CONTENTS

ACKNOWLEDGMENTS

Writing a textbook to put the best information about the latest diesel technology in the hands of technicians could not take place without the practical support, critical feedback, and assistance of many individuals. I'm grateful for those who have shared their hard-earned knowledge, insights, and skills derived from many years of trade-related experience. While preparing this textbook, it has also been a privilege to meet many remarkable people in the transportation industry with an infectious excitement for the technology, an interest in promoting skilled trades, and a passion for service excellence. I encountered many of those people teaching at Centennial College in Toronto, Canada. Centennial's School of Transportation, with its outstanding facilities and faculty, has provided a unique vantage point for writing this textbook. It is an honor to be surrounded by a group of incredibly talented colleagues and share in the warm support offered to one another. Their enthusiasm, natural inquisitiveness, and continual focus on raising the bar for teaching excellence a little higher with every new intake of learners are inspirational.

To Vern Anthony—a heartfelt thank you for seeing the potential of this textbook, giving it a home at CDX, and deftly steering this project to completion around some significant barriers. Thank you also Tony Resendes, friend in faith, for your special help and encouragement. And finally to my family—thank you Ingrid, Wesley, Hannah, Grace, and Noah for the immeasurable and unconditional support that you offered and the countless weekends, evenings, and family vacations you gave up to allow me to finish this work. Without your steadfast patience and esteem, the task would have been impossible. I hope that now you will look at this textbook and understand why I spent so much time in front of my computer.

In addition, along with the CDX editorial team, I'd like to thank the following individuals for their contributions to and feedback about this textbook:

Ian W. Andrew
Queensland, Australia

Abraham P. Arispe
Tidewater Community College

Jim Baird
Jones Technical Institute

Larry Baker
Aims Community College

Ron Beaumont
Brisbane, Queensland, Australia

Joseph Berhausen
Fox Valley Technical College

Westin A. Blidy
Orleans Niagara BOCES

Clarence Brewer
Crowder College

Gary Bronson
Laurel Oaks Career Development Campus

Donnie Brown
Mid-South Community College

Pete Carpentier Jr.
Delmar College

Jerry Clemons
Elizabethtown Community and Technical College

David Conant
Lincoln College of Technology

Scott Dalby
GACTC

Leevell Dansby Jr.
Lawson State Community College

Brent Delfel
Sno-Isle TECH Skills Center

Jay Duca
Fox Valley Technical College

Tim Dunn
Sydney, New South Wales, Australia

Casey Eglinton
Western Technical College

Jason Gholston
Itawamba Community College

Travis Grubb
Northern Wyoming Community College District Gillette College

Curtis Happe
Richland Community College

Kevin Heimbach
Berks Career and Technology Center

Doyle Howard
West Kentucky Community and Technical College

Jim Hunnicutt
Jacksonville, Florida

Edward Jackson
ASE Certified Instructor

Tim Janello
Southern Illinois University Carbondale

Kevin Jesser
Member of Institute of Automotive Mechanical Engineers

Bob Johnson
Fred W. Eberle Technical Center

Ed Jolly
Gordon Cooper Technology Center

Dr. John F. Kershaw
Harrisburg Area Community College

Brian King
Boone County ATC

Kevin Knaebel
Ivy Tech Community College

Joseph Koposko
Fayette County Career &Technical Institute

Aaron A. Lemoine
South Louisiana Community College T.H. Harris Campus

Jason R. Lewis
Western Technical College

Robbie Lindhorst
Southeastern Illinois College

Terryl Lindsey
OSU Institute of Technology

Stefan Liszka
Chisholm Institute of TAFE

Michael Lott
Bishop State Community College

Ron Locandro
Chisholm Institute of TAFE

Ronald Luellen
Yavapai College

James Mack
Berks Career and Technology Center

Robert Marshal
University of Northwestern Ohio

Michael Mauntel
Ivy Tech Community College

Robert McCabe
Great Oaks JVSD (Retired)

Alan McClelland
Dean of Centennial College's School of Transportation, Toronto, Canada

Jed Metzler
South Branch Career and Technical Center

Daniel Mielczarek
Cheney Tech High School

John Miller
Valley Career and Technical Center

James Mitchell
Tampa Bay Technical High School

Jason Montini
Lincoln Tech/Nashville Auto Diesel College

Coy Morris
Francis Tuttle Technology Center

John Murphy
Centennial College

Brent Newville
Dakota County Tech College

Pat Osterhaus
Northeast Iowa Community College

Zack Otterstrom
UAW-LETC

Lyman Parsell
Lincoln College of Technology

Chad M. Parsons
Wyotech

Brian L. Particka
Huron Area Technology Center

Levi Perkins
College of Southern Idaho

Billy Phillips
Johnston Community College

Adam Prusakiewicz
University of Northwestern Ohio

Larry Seibel
Miami Valley Career Technology Center

Darren Smith
Professor, Centennial College's School of Transportation

Tyler Slettedahl
North Dakota State College of Science

Claude Townsend
Oakland Schools

J.W. Turnpaugh
Mid America Technology Center

Craig Weckman
American River College

Larry Wehunt
Gwinnett Technical College

John Yinger
Ozarks Technical Community College

SECTION 1

Foundation and Safety

CHAPTER 1
Introduction to Diesel Engines

NATEF Tasks

There are no NATEF tasks for this chapter.

Knowledge Objectives

After reading this chapter, you will be able to:

1. Identify applications for diesel engines. (p 5)
2. Explain the relationship of temperature and pressure to the principles of compression ignition. (pp 6–7)
3. Describe the development of diesel technology. (pp 6–9)
4. Explain the advantages of compression-ignition engines over spark-ignition engines. (pp 9–13)
5. Identify and explain factors that contribute to diesel engine fuel efficiency. (pp 10–11)
6. Identify and explain factors that contribute to the high torque output of diesel engines. (pp 11–12)
7. Identify legislation that influenced the development of diesel technology. (pp 13–15)
8. Identify the major technological changes of diesel engines and explain their significance. (pp 15–17)
9. Identify major technologies and strategies used to reduce diesel engine emissions. (pp 15–17)

Skill Objectives

After reading this chapter, you will be able to:

1. Identify and interpret a vehicle identification number. (p 18) **SKILL DRILL 1-1**
2. Identify and interpret an engine emission decal. (p 19) **SKILL DRILL 1-2**
3. Record engine and trip information. (p 19) **SKILL DRILL 1-3**

► Introduction

Diesel engines are the workhorses of the heavy-duty, commercial transportation industry. Their proven economy, rugged durability, and reliability have made them the engine of choice for more than 95% of buses, heavy trucks, and off-road machinery **FIGURE 1-1**. In the off-road construction, agriculture, and mining industries, the majority of equipment, including tractors, trains, stationary engines, and pumps, depends on diesel technology. The diesel engine's long service life, low maintenance costs, and high torque output have made it indispensable for transporting almost every manufactured product, building every structure, harvesting or excavating almost any material, and transporting people **FIGURE 1-2**. Diesel engines are used by virtually all emergency vehicles, such as ambulances, fire trucks, and tow trucks. Hospitals, data centers, and other critical service sectors rely on diesel generators for emergency standby power. Even the military depends on diesel engines to power the majority of their equipment. While diesel engines have long had a vital strategic role in the military, the advantages diesels offer have been acknowledged with the switchover in recent years of nearly all tactical ground vehicles and electrical generators to diesel. The use of a single fuel, Jet Propellant 8 (JP8), which is also used for military aircraft, has simplified the logistics of supplying fuel to diesel-powered equipment ranging in size from all-terrain vehicles and motorcycles to heavy tanks and personnel carriers.

In the light-duty automobile sector, a new generation of clean diesel technology has attracted the public's attention. This is evidenced by the fact that diesel engine sales in North America have more than doubled in recent years. In Europe, where fuel costs are higher, light-duty diesel engines have captured 50–80% of the vehicle market, depending on the country.

In Canada, models from Mercedes-Benz and Volkswagen have more than 80% of customers preferring diesels over gasoline-fueled engine power trains. In light-duty applications, diesel's appeal has traditionally been its superior fuel economy. Compared to similarly sized gasoline-powered engines, diesel engines are 25–60% more fuel efficient. In heavy-duty applications, the advantage is even greater. Another advantage offered by diesels is that <u>turbochargers</u>, which use exhaust energy to compress air and pressurize the air intake system of an engine, can be used more effectively in diesel engines than in spark-ignition (SI) engines. Turbocharging a diesel engine has numerous benefits, but the primary benefit is increasing <u>power density</u>, the amount of power generated by each liter (or cubic inch) of engine displacement. In addition, today's diesels have a substantially lower environmental impact than gasoline-fueled SI engines. Public opinion about diesels has shifted favorably as technological advances have transformed diesel engines from historically noisy, smelly, hard-to-start machinery into a sophisticated, powerful, clean, and environmentally friendly power train alternative.

In heavy-duty truck, bus, and off-road equipment applications, diesel engines are used almost exclusively because of the following advantages:

1. Superior fuel economy
2. Higher engine torque output
3. Greater durability and longevity

Each of these advantages will be examined in detail throughout the following chapters. But to begin to understand these features, it is helpful to first examine the origin and development of diesel technology.

Class 1 0–6000 lb (0–2722 kg)	
Class 2 6001–10,000 lb (2723–4535 kg)	Pick-up Trucks, Minivans, Small Buses, Sport Utility Vehicles, etc.
Class 3 10,001–14,000 lb (4536–6350 kg)	
Class 4 14,001–16,000 lb (6351–7257 kg)	City Delivery Trucks, Flatbed Towing Trucks, etc.
Class 5 16,001–19,500 lb (7258–8845 kg)	
Class 6 19,501–26,000 lb (8846–11,793 kg)	
Class 7 26,001–33,000 lb (11,794–14,968 kg)	Long-Haul Trucks, Dump Trucks, Refuse Haulers, etc.
Class 8 33,001+ lb (14,969 kg)	

FIGURE 1-1 Diesel's high torque output, superior fuel economy, and rugged durability make it the primary engine choice for commercial vehicles.

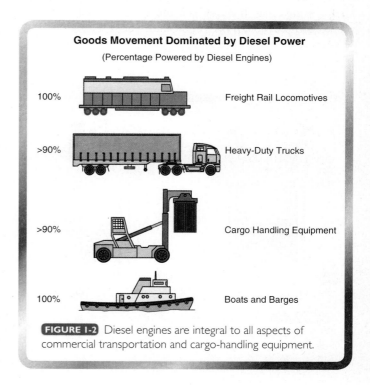

Goods Movement Dominated by Diesel Power

(Percentage Powered by Diesel Engines)

100% — Freight Rail Locomotives

>90% — Heavy-Duty Trucks

>90% — Cargo Handling Equipment

100% — Boats and Barges

FIGURE 1-2 Diesel engines are integral to all aspects of commercial transportation and cargo-handling equipment.

▶ Development of the Diesel Engine

Diesel engines are the most efficient combustion systems in use today. Compared to other engines, diesel engines convert burning fuel into the most mechanical energy. This has been the case from the time of their conception.

Engine Development

Engines are machines that convert energy produced from burning fuel into mechanical power. If an engine burns fuel outside a cylinder, it is an external combustion engine. Steam engines fall into this category. Steam engines were first widely used in the early 1700s. These early engines extracted only 1–8% of mechanical energy from burned fuel. This meant that they were heavy consumers of fuel in proportion to their power output. Very little of the heat energy produced by the fuel used to power steam engines was converted into mechanical power. Steam engines were also large and dangerous.

In 1861, Nikolaus Otto substantially improved engine efficiency by developing the four-stroke cycle internal-combustion engine. Internal-combustion engines burn fuel inside an engine's combustion chamber. Otto's four-stroke cycle engine used a spark to ignite kerosene-like fuel inside the engine cylinder. There are only two mechanisms used to ignite fuel in any engine: electric spark or heat generated through the compression of air **FIGURE 1-3**. Spark-ignited engines, such as Otto's, are designated as SI engines. Otto's four-stroke cycle engine won a gold medal in the Paris Exhibition of 1867 by utilizing the least amount of fuel to generate the greatest amount of power. **Otto cycle** engines, more commonly called four-stroke cycle engines, use two crankshaft rotations to complete an operating cycle. The cycle is made up of four piston strokes: intake, compression, power, and exhaust **FIGURE 1-4**.

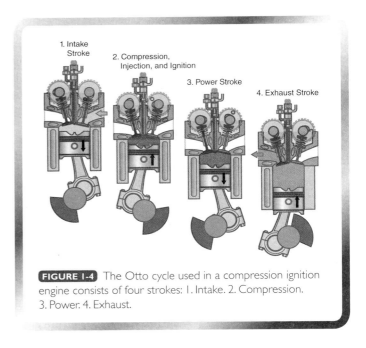

FIGURE 1-4 The Otto cycle used in a compression ignition engine consists of four strokes: 1. Intake. 2. Compression. 3. Power. 4. Exhaust.

1. Intake Stroke
2. Compression, Injection, and Ignition
3. Power Stroke
4. Exhaust Stroke

Rudolf Diesel and Compression-Ignition Combustion

When Rudolf Diesel (1858–1913) patented his engine in 1892, he envisioned a machine that would operate with dramatically improved **thermal efficiency** over the steam and Otto cycle engines of his day. Thermal efficiency is a comparison between the amount of energy released during combustion and the mechanical energy available at the engine flywheel. Both steam and Otto cycle engines had low thermal efficiency, and Rudolf Diesel believed that he had an idea for a more efficient engine. Anecdotally, it is believed that inspiration for the idea may have occurred when Rudolf Diesel observed a demonstration of an ancient device used to start fires. The device, called a fire piston, consists of a hollow, narrow tube sealed at one end and a plunger matched to the diameter of the tube. The plunger forms an air-tight seal in the tube and a ramrod handle is attached to the plunger, so the user can move the plunger in the tube. To start fires, the user places a small bit of wood or dried grass in the bottom of the tube and then repeatedly rams the plunger into the tube. Compressing the air with the plunger increases the pressure and temperature inside the tube, which ignites the kindling. Fascinated by this technique, Diesel conceived a new, more efficient engine ignition system: the **compression-ignition (CI)** combustion system. In this system, air alone, not a spark, would be the ignition source **FIGURE 1-5**. He had observed that the temperature of air, like any gas, would increase when it was compressed **FIGURE 1-6**. He correctly calculated that if fuel was injected into a cylinder when air was compressed sufficiently to reach a temperature hot enough to ignite the fuel, combustion would take place. He planned to inject fuel near the end of the compression stroke, when the combustion chamber of a typical CI engine will reach temperatures in excess of 1000°F (538°C). He hypothesized that heat produced after igniting and burning the fuel would

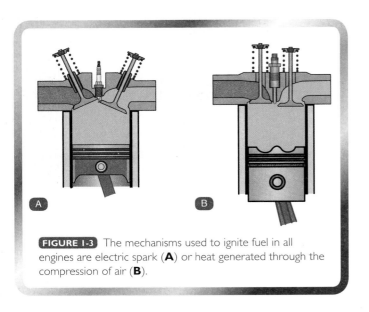

FIGURE 1-3 The mechanisms used to ignite fuel in all engines are electric spark (**A**) or heat generated through the compression of air (**B**).

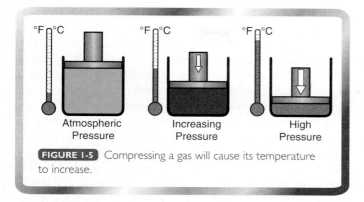

FIGURE 1-5 Compressing a gas will cause its temperature to increase.

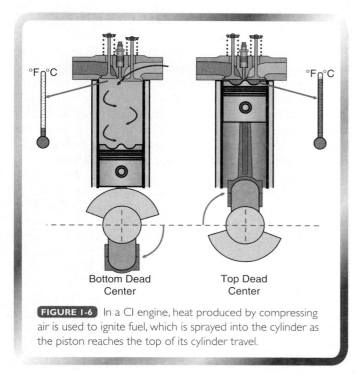

FIGURE 1-6 In a CI engine, heat produced by compressing air is used to ignite fuel, which is sprayed into the cylinder as the piston reaches the top of its cylinder travel.

FIGURE 1-7 Diesel engines inject liquid fuel under high pressure into the combustion chamber near the end of the compression stroke. Air, which is heated during compression stroke, becomes the ignition source.

FIGURE 1-8 This model, displayed in the Deutsches Museum, is a replica of Diesel's third experimental attempt at building a CI engine.

cause cylinder pressures to intensify due to gas expansion and that gas pressure would drive the piston downward just after the piston passed **top dead center (TDC)**, which is the highest point the piston reaches in the cylinder. Diesel believed this unique idea for a combustion mechanism would deliver higher engine efficiency and power output **FIGURE 1-7**.

In 1893, Diesel built the first working model of his patented design. The engine was fueled using coal dust, which was blasted into the combustion chamber using pressurized air. Injecting coal dust proved to be too complex and cumbersome, but in spite of these problems, the engine operated with 26% thermal efficiency, which means that 26% of the heat energy was converted into mechanical energy. This was more than three times the efficiency of steam engines of that day.

A later experimental attempt in 1897 at building a CI engine produced a reciprocating engine **FIGURE 1-8**. Reciprocating engines use a piston moving up and down in a cylinder to produce power. A crankshaft converts the reciprocating, or up-and-down, movement into rotational movement FIGURE 1-9 . Diesel's 1897 experiment stood more than 10 feet (3 meters) tall and was practical only in stationary applications such as ships and factories. It produced 18 horsepower (hp) (13 kilowatts [kW]) at 158 revolutions per minute (rpm), using a complex air injection system that blew liquid fuel into the cylinder near the end of the compression stroke. Liquid fuels were more practical and economical for use because CI engines could readily burn the waste oil by-product left after distilling gasoline from crude petroleum. Rudolf Diesel supported the use of renewable fuels to operate CI engines. Aggravated by the monopoly over oil production once held by American business interests, the French government in particular encouraged development of an engine that could operate using fuel grown and processed locally by farmers. At the 1897 Paris Exhibition, such an engine was displayed: an engine using peanut oil demonstrated the effective use of liquid **biodiesel**, which is a fuel derived from a plant or animal source.

▌ TECHNICIAN TIP

Diesel fuel is produced by boiling crude oil and condensing its vapors. Biodiesel, also referred to as biofuel, is fuel made from biological sources such as animal fats or vegetable oils. Biodiesel can reduce the noxious exhaust emissions from older diesel engines. Although it has many other advantages, biodiesel's emission advantage is irrelevant because today's diesel engines produce near zero emissions, even when using petroleum fuel.

Diesel's Continuing Development

Early diesel engines were large and cumbersome and were used primarily in stationary and industrial applications. Ships and submarines benefited the most from this technology. Prior to World War I, any country having military use of the diesel engine was believed to have an important strategic advantage. In fact, when Rudolf Diesel disappeared over the side of a ship in the English Channel in 1913, there was speculation that his death may have been politically motivated rather than an apparent suicide.

After his death, Diesel's original concept of a highly efficient engine design caught the attention of other inventors, who wanted to put it to use in smaller, lighter transportation applications. By the 1920s, Robert Bosch developed practical, compact injection pumps and governors that allowed the use of smaller diesel engines to power trucks, buses, and automobiles. Commercial vehicles first used diesel engines in Germany during the mid-1920s FIGURE 1-10 . In 1929, Clessie Cummins, founder of Cummins Engine Company, built North America's first production, diesel-powered car. Coincidentally, at this time the Great Depression began and, with it, the economic incentive for energy-efficient transportation that could be supplied by the diesel engine. Cummins popularized the reputation of the diesel as a fuel-thrifty engine by driving a seven-passenger Packard limousine retrofitted with his Model U diesel engine across the continental United States using only $11.22 worth of fuel. Later, in 1936, the diesel engine first found its way into a mass-produced passenger car, the Mercedes-Benz 260D. While other truck manufacturers had installed diesel engines in their trucks for decades, it wasn't until the mid-1950s that Volvo became the first manufacturer to mass-produce turbocharged diesel-powered engines like the kind used in today's vehicles.

The oil crisis of the early 1970s once again drove North American consumers to more fuel-efficient diesel engines in automobiles to offset the spike in gasoline prices. In the 1970s, every car manufacturer had several models of diesel-powered vehicles. However, after oil prices declined, consumers returned to gasoline-powered vehicles. Although interest was lost in placing diesel engines in small vehicles and light trucks, fleet operations such as school buses and delivery vehicles discovered the utility and economy of diesel engines during this time. The cost of fuel is still one of the largest business expenses in this category of vehicles. Here, the premium price paid for a diesel-powered vehicle compared to a gasoline-powered vehicle can be recovered in fuel cost savings in just a few months. The greatest reductions

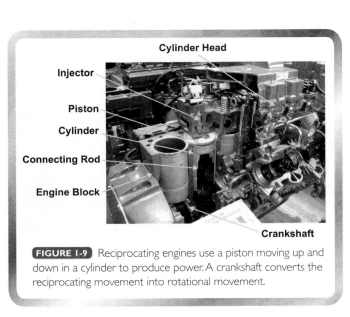

FIGURE 1-9 Reciprocating engines use a piston moving up and down in a cylinder to produce power. A crankshaft converts the reciprocating movement into rotational movement.

FIGURE 1-10 Mercedes-Benz was one of the earliest manufacturers of diesel-powered trucks.

in fuel consumption are also available for these larger vehicles—far more than in lighter, more compact vehicles. For example, if a vehicle's fuel economy was improved from 20 miles per gallon (mpg) (8.5 kilometers per liter [km/L]) to 25 mpg (10.6 km/L) with diesel (a 25% increase in economy), that improvement would yield a 120-gallon (454-liter) annual fuel savings based on driving 12,000 miles (19,312 km) per year. In contrast, improving from 30 mpg (12.8 km/L) to 37.5 mpg (15.9 km/L) (also a 25% increase) yields only an 80-gallon (303-liter) savings per year when traveling the same distance **FIGURE 1-11**.

Today, while some truck, bus, and off-road equipment manufacturers design and produce their own diesel engines, many depend on other manufacturers to produce diesel engines. In North America, the manufacturers of diesel engines include:

1. Cummins Inc.
2. Caterpillar
3. Detroit Diesel Corporation
4. Navistar
5. Volvo
6. Mack (a member of the Volvo Group)
7. PACCAR Inc.
8. Perkins (owned by Caterpillar)
9. Deere & Company
10. Kubota Corporation
11. Case Fiat Power Industrial (FPT) Yanmar America Corporation
12. Isuzu Motors America LLC
13. Ford Motor Company
14. General Motors

► Advantages of Diesel Engines

The history of the diesel engine shows how and why commercial vehicles use the engine so extensively today. There are also significant features and advantages of diesel-powered engines that are helpful for technicians to understand as they diagnose problems, develop maintenance practices, and make service recommendations to customers about diesel engines. Factors that influence engine efficiency, power output, durability, and emissions are particularly important to understand. In this next section, the operating principles of the diesel are examined to make the connection to a variety of distinctive diesel advantages that may not be obvious.

Engine Efficiency

The limiting factor to producing power from traditional gasoline-fueled, SI engines is the problem of combustion detonation caused by pre-ignition of the air–fuel mixture. Gasoline engines commonly draw the air–fuel mixture into the cylinder during the intake stroke, which can automatically ignite if it is

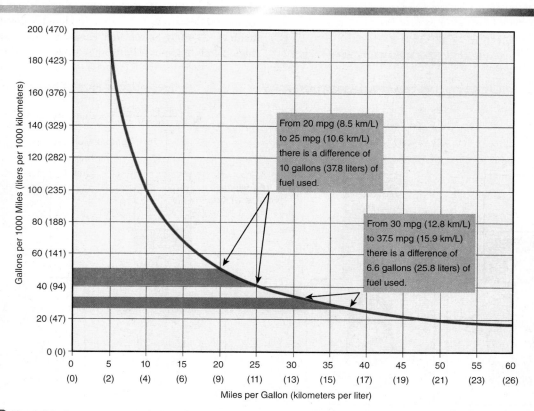

From 20 mpg (8.5 km/L) to 25 mpg (10.6 km/L) there is a difference of 10 gallons (37.8 liters) of fuel used.

From 30 mpg (12.8 km/L) to 37.5 mpg (15.9 km/L) there is a difference of 6.6 gallons (25.8 liters) of fuel used.

FIGURE 1-11 Even slight improvements in fuel economy in vehicles with high fuel consumption are more beneficial than making major fuel economy improvements in more fuel-efficient vehicles.

heated too much during the compression stroke. This is why gasoline engines traditionally have a lower limit to cylinder compression pressures. Diesel engines inject fuel into the cylinder at the end of compression stroke rather than during intake stroke. This unique diesel feature eliminates heating of the air–fuel mixture during compression stroke. Because heating does not take place, much higher compression pressures can be used in the engine cylinders. Higher **compression ratios** used by diesel engines extract more energy from burning fuel, which translates into increased power and lower fuel consumption **FIGURE 1-12**.

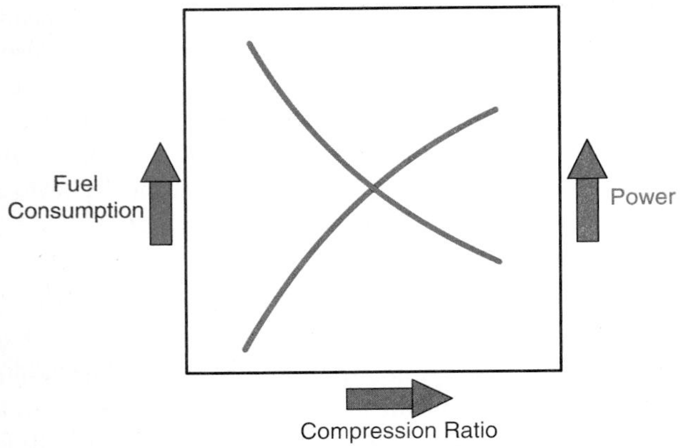

FIGURE 1-12 Higher compression ratios increase power output and decrease fuel consumption. The high compression ratio of diesels is the main reason for the various advantages of diesel engines.

The compression ratio measures how much air is compressed in a cylinder by comparing the clearance volume (the space left in the cylinder when the piston is at TDC) to the total cylinder volume **FIGURE 1-13**. With smaller clearance volumes, diesel engines compress air twice as much as SI engines.

Another factor contributing to increased efficiency in diesel engines is the use of **lean burn combustion**, which is the process of burning fuel using excess air. Diesel engines use more air than is necessary to burn fuel, unlike most gasoline-fueled, SI engines, which burn fuel at stoichiometric ratio. Burning fuel at stoichiometric ratio means that only enough air is mixed with fuel so that neither air nor fuel is left after the combustion process. Using turbocharging to fill the cylinders with even more air can further enhance engine efficiency in diesels **FIGURE 1-14**.

Fuel Economy

As noted previously, the use of higher compression ratios in diesel engines contributes not only to higher engine efficiency but also to lower fuel consumption, because more energy is released when air and fuel are squeezed into increasingly smaller combustion chambers. The higher pressure spike and longer stroke travel in diesel engines means more of the chemical energy stored in fuel converts to mechanical energy. Diesel fuel's 10–12% higher energy content also contributes to the fuel efficiency of diesel engines **FIGURE 1-15**.

Diesel engines use substantially less fuel than similarly displaced gasoline-fueled engines to produce the same horsepower (kilowatts). Typically, light-duty diesel engines will achieve 25–60% better fuel economy than similar gasoline-fueled, SI engines. In some instances, the improvement

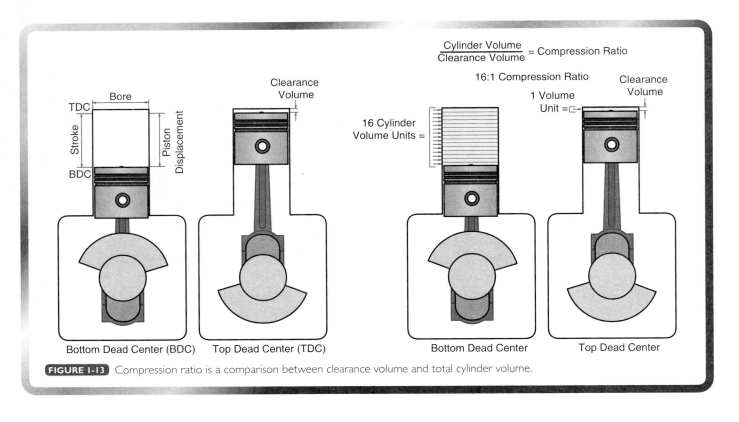

FIGURE 1-13 Compression ratio is a comparison between clearance volume and total cylinder volume.

$$\frac{\text{Cylinder Volume}}{\text{Clearance Volume}} = \text{Compression Ratio}$$

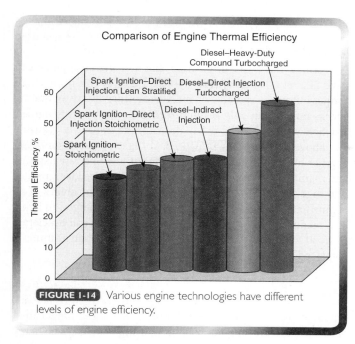

Comparison of Engine Thermal Efficiency

FIGURE 1-14 Various engine technologies have different levels of engine efficiency.

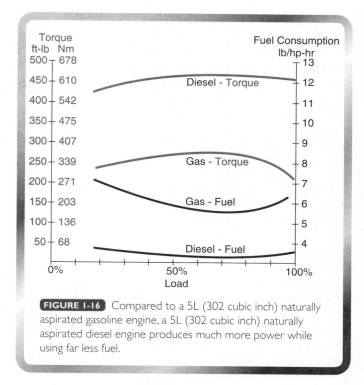

FIGURE 1-16 Compared to a 5L (302 cubic inch) naturally aspirated gasoline engine, a 5L (302 cubic inch) naturally aspirated diesel engine produces much more power while using far less fuel.

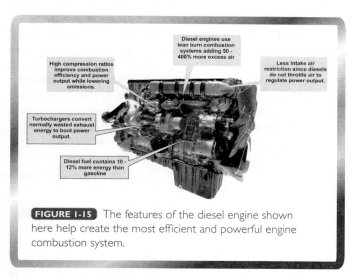

FIGURE 1-15 The features of the diesel engine shown here help create the most efficient and powerful engine combustion system.

will be as much as 75% **FIGURE 1-16**. However, common efficiency improvements are closer to 25–40% over gasoline engines in light- and medium-duty vehicles. In heavy-duty diesels, fuel efficiency is much higher. A typical late-model, on-highway, heavy-duty truck will obtain approximately 7.5 mpg (3.2 km/L) when towing a fully loaded trailer with extra rolling resistance from the tires and wind resistance from the larger vehicle profile. At 80,000 lb (36,287 kg) total vehicle weight, the truck-trailer combination's equivalent efficiency in a passenger car or truck weighing 4000 lb (1814 kg) would be 150 mpg (63.8 km/L) **FIGURE 1-17**. Today's engines that are compliant with greenhouse gas requirements are meeting higher fuel economy standards, yielding 11 mpg (5 km/L) or more.

Fuel costs for diesel-powered equipment are lower not only because of higher engine efficiency, which leads to better fuel mileage, but also because diesel fuel is usually cheaper than gasoline. Historically, diesel fuel has been less expensive because it is a by-product of gasoline production and requires less refining. Where large differences exist between gasoline and diesel fuel prices, taxes account for much of the difference. For example, in Europe, diesel fuel generally receives favorable taxation rates compared to gasoline. Demand for home heating fuel in North America drives up the price of diesel fuel during colder months.

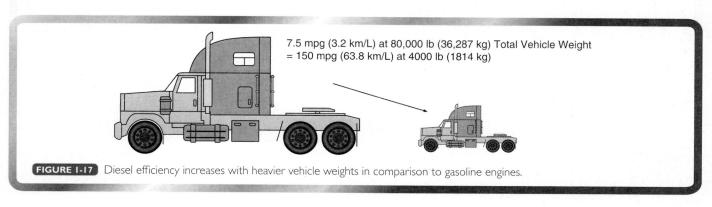

7.5 mpg (3.2 km/L) at 80,000 lb (36,287 kg) Total Vehicle Weight = 150 mpg (63.8 km/L) at 4000 lb (1814 kg)

FIGURE 1-17 Diesel efficiency increases with heavier vehicle weights in comparison to gasoline engines.

The benefits of diesel fuel efficiency extend to diesel generators; a diesel generator uses only half the amount of fuel that a gasoline-powered unit uses to produce the same amount of power. Motorbikes and all-terrain vehicles (ATVs), which manufacturers recently began building with diesel engines, also benefit from diesel fuel efficiency. Even aircraft are being built with diesel engines to improve fuel thriftiness. The high cost of aviation gasoline in North America and Europe, combined with concerns about its availability, has led to aviation's greater dependency on jet fuel, Jet-A, which is similar to #1D diesel fuel. Using reciprocating engines, the best gasoline-powered airplanes only achieve the equivalent of 15 mpg (6.4 km/L). However, a single-engine, two-seater aircraft powered by a Centurion common rail diesel achieves the equivalent of 123.8 mpg (52.6 km/L).

Torque Output

A diesel engine has significantly higher **torque** output than a similarly displaced gasoline-fueled engine. Torque is the twisting force applied through the crankshaft to the flywheel. Torque is generated by cylinder pressure and crankshaft leverage. Higher compression ratios produce higher torque output, and higher torque enables vehicles to accelerate powerfully and smoothly. Torque is particularly useful for quickly and smoothly merging onto busy highways, towing trailers, or climbing steep roads. Torque is also an important factor when moving a load. High torque output enables engines to not only move heavier loads, but also remain in higher gears while pulling loads up a hill. A driver will not need to shift down many gears, if any at all, when hauling heavy loads up steep grades using a high torque output diesel engine. Without the need to downshift to prevent an engine from stalling, the high torque output engine remains in a lower, more fuel-efficient operating range while maintaining road speed and fuel economy. Given that torque is the factor

that ultimately moves a vehicle and its load, diesel engines have a tremendous advantage in trucks, buses, and any equipment used for moving heavy loads.

Unlike most gasoline-fueled engines, diesel engines can have a flatter torque curve profile **FIGURE I-18**. This means high torque output is available at more useful driving or operating speeds rather than only at full throttle like throttled SI engines. For heavy-duty diesels, the highest torque output is available just above idle speed **FIGURE I-19**. At highway speeds, a diesel engine's ability to produce high torque at low operating speeds and maintain it over a wide range of operating speeds translates into high **torque elasticity**. Torque elasticity is the ability of an engine to accelerate at middle- and high-speed ranges. In light- and medium-duty applications, a diesel engine will accelerate from 50 to 80 mph (80 to 129 kph) much faster than a similarly displaced gasoline-powered engine.

Durability

Diesel engines typically operate three to five times longer than gasoline-powered engines before wearing out. In fact, many late-model, heavy-duty diesels are expected to exceed 1 million miles (1.6 million kilometers) of operation before needing an overhaul; for example Detroit Diesel's DD-15 and DD-16 engines have a B-50 bearing life (the distance where useful bearing wear has reached 50%) of 1.2 million miles (1.9 million kilometers). A diesel engine will travel farther and operate for a longer life cycle for several reasons. First, piston speed and piston travel is considerably reduced in a diesel engine compared to a gasoline-powered engine. Because the engine operates at lower rpm, the piston moves at a slower velocity and travels a shorter distance for every mile (kilometer) that the vehicle travels. While an automotive gasoline-powered engine typically operates between 2000 and 3000 rpm at cruising speed,

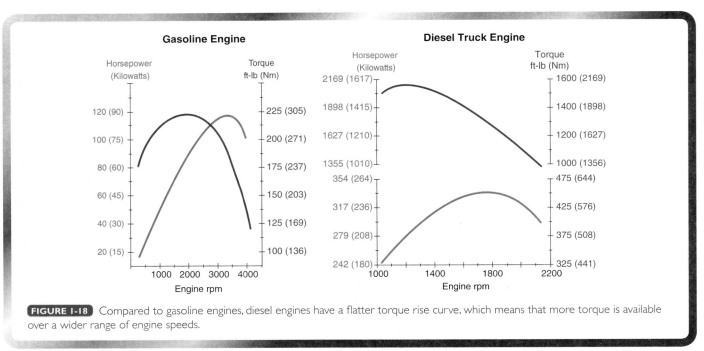

FIGURE I-18 Compared to gasoline engines, diesel engines have a flatter torque rise curve, which means that more torque is available over a wider range of engine speeds.

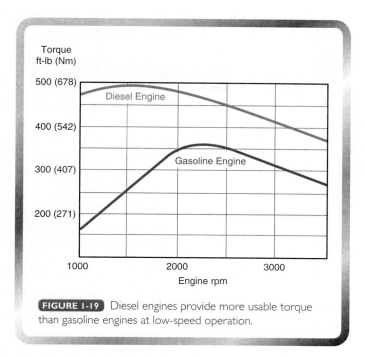

FIGURE 1-19 Diesel engines provide more usable torque than gasoline engines at low-speed operation.

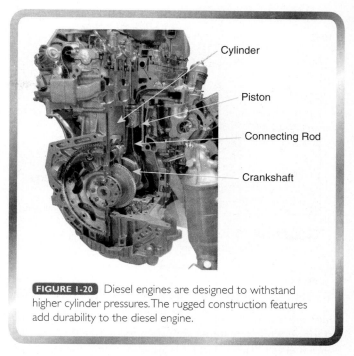

FIGURE 1-20 Diesel engines are designed to withstand higher cylinder pressures. The rugged construction features add durability to the diesel engine.

a diesel engine typically operates between 1100 and 1500 rpm. The "gear fast, run slow" strategy of heavy-duty, on-highway engines is also referred to as **down speeding**, and this strategy uses low axle differential gear ratios to take advantage of a diesel engine's high torque output at low engine speeds.

A second wear factor that is not as severe in diesel engines as in gasoline engines is the washing of lubrication from the cylinder wall with fuel. Because no fuel is present during the compression stroke in the diesel engine, lubrication oil on the cylinder walls can do a better job at minimizing engine friction.

Third, because diesel engines must withstand higher peak combustion chamber forces than gasoline-powered engines, more durable construction features are utilized in diesel engines **FIGURE 1-20**. These include heavier pistons and stronger crankshafts, valve trains, and gear trains. Crankshafts, cylinder sleeves, and blocks in a diesel engine are hardened using a specialized technique. In addition, many medium- and large-bore diesel engines are designed to be repeatedly rebuilt using replaceable cylinder sleeves. The speed and economy with which a diesel engine can be restored to original specifications is an important asset in commercial applications where long distances and long operating hours are quickly accumulated and where long chassis life cycles are the norm. A fourth factor contributing to the durability of diesel engines is that emissions legislation has established **useful life requirements** for diesel engines. Heavy-duty diesel engines must maintain emission compliance for their normal expected service life; currently, this standard is set at 435,000 miles (700,065 kilometers) or 10 years of service.

Related to a diesel engine's rugged durability is the need for less scheduled maintenance than a gasoline-powered engine. Without ignition system parts such as spark plugs to replace, diesel engine service mostly consists of changing the oil and filters as infrequently as two times a year, even with daily vehicle

use and normal driving distances. Adjustments to injectors and valve lash may take place as little as three or four times in an engine's useful operating life. Another benefit in addition to diesel engine durability and lower operating costs is higher resale value. Higher resale value makes diesel equipment even more economical over time.

▶ Technological Advancements for Diesels

The invisibility of exhaust and other emissions from today's diesel engines may leave the impression that the topic is of little importance, but the opposite is true. The need to reduce air pollution has driven innovation in diesel engine design for the past five decades and is the single-most important reason for the changes to the construction features and operation of nearly every engine system. Diesels also have an impact on air quality and energy policy that may seem disproportionate to the number of diesels on the road. That is due to the fact that although diesels make up only 5% of all the registered vehicles on the road, they burn close to 22% of all transportation fuels. This is in part why the latest emission standards not only require reductions in the output of noxious emissions to nearly zero, but also demand increased fuel efficiency and longer engine life and compliance with emissions standards.

Diesel Emissions Today

Emissions legislation, which has historically required increasing reductions in noxious emissions, has long driven diesel engine technological innovation. Emission reductions through technological innovation have the added benefit of increased power output for diesel engines **FIGURE 1-21**. Durability standards,

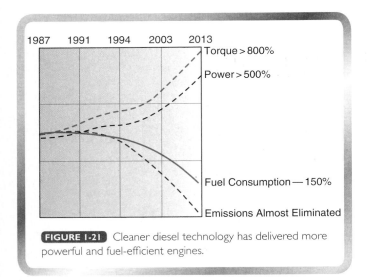

FIGURE I-21 Cleaner diesel technology has delivered more powerful and fuel-efficient engines.

which are a part of emissions legislation, require that engines last longer while remaining almost emission free through their useful lifecycle. These standards are also prompting significant engine design changes. Fuel economy standards introduced in 2014 are advancing further transformation of engine and fuel technology.

Evaporative and Cold Start Emissions

Some noxious emissions, such as carbon monoxide (CO) and hydrocarbon (HC) emissions, are much lower from diesel engines than from gasoline-powered engines. The discrepancy is greatest when engines are cold because gasoline-fueled engines produce the highest levels of emissions until the engine and exhaust catalysts are warmed up. Evaporative emissions from diesel-fueled vehicles are also lower than those from gasoline-fueled vehicles. In fact, diesel fuel evaporative emissions are insignificant because diesel fuel is much less volatile than gasoline. Because of this, fuel vapor recovery systems found on gasoline-fueled vehicles are not necessary on diesel engines. The production of carbon dioxide (CO_2), a **greenhouse gas (GHG)**, is 20–40% lower in diesel engines than in gasoline-fueled engines due to the fact that diesel engines extract more power from fuel and fuel economy improves. Moving people and freight with a diesel engine uses less fuel per pound per mile (or per kilogram per kilometer) than with a gasoline-fueled SI engine. GHGs are believed to trap heat in the atmosphere, which contributes to global warming. While diesel fuel contains more carbon than gasoline, this is offset by the fact that less energy is required to refine diesel fuel than gasoline **TABLE I-I**.

▶ **TECHNICIAN TIP**

While diesel engines consume approximately 22% of transportation fuels, a 2013 U.S. Environmental Protection Agency (EPA) study showed that 97% of North American and 83% of European emissions are produced from non-diesel sources.

TABLE I-I: Fuel Carbon Content and CO_2 Emissions

Category	Gasoline	Diesel
Carbon Content	5.3 lb per gallon of fuel (635 g per liter of fuel)	6.1 lb per gallon of fuel (731 g per liter of fuel)
CO_2 Emissions	19.4 lb per gallon of fuel (2325 g per liter of fuel)	22.2 lb per gallon of fuel (2660 g per liter of fuel)

Greenhouse Gas Emissions

Until recently, CO_2, a by-product of normal combustion, was not a regulated emission because it was not considered toxic to animal or plant life. However, much attention has been given to its role as a GHG, so much so that public interest in reducing the production of CO_2 has turned to regulating CO_2 emissions **TABLE I-2** and **TABLE I-3**. Beginning in January 2009, California was granted a waiver exempting it from U.S. federal emissions legislation, which permitted the state to establish its own mandatory limits on CO_2 emissions from motor vehicles.

TABLE I-2: 2007 GHG Standard for Carbon Dioxide Emissions from Vocational Applications of Diesel-Powered Vehicles

Category	EPA CO_2 Emissions (grams/ton-mile)	National Highway Traffic and Safety (NHTSA) CO_2 Emissions (gallons/1000 ton-mile)
Light Heavy-Duty Classes 2–5	373	36.7
Medium Heavy-Duty Classes 6–7	225	22.1
Heavy Heavy-Duty Class 8	222	21.8

TABLE I-3: GHG Standard for Carbon Dioxide Emissions from On-Highway Diesel-Powered Vehicles

Category	Year	EPA CO_2 Emissions (grams/ton-mile)	NHTSA CO_2 Emissions (gallons/1000 ton-miles)
Medium-Duty	2014	502	4.93
Medium-Duty	2017	487	4.78
Heavy-Duty	2014	475	4.67
Heavy-Duty	2017	460	4.52

In that state, beginning in 2012, passenger vehicles, light-duty trucks, and medium-duty passenger vehicles are required to meet an estimated combined average CO_2 emissions level of 250 g per mile (155 g per km). The remainder of North America indirectly regulates CO_2 through fuel economy standards. Ton-miles per gallon is the measuring unit used for the new fuel efficiency standards in the United States; other countries use grams per mile or kilometer. Ton-miles per gallon is calculated by measuring the vehicle weight in tons, multiplying by the distance traveled in miles, and then dividing by the volume of fuel consumed measured in gallons. The metric equivalent of ton-miles per gallon is grams per ton.

New fuel efficiency standards for EPA-certified diesel-powered commercial trucks and buses started in 2014 and will be phased in through 2017. While standards mandating reduced fuel consumption enable lower CO_2 emissions, technology to reduce GHGs also doubles the fuel mileage of vehicles compared to levels achieved just a few years ago. In 2014, manufacturers were already demonstrating fully loaded, on-highway, tractor-trailer combinations that achieved 10–14 mpg (4.3–6 km/L). Compare this with 5–7 mpg (2.1–3 km/L) just a few years earlier. While diesels comprise approximately 5% of vehicle registrations, they consume close to 22% of all transportation fuel, so diesel engine efficiency will have a major impact on the environment and energy use.

To achieve the largest decreases in GHG emissions, which the transportation sector is 70% responsible for, a major shift in diesel technology will be needed. Adopting diesel technology on this scale could reduce CO_2 emissions by as much as a 40%. Even larger reductions are achievable when biodiesel fuel, rather than petroleum-based diesel fuel, is used to power diesel engines. A 1998 study by the U.S. Department of Agriculture and the U.S. Department of Energy concluded that using biodiesel reduces net emissions of CO_2 from diesel engines by 78% compared to petroleum-based diesel. This large reduction is due to the plants and other biomasses used to produce biodiesel, which trap carbon as they grow. This carbon is released from combustion and is then reabsorbed by plants in a self-sustaining cycle.

Emission Reduction Strategies

Useful Life Requirements

Compliance with emissions standards over the useful life of a diesel engine was required beginning in 2004. This means that an engine cannot exceed the maximum legislated emissions limits during its expected normal service life. Useful life now includes not only noxious emissions, but CO_2 as well. Engines must be built more durably to meet these standards and use adaptive strategies to compensate for deterioration in components found in the fuel, air, and exhaust systems that could cause an engine to exceed maximum emission thresholds. In 2004, useful life was defined as:

1. Light-Duty: 110,000 miles (177,028 km) or 10 years
2. Medium-Duty: 185,000 miles (297,729 km) or 10 years
3. Heavy-Duty: 435,000 miles (700,065 km), 10 years, or 22,000 hours

Ultra-Low-Sulfur Fuel and Fuel Quality

A reduction of sulfur levels in diesel fuel began in mid-2006 to help manufacturers meet emissions standards. Exhaust after-treatment devices such as particulate traps, oxides of nitrogen (NO_x) adsorber catalysts, and other catalytic converters are poisoned by even the smallest quantities of sulfur in diesel fuel. European standards have dictated the removal of sulfur from diesel fuel for years, which has enabled the use of more advanced diesel injection systems that would be damaged by sulfur and other impurities. Starting in 2007, the EPA's diesel fuel regulations required fuel refineries to supply fuel containing fewer than 15 parts per million (ppm), or 0.0015%, of sulfur.

Additional changes to fuel properties can reduce engine emissions even further. An increase in the minimum cetane number, which is a measure of diesel fuel ignition quality, and a reduction in fuel's aromatic content (complex, hard-to-burn fuel molecules) also improve combustion and reduce emissions from diesel engines. Availability of good quality fuel is not a significant issue for operators of diesel-powered vehicles. Medium-duty and Class 2 truck sales have helped build diesel infrastructure to the point where a recent survey showed that 48% of fuel stations in the United States have diesel fuel available. In Canada and Europe, this percentage is much higher.

To further reduce emissions, the Renewable Fuel Standard (RFS), which is part of the Energy Independence and Security Act of 2007 (EISA), in the United States indirectly mandates the use of B-20 fuel for 2011. B-20 is a blend of 20% biologically derived fuel with 80% conventional diesel fuel. Fuels derived from biological sources produce fewer noxious emissions. The EISA also requires that 30% of all fuels originate from renewable sources by 2022. This legislation was passed to further encourage the use of alternative fuels, particularly biodiesel and ethanol.

High-Pressure Injection Systems

Injecting fuel at high pressure is one of the distinctive features of CI engines. Efficient diesel engine operation requires the injection of a precise quantity of fuel, at high pressure, and delivered at the correct time into the combustion chamber. In today's engines, injection pressures range from a low of 3200 pounds per square inch (psi) (221 bar) during idle conditions to more than 37,000 psi (2551 bar) at high speed under full engine loads. Even higher injection pressures are planned for future engines; developmental engines are now achieving pressures as high as 60,000 psi (4137 bar).

An enormous variety of high-pressure fuel systems are available for diesel engines. One of the most significant technological advances in diesel engines is the use of electronic controls in fuel systems. These electronic controls can rapidly vary the timing for beginning and ending of injection events while accurately measuring the correct quantity of fuel for each injection event based on continuously changing operating conditions. Switching injection events on and off at high pressures and with the accuracy required for diesel combustion is no small feat. The latest common rail injection systems electronically vary injection pressures and the duration of the injection event and produce multiple injection events during a combustion cycle **FIGURE 1-22**.

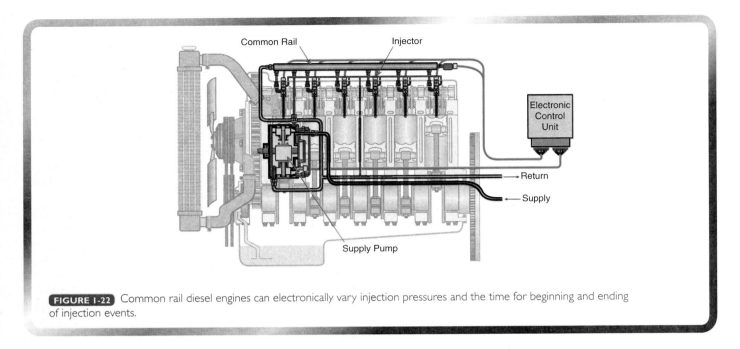

FIGURE I-22 Common rail diesel engines can electronically vary injection pressures and the time for beginning and ending of injection events.

Shot-to-shot and cylinder-to-cylinder changes are calculated continuously to achieve the best performance combined with the lowest emissions and fuel consumption using an injection strategy called injection rate shaping **FIGURE I-23**.

Exhaust Aftertreatment Systems

In addition to high-pressure injection systems with injection rate–shaping capabilities, microprocessor engine control, and changes to turbocharging, new exhaust aftertreatment technology has enabled today's diesel engines to achieve close to zero emissions. Some of the most visible changes enabling emission reductions are seen in exhaust system technology, which cleans up noxious emissions after they are produced in the cylinders. These technologies include diesel particulate filters, selective catalyst reduction, and soon-to-be-introduced plasma catalytic converters.

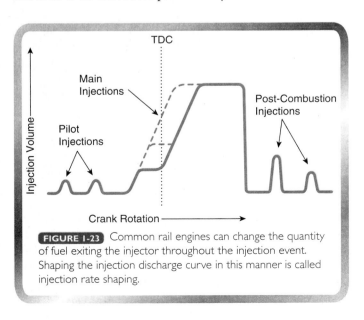

FIGURE I-23 Common rail engines can change the quantity of fuel exiting the injector throughout the injection event. Shaping the injection discharge curve in this manner is called injection rate shaping.

Diesel Particulate Filters

The **diesel particulate filter (DPF)** was introduced for all diesel engines beginning in 2007. DPFs use technology that filters and traps soot particles from the exhaust stream in a ceramic filter. To prevent the filter from completely plugging, an oxidation catalyst upstream of the DPF can heat relatively cool exhaust to help burn the soot off of the filter; this process is referred to as passive regeneration. If driving or operating conditions do not produce enough heat to naturally regenerate or clean the filter, the oxidation catalyst can be dosed with small amounts of diesel fuel, which produces chemical reactions that heat the exhaust gases and DPF filter. This is referred to as active regeneration of the filter. The by-products of regeneration can be harmlessly released into the atmosphere.

Selective Catalyst Reduction

In addition to soot, which is classified as **particulate matter (PM)**, NO_X is the other major emission from diesel engines. NO_X is produced by a diesel engine's hot combustion temperatures and naturally higher compression pressures. When atmospheric nitrogen reacts with oxygen under high-pressure and high-temperature conditions, NO_X emissions are formed, which contributes to the production of smog. The reddish-brown appearance of the atmosphere on hot, sunny, windless days is evidence of atmospheric NO_X emissions. The exhaust aftertreatment technology unique to diesel engines that specifically targets this emission is **selective catalyst reduction (SCR)** **FIGURE I-24**. NO_X-reducing technology in the exhaust system selectively targets NO_X to break it into nitrogen and oxygen. Lean NO_X traps (LNTs), NO_X adsorbing catalysts (NACs), and liquid SCR systems are examples of common NO_X-reducing technologies. Liquid SCR systems used on most heavy-duty diesels inject diesel exhaust fluid (DEF), which is a solution of water and urea, into the exhaust stream. Combined with a specialized catalytic converter, DEF eliminates NO_X from the exhaust. Light- and

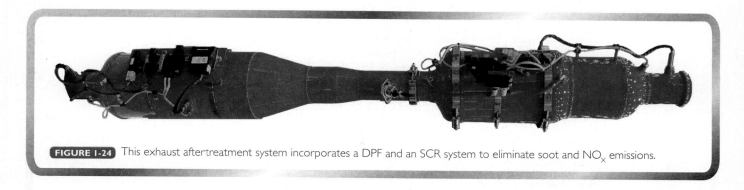

FIGURE 1-24 This exhaust aftertreatment system incorporates a DPF and an SCR system to eliminate soot and NO_x emissions.

medium-duty diesels use LNTs and NACs, which manufacture urea molecules inside a specialized catalyst on board the vehicle. Unlike systems used on heavy-duty diesels, the systems on light- and medium-duty diesels do not require a reservoir to store liquid DEF.

Plasma Catalytic Converters

A new aftertreatment technology expected for use beginning in 2016 is used in **plasma catalytic converters**. This new device breaks down exhaust emissions using a combination of specialized catalysts and high frequency AC electrical energy. It is expected to be so effective at destroying any noxious emission produced in the cylinders that major engine redesign can take place. Rather than attempting to prevent the formation of NO_x and other pollutants in the engine, combustion events can be optimized to produce the highest amount of power from the least amount of fuel while the plasma catalytic converter cleans up any noxious exhaust emissions. The goal of injection timing, fuel metering, and cylinder pressure control will be to produce the highest power output, which will reduce fuel consumption and GHG emissions such as CO_2.

▶ Vehicle Identification Numbers

Identifying a vehicle and its equipment is one of the first tasks a technician performs when preparing a work order for servicing commercial vehicles. To do this, the vehicle identification number (VIN) is used. A VIN is a combination of 17 numbers and letters that represent different pieces of information about the vehicle **FIGURE 1-25**. Locating and correctly recording the VIN for every vehicle is essential to obtaining parts and service information. Warranty claims also require VINs. VINs are formatted according to an international standard that arranges vehicle information into three groups: the World Manufacturer Identifier, the Vehicle Descriptor Section, and the Vehicle Identifier Section **FIGURE 1-26**. VINs can be read from specific locations on a vehicle and can also be scanned with barcode scanners or cell phone cameras. VINs can also be read using an electronic service tool such as a fault code scanner or original equipment manufacturer (OEM) software from one or more of the on-board network electronic control modules. Specific information about the vehicle can be decoded from the VIN and interpreted by many websites.

```
INCOMPLETE VEHICLE MANUFACTURED BY /
(VEHICULE INCOMPLET FABRIQUE PAR)
INTERNATIONAL TRUCK AND ENGINE CORPORATION
G / P
V / N    13154  KG
W / B
R / V    29000  LB )

G / P    FRONT              FR-REAR-RR
A / N    4535  KG          8618          KG
W / B
R / E    10000  LB )        19000        LB )
VIN  1HTMKAAN17H397874        DATE            3588277C2
```

FIGURE 1-25 A VIN on an OEM vehicle identification decal.

To identify and interpret a VIN, follow the steps in **SKILL DRILL 1-1**.

▶ Engine Emission Decals

Engine emission decals are required by law for any vehicle certified for on-highway use. Even off-highway engines use emission decals because the decal provides important information such as the engine serial number, arrangement number, or controlled parts list, which are needed by a technician to locate service information, order parts, and perform engine service. Engine power ratings and emission family information are found on the decal as well. Valve adjustment and engine speed specifications are pieces of emission decal information of particular usefulness to technicians. On newer engines, any emission control system the vehicle or engine is equipped with is listed on the decal. When vehicles are inspected for compliance with emission regulations, acronyms are used to verify that the equipment is in place and operating **TABLE 1-4**. It is important for technicians to be familiar with the acronyms on the decal.

To identify and interpret an engine emission decal, follow the steps in **SKILL DRILL 1-2**.

▶ Engine and Trip Information

The ECM is rich in information for technicians and those managing vehicles in a fleet. Accessing the portion of the ECM where engine-vehicle operating parameters and trip

Seventeen-Character Vehicle Identification Number (VIN)									
Typical VIN	IHT	M	K	AA	N	I	7	H	397874
Character Position	1, 2, 3	4	5	6, 7	8	9	10	11	12 thru 17
Code Description									
Manufacturer, Make, Vehicle Type									
Chassis, Front Axle Position, Brakes									
Vehicle Model Series, Cab									
Engine Model, Horsepower Range									
Gross Vehicle Weight Rating (GVWR)									
Check Digit									
Vehicle Model Year									
Plant of Manufacture									
Production Number									

FIGURE 1-26 A breakdown of a VIN, which identifies unique vehicle features.

SKILL DRILL 1-1 Identifying and Interpreting a Vehicle Identification Number

VEHICLE PRODUCTION YEAR VIN KEY

10th Digit in VIN	Production Year	10th Digit in VIN	Production Year
I	2001	C	2012
2	2002	D	2013
3	2003	E	2014
4	2004	F	2015
5	2005	G	2016
6	2006	H	2017
7	2007	J	2018
8	2008	K	2019
9	2009	L	2020
A	2010	M	2021
B	2011		

1. Inspect the vehicle for a VIN identification plate or stamping in the following locations: the driver-side door jamb, the top or side of right frame rail near the front of the vehicle, the left windshield post pillar, beneath the hood on either the driver or passenger side of the vehicle, under a panel on the dash on the passenger side of the vehicle (in the area where a glove box would be found). Most vehicles have a VIN in multiple locations.

2. Record the VIN and enter it into a website that identifies the VIN information, such as the type of braking system, gross vehicle weight, the type of engine, or the manufacturing plant where the vehicle was produced. Or, identify the vehicle's production year using the chart at the left.

3. Connect an electronic service tool to the vehicle's data link connector located next to the steering column below the dash panel. Switch the ignition key on, but do not start the engine (key on, engine off [KOEO]).

4. Navigate to a screen or window in the service tool where the VIN is located and record the information. Compare the chassis VIN to the VIN stored in the engine's electronic control module to check whether they correspond.

information are stored provides valuable insights into all aspects of vehicle operation **FIGURE 1-27**. Fuel economy and idle time, maintenance schedules, abuse conditions, and fault codes are just of few examples of common trip information available. Most late-model vehicles have driver information displays, which are LCD screens that are easily connected to the on-board vehicle network. Using this type of display makes it easy to navigate to a wide variety of engine and vehicle data. Quick access to this information is often required by a technician during road calls and routine service. Software is available to download trip information for analysis of vehicle operations by fleet managers.

To record engine and trip information, follow the steps in **SKILL DRILL 1-3**.

TABLE 1-4: Common Emission System Acronyms

Acronym	Emission System
CAC	Charge air cooler
CCV	Closed crankcase ventilation
DOC	Diesel oxidation catalyst
DPF	Diesel particulate filter
ECM	Electronic control module
EGR	Exhaust gas recirculation
LNC	Lean NO$_X$ catalyst
LNT	Lean NO$_X$ trap
SCR	Selective catalytic reduction
TC	Turbocharger

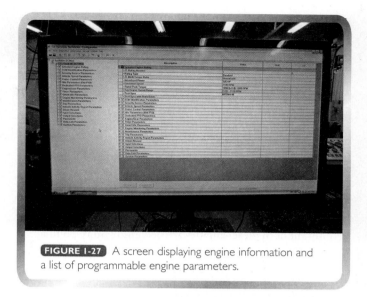

FIGURE 1-27 A screen displaying engine information and a list of programmable engine parameters.

SKILL DRILL 1-2 Identifying and Interpreting an Engine Emission Decal

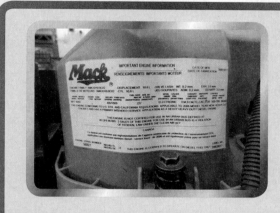

1. All medium- and heavy-duty emission decals are located on a vehicle's engine, not on the chassis as light-duty vehicle decals are. Inspect the valve cover and other engine surfaces for an EPA or EURO standard emission decal.

2. Record the engine serial number, horsepower, rated rpm, fuel rate, valve adjustment specifications, and the acronyms for emission control systems.

3. Use the acronyms along with OEM service literature, aftermarket manuals, or internet research to interpret what the acronyms mean, or use **TABLE 1-4**.

4. Inspect the vehicle and identify whether the vehicle is equipped with the systems listed on the decal.

5. List the systems and report your results.

SKILL DRILL 1-3 Recording Engine and Trip Information

1. Turn the ignition switch of the vehicle to the key-on-only position.

2. Using a driver's information display, navigate to find any fault codes, fuel consumption, and idle time data.

3. Using OEM software, connect to the vehicle's data link connector.

4. Download and store a vehicle trip report.

5. Record the engine's serial numbers and power ratings from the appropriate screens.

Wrap-Up

Ready for Review

▶ Diesel engines have widespread use in transportation, construction, mining, emergency services, military applications, and electric power generation.

▶ Diesel engines are the primary engines used in heavy-duty and commercial vehicles because they produce more power while using less fuel and last longer than other types of engines.

▶ Diesel engine use in automobiles has varied over the years, but modern diesel engines are becoming more popular in automobiles because they achieve 25–60% better fuel economy than gasoline-powered engines, and they have more power and provide quieter, smoother engine operation than older diesel technology.

▶ Diesel engines are the most efficient combustion system, converting burning fuel into the most mechanical energy in comparison to any other engine technology.

▶ Rudolf Diesel developed the concept of the CI combustion system. In his engine, heat produced from compressing air, not the heat of an electric spark, ignited fuel.

▶ Diesel's original concept of a highly efficient engine caught the attention of other inventors, who adapted it for use in smaller, lighter transportation applications. By the 1920s, Robert Bosch developed compact injection pumps and governors that enabled smaller diesels to power motor vehicles.

▶ Diesel engines today can meet and exceed the emissions standards of gasoline engines. Not only are the emissions of diesel engines as clean as, if not cleaner than, gasoline-fueled engines, but they also contain 20–40% less GHGs.

▶ A diesel engine uses substantially less fuel to produce the same horsepower (kilowatts) as a similarly displaced gasoline-fueled engine.

▶ The diesel engine has significantly higher torque output than a similarly displaced gasoline-fueled engine. Higher compression ratios produce even higher torque output.

▶ Diesel engines typically operate three to five times longer than gasoline-fueled engines before wearing out. Because diesel engines must withstand higher combustion chamber forces than gasoline-powered engines, more durable construction features are utilized in a diesel engine. Diesel engines turn slower than SI engines and have better cylinder wall lubrication.

▶ Some noxious emissions are much lower from diesel engines than from gasoline-fueled engines. Diesels produce lower amounts of CO and HCs.

▶ Diesel fuel contains more carbon than gasoline, but less energy is required to refine diesel fuel than gasoline.

▶ New fuel efficiency standards for commercial trucks and buses mean that CO_2 emissions will be lower; these standards will also enable heavy-duty engines to nearly double fuel mileage compared to just a few years ago.

▶ DPFs filter and trap soot in the exhaust system. The process of cleaning soot from a filter is called regeneration.

▶ Active DPF regeneration requires dosing of the exhaust stream with fuel, which is used to heat the exhaust system catalysts.

▶ Passive regeneration of the DPF filter uses the natural exhaust heat and other chemical reactions to oxidize or burn out soot.

▶ SCR is an exhaust aftertreatment technology that targets only NO_x emissions.

▶ RFS and Energy Security legislation require diesel engines to use more biologically derived fuel in future years.

▶ Common rail engines have fuel systems capable of electronically varying injection pressure, injection timing, and the injection rate.

▶ Ultra-low-sulfur fuels have fewer than 15 ppm of sulfur and are needed to enable the use of DPF and SCR exhaust system aftertreatment technology.

▶ Emission legislation requires diesel engines to meet minimum life expectancy standards and remain emission compliant during their useful life. The useful life requirement is measured by time in service, distance traveled, or accumulated engine hours.

Vocabulary Builder

biodiesel A fuel derived from a plant or animal source.

common rail A high-pressure injection system that electronically varies injection pressure, timing, and rate.

compression-ignition (CI) A combustion mechanism that ignites fuel by using the heat derived from compressing air as an ignition source.

compression ratio A comparison between total cylinder volume and clearance volume (the space left in the cylinder when the piston is at TDC).

diesel particulate filter (DPF) An exhaust emission aftertreatment device that filters soot particulate from the exhaust stream.

down speeding A strategy that takes advantage of a diesel engine's high torque output at low engine speeds by lowering drive axle gear ratios. The engine operates at lower rpm while operating at highway speeds.

greenhouse gas (GHG) Gases that are believed to contribute to global warming.

Technician Duties

Commercial vehicle technicians, are the people who inspect, repair, and diagnose mechanical, electrical, and electronic control systems in heavy-duty trucks, buses, trailers, and medium-duty commercial transportation trucks. They are employed by new truck and trailer dealerships, garages of commercial fleets, specialty repair shops, transit and bus companies, plus other service centers, which may include service shops. Technicians are also employed by vehicle manufacturers to perform diagnostic work and major repairs or replacement of components on new vehicles.

On any typical workday a truck-coach and trailer technician will be involved in any of the following:

- Road testing vehicles, performing diagnostic testing of vehicle systems and components using specialized equipment and diagnostic software to identify and pinpoint faults or validate their proper operation.
- Adjusting, repairing, or replacing parts and components of engine and chassis systems including the frame cab, body, air brakes, steering, transmissions, drive axles, fuel injection systems, hydraulic, exhaust aftertreatment, air conditioning, electrical, and electronic systems. **FIGURE 2-1** shows the parts department of a truck service center in a typical heavy-duty vehicle dealership.
- Testing and adjusting repaired systems to manufacturer's performance specifications.
- Performing inspections and preventative maintenance service, such as chassis lubrication, oil changes, and tire repairs.
- Making operating and service recommendations to customers about vehicle repairs.
- Completing reports, reviewing work orders, and discussing work with a supervisor.

While many technicians become skilled in diagnosing, servicing, and repairing most vehicle systems, specialization of skills can take place in the areas of engine and fuel systems, transmission and driveline, air conditioning, refrigeration and heating systems, brakes, steering, vehicle alignment, trailer repair, or diagnostic services.

Job Classifications

The commercial vehicle industry offers a range of employment opportunities. One need not be an experienced technician to enter this field. A variety of entry level jobs in service facilities provide a helpful starting point to get exposure to the trade. Cleaning vehicles, pick-up and delivery of vehicles, equipment, and/or parts, assisting other technicians performing chassis lubrication and oil change services, and washing parts are common activities that can provide useful experience when making a decision about whether to begin a career in the industry. The training and exposure provided by working and learning in a service facility or vocational college, such as that shown in **FIGURE 2-2**, can also lead to positions in management, sales, technical support, or teaching. Service managers, service writers, and technical advisors are typically recruited after they have demonstrated skill and expertise in the trade as technicians.

Service Technicians

Joining the commercial vehicle service industry in its repair and service sector as a service technician is the most popular trade pathway. This position allows for maximum exposure to the most recent technological developments and advancements in the industry. Becoming a service technician may require the completion of a college program. Many of these programs are run in partnership with truck manufacturers who provide prospective technicians with an in-depth education and some practical experience in the operation and service of all commercial vehicle systems. The experience gained working on the job provides students with the necessary skills to handle troubleshooting in service facilities while using the classroom instruction provided by the vocational school or manufacturer. Technicians are expected to be knowledgeable in machine shop processes, pneumatics, hydraulics, electronics, as well as in computer

FIGURE 2-1 Inside a parts department of a truck service center for a typical heavy-duty vehicle dealership.

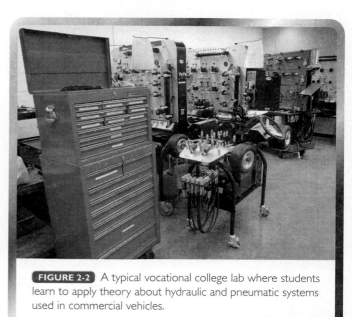

FIGURE 2-2 A typical vocational college lab where students learn to apply theory about hydraulic and pneumatic systems used in commercial vehicles.

skills required to perform many diagnostic and service procedures. **FIGURE 2-3** shows a technician performing repairs on a heavy-duty on-highway truck.

Job opportunities are currently predicted to grow at an annual rate of 15% between 2010 and 2020. Retirement by many older workers is also expected to increase demand for more technicians equipped with newer information about the latest technologically advanced equipment. Entry level positions in the industry include tire service, performing service maintenance, or simply assisting experienced technicians in the capacity of a trainee or apprentice, as they are correctly referred to.

Educational Requirements

Although not always compulsory, depending on your country of residence, service technicians are normally required to successfully complete trade related courses or a program at a college or vocational school in addition to having a high school diploma or completion certificate. In most countries, employers prefer technicians who have completed an apprenticeship or received certification from a vocational training program. Most employers only recruit technicians with educational qualifications from an accredited college certificate or associate degree program. For instance, in Canada, trade qualifications are mandatory to work on motor vehicles operated on public roads. A formal apprenticeship period must be served with an employer, as the students in **FIGURE 2-4** are doing, before applying for a final general certificate of qualification. After registering the apprenticeship contract with the provincial governing body, apprentices are required to meet performance-based learning outcomes and complete in-school trade-related classes before taking the final exam for a certificate of qualification. An inter provincial red seal is granted to technicians with qualifying exam results to work in all provinces in Canada.

FIGURE 2-3 A technician performing repairs on a heavy-duty on-highway truck.

FIGURE 2-4 Apprenticeship students at a vocational college learning to perform electrical diagnostic work on a school bus.

ASE Certification

In the United States, while certification is not a mandatory requirement to work in the trade, the National Institute for Automotive Service Excellence (ASE) offers credentialing to truck-coach and medium-duty truck technicians. Possessing ASE certification leads to better employment opportunities. To gain the ASE qualifications, candidates need a minimum of two year's working experience before taking an exam for each area of specialization. The National Institute for Automotive Service Excellence (ASE) administers certification procedures throughout the United States. Certification tests are scheduled throughout the year and taken at secure testing centers nationwide. The certification areas needed for heavy-duty truck technicians are the following:

- T-series for medium-/heavy-duty truck technicians
- S-series for school bus technicians
- H-series for transit bus technicians (as shown in **FIGURE 2-5**)

For those aspiring to be a master technician in medium- and heavy-duty trucks, successful completion in the following T-series certification areas is required: T2, T3, T4, T5, T6, and T7.

Master Technicians

In the United States, several years of experience and proper educational qualifications can fast-track a technician's career to that of a master technician status. To be certified as a T-, H-, or S-series ASE Master Technician, the following certification tests must be taken and passed:

- T-Series Master Tech: T2 through T7 inclusive
- S-Series Master Tech: S1 through S6 inclusive
- H-Series Master Tech: H2 through H7 inclusive

FIGURE 2-5 Inside a transit bus garage where repair and maintenance are performed on a fleet of urban transit buses.

Specialty Technicians

Electronics, engines, brakes, hybrid vehicle, and alternate fuels are just a few of the areas in commercial vehicle service and repair on which a technician can specialize. A specialized technician is engaged in an in-depth, continuous education to develop and refine skills to diagnose, service, and maintain the latest vehicle technologies. FIGURE 2-6 shows a recently overhauled S-50 Detroit engine. The engine is connected to a dynamometer in a test cell to validate its operation and performance. The overhaul and testing of diesel engines is generally performed by a specialist technician with advanced qualifications often obtained from the original equipment manufacturer.

S- and H-Series Certification

There are two certification series under Automotive Service Excellence (ASE) specifically for transit operations: the S-series (school bus) and the H-series (transit bus) certification. All ASE's heavy-duty certifications are designed in such a way that the number represents the subject matter and the letter represents the classification of the vehicle type. Examples of specific S- and H-tests are the following:

- H1 certification for compressed natural gas (CNG)–fueled bus engines
- H8 certification for preventive maintenance
- S1 certification for school bus body systems

Other Countries' Qualifications

Just as outlined above for the United States and Canada, many other countries also have qualifications and formal training specific to those locations. For example, countries like Australia, New Zealand, South Africa, and the United Kingdom also have their own formal qualification standards. If you are a budding technician in those countries, and indeed any other geographic location, you should seek information from the appropriate regulatory authorities about the specific requirements and training packages relevant to that country.

Working Conditions

Bus and truck technicians normally work in well-lit, well-ventilated shops, such as the one shown in FIGURE 2-7. Shop cleanliness, order, plus care and protection of customer/fleet vehicles are important to a successful and respected business. Health and safety legislation demand strict adherence by employers to regulations in the use of certified personal and shop safety equipment for all workers. Today, working conditions minimize exposure to any working conditions that have the

FIGURE 2-6 A recently overhauled engine connected to a dynamometer in a test cell.

FIGURE 2-7 This chassis inspection pit used by a fleet operation is typical of a clean, well-ventilated, and well-lit service facility.

potential to harm shop workers. Professional looking uniforms and or coveralls are always worn to protect clothing from grime, which can be picked up during some work operations. Work is occasionally performed outside a shop environment if a vehicle cannot be towed or moved inside for repairs. Some businesses even specialize in mobile service work where technicians will travel to a customer's workplace with tools and basic supplies to perform minor repair work. A mobile repair vehicle is shown in FIGURE 2-8 .

If you prefer hands-on work, like problem solving, and enjoy working with tools, repair technician is an ideal career. Having one's own tools and skills enables a technician amazing mobility to work anywhere there are trucks, buses, and trailers needing repair and maintenance.

▶ Employability Skills

Although we have been communicating all of our lives, most of us are not aware of the importance of the communication skills of listening, reading, writing, and speaking. In fact, they are critical skills in the workplace. Learning and applying good communication skills will save you time in the workplace and help you avoid or get through tricky situations. These skills will build over time, and you will find that you learn something new every day when you encounter new situations or meet new people. It is a lifelong learning process to perfect your communication skills.

Since communication is an essential workplace skill needed to function successfully in the commercial-vehicle service facility, this entire section is dedicated to communication. This chapter describes the steps to becoming an effective communicator, offers tips on how to be a good listener—the first step in good communication—and explains how to speak to both customers and your coworkers. Along the way, we will discuss the requirement for writing and preparing documentation used in the workplace.

Effective Listening

Effective listening is an essential skill. We may hear what someone is saying, but are we truly understanding what the person is trying to communicate? The listening process can be difficult to perfect, but is one of the most important skills to possess when gathering information from a customer or any other person. The active listener, like the technician shown in FIGURE 2-9 , focuses all of his or her attention on the speaker, including verbal and nonverbal messages. When appropriate, the active listener encourages the speaker to further communicate details that may have otherwise been left out.

The Listening Process

To be a good listener, we need to be aware of barriers that can disrupt the listening process. These barriers can be mental and physical.

Mental barriers are thoughts and feelings that interfere with our listening, such as our own assumptions, emotions, and prejudices. To fully absorb what someone is telling us, we need to learn to set these feelings aside. It takes effort and is not always easy, but it is important to keep an open mind throughout the listening process. For example, when listening to a customer who is describing his or her vehicle concern, it is good practice to allow the customer to fully complete what he or she is saying, even if you believe you have all the information you need.

Keeping an open mind is also an important first step in practicing empathy, discussed later.

As a listener and active participant, we can encourage the flow of communication by welcoming the speaker, letting him or her know that we care enough to want to understand the message, and acknowledging the speaker's feelings and concerns. To accomplish that, give the speaker your undivided attention by focusing on him or her. This means removing as many distractions as possible. Stop what you are doing, clear your mind of distractions, and look the speaker in the eye.

FIGURE 2-8 Mobile repair truck.

FIGURE 2-9 The active listener focuses all of his or her attention on the speaker.

As the person is speaking, you will also need to provide listening feedback, which indicates to the speaker that you are engaged in what he or she is saying. Feedback can be nonverbal (e.g., facial expressions, body posture) and verbal. Nonverbal language, such as nodding while listening and gesturing while speaking, is used to reinforce or add emphasis. If, while speaking, you send a conflicting message, such as looking annoyed while stating that you value the customer's opinion, the person may tend to believe the nonverbal message over the verbal one, even though it is only half of the total message. For example, consider a customer who contacts you because of a vehicle that will not start and who has his vehicle towed into your shop. The customer complains that the cause is a "bad headlight." Regardless of your personal opinion, you must, as a professional, maintain a sincere and attentive attitude toward the customer. Because nonverbal communication is perceived to be more spontaneous and less conscious, most people tend to believe the nonverbal message more than the actual words expressed.

Empathy

Empathy can help us to avoid selective hearing. To empathize with someone is to attempt to see the situation from his or her point of view. It requires good listening skills, which include an effective use of verbal and nonverbal listening feedback, in order to take in and consider the message without applying our own biases. True empathy means breaking down or putting aside existing mental barriers. For example, when a customer brings a vehicle in with a fault requiring an expensive repair that is not in his or her budget, we risk coming across as uncaring with a "take it or leave it" attitude if we expect the customer to do the repair regardless of the expense. Expressing your understanding of the customer's situation and seeking to explore valid options to resolve the issue will go a long way in building trust with the customer. Remember, we can empathize with people even if we do not agree with them. Also, we do not have to take responsibility for their problem. But we can at least attempt to help them find the best possible solution that will work for them. You will know that you have demonstrated empathy when no valid options were found but the customer thanks you deeply for your assistance.

Empathy not only helps you understand the message better, but also helps you to be less reactive in a negative way as you realize you could feel the same way in that person's position. It may also help to motivate you to find a better resolution of the situation, knowing that it could be you in the very same situation.

Nonverbal Feedback

Nonverbal feedback can be a very useful tool when listening. Your body position, eye contact, and facial expression can all set the direction of a conversation.

We use body language to help emphasize our message, and when listening, we can use it to provide listening feedback. When listening to a speaker, try to sit or stand upright, while making eye contact. Try to avoid folding your arms, as this can be perceived as either an aggressive stance or defensive. At the same time, do not act too casual, such as standing with your hands in your pockets. It may seem harmless, but a customer or supervisor would likely see such a posture as a sign of disrespect or disinterest. Imagine that you are talking to a service manager during a job interview and the manager leans back and puts his or her feet up on the desk. That one gesture would send you a message about the manager's level of professionalism and his or her respect for you and overall interest in the conversation, and in turn would have an effect on the way you viewed the meeting.

Maintaining some eye contact during the conversation, and not looking at something or someone else, will also let your speaker know you are paying attention. If you are taking notes, be sure to look up periodically and make eye contact with the person.

Just as our own facial expressions are being noted by the speaker, remember to pay attention to the speaker's facial expressions to get a clearer sense of his or her message. If, for example, a customer scrunches up her face while talking about the squealing noise the brakes are making, you can probably assume the customer would be happy if you could make that noise go away.

Verbal Feedback

Verbal feedback includes very simple signals that can enhance the conversation and let the person know you comprehend. Some examples are the use of validating statements and supporting statements.

A **validating statement** shows common interest in the topic being discussed. A phrase such as "I see" or "Tell me more" indicates that you are paying attention. A validating statement also helps show empathy for the person speaking and can be a simple "I understand" or "That must be frustrating for you."

A **supporting statement** can urge the speaker to elaborate on a particular topic. Statements like "Go on" and "Give me an example" let the speaker know you would like more detail because you are genuinely interested in finding a solution. This is a necessary part of communication when you are gathering information from the customer—by asking for more details, you are likely to obtain more thorough information, giving you a better starting point for solving the problem. For example, imagine you are talking with a customer about a noise his dump truck made while going over a bump. If you were to say "Tell me more," the customer would know that you understood but wanted a little more information.

Effective Speaking

Speaking is often referred to as an art. That is because there are so many facets to effectively communicate and/or gather information. Whether you are asking a customer about a vehicle or your boss for a raise, knowing how to "artfully speak" will benefit you.

Speaking is a three-step process:

1. Think about the message.
2. Accurately present the message.

3. Check whether the message is correctly understood. If it is not, we have to respond by rethinking and reiterating the message and rechecking with our listener. This process continues until we are satisfied that the listener correctly understands our message.

Think before you speak is easier said than done, but it is not impossible. In some situations, we have time to think and plan beforehand. Others require us to think on our feet. Thinking on your feet simply means you may be called upon to answer or handle a difficult situation quickly. Having to get things right in a fast-paced setting can result in rash decisions, but there are a few tactics you can use to make these situations easier:

1. **Relax.** It is not easy to do in an urgent situation, but attempting to remain calm is extremely beneficial, keeping your mind clear and helping you to embody the confidence needed in such a situation.

2. **Listen.** If the situation requires you to answer a tough question, make sure you fully understand the question before answering. You can always ask the questioner to repeat or, better yet, rephrase the question. This gives you more time to think about your answer and also another chance to read into the intent of the question. Remember that if someone is asking a question of you, then he or she is showing interest. Interest is a good thing!

3. **Pause.** Silence is golden—when used properly. Most people are uncomfortable with silence, but it is perfectly acceptable to take slight pauses before speaking to organize your thoughts. This will also give you the advantage of controlling the pace of the conversation. If a situation that you have been put in charge of is slipping out of control, regain control with slight pauses and thoughtful answers. It may be beneficial to say something like, "Let me think about that for a second." Or you may take a few seconds to restate your understanding of the problem and the person's question. Doing so can help the other person understand that you are devoting effort to the question while giving you a bit of time to decide on an answer.

Before speaking, take a moment to consider that your tone of voice reveals a lot about your feelings and adds significant meaning to your message. The tone of voice includes how high or low the pitch of our voice is, how fast or slow we speak, how soft or loud, and most importantly, what our voice characteristics or emotional indications are.

After thinking about what we want to say, and how to say it, we can then use the second step of the process by presenting a message using verbal and nonverbal language. Remember that when we say "verbal language," we mean the actual words that are being spoken. Nonverbal language includes how we speak those words—our tone of voice, body language, and appearance—and takes into consideration the environment. Imagine you are with a friend in a quiet café, drinking coffee, and she is telling you how much she values your opinion. Now imagine that she is clenching her fists, scowling, and screaming those same words to you. It would change the message a little, wouldn't it?

The last step of the speaking process is to make sure our message is correctly understood by the listener. Look to see that the listener is making eye contact with you. If you perceive a lack of understanding or confusion, be prepared to repeat yourself while trying to explain it in another way or by using an example. Make sure you suppress any outward irritation you may feel at needing to do so. In stressful situations, the parties involved are often not as open minded as in calmer moments and are therefore not as receptive to your words. This can also end with misunderstandings and expectations that go unmet. So take the extra step and ask clarifying questions or summarize the message.

> ### ▶ Caring for the Customer
>
> A calm and happy customer or coworker is normally easy to communicate with. Most people struggle with how to handle the angry one. In almost all cases, keeping a calm and steady tone of voice and overall demeanor is the best bet. Never lose your temper; doing so will only escalate the situation and lead to an unwanted outcome.

Asking Questions

Questioning is an important speaking skill that helps keep us out of a lot of trouble. We speak to deliver a message, but many times we need more information or we need to confirm the details of an agreement. Asking questions to gather more information can provide us with enough information to make good decisions. Or, once we come to an agreement with another person, we can use questions to confirm those details. In either of these situations, we have avoided trouble. In the first case, we gathered enough information to avoid a bad decision. And in the second, we confirmed the expectations that each person had regarding the agreement, helping to avoid disappointment and loss of trust.

To use questions effectively, we need to know how to ask the right questions. We can ask three types of questions:

- Open questions
- Closed questions
- Yes or no questions

Each type of question is beneficial when used appropriately. Good communicators know when and how to use the appropriate type. In dealing with customers, we usually start with open questions to gather general information about the issue. Then we use closed questions to find out specific details. We use yes/no questions to further check or confirm the listener's responses or to gain the customer's agreement to authorize a repair or diagnostic procedure.

Open Questions

An open question encourages people to speak freely so we can gather facts, insights, and opinions from them. It is a good way to start a conversation with a new acquaintance or even a customer. Open questions usually begin with the following words:

- What
- How
- Why
- Could you tell me

For example, if you were questioning a customer about their visit to a repair facility, you could ask, "What type of service did you receive from the XYZ repair center?" This question opens the topic up for discussion and allows the customer to give details about his or her visit.

Closed Questions

If we want to know more information, we can use closed questions to establish facts and details. Closed questions usually begin with the following words:

- When
- Where
- Which
- Who
- How many
- How much

This type of question requires a specific answer, and there is usually only one answer. For example, you could ask a customer, "How many times have you visited the XYZ repair center?" or, "When did you start going to them?" These closed questions allow for only one answer, without much room for discussion. These questions help you to narrow the topic and guide the discussion in the direction you would like it to go, which is helpful when talking with a customer.

Yes/No Questions

Yes/no questions allow individuals to answer with a simple yes or no. This type of question is useful for checking or confirming a person's responses. For example, "Would you recommend them?" gets to the point and helps clarify information. We should generally not start out with yes/no questions because they discourage further explanation or discussion. However, ending with yes/no questions is a good way to get confirmation. For example, after explaining the need for replacing the customer's water pump and answering the customer's questions about the job, it would be very appropriate to ask, "Can we go ahead and replace the faulty water pump for you?"

Telephone Skills

We have learned about the important aspects of the speaking process. A phone conversation presents some different challenges. Since we cannot see each other, we can rely only upon verbal messages and some nonverbal cues, such as the tone of voice. Other nonverbal cues that we miss are body language, appearance, and the environment.

On the phone, we are limited in how we present our messages, so we need to think about our words and tone more carefully perhaps than in person. It is a good idea to plan and even write down each of the points you want to say before even picking up the phone.

Phone communication consists of three parts: greeting, exchanging messages, and finishing the call.

We should always answer a phone call by first saying hello, identifying ourselves, and identifying our place of business, succinctly and clearly. An example could be, "Hello, this is John with the XYZ repair center. How may I help you?" Try to keep your greeting friendly and short.

The second part of the phone conversation is exchanging messages. This requires concise, clear communication followed by clarifying questions and summarizing any main points. At all times, we should be polite and considerate, and remember that the most important nonverbal clue we send out over the phone is our tone of voice, since it reveals a lot about our feelings. Here are a few tips to create a good impression:

- Do not sound bored. Try to keep some inflection in your voice; do not speak in a monotone.
- Sound calm and in control, even if you were caught at a busy moment.
- No matter what, never lose your temper or patience.
- If there is a need to keep someone on hold for an extended time, offer to call him or her back, and do it.

Finish a call by confirming actions both you and the caller will take to ensure that the messages on both sides were accurately received, and end, as shown in **FIGURE 2-10**, with a pleasant and friendly goodbye. Remember to thank all customers for their business, and invite them to come back. When taking a phone message for someone else, make sure you have the caller's name and organization, contact details, the date and time of the call, and a summary of the caller's message.

When making a phone call, use these same skills and always have necessary information available to give to the person you are calling. For example, if you need to order parts, relevant vehicle information should be shared with your parts supplier. You usually need to have vehicle make, model, year, engine size, and transmission type, and many times you will need the vehicle identification number (VIN).

Giving and Receiving Instructions

A critical aspect of an efficient and well-run workshop is the ability to give clear, logical instructions and to receive instructions. Usually, instructions should contain information about who, what, when, where, why, and directions for how a task should be completed. What is the job that needs to be done? Who should do it? When should the job be done? Apart from

FIGURE 2-10 Always end calls with a friendly goodbye.

knowing what information we should include in our instructions, we should also know how to present them.

When receiving instructions, we should make sure we can understand and follow the instructions successfully. For example, the instruction "Use the tire machine to change a tubeless tire" indicates what to do. Asking follow-up questions such as, "Should I install new valve stems?" or "Should I use a new tire or retread replacement" helps ensure we understood correctly what needs to be done. Such questions may not be needed every time an instruction is given, but by clarifying, the quality of work will be closer to the person's expectations and will save time in the long run.

Communication in a Team

Being part of a team can make working an enjoyable experience or a horrible experience, depending on the team. In large part, the ability of each team member to communicate effectively will determine the success of the team. A high-performing team can accomplish much. As the saying goes, the sum is greater than its parts. We can achieve more when we effectively work together. Being part of a team allows us to:

- Learn new things from other team members
- Share ideas, knowledge, and resources
- Complement each other's strengths and weaknesses
- Feel a sense of belonging

A poorly functioning team spends a lot of time and energy bickering and blaming, and not enough time and energy being productive. Transitioning from a poorly functioning team to a high-performing team requires commitment to the team along with self-discipline. When all team members are committed to a set of common goals, they can contribute in positive ways to the success of the team.

Developing such a team requires good leadership skills as well as good followership skills. Good leadership skills involve setting a clear vision of the goals, empowering each team member to contribute his or her best efforts, and recognizing each team member's strengths and weaknesses. Good leadership also provides training or mentoring to address any weaknesses in the team. Followership is just as important as leadership. Not much would get done if everyone were a leader. Good followership skills involve being fully engaged in the team and its goals, stepping in and performing the work that needs to be done, participating fully in all decision making, and giving honest feedback.

We need to be committed to the team and team goals to make teamwork successful. Each team member should have a defined role and responsibilities that go with that role. Each member is then able to rely on the others to do their part. Think of a team as a chain; one broken link can break the whole chain. A good team player is someone who commits to being a part of that team and contributes to its success by fulfilling his or her role. Each member is then able to rely on the others to do their part. Think of a team as a chain; one broken link can break the whole chain. A good team player is someone who commits to being a part of that team and contributes to its success by fulfilling his or her role.

Effective Reading

Every day we are faced with interpreting service information, emails, voicemails, and work orders with customer concerns. Understanding these messages without the verbal and nonverbal clues that come with face-to-face communication can be more difficult.

Reading Comprehension

Technicians are required to read a lot of information, including repair orders, service information, technical service bulletins (TSBs), and training materials. Many of these reading materials can be written at high grade levels. For example, many service manuals and TSBs are written at grade level 14 and higher. Technicians need to be proficient readers to be able to comprehend this information. Before we start reading, we need to know the purpose of the particular material and what we intend to do with the information once we understand it. In reading, the objective may be to:

- Access information quickly, such as a particular specification
- Understand the information, such as how to perform a particular series of tests on a system you are diagnosing
- Remember the information, such as learning about new technology that a manufacturer is introducing to its vehicles, how it works, and what kind of tests are used during diagnosis

Once we know our reading purpose, we can choose the suitable reading method, which can be selective, comprehending, or absorbing. Selective reading is reading only the parts we need to know. This method is useful when looking for a particular piece of information. The quickest way to use selective reading is to read through the table of contents, introduction, conclusion, headings, and index until we find what we are looking for. When we use comprehending reading, we need to interpret and understand the information. Understanding what is being communicated requires careful attention to the structure of the sentences and paragraphs. To use an absorbing reading method, we need to:

- Interpret and understand the information
- Absorb it into our memory
- Review the information regularly

When we talk about reading, we are not concerned only about how fast we can read but also how well we understand and retain what we have read. Unfortunately, the faster we try to read, the less we are likely to concentrate on the meaning, so these two objectives (speed and comprehension) work against each other. Reading is about practice, and the more we practice, the faster, more efficiently, and more accurately we can read.

defective equipment, you will need to complete both an accident report and a defective equipment report. On the report, you will record the date when the defect was detected, the location of the defective equipment, the name of the equipment, the serial number (if possible), and a description of the defect and the action you have taken. Then sign your name as the reporter. Finally, notify your supervisor.

Completing an Accident Report

Safety is the most important issue in the workplace. We must make a conscious decision to work safely and act responsibly to protect others and ourselves. Unfortunately, accidents do happen. When one occurs, an accident report should be completed by those involved, both the victim and witnesses, if possible. The information in the report is used to protect both employees and employers. It protects the employer and employee against false claims. And it protects future employees by calling attention to a situation that caused an accident, so hopefully measures can be taken to prevent it in the future. To ensure that the information is accurate, the accident report should be completed as soon as practically possible while the facts of the accident are still fresh in everyone's memory.

A typical accident report includes the date and time when the accident happened, the location where the accident happened, the name of the person who was injured, the name of any witnesses, the details of the accident, any first aid treatment provided, and any medical assistance rendered. It is also important to note if the accident will be subject to, or covered by, any insurance claims. Finally, the form needs to be signed by the person reporting the accident and turned in to the supervisor.

Completing a Vehicle Inspection Form

We provide customers with a very beneficial service when we perform a thorough inspection of their vehicles. When performing an inspection, we need to check that all major components and systems are operational, secured, and safe in accordance with the vehicle manufacturer's recommendations.

This means testing the operation of the electrical and mechanical systems, such as lights and brakes, and visual inspections of the components, such as tires and glass.

An inspection form is a useful guide when conducting a vehicle inspection. By following the checklist, a technician can test all the components in a systematic way and ensure that they are operational or serviceable. It also becomes a record for the shop to bring a customer's attention to needed service, or in the event that a customer declines repairs, shows that the repair shop made the customer aware of them. Many repair shops use their own inspection form that lists every item tested, which are known as points. Depending on the number of points covered, the inspection may be called by a particular name, these names are generally associated with either a time or distance travelled specification.

To complete the inspection form, you must inspect all the components and systems on the checklist, such as:

- Fluids, belts, and hoses
- Steering and suspension system
- Brakes

- Drive line
- Fuel system
- Exhaust system
- Tires
- Lighting system
- Electrical system
- Visibility
- Seat belts

General Components

Once the inspection is completed, the results should be presented to the customer so he or she can decide if any repairs are to be made. This is where verbal communication comes back into play, as it is important to accurately communicate with the customer so he or she has a good understanding of what the vehicle needs, why it is important to have it repaired, and the consequences of not repairing it. All of this conversation should be based on trust and the relationship you have built with the customer during his or her experience with you and the shop. And as you can see, successful communication includes good verbal, nonverbal, listening, clarifying, writing, and presentation skills.

Lockout/Tagout

There are many dangers in the repair facility that may need to be properly documented and tagged. One example could be a defective vehicle lift. If a problem is noticed with a piece of equipment, a lockout/tagout procedure should be followed. Lockout/tagout procedures have been developed to prevent avoidable and unnecessary workshop accidents. Most workshops have a defined process and steps to be followed which should be adhered to at all times. These procedures have many functions:

- The tag notifies other users that the tool or component is dangerous to use, as shown in **FIGURE 2-17**. Any equipment that is found to be faulty needs to be identified so that other users are not put at risk. Write the fault, the date, and your name on the tag. Attach the tag to the tool. Smaller equipment should also be tagged and placed in a

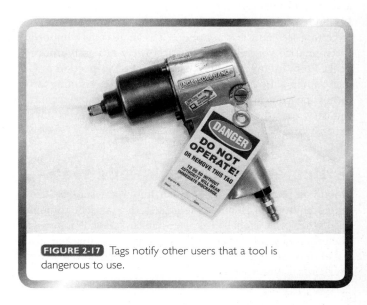

FIGURE 2-17 Tags notify other users that a tool is dangerous to use.

location where it is not forgotten. Notify your supervisor so that repairs or a replacement can be arranged.

- If a machine is faulty, the lockout procedure is used. Most large workshop equipment is permanently wired to the electrical supply and usually will have an isolation switch that will disconnect the electrical power. A lockout tag should be placed on the isolation switch as well as the equipment. Turn the machine off at the power and master switches, attaching the lockout tag in a manner that prevents the switches from being turned on. Once again, notify your supervisor so repairs can be arranged.
- The lockout/tagout procedure is also used to notify other technicians that a vehicle is not drivable.

Your workshop will have a procedure for vehicle lockout/tagout. Most workshops have a defined process and steps to be followed, which should be adhered to at all times. It may involve the technician filling out a "defective vehicle" label listing the nature of the defect, name of the technician, and date and time of the defect.

If you remove the vehicle keys, do not keep them in your pocket or on your workbench. Attach a label or tag to the keys that identify the vehicle they belong to and store them in a secure key organizer.

If a vehicle is going through a relearn process (i.e., the vehicle's computer communicating with another computer), it may be necessary to leave the ignition on for many hours. In this case, tag the vehicle with instructions to leave the ignition on; otherwise a passing technician may turn it off in an effort to be helpful. If a vital component has been removed for service, it may not be obvious to a casual observer, so it is necessary to tag the vehicle. The best place to tag the vehicle is in on the steering wheel or driver's window where others trying to operate the vehicle will see it. Also, remove the ignition key and store it in a safe place. Ask your supervisor to demonstrate the lockout/tagout process used in your workshop and to show you the location of the key organizer.

In conclusion, communication is a critical component of a successful business and an efficient workplace. Often overlooked in our current digital world, where face-to-face contact is getting less and less common, it is increasingly important to familiarize yourself with a wide variety of communication skills. From listening to simply filling out an inspection report, using and practicing these skills can be a big determining factor in how far you can go and how much money you make in the industry. And the good news is that it does not even require expensive tools!

▶ Professional Workplace Habits

Good communication skills are an important start to strong employability skills, but for true success, they must be combined with other professional workplace habits. Personal appearance and orderliness are important, as are respect for time and space. All of those skills and habits, then, can be applied to delivering excellent customer service.

Appearance and Environment

Our appearance is the image we present of ourselves to the public. All aspects of our physical appearance, including our clothes, jewelry, hairstyle, posture, and outward demeanor, culminate to create the first impression made in any encounter. That first impression often informs the judgment others make about us, which in turn affects the level of respect and trust you achieve. It is much harder to convey your message effectively if your audience is distracted by some aspect of your appearance or does not take you seriously. When working in a professional environment, always do your best to look professional. Remember that, while you are at work, you embody the image of your company. Shorts, improper footwear, or untucked or filthy clothes can all send negative signals to a customer. A customer will be much more willing to have his or her vehicle serviced by someone who looks well put together, such as the person shown in **FIGURE 2-18**, than someone who does not.

The surrounding environment is also worth consideration, as it can affect the outcome of our communication. A disorganized, cluttered, and dirty area leaves a negative impression with most customers, leading them to believe that you do not care about appearances or quality. Look around you and evaluate the housekeeping. Is it clean, organized, and inviting? Or is it neglected, dirty, and gross? A little housekeeping goes a long way toward making customers feel comfortable. You will also want to avoid distractions such as excessive background noise, a blaring radio, or inappropriate coworker conversations. **FIGURE 2-19** shows a professional, orderly environment.

Interruptions by both coworkers and phone calls can hinder communication. Whenever it is in your power to do so, work to keep these distractions at a minimum.

FIGURE 2-18 When working in a professional environment, always do your best to look presentable.

FIGURE 2-19 A professional and orderly work environment inspires customer confidence.

Be aware of dangers around you as well. While most insurance policies prohibit customers in the work area, there may be occasional times when they need to see a particular issue. If you have to take customers into the shop, always escort them, and be sure to keep them safe. Do they need safety glasses on? Escort them back out of the shop as soon as possible and continue the conversation in the customer write-up area.

Time and Space

We know that in the work environment, time is money. This is especially true in most repair shop environments, where every minute is costing somebody something—the customer, the shop owner, and/or the technician. Punctuality is an important nonverbal message in a business environment. When you are punctual, clocking in on time, for example, as shown in **FIGURE 2-20**, you demonstrate a good work attitude

and professionalism. Punctual means showing up on time (typically 5–10 minutes early to get ready to start work at the appointed time). If you have an unexpected delay, such as finding a flat tire when you get into your car to go to work, make sure you call your supervisor and let him or her know what happened and when you will be in. The same applies if you need to call in sick; do so as soon as you can so that other arrangements can be made.

Punctuality also means you will complete the job when you say you will. If you tell a customer his vehicle will be finished at 3:00, you should plan on finishing it prior to that just in case something goes wrong. Occasionally, there will be unforeseen events that keep you from completing a job on time, but those should be rare exceptions. If there is a delay, then you need to communicate that to your customers as quickly as possible so that they can make other arrangements.

Lastly, you should be giving a full measure of work for the time you are being paid. Routinely texting your friends or taking personal calls during work hours is stealing from your employer. Use your work time efficiently, just as you would want your own employees to do.

When we say that space is a part of nonverbal language, we are referring to the physical space between ourselves and the people with whom we are communicating, commonly known as "personal space" (generally 3 feet (0.9 m)). How we use personal space depends on how we feel about others; it is also a consideration for another person's comfort level. Familiarity, gender, status, and culture will determine the use of our personal space. Be aware of space as a nonverbal message and adjust accordingly.

Customer Service

Good customer service is vital in today's competitive business environment. As illustrated by **FIGURE 2-21**, the quality of our customer service influences people to choose us over our competitors; good service makes people feel good about continuing to buy our products or services, which is how the business gets the money to pay your wages. So, customer service has a direct impact on the ability of employers to hire employees, provide

FIGURE 2-20 Punctuality sends an important nonverbal message about professionalism.

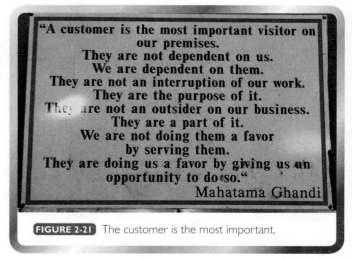

"A customer is the most important visitor on our premises.
They are not dependent on us.
We are dependent on them.
They are not an interruption of our work.
They are the purpose of it.
They are not an outsider on our business.
They are a part of it.
We are not doing them a favor by serving them.
They are doing us a favor by giving us an opportunity to do so."
Mahatama Ghandi

FIGURE 2-21 The customer is the most important.

wages, and offer promotions. In fact, most vehicle manufacturers place great importance on the customer satisfaction index (CSI) rating at their dealerships. The CSI rating is gathered from virtually all of the customers who have service work completed. The CSI rating is reported each month and used to evaluate individual technicians and the entire service facility. If the CSI rating is high, bonuses can be paid to everyone who contributed to that success. If the CSI rating slips, bonuses can be withheld, and new processes can be implemented to help restore the CSI rating.

To be able to provide good customer service, we must first understand who our customers are and then identify their needs. Internal customers, such as parts suppliers, are as important as external customers. By helping our coworkers with their jobs, it will ultimately help our external customers and our organization. It is helpful to remember that it is almost always external customers who bring resources into your organization when they trade their money for your service or product.

Being focused on customer service, as shown in **FIGURE 2-22**, means you are fully engaged in providing the highest level of service that you can. This includes clear, friendly communication to help prevent misunderstandings and helping to establish achievable expectations. It also includes simple things like not getting grease on the vehicle's steering wheel, upholstery, or paint. And it means taking extra steps such as washing the vehicle when the work is completed or vacuuming it out so it is cleaner than when you started working on it. Keep in mind, one of the most important parts of customer service is repairing the vehicle correctly the first time. This goes a long way toward maintaining customer satisfaction.

In most cases, we can divide our customers into three categories: those who are more concerned about getting things right; those who want to get things done; and those who just want to get along with people. Each of these customers is motivated by different factors. The person who wants the job done right will usually not be interested in lesser quality parts and will want you to take the time to make sure the job is not rushed. If the diagnosis was rushed and was incorrect, this person will likely not be happy.

People who are most interested getting things done will probably be very keen to have the repairs finished on schedule. If the vehicle is not finished on schedule, this person will likely not be happy. For the person who just wants to get along with people, it will be important that a level of trust is maintained. If trust is broken, it will be hard to regain. We have to identify what our customers' needs are, so we can serve them properly.

If you are the one in charge of questioning the customer about symptoms, be sure to get specific information from the customer about what happens, when it happens, and how often it happens. Take notes that will help to diagnose the problem. Then be sure that, when relaying this information to someone else, the other person understands the symptoms with the same level of detail that you do. For example, a customer is concerned about a particular noise in a vehicle. If the noise does not happen all the time, then we would ask when the noise happens or under what conditions the noise happens. We may need to prompt the customer with follow-up questions like, "Does it happen when it is cold or hot, or when going around a corner or over bumps, or when braking or accelerating?"

We may need to ask where he or she thinks the noise is coming from. Of course, if the noise can be reproduced, we may need to drive or ride with the customer so that he or she can identify the noise for us.

Protecting the Customer's Vehicle

Care should always be taken to protect the customer's vehicle during servicing by using fender covers and floor mats. Since the purpose of fender covers and floor mats is to protect the vehicle, you should always inspect them for damage prior to use. Ensure that fender covers and floor mats are clean on both sides and do not have any metal or hard objects stuck to them. Ensure that they fit securely and provide adequate protection.

Fender covers cannot generally be used on heavy vehicles because the fenders are attached to the hood. The covers would fall off upon raising the hood. On cab-over-engine (COE) tractors the hood folds forward for servicing, so there is no provision for using fender covers. If fender covers can be fitted to the vehicle you are servicing, then you should use them.

Some fender covers are made with a magnetic strip in them, which is designed to help hold the fender cover in place. Unfortunately, the magnet attracts metal particles, which can be held between the cover and the fender and scratch the paint. Always check these types of covers very thoroughly for metal particles.

Preparing the Vehicle for Customer Pickup

To ensure that the vehicle is prepared to return to the customer per school/company policy:

- Identify shop policy or procedures for returning a customer's vehicle.
- Check the vehicle for cleanliness.
- Clean the vehicle according to shop policy.

FIGURE 2-22 Focus on customer service and communicate clearly.

- Remove all vehicle protection prior to customer pickup.
- Dispose of any waste products in an environmentally safe manner, and clean and return fender covers, seat covers, and floor mats to the appropriate storage area.

Make sure all vehicle protection is removed prior to releasing the vehicle to the customer. After removing the vehicle protection, such as fender covers, floor mats, and steering and seat covers, ensure that no damage to the vehicle has been sustained during repair. Check the vehicle for cleanliness by ensuring that all trash has been removed and no oil or grease marks are on the vehicle prior to returning it to the customer. Check that all of the windows are crystal clear, that the dashboard, knobs, steering wheel, and center console are spotless and clean, that floor mats have no dirt, and that there are no fingerprints on the door latches, fenders, or the backs of the mirrors. Now go back through the vehicle and look for tools. Wear appropriate personal protective gear such as safety glasses and gloves when working with cleaning materials.

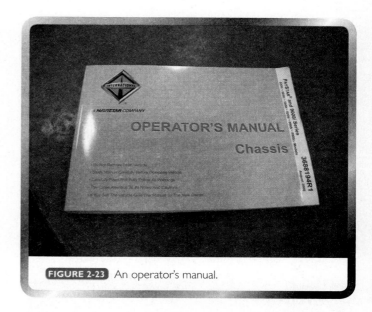

FIGURE 2-23 An operator's manual.

▶ Vehicle and Service Resources

Vehicle and customer information from various sources provides the fundamental knowledge required to conduct repairs and servicing. Today, the ability to properly perform maintenance and repair activities is increasingly dependent on the technician's ability to research and apply technical information. Vehicle information can come from a number of sources, including vehicle identification plates, operator's manuals, shop manuals, repair orders, service and parts programs, and technical service bulletins. The various sources of information can be published in books or manuals or made available through software packages or the Internet. It is important that you know how to research and apply this information correctly so you can properly repair and service vehicles.

Vehicle Operators' Manual

Manufacturers supply a vehicle operator's manual, which comes with every new vehicle purchased. The operator's manual is usually kept in the vehicle's glove compartment. Second-hand vehicles may or may not have the operator's manual in the glove compartment. The **operator's manual**, like that shown in **FIGURE 2-23**, contains information about the vehicle and is a valuable source of information for both the owner and the technician.

The information contained in the operator's manual will vary for each manufacturer. In general, it contains basic information on the safe operation and specifications of the vehicle. A typical operator's manual includes an overview of the controls and features of the vehicle; the proper operation, care, and maintenance of the vehicle; operator service procedures; and specifications or technical data. The operator's manual also details such elements as vehicle security PIN codes; warranty and service information; fuel, lubricant, and coolant capacities; tire changing specifications; jacking and towing information; and a list of service facilities. In addition, most include information

about warning light identification, how to reset maintenance minder functions, and fuse circuit breaker locations.

The layout and amount of detail in an operator's manual will vary according to the manufacturer and age of the vehicle.

Shop Manual

Shop or service manuals are available for just about every make and model of every vehicle made. Service manuals come in two types—factory and after market. Factory manuals are produced by vehicle manufacturers and specify the procedures to maintain, repair, and diagnose their vehicles. Usually a factory service manual is specific to one year and make/model of a particular vehicle.

Most manufacturers shop manuals are now available online. These services are usually provided through a daily, monthly, or yearly subscription. Electronic versions are becoming very popular because they allow shops to access the information they need without having to pay for and store large numbers of shop manuals. Also, it is easier for the publisher to update information as changes or corrections are needed, so the information is generally more accurate than printed materials, which require supplemental printed updates on a periodic basis.

TECHNICIAN TIP

In many heavy-vehicle applications (generally over one ton and due to the many engine options available), some additional information on engines cannot be normally sourced or generally found in the vehicle service manual. This information can be found in specific (engine) manufacturer manuals or databases such as the Cummins Quickserve system.

Typical shop manuals will be broken into a number of sections that relate to systems within the vehicle—for example, engine, transmission, drivetrain, suspension, and electrical.

The sections of the shop manuals will be further divided into topics or subject areas; for example, in the engine section, topics could be general description, engine diagnosis, and on-vehicle service. A typical shop manual page, like that shown in **FIGURE 2-24**, will have a task description broken into steps and diagrams or pictures to aid the technician. It is important to know that all service manuals arrange the content in their own way, so using a variety of different manuals will help you become familiar with finding the information you are looking for.

Service Information Programs

Service information programs are computer applications used to provide technical information for the repair and maintenance of vehicles. The software, as shown in **FIGURE 2-25**,

FIGURE 2-24 A typical shop manual page will have a task description broken into steps and diagrams or pictures to aid the technician.

1.8hr	1.9hr	1.0hr
1.1hr	1.7hr	1.0hr
1.6hr	2.7hr	1.6hr
2.0hr	2.7hr	1.1hr
1.5hr	1.5hr	1.0hr
2.0hr	2.7hr	1.5hr
1.2hr	1.9hr	1.2hr

FIGURE 2-25 Computer databases provide information on procedures, parts, and service problems.

can be installed on the computer, accessed via the Internet using a browser, or run from a CD or DVD.

Using a Service Information Program

To use a service information program, you need to have a basic understanding of how to start and use a computer. Usernames and passwords may be required to log in to the computer and the service information program, so make sure you have these available before you start. A printer is also helpful to print copies of the information so that you can use it when conducting service and repairs; alternatively, you may need to take notes.

To obtain the correct information, you will need vehicle identification information, such as the date of manufacture, model, engine and VIN numbers, and an understanding of the type of repair or scheduled service that is being performed. The repair order may provide you with this information, or you may have to research vehicle identification information from the vehicle. You may need to perform some initial diagnosis of the fault to further continue the search for information.

Information can usually be obtained by searching for the vehicle and then selecting from the list of systems such as brakes or maintenance, followed by subsystems such as disc brakes or fluid capacities. A keyword search may also be available; for example, use the keyword "service interval" to obtain a list of scheduled service intervals. Using a generic word like "engine" may return a very large list. If this occurs, the search can be narrowed further by entering more specific criteria such as "engine oil," "water pump," or "camshaft."

The information will be displayed on pages that will have a mixture of text and diagrams with explanations. Some of the diagrams may have detailed views so you can see how parts fit together, while links may be provided to other relevant information such as a schematic diagram. Most systems will contain help menus or training guides with examples to assist you in using the software, if required.

Technical Service Bulletins

Technical service bulletins (TSBs) are issued by manufacturers to provide information to technicians on unexpected problems, updated parts, or changes to repair procedures that may occur with a particular vehicle system, part, or component. The typical TSB contains step-by-step procedures and diagrams on how to identify if there is a fault and perform an effective repair.

At the time of production, manufacturers prepare service and technical information and attempt to anticipate the information the technicians will require to undertake service and repairs. Once the vehicle is in use, situations can arise when particular components or repair procedures may need either additional information or changes. This is where TSBs are most useful. For example, a TSB may provide details about a change to the procedure that bleeds air from the cooling system. In this situation, the manufacturer would issue a service bulletin explaining the problem and the changes to the current procedure performed to bleed air from the cooling system.

Using TSBs

To use a TSB, follow these guidelines. Locate where the TSBs are kept in your shop or look them up with your electronic service information system. Prior to performing repairs, look through the TSBs and get to know the type of information contained in them. Before working on a vehicle, it is good practice to check if a TSB has been issued for that vehicle and the type of fault or repair. This can save a lot of wasted time.

Compare the information contained in the TSB to that found in the shop manual. Note the differences, and if necessary, copy the TSB and take it with you to perform the repair. Perform the repair following the TSB where appropriate while also referring to the shop manual. If required in your shop policy, note the details of the service bulletin in the appropriate area on the repair order.

▶ TECHNICIAN TIP

Follow these guidelines when using a technical service bulletin (TSB):

- Locate where the TSBs are kept in your shop or look them up with your electronic service information system.
- Prior to performing repairs, look through the TSBs and become familiar with the type of information contained in them.
- Before working on a vehicle, check whether a TSB has been issued for that vehicle and the type of fault or repair.
- Compare the information contained in the TSB to the shop manual information and note the differences. You may copy the TSB and take it with you to perform the repair.
- Perform the repair following the TSB where appropriate while also referring to the shop manual.
- If required by your shop policy, note the details of the service bulletin in the appropriate area on the repair order.

Service Campaigns and Recalls

Service campaigns and recalls are usually conducted by manufacturers when a safety issue is discovered with a particular vehicle. Recalls are costly to manufacturers because they can require the repair of an entire model or production run of vehicles. Potentially, this could involve many thousands of vehicles. Depending on the nature of the problem, recalls can be mandatory and enforced by law, or manufacturers may choose to voluntarily conduct a recall to ensure the safe operation of the vehicle or minimize damage to their business and product image.

Safety

Each country has specific laws regarding product recalls. Find out the laws in your jurisdiction.

An example of a mandatory recall is a fault within the locking mechanism of a seat belt fitted to a vehicle that results in the seat belt operating not as a restraint when it should. In this case, the manufacturer would need to identify the problem, its cause, the vehicles affected, and the recertification requirements. A recall would then be issued and advertised in popular media. Letters would be sent from the manufacturer to known owners of the particular vehicle indicating that the vehicles should be returned for repair. Usually all costs associated with the recall are paid by the manufacturer.

Using Service Campaign Information

To utilize service campaigns or recall information, follow these guidelines. Locate where the special service messages, service campaigns/recalls, vehicle/service warranty applications, and service interval recommendations can be accessed in your shop. Look through the TSBs, service recalls, service warranty applications, and service interval recommendations, and get to know the type of information that is contained in them. Identify how they could be used in your daily tasks.

When working on vehicles, check to see if a TSB has been issued for that vehicle and type of repair. Perform service and repairs following the special service messages, service campaigns/recalls, vehicle/service warranty applications, and service interval recommendations. Fill in the required documentation as required in your shop policies. Note the details of the special service messages, service campaigns/recalls, vehicle/service warranty applications, and service interval recommendations in the appropriate area on the repair order.

Labor Guide

Labor guides list how much time will be involved in performing a standard or warranty-related service or repair. They are regularly updated as new models are released into the market and provide a basis for making job estimates and standard charges for the customer. Flat rate servicing costs are usually derived from a labor guide. For example, if a customer wants to know how much it will cost to replace a leaking intake manifold gasket on a particular vehicle, a technician can look up this procedure in a labor guide and find the information on the time and parts required for that particular repair on the specific vehicle.

With the advent of technology and the Internet, many providers of labor guides have started making them available online as well as in print. The online versions are paid for by subscription, which is usually a monthly or annual fee to access the information. Having access to online labor guides means the shop does not have to wait for a new version of the print publication to become available. Online versions of labor guides also can be updated as new models of vehicles are released or updates are made by the manufacturer.

Using a Labor Guide

The labor guide, like that shown in **FIGURE 2-26**, indicates how quickly an average technician can complete the task. Experienced technicians who have performed the task many times and who are working efficiently can usually perform the job quicker than the labor guide specifies. But since each task and vehicle has its small differences, the time is not always completely

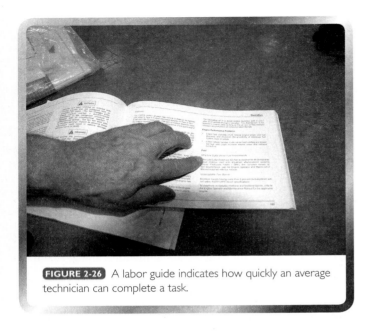

FIGURE 2-26 A labor guide indicates how quickly an average technician can complete a task.

accurate. The information contained within a labor guide is referenced in a similar manner as a repair manual or online service information system.

> **TECHNICIAN TIP**

Dealership technicians have one advantage over most independent technicians: they have an onsite parts department that stocks many of the parts needed for repairs. Many independent shops maintain a relatively small inventory of high-demand parts such as filters, belts, and light bulbs and use a local parts house to supply the less common parts. This can result in delays waiting for parts to arrive.

To use a labor guide, follow the steps in **SKILL DRILL 2-1**.

Parts Program

Parts programs are the modern-day version of parts manuals. They are essentially an electronic version of a parts manual.

 SKILL DRILL 2-1 Using a Labor Guide

1 Decide what specific labor operations you need to locate. Make sure you know the year, make, model, engine, and any other pertinent details of the vehicle.

2 Log in to the labor estimating system.

3 Enter the vehicle information into the system.

4 Find the labor operation either by working your way through the menu tree or by typing a keyword into the search bar.

5 Once you locate the labor operation, there are usually two columns that list the time. The first one is "warranty time." It is the amount of time the manufacturer would pay the shop for the operation under a customer warranty. The second time listed is the "customer pay" time. That is the amount of

time a customer would be billed for and is usually 20–40% longer than warranty time. The length of time is usually listed in tenths of an hour. So 0.6 hours represents 36 minutes. Every tenth of an hour equals 6 minutes.

6 Check for any "combination" time that would need to be added to the base job when a related job is also being completed. Combination time recognizes that combined tasks in many cases save a lot of time over individual tasks because the customer is already being charged for part of the job in the first task. This could be time needed to flush the brakes while the main operation is to replace the brake pads.

7 Check for an "additional" time. This is extra time needed to deal with situations that occur on a relatively common basis, such as vehicle-installed options that are not common to all vehicles, like wheel locks. If you are replacing an engine, swap with or without transfer of associated parts. Obviously transfer of parts would require additional time that would need to be factored in.

The customer should be charged for the extra time it takes to remove and replace the various additional components Thus, "additional" time needs to be added to the base operation time if the vehicle meets the criteria for the particular "additional" situation.

8 Calculate the total time and multiply it by the shop's hourly labor rate. You now have the correct figure to estimate the charge for the particular service.

Parts programs may be available via a CD/DVD, a computer network, or the Internet. Technicians and **parts specialists**, the individuals working at the parts counter, use these programs to identify parts and find order numbers.

Parts manuals are produced for all makes and models of vehicles and are essentially a catalogue of all the parts that make up a vehicle. The parts are catalogued by systems—for example, brake, engine, and transmission. Diagrams of each part are shown along with a part number, which is a unique identifying number for that particular part.

Using a Parts Program

To use a parts program, you need to have a basic understanding of how to start and use a computer. Usernames and passwords may be required to log in to the computer and the parts program, so make sure you have those available before you start. A printer is also helpful to print out copies of the information so that you can use it when ordering parts; alternatively, you may need to take notes.

To identify the correct part, you will need to know where on the vehicle the part is installed, what system or subsystem it comes from, and vehicle identification information, such as date of manufacture, model, and engine and VIN numbers. Make sure you have this information on hand before you use the system. Searches can be conducted by keywords. If the part is for the brake system, in the search criteria box, enter "brake." Using a generic word like "brake" may return a very large list. If this occurs, the search can be narrowed further by entering more specific criteria such as "disc brake."

The parts will be displayed in diagrams that are labeled and show individual parts in exploded view, making it easier to identify parts. The diagrams may number the parts and have a key on the page for reference to part numbers, or arrows may point to listed part numbers on the page. Most systems will contain help menus or training guides with examples to assist you in using the software, if required.

To locate parts information on the computer, follow the steps in **SKILL DRILL 2-2**.

Repair Order Information [Driver Vehicle Inspection Report (DVIR)]

A Driver Vehicle Inspection Report (DVIR) is a daily log filled out by the driver prior to operating a commercial vehicle. These are required by federal motor carrier standards to be filled out daily. One copy must be filed in the maintenance office and another copy kept in the vehicle. A driver notes any problems found on this form and decides whether or not a vehicle is safe to operate. If it is not safe, the driver should not operate the vehicle and the problem should be reported immediately. If the vehicle is safe to operate, the driver will turn the completed form in at the end of the day. The DVIR is a vital tool in communicating vehicle condition to the maintenance department. From that, a repair order can be generated to ensure that the required repairs are carried out.

A **repair order**, or work order, like that shown in **FIGURE 2-27**, is a form used by shops to collect information regarding a vehicle coming in for repair. Initial information for the repair order includes customer and vehicle details, along with a brief description of the customer's complaint(s). The repair order is used by the technician to guide him or her to the problem, and by the customer service staff to create the invoice when the work is completed.

Detailed information that will be on the repair order includes customer details such as name and address; the vehicle make, model, and year; the odometer reading; the date; customer concern information; the cause of the problem(s); the correction for the problem(s); the hours of labor; and the parts used for the repair. The repair order should always include all of the information pertaining to the customer, vehicle, and cost of repair. Repair orders are legal documents that can be used as evidence in the event of a lawsuit. Make sure the information is

SKILL DRILL 2-2 Locating Parts Information on the Computer

1. Log in to the application using the appropriate username and password.

2. Enter the year, make, model, and engine and VIN number information into the system in the appropriate places.

3. Search for the parts you require to conduct the service or repair.

4. The search engine will provide a list of possible matches for you to select from. If the initial search does not produce what you are looking for, try changing the search criteria. Keep searching until you find the information.

5. Gather information on the identified parts, including part numbers, location, availability, and cost.

6. Print, write down, or directly place an order for the desired parts.

DRIVER'S INSPECTION REPORT

Date: _____

TRACTOR/TRUCK NO.: _____   TRAILER(S) NO.(S): _____

TRACTOR/TRUCK	Defective?	Remarks	TRACTOR/TRUCK	Defective?	Remarks
Air compressor			Brake connections		
Air lines			Brakes		
Battery			Coupling chains		
Brake accessories			Coupling (kingpin)		
Brakes			Doors		
Carburetor			Hitch		
Clutch			Landing gear		
Defroster			Lights—all		
Drive line			Roof		
Engine			Springs		
Fifth wheel			Tarpaulin		
Front axle			Tires		
Fuel tank			Wheels		
Heater			OTHER		
Horn			Condition of vehicle is satisfactory? ○ Yes ○ No		
Lights					
Mirrors			Defects corrected? ○ Yes ○ No		
Muffler					
Oil pressure			Defects need not be corrected for vehicle safety. ○ Yes ○ No		
On-board recorder					
Radiator			DRIVER'S Signature:		
Reflectors					
Safety equipment			MECHANIC Signature:		
Springs					
Starter					
Steering					
Tachograph					
Tires					
Transmission					
Wheels					
Windows					
Windshield wipers					
OTHER					

FIGURE 2-27 A Driver Vehicle Inspection Report (DVIR).

complete and accurate whenever filling out a repair order, and store it in an organized safe place, such as in a file cabinet or electronically on a secure computer network.

To identify the information needed and the service requested on a repair order, follow the steps in **SKILL DRILL 2-3**.

Accounting

The accounting section contains information about the methods of payment, which can be cash, credit card, or account. An account system can be set up to handle all payments related to a customer or to a company that uses your service for a number of vehicles. When a vehicle on an account system comes in, you need to record both the account number and the order number.

To work out the total cost of the service, you need to know:

- The labor cost
- The cost of parts
- The tax amounts
- The cost of gas and consumables you used to service the vehicle

You also need to have the customer's authorization to carry out the service. Remember, before making any changes to this service invoice or work order after the authorization, you will need to receive the customer's approval.

TECHNICIAN TIP

A vehicle's service history is valuable for several reasons:

- It can provide helpful information to the technician when performing repairs.
- It allows potential new owners of the vehicle to know how well the vehicle and its systems were maintained.
- Manufacturers use the history to evaluate warranty claims.

SKILL DRILL 2-3 Identifying Information Needed and Service Requested

1. Locate a repair order used in your shop.
2. Familiarize yourself with the repair order, and identify the following information on the repair order:
   a. Date
   b. Customer details: name and address, daytime phone number
   c. Vehicle details: year, make, model, color, odometer reading, VIN
   d. Customer concern details: Note any additional information that is required on your shop's repair order.
3. Following the shop procedures, determine the workflow for the tasks that are listed.
4. Use the repair order to carry out the requested service or repair. Fill in the repair order with details of the cause of the customer concern(s) and the correction(s) conducted.

TECHNICIAN TIP

Always obtain the customer's authorization before servicing his or her vehicle, and also make sure you have the customer's approval before making any changes to the service invoice or the work order.

TECHNICIAN TIP

Repair orders are used also to inform the customer of needed repairs or service. This usually results in the customer agreeing to the needed repair, in which case all is well. But if he or she does not agree to the repair and the vehicle is involved in an accident because of the faulty components, having the customer's initials on the repair order signifying that he or she understands the safety issues can help prevent the shop from being held liable for the accident.

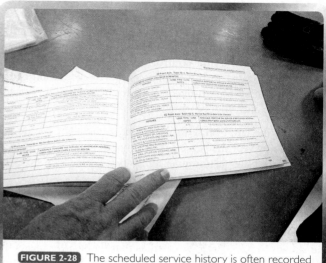

FIGURE 2-28 The scheduled service history is often recorded in a service booklet that is kept in the glove compartment.

Service History

Service history is a complete list of all the servicing and repairs that have been performed on a vehicle. The scheduled service history is often recorded in a service booklet or owner's manual, like that shown in **FIGURE 2-28**, that is kept in the glove compartment. The service history can provide valuable information to technicians when conducting repairs. It also can provide potential new owners of used vehicles an indication of how well the vehicle was maintained.

A vehicle with a regular service history is a good indication that all of the vehicle's systems have been well maintained and the vehicle will often be worth more during resale. Most manufacturers store all service history performed in their dealerships (based on the VIN) on a corporate server that is accessible from any of their dealerships. They will also use this vehicle service history when it comes to evaluating warranty claims. A vehicle that does not have a complete service history may not be eligible for warranty claims. Independent shops generally keep records of the repairs they perform. However, if a vehicle is repaired at multiple shops, repair history is much more difficult to track and, again, may result in a denial of warranty claims.

To review the vehicle service history, follow the steps in **SKILL DRILL 2-4**.

 SKILL DRILL 2-4 Reviewing Vehicle Service History

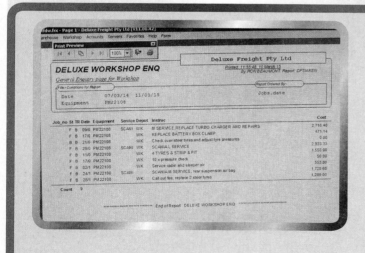

Locate the service history for the vehicle. This may be in shop records or in the service history booklet within the vehicle glove compartment. Some shops may keep the vehicle's service history on a computer.

Familiarize yourself with the service history of the vehicle.
a. On what date was the vehicle first serviced?
b. On what date was the vehicle last serviced?
c. What was the most major service performed?
d. Was the vehicle ever serviced for the same problem more than once?

Compare the vehicle service history to the manufacturer's scheduled maintenance requirements and list any discrepancies.
a. Have all the services been performed?
b. Have all the items been checked?
c. Are there any outstanding items?

Vehicle Information Labels

The **Vehicle Emission Control Information (VECI) label**, like the one shown in **FIGURE 2-29**, is used by technicians to identify engine and emission control information for the vehicle. It is usually located in the engine compartment on either the hood or radiator support or attached to the engine. It typically includes the following information:

- Engine family and displacement
- Model year the vehicle conforms to
- Spark plug part number and gap
- Evaporative emission system family
- Emission control system schematic
- Certification application

The **Vehicle Safety Certification (VSC) label**, like the one shown in **FIGURE 2-30**, certifies that the vehicle meets the Federal Motor Vehicle Safety, Bumper, and Theft Prevention Standards in effect at the time of manufacture. It is used by technicians to identify some basic types of information about the vehicle such as month and year of manufacture, Gross Vehicle Weight Rating (GVWR), and tire information. It is usually affixed to the driver's side door pillar or on the side of the door next to the pillar. It typically includes the following information:

- Month and year of manufacture
- GVWR and Gross Axle Weight Rating (GAWR)
- VIN
- Recommended tire sizes
- Recommended tire inflation pressures
- Paint and trim codes

Other labels include the refrigerant label, the coolant label, and the belt routing label. The **refrigerant label**, like that shown in **FIGURE 2-31**, lists the type and total capacity of refrigerant that is installed in the A/C system. The **coolant label**, as shown in **FIGURE 2-32**, lists the type of coolant installed in the cooling system. The **belt routing label**, like that shown in **FIGURE 2-33**. lists a diagram of the serpentine belt routing for the engine accessories.

FIGURE 2-31 Refrigerant label.

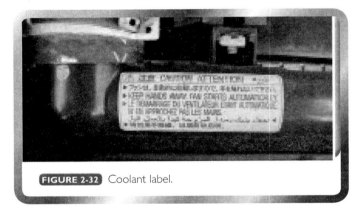

FIGURE 2-32 Coolant label.

FIGURE 2-29 VECI label.

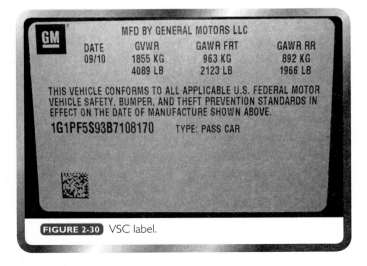

FIGURE 2-30 VSC label.

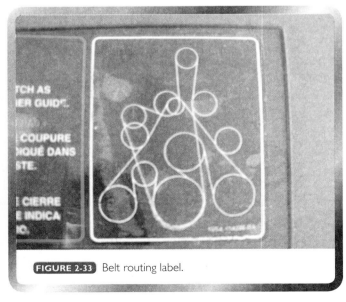

FIGURE 2-33 Belt routing label.

Wrap-Up

Ready for Review

▶ Careers in the commercial vehicle industry are numerous and range from basic technicians to technicians that hold specialty certifications.

▶ Communication includes listening, reading, writing, and speaking skills—soft skills that every good heavy-duty commercial vehicle technician needs to master over time.

▶ To empathize with someone is to attempt to see the situation from his or her point of view.

▶ Nonverbal feedback helps to emphasize our message.

▶ When listening, information gained can be used to provide feedback.

▶ Verbal feedback includes very simple signals that can enhance the conversation and let the person know you comprehend.

▶ A supporting statement can urge the speaker to elaborate on a particular topic.

▶ Speaking is often referred to as an art because there are so many facets involved in effectively communicating and/or information gathering.

▶ Speaking is a three-step process: think about the message, present it, and check that it was understood.

▶ When encountering an upset customer, empathize, de-escalate, do not argue, and stay calm.

▶ There are three types of questions: open, closed, and yes/no.

▶ A critical aspect of an efficient and well-run workshop is the ability to give clear, logical instruction and to receive instruction.

▶ Your appearance makes the first impression and informs others' judgment of who you are.

▶ In the work environment, time is money. Always strive to be on time, ready to do your part by being present, both physically and mentally.

▶ Good customer service is vital in today's competitive business environment.

▶ Every day we are faced with interpreting service information, emails, voicemails, and work orders with customer concerns.

▶ Researching is an important part of troubleshooting a vehicle. First define the problem, then gather clues, and then put all the pieces together to get the conclusion.

▶ When a technician is writing a repair order, the three Cs need to be included: concern, cause, and correction. The customer and vehicle information should also be included.

▶ The operator's manual provides information on how to operate the vehicle and basic maintenance to be performed.

▶ Manufacturers provide shop (or service) manuals for each make and model of truck; these manuals provide vehicle-specific instructions on service and repair.

▶ Service information programs allow users to access maintenance and repair information via computer.

▶ After market repair manuals are not produced by manufacturers and provide less detailed information for specific makes and models.

▶ Manufacturers provide technical service bulletins (TSBs) as updates to shop manuals when new problems or maintenance concerns arise for certain vehicle makes or models.

▶ If a safety issue is discovered on a certain make of vehicle, the manufacturer may issue a service campaign or recall.

▶ Labor guides provide up-to-date information on service repair times and cost estimates.

▶ Parts programs are electronic catalogues of vehicle parts.

▶ Repair or work orders detail customer concern information to guide the service technician, as well as information on services as they are performed.

▶ Account systems track repair costs and customer methods of payment.

▶ A vehicle's service history consists of records of all maintenance and repairs performed on the vehicle.

▶ Manufacturers also provide vehicle information labels to provide further specifications for each model of vehicle.

Vocabulary Builder

belt routing label A label that lists a diagram of the serpentine belt routing for the engine accessories.

coolant label A label that lists the type of coolant installed in the cooling system.

labor guide A guide that provides information to make estimates for repairs.

operator's manual A document that contains information about a vehicle, which is a valuable source of information for both the owner and the technician.

parts program A computer software program for identifying and ordering replacement vehicle parts.

parts specialist The person who serves customers at the parts counters.

primary sources People who have direct experience with the same or a similar problem.

refrigerant label A label that lists the type and total capacity of refrigerant that is installed in the A/C system.

repair order A form used by shops to collect information regarding a vehicle coming in for repair, also referred to as a work order.

secondary sources Secondhand information compiled from a variety of sources.

service campaign and recall A corrective measure conducted by manufacturers when a safety issue is discovered with a particular vehicle.

service history A complete list of all the servicing and repairs that have been performed on a vehicle.

shop or service manual Manufacturer's or after market information on the repair and service of vehicles.

supporting statement A statement that urges the speaker to elaborate on a particular topic.

technical service bulletin (TSB) Information issued by manufacturers to alert technicians of unexpected problems or changes to repair procedures.

three Cs Concern (the concern, or problem, with the vehicle); cause (the cause of the concern); and correction (fixing the problem).

validating statement A statement that shows common interest in the topic being discussed.

vehicle emission control information (VECI) label A label used by technicians to identify engine and emission control information for the vehicle.

vehicle safety certification (VSC) label A label certifying that the vehicle meets the Federal Motor Vehicle Safety, Bumper, and Theft Prevention Standards in effect at the time of manufacture.

Review Questions

1. A(n)_____ is a statement that urges the speaker to elaborate on a particular topic.
   a. introductory statement
   b. supporting statement
   c. concluding statement
   d. exclamatory statement

2. The _____ certifies that the vehicle meets the Federal Motor Vehicle Safety, Bumper, and Theft Prevention Standards in effect at the time of manufacture.
   a. vehicle safety certification (VSC) label
   b. vehicle emission control Information (VECI) label
   c. technical service bulletin (TSB)
   d. operator's manual

3. A _____ is secondhand information compiled from a variety of sources.
   a. primary source
   b. secondary source
   c. supporting source
   d. direct source

4. The _____ is used by technicians to identify engine and emission control information for the vehicle.
   a. parts specialist
   b. shop or service manual
   c. vehicle safety certification (VSC) label
   d. vehicle emission control information (VECI) label

5. The _____ is issued by manufacturers to alert technicians of unexpected problems or changes to repair procedures.
   a. shop or service manual
   b. operator's manual
   c. service campaign and recall
   d. technical service bulletin (TSB)

6. The _____ is a document that contains information about a vehicle and is a valuable source of information for both the owner and the technician.
   a. operator's manual
   b. shop or service manual
   c. technical service bulletin (TSB)
   d. vehicle safety certification (VSC) label

7. _____ are people who have direct experience with the same or similar problem.
   a. Secondary sources
   b. Primary sources
   c. Indirect sources
   d. Supporting sources

8. The _____ contains manufacturer's or after-market information on the repair and service of vehicles.
   a. technical support bulletin (TSB)
   b. service campaign and recall
   c. shop or service manual
   d. operator's manual

9. "Give me an example." is an example of a _____ statement.
   a. supporting
   b. concluding
   c. primary
   d. secondary

10. A(n) _____ question requires a specific answer, and there is usually only one answer.
    a. open
    b. closed
    c. direct
    d. simple

ASE-Type Questions

1. Technician A says all ASE's heavy-duty certifications are designed in a way that the number represents the subject matter and the letter represents the classification of the vehicle type. Technician B says the number represents the classification of the vehicle type and the letter represents the subject matter. Who is correct?
   a. Technician A
   b. Technician B
   c. Both Technician A and Technician B
   d. Neither Technician A nor Technician B

2. Technician A says an open question allows a person to answer with only a yes or a no. Technician B says a closed question allows a person to answer with more than a simple yes or no. Who is correct?
   a. Technician A
   b. Technician B
   c. Both Technician A and Technician B
   d. Neither Technician A nor Technician B

3. Technician A says instructions should include information about who, what, when, where and why. Technician B says instructions should also include directions for how a task should be completed. Who is correct?
   a. Technician A
   b. Technician B
   c. Both Technician A and Technician B
   d. Neither Technician A nor Technician B

4. Technician A says technical assistance hotlines put you in contact with professionals who can assist you in diagnosing a particularly difficult problem over the phone. Technician B says the technical assistance hotlines put you in contact with someone who will schedule an appointment for you to bring the vehicle in for inspection. Who is correct?
   a. Technician A
   b. Technician B
   c. Both Technician A and Technician B
   d. Neither Technician A nor Technician B

5. Technician A says an active listener focuses all of his or her attention on the speaker, including verbal and nonverbal messages. Technician B says an active listener encourages the speaker to further communicate details that may have otherwise been left out. Who is correct?
   a. Technician A
   b. Technician B
   c. Both Technician A and Technician B
   d. Neither Technician A nor Technician B

6. Technician A says a supporting statement such as "Tell me more" indicates to the customer that you are paying attention. Technician B says a validating statement such as "I tell me more" indicates to the customer that you are paying attention. Who is correct?
   a. Technician A
   b. Technician B
   c. Both Technician A and Technician B
   d. Neither Technician A nor Technician B

7. Technician A says most shops should have a safety inspection form that needs to be completed on a regular basis. Technician B says the safety inspection form needs to be completed weekly or monthly, but that some tasks need to be performed daily. Who is correct?
   a. Technician A
   b. Technician B
   c. Both Technician A and Technician B
   d. Neither Technician A nor Technician B

8. Technician A says being punctual is a demonstrates professionalism and a good work attitude. Technician B says clocking in only a few minutes late is still considered punctual. Who is correct?
   a. Technician A
   b. Technician B
   c. Both Technician A and Technician B
   d. Neither Technician A nor Technician B

9. Technician A says a typical operator's manual is issued by manufacturers and contains step-by-step procedures and diagrams on how to identify if there is a fault and perform an effective repair. Technician B says a technical service bulletin contains step-by-step procedures on how to identify if there is a fault and perform an effective repair. Who is correct?
   a. Technician A
   b. Technician B
   c. Both Technician A and Technician B
   d. Neither Technician A nor Technician B

10. Technician A says only a few aspects of our physical appearance culminate to create the first impression in any encounter. Technician B says our clothes, jewelry, hairstyle, posture, and outward demeanor do not the first impression made in any encounter. Who is correct?
    a. Technician A
    b. Technician B
    c. Both Technician A and Technician B
    d. Neither Technician A nor Technician B

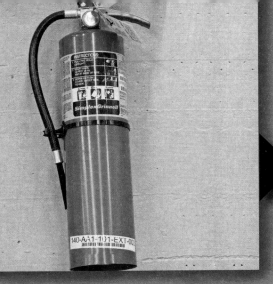

CHAPTER 3

Safety, Personal Protection Equipment, and First Aid

NATEF Tasks

Required Supplemental Tasks

Shop and Personal Safety
- Identify the location of the posted evacuation routes. (p 52)
- Identify general shop safety rules and procedures. (pp 53–54)
- Identify marked safety areas. (pp 53–54)
- Identify the location and the types of fire extinguishers and other fire safety equipment; demonstrate knowledge of the procedures for using fire extinguishers and other fire safety equipment. (pp 58–60)

- Identify the location and use of eye wash stations. (p 60)
- Locate and demonstrate knowledge of material safety data sheets (MSDS). (p 60–66)
- Comply with the required use of safety glasses, ear protection, gloves, and shoes during lab/shop activities. (p 68–73)
- Identify and wear appropriate clothing for lab/shop activities. (pp 68–73)
- Secure hair and jewelry for lab/shop activities. (pp 73–74)
- Utilize proper ventilation procedures for working within the lab/shop area. (p 74)

Knowledge Objectives

After reading this chapter, you will be able to:
1. Explain how the shop layout contributes to efficiency and safety. (pp 52–54)
2. Describe how to follow safe practices in the workplace. (pp 52–54)
3. Describe how the Occupational Safety and Health Administration (OSHA) and the Environmental Protection Agency (EPA) impact the workplace. (pp 52–54)
4. Explain how shop policies, procedures, and safety inspections make the workplace safer. (pp 52–54)
5. Describe the difference between a shop policy and a shop procedure. (p 53)

6. Describe how to identify hazardous environments and the safety precautions that should be undertaken in hazardous environments. (pp 53–54)
7. Identify workplace safety signs and their meanings. (pp 53–55)
8. Describe the standard safety equipment that should be in the workplace. (pp 54–55)
9. Describe how to maintain a safe level of air quality in the workplace. (pp 55–56)
10. Describe the safety precautions to be taken when working with electrical tools and equipment. (pp 56–57)
11. Describe how to reduce the risk of fires in the shop. (p 58)

Skills Objectives

After reading this chapter, you will be able to:
1. Identify hazardous environments and apply appropriate risk prevention strategies. (p 54) **SKILL DRILL 3-1**

2. Locate information on an SDS and apply appropriate safety measures. (p 66) **SKILL DRILL 3-2**
3. Safely clean and dispose of brake dust. (p 67) **SKILL DRILL 3-3**

► Introduction

Occupational safety and health is very important to ensure that everyone can work without being injured. Governments will normally have legislation in place with significant penalties for those who do not follow safe practices in the workplace. Potential hazards are in most workplaces, especially repair shops. It is important to learn about hazards so you can identify them and take action to protect yourself and your coworkers. Some hazards are obvious, such as vehicles falling from hoists or jacks or tires exploding during inflation. Other hazards are less obvious, such as the long-term effects of fumes from solvents. There are many things to learn about safety in the automotive shop, but it is impossible to cover every situation you will encounter. One of the most important skills to learn is the ability to recognize unsafe practices or equipment and put in place measures to prevent injuries from happening.

Occupational safety and health is everyone's responsibility. You have a responsibility to ensure that you work safely and take care not to put others at risk by acting in an unsafe manner. Your employer also has a responsibility to provide a safe working environment. To ensure the safety of yourself and others, make sure you are aware of the correct safety procedures at your workplace. This means listening very carefully to safety information provided by your employer and asking for clarification, help, or instructions if you are unsure how to perform a task safely. Always think about how you are performing shop tasks, be on the lookout for unsafe equipment and work practices, and wear the correct **personal protective equipment (PPE)**. PPE refers to items of safety equipment like safety footwear, gloves, clothing, protective eyewear, and hearing protection **FIGURE 3-1**.

► Safety Overview

Commercial vehicle servicing is one of the most common vocations worldwide. Hundreds of thousands of shops service millions of vehicles every day. That means many people are conducting servicing and there is a great potential for things to go wrong. It is up to you and your workplace to

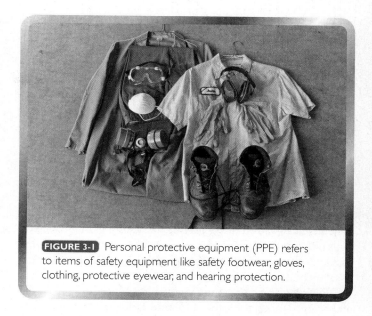

FIGURE 3-1 Personal protective equipment (PPE) refers to items of safety equipment like safety footwear, gloves, clothing, protective eyewear, and hearing protection.

make sure work activities are conducted safely. Accidents are not caused by properly maintained tools; accidents are caused by people.

Don't Underestimate the Dangers

Because vehicle servicing and repair are so commonplace, it is easy to overlook the many potential risks relating to this field. Think carefully about what you are doing and how you are doing it. Think through the steps, trying to anticipate things that may go wrong and taking steps to prevent them. Also be wary of taking shortcuts. In most cases, the time saved by taking a shortcut is nothing compared to the time spent recovering from an accident.

Accidents and Injuries Can Happen at Any Time

There is the possibility of an accident occurring whenever work is undertaken. For example, fires and explosions are a constant hazard wherever there are flammable fuels. Electricity can

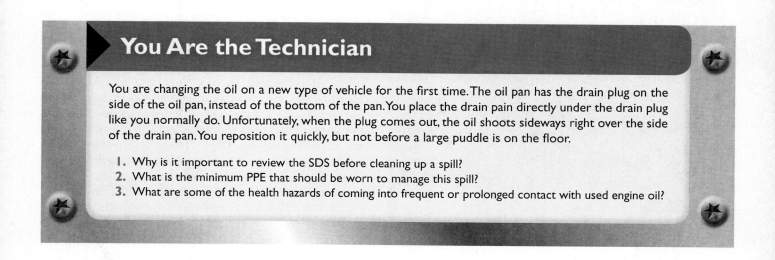

► You Are the Technician

You are changing the oil on a new type of vehicle for the first time. The oil pan has the drain plug on the side of the oil pan, instead of the bottom of the pan. You place the drain pain directly under the drain plug like you normally do. Unfortunately, when the plug comes out, the oil shoots sideways right over the side of the drain pan. You reposition it quickly, but not before a large puddle is on the floor.

1. Why is it important to review the SDS before cleaning up a spill?
2. What is the minimum PPE that should be worn to manage this spill?
3. What are some of the health hazards of coming into frequent or prolonged contact with used engine oil?

kill quickly, as well as cause painful shocks and burns. Heavy equipment and machinery can easily cause broken bones or crush fingers and toes. Hazardous solvents and other chemicals can burn or blind as well as contribute to many kinds of illness. Trips and falls can be caused by things such as oil spills and tools left lying around. Poor lifting and handling techniques can cause chronic strain injuries, particularly to your back **FIGURE 3-2**.

Accidents and Injuries Are Avoidable

Almost all accidents are avoidable or preventable by taking a few precautions. Think of nearly every accident you have witnessed or heard about. In most cases someone made a mistake. Whether involved in horse play or neglecting maintenance on tools or equipment, these instances lead to injury. Most of these accidents can be prevented if people follow policies and develop a "safety first" attitude.

By following regulations and safety procedures, you can make your workplace safe. Learn and follow all of the correct safety procedures for your workplace. Always wear the right PPE and stay alert and aware of what is happening around you. Think about what you are doing, how you are doing it, and its effect on others. You will also need to know what to do in case of an emergency. Document and report all accidents and injuries whenever they happen, and take the proper steps to make sure they never happen again.

Evacuation Routes

Evacuation routes are a safe way of escaping danger and gathering in a safe place where everyone can be accounted for in the event of an emergency. It is important to have more than one evacuation route in case any single route is blocked during the emergency. Your shop may have an evacuation procedure that clearly identifies the evacuation routes **FIGURE 3-3**.

Often the evacuation routes will be marked with colored lines painted on the floors. Exits should be highlighted with signs

FIGURE 3-2 Poor lifting and handling techniques can cause chronic strain injuries, particularly to your back.

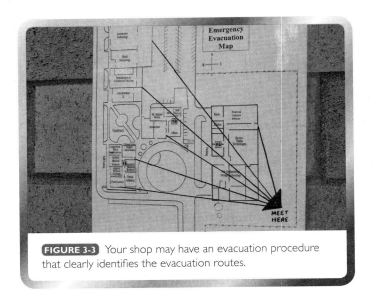

FIGURE 3-3 Your shop may have an evacuation procedure that clearly identifies the evacuation routes.

that may be illuminated. Always make sure you are familiar with the evacuation routes for the shop. Before conducting any task, identify which route you will take if an emergency occurs.

▶ TECHNICIAN TIP

Never place anything in the way of evacuation routes, including equipment, tools, parts, or vehicles.

Work Environment

The work environment can be described as anywhere you work. The condition of the work environment plays an important role in making the workplace safer. A safe work environment goes a long way toward preventing accidents, injuries, and illnesses. There are many ways to describe a safe work environment, but generally it would contain a well-organized shop layout, use of shop policies and procedures, safe equipment, safety equipment, safety training, employees who work safely, a workplace orientation, good supervision, and a workplace culture that supports safe work practices.

OSHA and EPA

OSHA stands for the <u>Occupational Safety and Health Administration (OSHA)</u>. It is a U.S. government agency that was created to provide national leadership in occupational safety and health. It finds the most effective ways to help prevent worker fatalities and workplace injuries and illnesses. It has the authority to conduct workplace inspections and, if required, fine employers and workplaces if they violate OSHA regulations and procedures. For example, a fine may be imposed on the employer or workplace if a worker is electrocuted by a piece of faulty machinery that has not been regularly tested and maintained.

EPA stands for the <u>Environmental Protection Agency</u>. This federal government agency deals with issues related to environmental safety. The EPA conducts research and monitoring, sets standards, and can hold employees and companies legally accountable in order to keep the environment protected. Shop activities will need to comply with EPA laws and regulations by ensuring that waste products are disposed of in an environmentally responsible way, chemicals and fluids are correctly stored, and work practices do not contribute to damaging the environment.

While the examples in this chapter refer to OSHA and EPA, most countries have equivalent organizations. If you are in a different geographic region to North America, you should check with your local government authorities for the appropriate regulations that apply to your location.

Shop Policies and Procedures

Shop policies and procedures are a set of documents that outline how tasks and activities in the shop are to be conducted and managed. They also ensure that the shop operates according to OSHA and EPA laws and regulations. A **policy** is a guiding principle that sets the shop direction, while a **procedure** is a list of the steps required to get the same result each time a task or activity is performed. An example of a policy would be an OSHA document for the shop that describes how the shop complies with legislation. A procedure would be a document that describes the steps required to safely use a commercial vehicle hoist.

Each shop will have its own set of policies and procedures and a system in place to make sure the policies and procedures are regularly reviewed and updated. Regular reviews ensure that new policies and procedures are developed and old ones are modified in case something has changed. For example, if the shop moves to a new building, then a review of policies and procedures will ensure that they relate to the new shop, its layout, and equipment. In general, the policies and procedures are written to guide shop practice; help ensure compliance with laws, statutes, and regulations; and reduce the risk of injury. Always follow your shop policies and procedures to reduce the risk of injury to your coworkers and yourself and to prevent damage to property.

It is everyone's responsibility to know and follow the rules. Locate the general shop rules and procedures for your workplace. Look through the contents or index pages to familiarize yourself with the contents. Discuss the policy and the shop rules and procedures with your supervisor. Ask questions to ensure that you understand how the rules and procedures should be applied and your role in making sure they are followed.

Identifying Hazardous Environments

A **hazardous environment** is a place where hazards exist. A **hazard** is anything that could hurt you or someone else, and most workplaces have them. It is almost impossible to remove all hazards, but it is important to identify hazards and work to reduce their potential for causing harm by putting specific measures in place. For example, operating a bench grinder poses a number of hazards. While it is not possible to eliminate the hazards of using the bench grinder, by putting specific measures in place, the risk of those hazards can be reduced.

A risk analysis of a bench grinder would identify the following hazards and risks: a high-velocity particle that could damage your eyesight or that of someone working nearby; the grinding wheel breaking apart, damaging eyesight or causing cuts and abrasion; electrocution if electrical parts are faulty; a risk to your hands from heat or high-velocity particles; a risk to your hearing due to excessive noise; and a risk of entrapment of clothing or body parts through rotating machinery. To reduce the risk of these hazards, the following measures are taken: position the bench grinder in a safe area away from where others work; make sure electrical items are regularly checked for electrical and mechanical safety; when operating the equipment, wear PPE such as protective eyewear, gloves, hearing protection, hairnets, or caps; and do not wear loose clothing that can be caught in the bench grinder.

An important first step in identifying hazardous environments is to familiarize yourself with the shop layout. There are special work areas that are defined by painted lines. These lines show the hazardous zone around certain machines and areas. If you are not working on the machines, you should stay outside the marked area.

Study the various warning signs around your shop. Understand the meaning of the signal word, the colors, the text, and the symbols or pictures on each sign. Ask your supervisor if you do not fully understand any part of the sign.

To identify hazardous environments, follow the steps in **SKILL DRILL 3-1**.

▶ Standard Safety Measures
Signs

Always remember that a shop is a hazardous environment. To make people more aware of specific shop hazards, legislative bodies have developed a series of safety signs. These signs are designed to give adequate warning of an unsafe situation. Each sign has four components:

- **Signal word**: There are three signal words—danger, warning, and caution. *Danger* indicates an immediately hazardous situation, which, if not avoided, will result in death or serious injury. Danger is usually indicated by white text with a red background **FIGURE 3-4 A**. *Warning* indicates a potentially hazardous situation, which, if not avoided, could result in death or serious injury. The sign is usually in black text with a yellow or orange background **FIGURE 3-4 B**. *Caution* indicates a potentially hazardous situation, which, if not avoided, may result in minor or moderate injury. It may also be used to alert against unsafe practices. This sign is usually in black text with a yellow background **FIGURE 3-4 C**.
- **Background color**: The choice of background color also draws attention to potential hazards and is used to provide contrast so the letters or images stand out. For example, a red background is used to identify a definite hazard; yellow indicates caution for a potential hazard. A green background is used for emergency-type signs, such as for first aid, fire protection, and emergency

SKILL DRILL 3-1 Identifying Hazardous Environments

1 Familiarize yourself with the shop layout. Study and understand the various warning signs around your shop. Identify exits and plan your escape route. Know the designated gathering point and go there in an emergency.

2 Check for air quality. Locate the extractor fans or ventilation outlets and make sure they are not obstructed in any way. Locate and observe the operation of the exhaust extraction hose, pump, and outlet used on the vehicle's exhaust pipes.

3 Check the location, type, and operation of fire extinguishers in your shop. Be sure you know when and how to use each type of fire extinguisher.

4 Find out where flammable materials are kept, and make sure they are stored properly.

5 Check the hoses and fittings on the air compressor and air guns for any damage or excessive wear. Be particularly careful when troubleshooting air guns. Never pull the trigger while inspecting one. Severe eye damage can result.

6 Identify caustic chemicals and acids associated with activities in your shop. Ask your supervisor for information on any special hazards in your particular shop and any special avoidance procedures, which may apply to you and your working environment.

equipment. A blue background is used for general information signs.

- **Text**: The sign will sometimes include explanatory text intended to provide additional safety information. Some signs are designed to convey a personal safety message.
- **Pictorial message**: In symbol signs, a pictorial message appears alone or is combined with explanatory text. This type of sign allows the safety message to be conveyed to people who are illiterate or who do not speak the local language.

Safety Equipment

Shop safety equipment includes items such as:

- **Handrails**: Handrails are used to separate walkways and pedestrian traffic from work areas. They provide a physical barrier that directs pedestrian traffic and also provide protection from vehicle movements.
- **Machinery guards**: Machinery guards and yellow lines prevent people from accidentally walking into the operating equipment or indicate that a safe distance should be kept from the equipment.

Portable Electrical Equipment

If you need to use an extension cord, make sure it is made of flexible wiring—not the stiffer type of house wiring—and that it is fitted with a ground wire. The cord should be neoprene-covered, as this material resists oil damage **FIGURE 3-7**. Always check it for cuts, abrasions, or other damage. Be careful how you place the extension cord so it does not cause a tripping hazard. Also avoid rolling equipment or vehicles over it, as doing so can damage the cord. Never use an extension cord in wet conditions or around flammable liquids.

Portable electric tools that operate at 240 volts are often sources of serious shock and burn accidents. Be particularly careful when using these items. Always inspect the cord for damage and check the security of the attached plug before connecting the item to the power supply. Use 110-volt or lower voltage tools if they are available.

All electric tools must be equipped with a ground prong or double-insulated. If they are not, do *not* use them. Never use any high-voltage tool in a wet environment. Air-operated tools cannot give you an electric shock, because they operate on air pressure instead of electricity; so they are safer to use in a wet environment.

Portable Shop Lights

Portable shop lights/droplights can be very useful tools to add light to a particular area or spot on the vehicle you are working on. Always make sure you follow the safety directions when using shop lights. Shop lights should have protective covers fitted to them to prevent accidentally breaking the lamp. If a lamp breaks, it can be an electrical hazard, particularly if a metal object comes in contact with exposed live electricity. For this reason, often low-voltage lamps or lamps with safety switches fitted are used to prevent accidental electrocution. Some shop lights are now cordless, particularly those with LEDs fitted as the light source. Cordless lights are a very safe option because they isolate you from the high voltage.

Electric droplights are a common source of shocks, especially if they are the wrong type for the purpose or if they are poorly constructed or maintained. All droplights should be designed in such a way that the electrical parts can never come into contact with the outer casing of the device. Such lights are called **double-insulated**. The bulb should be completely enclosed in a transparent insulating case or protected within a robust insulating cage **FIGURE 3-8**.

The bulbs used in electric droplights are very vulnerable to impact and must not be used without insulating cage protection. Incandescent bulbs present an extreme fire hazard if broken in the presence of flammable vapors or liquids and should not be used in repair shops. LED and fluorescent bulbs, while still hazardous, are much safer.

> ▶ **TECHNICIAN TIP**
>
> Always inspect the wiring for damage and check the security of the attached plug before connecting a droplight to the power supply. Always switch off and unplug a droplight before changing the bulb.

Shop Layout

The shop should have a layout that is efficient and safe with clearly defined working areas and walkways. Customers should not be allowed to wander through work areas unescorted. A good shop layout can be achieved by thinking about how the work is to be done, how equipment is used, and what traffic movements, both pedestrian and vehicular, occur within the shop. A well-planned shop should have clearly defined areas for various activities, like parts cleaning, parts storage, tool storage, flammable liquid storage, jacking or lifting, tire fitting, and painting. All flammable items should be kept in an approved fireproof storage container or cabinet, with firefighting equipment close at hand.

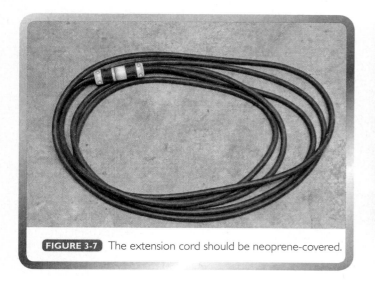

FIGURE 3-7 The extension cord should be neoprene-covered.

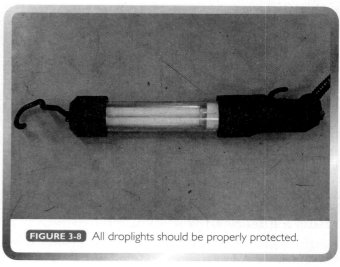

FIGURE 3-8 All droplights should be properly protected.

Preventing Fires

The danger of a fuel fire is always present in an repair shop. Most vehicles carry a fuel tank, often with large quantities of fuel on board, which is more than sufficient to cause a large, very destructive, and potentially explosive fire. Take precautions to make sure you have the correct type and size of extinguishers on hand for a potential fuel fire. Make sure you clean up spills immediately and avoid ignition sources, like sparks, in the presence of flammable liquids or gases.

Fuel Vapor

Liquid fuel vaporizes to different degrees, especially when spilled, and the vapor is generally easy to ignite. Because fuel vapor is invisible and heavier than air, it can spread unseen across a wide area, and a source of ignition can be quite some distance from the original spill. Fuel can even vaporize from the cloths or rags used to wipe up liquid spills. These materials should be allowed to dry in the open air, not held in front of a heater element. Any spark or naked flame, even a lit cigarette, can start an explosive fire.

Spillage Risks

Spills frequently occur when technicians remove and replace fuel filters. They also occur during removal of a fuel tank sender unit, which can be located on the side or top of the fuel tank, without first emptying the tank safely. Spills also can occur when fuel lines are damaged and are being replaced, when fuel systems are being checked, or when fuel is being drained into unsuitable containers. Avoid spills by following the manufacturer's specified procedure when removing fuel system components. Also, keep a spill response kit nearby to deal with any spills quickly. Spill kits should contain absorbent material and barrier dams to contain moderate-sized spills.

Draining Fuel

If there is a possibility of fuel spillage while working on a vehicle, then you should first remove the fuel safely. Do this only in a well-ventilated, level space, preferably outside in the open air. Make sure all potential sources of ignition have been removed from the area, and disconnect the battery on the vehicle. Do not drain fuel from a vehicle over an inspection pit. Make sure the container you are draining into is an approved fuel storage container (fuel retriever) and that it is large enough to contain all of the fuel in the system being drained.

Using a Fuel Retriever

Always use a fuel retriever, preferably removing the fuel through the filler neck. A fuel retriever will minimize the chance of sudden large spills occurring. You may need to use narrow-diameter hoses or adapters to drain fuel lines or to bypass anti-spillage devices. Check the service manual for details on how best to drain the fuel from the vehicle you are working on.

Extinguishing Fires

Three elements must be present at the same time for a fire to occur: fuel, oxygen, and heat. The secret of firefighting involves the removal of at least one of these elements, usually the oxygen or the heat, to extinguish the fire. For example, a fire blanket when applied correctly removes the oxygen, while a water extinguisher removes heat from the fire. In the shop, fire extinguishers are used to extinguish the majority of small fires. Never hesitate to call the fire department if you cannot extinguish a fire safely.

Fire Classifications

In the United States, there are five classes of fire:

- Class A fires involve ordinary combustibles such as wood, paper, or cloth.
- Class B fires involve flammable liquids or gaseous fuels.
- Class C fires involve electrical equipment.
- Class D fires involve combustible metals such as sodium, titanium, and magnesium.
- Class K fires involve cooking oil or fat.

Fire Extinguisher Types

Fire extinguishers are marked with pictograms depicting the types of fires that the extinguisher is approved to fight **FIGURE 3-9** :

- Class A: Green triangle
- Class B: Red square

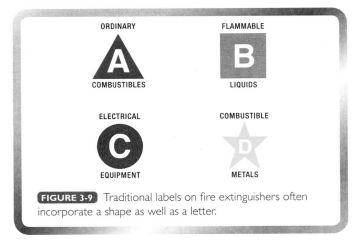

FIGURE 3-9 Traditional labels on fire extinguishers often incorporate a shape as well as a letter.

- Class C: Blue circle
- Class D: Yellow pentagram
- Class K: Black hexagon

Fire Extinguisher Operation

Always sound the alarm before attempting to fight a fire. If you cannot fight the fire safely, leave the area while you wait for backup. You will need to size up the fire before you make the decision to fight it with a fire extinguisher by identifying what sort of material is burning, the extent of the fire, and the likelihood of it spreading.

To operate a fire extinguisher, follow the acronym for fire extinguisher use: PASS (Pull, Aim, Squeeze, Sweep). *Pull* out the pin that locks the handle at the top of the fire extinguisher to prevent accidental use **FIGURE 3-10 A**. Carry the fire extinguisher in one hand, and use your other hand to aim the nozzle at the base of the fire **FIGURE 3-10 B**. Stand about 8–12′ (2.4–3.7 m) away from the fire and *squeeze* the handle to discharge the fire extinguisher **FIGURE 3-10 C**. Remember that if you release the handle on the fire extinguisher, it will stop discharging. *Sweep* the nozzle from side to side at the base of the fire **FIGURE 3-10 D**. Continue to watch the fire. Although it may appear to be extinguished, it may suddenly reignite.

If the fire is indoors, you should be standing between the fire and the nearest safe exit. If the fire is outside, you should stand facing the fire with the wind on your back, so that the smoke and heat are being blown away from you. If possible, get an assistant to guide you and inform you of the fire's progress. Again, make sure you have a means of escape, should the fire get out of control. When you are certain that the fire is out, report it to your supervisor. Also report what actions you took to put out the fire. Once the circumstances of the fire have been investigated, and your supervisor or the fire department has given you the all clear, clean up the debris and submit the used fire extinguisher for inspection.

Fire Blankets

Fire blankets are designed to smother a small fire and are very useful in putting out a fire on a person. They are also used in situations where a fire extinguisher could cause damage. For example, if there is a small fire under the hood of a vehicle, a fire blanket might be able to smother the fire without running the risk of getting fire extinguisher powder down the intake system. Obtain a fire blanket and study the how-to-use instructions on the packaging. If instructions are not provided, research how to use a fire blanket or ask your supervisor. You may require

FIGURE 3-10 To operate a fire extinguisher, follow PASS. **A.** Pull. **B.** Aim. **C.** Squeeze. **D.** Sweep.

instruction from an authorized person in using the fire blanket. If you do use a fire blanket, make sure you return the blanket for use or, if necessary, replace it with a new one.

Eye Wash Stations and Emergency Showers

Hopefully you will never need to use an eye wash station or emergency shower. The best treatment is prevention, so make sure you wear all the PPE required for each specific task to avoid injury. Eye wash stations are used to flush the eye with clean water or sterile liquid in the event that you get foreign liquid or particles in your eye. There are different types of eye washers; the main ones are disposable eye wash packs and eye wash stations. Some emergency or deluge showers also have an eye wash station built in FIGURE 3-11.

When individuals get chemicals in their eyes, they typically need assistance in reaching the eye wash station. Take their arm and lead them to it. They may not want to open their eyes even in the water, so encourage them to use their fingers to pull their eyelids open. If a chemical splashed in their eyes, encourage them to rinse their eyes for 15 minutes. While they are rinsing their eyes, call for medical assistance.

▶ Hazardous Materials Safety

A hazardous material is any material that poses an unreasonable risk of damage or injury to persons, property, or the environment if it is not properly controlled during handling, storage, manufacture, processing, packaging, use and disposal, or transportation. These materials can be solids, liquids, or gases. Most shops use hazardous materials daily, such as cleaning solvents, gasket cement, brake fluid, and coolant. Hazardous materials must be properly handled, labeled, and stored in the shop.

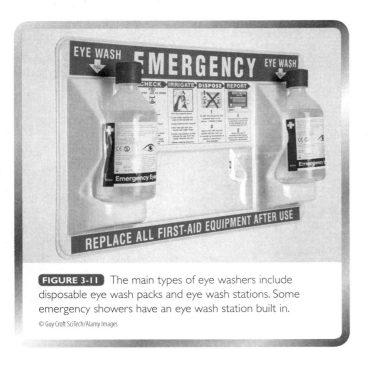

FIGURE 3-11 The main types of eye washers include disposable eye wash packs and eye wash stations. Some emergency showers have an eye wash station built in.
© Guy Croft SciTech/Alamy Images

Safety Data Sheets

Hazardous materials are used daily and may make you very sick if they are not used properly. Safety data sheets (SDS) contain detailed information about hazardous materials to help you understand how they should be safely used, any health effects relating to them, how to treat a person who has been exposed to them, and how to deal with them in a fire situation. An SDS can be obtained from the manufacturer of the material. The shop should have an SDS for each hazardous substance or dangerous product. In the United States it is required that workplaces have an SDS for every chemical that is on site.

Whenever you deal with a potentially hazardous product, you should consult the SDS to learn how to use that product safely. If you are using more than one product, make sure you consult all the SDS for those products. Be aware that certain combinations of products can be more dangerous than any of them separately.

SDS are usually kept in a clearly marked binder and should be regularly updated as chemicals come into the workplace. Generally the SDS must contain at least the following information FIGURE 3-12:

- Revision date
- Material and manufacturer ID
- Hazardous ingredients
- Health hazard data
- Fire and explosion data
- Details about the material mixing or reacting with other materials
- Special precautions

To identify information found on an SDS, follow the steps in SKILL DRILL 3-2.

Cleaning Toxic Dust Safely

Toxic dust is any dust that may contain fine particles that could be harmful to humans or the environment. If you are unsure as to the toxicity of dust, then you should always treat it as toxic and take the precautions identified in the SDS or shop procedures. Brake and clutch dust are potential toxic dusts that repair shops must manage. The dust is made up of very fine particles that can easily spread and contaminate an area. One of the more common sources of toxic dust is inside drum brakes and manual transmission bell housings.

It is a good idea to avoid all dust if possible, whether it is classified as toxic or not. If you do have to work with dust, never use compressed air to blow it from components or parts and always use PPE such as face masks, eye protection, and gloves. If you are cleaning up your area after a repair, do not dry sweep; instead, use a low-pressure wet cleaning method. Such methods include a soap and water solution used in a dedicated portable wash station, a low-pressure aerosol brake cleaning solution, or a pump spray bottle filled with water. You may also use a HEPA vacuum cleaner to collect dust and clean equipment. HEPA stands for high-efficiency particulate absorbing.

 **MATERIAL SAFETY DATA SHEET**

Section 1: Product & Company Identification

Product Name: **Brakleen® Brake Parts Cleaner** (aerosol)

Product Number (s):   **05089, 05089-6, 05089T, 75089, 85089, 85089AZ**

Product Use: Brake parts cleaner

Manufactured / Supplier Contact Information:

In United States:

CRC Industries, Inc.
885 Louis Drive
Warminster, PA 18974
www.crcindustries.com
1-215-674-4300 (General)
(800) 521-3168 (Technical)
(800) 272-4620 (Customer Service)

In Canada:

CRC Canada Co.
2-1246 Lorimar Drive
Mississauga, Ontario L5S 1R2
www.crc-canada.ca
1-905-670-2291

In Mexico:

CRC Industries Mexico
Av. Benito Juárez 4055 G
Colonia Orquídea
San Luís Potosí, SLP CP 78394
www.crc-mexico.com
52-444-824-1666

24-Hr Emergency – CHEMTREC: (800) 424-9300   or   (703) 527-3887

Section 2: Hazards Identification

Emergency Overview

DANGER: Vapor Harmful. Contents Under Pressure.
As defined by OSHA's Hazard Communication Standard, this product is hazardous.
Appearance & Odor: Colorless liquid, irritating odor at high concentrations

Potential Health Effects:

ACUTE EFFECTS:

EYE: May cause slight temporary eye irritation. Vapors may irritate the eyes at concentrations of 100 ppm.

SKIN: Short single exposures may cause skin irritation. Prolonged exposure may cause severe skin irritation, even a burn. A single prolonged exposure is not likely to result in the material being absorbed through skin in harmful amounts.

INHALATION: Dizziness may occur at concentrations of 200 ppm. Progressively higher levels may also cause nasal irritation, nausea, incoordination, and drunkenness. Very high levels or prolonged exposure could lead to unconsciousness and death.

INGESTION: Single dose oral toxicity is considered to be extremely low. Swallowing large amounts may cause injury if aspirated into the lungs. This may be rapidly absorbed through the lungs and result in injury to other body systems.

CHRONIC EFFECTS: Repeated contact with skin may cause drying or flaking of skin. Excessive or long term exposure to vapors may increase sensitivity to epinephrine and increase myocardial irritability.

TARGET ORGANS: Central nervous system. Possibly liver and kidney.

Medical Conditions Aggravated by Exposure: None known.

See Section 11 for toxicology and carcinogenicity information on product ingredients.

Page 1 of 7

FIGURE 3-12 An example of an SDS.
Courtesy of CRC Industries, Inc.

Continued on next page

Product Name: Brakleen® Brake Parts Cleaner (aerosol)
Product Number (s): 05089,05089-6, 05089T, 75089, 85089, 85089AZ

Section 3: Composition/Information on Ingredients

COMPONENT	CAS NUMBER	% by Wt.
Tetrachloroethylene (PERC)	127-18-4	> 95
Carbon Dioxide	124-38-9	< 5

Section 4: First Aid Measures

Eye Contact: Immediately flush with plenty of water for 15 minutes. Call a physician if irritation persists.

Skin Contact: Remove contaminated clothing and wash affected area with soap and water. Call a physician if irritation persists. Wash contaminated clothing prior to re-use.

Inhalation: Remove person to fresh air. Keep person calm. If not breathing, give artificial respiration. If breathing is difficult give oxygen. Call a physician.

Ingestion: Do NOT induce vomiting. Call a physician immediately.

Note to Physicians: Because rapid absorption may occur through lungs if aspirated and cause systemic effects, the decision of whether to induce vomiting or not should be made by a physician. If lavage is performed, suggest endotracheal and/or esophageal control. If burn is present, treat as any thermal burn, after decontamination. Exposure may increase myocardial irritability. Do not administer sympathomimetic drugs unless absolutely necessary. No specific antidote.

Section 5: Fire-Fighting Measures

Flammable Properties: This product is nonflammable in accordance with aerosol flammability definitions.
(See 16 CFR 1500.3(c)(6))
Flash Point: None (TCC)   Upper Explosive Limit: None
Autoignition Temperature: None   Lower Explosive Limit: None

Fire and Explosion Data:

Suitable Extinguishing Media: This material does not burn. Use extinguishing agent suitable for surrounding fire.

Products of Combustion: Hydrogen chloride, trace amounts of phosgene and chlorine

Explosion Hazards: Aerosol containers, when exposed to heat from fire, may build pressure and explode.

Protection of Fire-Fighters: Firefighters should wear self-contained, NIOSH-approved breathing apparatus for protection against suffocation and possible toxic decomposition products. Proper eye and skin protection should be provided. Use water spray to keep fire-exposed containers cool and to knock down vapors which may result from product decomposition.

Section 6: Accidental Release Measures

Personal Precautions: Use personal protection recommended in Section 8. Do not breathe vapors.

Environmental Precautions: Take precautions to prevent contamination of ground and surface waters. Do not flush into sewers or storm drains.

Methods for Containment & Clean-up: Dike area to contain spill. Ventilate the area with fresh air. If in confined space or limited air circulation area, clean-up workers should wear appropriate

Continued on next page

Product Name: Brakleen® Brake Parts Cleaner (aerosol)
Product Number (s): 05089, 05089-6, 05089T, 75089, 85089, 85089AZ

respiratory protection. Recover or absorb spilled material using an absorbent designed for chemical spills. Place used absorbents into proper waste containers.

Section 7: Handling and Storage

Handling Procedures:	Vapors of this product are heavier than air and will collect in low areas. Make sure ventilation removes vapors from low areas. Do not eat, drink or smoke while using this product. Use caution around energized equipment. The metal container will conduct electricity if it contacts a live source. This may result in injury to the user from electrical shock and/or flash fire. For product use instructions, please see the product label.
Storage Procedures:	Store in a cool dry area out of direct sunlight. Aerosol cans must be maintained below 120 F to prevent cans from rupturing.
Aerosol Storage Level:	I

Section 8: Exposure Controls/Personal Protection

Exposure Guidelines:

COMPONENT	OSHA		ACGIH		OTHER		
	TWA	STEL	TWA	STEL	TWA	SOURCE	UNIT
Tetrachloroethylene	100	N.E.	25	100	N.E.		ppm
Carbon dioxide	5000	30000 v	5000	30,000	N.E.		ppm
N.E. – Not Established		(c) – ceiling		(s) – skin		(v) – vacated	

Controls and Protection:

Engineering Controls:	Area should have ventilation to provide fresh air. Local exhaust ventilation is generally preferred because it can control the emissions of the contaminant at the source, preventing dispersion into the general work area. Use mechanical means if necessary to maintain vapor levels below the exposure guidelines. If working in a confined space, follow applicable OSHA regulations.
Respiratory Protection:	None required for normal work where adequate ventilation is provided. If engineering controls are not feasible or if exposure exceeds the applicable exposure limits, use a NIOSH-approved cartridge respirator with organic vapor cartridge. Air monitoring is needed to determine actual employee exposure levels. Use a self-contained breathing apparatus in confined spaces and for emergencies.
Eye/face Protection:	For normal conditions, wear safety glasses. Where there is reasonable probability of liquid contact, wear splash-proof goggles.
Skin Protection:	Use protective gloves such as PVA, Teflon, or Viton. Also, use full protective clothing if there is prolonged or repeated contact of liquid with skin.

Section 9: Physical and Chemical Properties

Physical State: liquid
Color: colorless
Odor: irritating odor
Odor Threshold: 50 ppm
Specific Gravity: 1.619

Continued on next page

Product Name: Brakleen® Brake Parts Cleaner (aerosol)
Product Number (s): 05089, 05089-6, 05089T, 75089, 85089, 85089AZ

Initial Boiling Point: 250 F
Freezing Point: ND
Vapor Pressure: 13 mmHg @ 68 F
Vapor Density: 5.76   (air = 1)
Evaporation Rate: very fast
Solubility: 0.015 g/ 100 g @ 77 F in water
Coefficient of water/oil distribution (log P_{ow}):   2.88
pH: NA
Volatile Organic Compounds: <u>wt %</u>:   0   <u>g/L</u>:   0   <u>lbs./gal</u>:   0

Section 10: Stability and Reactivity

Stability: Stable

Conditions to Avoid: Avoid direct sunlight or ultraviolet sources. Avoid open flames, welding arcs, and other high temperature sources which induce thermal decomposition.

Incompatible Materials: Avoid contact with metals such as: aluminum powders, magnesium powders, potassium, sodium, and zinc powder. Avoid unintended contact with amines. Avoid contact with strong bases and strong oxidizers.

Hazardous Decomposition Products: Hydrogen chloride, trace amounts of chlorine and phosgene

Possibility of Hazardous Reactions: No

Section 11: Toxicological Information

Long-term toxicological studies have not been conducted for this product. The following information is available for components of this product.

Acute Toxicity:

Component	Oral LD50 (rat)	Dermal LD50 (rabbit)	Inhalation LC50 (rat)
Tetrachloroethylene	2629 mg/kg	> 10 g/kg	5200 mg/kg/4H
Carbon dioxide	No data	No data	470,000 ppm/30M

Chronic Toxicity:

Component	OSHA Carcinogen	IARC Carcinogen	NTP Carcinogen	Irritant	Sensitizer
Tetrachloroethylene	No	Group 2A	Reasonably Anticipated to be a Carcinogen	E (mild) / S (severe)	No
Carbon dioxide	No	No	No	None	No

E – Eye	S – Skin	R - Respiratory

Reproductive Toxicity: No information available
Teratogenicity: No information available
Mutagenicity: Tetrachloroethylene: in vitro studies were negative
                                                 animal studies were negative
Synergistic Effects: No information available

Section 12: Ecological Information

Ecological studies have not been conducted for this product. The following information is available for components of this product.

Page 4 of 7

Continued on next page

Product Name: Brakleen® Brake Parts Cleaner (aerosol)
Product Number (s): 05089,05089-6, 05089T, 75089, 85089, 85089AZ

Ecotoxicity: Tetrachloroethylene -- 96 Hr LC50 Rainbow Trout: 5.28 mg/L (static)
                                              96 Hr LC50 Fathead minnow: 13.4 mg/L (flow-through)
Persistence / Degradability: Biodegradation under aerobic conditions is below detectable limits.
                        Biodegradation may occur under anaerobic conditions. Biodegradation rate may
                        increase in soil and/or water with acclimation.
Bioaccumulation / Accumulation: Bioconcentration potential is low (BCF less than 100).
Mobility in Environment: Potential for mobility in soil is medium.

Section 13: Disposal Considerations

<u>Waste Classification:</u> The dispensed liquid product is a RCRA hazardous waste for toxicity with the following potential
                    waste codes: U210, F001, F002, D039. Pressurized containers are a D003 reactive waste.
                    (See 40 CFR Part 261.20 – 261.33)
                    Empty aerosol containers may be recycled. Any liquid product should be managed as a
                    hazardous waste.

All disposal activities must comply with federal, state, provincial and local regulations. Local regulations may be more
stringent than state, provincial or national requirements.

Section 14: Transport Information

US DOT (ground):   Consumer Commodity, ORM-D

ICAO/IATA (air):   Consumer Commodity, ID8000, 9

IMO/IMDG (water):   Aerosols, UN1950, 2.2, Limited Quantity

Special Provisions: None

Section 15: Regulatory Information

<u>U.S. Federal Regulations:</u>

<u>Toxic Substances Control Act (TSCA):</u>
    All ingredients are either listed on the TSCA inventory or are exempt.

<u>Comprehensive Environmental Response, Compensation and Liability Act (CERCLA):</u>
    Reportable Quantities (RQ's) exist for the following ingredients: Tetrachloroethylene (100 lbs)

    **Spills or releases resulting in the loss of any ingredient at or above its RQ require immediate notification to
    the National Response Center (800-424-8802) and to your Local Emergency Planning Committee.**

<u>Superfund Amendments Reauthorization Act (SARA) Title III:</u>
    Section 302 Extremely Hazardous Substances (EHS):   None

    Section 311/312 Hazard Categories: Fire Hazard   No
                                            Reactive Hazard   No
                                            Release of Pressure Yes
                                            Acute Health Hazard Yes
                                            Chronic Health Hazard Yes

    Section 313 Toxic Chemicals: This product contains the following substances subject to the reporting requirements
                                of Section 313 of Title III of the Superfund Amendments and Reauthorization Act of
                                1986 and 40 CFR Part 372:

Page 5 of 7

Continued on next page

Product Name: Brakleen® Brake Parts Cleaner (aerosol)
Product Number (s): 05089,05089-6, 05089T, 75089, 85089, 85089AZ

Tetrachloroethylene (97.7%)

Clean Air Act:
  Section 112 Hazardous Air Pollutants (HAPs):   Tetrachloroethylene

U.S. State Regulations:

California Safe Drinking Water and Toxic Enforcement Act (Prop 65):
  This product may contain the following chemicals known to the state of
  California to cause cancer, birth defects or other reproductive harm: Tetrachloroethylene

Consumer Products VOC Regulations: This product cannot be sold for use in California and New Jersey. In other
                                      states with Consumer Products VOC regulations, this product is compliant as a
                                      Brake Cleaner.

State Right to Know:
New Jersey: 127-18-4, 124-38-9
Pennsylvania: 127-18-4, 124-38-9
Massachusetts: 127-18-4, 124-38-9
Rhode Island :   127-18-4, 124-38-9

Canadian Regulations:

Canadian DSL Inventory: All ingredients are either listed on the DSL Inventory or are exempt.

WHMIS Hazard Class: A, D1B, D2A, D2B

European Union Regulations:

RoHS Compliance: This product is compliant with Directive 2002/95/EC of the European Parliament and of the
                      Council of 27 January 2003. This product does not contain any of the restricted substances as
                      listed in Article 4(1) of the RoHS Directive.

Additional Regulatory Information: None

Section 16: Other Information

HMIS® (II)	
Health:	2
Flammability:	0
Reactivity:	0
PPE:	B

Ratings range from 0 (no hazard) to 4 (severe hazard)

NFPA

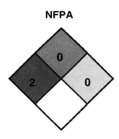

Prepared By: Michelle Rudnick
CRC #:   491G
Revision Date: 01/25/2010

Changes since last revision: MSDS reformatted to meet the requirements of the Canadian Controlled Products
                                Regulations.

Page 6 of 7

Continued on next page

Product Name: Brakleen® Brake Parts Cleaner (aerosol)
Product Number (s): 05089,05089-6, 05089T, 75089, 85089, 85089AZ

The information contained in this document applies to this specific material as supplied. It may not be valid for this material if it is used in combination with any other materials. This information is accurate to the best of CRC Industries' knowledge or obtained from sources believed by CRC to be accurate. Before using any product, read all warnings and directions on the label. For further clarification of any information contained on this MSDS consult your supervisor, a health & safety professional, or CRC Industries.

ACGIH:	American Conference of Governmental Industrial Hygienists	NA:	Not Applicable
CAS:	Chemical Abstract Service	ND:	Not Determined
CFR:	Code of Federal Regulations	NIOSH:	National Institute of Occupational Safety & Health
DOT:	Department of Transportation	NFPA:	National Fire Protection Association
DSL:	Domestic Substance List	NTP:	National Toxicology Program
g/L:	grams per Liter	OSHA:	Occupational Safety and Health Administration
HMIS:	Hazardous Materials Identification System	PMCC:	Pensky-Martens Closed Cup
IARC:	International Agency for Research on Cancer	PPE:	Personal Protection Equipment
IATA:	International Air Transport Association	ppm:	Parts per Million
ICAO:	International Civil Aviation Organization	RoHS:	Restriction of Hazardous Substances
IMDG:	International Maritime Dangerous Goods	STEL:	Short Term Exposure Limit
IMO:	International Maritime Organization	TCC:	Tag Closed Cup
lbs./gal:	pounds per gallon	TWA:	Time Weighted Average
LC:	Lethal Concentration	WHMIS:	Workplace Hazardous Materials Information
LD:	Lethal Dose		System

Canadian Regulations

Canadian DSL Inventory: All ingredients are either listed on the DSL Inventory or are exempt.

SKILL DRILL 3-2 Identifying Information on a Safety Data Sheet

limit values (TLVs). The concentration of this material in the air you breathe in your shop must not exceed these figures. There could be physical symptoms associated with breathing harmful chemicals. Find out what will happen to you if you suffer overexposure to the material, either through breathing it or by coming into physical contact with it. This will help you take safety precautions, such as eye, face, or skin protection, wearing a mask or respirator while using the material, or washing your skin afterwards.

4 Note the flash point for this material so that you know at what temperature it may catch fire. Also note what kind of fire extinguisher you would use to fight a fire involving this material. The wrong fire extinguisher could make the emergency even worse.

5 Study the reactivity for this material to identify the physical conditions or other materials that you should avoid when using this material. It could be heat, moisture, or some other chemical.

6 Find out what special precautions you should take when working with this material. This will include personal protection for your skin, eyes, or lungs and storage and use of the material.

7 Be sure to refresh your knowledge of your SDS from time to time. Be confident that you know how to handle and use the material and what action to take in an emergency, should one occur.

1 Once you have studied the information on the container label, find the SDS for that particular material. Always check the revision date to ensure that you are reading the most recent update.

2 Note the chemical and trade names for the material, its manufacturer, and the emergency telephone number to call.

3 Find out why this material is potentially hazardous. It may be flammable, it may explode, or it may be poisonous if inhaled or touched with your bare skin. Check the threshold

HEPA filters can trap very small particles and prevent them from being redistributed into the surrounding air.

After completing a servicing or repair task on a vehicle, there is often dirt left behind. The chemicals present in this dirt usually contain toxic chemicals that can build up and cause health problems. To keep the levels of dirt to a minimum, clean up dirt immediately after the task is complete. The vigorous action of sweeping causes the dirt to rise; therefore, when sweeping the floor, use a soft broom that pushes, rather than flicks, the dirt forward. Create smaller dirt piles and dispose of them frequently. Another successful way of cleaning shop dirt is to use a water hose. The waste water must be caught in a settling pit and not run into a storm water drain.

Various tools have been developed to clean toxic dust from vehicle components. The most common one is the brake wash station. It uses an aqueous solution to wet down and wash the dust into a collection basin. The basin needs periodic maintenance to properly dispose of the accumulated sludge. This tool is probably the simplest way to effectively deal with hazardous dust because it is easy to set up, use, and store.

Another such tool uses a vacuum cleaner that has a large cone attachment at the nozzle end. The base of the cone is open so the brake assembly can fit into the cone. A compressed air nozzle, which is also attached to the inside of the cone, is used to loosen dirt particles. The particles are drawn into the cleaner via a very fine filter. Domestic vacuum cleaners are not suitable for this application because their filters are not fine enough to capture very small dust particles.

To safely clean brake dust, follow the steps in **SKILL DRILL 3-3**.

Used Engine Oil and Fluids

Used engine oil and fluids are liquids that have been drained from the vehicle, usually during servicing operations. Used oil and fluids will often contain dangerous chemicals and impurities and need to be safely recycled or disposed of in an environmentally friendly way **FIGURE 3-13**. There are laws and regulations that control the way in which they are to be handled and disposed. The shop will have policies and procedures that describe how you should handle and dispose of used engine oil and fluids. Be careful not to mix incompatible fluids such as used engine oil and used coolant. Generally speaking, petroleum products can be mixed together. Follow your local, state, and federal regulations when disposing of waste fluids.

Used engine oil is a hazardous material containing many impurities that can damage your skin. Coming into frequent or prolonged contact with used engine oil can cause dermatitis and other skin disorders, including some forms of cancer. Avoid

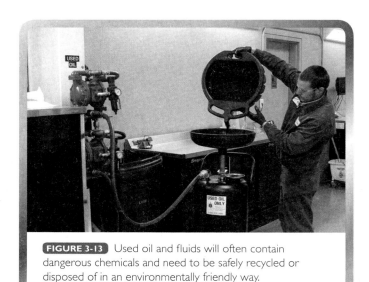

FIGURE 3-13 Used oil and fluids will often contain dangerous chemicals and need to be safely recycled or disposed of in an environmentally friendly way.

SKILL DRILL 3-3 Safely Cleaning Brake Dust

1. When performing any cleaning tasks on brake or clutch components, always wear a face mask, gloves, and eye protection.

2. Position the brake wash station under the bottom of the backing plate. When cleaning brakes, remove the brake drum and check for the presence of dust and brake fluid. When cleaning a clutch, position the wash station underneath the bell housing.

3. Turn on the wash station pump and paint the solution over the components to wet and clean the components and remove the dust. Any toxic dust will be washed down and caught in the wash station.

4. Periodically dispose of the residue in an approved manner.

direct contact as much as possible by always using gloves and other protective clothing, which should be cleaned or replaced regularly. Using a barrier-type hand lotion will also help protect your hands as well as make cleaning them much easier. Also follow safe work practices, which minimize the possibility of accidental spills. Keeping a high standard of personal hygiene and cleanliness is important so that you get into the habit of washing off harmful materials as soon as possible after contact. If you have been in contact with used engine oil, you should regularly inspect your skin for signs of damage or deterioration. If you have any concerns, see your doctor.

▶ **TECHNICIAN TIP**

- Some vehicle components, including brake and clutch linings, contain asbestos, which, despite having very good heat properties, is toxic. Asbestos dust causes lung cancer. Complications from breathing the dust may not show until decades after exposure.
- Airborne dust in the shop can also cause breathing problems such as asthma and throat infections.
- Never cause dust from vehicle components to be blown into the air. It can stay floating for many hours, meaning that other people will breathe the dust unknowingly.
- Wear protective gloves whenever using solvents.
- If you are unfamiliar with a solvent or a cleaner, refer to the SDS for information about its correct use and applicable hazards.
- Always wash your hands thoroughly with soap and water after performing repair tasks on brake and clutch components.
- Always wash work clothes separately from other clothes so that toxic dust does not transfer from one garment to another.
- Always wear protective clothing and the appropriate safety equipment.

▶ **TECHNICIAN TIP**

Whenever using an atomizer with solvents and cleaners, make sure there is adequate exhaust ventilation. Wear appropriate breathing apparatus and eye protection.

▶ Shop Safety Inspections

Shop safety inspections are valuable ways of identifying unsafe equipment, materials, or activities so they can be corrected to prevent accidents or injuries. The inspection can be formalized by using inspection sheets to check specific items, or they can be general walk-arounds where you consciously look for problems that can be corrected. Some of the commons things to look for would be items blocking emergency exits or walkways, poor safety signage, unsafe storage of flammable goods, tripping hazards, faulty or unsafe equipment or tools, missing fire extinguishers, clutter, spills, unsafe shop practices, and people not wearing the correct PPE. Formal and informal safety inspections should be held regularly. For example, an inspection sheet might be used weekly or monthly to formally evaluate the shop, while informal inspections might be held daily to catch issues that are of a more immediate nature.

▶ Personal Protective Equipment

Personal protective equipment (PPE) is equipment used to block the entry of hazardous materials into the body or to protect the body from injury. PPE includes clothing, shoes, safety glasses, hearing protection, masks, and respirators **FIGURE 3-14**. Before you undertake any activity, think about all potential hazards and select the correct PPE based on the risk associated with the activity. For example, if you are going to change hydraulic brake fluid, put on some gloves to protect your skin from chemicals.

As you go through this chapter, you will learn how to identify the correct PPE for a given activity and how to wear it safely. It is important that the PPE you use fits correctly and is appropriate for the task you are undertaking. For example, if the task requires you to wear eye protection and specifies that you should use a full face shield, do not try to cut corners and only wear safety glasses. You also need to make sure the PPE you are using is worn correctly. For example, a hairnet that does not capture all of your hair is not protecting you adequately.

Protective Clothing

Protective clothing includes items like shirts, pants, shoes, and gloves. These items are your first line of defense against injuries and accidents and must be worn when performing any work. Always make sure protective clothing is kept clean and in good condition. You should replace any clothing that is not in good condition, since it is no longer able to fully protect you.

Work Clothing

Always wear appropriate work clothing. Whether this is a one-piece coverall/overall or a separate shirt and pants, the clothes you work in should be comfortable enough to allow you to move, without being loose enough to catch on machinery. The material must be flame retardant and strong enough that it

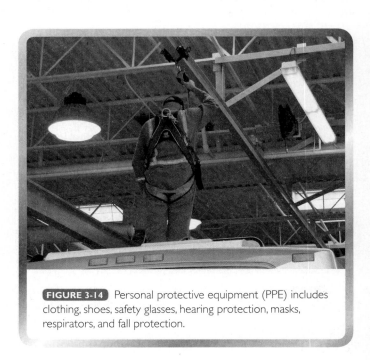

FIGURE 3-14 Personal protective equipment (PPE) includes clothing, shoes, safety glasses, hearing protection, masks, respirators, and fall protection.

cannot be easily torn. A flap must cover buttons or snaps. If you wear a long sleeve shirt, the cuffs must be close fitting, without being tight. Pants should not have cuffs, so that hot debris cannot become trapped in the fabric.

> ### ▶ TECHNICIAN TIP
>
> Each shop activity will require specific clothing depending on its nature. Research and identify what specific type of clothing is required for every activity you undertake. Wear appropriate clothing for various activities according to the shop's policy and procedures.

Care of Clothing

Always wash your work clothes separately from your other clothes. Start a new working day with clean work clothes and change out of contaminated clothing as soon as possible. It is a good idea to keep a spare set of work clothes in the shop in case a toxic or corrosive fluid is spilled on the clothes you are wearing.

Footwear

The proper footwear provides protection against items falling on your feet, chemicals, cuts, abrasions, and slips. The soles of your shoes must be acid and slip resistant, and the uppers must be made from a puncture-proof material such as leather. Some shops and technicians prefer safety shoes with a steel cap to protect the toes **FIGURE 3-15**. Always wear shoes that comply with your local shop standards.

Headgear

Headgear includes items like hairnets, caps, and hard hats. They help protect you from getting your hair caught in rotating machinery and protect your head from knocks or bumps.

For example, your hard hat can protect you from bumping your head on a vehicle when the vehicle is raised on a hoist. It is also good practice to wear a cap to hold longer hair in place and to keep it clean when working under a vehicle. Some caps are designed specifically with additional padding on the top to provide extra protection against bumps.

Hand Protection

Hands are a very complex and sensitive part of the body with many nerves, tendons, and blood vessels. They are susceptible to injury and damage. Nearly every activity performed on vehicles requires the use of your hands, which provides many opportunities for injury. Whenever possible, wear gloves to protect your hands. There are many types of gloves available and their applications vary greatly. It is important to wear the correct type of glove for the various activities you perform.

Chemical Gloves

Heavy-duty and impenetrable chemical gloves should always be worn when using solvents and cleaners. They should also be worn when working on batteries. Chemical gloves should extend to the middle of your forearm to reduce the risk of chemicals splashing onto your skin **FIGURE 3-16**. Always inspect chemical gloves for holes or cracks before using them, and replace them when they become worn.

Some chemical gloves are also slightly heat resistant. This type of chemical glove is suitable for use when removing radiator caps and mixing coolant.

Leather Gloves

Leather gloves will protect your hands from burns when welding or handling hot components **FIGURE 3-17**. You should also use them when removing steel from a storage rack and when handling sharp objects. When using leather gloves for handling hot components, be aware of the potential for heat buildup.

FIGURE 3-15 The proper footwear provides protection against items falling on your feet, chemicals, cuts, abrasions, and slips.

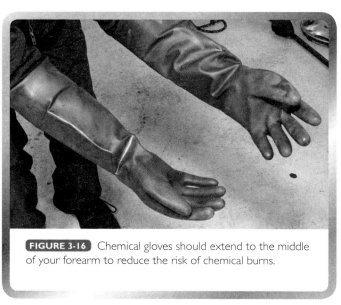

FIGURE 3-16 Chemical gloves should extend to the middle of your forearm to reduce the risk of chemical burns.

FIGURE 3-17 Leather gloves will protect your hands from burns when welding or handling hot components.

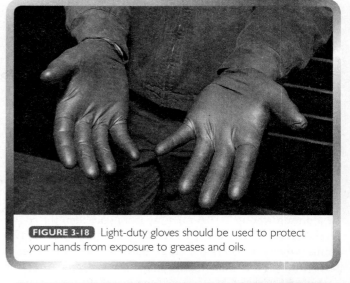

FIGURE 3-18 Light-duty gloves should be used to protect your hands from exposure to greases and oils.

Heat buildup occurs when the leather glove can no longer absorb or reflect heat, and heat is transferred to the inside of the leather glove. At this point, the leather gloves' ability to protect you from the heat is reduced and you will need to stop work, remove the leather gloves, and allow them to cool down before continuing to work. Also, avoid picking up very hot metal with leather gloves because it causes the leather to harden, making it less flexible during use. If very hot metal must be moved, it would be better to use an appropriate pair of pliers.

Light-Duty Gloves

Light-duty gloves should be used to protect your hands from exposure to greases and oils **FIGURE 3-18**. Light-duty gloves are typically disposable and can be made from a few different materials, such as nitrile, latex, and even plastic. Some people have allergies to these materials. If you have an allergic reaction when wearing these gloves, try using a glove made from a different material.

General-Purpose Cloth Gloves

Cloth gloves are designed to be worn in cold temperatures, particularly during winter, so that cold tools do not stick to your skin **FIGURE 3-19**. Over time, cloth gloves will accumulate dirt and grime so you will need to wash them regularly. Regularly inspect cloth gloves for damage and wear, and replace them when required. Cloth gloves are not an effective barrier against chemicals or oils, so never use them for that purpose.

Barrier Cream

<u>Barrier cream</u> looks and feels like a moisturizing cream, but it has a specific formula to provide extra protection from chemicals and oils. Barrier cream prevents chemicals from being absorbed into your skin and should be applied to your hands before you begin work **FIGURE 3-20**. Even the slightest exposure to certain chemicals can lead to dermatitis, a painful skin irritation. Never use a standard moisturizer as a replacement for proper barrier cream. Barrier cream also makes it easier to clean your hands because it can prevent fine particles from adhering to your skin.

FIGURE 3-19 Cloth gloves work well in cold temperatures, particularly during winter, so that cold tools do not stick to your skin.

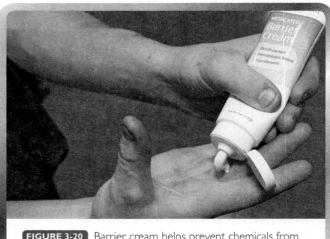

FIGURE 3-20 Barrier cream helps prevent chemicals from being absorbed into your skin and should be applied to your hands before you begin work.

Cleaning Your Hands

When cleaning your hands, use only specialized hand cleaners, which protect your skin FIGURE 3-21. Your hands are porous and easily absorb liquids on contact. Never use solvents such as gasoline or kerosene to clean your hands, because they can be absorbed into the bloodstream and remove the skin's natural protective oils.

Ear Protection

Ear protection should be worn when sound levels exceed 85 decibels, when you are working around operating machinery for any period of time, or when the equipment you are using produces loud noise. If you have to raise your voice to be heard by a person who is 2′ (0.6 m) away from you, then the sound level is about 85 decibels or more. Ear protection comes in two forms: One type covers the entire outer ear, and the other is fitted into the ear canal FIGURE 3-22. Generally speaking, the

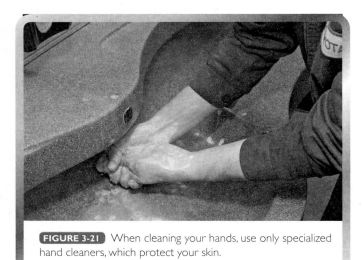

FIGURE 3-21 When cleaning your hands, use only specialized hand cleaners, which protect your skin.

FIGURE 3-22 Ear protection comes in two forms: One type covers the entire outer ear, and the other is fitted into the ear canal.

in-the-ear style has higher noise-reduction ratings. If the noise is not excessively loud, either type of protection will work. If you are in an extremely loud environment, you will want to verify that the option you choose is rated high enough.

Breathing Devices

Dust and chemicals from your workspace can be absorbed into the body when you breathe. When working in an environment where dust is present or where the task you are performing will produce dust, you should always wear some form of breathing device. There are two types of breathing devices: disposable dust masks and respirators.

Disposable Dust Mask

A disposable dust mask is made from paper with a wire-reinforced edge that is held to your face with an elastic strip. It covers your mouth and nose and is disposed of at the completion of the task FIGURE 3-23. This type of mask should only be used as a dust mask and should not be used if chemicals, such as paint solvents, are present in the atmosphere.

Respirator

A respirator has removable cartridges that can be changed according to the type of contaminant being filtered. Always make sure the cartridge is the correct type for the contaminant in the atmosphere. For example, when chemicals are present, use the appropriate chemical filter in your respirator. The cartridges should be replaced according to the manufacturer's recommendation to ensure their effectiveness. To be completely effective, the respirator mask must make a good seal onto your face FIGURE 3-24.

Eye Protection

Eyes are very sensitive organs and they need to be protected against damage and injury. There are many things in the shop

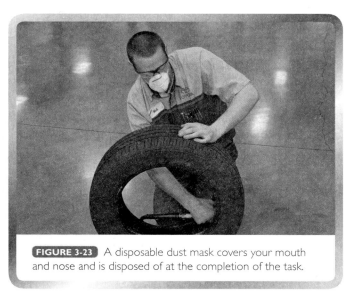

FIGURE 3-23 A disposable dust mask covers your mouth and nose and is disposed of at the completion of the task.

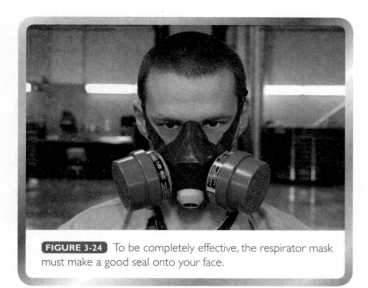

FIGURE 3-24 To be completely effective, the respirator mask must make a good seal onto your face.

environment that can damage or injure eyes, such as high-velocity particles coming from a grinder or high-intensity light coming from a welder. In fact, the American National Standards Institute (ANSI) reports that 2000 workers per day suffer on-the-job eye injuries. Always select the appropriate eye protection for the work you are undertaking. Sometimes this may mean that more than one type of protection is required. For example, when grinding, you should wear a pair of safety glasses underneath your face shield for added protection.

Safety Glasses

The most common type of eye protection is a pair of safety glasses, which must be marked with "Z87" on the lens and frame. Safety glasses have built-in side shields to help protect your eyes from the side. Approved safety glasses should be worn whenever you are in a shop. They are designed to help protect your eyes from direct impact or debris damage **FIGURE 3-25**. The only time

they should be removed is when you are using other eye protection equipment. Prescription and tinted safety glasses are also available. Tinted safety glasses are designed to be worn outside in bright sunlight conditions. Never wear them indoors or in low light conditions because they reduce your ability to see.

Welding Helmet

Wear a <u>welding helmet</u> when using or assisting a person using an electric welder. The light from a welding arc is very bright and contains high levels of ultraviolet radiation. The lens on a welding helmet has heavily tinted glass to reduce the intensity of the light from the welding tip, allowing you to see the task you are performing more clearly **FIGURE 3-26**. Lenses come in a variety of ratings depending on the type of welding you are doing; always make sure you are using a properly rated lens.

The remainder of the helmet is made from a durable material that blocks any other light from reaching your face. Welding helmets that tint automatically when an arc is struck are also available. Their big advantage is that you do not have to lift and lower the lens by hand.

Safety

Be aware that the ultraviolet radiation can burn your skin like a sunburn, so wear the appropriate welding apparel to protect yourself from this hazard.

Gas Welding Goggles

<u>Gas welding goggles</u> can be worn instead of a welding mask when using or assisting a person using an oxyacetylene welder **FIGURE 3-27**. The eyepieces are available in heavily tinted versions, but not as tinted as those used in an electric welding helmet. There is no ultraviolet radiation from an oxyacetylene flame, so the welding helmet is not required. However, the flame

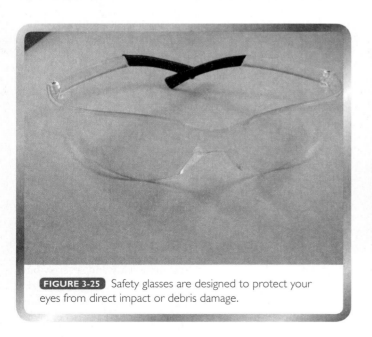

FIGURE 3-25 Safety glasses are designed to protect your eyes from direct impact or debris damage.

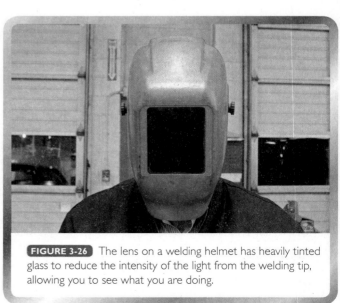

FIGURE 3-26 The lens on a welding helmet has heavily tinted glass to reduce the intensity of the light from the welding tip, allowing you to see what you are doing.

FIGURE 3-27 Gas welding goggles can be worn instead of a welding helmet when using or assisting a person using an oxyacetylene welder.

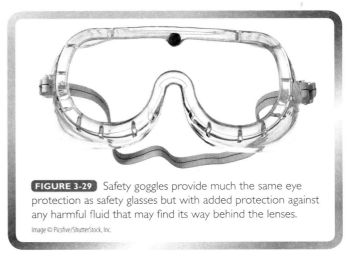

FIGURE 3-29 Safety goggles provide much the same eye protection as safety glasses but with added protection against any harmful fluid that may find its way behind the lenses.

Image © Picsfive/ShutterStock, Inc.

is bright enough to damage your eyes, so always use goggles of the correct rating.

Full Face Shield

It is necessary to use a full face shield when using solvents and cleaners, epoxies, and resins or when working on a battery **FIGURE 3-28**. The clear mask of the face shield allows you to see all that you are doing, but will protect your entire face from chemical burns should there be any splashes or battery explosions. It is also recommended that you use a full face shield combined with safety goggles when using a bench or angle grinder.

Safety Goggles

Safety goggles provide much the same eye protection as safety glasses but with added protection against harmful chemicals that may splash up behind the lenses of glasses **FIGURE 3-29**. Goggles

FIGURE 3-28 It is necessary to use a full face shield when using a grinder, solvents and cleaners, epoxies, and resins or when working on a battery.

also provide additional protection from foreign particles. Safety goggles must be worn when servicing air-conditioning systems or any other system that contains pressurized gas. Goggles can sometimes fog up when in use; if this occurs, use one of the special anti-fog cleaning fluids or cloths to clean them.

TECHNICIAN TIP

Each lab/shop activity will require at least the safe use of safety glasses, clothing, and shoes depending on its nature. Research and identify whether any additional safety devices are required for every activity you undertake.

Hair Containment

It is easy to get hair caught in rotating machinery, such as drill presses or running engines, and it can happen very quickly. If your hair gets caught in the machinery, you can be pulled into the machinery and injured or killed. Hair should always be tied back and contained within a hairnet or cap.

Your shop will have policies and procedures relating to appropriate hairstyles for shop activities. Research the policy and procedures to determine appropriate hairstyles for activities. Always wear your hair according to the policy and procedures. Use hairnets, caps, or elastic bands as required for each activity.

Watches and Jewelry

When in a shop environment, watches, rings, and jewelry present a number of hazards. They can get caught in rotating machinery, and because they are mainly constructed from metal, they can conduct electricity. Imagine leaning over a running engine with a dangling necklace; it could get caught in the fan belt and be ripped from your neck; not only will it get destroyed, but it could seriously injure you. A ring or watch could inadvertently short out an electrical circuit, heat up quickly and severely burn you, or cause a spark that may make the battery explode. A ring can also get caught on moving parts, breaking the finger bone or even ripping the finger out of the hand. To be safe, always remove watches, rings, and jewelry before starting work. Not only is it safer to remove these items, but your valuables will not get damaged or lost.

▶ Injury Protection Practices

Safe Attitude

Develop a safe attitude toward your work. You should always think "safety first" and then act safely. Think ahead about what you are doing, and put in place specific measures to protect yourself and those around you. For example, you could ask yourself the following questions:

- What could go wrong?
- What measures can I take to ensure that nothing goes wrong?
- What PPE should I use?
- Have I been trained to use this piece of equipment?
- Is the equipment I'm using safe?

Answering these questions and taking appropriate action before you begin will help you work safely.

Proper Ventilation

Proper ventilation is required for working in the shop area. The key to proper ventilation is to ensure that any task or procedure that may produce dangerous or toxic fumes is recognized so that measures can be put in place to provide adequate ventilation. Ventilation can be provided by natural means, such as by opening doors and windows to provide air flow for low-exposure situations. However, in high-exposure situations, such as vehicles running in the shop, a mechanical means of ventilation is required; an example is an exhaust extraction system.

Parts cleaning areas or areas where solvents and chemicals are used should also have good general ventilation, and if required, additional exhaust hoods or fans should be installed to remove dangerous fumes. In some cases, such as when spraying paint, it may be necessary to use a personal respirator in addition to proper ventilation.

Lifting

Whenever you lift something, there is always the possibility of injury; however, by lifting correctly, you reduce the chance of something going wrong. Before lifting anything, you can reduce the risk of injury by breaking down the load into smaller quantities, asking for assistance if required, or possibly using a mechanical device to assist the lift. If you have to bend down to lift something, you should bend your knees to lower your body; do not bend over with straight legs because this can damage your back FIGURE 3-30. Place your feet about shoulder width apart and lift the item by straightening your legs while keeping your back as straight as possible.

Housekeeping and Orderliness

Good housekeeping is about always making sure the shop and your work surroundings are neat and kept in good order. Trash and liquid spills should be quickly cleaned up, tools need to be cleaned and put away after use, spare parts need to be stored correctly, and generally everything needs to have a safe place to be kept. You should carry out good housekeeping practices while working, not just after a job is completed. For example, get rid of trash as it accumulates, clean up spills when they happen, and put tools away when you are finished working with them. It is also good practice to periodically perform a deep clean of the shop so that any neglected areas are taken care of.

Slip, Trip, and Fall Hazards

Slip, trip, and fall hazards are ever present in the shop, and they can be caused by trash, tools and equipment, or liquid spills being left lying around. Always be on the lookout for hazards that can cause slips, trips, or falls. Floors and steps can become slippery so they should be kept clean and have anti-slip coatings applied to them. High-visibility strips with anti-slip coatings can be applied to the edge of step treads to reduce the hazard.

Clean up liquid spills immediately and mark the area with wet floor signs until the floor is dry. Make sure the shop has good lighting so hazards are easy to spot, and keep walkways clear from obstruction. Think about what you are doing and make sure the work area is free of slip, trip, and fall hazards as you work.

FIGURE 3-30 Prevent back injuries when lifting heavy objects by crouching with your legs slightly apart, standing close to the object, and positioning yourself so that the center of gravity is between your feet.

► First Aid Principles

The following information is designed to provide you with an awareness of basic first aid principles and the importance of first aid training courses. You will find general information about how to take care of someone who is injured. However, this information is only a guide. It is not a substitute for training or professional medical assistance. Always seek professional advice when tending to an injured person.

First aid is the immediate care given to an injured or suddenly ill person. Learning first aid skills is valuable in the workplace in case an accident or medical emergency arises. First aid courses are available through many organizations, such as the Emergency Care and Safety Institute (ECSI). It is strongly advised that you seek out a certified first aid course and become certified in first aid. The following information highlights some of the principles of first aid.

In the event of an accident, the possibility of injury to the rescuer or further injury to the victim must be assessed. The first step is to survey the scene. While doing this, try to determine what happened, what dangers may still be present, and the best actions to take. Remove the injured person from a dangerous area only if it is safe for you to do so. When dealing with electrocution or electrical burns, make sure the electrical supply is switched off before attempting any assistance.

Always perform first aid techniques as quickly as is safely possible after an injury. When breathing or the heart has stopped, brain damage can occur within 4 to 6 minutes. The degree of brain damage will increase with each passing minute, so make sure you know what to do, and do it quickly.

First Aid Concepts

Prompt care and treatment prior to the arrival of emergency medical assistance can sometimes mean the difference between life and death. The goals of first aid are to make the immediate environment as safe as possible, preserve the life of the patient, prevent the injury from worsening, prevent additional injuries from occurring, protect the unconscious, promote recovery, comfort the injured, prevent any delay in treatment, and provide the best possible care for the injured person.

When attending to an injured victim, always send for assistance. Make sure the person who stays with the injured victim is more experienced in first aid than the messenger. If you are the only person available, request medical assistance as soon as reasonably possible. When you approach the scene of an accident or emergency, do the following:

1. **Danger**: Make sure there are no other dangers, and assist only if it is safe to do so.

2. **Response**: Check to see if the victim is responsive and breathing. If responsive, ask the victim if he or she needs help. If the victim does not respond, he or she is unresponsive.

3. Have a bystander call 9-1-1. If alone, call 9-1-1 yourself (or, if in another country, the relevant emergency assistance phone number).

4. If the victim is unresponsive and not breathing, place your hands in the center of the victim's chest and provide 30 chest compressions hard and fast **FIGURE 3-31**.

5. Tilt the victim's head back and lift the chin to open the airway. Give one rescue breath lasting 1 second, take a normal breath for yourself, and then give the victim another breath lasting 1 second. Each rescue breath should make the victim's chest rise.

6. Repeat the compression and breath cycles until an AED is available or EMS personnel arrive.

7. Once an automated external defibrillator (AED) arrives, expose the victim's chest and turn on the AED. Attach the AED pads. Ensure that no one touches the victim. Follow the audio and visual prompts from the AED. If no shock is advised, resume CPR immediately (five sets of 30 compressions and two breaths). If a shock is advised, do not touch the victim and give one shock. Or, shock as advised by AED. Resume immediately 30 compressions and two breaths.

FIGURE 3-31 Chest compressions.

Bleeding

A wound that is severely bleeding is serious. If the bleeding is allowed to continue, the victim may collapse or die. Bleeding is divided into two categories: external and internal. **External bleeding** is the loss of blood from an external wound where blood can be seen escaping. **Internal bleeding** is the loss of blood into a body cavity from a wound with no obvious sign of blood.

Before providing first aid, make sure you are not exposed to blood. Wear latex gloves or an artificial barrier. Lay the victim down, then apply a gauze pad and direct pressure to the wound **FIGURE 3-32**. Apply a pressure bandage over the gauze. If blood soaks through the bandage, apply additional dressings and pressure bandage **FIGURE 3-33**. Call 9-1-1 if bleeding cannot be controlled. Give nothing by mouth and seek medical aid immediately.

If an object punctures the victim's skin and becomes embedded in the victim's body, do not attempt to remove the object. Stabilize the object with a bulky dressing. Seek medical care immediately.

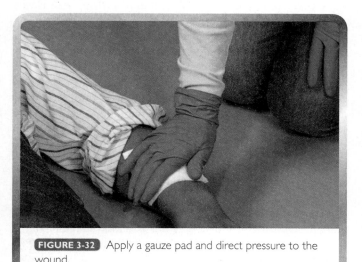

FIGURE 3-32 Apply a gauze pad and direct pressure to the wound.

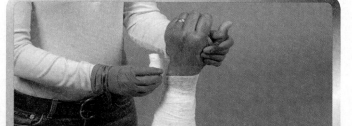

FIGURE 3-33 If blood soaks through the bandage, apply additional dressings and pressure bandage.

If the injured person has internal bleeding, it may not be immediately obvious. Symptoms of internal bleeding are bruising, a painful or tender area, coughing frothy blood, vomiting blood, stool that is black or contains bright red blood, and passing blood with urine. To assist an injured victim with internal bleeding, lay the victim down, loosen tight clothing, give nothing by mouth, and seek medical aid immediately.

Eye Injuries

Foreign objects can become embedded in the eye or chemicals can splash into the eye. If an object penetrates and becomes embedded in the eye, do not attempt to remove it. Lay the victim down, stabilize the object with a bulky dressing or clean cloths, ask the victim to close the other eye, and call 9-1-1 (or relevant emergency assistance phone number) **FIGURE 3-34**.

If an object is loose on the surface of the eye, pull the upper lid over the lower lid. Hold the eyelid open and gently rinse with water. Examine the lower lid by pulling it down gently. If you can see the object, remove it with a moistened sterile gauze, a clean cloth, or a moistened cotton swab. Examine the underside of the upper lid by grasping the lashes of the upper lid and rolling the lid upward over a cotton swab. If you can see the object, remove it with a moistened sterile gauze or a clean cloth **FIGURE 3-35**.

If a chemical splashes into the eyes, you may be able to flush it out using an eye wash station **FIGURE 3-36**. Hold the eye wide open and flush with warm water for at least 20 minutes, continuously and gently. Irrigate from the nose side of the eye toward the outside to avoid flushing material into the other eye. Loosely bandage the eyes with wet dressings. Call 9-1-1 (or the relevant emergency assistance phone number).

Fractures

A fracture is a broken or cracked bone. Always seek medical care for all fractures. There may be symptoms you are not aware of that may make the injury more complex than first thought. There are

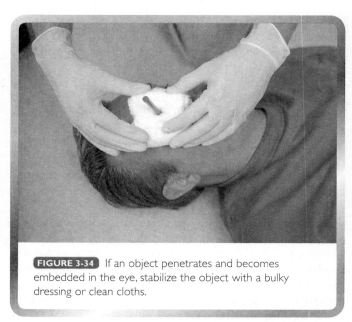

FIGURE 3-34 If an object penetrates and becomes embedded in the eye, stabilize the object with a bulky dressing or clean cloths.

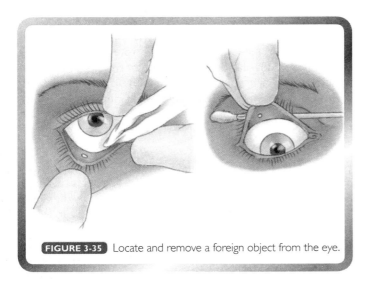
FIGURE 3-35 Locate and remove a foreign object from the eye.

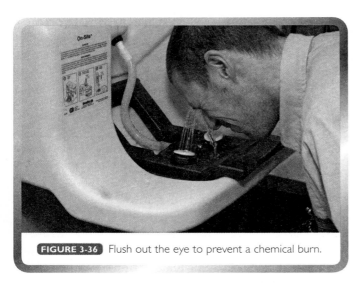
FIGURE 3-36 Flush out the eye to prevent a chemical burn.

three types of bone fractures: A **simple fracture** involves no wound or internal or external bleeding, an **open fracture** involves bleeding or the protrusion of bone through the skin, and a **complicated fracture** involves penetration of a bone into a vital organ.

The symptoms of a fracture include hearing a snapping noise when the injury occurred, pain or tenderness at or near the injury, inability to move the limb, loss of strength in the limb, shortening of the limb or an abnormally shaped limb, swelling and/or bruising around the area, and a grinding noise if the limb is moved. Allow the victim to support the injured area in the most comfortable position. Stabilize the injured part with your hands or a splint to prevent movement. If the injury is an open fracture, do not push on any protruding bone. Cover the wound and exposed bone with a dressing. Apply ice or a cold pack if possible to help reduce swelling or pain. Call 9-1-1 (or the relevant emergency assistance phone number) for any open fractures or large bone fractures. Do not move the victim unless there is an immediate danger. Be aware of the onset of **shock**, which may present as the victim vomiting or fainting. Shock is when the body's tissues do not receive enough oxygenated blood.

Sprains, Strains, and Dislocations

When a joint has been forced past its natural range of movement, or a muscle or ligament has been overstressed or torn, a sprain, strain, or dislocation may occur. A **sprain** occurs when a joint is forced beyond its natural movement limit. This causes stretching or tearing in the ligaments that hold the bones together. The symptoms of a sprain include pain and loss of limb function, with swelling and bruising present. When a sprain occurs, apply covered ice packs every 20 minutes, elevate the injured limb, and apply an elastic compression bandage to the area and beyond the affected area. You should always treat a sprain as a fracture until medical opinion says otherwise.

A **strain** is an injury caused by the overstretching of muscles and tendons. Symptoms of a strain are sharp pain in the area immediately after the injury occurs, increased pain when using the limb, or tenderness over the entire muscle. The muscle may also have an indentation at the strain location. When a strain occurs, have the victim rest, elevate the injured limb, apply covered ice packs every 20 minutes, and apply an elastic compression bandage.

A **dislocation** is the displacement of a joint from its normal position; it is caused by an external force stretching the ligaments beyond their elastic limit. Symptoms of a dislocation are pain or tenderness around the area, inability to move the joint, deformity of the joint, and swelling and discoloration over the joint. If a dislocation occurs, try to immobilize the limb and seek medical attention. Do not try to put the joint back in place.

Burns and Scalds

Burns are injuries to body tissues, including skin, that are caused by exposure to heat, chemicals, and radiation. Burns are classified as either superficial, partial thickness, or full thickness. Superficial burns, or **first-degree burns**, show reddening of the skin and damage to the outer layer of skin only **FIGURE 3-37**. Partial-thickness burns, or **second-degree burns**, involve blistering and damage to the outer layer of skin **FIGURE 3-38**. Full-thickness burns, or **third-degree burns**, involve white

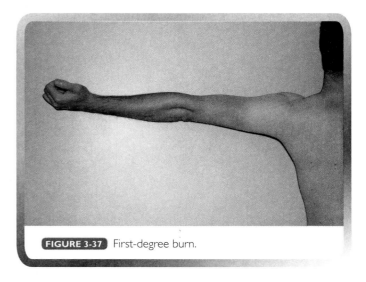
FIGURE 3-37 First-degree burn.

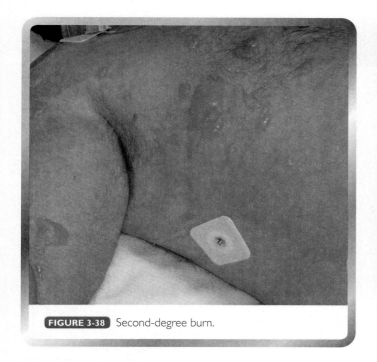

FIGURE 3-38 Second-degree burn.

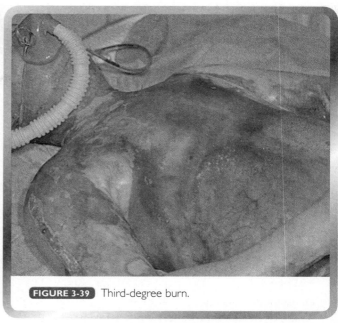

FIGURE 3-39 Third-degree burn.

or blackened areas and include damage to all skin layers and underlying structures and tissues **FIGURE 3-39**.

Burns can be caused by excessive heat, such as from fire; friction, such as from a rope burn; radiation, such as from a welding flash or a sunburn; chemicals, including acids and bases; or electricity, such as from faulty appliances. Scalds are injuries to the skin caused by exposure to hot liquids and gases. The effects of burns and scalds can include permanent skin and tissue damage, blisters caused by damage to surface blood vessels, severe pain, and shock.

Remove the victim from any danger. If clothing is burning, have the victim roll on the ground using the "stop, drop, and roll" method. Smother the flames with a fire blanket or douse the victim with water. For minor burns, cool the burn with cool water until the body part is pain free. After the burn has cooled, apply antibiotic ointment. Do not apply lotions or aloe vera. Cover the burn loosely with a dry, nonstick, sterile or clean dressing. Do not break any blisters. Give an over-the-counter pain medication such as ibuprofen. Seek medical care. Any large or third-degree burn must be treated by a qualified medical practitioner. Serious burns include skin that is blackened, whitened, or charred; a burn that is larger than 0.75″ (2 cm) in diameter; or a burn that is in the airway or on the face, hands, or genitals. When presented with such burns, call 9-1-1 immediately.

Wrap-Up

Ready for Review

▶ Your employer is responsible for maintaining a safe work environment; you are responsible for working safely.

▶ Always wear the correct personal protective equipment, such as gloves or hearing protection. Personal protective equipment (PPE) protects the body from injury but must fit correctly and be task appropriate.

▶ Accidents and injuries can be avoided by safe work practices.

▶ Every shop should mark evacuation routes; always know the evacuation route for your shop.

▶ OSHA is a federal agency that oversees safe workplace environments and practices.

▶ The EPA monitors and enforces issues related to environmental safety.

▶ Shop policies and procedures are designed to ensure compliance with laws and regulations, create a safe working environment, and guide shop practice.

▶ Identify hazards and hazardous materials in your work environment.

▶ Safety signs include a signal word, background color, text, and a pictorial message.

▶ Shop safety equipment includes handrails, machinery guards, painted lines, soundproof rooms, adequate ventilation, gas extraction hoses, doors and gates, and temporary barriers.

▶ Air quality is an important safety concern. Carbon monoxide and carbon dioxide from running engines can create a hazardous work environment.

▶ Electrical safety in a shop is important to prevent shocks, burns, fires, and explosions.

▶ Portable electrical equipment should be the proper voltage and should always be inspected for damage.

▶ Shop layouts should be well planned to maximize safety.

▶ Fuels and fuel vapors are potential fire hazards.

▶ Use fuel retrievers when draining fuel and have a spill response kit nearby.

▶ Types of fires are classified as A, B, C, D, or K, and fire extinguishers match them accordingly.

▶ Do not fight a fire unless you can do so safely.

▶ Eye wash stations and emergency showers allow flushing of chemicals or other irritants.

▶ Safety data sheets contain important information on each hazardous material in the shop.

▶ Vacuuming and using water are the safest methods of cleaning dust or dirt that may be toxic.

▶ Used engine oil and fluids must be handled and disposed of properly.

▶ Shop safety inspections ensure that safety policies and procedures are being followed.

▶ Hazardous chemicals and oils can be absorbed into your skin.

▶ Breathing devices include disposable dust masks and respirators.

▶ Forms of eye protection are safety glasses, welding helmet, gas welding goggles, full face shield, and safety goggles.

▶ Before starting work, remove all jewelry and watches, and make sure your hair is contained.

▶ Thinking "safety first" will lead to acting safely.

▶ All shops require proper ventilation.

▶ Lifting correctly or seeking assistance will prevent back injuries.

▶ First aid involves providing immediate care to an ill or injured person.

▶ Do not perform first aid if it is unsafe to do so.

Vocabulary Builder

barrier cream A cream that looks and feels like a moisturizing cream but has a specific formula to provide extra protection from chemicals and oils.

complicated fracture A fracture in which the bone has penetrated a vital organ.

dislocation The displacement of a joint from its nor- mal position; it is caused by an external force stretching the ligaments beyond their elastic limit.

double-insulated Tools or appliances that are designed in such a way that no single failure can result in a dangerous voltage coming into contact with the outer casing of the device.

ear protection Protective gear worn when the sound levels exceed 85 decibels, when working around operating machinery for any period of time, or when the equipment you are using produces loud noise.

Environmental Protection Agency (EPA) Federal government agency that deals with issues related to environmental safety.

external bleeding The loss of blood from an external wound; blood can be seen escaping.

first aid The immediate care given to an injured or suddenly ill person.

first-degree burns Burns that show reddening of the skin and damage to the outer layer of skin only.

gas welding goggles Protective gear designed for gas welding; they provide protection against foreign particles entering the eye and are tinted to reduce the glare of the welding flame.

hazard Anything that could hurt you or someone else.

hazardous environment A place where hazards exist.

hazardous material Any material that poses an unreasonable risk of damage or injury to persons, property, or the environment if it is not properly controlled during handling, storage, manufacture, processing, packaging, use and disposal, or transportation.

headgear Protective gear that includes items like hairnets, caps, or hard hats.

heat buildup A dangerous condition that occurs when the glove can no longer absorb or reflect heat and heat is transferred to the inside of the glove.

internal bleeding The loss of blood into the body cavity from a wound; there is no obvious sign of blood.

Occupational Safety and Health Administration (OSHA) Government agency created to provide national leadership in occupational safety and health.

open fracture A fracture in which the bone is protruding through the skin or there is severe bleeding.

personal protective equipment (PPE) Safety equipment designed to protect the technician, such as safety boots, gloves, clothing, protective eyewear, and hearing protection.

policy A guiding principle that sets the shop direction.

procedure A list of the steps required to get the same result each time a task or activity is performed.

respirator Protective gear used to protect the wearer from inhaling harmful dusts or gases. Respirators range from single-use disposable masks to types that have replaceable cartridges. The correct types of cartridge must be used for the type of contaminant encountered.

safety data sheet (SDS) A sheet that provides information about handling, use, and storage of a material that may be hazardous.

second-degree burns Burns that involve blistering and damage to the outer layer of skin.

shock Inadequate tissue oxygenation resulting from serious injury or illness.

simple fracture A fracture that involves no open wound or internal or external bleeding.

sprain An injury in which a joint is forced beyond its natural movement limit.

strain An injury caused by the overstretching of muscles and tendons.

third-degree burns Burns that involve white or blackened areas and damage to all skin layers and underlying structures and tissues.

threshold limit value (TLV) The maximum allowable concentration of a given material in the surrounding air.

toxic dust Any dust that may contain fine particles that could be harmful to humans or the environment.

welding helmet Protective gear designed for arc welding; it provides protection against foreign articles entering the eye, and the lens is tinted to reduce the glare of the welding arc.

Review Questions

1. Threshold limit value (TLV) is _____ allowable concentration of a given material in the surrounding air.
   a. the minimum
   b. the maximum
   c. half the
   d. twice the

2. A _____ is an injury caused by the overstretching of muscles and tendons.
   a. strain
   b. tear
   c. pull
   d. sprain

3. Ear protection should be worn when the sound levels exceed _____ decibels.
   a. 65
   b. 70
   c. 80
   d. 85

4. The _____ is a government agency created to provide national leadership in occupational safety and health.
   a. Environmental Protection Agency
   b. Automotive Safety Council
   c. Occupational Safety and Health Administration
   d. National Transportation Safety Board

5. _____ is inadequate tissue oxygenation resulting from serious injury or illness.
   a. Strain
   b. Internal bleeding
   c. Shock
   d. Bruising

6. A fire extinguisher marked with a _____ is approved to fight a class A fire.
   a. red triangle
   b. green triangle
   c. red square
   d. green square

7. _____ gloves should be used to protect your hands from exposure to gases and oils.
   a. Light-duty
   b. Cloth
   c. Leather
   d. Chemical

8. If a chemical splashes into the eye, hold the eye wide open and flush it with _____ water.
   a. cool
   b. cold
   c. warm
   d. hot

9. A machinery guard or a _____ painted line on the floor usually borders large, fixed machinery such as lathes and milling machines to prevent accidents.
   a. red
   b. orange
   c. black
   d. yellow

10. Properly constructed drop lights are _____.
    a. double insulated
    b. single insulated
    c. metal only
    d. plastic only

ASE-Type Questions

1. Technician A says a pictorial message allows a safety message to be conveyed to people who are illiterate. Technician B says that a pictorial safety message allows people who speak different languages to understand a safety message. Who is correct?
   a. Technician A
   b. Technician B
   c. Both Technician A and Technician B
   d. Neither Technician A nor Technician B

2. Technician A says almost all accidents can be avoided or prevented by taking a few precautions. Technician B says taking a few precautions doesn't prevent many accidents from happening. Who is correct?
   a. Technician A
   b. Technician B
   c. Both Technician A and Technician B
   d. Neither Technician A nor Technician B

3. Technician A says that it's a good idea for electric tools to be equipped with a ground prong or double-insulated, but you can proceed to use them with caution if they are not. Technician B says that all electric tools must be equipped with a ground prong or double-insulated or you should not use them. Who is correct?
   a. Technician A
   b. Technician B
   c. Both Technician A and Technician B
   d. Neither Technician A nor Technician B

4. Technician A says that fuel, oxygen, and heat need to be present in order for a fire to occur. Technician B says that fires can occur with just fuel and oxygen. Who is correct?
   a. Technician A
   b. Technician B
   c. Both Technician A and Technician B
   d. Neither Technician A nor Technician B

5. Technician A says that the shop should have a safety data sheet for each hazardous substance. Technician B says that each shop should have a safety data sheet for each dangerous product. Who is correct?
   a. Technician A
   b. Technician B
   c. Both Technician A and Technician B
   d. Neither Technician A nor Technician B

6. Technician A says that frequent and prolonged contact with used engine oil is not harmful to your health. Technician B says that prolonged and frequent contact with used engine oil can cause skin disorders and cancer. Who is correct?
   a. Technician A
   b. Technician B
   c. Both Technician A and Technician B
   d. Neither Technician A nor Technician B

7. Technician A says safety goggles are sufficient protection when using solvents and cleaners, epoxies, and resins. Technician B says safety goggles are the appropriate safety gear for working on a battery. Who is correct?
   a. Technician A
   b. Technician B
   c. Both Technician A and Technician B
   d. Neither Technician A nor Technician B

8. Technician A says it's important to remove a wedding ring before beginning work but not a watch. Technician B says it's important to remove a watch but not a necklace before beginning work. Who is correct?
   a. Technician A
   b. Technician B
   c. Both Technician A and Technician B
   d. Neither Technician A nor Technician B

9. Technician A says that most shops use hazardous materials daily. Technician B says most shops use cleaning solvents, gasket cement, brake fluid, and coolant on a daily basis. Who is correct?
   a. Technician A
   b. Technician B
   c. Both Technician A and Technician B
   d. Neither Technician A nor Technician B

10. Technician A says that the acronym PAST should be used when operating a fire extinguisher. Technician B says the acronym for using a fire extinguisher is PASS. Who is correct?
    a. Technician A
    b. Technician B
    c. Both Technician A and Technician B
    d. Neither Technician A nor Technician B

CHAPTER 4
Basic Tools and Lubricants

NATEF Tasks

Required Supplemental Tasks

Shop and Personal Safety
- Utilize safe procedures for handling of tools and equipment. (pp 83–84)

Tools and Equipment
- Identify tools and their usage in automotive applications. (pp 83–112)

- Identify standard and metric designation. (p 84)
- Demonstrate safe handling and use of appropriate tools. (pp 83–112)
- Demonstrate proper cleaning, storage, and maintenance of tools and equipment. (pp 83–112)
- Demonstrate proper use of precision measuring tools (i.e., micrometer, dial-indicator, dial-caliper). (pp 84–92)

Knowledge Objectives

After reading this chapter, you will be able to:
1. Discuss basic tool preparation and safety. (p 83)
2. Discuss tools and equipment fundamentals. (pp 83–84)
3. Discuss tool location. (pp 83–84)
4. List and describe precision measuring tools. (pp 84–91)
5. List and describe power tools. (pp 90–93)
6. List and describe air tools. (pp 93–94)
7. List and describe common shop tools. (pp 107–114)
8. List and describe diagnostic equipment. (pp 107–109)
9. List and describe servicing equipment. (pp 109–111)
10. Discuss the use of oxyacetylene torches. (p 111)
11. List and describe cleaning equipment. (pp 111–112)
12. List and describe electrical equipment. (pp 112–115)
13. Identify fluids and lubricants commonly used in the industry. (pp 115–120)
14. Identify metals commonly used in the industry. (pp 120–122)
15. Identify materials commonly used in the industry. (pp 122–124)

Skills Objectives

After reading this chapter, you will be able to:
1. Measure using an outside micrometer. (p 90)
   SKILL DRILL 4-1
2. Measure using a dial bore gauge. (p 91)
   SKILL DRILL 4-2
3. Measure using vernier calipers. (p 92)
   SKILL DRILL 4-3
4. Measure using a dial indicator. (p 93)
   SKILL DRILL 4-4
5. Select and use feeler gauge sets. (p 94)
   SKILL DRILL 4-5

► Introduction

Heavy vehicles are the result of a number of engineering sciences. Not only are they structurally complex, but they also combine a number of unique characteristics that unite together to provide passenger comfort in sometimes harsh environments.

Engine blocks and components are made of metals that are able to withstand very high temperatures and stresses. Lubricants keep the engine and its cooling systems functioning smoothly by reducing friction on moving parts and allowing the engine to perform reliably. The vehicle body is made of materials that are durable and strong enough to withstand harsh conditions and repeated use.

In addition to understanding the basic materials used in heavy-duty vehicle construction and the fluids used to keep them operating safely and efficiently, technicians must know which tools to use for different types of service applications. Tools and equipment are vital components of an efficient and effective shop operation. Nearly all shop tasks involve the use of some sort of tool or piece of equipment.

In this chapter, you will learn about the basic tools found in a shop and how to identify the correct tool for a particular application, how to use the tool correctly, and how to clean, inspect, and store it properly after using it. You will also learn about the fluids, lubricants, materials, and metals that make a vehicle what it is.

► Basic Tool Preparation and Safety

Although it is important to be trained on the safe use of tools and equipment, it is even more critical to have a safe attitude. A safe attitude will help you avoid being involved in an accident. Students who think they will never be involved in an accident will not be as aware of unsafe situations as they should be, and such an attitude could lead to accidents. Therefore, as we discuss the various tools and equipment you will encounter in the shop, pay close attention to the safety and operation procedures. Tools are a technician's best friend, but if used improperly, they can injure or kill.

Work Safe and Stay Safe

Always think "safety first" whenever you use tools. There is nothing more important than your personal safety. If you use tools (both hand and power) incorrectly, you could potentially injure yourself and others. Always follow equipment and shop instructions, including the use of recommended personal protective equipment (PPE). Accidents take only a moment to occur, but can take a lifetime to recover from. You are ultimately responsible for your own safety, so remember to work safe and stay safe.

Handling and Using Tools Safely

Tools must be safely handled and used to prevent injury and damage. Always inspect tools prior to use and never use damaged tools or any replacement tool. Check the manufacturer documentation and the shop procedures, or ask your supervisor if you are uncertain about how to use any tool. Inspect and clean tools when you have finished using them. Always return tools to their correct storage location. Some tools are heavy or awkward to use, so seek assistance if necessary, and use correct manual handling techniques.

► Tools and Equipment Fundamentals
Why Proper Tool Usage Is Critical

Every tool is designed to be used in a certain way to do the job safely. It is critical to use a tool in the way it is designed to be used and to do so safely. For example, a screwdriver is designed to tighten and loosen screws, not to be used as a chisel. <u>Ratchets</u> are designed to turn <u>sockets</u>, and are not to be used as a hammer. Think about the task you are undertaking, select the correct tools for the task, and use each tool for what it was designed.

► **TECHNICIAN TIP**

The correct tools make you much more efficient and effective in performing your job. Without tools, it would be very difficult to carry out vehicle repairs and servicing. This is the reason many technicians invest thousands of dollars in their personal tools. If purchased wisely, tools will help you perform more work in a shorter amount of time, thereby making you more productive. Therefore, think of your tools as an investment that pays for itself over time.

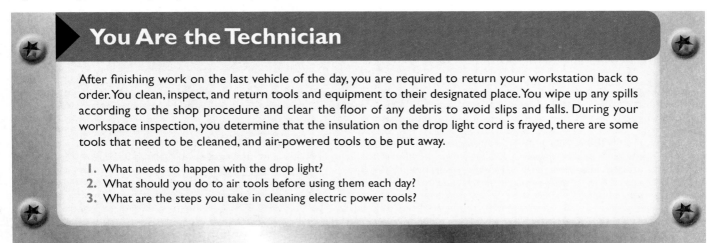

► You Are the Technician

After finishing work on the last vehicle of the day, you are required to return your workstation back to order. You clean, inspect, and return tools and equipment to their designated place. You wipe up any spills according to the shop procedure and clear the floor of any debris to avoid slips and falls. During your workspace inspection, you determine that the insulation on the drop light cord is frayed, there are some tools that need to be cleaned, and air-powered tools to be put away.

1. What needs to happen with the drop light?
2. What should you do to air tools before using them each day?
3. What are the steps you take in cleaning electric power tools?

Lockout/Tagout

Lockout/tagout is an umbrella term that describes a set of safety practices and procedures. These practices and procedures are intended to reduce the risk of technicians inadvertently using tools, equipment, or materials that have been determined to be unsafe or potentially unsafe, or that are in the process of being serviced. An example of lockout is physically securing a broken, unsafe, or out-of-service tool so that it cannot be used by a technician (FIGURE 4-1A). In many cases, the item is also tagged out so it is not inadvertently placed back into service or operated. An example of tagout is affixing a clear and unavoidable label to a piece of equipment that describes the fault found, the name of the person who found the fault, and the date that the fault was found, and that warns not to use the equipment (FIGURE 4-1B).

> **▶ TECHNICIAN TIP**
>
> Standardized lockout/tagout procedures are a mandatory part of workplace safety regulations in most countries. Familiarize yourself with your local legislation and with the specific lockout/tagout practices that apply in your workplace.

Identifying Metric and Imperial Designation

Many tools, measuring instruments, and fasteners come in metric and imperial sizes. Tools are identified as metric or imperial by markings identifying their sizes, or by the increments on measuring instruments. Fasteners bought new will have their designation identified on the packaging. Other fasteners may have to be measured by a ruler or vernier caliper to identify their designation. Manufacturers' charts showing thread and fastener sizing will assist in identifying standard or metric sizing.

To identify metric or imperial designation, follow these steps:

1. Examine the component, tool, or fastener to see whether any marking identifies it as metric or imperial. Manufacturer specifications and shop manuals may be referred to and may identify components as metric or imperial.

2. If no markings are available, use measuring devices to gauge the size of the item and compare thread and fastener charts to identify the sizing. Inch-to-metric conversion charts will assist in identifying component designation.

▶ Precision Measuring Tools

Technicians are required to perform a variety of measurements while carrying out their job. This requires knowledge of what tools are available and how to use them. Measuring tools can generally be classified according to what type of measurements they can make. A measuring tape is useful for measuring longer distances and is accurate to a millimeter or fraction of an inch (FIGURE 4-2A). A steel rule is capable of accurate measurements on shorter lengths, down to a millimeter or a fraction of an inch (FIGURE 4-2B). Precision measuring tools are accurate to much smaller dimensions: a micrometer, for example, can accurately measure down to 1/1000 of a millimeter (0.001 mm) in some cases.

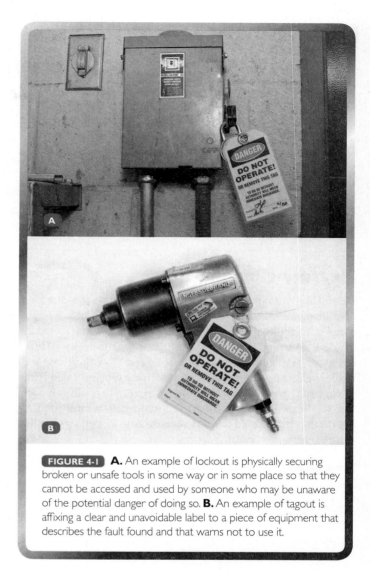

FIGURE 4-1 **A.** An example of lockout is physically securing broken or unsafe tools in some way or in some place so that they cannot be accessed and used by someone who may be unaware of the potential danger of doing so. **B.** An example of tagout is affixing a clear and unavoidable label to a piece of equipment that describes the fault found and that warns not to use it.

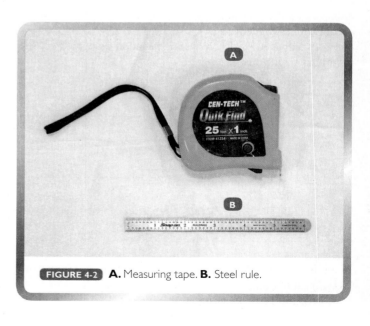

FIGURE 4-2 **A.** Measuring tape. **B.** Steel rule.

The metric and imperial systems are two sets of standards for quantifying weights and measurements. Each system has defined units. For example, the metric system uses millimeters, centimeters, and meters, whereas the imperial system uses inches, feet, and yards. Conversions can be undertaken from one system to the other. For example, 25.4 mm is equal to 1 inch, and 304.8 mm is equal to 1 foot.

Tools that make use of a measuring system, such as wrenches, sockets, drill bits, micrometers, rulers, and many others, come in both metric and imperial measurements. In many countries, metric measurements are the standard. However, conversion tables can be used to convert from one system to the other if needed.

Measuring Tape

Measuring tapes are a flexible type of ruler and are a common measuring tool. The most common type found in shops is a thin metal strip about 0.5″ to 1″ (13 to 25 mm) wide that is rolled up inside a housing with a spring return mechanism. Measuring tapes can be of various lengths, 16 to 25 feet (5 or 8 meters) and longer being very common. The measuring tape is pulled from the housing to measure items, and a spring return winds it back into the housing. The housing will usually have a built-in locking mechanism to hold the extended measuring tape against the spring return mechanism.

Stainless Steel Rulers

As the name suggests, a stainless steel ruler is a ruler that is made from stainless steel. Stainless steel rulers commonly come in 12″, 24″, and 36″ (30 cm, 61 cm, and 1 meter) lengths. They are used like any ruler to measure and mark out items. They are very strong, have precise markings, and resist damage. When using a stainless steel ruler, you can rest it on its edge so the markings are closer to the material being measured, which helps to mark the work precisely. Always protect the steel ruler from damage by storing it carefully; a damaged ruler will not give an accurate measurement. Never take measurements from the very end of a damaged steel ruler, as damaged ends may affect the accuracy of your measurements.

If the end of a ruler is damaged, you may be able to measure from the 25-mm mark and subtract 25 mm from the measurement.

Outside, Inside, and Depth Micrometers

Micrometers are precise measuring tools designed to measure small distances, and are available in both millimeter (mm) and inch (″) calibrations. Typically, they can measure down to a resolution of 1/1000 of an inch (0.001″) for a standard micrometer or 1/100 of a millimeter (0.01 mm) for a metric micrometer. Vernier micrometers equipped with the addition of a vernier scale can measure down to 1/10,000 of an inch (0.0001″) or 1/1000 of a millimeter (0.001 mm).

The most common types of micrometers are the outside, inside, and depth micrometers. As the name suggests, an **outside micrometer** FIGURE 4-3A measures the outside dimensions of an item. For example, it could measure the diameter of a valve stem. The **inside micrometer** measures inside dimensions. For example, the inside micrometer could measure an engine cylinder bore FIGURE 4-3B. **Depth micrometers** measure the depth of an item, such as how far a piston is below the surface of the block FIGURE 4-3C.

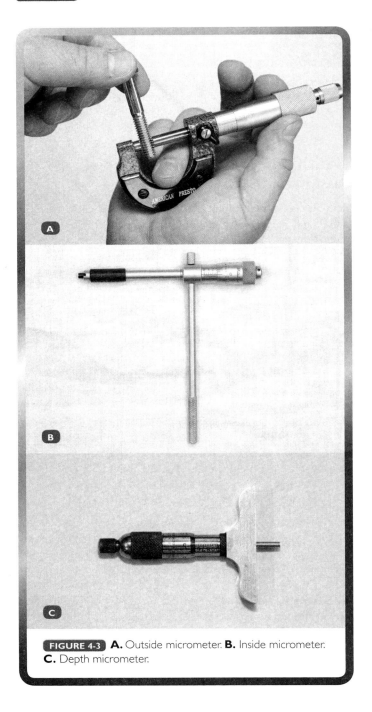

FIGURE 4-3 **A.** Outside micrometer. **B.** Inside micrometer. **C.** Depth micrometer.

Micrometers are precision measuring instruments and must be handled and stored with care. They should always be stored with a gap between the spindle and anvil so metal expansion does not interfere with their calibration.

All micrometers need to be checked for calibration (also called "zeroing") before each use. A 0–1" or 0–25 mm outside micrometer can be lightly closed all of the way. If the anvil and spindle are clean, the micrometer should read 0.000, indicating the micrometer is calibrated correctly. If the micrometer is bigger than 1" or 25 mm, then a "standard" is used to verify the calibration. A standard is a hardened machined rod of a precise length, such as 2" or 50 mm. When inserted in the same-sized micrometer, the reading should be exactly the same as listed on the standard. If a micrometer is not properly calibrated, it should not be used until it is recalibrated. See the tool's instruction manual for the calibration procedure.

The most common micrometer is an outside micrometer. The horseshoe-shaped part is the frame. It is built to make sure the micrometer holds its shape. Some frames have plastic finger pads so that body heat is not transferred to the metal frame as easily because heat can cause the metal to expand slightly and affect the reading. On one end of the frame is the anvil, which contacts one side of the part being measured. The other contact point is the spindle. The micrometer measures the distance between the anvil and spindle, so that is where the part being measured fits.

The measurement is read on the sleeve/barrel and thimble. The sleeve/barrel is stationary and has linear markings on it. The thimble fits over the sleeve and has graduated markings on it. The thimble is connected directly to the spindle, and both turn as a unit. Because the spindle and sleeve/barrel have matching threads, the thimble rotates the spindle inside of the sleeve/barrel, and the thread moves the spindle inwards and outwards. The thimble usually incorporates either a ratchet or a clutch mechanism, which prevents overtightening of the micrometer thimble when taking a reading. A lock nut, lock ring, or lock screw is used on most micrometers and locks the thimble in place while you read the micrometer.

To read a standard micrometer, perform the following steps:

1. Verify that the micrometer is properly calibrated.
2. Verify what size of micrometer you are using. If it is a 0–1" micrometer, start with 0.000. If it is a 1–2" micrometer, start with 1.000". A 2–3" micrometer would start with 2.000", and so on. (To give an example, let's say it is 2.000".)
3. Read how many 0.100" marks the thimble has uncovered. (Example: 0.300")
4. Read how many 0.025" marks the thimble has uncovered past the 0.100" mark in step 3. (Example: $2 \times 0.025 = 0.050"$)

5. Read the number on the thimble that lines up with the zero line on the sleeve. (Example: $13 \times 0.001 = 0.013"$)
6. Lastly, total all of the individual readings. (Example: $2.000 + 0.300 + 0.050 + 0.013 = 2.363"$)

A metric micrometer uses the same components as the standard micrometer. However, it uses a different thread pitch on the spindle and sleeve. It uses a 0.5-mm thread pitch (2.0 threads per millimeter) and opens up approximately 25 mm. Each rotation of the thimble moves the spindle 0.5 mm, and it therefore takes 50 rotations of the thimble to move the full 25-mm distance. The sleeve/barrel is labelled with individual millimeter marks and half-millimeter marks, from the starting millimeter to the ending millimeter, 25 mm away. The thimble has graduated marks from 0 to 49.

Reading a metric micrometer involves the following steps:

1. Read the number of full millimeters the thimble has passed. (To give an example, let's say it is 23 mm.)
2. Check to see if it passed the 0.5-mm mark. (Example: 0.50 mm)
3. Check to see which mark the thimble lines up with or has just passed. (Example: 37×0.01 mm $= 0.37$ mm)
4. Total all of the numbers. (Example: 23 mm + 0.50 mm + 0.37 mm = 23.87 mm)

If the micrometer is equipped with a vernier gauge, meaning it can read down to 1/1000 of a millimeter (0.001 mm), you need to complete one more step. Identify which of the vernier lines is closest to one of the lines on the thimble. Sometimes it is hard to determine which is the closest, so decide which three are the closest and then use the center line. At the frame side of the sleeve will be a number that corresponds to the vernier line. It will be numbered 1 to 0. Take the vernier number and add it to the end of your reading. For example: 23.77 + 0.007 = 23.777 mm.

For inside measurements, the inside micrometer works on the same principles as the outside micrometer, and so does the depth micrometer. The only difference is that the scale on the sleeve of the depth micrometer is backward, so be careful when reading it.

Using a Micrometer

To maintain accuracy of measurements, it is important that both the micrometer and the items to be measured are clean and free of any dirt or debris. Also make sure the micrometer is zeroed before taking any measurements. Never overtighten a micrometer or store it with its measuring surfaces touching, as this may damage the tool and affect its accuracy. When measuring, make sure the item can pass through the micrometer surfaces snugly and squarely. This is best accomplished by using the ratchet to tighten the micrometer. Always take the measurement a number of times and compare results to ensure you have measured accurately.

To correctly measure using an outside micrometer, follow the guidelines in **SKILL DRILL 4-1**.

SKILL DRILL 4-1 Measuring Using an Outside Micrometer

3 In your right hand, hold the frame of the micrometer between your little finger, ring finger, and palm of your hand, with the thimble between your thumb and forefinger.

4 With your left hand, hold the part you are measuring and place the micrometer over it.

5 Using your thumb and forefinger, lightly tighten the ratchet. It is important that the correct amount of force is applied to the spindle when taking a measurement. The spindle and anvil should just touch the component, with a slight amount of drag when the micrometer is removed from the measured piece. Be careful that the part is square in the micrometer so the reading is correct. Try rocking the micrometer in all directions to make sure it is square.

6 Once the micrometer is properly snug, tighten the lock mechanism so the spindle will not turn.

7 Read the micrometer and record your reading.

1 Select the correct size of micrometer. Verify that the anvil and spindle are clean and that it is calibrated properly.

8 When all readings are finished, clean the micrometer, position the spindle so it is backed off from the anvil, and return it to its protective case.

2 Clean the surface of the part you are measuring.

Telescoping Gauge

For measuring distances in awkward spots, such as the bottom of a deep cylinder, the **telescoping gauge** has spring-loaded plungers that can be unlocked with a screw on the handle so they slide out and touch the walls of the cylinder **FIGURE 4-4**. The screw then locks them in that position, the gauge can be withdrawn, and the distance across the plungers can be measured with an outside micrometer or calipers to convey the diameter of the cylinder at that point. Telescoping gauges come in a variety of sizes to fit various sizes of holes and bores.

Split Ball Gauge

A **split ball gauge (small hole gauge)** is good for measuring small holes where telescoping gauges cannot fit. They use a similar principle to the telescoping gauge, but the measuring head uses a split ball mechanism that allows it to fit into very small holes. Split ball gauges are ideal for measuring valve guides on a cylinder head for wear.

A split ball gauge can be fitted in the bore and expanded until there is a slight drag. Then it can be retracted and measured with an outside micrometer. Like some of the other measuring instruments discussed, the split ball gauge may have a dial or digital measurement scale fitted for direct reading purposes.

Dial Bore Gauge

A **dial bore gauge** is used to measure the inside diameter of bores with a high degree of accuracy and speed **FIGURE 4-5**.

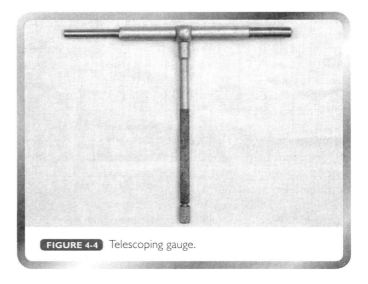

FIGURE 4-4 Telescoping gauge.

The dial bore gauge can measure a bore directly by using telescoping pistons on a T-handle with a dial mounted on the handle. The dial bore gauge combines a telescoping gauge and dial indicator in one instrument. A dial bore gauge determines whether the diameter is worn, tapered, or out-of-round according to the manufacturer's specifications. The resolution of a dial bore gauge is typically accurate to 5-10,000 of an inch (0.0005″) or 1/100 of a millimeter (0.01 mm).

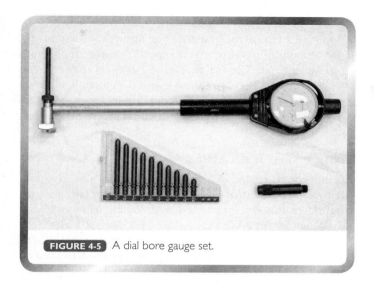
FIGURE 4-5 A dial bore gauge set.

Store a bore gauge carefully in its storage box and ensure the locking mechanism is released while in storage. Bore gauges are available in different ranges of size. It is important to select a gauge with the correct range for the bore you are measuring. When measuring, make sure the gauge is at a 90° angle to the bore and read the dial. Always take the measurement a number of times and compare results to ensure you have measured accurately.

To correctly measure using a dial bore gauge, follow the guidelines in **SKILL DRILL 4-2**.

Vernier Calipers

Vernier calipers are a precision instrument used for measuring outside dimensions, inside dimensions, and depth measurements, all in one tool. They have a graduated bar with markings like a ruler. On the bar, a sliding sleeve with jaws is mounted for taking inside or outside measurements. Measurements on older versions of vernier calipers are taken by reading the graduated bar scales, while fractional measurements are read by comparing the scales between the sliding sleeve and the graduated bar. Technicians will often use vernier calipers to measure length and diameters of bolts and pins or the depth of blind holes in housings.

Newer versions of vernier calipers have dial and digital scales. The dial vernier has the main scale on the graduated bar, while fractional measurements are taken from a dial with a rotating needle. These tend to be easier to read than the older versions. More recently, digital scales on vernier calipers have become commonplace. The principle of their use is the same as any vernier caliper; however, they have a digital scale that reads the measurement directly.

Using a Dial Bore Gauge

To use a dial bore gauge, select an appropriately sized adapter to fit the internal diameter of the bore, and install it to the measuring head. Many dial bore gauges also have a fixture to calibrate the tool to the size you desire. The fixture is set to the size desired, and the dial bore gauge is placed in it. The dial bore gauge is then adjusted to the proper reading. Once it is calibrated, the dial bore gauge can be inserted inside the bore to be measured. Hold the gauge in line with the bore and slightly rock it to ensure it is centered. Read the dial when it is fully centered and square to the bore to determine the correct measurement.

SKILL DRILL 4-2 Measuring Using a Dial Bore Gauge

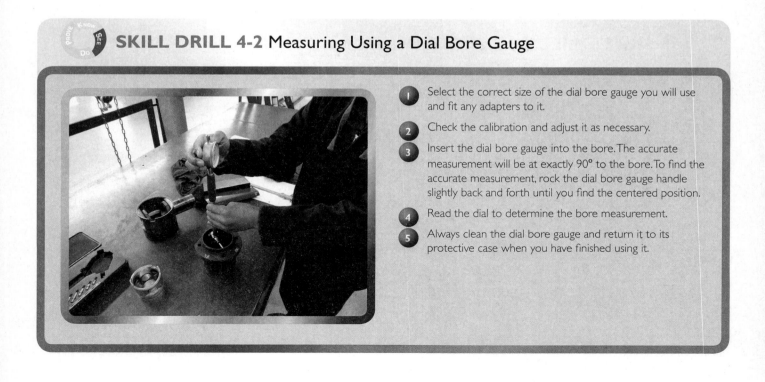

1. Select the correct size of the dial bore gauge you will use and fit any adapters to it.

2. Check the calibration and adjust it as necessary.

3. Insert the dial bore gauge into the bore. The accurate measurement will be at exactly 90° to the bore. To find the accurate measurement, rock the dial bore gauge handle slightly back and forth until you find the centered position.

4. Read the dial to determine the bore measurement.

5. Always clean the dial bore gauge and return it to its protective case when you have finished using it.

Using Vernier Calipers

Always store vernier calipers in a storage box to protect them and ensure the measuring surfaces are kept clean for accurate measurement. If making an internal or external measurement, make sure the caliper is at right angles to the surfaces to be measured. You should always repeat the measurement a number of times and compare results to ensure you have measured accurately.

To correctly measure using vernier calipers, follow the guidelines in SKILL DRILL 4-3 .

Dial Indicators

Dial indicators can also be known as dial gauges, and, as the name suggests, they have a dial and needle where measurements are read. They have a measuring plunger with a pointed contact end that is spring-loaded and connected via the housing to the dial needle. The dial accurately measures movement of the plunger in and out as it rests against an object. For example, they can be used to measure the trueness of a rotating disc brake rotor.

A dial indicator can also measure how round something is. A crankshaft can be rotated in a set of V blocks. If the crankshaft is bent, it will show as movement on the dial indicator as the crankshaft is rotated. The dial indicator senses slight movement at its tip and magnifies it into a measurable swing on the dial.

Dial indicators typically measure ranges from 0.010″ to 12″ or 0.25 mm to 300 mm and have graduation marks of 0.0005″ to 0.01″ or 0.001 mm to 0.01 mm. The large needle is able to move numerous times around the outer scale. One full turn may represent 1 mm or 0.1″. The small inner scale indicates how many times the outer needle has moved around its scale. In this way, the dial indicator is able to read movement of up to 1″ or 2 cm.

Dial indicators can measure with an accuracy of 0.001″ or 0.01 mm. The type of dial indicator you use will be determined by the amount of movement you expect from the component you are measuring. The indicator must be set up so that there is no gap between the dial indicator and the component to be measured. Most dial indicator sets contain various attachments and support arms so they can be configured specifically for the measuring task.

Using a Dial Indicator

Dial indicators are used in many types of service jobs. They are particularly useful in determining run-out on rotating shafts and surfaces. Run-out is the side-to-side variation of movement when a component is turned.

When attaching a dial indicator, keep support arms as short as possible. Make sure all attachments are tightened to prevent unnecessary movement between the indicator and the component. Make sure the dial indicator pointer is positioned at 90 degrees to the face of the component to be measured. Always read the dial face straight on, as a view from the side can give a considerable parallax error. The outer face of the dial indicator is designed so it can be rotated so that the zero mark can be positioned directly over the pointer. This is how a dial indicator is zeroed.

To correctly measure using a dial indicator, follow the guidelines in SKILL DRILL 4-4 .

Straight Edge

Straight edges are usually made from hardened steel and are machined so that the edge is perfectly straight. A straight edge is used to check the flatness of a surface. It is placed on its edge against the surface to be checked. The gap between the straight

SKILL DRILL 4-3 Measuring Using Vernier Calipers

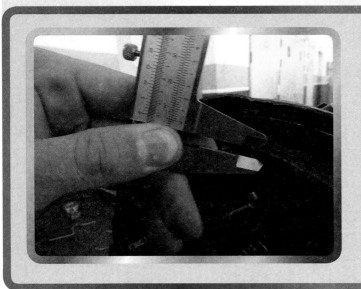

1. Verify that the vernier caliper is calibrated (zeroed) before using it. If it is not zeroed, notify your mentor, who will get you a replacement vernier caliper.

2. Position the caliper correctly for the measurement you are making. Internal and external readings are normally made with the vernier caliper positioned at 90° to the face of the component to be measured. Length and depth measurements are usually made parallel to or in line with the object being measured. Use your thumb to press or withdraw the sliding jaw to measure the outside or inside of the part.

3. Read the scale of the vernier caliper, being careful not to change the position of the movable jaw. Always read the dial or face straight on. A view from the side can give a considerable parallax error. Parallax error is a visual error caused by viewing measurement markers at an incorrect angle.

SKILL DRILL 4-4 Measuring Using a Dial Indicator

1. Select the gauge type, size, attachment, and bracket that fit the part you are measuring. Mount the dial indicator firmly to keep it stationary.

2. Adjust the indicator so that the plunger is at 90° to the part you are measuring and lock it in place.

3. Rotate the part one complete turn and locate the low spot. Zero the indicator.

4. Find the point of maximum height and note the reading. This will indicate the run-out value.

5. Continue the rotation and make sure the needle does not go below zero. If it does, reverse the indicator and remeasure the point of maximum variation.

6. Check your readings against the manufacturer's specifications. If the deviation is greater than the specifications allow, consult your supervisor.

edge and the surface can be measured by using feeler gauges. Sometimes the gap can be seen easily if light is shone from behind the surface being checked. Straight edges are often used to measure the amount of warpage the surface of a cylinder head has.

Feeler Gauges

Feeler gauges (also called *feeler blades*) are used to measure the width of gaps, such as the clearance between valves and rocker arms. Feeler gauges are flat metal strips of varying thicknesses. The thickness of each feeler gauge is clearly marked on each one. They are sized from fractions of a millimeter or fractions of an inch. They usually come in sets with different sizes and are available in metric and imperial measurements. Some sets contain feeler gauges made of brass. These are used to take measurements between components that are magnetic. If steel gauges were used, the drag caused by the magnetism would mimic the drag of a proper clearance. Brass gauges are not subject to magnetism, so they work well in that situation.

Some feeler gauges come in a bent arrangement to be more easily inserted in cramped spaces. Others come in a stepped version. Two or more feeler gauges can be stacked together to make up a desired thickness. Alternatively, if you want to measure an unknown gap, you can interchange feeler gauges until you find the one or more that fit snugly into the gap, and total their thickness to measure the gap. In conjunction with a straight edge, they can be used to measure surface irregularities in a cylinder head.

Using Feeler Gauges

If the feeler gauge feels too loose when measuring a gap, select the next size larger and measure the gap again. Repeat this procedure until the feeler gauge has a slight drag between both

parts. If the feeler gauge is too tight, select a smaller size until the feeler gauge fits properly. When measuring a spark plug gap, feeler gauges should not be used because the surfaces are not perfectly parallel, so it is preferable to use wire feeler gauges. Wire feeler gauges use accurately machined pieces of wire instead of metal strips.

To select and use feeler gauge sets, follow the guidelines in **SKILL DRILL 4-5**.

TECHNICIAN TIP

Never use feeler gauges on operating machinery.

Safety

Feeler gauges are strips of hardened metal that have been ground or rolled to a precise thickness. They can be very thin and will cut through skin if not handled correctly.

▶ Power Tools

Power tools are typically powered by an electric motor or compressed air. They may also be powered by burning of propellant, as in the case of a nail gun, or by a petroleum engine, as in the case of a portable compressor. A power tool may be stationary, such as a bench grinder, or portable, such as a portable electric drill. There are many different power tools designed to perform specific tasks. Some are corded and have to be plugged in, and others are cordless and have batteries. Power tools make many tasks quicker and easier to perform, and they can save many hours of work when used and maintained correctly.

SKILL DRILL 4-5 Selecting and Using Feeler Gauge Sets

1 Select the appropriate type and size of feeler gauge set for the job you are working on.

2 Inspect the feeler gauges to make sure they are clean, rust-free, and undamaged, but slightly oiled for ease of movement.

3 Choose one of the smaller wires or blades, and try to insert it in the gap on the part. If it slips in and out easily, choose the next size up. When you find one that touches both sides of the gap and slides with only gentle pressure, then you have found the exact width of that gap.

4 Read the markings on the wire or blade, and check these against the manufacturer's specifications for this component. If gap width is outside the tolerances specified, inform your supervisor.

5 Clean the feeler gauge set with an oily cloth to prevent rust when you store the set.

Drills and Drill Bits

A portable drill may be corded or cordless **FIGURE 4-6A**. A corded drill has a lead that has to be plugged into an electrical supply. The operating voltage of a drill depends on the country's supply. Corded drills are a good choice when moderate power is needed or when extended drilling is required. Cordless drills use their own internal batteries **FIGURE 4-6B**. Use a cordless drill when you cannot bring the work to the drill; instead, take the drill to the work. However, do not expect a cordless drill to be able to drill large holes through hard metal. Although they are very versatile, the amount of work they can do is limited by their power rating. The biggest drill bit that will fit into the chuck of these drills is usually marked on the body of the drill or chuck, along with the speeds at which it will turn. Some portable drills have two operating speeds, but most have a variable speed rating

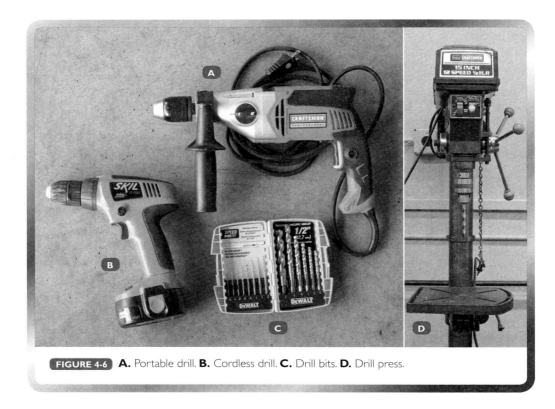

FIGURE 4-6 **A.** Portable drill. **B.** Cordless drill. **C.** Drill bits. **D.** Drill press.

that is determined by how much pressure is placed on the trigger and which may be set to any speed within the drill's range.

Drill bits come in many closely spaced sizes and types FIGURE 4-6C. The most common is the twist drill. It has a point with cutting flutes that form a common angle of 118°. Its body, which usually has two spiral grooves, and its shank are gripped in the jaws of the drill chuck. A drill chuck is a device for gripping drill bits securely in a drill. The twist drill is a good all-purpose bit for drilling metals.

A drill press allows for accurate drilling and has more control than is offered by a portable drill—which, although convenient, can be difficult to guide accurately FIGURE 4-6D. A mounted drill can feed the drill bit at a controlled rate, and the worktable on the drill typically has a vice to secure the job at a constant angle to the drill bit. This type of drill can also be set to run at different drilling speeds. Most drill presses have a drill chuck that takes bits up to 0.5″ (13 mm) or more in diameter.

Morse taper is a system for securing drill bits to drills. The Morse taper size changes according to drill size. The shank of the drill bit is tapered and looks like the tang of a file. It fits snugly into the drill spindle, which has a similar taper on its inside. The tang on the drill bit is located in the spindle, and it drives the drill. It is a quick way to change drills without constantly adjusting the chuck.

When there is a hole already drilled in sheet metal that needs enlarging, a multifluted tapered-hole drill will do the job in practically the same time it takes to say the name of this tool. A drilling speed chart is usually supplied with the drill press and should be kept nearby for handy reference. It compares drill sizes and metals to show the proper speed. For example, to drill a 0.5″ (10-mm) hole through a piece of aluminum, the drill speed should be 1800 rpm. Note also that drilling metals is best performed with the aid of a lubricant. The lubricant helps cool the cutting edges of the drill bit as well as lubricate it. Each metal requires its own type of lubricant, so check a drilling guide to identify the correct lubricant for the metal you are working on.

> **TECHNICIAN TIP**
>
> Drills are also used to drive other accessories, such as rotary files, screwdriver bits, and sockets.

Bench and Angle Grinders

Power grinders are available in a range of sizes and speeds. The size of a power grinder is usually determined by the diameter of the largest grinding wheel or disc that can be fitted to it. Some grinders are fixed to a bench or pedestal and the work is brought to the grinder; others are portable devices that may be taken to the work. Bench or pedestal grinders are generally powered by electricity, whereas portable grinders may be electric or air powered.

Grinding wheels and discs usually have a maximum safe operating speed printed on them. This maximum speed must never be exceeded, or the wheel or disc could disintegrate. Every well-equipped shop has a solidly mounted grinder, either on a pedestal bolted to the shop floor or securely attached to the workbench. Appropriate eye protection must be worn when grinders are being used, and the wheel guards, tool rests, and shields must be correctly and firmly in place.

A bench grinder (pedestal grinder) usually has a rating specifying the size of the grinding wheel it can take FIGURE 4-7A. Do not attempt to install a grinding wheel larger or smaller than the grinder's rating. Grinding wheels come in grades from coarse to very fine, depending on the size of the abrasive grains that are bonded together to make the wheel. They also range in hardness, depending on the abrasive used and the material used to bond the particles together. When a particular grinding application is required, a check should be done to verify the most suitable grinding wheel for the application.

An angle grinder is usually needed when the bench grinder is not appropriate FIGURE 4-7B. The angle grinder uses discs rather than wheels. During grinding, the face of the disc is used instead of the edge. An angle grinder can emit sparks to a distance of a few meters, so direct the sparks in a safe direction or set up a guard to catch them. Use hearing protection whenever grinding, as it is very noisy and can damage your ears.

Although not as common in an automotive shop, the straight grinder accepts conventional grinding wheels, just as stationary grinders do. However, the grinding wheel diameter is limited to about 126 mm. In many cases, the grinder has a long

FIGURE 4-7 **A.** Bench grinder. **B.** Angle grinder.

shaft that moves the grinding wheel away from the motor. This makes it useful for getting into recessed areas.

Hand-held cut-off wheels are powered either by electricity or by air. They use a special thin grinding disk to enable them to cut. They use the edge of the wheel for cutting and are useful for jobs that cannot be reached with a hacksaw.

▶ Air Tools

Air tools operate by using compressed air at high pressure. Air compressors in automotive shops typically run at greater than 90 psi (621 kPa), so exercise caution around them. Compressed air is transported through pipes and hoses. Air tools have quick-connect fittings so that various air tools can easily be used on the same air hose. There are several styles of quick-connect fittings; a shop usually uses one style throughout the entire shop.

An **air ratchet** uses the force of compressed air to turn a ratchet drive **FIGURE 4-8A**. It is used on smaller nuts and bolts. Once the nut is loosened, the air ratchet spins it off in a fraction of the time it would take by hand. The air ratchet also works well when there is not much room to swing a ratchet handle.

An **air nozzle** is probably the simplest air tool **FIGURE 4-8B**. It simply controls the flow of compressed air. It is controlled by a lever or valve and is used to blast debris and dirt out of confined spaces. Blasting debris and dirt can be dangerous, so eye protection must be worn whenever this tool is used. Noise levels are usually high, so ear protection should also be worn. It is dangerous to use an air nozzle to clean yourself off. Its blast should always be directed away from the user and anyone else working nearby.

An **air hammer**, sometimes called an *air chisel*, is useful for driving and cutting **FIGURE 4-8C**. The extra force that is generated by the compressed air makes it more efficient than a hand chisel and hammer. Just as there are many chisels, there are many bits that fit into the air hammer. Their selection depends on the job at hand.

An **air drill** has some important advantages over the more common electric power drill **FIGURE 4-8D**. With the right attachment, an air drill can drill holes, grind, polish, and clean parts. Unlike the electric drill, it does not carry the risk of producing sparks, which is an important consideration around flammable liquids or petroleum tanks. An air drill does not trail a live electric lead behind it that could be cut and possibly cause shock and burns. Neither does it become hot with heavy use.

The most common air tool in an automotive shop is the **air-impact wrench** **FIGURE 4-8E**. It is also called an *impact gun* or **rattle gun**, and it is easy to understand why when you hear one. Taking the wheels off a vehicle to replace the tires is a typical application for this air tool. Removing lug nuts often requires a lot of torque to twist the nuts free, and air-impact wrenches work well for that.

The air-impact wrench may be set to spin in either direction, and a valve controls roughly how much torque it applies. It should never be used for final tightening of wheel nuts. There is a danger in overtightening the wheel nuts, as this could cause the bolts to fail and the wheel to separate from the vehicle while it is moving. Another rule to remember about the air-impact wrench is that you have to use special hardened impact sockets, extensions, and joints. The sockets are special heavy-duty, six-point types, and the flats can withstand the hammering force that the impact wrench subjects them to.

FIGURE 4-8 **A.** Air ratchet. **B.** Air nozzle. **C.** Air hammer. **D.** Air drill. **E.** Air-impact wrench.

Grease Gun

Air can also be used to power a grease gun, which is used to lubricate components with grease fittings. The air power forces the grease through the aperture.

Creeper

To work underneath a vehicle, technicians use creepers, which are platforms on rollers that allow the technician to roll under the vehicle while on his or her back.

▶ Hand Tools

A large percentage of your personal tools will be hand tools. These are available in a variety of shapes, sizes, and functions and, like all tools, they extend your ability to do work. Over the years, manufacturers have introduced new fasteners, wire harness terminals, quick-connect fittings for fuel and other lines, and additional technologies that require their own specific types of hand tools. This means that technicians need to add tools to their toolboxes all of the time.

Wrenches

Wrenches (often referred to as spanners in some countries) are used to tighten and loosen nuts and bolts, which are two types of fasteners. There are three commonly used wrenches: the closed-end wrench, the open-end wrench, and the combination wrench. The *closed-end wrench* fits fully around the head of the bolt or nut and grips each of the six points at the corners, just as a socket does. This is precisely the kind of grip needed if a nut or bolt is very tight, and it gives you a better chance of loosening very tight fasteners. Its grip also makes the closed-end wrench less likely than the open-end wrench to round off the points on the head of the bolt **FIGURE 4-9A**. The ends of closed-wrenches are bent or offset so they are easier to grip, and have different-sized heads at each end. One disadvantage of the closed-end wrench is that it can be awkward to use once the nut or bolt has been loosened a little because you have to lift it off the head of the fastener and move it to each new position.

The *open-end wrench* is open on the end, and the two parallel flats grip only two points of the fastener **FIGURE 4-9B**. Open-end wrenches usually have either different-sized heads on each end of the wrench, or heads the same size but with different angles. The head is at an angle to the handle, and is not bent or offset, so it can be flipped over and used on both sides.

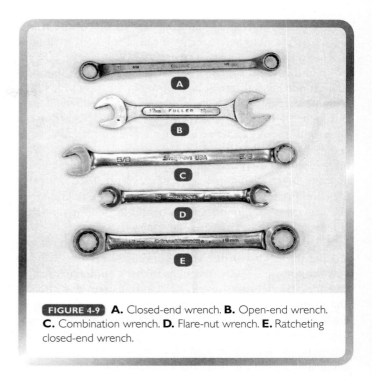

FIGURE 4-9 **A.** Closed-end wrench. **B.** Open-end wrench. **C.** Combination wrench. **D.** Flare-nut wrench. **E.** Ratcheting closed-end wrench.

This is a good wrench to use in very tight spaces as you can flip it over at the end of its travel and get a new angle, so the head can catch new points on the fastener. Although an open-end wrench often gives the best access to a fastener, it should not be used if the fastener is extremely tight, as this type of wrench grips only two points. If the jaws flex slightly or the flats do not fit tightly around them, the wrench could suddenly slip when force is applied. This slippage can round off the points of the fastener. The best way to tackle a tight fastener is to use a closed-end wrench to break the bolt or nut free; then use the open-end wrench to finish the job. The open-end wrench should be used only on fasteners that are no more than firmly tightened.

The *combination wrench* has an open-end head on one end and a closed-end head on the other **FIGURE 4-9C**. Both ends are usually the same size, so the closed end may be used to break the bolt loose and the open end to turn the bolt. Because of its versatility, this is probably the most popular wrench for technicians.

A variation on the open-end wrench is the flare-nut wrench, also called a flare-tubing wrench **FIGURE 4-9D**. This type of wrench gives a better grip than the open-end wrench because it grabs all six points of the fastener, instead of two. However, because it is open on the end, it is not as strong as a closed-end wrench. The partially open sixth side allows the wrench to be placed over tubing or pipes so it can be used to turn the tube fittings. Do not use the flare-nut wrench on extremely tight fasteners as the jaws may spread, damaging the nut.

Another open-end wrench is the *open-end adjustable wrench*, or *crescent wrench*. This wrench has a movable jaw that, by turning an adjusting screw, can be adjusted to fit any fastener within its range. It should be used only if other wrenches are not available because it is not as strong as a fixed wrench, and could slip off of and damage the heads of tight bolts or nuts. Still, it is a handy tool to have because it can be adjusted to fit most fastener sizes.

A *ratcheting closed-end wrench* is a useful tool for some applications because it can be repositioned without having to be removed **FIGURE 4-9E**. It has an inner piece that fits over and grabs the fastener points and is able to rotate within the outer housing. A ratcheting mechanism allows it to rotate in one direction and lock in the other direction. In some cases, the wrench needs simply to be flipped over to be used in the opposite direction. In other cases, it has a lever that changes the direction from clockwise to counterclockwise. Be careful to not overstress this tool by using it to tighten or loosen very tight fasteners, as the outer housing is not very strong.

There is also a *ratcheting open-end wrench*, but it uses no moving parts. One of the sides is partially removed so that only the bottom one-third remains to catch a point on the bolt. The normal side works just like a standard open-end wrench. The shorter side of the open-end wrench catches the point on the fastener so it can be turned. When moving the wrench to get a new bite, the wrench is pulled slightly outwards, disengaging the short side while leaving the long side to slide along the faces of the bolt. The wrench is then rotated to the new position and pushed back in so the short side engages the next point. This wrench, like other open-end wrenches, is not designed to tighten or loosen tight fasteners, but it does work well in blind places where a socket or ratcheting closed-end wrench cannot be used.

> ### ▶ TECHNICIAN TIP
>
> Wrenchs do a job properly only if they are the right size for the given nut or bolt head. The size used to describe a wrench is the distance across the flats of the nut or bolt. There are two systems in common use—metric (in millimeters) and imperial (in inches). Each system provides a range of sizes, which are identified either by a number, which indicates millimeters for the metric system, or by a fraction, which indicates fractions of an inch for the imperial system.

The *pipe wrench* grips pipes and can exert a lot of force to turn them **FIGURE 4-10A**. Because the handle pivots slightly, the more pressure put on the handle to turn the wrench, the more the grip tightens. The jaws are hardened and serrated, so increasing the pressure increases the risk of marking or even gouging the metal of the pipe. The jaw is adjustable so it can be threaded in or out to fit different pipe sizes. Pipe wrenches are also available in different lengths, allowing increased leverage to be applied to the pipe.

A specialized tool called an *oil-filter wrench* grabs the filter and gives you extra leverage to remove an oil filter when it is tight **FIGURE 4-10B**. These are available in various designs and sizes. Some oil-filter wrenches are adjustable to fit many filter sizes. Note also that an oil-filter wrench should be used *only* to remove an oil filter, never to install it. Almost all oil filters should be installed by hand.

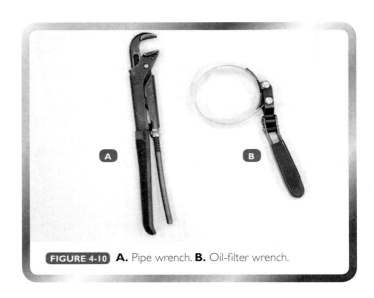

FIGURE 4-10 **A.** Pipe wrench. **B.** Oil-filter wrench.

Sockets

Sockets are very popular because of their adaptability and ease of use **FIGURE 4-11**. Sockets are a good choice when the top of the fastener is reasonably easily accessible. The socket fits onto the fastener snugly and grips it on all six corners, providing the type of grip needed on any nut or bolt that is extremely tight. They are available in a variety of configurations, and technicians

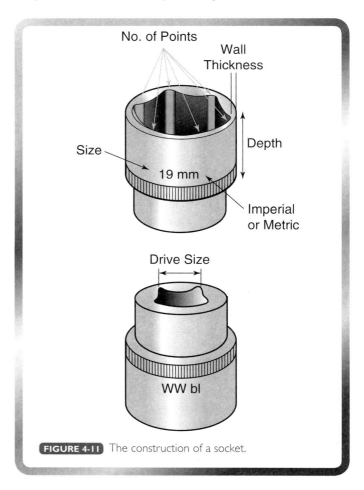

FIGURE 4-11 The construction of a socket.

usually have a lot of sockets so they can access a multitude of tight places. Individual sockets fit a particular size of nut or bolt, so they are usually purchased in sets.

Sockets are classified by the following characteristics:

- Metric or imperial depending on the vehicle manufacturer.
- Size of drive used to turn them: 1/2″, 3/8″, and 1/4″ are most common; 1″ and 3/4″ are less common.
- Number of points: 6 and 12 are most common; 4 and 8 are less common.
- Depth of socket: Standard and deep are most common; shallow is less common.
- Thickness of wall: Standard and impact are most common; thin wall is less common.

Sockets are built with a recessed square drive that fits over the square drive of the ratchet or other driver. The size of the drive determines how much twisting force can be applied to the socket. The larger the drive, the larger is the twisting force. Small fasteners usually need only a small torque, so do not use a drive larger than you need, because too large a drive may impede the socket's access to the bolt. For fasteners that are really tight, an impact wrench exerts a lot more torque on a socket than turning it by hand. Impact sockets are usually thicker walled than standard wall sockets and have six points so they can withstand the forces generated by the impact wrench, as well as grip the fastener securely.

Six- and 12-point sockets fit the heads of hexagonal-shaped fasteners. Four- and 8-point sockets fit the heads of square-shaped fasteners. Because 6-point and 4-point sockets fit the exact shape of the fastener, they have the strongest grip on the fastener, but they fit on the fastener in only half as many positions as a 12-point or 8-point socket.

> ### ▶ TECHNICIAN TIP
>
> Because sockets are usually purchased in sets, with each set providing a slightly different capability, you can see why technicians could easily have several hundred sockets in their toolbox.

Another factor in accessing a fastener is the depth of the socket. If a nut is threaded quite a distance down a stud, then a standard-length socket will not fit far enough over the stud to reach the nut. In this case, a deep socket will usually reach the nut **FIGURE 4-12A**.

Turning a socket requires a handle. The most common socket handle, the *ratchet*, makes easy work of tightening or loosening a nut when not a lot of pressure is involved **FIGURE 4-12B**. A ratchet may be set to turn in either direction and does not need much room to swing. It is built to be convenient, not super strong, so too much pressure could damage it. For heavier tightening or loosening, a breaker bar gives the most leverage **FIGURE 4-12C**. When that is not available, a **sliding T-handle** may be more useful. With this tool, both hands may be used, and the position of the tee piece is adjustable to clear any obstructions when turning it **FIGURE 4-12D**.

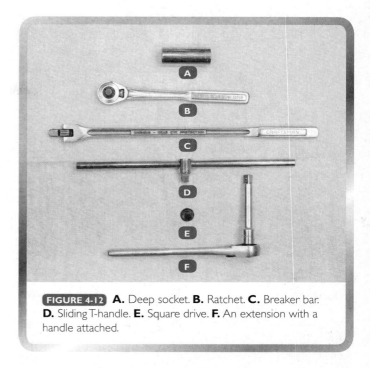

FIGURE 4-12 **A.** Deep socket. **B.** Ratchet. **C.** Breaker bar. **D.** Sliding T-handle. **E.** Square drive. **F.** An extension with a handle attached.

The connection between the socket and the accessory is made by a square drive **FIGURE 4-12E**. The larger the drive, the heavier and bulkier the socket. The 1/4-inch drive is for small work in difficult areas. The 3/8-inch drive accessories handle a lot of general work where torque requirements are not too high. The 1/2-inch drive is required for all-round service. The 3/4 inch and 1 inch are required for large work with high-torque settings. Many fasteners are located in positions where access can be difficult. There are many different lengths of extensions available to allow the socket to be on the fastener while extending the drive point out to where a handle can be attached **FIGURE 4-12F**.

A **speed brace** or speeder handle is the fastest way to spin a fastener on or off a thread by hand, but it cannot apply much torque to the fastener; therefore, it is used mainly to remove a fastener that has already been loosened, or to run the fastener onto the thread until it begins to tighten **FIGURE 4-13A**. A universal joint takes the turning force that needs to be applied to the socket through an angle **FIGURE 4-13B**.

Pliers

Pliers are a hand tool designed to hold, cut, or compress materials **FIGURE 4-14**. They are usually made out of two pieces of strong steel joined at a fulcrum point, with jaws and cutting surfaces at one end and handles designed to provide leverage at the other. There are many types of pliers, including slip-joint, combination, arc joint, needle-nosed, and flat-nosed.

Quality **combination pliers** **FIGURE 4-15A** are the most commonly used pliers in a shop. They are made from two pieces of high-carbon or alloy steel. They pivot together so that any force applied to the handles is multiplied in the strong jaws. Some pliers provide a powerful grip on objects, whereas others are designed to cut. Combination pliers can do both, which is

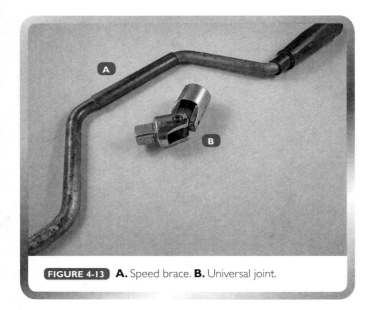

FIGURE 4-13 **A.** Speed brace. **B.** Universal joint.

FIGURE 4-14 Pliers are used for grasping and cutting.

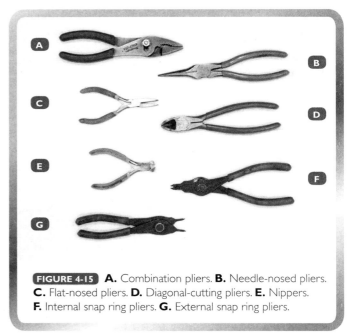

FIGURE 4-15 **A.** Combination pliers. **B.** Needle-nosed pliers. **C.** Flat-nosed pliers. **D.** Diagonal-cutting pliers. **E.** Nippers. **F.** Internal snap ring pliers. **G.** External snap ring pliers.

example, they can pick up a small bolt that has fallen into a tight spot **FIGURE 4-15B**. Flat-nosed pliers have an end or nose that is flat and square; in contrast, combination pliers have a rounded end. A flat nose makes it possible to bend wire or even a thin piece of sheet steel accurately along a straight edge **FIGURE 4-15C**. Diagonal-cutting pliers are used for cutting wire or cotter pins **FIGURE 4-15D**. Diagonal cutters are the most common cutters in the toolbox, but they should not be used on hard or heavy-gauge materials because the cutting surfaces will be damaged. End cutting pliers, also called nippers, have a cutting edge at right angle to their length **FIGURE 4-15E**. They are designed to cut through soft metal objects sticking out from a surface.

Snap ring pliers have metal pins that fit in the holes of a snap ring. Snap rings can be of the internal or external type. If internal, then internal snap ring pliers compress the snap ring so it can be removed from and installed in its internal groove **FIGURE 4-15F**. If external, then external snap ring pliers are used to remove and install the snap ring in its external groove **FIGURE 4-15G**. Always wear safety glasses when working with snap rings, as the rings can easily slip off the snap-ring pliers and fly off at tremendous speeds, possibly causing severe eye injuries.

▶ TECHNICIAN TIP

When applying pressure to pliers, make sure your hands are not greasy, or they might slip. Select the right type and size of pliers for the job. As with most tools, if you have to exert almost all your strength to get something done, then you are using either the wrong tool or the wrong technique. If the pliers slip, you will get hurt. At the very least, you will damage the tool and what you are working on. Pliers get a lot of hard use in the shop, so they do get worn and damaged. If they are worn or damaged, they will be inefficient and can be dangerous. Always check the condition of all shop tools on a regular basis.

why they are the most commonly used (please note that pliers are job specific).

Combination pliers offer two surfaces, one for gripping flat surfaces and one for gripping rounded objects, and two pairs of cutters. The cutters in the jaws should be used for softer materials that will not damage the blades. The cutters next to the pivot can shear through hard, thin materials, such as steel wire or pins.

Most pliers are limited by their size in what they can grip. Beyond a certain point, the handles are spread too wide, or the jaws cannot open wide enough, but water-pump pliers overcome that limitation with a movable pivot. These are often called Channellocks, after the company that first made them. These pliers have parallel jaws that allow you to increase or decrease the size of the jaws by selecting a different set of channels. They are useful for a wider grip and a tighter squeeze on parts too big for conventional pliers.

There are a few specialized pliers in most shops. Needle-nosed pliers, which have long, pointed jaws, can reach tight spots or hold small items that other pliers cannot. For

Locking pliers, also called *vice grips*, are general-purpose pliers used to clamp and hold one or more objects **FIGURE 4-16**. Locking pliers are helpful because they free up one or more of your hands when working; they clamp something and lock themselves in place to hold it. They are also adjustable, so they can be used for a variety of tasks. To clamp an object with locking pliers, put the object between the jaws, turn the screw until the handles are almost closed, then squeeze them together to lock them shut. You can increase or decrease the gripping force with the adjustment screw. To release them, squeeze the release lever and they should open up.

Cutting Tools

Bolt cutters cut heavy wire, nonhardened rods, and bolts **FIGURE 4-17A**. Their compound joints and long handles give the leverage and cutting pressure needed for heavy-gauge materials. **Tin snips** are the nearest thing in the toolbox to a pair of scissors **FIGURE 4-17B**. They cut thin sheet metal, and lighter versions make it easy to follow the outline of gaskets. Most snips come with straight blades, but if there is an unusual shape to cut, there is a pair with left- or right-hand curved blades. **Aviation snips** are designed to cut soft metals **FIGURE 4-17C**. They are easy to use because the handles are spring-loaded open and double-pivoted for extra leverage.

Allen Wrenches

Allen wrenches, sometimes called Allen keys or hex keys, are tools designed to tighten and loosen fasteners with Allen heads **FIGURE 4-18**. The Allen head has an internal hexagonal recess that the Allen wrench fits into. Allen wrenches come in sets, and there is a correct wrench size for every Allen head. They give the best grip on a screw or bolt of all the drivers, and their shape makes them good at getting into tight spots. Care must be utilized to make sure the correct size of Allen wrench is used, or the wrench and/or socket head will be rounded off. The traditional Allen wrench is a hexagonal bar with a right-angle bend at one end. They are made in various sizes in both metric and imperial. As their popularity has increased, so too has the number of tool variations. Now Allen sockets are available, as are T-handle Allen wrenches.

Screwdrivers

The correct screwdriver to use depends on the type of slot or recess in the head of the screw or bolt, and how accessible it is. Most screwdrivers cannot grip as securely as wrenches, so it is very important to match the tip of the screwdriver exactly with the slot or recess in the head of a fastener; otherwise the tool might slip, damaging the fastener or the tool and possibly injuring you. When using a screwdriver, always check where the screwdriver tip could end up if it slipped off the head of the screw. Many technicians who have not taken this precaution have stabbed a screwdriver into or through their hand.

The most common screwdriver has a flat tip, or blade, which gives it the name **flat-tip screwdriver** **FIGURE 4-19A**. The tip should be almost as wide and thick as the slot in the fastener, so that twisting force applied to the screwdriver is transferred

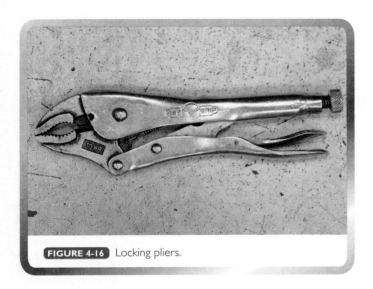
FIGURE 4-16 Locking pliers.

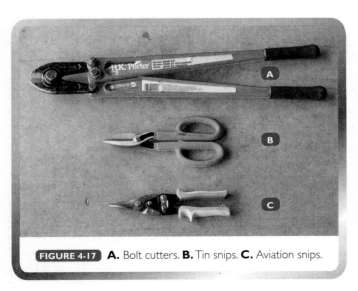
FIGURE 4-17 **A.** Bolt cutters. **B.** Tin snips. **C.** Aviation snips.

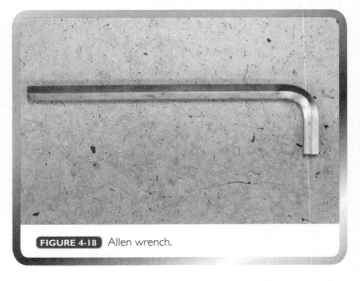
FIGURE 4-18 Allen wrench.

right out to the edges of the head where it has the most effect. The tip should be a snug fit in the slot of the screw head. Then the twisting force is applied evenly along the sides of the slot. This will guard against the screwdriver suddenly chewing a piece out of the slot and slipping just when the most force is being exerted. Flat-tip screwdrivers are available in a variety of sizes and lengths, so find the right one for the job.

If viewed from the side, the tip should taper slightly until the very end where the tip fits into the slot. If the tip is not clean and square, it should be reshaped or replaced.

When you use a flat-tip screwdriver, support the shaft with your free hand as you turn it (but keep it behind the tip). This helps keep the tip square on the slot and centered. Screwdrivers that slip are a common source of damage and injury in shops.

A screw or bolt with a cross-shaped recess requires a **Phillips screwdriver**, or a *Pozidriv screwdriver* **FIGURE 4-19B**. The cross-shaped slot holds the tip of the screwdriver securely on the head. The Phillips tip fits a tapered recess, whereas the Pozidriv fits into slots with parallel sides in the head of the screw **FIGURE 4-19C**. Both a Phillips and a Pozidriv screwdriver are less likely to slip sideways because the point is centered in the screw, but again, the screwdriver must be the right size. The fitting process is simplified for these two types of screwdrivers because four sizes are enough to fit almost all fasteners with this type of screw head.

The **offset screwdriver** fits into spaces where a straight screwdriver cannot and is useful where there is not much room to turn it **FIGURE 4-20A**. The two tips look identical, but one is set at 90° to the other. This is because sometimes there is room to make only a quarter turn of the driver. Thus, the driver has two tips on opposite ends, so that offset ends of the screwdriver can be used alternately.

The **ratcheting screwdriver** is a popular screwdriver handle that usually comes with a selection of flat and Phillips tips **FIGURE 4-20B**. It has a ratchet inside the handle that turns the tip in only one direction depending on how the slider is set. When set for loosening, a screw can be undone without removing the tip from the head of the screw. When set for tightening, a screw can be inserted just as easily.

An **impact driver** is used when a screw or a bolt is rusted/corroded in place, or overtightened, and needs a tool that can apply more force than the other members of this family **FIGURE 4-20C**. Screw slots could easily be stripped with the use of a standard screwdriver. The force of the hammer pushing the bit into the screw, and at the same time turning it, makes it more likely the screw will break loose. The impact driver accepts a variety of special, impact tips. Choose the right one for the screw head, fit the tip in place, and then tension it in the direction it has to turn. A sharp blow with the hammer breaks the screw free, and then it can be unscrewed.

Magnetic Pickup Tools and Mechanical Fingers

Magnetic pickup tools and **mechanical fingers** are very useful for grabbing items in tight spaces. A magnetic pickup tool is typically a telescoping stick that has a magnet attached to the end on a swivel joint **FIGURE 4-21A**. The magnet is strong enough to pick up screws, bolts, and sockets. For example, if a screw is

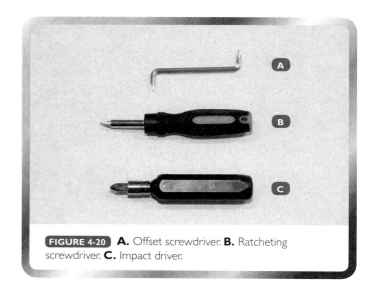

FIGURE 4-20 **A.** Offset screwdriver. **B.** Ratcheting screwdriver. **C.** Impact driver.

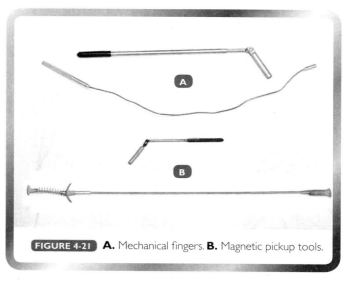

FIGURE 4-21 **A.** Mechanical fingers. **B.** Magnetic pickup tools.

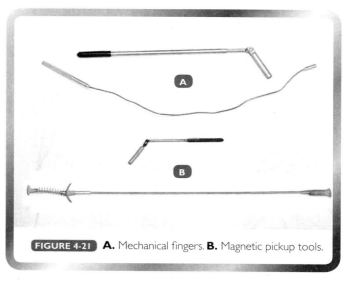

FIGURE 4-19 **A.** Flat-tip screwdriver. **B.** Phillips screwdriver. **C.** Pozidriv screwdriver.

dropped into a tight crevice where your fingers cannot reach, a magnetic pickup tool can be used to extract it.

Mechanical fingers are also designed to extract or insert objects in tight spaces **FIGURE 4-21B**. Because they actually grab the object, they can pick up nonmagnetic items, which makes them handy for picking up rubber or plastic parts. They use a flexible body and come in different lengths, but are typically about 12″ to 18″ (305 to 457 mm) long. They have expanding grappling fingers on one end to grab items, and the other end has a push mechanism to expand the fingers and a retracting spring to contract the fingers.

▶ **TECHNICIAN TIP**

The challenge is to get the magnet down inside some areas because the magnet wants to keep sticking to the sides. One trick in this situation is to roll up a piece of paper so that a tube is created. Stick that down into the area of the dropped part, then slide the magnet down the tube, which will help it get past magnetic objects. Once the magnet is down, you may want to remove the roll of paper. Just remember two things: First, patience is important when using this tool; and second, don't drop anything in the first place!

Hammers

Hammers are a vital part of the shop tool collection, and a variety are commonly used. The most common hammer in an automotive shop is the **ball-peen (engineer's) hammer** **FIGURE 4-22A**. Like most hammers, its head is hardened steel. A punch or a chisel can be driven with the flat face. Its name comes from the ball peen or rounded face. It is usually used for flattening and **peening** a rivet. The hammer should always match the size of the job, and it is better to use one that is too big than too small.

▶ **TECHNICIAN TIP**

The hammer you use depends on the part you are striking. Hammers with a metal face should almost always be harder than the part you are hammering. Never strike two hardened tools together, as this can cause the hardened parts to shatter.

Hitting chisels with a steel hammer is fine, but sometimes you need only to tap a component to position it **FIGURE 4-22B**. A steel hammer might mark or damage the part, especially if it is made of a softer metal such as aluminum. In such cases, a soft-faced hammer should be used for the job. Soft-faced hammers range from very soft, with rubber or plastic heads, to slightly harder, with brass or copper heads.

When a large chisel needs a really strong blow, it is time to use a **club hammer** **FIGURE 4-22C**. The club hammer is like a small mallet, with two square faces made of high-carbon steel. It is the heaviest type of hammer that can be used one-handed. The club hammer is used in conjunction with a chisel to cut off a bolt where corrosion has made it impossible to remove the nut.

FIGURE 4-22 **A.** Ball-peen hammer. **B.** Steel hammer. **C.** Club hammer. **D.** Nylon/brass tip mallet. **E.** Dead-blow hammer.

The most common small-headed mallet in the shop has a head made of hard nylon **FIGURE 4-22D**. It is a special-purpose tool and is often used for moving things into place where it is important not to damage the item being moved. For example, it can be used to tap a crankshaft, to measure end play, or to break a gasket seal on an aluminum casing.

A **dead-blow hammer** is designed not to bounce back when it hits something **FIGURE 4-22E**. A rebounding hammer can be dangerous or destructive. A dead-blow hammer may be made with a lead head or, more commonly, a hollow polyurethane head filled with lead shot or sand. The head absorbs the blow when the hammer makes contact, reducing any bounce-back or rebounding. This hammer can be used when working on the vehicle chassis or when dislodging stuck parts.

Safety

When using hammers and chisels, safety goggles must always be worn.

Chisels

The most common kind of chisel is a cold chisel **FIGURE 4-23A**. It gets its name from the fact that it is used to cut cold metals, rather than heated metals. It has a flat blade made of high-quality steel and a cutting angle of approximately 70 degrees. The cutting end is tempered and hardened because it has to be harder than the metals to be cut. The head of the chisel needs to be softer so it will not chip when it is hit with a hammer. Technicians sometimes use a cold chisel to remove bolts whose heads have rounded off. A **cross-cut chisel** is so named because the sharpened edge is across the blade width. This chisel narrows down along the stock, so it is good for getting in grooves **FIGURE 4-23B**. It is used for cleaning out or even making key ways. The flying chips of metal should always be directed away from the user.

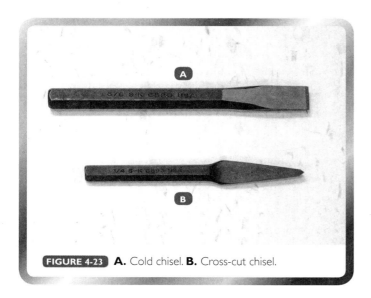

FIGURE 4-23 **A.** Cold chisel. **B.** Cross-cut chisel.

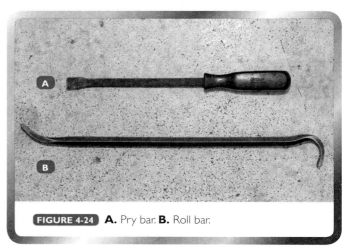

FIGURE 4-24 **A.** Pry bar. **B.** Roll bar.

FIGURE 4-25 A gasket scraper.

TECHNICIAN TIP

Chisels and punches are designed with a softer striking end than hammers. Over time, this softer metal "mushrooms," and small fragments are prone to breaking off when hammered. These fragments could cause eye or other penetrative injuries to people in the area. Always inspect chisels and punches for mushrooming and dress them on a grinder when necessary.

Pry Bars

Pry bars (also known as crowbars) are composed of a strong metal and are used as levers to move, adjust, or pry. Pry bars are available in a variety of shapes and sizes. Many have a tapered end that is slightly bent, with a plastic handle on the other end FIGURE 4-24A. This design works well for applying force to tension belts or for moving parts into alignment. Another type of pry bar is the roll bar FIGURE 4-24B. One end is sharply curved and tapered and is used for prying. The other end is tapered to a dull point and is used to align larger holes, such as transmission bell housings or engine motor mounts. Because pry bars are made of hardened steel, care should be taken when using them on softer materials to avoid any damage.

Gasket Scrapers

A gasket scraper has a hardened, sharpened blade. It is designed to remove a gasket without damaging the sealing face of the component, when used properly FIGURE 4-25. On one end, it has a comfortable handle to grip like a screwdriver handle; on the other end, a blade is fitted with a sharp edge to assist in the removal of gaskets. The gasket scraper should be kept sharp to make it easy to remove all traces of the old gasket and sealing compound. The blades come in different sizes, with a typical size being 1″ (25 mm) wide. Whenever you use a gasket scraper, be very careful not to nick or damage the surface being cleaned.

TECHNICIAN TIP

Many engine components are made of aluminum. Because aluminum is quite soft, it is critical that you use the gasket scraper very carefully so as not to damage an aluminum surface. This can be accomplished by keeping the gasket scraper at a fairly flat angle to the surface. The gasket scraper should also be used only by hand, not with a hammer.

Files

Files are cutting devices designed to remove small amounts of material from the surface of a workpiece. Files are available in a variety of shapes, sizes, and coarseness, depending on the material being worked on and the size of the job. Files have a pointed tang on one end that is fitted to a handle. Files are often sold without handles, but they should not be used until a handle of the right size has been fitted. A correctly sized handle fits snugly without working loose when the file is in use. Always check the handle before using the file. If the handle is loose, give it a sharp rap to tighten it up, or if it is the threaded type, screw it on tighter. If it fails to fit snugly, you must use a different-sized handle.

Safety

Hands should always be kept away from the surface of the file and the metal that is being worked on. Filing can produce small slivers of metal that can be difficult to remove from a finger or hand. Clean hands will help avoid slipping and lessen the corrosion caused by acids and moisture from the skin.

What makes one file different from another is not just the shape but also how much material it is designed to remove with each stroke. The teeth on the file determine how much material will be removed **FIGURE 4-26** . Since the teeth face in one direction only, the file cuts in only one direction. Dragging the file backwards over the surface of the metal only dulls the teeth and wears them out quickly.

Teeth on a coarse-grade file are longer, with a greater space between them. A coarse-grade file working on a piece of mild steel will remove a lot of material with each stroke, but it leaves a rough finish. A smooth-grade file has shorter teeth cut more closely together. It removes much less material on each stroke, and the finish is much smoother. The coarse file is used first to remove material quickly, then a smoother file gently removes the last of it and leaves a clean finish to the work.

The full list of grades in flat files, from rough to smooth, follows **FIGURE 4-27** :

- *Rough files* have the coarsest teeth, with approximately 20 teeth per 1 inch (25 mm). They are used when a lot of material must be removed quickly. They leave a very rough finish and have to be followed by finer files to produce a smooth final finish.

- *Coarse bastard files* are still coarse files, with approximately 30 teeth per 1 inch (25 mm), but they are not as coarse as the rough file. They are also used to rough out or remove material quickly from a job.
- *Second-cut files* have approximately 40 teeth per 1 inch (25 mm), and provide a smoother finish than the rough or coarse bastard file. They are good all-round intermediary files and leave a reasonably smooth finish.
- *Smooth files* have approximately 60 teeth per 1 inch (25 mm), and are a finishing file used to provide a smooth final finish.
- *Dead-smooth files* have 100 teeth per 1 inch (25 mm), or more, and are used where a very fine finish is required.

Some flat files are available with one smooth edge and are called *safe-edge files*. They allow filing up to an edge without damaging it.

Flat files are fine on straightforward jobs, but you need files that work in some awkward spots as well. A **warding file** is thinner than other files and comes to a point; it is used for working in narrow slots **FIGURE 4-28A** . A **square file** has teeth on all four sides, so you can use it in a square or rectangular hole **FIGURE 4-28B** . A square file can make the right shape for a squared metal key to fit in a slot. A triangular file has three sides **FIGURE 4-28C** . Because it is triangular, it can get into internal corners; it is able to cut right into a corner without removing material from the sides.

Curved files are either half-round or round. A half-round file has a shallow convex surface that can file in a concave hollow or in an acute internal corner **FIGURE 4-29A** . The fully round file, sometimes called a *rat-tail file*, can make holes bigger. It can also file inside a concave surface with a tight radius.

The thread file cleans clogged or distorted threads on bolts and studs **FIGURE 4-29B** . Thread files are available in either metric or imperial configurations, so make sure you use the correct file. Each file has eight different surfaces that match different thread dimensions, so the right face must be used.

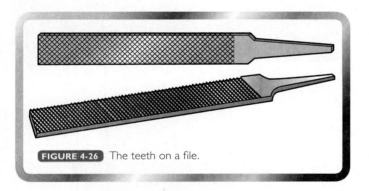

FIGURE 4-26 The teeth on a file.

FIGURE 4-27 Common flat files.

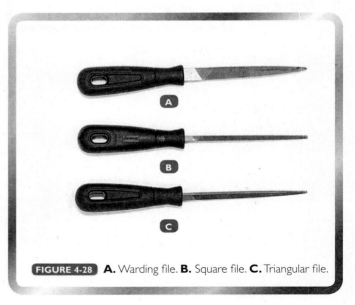

FIGURE 4-28 **A.** Warding file. **B.** Square file. **C.** Triangular file.

Files should be cleaned after each use. If they are clogged, they can be cleaned by using a file card or file brush FIGURE 4-29C. This tool has short steel bristles that clean out the small particles that clog the teeth of the file. Rubbing a piece of chalk over the surface of the file prior to filing will make it easier to clean.

Hacksaw

The hacksaw is used for the general cutting of metals for a crude cut FIGURE 4-30. The frames and blades are adjustable and rated according the number of teeth and hardness of the saw.

Clamps

The **bench vice** is a useful tool for holding anything that can fit into its jaws FIGURE 4-31A. Some common uses include sawing, filing, or chiselling. The jaws are serrated to give extra grip. They are also very hard, which means that when the vice is tightened, the jaws can mar whatever they grip. To prevent this, a pair of soft jaws may be fitted whenever the danger of damage arises. These are usually made of aluminum or some other soft metal, or can have a rubber-type surface applied to them.

When materials are too awkward to grip vertically in a plain vice, it may be easier to use an **offset vice**. The offset vice has its jaws set to one side to allow long components to be held vertically. For example, a long threaded bar can be held vertically in an offset vice to cut a thread with a die.

A **drill vice** is designed to hold material on a drill worktable. The drill worktable has slots cut into it to allow the vice to be bolted down on the table to hold material securely FIGURE 4-31B. To hold something firmly and drill it accurately, the object must be secured in the jaws of the vice. The vice can be moved on the bed until the precise drilling point is located, and then tightened down by bolts to hold the drill vice in place during drilling.

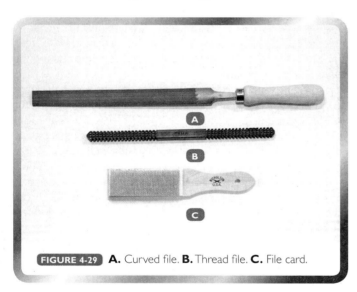

FIGURE 4-29 **A.** Curved file. **B.** Thread file. **C.** File card.

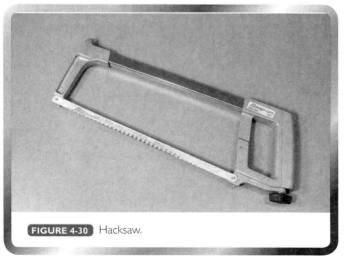

FIGURE 4-30 Hacksaw.

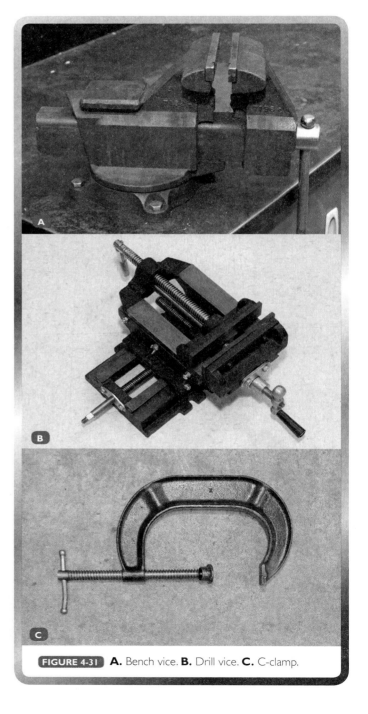

FIGURE 4-31 **A.** Bench vice. **B.** Drill vice. **C.** C-clamp.

The name for the C-clamp comes from its shape FIGURE 4-31C. It holds parts together while they are being assembled, drilled, or welded. It can reach around awkwardly shaped pieces that will not fit in a vice. It is also commonly used to retract disc brake caliper pistons. This clamp is portable, so it can be taken to the work.

Taps and Dies

Taps cut threads inside holes or nuts FIGURE 4-32A. They usually are available in three different types. The first is known as a taper tap. It narrows at the tip to give it a good start in the hole where the thread is to be cut. The diameter of the hole is determined by a tap drill chart, which can be obtained from engineering suppliers. This chart shows what hole size has to be drilled and what tap size is needed to cut the right thread for any given bolt size. Remember that if you are drilling a 0.250″ (6 mm) or larger hole, you should use a smaller pilot drill first. Once the properly sized hole has been drilled, the taper tap can tap a thread right through a piece of steel to enable a bolt to be screwed into it.

The second type of tap is an intermediate tap, also known as a *plug tap*, and the third is a bottoming tap. They are used to tap a thread into a hole that does not come out the other side of the material, called a blind hole. A taper tap is used to start the thread in the hole and then the intermediate tap is used, followed by a bottoming tap to take the thread right to the bottom of the blind hole.

A tap handle FIGURE 4-32B has a right-angled jaw that matches the squared end that all taps have. The jaws are designed to hold the tap securely, and the handles provide the leverage for the operator to rotate the tap comfortably to cut the thread. To cut a thread in an awkward space, a T-shaped tap handle is very convenient. Its handles are not as long, so it fits into tighter spaces; however, it is harder to turn and to guide accurately.

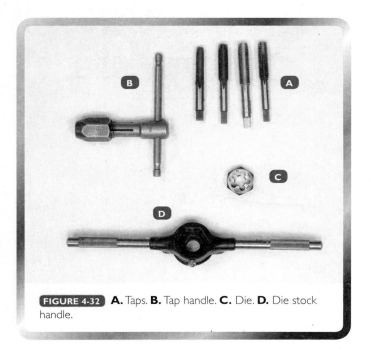

FIGURE 4-32 **A.** Taps. **B.** Tap handle. **C.** Die. **D.** Die stock handle.

To cut a brand-new thread on a blank rod or shaft, a die FIGURE 4-32C held in a die stock handle FIGURE 4-32D is used. The die may be split so that it can be adjusted more tightly onto the work with each pass of the die, as the thread is cut deeper and deeper, until the nut fits properly. The thread chaser is also common in the shop. It is hexagonal-shaped to fit a wrench, and it is commonly used to clean up threads that are rusty or have been damaged.

Screw extractors are devices designed to remove screws, studs, or bolts that have broken off in threaded holes. A common type of extractor uses a coarse, left-hand tapered thread formed on its hardened body. Usually, a hole is drilled in the center of the broken screw and then the extractor is screwed into the hole. The left-hand thread grips the broken part of the bolt and unscrews it. The extractor is marked with the sizes of the screw it is designed to remove and the hole that needs to be drilled. It is important to drill the hole carefully in the center of the bolt or stud in case you end up having to drill the bolt out. If you drill the hole off-center, you will not be able to drill it out all the way to the inside diameter of the threads, and removal will be nearly impossible.

Thread Repair

Thread repair is used in situations where it is not possible to replace a damaged component. This may be because the thread is located in a large, expensive component, such as the engine block or cylinder head, or because parts are not available. The aim of thread repair is to restore the thread to a condition that restores the fastening integrity. It can be performed on internal threads, such as in a housing, engine block, or cylinder head, or on external threads, such as on a bolt.

Types of Thread Repair

Many different tools and methods can be used to repair a thread. The least invasive method is to reshape the threads. If the threads are not too badly damaged—for example, if the outer thread is slightly damaged from being started crooked (cross-threaded)—then a thread file may be used to clean them up, or a restoring tool may be used to reshape them. Each thread file has eight different sets of file teeth that match various thread pitches. Select the set that matches the bolt you are working on and file the bolt in line with the threads. The file removes any distorted metal from the threads. File only until the bad spot is reshaped. The thread-restoring tool looks like an ordinary tap and die set, but instead of cutting the threads, it reshapes the damaged portion of the thread.

Threads that have substantial damage require other methods of repair. A common method for repairing damaged internal threads is a thread insert. A number of manufacturers make thread inserts, and they all work in a similar fashion. The thread insert is a sleeve that has both an internal and external thread. The internal thread on the insert matches the original damaged thread size. The hole with the damaged thread is made larger and a fresh, larger-diameter thread is cut. This thread matches the external thread on the insert. The thread insert can then be screwed and secured into the prepared hole. The insert provides a brand-new threaded inside thread that matches the original size.

Pullers

Pullers are a very common, universal tool that are used for removing bearings, bushings, pulleys, and gears **FIGURE 4-33A**. Specialized pullers are also available for specific tasks where a standard puller is not as effective. The most common pullers have two or three legs that grip the part to be removed. A center bolt, called a forcing screw or jacking bolt, is then screwed in, producing a jacking or pulling action, which extracts the part.

Gear pullers come in a range of sizes and shapes, all designed for particular applications **FIGURE 4-33B**. They consist of three main parts: jaws, a **cross-arm**, and a forcing screw. There are generally two or three jaws on a puller. They are designed to work either externally around a pulley or internally. The **forcing screw** is a long, fine-threaded bolt that is applied to the center of the cross-arm. When the forcing screw is turned, it applies many tons of force through the component you are removing. The cross-arm attaches the jaws to the forcing screw. There may be two, three, or four arms. If the cross-arm has four arms, three of the arms are spaced 120° apart. The fourth arm is positioned 180° apart from one arm. This allows the cross-arm to be used as either a two- arm or a three-arm puller.

FIGURE 4-33 **A.** Puller. **B.** Gear puller.

Flaring Tools

A **tube-flaring tool** is used to flare the end of a tube so it can be connected to another tube or component. One example of this is where the brake line screws into a wheel cylinder. The flared end is compressed between two threaded parts so that it will seal the joint and withstand high pressures. The three most common shapes of flares are the **single flare**, for tubing carrying low pressures, such as a fuel line; the **double flare**, for higher pressures, such as in a brake system; and the ISO flare (sometimes called a bubble flare), which is the metric version used in brake systems **FIGURE 4-34A**.

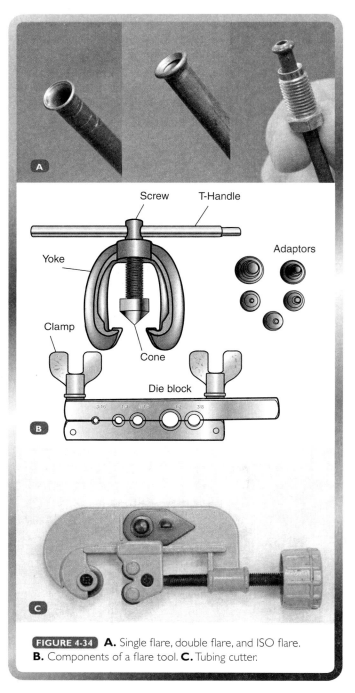

FIGURE 4-34 **A.** Single flare, double flare, and ISO flare. **B.** Components of a flare tool. **C.** Tubing cutter.

Flaring tools have two parts: a set of bars with holes that match the diameter of the tube end that is being shaped and a yoke that drives a cone into the mouth of the tube **FIGURE 4-34B**. To make a single flare, the end of the tube is placed level with the surface of the top of the flaring bars. With the clamp screw firmly tightened, the feed screw flares the end of the tube.

Making a double flare is similar, but an extra step is added and more of the tube is exposed to allow for the folding over into a double flare. A double-flaring button is placed into the end of the tube, and when it is removed after tightening, the pipe looks like a bubble. Placing the cone and yoke over the bubble allows you to turn the feed screw and force the bubble to fold in on itself, forming the double flare.

An ISO flare uses a flaring tool made specifically for that type of flare. It is similar to the double-flare process but stops with the use of the button. It does not get doubled back on itself. It should resemble a bubble shape when you are finished.

A <u>tubing cutter</u> is more convenient and neater than a saw when cutting pipes and metal tubing **FIGURE 4-34C**. The sharpened wheel does the cutting. As the tool turns around the pipe, the screw increases the pressure, driving the wheel deeper and deeper through the pipe until it finally cuts through. There is a larger version that is used for cutting exhaust pipes.

> ▶ **TECHNICIAN TIP**
>
> A flaring tool is used to produce a pressure seal for sealing brake lines and fuel system tubing. Make sure you test the flared joint for leaks before completing the repair; otherwise, the brakes could fail or the fuel could catch on fire.

▶ Additional Tools
Punches

<u>Punches</u> are used when the head of the hammer is too large to strike the object being hit without causing damage to adjacent parts. A punch transmits the hammer's striking power from the soft upper end down to the tip that is made of hardened high-carbon steel. A punch transmits an accurate blow from the hammer at exactly one point, something that cannot be guaranteed using a hammer on its own.

When marks need to be drawn on an object such as a steel plate to help locate a hole to be drilled, a <u>prick punch</u> is used to mark the points so they will not rub off **FIGURE 4-35A**. They can also be used to scribe intersecting lines between given points. The prick punch's point is very sharp, so a gentle tap leaves a clear indentation. The center punch is not as sharp as a prick punch and is usually bigger **FIGURE 4-35B**. It makes a bigger indentation that centers a drill bit at the point where a hole needs to be drilled.

A <u>drift punch</u> is also named a starter punch because you should always use it first to get a pin moving **FIGURE 4-35C**. It has a tapered shank, and the tip is slightly hollow so it does not spread the end of the pin and make it an even tighter fit. Once the starter drift has got the pin moving, a suitable pin punch will drive the pin out or in. A drift punch also works well

for aligning holes on two mating objects, such as a valve cover and cylinder head. Forcing the drift punch in the hole will align both components for easier installation of the remaining bolts.

<u>Pin punches</u> are available in various diameters. A pin punch has a long, slender shaft with straight sides. It is used to drive out rivets or pins **FIGURE 4-36A**. A lot of components are either held together or accurately located by pins. Pins can be pretty tight, and a group of pin punches is specially designed to deal with them.

Special punches with hollow ends are called <u>wad punches</u> or <u>hollow punches</u> **FIGURE 4-36B**. They are the most efficient tool to make a hole in soft sheet material, such as shim steel, plastic and leather or, most commonly, in a gasket. When they are used, there should always be a soft surface under the work, ideally the end grain of a wooden block. If a hollow punch loses its sharpness or has nicks around its edge, it will make a mess instead of a hole.

Numbers and letters, like the engine numbers on some cylinder blocks, are usually made with number and letter

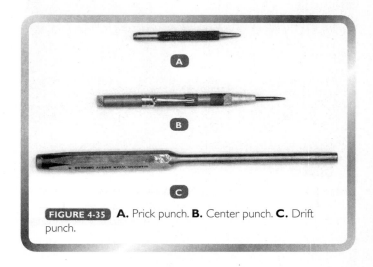

FIGURE 4-35 **A.** Prick punch. **B.** Center punch. **C.** Drift punch.

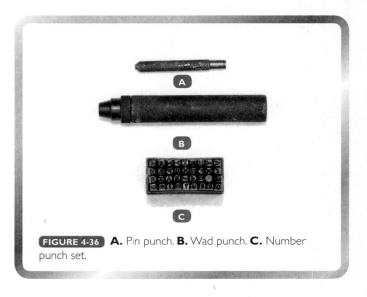

FIGURE 4-36 **A.** Pin punch. **B.** Wad punch. **C.** Number punch set.

punches that come in boxed sets **FIGURE 4-36C**. The rules for using these punches are the same as for all punches. The punch must be square with the surface being worked on, not on an angle, and the hammer must hit the top squarely.

Riveting Tools

There are many applications for blind rivets, and various rivet types and tools may be used to do the riveting. **Pop-rivet guns** are convenient for occasional riveting of light materials **FIGURE 4-37**. A typical pop or **blind rivet** has a body, which forms the **finished rivet**, and a **mandrel**, which is discarded when the riveting is completed **FIGURE 4-38**. It is called a blind rivet because there is no need to see or reach the other side of the hole in which the rivet goes to do the work. In some types, the rivet is plugged shut so that it is waterproof or pressure-proof.

FIGURE 4-37 Pop-rivet guns.

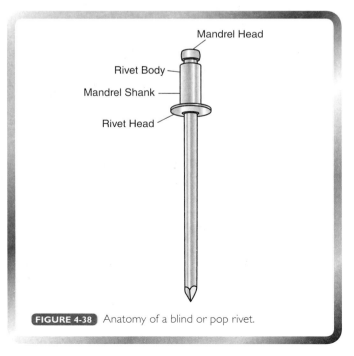

FIGURE 4-38 Anatomy of a blind or pop rivet.

Mandrel Head
Rivet Body
Mandrel Shank
Rivet Head

TECHNICIAN TIP

A rivet is a one-time-use fastener. Unlike a nut and bolt, which can generally be disassembled and reused, a rivet cannot. The metal shell that makes up a pop rivet is crushed into place so that it holds the parts firmly together. If it ever needs to be removed, it must be drilled out.

The rivet is inserted into the riveting tool, which, when squeezed, pulls the end of the mandrel back through the body of the rivet. Because the **mandrel head** is bigger than the hole through the body, it swells out as it comes through the body. Finally, the mandrel head will snap off under the pressure and fall out, leaving the rivet body gripping the two sheets of material together.

▶ Diagnostic Equipment

The trucks people drive today have certainly evolved significantly, even over just the last few years. Yet despite all the innovations, emissions from vehicles still harm the environment, as well as human health, and therefore need to be monitored and kept in check.

Truck repair technicians know that vehicle emissions testing and repair remedies are a big part of day-to-day business. In the interest of public health, keeping trucks running clean is a mandate. Low tailpipe emissions also mean a truck is running efficiently, which helps to conserve energy.

Dynamometer

A dynamometer is a machine that measures the torque and power produced by an engine **FIGURE 4-39**. It applies various loads to an engine and is usually connected to a computer that can analyze and calculate all the aspects of engine operation measured.

FIGURE 4-39 A chassis dynamometer. Notice the rollers on the floor to drive the vehicle's wheels.

Dynamometers are particularly useful in designing and refining engine technology. They can help identify how an engine or its drivetrain needs to be modified or tuned to achieve more efficient power transfer.

There are two types of dynamometer:

- **Engine dynamometer**. The engine dynamometer measures engine performance only, usually when the engine is removed from the vehicle and mounted onto a special frame. It is coupled directly to the engine flywheel and measures performance independent of the vehicle's drivetrain, such as its gearbox, transmission, or differential.
- **Chassis dynamometer**. The chassis dynamometer measures the power from the engine through a vehicle's driven wheels. The whole vehicle is mounted on rollers and fixed to the ground to prevent it jumping when it is driven during testing. The vehicle is driven in gear, and turns the rollers without moving, while its power output is measured.

Safety

In many cases, the vehicle is being operated at full throttle and making maximum horsepower. Always make sure the vehicle is secured effectively and the area is clear of tools, equipment, and people before using a chassis dynamometer. If the vehicle were ever to break free, the resulting accident would be catastrophic.

Pressure Testers/Tire Inflators

There is a range of pressure testers, or gauges, used in the automotive industry. All are used to provide information about the potential condition of various systems and components.

All gauges consist of a measurement scale, from which a reading is taken. Depending on its type of fitting, the gauge is normally fitted to the vehicle component via a pipe or tube. Instructions provided with the gauge describe how to take a correct reading. These should include the specific operational circumstances under which the reading should be taken, to enable correct interpretation of the condition of the item being tested.

Most gauges are designed to read "zero" at atmospheric pressure (1 bar at sea level or 14.7 psi) as a base measurement.

Here are some common types and applications:

- **Tire pressure gauge with attached inflation device**. This type of gauge is the one familiar to most people. Tire pressure gauges are normally part of a tire inflation device and are used to ensure that the air pressure inside a vehicle's tires is maintained at the recommended setting.
- **Tire pressure gauge with no inflation device**. Gauges that only measure—that is, they just check the pressure without being able to inflate as well—are also quite common. **FIGURE 4-40** is an example of this type, known as a "pencil-type" pressure gauge.
- **Pressure vacuum gauge**. Pressure vacuum gauges are a particular type of pressure gauge that measures "negative" pressure below atmospheric pressure **FIGURE 4-41**. They are normally used to determine an engine's general

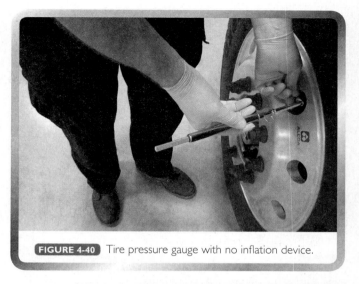

FIGURE 4-40 Tire pressure gauge with no inflation device.

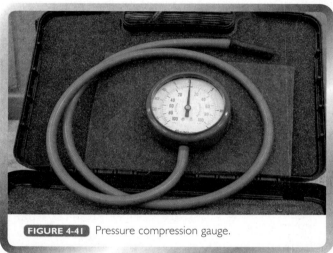

FIGURE 4-41 Pressure compression gauge.

operational condition. Depending on the reading, a number of engine faults can be identified.
- **Pressure compression gauge**. Pressure compression gauges are used to measure the compression pressures inside an engine cylinder and can identify overall condition and pressure leakage situations that could be caused by a range of engine faults **FIGURE 4-42**.
- **Cooling system pressure gauge**. Cooling system pressure gauges are used to identify faults in cooling systems and components such as pressure caps **FIGURE 4-43**.

Scan Tools

Essentially, a scan tool ("scanner") is a device able to communicate electronically with and extract data from the vehicle's one or more on-board computers. On-board computer modules include the power control module (PCM), electronic brake control module (EBCM), body control module (BCM), the transmission control module (TCM), and perhaps numerous others. Simple scan tools from the 1980s could read and erase fault codes and little more. Today, such scanners are sold to consumers. But as

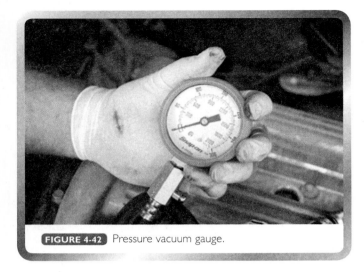

FIGURE 4-42 Pressure vacuum gauge.

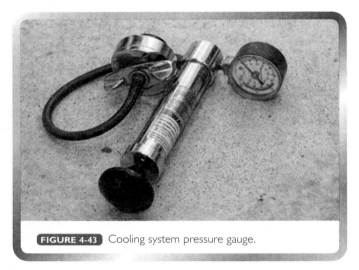

FIGURE 4-43 Cooling system pressure gauge.

on-board systems have become more complex, so too have professional-grade scan tools used in the service bay.

Cost and complexity increase commensurate with the bells and whistles desired in a scanner. Technicians today are finding that they must use faster and more accurate diagnostic instruments—like graphing scan tools—to see hidden faults in component or system waveforms. Scanners are now used to monitor engine compression, vacuum, internal engine anomalies, and so forth. They are used to "drive" various components and systems to test for their proper function. Scanners are used—along with digital storage oscilloscopes, portable emissions analyzers, and much more—for effective time-saving diagnostic routines.

Training and experience play a major role in using these modern information-gathering tools effectively. Understanding the principles of combustion theory, internal combustion engine operation, and emissions are essential ingredients for success. Indeed, the field demands extensive training—and also a sizeable investment! As one tool manufacturer has said, "It takes a lot to be a technician!" Opportunities abound for the technician who understands the theory and masters the use of the scanner

to quickly and efficiently analyze, diagnose, and solve problems on today's advanced vehicle engine systems.

▶ Servicing Equipment

Shops are equipped with machines that help technicians carry out servicing procedures. Those machines include computerized wheel alignment machines, pneumatic tire changing machines, and engine analyzers, which pinpoint faults in engine systems. For disc skimming, there is an on-vehicle lathe, but other skimming jobs are outsourced.

Engine Scanner

An engine scanner is a diagnostic or service tool that is used to view data from the vehicle electronic control systems **FIGURE 4-44**. They will have a screen for displaying data, test results and in some cases waveforms. The scanner will have a lead that is connected to the vehicle's diagnostic plug. They are used to check the performance of a vehicle's electrical and electronic systems. Some systems will also allow data to be stored on a computer and printed for later analysis or added to vehicle service history.

Wheel Alignment Machine

Wheel alignment systems are often incorporated into a special-purpose vehicle hoist and use light beams with calibration equipment to check vehicle wheel alignment **FIGURE 4-45**. The hoist allows easy access for the technician to adjust under body components where necessary. The wheel aligner enables technicians to check and adjust for caster, camber, toe in, and toe out. Most modern wheel alignment machines also produce printouts for the technician and customer showing before and after settings.

On-Vehicle Wheel Balancer

On-vehicle wheel balancers do not require the wheel to be removed from the vehicle. The balancer uses an electric motor

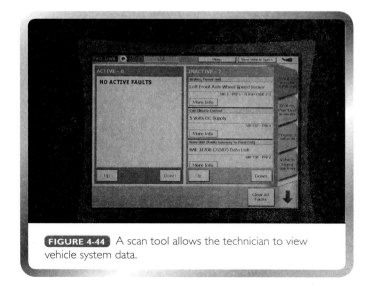

FIGURE 4-44 A scan tool allows the technician to view vehicle system data.

FIGURE 4-45 A wheel alignment machine is often incorporated into a hoist to allow the technician easy access to make vehicle adjustments.

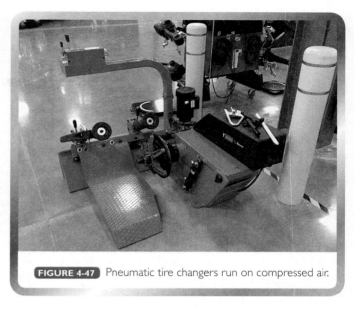

FIGURE 4-47 Pneumatic tire changers run on compressed air.

to run the wheel at speed, and analyzes the wheel's balance, providing a report to the technician on the amount of weights required and their position on the wheel **FIGURE 4-46** .

Pneumatic Tire Changer

Tire changers are designed to break the bead of the tire and remove and reinstall it on the rim. Pneumatic foot controls are usually used on the tire changer to allow both hands of the technician to be free to work on the tire. Tire changers usually incorporate a tire inflating device and pressure gauge **FIGURE 4-47** .

Drum Disc Lathe

Drum and disc lathes are special purpose lathes designed specifically to machine brake drums and discs **FIGURE 4-48** . They remove small amounts of metal to refinish the drum or

FIGURE 4-48 Brake lathes are used to machine discs and drums. Always refer to manufacturer's minimum machining specifications.

FIGURE 4-46 An on-vehicle wheel balancer spins the wheel at speed. The safety shield should always be lowered while the wheel is spinning.

disc surface. It's important not to remove too much material from the drum or disc. Always check manufacturers' specifications for minimum allowable thicknesses of drum and disc.

▶ Oxyacetylene

Oxyacetylene torches are occasionally used by technicians to heat, braze, weld, and cut metal. Acetylene is a highly combustible gas, and when combined with oxygen, it produces a very hot temperature of 6300°F to 6800°F (3480°C to 3760°C). Heating is used to loosen rusted fasteners to help remove them. Brazing uses brass filler rod, which is melted by the torch to join or patch metals.

The torch consists of an acetylene cylinder, an oxygen cylinder, a pressure regulator for each cylinder, hoses, a flashback arrestor for each hose, the torch handle, and the tip. The cylinders hold the gases. Each pressure regulator has two pressure gauges. One gauge shows how much pressure is in the cylinder, and the other gauge shows how much pressure is in the line. The line (hose) pressure is adjusted on the pressure regulator by the operator. The hoses run from each regulator to the flashback arrestors on the torch handle. The acetylene hose is red, and the oxygen hose is blue. The flashback arrestors are spring-loaded check valves that allow flow through the hoses in one direction only—from the cylinders to the torch handle. They prevent flame from travelling back up the hose in the case of a flashback, which is when the oxygen and acetylene ignite inside the torch handle. Flashback happens if the torch valves are set lower than they should be for a particular tip, which produces low gas flow out of the tip; if a welding spark jumps up into the tip; or if the torch is set with too much oxygen flowing. The torch handle usually has the flashback arrestors screwed into it. The gas flow valves are also near the base of the handle. The top of the handle is threaded so that different tips can be installed.

Oxyacetylene Torch Safety

Safety needs to be first and foremost when working with an oxyacetylene torch. Oxyacetylene cylinders carry very high pressures. The acetylene pressure in a full cylinder is approximately 250 psi (1724 kPa), and the oxygen cylinder is approximately 2200 psi (15,168 kPa). If an oxygen cylinder falls over and breaks the main valve off, the cylinder will become a missile and can even go through concrete block walls, so always secure the cylinders properly to the wall or an approved welding cart.

Wear a leather apron or similar protective clothing and welding gloves when using an oxyacetylene torch. T-shirts or nylon- and polyester-blend clothing will not provide enough protection because ultraviolet light and sparks of hot metal will pass through them. Always use proper welding goggles. Do not use sunglasses because they do not filter the extreme ultraviolet light as effectively and the plastic used in the lenses of sunglasses will not protect your eyes from sparks.

Never point the lighted flame towards another person or any flammable material. Always light the oxyacetylene torch with the striker. A cigarette lighter could explode, and a match would put your hand too close to the igniting tip. Wherever possible, use a heat shield behind the component you are heating.

This will prevent nearby objects from becoming hot. After heating a piece of metal, label it as "HOT" with a piece of chalk so that others will not attempt to pick it up.

▶ Cleaning Equipment
Pressure Washers and Cleaners

Pressure washers/cleaners are a valuable tool in the shop for cleaning vehicles, engine compartments, and components. They can be powered by an electric motor or a petroleum engine fitted to a high-pressure pump. The pressure washer takes water at normal pressure and boosts it through the high-pressure pump to exit through a cleaning gun, which has a control trigger. The cleaning gun has a high-pressure nozzle that focuses high-pressure water (possibly over 2000 psi or 13,790 kPa) to clean accumulated dirt and grease from components quickly. Some pressure washers have a provision for detergent to be injected into the high-pressure output to clean more effectively. Others have the ability to heat the water, in some cases hot enough to turn it to steam. Hot water and steam help loosen oil and grease buildup.

Pressure washers are dangerous because of their high pressure and possibly high temperature. Always wear appropriate PPE when working with pressure cleaners—for example, goggles or face shield, protective gloves, close-fitting clothes with long sleeves, full-length trousers, and leather-type boots or shoes.

Because pressure washers spray water at very high pressures, it is important that the water jet is directed properly. It can peel the paint off painted surfaces if the nozzle is brought too close to the surface. It can also damage soft parts such as labels and rubber hoses. Some components can be harmed by water, such as paper filters and some electronic components, including electronic control units, and ignition coils. You may need to cover those devices with plastic bags.

Spray-Wash Cabinets

Spray-wash cabinets spray high-temperature, high-pressure cleaning solutions onto parts inside a sealed cabinet. They are automated and act like a dishwasher for parts. This significantly reduces the labor required to clean parts because once the door is closed and they are turned on, the technician is free to move on to other tasks. They are available in a variety of sizes to cater to different-sized parts, and provide a high level of cleaning performance. The cleaning solution is designed to clean effectively without leaving residue on the parts, and most spray cabinets are fitted with a filtering system to reduce the frequency of cleaning solution changes.

Solvent Tanks

A solvent tank is a cleaning tank that is filled with a suitable solvent to clean parts by removing oil, grease, dirt, and grime. Solvent tanks are available in different sizes. Many solvent tanks have a pump that pushes solvent out of a nozzle into a sink, where it can be directed to the parts being cleaned. A brush either on the nozzle or separate from it can be used to loosen the grease and grime. The solvent falls back into the bottom of the solvent tank, where the heavier residue settles to the bottom. Other solvent tanks are designed so that parts can be immersed into the tank on racks or suspended on pieces of wire, and slowly lowered and soaked in the tank for a period of time. Some solvent tanks may have an agitation system or use a heated cleaning fluid to speed up the process. They may also have a circulation system and filters to remove debris and residue in the solvent to extend its life between changes.

Brake Washers

Brake washers are used to wash brake dust from wheel brake units and their components. Because it is possible that the brake dust may contain asbestos, which is a cancer-causing agent, and because dust in general is a lung irritant, brake washers are designed to capture the brake dust before it enters the shop environment. It does so by wetting down the dust on the brake parts and then washing it into the cleaning tray. Brake washers incorporate a built-in waste recovery system where the contaminated washer fluids can be captured to enable disposal in an environmentally friendly manner.

Brake washers are normally designed to operate at low pressure and use a range of cleaning agents. The most popular agent is an aqueous solution made up of water and a water-soluble detergent. A low-pressure air blower may be provided to remove the fluid from the component into the tray area and then back to the tank by gravity.

Avoid using solvent when cleaning brake components, as it contaminates friction materials and may cause seals to swell. Never use paraffin oil as a general cleaning agent to clean brake components, as it does not clean away brake fluid, can be absorbed into lining materials, and can cause seals to swell. Water is a good cleaning agent for brake components.

Sand or Bead Blasters

Sand or bead blasters use high pressure to blast small abrasive particles to clean the surface of parts. The most common method of propelling the sand or glass beads is with compressed air. In shops, sand or bead blasting can occur in a specially designed cabinet, or there are portable models that are available for use in open-air situations. The cabinets contain the blasting operation in a controlled, safe environment and are best for smaller parts that can fit into the cabinet. Portable systems that do not operate within a cabinet can blast larger parts but do require more protection for the operator and surrounding environment.

The sand or bead blaster cabinet is fitted with a hand-operated blasting nozzle, a viewing port, and an on/off switch (often this may be a foot-operated switch), and it has openings with tough rubber gloves sealed into them to allow a technician's hands to be inside the cabinet while being protected from the abrasive sand or beads. Wet sand or bead blasters are also available, and have the additional advantage of reducing the amount of dust and providing additional cleaning to the part being cleaned.

▶ Electrical Equipment

Multimeters **FIGURE 4-49**, which are also known as digital volt-ohmmeters (DVOMs), and oscilloscopes **FIGURE 4-50** are electrical measuring tools frequently used to diagnose and

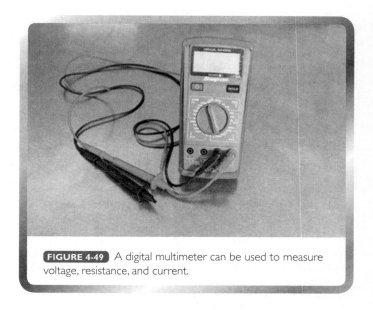

FIGURE 4-49 A digital multimeter can be used to measure voltage, resistance, and current.

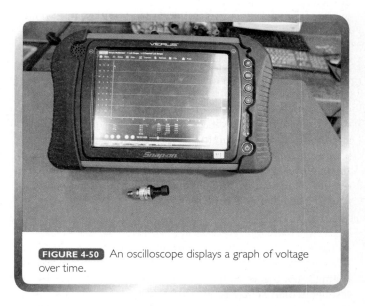

FIGURE 4-50 An oscilloscope displays a graph of voltage over time.

repair electrical faults. Like many diagnostic tools, practice is required to understand how the multimeter and oscilloscope are used to take electrical measurements, and how to connect them into electrical circuits to ensure correct readings are obtained. Once a reading is obtained, it needs to be interpreted and applied to diagnose the circuit under test. This section provides an explanation of how to use and set up a multimeter for measuring voltage, current, and resistance.

Using Ohm's Law to Diagnose Circuits

Ohm's law is used to calculate electrical quantities in an electrical circuit and is valuable as a way of cross-checking actual measured results within a circuit. For example, if the resistance and voltage of a circuit is known, then the theoretical current can be calculated using Ohm's law. The calculated result can then be compared to the measured results from an ammeter to determine whether the circuit is functioning correctly. Technicians will often do a quick calculation, in their heads, to obtain an approximate value of an electrical quantity before they take actual measurements. This gives them a good indication of what they will be measuring and allows them to set the measuring tool to the correct range. Always remember that a calculation may be only an approximate value because, in actual circuits, variation or tolerances exist in components, causing some variation between calculated values and actual measurements.

▶ TECHNICIAN TIP

When checking continuity with a multimeter, the power supplied to the circuit during operation must be switched **off**.

Electrical Testing Equipment

Using a Multimeter to Measure Voltage

The electrical system is becoming increasingly complex on modern vehicles, and measuring voltages with a multimeter is a very common task when diagnosing electrical faults. For most measurements, set the multimeter to auto range for ease of use. Select multimeter leads and probe ends to match the task at hand; for example, if you need to take a measurement but require both hands to be free, use probe ends with crocodile clips. Ensure that you do not exceed the maximum allowable voltage or current for the multimeter. If you are measuring high voltages, ensure you wear appropriate personal protective equipment, such as high-voltage safety gloves, long-sleeved shirts, long trousers and protective eyewear, and remove any personal jewelry, or items that may cause an accidental short circuit.

Checking a Circuit with a Test Light

Nonpowered test lights are useful in determining the live part of a circuit; however, make sure that the circuit voltage you are testing is not higher than the test light is rated for, otherwise the test light could be damaged. Most test lights are rated for 6- or 12-volt systems, and using them in a 24-volt system will usually blow out the bulb. You should never use a test light to test Supplemental Restraint Systems (SRS), as unintended deployment of the airbags could result—a very dangerous and costly mistake. In addition, using a test light on a computer circuit designed for very small amounts of current flow can damage the circuit.

Checking a Circuit with Fused Jump Leads

Jump leads may be used in a number of ways to assist in checking circuits. They can be created by the technician or purchased in a range of sizes, lengths, and fittings, or connectors. They are used to extend connections to allow circuit readings or tests to be undertaken with a multimeter, scope, current clamps on fuses, relays, and connector plugs on components. In some circumstances, jump leads may provide an alternative current or ground source for components under test. Regardless of their application, it is important that the circuit remain protected by a fuse of the correct size. To determine the correct size of fuse

required for any particular application, refer to the manufacturer's information.

Locating Opens, Shorts, Grounds, and High Resistance

Multimeters, test lights, and simulated loads tend to be the tools used most often for locating opens, shorts, grounds, and high-resistance faults. An **open circuit** is a break in the electrical circuit where either the power supply or ground circuit has been interrupted. Most open circuits can be located by testing along the circuit at various points to test for power, and at the ground point to check for an effective ground. Perform a systematic check of the circuit by first checking the voltages at the component, if possible. Analysis of the readings will usually dictate the next point to be checked.

Shorts or **short circuits** may occur anywhere in the circuit and can be difficult to locate, especially if they are intermittent. A short is a circuit fault where current travels along an accidental or unintended route. The short may occur to ground or to supply voltage. A short to ground causes low circuit resistance. The low-resistance fault would cause an abnormally high current flow in the circuit and could cause the circuit-protection devices, such as fuses or circuit breakers, to open circuit. A short to supply voltage may cause the circuit to remain live even after the switch is turned off. For example, a short between a fuse with power on all the time and a fuse switched by the ignition switch would cause the circuit controlled by the ignition switch to remain on after the switch is turned off. Shorts may be caused by faulty components or damaged wiring.

Grounds is a term often used in conjunction with shorts and is usually a reference to a short to ground. An initial test may be conducted by carrying out resistance checks or by disconnecting the load. To test the blower motor, for example, disconnect the blower motor and, if the short is still in place, then the wiring between the fuse or circuit breaker and the load must be at fault. To further narrow down the site of the short to ground, inspect the wiring harness, looking for obvious signs of damage. Another test may be conducted by connecting a test lamp or buzzer in place of a fuse: current will flow through the test lamp or buzzer and find a ground through the short; parts of the circuit may then be disconnected along the wiring harness to narrow down the location of the short. Specialized short-circuit detection tools are also available. They work by injecting a signal into the wiring where a short is suspected. A receiving device is then moved along the wiring loom and indicates where a short is located. This type of device is very useful in situations where it is difficult to access the wiring; for example, under guards or vehicle trim.

High resistance refers to a circuit where there is unintended resistance, which then causes a fault. It can be caused by a number of problems; for example, corroded or loose harness connectors, incorrectly sized cable for the circuit current flow, incorrectly fitted terminals, and poorly soldered joints. The high resistance causes an unintended voltage drop in a circuit when the current flows. The high-resistance fault reduces the current flow in the circuit, affecting its performance. It can be located by conducting a resistance check with a multimeter, or by checking for voltage drop in the power and ground circuits. Resistance checks are initial tests undertaken on components—for example, testing the resistance of a fuel injector or ignition coil—but should always be followed up with working tests, using a multimeter or oscilloscope. Due to the relatively low resistance of wires, it is usually more effective to conduct voltage-drop tests while the load current is flowing through the circuits.

To locate opens, shorts, grounds, and high resistance, follow these steps:

1. Identify the circuit to be checked and conduct a visual inspection.
2. Select and set up appropriate test equipment, and determine the type and location of the fault: opens, shorts, grounds, or high resistance.
3. Determine and perform the necessary actions.

Using an Alternator Test Bench

An alternator test bench is normally compact and should be easy to use for fast and accurate testing of a wide range of alternators and starter motors. The test bench can be operated at two speeds, ensuring thorough testing both at higher and lower speeds. It can also include vacuum testing.

A good test bench should have many of the specific features, such as a built-in power source, thus eliminating the need for external batteries. It must be capable of testing 12-volt and 24-volt systems with a digital ammeter/voltmeter FIGURE 4-51.

Battery Chargers

There are many different types of **battery chargers**, and each is designed for a particular purpose and application. **Fast chargers** have high current output to charge a **battery** quickly. **Slow chargers** take longer to charge a battery and have lower current outputs; they put less stress on the battery, which is ideal if time is not a consideration. **Smart chargers** incorporate

microprocessors to monitor and control the charge rate so that the battery receives the correct amount of charge according to its state of charge. These types of chargers are becoming more popular; they ensure that the battery receives the optimal charge, thus promoting longer battery life.

Even though a motor vehicle battery is typically 12 volts, it stores a lot of energy. The high-current supply from a battery can be very dangerous. Remember, batteries have to deliver enough power to crank over a cold engine. They also produce enough power to melt a metal rod resting across the terminals. High-voltage battery packs, like those fitted to hybrid vehicles, are even more dangerous because of the potential for high voltage and current, so special precautions for dealing with high-voltage systems must be taken FIGURE 4-52. Always treat batteries with care and respect.

Safety

High voltages used in a hybrid vehicle are extremely dangerous. The voltage and current flow is several times greater than that needed to kill a person. Most hybrid manufacturers require technicians to undergo special factory training before they will allow them to service a hybrid vehicle. They usually allow only very experienced technicians to undergo the training, not novices. In fact, one of the tools that Toyota requires of their shops for working on a hybrid vehicle is a nonconductive shepherd's hook. This can be used to drag a technician away from high voltage if the technician is electrocuted while working on the vehicle.

Battery Safety

Batteries give off hydrogen gas while they are being charged, and for some time afterwards. Hydrogen is a light and highly explosive gas that is easily ignited by a simple spark. Batteries are filled with **sulfuric acid**, so if the hydrogen does explode, the battery case can then rupture and spray everything and everyone nearby with this dangerous and corrosive liquid.

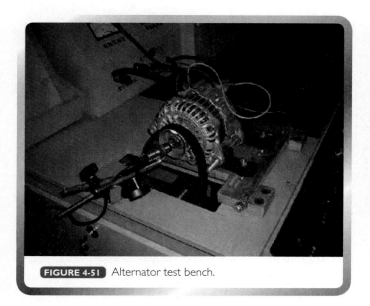

FIGURE 4-51 Alternator test bench.

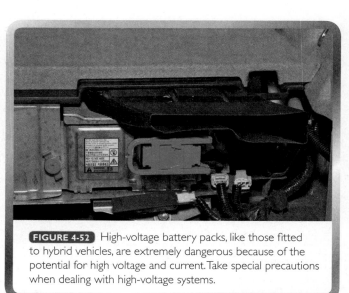

FIGURE 4-52 High-voltage battery packs, like those fitted to hybrid vehicles, are extremely dangerous because of the potential for high voltage and current. Take special precautions when dealing with high-voltage systems.

Be very careful not to create a spark when you are connecting or disconnecting battery cables or hooking up a charger to the battery terminals. Switch off the charger before connecting and disconnecting them from the battery **FIGURE 4-53**.

Do not try to charge a battery faster than the battery manufacturer recommends, and never use a battery load tester immediately after charging a battery. This is because both charging and rapidly discharging a battery generate heat and hydrogen. If you load-test a battery after charging it without waiting for it to cool down, you will increase the risk of distorting the plates inside the battery, as well as increase the risk of explosion.

▶ Fluids and Lubricants

Reducing friction and cooling are the primary functions of fluids and lubricants. This section outlines the key fluids used to keep vehicles running smoothly and introduces the use of alternative fuels.

Antifreeze

All truck engines currently on the market are liquid-cooled engines. A liquid-cooled system uses **coolant**, a fluid that contains special antifreezing and anticorrosion chemicals mixed with water **FIGURE 4-54**.

Water alone is by far the best coolant there is because it can absorb a larger amount of heat than most other liquids. But water has some drawbacks. It freezes if its temperature drops to 0°C (the temperature at which water becomes a solid). As water freezes, it expands into a solid. If it expands in the coolant passages inside the engine, these passages—typically made of cast aluminum or cast iron—will not flex to allow expansion and will break. This renders the engine inoperative and unrepairable in most cases.

Another thing to realize about using water alone as a coolant is that water is corrosive and causes metal to rust. Antifreeze prevents corrosion and rusting through anticorrosion additives (called corrosion inhibitors) mixed into the solution. Another important note on water is that water contains minerals and will potentially lead to excessive deposits, even when added to antifreeze. Because of this, most manufacturers recommend using distilled water for cooling systems.

Antifreeze is mixed with water to lower the freezing point of water and reduce the chances of cracking the engine block, cylinder heads, and other cooling system components. Antifreeze is made from one of two base chemicals—ethylene glycol or propylene glycol—plus a mixture of additives to protect against corrosion and foaming. Ethylene and propylene glycol may achieve a maximum very low freezing point of –71°F (–57°C) when mixed with the appropriate amount of water. **Ethylene glycol** is a chemical that resists freezing but is very toxic to people and animals. **Propylene glycol** is another chemical that resists freezing but is not toxic and is used in nontoxic antifreezes. Either of these antifreezes will actually freeze at around –0.4°F (–18°C) if not mixed with water, so water is a necessary part of coolant. The freezing point of coolant will vary depending upon how much water is added to the antifreeze. Because antifreeze does not absorb heat as effectively as water, it should not be mixed at a ratio higher than 65% antifreeze and 35% water. Using a higher proportion of antifreeze will actually

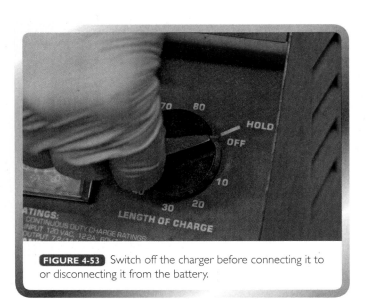
FIGURE 4-53 Switch off the charger before connecting it to or disconnecting it from the battery.

FIGURE 4-54 Coolant is a fluid that contains special antifreezing and anticorrosion chemicals mixed with water.

reduce the cooling quality of the mixture and raise the operating temperature of the engine **FIGURE 4-55**.

The best coolant is a 50/50 balance of water and antifreeze, making it an ideal coolant for both hot and cold climates and providing adequate corrosion protection. In addition, when antifreeze is added at a 50% mixture, the boiling point increases to around 228°F (109°C). As you can see, this is an extremely beneficial characteristic of antifreeze as manufacturers continue to build engines that are more powerful, create more heat, and operate at higher temperatures.

Antifreeze can be purchased as straight antifreeze (100%) or as a 50/50 premix with water. Straight antifreeze that you buy from the dealer or parts store consists of three parts: glycol (around 96%), corrosion inhibitors and additives (around 2–3%), and water (around 2%). Glycol, as discussed previously, keeps the freezing point low and the boiling point high. Corrosion inhibitors and additives prevent corrosion and erosion, resist foaming, ensure coolant is compatible with cooling system component materials and hard water, resist sedimentation, and balance the acid-to-alkaline content of the antifreeze. Water is added to blend the inhibitors with the glycol.

Antifreeze is an amazing chemical that performs a monumental task in the operation of our vehicles. It works so well that it is often overlooked for maintenance by the customer. However, because the additives wear out and become less effective over time, coolant does need to be changed at recommended intervals. Doing so reduces the possibility of engine damage and failure over time. Similarly, lubrication enhancers, which keep the water pump and seals functioning properly, wear out and need to be replaced.

Automatic Transmission Fluid

Automatic transmission fluid (ATF) is a specialized fluid that has been designed for a specific job. The ATF must be able to transfer heat from the internal components of the transmission to the transmission cooler to prevent damaging the internal seals of the transmission **FIGURE 4-56**. The fluid must also lubricate the internal gears, bearings, and bushes (also known as bushings) of the transmission, yet have a large enough <u>**coefficient of friction**</u> to allow the clutches to grab and not slip. Coefficient of friction is the force required to move two sliding surfaces over each other. ATFs are typically dyed red for easy identification and contain many additives such as:

- Rust and corrosion inhibitors: These additives prevent the internal parts of the transmission from developing rust and corrosion on metal components. Rust and corrosion can affect the shift quality and longevity of the transmission. As rust particles break off, they become an abrasive in the fluid, causing increased wear.
- Friction modifiers: Manufacturers add friction modifiers to the fluid to ensure that the fluid has the proper coefficient of friction to produce the desired shift quality. A fluid with a lower coefficient of friction will produce softer, longer shifts, causing an increase in clutch slippage. A fluid with a higher coefficient of friction will cause shorter, harsher shifts, reducing clutch slippage but increasing driveline shock.
- Seal conditioners: These additives are designed to help protect the seals inside a transmission and cause the seals to swell slightly to help prevent leaks and clutch slippage.
- Detergents: ATF has a large amount of detergent to prevent dirt and other foreign particles from becoming trapped inside the transmission. The detergent causes the dirt and other particles to be attracted to the fluid

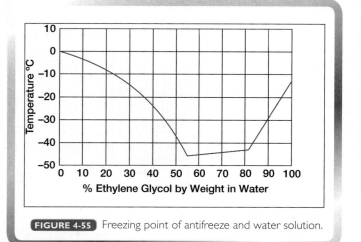

FIGURE 4-55 Freezing point of antifreeze and water solution.

FIGURE 4-56 Automatic transmission fluid (ATF).

so they transfer with the fluid. When the fluid passes through the filter, the large particles become trapped in the filter; the small particles are removed during the next transmission fluid change.

- Antifoam: These additives help to prevent foaming of the transmission fluid. When moving parts spin through a fluid, they tend to produce air bubbles. These air bubbles can quickly multiply and become foam. Foam is compressible and can cause a transmission to slip because insufficient pressure is applied to the clutches.
- Viscosity modifiers: These additives are similar to the engine oil additives that allow us to have multiviscosity engine oils such as 5W-30. These additives allow the fluid to remain thin when the temperature is cold and prevent the fluid from becoming too thin as the transmission fluid warms up.

ATFs can be mineral oil based or a synthetic lubricant. Many late-model trucks recommend a specific synthetic ATF. In the past few decades, most vehicle manufacturers have developed their own fluids for use in their transmissions. This practice has required repair facilities to carry many different types of fluids. Some shops carry a few major types of fluids and use those in every vehicle, but that is not recommended as it may cause undesirable transmission operation and may void the transmission warranty. Several vehicle manufacturers have published technical service bulletins (TSBs) related to incorrect fluid use and the negative effects on the transmission.

ATF needs to be changed periodically to remove dirt and contaminants from the transmission. Technicians used to tell whether the transmission fluid needed to be changed by looking at and smelling the fluid. If the fluid was dark or smelled burnt, it needed to be changed. You cannot determine the condition of modern ATF by looks and smell. Some newer synthetic fluids will have a burnt smell when they are brand new and are often darker than mineral-based ATF. To check ATF for contaminants, drop a few drops of transmission fluid onto a white paper towel. The fluid will spread out on the paper towel, but the contaminants will remain where the fluid was dropped.

Acid and Alkali

The main use of sulfuric acid in the industry is in the construction of batteries. Sulfuric acid is mixed with distilled water to create an electrolyte, which is used in a lead-acid battery to store electrical energy. Batteries were developed in the early 1800s, and since that time many varieties and designs have been developed. The battery is part of everyday life and is widely used in modern electrical and electronic devices. Batteries store electricity in chemical form, which is possible because electricity causes a chemical reaction within the battery. In other words, the electrical energy is transformed into chemical energy **FIGURE 4-57**.

The traditional vehicle battery type is the lead-acid battery. Although it is available in many types, all types have the same basic components as shown in **FIGURE 4-58** including two dissimilar metals, an insulator material separating the metals, and an electrolyte.

Lead-Acid Flooded Cell Battery

The wet cell lead-acid battery is the main storage device in use. It is called a flooded cell battery because the lead plates are immersed in a water-acid electrolyte solution. A typical battery can supply very high discharge currents while maintaining a high voltage, which is useful when cold starting. It gives a high power output for its compact size, and it is rechargeable.

The standard 12-volt battery consists of six cells connected in series. Each cell has a nominal 2.1 volts, for a total of 12.6 volts for a fully charged "12-volt" battery. Each cell contains two sets of electrodes (called plates), one set of lead (Pb) and the other set of lead dioxide (PbO_2), in an electrolyte solution of diluted sulfuric acid (H_2SO_4). As the battery discharges, the sulfuric acid is absorbed into the lead plates and both of the plates slowly turn into lead sulfate. At the same time, the strength of the electrolyte becomes less acidic as the acid is absorbed into the plates. Recharging the battery reverses this process.

FIGURE 4-57 Batteries store electricity in chemical form.

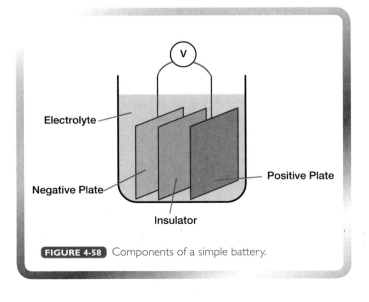

FIGURE 4-58 Components of a simple battery.

<u>Alkalis</u> are a chemical compound—bicarb of soda is an example—which are used to neutralise acidic compounds. For example, bicarb is used to clean battery terminals. A substance is rated acidic or alkaline on a pH scale. Alkalis have a pH value greater than 7.

Brake Fluid

Hydraulic and air-over-hydraulic brakes use a special brake fluid, which is a special-purpose high-boiling-point fluid. It transmits the hydraulic pressure generated by the master cylinder to the brake units **FIGURE 4-59**.

Brake fluid is hydraulic fluid that has specific properties. The fluid is used to transfer force while under pressure through hydraulic lines to the wheel braking system.

Braking applications produce heat, so the fluid used must have both a high boiling point to remain effective and a low freezing point so as not to freeze or thicken in cold conditions.

Brake fluid is <u>hygroscopic</u>, which means it absorbs water from the atmosphere. This will gradually reduce its boiling point, so the fluid should be changed periodically to remove water and other contaminants and to ensure the continued effectiveness of the braking system **FIGURE 4-60**.

Brake Fluid DOT Specifications

The properties of different types of brake fluids are tested for many different characteristics, such as pH value, viscosity, resistance to oxidation, and stability, and graded against compliance standards set by the U.S. Department of Transportation (DOT):

- DOT 2 is castor oil based.
- DOT 3 is composed of various glycol esters and ethers. Boiling point: 284°F (140°C)
- DOT 4 is also composed of glycol esters and ethers. Boiling point: 311°F (155°C)
- DOT 5 is silicone based. It is not recommended for any vehicle equipped with antilock brakes (ABS). It gives better

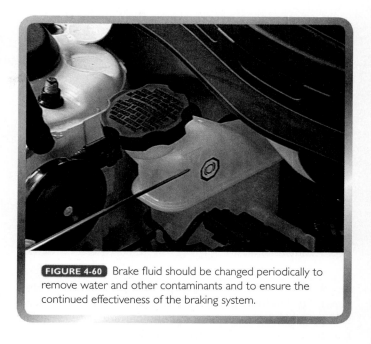

FIGURE 4-60 Brake fluid should be changed periodically to remove water and other contaminants and to ensure the continued effectiveness of the braking system.

protection against corrosion, and is more suitable for use in wet driving conditions. Boiling point: 356°F (180°C)
- DOT 5.1 is a high-boiling-point fluid that is suitable for ABS-equipped vehicles. It contains polyalkylene glycol ether, but is more expensive than other brake fluids. Boiling point: 375°F (190.6°C).

TECHNICIAN TIP

Even if they have similar base composition, fluids with different DOT ratings must not be mixed.

Diesel Oil

Diesel fuel oil is a derivative of crude oil that is used to power diesel engines, also known as compression ignition, or CI, engines **FIGURE 4-61**. Diesel fuel is produced as a fractional distillate of crude oil between 392°F and 662°F (200°C and 350°C). Ultra-low sulfur diesel (ULSD) is commonly used in passenger vehicles in Europe, the United States, and Canada. The principal measure of diesel fuel quality is its cetane number. A higher cetane number indicates that the fuel ignites more readily when sprayed into hot compressed air. European (EN 590 standard) road diesel has a minimum cetane number of 51. Fuels with higher cetane numbers, normally "premium" diesel fuels with additional cleaning agents and some synthetic content, are available in some markets.

Biodiesel

<u>Biodiesel</u> is renewable fuel made by chemically combining natural oils from soybeans (or cottonseeds, canola, etc.; animal fats; or even recycled cooking oil) with an alcohol such as methanol (or ethanol).

FIGURE 4-59 Brake fluid transmits hydraulic pressure to the brake units.

FIGURE 4-61 Diesel oil is a derivative of petrol oil that is used to power diesel engines.

Biodiesel fuels are usually more expensive than petro-diesel, but biodiesel burns with less particulate and with no sulfur or aldehydes, producing less harmful and irritating tailpipe emissions. NO_x sometimes increases with biodiesel, but after-treatment devices benefit from the lack of sulfur in biodiesel. The improved lubricity and zero sulfur content of biodiesel result in longer maintenance intervals, longer engine, and fuel system life and lower emissions.

Biodiesel fuel is compatible with petrodiesel and may be used 100% (B100) in place of petrodiesel, or may be blended with petrodiesel. A typical blend would be 20% biodiesel with 80% petrodiesel fuel (B20).

Biodiesel tends to clean petrodiesel residues from the fuel system, so fuel filters may require frequent servicing for the first few tank fills. Alcohol-based alternative fuels are used extensively in light duty passenger vehicles but have not found widespread acceptance in the heavy vehicle industry. In some countries, the trucking industry instead is more reliant on bio-diesel blends, such as B20.

In South Africa, heavy vehicles run only on diesel.

Engine Oil

Engine oil reduces unwanted friction. It reduces wear on moving parts, and helps cool an engine. It also absorbs shock loads and acts as a cleaning agent **FIGURE 4-62**:

- Clearances fill with oil so that engine parts move or float on layers of oil instead of directly on each other. Much less power is needed to move them.
- Oil helps cool an engine. It collects heat from the engine, and then returns to the sump, where it cools.
- It helps absorb shock loads. A diesel engine's power stroke can suddenly put as much as 15 tons of force on main bearings. Layers of oil cushion this loading.
- Oil is also a cleaning agent. It collects particles of metal and carbon and carries them back to the oil filter to be suspended until the filter is replaced.

For oil to do all of the work that is expected of it, it must have special properties. Its viscosity is crucial. Viscosity is a

FIGURE 4-62 Engine oil reduces unwanted friction, reduces wear on moving parts, helps cool an engine, and acts as a cleaning agent.

measure of how easily a liquid flows. Low-viscosity liquid is thin and flows easily. High-viscosity liquid is thick and flows slowly. Lubricating oil must be thin enough to circulate easily between moving parts, but not so thin that it will be forced out from between them. If it is forced out, parts will be left in direct contact and they will be damaged.

Synthetic Oils

Synthetic lubricating oils are more costly to manufacture and to use but they have a number of advantages over conventional mineral oils.

They offer better protection against engine wear and can operate at the higher temperatures needed by performance engines; they have better low-temperature viscosity, without the wax impurities that coagulate at low temperatures; they are chemically more stable; and they are generally thinner, so they allow for closer tolerances in engine components without loss of lubrication. They also last considerably longer, extending oil change intervals out to 20,000 miles (30,000 km) or more, which benefits the environment by reducing the used oil stream.

True synthetic oils are based on man-made hydrocarbons, commonly polyalphaolefin, or PAO, but very few of the synthetic oils on the market are full PAO oils. Many of the oils allowed to be labeled as synthetic are in fact blends of processed mineral oil and PAO, or even just heavily processed natural crude oil.

Gear Oil

Gear oil is the lubricant used in transmissions, transfer cases, and differentials FIGURE 4-63. It is of a higher viscosity than engine oil because it needs to protect meshing gears, which are in enclosed cases without the benefit of pumps. Most lubricants for manual gearboxes and differentials contain extreme pressure and antiwear additives to cope with the sliding action of bevel gears.

Paint

Paint is used to cover metal parts of vehicles to provide protection and an attractive color. Once applied, a clear coat is often applied to the surface of the paint to protect the paint from damage FIGURE 4-64.

FIGURE 4-63 Gear oil is of a higher viscosity than engine oil because it needs to protect meshing gears.

FIGURE 4-64 Paint covers metal parts to provide protection and add color.

Paraffin

Paraffin, also known as mineral oil, is used mainly as a cleaning agent in the automotive industry. It is a liquid by-product of the petroleum distillation process of crude oil. It is a transparent, colorless oil, which is produced in light and heavy grade.

Solvents

A solvent is a highly flammable liquid that can dissolve other substances. Examples of solvents are turpentine, methylated spirits, and lacquer thinners used as an additive to paints.

Water

Water is the universal solvent. Given a long enough time, water will dissolve any material. In this industry, distilled water is often used to top off batteries. Water is also used in windshield washers and radiators and to wash vehicles.

▶ Metals

Metals play an integral role in the construction of major vehicle components, particularly engine components and the vehicle body itself. Metals can roughly be divided into ferrous and nonferrous categories. Ferrous metals use iron as an alloying agent. Cast iron, steel, and stainless steel are the main categories of iron alloys used in the industry. Nonferrous metals, such as copper, are pure metals that can be used in alloys as well.

Cast Iron

Cast iron is an alloy, or combination, of materials. There are many different kinds of cast iron, depending on the particular materials they contain.

Gray iron, for example, is a cast iron that contains carbon in the form of graphite, plus silicon, manganese, and phosphorus. The fractured surface of a cast iron with graphite appears gray, hence the name. It is brittle and cannot absorb shocks. It resists heat and corrosion, and can be cast into many different shapes. It is used for many components, such as engine cylinder blocks and crankcases.

Steel

When carbon and other materials are alloyed with iron they form steel. The amount of carbon is very small; it can be less than 1%. Changing the amount of carbon, even by small amounts, will dramatically change properties, such as hardness, ductility, and toughness.

Different properties mean different uses. Generally, low-carbon steels, also known as mild steels, are used where toughness is needed, such as in the frame, body, bolts, nuts, and washers. Increasing the amount of carbon increases hardness, so high-carbon steels are used where hardness is needed, such as in engine parts, springs, dies, and punches.

Stainless steels are also used in vehicle applications for their resistance to corrosion and toughness **FIGURE 4-65**. Stainless steel has a shiny appearance and can be polished to a bright, mirror-like finish. Stainless steel is used in the construction of valves, pipes, bolts, and screws.

Copper

Copper is a nonferrous, pure metal that can be alloyed (combined) with other metals but is not combined with iron. Copper is often alloyed with brass or bronze for bearings and bushes **FIGURE 4-66**. It is also used in vehicle wiring because of its electrical conducting properties.

Lead

Lead is used in the construction of vehicle batteries. The wet cell lead-acid battery is the main storage device in vehicle use **FIGURE 4-67**. A vehicle battery can supply very high discharge currents while maintaining a high voltage—which is useful for cold starting. It gives a high power output for its compact size, and it is rechargeable.

The most common standard 12-volt truck batteries consist of six cells, each of a nominal 2 volts. Each cell contains two electrodes, one of lead (Pb) and the other of lead peroxide (PbO_2), in an electrolyte of dilute sulfuric acid (H_2SO_4). As the battery discharges, both electrodes turn into lead sulfate and the acid turns into water. Recharging the battery reverses this process.

Brass

Brass is an alloy of zinc and copper and is used in the automotive field for hose connections and fittings. Low-pressure fuel-line connections are commonly made from brass **FIGURE 4-68**. In the past, brass was used extensively in cooling system radiators because of its excellent heat dissipation properties. Today, radiators are constructed primarily from aluminum because of the high cost and heavy weight of brass.

Chrome

Chrome may be confused with stainless steel. Like stainless, it is a bright, shiny corrosion-resistant metal and is used mostly for decorative purposes, such as on hubcaps.

FIGURE 4-65 Stainless steel is resistant to corrosion and toughness.

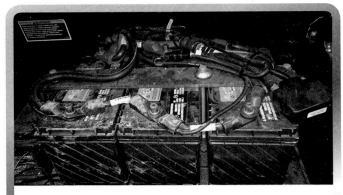

FIGURE 4-67 The wet cell lead-acid battery is the main storage device in vehicle use.

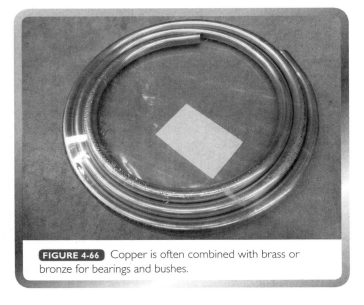

FIGURE 4-66 Copper is often combined with brass or bronze for bearings and bushes.

FIGURE 4-68 Brass is an alloy of zinc and copper and is used to make fuel-line fittings and connectors.

Aluminum

As more manufacturers try to make vehicles lighter and more fuel efficient, more and more components are being cast from aluminum such as fuel tanks, wheels, and some suspension components.

Tin

Tin is most often used as a corrosion-resistant coating in vehicle applications. Fuel tanks, for example, are made of tinned sheet steel that has been pressed into shape. Tin is also used as a coating. Solder used in vehicle electrical applications is an alloy typically made up of 60% tin and 40% lead. Fuel lines in light diesel systems are usually made of stainless steel tubing coated with tin to prevent rust.

▶ Materials

Materials used in the commercial vehicle industry are used in everything from dashboard coverings to interior trim. They often determine the look of the vehicle but also have important structural elements that can be applied to vehicle components
TABLE 4-1.

Safety

Asbestos is a name used to describe a number of naturally occurring noncombustible fibrous mineral compounds, mostly iron or magnesium silicates.

Because of its heat- and fire-resistant qualities, asbestos was used in brake shoes, silencer systems, and some gaskets for many years. Asbestos fiber or powder inhalation is now known to cause some very serious respiratory diseases, such as a lung fibrosis called "asbestosis," and a very aggressive form of cancer called "mesothelioma." As a result, the use of asbestos has been banned in many countries.

Manufacturers of vehicle brake components now use a range of alternative materials in the manufacturing process depending on the particular braking application. These can be various ceramic compounds; semi-metallic, low-metallic, synthetic fibers such as Kevlar; and nonasbestos organic compounds.

▶ TECHNICIAN TIP

PVC, or polyvinyl chloride, is in the top three worldwide-produced plastics.

TABLE 4-1: Materials Used in the Vehicle Industry

Material	Definition
Bakelite	A synthetic resin that was used primarily in the construction of distributor caps and rotors. It is easily molded and machined.
Cloth	A fabric used as internal trimming on some vehicles.
Cork	Often used in combination with rubber to form gaskets for engine blocks. It is lightweight and prevents oil and water from leaking into cylinders, which makes it ideal for use as a gasket material.
Felt	A woven material that is used as an underlay in floor mats.
Fiberglass	A metal glass that is used in some timing belts. Fiberglass is a lightweight, extremely strong, and robust material.
Formica	Often used in public transport vehicles as a decorative, laminated board.
Glass	Used for windshields, windows, and headlight coverings. Glass technology has resulted in shatter-proof windshields that help protect drivers and passengers.
Graphite	Used as a lubricant in vehicle applications. It is a black substance that is often used as an additive to grease or it can be sprayed on.
Leather	Expensive vehicles use leather, which is a tanned animal hide, for seat covers and other vehicle trim.
Melamine	A compound used to make synthetic resins and used for molding some lightweight vehicle body parts.
Nylon	A synthetic plastic material that is used in the construction of some bushings.

Continued on next page

TABLE 4-1: Materials Used in the Vehicle Industry, continued

Material	Definition
Perspex	A tough, clear plastic used as partitions on instrument panels. It resembles glass by its transparency.
Polish	A wax liquid that is spread onto a vehicle body surface after washing. It is buffed to a high-gloss polish.

Material	Definition
Polyurethane	A fire-resistant plastic resin that is used in the manufacture of vehicle seats.
Polyvinyl chloride (PVC)	Lightweight, strong, and flexible with acid-resistant properties. You can find PVC being used as piping in plumbing applications such as water distribution. In vehicle applications, it is used for oil seals and other flexible gaskets. It can also be found incorporated into floor mats because of its toughness and wear resistance.

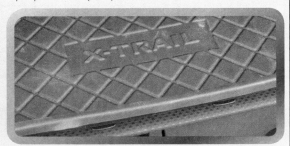

Material	Definition
Rubber	A versatile, elastic material that has dozens of applications in the motor trade industry. It is used in the manufacture of tires, for example. The rubber is mostly synthetic, with carbon black added to increase strength and toughness. When used in the tread, this combination gives a long life: Natural rubber is weaker than the synthetic version. It is used mainly in sidewalls. The plies are made from cords of fabric, coated with rubber. Early tires used cords of cotton, but with increased vehicle speeds and loads, rayon and nylon cords are now common. Cords of synthetic fabric have high tensile strength. They resist stretching, but are flexible under load. The cords are placed in parallel and impregnated with rubber to form sheets called plies. Plies have high strength in one direction, and are flexible in other directions. Steel-reinforced rubber is also used in the manufacture of radiator hoses.

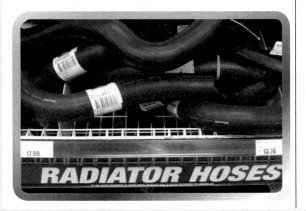

Continued on next page

TABLE 4-1: Materials Used in the Vehicle Industry, continued

Material	Definition
Silicone rubber	A synthetic rubber that is used for spark plug high-tension leads, seals, and gaskets.
Vinyl	A synthetic plastic material used for interior vehicle upholstery. Because it resembles leather, it is a cheaper alternative to the animal hide product.
Wax	The base substance used for polish.
Wood	Often used as an interior trim material. In super-luxury vehicles, such as the Rolls Royce or Bentley, highly polished, rare wood is used throughout the interior.

Wrap-Up

Ready for Review

- Tools and equipment should be used only for the task they were designed to do.
- Always have a safe attitude when using tools and equipment and wear necessary personal protection equipment.
- Do not use damaged tools; inspect before using, then clean and inspect again before putting them away.
- Lockouts and tagouts are meant to prevent technicians from using tools and equipment that are potentially unsafe.
- Many tools and measuring instruments have USCS or metric system markings to identify their size.
- Micrometers can be outside, inside, or depth.
- Gauges are used to measure distances and diameters; types include telescoping, split ball, and dial bore.
- Vernier calipers measure outside, inside, and depth dimensions; newer versions have dial and digital scales.
- Dial indicators are used to measure movement.
- A straight edge is designed to assess the flatness of a surface.
- Feeler blades are flat metal strips that are used to measure the width of gaps.
- Power tools can be stationary or portable, corded, or cordless and are powered by electricity, batteries, compressed air, a propellant, or a gasoline engine.
- Drills are designed to drive a drill bit into metal (or other material) to create a hole; check drilling speed charts for proper drilling speed.
- Portable grinders are designed to grind down metals, but can also be fitted with a cutting disc to cut sheets of metal.
- Air tools use compressed, pressurized air for power; types include the air impact wrench, air ratchet, air hammer, air drill, and blowgun/air nozzle.
- Common wrenches include box end, open end, combination (most popular), flare nut (or flare tubing), open-end adjustable, and ratcheting box end.
- Use the correct wrench for the situation, so as not to damage the bolt or nut.
- Sockets grip fasteners tightly on all six corners are classified as follows: standard or metric, size of drive used to turn them, number of points, depth of socket, and thickness of wall.
- Fasteners can be spun off or on (but not tightened) by a speed brace or speeder handle.
- Pliers hold, cut, or compress materials; types include slip-joint, combination, arc joint, needle nose, flat, diagonal cutting, snap ring, and locking.
- Cutting tools include bolt cutters, tin snips, and aviation snips.
- Allen wrenches are designed to fit into fasteners with recessed hexagonal heads.
- Screwdriver types include flat blade (most common), Phillips, Pozidriv, offset, ratcheting, and impact.
- The tip of the screwdriver must be matched exactly to the slot or recess on the head of a fastener.
- Types of hammers include ball peen (most common), sledge, mallet, and dead blow.
- Chisels are used to cut metals when hit with a hammer.
- Punches are used to mark metals when hit with a hammer and come in different diameters and different points for different tasks; types of punches include prick, center, drift, pin, ward, and hollow.
- Pry bars can be used to move, adjust, or pry parts. Gasket scrapers are designed to remove gaskets without damaging surrounding materials.
- Files are used to remove material from the surface of a truck part.
- Types of files include flat, warding, square, triangular, curved, and thread.
- Bench vices, offset vices, drill vices, and G-clamps all hold materials in place while they are worked on.
- Taps are designed to cut threads in holes or nuts; types include taper, intermediate, and bottoming.
- Gear and bearing pullers are designed to remove components from a shaft when considerable force is needed.
- Flaring tools create flares at the end of tubes to connect them to other components; types include single, double, and ISO.
- Rivet tools join together two pieces of metal; each rivet can be used only once.
- Most shops will have diagnostic equipment such as dynamometers, scanning tools, and various pressure testing equipment.
- Other shop equipment may be wheel alignment machines, tire changers, and/or brake drum/disc lathes.
- Oxyacetylene torches are designed to heat, braze, weld, and cut metal by combining acetylene with oxygen at a high temperature.
- Pressure washers/cleaners use focused, pressurized water to clean accumulated dirt and grease from vehicle components; water must be directed properly so as not to damage other parts.
- Spray wash cabinets are designed to clean automotive parts in a sealed cabinet, much like a dishwasher.
- Solvent tanks are designed for immersion of vehicle parts to remove oil, dirt, grease, and grime.
- Brake washers are designed to remove brake dust from wheel brake units and their components.
- Sand or bead blasters are designed to clean paint, corrosion, or dirt from metal parts by blasting small abrasive particles onto the surface.

- ▸ Electrical testing equipment used in the shop include multimeters, oscilloscopes, and graphing meters.
- ▸ Battery chargers can be fast chargers, slow chargers, or smart chargers that analyze the battery and select the best charging method.
- ▸ Vehicle batteries can be dangerous due to their high voltage; hybrid vehicle batteries have extremely high voltage and current flows.
- ▸ Many fluids are used in vehicles as coolants and lubricants.
- ▸ Engine coolants prevent freezing in the winter and increase the engine coolant's boiling point in the summer.
- ▸ ATF automatic transmission fluid can be specific to the vehicle, so always check and use the OEM-recommended fluid.
- ▸ Brake fluid is hygroscopic meaning that it readily absorbs water.
- ▸ Diesel fuel is a crude oil distillate used in CI engines.
- ▸ Biodiesel is made from either soybeans or canola or animal fats.
- ▸ Engine oil and gear oil can be petroleum or synthetic based.
- ▸ Many different metals and substances are used in vehicle manufacture; technicians should work on being able to identify these materials.

Vocabulary Builder

air drill A compressed air-powered drill.

air hammer A tool powered by compressed air with various hammer, cutting, punching, or chisel attachments. Also called an air chisel.

air-impact wrench An impact tool powered by compressed air designed to undo tight fasteners.

air nozzle A compressed-air device that emits a fine stream of compressed air for drying or cleaning parts.

air ratchet A ratchet tool for use with sockets powered by compressed air.

alkalis Chemical compounds that have a pH value greater than 7. They are commonly used in toy batteries and bleaches.

Allen wrench A type of hexagonal drive mechanism for fasteners.

angle grinder A portable grinder for grinding or cutting metal.

aviation snips A scissor-like tool for cutting sheet metal.

ball-peen (engineer's) hammer A hammer that has a head that is rounded on one end and flat on the other; designed to work with metal items.

battery A device that converts and stores electrical energy through chemical reactions.

battery charger A device that charges a battery, reversing the discharge process.

bench grinder (pedestal grinder) A grinder that is fixed to a bench or pedestal.

bench vice A device that securely holds material in jaws while it is being worked on.

biodiesel A renewable fuel made by chemically combining natural oils from soybeans (or cottonseeds, canola, etc.; animal fats; or even recycled cooking oil) with an alcohol such as methanol (or ethanol).

blind rivet A rivet that can be installed from its insertion side.

bolt cutters Strong cutters available in different sizes, designed to cut through nonhardened bolts and other small-stock material.

bottoming tap A thread-cutting tap designed to cut threads to the bottom of a blind hole.

C-clamp A clamp shaped like the letter C; it comes in various sizes and can clamp various items.

chassis dynamometer A machine with rollers that allows a vehicle to attain road speed and load while sitting still in the shop.

chrome A bright, shiny corrosion-resistant metal; it is mostly used for decorative purposes, such as on hubcaps.

cleaning gun A device with a nozzle controlled by a trigger fitted to the outlet of pressure cleaners.

closed-end wrench A wrench with a closed or ring end to grip bolts and nuts.

club hammer The club hammer is like a small mallet, with two square faces made of high-carbon steel. It is the heaviest type of hammer that can be used one-handed.

coefficient of friction (CoF) The amount of friction between two particular objects in contact; calculated by dividing the force required to move the object by the weight of the object.

combination pliers A type of pliers for cutting, gripping, and bending.

combination wrench A type of wrench that has an open end on one end and a closed-end wrench on the other.

coolant A fluid that contains special antifreezing and anticorrosion chemicals mixed with water.

copper A nonferrous, pure metal that can be alloyed (combined) with other metals but is not combined with iron.

crankshaft A vehicle engine component that transfers the reciprocating movement of pistons into rotary motion.

cross-arm A description for an arm that is set at right angles or 90° to another component.

cross-cut chisel A type of chisel for metal work that cleans out or cuts key ways.

curved file A type of file that has a curved surface for filing holes.

dead-blow hammer A type of hammer that has a cushioned head to reduce the amount of head bounce.

depth micrometers A micrometer that measures the depth of an item such as how far a piston is below the surface of the block.

diagonal-cutting pliers Cutting pliers for small wire or cable.

dial bore gauge A gauge that is used to measure the inside diameter of bores with a high degree of accuracy and speed.

dial indicators A dial that can also be known as a dial gauge, and, as the name suggests, has a dial and needle where measurements are read.

die A device used to cut threads on a bolt or shaft.

die stock handle A handle for securely holding dies to cut threads.

double flare A seal that is made at the end of metal tubing or pipe.

drift punch A type of punch used to start pushing roll pins to prevent them from spreading.

drill chuck A device for securely gripping drill bits in a drill.

drill press A device that incorporates a fixed drill with multiple speeds and an adjustable worktable. It can be free-standing or fixed to a bench.

drill vice A tool with jaws that can be attached to a drill press table for holding material that is to be drilled.

ethylene glycol A chemical that resists freezing but is very toxic to people and animals.

fast chargers A type of battery charger that charges batteries quickly.

feeler gauges Also called feeler blades; flat metal strips used to measure the width of gaps, such as the clearance between valves and rocker arms.

ferrous metals Metals that use iron as an alloying agent. Cast iron, steel, and stainless steel are the main categories of iron alloys used in the automotive industry.

finished rivet A rivet after the completion of the riveting process.

flare-nut wrench A type of closed-end wrench that has a slot in the box section to allow the wrench to slip through a tube or pipe. Also called a flare tubing wrench.

flashback arrestor A spring-loaded valve installed on oxyacetylene torches as a safety device to prevent flame from entering the torch hoses.

flat-nosed pliers Pliers that are flat and square at the end of the nose.

flat-tip screwdriver A type of screwdriver that fits a straight slot in screws.

forcing screw The center screw on a gear, bearing, or pulley puller. Also called a jacking screw.

fuel (gasoline, diesel) A derivative of crude oil.

gasket scraper A broad, sharp, flat blade to assist in removing gaskets and glue.

gear pullers A tool with two or more legs and a cross-bar with a center forcing screw to remove gears.

grinding wheels and discs Abrasive wheels or flat discs fitted to bench, pedestal, and portable grinders.

ground The return path for electrical current in a vehicle chassis, other metal of the vehicle, or dedicated wire.

high resistance Describes a circuit or components with more resistance than designed.

hygroscopic When brake fluid absorbs water from the atmosphere.

hollow punch A punch with a center hollow for cutting circles in thin materials such as gaskets.

impact driver A tool that is struck with a blow to provide an impact turning force to remove tight fasteners.

inside micrometer Micrometer that measures inside dimensions.

intermediate tap One of a series of taps designed to cut an internal thread. Also called a plug tap.

locking pliers A type of plier where the jaws can be set and locked into position.

lockout/tagout A safety tag system to ensure that faulty equipment or equipment in the middle of repair is not used.

magnetic pickup tools An extending shaft, often flexible, with a magnet fitted to the end for picking up metal objects.

mandrel The shaft of a pop rivet.

mandrel head The head of the pop rivet that connects to the shaft.

measuring tapes A flexible type of ruler and a common measuring tool.

mechanical fingers Spring-loaded fingers at the end of a flexible shaft that pick up items in tight spaces.

micrometers Precise measuring tools designed to measure small distances and are available in both millimeter (mm) and inch calibrations.

Morse taper A tapered mounting shaft for drill bits and chucks in larger drills and lathes.

needle-nosed pliers Pliers with long tapered jaws for gripping small items and getting into tight spaces.

nippers Pliers designed to cut protruding items level with the surface.

nonferrous metals Pure metals such as copper; can also be used in alloys.

offset screwdriver A screwdriver with a 90° bend in the shaft for working in tight spaces.

offset vice A vice that allows long objects to be gripped vertically.

open circuits Describes a circuit that has a break and no current can flow.

open-end wrench A wrench with open jaws to allow side entry to a nut or bolt.

outside micrometer Measures the outside dimensions of an item.

oxyacetylene torch A gas welding system that combines oxygen and acetylene.

paraffin (mineral oil) Used mainly as a cleaning agent in the commercial vehicle industry.

parallax error A visual error caused by viewing measurement markers at an incorrect angle.

peening A term used to describe the action of flattening a rivet through a hammering action.

Phillips screwdriver A type of screwdriver that fits a head shaped like a cross in screws; also called Phillips head screwdriver.

pin punch A type of punch in various sizes with a straight or parallel shaft.

pliers A hand tool with gripping jaws.

pop-rivet gun A hand tool for installing pop rivets.

power tools Tools powered by electricity or compressed air.

pressure washer/cleaner A cleaning machine that boosts low-pressure tap water to a high-pressure output.

prick punch A punch with a sharp point for accurately marking a point on metal.

Propylene glycol An organic-based chemical that resists freezing and, unlike ethylene glycol, is nontoxic.

pry bars (crowbars) A high-strength carbon-steel rod with offsets for levering and prying.

pullers A generic term to describe hand tools that mechanically assist the removal of bearings, gears, pulleys, and other parts.

punches A generic term to describe a high-strength carbon-steel shaft with a blunt point for driving. Center and prick punches are exceptions and have a sharp point for marking or making an indentation.

ratchet A generic term to describe a handle for sockets that allows the user to select direction of rotation. It can turn sockets in restricted areas without the user having to remove the socket from the fastener.

ratcheting screwdriver A screwdriver with a selectable ratchet mechanism built into the handle that allows the screwdriver tip to ratchet as it is being used.

rattle gun The most common air tool in a shop; also called the air-impact wrench or impact gun.

sand or bead blasters A cleaning system that uses high-pressure fine particles of glass bead or sand.

screw extractor A tool for removing broken screws or bolts.

short circuits Describe a condition in which the current flows along an unintended route.

single flare A sealing system made on the end of metal tubing.

sliding T-handle A handle fitted at 90° to the main body that can be slid from side to side.

slow charger A battery charger that charges at low current.

smart charger A battery charger with microprocessor-controlled charging rates and times.

snap ring pliers A pair of pliers for installing and removing internal or external snap rings.

socket An enclosed metal tube commonly with 6 or 12 points to remove and install bolts and nuts.

solvent A highly flammable liquid that can dissolve other substances.

solvent tank A tank containing solvents to clean vehicle parts.

speed brace A U-shaped socket wrench that allows high-speed operation. Also called a speeder handle.

split ball gauge (small hole gauge) A gauge that is good for measuring small holes where telescoping gauges cannot fit.

spray-wash cabinet A cleaning cabinet that sprays solvent under pressure to clean vehicle parts.

square file A type of file with a square cross section.

steel ruler A ruler that is made from stainless steel. Stainless steel rulers commonly come in 30 mm, 60 mm, and 1 meter lengths.

straight edges A measuring device generally made of steel to check how flat a surface is.

straight grinder A powered grinder with the wheel set at 90° to the shaft.

sulfuric acid A type of acid that when mixed with pure water forms the basis of battery acid or electrolyte.

tap A term used to generically describe an internal thread-cutting tool.

tap handle A tool designed to securely hold taps for cutting internal threads.

taper tap A tap with a tapper; it is usually the first of three taps used when cutting internal threads.

telescoping gauge Gauge used for measuring distances in awkward spots such as the bottom of a deep cylinder.

thread repair A generic term to describe a number of processes that can be used to repair threads.

thread chaser A device similar to a die that cleans up rusty or damaged threads.

tin A metal most often used as a corrosion-resistant coating in automotive applications.

tin snips Cutting device for sheet metal; works in a similar fashion to scissors.

tube-flaring tool A tool that makes a sealing flare on the end of metal tubing.

tubing cutter A hand tool for cutting pipe or tubing squarely.

twist drill A hardened steel drill bit for making holes in metals, plastics, and wood.

V blocks Metal blocks with a V-shaped cutout for holding shafts while working on them. Also referred to as vee blocks.

vernier caliper An accurate measuring device for internal, external, and depth measurements that incorporates fixed and adjustable jaws.

volatile organic compounds (VOCs) Evaporative emissions that vehicles emit.

wad punch A type of punch that is hollow for cutting circular shapes in soft materials, such as gaskets.

warding file A type of thin, flat file with a tapered end.

water-pump pliers Adjustable pliers with parallel jaws that allow you to increase or decrease the size of the jaws by selecting a different set of channels.

wrench A generic term to describe tools that tighten and loosen fasteners with hexagonal heads.

Review Questions

1. A _____ is an accurate measuring device for internal, external, and depth measurements that incorporates fixed and adjustable jaws.
   a. telescoping gauge
   b. vernier caliper
   c. chassis dynamometer
   d. morse taper

2. _____ are chemical compounds that have a pH value greater than 7.
   a. Alkalis
   b. Acids
   c. Liquids
   d. Metals

3. The _____ is the most common air tool in an automotive workshop.
   a. air-impact driver
   b. bench vice
   c. air-impact wrench
   d. flashback arrestor

4. Like stainless steel, _____ is a bright, shiny corrosion-resistant metal and is used mostly for decorative purposes.
   a. aluminum
   b. chrome
   c. tin
   d. graphite

5. Pressure _____ gauges are a particular type of pressure gauge that measures "negative" pressure below atmospheric pressure.
   a. impact
   b. magnet
   c. hydraulic
   d. vacuum

6. A measuring _____ is a flexible type of ruler that is useful for measuring longer distances and is accurate to a millimeter or a fraction of an inch.
   a. tape
   b. rod
   c. micrometer
   d. ruler

7. _____ is a term used to describe the action of flattening a rivet through a hammering action.
   a. Smashing
   b. Grinding
   c. Peening
   d. Tweeking

8. _____ is a system for securing drill bits to drills.
   a. Morse taper
   b. Lockout/tagout
   c. Double flare
   d. Tap

9. _____ torches are used by technicians to heat, braze, weld, and cut metal.
   a. Methane
   b. Butane
   c. Propane
   d. Oxyacetylene

10. Screw _____ are devices designed to remove screws, studs, or bolts that have broken off in threaded holes.
    a. extractors
    b. pullers
    c. grippers
    d. fingers

ASE-Type Questions

1. Technician A says an air hammer is not as efficient as a hand chisel and hammer for driving and cutting. Technician B says an air hammer works just as well or better. Who is correct?
   a. Technician A
   b. Technician B
   c. Both Technician A and Technician B
   d. Neither Technician A nor Technician B

2. Technician A says six- and 12-point sockets fit the heads of hexagonal-shaped fasteners. Technician B says four- and 8-point sockets fit the heads of square-shaped fasteners. Who is correct?
   a. Technician A
   b. Technician B
   c. Both Technician A and Technician B
   d. Neither Technician A nor Technician B

3. Technician A says Propylene glycol is a chemical that resists freezing but is very toxic to people and animals. Technician B says Propylene glycol resists freezing but is non-toxic. Who is correct?
   a. Technician A
   b. Technician B
   c. Both Technician A and Technician B
   d. Neither Technician A nor Technician B

4. Technician A says gear oil is the lubricant used in transmissions, transfer cases, and differentials. Technician B says motor oil is the lubricant used in transmissions, transfer cases, and differentials. Who is correct?
   a. Technician A
   b. Technician B
   c. Both Technician A and Technician B
   d. Neither Technician A nor Technician B

5. Technician A says the engine dynamometer measures engine performance through a vehicle's driven wheels. Technician B says the chassis dynamometer measures engine performance through the engine's crankshaft while the engine is removed from the vehicle. Who is correct?
   a. Technician A
   b. Technician B
   c. Both Technician A and Technician B
   d. Neither Technician A nor Technician B

6. Technician A says a micrometer should always be stored with its measuring surfaces touching in order to maintain its calibration. Technician B says to leave a gap between measuring surfaces to maintain calibration. Who is correct?
   a. Technician A
   b. Technician B
   c. Both Technician A and Technician B
   d. Neither Technician A nor Technician B

7. Technician A says a pry bar is designed to remove a gasket without damaging the sealing face of the component. Technician B says a cold chisel will work just as well. Who is correct?
   a. Technician A
   b. Technician B
   c. Both Technician A and Technician B
   d. Neither Technician A nor Technician B

8. Technician A says an angle grinder uses discs. Technician B says an angle grinder uses wheels. Who is correct?
   a. Technician A
   b. Technician B
   c. Both Technician A and Technician B
   d. Neither Technician A nor Technician B

9. Technician A says diesel fuel oil is used to power diesel engines. Technician B says diesel fuel oil is used to power compression ignition engines. Who is correct?
   a. Technician A
   b. Technician B
   c. Both Technician A and Technician B
   d. Neither Technician A nor Technician B

10. Technician A says when a brake fluid absorbs moisture from the atmosphere it is hygroscopic. Technician B says when a brake fluid absorbs moisture from the atmosphere it is hydrophobic. Who is correct?
    a. Technician A
    b. Technician B
    c. Both Technician A and Technician B
    d. Neither Technician A nor Technician B

CHAPTER 5
Fasteners, Locking Devices, and Lifting Equipment

NATEF Tasks

Supplemental Task List

Shop and Personal Safety Page
- Identify and use proper placement of floor jacks and jack stands. (pp 154–156)

- Identify and use proper procedures for safe lift operation. (pp 156–158)

Knowledge Objectives

After reading this chapter, you will be able to:
1. Identify locking devices and tools. (pp 132–138)
2. Describe fasteners and torque. (pp 138–142)
3. Identify locking device measuring tools. (138–142)
4. Describe helical inserts. (p 142)
5. Identify locking pins and keys. (pp 142–144)
6. Discuss the design and function of head gaskets. (pp 144–145)
7. Discuss the design and function of lip-type seals. (pp 145–148)
8. Discuss the design and function of ring seals. (p 148)
9. Discuss the design and function of crankshaft seals. (pp 148–149)
10. Discuss the design and function of mechanical seals. (pp 149–150)
11. Discuss the use of adhesives and sealants. (pp 150–151)
12. Describe the correct procedure for manual lifting. (p 152)
13. Describe the application and purpose of lifting equipment. (pp 152–153)
14. Describe the safe use of lifting equipment. (p 153)
15. Identify types of lifting and moving equipment. (pp 153–159)
16. Know how to use lifting equipment. (pp 159–161)

Skills Objectives

After reading this chapter, you will be able to:
1. Use a torque wrench and torque angle gauge. (p 145) **SKILL DRILL 5-1**
2. Remove and install split pins. (p 146) **SKILL DRILL 5-2**
3. Fit a formed head gasket. (p 149) **SKILL DRILL 5-3**
4. Assemble and make a user-formed gasket. (p 149) **SKILL DRILL 5-4**
5. Assemble and make a user-formed gasket—tap method. (p 150) **SKILL DRILL 5-5**
6. Remove and replace lip-type seals. (p 152) **SKILL DRILL 5-6**
7. Remove and replace ring seals. (p 153) **SKILL DRILL 5-7**
8. Lift and secure a vehicle with a vehicle floor jack and stands. (p 160) **SKILL DRILL 5-8**
9. Lift a vehicle using a hydraulic hoist. (p 163) **SKILL DRILL 5-9**
10. Use engine hoists and stands. (p 164) **SKILL DRILL 5-10**

▶ Introduction

Locking devices used in this industry are primarily designed to hold things in a particular location or to hold things together. These devices come in many forms, and depending on the particular application, one or more types of locking devices may be used. They can be in the form of a physical fastener and/or chemical adhesive. This chapter provides a description of the types of locking devices and fasteners found in automotive design vehicle applications. We will also discuss the safe use of lifting equipment.

▶ Locking Devices and Tools

Fasteners

There are many different __fasteners__ used in vehicle applications, including screws, bolts, studs and nuts. Washers and chemical compounds can be used to help secure these fasteners.

Screws

__Screws__ are generally smaller than bolts and are sometimes referred to as metal threads **FIGURE 5-1**. They can have a variety of heads, they're used on smaller components, and often their thread extends right from the tip to the head so they can hold together components of different thickness.

Different screws can be tightened with a range of tools. An __Allen head screw__ has a recess for an __Allen wrench__ **FIGURES 5-2A and 2B**. An Allen head screw is sometimes called a cap screw. It usually screws into a hole rather than a nut, and it needs tightening with an Allen wrench.

A __machine screw__ has a slot for a screwdriver **FIGURE 5-3**. Screwdrivers come in many sizes, and you should always use the correct size blade for the particular machine screw slot.

There are a number of special screws that cut their own threads as they go. This is called *tapping a thread*. Pictured in **FIGURE 5-4A** is a __self-tapping screw__. It is made of hard material that cuts a mirror image of itself into the hole as you turn it.

FIGURE 5-1 Generally smaller than bolts and are sometimes referred to as metal threads.

The screw in **FIGURE 5-4B** is also known as a self-tapping screw, but it is designed for cutting and holding thin sheet metal, so it is often used on car bodies.

▶ TECHNICIAN TIP

Threads are cut on screws, bolts, nuts, and studs and inside holes to allow components to be attached and assembled. There was a time when there were many different thread designs used throughout the world. Modern vehicles still use a range of thread patterns, but due to standardization, it is getting much simpler **FIGURE 5-5**. Nearly all the nuts, bolts, screws, and studs on a vehicle have a V-thread cut into them.

A screw jack or a clamp has __square threads__ cut into it. The square thread is more difficult to machine and is used mainly in situations where rotational movement needs to be transferred into lateral movement—for example, the screw in a vice where the rotary movement of turning the handle is translated into the lateral movement of the jaws closing.

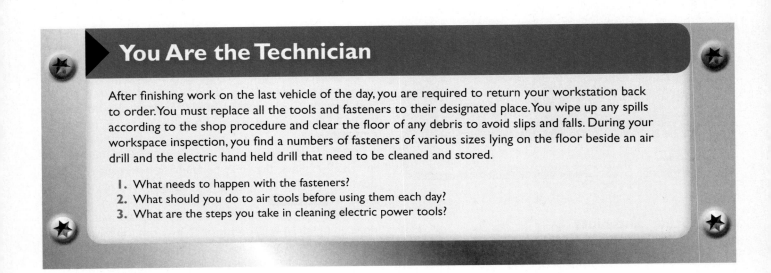

▶ You Are the Technician

After finishing work on the last vehicle of the day, you are required to return your workstation back to order. You must replace all the tools and fasteners to their designated place. You wipe up any spills according to the shop procedure and clear the floor of any debris to avoid slips and falls. During your workspace inspection, you find a numbers of fasteners of various sizes lying on the floor beside an air drill and the electric hand held drill that need to be cleaned and stored.

1. What needs to happen with the fasteners?
2. What should you do to air tools before using them each day?
3. What are the steps you take in cleaning electric power tools?

FIGURE 5-2 **A.** An Allen head screw. **B.** An Allen wrench set.

FIGURE 5-4 Self-tapping screws.

FIGURE 5-3 A machine screw.

Bolts, Studs, and Nuts

Bolts, studs, and nuts are fasteners designed for heavier jobs than screws and tend to be made of metal or metal alloys.

Bolts are cylindrical pieces of metal with a hexagonal head on one end and a thread cut into the shaft at the other end **FIGURE 5-6** . They are often bigger than screws and are used for heavier jobs. Bolts are always threaded into a nut or hole that has an identical thread cut inside. The thread acts as an inclined plane; as the bolt is turned, it is drawn into or out of the matching thread.

Nuts are often used with bolts. A nut is a piece of metal, usually hexagonal, with a thread cut through it to fit the bolt thread. The hexagonal heads for the bolt and nut are designed to fit tools such as combination wrenches and sockets **FIGURE 5-7** .

Torx drivers are used for **torx bolts** and are often found in vehicle engines; they may be found in places such as cylinder heads to blocks, where particular tightening sequences are required **FIGURE 5-8** .

There are many different ways to keep the nut and bolt done up tightly. A self-locking or **Nylock nut** can have a plastic or nylon insert. Tightening the bolt squeezes it into the insert, where it resists any movement. The self-locker is highly resistant

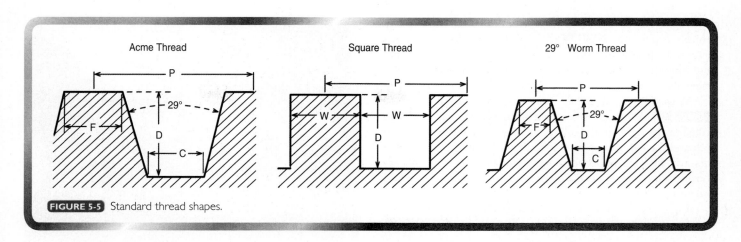

FIGURE 5-5 Standard thread shapes.

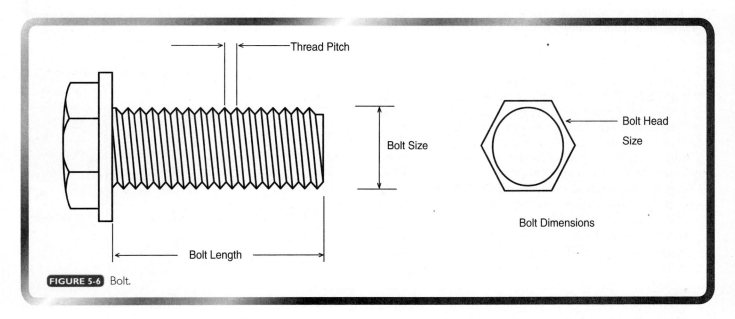

FIGURE 5-6 Bolt.

FIGURE 5-7 Bolts usually have hexagonal heads.

FIGURE 5-8 Torx bolts are often found in many vehicle locations; they may be found in places such as cylinder heads to blocks, where particular tightening sequences are required.

to being loosened by the kind of vibration that engines and vehicles experience **FIGURE 5-9**. Tightening this style of nut distorts the insert, so it provides its locking effect only the first time you use it. If you remove the nut, it should be replaced with a new one.

A <u>castellated nut</u> has slots like towers on a castle **FIGURE 5-10**. When it is screwed onto a bolt that has been drilled in the right spot, a split pin can be passed through them both and then spread open to lock the nut in place. Castellated nuts are used where scheduled maintenance requires inspection and adjustments to take place for items such as front wheel bearings.

A <u>speed nut</u> is not as strong as the other types, but it can be a fast and convenient way to secure a screw **FIGURE 5-11**. Once the speed nut is started, it does not need to be held. These are often used in places like body component fixings.

Some bolts and nuts need washers. Washers can be made from a number of materials depending on their application, including aluminum, copper, fiber, and steel. Here are some brief descriptions of the more common washers:

- <u>Flat washers</u> spread the load of a bolt head or a nut as it is tightened and distribute it over a greater area **FIGURE 5-12A**. This protects the surface underneath from being marked by the nut or head as it turns and tightens down. Flat washers should always be used to protect aluminum alloy.
- A <u>spring (lock) washer</u> compresses as the nut tightens, and the nut is spring loaded against this surface, which makes it unlikely to work loose **FIGURE 5-12B**. The ends of the spring washer also bite into the metal. Spring washers are used more for bolts and nuts.
- Screws mostly rely on smaller <u>serrated edge shake-proof washers</u> **FIGURE 5-12C**. The external ones have teeth on the outside, and the internal ones have teeth on the inside; one type has both.

FIGURE 5-10 Castellated nut.

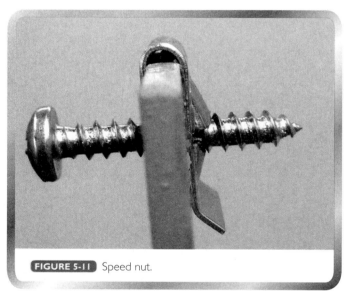

FIGURE 5-11 Speed nut.

FIGURE 5-9 A self-locking nut is highly resistant to being loosened by engine vibrations.

- <u>Spindle washers</u> are used behind a wheel bearing. The key or tab on the washer **FIGURE 5-12D** prevents the washer from spinning due to bearing rotation.

Often, the thread on a stud is only as long as it needs to be to tighten onto the nut or into the threaded hole. Some special versions have both a left- and right-hand thread on them. A <u>stud</u> **FIGURE 5-13** is like two bolts in one; for instance, an exhaust manifold on the cylinder head is normally located and held by studs and nuts.

A stud does not have a fixed hexagonal head; rather, it has a thread cut on each end. It is threaded into one part, where it stays. The mating part is then slipped over it and a nut is threaded onto the end of the stud to secure the part. Studs are commonly used to attach a throttle body to the intake manifold. Studs can have different threads on each end.

FIGURE 5-12 Types of washers. **A.** Flat washer. **B.** Spring washer. **C.** Serrated edge shake-proof washers. **D.** Spindle washer.

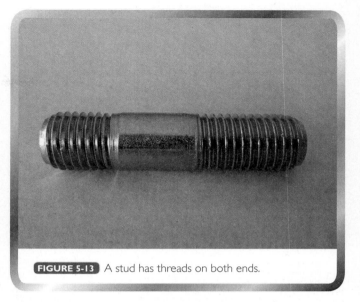

FIGURE 5-13 A stud has threads on both ends.

Bolts, nuts, and studs can have either standard or metric threads. They are designated by their thread diameter, thread pitch, length, and grade. The diameter is measured across the outside of the threads; it is measured in fractions of an inch for standard-type fasteners and millimeters for metric-type fasteners. A 3/8" (9.5 mm) bolt has a thread diameter of 3/8" (9.5 mm); 3/8" (9.5 mm) is not the size of the bolt head.

The **standard (imperial) system** also uses a marking system to indicate tensile strength, as shown in **FIGURE 5-14**. This is a grade 5 bolt, and can be tightened to specific torque as specified by the manufacturer. **Torque** is a way of defining how much a fastener should be tightened.

The metric system uses numbers stamped on the heads of metric bolts and on the face of metric nuts **FIGURE 5-15**. Even studs have a marking system to make sure they are not over-stressed when you tighten them. The numbers indicate the *tensile strength* of the bolt. The number does *not* mean the size of the bolt. NOTE: The distance between flats on the bolt or nut heads generally indicates wrench size to be used.

The coarseness of any thread is called its **thread pitch** **FIGURE 5-16A**. In the standard system, the thread pitch is measured in threads per inch (tpi) which is the distance between the peaks of the threads in inches **FIGURE 5-16B**. Each bolt diameter in the metric system can have up to four thread pitches. Metric threads, designated with a capital M, are rated according to their outer diameter and their pitch **FIGURE 5-16C**.

The length of a bolt is fairly straightforward. It is measured from the end of the bolt to the bottom of the head and is listed in inches or millimeters. The grade of a fastener relates to its strength. The higher the grade number, the higher the **tensile strength**, which refers to how much tension it can withstand before it breaks. Tensile strength for fasteners is generally listed in pounds per square inch (megapascals, or MPa), of bolt shaft area.

FIGURE 5-14 Tensile strength markings using the standard system—Grade 5 bolt.

FIGURE 5-15 Bolts and nuts are often marked to indicate how much torque can be safely applied to them. Markings using the metric system are shown here.

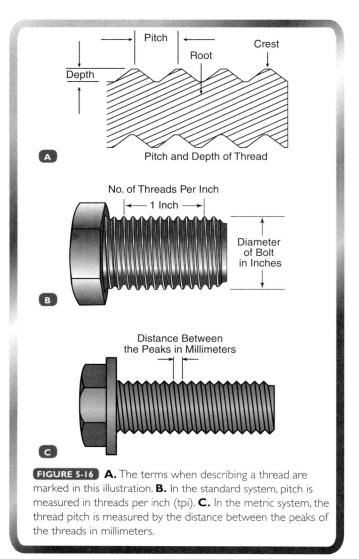

FIGURE 5-16 **A.** The terms when describing a thread are marked in this illustration. **B.** In the standard system, pitch is measured in threads per inch (tpi). **C.** In the metric system, the thread pitch is measured by the distance between the peaks of the threads in millimeters.

TECHNICIAN TIP

The global version of metric is called the International System of Units, or SI. The standard system of inch-pounds is still used by some manufacturers, particularly in the United States.

The metric system, however, has produced some competing classifications for fasteners. For example, metric hex cap screws may have three different standards:

1. DIN 931 (DIN 933 fully threaded)
2. ISO 4014 (ISO 4017 fully threaded)
3. ANSI/ASME B18.2.3.1M

These three standards are interchangeable, differing primarily in the width across the flat dimensions.

TECHNICIAN TIP

Many automotive bolts and nuts need to be tightened to a specified level—tight enough to hold components together but not so tight that the component or the fastener could fail. This level of tightness is called the **torque specification**. Bolts and nuts are often marked with grades to tell you their strength, which determines how much torque can safely be applied to them. For example, a grade 8 bolt is stronger than a grade 5 bolt and can be tightened to a higher torque. The specific torque required for every bolt on the vehicle should always be obtained from the manufacturer's technical information system. Once bolts are tightened, there are different ways to ensure they stay tight. For example, a locking washer, a locking chemical compound, or a nylon locking device built into the nut may be used.

Chemical Compounds

Chemical compounds (such as Loctite) help prevent fasteners from loosening **FIGURE 5-17**. They are applied to one thread, and then the other is screwed onto it. This creates a strong bond

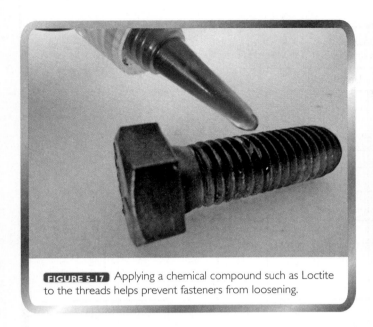

FIGURE 5-17 Applying a chemical compound such as Loctite to the threads helps prevent fasteners from loosening.

FIGURE 5-18 Applying an antiseize compound prevents threads and fasteners from sticking together.

between them, but one that stays plastic, so in future they can be separated with a wrench if necessary.

Some metals react with each other and bind together—for instance, spark plugs when they are in aluminum cylinder heads. An **antiseize compound** neutralizes the chemical reaction that can make this happen and prevents threads and fasteners from sticking together **FIGURE 5-18**.

▶ Fasteners and Torque

Fasteners are designed to secure parts that are under various tension and shear stresses. The nature of the stresses placed on parts and fasteners depends on their use and location. For example, head bolts withstand *tension stresses* by clamping the head gasket between the cylinder head and the block. The bolts must withstand the very high combustion pressures trying to push the head off the engine block in order to leak past the head gasket. An example of fasteners withstanding *shear stresses* is wheel studs and wheel nuts. They clamp the wheel assembly to the suspension system, and the weight of the vehicle tries to shear the lug studs. If this were to happen, the wheel would fall off the vehicle, leading to an accident.

To accomplish their job, fasteners come in a variety of diameters and hardnesses, which are defined in tensile strength grades. Fasteners with screw threads are designed to be tightened to a specific torque depending on the job at hand, the tensile strength or hardness of the material they are made from, their size, and the thread pitch. If a fastener is overtightened, it could become damaged or could break. If it is undertightened, it could work loose over time.

Torque Charts

Torque specifications for bolts and nuts in vehicles will usually be contained within shop manuals. Bolt, nut, and stud manufacturers also produce torque charts, which contain all the information you need to determine the maximum torque of bolts

or nuts **FIGURE 5-19**. For example, most charts include the bolt diameter, threads per inch (mm), grade, and maximum torque setting for both dry and lubricated bolts and nuts **TABLE 5-1**. A lubricated bolt and nut will reach maximum torque value at a lower setting. In practice, most torque specifications call for the nuts and bolts to have dry threads prior to tightening. There are some exceptions, so close examination of the torque specification chart is critical.

▶ Locking Device Measuring Tools
Torque Wrenches

A **torque wrench** is also known as a tension wrench **FIGURE 5-20**. It is used to tighten fasteners to a predetermined torque. It is designed to tighten bolts and nuts using the drive on the end, which fits with any socket and accessory of the same drive size found in an ordinary socket set. Although manufacturers do not specify torque settings for every nut and bolt, it is important to follow the specifications when they do. For example, manufacturers specify a torque for cylinder head bolts. The torque specified will ensure that the bolt provides the proper clamping pressure and will not come loose, but will not be so tight as to risk breaking the bolt or stripping the threads **FIGURE 5-21**.

The torque value will be specified in foot pounds (ft lbs) or newton meters (Nm). The torque value is the amount of twisting force applied to a fastener by the torque wrench. For example, foot-pound (newton meter) is described as the amount of twisting force applied to a shaft by a perpendicular lever 1 foot (meter) long with a force of 1 pound (newton) applied to the outer end. A torque value of 100 ft-lb will be the same as applying a 100-pound force to the end of a 1-foot-long lever. *(One ft-lb is equal to 1.35 Nm.)*

Torque wrenches come in various types: beam style, clicker, dial, and electronic **FIGURE 5-22**. The simplest and least expensive is the *beam-style* torque wrench. It uses a spring steel beam that flexes under tension. A smaller fixed rod then indicates the

In the absence of torque specifications, the values below can be used as a guide to the maximum safe torque for a specific diameter/grade of fastener. The torque specification is for clean dry threads; if the threads are oiled, reduce the torque by 10%.

Bolt Diameter	Bolt Grade Marking									
	4.6		4.8		8.8		10.9		12.9	
	Maximum Torque		Maximum Torque		Maximum Torque		Maximum Torque		Maximum Torque	
	lb-ft	Nm	lb-ft	Nm	lb-ft	Nm	lb-ft	Nm	lb-ft	Nm
M4	0.8	1.1	1	1.5	2	3	3	4.5	4	5
M5	1.5	2.5	2	3	4.5	6	6.5	9	7.5	10
M6	3	4	4	5.5	7.5	10	1.1	15	13	18
M8	7	9.5	10	13	18	25	26	35	33	45
M10	14	19	18	25	37	50	55	75	63	85
M12	26	35	33	45	63	85	97	130	111	150
M14	37	50	55	75	103	140	151	205	177	240
M16	59	80	85	115	159	215	232	315	273	370
M18	81	110	118	160	225	305	321	435	376	510
M20	118	160	166	225	321	435	457	620	535	725
M22	159	215	225	305	435	590	620	840	726	985

FIGURE 5-19 Torque specification chart.

TABLE 5-1: U.S. Bolt Torque Specifications

Bolt Diameter	SAE Grade Threads Per Inch	5 (Dry) Torque (lb-ft)	7 (Dry) Torque (lb-ft)	8 (Dry) Torque (lb-ft)
1/4"	20	8	10	12
1/4"	28	10	12	14
5/16"	18	17	21	25
5/16"	24	19	24	29
3/8"	16	30	40	45
3/8"	24	35	45	50
7/16"	14	50	60	70
7/16"	20	55	70	80
1/2"	13	75	95	110
1/2"	20	90	100	120
9/16"	12	110	135	150
9/16"	18	120	150	170
5/8"	11	150	140	220
5/8"	18	180	210	240

Continued on next page

TABLE 5-1: U.S. Bolt Torque Specifications, continued

Bolt Diameter	SAE Grade Threads Per Inch	5 (Dry) Torque (lb-ft)	7 (Dry) Torque (lb-ft)	8 (Dry) Torque (lb-ft)
3/4"	10	260	320	380
3/4"	16	300	360	420
7/8"	9	430	520	600
7/8"	14	470	580	660
1"	8	640	800	900
1"	12	710	860	990

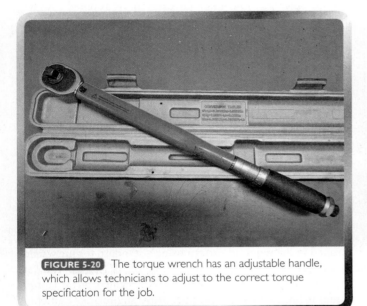

FIGURE 5-20 The torque wrench has an adjustable handle, which allows technicians to adjust to the correct torque specification for the job.

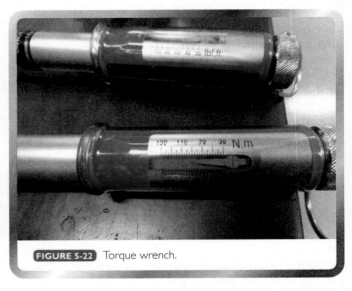

FIGURE 5-22 Torque wrench.

FIGURE 5-21 The torque wrench is fitted over the wheel locking nuts and tightened to the specified torque.

amount of torque on a scale mounted to the bar. The amount of deflection of the bar coincides with the amount of torque on the scale. One drawback of this design is that you have to be positioned directly above the scale so you can read it accurately. That can be a problem when working under the hood of a vehicle.

The *clicker-style* torque wrench uses an adjustable clutch inside that slips (clicks) when the preset torque is reached. You can set it for a particular torque on the handle. As the bolt is tightened, once the preset torque is reached, the torque wrench will click. This makes it especially handy in situations where the scale of a beam-style torque wrench cannot be read. The higher the torque, the louder the click; the lower the torque, the quieter the click. Be careful when using this style of torque wrench, especially at lower torque settings. It is easy to miss the click and overtighten, break, or strip the bolt. Once the torque wrench clicks, stop turning it, as it will continue to tighten the fastener if you turn it past the click point.

The *dial* torque wrench turns a dial that indicates the torque based on the torque being applied. Like the beam-style torque wrench, you have to be able to see the dial to know how much torque is being applied. Many dial torque wrenches have a movable indicator that is moved by the dial and stays at the highest reading. That way, you can double-check the torque achieved once the torque wrench is released. Once the proper torque is reached, the indicator can be moved back to zero for the next fastener being torqued.

The *digital* torque wrench usually uses a spring steel bar with an electronic strain gauge to measure the amount of torque being applied. The torque wrench can be preset to the desired torque. It will then display the torque as the fastener is being tightened. When it reaches the preset torque, it will usually give an audible signal, such as a beep. This makes it useful in situations where a scale or dial cannot be read.

Torque wrenches fall out of calibration over time or if they are not used properly, so they should be checked and calibrated annually. This can be performed in the shop if the proper calibration equipment is available, or the torque wrench can be sent to a qualified service center. Most quality torque wrench manufacturers provide a recalibration service for their customers.

Using a Torque Wrench and a Torque Angle Gauge

To help ensure that the proper amount of torque gets from the torque wrench to the bolt, support the head of the torque wrench with one hand **FIGURE 5-23**. When using a torque wrench, it is best not to use extensions. Extensions make it harder to support the head, which can end up absorbing some of the torque. If possible, use a deep socket instead.

Torque is not always the best method of ensuring that a bolt is tightened enough to give the proper amount of clamping force. If the threads are rusty, rough, or damaged in any way, the amount of twisting force required to tighten the fastener increases. Tightening a rusty fastener to a particular torque will not provide as much clamping force as a smooth fastener torqued the same amount. All threads must be clean before tightening the

fastener to a specified torque. This also brings up the question of whether threads should be lubricated. In most cases, the torque values specified are for dry, nonlubricated threads, but always check the manufacturer's specifications.

When bolts are tightened, they are also stretched. As long as they are not tightened too much, they will return to their original length when loosened. This is called **elasticity**. If they continue to be tightened and stretched beyond their point of elasticity, they will not return to their original length when loosened. This is called the **yield point**. **Torque-to-yield (TTY)** means that a fastener is torqued to, or just beyond, its yield point.

With the changes in engine metallurgy that manufacturers are using in modern vehicles, bolt technology has had to change as well. To help prevent bolts from loosening over time and to maintain an adequate clamping force when the engine is both cold and hot, manufacturers have adopted "stretch" or **torque-to-yield (TTY) bolts**. TTY bolts are designed to provide a consistent clamping force when torqued to their yield point or just beyond. The challenge is that the torque does not increase very much, or at all, once yield is reached, so using a torque wrench by itself will not indicate the point at which the manufacturer wants the bolt tightened. Consequently, TTY bolts generally require a new torqueing procedure called **torque angle**. It is important to note that, in virtually all cases, TTY bolts cannot be reused because they have been stretched into their yield zone and would very likely fail if retorqued. Always check the manufacturer's specifications when doing this as some manufacturers say that the bolt must be changed once a maximum length has been reached.

Torque angle is considered a more precise method to tighten TTY bolts and is essentially a multistep process. Bolts are first torqued in the required pattern using a standard torque wrench to a required moderate torque setting **FIGURE 5-24**. They are then further tightened an additional specified angle (torque angle) using an angle gauge, thus providing further tightening to tighten the bolt to, or beyond, its yield point. In some cases, after torqueing, the manufacturer first wants all of the bolts to be turned to an initial angle, and then turned an additional angle **FIGURE 5-25**. In other cases, the manufacturer wants all of

FIGURE 5-23 Ensure the proper amount of torque gets from the torque wrench to the bolt by supporting the head of the torque wrench with one hand.

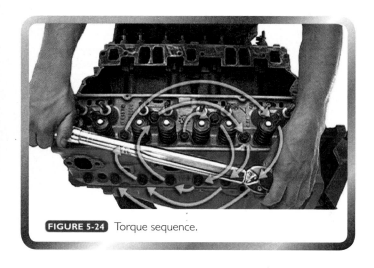

FIGURE 5-24 Torque sequence.

FIGURE 5-25 Angle gauge.

▶ Helical Inserts

No matter how strong a bolt is, it can break. There are a number of techniques used to remove broken bolts and repair threads. Those techniques will be demonstrated in later chapters. One of the tools used to repair damaged bolt holes is the helical insert, more commonly known by its trademark *Heli-coil* **FIGURE 5-26**. Heli-coils are made of coiled wire and are inserted into a tapped hole that is larger than the desired hole. Heli-coils are self-anchoring, and special tools are required to install them. Once in place, a new bolt or spark plug is threaded into the heli-coil insert.

▶ Locking Pins and Keys

A split pin is used to secure other fasteners, typically castellated nuts **FIGURE 5-27**. Split pins are often made of soft metal, making them easy to install or remove. They should never be used more than once, and they should not be used in applications

the bolts torqued in a particular sequence, then de-torqued in a particular sequence, then retorqued once again in a particular sequence, and finally tightened an additional specified angle. You must therefore always check the manufacturer's specifications and procedure before torqueing TTY bolts.

To use a torque wrench and torque angle gauge, follow the guidelines in **SKILL DRILL 5-1**.

 SKILL DRILL 5-1 Using a Torque Wrench and Torque Angle Gauge

1 Identify the stretch bolt through the manufacturer's specifications. (In some cases, stretch bolts themselves have a specific marking on the head of the bolt.) In addition, the diameter of the shank of the bolt is thinner than the threaded diameter.

2 Check the specifications. Determine the correct torque value and sequence for the bolts or fastener you are using. This will be in foot-pounds (ft-lb). Also, check the torque angle specifications for the bolt or fastener, and whether the procedure is one step or more than one step.

3 Tighten the bolt to the specified torque. If the component requires multiple bolts or fasteners, make sure to tighten them all to the same torque value in the sequence and follow the steps that are specified by the manufacturer. Some torqueing procedures could call for four or more steps to complete the torqueing process.

For example, vehicle specifications as follows:

a. Step 1: Torque bolts to 30 foot pounds (40 newton meters).

b. Step 2: Torque bolts to 44 foot pounds (60 newton meters)

c. Step 3: Finally, tighten the bolt a further 90°.

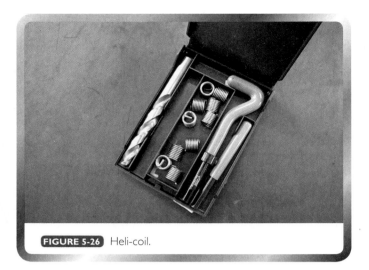

FIGURE 5-26 Heli-coil.

where there are strong shearing forces at play. Split pins are also used to keep other components, such as nuts, from coming off shafts. To remove and install split pins, follow the guidelines in **SKILL DRILL 5-2**.

Locking Pins

<u>Dowel pins</u> are used to keep components in place where shearing forces are high **FIGURE 5-28**. For example, they are used in high-pressure pumps to keep valve plates anchored in position. Pins should never be directly struck by a hammer; a pin punch should be used instead.

<u>Taper pins</u> are used to position parts on a shaft, for example gears, pulleys, and collars. They are steel rods with one end having a slightly larger diameter than the other.

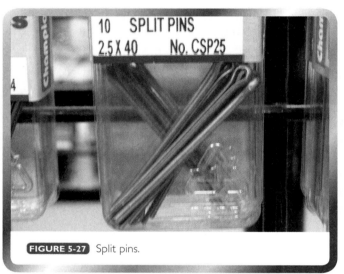

FIGURE 5-27 Split pins.

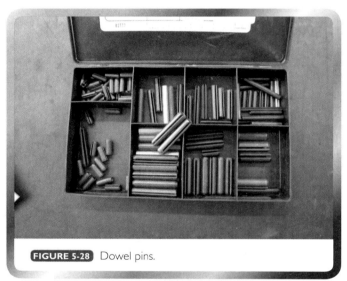

FIGURE 5-28 Dowel pins.

SKILL DRILL 5-2 Removing and Installing Split Pins

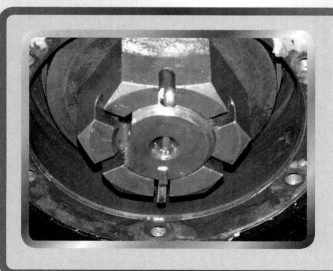

1. Ensure you have the correct size of split pin for the relevant hole size.
2. Use an appropriate pair of pliers to straighten the legs of the split pin.
3. Grip the pin head and pull it out of the nut or bolt.
4. Make the required repair/adjustment and reassemble and adjust accordingly.
5. Insert the new pin, legs first, as far as it will go.
6. Bend the legs back and cut them to the required size if necessary.

Rawl pins are often used to hold components on rotating shafts. They are a type of shear pin, used when excessive force is applied to avoid further damage to a component. They are normally made from a spring-type steel.

Locking Keys

Locking keys are used to prevent the free rotation of gears or pulleys on a shaft (FIGURE 5-29). Keys come in various shapes depending on their use:

- Parallel keys, for example, can be used to secure a gear wheel on its shaft (FIGURE 5-30).
- Taper keys are used to anchor a pulley to a shaft or a disc to a driving shaft (FIGURE 5-31).
- A feather key is usually attached to levers that have to slide along a shaft to allow engagement of a part (FIGURE 5-32). A feather key is an extra component used with a shaft-to-collar connection. The connection is positive fitting and serves to transmit torques and revs, for example, on the drive shaft of a belt pulley.
- Gibb-head keys are designed to be pulled out easily and are used when a gear or a pulley has to be attached to a shaft (FIGURE 5-33).

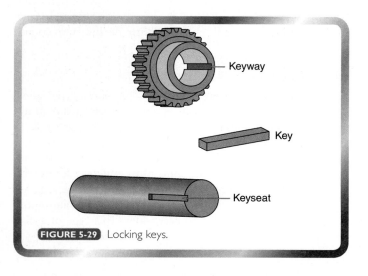

FIGURE 5-29 Locking keys.

Keyway

Key

Keyseat

FIGURE 5-30 Parallel keys.

FIGURE 5-31 Taper key.

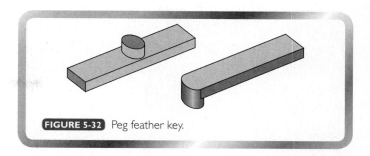

FIGURE 5-32 Peg feather key.

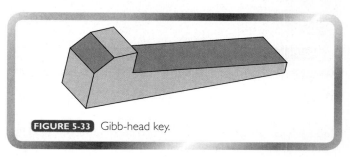

FIGURE 5-33 Gibb-head key.

▶ Gaskets and Seals

Gaskets and seals are critical in stopping leaks of critical fluids and lubricants in all mechanical systems that often operate under extremely high temperatures and pressures. So they have to be durable and made of materials that withstand extreme conditions. Gaskets are generally used in static conditions where components need to be sealed. Seals are used in dynamic operations where there are moving parts such as shafts. Both gaskets and seals operate on the same principle: keep critical fluids in and contaminants out.

Machinery vibration, heat, and expanding metal would make it virtually impossible to stop leaks if it were not for the critical performance of gaskets and seals.

Gaskets form a seal by being compressed between stationary parts where liquid or gas could pass. Most gaskets are made to be used only once. They can be made of soft materials such as cork, rubber, nitrile, paper, heat-resistant materials, or graphite; or they can be made of soft alloys and metals such as brass, copper, aluminum, or soft-steel sheet metal. Such materials may be used individually or, in some cases, as blends, to produce the required functional material.

Choosing which material and design to use depends on the substance to be sealed, the pressures and temperatures involved and the materials and mating surfaces to be sealed.

Gaskets are often purchased premanufactured, or they can be made by hand, a procedure that will be demonstrated in this chapter (FIGURE 5-34).

Head Gaskets

One of the most critical gaskets in automotive applications is the head gasket. Head gaskets seal and contain the pressures of combustion within the engine, between the cylinder head and the engine block. They also seal oil passages between the engine block and the cylinder head. Finally, head gaskets control the flow of coolant between the engine block and the cylinder head.

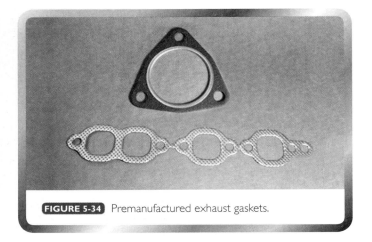
FIGURE 5-34 Premanufactured exhaust gaskets.

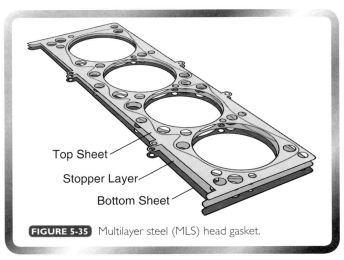
Top Sheet
Stopper Layer
Bottom Sheet
FIGURE 5-35 Multilayer steel (MLS) head gasket.

Modern head gaskets have to be constructed to resist high temperatures and engine detonation.

With the increasing emphasis on environmental considerations and the reduced use of asbestos, a known carcinogen, replacement materials have been developed. Some of these modern special materials that are now used for the side layers of head gaskets are designed to withstand temperatures up to 2100°F (1150°C). Such materials are also designed to allow the cylinder head and block, some of which have considerable distortion rates, to move slightly on the head gasket as they expand during engine warm-up. This feature is vital for preventing head gasket failure.

Some high-temperature head gaskets are called **anisotropic** in nature. *Anisotropic* means that the gasket is designed to conduct heat laterally to transfer heat from the combustion chamber to the coolant faster. These gaskets are normally constructed with a steel core. Special facing materials are added to both sides of the gasket core to provide a comprehensive seal under varying expansion conditions.

On some engines, the head gasket provides or adjusts the proper clearances between the piston and the cylinder head by the thickness of the gasket. The service information (or repair information) for a vehicle will specify how to select the proper thickness of gasket and why that thickness is needed. Sometimes, it is as simple as looking for a mark denoting the thickness of the old gasket and using that to order the new gasket.

Other head gaskets incorporate stainless steel **fire rings** to help contain heat and pressure within the cylinder. Fire rings are steel rings built into the cylinder head gasket. The rings provide extra sealing on the top of the cylinder to help seal in the high-combustion pressures (hence the name "fire ring"). For high-performance use, such as in racing cars, some engine builders use soft metal O-rings, which fit in shallow grooves cut in the head around the cylinders and passageways to seal the compression and fluids. The O-rings are crushed in place when the head bolts are torqued into place. This is a very effective but expensive way to seal the heads.

For many late-model vehicles, the preferred head gasket is a **multilayer steel (MLS) head gasket** FIGURE 5-35 . These gaskets offer a wide range of benefits, such as strategically placed sealing beads that help eliminate leak paths; extra-strong layers that provide superior combustion sealing; and a stainless steel material that maintains its shape despite thermal expansion and scrubbing between the engine block and the cylinder head. Many MLS and other head gaskets have an added silicone-based outer coating on both sides of the side material layers to provide additional cold-sealing ability during start-up and warm-up.

Installing Head Gaskets

Before installing a head gasket, look for "this side up" or "front" labels on the head gaskets. If there are no labels, it should not matter which side goes up. Double-check that for every hole in the block or heads there is a corresponding hole in the gasket.

Most engines use a composition-type gasket that does not require sealant on either side. Some older engines use a metal-shim gasket that requires an even coat of a high-tack gasket sealant to be sprayed on both sides, or high-heat aluminum paint to be sprayed lightly on both sides. This type of gasket coating should dry before the gasket is installed.

To fit a formed head gasket, follow the guidelines in SKILL DRILL 5-3 .

To assemble and make a user-formed gasket, follow the guidelines in SKILL DRILL 5-4 .

To assemble and make a user-formed gasket—tap method, follow the guidelines in SKILL DRILL 5-5 .

Lip-Type Seals

Gaskets cannot be used around a rotating part, such as where the camshaft protrudes through the front of the cylinder head, because they would quickly wear out and leak. To seal the rotating parts of an engine, **oil seals** are needed. Oil seals are round seals made of rubber or rubber-type compounds of silicone, ethylene propylene diene monomer (M-class), rubber (EPDM)—a type of synthetic rubber—or another durable, flexible material, placed in a metal housing TABLE 5-2 . These seals are typically driven into a machined bore around

SKILL DRILL 5-3 Fitting a Formed Head Gasket

1. Obtain an assembly that will need a gasket replaced, in this case the head gasket.

2. Remove the head cover and keep track of the head bolts.

3. Remove the old gasket.

4. Clean the mating surfaces with the proper cleaning fluid.

5. Select a gasket according to the manufacturer's specifications.

6. Inspect the gasket for cracks or other deformities.

7. Select a sealant that is manufacturer recommended.

8. Spread the sealant on the mating surfaces according to the manufacturer's specifications.

9. Align the gasket with the mating surface.

10. Assemble the components and tighten the bolts to their torque specification and tightening sequence.

SKILL DRILL 5-4 Assembling and Making a User-Formed Gasket

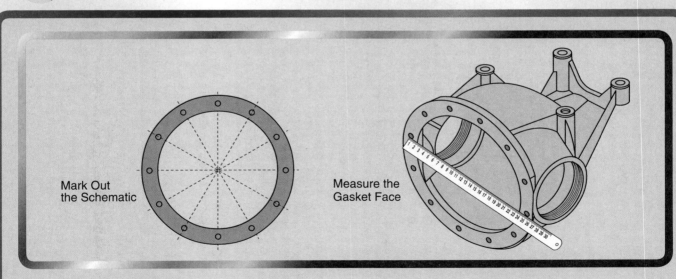

Mark Out the Schematic

Measure the Gasket Face

1. Use the object that the gasket is being made for as the die for forming the new gasket.

2. Select a suitable gasket material. (In this case, paper is being used as an example.)

3. Inspect and clean the mating surfaces.

4. Measure the sealing surface to assure coverage of your gasket material.

5. Use tin snips to cut the gasket shape and a punch to open the gasket holes.

SKILL DRILL 5-5 Assembling and Making a User-Formed Gasket—Tap Method

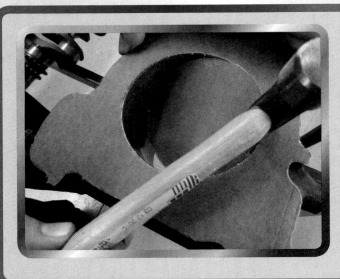

1. Select the correct gasket material.

2. Clean the component mating surfaces.

3. Place the gasket over the face of the component and use your fingers to rub along the outer profiles of the component. Use tin snips to cut along the profile.

4. Once you have the general shape of the gasket, use your thumb to make small indentations in the component holes.

5. Using the round end of the ball-peen hammer, tap along the surfaces of the holes and lift the gasket often to make sure it matches the mating surfaces and holes.

6. Continue this process of tapping and inspecting until the gasket is made.

TABLE 5-2: Common Materials for Manufacturing Seals

Material	Material suitable for:	Material not suitable for:	Operating Temperature
Ethylene Propylene	• Atmospheric agents • Diluted acids • Good resistance to heat • Good resistance to permanent deformation • Steam	• Oils • Gasoline	−40°F to +320°F (−40°C to +160°C)
Neoprene (synthetic rubber)	• Atmospheric agents • Good mechanical properties • Good resistance to acid • Oils with high aniline point • Oxygen	• Hot water • Oils with low aniline point • Gasoline	−40°F to +248°F (−40°C to +120°C)
Nitrile	• Extreme weather conditions • Hydraulic fluids • Mineral oils • Resistance to permanent deformation	• Aromatic hydrocarbons • Inorganic acids • Organic acids	−40°F to +248°F (−40°C to +120°C)
Silicone	• Air • Atmospheric agents • Gas • Good resistance to very high temperature • Good resistance to very low temperature	• Oils with low aniline point • Water vapor	−76°F to +482°F (−60°C to +250°C)
Viton	• Acids • Good resistance to high temperatures in the presence of oils and lubricants • Oxygen	• Dynamic uses	−22°F to +446°F (−30°C to +230°C)

a rotating part **FIGURE 5-36**. A metal spring, called a <u>garter spring</u>, is wrapped circularly around the inside of the seal and applies a small, constant pressure to keep the lip in contact with the rotating part it is sealing. The most widely used seal for rotating parts is the <u>lip-type dynamic oil seal</u>. This seal is a precisely shaped, dynamic rubber lip. Like other oil seals, the lip-type dynamic oil seal also uses a garter spring to help keep the lip of the seal in contact with the shaft **FIGURE 5-37**.

▶ TECHNICIAN TIP

As a general rule, oil seals must be replaced with new ones when they are removed or when a component is overhauled or replaced.

FIGURE 5-36 Lip-type seals provide extra sealing pressure and are used in high-pressure, heavy-duty applications.

FIGURE 5-37 A garter spring.

A similar sealing principle is used to seal the valve stem to prevent oil from entering the engine combustion chamber. Like the oil seals, the valve stem seal is pressed onto the valve guide. It allows the valve to be wiped almost clean of oil on its opening trip, keeping a minimum amount of oil pulled down between the valve stem and the guide for lubrication purposes.

To remove and replace lip-type seals, follow the guidelines in **SKILL DRILL 5-6**.

▶ TECHNICIAN TIP

Like the oil seals, the valve stem seal is pressed onto the valve guide. It allows the valve to be wiped almost clean of oil on its opening trip, keeping a minimum amount of oil pulled down between the valve stem and the guide for lubrication purposes.

Ring Seals

Stationary and slowly rotating or sliding shafts can also be sealed by using an O-ring, a simple sealing device consisting of a rounded ring of rubber or plastic. O-rings are typically used to seal a joint against high pressure or the circumference of a rotating shaft from high- or low-pressure fluid leakage. O-rings come in a wide variety of sizes with reference numbers giving the internal and external diameter. Their selection depends on the speed of moving parts, the type of lubricant and fluid being used, working pressures (minimum and maximum), and the size and finish of working components.

The O-ring is inserted around the part to be sealed and held in place by an external housing. The O-ring seals the two surfaces **FIGURE 5-38**. In many cases, the housing supplies the force to keep the ring in direct contact with the shaft. O-rings are generally effective at sealing high pressures where the differential speed between the opposing surfaces is minimal. In contrast, a lip seal is effective at sealing low pressures, but the differential speed of the opposing surfaces can be substantial. As the lip-type seal wears, the garter spring holds tension on the seal, keeping it against the part it is sealing. The O-ring seal has no mechanism for self-adjustment. Once worn, its sealing ability is compromised.

Two other types of ring seals are the D-ring and square ring. The square ring seal in **FIGURE 5-39** is being removed from an oil filter cartridge.

To remove and replace ring seals, follow the guidelines in **SKILL DRILL 5-7**.

Crankshaft Seals

Crankshaft seals are located at each end of the crankshaft assembly where it projects through the crankcase. The seals help contain the lubricating oils inside the lower part of the crankcase and prevent them from leaking out. A rear main seal is located just after the rear main bearing **FIGURE 5-40**. In engines that use a <u>timing chain</u> or <u>timing gears</u>, the front main seal is located in the front timing cover. In engines equipped with a timing belt, the front main seal is located in a housing bolted to the front of the engine block **FIGURE 5-41** and sits between the block and

SKILL DRILL 5-6 Removing and Replacing Lip-Type Seals

1. Use a component that requires a lip-type seal, usually a shaft.
2. Inspect the assembly for leaks, sharp edges, or burrs.
3. Clean the assembly and assess seal failure.
4. Seal failure can include a broken garter spring or a damaged component at the sealing surface.
5. Remove the seal with an oil seal puller.
6. Measure and record the housing bore diameter, the shaft diameter, and depth of the seal landing.
7. Select the recommended replacement seal.
8. Compare the new seal with the old to make sure they are the same size.
9. Lubricate the shaft and the seal with clean grease before fitting the new seal over the shaft, making sure that the seal spring faces into the housing.
10. Locate the seal in the housing according to the manufacturer's specifications.
11. Press the seal into the housing with the sealing lip toward the fluid being sealed.
12. Use a hammer to make sure the seal is snugly fit.
13. Check the installation and make sure the fluid level is correct.

FIGURE 5-38 O-ring seal.

FIGURE 5-39 Square ring seal from an oil filter.

the timing belt. Most modern crankshaft seals are of a circular one-piece style with a sealing lip. Some seals use a small spring, called a *garter spring*, around the inside of the sealing lip to tension the lip against the sealing surface of the crankshaft or harmonic balancer.

Mechanical Seals

Mechanical seals are used to seal between two working fluids or to prevent leakage of working fluids to the atmosphere past a rotating shaft. This rotary motion is a feature of mechanical

seals. Mechanical seals are capable of sealing pressures of up to 7250 psi (500 bar). The core parts of the seal are the rotating "floating" seal ring and the stationary seat.

The rotating floating seal ring and the stationary seat are made of wear-resistant materials. The floating ring is kept under force from a spring or bellows to force it into contact with the seat face. This "face seal" is commonly used in vehicle applications such as water pumps and automatic transmission gearboxes.

Welch plugs, also known as *core plugs*, are used to seal holes in the engine block that were left during original manufacture to remove the sand core during the casting process. Made from

SKILL DRILL 5-7 Removing and Replacing Ring Seals

1. Select the component where the seal needs replacing and assemble the correct tools and solvents.
2. Clean and inspect the assembly.
3. Remove the ring seal.
4. Clean and deburr the groove and inspect for damage.
5. Measure and record the width of the groove and inspect for damage.
6. Select the recommended seal.
7. Coat the new seal with clean lubricant.
8. Fit the seal into the appropriate groove.
9. Assemble the component and check for leaks.

FIGURE 5-40 An example of a smaller engine rear main seal.

FIGURE 5-41 An example of a smaller engine front main seal.

brass and steel, welch plugs are designed to prevent water and oil leaks during use FIGURE 5-42.

Adhesives and Sealants

When installing engine covers, manifolds, and oil sumps, sealants are often used to ensure there are no leaks. There are many different engine applications and engine designs, which require various sealants. Refer to the service information for your specific engine. There are also many types of adhesives and brands of room temperature vulcanizing (RTV) oxygen-safe silicone produced. Always follow the manufacturer's instructions when deciding which adhesive or sealant to use. Generally, silicone sealants should never be used in fuel tanks or any place where solvents are present.

Adhesives

To help hold the gaskets in place, you can use contact cement in a liquid or spray form; sometimes manufacturers recommend the use of such materials. It does a good job of holding a gasket to a smooth metal surface while the parts are being assembled. The spray type has a spray nozzle that can be controlled and directed in a specific fan direction. However, use caution when you apply it around areas that you do not want any spray adhesive to get inside or on. Sealants may be used in different locations dependent on use. Always be sure to use only such materials that the manufacturer specifies, as damage can occur if used incorrectly and in the wrong location.

FIGURE 5-42 Welch plugs, also known as core plugs.

Silicone Sealants

There are many different silicone sealants, with variants based on the temperature range the silicone can withstand or the type of fluid it is designed to seal. RTV is used to help seal fiber gaskets and gasket joints, and sometimes on surfaces designed to be assembled with no gasket. Make sure the RTV is labelled oxygen-sensor safe. Otherwise, it could harm the sensors on the engine by coating them with a silicone film, which, after a short time of engine operation, would negatively affect the operation of the sensor. Be sure to use the appropriate product and follow its instructions.

Applying Gaskets with Adhesive

For cork, felt or neoprene gaskets, a light coat of adhesive spray is used on each surface of the block and the gasket. Be sure no overspray gets into the engine—that can be done in two different ways. One way is to spray the gasket only with a heavy coat and then put the sprayed side of the gasket on the block surface and slide it around to smear the adhesive on the block surface. Then pull the gasket off, making sure there is adhesive on both surfaces. Let both the gasket and the block area dry. Position the gasket and make sure it is aligned, because you will not be able to move the gasket after you set it in place. The other way is to spray the gasket and then spray the block carefully, not allowing any overspray to get into the engine. You might have to use thin cardboard or rags to block any overspray. Let the adhesive dry and position the gasket, making sure all holes are aligned. Once in place, the gasket will not move.

Applying RTV Silicone

It is debatable whether silicone RTV should be used on gaskets. Most technicians agree that RTV can be used on paper gaskets. Some technicians say that cork and cork/rubber gaskets should be installed dry. Other technicians say that neoprene gaskets should use an adhesive other than RTV because RTV can make the neoprene slippery and cause the gasket to slip out of place during assembly. Do not use RTV on neoprene gaskets with multisealing edges. These gaskets are designed so that when one edge fails another edge will seal. If you use RTV on this style of gasket, the RTV fills up the multisealing edges and leaves only one sealing edge. In addition, RTV should be used in appropriate amounts. Using too much RTV will cause excess RTV to be squeezed out from between the surfaces and form ribbons inside the engine. This excess RTV can then tear away and be carried by oil or coolant throughout the system and clog up the oil pickup screen or passages in the lubrication or cooling system **FIGURE 5-43** .

Applying RTV Where the Manufacturer Specifies No Gaskets

On some engines, the manufacturer has designed some sealing surfaces that do not require a gasket, only RTV. When using only RTV and no gasket, a moderately larger bead of RTV is required to seal between the two surfaces. An example of this application is an oil sump; the manufacturer may have designed the engine to use no gasket. This is another reason that checking the manufacturer's specifications is so important.

▶ Lifting in the Shop

Technicians do a lot of lifting in a shop. While they do some lifting with raw muscle power, they do the remainder with the aid of lifting equipment. Lifting equipment is an essential tool in any heavy vehicle shop. It allows technicians to more easily access a vehicle's difficult-to-reach areas for repairs. To use lifting equipment properly ensures technicians' physical safety, as well as preventing damage to a customer's vehicle. This section focuses on the types of lifting equipment you will use in a shop and their proper use.

A professional shop always takes precautions to guarantee that all work is conducted safely and efficiently, as well as making certain that a customer's vehicle is treated with respect to protect it against accidental damage. Therefore, before you start repairs, pause for a moment to identify good work practices. This will prevent injury to yourself and coworkers, as well as accidental damage to a customer's vehicle.

FIGURE 5-43 Applying silicone sealant.

For your personal safety, it is important that lifting equipment such as vehicle lifts, jack stands (also known as jack stands), engine hoists, slings, and chains be inspected before each use and be well maintained. Most countries require annual certification inspections of all lifting equipment such as vehicle lifts and hydraulic jacks to help ensure their safety.

The Correct Procedure for Manual Lifting

The most elementary piece of lifting equipment is the muscle. But human muscles can be easily injured, affecting your ability to work. You can prevent many debilitating back and knee injuries by using proper lifting techniques. When bending down to lift an object, for example, always bend at the knees before attempting to lift. Never bend from the waist **FIGURE 5-44**, which is the surest way to strain your back or, in a worst-case scenario, rupture a disc in your back. Place your feet on either side of the object you want to lift and point them in the direction you wish to travel. If an item is too awkward or large for you to lift on your own, ask someone to help you lift it **FIGURE 5-45**.

FIGURE 5-44 Do not lift something without bending your knees.

FIGURE 5-45 Bend at the knees and ask for help.

> **TECHNICIAN TIP**
>
> Never attempt to lift heavy objects that may damage your body. Use the proper lifting equipment instead.

Selecting Appropriate Lifting Equipment

You may end up using many different types of lifting equipment in a shop. Lifting equipment is designed to lift and securely hold loads. Some examples of lifting equipment include vehicle hoists, floor jacks, jack or jack stands, engine and component hoists, mobile gantries, chains, slings, and shackles **FIGURE 5-46**.

Each piece of lifting equipment has a maximum weight it can support. The maximum operating capacity is usually expressed as the **safe working load (SWL)**. For example, if the SWL is 1 ton, the equipment can safely lift up to 2000 pounds (907 kilograms). When using lifting equipment, never exceed its capacity and always maintain some reserve capacity as an extra safety margin.

In addition, you should use each piece of lifting equipment for its designed purpose only. For example, use a vehicle hoist only to lift vehicles within its capacity. Using lifting equipment incorrectly may lead to equipment failure that can cause serious injury and damage.

> **TECHNICIAN TIP**
>
> When using multiple pieces of lifting equipment, the SWL is limited to the lowest rated piece of equipment. Remember that "a chain is only as strong as its weakest link." Whatever fittings you are using on a piece of lifting equipment, the lifting equipment's capacity is limited by the strength of any single component. For example, a 5-ton chain with a 3-ton D-shackle has a maximum lifting capacity of 3 tons or less.

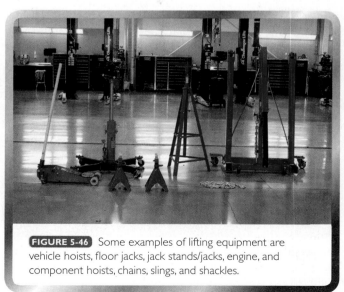

FIGURE 5-46 Some examples of lifting equipment are vehicle hoists, floor jacks, jack stands/jacks, engine, and component hoists, chains, slings, and shackles.

The Safe Use of Lifting Equipment

In addition to double-checking safe working loads and using equipment only for its intended purpose, technicians can take a number of other steps to ensure a safe operating environment. These include testing and test certification. Requirements can vary by country and your local area so be sure to check with your supervisor if you have any questions.

Testing Lifting Equipment

Lifting equipment should be periodically checked and tested to make sure it is safe, in accordance with local regulatory requirements. The testing should be recorded for each piece of lifting equipment and clearly labeled with a sticker affixed to the equipment with its inspection date and SWL. Inspections should identify any damage, such as cracks, dents, marks, cuts, and abrasions, that could prevent the lifting equipment from performing as designed.

Refer to the manufacturer's manual to find out how often maintenance inspections are recommended. The time frame is usually every 12 months in the case of hoists and lifts, but may be longer for lifting equipment such as chains and slings. Always check local regulations to determine the requirements for periodic testing of lifting equipment.

Checking the Test Certificate

In most countries, lifting equipment is subject to statutory testing and certification. If this is the case where you work, the **test certificate** should be attached to or displayed near the lifting equipment **FIGURE 5-47**. Before using a piece of lifting equipment, make sure the most recent inspection recorded on the test certificate is within the prescribed time limit. If it is not, the test certificate has expired and you should notify your supervisor.

▶ Types of Lifting and Moving Equipment

Once you have verified that a piece of equipment is safe to use, you can get to work. You will use your shop's lifting equipment not only to raise heavy components but to move and lower pieces into place as well. Which equipment you use depends on a part's size, weight, and type as well as the job you intend to perform. This section looks at a number of different types of lifting and moving equipment.

Chain Blocks and Mobile Gantries

Chain blocks and mobile gantries are often used together to lift larger components inside heavy vehicle shops. Chain blocks can be attached to and hang from mobile gantries. Chain blocks lift parts and mobile gantries move wherever the work needs to be done.

Chain blocks have a safety latch and hook fittings that attach to lifting points on a component. Once attached to a load, the chain block lifts large components when the technician pulls the chain through a rotating wheel.

Mobile gantries can either be wheeled into place on a floor or are mounted on tracks near the roof of the shop and operated with hand controls that move the gantry into position and lower the chain block with a hook **FIGURE 5-48**.

Both of these lifting devices relieve the technician of having to exert a lot of effort to remove heavy components and lower them into an area where they can be serviced or replaced. Carefully check the lifting hooks on these devices before use to make sure the end of the hook hasn't opened beyond the standard limit. Inspect chains for any mud or grit, and examine safety latches to be sure they are working properly.

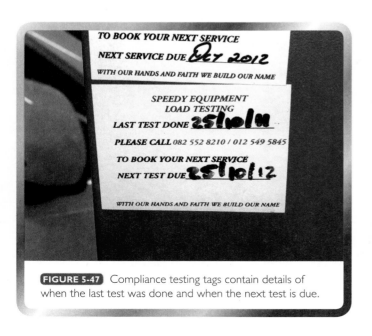

FIGURE 5-47 Compliance testing tags contain details of when the last test was done and when the next test is due.

FIGURE 5-48 This overhead gantry in a heavy vehicle shop is rated for lifting components that weigh up to 10 tons.

Slings and Shackles

Slings are another type of lifting equipment. Technicians use them to lift and lower many things in the shop, for example, transmissions **FIGURE 5-49**, engines, and differentials. They can be made from strong webbing material, wire rope, or chain.

Webbed slings have an eye at each end for the connection of shackles (discussed later in this section) to attach loads. Wire rope and chain slings may have any number of different fittings for different applications. Regardless of the sling type and its fittings, each will have a maximum working load that you cannot exceed. As with all lifting equipment, you must test slings regularly to ensure they are safe to use. If you suspect that any piece of lifting equipment is damaged, *do not use it.* Have it tested before placing it into service.

FIGURE 5-49 Chains and an overhead gantry can be used to lift a transmission.

Webbed slings are usually flat in appearance and made from strong synthetic materials such as polyester. Synthetic slings can be more susceptible to cutting or abrasive damage than harder materials, such as chains or wire, and should be checked before each use to ensure they are not damaged. Web slings are available in a variety of lifting capacities for different lifting tasks. When using synthetic slings, always ensure they are protected from sharp corners, which may damage the slings and reduce lifting capacity.

Wire rope slings are made from many strands of fine wire and a core. The size, number, and arrangement of the wires determine the sling's lifting capacity. Wire rope slings are less susceptible to abrasion and cutting than synthetic slings but always check them for any damage, such as kinks and broken or cut wires, as these will reduce their lifting capacity.

Chains are made from hardened steel and are not as susceptible to damage as synthetic or wire rope slings. Chains can have a number of different types of fittings attached to the ends, such as eyes, shackles, and hooks **FIGURE 5-50**. Chains, like all lifting equipment, should be checked for damage before being used and regularly tested and tagged.

Shackles are attached to slings and chains to use as connectors between a component and various applications, such as lifting equipment **FIGURE 5-51**. In lifting equipment, shackles are secured with a pin through the bottom of the shackle. Secure D-shackles, a common type of shackle, with a piece of wire through the shackle's eye to lock the pin and prevent it from working loose. The same applies to bow shackles. As with all lifting equipment, inspect shackles to make sure they are in good condition and free from dirt and grime.

Jacks and Jack Stands

Jacks and **jack stands** are used every day in heavy vehicle shops to safely lift and secure vehicles. As with other shop equipment, it's important to check jacks and jack stands for safety reasons

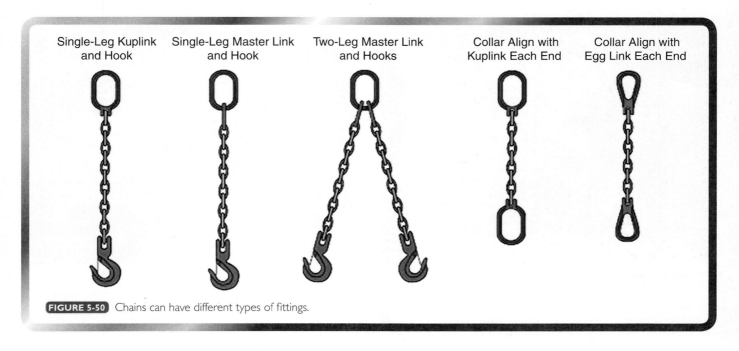

Single-Leg Kuplink and Hook   Single-Leg Master Link and Hook   Two-Leg Master Link and Hooks   Collar Align with Kuplink Each End   Collar Align with Egg Link Each End

FIGURE 5-50 Chains can have different types of fittings.

before use. If you suspect that they are faulty, *do not use them.* Take them out of service and have them tested and serviced.

Jacks

A vehicle jack is a lifting tool that can raise part of a vehicle from the ground prior to removing or replacing components or raise heavy components into position. While you can use a vehicle's emergency jack to raise and support a vehicle to change a wheel on the side of the road, you must not use a vehicle jack to support a vehicle's weight during any task that requires you to get underneath any part of the vehicle. For any shop tasks that call for you to crawl under a vehicle, only use the vehicle jack to raise the vehicle so that it can then be lowered onto suitably rated and carefully positioned stable jack stands **FIGURE 5-52** .

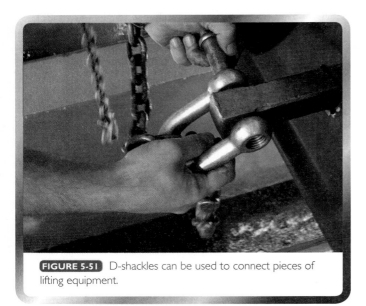

FIGURE 5-51 D-shackles can be used to connect pieces of lifting equipment.

The three main types of vehicle jacks are the **hydraulic jack**, **pneumatic jack**, and **mechanical jack**. Hydraulic and pneumatic jacks are the most common types. They can be mounted on slides or on a wheeled floor. In hydraulic jacks, pressurized oil acts on a piston to provide the lifting action; in pneumatic jacks, compressed air lifts the vehicle; in mechanical jacks, a screw or gears provide the mechanical leverage required for lifting.

Different jacks are available for different purposes, including **FIGURE 5-53** :

- *Floor jacks* are a common type of hydraulic jack that is mounted on four wheels, two of which swivel to provide a steering mechanism. The floor jack has a long handle that is used both to operate the jacking mechanism and to move and position the jack. Floor jacks have a low profile, making them suitable to position under vehicles.
- *Bottle jacks* are portable jacks that usually have either a mechanical screw or a hydraulic ram mechanism that rises vertically from the jack's center as you operate the handle. They are relatively inexpensive and may be provided with vehicles for the purpose of changing flat tires.
- *Air jacks* use compressed air either to operate a large ram or to inflate an expandable air bag to lift the vehicle. Often the air jack is fitted to a movable platform with a long handle. You use air jacks to lift vehicles as an alternative to floor jacks. Because they require a compressed air supply, air jacks are usually used in the shop rather than for mobile operations.
- *Sliding-bridge jacks* are usually fitted in pairs to four-post hoists as an accessory to allow the vehicle to be lifted off the drive-on hoist runways. Operated by a hydraulic mechanism or compressed air, they use a platform mounted to a scissor-action jack to lift the vehicle along the length of the runway, thus making it more convenient to work on wheels and brakes.

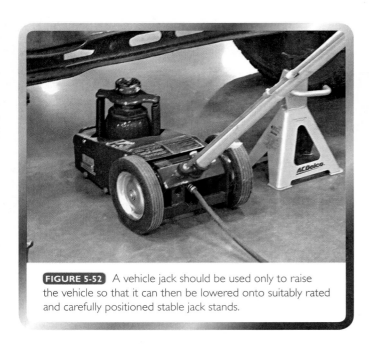

FIGURE 5-52 A vehicle jack should be used only to raise the vehicle so that it can then be lowered onto suitably rated and carefully positioned stable jack stands.

FIGURE 5-53 A floor jack. These should always be used with stands or jacks. The jack is used to raise or lower the vehicle. The stands, or jacks, are designed to support the vehicle.

- *Transmission jacks* are specialized jacks for lifting and lowering transmissions during removal and installation. Transmission jacks are usually mounted on a floor with wheels and have a large flat plate area on which the transmission rests securely. They are usually operated by a hydraulic mechanism but can also be powered by compressed air.

Jack Stands

Jack stands, also known as just *stands*, are adjustable supports used with vehicle jacks. They are designed to support a vehicle's weight once a vehicle has been raised by a vehicle jack. They normally come in matched pairs and should always be used as a pair **FIGURE 5-54**.

Jack stands are mechanical devices, meaning they mechanically lock in place at the height selected. Stands are load rated, so you should only use them for loads less than the rating indicated on the jack stand. They are very dependable, if you use them properly.

Always grip jack stands by the sides to move them. Never grip them by the top or the bottom to move them, as they can slip and pinch or injure you. Check that a stand's base is flat on the ground before lowering a vehicle onto it; otherwise, the stand might tip over, causing the vehicle to slip off. Once you have the jack stands positioned correctly, you can lower the vehicle onto the stands and move the vehicle jack out of the way.

TECHNICIAN TIP

For safety's sake, always place the jack stand locking pins into the aligned holes of the jack stand frame and the movable support platform.

Vehicle stands provide a stable support for a raised vehicle that is safer than the jack because the vehicle cannot be accidentally lowered while the stands are in place. Once you are ready to lower a vehicle that is on stands, you first raise it again with a vehicle jack so you can remove the stands. Since lifting devices are also lowering devices, remember that it's unsafe to

work underneath a vehicle that is supported only by a vehicle jack because it could give way or be accidentally lowered. Never use stands for a job for which they are not recommended.

TECHNICIAN TIP

Never support a vehicle on anything other than jack stands. Do not use wood or steel blocks to support a vehicle; the blocks might slide or split under the vehicle's weight. Do not use bricks or concrete blocks to support a vehicle either; they will crumble under the weight.

Some shops have tall stands that are used along with a vehicle hoist; they are much taller than standard stands. Shops use tall stands to stabilize a vehicle up on a hoist that is having a heavy component, such as a transmission, removed or installed. Do not try to lower the vehicle with the tall stands still in place; doing so can cause the vehicle to slip off the hoist.

Using Vehicle Jacks and Jack Stands

The weight of the vehicle you want to lift will determine the size of the vehicle jack you use. Always check the capacity of the jack before lifting a vehicle. If the end of the vehicle is heavier than usual, or if the vehicle is loaded, you will need to use a vehicle jack with a larger lifting capacity.

Make sure the stands are in good condition and that their size and capacity are adequate before you use them to support the vehicle. If they are cracked or bent, they will not support the vehicle safely. Always use matched pairs of jack stands. To lift and secure a vehicle with a vehicle floor jack and stands, follow the guidelines in **SKILL DRILL 5-8**.

Safety

Air bags, shocks, and other suspension components can be damaged if a vehicle is lifted incorrectly. Make sure you always use the specified lift points to lift the vehicle.

Vehicle Hoists

A **vehicle hoist** raises a whole vehicle off the ground so that a technician can easily work on the vehicle's underside. The vehicle hoist is also useful for raising a vehicle to a height that removes the need for the technician to bend down. For example, when changing wheels, you can raise the vehicle to waist height to avoid excessive bending.

Vehicle hoists are available in a number of different designs. They also come in a range of sizes and configurations to meet a shop's particular needs. For instance, some vehicle hoists are mobile and others are designed for use where the ceiling height is limited. You can electronically link together some vehicle hoists to use on longer vehicles, such as trucks and buses.

Hydraulic Hoist

One type of vehicle hoist, the **hydraulic hoist**, is very easy to use with most vehicles. You drive a vehicle onto a platform so that the wheels rest on two long, narrow platforms, one on each side

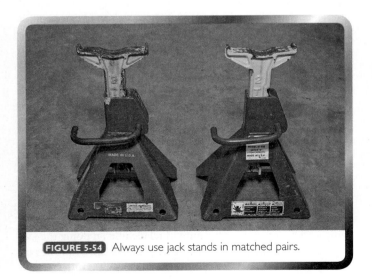
FIGURE 5-54 Always use jack stands in matched pairs.

SKILL DRILL 5-8 Lifting and Securing a Vehicle with a Vehicle Floor Jack and Stands

1 Position the vehicle on a flat, solid surface. Put the vehicle into neutral or park and set the emergency or hand brake. Place wheel chocks in front of and behind the wheels that are not going to be raised off the ground.

2 Select two stands of the same type, suitable for the vehicle's weight. Place one stand on each side of the vehicle at the same point, and adjust them so that they are both the same height.

3 Roll the vehicle jack under the vehicle, and position the lifting pad correctly under the frame, cross member, or

specified jacking point. Turn the jack handle clockwise, and begin pumping the handle up and down until the lifting pad touches and begins to lift the vehicle. If jacking on the truck frame, always use a wooden block or similar device between the jack and the frame to protect the frame from gouges.

4 Once the wheels lift off the floor, stop and check the placement of the lifting pad under the vehicle to make sure there is no danger of slipping. Double-check the position of the wheel chocks to make sure they have not moved. If the vehicle is stable, continue lifting it until it is at the height at which you can safely work under it.

5 Slide the two stands underneath the vehicle and position them to support the vehicle's weight. Slowly turn the jack handle counterclockwise to open the release valve and gently lower the vehicle onto the stands. When the vehicle has settled onto the stands, lower the vehicle jack completely and remove it from under the vehicle. Gently push the vehicle sideways to make sure it is secure. Repeat this process to lift the other end of the vehicle.

6 When the repairs are complete, use the jack to raise the vehicle off the stands. Slide the stands from under the vehicle. Make sure no one goes under the vehicle or puts any body parts under the vehicle, since the jack could fail or slip.

7 Slowly turn the jack handle counterclockwise to gently lower the vehicle to the ground. Return the jack, stands, and wheel chocks to their storage area before you continue working on the vehicle.

FIGURE 5-55 A hydraulic hoist.

of the vehicle **FIGURE 5-55**. The platforms are then raised, taking the vehicle with them. The vehicle's underside is then accessible to the technician. Since the vehicle rests on its wheels on the hoist, you can't remove the wheels unless the hoist is fitted with sliding-bridge jacks.

Portable Lifting Hoists

Another type of vehicle hoists is **portable lifting hoists**—or *portalift mobile hoists* as they are sometimes referred to—which offer an economical and flexible solution to shop servicing and maintenance requirements. They offer a lifting system that is simple to operate and allow complete underbody access for maintenance and repair. Portable lifting hoists provide shop flexibility as they are fully portable and can be easily moved to any area of a standard shop floor.

You can raise or lower the hoist posts individually, in pairs, or all together. When used as a group, they are coupled together with cables to ensure that they operate in sync with each other and the vehicle is raised equally on each leg of the hoist **FIGURE 5-56**. Many types have cable hangers allowing you to keep your cables off the shop floor.

The vehicle being worked on can always be put in the best possible position to suit the type of work being done. This can save time and provide the correct working condition for the technician. The vehicle can be set at the best height for the task being performed and for the individual technician doing the job.

Some types of portable lifting hoists have the controller on one of the pedestal legs, and others have a mobile controller that

FIGURE 5-56 Portable lifting hoists.

FIGURE 5-57 Inspection pits have safety lines clearly marking their position.

gives the operator complete lifting control away from the lifting zone. Both types of hoists have a remote pendant that allows the operator to safely inspect the lifting operation from any point around the vehicle.

Safety Locks

Every vehicle hoist in the shop must have a built-in mechanical locking device so the vehicle hoist can be secured at the chosen height after the vehicle is raised. This locking device prevents the vehicle from being accidentally lowered and holds the vehicle in place, even if the lifting mechanism fails. You should never physically go under a raised vehicle for any reason unless the safety locking mechanism has been activated.

Ratings and Inspections

All vehicle hoists are rated for a particular weight and type of vehicle. Never use them for any task other than that recommended by the manufacturer. In particular, never use a vehicle hoist to lift a vehicle that is heavier than its rated limit. Most countries have regulations that require hoists to be periodically inspected, typically annually, and certified as fit for use. Before you use a vehicle hoist, check the identification plate for its rating, and make sure it has a current registration or certification label.

Inspection Pits

An alternative to vehicle hoists is a pit. These are very common in purpose-built heavy-duty vehicle servicing facilities. Pit walls often have lubrication and air tool outlets. Once you drive the vehicle over the pit, you can inspect and service the underside without fear of the vehicle toppling over. Beware some hazards associated with pits, however, as they require special attention. Pits must be appropriately marked to prevent a falling hazard for staff **FIGURE 5-57**. Pits must also be well ventilated as chemical vapors can cause a fire or pose health hazards to those working in the pit, where harmful vapors can gather.

Engine Hoists

Engine hoists, or mobile floor cranes, are capable of lifting very heavy objects, such as engines, while the engines are being removed from a vehicle or refitted. The engine hoist's lifting arm is moved by a hydraulic cylinder and is adjustable for length. However, extending the lifting arm reduces its lifting capacity, because it moves the load farther away from the supporting frame. You can extend the supporting legs for stability, but the more you extend the arm and the legs, the lower the engine hoist's lifting capacity. The safe lifting capacity at various extensions is normally marked on the lifting arm.

The engine or component to be lifted is attached to the lifting arm by a sling or a lifting chain. The sling and lifting chain must be rated as capable of lifting weights in excess of the engine or component being lifted and must be firmly attached before the engine hoist is raised. When the engine or other component has been lifted and slowly and carefully moved away from the vehicle, it should be lowered onto an engine stand or onto the floor **FIGURE 5-58**. The farther off the ground an engine is lifted, the less stable the engine hoist becomes.

When using these types of hoists or cranes, always make sure that the slings and rope, cables, and chains that are used are compliant with relevant regulations and do not exceed the load ratings **FIGURE 5-59**.

FIGURE 5-58 A folded engine hoist.

FIGURE 5-60 Overhead cranes are commonplace in heavy vehicle shops.

FIGURE 5-59 Make sure that all chains and fixtures are in good condition.

Overhead Cranes

Many heavy vehicle shops are equipped with overhead cranes FIGURE 5-60. These must be used in accordance with local regulations and with the correct slings, ropes and chains. The crane is only as good as the slings connecting it to the equipment to be moved. Operate the crane smoothly, slowly, and with caution. Don't rush. Always ask for assistance, if required. In many cases, two people will be required to operate an overhead crane—one to operate the crane, the other as a lookout—to watch the load and guide it if necessary.

Safety

Never use a hoist to lift any weight greater than the lifting capacity of the hoist, sling, chains, or bolts.

▶ Using Lifting Equipment

Like many shop activities, using lifting equipment involves managing risks. Think carefully about what you are going to do, plan your activities, and check the equipment to make sure it is safe to use.

Using a Hydraulic Hoist

Four-post hoists are often used to lift a vehicle for wheel alignment services. Make sure you know how to operate the hydraulic hoist, taking particular care to know where the stop control is so you can use it quickly in an emergency. Always refer to the operations manual for the correct procedure for stopping the hoist. To lift a vehicle using a hydraulic hoist, follow the guidelines in SKILL DRILL 5-9.

Using Engine Hoists and Stands

Engine hoists are capable of lifting very heavy objects, which make them suitable for lifting engines. Make sure the lifting attachment at the end of the lifting arm is strong enough to lift the engine and is not damaged or cracked. When attaching the lifting chain or sling to an engine, make sure it is firmly attached and that the engine hoist is configured to lift that weight. Make sure the fasteners attaching the lifting chain, or sling, have a tensile strength that is in excess of the engine's weight. To keep from overstressing the sling, leave enough length in the sling so that when the engine is hanging, the angle at the top of the sling is close to 45° and not exceeding 90°.

In areas where space is limited for lifting, you should use a spreader bar to aid the lifting operation FIGURE 5-61. The bar is a straight piece of reinforced steel that bridges across the lifting eyes and is connected by D-shackles. The bar's center has a ring or D-shackle that is attached to the crane for lifting.

SKILL DRILL 5-9 Lifting a Vehicle Using a Hydraulic Hoist

1 Read and follow the safety instructions that are provided with the hoist. They should be displayed near the lift operating controls. Also verify the vehicle's weight and compare it against the hoist's safe load capacity. Check the hydraulic system for any leaks and the steel cables for any sign of damage. Make sure there are no oil spills around or under the hoist. The hoist should be completely down before you attempt to drive the vehicle onto it.

2 The platform may have built-in wheel restraints or attachments for wheel alignment equipment. A set of bars is normally mounted at the front of each ramp to prevent the vehicle from being driven off the front of the hoist. At the back will be ramps that allow the vehicle to be driven onto the hoist. The back of the ramps will pivot upwards when the hoist is raised and prevent the vehicle from rolling off the back.

3 Prepare to use the vehicle hoist safely. With the aid of an assistant guiding the driver, or a large mirror in front of the hoist, drive the vehicle slowly and carefully onto the hoist and position it centrally. If the vehicle has front wheel restraints, drive the vehicle forward until the wheels lock into the brackets.

4 Get out of the vehicle and check that it is correctly positioned on the platform. If it is, apply the emergency brake.

5 Make sure the hydraulic hoist area is clear. Move to the controls and lift the vehicle until it reaches the appropriate work height. If the hoist has a manual safety mechanism, lock it in place to engage whatever safety device is used.

6 Before the hoist is lowered, remove all tools and equipment from the area and wipe up any spilled fluids. Remove the safety device or unlock the lift before lowering it. Make sure no one is near the area. Once the hoist is fully lowered, carefully back the vehicle off the hoist with the help of a guide.

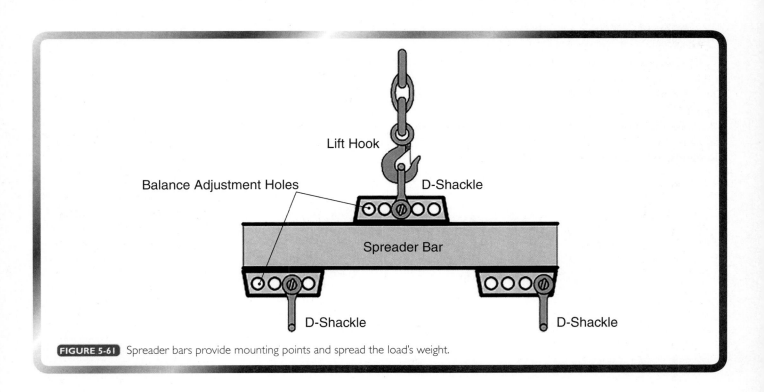

FIGURE 5-61 Spreader bars provide mounting points and spread the load's weight.

SKILL DRILL 5-10 Using Engine Hoists and Stands

1 Prepare to use the engine hoist. Lower the lifting arm and position the lifting end and chain over the center of the engine.

2 Wear appropriate PPE, such as leather gloves, during the entire operation, beginning with inspecting the chain, steel cable, or sling, and bolts to make sure they are in good condition. Before you use the crane, make sure the chain/ sling is rated higher than the weight of the item to be lifted. Also ensure that the lifting arm is only extended to the length of its lifting capacity applicable to the weight of the item to be lifted. Only use approved lifting equipment, nothing homemade. Look carefully around the component, which is about to be lifted, to determine if it has lifting eyes or other anchor points.

3 If the engine or component has lifting eyes, attach the sling with D-shackles or chain hooks. If you need to screw in bolts and spacer washers to lift the engine, make sure you use the correct bolt and spacer size for the chain or cable. Screw the bolts until the sling is held tight against the component.

4 Attach the hoist's hook under the center of the sling and raise the engine hoist just enough to lift the engine to take the slack up on the cable, chain, or sling. Double-check the sling and attachment points for safety. The engine's or component's center of gravity should be directly under the engine hoist's hook, and there should be no twists or kinks in the chain or sling.

5 Raise the engine hoist until the engine is clear of the ground and any obstacles. Slowly and gently move the engine hoist and lifted component to the new location with minimum ground clearance to prevent swinging and potential tilting of the whole crane.

6 Make sure the engine is positioned correctly. You may need to place blocks under the engine to stabilize it. Once you are sure the engine is stable, lower the engine hoist and remove the sling and any securing fasteners. Finally, return the equipment to its storage area.

If removing an engine from an engine bay, lower the engine so that it is close to the ground after removal. If the engine is lifted high in the air, the engine hoist will be unstable. When moving a suspended engine, move the engine hoist slowly. Do not change direction quickly because the engine will swing and may cause the whole apparatus to tumble. To use engine hoists and stands, follow the guidelines in SKILL DRILL 5-10.

TECHNICIAN TIP

- The engine hoist's load rating must be greater than the weight of the object to be lifted.
- Never leave an unsupported engine hanging on an engine hoist. Secure the engine on an engine stand, or on the ground, before starting to work on it.
- If using an engine stand, make sure it is designed to support the weight of the engine and that you have the correct number of bolts to hold the engine to the stand.
- Always extend the engine hoist's legs in relation to the lifting arm to ensure adequate stability.

Wrap-Up

Ready for Review

▶ Threaded fasteners include bolts, studs, and nuts, and are designed to secure vehicle parts under stress.

▶ Torque defines how much a fastener should be tightened.

▶ Bolts, nuts, and studs use threads to secure each part; these threads can be in standard or metric measures.

▶ Flat washer spread the load on a bolt or nut.

▶ Spring, (or lock washers) and, serrated edge washers are designed to prevent the bolt or nut from loosening.

▶ Metric bolts have a numbering system stamped on the bolt head that indicates the tensile strength of the bolt.

▶ The imperial system uses symbols to indicate the tensile strength or grade of a bolt.

▶ Metric bolts are sized and classified by millimeters in diameter and the distance in millimeters between the thread peaks.

▶ Imperial system bolts are sized and classified by the diameter and the number of threads per inch.

▶ Torque wrenches and torque angle gauges are used to ensure the bolts torque.

▶ Torque to yield bolts are usually not reusable as they stretch when they are tightened correctly.

▶ Keys and lock pins are used to prevent bolts or components from turning after assembly.

▶ Gaskets and seals are used to prevent fluid or gas escape and to prevent contamination from entering.

▶ Gasket and or seal may or may not require adhesives or RTV sealant during replacement; check OEM literature.

▶ Always use the proper lifting techniques when moving heavy objects.

▶ The safe working load indicates the operating capacity for lifting equipment.

▶ Lifting equipment includes vehicle hoists, floor jacks, jack stands, engine and component hoists, chains, slings, and shackles.

▶ Periodically check and test lifting equipment; consult the test certificate if available.

▶ Vehicle jacks can be classified by the type of lifting mechanism they use: hydraulic, pneumatic, or mechanical.

▶ Jack types include floor jacks, high-lift (farm) jacks, bottle jacks, air jacks, scissor jacks, sliding bridge jacks, and transmission jacks.

▶ Choose vehicle jacks according to size and lifting capacity.

▶ Jack stands support a vehicle's weight when it has been raised; always use jack stands in pairs.

▶ Vehicle hoists raise the vehicle to allow technicians underside access.

▶ Never use a vehicle hoist without activating the safety lock or for lifting a vehicle heavier than the rated limit.

▶ Make sure a vehicle has enough clearance over the lifting mechanism.

▶ Engine hoists can lift heavy objects out of a vehicle and onto an engine stand.

▶ Vehicle inspection pits allow access to the vehicle's underside without using a hoist or jack.

▶ Cover or fence inspection pits when not in use to prevent others from falling in.

▶ Check for damage before using an engine hoist, and make sure all components have the lifting capacity needed for the task.

Vocabulary Builder

Allen head screw Sometimes called a cap screw, it has a hexagonal recess in the head which fits an Allen key. This type of screw usually anchors components in a predrilled hole.

Allen wrench A type of hexagonal drive mechanism for fasteners.

anisotropic An object that has unequal physical properties along its various axes. Used in head gaskets to pull heat laterally from the edge surrounding the combustion chamber to the water jacket.

antiseize compound Neutralizes a chemical reaction that can prevent threads and fasteners from sticking together and freeze spark plugs in place in aluminum cylinder blocks.

bolt A type of threaded fastener with a thread on one end and a hexagonal head on the other.

castellated nut A nut with slots, similar to towers on a castle, that is used with split pins; it is used primarily to secure wheel bearings.

chemical compound Helps prevent fasteners from loosening; it is applied to one thread, then the other fastener is screwed onto it. This creates a strong bond between them, but one that stays plastic, so they can be separated by a wrench.

dowel pins Used to keep components in place where shearing forces are high, such as valve plates on high-pressure pumps.

elasticity The amount of stretch or give a material has.

engine hoist A small crane used to lift engines.

fasteners Devices that securely hold items together, such as screws, cotter pins, rivets, and bolts.

feather key Used to prevent the free rotation of gears or pulleys on a shaft; usually attached to levers that have to slide along a shaft to allow engagement of a part. The connection is a positive fitting and serves to transmit torques and revs, for example, on the drive shaft of a belt pulley.

fire rings Steel rings integrated into the cylinder head gasket nearest the combustion chambers that provide extra sealing to seal in the high combustion pressures.

flat washers Spread the load of bolt heads or nuts as they are tightened and distribute it over a greater area. They are particularly useful in protecting aluminum alloy.

garter spring A metal spring wrapped circularly around the inside of a lip seal to keep it in constant contact with the moving shaft.

Gibb-head key Used to prevent the free rotation of gears or pulleys on a shaft; designed to be pulled out easily and are used when a gear or a pulley has to be attached to a shaft.

hydraulic hoist A type of hoist that the vehicle is driven onto that uses two long, narrow platforms to lift the vehicle.

hydraulic jack A type of vehicle jack that uses oil under pressure to lift vehicles.

jack stands Metal stands with adjustable height to hold a vehicle once it has been jacked up.

lip-type dynamic oil seal A seal with a precisely shaped dynamic rubber lip that is held in contact with a moving shaft by a garter spring. An example would be a valve seal or camshaft seal.

machine screw A screw with a slot for screwdrivers.

mechanical jacks A type of vehicle jack that uses mechanical leverage to lift a vehicle.

multilayer steel (MLS) head gasket A gasket composed of multiple layers of steel and coated with a rubberlike substance that adheres to metal surfaces. They are typically used between the cylinder head and the cylinder block.

nut A fastener with a hexagonal head and internal threads for screwing on bolts.

Nylock nut Keeps the nut and bolt done up tightly; can have a plastic or nylon insert. Tightening the bolt squeezes it into the insert, where it resists any movement. The self-locker is highly resistant to being loosened.

oil seal Any seal used to seal oil in and dirt, moisture, and debris out.

parallel keys Used to prevent the free rotation of gears or pulleys on a shaft and can be used to secure a gear wheel on its shaft.

pneumatic jacks A type of vehicle jack that uses compressed gas or air to lift a vehicle.

portable lifting hoists A type of vehicle hoist that is portable and can be moved from one location to another.

rawl pins Often used to hold components on rotating shafts. They are a type of shear pin, used when excessive force is used to avoid further damage to a component.

safe working load (SWL) The maximum safe lifting load for lifting equipment.

screws Usually smaller than bolts and are sometimes referred to as metal threads. They can have a variety of heads and are used on smaller components. The thread often extends from the tip to the head so they can hold together components of variable thickness.

self-tapping screw A screw that cuts down its own thread as it goes. It is made of hard material that cuts a mirror image of itself into the hole as you turn it.

serrated edge shake-proof washer A washer that is used to anchor smaller screws.

speed nut A nut usually made of thin metal; it does not need to be held when started, but it is not as strong as a conventional nut. A fast and convenient way to secure a screw.

spring washer A washer that compresses as the nut tightens; the nut is spring loaded against this surface, which makes it unlikely to work loose. The ends of the spring washer also bite into the metal.

square thread A thread type with square shoulders used to translate rotational to lateral movement.

standard (imperial) system Bolts, nuts, and studs can have either metric or imperial threads. They are designated by their thread diameter, thread pitch, length, and grade. Imperial measures are in feet, inches, and fractions of inches. Most countries use metric.

stud A type of threaded fastener with a thread cut on each end, as opposed to having a bolt head on one end.

tab washer A washer that gets its name from the small tabs that are folded back to secure the washer. After the nut or bolt has been tightened, the washer remains exposed and is folded up to grip the flats and prevent movement.

taper key Used to prevent the free rotation of gears or pulleys on a shaft; used to anchor a pulley to a shaft or a disc to a driving shaft.

taper pins Used to position parts on a shaft; for example, gears, pulleys, and collars.

tensile strength The amount of force required before a material deforms or breaks.

test certificate A certificate issued when lifting equipment has been checked and deemed safe.

thread pitch The coarseness or fineness of a thread as measured by the distance from the peak of one thread to the next, in threads per inch.

timing chain A steel chain connecting the crankshaft assembly to the camshaft assembly.

timing gear A sprocket attached to the crankshaft assembly and the camshaft assembly.

torque The twisting force applied to a shaft that may or may not result in motion.

torque angle A method of tightening bolts or nuts based on angles of rotation.

torque specification Describes the amount of twisting force allowable for a fastener or a specification showing the twisting force from an engine crankshaft; supplied by manufacturers.

torque-to-yield (TTY) A method of tightening bolts close to their yield point or the point at which they will not return to their original length.

torque-to-yield (TTY) bolts Bolts that are tightened using the torque-to-yield method.

torque wrench A tool used to measure the rotational or twisting force applied to fasteners.

torx bolt Often found in vehicle engines in places such as cylinder heads to blocks, where particular tightening sequences are required.

vehicle hoist A type of vehicle lifting tool designed to lift the entire vehicle.

yield point The point at which a bolt is stretched so hard that it fails; it is measured in pounds per square inch (psi) or kilopascals (kPa) of bolt cross-section.

Review Questions

1. _____ are devices that securely hold items together, such as cotter pins, rivets, and bolts.
   a. Fasteners
   b. Flat washers
   c. Screws
   d. Taper keys

2. _____ is the twisting force applied to a shaft that may or may not result in motion.
   a. Tensile strength
   b. Hoist
   c. Torque
   d. Fastening

3. A _____ is used to prevent the free rotation of gears or pulleys on a shaft; used to anchor a pulley to a shaft or a disk to a driving shaft.
   a. taper key
   b. torx bolt
   c. fasteners
   d. flat washers

4. A mobile floor crane is also referred to as a(n) _____.
   a. floor jack
   b. engine hoist
   c. bottle jack
   d. air jack

5. Newton meters are used to specify _____.
   a. torque angle
   b. torque value
   c. torque gauging
   d. pitch gauging

6. _____ pins are often used to hold components on rotating shafts.
   a. Taper
   b. Dowel
   c. Split
   d. Rawl

7. The metric system uses _____ stamped on the heads of metric bolts and on the face of metric nuts.
   a. numbers
   b. letters
   c. symbols
   d. codes

8. If a bolt continues to be tightened and stretched beyond its _____ point, it will not return to its original length when loosened.
   a. stretch
   b. yield
   c. elasticity
   d. torque

9. Pitch is the _____ of any thread.
   a. tensile strength
   b. coarseness
   c. elasticity
   d. grade

10. _____ help contain heat and pressure within an engine's cylinder.
   a. Fire rings
   b. Sealing beads
   c. Anisotropic sealers
   d. O-rings

ASE-Type Questions

1. Technician A says that bolts are always threaded into a nut or hole that has an identical thread cut inside. Technician B says that bolts are designated by their thread diameter, grade, and pitch. Who is correct?
   a. Technician A
   b. Technician B
   c. Both Technician A and Technician B
   d. Neither Technician A nor Technician B

2. Technician A says studs can have different threads on each end. Technician B says studs always have the same threads on each end. Who is correct?
   a. Technician A
   b. Technician B
   c. Both Technician A and Technician B
   d. Neither Technician A nor Technician B

3. Technician A says torque-to-yield bolts can be reused because they have not been stretched into their yield zone. Technician B says if a bolt continues to be tightened beyond its yield point, will not return to its original length when loosened. Who is correct?
   a. Technician A
   b. Technician B
   c. Both Technician A and Technician B
   d. Neither Technician A nor Technician B

4. Technician A says a spherical insert is used to repair damaged bolt holes. Technician B says a helical insert is used to repair damaged bolt holes. Who is correct?
   a. Technician A
   b. Technician B
   c. Both Technician A and Technician B
   d. Neither Technician A nor Technician B

5. Technician A says the most widely used seal for rotating parts is the sealing bead. Technician B says the most widely used seal for rotating parts is the core plug. Who is correct?
   a. Technician A
   b. Technician B
   c. Both Technician A and Technician B
   d. Neither Technician A nor Technician B

6. Technician A says O-rings are generally effective at sealing high pressures where the differential speed between the opposing surfaces is minimal. Technician B says fire rings are generally effective at sealing high pressures where the differential speed between opposing surfaces is minimal. Who is correct?
   a. Technician A
   b. Technician B
   c. Both Technician A and Technician B
   d. Neither Technician A nor Technician B

7. Technician A says a light coat of adhesive spray is used on each surface of the block and the gasket for cork and felt. Technician B says a light coat of adhesive spray is also used on neoprene gaskets. Who is correct?
   a. Technician A
   b. Technician B
   c. Both Technician A and Technician B
   d. Neither Technician A nor Technician B

8. Technician A says it is recommended that all workshops have a built-in mechanical locking device on every vehicle hoist in the shop. Technician B says the built-in mechanical device on the hoist is to keep vehicles secured at the chosen height after the vehicle is raised. Who is correct?
   a. Technician A
   b. Technician B
   c. Both Technician A and Technician B
   d. Neither Technician A nor Technician B

9. Technician A says a crane is only as good as the slings connecting it to the equipment to be used. Technician B says slings are normally made out of chain, wire rope, or webbing material. Who is correct?
   a. Technician A
   b. Technician B
   c. Both Technician A and Technician B
   d. Neither Technician A nor Technician B

10. Technician A says the minimum operating capacity of lifting equipment is usually expressed as the safe working load. Technician B says the maximum operating capacity of lifting equipment is usually expressed as the safe working load. Who is correct?
    a. Technician A
    b. Technician B
    c. Both Technician A and Technician B
    d. Neither Technician A nor Technician B

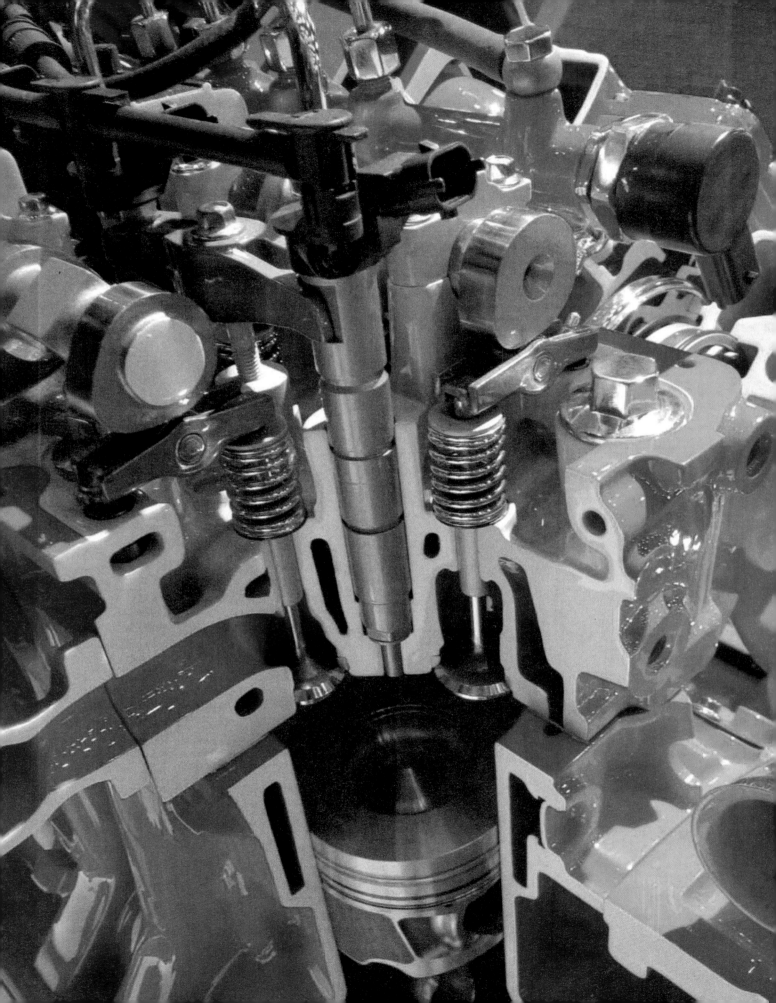

SECTION II

Diesel Engine Fundamentals

CHAPTER 6
Basic Engine Terminology and Operating Principles

NATEF Tasks

There are no NATEF tasks for this chapter.

Knowledge Objectives

1. Explain the differences between motors and engines. (p 167)
2. Define and explain terminology associated with engine operating principles. (pp 168–169)
3. Identify and explain the purpose of major engine components. (pp 169–173)
4. Perform calculations of horsepower and torque. (pp 173–177)
5. Identify and classify engines. (pp 178–186)
6. Identify and explain four-stroke engine operation and valve timing. (pp 179–183)
7. Identify and describe Miller cycle engine operation. (pp 183–185)
8. Identify and describe two-stroke engine operation. (pp 185–186)
9. Identify and describe unique construction features, operating features, and characteristics of diesel engines. (pp 186–187)

Skill Objectives

1. Measure torque rise. (p 182) **SKILL DRILL 6-1**
2. Perform a stall test. (p 182) **SKILL DRILL 6-2**
3. Understand valve and injector timing in a four-stroke cycle diesel. (p 190) **SKILL DRILL 6-3**

► Introduction

The simplest definition for an engine is that it is a machine used to convert heat energy produced from burning fuel into mechanical power **FIGURE 6-1**. Burning fuel, a process technically known as **combustion**, is a chemical reaction between fuel and oxygen that releases heat. During combustion, oxygen atoms contained in air will combine with atoms in fuel molecules such as hydrogen and carbon. When the chemical bonds between a fuel's hydrogen and carbon atoms are broken and oxygen attaches to fuel molecules, heat is released **FIGURE 6-2**. An engine uses pistons moving up and down in cylinders to convert the force of combustion into rotational motion at the flywheel **FIGURE 6-3**. In other words, an engine harnesses the heat from combustion.

The terms **prime mover** and *power unit* are sometimes used to describe engines used in off-road equipment, locomotives, and electrical generators. While these terms can be used interchangeably with the term *engine*, the term *motor* cannot.

Engines and motors are different from one another. Motors do not use combustion as an energy source. Instead, motors convert other sources of energy, such as hydraulic pressure, electricity, or compressed air, into mechanical energy.

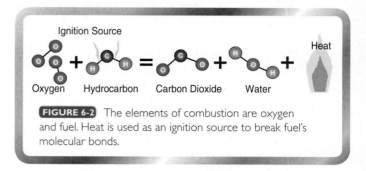

FIGURE 6-2 The elements of combustion are oxygen and fuel. Heat is used as an ignition source to break fuel's molecular bonds.

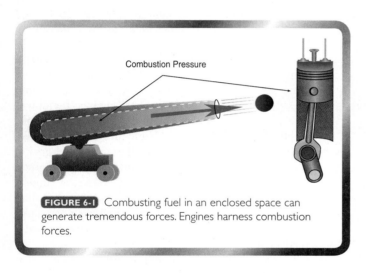

FIGURE 6-1 Combusting fuel in an enclosed space can generate tremendous forces. Engines harness combustion forces.

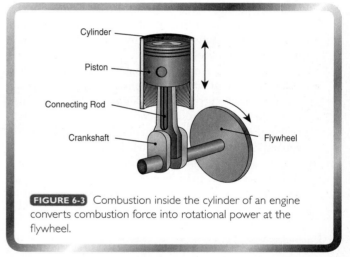

FIGURE 6-3 Combustion inside the cylinder of an engine converts combustion force into rotational power at the flywheel.

► You Are the Technician

A relatively new bus arrives at your shop and the driver complains that the engine lacks power. For three weeks, the driver has driven the vehicle between cities, over long stretches of highway with many hills. The driver reports that he needed to downshift the transmission several more gear steps than he has ever needed to in any other bus operated over the past 20 years. Fuel consumption seems to be above average in spite of light passenger loads. You perform a preliminary inspection to check for potential causes of low power complaints, but no fault is found with the bus engine, its customer programmable parameters, the manual transmission, or the clutch. A road test around a few city blocks indicates that the bus has plenty of power to accelerate between traffic lights and to keep up with other traffic. Before you dismiss the complaints as unfounded, you consider measuring the engine's power output at various road speeds.

1. What method would you recommend to measure the engine's power output?
2. Ideally, what kind of torque rise would a vehicle used for this purpose have?
3. What kind of transmission would properly match an engine suitable for this application?

▶ Engine Terminology

When you are learning the fundamentals about anything, including engines, it is helpful to start with common vocabulary and terminology. Understanding the following terms and concepts will help you understand this and the following chapters.

- **Bore**: The diameter of a cylinder **FIGURE 6-4A**. This measurement is used as a reference point for measuring cylinder wear.
- **Stroke**: The distance traveled by the piston from the top to the bottom of the cylinder **FIGURE 6-4B**.
- **Stroke ratio**: The ratio between a cylinder's bore and stroke, also referred to as squareness. This figure can be found using the following formula:

    Bore/Stroke = Stroke Ratio

    Engine application characteristics, or what types of work an engine is best suited for, are determined by the bore/stroke relationship **FIGURE 6-5**. Breathing characteristics and valve timing characteristics of engines also change due to the shape of the areas where gas is exchanged between the intake and exhaust valves and the time the pistons take to move through the top and bottom of their strokes.

- **Square engine**: An engine that has equal, or nearly equal, bore and stroke dimensions. Square engines are commonly used in spark-ignition (SI) passenger cars. They are a reasonable compromise between high-revving, over-square performance engines and under-square, high-torque diesel or truck engines.

- **Under-square engine**: An engine with a stroke dimension that is longer than the bore dimension, also known as a long-stroke engine. These engines are used to

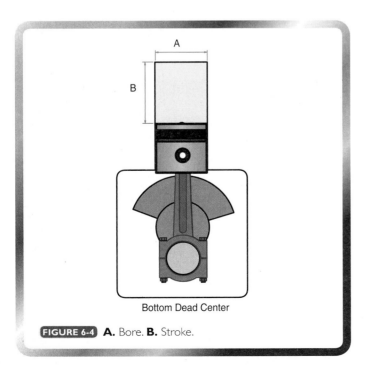

FIGURE 6-4 **A.** Bore. **B.** Stroke.

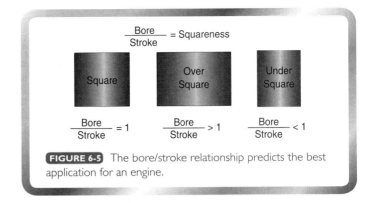

FIGURE 6-5 The bore/stroke relationship predicts the best application for an engine.

perform heavy hauling and vocational work, such as diesel or SI engines used in pick-up trucks. Under-square engines have a stroke ratio more useful for operating at low speed and developing **peak torque**, the engine speed where cylinder pressures are highest, at lower engine speeds. In under-square engines the **crankshaft throw**, which is the distance between the centerline of the crankshaft main bearing journals and the crankpin, is longer. This naturally produces more **torque**, a measurement of rotational force transmitted from the crankshaft to the flywheel, from the same cylinder pressure as a square or over-square engine. The downside of an under-square engine is that the long stroke length increases friction and mid-stroke piston speed. More cylinder side thrust from the piston and greater crankshaft stress takes place in under-square engines. Under-square engines need wider crankcase dimensions to accommodate longer throws on the crankshaft compared to over-square engines, which are not as large perpendicularly to the crankshaft (they have a smaller vertical height).

- **Over-square engine**: An engine with a stroke that is shorter than the bore diameter. Over-square engines are best suited to high-speed operation. Stroke ratios in over-square engines are better adapted to use in high-speed applications where engines need to develop the highest torque at high speed. Over-square engines, also called short-stroke engines, are commonly used by cars with SI systems. The short stroke allows the piston to change direction quickly at top dead center (TDC) and bottom dead center (BDC), which allows higher revolutions per minute (rpm) without excessive piston speed.

- **Cylinder displacement**: The volume displaced by the piston as it moves from TDC to BDC **FIGURE 6-6**. Cylinder displacement is also called swept volume. Cylinder displacement can be found using the following formula:

    $$\text{Cylinder Displacement} = \pi \times \text{Radius}^2 \times \text{Stroke}$$

- **Total cylinder displacement**: The volume of all of the cylinders in an engine **FIGURE 6-7**. Total cylinder

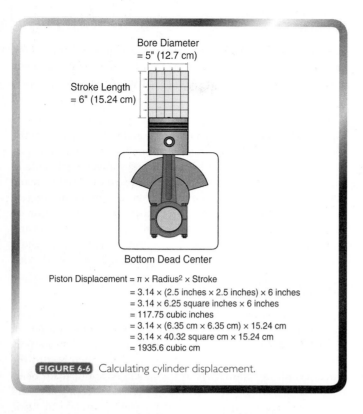

Piston Displacement = π × Radius² × Stroke
    = 3.14 × (2.5 inches × 2.5 inches) × 6 inches
    = 3.14 × 6.25 square inches × 6 inches
    = 117.75 cubic inches
    = 3.14 × (6.35 cm × 6.35 cm) × 15.24 cm
    = 3.14 × 40.32 square cm × 15.24 cm
    = 1935.6 cubic cm

FIGURE 6-6 Calculating cylinder displacement.

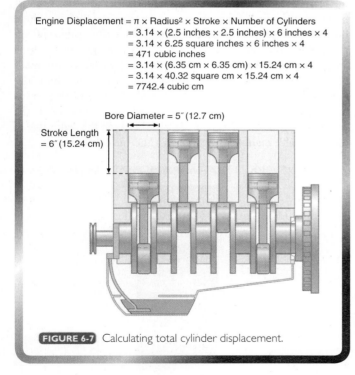

Engine Displacement = π × Radius² × Stroke × Number of Cylinders
    = 3.14 × (2.5 inches × 2.5 inches) × 6 inches × 4
    = 3.14 × 6.25 square inches × 6 inches × 4
    = 471 cubic inches
    = 3.14 × (6.35 cm × 6.35 cm) × 15.24 cm × 4
    = 3.14 × 40.32 square cm × 15.24 cm × 4
    = 7742.4 cubic cm

FIGURE 6-7 Calculating total cylinder displacement.

displacement, also known as engine displacement, can be found using the following formula:

Total Cylinder Displacement =
    π × Radius² × Stroke × Number of Cylinders

- **Clearance volume**: The space remaining in a cylinder when the piston is at TDC.
- **Total cylinder volume**: The sum of the cylinder displacement plus clearance volume.
- **Compression ratio**: A comparison of total cylinder volume to clearance volume. In other words, compression ratio is a comparison between the cylinder volume when the piston is at BDC and when it reaches TDC **FIGURE 6-8**. Compression ratio can be found using the following formula:

$$\text{Cylinder Ratio} = \frac{\text{Cylinder Volume}}{\text{Clearance Volume}}$$

As compression ratios increase in an engine, fuel consumption decreases and power increases exponentially. Higher compression ratios convert more combustion energy into mechanical force. This is because the push on the piston is harder and the stroke length is usually longer in engines with high compression ratios. Diesel engines with high compression ratios use very small clearance volumes, which is primarily in the piston-formed combustion chamber. In direct injection (DI) diesel engines, most of this volume is contained in the piston-formed combustion chamber, with a space between the piston and cylinder head measured in as little as a few thousandths of an inch. While engines with high compression ratios produce more power, burn less fuel, and mix air and fuel better, the downside is that they require more cylinder head clamping force, better head gaskets, and heavier, high-torque starting systems.

▶ Engine Components

Diesel engine components are exposed to operating temperatures, pressures, and other forces that are higher than those found in gasoline engines of similar displacement. Because of the higher temperatures and compression ratios encountered,

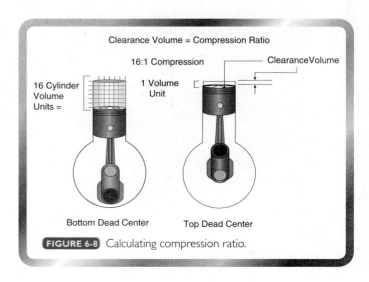

FIGURE 6-8 Calculating compression ratio.

diesel engine parts are usually heavier and built more ruggedly than parts for comparable gasoline-fueled engines **FIGURE 6-9**.

Cylinder Block

The **cylinder block** is the largest structure of an engine. It encloses the cylinders and provides a rigid frame to support the cylinders or cylinder liners, crankshaft, oil and coolant passages, and, in many engines, the camshaft **FIGURE 6-10**.

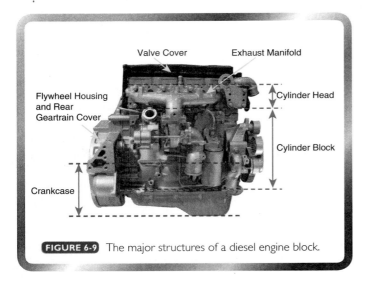

FIGURE 6-9 The major structures of a diesel engine block.

FIGURE 6-10 The cylinder block encloses the cylinders and is an attachment point for most other engine parts.

Crankcase

The crankcase is the lower portion of the engine. It contains the crankshaft. It is usually defined as the area of the cylinder block below the cylinders, and it includes the oil pan/sump.

Cylinder Head

The cylinder head is usually a heavy metal casting that seals the top of the engine to form a combustion chamber above the pistons. The cylinder head is bolted to the cylinder block. Due to the high combustion chamber pressures of a diesel engine, many cylinder head bolts are required to clamp and maintain the seal between the cylinder head and cylinder block. In addition to supporting and enclosing the valve mechanisms, the air, coolant, and exhaust coolant passages, the injectors, and often a camshaft, the cylinder head has intake and exhaust manifolds bolted to it.

Crankshaft

Within the crankcase is the crankshaft. The **crankshaft** converts the reciprocating action of the pistons into rotational movement **FIGURE 6-11**. The crankshaft revolves inside the crankcase portion of the engine block. Main bearing caps, which bolt to the block, clamp the crankshaft to the block. A round main bearing bore, or crank bore, is formed by the main bearing caps and block. Plain bearing inserts called main bearings are placed inside the main bearing bore to provide a replaceable, low-friction surface to enable the crankshaft to freely rotate. The surfaces where the main and connecting rod bearings contact the crankshaft are called the crank journal surfaces. **Main bearing journals**, which are the surfaces where the crankshaft is supported by the main bearing caps, are located along the crankshaft center line. The part of the crankshaft that connects with the connecting rod is the **crankpin**. An important dimension of the crankshaft is the crankshaft throw, which is the distance between the centerline of the crankshaft main bearing journals and the crankpin.

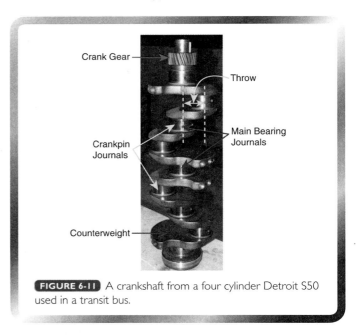

FIGURE 6-11 A crankshaft from a four cylinder Detroit S50 used in a transit bus.

Cylinder Components

Cylinder components consist of the engine parts enclosed by the cylinders. These include the piston, piston rings, wrist pin, and connecting rod FIGURE 6-12. The piston is attached to one end of a connecting rod by a pin called a piston pin, or a wrist pin. The other end of the rod is attached to the crankshaft. Connecting rod bearings, similar to the split-insert, plain main bearings, are used to minimize friction between the connecting rod and the crankshaft.

Pistons

Pistons are moving cylinder parts that are directly acted upon by combustion forces. These round metal components fit snuggly in the cylinder, but there is clearance between the piston and cylinder walls to allow for heat expansion and prevent piston seizure inside the cylinder when the engine is at operating temperature.

Piston Rings

Engines have replaceable piston rings to minimize gas leakage past the piston FIGURE 6-13. These rings function as the seal between the piston and the cylinder wall and also act to reduce friction by reducing the contact area between the piston and the cylinder wall. Most diesel pistons use several rings, each performing a distinct function. The top ring operates primarily as the gas-tight compression seal to prevent gas leakage past the piston. An intermediate ring has oil control and compression-sealing functions. An oil control ring maintains an oil film on the cylinder wall to minimize friction.

Valves and Ports

Poppet-type valves are used to control the movement of gases into and out of the cylinder. The intake and exhaust valves open at the correct times to admit air into the cylinder and expel combustion exhaust. Separate intake and exhaust valves direct gases through cylinder head passageways called ports. In diesels, intake ports are shaped to cause air to become highly turbulent, or swirl, as it enters the cylinders. Clean diesel engines generally use two pairs of intake and exhaust ports for improved engine breathing and combustion quality FIGURE 6-14. Older engines use a single intake and exhaust valve pair. A few engine types use two intake valves and a single exhaust valve to improve engine breathing.

Camshaft

A camshaft is used to operate the valves in the correct sequence. Eccentric lobes on the camshaft actuate valves through the valve train FIGURE 6-15. When the camshaft is located in the block, the valve train may consist of valve lifters, pushrods, rocker

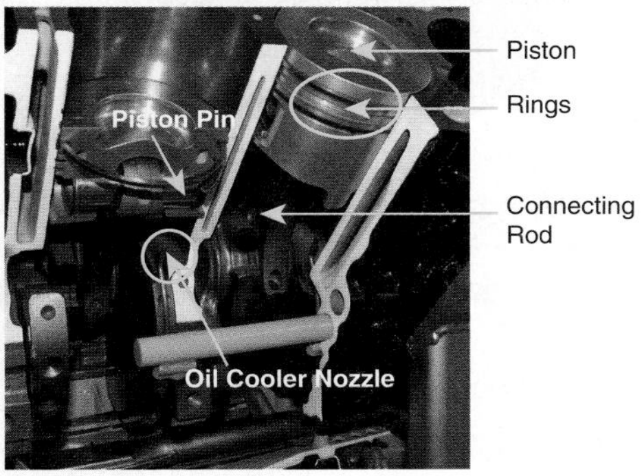

FIGURE 6-12 Typical cylinder components in a parent bore cylinder block.

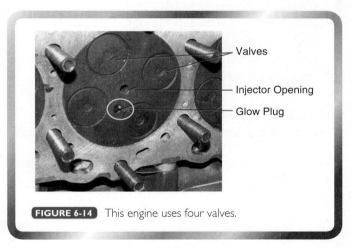

FIGURE 6-14 This engine uses four valves.

FIGURE 6-13 A trunk-type piston with rings.

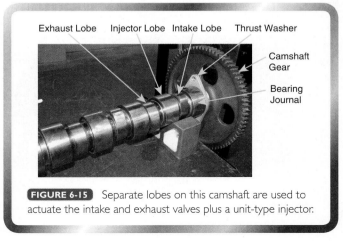

FIGURE 6-15 Separate lobes on this camshaft are used to actuate the intake and exhaust valves plus a unit-type injector.

levers, and bridges **FIGURE 6-16**. In overhead camshaft engines, the camshaft is located in the cylinder head. While there is a reduction of parts and complexity to the valve train mechanism associated with overhead camshaft engines, they are used primarily to enable higher pressurization of fuel by injectors, which can directly contact an injector lobe on the camshaft.

Valve and Gear Train Mechanism

A gear train or valve timing mechanism is used to coordinate the movement of the crankshaft with the camshaft and the valves.

The gear train may also operate fuel injection apparatus, lubrication, power steering, and coolant pumps, accessory drive mechanisms, and even power take-off (PTO) pumps **FIGURE 6-17**. Belts, chains, or gears are typical components used to transfer power in the gear train **FIGURE 6-18**. The stronger, more durable gear-type valve train mechanism is used on most commercial diesel vehicles. This strength is required because firing impulses accelerate the crankshaft much faster, and high compression forces momentarily slow the engine, which increases stress on the valve train mechanism. A thrust washer between the engine block and rotating cam gear prevents the cam gear from wearing into the block. This can occur due to the thrust loads generated by the helical teeth of the cam gear, which tend to push the driving gear forward and the driven gear backward. Overhead camshaft engines locate the camshaft in the cylinder head. Overhead cam

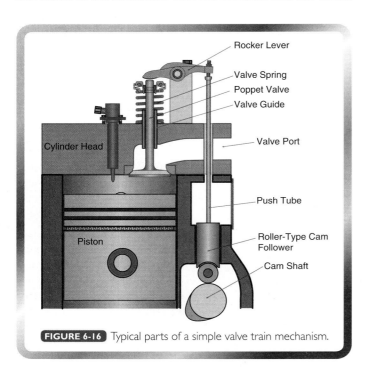

FIGURE 6-16 Typical parts of a simple valve train mechanism.

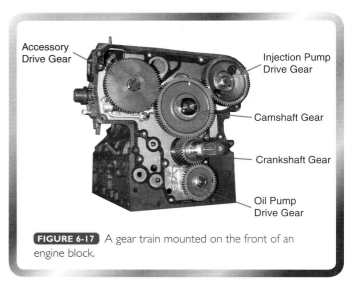

FIGURE 6-17 A gear train mounted on the front of an engine block.

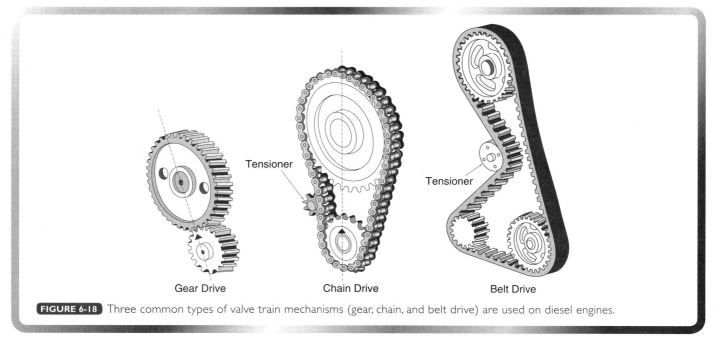

FIGURE 6-18 Three common types of valve train mechanisms (gear, chain, and belt drive) are used on diesel engines.

engines can apply more force directly to the injector for higher injector spray-in pressures. Rollers on the camshaft followers reduce friction and increase camshaft durability FIGURE 6-19 .

Flywheel

The flywheel is a heavy, round casting bolted to the end of the crankshaft. The heavy mass of the flywheel develops considerable inertia that is used to smooth out the intermittent impulses of the firing strokes. The flywheel keeps the engine turning because it resists a decrease in speed. A ring gear is attached to the outside diameter of the flywheel; it engages the starting motor to rotate the engine during starting FIGURE 6-20 .

When an automatic transmission is used, a torque converter is bolted to the flywheel. Because the torque converter is heavy, the flywheel can be much lighter. The type of flywheel that is used with a torque converter is called a flex plate. The total weight of

FIGURE 6-19 An overhead camshaft is positioned in the cylinder head.

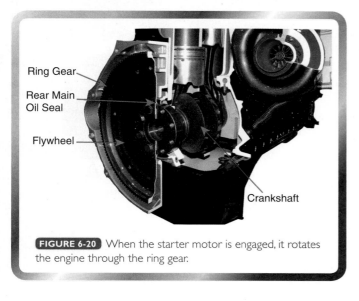

FIGURE 6-20 When the starter motor is engaged, it rotates the engine through the ring gear.

a torque converter and flex plate is approximately the same as a flywheel and clutch on a manual transmission engine.

▶ Measuring Engine Power

Engines are machines that convert heat energy into mechanical power, which is used to perform work. Understanding how engines produce power is important for engine technicians because they maintain engines to keep them effective and efficient at producing power and diagnose problems with engines when they don't efficiently, efficiently produce power. In this next section, important foundational concepts about engine power are introduced. These are very helpful when you are identifying and troubleshooting power-related complaints. Two major power-related concepts to differentiate between are torque and horsepower.

Torque

Torque is a measurement of rotational force, or twisting force. Torque is calculated by multiplying the force applied to a lever by its length FIGURE 6-21 . In an engine, torque is transmitted from the crankshaft to the flywheel and used to drive the wheels of a vehicle. Applying the lever concept of torque to an engine, the amount of torque produced by an engine is determined by multiplying cylinder pressure by the length of the crankshaft throw (the distance between the crankshaft crankpin and main bearing journal) FIGURE 6-22 . This means that when combustion pressure increases, the force of cylinder pressure against the top of the piston is like the force applied to the end of a wrench. Engine torque increases proportionally with the cylinder pressure produced by the force of combustion. This relationship can be easily understood by anyone who has tightened a bolt or wheel nut. When more force is applied to a fastener through a wrench, more torque is available to tighten or loosen the fastener.

Engine torque output is regulated by the amount of air and fuel burned in the combustion chamber, which is controlled primarily by driver demand. If more fuel is burned, engine torque output increases because combustion force also rises. If less fuel is burned, engine torque output decreases. In a spark ignition (SI) engine, which uses a throttle plate to regulate airflow, maximum or peak torque can only be reached only when the throttle is wide open; this is because maximum airflow into the engine takes place

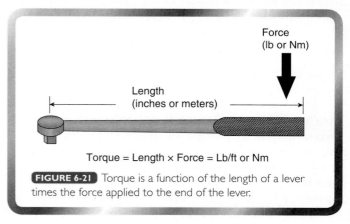

Force (lb or Nm)

Length (inches or meters)

Torque = Length × Force = Lb/ft or Nm

FIGURE 6-21 Torque is a function of the length of a lever times the force applied to the end of the lever.

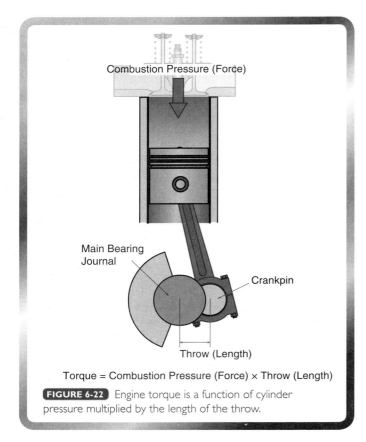

Torque = Combustion Pressure (Force) × Throw (Length)

FIGURE 6-22 Engine torque is a function of cylinder pressure multiplied by the length of the throw.

only then. Diesels, which do not throttle intake air, regulate torque by varying the amount of fuel injected directly into the cylinders. In a turbocharged diesel engine, very high torque can easily be reached at engine speeds not far above **idle** (an engine's minimum operational speed). In fact, most diesel engines reach peak torque at two-thirds of rated rpm. For example, in an engine governed to 1800 rpm, peak torque would occur around 1200 rpm. That's just 400–500 rpm above a typical idle speed of 600–700 rpm.

To calculate torque using imperial measurements, the following formula is used:

$$\text{Torque} = \text{Force (pounds)} \times \text{Length of lever (feet)}$$

Torque, in imperial measurements, is expressed in units called foot-pounds (ft-lb). This unit is also sometimes referred to as a pound-foot (lb-ft). To calculate torque using metric measurements, the following formula is used:

$$\text{Torque} = \text{Force (newtons)} \times \text{Length of lever (meters)}$$

In the metric system, torque is expressed in units of newton meters (Nm).

Torque is the most important force required to move a load. Note that engine speed is not included in the mathematical formula used to calculate torque. This means torque can be exerted with no rotational speed (think of loosening a seized fastener or a stalled electric motor where torque is present but no movement takes place). An engine's torque output will also vary proportionally with load. This means that high or low torque can be exerted by an engine at any engine speed. For example, if

an engine is under load, the operator will push on the throttle to prevent the engine from stalling. As the throttle is opened further, more air and fuel are burned during each combustion event and the engine will produce increasing amounts of torque.

Under heavy load, torque reaction can occur. This occurs because every action has an equal and opposite reaction; as load increases, the engine's cylinder block will lean in the opposite direction of engine rotation. Under heavy load, the torque reaction of the truck body to engine torque will lift the vehicle's left front tire and right rear tire; this can produce uneven tire wear. This phenomenon explains why the right front tire will often have more wear than the left front tire on heavily loaded trucks **FIGURE 6-23**.

▶ TECHNICIAN TIP

When determining which side of a vehicle is left or right, the position of the driver in the driver seat is always the point of reference. For engines, the Society of Automotive Engineers (SAE) uses the flywheel as the reference point for determining the front and rear of the engine as well as the direction of rotation.

A diesel engine produces virtually no torque at idle or **high idle** (the maximum speed an engine turns without a load). Under these conditions, only enough power is produced to overcome internal friction and inertia and rotate the engine. When crankshaft or flywheel movement is resisted (such as when the engine is put into gear, an accessory like the alternator increases

FIGURE 6-23 Under heavy load, the torque reaction of the truck body to engine torque will lift the left front tire and the right rear tire.

output current, or the compressor begins to load), the governor, which regulates fueling by the high-pressure injection system, adds the additional fuel needed to maintain engine speed. In this case, engine torque increases.

Torque Rise

Torque rise is the difference between engine torque at its peak compared to torque at the maximum or rated rpm the engine. Torque back-up is another term for torque rise. A high torque rise engine has a large difference between torque measured at rated rpm and peak torque rpm. A high torque rise engine will quickly build torque when it is under load because engine speed drops when approaching peak torque rpm. High torque rise engines are best suited for line haul vehicles where engines are operated at fast highway speeds for long distances. Drivers of these vehicles will sense that high torque rise engines have more power when climbing hills because torque increases substantially as rpm drops. With high torque rise engines, fewer transmission gear steps are needed because the driver can remain in gear longer before downshifting while climbing a hill.

An engine with low torque rise or torque back-up will begin to drop rpm quickly, which can produce the sensation that there is little power available. This happens because torque does not increase very much as engine rpm falls off. Urban buses, delivery vehicles, and off-road equipment use low torque rise engines. The advantage of a low torque rise engines is that more torque is available over a wider engine rpm range and fuel efficiency is better over a wider engine speed range. Vocational applications use flatter torque rise profiles and have more gear steps for the transmission to compensate for lower torque rise FIGURE 6-24 . More information about torque rise is covered in the Governors chapter.

Measuring Torque Rise

Peak torque and maximum torque at rated rpm are best measured on a dynamometer, but original equipment manufacturer (OEM) software on late-model engines can be used to help accurately measure torque during a road test. Torque values reported in the software are estimates based on fuel rates, boost pressure, and other variables unique to the engine that are known only by the OEM.

To measure torque rise, follow the steps in SKILL DRILL 6-1 .

Stall Testing

When low power or poor engine performance is reported, an engine stall test can be used to determine whether the problem is in the engine or transmission. A stall test puts maximum load on the engine; during the test, a variety of engine parameters, such as boost pressure and rpm, can be measured. This test is commonly performed on transit buses to investigate low-power and transmission-related complaints.

To perform a stall test, follow the steps in SKILL DRILL 6-2 .

Horsepower

Horsepower (hp) is a calculation of the rate at which work is performed; it measures an engine's power output as a function of both torque and engine speed. James Watt (1736-1819), an engineer who helped make significant improvements to the

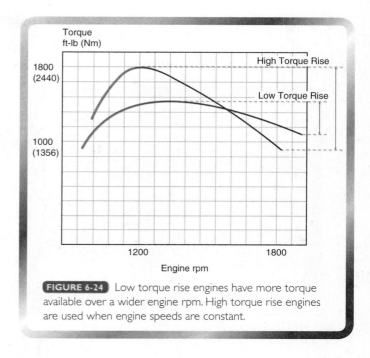

FIGURE 6-24 Low torque rise engines have more torque available over a wider engine rpm. High torque rise engines are used when engine speeds are constant.

steam engine, developed the formula to determine an engine's hp. Watt wanted to compare the power of a steam engine to the number of horses required to perform the same amount of work. He based his calculation on observations of horses pulling skids of coal up mine shafts. He observed that 1 hp was equal to the amount of power required from a horse to pull 150 lb out of a hole that was 220 feet deep in 1 minute. That same standardized measurement of horsepower today is expressed mathematically two different ways. In the first, 1 hp is the amount of work performed to lift 550 lb per second, or 33,000 lb per minute (550 pound × 60 seconds). The measurement of engine hp is calculated from the amount of torque at the crankshaft and the speed at which it is turning. The formula for engine hp is:

$$\text{Horsepower} = \frac{\text{Force (pounds)} \times \text{Distance (feet)}}{\text{Times (minutes)}/33,000}$$

Stated more simply:

$$\text{Horsepower} = \frac{\text{Torque} \times \text{rpm}}{5252 \text{ rpm}}$$

Or:

$$\text{hp} = \text{rpm} \times \text{ft-lb} \div 5252$$

For example, if an engine creates 1500 ft-lb of torque at 1200 rpm, then the amount of hp is:

$$\text{hp} = 1500 \times 1200 \div 5252$$

$$\text{hp} = 342.7 \text{ hp at 1200 rpm}$$

$$\text{Torque} = \frac{5252 \times \text{hp}}{\text{rpm}}$$

SKILL DRILL 6-1 Measuring Torque Rise

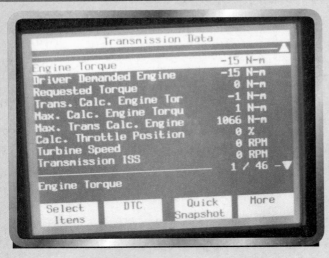

① Using a chassis dynamometer or a vehicle connected to a laptop with OEM software, run the vehicle through its entire engine operating range under load. Use a data recorder or take snapshots of the engine data list during the trip using the feature in the OEM software.

② During a road test, a vehicle that is lugged by using a gear that is one or two steps above where it should operate will move through peak torque with a full throttle application. Record the trip using a data logger feature within the OEM software.

③ Operate the vehicle at highway speed one or two gears down from where it should be while the vehicle is under load, such as traveling up a hill. Again, record the data.

④ Find the highest peak torque value recorded.

⑤ Find the highest torque value reached while the engine was at rated speed.

⑥ Calculate the torque rise using the following formula:

$$\frac{\text{Peak Torque} - \text{Rated Torque}}{\text{Rated Torque}} \times 100 = \text{Torque Rise}$$

⑦ Determine whether the torque rise is more suited to vocational or on-highway use and compare your findings with the vehicle's actual application.

SKILL DRILL 6-2 Performing a Stall Test

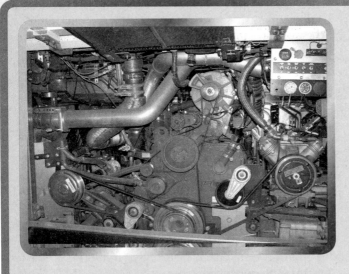

① Warm the engine to operating temperature.

② Chock the wheels with purpose made blocks and apply the park brakes.

③ Using an appropriate electronic service tool or OEM software, navigate to an engine data display screen and prepare a custom data list including engine rpm and boost pressure. If fuel rates and exhaust back pressure are available, measure those, too.

④ With the park brakes applied, depress the accelerator until the engine reaches its maximum speed. Observe and record the engine rpm and compare it to the OEM specifications. Engine rpm that is lower than the OEM specified rpm indicates that the engine is not producing enough power.

⑤ Make service recommendations to investigate other causes of low engine power if the engine stall speed is more than 150 rpm below the OEM specifications.

Because hp would change with rpm, it is necessary to express not only the power value, but also to include the engine speed, in rpm, at which it occurs. Using metric units of measurement, power is measured in kilowatts. A kilowatt (1000 watts) is equivalent to 1000 Nm per second. One hp is equal to 0.746 kilowatts, or 746 watts.

Brake Horsepower

Brake horsepower (BHP) is the actual hp available at the flywheel. It is measured with a dynamometer using a brake-like device called a prony brake to apply a load. Other calculations of hp are made using different pieces of data and measuring instruments. For example, indicated horsepower (IHP) refers to power developed in a cylinder based on the amount of heat released during combustion. To measure IHP, a special pressure gauge is installed in the cylinder and the maximum firing pressure is recorded. Using the surface area of the piston to calculate the force applied to the crankshaft, IHP is calculated. Frictional losses are not accounted for in this calculation. When IHP is subtracted from BHP measured at the engine flywheel, friction losses can be estimated and the engine's mechanical efficiency can be determined.

Measuring Power Using a Dynamometer

A dynamometer is a device that measures engine or vehicle road speed and torque to calculate engine power. A dynamometer applies a load to the engine or drive tires and collects speed and torque data. A common method used to collect data uses a strain gauge and an engine rpm or dynamometer roller speed sensor. The strain gauge operates like a weight scale and measures the force of reaction torque. When loaded, the strain gauge supplies an output signal that is proportional to weight measured in pounds or newtons of force. When the strain gauge is placed beneath a calibrated length of bar, an electronic calculator measures engine torque in ft-lb (Nm) and speed to calculate horsepower **FIGURE 6-25**. The dynamometer can also provide separate measures of horsepower, torque, and engine speed **FIGURE 6-26**.

Rated Horsepower

Rated horsepower is the power output of an engine measured at the maximum engine speed under SAE-defined standardized atmospheric pressure, humidity, and temperature. Rated speed is the maximum speed an engine will reach while under full load. Rated hp appears on the emissions decal, and the engine must operate within 5% of its stated value **FIGURE 6-27**.

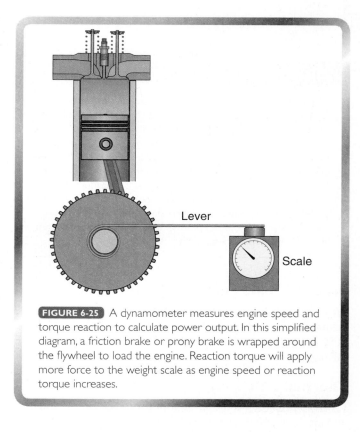

FIGURE 6-25 A dynamometer measures engine speed and torque reaction to calculate power output. In this simplified diagram, a friction brake or prony brake is wrapped around the flywheel to load the engine. Reaction torque will apply more force to the weight scale as engine speed or reaction torque increases.

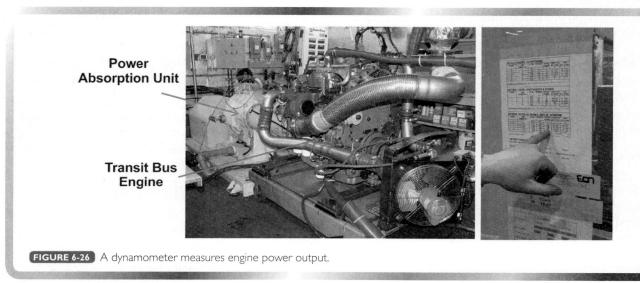

FIGURE 6-26 A dynamometer measures engine power output.

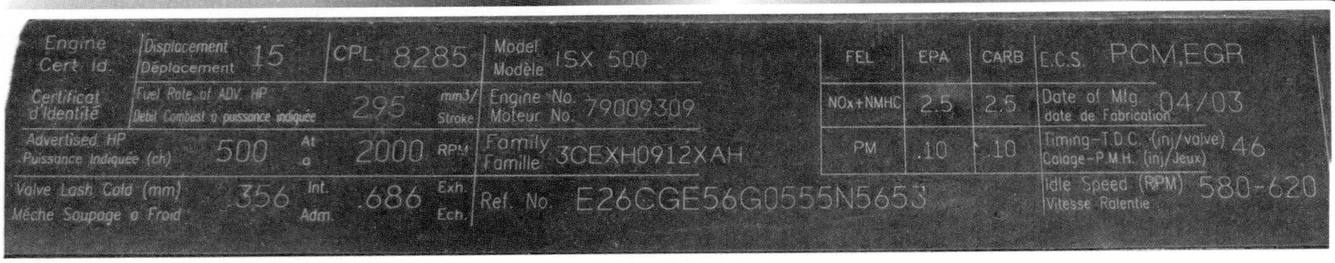

FIGURE 6-27 Rated horsepower appears on the emission decal. It is useful to compare the decal ratings with power measured on a dynamometer.

TECHNICIAN TIP

When comparing the power output of two engines, using hp only can be misleading. Consider two engines: the first is a diesel with 300 hp (224 kW) reaching peak torque at 1200 rpm; the other is an SI engine producing 300 hp (224 kW) reaching peak torque at 5000 rpm. The diesel engine would produce 1313 ft-lb (1780 Nm) of maximum torque while the SI engine would produce only 315 ft-lb (427 Nm) of torque. Both engines can produce identical amounts of power, but they have very different applications. The diesel, producing torque at a much lower and usable rpm range, could accelerate faster, and pull much heavier loads. It could not, however, reach road speeds as fast as the SI engine.

Brake Specific Fuel Consumption

Brake specific fuel consumption (BSFC) is the weight of fuel required to produce 1 hp for 1 hour, expressed as lb per hp per hour. BFSC can be determined by weighing fuel consumed in an hour on a dynamometer and dividing the consumption by the output hp.

Thermal Efficiency

Thermal efficiency is the amount of energy an engine converts into mechanical energy compared to what could theoretically be extracted from a pound of fuel. Newer, electronically controlled DI diesel engines are now producing efficiencies of 45–52%. This compares with SI port fuel-injected gasoline engines at 25–30%.

Brake Mean Effective Pressure

Brake Mean Effective Pressure (BMEP) is the average pressure exerted on the crown of a piston during power stroke. It is a factor that measures how efficiently an engine is using its piston displacement to do work.

Volumetric Efficiency

Volumetric efficiency is a comparison between the volume of air actually filling a cylinder and what it is theoretically capable of holding. Volumetric efficiency is expressed as a percentage; this percentage is found by dividing the actual filled volume of a cylinder by physical dimensions of the cylinder. For example, if a cylinder is filled to three-quarters of its total volume with air, it has 75% volumetric efficiency. The greater an engine's volumetric efficiency, the higher the amount of air mass entering the cylinders. As air mass increases, so does the potential weight of fuel an engine can burn. When an engine can extract more power from each cubic inch (or centimeter) of air it takes in, its power density increases. Some diesels today are capable of running more than 300% volumetric efficiency with high-pressure turbocharging. Ideally, the highest volumetric efficiency from an engine is desirable because it allows the engine to produce more power for ever cubic inch (or centimeter) of displacement. Engine size can be reduced with improvements to volumetric efficiency. Filling the cylinders with the maximum air mass has technical challenges, though. For example:

1. As engine speed increases, less time is available to fill the cylinders with air. This is because the duration of the intake valve opening becomes progressively shorter.
2. Atmospheric pressure is the only pressure that is available to push air into the cylinders for **naturally aspirated** engines (engines without turbochargers or pressurized air intake systems). At higher altitudes, engine power diminishes with decreasing atmospheric pressure. With modifications, engines can pressurize the air intake system above atmospheric pressure to charge the cylinders with more air; these engines are referred to as **supercharged**.
3. Intake and exhaust valve opening diameters are limited, along with the intake and exhaust port dimensions. Smaller ports and valves restrict air flow into an engine.
4. Valve timing can affect the ability to fill a cylinder. Leaving an intake or exhaust valve open or closed for a longer or shorter duration has significant effect on the torque an engine produces and at what rpm the most torque is produced.

Many design changes are regularly made to improve volumetric efficiency. Adding turbochargers, using four instead of two intake and exhaust valves per cylinder, and the use of variable valve timing are some of the many innovations to improve engine breathing efficiency.

► Engine Classification

Engines are classified using a wide variety of criteria. Common categories are defined according to:

- the engine's operating cycle
- the type of fuel an engine burns

- whether an engine is rotary or reciprocating
- the engine's ignition system
- the engine's cylinder arrangement and number of cylinders
- the engine's construction material
- the engine's cylinder bore diameter and displacement
- the engine's horsepower, torque, and speed range
- the type of cooling system used
- the location of the camshaft
- the engine's air induction system

One major classification is made according to where fuel is burned. If an engine burns fuel outside a cylinder, it is an **external combustion engine**. Steam engines fall into this category FIGURE 6-28. An **internal combustion engine** burns fuel inside an engine's cylinder. In both instances, heat is used to increase the pressure of a gas and the force of expansion is used to drive pistons operating in cylinders. **Reciprocating engines** are the most common type of internal combustion engine. These engines use pistons moving up and down in cylinders to convert the force of combustion into rotational motion at the flywheel FIGURE 6-29.

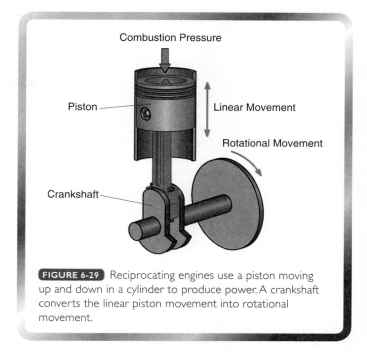

FIGURE 6-29 Reciprocating engines use a piston moving up and down in a cylinder to produce power. A crankshaft converts the linear piston movement into rotational movement.

Classification of Engines by Operating Cycle

Engine operating cycle refers to the number of piston strokes needed to complete a combustion cycle. Air will be drawn into the engine, compressed, mixed with fuel, burned, and finally exhausted to complete an operating cycle. The four-stoke cycle has been used in the majority of diesel engines, but two other operating cycles are used: two-stroke, popularized by Detroit Diesel from the 1930s to the late 1980s, and the Miller cycle used by Caterpillar's **Advanced Combustion Emission Reduction Technology (ACERT)** engines. ACERT is a marketing term used by Caterpillar to describe a variety of technologies used to lower emissions and increase engine efficiency.

Four-Stroke Cycle Diesels

A cycle is the repetition of a set of events in a periodic pattern. In the four-stroke cycle, four strokes of the piston complete one cycle. The four strokes of the operating cycle are intake, compression, power, and exhaust FIGURE 6-30. The four-stroke engine cycle in a diesel, while similar to an SI engine, has different operational characteristics due to the following factors:

- longer piston stroke required to produce higher compression
- little piston movement at BDC and TDC in comparison to crank rotation because of the long stroke
- adaptations for turbocharging
- large valve overlap period FIGURE 6-31

The following sections describe the events of the four-stroke engine operating cycle with an emphasis on the unique features of diesel engines.

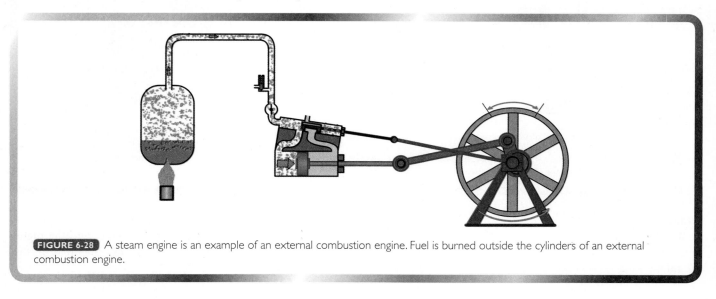

FIGURE 6-28 A steam engine is an example of an external combustion engine. Fuel is burned outside the cylinders of an external combustion engine.

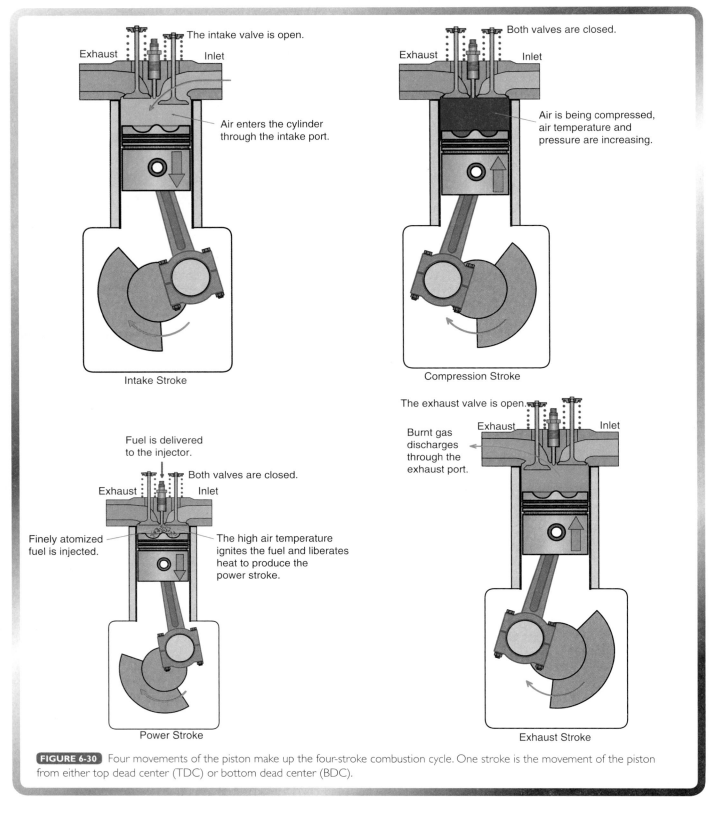

The intake valve is open.

Exhaust   Inlet

Air enters the cylinder through the intake port.

Intake Stroke

Both valves are closed.

Exhaust   Inlet

Air is being compressed, air temperature and pressure are increasing.

Compression Stroke

Fuel is delivered to the injector.

Both valves are closed.

Exhaust   Inlet

Finely atomized fuel is injected.

The high air temperature ignites the fuel and liberates heat to produce the power stroke.

Power Stroke

The exhaust valve is open.

Exhaust   Inlet

Burnt gas discharges through the exhaust port.

Exhaust Stroke

FIGURE 6-30 Four movements of the piston make up the four-stroke combustion cycle. One stroke is the movement of the piston from either top dead center (TDC) or bottom dead center (BDC).

Intake Stroke

To draw air into the cylinders, the piston moves down the cylinder, from TDC to BDC, after the camshaft has begun opening the intake valve. Piston movement increases cylinder volume, creating a low-pressure area within the cylinder. A pressure differential between the low cylinder pressure and the higher atmospheric pressure, or pressurized intake manifold, pushes air into the cylinder.

Valve Timing

An engine would operate if the intake valve simply opened and closed at TDC and BDC. However, changing the time when the intake valve opens and closes can improve engine performance and increase volumetric efficiency. Today's engines do not simply open and close the intake or exhaust valves at the top and bottom of each stroke. Instead, various factors influence the precise timing of valve opening and closing FIGURE 6-32 . These factors include:

1. The momentum or gas inertia of incoming intake air: Air may seem to have relatively little weight, but it does have some. Air velocities can easily achieve as much as 150 mph (241 kph) in the intake manifold and have significant inertia due to the mass of airflow. Making adjustments to valve timing outside of simply opening and closing the valve at TDC and BDC can take advantage of air's gas inertia. For the intake valve, this typically means closing the intake valve after the piston begins an upward stroke. Even though the piston begins to move upward, piston movement is initially slow, and gas inertia is high, which enables the cylinder to fill with more air.

2. Late valve closing after TDC for the exhaust valve: This allows moving exhaust gas momentum to pull more exhaust gases out of the cylinder. Clearance volume pressure can actually become negative as the departing exhaust gas pulse pulls exhaust gases, which might ordinarily linger in the clearance volume area, out the exhaust port. Leaving the exhaust valve open after TDC at the end of the exhaust stroke helps empty, or scavenge, exhaust gases from the cylinder and make room for the fresh intake air charge.

3. A small amount of piston movement relative to crankshaft rotation at the bottom and top of each stroke: Little movement of the piston takes place in long-stroke engines at TDC

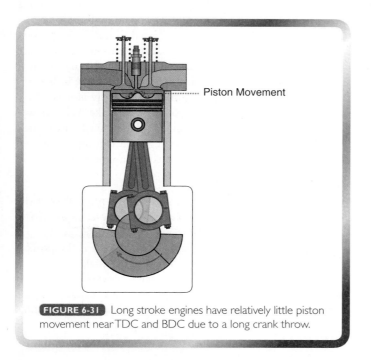

FIGURE 6-31 Long stroke engines have relatively little piston movement near TDC and BDC due to a long crank throw.

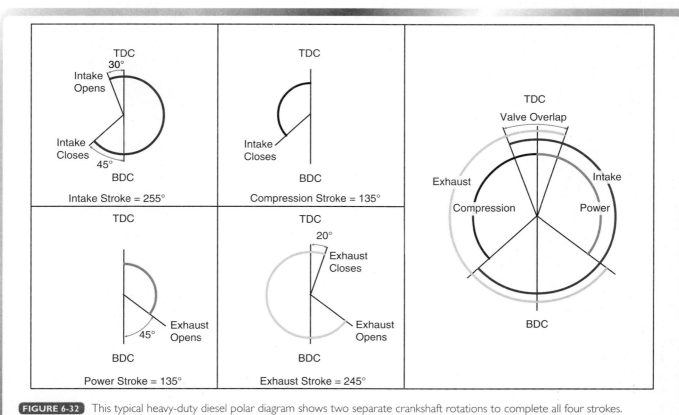

FIGURE 6-32 This typical heavy-duty diesel polar diagram shows two separate crankshaft rotations to complete all four strokes.

and BDC compared to short-stroke engines. Piston speed in a diesel is highest at mid-stroke rather than at TDC or BDC. Because piston speed is slow when changing direction, the intake and exhaust valves are held open longer to take advantage of gas inertia or intake manifold pressure produced through turbocharging. For example, opening the intake valve as the piston approaches TDC at the end of the exhaust stroke will not cause large quantities of exhaust gases or intake air to push back into the intake manifold. Instead, the intake valve will have a head start opening, enabling unrestricted air intake flow past the intake valve and into the cylinder when the piston begins its downward stroke.

Compression Stroke

After the intake valve closes, the compression and heating of the air charge begins. Because cylinder volume is reduced by upward piston movement, cylinder pressure and temperature increases. These values will depend on the compression ratio, the amount of air volume drawn on intake stroke, and the air inlet temperature. Compression stroke ends when the piston reaches TDC.

Power and Exhaust Stroke

When fuel is injected into the hot air mass near the end of compression stroke, the combustion event begins. Cylinder pressure will begin to rise rapidly just after TDC and should peak 10°-15° after TDC. No power can be made in the engine until the piston crosses over TDC and a crank angle is present to rotate the crankshaft. Cylinder pressures and volumes expand during the power stroke, forcing the piston down with a peak pressure as high as 3750 psi (259 bar) **FIGURE 6-33** . This compares to approximately 900 psi (62 bar) in a gasoline-fueled engine. At 90° after TDC, maximum leverage on the crankshaft is reached. Beyond this point, the amount of power diminishes rapidly because cylinder volume is increasing and the angle between the connecting rod and crank throw is reduced. The exhaust valve is typically opened at 100°-140° of crank rotation after TDC. Compared to the other engine strokes, power stroke is the shortest stroke. Opening the exhaust valve long before BDC, which ends the power stroke, improves engine efficiency for a couple of reasons. First, opening the valve at this time ensures more exhaust gas is allowed to leave the cylinder. By the time the piston reaches BDC, most combustion pressure is released and the exhaust valve is fully opened. By opening the exhaust valve at this point, diminished pressure in the cylinder will ensure a minimum amount of energy is needed for the upward travel of the piston during the stroke. What power may have been lost by an opening of the exhaust valve when the cylinder is still pressurized is regained through improved exhaust scavenging and reduced backpressure on the piston.

Valve Overlap

When both intake and exhaust valves are open together at the beginning of the intake stroke and end of the exhaust stroke, the condition is known as **valve overlap** **FIGURE 6-34** . Longer overlap periods enhance scavenging. Scavenging is the process of cleaning exhaust gases from the cylinder. Intake air passing across pistons and exhaust valves, which leaves with the departing exhaust, helps cool the piston crown and exhaust valves. Turbocharged engines will use a longer overlap period to take advantage of higher intake pressure and gas inertia.

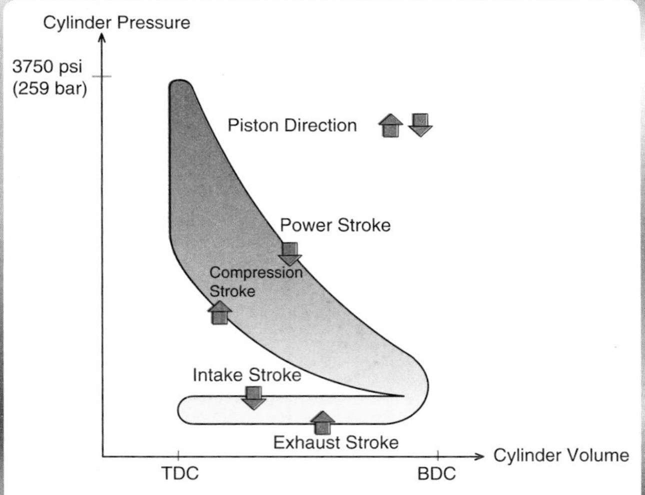

FIGURE 6-33 Cylinder pressure compared to volume for a late-model 12L (732 cubic inch) four-stroke cycle diesel. Note that recent heavy-duty on-highway diesel combustion pressures are now exceeding 3750 psi (259 bar) of cylinder pressure.

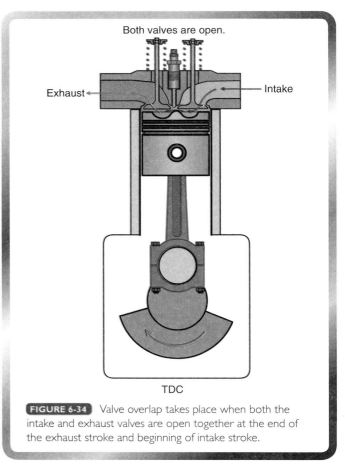

FIGURE 6-34 Valve overlap takes place when both the intake and exhaust valves are open together at the end of the exhaust stroke and beginning of intake stroke.

Valve overlap is an important engine reference point for diesel engines. When diesel engines require adjustment of valves and injectors, the engine must be first correctly positioned so that the valve requiring adjustment is closed. Manufacturers generally provide some method to externally identify TDC or a procedure to identify some other adjustment position, but some do not. Instead, valve overlap in a cylinder is used to identify a cylinder with its piston at TDC. In a six cylinder engine, cylinder piston travel is paired with a companion cylinder for smooth engine balance. As one piston travels upward or downward, its companion movement is synchronized and has the same position in terms of crankshaft rotation. Both pistons will reach TDC at the same time. However, only one of the two cylinders can be adjusted because only one cylinder will have both valves closed at TDC—the end of compression stroke or beginning of power stroke. The paired or companion cylinder will have both valves open during valve overlap period. If the valves of the overlapped cylinder are adjusted incorrectly at TDC, and not 360° later, the engine will be severely, if not catastrophically, damaged.

TECHNICIAN TIP

It is vital to understand valve overlap when working on diesel engines. When diesel engines require adjustment of valves and injectors, the engine must be first positioned so that the valve that requires adjustment is closed. Technicians must verify that the engine is correctly positioned at TDC using the valve overlap method. During overlap, the first cylinder requiring adjustment will have two valves closed; a companion cylinder will have two open valves.

TECHNICIAN TIP

Any engine that pressurizes intake air above atmospheric pressure is referred to as supercharged. Engines without pressurized intake systems are classified as naturally aspirated. Because diesel engines charge the cylinders with just air and no fuel during compression stroke, diesel engines are well adapted to supercharging.

Understanding Valve and Injector Action in a Four-Stroke Cycle Diesel

A hands-on understanding of the relationship between valve position and crankshaft position in a four-stroke cycle diesel engine is foundational to performing any significant type of engine work. The timing of valve opening and closing is especially critical to a technician when adjusting valves and unit injectors; determining engine TDC; installing injection pumps, gear trains, or camshafts; and many other common service tasks. Failure to understand and use the correct service procedures for adjusting valves and performing other engine operations which have a foundation in an understanding of valve action will result in significant damage to valve trains, pistons, and injectors; performance complaints; and installation errors with engine brakes, camshafts, and high-pressure injection systems.

The positioning of valves, injectors, and pistons during engine cycle operation can vary widely depending on an engine's displacement, manufacturer, and application, as well as whether the engine uses exhaust gas recirculation. Naturally aspirated or supercharged air intake systems also use different valve and injector action.

To understand valve and injector action in a four-stroke cycle diesel, follow the steps in SKILL DRILL 6-3. While this skill drill does not directly apply to engine service, it provides critical insights required to develop the skills needed to undertake any engine work.

TECHNICIAN TIP

The SAE references engine rotation from the flywheel end of the engine. Engines can rotate in either a clockwise (CW) or counter-clockwise (CCW) direction. Right-hand rotation is CW, left-hand rotation is CCW. Both systems of notation are found in service manuals. Most engines are CCW or left-hand rotation. Marine engines, some industrial engines, and many rear-mounted coach engines are CW or right-hand rotation. This direction of engine rotation affects the location and direction of rotations of starters, injection pumps, and water-pumps.

Miller Cycle Diesels

In the 1940s, a variation of the four-stroke cycle used in diesel engines was invented by Ralph Miller; it is called the **Miller cycle**. Some refer to it as a five-stroke cycle because the compression stroke is divided into two separate events. Engines using Miller cycle principles essentially change the length of the compression stroke by varying when intake valves close in response to engine load changes FIGURE 6-35. By closing the intake valve

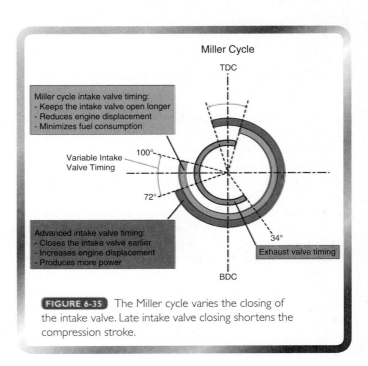

FIGURE 6-35 The Miller cycle varies the closing of the intake valve. Late intake valve closing shortens the compression stroke.

SKILL DRILL 6-3 Understanding Valve and Injector Action in a Four-Stroke Cycle Diesel

1 Select an inline six cylinder assembled engine in the lab with the valves correctly adjusted and the flywheel exposed.

2 Remove a valve cover and identify the intake and exhaust rocker levers.

3 Using a shop manual, OEM service information, or other directions, position the engine at TDC for cylinder 1. The use of timing pins, aligning markers on the front engine dampener, flywheel, or accessory drive pulley are just a few of the many ways TDC can be identified.

4 Use a piece of white chalk to mark the bell housing and the flywheel at the 12 o'clock position with the engine at TDC.

5 Inspect the rocker levers on cylinders 1 and 6. One pair of levers should both be tight and the other pair loose. This happens because one of the cylinders is on valve overlap while its paired cylinder is ending compression stroke and beginning power stroke.

6 Rotate the engine in the correct direction of rotation using a ¾" (19 mm) bar and socket or barring adapter suitable to rotate the engine. Have a partner observe the operation of the rocker levers on one cylinder. When rotating the engine in the correct direction of rotation, the exhaust valve in the cylinder with both valves closed should open first within half of an engine rotation. If the intake valve opens first and more than half of a rotation is needed, the engine is being turned in the wrong direction. Any time valves and injectors are adjusted, the engine must be turned in the correct direction of rotation to adjust the correct cylinder in its proper valve position. Failure to do this could potentially result in catastrophic engine damage.

7 When the exhaust valve just begins to open, as indicated by the disappearance of exhaust valve lash, mark the flywheel with a chalk line and the letters EO (for exhaust opening).

8 Continue to rotate the engine while observing the exhaust valve and note the point in the rotation when it closes. This is indicated by the appearance of valve lash. Mark the flywheel with a chalk line and the letters EC (for exhaust closing).

9 Continue to rotate the engine and observe the intake valve opening and closing. Mark the flywheel with a chalk line and the letters IO (for intake opening) when the intake valve lash appears. Mark the flywheel with another chalk line and the letters IC (for intake closing) when the intake valve lash disappears.

10 If the engine uses unit injectors, mark the flywheel at the approximate time the injector plunger begins to move downward and upward.

11 Record the engine manufacturer and model. Estimate the approximate length of each stroke (intake, compression, power, and exhaust) in degrees using the bolt hole spacing on the flywheel.

12 Summarize your findings by drawing a polar valve diagram like Figure 6-32.

later as the engine load increases, Miller cycle engines reduce NO_x emissions by as much as 30% using a cooler intake air charge. Miller cycle engines provide increased engine efficiency by enabling more advanced injection timing and reducing the energy needed to compress air during the shortened compression stroke.

In diesel engines such as Caterpillar ACERT engines, which use the Miller cycle, series turbocharging is used to transfer some of the work of compressing the air intake charge during compression stroke from the engine to the turbochargers. In other words, the turbochargers compress air more, and less energy is derived from the crankshaft to compress intake air charge. ACERT engines increase turbocharger boost to close to 65 psi (448 kPa) in some models. At this pressure, more air can be packed into the cylinders in a shorter amount of time. Instead of closing the intake valve at 120°–140° before TDC,

the intake may close at 90° and still pack enough air mass into the cylinder. Under those conditions, the engine does not need to work as hard compressing air. Cooling the air before it enters the cylinder also means the pre-ignition air temperatures are cooler, which lowers peak combustion temperatures; lower peak combustion temperatures reduce the formation of NO_x.

Transferring the work of compressing the intake air charge from the crankshaft to the exhaust system uses exhaust energy that would normally be wasted by repurposing the energy to build boost pressure. However, the increased efficiencies are not always available. Late intake valve closing is only beneficial under conditions where boost pressure is high enough. The Miller cycle does not work at low-speed, low-load operation. Electronic controls are needed to change the timing of the intake valve closing to enable conventional valve timing at low speeds and shorten the intake stroke length at high-speed, high-load conditions when turbocharger boost pressure is high. In ACERT engines, a **variable intake valve actuator (VIVA)** mechanism uses oil pressure to actuate a small piston used to hold the intake valve open. The VIVA actuator is currently the closest device used on medium- and heavy-duty diesel engines to produce variable valve timing.

Two-Stroke Diesel Engines

Most CI engines use the four-stroke cycle. However, many applications, both on- and off-road, have benefitted from the use of the two-stroke cycle diesel engine. The **two-stroke engine** performs all of the same combustion cycle events of a four-stroke engine, but they are accomplished with two strokes of the piston and one revolution of the crankshaft **FIGURE 6-36**. Remember, the five events common to all internal combustion engines are intake, compression, ignition, power, and exhaust. The challenge of the two-stroke cycle is to accomplish all five of these events in half the time it takes to complete the same operations in a four-stroke engine.

The two-stroke diesel engine cycle works as follows: As the air–fuel mixture compressed in the cylinder ignites, high combustion pressure pushes the piston downward to produce power stroke. Before the piston reaches BDC, the exhaust valve(s) opens and begins exhausting burned cylinder gases. Next, as the piston continues downward, the intake ports, located in the cylinder wall near the bottom of the cylinder stroke, are uncovered. As the intake ports are uncovered, pressurized air is forced into the cylinder by an engine-driven blower, filling the cylinder with fresh intake air and pushing the exhaust out at the same time., As the piston begins moving upward, it covers the intake ports, and the compression stroke begins. As the

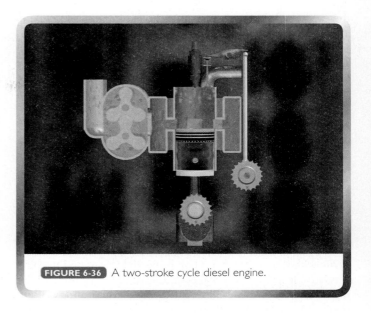

FIGURE 6-36 A two-stroke cycle diesel engine.

piston approaches TDC, fuel is injected into the highly compressed air in the cylinder and the ignition process begins near TDC. When examining the operating cycle, it is essentially the combination of the intake and exhaust strokes that reduces the number of strokes. Like the four-stroke cycle CI engine, the fuel is ignited by the heat of compression. The burning fuel mixture rapidly expands, producing maximum combustion force on the piston at about 10°–15° after TDC, and pushes the piston down **FIGURE 6-37**. The cycle repeats as long as the engine is running. In Detroit two-stroke engines, the intake air blower is driven by

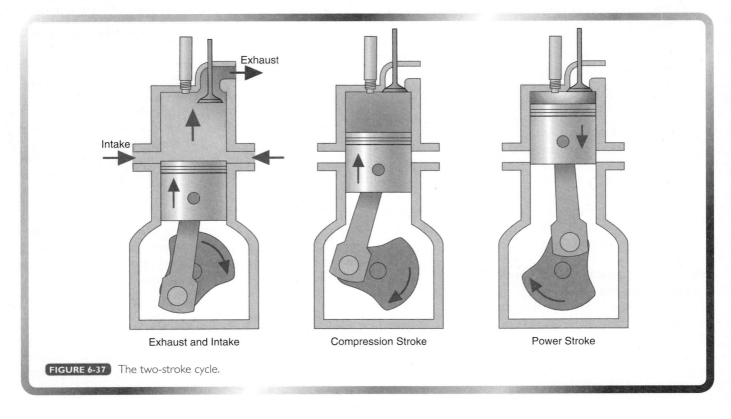

Exhaust and Intake   Compression Stroke   Power Stroke

FIGURE 6-37 The two-stroke cycle.

the crankshaft. Turbochargers are also on high output engines along with the supercharger to improve volumetric efficiency.

Detroit Diesel

General Motors' Detroit Diesel division originally developed the most popular version of two-stroke diesels in the 1930s for US military patrol boats; millions of these 71 series engines were produced and used around the world. Until the late 1970s, this engine represented astounding, advanced construction and operating concepts, which remained mostly unchanged until it was discontinued in the late 1980s. This engine still has, by far, the best hp-to-weight ratio of any diesel. It included innovative features, like modular engine construction with cylinder kits in standard displacements of 51″ (130 cm), 53″ (135 cm), 71″ (180 cm), and 92″ (234 cm) that were used to make inline or V-block engines in 4, 6, 8, and 12 cylinder configurations. A roots blower, a device used on farms to blow grain into silos, was used to pressurize intake air almost half a century before turbocharging became common place. Other features of the two-stroke Detroit Diesel include:

- Weight and power: With twice as many power strokes per engine revolution as a four-stroke cycle engine, the Detroit Diesel two-stroke engine produces more power than a four-stroke diesel of the same displacement
- Response and acceleration: Because each cylinder of a two-stroke engine produces a power stroke every revolution, there is a quick response to load changes. These engines have no turbocharger lag and change speed quickly. The engine is a high-speed diesel, which made it ideal for marine and urban transit bus operation when connected to an automatic transmission.
- Smoothness: Two-stroke engines run smoother than four-stroke engines. The two-stroke cycle distributes the combustion force each cylinder produces, using two lighter power impulses per two revolutions instead of the single heavy impulse of a four-stroke engine. The lighter, more frequent power impulses mean less torsional dampening (the rapid speeding up and slowing down of the crankshaft) is required from the flywheel or torsional vibration dampener.
- Lower exhaust temperatures: More air goes through a two-stroke engine than a four-stroke engine for the same amount of fuel consumed. In fact, in a two-stroke engine up to 30% of the engine cooling is performed by pushing air through the cylinders during scavenging. Additional airflow produces lower exhaust temperature and longer exhaust valve life.

EcoMotors Opposed-Piston Opposed-Cylinder Two-Stroke Engines

New, innovative two-stroke engines developed by EcoMotors use opposed-piston opposed-cylinder (OPOC) technology FIGURE 6-38. Navistar is currently collaborating in the development of this engine technology. Navistar's EcoMotors EM100 design uses two cylinders and four pistons. Outboard pistons take the place of the cylinder head, and each piston only travels

FIGURE 6-38 A prototype of Navistar's EcoMotors EM100.

half the distance needed for a complete stroke FIGURE 6-39. Short stroke lengths enable higher engine speeds. The engine uses a turbocharger with an electric assist that can supply boost pressure during starting. Using a modular engine design, more cylinders can be added in pairs with a clutch between additional cylinder modules. This configuration allows one cylinder pair to start the engine or provide power at light loads. Using a clutch to engage other cylinders keeps power losses, which are caused by moving gases in and out of the engine, to a minimum. Current test engines have achieved 100 mpg (43 km/L) in automotive applications. This technology is likely to be used in trucks and buses for medium-duty engine applications.

The advantages of Navistar's EcoMotors EM100 include:

- 50% fewer parts than an equivalent four-stroke cycle engine
- lower production costs due to few parts
- the cylinder head and valve train are eliminated, which reduces engine complexity
- 15–50% improvement to fuel economy
- high thermal efficiency for a reduced cooling system capacity
- ultra-low exhaust emissions, which may eliminate the need for exhaust aftertreatment systems

▶ Engine Systems

Engine operation also requires other subsystems, which are covered in detail in later chapters. These systems include cooling systems, engine brake systems, fuel systems, lubrication systems, and air induction and exhaust systems.

Cooling Systems

Cooling systems are used to remove excess heat (produced by the combustion process) from the engine. It also has two other purposes: heating the passenger compartment and removing excess heat from the airflow into the intake manifold.

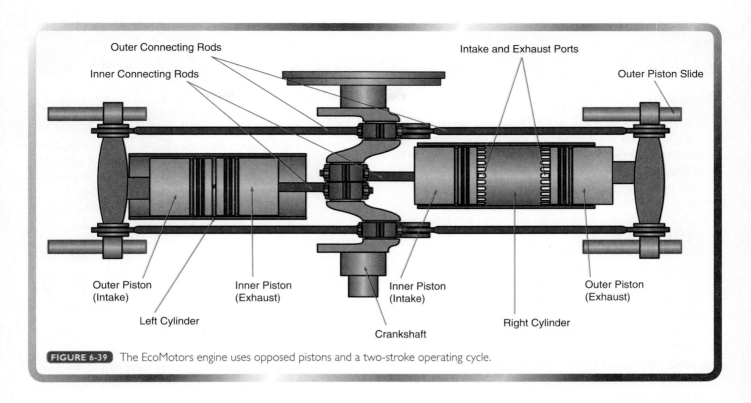

FIGURE 6-39 The EcoMotors engine uses opposed pistons and a two-stroke operating cycle.

Engine Brake Systems

Because diesel engines have less natural retarding force to slow a vehicle than a throttled SI engine, diesels often have an engine-based braking system to supplement service brake operation. Compression release brakes slow the vehicle by releasing compressed air from the cylinder near TDC. Exhaust brakes use exhaust backpressure to slow the vehicle by increasing resistance to engine rotation. When the flow of the exhaust gas through the exhaust system is restricted, the cylinders must work harder to force gases out the exhaust pipe.

Fuel Systems

Diesel engines use high- and low-pressure fuel systems. Low-pressure fuel systems transfer fuel to high-pressure injection systems after cleaning and conditioning the fuel. High-pressure systems essentially meter and pressurize the amount of fuel required for injection. Pressurized fuel is sprayed into the cylinders where it is atomized at the correct time to achieve optimal combustion.

Lubrication Systems

The primary purpose of lubrication systems is to lubricate moving engine parts to reduce friction. Lubrication systems also:

- clean and carry away soot and contamination from cylinder walls and internal engine parts
- cool engine parts such as pistons
- enhance the gas-tight sealing of piston rings to cylinder walls
- reduce engine noise from metal engine part contact

Air Induction and Exhaust Systems

Gas or air flow through an engine is another major engine subsystem. The air induction system is responsible for providing fresh, clean, cool, dry, filtered air to the engine. The exhaust system removes the excess heat and combustion gases from the engine's cylinders.

Wrap-Up

Ready for Review

- An engine is a machine used to convert heat energy produced from burning fuel into mechanical power. Unlike engines, motors do not use combustion to produce energy.
- Combining oxygen with fuel molecules releases heat through a chemical reaction called combustion.
- Engines are classified in a variety of ways, but two of the major classifications are the type of ignition system and operating cycle.
- Most engines used in commercial vehicles are reciprocating engines, which convert the up-and-down motion of pistons in cylinders to rotational motion using a crankshaft.
- Piston rings seal gases in a cylinder, control oil distribution on a cylinder wall, and reduce engine friction.
- Intake and exhaust valves control gas flow in and out of a cylinder. Valve operation is controlled by the camshaft, which lifts and lowers valves with a lobe.
- The valve train mechanism consists of gears, chains, or belts; it synchronizes the valve timing with the crankshaft.
- Flywheels help smooth crankshaft power impulses. Flex plates are used to couple the engine with automatic transmissions.
- The stroke ratio of an engine determines whether the engine is used to haul heavy loads at low speeds or operate at high rotational speeds.
- The small clearance volume of a diesel engine is mostly contained in the piston-formed combustion chamber. Small clearance volumes contribute to high compression ratios.
- A diesel engine's high compression ratio converts more fuel energy into combustion force. Increasing compression ratios reduce fuel consumption while increasing power and thermal efficiency.
- Engine torque, the twisting force an engine produces at the flywheel, is a function of cylinder pressure and the length of the crankshaft throw. High-torque engines can carry heavier loads in higher gears and more quickly accelerate a vehicle.
- Torque output from an engine is varied by changing the amount of air and fuel burned in the engine's cylinders.
- Torque rise is the difference between maximum torque and torque at rated speed. Low torque rise engines are best used where vehicle load and speed constantly vary, such as in urban driving conditions. High torque rise engines are used mostly on highways, where vehicle and engine speed are relatively constant.
- Horsepower measures how much work can be performed in a specified amount of time.
- Brake horsepower is measured at the flywheel. Rated horsepower is the power output of the engine measured at the flywheel at rated rpm or the maximum engine speed under load.

- Fuel economy of a diesel engine is measured as brake specific fuel consumption. BSFC refers to the weight of fuel required to produce one horsepower for 1 hour.
- Engines with high volumetric efficiency fill the cylinders with more air than engines with low volumetric efficiency. Adding turbochargers, increasing the number of valves, and valve timing can improve volumetric efficiency.
- The four parts of the four-stroke engine operating cycle, in sequence, are intake stroke, compression stroke, power stroke, and exhaust stroke.
- Valve overlap is the time in the operating cycle when both the intake and exhaust valves are open together. Large amounts of valve overlap improves an engine's volumetric efficiency, particularly when an engine is turbocharged. Valve overlap is an important reference point used to determine whether the engine is correctly positioned to adjust valves and injectors.
- Miller cycle engines use late intake valve closing to improve engine efficiency and reduce emissions.
- Detroit Diesel and EcoMotors OPOC engines are two examples of two-stroke engines.

Vocabulary Builder

Advanced Combustion Emission Reduction Technology (ACERT) A marketing term used by Caterpillar to describe a variety of technologies used to lower emissions and increase engine efficiency.

bore The diameter of a cylinder.

brake horsepower (BHP) The actual useful horsepower available at the flywheel.

brake specific fuel consumption (BSFC) The amount of fuel required to produce one horsepower for 1 hour, expressed as lb per hp per hour.

clearance volume The space remaining in a cylinder when the piston is at top dead center.

combustion A chemical reaction between fuel and oxygen that releases heat.

compression ratio A comparison between cylinder volume and clearance volume.

crankpin The crankshaft journal which attaches the connecting rod to the crankshaft.

crankshaft The component that converts the reciprocating action of the pistons to a rotational movement and revolves inside the crankcase portion of the engine block.

crankshaft throw The distance between the centerline of the main bearing journal and crankpin journal.

cylinder block The largest structure of an engine, which encloses the cylinders and provides a rigid frame to support the cylinders or cylinder liners, crankshaft, oil and coolant passages, and, in many engines, the camshaft.

cylinder displacement The volume displaced by the piston as it moves from TDC to BDC.

dynamometer A device that measures engine or vehicle road speed and torque to calculate engine power.

external combustion engine An engine that burns fuel outside the engine cylinders.

high idle The maximum speed an engine turns without a load.

horsepower (hp) A measure of engine power, which is a function of both torque and engine speed.

idle An engine's minimum operational speed.

internal combustion engine An engine that burns fuel inside the cylinders.

main bearing journals The crankshaft surfaces located along the crankshaft centerline supported by the main bearing caps.

Miller cycle An operating cycle that uses late intake valve closing and varies the closing of the intake valve.

naturally aspirated An engine that uses only atmospheric pressure, not pressurized air, to charge the cylinders with air.

over-square engine An engine with a stroke that is shorter than the cylinder bore dimension.

peak torque The engine speed where cylinder pressures are highest.

prime mover A term used for engines in off-road equipment, locomotives, and electrical generators.

rated horsepower The power output of an engine measured at the maximum engine speed.

reciprocating engine An engine that uses pistons moving up and down in a cylinder. A crankshaft converts the up-and-down motion into rotational movement.

square engine An engine with an equal stroke and bore dimensions.

stroke The distance traveled by the piston from the top to the bottom of the cylinder

stroke ratio A comparison between the bore diameter and stroke distance of a cylinder, also known as squareness.

supercharged An engine that pressurizes the air intake system to charge the cylinders with air.

thermal efficiency The amount of energy an engine converts into mechanical energy compared to what could theoretically be extracted from a pound of fuel.

torque A measurement of rotational force, or twisting force, transmitted from the crankshaft to the flywheel.

torque rise The difference between peak torque and torque at rated speed.

total cylinder displacement The volume of all of the cylinders in an engine. To find total cylinder displacement, multiply the displacement of one cylinder by the total number of cylinders.

total cylinder volume The sum of the cylinder displacement plus clearance volume.

two-stroke engine An engine that uses an operating cycle that is completed using two piston strokes and one crank rotation.

under-square engine An engine with a stroke that is longer than the cylinder bore.

valve overlap The number of degrees of crankshaft rotation when both the intake and exhaust valves are open.

variable intake valve actuator (VIVA) A device used by Caterpillar ACERT engines to vary the timing of intake valve closing.

volumetric efficiency A comparison between the measured cylinder volume and the volume of air actually filling a cylinder; this measurement is expressed as a percentage.

Review Questions

1. A(n) _____ has equal stroke and bore dimensions.
   a. square engine
   b. over-square engine
   c. under-square engine
   d. camshaft

2. A _____ is a device that measures engine or vehicle road speed and torque to calculate engine power.
   a. bore
   b. crankshaft throw
   c. dynamometer
   d. crankpin

3. _____ is the number of degrees of crankshaft rotation when both the intake and exhaust valves are open.
   a. Total cylinder volume
   b. Partial cylinder volume
   c. Total efficiency
   d. Valve overlap

4. _____ is a chemical reaction between fuel and oxygen that releases heat.
   a. Combustion   c. Compression
   b. Displacement   d. Consumption

5. High idle is the engine's maximum operational _____ without a load.
   a. speed
   b. torque
   c. compression ratio
   d. cylinder volume

6. The _____ is an engine with a stroke that is longer than the cylinder bore.
   a. over-square engine
   b. under-square engine
   c. square engine
   d. semi-square engine

7. _____ is the diameter of the cylinder.
   a. Bore
   b. Combustion
   c. Clearance volume
   d. Total cylinder volume

8. _____ is the sum of the cylinder displacement plus the clearance volume.
   a. Volumetric efficiency
   b. Total cylinder volume
   c. Partial cylinder volume
   d. Clearance volume

9. The _____ is an engine with a stroke that is shorter than the cylinder bore dimension.
   a. over-square engine
   b. under-square engine
   c. square engine
   d. rectangular engine

10. _____ is the distance between the centerline of the main bearing journal and the crankpin journal.
    a. Diameter
    b. Dynamometer
    c. Compression zone
    d. Crankshaft throw

ASE-Type Questions

1. Technician A says an engine harnesses heat from combustion. Technician B says combustion releases heat because of a chemical reaction between fuel and oxygen. Who is correct?
   a. Technician A
   b. Technician B
   c. Both Technician A and Technician B
   d. Neither Technician A nor Technician B

2. Technician A says the bore/stroke relationship predicts the best application for an engine. Technician B says the bore/stroke relationship does not tell us much about the best application for an engine. Who is correct?
   a. Technician A
   b. Technician B
   c. Both Technician A and Technician B
   d. Neither Technician A nor Technician B

3. Technician A says idle is the maximum speed an engine can turn without a load. Technician B says idle is an engine's minimum operational speed. Who is correct?
   a. Technician A
   b. Technician B
   c. Both Technician A and Technician B
   d. Neither Technician A nor Technician B

4. Technician A says combustion ratio is a comparison between the cylinder volume when the piston is at BDC and when it reaches TDC. Technician B says compression zone is the comparison between the cylinder volume when the piston is at BDC and when it reaches TDC. Who is correct?
   a. Technician A
   b. Technician B
   c. Both Technician A and Technician B
   d. Neither Technician A nor Technician B

5. Technician A says brake horsepower is measured with a dynamometer using a brake-like device called a pony brake to apply a load. Technician B says a dynamometer is a device that measures engine or vehicle road speed and horsepower to calculate engine power. Who is correct?
   a. Technician A
   b. Technician B
   c. Both Technician A and Technician B
   d. Neither Technician A nor Technician B

6. Technician A says diesel engines have less natural retarding force to slow a vehicle than a throttled SI engine. Technician B says diesels often have an engine-based braking system to supplement service brake operation. Who is correct?
   a. Technician A
   b. Technician B
   c. Both Technician A and Technician B
   d. Neither Technician A nor Technician B

7. Technician A says that Navistar's EcoMotors EM 100 design uses two cylinders and four pistons. Technician B says that Navistar's EcoMotors EM 100 design uses two cylinders and two pistons. Who is correct?
   a. Technician A
   b. Technician B
   c. Both Technician A and Technician B
   d. Neither Technician A nor Technician B

8. Technician A says the Miller cycle is sometimes referred to as a five-stroke cycle. Technician B says the Miller cycle compression stroke is divided into two separate events. Who is correct?
   a. Technician A
   b. Technician B
   c. Both Technician A and Technician B
   d. Neither Technician A nor Technician B

9. Technician A says changing the time when the intake valve opens and closes cannot impact engine performance. Technician B says that changing the time when the intake valve opens and closes can increase volumetric efficiency. Who is correct?
   a. Technician A
   b. Technician B
   c. Both Technician A and Technician B
   d. Neither Technician A nor Technician B

10. Technician A says the crankcase is usually defined as the area of the cylinder block below the cylinders. Technician B says the crankcase includes the oil pan/sump. Who is correct?
    a. Technician A
    b. Technician B
    c. Both Technician A and Technician B
    d. Neither Technician A nor Technician B

CHAPTER 7
Diesel Engine Emissions

NATEF Tasks

Diesel Engines

General
- Observe engine exhaust smoke color and quantity; determine needed action. (pp 205–206).

Knowledge Objectives

After reading this chapter, you will be able to:
1. Identify and describe the categories of noxious emissions from diesel engines. (pp 199–202)
2. Describe the mechanisms that form noxious emissions in diesel engines. (pp 202–206)
3. Explain common strategies used to reduce noxious emissions from diesel engines. (pp 202–206)
4. Describe emissions standards for diesel engines. (pp 206–211)
5. Identify and describe the major emission monitoring and control systems used to reduce noxious emissions from diesel engines. (pp 211–214)

Skills Objectives

There are no Skill Objectives for this chapter.

► Introduction

Technological innovations in today's diesel are driven by emissions legislation. These legal standards aim to reduce and eliminate the production of noxious substances from all internal combustion engines, including diesel-powered vehicles **FIGURE 7-1**. Technological advances made to meet these standards have not sidelined diesels but instead have produced cleaner engines that are more efficient and powerful. Today's engines also have greater driving refinement and noise reduction than any previous generation of engines.

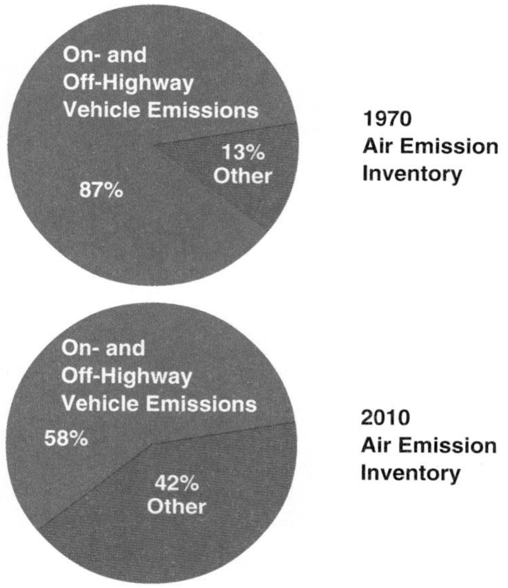

Emissions reduction is a crucial part of engine technology. Identifying the emissions unique to diesels, and how those emissions are formed, enables technicians to better understand engine and emission system operation. Emissions standards also have implications for service practices and procedures because technicians are required to maintain vehicles in compliance with emissions standards. Familiarity with emissions legislation that outlines standards for engine durability, service tool capabilities, on-board communication between electronic control modules, and self-diagnostic capabilities of emission control system operation is also helpful to technicians.

Is Diesel Dirty?

The public perception of dirty diesel is not without foundation **FIGURE 7-2**. Emissions legislation for diesel engines has lagged behind legislation for gasoline engines. Although passenger vehicles were equipped with emissions controls beginning in the late 1950s, the first emissions standards for heavy-duty diesels were not established until the 1970s. One reason for lagging emission standards is that the number of diesel engines in use is small compared to the number of gasoline engines in use. In fact, diesel engines are used primarily in heavy-duty

FIGURE 7-1 Technological innovations that reduce and eliminate emissions have led to a substantial drop in pollution from motor vehicles.

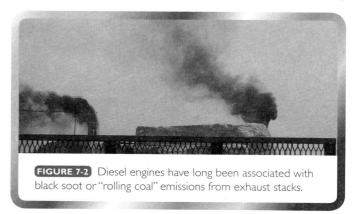

FIGURE 7-2 Diesel engines have long been associated with black soot or "rolling coal" emissions from exhaust stacks.

You Are the Technician

A 2005 truck arrives at your shop with the complaint that the exhaust is blowing excessive black smoke and the engine has low power. The driver has also received a fine for the excessive emissions and has an order to have the vehicle's emission-related defects repaired. You begin to prepare a repair estimate by identifying and diagnosing the possible causes of the power loss and black smoke. One concern you have is whether the engine is too worn out to repair and needs rebuilding. You investigate this possibility by performing a crankcase pressure test according to the manufacturer's recommendations. It turns out that the engine does have excessive crankcase blow-by and the engine is likely too worn to perform any repairs that would reduce the emission- and power-related problems.

1. What parts would you replace during an engine overhaul to minimize blow-by emissions from the crankcase?
2. What other parts would you recommend replacing or testing that may also impact the emissions and power complaints?
3. How are the emissions-related problems possibly related to the reduced power output from the engine?

Diesel engines built after 2010 are approaching near zero emissions in real-world measurements. More particulate is left on the road by a truck's tires than is emitted from its exhaust. One study of late-model diesel engine emissions found that the number of particles in the air of the average living room is higher than in late-model diesel exhaust. A recent study completed by the University of California found that more particulate is produced by charbroiling a single hamburger patty than by driving a MY2007–2010 diesel truck. The study noted that a fully loaded 18-wheeler diesel engine truck would have to drive 143 miles (230 km) at highway speed to produce a mass of particulate equivalent to that produced by cooking a single charbroiled hamburger patty.

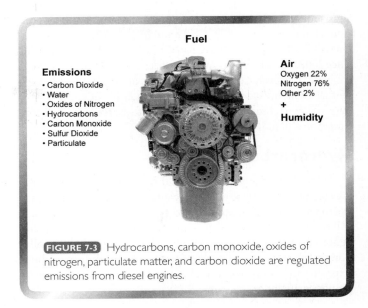

FIGURE 7-3 Hydrocarbons, carbon monoxide, oxides of nitrogen, particulate matter, and carbon dioxide are regulated emissions from diesel engines.

buses and trucks and make up approximately 5% of the vehicle registrations in North America. Emission standards for diesel engines began to become more noticeable as emissions from gasoline-fueled vehicles dropped which made the proportion of emissions produced by diesels rise. Data estimates from the 1980s and 1990s show that diesel contributed more than 50% of the emissions in overall emissions inventories—a disproportionate amount when you consider that diesels are only 5% of the vehicles on the road.

These numbers do not paint the whole picture, however. Actual measurements showed that diesel exhaust made up only 24% of overall air emissions, far lower than estimates predicted by EPA models. Longer distances are traveled by heavy-duty diesels; 40% of total accumulated trip distances are made by diesel-powered commercial vehicles such as buses, heavy trucks, and delivery vehicles. Also, diesel-powered vehicles carry much heavier loads than gasoline-fueled vehicles. And, since 2005, there has been a dramatic increase in the use of diesel-fueled vehicles used for transportation.

For instance, according to statistical data, in the United States in 2011, 23% of fuel used for transportation was diesel. When all of these factors are brought together, the full picture shows that diesels travel much farther, carrying heavier loads, while using less fuel. A diesel-powered vehicle will produce lower emissions than gasoline-powered vehicles for every ton of weight transported per mile. Today's diesels are in fact as clean as, if not cleaner than, gasoline engines. In fact, modern diesels emit close to zero emissions; sensitive, research-grade instruments are now required to even measure emissions emitted from today's diesel vehicles.

▶ Classification of Emissions

All internal combustion engines produce emissions, which are by-products of the combustion of fuel **FIGURE 7-3**. Close to 2000 substances are identified as engine emissions. Not all of these emissions are harmful to humans or plant life. Emissions that are hazardous to human or plant life are identified as noxious and classified into four main categories: hydrocarbons (HCs), carbon monoxide (CO), oxides of nitrogen (NO_x), and particulate

matter (PM). These categories of noxious emissions are referred to as regulated emissions because legislation limits their production from motor vehicles and equipment. Other emissions are not referred to as noxious, but some do fall into the category of **greenhouse gases (GHGs)**. GHGs are believed to trap heat in the atmosphere which contributes to global warming **FIGURE 7-4**.

Carbon Dioxide

An additional emission, carbon dioxide (CO_2), has also been garnering attention recently.

Until 2009, **carbon dioxide (CO_2)**, a by-product of normal combustion, was not a regulated emission because it was not considered toxic to animal or plant life. However, much attention has been given to its role as a GHG, so much so that public interest in reducing the production of CO_2 has turned to regulating CO_2 emissions. Beginning in the United States in January 2009,

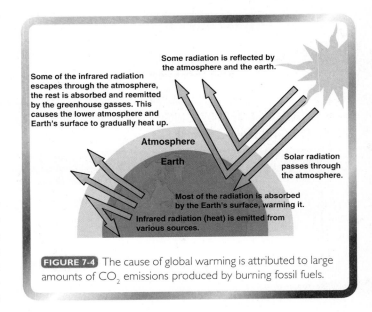

FIGURE 7-4 The cause of global warming is attributed to large amounts of CO_2 emissions produced by burning fossil fuels.

legislation passed imposing mandatory limits on carbon emissions from all motor vehicles **TABLE 7-1** and **TABLE 7-2**. The European Union's EURO standards have had direct limits on carbon dioxide since 2007 but only for passenger vehicles and not trucks. In North America, however, carbon dioxide limits are indirectly regulated by fuel-economy standards. Because carbon dioxide is a normal by-product of combusting carbon-based fuels, reducing fuel consumption will in turn lower CO_2 output.

Hydrocarbons

Hydrocarbon emissions are formed from unburned fuel. Fuels are classified as hydrocarbons because they are made of mostly hydrogen and carbon atoms. Hydrocarbons in the atmosphere will react with NO_2, an oxide of nitrogen, in the presence of sunlight to form **photochemical smog**, which is a form of air pollution resembling a hazy brown or reddish fog in the atmosphere. Exposure to hydrocarbons is also associated with human health problems, including cancer.

Carbon Monoxide

Carbon monoxide is a colorless, odorless, and tasteless gas that is poisonous in concentrations of as little as 0.3%. Carbon monoxide is created as a result of incomplete combustion of carbon-based fuels. This gas was once prevalent in vehicle exhaust gas, in particular when lead was used as a fuel additive. Contrary to common belief modern gasoline-powered vehicles still produce carbon monoxide (even those using electronically controlled combustion systems and catalytic converters) and

can still cause severe poisoning and even death if a person is exposed to exhaust gases in confined spaces where the exhaust gases cannot escape freely into the atmosphere.

Higher compression pressures and excess air used in diesel combustion limits carbon monoxide formation in diesels. Under most conditions, fuel is able to find enough oxygen molecules to react with, and higher compression pressures push molecules more closely together which increases the likelihood of chemical reactions.

Oxides of Nitrogen

Oxides of nitrogen and NO_x are terms for the same category of emissions formed from combining nitrogen with oxygen. There are several different oxides of nitrogen, which the x in NO_x designates, but two are most commonly found in engine emissions. The first is nitric oxide (NO), a colorless, odorless, and tasteless gas that quickly converts to nitrogen dioxide (NO_2) in the presence of oxygen. NO_2 is a reddish-brown, poisonous gas, and it is a major contributor to smog. These gases should not be confused with nitrous oxide (N_2O)—also known as laughing gas—which is used as an anesthetic. Nitrous oxide is also used to boost engine performance when delivered to the combustion chamber through the intake manifold.

NO$_x$ and Smog

Oxides of nitrogen are particularly harmful engine emissions for a couple of reasons. First, NO_x is an essential ingredient to the formation of smog. On warm days in the presence of sunlight,

TABLE 7-1: GHG Standard for Carbon Dioxide Emissions from On-Highway Diesel-Powered Vehicles

Category	Year	EPA CO_2 Emissions (grams/ton/mile)	National Highway Traffic and Safety Administration (NHTSA) Gallons/1000 miles/ton
Medium-Duty	2014	502	4.93
Medium-Duty	2017	487	4.78
Heavy-Duty	2014	475	4.67
Heavy-Duty	2017	460	4.52

TABLE 7-2: 2007 GHG Standard for Carbon Dioxide Emissions from Vocational Applications of Diesel-Powered Vehicles

Category	EPA CO_2 Emissions (grams/ton/mile)	NHTSA CO_2 Emissions Gallons/1000 miles/ton
Light Heavy-Duty Classes 2–5	373	36.7
Medium Heavy-Duty Classes 6–7	225	22.1
Heavy Heavy-Duty Class 8	222	21.8

volatile organic compounds (VOCs), which are chemically reactive molecules containing carbon, cause NO_x to break down and form ground-level ozone (O_3), a noxious gas molecule. Like NO_x, ozone can damage lung tissue, sting eyes, irritate the nose, and aggravate respiratory problems such as asthma and bronchitis. In addition, NO_x emissions can also form nitric acid, contributing to acid rain. Without NO_x emissions from the engine, photochemical smog would simply not form.

Particulate Matter

As the name suggests, particulate matter refers to the combination of liquids and solid particles emitted from the exhaust pipe and crankcase of a diesel engine. Particulate matter originating from the exhaust is observed as soot particles emitted during engine acceleration FIGURE 7-5A. Black carbon mostly makes up this emission. In newer diesel-powered vehicles, particulate emissions are almost undetectable FIGURE 7-5B. Though

less visible, liquids in the exhaust, such as oil droplets and sulfate compounds, are also considered to be particulate matter. Oil droplets make up the bulk of particulate matter originating from the engine crankcase.

Particulate matter is regulated and classified by particle size FIGURE 7-6. Four categories exist: PM-50, PM-10, PM-2.5, and ultrafine PM. PM-50, which is particulate matter smaller than 50 microns in diameter, is the only particulate matter visible to the naked eye, and it falls quickly to the ground. PM-10 is particulate matter smaller than 10 microns in diameter, and PM-2.5 is particulate matter smaller than 2.5 microns in diameter. PM-2.5 is a subset of PM-10, but it is categorized separately because it is considered more hazardous and requires separate accounting. Ultrafine, or nano, particles are those between 5 and 50 nanometers (nm) in diameter. While ultrafine PM accounts for 50–90% of the number of particles in diesel exhaust, it is only 1–20% of the total particulate mass. Fine particles (PM-10 or smaller) remain airborne for days or even months.

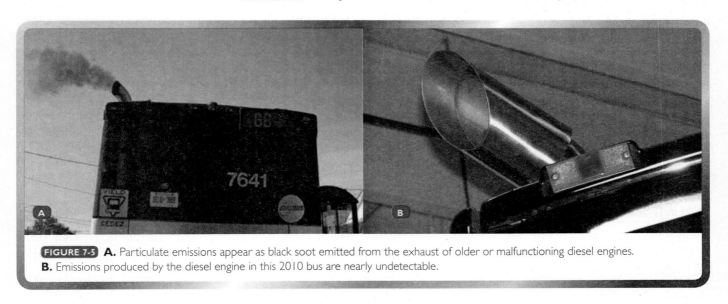

FIGURE 7-5 A. Particulate emissions appear as black soot emitted from the exhaust of older or malfunctioning diesel engines. B. Emissions produced by the diesel engine in this 2010 bus are nearly undetectable.

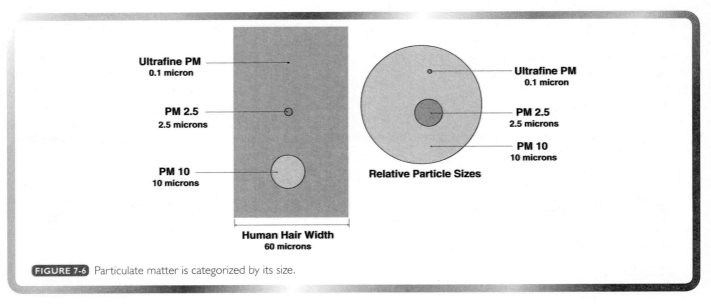

FIGURE 7-6 Particulate matter is categorized by its size.

Airborne particulate matter has many sources; it is estimated that transportation produces nearly a third of total particulate matter. Particulate matter in the atmosphere is responsible for the hazy appearance of the sky on smoggy days. However, the largest proportion of exhaust, ultrafine PM and PM-2.5, is not even visible to the eye because it is microscopic. The small size of these particles is what makes diesel particulate hazardous.

Sulfates

When diesel fuel is refined from petroleum oil that is pumped from the ground, varying quantities of sulfur naturally combine with oil. Burning sulfur contained in fuel produces **sulfate (SO_x)** emissions, which can contribute to air pollution and acid rain. The biggest hazard of burning fuel containing sulfur is that it reacts with other combustion by-products to increase the formation of particulate matter.

Formation of Emissions

Understanding where and how emissions are formed provides helpful insight into the design and operation of various engine systems and strategies that manufacturers have developed to reduce and eliminate emissions from diesel engines. Manufacturers attempt to either prevent the formation of emissions by altering combustion conditions that lead to the production of emissions, or clean up emissions after they are produced. Crankcase controls and exhaust aftertreatment systems are examples of systems used to prevent noxious emissions from entering the atmosphere after they are formed. Most other engine and fuel system technologies are designed to target in-cylinder formation of emissions.

Emission Sources

Diesel vehicles produce emissions from two sources: the exhaust system and the crankcase. Regulatory attention until recently has been given only to exhaust emissions. There are no regulations for evaporative emissions from diesels because negligible emissions are produced from the evaporation of diesel fuel. Crankcase emissions from diesels were regulated beginning under EURO 5 and EPA 07 emission standards, about 40 years after similar regulations began for gasoline engines. This delay in regulations was because emissions from this area of the engine are different and have a smaller environmental impact compared to gasoline engines.

Safety

Exhaust particles smaller than 10 microns are especially dangerous because they remain airborne for a long time and can penetrate into the deepest parts of the lung when breathed in. These small particles within the lungs aggravate respiratory conditions such as asthma and bronchitis. Particulate matter is also believed to carry other toxic, combustion-formed compounds with it into the lungs and bloodstream. Compounds found in soot such as polycyclic aromatic hydrocarbons (PAHs) are carcinogenic; in fact, diesel soot itself is classified by many government agencies as either a probable or known cancer-causing agent. According to reports by the California Air Resources Board (CARB) diesel soot has been responsible for a significantly high level of risk of cancer caused by air pollution.

Exhaust Emissions

Exhaust emissions, also occasionally referred to as tailpipe emissions, consist of waste combustion gases **FIGURE 7-7**. Water, carbon dioxide, and nitrogen make up the bulk of the exhaust content, but harmful carbon monoxide, hydrocarbons, oxides of nitrogen, and particulates accompany the relatively harmless substances. Noxious emissions from diesel exhaust make up 0.2–0.3% of all combustion by-products. In comparison, untreated emissions from spark-ignition engines burning gasoline comprise 1–3%. Exhaust emissions are formed during the combustion process. Injector spray characteristics have a major influence on combustion quality, which in turn influences the types and quantities of emissions produced **FIGURE 7-8**. Diesel engine exhaust emissions are unique due to the higher combustion temperatures and pressures produced through turbocharging and high compression ratios. Diesel fuel properties and the nature of compression ignition operation also change the type of emissions formed and the processes forming them.

Crankcase Emissions

Crankcase emissions are mainly composed of cylinder **blow-by** gas and oil droplets **FIGURE 7-9**. Blow-by is the leakage of air past the piston rings into the crankcase. In any engine, blow-by occurs mostly during the compression stroke. This happens because the piston rings cannot form a perfect gas-tight seal,

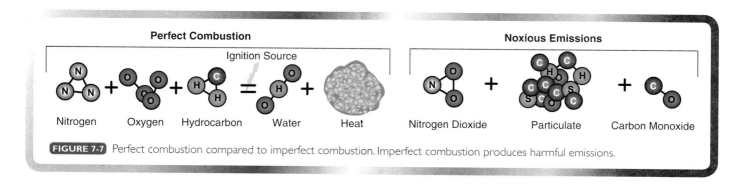

Perfect Combustion

Nitrogen   Oxygen   Hydrocarbon   Water   Heat

Noxious Emissions

Nitrogen Dioxide   Particulate   Carbon Monoxide

FIGURE 7-7 Perfect combustion compared to imperfect combustion. Imperfect combustion produces harmful emissions.

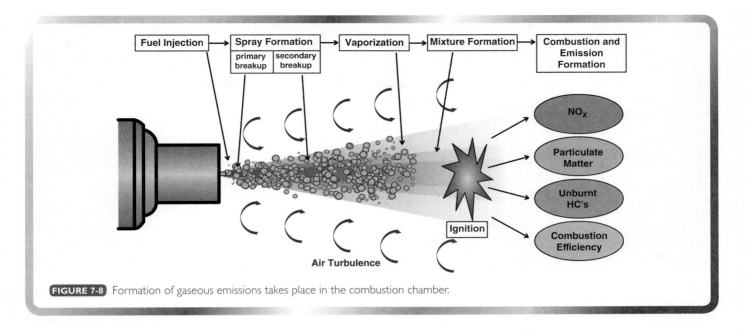

FIGURE 7-8 Formation of gaseous emissions takes place in the combustion chamber.

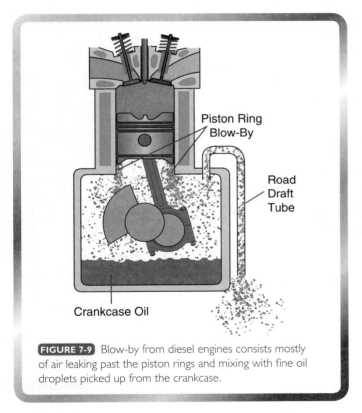

FIGURE 7-9 Blow-by from diesel engines consists mostly of air leaking past the piston rings and mixing with fine oil droplets picked up from the crankcase.

FIGURE 7-10 This 7.3L (445 cubic inch) turbocharged IDI diesel engine has excessive blow-by due to cylinder wear.

which permits some air to leak past the rings. In diesels, only air is present in the cylinder during the compression stroke. This means most blow-by consists of air. During the power stroke when cylinder pressure is highest, little blow-by takes place because the compression rings are tightly sealed. Almost no blow-by takes place during the exhaust and intake strokes. While some blow-by is normal, the volume of blow-by will increase as cylinder walls and piston rings wear **FIGURE 7-10**. In fact, measuring crankcase pressure to evaluate the volume

of blow-by is one of the best measurements of engine wear. Engines with excessively high crankcase pressure typically have a poor piston ring-to-cylinder wall seal, which in turn increases blow-by.

Unless vented to the atmosphere, blow-by gases built up in the crankcase would cause seals and gaskets to leak oil from the engine. Blow-by only becomes a problem when it travels through the crankcase to the atmosphere and picks up droplets of oil thrown from the crankshaft and piston cooling jets. Blow-by containing liquid oil droplets is categorized as a particulate emission. Until 2006, diesel engines could vent crankcase blow-by directly to the atmosphere **FIGURE 7-11A**. Today, diesels are equipped with crankcase controls **FIGURE 7-11B**. Crankcase controls are covered in more detail later in the book.

FIGURE 7-11 **A.** An open crankcase ventilation system used by a 3126B Caterpillar engine. **B.** This Cummins C series engine uses a crankcase ventilation system that separates oil from air using a coalescing filter located inside the housing over the valve cover.

Hydrocarbon Production

Hydrocarbon emissions are composed of unburned fuel and are produced from the evaporation of fuel or from incomplete combustion. Diesel engines produce comparatively little hydrocarbon emissions in contrast to gasoline-fueled engines. With almost no evaporative fuel vapors, hydrocarbon emissions due to fuel evaporation are drastically lower from diesels than from gasoline-fueled vehicles. Diesel cold-start emissions are also negligible in comparison to gasoline engines. Excess air and higher combustion temperatures and pressures ensure more complete combustion of fuel in a diesel.

Evaporative Emissions

Fuel evaporation, such as from a fuel tank, can be a major source of hydrocarbon emissions from gasoline vehicles. However, diesel fuel vaporizes at a higher temperature than gasoline. Diesel fuel's low volatility means little evaporation of fuel takes place from diesel fuel tanks **FIGURE 7-12**. When diesel fuel does evaporate, it exerts very little pressure in comparison to gasoline. For these reasons, there is no requirement for evaporative emissions controls on diesel engines. Diesel fuel does not easily vaporize. This tendency can be easily observed at fuel-pump islands where spilled fuel lingers for days and weeks before disappearing. Lighter, more volatile fractions of the fuel evaporate more quickly. Heavier, more viscous fuel molecules linger on pumps and concrete surfaces longer than spilled gasoline molecules do.

Incomplete Combustion

Incomplete combustion is responsible for the majority of hydrocarbon emissions from diesels. The most common causes for incomplete combustion are:

- Inadequate combustion time
- Improperly mixed air and fuel

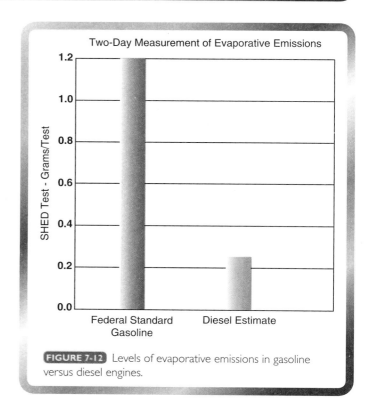

FIGURE 7-12 Levels of evaporative emissions in gasoline versus diesel engines.

- Coarse spray droplets
- Insufficient combustion heat and pressure

Fuel can also sometimes avoid combustion in certain areas around the combustion chamber. One major area where hydrocarbons and carbon monoxide form is above the top compression ring between the piston crown and the cylinder wall in an area called the **crevice volume** **FIGURE 7-13**. Manufacturers' research has discovered that close to 50% of hydrocarbon emissions from diesels originate from fuel trapped in this region.

FIGURE 7-13 Crevice volume.

Carbon Monoxide Production

Carbon monoxide is formed when fuel has only partially reacted with oxygen. With adequate heat, pressure, and combustion time, carbon monoxide would change into carbon dioxide. Low combustion temperatures and pressure, lack of oxygen, or insufficient burn time typically contribute to increased carbon monoxide production from an engine.

Diesel engines produce only very small amounts of carbon monoxide compared to gasoline-fueled engines. Unlike gasoline-fueled engines, diesel-fueled engines do not operate near stoichiometric air–fuel ratios. Generally, diesel combustion uses excess air, which means a greater likelihood of complete reactions between fuel and oxygen; this limits carbon monoxide production. High compression ratios and turbocharging, which increase combustion pressure and push molecules closer together in the diesel combustion chamber, also enable greater likelihood of chemical reactions between oxygen and fuel.

This region prevents proper heating and mixing of fuel with air. The gap between the cylinder head gasket, block deck, and cylinder head is another region contributing to hydrocarbon emissions. In today's diesels, manufacturers have moved the top compression ring closer to the piston crown, and made other modifications to piston design, to minimize crevice volume. The fire ring of the head gasket has also been moved closer to the cylinder in modern engines.

Difficult-to-burn fuel molecules called aromatic molecules cause a characteristic smell from diesel exhaust at idle and low speed. These molecules are complex hydrocarbons which are unusually shaped and sometimes not completely combusted, especially during low speed and load conditions when cylinder pressure and temperatures are reduced **FIGURE 7-14**. Diesel fuel aromatic content is limited by legislation to reduce hydrocarbon emissions and carbon monoxide production.

Oxides of Nitrogen Production

Nitrogen is a relatively inert gas and has many industrial applications where that property is useful (e.g., shock absorbers, welding shielding gas, AC leak detection). In engines, however, high combustion temperatures and pressures eventually cause reactions between nitrogen and oxygen **FIGURE 7-15**. Because nitrogen makes up 78% of air, its sheer volume means a great potential exists to enter combustion reactions. Even though diesel engines produce relatively low levels of HCs and CO emissions, diesel engines have a natural capability to produce far more NO_x than gasoline-fueled engines. Combustion temperatures above 2500°F (1370°C) contribute to NO_x formation. Because diesel fuel burns at close to 4000°F (2200°C), increases in temperatures above 2500°F (1370°C) are easily achieved. Combustion temperature increases above 2500°F (1370°C) also cause NO_x production to increase exponentially. The three main reasons that diesel engines produce higher levels of NO_x are their higher compression ratios, cylinder pressures, and temperatures which accelerate the speed of chemical reactions.

Particulate Matter Production

Particulate matter is formed in the diesel combustion chamber from the tiny drops of fuel sprayed into the chamber near the end of the compression stroke. It's important to remember that these are liquids and not vapors. Vapors—not liquids—burn. Time and heat are needed to convert diesel fuel into vapor.

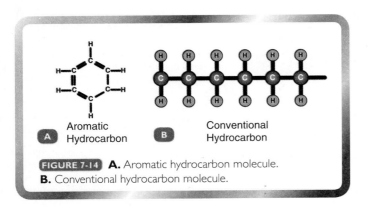

A Aromatic Hydrocarbon   **B** Conventional Hydrocarbon

FIGURE 7-14 **A.** Aromatic hydrocarbon molecule. **B.** Conventional hydrocarbon molecule.

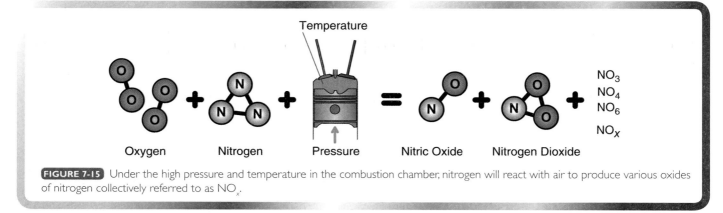

FIGURE 7-15 Under the high pressure and temperature in the combustion chamber, nitrogen will react with air to produce various oxides of nitrogen collectively referred to as NO_x.

The low volatility of diesel fuel promotes poor vaporization, but vaporization is needed for complete combustion. In diesel combustion, there is a limited amount of time for vaporization to take place because fuel is injected near the end of the compression stroke. Because diesel fuel vaporization is poor, liquid fuel burns from the outside in **FIGURE 7-16**. Burning fuel from the outside in, with limited time, heat, and air, will produce a small carbon nucleus; this is the primary component of particulate.

Diesel fuel chemistry also contributes to particulate formation. Carbon, rather than hydrogen, tends to be left over after combustion because it reacts more slowly with oxygen due to the greater number of bonds in a carbon atom. Four bonds are formed by carbon atoms in comparison to a single bond formed by hydrogen. The carbon-to-carbon bonds are especially strong and difficult to break. When carbon-to-carbon bonds are unbroken, black carbon will agglomerate, or chain together, to form black sooty particulate.

The short amount of time to inject, vaporize, distribute, mix, and burn the fuel at the end of diesel's compression stroke means particulate matter production is higher from a diesel engine than in a gasoline engine. Gasoline will vaporize and mix with air quickly during the intake and compression strokes, which also permits more time for improved mixture preparation. A common strategy to reduce particulate formation is to make fuel droplets smaller by using finer atomization.

This is done by using higher pressurization of fuel through an injector with smaller, more numerous spray holes. Particulate matter production can also be reduced by using higher combustion pressures and temperatures to accelerate the burn rate, which causes more complete oxidation of the carbon content of diesel fuel.

Sulfate Production

When diesel fuel is refined from petroleum that is pumped from the ground (mineral petroleum), varying quantities of sulfur naturally combine with the oil. When sulfur burns in the combustion chamber, sulfate (SO_x) emissions are formed. Since the mid-1990s, in North America and around the world, sulfur content has been progressively reduced to minimize SO_x production. In 2007, sulfur content in North America dropped from a high of 500 parts per million (ppm) to a low of 15 ppm. This change followed the use of ultra-low-sulfur fuel used for many years in Europe. Further reductions are scheduled for 2015. No exhaust emission standard currently exists for sulfur compounds alone. Instead, sulfur content in fuel is limited. Regulating sulfur content out of fuel enables the use of sophisticated exhaust emissions aftertreatment systems such as particulate filters, selective catalyst reduction, and NO_x adsorbers. High fuel-sulfur content destroys the ability of these devices to convert noxious emissions into other harmless combustion by products **FIGURE 7-17**.

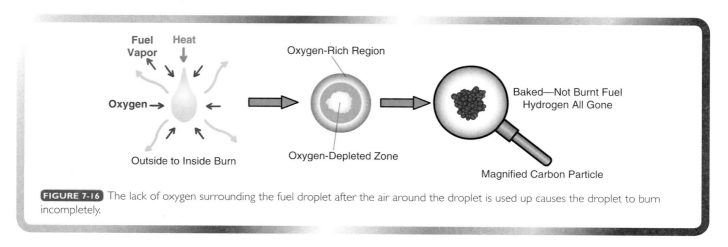

FIGURE 7-16 The lack of oxygen surrounding the fuel droplet after the air around the droplet is used up causes the droplet to burn incompletely.

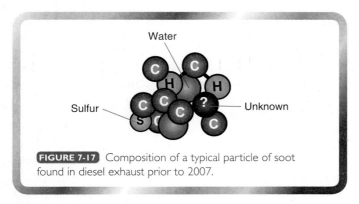

FIGURE 7-17 Composition of a typical particle of soot found in diesel exhaust prior to 2007.

Particulate Emissions and Engine Speed

Maximum engine speed is part of the emissions information on diesel engines. Tachometers in diesel-powered vehicles have a lower maximum engine speed limit than gasoline-fueled engines. Diesel engines cannot turn as fast as gasoline engines because they will not completely burn fuel at high speed. The pre-combustion processes of atomizing, distributing, vaporizing, and mixing fuel with air in the few degrees of engine rotation near the end of the compression stroke requires time. If an engine's piston is rotated too fast through the cylinders top dead center (TDC), not enough time is available to properly complete the pre-combustion mixture preparation stages. In that situation, the engine simply runs out of time to properly prepare and burn the fuel air mixture. If the maximum engine speed limits are exceeded, diesel engines will produce excessive noxious exhaust emissions **FIGURE 7-18**. This is why diesel emission decals have a maximum rated speed and the fuel system governor must limit top engine speed.

▶ **TECHNICIAN TIP**

The maximum engine speed listed on the emission decal is part of the regulatory emission certification for an engine family. Technicians are required to ensure that engine speeds cannot be exceeded through any fuel system malfunction, tampering, service practices, or procedures.

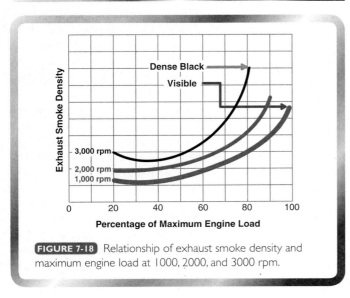

FIGURE 7-18 Relationship of exhaust smoke density and maximum engine load at 1000, 2000, and 3000 rpm.

Carbon Dioxide Production

As with all exhaust emissions that can damage the atmosphere and the environment, carbon dioxide is best known as a greenhouse gas. Internationally, legislation requires vehicle manufacturers to limit CO_2 emissions from their vehicles. Carbon dioxide is a normal byproduct of combustion of carbon-based fuels. Diesel engines offer a good solution to meet both fuel mileage standards and reduce overall CO_2 emissions. Typically, CO_2 emissions from diesels are 30–40% lower than an equivalently powered gasoline-fueled engine. Factoring in the use of biodiesel, a 100% renewable fuel source, the environmental footprint of the diesel engine can be even smaller.

▶ Emissions Standards

Around the world, concerns about the negative environmental and health impacts of vehicle emissions have produced legislated standards for noxious emissions.

The European Union (EU) and the United States have developed two emission standards adopted by most other countries in the world. The greatest number of countries use emission legislation made law by the European Parliament which was phased in between 1993 and 2014. In the EU, there are six progressive stages for reducing emissions beginning with EURO 1 until the most current EURO 6 from 2014. In the United States, the Environmental Protection Agency (EPA) has developed emission standards. The United States and Canada use U.S. EPA standards. China has developed its own standards that closely approximate EURO standards. Japan follows Japanese Ministry of Land, Infrastructure and Transportation (JMLIT) standards **FIGURE 7-19**.

Both EPA and EURO standards regulate nearly the same noxious emissions; the only difference is the classification of hydrocarbons into several different subcategories. GHG emissions, which are vehicle emissions believed to contribute to global warming, are a recent EPA regulation. The EPA has set fuel economy standards for heavy-duty vehicles to reduce carbon dioxide emissions, a major GHG gas, while the EURO standard currently limits carbon dioxide only in light-duty vehicles. While both standards vary in the regulation of light-, medium-, and heavy-duty vehicles, the EPA and EURO emission standards for off-road engines are harmonized with identical standards applying to engines used in heavy equipment, mining, locomotives, and other no-road vehicle applications.

Emission limits and testing procedures are the significant differences between EURO and EPA standards. For heavy-duty engines, EURO and EPA emissions are measured on a dynamometer, which runs the engine only through a precise sequence of changing speed and load conditions to simulate driving in urban and on-highway conditions. Heavy-duty emissions are measured in grams per horsepower per hour, while light-duty emissions are measured in grams per mile or kilometer. Engine testing only, rather than testing the entire vehicle, is necessary because a heavy-duty engine may go into a wide variety of chassis, such as a truck or bus. A more

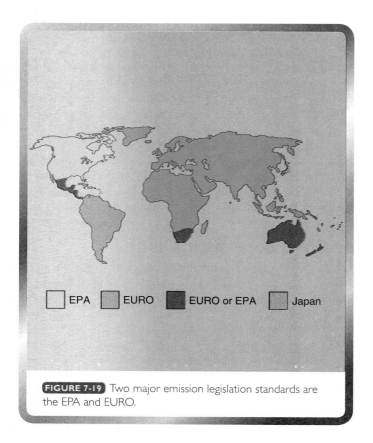

FIGURE 7-19 Two major emission legislation standards are the EPA and EURO.

EPA EURO EURO or EPA Japan

comprehensive and rigorous test procedure performed by the EPA measures emissions under a wider variety of operating conditions with slightly lower maximum emission threshold than the EURO standards.

Sometimes, within an individual country, multiple emissions standards are in force. For example, two sets of emissions standards are used in the United States—a federal standard and a state standard (California). Federal standards are set by the EPA; California standards are set by the California Air Resources Board (CARB). California standards are stricter than federal standards; this is due in part to high population density and geographical factors that contribute to poor air quality in California. California is the only U.S. state permitted by federal law to enact vehicle emissions standards stricter than those set by the federal government. Other states can choose to adopt California's standards, but only California can be the first to surpass standards set by the federal government. The following sections will detail the development of North American emissions standards, applied to diesel vehicles sold there (such as emissions decals and useful life requirements), and specialized standards for different types of diesel-fueled vehicles.

Standards Development

Emissions standards for diesel-fueled vehicles are constantly evolving with emission reductions required by each new standard, causing the development of new technology to reduce emissions. The first emissions standards for diesels were not

established until 1970. These first standards limited peak smoke opacity for heavy-duty diesels. A diesel emissions standard for oxides of nitrogen followed in 1984, and a particulate matter standard was first established in 1988.

In 1993, a new standard required that diesel fuel's typical 5–7% sulfur content be reduced to less than 1%. Reducing fuel's sulfur content helped reduce particulates and minimize corrosion and deposit formation in fuel system components. Maximum aromatic content was limited simultaneously in 1993. European manufacturers reduced sulfur content much earlier and introduced <u>selective catalytic reduction (SCR)</u> systems. SCR allowed optimization of engine power output while reducing particulate emissions close to North American standards without a fuel penalty. Because sulfur content in fuels can poison the most recent converter substrates, ultra-low-sulfur fuel was introduced for the 2007 emission systems; this dropped sulfur content. European manufacturers reduced sulfur content much earlier and introduced SCR systems, an exhaust aftertreatment system for removing NO_x emissions, before using particulate filters. SCR allowed optimization of engine power output while reducing particulate emissions to levels close to North American standards without the fuel penalty in this market which is sensitive to higher fuel prices.

Minimizing the production of emissions produced in the cylinders, rather than exhaust-based reduction, was the traditional control strategy until 2007. Until that point, the problem of diesel exhaust's relatively cool temperatures and air-rich output prevented the use of conventional catalytic converter technology, which is used in automobiles. However, when <u>diesel particulate filters (DPFs)</u>, another exhaust aftertreatment system designed to filter soot particles from the exhaust, were introduced for all on-highway heavy-duty diesels, exhaust-based reduction became a major strategy for reducing diesel emissions.

Until 2009, carbon dioxide (CO_2), a by-product of normal combustion, was not a regulated emission because it is was not considered toxic to animal or plant life. However, because of its role as a GHG, public interest in reducing the production of CO_2 has turned to regulating CO_2 emissions. Rather than regulate CO_2 standards directly, which the EURO standard does only on light-duty vehicles, fuel economy standards are established to indirectly limit CO_2 production. The reasoning is that with reduced fuel consumption, less CO_2 is produced.

Fuel economy standards targeting CO_2 for 2014–2017 are the most recently scheduled emission standards. For tractor-trailer combinations, vehicle emissions standards for 2014–2017 target 7–20% reduction in CO_2 emissions over the 2010 baselines. Vocational vehicles, heavy-duty pickup trucks, and vans must achieve at least a 10% reduction in CO_2.

To meet the 90% reduction in NO_x output for 2010, several SCRs were introduced **FIGURE 7-20**. The most common SCR systems on heavy-duty trucks and buses is liquid SCR. This system uses a urea molecule dissolved in water to break down NO_x. A few light- and medium-duty vehicles manufacture urea molecules in a uniquely designed catalyst.

EPA Standards for New Trucks and Buses

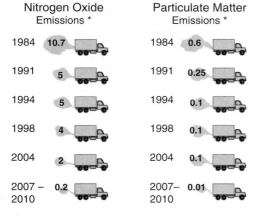

Nitrogen Oxide Emissions *		Particulate Matter Emissions *	
1984	10.7	1984	0.6
1991	5	1991	0.25
1994	5	1994	0.1
1998	4	1998	0.1
2004	2	2004	0.1
2007–2010	0.2	2007–2010	0.01

* EPA's emission standards for trucks and buses are based on the amount of pollution emitted per unit of energy (expressed in grams per brake horsepower hour).

FIGURE 7-20 A comparison between old and new clean diesel technology.

Emissions Decals

One way that countries ensure compliance to emissions standards is by issuing decals. For example, vehicles and equipment sold for on- or off-highway use in North America must have an emission decal affixed to the vehicle or engine **FIGURE 7-21**. The decal contains emissions information indicating to what standard the vehicle or engine is certified. The decal also includes important information for the technician about part replacement and adjustment procedures, software calibration files, and other relevant data that could affect emissions production. For example, on a diesel engine, the decal will contain information about valve lash settings, injection timing, fuel rates, and the presence of emissions system components. Because heavy-duty engines are certified for emissions output in grams per horsepower-hour, decals are affixed to the engine. These engines are used in a variety of chassis configurations, so measuring emissions for distance traveled is impractical. Light-duty vehicle emissions are certified by vehicle type, and emissions are measured in mass units for every mile or kilometer traveled. Emissions decals for light-duty vehicles are placed on the chassis in the vicinity of the engine compartment.

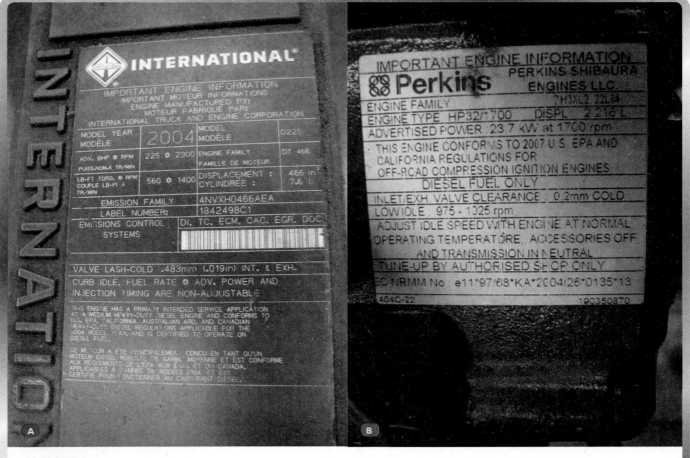

FIGURE 7-21 **A.** An emission decal from a heavy-duty diesel engine. **B.** An emission decal from an off-road diesel engine.

Useful Life Requirement

Starting in 2004, diesel engines must meet emissions standards over what is termed the "useful life" of the engine. The definition of "useful life" depends on the type of engine. In 2004, useful life was defined as:

- Light-Duty: 110,000 miles (177,000 km) or 10 years
- Medium-Duty: 185,000 miles (297,728 km) or 10 years
- Heavy-Duty: 435,000 miles (700,065 km) or 10 years

Useful life now includes not only regulated emissions, but CO_2 as well, so engines must be built more durably to meet these standards. Adaptive strategies must be used to compensate for deterioration factors which could push an engine out of compliance.

Heavy-Duty Standards

Emissions milestones for heavy-duty diesels were updated beginning in 1991 through to 1994; they were also updated in 1998, 2002, 2007, and 2010. This series of updates led to dramatic drops in emissions, with particulate emissions dropping 90% from 2004 to 2007 and both NO_x and particulate dropping 90% from 2007 to 2010 **FIGURE 7-22**. For example, engine manufacturer diagnostics (EMD) apply to all MY2007 and newer heavy-duty engines used in vehicles over 14,000-lb (6350-kg) gross vehicle weight rating (GVWR). Also starting in MY2007, crankcase emission controls were required. On turbocharged engines, the crankcase could be vented to the atmosphere, but the weight of crankcase emissions was totaled with exhaust emissions. However, crankcase controls are more practical for heavy-duty diesels because deterioration of crankcase emissions with engine wear was added to the exhaust deterioration factors. Emission standards for 2010, EPA 10, heavy-duty diesels were:

- Particulate matter: 0.01 g/bhp-hr
- Oxides of nitrogen: 0.20 g/bhp-hr
- Non–methane hydrocarbon (NMHC): 0.14 g/bhp-hr

Heavy-duty on-board diagnostics (HD-OBD) are part of the newest emission legislation and use a more sophisticated set of emission standards that were introduced in 2010. A phase-in period from one engine family from a manufacturer to all engine families was required by 2013. HD-OBD standards are developed continuously by the Society of Automotive Engineers (SAE) and adopted on a yearly basis by the EPA as a legislated standard. The HD-OBD system is designed to detect potential conditions which could lead to excessive emissions **FIGURE 7-23**.

Off-Road Standards

Standards for off-road equipment are different than those for on-highway equipment **FIGURE 7-24**. These standards are referred to as Tier 1, 2, 3, and 4 emission standards and are harmonized worldwide with European standards. Tier 1, established in 1994 and phased in between 1996 and 2000, represents the earliest phase in increasingly stricter emission limits, with Tier 4 being the final, cleanest, standard of the four phases. These standards are based on horsepower ratings, with larger horsepower engines taking longer to implement emissions standards. Off-road diesels have emission standards applied depending on the power and year the engine is produced. Emission standards lag on-highway engines but approach the same levels by the 2015–2020 phase-in period. Tier 1 standards remained in effect until the Tier 2 and/or Tier 3 standards took effect. Tier 2 and Tier 3 standards were established in 1998 to be phased-in for various horsepower ratings between 2001 and 2008. An interim Tier 4 standards phase-in began in 2011, and a final standard began being implemented in 2013. Emission standards for off-road equipment lag on-highway engines but will eventually approach the same levels **FIGURE 7-25**.

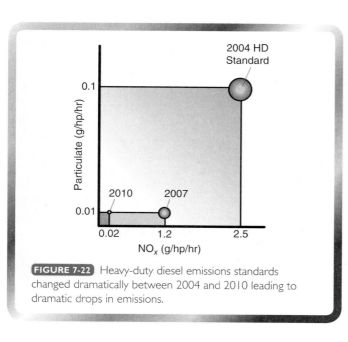

FIGURE 7-22 Heavy-duty diesel emissions standards changed dramatically between 2004 and 2010 leading to dramatic drops in emissions.

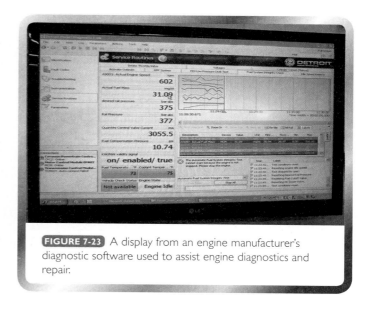

FIGURE 7-23 A display from an engine manufacturer's diagnostic software used to assist engine diagnostics and repair.

U.S. EPA On-Highway Standards

	2004–2006	2007–2009	2010
>33,000 lb GVWR	United States '04	United States '07	United States '10
19,500 to 33,000 lb GVWR			
8500 to <19,500 lb GVWR*			
Light Duty**	Tier 2 (phase-in 2004–2009)		

* Note: Heavy-duty vehicles between 8500–14,000 lb GVW have the option of certifying engine or doing a whole certification using a chassis dynamometer (starting 2008).

**Note: Medium-duty passenger vehicles in the 8500–14,000 lb GVW are included in the Tier 2 arrangements.

U.S. EPA Off-Highway Standards

	2006	2007	2008	2009	2010	2011	2012	2013	2014	2015
175 + hp	Tier 3					Tier 4				
100 to 175 hp	Tier 2	Tier 3					Tier 4			
75 to 100 hp	Tier 2		Tier 3				Tier 4			
<75 hp	Tier 2		Tier 4							

FIGURE 7-24 Tier standards for off-highway and on-highway engines.

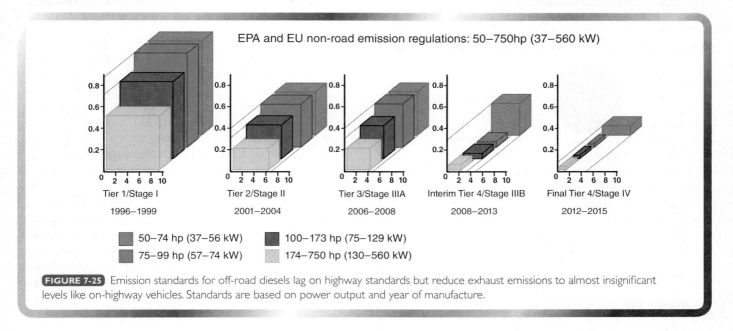

FIGURE 7-25 Emission standards for off-road diesels lag on highway standards but reduce exhaust emissions to almost insignificant levels like on-highway vehicles. Standards are based on power output and year of manufacture.

Testing Emissions

EURO and EPA emission standards measure emission outputs recorded when a dynamometer is placed on either an engine or chassis **FIGURE 7-26**. Chassis dynamometers measure emissions based on distance traveled by the complete vehicle. Before a vehicle or engine can be certified for use on or off highway, the test protocol, which is a precise schedule of varying speed and load conditions, must be completed to determine whether the vehicle or engine emissions remain below the maximum limits through the test cycle. The mass of emissions produced by the engine or vehicle is collected and measured during the driving cycle.

Opacity Testing

Opacity testing is the common measurement for evaluating smoke density from diesel engines. This is based on the principle of light extinction by exhaust smoke. A beam of light of a particular wavelength is passed through a sample of smoke **FIGURE 7-27**. Opacity, the measure of smoke density, is based

on the percentage of light blocked. The darker the smoke, the higher the percentage of opacity. A measure of 75% opacity means 75% of the light is blocked, while 25% is transmitted. The procedure used by law enforcement agencies to measure smoke emissions is based on the SAE J1667 Snap Acceleration Test. This is a non-moving vehicle test which can be conducted along the roadside, in a truck stop, at a vehicle repair facility, or at inspection maintenance test facilities. The Snap Acceleration Test is intended to be used on heavy-duty trucks and buses powered by diesel engines. The procedure is intended to provide an indication of the state of maintenance and/or tampering of the engine and fuel system relative to the factors that affect exhaust smoke.

▶ Emission Control and Monitoring Systems

Emissions standards require that manufacturers monitor and control diesel engine emissions. While certain monitoring systems are required for diesel engines, manufacturers are relatively free to

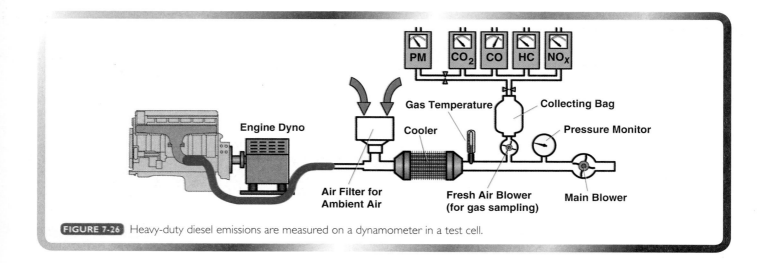

FIGURE 7-26 Heavy-duty diesel emissions are measured on a dynamometer in a test cell.

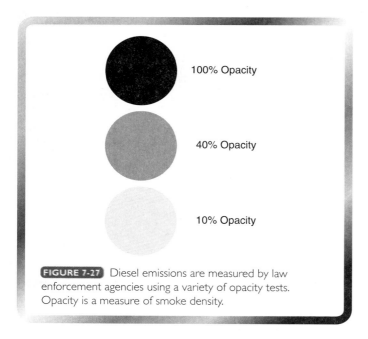

100% Opacity

40% Opacity

10% Opacity

FIGURE 7-27 Diesel emissions are measured by law enforcement agencies using a variety of opacity tests. Opacity is a measure of smoke density.

determine how they will control emissions to meet standards, as long as they do meet the standards. They design systems and processes that will effectively and cost-efficiently meet the standards. This section will detail several common emission monitoring and control systems.

Diesel Engine Emission Controls

Diesel emissions can be controlled in a variety of ways. Common emissions controls will be discussed in detail in other chapters in this volume. Some examples of engine technology required to meet the 2007–2010 Engine Manufacturers Diagnostics or EPA-07 standards include:

- Common rail injection with injection rate shaping
- Unit injection with injection rate shaping capabilities
- Low- and high-pressure cooled exhaust gas recirculation (EGR)

- Variable geometry turbochargers (VGTs)
- Charge air cooling (CAC)
- Two-way oxidation converters (DOCs)
- Diesel particulate filters (DPFs)
- Selective catalyst reduction (SCR)
- NO_x traps and NO_x adsorbers
- Exhaust gas sensors—wide range oxygen and NO_x

Diesel Engine Emission Monitors

Major engine systems which influence the production of emissions are monitored by the EMD or HD-OBD systems. These monitors are essentially diagnostic strategies used to determine if an emission system is functioning correctly. As detailed earlier, EMD, a pre HD-OBD emission monitoring system, and HD-OBD are used on heavy-duty diesels.

Engine Manufacturer Diagnostics

EMD systems are required in all MY2007 and newer heavy-duty engines used in vehicles over 14,000-lb (6350-kg) GVWR. EMD systems check the functioning of the fuel delivery system, exhaust gas recirculation system, particulate filter, and emissions-related circuit continuity and rationality for the engine control module (ECM) inputs and outputs. To detect emission system malfunctions, the diagnostic manager, a piece of software installed in the ECM, checks to detect any condition which could potentially cause emissions to exceed maximum threshold limits. Major **emission monitors** in EMD systems are listed in **TABLE 7-3**.

A diagnostic data link connector located below the dash and to the left of the steering column has six or nine pins and is used to access SAE fault codes from on-highway trucks and buses. The fastest and most modern communication protocol between service tools and vehicle networks is J-1939. Data is transmitted in both directions between the vehicle and service tool using a nine-pin data link connector.

TABLE 7-3: Engine Manufacturer Diagnostics

Engine System	System Analysis
Fuel system	• Fuel pressure • Fuel-injection quantity • Multiple fuel-injection event performance • Fuel-injection timing • Exhaust gas sensor monitoring (NO_x and O_2 only)
Misfire monitoring	• Must detect misfire occurring continuously in one or more cylinders during idle.
EGR system	• EGR flow rate • EGR response rate • EGR cooling system • Mass air flow rate
Boost-pressure control systems	• Under- and over-boost malfunctions • Wastegate operation • Slow turbocharger response • Charge air cooler efficiency
Glow plugs	• On-time • Glow plugs enabled • Intake heater operation
Diesel exhaust aftertreatment systems (Monitor requires potential faults to be detected before emissions exceed standards for any of the following systems)	• Oxidation catalyst • Lean NO_x catalyst • SCR catalyst • NO_x trap • PM trap

Heavy-Duty On-Board Diagnostics

HD-OBD emissions standards for heavy-duty diesel-fueled engines began in 2010. HD-OBD has many specific standards governing everything from the style, type, and location of electrical and diagnostic connections, to communication standards, emissions thresholds, fault code structure and emission monitoring strategies. The **malfunction indicator lamp (MIL)** joined other lamps on the instrument panels of heavy-duty vehicles to meet HD-OBD requirements **FIGURE 7-28**. Whenever an emission-related fault exceeds a threshold level, the MIL is required to switch on to alert the driver of a potential fault **FIGURE 7-29**. More about HD-OBD system operation is found in other chapters in this volume. HD-OBD monitors include the features listed in **TABLE 7-4**.

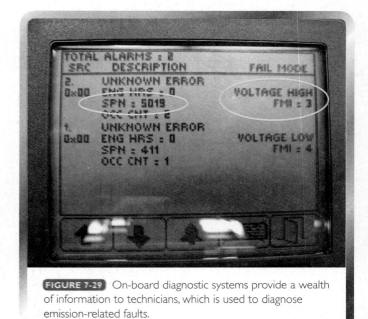

FIGURE 7-29 On-board diagnostic systems provide a wealth of information to technicians, which is used to diagnose emission-related faults.

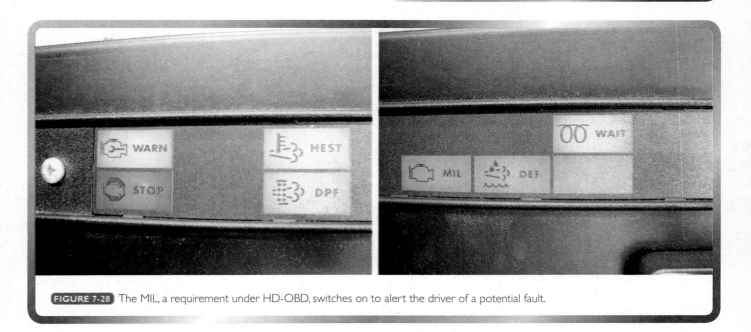

FIGURE 7-28 The MIL, a requirement under HD-OBD, switches on to alert the driver of a potential fault.

TABLE 7-4: On-Board Diagnostics (OBD)

Engine System	System Analysis
NMHC	
Catalyst conversion monitors	• Diesel oxidation catalyst • Diesel oxidation catalyst efficiency monitor • DPF regeneration assistance monitor • Diesel oxidation catalyst SCR assistance monitor
NO_x converting catalyst monitoring	• Selective catalyst reduction catalyst • Efficiency monitor • Selective catalyst reduction feedback • Control monitors • Selective catalyst reduction tank level
Misfire monitor	• Similar in function to EMD but does not set the MIL
Fuel system monitor	• Fuel rail pressure sensor circuit • Fuel rail pressure sensor range • Injector code missing or invalid • Fuel system injection pressure control • Fuel rail pressure monitors • Injection timing • Injection quantity • Zero fuel calibration • Feedback controls
Exhaust gas sensor monitor	• Air–fuel ratio sensors: tailpipe NO_x • O_2 sensor control module
EGR system monitor	• EGR rate system monitor • EGR cooler/EGR cooler bypass monitor • EGR system slow response • EGR closed-loop control limits monitor • Mass airflow closed-loop control limits monitor
Boost-pressure control system monitor	• Intrusive turbo position and response monitoring • Intrusive wastegate monitoring • Functional overboost monitoring • Functional underboost monitoring • Threshold underboost monitoring • Charge air cooler monitoring
Particulate filter monitor	• DPF filter efficiency and missing substrate monitors • DPF frequent regeneration monitor • DPF incomplete regeneration monitor • DPF feedback control monitors • DPF restriction monitor
Crankcase ventilation pressure	• Crankcase pressure is monitored but faults do not set the MIL.
Cold start and warm-up monitoring	
Glow plug resistance monitor	• Glow plugs enabled • Glow plug resistance • Intake heater operation
Comprehensive component monitor (CCM)	• All circuit monitoring for components supporting other monitors and powertrain control operation are the same as EMD.

Comprehensive Component Monitoring (CCM)

The CCM is part of the HD-OBD system. Its function is to monitor electrical circuits operating powertrain components that:

- Can cause a measurable emissions increase during any reasonable driving conditions
- Are used for other OBD monitors
- Are required to monitor input components for circuit and rationality faults
- Are required to monitor output components for functional faults

The CCM is not tied to emission thresholds. Any electrical problem related to emission systems will cause the MIL to illuminate.

Wrap-Up

Ready for Review

▸ Emissions legislation requiring reduction of vehicle emissions drives most changes in engine technology.

▸ Emissions from modern diesel engines are so low that only test instruments with the highest sensitivity can measure their exhaust emissions.

▸ Diesel engines produce lower emissions per ton of weight carried than gasoline engines.

▸ Noxious emissions from diesels comprise 0.2–0.3% of untreated exhaust compared to as much as 3% from spark-ignition, gasoline-fueled engines.

▸ Diesel-powered vehicles travel farther carrying heavier loads while using less fuel than spark-ignition engines.

▸ If motor vehicles produced no NO_x emissions, photo-chemical smog would not exist.

▸ Diesel engines produce more NO_x and particulate emissions than spark-ignition engines, but they produce lower levels of hydrocarbons and carbon monoxide emissions.

▸ Most diesel exhaust particulate emissions is composed of black carbon or soot.

▸ NO_x formation is a major emission problem plaguing diesel engines due to their higher compression ratios, cylinder pressures, and temperatures.

▸ Diesel fuel does not produce significant evaporative emissions, and diesel fuel systems are not regulated for evaporative emissions.

▸ Crankcase emissions are classified as particulates because they contain oil droplets.

▸ Excess air, higher combustion temperatures, and pressure in diesel engines means lower amounts of hydrocarbons and carbon monoxide emissions are produced.

▸ Diesel fuel properties and the short time fuel has to mix with air and burn contribute to higher amounts of particulate formed in engine cylinders.

▸ Hard-to-burn fuel molecules called aromatic molecules produce the distinctive odor of diesel exhaust.

▸ Reducing sulfur content in fuel reduces particulate formation.

▸ Finer atomization of fuel reduces particulate formation.

▸ Carbon dioxide emissions constitute a greenhouse gas (GHG) and as such are regulated indirectly through fuel economy standards.

▸ The Environmental Protection Agency (EPA) and the EURO 1–6 set the emission standards for most of the world.

▸ The use of ultra-low-sulfur diesel fuel has enabled the use of exhaust aftertreatment systems such as Selective Catalyst Reduction (SR) systems and particulate filters.

▸ Emission decals indicating compliance with emission standards are required by all on- and off road diesel engines.

▸ Heavy-duty diesels have a durability requirement to remain emission compliant and not exceed certification limits for 10 years or 435,000 miles (700,065 km).

▸ EPA and EURO (EEA) emission standards are harmonized for off-road diesel engines.

▸ Exhaust opacity is a measurement of exhaust smoke density. Higher opacity means the smoke is darker.

▸ On-board diagnostic system monitor the engine operation to detect the presence of any fault which could potentially cause increased emissions.

▸ The malfunction indicator lamp (MIL) illuminates whenever an emission-related fault is detected by the on-board diagnostic system.

Vocabulary Builder

<u>blow-by</u> The leakage of air past the piston rings into the crankcase.

<u>carbon dioxide (CO_2)</u> A harmless, colorless, odorless gas which is a by-product of combustion. It is also classified as a greenhouse gas (GHG).

<u>carbon monoxide (CO)</u> A regulated poisonous gas emission which is odorless, colorless, and tasteless. It is a by-product of incomplete combustion.

<u>crevice volume</u> The area above the top compression ring between the piston crown and the cylinder wall.

<u>diesel particulate filter (DPF)</u> A device installed in the exhaust system to filter out black carbon soot and other particulate from the exhaust stream.

<u>emission monitor</u> A diagnostic strategy used by the engine control module to evaluate whether emission-related systems are functioning correctly.

<u>engine manufacturer diagnostics (EMD)</u> A pre HD-OBD standard for an on-board diagnostic system used to detect emission related faults.

<u>greenhouse gas (GHG)</u> A gas classified as contributing to global warming because it traps heat in the atmosphere.

<u>heavy-duty on-board diagnostics (HD-OBD)</u> The most recent EPA standard for detecting emission-related faults in heavy-duty vehicles.

<u>hydrocarbon (HC)</u> A molecule, often a fuel, composed of hydrogen and carbon atoms.

<u>malfunction indicator lamp (MIL)</u> A dash-mounted warning light used to alert the driver when an emission-related fault is detected by the on-board diagnostic system.

<u>opacity</u> A measure of the percentage of light blocked by exhaust smoke which is used to evaluate exhaust gas density.

<u>oxides of nitrogen (NO_x)</u> A category of noxious emissions made up of oxygen and nitrogen.

<u>ozone</u> A noxious gas molecule composed of three oxygen molecules.

particulate matter (PM) A category of noxious emissions composed of a combination of very small solid or liquid particles.

photochemical smog A type of air pollution that gives the atmosphere a hazy, reddish-brown color.

selective catalyst reduction (SCR) An exhaust aftertreatment system designed to break down NO_x gases in the exhaust system into harmless substances.

Tier 1, 2, 3, and 4 emission standards Consecutive phases of increasingly cleaner off-road emission standards.

volatile organic compound (VOC) Any carbon-containing molecule that is highly reactive.

Review Questions

1. _____ is a gas classified as contributing to global warming because it traps heat in the atmosphere.
   a. Carbon monoxide (CO)
   b. Greenhouse gas (GHG)
   c. Carbon dioxide (CO_2)
   d. Ozone

2. _____ is a type of air pollution that gives the atmosphere a hazy, reddish-brown color.
   a. Fog
   b. Soot
   c. Photochemical smog
   d. Ozone

3. _____ is a harmless, colorless, odorless gas which is a by-product of combustion.
   a. Carbon dioxide (CO_2)
   b. Carbon monoxide (CO)
   c. Nitrous oxide
   d. Hydrocarbon

4. _____ is a noxious gas molecule composed of three oxygen molecules.
   a. Photochemical smog
   b. Greenhouse gas
   c. Hydrocarbon
   d. Ozone

5. Close to _____ of hydrocarbon emissions from diesel engines originate from the crevice volume.
   a. 25%
   b. 40%
   c. 50%
   d. 75%

6. Particulate matter between _____ nanometers in diameter is classified as nano or ultrafine.
   a. 5 and 50
   b. 0 and 50
   c. 10 and 50
   d. 5 and 60

7. Emission standards for off-road equipment are referred to as _____ 1, 2, 3, and 4 emission standards.
   a. level
   b. tier
   c. grade
   d. stage

8. Hydrocarbons in the atmosphere react with _____ in the presence of sunlight to form photochemical smog.
   a. CO_2
   b. NO_2
   c. CO
   d. GHG

9. Volatile organic compounds cause _____ to break down and form ground-level ozone.
   a. NO_x
   b. CO_2
   c. hydrocarbon
   d. CO

10. The first emissions standards limited peak smoke _____ for heavy-duty diesels.
    a. opacity
    b. density
    c. volume
    d. smog

ASE-Type Questions

1. Technician A says that technological advances made to meet emissions standards have produced cleaner engines. Technician B says these technological advances have also made engines more efficient and powerful. Who is correct?
   a. Technician A
   b. Technician B
   c. Both Technician A and Technician B
   d. Neither Technician A nor Technician B

2. Technician A says a truck's tires leave more particulate on the road than late-model diesel engine emissions. Technician B says late-model diesel engines leave more particulate on the road than a truck's tires. Who is correct?
   a. Technician A
   b. Technician B
   c. Both Technician A and Technician B
   d. Neither Technician A nor Technician B

3. Technician A says ozone does not damage the human body. Technician B says ozone is not harmful to organs, but can sting the eyes and irritate the nose. Who is correct?
   a. Technician A
   b. Technician B
   c. Both Technician A and Technician B
   d. Neither Technician A nor Technician B

4. Technician A says fuel injector spray characteristics do not impact the exhaust emissions produced. Technician B says fuel injector spray characteristics influence the type and quantity of exhaust emissions produced. Who is correct?
   a. Technician A
   b. Technician B
   c. Both Technician A and Technician B
   d. Neither Technician A nor Technician B

5. Technician A says difficult-burn fuel molecules called aromatic molecules cause a characteristic smell from diesel exhaust at high speed. Technician B says the smell is caused from diesel exhaust at idle and low speeds. Who is correct?
   a. Technician A
   b. Technician B
   c. Both Technician A and Technician B
   d. Neither Technician A nor Technician B

6. Technician A says diesel engines have a higher maximum engine speed than gasoline engines because of how well they burn fuel at high speed. Technician B says diesel engines have a lower engine speed than gasoline engines because they completely burn fuel at high speed. Who is correct?
   a. Technician A
   b. Technician B
   c. Both Technician A and Technician B
   d. Neither Technician A nor Technician B

7. Technician A says vehicles sold for on- or off-highway use in North America must have an emission decal affixed to the vehicle or engine. Technician B says the same is true for equipment sold for on- or off-highway use in North America. Who is correct?
   a. Technician A
   b. Technician B
   c. Both Technician A and Technician B
   d. Neither Technician A nor Technician B

8. Technician A says opacity testing is the common measurement for evaluating greenhouse gases from diesel engines. Technician B says opacity testing is the common measurement for evaluating smog density from diesel engines. Who is correct?
   a. Technician A
   b. Technician B
   c. Both Technician A and Technician B
   d. Neither Technician A nor Technician B

9. Technician A says EMD systems check the functioning of the fuel delivery system, exhaust gas recirculation system, and particulate filter. Technician B says EMD systems also check the emissions-related circuit continuity and rationality for the engine control module inputs and outputs. Who is correct?
   a. Technician A
   b. Technician B
   c. Both Technician A and Technician B
   d. Neither Technician A nor Technician B

10. Technician A says particulate matter is a category of noxious emissions composed of a combination of very small solid or liquid particles. Technician B says particulate matter is a category of noxious emissions composed of only very small liquid particulates. Who is correct?
    a. Technician A
    b. Technician B
    c. Both Technician A and Technician B
    d. Neither Technician A nor Technician B

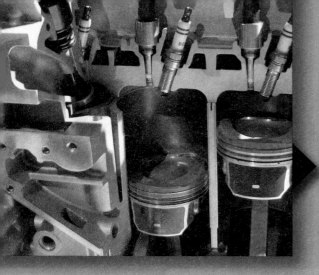

NATEF Tasks

Diesel Engines

General

- Listen for engine noises; determine needed action. (pp 224, 226, 228–229)
- Observe engine exhaust smoke color and quantity; determine needed action. (pp 216–218, 223)
- Check engine no cranking, cranks but fails to start, hard starting, and starts but does not continue to run problems; determine needed action. (pp 216–217, 223)

- Identify engine surging, rough operation, misfiring, low power, slow deceleration, slow acceleration, and shutdown problems; determine needed action. (pp 224, 226)
- Identify engine vibration problems. (pp 218, 229)

Air Induction and Exhaust System

- Inspect and test preheater/inlet air heater, or glow plug system and controls; perform needed action. (pp 232–233)

Knowledge Objectives

After reading this chapter, you will be able to:

1. Classify and describe types of diesel engine combustion chambers. (pp 221–222, 224)
2. Identify and describe the unique operating features and characteristics of diesel engines. (pp 214–215)
3. Describe and explain factors which influence compression ignition combustion characteristics. (pp 215–217)
4. Identify limiting factors for spark and compression ignition system efficiency. (pp 213, 216–217)
5. Identify and explain the effects of fuel system properties on diesel combustion. (pp 220–221)
6. Predict factors that will negatively affect combustion efficiency. (pp 217–218)
7. Identify technology and operating strategies which reduce combustion chamber noise. (pp 224, 226)
8. Identify and explain the effects of abnormal combustion. (pp 226–229)
9. Recommend practices to follow when making performance upgrades and improving cold-starting. (pp 223–224)
10. Define and explain terminology associated with combustion principles and compression ignition. (pp 212, 214–233)

Skills Objectives

After reading this chapter, you will be able to:

1. Measure idle time. (p 236) **SKILL DRILL 8-1**
2. Adjust idle speed and the shut-down timer. (p 236) **SKILL DRILL 8-2**
3. Inspect air intake heaters and glow plugs. (p 240) **SKILL DRILL 8-3**

▶ Introduction

<u>Combustion</u> is a chemical reaction between oxygen and fuel molecules in which heat is released. For technicians, understanding engine combustion principles is fundamental to comprehending engine design and operation. Combustion systems, which are the mechanisms an engine uses to burn fuel, are the basis of how engines are constructed and operate. In fact, combustion chamber design is the most significant factor determining an engine's construction features; type of fuel system; and operational, emissions, and performance characteristics. Learning the principles of engine combustion is also essential to developing good observational and diagnostic skills. When irregular combustion takes place, a technician needs to be able to identify possible causes and observe the effects of irregular combustion on engine operation. Identifying conditions that are potentially contributing to irregular combustion is essential to developing service and repair strategies.

This chapter first examines combustion reactions that occur in all engines, and then moves to combustion systems used in diesels. Combustion support systems, such as intake air heating, glow plugs, and other combustion starting aids, are also included in this chapter.

▶ Combustion Fundamentals

Engines are machines that burn fuel to produce mechanical energy. Fuel is burned through the process of combustion. During combustion, fuel, which is made up primarily of hydrogen and carbon atoms, reacts with oxygen; this reaction releases heat. To begin the combustion process, the bonds between fuel's hydrogen and carbon molecules must be broken to enable oxygen to bind with the broken and exposed carbon and hydrogen bonds. When hydrogen and carbon bond with oxygen, heat is released. To break fuel's molecular bonds, heat is also needed. A heat source, whether it is the electric arc of a spark plug or hot compressed air, provides the initial energy needed to begin to break apart hydrogen-to-carbon and carbon-to-carbon bonds so those atoms can recombine with oxygen **FIGURE 8-1**. Think of the ignition source like a match put to a pile of dry wood. Once the match begins to burn some wood, it is no longer needed, because the heat-releasing process can be self-sustaining if the correct conditions are available.

Engines can be categorized by the type of combustion process used to produce mechanical energy. The most basic classification is whether combustion takes place inside or outside a cylinder. Most of today's engines are internal combustion engines, in which an air–fuel mixture is prepared and burned inside a cylinder. External combustion engines burn fuel outside a cylinder. A steam engine is an example of an external combustion engine. Another engine combustion classification is based on the mechanism or heat source used to initiate the combustion process. Electric sparks are used to ignite air–fuel mixtures in spark ignition (SI) systems. <u>Compression ignition (CI)</u> systems initiate combustion using heat derived from the compression of air **FIGURE 8-2**.

▶ You Are the Technician

While reviewing the maintenance records of long-haul highway tractors, you've noticed a pattern among several trucks. When scheduled oil sampling has been performed, the analysis report has recommended a shorter service interval because soot loading of the oil was high and the oil viscosity had increased. Idle time on those engines was as much as 50% on some units, with the majority well above 20%. Fuel dilution of oil and accelerated wear were also evident in those engines; particle counts of iron and other metals were above average. These engines, meant to haul heavy loads, were not designed for so much idling. In addition to the shortened engine life caused by excessive engine idle, high fuel costs are associated with idling. These particular trucks cross many jurisdictions with varying anti-idle laws; excessive idling can incur fines because the noise, vibration, and emissions produced during idle are a nuisance and health hazard. The easiest solution would be to program idle shutdown timers to limit idle time to 5 minutes. However, the drivers explained that during enforced rest periods they need to idle the engines to supply heat or air conditioning to the cab while they are sleeping. They also had fears that an engine might fail to start again if it was shut down when hauling time-sensitive loads. Given these circumstances, purchasing auxiliary power units would be a better alternative. These devices have small, fuel-efficient engines that can supply electrical current, heat, and air conditioning when a truck's engine is shut down. They would also quickly provide a return on investment through fuel savings.

1. Explain why idling contributes to excessive soot loading and engine wear.
2. Why would truck engines operate at a high idle speed rather than low idle speed to provide heat to the cab when drivers are taking legally mandated rest breaks?
3. Recommend several maintenance practices to minimize problems associated with excessive low-speed engine idling.

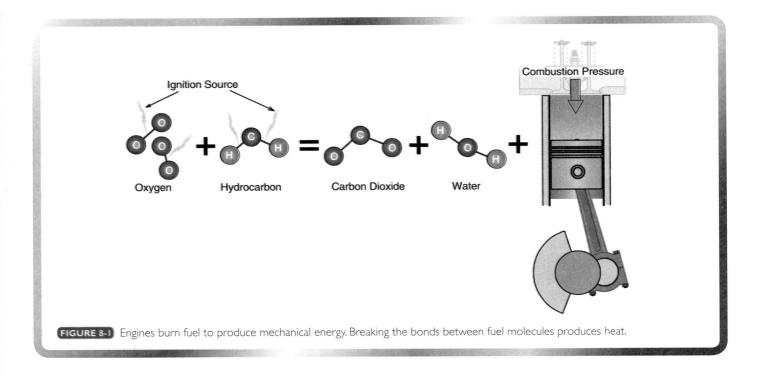

FIGURE 8-1 Engines burn fuel to produce mechanical energy. Breaking the bonds between fuel molecules produces heat.

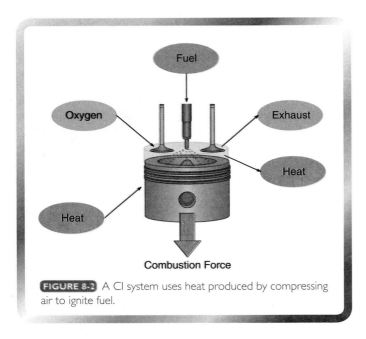

FIGURE 8-2 A CI system uses heat produced by compressing air to ignite fuel.

▶ Spark Ignition Systems

SI systems are used to initiate combustion between oxygen and a variety of fuels, including gasoline, propane, natural gas, or alcohol (methanol or ethanol). An ignition system using electric sparks produces heat by forcing electric current across the gap of a spark plug. The heat produced by the spark at the spark plug's electrodes ignites fuel between the spark plug electrodes. Like a match placed into a pile of dry wood, this "kernel" of combustion at the electrode causes the fuel to ignite at the plug air gap and burn across the combustion chamber like a wave. Combustion ends when either the fuel or air (or both) are consumed.

Limitations of Spark Ignition Systems

The major drawback of SI engines is that high compression pressures can prematurely ignite the air–fuel mixture drawn into the cylinders during the intake stroke. This condition, known as pre-ignition detonation, will take place when cylinder pressures and temperatures exceed the ignition temperature of the air–fuel mixture before the spark can ignite the mixture **FIGURE 8-3**. When this happens, cylinder pressure, rather than spark timing, controls the start of combustion. If fuel is ignited prematurely, a pinging noise or sharp, powerful knocking sound can be heard due to a rapid, uncontrolled increase in cylinder pressure. If pre-ignition detonation occurs early enough during the compression stroke, the engine can not only be damaged but also fail to produce any power.

Until the development of antiknock additives for gasoline, such as tetraethyl lead, in the late 1920s, compression of the air–fuel mixture in SI engines was limited to a 4:1 compression ratio. Stated another way, the air–fuel mixture was compressed to only one-quarter of the cylinder's total volume. Antiknock additives, also known as octane boosters, increase the temperature-pressure thresholds where pre-ignition takes place and enables an SI engine to use higher compression ratios. Today's SI engines commonly operate with compression ratios between 8:1 and 11.5:1 with octane boosters. A theoretical limit to the compression ratio in SI engines using gasoline is 13.5:1. While compression ratios like 8:1 or 11.5:1 might appear acceptable, these compression ratios do not extract the maximum potential energy from combustion. Higher compressions ratios are essential to converting fuel into the maximum amount of power for the best engine efficiency. With a higher compression ratio, more power is produced from the same amount of fuel **FIGURE 8-4**.

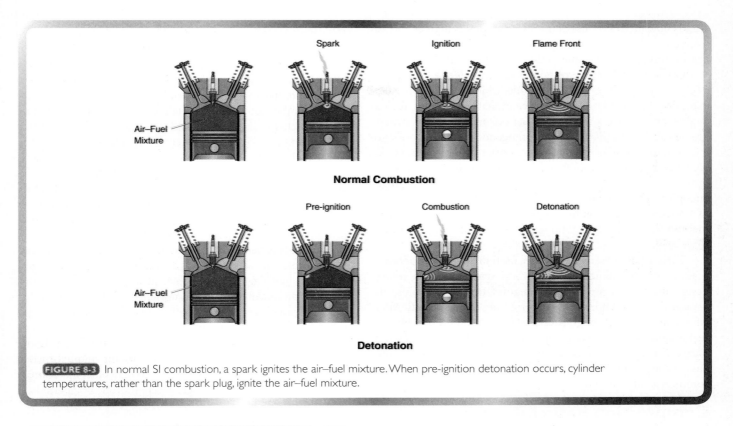

FIGURE 8-3 In normal SI combustion, a spark ignites the air–fuel mixture. When pre-ignition detonation occurs, cylinder temperatures, rather than the spark plug, ignite the air–fuel mixture.

Advantages of Compression Ignition Systems

Steam engines and early internal combustion engines converted only 1–8% of fuel's heat energy into mechanical energy. This means that for every 100 gallons (379 liters) of fuel used in these engines, only 1–8 gallons (4–30 liters) produced energy that was harnessed by the engine, while the other 92–99 gallons (348–375 liters) were wasted. When Rudolf Diesel developed his "rational combustion engine," the name he gave to the engines we now refer to as diesels, he enabled the development of engines with over 50% thermal efficiency (thermal efficiency is a measure of an engine's ability to convert heat energy into mechanical energy).

Of all engines, the diesel engine is the most efficient combustion system due to its ability to extract the greatest amount of mechanical energy from burning fuel. While there are a number of factors that account for the diesel's increased efficiency, the most significant is its higher compression ratios. Today's on-highway diesel engines have compression ratios that are twice that of traditional SI engines; the average compression ratio of diesel engines is approximately 16:1. On-highway, heavy-duty diesels with **direct injection (DI)** combustion chambers, which have a piston-formed combustion chambers and a multi-orifice nozzle, typically have compression ratios between 15.5:1 and 17.5:1. **Indirect injection (IDI)** combustion chambers, which have a pre-combustion chamber formed in the cylinder head, are used in smaller high-speed engines; they usually have compression ratios between 19:1 and 23:1. Slower turning, heavy-duty engines exceeding displacement of 20L

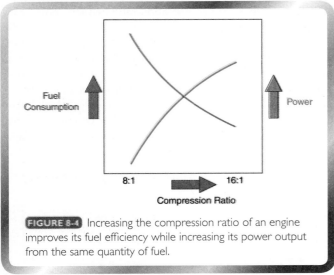

FIGURE 8-4 Increasing the compression ratio of an engine improves its fuel efficiency while increasing its power output from the same quantity of fuel.

▶ Compression Ignition Systems

CI engines use heat derived from compressing air to ignite fuel. Near the end of the compression stroke, fuel is sprayed into the cylinder where it ignites and burns. Burning fuel heats the air charge, which then expands to increase cylinder pressure. Combustion force is converted into mechanical energy by the engine. Because fuel and air do not mix in the cylinder until the very end of the compression stroke, diesel's efficiency is not limited to lower compression ratios used by SI engines.

(1220 cubic inch) may use compression ratios as high as 25:1 to compensate for compression pressure losses from cylinder leakage around piston rings due to slow piston movement.

One other CI engine of note is the <u>**homogeneous charge compression ignition (HCCI)**</u> engine, which is a low-emission experimental engine. Like a conventional SI gasoline-fueled engine, an HCCI engine injects fuel during the intake stroke. The air and fuel are evenly, or homogenously, mixed prior to ignition. Instead of using an electric spark to ignite the mixture, HCCI engines use compression ignition to begin combustion. Ignition occurs when the cylinder temperatures are high enough to ignite the air–fuel mixture. Microprocessor control of pre-combustion conditions (such as mixture density, air–fuel ratios, and other factors) determine when ignition occurs **FIGURE 8-5**.

Turbine engines, or jet engines, used in aircraft are another example of CI engines. While turbine engines have a rotary design and are not reciprocating engines, they do compress air using a series of compressor blades rotating at high speeds. After air is compressed through several stages of compressor blades, fuel is sprayed into the hot compressed air, where it ignites and burns. The burning gases expand as they leave the engine and pass through another series of turbine blades, which drive a common shaft shared by the compressor blades.

Compression Ratio Effects

The high compression ratios used by diesel engines is the most significant factor contributing to their superior power output, high fuel efficiency, and low emission characteristics. Compression pressure is the also most vital factor needed to ignite fuel. Examining the role of compression ratio and compression pressure in a diesel is a lot like studying the ignition system of a gasoline engine—there's quite a bit of detail that is useful for understanding engine operating characteristics and diagnosing a wide range of engine problems when they do occur.

Temperature and Pressure

To understand the advantages of high compression ratios, it is important to remember that pressure and temperature increase proportionally when compression ratio rises. Pressure and temperature have a major influence on the chemical reactions of the combustion process. High pressure and temperature speed up chemical reactions and increase the likelihood that fuel and oxygen will react. When the temperature in a cylinder is high, molecules collide with greater velocity because they have increased energy. Higher pressure pushes molecules closer together, which also increases the likelihood of chemical reactions **FIGURE 8-6**. This means that fuel is burned faster in an engine with a high compression ratio, which shortens combustion time. Injecting more fuel to accelerate a vehicle or carry heavier loads generates more combustion heat. When increasing quantities of fuel are injected, combustion time is actually shortened, not lengthened. It may seem counterintuitive that adding additional fuel results in shortened combustion time, but the effect can observed when building any fire. Small fires with only a few pieces of wood will burn more slowly and consume less wood every minute than very large, hot fires. Just as hotter fires burn wood faster and require a constant supply of wood to sustain them, diesel combustion chambers burn increasingly larger quantities of fuel in progressively shorter time periods.

Power Output

An engine with a high compression ratio extracts more power using the same amount of fuel compared to an engine with a lower compression ratio. Compacting air into a smaller volume at a higher temperature causes combustion to take place more rapidly because molecules are pressed together more closely and have higher energy levels. This leads to a much sharper pressure spike in the cylinder during combustion, which applies greater force to the top of a piston. Higher compression ratio engines also typically use a longer piston stroke. Because higher

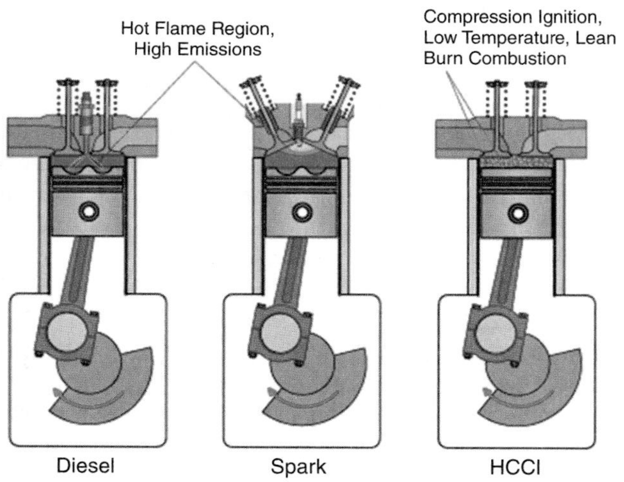

Diesel   **Spark**   **HCCI**

FIGURE 8-5 Compression or electric sparks are the only ignition sources used by engines to begin combustion.

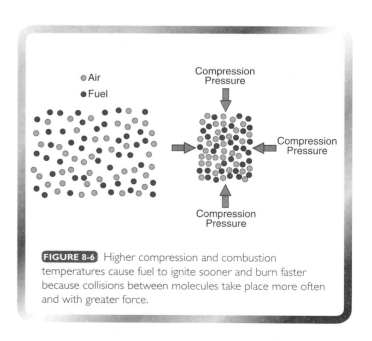

FIGURE 8-6 Higher compression and combustion temperatures cause fuel to ignite sooner and burn faster because collisions between molecules take place more often and with greater force.

pressures are applied to the piston and the piston travels over a longer stroke, the longer, harder push on the crankshaft enhances the conversion of combustion pressure into mechanical energy. To obtain a longer stroke in any engine, an increase in the length of the crankshaft throw is required. Because torque is a function of the length of a lever times the force applied to it, a diesel engine's longer crankshaft throw will produce more torque for the same combustion force FIGURE 8-7.

Higher compression ratios also lead to better mixing of air and fuel, which results in improved combustion and increased power output. Because air and fuel are more tightly packed together in a combustion chamber with a high compression ratio, the air and fuel molecules have the potential for better contact. Additionally, smaller clearance volumes in diesel engines improve scavenging of exhaust gases from the cylinder. This means more exhaust gas is pushed from the cylinder because a small clearance volume provides little space for exhaust gases to linger at the end of the exhaust stroke.

Temperature, Pressure, and Hard Starting of Diesel Engines

CI systems make diesels sensitive to changes in air temperature and compression pressures. Hard starting and prolonged cranking times for diesels have many possible causes, but conditions that result in inadequate compression temperature are at the top of the list. For example, engines that crank slowly and are worn out allow more air to leak past the piston rings, which reduces cylinder temperatures at the end of the compression

stroke. When this happens, fuel will take longer to ignite and may not burn at all. If fuel is injected and the engine will not start, white smoke, which consists of vaporized fuel, will emerge from the exhaust pipe during cranking. This problem is made worse when air temperatures are cold FIGURE 8-8. Starting aids, including heating flames or electric intake heaters, can warm intake air. This increases pre-ignition temperatures to improve combustion quality and shorten the period of ignition delay, which is the time period between the beginning of fuel injection and the actual ignition of fuel in a combustion chamber. Ethyl ether, also referred to as ether or starting fluid, ignites at a lower temperature than diesel fuel. Ethyl ether can increase cylinder temperatures and pressures enough to help ignite fuel when it is injected. Electric coolant heaters increase compression temperatures by reducing the quantity of heat absorbed by cold cylinder components. Oil pan heaters can minimize the drag of thick lubricant in an engine and increase cranking revolutions per minute (rpm), which in turn produces higher cylinder temperatures. Adequate battery cranking power is important, too, because it will help the starter motor produce more torque and turn the engine faster.

Diesel Cranking Speed and Compression Pressures

Most four-stroke diesels generally require a minimum cranking speed of 125 rpm to start. Without adequate cranking speed, insufficient compression pressure and accompanying heat is available to start combustion. Normal cranking speeds for medium- and large-bore diesels are between 150 and 250 rpm.

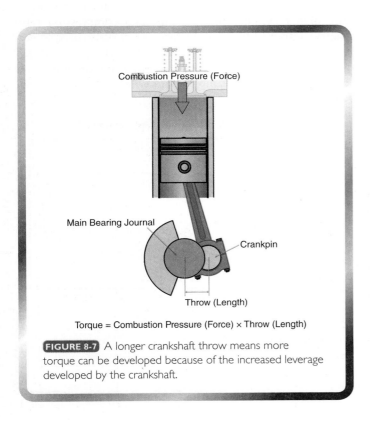

Torque = Combustion Pressure (Force) × Throw (Length)

FIGURE 8-7 A longer crankshaft throw means more torque can be developed because of the increased leverage developed by the crankshaft.

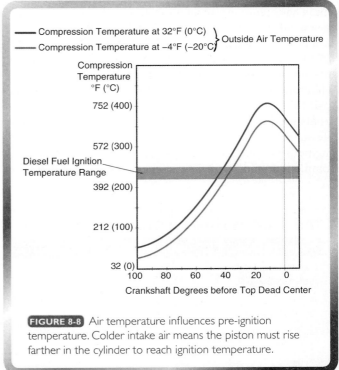

FIGURE 8-8 Air temperature influences pre-ignition temperature. Colder intake air means the piston must rise farther in the cylinder to reach ignition temperature.

Diesel Fuel Properties and Compression Ignition

Depending on the quality and grade of the fuel, diesel fuel's **auto-ignition temperature**, or the temperature at which a fuel will ignite when heated, is approximately 380–500°F (193–260°C). These temperatures are well above diesel fuel's **flash point** of 100–125°F (38–52°C) (flash point is the temperature at which fuel will produce adequate vapor to ignite if exposed to an open source of ignition such as a spark or flame). Diesel fuel will ignite under conditions that are more air lean than gasoline **TABLE 8-1**.

Pre-ignition heat adequate to ignite fuel must be present in the combustion chamber. Pre-ignition temperatures, or the heat present in the cylinder before the fuel ignites, depend on a variety of factors. These include the compression ratio, ambient air temperatures, inlet air temperature, boost pressure, use of charge air cooling, valve timing, combustion chamber design, engine speed, and other variables. However, a pre-ignition temperature of 1000°F (538°C) or more is common. The maximum auto-ignition temperature required by North American fuel standards for retailed diesel fuel is 558°F (292°C). This means if fuel requires any higher temperature than 558°F (292°C) to ignite, it cannot be retailed because the engine may not start or run at all. During cranking, most DI engines will produce a minimum of 280–300 pounds per square inch (psi) (19–21 bar) of compression pressure. IDI engines commonly produce over 500 psi (34 bar) of cylinder compression pressure. These compression pressures will increase when the engine is running and when engines are turbocharged. It is common for mid-range diesels (engine displacement of 6–10L [366–610 cubic inch]) to have 500–1200 psi (34–83 bar) of compression pressure at maximum rpm or rated speed. At peak torque, when the turbocharger airflow into the engine is high, compression pressures in high-horsepower, on-highway diesels commonly reach 1000–1800 psi (69–124 bar). Miller cycle engines are capable of reducing the energy required to compress air to these pressures by leaving the intake valve open longer as boost pressure increases.

Disadvantages of High Compression Ratios

Compression ratios above 16:1 begin to return diminishing power increases compared to increasing compression pressure. In fact, any increase of compression ratio beyond 23:1 results in a decrease in engine efficiency **FIGURE 8-9**. This happens because more energy is used to compress the air than is yielded from combustion force. In spite of this effect, many engines do operate with compression ratios above 16:1. IDI combustion chambers use higher compression ratios to compensate for the lower thermal efficiency of that type of combustion chamber. Slower-moving engines also use higher compression ratios to compensate for blow-by past the piston rings during a longer compression stroke.

Engines that use high compression ratios also have reduced mechanical efficiency due to increased frictional losses. Longer piston strokes mean more energy is used because of friction between pistons, rings, and cylinder walls. Higher compression pressures also require the strengthening of engine components, including pistons, cranks, and rods; strengthening makes components heavier, which means they require more power to get them and keep them in motion. The higher cylinder pressures of high compression ratio engines also lead to the need for head gaskets (used to seal the joint between the cylinder block and cylinder head) that are manufactured to seal better. Larger and more numerous bolts are required to clamp a cylinder head to the block; for

TABLE 8-1: Properties of Gasoline and Diesel Fuel		
Property	**Gasoline**	**Diesel**
Flammability Limits (volume % in air)	1.4–7.6	0.6–5.5
Auto-ignition Temperature (°F [°C], averaged)	572°F (300°C)	446°F (230°C)
Flash Point (averaged)	−45°F (−43°C)	100°F–125°F (38–52°C)

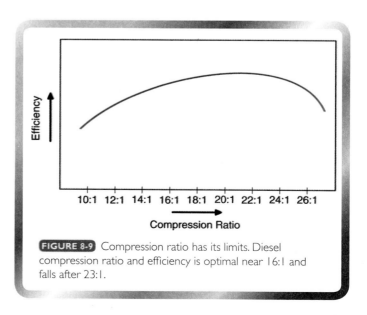

FIGURE 8-9 Compression ratio has its limits. Diesel compression ratio and efficiency is optimal near 16:1 and falls after 23:1.

example, an SI gasoline-fueled engine typically uses two bolts per cylinder, while a diesel uses four to six bolts per cylinder. Heavier, more expensive starting systems with greater cranking torque are also required because of high compression ratios.

Torsional Vibration and Compression Pressure

Engines with very high compression ratios have the disadvantage of producing more **torsional vibration** than engines with lower compression ratios **FIGURE 8-10**. Torsional vibration occurs when the crankshaft speeds up and slows down. During compression stroke, pistons slow down because of increasing cylinder pressure as they approach top dead center (TDC). The rapid rise in combustion pressure after TDC then accelerates the crankshaft. The alternating effects of compression and combustion produce a constant speeding up and slowing down of the crankshaft. The constantly changing crankshaft speed produces torsional vibration. Forces produced from torsional vibration are a major problem in diesel engines. Specialized features prevent engine damage and the transmission of torsional vibration to the driveline. For example, most new diesels use rear-mounted gear trains to reduce noise and excessive gear wear caused by torsional vibrations. Gear rattle is minimized at the rear of the engine because the flywheel smooths out crankshaft speed changes. Torsional vibration dampeners can also be used to smooth out torsional impulses at the front of the engine; this prevents crankshaft damage and other problems associated with torsional vibration. Many smaller automotive diesel engines have low compression ratios to avoid producing these vibrations.

▶ Combustion in Diesel Engines

Among all engines, diesel engines are the most efficient combustion systems. A variety of factors contribute to diesel's ability to convert burning fuel into the most mechanical energy. It is important to examine these factors in order to understand not only how a diesel operates so efficiently, but also what can go wrong when an engine's performance has declined. As air-breathing machinery, diesels are sensitive to air quality and quantity. Air–fuel ratio, compression pressure, temperature, injection timing, and combustion chamber design are all critical variables that affect engine operation. Understanding these variables is important when diagnosing problems affecting engine performance, efficiency, and emissions.

Stoichiometric Versus Lean Burn Combustion

Gasoline-fueled engines burn fuel at close to **stoichiometric ratio**, which occurs when the minimum quantity of air is present in the combustion chamber to completely burn all fuel with neither air nor fuel remaining after the combustion event. Diesel engine air–fuel ratios are unlike those found in gasoline-fueled engines. Diesel engines use **lean burn combustion**, which uses more air than necessary to burn fuel and has the advantage of reducing fuel consumption **FIGURE 8-11**. This is because the burning fuel can heat a larger mass of air and develop higher cylinder pressures. During full-load, high-speed operation, diesels will smoke heavily if air–fuel ratios fall below 100:1. A common air–fuel ratio under moderate load is 300:1.

In diesels, intake air is not throttled for the purpose of controlling power; intake air passages are generally designed to flow the maximum amount of air. Instead of using a throttle plate to control power, diesel engines meter, or regulate, the quantity of fuel injected into the engine. The quantity of fuel injected is controlled by a governor, which first measures engine speed, throttle pedal position, and engine load to determine how much fuel should be injected. In diesels, fuel is not measured by air–fuel ratios like it is in SI engines, but by volume or fuel mass injected per stroke. The absence of a throttle plate increases

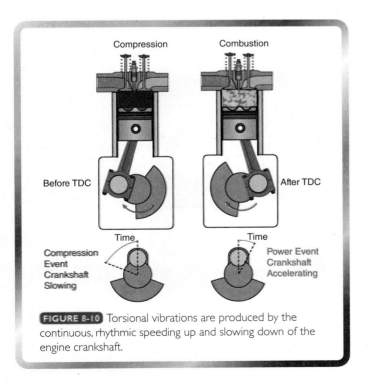

FIGURE 8-10 Torsional vibrations are produced by the continuous, rhythmic speeding up and slowing down of the engine crankshaft.

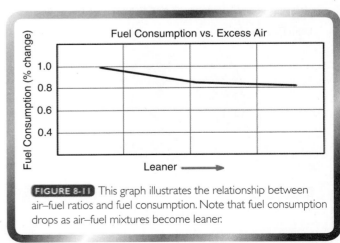

FIGURE 8-11 This graph illustrates the relationship between air–fuel ratios and fuel consumption. Note that fuel consumption drops as air–fuel mixtures become leaner.

the efficiency of diesel engines because it eliminates <u>pumping loss</u>, which is energy expended by an engine to move air in and exhaust out of the cylinders. Pumping losses are increased when an engine has to pull air past a narrow throttle plate. This advantage is offset by the disadvantage that without a throttle plate, diesel engines have little natural retarding force to slow a vehicle and therefor need engine-based braking systems.

Stratified Combustion

<u>Stratified combustion</u> occurs when combustion chambers burn fuel in layers that vary in air–fuel ratios. Overall, air–fuel ratios in diesel engines are very high, but concentrations of air and fuel vary widely throughout the combustion chamber. Areas near the fuel spray from injector nozzles will be fuel rich, while other regions have little or no fuel and are all air. Combustion begins in the regions where the temperature of the air and fuel are above the auto-ignition temperature, and the air–fuel ratio is close to 15:1. During the rest of the combustion period, heat and pressure push the remaining fuel molecules together in lean regions where they are rapidly ignited **FIGURE 8-12**.

Requirement for Excess Air

Excess air supply for combustion is required by diesels for a number of reasons. First, because the flame temperature of diesel fuel is approximately 4000°F (2204°C), diesel fuel burned at stoichiometric ratio would easily melt aluminum alloy pistons, which have a melting point of 1400°F (760°C) **FIGURE 8-13**. During full-load conditions, when maximum quantities of fuel are injected, excess air dilutes the heat of combustion, which prevents damage to cylinder components and valves. Valve and piston life is extended because they operate cooler in cylinders with excess air. Excess air is also critical to complete, clean combustion because it guarantees good contact between the fuel and air. In lean burn combustion, fuel is able to find enough air to combine with in a very short amount of time. The absence of a throttle plate enables diesels to achieve greater intake airflow.

FIGURE 8-13 This diesel piston melted because there was an insufficient amount of excess air in the combustion chamber to dilute the combustion heat.

Excess combustion air also keeps diesel exhaust temperatures much cooler than SI engines burning fuel at stoichiometric ratio. For example, without a load, a typical DI diesel's exhaust temperature is between 130°F and 150°F (54°C and 66°C) at idle. Cooler combustion temperatures also mean that a diesel engine will not warm up if the engine is only operated at idle speed without a load. One typical strategy used to speed warm up is the use of exhaust back-pressure regulators. These devices restrict exhaust flow from the engine and increase combustion temperatures **FIGURE 8-14**. Exhaust back pressure is the exhaust pressure built

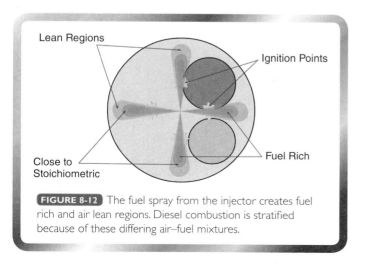

FIGURE 8-12 The fuel spray from the injector creates fuel rich and air lean regions. Diesel combustion is stratified because of these differing air–fuel mixtures.

FIGURE 8-14 This turbocharger uses an exhaust back-pressure regulator to restrict exhaust gases and increase exhaust back pressure while at idle to speed engine warm up.

up in the exhaust system or engine by reducing exhaust flow out of the engine. By restricting air-rich exhaust gases, higher cylinder pre-ignition pressures are achieved, which translate into high combustion temperatures.

▶ TECHNICIAN TIP

When additional fuel is injected to develop greater power output, the airflow into the engine needs to be increased proportionally. Without additional airflow, exhaust temperatures and cylinder temperatures will increase, resulting in engine damage and shortened engine life. Performance modification to increase power should always be accompanied by increased air intake and exhaust system flow. Turbocharger boost pressure can be increased to maintain exhaust and cylinder temperatures in a safe operating range.

▶ TECHNICIAN TIP

DI diesel engines do not warm up quickly and will not reach operating temperature when idled. This is because excess air supplied during combustion dilutes combustion heat, which in turns lowers the amount of heat transferred to the engine coolant. Excess combustion air is the reason why diesel exhaust temperatures are cool and why it is impossible for diesels to use the same catalytic converter technology used by gasoline-fueled engines. To verify an overcooling or overheating complaint, a diesel engine must be operated under a moderate load and not idled.

Injection Timing

Changes to combustion speed, which varies with temperature and pressure, are why it is necessary to vary the timing of the beginning of fuel injection events when changes to engine speed and load conditions take place. Under light-load conditions, less fuel is injected and combustion takes place more slowly because combustion temperatures and pressures are lower. The opposite is true when combustion temperatures and pressures are higher and combustion time is shortened. Because engines are designed to produce peak combustion pressure at approximately 10° to 15° of crankshaft rotation after TDC, it is important to begin combustion at the correct moment. A slight angle between the piston's connecting rod and crankshaft at 10° after TDC provides some leverage to begin rotating the crankshaft. Having peak pressure occur at this point ensures that combustion forces will push the crankshaft early in the combustion cycle, with the highest available cylinder pressure, for the longest time. The longer and harder the push on the piston by combustion forces, the greater the combustion efficiency becomes **FIGURE 8-15**.

Advancing Injection Timing

To maintain peak combustion pressure at 10° after TDC, timing of the injection event needs to vary with engine speed and load change. Generally, the injection event will take place progressively earlier as engine speed increases with no change to engine load. This happens because the piston moves through TDC faster at higher engine speed, but combustion time does not change if the same amount of fuel is injected. When injection takes

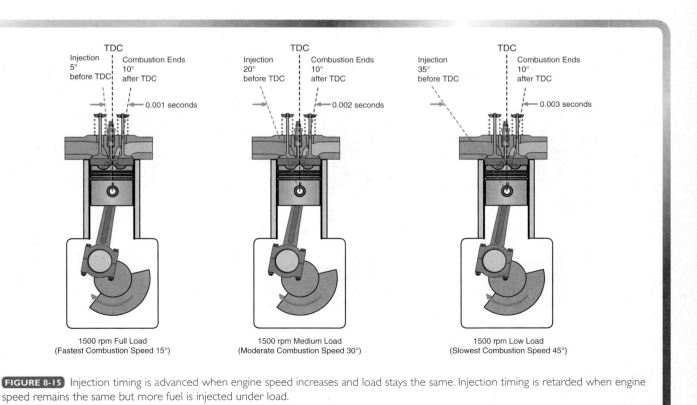

TDC	TDC	TDC
Injection 5° before TDC — Combustion Ends 10° after TDC — 0.001 seconds	Injection 20° before TDC — Combustion Ends 10° after TDC — 0.002 seconds	Injection 35° before TDC — Combustion Ends 10° after TDC — 0.003 seconds
1500 rpm Full Load (Fastest Combustion Speed 15°)	1500 rpm Medium Load (Moderate Combustion Speed 30°)	1500 rpm Low Load (Slowest Combustion Speed 45°)

FIGURE 8-15 Injection timing is advanced when engine speed increases and load stays the same. Injection timing is retarded when engine speed remains the same but more fuel is injected under load.

place earlier than, or further away from, TDC at the end of the compression stroke, injection timing is referred to as advancing FIGURE 8-16.

Air inlet temperature requires a change to injection timing, too. Cool air inlet temperatures mean lower pre-ignition cylinder temperatures, which require more time to ignite fuel. Under this condition, injection timing is advanced. Conversely, hotter inlet temperatures with higher pre-ignition temperatures will ignite fuel sooner and require retarding of injection timing.

Retarding Injection Timing

When engine load is increased, and it is not accompanied by a change in engine speed, injection timing needs to take place later than it did before the load was applied to the engine. When injection takes place later than normal, the injection event is referred to as having retarded timing. Engine load increases when more fuel is injected into the engine under load to maintain vehicle speed. Increasing injection quantity in turn causes cylinder temperatures and pressures to rise. This shortens combustion time because fuel burns faster under these conditions. If timing was not retarded and remained unchanged, peak cylinder pressures would not take place at 10° after TDC but would instead take place closer to TDC. During cranking, injection timing is retarded further than normal. Retarding the injection timing during cranking increases the likelihood of starting the engine, because the piston rises farther in the cylinder, increasing the cylinder temperatures before fuel is injected.

Combustion Chambers

Combustion chamber design is the most significant factor determining an engine's construction features; type of fuel system; and operational, emissions, and performance characteristics. The chamber is responsible for promoting good mixing of air and fuel to achieve efficient engine operation, low emissions, and other favorable operational characteristics. A good combustion chamber design will:

- promote efficient combustion by enabling the formation of good air–fuel mixtures
- promote the maximum conversion of combustion energy into mechanical force
- minimize the production of noxious emissions, including hydrocarbons (HCs), oxides of nitrogen (NO_x), carbon monoxide (CO), and particulate matter (PM)
- minimize noise
- provide good fuel economy
- smooth engine operation

Combustion Chamber Classification

There are two basic combustion chamber designs for diesel engines, with numerous variations on each of these designs. All diesel engines can be categorized as having either an IDI combustion chamber or DI combustion chamber FIGURE 8-17. Each chamber design has its own unique fuel system and operational characteristics. The DI chamber is currently the most popular

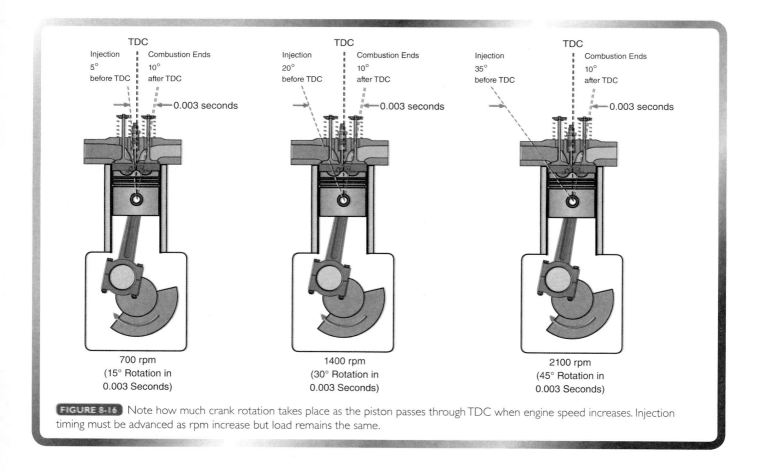

TDC
Injection 5° before TDC   Combustion Ends 10° after TDC   ← 0.003 seconds

TDC
Injection 20° before TDC   Combustion Ends 10° after TDC   ← 0.003 seconds

TDC
Injection 35° before TDC   Combustion Ends 10° after TDC   ← 0.003 seconds

700 rpm
(15° Rotation in
0.003 Seconds)

1400 rpm
(30° Rotation in
0.003 Seconds)

2100 rpm
(45° Rotation in
0.003 Seconds)

FIGURE 8-16 Note how much crank rotation takes place as the piston passes through TDC when engine speed increases. Injection timing must be advanced as rpm increase but load remains the same.

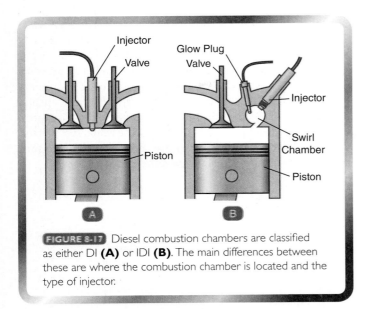

FIGURE 8-17 Diesel combustion chambers are classified as either DI **(A)** or IDI **(B)**. The main differences between these are where the combustion chamber is located and the type of injector.

chamber in all applications because of its simplicity, superior fuel economy, and good emission characteristics when combined with an electronically controlled high-pressure fuel system. Until the early 1990s, the IDI chamber was the most popular chamber design in automotive applications because of its high-speed capabilities and favorable emission characteristics. IDI engines use simple, inexpensive fuel injection systems because injection pressures are lower than in DI chambers. Because the performance characteristics of IDI engines are similar to gasoline-fueled engines, IDI chambered diesels could directly replace gasoline-fueled engines without major changes to the drive train configuration.

Combustion Chamber Turbulence

Air motion in the combustion chamber is a critical factor to combustion mixture preparation in diesel engines. Cylinder turbulence in a combustion chamber is created by the shape of the combustion bowl **FIGURE 8-18**. Without adequate air turbulence, proper mixing of air and fuel will not take place, resulting in lost performance and efficiency and increased emissions. The semi-toroidal shape common to almost all DI chambers is designed to mix air and fuel. Because fuel is injected near the end of the compression stroke, very little time is available

to prepare the mixture for combustion; the turbulence created by the chamber must quickly mix air and fuel **FIGURE 8-19**. The shape of the combustion bowl converts the toroidal airflow created during intake into smaller rolling or tumbling balls of air that best mix air and fuel.

Matching the injector spray pattern with the combustion bowl is also required to obtain proper mixing **FIGURE 8-20**. The geometric configuration of the piston bowl will be determined by fuel spray penetration, spray angle, droplet sizing, and turbulence. Precisely matched injectors and piston-formed combustion chambers ensure good performance and emission compliance. Using a piston with the wrong bowl shape will drastically affect engine operation. For example, overlapping spray will create denser air–fuel mixtures and increase emission levels of HCs, CO, and PM.

Deep bowls tend to create high turbulence. Fuel in a high-turbulence chamber can readily impinge or condense onto the cylinder walls and enter the crevice volume space between the piston and cylinder wall. In those locations, fuel will not burn. Shallow bowls tend to have less turbulence. Shallow, wide bowls are called quiescent bowls because they create relatively little turbulence

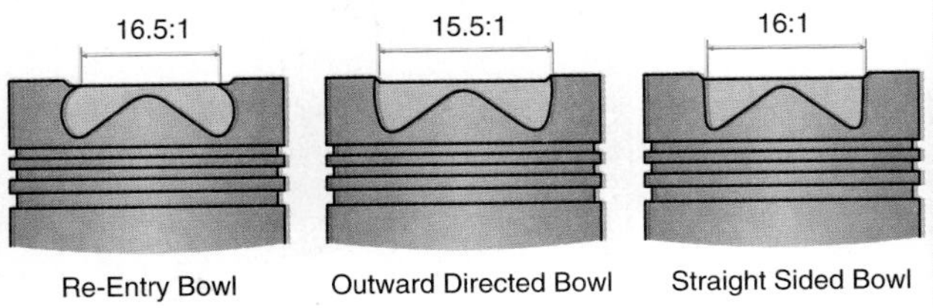

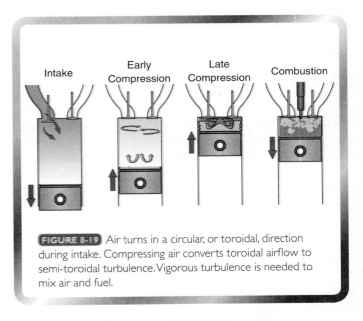

FIGURE 8-19 Air turns in a circular, or toroidal, direction during intake. Compressing air converts toroidal airflow to semi-toroidal turbulence. Vigorous turbulence is needed to mix air and fuel.

FIGURE 8-18 The direction of the sides of the piston bowl determines how much turbulence is achieved.

FIGURE 8-20 These three pistons fit the same engine but have different combustion chamber shapes. The bowl shapes must match the spray pattern of the injectors.

FIGURE 8-21. The formation of emissions is reduced in these low-swirl quiescent bowls by increasing injection pressures and the number of spray holes at the injector tip. Most late-model engines use quiescent bowls combined with high-injection pressurization to mix air and fuel to achieve lower NO_x emissions.

▶ Direct Injection

In a DI combustion chamber, fuel is injected directly into the combustion chamber, which is located between the top of the piston and the cylinder head. The combustion chamber is formed primarily in the piston and the cylinder head is flat. The fuel injector or spray nozzle, and the intake and exhaust valves, are located in the combustion chamber, directly above the piston.

Higher engine thermal efficiencies are achieved using DI chambers because there is a small ratio between combustion chamber surface area and combustion volume. This results in 10–15% better fuel efficiency compared to IDI chambers because less heat is rejected or absorbed by the cooling system. Current thermal efficiencies are higher than 45% in newer on-highway engines and 50% or more in slower-turning industrial engines. Until the introduction of very high-pressure fuel injection systems and electronic control of injection timing, emissions from DI chambers were higher than IDI designs.

Compression ratios in a DI chamber typically range between 15.5:1 and 17.5:1 for most on-highway diesel engines. The average compression ratio for on-highway vehicles is 16:1. At these compression ratios, pre-ignition air temperatures of 800–1200°F (427–649°C) are produced, with an average pre-ignition temperature of 1000°F (538°C). When using air-to-air charge air cooling and a turbocharger, the typical compression pressure range is 300–1800 psi (21–124 bar). Peak cylinder combustion pressures may reach as high as 1800–2300 psi (124–159 bar) in small late-model diesel engines, and 3000 psi (207 bar) in large engines. This compares with maximum pressure of approximately 900 psi (62 bar) found in gasoline-fueled engines.

DI chambers use injectors with multi-orifice nozzles, which spray fuel in at high pressure **FIGURE 8-22**. Very small holes in the nozzles spray fuel in a fine fog-like air–fuel mixture. Fuel begins spraying from the latest injectors when nozzle opening pressures are 3200–5500 psi (221–379 bar). Electronic control of nozzle opening pressures in a unit injector with variable nozzle opening pressure capability opens the nozzle at pressures between approximately 5500–20,000 psi (379–1379 bar). The actual fuel pressure during an injection will be higher than nozzle opening pressures and have velocities that easily exceed the speed of sound.

▶ TECHNICIAN TIP

Fuel vapors, not liquids, ignite and burn. Fuel is injected first as small liquid droplets. Only after the fuel droplets absorb heat can they vaporize and ignite. High pressurization of fuel is needed to form the finest droplets, which will quickly vaporize and burn. Slow cranking speeds and worn-out injection systems that cannot adequately pressurize fuel will often lead to complaints by causing hard starting and prolonged cranking times. Worn-out engines and fuel injection systems can easily be detected by recognizing these symptoms.

Direct Injection Starting Aids

DI chambers generally require no starting aids such as glow plugs or air intake heaters. However, glow plugs and air intake heaters are used in some DI engines to minimize cold-start emissions and white smoke caused by low cylinder temperatures, poor fuel atomization, and cylinder misfires during the warm-up period. Higher pre-ignition temperatures are obtained by using air intake heaters, which provide faster start-up in colder ambient temperatures with less soot and other emissions **FIGURE 8-23**. Because some fuel systems do not effectively pressurize fuel at cranking speeds, a glow plug placed near the fuel nozzle will speed up fuel vaporization to ensure that the time

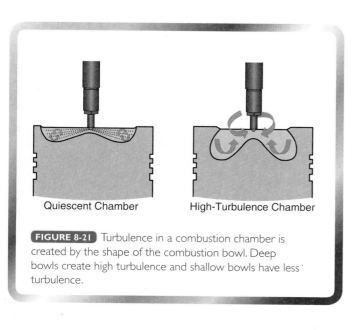

FIGURE 8-21 Turbulence in a combustion chamber is created by the shape of the combustion bowl. Deep bowls create high turbulence and shallow bowls have less turbulence.

Quiescent Chamber   High-Turbulence Chamber

FIGURE 8-22 DI chambers use multi-orifice nozzles, which finely atomize and distribute fuel in piston-formed combustion chambers.

FIGURE 8-23 A high current flow electric air intake heater warms intake air during starting and warm-up. Note the location of the high current relay.

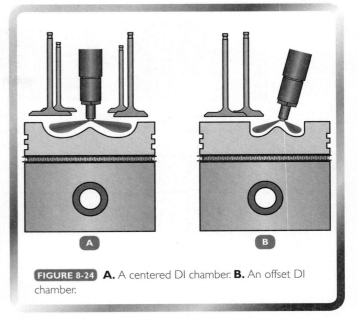

FIGURE 8-24 **A.** A centered DI chamber. **B.** An offset DI chamber.

when fuel ignites remains consistent. This is necessary because large fuel droplets produced by the injectors during cranking will not produce enough vapor to start the engine. The use of a hot glow plug will vaporize fuel and promote faster ignition.

Classification of Direct Injection Chambers

There are two common types of DI chambers: centered and offset **FIGURE 8-24**. The names refer to the location of the injector in the combustion chamber. Centered DIs use four valves per cylinder, and the injector is centrally located. The centralized placement of the injector allows centered DIs to distribute fuel more symmetrically for better emission characteristics. The four-valve intake and exhaust configuration also improves the engine's ability to breathe, which increases volumetric efficiency.

Offset DIs use two valves per cylinder. Due to larger valves, this setup does not provide room to accommodate the centrally located injector. Instead, the injector is leaned to one side of the cylinder head, making room for the valves. Offset combustion chambers, while less expensive to manufacture, create uneven piston crown temperatures and thrust loads in addition to higher emissions from asymmetrical fuel distribution. In recent years, offset combustion chambers have disappeared from all clean diesels.

Direct Injection Pressure Volume Cycle

The pressure volume curve in an engine is a comparison between the cylinder pressure and engine position. Pressure volume curves of combustion chambers are helpful in understanding the characteristics of combustion in different combustion chambers **FIGURE 8-25**. Four distinct phases of combustion are observed in DI chambers **FIGURE 8-26**. These phases are:

- injection delay
- uncontrolled burn
- controlled burn
- afterburn

Ignition Delay

Ignition delay, also called ignition lag, refers to the time period between the beginning of the injection event and the point when ignition takes place. Ignition delay takes place because fuel needs to distribute, atomize, absorb heat, vaporize, and mix with air in the proper concentration before it can begin to burn.

Ignition delay is the factor responsible for the characteristic "knock" or combustion noise from diesel engines. This delay period and noise associated with it is more pronounced at idle. During the delay period, fuel will accumulate in the cylinder while mixing and vaporizing. The combustion noise does not occur during the delay period but immediately afterward in the uncontrolled burn phase. When fuel does begin to burn during the uncontrolled combustion period, a sharp increase in pressure produces a sound wave known as fuel knock. Ideally, the shorter the ignition delay period, the quieter the engine will operate because less fuel is built up in the chamber during a shorter delay period. A small delay is approximately 0.001 second. A delay of 0.003 seconds or more results in a rough running engine and an exaggerated fuel knock, as more fuel accumulates during the delay period. When the fuel does ignite, the larger amount of fuel accumulated during the longer delay period causes the pressure to spike higher than during a shorter delay period.

There are several factors that affect ignition delay **FIGURE 8-27**. These include:

- Fuel quality: Fuel with a high cetane value ignites more quickly to produce a shorter delay time.
- Compression ratio: High compression ratios produce shorter ignition delay times.
- Degree of fuel atomization: Finer atomization will shorten ignition delay because finer droplets vaporize, ignite, and burn faster.

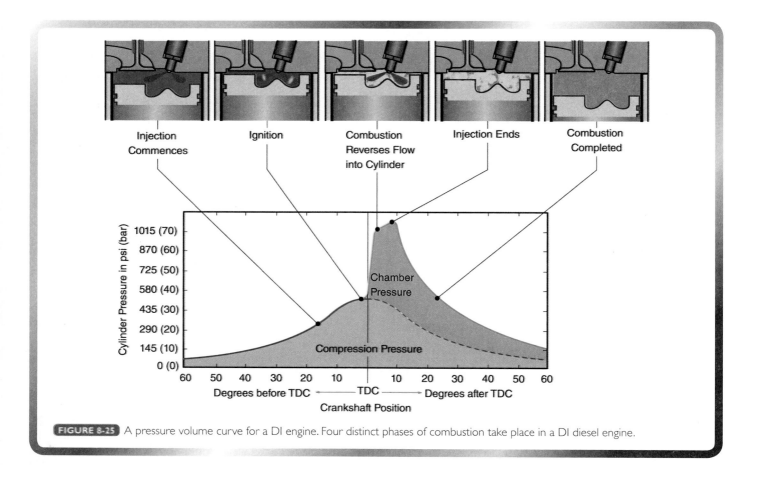

FIGURE 8-25 A pressure volume curve for a DI engine. Four distinct phases of combustion take place in a DI diesel engine.

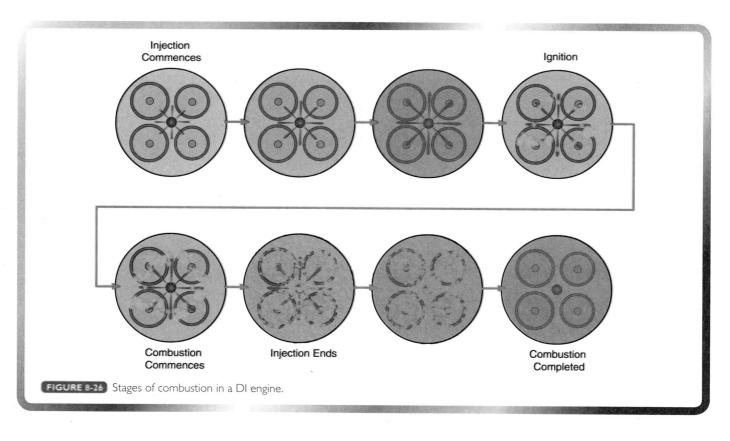

FIGURE 8-26 Stages of combustion in a DI engine.

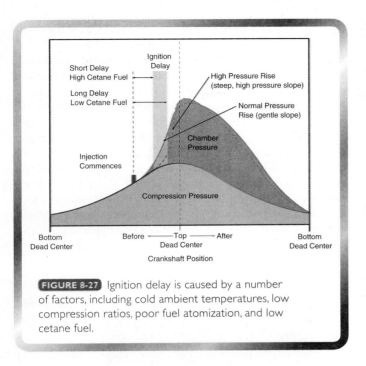

FIGURE 8-27 Ignition delay is caused by a number of factors, including cold ambient temperatures, low compression ratios, poor fuel atomization, and low cetane fuel.

- Pre-ignition temperature: Colder ambient and engine temperatures will create a longer ignition delay; diesels are noisier when cold.

Uncontrolled Burn

The uncontrolled burn phase, also called the flame propagation phase, is characterized by uncontrolled combustion in a cylinder until fuel accumulated during ignition delay is burned. Many points in the combustion chamber will simultaneously reach the threshold values required for ignition, and multiple flame fronts will move through the air–fuel mixture. This rapid progression of multiple flame fronts causes a very sharp pressure spike in the cylinder while all fuel accumulations are consumed. The high compression ratio and supercharging of diesel engines will speed up combustion processes taking place during this period, because molecules are packed together more tightly at higher temperatures. Multiple ignition points and high cylinder pressures cause the fuel to burn much faster in comparison to SI engines.

Controlled Burn

The controlled burn phase of combustion occurs when the remaining injection quantity is delivered. Combustion during this phase causes a gradual controlled rise in cylinder pressure after TDC. Depending on the injection rate, fuel delivery will not stop until just after TDC.

Afterburn

The afterburn phase of combustion occurs when any remaining injected fuel is completely burned. This event produces pressure on the piston to keep it moving during its power stroke. The afterburn period can affect formation of PM emissions. Having

adequate afterburn time is important to completely consume any unused or partially burned fuel. Poor mixing of air and fuel prior to this phase, or extended ignition delay, will not enable complete combustion during the afterburn phase, because cylinder pressure and temperature are decreasing as the piston moves downward on the power stroke. If these poor combustion conditions exist, more PM will form. Some manufacturers that use common rail fuel systems will inject additional fuel during this period to increase afterburn temperatures in order to reduce the formation of soot.

▶ TECHNICIAN TIP

The combustion pressure spike produces a noise that characterizes diesel engines. Sometimes called fuel knock, it is the result of a prolonged time period between the injection of fuel and its ignition. During the ignition delay period, formation of the air–fuel mixture is taking place. When fuel does ignite, the high compression pressure and temperature in the combustion chamber causes the fuel to rapidly ignite and burn. Long ignition delay produces unstable engine operation, results in more combustion noise, and indicates fuel or base engine system problems.

Operational Characteristics of Direct Injection Combustion

Diesel's use of excess air, high compression ratios, and fuel properties combine to create some unusual engine operating characteristics. Some of these operational characteristics are exceptionally destructive and require technical solutions to extend engine life. Most importantly, having the skill to differentiate between normal and abnormal DI operational features is essential to diagnosing combustion-related engine problems and making sound service recommendations to operators.

Cold Idle

Injection quantities of fuel in a diesel engine at idle are very small. Combined with the cooling effect of excess air, prolonged idle has detrimental effects on the engine. A typical idle injection quantity in a diesel engine is 2–10 cubic millimeters (mm³). Compare this to the size of a normal fuel droplet, which is approximately 25–28 mm³ **FIGURE 8-28**. Small quantities of fuel are adequate to create enough cylinder pressure to rotate the crankshaft but produce very little heat, which is transferred to engine coolant and cylinder components.

Because the use of excess air in diesels dilutes the heat of combustion and lowers average cylinder temperatures, less heat energy is transmitted to the cooling system. The small combustion chamber surface area of the DI chamber further exaggerates this problem. DI chambers do not allow the engine to warm up from idle; in fact, an engine will cool down below operating temperature when idled. Passenger compartments heated with engine coolant will be cold. For this reason, some

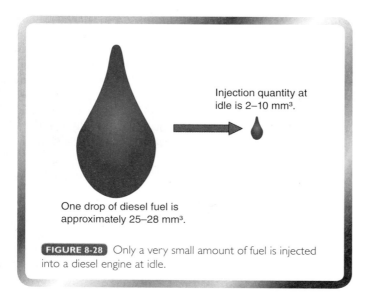

Injection quantity at idle is 2–10 mm³.

One drop of diesel fuel is approximately 25–28 mm³.

FIGURE 8-28 Only a very small amount of fuel is injected into a diesel engine at idle.

manufacturers utilize exhaust back-pressure devices to speed engine warm up. These devices operate by restricting exhaust gases leaving the engine. Exhaust back-pressure regulators increase exhaust temperature and cause more heat retention by the engine around the exhaust ports, which transfers more heat to the cooling system. Piston rings will seal better with increased exhaust pressure. Under load, much higher injection rates are used by diesels **FIGURE 8-29**.

Combustion Slobber and Wet Stacking

Due to low cylinder pressures and the absence of heat, DI combustion quality at idle tends to be very poor. Excess air supplied for combustion lowers cylinder temperatures even more. The excess air can make the air–fuel ratio exceed 500:1. Not all of the injected fuel will burn when temperatures and pressures are low. Fuel may condense or be quenched in regions of the chamber, such as between the piston crown and cylinder wall. Low piston temperatures also lead to the piston not fully expanding; this allows lube oil into the combustion chamber. When soot produced by partially burned fuel mixes with liquids, such as lube oil, it produces **combustion slobber**, a black gooey liquid that leaks from exhaust manifold joints and exhaust pipes when engines are excessively idled; this is also called engine slobber or turbo slobber **FIGURE 8-30**. The appearance of combustion slobber on an exhaust stack as a result of prolonged engine idle is known as **wet stacking** **FIGURE 8-31**. Excess idle time, which causes the engine oil to thicken with soot and slobber, will cause piston rings to stick. Abrasive deposits will also accumulate quickly on pistons; this can lead to premature cylinder wear **FIGURE 8-32**.

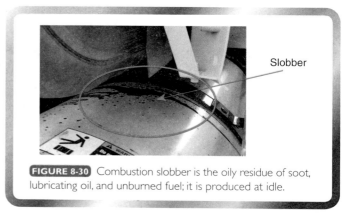

Slobber

FIGURE 8-30 Combustion slobber is the oily residue of soot, lubricating oil, and unburned fuel; it is produced at idle.

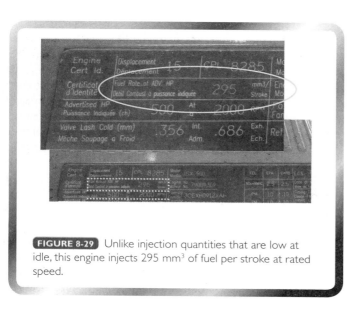

FIGURE 8-29 Unlike injection quantities that are low at idle, this engine injects 295 mm³ of fuel per stroke at rated speed.

FIGURE 8-31 Wet stacking is the appearance of combustion slobber on an exhaust stack as a result of prolonged engine idle.

FIGURE 8-32 These pistons are from two different engines that were excessively idled. The piston rings and lands on the piston on the left are completely carbon filled from baked combustion slobber.

► TECHNICIAN TIP

Diesel combustion produces soot, which can stick to the oil film on the cylinder wall. When oil is scraped from the cylinder wall, soot contaminates the oil. Engines that are excessively idled will quickly soot load the oil. Shorter service intervals are required for the oil to prevent it from thickening and increasing engine-abrasive wear. Soot-thickened oil will plug oil filters quickly, too, leading to more frequent service.

Measuring Idle Time

Because idle is so inefficient and destructive to an engine, all engine manufacturers provide a system to report engine idle time **FIGURE 8-33**. Idle time, which uses 0.9–1.6 gallons (3.5–6 liters) of fuel per hour, is an unnecessary operating expense

FIGURE 8-33 This screen displays the total amount of fuel consumed at idle on this vehicle's last trip.

that accelerates engine wear and shortens the service interval required between oil changes. To determine if oil change intervals require adjustment or investigate complaints about high fuel consumption or engine slobber appearing from exhaust manifold joints, turbochargers, and the exhaust pipe outlet, the percentage of time a truck is idling is an important piece of data to collect.

To measure idle time, follow the steps in **SKILL DRILL 8-1**.

Adjusting Idle Speed and the Shut-Down Timer

Most engine manufacturers recommend that late-model diesel engines should idle for no more than 3 minutes. Unnecessary idling accelerates engine wear, increases soot loading of oil, and wastes fuel. Allowing an engine to idle is more detrimental to an engine than starting and stopping. To limit the amount of idle time and its negative effects, an engine's idle speed, fast idle speed, and a shut-down timer can be adjusted to limit idle time. Most manufacturers provide a recommended idle speed on the emission decal. Generally. idle speed is kept at 550–650 rpm. On electronically controlled engines, fast idle speed can be adjusted so that whenever the cruise control or PTO switches are actuated, the engine will speed to fast idle. Each movement of the PTO or cruise control button can increase or decrease fast idle speed in increments; these increments are also adjustable.

To adjust idle speed and the shut-down timer, follow the steps in **SKILL DRILL 8-2**.

Direct Injection Combustion Noise and Pilot Injection

One strategy to minimize combustion noise from DI chambers is the use of **pilot injection**. Pilot injection shortens the ignition delay period using one, two, or even three small injections of fuel before the main injection event. A pilot injection of fuel 8°–10 °

SKILL DRILL 8-1 Measuring Idle Time

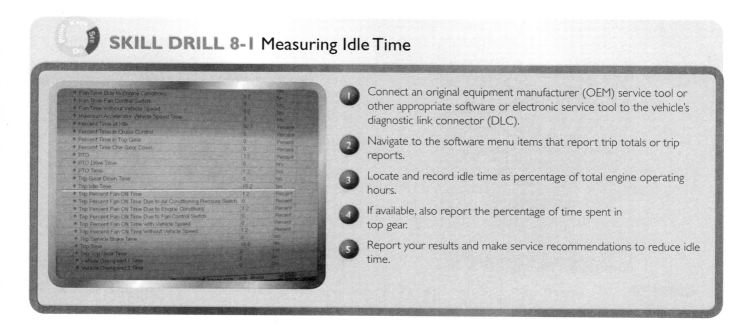

1. Connect an original equipment manufacturer (OEM) service tool or other appropriate software or electronic service tool to the vehicle's diagnostic link connector (DLC).

2. Navigate to the software menu items that report trip totals or trip reports.

3. Locate and record idle time as percentage of total engine operating hours.

4. If available, also report the percentage of time spent in top gear.

5. Report your results and make service recommendations to reduce idle time.

SKILL DRILL 8-2 Adjusting Idle Speed and Shut-Down Timer

1. Identify the correct idle speed for the engine.

2. Using OEM software or other electronic service tools, navigate to the programmable engine parameter screen.

3. Review the idle speed. Enter a new idle speed if the current setting is unacceptable. If a truck's mirrors vibrate and other cab noises are a problem, idle speed can be increased. If the vehicle easily stalls when engaging the clutch or runs rough due to too low an idle speed, increase the engine rpm speed at idle. Customer passwords may be required to make changes to customer programmable parameters.

4. Navigate to the programmable engine parameter screen for the idle shut down timer. The time setting in minutes on this feature will shut down the engine, but the vehicle electrical system and accessories will remain active until the key switch is turned off. When engine operation is required again, the driver must simply either push the clutch or turn the ignition to start the engine again. Touching the clutch or brake pedal will reset the timer to 0 minutes.

5. A cold or hot ambient temperature protection feature may accompany the shut-down timer adjustment. In very hot weather, the air conditioner may be required by the driver; in very cold weather, the engine may need to idle to help keep the engine from cooling off too much.

before the main injection event shortens, and can almost eliminate, ignition delay FIGURE 8-34 . Shortening the ignition delay period can help reduce engine emissions. For example, when cylinder pressure is reduced, especially near TDC, less NO_x is formed. Also, when the ignition delay period is shortened, more time in the combustion cycle is available to burn fuel during the other combustion phases; this results in more complete, cleaner combustion. Shortening the ignition delay period also means that the pressure spike during the uncontrolled burn period is minimized.

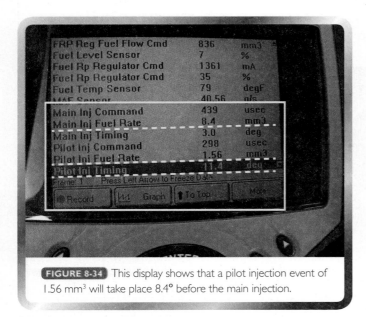

FIGURE 8-34 This display shows that a pilot injection event of 1.56 mm³ will take place 8.4° before the main injection.

Rate-Shaped Injection

At each stage of combustion, and for any given speed and load condition, injecting an ideal quantity of fuel at a specific pressure will produce optimal fuel economy, power, and the lowest amount of emissions. Rate-shaped injection is an injection strategy that carefully regulates the amount of fuel injected into a cylinder per degree of crank angle rotation **FIGURE 8-35**. Split shot or pilot injection are part of the injection rate shape. This is covered in greater detail in the "Functions of High-Pressure Fuel Systems" chapter.

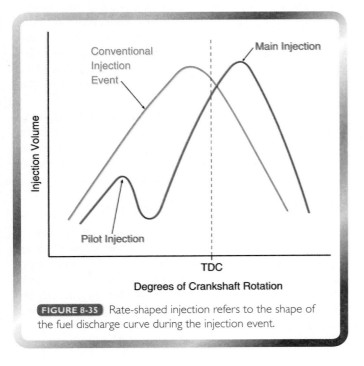

FIGURE 8-35 Rate-shaped injection refers to the shape of the fuel discharge curve during the injection event.

▶ Indirect Injection

The IDI combustion chamber is the other of the two main types of diesel combustion chambers **FIGURE 8-36**. This chamber was traditionally most common in automotive applications because of its high-speed capabilities and low-emission characteristics relative to the DI chamber. Pick-up trucks, vans, and small displacement engines used this chamber design because it offered the performance of a gasoline-fueled vehicle with the durability and fuel economy of a diesel. The Comet and the Ricardo Comet are names for the IDI chamber that capture its physical and operational characteristics **FIGURE 8-37**. The comet-like dynamics of the combustion chamber led to the name to this type of IDI chamber. As fuel is sprayed from the single spray hole of the pintle injector, the spherical shape of the chamber rolls the fuel into burning balls of fire that resemble comets. Henry Ricardo developed this comet chamber in the late 1920s.

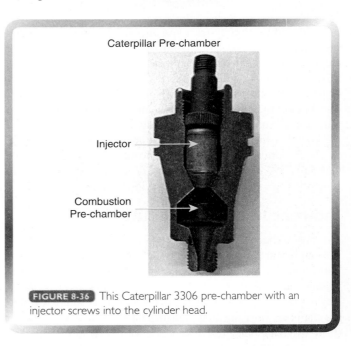

FIGURE 8-36 This Caterpillar 3306 pre-chamber with an injector screws into the cylinder head.

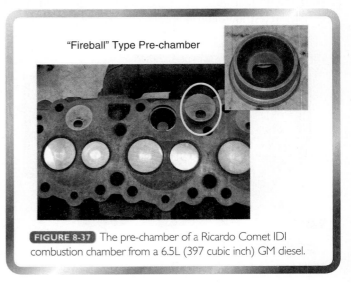

FIGURE 8-37 The pre-chamber of a Ricardo Comet IDI combustion chamber from a 6.5L (397 cubic inch) GM diesel.

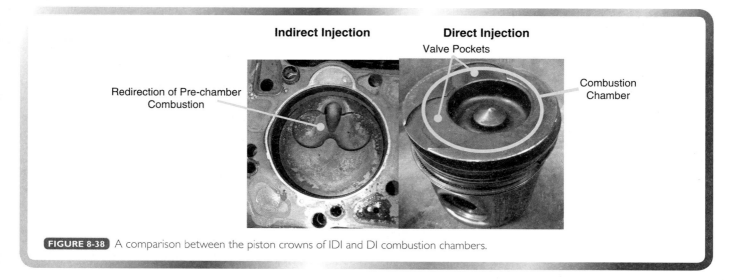

FIGURE 8-38 A comparison between the piston crowns of IDI and DI combustion chambers.

IDI combustion systems use fuel injected into a smaller, spherical, highly turbulent chamber that is connected to a main chamber through a narrow passageway called the venturi. Fuel is mixed with air and ignited in this pre-chamber. The fireball then expands into the main chamber where combustion is completed. The shape of the piston is different from those used in DI engines. Only a small contour in the piston redirects combustion from the pre-chamber into the main combustion chamber **FIGURE 8-38**. In North America, the last engine to use this design was the GM 6.5L (397 cubic inch) diesel in "G" vans, in 2001. Buses in London, England, first used this type of chamber in the 1930s.

Indirect Injection Features

The major characteristics of IDI chambers are that they use a pre-combustion chamber formed in the cylinder head, that the chamber typically holds approximately 70% of the cylinder volume, and that they use <u>pintle nozzles</u>. Pintle nozzles have a single orifice at the tip to spray a single, coarse stream of fuel into the chamber. Their opening pressures range from 900 to 5000 psi (62 to 345 bar). Pintle nozzles operate with lower nozzle opening pressure (NOP) than <u>multi-orifice nozzles,</u> which use multiple spray holes to distribute and atomize fuel **FIGURE 8-39**.

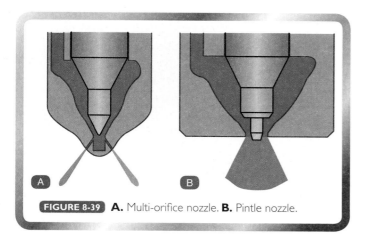

FIGURE 8-39 **A.** Multi-orifice nozzle. **B.** Pintle nozzle.

The atomization of fuel critical to the DI chamber is not required in an IDI chamber due to the high degree of turbulence in the pre-chamber. The turbulent pre-chamber is responsible for mixing the air and fuel. It performs this job much better than the DI chamber, accounting for its high-speed and low-emission characteristics. Vaporization of the coarse fuel droplets is accomplished when fuel initially contacts the incandescent glow plug during start-up and then the hot walls of the pre-chamber during regular operation.

IDIs are capable of faster top engine rpm limits due to a higher degree of turbulence, which produces more rapid and even mixing of air and fuel. The use of a pre-chamber allows the engine to tolerate poorer grades of fuels without significantly longer ignition delay. The mixing of fuel in the pre-chamber and its passage into the main chamber through a venturi enhances mixing and complete combustion. The two-chamber design creates a quieter engine with less knock because ignition delay is minimized. The turbulent pre-chamber, which promotes faster mixing and vaporization of fuel, is the reason for this, because it ensures a rapid combustion sequence from injection to afterburn. Noise is further reduced because the expansion of the burning fuel is regulated as it passes through the venturi, thus smoothing the rapid rise in cylinder pressure.

Indirect injection combustion chambers had the advantage of being a high-speed, clean-burning, quieter sounding engine in comparison to DI chambers. Electronics and the introduction of high-pressure injection system capabilities erased the advantages of IDI engines **FIGURE 8-40**.

Glow Plugs and IDI Chambers

One of the most significant features of the IDI chamber is the requirement for a glow plug starting aid. Glow plugs are required to produce fuel vapor from the coarse fuel spray, which does not generate sufficient fuel vapor for ignition on its own. When energized with electric current, the glow plug heating element causes the fuel to vaporize on contact with the element. The heat from the glow plug must affect the fuel, not the air; only by vaporizing enough fuel will the glow plug enable the

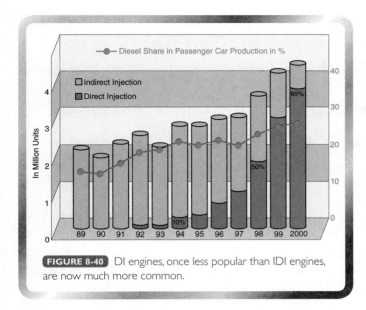

FIGURE 8-40 DI engines, once less popular than IDI engines, are now much more common.

engine to start. After a few minutes of engine operation, glow plug operation is not required—at that point, the combustion chamber walls provide the hot surface needed to vaporize fuel.

Glow Plug Control

Control of glow plug operation in modern engines is delegated to a separate electronic module on both IDI and DI engines **FIGURE 8-41**. Glow plug failure will produce excessive emissions, so it therefore has a diagnostic monitor associated with it on on-board diagnostic II (OBD-II) and heavy-duty on-board diagnostic (HD-OBD) compliant vehicles. Glow plugs must be heated before the operator begins cranking the engine over to start. High amperage current is best switched through a relay commonly used by glow plug controllers. Coolant, ambient air, and oil temperatures, and even barometric pressure, are sensed by the control circuit to determine the length of time the glow plug will be heated before the operator is prompted to crank the engine. An instrument panel–mounted wait-to-start light usually remains illuminated until the correct amount of time has elapsed for the plugs to reach starting temperature. Once the

engine is operational, the controller will cycle the plugs on and off during an afterglow period, which lasts until the engine has warmed up. Subsequent to the afterglow period, the plugs are switched off to prevent burning out **FIGURE 8-42**.

Inspecting Air Intake Heaters and Glow Plugs

In OBD-II and HD-OBD engines, a cold-start emission reduction strategy monitors air intake heaters and glow plugs to ensure that they operate properly. Voltage drops and current flow through the devices are continuously checked when they are operational.

If fault codes for the air intake heaters and glow plugs are logged, follow the steps in **SKILL DRILL 8-3** to pinpoint the type of failure.

Instant Start Systems

To reduce wait-to-start times, newer glow plugs have been developed that heat to operating temperature very quickly. An **instant start glow plug system (ISS)** uses two heating elements connected together in series **FIGURE 8-43**. A sheath covering the heating elements rapidly heats to starting temperature in as little as 2 seconds. ISS plugs are now used in most automotive applications. These systems are much faster than older plugs, which contained a single heating element and took 10–30 seconds to heat to starting temperature. The use of silicon nitrate ceramics to form the glow plug sheath and dual coil heating elements have enabled this rapid cycle time. Silicon nitrate is a better heat conductor than other ceramics. A second "intelligent" control heating element connected in series with the heating coil limits current by changing resistance as it heats, depending on temperature. The variable resistance of this second coil prevents damage to the plug through overheating. The newest innovations to glow plug mechanisms include an **integrated pressure-sensing glow plug**, which is a glow plug that includes a pressure sensor that measures cylinder pressure for closed-loop feedback of combustion pressure.

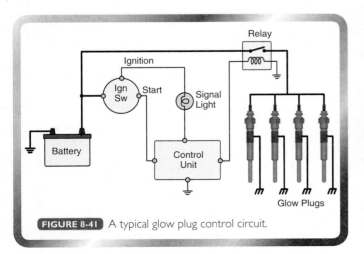

FIGURE 8-41 A typical glow plug control circuit.

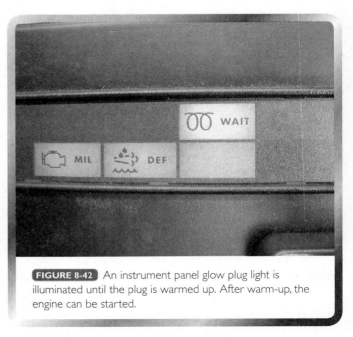

FIGURE 8-42 An instrument panel glow plug light is illuminated until the plug is warmed up. After warm-up, the engine can be started.

SKILL DRILL 8-3 Inspecting Air Intake Heaters and Glow Plugs

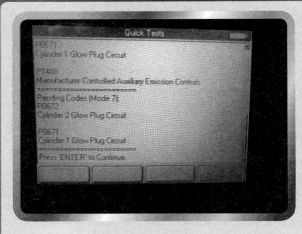

1 Obtain the fault codes to determine whether the fault is with the air intake heater or the glow plugs.

2 With the key off, disconnect the leads to the intake air heater and measure the resistance of the electrical heating elements. If any circuit has high resistance (generally no more than a few ohms) the circuit is defective.

3 If the air intake heater circuit resistance is satisfactory, switch the ignition key on while measuring the voltage to the air intake heater. To simulate a cold start condition, the engine should be cold or the intake air and coolant sensors should disconnected. A high amperage relay will supply current flow to the electric heating element.

4 If no current is supplied by the relay, check the relay terminal, which is switched to ground through the electronic control module (ECM). Use a jumper wire to ground the terminal to determine if the relay will switch and supply current to the heater.

5 Using a voltmeter, check the battery supply cables to the relay to determine whether current is supplied to the relay. Battery voltage should appear at the relay at all times.

6 For glow plugs, measure the electrical resistance of each plug. Connect the test lead of a test light to the battery positive. When the probe is touching the terminal tip of the plug, the test light will faintly glow if the glow plug has continuity.

7 Report your findings and make service recommendations for repairs.

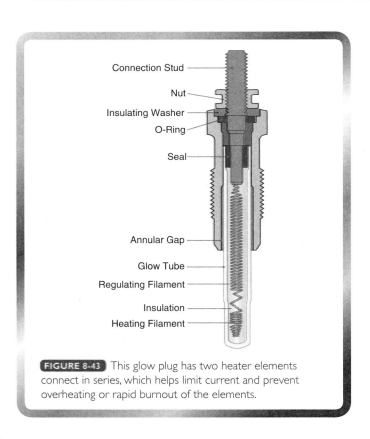

Connection Stud
Nut
Insulating Washer
O-Ring
Seal
Annular Gap
Glow Tube
Regulating Filament
Insulation
Heating Filament

FIGURE 8-43 This glow plug has two heater elements connect in series, which helps limit current and prevent overheating or rapid burnout of the elements.

Wrap-Up

Ready for Review

▶ Learning the principles of engine combustion is essential to making useful observations about engine operation and the effects of abnormal combustion, and developing effective diagnostic and repair skills.

▶ Combustion is a chemical process in which fuel, made up primarily of hydrogen and carbon atoms, reacts with oxygen. When chemical bonds between fuel atoms are broken, oxygen combines with hydrogen and carbon and heat is released.

▶ A heat source is required to begin the combustion process. In engines, ignition heat is derived from only two sources: an electric spark or heat produced by compressing air.

▶ Diesels use a compression ignition (CI) system, which makes them sensitive to changes in air temperature and compression pressures. Hard starting and prolonged cranking time can be caused by low cylinder pressures and temperatures.

▶ Spark ignition (SI) engines are limited to lower compression ratios because high compression pressures can heat and prematurely ignite the air–fuel mixture drawn into the cylinders during the intake stroke. Prematurely igniting the air–fuel mixture is called pre-ignition detonation; this is a condition that reduces engine power and can severely damage an engine.

▶ Detonation due to a rapid, uncontrolled increase in cylinder pressure is recognized by a pinging noise or a sharp, powerful knocking sound in SI engines. Antiknock additives, called octane boosters, enable higher compression ratios in today's SI engines, but they still operate below the compression ratios used commonly by diesels.

▶ Thermal efficiency is an engine's ability to convert heat into mechanical energy. The higher compression ratios used by diesel engines extract more energy from combustion and enable much higher thermal efficiency than other engine types.

▶ Diesel engines operate at twice the compression ratio of traditional SI engines. The average compression ratio of today's on-highway diesel engines is approximately 16:1. After 16:1, power increases are smaller with increasing compression ratios. At 23:1, engines will begin lose power if the compression ratios are increased.

▶ The two types of diesel combustion chambers are direct injection (DI) and indirect injection (IDI) chambers. DI combustion chambers are the most common type of diesel engine combustion chamber used today.

▶ Typical DI combustion chambers in on-highway heavy-duty diesels have compression ratios between 15.5:1 and 17.5:1. DI chambers use multi-orifice nozzles.

▶ IDI combustion chambers use combustion pre-chambers located in the cylinder head and are used by smaller engines. Compression ratios for IDI engines are commonly between 19:1 and 23:1.

▶ Large-bore diesels may use compression ratios as high as 25:1 to compensate for compression pressure losses from cylinder leakage around piston rings due to slow piston movement. Slower-moving diesel engines use more compression rings to minimize gas leakage past the rings during compression stroke.

▶ Higher compression ratio engines have increased thermal efficiency because they have higher power output, are more fuel efficient, and mix air and fuel better. A harder, longer push against the piston is possible in higher compression ratio engines, which also increases thermal efficiency.

▶ Higher compression ratios improve combustion quality by speeding up chemical reactions through higher temperatures and pressures. Fuel is burned more cleanly and completely because chemical reactions are enhanced.

▶ Injecting more fuel into a combustion chamber shortens the combustion time due to higher cylinder temperatures and pressures. Smaller injection quantities require a longer time to burn than larger quantities.

▶ Torsional vibration occurs when the crankshaft speeds up and slows down. During compression stroke, pistons will slow down as they approach top dead center (TDC) due to increasing cylinder pressures. After combustion begins, the crankshaft will accelerate quickly. Torsional vibration can cause engine damage and produce unpleasant vibration in the driveline.

▶ The absence of a throttle plate increases diesel efficiency.

▶ Energy expended by an engine to move air in and exhaust out of the cylinders is known as pumping loss.

▶ Diesel engines are lean burn combustion systems that use excess air to burn fuel. The heat of combustion is diluted by excess air, which produces cool exhaust temperatures but also prevents the engine from reaching operating temperature at idle. Without an auxiliary device to speed up engine warming, DI engines need to be placed under load to quickly reach operating temperature.

▶ Prolonged idling of DI engines produces combustion slobber, which is a mixture of soot, unburned fuel, and oil. Slobber can sometimes be observed leaking from the exhaust manifold joints and exhaust system joints. Wet stacking refers to the dark, oily appearance of the exhaust stack.

▶ To maintain peak combustion pressures at 10°–15° after TDC, injection timing needs to be advanced in an engine when its speed increases and the load remains the same. Timing is retarded when the load increases and the speed remains the same.

▶ Pilot ignition is an injection event that takes place 8°–10° before the main injection event. The use of one, two, or three pilot injections reduces and almost eliminates combustion noise caused by ignition delay. When pilot injection shortens and eliminates ignition delay, a longer combustion period produces fewer noxious emissions.

▶ A prolonged ignition delay period in a diesel leads to an increase in engine combustion noise. Low cetane fuel, cold ambient and engine temperatures, low compression, and poor fuel atomization are common causes of long ignition delay.

▸ IDI combustion chambers require glow plugs to start, because fuel spray from pintle nozzles is heavy and coarse. The glow plug produces fuel vapor for starting until the walls of the combustion chamber are hot enough to vaporize fuel.

Vocabulary Builder

auto-ignition temperature The temperature at which a fuel will ignite when heated.

combustion A chemical reaction between oxygen and fuel molecules in which heat is released.

combustion slobber A combustion by-product from diesel engines consisting of unburned fuel, soot, and lubricating oil; also known as engine slobber or turbo slobber.

compression ignition (CI) An ignition system that initiates combustion using heat derived from only the compression of air.

direct injection (DI) A diesel combustion chamber design that has a piston-formed combustion bowl and a multi-orifice nozzle.

flash point The temperature at which fuel will produce adequate vapor to ignite if exposed to an open source of ignition such as a spark or flame.

homogeneous charge compression ignition (HCCI) engine A low-emission, experimental type of CI combustion system that pulls air and fuel into the cylinder during intake stroke.

ignition delay The time period between the beginning of fuel injection and actual ignition of fuel in a combustion chamber.

indirect injection (IDI) A diesel combustion chamber that uses a pre-combustion chamber formed in the cylinder head and a pintle nozzle.

instant start glow plug system(ISS) A recent development in glow plug technology that uses two heating elements connected together in series. A steel-like sheath covers the heating elements and rapidly heats to starting temperature in as little as 2 seconds.

integrated pressure-sensing glow plug A glow plug that includes a pressure sensor that measures cylinder pressure for closed-loop feedback of combustion pressure.

lean burn combustion A combustion system that uses excess air so that it is air rich and fuel lean. Air–fuel ratios are above stoichiometric ratio.

multi-orifice nozzle A fuel nozzle that uses multiple spray holes to distribute and atomize fuel.

pilot injection A small injection event taking place 8°–10° before the main injection event.

pintle nozzle A fuel nozzle that sprays fuel through a single hole.

pumping loss The energy used by an engine to move intake and exhaust gases in and out of the cylinders.

rate-shaped injection An injection strategy that carefully regulates the amount of fuel injected into a cylinder per degree of crank angle rotation.

stoichiometric ratio The minimum mass of air required to completely burn all fuel in the combustion chamber so that no fuel or air remains after combustion.

stratified combustion Combustion that burns fuel in layers of varying air–fuel ratios.

torsional vibration The rhythmic speeding up and slowing down of a crankshaft due to alternating compression and power events in an engine's cylinders.

wet stacking The appearance of engine slobber on an exhaust stack as a result of prolonged engine idle.

Review Questions

1. _____ is a diesel combustion chamber design that has a piston-formed combustion chamber and a multi-orifice nozzle.
   a. Direct injection
   b. Indirect injection
   c. Compression ignition
   d. Rate-shaped injection

2. _____ is an ignition system that initiates combustion using heat derived from only the compression of air.
   a. Indirection injection
   b. Compression ignition
   c. Direct injection
   d. Rate-shaped injection

3. _____ is the minimum mass of air required to completely burn all fuel in the combustion chamber so that no fuel or air remains after combustion.
   a. Lean burn
   b. Auto-ignition temperature
   c. Flash point
   d. Stoichiometric ratio

4. _____ is a diesel combustion chamber that uses a precombustion chamber in the cylinder head and a pintle nozzle.
   a. Direct injection
   b. Indirect injection
   c. Rate-shaped injection
   d. Compression ignition

5. _____ is an injection strategy that carefully regulates the amount of fuel injected into a cylinder per degree of crank angle rotation.
   a. Rate-shaped injection
   b. Direct injection
   c. Indirect injection
   d. Compression ignition

6. An engine with a high compression ratio extracts more _____ using the same amount of fuel compared to an engine with a lower compression ratio.
   a. torque
   b. power
   c. turbulence
   d. efficiency

7. _____ is the time period between the beginning of fuel injection and the actual ignition of fuel in a combustion in a combustion chamber.
   a. Overlap
   b. Engine load
   c. Stoichiometric ratio
   d. Ignition delay

8. Pilot injection is a small injection event taking place _____ degrees before the main injection event.
   a. 2-4
   b. 6-8
   c. 8-10
   d. 10-12

9. _____ spray fuel through a single hole.
   a. Single-orifice nozzles
   b. Multi-orifice nozzles
   c. Pintle nozzles
   d. Fuel injectors

10. Pressure and temperature _____ when compression ratio rises.
   a. increase proportionally
   b. increase at slightly different rates
   c. increase at extremely different rates
   d. increase unpredictably in comparison to one another

ASE-Type Questions

1. Technician A says when preignition detonation occurs in an SI system, cylinder temperatures ignite the air-fuel mixture. Technician B says the spark plug ignites the air-fuel mixture when preignition detonation occurs in an SI system. Who is correct?
   a. Technician A
   b. Technician B
   c. Both Technician A and Technician B
   d. Neither Technician A nor Technician B

2. Technician A says pressure and temperature increase at different rates when compression ratio rises. Technician B says they increase proportionally when compression ratio rises. Who is correct?
   a. Technician A
   b. Technician B
   c. Both Technician A and Technician B
   d. Neither Technician A nor Technician B

3. Technician A says 150 rpm is a normal cranking speed for medium- and large-bore diesels. Technician B says 250 rpm is a normal cranking speed for medium- and large-bore diesels. Who is correct?
   a. Technician A
   b. Technician B
   c. Both Technician A and Technician B
   d. Neither Technician A nor Technician B

4. Technician A says during full-load conditions, when maximum quantities of fuel are injected, excess air dilutes the heat of combustion. Technician B says that process prevents damage to cylinder components and valves. Who is correct?
   a. Technician A
   b. Technician B
   c. Both Technician A and Technician B
   d. Neither Technician A nor Technician B

5. Technician A says engines that use high compression ratios also have increased mechanical efficiency. Technician B says in diesel engines, intake air is throttled for the purpose of controlling power. Who is correct?
   a. Technician A
   b. Technician B
   c. Both Technician A and Technician B
   d. Neither Technician A nor Technician B

6. Technician A says that when injection takes place later than normal, the injection event is referred to as having retarded timing. Technician B says that when injection takes place later than normal, the injection event is referred to as having delayed timing. Who is correct?
   a. Technician A
   b. Technician B
   c. Both Technician A and Technician B
   d. Neither Technician A nor Technician B

7. Technician A says offset combustion chambers create even piston crown temperatures. Technician B says offset combustion chambers create uneven piston crown temperatures. Who is correct?
   a. Technician A
   b. Technician B
   c. Both Technician A and Technician B
   d. Neither Technician A nor Technician B

8. Technician A says most engine manufacturers recommend that late-model diesel engines should idle for no more than one minute. Technician B says most engine manufacturers recommend that late-model diesel engines should idle for no more than two minutes. Who is correct?
   a. Technician A
   b. Technician B
   c. Both Technician A and Technician B
   d. Neither Technician A nor Technician B

9. Technician A says an injection strategy that carefully regulates the amount of fuel injected into a cylinder per degree of crank angle rotation is called rate-shaped injection. Technician B says an injection strategy that carefully regulates the amount of fuel injected into a cylinder per degree of crank angle rotation is called a stratified injection. Who is correct?
   a. Technician A
   b. Technician B
   c. Both Technician A and Technician B
   d. Neither Technician A nor Technician B

10. Technician A says the appearance of combustion slobber on an exhaust stack as a result of prolonged engine idle is known as spittle streaking. Technician B says the appearance of combustion slobber on an exhaust stack as a result of prolonged engine idle is known as wet stacking. Who is correct?
   a. Technician A
   b. Technician B
   c. Both Technician A and Technician B
   d. Neither Technician A nor Technician B

SECTION III

Engine Construction and Operation

NATEF Tasks

Diesel Engines

General

- Listen for engine noises; determine needed action. (pp 243, 249–250)
- Identify engine surging, rough operation, misfiring, low power, slow deceleration, slow acceleration, and shutdown problems; determine needed action. (p 254)
- Identify engine vibration problems. (pp 243, 251, 253)

Engine Block

- Perform crankcase pressure test; determine needed action. (pp 258–260)
- Remove, inspect, service, and install pans, covers, gaskets, seals, wear rings, and crankcase ventilation components. (pp 254–258)

- Clean, inspect, and measure cylinder walls or liners for wear and damage; determine needed action. (pp 258–259)
- Inspect connecting rod and bearings for wear patterns; measure pistons, pins, retainers, and bushings; perform needed action. (pp 254–257)
- Determine piston-to-cylinder wall clearance; check ring-to-groove fit and end gap; install rings on pistons. (pp 255–256)
- Assemble pistons and connecting rods; install in block; install rod bearings and check clearances. (pp 251–252)
- Check condition of piston cooling jets (nozzle); determine needed action. (p 253)

Knowledge Objectives

After reading this chapter, you will be able to:

1. Identify and describe emission-related features of cylinder components. (pp 238–244)
2. Define and explain terminology associated with cylinder components. (pp 238–253)
3. Classify pistons according to their application and design. (pp 239–242)
4. Identify the types of diesel engine pistons rings, piston pins, and connecting rods and their applications. (pp 245–253)
5. Describe the construction features and functions of diesel engine pistons rings, piston pins, and connecting rods. (pp 245–253)

6. Recommend practices to enhance the durability and reliability of cylinder components. (pp 253–257)
7. Select appropriate tools for performing diagnostic tests and repairs on cylinder components. (pp 253–260)
8. Predict and identify component failures based on operating conditions and wear factors. (pp 253–260)
9. Interpret the results of diagnostic tests and measurements of cylinder components. (pp 253–260)
10. Recommend common reconditioning or repairs to cylinder components. (pp 254–257)
11. Identify and explain common causes of abnormal wear, bending, or torsional stresses of cylinder components. (pp 256–257)

Skills Objectives

After reading this chapter, you will be able to:
1. Perform a crankcase blow-by test. (p 269) **SKILL DRILL 9-1**

► Introduction

Cylinder components are the engine components first used to convert combustion forces into mechanical power, which makes them a logical starting point to examine diesel engine construction **FIGURE 9-1**. These components include pistons, piston rings, piston pins (also called wrist pins), piston pin bushings, and connecting rods (also called con-rods) **FIGURE 9-2**. These components convert and transfer the forces of combustion to the crankshaft. They are the most highly stressed parts of the diesel engine. Flame temperature of diesel fuel is over 3900°F (2149°C), and cylinder pressures can now exceed 3000 pounds per square inch (psi) (20,684 kilopascals [kPa]) of force. Because of these stresses, the design, construction, and operation of cylinder components are critically important to engine performance and durability. In addition, cylinder components, together with other engine systems, are used to reach emissions targets.

Emission legislation from the US Environmental Protection Agency (EPA) imposes new design features on cylinder components through **durability requirements**, which are legislated standards for engine durability that require noxious engine emissions to remain below specific thresholds through the expected useful life of an engine. To keep emissions low throughout an engine's anticipated life cycle, cylinder components are now constructed to last longer than ever. EPA standards require medium-duty diesels to remain emission compliant for a useful life of 10 years or 185,000 miles (297,729 km). Heavy-duty diesels must have a useful life of 10 years or 435,000 miles (700,065 km). EURO 4 and EURO 5 mandate a useful life of up to 6 years and between 62,137 and 186,411 miles (100,000 and 300,000 km) for medium-duty diesels. The latest EURO 6 heavy-duty diesel standards are 7 years of useful life or 434,960 miles (700,000 km).

Cylinder components in contemporary diesels have undergone numerous refinements to help meet higher standards for performance, life expectancy, and low emission output. Major engine repairs and overhaul involve replacing or determining the serviceability (remaining service life) of these parts, so technicians need to familiarize themselves with the construction, operating principles, and failure modes of these parts. Engine failures often involve damage to these components, so understanding failure modes is necessary in order to correct root causes of damage to these components.

You are the Technician

An older truck arrives at your shop, and the driver complains that the engine lacks power and is running rough. During an inspection, you observe a knocking sound in the engine. There are many significant oil leaks from the gaskets and seals on the engine. In addition, a considerable amount of oil-laden blow-by is being emitted from the road draft tube; this has left a large amount of oil on the vehicle frame. The engine oil level is low as well. When the throttle is snapped to accelerate the engine, visible black and grey smoke are observed at the exhaust pipe. While the odometer reading is only 279,617 miles (450,000 kilometers [km]), the vehicle is close to 10 years old and is used primarily to pick up and deliver scrap metal in and around the city on a daily basis. Before you can prepare an estimate for the cost of repairs, you need to validate whether the base engine system is in satisfactory condition to justify any repairs or adjustments to the fuel system and other engine systems.

1. What techniques would you use to estimate the remaining service life of the engine, and why would you recommend them?
2. The accumulated distance on the odometer is relatively low for the engine to be worn out and in need of an overhaul. What factors could contribute to premature wear of this truck's engine? What observations could you make that would support your answer?
3. If the engine is overhauled and the vehicle is returned to service, what operating recommendations would you make to the driver to extend the life of the engine?

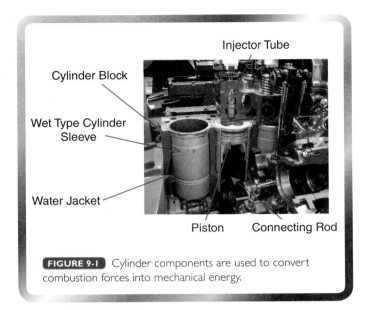

FIGURE 9-1 Cylinder components are used to convert combustion forces into mechanical energy.

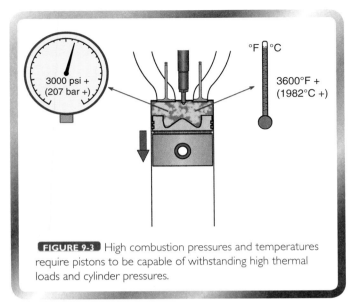

FIGURE 9-3 High combustion pressures and temperatures require pistons to be capable of withstanding high thermal loads and cylinder pressures.

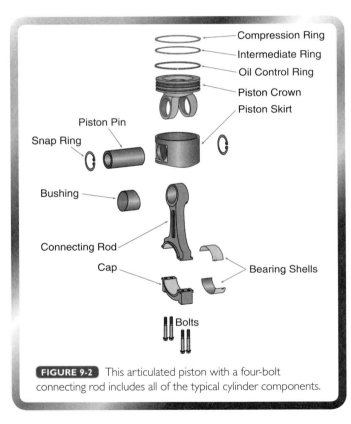

FIGURE 9-2 This articulated piston with a four-bolt connecting rod includes all of the typical cylinder components.

▶ Pistons

One of the most significant components in a reciprocating engine is the piston. Tremendous heat, pressure, and inertia forces are endured by the pistons as they capture combustion energy and transmit it to the other reciprocating and rotating parts of the engine **FIGURE 9-3**. In order to operate reliably for many hours under extreme conditions, pistons require some important construction features. Piston design is a major factor in determining a variety of engine characteristics such as power output, emission characteristics, speed, oil consumption, and durability.

Piston Design

Pistons have three main parts **FIGURE 9-4**. They are:

- The crown, or top of the piston, which is subjected to cylinder pressure and heat
- The ring belt, which is where piston grooves are located
- The skirt, which is the surface that slides directly against the cylinder wall to stabilize piston movement

In the uppermost part of the skirt is the piston pin. Additional piston material, called the pin boss, reinforces the area around the pin. Steel struts are often cast into the pin boss for improved strength.

Several basic piston designs are used in today's diesels, including slipper skirt, cam ground, trunk, articulating, and MONOTHERM® **FIGURE 9-5**.

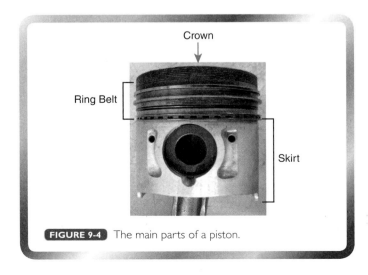

FIGURE 9-4 The main parts of a piston.

FIGURE 9-5 Major types of piston designs used in today's diesel engines include MONOTHERM, trunk, articulating, and more.

Slipper Skirt Pistons

In the design of a **slipper skirt piston**, a portion of the skirt is removed on both non-thrust sides of the piston. This provides clearance for the turning radius of the crankshaft counterweight when the piston approaches bottom dead center (BDC) **FIGURE 9-6**. Slipper skirt pistons enable the use of shorter connecting rods, which permits the manufacture of vertically smaller, lighter, more compact engines. This is important when the profile of the engine must be kept short to fit in a smaller vehicle. More compact engines also translate into lighter designs for better vehicle dynamics. Slipper skirt pistons are often used in smaller V-block diesels where compact engine design is vital.

Cam Ground Pistons

A number of strategies are used to help to minimize the expansion problems of pistons; for example, the shape of the piston is carefully machined to allow expansion in the cylinder. The shape that is almost universally used to enable expansion without seizing is an elliptical, or oval, shape. When pistons are manufactured this way, the piston expands to form a symmetrical, round shape after it is warmed up **FIGURE 9-7**. This piston configuration is commonly known as a **cam ground piston**.

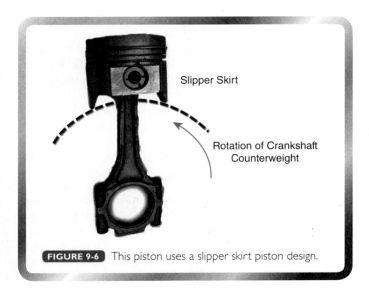

FIGURE 9-6 This piston uses a slipper skirt piston design.

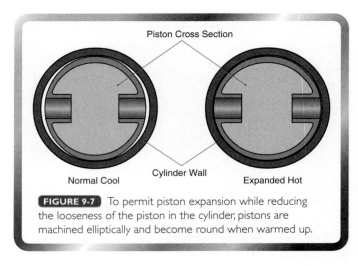

FIGURE 9-7 To permit piston expansion while reducing the looseness of the piston in the cylinder, pistons are machined elliptically and become round when warmed up.

Trunk Pistons

Trunk pistons have a full skirt and are longer than they are wide. The full skirt design is stronger than a slipper skirt piston. This enables the cylinders to support higher cylinder pressures and accompanying side thrust. Side thrust is the force of a piston against the side of a cylinder wall produced by the angle of the connecting rod, which pushes the piston sideways when cylinder pressures are high. Cylinder pressure during power stroke produces **major side thrust**, while compression pressure produces **minor side thrust**. Trunk pistons are used in more rugged diesel engine applications and are almost always made from aluminum alloys. As trunk piston design has developed, pistons are being shortened to minimize cylinder wear, noise, mass, and friction, and the likelihood oil can be pumped into the combustion chamber **FIGURE 9-8**.

Articulating Pistons

Another innovation to piston technology is the use of **articulating pistons** in many medium- and heavy-duty diesel engines. These pistons are constructed using two pieces: a separate aluminum skirt connected to an alloy steel crown by a piston pin **FIGURE 9-9**. The use of steel as a construction material

FIGURE 9-8 The evolution of trunk pistons.

FIGURE 9-9 Articulating pistons use steel crowns to withstand high cylinder temperatures and pressures. These pistons have low crevice volume crowns.

FIGURE 9-10 Crevice volume is the area between the crown and cylinder wall. A larger crevice volume area produces more noxious emissions.

helps these pistons resist damage from high temperatures while supporting greater cylinder pressures. Steel piston crowns also enable a reduction in the volume of the area above the top ring and between the piston and cylinder wall. This region between the piston crown and cylinder wall above the top compression ring is called the **crevice volume**. The strength of a steel crown enables the top ring to be placed closer to the crown without causing a fracture between the ring groove and crown, which would occur if an aluminum piston crown was used. Pistons with this feature are referred to as low crevice volume (LCV) pistons. Manufacturers' studies have found this change alone improves fuel economy as much as 5%. Eliminating the dead air of the crevice volume area lowers hydrocarbon (HC) exhaust emissions by as much as 50% **FIGURE 9-10**. Trunk pistons are also made with reduced crevice volume, but aluminum pistons cannot reduce the crevice volume to the same extent as pistons with steel crowns.

MONOTHERM Pistons

MONOTHERM pistons, also known as ecotherm pistons, are the newest innovation in diesel piston design **FIGURE 9-11**. The most noticeable feature of these pistons is the one-piece alloy steel design, which uses less material between the piston crown and piston pin **FIGURE 9-12**. Shortening the piston achieves nearly a 50% reduction in the distance between the centerline of the pin bore and the top of the piston—a dimension referred to as the compression height. MONOTHERM pistons are also LCV pistons. The MONOTHERM piston design offers the following advantages:

- Alloyed steel, although heavier than aluminum, is stronger than aluminum. The strength of the alloyed steel allows less material to be used in the construction of the piston, resulting in an alloyed steel piston comparable in weight to an aluminum piston. The fact that MONOTHERM pistons are short also makes them lighter.

- One-piece steel design increases load-carrying capacity. This means higher peak combustion pressures are sustainable. The current maximum cylinder pressure for MONOTHERM pistons is 4000 psi (27,579 kPa).
- Higher load-bearing capabilities enable the use of larger cylinder bores for higher displacement volume and power output within the same engine block. Originally, these pistons were used in engines with approximately 15L (915 cubic inch) displacement. However, increasing numbers of mid-bore engines are now using these one-piece steel pistons.
- Reduction of the size of the piston skirt and the corresponding reduction in friction, plus the tighter operating clearances of steel, provides 1% higher power output and a 1% reduction in fuel consumption. This improvement also allows turbocharger speed to decrease by 1000 revolutions per minute (rpm) in some engines, which leads to improved turbocharger durability.
- A smaller skirt area results in reduced cylinder wear.
- The strength of the alloyed steel reduces tear-apart forces during catastrophic failure; this leads to less engine destruction.
- No piston pin bushing is required by the steel construction. Instead, the wrist pin bore is coated with phosphate for reduced friction. A black phosphate coating reduces the possibility of corrosion in exhaust gas recirculation (EGR) engines.
- One-piece design makes assembly and service simpler.

Piston Construction

A piston can be made using either a casting process or a forging process. In a casting process, molten metal is injected into a mold from the bottom up. This minimizes the likelihood of trapped air pockets forming in the casting. Various components can be fixed in the piston during the casting process, including reinforcing steel struts in the pin boss area or hardened nickel alloy inserts for ring grooves. When cooled, the piston features are machined to the correct dimensions and to accept rings and wrist pins.

Most diesel pistons are forged. **Forged pistons** are made from aluminum alloy billets that are stamped into shape by forging dies. In the forging process, the billet is heated to a plastic-like state. The material is placed into a mold, and it is hammered or squeezed under high pressure into a finished shape **FIGURE 9-13**. The forging process realigns the grain structure of the metal and compacts the metal structure to form a denser, heavier piston. Forged pistons are able to withstand higher cylinder pressures and temperatures than cast pistons. However, the denser structure of a forged piston will not conduct heat away as fast as a cast piston, so a forged piston will run 20% hotter. Forged pistons also have a greater expansion coefficient than cast pistons, and therefore require larger running clearances in cold engines.

A few pistons may have the crown and skirt manufactured in two separate processes. The skirt may be forged and the crown cast, but both will be bonded together by welding or by simply casting the crown onto the forged skirt.

After shaping, the skirts of aluminum pistons are anodized to resist wear. **Anodizing** is a process used to harden

FIGURE 9-11 Ecotherm pistons are single-piece alloyed steel pistons used in medium-duty diesel engines.

FIGURE 9-12 A MONOTHERM piston is a one-piece alloyed steel design.

- Steel expands at a lesser rate than aluminum, so operating clearances are much smaller for MONOTHERM pistons. This reduces piston noise at cold-start and low-load conditions when operating clearances are greatest. Tighter operating clearances also reduce blow-by and oil consumption.

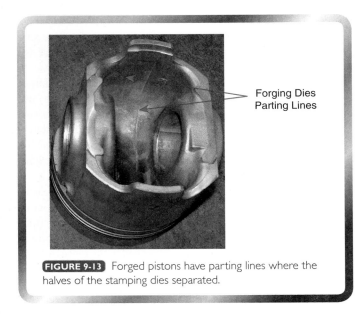

FIGURE 9-13 Forged pistons have parting lines where the halves of the stamping dies separated.

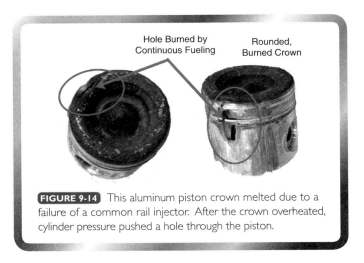

FIGURE 9-14 This aluminum piston crown melted due to a failure of a common rail injector. After the crown overheated, cylinder pressure pushed a hole through the piston.

aluminum by electrochemically reacting oxygen with aluminum. A **micro-finish etching**, or machining of fine lines, is commonly imparted to the piston skirt to retain oil. Oil trapped on the skirt is used to help lubricate the piston.

Piston Materials

Due to the high speed of a reciprocating engine and the tremendous inertial forces of the piston at the end of each stroke, easily machined aluminum alloys are the material of choice for pistons. The lower inertial force of aluminum alloy pistons translates into less stress on other engine components, including connecting rods and crankshafts, which extends engine life. Engine vibration and harshness are also minimized with the use of aluminum alloy pistons. In addition to being one-third lighter than steel or iron, aluminum alloy conducts heat approximately four times faster than iron. This means more heat will be transferred from the piston to the cylinder wall and engine oil.

Disadvantages of Aluminum Pistons

Advances in material and manufacturing technology have enabled the use of more rugged steel alloyed pistons, which were once unthinkable to use. Alloyed steel pistons have not completely displaced the use of aluminum, but are used more widely now due to several disadvantages of aluminum. These disadvantages include:

- Low melting point: Aluminum has a melting temperature of approximately 1250°F (677°C), and the flame temperature of diesel fuel is much higher at 3900°F (2149°C). High compression pressures and combustion temperatures would easily melt aluminum pistons if fuel was burned at stoichiometric ratio and did not have excess combustion air **FIGURE 9-14** . To overcome this problem, aluminum is alloyed with approximately 10% of other materials, including silicon, copper, zinc, or chromium. Silicon, which can be found in quartz or beach sand, gives the alloy higher temperature resistance and minimizes

thermal expansion. A **hypereutectic piston**, used by almost all diesel engines with aluminum pistons, has high silicon content (approximately 16–20% silicon). Other silicon pistons are 8–11% silicon.

- Poor wear characteristics: Because aluminum is soft, it does not stand up well to wear. This problem can be partially overcome by alloying aluminum. One of the areas on a piston that experiences the greatest wear is the top ring groove. The high combustion temperatures combined with ring movement in the top ring groove can cause rapid wear of this area. To prevent this, a band of special stainless steel–nickel alloy is cast into the top ring groove or even the top two ring grooves. The band is machined with a groove to accept the piston ring. This band is commonly known as a **Ni-Resist insert**. A Ni-Resist insert further reinforces the top ring piston land, which will prevent the top of the weaker aluminum of the ring land from fracturing and breaking away **FIGURE 9-15** . Installing this nickel insert has the disadvantage of adding complexity and cost to the manufacturing process.

- High expansion coefficient: Aluminum, when heated, will expand four to seven times more than ferrous metal. If this

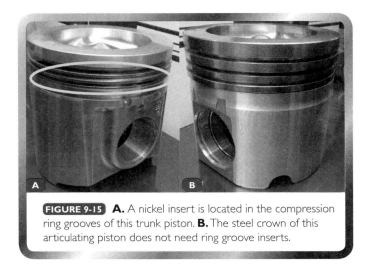

FIGURE 9-15 **A.** A nickel insert is located in the compression ring grooves of this trunk piston. **B.** The steel crown of this articulating piston does not need ring groove inserts.

expansion is not controlled, the piston will expand and score the cylinder and piston or even seize in the cylinder. Using excessive clearances is not a good alternative because this will result in __piston slap__, a noise most often heard when the engine is cold. This noise is the result of large operating clearances between a piston and cylinder wall. Collapsed skirts, poor sealing, and oil control are other undesirable results of running excessive clearances.

> ### TECHNICIAN TIP
>
> Piston slap is a noise that can be heard in an engine during warm-up and light-load operation when the piston has not fully expanded in the cylinder bore. The noise is normal, but should disappear quickly when the piston is warmed up. Heavy loads applied to cold engines with large operating clearances will allow the piston skirt to hammer the cylinder walls and cause the skirt to collapse.

> ### TECHNICIAN TIP
>
> Diesel pistons operate with larger clearances between the cylinder walls when the engine is cold. Because of this, it is important to warm up the pistons before heavily loading an engine in order to prevent piston damage from collapsed piston skirts. This is done by operating the engine at high idle for several minutes. Many electronically controlled engines use a cold-weather protection strategy that reduces power and engine speed until the cylinders are warmed up.

Aluminum Pistons and Emissions

Aluminum trunk-type pistons were satisfactory for many years and continue to be used today in many engines. However, other disadvantages of aluminum pistons have come to light as manufacturers strive to reduce engine emissions and increase engine longevity and horsepower at the same time. Because aluminum pistons cannot withstand the high cylinder pressures and temperatures produced by high engine power output, new materials have been sought as replacements. Ceramic-coated pistons and ceramic alloy crowns are among the replacement materials. These pistons not only withstand greater thermal loading but also help reduce heat rejection loss from the combustion chamber. Reducing heat transfer to the coolant or oil means more fuel energy is converted into mechanical energy.

Piston Cooling

The high cylinder temperatures and pressures in diesel engines place high heat loads on pistons. To prevent piston failure, several mechanisms are used to transfer heat away from the pistons. First, piston rings can transfer some heat to the cylinder walls. As much as one-third of the heat can be removed from pistons this way. Heat is also removed from pistons during the valve overlap period. During the valve overlap period, when the intake and exhaust valves are both open at the end of the exhaust stroke and the beginning of intake, the fresh, cool air mass flowing out of the exhaust valve also passes over and cools the piston crown. An engine with a restricted air filter or inadequate valve overlap period will cause only the crown to crack from excessive heat **FIGURE 9-16**. However, the most cooling of diesel engine pistons comes by way of oil being sprayed at the bottom surface of the crown. Passageways formed in the pistons also help transfer more heat to the oil **FIGURE 9-17**. Heat absorbed by oil is transferred to the cooling system through an oil cooler. Directional aim of the oil cooling nozzles to the piston is critical to ensure adequate heat transfer. One or two cooling nozzles may be used. If only one piston in an engine overheats, it may indicate a misaligned, damaged, or blocked cooling nozzle.

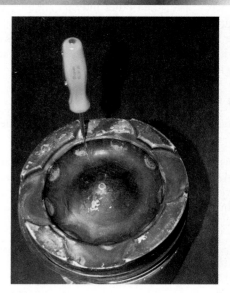

FIGURE 9-16 This piston crown cracked due to inadequate cooling during valve overlap. The engine this piston was in had a restricted air filter.

Oil Cooling Gallery

Oil Spray from Cooling Nozzle

FIGURE 9-17 Passageways inside the piston allow oil to circulate and remove heat from the piston.

More pistons fail due to heat damage when an engine overheats because of a lack of coolant. In that instance, the piston skirt and rings cannot transfer heat to the cylinder wall from the crown. Excessive skirt expansion causes the piston operating clearances to disappear, which then causes the piston to seize in the cylinder bore or score the cylinder wall. Metal-to-metal transfer takes place between the cylinder wall and piston during an overheating failure, and only the skirt is damaged, not the crown **FIGURE 9-18**.

▶ Piston Rings

Piston rings are among the most critical components for engine durability and efficient operation. Worn rings cause high oil consumption and a loss of compression that results in low power and excessive blow-by **FIGURE 9-19**. Rings, along with cylinder walls, will wear faster than other internal engine parts, which limits engine life. In fact, one of the primary determinants of engine life is the ability of the piston rings to work efficiently. Long ring life is a function of ring design, service practices, and proper engine operation.

Piston Ring Functions

Piston rings must perform the following jobs under extreme temperatures for the life of the engine:

- Form of a gas-tight seal between the piston and the cylinder wall: Gas-tight sealing of the cylinder is necessary to provide adequate compression pressure. It also minimizes blow-by, which reduces power and leads to oil contamination and excessive crankcase emissions. An oil film on the cylinder walls enhances the sealing between the ring and cylinder wall.

- Assist in cooling the piston: Piston rings transfer heat to the cylinder wall, which helps keep pistons cool.
- Apply a film of lubrication oil on the cylinder wall: Piston rings must apply a film of oil that provides adequate lubrication properties. However, the film of oil cannot be excessive and thus cause high oil consumption and excessive emissions.
- Form a compatible, replaceable wear surface with the cylinder wall: Piston rings must be compatible with the cylinder wall. <u>Compatibility</u> is a property that allows two metals to slide against one another with minimal friction or wear.

EGR and Piston Ring Longevity

Refinements to ring design, cylinder bore finishing techniques, and engine oils have helped produce engines that can operate for thousands of hours and more than 1,000,000 miles (1,609,344 km) of use before the piston rings need to be replaced. Ring design and the performance of engine oil are even more critical with the use of EGR-equipped engines. Higher cylinder temperatures and pressures, combined with the reintroduction of soot and corrosive exhaust gases found in recirculated exhaust gases, can affect ring longevity **FIGURE 9-20**. Diesel EGR rates are more than three times that of gasoline-fueled engines. For this reason, ring technology has changed to compensate for this new engine wear factor. New materials such as alloyed steel or ceramic-faced rings and manufacturing techniques such as plasma-sprayed ring faces have produced some of the most sophisticated and durable rings ever made.

FIGURE 9-18 This piston skirt was scored due to a coolant overheating failure.

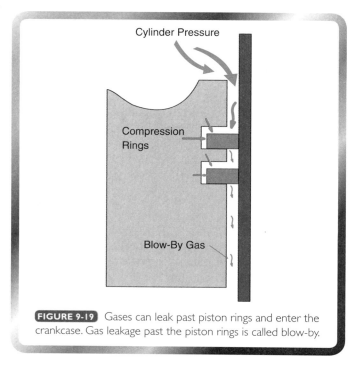

FIGURE 9-19 Gases can leak past piston rings and enter the crankcase. Gas leakage past the piston rings is called blow-by.

FIGURE 9-20 The use of EGR reintroduces soot, an abrasive compound, back into cylinders.

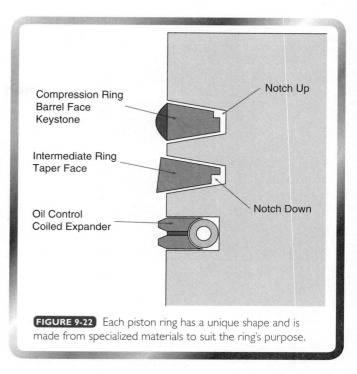

FIGURE 9-22 Each piston ring has a unique shape and is made from specialized materials to suit the ring's purpose.

Ring Types

Three basic types of piston rings are found in all diesel engines: compression, intermediate (a combination of compression and oil control), and oil control **FIGURE 9-21**. Each ring has a unique shape and is made from specialized materials to suit the ring's particular function **FIGURE 9-22**. The top ring is the compression ring, and it helps seal the cylinder. This ring is sometimes called the fire ring because it is directly exposed to combustion heat. The second ring is the intermediate ring; it has both compression and oil control functions. The third ring is the oil control ring.

Compression Rings

Compression rings are located nearest the piston crown. Their primary job is to prevent gases from leaking past the piston during compression and power stroke. Gas leakage past these rings, or blow-by, robs the engine of power because it reduces

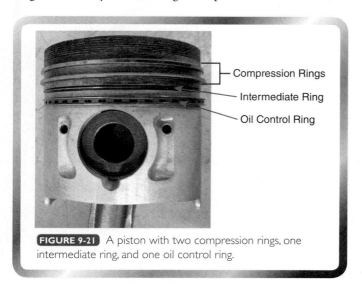

FIGURE 9-21 A piston with two compression rings, one intermediate ring, and one oil control ring.

compression pressures. It may even allow combustion gases to leak into the crankcase.

Compression rings perform a sealing function in a number of ways. One way is through the static force of ring tension against the cylinder wall. Because rings are manufactured to have a larger relaxed diameter than the diameter of the cylinder they are to be installed in, sealing is accomplished by the ring's spring tension expanding out against the cylinder wall. In older rings, static ring force could easily be over 20 lb (9.1 kg). However, to minimize friction losses in an engine, high ring tension is not desirable. Thinner rings can actually seal better using their knife-like edge for sealing. A thinner ring directs more pressure against a small surface area. Today, ring tension may be as low as 4–8 lb (1.8–3.6 kg). These low-tension rings significantly increase fuel economy by decreasing internal friction and cylinder wear.

Another way compression rings seal is through the use of gas pressure during compression and power stroke, which pushes the ring out harder against the cylinder wall. To accomplish this, the thickness of the ring is made slightly less than the height of the ring groove. With this arrangement, gas pressure is able to get behind the ring and push the ring out against the cylinder wall harder than ring static tension **FIGURE 9-23**. Gas pressure also pushes the ring down against the bottom of the groove for better sealing. This means that the higher the cylinder pressure, the greater the sealing capability of the ring. During power stroke, the compression and intermediate rings seal more effectively. (This is also the reason why most blow-by occurs during compression stroke.)

Piston speed and size are factors in determining how many compression rings are used on a piston. Engines with slower speeds require more rings to minimize the loss of compression pressure because more time is available for gases to leak past the rings. Compression rings, like all piston rings, are split for installation and to accommodate thermal expansion. Because

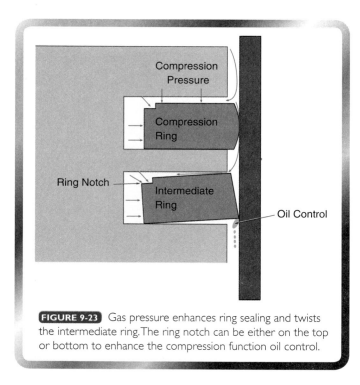

FIGURE 9-23 Gas pressure enhances ring sealing and twists the intermediate ring. The ring notch can be either on the top or bottom to enhance the compression function oil control.

gases can escape through the ring end gap, two compression rings are used on some pistons.

Compression Ring Materials

Cast iron was used to make piston rings in early automotive days. The ability of iron to break in easily, to conform to cylinder irregularities, and resist high heat made it an ideal material. Today, cast iron rings are used occasionally during the rebuild of gasoline-fueled engines, but never for diesel engines. Ductile iron and steel are the most common ring materials now used **TABLE 9-1**. Special coatings are applied to the ring face to improve hardness or oil retention.

Turbocharged diesel engines with high temperatures and cylinder pressures require more durable ring materials. Malleable iron was often used as a ring base material because it will bend and not fracture like cast iron rings. Chrome plating was used on the ring face of malleable iron rings to improve wear and heat resistance. This material was first used during World War II to prevent the engines in desert tanks from dusting out from ingestion of desert sand. **Dusting out** occurs when dirt is drawn into an engine; this causes premature abrasive wear of the cylinder walls and rings. When cylinder walls and compression rings wear due to dusting out, the ends of the piston ring will become tapered **FIGURE 9-24**.

TABLE 9-1: Comparison of Piston Ring Alloys

Material Hardness	Tensile Strength	Fatigue Strength
Gray cast iron	45,000 psi (3103 bar)	30,500 psi (2103 bar)
Ductile iron	180,000 psi (12,410 bar)	87,300 psi (6019 bar)
Steel (SAE9254)	240,000 psi (16,547 bar)	138,600 psi (9556 bar)

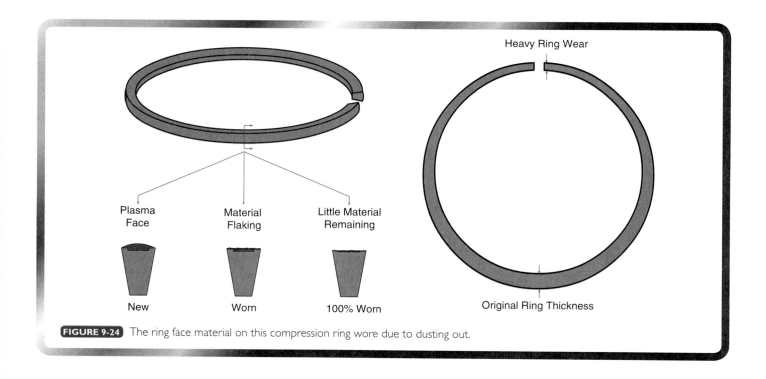

FIGURE 9-24 The ring face material on this compression ring wore due to dusting out.

Chrome ring face material has one disadvantage: Its smooth face will not retain oil for lubrication. The consequence of this is higher cylinder wall wear in the ring turnaround area, the area traveled only by the compression ring, because upper cylinder wall lubricant is nonexistent above the intermediate ring. During the 1970s, ring manufacturers found that a coating of molybdenum on the compression ring improves wear characteristics. Wear resistance is improved because moly-faced rings have a porous finish. This porosity permits oil retention on the ring face, which allows oil to be carried there, thus reducing upper cylinder wall wear. After this discovery, a combination of chrome and molybdenum was used for decades for compression rings.

A much better material for compression rings than cast iron and ductile iron is steel, which is twice as strong as ductile iron. Because steel is the best material for withstanding the pressure and temperature loads found inside high-compression turbocharged diesels, this material has been used for over 30 years in many heavy-duty diesel applications. Generally, steel compression rings have the following advantages:

- Improved breakage resistance
- Improved heat resistance
- Improved mechanical stress resistance
- Reduced ring-side wear
- Reduced groove-side wear
- Longer service life
- Simpler and less expensive to manufacture (made from coiled wire)

With the introduction of EGR, ring face materials need to be even harder, so combinations of ceramic metal alloys are now being used. Further hardening of ring material is accomplished by nitriding the rings. **Nitriding** is a hardening process that impregnates the surface of the steel rings with nitrogen. The hardening extends into the ring to a depth of about 0.001″ (0.025 mm). This hardening technique produces rings that have almost 50% greater wear resistance than non-hardened steel rings and 400% greater wear resistance than gray cast iron rings. Nitriding improves the ring resistance to side wear and face wear to the point where ring wear is negligible. Cylinder walls will wear out before these rings do.

One other diesel engine ring material uses a combination of plasma sprayed-moly and ceramics, such as chromium carbide or silicon carbide. Ceramics are extremely hard and wear resistant but do not conduct heat well. Molybdenum Cermet is one such material. It is comprised of 80% molybdenum and 20% chromium carbide ceramic, which makes for durable ring face material in a turbocharged diesel engine.

Compression Ring Shapes

Rectangular rings were once the standard piston ring shape, but they had a problem with sticking when oil and fuel residues carbonized in the ring groove. The keystone ring is the ring shape of choice for most engine manufacturers today **FIGURE 9-25**. Keystone ring action helps keep the ring land clean and prevents the ring from sticking. To obtain good sealing and minimize friction, a barrel face is often ground on the face of compression

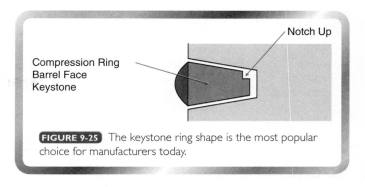

FIGURE 9-25 The keystone ring shape is the most popular choice for manufacturers today.

rings. The barrel face forms line contact with the cylinder wall for tight and relatively friction-free contact. Prior to packaging compression rings, the manufacturer laps rings in a cylinder identical to the one in which the rings will run. A witness line left by the lapping process shows the contact with the cylinder. This same line will grow wider as the ring wears into its installed cylinder. The width of the witness line can be used as a visual indication to determine the amount of ring wear **FIGURE 9-26**.

Intermediate Rings

Intermediate rings may also be called compression rings, even though they perform more than just a compression and sealing function. While intermediate rings seal compression gases that escape past the top rings, they also assist in oil control. A small, metered quantity of oil is required on the cylinder walls for the piston and rings, but any excess quantity will lead to high oil consumption and emissions. The ring shape of choice for the intermediate ring is a taper-faced ring. This shape allows the ring to glide over the oil film on the upstroke, enhancing the sealing effect of oil between the ring and cylinder wall. On the down stroke, the ring will scrape oil from the cylinder back into the crankcase. A variation of this design is to allow the ring to twist in the groove. Using a ring with a groove machined in the bottom or top inside edge of the ring permits gas pressure to cause the ring to twist during compression and power strokes. Either compression sealing or oil control can be enhanced depending on the direction of twist. An intermediate ring, if installed upside down, will pump oil into the combustion chamber rather than scraping it from the cylinder wall.

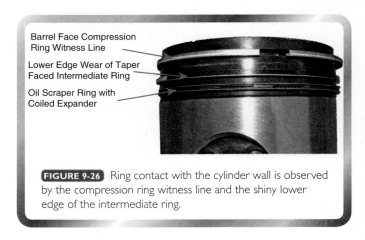

FIGURE 9-26 Ring contact with the cylinder wall is observed by the compression ring witness line and the shiny lower edge of the intermediate ring.

Oil Control Rings

The last ring type found on a ring pack is the oil control ring. This ring is usually cast iron with scraper rails that remove excess oil from the cylinder wall while leaving a metered quantity of oil for lubrication. This oil film thickness is typically no more than 0.000004″ (0.000102 mm) thick.

The oil control ring is usually a low-tension type of ring and has no significant gas pressure acting upon it. For this reason, a metal expander is placed behind the ring to maintain a constant, uniform pressure against the cylinder walls by the scraper rails **FIGURE 9-27**. The expander ring may be corrugated, slotted, or a wire coil. Like the intermediate and compression rings, the oil control ring is vulnerable to premature wear from dirt ingestion into the engine. Scraper rails will show premature wear if abnormal amounts of dirt contaminate the oil through the intake air.

▶ Piston Pins

Piston pins, also called wrist pins, are the connecting joint between the piston and the connecting rod (see the Connecting Rods section). Piston pins are fabricated from high-alloy steel and may be either hollow or solid.

The area of the piston around the piston pin bore is the pin boss. This area is reinforced because the thrust forces of

combustion are transmitted through the piston to the piston pin in that area. The piston pin bore is usually offset toward the major side thrust portion of the cylinder **FIGURE 9-28**. This is done to minimize the noise caused when the thrust side of the piston crosses over near top dead center (TDC). Because there is more clearance between the piston and cylinder wall on one side of the piston compared to the other, side thrust on the piston will cause the clearance to switch sides at TDC, producing a knocking sound. Placing the pin bore slightly offset to the centerline results in a slight tilt of the piston around the pin axis during directional change of the piston at TDC **FIGURE 9-29**. Instead of hitting the cylinder wall with its entire length, it tilts before it crosses over, touching the cylinder wall first with its lower skirt end as it changes sides. The rest of the piston then makes contact with the cylinder wall before beginning its slide downward against the opposite side of the cylinder.

Full Floating Piston Pins

The pin design most common to diesel engines is a full floating piston pin. In this design, both the piston and the connecting rod rotate on the pin. Although this requires a bushing in the small end of the connecting rod, more surfaces are rotating with an oil film to better distribute wear. A full floating pin is held in place by spring clips. A **trapezoidal pin bushing** is most commonly used with this design because the bearing surfaces that

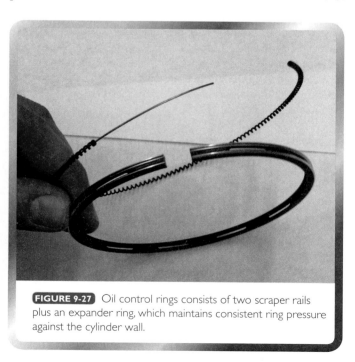

FIGURE 9-27 Oil control rings consists of two scraper rails plus an expander ring, which maintains consistent ring pressure against the cylinder wall.

FIGURE 9-28 Note the directional arrow on this piston crown. The offset centerline of the piston pins requires the pistons to have a specific orientation in the engine.

absorb combustion forces are wider on the connecting rod and piston; this improves piston and connecting rod load-bearing capabilities FIGURE 9-30.

Connecting Rods

A connecting rod links a piston to the crankshaft, which enables the conversion of the piston's reciprocating motion into rotational movement of the crankshaft. Connecting rods are the most stressed component of the engine because they experience tensional loading or compression loading every time the piston changes direction.

Tensional loading occurs at the end of the upstroke at TDC, when the weight of the piston assembly would naturally continue in a straight line through the cylinder head but is stopped by the connecting rod. Without the cushioning effect of pushing exhaust gases out or compressing the gases in the cylinder, the tensional forces would be even greater. Compression loading occurs during power stroke when the combustion forces push the connecting rod down with forces in excess of 30,000 lb (13,608 kg). Because of these forces, connecting rods are built to typically withstand forces more than 16 times greater than those expected during normal operation. These forces could be from abnormal combustion conditions or engine overspeeding. Engines that use heavier articulating pistons have larger connecting rods to handle the increased tensional forces.

Connecting Rod Materials

Because connecting rods are highly stressed, they are commonly forged from high-alloy steel. Rods are then **shot-peened** to relieve stress risers—points where the rod can easily break—and add additional fatigue strength. This technique involves shooting thousands of small steel balls at the rod using compressed air. The balls make small dents in the rod surface and smooth,

or peen, over any microscopic cracks or pores in the rod that could form stress risers. Bolts used on the caps are made from proprietary alloys of grade 8 or higher metals. Rolled threads are used on these bolts to increase their strength FIGURE 9-31. Rolled threads have a wider root diameter and are pressed into the bolt, not machine cut. The machine cut of a die making threads leaves stress risers. Rolling threads does not remove metal or disturb the metal's grain structure. Bolts with rolled threads can withstand more stretching or preload than machine-cut threads.

Connecting Rod Features

Connecting rods use an I-beam cross section, which has good weight-to-strength characteristics and resists bending

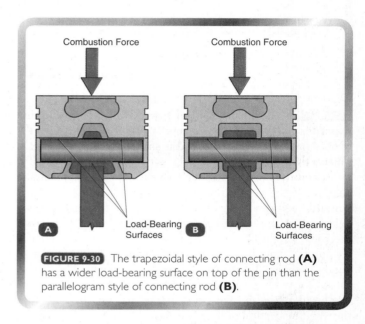

FIGURE 9-30 The trapezoidal style of connecting rod **(A)** has a wider load-bearing surface on top of the pin than the parallelogram style of connecting rod **(B)**.

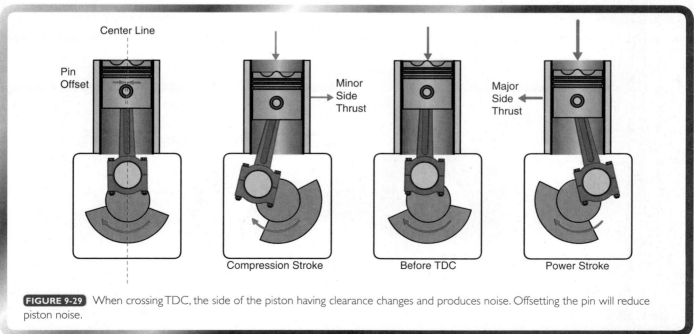

FIGURE 9-29 When crossing TDC, the side of the piston having clearance changes and produces noise. Offsetting the pin will reduce piston noise.

FIGURE 9-31 Connecting rods use bolts with rolled threads. Note that on the bolt with rolled threads, the root diameter of the threaded section is as large as the bolt's shank.

Rolled Thread

Conventional Thread

an engine. If a service rod is required, it will often have a different paint marking that is in the middle of the weight distributions. Because the final finish bore dimensions of the big end of the rod are made after the parting halves of the rod and cap are completed, the two parts must be assembled together in the same way as they were finished. If the cap is fastened to the rod 180° away from the original position, the bore will not be concentric, even though the two pieces can be bolted together. Matching marks on a connecting rod identify the assembled position. Failure to align these marks will result in improper bearing clearances, and the engine may not rotate after the pieces are assembled. If the engine is operated when the components are assembled incorrectly, a tight connecting rod bearing will result in an insufficient oil film on the connecting rod journal, which will produce catastrophic engine damage **FIGURE 9-33**. To further ensure a concentric bore in the big end of the connecting rod, the parting halves of the cap and rod will have various machined features, serrations, or alignment dowels **FIGURE 9-34**.

FIGURE 9-32. The smaller end of the rod will have a bushing pressed into it if it is used with a full-floating piston. When the small end of the connecting rod is shaped like a triangle, it is called a trapezoidal rod.

The weight of a set of connecting rods is critical to engine balance. If the connecting rods vary in their mass, engine vibration will result. To adjust the weight of connecting rods, balance pads are located at each end for grinding to balance the rod's weight between the rod ends and around its center point. Often, select fit rods are used together in sets in an engine. In select fit rod sets, rods are weighed after fabrication; those closest in weight are used together in sets. These sets can be identified by the paint marks that uniquely identify the weight variation of the rod (that is, a group of connecting rods may have white, yellow, red, or other paint markings to identify them as belonging to a particular weight classification). Such rod sets should be kept together when assembling

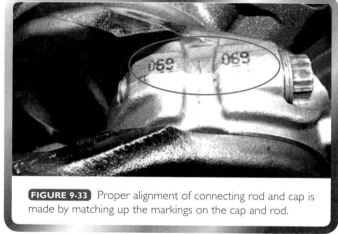

FIGURE 9-33 Proper alignment of connecting rod and cap is made by matching up the markings on the cap and rod.

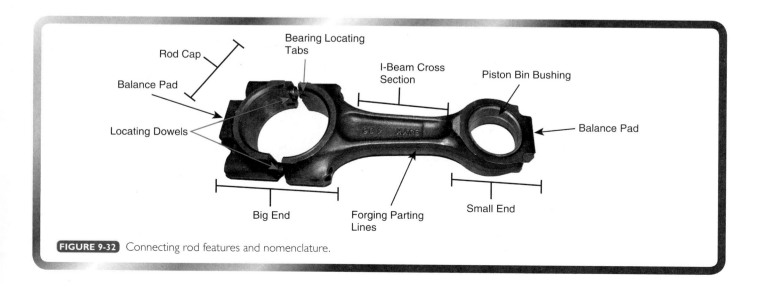

FIGURE 9-32 Connecting rod features and nomenclature.

Rod Cap

Balance Pad

Locating Dowels

Bearing Locating Tabs

I-Beam Cross Section

Piston Bin Bushing

Balance Pad

Big End

Forging Parting Lines

Small End

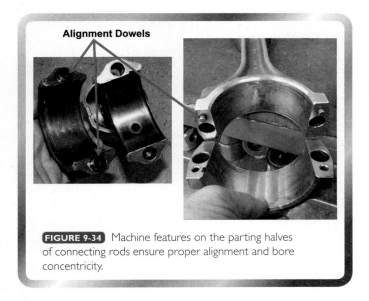

FIGURE 9-34 Machine features on the parting halves of connecting rods ensure proper alignment and bore concentricity.

FIGURE 9-35 An offset split rod permits a larger crankpin diameter and a stronger rod cap retention.

Diesel engines can have a passageway drilled through the connecting rod to the piston pin bushing to supply oil to the piston pin. In V6 and V8 engines, connecting rods share a common crankpin journal, which means rods must also be correctly oriented. A chamfered edge in the rod cap is installed toward the crankshaft fillet radius—that is, the edge between the journal and crank cheek. The flat sides of each rod match one another, providing a surface for each rod to glide over one another. Even in inline engines, the connecting rod must be correctly oriented front and back due to piston pin and rod cap split offsets.

Split Fracture Connecting Rods

One common feature of connecting rods is that rod ends can have a 45° to 60° offset, or split, of the rod cap to accommodate larger connecting rod journal sizes while still allowing the connecting rod to pass through the cylinder during assembly **FIGURE 9-35**. If the rod were not split at an offset angle, the big end would not pass through the cylinder due to the dimensions of the rod. The mass of the big end can be somewhat minimized by using this feature. **Split fracture connecting rods** are the most commonly manufactured type of connecting rods today. These connecting rods have the big end of the connecting rod parting surfaces split by fracturing, rather than machining, the mating surfaces between the rod and bearing cap **FIGURE 9-36**.

Using a split fracture connecting rod offers the following advantages:

- More precise alignment of the rod and cap than a machined rod and cap
- Improved control of oil clearances
- Reduced production cost because machining steps are eliminated
- Greater retention strength between the cap and rod

Split fracture connecting rods allow the rod and cap to be separated along a predetermined fracture line. Instead of

FIGURE 9-36 Split fracture rods give a coarse, grainy appearance to both rod cap surfaces.

cutting the rod cap away from the rod and then machining and reboring the rod and cap, a hydraulically operated wedge pushes the two pieces away from one another. A line scribed where the split should take place provides a weakened point to control the split. Because the big end of the connecting rod is fracture-split, the rough-edged big end and cap will resist movement better and are aligned more precisely than a conventional flat machined surface. Split fracture rods can be made about 17% lighter, which reduces engine vibration while maintaining the strength of traditionally manufactured rods. Split fracture rods are produced more economically and with less energy.

▶ Maintenance of Cylinder Components

While diesel engine cylinder components are ruggedly built to last for very long distances and many years of operation, they are intentionally designed for rebuilding. Specialized tools, techniques, and service procedures prescribed by the original equipment manufacturer (OEM) must be used to ensure engine overhaul and repairs are reliably completed to maximize service life and customer satisfaction. Technicians also need to be aware of particular operating conditions that can dramatically shorten engine life. Excessive idle time is particularly destructive to diesel engines. Understanding failure modes of cylinder components can help technicians make proper service recommendations to customers and identify operating conditions and practices that require correction.

Engine Damage at Idle

It is important to know that prolonged idling of diesel engines shortens engine life and is particularly damaging to cylinder components. Idling damages cylinder components through slobber production, excessive soot loading of engine oil, and cylinder glazing.

Slobber Production

Combustion at idle in diesels is cool and sooty. This happens because excess air and small quantities of fuel injected at idle produce low cylinder temperatures and pressures. Pistons do not expand properly when cold, which results in poor cylinder sealing. Poor sealing not only permits compression pressure to slip past the rings but also allows more lubricating oil to enter the combustion chamber. Accumulations of unburnt oil, fuel, and soot are produced during low-temperature, low-pressure combustion, and they mix to form engine slobber **FIGURE 9-37**. This slobber will accumulate in the exhaust system and stick around the exhaust valves, on piston rings, and in the ring belt area. If this slobber gets around the piston rings and hardens, the rings will stick in their grooves and become ineffective **FIGURE 9-38**.

Excessive Soot Loading of Engine Oil

Soot loading of engine oil is the result of poor combustion quality at idle. Soot clings to the cylinder wall and is scraped down into the crankcase to contaminate lubrication oil. High soot loading thickens the oil and reduces the required time or distance service intervals between oil changes. Soot is also an abrasive compound, which will cause premature engine wear, especially if oil is allowed to reach more than 5% contaminant loading.

FIGURE 9-37 Engine slobber produced during engine idle dripped from the exhaust pipe joints of this truck.

FIGURE 9-38 This steel alloy piston shows indications of excessive idle. The ring belt and grooves have engine slobber baked in, preventing proper sealing of the cylinder.

▶ TECHNICIAN TIP

Engines operating under severe service, such as prolonged idle conditions in cold weather, require shorter service intervals between oil changes. Under these conditions, engine lubricating oil will contaminate with soot, which is produced by poor-quality combustion. Soot contamination of lubricating oil thickens the oil. While late-model diesels have better combustion quality, the use of EGR, which puts exhaust back into cylinders, also increases soot loading of oil.

Cylinder Glazing

<u>Cross-hatch</u> is the fine intersecting lines on the cylinder walls; it provides a cylinder wall finish that retains engine oil, which is needed for piston lubrication and to promote a gas-tight piston ring seal **FIGURE 9-39**. Oil can fill the cross-hatch finish of the cylinder walls during idle and become baked onto the cylinder wall. Piston and ring travel smooths the baked oil into a mirror-like finish that is unable to retain oil. This process, called <u>cylinder glazing</u>, prevents the piston rings from effectively sealing and leads to a loss of compression through blow-by. This process of cylinder glazing is different from the glazing produced by cylinder wear, which also produces a mirror-like finish on the cylinder wall.

▶ TECHNICIAN TIP

Diesel engines should never be operated at idle for prolonged periods. If an engine must be idled, it is best to operate it at high idle. Manufacturers are using engine calibrations to increase engine speed and change injection timing when oil and coolant temperatures are low. Similarly, many late-model diesels limit engine speed when cold. This ensures that cold, thickened oil is flowing to critical engine parts and the pistons are adequately warmed before fully loading the engine.

Cylinder Component Service

Cylinder component servicing consists of testing, removing, disassembling, inspecting, and replacing pistons, piston rings, and connecting rods. A worn engine may be indicated when oil consumption is increased; engine power is reduced; fuel consumption is increased; or the engine runs rough, misfires, produces excessive exhaust emissions, or has excessive crankcase blow-by. While time and distance are the typical wear factors, there are many causes for premature wear and failure of cylinder components, including problems with oil quality, the air induction system leaking dirt into the engine, internal coolant and fuel leaks, or failures in the EGR system that allow excess recirculation of exhaust gas into the cylinders. Inspecting and diagnosing worn or damaged cylinder components should begin with evaluating the cylinder wear and ring-to-cylinder wall sealing. This can be performed non-intrusively, without disassembling the engine. Inspection of cylinder components can also take place after disassembly.

Most cylinder wear takes place at the top of the cylinder and tapers toward the bottom **FIGURE 9-40**. Lack of lubrication oil above the oil control ring and intermediate ring is the primary reason for most wear taking place in the ring turnaround area. This means cylinder wear is usually tapered, with the widest dimension of the cylinder near the top in a worn-out engine. Major side thrust force is responsible for wear in the middle of the cylinder wall, where the angle between the connecting rod and the piston, combined with high cylinder pressures during power stroke, force the piston against the cylinder wall **FIGURE 9-41**.

Piston Service

A piston has a micro-finish on the skirt that allows it to retain oil, which improves wear characteristics. It is important to remember that this finish should not be damaged during servicing. Do not clean pistons with abrasive cleaners, wire wheels, or other items that can damage the finish of the piston skirt. The best method for cleaning aluminum pistons is to soak them in a mild aluminum-compatible cleaner followed by steam cleaning. Hard carbon deposits on the crown may be scraped with a plastic scraper.

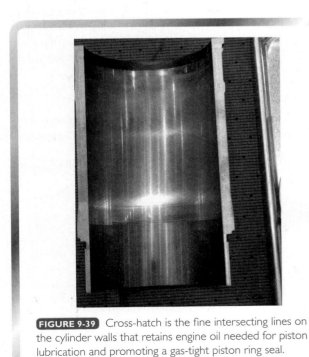

FIGURE 9-39 Cross-hatch is the fine intersecting lines on the cylinder walls that retains engine oil needed for piston lubrication and promoting a gas-tight piston ring seal.

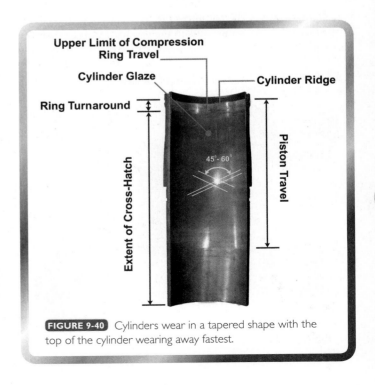

FIGURE 9-40 Cylinders wear in a tapered shape with the top of the cylinder wearing away fastest.

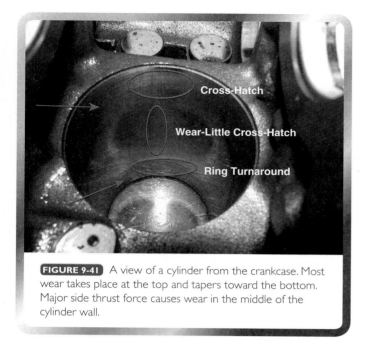

FIGURE 9-41 A view of a cylinder from the crankcase. Most wear takes place at the top and tapers toward the bottom. Major side thrust force causes wear in the middle of the cylinder wall.

Visual inspection of pistons should be made for evidence of cracking, overheating, and wear **FIGURE 9-42**. The presence of vertical or horizontal cracks in the piston bowl or piston pin bore give important clues when performing failure analysis. Horizontal cracks usually indicate a bonding problem between the piston skirt and crown. Vertical cracks in the bowl often indicate high cylinder temperatures. Cracking between the crown and the piston pin bore indicate excessive cylinder pressure.

Worn ring grooves will cause excessive oil consumption. Wear in the piston's ring grooves is typically checked with specialized OEM gauge pins **FIGURE 9-43**. Specialized OEM gauge pins snuggly fit into the compression piston ring groove. A pair of springs holds two gauge pins in the grooves, and the distance between the gauge pins is measured with a micrometer. If the

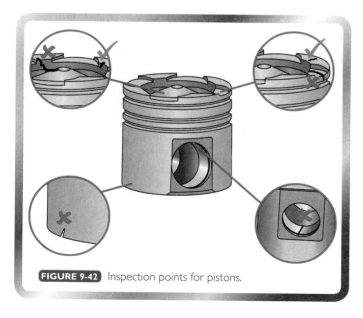

FIGURE 9-42 Inspection points for pistons.

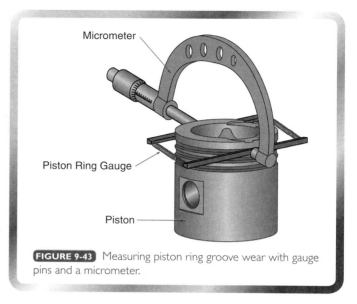

FIGURE 9-43 Measuring piston ring groove wear with gauge pins and a micrometer.

piston ring groove wear is excessive, the pins will sit farther into the groove and the dimension between the pins will become smaller. Comparing actual, measured dimensions with manufacturer specifications will determine whether the piston can be reused. Another way to measure wear in a the piston's ring grooves is with a go, no-go gauge **FIGURE 9-44**.

The clearances between a piston and cylinder wall are best measured with a long feeler blade **FIGURE 9-45**. This is done by placing the piston in the cylinder. The thickest possible feeler blade is then slid in between the piston and the cylinder wall 90° to the wrist pin. The blade should not be forced into the clearance, but a 5–8 lb (2.3–3.6 kg) drag should be felt when pulling the blade out of the clearance. Generally, clearances of between 0.003 and 0.006" (0.076 and 0.152 mm) are normally encountered in cylinders that fit well. Less clearance than this prevents the piston from properly expanding, while more clearance will create noise, cause high oil consumption, and indicates excessive wear or damage to the piston and cylinder wall.

Ring Service

When replacing piston rings, the end gaps of all piston rings should be placed 120° apart in a three-ring pack. If the end gaps

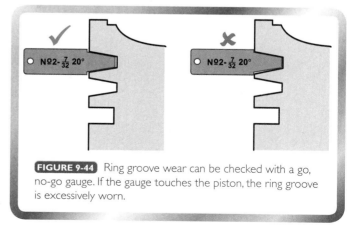

FIGURE 9-44 Ring groove wear can be checked with a go, no-go gauge. If the gauge touches the piston, the ring groove is excessively worn.

FIGURE 9-45 Measuring piston-to-cylinder wall clearance is performed using a long feeler blade between the piston and cylinder wall.

FIGURE 9-46 To break cylinder glazing and reestablish cross-hatch, a ball hone is rapidly moved up and down the cylinder bore using an electric or air drill.

are lined up, excessive blow-by will take place through the gaps. Rings should be removed and installed with a pair of ring pliers to prevent unnecessary stress from breaking or distorting the ring. When installing rings, several types of ring compressors are used to push the piston rings into the grooves; this assists in the installation of the piston into the cylinder. Both the cylinder wall and compressor should be well lubricated during the installation procedure. A soft hammer handle can be used to gently tap a piston into the cylinder bore.

When new rings are installed into the cylinder, a new cross-hatch finish needs to be made on the cylinder wall. As long as taper wear is within specifications, a ball hone or straight-sided honing stone can be used to put cross-hatch finish into the cylinder **FIGURE 9-46**. About one stroke per second is required at 60 rpm to establish the correct angle on the cross-hatch finish. Cylinders are rarely honed dry; usually fuel or special cutting oil is used to lubricate the stone. Coarse-, medium-, and fine-grit stones are available, depending on whether a new cross-hatch is needed to help seat the new rings and retain oil, or to remove some taper wear. If excessive scoring or taper wear is present in a cylinder, the cylinder may require boring out to an oversize dimension. The final dimension depends on the availability of oversize pistons and rings. Oversize pistons in sizes 0.01″ (0.25 mm), 0.02″ (0.5 mm), 0.03″ (.76 mm), and 0.04″ (1 mm) are typically available for popular engines constructed without cylinder sleeves.

Ring Break-In

When piston rings are initially installed with a new cross-hatch finish on the cylinder walls, the rings will need to seat, or slightly wear, into the cylinder wall and conform to wall irregularities.

A time period, called the **break-in period**, is needed to seat rings as well as other engine parts, including bearings, valve guides, piston pins, cam bushings, and other moving parts. During the break-in period, cross-hatch is slightly worn away to conform to the shape of the piston rings, enabling the rings to seat better on the cylinder wall. It is important to operate the engine under heavy load for a short time after an engine is overhauled to seat rings and prevent formation of cylinder glaze in the engine. Under load, the cylinder gas pressure will push the rings against the cylinder wall hardest, which best helps rings to seat. This procedure is important especially during the initial break-in period. Manufacturers will often provide a schedule in their service manual that outlines specific break-in procedures, including what percentage of load to place the engine under for a prescribed amount of time.

▶ TECHNICIAN TIP

Rings can be made harder for improved wear resistance, but the downside is prolonged break-in periods. Both the ring and the cylinder wall must conform to each other's shape for optimum cylinder sealing. At one time, with softer ring materials, break-in would take place in a matter of hours. Some heavy-duty engines now take as long as 12,000 miles (19,312 km) for break-in. Blow-by, low power, and engine slobber are complaints expected during longer break-in periods.

Connecting Rod Service

Connecting rods should be checked for twists, bends, wear, nicks, and cracks. The oil passageways drilled through the connecting rod should also be checked to ensure that they are clear of any obstructions. Twists and bends in connecting rods are usually due to **hydrostatic locking**. A hydrostatic lock occurs when liquids enter the combustion chamber, eliminating the little clearance volume remaining in a diesel engine. When the piston compresses the liquid, it will stop moving while the crankshaft continues to move, causing the connecting rod to bend and twist. Sources of liquids entering the combustion chamber include head gasket leakage; block porosity (from cavitation erosion); leaking injectors or injector tubes; water entering the exhaust system through an open exhaust stack; or water, snow, oil, or fuel entering through the intake system.

A hydrostatically locked engine will turn freely when rotated backward, because fluids are pushed out of the intake valve. When the engine is rotated again in the correct direction, the engine will lock up once more. Never use a starter motor to break free a hydrostatically locked engine. The cylinder components, valves, and starter motor can be easily damaged by the starter motor torque.

Bent connecting rods in diesels can be checked for by seeing how far above the block deck a piston protrudes. Most pistons do rise into the area occupied by the cylinder head gasket. A comparison can be made between the manufacturer's specifications and the actual observed measurement. All pistons should rise uniformly to the same dimension when measured using a dial indicator **FIGURE 9-47**. Connecting rods can also be checked by a machine shop specialist using a fixture to determine if the rod is bent, twisted, and whether the small and large bores are parallel. If a bent or twisted rod is found, the replacement rod should be matched to the same weight classification as the other rods in the engine. The weight classification is usually indicated by a paint mark on the rod.

Assembling Split Fracture Rods

If the connecting rod cap of a split fracture rod is fitted incorrectly and tightened, then the connecting rod must be replaced. This is necessary because the unique profile of the mating surfaces will be damaged when the cap is tightened, causing distortion of the two mating surfaces. The cap will no longer locate correctly, even if it

is returned to its original position. To minimize the possibility of this error, connecting rod bolts or cap screws are located off center to ensure that the cap is fitted to the rod in the correct orientation.

TECHNICIAN TIP

When major engine work is performed, always turn the engine over manually before using the starter. This procedure can identify incorrectly installed or misadjusted components or the presence of hydraulic locks, which could potentially damage the engine if the starter is used.

Ring-to-Cylinder Wall Seal Testing

Evaluating the piston ring-to-cylinder wall seal is an important indicator of engine life. Poor sealing means the engine is worn out or has internal damage. Three methods can be used to evaluate the condition of piston ring-to-cylinder wall seal: compression testing, cylinder leak-down testing, and crankcase pressure testing.

Compression Testing

Compression testing is a measure of the maximum pressure of the engine cylinders when they are cranking. It is rarely used on diesel engines due to the small clearance volume of the cylinders and the prospect of hydraulic locking with oil when wet testing. Wet testing is a procedure used to check for worn rings. It is done by squirting oil into the cylinders. If compression pressures significantly increase after adding more cylinder wall lubricant, it usually indicates worn rings. Oil may also ignite during compression testing. Large variations between compression pressure measurements in an engine's cylinders at cranking speed can be the result of keystone ring design, in which high cylinder pressure is needed to help rings seal effectively. Furthermore, it's cumbersome and time consuming to remove an injector to install a compression pressure gauge into a cylinder. However, smaller

FIGURE 9-47 Measure piston protrusion above the block deck to check for a bent or twisted connecting rod.

light-duty diesels can allow for the removal of glow plugs to measure cylinder compression pressure. Other methods to evaluate cylinder sealing are more effective.

Cylinder Leak-Down Testing

<u>Cylinder leakage</u> is the percentage of gas leakage past the piston rings. High leakage rates are usually due to worn cylinders and rings. Cylinder leakage testing is an accurate and meaningful measurement of the cylinders' sealing capabilities. The leak-down test can be performed separately or together with compression testing. Cylinder leak-down testing is more practical for diesel engines than compression testing. During cylinder leak-down testing, air is fed into the cylinder at pressures of 80–120 psi (552–827 kPa). During cylinder leak-down testing, the engine should be warm to minimize the clearance between the cylinder wall and piston. With the valves closed, the piston is first positioned at TDC and then the engine is locked there. The cylinder leakage tester is connected to the cylinder and pressurized with regulated shop air. A second gauge on the leakage tester will measure actual cylinder pressure, which varies with the amount of cylinder leakage. A worn cylinder will allow more air leakage past the rings. Leakage is calculated as a percentage of measured cylinder pressure compared with regulated air pressure. The rate of leakage is compared against the manufacturer's specification to determine if the amount of leakage is acceptable. Engine problems can be detected by listening for large volumes of air leaking out of the turbocharger, the intake or exhaust system, or even the oil filler tube. Excess air leakage in these areas may indicate burnt or broken valves, damaged pistons, or simply worn cylinders. An engine in good condition should generally show only 5–10% leakage of the pressure of the air supplied to the cylinder after 1 minute. Some engines in acceptable condition may have leakage as high as 20%, but more than 30% leakage indicates a severe problem.

Crankcase Pressure Testing

One of the best practices for evaluating the condition of piston rings in a diesel engine is a <u>crankcase pressure test</u>. This is a measurement of the amount of cylinder blow-by, which is proportional to the sealing ability of the piston rings and cylinder walls. Because blow-by gas pressure in the crankcase is a function of the effectiveness of the piston ring-to-cylinder wall seal, the quantity of blow-by and crankcase pressure is a good measure of piston ring and cylinder wall condition. Excessive blow-by and crankcase pressure means there is poor sealing and the cylinders are worn out. Crankcase blow-by pressure is usually very low—just a few inches (centimeters) of water column pressure when the engine is under full load and the rings are seated well by high cylinder pressure. When the piston rings and cylinder walls are worn, blow-by volume increases, driving up the crankcase pressure. Blow-by testing is a fast, simple, and nonintrusive technique to evaluate the condition of piston ring-to-cylinder wall sealing. Pressure is measured at high-idle, no-load operation. When piston rings seal well, little blow-by gas enters the crankcase. When cylinder pressures are higher, such as during high idle rpm operation, the rings seal much better than they would at low engine rpm. Crankcase pressure is typically higher at idle than at high idle in good engines. However, glazed

cylinders are indicated when crankcase pressure is significantly higher at idle and drops as engine speed increases.

Pressure in the crankcase is measured in inches (centimeters) of water column using a water manometer or <u>Magnehelic gauge</u> **FIGURE 9-48**. A calibrated restriction fitting is placed over the crankcase breather tube. If equipped, the crankcase depression regulator, a device that limits how low crankcase pressure can fall, is blocked during the test. After the engine coolant and oil are warmed to operating temperature, the engine is put to full throttle, no load, and crankcase pressure is measured. Usually only a few inches (centimeters) of pressure are measured in an engine in good condition. Small-bore diesels will typically have a maximum limit of 10″ (25 cm) of water column pressure indicating 0% service life. Larger engines may be allowed as much as 15–18″ (38–46 cm) of water column pressure.

Inspecting for Cylinder Wear

Several methods are used to measure engine wear when an engine is partially or fully disassembled. One effective method to visually evaluate cylinder wear is to examine the ring turnaround area **FIGURE 9-49**. Using a piece of paper to reflect light directly into the cross-hatch helps make the cylinder wear more visible. If 20% or more of the cross-hatch is missing, 0% service life remains. If 10% of the cross-hatch is missing, 50% service life remains. An engine with a 5″ (13 cm) stroke and 0.25″ (6 mm) of polish has 75% service life remaining.

A second method is to measure the piston ring end gap at three points in the cylinder swept by the piston rings: top, middle, and bottom **FIGURE 9-50**. After squaring a used compression ring in the cylinder, a feeler blade is placed in the end gap of the ring. The maximum clearance in the end gap is measured at three points. Because the circumference of a circle is found by multiplying π (3.14) and the circle's diameter, the end gap differences are divided by 3.1 (which is rounded from π, which is 3.14). That means a difference of 0.003″ (0.076 mm) between the widest and smallest end gap equals 0.001″ (0.025 mm) of taper wear. A general rule for engine wear is that no more than 0.001″ (0.025 mm) of taper wear is permissible for every 1″ (25 mm) of cylinder bore up to 0.005″ (0.127 mm). If wear exceeds this amount, two problems will occur. The first is that the cylinder wall will not be able to retain

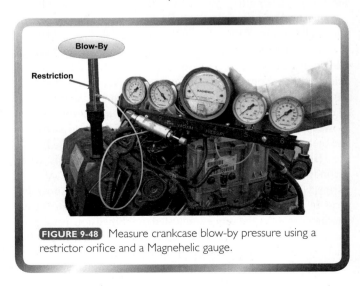

FIGURE 9-48 Measure crankcase blow-by pressure using a restrictor orifice and a Magnehelic gauge.

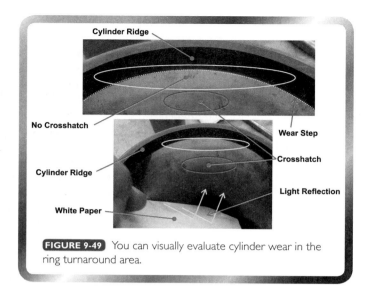

FIGURE 9-49 You can visually evaluate cylinder wear in the ring turnaround area.

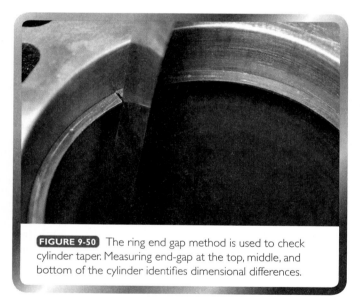

FIGURE 9-50 The ring end gap method is used to check cylinder taper. Measuring end-gap at the top, middle, and bottom of the cylinder identifies dimensional differences.

an oil film for lubricating and sealing the rings because the cross-hatch is worn from the cylinder wall. The second problem is that the rings will open and close too far during each stroke; they will eventually become fatigued from the continual flexing and break.

The dimensions of the cylinder can also be measured using a telescoping gauge set. This is done in three places as well—the top, middle, and bottom of the cylinder where it is swept by the piston rings. An experienced and skilled technician can measure the bore diameter with a telescoping gauge and an outside micrometer. However, due to the difficulty of developing the skills to accurately use these types of measurement tools, they are seldom used.

The method used most commonly by machinists when reconditioning cylinder bores involves the use of a <u>dial bore gauge</u>, which is a precision measuring tool used to measure taper wear in a cylinder. This tool has a dial indicator-like measuring mechanism. After the gauge is adjusted to a dimension just slightly more than the bore diameter, it is placed in the cylinder and rocked back and forth to sweep the gauge through a perpendicular point,

or at a right angle, to the cylinder wall. The smallest dimension of the bore gauge indicates when the gauge has found the narrowest point in the cylinder. The gauge is moved to several more points in the cylinder to determine what the narrowest dimensions are and then a comparison is made between the measurements. Once again, the maximum permissible variation between the smallest and largest measurements should be less than 0.005″ (0.127 mm), which indicates 0% remaining service life.

Performing a Crankcase Blow-By Test

One of the best practices for evaluating the condition of piston rings in a diesel engine is a crankcase blow-by test. Blow-by gas pressure in the crankcase is a function of the effectiveness of the ring–to–cylinder wall seal. Because of this, the quantity of blow-by and crankcase pressure is indicative of the condition of the piston rings and cylinder walls. Crankcase blow-by pressure is usually very low—just a few inches (millimeters) of water column pressure when the engine is under full load (when the rings are seated). When the rings and cylinder walls are worn, blow-by volume increases, which drives up crankcase pressure.

This non-intrusive technique to evaluate the effectiveness of piston ring–to–cylinder wall sealing involves measuring crankcase pressure at high idle (high-speed, no-load operation). When piston rings are able to seal well because of good cylinder wall condition, ring operation allows little blow-by gas into the crankcase. When cylinder pressures are higher, such as during high idle rpm operation, the rings seal much better than they would at low idle rpm. Pressure in the crankcase is measured in inches (millimeters) of water column using a water manometer or Magnehelic gauge **FIGURE 9-51**. Small-bore diesels will have a maximum limit of 10″ (254 mm) of water column pressure. Larger engines may have as much as 15–18″ (381–457 mm) of pressure.

To perform a crankcase blow-by test, follow the guidelines in **SKILL DRILL 9-1**.

FIGURE 9-51 A Magnehelic gauge measures pressure in inches (millimeters) of water column.

SKILL DRILL 9-1 Performing a Crankcase Blow-By Test

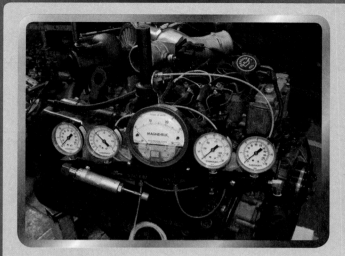

3 Ensure that the oil dipstick tube seal and any other gaskets and seals on the engine are performing properly.

4 Connect the Magnehelic gauge with plastic tubing to the restriction tool. There are two ports on the gauge, pressure and vacuum; connect to the pressure port.

5 Make sure the gauge tubing is clean and dry, so that the gauge does not become damaged. It is good practice to blow clean, dry compressed air through the tubing with before each use.

6 Zero the Magnehelic gauge.

7 Chock the wheels of the vehicle and apply the brakes. Place the transmission in neutral or park.

8 Start the vehicle's engine and run it at wide-open throttle under no load. Maintain this engine speed for at least 30 seconds and take a stabilized reading. Make sure the hole in the top of the crankcase orifice restrictor tool is never blocked when the engine is running.

9 Record your results and compare against specifications. Any reading of more than 4" (102 mm) of water during the crankcase pressure test indicates a worn engine. It is likely that base engine mechanical concerns exist. Make a service recommendation to overhaul the engine if engine hours and distance traveled are high.

1 Before starting the crankcase pressure test, it is important to run the engine until it reaches normal operating temperature. A cold engine will produce an abnormally high pressure reading.

2 Install the crankcase orifice restrictor tool in a road draft tube or a crankcase pressure test adapter in the oil fill hole. Use the manufacturer's prescribed tool and restriction diameters.

Wrap-Up

Ready for Review

▸ Cylinder components consist of the pistons, piston rings, piston pins, and connecting rods. Because these components convert combustion energy into mechanical power, they are the most highly stressed parts of the diesel engine.

▸ Cylinder components need to have a useful life that meets or exceeds EURO 6 and EPA emission standards for durability. EPA requires 435,000 miles (700,065 km) or 10 years for engines to remain emission compliant. The latest EURO 6 heavy-duty diesel standards are 434,960 miles (700,000 km) or 7 years of useful life.

▸ Basic piston designs used in diesels include slipper skirt, trunk, articulating (medium- and heavy-duty only), and MONOTHERM (medium- and heavy-duty only) pistons.

▸ Slipper skirt pistons are used in lighter, more compact diesels, while MONOTHERM pistons are used in the latest heavy-duty engines. Articulating pistons have a two-piece design and use an aluminum skirt attached to a steel crown with a piston pin. Trunk pistons are longer than they are wide.

▸ LCV pistons reduce emissions by minimizing the space between the piston crown and cylinder wall above the compression ring. Articulating and MONOTHERM pistons are classified as LCV pistons because the top ring is closer to the crown and the clearance between the cylinder wall and crown is reduced.

▸ While aluminum pistons are traditionally lighter than steel pistons, which minimizes inertia forces at the end of each stroke, aluminum pistons have several disadvantages. Aluminum pistons' needs for high crevice volume and larger operating clearances have enabled pistons with steel alloy crowns, which can withstand higher cylinder temperatures and pressures, to displace aluminum pistons in many applications.

▸ Pistons are cooled by several mechanisms, including transferring heat through the piston rings, during valve overlap when the intake air mass crosses over the piston, and by oil cooler nozzles, which spray engine oil, aimed at the underside of the piston.

▸ Piston rings help form a gas-tight seal in a cylinder, distribute oil over the cylinder wall, transfer heat from the piston, and provide a low-friction, replaceable wear surface.

▸ Three types of piston rings are used in an engine: a compression ring, an intermediate ring, and an oil control ring. Each ring has its own unique shape and materials based on its primary function.

▸ Compression rings help form a gas-tight seal in the cylinder. Intermediate rings form a compression seal and control oil distribution. Oil control rings distribute a thin coat of oil on the cylinder walls.

▸ The introduction of low-tension, low-friction piston rings is the most recent change in ring technology to reduce engine wear and friction.

▸ Steel piston rings are more commonly used. Longer break-in periods are required due to harder ring materials.

▸ Piston pins are offset from the piston's centerline to reduce noise when the piston crosses over TDC.

▸ Piston rings, pistons, and connecting rods all have directional markings that indicate which way they should be installed in an engine.

▸ Rolled threads, which are stronger than machine-cut threads, are used on connecting rod cap bolts.

▸ Prolonged engine idle produces engine slobber, which is a combination of lubricating oil, unburnt fuel, and soot. Slobber can cause piston rings to stick and leaves damaging deposits on pistons.

▸ Prolonged engine idle time can also increase cylinder glazing and soot loading of engine oil. Glazing takes place when the fine lines on the cylinder wall, called cross-hatch, are filled with oil that is then baked and smoothed over by the piston rings. When glazed, cylinder walls cannot properly retain oil, which leads to increased cylinder blow-by and power loss.

▸ Crankcase pressure testing is the most effective way to non-intrusively evaluate how much an engine's cylinders are worn.

▸ Most wear takes place in the cylinders in the ring turnaround area, which is the place in the cylinder above the highest point of travel of the oil control rings and below the compression ring. Cylinder wear is tapered, with the greatest wear at the top of the cylinders.

▸ No service life remains in a cylinder when the percentage of cross-hatch that is worn away exceeds 20% of the stroke length. Maximum taper wear is 0.001" (0.025 mm) per 1" (25 mm) of cylinder bore diameter to a maximum of 0.005" (0.127 mm).

▸ After rebuilding an engine, the engine must be run-in under a heavy load to seat piston rings and minimize the likelihood of cylinder glazing.

Vocabulary Builder

anodizing A process used to harden aluminum by electro-chemically reacting oxygen with aluminum.

articulating piston A two-piece piston design that uses a separate aluminum skirt connected to an alloy steel crown through a piston pin.

break-in period The operation of an engine after it is initially assembled or rebuilt when piston ring, cylinder wall, bushing, and bearing surfaces have high initial wear as the moving surfaces conform to each other.

cam ground piston An elliptically shaped piston that expands to a round, symmetrical shape after it is warmed up.

compatibility A property that allows two metals to slide against one another with minimal friction or wear.

compression testing A measure of the maximum pressure of engine cylinders when cranking.

crankcase pressure test A measurement of the amount of cylinder blow-by; this indicates the sealing ability of the piston rings and cylinder walls.

crevice volume The area between the piston crown and cylinder wall above the top compression ring.

cross-hatch A cylinder wall finish of fine intersecting lines that are used to retain oil.

cylinder glazing A condition that occurs when lubricating oil is first baked and then smoothed into the cross-hatch of the cylinder wall. Cylinder glazing prevents the cylinder wall from retaining oil and reduces the ability of rings to seal.

cylinder leakage The percentage of gas leakage past the rings. High leakage rates are usually due to worn cylinders and rings.

dial bore gauge A precision measuring tool used to measure taper wear in a cylinder.

durability requirements Legislated standards for engine durability that require noxious engine emissions to remain below set thresholds through the expected useful life of an engine.

dusting out A condition where dirt is drawn into an engine; this causes premature abrasive wear of the cylinder walls and rings.

forged pistons Pistons made from aluminum alloy billets that are stamped into shape by forging dies.

hydrostatic lock A condition that occurs when fluids in the cylinder of an engine prevent the engine from rotating.

hypereutectic piston A piston that has high silicon content (16–20% silicon).

Magnehelic gauge A gauge that measures both pressure and vacuum using inches or a water column as a measuring unit.

major side thrust Piston side thrust caused by cylinder pressure and the angle of the connecting rod during power.

micro-finish etching A piston skirt finish where many fine lines are machined into the skirt to retain oil.

minor side thrust Piston side thrust caused by compression pressure and the angle of the connecting rod.

MONOTHERM piston A one-piece piston design made entirely of alloyed steel, which has a compact height and a large reduction of material between the skirt and crown.

Ni-Resist insert A stainless steel–nickel alloy insert placed in aluminum pistons in the compression ring groove. The insert minimizes groove wear caused by ring movement.

nitriding The process of hardening a metal's surface by heating the metal and quenching it with cyanide salts.

piston slap A noise in the engine produced by large operating clearances between a piston and cylinder wall. Piston slap is most often heard when an engine is cold.

shot-peened A technique that uses small steel balls to blast metal surfaces in order to close up any small cracks or pores, which have the potential to become larger.

slipper skirt piston A piston design that has a portion of the skirt removed on both non-thrust sides of the piston to provide clearance for the crankshaft counterweights.

soot loading A condition that occurs when engine oil dissolves combustion soot.

split fracture connecting rod A technique used to form a mating surface between a connecting rod and cap. The mating surfaces are not machined but are produced by fracturing the big end of the rod along a line scribed into the rod.

trapezoidal pin bushing A pin bushing design in which the bearing surfaces absorbing combustion forces are wider on the connecting rod and piston to improve piston and connecting rod load bearing capabilities.

trunk piston A piston design that is dimensionally longer than it is wide, with a full piston skirt.

Review Questions

1. A(n) _____ is a two-piece piston design that uses a separate aluminum skirt connected to an alloy steel crown through a piston pin.
   a. cam ground piston   c. trunk piston
   b. articulating piston   d. slipper skirt piston

2. A _____ is a piston design that is dimensionally longer than it is wide, with a full piston skirt.
   a. trunk piston   c. hypereutectic piston
   b. slipper skirt piston d. cam ground piston

3. A _____ is a piston design that has a portion of the skirt removed on both non-thrust sides of the piston to provide clearance for the crankshaft counterweights.
   a. trunk piston   c. articulating piston
   b. hypereutectic piston d. slipper skirt piston

4. A(n) _____ is an elliptically shaped piston that expands to a round, symmetrical shape after it is warmed up.
   a. cam ground piston   c. slipper skirt piston
   b. articulating piston   d. trunk piston

5. A(n) _____ is a piston that has high silicon content.
   a. trunk piston   c. hypereutectic piston
   b. articulating piston   d. cam ground piston

6. The _____ is the top of the piston and is subjected to cylinder pressure and tremendous heat.
   a. cap   c. rod cap
   b. crown   d. balance end

7. Eliminating the dead air of the crevice volume area can lower hydrocarbon exhaust emissions by as much as _____%.
   a. 25   c. 65
   b. 50   d. 75

8. A _____ is made from aluminum alloy billets that are stamped into shape using dies.
   a. slipper skirt piston c. trunk piston
   b. cam ground piston   d. forged piston

9. A(n) _____ seals in compression gases that escape past the top rings and assist in oil control.
   a. intermediate ring   c. snap ring
   b. O-ring   d. oil control ring

10. The _____ is usually a low-tension type of ring and has no significant gas pressure acting upon it.
    a. intermediate ring   c. oil control ring
    b. O-ring   d. piston ring

ASE-Type Questions

1. Technician A says slipper skirt pistons enable the use of shorter connecting rods. Technician B says the use of shorter connecting rods permit the manufacture of vertically smaller, lighter, more compact engines. Who is correct?
   a. Technician A
   b. Technician B
   c. Both Technician A and Technician B
   d. Neither Technician A nor Technician B

2. Technician A says aluminum, when heated, will expand to three times more than ferrous metal. Technician B says aluminum, when heated, will expand to eight times more than ferrous metal. Who is correct?
   a. Technician A
   b. Technician B
   c. Both Technician A and Technician B
   d. Neither Technician A nor Technician B

3. Technician A says refinements to ring design, cylinder bore finishing techniques, and engine oils have helped produce engines that can operate for more than a million miles of use before the piston rings need to be replaced. Technician B says refinements to ring design, cylinder bore finishing techniques, and engine oils have helped produce engines that can operate for more than about a half a million miles of use before the piston rings need to be replaced. Who is correct?
   a. Technician A
   b. Technician B
   c. Both Technician A and Technician B
   d. Neither Technician A nor Technician B

4. Technician A says the piston pin bore is usually offset toward the major side thrust portion of the cylinder. Technician B says a compression test is used to measure the percentage of gas leakage past the piston rings. Who is correct?
   a. Technician A
   b. Technician B
   c. Both Technician A and Technician B
   d. Neither Technician A nor Technician B

5. Technician A says a break-in period is not needed to seat rings. Technician B says a break-in period is needed for seat rings, in addition to other engine parts including bearings, valve guides, piston pins, and cam bushings. Who is correct?
   a. Technician A
   b. Technician B
   c. Both Technician A and Technician B
   d. Neither Technician A nor Technician B

6. Technician A says split fracture connecting rods allow the rod and cap to be separated along a predetermined fracture line. Technician B says proper alignment of the connecting rod and cap is made by matching up the markings on the cap and rod to identify the assembled position. Who is correct?
   a. Technician A
   b. Technician B
   c. Both Technician A and Technician B
   d. Neither Technician A nor Technician B

7. Technician A says the presence of vertical cracks in the piston bowl usually indicates a bonding problem between the piston skirt and crown. Technician B says the presence of vertical cracks in the piston pin usually indicates a bonding problem between the piston skirt and crown. Who is correct?
   a. Technician A
   b. Technician B
   c. Both Technician A and Technician B
   d. Neither Technician A nor Technician B

8. Technician A says when replacing piston rings, the end gaps of all piston rings should be placed 180° apart in a three-ring pack. Technician B says when replacing piston rings, the end gaps of all piston rings should be placed 120° apart in a three-ring pack. Who is correct?
   a. Technician A
   b. Technician B
   c. Both Technician A and Technician B
   d. Neither Technician A nor Technician B

9. Technician A says prolonged idling of diesel engines can cause excessive soot loading and slobber production. Technician B says prolonged idling of diesel engines can cause cylinder glazing. Who is correct?
   a. Technician A
   b. Technician B
   c. Both Technician A and Technician B
   d. Neither Technician A nor Technician B

10. Technician A says the US Environmental Protection Agency imposes new design features on cylinder components through legislated standards called durability requirements. Technician B says the US Environmental Protection Agency imposes new design features on cylinder components through legislated standards called longevity standards. Who is correct?
    a. Technician A
    b. Technician B
    c. Both Technician A and Technician B
    d. Neither Technician A nor Technician B

CHAPTER 10
Cylinder Blocks and Crankshafts

▶ NATEF Tasks

Diesel Engines

General
- Identify engine vibration problems. (pp 267–268, 275–280)

Engine Block
- Disassemble, clean, and inspect engine block for cracks/damage; measure mating surfaces for warpage; check condition of passages, core/expansion, and gallery plugs; inspect threaded holes, studs, dowel pins, and bolts for serviceability; determine needed action. (p 269)
- Inspect cylinder sleeve counter bore and lower bore; check bore distortion; determine needed action. (pp 292–294)
- Clean, inspect, and measure cylinder walls or liners for wear and damage; determine needed action. (pp 295–296)
- Replace/reinstall cylinder liners and seals; check and adjust liner height (protrusion). (pp 292–294)
- Inspect in-block camshaft bearings for wear and damage; determine needed action. (pp 288–290)

- Inspect, measure, and replace/reinstall in-block camshaft; measure/adjust end play. (pp 275, 284, 299–300)
- Clean and inspect crankshaft for surface cracks and journal damage; check condition of oil passages; check passage plugs; measure journal diameter; determine needed action. (pp 280–284)
- Inspect main bearings for wear patterns and damage; replace as needed; check bearing clearances; check and correct crankshaft end play. (pp 290–291, 296–297)
- Inspect, install and time gear train; measure gear backlash; determine needed action. (pp 275–276)
- Inspect crankshaft vibration damper; determine needed action. (pp 275–278)
- Install and align flywheel housing; inspect flywheel housing(s) to transmission housing/engine mating surface(s) and measure flywheel housing face and bore runout; determine needed action. (pp 279–281)
- Inspect flywheel/flexplate (including ring gear) and mounting surfaces for cracks and wear; measure runout; determine needed action. (pp 286–289)

▶ Knowledge Objectives

After reading this chapter, you will be able to:
1. Identify and describe the functions, construction, composition, types, styles, and applications of diesel engine cylinder block and crankshaft assemblies. (pp 266–288)
2. Identify and describe inspection, testing, and diagnostic procedures on diesel engine cylinder block assemblies. (pp 292–295)

3. Recommend reconditioning or repair procedures for diesel engine cylinder block and crankshaft assemblies. (pp 292–297)
4. Identify common causes of abnormal wear, bending, and torsional stress of crankshafts. (pp 275–276)
5. Describe construction features of crankshafts. (pp 272–275)

Skills Objectives

After reading this chapter, you will be able to:

1. Reinstall a flywheel housing. (p 289) SKILL DRILL 10-1

2. Measure liner protrusion. (p 302) SKILL DRILL 10-2
3. Measure crankshaft endplay. (p 305) SKILL DRILL 10-3

▶ Introduction

The cylinder block, which encloses the cylinder bores, is the largest part and main structure of the diesel engine FIGURE 10-1 . Because the diesel's high cylinder pressure generates substantially more power output per cubic inch of displacement, it produces extraordinary vibration that requires unique design and construction features. The block's design and other major engine components integral to the block such as crankshafts, balance shafts, vibration dampeners, and flywheels are examined in this chapter as well.

▶ Fundamentals of Cylinder Blocks

The cylinder block can be described as the largest single part and backbone of the diesel engine. Its primary function is to support cylinders and liners (if equipped) as well as major engine components such as the crankshaft and camshaft. The transmission, cylinder head(s), and all other major engine parts are bolted or connected to the cylinder block. The cylinders on diesel engine blocks are arranged inline, V banked, or horizontally opposed FIGURE 10-2 . The numbers of cylinders within a block are commonly configured in four, five, six, eight, and even ten and twelve cylinder bores; however, many single, two, and three cylinder blocks are produced as well. High cylinder pressures combined with a rapid combustion phase

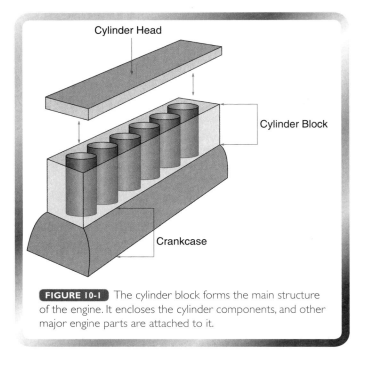

FIGURE 10-1 The cylinder block forms the main structure of the engine. It encloses the cylinder components, and other major engine parts are attached to it.

create unusual vibration and torsional twisting forces in diesel blocks. These diesel characteristics require specialized features to reduce noise, vibration, and harshness from diesels. Strong,

You Are the Technician

You work for a fleet operation that is beginning a program to overhaul and rebuild all engines in-house rather than subcontract the work to an independent engine repair facility. The fleet is a mixed operation with a third of the trucks large-bore on-highway tractors, another third medium-duty pick-up and delivery vehicles, and finally some vocational vehicles such as flat-bed delivery trucks and haulers. You are tasked with preparing an overhaul guideline for the variety of the fleet's engines. Using the guidelines, technicians will perform inspection procedures when dissembling the engines to determine whether parts will be replaced. As you set out to prepare the guidelines, consider the following:

1. What type of engine blocks do you expect to encounter? Explain your answer.
2. Outline the inspection and overhaul procedures you can expect to perform for each category of engines encountered in the fleet.
3. Outline the service procedures you expect all the engines to undergo during overhaul and rebuild.

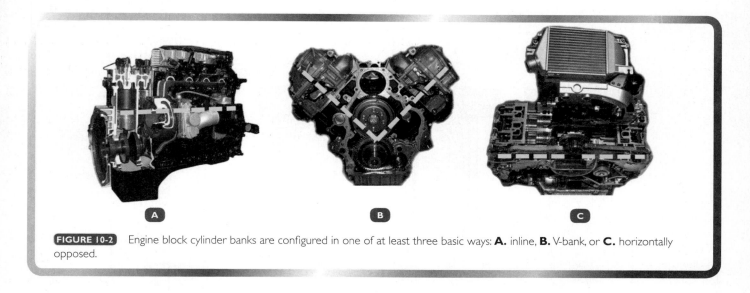

FIGURE 10-2 Engine block cylinder banks are configured in one of at least three basic ways: **A.** inline, **B.** V-bank, or **C.** horizontally opposed.

rigid, vibration-free, lightweight, durable designs are necessary for engines to perform well under all operating conditions.

Cylinder Block Structure

The diesel engine cylinder block consists of these three distinct sections:

1. Main block structure—encloses the cylinder components
2. Cylinder component assemblies—includes the pistons, rings, wrist pins, and connecting rods
3. Crankcase—the area below the cylinders enclosing the crankshaft and its bearings

The gear train may be located on either the front or the rear of the engine **FIGURE 10-3**. Gear train rattle is an issue in diesel engines, affecting not only noise but also engine durability. Using scissor gears minimizes gear rattle, a common problem in the long gear trains of overhead camshaft engines. A **scissor gear** is actually two separate gears incorporated into a single unit. Zero lash between the gears teeth is maintained by a tensioned set of springs. High torsional forces contribute to gear rattle and gear train wear **FIGURE 10-4**. Firing impulses applied to the crankshaft cause sharp variations to its rotational velocity. The rhythmic change in crankshaft speed is referred to as **torsional vibration** **FIGURE 10-5**. With each alternating power and compression stroke, the crankshaft will slow then accelerate several times during each revolution. The results are camshaft and crankshaft speed variation of between 3% and 6% during each crank rotation, which affects gear train durability and noise emissions. Moving the gear train to the rear of the engine where torsional vibrations are reduced due to the heavier flywheel mass can dramatically reduce gear train noise. Gear life and valve timing accuracy are improved.

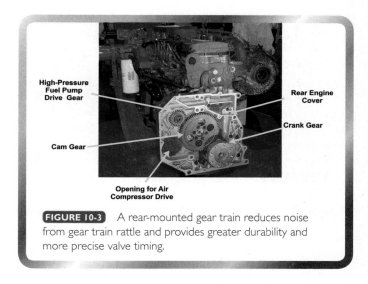

FIGURE 10-3 A rear-mounted gear train reduces noise from gear train rattle and provides greater durability and more precise valve timing.

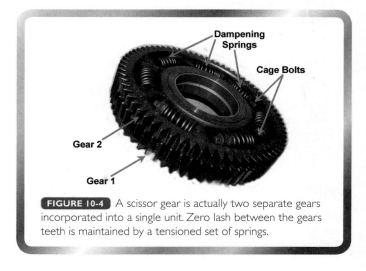

FIGURE 10-4 A scissor gear is actually two separate gears incorporated into a single unit. Zero lash between the gears teeth is maintained by a tensioned set of springs.

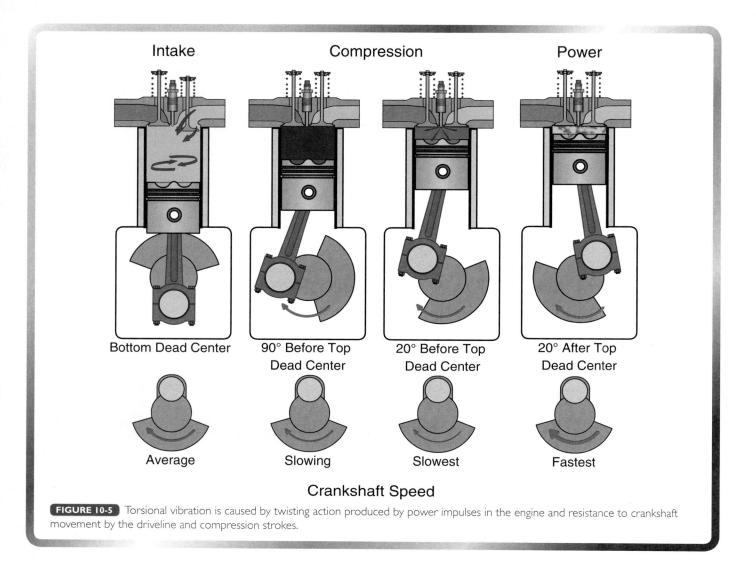

FIGURE 10-5 Torsional vibration is caused by twisting action produced by power impulses in the engine and resistance to crankshaft movement by the driveline and compression strokes.

▶ TECHNICIAN TIP

High compression ratios and even higher cylinder pressures of a diesel engine produce intense torsional vibration. Torsional vibration is observed by watching the back-and-forth oscillation of belt tensioners. The change in speed of the crankshaft causes drive belts to alternately stretch and shorten, thus causing tensioner movement and belt vibration. Severe torsional vibration can result in damaged or broken crankshafts, camshafts, and severe wear of gear train mechanisms. Taming torsional vibration is necessary to avoid not only engine damage but also unpleasant driveline noise, vibration, and harshness (NVH) in a vehicle.

Cylinder Block Materials

Most cylinder blocks are manufactured from cast iron, but aluminum is popular in many light-duty European diesels from Mercedes and Volkswagen.

Cast Iron

Cast iron refers to metal made from iron ore with a carbon content of 3–5%. The carbon is scattered throughout the metal in flakes, creating metal with a crystalline-like structure. The metal is poured or cast into molds commonly made from sand or fiberglass. The advantages of cast iron are that it is easy to manufacture and machine, it absorbs vibration well, it is inherently strong, and it is corrosion and heat resistant. The high carbon graphite content of iron makes it a compatible, wear-resistant surface for moving parts such as pistons and piston rings. To improve strength, hardness, and corrosion resistance, manufacturers may add nickel, molybdenum, and chromium alloys. Cast iron is still not as strong as steel, so machine threads usually have a coarse thread pitch to minimize the problem of stripping threads. Main bearing caps are often hardened or use special alloys to improve block strength.

Casting and Block Seasoning

Sand casting cylinder blocks requires the removal of sand from inner passageways. Core plugs, sometimes called frost plugs because they are pushed out by frozen coolant, are used to cover holes made in the block to flush sand out of small passageways during casting **FIGURE 10-6**. After rough casting, blocks tend to warp. To prevent this, diesel blocks are often stored at high temperatures for a day or two to heat treat and "season" them. Heating the blocks hardens them, making them resistant to stress and minimizing future distortion. Subsequent to seasoning, castings are bored, tapped, and machined to finish. Induction hardening may also be performed to increase the hardness and durability of cast iron cylinder blocks. **Induction hardening** is a heat treatment process that involves passing alternating electrical current through coils of heavy-gauge wire surrounding the material to be hardened. Through magnetic induction, heat is produced in the metal, which is then quenched with water to produce a hard, wear-resistant, metal surface **FIGURE 10-7**.

Disadvantages of Cast Iron

Cast iron is heavy, and engines made from cast iron therefore add considerable weight to the vehicle in comparison to lighter materials such as aluminum. This can negatively affect vehicle handling and braking characteristics. Cast iron does not transfer heat as readily as aluminum. Cast iron cannot be as easily repaired as

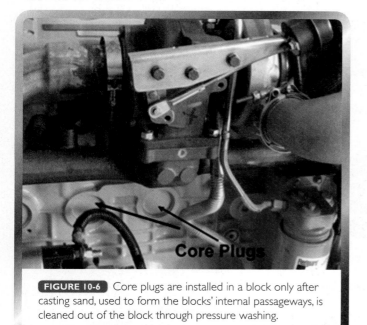

FIGURE 10-6 Core plugs are installed in a block only after casting sand, used to form the blocks' internal passageways, is cleaned out of the block through pressure washing.

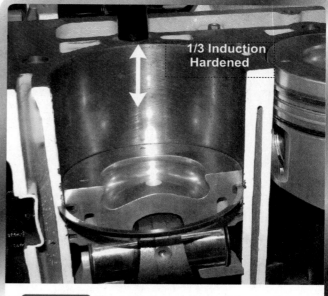

FIGURE 10-7 The arrow shows an area of discoloration where the upper third of this cylinder has been induction hardened. Induction hardening increases engine life by minimizing cylinder wall wear in the ring turnaround area where there is the least amount of cylinder lubrication.

steel or other metals. Whenever repairs to damaged blocks are made, welding techniques to repair cracks involve preheating the block and using a welding rod with high nickel content or a powdered iron welding rod. An original equipment manufacturer (OEM) repair recommendation for block porosity is to use epoxy in areas where mechanical stress is not significant.

Aluminum

Aluminum is being used more commonly as a block material in high-performance diesels; and while improving performance, it also saves on weight. When used in small, six cylinder diesel engines, aluminum can eliminate more than 77 lb (35 kg) of weight compared to a similar engine block made from cast iron.

Aluminum does have its disadvantages, however. Until the 1990s, aluminum engine blocks were only used in gasoline-fueled engines because high-performance diesel engines were required to withstand high temperatures and three times more cylinder pressure than spark ignition engines. Aluminum also has challenges with rigidity, strength, and reliable bolting of the cylinder head and main bearings. Although it transmits heat well, aluminum has an expansion coefficient of about four to seven times the rate of iron. This causes enlargement of critical dimensions such as the crankshaft bearing bores and cylinder bore diameters. Soft aluminum cannot sustain the friction between pistons and the cylinder wall without wearing rapidly.

However, because of aluminum's significant weight-saving advantage, manufacturing techniques have been employed to overcome these difficulties. For example, aluminum cylinder blocks use a **warp anchor** principle to prevent distortion of the block from cylinder head bolts. This means the cylinder head and the cylinder block are bolted together by tie bolts. Sliding steel sleeves that are locked in the block accept the cylinder head bolt from one side and the tie bolt from the other **FIGURE 10-8**. Also, cylinder walls and bearing bores are fabricated from casting iron liners into the aluminum block structure to provide durable, low-friction wear surfaces. Another technique is to apply another harder material to cylinder wall surfaces. Spray welding, also called plasma welding, applies an alloyed iron coating over the cylinder wall. Coatings of tool-grade hardness iron carbon alloys can be achieved by a plasma-spraying technique called by **Nanoslide technology** **FIGURE 10-9**. Using a rotating plasma torch and metal alloy powder, parent bore block walls are sprayed with a coating a few tenths of a millimeter thick to give the cylinder walls great wear resistance and durability **FIGURE 10-10**.

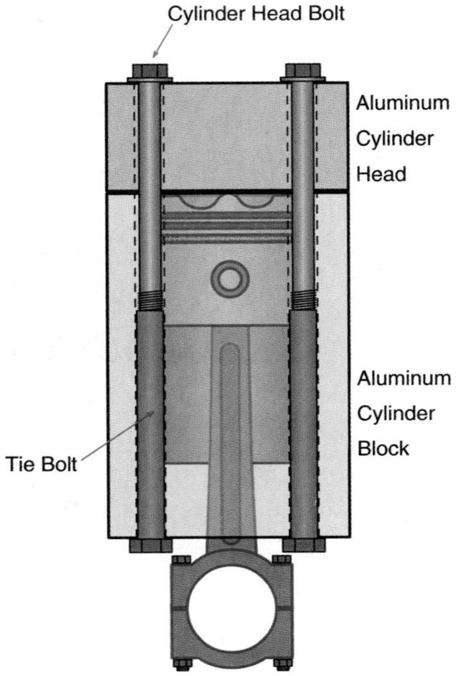

▶ TECHNICIAN TIP

Mercedes-Benz has developed a plasma spray welding technique called Nanoslide technology to coat cylinder walls of the 3L (183 cubic inch) block with a tool-grade hardness iron alloy. The technique first melts wires of iron–carbon alloy in an electric arc. Pressurized gas deposits the melted material onto the cylinder walls to only 0.004–0.006" (0.102–0.152 mm) thickness. This ultrafine nanocrystalline coating is then finished to a smooth mirror-like surface using a special honing process. In spite of the extreme smoothness, the honing process opens pores in the material that retain oil for lubricating the piston and cylinder wall. The result is a low-friction surface that reduces mechanical losses due to friction by up to 50% in comparison to cast-iron cylinder liners. In addition, extremely high wear resistance is imparted to the cylinder walls. Other advantages include lower engine weight, reduced fuel consumption, and lower emissions.

Compacted Graphite Iron

Using **compacted graphite iron (CGI)**, or sintered graphite, is an engine block building technique that starts with squeezing powdered iron alloys into molds at high pressures and then heating them to bond the metal particles together. This construction

FIGURE 10-8 Warp anchor principle. The cylinder head and the cylinder block are bolted together by tie bolts. Sliding steel sleeves locked in the block accept the cylinder head bolt from one side and the tie bolt from the other, preventing distortion of the block.

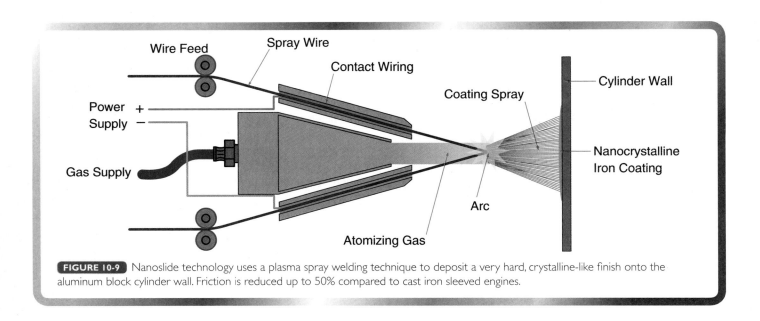

FIGURE 10-9 Nanoslide technology uses a plasma spray welding technique to deposit a very hard, crystalline-like finish onto the aluminum block cylinder wall. Friction is reduced up to 50% compared to cast iron sleeved engines.

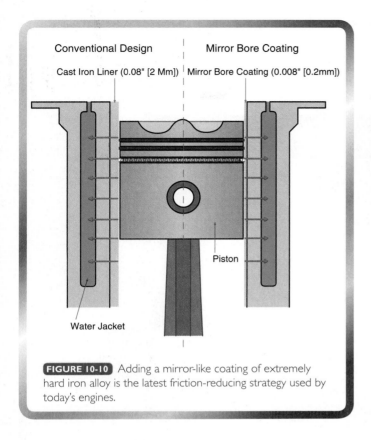

FIGURE 10-10 Adding a mirror-like coating of extremely hard iron alloy is the latest friction-reducing strategy used by today's engines.

FIGURE 10-11 A popular example of a CGI engine block is the Scorpion 6.7L (409 cubic inch) PowerStroke. CGI block material provides for a quieter, stronger, and lighter design.

technique yields blocks with at least 80% higher tensile strength, 45% greater stiffness, and approximately double the fatigue strength of conventional cast iron and aluminum. The weight of an engine block made from CGI alone can be reduced by 22% through a 15% reduction in the thickness of the block walls. Noise transmission through the block is dramatically reduced as well because the vermicular (wormlike) grain structure of CGI has sound-absorbing properties. CGI also allows engine designers to improve power density, performance, fuel economy, and durability in addition to reducing engine weight and noise.

A number of heavy-duty diesel engine blocks currently use this material, including International 7L (427 cubic inch), 13L (793 cubic inch) MaxxForce, John Deere 9L (549 cubic inch), Paccar MX13 (in which both block and cylinder head are made from CGI), Caterpillar, Volvo, HD Mercedes engines, and the Ford 6.7L (409 cubic inch) PowerStroke introduced in 2010 **FIGURE 10-11** . The Ford 6.7L (409 cubic inch) PowerStroke uses a patented SinterCast CGI material and is 40% more rigid and 100% more fatigue resistant than cast iron. CGI has allowed Ford designers to reduce the engine wall thickness by 15% in comparison to cast iron. A weight reduction of 160 lb (70 kg) is achieved in comparison to the earlier 6.4L (391 cubic inch) engine.

Engine Balance

Inline engines are preferred in vocational and heavy-duty diesel engines because the crankshaft is supported by more main bearings than in V-block configurations. This means the inline block is better able to handle higher cylinder pressure with greater durability than V-block configurations. The advantage of a V-block lies in its more compact design, which permits lower hood profiles. Cylinder banks leaned 60°, 72°, or 90° result in an engine with less overall height. However, an inline six cylinder engine is also among the best balanced configurations for the internal combustion engine, possessing excellent primary and secondary balance characteristics.

Primary Balance

Primary balance is achieved when the crankshaft counterweights offset the weight of the piston and connecting rod assembly **FIGURE 10-12** . Most engines use a counterweight on the crankshaft for each cylinder to counteract the inertia of the piston and connecting rod assemblies to minimize engine vibration. In inline six cylinder engines, the crankshaft counterweight is usually absent for cylinders 2 and 5.

Secondary Balance

Secondary balance is achieved when the movement of one piston counterbalances the movement of another. Secondary balance is easily achieved in inline engines, because all the pistons are in one plane. Inherent in the inline six cylinder design is the advantage of pairing pistons that move simultaneously in the same direction and plane to be counterbalanced by pairs of pistons moving in the opposite direction. The dynamic forces of piston weight can be canceled out by the forces of pistons moving

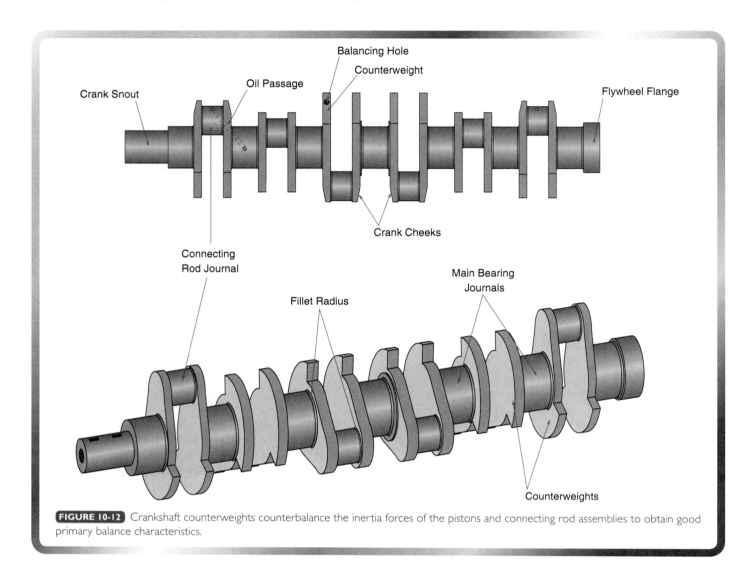

FIGURE 10-12 Crankshaft counterweights counterbalance the inertia forces of the pistons and connecting rod assemblies to obtain good primary balance characteristics.

in the opposite direction. Paired cylinders are 1 and 6, 2 and 5, and 3 and 4. The 1-6 pair rotates 240° away from 3-4, which enables counterbalancing of each of those pairs. The 2-5 cylinder pair is 120° opposite in rotation to the 1-6 and 3-4 cylinder pairs **FIGURE 10-13**. Horizontally opposed engines also have good secondary balance. In contrast, V-block engines have a natural secondary imbalance that may cause engine vibration. This occurs because pistons do not move in the same plane. The direction of movement may be 60°, 72°, or 90° apart.

Good inherent primary and secondary balance translates into smoother running engines. Firing orders are arranged to produce even spacing between power impulses and to distribute loads evenly along the crankshaft **FIGURE 10-14**. An even number of degrees of crankshaft rotation between cylinder power impulses minimizes engine vibration.

▶ Fundamentals of Crankshafts

Crankshafts convert the up-and-down, or reciprocating, movement of pistons to rotational movement. Engine power is transmitted through the crankshaft to the flywheel where the

power train connects to the engine. The higher cylinder pressures and rapid combustion phase of a diesel engine require crankshaft design, construction, and service procedures to be unique and sophisticated. The rugged sophistication of the crankshaft is reflected in manufacturing costs, which makes the component one of the most expensive parts of an engine after the fuel system and turbocharger. Understanding the construction details of crankshafts will help a technician realize the importance of the skills related to handling and servicing of a crankshaft to ensure the best engine reliability and longevity.

Purpose and Construction

The main purpose of the crankshaft in a reciprocating engine is to convert the linear motion of the connecting rod assemblies into rotational movement **FIGURE 10-15**. The mechanical stress caused by rotational speeds, combustion pressure, thrust loads, and vibrations require the crankshaft to be exceptionally strong and precisely manufactured. The two connecting surfaces to the crankshaft are the main and rod bearing journals

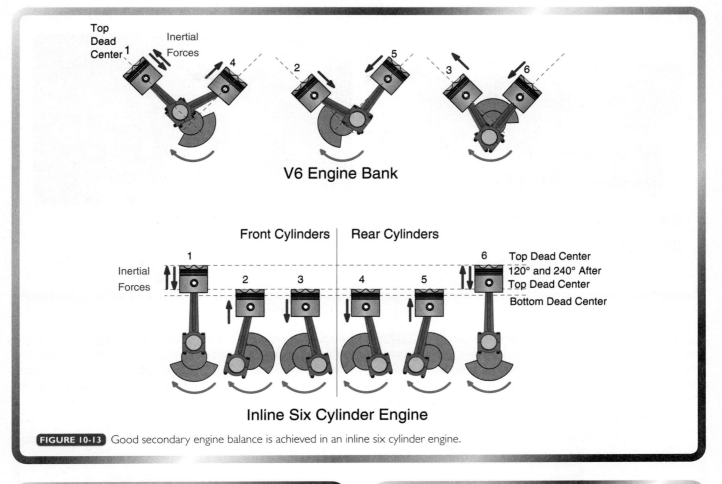

FIGURE 10-13 Good secondary engine balance is achieved in an inline six cylinder engine.

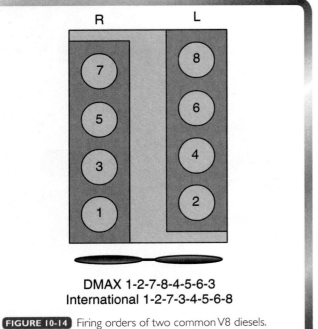

DMAX 1-2-7-8-4-5-6-3
International 1-2-7-3-4-5-6-8

FIGURE 10-14 Firing orders of two common V8 diesels. The leading bank of an engine identifies cylinder 1. The firing order is designed to distribute firing impulses evenly over the crankshaft to minimize damaging torsional or twisting forces along the crankshaft.

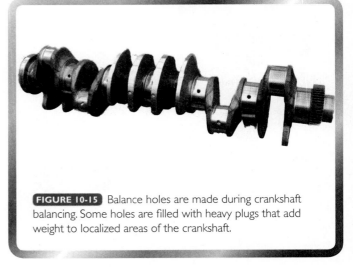

FIGURE 10-15 Balance holes are made during crankshaft balancing. Some holes are filled with heavy plugs that add weight to localized areas of the crankshaft.

FIGURE 10-16. Main bearing journals are located along the crankshaft centerline. Main bearing caps support the crankshaft as it rotates. Rod journals are offset from the crankshaft centerline main journals. The distance of rod journal offset from the main bearing journals is known as the throw. The length of throw determines the stroke length of the engine. The arrangement of the rod journals, or throws,

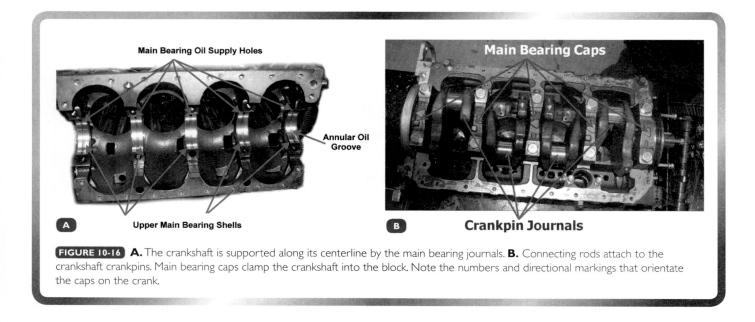

FIGURE 10-16 **A.** The crankshaft is supported along its centerline by the main bearing journals. **B.** Connecting rods attach to the crankshaft crankpins. Main bearing caps clamp the crankshaft into the block. Note the numbers and directional markings that orientate the caps on the crank.

allows for even spacing between power impulses **FIGURE 10-17**. For example, a six cylinder engine will have 120° of spacing between the rod journals (720° of rotation over six cylinders). The throws are further arranged to evenly distribute the firing order over the length of the shaft to balance out vibration and stresses. For example, in inline six cylinder engines, the throws of cylinders are paired one and six, two and five, and three and four. Using a standard firing order of 1-5-3-6-2-4 distributes power impulses evenly throughout the crankshaft during the two rotations it makes to complete a combustion cycle.

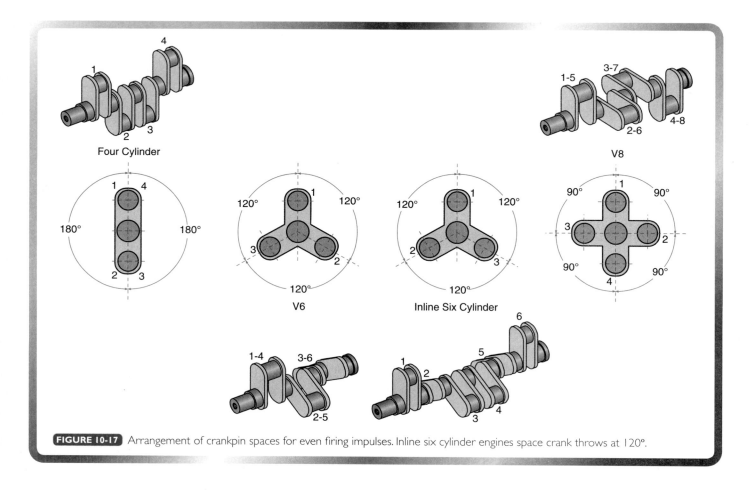

FIGURE 10-17 Arrangement of crankpin spaces for even firing impulses. Inline six cylinder engines space crank throws at 120°.

When the engine is operating, tremendous inertia is generated by the reciprocating mass of the connecting rod and piston assembly. To balance these forces, large counterweights are formed on the crankshaft 180° opposite the rod journal.

A <u>fillet radius</u> is a critical feature unique to a diesel crankshaft. It is a circular-shaped machining applied to the rod and main journal surface between the journal and the crankshaft cheek. Because this region is one of the most stressed areas of the crankshaft, leaving a sharp 90° angle between them could induce a crack through a stress riser. Imparting a smooth circular radius to this area strengthens the crankshaft and minimizes the possibility of a fracture.

Crankshaft Journal Hardening

Crankshafts in diesel engines are commonly forged from high carbon steel alloys, which produces a denser and stronger component. Following the machining of crankpins, counterweights, and other surfaces, journal surfaces are hardened to improve the durability of a diesel crankshaft. The two most common processes used to harden bearing surfaces of the crankshaft are induction hardening and nitriding.

Induction Hardening

To induction harden a crankshaft, the journal is wrapped in a coil of wire that has high-amperage alternating current passed through it. The journal surface will have current induced into it by mutual induction, much like the secondary winding of an ignition coil. This current flows over the journal surface, heating the metal surface and changing its molecular structure. Quenching the heated surfaces with water produces a very hard surface finish. Induction hardening causes discoloration of the metal surfaces hardened through this process **FIGURE 10-18**. Typically, induction hardening is effective to no more than 0.03″

FIGURE 10-18 This crankshaft has discoloration around hardened journals, which is not evidence of damage from overheating but is caused by heating during induction hardening.

(0.76 mm) deep. It may go deeper, but the surface will be less hard with increasing depth. This is one reason why machining diesel cranks is typically not an accepted practice; the hardening material is removed by machining and most rebuilders are not able to restore it during rebuilding and repair. This is why replacement bearings are generally unavailable for crankshafts with journals machined smaller or undersized to repair damaged journal surfaces. However, at an OEM rebuild level, plasma spray welding of the crankshaft with high alloy steel, which is then machined to the correct journal dimension, is an accepted technique for diesel engine crankshaft restoration.

> ▶ **TECHNICIAN TIP**
>
> Grinding of diesel crankshafts to undersize dimensions to repair damaged journal surfaces is common in spark ignition (SI), gasoline-fueled engines. Diesel cranks, however, are almost always hardened, and grinding to repair journal damage will remove the surface hardening. Furthermore, a fillet radius ground into each crankshaft journal is difficult for most machine shops to restore. For these reasons, most manufacturers do not recommend the practice, and undersize crankshaft bearings are not commonly available for diesel crankshafts.

Nitriding

Another crankshaft hardening technique is <u>nitriding</u>. Chevy diesels, including the Duramax, use this technique. The process involves heating the shaft and introducing cyanide salt or liquid into the heating chamber with the crankshaft. Slowly cooling or quenching the crank with these substances in its heated condition causes the nitrogen and carbon to molecularly bond with metal surfaces to create an extremely hard journal. This hardened finish does not extend more than 0.012″ (0.305 mm) deep, but is one of the hardest journal surface finishing techniques.

Crankshaft Lubrication

To lubricate the main and rod bearings, engine oil needs to be directed in sufficient quantities to lubricate, cool, and clean the crankshaft journals and bearings. Engine oil is delivered to the oil galleries in the block and then distributed to the main bearings using holes present in the upper main bearing shells **FIGURE 10-19**. A cross-drilled hole in the crank's main bearing journal uniformly distributes oil around the crankshaft journal. The crankshaft also has holes drilled from the main bearing cross-drilling to the rod journal, connecting each main bearing to an adjacent rod bearing through an oil passageway. The exception to this is the rear main, which, in some cases, has a slightly smaller oil hole into the block for lubrication of only one main journal. This relieves lubrication oil pressure exerted against the rear main seal, which minimizes potential leaks and oil weepage from the rear main seal.

Vibration Dampeners

Torsional vibration is observed as the crankshaft decelerates and accelerates during rotation and is caused by the alternating

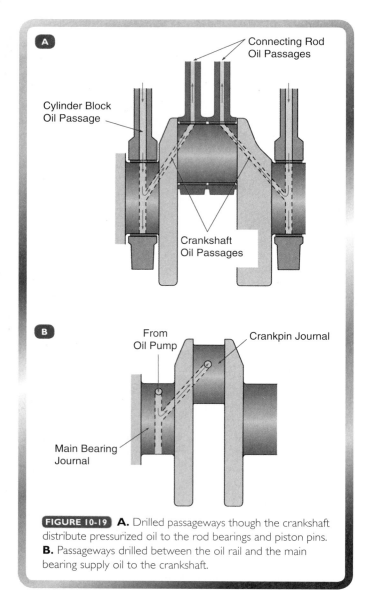

FIGURE 10-19 **A.** Drilled passageways though the crankshaft distribute pressurized oil to the rod bearings and piston pins. **B.** Passageways drilled between the oil rail and the main bearing supply oil to the crankshaft.

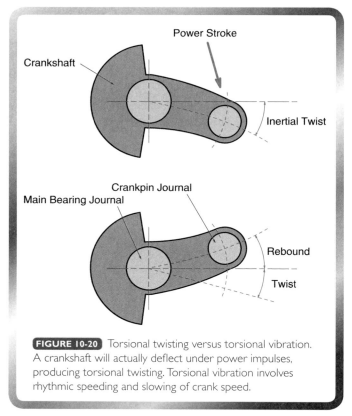

FIGURE 10-20 Torsional twisting versus torsional vibration. A crankshaft will actually deflect under power impulses, producing torsional twisting. Torsional vibration involves rhythmic speeding and slowing of crank speed.

combustion and compression pressure in each cylinder. At specific rpm, accessory drive belts can be spontaneously thrown and driveline vibration can occur due to torsional vibration. Alternators, A/C compressors, and other accessories will loosen and fall off due to excessive torsional twisting of the crankshaft. Cylinder pressure applied against the piston and connecting rod assembly is intense enough to also deflect and twist the crankshaft while it turns **FIGURE 10-20**. The twisting event eventually results in a rebound of the crankshaft as the journal snaps back in the opposite direction of rotation. The effect of this torsional stress is telegraphed through the gear train and driveline and, if not properly controlled, can cause rapid main bearing and gear train wear and possible breakage of the camshaft and the crankshaft itself. These forces produce harmonic waves as well, which are like the vibration of a guitar string with pressure waves moving back and forth along the crankshaft. The appearance of these waves is similar to sound

waves and in fact sounds like a ringing bell. This wave motion, called **harmonic vibration**, is another potentially destructive force to the engine crankshaft. Nodal points along the crank are points of potential failures due to harmonic vibration.

To control the destructive effects of both torsional and harmonic vibrations, diesel engines are equipped with a vibration dampener that reduces both. The mass of the flywheel can substantially suppress torsional vibration at its end of the crankshaft. At the flywheel, changes in crankshaft velocity are minimized by the inertia of the flywheel, which resists speeding up and slowing down with each change in cylinder pressure. To reduce torsional twisting at the opposite end of the crank, a vibration damper is located at the front of the crank where it is needed to reduce both torsional and harmonic vibrations.

Five types of dampener construction are used on diesel engines.

- Elastomer dampeners
- Viscous or fluid dampeners
- Combination dampeners
- Rotating pendulum vibration absorber
- Balance shafts

Elastomeric Dampeners

Elastomer dampeners refer to vibration dampeners that use rubber as the primary material to absorb harmonic vibrations and reduce torsional stress on the crankshaft. These are made of three parts: The inner hub is attached to the crankshaft, which connects to a heavier, outer iron inertia ring through a rubber or elastomeric ring. The dampening action occurs as the outer ring oscillates alternately with speed changes in the inner ring's movement **FIGURE 10-21**. For example, when the crankshaft slows, the inner ring is sped up by the inertia of the outer ring. When the inner ring slows down, the outer ring transmits inertial force through the rubber ring to speed up the inner ring. The opposite action occurs as the inner ring accelerates and transmits resistance to the sudden speed change through the rubber ring. The elastomeric dampener is tuned to vibrate out of phase with the lowest torsional frequency of the engine. Alignment and verification of the proper operation of the two inertia rings is confirmed by the use of a mark scribed in the face of the outer and inner ring. If the marks are not aligned, the rings have debonded from the elastomer ring and the dampener is defective **FIGURE 10-22**.

▶ TECHNICIAN TIP

Timing marks located on the outside of elastomer vibration dampeners may be incorrect if the outer hub has slipped relative to the inner hub. Oil on the dampener and age are common deterioration factors causing slippage, and a technician must carefully inspect the dampener for such evidence.

Viscous Dampeners

Silicone fluid is used in viscous dampeners to tune out harmonic and torsional vibrations. Higher horsepower engines (those over 300 hp [224 kW]) possess higher vibrational energy, which can lead to overheating and shorten an elastomer dampener's life. In a viscous dampener, the inertia ring rotates inside a sealed case connected to the crankshaft **FIGURE 10-23**. A thin film of

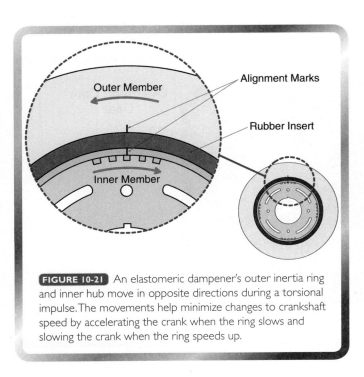

FIGURE 10-21 An elastomeric dampener's outer inertia ring and inner hub move in opposite directions during a torsional impulse. The movements help minimize changes to crankshaft speed by accelerating the crank when the ring slows and slowing the crank when the ring speeds up.

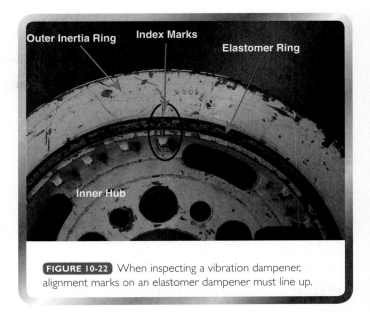

FIGURE 10-22 When inspecting a vibration dampener, alignment marks on an elastomer dampener must line up.

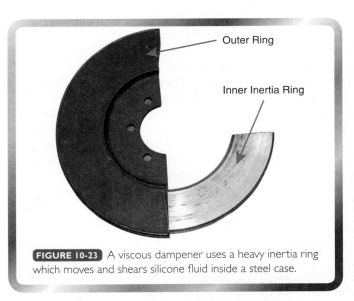

FIGURE 10-23 A viscous dampener uses a heavy inertia ring which moves and shears silicone fluid inside a steel case.

highly viscous silicone fluid fills the small gap between the inner inertia ring and the outer case. During changes in crankshaft speed, the silicone fluid drags the inertia ring, permitting it to rotate at approximately the same rpm as the crankshaft. If no torsional vibration is present, the inertia ring and outer casing rotate at identical speeds. However, changes to crankshaft speed due to harmonic and torsional vibrations cause the inertia ring and outer case to shear the silicone fluid. This converts the relative motion between the inertia ring and outer case into heat energy, which effectively dampens torsional and harmonic vibrations. The oscillating (back and forth) movement between the ring and case allows the viscous dampener to dissipate more energy than the same size elastomeric dampener, permitting more effective dampening of torsional vibrations.

Combination Dampeners

These dampeners combine the dampening advantages of both viscous and elastomeric dampeners. Elastomeric dampeners provide good low-speed harmonic dampening in comparison to viscous dampeners. However, at higher engine speeds, the reverse is true, and viscous dampeners provide better harmonic vibration dampening.

Rotating Pendulum Vibration Absorber

Unlike regular balancers, <u>pendulum vibration absorbers</u> provide torsional control by producing forces that directly cancel the forces that produce torsional vibration. Steel rollers called centrifugal pendulums fit loosely into a specific number of holes in either a harmonic balancer or overhead cam drive gear. The rollers store and release energy back into the crankshaft rather than converting the mechanical energy into heat energy as dampeners do **FIGURE 10-24**. A patented mathematical algorithm is used to calculate roller size, hole size, and gear size to control how the rollers move forward during compression strokes when the crank slows and roll backward during the power stroke. Movement of the rollers back and forth minimizes engine speed changes, keeping torsional vibration low. Manufacturers claim the pendulum dampener provides a smoother-running engine, increased valve train stability, and more accurate injection timing.

Pendulum dampeners have the advantage of being lighter than conventional dampeners.

Balance Shafts

Balance shafts are used to dampen secondary engine vibration made by piston movement. When two balance shafts are used, they rotate in opposition to one another at twice the engine speed, countering secondary imbalance forces. Balance shafts help eliminate vibrations that drivers and passengers might otherwise feel transmitted through the engine mounts to the steering wheel, seats, floor pan, or instrument panel. Three- and four cylinder engines commonly use balance shafts. A more popular example of their use is in the S-50 Detroit Diesel. This four cylinder engine block is nearly identical to the larger S-60 six cylinder block. Removing two cylinders created abnormal engine vibration, which is dampened with the use of a counterbalance shaft mechanism bolted to the crankcase **FIGURE 10-25**.

Flywheels

Flywheels are like large plates bolted to the rear of the engine, and they serve several purposes. Their primary purpose is to provide some inertia between power impulses to keep the engine rotating. Storing energy in the heavy flywheel produced during each power impulse helps smooth out engine speed. A toothed ring gear fastened to the circumference of the flywheel provides a drive point for the starting motor pinion gear. To crank the engine, the starter will engage the engine through the flywheel ring gear. Turning tools are often temporarily attached to the flywheel to rotate the engine when performing service procedures **FIGURE 10-26**.

A flywheel also provides a mounting surface for a clutch in the case of a manual transmission and a torque converter for

FIGURE 10-24 A rotating pendulum vibration dampener is used by Caterpillar in overhead camshaft ACERT engines.

Overhead Cam Gear

Rollers

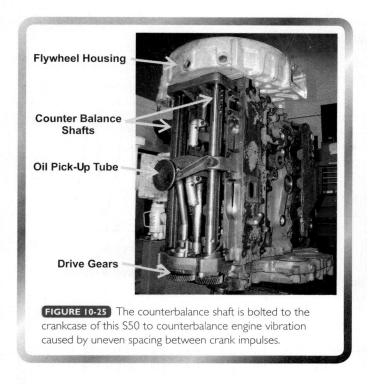

FIGURE 10-25 The counterbalance shaft is bolted to the crankcase of this S50 to counterbalance engine vibration caused by uneven spacing between crank impulses.

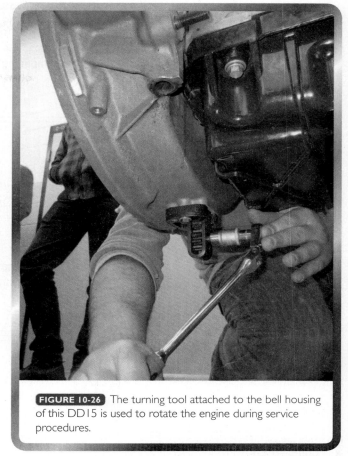

FIGURE 10-26 The turning tool attached to the bell housing of this DD15 is used to rotate the engine during service procedures.

automatic transmissions. Flywheel shape and construction can vary depending on the type of clutch used and whether torsional dampening capabilities are built into the flywheel.

Dual Mass Flywheels

Torsional vibration dampening is important to drivetrain durability and reduction of noise, vibration, and harshness. A number of medium-duty engines incorporate specialized torsional vibration dampening springs in the flywheel construction called <u>dual mass flywheels (DMFs)</u>. When connected to manual transmissions, DMFs enable the use of lighter transmissions and drivelines by minimizing torque spikes produced by torsional vibration **FIGURE 10-27** . Transmissions shift easier and transmission gear rattle is virtually eliminated with DMFs.

DMFs are made from two separate sections that can be disassembled and inspected during clutch servicing. The clutch surface and ring gear are each separate halves of the flywheel. DMFs are further recognized by a series of springs located around the flywheel circumference on the engine side of the flywheel. One set of bolts near the center hub connect the flywheel to the crankshaft and another set hold both halves of the flywheel together **FIGURE 10-28** .

Power is transmitted to the flywheel clutch mounting surface through a series of springs located around the circumference of the inner plate, which attaches to the crankshaft. These springs act like the dampening springs of a clutch disc to reduce torsional vibration. Between the inner and outer sections of the flywheel is a friction ring that permits the inner and outer parts of the flywheel to slip. This friction ring will slip under high torque input, which prevents transmission damage from

excessively high torque inputs caused by loading the vehicle beyond its gross vehicle weight (GVW) capacity. The friction ring is made of a material similar to brake lining and can wear out if excessive torque loads are continuously applied. If this occurs, there is a loss of torque transfer to the powertrain.

Reinstalling a Flywheel Housing

When a flywheel is transferred from one engine block to another, such as during engine replacement, the flywheel housing and crankshaft must share a common center line. When a flywheel housing is reinstalled, the housing center line often does not match the centerline of the crankshaft, even if alignment dowels are used. If the center lines are not correctly aligned, a number of significant problems can develop. First, the rear main seal may leak. Also, on manual transmissions the input shaft bearing and seal will quickly fail because the input shaft is operating at an angle. Vibrations produced by the non-aligned input shaft will travel up the main shaft in direct gear and cause gear jump-out in a non-synchronized transmission. Clutch plate splines and the input shaft will wear rapidly. With automatic transmissions, the transmission input seal will also leak. The starter motor may even be excessively noisy.

To reinstall a flywheel housing, follow the guidelines in **SKILL DRILL 10-1** .

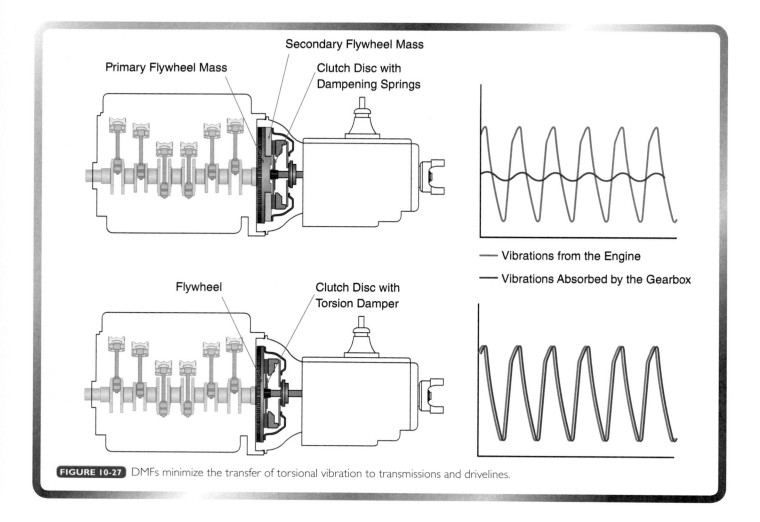

FIGURE 10-27 DMFs minimize the transfer of torsional vibration to transmissions and drivelines.

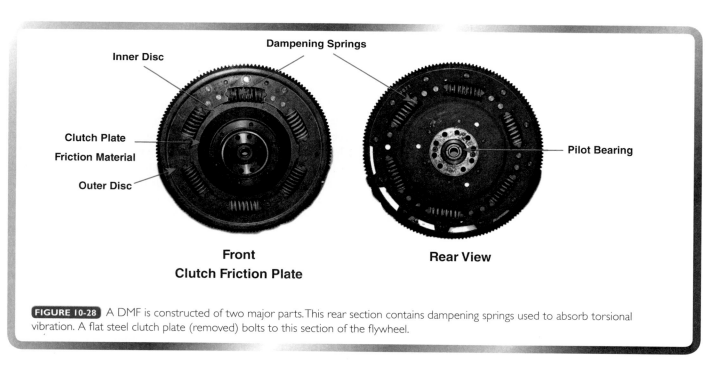

FIGURE 10-28 A DMF is constructed of two major parts. This rear section contains dampening springs used to absorb torsional vibration. A flat steel clutch plate (removed) bolts to this section of the flywheel.

SKILL DRILL 10-1 Reinstalling a Flywheel Housing

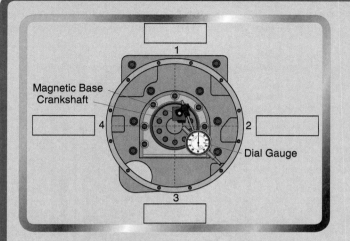

Magnetic Base
Crankshaft

1

4

2

3

Dial Gauge

crankshaft rotation, measure how far the dial indicator moved at each of the reference points and whether it moved in or out.

6 Record the dial indicator movement in four places using the chart in this box.

7 Identify the Society of Automotive Engineers (SAE) size of the flywheel housing that the engine uses by measuring its opening diameter.

8 After identifying the SAE flywheel size, determine the maximum permissible run out for the flywheel housing size. Larger housings are allowed more run out than smaller housings.

9 Compare the total indicated run out (TIR) measured on the flywheel with the specifications in **TABLE 10-1**. TIR is calculated by subtracting the maximum movement at each position from its opposite minimum measure. For example, if the dial indicator moved 0.010″ (0.254 mm) out at 3 o'clock and −0.004″ (0.101 mm) in at the 9 o'clock position, the TIR is 0.006″ (0.152 mm).

10 If the TIR is more than the allowed specification, the housing needs to be moved. To move a housing a small amount (less than 0.020″ [5.08 mm]), loosen all but two bolts in the housing. Tap the housing with a heavy hammer (a 5–10 lb [2–5 kg] sledge) in the correct direction to compensate for the off-center position. Recheck the bell housing run out once again to determine whether it is within specifications. On a housing that requires significant movement, remove the alignment dowels to move the housing. After the housing is aligned, redrill the dowel holes and reinstall the dowels.

1 Clean the flywheel housing and inspect it for damage caused by a previously loose transmission mounting.

2 Mount a dial indicator on the face of the flywheel or crankshaft.

3 Place the indicator pointer on the inside circumference of the housing.

4 Mark the flywheel housing at 12 o'clock, 3 o'clock, 6 o'clock, and 9 o'clock.

5 Zero the dial indicator at 12 o'clock. Turn the engine through 90° of crankshaft rotation. After stopping the

TABLE 10-1: Flywheel Housing Bore Location

SAE No.	Bore ID		Bore Location TIR (MAX)	
	Inches	Millimeters	Inches	Millimeters
00	31.0	788	0.012	0.31
0	25.5	648	0.010	0.25
1/2	23.0	584	0.010	0.25
1	20.0	511	0.008	0.20
2	17.6	448	0.008	0.20
3	16.1	410	0.008	0.20

▶ Types of Cylinder Blocks

The engine block is the main structure of the engine and encloses the cylinders and crankshaft. The block has two main sections: the cylinder block, which contains the cylinders, and the crankcase, which contains the crankshaft. Because diesel engines produce tremendous amounts of force—enough to literally push the crankshaft away from the cylinder block—specialized construction techniques are used to increase block strength. Noise vibration and harshness produced by diesels' high combustion pressures are also controlled through a variety of block construction features. And because the reciprocating action of pistons within the cylinder bores can eventually wear out the engine, blocks are designed with replaceable cylinder liners to restore engines to their original specifications.

Block Construction

Blocks must be designed as compact as possible to reduce weight and size while maintaining strength and rigidity. Unnecessary weight is the enemy of hauling heavier revenue generating payloads, good vehicle braking, and precise handling characteristics **FIGURE 10-29**.

Deep-Skirt Blocks

A **deep-skirt block** design refers to a block configuration in which the bottom edge of the block extends well below the crankshaft's centerline **FIGURE 10-30**. The sides of the crankcase

are separated from the main bearing caps to minimize transmission of noise produced by vibrations from the main bearing caps. Bearing caps are held in place with two or four vertically placed bolts. Lengthening the block walls enhances structural rigidity and operating smoothness, and allows for a larger mating surface with the transmission. A reinforcing bedplate

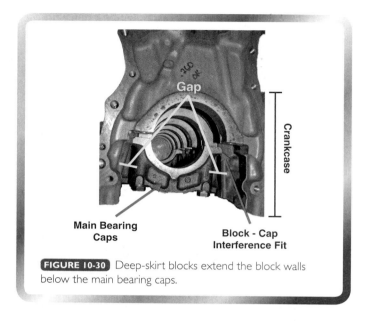

FIGURE 10-30 Deep-skirt blocks extend the block walls below the main bearing caps.

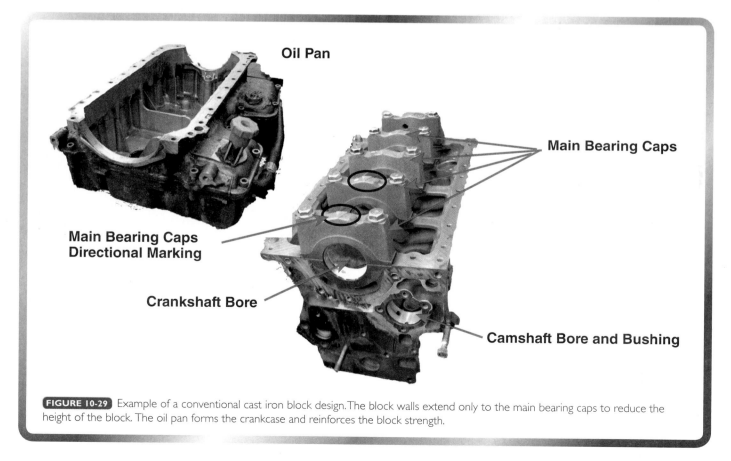

FIGURE 10-29 Example of a conventional cast iron block design. The block walls extend only to the main bearing caps to reduce the height of the block. The oil pan forms the crankcase and reinforces the block strength.

may also be attached to the oil pan rails and main bearing caps to enhance the rigidity and strength of the block's crankcase **FIGURE 10-31** .

Cross-Bolted Blocks

A variation of the deep-skirt block is a **cross-bolted block**. Also known as tie-bolted or bolster-bolted blocks, this design uses additional horizontally placed bolts to connect crankcase walls of the block to the main bearing caps. Cross-bolted blocks permit the use of more than the traditional two or four vertical bolts to hold the main bearing caps **FIGURE 10-32** . Cross bolting limits crankshaft flexing, stiffens the engine's structure, and reduces overall vibration. This type of block reinforcement technique permits further weight reductions.

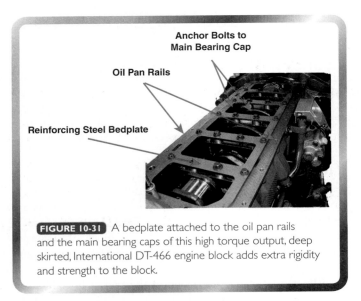

FIGURE 10-31 A bedplate attached to the oil pan rails and the main bearing caps of this high torque output, deep skirted, International DT-466 engine block adds extra rigidity and strength to the block.

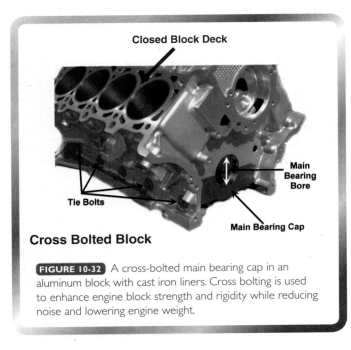

Cross Bolted Block

FIGURE 10-32 A cross-bolted main bearing cap in an aluminum block with cast iron liners. Cross bolting is used to enhance engine block strength and rigidity while reducing noise and lowering engine weight.

Ladder-Frame Blocks

A number of newer engine designs are incorporating ladder-frame construction features, which can strengthen a block while reducing weight, noise, and vibration. In **ladder-frame blocks**, the sides of the block extend exactly to the centerline of the crankshaft bearings. A separate additional ladder-like section of the block structure, called a ladder frame, attaches to the crankcase on one side and the other to the oil pan. The main bearing caps are integrated into this lower section of the block **FIGURE 10-33** and **FIGURE 10-34** . Removing one bearing cap requires removing the entire ladder frame, because it contains all the bearing caps. The ladder frame may also contain balance shaft housings and the oil pump. Ladder frames considerably improve block rigidity and strength, but they also can add to the cost and complexity of an engine. Another drawback, depending on construction technique, is the potential for leakage in the gasket joint created by the device. Engine bearings cannot be serviced in frame or in chassis. Removal and replacement of a bearing requires complete removal of the engine from the vehicle.

Tunnel-Bore Blocks

Tunnel-bore blocks are one of the smoothest operating and strongest block designs. Integrating the main bearing bores into a single solid block structure makes this block the strongest and most rigid. The crankshaft and main bearing enclosures are dropped into the block's tunnel during assembly. Locating bolts in the block align oil passageways to the crankshaft and lock the main bearing supports into position **FIGURE 10-35** . Kubota supplies these blocks for use in compact off-road equipment.

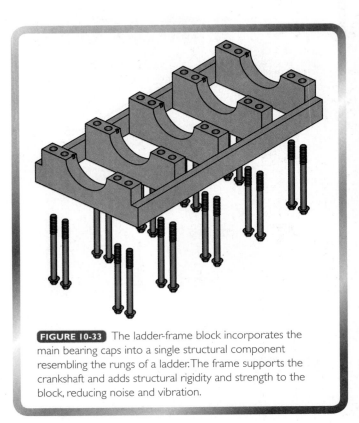

FIGURE 10-33 The ladder-frame block incorporates the main bearing caps into a single structural component resembling the rungs of a ladder. The frame supports the crankshaft and adds structural rigidity and strength to the block, reducing noise and vibration.

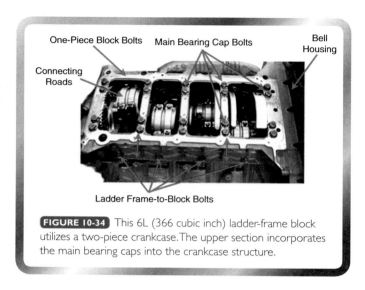

One-Piece Block Bolts   Main Bearing Cap Bolts   Bell Housing

Connecting Roads

Ladder Frame-to-Block Bolts

FIGURE 10-34 This 6L (366 cubic inch) ladder-frame block utilizes a two-piece crankcase. The upper section incorporates the main bearing caps into the crankcase structure.

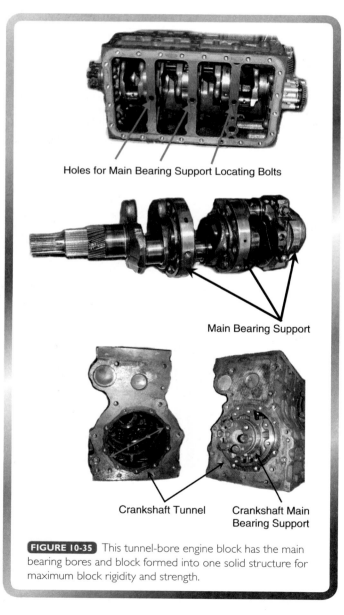

Holes for Main Bearing Support Locating Bolts

Main Bearing Support

Crankshaft Tunnel   Crankshaft Main Bearing Support

FIGURE 10-35 This tunnel-bore engine block has the main bearing bores and block formed into one solid structure for maximum block rigidity and strength.

▶ TECHNICIAN TIP

Diesel engines have a unique problem known as **cavitation erosion**, which is caused by the collapse of tiny water vapor bubbles formed when coolant vaporizes on hot cylinder walls. Liner vibration and flexing during the combustion phase and power stroke are the primary causes of vapor bubble formation. These vapor bubbles collapse when cooled or when pressure increases around the bubble. Pressure exerted by the force of bubble collapse is reported to be as high as 60,000 psi (413,685 kPa). The force of vapor bubble implosion against cylinder walls, cylinder liners, and other components can eventually cause pitting and quickly destroy cylinder walls and liners. Diesel engines therefore require the addition of supplemental coolant additives containing nitrite. These additives form a sacrificial barrier to protect the coolant side of the cylinder wall and liner against pitting.

Cylinder Block Configurations

Several configurations for manufacturing cylinder blocks exist to accommodate different applications, production costs, and expected vehicle life cycles. Common cylinder construction types include parent bore, wet sleeve, and dry sleeve.

Parent Bore Block

A **parent bore block**, also commonly called a no-sleeve block, has holes cast and bored into the block, and the pistons are inserted directly into these holes **FIGURE 10-36** . No provision is made to add a cylinder sleeve to this type of block. The cylinder walls form a part of the block structure, giving it rigidity and strength.

The most notable advantage of the parent bore block is that it costs less to construct, because machining and fitting of cylinder sleeves is not required. Unlike sleeved blocks, the cylinder walls are structural members of the casting and add strength and rigidity to the block while using less block mass. Thin cylinder walls with minimal material thickness between cylinders permit compact, lightweight construction. These blocks are best used in applications in which chassis life and expected engine life are approximately equal. Water jackets formed inside the block permit cooling of cylinder walls all the way to the top of the block, unlike sleeved engines. This feature reduces carbon formation on pistons and other problems related to excess heat near the top of the cylinder.

A major disadvantage of parent bore blocks is that during rebuild or repair of the engine, a worn cylinder must be rebored or honed. Reboring requires special equipment available only at a machine shop. Usually, the engine must be removed from the chassis and disassembled completely to perform the machining process. The number of times the engine can be rebuilt is limited to available piston oversizes and the thickness of the cylinder walls. Parent bore blocks are not as durable as sleeved engines. Part of the reason is the block materials form the cylinder walls. Cylinder wall surfaces are not as easily hardened as sleeved engines. Without costly alloys and hardening techniques, the

FIGURE 10-36 This 6.7L (409 cubic inch) Cummins is an example of a parent bore block. A parent bore block forms the cylinders and block from a single casting. Water jackets and other internal passageways are cast into the block.

cylinder walls will wear at a faster rate than hardened replaceable cylinder sleeves. Because cylinder walls are irregularly thick, heat transfer differentials cause varying cylinder dimensions and accelerated wear.

> ### TECHNICIAN TIP
>
> Coolant temperatures are hotter at the rear of the engine where coolant has to travel the farthest to remove heat. Some engine rebuilders recommend a larger piston to cylinder wall clearance in the rearmost cylinders of some V-8 diesel engines to accommodate the greater thermal expansion of parts.

Cylinder Sleeves

The replaceable wear surfaces making up the cylinder wall are called sleeves or liners. Constructed to the identical inside diameter and length of the cylinder found in a parent bore block, sleeves may be replaced individually if they become worn or damaged prematurely. Cylinder sleeves may be induction hardened and manufactured using special alloys to produce durable, wear-resistant surfaces. Sleeves are commonly used in medium- to large-bore engines operating under extended service conditions and high engine hours. This means an engine will wear out faster than the chassis. Replacing the liner sleeves using cylinder kits made up of new pistons, rings, and liners enables rapid restoration of an engine to factory specifications **FIGURE 10-37** . There are several different types of cylinder liners in use, including dry liners, mid-stop liners, also called half- or full-stop liners, and wet liners **FIGURE 10-38** .

Dry Sleeve Block

A **dry sleeve block** is designed with a bored or honed hole in the block that allows no coolant contact with the cylinder sleeve. The sleeve is inserted into the bored hole as either a slip or press fit. If the liner is installed with an interference fit, meaning the liner is slightly larger than the cylinder bore, it does not usually have a top flange, but is machined flush with the block deck. A slip fit liner will use a counterbore machined into the block to accommodate the liner flange. Pressure applied by the cylinder head to a slight protrusion of the liner flange will prevent liner movement.

Using a dry cylinder sleeve provides the great advantage of quick restoration of the cylinder block to original specification through the installation of new sleeves. Because the sleeve is fitted into a bored hole in the block, it does not have contact with coolant that could cause sleeve deterioration. Additionally, the absence of coolant contact means there is not a requirement to seal the sleeve to prevent coolant leakage into the crankcase. Cylinder sleeves may be replaced individually if they become worn prematurely or damaged.

Dry sleeves do have some disadvantages. Because the coolant is not in direct contact with the dry sleeve, heat transfer from the combustion chamber to the coolant water is not as rapid as it would be with a wet sleeve. This slow heat transfer may potentially result in limitations on power output per

FIGURE 10-37 Replaceable cylinder sleeves enable a worn-out engine to be quickly rebuilt and restored to factory specifications.

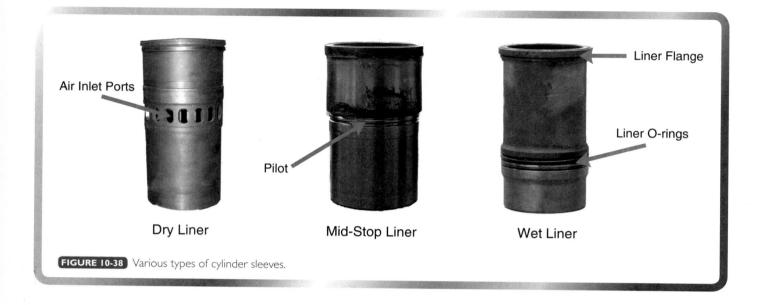

FIGURE 10-38 Various types of cylinder sleeves.

cylinder, short engine life, and cylinder damage. Extra steps in manufacturing and machining the block are required for sleeve installation. Dry sleeved blocks tend to weigh more than parent bore blocks.

Wet Sleeve Block

A **wet sleeve block** is designed with a number of large holes into which the cylinder sleeves are inserted. Coolant has direct contact with the outside of the sleeve and there is no supporting cylinder bore structure like a dry sleeve around the wet sleeve. O-rings prevent coolant from leaking out of the water jackets and into the oil pan. Wet sleeves are thick enough to withstand the higher heat loads and combustion forces in high horsepower engines.

The major advantage of wet sleeve liners is the direct contact of coolant with the sleeve that enables rapid heat transfer from the cylinder to the coolant. Sleeves are easily removed and installed during engine rebuilding to restore the cylinders to original specifications.

The major disadvantages with wet sleeve liners are the problems associated with preventing internal engine coolant leaks. The O-ring seal (if used) at the lower part of the liner can deteriorate and leak coolant into the lubrication oil. Some engines have weep holes to drain the leaked coolant and prevent it from entering the oil pan **FIGURE 10-39**. Additionally, liner vibration caused by combustion forces can exaggerate the effects of cavitation. Greater attention to maintenance of the cooling system is required in wet sleeve engines to prevent cavitation. Cavitation can cause pinholes to perforate the sleeve, allowing coolant to enter the cylinder or combustion gases to enter and pressurize the cooling system. A second problem is ensuring liner protrusion above the block deck is within specification and even across all cylinders **FIGURE 10-40**. Without correct protrusion, combustion gases will leak into the coolant, head gaskets will leak, and other structural problems can result.

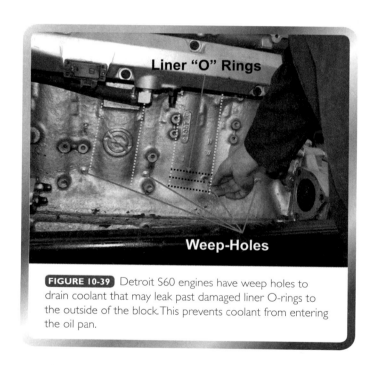

FIGURE 10-39 Detroit S60 engines have weep holes to drain coolant that may leak past damaged liner O-rings to the outside of the block. This prevents coolant from entering the oil pan.

Mid-Stop Liners

Liners use a flange surface on the sleeve to prevent the liner from sliding down into the crankcase and to serve as a surface to clamp or hold the liner in place through force transmitted by the cylinder head. As the name suggests, a top-stop liner has a flange at the top of the liner. The flange will rest in a counterbore machined into the block deck. An interference fit between the top of the flange or the area just below the flange and the block helps seal the coolant from leaking around the liner and onto the block deck. The lower part of the liner typically uses a series of O-rings between the liner and block to prevent coolant from leaking into the crankcase. Counterbores and liner O-rings are

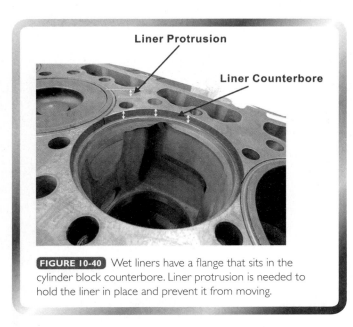

FIGURE 10-40 Wet liners have a flange that sits in the cylinder block counterbore. Liner protrusion is needed to hold the liner in place and prevent it from moving.

prone to leakage due to O-ring seal deterioration, liner movement, and other defects of the counterbore. To eliminate the problems with the traditional top-stop flange liner, another liner design has emerged that's termed a mid-stop, half-stop, or wet-dry liner.

These mid-stop liners do not have a flange at the top of the liner that fits into the block deck, which provides several advantages. First, the counterbore is approximately halfway or midway down the liner FIGURE 10-41 . In this area the ledge or counterbore that the liner flange or pilot sits on is much stronger because it is surrounded by more rigid block structure. Pilot breakage is unheard of, and expansion of the pilots will not crack the block deck, like top-stop liners will often do.

Using a ledge in this area also eliminates the need for O-rings to seal coolant around the liner. While a seal may be used on some liner designs, more often only a bead of silicone is used to prevent leakage around the liner pilots. Mid-stop liners

can minimize engine block weight by requiring smaller water jackets. Top-stop liners, however, have the advantage of having less distortion when installed in the block due to fit between an upper flange and the block that does not squeeze the liner in the middle like mid-stops do. Top-stops will also occupy less overall space than mid-stops, thus allowing the block to be a few millimeters shorter.

Cylinder Wall Finish

Cross-hatching is a special machined finish for cylinder walls used to provide a surface to retain oil and break in piston rings FIGURE 10-42 . Because a cylinder is not perfectly symmetrical, the cross-hatch will initially wear into the rings and vice versa to produce a tighter seal between the two parts.

Highly polished cylinder walls having no cross-hatch will not allow residual oil to cling to the cylinder walls. Without the oil film on the cylinder walls, a gas-tight piston ring seal cannot be achieved. Consequently, poor sealing between the piston ring and cylinder wall causes piston and ring scuffing as well as compression and power loss due to blow-by. Poor ring sealing also leads to high oil consumption.

Cylinder cross-hatch is produced when an engine is manufactured and during proper cylinder reconditioning processes during engine rebuild. Honing stones are used to produce the cross-hatch finish of the cylinder walls.

To reduce the time and distance required for engine break-in, manufacturers use a process called plateau honing.

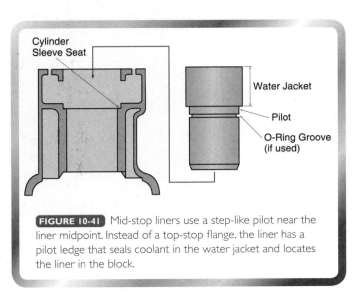

FIGURE 10-41 Mid-stop liners use a step-like pilot near the liner midpoint. Instead of a top-stop flange, the liner has a pilot ledge that seals coolant in the water jacket and locates the liner in the block.

FIGURE 10-42 Cylinder walls have a special machined finish called cross-hatching. The cross-hatch provides a surface for piston rings to wear into during break-in period and retains oil for lubrication of the piston to cylinder wall.

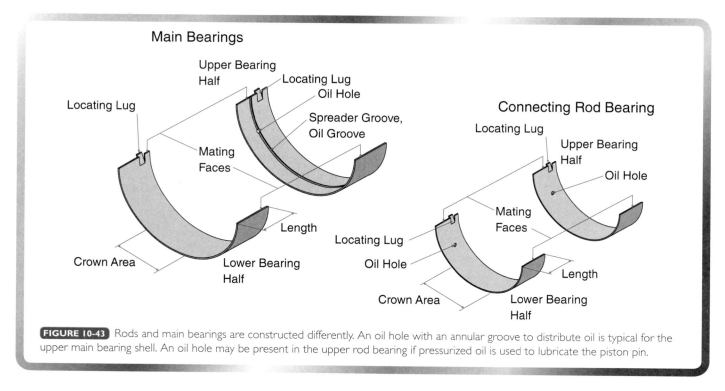

FIGURE 10-43 Rods and main bearings are constructed differently. An oil hole with an annular groove to distribute oil is typical for the upper main bearing shell. An oil hole may be present in the upper rod bearing if pressurized oil is used to lubricate the piston pin.

This involves honing the cylinders and then removing the peaks of the cylinder cross-hatch with specialized brushes generally made of nylon-like material. Plateau honing also reduces engine oil consumption during break-in.

▶ Types of Engine Bearings

Engine bearings are replaceable wear surfaces used on the rotating journals of the crankshaft and camshaft. Bearings used on the crankshaft journals are referred to as main bearings. The upper shell of a main bearing always has a hole to receive lubrication and a circumferential groove to channel oil from the oil supply hole to the bearing. Rod bearings are used on the crankpin journals or connecting rod journal surfaces **FIGURE 10-43**. The engine's connecting rods and main bearing caps could be designed to operate without bearings, but those parts would require much more expensive and intensive labor to replace. The materials bearings are made from are also chosen to extend the life of the engine by reducing friction between the moving surfaces. Experimentation with various types of bearing materials and construction techniques have helped diesel engines evolve to the point where more than a million and a half miles can accumulate on heavy-duty diesels before the bearings need replacement. For example, Detroit Diesel's DD series engines use **sputter bearings**. This is a construction technique that hardens the bearings to increase their durability **FIGURE 10-44**. The hardened sputter overlay is much harder than lead-tin alloys **FIGURE 10-45**. Operating clearances on these bearings are also much smaller—typically just over 0.001″ (0.025 mm) of oil film. While bearings have increased engine longevity, technicians still need to be aware

FIGURE 10-44 This set of sputter bearings from a Detroit Diesel DD15 has more than 497,097 miles (800,000 km). The hardened half of the bearing is darker.

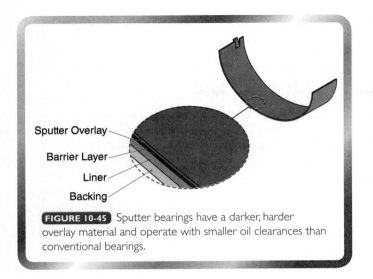

FIGURE 10-45 Sputter bearings have a darker, harder overlay material and operate with smaller oil clearances than conventional bearings.

of different types of bearings and their construction to be ready to diagnose problems with bearings and replace them when necessary.

Plain Insert Bearings

Engine bearings are known by a number of terms, including precision inserts, plain bearings, tri-metal bearings, and so on. Bearings used around the crankshaft are split insert bearings, so called because the bearing is made in two pieces. Manufacturing the bearing in halves allows it to be easily serviced and the use of a one-piece crankshaft (as opposed to a crankshaft made of multiple pieces and one-piece bearings). Camshaft bushings are examples of one-piece plain bearings. Plain bearings are lighter and more compact for their load-bearing capacity than roller bearings.

Bearings perform a number of important functions inside the engine:

- Reduce friction
- Support moving parts under load
- Serve as replaceable wear surfaces

Reducing friction is one of the most obvious functions bearings perform along with the lubrication system. Bearing surfaces should minimize friction and heat generation. It should be noted that plain bearings with a pressurized oil film have less high-speed friction than antifriction bearings (e.g., rollers, ball bearings).

Plain bearings are best to achieve long engine life. Today a typical B-50 bearing life is approaching 1,500,000 miles (2,414,016 km) for heavy-duty diesels, meaning that at that mileage there is still 50% bearing life remaining.

Bearings can last so long but wear so little due to something called the hydrodynamic wedge. Essentially the oil, bearing, and rotating shaft are separated from one another by hydraulic pressure. At rest, the shaft and bearing are in contact. On startup, the shaft contacts the bearing briefly. As it runs, the shaft pulls oil from the clearance space into the wedge-shaped area between the shaft and bearing. Oil is literally pulled in because of the electrical

attraction oil has to the metal shaft. The oil wedge lifts the shaft off its bearing and supports it during engine operation. During normal operating conditions, a continuous supply of clean oil will keep the shaft and bearing surfaces separated. Bearings fail when the oil film breaks down or when the bearing is overloaded. The oil film pressure is generated by shaft rotation **FIGURE 10-46**.

Bearing Construction

In early automotive history, bearings were made of a lead-tin alloy called babbitt. This alloy was effective because of its low frictional characteristics and its ability to distort under severe load and embed dirt into its shell so the crankshaft would not be damaged. However, one characteristic these bearings did not have was fatigue strength, the ability to withstand high loading for long periods of time.

To summarize, the most important bearing characteristics include the following:

- **Compatibility**: The ability of a bearing to allow friction without excessive wear or friction. Dissimilar metals have better compatibility. Copper and steel have good compatibility and l ower wear, as do bronze or lead and steel. A bronze crankshaft with steel bearings could be combined to minimize wear, except bronze isn't as strong as steel or cast iron.
- **Fatigue Strength**: The ability of a bearing to carry a load. A bearing will crack or be wiped away if overloaded by shaft pressure.
- **Conformability**: The ability of a bearing to conform to irregularities on a journal surface. Poor conforming will work against fatigue strength, limiting load-bearing ability.
- **Embedability**: The ability of a bearing to absorb particle contamination. Dirt particles will scratch a shaft and ruin it **FIGURE 10-47**.

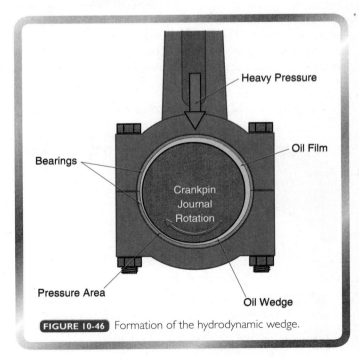

FIGURE 10-46 Formation of the hydrodynamic wedge.

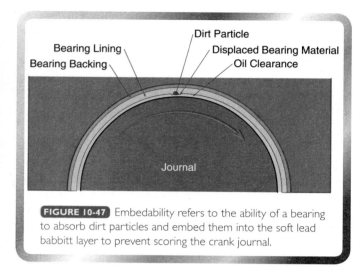

FIGURE 10-47 Embedability refers to the ability of a bearing to absorb dirt particles and embed them into the soft lead babbitt layer to prevent scoring the crank journal.

A variety of construction techniques are used to achieve different balances among the characteristics that will adapt to each engine's unique operating conditions. Tri-metal bearings with copper alloys for the intermediate layer are used in diesels **FIGURE 10-48**. A steel back with a copper alloy intermediate layer gives the strength, fatigue resistance, and conformability characteristics required of a diesel engine bearing. The lead tin babbitt layer provides good wear and compatibility features. Nickel barrier plating prevents galvanic reactions between the babbitt and copper or lead that would lead to corrosion. Flash lead or tin plating protects and provides a finish for the engine's break-in period. This finish can be easily removed when new by touching the bearing or wiping it with a shop rag.

Bearing Lubrication

Every bearing receives lubrication through holes drilled into the crankshaft. Main bearings receive oil first from the oil pump and main oil gallery. The oil enters the main bearing journal and drilled passages connecting to the rod bearing journals. Most journals are crossed drilled so the oil holes align twice for every

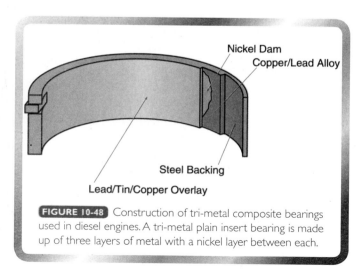

FIGURE 10-48 Construction of tri-metal composite bearings used in diesel engines. A tri-metal plain insert bearing is made up of three layers of metal with a nickel layer between each.

crankshaft revolution. Oil is otherwise cut off, so many main bearings have a groove down the center of the main bearing that allows oil to flow around the main bearing journal. The amount of oil clearance is important to maintaining the hydraulic pressure of the oil wedge separating the rotating shaft and bearing. Too little clearance and inadequate oil will flow into the bearing for lubrication and cooling. Too much clearance and the oil wedge will collapse, resulting in contact between the shaft and bearing. Excessive bearing clearance is a primary reason to maintain low oil pressure. If the oil pump is required to pump extra volume to fill the clearances while even greater quantities of oil are thrown off a shaft, loss of pressure will result. (Pumps produce volume not pressure; lubrication systems require restrictions to produce pressure.) Higher shaft speeds also produce greater oil wedge pressure.

Plastigauging

To evaluate the oil clearances of engine bearings, the use of Plastigauge is recommended. Plastigauge is a measuring tool consisting of a strip of oil-soluble plastic material and packaging printed with a thickness gauge.

Measuring bearing clearances with Plastigauge is very simple. After the bearing cap has been removed and the oil wiped from the crankshaft and bearing shell, a piece of Plastigauge is laid across the bearing insert. The bearing cap is reinstalled with a torque recommended by the engine manufacturer. When the bearing cap is tightened, the pressure causes the Plastigauge to be flattened. The less clearance there is, the flatter and wider the Plastigauge will be. When the bearing cap is removed, the width is measured with the graduated scale on the Plastigauge envelope **FIGURE 10-49**. The numbers on the graduated scale indicate bearing clearance in thousandths of an inch or in millimeters. Plastigauge is available in four different sizes, each covering a particular bearing clearance range.

Bearing Location

Bearings must not move within the bearing bore and must have good contact within the bore for good heat transfer. Several construction features of a bearing are common to ensure these functions.

Bearing Spread

To assist bearing retention and good contact with the cap or web of the bearing bore for heat transfer, the parting face of a bearing is wider than the diameter of the cap or web. Bearings must be snapped or pushed into place **FIGURE 10-50**.

Bearing Crush

The diameter of the bearing shells is larger than the bearing bore, and the difference in height between the bearing and the cap or web is called bearing crush. This feature assists retention and heat transfer. The dark spots observed on the back of a bearing indicate where the greatest heat transfer takes place. For this reason, bearings should go in dry on the backside with no grease or thread lockers applied to the back of the shell. Using this material would impede the transfer of heat from the bearing.

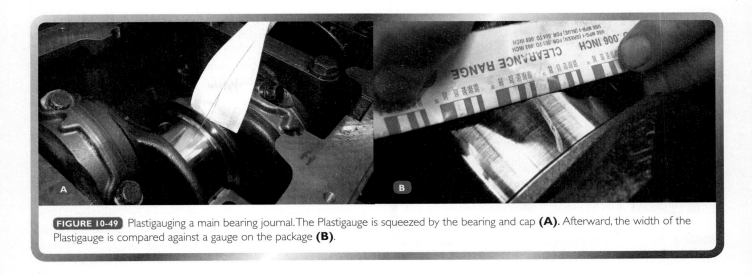

FIGURE 10-49 Plastigauging a main bearing journal. The Plastigauge is squeezed by the bearing and cap **(A)**. Afterward, the width of the Plastigauge is compared against a gauge on the package **(B)**.

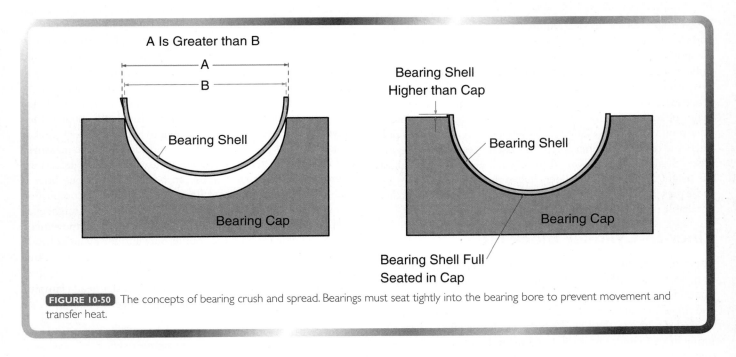

FIGURE 10-50 The concepts of bearing crush and spread. Bearings must seat tightly into the bearing bore to prevent movement and transfer heat.

Locating lugs are used on bearings to prevent movement and to properly center the bearing in the bore. To ensure correct matching of bearing caps and lugs, assemble caps together locating tab to tab. Make sure identification numbers match for main bearing location in block and on connecting rod bearings.

Undersize and Oversize Bearings

An undersize bearing is thicker than a standard bearing. It does not describe the bearing, but the shaft it fits. If a crankshaft is worn or ground to undersize, an undersize bearing is used to fit the journal. If a spun main bearing damages a block, the bearing bore can be re-bored to an oversize, and an oversized bearing can be installed.

Camshaft bushings typically can outlast two sets of main bearings because there is less loading. However, excessively worn and bleeding cam bearings can starve main bearings of oil and lead to premature crankshaft bearing failure.

Thrust Bearings

Thrust bearings are used to control end play in a crankshaft **FIGURE 10-51**. The forces of disengaging the clutch, helical gearing on the gear train, and automatic torque converters can easily push or pull a crankshaft to the point where severe damage to the connecting rods and journals occur. If thrust bearings are worn out, it will be difficult to maintain a proper clutch adjustment when pressure plates are separated by just a few thousandths of an inch. Thrust washers or bearings with flanges ride against a specially machined journal on usually only one cheek of a main bearing journal.

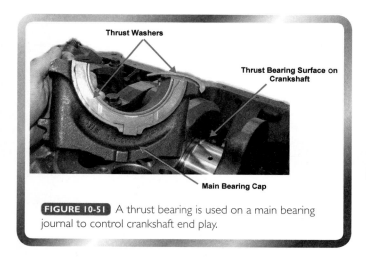

FIGURE 10-51 A thrust bearing is used on a main bearing journal to control crankshaft end play.

► Engine Block Service

Diesel engine block service requires a high degree of skill and knowledge due to the sophisticated and exacting precision fit of components such as liners, pistons, cylinder sleeves, and bearings. Little margin for error is permissible and mistakes in fitting closely machined tolerances or failure to follow acceptable service procedures can result in costly catastrophic engine failures. A major operation during engine overhaul and rebuild is cylinder liner removal and installation. A variety of tools are used to pull liners and or complete liner and piston assemblies from the engine block. Similarly, the tools used to reinstall and correctly adjust the height or protrusion of liners above the block deck must be those prescribed by the manufacturer to deliver consistent quality of reliable repairs to ensure trouble-free engine operation.

Liner-to-Cylinder Block Fit

The fit of a liner into the cylinder block is critical to engine operation, because it can produce various leaks and cause premature if not catastrophic damage to cylinder components such as pistons and rings. For example, a dry liner with an excessively loose fit will not transfer heat to the cylinder block as effectively as a correctly fitting liner. Cylinder heat will build up and cause scuffing, scoring, and eventual seizure of the piston. An excessively tight-fitting liner will collapse and distort, reducing the piston-to-liner clearance and causing hot spots. Consequently, the piston and liner can become scored, which could lead to eventual failure.

In wet liners, interference fit between the top-stop flange and counterbore, or lower part of the counterbore, is a coolant seal. A loose fit will allow coolant to leak above the block deck or into the cylinder.

Piston-to-Liner Sleeve Fit

Adequate piston skirt clearance must be maintained between the liner and the piston to allow for normal expansion of the piston when running at operating temperature. Insufficient skirt clearance will reduce the running clearance and could lead to scuffing or scoring. Excessive clearance will result in piston

knock or slap. To measure the clearance between the piston and cylinder wall, the largest thickness of feeler blade is slid between the skirt and liner at 90° to the wrist pin. A typical specification in a 10–15L (610–915 cubic inch) engine is 0.004–0.006″ (0.102–0.152 mm) clearance.

Liner Protrusion

Wet liners protrude or extend 0.001–0.01″ (0.025–0.254 mm) above the cylinder block deck **FIGURE 10-52**. This extension is necessary to project clamping forces from the cylinder head onto the liner flange and hold it in place. Measuring and adjusting protrusion is one of the most critical operations when rebuilding a sleeved engine. In most engines, liner protrusion must be no more than 0.002–0.005″ (0.051–0.127 mm) between the highest and lowest liner. Liner flanges must also be perfectly parallel with the block deck, typically within 0.001–0.002″ (0.025–0.051 mm). Problems with the liner flange or counterbore or a twisted O-ring will tilt a liner. The liner must be removed and re-inspected before reinstalling.

A liner must be clamped into place after installation in order to measure protrusion **FIGURE 10-53**. After installing and correctly torqueing hold-down clamps on engine block liners to specifications, a dial indicator on a sled is used to measure the projections **FIGURE 10-54**. When placed on the block deck, the dial indicator depth gage is set to zero. The depth gauge is then moved to the liner flange and its height above the block deck is measured. Three or four points around each liner are measured and recorded. After all liners are measured and no defects are found, the hold-down clamps can be removed. If one liner is slightly lower than adjacent liners, a leak path for combustion gases and coolant can form. If the variation is great, it might even warp the cylinder head. Variation will cause liner movement, which will damage both the counterbore and the cylinder head.

If one liner is slightly higher than the others, the same results will take place regarding leakage and warpage. The liner will not move, but the concentration of cylinder head clamping forces on the higher liner can crack the flange.

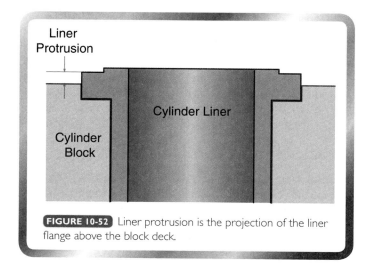

FIGURE 10-52 Liner protrusion is the projection of the liner flange above the block deck.

FIGURE 10-53 Liners need to be clamped in place before measuring protrusion.

Liner counterbores can be repaired with cutting and machining. A liner with inadequate protrusion can be raised with the installation of a shim beneath the liner flange **FIGURE 10-55**. Unlike counterbores and pilots, liner flanges are never machined. A liner that sits too high can be swapped with a liner that may be sitting to low. Rarely if ever will a cylinder block require machining to lower a liner protrusion.

Measuring Liner Protrusion

Ensuring that cylinder liners protrude or extend above the block deck the correct amount is one of the most critical operations for engine technicians. Without enough protrusion, a liner can move in the block resulting in rapid wear, leaks, and block damage. If there is too much protrusion, the cylinder head gasket cannot seal properly. Uneven protrusion between liners results in compression and coolant leaks, cracked liner flanges, liner movement, and warped cylinder heads. Liner counterbores or ledges where the liner sits in the block must be carefully inspected before liners are installed to ensure that they are square and cut to the correct depth. The counterbore may need to be shimmed

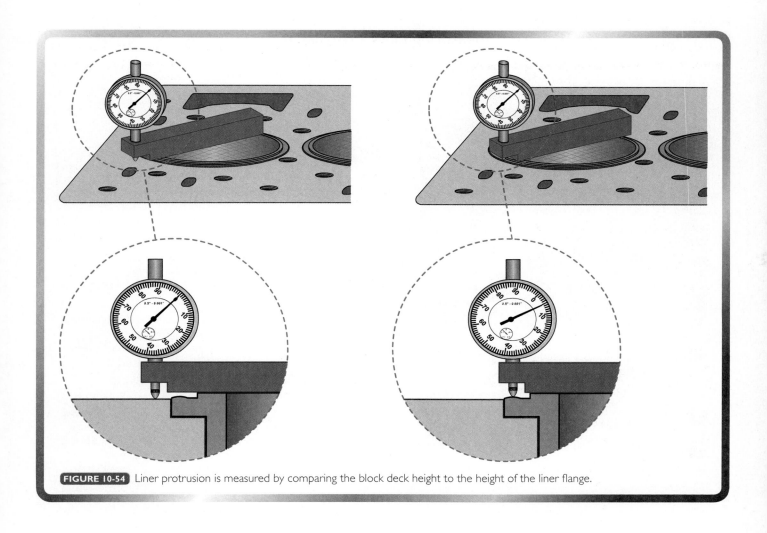

FIGURE 10-54 Liner protrusion is measured by comparing the block deck height to the height of the liner flange.

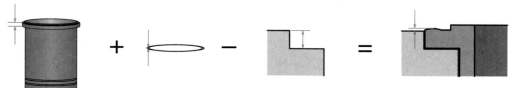

Liner Flange Height $+$ Shim Thickness $-$ Counterbore Depth $=$ Cylinder Liner Protrusion

Minimum 0.004″ (0.10 mm)
Maximum 0.007″ (0.18 mm)

FIGURE 10-55 A liner with insufficient protrusion or a block that has a machined counterbore can be raised with a shim beneath the liner flange. Shim thickness is calculated after measuring counterbore depth, liner flange, and desired protrusion.

if liner protrusion is too low or cut and shimmed if the liner sits too high and the counter bore is damaged in any way. Anytime a liner is installed, the protrusion must be measured.

To measure liner protrusion, follow the guidelines in **SKILL DRILL 10-2**.

Flange Breakage

Top-stop flange breakage is usually caused by excessive flange loading because of excessive pressure that was applied to the flange through the cylinder head clamping forces. The cylinder

SKILL DRILL 10-2 Measuring Liner Protrusion

make sure the ring is not twisted. Generally, seals are not lubricated with petroleum-based products; this prevents rapid deterioration if the seals are not oil compatible. Antifreeze is often used as an effective lubricant.

4. Insert the liners into the engine block. Do not force the liners into the block. Instead, use the OEM prescribed tool to press the liner into the block. Hammering or hitting the flange can dent the flange surface, which causes a leak path. The OEM prescribed tools will protect the liner flange and sealing surfaces from damage. They can be used to install the liner squarely into the block and, in some cases, clamp the liner into the block.

5. Clamp the liner in the block with the OEM prescribed holding or clamping fixture, following the manufacturer's procedures.

6. Using a dial indicator and sled, measure the liner protrusion in three or four places. Protrusion is measured as the distance between the block deck and a very specific point on the flange; this point varies between manufacturers.

7. Compare the measured protrusion against the manufacturer's specifications values. Variation from side to side should not exceed 0.001″ (0.025 mm). If it does, it is usually due to a piece of debris beneath the flange or a twisted O-ring. Remove, check, and reinstall the liner if the liner variations are excessive from side to side. Install a selective shim beneath any liner flange that sits too low.

1. Inspect the liner counterbores for squareness, cracks, and the correct machined depth. Generally, the machined depth is only measured if there has been a problem with protrusion or the counterbore has been machined.

2. Thoroughly clean the liner and counterbores. Any dirt or other material will prevent the liner from seating properly.

3. Install and lubricate the liner seals. Seals are lubricated only after they are installed to prevent twisting and rolling when the liner is installed. Slide a small pick beneath the O-ring and move around the liner circumference several times to

head gasket distributes a large amount of clamping force over the block deck, but if it is accidently left uninstalled when the cylinder head is tightened, all the liner flanges will crack and break due to the localized clamping forces. Flange breakage can result from the following:

- Improper torqueing of cylinder head during a rebuild
- Uneven flange height above deck
- Uneven wear in cylinder block flange counterbore if liners are not uniform in protrusion or out of parallel to the block deck
- Worn inner edge of flange counterbore seat (in cylinder block), causing the flange to tilt downward
- Improper positioning of head gasket fire ring

► TECHNICIAN TIP

When a cylinder liner or cylinder component is to be removed, the cooling nozzle should always be removed first. Even slight damage or bending of the cooler nozzle will overheat the piston in that cylinder and lead to catastrophic engine damage. Servicing of the cylinder components will cause contact between the nozzle and components, so resist the temptation to save a few minutes and shortcut nozzle removal.

► Maintenance of Cylinder Walls and Bearings

Cylinder walls and engine bearings are the two areas that have the highest degree of wear. As a consequence, they are the most significant factors limiting engine service life. For this reason, servicing and maintaining these two parts of an engine are commonly performed during major and minor overhauls. It is important for technicians to understand the factors influencing wear to anticipate features of these areas to inspect. Understanding wear factors helps form a foundation for service practices.

Cylinder Wall Wear

Diesel engine cylinder walls last longer than their gasoline counterparts for several reasons. Slower engine speeds reduce the amount of piston travel. Diesel fuel acts like a lubricant to minimize wear from friction. The hardening process and special alloys further increase the durability of diesel blocks. However, cylinder block walls progressively wear with increasing engine hours and distance traveled. The greatest amount of wear occurs near the uppermost part of the compression ring travel path and diminishes down the cylinder to the bottom **FIGURE 10-56**. This gives a worn cylinder a bell-shaped wear pattern observed at the top of the cylinder sleeve. The reasons for the greatest amount of wear near the top of the cylinder wall causing the cylinder wall to taper include the following:

- Higher cylinder pressures near the top part of piston's travel path increase ring pressure against the cylinder walls. (Gas pressure behind the rings forces the piston rings outward from their grooves.)
- Higher cylinder temperatures make the cylinder wall softer and more prone to wear.

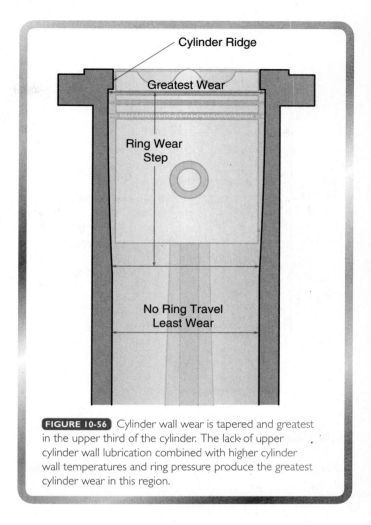

FIGURE 10-56 Cylinder wall wear is tapered and greatest in the upper third of the cylinder. The lack of upper cylinder wall lubrication combined with higher cylinder wall temperatures and ring pressure produce the greatest cylinder wear in this region.

- There is a lack of upper cylinder wall lubricant due to the fact that lubrication oil can only be carried into this area on the face of the compression ring.

Long stoke engines will have more wear mid-stoke as well due to a higher amount of major thrust. The side thrust is produced by the angle of the connecting rod with the piston, which tends to push the piston sideways into the cylinder wall when cylinder pressures are high. The angle formed between the connecting rod and the piston forces the piston against the cylinder wall during compression and power stroke. During power stroke the force is greatest, producing a major thrust force and a minor thrust force during compression stroke. The longer stroke distance of the diesel makes for higher thrust angle forces **FIGURE 10-57**.

Measuring Cylinder Wall Wear

Several methods can be used to measure the amount of taper within a cylinder.

1. Measure the amount of piston ring end gap in a cylinder. By measuring the end gap at the top of the cylinder, in the ring turnaround area, in the middle, and at the bottom, cylinder taper can be calculated. End gap is measured after squaring the

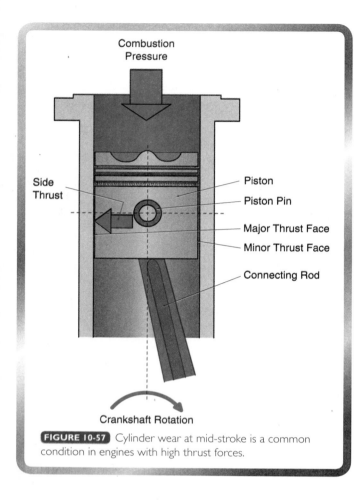

FIGURE 10-57 Cylinder wear at mid-stroke is a common condition in engines with high thrust forces.

FIGURE 10-58 Cylinder polish or the loss of cross-hatch is a good indicator of cylinder wear. A cylinder with 20% or more wear has 0% service life.

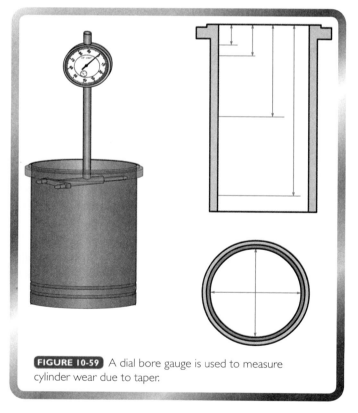

FIGURE 10-59 A dial bore gauge is used to measure cylinder wear due to taper.

ring with a piston inside the cylinder. A 0.001″ (0.0254 mm) increase in cylinder wall diameter will produce approximately a 0.003″ (0.0762 mm) increase in ring end gap. A typical maximum taper wear of a cylinder is 0.001″ (0.0254 mm) per inch of cylinder diameter, up to 0.005″ (0.127 mm) maximum wear in larger cylinders.

2. Look for loss of cross-hatch. Cylinder cross-hatch is produced when an engine is manufactured and during reconditioning. The presence of cross-hatch on the cylinder wall is important to provide a surface to seat piston rings and to retain oil for piston and ring lubrication. Highly polished liners will not allow residual oil to cling to the cylinder walls, causing scuffing and piston wear. Highly polished liners indicate worn cylinders **FIGURE 10-58**.

3. Use a dial bore gauge to measure cylinder taper but not cylinder diameter. These gauges are used when honing or performing other marching processes to ensure a consistent, symmetrical dimension is produced **FIGURE 10-59**.

4. Use a micrometer and inside telescoping gauges. An inside telescoping gauge is used to gauge the cylinder diameter. An outside micrometer is then used to measure the width of the inside telescoping gauge.

Bearing Failures

Most bearing failures are caused by problems with lubrication **FIGURE 10-60**. Bearing failures are indicated by:

- A drop in lubricating oil pressure
- Excessive oil consumption (excessive oil thrown onto the cylinder walls)

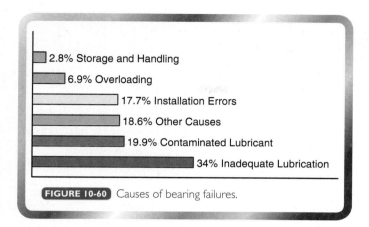

2.8% Storage and Handling
6.9% Overloading
17.7% Installation Errors
18.6% Other Causes
19.9% Contaminated Lubricant
34% Inadequate Lubrication

FIGURE 10-60 Causes of bearing failures.

■ Noises that can be diminished during a cylinder cut-out procedure

Bearing roll-ins are performed during engine overhaul. Because the crankshaft is not removed when the engine is repaired in

chassis, the upper main bearing shell must be pushed out and another bearing rolled into position.

Measuring Crankshaft Endplay

Occasionally, crankshaft thrust bearings may become excessively worn or even broken. A sudden, sharp release of the clutch or a driver's foot resting on the clutch can apply excessive force against the thrust bearing leading to premature wear or breakage. The result is a slipping clutch or difficulty adjusting a clutch with the free play continually changing after a manual adjustment. Crank position sensor codes may also be logged if endplay is excessive. Insufficient endplay can be the result of a misaligned main baring cap.

To measure crankshaft endplay, follow the guidelines in **SKILL DRILL 10-3**.

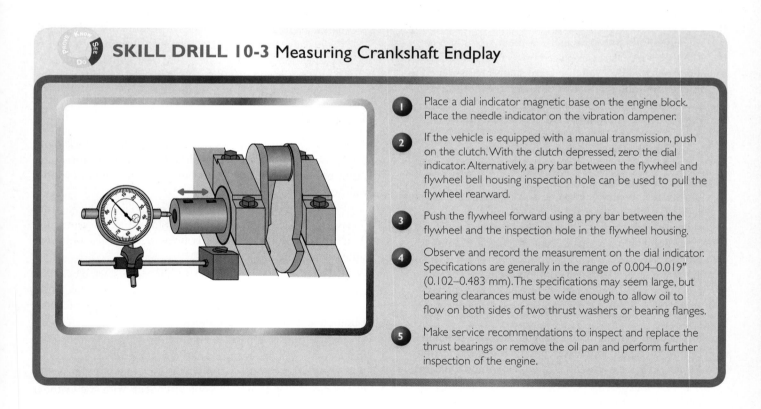

SKILL DRILL 10-3 Measuring Crankshaft Endplay

1. Place a dial indicator magnetic base on the engine block. Place the needle indicator on the vibration dampener.

2. If the vehicle is equipped with a manual transmission, push on the clutch. With the clutch depressed, zero the dial indicator. Alternatively, a pry bar between the flywheel and flywheel bell housing inspection hole can be used to pull the flywheel rearward.

3. Push the flywheel forward using a pry bar between the flywheel and the inspection hole in the flywheel housing.

4. Observe and record the measurement on the dial indicator. Specifications are generally in the range of 0.004–0.019" (0.102–0.483 mm). The specifications may seem large, but bearing clearances must be wide enough to allow oil to flow on both sides of two thrust washers or bearing flanges.

5. Make service recommendations to inspect and replace the thrust bearings or remove the oil pan and perform further inspection of the engine.

Wrap-Up

Ready for Review

▶ The cylinder block is the largest single part and main structure of the diesel engine, and its primary function is to support cylinders and liners (if equipped) and major engine components, including the crankshaft and camshaft.

▶ Diesel engine blocks have cylinders arranged either inline, V-banked, or horizontally opposed, and can be configured with different numbers of cylinder bores.

▶ Cylinder blocks can be constructed from cast iron, aluminum, or compacted graphite iron (CGI); each of these materials has advantages and disadvantages.

▶ Primary balance, which is achieved when the crankshaft counterweights offset the weight of the piston and connecting rod assembly, and secondary balance, which is achieved when the movement of one piston counterbalances the movement of another, result in smoother running engines.

▶ The main purpose of the crankshaft in a reciprocating engine is to convert the linear motion of the connecting rod assemblies to rotational movement.

▶ The mechanical stresses placed on a crankshaft require it to be especially strong, so crankshafts are hardened to improve durability; the two most common processes are induction hardening and nitriding.

▶ Engine oil is used to lubricate, cool, and clean the crankshaft journals and bearings.

▶ To control the destructive effects of both torsional and harmonic vibrations, diesel engines are equipped with vibration dampeners.

▶ Blocks must be designed to be as compact as possible to reduce weight and size while maintaining strength and rigidity; common block designs include deep-skirt blocks, cross-bolted blocks, ladder-frame blocks, and tunnel-bore blocks.

▶ There are several different configurations for engine block cylinders; which one is best depends on the vehicle's application, production cost, and expected vehicle lifecycle.

▶ Replaceable cylinder sleeves enable a worn-out engine to be quickly rebuilt and restored to factory specifications.

▶ Bearings perform a number of important functions inside the engine, including reducing friction, supporting moving parts under load, and serving as replaceable wear surfaces.

▶ The characteristics important for engine bearings are compatibility, fatigue strength, conformability, and embedability; a variety of construction techniques are used to achieve different balances among the characteristics that will adapt to each engine's unique operating conditions.

▶ The amount of oil clearance between the rotating shaft and the engine bearing is important to maintaining the hydraulic pressure of the oil wedge that cools and lubricates these parts.

▶ Bearings must not move within the bearing bore and must have good contact within the bore for proper heat transfer.

▶ Thrust bearings control end play in a crankshaft.

▶ The fit of a liner into the cylinder block is critical to engine operation; improper fit can produce various leaks and cause premature, if not catastrophic, damage to cylinder components such as pistons and rings.

▶ Adequate piston skirt clearance must be maintained between the liner and the piston to allow for normal expansion of the piston when the engine is running at operating temperature.

▶ Wet liners protrude or extend above the cylinder block deck to project clamping forces from the cylinder head onto the liner flange and hold it in place; measuring and adjusting protrusion is one of the most critical operations when rebuilding a sleeved engine.

▶ Top-stop flange breakage is usually caused by excessive flange loading because of excessive pressure that was applied to the flange through the cylinder head clamping forces.

▶ Cylinder block walls progressively wear with increasing engine hours and distance traveled; a dial bore gauge is used to measure cylinder wear due to taper.

Vocabulary Builder

<u>cavitation erosion</u> Pinholes produced in cylinder block walls, heads, and liner sleeves as a result of the collapse of tiny water vapor bubbles formed when coolant vaporizes on hot cylinder wall surfaces.

<u>compacted graphite iron (CGI)</u> A material produced from powdered iron alloys squeezed into molds at high pressures and then heated to bond the metal particles together; also known as sintered graphite.

<u>cross-bolted block</u> A variation of the deep-skirt block that uses additional horizontally placed bolts to connect the crankcase walls of the block to the main bearing caps; also known as a tie-bolted or bolster-bolted block.

<u>deep-skirt block</u> A block configuration with a bottom edge that extends well below the crankshaft's centerline.

<u>dry sleeve block</u> A block designed with a bored or honed hole in the block that allows no coolant contact with the cylinder sleeve.

<u>dual mass flywheel (DMF)</u> A two-piece flywheel design that incorporates specialized torsional dampening springs.

<u>fillet radius</u> A circular machining applied to the surface between the journal and the crankshaft cheek that strengthens the crankshaft and minimizes the possibility of a fracture.

<u>harmonic vibration</u> A vibration that sends pressure waves moving back and forth along the crankshaft.

induction hardening A heat treatment process that involves passing alternating electric current through coils of heavy-gauge wire surrounding the material to be hardened; through magnetic induction, heat is produced in the metal, which is then quenched with water to produce a hard, wear-resistant metal surface.

ladder-frame block A block design with sides that extend exactly to the centerline of the crankshaft bearings and a separate, additional section that attaches to the crankcase and the oil pan and incorporates the main bearing caps into one unit.

Nanoslide technology A plasma spray welding technique developed by Mercedes-Benz to coat cylinder walls with a tool-grade hardness iron alloy.

nitriding A crankshaft hardening technique that involves heating the shaft and introducing cyanide salt or liquid into the heating chamber with the crankshaft; slowly cooling or quenching the crank with these substances in its heated condition causes the nitrogen and carbon to molecularly bond with metal surfaces to create an extremely hard journal.

parent bore block A block design that has holes cast and bored in the block for the cylinders with the pistons inserted directly into these holes; also known as a no-sleeve block.

pendulum vibration absorber A dampener that provides torsional vibration control by producing forces that directly cancel the forces producing torsional vibration.

primary balance Balance achieved when the crankshaft counterweights offset the weight of the piston and connecting rod assembly.

scissor gear Two separate spring-loaded gears incorporated into a single unit to reduce gear rattle caused by torsional vibration.

secondary balance Balance achieved when the movement of one piston counterbalances the movement of another, result in smoother running engines.

sputter bearing The latest technology in bearing overlay material, which deposits a metal overlay surface onto a bearing backing that is three times harder than conventional overlay. This complex process involves spray welding in a vacuum and is used to make a bearing that has the highest ability to carry a load over any other bearing.

torsional vibration The speeding up and slowing down of the crankshaft caused by alternating compression and power strokes of the engine cylinder.

tunnel-bore block A block that has the main bearing bores and block formed into one solid structure for maximum block rigidity and strength.

warp anchor A block design that has the cylinder head and the cylinder block bolted together by tie bolts; sliding steel sleeves, which are locked in the block, accept the cylinder head bolt from one side and the tie bolt from the other.

wet sleeve block A block designed with a number of large holes into which the cylinder sleeves are inserted; coolant has direct contact with the outside of the sleeve and there is no supporting cylinder bore structure.

Review Questions

1. A _____ is a block design that has holes cast and bored in the block for the cylinders with the pistons inserted directly into these holes.
   a. deep-skirt block
   b. parent bore block
   c. ladder-frame block
   d. tunnel-bore block

2. Cast iron is a metal made from iron ore with a carbon content of _____.
   a. 10-15%
   b. 6-9%
   c. 3-5%
   d. 2%

3. The transmission, cylinder head(s), and all other major engine parts are bolted or connected to the _____.
   a. cylinder block
   b. crankshaft
   c. chassis
   d. liner

4. Coatings of tool-grade hardness iron carbon alloys can be achieved by a plasma-spraying technique developed by Mercedes-Benz called _____ technology.
   a. nanoslide
   b. induction hardening
   c. nitriding
   d. sintering

5. Silicone fluid is used in _____ dampeners to tune out harmonic and torsional vibrations.
   a. friction   c. sputter
   b. mass   d. viscous

6. The crankshaft is supported along its centerline by the main bearing _____.
   a. pendulum   c. journals
   b. wet sleeve   d. protrusion

7. The main purpose of the _____ in a recipro-cating engine is to convert the linear motion of the connecting rod assemblies into rotational movement.
   a. counterweight
   b. crankshaft
   c. pendulum
   d. bearing flange

8. Measuring and adjusting _____ is one of the most critical operations when rebuilding a sleeved engine.
   a. fillet radius
   b. counterweights
   c. oil passages
   d. protrusion

9. A _____ vibration sends pressure waves moving back and forth along the crankshaft.
   a. viscous
   b. harmonic
   c. torsional
   d. ductile

10. _____ are two separate spring-loaded gears incorporated into a single unit to reduce gear rattle caused by torsional vibration.
    a. Scissor gears
    b. Pilot bearings
    c. Crank cheeks
    d. Warp anchors

ASE-Type Questions

1. Technician A says that moving the gear train to the front of the engine can dramatically reduce gear train noise. Technician B says gear train placement has no effect on noise. Who is correct?
   a. Technician A
   b. Technician B
   c. Both Technician A and Technician B
   d. Neither Technician A nor Technician B

2. Technician A says one of the most common processes used to harden bearing surfaces of the crankshaft is induction hardening. Technician B says one of the most common processes used to harden bearing surfaces of the crankshaft is nitriding. Who is correct?
   a. Technician A
   b. Technician B
   c. Both Technician A and Technician B
   d. Neither Technician A nor Technician B

3. Technician A says that an interference fit dry cylinder sleeve never has a top flange. Technician B says that a slip fit dry cylinder sleeve has a counterbore. Who is correct?
   a. Technician A
   b. Technician B
   c. Both Technician A and Technician B
   d. Neither Technician A nor Technician B

4. Technician A says the ability of a bearing to carry a load is known as conformability. Technician B says the ability of a bearing to carry a load is known as dual mass. Who is correct?
   a. Technician A
   b. Technician B
   c. Both Technician A and Technician B
   d. Neither Technician A nor Technician B

5. Technician A says excessive skirt clearance will result in piston knock. Technician B says excessive skirt clearance will result in piston slap. Who is correct?
   a. Technician A
   b. Technician B
   c. Both Technician A and Technician B
   d. Neither Technician A nor Technician B

6. Technician A says diesel engine cylinder walls wear out faster than their gasoline engine counterparts. Technician B says gasoline engine cylinder walls wear out faster than their diesel engine counterparts. Who is correct?
   a. Technician A
   b. Technician B
   c. Both Technician A and Technician B
   d. Neither Technician A nor Technician B

7. Technician A says most bearing failures are caused by problems with lubrication. Technician B says most bearing failures are caused by normal wear and tear. Who is correct?
   a. Technician A
   b. Technician B
   c. Both Technician A and Technician B
   d. Neither Technician A nor Technician B

8. Technician A says Detroit Diesel's DD series engines use sputter bearings. Technician B says Detroit Diesel's DD series engines use pilot bearings. Who is correct?
   a. Technician A
   b. Technician B
   c. Both Technician A and Technician B
   d. Neither Technician A nor Technician B

9. Technician A says long stoke engines will have more wear mid-stoke as well due to a higher amount of minor thrust. Technician B says long stoke engines will have more wear mid-stoke as well due to a higher amount of major thrust. Who is correct?
   a. Technician A
   b. Technician B
   c. Both Technician A and Technician B
   d. Neither Technician A nor Technician B

10. Technician A says thrust bearings are used to control endplay in a crankshaft. Technician B says thrust bearings are used to control torsion in a crankshaft. Who is correct?
    a. Technician A
    b. Technician B
    c. Both Technician A and Technician B
    d. Neither Technician A nor Technician B

NATEF Tasks

Diesel Engines

General

- Identify engine fuel, oil, coolant, air, and other leaks; determine needed action. (pp 319–322)
- Listen for engine noises; determine needed action. (p 322)

Cylinder Head and Valve Train

- Inspect cylinder head for cracks/damage; check mating surfaces for warpage; check condition of passages; inspect core/expansion and gallery plugs; determine needed action. (pp 319–323)
- Disassemble head and inspect valves, guides, seats, springs, retainers, rotators, locks, and seals; determine needed action. (pp 307–311)
- Measure valve head height relative to deck and valve face-to-seat contact; determine needed action. (p 310)

- Inspect valve train components; determine needed action. (pp 313–314)
- Reassemble cylinder head. (p 319)
- Inspect, measure, and replace/reinstall overhead camshaft; measure/adjust end play and back lash. (pp 322–323)
- Adjust valve bridges (crossheads); adjust valve clearances and injector settings. (pp 322–324)

Engine Block

- Remove, inspect, service, and install pans, covers, gaskets, seals, wear rings, and crankcase ventilation. (pp 327–328)
- Inspect, measure, and replace/reinstall in-block camshaft; measure/adjust end play. (p 314)
- Inspect, install, and time gear train; measure gear backlash; determine needed action. (pp 322, 329–331)

Knowledge Objectives

After reading this chapter, you will be able to:

1. Identify and classify cylinder heads and associated components. (pp 310–323)
2. Describe the functions, construction, composition, types, styles, and applications of diesel engine cylinder head assemblies. (pp 310–323)
3. Describe common inspections and testing and diagnostic procedures on diesel engine cylinder head assemblies. (pp 318–319, 323–332)
4. Recommend common reconditioning or repairs of diesel engine cylinder heads. (pp 323–332)
5. Identify common causes of abnormal wear and failure of cylinder heads. (pp 326–331)

Skills Objectives

After reading this chapter, you will be able to:

1. Measure cylinder head warpage. (p 330) **SKILL DRILL 11-1**
2. Perform a valve adjustment. (p 331) **SKILL DRILL 11-2**

► Introduction

The cylinder head is a metal casting that forms a major engine part and attaches to the top of the cylinder block **FIGURE 11-1**. Cylinder heads are needed to seal the combustion chamber so the engine can develop and contain compression and combustion pressure. Because compression and combustion pressures are much higher inside a diesel engine, cylinder heads are ruggedly designed and use high clamping forces to secure the head to the block. Many of the components of the valve train and fuel injection mechanism are incorporated into the cylinder heads, which adds complexity to their design and service. As a major structural element of the engine, the cylinder head also supports other components critical to the operation of the engine.

Components that attach to the cylinder head include the following:

- Valve train components
- Fuel injectors
- Camshaft (in overhead cam engines)
- Valve guides and seats for valves
- Intake and exhaust manifolds

The cylinder head also contains drilled bores or seats for injectors, nozzles, injector tubes, coolant, fuel, and oil passageways; provides intake and exhaust passageways; and incorporates precombustion chambers **FIGURE 11-2**. Various sensors, such as the coolant temperature and cam position sensor, may be located in the head as well.

Cylinder heads are classified by the type of material used, by the way exhaust and intake ports are arranged, by the number of cylinder heads used on an engine, and by the valve train arrangement.

► Types of Cylinder Heads and Valve Trains

Because the cylinder head has to withstand high combustion temperatures and pressures without distortion, it is essential that it be constructed with high levels of strength and temperature

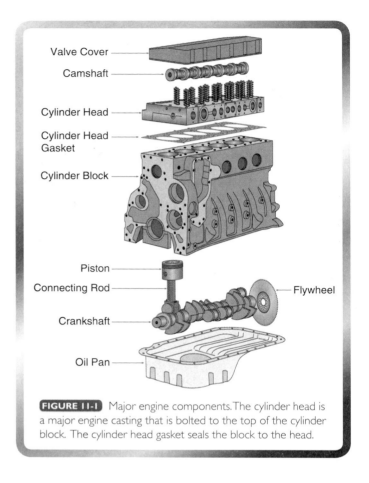

FIGURE 11-1 Major engine components. The cylinder head is a major engine casting that is bolted to the top of the cylinder block. The cylinder head gasket seals the block to the head.

resistance. Cooling of the head to keep NO_x emissions low and the addition of temperature-sensitive components, such as injectors and electronic sensors, have also become particularly important in the latest engines. Air and exhaust gas flow through the cylinder head is another design concern. The shape and position of the intake and exhaust ports, the position of the valves, and the location of the camshaft determine the overall geometry of the cylinder head. In addition to these considerations,

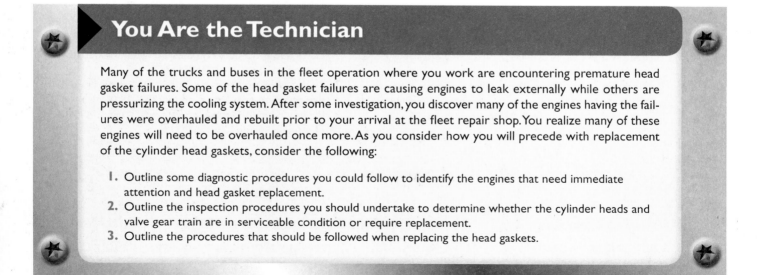

You Are the Technician

Many of the trucks and buses in the fleet operation where you work are encountering premature head gasket failures. Some of the head gasket failures are causing engines to leak externally while others are pressurizing the cooling system. After some investigation, you discover many of the engines having the failures were overhauled and rebuilt prior to your arrival at the fleet repair shop. You realize many of these engines will need to be overhauled once more. As you consider how you will precede with replacement of the cylinder head gaskets, consider the following:

1. Outline some diagnostic procedures you could follow to identify the engines that need immediate attention and head gasket replacement.
2. Outline the inspection procedures you should undertake to determine whether the cylinder heads and valve gear train are in serviceable condition or require replacement.
3. Outline the procedures that should be followed when replacing the head gaskets.

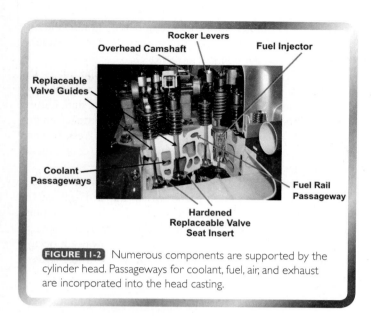

FIGURE 11-2 Numerous components are supported by the cylinder head. Passageways for coolant, fuel, air, and exhaust are incorporated into the head casting.

manufacturers must be able to construct cylinder heads that require the least amount of maintenance, are economical to produce, and promote outstanding performance and low emissions and fuel consumption. To meet the constantly improving benchmarks of engine performance, a wide variety of cylinder head design, construction techniques, and service procedures are currently in use.

Classification by Materials

Potentially corrosive coolants, flow of viscous oils, high horsepower engine applications (in which cylinder temperatures and pressures are high), and the demand for lightweight engine designs are just a few of the many factors involved in the selection of cylinder head materials. While traditional materials such as cast iron have provided good strength and wear characteristics for valve train mechanisms, new materials and construction techniques are enabling improved engine performance. Lighter weight designs now have greater durability and lower maintenance requirements while improving fuel economy.

Aluminum Versus Cast Iron

Cylinder heads are commonly made of cast iron alloy because of its superior strength, ease of manufacture, machinability, and capability to withstand high temperatures. Aluminum is another material now gaining widespread use as a material of choice. At one time aluminum was not considered for several reasons:

- Tendency to warp and crack especially when overheated
- Difficulty in tolerating dirty oil, which can quickly wear away softer aluminum friction surfaces
- Extra manufacturing steps required to install cast iron valve guides, valve seats, and bushings for camshaft (if used)
- Greater electrochemical corrosion in engines containing high aluminum content, making them unable to tolerate old contaminated coolant in the same way as cast iron
- More costly to cast than iron

Aluminum's higher expansion rate at operating temperature compared to iron's is another problem. The expansion coefficient of aluminum, which is four to seven times greater than that of cast iron, demands improvements in the selection and replacement of head gasket materials and greater precision in cylinder head fastener tightening procedures. Valve lash can be similarly affected by expansion. Cylinder head bolts must stretch, too, and require non-reusable torque yield bolts.

Aluminum's primary advantage, however, is that it is lightweight. Unnecessary engine weight is the enemy of good braking, handling, and quick acceleration and it displaces the vehicle's capacity to carry load. Because aluminum is 50% lighter than cast iron, aluminum cylinder heads can easily save more than 60–100 lb (27–45 kg) in some larger diesel engines. Aluminum also lends itself well to the manufacture of head casting with large intake and exhaust ports to create more powerful engines.

Another favorable attribute of aluminum is its higher heat conductivity, which improves heat transfer from the combustion chamber to coolant. This is especially important for emissions. Valve temperatures can be as much as 200°F (93°C) cooler in aluminum cylinder heads. This not only lowers the variations in valve lash, but also enhances durability of the valve seats and increases reliability of the engine as a whole. Aluminum carries away excess heat more rapidly, and localized hotspots are eliminated with aluminum cylinder heads; thus, higher combustion pressures and temperatures can be sustained. Similarly, because high combustion chamber temperatures cause increases to NO_X production, this emission can be reduced with the use of aluminum heads.

Aluminum is now a material of choice primarily because revised hardening techniques make it very durable and heat resistant. A hardening process performed shortly after the head is cast, called T6 treatment, relieves casting stresses and creates a more uniform metallurgical structure. T6 treatment involves heating the casting to 1000°F (538°C) for about six hours and then quenching the casting in water for a few seconds. The cooled casting is then seasoned in a 320°F (160°C) oven for approximately five hours and then allowed to cool to ambient temperature. The result is a casting with Rockwell hardness (HRC) on the B scale of approximately 84–88.

Compacted Graphite Iron

A material forming many new diesel cylinder block designs, **compacted graphite iron (CGI)** is also used for cylinder heads. CGI, also called sintered graphite, is a material produced from powdered iron alloys squeezed into molds at high pressures and then heated to bond the metal particles together. When made from CGI, diesel cylinder heads have approximately the same weight as aluminum but also possess higher strength and rigidity than steel and have the sound-dampening characteristics of CGI. Paccar's MX13 diesel engine uses a CGI cylinder block and cylinder head. Paccar reports an increase of 75% in both strength and rigidity, a 200% increase in thermal fatigue resistance, and 150 lb (68 kg) of weight reduction compared to conventional cast iron **FIGURE 11-3**.

FIGURE 11-3 Paccar's MX13 diesel engine uses a CGI cylinder block and cylinder head.

Classification by Intake and Exhaust Port Arrangement

Because intake and exhaust port arrangements influence gas flow and turbulence or swirl into the cylinders, configuration of these ports affects engine performance and emissions. The **cross-flow cylinder head** design is the most popular **FIGURE 11-4**. In this configuration, the intake and exhaust manifolds are located on opposite sides of an inline engine to improve engine breathing characteristics. Air enters one side of the engine and exhaust exits the other side. Also, because the exhaust ports and manifolds are opposite one another, little heating of intake air occurs. This design provides cooler air for efficient combustion, improved fuel economy, maximum efficiency, and reduced emissions. The drawback to this configuration is that exhaust and intake manifolds on opposite sides

of the cylinder head create a wider temperature gradient across the head with the exhaust side having much higher temperatures than the intake side.

The **parallel flow head**, sometimes referred to as the uniflow design, places the intake and exhaust manifolds on the same side of the engine **FIGURE 11-5**. In this design, joining together short, large ports provides a more compact engine design with adequate airflow to the cylinders. Less thermal stress of the cylinder head takes place because the cooler intake ports are placed alongside the exhaust ports.

A **reverse-flow cylinder head**, which is used on a V-block engine, places the exhaust ports on the inboard side of the engine. This shortens the connection between the exhaust ports and turbocharger, resulting in quicker turbocharger response. Without outboard exhaust manifolds, reverse flow heads occupy a smaller footprint beneath the hood of a vehicle where space is limited **FIGURE 11-6**.

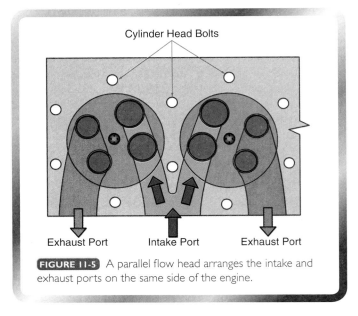

FIGURE 11-5 A parallel flow head arranges the intake and exhaust ports on the same side of the engine.

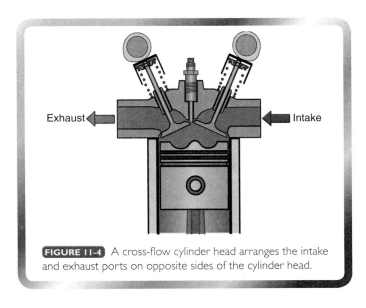

FIGURE 11-4 A cross-flow cylinder head arranges the intake and exhaust ports on opposite sides of the cylinder head.

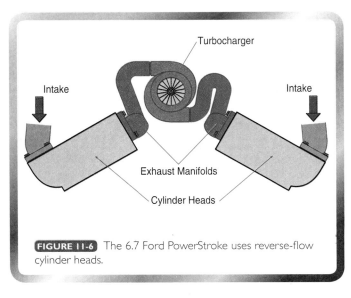

FIGURE 11-6 The 6.7 Ford PowerStroke uses reverse-flow cylinder heads.

Variable Swirl Intake Ports

Variable intake charge and motion systems have a flap deactivation system to change swirl characteristics of intake air. This provides for a variable swirl design to match intake swirl to engine load and fuel rate. The shape of the intake port of most diesels is designed to impart a twisting or spinning motion to the air as it enters the cylinder to increase turbulence FIGURE 11-7. The diagonal placement of the valves in the cylinders spins the air entering the cylinders. Turbulence is critical to improved air fuel mixture formation at low engine speeds.

Classification by Number

The number of cylinder heads used by a diesel engine is influenced by a variety of factors. Strength and rigidity of the engine is enhanced by a single-piece casting, but this type of cylinder head does not have the flexibility to adapt to multiple engine platforms. Single-piece heads also have unique problems with sealing combustion gases; multiple-piece cylinder heads also have problems with sealing combustion gases, but each situation is dependent on engine application. The location of the camshaft, gas flow, and serviceability are other considerations when selecting the type of cylinder head casting.

Single-Piece Cylinder Heads

Single-piece cylinder head castings cover the engine block completely by using one head. One-piece castings are relatively easy to manufacture, and their rigidity adds structural strength to a block.

Single-piece castings do, however, have the greatest amount of creep when thermally cycled, which means they expand and contract significantly across the block deck by sliding over the head gasket. This can translate into more head gasket failures at the rear of the engine where coolant temperatures are hottest. Servicing a single-piece casting can be labor intensive if not all engine cylinders require service. Care in maintaining a liner projection is critical on sleeved engines using single-piece castings. Warping and cracking of heads and liner flanges will result, because clamping forces are concentrated on the higher cylinder liner projection. On high-horsepower (high-kilowatt) Caterpillar engines, a spacer plate between the cylinder head and block deck minimizes the loads exerted by the cylinder head against the liner flange for improved reliability FIGURE 11-8.

Multiple-Piece Cylinder Heads

Multiple-piece cylinder heads use a separate cylinder head for a group of two or three cylinders in a multiple-cylinder engine FIGURE 11-9. Multiple-piece cylinder heads are ideal for modular engine designs where part castings shared between different engines can be used to construct various engine configurations. This allows the same head to be used on a variety of cylinder arrangements. For example, a single cylinder head can be used to build single, two, four, six, or eight cylinder engines. Servicing is simplified if only one or a few cylinders of an engine are being serviced. However, multiple cylinder heads tend to move around more, wearing the top of liners or block decks.

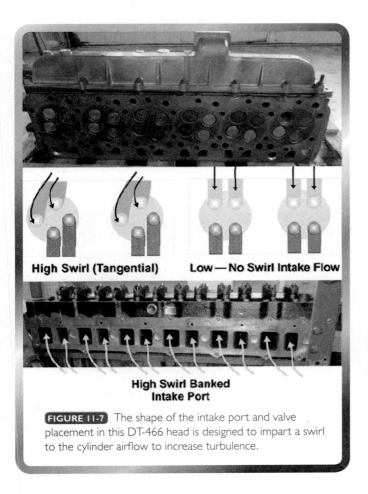

High Swirl (Tangential)　　**Low—No Swirl Intake Flow**

High Swirl Banked Intake Port

FIGURE 11-7 The shape of the intake port and valve placement in this DT-466 head is designed to impart a swirl to the cylinder airflow to increase turbulence.

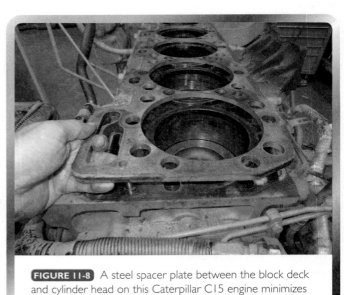

FIGURE 11-8 A steel spacer plate between the block deck and cylinder head on this Caterpillar C15 engine minimizes cylinder head clamping forces applied to the liner flanges.

FIGURE 11-9 Multiple-piece cylinder heads may cover one, two, or even three separate cylinders.

Classification by Valve Train Arrangement

Cylinder heads are further classified by the arrangement of the valve train mechanism. For example, the camshaft arrangements in diesel engines are commonly one of two types—overhead camshaft or in-block camshaft. <u>Overhead camshaft engines</u> have the camshaft located in the cylinder head. This allows push rods, which can bend during high-pressure injections, to be eliminated, enabling the highest injection pressures using unit injectors. Valve timing is more accurate in this configuration **FIGURE 11-10**. <u>In-block camshafts</u> have only the valves, rocker levers, and bridges located in the cylinder heads above the piston, and the camshaft is located in the engine block **FIGURE 11-11**. Another term for this camshaft arrangement is a pushrod engine because the camshaft actuates the valves through a pushrod and rocker lever **FIGURE 11-12**.

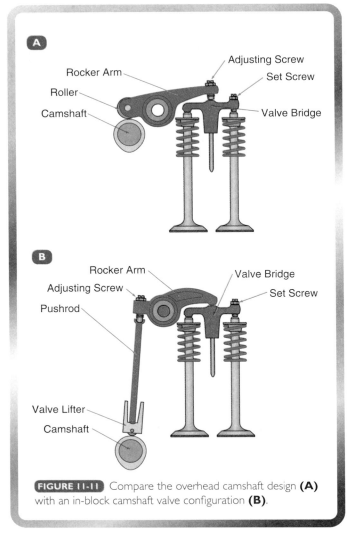

FIGURE 11-11 Compare the overhead camshaft design **(A)** with an in-block camshaft valve configuration **(B)**.

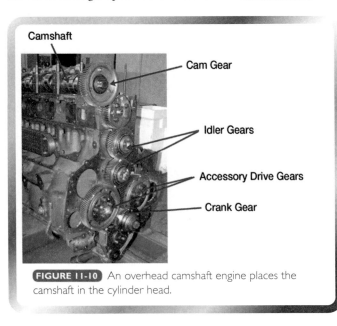

FIGURE 11-10 An overhead camshaft engine places the camshaft in the cylinder head.

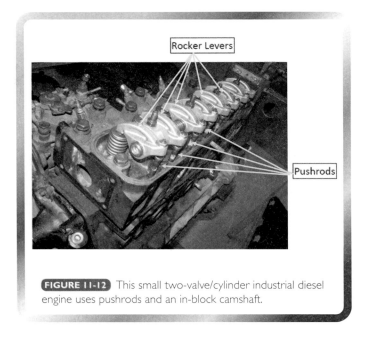

FIGURE 11-12 This small two-valve/cylinder industrial diesel engine uses pushrods and an in-block camshaft.

Overhead Cam Advantages

Overhead cam engines are now a popular design with a number of advantages:

1. Simplicity. Pushrods and several other valve train components are eliminated. This also means there are fewer wearing surfaces, with the elimination of parts resulting in fewer adjustments required to maintain valve clearances.

2. Easier inspection and service. All the components are easier to inspect and remove. For example, camshaft inspection can be performed visually, and it can be replaced without disassembling the engine front cover, removing the cylinder head, and performing other steps FIGURE 11-13.

3. More accurate valve train action. Shortening the length of the valve train minimizes its thermal expansion and reduces its inertia. This permits higher engine speeds and closer valve train clearances, resulting in more accurate valve timing. Stiffer and heavier components can be used without the penalty of added mass and length associated with a pushrod.

4. Optimized intake and exhaust passageways for easier breathing. Because there is no obstruction from push tubes to interfere with intake and exhaust port design, the size, location, and shape of intake and exhaust ports are optimized to improve engine breathing ability.

5. Higher injection pressures. A shorter, stiffer valve train permits unit injectors to be actuated to higher injection pressures (34,000 psi [234,422 kPa]) with more accurate injection timing. When pushrods are used to transfer movement from the camshaft to injectors, they tend to bend and add considerable inertia to injector actuation. For this reason, overhead cam diesel engines that do not use pushrods will have minimal injection lag, which is an important consideration for emissions.

FIGURE 11-13 Installing the rocker arm shaft on an overhead camshaft MP-10 Mack engine using the manufacturer-prescribed lifting tool.

► Components of Cylinder Heads and Valve Trains

Valves

Poppet valves are the most common type of valve used in diesel engines. Poppet valves are characterized by a large head and a long stem. Intake valves are usually larger than exhaust valves, because pressure forcing the air charge into the cylinder is much lower than forces pushing exhaust gases out FIGURE 11-14. On diesel engines, the valves are often designed in two pieces that are spun-welded together. The weld, though durable under most operating conditions, can break when valves become overheated. The valve head will separate from the stem and the head will embed itself in a piston if a weld failure occurs FIGURE 11-15. The valve stem is typically chrome-plated steel to reduce its requirement for lubrication and minimize wear and friction. The head is made of specialized alloys to withstand high temperatures and mechanical forces that slam the head into the valve seat. Stellite® or Inconel® are alloys commonly used to make the valve head. These are materials made from a combination of chromium, nickel, tungsten, and cobalt to give the metal great strength and wear resistance at high temperatures.

Two and four valves per cylinder are common, but a number of engines may use three and five valves. An extra intake valve, usually the third valve (such as used in the Caterpillar 3126b or C9), is used to improve intake flow for improved engine airflow and lower emissions. Four smaller valves rather than two large intake and exhaust valves are used in central DI combustion chambers to accommodate an injector nozzle. A centrally located injector provides better uniform fuel distribution for lower emissions FIGURE 11-16. In two-valve engines, the injector is offset to one side and leaned over to make room for the exhaust and intake valves.

Valve Angles

Valve faces are machined at an angle to wedge themselves into the seat to improve sealing. The degree of angle determines the valve port's flow characteristics. Valve face angles are measured from the horizontal. A 45-degree angle is common and is better at self-centering the valve at closure while wedging the valve tighter to the valve seat. Some manufacturers use alternate angles. Flatter angles of 30 or 40 degrees can be used on diesel exhaust valve faces to provide for better heat transfer. Some exhaust and intake valve face angles are between 20 and 40 degrees to permit better flow over the edge of the seat. This flatter angle also creates less wear, resulting in fewer overhead adjustments.

Valve Guides

Valves are located in guides that are either integral, meaning they are cast into the cylinder head, or removable, which means they can be replaced FIGURE 11-17. Premium engines have replaceable valve guides that can be easily replaced during overhaul. The condition of a valve guide is critical to oil consumption control. A limited amount of lubrication oil must pass between the guide and valve. However, worn guides can allow oil to be drawn

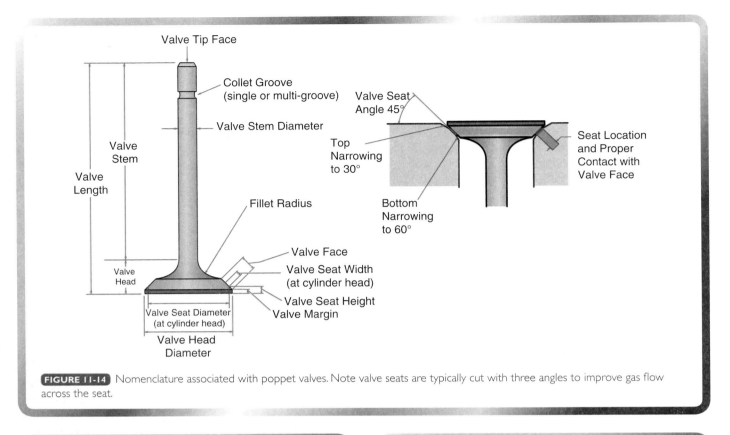

FIGURE 11-14 Nomenclature associated with poppet valves. Note valve seats are typically cut with three angles to improve gas flow across the seat.

FIGURE 11-15 A broken weld of a two-piece valve is evidenced by a valve head embedded in the top of a piston. Overheating a valve can cause the weld to break.

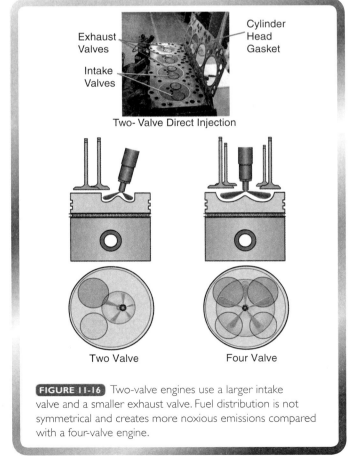

FIGURE 11-16 Two-valve engines use a larger intake valve and a smaller exhaust valve. Fuel distribution is not symmetrical and creates more noxious emissions compared with a four-valve engine.

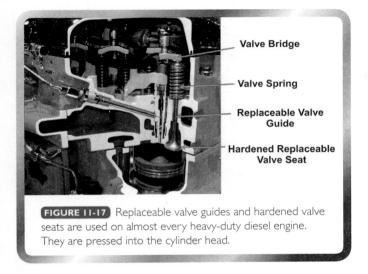

FIGURE 11-17 Replaceable valve guides and hardened valve seats are used on almost every heavy-duty diesel engine. They are pressed into the cylinder head.

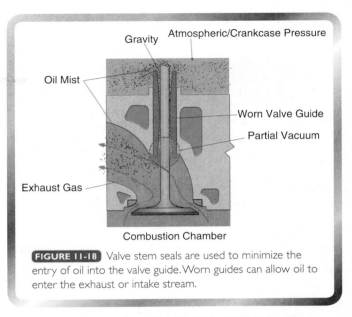

FIGURE 11-18 Valve stem seals are used to minimize the entry of oil into the valve guide. Worn guides can allow oil to enter the exhaust or intake stream.

into the combustion chamber or exhaust stream because of the Venturi effect. This happens as a low-pressure area is created at the base of the valve guide by high-velocity gases that draw oil into the exhaust or intake stream, causing high oil consumption that may be accompanied by blue smoke **FIGURE 11-18**. Older diesel engines, particularly turbocharged engines, did not use seals on the intake guides because the intake manifold was pressurized and had little or no vacuum. However, positive umbrella seals are now used on all valve guides and stems to minimize the entrance of oil into the guide **FIGURE 11-19**. The high temperatures of the guide can cause oil to coke and accelerate abrasive wear. Oil entering the exhaust stream can contribute to engine emissions. The newest guides are made from sintered iron, which is porous and can retain oil in the guide better while using smaller stems to guide clearances.

TECHNICIAN TIP

Worn guides and missing valve stem seals lead to high oil consumption and blue smoke during deceleration. Oil in the guides can carbonize, accelerating stem wear. Also, any oil consumption in an engine leads to formation of particulate emissions. Long exhaust systems, such as those found on school buses, create a longer and more intense period of low pressure at the valve guide in the exhaust port, especially during deceleration. More oil can be dragged down the stem during this time, increasing oil consumption.

TECHNICIAN TIP

Combustion quality in diesels at idle is often poor due to low combustion pressures and temperatures. Engine slobber, a residue consisting of unburnt fuel, soot, and engine oil, can coat the back face of valves during prolonged idle. When left to cool, slobber will solidify on the back face of an open valve, preventing the valve from closing during engine start-up.

FIGURE 11-19 A positive valve stem seal prevents oil from entering the valve guide.

Valve Seat Inserts

All premium diesel engines use replaceable valve seat inserts. Typically, these are manufactured from material such as Stellite or Iconel. Replaceable inserts eliminate the need for complex machining processes to install a new valve seat into a damaged or rebuilt head. Their wear-resistant hardness and heat resistance add considerable durability and prolong an engine's operating life. Valve seats have a minimum of three angles to ensure good gas flow and proper transfer of heat from the valve face. A narrow 45-degree seat promotes clean valve seats and good sealing. Three angle cuts on the seat provide improved gas flow and a narrow contact between the valve face and seat to promote heat transfer **FIGURE 11-20**.

Valve face to seat contact width must be adjusted to within typically 0.0625–0.125″ (1.5875–3.175 mm) for optimal heat transfer. Too wide a seat contact diminishes pressure per square

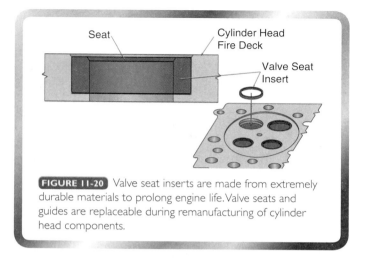

FIGURE 11-20 Valve seat inserts are made from extremely durable materials to prolong engine life. Valve seats and guides are replaceable during remanufacturing of cylinder head components.

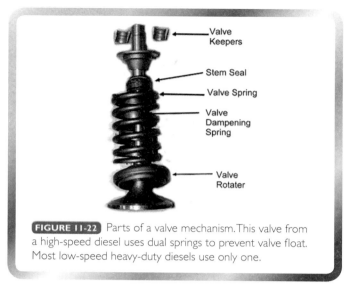

FIGURE 11-22 Parts of a valve mechanism. This valve from a high-speed diesel uses dual springs to prevent valve float. Most low-speed heavy-duty diesels use only one.

unit of area and will result in less heat transfer from the face to the seat. This may seem counterintuitive, but high-pressure contact transfers heat better than low-pressure contact.

When servicing valve seats and faces, the technician must ensure the correct amount of valve protrusion or intrusion exists **FIGURE 11-21**. A valve sunk too low into the head will prevent proper gas flow and require a new valve seat. A valve sitting too high in the seat could potentially contact the piston, causing catastrophic engine damage. If valve protrusion is excessive, the valve seat requires grinding to lower the valve.

Valve Springs

Valve springs hold the valve closed on the seat and must maintain tension on the valve train when the valve is open **FIGURE 11-22**. If inertia of the valve train is great enough, weak valve springs will allow the valve to stay open after the cam rotates to its inner base circle. This is known as valve float. However, excessive spring tension will slam the valve against the seat, prematurely wearing the valve, stretching the stem, and wearing cam lobes and other parts due to high valve opening pressures. Valve springs should be inspected for free length, cracks, nicks, pitting, straightness, and spring tension. A valve spring testing apparatus, which operates

like a weigh scale, is used to check spring tension. The spring is compressed to a specified height and the spring scale reports the valve spring's tension. For example, if a spring is compressed to 1″ (2.5 cm), a corresponding manufacturer's specifications would indicate that an acceptable valve spring pressure of 150 lb (68 kg) or greater is required. If spring tension falls below this, the valve spring is discarded **FIGURE 11-23**.

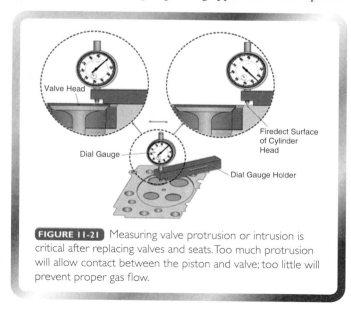

FIGURE 11-21 Measuring valve protrusion or intrusion is critical after replacing valves and seats. Too much protrusion will allow contact between the piston and valve; too little will prevent proper gas flow.

FIGURE 11-23 A valve spring tester measures a spring's free length and compressed tension.

Valve Cooling

Because exhaust valve temperatures can momentarily exceed 1200°F (649°C), the temperature at which valve damage can occur, excess heat must be removed to prevent burning, warping, and leaking. Good seat contact provided by a three-angle valve grind is important for heat transfer. Also, rotating the valve slightly each time it opens can eliminate localized hot spots that can lead to valve burning. Valve rotators installed on either the bottom or top of the valve produce this rotation FIGURE 11-24.

FIGURE 11-24 The top of a dual valve spring. The inner spring rubs against the outer spring to minimize valve float, and the rotator turns the valve each time it opens and closes to help cool the valve.

Valve Actuating Mechanisms

Transfer of movement of the camshaft to the valves is accomplished through the valve train. For in-block camshaft engines, the camshaft will initiate valve action by transferring force through the cam follower, then to the pushrod, rocker lever, and valve. Multivalve setups will use a valve bridge to open two valves with one rocker lever FIGURE 11-25. Most valve actuating mechanisms will use a roller-type cam follower or lifters and roller rocker levers to reduce friction. Not only does this reduction in friction increase the durability of the components, but it also can add 1.5–3% higher power output. Reducing valve actuation friction is especially important in diesel engines because high loading of the camshaft occurs when the exhaust valve opens against cylinder pressure. Cylinder pressures remaining at the end of the power stroke are still high and tremendous pressure must be exerted by the camshaft to open the valve and begin the exhaust stroke. The combination of pressure and friction in the exhaust valve train causes premature valve train wear and camshaft failures unless extra features are designed into the exhaust valve train mechanisms. Excessive cam lobe wear is measured using a dial indicator when the camshaft is still in the engine. The amount of lift each lobe has is compared against specifications; a worn lobe will produce an engine misfire or popping sound through the intake air system because the exhaust gas cannot leave the cylinder through the exhaust port.

Roller type followers and larger diameter and wider cam lobes are used in combination with exhaust longer rocker arm ratios to multiply the force of camshaft lift and increase the durability of exhaust valve train components. Roller-type lifters and followers reduce friction between the camshaft and follower. When hip or flat lifters are used, the cam may have a special angle ground to rotate the lifter as the cam wipes along the bottom of the lifter FIGURE 11-26. This rotation minimizes premature lifter wear. Offsetting the lifter slightly from the lobe centerline will cause lifter rotation FIGURE 11-27.

FIGURE 11-25 Valve bridges actuate two valves with a single rocker lever. Older bridges were adjustable. Newer engines use nonadjustable bridges.

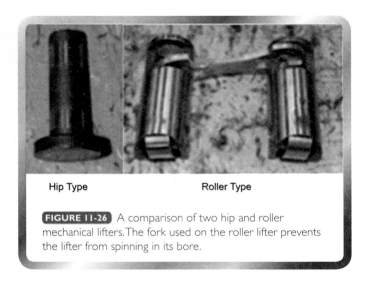

FIGURE 11-26 A comparison of two hip and roller mechanical lifters. The fork used on the roller lifter prevents the lifter from spinning in its bore.

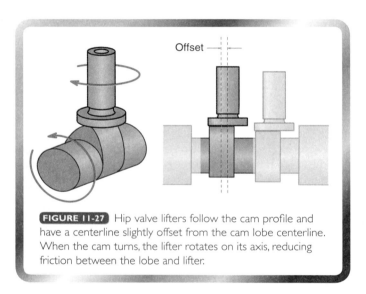

FIGURE 11-27 Hip valve lifters follow the cam profile and have a centerline slightly offset from the cam lobe centerline. When the cam turns, the lifter rotates on its axis, reducing friction between the lobe and lifter.

▶ TECHNICIAN TIP

Adjustments to valve bridges are generally not performed during scheduled valve and injector adjustments. Whenever they are adjusted, they must never be loosened or tightened while on the valve stems. Pulling a wrench to loosen the lock nuts will bend the valve stems, causing the valves to stick open. Always remove the bridge and loosen it in a soft-jawed vice. After setting proper clearances on the engine, the lock nut should be only lightly tightened and only firmly torqued while in a vice.

Valve Overlap

Valve overlap is the angle in crankshaft degrees that both the intake and exhaust valves are open **FIGURE 11-28**. Overlap occurs at the end of the exhaust stroke and the beginning of the intake

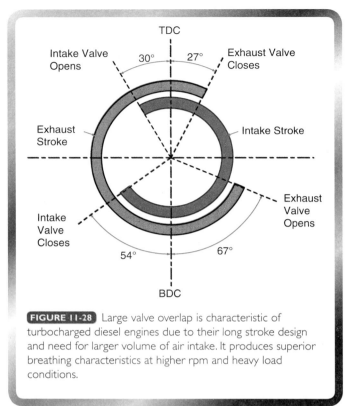

FIGURE 11-28 Large valve overlap is characteristic of turbocharged diesel engines due to their long stroke design and need for larger volume of air intake. It produces superior breathing characteristics at higher rpm and heavy load conditions.

stroke. Because fuel does not enter the cylinders with air during intake stroke, diesels can use large amounts of valve overlap and not waste fuel or generate hydrocarbon emissions. A large valve overlap helps create a power profile that delivers higher torque at high speed and heavy load. Large overlap helps an engine to breathe better, but it also produces soot loading of the intake manifold and more intake noise as exhaust pulses can travel into the intake manifold at low speed. The use of turbochargers also helps pack more air into cylinders using large amounts of valve overlap. Small valve overlap delivers higher torque at lower engine speeds, but the power will drop off as the engine speed and load increase.

Valve Timing in a Diesel Engine

Valve timing is another important feature that gives diesel engines their superior performance characteristics. The addition of a turbocharger and the absence of fuel in the intake air during intake stroke provide the diesel with the capability to increase power output using a prolonged valve overlap period, thus increasing engine torque without increasing displacement.

Because most gasoline-fueled engines have fuel in the intake air charge, longer valve overlap is not possible. With fuel entering the intake air, long overlap would result in wasted fuel and high emissions. A turbocharged diesel engine requires a larger valve overlap to allow more time for charging and scavenging a cylinder.

Soot loading of an intake manifold is common on diesel engines even without an exhaust gas recirculation (EGR) system. During low-speed, low-load operation, some exhaust gases will back up into the intake manifold when both intake and exhaust valves are open. Soot can accumulate on the intake, which is a relatively harmless condition unless buildup is excessive. EGR and closed crankcase ventilation systems can also contribute to soot loading and sludge formation in the intake manifold.

Pushrods

Pushrods transmit the cam actuation force from the followers to the rocker levers. To reduce weight and inertia at high speeds, longer pushrods are usually hollow. When servicing, the pushrods should be checked for wear at each end and bending caused by maladjustment or high-speed valve float. Some pushrods will use a hardened end at the rocker lever to withstand greater friction at this point. If the weld at the ball socket end fractures, oil can enter and accumulate inside the pushrod. The easiest way to check for oil entering the pushrod is to listen to the sound made when dropped. A pushrod filled with oil will make a distinctively different clunking sound when it is dropped and will not bounce as much as a good pushrod. Shorter, solid pushrods capable of transmitting larger forces with less flexing are also commonly used with high-mounted camshafts (FIGURE 11-29). Solid, short pushrods allow for higher injection pressures and reduced injection lag.

Rocker Arms

Rocker arms convert the linear change of the cam profile to the reciprocating motion used to open and close the valves. The arms may be constructed of stamped steel, cast, or forged steel. A roller is incorporated into the levers of overhead cam engines to reduce friction. A much wider roller is used on the exhaust valve rocker lever, because cylinder pressures are higher when the exhaust valve opens and the loading of the roller is much higher than on the intake valve. The roller for an injector lobe is the widest; injection pressures can reach as high as 33,000 psi (2275 bar) on engines such as Cummins ISX. Hardened wear pads may be welded to the arm, or the arm may be induction hardened for increased durability. If rocker arms are of different lengths on the engine, the exhaust rocker lever is often longer than the intake lever (FIGURE 11-30). This is due to the cam profile of the exhaust cam lobe. A less aggressive profile with a smaller lift is used on the camshaft's exhaust lobe to minimize wear. The rocker arm ratio means a greater mechanical advantage is used on the lever to multiply the cam lobe lift and lift it more rapidly. This translates into less friction on the exhaust cam lobe. A larger exhaust rocker arm lever ratio is not a rule though—there are exceptions.

Crossheads, Yokes, and Valve Bridges

To actuate more than one valve with a single rocker lever, most four-valve engines use a crosshead to exert the camshaft force against the valve stem. Crossheads are also called yokes and bridges. There are two varieties of crossheads: guideless crossheads are nonadjustable, and adjustable crossheads use a guide pin to locate the device in the cylinder head.

Camshafts

Camshafts are critical components to engine performance because they control the gas dynamics or engine breathing characteristics (FIGURE 11-31). They are commonly made from nodular cast iron. Camshaft lobes may be occasionally induction hardened or even nitrided to withstand high unit loading. Cam profiles are ground to create quieting ramps that prevent high velocities when seating valves (FIGURE 11-32). Valve timing (opening and closing in relation to crank position), valve lift, duration, and lobe separation are controlled by the cam profile. If a camshaft is shared between different power ratings of the same engine model, offset keyways on the cam gear may change valve timing. Cam bushings

FIGURE 11-29 A high-mounted camshaft is located as close to the cylinder head as possible to shorten the length, inertia, and weight of the pushrods. Solid, short pushrods will not flex easily.

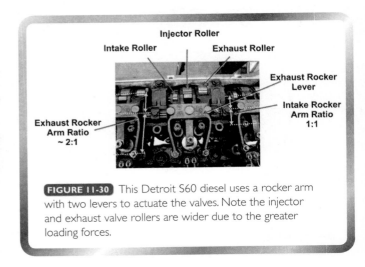

FIGURE 11-30 This Detroit S60 diesel uses a rocker arm with two levers to actuate the valves. Note the injector and exhaust valve rollers are wider due to the greater loading forces.

FIGURE 11-31 A typical diesel camshaft. Note the three lobes per cylinder. One is for the injector, and the other two are for the valves.

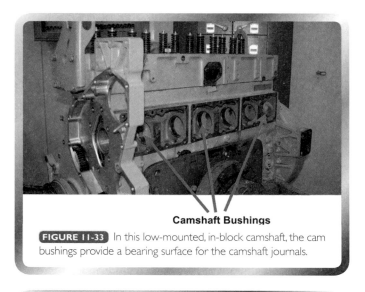

Camshaft Bushings

FIGURE 11-33 In this low-mounted, in-block camshaft, the cam bushings provide a bearing surface for the camshaft journals.

are used to provide a bearing surface for camshaft journals **FIGURE 11-33**.

All camshafts require correct timing to the engine to ensure the valves open at precisely the correct time in relation to piston position. Timing marks are stamped into the gear train and are aligned during assembly to establish correct camshaft-to-engine timing **FIGURE 11-34**. A low-mounted camshaft will typically use a single camshaft gear that rotates at half the engine speed to link to the engine's crank gear.

Overhead camshaft engines often use two camshafts. The Detroit DD13 and DD15 engines use one camshaft for the intake valves, a second camshaft for the exhaust valves, and an additional lobe on the exhaust cam to operate the compression release brake. The rear-mounted gear train does not use timing marks to synchronize cam-to-crank operation. Instead, it uses special fixtures to lock the camshaft and gear train in place **FIGURE 11-35**. Cummins ISX uses two camshafts as well. One camshaft operates the valves having lobes for the intake, exhaust, and compression release brake. The other, larger-diameter camshaft contains the injector

FIGURE 11-34 Timing marks on the gear train are used to synchronize the valve operation with the piston position.

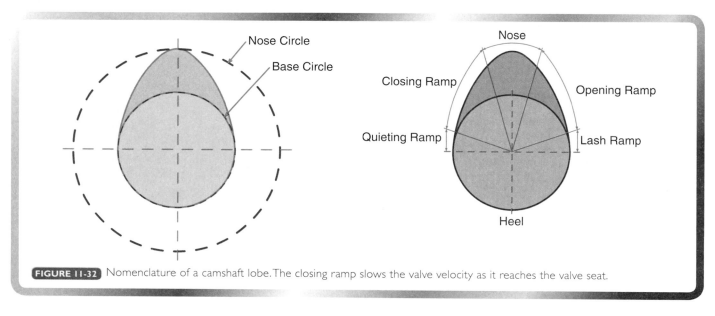

FIGURE 11-32 Nomenclature of a camshaft lobe. The closing ramp slows the valve velocity as it reaches the valve seat.

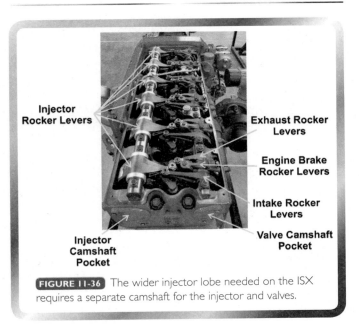

FIGURE 11-35 **A.** The DD15 engine crankshaft is positioned at top dead center and the gear train is locked in place to synchronize cam and crank operation. **B.** This wedge tool is placed between the two DD15 camshafts to properly phase camshaft operation.

lobes FIGURE 11-36. The high pressurization of fuel requires a wider lobe to distribute the injection actuation force. Space on the camshaft would not allow the use of three or four lobes on a single camshaft.

▶ TECHNICIAN TIP

Exhaust cam lobes and exhaust valve train mechanisms have the greatest loading pressure, which produces comparatively greater wear in these components. The loading pressure is caused by the high force required to open the exhaust valves at the end of the power stroke, and several hundred pounds (bar) of pressure remains present in the cylinders after power stroke in some engines. The wide profile of exhaust cam lobes and rollers help distribute the mechanical forces over a larger surface area. Injector lobes are even wider to pressurize fuel and prevent camshaft wear.

Injector Rocker Levers

Exhaust Rocker Levers

Engine Brake Rocker Levers

Intake Rocker Levers

Valve Camshaft Pocket

Injector Camshaft Pocket

FIGURE 11-36 The wider injector lobe needed on the ISX requires a separate camshaft for the injector and valves.

▶ Maintenance of Cylinder Heads and Valve Trains

Maintenance of cylinder heads is often required when coolant or combustion leaks occur. In addition, valve seats and faces can become worn or damaged, which requires replacement during a cylinder head overhaul and service FIGURE 11-37. Continual pounding of the valve faces and seats can take place whenever valves are out of adjustment; this prevents effective performance of the quieting ramps on the camshaft, which slow down valve velocity as they seat. Valve faces become recessed when worn out. Excessive oil consumption and extended idle time can contribute to valve seat and face pitting, which eventually results in valve leakage FIGURE 11-38. Very long periods of extended idle can lead to excessive formation of slobber on the back of the valve FIGURE 11-39. If the slobber solidifies during a cold shut-down period while the valve is open, the valve and piston will make contact and the valve will bend.

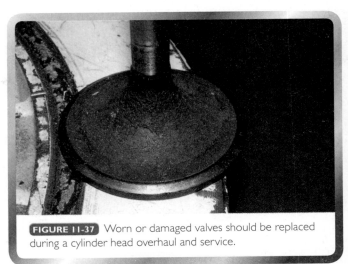

FIGURE 11-37 Worn or damaged valves should be replaced during a cylinder head overhaul and service.

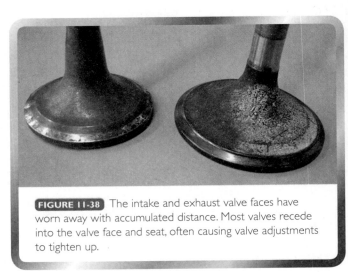

FIGURE 11-38 The intake and exhaust valve faces have worn away with accumulated distance. Most valves recede into the valve face and seat, often causing valve adjustments to tighten up.

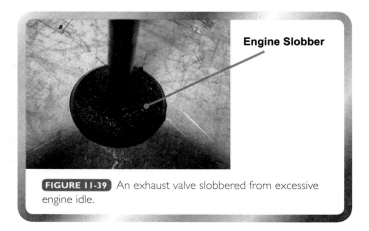

FIGURE 11-39 An exhaust valve slobbered from excessive engine idle.

Cylinder Head Bolts

Because of their higher cylinder pressures, consistent bolt clamping force is a critical maintenance issue for diesel engines. The size, number, and grade of bolts are increased in four-stroke diesels in comparison to two-stroke diesels and spark-ignition engines. Typically, five to seven bolts are used per cylinder, but as few as four may be used.

Cylinder head bolts use specialized rolled threads like those used to retain main and rod bearing caps. Unlike machine-cut threads, which have material removed during fabrication, rolled threads are instead formed using a tool that pushes into and displaces the metal while the bolt is turned. This technique does not reduce the root diameter of a bolt. Because no material is removed and the metal grain of the bolt is uninterrupted by cutting, rolled threads are stronger and less prone to damage **FIGURE 11-40**. Usually, the bolt, thread, and grade are proprietary, which means the bolt diameter, thread pitch, and strength are unique to the manufacturer.

Care must be taken to inspect bolts for damage before reuse. Nicks, corrosion, or thread damage can lead to stress risers and breakage. Bolts should also be inspected for necking out or stretching using a go-no-go gauge **FIGURE 11-41**. If the bolt is longer than the gauge permits, the bolt is stretched and should be discarded.

Bolt threads should be cleaned and lightly oiled before installation to ensure maximum and consistent clamping force **FIGURE 11-42**. Lubricating the bolts ensures that more of the twisting force used to tighten a bolt turns the bolt and is not instead lost to friction on the bolt threads. Variations between clamping forces of bolts can lead to premature head gasket

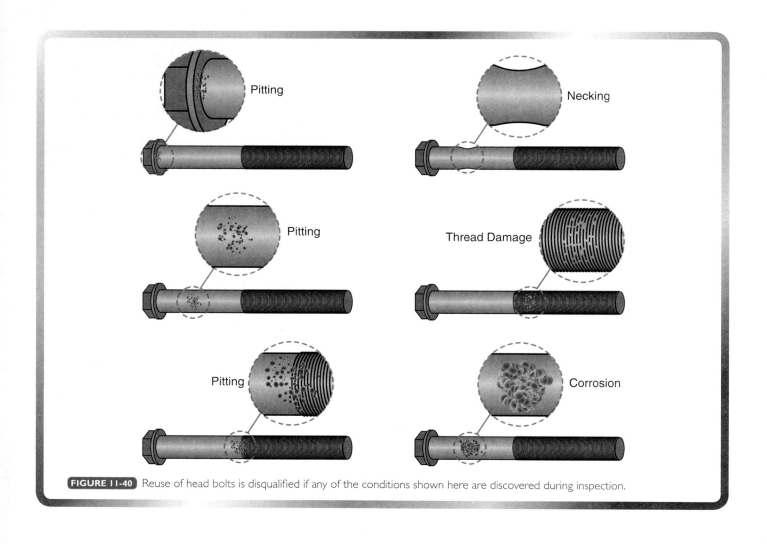

FIGURE 11-40 Reuse of head bolts is disqualified if any of the conditions shown here are discovered during inspection.

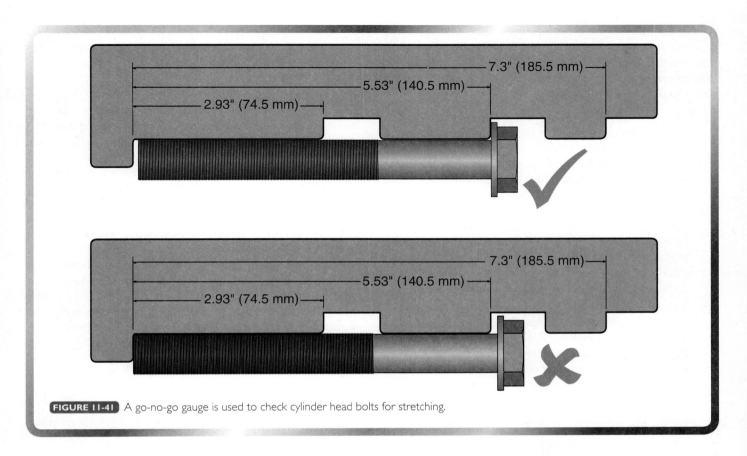

FIGURE 11-41 A go-no-go gauge is used to check cylinder head bolts for stretching.

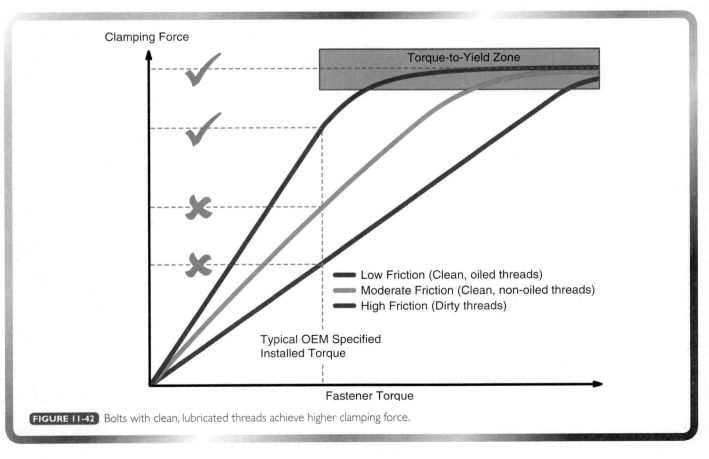

FIGURE 11-42 Bolts with clean, lubricated threads achieve higher clamping force.

failure and head warping. Research has revealed that tightening the head bolts with only a torque wrench to the torque specification results in over 30% variation in clamping force. Because of this, several service techniques have evolved for ensuring consistent gasket clamping forces.

1. **Torque to yield (TTY) bolts** are cylinder head bolts that have been tightened past their yield strength or elastic point. When tightened to specification, they stretch to a point just over precisely calibrated yield strength and not to the tensile where the bolt will break. When stretched to its yield point, the bolt becomes more elastic, allowing it to accommodate changes in the dimensions of the cylinder head caused by temperature fluctuations between cold and high operating temperature. The grade of the metal and root diameter determines its clamping force. All engines with aluminum cylinder heads use TTY bolts, as do some cast iron engines. These bolts must be discarded after a single use.

2. The torque plus angle or **torque-turn method** requires initial bolt tightening with a torque wrench and then turning the bolt an additional number of degrees past this point **FIGURE 11-43**. This may be measured in degrees of rotation, turns, or a specified number of flats on the bolt. Clamping forces with this method are the most consistent and widely preferred method. When tightening down a bolt using the torque plus angle method, it is helpful to mark a socket with white-out to gauge the amount of turning. Special markings are embossed into the cap of torque plus angle bolts designating the specialized tensile strength of the

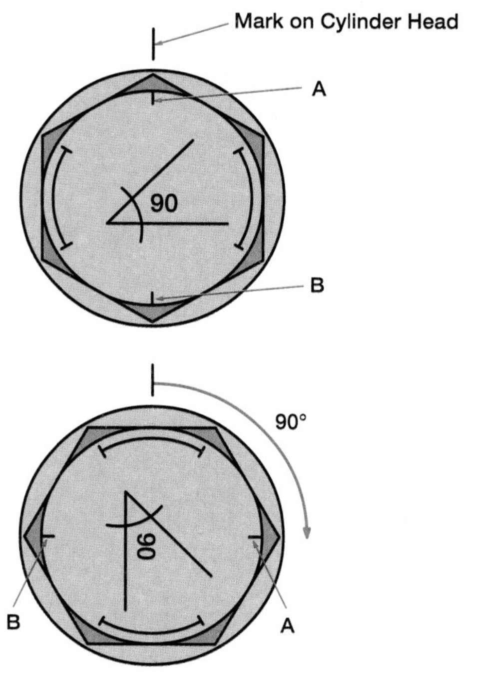

FIGURE 11-43 The torque-turn method requires a bolt to receive an initial preload using a torque wrench. Then the bolt is turned several additional degrees, flats, or turns.

bolt. While the bolt usually is higher than a grade 8 tensile strength, the threads are annealed to soften them so they strip less easily.

Studs Versus Bolts

Some applications or high-performance modifications use studs rather than bolts. There are several advantages to using studs. First, studs are often made to higher tensile strengths than stock bolts, permitting higher clamping forces. Also, a stud installed in the cylinder head is far less likely to break when removed.

Studs also can provide an even more consistent clamping force than bolts. With threads at each end, studs are initially finger tightened into the block. After the cylinder head and gasket are installed, torque is applied to a nut. Unlike a bolt, which is reacting to two separate twisting forces on the bolt head and threads in the block, the stud will stretch only on the vertical axis when the nut is tightened. Rotational force on the stud is avoided and clamping force is directly translated from the torque applied to the nut. This provides a more even clamping force on the cylinder head.

Cylinder Head Gaskets

The **cylinder head gasket** is arguably the most important seal in the diesel engine. The head gasket must maintain the seal around the combustion chamber at peak operating temperatures and pressures as well as seal compression air, coolants, and engine oil at their respective peak temperatures and pressures. The design and materials used must be thermally and chemically resistant to the products of combustion and to the coolants and oils used in the engine.

The most widely used materials include:

- Steel
- Stainless steel
- Fiber-based composition materials
- Graphite
- Numerous chemical formulations containing silicone, fluoropolymers, nitriles, neoprenes, polymeric resins, polytetrafluorothylene (PTFE or Teflon®), and others

Traditional copper and brass were replaced by metal and asbestos gaskets during the 1950s. Composite metal fiber or graphite composite gaskets superseded these gaskets in the 1980s. Since the early 1990s, those gasket systems have largely been replaced by the development of the **multilayer steel (MLS) gasket**. An MLS gasket is the preferred method of sealing between cylinder head and engine block. Today an estimated 80% of new engines are designed with MLS gaskets as standard equipment. In the MLS system, multiple thin layers of cold-rolled, spring-grade stainless steel are coated with elastomeric (rubber) material. The resilient elastomer is necessary to the gasket structure to provide microsealing of metal surface imperfections while making the gasket chemically resistant to aggressive combustion gases, oils, and coolants **FIGURE 11-44**.

Advantages of an MLS gasket include the following:

- Uniform loading distribution on sealing beads
- Constant operation thickness

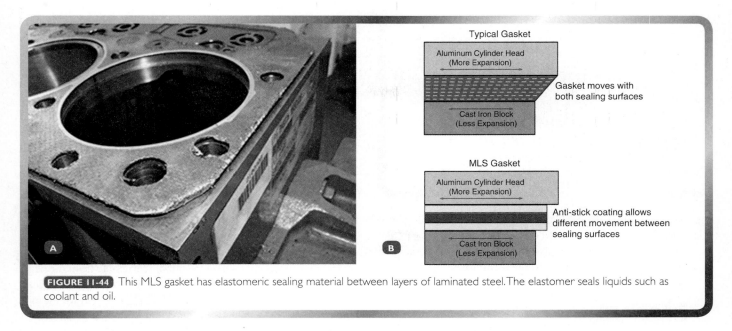

FIGURE 11-44 This MLS gasket has elastomeric sealing material between layers of laminated steel. The elastomer seals liquids such as coolant and oil.

- High crush strength
- Low relaxation coefficient
- Reduced clamp load requirement resulting in diminished cylinder bore distortion
- High strength for increased durability
- Do not require retorquing after engine run-in

Cylinder bores are commonly sealed by a ring of stainless steel positioned over a wire around the perimeter of the combustion chamber. This is known as the fire ring because it is directly exposed to combustion. This ring is critical to sealing the combustion chamber in high-pressure situations. Graphite or rubber facings are applied to a head gasket for sealing liquids. Graphite is especially useful on aluminum-headed engines because it allows the head to slide or creep easily. This is especially important when an aluminum head is used over a cast iron block because they have different expansion coefficients. Surface finish of the block deck and cylinder head is a critical factor when installing gaskets. If the surface is too smooth, the gasket will be unable to properly grip the cylinder head and block deck surfaces, and the gasket will tend to slip, resulting in combustion leaks. If the surface is too rough, the gasket may be unable to fill in the voids between the metal peaks and valleys. These voids can form leak paths for fluids and combustion gases.

Head Gasket Replacement

To prevent warping of cylinder heads, damaged bolts and threads, and gasket leakage, consistent and adequate clamping of cylinder heads is necessary. A traditional technique for clamping cylinder heads to the block requires the use of a torque wrench and a spiral pattern sequence for torqueing the head bolts down in the correct sequence. Starting at the center of the cylinder head and working out, this technique prevents pinching of the head gasket by ensuring an even spreading out of the gasket along the block deck surface. Any bolt-tightening sequence should take the cylinder head down in a minimum of three progressive steps of torque, and five or six steps is not uncommon **FIGURE 11-45**. Reversing this pattern when removing a cylinder head will prevent warping of the head. It is especially important to follow this practice in the case of aluminum cylinder heads.

After removing a cylinder head, it should be checked for warping. No more than generally 0.006″ (0.015 mm) of warping is allowed on a cylinder head. Manufacturers' specifications and techniques will vary. Diesel engines are allowed very little removal of material from the cylinder head or block deck during resurfacing because machining will cause valve-to-piston interference **FIGURE 11-46**.

While diesel engine cylinder heads are ruggedly built, they can be warped and cracked by incorrect liner protrusions. A liner flange that protrudes too far above the block deck can allow combustion gases and coolant to leak because the head gasket doesn't seal properly, and it can also distort the cylinder head. Remember that the clamping forces of 36–42 head bolts can add up to over 1,000,000 lb (453,592 kg) of force applied by

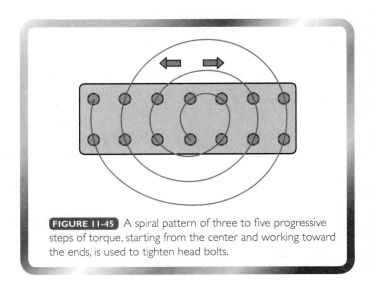

FIGURE 11-45 A spiral pattern of three to five progressive steps of torque, starting from the center and working toward the ends, is used to tighten head bolts.

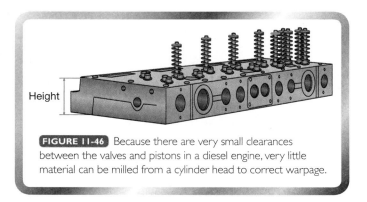

FIGURE 11-46 Because there are very small clearances between the valves and pistons in a diesel engine, very little material can be milled from a cylinder head to correct warpage.

the head to the block deck through the gasket. A protruding liner allows those forces to be exerted on a small area **FIGURE 11-47**.

Cylinder heads should also be inspected for cracking. Several techniques are available to the technician:

- Dye penetrant
- Magnetic flux
- Pressure testing

An effective method for checking for head gasket and combustion leakage into coolant from a cracked cylinder head is to check for a continuous release of gas bubbles from the cooling system **FIGURE 11-48**. After warming up the engine, a hose is connected to the coolant overflow pipe at the pressure cap. The other end of the hose is then submerged in a bottle of water and the amount of gases continuously released from the surge tank or radiator overflow is observed. In a normal engine, there will be a small amount of gas bubbles released in a steady stream as some coolant continuously vaporizes. However, a large and steady stream of bubbles indicates combustion leakage into the cooling system, which requires further diagnosis. A defective air compressor head gasket or air-operated device connected to the cooling system can be eliminated as a cause by opening the air tank drain valves while the engine is operating. Because system air pressure cannot build, little or no air will enter the cooling system if a defect exists in one of these accessories. Cavitated liners can also leak combustion gases into the cooling system, but they tend to produce hydrostatic locks after the engine is shut down when hot.

A head gasket leaking coolant into the engine can quickly cause catastrophic engine damage because coolant will easily displace and allow oil film shearing or separation on engine bearings. To check for an internal head gasket leak, a scheduled oil sampling can detect coolant in the oil. However, to pinpoint the source of a leak such as a leaking liner O-ring or head gasket, the engine oil is drained and the oil pan removed. After pressurizing the cooling system with a radiator pressure tester, one can easily inspect the internal parts of an engine from the crankcase and identify where coolant is leaking.

If a cylinder head is suspected of being cracked or leaking, often the over-pressurization of the cooling system presents itself only after an engine has run very hard for some time and thermal expansion opens a crack. If this is the case, the cylinder head can be removed and pressure tested in a hot tank with special fixtures that supply pressurized air into the intake and exhaust ports where leak paths are formed. In the tank, the head is sealed by the fixtures to prevent leakage out the valve ports and then it is carefully inspected for any leaking air bubbles. Cracks are easily detected by observing where the bubbles originate from the head.

Cylinder head cracks often develop between the valve seats after an engine has overheated **FIGURE 11-49**. When the head is removed, the valves are also removed and the seat areas visually inspected. Always use an appropriate lifting sling to remove and reinstall cylinder heads **FIGURE 11-50**. Dye penetrant testing, which is a three-step process that allows dye to penetrate cracks to make them more visible, is a convenient way to identify casting cracks. A magnetic flux technique is another method that uses a powerful magnet and iron filings to identify cracks. In this method, a cylinder head is magnetized by either AC current using a specialized piece of equipment or a strong magnet placed on either side of a suspected crack. Iron filings are then blown onto the area using a small squeeze bulb filled with filings. Because cracks will develop a north and south polarity, the filings will line up end to end along a crack, which enables the crack to be easily observed.

▶ TECHNICIAN TIP

When removing a cylinder head, the best technique to prevent warping a cylinder head is to remove the head bolts starting at each end of the cylinder head. Alternately removing a bolt from each end while working toward the center in a spiral-like pattern minimizes the likelihood of the cylinder head lifting, twisting, and warping. This sequence is the reverse of the sequence used to torque a cylinder head.

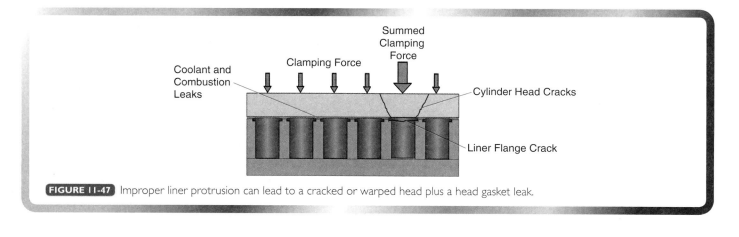

FIGURE 11-47 Improper liner protrusion can lead to a cracked or warped head plus a head gasket leak.

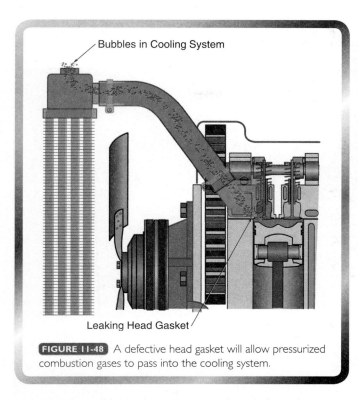

FIGURE 11-48 A defective head gasket will allow pressurized combustion gases to pass into the cooling system.

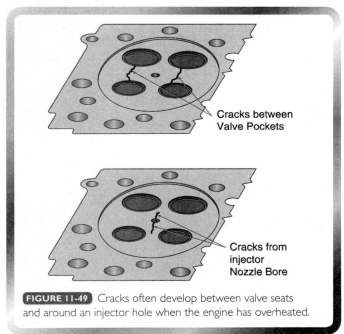

FIGURE 11-49 Cracks often develop between valve seats and around an injector hole when the engine has overheated.

Measuring Cylinder Head Warpage

Before installing a cylinder head, the casting should be checked for warpage to prevent a head gasket leak FIGURE 11-51. A warped cylinder head will not clamp against the block deck properly and allow the gasket to seal properly. If an engine has overheated, a leak has occurred, or liner protrusions have not been properly established after the head has been installed, it is particularly important to check the deck surface for warpage.

To measure cylinder head warpage, follow the steps in SKILL DRILL 11-1.

FIGURE 11-50 A lifting sling is used to remove and reinstall cylinder heads. The sling is adjustable to keep the head balanced and level.

Gear Train Mechanisms

To coordinate the movement of the crankshaft with the camshaft and the valves, a gear train or valve timing mechanism is used. The gear train may also transfer power from the crankshaft to operate fuel injection apparatuses, lubrication, power steering and coolant pumps, accessory drive mechanisms, and even power takeoff pumps. The high driving forces and **torsional vibration**, which is the speeding up and slowing down of the crankshaft caused by alternating compression and power strokes of the engine cylinder, of heavy-duty diesels means gears are the mechanisms of choice. Chains and even belts are used on automotive light-duty diesels.

Noise from gear rattle caused by torsional vibration can be dampened by **scissor gears**. These are two-piece gears that are spring loaded to keep the gears meshed in a constant state of tension. Spring loading the drive gears eliminates gear lash,

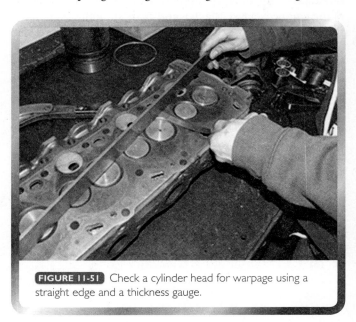

FIGURE 11-51 Check a cylinder head for warpage using a straight edge and a thickness gauge.

SKILL DRILL 11-1 Measuring Cylinder Head Warpage

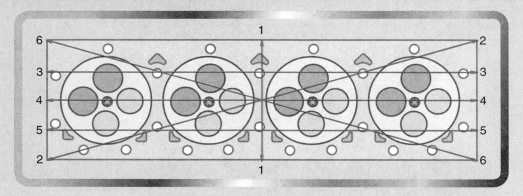

① Thoroughly clean the cylinder head and block deck surfaces with solvent. Remove any foreign material, gasket, or silicone with a cleaning pad. Choose a cleaning pad that removes soft material but not metal; this will protect the casting surfaces from damage that more aggressive abrasives and tools can cause.

② Use a purpose-made straight edge. Lay the straight edge along the flat cylinder head surface. Try to slide a feeler gauge or thickness gauge between the straight edge and the casting. Any gaps between the straight edge and the surface indicate warpage of the head deck. A general specification allows no more than 0.006" (0.152 mm) of warpage in 12" (30 cm) of casting surface when using MLS gaskets. This means a 0.006" (0.152 mm) thickness gauge should generally be used to check for warpage, but check the manufacturer's specifications to be sure. Much smaller

clearances are permissible on smaller heads used in automobile engines.

③ Check for warpage in the longitudinal and diagonal directions as well as across the head deck. Follow the chart in this box when measuring.

④ If the feeler blade slipped beneath the straight edge and there is little resistance when pulling on the blade, it has indicates a depression or warpage of the head surface. If the clearance is beyond specifications, make a service recommendation for the cylinder head to be resurfaced by a machine shop. Note, though, that due to the small clearance space between valves and pistons on diesel engines, very little, if any, material can be machined from the cylinder head to correct warpage. Always check specifications for head thickness if a head has been machined.

⑤ Check the cylinder block deck using the same procedures as checking the cylinder head.

which minimizes gear train noise **FIGURE 11-52**. Rear gear trains are the most common gear train available on contemporary diesels. Torsional vibration is reduced at the flywheel end of the engine because the flywheel mass smoothes out crankshaft velocity changes. Gear train noise and gear wear is kept to a minimum with a rear gear train. More accurate valve timing and injection action is possible because more consistent camshaft speed is possible with reduced gear rattle keeps.

▶ TECHNICIAN TIP

Loss of engine coolant or excessive cooling system pressure can often be attributed to a cylinder head gasket leaking externally or internally or a cracked cylinder head. Air bubbles originating from the engine block will appear in the radiator, and pressure will build rapidly in the cooling system, which will cause the engine to lose coolant or even push coolant out of the engine under heavy load. Technicians can check for hydrocarbons or carbon monoxide in the gas bubbles on gasoline engines but not diesels, because only air is present in the cylinders during compression stroke. Test kits that measure carbon dioxide gas in coolant are used to evaluate gas bubbles in diesels.

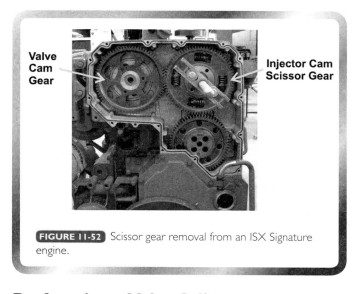

FIGURE 11-52 Scissor gear removal from an ISX Signature engine.

Performing a Valve Adjustment

As valve seats, faces, and the tip of a valve stem wear, the clearances between the valve stem and rocker lever change. The camshaft and other valve train parts can wear as well, which changes the timing of valve opening and closing. As this happens, the engine's ability to move air in and exhaust gases out changes. The length of each stroke changes and engine operation deteriorates, with power output dropping, engine brakes not working as effectively, and fuel consumption and emissions increasing. Today's engines use valve angles and valve train materials that are extremely wear resistant, which means the need to adjust the valves is less frequent that just a few years ago. In fact, adjusting valve lash is a procedure done less frequently than simply checking the valve lash. Today's valve bridges are universally nonadjustable and few engines in service use adjustable bridges or crossheads.

To perform a valve adjustment for an inline six cylinder engine with a firing sequence of 1-5-3-6-2-4, follow the steps in **SKILL DRILL 11-2**. This procedure is outlined with the assumption that there is no engine compression release brake on the engine.

Pendulum Vibration Absorbers

In addition to scissor gears and viscous dampeners, which are used to provide torsional vibration dampening for the gear train and camshaft, pendulum dampeners are a unique torsional

SKILL DRILL 11-2 Performing a Valve Adjustment

Cylinder	1		2		3		4		5		6	
Valves	E	I	E	I	E	I	E	I	E	I	E	I
Cylinder 1 TDC	X	X	O	X	X	O	O	X	X	O	O	O
Cylinder 6 TDC	O	O	X	O	O	X	X	O	O	X	X	X

1. Clean the upper engine with a pressure washer.

2. Locate original equipment manufacturer (OEM) service literature for valve adjustment procedures.

3. Unless the manufacturer indicates that their valve adjustment specifications are for warmed engines, lash should adjusted on a cold engine. If the OEM indicates a warm engine is required, bring the engine operating temperature to 140°F (60°C).

4. Remove the valve cover or rocker housing cover(s). Position the engine at top dead center (TDC) unless otherwise indicated. Use the companion cylinder method to find TDC for the end of compression stroke for cylinder 1. This is done by positioning the engine at TDC. Cylinder 6, the companion of cylinder 1, should have two tight rocker levers because the valves should both be open as the engine moves through overlap position. If not, rotate the engine 360 degrees and recheck. Cylinder 1 should have both valves closed because it is finishing compression stroke and beginning power stroke. At TDC position, half of the valves can be adjusted. Use the chart in this box to find the adjustable valves.

5. With the engine at cylinder 1 TDC (end of compression stroke), check the valve clearance by inserting the correct thickness gauge between the rocker lever and the valve stem or bridge. The blade should slide between the two machined surfaces easily, but a light amount of drag should be felt when pulling and removing the blade. If the setting is correct, mark the rocker with a yellow crayon marker. Follow this sequence for all valves that can be adjusted at cylinder 1 TDC.

6. Rotate the engine 360 degrees in the correct direction of rotation until cylinder 6 is at TDC (end of compression

stroke). Cylinder 1 should be on overlap and both rocker levers should be tight because the valves are both open. Both rocker levers should be loose on cylinder 6.

7. Repeat the procedure for checking the adjustment for the remaining intake and exhaust valves.

8. If the lash is too loose or tight, it needs to be adjusted to the correct clearance. To adjust valve lash, loosen and back off the locknut on the rocker adjusting screw. Initially back off the adjusting screw for the rocker lever as well.

9. Screw down the adjusting screw until the rocker lever clearance just disappears. Next, back off the adjusting screw sufficiently to insert the correct size thickness gauge.

10. Turn the adjusting screw down again until a moderate amount of resistance is felt after the screw makes contact with the valve stem or bridge. This step actually overtightens the screw and reduces the amount of valve clearance.

11. Check the thickness gauge drag. If the drag is acceptable, snug up the locknut while holding the screwdriver to prevent rotation of the adjusting screw and maintain correct lash clearance. Tightening the lock nut will pull on the threads of the adjusting screw and increase clearances slightly. After tightening the lock nut, the correct valve lash clearance should be established.

12. Torque the lock nut to the correct OEM specifications.

13. Reinstall rocker housing cover(s) following manufacturer's procedure. Most current on-highway diesel engines use rocker housing cover gaskets that are reusable provided they are installed clean and torqued correctly.

dampener. Unlike regular balancers, pendulum vibration absorbers provide torsional control by producing forces that directly cancel the forces producing torsional vibration. Steel rollers called centrifugal pendulums fit loosely into a specific number of holes in either a harmonic balancer or overhead cam drive gear. The rollers store and release energy back into the crankshaft rather than converting the mechanical energy into heat energy as dampers do. A patented mathematical algorithm is used to calculate roller size, hole size, and gear size to determine how the rollers will move forward during compression strokes when the crank slows and roll backward during the power stroke. Movement of the rollers back and forth minimizes engine speed changes to the camshaft, keeping torsional vibration low. Manufacturers claim the pendulum dampener provides a smoother-running engine and increases valve train stability while offering more accurate injection timing. Pendulum dampeners have the added advantage of being lighter than conventional dampeners.

Wrap-Up

Ready for Review

▶ The cylinder head is a metal casting that attaches to the top of the cylinder block and seals the combustion chamber so the engine can develop and contain compression and combustion pressure.

▶ Cylinder heads are commonly made of cast iron alloys because of their superior strength, ease of manufacture, machinability, and capability to withstand high temperatures; aluminum and compacted graphite iron are other materials commonly used for cylinder heads.

▶ Because intake and exhaust port arrangements influence gas flow and turbulence, or swirl, into the cylinders, the configuration of these ports is important for reducing emissions and used to classify cylinder heads.

▶ Cylinder heads can also be classified by their number of pieces; single-piece cylinder head castings and multiple-piece cylinder heads both have advantages and disadvantages.

▶ Cylinder heads are further classified by the arrangement of the valve train mechanism; the camshaft arrangements in diesel engines are commonly one of two types—overhead camshaft or in–block camshaft.

▶ Intake and exhaust valves allow air into and out of an engine; diesel engines usually have two or four valves per cylinder, but a number of engines may use three or five valves.

▶ Pushrods transmit the cam actuation force from the followers to the rocker levers.

▶ Rocker arms convert the linear change of the cam profile to the reciprocating motion used to open and close the valves.

▶ To actuate more than one valve with a single rocker lever, most four-valve engines use a crosshead, also called a yoke or bridge, to exert the camshaft force against the valve stem.

▶ Camshafts are critical components to engine performance because they control the gas dynamics or engine breathing characteristics.

▶ Because of the higher cylinder pressures, consistent bolt clamping force is a critical maintenance issue for diesel engines.

▶ In some applications or high-performance modifications, studs rather than bolts are used.

▶ The cylinder head gasket is arguably the most important seal in the diesel engine; to prevent warping of cylinder heads, damaged bolts and threads, and gasket leakage, adequate and consistent clamping force of the cylinder head is necessary.

▶ To coordinate the movement of the crankshaft with the camshaft and the valves, a gear train or valve timing mechanism is used; the gear train may also transfer power from the crankshaft to operate fuel injection apparatuses,

lubrication, power steering and coolant pumps, accessory drive mechanisms, and even power takeoff pumps.

▶ Pendulum dampeners provide torsional control by producing forces that directly cancel the forces producing torsional vibration.

Vocabulary Builder

compacted graphite iron (CGI) A material produced from powdered iron alloys squeezed into molds at high pressures and then heated to bond the metal particles together; also known as sintered graphite.

cross-flow cylinder head A head design with the intake and exhaust manifolds located on opposite sides of an inline engine to improve engine breathing characteristics.

cylinder head gasket The component that maintains the seal around the combustion chamber at peak operating temperatures and pressures and keeps air, coolants, and engine oil in their respective passages over all temperatures and pressures.

in-block camshaft An engine that has only the valves, rocker levers, and bridges located in the cylinder heads above the piston; the camshaft is located in the engine block. The cam may be a low or high mounted type. Also called a pushrod engine.

multilayer steel (MLS) gasket A method of sealing the cylinder head to the engine block using multiple thin layers of cold-rolled, spring-grade stainless steel coated with elastomeric (rubber) material.

overhead camshaft engine An engine that has the camshaft located in the cylinder head.

parallel flow head A head design that features intake and exhaust manifolds on the same side of the engine and short, large ports that are joined together to provide a more compact engine design with adequate airflow to the cylinders; also known as the uniflow design.

reverse-flow cylinder head A cylinder head with no exhasut manifolds on the outside of the cylinder head; instead, short exhaust runs are fed directly to the turbocharger located in the V between the cylinder banks.

scissor gear Two separate spring-loaded gears incorporated into a single unit to reduce gear rattle caused by torsional vibration.

torque-turn method A method that requires a bolt to receive an initial preload using a torque wrench; afterward, the bolt is turned several additional degrees, flats, or turns. Also called the torque plus angle method.

torque-to-yield (TTY) bolts Cylinder head bolts that are tightened past their yield strength or elastic point; when tightened to specification, they stretch to a point just over precisely calibrated yield strength and not to the tensile where the bolt will break.

torsional vibration The speeding up and slowing down of the crankshaft caused by alternating compression and power strokes of the engine cylinder.

valve overlap The angle in crankshaft degrees that both the intake and exhaust valves are open; overlap occurs at the end of the exhaust stroke and the beginning of the intake stroke.

Review Questions

1. The _____ is an engine that has only the valves, rocker levers, and bridges located in the cylinder heads above the piston; the camshaft is located in the engine block.
   a. in-block camshaft
   b. overhead camshaft engine
   c. cross-flow cylinder head
   d. reverse-flow cylinder head

2. A(n) _____ is a head design that features intake and exhaust manifolds on the same side of the engine and short, large ports that are joined together to provide a more compact engine design with adequate airflow to the cylinders.
   a. reverse-flow cylinder head
   b. parallel flow head
   c. cross-flow cylinder head
   d. in-block camshaft

3. A(n) _____ is a head design with the intake and exhaust manifolds located on opposite sides of an engine to improve engine breathing characteristics.
   a. reverse-flow cylinder head
   b. parallel cylinder head
   c. cross-flow cylinder head
   d. in-block camshaft

4. The _____ is an engine that has the camshaft located in the cylinder head.
   a. overhead camshaft engine
   b. in-block camshaft engine
   c. in-head camshaft engine
   d. top-head camshaft engine

5. The _____ is a cylinder head with no exhaust manifolds on the outside of the cylinder head; instead, short exhaust runs are fed directly to the turbocharger located in the V between the cylinder banks.
   a. parallel flow head
   b. in-block camshaft
   c. cross-flow cylinder head
   d. reverse-flow cylinder head

6. The size, number, and grade of bolts are increased in _____.
   a. four-stroke diesels
   b. two-stroke diesels
   c. spark-ignition engines
   d. gasoline-fueled engines

7. On a four-stroke engine, the cam gear rotates at _____ the engine speed as the crank gear.
   a. half
   b. two times
   c. equal
   d. two and a half times

8. Cylinder head bolts use specialized _____.
   a. formed threads
   b. cut threads
   c. forged threads
   d. rolled threads

9. When made from compacted graphite iron, diesel cylinder heads weigh _____ aluminum.
   a. significantly more than
   b. slightly more than
   c. less than
   d. approximately the same as

10. _____ premium diesel engines use replacement valve seat inserts.
    a. All
    b. Some
    c. Many
    d. None of the above

ASE-Type Questions

1. Technician A says single-piece cylinder head castings are more likely to experience head gasket failure at the rear of the engine where coolant temperatures are hottest. Technician B says the castings are not any more likely to experience head gasket failure at the rear of the engine. Who is correct?
   a. Technician A
   b. Technician B
   c. Both Technician A and Technician B
   d. Neither Technician A nor Technician B

2. Technician A says that all diesel engines use replaceable valve guides. Technician B says all premium diesel engines use replaceable valve guides. Who is correct?
   a. Technician A
   b. Technician B
   c. Both Technician A and Technician B
   d. Neither Technician A nor Technician B

3. Technician A says that rotating a valve slightly each time it opens can eliminate hot spots that can lead to valve burning. Technician B says that rotating there is nothing that can be done to effectively eliminate hot spots. Who is correct?
   a. Technician A
   b. Technician B
   c. Both Technician A and Technician B
   d. Neither Technician A nor Technician B

4. Technician A says overhead camshaft engines often use two camshafts. Technician B says some overhead camshaft engines will use a separate camshaft for the injectors. Who is correct?
   a. Technician A
   b. Technician B
   c. Both Technician A and Technician B
   d. Neither Technician A nor Technician B

5. Technician A says a traditional technique for clamping cylinder heads to the block requires the use of a torque wrench to tighten the head bolts. Technician B says the head bolts must be tightened in a spiral pattern sequence. Who is correct?
   a. Technician A
   b. Technician B
   c. Both Technician A and Technician B
   d. Neither Technician A nor Technician B

6. Technician A says that an in-block camshaft arrangement has rockers that directly contact the camshaft. Technician B says that an in-block camshaft arrangement does not use pushrods. Who is correct?
   a. Technician A
   b. Technician B
   c. Both Technician A and Technician B
   d. Neither Technician A nor Technician B

7. Technician A says that to thoroughly clean cylinder head and block surfaces, you must choose a cleaning pad that removes both soft material and metal. Technician B says that to clean the cylinder head and block surfaces, you must choose a cleaning pad that removes soft material but not metal in order to protect the casting surfaces from damage. Who is correct?
   a. Technician A
   b. Technician B
   c. Both Technician A and Technician B
   d. Neither Technician A nor Technician B

8. Technician A says to measure cylinder head warpage, you should check in the longitudinal and diagonal directions as well as across the head deck. Technician B says to measure cylinder head warpage, you should check in the latitudinal and diagonal directions as well across the head deck. Who is correct?
   a. Technician A
   b. Technician B
   c. Both Technician A and Technician B
   d. Neither Technician A nor Technician B

9. Technician A says dye penetrant and pressure testing are used to check cylinder heads for cracks. Technician B says that magnetic flux and is used to check cylinder heads for cracks. Who is correct?
   a. Technician A
   b. Technician B
   c. Both Technician A and Technician B
   d. Neither Technician A nor Technician B

10. Technician A says an estimated 50% of new engines are designed with multilayer steel gaskets as standard equipment. Technician B says that all new engines are designed with multilayer steel gaskets as standard equipment. Who is correct?
    a. Technician A
    b. Technician B
    c. Both Technician A and Technician B
    d. Neither Technician A nor Technician B

CHAPTER 12
Diesel Engine Lubrication Systems

NATEF Tasks

Diesel Engines

General

- Inspect fuel, oil, Diesel Exhaust Fluid (DEF) and coolant levels, and condition; determine needed action. (pp 349–354)
- Identify engine fuel, oil, coolant, air, and other leaks; determine needed action. (pp 352–356)

Lubrication Systems

- Test engine oil pressure and check operation of pressure sensor, gauge, and/or sending unit; test engine oil temperature and check operation of temperature sensor; determine needed action. (pp 342–343, 352–353)
- Check engine oil level, condition, and consumption; determine needed action. (pp 339, 349–353)
- Inspect and measure oil pump, drives, inlet pipes, and pick-up screens; check drive gear clearances; determine needed action. (pp 340–341)
- Inspect oil pressure regulator valve(s), bypass and pressure relief valve(s), oil thermostat, and filters; determine needed action. (pp 341–347)
- Inspect, clean, and test oil cooler and components; determine needed action. (pp 342–343)

Knowledge Objectives

After reading this chapter, you will be able to:

1. Explain the operating principles of diesel engine lubrication systems. (pp 337–338)
2. Describe the purpose, properties, function, composition, types, and applications of diesel engine lubricating oils. (pp 338–343)
3. Identify and describe the types, functions, construction features, and applications of diesel engine lubrication system components. (pp 346–355)
4. Recommend service and maintenance of lubrication oils. (pp 355–360)
5. Describe the inspection and testing procedures for a diesel engine lubrication system. (pp 360–364)

Skills Objectives

After reading this chapter, you will be able to:

1. Replace a spin-on oil filter. (p 358) **SKILL DRILL 12-1**
2. Locate an oil leak. (p 363) **SKILL DRILL 12-2**
3. Replace a rear main oil seal. (p 364) **SKILL DRILL 12-3**

► Introduction

Friction produced by moving engine parts at high speed under load for even a few minutes can generate enough heat to melt and severely damage engine parts **FIGURE 12-1**. Without lubricant to minimize the effects of friction, the engine would be quickly destroyed and or seize. The lubrication system performs not only the obvious requirement to reduce friction between moving parts but is essential for cooling, cleaning, assist sealing piston rings, and absorbing shock loads inside the engine **FIGURE 12-2** and **FIGURE 12-3**. Lubrication systems in today's diesels also have new demands imposed by emission legislation accompanied by increased durability requirements. Oils also now need to be compatible with the latest exhaust aftertreatment systems and biofuels while meeting customers' expectations for longer oil drain intervals to reduce operating

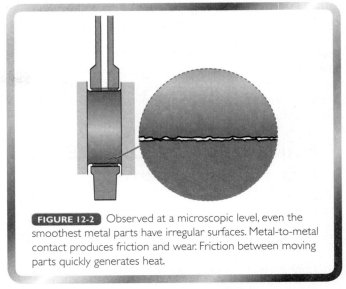

FIGURE 12-2 Observed at a microscopic level, even the smoothest metal parts have irregular surfaces. Metal-to-metal contact produces friction and wear. Friction between moving parts quickly generates heat.

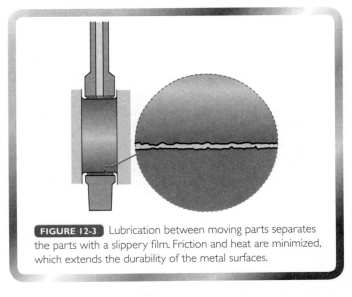

FIGURE 12-3 Lubrication between moving parts separates the parts with a slippery film. Friction and heat are minimized, which extends the durability of the metal surfaces.

FIGURE 12-1 This crankshaft journal was damaged because of lack of lubrication. The oil feed hole is plugged with bearing material, which melted during engine operation.

You Are the Technician

A number of trucks you service at your repair center haul time-sensitive loads, which means there is almost no tolerance for breakdowns on the road. To ensure these vehicles do not experience any kind of mechanical problems when in service, you have been tasked with developing a preventative maintenance (PM) schedule and identifying inspection and service criteria to present to customers as part of a maintenance agreement. Part of PM involves lubrication system service. As you prepare the maintenance schedule, consider the following:

1. Identify potential problems with the lubrication system that could lead to a breakdown or road service call.
2. Outline maintenance practices and inspection points of the lubrication system requiring attention during PM services. Explain your service recommendations.
3. Outline some of the more important factors of lubrication system maintenance that promote extending engine life and reliability.

costs. In this chapter, the function of the lubrication system is examined along with the operation of components performing the various tasks required of the lubrication system. A thorough knowledge of the operation of the lubrication system will assist the repair technician in making correct recommendations for service and maintenance of this important engine system to ensure reliable engine operation and maximum vehicle durability.

▶ Fundamentals of Diesel Engine Lubrication Systems

Lubrication systems in a diesel engine are designed to operate and accomplish the following tasks:

1. Reduce friction between moving parts to minimize engine wear and the creation of heat.

2. Cool a variety of internal engine parts and remove some heat from the engine.

3. Remove dirt, abrasives, and contaminants from inside the engine.

4. Assist sealing of the combustion chamber by forming a film between the piston rings and the cylinder wall. Some seals perform better with a film of lubricant on rotating surfaces.

5. Absorb shock loads between bearings and gears, thus cushioning and protecting engine parts while minimizing engine noise production.

6. Store an adequate supply of oil for lubricating internal engine parts.

7. Minimize corrosion of internal engine components.

▶ Fundamentals of Engine Oil
Friction and Lubrication

A typical lubricant molecule consists of a long chain of carbon and hydrogen atoms. Because even the most highly polished metal surfaces are rough and irregular at a microscopic level, moving surfaces need to be separated to avoid wear and friction. Oil works by forming a separating film between parts to minimize direct contact between moving parts. Because

oil is slippery, it reduces friction and heat build-up caused by friction. Oil is capable of separating moving parts because its molecules behave like billions of tiny ball bearings that physically separate moving metal surfaces **FIGURE 12-4**. At a molecular level, the forces attracting oil molecules to metal surfaces are greater than the forces causing oil molecules to adhere to one another. This permits lubricants to adhere to the irregular surface of metal yet easily slide over other lubricant molecules.

Oil Classification

Oil is commonly classified by its application. Depending on its use, oil may be derived from biological sources such as fish, vegetables, or animal fat. More often lubricating oil, even synthetic oil, is primarily a product of petroleum refined from crude oil, also called mineral oil, which originates from the ground. <u>Base stock</u> is the raw mineral processed from crude oil, while <u>synthetic oil</u> is made from base stock that is synthetically derived or manufactured.

Mineral oils contain a variety of different hydrocarbon molecules that have different sizes, shapes, and lubricating qualities. This means they will perform and respond differently to heat, pressure, and other engine operating factors. To be approved for the operating conditions and the unique technologies of various manufacturers, engines oils are classified by the <u>American Petroleum Institute (API)</u> and will carry the API designation indicating their suitability for an engine application. Given the variations of engine technology plus potentially different oil characteristics and qualities, the API has developed specifications to define what engine oil performance standards are. For example, engines using high-speed turbochargers and recirculating exhaust gases into the combustion chamber will place different demands on oil than that used to lubricate a naturally aspirated engine with little or no emission controls.

Two distinct classifications of oils are recognized by API performance specifications. S-series oils are designed to meet performance standards for spark ignition systems, while C-series oils meet compression ignition engine performance requirements. C- and S-series oils are distinctly formulated due to the combustion by-products of gasoline and diesel fuel combustion.

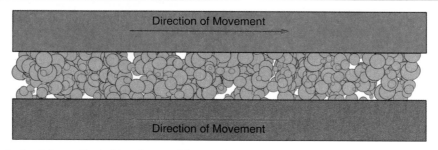

FIGURE 12-4 Oil lubrication behaves like ball bearings, enabling metal surfaces to slide over one another without metal-to-metal contact.

TECHNICIAN TIP

When changing engine oil, the recommended API service classification must be used. The API service classification is marked on any bottle or jug of engine oil suitable for internal combustion engines. Diesel engine API classifications always begin with the letter C. The most recent API designation is CJ-4, which is required by all light-duty tier 5 bin 2, medium-duty, and heavy-duty diesels manufactured in North America since 2007 that use exhaust particulate filters. There is a new oil due out in January 2016 that is currently called PC-11—the PC stands for proposed category. PC-11 will improve oil performance qualities beyond the current API CJ-4 engine oils. First proposed in 2011, this new oil, which will be designated as a CK series, will help meet new greenhouse gas regulations. It will be compatible with new biofuels and reduce engine wear for enhanced engine durability.

These API standards have progressively evolved since they were first conceived in the 1940s to meet advances in engine technology and engine manufacturers' performance requirements. The earliest API classification developed in the 1940s, which is now obsolete, was CA. Successive standards are indicated by progressive alphabetic designations: CB, CE, CD, and so on. Today's oils are highly refined petroleum products with a package of chemicals called **additives** that enable lubricating oil to meet engine operational requirements FIGURE 12-5 and FIGURE 12-6. The engine manufacturer will make the recommendation for the API classification of oil to be used in their engine. This information can be found in the vehicle's operator manual or manufacturer's service manual.

The API Service Symbol

The API service symbol and certification mark, which resembles a donut, identifies the performance standards of engine oils used in gasoline- and diesel-powered vehicles FIGURE 12-7. Engine oil carrying the API designations must be certified after specialized testing to determine whether they meet minimum API standards. Oils meeting minimum API criteria are permitted to carry the API service symbol. The donut symbol is divided into three parts:

- The top half designates the oil's performance standard set by the API test criteria.
- The center identifies the oil's <u>Society of Automotive Engineers (SAE) viscosity rating</u>. <u>Viscosity</u> is the measure of oil's thickness or resistance to flow.
- The bottom half is the API certification mark. A separate API designation is used for gasoline and diesel engines. Gasoline engines may carry a starburst symbol, whereas diesels do not. In gasoline engines, the mark or starburst symbol indicates whether the oil has demonstrated energy-conserving properties in a standard test in comparison to reference oil. The use of friction-reducing additives such as graphite, molybdenum disulfide, or other suspended materials provides energy-saving enhancements to the oils.

The API Certification Mark for Diesels

The API certification mark identifies engine oil as recommended for a specific application such as diesel or gasoline service. A global standard is also used for engine oil. DLD-1, DLD-2, and DLD-3 are global standard designations. API-rated oil qualifies to display the certification mark only if it meets the most current requirements for minimum performance standards and is licensed by the API. Intended for 2010 and later

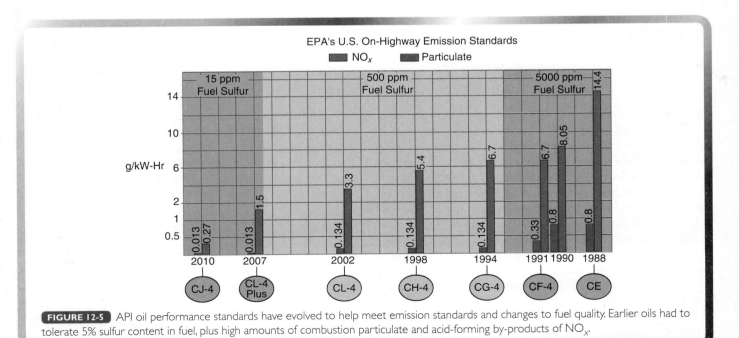

FIGURE 12-5 API oil performance standards have evolved to help meet emission standards and changes to fuel quality. Earlier oils had to tolerate 5% sulfur content in fuel, plus high amounts of combustion particulate and acid-forming by-products of NO$_x$.

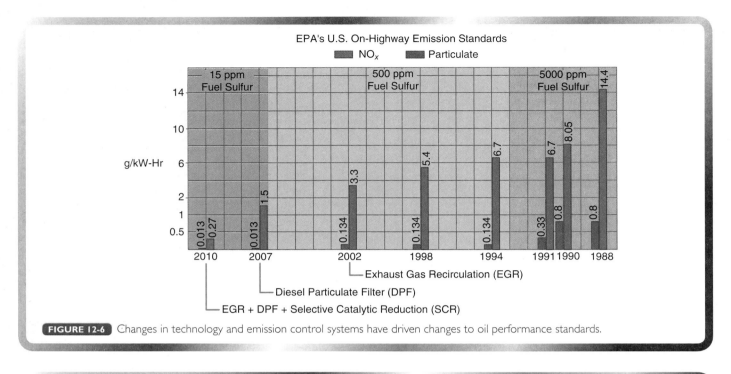

EPA's U.S. On-Highway Emission Standards
NOₓ   Particulate

FIGURE 12-6 Changes in technology and emission control systems have driven changes to oil performance standards.

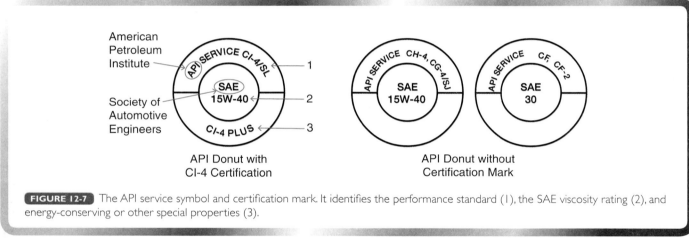

FIGURE 12-7 The API service symbol and certification mark. It identifies the performance standard (1), the SAE viscosity rating (2), and energy-conserving or other special properties (3).

diesel engines, oils meeting the API CJ-4 standard are permitted to carry the certification mark. CJ-4 was developed in the 2010 model year for engines using exhaust gas recirculation (EGR), diesel particulate filters (DPF), and selective catalyst reduction (SCR) systems. The PLUS suffix (e.g., CI-4 PLUS and CJ-4 PLUS) indicates that the oil provides a higher level of protection against changes to viscosity related to soot loading and viscosity loss due to oil molecule shear in diesel engines. This 2010 oil standard is also formulated to be compatible for diesel engine applications burning ultra-low-sulfur diesel (ULSD) fuel and to prevent poisoning and plugging of the new catalytic converter technology. Because combustion products entering the oil from blow-by around the rings is different in engines using ULSD and EGR, these oils must be capable of holding more soot with less acidic properties than high-sulfur fuel. Additionally, oil consumed in the cylinders end up in the particulate filter, where

oil additives leave ash residue that must be physically cleaned out of the filter. Since 2007 oils produce minimal ash residue that blocks exhaust gas flow through the DPF and cannot be removed by regeneration. When the DPF is loaded with ash, the filter requires removal and cleaning.

► TECHNICIAN TIP

Oil used in diesel engines turns darker more quickly than oil used in gasoline engines. Soot produced during diesel combustion will cling to the oil film on the cylinder walls and is scraped into the oil pan. Soot, which is composed primarily of black carbon, turns engine oil black. Newer engines with finer fuel atomization and engines operating consistently at high load and speed conditions will take longer to turn dark because less soot is produced.

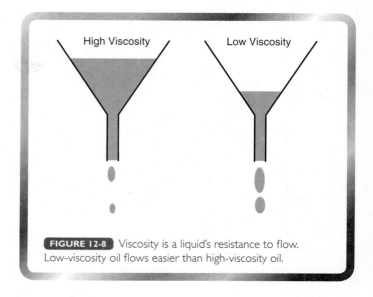

FIGURE 12-8 Viscosity is a liquid's resistance to flow. Low-viscosity oil flows easier than high-viscosity oil.

Oil Viscosity

Oil viscosity is a performance criteria defined by the SAE and not the API. Until API standards were first developed in 1947, viscosity was the only way oil was rated. The term viscosity refers to a liquid's resistance to flow **FIGURE 12-8**. A numerical designation developed by the SAE is used to measure oil viscosity. The numbers basically indicate whether a particular oil flows quickly or slowly. For example, engine oils having a viscosity with low numbers such as 0, 5, or 10 flow more easily than viscosities of 20, 30, or 50. In other words, the higher the number, the thicker the viscosity.

When it is hot, oil thins and becomes less viscous. Likewise, oil thickens and the viscosity increases as its temperature decreases **FIGURE 12-9**. When an oil's viscosity is measured at 0°F (−18°C), it is given the suffix W, indicating that it has a winter viscosity rating. This scale for measuring viscosity is known as the absolute viscosity rating. Oils tested at 212°F (100°C) are referred to as a hot or summer viscosity and no letter accompanies the viscosity grade. When tested at this temperature, the viscosity rating is known as a kinematic viscosity rating.

Multigrade Oils

Oils with only a single viscosity number are designated single-grade or single-weight oils. Single-grade oils have been made obsolete for use in any modern diesel by multiweight or **multigrade oils**. Multigrade oils can be a blend of several different oils with different viscosities or blended oil with viscosity changing additives **FIGURE 12-10**. Oil viscosity today is indicated by two numbers (e.g., 15W-40), which means they have their viscosity measured under both hot and cold conditions. The numbers provide viscosity information about the oil's performance under a wide range of operating conditions.

The first number (e.g., 15W in 15W-40) is the low-temperature viscosity, and it helps predict how well an engine might crank in cold temperatures when the oil is thick and

FIGURE 12-9 Temperature changes an oil's viscosity. Multigrade oils have a lower viscosity index than single-weight oils. That means multigrade oil viscosity does not change as dramatically with temperature.

resistance to cranking is high. Generally, a lower number means the engine will start easier in cold weather. The low-temperature or winter number also indicates how well the oil will flow to lubricate critical engine parts at cold temperatures

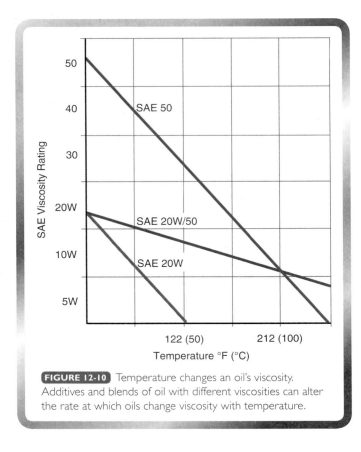

FIGURE 12-10 Temperature changes an oil's viscosity. Additives and blends of oil with different viscosities can alter the rate at which oils change viscosity with temperature.

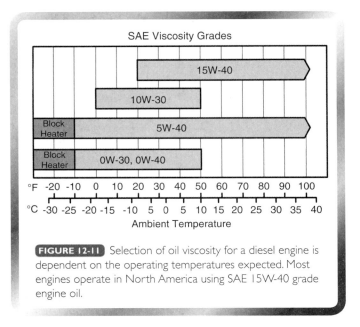

FIGURE 12-11 Selection of oil viscosity for a diesel engine is dependent on the operating temperatures expected. Most engines operate in North America using SAE 15W-40 grade engine oil.

FIGURE 12-11. Colder temperatures require oil with thinner viscosity and the use of an engine block and an oil heater when the engine is shut down. The second number (40 in 15W-40 oil) is the high-temperature viscosity, and it indicates the oil's thickness or body when it is heated. Thick oil provides good lubrication and load-bearing characteristics at normal engine operating temperatures.

Multigrade oil's main advantage is improved cold-starting characteristics with less engine drag. At operating temperature, multigrade oils decrease rotational resistance in an engine due to drag from lubricating oil. Modern engines typically operate with low oil viscosities without any detrimental effects to the engine. Many engines today are operated with 10w-30 viscosity, whereas mainly 15w-40 was used several years ago. Specialized anti-wear additives permit the use of lower viscosity oils without causing metal-to-metal contact.

▶ **TECHNICIAN TIP**

Oil classification for heavy-duty diesels and light-duty diesels is the same. However, the International Lubricant Standardization and Approval Committee (ILSAC) is working on a new light-duty specification for diesel engine oil. Both heavy- and light-duty diesels are now using oils with lower viscosity to improve fuel economy. For example, heavy-duty diesels have traditionally used 15W-40, but many now use 10W-30. Light-duty diesels typically require synthetics with viscosities of 5W-30 or 5W-40.

Viscosity Change and Viscosity Index Improver

Looking at the viscosity numbers of multigrade oil, 15W-40, it appears that the oil is thicker when hot and thinner when cold. However, this grade of oil is still thicker when cold than when hot, because a cold 15W winter viscosity scale measures differently than the 40 summer scale. Multigrade oils are formulated with a feature to control viscosity change. Because oil is made of a variety of hydrocarbon molecules, some of which are light and thin while others are thick and tar-like, changes to viscosity with temperature can occur more dramatically with some oils than others. This change is measured by the **viscosity index (VI)**, which refers to the change in oil viscosity with temperature **FIGURE 12-12**. Oil with a low VI will change viscosity faster than oil with a high VI. Oil with a low VI thickens and thins

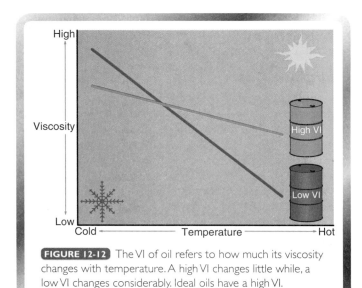

FIGURE 12-12 The VI of oil refers to how much its viscosity changes with temperature. A high VI changes little while, a low VI changes considerably. Ideal oils have a high VI.

too much with temperature change, giving it an undesirable, uneven lubrication performance. An additive ingredient called **viscosity index (VI) improver** can be used to control the VI properties of lubrication oil. The VI improver is a special hydrocarbon polymer or, more simply, a chain of atoms that changes shape with temperature. The additive prevents oil from thickening when cold and thinning when hot.

The unique property of the VI improver polymer molecule is that when cold, it coils into a ball-like shape. This means that when cold, the oil will tend to be less viscous than oil without the VI improver additive **FIGURE 12-13**. When heated, the polymer molecule stretches into a long rod, which thickens the oil. When added to oil, VI improver will counteract the oil's natural tendency to thin when hot and thicken when cold. Eventually VI improver additives wear out as the polymer chains are broken through mechanical action of shearing the oil molecules.

> ### ▶ TECHNICIAN TIP
>
> Because soot is produced during diesel combustion, diesel engine oil turns blacker more quickly than oil in gasoline engines. Soot sticks to the oil film in the cylinders and is scraped off the cylinder walls and into the crankcase by the rings. Diesel engines require more detergent and dispersant additives to prevent the soot from clumping and thickening the oil, which in turn can block oil passageways to bearings. Filters are able to remove soot from the oil when it stays in suspension.

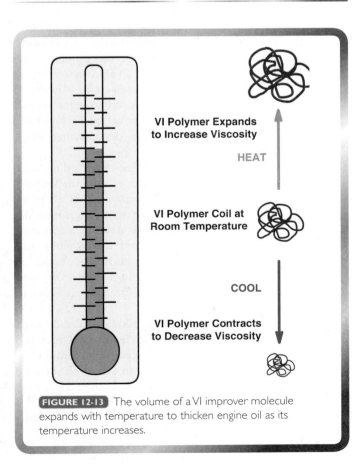

FIGURE 12-13 The volume of a VI improver molecule expands with temperature to thicken engine oil as its temperature increases.

> ### ▶ TECHNICIAN TIP
>
> Some diesel engines suddenly start to use more oil as the oil change interval is extended. Moving oil through pumps and between bearings at high pressure, and scraping oil from cylinder walls literally chops or shears the molecules of VI improver. Smaller VI improver molecules means the oil loses its viscosity faster as it warms up, resulting in increased oil consumption. Higher viscosity enables the oil to support heavy loads without damage, but it increases the energy required to pump oil. Newer engine oils contain additives that prevent metal-to-metal contact, which in turn permit the use of energy-saving lower-viscosity oil.

Oil Additives

Motor oils are comprised typically of 75–85% base stock, which is the raw mineral processed from crude oil. The remainder of the oil volume is made of chemical additives **FIGURE 12-14**.

Advantages of Oil Additives

Additives improve the original properties of base stock oil. Enhancing the performance of motor oil base stocks is necessary to adjust the performance of the oil to suit its intended application. For example, diesel engines produce higher levels of soot than gasoline engines, which is why engine oil turns black more quickly in diesels than in gasoline engines. This soot tends to clump together, leaves deposits inside the engine, and even thickens the oil. To prevent this, more detergent is added to diesel engine oil causing the soot to stay suspended in the oil **FIGURE 12-15**. To understand the function of detergents, consider washing dishes with and without detergent. Dishwater will stay dirty if it has detergent keeping the dirt suspended in the water. Without detergent, the dirt eventually settles out of the water to the bottom of the sink. By keeping soot (dirt) suspended, the filters can remove more soot from the oil and leave the engine less susceptible to sludge deposits.

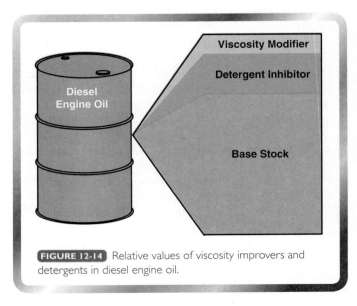

FIGURE 12-14 Relative values of viscosity improvers and detergents in diesel engine oil.

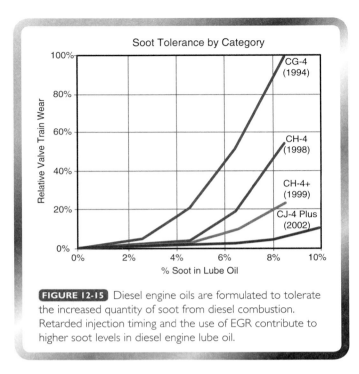

FIGURE 12-15 Diesel engine oils are formulated to tolerate the increased quantity of soot from diesel combustion. Retarded injection timing and the use of EGR contribute to higher soot levels in diesel engine lube oil.

Additives also add performance characteristics to base stock oils to suit a particular application. The use of VI improvers is an example previously mentioned. Antifoaming additives are critical to oil used in engines with hydraulically actuated unit injectors (HEUI) to prevent aeration of engine oil. Aerated oil causes changes to injection timing and pressurization of fuel, resulting in low power and poor fuel economy. Aerated oil does not lubricate parts very well and interferes with delivery of the correct oil volume to engine components.

Common Oil Additives

There are many additives commonly used in diesel engine oil:

- Pour point depressants lower oil's freezing point in cold conditions.
- Anti-wear additives protect against metal-to-metal contact under high pressure conditions when oil viscosity is low.
- Detergents and dispersants keep internal engine components clean and prevent thickening and sludging of oil.
- Oxidation inhibitors maintain oil viscosity stability between service intervals. Oil reacts with oxygen in the air by thickening, particularly with higher temperatures and form deposits.
- Corrosion and rust inhibitors protect engine parts against the effects of condensation.
- Antifoaming additives minimize oil foaming and cavitation erosion of metal parts.
- VI improvers prevent oil from thickening when cold and thinning out when hot.
- Emulsifiers prevent water from combining with engine oil.

- Reserve alkalinity additives ensure the oil does not become acidic from products of combustion. Sulfur in diesel fuel will produce corrosive effects of acids over an extended period of time.

Aftermarket Oil Additives

The cost for an oil manufacturer to test and certify engine oil to API standards easily runs into the range of hundreds of thousands of dollars. Profits made from API-certified oil, which retails for a few dollars a liter, is small in comparison to the huge profits made by aftermarket additive marketers on a single bottle of additive. Despite the carefully exacting standards engine oil is refined to, the advertising of engine oil aftermarket additives leaves the impression that regular engines oils are inadequate. Claims made by aftermarket additive makers range from substantial increases in fuel economy to reduced engine wear, increased horsepower, cleaner engines, and eliminated engine oil leaks. Substantiation for these claims rests heavily on customer testimonials and little on verifiable testing of products by independent labs. In fact, in recent years a number of high-profile additive marketers have been prosecuted for making unsubstantiated claims about their products.

Oil Additive Categories

Common aftermarket oil additives include the following:

- Products that are simply heavier viscosity oil or VI additive that can reduce oil consumption.
- Products containing polytetrafloeraethylene (PTFE), otherwise known as Teflon®, mixed with high-viscosity motor oil. This powdery substance was claimed to be capable of coating engine parts with a protective film to reduce friction. However, a substantial body of evidence indicates that PTFE additive dumped into engine oil can in fact plug filters and small internal oil passageways. Many other tests and studies have demonstrated PTFE additives actually increase engine wear.
- Products containing regular engine oil including standard additives with the addition of zinc dialkyldithiophosphate (ZDP). This zinc compound is added to many oil products already as an extreme pressure additive to minimize damage when metal-to-metal contact occurs. ZDP must be kept to minimal values; field testing of engines with excess additive has found the intermediate copper layer of bearings is often corroded through galvanic reactions when extra zinc is added to the engine oil.
- Products containing the same additives already used in major brands of oil but in different quantities and combinations. Engine industry experts object to the use of these additives, because they can disturb the delicate balance between base stock oil and additives already contained in the certified oil. Unintended chemical reactions can take place between these additional additives and engine parts or additives already in the oil.

TECHNICIAN TIP

ZDP is not compatible with biodiesel. Biodiesel will interact with ZDP and destroy the important additive. Newer formulations of engine oil no longer contain ZDP, but it is still popular as an aftermarket additive. Note also, excess ZDP in engine oil will attack copper and damage engine bearings.

Synthetic Oils

Synthetic-base lubricants have been used in aviation and special-purpose engines since World War II. Tanks used in World War II needed synthetics to allow the oil to properly lubricate the engines in extreme cold. High temperatures encountered in jet engines would burn petroleum-based oils, necessitating the use of synthetics. Synthetic lubricants did not begin to make inroads into automotive applications, however, until the late 1970s.

Synthetic oils generally refer to oils whose base stock is synthetically derived or manufactured. While some brands of synthetic oils are derived from ultra-refined petroleum oil, the most popular base stock for synthetic oil is made from a manmade material called **polyalphaolefin (PAO)** `TABLE 12-1`. PAO molecules are smaller and more consistent in size, and no impurities are found in this oil because it is derived through chemical process, making it very chemically stable and flexible compared to conventional oil. Approximately 70% of the base stock of synthetic oils is made from POA. Chemical additives are then blended with the synthetic oil base stock, similar to the process of making conventional oils. However, synthetic oils usually have more additives than conventional oils. No API or SAE standards exist yet for defining what synthetic oil is, but they do need to meet minimum API and SAE criteria if they carry the API symbols. Oil additives go through no testing except by the U.S. Environmental Protection Agency (EPA) to certify they are not environmentally noxious.

Benefits of Synthetic Oil

Manufacturers claim the following benefits for synthetic oils:

- Lower coefficient of friction (slipperier): Users of synthetic oil have claimed increases in their fuel mileage ranging from 2% to 5%.
- Improved low-temperature viscosities: Conventional oils tend to include wax molecules that thicken oil at lower temperatures. Typical synthetic 15W-40 oil remains liquid even at −58°F (−50°C).
- Improved high-temperature performance: Synthetic oils have few light or thin hydrocarbon molecules, which tend to evaporate at high temperatures.
- Greater resistance to chemical breakdown, oxidation, coking, and deposit formation.
- Decreased oil consumption: When synthetic oil is used, 42% less oil consumption occurs. This is due to less evaporation and resistance to deposit formation.
- Fewer chemical impurities: This means additives do not adversely react with impurities, prolonging the usefulness of the additive package.
- Reduced friction and engine wear because of a lower coefficient of friction.
- Longer intervals between oil changes due to higher resistance to oxidation `TABLE 12-2`.

Disadvantages of Synthetic Oil

The primary disadvantage of synthetic oils is that they cost significantly more than mineral oils. Synthetic oil manufacturers, however, suggest this problem is offset by long service life and improved performance. Less wear is likely during cold start-ups, because oil will reach turbocharger and camshaft bearings faster than conventional oil. Synthetic POA-based oil is also less likely to deteriorate during high-speed high-load operation in smaller displacement diesels.

Another problem with synthetics is the molecules are more uniform in size and thus more likely to leak or weep through

TABLE 12-1: Sources of Base Stock Lubrication Oil

Oil Base Stock	Source	Disadvantages
Conventional mineral oil	Mineral oil derived from crude oil	Contain undesirable impurities such as oxygen, sulfur, nitrogen compounds, trace metals, and carbon residues. Additive package cannot operate effectively because the additive has to compete with the impurities when bonding with base oil molecules. These oils break down under extreme heat and form solids under extreme cold.
Hydro-processed mineral oil	Highly refined mineral oil	Some undesirable chemical impurities but is more refined than conventional mineral oil.
Severe hydro-processed mineral oil (considered synthetic oil in North America only).	Ultra-refined mineral oil (may be also blended with POA to make semi-synthetic oils)	Requires additional processing and removal of more impurities than hydro-processed mineral oil, but some impurities still exist.
Fully synthetic oil (chemically derived)	Chemically manufactured PAO	Expensive

TABLE 12-2: A Comparison Between Two Leading Brands of Oil

Measurement of oil performance	Synthetic 10W-40 (POA base stock)	Petroleum 10W-40 (Poor quality)
Effective lubrication range	−60–400°F (−51–204°C)	0–300°F (−18–149°C)
Viscosity increase after 64-hour running test	> 9%	> 102–400%
Volatility (evaporation at 300°F [149°C] after 22 hours)	1%	28%
Crankcase temperature (track test)	240°F (116°C)	290°F (143°C)
Flash point (D92 test)	470°F (243°C)	400°F (204°C)
Film strength	3000 psi (207 bar) routinely observed	500–2000 psi (345–138 bar)

worn seals and lose gaskets. This explains why more engine oil leaks are observed when changing over to synthetic oil after using conventional engine oils.

Because synthetic oils have a lower coefficient of friction, they are not recommended for break-in periods. Synthetics' best application is in extreme operating conditions such as heat and cold. Equipment with high initial cost and long chassis life such as diesel engines can also benefit from the extended engine longevity that can result from using synthetics. In other words, synthetics would protect high-value investments through longer vehicle life.

Biodiesel and Engine Oil

For years biodiesel has been considered as a lubricity additive to keep moving parts operating smoothly inside fuel injection systems. Dilution of engine oil with biodiesel is another matter. Biodiesel promotes fuel dilution of engine oil to a much greater extent than mineral diesel fuel. Oil dilution with biodiesel occurs when a post-combustion injection of fuel into the cylinders is used to regenerate the particulate trap or NO_x absorber. All the fuel is expected to vaporize in the cylinder and not combust until it reaches the exhaust catalysts. Heavier, less volatile fractions of fuel, however, do not vaporize during post-combustion injection and liquid fuel clings to the cylinder walls.

Because biodiesel has a higher distillation temperature and boiling point, it tends to dilute the engine oil disproportionately to its blend ratio in the fuel. Biodiesel blends higher than B20 (20% bio source) cause larger amounts of unburned fuel to slip by the piston rings. Fuel passes by the pistons and accumulates

Synthetic oils are of tremendous benefit to high-speed turbocharged diesels for several reasons:

1. Turbochargers and rocker shafts receive lubrication quicker in comparison to petroleum-based oils. Because synthetics flow easily at cold temperatures, engine components do not starve for oil.
2. Synthetic oils are resistant to coking. During hot shutdown of turbocharged engines, exhaust heat in the turbine housing moves into the center bearing housing, which can cause turbine shaft bearings to burn and coke. The abrasive carbon residue from coked oil can damage shaft bearings and score the turbine shaft.
3. More flexible molecules provide improved shear strength. Engines using unit injectors exert greater stress on oil through shearing, causing oil to thin out. The smaller synthetic oil molecule is less affected by shear, and enables viscosity to remain stable over a longer period of time.

in the crankcase. Once there, fuel polymerizes (joins together to form long, complexly shaped molecules) with oil, producing sludge. Engine damage can result from oil passageways being blocked by sludge. Deposits also form in the ring belt area, causing the rings to stick and crankcase blow-by to increase, which further aggravates oil contamination with increased levels of soot.

Raw or refined vegetable oils produce the greatest harm, which may not become evident until a significant amount of damage has occurred over an extended period. Engine oil change intervals may need to be shortened significantly if using blends of biodiesel higher than B20. Detergents and specific anti-wear additives do not work as well when oil is diluted with biodiesel, either.

▶ Components of Lubrication Systems

In addition to the oil itself, the lubrication system accomplishes its tasks through a number of major components, including:

- Oil pan
- Oil pump
- Pressure regulating and relief valves
- Oil cooler
- Oil filter

Oil Pan

The function of the oil pan is to store an adequate supply of oil for the lubrication system **FIGURE 12-16**. While more than enough oil is available in the oil pan to supply the lubrication requirements of the engine, excess oil is needed to distribute contaminant loading of lubrication oil and to compensate for oil consumption. The location of the oil pan provides some cooling

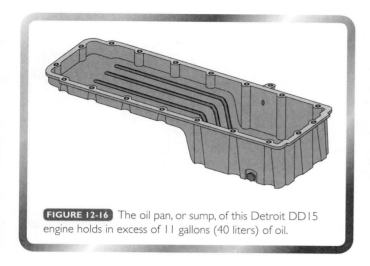

FIGURE 12-16 The oil pan, or sump, of this Detroit DD15 engine holds in excess of 11 gallons (40 liters) of oil.

FIGURE 12-18 The engine oil dipstick measures the level of the oil when the engine is off. The oil level should be between the hash marks. Overfilling will cause seals to leak and aerate the oil.

of engine oil, which normally is at temperatures above coolant operating temperature. An oil pan may be made of fiberglass, stamped steel, or aluminum **FIGURE 12-17**. Significant engine noise originates from the oil pan, so it is often covered in sound-insulating material.

The sump is the deepest part of the oil pan where the oil pump pick-up tube is located. Depending on the chassis configuration, the sump may be located at the rear, front, or middle of the engine to accommodate suspension of frame component clearances.

An oil dipstick measures the level of engine oil when the engine is off **FIGURE 12-18**. A windage tray may also be incorporated into the oil pan. Windage trays separate the crankcase from the oil pan reservoir to prevent the crankshaft from whipping engine oil stored in the pan **FIGURE 12-19**. The primary advantage of the tray is it increases fuel economy by as much as 1–2%. The tray also prevents complaints such as engine thumping and stumbling during cornering or braking, when oil can surge up into the crankcase. Additionally, an oil level sensor is used in the lower pan.

Slosh Baffles

FIGURE 12-17 The aluminum oil pan of this off-road diesel contains baffles to prevent the sloshing of oil. Aluminum helps reduce engine weight and improves heat transfer from oil.

FIGURE 12-19 The windage tray from a Mack MP7 engine. A windage tray prevents oil from interfering with crankshaft motion and causing oil foam.

Oil Pumps

Oil pumps are used to pressurize the lubrication system of a diesel engine. They are positive displacement pumps, usually constructed with a closed gear or gerotor design. A gerotor pump is constructed of an inner rotor and an outer rotor. The inner rotor turns inside the outer rotor ring, which also turns. The inner rotor has one less lobe than the outer ring and is positioned off center from the outer ring. As the lobes slide up and over one another, oil is drawn through a fixed passageway connected to the oil pan pick-up tube. Oil is squeezed out into the main oil gallery through the outlet passageway behind the rotors **FIGURE 12-20**. The external gear pump is another common configuration for an engine oil pump. This pump has two opposing gears. A drive shaft turns one gear, which in turn rotates the opposite gear. Oil is trapped and carried around the pump between the gear teeth. A seal is formed between the gear teeth and the oil pump housing **FIGURE 12-21**.

The lube oil is supplied under pressure to moving parts through drilled passageways in the engine called oil galleries **FIGURE 12-22**. Most moving parts are supplied pressurized oil for lubrication. However, cylinder walls are lubricated by oil thrown off of engine bearings and from oil cooler nozzles. Oil is drawn into the pump through a pick-up tube and screen located in the oil pan sump **FIGURE 12-23**. When replacing oil pumps, they should be primed to shorten the time required to develop engine oil pressure.

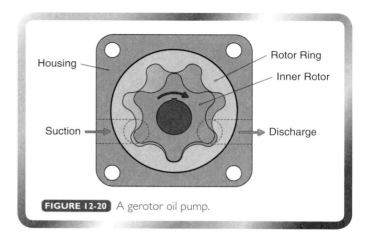

FIGURE 12-20 A gerotor oil pump.

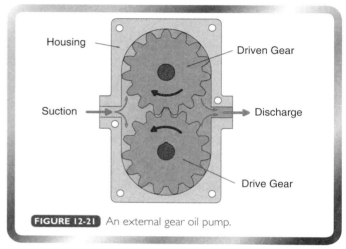

FIGURE 12-21 An external gear oil pump.

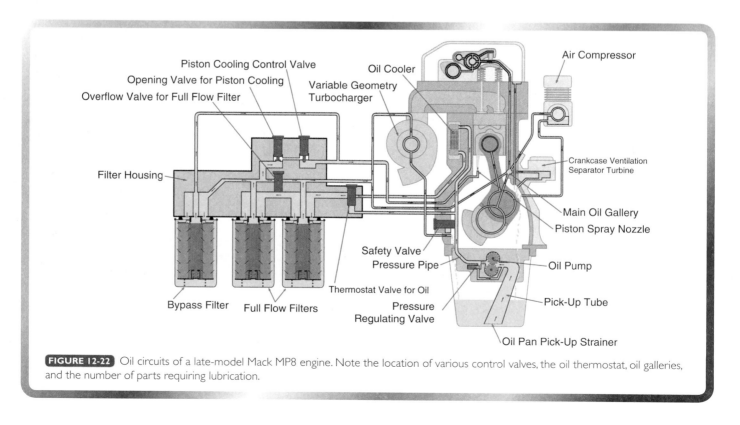

FIGURE 12-22 Oil circuits of a late-model Mack MP8 engine. Note the location of various control valves, the oil thermostat, oil galleries, and the number of parts requiring lubrication.

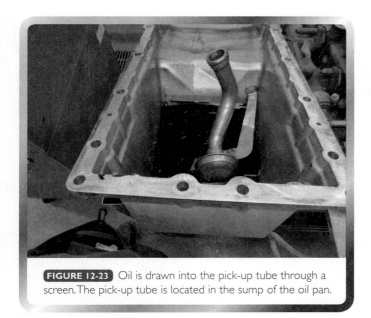

FIGURE 12-23 Oil is drawn into the pick-up tube through a screen. The pick-up tube is located in the sump of the oil pan.

Pressure Regulating and Pressure Relief Valves

Because the oil pump can produce more oil flow than the engine can use, an oil pressure regulating valve is used to control oil pressure. Oil pressure that is too high can blow gaskets on the spin-on oil filter and burst or swell the oil filter into a pumpkin shape. Excessively high oil pressure can also erode engine bearings. Keeping the oil pressure regulated to between 20 and 40 psi (138 and 276 kPa) when the engine oil is warm can reduce parasitic power loss caused by pumping more oil than is necessary to regulate oil at a higher pressure **TABLE 12-3**.

The oil pressure regulating valve is usually located in the main oil gallery or at the outlet of an oil pump **FIGURE 12-24**. Using a conventional spring-loaded bypass valve arrangement permits maximum oil pressure control by the valve. When oil pressure reaches a value equal to spring tension of a pressure regulating valve, spring pressure is overcome by oil pressure, which moves a spool valve to a bypass position. Oil returns to the sump in quantities proportional to the excess volume produced by the oil pump **FIGURE 12-25**. As long as clearances between engine bearings and other components using oil remain close, adequate oil pressure is maintained by the oil pump and pressure regulating valve. If an engine has excessive wear or internal

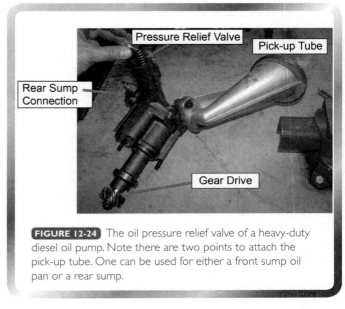

FIGURE 12-24 The oil pressure relief valve of a heavy-duty diesel oil pump. Note there are two points to attach the pick-up tube. One can be used for either a front sump oil pan or a rear sump.

TABLE 12-3: Typical Lubricating System Specifications for a Medium-Duty Diesel Engine

Lubricating Oil System			
Oil Pressure	At Low Idle (minimum allowable)		10 psi (69 kPa)
	At Rated Speed (minimum allowable)		30 psi (207 kPa)
Oil Regulating Value Opening Pressure Range			65 psi (448 kPa) to 75 psi (517 kPa)
Oil Filter Differential Pressure to Open Bypass			50 psi (345 kPa)
Lubricating Oil Filter Capacity			1 qt (0.950 liters)
Lubricating Oil Capacity of Standard Engine	Standard Oil Pan	Pan Only	15 qt (14.2 liters)
		Total System	17.6 qt (16.7 liters)
		High to Low (dipstick)	2 qt (1.9 liters)
	High-Capacity Oil Pan	Pan Only	19 qt (18 liters)
		Total System	21.4 qt (20.3 liters)
		High to Low (dipstick)	2 qt (1.9 liters)
Maximum Oil Temperature			280°F (138°C)

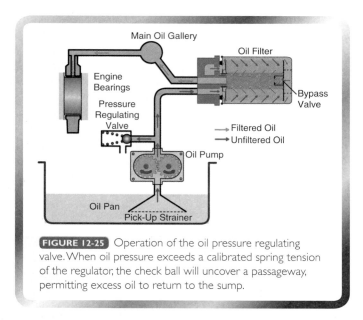

FIGURE 12-25 Operation of the oil pressure regulating valve. When oil pressure exceeds a calibrated spring tension of the regulator, the check ball will uncover a passageway, permitting excess oil to return to the sump.

oil leaks, oil pressure will drop as the pump tries to make up for the additional volume required by the leaks and larger operating clearances in the engine lubrication system.

In the event, the pressure regulating valve cannot relieve oil pressure fast enough, such as when the oil is cold and thick or the regulator is not properly working, a pressure relief valve is connected in series with the pressure regulator. This valve will open at typically 100 psi (689 kPa) and return oil to the sump **FIGURE 12-26** .

Oil Coolers

Oil coolers are heat exchangers used to remove excess heat from engine oil **FIGURE 12-27** . Virtually all diesel engines use oil coolers because cooling of pistons and other internal engine parts is performed using lubrication oil. Engine oil can easily become overheated while absorbing heat from turbochargers and other internal parts, particularly when the engine is heavily loaded. Nozzles or drilled passageways in the connecting rods direct oil

FIGURE 12-27 The oil cooler of this Detroit S60 engine is located above the oil filters. Note the coolant pipe attached directly to the water pump outlet.

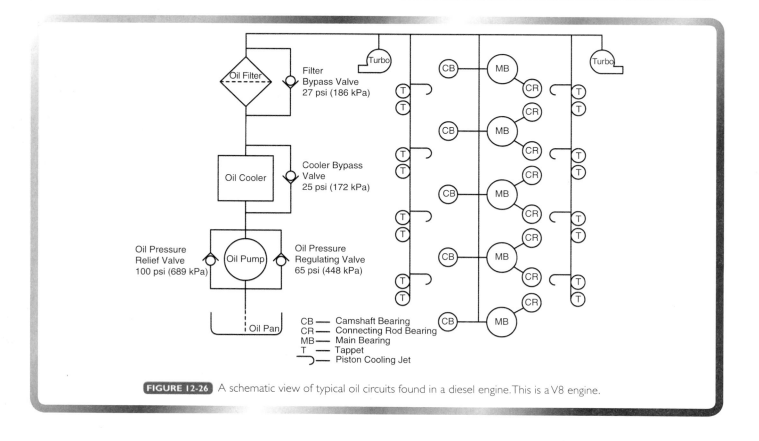

FIGURE 12-26 A schematic view of typical oil circuits found in a diesel engine. This is a V8 engine.

to the underside of the piston crown to prevent heat damage and ring seizure FIGURE 12-28. Engine oil should never exceed 250°F (139°C). Many electronic engines use oil temperature sensors to shut down or derate engine power if oil temperatures exceed 250–260°F (139–143°C). When under load, normal engine oil temperature should not exceed the temperature of the coolant by more than 30–40°F. This means an engine operating at 190–205°F (88–96°C) should have a maximum oil temperature of 220–245°F (122–136°C).

Oil coolers are usually thermostatically controlled and will not allow either oil or coolant to flow through it until the oil or coolant has warmed up. This feature prevents prolonged circulation of poorly lubricating, highly viscous oil during warm-up. When the oil or coolant reaches operating temperature, oil will divert into the cooler where it releases heat to the cooling system FIGURE 12-29. The cooler may also be equipped with a pressure relief valve that allows oil to bypass the cooler if it becomes plugged. The bypass valve will open if a substantial pressure drop occurs across the cooler.

Engine coolant will usually remove heat from an oil cooler. Plate and tube oil coolers are the most commonly used design FIGURE 12-30 and FIGURE 12-31. Defective coolers or poor maintenance of the cooling system can lead to cooler corrosion, which will cause oil to enter the engine coolant. A suspected leaking cooler can be removed from the engine and pressurized with air to check for leaks.

Another problem with coolers is they can become contaminated and plugged with crankcase debris. Often, manufacturers send unfiltered oil through a cooler before it enters the oil filters. Soot, oil sludge, and debris such as pieces of gaskets, silicone sealant used as a gasket material, and dirt can clog cooler passageways. For this reason, a cooler bypass valve is used to prevent oil starvation if the cooler becomes plugged. Engine bearing failures will also fill the cooler with metal debris, which requires the cooler to be backward flushed out with solvent

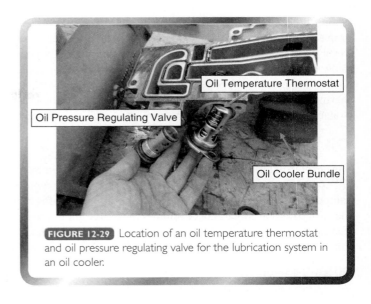

FIGURE 12-29 Location of an oil temperature thermostat and oil pressure regulating valve for the lubrication system in an oil cooler.

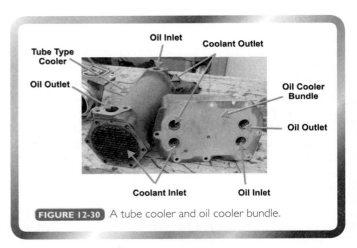

FIGURE 12-30 A tube cooler and oil cooler bundle.

FIGURE 12-28 The cooling nozzle is aimed at the underside of the piston crown. A notch in the piston prevents contact with the oil cooler nozzle.

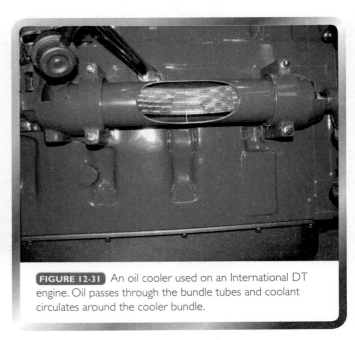

FIGURE 12-31 An oil cooler used on an International DT engine. Oil passes through the bundle tubes and coolant circulates around the cooler bundle.

before the cooler is returned to service after an engine repair or overhaul. One symptom of a plugged cooler is a sudden drop in oil pressure during engine warm-up. Because coolers normally do not allow oil through the core until the oil or coolant is warmed up, oil pressure will be normal until the cooler thermostat diverts oil to pass through the cooler. If the cooler is clogged, oil pressure will suddenly drop after engine warm-up.

Oil Filters

The purpose of lubrication oil filtration is contamination removal. Oil contamination can cause abrasives to rapidly wear engine components if not properly controlled. Soot, sludge, and dirt are the most common contaminants removed by the filtration system. The choice of filter capacity and type of filter media are determined by the degree of cleanliness desired for the lubrication oil.

Filter Media

The type of filter media used inside the oil filter depends on a number of variables, including particle removal efficiency, contaminant holding capacity, resistance to flow, and corresponding pressure drop. There are between 50 and 75 different media grades designed for oil filtration available to filter manufacturers. Media used for air, coolant, and oil filtration cannot be used interchangeably. Types of media range from mesh-like screens to thread or chopped paper to 100% natural cellulose and 100% synthetic microfibers.

When only large particles are to be removed, a cellulose or paper media is used. To remove progressively smaller particles, the type of media changes from complex cellulose to blended media containing cellulose and microfiber materials. Cellulose or paper typically provide filtration down to 13–20 microns **FIGURE 12-32** .

Glass microfiber, or micro-glass, will provide the most efficient filtration with the least amount of restriction but usually is the most expensive to manufacture. Micro-glass filtration is capable of removing particles as small as 2–5 microns **FIGURE 12-33** . Pleated filters provide more surface area for holding contaminants. However, too many pleats can swell and prevent oil flow.

Because diesel engine oil contains a substantial amount of soot, more than one filter is used, and bypass filters are commonly used in addition to the full-flow filters that supply oil directly to engine bearings **FIGURE 12-34** . Bypass filters supplement regular filtration by filtering oil and returning it to the oil pan. Paper depth filters and spinner or centrifugal bypass filters are commonly used. Centrifugal bypass filters use a replaceable paper filter that separates soot by spinning a filter core at high speeds using oil pressure to drive the spinner core **FIGURE 12-35** . The thin paper, which is replaceable in many bypass spinners, separates soot from oil.

> ▶ **TECHNICIAN TIP**
>
> Always prime oil pumps before installation to minimize the time required to pick-up oil from the sump. After an overhaul, always prime an engine with oil before starting to prevent any damage due to lack of oil during start-up and cranking.

Anti-Drain Back Valve

Many **cartridge filters**, which are filter elements consisting simply of filter media unenclosed by metal containers, have an **anti-drain back valve** built into the filter element. The purpose of the anti-drain back valve is to prevent the oil in the engine from returning

FIGURE 12-32 Two oil filters. **A.** A paper filter with yellow media. **B.** A micro-glass filter with white media.

FIGURE 12-33 Cutaway of a bypass filter that uses cellulose micro-glass filter media. Unfiltered oil enters the case on the outside of the filter and must pass through the filter media to the filter center. The bypass filter has two different types of media supplied with one inlet but two separate outlets.

FIGURE 12-34 This engine uses two full-flow filters and one bypass filter.

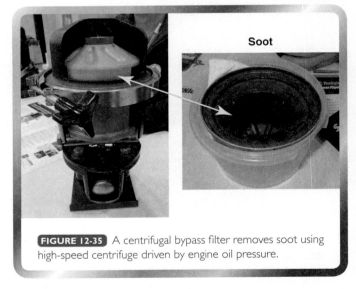

FIGURE 12-35 A centrifugal bypass filter removes soot using high-speed centrifuge driven by engine oil pressure.

to the crankcase when the engine is shut down. This permits the instantaneous build-up of oil pressure and oil supply to the engine after start-up. This valve usually consists of a one-way flow valve in the center tube of the filter. Many drain back valves are made of nitrile rubber. However, nitrile rubber diaphragms stiffen in extreme cold and may fail to seal in those conditions. Silicone rubber seals or steel valves are not prone to this problem. Detroit Diesel DD-series engines and other original equipment manufacturers (OEMs) use a check valve in the oil pick-up tube to prevent drain back to the pan when the engine is shut down.

Oil Filter Bypass Valves

The bypass valve is a feature incorporated into the filter to allow oil to pass from the dirty side to the clean side of the filter if resistance or restriction is excessive across the filter media **FIGURE 12-36**. This prevents oil starvation to the engine in the event of a plugged filter. The simplest design uses a spring-loaded filter element that causes the spring located beneath the element to compress if the oil pressure differential across the filter element becomes too high **FIGURE 12-37**. This design permits oil to move through the dirty outside of the filter straight through to the filtered center of the element without passing through the filter media.

To supplement the filter bypass valve, an oil filter bypass relief valve is often found in the oil filter header of many engines. Its purpose is identical to the filter bypass valve in a cartridge filter: it allows pressurized oil to bypass a plugged filter. The filter bypass valve operates on principles of pressure differential.

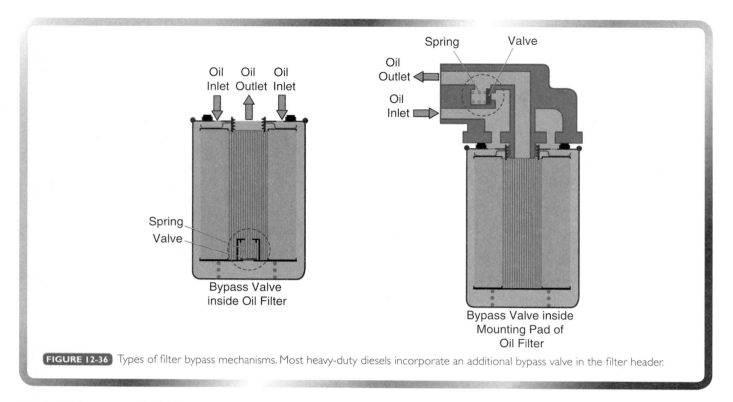

FIGURE 12-36 Types of filter bypass mechanisms. Most heavy-duty diesels incorporate an additional bypass valve in the filter header.

FIGURE 12-37 A bypass valve located in the header of the oil filter. The bypass valve opens when filter restriction is too high, and dirty oil is then circulated through the engine.

Usually, when a new oil filter is installed, very little pressure drop occurs across the filter media. With increasing contamination, however, the filter will become restrictive and a pressure drop across the filter occurs. Typically, when the pressure drop exceeds approximately 3–30 psi (21–207 kPa), the bypass valve will open and allow unfiltered oil to move through the main oil gallery. Without the bypass valve, the pressure differential across the filter media would burst or tear the filter. The operation of the filter bypass valve is performed in addition to the normal bypass relief feature incorporated into most oil filters.

Filtration Systems

Almost all diesel engine lubrication systems use full-flow lubrication. This means any oil reaching engine parts has passed through an oil filter. Some lubrication systems use a supplemental partial-flow, or bypass, lubrication system that filters oil through a bypass filter and returns the filtered oil to the sump. No oil passing through the bypass filter actually reaches moving engine parts.

Types of Oil Filters: Cartridge Versus Spin-On

Spin-on filters, which are enclosed in a metal can that is threaded onto a filter header, were introduced during the 1950s and made changing oil easier and less messy. Since the late 1980s however, European and North American engine manufacturers are reverting to the cartridge filter because there are a number of problems associated with the use of spin-on filters. One problem is the availability of engine compartment space for filters. Because space is at a premium in the engine compartment of today's vehicles, the oil filter can be very difficult to locate and change. New cartridge filter housings are usually conveniently located on the top or side of the engine compartment, making them easily accessible. Cartridge filter housings are typically designed with a screw-on cap and a single sealing gasket **FIGURE 12-38**. The housings are ventilated when opened and the oil flows out of the

FIGURE 12-38 Cartridge filters are quickly replacing spin-on filters for space and accessibility reasons.

filter cavity and back to the sump through a separate drain system. Messy spills associated with spin-on filters are minimized this way.

Another advantage of the cartridge filter that it costs significantly less than a spin-on filter. It is reported that almost 80% of the cost of a spin-on filter is due to the steel canister and valves. With a cartridge filter, only the pleated media and a gasket are replaced during filter service. Not only does this reduce the cost, but it also eliminates unnecessary waste of natural resources. They also allow OEMs to establish standardized oil filter cartridge sizes, reducing the number of different cartridges required to service a particular brand of vehicle or engine.

Filter Disposal and the Environment

The most important reason for the transition from spin-on to cartridge filters is spin-on filter disposal. The disposal cost of a cartridge filter is far less than that of a spin-on filter, which requires special handling procedures to be exempt from EPA regulations regarding hazardous waste. In many jurisdictions, manufactured oil filters are exempt from hazardous waste regulation if the oil filter is:

- Punctured through the dome end or anti-drain back valve and hot-drained (the anti-drain back valve usually prevents sludge from draining out of the filter)
- Hot-drained and crushed
- Hot-drained and dismantled
- Hot-drained using an equivalent method to remove used oil

Hot-draining is defined as draining the oil filter at or near engine operating temperature. This means the filter is removed from the engine while it is still warm, then punctured or crushed and drained. Most of the oil is removed from the filter during hot-draining. The EPA further recommends hot-draining for a minimum of 12 hours.

▶ Maintenance of Lubrication Systems

While the properties of oil and the lubricating system can seem complex, the most common considerations a technician will encounter are when and how to change the oil. A technician will need to diagnose problems with oil circuits and control valves very few times, but failing to service engine oil can dramatically shorten engine life and lead to catastrophic and costly component failures. Over-servicing an engine is often viewed as an effective maintenance strategy, but the quantity of oil used during a service and the accompanying cost of replacing oil and filters too frequently is inefficient. It also yields few, if any, meaningful benefits compared to timely service intervals. Understanding the factors that limit oil life and the methods used to evaluate the optimal service schedule are the most helpful service recommendations technicians can provide when advising customers.

Other relatively common conditions encountered by technicians are situations where a customer reports high oil consumption and excess engine oil in the crankcase or low oil pressure. These conditions often point to potentially imminent engine failure, which can be prevented with perceptive diagnostic checks and interventions.

Limiting Factors to Engine Oil Life

Today's diesel engine technology requires lubrication oils to meet a variety of operating conditions and provide for long service intervals and engine durability. To understand what additives are needed to provide acceptable service, and when oil should be changed, it is helpful to consider the main factors that can limit oil life.

The Percentage of Solids

The percentage of solids refers to the total amount of particles that are suspended in the oil. Combustion soot, dirt, and oxidized oil are typically the major solids found in oil. The percentage of solids becomes a limiting factor to oil life when the particles interfere with the oil's lubricating abilities. Engine manufacturers suggest an oil change to remove dissolved solids before they rise above 5% by weight. However, improvements in wear reduction are best achieved if the solids are kept below 2%. Detergents are added to the oil to prevent the solids from clumping and forming damaging deposits inside the engine.

Detergents surround the particles and suspend them in the oil until it is drained or until the filter removes the particles. Synthetic oils require change intervals just like conventional oils if the percentage of solids is the limiting factor to engine oil life.

Sulfur and Combustion Acids

Sulfuric acids are present in engine oil whenever there is sulfur in the diesel fuel and corrosive acids produced using recirculated exhaust gas in the cylinders. Because sulfur combines with water produced during combustion, highly corrosive acids are formed in the oil. To counteract this condition, oil manufacturers add alkali or base substances such as calcium and ash to the oil to neutralize the effect of sulfuric acids. This property distinguishes oils used in spark ignition engines from compression ignition engines. **Total acid number (TAN)** refers to the acidity of an oil, whereas **total base number (TBN)** is the measurement of a lubricant's reserve alkalinity, which aids in the control of acids formed during the combustion process. The higher an oil's TBN, the more effective it is in preventing the formation of wear-causing contaminants. Diesel engines will use a TBN of between 6 and 10 points. When the TBN is below half its new value, the engine oil should be changed.

TECHNICIAN TIP

The most recent classification for diesel engine oil is CJ-4. This is required for engines using EGR and diesel particulate traps. Sulfated ash, the additive used to increase the TBN of diesel lubrication oil, is reduced in CJ-4. Removal of sulfur from fuel in recent years is important to extend the life of the catalyst material in the diesel particulate filter (DPF), so less ash and other alkaline substances are now used in engine oil. Additionally, as the engine uses oil, the ash will burn and deposit in the DPF. The DPF will require more frequent cleaning (not regeneration) if any engine oil other than CJ-4 is used. Algorithms used by OEMs estimate ash loading of DPFs base calculations on the use of CJ-4 oil.

TECHNICIAN TIP

Whenever a diesel has had contaminated fuel or an internal fuel or coolant leak, it is critical to drain and flush the fuel system, change fuel filters, and change the engine oil and filters. Oil dilution and contamination is likely to have occurred. Always change the engine oil after any major repair to an engine, because the oil can be contaminated with dirt, coolant, or fuel. Never use an air gun to blow contaminants away from inside an engine, as the contaminants are usually blown into the oil; use a vacuum cleaner instead. Always cover an engine under repair between work shifts to prevent contamination of parts and oil with dirt. Leave parts in bags or boxes until just prior to installation to prevent carrying dirt into an engine's oil or fuel system.

Oxidized Oil

Oil is oxidized when it is exposed to air and oxygen joins the oil. Conventional oils generally thicken, turn brown, and form deposits if highly oxidized. This process occurs more rapidly at high temperatures. The problem with oxidation is oil loses some of its lubricating properties as it oxidizes, thus accelerating engine wear. Synthetic oils are at an advantage because they do not oxidize as quickly as conventional oils. Therefore, if oil oxidation due to high engine operating temperatures is the limiting factor of oil life, the use of synthetic oil can extend the oil change interval.

Other Limiting Factors

Engine problems such as coolant leaks into the oil from sources such as leaking heads require oil change after a repair. Defective air filters that permit dirt to enter the engine, fuel leaking into the oil, wrong fuel (i.e., gasoline contamination of diesel fuel), water in the oil, or a mechanical failure producing internal debris are all circumstances that require an oil change subsequent to engine repair. Many engines have experienced catastrophic failures subsequent to seemingly minor repairs when the oil has not been changed.

When oil turns milky white, brown, or gray, it is usually a sign that coolant has leaked into it. Minor internal coolant leaks are not easily detected, and an oil sample should be obtained for analysis **FIGURE 12-39**. Conventional antifreeze leaks will show up on an oil analysis as high silicate levels in the oil. Long-life antifreeze has other chemical signatures. Fuel contamination of oil can often be detected by simply smelling the fuel in the oil or performing an oil analysis.

Oil Change Interval

Oil change intervals are based on the operating conditions an engine encounters and the amount of fuel consumed. Several

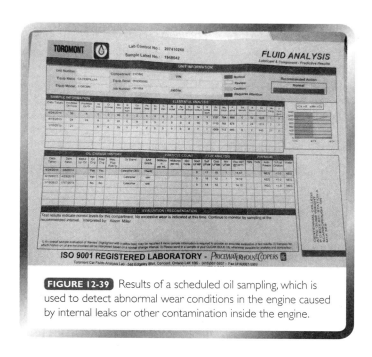

FIGURE 12-39 Results of a scheduled oil sampling, which is used to detect abnormal wear conditions in the engine caused by internal leaks or other contamination inside the engine.

formulas are used to calculate the correct service interval, but generally, every 45 gallons (170 liters) of fuel consumed by the diesel engine produces enough contaminants to use up 1 quart (1 liter) of oil. The recommended oil change interval is calculated by multiplying the quantity of oil in the oil pan by the number of barrels of fuel burned (45 gallons [170 liters]). This means a vehicle with 7-mpg (3-km/L) fuel consumption will need changing at 12,600 miles (20,117 km). Extended service intervals can be achieved using good quality lubricating oil, such as synthetics, and filters that minimize the effects of oil life limiting factors such as soot loading of the oil, oxidation, and acid formation. An engine electronic control module (ECM) can be configured to prompt the driver to have the engine oil changed. A maintenance monitor light in the dash can alert the driver when oil is at the end of its service life. Technicians need to reset the monitor after service **FIGURE 12-40** .

Operating an engine in stop-and-go conditions, under heavy load, in cold weather, with extended idle, and so on are severe operating conditions that shorten the oil service interval. Moderate temperatures and steady state driving conditions on highway are normal service conditions that extend oil life **TABLE 12-4** . The best practice to extend oil change intervals is to use engine oil sampling analysis to determine levels of solids, the TBN, and limits of oil oxidation.

▶ TECHNICIAN TIP

Oils must be changed when soot levels reach a maximum of 3–5%. Failing to change oil at these levels will cause excessive wear and soot thickening of oil. Soot-thickened oil does not move well through oil passages, especially when cold. Soot is also an abrasive that will accelerate engine wear.

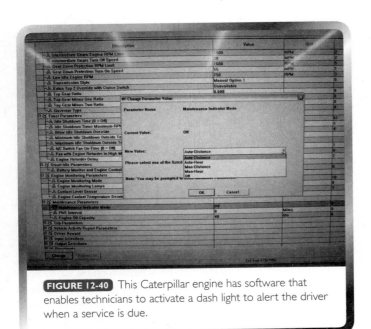

FIGURE 12-40 This Caterpillar engine has software that enables technicians to activate a dash light to alert the driver when a service is due.

▶ TECHNICIAN TIP

Engines built in 2007 and later are not permitted to allow oil carryover to the atmosphere. Many engines use a closed crankcase system, which means the crankcase has no direct connection to the atmosphere. When draining oil from these engines, removing the oil fill cap during oil drain will help the oil drain faster.

Safety Tip

Remember hot engine oil can easily exceed the temperature of boiling water. Hot engine oil can scald, and extreme care is necessary to prevent injury when performing what may be considered the simple process of removing an oil pan drain plug or filter when changing engine oil.

TABLE 12-4: Maximum Oil Drain Intervals

Severe Service	Normal Service
Average fuel economy is less than 7 mpg (3 km/L)	Average fuel economy is better than 7 mpg (3 km/L)
Refuse hauler Concrete mixer Dump truck	Pick-up & delivery On-highway tractor

Replacing a Spin-On Oil Filter

Oil filters on diesel engines are changed every time the oil is changed. Unlike some gasoline-fueled, spark-ignited engines that can have the oil filter changed during every other oil change, diesel engine oil filters load faster with contaminants. The majority of contaminants in diesel engine oil are combustion by-products, such as soot. Some manufacturers even recommend changing the oil filters between oil changes if a vehicle uses synthetic oil. More frequent filter changes help keep soot loading of oil low, which enables extended oil change intervals. Multiple spin-on filters with high capacity require simple precautions during installation.

To replace a spin-on oil filter, follow the steps in **SKILL DRILL 12-1** .

Measuring Oil Quality

It is in the best interest of owners and the environment to extend oil change intervals. Owners are motivated to sample engine oil to determine if any oil properties are depleted. Oil need not be changed if oil properties are intact. Operating costs are another benefit and so is the fact that important clues about impending engine failures can be detected before a catastrophic failure occurs.

SKILL DRILL 12-1 Replacing a Spin-On Oil Filter

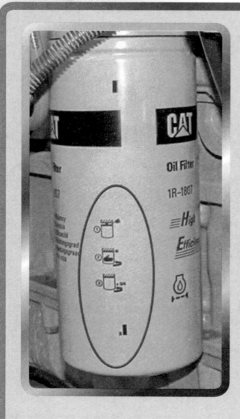

1. With the engine off, remove the filter with a filter wrench. A large belt-type filter wrench assisted with a power bar can be used to remove a tight filter. Occasionally, chain-type belt wrenches are used to remove tight filters. To prevent hot oil from scalding your hand when the filter is removed, the filter may have an hole punched into the bottom to allow oil to drain before removal.

2. Visually inspect the filter base for any damage or warpage. Ensure that the old filter gasket is removed.

3. Fill the new filter with oil. Put oil in the unfiltered outer holes of the cartridge (the center filter hole returns filtered oil to the engine).

4. Lubricate the filter gasket with oil or a smear of grease. This will allow the gasket to slide on the filter base and prevent the gasket from buckling when the filter is tightened. It is also necessary to lubricate the gasket to enable easy removal during the next service.

5. Spin the new filter on hand tight. Note the arrows or markings at the top of the filter canister, which indicate how far the new filter should be tightened after snugging the filter to the base using hand force only. Most filters are tightened a quarter to 3/4 of a turn beyond hand tight. Tightening the filter further could potentially distort the filter base, which is often aluminum. The filter element to canister seal can also be damaged and internal leaks paths formed if it is overtightened. If the filter is too loose, it will leak.

6. If the engine is being started for the first time after an overhaul, the engine should be prelubricated with pressurized oil through an oil gallery plug. As an additional precaution to prevent damage to bearings and other moving parts from oil starvation, disable the fuel system by disconnecting an ignition fuse or crank and cam sensor, or using a remote starter button. Crank, but do not start, the engine until oil pressure appears on the direct reading gauge in the instrument cluster.

7. After the engine is started and oil pressure is stabilized, check for leaks. Reset any maintenance monitor to indicate when the next scheduled filter and oil service is required.

From an environmental viewpoint, extending oil change intervals reduces environmental waste. According to the U.S. EPA, of the 1 billion gallons of engine oil consumed every year, about 185 million gallons (700 million liters) of used engine oil are improperly disposed of. Likely the oil is dumped into the ground, tossed into landfills, or poured into sewers. The EPA now encourages vehicle owners to follow OEMs' oil change recommendations and not those of the oil change industry. Research has demonstrated that oil changes can be extended by using higher quality oil and oil analysis for heavy-duty diesels.

Scheduled Oil Sampling

Oil quality sensors, which are electrical devices that measure the amount of soot loading in engine oil, are now available to measure the condition of lubrication oil but are not mature in terms of technological sophistication to perform condition-based oil changes. Such a sensor also helps alert the operator when oil quality falls outside specified parameters, which could be due either to the oil exceeding its useful life or a symptom of an engine problem. One of several

sensor technologies accurately measures soot, which absorbs oil additives and contributes to engine wear. The sensor operates like a variable capacitor using oil as the dielectric element. By measuring AC conductivity across the sensor at frequencies of 2–5 MHz, the sensor evaluates the dielectric strength of oil. This variable will change in proportion to oil quality.

In the absence of any sensor capable of comprehensively measuring oil quality, scheduled oil sampling (SOS) is recommended. In SOS, a sample of engine oil is obtained from the engine and sent out for analysis **FIGURE 12-41**, **FIGURE 12-42**, and **FIGURE 12-43**. SOS can provide extremely detailed analysis of the condition of the engine and quality of the engine oil **TABLE 12-5**.

Oil Life Algorithm Systems

An internal computer continuously monitors engine operating conditions to determine when to change oil. Software-based calculations use a formula or algorithm with input variables for engine operating conditions to determine oil life. Because oil degradation is associated with combustion events, analyzing combustion conditions can accurately determine

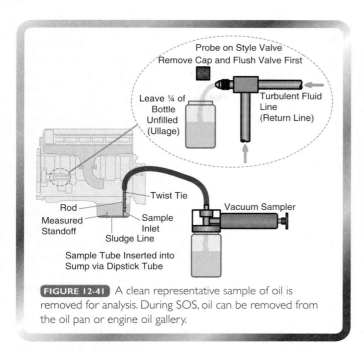

FIGURE 12-41 A clean representative sample of oil is removed for analysis. During SOS, oil can be removed from the oil pan or engine oil gallery.

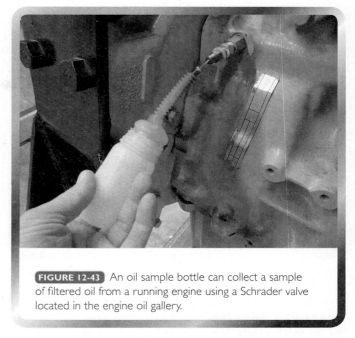

FIGURE 12-43 An oil sample bottle can collect a sample of filtered oil from a running engine using a Schrader valve located in the engine oil gallery.

FIGURE 12-42 An SOS bottle is mailed for analysis. Results are available through reports accessed on the Internet.

TABLE 12-5: Measures of Oil Quality for Analysis

Indication in Oil	Possible Cause
Viscosity increase	Soot loading
	Oxidation
	Water contamination
Viscosity decrease	Fuel dilution
	VI depletion from shear
	Overheated oil
Depleted additive	High operating temperature
	Extended oil change intervals
	Addition of aftermarket additives
	Incorrect oil
High solids content	Dirt contamination
	Excessive metal wear
Water contamination	Extended idle time
	Coolant leak
Antifreeze contamination	Head gasket leakage
	Cylinder liner
	O-ring leak
Fuel contamination	Injector damaged
	Cylinder misfire
	Injector O-ring damage
Metal contamination	Excessive wear or damage indicated by type of metal contaminant (i.e., lead from bearings, chrome from rings, tin from pistons, iron from gears or block material, silicon from coolant additive, etc.)

when oil life has reached its maximum value **FIGURE 12-44**. For example, when a cylinder fires, a small amount of oil is exposed to combustion and destroyed. Combustion gases containing acids, unburned fuel, water, and other by-products leak past the piston rings and react with engine oil. Diesels tend to generate much more soot and acidic combustion

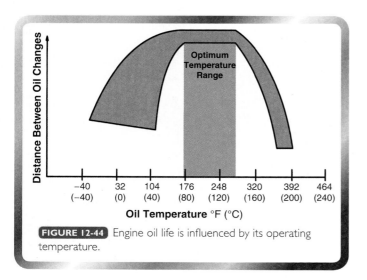

FIGURE 12-44 Engine oil life is influenced by its operating temperature.

blow-by into the crankcase. It is also known that oil temperature exerts a strong influence on deterioration of oil quality. As oil temperature increases, the rate of oxidation accelerates, which can lead to oil thickening. Turbochargers subject motor oils to high temperatures and are more prone to form engine deposits. Colder oil temperatures increase the concentration of oil contaminants such as fuel and water. Depending on the vehicle and engine type, each engine receives its own unique algorithm to determine engine oil life.

Excessively Low and High Oil Pressure

Virtually all heavy-duty diesel-powered vehicles use a dash-mounted oil pressure gauge. Although engine protection systems will shut down the engine, derate, or at least warn the driver of excessive oil temperature or low oil pressure, the presence of a prominent dash gauge underlines the importance for the driver and technician to monitor this engine parameter.

Low oil pressure can lead to oil starvation of critical engine components, which can cause seizure or rapid, premature wear. It is important to differentiate between low and abnormally low oil pressure. As engines wear normally, bearing clearances will become wider, which will result in more oil pump volume and lower oil pressure. This happens because pumps move oil volume while restrictions to volume produce pressure. Low oil pressure, or a drop in oil pressure from operating speed, is not necessarily abnormal. When oil becomes hot, it thins and causes a normal drop in pressure. Abnormal pressure is defined by the manufacturer and measured when the engine oil is at operating temperature, preferably with an accurate direct reading mechanical gauge. The potential for reporting the wrong oil pressure due to a defective sending unit or dash gauge requires another independent measuring device to validate a dash gauge measurement. Before confirming a low oil pressure complaint, the OEM specification must be consulted; technicians and drivers alike may be surprised by these numbers because they are often lower than expected. The oil level, viscosity, and presence of dilution with fuel should be checked when investigating low oil pressure complaints.

Subsequent to preliminary checks, diagnosis of low oil pressure should follow an OEM fault tree to differentiate problems caused by blocked oil filters, plugged oil coolers, internal oil leaks, worn oil pumps, and faulty pressure-regulating valves and thermostats. Worn engine bearings are best checked by removing several main and rod bearing caps to determine whether the top layer of babbitt is worn away. Some engines may use an oil viscosity regulating valve to correct oil pressure when the oil is cold or thickened. These valves can fail and produce a rapid drop in oil pressure only after the engine begins to warm up.

When investigating any oil pressure complaint, a technician should note where the dash sending unit is located in the lubricating system circuits. Generally, most sending units are located after the oil pump and before the oil filter. This minimizes the alarm a driver might have when watching little or low oil pressure for many minutes that only slowly rises after an engine starts cold.

Complaints about low oil pressure should be verified when the engine is at operating temperature. Idle oil pressure and high-idle oil pressure can be compared against the manufacturer's specifications **FIGURE 12-45**.

High oil pressure and abnormally high oil pressure need to be differentiated from normal oil pressure following procedures similar to those used to investigate low oil pressure. The high system pressure needs validation with an independent, accurate pressure gauge. While plugged filters, thick oil, and even tight engine bearings or cam bushings can produce high oil pressure, abnormally high pressure is defined by OEM specifications. Generally, abnormally high oil pressure is caused by a defective oil pressure regulating valve. Replacing the valve after visually inspecting it is often the only effective diagnostic procedure in this case. Operation of the valves and oil pump are evaluated using a pressure gauge in the main oil gallery. High oil pressure can cause foaming of oil since the oil contacts the rotating crankshaft producing aerated oil. Oil cannot properly pressurize and will produce erratic readings as well as rough running, stalling and other related drivability problems with HEUI fuel systems.

High Oil Consumption

Engines can experience high oil consumption for a multitude of reasons, but ultimately oil is either being burned in the combustion chamber or leaking from the engine. When engine oil is leaking, the common procedure to test for leaks is to steam clean or power wash the engine. Then, ultraviolet dye is added to engine oil and the engine is run at operating temperature for at least 20 minutes. A black light is then used to pinpoint the source of the leak. Gaskets, rear main seals, and turbochargers are common leak paths for engine oil. Air compressors are frequently known to pump oil into the engine's intake when unloaded; this will produce mysteriously high oil consumption. The air intake pipe to the compressor should be checked as well as the air reservoirs and air dryer for passing excessive amounts of oil.

Worn rings and valve guides are another point where oil can disappear into the engine. Worn rings will allow oil

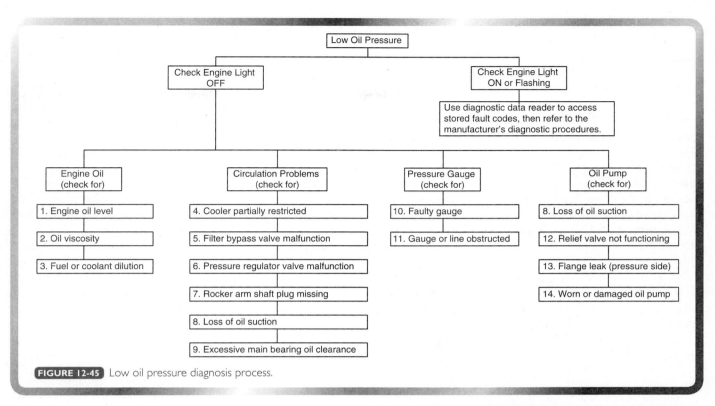

FIGURE 12-45 Low oil pressure diagnosis process.

into the combustion chamber. Piston rings that are coated in carbon, stuck, or seized can provide little to no oil control as well. These conditions will be accompanied by excessive crankcase blow-by, and if a road draft tube ventilates the crankcase, the area below and in the tube air stream will show heavy oil contamination. High crankcase pressure can also push more oil from a closed crankcase ventilation system into a turbocharger or engine intake system. Thin oil or oil that does not have the correct viscosity will more easily pass between tight clearances between valve guides, the piston, and cylinder walls.

Related to high oil consumption is a high oil level. In this situation, the engine appears to "make" oil. Often, the source of this complaint is fuel leakage into the engine. A misfiring injector will allow fuel to wash into the crankcase. A low-pressure fuel system jumper tube beneath the valve cover or a high-pressure tube for a common rail injector can quickly leak fuel into the engine. Leaking injector O-rings, which are caused by loose injectors or cut rings, will cause fuel to flow from around the injectors and into the deck of the cylinder head. Ultraviolet dyes can be used to inspect for fuel system leaks. However, visual inspection of fuel lines when the engine is running is the most common technique to identify internal fuel system leaks. A technician should never use his or her hand to check for leaks because fuel under high pressure can easily penetrate skin and cause blood poisoning.

When checking the engine oil level, the acceptable oil level range is stamped on the oil dipstick **FIGURE 12-46**. An excessive oil level will cause the oil to foam when it contacts the crankshaft or simply leak out of the engine through the rear main oil seal located at the end of the crankshaft **FIGURE 12-47**.

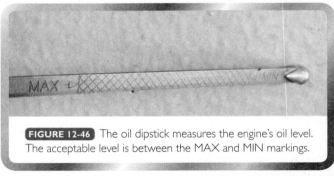

FIGURE 12-46 The oil dipstick measures the engine's oil level. The acceptable level is between the MAX and MIN markings.

FIGURE 12-47 The rear main seal of the engine prevents oil from leaking out of the crankcase from around the end of the crankshaft.

High oil consumption complaints need to be verified by actual measurement of oil used for a given distance FIGURE 12-48 . Usually the technician diagnosing the complaint, and not the customer, will add oil to the engine in order to provide a verifiable and accurate record for oil consumption.

Locating an Oil Leak

Quickly and accurately pinpointing oil leaks is an important skill technicians need to develop. Engines oil leaks are an offense under environmental and U.S. Federal Motor Carrier Safety Administration (FMCSA) legislation. An oil leak qualifies as an out-of-service criteria and is strictly enforced in many jurisdictions. Leaks can often be identified by the color of the leaking fluid. Diesel lubricating oil is black, while transmission fluid, antifreeze, power steering fluid, and washer fluid can be red, green, gold, orange, brown, or blue. Once a leak is determined to be engine oil, it can be difficult to identify where it is leaking from because of gravity, air blown across the engine, and the creeping of oil along an edge of a component. The best method to use to identify the location of an oil leak is tracing dye, which is easily detected with an ultraviolet (UV) light.

To locate an oil leak, follow the steps in SKILL DRILL 12-2 .

Replacing a Rear Main Oil Seal

Engine gaskets and seals are designed to keep liquids, such as oil, from leaking between component surfaces. One particularly important seal is the rear main oil seal located at the end of the crankshaft behind the flywheel FIGURE 12-49 . This dynamic seal, which is a type of seal that prevents leakage around moving parts, blocks oil from leaking from the crankcase. It surrounds the rear snout of the crankshaft and is located in front of the flywheel, pressed into the flywheel housing FIGURE 12-50 .

The seal can begin to leak as a result of wear, excessive bearing clearances, abrasive dirt, or even metal filings in the crankcase, which quickly tear up the seal's soft materials. Because the seal sits just above the crankcase oil level, even a small amount of seal wear can allow a significant amount of oil to leak out into the housing and onto the clutch or torque converter. Oil will cover the underside of a vehicle when the seal is leaking and can even allow the engine to lose most of its oil in a single trip.

To replace a rear main oil seal, follow the steps in SKILL DRILL 12-3 . This procedure is generally performed on an as-needed basis and is not a part of any service recommendation or overhaul procedure.

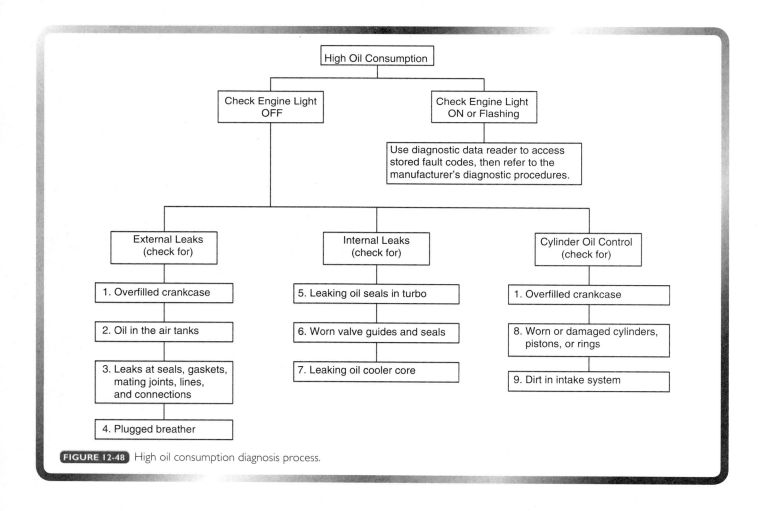

FIGURE 12-48 High oil consumption diagnosis process.

SKILL DRILL 12-2 Locating an Oil Leak

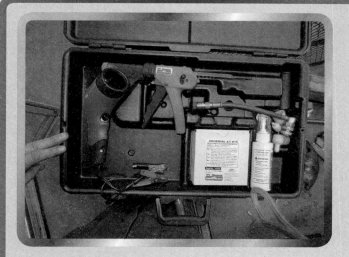

1 Obtain the correct type of fluorescent tracing dye. There are dyes that are only compatible with oil, fuel, coolant, or refrigerant. Choose the correct type.

2 Bring the engine to operating temperature and add the prescribed amount of dye to the engine oil as recommended by the dye manufacturer.

3 Road test the vehicle with the engine under load. When checking for a leak, it is important to get the engine oil to operating temperature. High oil pressure and hot oil will reveal leaks quicker than cold, low-pressure oil.

4 After running the engine for 20–40 minutes, shut the engine off and examine the engine using a UV light. Some kits use alligator clips to power compact 12-volt lights. The newest dyes reflect a bright yellow-green at a leak path when using the UV light. The use of glasses with yellow lenses further enhances the appearance of the dye, making even small leaks easier to detect in tight spots.

5 If uncertain about the actual spot leaking, clean the area with an aerosol solvent and recheck the area with the engine running.

6 Record your observations and make a repair recommendation based on your findings.

FIGURE 12-49 The seal surface for the rear main seal on this DD15 engine is not on the crankshaft, where seals commonly are, but is instead on the flywheel. The seal should be replaced any time the flywheel is removed.

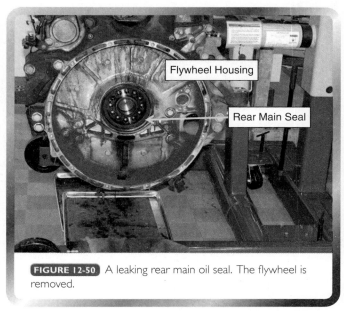

FIGURE 12-50 A leaking rear main oil seal. The flywheel is removed.

SKILL DRILL 12-3 Replacing a Rear Main Oil Seal

1 Verify that the rear main seal is leaking; if it is, oil will originate from inside the flywheel housing. This should not be confused with an oil pan leak or other engine leaks which end up dripping from outside the flywheel housing. A fluorescent dye can be added to the engine oil to help easily pinpoint the source of any oil leak.

2 Disconnect and remove the transmission, clutch, and flywheel.

3 Ensure that the flywheel and bell housing are centered by performing the Re-Installing a Flywheel Housing Skill Drill in the Cylinder Blocks and Crankshafts chapter. An improperly centered flywheel or bell housing will cause premature wear on one side of the seal. Correct any flywheel run out before removing or reinstalling the new rear main seal.

4 Remove the old seal using a heel bar to pry on a self-tapping screw installed in the seal.

5 Remove any seal wear ring installed on the crankshaft, which most manufacturers use on heavy-duty diesels.

6 Inspect the crank sealing surface for damage and clean up the seal surface with crocus cloth.

7 Clean the seal bore in the bell housing.

8 Using a pry bar placed between the crankshaft and bell housing, gently pry up on the crankshaft to observe whether there is any visible movement of the crankshaft that would indicate excessive bearing wear. There should be no movement detected. Take special precautions to prevent damaging the crankshaft with the pry bar. Any detectable vertical movement of the crankshaft will require a main bearing replacement and further investigation regarding the remaining service life of the engine. Any movement will cause the seal to prematurely wear and leak.

9 Using the OEM prescribed seal installation tool, mount the seal on the seal driver and follow any special instructions recommended by the OEM.

10 Center the seal driver on the end of the crankshaft and set the seal to the correct depth required by the OEM. (This is usually achieved as a feature of the installation tool's design.) A wear ring is installed at the same time as the seal. Use special care to drive the seal into the bore squarely because gravity will tilt the driver and seal, which will cause damage to both if the seal is misaligned while tightening it into the bore.

11 Clean, reinstall, and torque the flywheel. Run the engine and check for oil leakage from the rear main oil seal.

Wrap-Up

Ready for Review

▶ The lubrication system reduces friction between moving parts in an engine and is essential for cooling, cleaning, sealing, and absorbing shock loads inside the engine.

▶ Lubrication systems in today's diesels have new demands because of emission legislation and durability requirements.

▶ Oil works by forming a separating film between parts, which minimizes direct contact between moving parts, reducing friction and heat buildup caused by friction.

▶ Oil may be derived from biological sources, but lubricating oils, even synthetics, are primarily a product of petroleum refined from crude oil.

▶ Engine oils are classified by the American Petroleum Institute (API) and carry an API designation indicating their suitability for an engine application.

▶ Viscosity is a liquid's resistance to flow; a numerical designation developed by the Society of Automotive Engineering (SAE) is used to measure oil viscosity.

▶ Motor oils are typically 75–85% base stock, which is the raw mineral processed from crude oil; the remainder of the oil volume is chemical additives.

▶ Additives improve the original properties of the base stock oil; enhancing the performance of motor oil base stocks is necessary to adjust the performance of the oil to suit its intended application.

▶ Synthetics oils are oils with base stock that was synthetically derived or manufactured.

▶ For years, biodiesel has been considered a lubricity additive to keep moving parts operating smoothly inside fuel injection systems, but dilution of engine oil with biodiesel is another matter; biodiesel actually promotes fuel dilution to a much greater extent than mineral diesel fuel.

▶ The lubrication system accomplishes its tasks as a function of a number of major lubrication system components, including the oil pump, oil pan, oil cooler, oil filter(s), and pressure regulating and relief valves.

▶ The function of the oil pan is to store an adequate supply of oil for the lubrication system.

▶ Oil pumps are used to pressurize the lubrication system of a diesel engine.

▶ The oil pump can produce more oil flow than the engine can use; an oil-pressure regulating valve is used to control oil pressure.

▶ Oil coolers are heat exchangers used to remove excess heat from engine oil.

▶ The purpose of lubrication oil filtration is contamination removal; oil contamination can cause abrasives to rapidly wear engine components if not properly controlled.

▶ Today's diesel engine technology requires lubrication oils to meet a variety of operating conditions and provide for long service intervals and engine durability.

▶ The main factors that can limit oil life are the percentage of solids suspended in the oil, sulfur and combustion acids, and oxidized oil.

▶ Oil changes intervals are based on the operating conditions an engine encounters and the amount of fuel consumed; as a general rule, every 45 gallons (170 liters) of fuel consumed by the diesel engine produces enough contaminants to use up 1 quart (1 liter) of oil.

▶ It's in the interest of owners and the environment to extend oil change intervals.

▶ Operation of the valves and oil pump are evaluated using a pressure gauge in the main oil gallery.

Vocabulary Builder

additives Chemicals that improve the original properties of the base stock oil.

American Petroleum Institute (API) An organization that has developed specifications to define engine oil performance standards.

anti-drain back valve A valve that prevents the oil in the engine from returning to the crankcase when the engine is shut down.

base stock The raw mineral processed from crude oil.

cartridge filter A filter element consisting simply of filter media unenclosed by a metal container.

multigrade oil A blend of a several different oils with different viscosities; also known as multiweight oil.

oil quality sensor An electrical device that measures the amount of soot loading in engine oil.

polyalphaolefin (PAO) A manmade base stock (synthetic) used in place of mineral oil. PAO molecules are smaller and more consistent in size, and no impurities are found in this oil because it is derived through chemical process.

scheduled oil sampling (SOS) An extremely detailed analysis of the condition of the engine and quality of the engine oil.

Society of Automotive Engineers (SAE) viscosity ratings An oil performance criteria that indicates oil's flow characteristics.

spin-on filter Filter media enclosed in a metal can that is threaded onto a filter header.

synthetic oil Oil made from base stock that is synthetically derived or manufactured.

total acid number (TAN) The acidity of an oil. Certain contaminants cause engine oil to increase in acidity, which is measured using the TAN index.

total base number (TBN) The measurement of a lubricant's reserve alkalinity, which aids in the control of acids formed during the combustion process.

viscosity A measure of oil's resistance to flow.

viscosity index (VI) A measurement of the total amount of change in an oil's viscosity due to temperature.

viscosity index (VI) improver An additive that prevents oil from thickening when cold and thinning when hot.

Review Questions

1. _____ are a blend of several different oils with different viscosities.
   a. Base stocks
   b. Multigrade oils
   c. Addittives
   d. Synthetic oils

2. Every 45 gallons of fuel consumed by a diesel engine produces enough contaminants to use up to _____ quart(s) of oil.
   a. 0.5
   b. 1
   c. 1.5
   d. 2

3. _____ is a measure of oil's resistance to flow.
   a. Viscosity
   b. Velocity
   c. Positive displacement
   d. Impulse

4. Approximately _____ of the base stock of synthetic oils is made from polyalphaolefin.
   a. 50%
   b. 60%
   c. 70%
   d. 80%

5. _____ is a raw mineral processed from crude oil.
   a. Multigrade oil
   b. Polyalphaolefin
   c. Additive
   d. Base stock

6. Engine oils are classified by the _____ and will carry a designation indicating their suitability for engine applications.
   a. Society of Automotive Engineers
   b. American Petroleum Institute
   c. U.S. Environmental Protection Agency
   d. American Fuel Institute

7. Motor oils are comprised typically of _____ base stock.
   a. 60-70%
   b. 65-75%
   c. 70-80%
   d. 75-85%

8. When performing an oil change, the acceptable oil level range is stamped on the oil _____.
   a. oil pan
   b. dipstick
   c. oil pump
   d. engine

9. When oil turns gray, milky white, or brown, it is usually a sign that _____ has leaked into it.
   a. coolant
   b. base stock
   c. additive
   d. water

10. Because the oil pump can produce more oil flow than the engine can use, an oil pressure _____ is used to control oil pressure.
    a. bypass valve
    b. regulating valve
    c. safety valve
    d. thermostat valve

ASE-Type Questions

1. Technician A says oils with a lower viscosity flow easier than higher viscosities. Technician B says oils with a higher viscosity flow easier than lower viscosities. Who is correct?
   a. Technician A
   b. Technician B
   c. Both Technician A and Technician B
   d. Neither Technician A nor Technician B

2. Technician A says engine oils tested at 212°F are referred to as a summer viscosity. Technician B says engine oils tested at 100°F are referred to as a hot viscosity. Who is correct?
   a. Technician A
   b. Technician B
   c. Both Technician A and Technician B
   d. Neither Technician A nor Technician B

3. Technician A says the best method used to identify the location of an oil leak is tracing dye. Technician B says the best method used to identify the location of an oil leak is to use a towel to check for oil deposits. Who is correct?
   a. Technician A
   b. Technician B
   c. Both Technician A and Technician B
   d. Neither Technician A nor Technician B

4. Technician A says engine oils are classified by the American Petroleum Institute. Technician B says engine oils carry a designation indicating their suitability for engine applications. Who is correct?
   a. Technician A
   b. Technician B
   c. Both Technician A and Technician B
   d. Neither Technician A nor Technician B

5. Technician A says reserve alkalinity additives ensure the oil does not become alkaline from products of combustion. Technician B says reserve alkalinity additives ensure the oil does not become acidic from products of combustion. Who is correct?
   a. Technician A
   b. Technician B
   c. Both Technician A and Technician B
   d. Neither Technician A nor Technician B

6. Technician A says the percentage of liquids refers to the total amount of particles that are suspended in the oil. Technician B says the percentage of gasses refers to the total amount of particles that are suspended in the oil. Who is correct?
   a. Technician A
   b. Technician B
   c. Both Technician A and Technician B
   d. Neither Technician A nor Technician B

7. Technician A says the recommended oil change interval is calculated by subtracting the quantity of oil in the oil pan from the number of barrels of fuel burned. Technician B says the recommended oil change interval is calculated by multiplying the quantity of oil in the oil pan by the number of barrels of fuel burned. Who is correct?
   a. Technician A
   b. Technician B
   c. Both Technician A and Technician B
   d. Neither Technician A nor Technician B

8. Technician A says polyalphaolefin is a man-made base stock used in place of mineral oil. Technician B says a base stock is the raw mineral processed from crude oil. Who is correct?
   a. Technician A
   b. Technician B
   c. Both Technician A and Technician B
   d. Neither Technician A nor Technician B

9. Technician A says that at a molecular level, the forces attracting oil molecules to each other are greater than the forces causing oil molecules to adhere to metal surfaces. Technician B says that at a molecular level, the forces attracting oil molecules to metal surfaces are weaker than the forces causing oil molecules to adhere to one another. Who is correct?
   a. Technician A
   b. Technician B
   c. Both Technician A and Technician B
   d. Neither Technician A nor Technician B

10. Technician A says spin-on filters are exempt from EPA regulations regarding hazardous waste. Technician B says spin-on filters are regulated by the EPA regarding hazardous waste. Who is correct?
    a. Technician A
    b. Technician B
    c. Both Technician A and Technician B
    d. Neither Technician A nor Technician B

CHAPTER 13
Diesel Engine Cooling Systems

NATEF Tasks

Diesel Engines

General
- Inspect fuel, oil, Diesel Exhaust Fluid (DEF) and coolant levels, and condition; determine needed action. (pp 387–388)
- Identify engine fuel, oil, coolant, air, and other leaks; determine needed action. (pp 388–390)

Cooling System
- Check engine coolant type, level, condition, and consumption; test coolant for freeze protection and additive package concentration; determine needed action. (pp 374–377, 387–388, 392–393)
- Test coolant temperature and check operation of temperature and level sensors, gauge, and/or sending unit; determine needed action. (p 390)
- Inspect and reinstall/replace pulleys, tensioners, and drive belts; adjust drive belts and check alignment. (p 387)
- Inspect thermostat(s), bypasses, housing(s), and seals; replace as needed. (pp 381–383)
- Recover coolant, flush, and refill with recommended coolant/additive package; bleed cooling system. (pp 387–393)
- Inspect coolant conditioner/filter assembly for leaks; inspect valves, lines, and fittings; replace as needed. (pp 389–390)

- Inspect water pump and hoses; replace as needed. (pp 379–381, 391–392)
- Inspect, clean, and pressure-test radiator. Pressure-test cap, tank(s), and recovery systems; determine needed action. (pp 388–389)
- Inspect thermostatic cooling fan system (hydraulic, pneumatic, and electronic) and fan shroud; replace as needed. (pp 383–386, 391)

Heating, Ventilation, & Air Conditioning

Heating and Engine Cooling Systems
- Inspect and test radiator, pressure cap, and coolant recovery system (surge tank); determine needed action. (pp 388–389)
- Inspect water pump; determine needed action. (pp 379–381)
- Inspect and test thermostats, by-passes, housings, and seals; determine needed repairs. (pp 381–383)
- Recover, flush, and refill with recommended coolant/additive package; bleed cooling system. (pp 387–393)

Preventive Maintenance and Inspection

Engine System
Cooling System
- Inspect water pump. (pp 379–381)

Knowledge Objectives

After reading this chapter, you will be able to:
1. Explain the operating principles of the diesel engine cooling system and its components. (pp 369–379)
2. Describe the purpose, types, function, composition, and applications of diesel engine coolant. (pp 379–385)
3. Identify and describe the construction features, types, and applications of the diesel engine cooling system and its components. (pp 386–394)
4. Describe the inspection and testing procedures for a diesel engine cooling system and its components. (pp 395–400)
5. Recommend service and maintenance of diesel engine cooling system and its components. (pp 400–402)

Skills Objectives

After reading this chapter, you will be able to:

1. Pressure test the cooling system and inspect for leaks. (p 397) SKILL DRILL 13-1
2. Verify the engine operating temperature. (p 398) SKILL DRILL 13-2
3. Inspect for a leaking EGR cooler. (p 398) SKILL DRILL 13-3
4. Test coolant nitrite or DCA/SCA levels. (p 399) SKILL DRILL 13-4
5. Use a hydrometer to test the freeze point of the coolant. (p 401) SKILL DRILL 13-5
6. Use a refractometer to test the freeze point of the coolant. (p 401) SKILL DRILL 13-6

► Introduction

The cooling system may not receive much interest as an engine subsystem, but its operation and maintenance is critical to engine durability and reliability. Manufacturer studies report as much as 40% of all engine maintenance or breakdown is related directly or indirectly to cooling system maintenance. Over 50% of catastrophic engine failures can be attributed to cooling system failure, and 60% of water pump failures are caused by preventable seal leakage. Diesel cooling systems also need specialized attention because of unique heat loads and combustion characteristics that affect coolant maintenance practices.

In this chapter the function of the diesel engine cooling system is examined along with the operation and maintenance of components in the system. A thorough knowledge of the operation and unique features of the diesel cooling system will assist technicians in making correct recommendations for service and maintenance of this critical engine system.

► Fundamentals of Cooling Systems

Cooling systems perform a variety of functions, which are outlined in the sections below.

Removal of Excess Heat

The flame temperature of diesel fuel is approximately 3900°F (2149°C). Sustained operation of the engine at temperatures like this without some means to remove heat would quickly result in damaged and destroyed engine components. Operating

You Are the Technician

You have started to work at a school bus fleet operation. The operation has close to two hundred units from different manufacturers using a variety of diesel engines, but most are less than ten years old. While the goal is to keep the vehicles in a good state of repair, the company is cost conscious and you understand that any service recommendation multiplied two hundred times translates into a significant amount of money either spent or saved. As you review the service records and preventive maintenance schedule you notice that the engine coolant has never been changed in any of the vehicles. When you ask about this, you hear conflicting information. Some technicians say the buses use coolant that doesn't need changing. Others say it needs changing, but the company doesn't want to spend the money on labor to flush and fill the cooling system, on disposal costs to recycle old coolant, or on purchasing good-quality long-life coolant. You will need to make a service recommendation about the coolant as part of inspection reports you are completing. As you think about a service recommendation, consider the following:

1. What specific information would you collect about a vehicle, the fleet, and its equipment to make a recommendation to leave the coolant in the engines; drain, flush, and refill the cooling systems; or switch to stocking a single type of coolant or multiple types of coolant?
2. List and explain the factors that are important to take into consideration when making a decision about the selection of coolant or coolants you would use if the coolant was to be replaced.
3. What risks might there be and what kind of repairs would you anticipate after leaving coolant in the engines if it is a type I or type III coolant?

clearances between moving engine parts would disappear and cause engine seizure. Components such as pistons and valves would burn, or soften and permanently distort, under the high temperatures. Lubrication oil would also burn upon contact with hot engine. Its viscosity would become too thin to properly support bearing loads and lubricate parts. To prevent these adverse conditions, the cooling system removes excess heat from the engine and releases it to the atmosphere through the radiator **FIGURE 13-1**.

In today's engines, more than half the heat energy produced from combustion is wasted through heat radiated from engine surfaces and dissipated from the engine through the cooling system and exhaust gases. The measure of an engine's ability to convert the energy content of fuel into mechanical force is called <u>thermal efficiency</u> **FIGURE 13-2**. Thermal efficiency is measured as a percentage of the potential energy content in fuel compared with the engine's ability to convert the potential energy into mechanical energy. A simplified way of stating thermal efficiency would be to compare the mechanical energy available at the flywheel to the cost of fuel. If $100 of fuel is burned by an engine and only $40 of mechanical energy is produced at the flywheel, the engine would have 40% thermal efficiency. Currently, the best heavy-duty on-highway diesel engines operate at approximately 45% thermal efficiency, which means that 45% of the fuel energy released during combustion is converted into mechanical energy and available at the flywheel. The remaining energy is absorbed by the cooling system (30–35%), emitted by the exhaust system (20–25%), or radiated to the atmosphere through hot engine parts (5%). Friction and the energy required to move gases in and out of the engine account for the remaining losses in thermal efficiency. Larger, slow-speed industrial diesel engines used on ships and for electric power generation can operate at more than 50% thermal efficiency. Greenhouse gas (GHG) emission standards for heavy-duty diesels require a 17% increase in thermal efficiency for diesel engines by 2025. The thermal efficiency of today's diesel engines is almost double that of spark-ignited gasoline engines, which operate at up to approximately 25–30% thermal efficiency. Recapturing energy that would normally be lost in the exhaust system to power a turbocharger can increase the thermal efficiency of a diesel engine; this is just one way that heat energy is recovered by diesels. Higher compression ratios, the absence of a throttle valve, and other mechanical factors also help diesels achieve better thermal efficiency.

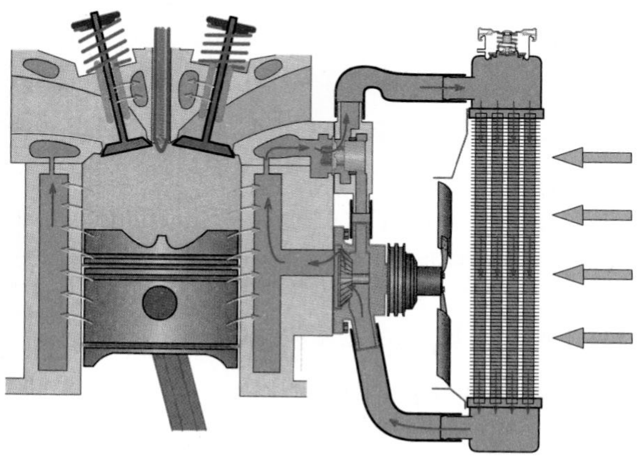

FIGURE 13-1 The cooling system removes excess heat from the engine and releases it to the atmosphere through the radiator.

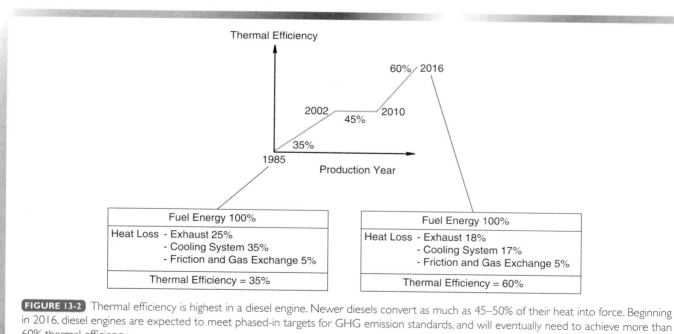

FIGURE 13-2 Thermal efficiency is highest in a diesel engine. Newer diesels convert as much as 45–50% of their heat into force. Beginning in 2016, diesel engines are expected to meet phased-in targets for GHG emission standards, and will eventually need to achieve more than 60% thermal efficiency.

Diesel Engine Heat Loads

While compression-ignition combustion is one of the most thermally efficient processes for converting fuel energy into mechanical energy, it still involves a substantial amount of heat being released to the cooling system. The release of heat to the cooling system is called <u>heat rejection</u>. Diesel engines have several unique systems and components that require additional cooling systems not found in automotive engines. These systems use engine coolant to transfer heat away from the engine and into the atmosphere.

Exhaust Gas Recirculation

Cooled exhaust gas recirculation (EGR), which has been used by diesels for the past decade and a half, places an even larger heat load on the cooling system **FIGURE 13-3**. Up to 30% of intake air mass in most current diesels will include exhaust gases, which can reach 1200°F (649°C). These temperatures are reduced to 400°F (204°C) or less before being mixed with intake air originating from the outlet of the charge-air cooler. This means the diesel-powered vehicle's cooling system needs to dissipate 15–40% more heat absorbed from the exhaust gas. Until model year 2002, when cooled EGR was introduced, most diesels had 100% of exhaust heat passed into the atmosphere. Now, larger heat loads are handled by the cooling system to accommodate EGR. Engine modifications to deal with the increased heat loads include larger water pumps, cooling fans, and radiator cross-sectional areas combined with increased underhood airflow are needed to remove the additional heat from the cooling system.

Lubrication Oil

Heat generated by combustion is rejected and transferred to engine parts and lubrication oil. If excess heat is not removed from the oil it can lose its viscosity and thin too much to support bearing loads and properly lubricate parts. At temperatures above 250°F (121°C), oil can quickly oxidize and even burn. Because every turbocharged engine cools the underside of the piston with engine oil, higher heat loads are imposed on the lubrication system. To remove this heat from the oil, virtually all diesel engines use oil coolers that circulate engine coolant to remove heat from the engine oil **FIGURE 13-4**.

Air Intake System

Intake air compressed by the turbocharger easily heats to over 400°F (204°C). Temperatures are even higher than this in engines using series turbocharging. Cooling heated intake air is necessary to reduce emissions and prevent thermal overloading of cylinder components such as piston crowns and valves. While most engines use air-to-air aftercooling (ATAAC), engine coolant is often used to help reduce charge air temperatures. Liquid heat exchangers, charge air coolers, or aftercoolers may be located in the intake manifold to circulate coolant, which lowers air inlet temperatures **FIGURE 13-5**. More commonly, liquid interstage coolers are used on series turbocharged engines to reduce air temperatures between the low- and high-pressure turbochargers. Heat removed from intake air is simply transferred to the atmosphere through the radiator.

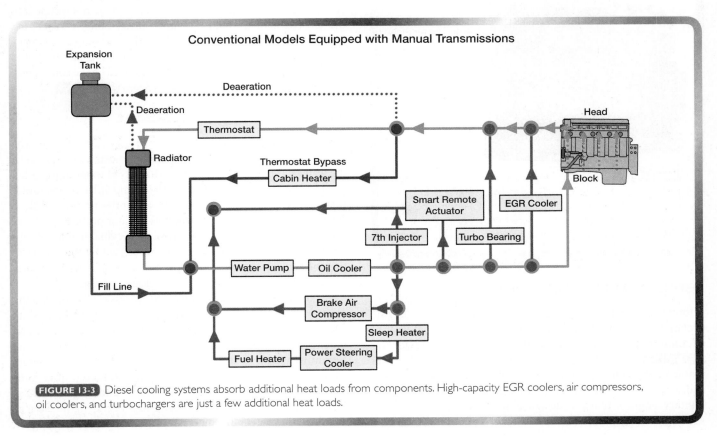

FIGURE 13-3 Diesel cooling systems absorb additional heat loads from components. High-capacity EGR coolers, air compressors, oil coolers, and turbochargers are just a few additional heat loads.

FIGURE 13-4 Oil cooler nozzles spray the underside of all engine piston crowns with oil to remove heat. The heat absorbed by the oil is removed by the cooling system through the oil cooler.

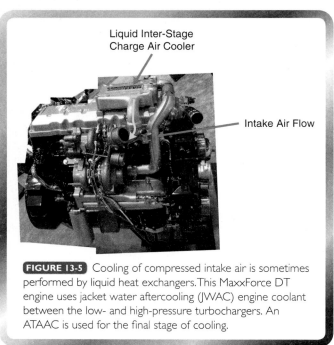

Liquid Inter-Stage Charge Air Cooler

Intake Air Flow

FIGURE 13-5 Cooling of compressed intake air is sometimes performed by liquid heat exchangers. This MaxxForce DT engine uses jacket water aftercooling (JWAC) engine coolant between the low- and high-pressure turbochargers. An ATAAC is used for the final stage of cooling.

Temperature Regulation

Another important job of the cooling system is to raise engine coolant temperature quickly to keep engine component wear to a minimum by circulating through the engine **FIGURE 13-6** and **FIGURE 13-7**. Machined parts operating with close tolerances require consistent operating temperatures of between 180°F and 200°F (82°C and 93°C). (An exception is emergency and military engines that are designed to withstand as much as 230°F [110°C].)

Higher operating temperatures will lower the amount of heat rejected, but if temperatures climb even as little as 12°F beyond normal range, cylinder wall wear begins to dramatically increase. Conversely, cold cylinders will prevent engine parts from operating at optimal clearances and lead to excessive oil consumption, carbon deposits on pistons, poor combustion quality, and oil sludging due to water condensation. In current diesels, the coolant must reach a minimum temperature necessary within a reasonable time to enable other on-board diagnostic (OBD) monitors to run.

▶ **TECHNICIAN TIP**

Short run operation of any engine will cause sludging of the engine oil. If oil is not allowed to properly heat up, water condensation from blow-by gases will contaminate the oil, which could eventually clog the oil pick-up tube for the oil pump and other oil passages in the engine. Always ensure that engine oil is frequently brought to operating temperature during daily equipment operation to vaporize any water condensation in the lubrication oil.

Provide for Coolant Expansion

Cooling systems must provide for the expansion of coolant. As engine coolant warms, it expands. An overflow reservoir is needed to contain the coolant pushed out of the radiator and engine. Surge tanks, overflow reservoirs, and large radiator tanks are used to buffer coolant expansion **FIGURE 13-8**. Most anti-freezes are made from a base chemical called **ethylene glycol**, and because ethylene glycol is considered toxic, coolant must not escape into the environment through overflow hoses. (Some coolants are made with **propylene glycol**, which is nontoxic and environmentally friendly.) When the engine cools, coolant is drawn back into the radiator through negative pressure induced by the contraction of cool coolant in the closed cooling system **FIGURE 13-9**.

Pressurize Engine Coolant

Cooling systems are pressurized for two important reasons. The first is to maintain pressure greater than atmospheric pressure at the water pump inlet. Without pressure to the water pump inlet, pumps operate less efficiently. If the pump inlet is not under pressure, it can become air-bound and prevent coolant flow. Related to this is **cavitation**, which is a major problem in diesel cooling systems. Cavitation is erosion in cylinder block walls, heads, injector tubes, and liner sleeves caused by the vaporization of coolant that is under low pressure. Cavitation occurs more easily if cooling system pressures are abnormally low.

The second important reason for pressurizing the cooling system is that it increases the boiling point of water. Permitting water to turn to vapor or steam near the cylinders and in the cylinder heads would dramatically lower the ability of the cooling system to absorb heat. Even momentary loss of direct contact with coolant would cause severe thermal stress on these components, resulting in cracking of heads and engine blocks. Increasing cooling system pressure will prevent engine damage and loss of coolant by increasing the temperature at which

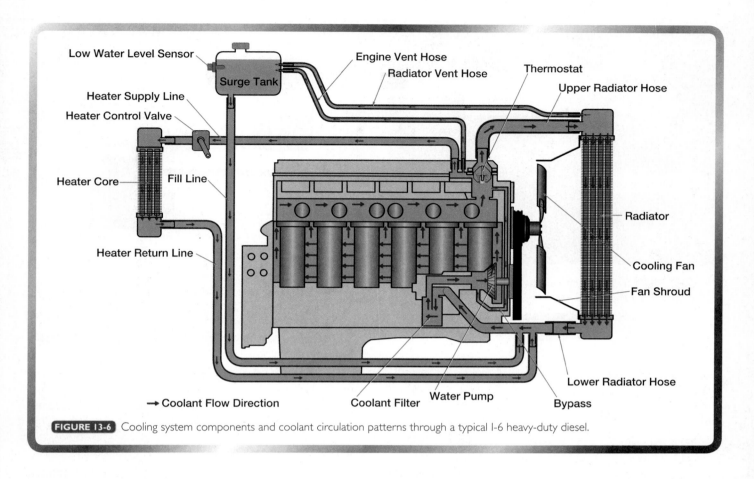

FIGURE 13-6 Cooling system components and coolant circulation patterns through a typical I-6 heavy-duty diesel.

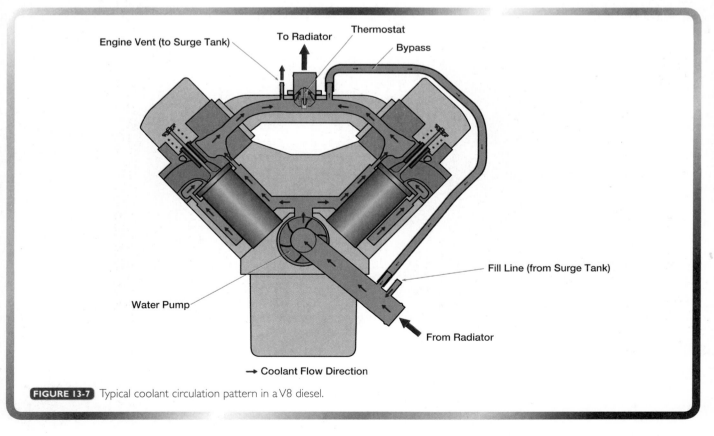

FIGURE 13-7 Typical coolant circulation pattern in a V8 diesel.

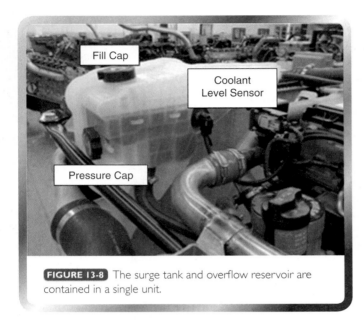

FIGURE 13-8 The surge tank and overflow reservoir are contained in a single unit.

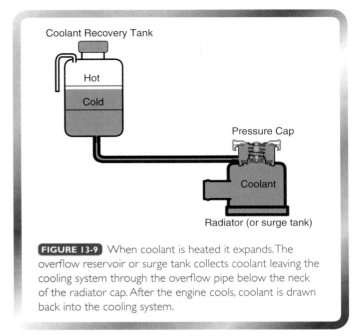

FIGURE 13-9 When coolant is heated it expands. The overflow reservoir or surge tank collects coolant leaving the cooling system through the overflow pipe below the neck of the radiator cap. After the engine cools, coolant is drawn back into the cooling system.

coolant will boil. Every 1-psi (7-kPa) increase in cooling system pressure increases the boiling point by approximately 3°F. This means 10 psi (69 kPa) of pressure on the cooling system raises its boiling point to 242°F (117°C) **FIGURE 13-10**.

Pressurizing the cooling system also prevents water from boiling away from the cooling system. The cooling system is pressurized by both coolant expansion and trapped air, including steam trapped in the radiator during heating.

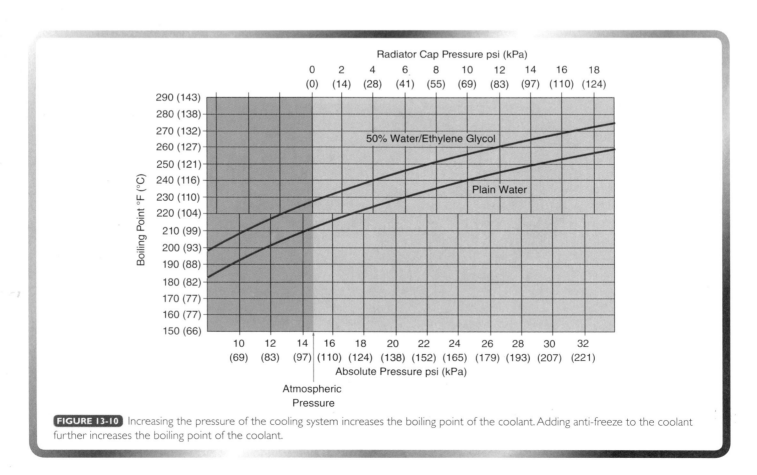

FIGURE 13-10 Increasing the pressure of the cooling system increases the boiling point of the coolant. Adding anti-freeze to the coolant further increases the boiling point of the coolant.

▶ TECHNICIAN TIP

Diesel engine cooling systems have traditionally operated at pressures between 7 and 10 psi (48 and 69 kPa), which is lower than gasoline engines. The primary reason for this lower pressure is to prevent overheating the oil in the oil cooler. At higher coolant temperatures, the lubricating oil will lose its viscosity, which could potentially cause a loss in lubricating abilities. At a lower boiling point, coolant escaping as steam will carry heat away from the engine and keep the oil temperature in the oil coolers lower. Higher operating temperatures would allow the oil to potentially overheat. Newer engines using cooled EGR have higher cooling system pressures to prevent boiling of coolant in the EGR cooler.

▶ TECHNICIAN TIP

Galvanic activity in a cooling system is easily measured with a digital multimeter. After setting the meter to a low-voltage DC scale, one test lead is placed in the coolant. The other test lead can be placed anywhere on the engine where there is metal exposed for a good ground. A cooling system with a level of additives that is adequate to protect metals from corrosion will test at 0.2 volts or less. Coolant that has become depleted of additives or highly acidic or alkaline (basic) will produce more voltage. If voltage exceeds 2 volts, the cooling system should be drained and flushed, and new coolant that contains the recommended level of conditioners should be added.

Deaeration of Coolant

Aeration is the condition in which excessive amounts of air or steam bubbles are dissolved in coolant, diminishing the coolant's effectiveness. Cooling systems must provide for deaeration of coolant to prevent pumps and coolant passageways in the cylinder head from becoming air bound, or blocked by an accumulation of steam **FIGURE 13-11**. As coolant warms, some vaporization occurs, forming bubbles and vapor pockets. Even when coolant is relatively cold, coolant next to hot interior engine surfaces becomes hotter than surrounding coolant and vaporizes. If the vapor collects into large steam pockets, the engine cannot transfer heat to the coolant, causing localized hot spots and potential damage from overheating.

Minimize Corrosion

Dissimilar metals in contact with engine coolant causes electrochemical reactions **FIGURE 13-12**. The coolant is an **electrolyte**, which means it can conduct current. In a sense, the cooling system can behave like a primary battery in which dissimilar metals in the presence of an electrolyte will produce a flow of electric current. This principle of inducing current flow by using dissimilar metals and an electrolyte is called the galvanic effect. Eventually, some metals in contact with coolant will be severely and quickly corroded through these chemical reactions unless some strategy is used to prevent these reactions. For this reason, anti-freeze contains a number of additives that minimize electrochemical reactions, prolonging the durability of engine and cooling system components.

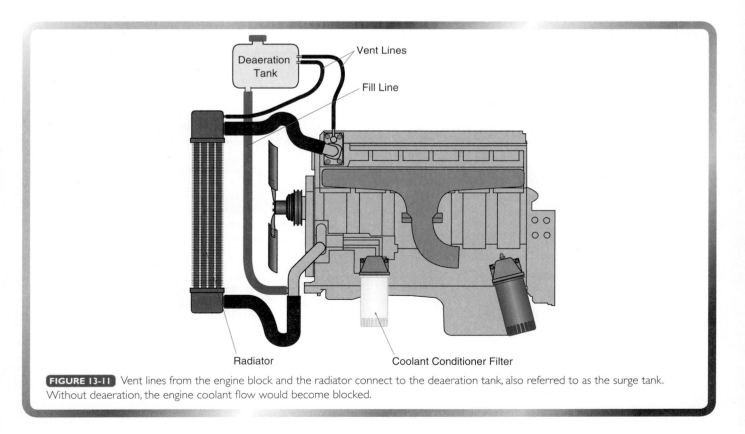

FIGURE 13-11 Vent lines from the engine block and the radiator connect to the deaeration tank, also referred to as the surge tank. Without deaeration, the engine coolant flow would become blocked.

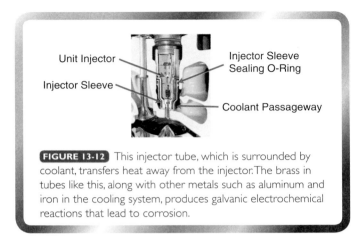

FIGURE 13-12 This injector tube, which is surrounded by coolant, transfers heat away from the injector. The brass in tubes like this, along with other metals such as aluminum and iron in the cooling system, produces galvanic electrochemical reactions that lead to corrosion.

Minimize Scaling and Deposits

Scale and deposits on internal surfaces within the engine and cooling system can sharply reduce heat transfer. In fact, a 0.06" (1.6 mm) deposit will reduce heat transfer by 40%. Scale can come from calcium and magnesium in the water used for cooling, but some scale is produced by additives in the anti-freeze such as phosphate, silicate, and nitrite. Scaling and deposit formation commonly occur on hot engine surfaces where coolant turbulence is low. Maintenance practices and formulations of engine coolant should be designed to minimize the formation of these engine-damaging deposits **FIGURE 13-13**.

Freeze and Boil Protection

Because water is the primary ingredient of engine coolant, the engine requires protection from freezing and boiling coolant. Frozen coolant can easily break and crack cylinder heads, blocks,

water pumps, and radiators. Core plugs, sometimes called frost plugs, are pushed out by frozen coolant, which causes a major loss of coolant. It should be noted that core plugs are not designed to relieve pressure from frozen coolant to prevent engine damage. When coolant is frozen, it will not flow, which causes the cylinder components to rapidly overheat, thermally stressing the cylinder block and head to the point of cracking. Conversely, boiling coolant is not able to effectively absorb heat, because it is not in a liquid state. Freeze and boil protection are both provided to the engine by the use of anti-freeze (also referred to as coolant in some regions) **TABLE 13-1**. Additional boiling protection is accomplished through pressurizing the cooling system.

Concentration of Anti-freeze by % Volume	Freeze Point of Coolant			
	Ethylene Glycol		Propylene Glycol	
0% (water only)	32°F	0°C	32°F	0°C
20%	16°F	−0°C	19°F	−7°C
30%	4°F	−16°C	10°F	−12°C
40%	−12°F	−24°C	−6°F	−21°C
50%	−34°F	−37°C	−27°F	−33°C
60%	−62°F	−52°C	−56°F	−49°C
80%	−57°F	−49°C	−71°F	−57°C
100%	−5°F	−22°C	−76°F	−60°C

TABLE 13-1: Freezing Points of Ethylene Glycol and Propylene Glycol Anti-freeze

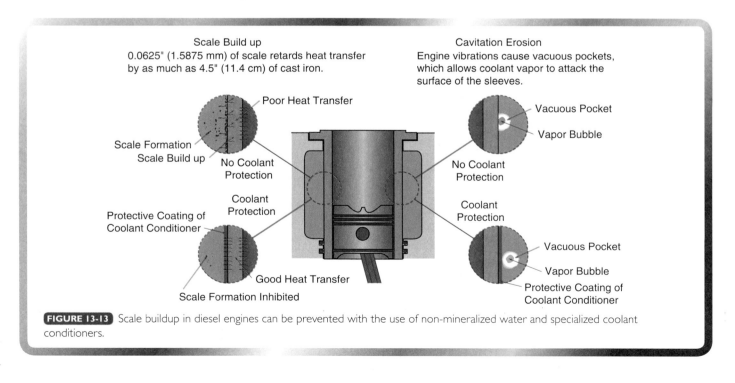

FIGURE 13-13 Scale buildup in diesel engines can be prevented with the use of non-mineralized water and specialized coolant conditioners.

Minimize Cavitation Erosion

A condition unique to diesel engines is cavitation of the cylinder wall and liner **FIGURE 13-14**. Cavitation erosion is caused by the collapse of tiny water vapor bubbles formed when coolant rapidly heats next to hot surfaces, or the coolant is subjected to a rapid drop in pressure. Liquid will vaporize in both these situations, producing air bubbles. This phenomenon is easily observed while watching and listening to a pot of water sitting on the heating element of a stove. In a pot of cold water, bubbles will appear on the bottom of the pot where it is in contact with the hot heating element. These vapor bubbles collapse back into liquid when cooled by the surrounding cold water, or when pressure increases around the vapor bubble. The snapping and popping sound initially heard from the cold pot of is evidence of vapor bubble collapse, which can lead to cavitation in an engine. Pressure exerted by the force of bubble collapse is reported to be as high as 60,000 psi (4137 bar). The force of implosion against cylinder walls, cylinder liners, water pump inlets, injector tubes, and other such components can easily blast holes into the components and eventual destroys them **FIGURE 13-15**. Cylinder liners have an exaggerated pattern of cavitation erosion on the major thrust surfaces, because that particular liner surface flexes and relaxes during and after the piston's power stroke. This expansion–contraction vibration creates a temporary low-pressure area on the outside of the liner, producing even more vapor bubbles and thus more cavitation erosion **FIGURE 13-16**. Chemical treatment of the cooling system is the preferred method for minimizing cavitation erosion. Both new and old formulations of anti-freeze for diesel engines use a critical additive, nitrite, to minimize cavitation erosion. Today, most OEMs use and recommend the use of long-life anti-freeze formulated with nitrite at the point of production.

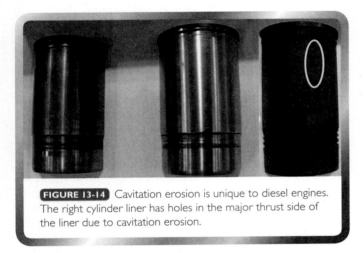

FIGURE 13-14 Cavitation erosion is unique to diesel engines. The right cylinder liner has holes in the major thrust side of the liner due to cavitation erosion.

Cavitation and Engine Damage

Cavitation erosion is particularly destructive because it can produce pin-sized holes in the cylinder wall that allow coolant to leak into the cylinders or compression gases to leak into the cooling system. Hydrostatic lock of the engine is caused when pressurized coolant is pushed through these holes and into the cylinder during engine hot soak period. (Hot soak is the time when a hot

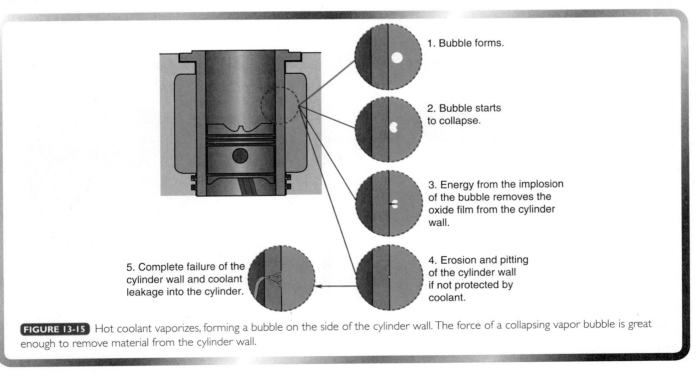

1. Bubble forms.

2. Bubble starts to collapse.

3. Energy from the implosion of the bubble removes the oxide film from the cylinder wall.

4. Erosion and pitting of the cylinder wall if not protected by coolant.

5. Complete failure of the cylinder wall and coolant leakage into the cylinder.

FIGURE 13-15 Hot coolant vaporizes, forming a bubble on the side of the cylinder wall. The force of a collapsing vapor bubble is great enough to remove material from the cylinder wall.

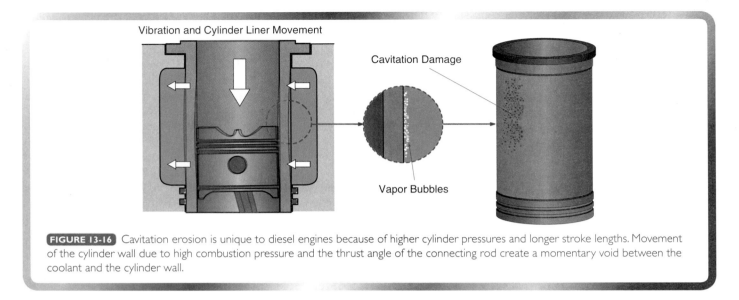

FIGURE 13-16 Cavitation erosion is unique to diesel engines because of higher cylinder pressures and longer stroke lengths. Movement of the cylinder wall due to high combustion pressure and the thrust angle of the connecting rod create a momentary void between the coolant and the cylinder wall.

engine is cooling down after it is shut off.) If the cavitation erosion has created a hole in the cylinder below the point where the piston normally rests, coolant will leak into the crankcase causing what may appear to be a loss of coolant.

Parent bore engines, or engines without liners, are not immune to the problem of cavitation erosion as some engine sales literature tries to suggest. The sharp increase in combustion pressure also creates temporary pressure voids on the coolant side of the block's cylinder walls, which produces cavitation erosion. For this reason, all diesel engine cooling systems need to use special conditioners to prevent or minimize cavitation erosion. There are two categories of conditioner: **organic acid technology (OAT)** and **inorganic additive technology (IAT)** **FIGURE 13-17**. IAT is commonly marketed using the terms **supplemental coolant additive (SCA)** and **diesel coolant additive (DCA)**. Both OAT and IAT were developed primarily

to treat or condition the cooling system to reduce the effects of cavitation erosion. The most significant additive that prevents cavitation erosion is nitrite. Nitrite, when added to coolant, forms a thin, protective film on the coolant side of the engine cylinder walls and other surfaces to reduce cavitation erosion. Vapor implosion in an engine protected by nitrite will damage only the nitrite layer, which can be replenished from the nitrite dissolved in the coolant **FIGURE 13-18**. Nitrite also combines with the iron in liners and block walls to form very hard, micro-thin alloys that minimize damage from vapor implosion. Regardless of the formulation of the anti-freeze used in a diesel engine, cooling system maintenance must include the measurement of the level of nitrite to evaluate the level of this important additive. In older Type I anti-freeze, there is a recommended service interval for testing and adding a prescribed amount of DCA or SCA.

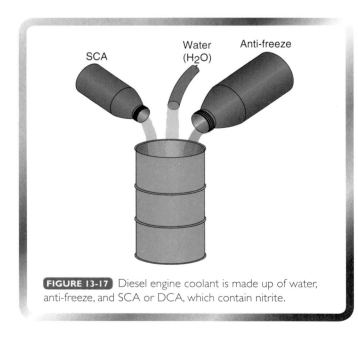

FIGURE 13-17 Diesel engine coolant is made up of water, anti-freeze, and SCA or DCA, which contain nitrite.

FIGURE 13-18 A coolant filter that uses powdered DCA containing nitrite.

Cooling System Circulation Patterns

In all liquid-cooled engines, the thermostat controls the flow of coolant through the radiator. In high-capacity cooling systems, more than one thermostat is often used. When cold, the coolant circulates through the water pump and flows out through a bypass hose or passageway, recirculating coolant back into the block. The bypass passageway is needed to circulate coolant through the engine and cylinder head while the thermostat is closed. When the thermostat opens, coolant leaves the cylinder head, flows through the radiator, and returns via the lower radiator hose to the water pump inlet. Depending on the manufacturer, coolant generally flows through the oil cooler first after leaving the water pump. Coolant then flows through the cylinder block water jackets, through the cylinder head and finally out through the thermostat to the radiator. The direction of coolant flow from the block to the head is controlled by coolant holes in the head gaskets. One side of the head gasket typically has more or larger holes than the other. The largest holes are located on the opposite side of the gasket from the thermostat. This requires coolant to flow across the head to properly cool the head before reaching the thermostat housing.

▶ Types of Coolant

Heavy-duty and automotive diesel engines depend almost exclusively on the efficiency of liquid cooling systems. Water, mixed with anti-freeze and other ingredients, is the primary coolant medium to absorb engine heat. A **heat exchanger** or radiator transfers heat from the coolant to the atmosphere. Some engines are air cooled; they are used primarily in off-road, agricultural, and heavy-equipment applications. Liquid cooling systems consist of a number of components operating together to perform the cooling system functions.

Coolant

Though they are similar in some respects, coolant for diesel-fueled engines and coolant for gasoline-fueled engines are quite different. Diesel coolant consists of water, anti-freeze that contains a special corrosion-inhibitor package, and supplemental coolant additives to minimize cavitation erosion.

Coolant pH

One major factor affecting the corrosion rate of the metals in an engine is the coolant's pH level, its alkaline or acidic chemical property. A material's pH is measured on a scale of 0–14, with 7 being neutral. A coolant with a pH less than 7 is acidic, and a coolant with a pH more than 7 is alkaline. Coolant pH should be maintained between 8.5 and 10.5. Shifts in coolant pH will affect the rate of corrosion of different metals **FIGURE 13-19**. If a coolant's pH drops below 8.5, it will become aggressive to ferrous metals (cast iron and steel), aluminum, copper, and brass. If it increases above 11, it will become aggressive to aluminum and solder in a cooling system. Maintaining optimum pH in a coolant is a critical function of a coolant additive (DCA/SCA). Ethylene glycol anti-freeze will become more acidic when exposed to air. Combustion gas leakage into coolant can also make it acidic. Overconcentration and overuse of conditioner that contains pH buffers to make coolant alkaline will cause coolant to become destructive to engine metal.

Water

Water is the most efficient fluid to transfer heat. However, water will cause corrosion of metal parts in contact with the cooling

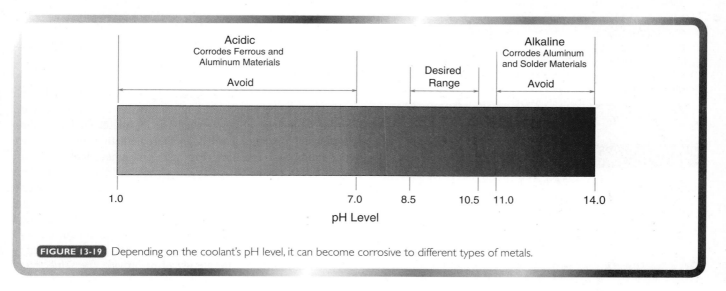

FIGURE 13-19 Depending on the coolant's pH level, it can become corrosive to different types of metals.

system and therefore requires the addition of corrosion inhibitors. Pure water will boil and freeze at temperatures within the operating range of the cooling system. Anti-freeze is added to water to increase the boiling point and lower the freezing temperature of water.

Distilled water is best for cooling systems because it has no mineral content to scale, or deposit, on a cooling system. Chlorine, which forms corrosive chloride chemical compounds, is also absent from distilled water. The percentage of anti-freeze in the water mixture should never be higher than 60% or lower than 40%. Coolant with less than 40% concentration of anti-freeze may not contain enough corrosion inhibitors. Over 65% concentration and the coolant will not remove heat effectively and will in fact lose its freeze protection. A 50/50 mixture is optimal for removing heat and providing corrosion protection. However, extremely cold operating conditions may need a higher concentration of anti-freeze. Similarly, higher concentration of water in extreme heat conditions improves heat transfer. In hot climates, a concentration of less than 40/60 is not recommended because insufficient amount of additives are present to protect the cooling system. For boil protection, anti-freeze concentrations in engines operating above 195°F (91°C) should not be less than 50%.

It's important to remember that too high a concentration of anti-freeze will reduce the ability of coolant to absorb and release heat. An anti-freeze–water preparation is capable of absorbing and releasing as little as 50–70% as much heat as pure water. Poor engine cooling, overheating, and inadequate passenger warm air heating results when anti-freeze is over concentrated. Propylene glycol–based anti-freeze requires higher concentration to achieve the same freeze protection as ethylene glycol–based anti-freeze.

▶ TECHNICIAN TIP

Too much of a good thing is bad. In the case of anti-freeze, overconcentration can lead to engine overheating because anti-freeze does not remove and release heat as quickly as water. Even though the cooling system temperature may be normal, in-cylinder temperatures will be higher. Less heat is released by the heater core and radiator which can lead to overheating in some instances. Over concentrating ethylene glycol anti-freeze will cause an increase rather than a decrease in the coolant's freeze point protection.

▶ TECHNICIAN TIP

Ethylene glycol, which is the base from which the majority of anti-freezes are made, is toxic. Less than 4 ounces (113 grams) will kill a 150-lb person (68 kg). Because ethylene glycol is toxic, anti-freeze is an environmental hazard and must be properly disposed of. Old anti-freeze is typically picked up and recycled by licensed recyclers.

Anti-freeze

Using water alone as an engine's only coolant may be efficient, but it is detrimental to engine operation. Not only can water freeze and crack engine castings, but it will quickly corrode the engine internally. Adding anti-freeze to water can eliminate these problems and extend engine life, plus it will increase the boiling temperature of the coolant. In addition, new anti-freeze formulations have dramatically improved the ability of anti-freeze to perform its basic functions with the additional benefits of reducing the cooling systems maintenance requirements, maintenance costs, and the impact on the environment of disposing of used coolant.

Ethylene Glycol

Coolant has evolved considerably since the early days of automotive technology. In the past, coolant has included mixtures of alcohol and water as well as water mixed with honey and soluble oils. In the 1940s, ethylene glycol was developed for use to provide both freeze and boil-over protection. When initially manufactured, ethylene glycol is a clear, colorless, syrupy fluid. Green dye is later added for identification. One of the most significant reasons ethylene glycol is dyed is to clearly distinguish it from other coolants, because it is extremely poisonous. If ingested, 4 ounces (113 grams) of ethylene glycol will cause fatal kidney failure in humans after a couple of days. Many animals die from anti-freeze poisoning every year, because they are attracted to the anti-freeze's sweet odor and taste. Ethylene glycol–based coolants must be recovered and recycled to prevent environmental contamination.

▶ TECHNICIAN TIP

Understanding which type of anti-freeze to use can be confusing to even the most well-informed technician. The various bases, chemical formulations, and colors of anti-freeze available today are chosen primarily for compatibility with materials in the cooling system and environmental concerns. The wrong anti-freeze can cause severe corrosion in the cooling system, gaskets, and cylinder head gaskets, as well as damage coolant hoses. To avoid problems and confusion, always check the manufacturer's recommendations for anti-freeze noted on surge tank decals or service bulletins. In emergencies, no more than 5% contamination is permissible by most manufacturers.

Propylene Glycol

To minimize the problems associated with the toxicity of ethylene glycol, a relatively new environmentally friendly anti-freeze base called propylene glycol is available for diesel engine cooling systems. Propylene glycol is an ingredient in many cosmetics and foods, from moisturizer to ice cream. It has slightly different physical properties than ethylene glycol, and therefore the density and concentration required for freeze protection is different. As such, care must be taken to differentiate between ethylene glycol and propylene glycol anti-freeze bases and the amount of propylene glycol mixed with water to obtain adequate freeze protection FIGURE 13-20. Propylene glycol requires a higher concentration than ethylene glycol to provide the same freeze

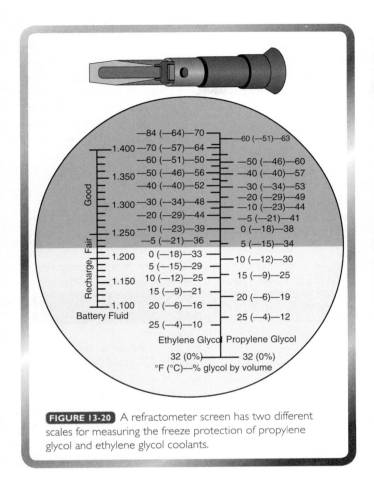

FIGURE 13-20 A refractometer screen has two different scales for measuring the freeze protection of propylene glycol and ethylene glycol coolants.

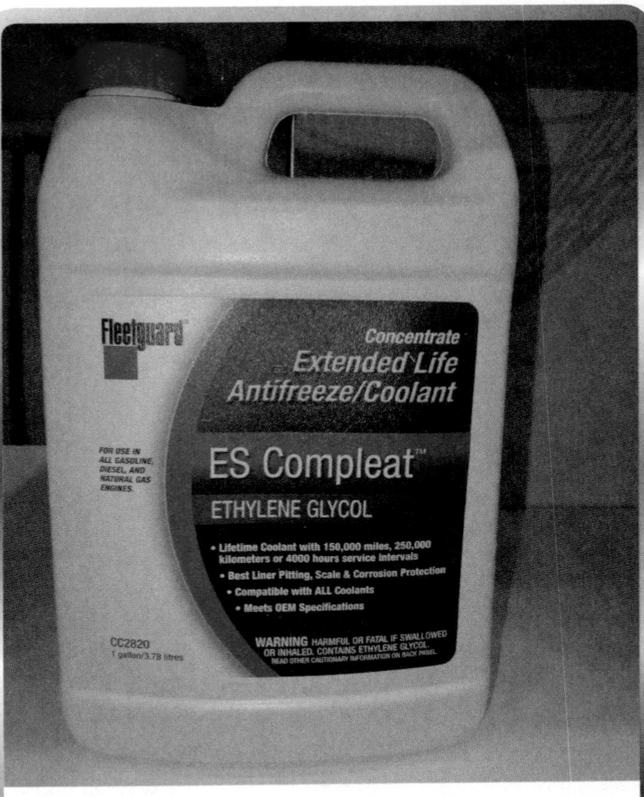

FIGURE 13-21 Compleat is one of the few glycerin-based anti-freezes compatible with diesel engine cooling system requirements.

protection. Higher concentrations may reduce the cooling effectiveness of propylene glycol mixtures. The slippery, greasy texture of both ethylene glycol and propylene glycol anti-freeze bases makes it an excellent lubricant for the water pump seal.

Glycerin-Based Anti-freeze

Glycerin is another non toxic base for anti-freeze. Glycerin was used as a heat transfer agent in anti-freeze formulations as early as the 1920s, but was eventually displaced by ethylene glycol. Interest in this anti-freeze base has been revived due to the biofuel industry, which produces huge amounts of glycerin as a byproduct of biofuel production. Glycerin, which is also sometimes called propanetriol or glycerol, has a number of distinct advantages, including:

- It is close to neutral on the pH scale.
- It is inexpensive, or at least cost competitive with other coolants.
- Its nontoxic properties make it an environmentally friendly choice.
- It supports the renewable fuel industry.
- It is compatible with most cooling system materials.

Cummins currently produces a glycerin-based anti-freeze, Compleat, that meets the recently developed ASTM International standard for the latest anti-freeze technology **FIGURE 13-21**.

The primary disadvantage of glycerin is that its freeze protection temperature is high in comparison to ethylene glycol. Diluted to a 30/70 water-to-glycerin concentration, glycerin can only provide freeze protection to −36°F (−37.8°C). At that concentration, glycerin-based coolant is not able to remove as much heat as a mixture with a higher amount of water. The different density of the anti-freeze also requires new test instruments to evaluate freeze protection.

Anti-freeze Formulations

The mixing of ethylene glycol or propylene glycol anti-freeze and water alone is not effective to prevent corrosion or erosion of cooling system components. In fact, the addition of anti-freeze to water causes additional chemical reactions that require control. For example, ethylene glycol when exposed to air will become acidic, and propylene glycol is highly corrosive to a few metals. Development of anti-freeze formulation is an evolutionary process driven by the requirements to minimize corrosion and erosion in the cooling system, ensure material compatibilities, and minimize maintenance requirements **TABLE 13-2**. While the bases of all modern anti-freezes are propylene glycol or ethylene glycol, the additive package vary considerably, which can lead to confusion and severe maintenance problems if not properly understood and executed. The additive package essentially differentiates between the various types of coolants **TABLE 13-3**.

Type I: Conventional Low-Silicate Anti-freeze

To protect cooling system materials such as cast iron, aluminum, copper, brass, solder, steel, and many non-metallics like nylon and silicone, anti-freeze contains corrosion inhibitors. Type I conventional anti-freeze uses older additive technology and contains corrosion inhibitors such as boron, phosphate, and sodium silicate (**TABLE 13-4**). These types of inhibitors are known as inorganic additive technology (IAT) and are identified by the green-colored coolant. Sodium silicate is primarily used to protect aluminum and is found in much higher concentration when used in gasoline engines with aluminum cylinder heads. A problem with sodium silicate in diesels, however, is the incompatibility of silicate with high levels of nitrite, which is added to protect cylinder walls from cavitation erosion. High concentration of both these additives together will cause a condition known as silicate dropout (**FIGURE 13-22**). Silicate dropout is characterized by the appearance of green "goo" or gel that plugs radiator and heater core tubes, leading to overheating of the engine and even catastrophic failure. For this reason, type I anti-freeze is blended differently for gasoline and diesel engines. Foam suppressants

TABLE 13-2: Anti-freeze Types

Anti-freeze Type	Performance Specification	Suggested Color
Type I Conventional low-silicate using IAT	Technology & Maintenance Council (TMC) RP-302a	Green
Type II Fully formulated ethylene glycol extended-life using OAT	Technology & Maintenance Council (TMC) RP-3298	Purple or pink
Type III Fully formulated propylene glycol extended-life using OAT	Technology & Maintenance Council (TMC) RP-330	Blue
Type IV OAT	Technology & Maintenance Council (TMC) RP-338	Red
Hybrid organic acid technology (HOAT)	Combination of IAT and OAT with nitrites added	Ford: yellow Daimler-Chrysler: orange
Nitrated organic acid technology (NOAT)	Similar to HOAT	No color designated

TABLE 13-4: Type I Anti-freeze Inhibitor Additives

Type I Anti-freeze Inhibitor	Protects
Phosphate	Iron pH control (keeps coolant alkaline between 8.5 and 10.5 pH)
Borate	Iron pH control (keeps coolant alkaline)
Sodium silicate	Aluminum
Nitrite	Cast iron Steel Aluminum Solder
Mercaptobenzothiazole (MBT) and tolytriazole (TT)	Copper Brass

TABLE 13-3: Cooling System Maintenance Concerns and the Additives Used for Prevention

Condition	Causes	Effects	Prevention
Scale	Minerals present in water added to cooling system, particularly calcium and magnesium, can solidify and stick to hot metal surfaces	Plugged cooling system passageways Prevents heat transfer from cylinders, eventually causing uneven metal expansion, scuffing, scoring, accelerated ring wear, and depending on severity, cracked cylinder heads and/or blocks	Use of supplemental coolant additives to form a thin barrier on metal parts preventing the adhesion of scale
Rust	Oxidized iron in cooling system Damaged oxidation inhibitors caused by overheated coolant	Plugged coolant passageways	Use of SCA/DCA with rust inhibitor
Acidity (low pH)	Chemical reaction between air and ethylene glycol anti-freeze Combustion gas leakage into the coolant	Corrosion of iron, steel, and aluminum	Use of SCA/DCA with a pH buffer to maintain a slightly alkaline pH of the coolant
Cavitation	Implosion of vapor bubbles against the cylinder walls	Perforation of cylinder walls Leakage of combustion gases into the coolant and/or leaking coolant into the engine	Use of nitrite as a sacrificial barrier to cavitation

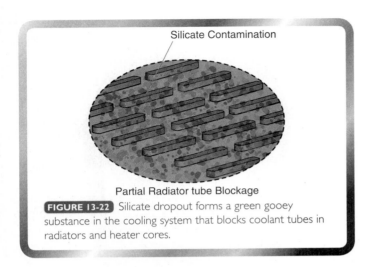

FIGURE 13-22 Silicate dropout forms a green gooey substance in the cooling system that blocks coolant tubes in radiators and heater cores.

need to be added to maintain coolant contact with engine parts, because steam and other vapor bubbles do not cool well.

Type I additives deplete quickly and require monitoring. With time, many of the additive's other components, such as phosphorous, drop out with the silicate, coating cooling system components with a layer of slime and deposits. This is why it is important to drain and replace Type I anti-freeze containing this corrosion inhibitor package every two years. To maintain the correct level of additives, Type I coolant requires testing to ensure the correct levels of nitrite and other inhibitors are present.

Between 3% and 5% of DCA or SCA is added after the initial mixing of anti-freeze and water to bring the additive package for diesel engines to the correct protection level **FIGURE 13-23**.

FIGURE 13-23 This bottle of liquid additive is added to approximately 1 gallon (4 liters) of type I coolant to properly condition the coolant. Note the dried silicate appearing around the cap of the bottle.

Monitoring the additive package is necessary at every service to maintain the correct levels of the various corrosion inhibitors **FIGURE 13-24** and **FIGURE 13-25**.

▶ TECHNICIAN TIP

Type I anti-freeze for diesel engines is different from Type I anti-freeze for gasoline engines and the two should never be interchanged. Gasoline engines use Type I anti-freeze that contains higher silicate levels. Only low-silicate anti-freeze should be used in diesel engines because the addition of nitrite to diesel coolant will cause silicate dropout, which can lead to plugged radiators, water pump seal leaks, and overheated engines.

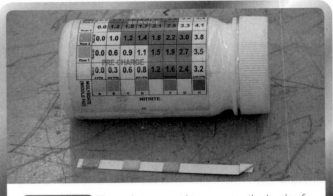

FIGURE 13-24 Test strips are used to measure the levels of various cooling system additives. This test strip measures the levels of nitrite and molybdates, another type of corrosion inhibitor, in anti-freeze.

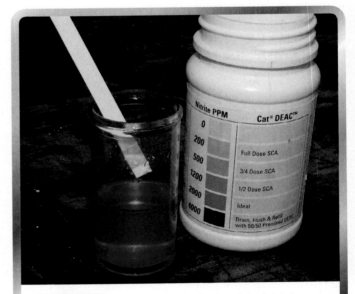

FIGURE 13-25 This test strip checks the nitrite levels in either type I or extended-life coolant. A different scale on the side of the bottle is used for each type of anti-freeze.

Extended-Life Coolant

Given the high maintenance requirements of Type I anti-freeze and its short two-year service interval, manufacturers have sought to develop new coolant technology to minimize cooling system maintenance and extend the service interval. To achieve this, a new category of anti-freezes, called **extended-life coolant (ELC)** or long-life coolant, has been developed with corrosion inhibitors made from organic acids. These inhibitors use OAT and generally contain low levels or are free of nitrite, nitrate, phosphate, silicate, and borate. Instead, they use carboxylate acids, which are neutralized versions of acids containing carbon.

OAT anti-freeze has the advantage of being more chemically stable, which allows for exceptionally long service intervals. The formulation provides maximum protection of the six basic metal alloys found in most cooling systems. Because the coolant generally contains no phosphates or silicates, deposits in the cooling system are almost eliminated. The low level of IAT abrasive solids dissolved in anti-freeze results in improved water pump seal life. Anti-freezes using this coolant chemistry are also referred to as long-life, fully formulated, OAT and nitrited organic acid technology (NOAT) coolant. Variations in the inhibitor package differentiate between these types of anti-freezes.

Type II and III: Fully Formulated Anti-freeze

Type II and type III anti-freeze are differentiated by the type of base used. Type II is made from ethylene glycol, and type III is made from propylene glycol. These anti-freezes generally do not require an initial charge of DCA or SCA because it is incorporated into the solution during manufacture **TABLE 13-5**. The corrosion inhibitors in these types of ELC anti-freeze are designed to last 600,000 miles (965,600 km) on-road or 12,000 hours off-road. However, a **coolant extender** that contains nitrite for protection against cavitation erosion has an additive package similar to SCA/DCA **FIGURE 13-26**. This must be added only once at 300,000 miles (482,800 km) or 6000 hours, which is about halfway through the anti-freeze's service life, if a longer service life is expected.

FIGURE 13-26 The use of an extender additive package halfway through an ELC's service life can lengthen the time that long-life coolant remains in service.

To maintain these fully formulated anti-freezes at every preventive maintenance or at least twice per year, the color and freeze point of the coolant is checked. If coolant is the correct color, has no deposits, and has a freeze point between −15°F (−26°C) and −60°F (−51°C), then the coolant is considered in suitable condition for further use.

Type IV OAT Anti-freeze

This type of anti-freeze uses non-carboxylate acids, such as benzoate, from benzoic acid, to form the additive package. This red-colored anti-freeze is commonly used in today's diesel and gasoline engines.

Hybrid Organic Acid Technology

Hybrid organic acid technology (HOAT) is a combination of IAT and OAT with nitrites added. This makes HOAT compatible with both light- and heavy-duty system materials. Different versions of this anti-freeze are dyed colors between orange and straw yellow. This anti-freeze is often marketed as a universal anti-freeze.

Nitrated Organic Acid Technology

Nitrated organic acid technology (NOAT) is an OAT with nitrates added, similar to HOAT. This chemical combination is expected to make the anti-freeze suitable for use in both light- and heavy-duty diesel cooling systems, and it is often marketed as a universal anti-freeze. NOAT and HOAT are very similar in performance characteristics, but currently no vehicle OEM

TABLE 13-5: Type II Anti-freeze Additives and Their Purposes

Type II Anti-freeze Inhibitor	Protects
Potassium soap of dibasic carboxylic acid	Iron Solder Aluminum
Potassium soap of monobasic carboxylic acid	Aluminum Iron
Nitrite	Cast iron Steel
Molybdate	Iron
Tolytriazole	Copper

uses a factory fill of NOAT anti-freeze. The normal NOAT service life is five years or 150,000 miles (250,000 km) and uses an extender package halfway through the service life.

Mixing IAT with OAT, HOAT, and NOAT anti-freezes will not damage the engine's cooling system. However, mixing anti-freezes nullifies the extended-life attributes of these formulations. Depending on the type of formulation, acceptable contamination can range from 5% to 25%, though Most OEMs do not recommend contamination above 5%.

It is easy to be confused with the variety and complexity of anti-freeze formulations available for use. Therefore, it is imperative the technician and diesel engine owner be fully aware of what the vehicle manufacturer's requirements for anti-freeze are and for those recommendations to be carefully followed.

▶ TECHNICIAN TIP

Sensors and other electrical devices that are exposed to engine coolant have the potential to short out. Electrical current passing though the coolant will quickly corrode brass and aluminum oil coolers, injector tubes, and other metals in the cooling system. To minimize this problem, engine blocks use a number of ground straps to not only lower resistances for engine-mounted electrical devices but also to minimize electrical conduction through engine coolant. Electrical conduction through coolant quickly eliminates nitrite additives in coolant, leading to further engine damage.

▶ TECHNICIAN TIP

If coolant is brown in color, it often indicates the presence of rust in the coolant. Some corrosion inhibitors used to prevent rust are easily damaged by overheating coolant. Coolant that has overheated should not be reused during service.

▶ Components of Cooling Systems

Transferring heat absorbed from the engine to the atmosphere is the primary function of the cooling system. To do this, radiators, which allow air to pass though cooling fins to release heat, are used. A wide variety of radiators are designed and used to accommodate various heat transfer requirements and chassis applications. Radiator technology continues to change to extend service life and operate more efficiently while reducing construction costs and maintenance requirements.

Radiators

Radiators are heat-exchanging devices that release heat absorbed from the engine to the air. Coolant can flow through a radiator two ways. In down-flow radiators, the coolant will enter through a hose connected to the top tank that is carrying hot coolant from the water pump outlet. The coolant will then flow from the top tank, through cooling tubes, and into the bottom tank. Alternatively, in cross-flow radiators, coolant will flow from a top-connected hose, through a side-mounted tank, into cooling tubes, and across the radiator to another side-mounted tank. **FIGURE 13-27**. Cross-flow radiators are preferred in vehicles with low-profile aerodynamic hoods because they can be made wider with a lower height profile.

Tubes within the radiator core provide the surface area to exchange heat. Heat dissipates from the coolant through the tube wall and then through the fins. Air passing through the fins carries away heat, thereby allowing tubes and fins to absorb more heat from the coolant **FIGURE 13-28**.

Early radiator construction used copper brass radiator components. Copper brass construction seemed the obvious choice for the radiators because of its superior heat conductivity, ease of forming, and ease of repair. However, it was learned that increasing diameter of tubes in a radiator made radiators more efficient. This required thicker tube walls to

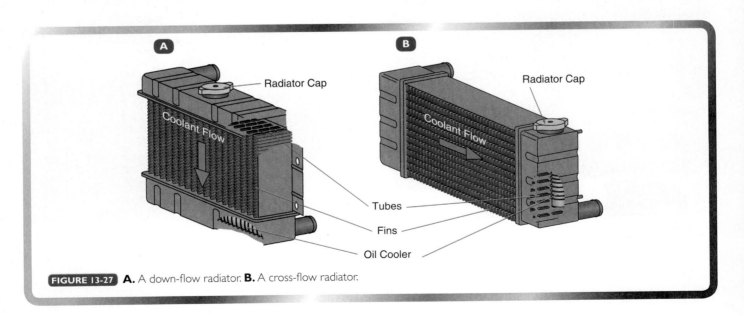

FIGURE 13-27 **A.** A down-flow radiator. **B.** A cross-flow radiator.

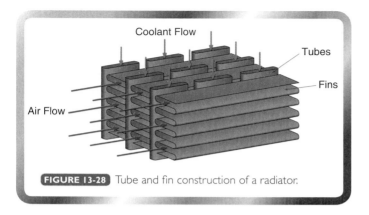

FIGURE 13-28 Tube and fin construction of a radiator.

prevent ballooning of the tubes from internal pressure, which in turn created unacceptably heavier radiators. Beginning in the 1980s, most manufacturers began to use aluminum tube radiators **FIGURE 13-29**. A two-row aluminum radiator core (also referred to as double core radiator) with 1″ (25 mm) circumference tubes is equivalent to a five-row copper brass radiator with 1/2″ (13 mm) circumference tubes. The 1″ (13 mm) tube size also increased tube-to-fin contact and cooling capacity by roughly 25%.

Copper is a good heat conductor but solder required to bond the tubes to the fins creates an insulation point that prevents some heat transfer. All the mechanical stresses are borne by the solder in the joints between the radiator tank and the tube core. Solder can be attacked if the coolant pH level becomes too alkaline through the excessive use of DCA/SCA. Aluminum tubes are welded or crimped rather than soldered to the aluminum or plastic tanks. This provides a more efficient conductor for cooling efficiency.

Radiator Caps

While early radiator caps simply prevented coolant from spilling out of the cooling system, today's radiator caps have several additional functions. First, the calibrated pressure valve inside the cap increases the pressure of the cooling system to raise the boiling point of coolant. This feature prevents coolant loss through boil over **FIGURE 13-30**.

Second, a vacuum valve incorporated into the cap allows air or coolant to re-enter the cooling system when the pressure drops after the engine cools **FIGURE 13-31**. Faulty vacuum valves are often identified when the upper radiator hose collapses after the engine cools or when coolant is lost. A coiled spring inside the lower radiator hose, or a solid metal tube, is required to prevent its collapse.

The radiator cap is also important to water pump efficiency. When the cooling system is pressurized, the pump operates much better than the 85% efficiency without pressure cap.

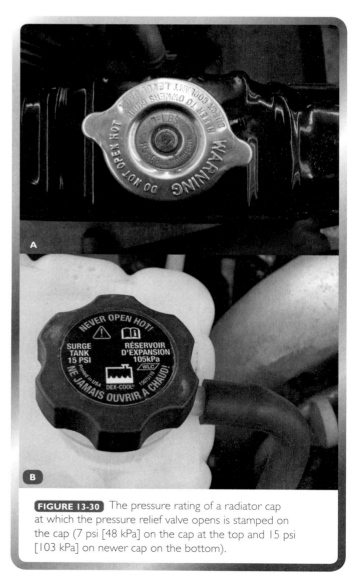

FIGURE 13-30 The pressure rating of a radiator cap at which the pressure relief valve opens is stamped on the cap (7 psi [48 kPa] on the cap at the top and 15 psi [103 kPa] on newer cap on the bottom).

FIGURE 13-29 This radiator is a common design in which plastic tanks are crimped to an aluminum cooling core. A silicone gasket between the tank and radiator core prevents leaks.

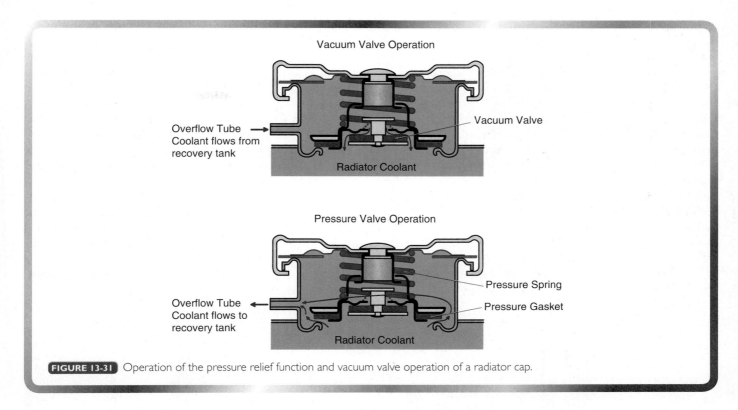

Vacuum Valve Operation

Overflow Tube
Coolant flows from
recovery tank

Vacuum Valve

Radiator Coolant

Pressure Valve Operation

Overflow Tube
Coolant flows to
recovery tank

Pressure Spring

Pressure Gasket

Radiator Coolant

FIGURE 13-31 Operation of the pressure relief function and vacuum valve operation of a radiator cap.

Finally, pressurizing the cooling system minimizes cavitation of the entire cooling system because vapor bubbles caused by low pressure in the cooling system are less likely to form.

Safety Tip

Never open the radiator cap of a hot engine, as the coolant will be depressurized and boil over. The sudden conversion of hot water into steam pressure in the engine will cause water to explosively erupt from the radiator with projectile force. Anyone near the radiator can be scalded.

Surge Tanks

Additional expansion volume for the cooling system is necessary to allow for the expansion of coolant. Surge or overflow tanks provide the space for coolant and vapor to move into when the engine coolant is hot. When the engine cools, the stored overflow volume returns to the radiator. Sometimes, large radiator top tanks will accomplish the same purpose as a separate reservoir. Overflow tanks use a line connected to the radiator just below the pressure cap, allowing the movement of coolant back and forth during the cooling system's thermal cycles.

Surge and overflow tanks provide a coolant reserve for gradual loss of coolant. One study found that new trucks in their first year of service lost almost one gallon of coolant about a drop of coolant per mile. Most of the leakage was determined to come from radiator hose clamps. Constant torque spring clamps are the best clamps to use to minimize coolant loss, because they change dimensionally with the expansion and contraction of hoses and connections.

Vent Lines

Vent lines located at the highest points on the engine and radiator bleed any steam and air out of the engine and into the surge tank. If these gases are allowed to remain in the engine, they will accumulate in the cylinder head, causing overheating and an air bind within the water pump.

Water Pumps

To ensure positive circulation of coolant, an engine-driven water pump moves coolant through the cooling system. Pumps can be belt- or gear-driven **FIGURE 13-32**. Although a gear-driven pump does not rely on a belt, which minimizes service

FIGURE 13-32 A gear-driven water pump.

requirements and is more reliable than a belt for long distances, failure of the weep hole to drain leaking coolant away from the pump can allow coolant to enter the engine. All water pumps are centrifugal turbine pumps, which means they become more efficient the faster they turn. The inlet to the water pump is the lower radiator hose or some point located near the lower radiator hose. Water drawn into the pump is discharged into the engine. Under fast acceleration, internal engine block pressures between the pump and thermostat can reach as high as 40 psi (276 kPa). To reduce energy losses from driving water pumps, manufacturers are introducing electrically controlled variable speed water pumps to help meet GHG targets. **FIGURE 13-33**. A clutch that controls the speed of the water pump is signaled by the electronic control module (ECM) using a pulse-width modulated (PWM) electrical signal. A speed sensor on the

pump provides data for closed loop feedback control of the water pump speed **FIGURE 13-34**.

The impeller, which transfers the pump's energy to the coolant, is located in the coolant and may be made of plastic or metal **FIGURE 13-35**. Impellers can wear if a significant amount of abrasive circulates through the cooling system. Impellers can also become separated from the shaft and cause poor coolant flow. This problem is usually identified when the engine overheats but the lower radiator hose, which is normally hot to the touch, is instead cold or lukewarm because radiator coolant is not being pulled by the pump into the engine.

A special seal separates coolant from the bearings supporting the water pump shaft **FIGURE 13-36**. If coolant reaches the bearings, a major failure of the water pump will occur. To prevent this from happening, manufacturers add a weep hole between the

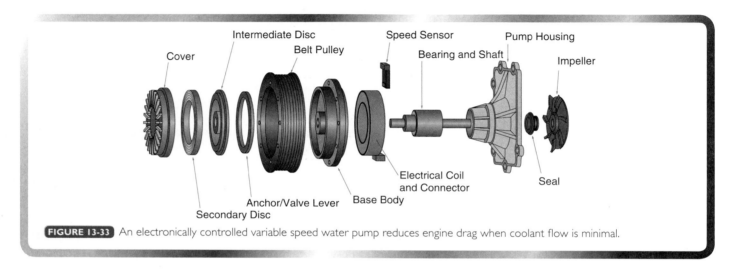

FIGURE 13-33 An electronically controlled variable speed water pump reduces engine drag when coolant flow is minimal.

FIGURE 13-34 This 2015 Paccar MX engine uses an electrically controlled variable speed water pump. Note the speed sensor and another connector supplying a PWM signal, which regulates water pump speed to minimize parasitic loads on the engine.

FIGURE 13-35 A centrifugal metal water pump impeller.

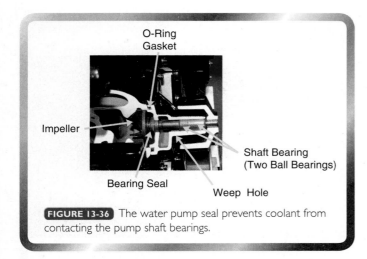

FIGURE 13-36 The water pump seal prevents coolant from contacting the pump shaft bearings.

seal and the bearing **FIGURE 13-37**. If the seal is worn and damaged, the weep hole allows coolant to leak from the cavity inside the water pump to prevent bearing damage. Some coolant leakage from a weep hole is normal, and some water pumps hold any small leakage of coolant in a small reservoir, where it evaporates.

Adding cold water to hot engine operating with low coolant will thermally shock the engine and damage ceramic or sintered metal water pump seals. This can create cracks in all of the engine castings. If an engine cannot be left to cool down before adding water, it should be added only when the engine is running.

TECHNICIAN TIP

A coolant leak from the weep hole of a water pump indicates that the water pump seal is leaking. The weep hole is necessary so coolant cannot reach the water pump shaft's support bearing. If coolant should reach the bearing, a catastrophic bearing failure can occur. On gear-driven pumps, the weep hole prevents coolant from entering the engine and mixing with lubrication oil. When inspecting an engine for leaks, or when pressure testing a cooling system, keep in mind a small amount of coolant leakage from a pump is acceptable because the seal cannot form a perfect liquid-tight barrier.

FIGURE 13-37 The weep hole of a water pump on Mack E-7.

TECHNICIAN TIP

Silicate, phosphates, and borates used as corrosion inhibitors are dissolved solids. In time they crystallize and fall out, or precipitate out, of the glycol and water solution. These crystals can enter the area between the water pump shaft and seal, acting as an abrasive and causing premature wear of the seal. The result is a coolant leak from the weep hole of the water pump.

Water Filters

Water filters on diesel engines, if equipped, perform two primary purposes. First, they can remove sediment rust and dissolved particles that can cause abrasive damage to the cooling system. This will contribute to longer water pump life and minimize cooling system deposits. The water filter's second important function is to supply DCAs to the coolant. Filters contain pucks of DCA additive, which is dissolved within minutes of coolant circulating through the filter. The quantity of additive required for the maintenance of the cooling system is adjusted by selecting the appropriate filter. For example, some filters are prepared with no DCA, while others may have two, four, or eighteen units of DCA. So when servicing the vehicle, the technician must select the appropriate filter for the cooling system capacity and the DCA requirement. This information is located in the vehicle service manual.

Diesel engines without water filters usually use SCA in long-life coolant that does not require additives when it is fully formulated. SCA is a liquid used to condition the cooling system if required. With the increased use of ELC, which only requires extender halfway through the coolant's service life, generally no coolant filters are installed to prevent contamination of the coolant with powdered DCA.

Thermostats

Thermostats regulate the temperature of the engine coolant by modulating or controlling the volume of coolant circulated to the radiator. When the engine is below its normal operating temperature, the thermostat prevents coolant flow to the radiator. At a predetermined point, i.e., 180°F (82°C), the thermostat will begin to open, and it will continue to open further if the coolant temperature continues to increase.

A variety of thermostats are commonly used in diesel engines. Blocking or partial blocking thermostats stop the flow of coolant to the top radiator hose, causing coolant to be redirected through a bypass passageway and back to the water pump inlet for recirculation into the engine **FIGURE 13-38** and **FIGURE 13-39**. A damaged or missing seal located around the circumference of these types of thermostats will cause overcooling or the failure of the engine to warm up because cold coolant will have a flow path around the seal to the upper radiator hose **FIGURE 13-40**. In engines not equipped with vent lines, a small jiggle or venting valve is located in a chocking thermostat to allow air and steam to escape past the thermostat and into the radiator **FIGURE 13-41**.

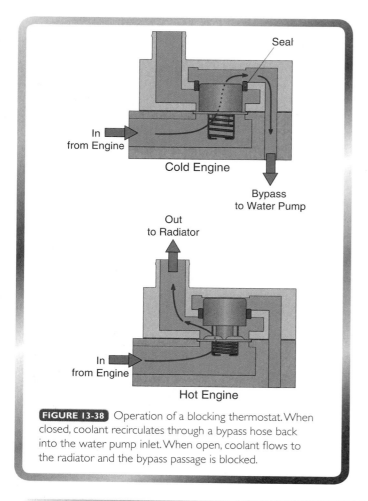

FIGURE 13-38 Operation of a blocking thermostat. When closed, coolant recirculates through a bypass hose back into the water pump inlet. When open, coolant flows to the radiator and the bypass passage is blocked.

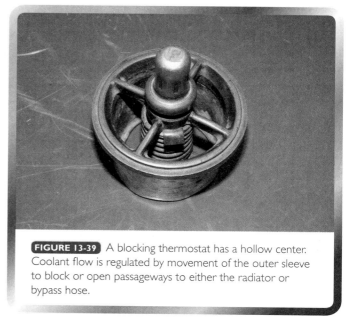

FIGURE 13-39 A blocking thermostat has a hollow center. Coolant flow is regulated by movement of the outer sleeve to block or open passageways to either the radiator or bypass hose.

Choking and full blocking thermostats operate by using a special wax pellet combined with a powdered metal tightly squeezed into a copper cup that is equipped with a piston inside a rubber boot **FIGURE 13-42**. Heat causes the wax pellet to expand, which pushes the piston upward, opening the valve **FIGURE 13-43**.

Faulty thermostats will cause overcooling of the engine by partially staying open. An engine that will not warm up to operating temperatures, is very slow to warm up, or warms only

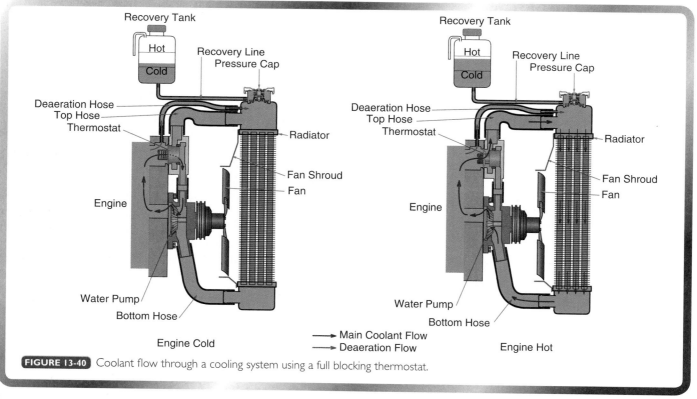

FIGURE 13-40 Coolant flow through a cooling system using a full blocking thermostat.

FIGURE 13-41 A jiggle valve in a choking thermostat enables trapped steam to vent through a closed thermostat.

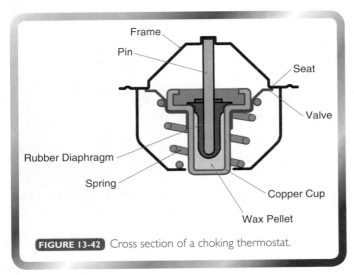

FIGURE 13-42 Cross section of a choking thermostat.

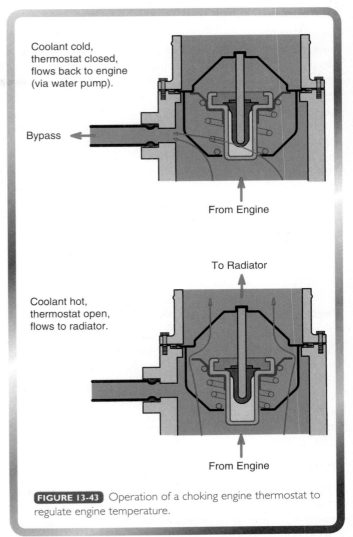

Coolant cold, thermostat closed, flows back to engine (via water pump).

Bypass

From Engine

To Radiator

Coolant hot, thermostat open, flows to radiator.

From Engine

FIGURE 13-43 Operation of a choking engine thermostat to regulate engine temperature.

under heavy load likely has a thermostat partially stuck open or a blocking thermostat with a leaking seal. Thermostats may occasionally fail to fully open or be fully open at a particular temperature. This condition will cause an engine to overheat when under load.

Fans and Fan Drives

Engine fans are designed to increase the airflow across the radiator, which improves the efficiency of heat removal from coolant **FIGURE 13-44**. The number of blades, fan speed, and fan pitch will determine the volume of air moved by the fan. For most vehicles, engine fans pull air through the radiator in the same direction as airflow when traveling in a forward direction. When the vehicle is traveling, its movement usually creates enough airflow and the fan is not required. At low-speed operation and at idle, air movement is often inadequate and a fan is required for the cooling system and to move air across the air conditioning condenser and any other front-mounted heat exchangers. To reduce the parasitic loss of power from the engine, which is often

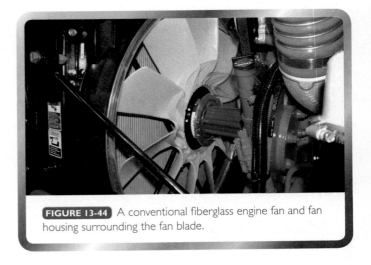

FIGURE 13-44 A conventional fiberglass engine fan and fan housing surrounding the fan blade.

more than 25 horsepower (hp) (19 kilowatts [kW]) on some heavy-duty fans, a fan drive mechanism is used to decouple the fan from the engine when airflow is not required.

Viscous Fan Clutches

One of several common methods of controlling fan operation is though a temperature-controlled modulating fan clutch. These fans are coupled to the drive through a highly viscous silicone fluid. The amount of slippage of the clutch is determined by a temperature-sensitive, bi-metal control valve regulating the quantity of silicone fluid in the clutch coupling mechanism. When the clutch is cool, little silicone fluid enters the clutch and the fan freewheels. As the temperature of air in the fan clutch area increases, more fluid enters the clutch mechanism, thus creating more drag or silicone fluid shear within the coupling mechanism. The fan speed does not correspond to engine speed and is thus modulated or adjusted according to the heat load across the radiator (FIGURE 13-45). These clutches are quieter, because fan speed is kept proportional to heat load. Because their operational speed is proportional to engine temperature, they conserve energy and extract significantly less energy from an engine with a directly coupled fan.

Variable Speed Engine Fan

To reduce parasitic loss caused by operating a cooling fan, many late-model medium- and heavy-duty engines use a variable speed cooling fan. Operation of the fan is controlled by the ECM using a PWM signal to control the fan speed. An electrically operated control valve is used instead of the bimetallic heat sensing spring in conventional viscous cooling fans. Slower fan speed also translates into less engine noise (FIGURE 13-46) and (FIGURE 13-47).

Hydraulic Fan Drive

A hydraulic fan drive system enables variable fan speed independent of the engine speed. These fan drive mechanisms are commonly found in off-road equipment and transit buses where cooling demands can exceed the ability of a conventional fan drive system to move air through a radiator and

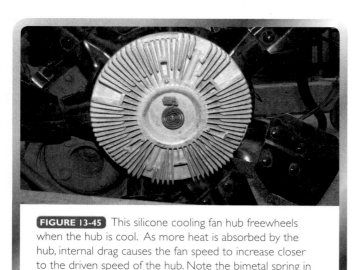

FIGURE 13-45 This silicone cooling fan hub freewheels when the hub is cool. As more heat is absorbed by the hub, internal drag causes the fan speed to increase closer to the driven speed of the hub. Note the bimetal spring in the center of the hub, which is connected to a valve that controls fluid movement.

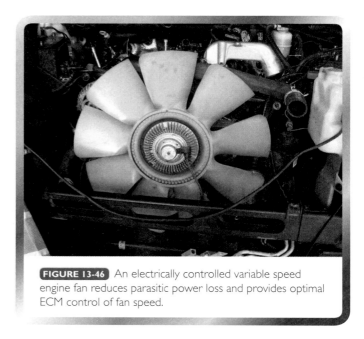

FIGURE 13-46 An electrically controlled variable speed engine fan reduces parasitic power loss and provides optimal ECM control of fan speed.

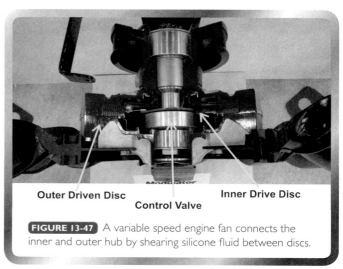

Outer Driven Disc   Inner Drive Disc
Control Valve

FIGURE 13-47 A variable speed engine fan connects the inner and outer hub by shearing silicone fluid between discs.

other heat exchangers. A hydraulic pump and an electronically controlled pressure control valve supply hydraulic pressure to a hydraulic motor that drives the cooling fan. Because airflow across radiators in these applications is not provided by forward vehicle movement due to a rear- or side-of-vehicle location, the fans can actually be driven at much higher speeds than an engine could provide at idle or high-load, low-speed engine operation. Like electronically variable speed fans using air or silicone fluid, cooling speeds can be ramped to avoid shock loading of the engine or belt drive system. Electronically controlled fan speed yields significant power and fuel savings (FIGURE 13-48) and (FIGURE 13-49).

On/Off Fan Hubs

A more traditional fan engagement mechanism is an on/off fan hub, which uses air pressure to either engage or release a

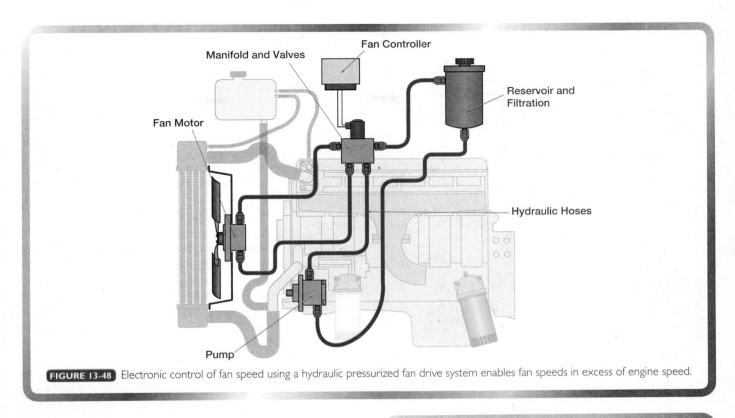

FIGURE 13-48 Electronic control of fan speed using a hydraulic pressurized fan drive system enables fan speeds in excess of engine speed.

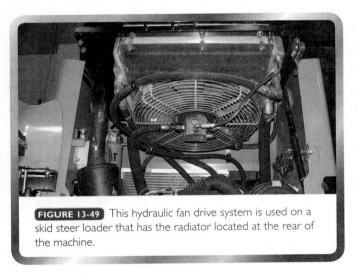

FIGURE 13-49 This hydraulic fan drive system is used on a skid steer loader that has the radiator located at the rear of the machine.

spring-loaded friction clutch **FIGURE 13-50** and **FIGURE 13-51**. The air supplied to the fan hub is electrically signaled through an electric over-air control valve. Either the engine ECM will provide an electrical signal to open or close the air supply solenoid, or a temperature-sensitive switch in the cooling system will activate the solenoid. An air-conditioning high-pressure switch also supplies an input signal to operate the fan to pull air across the condenser if the refrigerant pressures in the condenser become too high. Typically a timer will be connected to the circuit to keep the fan engaged for 90–120 seconds to prevent excessive cycling between on and off, which will wear out the friction clutch faster. The temperature at which the fan

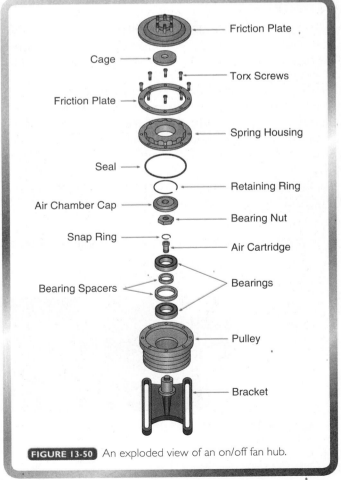

FIGURE 13-50 An exploded view of an on/off fan hub.

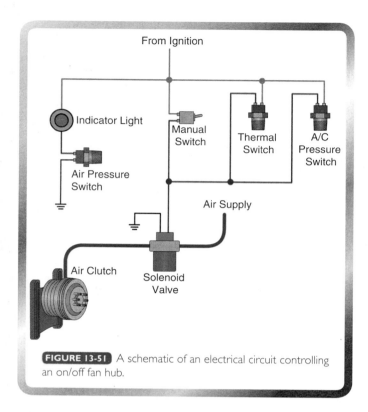

FIGURE 13-51 A schematic of an electrical circuit controlling an on/off fan hub.

Radiator Fan Shroud

Fan shrouds seal the gap around the fan and radiator to ensure cooling air runs through the radiator rather than leaking around its sides or past the headlights. Recirculating air that has already passed through the radiator decreases cooling efficiency. Fan shrouds minimize the likelihood of air passing through the fan and back into the radiator again. Fans for on-highway vehicles are usually pulling fans, which means they pull in air in the direction the vehicle is traveling. Transit buses and highway coaches with side-mounted radiators, particularly AC condensers, use pusher fans instead.

Hoses

The upper and lower radiator hoses and heater hoses require flexible connections between the engine radiator and heater core due to engine vibration and torque flexion. These hoses must be able to withstand the hot underhood environment as well as up to 20 psi (138 kPa) of internal pressure. Because cooling systems operate under a wide range of temperatures, hoses must be compatible with operating conditions from well below zero to over 250°F (121°C) without failing. Two common hose materials are a silicone-based material and an ethylene propylene rubber compound known for its resilience and flexibility. Silicone-based hoses are more chemically resistant to deterioration and able to withstand wider temperature variations, which makes them premium quality. Silicone hoses, however, are generally not compatible with oil and will soften if exposed to fuel and lubrication oil. Silicone hoses are not compatible with all types of long-life anti-freeze and will quickly deteriorate if the wrong type of coolant is used.

Hose Clamps

Hose clamps help the hose seal at its connections. Constant torque spring clamps allow hose ends to thermally expand and contract, which minimizes coolant loss from loose clamps. Some vehicles are manufactured with shrink bands, which perform like electrical shrink tube instead of hose clamps. Shrink bands are designed to prevent cold weather leaks, and they do not require any adjustment after installation **FIGURE 13-52**.

will engage is 10–15°F above the coolant operating temperature, which allows vehicle movement to first move air across the radiator and ATAAC and only engage if airflow provided by vehicle speed is insufficient. Because engine fans consume a lot of engine power (easily 25 hp [19 kW] on heavy-duty engines), the fan is often activated with the engine brake to increase the engine's resistance to driveline rotation. During engine warm-up operation, the fan may also engage to apply a load to the engine when the transmission is in neutral. A two-speed fan hub is also available, which provides a combined variable speed operating mechanism and spring-engaged on–off operation.

FIGURE 13-52 Constant torque hose clamps use a spring to maintain continual torque around the hose clamp. Tightening the clamp increases the torque applied continually by the clamp. A spring hose clamp uses spring pressure to maintain a continual pressure. Tension is not adjustable.

► Maintenance of Cooling Systems

This chapter on cooling systems is lengthy not only because of the wide range of technology used in cooling system, but also due to the disproportionate influence the cooling system has on potential engine failures and maintenance. Approximately 40% of all engine maintenance or breakdown is related directly or indirectly to cooling system maintenance, so technicians need to be familiar with common service practices and diagnostic procedures.

Tools

A properly trained and experienced technician will use special tools for diagnosing and servicing the engine cooling system. These tools include **FIGURE 13-53** :

- **Coolant system pressure tester**: A pressure tester is used to apply pressure to the cooling system to diagnose leakage complaints. Under pressure, coolant may leak internally to the combustion chamber, intake or exhaust system, or the engine lubrication system. It can also leak externally to the outside of the engine.
- **Hydrometer**: A hydrometer is used to test coolant mixture and freeze protection by testing the specific gravity of the coolant. You must use a hydrometer designed specifically for the anti-freeze you are testing.
- **Refractometer**: A refractometer is used to test coolant mixture and freeze protection by testing the fluid's ability to bend light. This tester can be used with any type of anti-freeze.
- **Coolant pH test strips**: These are used to test the acid-to-alkalinity balance of the coolant.
- **Coolant dye kit**: This is used to aid leak detection by adding dye to coolant and using an ultraviolet light source (black light) to trace to the source of the leak; the dye glows fluorescent when a black light is shined on it.
- **Infrared temperature sensor**: This is a non-contact thermometer used to check actual temperatures and variations of temperature throughout the cooling system to help pinpoint faulty parts and system blockages.
- **Thermometer**: A thermometer is used to check the temperature of air exiting the heating ducts.
- **Voltmeter**: A voltmeter is used to check for electrical problems, such as cooling fan and temperature gauge issues.
- **Belt-tension gauge**: This gauge is used to check belt tension in older V-belt drive systems.
- **Serpentine belt wear gauge**: This gauge is used to check whether the serpentine belt grooves are worn past their specifications.
- **Alkaline cleaning agents**: These are used to clean cooling systems of oil and fuel contamination. They are generally many times more effective than powdered detergents. These are safe for aluminum radiator and heater cores. This type of cleaner also removes silicate gel.

FIGURE 13-53 Common tools needed to service cooling systems. **A.** Pressure tester. **B.** Refractometer.

- **Mild acid-based cleaning agents**: These are used to safely remove rust, corrosion, scale, and solder without disassembling the cooling system.
- **Electronic Service Tools (ESTs)**: A scan tool is used to activate the cooling fan through bidirectional communication. Fan timers are used to control minimum fan run-time speeds to reduce on–off fan clutch wear and are adjusted using OEM software. Diagnostic trouble codes related to the cooling system are read and cleared using OEM software

Visual Inspection

A visual inspection of the cooling system is performed first to identify obvious system defects. Check the level of the coolant in the overflow bottle and radiator. At the same time, check the color and condition of the coolant to see whether it is cloudy due to silicate drop-out or contaminated with fuel or oil. Similarly, if there is a complaint about the loss of coolant, check the engine oil level and the color of the engine oil. Drain the air tank reservoirs to check for coolant leakage. Inspect the water pump weep hole for a leak or dried coolant track. Also check the cooling system hoses and clamps for any collapsed hoses, deterioration, leaks, or chaffing. If the characteristically sweet smell of ethylene glycol–based coolant is detected when the cab ventilation system fan is switched on, check for a leaking heater core by inspecting for coolant leaking from the heater box drain. White exhaust smoke may indicate coolant leaks into the combustion chamber through a defective head gasket, cracked cylinder head, or a leaking EGR cooler. Additionally, run the engine with the radiator cap off or look into the surge tank, which is often translucent, for excessive bubbles. Some vaporized steam bubbles should be present from the vent lines connecting the tank to the engine, but excessive bubbling may indicate a cavitated liner or block or a cracked cylinder head. Air-operated switches and valves connected to the cooling system, such as water control valves for the cab and bunk heaters, may give a false positive for an internal engine leak. A cracked air compressor casting may give the same indication. Open the air reservoir drain valves while running the engine to eliminate the likelihood of a defective air compressor pressurizing the cooling system. The gaskets and seals on the radiator cap should be inspected for any cracks or damage. Any damage to the seals requires cap replacement.

Safety Tip

When working around the cooling system, care must be taken, particularly if the engine is at operating temperature, because the coolant may be hot enough to scald. If possible, allow the system to cool before removing the cooling system pressure cap, and use extreme caution when removing the pressure cap. If you must remove the radiator cap from a hot system, wear protective gloves and eyewear. A safety stop on the cap allows the pressure to be released slowly, to a safety point, which will slow the flow of coolant forced out by hot coolant. Hot liquid coolant converts and expands into steam deep in the engine block as system pressure is suddenly reduced.

Pressure Testing the Cooling System and Checking for Leaks

Pressure testing the cooling system for leaks is an effective way to locate external and internal coolant leaks. High cooling system pressure causes coolant to leak out much more quickly from a crack, hole, leaking gasket, or seal, which makes leaks easier to locate. The use of a droplight and a mirror may be necessary to see behind the engine or in tight, hard-to-access areas. Adding dye to the engine coolant that can be detected with an ultraviolet light can make it even easier to pinpoint coolant leaks. Loose hose clamps are often cold leaks and can be detected more easily

when the engine is off. Other leaks, such as head gasket leaks, may show up only after the engine is warmed up. The cooling system pressure cap should also be tested because a defective or leaking cap will fail to pressurize the cooling system, resulting in coolant loss **FIGURE 13-54**.

To pressure test the cooling system and check for leaks, follow the guidelines in **SKILL DRILL 13-1**.

▶ TECHNICIAN TIP

If you need to replace a pressure cap, use only a cap with the recommended pressure, not a higher pressure cap. Diesel engines often use lower cooling system pressure caps to protect engine oil from overheating in the oil cooler. Lower pressure caps will allow coolant to boil at a lower temperature, enabling escaping steam to carry away excess heat.

Verifying the Engine Operating Temperature

Technicians need to verify whether an engine is reaching operating temperature whenever there is a complaint about an engine overheating or overcooling. Overcooling takes place when the engine is not reaching operating temperature. Observations about how long the engine takes to reach operating temperature and

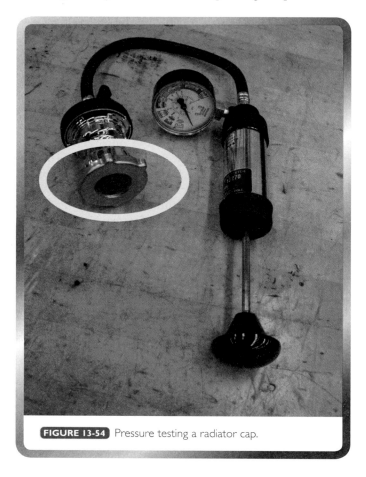

FIGURE 13-54 Pressure testing a radiator cap.

SKILL DRILL 13-1 Pressure Testing the Cooling System and Checking for Leaks

1 With the engine off, top up the engine coolant level with premixed coolant.

2 With the engine off, connect the radiator pressure tester in place of the pressure cap. Larger caps, which are found on heavy-duty cooling systems, or unique OEM pressure cap designs may not fit with a standard pressure cap tester. An adapter may be required to seal the tool to the neck of the surge tank or radiator. Pressurize the system to 15–17 psi (103–117 kPa).

3 Observe the pressure readings for 30 minutes. During this time, visually inspect the cooling system hoses, all hose connections, auxiliary coolant heaters, bunk and cab heaters, EGR coolers, EGR valves, turbocharger coolant lines, the water pump weep hole, all gasket sealing surfaces, and any other components that have coolant flow.

4 Check the engine oil level and verify that the oil has a normal color. Oil that looks milky likely has a coolant leaking into it.

5 Inspect the seals on the pressure cap and pressure test the cap. The seals should be intact and in good condition without any cracks. The same pressure tester used for the engine is used to test the cap. An adapter is placed between the cap and test tool and the tester is pumped once again. The cap's release pressure should be indicated on the cap and it should hold pressure until the tester applies the amount of pressure specified on the cap.

6 Refer to the OEM service information to check whether the pressure cap is the correct pressure rating for the vehicle. If the cap will not hold or cannot reach specified pressure, or if it does not vent at the specified pressure, then replace it with a new cap with the correct pressure rating.

7 Record and report your results.

8 If there is a significant drop in pressure and the complaint investigated is coolant loss, the engine may have an internal coolant leak. The engine should be first checked to determine if the cooling system is excessively pressurized using a separate procedure. The EGR cooler should be inspected as well using a separate procedure.

9 To check for internal leaks, drain the engine oil and remove the oil pan.

10 While the cooling system continues to be pressurized, observe whether the liner O-rings are leaking or if coolant is originating from a head gasket leak. In push tube engines, head gasket leaks will drip coolant from the cam side of the engine.

---

maximum coolant temperature are required in these instances, such as when an engine protection system logs faults for high engine temperature or if there is inadequate heat from the cab heater. The HD-OBD cooling system monitor will also log codes if the engine does not warm to operating temperature quickly enough to enable other monitors to run. Validating the operating temperature reported by the coolant temperature gauge in the instrument cluster should be performed at the same time.

To verify the engine operating temperature, follow the guidelines in **SKILL DRILL 13-2**.

Inspecting for a Leaking EGR Cooler

Loss of engine coolant without any visible external leaks may be caused by a variety of internal leaks or over-pressurizing of the cooling system forcing coolant out the over flow tank. Leaking

head gaskets, or air compressors can consume coolant. A more common problem is a cracked EGR cooler which can either over-pressurize the cooling system or allow engine coolant to leak into the cooler where it is mixed with exhaust gas and delivered to the engine intake. White exhaust smoke that smells sweet is an indication of an EGR cooler leak. The problem can worsen under hard acceleration.

To inspect for a leaking EGR cooler, follow the guidelines in **SKILL DRILL 13-3**.

Testing Coolant Nitrite or DCA/SCA Levels

Nitrite is the most important additive used in diesel coolant because it prevents cavitation damage in the cooling system. Nitrite is one of the ingredients present in DCA and SCA

SKILL DRILL 13-2 Verifying the Engine Operating Temperature

1. Perform a visual inspection of the engine and cooling system. Top up the coolant level if it is low.

2. Because a diesel engine will not reach operating temperature if it is only run at idle, the engine needs to be placed under load and run until the cooling system temperature no longer increases. Alternatively, the engine can be operated at high idle for 45 minutes.

3. After reaching maximum operating temperature, aim a non-contact infrared (IR) temperature gun at the thermostat housing and record the temperature.

4. If the engine is equipped with an on–off engine fan, also record the coolant temperature that is activating and deactivating the fan to validate correct fan operation.

5. Using an EST, such as a scanner or OEM software, observe and record the engine coolant temperature parameter data provided by the temperature sensor.

6. Compare the IR thermometer reading with the coolant sensor data to check whether the sensor data is valid and accurate. Also compare the data with the instrument cluster display to verify the correct gauge operation.

7. If the engine is equipped with an electronically controlled variable speed engine fan, activate the cooling fan using OEM software to verify that the fan is operating correctly.

9. Report your results and provide service recommendations for further repairs or diagnosis.

 SKILL DRILL 13-3 Inspecting for a Leaking EGR Cooler

1. Pressurize the cooling system and inspect for obvious external leaks.

2. Remove the EGR valve and inspect it to see if it looks wet and shiny. If the EGR valve is located after the EGR cooler, coolant leaks will wet the valve. EGR valves on the hot side of the EGR system will not become wetted with coolant.

3. While the cooling system is pressurized, disconnect the outlet pipe of the cooler and check for visible leaks.

4. Disconnect the EGR cooler inlet and outlet exhaust pipe. Using a block-off kit with a pressure adapter, plug the exhaust inlet and outlets and tighten the block-off plate adapters using the EGR clamps.

5. Pressurize the exhaust side of the EGR cooler using the block-off kit with shop air supplied at 30 psi (207 kPa).

6. Shut off the compressed air to the cooler while it is pressurized and wait 30 minutes. There should be no pressure drop in 30 minutes. Any drop indicates the cooler is defective.

7. Check for air bubbles in the surge tank and from the vent lines. If air bubbles are present, replace EGR cooler.

coolant conditioner packages. Coolant filters also have a specific level of nitrite that requires matching a coolant filter with the cooling system maintenance requirements. In engines that use conventional type 1 anti-freeze, nitrite levels should be checked at every oil change. For engines using extended life anti-freeze, nitrite levels should be checked once a year. Different nitrite levels are required depending on the anti-freeze formulation used. Type 1 requires 3–5% nitrite levels, but long-life formulations require substantially less. A coolant test strip that contains at least three kinds of chemically treated testing pads should be used. One is for anti-freeze concentration, another for nitrite levels, and another for pH. Additional pads can be found on test strips for testing other corrosion inhibitors.

To test coolant nitrite or DCA/SCA levels, follow the guidelines in **SKILL DRILL 13-4**.

Maintenance Tips

The unique requirements of diesel engine cooling systems make it important to keep in mind a number of points when servicing diesel engine cooling system. These include:

- The cooling system must be maintained on a regular basis to prevent overheating, cavitation, corrosion, scale, and gelation due to silicate dropout.
- Cracked cylinder heads and leaking head gaskets can cause coolant leakage into the engine, leading to catastrophic engine failure.

SKILL DRILL 13-4 Testing Coolant Nitrite or DCA/SCA Levels

Water Shut-off Valve

1. Identify the type of coolant formulation using coolant color. The decal next to the surge tank may not be correct if the coolant has been changed or contaminated with other coolant formulations.

2. Using a manufacturer or aftermarket test strip, dip the strip into the coolant and shake any excess coolant off of the strip.

3. Using the chart on the test strip bottle, compare the color of the nitrite pad on the test strip against the chart scales.

4. Determine the level of nitrite in the cooling system in parts per million or as a percentage.

5. Using the service manual or test strip manufacturer's recommendations, determine the amount of nitrite that may be needed based on the coolant formulation. The level may be acceptable, too high, or too low.

6. Drain the coolant to correct excessive nitrite levels, which can lead to deterioration of cooling system components, particularly hoses. Add the correct amount of extender, DCA, or SCA based on the cooling system capacity and coolant anti-freeze formulation.

- Overconcentration of DCA or overconcentrated anti-freeze can lead to silicate dropout.
- Conventionally formulated coolant should be changed and the cooling system flushed every two years.
- Corrosion inhibitor packages contained in engine coolant can be damaged though overheating and should be discarded and not reused.
- It is recommended to pressure test cooling systems at 15–18 psi (103–124 kPa) to check for leaks. The pressure should hold for several minutes without significantly dropping. The engine should be inspected for external leaks after pressure testing. The circled adapter is used by the pressure tester to check the radiator cap. The radiator cap should release pressure only at the rating on the cap.
- The concentration of anti-freeze should be checked not only to ensure freeze protection but because adequate anti-freeze is needed to provide enough corrosion and cavitation inhibitors to the cooling system.

Radiator Cap Inspection

The rubber gasket that seals the pressure valve at the bottom of the radiator neck should be inspected. Cracked, deteriorated, or damaged gaskets will leak, and caps with such gaskets should be discarded. When pressure testing cooling systems, the radiator cap should be simultaneously pressure checked. The cap should not leak until the pressure rating imprinted on the cap is reached.

The vacuum valve spring should also hold the vacuum valve closed when the cap is removed and no pressure is applied to the cap. A dangling vacuum valve observed when the cap is removed is evidence of a defective vacuum valve.

Evaluating Thermostatic Fan Clutches

Checking by hand the amount of drag the thermostatic fan clutch has will not provide any indication of whether the clutch is operating. To evaluate these silicone fluid thermostatic fan clutches, the amount of slippage is measured. This is best done with an optical tachometer. Manufacturer's specifications will provide a measure for the percentage of the fan speed relative to engine speed when the engine is cold. This percentage will increase proportional to the temperature of the thermostatic fan clutch. Measuring both the fan speed and engine speed with the optical tachometer will yield accurate data. Any fluid leakage and damaged hubs should be taken out of service.

Hose Inspection

Air, coolant chemical attacks, and extreme temperatures all contribute to hose deterioration. As hoses age, they can become hardened and crack. Electrochemical attacks on hoses tend to affect the hose nearest the radiator and engine ends. Internally, hoses can soften and crack, causing lining failure and eventual hose rupture. Rubber particles loosened from the hose linings can clog radiators and thermostats. A weakened hose may collapse and restrict coolant flow. The bottom radiator hose has an internal spring that prevents the hose collapsing when the engine is suddenly accelerated and the water pump draws more coolant.

The following is a recommended procedure to inspect coolant hoses for the effects of electrochemical degradation (ECD):

1. Make sure the engine is cool.

2. Use fingers and thumb to partially squeeze the hose near the clamps or connectors while checking for weakness. Do not use your whole hand. ECD usually occurs within two inches of the ends of the hose and not in the middle. Do not completely squeeze the hose—too much compression can crack the inside of the hose.

3. While squeezing, feel for voids, cracks, mushiness, or weak spots near the hose ends where it may be weakened by ECD. Heaviest damage occurs where the temperature is hottest and air is present with the coolant. Upper radiator hoses more commonly fail first.

Preventative Maintenance for Cooling Systems

The following tasks will help keep a diesel engine's cooling system in good working order:

- Pressure test the radiator cap to check for the recommended system pressure level.
- Check the thermostat for proper opening and closing.
- Pressure test the system to identify any external leaks to the cooling system including the radiator, water pump, engine cooling passages, radiator and heater hoses, cylinder head gasket, and heater core.
- Visually inspect the coolant color and condition to check for oil cooler, transmission cooler, and fuel leaks into the cooling system.
- Visually inspect all cooling system components, including belts, hoses, and belt tensioners.
- Test the engine fan clutch for proper operation.
- Measure the freeze protection of the coolant using a refractometer or hydrometer **FIGURE 13-55**.
- When using conventionally formulated Type I anti-freeze, measure nitrite/nitrate levels to indicate correct levels or DCA/SCA. This can be done using coolant test strips or other chemical tests at every oil change interval. Test strips are dipped into the coolant through the radiator opening and will indicate ratios of nitrates/nitrites. Test strips may also indicate pH level, ratio of glycol, and other levels of corrosion inhibitors.
- Complete a lab analysis of additive package in ELC at 300,000 miles (482,800 km). Field test kits are currently not available to evaluate levels of SCA/DCA.
- If preferred, add extender to HOAT and NOAT ELC at 300,000 miles (482,800 km).
- Flush and fill cooling system every 200,000 miles (321,900 km) or 2 years if conventionally formulated type I anti-freeze is used and every 600,000 miles (965,600 kms) if ELC is used.

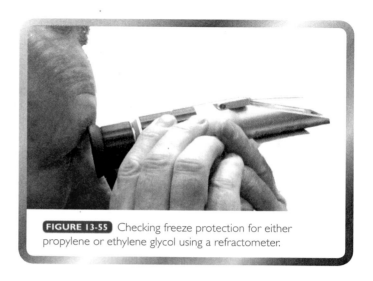

FIGURE 13-55 Checking freeze protection for either propylene or ethylene glycol using a refractometer.

Preventative Maintenance Schedules

Preventive maintenance of the cooling system is critical for long life and reliability of the engine. Failure to perform required maintenance will result in cooling system failure, which can lead to breakdowns and major engine damage. Manufacturers publish the required maintenance for a vehicle in the owner's manual and in the service information. The maintenance schedule lists which services are due at a particular number of miles (kilometers) or date. Different types of coolant will have different service intervals and can range from a low of 24,855–93,206 miles (40,000–150,000 km) or more. Always check the manufacturer's service interval to ensure effective coolant operation. Belts and hoses have similar inspection and maintenance requirements. It is critical to follow these service intervals, so always check the preventive maintenance schedule for the vehicle you are working on.

Measuring Freeze Protection

The use of a hydrometer or refractometer is necessary when testing the freeze protection of the coolant in the cooling system. The customer may request this service as part of a winterization package performed by the workshop. Any time coolant is replaced in the cooling system, the freeze point should be verified.

The hydrometer is a tool that measures the specific gravity of a liquid. When coolant is drawn into the hydrometer, a float will rise to a certain level depending upon the density of the coolant. Anti-freeze has a higher specific gravity than water, so the higher the float rises in the liquid, the greater the percentage of anti-freeze in the mix. One drawback to hydrometers is that they are typically anti-freeze specific. This means you will need one for ethylene glycol and one for propylene glycol, as the specific gravities of the two chemicals are different. Another drawback is that as the temperature of the coolant goes up, the specific gravity goes down. Some hydrometers have a built-in thermometer and a chart, allowing you to compensate for the temperature of the coolant.

A refractometer can also be used to test the proportions of anti-freeze and water in the coolant mix (or the level of freeze protection) by measuring a liquid's specific gravity. It works by allowing light to shine through the fluid. The light bends in accordance with the particular liquid's specific gravity. The bending of the light displays on a scale inside the tool, indicating the specific gravity of the fluid. One nice feature of a refractometer is that it has a scale for both types of anti-freeze and reads the freeze point accurately.

To use a hydrometer to test the freeze point of the coolant, follow the guidelines in SKILL DRILL 13-5. To use a refractometer to test the freeze point of the coolant, follow the guidelines in SKILL DRILL 13-6.

Possible Causes of Overcooling

Overcooling can be caused by several different issues, including:

- A thermostat sticking open
- A blocking thermostat that is leaking
- A malfunctioning temperature gauge
- Fan drives that are operating continuously

Possible Causes of Overheating

There are many causes of overheating as well. The following are common reasons for overheating:

- Low coolant
- Blocked or restricted airflow through radiator, charge air cooler, or AC condenser

SKILL DRILL 13-5 Using a Hydrometer to Test the Freeze Point of the Coolant

1. Remove the pressure cap. Be sure the cooling system is cool before removing the cap.

2. Determine the type of anti-freeze and verify that the hydrometer is designed to be used with it.

3. Place the hydrometer tube into the coolant and squeeze the ball on top of the tool.

4. Release the ball to draw in a sample of coolant. Make sure the level of coolant drawn in is above the minimum line.

5. Read the scale on the tool to verify the freeze protection of the coolant.

6. Return the coolant sample to the radiator or surge tank.

SKILL DRILL 13-6 Using a Refractometer to Test the Freeze Point of the Coolant

1. Remove the pressure cap. Be sure the cooling system is cool before removing it.

2. Determine the type of anti-freeze and verify that the refractometer is designed to be used with it.

3. Place a few drops of coolant on the sample plate on the top of the tool.

4. Hold the refractometer roughly level under a light, look through the viewfinder and read the scale to verify the freeze protection of the coolant.

5. Return the coolant sample to the radiator or surge tank.

- Fan drive not working
- Missing or damaged fan shroud
- Blocked or restricted radiator
- Incorrect radiator cap
- Overconcentrated anti-freeze
- Water pump impeller broken, slipping, or damaged
- Overfueling engine
- High ambient operating temperature
- Over-pressurized cooling system from cracked cylinder head, cavitated block, defective air compressor, etc. pushing coolant out of radiator

HD-OBD and Cooling Systems

An OBD system for diesels is required to monitor the cooling system for proper operation so that other OBD monitors and any emission control strategy that is dependent on proper cooling system temperature is reached within a reasonable time. Data derived from the engine coolant temperature (ECT) sensor will indicate whether the engine has reached near thermostat regulating temperature within a predetermined amount of time. Slow or inadequate engine warm-up will log fault codes.

Wrap-Up

Ready for Review

▶ The operation and maintenance of the cooling system is critical to engine durability and reliability.

▶ The flame temperature of diesel fuel is approximately 3900°F (2149°C); sustained operation of the engine at this temperature without some means of removing heat would quickly result in damaged or destroyed engine components.

▶ Diesel engine heat loads include exhaust gas recirculation, lubrication oil, and the air intake system.

▶ An important job of the cooling system is to raise engine coolant temperature quickly to keep engine component wear to a minimum.

▶ Machined parts operating with close tolerances require consistent operating temperatures of 180–200°F (82–93°C); some exceptions are emergency and military engines that are designed to withstand as much as 230°F (110°C).

▶ As engine coolant warms, it expands, and cooling systems must provide for this expansion.

▶ Cooling systems are pressurized to maintain greater-than-atmospheric pressure at the water pump inlet and increase the boiling point of water.

▶ Cooling systems must provide for deaeration of coolant to prevent pumps and coolant passageways in the cylinder head from becoming air bound.

▶ Anti-freeze contains a number of additives that minimize electrochemical reactions, which prolongs the durability of engine and cooling system components.

▶ Maintenance practices and engine coolant formulations should be designed to minimize the formation of engine-damaging deposits like calcium and magnesium.

▶ Freeze and boil protection are both supplied to the engine through the use of anti-freeze; additional boiling protection is accomplished through pressurizing the cooling system.

▶ Cylinder wall and liner cavitation is a condition unique to diesel engines; chemical treatment of cooling system is a preferred method for minimizing cavitation erosion.

▶ Coolant generally flows through the oil cooler first, then the cylinder block water jackets and intercooler, and then through the cylinder head.

▶ Heavy-duty and automotive diesel engines depend almost exclusively on the efficiency of liquid cooling systems.

▶ Diesel coolant consists of water, anti-freeze (which contains a special corrosion inhibitor package), and supplemental coolant additives that minimize cavitation erosion.

▶ One major factor in the corrosion rate of an engine's metals is the coolant's pH.

▶ Water is the most efficient fluid to transfer heat; however, water will cause corrosion of metal parts in contact with the cooling system and therefore needs addition of corrosion inhibitors.

▶ Anti-freeze is added to water, which increases the boiling point and lowers the freezing temperature of water.

▶ Most anti-freezes are made with a base of either ethylene glycol or propylene glycol.

▶ Mixing ethylene glycol or propylene glycol anti-freeze with water alone is not effective to prevent corrosion or erosion of cooling system components; the additive packages are used to enhance anti-freeze.

▶ Radiators are heat-exchanging devices that release heat absorbed from the engine to the air.

▶ While early radiator caps simply prevented coolant from spilling out of the cooling system, today's radiator caps have additional functions, such as increasing the pressure of the cooling system to raise the boiling point of coolant and allowing air or coolant to re-enter the cooling system when the pressure drops after the engine cools.

▶ Surge or overflow tanks provide the space for coolant and vapor to move when the engine coolant is hot.

▶ Vent lines located at the highest points on the engine and radiator bleed any steam and air out of the engine and into the surge tank.

▶ To ensure positive circulation of coolant, an engine-driven water pump is used move coolant through the cooling system.

▶ Water filters on diesel engines, if equipped, perform two primary purposes: they remove sediment, rust, and dissolved particles that can cause abrasive damage to the cooling system, and they supply additives to the coolant.

▶ Thermostats regulate the temperature of the engine coolant by modulating or controlling the volume of coolant circulated to the radiator.

▶ Engine fans are designed to increase the airflow across the radiator, which improves the efficiency of heat removal from coolant.

▶ Fan shrouds seal the gap around the fan and radiator to ensure that cooling air runs through the radiator rather than leaking around its sides or past the headlights.

▶ The upper and lower radiator hoses and heater hoses require flexible connections between the engine radiator and heater core due to engine vibration and torque flexion.

▶ The cooling system must be maintained on a regular basis to prevent overheating, cavitation, corrosion, scale, and gelation due to silicate dropout.

▶ On-board diagnostic (OBD) systems are required to monitor the cooling system for proper operation.

Vocabulary Builder

aeration A condition in which excessive amounts of air or steam bubbles are dissolved in coolant, diminishing the coolant's effectiveness.

cavitation Erosion in cylinder block walls, heads, and liner sleeves as a result of the collapse of tiny water vapor bubbles formed when coolant vaporizes on hot cylinder wall surfaces.

coolant extender An additive package that is only used with ELC, which is added at the midpoint of the coolant's life.

diesel coolant additive (DCA) An additive used to treat cooling systems to reduce the effects of cavitation erosion.

electrolyte A substance that can conduct current.

ethylene glycol The base chemical from which the majority of anti-freezes are made.

extended-life coolant (ELC) Several types of long-life coolant formulations containing an anti-corrosion additive package that does not deplete; also known as long life coolant (LLC).

heat exchanger A system that transfers heat from coolant to the atmosphere.

heat rejection The transfer of heat into the cooling system from the combustion chamber.

hybrid organic acid technology (HOAT) A combination of IAT and OAT with nitrites added, making it suitable for use in both light- and heavy-duty systems.

inorganic additive technology (IAT) A diesel engine cooling system conditioner containing non-carbon-based corrosion inhibitors such as phosphates, borates, and silicate.

nitrated-organic acid technology (NOAT) An ELC using OAT with nitrates added.

organic acid technology (OAT) A category of ELC containing carbon-based corrosion inhibitors.

propylene glycol An anti-freeze base that is non-toxic and environmentally friendly.

supplemental coolant additive (SCA) An additive used to treat cooling systems to reduce the effects of cavitation erosion and optimize cooling system performance.

thermal efficiency The ability of an engine to convert the energy content of fuel into mechanical force.

Review Questions

1. If ingested, _____ of ethylene glycol will cause fatal kidney failure in humans after a couple of days.
   a. 2 ounces
   b. 4 ounces
   c. 6 ounces
   d. 8 ounces

2. Surge tanks, overflow reservoirs, and large radiator tanks are used for accommodating coolant _____.
   a. expansion
   b. pressure
   c. temperature
   d. leakage

3. A coolant with a pH of _____ is considered neutral.
   a. 5
   b. 6
   c. 7
   d. 8

4. Type IV OAT anti-freeze is _____ and uses non-carboxylate acids, such as benzoate, from benzoic acid, to form the additive package.
   a. pink
   b. red
   c. green
   d. orange

5. The _____ is a system that transfers heat from coolant to the atmosphere.
   a. liquid heat exchanger
   b. heat exchanger
   c. charge air cooler
   d. air-air aftercooling

6. _____ is the base chemical from which the majority of anti-freezes are made.
   a. Propylene glycol
   b. Ethylene glycol
   c. Phosphate
   d. Water

7. The best heavy-duty on-highway diesel engines operate at approximately _____ thermal efficiency.
   a. 30%
   b. 35%
   c. 40%
   d. 45%

8. In all liquid-cooled engines, the _____ controls the flow of coolant through the radiator.
   a. thermostat
   b. water pump
   c. scale
   d. lower radiator hose

9. _____ is an anti-freeze base that is nontoxic and environmentally friendly.
   a. Phosphate
   b. Ethylene glycol
   c. Propylene glycol
   d. Water

10. _____ is the primary ingredient of engine coolant.
    a. Phosphate
    b. Water
    c. Propylene glycol
    d. Ethylene glycol

ASE-Type Questions

1. Technician A says that cavitation erosion is unique to diesel engines. Technician B says that cavitation erosion is unique to gasoline engines. Who is correct?
   a. Technician A
   b. Technician B
   c. Both Technician A and Technician B
   d. Neither Technician A nor Technician B

2. Technician A says coolant for diesel-fueled engines and coolant for gasoline-fueled engines are identical. Technician B says coolant for diesel-fueled engines and coolant for gasoline-fueled engines are different. Who is correct?
   a. Technician A
   b. Technician B
   c. Both Technician A and Technician B
   d. Neither Technician A nor Technician B

3. Technician A says that in the past, coolant has included mixtures of alcohol and water. Technician B says that in the past, coolant has included water mixed with honey and soluble oils. Who is correct?
   a. Technician A
   b. Technician B
   c. Both Technician A and Technician B
   d. Neither Technician A nor Technician B

4. Technician A says propylene glycol requires a higher concentration than ethylene glycol to provide the same freeze protection. Technician B says propylene glycol requires a lower concentration than ethylene glycol to provide the same freeze protection. Who is correct?
   a. Technician A
   b. Technician B
   c. Both Technician A and Technician B
   d. Neither Technician A nor Technician B

5. Technician A says ethylene glycol is both nontoxic and environmentally friendly. Technician B says propylene glycol is very toxic and bad for the environment. Who is correct?
   a. Technician A
   b. Technician B
   c. Both Technician A and Technician B
   d. Neither Technician A nor Technician B

6. Technician A says core plugs are designed to relieve pressure from frozen coolant to prevent engine damage. Technician B says core plugs are designed to relieve pressure from heated coolant to prevent engine damage. Who is correct?
   a. Technician A
   b. Technician B
   c. Both Technician A and Technician B
   d. Neither Technician A nor Technician B

7. Technician A says the cooling system removes excess heat from the engine and releases it to the atmosphere through the thermostat. Technician B says the cooling system removes excess heat from the engine and releases it to the atmosphere through the radiator. Who is correct?
   a. Technician A
   b. Technician B
   c. Both Technician A and Technician B
   d. Neither Technician A nor Technician B

8. Technician A says the principle of inducing current flow by using dissimilar metals and an electrolyte is called the cavitation effect. Technician B says the principle of inducing current flow by using dissimilar metals and an electrolyte is called the galvanic effect. Who is correct?
   a. Technician A
   b. Technician B
   c. Both Technician A and Technician B
   d. Neither Technician A nor Technician B

9. Technician A says that some of the scale that collects in the cooling system comes from calcium and magnesium in the water used for cooling. Technician B says that some of the scale that collects in the cooling system is produced by additives in the anti-freeze. Who is correct?
   a. Technician A
   b. Technician B
   c. Both Technician A and Technician B
   d. Neither Technician A nor Technician B

10. Technician A says that, if ingested, 4 ounces of ethylene glycol will cause fatal kidney failure in humans after a couple of days. Technician B says that, if ingested, 4 ounces of propylene glycol will cause fatal kidney failure in humans after a couple of days. Who is correct?
    a. Technician A
    b. Technician B
    c. Both Technician A and Technician B
    d. Neither Technician A nor Technician B

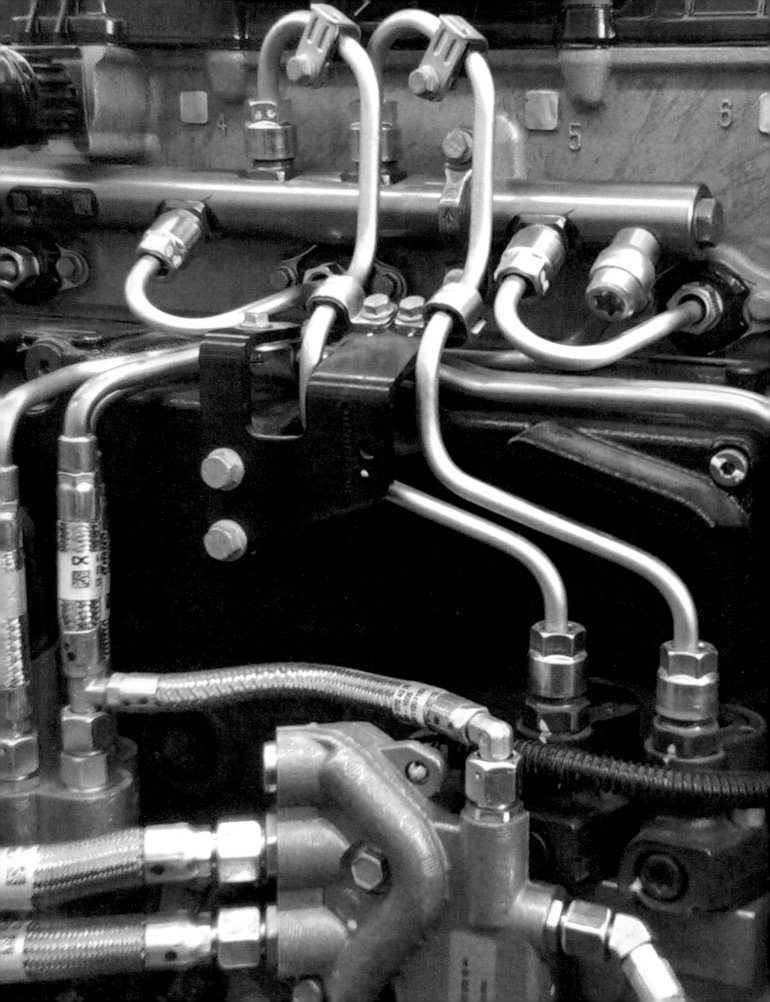

SECTION 4

Diesel Fuel and Fuel Systems

CHAPTER 14
Diesel Fuel Properties and Characteristics

NATEF Tasks

There are no NATEF tasks for this chapter.

Knowledge Objectives

After reading this chapter, you will be able to:

1. Identify and describe the purpose, functions, properties, and characteristics of diesel fuel. (pp 409–418)
2. Describe the processes for production of diesel fuels. (pp 411–412)
3. Identify and describe grades of petroleum- and biological-based fuels. (pp 422–425)
4. Make recommendations for selecting the appropriate grade of diesel fuel according to vehicle application and operating conditions. (pp 422–425)

5. Describe and explain the purpose, functions, and characteristics of diesel fuel additives. (pp 426–428)
6. Identify and explain fuel system failures and performance problems associated with poor quality diesel fuel. (pp 428–430)
7. Recommend service and maintenance practices related to correct handling of fuel and fuel additives. (pp 428–430)
8. Identify the causes of fuel contamination. (pp 429–430)

Skills Objectives

After reading this chapter, you will be able to:

1. Determine a fuel's ASTM grade. (p 423) **SKILL DRILL 14-1**

2. Detect water in diesel fuel. (p 429) **SKILL DRILL 14-2**
3. Evaluate fuel quality. (p 430) **SKILL DRILL 14-3**

▶ Introduction

An understanding of diesel fuel properties and characteristics is essential for selecting appropriate fuel and fuel additives for the wide variety of applications for diesel engines. Fuel properties exert a major influence on engine performance. Operating conditions and location of engine operation—stationary, marine, on- or off-highway applications—significantly change the correct selection of fuel and choice of additives. The rising cost of diesel fuel, too, should always be a consideration in getting the best performance **FIGURE 14-1**.

Environmental considerations and legislative requirements for renewable fuels are adding complexity to today's fuel characteristics. This complexity can potentially lead to an incorrect selection of fuel that can have dramatic negative effects on engine durability and reliability. Diesel technicians should also be familiar with identifying performance problems and engine failures associated with fuel quality as well as the impact of fuel additives on treated fuel. To help the technician understand the function and purpose of diesel fuel properties and characteristics, this chapter presents relevant and practical information about diesel fuel production, specifications, and performance standards. Information regarding fuel handling, fuel additives, and the problems associated with fuel quality are included to enhance technician understanding of fuels as they are related to service and maintenance practices associated with diesel engines **FIGURE 14-2**.

▶ Diesel Fuel Fundamentals

Diesel fuel properties and characteristics are matters a technician can do little to change. It is important, however, to understand the impact fuel quality has on engine operation, especially when diagnosing and servicing performance-related problems. Also, a competent diesel technician should have the expertise to make recommendations about the use of different grades of diesel fuel and fuel additives.

Development of Diesel Fuel

While the term "diesel fuel" bears the name of the engine's inventor, it is a generic term that refers to a range of fuels burned in compression ignition (CI) engines. Each has its own uniform designation as well as its own formulation. Some diesel fuel products are made from petroleum, while others are processed from biological sources and even waste products. The following section surveys the development of diesel fuel since the invention of the diesel engine.

Early Fuels

Coal dust was the original diesel fuel. Rudolf Diesel's prototype engine, based on his 1892 patent for a CI engine, used this resource found in plentiful quantities in the mines and factories of Germany's industrialized Ruhr Valley. The fuel did not work well, and Diesel searched for an alternative liquid fuel.

▶ You Are the Technician

Over the years that you have serviced diesel engines, you've accumulated experience working with a variety of fuel quality problems and many customers and drivers seek you out for advice about the purchase of fuel and fuel additives. Because your repair shop is located in a colder region of the country that has dramatic seasonal temperature changes, you can anticipate a number of fuel-related problems due to colder temperatures. Some of the problems you have encountered include:

- Drivers entering the region with fuel purchased in warmer regions
- Performance problems such as low power and hard starting using fuel purchased locally in the winter
- Drivers unnecessarily using fuel additives and incorrectly using those additives
- Stale fuel
- The use of biodiesel purchased in regions where biodiesel is inexpensive and widely available
- Water and asphaltene contamination
- Obstructed fuel filters and lines when the temperatures are very low

1. For each of the above situations, outline the advice you would provide to a customer, explaining either the potential fuel-related operating problems a driver could expect to encounter, or the reasons that cause each of the service conditions.
2. Outline the procedures you would follow to evaluate the fuel quality used by an engine you suspect has a problem related to fuel quality. Explain your reasons for using each of those procedures.
3. Make a list of service recommendations to help drivers and owners avoid fuel quality–related problems with diesel engines.

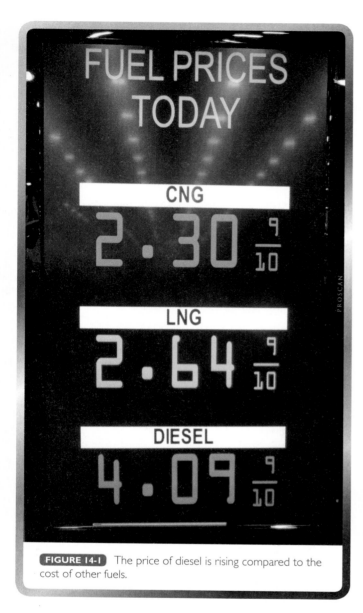

FIGURE 14-1 The price of diesel is rising compared to the cost of other fuels.

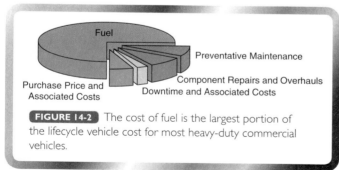

FIGURE 14-2 The cost of fuel is the largest portion of the lifecycle vehicle cost for most heavy-duty commercial vehicles.

In 1900, demonstration of an early prototype engine took place at the Paris World Exhibition in France. This engine was fueled by the first biodiesel fuel made of peanut oil. Encouraged by the French government to support its colonies around the world, the intention was to develop a renewable nonpetroleum-based fuel that would permit small industry, farmers, and other producers to effectively compete with the monopolized oil industry of the time. In fact, until the 1920s, many diesel and other CI engines were powered by biologically derived fuels.

▶ **TECHNICIAN TIP**

Biodiesel refers to diesel fuel derived from biological sources such as vegetable oils or animal fats. In contrast, petroleum diesel is refined from crude oil. Crude oil is considered a mineral oil because it is extracted from the earth.

ASTM Diesel Fuel Standard

For a number of reasons, the more favored alternative to biologically based diesel engine fuels are derived from petroleum. <u>Petroleum distillates</u>, that is, fuel recovered from distilling crude oil, could readily burn in the diesel engine and were widely available because there was plenty of this by-product left over after refining gasoline used to fuel automobiles and other vehicles. The same fuels commonly used for lanterns and heating homes (kerosene and other light hydrocarbons) could also be used to operate diesel engines. Until the 1930s, these petroleum products varied widely in composition and quality, so their performance was unpredictable. Manufacturers began to develop diesel fuel specifications after observing numerous engine failures associated with fuel composition. Today, <u>ASTM International</u> (formerly known as the American Society for Testing Materials) establishes diesel fuel standards. While most countries possess their own separate and distinct performance standards for diesel fuel, the ASTM-defined fuel standards are widely recognized around the world. Petroleum diesel fuel is defined in ASTM standard D975, and biodiesel specifications are set in ASTM standard D6751. ASTM diesel fuel grades are denoted as 1-D (for Diesel #1) and 2-D (for Diesel #2); 1-D and 2-D are both commonly used by on- and off-road diesel engines. In North America, 2-D is commercially retailed at pumps and 1-D and 2-D are both available at pumps outside North America **FIGURE 14-3** . ASTM grade 4-D is used primarily as home heating oil, but it is also used by some large-displacement, stationary, low-speed diesel engines in applications predominantly involving constant speed and load, such as water pumps and power generators. Because 4-D is not as refined in the same manner as 1-D and 2-D, it has impurities and other characteristics that will quickly damage on-highway engines, so it should never be used in them. There is no ASTM 3-D designation.

▶ **TECHNICIAN TIP**

In the United States, diesel fuel properties are regulated by ASTM International and the Environmental Protection Agency (EPA). While most characteristics of diesel fuel are ASTM defined, the EPA also imposes additional environmental standards to minimize formation of toxic emissions.

FIGURE 14-3 The two common ASTM diesel fuel grades for on-highway use are 1-D and 2-D.

Production of Diesel Fuel

Fuels such as diesel or gasoline are derived from crude oil. Crude oil is a mixture of various types of hydrocarbon molecules composed of hydrogen and carbon **FIGURE 14-4**. Some of the molecules are small, having higher ratios of hydrogen to carbon, and therefore lighter. Others are heavier, having greater carbon-to-hydrogen ratios. High-carbon molecules are typically larger and heavier molecules. By boiling the oil and collecting oil vapors through a process known as **distillation**, oil molecules are separated into **fractions**, or cuts, based on the boiling point temperature of each fraction. Smaller, lighter hydrocarbon molecules have a lower boiling point and larger, heavier molecules have a higher boiling point. The boiling and vapor separation process produces petroleum products ranging from propane and butane (called light ends) to gasoline and **middle distillates**, which includes diesel fuel **FIGURE 14-5**.

Diesel and gasoline fuels are different in that diesel fuels contain heavier hydrocarbon molecules, which have a higher boiling point than gasoline, and a higher carbon-to-hydrogen ratio. Kerosene, home heating, and jet fuel account for another proportion of middle-distillate production, and they have specifications and physical properties similar to diesel fuel. However, while similar in properties, they must be used for their specific applications. Fuel specifications developed to operate a camp stove, fly an aircraft, and power an on-highway engine are different and are not interchangeable.

Diesel fuel is also produced by liquefying hydrocarbon gases such as methane and modifying the chemical structure of the hydrocarbon molecules. Such **gas-to-liquid (GTL) diesel fuel** is manufactured by using a chemical process invented in Germany during the 1920s called the **Fischer-Tropsch reaction**. Coal, carbon monoxide (CO), and gases produced by decomposing wood and other plant material can all be used

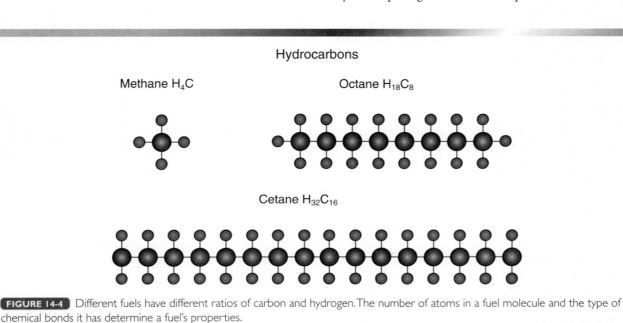

FIGURE 14-4 Different fuels have different ratios of carbon and hydrogen. The number of atoms in a fuel molecule and the type of chemical bonds it has determine a fuel's properties.

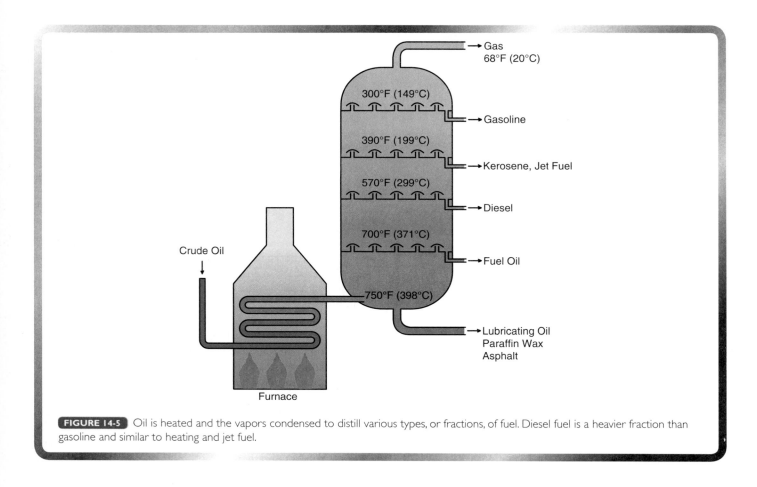

FIGURE 14-5 Oil is heated and the vapors condensed to distill various types, or fractions, of fuel. Diesel fuel is a heavier fraction than gasoline and similar to heating and jet fuel.

to manufacture this kind of <u>synthetic diesel</u> fuel (that is, diesel fuel not derived from petroleum). Testing of such fuels manufactured from this process have successfully demonstrated the viability of this fuel. However, the high operation and maintenance costs associated with its use, plus volatile oil prices, have prevented greater commercial production of this fuel.

> ▶ **TECHNICIAN TIP**
>
> Biodiesel is fuel made exclusively from biological sources, such as plant oil or animal fat, or a combination of petroleum-based fuel and biological fuel sources. The number following the letter "B" indicates the percentage of biologically sourced fuel combined with petroleum fuel. Thus, biodiesel made from 20% biological fuel sources and 80% petroleum fuel sources would be designated B20.

Historically, diesel fuel has been cheaper to buy than gasoline because it is a by-product of gasoline production. With new standards required to produce diesel fuel with lower emissions, its production costs have increased in recent years in North America. In Europe, diesel fuel is typically still cheaper than gasoline because it has favorable taxation policies to encourage diesel's use as a more economical fuel source.

Quality commercial diesel fuel is normally clear to light amber in color depending on the refining process and the source of the oil **FIGURE 14-6**. Certain diesel fuels are dyed to differentiate their sources and applications. Aviation fuel, for example, is dyed blue. Diesel fuels intended for home heating oil and agricultural machinery are dyed red because they are taxed at a lower rate and not to be used in vehicles for on-highway use. The dyes have no effect on fuel performance or emission.

Diesel fuel may darken after prolonged storage, due to oxidation. This darkening is often accompanied by performance problems due to a change in the ignition quality of the fuel. If the darkening is accompanied by the formation of sediment, the fuel can foul and plug fuel filters **FIGURE 14-7**.

Sulfur and Diesel Fuel

Sulfur naturally occurs in much of the crude oil that is pumped from underground deposits. (Biodiesel has no sulfur content.) Sulfur not removed during the refining process is present when the fuel burns. The sulfur content of diesel fuel affects particulate matter (PM) emissions because some of the sulfur in the fuel is converted to sulfate particles in the exhaust. How much sulfur is converted to PM varies from one engine to another, but reducing sulfur decreases PM in almost all engines. For this reason, the EPA began to limit the sulfur content of on-road diesel fuel in 1993 to 0.05% mass or 500 ppm maximum, which mandated

Retailed Clear Diesel $0.88/L

Red Dyed-Diesel $0.77/L

FIGURE 14-6 Fresh, clean petroleum-based diesel fuel is clear when commercially retailed in North America. Dyed fuels are intended for specific uses and taxation categories.

FIGURE 14-7 Older fuel darkens and becomes cloudy as it absorbs water. It will also develop a varnish- or turpentine-like odor.

Ultra-Low-Sulfur Diesel

Ultra-low-sulfur diesel (ULSD) fuel has its sulfur content reduced from approximately 500 ppm to 15 ppm. This cleaner diesel fuel, designated S15, which is appended to the fuel grade (e.g., 1-D S15), became available beginning in 2006 before new diesel vehicles were introduced to meet the EPA 2007 emissions standards **FIGURE 14-8**. Emissions reductions in heavy-duty diesel trucks and buses require the use of exhaust aftertreatment devices such as particulate filters (DPFs), NO$_x$ adsorbers (NACs), liquid selective catalyst reduction (SCR), and oxidation catalysts. ULSD is necessary to avoid damaging or "poisoning" the catalytic materials in these devices. There are benefits to using diesel fuel that has reduced sulfur content **TABLE 14-1**.

the production of **low-sulfur diesel (LSD)** fuel. Such regulations are not necessary for biodiesel, for it has no sulfur content.

Reducing sulfur content of fuel can increase engine longevity. Sulfur can deposit on rings, which causes premature wear and sticking. Sulfur can also combine with water and other substances to damage fuel injectors and contaminate engine oil, resulting in the production of corrosive compounds that damage bearings and other metal parts. Lower sulfur content of the exhaust stream also translates into less corrosion of the exhaust system.

▶ TECHNICIAN TIP

When evaluating diesel fuel quality, in addition to color and the API rating, the fuel's odor is another indicator of its quality. Fresh fuel has a strong, pungent, characteristic odor. Old or stale fuel lacks a strong odor when exposed to air and smells like varnish or turpentine.

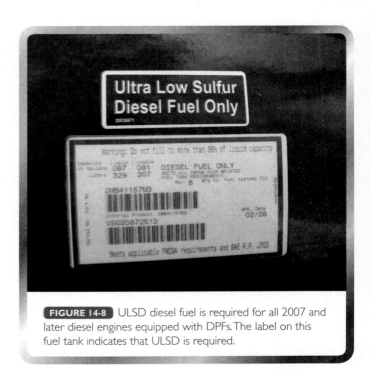

FIGURE 14-8 ULSD diesel fuel is required for all 2007 and later diesel engines equipped with DPFs. The label on this fuel tank indicates that ULSD is required.

TABLE 14-1: Benefits of Using Sulfur-Reduced Fuel

Diesel Fuel Type	Sulfur Limit	U.S. EPA Year of Mandate
On-highway	500 ppm	1993
	30 ppm	2004
	15 ppm	Mid-2006
	2500+ ppm	Pre-1993
Off-road	500 ppm	Mid-2007
	15 ppm	Mid-2010
	500 ppm	Mid-2007
Railway and Marine	15 ppm	Mid-2012

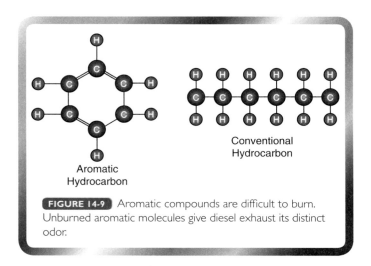

FIGURE 14-9 Aromatic compounds are difficult to burn. Unburned aromatic molecules give diesel exhaust its distinct odor.

Aromatic Content

Aromatic content refers to a particular type of hydrocarbon molecule containing sulfur and nitrogen. Aromatic molecules are large, complex, and difficult to burn. The characteristic odor of diesel exhaust is attributed to the aromatic content of diesel fuel. Because aromatic fuel molecules are hard to break apart and burn, their presence in fuel contributes to increases of emissions **FIGURE 14-9**. Current environmental legislation limits aromatic content to 15% by volume, with some jurisdictions opting for 10%. California has limited aromatic content to 10% since 1993, with a 20% exemption for small refineries. ASTM standards limit aromatic content to a maximum of 35%.

> ### ▶ TECHNICIAN TIP
>
> Hydro-treating fuel, which is a chemical process used by refineries to remove sulfur, simultaneously reduces the aromatic content of fuel. Fuels with lower aromatic content may cause fuel system leaks if fuel system components have operated and absorbed fuels with high aromatic content. High aromatic content fuels have molecules that may be absorbed by some fuel system seals and O-rings. The use of low aromatic fuels may cause the some seals and O-rings to lose these molecules and shrink, which causes fuel system leaks. B-100 biodiesel has no aromatic content.

Performance Requirements for Diesel Fuel

Diesel engines place a number of performance requirements on the fuels:

1. **Starting ease**: Diesel fuel needs to ignite at low temperatures and pressures found in the combustion chamber during cranking. Immediately after the engine starts, a relatively cool combustion chamber can extinguish combustion flames, which causes small fuel droplets to be left unburned and forms white smoke. Diesel fuel should have properties that promote complete combustion at low pressures and temperatures.

2. **Lubricating properties**: The lubricating quality of fuel must aid in reducing engine and fuel system wear. For example, high-pressure injection systems have many moving parts that operate with very small clearances, which are lubricated only by diesel fuel. Fuel should minimize wear by possessing good lubricating properties. (See the Lubricity section.)

3. **Efficient production of power**: Engine design factors are the most critical for extracting energy from the combustion process. Diesel fuel requires sufficient heat content to produce power ratings published by the manufacturer. Waxes and other heavy hydrocarbon compounds contained in diesel fuel produce the greatest heat release from diesel fuel.

4. **Operation during low-temperature conditions**: Diesel fuels contain wax-like molecules that solidify at low temperatures. Gelled fuel will foul or plug filters and fuel lines and prevent fuel from reaching the engine. To minimize this problem, refiners of diesel fuel blend fuels and additives to suit local climate conditions where engines are operated.

5. **Low noise production**: Prolonged ignition delay time leads to increased combustion noise from the diesel engine. Diesel fuel properties can affect noise by increasing or decreasing ignition delay time.

6. **Long filter life**: Diesel fuel should be free of particles causing abrasive wear of the fuel system. Other particles not dissolved in fuel include gums, resins, and asphaltenes that can quickly foul and plug filters.

7. **Good fuel economy**: Fuel economy and power are proportional to the heat content of diesel fuel. Increasing the density of fuel will increase its heat content and improve fuel economy.

8. **Low emissions**: Fuel chemistry can have an impact on engine emissions. Aromatic and sulfur content of fuel as well as other chemical properties can change an engine's emission output.

Diesel fuel contains higher paraffin and other wax-like compounds than gasoline. These waxes will congeal when the fuel is cool and affect engine performance. For this reason, additives are blended into fuel by refineries according to geographical and seasonal requirements. This means fuel purchased in a cold region may not perform well if the vehicle travels to a warmer, distant geographical location. (See the Pour Point and Cloud Point section.)

Flash Point

The **flash point** of a fuel is defined as the temperature to which the fuel must be heated to produce a vapor that will ignite when exposed to a spark or open flame **FIGURE 14-10**. If the flash point of a fuel is too low, the fuel is a fire hazard that is prone accidental ignition and even explosion. For most diesel fuels, the flash point is 100–125°F (38–52°C) depending on the grade of diesel fuel. This contrasts with gasoline, which has a flash point of at least −45°F (−43°C) or lower. If both diesel and gasoline are at room temperature, a lighted match could likely be extinguished in the diesel fuel. The same action with gasoline would likely produce an immediate fire. (Do not attempt to try this!) Because the flash point of diesel is so high, it is a safer fuel to handle and store (unless it is contaminated with gasoline or alcohol). Diesel fuel's low volatility and high flash point are why diesel fuel pump islands often appear dirty and greasy. Diesel fuel is slow to evaporate, while gasoline turns quickly to a vapor **FIGURE 14-11**.

Auto-Ignition Temperature

The **auto-ignition temperature** of diesel fuel is different from the flash point. This is the temperature at which a fuel will

FIGURE 14-11 Unevaporated diesel fuel makes diesel fuel pump islands appear dirty and greasy.

Mixing alcohols or gasoline with diesel fuel is not only a harmful practice for the engine and fuel system, it also lowers the flash point of the fuel. This means the fuel will ignite easier if exposed to an open flame and will become more hazardous to store and handle. Alcohols are also reactive and can cause corrosion of metal within the fuel system and compromise the lubricating characteristics of diesel fuel.

ignite when heated. The lowest permissible auto-ignition temperature of diesel fuel sold in North America is 292°F (144°C). Typically, diesel fuel ignites at temperatures of 392–482°F (200–250°C). Ignition temperatures are even lower when under combustion chamber compression pressure. It should be noted again that although gasoline is more volatile and possesses a lower flash point than diesel fuel, it has a higher auto-ignition temperature **FIGURE 14-12**. Thus, if gasoline is mixed with diesel fuel, it produces a longer ignition delay time causing excessive combustion noise, excessive exhaust smoke, and other problems.

Volatility

Volatility refers to the quantity of fuel evaporating at a particular temperature. Diesel fuel boils at 302–662°F (150–350°C). Volatility is expressed as a percentage of the fuel evaporating between those boiling temperatures. For example, to express the volatility standard of 2-D fuel, 90% would be evaporated at 550–650°F (288–343°C).

Evaporative emission systems are not required on diesel-fueled vehicles because its volatility is low. Even in warm weather, the vapor pressure that diesel fuel exerts inside a storage tank is insignificant in comparison to gasoline **FIGURE 14-13**.

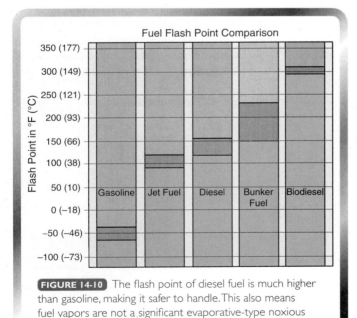

FIGURE 14-10 The flash point of diesel fuel is much higher than gasoline, making it safer to handle. This also means fuel vapors are not a significant evaporative-type noxious emission.

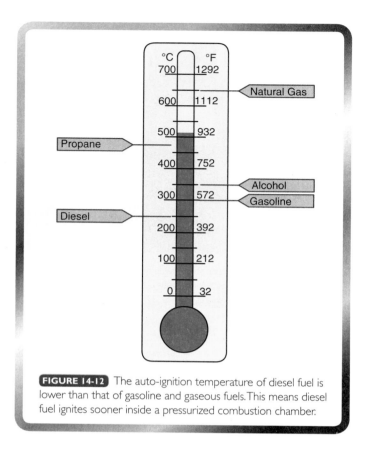

FIGURE 14-12 The auto-ignition temperature of diesel fuel is lower than that of gasoline and gaseous fuels. This means diesel fuel ignites sooner inside a pressurized combustion chamber.

FIGURE 14-13 Unlike gasoline tanks, diesel fuel tanks are vented directly to the atmosphere because diesel fuel is not volatile.

TECHNICIAN TIP

Diesel fuel filling stations may often have a lingering smell of diesel fuel because of the higher flash point and distillation temperature. A diesel fuel spill takes days to vaporize and dissipate, unlike gasoline, which takes minutes.

Pour Point and Cloud Point

Pour point and cloud point refer to the temperatures at which wax molecules in fuel crystallize. More specifically, cloud point, as the name suggests, is the temperature at which wax begins to give fuel a hazy or milky appearance. The pour point occurs when the fuel becomes even colder. Pour point is the temperature at which diesel fuel thickens—the so-called fuel-gelling phenomenon—and no longer pours. When fuel reaches pour point, it cannot pass though lines and filters FIGURE 14-14 .

While some engines fail to run at the cloud point, all engines will fail to operate at the pour point temperature. Depending on cloud composition, the cloud points and pour points can be anywhere from just a few degrees apart to as much as 20°F. Without additives and conditioners, the cloud point for 2-D fuels occurs at approximately 40°F (4°C) and the pour point at 15°F to 20°F (−9 °C to −7°C). In a cold climate, winterized fuel is a blend of 1-D and 2-D or jet aviation fuel (JET A), which is designed to operate at high altitudes in very cold temperatures. Diesel 1-D has a lower pour point, which allows it to move through lines and filters easier, but it also has a lower viscosity, which means it can more easily leak past operating clearances between high-pressure injection system components. Low-power problems can occur with the use of winter grade fuel because it has less energy content. The cloud and pour points of different grades of diesel and biodiesel vary TABLE 14-2 .

Low-End Design Temperature

To operate diesels year round and in cold temperatures, the properties of seasonal diesel fuel are adjusted throughout the year according to historical temperature data of the region where the fuel is sold. For example, in Ontario, Canada, a "Muskoka blend" is prepared for southern Ontario and an "Arctic blend" is used in northern Ontario.

Lubricity

Lubricity refers to a fuel's lubricating quality. Many fuel system components rely on the lubricating properties of the fuel to prevent "galling" (i.e., the scarring of metal surfaces) and seizure of moving parts. It is important that fuel have good lubricating

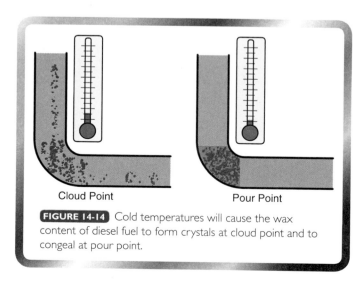

Cloud Point   Pour Point

FIGURE 14-14 Cold temperatures will cause the wax content of diesel fuel to form crystals at cloud point and to congeal at pour point.

TABLE 14-2: Cold Flow Properties of Three Grades of Diesel and Biodiesel

Diesel Fuel	Cloud Point	Pour Point	Cold Filter-Plugging Point
2-D	5°F (−15°C)	−31°F (−35°C)	−4°F (−20°C)
B100 (Canola formulated)	26°F (−3°C)	25°F (−4°C)	24°F (−4°C)
B100 (Soybean formulated)	38°F (3°C)	25°F (−4°C)	28°F (−2°C)

properties to enhance the fuel system's durability. The lubricating properties of diesel fuel are provided by compounds such as fats and waxes that are already naturally present in diesel fuel.

A Scuffing Load Ball-On-Cylinder Lubricity Evaluator (SLBOCLE) test evaluates a fuel's ability to lubricate, which is expressed in grams of load. The higher the SLBOCLE value, the better the lubricating ability. Another test that determines lubricity is the High Frequency Reciprocating Rig (HFRR). This test measures the depth and width of a scar left on a metal surface after repeated friction with another metal instrument. Depending on the lubricating properties of a fuel sample, a larger or smaller scar is produced.

▶ **TECHNICIAN TIP**

Removing sulfur from diesel fuel does not directly cause fuel to loose lubricating qualities. The process used in North America to remove sulfur from diesel fuel also removes molecules from the fuel that give it its natural lubricating qualities. Low-sulfur (LSD S-500) and ultra-low-sulfur diesel fuel (ULSD S-15) are associated with greater fuel system component wear. Manufacturers have hardened fuel system components with a variety of ceramic alloy metals to better withstand the effects of the poorer lubricating properties of fuel with lower sulfur content.

Fuel Viscosity Affects Spray Patterns

Correct Viscosity Fuel (good dispersion)

High Viscosity Fuel (poor dispersion)

FIGURE 14-15 Fuel viscosity can affect the spray pattern and fuel droplet size from an injector. Highly viscous fuel will not atomize well and will negatively affect combustion quality.

Kinematic Viscosity

Viscosity refers to a liquid's resistance to flow. High viscosity means the liquid is thick and slow flowing; low viscosity means the opposite. Fuel viscosity is measured in centistokes. The higher the centistoke measure of a liquid, the thicker and more viscous it is. For example, water has a centistoke of value of 1 and 20w oil is 4.3 centistokes. The property of fuel viscosity affects injector lubrication and fuel atomization **FIGURE 14-15**. Fuels with low viscosity may not provide adequate lubrication for the close clearances of precision-fit fuel system components, because parts are separated with only thin lubricating film barriers. If fuel's viscosity is too low, it can easily leak and slip around the high-pressure system's plunger and barrels. The result is that less fuel is injected, which reduces power output and increases wear of the fuel system's components. Fuels that are too thick or viscous will also cause other performance-related problems. Because fuel atomization is affected by fuel viscosity, fuel with high viscosity forms larger droplets during atomization. Larger droplets take longer to burn and mix poorly with air, which leads to poor combustion quality and increased exhaust emissions.

Mixing Gasoline and Diesel Fuel

Gasoline and diesel fuels should never be mixed. One percent or less gasoline will lower the flash point of a gasoline-diesel fuel blend below the minimum specification for diesel fuel. This does not dramatically affect the engine performance, but the fuel is more hazardous to handle **TABLE 14-3**.

TABLE 14-3: Ignition Quality of Gasoline and Diesel Fuel

Property	Gasoline	Diesel
Flammability Limits (volume in air)	1.4–7.6%	0.6–5.5%
Auto-Ignition Temperature	700–840°F (371–449°C)	600°F (316°C)
Flash Point	−45°F (−43°C)	100–125°F (38–52°C)

Occasionally, an incorrect recommendation is made to mix gasoline or alcohol and diesel fuel together to minimize fuel gelling and improve combustion. There are several problems with this. First, while gasoline and alcohols do have an anti-gelling effect on diesel fuel, they reduce diesel fuel lubricity. Reduced lubricity can increase fuel system wear and shorten fuel system life. The second problem is that the cetane index or ignition qualities of these fuels are inversely related to one another. Gasoline contamination, even in small amounts, will dramatically reduce diesel fuel's ability to ignite, causing longer ignition delay and engine knock. This is why gasoline contamination of diesel fuel produces a lot of smoke, causes engines to run roughly, and increases engine noise. Diesel fuel that is mixed with gasoline or alcohol does not have enough time to completely burn because ignition begins later in the combustion cycle. The pressure spike caused by prolonged ignition delay will break glow plugs and possibly cause other engine damage. Lastly, diesel fuel mixed with gasoline will not vaporize quickly, causing poor engine performance. Gasoline has a higher ignition temperature than diesel, which contributes to further ignition delay. So, while some may think mixing diesel fuel with gasoline, which has higher volatility, will improve a diesel's ability to start, the opposite is true. Gasoline needs more heat to convert to a vapor in the combustion chamber, which produces a longer ignition delay period.

TECHNICIAN TIP

If diesel fuel is accidentally contaminated with gasoline, it should be drained from vehicle storage tanks, lines, and filters. After replacing the tainted fuel with good-quality diesel fuel, the engine lube oil should be changed if the engine has been operated with contaminated fuel. This step is needed because engine misfires and poor combustion quality will dilute engine oil with unburned fuel that has washed down the cylinder walls and into the crankcase oil.

▶ Biodiesel Fundamentals

Not only can diesel engines burn fuel made from petroleum oils, but also fuels made from biological sources such as animal fat or plant matter. Some diesel engines will run using pure vegetable oil for fuel. With legislation requiring the use of more renewable fuels, the use of biodiesel will become more widespread. Prior to 2011, almost all manufacturers endorsed the use of B5 blends of fuel, but B20 biodiesel was commonly available. Many countries have mandated the use of biodiesel fuel. In the United States, for example, the Renewable Fuel Standard (RFS), part of the Energy Independence and Security Act (EISA) of 2007, encourages the use of biofuel by requiring manufacturers to certify engine emissions using B20 biodiesel fuel. The EISA also requires that 30% of all fuels originate from renewable sources by 2022.

Pure biodiesel can be used as fuel (such as B100) or blended with any amount of petroleum diesel to add the beneficial characteristics of biodiesel to petroleum diesel (such as B5 and B20).

Biodiesel Advantages

Biodiesel offers a number of benefits, both economically and environmentally, for energy security, job creation, agriculture, rural development, energy supply, and public health. Although there are drawbacks to biodiesel, studies indicate that biodiesel can achieve as much as a 78% reduction in the amount of carbon dioxide (CO_2), a greenhouse gas, over the lifecycle of production and use. Furthermore, while production of biodiesel requires more energy input than petroleum-derived diesel fuel, biodiesel yields 3.24 units of energy for every 1 unit of biodiesel used during production. Additional benefits of biodiesel include:

- It is a renewable resource.
- It is biodegradable.
- It is not toxic to the environment if spilled.
- It contains little or no sulfur.
- No engine modifications are required to use it.
- It produces lower hydrocarbon (HC), CO, and PM emissions than petroleum-based diesel.
- It has enhanced lubricating properties in comparison with LSD and ULSD petroleum diesel.
- It has no aromatic content.
- It has a naturally high cetane number (CN), a measure of the ignition quality of fuel.

Biodiesel Performance

Operationally, biodiesel performance is similar to conventional diesel in terms of power, torque, and fuel consumption without any modification of the fuel system. Biodiesel can also be blended into petroleum-based diesel, and for the most part, no engine modifications are required to use blends of biodiesel and petroleum diesel. The shape and composition of biodiesel fuel molecules provide other advantages that make it appealing as an alternative to conventional diesel fuel:

- Biodiesel has no sulfur content. This means fewer emissions and increased engine longevity.
- Biodiesel has no aromatic content; this improves emissions and reduces the risk of carcinogens.
- Biodiesel has about 11% oxygen content (petroleum-based diesel contains no oxygen) for improved combustion characteristics.
- Biodiesel has a naturally higher CN, commonly 50–55.
- Biodiesel has better lubricity. Conventional diesel fuel has a minimum standard of 109 ounces (3090 grams) SLBOCLE, whereas biodiesel has 176 ounces (4990 grams). Even mixing biodiesel with conventional fuel in a concentration as low as 1% can improve lubricity by 65%.
- Biodiesel has a higher flash point, which means the fuel is safer to handle.

- Because biodiesel is made from vegetable oil or animal fat, it is comparable to table salt in toxicity and biodegrades as fast as sugar. This means it is not hazardous to the environment if it is spilled or leaks from an underground storage tank.
- Biodiesel has favorable emission characteristics **FIGURE 14-16**. Biodiesel fuel has been rigidly evaluated for its production of emissions and potential health effects, as required of all alternate fuels by the U.S. EPA under the Clean Air Act.

Using B100 fuel, for example, will result in the following emission benefits:

- A 67% reduction in unburned HCs
- A 48% reduction in CO
- A 47% reduction in PM emissions

▶ TECHNICIAN TIP

Before switching to biodiesel, technicians should check with a vehicle manufacturer to ensure materials used in the fuel system are compatible with biodiesel use. When biodiesel fuels are used in vehicles built prior to 2010, seals, hoses, gaskets, and even wire coatings require regular monitoring. Currently, most vehicle manufacturers will repair fuel-related failures under warranty only if B5 fuel (conventional diesel plus a 5% mixture of biodiesel) is used.

Biodiesel Disadvantages

While biodiesel has many advantages, it also has certain disadvantages, including:

- Cost: Biodiesel is currently more expensive than petroleum diesel fuel due to the oil content of its sources, such as the soybean, which is only 20% oil.
- Energy input: Biodiesel requires a high input of energy to produce compared to conventional diesel fuel. For example, soybeans require energy to sow, fertilize, and harvest.
- Fuel system incompatibility: Biodiesel is an excellent solvent and leaves fuel systems cleaner. However, biodiesel fuel can damage some types of rubber found in fuel hoses, gaskets, and wire insulation used in some vehicles, particularly in vehicles built before 1994. Currently, fuel system part manufacturers are switching to components suitable for use with low-sulfur and biodiesel fuel.
- Filter plugging upon switching: Plugging typically occurs when switching from conventional diesel fuel to biodiesel. Due to the solvent action of biodiesel, the dirt removed can quickly foul filters, which should be changed several hours after engine operation.
- Distribution infrastructure: Biodiesel is not distributed as widely as traditional petroleum diesel. Production, blending, and distribution are performed on a smaller

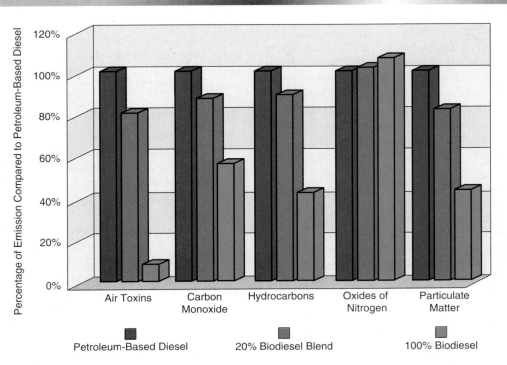

FIGURE 14-16 Biodiesel generally produces fewer noxious emissions compared to conventional diesel fuel. Note the increase in NO_x emissions with biodiesel.

scale than conventional petroleum diesel. However, distribution infrastructure is improving, and many fleets use a blend of biodiesel for their operations.

- American Petroleum Institute (API) standards: Despite attempting to meet ASTM D6751 standards, numerous problems with biodiesel stem from its manufacturing processes. For example, if too much methanol is used, it will cause corrosion of aluminum and zinc components in the fuel system.
- Aromatic content: Because there is no aromatic content in biodiesel fuel, it can cause rubber and elastomer components to crack and deteriorate.
- Heat content: Biodiesel has less heat content than petroleum diesel fuel. Fuel economy can be reduced by as much as 10% for pure biodiesel.
- Pour point: Biodiesel has a higher pour point (5°F to 10°F [−15°C to −12°C]) than conventional diesel fuel. This means it can thicken and gel more readily in cold weather. To remedy this condition, biodiesel can be blended with conventional 2-D or 1-D diesel fuel. Biodiesel can also be treated with pour point depressants. (Fuel system heaters and heated storage are also recommended.)
- Shelf life: The shelf life of biodiesel is not as long as conventional diesel. What makes biodiesel biodegradable also makes that biodiesel fuel—in its pure form—unstable. Over time, its acid content increases, which can damage metal components. Fuel ageing is also accelerated in the presence of heat, oxygen, water, and metal ions. Storage of biodiesel longer than 6 months is not recommended. If biodiesel is stored for longer than 6 months, it should be reevaluated to ensure that it meets ASTM D6751.
- Polymerization (gelling) of engine oil: The most serious problem with the use of biodiesel is its effect on engine oil. On engines built in 2007 and later that are equipped with DPFs, which are actively regenerated by an additional injection event during the exhaust stroke, some fuel will cling to the cylinder walls. Rings will sweep the fuel into the oil where it will accumulate because biodiesel's higher flash point will not allow it to boil out of oil like petroleum-based fuel. The fuel will cause chemical changes to take place in the oil that will link up chains of hydrocarbons and turn the oil into gel. Lacking proper lubrication, the engine will catastrophically fail. The biodiesel also attacks an important oil additive, zinc disulfide. Even before the engine is damaged, the oil loses some of its lubricating properties. Dosing the DPF using an external dosing valve located after the turbocharger is the solution for this problem. The DPF will need to be dosed frequently to produce enough biodiesel in the crankcase to cause engine failure.

Biodiesel and NO_x Emissions

One notable exception to the emission benefits of biodiesel is that it can produce higher levels of NO_x from some engine families. Because engines built prior to 2010 were not certified to operate using biodiesel, some engines may in fact produce more NO_x emissions using biodiesel than conventional petroleum-based diesel.

Production of Biodiesel

Biodiesel is primarily manufactured from seeds or grains. Such vegetable oil sources include peanuts, soybeans, rapeseeds (i.e., canola oil), cottonseeds, safflower seeds, linseeds, corn, and sunflower seeds, among others. Animal fats such as beef tallow, recycled cooking oil, and the like, are also used in some formulations. Using **straight vegetable oil (SVO)**, or unrefined vegetable oil, poses two problems for using it as an acceptable alternate biodiesel fuel source. First, it can lead to coking of the injectors. Coking is the build-up of carbon in the injector nozzle that in turn leads to reduced fuel flow and irregular injector spray pattern. Second, at approximately eight times the viscosity of conventional diesel fuel, SVO is too viscous to move effectively through lines, filters, and other fuel system components. Heating the fuel to thin it out is one solution to this problem **FIGURE 14-17**. Another is to remove glycerin from the vegetable oil molecule and replace it with an alcohol molecule, which is what happens during the process of transesterification.

Biodiesel Processing

Typically, for biodiesel derived from soybeans and like sources, the vegetable oil is extracted from grains after crushing them and separating solids from oils using solvents such as hexane. Gummy substances and impurities are removed by mixing the oil with 2–3% water and heating to 122°F (50°C) while mixing the material. Heavier gums, water, and impurities will settle out of the mixture, and the process of removing the fatty acids for fuel production can take place. In this step, the vegetable oil is reacted with an alcohol such as **methanol** or **ethanol** using a catalyst **FIGURE 14-18**.

Transesterification

Several techniques are used to convert animal fats and vegetable oils into biodiesel fuel. Even algae are considered a viable source of oil to produce biofuels. Microproducers, from small companies to individuals, also have processes and formulations to make biodiesel fuel for agricultural use and even private, home use.

In the most common method to produce biodiesel, methanol alcohol is used to react with vegetable oils and replace glycerin with alcohol. A catalyst such as sodium or potassium hydroxide speeds the process. The glycerin separates usable fuel from the oil and sediment after some cleaning processes. Replacing the glycerin with alcohol molecules is a process called **transesterification**, that is, the substitution of methanol for fatty acids to change the oil into fuel. **Fatty acid methyl ester fuels (FAME)** is another name given to biodiesel produced through transesterification. FAME processes that use potassium hydroxide or sodium hydroxide as a catalyst, however, can cause fuel system corrosion, injector plugging, and deposit formation if any catalyst is left in the fuel.

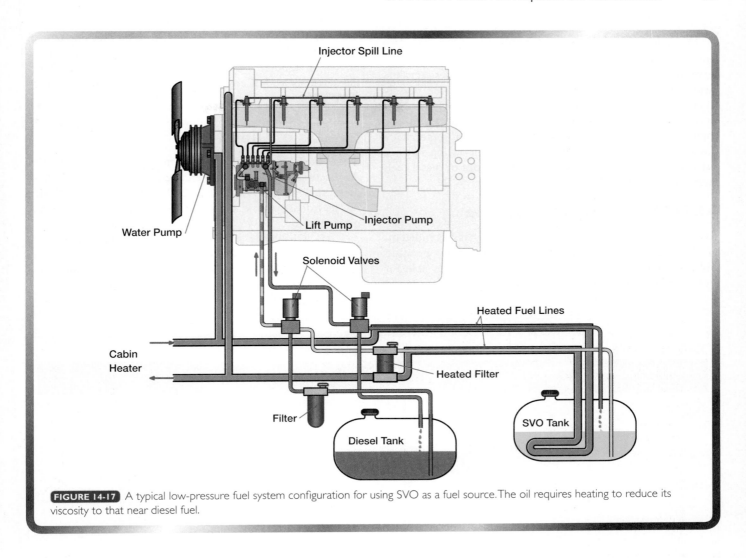

FIGURE 14-17 A typical low-pressure fuel system configuration for using SVO as a fuel source. The oil requires heating to reduce its viscosity to that near diesel fuel.

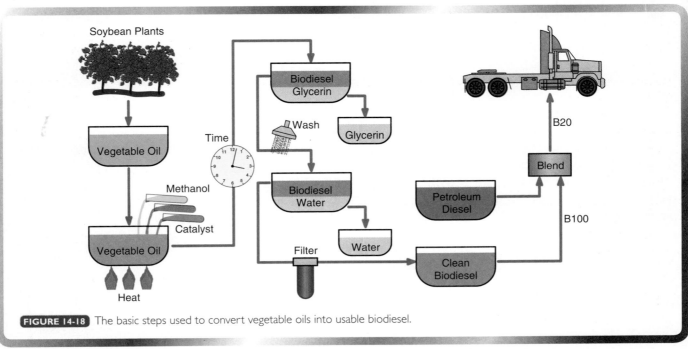

FIGURE 14-18 The basic steps used to convert vegetable oils into usable biodiesel.

▶ Types of Diesel Fuel

Diesel fuel is manufactured in a variety of formulations to serve different kinds of on- or off-highway vehicles, agricultural equipment, railroad locomotives, and marine vessels (such as river barge tugs, pleasure craft, ocean-going vessels), among others. Special diesel fuels are also used for stationary engines used to power irrigation equipment and emergency generators, such as those that hospitals rely on during a power outage. This section surveys the different types of diesel fuel, including biodiesel.

ASTM Diesel Fuel Properties

To a large extent, diesel engine development has depended on the development of fuels that contribute to reliable operation and satisfactory performance. The ASTM is responsible for diesel fuel specifications and test methods for petroleum-based diesel fuel and biodiesel fuel (see the Biodiesel Fundamentals section). These specifications are defined and explained in ASTM standard D975 and they can differ in characteristics such as sulfur content, flash point, and auto-ignition **TABLE 14-4**.

Grades of Diesel Fuel

Diesel fuel is classified according to its viscosity and density. As discussed earlier in this chapter, commercially available diesel fuel is numbered as 1-D, 2-D, and 4-D, with 1-D being the less dense and viscous and 4-D being the heaviest and most viscous.

1-D is usually a special purchase by bulk users such as transit fleets and municipalities with their own fuel distribution systems. It is preferred whenever the lowest emission output and superior cold weather performance is required.

TABLE 14-4: Specifications for Diesel Fuel Grades and Gasoline

Diesel Fuel Grade	1-D low Sulfur	2-D Low Sulfur	B100 Biodiesel	2-D ULSD	Gasoline	4-D
Auto-Ignition Temperature	350–714°F (177–379°C)	490–545°F (254–285°C)	550°F (288°C)	604–662°F (318–350°C)	700–840°F (371–449°C)	N/A
CN[a] (minimum)	40	40	48–65	40	N/A	30
Flash Point (minimum)	100°F (38°C)	126°F (52°C)[b] 109°F (43°C)[c]	302–338°F (150–170°C)	266°F (130°C)	−49°F (−45°C)	131°F (55°C)
Heat Value	135,000 Btu	140,000 Btu	117,000 Btu	134,000 Btu	124,000 Btu	N/A
Aromatic Content by Volume (maximum)	35%[d]	35%[d]	N/A	27–32%	N/A	N/A
Sulfur Content (by weight)	0.05%	0.05%	NA	0.0015%	N/A	2.00%
Water Content (maximum volume)	0.05%	0.05%	0.05%	0.05%	N/A	0.50%
Distillation Temperature[e]	550°F (288°C)	730°F (388°C)	680°F (360°C)	730°F (388°C)	N/A	N/A
Viscosity at 104°F (40°C) (maximum)[f]	1.3–2.4 cSt	1.9–4.1 cSt	4.7–6.0 cSt	1.9–4.1 cSt	N/A	13.1–29.8 cSt
Lubricity (maximum microns)[g]	0.018″ (460 microns)	0.018″ (460 microns)	0.012″ (314 microns)	0.018″ (450 microns)	N/A	N/A
Density at 59°F (15°C)	6.76 lb/gal. (810 g/L)	7.05 lb/gal. (845 g/L)	7.328 lb/gal. (878 g/L)	7.206 lb/gal. (863 g/L)	6.14 lb/gal. (736 g/L)	N/A
API rating	35–40	26–37	28–40	32–37	56–59	N/A
Reid Vapor Pressure at 100°F (38°C)	N/A	<0.2 psi (<1.4 kPa)	<0.04 psi (<0.28 kPa)	N/A	8–15 psi (55–103 kPa)	N/A

a. See Cetane Number section.
b. May through October.
c. November through April.
d. 90% volume recovered.
e. 10% California Air Resource Board standard in California.
f. The HFRR test is at 140°F (60°C); cSt stands for centistoke, the standard measurement for viscosity.
g. Lower numbers have better lubricating properties.

2-D is the most commonly retailed grade of diesel fuel. The higher heat content of 2-D provides better fuel economy. More 2-D is produced from a barrel than 1-D, which translates into lower prices at the pump.

4-D is heating fuel for oil burner furnaces, but it can be tolerated by indirect injection combustion chambers. 4-D has numerous other properties making it undesirable for use as an engine fuel. Because it is not taxed like 1-D and 2-D, it is not permitted to be used for on-highway transportation and is not for sale at retail fuel pumps.

Biodiesel is defined as a fat-based fuel made from vegetable and animal sources. Pure biodiesel is termed B100, with the "B" designating it as biologically derived and the 100 as the percentage of bio-based source. A 20% mixture of biodiesel with conventional diesel would be identified as B20. Biodiesel is most commonly blended with conventional diesel fuel; it is uncommon to see B100 retailed. (See the Biodiesel Fundamentals section.)

Determining a Fuel's ASTM Grade

Determining the ASTM grade and API number of a fuel is an important starting point when diagnosing low-power complaints. Seasonally blended fuels with low density will not have the same energy content or characteristics as fuels prepared for warmer seasons and regions. Low-density fuels also typically have low fuel viscosity, which can allow fuel to more easily leak past clearances between plungers and barrels in high-pressure injection systems, which results in reduced fuel delivery. To determine the grade and density of fuel, a temperature compensated hydrometer is used, which measure a fuel's API number **FIGURE 14-19**.

To determine a fuel's ASTM grade, follow the steps in **SKILL DRILL 14-1**.

FIGURE 14-19 Reading the API number from the hydrometer.

Cetane Number

The CN is one of the most significant properties of diesel fuel. The CN is a measure of the ignition quality of fuel and refers to the fuel's ignitability under compression. CN can be compared to the <u>octane number</u> used to measure gasoline's ignition characteristics **FIGURE 14-20**. Fuel with a high CN ignites sooner and burns faster than a fuel with a low CN. When combustion chamber pre-ignition temperatures are reduced by variables such as lower compression pressure, ambient temperature, and coolant temperature, an engine requires an increasingly higher CN fuel to start easily and burn quickly **FIGURE 14-21**.

SKILL DRILL 14-1 Determining a Fuel's ASTM Grade

ASTM Grade	API Number	Density	Btu Heating Value
1-D	38–45	6.675–6.950 lb/gal. (800–833 g/L)	132,900–137,000 per gallon (35,108–36,192 per liter)
2-D	30–38	6.960–7.296 lb/gal. (834–874 g/L)	137,000–141,800 per gallon (36,192–37,460 per liter)
4-D	20–28	7.396–7.787 lb/gal. (886–933 g/L)	143,100–148,100 per gallon (37,803–39,124 per liter)

1. Obtain a fuel sample from the vehicle or equipment fuel tank and place the sample in a graduated cylinder.

2. Using a purpose-made fuel hydrometer, measure the fuel's temperature and API number.

3. Using a chart provided by the hydrometer's manufacturer, look up the temperature-corrected API number for the fuel. Because the density of a fuel is affected by temperature, the corrected API value provides the API number that the fuel would have at room temperature.

4. Using the ASTM standard, compare the API number with the ranges for 1-D, 2-D, and 4-D ASTM grades of fuel.

5. Report the information on a worksheet or work order.

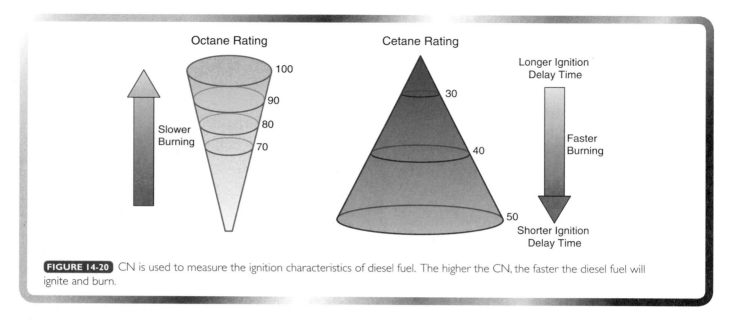

FIGURE 14-20 CN is used to measure the ignition characteristics of diesel fuel. The higher the CN, the faster the diesel fuel will ignite and burn.

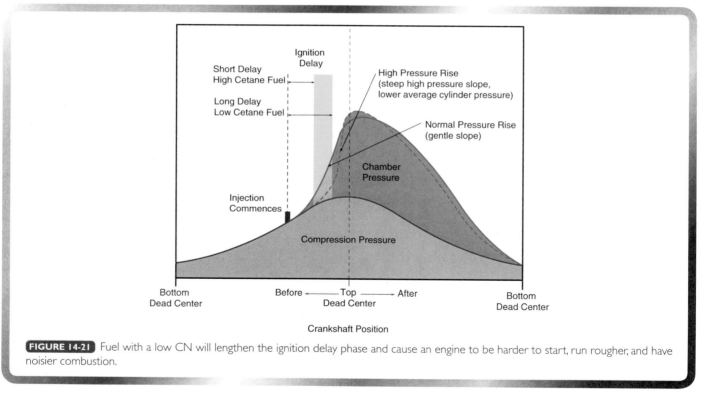

FIGURE 14-21 Fuel with a low CN will lengthen the ignition delay phase and cause an engine to be harder to start, run rougher, and have noisier combustion.

The CN of a particular diesel fuel is calculated by comparing the sample fuel against a reference fuel with a CN of 100. This means if the fuel has a CN of 45, then the fuel will ignite 45% as well as 100% pure cetane. Ignition quality of the fuel is analyzed using a single piston engine operated on the sample fuel.

The CN for a fuel can only be determined by using specialized test equipment measuring ignition quality. (A correlation between the weight or API number of the fuel measured with a hydrometer and cetane is not an accurate measure.) CN ratings apply only to diesel and mid-distillate fuels, not gasoline.

Octane rating for gasoline is a measure of ignition quality, but the numbering system moves in the opposite direction of CN. Slower igniting and burning gasoline used in high compression ratio gasoline engines have high octane numbers, while slower igniting and burning diesel fuels have lower CNs.

The 2011 ASTM minimum requirement for 1-D and 2-D diesel fuel is CN 40. For biodiesel, the ASTM standard is a minimum CN of 47. When engines operate below 32°F (0°C), a higher CN is recommended. Engines that operate at slower speeds can use lower CN fuel. Large, low-speed engines can operate on fuels with a CN as low as 20, while most late-model, high-speed passenger car diesel engines operate best using CN 55 fuel. The higher CN fuel results in shorter ignition delay, providing improved combustion, lower combustion noise, easier cold starting, faster warm-up, less white smoke, and, in many engines, reduction of emissions. The type of fuel molecules in high CN fuel break apart easier, too, but tend to release less energy. This means that a naturally high-cetane fuel, such as 1-D, produces less power and increases fuel consumption relative to 2-D. In fact, as of 2011, 2-D fuels sold at retail pumps in the United States have an average CN of approximately 47–52, depending on seasonal variations. In Europe, the minimum CN used for passenger automobiles is 55.

High aromatic content lowers the natural CN of fuel. Removing aromatic content increases the CN of diesel fuel. B100 biodiesel, for example, has no aromatic content.

Previously, many engine manufacturers did not perform testing of engines using biodiesel. Failures caused by or attributed to the use of the fuel above a B5 blend were not covered by warranty by parts original equipment manufacturers (OEMs). Because engine and emission compatibility is legislated for B20 blends (beginning in 2011), warranties are now honored.

TECHNICIAN TIP

Fuels with a higher CN have lighter, less complex molecules that are easier to burn than molecules found in low-cetane fuels. Complex and heavier fuel molecules, on the other hand, have more molecular bonds that release greater amounts of heat when burned. Complex, difficult-to-burn fuel molecules are collectively referred to as aromatic fuel molecules. Fuels with a *higher* natural CN generally have *less* aromatic content, will produce *less* power and have slightly *poorer* fuel economy in comparison to low-cetane fuels. Fuels with high aromatic content, that is, fuels with larger heavier more difficult to burn fuel molecules, will have a lower CN but have greater heat content.

Safety Tip

Mixing alcohols or gasoline with diesel will also lower the flash point and the CN of diesel fuel, but it is dangerous and not recommended.

▶ Diesel Fuel Additives

A wide variety of diesel fuel additives are used to generally improve quality and performance of diesel fuel when fuel quality is compromised. Normally, when clean, good-quality fuel is used there is no need to add anything to fuel. Nevertheless, many aftermarket additives are sold to meet many different applications. Most of these products are added to the diesel fuel to improve engine performance and increase mileage. The formulations tend to be highly concentrated, and for this reason a little goes a long way **FIGURE 14-22**.

FIGURE 14-22 Additives are generally used sparingly. This 32 oz. 0 (1 liter) bottle treats almost 250 gallons (946 liters) of fuel.

TECHNICIAN TIP

Many fuel producers and OEM engine manufacturers do not recommend the use of any fuel additives to their fuels.

Additive Maker Claims

In the United States, all manufacturers of fuel additives must register their product with the EPA, which, in turn, evaluates the products for adverse human health or negative environmental impact.

However, registration with the EPA does not substantiate marketing claims made by additive manufacturers. Many of the claims of additive manufacturers cannot be proven. For example, a group of combustion catalysts, which claim to increase fuel economy and lower emissions, were evaluated by an independent research facility and revealed no significant differences in fuel economy or exhaust soot levels. Such results are not surprising, because diesel engine combustion efficiency is typically greater than 98% even when using fuel without additives. If you believe an additive is necessary, thoroughly research the product before you purchase and use it.

Types of Additives

The large numbers of available additives can be simply grouped according to function (TABLE 14-5). Four major categories include:

- Engine performance enhancers
- Fuel stability
- Fuel handling
- Contaminant control

Engine Performance Enhancers

Additives in this category are commonly cetane boosters, detergents, lubricity additives, and smoke suppressants.

Cetane Boosters

Cetane boosters, also called ignition accelerators, are supposed to reduce combustion noise and smoke, improve starting in cold weather, and increase acceleration response. Boosters

accomplish this by increasing the CNs of diesel fuel. This means fuel will ignite and burn faster. By minimizing the ignition delay, improvements to cold starting and acceleration, along with reduced smoke emissions, are accomplished. However, user reports indicate that overconcentration of cetane boosters can also produce the opposite effects—excessive exhaust smoke emissions, low power, and poor fuel economy.

The majority of these CN booster compounds are nitrate based, which can increase the CN of the fuels by as much as seven points in small concentrations (0.2%). Cetane boosters may be added by fuel refiners or end users.

TECHNICIAN TIP

A lot of a good thing is not always better. Excessive concentration of fuel additives in fuel can cause adverse and unintended changes to fuel chemistry. For example, overconcentration of some cetane boosters may in fact cause excessive black smoke. Some additives will damage fuel system materials such as elastomer seals and nylon components.

Detergents

Fuel and crankcase lubricants can leave gummy carbon deposits in the fuel system that can decrease engine performance. This is especially true of nozzle valve deposits. Detergent additives operate as solvents to dissolve these resins, allowing them to be flushed through the fuel system. Optimal concentrations of detergents are typically 50–300 ppm.

Detergent additives are also used to treat asphaltene, a contaminant that is increasingly common as refineries use new methods to increase yield from a barrel of oil (FIGURE 14-23). Asphaltene formation increases when fuel is stored for a long period of time and when the fuel is heated after circulating through an engine. Asphaltene can cause abrasive wear and fuel filter plugging (FIGURE 14-24).

Lubricity Additives

When fuel is severely hydro-treated to remove sulfur, other compounds, which provide lubricating properties, are also removed.

TABLE 14-5: Fuel Additive Types and Benefits

Additive	Benefit
Cetane Number Boosters	Improve ignition quality by increasing the CN for improved starting and reduced white smoke
Lubricity Improvers	Improve lubricating properties of fuel
Detergents, Dispersants, and Antioxidants	Prolong storage life; minimize oxidation; reduce gums, resins, and sediments; and improve injector spray patterns
Stabilizers	Inhibit oxidation to extend storage life
Metal Deactivators	Deactivate metal ions such as copper compounds in fuel, to promote longer storage life
Biocides	Minimize bacteria and fungi growth, which helps prevent fuel filter plugging
Pour Point Depressants	Lower temperature operation Improve cold-flow properties Reduce pour and cloud point
Defoamers	Reduce foaming when filling tanks and transferring fuels through pipelines
Smoke Suppressants	Promote more complete combustion and reduce exhaust smoke
Rust Inhibitors	Reduce formation of rust in fuel storage

Clear Sample   Ashphaltenes

FIGURE 14-23 Ashphaltenes are small, hard particles of asphalt that develop in diesel fuel when it is exposed to high temperatures for an extended time period. Stagnant fuel will also develop ashphaltenes.

The service life of injection pumps, injectors, fuel transfer pumps, and other fuel system components can be prolonged through the use of lubricity additives.

Smoke Suppressants

To minimize black smoke, a number of products have been used. In the 1960s, a barium-based substance was used before the Clean Air Act became effective. This compound was later banned because of concerns about the human health impact of barium. Other suppressants, such as cerium or platinum, have been added to fuel as combustion catalysts, although these have not yet been approved by the EPA.

Fuel-Handling Additives

End-user applications of these additives are primarily for de-icing and pour point depressants. At refineries, additives to minimize fuel foaming and reduce drag in pipelines are also used. Antifoaming additives are used to minimize foam while filling fuel tanks.

De-icing Additives

Diesel fuel is both hygroscopic and hydrophilic, this means it attracts water and absorbs water **FIGURE 14-25**. Because water dissolved in diesel fuel can freeze, fuel lines and filters can plug with ice. To prevent this, small quantities of glycol can be added to fuel. This substance dissolves in water rather than fuel, resulting in a lower icing temperature of the water in diesel.

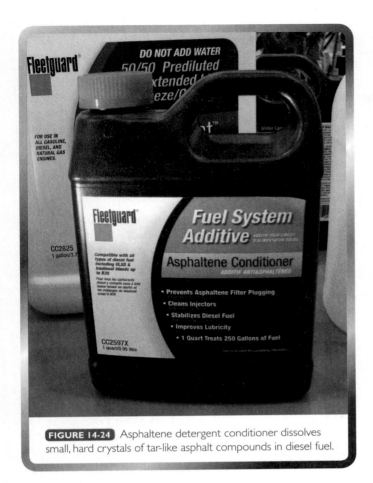

FIGURE 14-24 Asphaltene detergent conditioner dissolves small, hard crystals of tar-like asphalt compounds in diesel fuel.

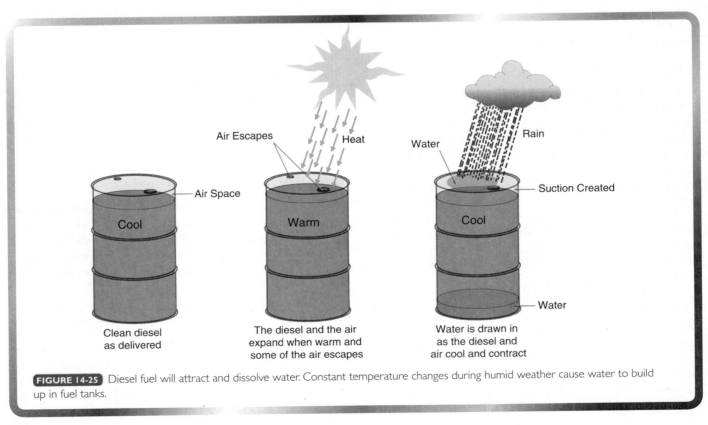

Air Escapes   Heat   Rain   Water

Air Space   Suction Created

Cool   Warm   Cool

Water

Water

Clean diesel as delivered

The diesel and the air expand when warm and some of the air escapes

Water is drawn in as the diesel and air cool and contract

FIGURE 14-25 Diesel fuel will attract and dissolve water. Constant temperature changes during humid weather cause water to build up in fuel tanks.

TECHNICIAN TIP

Water is a fuel system's biggest enemy, because it reduces fuel's lubricating ability and causes corrosion. Moisture will readily condense on cooler surfaces of diesel fuel, which subsequently absorbs water. Keeping fuel tanks topped up will minimize the condensation of warm, moist air inside a fuel tank. The best practice to prevent fuel from absorbing water content is to fill a fuel tank in the evening or late afternoon rather than in the morning. This prevents large quantities of warm, moist air from condensing in the fuel tank.

Pour Point Depressants

Paraffin is one of the major types of hydrocarbons that make up diesel fuel. At low temperatures, these wax molecules can clump together clouding and eventually gelling diesel fuel. The typical temperature range at which fuels thicken and no longer flow is approximately 20°F below the cloud point. To solve this problem, fuel can be blended with kerosene or 1-D. Additives are manufactured that can change the size and shape of wax crystal formation.

Fuel Stabilizers

After refining diesel fuel, chemical reactions between air and compounds in the fuel can take place. Heat will, in turn, speed up some of these reactions, which can lead to darkening, formation of particles in the fuel, and general deterioration of fuel quality.

Fuel refineries use fuel stabilizers to reduce oxidation and other chemical reactions between compounds in the fuel. Dispersants can also be added to keep particles dissolved in fuel rather than clustered together eventually fouling and plugging filters.

Corrosion Inhibitors

Because many fuel tanks and lines are made of steel, rusting and corrosion of the interior as well as metal fittings and filter housings can take place. Eventually, corrosion can penetrate steel walls, creating fuel leaks. Rust particles can also plug fuel filters and cause abrasive wear to fuel system components. Corrosion inhibitors are compounds that form a barrier on metal surfaces that prevents chemical reactions between corrosive substances in the fuel.

Copper is another metal that diesel fuel should not corrode. Due to the sulfur content of diesel fuel, it can darken materials made of copper and bronze, forming a black, gooey coating on these parts. ASTM standard D975 has specifications for diesel fuel compatibility with copper.

Contaminant Control

Contaminant control additives are remedies to problems associated with prolonged fuel storage. Fuel can absorb water if it remains stagnant for long periods in humid conditions. As fuel absorbs more water and remains in suspension, it is referred to as bound fuel. Rusting and corrosion of fuel tanks can take place as fuel absorbs water where it remains either free or bound.

Biocides

Additives that control biological contaminants are also marketed. The most important, and useful, are **biocides**, which are poisons that kill bacteria and microorganisms that thrive in fuel containing free water. Free water is water that is visible in fuel, which is unlike water that is bound or dissolved in fuel and is invisible. Typically, fuel that has been stored for prolonged periods and in warm humid climates are most vulnerable to this kind of contamination. When organisms are present inside a fuel tank or system, they can foul fuel filters and fuel lines.

Detecting Water in Diesel Fuel

A small amount of bound and free water in diesel fuel is normal. Some fuel specifications allow for up to 2.5% water contamination and some OEMs allow 4%. However, large amounts of water in fuel tanks, lines, injectors, and filters will freeze more readily than fuel without water. Microorganisms can also grow in water in diesel fuel. Excessive injector wear, filter plugging, power loss, and corrosion of engine fuel system parts can also take place when there is too much water in diesel fuel. Injector tips can be blown off if excessive water is present in the fuel. Checking for water in diesel fuel is an important part of monitoring fuel quality at the point of supply or distribution, as well as in the fuel tanks of equipment. Fuel deliveries should be checked before fuel is supplied to the engines used in critical vehicles or equipment, such as back-up power generators.

To detect water in diesel fuel, follow the steps in **SKILL DRILL 14-2**.

▶ Maintenance and Diesel Fuel

Diesel fuel, whether it is petroleum derived or biodiesel, has specialized maintenance needs that the technician should take into consideration for the kinds of vehicles and engines that he or she maintains. Fuel suspected of causing problems must be analyzed properly not only for servicing the fuel system but also when informing fuel suppliers of a problem. This can be especially crucial when fuel is purchased in bulk. The operation of an entire company—both in costs and efficiency—can be jeopardized by bad fuel and the problems it can cause.

Specific Gravity: API Index

For diesel service technicians, the specific gravity or density of a fuel is a good indication of the grade of fuel—but not its CN. Fuel density is an important property of fuel because it affects engine power and fuel economy. Less dense fuel, which has lower specific gravity, weighs less than denser fuel and has less energy content.

Fuel density is measured with a **fuel hydrometer** **FIGURE 14-26**. A fuel hydrometer will report the density in API units, that is, the **API number**. API stands for the **American Petroleum Institute**, a regulatory body that develops standards for measuring fuel density. The API index corresponds to the grade of fuel and its heat content. Generally, there is a 3–5% decrease in the thermal energy content, measured using the unit Btu, of fuel for every 10-point increase in API specific gravity.

SKILL DRILL 14-2 Detecting Water in Diesel Fuel

1 Take a fuel sample and examine it against a lighted background. Look for haziness, which indicates high amounts of bound water in fuel.

2 Using a good quality water paste, dip the paste into a fuel sample to check for water. For vehicle fuel tanks and underground reservoirs, the paste can be applied to the end of a long dipping rod or stick. The color of the paste will change instantly when it contacts water.

3 Place a 16.9 ounce (500 mL) sample of fuel in a clear glass beaker or jar. Slowly add 1.7–3.4 ounces (50–100 mL) of methanol to the jar. Only methyl alcohol (methanol) should be used because it does not mix with diesel fuel. (Ethanol can be mixed with diesel fuel and will dissolve water in the fuel.) The methanol will float on the diesel fuel.

4 Allow the two liquids to settle and separate.

5 Mark the container wall with a line at the point of liquid separation.

6 Vigorously shake and mix the alcohol and fuel together for 1 minute. Let the sample stand and settle for approximately 5 minutes.

7 Note the new separation line between the alcohol and fuel and mark it with another line on the container wall.

8 Because methanol will absorb water, its volume will expand if it dissolves any water from the fuel. If water was present in the fuel sample, the line of liquid separation after mixing will be below the first marked line on the container wall. The difference between the two lines of separation is proportional to the fuel's water content. The water is now irreversibly bound with the alcohol.

9 Report you findings. If necessary, make a service recommendation to drain free water from fuel tanks.

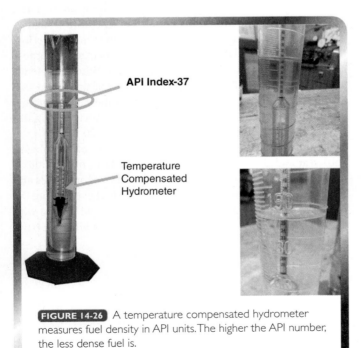

API Index-37

Temperature Compensated Hydrometer

FIGURE 14-26 A temperature compensated hydrometer measures fuel density in API units. The higher the API number, the less dense fuel is.

Determining the API index is important when investigating symptoms of low power or high fuel consumption. Lower specific gravity can indicate whether the fuel is blended with kerosene or 1-D. Blended fuels will have a high API number, meaning the fuel is lighter or less dense. API number will change with seasons and geography. For example, during the summer months in Ontario, Canada, retailed 2-D diesel will weigh between 6.951 lb/gal. (833 g/L) (API 38) and 7.076 lb/gal. (848 g/L) (API 35). In winter, the same diesel may weigh as little as approximately 6.87 lb/gal (823 g/L) (API 40).

Evaluating Fuel Quality

Diesel fuel can become stale and contaminated with water, oil, microorganisms, dirt, sediment, ashphaltenes, and particles of corroded metal. If fuel has become stale and contaminated, its smell and color will change. Filters will quickly plug with contaminated fuel and overwhelm the fuel-water separator. More significantly, diesel fuel's ignition quality will change when it becomes stale and adversely affect engine operation. While a fuel sample can be taken and sent to a lab for analysis, technicians can make some simple observations to quickly evaluate the quality of fuel.

To evaluate fuel quality, follow the steps in **SKILL DRILL 14-3**.

SKILL DRILL 14-3 Evaluating Fuel Quality

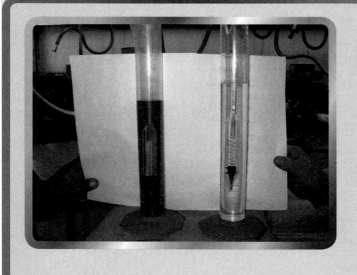

1. Obtain a fuel sample and allow the fuel to settle in a beaker for a few minutes

2. Place a piece of white paper behind the beaker to reflect through the fuel and visually examining the fuel.

3. Record the color and clarity of the fuel. Observe any sedimentation or separation of fuel from other liquids or particles in the beaker. Fuel becomes darker as it ages. Fuel contaminated with bound water that has also gone stale turns brown. Microorganisms may even be visible in fuel.

4. Use a rapid hand motion to draw a sample of the fuel vapors toward you. Smell the vapors and note the odor of the fuel. Fuel, as it ages, will gradually loose its intense smell and begin to change to having a smell similar to turpentine, varnish, plasticine, or paint. The presence of microorganisms will give the fuel a foul rotten smell.

5. Record you observations and make a service recommendation. A fuel system with significant contamination should be drained and flushed and the filters replaced. A cetane booster may be recommended for fuel that has become slightly stale but not contaminated. Recommend a fuel stabilizer if fuel is to remain stored for several months, but do not recommend long-term storage of biodiesel.

Biodiesel and Engine Oil

After the introduction of low-sulfur fuels, biodiesel has been considered for use as a lubricity additive to keep moving parts operating smoothly inside fuel injection systems. The dilution of engine oil with biodiesel is another matter. Biodiesel actually promotes fuel dilution of engine oil to a much greater extent than petroleum-based fuel. Oil dilution with biodiesel occurs when a post-combustion injection of fuel into the cylinders is used to reduce combustion soot, regenerate a particulate trap or NO_x adsorber. Heavier, less volatile fractions of fuel, however, do not vaporize during post-combustion injection and liquid fuel clings to the cylinder walls. Because biodiesel has a higher boiling temperature, it tends to dilute the engine oil disproportionately to its blend ratio in the fuel.

Fuel passes by the pistons and accumulates in the crankcase. Once there, fuel polymerizes (joins together to form long, complex-shaped molecules) with oil and produces sludge. Engine damage can result from oil passageways blocked by sludge. Deposits also form in the ring-belt area leading to ring stickage and increased crankcase blowby, which further aggravates oil contamination with increased levels of soot.

Raw or refined vegetable oils produce the greatest harm. However, the harm may not become evident until a significant amount of damage has occurred over an extended period. Petroleum-based fuel does not produce this effect at all, because it readily evaporates when the oil is heated. Biodiesel blends higher than B20 will enable larger amounts of unburned fuel to slip by the piston rings and condense in the lubricating oil. Engine oil change intervals may need to be shortened significantly if using blends of biodiesel higher than B20.

Biodiesel also interferes with the action of zinc-based anti-wear additives and detergents used in engine oil. Engine oil diluted with biodiesel can displace such additives on metals and chemically destroy the additive. This means that even before the engine oil thickens and turns to gel, lubricating oil diluted with biodiesel will begin to lose its ability to properly lubricate parts under extreme pressure.

Wrap-Up

Ready for Review

▶ An understanding of diesel fuel properties and characteristics, which exert a major influence on engine performance, is essential for selecting appropriate fuel and fuel additives for the wide variety of applications for diesel engines.

▶ Environmental considerations and legislative requirements for renewable fuels are adding complexity to today's fuel characteristics; for example, in addition to ASTM standards for diesel fuel, the U.S. EPA regulates diesel fuel to limit engine emissions, including sulfur content, aromatic content, and cetane number. Additives are tested to ensure they have no negative health or environmental impact.

▶ Most countries possess their own separate and distinct performance standards for diesel fuel, but the ASTM standards for fuel are widely recognized.

▶ Fuels, such as diesel or gasoline, are derived from crude oil, which is a mixture of various types of hydrocarbon molecules. Through the processes of distillation and condensation, oil molecules are separated into fractions or cuts based on the boiling point temperature of each fraction.

▶ The performance requirements of fuels include starting ease, low wear characteristics, providing sufficient power, low-temperature operability, low combustion noise, long filter life, good fuel economy, and low emissions.

▶ The grade of diesel fuel can be identified by a technician by measuring fuel's density with a hydrometer, which determines its API number.

▶ Cetane number is one of the most significant properties of diesel fuel; this rating is a measure of the ignition quality of fuel and refers to the fuel's ignite and burn speeds.

▶ Biodiesel is fuel made from biological sources such as plant oil or animal fat or a combination of petroleum-based fuel and biological fuel sources.

▶ The use of biodiesel offers a number of benefits both economically and environmentally, including energy security, job creation, agriculture, rural development, energy supply, and public health.

▶ Operationally, biodiesel performs very similar to conventional diesel in terms of power, torque, and fuel consumption without any modification of the fuel system required.

▶ Biodiesel has several disadvantages, including cost, gelling of lubricating oil, poor cold weather performance, lower power output, and reduced fuel economy.

▶ Because of their abundance, vegetable oils are the preferred biological source for bio diesel fuel; oil derived from seeds or grains are most common sources for fuel production.

▶ A wide variety of diesel fuel additives are used to generally improve quality and performance of diesel fuel when fuel quality is compromised; when clean, good-quality fuel is used, there is no need to introduce additives to fuel.

▶ Many of the claims of additive manufacturers cannot be properly substantiated.

▶ The large numbers of available additives are grouped according to function; the four major categories include engine performance enhancers, fuel stability, fuel handling, and contaminant control.

▶ Determining a fuel's API index is important when investigating a low-power or high fuel consumption problem.

Vocabulary Builder

American Petroleum Institute (API) A regulatory body that develops standards for a measuring fuel density.

ASTM International An organization that establishes today's diesel fuel standards; formerly known as the American Society for Testing and Materials (ASTM).

API number A measurement of a fuel's density.

aromatic content The portion of fuel composed of a particular type of hydrocarbon molecule that is difficult ignite and burn.

auto-ignition temperature The temperature at which a fuel will ignite when heated.

biocide A fuel treatment that kills microorganisms.

cetane booster An additive that is marketed to reduce combustion noise and smoke, improve startability in cold weather, and increase acceleration response; also known as ignition accelerator.

cetane number (CN) A measure of the ignition quality of fuel; also known as cetane rating or cetane value.

cloud point The temperature at which the wax in diesel fuel begins to congeal.

distillation The process of boiling petroleum oil to separate oil molecules into fractions or cuts based on the boiling point temperature of each fraction.

Energy Independence and Security Act (EISA) Legislation that requires the increased use of renewable fuels.

ethanol Alcohol-based fuel made from starches and sugars.

fatty acid methyl ester (FAME) Biodiesel produced through transesterification.

Fischer-Tropsch reaction A process used to create synthetic liquid diesel fuel from vaporized hydrocarbons.

flash point The temperature to which a fuel must be heated to produce a vapor that will ignite when exposed to a spark or open flame.

fractions The different petroleum products that make up a barrel of oil, which are separated by the distillation process.

fuel hydrometer A tool used to measure fuel density and identify its API number.

gas-to-liquid (GTL) fuel Fuel derived from using the Fischer-Tropsch reaction.

low-sulfur diesel (LSD) Diesel fuel with a maximum sulfur content of 0.05% mass or 500 ppm.

lubricity A fuel's lubricating quality.

methanol A fuel made from wood or cellulose.

middle distillates A fraction or cut produced in the distillation process, such as jet fuel or diesel.

octane number A measurement of the ignition characteristics of gasoline.

petroleum distillates Fuel produced from distilling crude oil.

pour point The temperature at which fuel will no longer flow through lines and filters because of wax.

Renewable Fuel Standard (RFS) Part of EISA passed in the United States in 2007 that indirectly mandates the use of B20 fuel starting in 2011.

straight vegetable oil (SVO) Unrefined vegetable oil used as fuel made from plants such as soybeans, jatropha, and palms.

synthetic diesel Fuel made through the Fischer-Tropsch reaction.

transesterification A process that replaces glycerin in vegetable oil or animal fat with alcohol molecules.

ultra-low-sulfur diesel (ULSD) Fuel that has a maximum sulfur content of 15 ppm.

viscosity A measure of a fluid's flow characteristics, or thickness.

volatility The quantity of fuel evaporating at a particular temperature.

Review Questions

1. _____ is a process that replaces glycerin in vegetable oil or animal fat with alcohol molecules.
   a. Transesterification
   b. Fischer-Tropsch reaction
   c. Distillation
   d. Compression

2. _____ is a process used to create synthetic liquid diesel fuel by liquefying hydrocarbon gases.
   a. Distillation
   b. Fischer-Tropsch reaction
   c. Transesterification
   d. Compression

3. _____ is an alcohol-based fuel made from starches and sugars.
   a. Distillation
   b. Transesterification
   c. Ethanol
   d. Methanol

4. _____ is a fuel made from wood or cellulose.
   a. Ethanol
   b. Distillation
   c. Methanol
   d. Transesterification

5. _____ is the process of boiling petroleum oil to separate oil molecules into fractions or cuts based on the boiling point temperature of each fraction.
   a. Compression
   b. Fischer-Tropsch reaction
   c. Transesterification
   d. Distillation

6. The cloud point is the temperature at which wax begins to give fuel a _____ appearance.
   a. bluish
   b. hazy or milky
   c. clear
   d. amber

7. A chemical process called _____ was invented in Germany during the 1920s to manufacture gas-to-liquid diesel fuel.
   a. distillation
   b. Fischer-Tropsch reaction
   c. transesterification
   d. compression

8. _____ was used to make the first biodiesel fuel.
   a. Soybean
   b. Corn
   c. Vegetable oil
   d. Peanut oil

9. _____ was the original diesel fuel.
   a. Soybean
   b. Coal dust
   c. Beef tallow
   d. Algae

10. ULSD has a sulfur content of _____
    a. 500 ppm
    b. 15 ppm
    c. 150 ppm
    d. 5 ppm

ASE-Type Questions

1. Technician A says coal dust was the original diesel fuel. Technician B says the first biodiesel fuel was made out of peanut oil. Who is correct?
   a. Technician A
   b. Technician B
   c. Both Technician A and Technician B
   d. Neither Technician A nor Technician B

2. Technician A says coal and carbon monoxide can be used to manufacture synthetic diesel fuel. Technician B says gases produced by decomposing wood and other plant material can also be used to manufacture synthetic diesel fuel. Who is correct?
   a. Technician A
   b. Technician B
   c. Both Technician A and Technician B
   d. Neither Technician A nor Technician B

3. Technician A says cetane boosters, detergents, lubricity additives, and smoke suppressants are considered fuel handling additives. Technician B says they are considered fuel stability enhancers. Who is correct?
   a. Technician A
   b. Technician B
   c. Both Technician A and Technician B
   d. Neither Technician A nor Technician B

4. Technician A says the NTSB is responsible for diesel fuel specifications and test methods for petroleum-based diesel fuel and biodiesel fuel. Technician B says the ASTM is responsible for diesel fuel specifications and test methods for petroleum-based diesel fuel and biodiesel fuel. Who is correct?
   a. Technician A
   b. Technician B
   c. Both Technician A and Technician B
   d. Neither Technician A nor Technician B

5. Technician A says the American Petroleum Institute is a regulatory body that develops standards for measuring fuel density. Technician B says fuel density is measured by a hydrometer. Who is correct?
   a. Technician A
   b. Technician B
   c. Both Technician A and Technician B
   d. Neither Technician A nor Technician B

6. Technician A says biodiesel is manufactured from algae. Technician B says biodiesel is manufactured from beef tallow and soybeans. Who is correct?
   a. Technician A
   b. Technician B
   c. Both Technician A and Technician B
   d. Neither Technician A nor Technician B

7. Technician A says using B100 fuel will result in 67% reduction in CO. Technician B says using B100 fuel will result in a 47% reduction in unburned HCs. Who is correct?
   a. Technician A
   b. Technician B
   c. Both Technician A and Technician B
   d. Neither Technician A nor Technician B

8. Technician A says that in the United States, all manufacturers of fuel additives must register their product with the Environmental Protection Agency. Technician B says the Environmental Protection Agency evaluates products for adverse negative environmental impact only. Who is correct?
   a. Technician A
   b. Technician B
   c. Both Technician A and Technician B
   d. Neither Technician A nor Technician B

9. Technician A says the sulfur content of diesel fuel affects particulate matter emissions. Technician B says particulate matter emissions is not impacted by the sulfur content. Who is correct?
   a. Technician A
   b. Technician B
   c. Both Technician A and Technician B
   d. Neither Technician A nor Technician B

10. Technician A says when fuel reaches its brume point, it can no longer pass through the lines and filters. Technician B says when fuel reaches its pour point, it can no longer pass through the lines and filters. Who is correct?
    a. Technician A
    b. Technician B
    c. Both Technician A and Technician B
    d. Neither Technician A nor Technician B

NATEF Tasks

Diesel Engines

General

- Inspect fuel, oil, Diesel Exhaust Fluid (DEF) and coolant levels, and condition; determine needed action. (pp 431, 433–434, 451–452)
- Identify engine fuel, oil, coolant, air, and other leaks; determine needed action. (pp 448, 450–451)
- Check engine no cranking, cranks but fails to start, hard starting, and starts but does not continue to run problems; determine needed action. (pp 450–454)
- Identify engine surging, rough operation, misfiring, low power, slow deceleration, slow acceleration, and shutdown problems; determine needed action. (pp 448–450)
- Check and record electronic diagnostic codes. (pp 433, 447)

Fuel System

Fuel Supply System

- Check fuel level, and condition; determine needed action. (pp 431, 433–434, 451–452)
- Perform fuel supply and return system tests; determine needed action. (pp 446–447)
- Inspect fuel tanks, vents, caps, mounts, valves, screens, crossover system, and supply and return lines and fittings; determine needed action. (pp 446–447)
- Inspect and test pressure regulator systems (check valves, pressure regulator valves, and restrictive fittings); determine needed action. (pp 451–452, 458)
- Inspect, clean, and test fuel transfer (lift) pump, pump drives, screens, fuel/water separators/indicators, filters, heaters, coolers, ECM cooling plates, and mounting hardware; determine needed action. (pp 440–446)
- Check fuel system for air; determine needed action; prime and bleed fuel system; check primer pump. (pp 446–447, 453–454)

Knowledge Objectives

After reading this chapter, you will be able to:

1. Identify and describe the low-pressure fuel supply system, construction, delivery circuits, and components of the low-pressure fuel system. (pp 436–454)
2. Explain the operating principles, functions, and application of the low-pressure fuel system and its components. (pp 436–454)
3. Identify and explain procedures for inspection, servicing, testing, and diagnosing problems associated with low-pressure fuel systems. (pp 454–462)
4. Recommend maintenance, reconditioning, or repairs of the low-pressure fuel system. (pp 454–462)

Skills Objectives

After reading this chapter, you will be able to:

1. Perform a primary fuel filter suction-side pressure test. (p 458) SKILL DRILL 15-1
2. Measure primary filter restriction. (p 459) SKILL DRILL 15-2
3. Perform a primary fuel filter suction-side restriction test. (p 460) SKILL DRILL 15-3
4. Measure secondary filter output pressure. (p 461) SKILL DRILL 15-4
5. Replace a fuel filter and prime a fuel system. (p 462) SKILL DRILL 15-5

▶ Introduction

Diesel engines need a low-pressure fuel supply to transfer fuel, with adequate volume and pressure, from the fuel tank to the high-pressure injection stage of the fuel system. Fuel tanks, pumps lines, and filters are the most visible components of the low-pressure fuel system. But fuel supply and storage are not the only important functions. Properties of diesel fuel and the sensitivity of the injection system to dirt, water, and contaminants means fuel must be conditioned to ensure long-term durability of the high-pressure injection system FIGURE 15-1 Removing vapor bubbles and supplying fuel at the correct temperature range is as vital as cleaning contaminants and abrasives from fuel.

Low-pressure fuel systems also include features that inform the operator of fuel tank levels and the need to service fuel filters and filters that separate water from fuel (see the

You Are the Technician

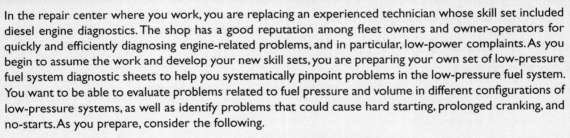

In the repair center where you work, you are replacing an experienced technician whose skill set included diesel engine diagnostics. The shop has a good reputation among fleet owners and owner-operators for quickly and efficiently diagnosing engine-related problems, and in particular, low-power complaints. As you begin to assume the work and develop your new skill sets, you are preparing your own set of low-pressure fuel system diagnostic sheets to help you systematically pinpoint problems in the low-pressure fuel system. You want to be able to evaluate problems related to fuel pressure and volume in different configurations of low-pressure systems, as well as identify problems that could cause hard starting, prolonged cranking, and no-starts. As you prepare, consider the following.

1. Draw out several different low-pressure fuel systems configurations:
   - One containing a primary and secondary filter with a transfer pump between them
   - One with a primary and secondary filter system and a fuel–water separator with a transfer pump between the water separator and filters
   - Finally, a system with a single final filter and an in-tank fuel pump

   For each of the systems, indicate the following:
   - Where pressure measurements are made
   - Where fuel filter restrictions are measured
   - Where fuel volume measurements are measured
   - Where vapor bubbles should not be detected and where they may be acceptable

2. List what features and components of a low-pressure fuel system you would recommend to customers to ensure long-term durability of the high-pressure fuel system components.
3. Consider a vehicle that has a gradual loss of power when driving at highway speeds and then stalls. List several possible causes of excessively negative, suction-side pressure between the transfer pump and a fuel tank that could cause the vehicle to stall.

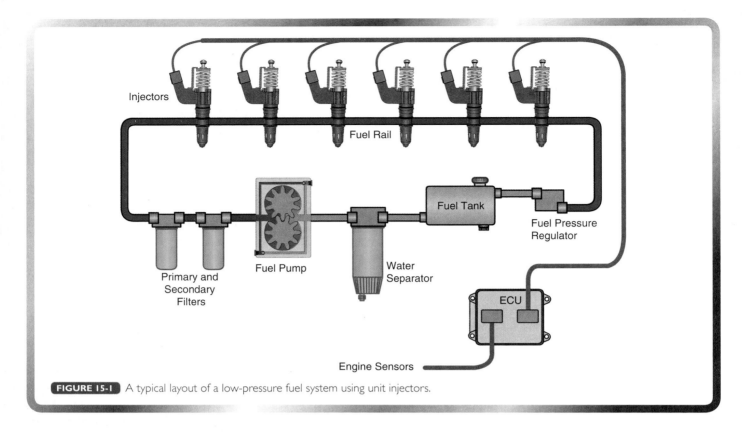

FIGURE 15-1 A typical layout of a low-pressure fuel system using unit injectors.

Fuel–Water Separators section). Proper operation and service of the low-pressure supply system is critical to quick starting, maximum engine power output, engine durability, and reliable, trouble-free operation of diesel-powered vehicles.

▶ Fundamentals of Low-Pressure Fuel Systems

Much of the work an engine technician performs is often directly or indirectly related to the low-pressure fuel system. Diagnosing low-power complaints, identifying problems and failures with components in the high-pressure injection system, and day-to-day work performing preventative maintenance service all require a comprehensive understanding of low-pressure fuel system components and operating principles. This next section outlines the construction and operation of the low-pressure fuel system and provides a sound understanding of the system, which is essential to developing good service practices and skills.

Requirements of Low-Pressure Fuel Systems

The function of the low-pressure fuel system is to:

1. Store and supply fuel free of contaminants and vapor
2. Supply an adequate volume of fuel at the correct pressure to the high-pressure injection system
3. Remove water contamination
4. Prevent wax gelling
5. Regulate fuel temperature

Fuel Temperature

Because fuel is used to cool and lubricate high-pressure system components, high fuel temperatures can change fuel viscosity and density to the point where fuel loses its ability to lubricate and cool components. High fuel temperatures also affect engine power output as fuel density decreases. Power loss happens because fewer fuel molecules are present in the now lower-density fuel **FIGURE 15-2**. At low temperatures, the **paraffin** content, that is, the wax that exists in the fuel, can cause the fuel to become too viscous to properly flow through filters and lines. Restricted and plugged supply system passages also lead to power loss and engine stalling. This condition, called **gelling**, is prevented by warming the diesel fuel.

▶ Components of Low-Pressure Fuel Systems

Components of the fuel transfer system typically include:

1. Fuel tank(s)
2. Low-pressure fuel lines
3. Fuel level sending units and tank pickup
4. Fuel filters
5. Fuel heaters
6. Water filtration
7. Fuel coolers
8. Fuel transfer pumps

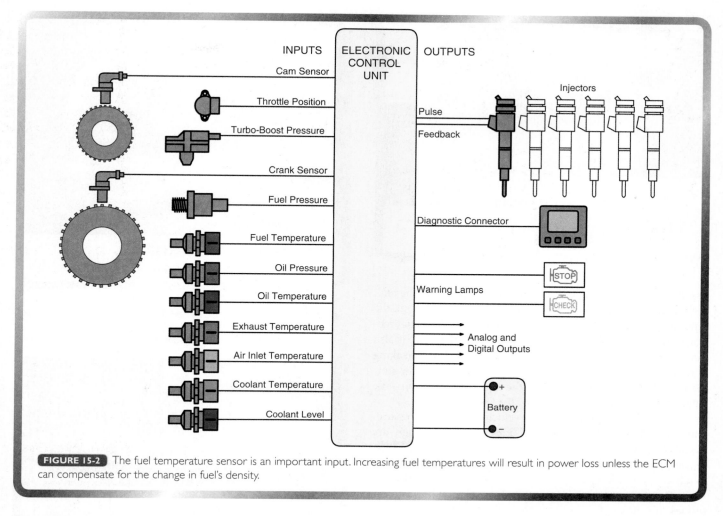

FIGURE 15-2 The fuel temperature sensor is an important input. Increasing fuel temperatures will result in power loss unless the ECM can compensate for the change in fuel's density.

Fuel Tanks

The most obvious function of the fuel tank is to store an adequate supply of fuel for the engine to operate. A secondary function is to allow fuel returned from the engine to cool after absorbing heat from the engine and fuel injectors. Cooling hot fuel is important for a number of reasons. First, fuel loses its viscosity and density as it becomes hotter. This translates into a loss of film strength necessary to lubricate injection system components. More significantly, the change in density will correspond to smaller injection quantities causing power loss. Thus, a 2% power loss occurs for every 10°F of fuel temperature above 115°F (46°C). Most electronically controlled injection systems have the capacity to monitor fuel temperature and compensate injection rates for changes in fuel density.

Tank Materials

Fuel tanks should be made of a noncorrosive material that remains free of leaks and is chemically compatible with diesel fuel. Aluminum, plastics, and steel alloy are popular materials. Fiberglass is a strong, long-lasting, and resilient material that is immune to corrosion and easily formed into custom designs. However, the potential exists for fiberglass to disintegrate and plug fuel filters. For this reason, fiberglass is not a material of choice for tanks in mobile applications. Copper is not suitable for tanks or lines because chemical reactions between diesel fuel and copper cause corrosion that produces a gum-like resin that clogs injectors. Galvanized steel and zinc are also not suitable materials because diesel fuel reacts with the zinc to form a powdery abrasive residue that clogs and damages the fuel system.

The fuel tank should be located far enough from the engine to prevent ignition and any fire hazard in the event of an accident. The Federal Motor Vehicle Safety Standards (FMVSS) and Canadian Motor Vehicle Safety Standards (CMVSS) are safety regulations that include standards for the protection and shielding of fuel tanks, ground clearance, and the like on truck, bus, and light-duty vehicle chassis. A decal for the safety standards a tank must meet must be attached to the tank **FIGURE 15-3**.

Fuel Tank Ventilation

A completely sealed fuel tank may prevent leaks, but tanks require venting to the atmosphere. The reasons for this are simple: First, returning fuel may contain fuel vapor in the form of bubbles, which are released inside the fuel tank. Secondly, when the level of fuel drops in the tank as the engine uses it, a negative pressure is created, which can slow, if not stop, fuel delivery to the engine. Tank venting is necessary to allow air into the tank and some fuel vapors to escape. A vent or pressure-compensating valve is

FIGURE 15-3 The decal on this tank includes the government safety standards a fuel tank must meet.

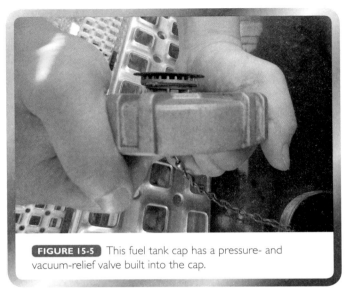

FIGURE 15-5 This fuel tank cap has a pressure- and vacuum-relief valve built into the cap.

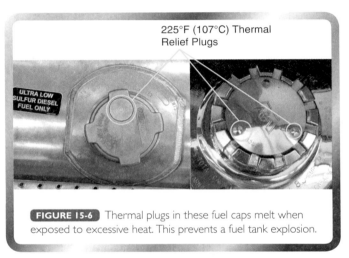

225°F (107°C) Thermal Relief Plugs

FIGURE 15-6 Thermal plugs in these fuel caps melt when exposed to excessive heat. This prevents a fuel tank explosion.

usually located at the highest point in the tank, often in the tank fuel cap **FIGURE 15-4**. Venting, too, can be incorporated into the sending unit pump module. While the vent valve allows bidirectional movement of air and tank vapors from the tank, it also must prevent dirt from entering the tank and fuel from leaking out. In the event of an accident and a vehicle rollover—or simply when fuel sloshes around while the vehicle is in motion—the valve must prevent fuel leakage from the fuel vent line.

Fuel tank caps on heavy-duty vehicles often use pressure- and vacuum-vent valves **FIGURE 15-5**. Thermal plugs are installed to release fuel if a fire heats the tanks **FIGURE 15-6**. Releasing liquid fuel, rather than allowing pressure to build up in a fire, also minimizes the likelihood of an explosion. The fuel tank **rollover valve**, which connects to the tank vent line, accomplishes this. It is a pressure-sensitive valve attached to a rubber hose. The valve may be clipped to the frame or near the tank. The rollover valve vents the tank to the atmosphere as long as no fuel is in contact with the rollover valve. Contact with fuel closes the valve to prevent fuel from leaking from the tank.

Fuel tanks are designed to have an air pocket near the top to allow for expansion of fuel that naturally takes place as it warms.

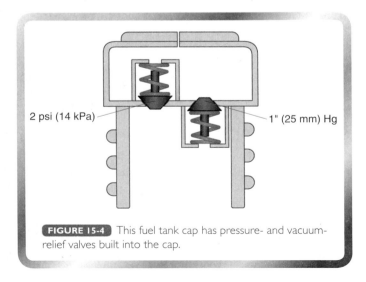

2 psi (14 kPa)   1" (25 mm) Hg

FIGURE 15-4 This fuel tank cap has pressure- and vacuum-relief valves built into the cap.

The volume is 5–10% of the total tank volume. On medium-duty trucks and pickups, the filler neck may have an inner and outer tube that is designed to prevent complete filling of the tank and allow air to channel between the two tubes and to escape from the tank as it is being filled with fuel. A separate tank vent line is most often used on these tanks.

Safety Tip

Gasoline and diesel fuels have very different flash points and volatility characteristics. Diesel fuel requires almost 100°F (38°C) to produce enough vapor to burn when exposed to an open ignition source such as a match or spark. Gasoline will easily vaporize and burn at −45°F (−43°C) or colder. Gasoline will also completely evaporate at much lower temperatures than diesel fuel and exert higher vapor pressure than diesel fuel. Because fuel vapors are a source of hydrocarbon (HC) emissions, gasoline fuel systems require evaporative emission systems to prevent fuel vapor from escaping into the atmosphere—diesel fuel systems do not.

Fuel Lines

The low-pressure fuel system is connected by low-pressure fuel transfer lines. These can be constructed of braided steel, corrosion-resistant metal tubes, and diesel fuel–compatible rubber material. Such flexible tubing is designed to pass through the different sections of chassis to transfer fuel from the fuel tank to the engine. Compared to existing rubber and steel fuel lines, new grades of nylon plastic fuel lines (e.g., Synflex) are durable, lightweight, lower in cost, and corrosion, vibration, and impact resistant. Nylon plastic lines are chemically compatible with diesel fuel and mold well with specialized connectors for ease of assembly and service **FIGURE 15-7**.

Fuel lines used on low-pressure systems must be routed where they cannot be mechanically damaged. As well, if fuel leaks do occur, dripped or evaporated fuel must not be allowed to accumulate or ignite. For safety reasons, fuel lines are not allowed to be routed through a vehicle's passenger or driver compartment. When a vehicle or engine twists and bends, the fuel line must be flexible enough to repeatedly allow this without deteriorating.

Fuel Tank Pickup and Sending Unit

Fuel tank pickups are usually integrated with a fuel level **sending unit** (an electrical device, usually a variable-resistance rheostat, that supplies a voltage signal to an analog-type dash gauge proportional to the fuel level) in medium-duty applications **FIGURE 15-8**. In medium-duty applications, an electrically operated fuel pump is also incorporated with the pickup and sending unit to form a module. Modules may include some or all of the following components, which may or may not be separately serviceable:

- Fuel filter
- Fuel pressure regulator
- Electric fuel pump
- Fuel pump reservoir

FIGURE 15-7 These snap-to-connect (STC) plastic supply and return lines are typical for diesels.

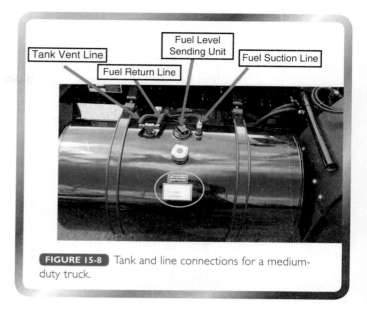

FIGURE 15-8 Tank and line connections for a medium-duty truck.

- A separate in-tank fuel pickup filter (strainer)
- Pressure relief/rollover valve
- Fuel gauge sending unit (i.e., fuel level sensor)
- An auxiliary non-pressurized fuel supply fitting

Tank Pickup

Diesel fuel pickup units almost touch the bottom of fuel tanks that range in size from 75 to 300 gallons (284 to 1136 liters). Their design prevents the accumulation of contaminants, such as water, sediment, and microorganisms in the fuel tank. They work by means of a Venturi effect—created by rubber nibs that contain small restrictions—which draws the fuel. As the fuel passes through the nibs, the pressure drops and draws water as well **FIGURE 15-9**. Water is later removed from the fuel by the fuel–water separator.

Heavy-duty vehicles tend to use tank pickups located at the top of the tank **FIGURE 15-10**. The higher fuel consumption and longer operating distances traveled by these vehicles require larger capacity fuel tanks that use thousands of gallons (liters) per year. Heavy-duty vehicle fuel tanks typically have a drain plug to regularly drain accumulations of sediments. The drain plug is located at the lowest point and at the rear of the tank. Medium-duty vehicles typically rely on the tank pickup to keep their tanks relatively free of sediments. The contaminants are then removed by the fuel and water filters.

Dual Fuel Tank Pickups

Heavy-duty diesel-powered vehicles may have two separate fuel tanks with each having a pickup tube **FIGURE 15-11**. The problem with two tanks is that one tank may be drawn down faster than the other. Too much return fuel may be diverted to one tank and less to another, causing one tank to drain faster and introducing air into the fuel system. To solve this problem, a return flow splitter valve is used **FIGURE 15-12**. The return flow splitter valve is designed to eliminate the crossover line between

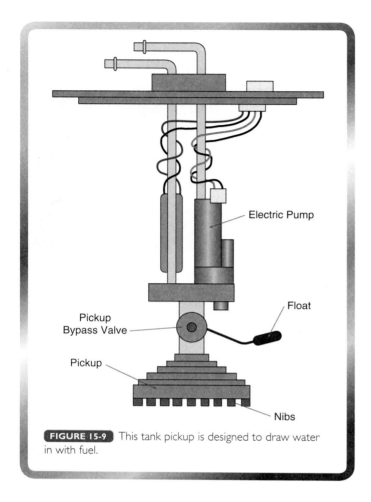

FIGURE 15-9 This tank pickup is designed to draw water in with fuel.

the fuel tanks of on-highway vehicles. It operates by equally dividing return fuel flow from the engine to each tank. Even if one tank is being drawn down faster, the volume of the return flow plus the operation of the valve will maintain identical fuel levels in each tank. The return flow splitter valve uses patented variable flow valve openings with a spring-centered spool valve to control return fuel flow. Slight pressure difference between each tank changes return flow. It should be noted that the return flow splitter will not correct problems in the suction side of the system. Its only function is to correct flow rates in the system's return side.

Most systems are configured using equal-length draw lines from each tank to a supply tee often mounted on the transmission. The suction supply line connects to the fuel filter. A single return line connects to the flow splitter valve. Two fuel-return lines run from the flow splitter valve to the fuel tanks. Some dual draw tanks also have the option of using a manual shut-off valve located beneath the cab that controls the flow of fuel from either tank.

Fuel Return Circuits

Diesel fuel systems almost universally allow fuel to circulate through the injectors and other fuel system components to remove vapor and lubricate and cool fuel system components. Pressurizing fuel also increases its temperature. It is normal for **fuel return circuits**, which is the fuel circuit that collects fuel from the injectors, fuel pump, and relief valves and returns the fuel to the tank, to have a slight amount of vapor present, which is mostly light fuel fractions that have converted to vapor. The latest fuel systems minimize the

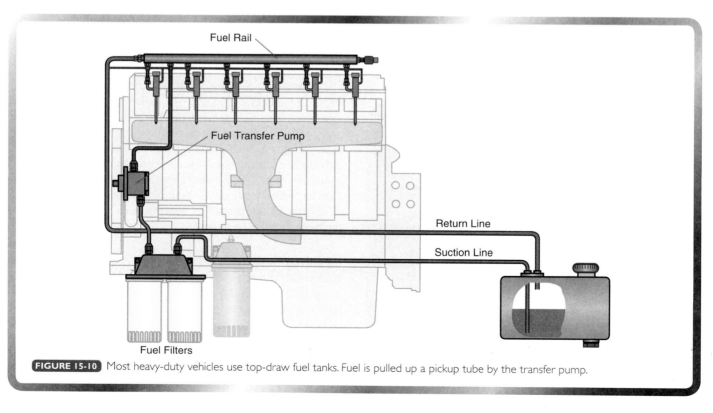

FIGURE 15-10 Most heavy-duty vehicles use top-draw fuel tanks. Fuel is pulled up a pickup tube by the transfer pump.

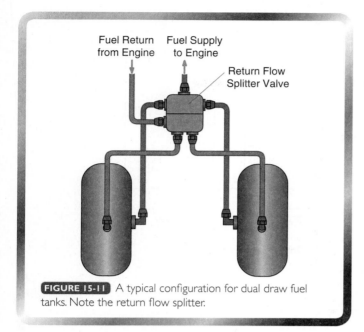

FIGURE 15-11 A typical configuration for dual draw fuel tanks. Note the return flow splitter.

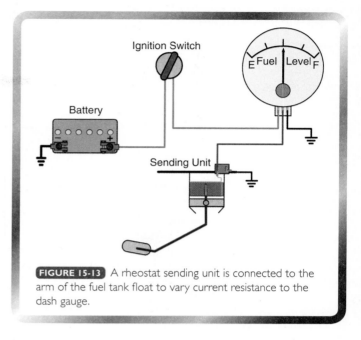

FIGURE 15-13 A rheostat sending unit is connected to the arm of the fuel tank float to vary current resistance to the dash gauge.

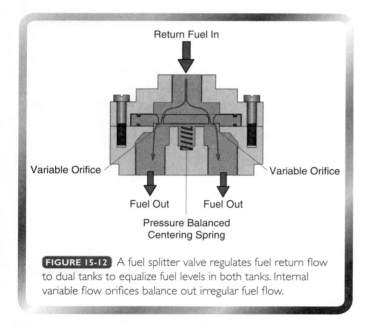

FIGURE 15-12 A fuel splitter valve regulates fuel return flow to dual tanks to equalize fuel levels in both tanks. Internal variable flow orifices balance out irregular fuel flow.

amount of fuel returned to the tank to improve fuel economy and meet greenhouse gas (GHG) emission standards. No return flow means less energy is used pumping fuel that the engine doesn't use. Reducing this parasitic power loss improves engine efficiency, enables pump downsizing, and eliminates the need for the additional expense of a return flow fuel cooler.

Sending Units

Each fuel tank is equipped with an electrical sending unit—typically a variable-resistance rheostat—attached to a float that transmits the fuel level to the instrument panel in the operator's cab **FIGURE 15-13**. Current from the instrument

panel or fuel gauge module will connect to the sending unit. The resistance to the ground to complete this circuit is determined by the position of the float. One end of the float arm operates an electrical wiper moving across resistive wires connected to the chassis ground. Current will pass through the wiper and then to ground through the resistive wires. On most sending units, high resistance to ground corresponds to a full tank, while low resistance signals an empty tank. Disconnecting the wire to the sending unit should cause the fuel gauge to register full because circuit resistance is high. Grounding the wire will cause the fuel gauge to indicate empty because resistance is low.

For HD-OBD–compliant vehicles, fuel level data is more critical because input from the sending unit is used to differentiate engine misfires caused by low fuel level from other kinds of misfires. For example, if the fuel level is too low on some HD-OBD vehicles, a misfire code will not be sent because it may have been caused by the engine running out of fuel. Because most instrument clusters use stepper motor-type gauges and receive signals to operate from the controlled area network data bus (CAN bus), an input is required to an electronic control module (ECM), electrical system or body controller about fuel level **FIGURE 15-14**. Using this input, an audible alert with a warning light informs the operator that the fuel level is low. (Newer circuits use stepper-type motors for a dash gauge but still use a variable-resistance sending unit.) On-board telematics can also use the data to help plot a route to the nearest fuel station.

Fuel Filters

Fuel filters are one of the most common intersection points between the technician and the low-pressure fuel system. Although the concept of using a fuel filter is straightforward, it is important to understand how vital they are for the fuel

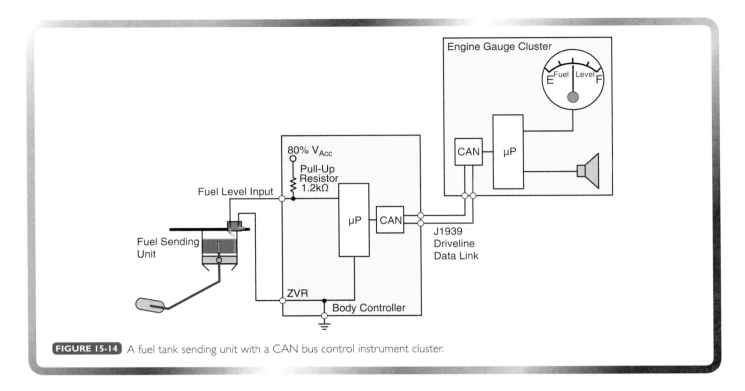

FIGURE 15-14 A fuel tank sending unit with a CAN bus control instrument cluster.

system, what contaminants they remove, and how the contaminants are removed by fuel filtration components.

Requirements

The reliability and durability of diesel fuel injection systems depends largely on the quality of fuel, which can often be contaminated by fine abrasive wear **FIGURE 15-15**. Left free in the high-pressure injection system, dirt contaminants cause abrasive wear of injection components operating at tolerances of only a few thousandths of a millimeter. Damage-causing dirt contamination is not readily apparent with a casual visual inspection of fuel. Studies have shown that most fuel system wear takes place with particle contamination of 5–7 microns in diameter, a **micron (μ)** being 0.001 millimeters (mm). The smallest particle visible to the human eye is 40 μ. A grain of salt is about 70 μ in diameter; 5 μ is 0.0002″ or 0.005 mm in diameter **FIGURE 15-16**.

Wear of fuel system components results in poor pressurization and atomization of fuel, eventually causing:

- High fuel consumption
- Hard starting
- Rough idle
- Reduced engine power
- Increased smoke and other exhaust emissions

Contamination Sources

Contamination usually occurs after fuel is pumped into a vehicle's fuel tank and during the course of operations. For example,

FIGURE 15-15 Abrasive particles that are 5–7 μ cause the greatest damage to a fuel system.

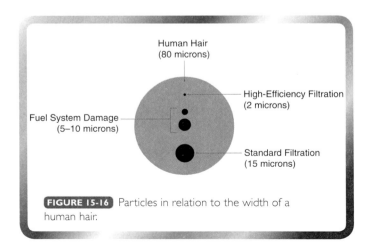

FIGURE 15-16 Particles in relation to the width of a human hair.

in off-road use around construction sites, airborne contaminants can be drawn into a fuel tank through its vent tube if the vent tube lacks an air filter. Likewise, a fuel tank cap vent can ingest dust if it is not properly sealed.

In the following sections, common contaminants are surveyed that affect the low-pressure fuel supply system. Asphaltenes, which are hard carbon crystals found in the bottom of fuel tanks and filters, are becoming a more common form of abrasive. This abrasive forms naturally when fuel is heated and stored over time. Changes in refining techniques to produce greater yields of fuel from a barrel of oil are also contributing to more asphaltene formation. Water not only damages fuel systems but when high amounts of water are in fuel, it encourages the growth of various organisms in fuel. A warm climate, where moisture condenses in fuel, contributes to the formation of biological contaminants. Biodiesel also lends itself well to the formation of biological contaminants, because biodiesel can support the growth of various organisms.

Asphaltenes

Asphaltenes are black tar-like organic particles that naturally occur in 2-D diesel fuels. Asphaltene particles are soft, deformable, and approximately 1.5–2 μ in diameter. Concentrations can increase through fuel oxidation and high heat. Although large asphaltenes are considered harmless to the injection system components, they constitute the most abundant of all substances plugging fuel filters. Smaller asphaltenes can produce abrasive damage in the fuel system.

Water

Water is arguably the greatest problem to fuel systems not only because it is the most common type of contaminant, but because it is also the most destructive. Water exists either in emulsion, meaning it is dissolved and mixed with fuel, or freely as droplets. Water is often introduced into the fuel supply as warm moisture-laden air that condenses on the cold metal walls of fuel tanks or condenses on the surface of cooler diesel fuel **FIGURE 15-17** . Diesel fuel has hydrophilic and <u>hydroscopic</u> properties, which means it attracts and dissolves water. The effects of water in diesel fuel are serious. Because water cannot pass easily through nozzle orifices, water will accumulate, vaporize, and cause a fuel injector tip to blow off. Water will also seize up injector plungers **FIGURE 15-18** .

- Water also causes the film strength of fuel to separate in close tolerance assemblies such as plungers and barrels.
- The loss of fuel lubricity caused by water contamination can cause seizure and scoring of moving metal surfaces.
- Water can combine with sulfur in the fuel to form strong corrosive acid.
- Water causes rusting of iron components, which in turn produces abrasive iron oxide particles. Significant quantities of these particles contribute to premature wear moving fuel system components with close tolerances.
- Water in fuel contributes to the growth of microorganisms that can multiply and eventually plug fuel filters.

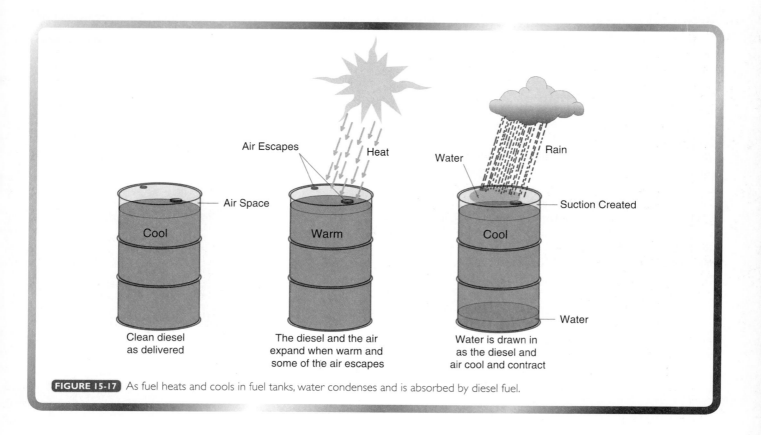

FIGURE 15-17 As fuel heats and cools in fuel tanks, water condenses and is absorbed by diesel fuel.

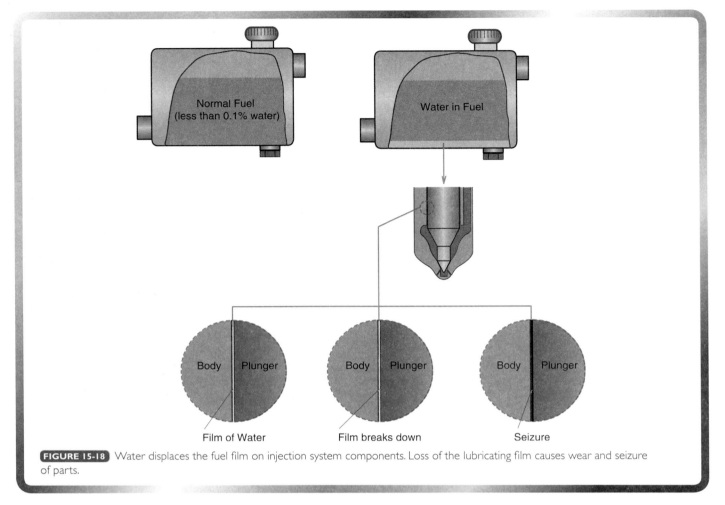

FIGURE 15-18 Water displaces the fuel film on injection system components. Loss of the lubricating film causes wear and seizure of parts.

Fuel and water are separated by specialized filter media and coalescing filters. In a regular canister filter, unfiltered fuel enters the filter through holes located near the outer edge of the filter, passes through the media, and clean fuel leaves through an opening in the filter's center. Dirt and water settle in the housing at the bottom if they are not trapped in the filter media **FIGURE 15-19**. Coalescence can be achieved by spinning fuel in a fuel bowl, which separates emulsified water from fuel using centrifugal force **FIGURE 15-20** and **FIGURE 15-21**. Filter media can also remove emulsified water by coalescence, a process where smaller water droplets merge to form heavier droplets **FIGURE 15-22**. Because water is heavier than diesel fuel, it collects

▶ TECHNICIAN TIP

Alcohol should never be added to diesel fuel systems. Alcohol dramatically lowers the cetane number of diesel fuel, which makes it more difficult to ignite and more dangerous to handle. Alcohols are volatile and they ignite at low temperatures. Diesel fuel can be easily ignited if it contains alcohol. The most hazardous issue caused by alcohol in fuel is that it can dissolve water in fuel and carry it through the fuel system. Ethanol, which dissolves easily in diesel fuel, will irreversibly mix with water, which then cannot be removed from the diesel fuel.

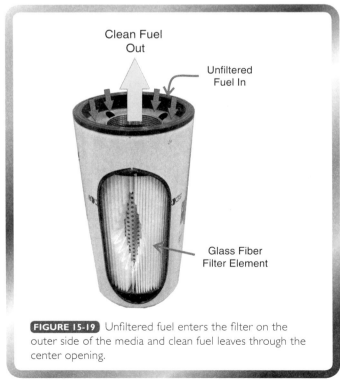

FIGURE 15-19 Unfiltered fuel enters the filter on the outer side of the media and clean fuel leaves through the center opening.

FIGURE 15-20 Water and fuel are spun by a baffle in the sediment bowl of this fuel–water separator to separate fuel and water using centrifugal force.

FIGURE 15-22 Specialized fuel filter media in this fuel–water separator helps convert emulsified water into larger, free droplets.

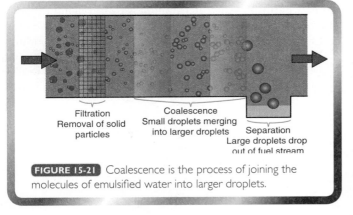

FIGURE 15-21 Coalescence is the process of joining the molecules of emulsified water into larger droplets.

FIGURE 15-23 This electronic water-in-fuel module uses two LED lights, which are green and red, to indicate whether the module needs draining.

in a sediment bowl or in the bottom of the filter. A drain valve on the bottom of a standard fuel filter or **fuel–water separator**, a filtration device that removes water from fuel, extends the life of a filter. To alert the operator via the instrument display of too much water in the fuel filter housing or fuel–water separator filter, a **water-in-fuel (WIF) sensor** is used FIGURE 15-23.

One type of sensor uses a float that can only be lifted by water, which is denser than fuel. When high enough, the float will electrically activate a warning light on the instrument display. Other sensors measure the electrical conductivity in the bottom of the filter **FIGURE 15-24**. Because water is more electrically conductive than fuel, the electrical signal can differentiate water from fuel.

Bacteria and Fungi

Unique microorganisms—typically bacteria but also fungi—are supported by water in fuel and feed on the HCs found in fuel. Sometimes referred to as "humbugs," these organisms can multiply throughout a fuel system and eventually clog fuel filters. Fuel left stagnant for long periods of time, such as that in stand-by electric power generators, is often affected by fungus and bacteria. Treating the fuel system with a biocide is recognized as the best means to eliminate microbial growth. Biodiesel is especially vulnerable to the formation of microorganisms that feed on the vegetable or animal derivatives in the fuel.

Wax

Wax or paraffin is desirable as a source of energy in fuel. However, in cold weather, wax that is normally dissolved in the fuel as a liquid begins to congeal, forming crystals. Unless properly treated or blended, 2-D fuel begins to cloud at 40°F (4.4°C). When these wax crystals form, it is known as the cloud point (see Cloud Point and Pour Point section in the Diesel Fuel Properties and Characteristics chapter). Fuel temperatures below the cloud point will result in wax precipitation and filter plugging.

To prevent wax formation, the cloud point of fuel must be at least 10°F below the lowest outside temperature. Fuel suppliers normally blend diesel fuel based on local cold weather conditions. However, particular attention should be given to diesel fuel purchased outside an area where the equipment is to be operated. For example, fuel purchased in the southern United States during the winter is not likely to be suitable for operating conditions in the American Midwest or Canada. Various types of <u>fuel heaters</u> are used to heat the fuel. These are thermostatically controlled devices that prevent the fuel from waxing and gelling (see the Fuel Heater section). Electric fuel heaters are often located in fuel filter housings **FIGURE 15-25**. These thermostatically controlled heaters uses hot engine coolant to warm the fuel **FIGURE 15-26**. Most diesel engines will recirculate up to 300 gallons (1136 liters) of fuel an hour through a cylinder head that also keeps fuel warm in cold weather operation.

> ### ▶ TECHNICIAN TIP
>
> Unlike gasoline fuel systems, alcohol should never be added to diesel fuel. Alcohol has wax-dissolving properties and an ability to mix and absorb water (i.e., its hydroscopic property); however, it has several detrimental effects:
>
> 1. It promotes the passage of water through the fuel system. This can damage injectors and other fuel system components. Water should be separated not dissolved.
> 2. Alcohol has very poor lubricity and leads to galling seizure and premature wear of the fuel system.
> 3. Alcohol lowers the cetane rating of the fuel, which is especially important in cold weather operation, because low cetane contributes to poor combustion quality.

Filter Media

A variety of materials are used to fabricate filters. Materials include paper (cellulose), microglass, cotton, felt, wood, and the like. The material should be made thick enough to trap and absorb contaminants in the filter fibers as fuel passes through filter pores. Pleating the filter media increases the surface area and adds to a filter's ability to retain contaminants. Indeed, ideal filter media remove the smallest particles with great efficiency while having tremendous capacity to store these particles to prevent filter restrictions. Paper or cellulose media are chemically treated with resin to repel water. The coating is used primarily to prevent damage to filter media and does not necessarily prevent water from passing through the media. Microglass or glass-fiber, a synthetic media, is considered the best filter media, trapping the smallest particles and absorbing

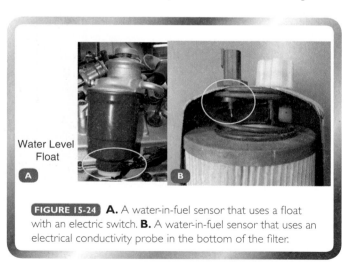

FIGURE 15-24 **A.** A water-in-fuel sensor that uses a float with an electric switch. **B.** A water-in-fuel sensor that uses an electrical conductivity probe in the bottom of the filter.

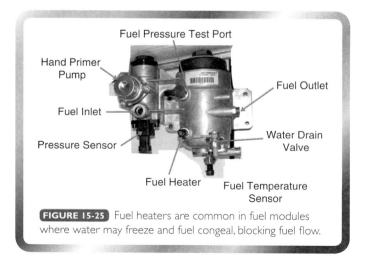

FIGURE 15-25 Fuel heaters are common in fuel modules where water may freeze and fuel congeal, blocking fuel flow.

FIGURE 15-26 This fuel–water separator circulates coolant in the lower housing to prevent accumulations of gelled fuel and ice crystals from blocking fuel flow.

with the greatest capacity. Paper cellulose filters, however, are usually the least expensive FIGURE 15-27.

Efficiency

Filters are classified not only by filtration media but by efficiency, too. The quality of a filter is based on the μ size of the particles it traps and its efficiency (the percentage of particles the filter can trap for a given size). Each filter has an __absolute micron rating__, which is a rating of a fuel filter that refers to the largest sized

FIGURE 15-27 Comparison of microglass and paper fuel filters. The drain valve enables water and sediment removal from the filter housing.

particle that the fuel filter media will allow to pass. For example, a 5 μ filter operating at 50% efficiency will only trap half the particles 5 μ and larger. A 5 μ filter operating at 100% efficiency will trap all the particles 5 μ and larger FIGURE 15-28.

Primary and Secondary Filters

Filters are also classified by location in the fuel stream FIGURE 15-29. The first filter in the fuel stream after the fuel tank is the __primary filter__. Primary filters are usually placed before any transfer pump in the system to remove any large particles that could prematurely wear the pump and cause check-valve damage. The job of a primary filter is to remove the bulk of free water and contaminants from the fuel. Using a primary filter extends the life of the secondary filter, which needs to be effective for finer contaminants, by preventing premature clogging. Typical primary filter efficiency is 95–98% at 10–100 μ.

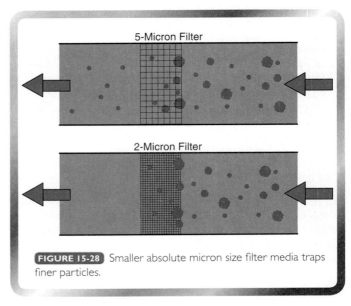

FIGURE 15-28 Smaller absolute micron size filter media traps finer particles.

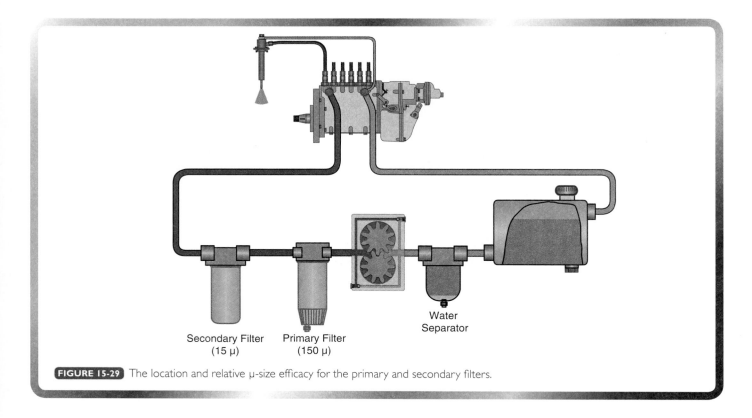

FIGURE 15-29 The location and relative μ-size efficacy for the primary and secondary filters.

Secondary Filter
(15 μ)

Primary Filter
(150 μ)

Water
Separator

The <u>secondary filter</u> provides additional filtration for particles that are even smaller. The secondary filter is located between the primary filter and the high-pressure fuel injection system. Typical secondary filter efficiency is 95–98% at 2–10 μ. Newer high-pressure fuel injection systems require removal of the smallest measurable hard particles—less than 5 μ. A properly sized two-filter system will often last longer and operate more efficiently than a similarly rated single-filter system.

▶ **TECHNICIAN TIP**

Whenever a fuel filter is replaced, the fuel system most often requires **priming** to remove any air that may have entered the fuel system. Fuel filters should generally be installed empty (without fuel) and the fuel system primed with either an electric or hand primer pump (depending on the system) to prevent introduction of unfiltered fuel into the system, which can cause damage. Some systems use a hand primer pump to prime, others an electric pump. A **bleeder screw** is sometimes located in the fuel system to allow entrapped air to escape from the filter when priming.

Cartridge Filters

While the use of spin-on fuel filters has been popular for decades, many jurisdictions have banned their disposal from landfills for environmental reasons. Today, spin-on metal-cased filters, at a minimum, must be drained of all free-flowing fuel and oil before they are disposed. Currently, in the United States, spin-on fuel and oil filters are exempt from hazardous waste regulations if the oil filter is:

- Punctured through the dome end or anti-drain back valve and hot-drained
- Hot-drained and crushed
- Hot-drained and dismantled
- Hot-drained using an equivalent method to remove used oil

Hot draining refers to draining engine oil at near operating temperatures but no less than 60°F (16°C). Because most spin-on fuel filters are indistinguishable from oil filters and are disposed together, cartridge-type filters have become far more popular with manufacturers. In addition to issues associated with their disposal, cartridge filters have other advantages. For example, most cartridge-type fuel filter housings are designed to prevent the fuel system from operating without a fuel filter. Also, because no metal components are usually involved in manufacturing cartridges, the likelihood of metal entering the fuel system and causing damage is diminished.

Fuel–Water Separators and Heaters

To prepare fuel for cold weather use and thus avoid operating difficulties, the low-pressure supply system is often equipped with a variety of devices to condition the fuel by removing water and dissolving wax.

Fuel Heaters

Engine power loss during winter operation conditions is a relatively frequent problem for operators of diesel-powered vehicles. When properly diagnosed, the power loss is often associated with gelled fuel caused by fuel wax that forms a restrictive coating on the filter element resulting in low fuel pressure. The same process occurs when starting an engine in cold weather. Fuel filters can become covered with a restrictive layer of wax.

This layer may permit enough fuel to flow and allow the engine to idle, but at full load, the engine cannot maintain operating revolutions per minute (RPMs) and may stall due to inadequate fuel pressure. Filter media impregnated with contaminants will result in this condition, and any clogged filter must be changed as the remedy. Often too, the root cause can be the temperature of the diesel fuel and its effects.

To prevent gelling of fuel two methods are available. One is to chemically treat the fuel with pour-point depressants (discussed in the Diesel Fuel Properties and Characteristics chapter). Another is to install a fuel heater, a thermostatically controlled device that prevents fuel from gelling as well as overheating. A fuel filter simply warms the fuel and keeps the wax in a dissolved state.

Fuel heaters can use electric current or warm coolant to heat fuel. Electric in-line heaters can also be placed inline just before fuel enters the filter housing. Other electric heaters use heating elements located within the fuel–water separator to warm fuel and to prevent icing.

Coolant-type heaters provide greater temperature increases but only after the engine coolant has warmed-up.

Fuel–Water Separators

When water in fuel turns to ice due to freezing cold weather, like gelling, it too can cause filters to clog. In general, water removal is critical to extending fuel system service life. Most water separator designs operate by coalescing or clumping smaller water droplets into larger ones that eventually fall out of the less-dense fuel into a sump. Gravity or centrifugal force facilitates this process of coalescence in many separator designs. Specialized filters, treated with silicone to repel water, also assist in filtering out fine droplets of water dissolved in fuel. It should be remembered that alcohol-based fuel additives will degrade fuel–water separator performance.

Water-in-Fuel Sensors

Water-in-fuel (WIF) sensors use an electrical conductivity probe to sense a specific level of water in fuel and cause a dash-mounted light to illuminate. This light alerts the operator of the need to drain water from the fuel–water separator. Because the electrical conductivity of water is greater than fuel, the small current passing between the fuel–water sensor probes needs to be amplified by an electronic module. The **water-in-fuel (WIF) module** is the actual device that illuminates a warning light informing the operator to drain or service the fuel–water separator **FIGURE 15-30**.

Fuel–Water Separator and Heater Modules

Fuel–water separators, water-in-fuel sensors, fuel heaters, and filters are often integrated into a single compact unit. These units reflect the importance of space conservation as design criteria. In fact, some modules also incorporate fuel pumps and pressure regulators. Heating combined with fuel cooling functions are

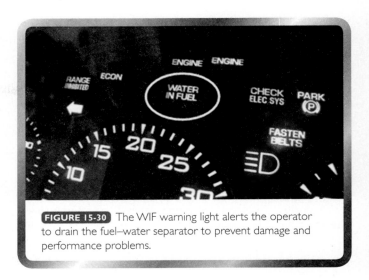

FIGURE 15-30 The WIF warning light alerts the operator to drain the fuel–water separator to prevent damage and performance problems.

commonly incorporated into the modules. Warm return fuel is blended with cooler tank fuel to ensure fuel at the correct temperature reaches the injectors.

Fuel Transfer Pumps

Fuel transfer pumps are used to move fuel from the fuel tanks to the high-pressure fuel system. The fuel must be supplied with adequate volume and at the correct pressure for every operating condition. A variety of pump types exist to match the unique requirements of each high-pressure fuel system.

Gear Pumps

A **gear pump** is a positive displacement pumps (a pump that deliver a fixed quantity of fluid for every revolution) with two counterrotating gears that mesh as they rotate **FIGURE 15-31**.

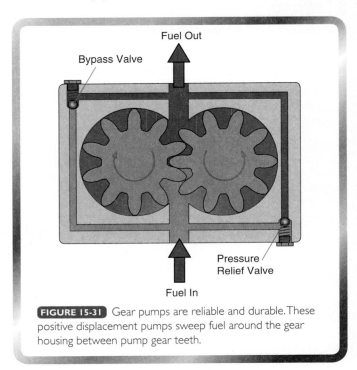

FIGURE 15-31 Gear pumps are reliable and durable. These positive displacement pumps sweep fuel around the gear housing between pump gear teeth.

Fuel is drawn into the circumference of the pump gears and then trapped between the pump gears and walls when the pump rotates. Fuel is then delivered to the pump outlet as the gears mesh again. Gear pumps produce volume. However, if restrictions to space or volume at the pump outlet diminish, the pump will build pressure proportional to the force driving the pump. The seal contact point between the gear teeth and pump housing act as a one-way check valve to prevent fuel from draining back into the tank. This means a one-way flow of fuel is integral to this pump design. Check valves at the pump inlet allow fuel to bypass the pump when a hand primer pump is installed.

A positive displacement pump depends on engine speed. The most suitable applications for gear pumps are injection systems that depend on increasing pump pressure as the engine speed increases. Unit injection systems typically use gear pumps. Hundreds of pounds of pressure are capable of being produced by this pump, so pressure regulation is required. A restriction orifice or pressure-regulating valve on the fuel-return side of the system or the use of a pressure regulator generally accomplishes this **FIGURE 15-32** and **FIGURE 15-33**. Failure of this valve will cause the engine to lose its fuel prime, which means fuel drains from the injectors. Air will enter the injectors, and the engine will be hard to start.

Advantages of the gear pump include both its high volume and pressure output and its simple design and durability. Gear pumps are usually maintenance-free, but they need priming if no fluid is in contact with the gears **FIGURE 15-34**. Injection

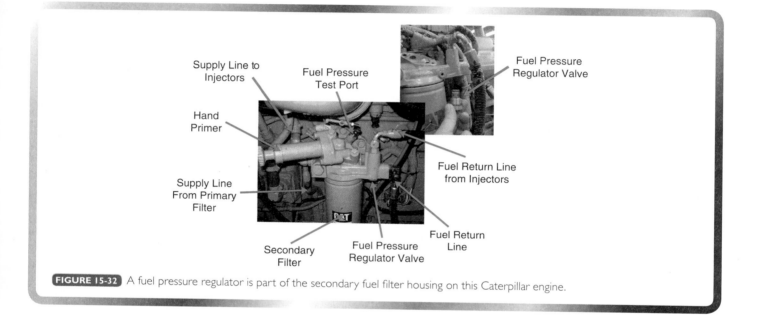

FIGURE 15-32 A fuel pressure regulator is part of the secondary fuel filter housing on this Caterpillar engine.

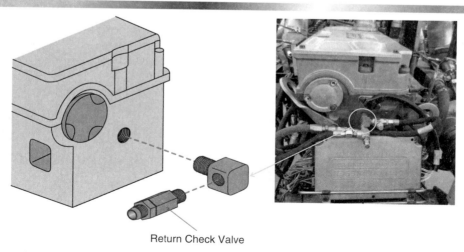

Return Check Valve

FIGURE 15-33 A restriction fitting with a check valve prevents fuel from draining from the cylinder head of the S50 and S60 Detroit engines.

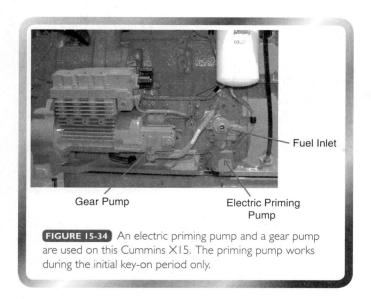

FIGURE 15-34 An electric priming pump and a gear pump are used on this Cummins X15. The priming pump works during the initial key-on period only.

systems that rely on gear pumps may be difficult to prime and restart if the vehicle has run out of fuel.

Mechanical Diaphragm Pump

Another common type of fuel transfer pump is the mechanically operated **diaphragm pump**. This pump is used to supply fuel at low pressure, usually not more than 7 pounds per square inch (psi) (48 kilopascals [kPa]) with a variable output volume **FIGURE 15-35**.

The engine camshaft activates this pump through a push-rod or lever operating against an eccentric cam lobe. As the eccentric moves the rod or lever back and forth, its linkage pulls down a diaphragm located between the upper and lower pump halves. While the reciprocating lever or rod movement stretches the diaphragm, the spring pressure beneath the diaphragm forces it to return to a relaxed position. This reciprocating motion of the diaphragm causes the chamber volume above the diaphragm to alternately increase and decrease, thus creating both a high- and low-pressure area above the diaphragm. Two one-way check valves, each located at the inlet and outlet of the pump, operate to control the direction of fuel flow through the pump. When the diaphragm is pulled down, the inlet check valve opens and the outlet closes. Relaxing the diaphragm causes the inlet valve to close and outlet valve to open and deliver fuel at pressure no greater than the spring force.

Variable Displacement in a Diaphragm Pump

The output pressure from the pump is determined by spring pressure. When output volume from the pump exceeds fuel system requirements, the pump utilizes a unique arrangement of its internal linkage that allows the diaphragm to remain in a stretched or extended position while, in turn, allowing the reciprocating action of the linkage. (An elongated slot on the diaphragm pull rod allows the pump lever to move back and forth.) No additional volume of fuel is delivered in this position. This means that the pump pressure and output is

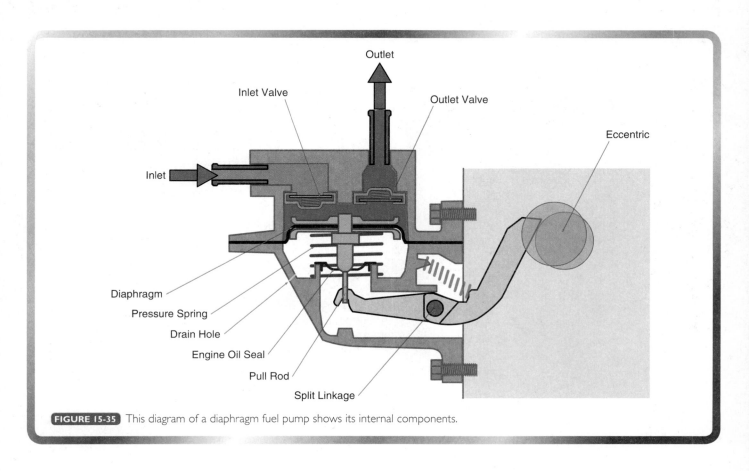

FIGURE 15-35 This diagram of a diaphragm fuel pump shows its internal components.

self-regulating, and it will only deliver fuel at the volumes required and at no more pressure than the force supplied by the spring.

Many fuel transfer pumps have an integral hand-prime button or, in the case of a diaphragm type, a lever. In the case of an external lever, it is connected to internal pump linkage that mechanically pulls down the diaphragm to draw fuel into the pump. Spring pressure pushes back the diaphragm, and the lever can be pulled down once more again to charge the fuel system. After the fuel system has been serviced, the technician can use this lever to fill fuel filters and manually prime the injection pump or purge trapped air from the system.

Piston-Type Pumps

Piston-type pumps are similar in operation to the diaphragm pump and use a similar system of check valves and spring operation **FIGURE 15-36**. However, instead of a diaphragm to develop pressure differentials, a piston is used, which allows these pumps to operate at a higher pressure and with greater durability than diaphragm pumps.

Common applications of this pump style include fuel transfer pumps—for which power is supplied by a cam lobe—and hand-operated primer pumps. Combination primer pumps and transfer pumps are used on mechanical inline pumps.

Output pressure will be determined by spring pressure beneath the piston. Output volume will depend on engine speed and spring pressure. The piston, as in the diaphragm pump, will rest in a position where output pressure is balanced against spring pressure. This means that as outlet pressure increases, there will be less piston movement in these kinds of pumps.

Hand Primers and Priming Buttons

When the engine is not running and the fuel system requires purging of air or filling of a filter, a hand primer or priming button, depending on the design, provides the piston action to develop pressure differentials needed to move the fuel **FIGURE 15-37**.

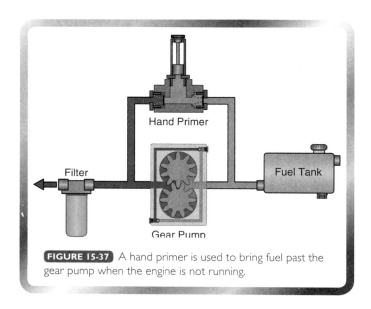

FIGURE 15-37 A hand primer is used to bring fuel past the gear pump when the engine is not running.

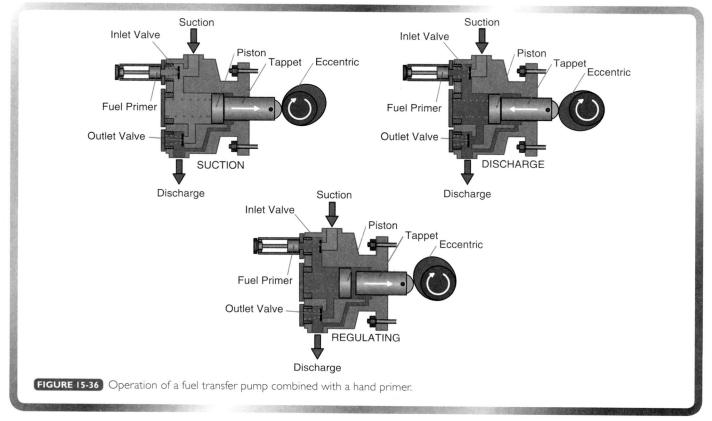

FIGURE 15-36 Operation of a fuel transfer pump combined with a hand primer.

Hand primers are also required for priming newly installed (i.e., dry, unfilled) fuel filters. This procedure minimizes the possibility of dirt contamination of the high-pressure fuel when using potentially dirty fuel from a can or other apparatus to fill fuel filters.

In-Tank Electric Pumps

Some kinds of medium-duty vehicles use electrically operated transfer pumps located in the fuel tank or on the frame near the tank. Locating the pump inside the tank has the advantage of pressurizing the entire delivery system. This minimizes the likelihood of suction-side leaks, which cause air to enter the fuel. Fuel filters are also able to operate with longer life because pressurized fuel delivery will render them less sensitive to pressure loss from restrictions FIGURE 15-38 .

Electrically operated fuel pumps have the other advantage of reducing the inconvenience of priming filters manually during filter changes. Cycling the ignition on and off or bypassing the fuel pump relay allows dry installation of filters with far less service time. Furthermore, when switching from one fuel tank to another, an electric pump is simply turned off while another is activated.

Because diesel fuel is less volatile than gasoline, pressurization is not necessary to prevent vapor locks in diesel fuel.

Fuel Coolers

High-pressure common rail systems pressurize fuel, which results in a large temperature increase for the fuel. Because heating fuel causes it to lose its viscosity and density, resulting in low power and poor atomization, fuel coolers are often used. The greatest danger of overheating fuel is changing its properties and causing the formation of ashphaltenes. Return fuel temperatures can exceed 140°F (60°C), which is the lower end of the flash point for diesel fuel. It is important to keep fuel temperatures lower than this. Some fuel-conditioning modules regulate fuel temperature by mixing cooler fuel from the tank with warmer return fuel. This strategy helps warm up cooler fuel pulled from the tank. But to lower the temperature of fuel returning from the engine, fuel coolers are used. Detroit Diesel DD series engines use fuel coolers located behind the fuel filter module FIGURE 15-39 . These coolers use engine coolant to reduce fuel's temperature and heat cold fuel. Fuel temperature is kept in a consistently even range using jacket water coolant.

Roller Vane Pumps

Most in-tank electric pumps are the positive displacement, roller vane–type using permanent magnet–type electric

FIGURE 15-39 Before returning to the tank, return fuel flows through the fuel cooler located in the engine block.

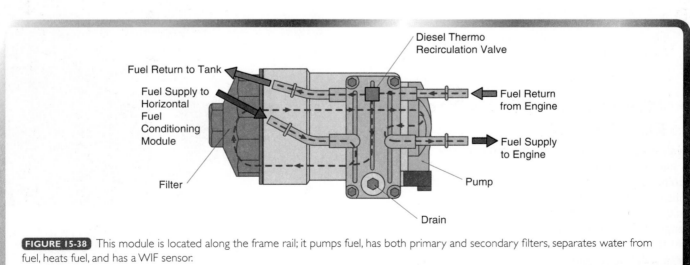

FIGURE 15-38 This module is located along the frame rail; it pumps fuel, has both primary and secondary filters, separates water from fuel, heats fuel, and has a WIF sensor.

motors. A permanent magnet electric motor rotates rollers or vanes that are spring-loaded and moveable in the slots on a rotor shaft. These vanes operate in an offset position inside a circular cavity. As the rotor shaft rotates, the pressure of fuel forces the vanes to trap fuel in a decreasing volume of the pump cavity. The result is fuel pressurization and movement of fuel from the inlet to outlet of the pump. Two check valves are usually located in the pump, one each on the pump inlet and outlet to ensure one-way flow of fuel and to prevent drainback of fuel, which can lead to hard and prolonged starting. A centrifugal impeller may also be used in parallel with these pumps to improve fuel delivery.

Vane-Type Pumps

Some engines use mechanical <u>vane-type pumps</u> located inside the injection pump (distributor-type pumps) or electric vane external transfer pumps. When controlled by the ECM, the external electric vane transfer pump uses a pulse-width modulation signal to provide two duty cycles: full speed when the engine is running and half speed during cranking to prevent overpressurization of the injection pump that can keep the injection pump from operating. Excessive internal pump pressure during cranking can prevent the plungers in some distributor-type pumps from being forced outwards, which limits the full delivery quantity during cranking.

During cranking, the pump pressure is limited to 7 psi (48 kPa) and then increases to 10 psi (69 kPa) after the engine starts. If the engine shuts down without the key being shut off, a safety feature prevents the pump from operating to prevent fuel leaks if a broken fuel line had been the cause of the shut down.

▶ TECHNICIAN TIP

If a diesel fuel system is inadvertently contaminated with gasoline, the engine should not be operated. Fuel should be drained from the tank and all fuel filters replaced. Electric tanks can be drained by bypassing the fuel pump relay to operate the in-tank or frame-mounted pump. When completed, the system and filters should be refilled with clean fresh diesel fuel. If an engine has operated for some time with contaminated fuel, lube oil and filters should also be changed.

▶ Maintenance of Low-Pressure Fuel Systems

Evaluating the operation of the low-pressure supply system is necessary when investigating low-power problems, hard or prolonged starting, rough engine operation, and high-pressure injection component failure. You can check fuel pressure and volume with a variety of mechanical or electronic pressure gauges to measure transfer pump output—as well as check specific locations in the low-pressure fuel system. Volume from mechanical pumps is measured by cranking the engine with the ignition disabled and measuring the quantity of fuel

delivered—usually a 30-second cranking interval—into an appropriate and graduated receptacle **FIGURE 15-40**.

Checks of the low-pressure suction system include vacuum testing and leak testing using a site glass to visually inspect for air bubbles in the fuel **FIGURE 15-41**. A clear plastic fuel line installed after a filter will indicate whether bubbles are present in the fuel caused by air leaks in the suction side of the fuel system. It is normal to have bubbles in the return fuel line. Fuel

FIGURE 15-40 Measuring fuel volume using a graduated cylinder. Fuel collected during a timed test is compared against specifications.

FIGURE 15-41 A site glass installed in-line with a fuel line can help detect air introduced though loose fittings, cracked or broken lines, and pickup tubes.

heated in the injectors or cylinder head will vaporize and return to the tank.

Filter restrictions can be evaluated using a pressure gauge for primary filters on the suction side of the transfer system or output pressure from filters located on the outlet side of transfer pumps FIGURE 15-42 . Measurements should be compared with manufacturer's specifications. FIGURE 15-43 .

Detroit Diesel FSIC Test

Detroit Diesel's DD series engines can perform an automated fuel system test that includes an evaluation of the low-pressure system. Called the Fuel System Integrity Check (FSIC), the test uses Detroit Diesel diagnostic software, Detroit Diesel Diagnostic Link (DDDL), to run the fuel system through several operational states. FSIC records critical information that is then used to diagnose an improperly functioning fuel system or failed components without removing any components from the engine. For example, to check for restriction in the return fuel line or a fuel inlet restriction at the low-pressure fuel pump the engine will monitor the low-pressure fuel sensor and fuel temperature sensor. Running the engine at several different speeds while opening and closing a fuel valve for the exhaust aftertreatment system—plus increasing and decreasing the engine's fuel rail pressure—will produce predictable changes in the sensor data. Data that is outside expected ranges can identify system problems FIGURE 15-44 .

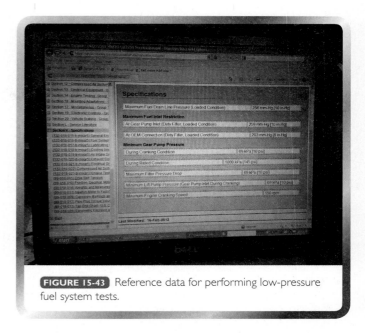

FIGURE 15-43 Reference data for performing low-pressure fuel system tests.

Malfunctioning Fuel Tank Vent

A malfunctioning fuel tank vent can cause negative pressure inside the tank that is apparent when removing the filler cap. Air rushes into the tank and, in some cases, the tank can be heard to expand

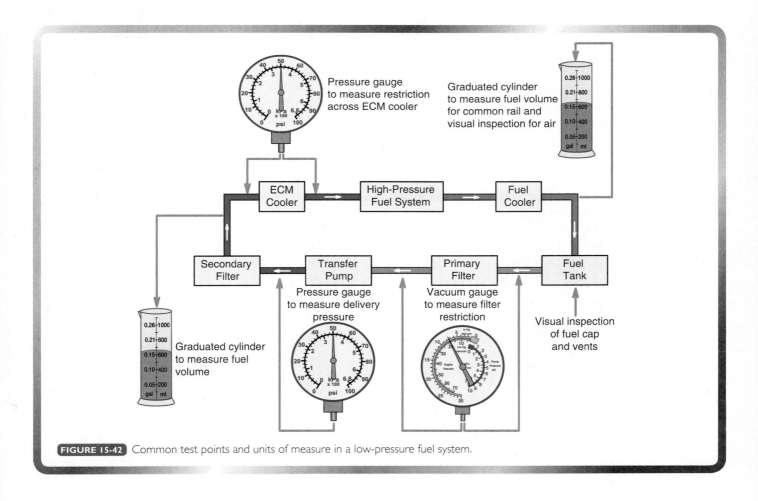

FIGURE 15-42 Common test points and units of measure in a low-pressure fuel system.

FIGURE 15-44 A screen from Detroit Fuel System Integrity Check (FSIC).

when the cap is released. This condition can lead to low power and stalling after a few minutes or hours of vehicle operation. Releasing the tank cap restores normal power to the engine.

Air Leaks on Suction Lines

The lines connecting the tank pickup to the transfer pump must have airtight seals because any leak on the negative-pressure or suction side of the fuel system will draw air into the system. Because air expands and compresses, air in fuel will affect fuel flow to the transfer pump that, in turn, causes hard starting, low power, and unstable engine-operating conditions.

Air can lead to damaged injector tips of newer high-pressure nozzles. When fuel that would normally cushion the seating of the nozzle valve within the injector is absent, the nozzle valve impacts the nozzle seat with tremendous force, damaging the nozzle tip **FIGURE 15-45** .

> ### TECHNICIAN TIP
>
> Air can easily enter the suction side of a fuel system through cracked fuel tank pickup tubes, leaking filter base gaskets, and loose fuel line connections. Not only will air in fuel cause low-power complaints, the engine will run rough, stall, and be hard to start.

Filter Service

Fuel filters naturally build resistance to the flow of fuel as they remove unwanted contaminants from the fuel system. Larger pores fill with particles first, leaving smaller pores open for filtration. Thus, filter efficiency improves with use. Fuel filters, unlike engine oil filters, have no bypass when they become restricted. Consequently, fuel flow through the filter decreases until the point is reached where the fuel supply system does not provide enough fuel at the correct pressure to properly operate the engine **FIGURE 15-46** . This results in reduced power output from the engine, which is usually noticed first when the engine is placed under load, such as during hard acceleration or climbing a hill.

Common Fuel System Problems

Fuel filters should be replaced at their recommended service interval. Alternatively, to avoid overservicing of filters, measuring filter restriction is the best indication of when a filter requires replacement. Restriction is the pressure differential created between the clean and dirty side of the filter when the filter begins to load with contaminants. Some vehicles include a restriction gauge or warning lamp for excessive filter restriction built into the dash. For the technician, a vacuum gauge connected with a T-fitting or service port between the transfer pump and primary filter provides an accurate indication of filter contamination. Manufacturer's specification should be compared with actual data. Generally, restrictions should not be more than 12″ (305 mm) of mercury (Hg) when the engine

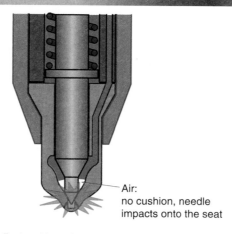
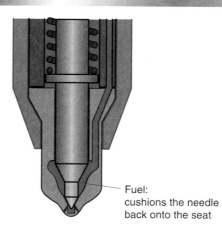

Air:
no cushion, needle impacts onto the seat

Fuel:
cushions the needle back onto the seat

FIGURE 15-45 Fuel cushions the nozzle valve on the nozzle seat at the end of injection. Air in fuel causes the nozzle valve to damage the nozzle tip.

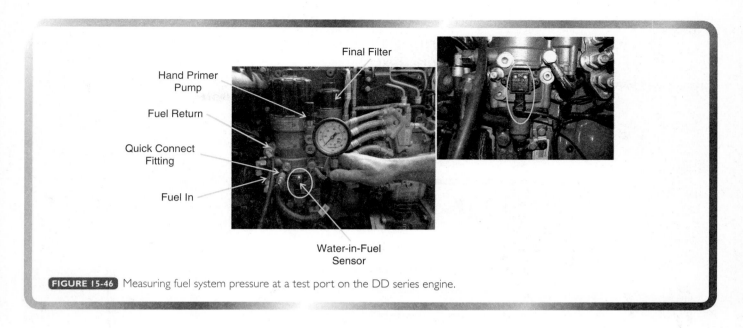

Hand Primer Pump

Fuel Return

Quick Connect Fitting

Fuel In

Final Filter

Water-in-Fuel Sensor

FIGURE 15-46 Measuring fuel system pressure at a test port on the DD series engine.

is operated at high idle. Most systems will run at a maximum of 4–8″ (102–203 mm) Hg. Similarly, restrictions of the fuel tank lines and the pickup can be measured by connecting a vacuum gauge to a T-fitting on the suction side of the primary filter. Restrictions at this point should be generally less than 1″ (25 mm) Hg. Kinked fuel lines or a restricted fuel pickup will increase negative pressure in the line to the point where fuel flow slows or exceeds a pump's ability to pull fuel from the tank. Output pressure of the secondary filter is measured to evaluate its restriction.

Performing a Primary Fuel Filter Suction-Side Pressure Test

Most heavy-duty diesel engines use both primary and secondary fuel filters to provide long service intervals between filter changes while providing the cleanest fuel to the high-pressure system. The primary filter incorporates a fuel–water separator, and occasionally an additional fuel–water separator is used before the primary filter. A primary fuel filter has several important jobs to perform. First, it must protect the transfer pump from damage caused by fuel contaminants. Second, it removes larger contaminant particles and both free and bound water from fuel, which reduces the loading in the finer secondary filter. It is important that the primary filter provides low restriction to fuel flow because it is located on the suction side of the fuel transfer pump. This means only atmospheric pressure pushes fuel through the primary filter and contaminant buildup will reduce fuel flow more drastically than a secondary filter restriction because the secondary filter is located on the pressure side of the transfer pump. In fact, a pressure drop as little as 0.5 psi (3 kPa) will reduce fuel output volume by approximately half. Primary fuel filters typically have a **nominal micron rating**, which is the minimum particle size a fuel filter is expected to remove, of 10–30 microns, but 40- and 100- micron filters are also used in the fuel–water separator. Filter restriction is measured to determine whether the filter needs servicing and to pinpoint a cause for low-power complaints.

To perform a primary fuel filter suction-side pressure test, follow the steps in **SKILL DRILL 15-1**.

Measuring Primary Filter Restriction

If the primary filter suction test indicates an excessively high negative pressure, the primary filter is restricted, or a restriction exists between the filter and the fuel tank. A more comprehensive test is required to compare the outlet pressure with the inlet pressure of the primary filter.

To measure primary filter restriction, follow the steps in **SKILL DRILL 15-2**.

Performing a Primary Fuel Filter Suction-Side Restriction Test

If the pressure drop across the primary filter is acceptable, but the suction-side pressure is too low, a suction-side restriction test should be performed. Pinched lines, undersized lines, or a pickup tube with more than one fuel line attached will produce suction-side pressures that are too low to provide adequate fuel flow.

To perform a primary fuel filter suction-side restriction test, follow the steps in **SKILL DRILL 15-3**.

Measuring Secondary Filter Output Pressure

Secondary fuel filters are connected between the pressurized transfer pump outlet and the high-pressure fuel system, which means they operate with higher pressures than primary filters. Secondary fuel filters are designed to remove finer particles of dirt and other contaminants than primary filters and typically have a nominal micron rating of 2–10 microns. Because secondary filters operate at a higher pressure and the primary filters generally remove the bulk of contaminants, some fleets choose to replace secondary filter after every other service interval in which the primary filter is replaced. Changing a filter sooner than necessary does not help keep fuel cleaner because filters become more efficient with use. This happens because larger pores and openings in the filter media plug up first, and then progressively smaller

SKILL DRILL 15-1 Performing a Primary Fuel Filter Suction-Side Pressure Test

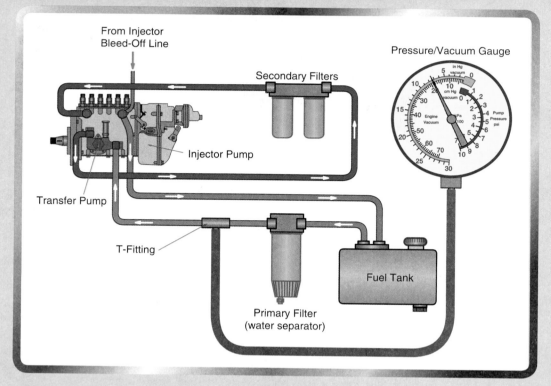

From Injector Bleed-Off Line

Secondary Filters

Pressure/Vacuum Gauge

Injector Pump

Transfer Pump

T-Fitting

Primary Filter (water separator)

Fuel Tank

1 Obtain an accurate, high quality pressure-vacuum gauge capable of measuring pressure in inches (millimeters) of Hg and psi in tenths of inches, or a Magnehelic gauge that measures in inches (millimeters) of water (H$_2$O). An electronic pressure transducer or a mechanical vacuum-pressure gauge are best.

2 Connect the gauge to the outlet side of the primary filter using a quick-connect fitting, which may need to be installed in the system if one was not equipped by the OEM. A T-fitting may also be used in the fuel line between the primary filter and transfer pump, but there is usually a test port and plug in the filter system.

3 Start the engine and run it at high-idle (full throttle, no load). Observe and record the pressure reading. A slight negative pressure is normal, but a high negative pressure means the filter is restricted or there is a suction-side restriction before the filter. Generally, if the negative pressure is less than 8–10" (203–254 mm) Hg or 4–5 psi (28–34 kPa), the filter is operating satisfactorily and still has service life remaining. If the restriction is between 12–18" (305–457 mm) Hg, recommend that the filter be replaced. Always refer to manufacturer's specifications.

---

pores are blocked by dirt and contaminants as the filter remains in service. The best method to determine when a secondary filter requires replacement is to measure the output pressure.

To measure secondary filter output pressure, follow the steps in SKILL DRILL 15-4.

Diaphragm Pump Problems

Pump volume and pressure decreases when the check valves deteriorate or have trapped dirt preventing them from closing, or when there are broken springs. More significantly, fuel can drain back from the fuel system, which leads to prolonged cranking and hard-starting conditions. Some pumps with this condition will allow the engine to briefly start on fuel contained

in the high-pressure system and then quit. More cranking is necessary to supply fuel and bleed air from the high-pressure system before the engine can restart.

Drain-back valves are often installed in filter modules and cylinder head fuel line fittings to prevent hard or prolonged starting caused by fuel draining back to the tank.

Other service problems with these pumps include weak or broken diaphragm springs causing low pump output pressure and volume. A quieting spring on the rocker lever can break causing a noise when the diagram is not retracted.

Check valves may also leak and allow fuel to drain back to the tank causing a loss of fuel priming. Fuel system additives are often the culprit for valve deterioration as well as dirt beneath the valve seats.

SKILL DRILL 15-2 Measuring Primary Filter Restriction

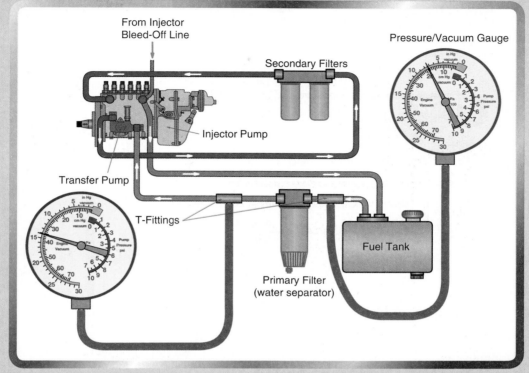

From Injector Bleed-Off Line

Pressure/Vacuum Gauge

Secondary Filters

Injector Pump

Transfer Pump

T-Fittings

Fuel Tank

Primary Filter (water separator)

1 Install quick-connect fittings and attach pressure vacuum gauges to both the inlet and outlet sides of the primary filter. An electronic pressure transducer can be used. Alternately, use the same gauge and take measurements on both sides of the filter during two separate sequences.

2 Start the engine and operate it at rated speed.

3 Observe and record the pressure difference between the two gauges. Most clean filters will have less than 0.1 psi (0.7 kPa) difference between the two readings.

4 If the filter restriction is approaching 5–8" (127–203 mm) Hg or 2.5–4 psi (17–28 kPa), recommend filter replacement.

Detection of a perforated diaphragm is done when fuel is detected leaking out the weep hole, which is designed to prevent fuel from running into the crankcase **FIGURE 15-47**. Oil leakage from the weep hole is normal. Heavy leaks may indicate excessive crankcase blow-by.

Oil Contamination of Fuel

Oil contamination of fuel can occur from a number of sources. Gear-type fuel transfer pumps with damaged seals can draw engine lube oil into the pump and recirculate it with fuel. Return fuel will in turn contaminate the fuel tank with lube oil. Hydraulically actuated electronic unit injection (HEUI) injectors and their O-rings can also fail, causing oil contamination of fuel. If oil contamination of fuel is suspected, the condition can be verified by dropping a sample of fuel on a paper towel. Oil and fuel will diffuse at different rates into the paper, with lube oil leaving a darker blotch in the center and the fuel, which is lighter, will leave a clear stain on the outside of the stain. Scheduled oil sampling (SOS) can also be used to detect the presence of fuel in oil.

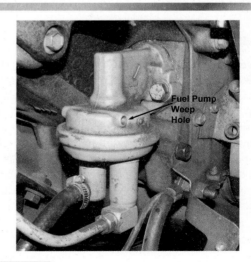

Fuel Pump Weep Hole

FIGURE 15-47 The weep hole prevents fuel from entering the crankcase. When it leaks fuel, this often indicates a ruptured diaphragm.

SKILL DRILL 15-3 Performing a Primary Fuel Filter Suction-Side Restriction Test

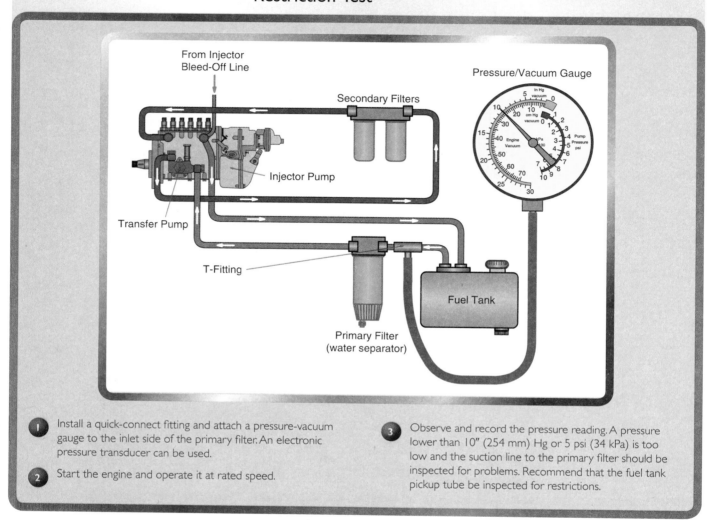

1. Install a quick-connect fitting and attach a pressure-vacuum gauge to the inlet side of the primary filter. An electronic pressure transducer can be used.

2. Start the engine and operate it at rated speed.

3. Observe and record the pressure reading. A pressure lower than 10" (254 mm) Hg or 5 psi (34 kPa) is too low and the suction line to the primary filter should be inspected for problems. Recommend that the fuel tank pickup tube be inspected for restrictions.

Priming Fuel Systems

Whenever fuel filters are replaced, or if an engine has run out of fuel, the system usually needs to have air purged from the filter and lines in order to start. On mechanical transfer systems, this involves locating and opening a bleeder valve on the pressure side of the fuel filter. The technician should operate the hand pump until fuel flows continuously from the bleeder screw with no air and then close the bleeder screw **FIGURE 15-48**. Electric systems often involve the same procedure, but the key can be cycled on and off or fuel pump relays jumped until the electric pump purges air from an opened bleeder screw.

Replacing a Fuel Filter and Priming a Fuel System

When a cartridge fuel filter is replaced, on some engines the filter housing will contain air after the cartridge is installed. Any air in the fuel system will prevent the fuel from properly pressurizing, which will cause the engine to quit, if it starts at

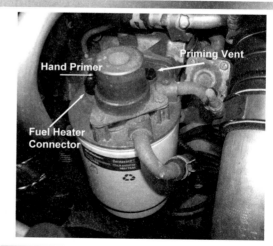

FIGURE 15-48 A bleeder screw or vent is slightly opened when priming a filter. Air is removed from the fuel by the primer pump and the screw is opened until only fuel flows.

SKILL DRILL 15-4 Measuring Secondary Filter Output Pressure

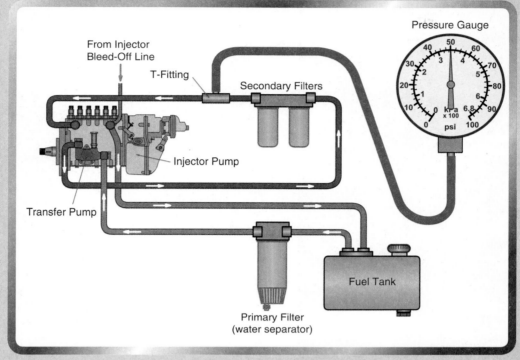

1. Obtain an accurate, high-quality pressure gauge capable of measuring pressure in psi (kPa). An electronic pressure transducer or a mechanical pressure gauge are best.

2. Connect the gauge to the outlet side of the secondary filter using a quick-connect fitting, which may need to be installed in the system if one was not equipped by the OEM. There is always a test port or plug to access measurement of the secondary fuel pressure.

3. Start the engine and run it at high-idle (full throttle, no load). Observe and record the pressure reading. Most secondary filters operate at pressures of 50–80 psi (345–552 kPa). Compare the observed pressures with the manufacturer's specifications.

4. Make a service recommendation to replace the secondary filter if the output pressures are approaching or below the manufacturer's specifications.

all. It is particularly important to bleed air from the fuel system because many systems today use very little fuel return to the tank, which can carry air and vapors back to the tank. Any air trapped in fuel lines requires a significant amount of service time and line replacement once air has been allowed to enter high-pressure lines. These low-return fuel systems are designed to prevent parasitic power loss from pumping more fuel than is needed and overheating the fuel in the tank by continuously returning fuel with heat picked up from the engine.

To replace a fuel filter and prime a fuel system, follow the steps in (SKILL DRILL 15-5). These steps are for a canister fuel system on a Detroit DD series engine.

Hard Starting Problems

Prolonged cranking or no-starts related to the fuel transfer system typically involve:

- Fuel leak back to the tank
- Air in the fuel system
- Low or no fuel pressure
- Inadequate fuel delivery volume

Loose lines, cracked or blocked pickup tubes, and loose fuel filters can be common points that allow air into the fuel system. If air is present, fuel cannot be properly pressurized. Priming pumps become "spongy," and engines run irregularly and rough at idle when air is in the low-pressure system.

Fuel can bleed back to the tank because of defective transfer pump or priming pump check valves. An important point to inspect on unit-injected and common rail engines is the check valve for the fuel return from the cylinder head. Valves that are stuck open allow fuel to drain from the fuel rail in the cylinder head, which enables air to enter the injectors.

System restrictions can lead to performance problems under load when the engine requires maximum fuel delivery. For example, a kinked or undersized fuel line will allow fuel pressure to drop drastically when high volumes of fuel are needed. Fuel lines tied to accessories, such as refrigeration units or supplemental power systems, can drop fuel pressure for the engine supply.

SKILL DRILL 15-5 Replacing a Fuel Filter and Priming a Fuel System

Hand Primer

Quick-Connect

Priming Reservoir

3 Install new filter media for the filters; there are usually two or three depending on the system. Some cartridges will install by turning the filter until a click is heard, which indicates that the filter is locked in place.

4 Lubricate the sealing O-rings for the canister caps. Install and torque the caps.

5 A purpose-made priming reservoir is needed to fill the canisters with fuel. Fill the canister with fuel and pump the priming tool with the integrated hand pump until the reservoir is pressurized.

6 Connect the priming reservoir to the quick-connect coupling on the filter housing. Open a shut-off valve on the priming reservoir's fuel line and allow the fuel to fill the filter housing; this should take approximately 30 seconds.

7 Close the fuel shut-off valve in the priming reservoir line and disconnect.

8 Use the hand primer pump on the fuel module to finish pressurizing the fuel system. Pumping for close to 1 minute should increase the filter housing pressure enough that significant resistance will be felt when operating the hand primer.

9 Start the engine and run it until the oil pressure has reached approximately 15 psi (103 kPa). Run the engine for 1 more minute. Check the filter housing for leaks.

10 Increase the engine speed to 1800 rpm for 3 minutes and then return the engine to idle. Allow the engine to idle for approximately 1 minute.

11 Shut down the engine and recheck for leaks.

1 Remove the filter cap covers with the appropriate wrench or socket.

2 Remove the filters and inspect the housings for large pieces of contaminants. Clean as necessary.

Wrap-Up

Ready for Review

▸ Diesels need a low-pressure fuel supply to transfer fuel from the fuel tank with adequate volume and pressure to the high-pressure injection stage of the fuel system.

▸ Proper operation and service of the low-pressure fuel supply system is critical to quick starting, engine durability, and reliable, trouble-free operation of diesel-powered vehicles.

▸ The functions of the low-pressure fuel system include storing and supplying fuel free of contaminants and vapor at the correct pressure to the high-pressure injection system, removing water contamination, preventing fuel wax from gelling, and regulating fuel temperature.

▸ While the most obvious function of the fuel tank is to store an adequate supply of fuel for the engine's application, a secondary function is to allow fuel returned from the engine to cool after absorbing heat from the engine and fuel injectors.

▸ Low-pressure fuel transfer lines connect the fuel circuits of the low-pressure transfer system.

▸ Fuel tank pickups can be integrated with a fuel level–sending unit and fuel transfer pump; these modules may include several components that may or may not be separately serviceable.

▸ Fuel filters remove dirt contamination from fuel that could cause abrasive wear of injection components.

▸ The most common contaminants found in today's fuels are asphaltene, air, water, microorganisms, and wax.

▸ To prepare fuel for cold weather use and avoid operating difficulties, the low-pressure supply system is often equipped with a variety of devices to condition the fuel by removing water and dissolving wax.

▸ Fuel transfer pumps are used to move fuel from the fuel tanks to the high-pressure fuel system; the fuel must be supplied with adequate volume at the correct pressure for every operating condition.

▸ A variety of pump types exist to match the unique requirements of each high-pressure fuel system.

▸ Evaluating the operation of the low-pressure supply system is indicated when investigating complaints regarding low power, hard or prolonged starting, rough engine operation, and failures of high-pressure injection components.

▸ Whenever fuel filters are replaced, or if an engine has run out of fuel, the system usually needs to have air purged from the filter and lines in order to start.

Vocabulary Builder

absolute micron rating A rating of a fuel filter that refers to the largest sized particle that the fuel filter media will allow to pass.

bleeder screw A component located in the fuel system that allows trapped air to escape from the filter when priming.

diaphragm pump A common type of fuel transfer pump used to supply fuel at low pressure.

fuel heater A device that warms fuel to keep wax dissolved in the fuel.

fuel return circuit The fuel circuit that collects fuel from the injectors, fuel pump, and relief valves and returns the fuel to the tank.

fuel–water separator A device that removes water from fuel by coalescing small water droplets into large ones that eventually fall out of the less-dense fuel into a sump.

gear pump A positive displacement fuel supply pump that sweeps fuel around the gear housing between pump gear teeth and can pressurize the output side to very high pressure.

gelling When the paraffin or wax content of the fuel causes fuel to become too viscous to properly flow through filters and lines due to low temperatures.

hydroscopic The ability to mix and absorb water.

micron (µ) A unit of measure equal to 0.001 mm.

nominal micron rating The minimum particle size a fuel filter is expected to remove.

paraffin A type of wax dissolved in diesel fuel.

primary filter The first filter in the fuel stream from the fuel tank.

priming A process that removes any air that may have entered the fuel system and prevents introduction of unfiltered fuel into the system

rollover valve A valve located on the fuel tank that prevents fuel from draining from the fuel tank vent line in the event of a rollover accident.

secondary filter The second filter in the fuel stream from the fuel tank.

sending units An electrical device, usually a variable-resistance rheostat, that supplies a voltage signal to an analog-type dash gauge proportional to the fuel level.

vane-type pump A pump that uses rotating vanes or rollers to pressurize fuel.

water-in-fuel (WIF) module A device that illuminates a warning light that informs the operator to drain or service the fuel–water separator.

water-in-fuel (WIF) sensor A detector that uses an electrical conductivity probe to sense a specific level of water in fuel and cause a dash-mounted light to illuminate; this light or warning alerts the vehicle operator of the need to drain water from the fuel–water separator.

Review Questions

1. The _____ is an electrical device, usually a variable-resistance rheostat, that supplies a voltage signal to an analog-type dash gauge proportional to the fuel level.
   - **a.** sending unit
   - **b.** bleeder screw
   - **c.** priming unit
   - **d.** fuel filter

2. The _____ is a component located in the fuel system that allows trapped air to escape from the filter when priming.
   - **a.** sending unit
   - **b.** bleeder screw
   - **c.** fuel filter
   - **d.** pressure relief valve

3. At low temperatures, the _____ content in diesel fuel can cause it to become too viscous to properly flow through filters and lines.
   - **a.** coolant
   - **b.** water
   - **c.** paraffin
   - **d.** bacteria

4. A _____ is necessary to allow air into the tank and some fuel vapors to escape.
   - **a.** tank vent
   - **b.** fuel return circuit
   - **c.** sending unit
   - **d.** cooler

5. The smallest particle visible to the human eye is _____ microns.
   - **a.** 30
   - **b.** 35
   - **c.** 40
   - **d.** 45

6. The _____ is located between the primary filter and the high-pressure fuel injection system.
   - **a.** fuel pump
   - **b.** sending unit
   - **c.** secondary filter
   - **d.** secondary filter

7. A diaphragm pump is used to supply fuel at low pressure, usually not more than _____ psi.
   - **a.** 5
   - **b.** 6
   - **c.** 7
   - **d.** 8

8. The _____ allows fuel returned from the engine to cool after absorbing heat from the engine and fuel injectors.
   - **a.** fuel tank
   - **b.** fuel heater
   - **c.** fuel outlet
   - **d.** fuel rail

9. The _____ collects fuel from the injectors, fuel pump, and relief valves and returns the fuel to the tank.
   - **a.** fuel temperature sensor
   - **b.** fuel return circuit
   - **c.** fuel pressure test port
   - **d.** fuel pressure regulator

10. A _____ separator is a filtration device that removes water from fuel and extends the life of a filter.
    - **a.** fuel-water
    - **b.** water-in-fuel
    - **c.** fuel return
    - **d.** cooler

ASE-Type Questions

1. Technician A says the fuel tank allows fuel returned from the engine to cool after absorbing heat from the engine and fuel injectors. Technician B says fuel tank pickups used in medium-duty applications are usually integrated with a fuel level sending unit. Who is correct?
   - **a.** Technician A
   - **b.** Technician B
   - **c.** Both Technician A and Technician B
   - **d.** Neither Technician A nor Technician B

2. Technician A says contact with fuel will close the rollover valve to prevent fuel from leaking from the tank. Technician B says contact with fuel will close the pressure relief valve to prevent fuel from leaking from the tank. Who is correct?
   - **a.** Technician A
   - **b.** Technician B
   - **c.** Both Technician A and Technician B
   - **d.** Neither Technician A nor Technician B

3. Technician A says that fuel lines are routed through a vehicle's passenger and driver compartments. Technician B says that fuel lines are not allowed to be routed through a vehicle's passenger or driver compartment. Who is correct?
   a. Technician A
   b. Technician B
   c. Both Technician A and Technician B
   d. Neither Technician A nor Technician B

4. Technician A says when two fuel tanks are used, the return flow splitter valve equally divides return fuel flow from the engine to maintain identical fuel levels in each tank. Technician B says when two fuel tanks are used, the flow splitter valve divides return fuel flow from the engine, but is unable to do so equally. Who is correct?
   a. Technician A
   b. Technician B
   c. Both Technician A and Technician B
   d. Neither Technician A nor Technician B

5. Technician A says bacteria and fungi can multiply throughout a fuel system and eventually clog fuel filters. Technician B says that bacteria and fungi are sometimes referred to as "humbugs." Who is correct?
   a. Technician A
   b. Technician B
   c. Both Technician A and Technician B
   d. Neither Technician A nor Technician B

6. Technician A says few in-tank electric pumps are the positive displacement, roller vane-type using permanent magnet-type electric motors. Technician B says most in-tank electric pumps are the positive displacement, roller vane-type using permanent magnet-type electric motors. Who is correct?
   a. Technician A
   b. Technician B
   c. Both Technician A and Technician B
   d. Neither Technician A nor Technician B

7. Technician A says the Detroit Diesel's DD series engines can perform an automated fuel system test. Technician B says the automated fuel system test includes an evaluation of the low-pressure system called the Fuel System Integrity Check. Who is correct?
   a. Technician A
   b. Technician B
   c. Both Technician A and Technician B
   d. Neither Technician A nor Technician B

8. Technician A says fuel heaters use engine oil to warm the fuel. Technician B says fuel heaters use electric current or engine oil to warm the fuel. Who is correct?
   a. Technician A
   b. Technician B
   c. Both Technician A and Technician B
   d. Neither Technician A nor Technician B

9. Technician A says a piston-type pump is used to supply fuel at low pressure, usually not more than 7 pounds per square inch. Technician B says a gear pump is used to supply fuel at low pressure, usually not more than 7 pounds per square inch. Who is correct?
   a. Technician A
   b. Technician B
   c. Both Technician A and Technician B
   d. Neither Technician A nor Technician B

10. Technician A says it is the job of the primary filter to remove the bulk of free water and contaminants from the fuel. Technician B says it is the job of the secondary filter to remove the bulk of free water and contaminants from the fuel. Who is correct?
    a. Technician A
    b. Technician B
    c. Both Technician A and Technician B
    d. Neither Technician A nor Technician B

CHAPTER 16

Functions of High-Pressure Fuel Systems

NATEF Tasks

Diesel Engines

Fuel System

Electronic Fuel Management System

- Interface with vehicle's on-board computer; perform diagnostic procedures using electronic service tool(s) (to include PC-based software and/or data scan tools); determine needed action. (pp 475–478)

- Check and record electronic diagnostic codes and trip/operational data; monitor electronic data; clear codes; determine further diagnosis. (pp 475–478)
- Perform cylinder contribution test utilizing electronic service tool(s). (p 478)

Knowledge Objectives

After reading this chapter, you will be able to:

1. Identify types of high-pressure injection systems found in heavy- and medium-duty diesel applications. (p 467)
2. Describe the functions, construction, and application of high-pressure fuel injection systems. (pp 468–493)
3. Identify and explain the purpose and operating principles of a high-pressure fuel injection system. (pp 468–493)
4. Identify characteristics of an improperly functioning high-pressure fuel system. (pp 479–480)
5. Recommend maintenance, reconditioning, or repairs of high-pressure fuel injection systems. (pp 479–480)

Skills Objectives

After reading this chapter, you will be able to:

1. Change an injector calibration code. (pp 479)
   SKILL DRILL 16-1
2. Perform a cylinder balance test. (pp 480)
   SKILL DRILL 16-2

► Introduction

Diesel engine fuel systems have two main divisions. One is the low-pressure transfer system that stores and supplies fuel for the injection system. The second is the high-pressure injection system that delivers fuel to the combustion chambers. An enormous variety of high-pressure injection systems exist and are radically different in terms of their construction, complexity, and operating principles **FIGURE 16-1**. Studying the differences between the various types of high-pressure injection systems can be overwhelming. High-pressure injection system operation is more easily understood by examining functions common to all high-pressure injection systems, rather than looking at each type individually. Analyzing high-pressure injection systems in terms of the functions described in this chapter is not only helpful in identifying and understanding injection system operations but also necessary to developing skills related to diagnosing, servicing, and maintaining diesel fuel injection systems. This chapter provides foundational information for understanding specific fuel injection systems presented in greater detail elsewhere in this textbook.

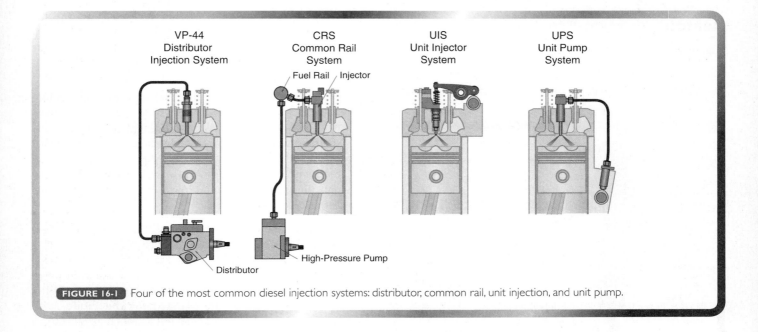

FIGURE 16-1 Four of the most common diesel injection systems: distributor, common rail, unit injection, and unit pump.

► You Are the Technician

A rough-running engine with a cylinder misfire and a noise is brought to your shop for diagnosis and repair. You begin various diagnostic tests after performing a number of visual inspections first—checking fuel and fluid levels and inspecting the engine for oil, fuel, and coolant leaks; the electrical harnesses for damage; and the exhaust system for leaks. A cylinder cut-out test performed at idle and at 1000 revolutions per minute (rpm) identifies a misfire in cylinder 3. A knocking sound in the engine also disappears when cylinder 3 is cut out. When following up the cylinder cut-out test with a relative compression test or cylinder balance test, cylinders 1 and 6 are discovered to be weak. While checking other operating parameters, the injector pulse width is a little longer in the weak cylinders, and the pilot injection event is taking place 8–10 degrees before the main injection event. As you decide the next steps to take, consider the following:

1. How could a defective injector be differentiated from a mechanical condition such as a damaged piston or noise caused by a loose wrist pin?
2. List some probable causes for a noise that would disappear from an engine when a cylinder is cut out for testing.
3. List and explain five possible reasons for low cylinder contributions from cylinders 1 and 6.

► Fundamentals of High-Pressure Fuel Systems

The high-pressure fuel injection system is a diesel engine's most distinctive feature—and one of the most fundamental functions of compression ignition (CI) engines **FIGURE 16-2**. Efficient diesel engine operation relies on a precise quantity of fuel being injected at high pressure at the correct time to the combustion chamber. In a sense, the injection system is the heart of diesel engine operation. The complexity and sophistication of the injection system is reflected in that it is the costliest engine system and requires the greatest technical refinement **FIGURE 16-3**.

Reasons for High-Pressure Fuel Systems

High pressurization of fuel is necessary for several reasons:

1. Fuel must have sufficient pressure to penetrate the dense combustion chamber air mass. Air at high pressure in the chamber makes it even more difficult to distribute fuel through tightly packed air molecules.

2. At high rotational speeds, only a short amount of time is available for the injection of fuel. Fuel must be atomized, distributed, and mixed with air; then it must absorb heat, convert to vapor, and begin burning near the end of the compression stroke, just before the piston reaches top dead center (TDC). Because fuel is injected only near the end of the compression stroke, these events must be performed quickly to allow adequate time for combustion. High-pressure injection enables the injection to take place in less time than it takes a camera to flash. This is especially important as engine speed increases. Time available for injection shortens as the engine speed increases, so increasing injection pressures proportionally with engine speed is necessary to quickly deliver fuel into the combustion chamber.

3. High pressure is necessary to break up the liquid fuel into a fine mist. This process, called **atomization**, is enhanced with high injection pressures **FIGURE 16-4**. Higher pressurization produces increasingly smaller droplets of fuel that readily absorb heat and burn. Improving atomization results in efficient combustion as well as better fuel economy, increased power, and lower emissions (see the Fuel Atomization section).

In today's engines, injection pressures range from a low around 4500 pounds per square inch (psi) (310 bar) during idle conditions to over 37,000 psi (2551 bar) at high speed under full engine loads. (Light-duty diesels have even lower pressures at idle speed to reduce combustion noise.) Higher peak injection pressures are planned for the future, with developmental engines now achieving as much as 60,000 psi (4137 bar). An enormous variety of high-pressure fuel systems are available to accomplish this task for the diesel engine. However, all these systems perform common tasks that, when recognized, can simplify the understanding of how a particular fuel system performs, as well as strategies to maintain, diagnose, and repair them.

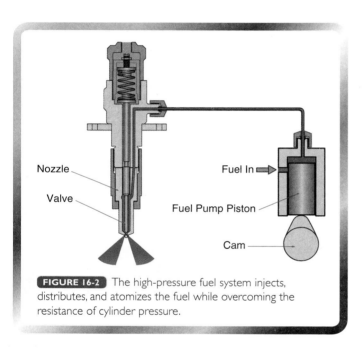

FIGURE 16-2 The high-pressure fuel system injects, distributes, and atomizes the fuel while overcoming the resistance of cylinder pressure.

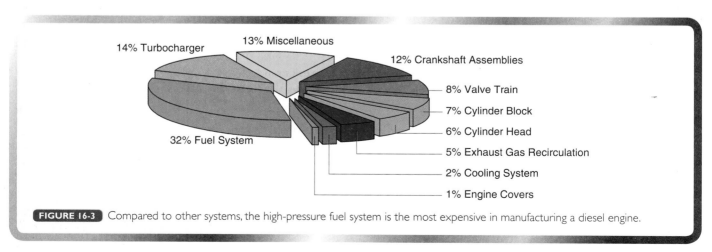

FIGURE 16-3 Compared to other systems, the high-pressure fuel system is the most expensive in manufacturing a diesel engine.

FIGURE 16-4 Better atomization of fuel into smaller, finer droplets produces cleaner and faster burn.

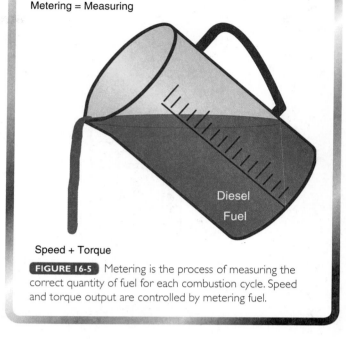

Metering = Measuring

Diesel Fuel

Speed + Torque

FIGURE 16-5 Metering is the process of measuring the correct quantity of fuel for each combustion cycle. Speed and torque output are controlled by metering fuel.

Functions of High-Pressure Fuel Systems

All high-pressure injection systems perform the following tasks:

- Meter the correct quantity of fuel for injection
- Time the injection of fuel
- Control the rate of fuel delivery
- Atomize the fuel
- Distribute the fuel throughout the combustion chamber

When any of these functions are deficient, engine performance- and emission-related problems are present and further mechanical problems will likely develop.

▶ Fuel Metering

Metering is the process of measuring and delivering the correct quantity of fuel to each cylinder required for various speed and load conditions from the engine **FIGURE 16-5**. Diesel engines only meter fuel and have no throttle plate in the air intake to regulate engine speed and power. Throttle plates, however, are used for other purposes, mostly for thermal control of exhaust aftertreatment systems on engines built since 2007. Restricting intake air with a throttle plate increases a diesel engine's naturally cool exhaust system temperature to enable heat-dependent chemical reactions to take place in the exhaust catalysts.

Unthrottled air intake into a diesel allows maximum airflow into the cylinders. To vary vehicle speed and power output, pressure in the cylinders must increase or decrease. To accomplish this, high-pressure systems adjust the quantity of fuel metered and delivered into the cylinders for combustion. Increasing combustion pressure inside the cylinders increases engine torque output **FIGURE 16-6**. So, if the operator demands

more power—e.g., when the road grade becomes steeper or additional freight and passengers are added to the vehicle—more fuel is injected to increase cylinder pressure.

Metering and Governors

All diesel engines use a governor to regulate the quantity of fuel injected into the cylinders **FIGURE 16-7**. Whether it is mechanical or electronic, the governor receives, at a minimum, inputs from the vehicle's throttle pedal, engine speed, and intake manifold or boost pressure. Based on input data, the governor uses linkage or software to calculate or move fuel control linkage to change the amount of fuel injected. A diesel governor's equivalent in a gasoline or Otto cycle engine is the throttle plate. In those engines, the operator opens and closes the throttle plate with a foot-operated accelerator pedal. The operator—or the cruise control system when engaged—determines engine power output. In a diesel engine, the operator's accelerator pedal or throttle lever is only one of several inputs to the engine governor, and the operator doesn't directly control the amount of fuel injected **FIGURE 16-8**. (See the Governors chapter for a further discussion of the governor and its functions.)

Electronic Metering Controls

An electronic governor in a high-pressure injection system is software-based and controls the injection of a precisely metered amount of fuel and also adjusts injection timing and injection rate **FIGURE 16-9**. For example, an electronic governor receives data from the fuel temperature sensor, which is used to calculate the quantity of fuel injected to compensate for changes to fuel density accompanying temperature changes. Engine speed and stroke identification for the cylinder 1 are performed by the cam and crank sensor. The crank position sensor will identify

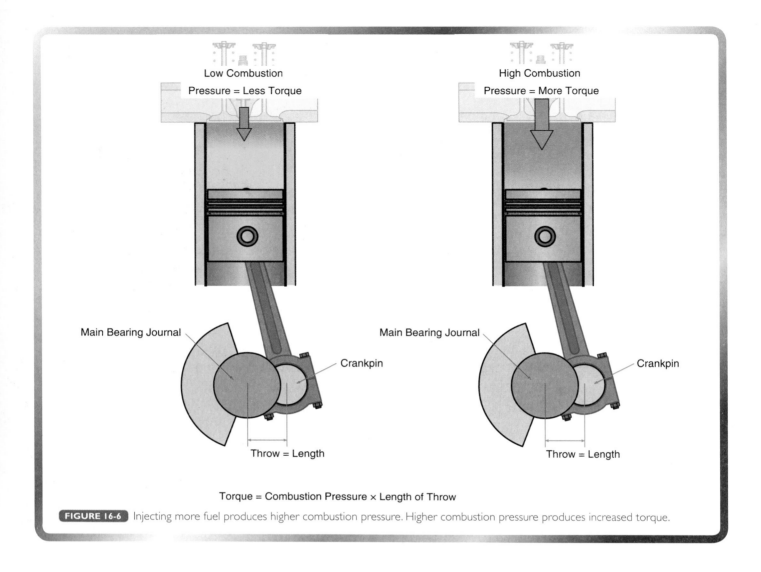

$$Torque = Combustion\ Pressure \times Length\ of\ Throw$$

FIGURE 16-6 Injecting more fuel produces higher combustion pressure. Higher combustion pressure produces increased torque.

FIGURE 16-7 Whether it is an electronic or hydro-mechanical injection system, the governor functions to control the operation of the high-pressure injection system.

piston position to accurately time the injection event for the remaining cylinders. The remaining inputs influence engine fueling, including protecting the engine through de-rating or shut down. Input data from the air temperature sensor assists in calculating changes to injection timing and protecting the engine from excessive intake temperatures, which can thermally overload cylinder components. Of course these sensors are involved in much more complex operational strategies, but these are the minimum contributions the sensor makes to governor operation.

The immediate benefit introduced by electronic refinement is lower engine emissions, improved fuel economy, increased engine reliability, and enhanced performance. Continual advances in engine control system design means these smarter engines deliver ever-increasing amounts of power from smaller displacements, with quieter operation and longer service intervals.

An electronic fuel governor relies on an **electronic control module (ECM)** to process electrical signals for the data it

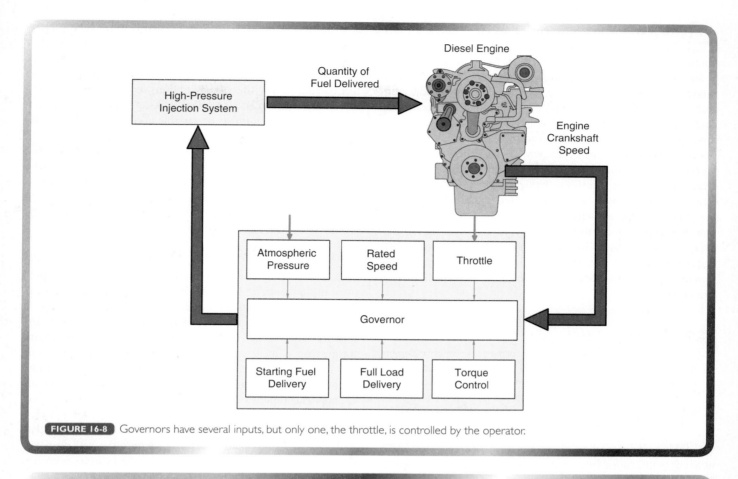

FIGURE 16-8 Governors have several inputs, but only one, the throttle, is controlled by the operator.

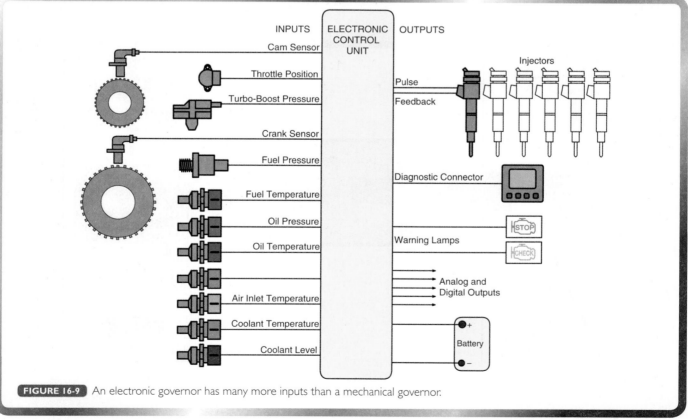

FIGURE 16-9 An electronic governor has many more inputs than a mechanical governor.

receives (inputs) and those that control fuel injection (outputs) **FIGURE 16-10**. The ECM contains a microprocessor, various microcontrollers, memory, and software to execute instructions to operate the engine. Information is collected from engine and vehicle sensors that are processed by the ECM to produce an output signal. Basic operational data regarding engine speed, load, driver commands, ambient conditions, and numerous other pieces of data are used to optimize engine operation to produce the lowest emissions while delivering the highest power output and the best fuel economy. For example, the ECM sends a command to electromechanical devices, such as the fuel injectors, using a pulse-width modulated signal. The length of the pulse corresponds with increased fueling by the injectors. The precise injection timing is set by an electrical signal that energizes the injectors. Optimal metering of injection quantities and fuel timing are calculated using mathematical **algorithms** (mathematical formulas used to solve a problem) developed by a manufacturer.

▶ **TECHNICIAN TIP**

An algorithm is simply a mathematical equation used to solve a problem. A simple example of an algorithm would be to calculate vehicle average speed. The mathematical formula Speed = Distance/Time is used to determine how fast a vehicle is traveling.

Taking the idea of an algorithm a little further, the ECM needs data indicating how many pulses from the vehicle's speed sensor make up a mile or kilometer of distance traveled. Tire size and rear-axle ratios are also needed to solve the problem. The ECM's internal clock also keeps track of the time, while a sensor measures pulses on the output shaft of the transmission that, in turn, supplies electrical pulses corresponding to drive-line rotation. All of these computations require algorithms and ECMs use data tables, also called look-up tables or calibration files, to supply the number or variable used to solve the mathematical equation for vehicle speed **FIGURE 16-11**.

The algorithms used by the ECM to calculate when to fire an injector, determine how long to energize an injector, detect a fault code, or calculate when to activate a malfunction indicator light are complex. In the end, however, they are simply large mathematical equations used by a complex calculator—the ECM—to control engine operation.

Metering and Torque Control

A question that is often asked is why a diesel engine can produce more torque at lower engine speeds than spark-ignition engine can using a throttle plate. Part of the explanation is that because diesels do not use a throttle plate, maximum airflow into the engine is always possible. In contrast, maximum torque from a four-stroke spark-ignition engine is only possible at wide-open throttle. That is because the maximum fuel rate needed to produce torque is limited by the mass of air available to support complete combustion. An additional point to understand about the throttle and engine efficiency is that without a throttle plate, less power is wasted trying to pull air past a partially closed throttle plate. The energy required to pull air past a throttle plate or move gases in and out of the cylinder is known as **pumping loss**.

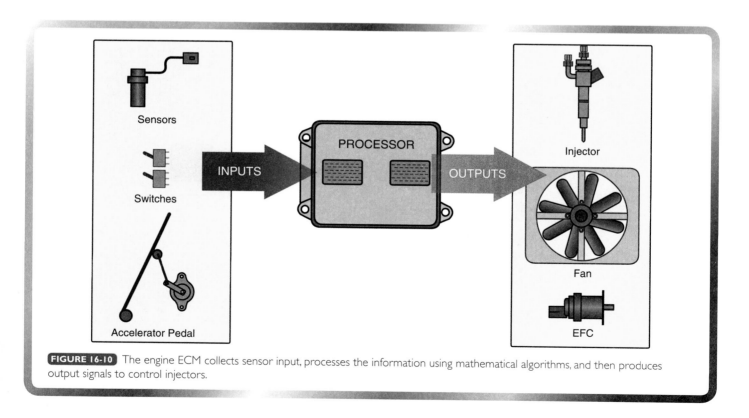

FIGURE 16-10 The engine ECM collects sensor input, processes the information using mathematical algorithms, and then produces output signals to control injectors.

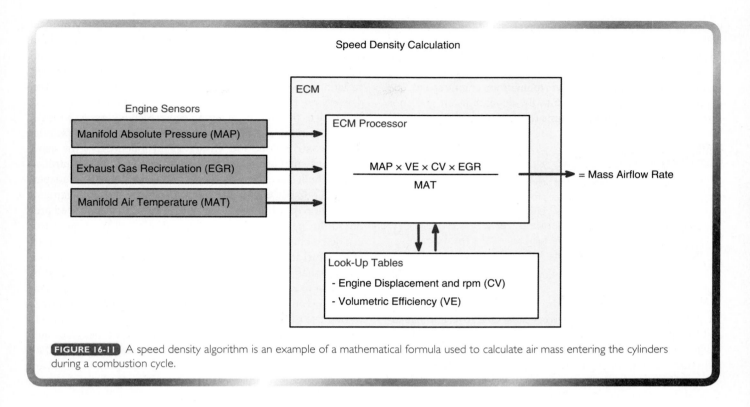

Speed Density Calculation

FIGURE 16-11 A speed density algorithm is an example of a mathematical formula used to calculate air mass entering the cylinders during a combustion cycle.

> ## TECHNICIAN TIP
>
> All diesel engines use a governor, whether it is mechanical or electronic. The most basic function of a governor is to regulate the amount of fuel injected into each cylinder. In a gasoline or Otto cycle engine, the throttle plate serves this purpose. In such engines, the operator opens and closes the throttle plate with a pedal in the cab. In a diesel engine, the driver's accelerator pedal (or throttle lever) is only one of several inputs to the engine governor and does not directly control the amount of fuel injected. Engine speed and load are two other inputs needed by all diesel governors to properly meter fuel into the cylinders.

> ## TECHNICIAN TIP
>
> High compression ratios, turbocharging, and longer crankshaft throws are just a few of the major reasons why diesels produce higher cylinder pressures and greater torque output. Another major reason for higher torque at low engine speed is the absence of a throttle plate. Without restriction to airflow, maximum air volume can enter the cylinders and provide more oxygen to properly combust greater amounts of fuel.

Metering and Compensation

All diesel engine governors function to maintain a minimum engine speed and limit maximum engine speed. For example, changing engine loads at idle, such as engaging the air compressor,

power take-off (PTO) pump, or switching on the air conditioning, results in the need for the governor to change fuel delivery to maintain a consistent idle speed.

Another unique feature common to all diesel governors is **compensation**. Compensation is observed when one or more cylinders are cut out and the engine maintains a set idle speed **FIGURE 16-12**. An increase or decrease in engine speed is sensed

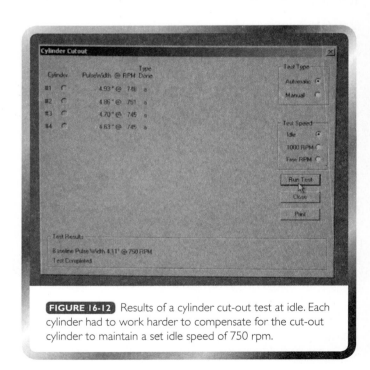

FIGURE 16-12 Results of a cylinder cut-out test at idle. Each cylinder had to work harder to compensate for the cut-out cylinder to maintain a set idle speed of 750 rpm.

by the governor, and fueling is changed accordingly. So, if fuel delivery is limited or blocked by a defective injector or a cylinder has low power contribution because of a mechanical condition, the governor responds to the loss of engine speed and increases fueling to the remaining cylinders to maintain engine speed. The engine's rpm may drop momentarily, depending on governor sensitivity, but will quickly resume the set idle rpm.

Hunting

Irregular or inconsistent fuel delivery causes the governor to readjust the quantity of fuel metered and correct the engine's speed. Called **hunting**, or loping, this correction may be experienced as a rhythmic change in engine rpm at idle speed. As the governor, electronic or mechanical, attempts to compensate for changes in engine rpm to maintain idle speed, it responds to a cylinder speeding up the engine by cutting back on fuel delivered to the next cylinder in the firing order. As a result, the engine rpm can fall below the set idle rpm. This, in turn, causes the governor to increase fuel delivery to the next cylinder, the one after, and so on. The problem is made worse if one cylinder is receiving more or less fuel and the engine has a highly sensitive and responsive governor that quickly corrects engine speed changes caused by the uneven metering. Once again, alternately reducing and increasing fuel delivery produces the rhythmic changes to engine speed.

Metering and Idle Adaptation

The smoothest engine idle is a goal of every diesel engine manufacturer, the end-users, and the technicians who repair diesel engines. Variations in the amount of power contributed from cylinders, caused by even the slightest changes to fueling, results in rough-running and uneven engine operation, vibration, and emissions. Uneven power contributions are caused by a wide variety of factors including:

- Differences to the quantity of fuel injected from cylinder to cylinder and injection shot to injection shot within the same cylinder.
- Variations in compression and combustion pressures caused by a large variety of mechanical conditions such as engine wear, valve action, and exhaust gas recirculation (EGR) delivery
- Manufacturing variations in injectors
- Fuel system component deterioration

Even very small changes to the injected quantities of fuel at idle produce rough running engines and unstable engine speed. Consider that a droplet of fuel has a volume of 25–30 cubic millimeters (mm^3). A typical idle quantity of injection for most engines is 3–8 mm^3 of fuel **FIGURE 16-13**. A variation of even 0.5 mm^3 corresponds to a 10% variation in delivery quantity and substantial changes in engine operation. In the newest engines, variations to the injection quantities at higher rates of fuel delivery are kept well below ±0.1 mm^3. Compare this metering accuracy to the volume of a pin head, which is close to 1 mm^3.

To minimize problems associated with uneven cylinder power contribution, and ensure all cylinders have the same consistent combustion pressure, most electronically controlled engines built since the early 2000s use a feature called idle adaptation **FIGURE 16-14**. Idle adaptation involves making adjustments to injection quantities based on changes to crankshaft speed produced during every power impulse. The crank position sensor can detect slight velocity changes that enable the ECM to subtract or add fuel to each cylinder based on the measured variations to crankshaft acceleration during power events. Data is used by the ECM to calculate and apply a correction factor to the quantity of fuel injected into a cylinder from one combustion cycle to the next **FIGURE 16-15** and **FIGURE 16-16**. If the correction to fuel delivery quantities becomes excessive, fault codes associated with cylinder contribution are generated. Codes are generated for loss of compression or uneven cylinder contribution, and power output depends on the measurement of the deceleration rate of the crankshaft during compression events as well as the acceleration rate during power stroke. Low power contributions from a cylinder do not accelerate a crankshaft as fast as a cylinder with good combustion quality. Cylinders with bent connecting rods or worn-out rings do not slow the crankshaft as fast during compression stroke either. When and how much the crankshaft speed changes are key to differentiating between cylinders with burnt valves, bent connecting rods, worn rings, or faulty injectors.

While the crank position sensor detects unbalanced cylinder contributions, the cam position sensor is used to calculate which cylinder is firing and which stroke each of the cylinders is moving through. Most engines built since 2002 generally have the capability to perform cylinder balance adaptation at

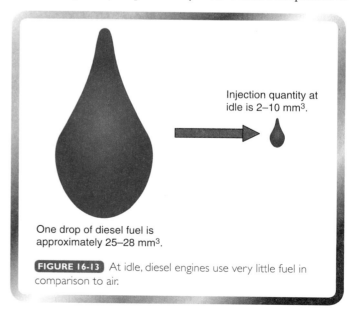

Injection quantity at idle is 2–10 mm^3.

One drop of diesel fuel is approximately 25–28 mm^3.

FIGURE 16-13 At idle, diesel engines use very little fuel in comparison to air.

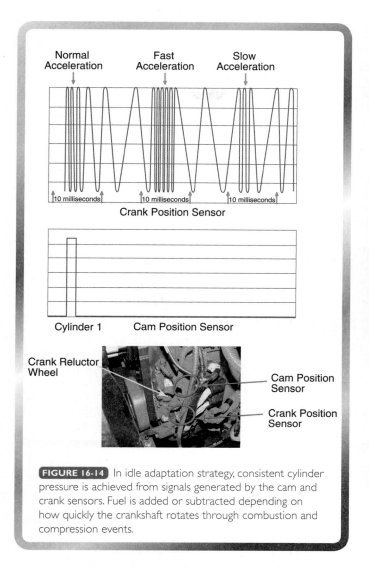

FIGURE 16-14 In idle adaptation strategy, consistent cylinder pressure is achieved from signals generated by the cam and crank sensors. Fuel is added or subtracted depending on how quickly the crankshaft rotates through combustion and compression events.

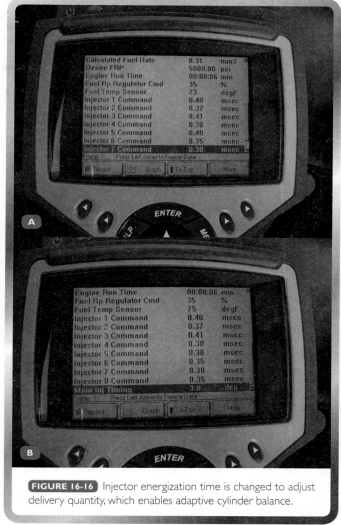

FIGURE 16-16 Injector energization time is changed to adjust delivery quantity, which enables adaptive cylinder balance.

FIGURE 16-15 Adaptive cylinder balancing allows the ECM to calculate a different injection quantity for each combustion event to maintain consistent cylinder pressures. This screenshot averages all cylinders to 100%.

idle. Since 2010, faster processor speeds and better ECMs enable adaptive balance to take place throughout the engine's entire operating range.

Cylinder firing order and stroke are calculated when data from the crank position sensor is synchronized with the cam sensor. Using a single raised pin on a cam gear, a missing tooth, or uniquely shaped window in the cam sensor that corresponds to TDC cylinder number 1 enables the ECM to precisely identify the position and stroke of each cylinder **FIGURE 16-17** and **FIGURE 16-18**. By measuring the time elapsed between each tooth passing by crank sensor, velocity changes caused by each compression and power event are measured.

Metering and Emissions

A more important problem of uneven cylinder pressures is the emissions they produce. Because formations of various noxious emissions, such as hydrocarbon (HC), oxides of nitrogen (NO$_x$), particulate matter (PM), and carbon monoxide (CO), are dependent on cylinder temperature and pressure, uneven cylinder pressures can exaggerate emission-related control strategies.

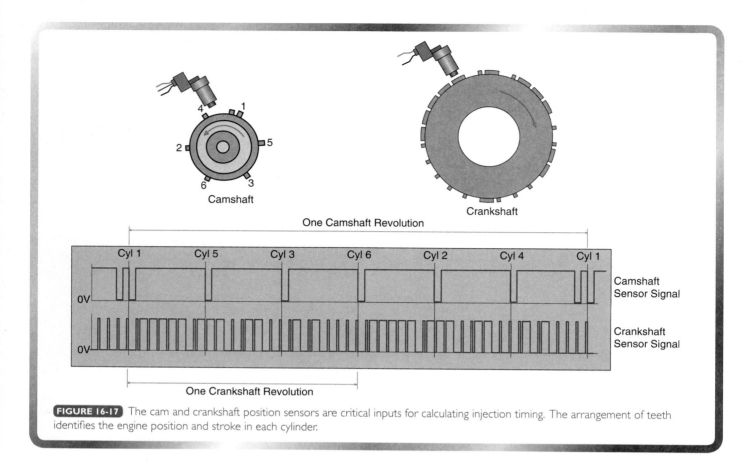

FIGURE 16-17 The cam and crankshaft position sensors are critical inputs for calculating injection timing. The arrangement of teeth identifies the engine position and stroke in each cylinder.

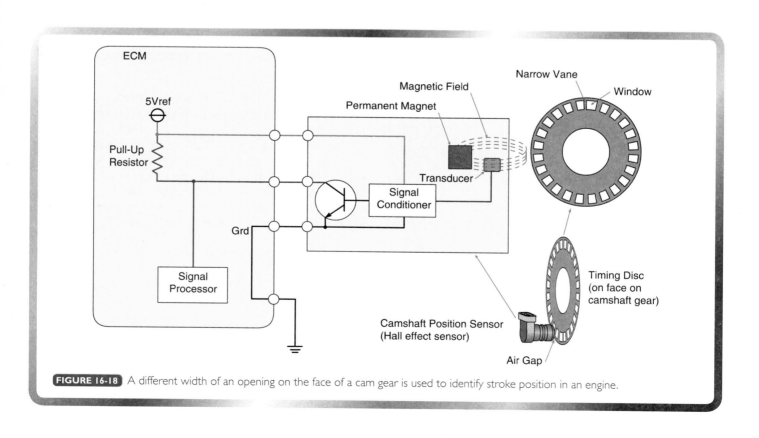

FIGURE 16-18 A different width of an opening on the face of a cam gear is used to identify stroke position in an engine.

For example, introducing EGR gas into a cylinder with lower-than-average combustion pressures increases HC, CO, and PM emissions. In a cylinder with above-average pressure, not enough EGR is delivered. To ensure good combustion quality and keep emissions minimal, consistent and even cylinder pressures are a critical factor to control in today's low-emission engines.

Safety Tip

Consistent combustion pressures from all cylinders are necessary to achieve low engine emissions. If pressure variations exist between cylinders, and from shot to shot in the same cylinder, the engine will produce different noxious emissions because pressure and temperature conditions change the combustion mechanisms that form NO_x, PM, CO, and HC emissions. Emission reduction strategies applied the same way to all cylinders, such as the use of EGR or injection timing, produce significantly different results if cylinder pressures and temperatures are uneven.

Adaptive Balance

Since 2010, almost all engines can adjust fueling not only at idle conditions, but throughout the entire engine operating range. Faster ECMs, operating with 32-bit microprocessors, provide the speed needed to make rapid calculations at high engine rpm. This means cylinder pressures are consistent all the way to maximum rpm and emissions, which form differently, depending on cylinder pressures and temperatures. Emission reduction strategies retarding injection timing or using EGR affects all cylinders the same way to reduce emissions rather than contributing to more production.

Metering and HD-OBD

Fuel pressure, misfiring, firing voltages, cylinder imbalance, timing, injector deterioration, and incorrect calibration codes are just a few of the high-pressure injection system variables monitored by the HD-OBD diagnostic system manager to detect conditions that could potentially lead to excessive emissions. Monitoring, too, must occur during the entire speed and load range of an engine. Failure of any fuel system component can permit emissions to exceed desired (and legal) levels.

Metering and Calibration Codes

During manufacturing, machining, and other production processes, tolerances, such as wire resistance in electrical actuators, result in deviations to fuel delivery quantities. Even when injectors are manufactured on the same assembly line, no two are exactly identical in terms of the quantity of fuel delivered for any particular energization time or fuel pressure supplied to the injector. To correct this problem, injectors are flow tested on a fuel bench after production at an original equipment manufacturer (OEM) facility and the characteristics of each injector is measured. Delivery quantities at different energization times and pressures are measured and graphed. With older injectors, a comparison is made between the nominal, or average, fuel delivery for hundreds or thousands of injectors and the actual delivery volume of the individual injector **FIGURE 16-19**.

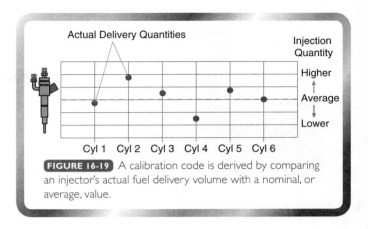

FIGURE 16-19 A calibration code is derived by comparing an injector's actual fuel delivery volume with a nominal, or average, value.

A calibration code is generated for each injector that is then stamped or etched on the injector **FIGURE 16-20** and **FIGURE 16-21**. When this code is uploaded to the engine or other fuel system–related ECM, the control unit can apply a correction factor to the calculated fuel quantity for each cylinder **FIGURE 16-22**. Variations to cylinder pressures are further minimized using this calibration code, which in turn smooths engine operation and reduces exhaust emissions. The appropriate calibration code must be entered into the ECM each time a new injector is installed or an injector is moved. Failure to do so will result in rough engine operation and fault codes associated with cylinder balance and injector calibration **FIGURE 16-23**. Calibration codes are given different names by manufacturers. Common names for this feature include **injection quantity adjustment (IQA)**, the E-Trim, the adaptation value, or simply the injector calibration code. Older mechanical unit injectors (that is, non-electronic injectors) on some engines can also be flow tested as well. The best practice for a hydro-mechanical injection systems requires injection replacement in matched sets, with injectors that have similar flow rates paired together.

FIGURE 16-20 The two-digit calibration code on this older Detroit injector helps correct for variations in fuel delivery quantities between injectors, which provides smoother engine operation and lower emissions.

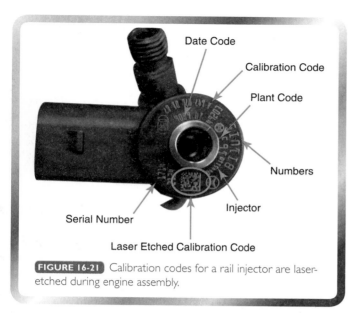

FIGURE 16-21 Calibration codes for a rail injector are laser-etched during engine assembly.

FIGURE 16-22 Injector calibration codes for each cylinder are programmed into control modules with codes obtained from each injector.

FIGURE 16-23 The calibration code on an injector must be entered into the master control module (MCM) on a DD series engine whenever injectors are replaced or relocated to another cylinder. (The MCM is another name for the ECM.)

Safety Tip

Some injectors with calibration codes can only be refurbished by the OEM that produced them. Equipment used to assign calibration codes and benchmark values are proprietary, meaning they are known only to the OEM. Replacement parts such as nozzles, springs, and other internal parts change the original calibration. Failure to accurately generate and assign a correct calibration code to an injector can cause the emissions to increase beyond legislated standards. Injection pumps are also carefully calibrated to ensure each cylinder delivers a precise fuel quantity under different speed and load conditions. Comparator benches are used at manufacturing and service facilities to measure the delivery volumes from injection pumps. Such benches, as their name suggests, compare delivery volumes from each delivery port of the pump after a fixed number of strokes or revolutions are made. Adjustments are made to ensure the delivery quantities match specifications and variations between cylinders are corrected.

Changing an Injector Calibration Code

Whenever an injector is replaced or relocated to another cylinder, its calibration code must be changed.

To change an injector calibration code, follow the steps in **SKILL DRILL 16-1**. The procedure shown is specific to Detroit

▶ **TECHNICIAN TIP**

Injection quantity adjustment numbers are assigned to each injector after flow testing during production. Codes are printed on the injector and are recorded by the technician when an injector is installed. The number code is stored in the ECM using a diagnostic service tool. Failure to store the correct value for each cylinder can result in rough running condition and a fault code that illuminates the malfunction indicator lamp (MIL). The injector calibration code is also used as a reference point for fueling adjustment factors due to deterioration and wear and requires replacement whenever an injector or ECM is replaced.

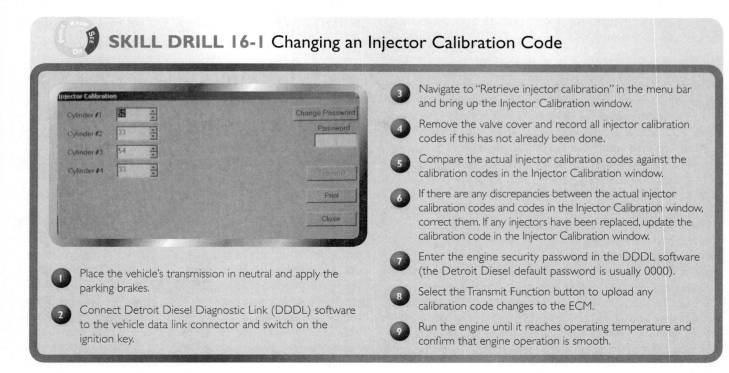

SKILL DRILL 16-1 Changing an Injector Calibration Code

3. Navigate to "Retrieve injector calibration" in the menu bar and bring up the Injector Calibration window.

4. Remove the valve cover and record all injector calibration codes if this has not already been done.

5. Compare the actual injector calibration codes against the calibration codes in the Injector Calibration window.

6. If there are any discrepancies between the actual injector calibration codes and codes in the Injector Calibration window, correct them. If any injectors have been replaced, update the calibration code in the Injector Calibration window.

7. Enter the engine security password in the DDDL software (the Detroit Diesel default password is usually 0000).

8. Select the Transmit Function button to upload any calibration code changes to the ECM.

9. Run the engine until it reaches operating temperature and confirm that engine operation is smooth.

1. Place the vehicle's transmission in neutral and apply the parking brakes.

2. Connect Detroit Diesel Diagnostic Link (DDDL) software to the vehicle data link connector and switch on the ignition key.

Diesel injectors. Follow the manufacturer's instructions for products from other OEMs.

Troubleshooting Misfires

To differentiate between a misfire caused by either a defective injector or damaged or worn cylinder components, the injector in a properly functioning cylinder can be swapped with the injector in the suspect cylinder. Movement of the misfire code to another cylinder that comes after the suspect injector is moved indicates a defective injector and not a problem with cylinder components.

To identify a misfiring cylinder that causes engine noise and vibration, a cylinder cut-out or balance test is useful. On hydro-mechanical engines using pump line nozzle fuel systems, an injector line can be loosened, which prevents injection of fuel to that cylinder. Scan tools or computers running software capable of bidirectional communication can also electronically cut out fuel delivery to individual cylinders. A measurement can then be made of the extent to which more or less fuel is injected by other cylinders to compensate for the lost contribution from a particular cylinder. The acceleration and deceleration speeds of the crankshaft are also monitored to identify cylinders with low combustion pressure.

A cylinder cut-out test detects misfiring or a cylinder with a low power contribution **FIGURE 16-24**. In Figure 16-24, the cylinder cut-out test displays the average number of degrees of crank rotation for four cylinders when each injector was energized. Energization time is reported in degrees of crankshaft rotation, which is also known as baseline pulse width. Baseline pulse width can then be compared with the pulse width of each injector when each cylinder is cut out. The remaining cylinders will need to contribute more fuel to maintain idle speed. A pulse-width number

FIGURE 16-24 A cylinder cut-out test from a Detroit S50 engine. Energization time is reported in degrees of crankshaft rotation.

that is higher than the baseline value beside a cylinder means the cylinder was contributing well. A lower number means less contribution from that cylinder. For example, note that when cylinder 1 is cut out, it has a pulse width of 5.14 degrees, which indicates that that is the new baseline when cylinder 1 is cut out. This means the remaining injectors had to stay energized longer to maintain engine speed only if cylinder 1 was contributing power before it was cut out. Cylinder 4, with 4.60 degrees of energization time, is the weakest cylinder because the loss of contribution from cylinder 4 required the smallest increase in energization time. If no change from baseline pulse width takes place when compared to the pulse width of a cylinder during a cut-out test, the cylinder is completely misfiring.

Performing a Cylinder Balance Test

To identify weak cylinders that are contributing to low power complaints and causing rough running conditions, the software diagnostic routines of all late-model diesel engines include some variation of a cylinder balance test. A cylinder balance test measures the crankshaft velocity changes for each cylinder compression and power stroke to identify cylinder misfiring, unbalanced power contributions, and mechanical problems with an engine, such as a bent connecting rod or burnt valve. Many fault conditions produce unique patterns of velocity changes in the crankshaft. For example, low compression due to a mechanical fault will fail to slow the crankshaft down on compression stroke in comparison to a good cylinder. The crank position when deceleration occurs will also be delayed. Weak injectors can be identified by measuring how much correction the ECM needs to make to injector pulse width by controlling the quantity of fuel each injector delivers. Crankshaft acceleration data during power stroke is used to calculate the correction factor. On a Detroit Diesel DD series engine, the Idle Speed Compensation number derived during a cylinder balance diagnostic routine indicates how much correction to the injector pulse-width signal is required to produce the same crankshaft acceleration from each cylinder.

To perform a cylinder balance test, follow the steps in SKILL DRILL 16-2.

▶ Injection Timing

For efficient combustion, clean emissions, and good engine performance, precisely timed injection events are critical. Efficient fuel systems must have the capability to change the point when fuel is injected based on a variety of engine-operating conditions and control algorithms.

Variables Affecting Timing

Operating and combustion conditions cause significant changes to the fuel burn rate and the time available for combustion. Temperature variables such as fuel, intake air, coolant, and oil affect combustion events, as do many other factors such as boost pressure, EGR rates, engine load, and speed.

To understand the factors influencing injection timing, consider that in most engines, peak cylinder pressure should occur approximately 10–15 degrees of crankshaft rotation after top dead cylinder (TDC) FIGURE 16-25. But before the piston can be pushed downward in its bore by combustion pressure, there is an ignition delay and a short uncontrolled combustion period that takes place before peak cylinder pressures occur. Several variables influence how long each of these periods are. Take for example the ignition delay period. This is the time period between the injection of fuel and its actual point of ignition. There is a time lag, expressed in degrees of crank rotation, for this period. Fuel must be injected, distributed, atomized, absorb heat, vaporize, mix with air in the correct proportions, and reach adequate temperature before it ignites. These

---

SKILL DRILL 16-2 Performing a Cylinder Balance Test

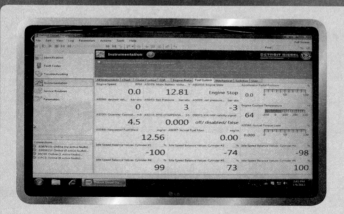

3 Navigate to the Instrumentation menu and then to the Fuel System tab.

4 Observe and record the Idle Speed Balance Values for each cylinder while the engine is at idle.

5 Analyze the results. The MCM will apply a positive or negative correction factor to the length of the injector pulse width. A positive value means more fuel is injected to compensate for low cylinder pressure. A negative value indicates a shortened pulse-width signal is used to remove some fuel from the cylinder. A 100% change means the MCM cannot add or remove any fuel and the cylinder contribution will not be the same as other cylinders. Generally, any value over 70% indicates a problem with the cylinder. These problems range from the need for a valve adjustment to defects in the injector, high-pressure fuel system, or a base engine mechanical condition.

1 Start and run the engine until it reaches operating temperature. Place the transmission in neutral and apply the parking brakes.

2 Connect DDDL software to the vehicle data link connector.

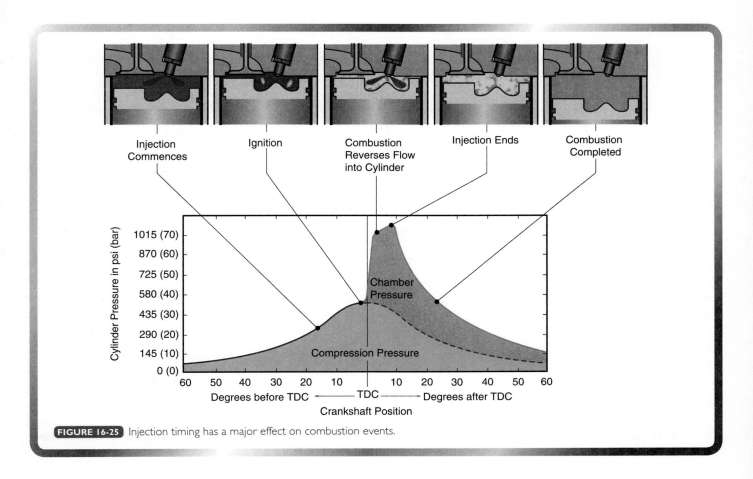

Injection Commences   Ignition   Combustion Reverses Flow into Cylinder   Injection Ends   Combustion Completed

Chamber Pressure

Compression Pressure

Degrees before TDC ←———— TDC ————→ Degrees after TDC

Crankshaft Position

FIGURE 16-25 Injection timing has a major effect on combustion events.

processes take time and are affected by factors such as pre-ignition temperatures in the cylinder, fuel droplet sizing, fuel properties, combustion chamber turbulence, EGR gas in the cylinders, and other factors. Because the ignition delay period is variable, changes to injection timing should be made to make sure cylinder pressures peak at the optimal crank position just after TDC. Without this, engine performance and emissions will be affected.

Engine Load and Injection Timing

The two most important factors influencing burn rate are cylinder pressure and temperature. Temperature and pressure affect the speed of any chemical reaction, including combustion. Higher pressure and temperatures tend to speed up reactions because molecules have more energy and are packed closer together. These conditions increase the likelihood of combustion reactions and speed of chain reactions. In the combustion chamber, the addition of fuel causes temperatures and pressures to rise proportionally to the quantity of fuel burned. This means the addition of fuel shortens combustion time. Naturally, the opposite is true—when small amounts of fuel are injected, combustion times are proportionally longer. Under load, more fuel is injected, and less fuel is injected when light loads or no loads are applied. To adjust for the variation in combustion time as engine load changes, the fuel system must have the capability to adjust injection timing based on fuel delivery quantities. When large quantities of fuel are injected, leaving initial timing unchanged would cause peak cylinder pressures to be reached sooner or even quite a few degrees before TDC. Similarly, under light load operation, when fuel burns slower, peak cylinder pressure occurs long after the optimal crank position. So, under load, fuel systems should retard the injection timing **FIGURE 16-26**. Retarding means fuel is injected later. Conversely, smaller quantities of injected fuel require advancing injection timing. Advancing injection timing means fuel is injected earlier **FIGURE 16-27**.

▶ TECHNICIAN TIP

High temperature and pressure accelerate chemical reaction of combustion. More fuel injected into a cylinder means higher temperature and pressure leading to shorter combustion times. Under load, higher cylinder pressures and temperatures cause fuel to burn more completely and only a "heat haze" or "shimmer" of hot air should be observed from an engine exhaust system. Observing any smoke from an engine, even without an exhaust aftertreatment, means the engine has a defect.

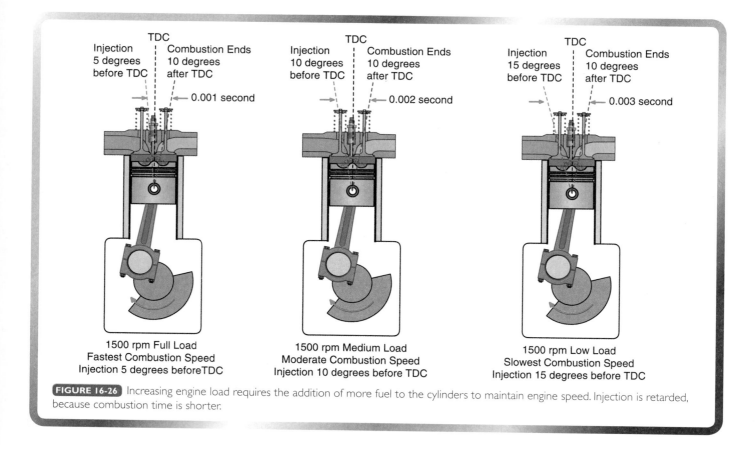

FIGURE 16-26 Increasing engine load requires the addition of more fuel to the cylinders to maintain engine speed. Injection is retarded, because combustion time is shorter.

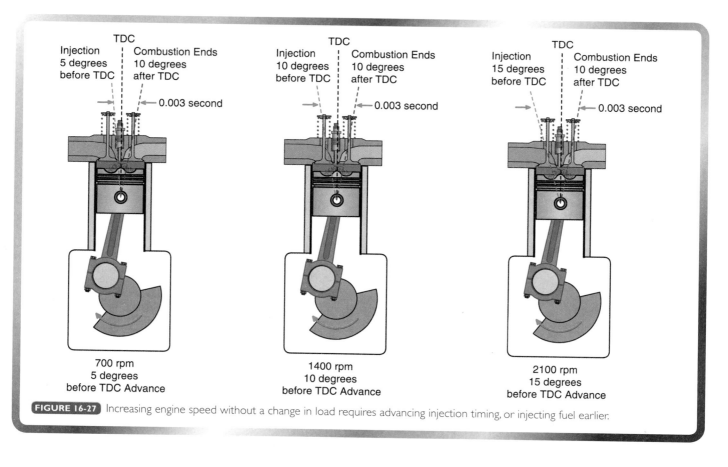

FIGURE 16-27 Increasing engine speed without a change in load requires advancing injection timing, or injecting fuel earlier.

Engine Speed and Injection Timing

As the engine speeds up, injection and combustion events do not speed up proportionally. So, while the crankshaft may be turning through more degrees of rotation per second, combustion and injection events cannot be completed as quickly because they require a fixed amount of time. To enable efficient combustion, an injection system needs the ability to change injection timing in response to engine speed changes.

To understand this, consider that the best engine efficiency is achieved when the peak cylinder pressures produce 10–15 degrees after TDC. If the time required for the combustion process stays the same, taking, for example, at 0.003 second, the injection of fuel should be timed to produce peak cylinder pressures just after TDC. At idle speed, the injection may require 15 degrees of crank rotation to finish ignition delay and burn to produce peak pressure. However, as the engine speed increases, the number of degrees of crank rotation per second is much greater. So, the crank turns farther, and the piston moves higher in one second at higher engine speed than at idle. To produce the peak cylinder pressure after TDC in this scenario, the injection needs to take place earlier, or advance. How much earlier for injection depends on the amount of time it takes for the fuel to burn.

Consider this example: Burn time is expressed in degrees of crankshaft rotation. The burn time would be subtracted from 10 degrees after TDC. So, if the fuel takes 0.003 second to burn and that translates into 15 degrees of crankshaft rotation, then injection should take place 5 degrees before TDC. If the engine turned faster, the number of degrees of crankshaft rotation would be greater per second, and the timing should move closer to TDC.

Example 1

Burn time of 0.003 second = 15 degrees of crankshaft rotation at idle 650 rpm

10 degrees after TDC − 15 degrees of burn time = injection beginning at 5 degrees before TDC

Example 2

Burn time of 0.003 second = 30 degrees of crankshaft rotation at 1300 rpm

10 degrees after TDC − 30 degrees of burn time = injection beginning at 20 degrees before TDC

When the engine speeds up with no change in load or injection quantity, timing is advanced. Similarly, when the engine slows down, timing is retarded.

Injection Timing and Cold Starting

Cold cylinder components and low ambient temperatures create exceptional operating conditions that require adjustments to injection timing. The primary problem of cold conditions is that they cause a longer ignition delay period. Cylinder pre-ignition temperatures are lower, so fuel requires more time to absorb sufficient heat to initiate combustion. The ignition delay causes a more pronounced knocking sound in the engine and affects combustion quality. Also, cold engine parts absorb compression

heat near TDC too. When running, injection timing is advanced to compensate for a longer ignition delay period caused by cold temperatures FIGURE 16-28.

When the engine is *running*, the time lag between injection and actual ignition can be so long as to cause black smoke. This is due to prolonged ignition delay, which shortens the total time available for combustion. Shorter combustion time and lower cylinder pressure produce more PM, CO, and HC emissions.

During *cranking*, initiating combustion is more difficult, because insufficient fuel vapor is produced inside cold cylinders. Heat content in the cylinders is low, and fuel tends to condense onto cold cylinder component surfaces; poor vaporization results. To minimize the effects of these conditions, two separate strategies are often used. Injection timing is retarded only when cranking and timing is advanced farther than normal during cold running conditions FIGURE 16-29.

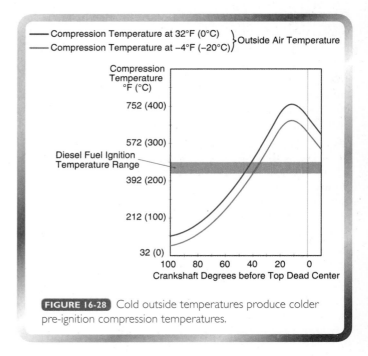

FIGURE 16-28 Cold outside temperatures produce colder pre-ignition compression temperatures.

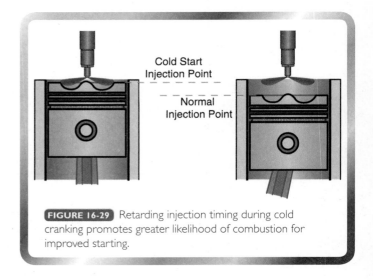

FIGURE 16-29 Retarding injection timing during cold cranking promotes greater likelihood of combustion for improved starting.

The benefit of retarding injection timing during cold cranking is that it allows for a longer amount of time for the piston to rise in the cylinder and generate increased pre-ignition temperatures. When fuel is finally injected, the cylinder is hotter and improved vaporization of fuel occurs. Thus, there is a greater likelihood of initiating combustion and starting the engine.

Once the engine starts, cold temperatures and cylinder components still demand additional time for ignition to occur after injection. It is necessary to advance the timing to prevent white smoke from misfiring and black smoke from incomplete combustion. Built into fuel timing maps—or the cold start mechanisms of mechanical systems—are the provision for advancing timing.

Injection Timing and Emissions

Diesel engine emissions and performance characteristics are significantly impacted by changes to injection timing **TABLE 16-1**. Slightly advancing the start of injection may reduce smoke, increase power, and reduce fuel consumption, however, it typically results in higher NO_x emissions **FIGURE 16-30**. (In fact, optimal timing for emissions negatively impacts fuel economy in North American engines.) The increase in NO_x emissions is due to the higher cylinder pressures and combustion temperatures produced when combustion is closer to TDC rather than 10–15 degrees after TDC. Because combustion chamber volume is smaller nearer TDC, further increased pressures and temperature take place above the threshold where NO_x is formed. Conversely, retarded timing increases the production of particulate and hydrocarbon emissions because combustion time is shortened.

To minimize both NO_x and particulate production, manufacturers aim for finer atomization of fuel that also shortens

ignition delay time. Timing can be retarded while, at the same time, the combustion process is more resistant to particulate formation. On electronically controlled engines, timing is still drastically retarded compared with older mechanically governed engines. Today, injection timing may occur at TDC or just a few

TABLE 16-1: Influence of Injection Timing on Combustion Events

Engine Parameter	Change to Injection Timing	
	Retarded	Advanced
Cylinder Pressure	Lowered	Raised
Oxides of Nitrogen (NO_x)	Reduced	Increased
Particulate Matter (PM) Peak Torque	Decreases	Increases
Particulate Matter (PM) Rated Speed	Increases	Decreases
Particulate Matter (PM) (low speed and load)	Increases	Decreases
Hydrocarbons (HC)	Increases	Decreases
Fuel Consumption (BSFC)	Increases	Decreases
Intake Manifold Boost Pressure	Increases	Decreases
Exhaust Temperature	Increases	Decreases
Starting	Easier	Harder
Coolant Temperature (heat rejection)	Increases	Decreases
Combustion Noise	Decreases	Increases

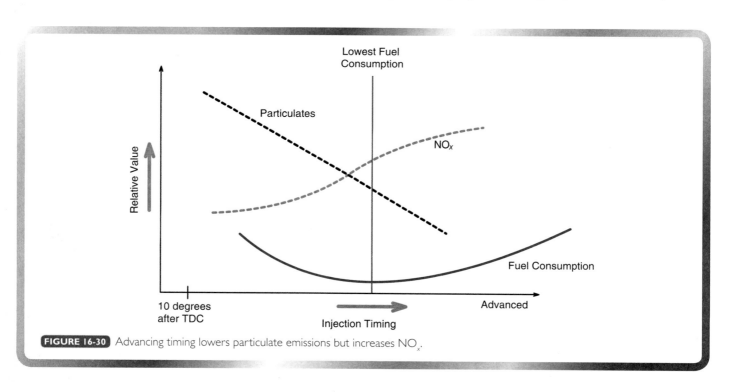

FIGURE 16-30 Advancing timing lowers particulate emissions but increases NO_x.

degrees before TDC, compared to the 15–20 degree range of earlier pre-emission standard engines. The retarded timing produces a gentler rise in cylinder pressure and lower peak cylinder pressures near TDC, which minimizes NO_x formation.

On mechanical systems injection, timing needs to be set to within one half degree of the manufacturer's specifications for correct emission control **FIGURE 16-31**. Electronic engines control injection timing variations to less than 0.1 degree of precision.

Injection Timing and OBD

Injection timing has always had a significant impact on emissions; injection timing is a part of the fuel system monitor on HD-OBD engines. A variety of strategies are used to determine the precise beginning of injection to ensure it coincides with expected values. Beginning in 2013, some engines have begun to use cylinder-pressure sensors to measure the rise in combustion pressure **FIGURE 16-32**. Knowing the cylinder pressure for every degree of crank rotation can provide feedback to the ECM, enabling it to change injection timing and rate to minimize emissions and increase engine efficiency. Other engines analyze electrical waveforms from the injector that change when control valves open and close. Most engines use data from the crank position sensor to detect the point when crankshaft acceleration begins due to a combustion event.

▶ Fuel Injection Rate Control

In modern fuel injection systems, the **injection rate** means the quantity of fuel injected per degree of crank angle rotation. Injection rate control is the most significant advancement of contemporary injection technology because it affects fuel consumption, exhaust emissions performance, and combustion

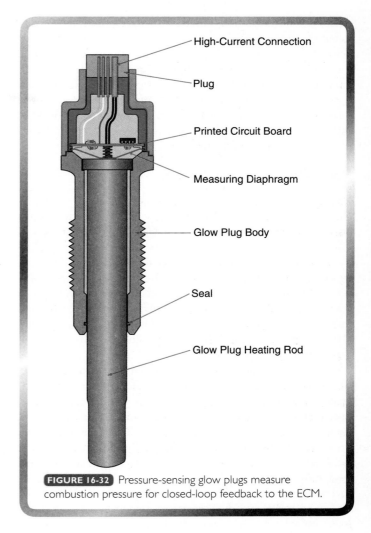

FIGURE 16-32 Pressure-sensing glow plugs measure combustion pressure for closed-loop feedback to the ECM.

- High-Current Connection
- Plug
- Printed Circuit Board
- Measuring Diaphragm
- Glow Plug Body
- Seal
- Glow Plug Heating Rod

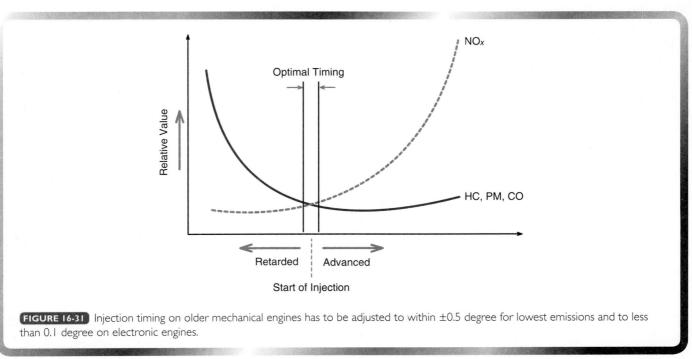

FIGURE 16-31 Injection timing on older mechanical engines has to be adjusted to within ±0.5 degree for lowest emissions and to less than 0.1 degree on electronic engines.

noise. When the ECM accounts for changes in fuel density due to temperature changes, injection rate is reported as milligrams per stroke. When referencing rate control of the injection system, the most meaningful definition is the quantity of fuel injected per degree of crank angle rotation. Rate control is different from fuel rate, which refers to fuel consumption expressed as the quantity of fuel burned per hour. Injection rate is reported in milliseconds or degrees of crankshaft rotation compared with the delivery volume of the injection event.

Rate-Shaped Injection

Rate-shaped injection refers to the shape of the injection discharge curve that is enabled through multiple injection events during a single combustion cycle **FIGURE 16-33**. The newest injection systems can provide several rate discharge profiles by varying injection pressures and the number of injection events. Manufacturers of common rail systems can currently provide as many as seven separate injection events during one combustion cycle. These events can include a post-combustion injection event that is used to dose the diesel particulate filter (DPF) or lean NO_x trap (LNT)—also called NO_x adsorber catalyst (NAC)—for regeneration.

To keep fuel consumption and soot emissions low, the injection quantity should be delivered as quickly as possible. This leads to a rapid build-up in cylinder pressure and a longer, harder push on the piston after TDC. Although combustion may be efficient and large quantities of power derived from gas expansion, greater NO_x emissions and noise are produced. To achieve lower noise and NO_x emissions, it is best to inject fuel slowly at the beginning of injection. After each piston travels past TDC, the fuel rate should rise and then abruptly stop. This rate of discharge leads to a relatively slow increase in combustion pressure and lower noise levels. The lower cylinder pressure and temperature produced from this injection rate minimizes NO_x formation.

Mechanical Rate Shaping

Earlier, mechanically governed fuel systems relied on throttle pintle injector nozzles to achieve rate shaping **FIGURE 16-34**. These nozzles generate a spray pattern that produces a gradually rising rate discharge curve. This discharge shape is achieved using a stepped type nozzle valve. When the nozzle valve begins to lift, a small narrow, low-volume spray jet is injected first into the combustion chamber. As the needle valve lifts higher because of increasing injection volume, more fuel is allowed out of the nozzle because the nozzle valve diameter narrows. At this point, the spray pattern changes into a wider, higher-volume cone pattern. Substantial noise reduction takes place using these nozzles along with improved emissions. A unique nozzle-valve shape is also used in the latest electronically controlled injectors to improve rate shaping.

Bosch and its licensees use a double spring nozzle to control the discharge rate. Each spring is calibrated to lift at a different level of fuel pressure. The first spring lifts, sprays fuel, drops injection line pressure, and seats again during the initial stage of injection. A control piston assists this process. As the injection volume increases for the remainder of the injection cycle, increased fuel volume and pressure to the nozzle is needed to lift both springs to supply a larger main injection. This injector operation is illustrated in the Hydraulic Nozzles chapter.

HEUI injectors built after 1996 utilize a groove machined into the plunger to pressurize fuel for injection. When fuel pressurization begins, the plunger travels downward and then uncovers a port that spills pressurized fuel. This momentarily stops fuel delivery. As the fuel plunger continues to move downward, the spill port is closed again and the main injection resumes. This feature is called pilot injection and is part of a rate shaping strategy. Variable pressurization of oil to the injectors, which supplies the force to operate the injector, also varies the injection rate. Gen II HEUIs produce three injection events using electrical signals applied to two solenoids rather than using mechanical control of the injection. This feature is illustrated in further detail in the Hydraulically Actuated Electronic Unit Injector Systems chapter.

Pilot Injection

Pilot or split-shot injection is another feature of rate shaping that is one of the most effective strategies for minimizing NO_x and noise emissions while optimizing engine performance. Like a pilot light in a gas appliance or furnace, this rate-shaping strategy delivers a small quantity of fuel to the combustion chamber 8–10 degrees before the main injection. Because the cylinder is

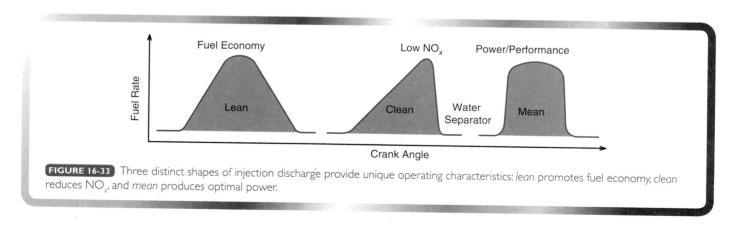

FIGURE 16-33 Three distinct shapes of injection discharge provide unique operating characteristics: *lean* promotes fuel economy, *clean* reduces NO_x, and *mean* produces optimal power.

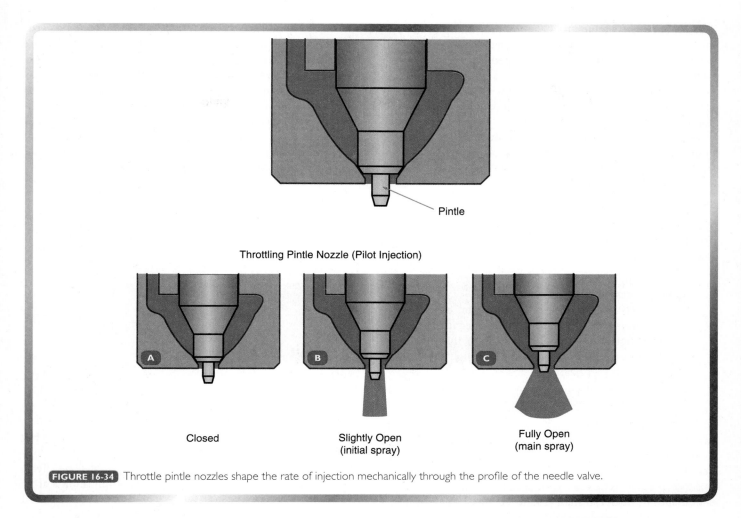

FIGURE 16-34 Throttle pintle nozzles shape the rate of injection mechanically through the profile of the needle valve.

warmed-up through a pre-injection of fuel, fuel injected during the larger main injection event is quickly ignited. Ignition delay is minimized and little combustion noise is produced. This approach to fueling produces exceptionally quiet engine operation such that the traditional diesel clatter is gone and the noise level is comparable to that of gasoline-powered vehicles. Because fuel is ignited more quickly using pilot injection, more time is available for combustion. The result is injection timing that can be retarded to lower NO_x emissions without a penalty to power or fuel economy. The most recent injection systems use two rather than a single pilot injection event for even greater improvements to combustion quality.

Post-Combustion Injections

Research proves that an injection after the main combustion event reduces the production of soot inside the cylinder **FIGURE 16-35**. The post–main injection event taking place shortly after the main injection adds additional heat and pressure to the power stroke that, in turn, consumes the carbon that forms soot.

The number and pressure of injection events vary with speed and load. At lower speeds, there is more time available for a couple of pilot injection events that are not possible to use at high-speed heavy load where injection timing is already

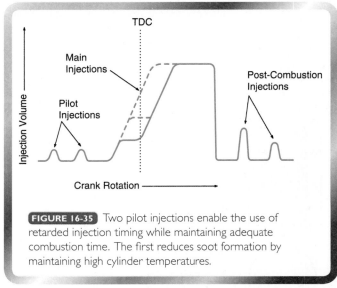

FIGURE 16-35 Two pilot injections enable the use of retarded injection timing while maintaining adequate combustion time. The first reduces soot formation by maintaining high cylinder temperatures.

retarded. High cylinder pressures and temperatures at high speed reduce the need for post–main combustion events.

Diesel particulate traps require supplemental heating to burn away trapped soot. Common rail fuel systems can supply an additional injection event during the exhaust stroke.

The HC in turn enables flameless combustion for supplemental heating of the exhaust oxidation catalyst. Heat in this catalyst is used to combust soot trapped in the downstream particulate filter.

NO_x adsorbers and lean NO_x traps require depletion of oxygen from the exhaust system and supplemental heating to break down stored NO_x emissions. When signaled by the engine or exhaust aftertreatment controller, additional fuel is injected in the post-combustion period in addition to other regeneration strategies.

▶ Fuel Pressurization

Why diesel engines need highly pressurize fuel has already been noted. High injection **pressurization** is necessary for the following reasons:

- Diesel engines compress dense air mass that requires higher pressure to penetrate with fuel.
- The brief time available for combustion events taking place near TDC requires rapid execution of pre-combustion events, such as **distribution**, that is, the mixing of fuel and air in the cylinders through atomization, mixing, and vaporization.
- Improved atomization requires higher pressurization for improved emissions and performance.

Traditional fuel systems have relied on some version of the camshaft-and-plunger system to pressurize fuel **FIGURE 16-36**. While this configuration worked well for decades, it has a number of drawbacks. The most significant is that the cam–plunger injection pressure is tied to engine speed. This means that at low engine speeds, when camshaft velocity and injection volume are low, only low fuel pressurization is possible. If an engine needs to rapidly accelerate, large injection quantities of high-pressure injection pressure are not available. Under other conditions, high engine speed and low injection quantities distribute fuel too far and fast in the combustion chamber to provide the best combustion conditions. To meet emission standards while optimizing engine performance, injection systems for on-highway use are now electronically controlled with variable injection pressure capabilities and with maximum injection pressure reached independent of engine speed **FIGURE 16-37**.

Safety Tip

Fuel pressurized to thousands of pounds per square inch (bar) can easily penetrate skin, causing bodily harm, blood poisoning, and even death. When checking for leaks from a high-pressure fuel system, use a small piece of cardboard or paper instead of a hand to detect the location of a leak.

▶ Fuel Atomization

As discussed earlier in the chapter, atomization refers to the breaking up of liquid fuel into smaller, finer liquid droplets. Atomization must take place in order to vaporize and ignite fuel. When liquid fuel leaves the nozzle tip, it breaks up into smaller droplets after encountering friction with air. Breaking the fuel into smaller droplets enhances the fuels ability to absorb heat, convert to vapor, and mix with air. Fuel droplet size affects combustion qualities, which makes proper atomization a critical injection system function. Just as a fire is kindled with small pieces of wood, efficient combustion requires exceedingly fine particles of fuel. Finer atomization means fuel ignites sooner, burns faster, and burns more completely.

This is why worn or damaged injector nozzles can result in such poor performance and emissions **FIGURE 16-38**.

The ignition delay period is also shortened, leading to lower levels of combustion noise. Better atomization promotes a more complete combustion of fuel while producing lower levels of particulate emissions and improving fuel economy. Finer atomization also means the air–fuel mixture is better able to tolerate the use of recirculated exhaust gas.

Fuel Droplet Size and PM Emissions

Vapor forms around the fuel droplet as it absorbs heat from the combustion chamber. This means fuel burns from the outside to inside. A smaller fuel droplet size produces faster conversion of liquid to vapor that, in turn, results in shorter ignition delay times and longer combustion time. To achieve the lowest particulate emissions, the finest atomization ensures that each droplet makes adequate contact with air for complete combustion. Fine droplets also allow the use of retarded injection timing for low NO_x production. The smallest droplets are produced using smaller and more numerous injector orifices along with high pressurization.

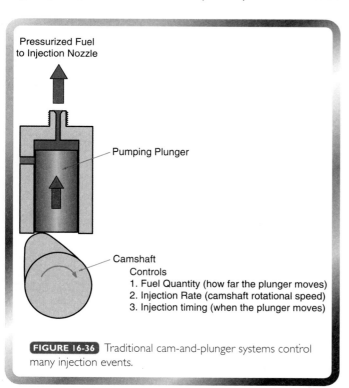

FIGURE 16-36 Traditional cam-and-plunger systems control many injection events.

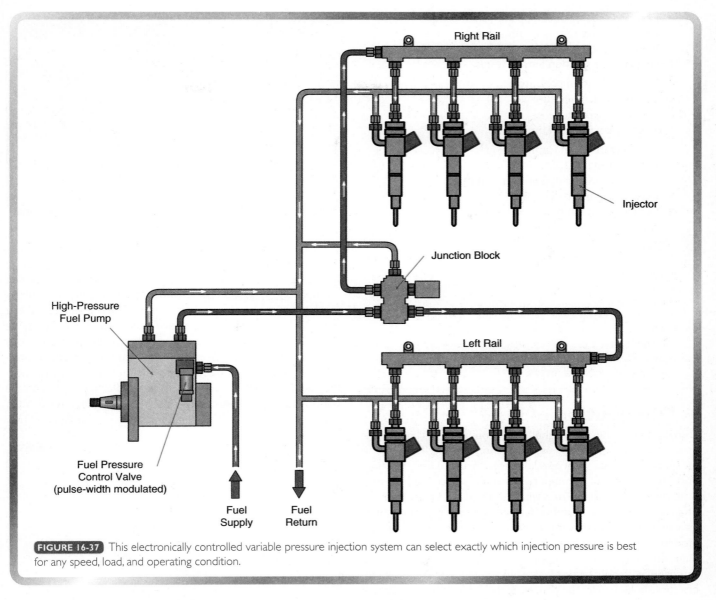

FIGURE 16-37 This electronically controlled variable pressure injection system can select exactly which injection pressure is best for any speed, load, and operating condition.

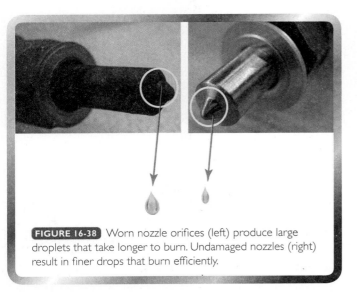

FIGURE 16-38 Worn nozzle orifices (left) produce large droplets that take longer to burn. Undamaged nozzles (right) result in finer drops that burn efficiently.

Particulate Formation

Ideally, only a heat wave should be observed from the exhaust pipe of a diesel engine when under load. When black or grey exhaust smoke is present, it is because of excessive particulate emissions. While they are the most common emission-related problem associated with diesel engines—and for that reason visible during on-highway operation—they also indicate a problem with engine operation.

Excessive particulate emissions are produced typically under the following conditions with their respective causes:

1. Large fuel droplet size
   - Worn nozzles and spray holes
   - Low injection pressures
   - Nozzle dribble
2. Poor mixing of air and fuel
   - Inadequate combustion turbulences
   - Restricted airflow

- Excessive fueling of combustion chamber
- Incorrect valve timing or adjustment
- Poor distribution of fuel in chamber
3. Inadequate pre-ignition temperatures
  - Low compression pressures
  - Low intake temperatures
  - Excessive ignition delay
4. Inadequate combustion time
  - Incorrect injection timing
  - Excessive engine speed
  - Incorrect valve timing or injection timing
  - Excessive ignition delay time
  - Cold ambient temperatures

> ### TECHNICIAN TIP
>
> Not all diesel smoke means engine trouble. Some older engines lack exhaust aftertreatment devices. During acceleration or when shifting gears, these engines momentarily produce a puff of smoke and, within a few seconds, produce a clear exhaust. Anything more than this indicates some engine fault. Law enforcement agencies often use standards of no more than 15 seconds of visible emissions during 1 minute of operation to assess emission-related penalties.

▶ Distribution of Fuel

Distribution of fuel throughout the combustion chamber is another function of high-pressure injection systems. The angle of the spray holes, number of nozzle orifices, their size, and injection pressure are some of the important variables affecting how fuel is distributed in order to mix with turbulent air. Larger, heavier droplets penetrate a chamber farther and faster because they have more mass, but they do not burn as well as smaller droplets. Modern diesel engines typically feature more injector spray holes than older engines—with as many as 13 holes in new engines, compared with only four or five in older engines. Even the length of a spray hole changes the velocity of fuel leaving the injector tip. Longer holes push fuel at a higher velocity than shorter holes. The angle of the spray holes are also important and must match the shape of the combustion bowl to prevent fuel from simply hitting the piston bowl. In this situation, fuel simply does not burn (see the Symmetrical Fuel Distribution section) **FIGURE 16-39**.

Problems with fuel distribution can have a significant impact on combustion quality. For example, in low-emission, high-speed engines, a slow start or ending of the injection period affects atomization of both the initial and final portions of the injected fuel. If fuel delivery is not stopped abruptly, the drop of injection pressures at the nozzle tip creates larger diameter spray droplets. The effect is poor atomization and penetration of fuel into the combustion chamber causing high emissions and poor combustion quality. Dribbling fuel due to low pressurization also wastes fuel. For this reason, the design of any fuel system incorporates features to ensure a sharp stop and beginning of injection that prevents lag (see the Injection Lag section) **FIGURE 16-40**. To properly distribute fuel, the beginning and ending of injection pressure must be consistent from beginning to end.

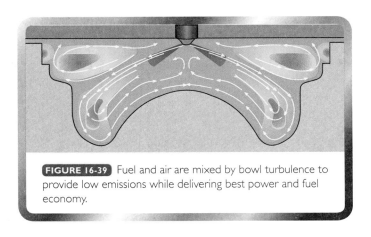

FIGURE 16-39 Fuel and air are mixed by bowl turbulence to provide low emissions while delivering best power and fuel economy.

Fuel systems incorporate design features to ensure abrupt beginning and ending of injection. The use of <u>delivery valves</u> in high-pressure lines connecting pumps and nozzles is one example **FIGURE 16-41**. These valves operate as one-way checks to allow fuel to remain at relatively moderate pressure in the fuel injection lines, typically around 800 psi (55 bar) when the engine is running. The design of the valves ensures fuel pressure drops far enough below nozzle opening pressure to prevent secondary injections caused by reflecting fuel pulsations in the injector line. These pulses occur when the needle valve in the nozzle closes, causing a pressure wave. The hammer sound heard when shutting off a water faucet in a house creates a similar condition

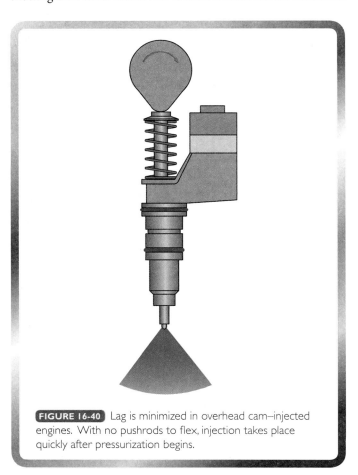

FIGURE 16-40 Lag is minimized in overhead cam–injected engines. With no pushrods to flex, injection takes place quickly after pressurization begins.

FIGURE 16-41 A delivery valve minimizes the back-flow of fuel into an injection system in order to maintain line pressure between injections.

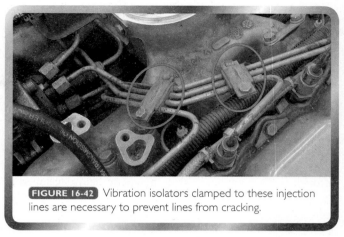

FIGURE 16-42 Vibration isolators clamped to these injection lines are necessary to prevent lines from cracking.

FIGURE 16-43 Vibration isolators clamped to these common rail fuel lines are necessary to prevent lines from cracking. Continuous expansion and contraction is caused by high-pressure injection pulsations.

found in the injection line when the needle valve closes. Delivery valves also prevent the nozzle from dribbling fuel.

Nozzles are designed to have higher pressure to lift the needle valve than is required to close the valve. So, whenever pressure begins to drop in the fuel line, the needle valve closes until injection pressure is increased high enough to reopen the valve.

Injection Lag

Injection lag describes the time delay that occurs between the start of fuel pressurization and the moment when injection actually occurs. In electronic systems, lag refers to the time between the time an injector is energized until the point when it begins to deliver fuel for the injection event. There is a substantial time lag unintentionally built into some injection systems. Injection lag influences the accuracy of injection timing controls and the ability of the fuel system to achieve an abrupt beginning and ending of injection.

A number of conditions cause lag, and good fuel system design minimizes those factors. For example, while fluids are not considered compressible, time is required to transmit the pressure wave from the pumping element to an injector nozzle. The wave does travel fast—approximately 4500 feet (1372 meters) per second—but it can make slight changes to timing at high-speed operation.

A more significant factor causing lag is the swelling of injection lines. In spite of lines having thick steel walls, lines do swell when pressurized fuel travels through them. Enough expansion and contraction of the lines can crack them if they are not properly secured with vibration-absorbing insulators **FIGURE 16-42** and **FIGURE 16-43**. Fuel volume intended for delivery is lost through swelling line walls. For this reason, high-pressure fuel lines are made not only thick but also the same length and diameter **FIGURE 16-44**. This minimizes variations to delivery quantities and injection timing.

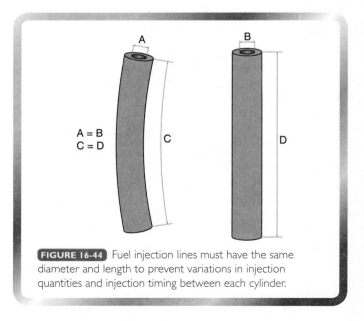

FIGURE 16-44 Fuel injection lines must have the same diameter and length to prevent variations in injection quantities and injection timing between each cylinder.

Unit injectors, which have no lines between the pressurization stage and the nozzle, have the least amount of lag caused by swelling injection lines because they have none. However, if unit injectors are actuated using camshaft-driven push rods, the flexion of the rods during injection causes lag.

One major source of injection lag is injectors that use magnetic actuators. A phenomenon, called reactive inductance or reactive resistance, causes a magnetic field to build up relatively slowly in the injector's electrical solenoid. The reactive inductance takes place because an opposing electrical current is induced in any coil of wire when an electrical current flows through it. This happens as the magnetic field developed by the initial inflow of current cuts across other conductors in the solenoid's windings and induces current flow in them. The two sources of current—initial and induced—travel in opposite directions, which produces a high initial resistance in the solenoid. Not only is the magnetic field slow to build up and open the injector's control valve, but the field also takes time to collapse and close the control valve in the injector. An injector's slow response means a large conventional electromagnetic actuator is capable of only one injection event in a combustion cycle **FIGURE 16-45** . Piezoelectric actuators, which have no magnetic fields, are replacing magnetic actuators in newer high-speed diesels.

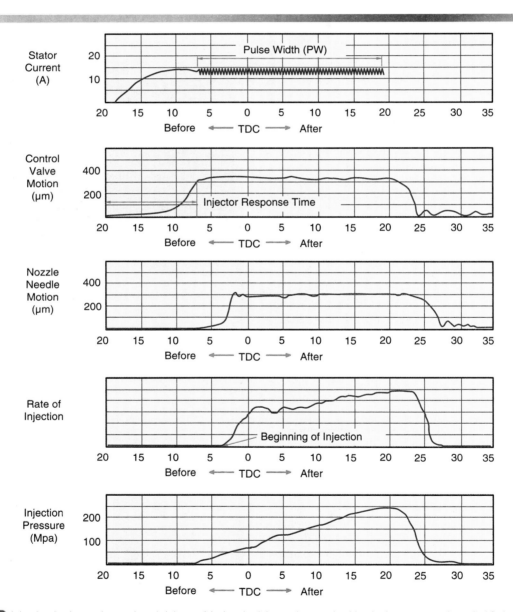

FIGURE 16-45 Injection lag in an electronic unit injector. Notice the injector is energized beginning at approximately 18 degrees before TDC. Actual injection takes place at approximately 3 degrees. Lag time is close to 15 degrees of crank rotation due to electrical and hydraulic characteristics of the injector.

Other factors contributing to injection lag include:

- The upward movement of the delivery valve in injection pumps, which causes fuel intended for delivery to the combustion chamber to be absorbed through displacement of the delivery valve.
- The upward movement of the needle valve in the nozzle, which causes the moving needle valve to consume some of the fuel intended for injection **FIGURE 16-46**.

Symmetrical Fuel Distribution

Fuel must penetrate the combustion chamber air mass evenly in all directions to mix correctly with air. Without even distribution, proper mixture formation cannot take place, resulting in areas of rich and lean air–fuel ratios and increased emissions.

To distribute fuel for optimal mixture preparation, the combustion chamber design and fuel system components must be correctly matched. Nozzle design, nozzle orifice sizing, combustion chamber turbulence, and specified fuel pressurization are some of the more significant factors affecting fuel distribution and mixture formation. Nozzles can also wear and be impaired given the hours of operation or distance travelled. Plugged nozzles cause uneven distribution patterns resulting in performance and emission problems.

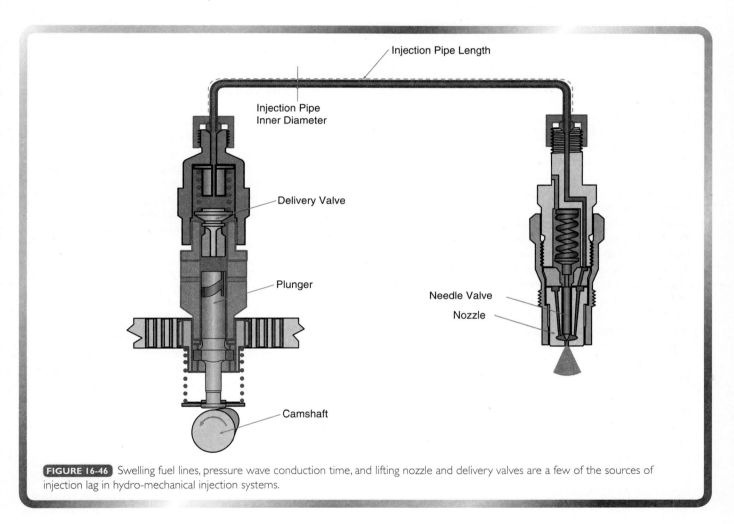

FIGURE 16-46 Swelling fuel lines, pressure wave conduction time, and lifting nozzle and delivery valves are a few of the sources of injection lag in hydro-mechanical injection systems.

Wrap-Up

Ready for Review

- Diesel engine fuel systems have two main divisions: the low-pressure transfer system, which stores and supplies fuel for the injection system, and the high-pressure injection system, which delivers fuel to the combustion chambers.
- Efficient diesel engine operation relies on the injection of a precise quantity of fuel, injected at high pressure, at the correct time, into the combustion chamber.
- High-pressure injection system operation is better understood by examining functions common to all injection systems.
- High pressurization of fuel is necessary for several reasons: fuel must have sufficient pressure to penetrate the dense combustion chamber air mass; at high rotational speeds, only a short amount of time is available for the injection of fuel; and high pressure is necessary to break up the liquid fuel into a fine mist.
- All high-pressure injection systems perform the following tasks: meter the correct quantity of fuel for injection, time the injection of fuel, control the rate of fuel delivery, atomize the fuel, and distribute the fuel throughout the combustion chamber.
- Diesel engines meter only fuel to control engine speed and torque. Metering is the process of measuring and delivering the correct quantity of fuel required for each cylinder for various speed and load conditions of the engine.
- To vary vehicle speed and power output, pressure in the cylinders must increase or decrease by changing the amount of fuel injected and burned. Increasing combustion pressure inside the cylinders increases engine torque output.
- All diesel engines use governors to regulate the quantity of fuel injected into the cylinders; a diesel governor equivalent in a gasoline or Otto cycle engine is the throttle plate controlled by a driver.
- Even very small changes to the quantities of fuel injected at idle produce rough running engines and unstable engine speed; to minimize problems associated with uneven cylinder power contribution, most new electronically controlled engines use idle adaptation to make cylinder pressures consistent.
- Consistent combustion pressures from all cylinders are necessary to achieve low engine emissions; emission reduction strategies achieve consistent results when they are applied the same way to all cylinders operating with identical pressure.
- To correct individual variations in flow rates, many newer injectors are assigned calibration codes to compensate for manufacturing tolerances to injector flow rates.
- For efficient combustion, clean emissions, and good engine performance, precisely timed injection events are critical; efficient fuel systems must have the capability to change the point when fuel is injected based on a variety of engine-operating conditions and control algorithms.
- The factors that influence injection timing include pre-ignition temperatures in the cylinder, fuel droplet size, combustion chamber turbulence, fuel quality, and more.
- To adjust for the variation in combustion time when an engine load or speed changes, the fuel system must have capability to change injection timing. When an engine load increases, injection timing is retarded. Speeding up an engine with no change in load requires advancing injection timing.
- Injection timing is a function of both speed and load changes. Both are opposing factors with increasing loads requiring a retarding of timing and speeding-up and engine-advancing timing.
- Cold cylinder components and low ambient temperatures create exceptional operating conditions that require adjustments to injection timing.
- Diesel engine emission characteristics are significantly impacted by changes to injection timing; for example, slightly advancing the start of injection may reduce smoke, increase power, and reduce fuel consumption, but it typically results in higher NO_x emissions.
- Injection timing is a part of the fuel system monitor on HD-OBD engines; a variety of strategies are used to determine the precise beginning of injection to ensure it coincides with expected values.
- Injection rate control is the most significant advancement of contemporary injection technology because it effects fuel consumption, exhaust emissions performance, and combustion noise.
- The shape of the injection discharge curve can be optimized for fuel economy, the low NO_x formation, and power. A unique injection rate shape is needed for each speed and load condition.
- Earlier, mechanically governed fuel systems use throttle pintle injector nozzles that generate a spray pattern that provided a gradually rising rate discharge curve.
- Pilot or split-shot injection is another method of rate shaping; it is one of the most effective strategies for minimizing NO_x and noise emissions while optimizing engine performance.
- An injection event after the main combustion event reduces the production of soot inside the cylinder by adding additional heat and pressure to the power stroke, which, in turn, consumes soot.
- To meet emissions standards while optimizing engine performance, electronically controlled, variable injection pressure independent of engine speed is used in all current on-highway engines.
- Atomization, or breaking fuel into smaller droplets, enhances the fuel's ability to absorb heat, convert to vapor, and mix with air.
- To achieve the lowest formation of particulate emissions, the finest atomization is required to ensure that each droplet makes adequate contact with air for faster and more complete combustion.
- To properly distribute fuel, the injection pressure must be consistent from beginning to end; fuel systems incorporate design features to ensure abrupt beginning and ending of injection.
- Injection lag is the time delay that may occur between the start of fuel pressurization and the moment when injection

actually occurs; this influences the ability of the fuel system to achieve an abrupt beginning and ending of injection.

▸ To distribute fuel for optimal mixture preparation, both the combustion chamber design and fuel system components must be correctly matched.

Vocabulary Builder

<u>algorithm</u> A mathematical formula used to solve a problem.

<u>atomization</u> The process of breaking up liquid fuel into a fine mist.

<u>compensation</u> A response by the fuel system governor to a loss of contribution from one or more cylinders. The governor increases the quantity of fuel injected into the other cylinders to maintain idle speed.

<u>delivery valve</u> Valves that operate as one-way checks and allow fuel to remain at moderately high pressure in the fuel injection lines. The valves prevent secondary injections and help reduce injection lag.

<u>distribution</u> The mixing of fuel and air in the cylinders during the injection event.

<u>electronic control module (ECM)</u> A device containing a microprocessor that processes electronic input signals according to software-based mathematical algorithms. The ECM then produces output signals based on processed information to control engine operation.

<u>fuel rate</u> Fuel consumption expressed as the quantity of fuel consumed per hour.

<u>governor</u> A device that regulates the quantity of fuel injected into the cylinders.

<u>hunting</u> A rhythmic change in engine rpm at idle speed caused by uneven delivery of fuel; also known as loping.

<u>injection lag</u> The time delay that occurs between the start of fuel pressurization and the moment when injection actually occurs.

<u>injection quantity adjustment (IQA)</u> A feature that allows software to compensate for pressure variations in cylinders; also known as the E-trim, adaptation value, or the injector calibration code.

<u>injection rate</u> The quantity of fuel injected per degree of crank angle rotation. It is reported as the position of the crankshaft when the injection begins.

<u>metering</u> Measurement of the correct quantity of fuel for each cylinder required for various speed and load conditions demanded of the engine.

<u>pressurization</u> Compressing fuel to the degree required for an injection event.

<u>pumping loss</u> The energy required to pull air past a throttle plate or move gases in and out of the cylinder.

<u>rate-shaped injection</u> An injection strategy that carefully regulates the amount of fuel injected into a cylinder per degree of crank angle rotation.

<u>timing</u> In the high-pressure injection system, the beginning of the injection event in the combustion cycle relative to crank rotation.

Review Questions

1. _____ is a rhythmic change in engine rpm at idle speed caused by uneven delivery of fuel.
   a. Distribution
   b. Hunting
   c. Atomization
   d. Metering

2. In the high-pressure injection system, _____ is the beginning of the injection event in the combustion cycle relative to crank rotation.
   a. timing
   b. metering
   c. hunting
   d. distribution

3. _____ is the mixing of fuel and air in the cylinders during the injection event.
   a. Atomization
   b. Timing
   c. Metering
   d. Distribution

4. _____ is the process of breaking up liquid fuel into a fine mist.
   a. Metering
   b. Distribution
   c. Atomization
   d. Hunting

5. _____ is the measurement of the correct quantity of fuel for each cylinder required for various speed and load conditions demanded of the engine.
   a. Timing
   b. Metering
   c. Hunting
   d. Distribution

6. Idle _____ involves adjusting injection quantities based on changes to crankshaft speed produced during every power impulse.
   a. adaptation
   b. atomization
   c. calibration
   d. delivery

7. The appropriate _____ code must be entered into the ECM each time a new injector is installed or an injector is moved.
   a. adaptation
   b. calibration
   c. delivery
   d. atomization

8. The two most important factors influencing _____ are cylinder pressure and temperature.
   a. injection rate
   b. burn rate
   c. pressurization rate
   d. fuel economy

9. Burn time is expressed in _____ of crankshaft rotation.
   a. degrees
   b. speed
   c. direction
   d. delivery

10. _____ describes the time delay that occurs between the start of fuel pressurization and the moment when injection actually occurs.
   a. Reactive inductance
   b. Inductive capacitance
   c. Reactive resistance
   d. Injection lag

ASE-Type Questions

1. Technician A says compensation is observed when one or more cylinders are cut out and the engine maintains a set idle speed. Technician B says irregular or inconsistent fuel delivery causes the governor to readjust the quantity of fuel metered and correct the engine's speed and that correction is called compensation. Who is correct?
   a. Technician A
   b. Technician B
   c. Both Technician A and Technician B
   d. Neither Technician A nor Technician B

2. Technician A says calibration codes are given different names by manufacturers including injection quantity adjustment. Technician B says manufacturers are also called E-Trims and the adaptation value. Who is correct?
   a. Technician A
   b. Technician B
   c. Both Technician A and Technician B
   d. Neither Technician A nor Technician B

3. Technician A says the two most important factors influencing burn rate are cylinder pressure and temperature. Technician B says burn rate is not influenced by cylinder pressure. Who is correct?
   a. Technician A
   b. Technician B
   c. Both Technician A and Technician B
   d. Neither Technician A nor Technician B

4. Technician A says optimal timing for emissions positively impacts the fuel economy in North American diesel engines. Technician B says optimal timing for emissions negatively impacts the fuel economy in North American diesel engines. Who is correct?
   a. Technician A
   b. Technician B
   c. Both Technician A and Technician B
   d. Neither Technician A nor Technician B

5. Technician A says fuel pressurized to hundreds of pounds per square inch can easily penetrate skin, causing bodily harm and blood poisoning. Technician B says fuel pressurized to hundreds of pounds per square inch can even cause death. Who is correct?
   a. Technician A
   b. Technician B
   c. Both Technician A and Technician B
   d. Neither Technician A nor Technician B

6. Technician A says injection rate describes the time delay that occurs between the start of fuel pressurization and the moment when injection actually occurs. Technician B says injection lag describes the time delay. Who is correct?
   a. Technician A
   b. Technician B
   c. Both Technician A and Technician B
   d. Neither Technician A nor Technician B

7. Technician A says poor mixing of air and fuel can cause nozzle dribble. Technician B says poor mixing of air and fuel can cause excessive ignition delay time. Who is correct?
   a. Technician A
   b. Technician B
   c. Both Technician A and Technician B
   d. Neither Technician A nor Technician B

8. Technician A says that in modern fuel injection systems, injection rate means the quantity of fuel injected per degree of crank angle rotation. Technician B says the fuel rate means the quantity of fuel injected per degree of crank angle rotation. Who is correct?
   a. Technician A
   b. Technician B
   c. Both Technician A and Technician B
   d. Neither Technician A nor Technician B

9. Technician A says peak cylinder pressure should occur 15-20 degrees of crankshaft rotation after top dead cylinder. Technician B says peak cylinder pressure should occur approximately 5-10 degrees of crankshaft rotation after top dead cylinder. Who is correct?
   a. Technician A
   b. Technician B
   c. Both Technician A and Technician B
   d. Neither Technician A nor Technician B

10. Technician A says a rate-shaping strategy called pilot injection delivers a small quantity of fuel to the combustion chamber 8-10 degrees before the main injection. Technician B says the rate-shaping strategy is called split-shot injection. Who is correct?
    a. Technician A
    b. Technician B
    c. Both Technician A and Technician B
    d. Neither Technician A nor Technician B

CHAPTER 17
Hydraulic Nozzles

NATEF Tasks

Diesel Engines

General
- Identify engine fuel, oil, coolant, air, and other leaks; determine needed action. (pp 511–513)
- Listen for engine noises; determine needed action. (pp 511–515)

- Observe engine exhaust smoke color and quantity; determine needed action. (pp 511–515)
- Identify engine surging, rough operation, misfiring, low power, slow deceleration, slow acceleration, and shutdown problems; determine needed action. (pp 511–515)

Knowledge Objectives

After reading this chapter, you will be able to:
1. Describe the purpose and operating principles of hydraulic nozzles. (pp 498–501)
2. Identify and describe hydraulic nozzles and associated components. (pp 498–502)
3. Define and explain terminology associated with hydraulic nozzles. (pp 498–516)
4. Identify and describe the types, styles, construction, and applications of hydraulic nozzles. (pp 508–510)

5. Identify and explain inspection and diagnostic procedures for evaluating hydraulic nozzles. (pp 510–515)
6. Recommend maintenance or repairs of hydraulic nozzles. (pp 515–519)
7. Identify performance modifications of hydraulic nozzles. (pp 515–519)
8. Identify nozzle failures. (p 517)

Skills Objectives

After reading this chapter, you will be able to:
1. Test nozzle spray patterns. (pp 512) **SKILL DRILL 17-1**
2. Measure NOP. (pp 513) **SKILL DRILL 17-2**

3. Measure valve seat leakage (forward leakage). (pp 515) **SKILL DRILL 17-3**
4. Measure back leakage. (pp 516) **SKILL DRILL 17-4**

► Introduction

Injector nozzles are a basic element of a diesel engine's fuel injection system. Used to spray fuel into the combustion chamber, nozzles are incorporated into every type of fuel injection system. The simplest function of the nozzle is to open and close, permitting highly pressurized fuel to squeeze through small orifices in the nozzle tip, which effectively atomizes and distributes fuel into the combustion chamber. Design and operation of a nozzle is therefore critical to combustion efficiency, fuel consumption, and emission formation. Because they operate using hydraulic pressure, nozzles are also termed hydraulic injector nozzles or simply injectors. Given the importance of injector nozzles, identifying nozzle types, construction features, and operating principles is necessary. With this information, diesel technicians can understand nozzle operation and develop diagnostic strategies and service and maintenance practices associated with these components.

► Fundamentals of Hydraulic Nozzles

The term injector is often used to encompass the operation of a hydraulic nozzle. More precisely though, a diesel engine's fuel injectors are larger components, which deliver fuel to the combustion chamber and operate using widely different high-pressure injection system technologies **FIGURE 17-1**. Examples of these systems include various types of common rail, unit injection, unit pumps, and hydraulically actuated unit injection. While vastly different in construction and operation, nearly all of these injectors have in common a hydraulic nozzle incorporated into their design. An open nozzle is another type of nozzle, and it is examined in the Cummins Unit Injection Systems chapter.

FIGURE 17-1 With rare exceptions, hydraulic nozzles are used by all types of injectors. Injectors are built using a wide variety of designs.

Functions of Nozzles

Hydraulic nozzles are composed of a nozzle valve and nozzle body. The **nozzle valve**, or needle valve, is the valve in the nozzle that seals the end of the nozzle tip when it is not injecting fuel. The two basic types of nozzles are the **multi-orifice nozzle**, which has multiple holes in the tip, and the **pintle nozzle**, which has a single hole **FIGURE 17-2**. A nozzle's primary function is to atomize and distribute fuel with combustion chamber turbulence. The performance, efficiency, and emissions of diesel engines are largely determined by the fuel **atomization** and distribution process. By breaking fuel into small droplets with

► You Are the Technician

When there is little repair work in your shop, technicians often use the time to rebuild engines and recondition a variety of engine components for use later. You have been asked to remove, test, and recondition the hydraulic nozzles from a number of scrap engines with pump-line-nozzle fuel systems. One of the things you do is carefully record injector part numbers and match them with the engine model and serial numbers. That will help match the injectors with the correct engine application later. After carefully cleaning the injectors with solvent and removing the copper sealing washers, you also clean the injector tips with a brass brush to avoid damaging the injector spray holes. You begin to test the nozzles in a pop tester to sort which injectors meet specifications and which require disassembly and parts replacement. Before starting your work, consider the following:

1. Outline all the tests you will need to perform to properly evaluate the hydraulic nozzles for serviceability.
2. What will be your service recommendation for nozzles that do not "chatter" when pop testing? Explain your answer.
3. Of the injectors that failed the pop tests, which parts do you believe will most likely need to be replaced? List parts in order of most likely to need replacement.

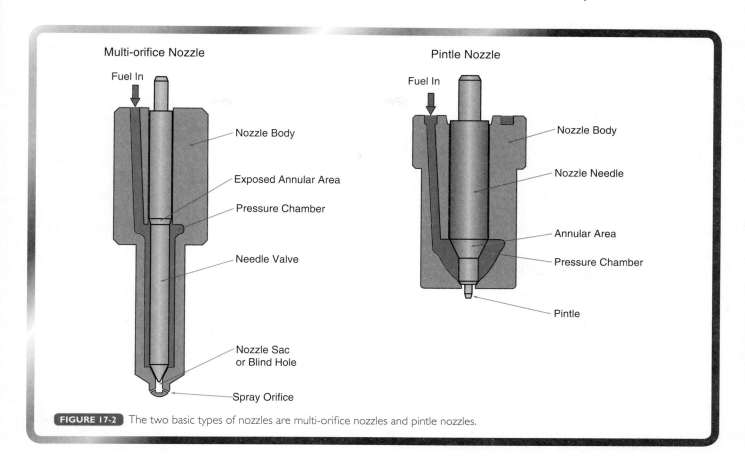

FIGURE 17-2 The two basic types of nozzles are multi-orifice nozzles and pintle nozzles.

more surface area, conversion of the fuel into a vapor state is enhanced, which increases combustion efficiency, reduces emissions, and improves fuel economy. While accomplishing the above, nozzles are required to provide an abrupt beginning and end of injection to prevent dribbling of fuel droplets into the combustion chamber.

Proper distribution of fuel is especially critical to reducing the formation of noxious emissions. Particulate matter (PM), including soot, and oxides of nitrogen (NO_x) are produced from uneven fuel distribution in the combustion chamber. Localized regions within the combustion chamber that are rich in fuel will typically produce higher temperatures and therefore more NO_x. Soot is also produced when the air–fuel ratio is excessive and there is not enough air making contact with fuel. Large fuel droplets that do not completely burn form soot, which is seen as black smoke emitted from the exhaust system.

Fuel Distribution

Fuel nozzles work with combustion chamber turbulence to distribute and mix fuel throughout the combustion chamber **FIGURE 17-3**. Because combustion chambers have different degrees of turbulence, the injector nozzle's job of distributing fuel to prepare an air–fuel mixture that burns well varies between engine designs. For example, indirect injection (IDI) combustion chambers have very high turbulence in comparison to direct injection (DI) chambers. This means the type of nozzles used and their operation are very different. Centrally

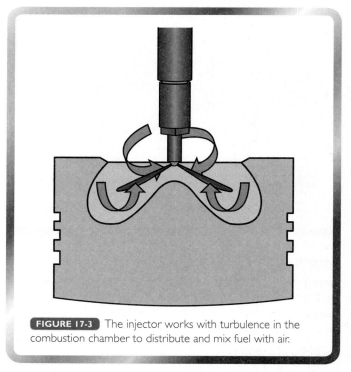

FIGURE 17-3 The injector works with turbulence in the combustion chamber to distribute and mix fuel with air.

located nozzles used by DI combustion chambers use four valves per cylinder and are more effective at symmetrically distributing fuel than offset nozzles found in two-valve cylinders **FIGURE 17-4** and **FIGURE 17-5**.

FIGURE 17-4 A DI chamber uses a multi-orifice nozzle to atomize and distribute fuel into the combustion chamber.

FIGURE 17-5 More spray holes provide better distribution of fuel, but smaller, finer droplets cannot penetrate the combustion chamber as thoroughly as heavier droplets.

Atomization

Atomization is the process of breaking large particles into smaller parts. In the case of the fuel nozzle, it breaks the injected quantity of fuel into a spray of very fine droplets that are better suited for combustion.

Fuel Droplet Size

The amount of time necessary for combustion is dependent on fuel quality, cylinder pre-ignition temperature, and atomization. Only a few degrees of crankshaft rotation are available for mixture formation prior to combustion, because fuel is injected at the end of compression stroke. Before fuel can burn, atomization,

distribution, heating, and vaporization of fuel droplets must quickly take place for the best combustion quality.

Finer atomization allows for the following benefits:

- Improved mixing of air and fuel for a faster and cleaner burn
- Shorter ignition lag time, resulting in lower combustion noise
- Greater tolerance for use of exhaust gas recirculation (EGR) and the use of retarded injection timing for reduced NO_x formation
- Higher engine speed; high-pressure injection systems with the ability to atomize fuel into finer droplets in a shorter time have enabled faster mixture formation with lower particulate emissions
- Improved fuel economy through more complete combustion of fuel
- Lower NO_x emissions, which are formed in fuel-rich regions of the combustion chamber

Combustible vapors will originate from the fuel droplet surface as it encounters air friction and absorbs heat produced during the compression stroke **FIGURE 17-6**. Liquid fuel droplets will vaporize and burn from the outside inward. Unless fuel droplets are broken into the smallest size, they will take longer to burn and make less contact with oxygen. Heated fuel with insufficient oxygen contact will cause the droplet to simply bake or carbonize, increasing soot production.

Not only are soot PM emissions accompanied by hydrocarbons (HCs) and carbon monoxide (CO) emissions, their production is reduced proportionally with smaller fuel droplet size.

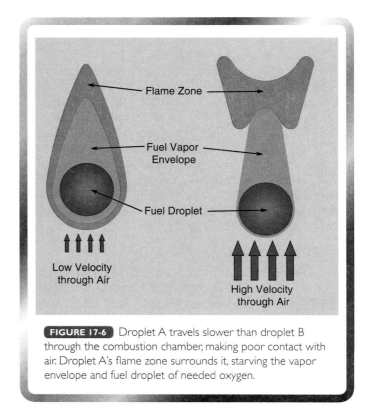

FIGURE 17-6 Droplet A travels slower than droplet B through the combustion chamber, making poor contact with air. Droplet A's flame zone surrounds it, starving the vapor envelope and fuel droplet of needed oxygen.

Improved atomization also enables NO$_x$ emission-reducing technology and strategies. For example, when the speed of air–fuel mixture formation and combustion increases due to finer atomization, injection timing can be retarded because less time is required for mixture preparation. The use of EGR is better tolerated by engines with finer atomization.

▶ TECHNICIAN TIP

Burning fuel in a diesel engine is like burning wood in a campfire. Small pieces of kindling start a campfire faster, and they burn more quickly and completely than large logs. Similarly, fine fuel droplets ignite easier and burn faster and more completely than large droplets. Just as hotter fires produce less smoke, clean engine emissions are achieved when fuel burns hot and has enough time to burn. Fine atomization helps fuel burn hot, fast, and more completely, leaving less residue.

Pressurization, Atomization, and Combustion

The quality of atomization and fuel distribution directly relates to the degree of pressurization. Pressurization is important to fuel distribution for a number of reasons. First, high pressure is necessary to impart adequate energy to fuel to penetrate dense turbulent charge air inside the combustion chambers as quickly as possible. The size or weight of the fuel droplet multiplied by its velocity determines the kinetic energy possessed by the droplet. When energy is higher, the distance traveled by fuel droplets will be farther. Droplets tend to break up and disperse faster at high rather than low velocities.

▶ TECHNICIAN TIP

Worn injector nozzles are a major cause of excessive PM emissions. As nozzles wear, their orifices become larger, producing larger fuel droplets, which in turn produce more smoke. Low injection pressures caused by worn plungers or leaking valves controlling **electronic unit injectors (EUIs)** can also increase droplet size. An EUI is an electrically controlled injector incorporating timing, metering, atomization, and pressurization functions into a single unit or injector.

To create smaller fuel droplets with more contact surface area for oxygen, finer diameter, more numerous nozzle orifices are required in addition to higher pressure. Smaller DI combustion chambers found in passenger vehicles will have between six and eight nozzle orifices, whereas larger commercial engines will use as many as 13 orifices. However, between five and eight spray holes are most common today. To inject all of the fuel required for the combustion cycle, higher pressure is required to deliver fuel through smaller spray holes in a short amount of time.

Basic Nozzle Construction

The most common type of injector used today is referred to as a closed nozzle. This means the needle valve in the nozzle seals the end of the nozzle tip when not injecting fuel. A nozzle consists of two main parts, the nozzle or needle valve and the nozzle body. The **hydraulic nozzle holder** encloses the nozzle assembly and contains a fitting or passageway connecting the high-pressure injection line to the nozzle valve **FIGURE 17-7**.

The nozzle body contains a spindle-like nozzle valve, also called a needle valve, which normally rests on a nozzle valve seat. Below the seat area are passages to the nozzle tip called orifices. Holding the nozzle valve closed against its seat is a nozzle spring that transmits its mechanical force through a pressure pin.

Within the nozzle holder, above the nozzle valve, is a chamber where small quantities of fuel can accumulate and then leak between the nozzle valve and body **FIGURE 17-8**. This leakage of fuel between the two parts, called **back leakage**, is a calibrated escape of fuel around the nozzle valve that lubricates and cools the valve. Back leakage is drained from the holder through a leak-off or return line connection and then flows back to the fuel tank.

Nozzle Manufacturing Techniques

An enormous degree of manufacturing expertise, specialized materials, and design work are involved in the production of injector nozzles. The principal techniques of making holes in injector nozzles are punching, electric discharge machining (EDM), twist drilling, and laser machining. EDM is the most common technique for newer nozzles. Hole geometry resulting from all these processes are still limited to shapes with straight walls or walls with varying degrees of taper. A technique used to enhance the flow characteristics and performance of injector nozzles is to smooth the ends of the spray holes by forcing

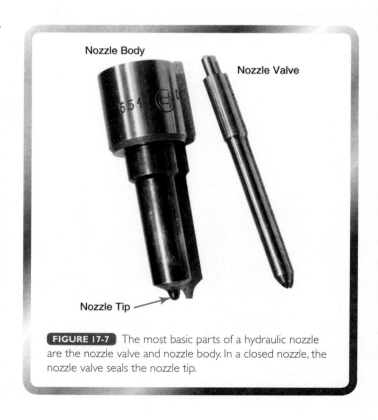

Nozzle Body

Nozzle Valve

Nozzle Tip

FIGURE 17-7 The most basic parts of a hydraulic nozzle are the nozzle valve and nozzle body. In a closed nozzle, the nozzle valve seals the nozzle tip.

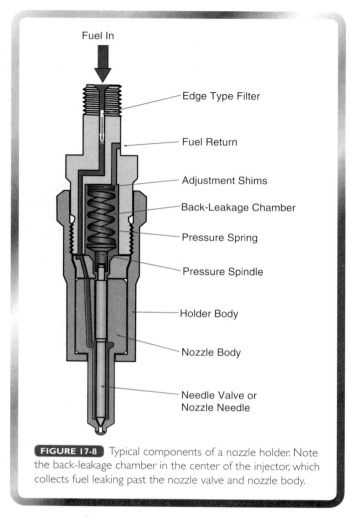

Fuel In

- Edge Type Filter
- Fuel Return
- Adjustment Shims
- Back-Leakage Chamber
- Pressure Spring
- Pressure Spindle
- Holder Body
- Nozzle Body
- Needle Valve or Nozzle Needle

FIGURE 17-8 Typical components of a nozzle holder. Note the back-leakage chamber in the center of the injector, which collects fuel leaking past the nozzle valve and nozzle body.

an abrasive compound through the nozzles. This smoothing process, known as **abrasive flow machining (AFM)**, not only enhances flow characteristics by removing resistance to fuel flow but permits, in performance applications, increased delivery of fuel **FIGURE 17-9**.

Durability Requirements

Nozzles must have high mechanical strength to tolerate the high injection pressures, to resist the stress and fatigue imposed by the fuel delivery cycle, and to ensure durability at high combustion temperatures to provide long engine life. Consider that the needle valve will open and close over a billion times during its service life, withstanding pressures higher at times than 38,000 pounds per square inch (psi) (2620 bar). This force is equivalent to the weight of a large tandem axle truck pressing on the area of a fingernail. If the nozzle is used in common rail fuel injectors operating with pre- and post-combustion injections, the needle valve will open and close as many as 10,000 times per minute. Main injection event durations of about 2 milliseconds means injection velocities of fuel can approach 1243 miles per second (2000 km per second) at full load. Operating clearances are kept as narrow as 2 microns or 1/30th the thickness of a human hair **FIGURE 17-10**.

Basic Nozzle Operation

Closed nozzles operate using a pressure differential principle. Normally, the nozzle valve rests on the valve seat, preventing fuel delivery through the nozzle orifices. High-pressure fuel will enter the nozzle holder though an inlet fitting and travel down through internally drilled passageways to a hollow, ring-shaped pressure chamber beneath the nozzle valve **FIGURE 17-11** and **FIGURE 17-12**.

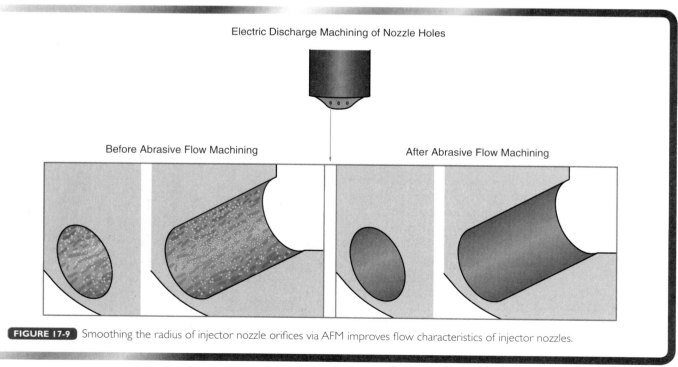

Electric Discharge Machining of Nozzle Holes

Before Abrasive Flow Machining   After Abrasive Flow Machining

FIGURE 17-9 Smoothing the radius of injector nozzle orifices via AFM improves flow characteristics of injector nozzles.

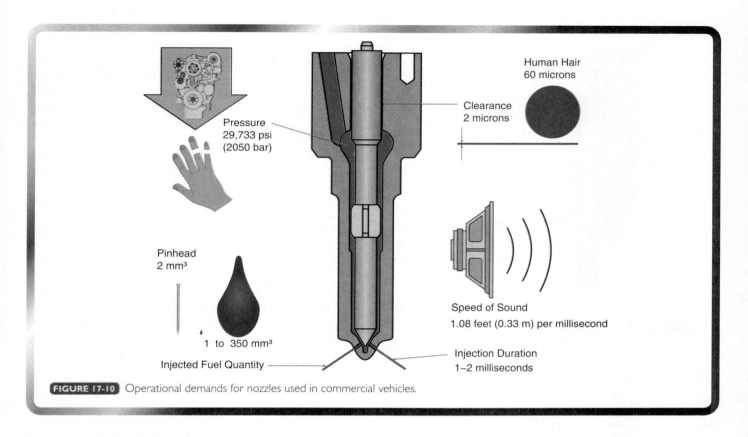

FIGURE 17-10 Operational demands for nozzles used in commercial vehicles.

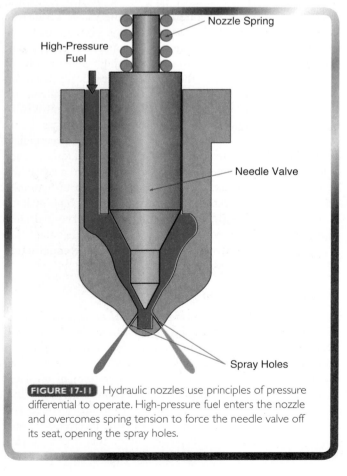

FIGURE 17-11 Hydraulic nozzles use principles of pressure differential to operate. High-pressure fuel enters the nozzle and overcomes spring tension to force the needle valve off its seat, opening the spray holes.

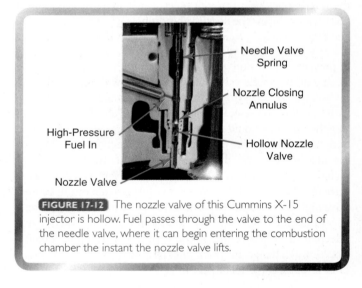

FIGURE 17-12 The nozzle valve of this Cummins X-15 injector is hollow. Fuel passes through the valve to the end of the needle valve, where it can begin entering the combustion chamber the instant the nozzle valve lifts.

This ring-shaped pressure chamber, called the annulus, will apply fuel pressure to the nozzle valve and force it from its seat when fuel pressure exceeds nozzle spring pressure. The hydraulic pressure required to open the nozzle valve is known as **nozzle opening pressure (NOP)** or valve opening pressure (VOP). NOP is determined by the pressure differential between the spring force holding the valve on the nozzle body seat and the surface area of the nozzle valve in the annulus. The nozzle spring will hold the nozzle valve against its seat until fuel pressure exerted against the annulus exceeds spring pressure FIGURE 17-13 .

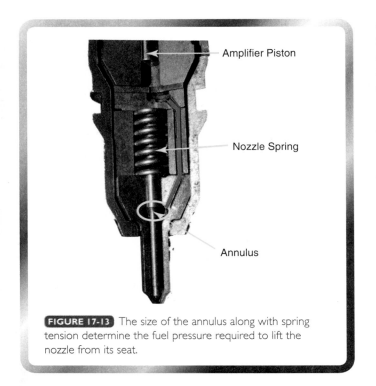

FIGURE 17-13 The size of the annulus along with spring tension determine the fuel pressure required to lift the nozzle from its seat.

Amplifier Piston

Nozzle Spring

Annulus

After high-pressure fuel unseats the nozzle, fuel passes between the end of the nozzle valve and the seat and then out of the nozzle body's tip through holes called spray orifices. When fuel pressure below the nozzle valve drops, such as when injection ends, the valve closes against the nozzle seat and blocks further fuel delivery. At the same time, the nozzle valve seals the injector tip to prevent combustion gases from entering the nozzle. The rapid closing of the nozzle valve cutting off the flow of fuel produces a **pressure wave reflection**. This simply means the direction of the hydraulic force reverses like ball bouncing off a wall or a wave hitting the sides of a liquid container. The pressure wave will bounce back and forth inside a high-pressure injection line between the nozzle valve and the pumping element. Injection systems include features such as injection pump delivery valves to minimize the likelihood of the nozzle valve lifting again due to consecutive high-pressure pulses produced by pressure wave reflection.

Adjustment of NOP is commonly accomplished using selective shims above the nozzle spring. For example, a 0.001" (0.025mm) change in shim thickness may result in a 50-psi (345-kilopascal [kPa]) change in NOP.

Nozzle Differential Ratio

Diesel engine fuel systems require an abrupt beginning and end of injection. **Beginning of injection (BOI)** is the point when fuel delivery begins and is referenced according to the position of the crankshaft measured in degrees of crankshaft rotation. Without an abrupt beginning and end of injection, a gradual loss of pressure at the nozzle tip would result in increasing spray droplet size and decreasing droplet penetration. To produce the sharp increase of pressure when the nozzle valve first lifts from its seat, it is necessary to ensure the valve moves rapidly. To accomplish this, nozzle valves are built with two different

surfaces that are acted upon by high-pressure fuel. The first surface is the area of the nozzle annulus. This area is smaller than the second surface, which is the entire area of the nozzle valve when it is unseated during injection. The difference between the two areas is referred to as the **nozzle differential ratio** **FIGURE 17-14**. In most nozzles, the area acted upon by highly pressurized fuel in the annulus is 20–80% smaller than the surface area exposed to pressurized fuel after the nozzle valve is lifted from its seat. This means that more fuel pressure is required to open the nozzle than is needed to close the nozzle. Because a larger nozzle valve surface area is exposed the instant the valve begins to lift, the valve will rapidly lift and remain unseated with less fuel pressure than was needed to initially move the valve.

Large and small nozzle differential ratios each have advantages and disadvantages. A small nozzle differential ratio means the nozzle valve will quickly reseat when a little fuel slips out the spray holes. This arrangement keeps fuel spray-in pressures high and droplet size small. However, it also produces a higher frequency of nozzle opening and closing, which accelerates nozzle valve and seat wear. Conversely, a large nozzle differential ratio produces less nozzle seat wear, but has the disadvantage of producing larger droplets because lower fuel pressure is required to keep the nozzle open.

Hydraulically Balanced Nozzle Valve Opening

The latest injectors control injection events by changing the balance of hydraulic pressure acting on the needle valve using electrically operated solenoids or control valves inside the injectors. Traditional fuel systems use high-pressure fuel only to unseat the nozzle valve and begin injection. Newer unit injectors and common rail injectors use high-pressure fuel to both open the and close the nozzle. Hydraulically balanced nozzle valves, also called hydraulically suspended valves, use the small mechanical control force of the injector control valve to trigger more powerful, faster acting hydraulic forces. Using comparatively small control valve movement to manipulate very high hydraulic pressure (that is, using a small force to control a much larger force) is called servo action. In a sense, the servo action in an injector is similar to an electric over-hydraulic relay; it uses small electrical forces to switch very high hydraulic pressures **FIGURE 17-15** and **FIGURE 17-16**. Servo-hydraulic injectors always use hydraulically balanced nozzle valves that are opened and closed by tipping the pressure differential acting above and below the nozzle valve.

Needle Lift Sensor

One disadvantage of the nozzle valve is its design, which contributes to injection lag. **Injection lag**, also known as injection delay, is the time between the start of injection pressurization and the point when fuel is actually delivered. Injection lag happens as the nozzle valve lifts and its movement displaces fuel volume originally intended for injection. This means that lifting the nozzle upwards uses some of the fuel metered and intended for delivery. So not all of the fuel metered for combustion is injected. The displacement of fuel accompanying nozzle lift movement delays the beginning of injection (BOI)

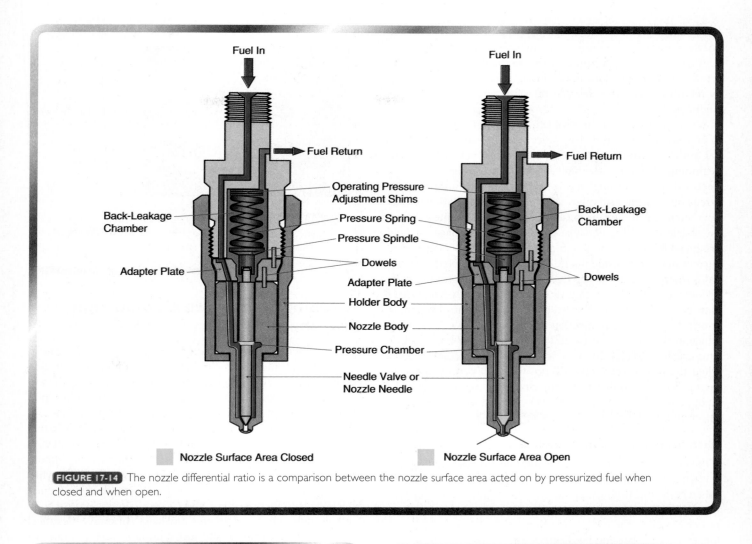

FIGURE 17-14 The nozzle differential ratio is a comparison between the nozzle surface area acted on by pressurized fuel when closed and when open.

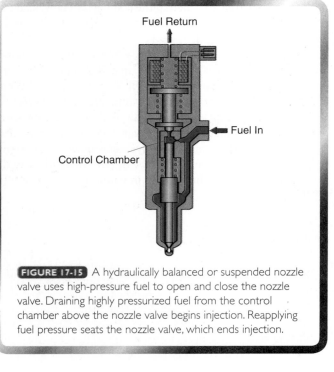

FIGURE 17-15 A hydraulically balanced or suspended nozzle valve uses high-pressure fuel to open and close the nozzle valve. Draining highly pressurized fuel from the control chamber above the nozzle valve begins injection. Reapplying fuel pressure seats the nozzle valve, which ends injection.

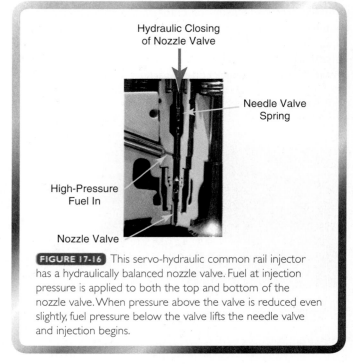

FIGURE 17-16 This servo-hydraulic common rail injector has a hydraulically balanced nozzle valve. Fuel at injection pressure is applied to both the top and bottom of the nozzle valve. When pressure above the valve is reduced even slightly, fuel pressure below the valve lifts the needle valve and injection begins.

since some of then intended delivery volume is used to lift the nozzle. A discrepancy always exists between the point when fuel delivery is expected to begin relative to crank rotation and the actual point of injection. Injection lag affects injection timing by retarding BOI. This delay in turn influences emissions and engine performance.

To compensate for this problem, a **needle lift sensor** is used to precisely identify BOI. This sensor provides an electrical signal to the electronic control module (ECM) that identifies the beginning of nozzle valve movement. This is done by passing electrical current through a wire coil surrounding an iron metal extension to the nozzle valve. When the nozzle is stationary, the flow of electrical current is smooth and uninterrupted. When the nozzle valve lifts, a change takes place in the magnetic field produced by the coil of wire that disrupts the flow of electrical current measured inside the ECM. The disrupted electrical signal is interpreted inside the ECM as the beginning of injection and adjustments to injection timing are made based on sensor data. Nozzle lift signals are used by the engine control system to eliminate variability in injection timing caused by injection lag, which enables more precise and consistent control of injection timing **FIGURE 17-17**. In other words, injection actually begins when the nozzle valve unseats, not when it is commanded to unseat. Typically, only a single injector in an engine needs to be equipped with an integrated nozzle valve lift sensor to correct injection timing for all cylinders **FIGURE 17-18**.

Nozzle Motion Failure Mode

If the needle lift sensor fails, a default injection timing program is started. Fuel injection is controlled according to values established in the fuel timing map stored in the engine control system. In addition, the injection quantity is reduced, resulting in engine power loss commonly known as limp mode. Lift sensors are no longer used in late-model diesel engines. Today's engines use cylinder pressure sensors or crankshaft acceleration rates, or monitor electrical signals from the injector solenoid windings. In an electronic unit injector, the movement of a metal control valve disrupts solenoid magnetic fields as in the lift sensor, which provides timing feedback control used by the ECM.

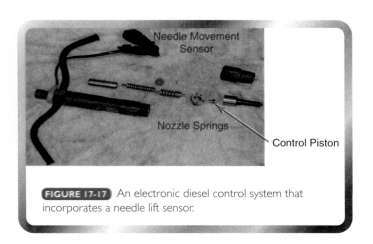

FIGURE 17-17 An electronic diesel control system that incorporates a needle lift sensor.

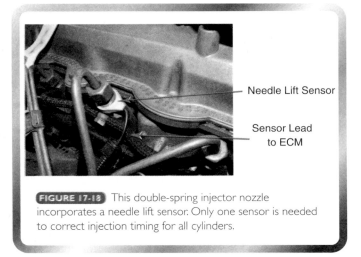

FIGURE 17-18 This double-spring injector nozzle incorporates a needle lift sensor. Only one sensor is needed to correct injection timing for all cylinders.

Matching Nozzles to Combustion Chambers

Precise matching of the injector to the shape of the piston bowl and turbulence of DI chambers is critical for efficient combustion. Ideally, homogenously mixed fuel and air will produce the lowest emissions and best combustion efficiency. However, diesel injection systems cannot currently achieve an even distribution of air and fuel in the few degrees of crankshaft rotation when the injection event takes place. Regions rich with excess fuel will produce soot and NO_x. Similarly, fuel should not spray directly against the walls of the piston bowl or cylinders, because this quenches or extinguishes combustion flames, which leads to increased HC and CO emissions. Because NOP and the angle, number, diameter, and length of spray holes affect atomization, penetration, and distribution of fuel, the injector needs to be precisely matched to the combustion bowl shape to provide optimum air–fuel mixing over the engine's entire operating range **FIGURE 17-19**.

It is important for technicians when rebuilding engines and servicing injectors to correctly match components using original equipment manufacturer (OEM) part numbers. While components might look identical, imperceptible differences in things like piston bowl depth or diameter, nozzle spray angle, or hole diameter or length can have a dramatic effect on mixture formation and negative consequences to engine operation. Numbers stamped on the nozzle's body identify the nozzle and help differentiate it from similarly shaped nozzles **FIGURE 17-20**.

▶ **TECHNICIAN TIP**

When replacing injectors or any other fuel system components, it is important to correctly match the parts to the engine. "Will fit" components are not precisely matched and can result in low power, excessive emissions, and engine failure. Technicians should use engine serial numbers to properly order fuel system components.

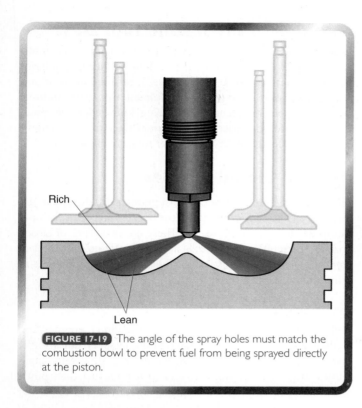

FIGURE 17-19 The angle of the spray holes must match the combustion bowl to prevent fuel from being sprayed directly at the piston.

FIGURE 17-20 A nozzle's spray angles, hole diameters, hole lengths, and other features are not easily visible. Identification numbers on nozzle body will identify the correct nozzle.

The orientation of an injector in the combustion chamber is also critical to good combustion. This is especially true when injectors are offset in the DI combustion chamber. A locating pin, ball, or other feature is required to ensure the injector spray pattern is positioned to produce the correct spray pattern over the piston bowl FIGURE 17-21 and FIGURE 17-22.

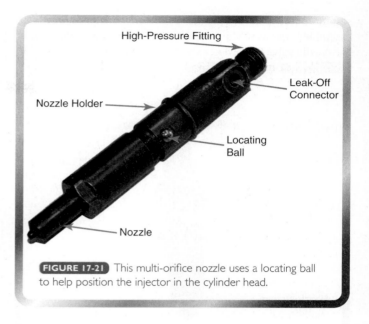

FIGURE 17-21 This multi-orifice nozzle uses a locating ball to help position the injector in the cylinder head.

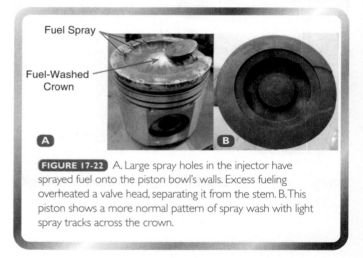

FIGURE 17-22 A. Large spray holes in the injector have sprayed fuel onto the piston bowl's walls. Excess fueling overheated a valve head, separating it from the stem. B. This piston shows a more normal pattern of spray wash with light spray tracks across the crown.

TECHNICIAN TIP

A vehicle operator may complain of low power subsequent to injector replacement in a diesel engine. This may happen for several reasons. Finer atomization and higher NOP may permit less fuel into the combustion chamber. This may lower power output slightly from what the driver was previously familiar with. New injectors, particularly some electronically controlled types, may need some use to break in and increase flow rates through the nozzle spray holes. NOP will typically lower after the injector has accumulated some hours in operation.

On many fuel nozzles, a spacer containing two locating pins is located between the nozzle and nozzle holder. This spacer ensures that the nozzle spray holes are correctly positioned within the combustion chamber. Because the locating pins are slightly offset from center, the nozzle and holder can only be assembled one way. The plate also limits upward movement of the needle valve to prevent excessive needle spring compression **FIGURE 17-23** and **FIGURE 17-24**.

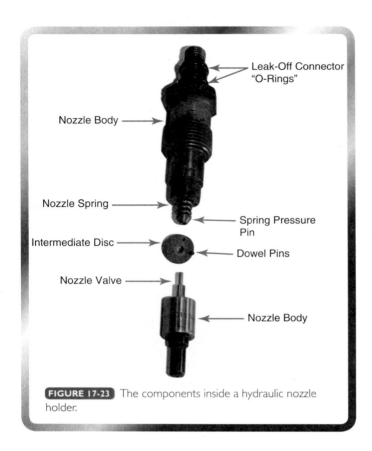

FIGURE 17-23 The components inside a hydraulic nozzle holder.

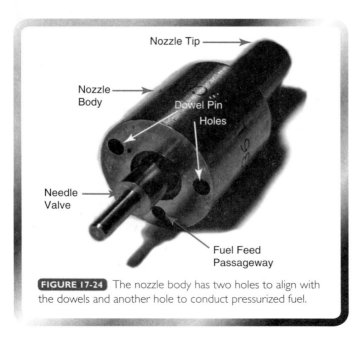

FIGURE 17-24 The nozzle body has two holes to align with the dowels and another hole to conduct pressurized fuel.

► Types of Hydraulic Nozzles

Today's on-highway diesel engines use direct injection multi-orifice nozzles. However, due to their long service life, millions of older diesel engines are still in use in off-road applications, power generation, and rental equipment that have indirect injection combustion chambers. Being knowledgeable about the design and construction of different injector helps engine technicians effectively service a wider range of engines.

Types of Closed Nozzles

Closed injector nozzles are the most popular nozzle type in use today. In a closed injector nozzle, the nozzle valve seals the nozzle tip when the valve is seated. There are two types of closed nozzles: the multi-orifice nozzle and the pintle nozzle. The two types are similar in construction but differ in the number of orifices and opening pressure.

Multi-orifice Nozzles

Multi-orifice, or multi-hole, nozzles are used in DI engines, and as their name suggests, they have multiple spray holes at the injector tip. Injectors used in DI engines require greater capabilities to pressurize, atomize, and distribute fuel than pintle nozzles, which only have a single spray hole in the tip. Older designs use four or five holes, while as many 13 are found in newer designs used in heavy-duty applications **FIGURE 17-25**.

NOP is higher in multi-orifice nozzles to produce the atomization, penetration, and distribution of fuel necessary for DI combustion chambers. Most multi-orifice nozzles are calibrated to an NOP of between 3300 and 5500 psi (228 and 379 bar). Newer engines use higher NOP, but higher pressure increases wear on nozzle valves and seats. Also, starting may be more difficult and low speed idling may be less stable with higher NOP. Some injectors not only use hydraulically balanced nozzle valves with servo actuators, but they can also electronically vary nozzle opening until injection pressures are as high as 17,000 psi (1172 bar). The Delphi E3 unit injector is an example of a nozzle with electronically controlled variable NOPs. The construction and operation of these injectors is covered in the Electronic Unit Injectors and Unit Pumps chapter.

Pintle Nozzles

Pintle nozzles are designed with a single orifice in the injector tip **FIGURE 17-26**. These nozzles are used only in IDI combustion chambers. Fuel leaves the nozzle tip as a single, relatively coarse, pencil-like spray plume. NOPs range from 900 to 5000 psi (62 to 345 bar). Most pintle nozzles have an average NOP of 1500–1950 psi (103–134 bar). NOPs are higher on turbocharged engines to seal the tip from the entry of combustion gases in these engines with increased cylinder pressures.

Fuel spray from a single opening and at this low pressure produces poor atomization compared to multi-orifice nozzles. Mixture preparation and distribution is therefore dependent primarily on cylinder turbulence. For this reason, pintle nozzles are used in IDI combustion chambers, where the more turbulent pre-chamber serves to mix and vaporize the coarse

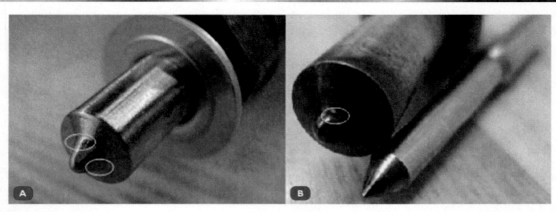

FIGURE 17-25 **A.** The injector tip of a multi-orifice injector used in a common rail engine. The naked eye cannot see its seven spray holes. **B.** The injector tip of this nozzle has four holes and is from an older engine.

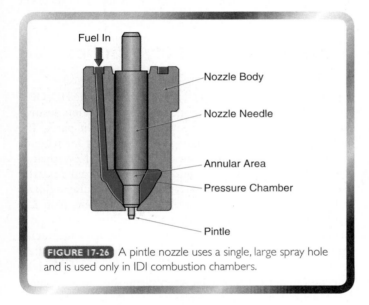

FIGURE 17-26 A pintle nozzle uses a single, large spray hole and is used only in IDI combustion chambers.

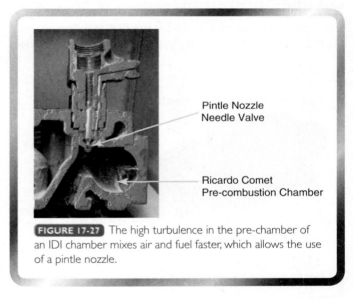

FIGURE 17-27 The high turbulence in the pre-chamber of an IDI chamber mixes air and fuel faster, which allows the use of a pintle nozzle.

spray droplets **FIGURE 17-27**. Hot pre-chamber walls operate to vaporize fuel on contact, while the comet or fireball shape of the combustion chamber configuration serves to mix fuel and air. The pre-chamber venturi further promotes mixing and vaporization of fuel as it is pushed by the expansion of burning gases into the main chamber. While the pintle nozzle, with its large, coarse spray hole, would appear to perform poorly at preparing a good combustible mixture, this chamber had the fastest mixture preparation and combustion time until the appearance of high-pressure electronically controlled DI systems. In fact, compared to non-electronic DI engines, IDI engines had the advantage of operating at higher speeds with lower air–fuel ratios, noise, and noxious emissions due to the ability of the IDI chamber to rapidly prepare the air and fuel mixture.

Rate-Shaping Nozzle Valves
Two varieties of pintle nozzles are commonly used. In standard pintle nozzles, the valve simply opens and closes, turning the

injection of fuel on or off with little change in the spray pattern or injection rate. Later pintle nozzles, called **throttle nozzles** or delay nozzles and identified by the cone-shaped nozzle body at the injector tip, have an injection rate-shaping feature that reduces the amount of fuel injected during the early stages of injection **FIGURE 17-28**. As injection progresses, the spray volume increases and the spray pattern changes from narrow and cylindrical to a conical-shaped distribution **FIGURE 17-29**. To accomplish this rate shaping, the nozzle valve profile has several machined steps producing variations in spray pattern and injection volume as the valve lifts from its seat.

The advantage of the throttle pintle nozzle is it limits the amount of fuel in the combustion chamber at the BOI, which in turn reduces the quantity of fuel accumulations during ignition delay period. Doing this minimizes the characteristic diesel knock and pressure spikes in a cylinder that produce NO_x. Less fuel means less heat and combustion noise when it ignites. This injection strategy is somewhat similar to pilot injection, but with a throttling pintle nozzle, injection takes place uninterrupted. The throttling effect on fuel delivery is most effective at idling when the valve lift is low.

Variable Orifice Injectors

Because nozzle geometry is a compromise to promote good mixture preparation over all operating ranges, manufacturers are working on **variable orifice nozzles**, or coaxial nozzles. Variable orifice injectors currently in development use two or more rows of orifices located around the tip of the injector. The two-row design would include one row of orifices around the nozzle tip that would deliver fuel at part-load low speeds when fuel injection volumes are smaller. Another row above the first would be added at full load when nozzle needle lift is greater. Using specialized electro-hydraulic control, the amount of needle lift is varied to uncover more or fewer spray holes injecting fuel at a different spray angles.

Double-Spring, Rate-Shaping Nozzles

Injecting small quantities of fuel at the BOI and then increasing the quantity of fuel injected as the injection event continues

lowers combustion noise and NO_x emissions. While various other injection strategies try to accomplish this, the two-spring two-stage injector nozzle is another innovation that mechanically controls injection rate by discharging fuel at two different rates.

Two nozzle springs made of different thicknesses and compression force are integrated one over the other inside the nozzle holder. A control valve on top of the nozzle valve between the lower and upper spring has a gap filled with fuel. When pressurized fuel begins to lift the nozzle valve, only the lighter top spring allows upward nozzle valve movement. A small amount of fuel is injected during this phase of operation, and a delay in the larger main injection event occurs.

While the upper spring lifts, fuel is squeezed slowly out of the control valve until the nozzle valve contacts the heavier lower spring. As a consequence, injection pressure must build even higher than before for any further fuel delivery to take place. The combined forces of the two nozzle springs will determine the second opening pressure for the main injection event **FIGURE 17-30**.

▶ Maintenance of Hydraulic Nozzles

When a problem with an injector is identified by the HD-OBD system or using cylinder cut-out and contribution testing, injectors are simply replaced with new or rebuilt parts. The faulty unit is returned as a parts core, potentially for rebuilding or remanufacturing in a specialized facility. Nevertheless, some service facilities do test and repair the hydraulic nozzles used inside injectors because cleaning and rebuilding a nozzle in-house is often more economical than replacement. Also, it is helpful to understand how injectors fail and the steps that can be taken to identify the failure mode. Even though a technician may never perform many of these diagnostic procedures, they provide valuable insights about potential causes and potential strategies to correct problems when diagnosing very sophisticated fuel system–related complaints.

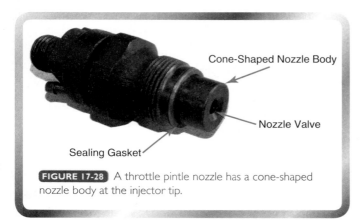

FIGURE 17-28 A throttle pintle nozzle has a cone-shaped nozzle body at the injector tip.

Cone-Shaped Nozzle Body

Nozzle Valve

Sealing Gasket

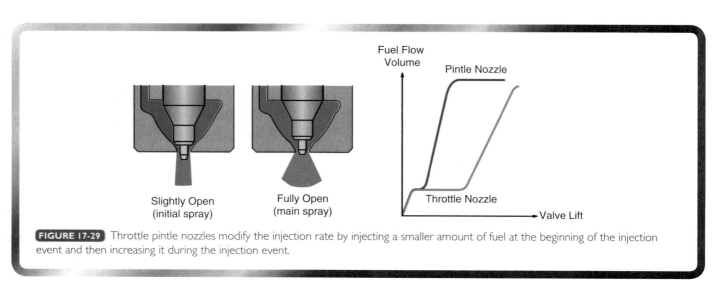

FIGURE 17-29 Throttle pintle nozzles modify the injection rate by injecting a smaller amount of fuel at the beginning of the injection event and then increasing it during the injection event.

Fuel Flow Volume

Pintle Nozzle

Throttle Nozzle

Valve Lift

Slightly Open (initial spray)

Fully Open (main spray)

Nozzle Testing

The most common problem associated with injector failures is worn, seized, or leaking hydraulic nozzles. Testing nozzles to detect these conditions can be performed using simple test equipment such as pop testers, which were once required tools for any dealership that serviced diesel engines **FIGURE 17-31**. Modern, more complex unit injectors are tested on specialized hydraulic test benches used by fuel system rebuilders. The following section outlines strategies and equipment used to diagnose problems with injectors.

Safety

The pressure that produces fuel spray from nozzle testers is high enough to penetrate skin, which can cause blood poisoning. Never bring your hands near the tip of an injector nozzle. Use a piece of cardboard or paper to check for wetting. Always wear eye protection.

Testing Nozzle Spray Patterns

To evaluate the condition of an injector nozzle, the spray pattern produced by a **pop tester** or another type of nozzle testing apparatus is used. A pop tester supplies pressurized fuel to an injector nozzle. A nozzle tester should be operated only with a

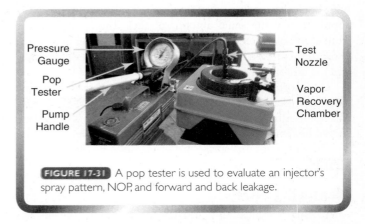

FIGURE 17-31 A pop tester is used to evaluate an injector's spray pattern, NOP, and forward and back leakage.

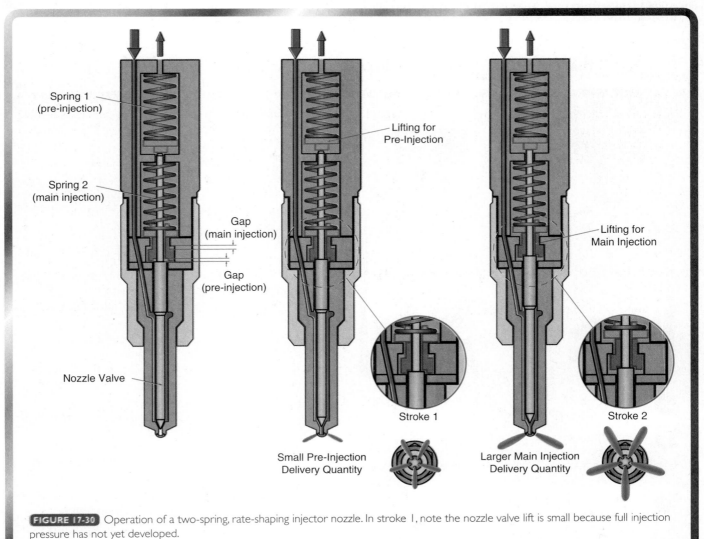

FIGURE 17-30 Operation of a two-spring, rate-shaping injector nozzle. In stroke 1, note the nozzle valve lift is small because full injection pressure has not yet developed.

spray chamber, which recovers fuel vapor produced from testing nozzles.

Spray patterns can be first evaluated visually on a nozzle tester to see if the injector spray pattern is uniform and symmetrical. The nozzle tester is hand operated and should be operated at approximately 15 strokes per minute. Atomized fuel should have a fine spray, and each spray hole should spray approximately the same amount of fuel. The spray patterns from each hole should be uniform. A piece of paper positioned beneath the nozzle may also be helpful to evaluate spray angle and the uniformity of the spray pattern.

A distorted spray pattern indicates a blocked or restricted spray hole, eroded nozzle tip, or worn nozzle orifice FIGURE 17-32 . Injectors with spray pattern distortions or poor atomization should be replaced or reconditioned.

To test nozzle spray patterns, follow the steps in SKILL DRILL 17-1 .

Measuring NOP

After visually evaluating a nozzle's spray pattern, the nozzle's opening and closing pressures are tested. NOP testing, also called pop testing, is used to determine whether a nozzle valve is opening and closing at the pressure recommended by the manufacturer. The test also determines whether the nozzle's valve is sticking. Electronically controlled nozzle testing is performed by doing a

FIGURE 17-32 One nozzle orifice in this injector is restricted and the spray pattern is not uniform. This is a defective nozzle.

 SKILL DRILL 17-1 Testing Nozzle Spray Patterns

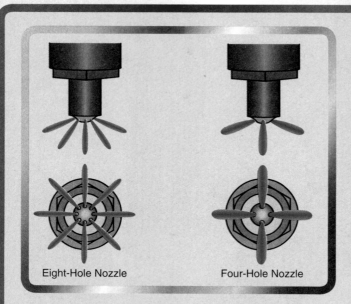

Eight-Hole Nozzle   Four-Hole Nozzle

1. Disconnect the high-pressure fuel line, then cap the nozzle fuel line inlet fittings with protective plastic caps.

2. Remove the nozzles from the engine. Inspect and clean the nozzles with solvent. Check for missing sealing washers or improperly installed nozzles, which will leak sooty combustion gases around the nozzle body.

3. Set up the nozzle pop tester by filling it with the appropriate test fluid. The fluid should be SAE calibration fluid or an equivalent test fluid, not diesel fuel.

4. Purge the nozzle tester of air by pumping the handle several times until clean fluid appears from the high-pressure line.

5. Ensure that the workbench area is clean and use clean solvent containers, clean tools, and clean hands to produce satisfactory results.

6. Install the proper nozzle–to–tester adapter that matches the high-pressure fitting on the nozzle. Connect the nozzle to the tester line.

7. Bleed air from the nozzle. This is done by opening the tester valve and pumping the tester handle 8–10 quick strokes to expel air from the injector nozzle. Test fluid should spray from the spray holes in the nozzle tip. If the nozzle is blocked or the needle is jammed, the nozzle should be replaced or rebuilt.

8. Carefully observe the spray pattern of the nozzle by pumping the tester handle rapidly and noting the characteristics of the spray pattern forming from the nozzle orifices.

9. Spray should originate from each orifice and the spray pattern from each orifice should be the same size and uniform in shape. The spray should be well atomized and cone-shaped as it leaves the injector nozzle. Injectors showing poor spray patterns should be replaced or rebuilt.

10. Listen for nozzle chatter and, if observed, note it along with your other observations. If one nozzle in a set doesn't chatter, and the rest do, recommend replacement or rebuilding of the nozzle.

cylinder cut-out test or using a purpose-built test bench generally found in fuel specialty shops. This test is performed by observing the pressure gauge located on the tester while slowly pressurizing the nozzle and observing the pressure at which the nozzle valve lifts from its seat and fuel delivery begins. Fuel should not leak from the nozzle when near NOP. The NOP should be consistent during each stroke of the nozzle tester. Continued observation will also indicate the closing pressure, which should be no more than 200 psi (14 bar) lower than NOP. Inconsistency in the NOP or too great a difference between NOP and closing pressures indicate a sticking nozzle valve, which would produce an intermittent misfire. Low opening pressure may indicate a nozzle valve that is sticking or not seating because it is seized or coked fuel has left carbon deposits in the seat area that are preventing the nozzle from sealing the spray holes. Weak, broken, misaligned, or improperly shimmed nozzle springs also produce low NOP. Nozzle valve recession caused by a worn nozzle valve and seat will also lower opening pressures. High opening pressure generally indicates a sticking nozzle or an improperly shimmed nozzle spring. Nozzle defects are usually indicated by one or more of the following symptoms:

- Black, gray, or white exhaust smoke
- Low power
- Misfire under load
- Rough engine operation after the engine is warmed up
- Excessive fuel consumption
- Engine will not reach high-idle or rated rpm
- Excessive combustion noise or fuel knock in one cylinder or more at idle

To measure NOP, follow the steps in **SKILL DRILL 17-2**.

Safety

Always wear approved safety glasses when testing nozzles. The liquid spray leaves the nozzle tip with sufficient velocity to penetrate the skin and cause serious injury. Make sure that the injector is mounted on the tester so that the spray is directed away from the operator and any other persons. Volatile liquids can be extremely flammable when vaporized—avoid any conditions (sparks, open flames, lit cigarettes, etc.) this might ignite the fluid used during the test procedure. Always use a vapor collector to prevent breathing carcinogenic hydrocarbons.

Measuring Valve Seat Leakage (Forward Leakage)

The sealing surface between the nozzle valve and body must prevent fuel from leaking past the valve and dripping into the combustion chamber. Carbon deposits, wear, or abrasion of the seat can cause **forward leakage**, which is fuel leakage from the nozzle tip. Tests that measure forward leakage evaluate the condition of the sealing surfaces between the nozzle valve and seat. Forward leakage is measured on a nozzle tester. If the sealing surfaces between the nozzle valve and seat are in good condition, no fuel leakage should be observed at the nozzle tip. After 5 seconds, some slight wetting of a multi-orifice nozzle tip is generally acceptable, but no droplet of fuel should form on a multi-orifice nozzle tip. If a droplet forms within 10 seconds, the valve seat is leaking **FIGURE 17-33**.

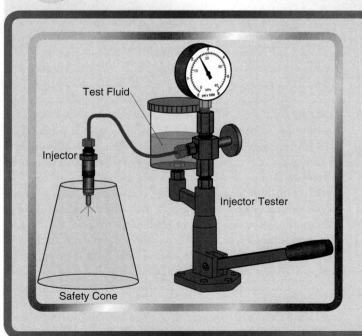

SKILL DRILL 17-2 Measuring NOP

1. Install the nozzle in the pop tester following Steps 1–7 in Skill Drill 17-1 Testing Nozzle Spray Patterns.

2. Observe and record the NOP by pumping the injector nozzle tester and noting the pressure at which the needle valve lifts and fuel begins to spray from the nozzle tip. Injector NOPs vary according to the type of nozzle and manufacturer's specifications.

3. Compare the injector's NOP with the manufacturer's specifications. Recommend replacement or overhaul if the NOP does not consistently fall within an acceptable range.

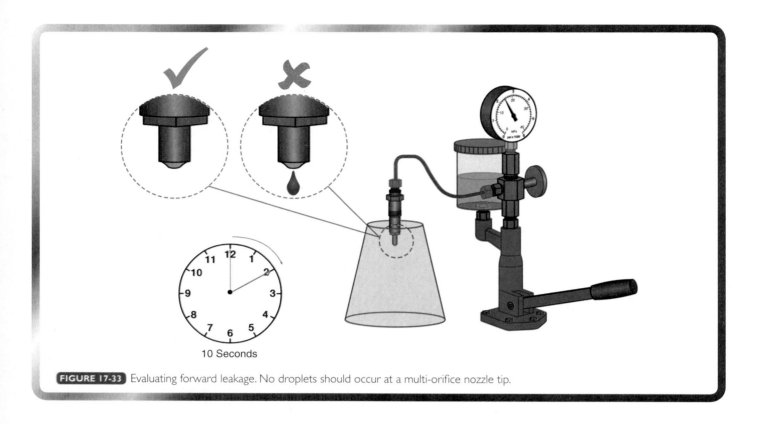

FIGURE 17-33 Evaluating forward leakage. No droplets should occur at a multi-orifice nozzle tip.

Because pintle nozzles generally open at much lower pressures than multi-orifice nozzles, less nozzle valve pressure is exerted against the valve seat. With pintle nozzles, fuel droplet formation is commonly acceptable, but if a droplet forms, it should not fall off the nozzle tip within 7 seconds **FIGURE 17-34**.

Worn seats or carbon deposits inside the injector will often cause forward leakage of the nozzle valve. Failure of the nozzle valve to properly seat is indicated by fuel leakage from the nozzle tip and an absence of chatter. Nozzles that leak tend to produce noisy combustion at idle, a loud,

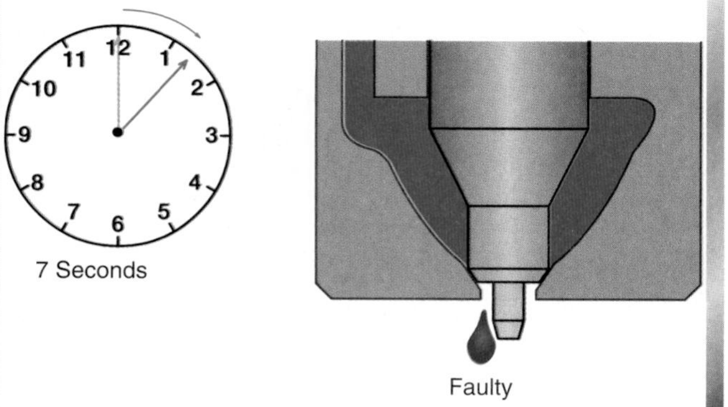

FIGURE 17-34 A pintle nozzle is allowed to leak only if the drop does not form within 7 seconds of reaching NOP.

sharp combustion knock in the affected cylinder, and smoke. When fuel sits in a nozzle, it will boil, which leaves carbon deposits that are commonly known as coke. Coked and worn nozzle valve seats are the most common causes of forward leakage.

To measure valve seat leakage (forward leakage), follow the steps in **SKILL DRILL 17-3**.

Measuring Back Leakage

The amount of back leakage, also known as leak-off or return leakage, from an injector can indicate problems with the clearances between the nozzle valve and the valve guide. Some manufacturers recommend this test if return flow pressure is high. Back leakage can be measured on the nozzle tester by observing the amount that the fuel pressure in the line to the nozzle drops. To perform this test, the nozzle is pressurized and the fuel pressure to the nozzle is sealed in the line by closing a valve on the nozzle tester. Fuel leakage between the nozzle valve and guide will cause a pressure drop in the line, which is observable on the tester's pressure gauge. Acceptable pressure drop varies from one manufacturer to another, but the amount of leakage from the return fitting of most injectors should not exceed 1.0 cc/minute at 1500 rpm. Back leakage at this rate would correspond to one drop forming at the leak-off fitting or line every minute during engine operation at idle. Back leakage on common rail injectors is much higher than this, however.

If injector line pressure drops too quickly during a back leakage test, excessive clearance likely exists between the nozzle

SKILL DRILL 17-3 Measuring Valve Seat Leakage (Forward Leakage)

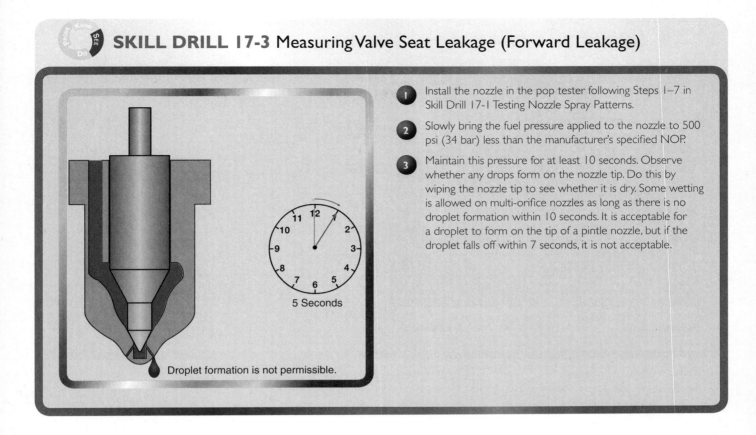

1. Install the nozzle in the pop tester following Steps 1–7 in Skill Drill 17-1 Testing Nozzle Spray Patterns.

2. Slowly bring the fuel pressure applied to the nozzle to 500 psi (34 bar) less than the manufacturer's specified NOP.

3. Maintain this pressure for at least 10 seconds. Observe whether any drops form on the nozzle tip. Do this by wiping the nozzle tip to see whether it is dry. Some wetting is allowed on multi-orifice nozzles as long as there is no droplet formation within 10 seconds. It is acceptable for a droplet to form on the tip of a pintle nozzle, but if the droplet falls off within 7 seconds, it is not acceptable.

5 Seconds

Droplet formation is not permissible.

valve and guide. If the pressure drops too slowly, inadequate clearance exists between the nozzle valve and guide. This condition can lead to nozzle sticking or seizure due to lack of lubrication.

Another technique used to evaluate a worn nozzle guide is the sliding nozzle test. This is done when the nozzle is disassembled. If the nozzle valve and body are lubricated with clean fuel, and the valve body is tilted at 60 degrees, the nozzle valve should drop smoothly out of the body due to its own weight after it has been initially pulled out about one-third of its length. This test should be performed several times while rotating the valve 120 degrees each time.

Dirt between the nozzle body and holder or misassembly of nozzles can also cause excessive back leakage. Fuel should not surge from leak-off port.

To measure back leakage, follow the steps in SKILL DRILL 17-4.

Chatter Test

The delivery of fuel causes a sudden drop in fuel pressure at the nozzle valve and causes the nozzle valve to close. Hundreds of times during a single injection event, the fuel pressure will rise and lift the nozzle valve and then fall, closing the valve again as fuel escapes from the spray holes. How often the valve opens and closes during an injection event is related to the nozzle differential ratio. The contact between the valve and seat that occurs during this high-frequency cycling of the nozzle valve opening and closing produces a high-pitched noise described as **nozzle chatter**. Nozzle chatter during

bench testing of an injector is an indication of a clean nozzle valve with good seat contact.

▶ TECHNICIAN TIP

Fuel is used to cushion the force of the needle valve as it moves into the nozzle seat. Running an engine low on fuel or with air entrained in the fuel can lead to damage in the nozzle valve seats and cause tip failure. A solid column of fuel is needed by injectors with high NOP values to absorb needle valve seating.

Chattering or high-pitched buzzing from the nozzle is heard as the nozzle valve contacts the seat during testing. The intensity of the noise will vary with the speed at which the nozzle tester lever is operated. Chattering is an indication that the nozzle valve and seat are in good condition if no leakage from the nozzle tip exists. While chatter is a positive indicator of a nozzle in good condition, the absence of chatter is not a reason to condemn or replace a nozzle.

Cleaning

Injector nozzles may be disassembled for cleaning and replacement of nozzle valves and bodies. Because they are lapped together, valves and bodies should always be replaced together and never interchanged.

The disassembled injector may be cleaned in a 15% caustic soda solution using an air-agitated solvent tank, or an ultrasonic cleaner. A brass brush can be used to clean a nozzle tip.

SKILL DRILL 17-4 Measuring Back Leakage

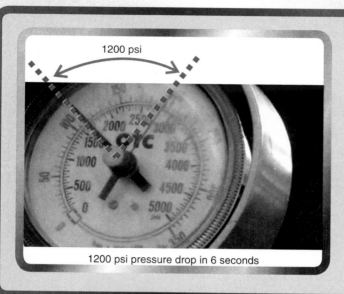

1200 psi

1200 psi pressure drop in 6 seconds

1. Install the nozzle in the pop tester following Steps 1–7 in Skill Drill 17-1 Testing Nozzle Spray Patterns.

2. Slowly bring the pressure applied to the nozzle to 100 psi (689 kPa) less than NOP.

3. Close the valve in the line to the nozzle. This seals the fuel in the nozzle under pressure.

4. Observe and record the pressure drop on the tester gauge 6 seconds after closing the tester valve.

5. Typically, a pressure drop of 300–875 psi (21–60 bar) in 6 seconds indicates that the mating surfaces inside the nozzle are not leaking excessively and that the nozzle valve-to-body clearances are acceptable. If the pressure drop is less than 300 psi (21 bar), the nozzle is not getting proper lubrication and should be replaced or rebuilt. If the pressure drop is more than 875 psi (60 bar), the nozzle is leaking excessively and should be replaced or rebuilt.

Nozzle Service

After an injector is identified as defective, the decision can be made to repair or replace the component. The following section outlines common symptoms and observations identifying defective nozzles and service strategies to correct the condition. TABLE 17-1 below is a summary of possible causes for various observations made during nozzle testing. Even without testing a nozzle, general symptoms will indicate a defective nozzle.

Forward Leakage

A well-sealing nozzle valve and seat is critical to proper engine operation. If the seal leaks, fuel can dribble out of the valve. Post-combustion fuel droplets can cause significant smoke exhaust emission and combustion noise, which is most often evident at idle. Engine performance diminishes as well, because nozzle dribble deteriorates the quality of atomization. No wetting or drop formation at the tip of a multi-hole nozzle is permissible after the nozzle is brought to 100 psi (689 kPa) below NOP. A pintle nozzle is allowed to leak only if the drop does not form within 7 seconds of reaching NOP.

▶ TECHNICIAN TIP

Leaking injector nozzle seats are most evident at idle, as they produce visible smoke emissions. Leaking nozzle seats can also result in leakage of combustion gases into the injector, eventually heating and carbonizing fuel there. Cylinder pressure can work its way through a leaking nozzle valve and into the injection system causing low power, rough running, engine stalling, and misfires.

Return Fuel—Back Leakage

A slight clearance exists between the nozzle valve and body. This clearance allows a calibrated leakage of fuel around the nozzle valve to lubricate and cool the valve FIGURE 17-35. Fuel passing into the nozzle holder containing the nozzle spring lubricates the spring seat. Eventually, leak-off lines in the nozzle holder above the valve accumulate fuel that is bled from the nozzle body to the fuel return line through a fitting attached to the nozzle FIGURE 17-36. Without this drain, fuel would eventually pressurize the area above the nozzle valve, preventing upward movement of nozzle valve.

▶ TECHNICIAN TIP

Excessive fuel leakage from the leak-off connector is evidence of an excessively worn nozzle valve or incorrectly assembled injector. Injectors showing evidence of more than a few drops of fuel per minute should be removed and properly evaluated using a tool such as a nozzle tester. On common rail systems, evaluating back leakage is an important diagnostic step to determine whether fuel system fault codes and performance problems have defective injectors as the root cause.

Factors That Can Reduce Injector Life

Nozzle service is indicated when poor fuel economy, rough running, low power, hard starting, misfiring, excessive combustion noise, or black, blue, or gray exhaust smoke are reported. Increasing fuel consumption and particulate emissions are the most common nozzle service indicators in heavier engines. Nozzle service for engines using electronic controls should take

TABLE 17-1: Evaluating Injector Nozzles

Nozzle Malfunction	Cause	Engine Symptom
NOP at 70–90% of minimum specification	• Uses additional fuel	• Excessive emissions of black or gray smoke • Slight horsepower increase (coarse droplets cause increased fuel delivery) • High fuel consumption • Excessive white smoke on start-up
NOP at 70% or less of minimum NOP	• Higher injection quantities at lower delivery pressure • Poor atomization and distribution • Combustion gases in fuel system	• Smoke • Misfiring • Poor fuel economy
Nozzle stuck open	• Over-fueling	• Excessive emissions of black or gray smoke • Cylinder misfiring at all load and speed conditions • Burned piston crowns • Oil dilution • Cylinder gases in fuel system at low speeds and loads • Nozzles have combustion gas pressure
Tip leakage	• Nozzle dribble • Poor atomization • Injection lag	• Misfiring • Light smoke, especially at idle • Excessive combustion noise • Nozzles may admit combustion • Combustion gases in fuel system
Excessive fuel return or leak-off	• Excessive clearance between nozzle valve and body	• Low power • Combustion noise • Smoke
Plugged orifices	• Improper fuel distribution	• Low power • Poor fuel economy • Rough running • White smoke on start-up • Black or gray smoke emissions while running

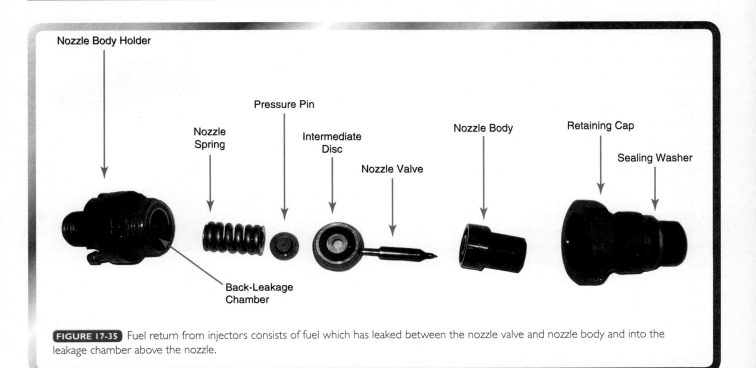

FIGURE 17-35 Fuel return from injectors consists of fuel which has leaked between the nozzle valve and nozzle body and into the leakage chamber above the nozzle.

FIGURE 17-36 Fuel leak-off lines at injectors collect fuel and return it to the fuel tank.

place whenever cylinder balance or contribution tests show excessive variations between cylinders or heavy-duty on-board diagnostics (HD-OBD) sets fault codes associated with the fuel system monitors.

Engine hours and distance traveled are factors in injector wear. While injector nozzles should provide thousands of hours of service, small-bore diesel engines using non-electronic fuel systems should be evaluated on a nozzle pop tester at 150,000 miles (241,402 km). Older heavy-duty diesels are expected to deliver between 300,000 (482,803 km) and 750,000 miles (1,207,008 km) of performance before it is necessary to evaluate with cylinder balance or contribution tests. Nozzle life on any engine should be a minimum of 5000 hours of operation using clean, good-quality fuel. Many can last as long as 30,000 hours—HD-OBD fuel systems have adaptive strategies that anticipate and compensate for nozzle wear. Emission legislation for late model engines sets durability requirements as long as 11 years of vehicle operation.

Several operating conditions can reduce the service life of diesel fuel injectors: Poor fuel quality and excessive idle time can lead to accelerated nozzle deterioration due to carbon and/or sulfur deposits forming in spray holes and other internal passageways. Sulfur in the presence of water forms corrosive acids. Even air can damage nozzles. Fuel below the nozzle valve dampens the valve against its seat, much like a shock absorber. Air will displace the fuel, leading to nozzle wear and damage.

Abrasives such as dirt in the fuel will accelerate wear of fuel system components. In injector nozzles, abrasives will enlarge the clearances between the nozzle valve and guide, damage the nozzle valve seat, and enlarge the spray hole openings. Scuffing of nozzle valves indicates poor lubrication inside the nozzle. This may be due to abrasives or poor fuel lubricity.

Excessive heat will accelerate wear between the nozzle valve and its guide. Increased back leakage of fuel will result when wear is excessive between the nozzle valve and nozzle body, thus reducing the quantity of fuel available for injection. Damage to

the hardened nozzle valve will also occur. Blued nozzle valves and tips are evidence of excessive heat. For this reason, proper clamping force and the use of a copper washer for an injector seal are necessary to remove heat from the injector. Improper installation can result in insufficient cooling and seizure of the nozzle valve **FIGURE 17-37** .

If the ends of the nozzle valves are dark or discolored, it is an indication that the nozzle valve is not properly sealing. The discoloration is due to combustion gasses blowing back through the spray holes, causing excessive temperatures and discoloration of the nozzle valve. Specialized cleaning brushes and scrapers are used to scrape carbon from injector tubes or cylinder head casting before reinstallation of injectors.

Water in the fuel will cause corrosion and galling of fuel system components. In addition, water does not easily pass through the spray holes in multi-orifice nozzles. Water accumulations can cause the injector tip to break due to the high pressures caused by steam expansion in the nozzle tip **FIGURE 17-38** .

Improper service procedures can cause nozzle damage. Nozzle removal should always be performed using correct tools. Cleaning nozzle tips with a steel wire wheel will damage the nozzle spray holes. Only brass brushes and recommended cleaning solvents should be used **FIGURE 17-39** .

▶ TECHNICIAN TIP

If nozzles are disassembled, only handle the nozzle valves by their stems. Oils on skin will cause corrosion and seizure of the nozzle valve.

FIGURE 17-37 An example of clean, well-sealing injector and an injector with a poorly sealing copper washer seal. Note carbon from the combustion chamber leakage has entered into the injector sleeve and deposited on the injector.

FIGURE 17-38 **A.** This nozzle tip is broken across the nozzle orifices. **B.** The same nozzle but with an intact tip.

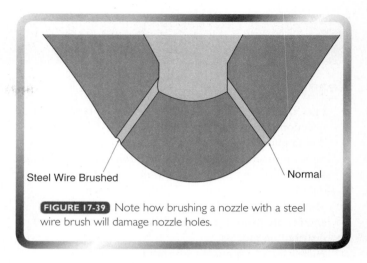

Steel Wire Brushed Normal

FIGURE 17-39 Note how brushing a nozzle with a steel wire brush will damage nozzle holes.

When injector lines are disconnected or when nozzles are removed for servicing, both the tips and inlet fittings should be capped with protective seals. Nozzles should never be handled by their tips with bare fingers, because oils and dirt can contaminate the spray holes.

Wrap-Up

Ready for Review

- Injector nozzles are incorporated into every type of fuel injection system.
- The simplest function of an injector nozzle is to permit highly pressurized fuel to squeeze through one or multiple small orifices in the nozzle tip, which atomizes and distributes fuel into the combustion chamber.
- The performance, efficiency, and emissions of diesel engines are major functions of the fuel atomization and distribution process.
- Fuel nozzles, combined with combustion chamber turbulence, distribute and mix fuel throughout the combustion chamber.
- The amount of time necessary for combustion is dependent on the quality of fuel, pre-ignition temperature, and degree of atomization.
- A nozzle consists of two main parts: the nozzle or needle valve and a larger assembly that encloses the nozzle, called the nozzle body.
- Closed nozzles operate using a pressure differential principle.
- Diesel engine fuel systems require an abrupt beginning and end of injection; without this, a gradual loss of pressure at the nozzle tip would result in increasing spray droplet size and decreasing penetration.
- Precise matching of the injector to the shape of the piston bowl and the turbulence of the combustion chamber is critical for efficient combustion.
- Closed injector nozzles are the most popular nozzle type in use today; there are two types of closed nozzles: the multi-orifice nozzle and the pintle nozzle.
- Multi-orifice, or multi-hole, nozzles are used in direct injection engines; they have four or more spray holes at the injector tip.
- Pintle nozzles are used in indirect injection engines; they have only one spray hole in the injector tip.
- Variable geometry injectors, which are currently under development, use two or more rows of orifices located around the tip of the injector.
- The two-spring, two-stage injector nozzle mechanically controls injection rate by using varying the amount of nozzle valve lift using two nozzle valve springs.
- Fuel spray from nozzle testers is under pressure high enough to penetrate skin, which can cause blood poisoning. Never bring hands near the end of injector nozzles, and always wear eye protection.

Vocabulary Builder

abrasive flow machining (AFM) A process of enhancing the flow characteristics and performance of injector nozzles by smoothing passageways through the injector and enlarging the spray holes by running an abrasive compound through the nozzles.

atomization The process of breaking up liquid fuel into a fine mist.

back leakage A calibrated leakage of fuel around the nozzle valve to lubricate and cool the valve.

beginning of injection (BOI) The point when fuel delivery begins and is referenced according to the position of the crankshaft measured in degrees of crankshaft rotation.

electronic unit injectors (EUI) An electrically controlled injector incorporating timing, metering, atomization, and pressurization functions into a single unit or injector.

forward leakage Leakage of an injector nozzle from the spray holes, which indicates that the nozzle valve-to-seat seal is poor.

hydraulic nozzle holder The nozzle body that encloses the nozzle assembly containing passageways connecting the high-pressure injection line to the nozzle valve.

injection lag The time delay that occurs between the start of fuel pressurization and the moment when injection actually takes place; also known as injection delay.

leak-off lines Lines at the injectors that collect fuel and return it to the fuel tank.

multi-orifice nozzle A fuel nozzle that uses multiple spray holes to atomize and distribute fuel.

needle lift sensor A sensor that provides a reference signal to the electronic control module for the beginning of injection (BOI) by providing information about movement of the nozzle valve.

nozzle chatter A high-pitched noise or chirping sound produced by the high-speed cycling of the nozzle valve opening and closing with contact between the valve and seat.

nozzle differential ratio The ratio between the surface area of the nozzle valve that is acted upon by high-pressure fuel when the valve is closed compared to the nozzle valve area when the nozzle valve is unseated.

nozzle opening pressure (NOP) The pressure required to unseat the nozzle valve and begin the injection of fuel. Also known as valve opening pressure (VOP).

nozzle valve A valve in the nozzle that seals the end of the nozzle tip when it is not injecting fuel; also known as a needle valve.

pintle nozzle A fuel nozzle which sprays fuel through a single hole.

pop tester A tool used by technicians that supplies pressurized fuel to injector nozzles which is used to evaluate the condition of fuel nozzles.

pressure wave reflection The movement of a pressure wave back and forth along the length of an injector line. Like the sloshing of water in a tub, the pressure wave bounces back and forth between the nozzle and high pressure pump.

throttle pintle nozzle A type of injector that changes the rate of injection from the nozzle through the shape of the nozzle valve; also called a delay nozzle.

variable orifice nozzle A type of nozzle that is under development, which has two rows of spray holes that regulate the delivery rate, spray angle, and spray hole size with a variable lift nozzle valve; also known as a coaxial nozzle.

Review Questions

1. The _____ is the nozzle body that encloses the nozzle assembly containing passageways connecting the high-pressure injection line to the nozzle valve.
   a. hydraulic nozzle holder
   b. throttle pintle nozzle
   c. electronic unit injector
   d. pintle nozzle

2. The _____ is a fuel nozzle which sprays fuel through a single hole.
   a. throttle pintle nozzle
   b. pintle nozzle
   c. multi-orifice nozzle
   d. hydraulic nozzle holder

3. The _____ is a fuel nozzle that uses multiple spray holes to atomize and distribute fuel.
   a. electronic unit injector
   b. throttle pintle nozzle
   c. pintle nozzle
   d. multi-orifice nozzle

4. The throttle pintle nozzle is a type of injector that changes the rate of injection from the nozzle through the shape of the nozzle valve, also called a _____.
   a. pintle nozzle
   b. throttle pintle nozzle
   c. delay nozzle
   d. multi-orifice nozzle

5. The _____ is an electrically controlled injector incorporating timing, metering, atomization, and pressurization functions into a single unit or injector.
   a. electronic unit injector
   b. pintle nozzle
   c. multi-orifice nozzle
   d. throttle pintle nozzle

6. The term _____ is often used to encompass the operation of a hydraulic nozzle.
   a. injector
   b. chatter
   c. connector
   d. distributor

7. Proper _____ of fuel is critical to reducing the formation of noxious emissions.
   a. compression
   b. distribution
   c. activation
   d. injection

8. Fine _____ helps fuel burn hot, fast, and more completely, leaving less residue.
   a. distribution
   b. pressure
   c. atomization
   d. chatter

9. An identification number stamped on a nozzle's _____ identifies the nozzle and helps differentiate it from similarly shaped nozzles.
   a. body
   b. needle
   c. sac
   d. tip

10. Nozzle _____ during bench testing of an injector is an indication of a clean nozzle valve with good seat contact.
    a. chatter
    b. leakage
    c. punching
    d. abrasive flow machining

ASE-Type Questions

1. Technician A says the size or weight of the fuel droplet divided by its velocity determines the kinetic energy processed by the droplet. Technician B says the size or weight of the fuel droplet must be multiplied by its velocity in order to determine the kinetic energy processed by the droplet. Who is correct?
   a. Technician A
   b. Technician B
   c. Both Technician A and Technician B
   d. Neither Technician A nor Technician B

2. Technician A says injection velocities of fuel can approach 2500 km per second at full load. Technician B says injection velocities of fuel can approach 2000 km per second. Who is correct?
   a. Technician A
   b. Technician B
   c. Both Technician A and Technician B
   d. Neither Technician A nor Technician B

522   **SECTION IV** DIESEL FUEL AND FUEL SYSTEMS

3. Technician A says if only a single injector in an engine is equipped with an integrated nozzle valve lift sensor, injection timing for all cylinders cannot be corrected. Technician B says that all of the injectors in an engine need to be equipped with an integrated nozzle valve lift sensor for injection timing in all cylinders to be corrected. Who is correct?
   a. Technician A
   b. Technician B
   c. Both Technician A and Technician B
   d. Neither Technician A nor Technician B

4. Technician A says newer multi-orifice nozzles may have as many as 13 spray holes in the tip. Technician B says the newer multi-orifice nozzles can have up to a dozen spray holes in the tip. Who is correct?
   a. Technician A
   b. Technician B
   c. Both Technician A and Technician B
   d. Neither Technician A nor Technician B

5. Technician A says the two-spring two-stage injector nozzle mechanically controls injection rate by discharging fuel at two different rates. Technician B says the fuel is discharged at the same rate. Who is correct?
   a. Technician A
   b. Technician B
   c. Both Technician A and Technician B
   d. Neither Technician A nor Technician B

6. Technician A says abrasive flow machining enhances flow characteristics by removing resistance to fuel flow. Technician B says abrasive flow machining permits increased delivery of fuel. Who is correct?
   a. Technician A
   b. Technician B
   c. Both Technician A and Technician B
   d. Neither Technician A nor Technician B

7. Technician A says nozzle geometry is a compromise to promote good mixture preparation across all operating ranges. Technician B says manufacturers are working on variable orifice nozzles. Who is correct?
   a. Technician A
   b. Technician B
   c. Both Technician A and Technician B
   d. Neither Technician A nor Technician B

8. Technician A says nozzle opening pressure is higher in multi-orifice nozzles to produce the atomization, penetration, and distribution of fuel necessary for direct injection combustion chambers. Technician B says the nozzle opening pressure is lower in multi-orifice nozzles. Who is correct?
   a. Technician A
   b. Technician B
   c. Both Technician A and Technician B
   d. Neither Technician A nor Technician B

9. Technician A says vapors originate from the fuel droplet surface as it encounters air friction and absorbs heat produced during the compression stroke. Technician B says these vapors are combustible. Who is correct?
   a. Technician A
   b. Technician B
   c. Both Technician A and Technician B
   d. Neither Technician A nor Technician B

10. Technician A says that particulate matter, including soot and oxides of nitrogen are produced from having too much fuel. Technician B says they are produced from having too much air. Who is correct?
    a. Technician A
    b. Technician B
    c. Both Technician A and Technician B
    d. Neither Technician A nor Technician B

CHAPTER 18
Governors

NATEF Tasks

Diesel Engines

General

- Observe engine exhaust smoke color and quantity; determine needed action. (pp 525–526, 536–537)
- Check engine no cranking, cranks but fails to start, hard starting, and starts but does not continue to run problems; determine needed action. (p 542)
- Identify engine surging, rough operation, misfiring, low power, slow deceleration, slow acceleration, and shutdown problems; determine needed action. (pp 544–546)

Fuel System

Electronic Fuel Management System

- Check and record electronic diagnostic codes and trip/operational data; monitor electronic data; clear codes; determine further diagnosis. (pp 538–541)
- Using electronic service tool(s) access and interpret customer programmable parameters. (pp 545–549)

Knowledge Objectives

After reading this chapter, you will be able to:

1. Describe the functions, construction, and operating principles of mechanical and electronic governors. (pp 526–534)
2. Identify and describe the types, styles, and applications of mechanical and electronic governors. (pp 534–546)
3. Recommend adjustments of mechanical governors. (pp 546–551)

Skills Objectives

After reading this chapter, you will be able to:

1. Test maximum engine speed for a mechanical governor. (p548) **SKILL DRILL 18-1**

2. Adjust maximum vehicle speed. (p 548) **SKILL DRILL 18-2**

3. Adjust engine protection fault response. (p551) **SKILL DRILL 18-3**

▶ Introduction

Diesel engines, unlike gasoline-fueled engines, do not use a throttle plate to regulate power output. Instead, engine speed and torque are controlled by the quantity of fuel injected into the cylinders by the high-pressure fuel system **FIGURE 18-1**. Monitoring the engine speed and adjusting the fuel quantity required by the engine for a given speed and load condition is the job of the diesel engine governor. The importance of these tasks makes the governor one of the most critical systems for providing responsive engine operation, performance, and emission control. Governors are an electronic control subsystem integrated into the engine ECM and operate according to programmed instructions in engine calibration software **FIGURE 18-2**. The sophistication of software-controlled governing on electronic engines has allowed the term *governor* to fall into disuse. Now governors operate invisibly using electronic signal processing strategies, and its operation is programmable **FIGURE 18-3**. Information provided in this chapter will enable diesel technicians and operators to properly understand the basics of governor operation in order to develop diagnostic strategies and make adjustments to electronic governors.

▶ You Are the Technician

A customer with a line-haul tractor has repeatedly returned to your shop complaining of low engine power. Other technicians have spent many hours checking the engine for possible causes of low power, such as restrictions in the low-pressure supply system, plugged air filters, damaged turbochargers, exhaust gas recirculation (EGR) system defects, and incorrect valve and injector adjustments. No problems were found, and the customer was told that there are no mechanical or electrical faults with the engine. The engine has also been tested on a chassis dynamometer, and the horsepower was measured at the rear wheels and was found to be even slightly better than specification. On yet another visit, the customer speaks with you, insisting something is wrong with the engine, and you ask her when the problems began. The customer tells you the problems began after the ECM was replaced. She also indicates that, in addition to experiencing low power, fuel consumption had significantly increased. But she believes this is due to the excessive downshifting of the transmission needed to get the tractor to climb hills. You now realize that there could likely be a problem with the calibration of the ECM or that perhaps some of the programmable parameters were not correctly adjusted. As you begin to investigate further, consider the following:

1. When measuring the power output of the engine on the chassis dynamometer, how is a single measurement of maximum horsepower misleading when investigating a low power complaint? What other important measures related to engine torque and power would be useful?

2. Identify some possible problems with programmable engine parameters that could possibly produce a low power complaint. Explain your answers.

3. List what you might do with a few programmable parameters before road testing to determine whether the low power complaint is due to incorrectly adjusted programmable parameters.

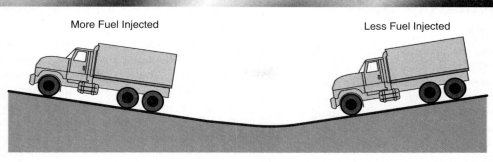

More Fuel Injected

Less Fuel Injected

FIGURE 18-1 Governors directly control changes to engine fueling. The operator only indirectly controls fueling through one of several inputs. Increasing quantities of fuel injected produces speed and torque changes.

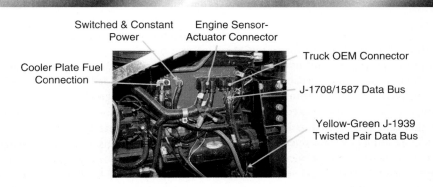

Switched & Constant Power

Engine Sensor-Actuator Connector

Cooler Plate Fuel Connection

Truck OEM Connector

J-1708/1587 Data Bus

Yellow-Green J-1939 Twisted Pair Data Bus

FIGURE 18-2 Governors are an engine control subsystem integrated into the engine ECM and operate according to programmed instructions in engine calibration software.

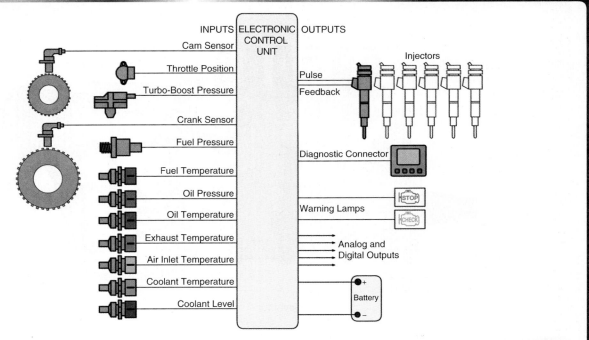

INPUTS   ELECTRONIC CONTROL UNIT   OUTPUTS

Cam Sensor
Throttle Position
Turbo-Boost Pressure
Crank Sensor
Fuel Pressure
Fuel Temperature
Oil Pressure
Oil Temperature
Exhaust Temperature
Air Inlet Temperature
Coolant Temperature
Coolant Level

Pulse
Feedback

Injectors

Diagnostic Connector

Warning Lamps

STOP
CHECK

Analog and Digital Outputs

Battery

FIGURE 18-3 While the high-pressure injection system meters the fuel supplied to the combustion chamber, the governor controls the quantity of fuel injected based on a variety of inputs and software instructions.

▶ Fundamentals of Diesel Governors

The governor is one of the most critical mechanical or electronic control subsystems needed by a diesel engine. Without the governors' capability to regulate fuel delivery for varying speed and load conditions, engine operation would be erratic at minimum and, at worst, would result in rapid engine destruction. While technicians typically do not often encounter governors in terms of service or repair like other engine systems, its influence on engine operation cannot be overestimated. The governor is essential to the functioning of the fuel system. Technicians can be expected to make adjustments to governors, so an understanding of governor functioning and terminology is vital.

Governor Functions

Because governors directly control fuel system operation, it's important to understand principles of governor operation and various terms associated with governor function. Comprehending governor terms and principles is helpful to technicians when analyzing engine performance or emission-related problems. When problems do arise that can be corrected with an adjustment or recalibration, understanding governor operating principles will help build effective diagnostic and service skills. The terminology and functions described in this next section apply to both electronic and mechanical governors.

Adjusting Fueling to Engine Load and Operator Demand

There are several reasons unique to diesel engine operation that make the use of governors necessary. First, on mechanical or electronically controlled high-pressure injection systems, very small changes in injection quantity produce very large changes in engine speed. And unlike gasoline engines with throttle plates, no single position of the fueling mechanism, such as a control rack inside an injection pump or the length of an electrical signal applied to an injector, is acceptable for particular speed and load conditions. If only throttle linkage was connected to directly control fuel delivery, such as a control rack inside a high-pressure pump, the slightest movements of the throttle pedal would produce excessively large changes in engine speed and power output **FIGURE 18-4**. It is impractical to have the vehicle operator continually make these fine adjustments through the throttle pedal to maintain engine speed and power output as load and speed vary.

The same holds true for electronic governors. The slightest change to engine loads or speeds require an adjustment to engine fueling, or the engine will either stall or accelerate rapidly and wildly. Consider for example a cold engine that has just started. Changes to engine friction take place continuously because lubricating oil thins, or the load changes when accessories such as the alternator, cooling fan, or air-conditioning compressor cycle on and off. If there were a direct mechanical linkage to the injection pump from the operator's pedal that controlled engine

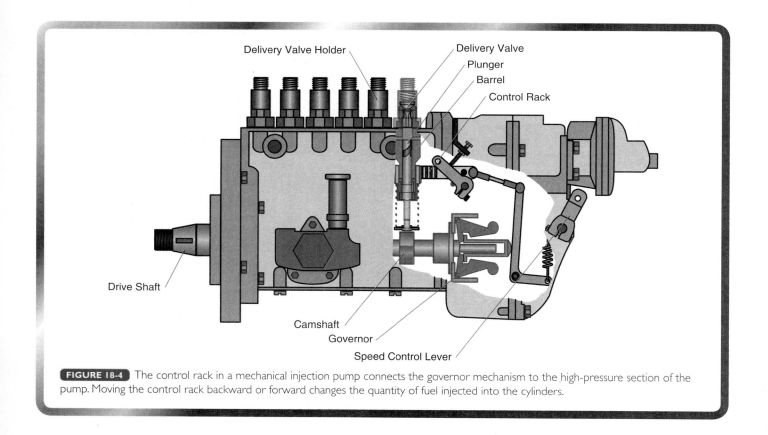

FIGURE 18-4 The control rack in a mechanical injection pump connects the governor mechanism to the high-pressure section of the pump. Moving the control rack backward or forward changes the quantity of fuel injected into the cylinders.

speed, the operator would be required to make too many small, incremental adjustments to maintain a constant, stable idle speed or any engine speed. To better understand this, consider engine operation at idle speed. **Idle** is an engine's minimum operational speed. Also remember that at idle, only a very small amount of fuel is injected, typically 2–8 mm^3. A droplet of fuel is approximately 25 mm^3. Increasing the engine speed to its maximum from idle only requires about 1 mm^3 of additional fuel for each combustion cycle in each cylinder. Controlling changes to such small injection quantities using a direct mechanical connection to the throttle pedal is simply not possible.

Controlling Engine Acceleration

A second important reason for the use of governors in diesel engines is that diesel engines possess a naturally high acceleration rate. Because the air intake is unrestricted and fuel injection rate can go to maximum delivery quantity almost instantly, the rate of acceleration of a diesel engine can be as much as 2000 rpm/sec. That means that for each second of uncontrolled fueling, the engine speed will increase 2000 rpm. This capability can easily cause the engine to go beyond critical rpm in a short time. To prevent this, governors have speed-sensing and fuel-regulating capabilities to minimize the likelihood of a runaway engine.

Limiting maximum engine speed and acceleration rate is also critical to emission control. A diesel will run out of time to complete combustion events when operating at excessive speed. As engine speed increases, the time available for diesel combustion

events is shorter. More exhaust smoke is produced at high engine speeds because combustion is incomplete FIGURE 18-5.

Maximum engine speed is limited by all types of diesel engine governors and the rate of acceleration is carefully regulated by a gradual increase in fueling. Emission decals on diesel engines indicate maximum engine speed or rated rpm. Exceeding rated rpm on a diesel can produce excessive particulate matter (PM) emissions because at higher rpm, the combustion process runs out of time to completely burn fuel FIGURE 18-6. Regulation of the engine's acceleration rate to minimize exhaust smoke production partly explains why diesel engines may seem "lazy" during acceleration.

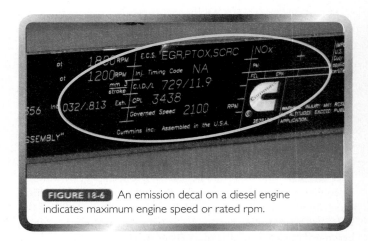

FIGURE 18-6 An emission decal on a diesel engine indicates maximum engine speed or rated rpm.

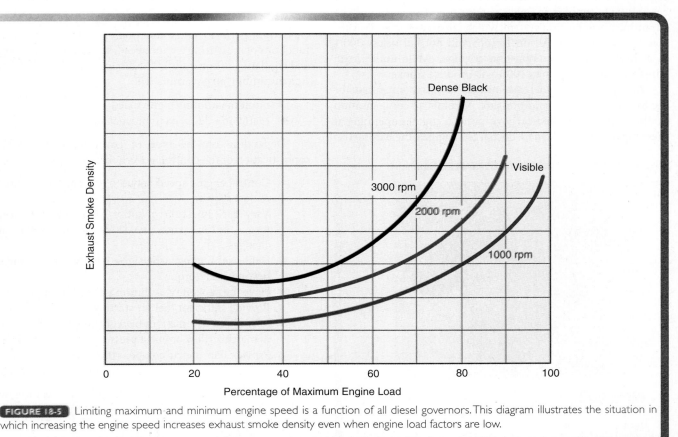

FIGURE 18-5 Limiting maximum and minimum engine speed is a function of all diesel governors. This diagram illustrates the situation in which increasing the engine speed increases exhaust smoke density even when engine load factors are low.

▶ TECHNICIAN TIP

Governors play an important role in minimizing the formation of PM emissions or smoke. The quantity of fuel injected to control engine speed and torque is regulated by the governor. Exceeding the rated speed of an engine will produce smoke emissions from incompletely burned fuel, because the time available for combustion events becomes too short at high speeds. Similarly, air–fuel ratios are also controlled by the governor to ensure an adequate mass of air is available to properly combust injected fuel. Air and fuel quantities are carefully calculated by the manufacturer. Tampering with governor controls to increase the quantity of fuel for a given speed or load condition will increase torque output but can also produce excessive emissions.

Managing Air–Fuel Ratio Controls

Governors perform a critical function in emission reduction. Incorporated into governor operation are emission-control mechanisms that regulate air–fuel ratio controls. Air–fuel ratio controls minimize the production of PM emissions or black smoke produced during engine acceleration **FIGURE 18-7** and **FIGURE 18-8**. Smoke occurs because airflow can lag behind the injection of pressurized fuel. To prevent smoke, the injection quantity of fuel cannot exceed the amount of air mass filling the combustion chamber needed to properly burn the fuel. A governor operates to limit the quantity of fuel injected if there is not enough air to support complete combustion. Diesel engines are a lean-burn combustion system, which means excess air is available for combustion. Air–fuel ratios will not fall below 300:1 in a direct injection combustion chamber while under load. Air–fuel ratios of less than 100:1 will produce smoke.

At high altitudes, fuel systems may need to compensate for the loss of air density and pressure. Barometric compensation can be built into mechanical governors on engines operating at these higher altitudes. On turbocharged engines, the barometric

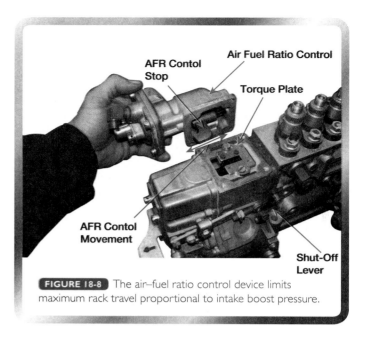

FIGURE 18-8 The air–fuel ratio control device limits maximum rack travel proportional to intake boost pressure.

sensor may also reduce fueling to prevent turbochargers from over–speeding, which occurs at high altitudes. Normalization of intake boost pressure by turbochargers (i.e., maintaining intake manifold boost pressure), which is a concept explained in the Fixed Geometry and Wastegated Turbochargers chapter, leads to turbocharger overspeed at high altitudes.

Other Governor Operations

Governors perform other functions in addition to the basic functions of measuring engine speed, sensing operator demand, and regulating the quantity of fuel injected into engine cylinders. At a minimum, all governors will:

- Limit maximum engine speed
- Maintain idle speed to prevent stalling

Depending on the type of governor, application, and sophistication of the control, governors may also:

- Control engine speed between idle and top engine limit or **rated speed**
- Vary fuel injection quantity to increase or decrease torque output when the load applied to the engine changes
- Decrease fueling when the engine speed increases beyond peak torque
- Have the capability of shutting down the engine
- Provide sufficient fuel for starting
- Minimize PM emissions by regulating the delivery of fuel to match airflow or boost pressure to engine cylinders
- Provide barometric compensation for fuel injection rate
- Dampen engine surge when engine loads rapidly change

Electronic governors can provide additional features, which include but are not limited to:

- Fast idle speed
- Shut-down timers

FIGURE 18-7 The torque plate limits maximum air–fuel ratio control movement. Steps on the plate set maximum control rack travel.

- Cruise control
- Limitation of vehicle speed
- **Programmable parameters** are measurable values about engine system operation that can be changed using service software; examples of common programmable parameters include idle speed, maximum engine and road speed, cruise control limits, engine protection limits, features that encourage efficient transmission shifting such as progressive shifting and gear-down protection, anti-tampering, load-based speed control, torque limiting, cold-weather protection, and adaptive terrain fueling (smart cruise)
- Remote throttle control for power take-off devices such as rear engine power take-off (REPTO) or power take-off (PTO)
- Surge or bucking dampeners, which provide smoother vehicle deceleration

► TECHNICIAN TIP

When learning to understand engine power measurements, the difference between engine torque and horsepower can be confusing. Horsepower is a function of torque and engine speed, whereas torque is only the result of cylinder pressure applied against the crankshaft throw. Stated another way, torque is a twisting force exerted by the crankshaft of an engine.

Governor Terminology

To understand principles of diesel engine governing, it is essential to recognize a number of basic terms associated with governor operation and control.

Torque

Ultimately, torque is the force that moves the vehicle or equipment load. It is the result of cylinder pressure applied against the crankshaft throw. Stated another way, torque is a twisting force exerted by the crankshaft of an engine. Expressed mathematically, torque = force (pounds) × length of lever (feet) = pounds per foot (or foot-pounds as it is more commonly called). The Imperial measuring unit for torque is the ft-lb; the SI measuring unit is the newton meter (Nm) (torque = force [newtons] × length of lever [meters] = Nm) **FIGURE 18-9**.

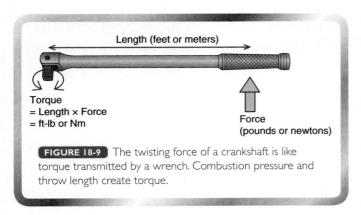

FIGURE 18-9 The twisting force of a crankshaft is like torque transmitted by a wrench. Combustion pressure and throw length create torque.

No motion is necessary to produce torque. Pushing on a one-foot-long wrench with 100 pounds of force will produce 100 ft-lb of torque, but if the bolt or nut is seized, no motion takes place. Torque is developed by the engine's crankshaft and is a function of the length of the crankshaft throw and the force or pressure inside the cylinder. A longer throw or stroke and/or greater cylinder pressure will produce increasing amounts of torque from the engine.

Diesel engines produce more torque compared to an equivalently displaced gasoline-fueled engine because higher compression ratios produce greater cylinder pressure (force) and longer crankshaft throws (lever length) due to longer stroke length.

It is helpful to understand that an engine produces virtually no torque at idle or high idle. Only enough cylinder pressure is produced to overcome engine friction and inertia to keep a crankshaft turning at idle rpm. When crankshaft or flywheel movement is resisted by applying a load to the engine, the fuel system is designed to produce torque or **torque rise**. Torque rise is the difference between peak torque and torque at rated speed. An increase in torque is the result of injecting greater quantities of fuel into the engine, which increases cylinder pressure.

Horsepower

Horsepower is a function of torque and engine speed. It is calculated by multiplying torque times engine rpm and dividing by a mathematical constant that represents one horsepower. What that means is horsepower has a unit of time in its measurement. For example, two engines can produce an identical amount of torque, but if one produces it at a faster speed, the horsepower increases.

High Idle Speed

Also known as maximum no-load speed, **high idle** speed is the highest rpm at which the governor permits the engine to operate with no load. This occurs when the throttle is at maximum fuel position or wide-open throttle (WOT), and the vehicle is in neutral. To improve engine efficiency, it is important to note that on many engines, a programmable feature limits engine speed when no vehicle speed is detected.

Low Idle Speed

Low idle speed is the rpm at which the engine operates when the throttle pedal is released. Idle speed is regulated by the governor, which operates to maintain a constant stable idle speed even as engine loads change. Stable, consistent idle speed uses the feature referred to as compensation, which is discussed in the Functions of High-Pressure Fuel Systems chapter. Compensation means that the loss or gain of power from one or more cylinders will cause the governor to increase or decrease fueling automatically to maintain idle speed. Compensation is one feature that all governors have.

Rated Speed

Rated speed is the rpm at which the most horsepower is produced from a diesel engine. Rated speed coincides with the maximum horsepower the engine will produce while under load.

Rated speed is required on the emissions decal because exceeding rated speed will produce excessive emissions. The injection quantity to produce rated speed is also usually indicated on the emission decal to help technicians make adjustments and diagnose low power complaints.

Speed Droop

Simply explained, upper speed <u>droop</u> is the change or difference in engine speed caused by an increase in load near rated speed. Upper speed droop occurs as engine fueling decreases when the engine approaches its rated speed. In mechanical governors, upper speed droop occurs because greater spring force inside the governor is required to move a control actuator, such as a control rack, in the full fuel position needed to operate an engine at rated speed. As the percentage of droop increases, fuel economy improves and emissions may drop; however, engine power is reduced **FIGURE 18-10**. While it may be possible to increase fueling of an engine as its speed drops, it can lead to increased emissions and poor fuel economy and cannot be adjusted beyond rated speed.

Droop is usually expressed as the difference in engine speed measured at high-idle rpm compared to engine rpm after a load is placed on the engine. This means that if an engine has a high idle speed of 2000 rpm and the speed drops by 200 rpm after it is loaded, the change from 2000 to 1800 rpm would mean it has a 10% speed droop.

Droop is an operating factor that has a significant impact on performance and fuel economy. Consider that during normal operation, as a vehicle climbs an uphill grade, the injection systems should provide progressively increasing fueling to the engine in order to maintain vehicle speed. Continued uphill climbing, with WOT, could eventually result in the maximum fueling rate being attained with little effect on vehicle speed. Fueling without a significant speed increase will result in wasted fuel and potentially excessive emissions. Allowing the engine speed to taper off, or droop, in this speed/load range will result in improved fuel economy. Any loss in power or performance is often disproportional to the improvement in fuel economy. Vehicle speed can be maintained but with a penalty to fuel economy by using a governor with little or no droop. Vehicles equipped with governors with a high percentage of droop (i.e.,

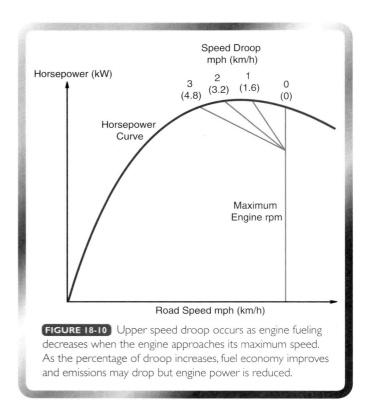

FIGURE 18-10 Upper speed droop occurs as engine fueling decreases when the engine approaches its maximum speed. As the percentage of droop increases, fuel economy improves and emissions may drop but engine power is reduced.

more than 5%) are perceived as having poor performance ("it won't pull") but achieve better fuel efficiency.

Lower speed droop is not as much of a concern because the setting is used to control engine speed on downhill grades. Increasing the lower speed droop will change how far a vehicle can go beyond its governed vehicle speed. Increasing lower droop by 1, 2, or 3 mph (1.6, 3.2, or 4.8 km/h) will allow the vehicle to travel faster. Faster downhill speed may help a truck or bus climb the next hill using less fuel. The trade-off of increasing lower droop speed is vehicle speed control **TABLE 18-1**.

Adjusting droop on an electronically controlled engine can be achieved through OEM software **FIGURE 18-11**. Increasing the amount of maximum upper speed droop will reduce the time the engine spends at maximum fueling, improving fuel

TABLE 18-1: Adjusting Droop Settings

Setting	Upper Droop Performance vs. Fuel Economy	Lower Droop Performance vs. Speed Control
0 mph (0 km/h)	Best Performance No Fuel Economy Benefit	Best Speed Control No Performance Benefit
1 mph (1.6 km/h)	Good Performance Moderate Fuel Economy Benefit	Good Speed Control Slight Performance Benefit
2 mph (3.2 km/h)	Decreased Performance Moderate Fuel Economy Benefit	Fair Speed Control Moderate Performance Benefit
3 mph (4.8 km/h)	Reduced Performance Best Fuel Economy Benefit	Reduced Speed Control Best Performance Benefit

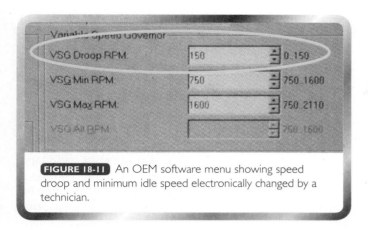

FIGURE 18-11 An OEM software menu showing speed droop and minimum idle speed electronically changed by a technician.

economy. Decreasing the amount of upper speed droop will allow an engine to maintain its speed but near its maximum fueling position. Performance, torque, and road speed, are increased or enhanced with less governor upper speed droop.

Droop Curve

Droop curve is the slope of the speed decrease near rated engine speed. Expressed as a percentage of high idle speed, the droop curve is the difference between an engine's high idle speed minus maximum engine speed without a load, and rated speed engine minus maximum speed with load. A 100-rpm difference in an engine with a high idle speed of 2000 rpm is a 5% droop. The droop curve can be managed both mechanically and electronically.

Governor Cut-Off

Governor cut-off is the speed at which the governor cuts off fueling, meaning no additional fuel is supplied for injection. Cut-off occurs at rated or high idle engine speed.

Hunting

Hunting refers to the rhythmic change in engine idle speed often caused by unbalanced fuel delivery in one or more engine cylinders. Engines using highly sensitive governors are prone to hunting. Both electronically and mechanically governed engines can hunt under a variety of operating conditions. Various fuel and engine system faults can cause hunting.

Overrun

Overrun is the inability of a governor to keep the engine speed below the high idle speed when it is rapidly accelerated.

Overspeed

Overspeed is any speed above high idle.

Peak Torque

Peak torque is the engine speed at which maximum cylinder pressure is produced. The highest cylinder pressures are produced during peak torque because the fuel injection rate is greatest. For on-highway diesel engines, peak torque is commonly found at two-thirds of the rated speed (i.e., 2000 rpm for a 3000 rpm rated speed engine or 1200 rpm for an 1800

rpm rated speed engine). This is the point in the **performance curve** (a line graph that plots engine torque, fuel consumption, and horsepower against engine speed) where the engine pulls best.

Torque Rise

Torque rise is the increase in engine torque as engine speed is decreased from rated speed to the engine speed where peak torque occurs. When an engine is operated at a speed above peak torque, the drop in engine speed results in increased torque or torque rise as the engine speed slows while encountering a hill or moving a heavier load. When measured, it is the difference between torque at rated engine speed and the engine speed where torque output is highest **FIGURE 18-12**. Because it is the slope of an engine's power curve that is measured, torque rise is expressed as a percentage. Cylinder pressure is highest at peak torque because the maximum amount of fuel is injected, which is supported by high turbocharger boost pressures. Highest turbocharger boost pressures, however, are matched with peak horsepower. A high percentage of torque rise means a greater amount of torque is generated as vehicle speed drops while under load, such as climbing a hill. In other words, torque rise is a measure of an engine's lugging ability to increase pulling power under load as engine rpm drops. A distinction should be made between lugging ability and lugging. Lugging ability is a non-precise, but common, phrase used to describe load-pulling abilities. As it is used here, **lugging** is a technical term that describes an abuse condition when an engine operates under heavy load below an acceptable operating speed range. Lugging an engine can damage engine bearings because high cylinder pressures are accompanied by low oil pressure that could allow metal-to-metal contact

Governors for engines used in line-haul on highway applications will produce a high torque rise, while vocational vehicles operating in the city or with mixed highway and city driving will use a smaller torque rise. Off-road equipment operating under varying speed and load conditions generally use low-torque rise

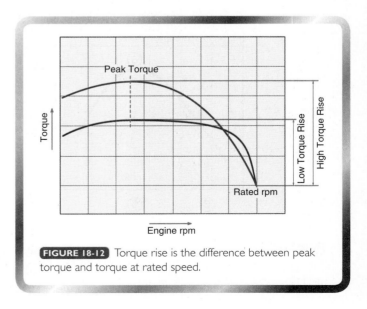

FIGURE 18-12 Torque rise is the difference between peak torque and torque at rated speed.

governing **FIGURE 18-13** and **FIGURE 18-14**. These figures illustrate the performance curves for two identical horsepower diesel engines, one for on-highway applications and the other for vocational use. Figure 18-13 calls out the following:

1. Peak torque. Expressed in ft-lb or Nm, this is where the maximum cylinder pressures occur because the quantity of injected fuel and air are greatest.

2. Peak torque rpm. The speed where the greatest torque is generated. Both the rpm and peak torque are listed together on the engine data plate.

3. Rated speed. The engine rpm at which maximum engine power is developed when the engine is under load. This number is also referenced on the engine data plate.

4. Maximum horsepower rpm. Also referred to as advertised horsepower.

5. Torque rise. This is the change in the engine torque from peak torque to rated speed. A small difference would be a low torque rise. A high torque rise engine develops more torque as it is loaded or lugged down from rated speed to peak torque.

6. Command point. The point where maximum fuel economy and horsepower coincide. Rear axle ratios and tire sizes are calculated to coincide with the point where the vehicle is most often at cruising speed.

High torque rise governing is preferred for on-highway line-haul trucks and buses, because it enables the use of transmissions with fewer gears. For a commercial vehicle, high torque rise allows the operator to downshift the transmission less often when climbing a grade or when under heavy load. This is important because downshifting increases fuel consumption as it causes the engine to turn faster and slows the vehicle. High torque rise can actually help increase fuel economy. Staying in a direct gear range longer (i.e., when engine rpm and transmission output shaft speed are the same) translates into lower fuel consumption. Because a vehicle's axle gear ratio and tire size are selected to enable the engine to cruise in an engine speed range for best fuel economy, which is above peak torque, a drop in speed while climbing a hill may cause engine speed to drop but torque to increase. And that increase in torque is what a driver needs in order to hold onto a gear longer before downshifting.

Vocational vehicles, city buses, and off-road equipment engines use governors with lower and flatter torque rise profiles. Compared to an engine with high torque rise, less torque is available at peak torque, but more torque is available over a wider engine operating range. Accelerating in city traffic or moving some dirt requires more torque availability at lower engine operating speeds and trading off reduced torque output at higher engine speeds to obtain a wider range of higher torque over all engine speeds. If high torque rise governing is used for a vocational application, the engine will feel powerless most of the time, because maximum torque is available only at top engine speeds. The same complaint is encountered if a low torque rise engine is used for an on-highway bus or line-haul truck application.

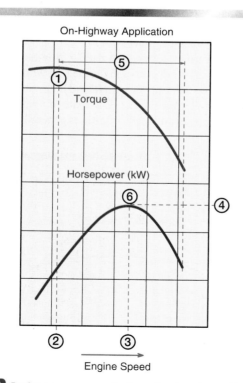
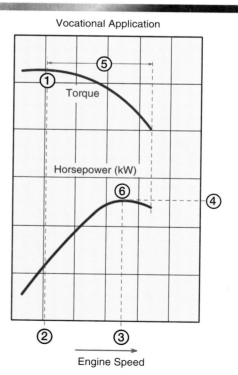

FIGURE 18-13 Performance curves for two diesel engines with identical horsepower. The left curve is for on-highway applications. The right is a flatter curve for vocational use. See the text for specific data points.

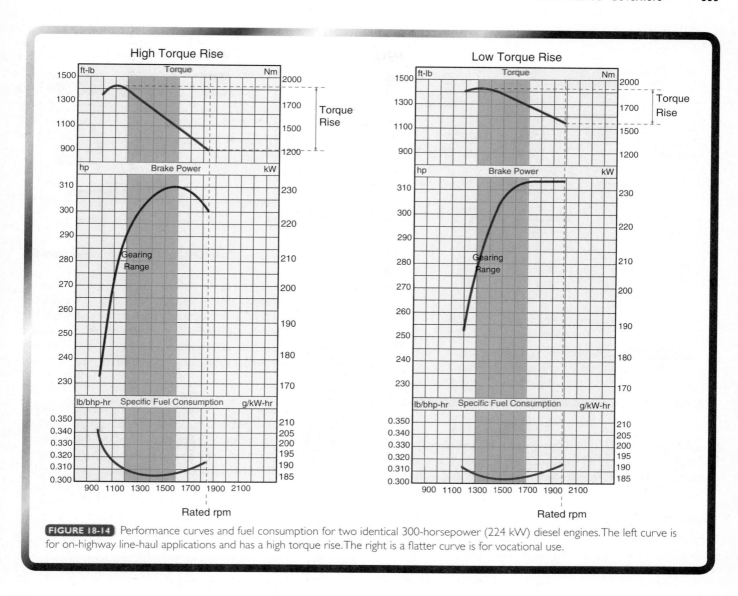

FIGURE 18-14 Performance curves and fuel consumption for two identical 300-horsepower (224 kW) diesel engines. The left curve is for on-highway line-haul applications and has a high torque rise. The right is a flatter curve is for vocational use.

The torque will not rise when the vehicle is under load, which leads to more downshifting and increased fuel consumption. Low torque rise engines use more transmission gear steps. Low speed gear ranges are split for greater gear reduction ratios, whereas on-highway line-haul engines commonly split the top gear ranges. For low torque rise engines, torque converters used by automatic transmissions can also multiply torque by allowing engine speed to rise. Electronic governors are easily adapted to suit a specific application to produce the best power output and lowest fuel consumption.

Increasing engine torque does require more fuel and is not always desirable for the most economical trucking operations. To help solve this problem, electronically controlled on-highway engines can use multiple torque rise profiles or split torque, also called multi-torque power profiles **FIGURE 18-15**. If an engine has multi-torque capabilities, additional engine torque can be supplied under specific conditions, such as climbing very long, steep hills; when in cruise control; or as a bonus from a driver reward system in which drivers are rewarded

with increased torque if they meet, for example, targets for fuel economy. Because the governor can control fueling better than most operators can, increasing torque output while only in cruise mode encourages drivers to use the cruise control more. Adaptive cruise controls called "Smart Power" allows the engine to learn the terrain, whether the vehicle is operating mostly on hilly roads or flat interstate highways. Higher torque output is provided if the engine ECM learns the vehicle is operating over hilly terrain. A variety of programmable parameters can be selected by a technician to determine when an increase or decrease in engine torque is beneficial.

A similar feature introduced more recently by engine manufacturers is something called **load-based speed control**. This feature will not only supply increased torque and sometimes more engine rpm when climbing hills with heavy loads, it will also reduce torque when it senses the vehicle is unloaded or only lightly loaded.

To calculate torque rise, the peak torque is divided by the torque available at rated speed or horsepower. It is expressed as a

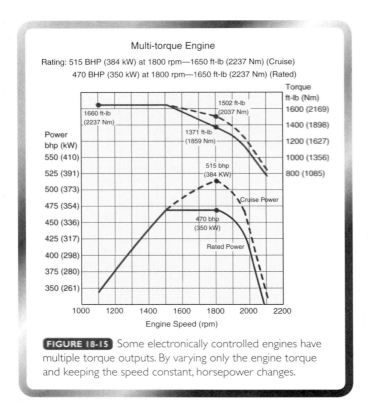

FIGURE 18-15 Some electronically controlled engines have multiple torque outputs. By varying only the engine torque and keeping the speed constant, horsepower changes.

Construction	Function	Vehicle
Mechanical	Minimum/Maximum Speed Control	
	Variable Speed All Speed Control	
Combined		
Pneumatic		

FIGURE 18-16 The type of governor used depends on the application.

percentage. As an example, if the torque rise is calculated at 15%, the engine develops 15% torque increase for every 100-rpm drop from rated speed to peak torque. High torque rise engines are generally considered to be those with more than 30% increase.

Governor Sensitivity

Governor sensitivity refers to the ability of the governor to respond and maintain a set rpm without fluctuation as load changes. In mechanical governors, sensitivity is often achieved at the expense of governor stability. This means engines with sensitive governors are prone to hunting conditions.

▶ Types of Governors

Governors are differentiated and classified a number ways. One is by type of construction. For example, a governor may be mechanical, electronic, hydraulic, or pneumatic. Another classification is by its function. Variable speed, isochronous, or all-speed governors are used in off-road equipment where the engine generally operates at steady states and needs to develop torque quickly when under load. Automotive governors, or min/max governors are used in on-highway vehicles **FIGURE 18-16**. While a large number and variety of governors exist, this section will review the construction and operation of mechanical and electronic governors commonly found in light- and medium-duty automotive applications.

Construction Classification

While mechanical governors have long been discontinued in on-highway applications due to their inability to meet emission

standards, their sheer numbers and continued use in off-road applications demands that a well-rounded engine technician be familiar with their construction, operation, and adjustment procedures. Electronic governors are integrated into the engine ECM electronics; their construction and operation are covered in the Electronic Signal Processing Principles chapter.

Mechanical

In **mechanical governors**, the functions of sensing engine speed, load, and driver input and processing and making changes to engine fueling are performed by mechanical mechanisms. A mechanical governor typically uses the **centrifugal force**, or the force pulling outward on a rotating body of flyweights to sense engine speed. Driver input is sensed by the governor through a mechanical throttle lever. Output to the injection system is performed through mechanical linkage.

Principles of Operation

Mechanical governors consist of two basic mechanisms:

- Speed-sensing mechanism
- Fuel-changing mechanism

The speed-sensing mechanism senses engine speed changes. The fuel-changing mechanism increases or decreases the amount of fuel supplied to the engine. Together, these governor mechanisms operate to vary the quantities of fuel metered into the engine.

Fuel Control Rack

Before you can understand the specifics of the governor mechanism, it is important to understand that engine fueling takes place by moving an actuator such as the fuel control rack, which in turn changes the quantity of fuel injected into the cylinders **FIGURE 18-17**. The governor is located at the rear of an inline injection pump. The governor changes fueling because it is connected to the injection pump through linkage to control fueling. This linkage, called a rack in in-line injection pumps, extends from the injection pump housing into the governor housing **FIGURE 18-18**. In the injection pump, the fuel control rack meshes with the injection pump's pinion gear segments. The control rack rotates the pumping plungers together in unison,

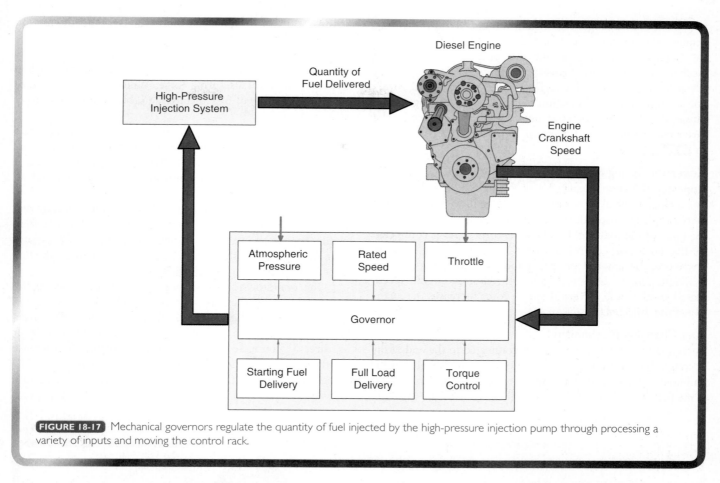

FIGURE 18-17 Mechanical governors regulate the quantity of fuel injected by the high-pressure injection pump through processing a variety of inputs and moving the control rack.

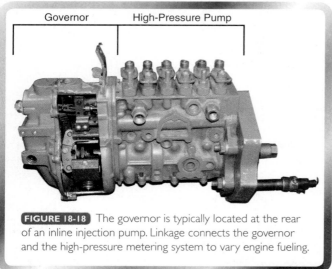

FIGURE 18-18 The governor is typically located at the rear of an inline injection pump. Linkage connects the governor and the high-pressure metering system to vary engine fueling.

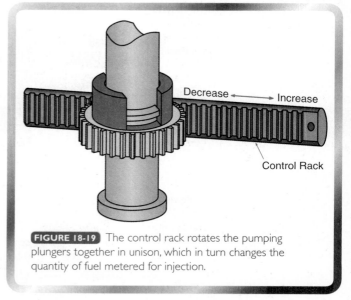

FIGURE 18-19 The control rack rotates the pumping plungers together in unison, which in turn changes the quantity of fuel metered for injection.

which in turn changes the quantity of fuel metered for injection **FIGURE 18-19**. Inputs from the operator, engine shut-off device, engine speed, and intake boost pressure (if equipped with a turbocharger) are received by the governor.

Because small volumes of fuel are delivered at low speed, even the slightest movement in the fuel rack will cause unstable engine operation. For this reason, precision operation and adjustment of the governor is critical to good vehicle performance.

Speed-Sensing Mechanism
Mechanically operated governors typically consist of three main parts:

- A gear drive from the engine
- Flyweights
- Governor spring

The speed-sensing mechanism is responsible for measuring engine speed accurately and sensing operator throttle input.

Centrifugal flyweights are the primary speed-sensing mechanism in mechanical governors. Flyweight force is proportional to engine speed. Flyweights inside a mechanical governor are rotated by the injection pump drive. Centrifugal force causes the flyweight to move outward, applying force to the thrust collar. The end of the rack is connected to the thrust collar **FIGURE 18-20** .

Governor Spring Force

Opposing the centrifugal force of the flyweight is the governor spring. The ball arms of the flyweights move outward with increasing engine speed. However, the spring force acts against the force of the rotating flyweights. A throttle lever connected to the governor control adds or removes spring tension. Therefore, the amount of spring force tension opposing the flyweight force is used to regulate the desired engine speed. Stated another way, governor spring force increases the quantity of fuel injected.

Fuel Changing Mechanism

There is a thrust collar mechanism connected to the end of the flyweight ball arms. The movement or force of the ball arms is summed or directed at this point. Connected to the thrust collar is the fuel control rack or linkage of the high-pressure injection

pump. Movement of the thrust collar will translate into motion in the fuel control rack.

Changing engine speed changes the force exerted by the flyweights against spring tension. A **state of balance** exists when flyweight force equals spring force. When a state of balance exists, the quantity of fuel injected, and therefore engine speed, remains steady.

If flyweight force is greater than spring force, *fueling will decrease*. This occurs when engine speed or power output exceed operator requirements. Because flyweight force increases, it overcomes spring force, thus moving the fuel control rack to decrease fuel to the engine.

If spring force is greater than flyweight force, *fueling will increase*. This occurs when operator demand is greater than engine speed or power output. Because spring force is greater than flyweight force, the control rack moves to increase the fuel injected into the engine **FIGURE 18-21** .

The operator adjusts spring force tension through the throttle lever, so there is no direct mechanical connection between the throttle lever and the control rack or governor output actuator. In some governors, the throttle lever is directly connected to the governor spring to increase or decrease spring tension. In a more popular Bosch RQ governor, changing the state of balance between spring and flyweight force is done by moving a **fulcrum** (the point

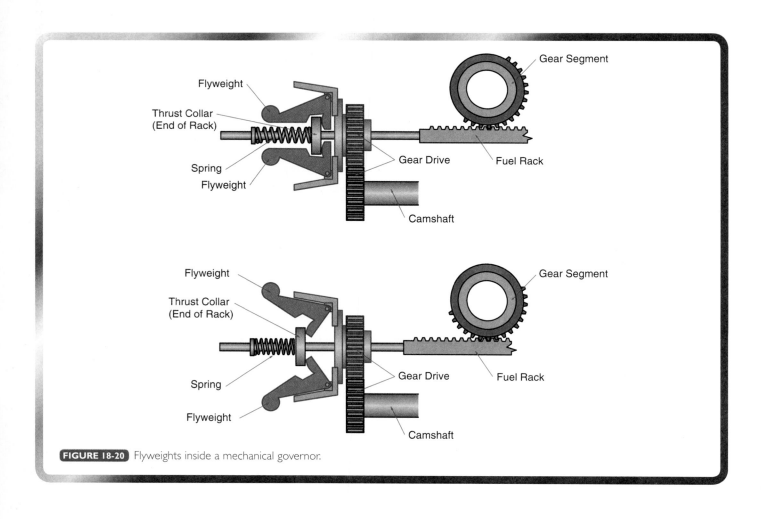

FIGURE 18-20 Flyweights inside a mechanical governor.

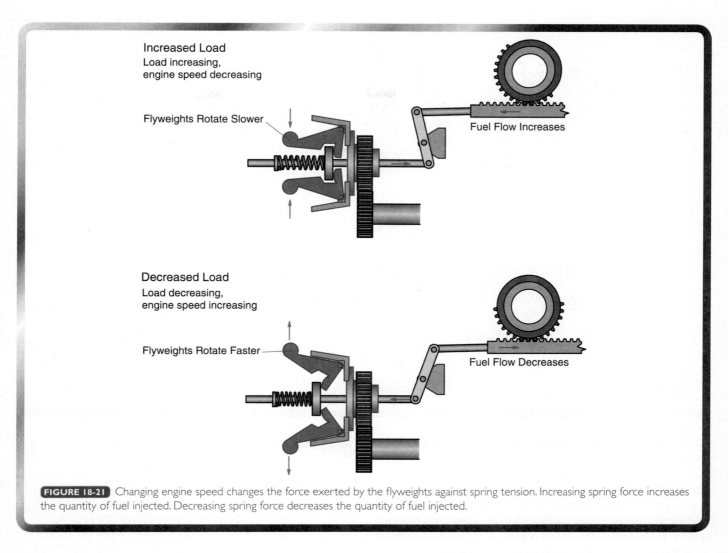

Increased Load
Load increasing,
engine speed decreasing

Flyweights Rotate Slower

Fuel Flow Increases

Decreased Load
Load decreasing,
engine speed increasing

Flyweights Rotate Faster

Fuel Flow Decreases

FIGURE 18-21 Changing engine speed changes the force exerted by the flyweights against spring tension. Increasing spring force increases the quantity of fuel injected. Decreasing spring force decreases the quantity of fuel injected.

around which a lever rotates and that supports the lever and the load) between the spring and flyweight forces using the throttle lever **FIGURE 18-22**.

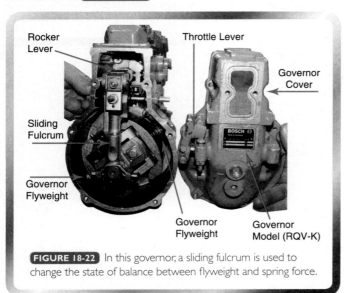

Rocker Lever

Throttle Lever

Governor Cover

Sliding Fulcrum

Governor Flyweight

Governor Flyweight

Governor Model (RQV-K)

FIGURE 18-22 In this governor, a sliding fulcrum is used to change the state of balance between flyweight and spring force.

The force exerted by the spring depends on the throttle lever position. Moving the throttle lever from idle to high idle will add increasing tension to the governor spring. Greater flyweight force or engine speed is necessary to overcome spring force/tension. At idle, the throttle exerts little tension on the governor spring. This means it is easier for flyweight force to be greater than spring force, which causes the control rack to move to a minimum-fuel position. Moving the throttle increases the governor spring tension, which becomes greater than flyweight force. The increased spring force causes the control rack to move to a position where more fuel is injected **FIGURE 18-23**.

Summary of Spring and Flyweight Force Dynamics

Mechanical governors use flyweights that act through mechanical linkage and respond to centrifugal force. As the engine speeds up, the flyweights will move out and operate to decrease engine fueling.

Acting against flyweight force is spring force. Spring force is indirectly varied by the position of the throttle pedal. As the throttle lever is moved to increase fueling, the spring force is increased. It is helpful to remember that flyweight force

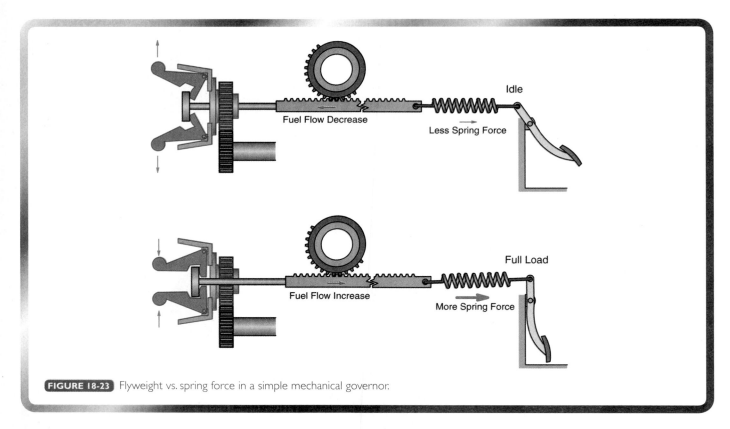

FIGURE 18-23 Flyweight vs. spring force in a simple mechanical governor.

always operates to reduce fueling and spring force operates to increase fueling.

Torque Control

<u>Torque control</u> refers to the governor's capability to regulate the maximum amount of fuel injected into the cylinders for a given engine speed. Generally, torque control is necessary to prevent black smoke caused by inadequate air or combustion chamber design limits. As an engine turns faster, less time is available for combustion; too much fuel will lead to visible emissions. However, addition of fuel above peak torque is provided by the operation of the torque control device **FIGURE 18-24**.

> ### TECHNICIAN TIP
>
> Some shops sell customized performance **torque plate** products, or full load stops, designed to increase fueling above the engine's stock power curve. These plates increase torque and power output by increasing allowable maximum control rack travel. However, alteration of injection pumps beyond engine manufacturers' design limits will increase engine emissions and can lead to driveline damage. Automatic transmissions unable to handle excessive torque will slip and burn. In standard transmissions, the excess torque will push the main and countershaft gears apart with enough force to split the transmission case.

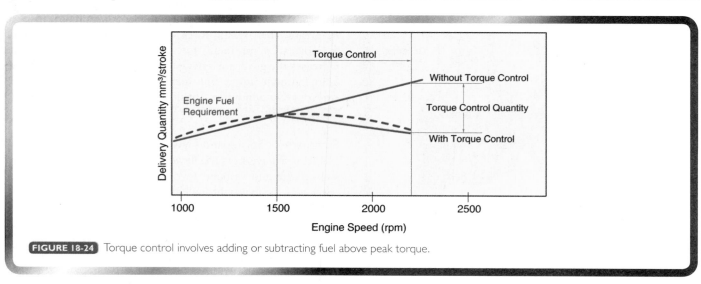

FIGURE 18-24 Torque control involves adding or subtracting fuel above peak torque.

Active Pulse Dampening

When the throttle pedal is pressed, the amount of fuel can quickly increase, causing sudden load change on the engine. The load changes generated during acceleration produce pulsing or jerking movements by the vehicle. To reduce the jerking, a governor mechanism will usually incorporate active pulse dampening to delay the full quantity of fuel delivered for a short time and gradually increase delivery (FIGURE 18-25). During vehicle deceleration, abruptly cutting off fuel supply will also cause the driveline to produce vehicle speed pulsations, causing it to jerk back and forth. In this case, the abrupt decrease in quantity of fuel injected is minimized to dampen driveline pulsations.

These devices simply slow down control rack travel during acceleration and deceleration. By slowing down the speed of change for injection rates, enough time is also provided for the turbocharger to spool and boost, ensuring air supply does not significantly lag behind fuel delivery. These mechanisms, known as **load controllers** or pulse dampeners, improve ride quality and reduce emissions. In electronic governors, the same function is performed by algorithms.

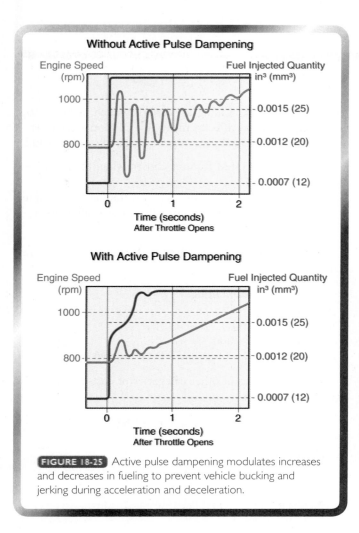

FIGURE 18-25 Active pulse dampening modulates increases and decreases in fueling to prevent vehicle bucking and jerking during acceleration and deceleration.

Air–Fuel Ratio Control

In turbocharged engines, the rate of fuel injection must be matched to the pressure in the intake manifold. Intake manifolds are connected via a line to air–fuel ratio controls (FIGURE 18-26). Without the correct matching of adequate air mass to fuel rate, overfueling will result in the production of black exhaust smoke. Essentially, air–fuel ratio controls limit full-load fuel delivery until air mass adequate for good combustion exists in the cylinders. A leaking or broken connector line will produce a low-power complaint, because without pressurized intake air the governor will not permit full fueling.

TECHNICIAN TIP

Air–fuel ratio controls prevent excess smoke production by limiting the quantity of fuel injected until adequate air supply is available to support combustion. While air–fuel ratio controls are used on naturally aspirated engines, they are even more critical on turbocharged engines. Because turbocharger boost pressure will lag delivery of fuel, excessive and prolonged production of black smoke can occur on engines with malfunctioning or incorrectly adjusted air–fuel ratio controls.

Electronic Governors

Electronic engine governors use principles of electronic signal processing to regulate fueling. Sensor inputs supply data to an ECM, where software stored in the ECM processes the information. Like other information processing systems, the governor collects sensor data and processes the signals using rules contained in software. The output is the amount of fuel required for each cylinder. The ECM produces an output signal used to control output devices such as injectors, fuel pressure regulators, and turbochargers (FIGURE 18-27). Electronic governors can be divided into two categories: partial and full authority systems.

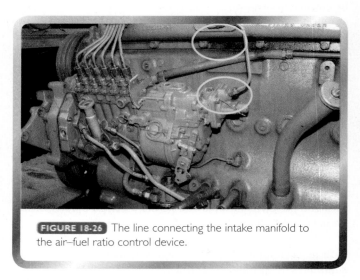

FIGURE 18-26 The line connecting the intake manifold to the air–fuel ratio control device.

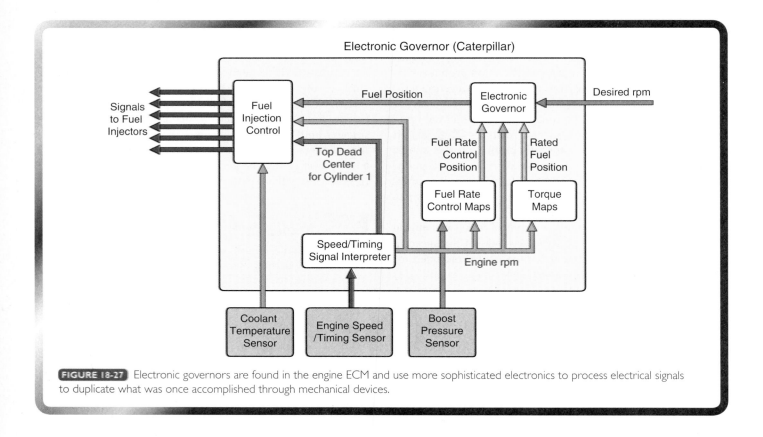

FIGURE 18-27 Electronic governors are found in the engine ECM and use more sophisticated electronics to process electrical signals to duplicate what was once accomplished through mechanical devices.

Programmable Electronic Governors

Today, electronic governors and engine controls do more than ensure combustion processes meet emission standards and expectations for power and fuel economy. Onboard networks communicate with other vehicle systems to improve or vehicle productivity, efficiency, and safety and enhance operator comfort. Software also enables monitoring of the vehicle and driving habits to meet business objectives.

Governors in electronically controlled engines can control fueling in more sophisticated ways that far exceed mechanical governor capabilities. In fact, the term *governing* has fallen out of use; the term used to describe the operation of making adjustments to the governor has been replaced with modifying *programmable parameters*. Now almost any measurable variable affecting either engine or vehicle operation can be adjusted through programmable software **TABLE 18-2**. Programmable governor features fall into two basic categories: factory specified and customer specified.

Factory-specified parameters and features include:

- Engine OEM manufacturer-specific features
- Truck or bus chassis manufacturer-specific features

Engine OEM manufacturer-specific features include variables such as horsepower, maximum torque output, and torque rise. These are not usually adjustable without factory authorization.

Chassis manufacturer specific parameters include features such as calibrations for the tachometer, integration of chassis controllers to the onboard vehicle network such as the ABS, traction control, or specialized equipment needed to operate a boom

truck **FIGURE 18-28**. Adding an accessory such as an exhaust brake may also be specified by the engine OEM manufacturer.

Customer-specified parameters and specifications include:

- Specialized OEM features chosen when the equipment is ordered
- Optional programmable features unique to the equipment application and normally adjusted after the truck or bus is delivered

The five most frequently used customer-specified parameters are:

- Vehicle speed limiting
- Progressive shift
- Cruise control
- Engine protection
- Idle shutdown timer and PTO shutdown

A few examples of other categories of customer-specified parameters include:

- Maintenance monitors **FIGURE 18-29**
- Vehicle security
- Vehicle activity
- Trip reports **FIGURE 18-30**
- Engine brake or retarder controls
- Dedicated PTO control features
- Driver reward
- Low gear torque reduction

TABLE 18-2: Typical Programmable Parameters for a Line Haul, On-Highway Vehicle with a 400 hp (298 kW) Engine

Feature	Range	Setting	Setting
Maximum Engine Speed	2120–2120 rpm		
Maximum Rated Speed	1800 rpm		
Rated Peak Torque	1200 ft-lb (1627 Nm) at 1800 rpm		
Torque at Rated Speed	1167 ft-lb (1582 Nm) at 1800 rpm		
Road Speed Governor			
Throttle Pedal Maximum Road Speed	30–120 mph (48–193 km/h)	65 mph (105 km/h)	1700 rpm
Maximum Engine Speed Without VSS	1400–3000 rpm	900 rpm	
Maximum Engine Speed with VSS	1400–3000 rpm	1800 rpm	Enabled
Lower Droop	0–3 mph (0–4.8 km/h)	1 mph (1.6 km/h)	
Upper Droop	0–3 mph (0–4.8 km/h)	3 mph (4.8 km/h)	
Transmission and Rear Axle			
Gear Down Protection Enabled			
Gear Down Protection rpm Limit	1200–1700 rpm	1600 rpm	
Gear down protection turn on speed	40–65 mph (64–105 km/h)	55 mph (89 km/h)	
Lower Gear Engine Speed Limit	700–2000 rpm	950 rpm	
Lower Gear Turn Off Speed Limit	5–15 mph (8–24 km/h)	9 mph (14 km/h)	
Torque Limit in First Gear	500–1000 ft-lb (678–1356 Nm)	800 ft-lb (1085 Nm)	
Rear Axle Ratio	1.92–15.97	4.11	
Tire Size	300–700 rev/mile	421 rev/mile	
Engine Idle			
Idle Engine Speed	600–850 rpm	700 rpm	
Idle Shutdown			Enabled
Idle Shutdown Timer	1–100 minutes	2 minutes	Enabled
Idle Shutdown Lower Ambient Temperature Air Temperature Override	0–100°F (−18–38°C)	32°F (0°C)	Enabled
Idle Shutdown Upper Ambient Temperature Air Temperature Override	0–100°F (−18–38°C)	85°F (29°C)	
ECM Fan Control			Enabled
Minimum Fan on Time	0–1000 seconds	120 seconds	
Fan Control Solenoid Logic		4.5 Volts ON	
Cruise Control/Engine Brakes			
Maximum Cruise Control Speed	30–102 mph (48–164 km/h)	65 mph (105 km/h)	
Cruise Control Upper Droop	0–3 mph (0–4.8 km/h)	0 mph (0 km/h)	
Cruise Control Lower Droop	0–3 mph (0–4.8 km/h)	2 mph (3.2 km/h)	
Engine Brake Cruise Control Activation	Enabled/Disabled	Enabled	
Engine Brake Minimum Vehicle Speed	0–35 mph (0–56 km/h)	15 mph (24 km/h)	
Engine Brake Delay	0–10 seconds		Disabled
Engine Brake Service Brake Activation	Enabled/Disabled		Enabled
J-1939/J-1587			
ABS Module		J-1939	Enabled
Engine Protection			
Engine Protection Shutdown Feature		Warning/Derate/Shutdown	Derate
Engine Protect Restart Inhibit		Enabled/Disabled	Enabled
Manual Override		Enabled/Disabled	Enabled

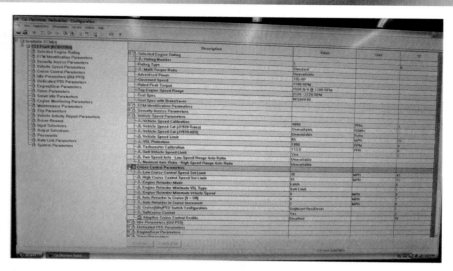

FIGURE 18-28 Chassis manufacturer programmable parameters reference chassis equipment such as axle two-speed shift motors, rear axle gear ratios, and tachometer calibrations.

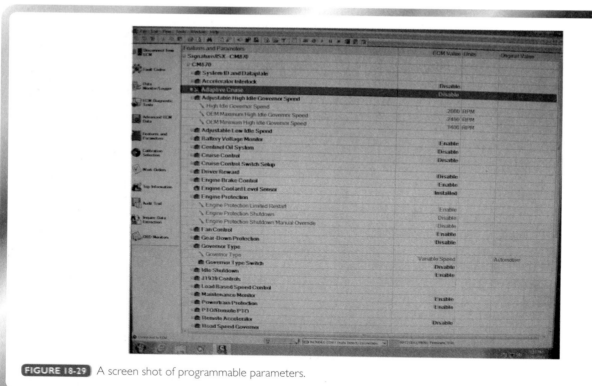

FIGURE 18-29 A screen shot of programmable parameters.

Partial-Authority Systems

Partial-authority fuel systems have adapted some electronic control to extend the fuel system and engine design usefulness where stricter emissions regulations require cleaner combustion. Partial-authority systems range from electronic control of just cruise control functions to electronic governing of all fuel metering and injection timing control with a mechanical high-pressure injection system. Electronic control of injection quantity is performed by a partial-authority governor, which uses a mechanical actuator, rather than a direct electrical signal, as an output device to move the metering control device inside a high-pressure pump. Moving the metering control device

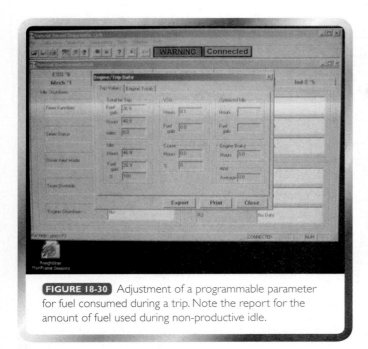

FIGURE 18-30 Adjustment of a programmable parameter for fuel consumed during a trip. Note the report for the amount of fuel used during non-productive idle.

signals. For example, an injector in a full-authority system will use a solenoid to determine the fuel quantity required and time for an injection event. Full-authority governing systems are also drive-by-wire, and electronic signal processing techniques are exclusively used to collect input data to control the injection event. All on-highway diesel engines manufactured today are full-authority systems. Some off-road engines are still manufactured with partial-authority systems.

Fueling Strategy Classification

Governors are further classified by their response to the throttle pedal. The common fueling strategies described in the following section can be achieved either mechanically or electronically.

Automotive Governor

Another name for the **automotive governor** is limiting speed (LS) or min/max (which refers to only minimum and maximum engine speed limiting governors). The automotive governor is common in passenger and commercial vehicle applications and has an accelerator response similar to throttle-plate controlled gasoline-fueled engines. When a load is applied to the engine,

increases or decreases fueling. More sophisticated partial-authority systems incorporate features to change injection timing as well. An electronically controlled solenoid can also be used to vary injection timing in a mechanical system **FIGURE 18-31** and **FIGURE 18-32**. All partial-authority systems are drive-by-wire, meaning a throttle position sensor or linkage is connected to a sensor that provides driver input to the governor.

Full-Authority Systems

Full-authority governing is more commonly referred to as electronic engine management. All metering and timing functions use principles of electronic signal processing to regulate engine fueling **FIGURE 18-33**. Rather than using a mechanical actuator to control output from a high-pressure injection pump, fueling is regulated using pulse-width modulated (PWM) electrical

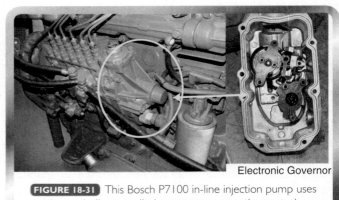

Electronic Governor

FIGURE 18-31 This Bosch P7100 in-line injection pump uses an electronically controlled actuator to move the control sleeve inside the high-pressure section of the pump.

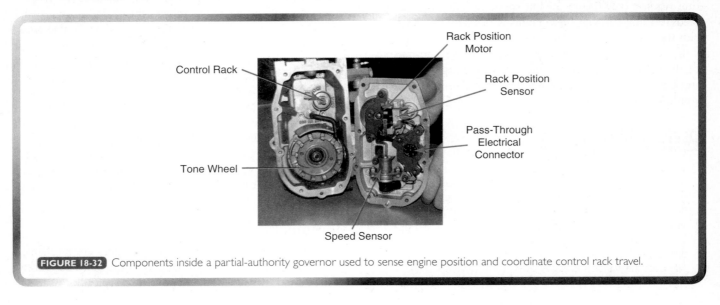

FIGURE 18-32 Components inside a partial-authority governor used to sense engine position and coordinate control rack travel.

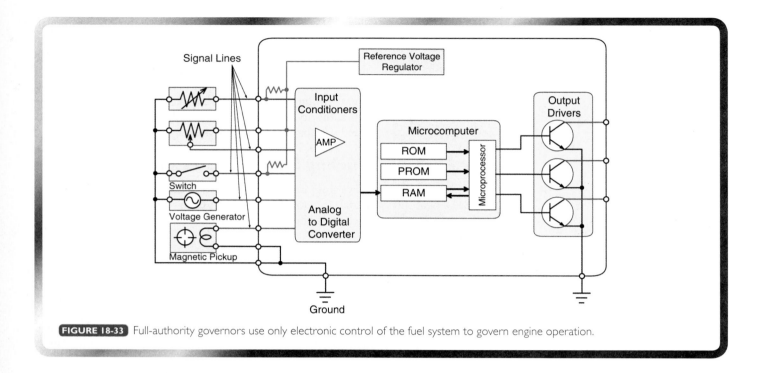

FIGURE 18-33 Full-authority governors use only electronic control of the fuel system to govern engine operation.

the engine speed will drop and the driver has to push the accelerator to increase injection fuel quantity. Likewise, to reduce speed or compensate for a load reduction, the throttle is backed off, which decreases fueling.

Automotive governors have the advantage of enabling better fuel economy in comparison to other types of governors. The explanation for this lies in the way fueling changes occur. With automotive governors, sudden load changes are responded to by the driver rather than a mechanism that automatically and instantly changes the quantity of fuel injected to maintain engine speed and torque. Typically, this results in less aggressive engine fueling. A driver who is "easier" on the throttle should obtain better fuel economy using this governor.

Mechanisms and adjustments within the automotive governor regulate only the engine idle speed and maximum engine speeds. Fueling between those points is regulated by the driver. With the automotive governor, the power output is determined by the position of the accelerator pedal. To increase torque output, the throttle is depressed farther. Decreased engine speed and torque requires the release of the throttle pedal or moving the throttle lever closer to a minimum speed position **FIGURE 18-34** .

TECHNICIAN TIP

When starting cold diesel engines, automotive governor mechanisms used by mechanical injection pumps often require the accelerator pedal to be partially or fully depressed to the floor once to achieve maximum fueling position for starting. Like setting the choke in old carbureted engines, the mechanical governor moves to a maximum fueling position only when the throttle is depressed. Maximum fueling is needed to ensure adequate fuel vapor is available during cold cranking/starting.

Variable Speed Governor

Sometimes referred to as an all-speed governor, the **variable speed governor** automatically changes the amount of fuel injected to regulate engine speed, which is based only on accelerator pedal position. With this type of governor, the operator can hold engine speed steady by maintaining a constant accelerator pedal position. A given amount of accelerator pedal travel will correspond to a specific engine speed. As engine loading increases or decreases, the governor, not the operator, will change fueling to attempt to maintain that engine speed **FIGURE 18-35** . The operation of a variable speed governor is best observed when a vehicle is using cruise control: the engine speed is set, and the governor changes fueling to maintain a consistent road speed. Torque control is managed by the governor and not the operator's movement of the throttle pedal. By fully depressing the accelerator pedal of a variable speed governor, the operator commands the maximum engine speed. Torque control is provided on an as-needed basis according to engine load. A variable speed governor establishes engine idle speed, high idle, and any speed in between these points proportional to accelerator pedal position.

Off-road equipment, stationary engine work, and some on-highway trucks are common applications for this type of governor. A PTO uses this type of governor because a change in load on the PTO will not produce wild swings in engine speed, which is an undesirable characteristic of an automotive type governor.

Combination Governors

As the name suggests, combination governors are mechanical governors that can combine the characteristics of the automotive governor and the variable speed governor. Typically, this means

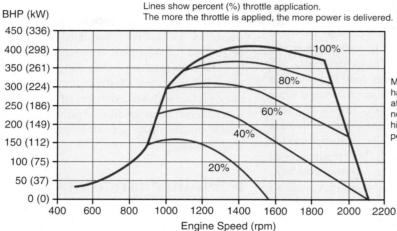

Min/Max Governor

Lines show percent (%) throttle application.
The more the throttle is applied, the more power is delivered.

Min/max governors can have responsive throttles at no load because the engine normally goes from low to high idle in less than 10% pedal movement.

Chart depicts a sample engine power curve and typical min/max governor response to throttle.
Actual engine settings may differ from this drawing.

FIGURE 18-34 A min/max governor, also called an automotive governor, increases or decreases fueling only in response to driver input. Governors shape the torque curve of an engine. This automotive governor shows some droop between 1990 and 2100 rpm.

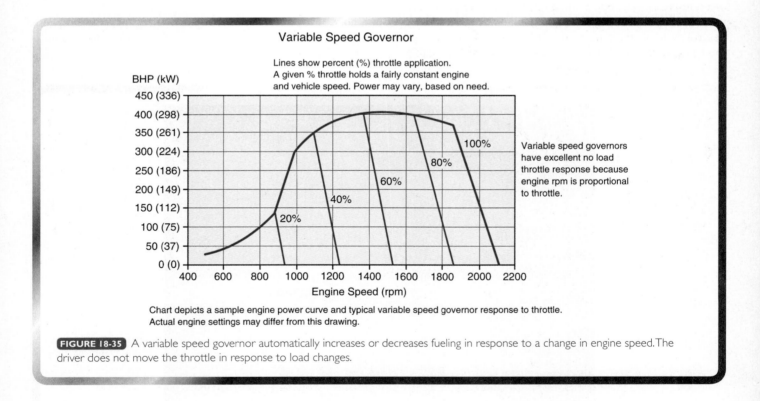

Variable Speed Governor

Lines show percent (%) throttle application.
A given % throttle holds a fairly constant engine and vehicle speed. Power may vary, based on need.

Variable speed governors have excellent no load throttle response because engine rpm is proportional to throttle.

Chart depicts a sample engine power curve and typical variable speed governor response to throttle.
Actual engine settings may differ from this drawing.

FIGURE 18-35 A variable speed governor automatically increases or decreases fueling in response to a change in engine speed. The driver does not move the throttle in response to load changes.

that at medium- to high-speed operation, the accelerator pedal will control fueling, because automotive governing takes over. At low- to mid-engine speeds the governor will behave like a variable speed governor. This configuration makes it convenient to adapt PTO devices to the engine devices. Because PTO devices are on or off and vary the load applied to the engine depending on the work they are doing, such as moving hydraulic cylinders or powering a water pump, it is desirable to use a governor with the ability to automatically adjust fueling to maintain a constant engine speed. Many medium- and heavy-duty on-highway diesel engines using mechanical governors are combination governors.

The choice between the automotive governor and the variable speed governor (which can often be selected on electronically controlled engines) is based on vehicle configuration and operator preference. While automotive governors generally get better fuel economy than variable speed governors, the disadvantage is that automotive governors tend to have poor startability, meaning they cause a sudden surge or lurch when the vehicle is loaded (e.g., when pulling away from a stop with a loaded trailer). Lurch or surge may cause driveline damage such as snapped drive shafts or broken axles. Automotive governors do not adapt well to the use of PTOs, because engine speed can rise and fall dramatically with varying load conditions imposed by the PTO device. Operators may perceive that an engine equipped with an automotive governor is not as responsive or as powerful as an engine with a variable speed governor. The use of a PTO switch separate from the engine throttle control on electronically controlled engines allows the use of variable speed and automotive governors.

To provide additional governor flexibility, some electronically controlled vehicles are equipped with a cab switch that allows the operator to switch from one type to the other in response to changing vehicle functions, operating conditions, or preferences (e.g., operating a PTO for a concrete mixer or moving a log trailer on a gravel road). On full-authority engine control systems, the type of governor and remote throttle for the PTO are selectable from a software menu **FIGURE 18-36** .

Isochronous Governor

The isochronous governor is able to maintain more precise engine speed control than other types of governors. A common application for this type of governor is in diesel-powered electrical generators used for AC power distribution. Here, AC frequency (i.e., 60Hz) is regulated by engine speed and has to be precisely maintained. Generally this means an engine has to hold 1800 rpm to produce 60Hz AC current from a three-phase AC generator (1550 rpm produces 50Hz AC). This governor operates with virtually zero droop. A zero-droop governor is very sensitive to speed change and corrects speed variations almost instantaneously, maintaining engine speed regardless of engine load.

▶ Maintenance of Governors

With a few exceptions, mechanical governors are not serviced in the field. They require specialized repair facilities equipped with sophisticated instruments and staffed with technicians with in-depth training on governors. It is useful, however, to learn what adjustments are made and how they are performed.

Mechanical Governor Adjustment and Testing

Smoke, low power, hunting, engine stalling, poor acceleration, and excessive engine speed are some of the complaints that indicate a governor may require evaluation.

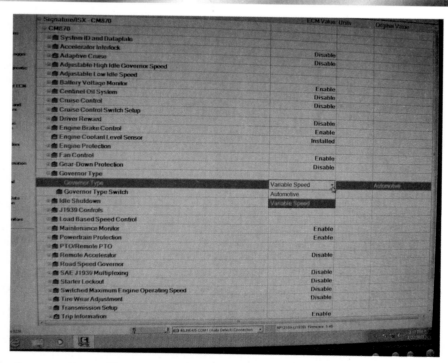

FIGURE 18-36 OEM software used to modify governor settings. Note the choice between variable and automotive governor settings.

In mechanical governors, springs can lose their tension and wear can occur between moving parts. Specialized injection repair shops will replace and adjust governor components such as flyweight assemblies, spring sets, spring retainers, bell cranks, fuel stops, and torques control devices. Wire ties sealed with lead tags cover critical governor adjustments to prevent tampering. The imprint on the lead seal identifies the manufacturer or repair shop servicing the pump **FIGURE 18-37**. Precision components like this should be disassembled and carefully inspected before major pump overhaul.

The most basic field test of governor wear is simply accelerating the engine gradually to its maximum no-load speed and comparing the engine speed to OEM specifications. If the engine does not reach maximum rpm, the governor spring is weakened. This happens because governor mechanisms are designed for wear and deterioration to reduce engine speed and torque, not increase it. Air–fuel ratio devices are pressure tested to check for diaphragm leaks. The devices typically have two adjustments. One adjustment is for limiting maximum fuel according to boost pressure. The second adjustment will control the initial starting point where maximum fuel limiting begins. If fuel limiting took place right at idle speed, the engine would accelerate very slowly.

Engine idle speed is externally adjustable on most mechanical governors. An adjustment screw on the pump linkage will move the throttle lever to produce a desired idle speed. Maximum engine speed is adjusted by increasing or decreasing the tension of governor flyweights **FIGURE 18-38**.

Most pumps also have an adjustment for torque control that is accessed externally. Moving the screw in and out will vary the maximum quantity of fuel provided for a given engine speed condition.

Testing Maximum Engine Speed for a Mechanical Governor

On mechanical governors with centrifugal flyweights, the governor springs can become weak because of age, heat, and fatigue from constant compression and release cycling. When this happens, the engine will fail to reach rated rpm and the driver will complain about low power. Before testing the governor, ensure that the throttle is reaching full throttle by observing the linkage with the accelerator pedal pressed to the floor. Most often, breakover linkage is used for the throttle lever. This linkage is a two-piece, spring-loaded lever, which, after contacting the maximum speed stop, will allow a little more movement of the lever through a spring. Configuring linkage like this minimizes throttle shaft force and bushing wear on the throttle shaft when a driver pushes the pedal to the floor. A properly adjusted throttle will allow the throttle linkage to break over and should be inspected when checking for full throttle accelerator pedal travel.

To test maximum engine speed for a mechanical governor, follow the steps in **SKILL DRILL 18-1**.

Adjusting Maximum Vehicle Speed

An electronically controlled engine has an adjustable vehicle speed limiting (VSL) parameter that sets the maximum speed of the vehicle. VSL cuts off fuel to the injectors when the engine exceeds the programmed parameter speed. On many engines, the VSL can be exceeded by adjusting the programmable cruise control limit to a higher value than the VSL parameter. This encourages more operation in cruise mode, which can better control engine fueling than the operator. Using the VSL feature allows the vehicle to take advantage of a diesel's high torque output at low engine speed. Another phrase that describes this type of operation is the gear fast, run slow strategy, which optimizes the balance between fuel economy and engine performance. Because most trucks are capable of very high vehicle speeds, setting VSL allows the operator to consistently drive at fuel efficient and safe vehicle speeds. However, VSL can be too hard a limit that cuts fueling until the

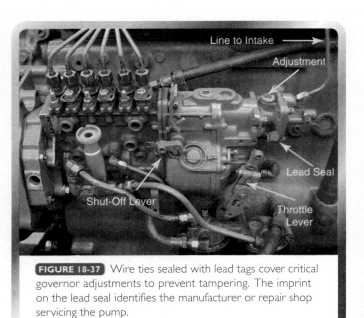

FIGURE 18-37 Wire ties sealed with lead tags cover critical governor adjustments to prevent tampering. The imprint on the lead seal identifies the manufacturer or repair shop servicing the pump.

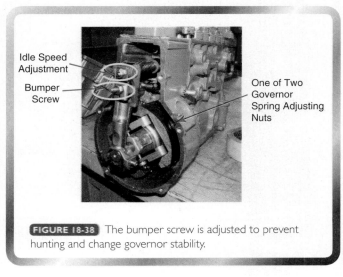

FIGURE 18-38 The bumper screw is adjusted to prevent hunting and change governor stability.

SKILL DRILL 18-1 Testing Maximum Engine Speed for a Mechanical Governor

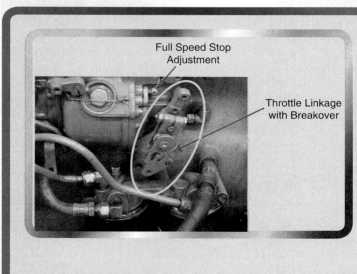

Full Speed Stop Adjustment

Throttle Linkage with Breakover

1. After checking for full accelerator pedal travel, start the engine and allow it to run at idle rpm.

2. Check the emission decal on the engine or the engine's service literature to find its high idle speed or rated rpm.

3. Slowly push on the throttle pedal to bring the throttle to full accelerator pedal travel.

4. Observe and record the maximum engine rpm and release the accelerator pedal.

5. Return the vehicle to idle, allow the turbocharger speed to slow, then turn off the engine.

6. If the engine reached high idle rpm, the governor spring condition is acceptable. The engine should typically reach 5–10% above rated rpm speed with no load acceleration. If the engine did not reach target speeds, recommend governor and injection pump overhaul.

---

vehicle slows to a speed below the programmed limit. This makes the practice of "running at hills" difficult.

To adjust maximum vehicle speed, follow the steps in **SKILL DRILL 18-2**.

Gearing Protection

While the concept of a governor tends to be limited to the idea of speed regulation, electronic governors have a seemingly endless number of variables to adjust that affect fueling. Many of these adjustments are application specific. For example, an electronic governor for a firetruck that pumps water and operates hydraulic equipment, such as boom buckets and outriggers to stabilize the vehicle, will have a completely different set of variables than an on-highway tractor or bus. A couple of simple examples are presented in this next section to introduce some key concepts about how governor variables behave and how adjustments can improve vehicle efficiency and protect the engine from damage.

SKILL DRILL 18-2 Adjusting Maximum Vehicle Speed

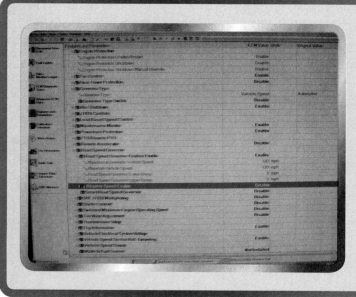

1. Connect a data link adapter to the vehicle's data link connector.

2. Using OEM software, locate the group of vehicle speed programmable parameters. A separate menu is provided for making adjustments in OEM software.

3. Identify the VSL that is appropriate for the vehicle and change the VSL limit number. A customer password may be required to lock and unlock the parameter.

4. Check that the chosen VSL is greater than or equal to peak torque rpm plus 100. If an acceptable vehicle speed is not attainable, recommend another axle ratio or transmission to increase engine rpm. If an acceptable vehicle speed is not attained, engine power and fuel economy will be adversely affected.

Progressive Shift

Two commonly changed customer programmable parameters concern engine speed and gearing. When a driver accelerates a vehicle to top engine speed limit before shifting to another gear, fuel is wasted. **Progressive shifting** limits engine rpm until a minimum road speed is reached. For example, if a vehicle is expected to accelerate to 3 mph (5 km/h) in first gear, the ECM can detect the transmission gear and road speed by measuring engine rpm and vehicle speed. A simple calculation will indicate to the ECM what gear the driver is using. To prevent wasteful engine overspeed, the governor can be programmed to limit engine speed to, say, 1100 rpm, rather than 1950 rpm, until a minimum road speed of 3 mph (5 km/h) is reached. If the driver wishes to go faster, a higher gear must be selected to increase vehicle speed. Low- and medium-speed gear ranges will have two adjustable parameters: a turn-off road speed and engine rpm. This means low-speed gear protection could be set to limit engine speed to 1100 rpm but would turn off the limit once the vehicle speed exceeds 3 mph (5 km/h). Above 3 mph (5 km/h), the next gear speed parameter is adjusted. That might be an engine rpm limit of 1500 rpm until road speed is 20 mph (32 km/h). Above 20 mph (32 km/h), the limit would switch off TABLE 18-3.

The disadvantage of progressive shifting is that an engine may not be able to climb a steep hill if engine speed is severely limited in lower gears, because the engine rpm is not available that is needed to multiply torque in a transmission in first gear.

Gear-Down Protection

Sometimes a driver will leave a truck in a lower gear while trying to maintain a cruising speed. The advantage this provides is quicker acceleration at the expense of wasted fuel. **Gear-down protection** enables the customer to set an engine rpm limit for the higher gears that ensures maximum cruising speed can only be reached in top gear.

Like progressive shifting, gear-down protection requires two parameters be changed: engine speed and road speed. Instead of turn-off speed, gear-down protection has a turn-on speed. This is the vehicle speed at which the engine rpm limit takes effect. If turn-on speed is set at 50 mph (80 km/h), engine speed is the second parameter to be set. Depending on transmission and rear-axle ratio gear combinations, 1600 rpm may be an appropriate engine speed limit adjustment. If the actual engine rpm at which the driver is operating is too high for that particular road speed—if, say, 2000 rpm is observed—the governor reduces engine speed to 1600 rpm to encourage the driver to upshift TABLE 18-4.

TABLE 18-3: Example of Progressive Shift Parameters

Low Gear Protection Range		Intermediate Gear Protection Range	
rpm Limit	Turn-Off Speed	rpm Limit	Turn-Off Speed
1100	3 mph (5 km/h)	1500	20 mph (32 km/h)

Engine Protection Parameters

Engine protection is a critical governor programmable setting. Faults that could potentially cause engine damage will cause the governor to do one of three things:

- Derate power
- Shut the engine down
- Warn the driver using an instrument cluster warning lamp

The engine will monitor important engine protection parameters such as fuel temperature, coolant level, oil pressure and temperature, intake air, fuel, oil, coolant, and particulate filter temperature. These values are compared to the allowable maximum limits to determine when a critical fault is reached. How the governor responds to the engine protection faults is adjusted using service software FIGURE 18-39.

If only a warning is specified, the vehicle operator has the responsibility to take action to avoid engine damage. No shutdown will occur. If shutdown is specified in response to a fault, the engine will stop after a short time of further operation. For example, coolant overheating might shut the engine down after 60 seconds. If it is a problem related to oil or the particulate filter, it might take only 30 seconds to shut down after the red engine protection system stop lamp is illuminated. Typically the

TABLE 18-4: Gear-Down Protection Range

rpm Limit	Turn-On Speed
1600	50 mph (80 km/h)

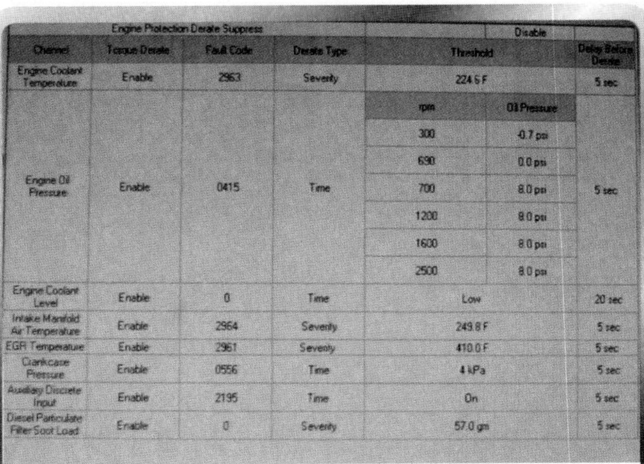

Engine Protection Derate Suppress — Disable

Channel	Torque Derate	Fault Code	Derate Type	Threshold		Delay Before Derate
Engine Coolant Temperature	Enable	2963	Severity	224.6 F		5 sec
Engine Oil Pressure	Enable	0415	Time	rpm	Oil Pressure	5 sec
				300	-0.7 psi	
				690	0.0 psi	
				700	8.0 psi	
				1200	8.0 psi	
				1600	8.0 psi	
				2500	8.0 psi	
Engine Coolant Level	Enable	0	Time	Low		20 sec
Intake Manifold Air Temperature	Enable	2964	Severity	249.8 F		5 sec
EGR Temperature	Enable	2961	Severity	410.0 F		5 sec
Crankcase Pressure	Enable	0556	Time	4 kPa		5 sec
Auxiliary Discrete Input	Enable	2195	Time	On		5 sec
Diesel Particulate Filter Soot Load	Enable	0	Severity	57.0 gm		5 sec

FIGURE 18-39 The governor will limit or cut off fueling when a programmable threshold for potential engine damage is reached.

stop lamp will flash for 20 to 30 seconds before engine shutdown occurs to give the operator time to pull the vehicle over to the shoulder of the road. A stop engine override (SEO) switch is available to delay engine shutdown if the operator believes safety is compromised without more time to maneuver the vehicle to a safe stopping point.

Derate warnings can be adjusted to progressively reduce engine power based on the severity of the condition. For example, if the coolant temperature reaches 225°F (107°C), the engine power may be reduced by 20%. At a higher coolant temperature like 235°F (113°C), a 60% derate will take place.

Adjusting Engine Protection Fault Response

The engine protection monitoring system provides surveillance of conditions that can lead to catastrophic engine failure. Generally, the system can detect and protect against abnormal oil pressure and high-temperature oil, intake manifold air, fuel, and coolant. If an optional coolant level sensor is installed, the engine can be protected against low coolant level. An additional warning lamp can be installed in the instrument panel for driver notification, but generally the yellow engine warning light will switch on if a fault is detected **FIGURE 18-40**.

To adjust engine protection fault response, follow the steps in **SKILL DRILL 18-3**.

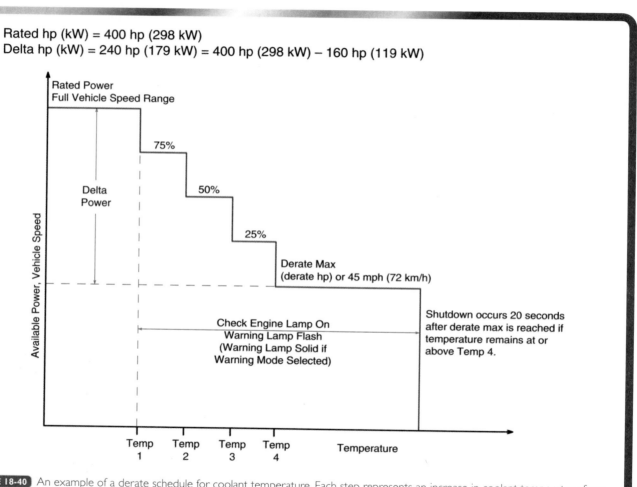

FIGURE 18-40 An example of a derate schedule for coolant temperature. Each step represents an increase in coolant temperature from 218°F (103°C) (25%), 220°F (104°C) (50%), and 224°F (107°C). Shutdown takes place after continuous temperatures of 224°F (107°C).

SKILL DRILL 18-3 Adjusting Engine Protection Fault Response

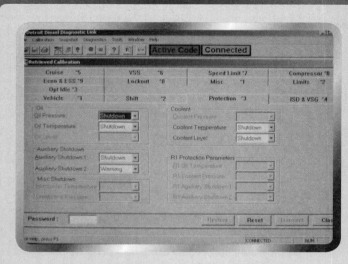

1. Connect OEM software to the vehicle's data link connector with the key on, engine off.

2. Navigate to the programmable parameters for engine protection faults.

3. Determine which parameters will be configured in the engine protection system.

4. Determine what threshold values will be used to warn, derate, or shutdown the engine.

5. Adjust the protection monitoring system to one of four different settings:
   - Off
   - Warning: The warning lamp on the dash turns on.
   - Derate: The warning lamp on the dash turns on and engine power is reduced.
   - Shutdown: The warning lamp on the dash turns on, engine power is reduced, and then the engine shuts down after 30 seconds. The≈red Stop Engine light will blink before shutdown occurs.

6. Adjust the programmable menu items for whether the override button will be allowed to override the shutdown feature and for the number of times the override button can override shutdown before cycling the key. This feature is not available in all software.

Wrap-Up

Ready for Review

▶ In diesel engines, engine speed and torque production are controlled entirely by the quantity of fuel injected into the cylinders by the high-pressure fuel system. Regulation of the high-pressure injection system is performed by the governor.

▶ The diesel engine governor monitors the engine speed and adjusts the fuel quantity required by the engine for given speed and load conditions.

▶ On mechanically or electronically controlled high-pressure injection systems, very small changes in injection quantity produce very large changes in engine speed.

▶ In a diesel engine, because the air intake is unrestricted and fuel injection rate can instantly go to maximum delivery quantity, the rate of acceleration can go as high as 2000 rpm/second; this capability can easily cause the engine to go beyond critical rpm in a few seconds.

▶ Governors perform a critical function in emission reduction by regulating air–fuel ratio control; air–fuel ratio controls minimize the production of particulate or black smoke produced during engine acceleration.

▶ At a minimum, all governors limit maximum engine speed and control idle speed to prevent stalling.

▶ Governors are differentiated and classified a number ways, including the governor's type of construction, operational characteristics, and fueling strategies.

▶ Mechanical mechanisms are used to accomplish the governor functions of sensing engine speed, load, and driver input, and making changes to engine fueling.

▶ Mechanical governors consist of two basic mechanisms: a speed-sensing mechanism and a fuel-changing mechanism.

▶ Engine fueling takes place by moving an actuator such as the fuel control rack, which in turn changes the quantity of fuel injected into the cylinders; the governor changes fueling because it is connected to the injection pump through linkage to control fueling.

▶ Typically, in mechanically operated governors the main parts are a gear drive from the engine, flyweights, and a governor spring.

▶ In a mechanical governor, flyweight force always operates to reduce fueling and spring force operates to increase fueling.

▶ Torque control is necessary to prevent black smoke caused by inadequate air or combustion chamber design limits.

▶ Electronic engine governing uses principles of electronic signal processing to regulate fueling. Electronic governors can be divided into two categories: partial- and full-authority systems.

▶ Partial-authority systems are fuel systems that have adapted some electronic control to extend the design usefulness of a mechanical fuel system, particularly where stricter emission regulations require cleaner combustion.

▶ In full-authority governing, all metering and timing functions use principles of electronic signal processing to regulate engine fueling.

▶ An automotive governor is the most common in medium- and heavy-duty commercial vehicle applications; it features an accelerator response similar to a throttle plate-controlled gasoline-fueled engine.

▶ A variable speed governor controls engine speed based only on accelerator pedal position.

▶ A combination governor combines characteristics of the automotive governor and the variable speed governor.

▶ An isochronous governor is used by diesel electric generators and is able to maintain more precise engine speed control than other types of governors.

▶ Smoke, low power, hunting, engine stalling, poor acceleration, and excessive engine speed are some of the complaints that indicate a governor may require evaluation.

Vocabulary Builder

automotive governor A governor that features an accelerator response similar to a throttle plate-controlled gasoline-fueled engine; also known as a limiting speed (LS) governor or a min/max governor. The operator has to change the throttle position in response to engine load and speed changes.

centrifugal force A force pulling outward on a rotating body.

droop The change or difference in engine speed caused by a change in load.

fulcrum The point around which a lever rotates and that supports the lever and the load.

full-authority governing A system in which all metering and timing functions use principles of electronic signal processing to regulate engine fueling; also known as electronic engine management.

gear-down protection A parameter that limits engine speed if the engine speed is too high for a particular road speed.

high idle The maximum speed at which an engine turns without a load.

hunting A rhythmic change in engine rpm at idle speed caused by uneven fueling of cylinders.

idle An engine's minimum operational speed.

isochronous governor A governor that is able to maintain more precise engine speed control than other types of governors.

load-based speed control A feature that supplies increased torque and sometimes more engine rpm when climbing hills with heavy loads, and also reduce torque when it senses the vehicle is unloaded or only lightly loaded.

load controller A mechanism that improves ride quality and reduces emissions by modulating increases and decreases in fueling to prevent vehicle bucking and jerking during acceleration and deceleration; also known as a pulse dampener.

lugging An abuse condition where an engine is operated under heavy load below an acceptable operating speed range.

mechanical governor A governor that regulates the quantity of fuel injected by the high-pressure injection pump using fly-weights and spring tension.

overrun The inability of a governor to keep the engine speed below the high idle speed when it is rapidly accelerated.

partial-authority fuel system A fuel system that has adapted some electronic control to extend the design usefulness, particularly where stricter emission regulations require cleaner combustion.

peak torque The engine speed at which cylinder pressures are highest.

performance curve A line graph that plots engine torque, fuel consumption, and horsepower against engine speed.

programmable parameter A measurable value about engine system operation that can be changed using service software (e.g., maximum vehicle speed).

progressive shifting A programmable parameter that limits engine speed until a minimum road speed is reached. Progressive shifting encourages a driver to shift gears sooner to save fuel.

rated speed An engine's maximum speed with a load.

state of balance The state of mechanical governor flyweights when flyweight force equals spring force.

torque control The regulation of fuel entering the cylinders to produce an appropriate amount of torque for a given engine speed.

torque plate A device that limits maximum control rack travel in a mechanical injection pump; also called a full load stop.

torque rise The difference between peak torque and torque at rated speed.

variable speed governor A governor that controls engine speed based only on accelerator pedal position; also known as an all-speed governor.

Review Questions

1. _____ is an engine's maximum speed with a load.
   a. High idle
   b. Peak torque
   c. Rated speed
   d. Torque rise

2. _____ is the regulation of fuel entering the cylinders to produce an appropriate amount of torque for a given engine speed.
   a. Torque control
   b. Peak torque
   c. Torque rise
   d. Rated torque

3. _____ is the engine speed at which cylinder pressures are highest.
   a. Torque rise
   b. Peak torque
   c. High idle
   d. Rated speed

4. _____ is the difference between peak torque and torque at rated speed.
   a. Rated torque
   b. High idle
   c. Torque control
   d. Torque rise

5. _____ is the maximum speed at which an engine turns without a load.
   a. High idle
   b. Rated speed
   c. Peak torque
   d. Torque rise

6. Programmable _____ are measurable values about engine system operation that can be changed using service software.
   a. decals
   b. performance curves
   c. parameters
   d. variables

7. A state of balance exists when flyweight force is _____ spring force.
   a. more than
   b. less than
   c. two times than
   d. equal to

8. Mechanical governors use _____ that act through mechanical linkage and respond to centrifugal force.
   a. flyweights
   b. speed sensors
   c. fuel gauges
   d. decals

9. Full-authority governing is more commonly referred to as _____ engine management.
   a. electronic
   b. mechanical
   c. automatic
   d. manual

10. Upper speed droop occurs as engine fueling decreases when the engine approaches its _____.
    a. peak horsepower
    b. fulcrum point
    c. rated torque
    d. rated speed

ASE-Type Questions

1. Technician A says air-fuel ratio controls minimize the production of PM emissions produced during engine acceleration. Technician B says air-fuel ratio controls minimize black smoke produced during engine acceleration. Who is correct?
   a. Technician A
   b. Technician B
   c. Both Technician A and Technician B
   d. Neither Technician A nor Technician B

2. Technician A says the droop curve can only be managed mechanically. Technician B says the droop curve can only be managed electronically. Who is correct?
   a. Technician A
   b. Technician B
   c. Both Technician A and Technician B
   d. Neither Technician A nor Technician B

3. Technician says engines using highly sensitive governors are prone to hunting. Technician B says engines using highly sensitive governors are not prone to hunting. Who is correct?
   a. Technician A
   b. Technician B
   c. Both Technician A and Technician B
   d. Neither Technician A nor Technician B

4. Technician A says mechanical engine governors use principles of electronic signal processing to regulate fueling. Technician B says electronic engine governors use principles of electronic signal processing to regulate fueling. Who is correct?
   a. Technician A
   b. Technician B
   c. Both Technician A and Technician B
   d. Neither Technician A nor Technician B

5. Technician A says combination governors are electronic governors that can combine the characteristics of the automotive governor and the variable speed governor. Technician B says combination governors are mechanical governors that can combine the characteristics of the automotive governor and the variable speed governor. Who is correct?
   a. Technician A
   b. Technician B
   c. Both Technician A and Technician B
   d. Neither Technician A nor Technician B

6. Technician A says the variable speed governor is able to maintain more precise engine speed control than other types of governors. Technician B says the automotive governor is able to maintain more precise engine speed control than other types of governors. Who is correct?
   a. Technician A
   b. Technician B
   c. Both Technician A and Technician B
   d. Neither Technician A nor Technician B

7. Technician A says mechanisms and adjustments within the automotive governor regulate only the engine idle speed and maximum engine speeds. Technician B says mechanisms and adjustments within the combination governor regulate only the engine idle speed and maximum engine speeds. Who is correct?
   a. Technician A
   b. Technician B
   c. Both Technician A and Technician B
   d. Neither Technician A nor Technician B

8. Technician A says for on-highway diesel engines, peak torque is commonly found at one-half of the rated speed. Technician B says for on-highway diesel engines, peak torque is commonly found at two-thirds of the rated speed. Who is correct?
   a. Technician A
   b. Technician B
   c. Both Technician A and Technician B
   d. Neither Technician A nor Technician B

9. Technician A says governors are designed to measure engine speed and sense operator demand. Technician B says governors are designed to regulate the quantity of fuel injected into the cylinders. Who is correct?
   a. Technician A
   b. Technician B
   c. Both Technician A and Technician B
   d. Neither Technician A nor Technician B

10. Technician A says command point is where maximum fuel economy and horsepower coincide. Technician B says fulcrum point is where fuel economy and horsepower coincide. Who is correct?
    a. Technician A
    b. Technician B
    c. Both Technician A and Technician B
    d. Neither Technician A nor Technician B

CHAPTER 19
Multiple Plunger Injection Pumps

NATEF Tasks

Diesel Engines

General

- Check engine no cranking, cranks but fails to start, hard starting, and starts but does not continue to run problems; determine needed action. (pp 562–563)
- Identify engine surging, rough operation, misfiring, low power, slow deceleration, slow acceleration, and shutdown problems; determine needed action. (pp 570–572)

Fuel System
Fuel Supply System

- Inspect and test pressure regulator systems (check valves, pressure regulator valves, and restrictive fittings); determine needed action. (pp 559–560, 567–569)

Electronic Fuel Management System

- Inspect high-pressure injection lines, hold downs, fittings, and seals; determine needed action. (pp 567–568)

Knowledge Objectives

After reading this chapter, you will be able to:

1. Describe the functions, construction, and application of port-helix metering injection pumps. (pp 556–560)
2. Explain the principles of operation of port-helix metering injection pumps. (pp 560–565)
3. Describe and explain methods for performing inspection and diagnostic procedures on port-helix metering injection pumps. (pp 565–574)
4. Recommend maintenance or repairs on port-helix metering injection pumps. (pp 565–574)
5. Identify performance modifications of port-helix metering injection pumps. (pp 565–574)

Skills Objectives

After reading this chapter, you will be able to:

1. Replace a delivery valve. (p 569) SKILL DRILL 19-1
2. Verify static timing for an inline injection pump. (p 572) SKILL DRILL 19-2
3. Adjust pump-to-engine timing. (p 573) SKILL DRILL 19-3

► Introduction

For decades, the most popular diesel engine fuel injection system was the multiple plunger fuel injection pump. This rugged, durable, compact fuel system enabled diesel engine design to transition from its original use in large, stationary applications to on-road and heavy-equipment service.

From light-duty car and truck engines to large industrial engines, multiple plunger injection pumps have been used in every diesel engine application. While millions of engines around the world still use this high-pressure injection system, the development of better, more sophisticated high-pressure injection systems has led to a discontinuation of inline injection

pumps for on-road applications. Despite technological changes that have displaced this pump from on-highway production, its durability and long, widespread use mean many are currently in service and will remain for years to come. This is especially the case for off-highway equipment, where, until recently, variations of these pumps dominated as the high-pressure injection system of choice **FIGURE 19-1**. As such, it is important to examine the construction features, operating principles, and mechanisms of multiple plunger injection pumps. With this information, diesel technicians can be well-rounded in their fuel system knowledge, and understand and develop diagnostic strategies to service and maintain this high-pressure fuel system.

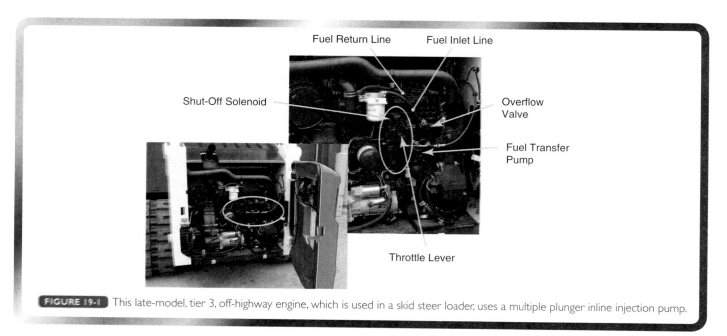

FIGURE 19-1 This late-model, tier 3, off-highway engine, which is used in a skid steer loader, uses a multiple plunger inline injection pump.

► You Are the Technician

At the diesel performance shop where you work, you install engine accessories and modify diesel engines to increase power output for racing and pulling competitions. Your customers' favorite injection pump is the P7100 Bosch used by Dodge Ram pick-up trucks until the late 1990s. In addition to installing injection pumps, you also install larger diameter plungers, replace full load stops or torque plates, and recalibrate the pumps for proper phasing and delivery volumes on a comparator bench. Over time, though, some of these vehicles have come back to the shop, the owners indicating that they are losing speed at the track or are not pulling as well as they once did. To differentiate between disappointed race enthusiasts and legitimate concerns, you have the vehicles' power output checked on a chassis dynamometer and compared to performance measured when the vehicles were delivered to the customer. In this particular case, the customer's complaints are verified and power output has dropped. Before taking any further diagnostic steps, consider the following:

1. Outline possible causes related to the injection pump mechanisms that might account for the loss of power.
2. How would the fuel pressure supplied by the low-pressure transfer system affect power output?
3. What effect would worn delivery valves have on power output?

What Are Multiple Plunger Injection Pumps?

A multiple plunger injection pump is a fuel system configuration that uses piston-like barrel and plunger assemblies that are actuated by a <u>camshaft</u> to pressurize fuel for injection. To vary the quantity of fuel required for injection, a <u>port-helix metering</u> system accurately meters the fuel used for each injection event. There is a pumping element, consisting of a barrel and plunger arranged inline in a pump housing, corresponding to each engine cylinder **FIGURE 19-2**. Some pumps are

Barrel

Plunger with Helix Groove

FIGURE 19-2 The plunger and barrel assembly for a P model inline injection pump.

constructed using a V-shaped housing with multiple plungers arranged inline in each bank of the pump **FIGURE 19-3**. Each pumping or pressurization element is connected to an injector nozzle through a rigid, high-pressure fuel line. Because of this arrangement of high-pressure components, these injection systems are referred to as pump-line-nozzle (PLN) fuel systems. The pumping elements share a common governor, camshaft, and fuel charging system that supplies low-pressure fuel to each pumping element **FIGURE 19-4**.

Multiple plunger injection pump systems consist of the following:

- A high-pressure injection pump having more than two pumping elements
- A mechanical or electronic governing system
- Air–fuel ratio controls
- A timing device to vary the beginning of injection (BOI) (optional)
- High-pressure fuel lines connecting the pumping elements to an injector in each cylinder
- Injection nozzles

Robert Bosch began mass production of this injection system in the 1920s, which facilitated the widespread use of diesel engines in mobile applications. Bosch licensed many of its designs to companies such as Lucas CAV, Nippondenso, American Bosch (AMBAC), Zexel, Diesel Kiki, and others. Variations on the basic designs have developed as each manufacturer enhanced or customized the initial pump design, but the parts commonality point to Bosch origins. On small displacement diesels used

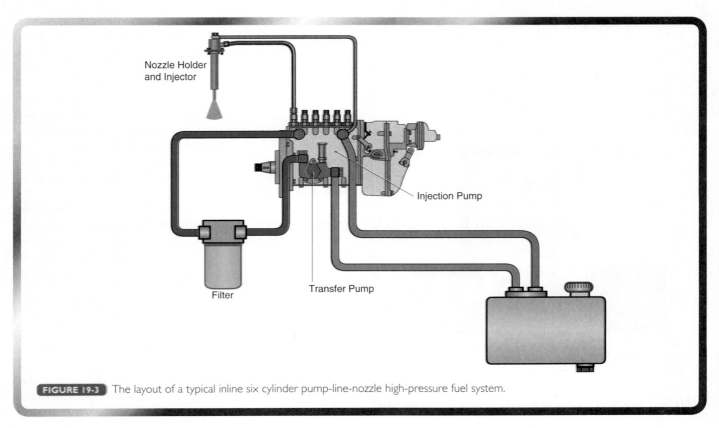

Nozzle Holder and Injector

Injection Pump

Filter

Transfer Pump

FIGURE 19-3 The layout of a typical inline six cylinder pump-line-nozzle high-pressure fuel system.

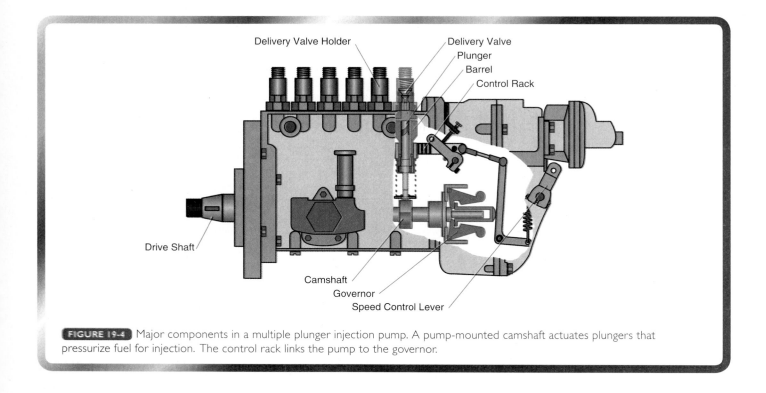

FIGURE 19-4 Major components in a multiple plunger injection pump. A pump-mounted camshaft actuates plungers that pressurize fuel for injection. The control rack links the pump to the governor.

off-road, the pump camshaft is often located in the engine block and is separate from the pump housing **FIGURE 19-5**.

Disadvantages and Obsolescence of Multiple Plunger Injection Pumps

Original equipment manufacturers (OEMs) have not used inline multiple plunger injection pumps for on-highway light- or medium-duty diesel applications in North America since the late 1990s, in spite of their earlier widespread popularity. The primary reason is that this injection system

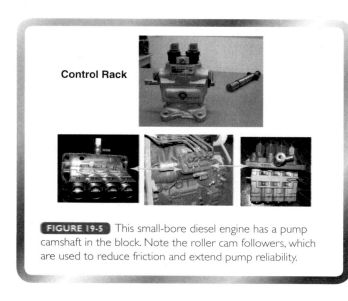

FIGURE 19-5 This small-bore diesel engine has a pump camshaft in the block. Note the roller cam followers, which are used to reduce friction and extend pump reliability.

is not capable of meeting strict emission requirements introduced in the late 1990s.

To achieve good emission characteristics from an engine, the most basic requirements are variable injection timing, which is the capability to change both the beginning and ending of injection timing, plus a high degree of very fine atomization of fuel. Fine atomization is also required to improve tolerance for exhaust gas recirculation (EGR) and complement other injection strategies such as retarded injection timing which lower the production of NO_x. Smaller droplet size, or finer atomization, is produced using smaller, more numerous nozzle spray orifices and higher injection pressures. The fuel pressure output of multiple plunger injection pumps simply cannot achieve the degree of atomization required to meet emission standards. This is especially evident at low-speed, high-load operation.

Aside from issues with atomization, there are two major problems present in the design of these pumps. First, these pumps have the disadvantage of fixed injection timing based on the unvarying shape of the cam profile in the injection pump and the fixed shape of the helix of the pumping plunger, which meters fuel. To extend the usefulness of their application, mechanical mechanisms to advance or retard injection timing have been added to some multiple plunger injection pump systems. Partial-authority electronic control of timing and metering functions has also been developed to improve exhaust emissions and fuel economy. However, these systems cannot match the capabilities of full-authority electronically controlled fuel systems in which all fuel metering, governing, and timing are electronically controlled.

TECHNICIAN TIP

A **partial-authority fuel system** is a mechanical-electrical hybrid fuel system design in which the governor and timing controls are typically electronic and not solely mechanical. Full-authority fuel systems refer to drive-by-wire fuel systems in which all metering and timing functions are electronically controlled.

Related to problems with injection timing is the long injection delay time, or lag, characteristic of the PLN system. A significant amount of fuel delivery volume is used up through expanding fuel lines and lifting the delivery and injector nozzle valves. Because some of the delivery volume is lost to these actions, variations to timing and delivery volume occur. The magnitude of these variations will also depend on engine speed and delivery quantity. However, some electronic controls used in PLN systems integrate nozzle valve lift sensors and engine position sensors to add precision to the control of injection timing and delivery volumes. These electronic controls can measure when injection actually begins and adjust injection timing accordingly.

The second major problem with multiple plunger injection pumps is their limited fuel pressurization. The smaller camshafts and pumping plunger diameters found in these pumps cannot match the force exerted by the much larger engine camshaft driving unit pumps and unit injectors. Unit injection and common rail systems can now deliver injection pressure as high as 38,000 psi (2620 bar), which allows better emission control than the PLN systems. In fact, the highest injection pressure available from an inline pump is approximately 19,500 psi (1344 bar) from a Bosch P7100, which was used on engines such as the Mack E7 and Cummins B and C series engines. These pressures, however, are dependent on engine speed, with the highest injection pressures achievable only with highest plunger velocities at maximum engine rpm **FIGURE 19-6** and **TABLE 19-1**.

Types of Multiple Plunger Injection Pumps

A variety of inline injection pumps are manufactured, but commonalities between all designs consist of the following:

- Plunger and barrel assemblies
- Control sleeves

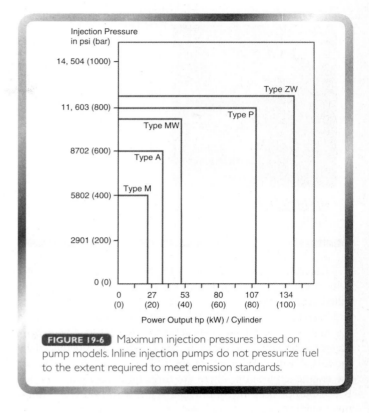

FIGURE 19-6 Maximum injection pressures based on pump models. Inline injection pumps do not pressurize fuel to the extent required to meet emission standards.

- Single housing integrating all pumping elements
- Integral pump camshafts
- Tappets
- Control racks
- Integrated governor controls
- Delivery valves
- Injection lines
- Fuel galleries
- Pressure-regulating overflow valves

Most multiple plunger pumps use a port-helix metering system, which uses a plunger assembly operating in a fixed barrel, called the **plunger and barrel assembly**. The plunger reciprocates inside the barrel assembly due to actuation force from a pump-mounted camshaft. Fuel pressurized in the barrel assembly is delivered to the nozzles through a high-pressure steel line **FIGURE 19-7**.

TABLE 19-1: Injection Pressures by Injection Pump Models

Pump Model	M Series	A Series	MW Series	P3000	P7100
Maximum injection pressure	8250 psi (569 bar)	11,250 psi (776 bar)	16,500 psi (1138 bar)	14,250 psi (983 bar)	19,500 psi (1344 bar)
Application	Passenger cars and vans	Light- to medium-duty commercial vehicles and industrial engines	Light- to medium-duty commercial vehicles and industrial engines	Light- to medium-duty commercial vehicles and industrial engines	Medium- to heavy-duty commercial vehicles
Maximum output/cylinder	27 hp (20 kW)	36 hp (26 kW)	48 hp (35 kW)	80 hp (59 kW)	214 hp (157 kW)

(Chart adapted from *Bosch Diesel Engine Management*, 2nd Edition, 1999.)

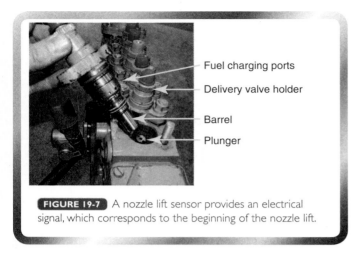

FIGURE 19-7 A nozzle lift sensor provides an electrical signal, which corresponds to the beginning of the nozzle lift.

Caterpillar is one exception to the common use of port-helix metering. Caterpillar uses an exclusive, patented system called scroll metering. In this system, the position of a plunger and barrel are switched with the position of the barrels changing the metered fuel quantity. However, in conventional port-helix metering systems, variations in the designs are influenced by the fuel volumes and pressure output required of the pumps for the engine application. There are three basic configurations for Bosch pumps used in commercial vehicles and off-road equipment applications: A, P, and MW. A smaller M pump is used in passenger cars and vans in Europe and in Mercedes cars in North America. Differences between these pumps include their size and construction features. Designs are based on injection quantity and pressure required for different engine power outputs and emission characteristics. Injected fuel quantity from each pump depends on the swept volume of the injection pump barrels and pump speed.

A-model pumps are for smaller horsepower (hp) engines **FIGURE 19-8**. Because of their compact size, A-model pumps do not deliver the highest possible injection volumes or pressures.

FIGURE 19-8 An A-model pump used on small displacement diesels. Note the cover plate, under which adjustments of lift to port closure and pump phasing are performed.

MW pumps have higher output volumes and pressures and are used in light- and medium-duty applications **FIGURE 19-9**. P models have the highest pressure and volume output and are commonly used for medium- and heavy-duty on- and off-highway applications **FIGURE 19-10**.

▶ Injection Volume Control Mechanisms

The metering of fuel for delivery is regulated by the pump governor using unique linkage, which requires synchronization of delivery quantities for all cylinders. It is helpful to observe how the governor interfaces with the high-pressure pump to achieve control of the injection events to deliver the precise quantity of fuel for all operating conditions. It is important to note that when pumps are calibrated in a specialized repair shop, these control mechanisms are adjusted. Wear, maladjustment, and tampering with these mechanisms can negatively impact engine performance and lead to catastrophic engine failure.

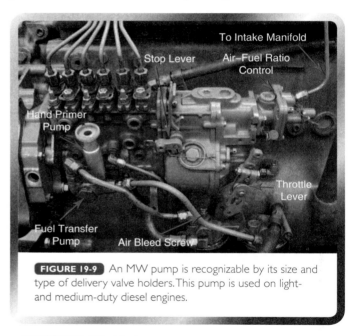

FIGURE 19-9 An MW pump is recognizable by its size and type of delivery valve holders. This pump is used on light- and medium-duty diesel engines.

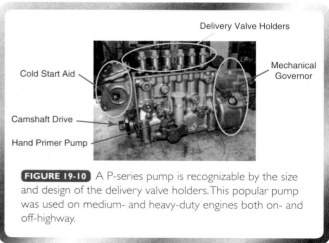

FIGURE 19-10 A P-series pump is recognizable by the size and design of the delivery valve holders. This popular pump was used on medium- and heavy-duty engines both on- and off-highway.

Plungers and Barrels

The pumping elements consist of a cylinder or barrel fitted with a reciprocating plunger. A locating pin will hold the barrel in the pump housing. In smaller pumps, the barrel has an inlet port near the top, and larger pumps have a discharge port as well. Located 180 degrees apart, these ports are also termed **fill and spill ports** (FIGURE 19-11).

Control Groove

A plunger's diameter is precisely matched to the barrel. It has a deep cut, shaped like a spiral, machined into its outer face. This spiral shape is known as a control groove, or helix, and it is vital to metering fuel for delivery. A vertical cut may also be machined into the outer surface of the plunger from the top of the plunger to the helix groove. If there is no vertical groove cut on the outer circumference of the plunger, a hole is drilled in the center of the plunger instead. This hole in the plunger intersects with another hole cross-drilled from the helix groove into the plunger, and connects the fuel in the control groove with the top of the plunger (FIGURE 19-12).

The fit of these parts must be ultra-precise in order to maintain a liquid-tight seal even at low speeds and high injection pressures. Some amount of controlled fuel leakage is allowed to bypass the plunger to lubricate the assembly. Sealing O-rings and a machined groove in the lower end of the barrel drain away fuel leaking past the plunger to minimize fuel leakage into the cam box, which could contaminate engine oil. The barrel and plunger must be replaced as matched sets during pump overhaul. On high hp engines, two helixes are commonly cut on barrels that are also separated by straight, vertically cut notches.

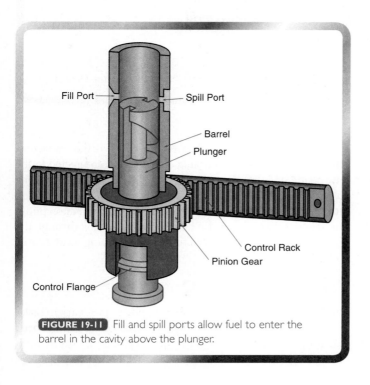

FIGURE 19-11 Fill and spill ports allow fuel to enter the barrel in the cavity above the plunger.

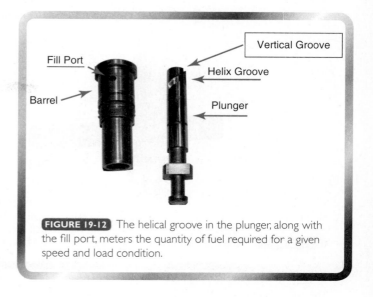

FIGURE 19-12 The helical groove in the plunger, along with the fill port, meters the quantity of fuel required for a given speed and load condition.

Control Vane, Sleeve, and Pinion Gears

The lower part of the plunger has a vane that engages a **control sleeve**. Attached to the control sleeve is a gear called a **pinion gear**. This gear meshes with the fuel pump **control rack**. When the control rack moves back and forth in a linear direction, this motion is transferred through the pinion gear to the driving vane, which rotates the plunger. The fuel control rack is connected to all the pinion gears, causing the pinions and plungers to rotate in unison (FIGURE 19-13). The governor is connected to the end of the control rack.

Fuel Supply to Pumping Elements

When the top of the plunger is below the inlet and spill ports, fuel completely fills the open spaces in the barrel. The supply pump delivers more fuel than is necessary so each barrel is always filled with fuel. Each plunger is attached to a roller that rides on a camshaft. A spring is located above the roller and operates to maintain contact between the roller and the camshaft, thus ensuring the plunger follows the camshaft profile.

▶ Fuel Metering

Multiple plunger injection pumps, like any other high-pressure injection system, must precisely meter, or measure out, the correct quantity of fuel required for any given engine speed and load condition. While the total quantity of fuel is regulated by governor controls, the multiple plunger section of the pump measures out the exact quantity of fuel delivered to each cylinder. The section on injection pump adjustments at the end of this chapter may seem beyond the scope of regular service procedures a field technician will perform, but it is included to help technicians understand the various external features of pumps, which are involved in overhauling and identifying potential problems associated with pump calibration done at specialty shops.

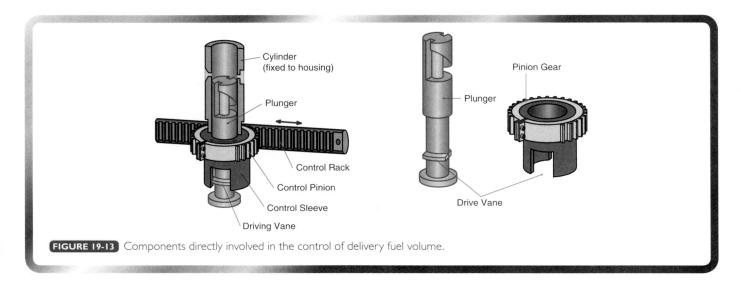

FIGURE 19-13 Components directly involved in the control of delivery fuel volume.

This next section will examine the supply of fuel to barrels and plungers and the operation of the port helix metering system. Many problems in multiple plunger injection pumps can be traced to these areas, so understanding the construction and operation of this part of pump operation is valuable for diagnostic and service purposes.

Fuel Charging

Fuel enters the injection pump from a low-pressure supply pump at anywhere between 10 and 65 psi (69 and 448 kPa). Pressures are usually in the vicinity of 35–55 psi (241–379 kPa). Fuel will enter the pump housing and circulate around the barrel assemblies to fill the chambers above the pumping plungers when the plunger is retracted below the charging ports. Surrounding the barrel are **charging galleries** that circulate fuel supplied by the low-pressure transfer pump **FIGURE 19-14**.

If a separate spill port is included, it can be found on the side of the pump opposite the fill port; this prevents pressure fluctuations that can interfere with precision fuel metering. Pressure pulsations in this fuel gallery, which can lead to cylinder misfires, are dampened by using a flexible piece of rubber hose connected to the fuel galleries. These hoses may be located on the charging or return side of the fuel flow through the pump. To regulate pressure within the injection pump housing, either an overflow valve or a restriction fitting must be used at the outlet of the fuel gallery, which returns excess fuel back to the fuel tank.

An **overflow valve** is similar to a pressure regulator. It uses a ball and spring assembly that will remain seated until sufficient pressure forces the ball off its seat, allowing fuel to flow out of the pump. Not only does this device maintain the correct transfer pump pressure inside the fuel chambers to charge the barrel/plungers, but it ensures air is purged from the injection pump housing's fuel galleries by allowing continuous flow of fuel out of the pump and back to the fuel tank. Excess fuel circulating through these fuel galleries aids in removal of heat and fuel vapor created through the continual pressurization of fuel within the pump. Fuel that leaves the pump returns to the tank through the overflow valve.

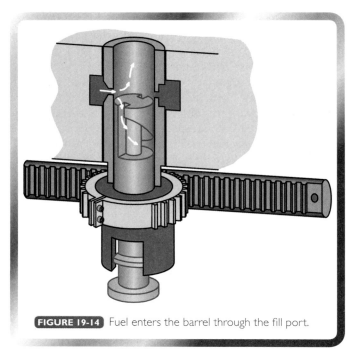

FIGURE 19-14 Fuel enters the barrel through the fill port.

Similar in function to the overflow valve is the restriction fitting. This is simply a calibrated orifice that is connected to the return side or injection pump outlet. As engine speed and the volume of transfer fuel pump output increases, the restriction fitting will cause fuel pressure to build inside the injection pump fuel galleries. Excess fuel also flows back to the tank through the return line through the restrictor fitting, carrying away heated fuel and vapor.

Varying Injection Quantity

The volume of fuel delivered to the cylinders must vary in order to start and stop the engine as well as to change the engine speed and torque output. To vary the delivery quantity, most multiple plunger pumps use port-helix fuel metering principles.

Summarized briefly, port-helix metering involves rotating the plunger and the helix groove orientation with the fill and spill port, effectively changing the point of plunger travel. This alters where the beginning and end of fuel pressurization for injection takes place. Changing the helix groove orientation to these ports increases or decreases the distance the plunger travels to produce the injection quantity. This distance, also known as effective stroke, ultimately controls the amount of fuel injected.

Effective Stroke

Effective stroke is the distance the plunger moves between the fill port closing and the spill port opening FIGURE 19-15. It occurs when fuel is pressurized during upward movement of the plunger in the barrel. When the helix groove uncovers the spill port, pressurized fuel drains back to the charging pressure and ends the injection event.

Start of Delivery

When the pumping plunger is at the bottom of its stroke, fuel fills the chamber above the plunger. As the plunger moves upward, past the fill and spill ports, the ports are sealed, thus trapping and pressurizing fuel on its upward stroke. During this upward plunger movement, fuel is delivered to the nozzles at high pressure for injection into the cylinders.

Lift to Port Closure

Lift to port closure is the position where the pumping plunger just begins to cover the fill and spill port. Lift to port closure is considered the beginning of the injection event when adjusting the pump to engine timing, either on a calibration bench or in the field FIGURE 19-16.

Injection

After the spill and fill ports are covered, the plunger continues its upward travel, pressurizing fuel as it moves. Fuel pressure above the plunger will lift the delivery valve from its seat, and fuel flows around the valve into the injection line which delivers it to the injector FIGURE 19-17. The delivery valve operates as a one-way check to allow fuel to remain at

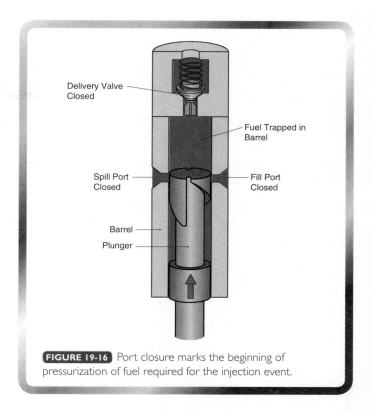

FIGURE 19-16 Port closure marks the beginning of pressurization of fuel required for the injection event.

relatively high pressure in the fuel injection line while ensuring that fuel pressure will drop far enough below nozzle opening pressure to prevent secondary injections caused by pressure wave reflections back and forth through the injector line.

End of Delivery

It is important to observe that pressurization of the fuel ends when the lower edge of the helix groove on the plunger uncovers

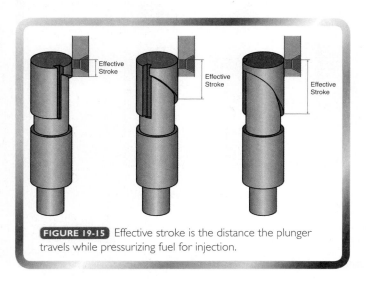

FIGURE 19-15 Effective stroke is the distance the plunger travels while pressurizing fuel for injection.

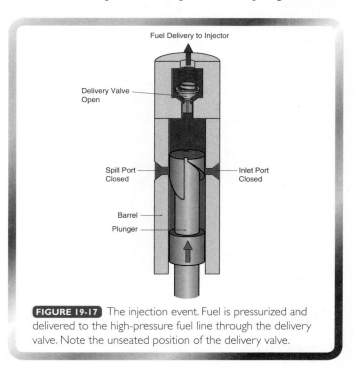

FIGURE 19-17 The injection event. Fuel is pressurized and delivered to the high-pressure fuel line through the delivery valve. Note the unseated position of the delivery valve.

the spill port. As the helix groove uncovers the spill port, fuel pressure above the plunger will vent down through the vertical slot in the side of the plunger and discharge fuel into the low-pressure spill port along the helix groove **FIGURE 19-18** .

Alternatively, a plunger with a hole drilled vertically from the top through the center line will vent fuel through the helix into the spill port via a horizontal hole cross-drilled between the helix groove and the vertical hole. As the helix uncovers the spill port, the groove will vent fuel pressure above the plunger to the spill port when the plunger has risen far enough to deliver the desired quantity of fuel **FIGURE 19-19** .

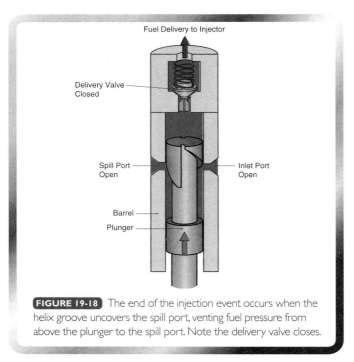

FIGURE 19-18 The end of the injection event occurs when the helix groove uncovers the spill port, venting fuel pressure from above the plunger to the spill port. Note the delivery valve closes.

Control of Fuel Delivery Volume

Rotational movement of the plunger relative to the fill and spill ports will vary fuel delivery quantity. To change the effective stroke, the control rack first rotates the pinions on the control sleeves that attach to each plunger. (Remember the governor is connected to one end of the control rack.) Rack travel, determined by the governor, will set the point at which the sleeve rotates and positions the plungers to cause the helix to uncover the spill ports. Rotating the plunger in one direction will cause the spill port to be uncovered later in the plunger's travel. When the effective stroke of the plunger becomes longer, delivery volume increases. To increase delivery volume, the control rack will always move *away* from the governor. Moving the control rack towards the governor in the opposite direction will cause the spill port to be uncovered sooner, which reduces delivery volume. A maximum fuel delivery quantity has the helix covering the spill port for the greatest distance of plunger travel, producing the longest effective stroke.

Stopping and Starting the Engine

To stop fuel delivery and engine operation, the vertical grooves in the sides of the pumping plunger are rotated to align with the fill and spill ports. This prevents any pressurization of fuel for injection **FIGURE 19-20** . The stop lever inside the governor will physically move the control rack to orient the plungers and spill ports to this position. On many engines, the stop lever is controlled using an electric shut-off solenoid **FIGURE 19-21** . The solenoid usually contains a pull-in winding and hold-in winding, which are both energized during the initial cranking period. Shortly after the engine starts, the solenoid is moved to the run position and held there only by the hold-in winding while the pull-in winding is disengaged. It is important to note that if the solenoid position is incorrectly adjusted, the pull-in winding will remain energized and quickly burn-out.

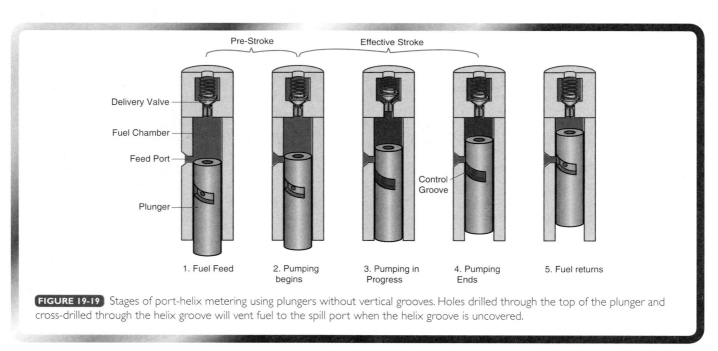

FIGURE 19-19 Stages of port-helix metering using plungers without vertical grooves. Holes drilled through the top of the plunger and cross-drilled through the helix groove will vent fuel to the spill port when the helix groove is uncovered.

Retard Notches

During cold starts, cylinder temperatures and pressures are lower than they are after the engine is warmed up, and maximum fuel quantity is required to produce sufficient vapor for combustion, as well as to produce enough energy to overcome the inertia of rotating an engine from cranking to idle speed. Under these conditions, the governor has the control rack in a full-fuel or excess-fuel position. To aid starting, some manufactures will retard injection timing to allow more crank rotation before injecting fuel. Delaying or retarding injection timing increases cylinder pre-ignition temperatures because the piston will rise to a higher point within the cylinder. To mechanically produce retarded injection timing, notches or slots are machined into the top of the pumping plungers. These notches correspond to the position the plunger will be moved to by the control rack for maximum fuel delivery during starting. The orientation of the notch causes fuel to be spilled longer as the plunger moves upward, usually approximately ten degrees of crank rotation. Spilling fuel delays the beginning of injection (BOI), allowing the engine piston to rise farther in the cylinder before injection begins. A piston which has risen farther in the cylinder will compress air to a higher temperature and pressure before injection begins FIGURE 19-22 .

Helix Shapes and Injection Timing

For efficient combustion and engine performance, injection timing should advance with increased engine speed without a load and retard with load increases without a change in speed. For multiple plunger pumps using port helix metering, a pump manufacturer can use several strategies to accomplish this. One is to change the shape of the helix to vary the beginning of injection (BOI) as fuel delivery quantities change. Because rotating the pumping plunger changes the lift to port closure dimension, the shape of the helix can also change injection timing FIGURE 19-23 and FIGURE 19-24 .

Timing Mechanisms

To modify injection timing beyond what is achieved by the helix profile, a timing advance or retard mechanism is used on some engines. These mechanisms modify the pump-to-engine timing relationship using a set of centrifugal flyweights enabling changes to injection timing relative to engine speed. The inner hub is splined to the pump camshaft while the housing is driven by the engine. Centrifugal flyweights, ramps, and rollers determine how much offset will occur between engine and pump position, which changes injection timing FIGURE 19-25 .

Automatic Timing Advance Mechanism

Automatic timing advance mechanisms are used to meet emission standards without compromising performance. These are located between the pump drive mechanism and the engine gear train FIGURE 19-26 . This location permits the alteration of pump-to-engine timing based on the use of centrifugal flyweight, spring tension, and cams located inside the mechanical timer. Manufacturers will determine the ideal timing advance/retard curve for their engines. Often the mechanisms operate to retard pump timing at speeds above idle when the engine is

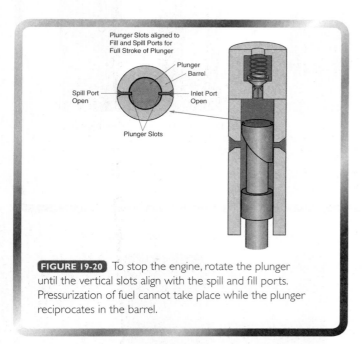

FIGURE 19-20 To stop the engine, rotate the plunger until the vertical slots align with the spill and fill ports. Pressurization of fuel cannot take place while the plunger reciprocates in the barrel.

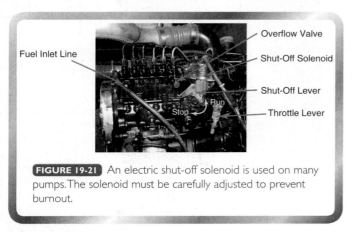

FIGURE 19-21 An electric shut-off solenoid is used on many pumps. The solenoid must be carefully adjusted to prevent burnout.

FIGURE 19-22 The retard notch causes the plunger to lift farther before beginning effective stroke, delaying the start of injection. Retarding injection timing is a strategy that increases the likelihood of starting a cold engine.

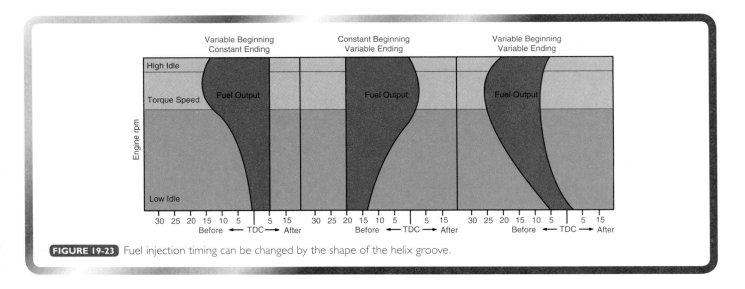

FIGURE 19-23 Fuel injection timing can be changed by the shape of the helix groove.

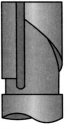

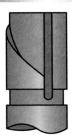
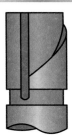
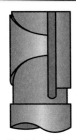
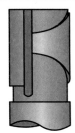

| Single Helix Lower Left Hand | Single Helix Lower Right Hand | Single Helix Upper Left Hand | Single Helix Upper Right Hand | Double Helix Lower Right Hand Upper Left Hand | Double Helix Lower Left Hand Upper Right Hand |

FIGURE 19-24 The shape of the helix grooves determines whether injection timing varies at the beginning or end of injection. Left- and right-hand helix terminology refers to the direction the plunger is rotated.

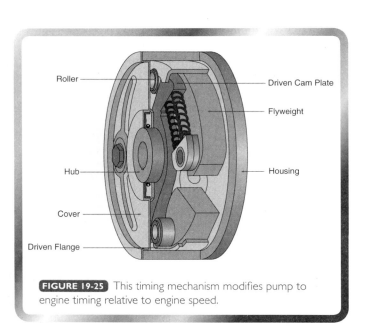

FIGURE 19-25 This timing mechanism modifies pump to engine timing relative to engine speed.

FIGURE 19-26 The mechanical automatic timing mechanism for a tier 3 injection pump camshaft.

usually under load. At higher rpm, the mechanism will allow injection timing to advance.

Partial-Authority Systems and Injection Timing Control

To extend the usefulness of multiple plunger injection pumps, electronic control of governing and, in some cases, injection timing has replaced mechanical controls. Because only some fuel system functions are electronically controlled, they are referred to as partial-authority injection systems. Additional factors such as air inlet, boost, and coolant temperature as well as engine speed and driver inputs are included in calculations for determining injection quantity and timing.

Partial-authority systems are drive-by-wire, which means they have a throttle position sensor and do not use mechanical linkage to connect the accelerator pedal to the pump. The use of an electronic governor also permits data exchange between other vehicle systems such as cruise and power take-off (PTO) controls plus electronically shifted transmissions. Partial-authority fuel systems use at least an electronic governor and may also incorporate a nozzle valve lift sensor and an injection timing control mechanism.

Nozzle Valve Sensor and Injection Lag

The nozzle valve sensor, also called a nozzle lift or needle valve sensor, will provide accurate data regarding the beginning of injection (BOI). This eliminates the unpredictable variable of injection relay in timing the combustion event. Integrating this data with the engine position sensor (e.g., top dead center [TDC]) or event marker provides an electronic control module (ECM) with precise information about when injection is taking place. The lift sensor enables electronic control of BOI. With inline injection systems, electromechanical control can be used to change the start of injection. This would involve the use of an electrically controlled timing mechanism, which would replace one using flyweights. One such mechanism used by the earliest Mack VMAC 1 and 2 systems electronically regulate oil pressure to the timing gear, which is composed of two sections: an outer hub, which is driven by the engine, and an inner section, which has internal helical-cut teeth on a spline connecting it to the injection pump drive shaft. Oil pressure to the mechanism can vary the pump-to-engine timing by changing the relation of the helical spline teeth to the engine-driven inner section connected to the pump camshaft.

Injection Pump Camshafts

Plunger speed and duration of injection are primarily dependent on the shape of the pump camshaft. For this reason, different camshaft shapes are used to regulate the injection rate and pressurization of the fuel delivery quantity. The slope of the outer base circle of the cam lobe is especially critical to fuel rate control. Asymmetrical profiles, or shapes that are irregular, are used to prevent the engine from starting and operating backward **FIGURE 19-27**. They also provide a very fast, high-pressure beginning to the injection event, followed by a gradual filling of the plunger barrels.

Roller **tappets** are lubricated by engine oil to reduce friction and wear. Engine oil enters the injection pump cambox through an oil supply line from the engine, and excess oil drains out of the front of the pump through passageways into the front cover.

> ### ▶ TECHNICIAN TIP
>
> Engines can be prevented from running backward by using an asymmetrically shaped injection pump cam profile. An engine running backward will push exhaust out the air intake and pull fresh air in through the exhaust system. When an engine runs backward, oil and fuel pumps do not supply the engine with either fluid.

> ### ▶ TECHNICIAN TIP
>
> Contamination of engine oil with fuel can take place when fuel leaks past plunger and barrel assemblies into the cambox of an injection pump. When investigating possible causes of oil dilution with fuel, do not overlook a leaking injection pump.

Delivery Valves

Delivery valves are required for each pumping plunger in a multiple plunger injection pump. The delivery valve is located at the outlet of the plunger and barrel assembly and consists of a spring, seat, and specially designed valve. Delivery valves are required

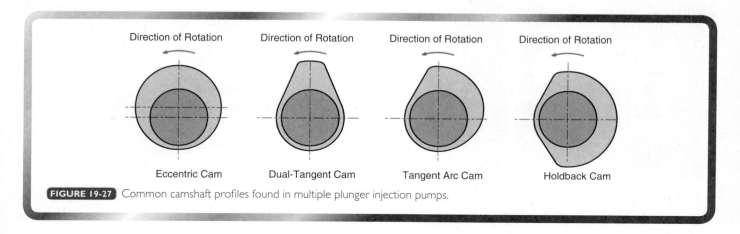

FIGURE 19-27 Common camshaft profiles found in multiple plunger injection pumps.

Direction of Rotation — Eccentric Cam

Direction of Rotation — Dual-Tangent Cam

Direction of Rotation — Tangent Arc Cam

Direction of Rotation — Holdback Cam

for two main purposes: to minimize injection lag and to prevent fuel dribbling caused by secondary injections.

Minimizing injection lag is accomplished by maintaining residual pressure in the fuel line of approximately 700–900 psi (48–62 bar) from injection event to injection event (shot to shot) when the engine is running. This remaining fuel volume allows the pressure to build up more quickly for the next injection. The head start on injection pressurization in the line minimizes the time delay needed to build injection pressure in a fuel line. Fuel is not permitted to quickly drain out of the injection lines and back into the pump because of the operation of this valve.

Secondary injections are caused by pressure wave reflections in the high-pressure system produced when the injector nozzle valve closes. A similar type of wave pattern is observed when a faucet in a house is suddenly shut off. What sometimes follows is a loud banging noise as the pressure wave reflects or ripples through the plumbing. The high pressures involved in fuel injection are much higher than water pressure in household plumbing, and the forces are magnified with the abrupt ending of injection. If the injector nozzle valve closes and fuel line pressure is near nozzle opening pressure, pressure waves will reflect up and down the length of the injection line, and fuel will dribble from the nozzle, causing secondary injections to take place. This nozzle dribble will cause excessive emissions and power loss.

To minimize the effect of pressure wave reflections, the delivery valve has a retraction function built into its shape **FIGURE 19-28**. As the delivery valve returns to its seat, it will pull a calibrated amount of fuel from the high-pressure fuel line, which varies with the shape of the valve **FIGURE 19-29**. This retraction volume sharply lowers line pressure from injection

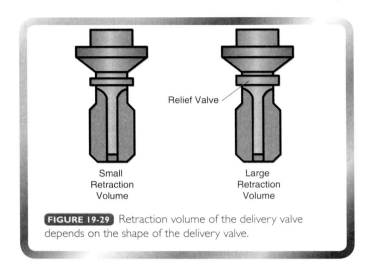

FIGURE 19-29 Retraction volume of the delivery valve depends on the shape of the delivery valve.

pressure to a residual pressure. Secondary injections and nozzle dribble are then minimized and a crisp, sharp ending to injection takes place **FIGURE 19-30**.

▶ **TECHNICIAN TIP**

Worn, stuck, scored, or poorly sealing delivery valves will interfere with injection timing and metering required for smooth engine operation. Problems with delivery valves lead to low power and rough running. In many commonly used injection pumps, delivery valves can be removed, inspected, and replaced without removing the pump from the engine or sending the pump out to a specialized repair shop.

FIGURE 19-28 The delivery valve of a P model pump.

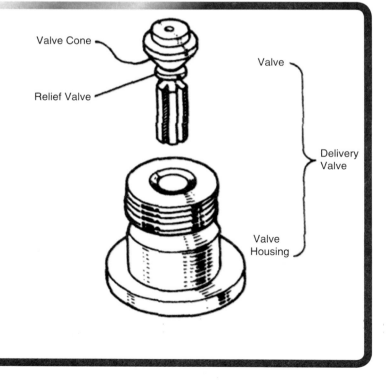

Replacing a Delivery Valve

If small particles of dirt enter the injection pump's delivery valves shortly after a filter replacement, the affected cylinder will misfire. When this happens, the valve, rather than the pump, can be removed and replaced. Delivery valves can wear out in an injection pump. Worn valves produce low power complaints and white exhaust smoke. On Bosch P7100 pumps, the valves are easily accessible for replacement.

To replace a delivery valve, follow the steps in SKILL DRILL 19-1.

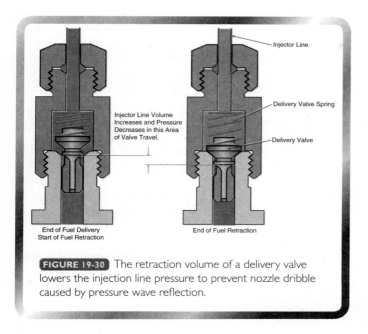

FIGURE 19-30 The retraction volume of a delivery valve lowers the injection line pressure to prevent nozzle dribble caused by pressure wave reflection.

High-Pressure Injection Lines

High-pressure fuel injection lines might seem quite simple in appearance, but their design is important to correct fuel system operation. Seamless steel tubing is most often used for their construction. Critical design features of injection lines are the size of the fuel nozzle inlet fitting, the length of the fuel line, and the inside diameter of the fuel line.

The inside diameter at each end of a fuel line is usually 0.010" (0.25 mm) larger than the inside diameter of the rest of the fuel line. This size difference is necessary to permit acceptable alignment between the injection nozzle inlet fitting and line. Also, each flared end of the fuel line is slightly larger than the rest of the injection line. Lines are made like this because this opening will decrease in diameter when the fuel line nuts are tightened.

Service Precautions with High-Pressure Fuel Lines

Injection lines are fabricated to be the same length to ensure that the fuel pressure wave arrives at each cylinder at exactly

SKILL DRILL 19-1 Replacing a Delivery Valve

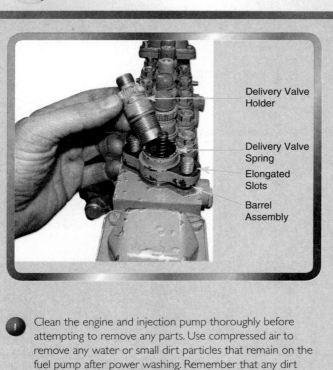

1. Clean the engine and injection pump thoroughly before attempting to remove any parts. Use compressed air to remove any water or small dirt particles that remain on the fuel pump after power washing. Remember that any dirt and debris inside the delivery valve will produce a misfire.

2. Disconnect the injector lines and cap them while performing this procedure.

3. Remove the delivery valve holder using a special 32-point socket. Some well-made 16-point sockets can also be effectively used for this work. A sealing O-ring may give some resistance when removing the holder from the pump body.

4. Remove the delivery valve seat from the holder if it is removed with the holder. Otherwise, use a magnet to remove the valve seat, delivery valve, and spring.

5. Using a pick, remove and discard the copper sealing washer located below the delivery valve holder.

6. Install a new copper sealing washer.

7. If the valve is being reused after dirt particles are removed, reinstall the delivery valve after cleaning it.

8. Install a new delivery valve, seat, and spring from a supply kit.

9. Reinstall the delivery valve holder with a new color-coded O-ring and torque to specifications.

10. Repeat the above procedure with the other pump plungers.

11. Reinstall the injection lines. Run the engine and inspect for leaks.

the same time, enabling identical injection timing between all cylinders in the engine. Changes in line length affects the time it takes to deliver the injection quantity of fuel. If one fuel line is longer than the others, the fuel will take extra time to travel in the lengthier line, which changes the timing of BOI. Similarly, the inside diameter of injection lines must be identical to prevent timing differences caused by different swell volumes of each line. While it may not be apparent, the bends and turns found in injection lines accommodate identical line length for each cylinder **FIGURE 19-31** . So, while cylinders 1 and 6 are different distances from the injection pump, more bends are placed in the shorter distance line to take up the slack. When installing a new line from stock material, bends must be no less than 50 mm in radius.

High-pressure fuel lines must be clamped at regular intervals with vibration-absorbing insulators. Line vibration produced from the injection swelling and lengthening of lines will quickly cause the lines to fatigue and break if they are not properly clamped **FIGURE 19-32** .

Precautions must be taken to not overtighten injection lines. Over-tightening creates grooves in the flared end, which can result in a poor seal between the fuel line and the nozzle or pump.

Stressing lines can occur through excessive handling and bending. An overstressed fuel line can easily break after a few hours or days in operation. A fuel line that is broken must be replaced and not brazed.

After initially installing an injection pump or running it out of fuel, a technician needs to bleed air out from internal fuel passageways. A small bleeder screw is often located on the pump, which can be loosened while the hand primer pump is operated. The screw is tightened after clean, bubble-free fuel flows from the bleeder screw **FIGURE 19-33** .

Injection Pump Timing

Timing on mechanical injections pump should be kept within ±0.5 degree of manufacturer specifications to maintain emission standard compliance and proper engine performance standards. Altering injection timing will produce changes in exhaust emissions, power output, fuel economy, and combustion temperatures.

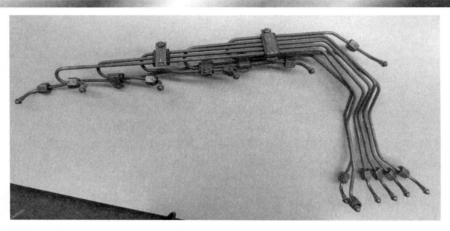

FIGURE 19-31 Injection lines for an engine are all the same length and diameter.

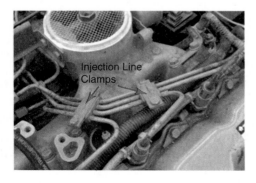

FIGURE 19-32 Line clamps use insulators to dampen vibrations caused by injection line swell during injection.

FIGURE 19-33 The bleeder screw on this MW model pump must be opened when using the hand primer to bleed the fuel system after filter installation.

Evaluating Injection Pump Timing to Engine Timing in Mechanical Systems

With increased distance and operating hours, gear trains can wear, causing excessive gear backlash which in turn alters injection timing. To evaluate pump timing, injection pumps can be checked when the engine is stopped (<u>static timing</u>) or running (<u>dynamic timing</u>). Pump timing is part of the important emission information and is included on the engine data plate.

Static Injection Pump Timing

A variety of methods can be used to set initial static pump to engine timing. <u>Timing pins</u>, timing indicators, pointers, and other aids will assist in the adjustment of the lift to port closure point to the appropriate engine position. To adjust static timing, for example, the BOI is established for cylinder 1's pumping plunger, and the pump position is locked. The engine is then rotated to the point where injection should begin, usually before TDC on cylinder 1. Some timing indicator is usually found on the engine to correctly identify the crank position needed to establish correct pump-to-engine timing. The valve cover of the engine should be removed to verify the engine is at the end of compression stroke and not exhaust stroke at cylinder 1 TDC. The pump drive and engine are then locked to one another to maintain this pump-to-engine timing. Alternatively, pump timing is often adjusted after positioning the engine or pump to manufacturer specifications for static timing (a specific number of degrees of crank rotation before TDC). Then the pump drive gear is adjusted and locked to fix the timing relationship **FIGURE 19-34**.

Another method to determine the correct pump-to-engine timing is to measure the plunger travel in the injection pump. The manufacturer will publish specifications for the plunger lift from BDC (bottom dead center), which corresponds to a specific injection timing position listed in degrees. For example, a 30mm plunger lift might correspond to injection beginning 12.0 degrees before TDC while a 50mm would be 9.5 degrees. The pump position is locked after measuring the appropriate plunger lift, and the pump is installed on the engine. The engine would be positioned at TDC and the pump drive gear locked in position.

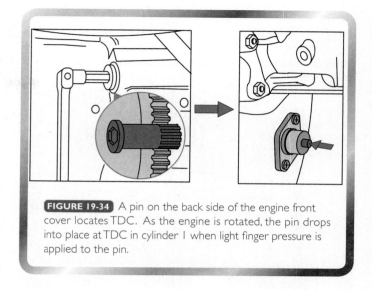

FIGURE 19-34 A pin on the back side of the engine front cover locates TDC. As the engine is rotated, the pin drops into place at TDC in cylinder 1 when light finger pressure is applied to the pin.

Verifying Static Timing for an Inline Injection Pump

Precise adjustment of pump-to-engine injection timing to ±0.5 degree is critical to obtaining good fuel economy, even for a mechanical injection system. Power and emissions are also affected by inaccurate injection timing. Advanced and retarded timing have similar symptoms, which include excessive black or gray exhaust smoke, increased combustion noise, poor fuel economy and power, and high exhaust temperatures. Normal gear train wear will cause timing to retard. Always verify pump-to-engine timing when investigating complaints with causes related to the high-pressure fuel system. Verification of pump timing can be performed using several methods: spill timing, static timing, and using a dial indicator to measure the correct amount of pump plunger lift for a specific crankshaft position.

To verify static timing for an inline injection pump, follow the steps in **SKILL DRILL 19-2**. These steps are for Cummins B and C series engines, which use P7100 pumps.

Adjusting Pump-to-Engine Timing

The most precise procedure for establishing correct pump-to-engine timing involves the use of a dial indicator to measure pumping plunger lift. Manufacturers such as Cummins and Dodge supply charts that provide a corresponding crankshaft position for a given pump plunger lift travel.

To adjust pump-to-engine timing, follow the steps in **SKILL DRILL 19-3**. These steps are for Bosch A model and P7100 injection pumps.

Spill Timing

High-pressure <u>spill timing</u> is a procedure that can be performed to verify or adjust pump-to-engine timing. With this procedure, a high-pressure pump fuel gallery is pressurized with fuel to the point where fuel pressure exceeds the pressure required to open the delivery valves, but not to open injector nozzles.

▶ **TECHNICIAN TIP**

One of the most common mistakes technicians make when installing inline injection pumps is when they attempt to establish the correct crankshaft position for cylinder 1 TDC. Because cylinder 1 TDC pointers can place the engine at either the end of power or exhaust stroke, it is essential the valve cover is removed and valve position verified. At TDC in a four-stroke cycle engine, clearance should exist between the rocker levers and both valves on cylinder 1, and no clearance should exist for cylinder 6. Cylinder 6 should be in valve overlap position with both valves open. If the valve positions are interchanged, the engine needs to turn one rotation because an inline injection pump will turn at half crank speed or the same speed as the camshaft.

SKILL DRILL 19-2 Verifying Static Timing for an Inline Injection Pump

TOC Plug
Indicator Hole

Pump Timing
Plug Holder

1 Position the engine near TDC for cylinder 1. To speed up this process, remove the valve cover for cylinder 6 and bar the engine over clockwise until the exhaust valve starts to close and the intake valve begins to open. Then, rotate the engine a few degrees counterclockwise. This procedure should place the engine near TDC for cylinder 1.

2 Rotate the engine clockwise slowly and gently while pushing the engine-mounted timing pin toward the front of the engine. Continue rotating the engine clockwise until the timing pin drops into the machined hole in the back of the camshaft gear. This engine position is TDC for cylinder 1.

3 Remove the 0.75" (19 mm) hex-head pump timing plug from the governor housing. The plug should have a plastic pin with a fork-shaped end.

4 Using a light, carefully look into the pump housing to check for a wire-like timing indicator that rotates with the pump camshaft.

5 If the wire indicator is centered in the hole, verify its correct position by gently pushing the forked end of the plastic plug into the hole, over the wire timing indicator. The plug should not be forced; it should slide over the wire indicator if the pump is correctly timed.

6 If the pump is timed correctly, reinstall the plug and valve cover to finish the procedure. If the pump timing is not correct, the pump needs to be reestablished.

7 To reestablish the pump, loosen the pump mounting bolts. The injection pump mounting bolts are in elongated slots on the pump.

8 Rotate the pump body until the wire timing indicator in the pump is centered in the plug hole and the plastic plug's forked end can slide over the wire. When moving the pump, the injection lines attached to the pump will resist pump body movement and cause the pump to spring back into position. Loosening the injection lines may help prevent this problem.

9 An alternative procedure that can be used when the injection pump is initially installed requires the pump timing wire to be aligned with the plastic fork in the pump body.

10 Lock the injection pump in position by removing a shim beneath a locking nut on the pump's adapter plate.

11 Install the pump onto the engine and torque the pump drive gear. Tighten the pump bolts to complete the timing phase of this procedure.

12 To remove the pump, undo the oil filler cap and unscrew the filler cap adapter from the engine's front cover.

13 Remove the pump drive gear nut and attach a T-bar puller to the timing gear using puller bolts between the T-bar and gear.

14 Using the T-bar puller, break the drive gear free from the pump's tapered shaft. Disconnect and remove the pump.

A pressure pump supplying fuel is connected to the fuel inlet and outlet ports of the injection pump. After all delivery valves are capped, except for cylinder 1, and the pump is rotated, fuel pressure will open the delivery valve whenever the spill and fill ports are uncovered. Fuel will then begin to leak from a gooseneck line connected to the delivery valve holder on the first cylinder of the pump. When the quantity of leaking fuel diminishes to only one or two drops per second, the lift to port closure is achieved, and the beginning of effective stroke or injection occurs. Comparing engine position to actual pump position using external timing indicators will determine whether adjustment to pump-to-engine injection timing is necessary **FIGURE 19-35**.

Dynamic Injection Timing

Dynamic timing can be checked using an injection pulse transducer device, called a diesel pulse adapter, attached to the fuel injection line. This procedure mirrors what is done when ignition timing is performed with a timing light on a spark ignition engine. However, instead of a high-voltage pulse, swelling of the line during injection can be detected with a piezoelectric pressure transducer. When the line swells, indicating BOI, a timing light connected to a piezoelectric signal amplifier will flash and illuminate a reference point on the crankshaft **FIGURE 19-36**.

Magnetic pick-up devices connected by probes attached near the harmonic balancer can also be used to reference engine position. Dynamic timing is especially useful to check for correct operation of an automatic pump-timing mechanism if the engine is equipped with one.

Injection Pump Testing and Adjustments

Problems with injection pumps are indicated by low engine power, rough idle, dark or white exhaust smoke (caused by

SKILL DRILL 19-3 Adjusting Pump-to-Engine Timing

Static Timing in Degrees Before TDC	Plunger Travel in mm
10.0	5.25
10.5	5.35
11.0	5.45
11.5	5.55
12.0	5.65
12.5	5.7
13.0	5.8
13.5	5.9
14.0	6.0

1. Follow Steps 1–2 in Skill Drill 19-2 to position the crankshaft at TDC for cylinder 1.

2. Follow Steps 1–4 in Skill Drill 19-1 to remove the delivery valve for cylinder 1.

3. Reinstall the delivery valve holder into the pump without the delivery valve.

4. Install a purpose-made dial indicator onto the delivery valve holder where the injection line would normally attach. Rest the dial indicator extension piece on the pumping plunger in the cylinder. The dial face is capable of indicating movement of ±20 mm with the dial marked in increments of 0.01 mm. An inner dial will measure 1 mm in one rotation with a total indicator travel of 10 mm.

5. With the engine at TDC for cylinder 1, back out the timing pin. Bar the engine over counterclockwise a quarter turn, or until the dial indicator needle movement stops. Zero in the dial indicator needle.

6. Bar the engine over in a clockwise rotation while pressing on the timing pin. Stop and note the dial indicator travel when the timing pin drops into the hole on the back of the camshaft.

7. Compare the dial indicator's movement with the manufacturer's specifications.

8. If the injection pump is not within specification, loosen the pump mounting bolts and rotate the pump housing until the dial indicator pointer matches the specifications for the correct engine position. For example, an engine with pump-to-injection timing of 10 degrees before TDC should have a dial indicator movement of 5.25 mm.

9. Tighten the pump mounting nuts and reinstall and reattach all pump parts.

10. Run the engine and recheck its operation.

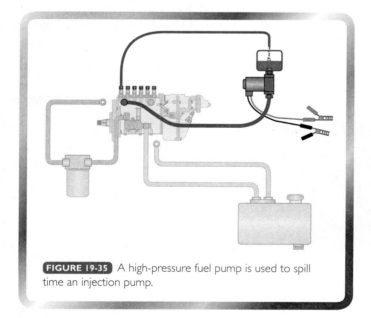

FIGURE 19-35 A high-pressure fuel pump is used to spill time an injection pump.

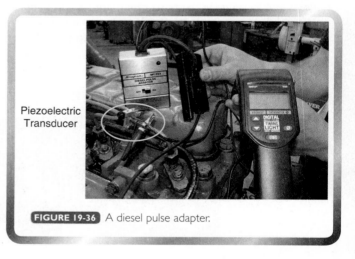

Piezoelectric Transducer

FIGURE 19-36 A diesel pulse adapter.

unburned fuel), misfiring, hard starting, poor fuel economy, and fuel in the oil. The root cause of these symptoms can be produced by other components or systems and these should be eliminated before removing an injection pump for testing.

Pumps are evaluated on test benches also known as **comparator benches** FIGURE 19-37 . When the pump is set up on the bench, it is first evaluated for external leaks and damage. Next, it is operated at several different rotational speeds to determine whether delivery quantity from each pumping element corresponds with manufacturer specifications. Barrel-to-barrel variations in delivery quantity can indicate worn pumping elements, plungers, or camshafts or simply miscalibration.

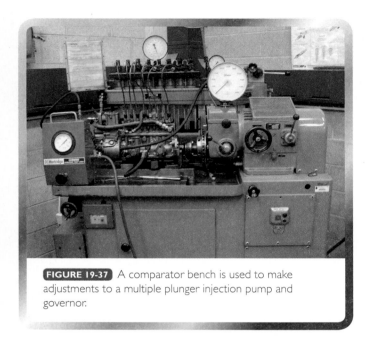

FIGURE 19-37 A comparator bench is used to make adjustments to a multiple plunger injection pump and governor.

To ensure proper performance when injection pumps are overhauled, adjustments should be made in the following sequence:

1. Establish lift to port closure adjustment first on cylinder 1 in the firing order of the injection pump. This establishes the beginning of effective stroke. The use of selective shims, adjustable tappets, or barrel rotation are methods commonly used to obtain the correct amount of plunger lift in relation to port closure of a pump **FIGURE 19-38**.

2. Continue by **phasing** the remaining pumping elements to obtain lift to port closure (in 60-degree intervals for six cylinder pumps) after making the initial lift to port closure setting on cylinder 1.

3. Perform **calibration** to ensure that that the delivery of fuel from each plunger is the same throughout the entire speed range of the pump. Uneven fuel delivery causes an engine to run rough run or cause other damage. Adjustments of the control rack to pinion, rack travel, or rotation of barrels generally accomplishes this set of adjustments.

4. Adjust the governor and air–fuel ratio device. A variety of adjustments are made to limit maximum fuel delivery for given boost pressure, speed, and load conditions. Final adjustments are made for adjusting rack travel to correctly position it to achieve the desired idle speed and stop the engine.

Low-Pressure System Testing

It is important to check the low-pressure fuel system for problems that would interfere with high-pressure injection pump operation. Fuel filters with restrictions, air in fuel caused by suction-side leaks, and low transfer pump pressure commonly cause problems that may incorrectly be attributed to the injection pump, which leads to unnecessary pump replacement or overhaul. Pressure output from the transfer pump should meet minimum specifications when measured at high idle engine speed. Volume and pressure tests after the fuel filters can indicate whether the injection system has restricted fuel filters. Low transfer pump pressure and volume indicate a low-pressure fuel system restriction or weak transfer pump. Erratic pump pressure often indicates air is in the fuel. The overflow valve will regulate fuel pressure between the transfer pump and injection pump. The use of a site glass or clear plastic line after the fuel filters and before the fuel enters the pump will indicate the presence of air in the fuel caused by a suction-side leak. Some air bubbles in the return fuel are acceptable because fuel returning to the tank is heated inside the injection pump, which produces fuel vapor in the return.

Elongated Slots

Selective Shims

FIGURE 19-38 Selective shims are used to adjust lift to port closure. Rotating the delivery valve holder varies delivery quantity; this should only be adjusted on a comparator bench.

Wrap-Up

Ready for Review

▸ The multiple plunger injection pump was the most popular diesel engine fuel injection system for nearly 70 years.

▸ A multiple plunger injection pump is a fuel system configuration that uses piston-like plungers actuated by a camshaft to pressurize fuel for injection.

▸ OEMs have not used multiple plunger injection pumps since the late 1990s in North America for light- or medium-duty on-highway diesel applications because they are not capable of meeting strict emission requirements introduced at that time.

▸ Most multiple plunger injection pumps use a port-helix metering system, which has a plunger with a machined helical groove operating in a fixed-position barrel.

▸ Variations between the designs of multiple plunger injection pumps have much to do with the fuel volumes and pressure output required of the pumps for the engine's application.

▸ The pumping elements of a multiple plunger injection pump consist of a cylinder or barrel containing a reciprocating plunger.

▸ A plunger has a deep cut, shaped like a spiral, machined in its outer face; this spiral shape is known as a control groove or helix, and it is vital to metering fuel for delivery.

▸ The lower part of the plunger has a drive vane; the control rack engages the pinion gear, which rotates the plunger drive vane. All the plungers are rotated in unison by the rack.

▸ Fuel enters the injection pump from a low-pressure supply pump after it is filtered through a secondary fuel filter.

▸ Varying the volume of fuel delivered to the cylinders is necessary to start and the stop the engine as well as change the engine speed and torque output; to vary the delivery quantity, port-helix fuel metering principles are used in most multiple plunger injection pumps.

▸ Port-helix metering involves rotating the plunger assemblies, which changes the orientation of the helix groove in relation to the fill and spill ports; this in turn regulates the change in injection quantity between the beginning and end of injection.

▸ To stop fuel delivery and engine operation, the vertical grooves in the sides of the pumping plunger are rotated to align with the fill and spill ports.

▸ During cold starting, maximum fuel quantity is required to produce sufficient pre-ignition cylinder vapor for combustion; under these conditions, the governor has the control rack in a full-fuel or excess-fuel position.

▸ To aid starting, some manufactures will retard injection timing to allow more crank rotation before injecting fuel. Additional heat in the cylinders before injection during cranking only helps ensure fast engine start-up.

▸ To obtain efficient combustion and engine performance, injection timing should advance with speed increases without a load and retard with load increases.

▸ To modify injection timing beyond what is achieved by the helix profile, a timing advance or retard mechanism is used on some engines.

▸ To extend the useful life of multiple plunger injection pumps, electronic control of governing and, in some cases, injection timing has replaced mechanical controls; these systems are referred to as partial-authority systems.

▸ Plunger speed and duration of injection are primarily dependent on the shape of the pump camshaft; for this reason, different camshaft shapes are used to regulate the fuel rate and pressurization of the fuel delivery quantity.

▸ Delivery valves are required for each pumping plunger in a multiple plunger injection pump to minimize ignition lag and prevent fuel dribbling caused by secondary injections.

▸ Critical design features of injection lines are the size of the fuel nozzle inlet fitting, the length of the fuel line, and the inside diameter of the fuel line.

▸ Timing on mechanical injections pumps should be kept within ½ a degree of manufacturer specifications to maintain emission and performance standards; altering injection timing will produce changes in exhaust emissions, fuel economy, and combustion temperatures.

▸ With increased distance and operating hours, gear trains can wear; this causes excessive gear backlash, which alters injection timing.

▸ High-pressure spill timing is a procedure that can be performed on an engine to verify or adjust pump-to-engine timing.

▸ Problems with injection pumps are indicated by rough idle, dark or white (unburned fuel) exhaust smoke, misfiring, hard starting, poor fuel economy, and fuel in oil.

Vocabulary Builder

__calibration__ Adjustments of the control rack to pinion, rack travel, or rotation of barrels to ensure that that the delivery of fuel from each plunger is the same throughout the entire speed range of the pump.

__camshaft__ A component used by multiple plunger injection pumps that actuates plungers that pressurize fuel for injection.

__charging gallery__ A passageway for fuel surrounding all the barrels of the injection pump.

__comparator bench__ A test bench used to evaluate pumps and make calibration adjustments to multiple plunger injection pumps and governors.

__control rack__ The mechanisms used to connect the mechanical governor to the plungers in order to rotate them in unison and meter correct quantities fuel.

__control sleeve__ The mechanisms used to connect the mechanical governor to the plungers in order to rotate them and meter fuel in the correct quantities.

delivery valve Valves that operate as one-way checks to allow fuel to remain at relatively high pressure in the fuel injection lines while ensuring that fuel pressure will drop far enough below nozzle opening pressure to prevent secondary injections caused by reflecting fuel pulsations in the injector line.

dynamic timing Changes in pump timing when an engine is running.

effective stroke The distance the plunger moves between fill port closing and spill port opening.

fill and spill ports Posts on either side of a barrel through which fuel enters or leaves the barrel's assemblies.

lift to port closure The position where the pumping plunger just begins to cover the fill and spill port.

overflow valve A low-pressure fuel system pressure regulating valve for an injection pump that uses a ball and spring assembly. The overflow valve helps purge vapor from fuel and keeps fuel temperatures cool inside the pump.

partial-authority fuel system A mechanical fuel system that has adapted some electronic controls to extend the design usefulness, particularly where stricter emission regulations require cleaner combustion.

phasing An injection pump adjustment procedure that is made when the remaining pumping elements are adjusted to obtain lift to port closure (in 60-degree intervals for a six cylinder pump) after the initial setting on cylinder 1.

pinion gear The component that is engaged by the control rack to rotate the plunger drive vane.

plunger and barrel assembly The elements making up the high-pressure pumps in a multiple plunger injection pump.

port-helix metering A mechanism to meter fuel that uses reciprocating plungers and a camshaft to pressurize fuel; rotating the helix groove in the pumping plungers in relation to the spill port controls fuel metered to the injectors.

spill timing A procedure that can be performed on an engine to verify or adjust pump-to-engine timing. The procedure is also used on a comparator bench to establish correct lift to port closure.

static timing Pump timing that is adjusted when an engine is stopped.

tappet A components used by multiple plunger injection pumps to produce low friction reciprocating motion of the plungers.

timing pins Tools used lock and injection pump or engine in position to obtain correct pump to engine timing.

Review Questions

1. _____ is the distance the plunger moves between fill port closing and spill port closing.
   a. Effective stroke   c. Static timing
   b. Spill timing   d. Dynamic timing

2. The _____ is a passageway for fuel surrounding all the barrels of the injection pump.
   a. effective stroke   c. charging gallery
   b. spill timing   d. dynamic timing

3. Changes in pump timing when an engine is running is called _____.
   a. effective stroke
   b. spill timing
   c. static timing
   d. dynamic timing

4. _____ is pump timing that is adjusted when an engine is stopped.
   a. Spill timing
   b. Static timing
   c. Dynamic timing
   d. Effective stroke

5. _____ is a procedure that can be performed on an engine to verify or adjust pump to engine timing.
   a. Spill timing
   b. Static timing
   c. Effective stroke
   d. Dynamic timing

6. A(n) _____ is similar to a pressure regulator.
   a. diesel pulse adapter
   b. overflow valve
   c. comparator
   d. plunger

7. The _____ operates as a one-way check to allow fuel to remain at relatively high pressure in the fuel injection line.
   a. barrel
   b. diesel pulse adapter
   c. delivery valve
   d. plunger

8. To mechanically produce _____ injection timing, notches or slots are machined into the top of the pumping plungers.
   a. high-pressure   c. retraction
   b. partial-authority d. retarded

9. Pumps are evaluated on test benches also known as _____ benches.
   a. comparator   c. overflow
   b. retraction   d. rack

10. To minimize the effect of pressure wave reflections, the delivery valve has a(n) _____ function built into its shape.
    a. delivery   c. comparator
    b. retraction   d. overflow

ASE-Type Questions

1. Technician A says that because of the arrangement of high-pressure components, multiple plunger injection systems are referred to as pump-line nozzle fuel systems. Technician B says some multiple plunger injection systems can match the capabilities of full-authority electronically controlled fuel systems. Who is correct?
   a. Technician A
   b. Technician B
   c. Both Technician A and Technician B
   d. Neither Technician A nor Technician B

2. Technician A says fill and spill ports allow fuel to enter the barrel. Technician B says the fuel enters the barrel in the space above the plunger. Who is correct?
   a. Technician A
   b. Technician B
   c. Both Technician A and Technician B
   d. Neither Technician A nor Technician B

3. Technician A says injection pump plunger speed and duration of injection are primarily dependent on the shape of the helix. Technician B says the shape of the helix can be used to change injection timing. Who is correct?
   a. Technician A
   b. Technician B
   c. Both Technician A and Technician B
   d. Neither Technician A nor Technician B

4. Technician A says injection lines are fabricated to be the same length and diameter. Technician B says that is done to ensure the fuel pressure wave arrives at each cylinder at exactly the same time. Who is correct?
   a. Technician A
   b. Technician B
   c. Both Technician A and Technician B
   d. Neither Technician A nor Technician B

5. Technician A says that when setting initial static pump to engine timing, the use of pointers can assist in the adjustment of the lift to port closure point to the appropriate engine position. Technician B says that the use of timing indicators and timing pins also assist in the adjustment of the lift to port closure point to the appropriate engine position. Who is correct?
   a. Technician A
   b. Technician B
   c. Both Technician A and Technician B
   d. Neither Technician A nor Technician B

6. Technician A says the highest injection pressure available from a Bosch P7100 inline pump is approximately 16,500 psi. Technician B says the highest injection pressure available from a Bosch P7100 inline pump is approximately 25,500 psi. Who is correct?
   a. Technician A
   b. Technician B
   c. Both Technician A and Technician B
   d. Neither Technician A nor Technician B

7. Technician A says Caterpillar uses an exclusive, patented system called scroll metering. Technician B says Caterprillar's patented system is called port-helix metering. Who is correct?
   a. Technician A
   b. Technician B
   c. Both Technician A and Technician B
   d. Neither Technician A nor Technician B

8. Technician A says inline multiple plunger injection pumps haven't been used on-highway light- or medium-duty diesel applications in North America since the late 1900s. Technician B says they haven't been used because they are not capable of meeting strict emissions requirements. Who is correct?
   a. Technician A
   b. Technician B
   c. Both Technician A and Technician B
   d. Neither Technician A nor Technician B

9. Technician A says Bosch type H pumps have the highest pressure and volume output and are commonly used for medium- and heavy-duty on-and off-highway applications. Technician B says Bosch type A pumps have the highest pressure and volume output and are commonly used for medium- and heavy-duty on- and off-highway applications. Who is correct?
   a. Technician A
   b. Technician B
   c. Both Technician A and Technician B
   d. Neither Technician A nor Technician B

10. Technician A says the governor is connected to the control vane. Technician B says the governor is connected to the control rack. Who is correct?
    a. Technician A
    b. Technician B
    c. Both Technician A and Technician B
    d. Neither Technician A nor Technician B

NATEF Tasks

Diesel Engines

General

- Check engine no cranking, cranks but fails to start, hard starting, and starts but does not continue to run problems; determine needed action. (pp 586–590)
- Identify engine surging, rough operation, misfiring, low power, slow deceleration, slow acceleration, and shutdown problems; determine needed action. (pp 583–595)

Fuel System

Fuel Supply System

- Inspect and test pressure regulator systems (check valves, pressure regulator valves, and restrictive fittings); determine needed action. (pp 586–592)

Knowledge Objectives

After reading this chapter, you will be able to:

1. Identify and describe the construction and application of mechanical distributor injection pumps and unit injection systems. (pp 579–581, 592–594)
2. Explain the operating principles of mechanical distributor injection pumps and unit injection systems. (pp 581–590, 594–596)
3. Identify and describe diagnostic procedures for mechanical distributor injection pumps and unit injection systems. (pp 590–592, 597–599)

Skills Objectives

After reading this chapter, you will be able to:

1. Measure dynamic injection pump timing. (p 592) **SKILL DRILL 20-1**
2. Measure pump housing pressure. (p 593) **SKILL DRILL 20-2**
3. Adjust static pump-to-engine timing. (p 598) **SKILL DRILL 20-3**

► Introduction

Mechanical distributor high-pressure injection pumps have provided the diesel engine with wider applications in automotive, agriculture, and heavy-duty equipment applications by significantly reducing the cost, size, and weight of diesel engines. The distributor pump achieves this by replacing the multiple plungers of inline pumps with a single pumping element supplying pressurized fuel for all the engine's cylinders. Until the development of the distributor injection pump, diesel engine production was limited to less than 5% of all engines produced in North America. Most notably, farm equipment operated exclusively using gasoline fuel until the 1950s, when compact injection systems put diesels on the farm. The popularity of the first successful light- and medium-duty diesels, such as the GM 6.2/6.5L (378/397 cubic inch), and the Ford 6.9/7.3L (421/445 cubic inch) used in pick-up trucks and vans, is also due to distributor pump technology. Distributor injection systems have fallen into disuse, supplanted by electronic unit injection and common rail systems. However, the number of these systems that are still in use in both on- and off-road applications justify an examination of the construction and operation of these important injection systems.

► Mechanical Distributor Injection Pumps

In the 1920s, compact multiple plunger injection pumps enabled diesel engine production to move from use exclusively in stationary engines and large-displacement diesel engines found in ships. The development of distributor injection pumps advanced diesel engine production even further into more widespread use. This next section will examine key developments of distributor injection pumps and two major pump designs used even today by off-road diesels.

Development of Distributor Pumps

Until the early 1950s, fewer than 5% of all engines produced in North America were diesels. Despite the demonstrated advantages of the diesel engine, the cost of the fuel system was the primary obstacle explaining the diesel engine's limited applications. After the first distributor pumps were introduced in 1952, farm equipment manufacturers who were already building their own gasoline engines saw they could provide the diesel advantage to their customers with little cost premium by converting many of their engines into diesels using the distributor pump. The compact size of the distributor pump, its low drive torque requirement, and the ability to mount the pump where an ignition distributor was normally located meant manufacturers could use the same engine block with few added manufacturing costs to produce diesel engines.

The first distributor pump, invented by Vernon Roosa, was manufactured around the world by its licensees to be used in a wide variety of applications, from automobiles, off-road equipment, and marine engines to trucks, buses, and stationary power generators. It was estimated that over 30 million of these high-pressure injection systems were produced by 1988 and were especially popular with farm equipment manufacturers like Allis-Chalmers, Ford, International Harvester, and John Deere. In 1976, General Motors first contracted Stanadyne Corporation's Roosa-designed pumps for its light trucks and passenger cars. GM's orders grew from an initial quantity of 75,000 pumps to about 300,000 annually during the oil crisis of the 1970s, when diesel production for automobiles increased dramatically.

Bosch also developed a distributor pump in the 1960s, using different operating and metering principles than the Roosa pump. The Bosch VE pump, whose model designation is an abbreviation of the German word *Verteiler*, which means distributor, has also been widely used around the world by many automobile

► You Are the Technician

At your equipment rental shop, a number of diesel-powered rental units use mechanical distributor injection pumps. While the equipment has been reliable after years of extensive use, there are an increasing number of complaints about hard starting, low power, and heavy black exhaust smoke. To investigate the complaints, you check pump-to-engine timing and find that the pump's static timing is not correct. However, the difference between the manufacturer's specifications and the observed timing can easily be explained by gear train wear, and the pump timing could be readjusted to fix the issue. When the dynamic timing is checked with a timing light while the engine is running, you find that the dynamic timing does not advance as it should when the engine is running. You conclude that the injection pumps are worn out internally and decide to replace them with rebuilt units. Before replacing the injection pumps, consider the following:

1. Suggest another test or further diagnostic work that might identify an issue that could be easily corrected without replacement of the pumps.
2. How does internal transfer pump pressure affect the injection timing of the pumps?
3. Why would gear train wear cause the static timing of the pumps to change?

and off-road equipment manufacturers **FIGURE 20-1**. Both distributor pump designs, the VE and the Stanadyne-Roosa, later owned by Delphi, evolved using electronic governor and metering controls to replace mechanical metering and timing mechanisms, which extended the usefulness of these basic pump designs past the year 2000 in light–duty, on-road vehicles. These designs are currently used today by many small-displacement, Tier 3, off-road engines **FIGURE 20-2**.

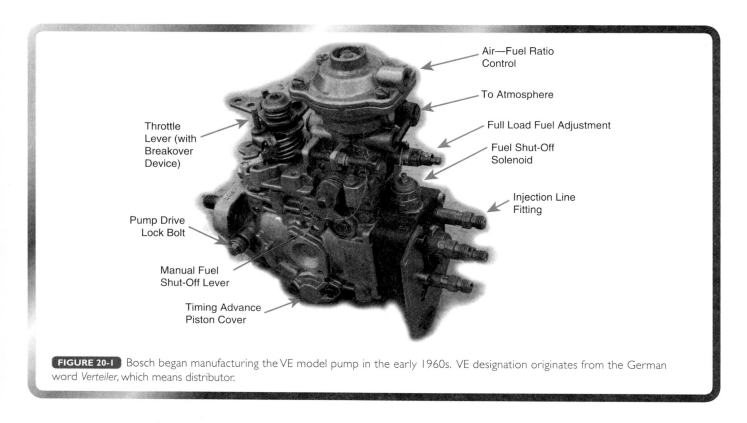

Air—Fuel Ratio Control

To Atmosphere

Full Load Fuel Adjustment

Fuel Shut-Off Solenoid

Injection Line Fitting

Throttle Lever (with Breakover Device)

Pump Drive Lock Bolt

Manual Fuel Shut-Off Lever

Timing Advance Piston Cover

FIGURE 20-1 Bosch began manufacturing the VE model pump in the early 1960s. VE designation originates from the German word *Verteiler*, which means distributor.

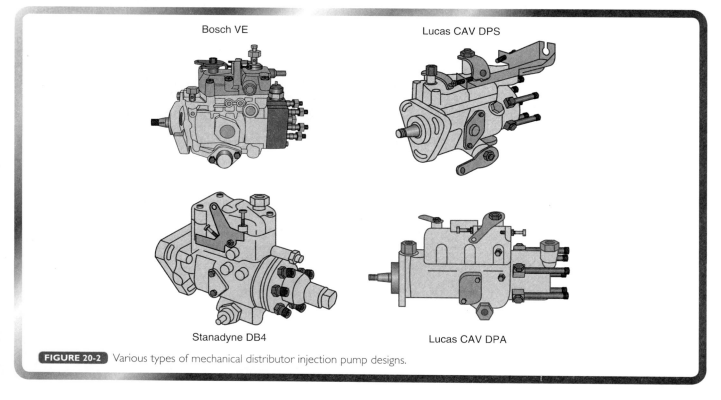

Bosch VE

Lucas CAV DPS

Stanadyne DB4

Lucas CAV DPA

FIGURE 20-2 Various types of mechanical distributor injection pump designs.

Distributor Pump Advantages

The design simplicity of distributor injection pumps accounts for the success of the distributor pumps **FIGURE 20-3**. As few as half the numbers of parts are required to manufacturer a distributor pump in comparison to inline versions producing the same engine horsepower. Unlike inline pumps or unit injectors, which use a separate fuel pressurization element for each cylinder, distributor pumps make use of a single pumping element to deliver fuel to all cylinders. This configuration greatly reduces the number of parts making for an economical, compact injection system design. Other fuel system components such as the governor, fuel transfer pump and injection-timing mechanisms are built into the pump body, which allows for increased production efficiency. Even when problems requiring pump repair are encountered, the associated repair costs are substantially less than those associated with rebuilding and recalibrating inline pumps. Unlike unit injector fuel systems, distributor pumps do not require periodic maintenance and adjustments.

Distributor Pump Disadvantages

Using a single pumping element not only limits power output and pressure but has the potential for wearing out sooner in comparison to multiple plunger injection systems. This is particularly troublesome when fuel quality is poor or if fuel is even slightly contaminated with water.

Injection pressures range from 5110 psi (352 bar) on older mechanical Bosch VE models to 6716 psi (463 bar) on a DB2 pump used on GM 6.2/6.5 (378/397 cubic inch) and Ford 6.9/7.3 (421/445 cubic inch) models at maximum engine speed. Compared to the higher pressure of inline pumps, common rail, and unit injectors, the lower injection pressures of distributor pumps makes them less favorable for emission control, because atomization and distribution of fuel in the cylinder is limited. Mechanical control of injection timing further limits the fuel system from adapting to a variety of operating conditions that affect emissions.

Using only a single fuel-pressurizing pumping element limits the distributor pump's fuel volume output. Distributor pumps typically have a maximum power output per cylinder of around 25–35 horsepower (hp) (19–26 kilowatts [kW]) per cylinder.

Distributor Pump Classification

Distributor injection pumps can be classified by the type of fuel-metering system they use. There are two designs commonly used:

1. Opposed plunger. Sometimes called radial piston, this design uses inlet metering principles. This pump is used by Stanadyne Corporation, later owned by Delphi, and its licensees are based on the Roosa Master pump design.

2. Axial piston. This design uses a sleeve metering system. In mechanical pumps, this is the configuration used by the Bosch VE pump and its licensees.

▶ Opposed Plunger Pressurization Principles

Two distinctly different metering and pressurization systems are used by axial and opposed plunger pump designs. Opposed plunger pumps are the earliest distributor pump design. They pressurize fuel between two, three, or four small, opposed pistons. In contrast, axial piston pumps use a single, larger plunger to pressurize fuel to injection pressure. In opposed plunger pumps, fuel for all the cylinders is pressurized by the

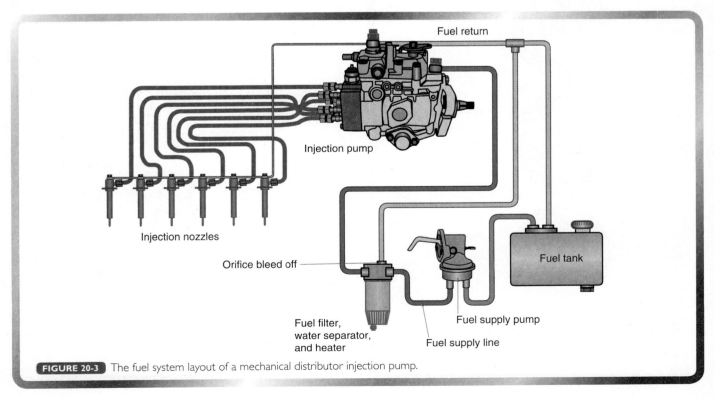

FIGURE 20-3 The fuel system layout of a mechanical distributor injection pump.

opposed pistons. Although fuel is not pressurized as high in these pumps because of the smaller pistons, the pumps' relatively simple, compact design made them arguably the most popular distributor pump. In this next section, pressurization metering principles used by these pumps are briefly examined.

Radial Piston Design

The **opposed plunger pressurization**, or radial piston pressurization, design uses pumping plungers arranged at 90-degree angles to the pump driveshaft, which operates inside a cam ring (hence the term *radial* plunger). The plungers alternately draw and then compress fuel into a single pressure chamber. Different opposed plunger designs use two, three, or four plungers depending on the number of cylinders and the pressure output required of the pump **FIGURE 20-4**.

The **cam ring** in a distributor pump is the equivalent of the camshaft in a multiple plunger pump. It is used to provide the actuation force needed to pressurize fuel. It can be described as a donut with a lumpy hole in the middle. Fuel is pressurized by the cam ring as it moves the pairs of opposed pistons over lobes inside the cam ring. The pump's rotor, which rotates inside the cam ring, carries the pistons **FIGURE 20-5**. Rotating the engine-driven rotor that contains the plungers inside the stationary cam ring causes the pumping plungers to reciprocate as they follow the profile of the cam ring. When the plungers follow the cam profile, fuel supplied to the cavity between the plungers is pressurized and pushed into the center of the pumping plungers. A hole in the rotor supplies the cavity when the plungers retract, which is in turn pressurized

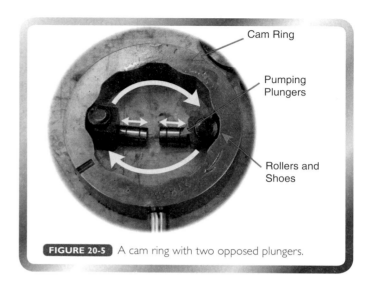

FIGURE 20-5 A cam ring with two opposed plungers.

as plungers move onto a cam lobe and are pushed toward the centerline of the rotor by the cam ring. The plungers are forced apart by the fuel pressure supplying the plungers when the plungers are between cam lobes. Fuel delivery takes place when the plungers are forced together by the cam lobes. Fuel pressurized between the plungers is forced out of the rotor through an outlet port. Continued rotor movement moves the plungers outward from the cam ring centerline and off the lobe, allowing a fresh, metered charge of fuel to enter the cavity between the plungers (also called the pressure chamber). Then, a new pressurizing cycle begins. Injection occurs when a passage in the outlet port corresponds with an opening in the distributor head of the injection pump **FIGURE 20-6**.

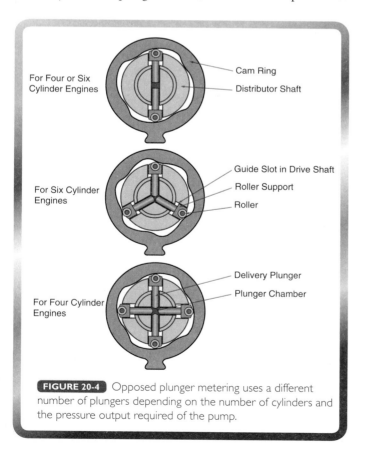

FIGURE 20-4 Opposed plunger metering uses a different number of plungers depending on the number of cylinders and the pressure output required of the pump.

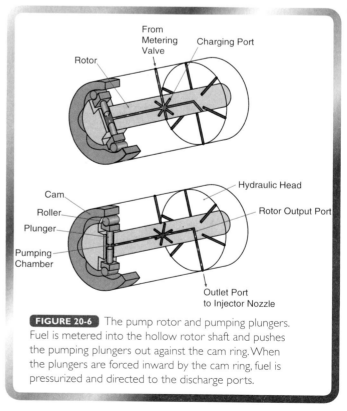

FIGURE 20-6 The pump rotor and pumping plungers. Fuel is metered into the hollow rotor shaft and pushes the pumping plungers out against the cam ring. When the plungers are forced inward by the cam ring, fuel is pressurized and directed to the discharge ports.

Popular models of opposed plunger or radial piston design include:

- Mechanical DB pumps by Stanadyne
- The D series Roosa Master models pumps used in many off-road applications. This pump was originally manufactured by the Hartford machine Screw Company, and later Stanadyne licensed the design to be built by Lucas/CAV, which was later acquired by Delphi
- Electronic versions of these pumps such as the Stanadyne–Delphi DS
- Bosch VP-44 used by Cummins for the 5.9L (360 cubic inch)

▶ Sleeve Metering Principles

Sleeve metering pumps use a large single pumping plunger that enables higher injection pressures to be achieved from these pumps. Unlike opposed plunger pumps, the quantity of fuel metered for injection is controlled by depressurizing, or spilling, fuel pressure from the pressure chamber of the pump plunger. Because the device that controls depressurization of the fuel is a sleeve that slides back and forth along the pump plunger, it is commonly referred to as sleeve metering.

Axial Piston Design

As its name suggests, the **axial piston pressurization** design uses a single reciprocating plunger located along the pump axis to pressurize fuel for injection. Instead of a cam ring, a **cam plate**, a multi-lobed rotating plate that looks like a disc with lumps, is used to actuate the plunger. Fuel is alternately drawn into a cavity created during one stroke of the plunger, and then pressurized on the next stroke. A sliding collar on the pump shaft opens and closes a spill port, which effectively ends injection. This process is called **sleeve metering** FIGURE 20-7 .

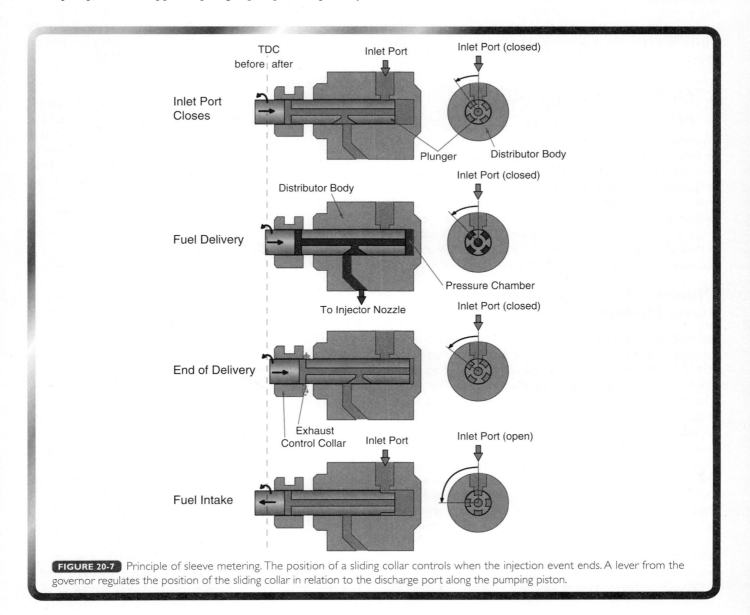

FIGURE 20-7 Principle of sleeve metering. The position of a sliding collar controls when the injection event ends. A lever from the governor regulates the position of the sliding collar in relation to the discharge port along the pumping piston.

Popular models of this pump design include the mechanical Bosch VE pump and those made by licensees such as Diesel Kiki, Zexel, and Denso.

Pump Commonality

While radial and axial piston distributor pump designs appear distinctly different, they have several features in common.

Among those commonalities is a rotating shaft with a fuel passageway drilled through its axis. This rotating shaft operates similarly to the rotor of a distributor used in a spark ignition system. The shaft delivers pressurized fuel to each cylinder in engine-firing sequence. Pressurized fuel will travel through the passageway in the shaft until it reaches an opening, drilled at 90 degrees to the passageway, and flows through a discharge port in the head of the pump. This pump head roughly corresponds to the distributor cap in an older electric spark ignition system. There is a discharge passageway in the pump head to correspond to each cylinder of the engine. This means a six-cylinder engine will have six passageways in the pump head fed by the single passageway in the rotor. Fuel injector lines connected to nozzles will carry the pressurized column of fuel from the discharge port fittings to the cylinders.

▶ Opposed Plunger–Inlet Metering System

Regulating the amount of fuel delivered to the pumping plungers to match engine speed and load conditions is the job of the governor. How that fuel is actually measured out and supplied to the plungers is performed by the metering systems. These next sections examine the construction of metering system components and how their operation regulates engine speed and torque output. Pumps used by Ford and GM are examined due to their immense popularity. These models have construction and operating features similar to those used by other models.

Opposed Plunger Metering Pump Models

The first opposed plunger distributor injection pump design that was developed by Roosa Master in the 1950s later became part of the line up of injection systems offered by Stanadyne Automotive. The pump's configuration evolved into several other models, including the DB model. Later, the Roosa Master pump was licensed to Lucas/CAV, which developed the popular industrial, off-road equipment DPA pump. Delphi acquired Lucas/CAV and continues to produce a number of variations of these radial piston, opposed plunger metering system pumps. The most popular application is the DB2 pump, which was used by GM in V8 automobile engines and by Ford in truck engines. The DB2 is still produced by Stanadyne for off-road products.

While the appearance and functions of these pumps are similar, some differences exist between the pumps used by GM and Ford. First, the direction of pump rotation is different in the two engines. The throttle shaft is also located on opposite sides of the pumps. The number of pumping plungers varies: a DB2 uses two opposed plungers while a DB4 uses four. Some electronic versions of this pump use three opposed plungers.

The following are typical specification for this pump:

- Model DB2 Mechanical Pump
- Capacities to 25 BHP (19 kW) cylinder
- Peak injection pressures to 6700 psi (462 bar)
- Two, three, four, five, six, and eight cylinder configurations
- Built-in automatic advance
- Electric shut-off
- Capable of producing injections for engine speeds to 5000 rpm (3400 rpm limit typical)
- Electric housing pressure cold-start advance (HPCA) mechanism to advance injection timing when engine is cold

Opposed Plunger Metering Pump Components

The main components of the DB2 and DB4 fuel injection pumps are the driveshaft, distributor rotor, cam ring, internal transfer pump, pumping plungers, hydraulic head, governor, and an injection timing advance mechanism **FIGURE 20-8**.

Driveshaft

The pump's driveshaft rotates inside a tube pressed into the pump housing. One end of the shaft engages the fuel distributor rotor and turns the rotor shaft. The other end is connected to the engine drive gear, which turns the pump at one-half engine speed. The driveshaft has two lip-like seals; one seal prevents engine oil from entering the pump, while the other prevents fuel from leaking out of the pump into the engine. Fuel is used to internally lubricate and cool all moving parts of the pump.

▶ **TECHNICIAN TIP**

Fuel could potentially enter the lubrication system through leaking pump seals. To prevent this condition, a weep hole is incorporated into the injection pump that allows fuel to leak externally if the oil seal on the pump driveshaft is defective. The external leak prevents fuel from diluting engine oil.

Distributor Rotor

The distributor rotor is the key component of the distributor pump. The two or four opposed pumping plungers housed within in the rotor are used to pressurize fuel for injection. A shoe and roller assembly are located between each pumping plunger and the cam ring. The roller contacts the cam ring in which the rotor turns, thus transferring the cam profile to produce a reciprocating action of pumping plungers that move in and out of the rotor. Through the center of the rotor shaft is a passageway connecting the pressure chamber formed at the end of the pumping plungers to two other hydraulic ports. One is the fuel charging port and the other is a fuel discharge port.

The hydraulic head in which the rotor turns has a number of charging and discharging ports. The ports will alternately align

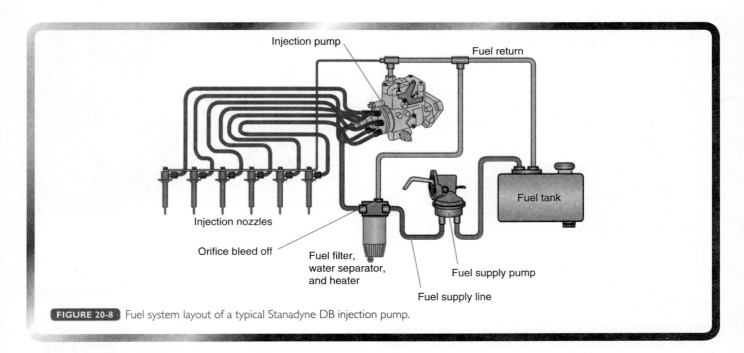

FIGURE 20-8 Fuel system layout of a typical Stanadyne DB injection pump.

with passageways in the head of the pump to allow a fresh charge of fuel into the rotor shaft or discharge pressurized fuel to the injectors. At the end of the rotor inside the distributor pump hydraulic head are slots used to locate spring-loaded transfer pump blades. Close-fitting clearances between the rotor shaft and the hydraulic head ensure a tight hydraulic seal between the moving parts. However, some leakage between the rotor and the distributor pump head is necessary to cool and lubricate the rotor.

> ### ▶ TECHNICIAN TIP
>
> Worn distributor rotor parts can lead to fuel leakage past the pumping plungers and poor pressurization of fuel. The results are low power complaints, poor acceleration, hard starting, and excessive emissions.

Cam Ring

The cam ring has lobes corresponding to the number of engine cylinders and surrounds the shoe and rollers of the rotor. This means that an eight-cylinder engine will have eight lobes. As the rotor turns, the rollers located in the shoes will contact the lobes of the cam ring and force the opposed pumping plungers inward. This will pressurize fuel between the plungers, forcing it through the rotor's central passageway, out the discharge port, and eventually to the injectors.

The cam ring can move several degrees inside the pump housing. Because the cam ring is only connected to the pump with a movable plunger at a single point near the pump's bottom, the beginning of injection (BOI) timing can be varied by moving the cam ring inside the pump housing.

Internal Transfer Pump

Filtered fuel is drawn into the pump by a **vane pump**, an internal transfer pump located at the end of the hydraulic head

FIGURE 20-9. This positive displacement pump consists of a stationary liner with spring-loaded blades that ride in slots at the end of the rotor shaft. The output capacity of the transfer pump is greater than the engine's fuel volume requirements. Transfer pump pressure also varies proportional to engine speed. A significant quantity of fuel is returned back to the fuel tank through a restriction fitting located on top of the injection pump. The continuous oversupply of fuel circulation through the pump helps cool the pump and remove any vapor from the fuel. The remaining excess pump output is bypassed through a

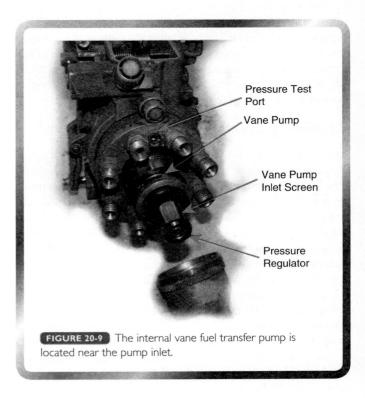

FIGURE 20-9 The internal vane fuel transfer pump is located near the pump inlet.

pressure-regulating valve back to the inlet side of the pump. The quantity and pressure of the fuel bypassed increases proportional to the pump's speed. The pressure regulator valve controls fuel pressure to a maximum of approximately 130 psi (9 bar).

This relationship between transfer pressure and engine speed is important to the operation of the hydraulically operated injection timing mechanism. Increasing transfer pump pressure is used to rotate the cam ring, producing changes to injection timing. During diagnostic testing of the fuel system, it is important to measure the output pressure of the internal vane pump though a fitting located in the hydraulic head of the pump. While at wide-open throttle, if the vane pump pressure falls outside of specifications, the pump must be replaced or reconditioned **FIGURE 20-10**. A worn vane pump results in low power and incorrect injection timing because the hydraulic timing mechanism uses internal pump pressure to vary the position of the cam ring.

Fuel Flow

Fuel is pulled from the fuel tank by either a mechanical or electrical lift pump. Fuel is pushed at a low pressure of between 3 and 6 psi (21 and 41 kPa) into the internal transfer pump, where it passes through a filter screen. Fuel pressurized by the transfer pump is then directed to the pressure regulator. Excess fuel is bypassed to the inlet side of the transfer pump.

Inlet Metering

In **inlet metering**, fuel flows from the internal transfer pump and around the rotor through a passage called the annulus. This passage connects to a helical-style metering valve. The quantity of fuel reaching the pumping plungers is regulated by varying the position of the helix in the metering valve to another passageway called the charging annulus, which surrounds the charging ports of the distributor rotor. Regulation of the engine speed and torque is accomplished by varying the quantity of fuel metered into the charging annulus during the charging cycle. This is why this pump's metering mechanism is often referred to as an inlet metering system.

Charging Cycle

As the rotor revolves, the two angled inlet passages connecting the pumping chamber between the pumping plungers align with the charging port annulus. Fuel under pressure from the transfer pump and measured by the metering valve flows into the pumping chamber, forcing the plungers outward. The pumping plungers' outward movement is a distance proportional to the amount of fuel required for injection. This means if a small quantity of fuel enters the pumping chamber, the plungers move out only a small distance **FIGURE 20-11**.

A limit to maximum fuel delivery is controlled by a leaf spring whose ends curve around the rotor to limit outward travel of the roller shoes. The tension on this spring is adjustable in order to alter maximum shoe travel and ultimately the maximum quantity of fuel metered for injection **FIGURE 20-12**. The fuel limiter leaf spring is accessed through the side of the injection pump. Tightening the screw retaining the curved spring

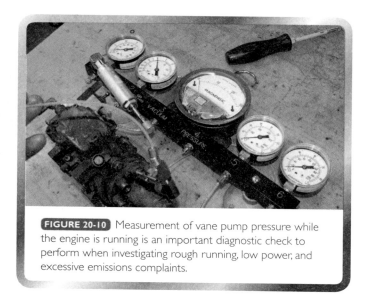

FIGURE 20-10 Measurement of vane pump pressure while the engine is running is an important diagnostic check to perform when investigating rough running, low power, and excessive emissions complaints.

increases the maximum quantity of fuel injected while loosening the retaining screw decreases fuel delivery **FIGURE 20-13**.

During the charging phase of injection, the rotor discharge port is not in alignment with outlets ports in the hydraulic head. Also, the rollers are off the lobes of the cam ring, which allows the pumping plungers to travel outward as far as metered fuel quantity and leaf spring position will permit **FIGURE 20-14**.

> ### ▶ TECHNICIAN TIP
>
> A fuel limiter adjustment screw accessed through the side of an injection pump can increase or decrease the maximum injection quantity for any given rpm. If the screw is turned too far clockwise (i.e., tightened too much), excess emissions will accompany an increase in power.

Discharge Cycle

As the pump rotor continues to turn, the inlet passages to the pumping chambers rotate away from the charging port or annulus. Next, both rollers begin contacting the lobes of the cam ring, forcing them toward each other. This action pressurizes the column of fuel, which can then be connected to the fuel nozzles. To do this, the rotor first turns and aligns a single angled passageway in the rotor to the discharge ports located in the hydraulic head that corresponding to each cylinder of the engine **FIGURE 20-15**.

A **delivery valve** located in the end of the rotor's axial passageway operates like a one-way check valve during the discharge of fuel. The valve is closed during the charging cycle and opens when high fuel pressure is produced as the plungers are forced together. The function of this delivery valve is similar to those in inline pumps. It provides for a sharp drop in injection line pressure at the end of injection to prevent secondary injection and nozzle dribble. It also permits a residual injection line pressure of approximately 500 psi (34 bar) to minimize injection lag for the next cylinder in the firing order while ensuring one-way movement of fuel out of the pump.

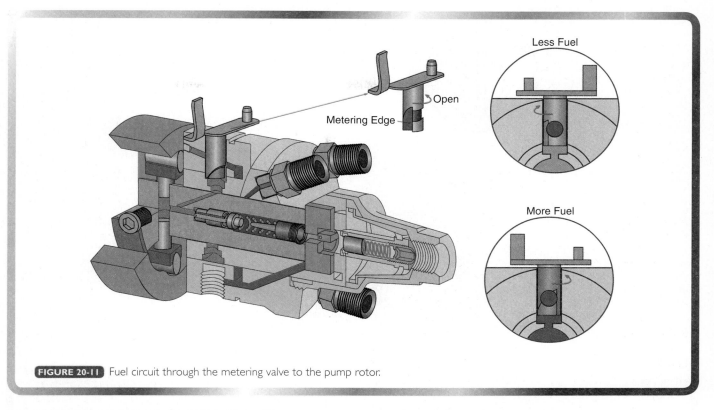

FIGURE 20-11 Fuel circuit through the metering valve to the pump rotor.

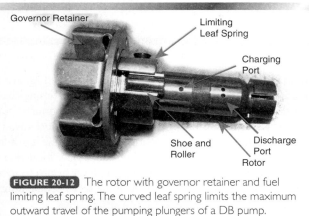

FIGURE 20-12 The rotor with governor retainer and fuel limiting leaf spring. The curved leaf spring limits the maximum outward travel of the pumping plungers of a DB pump.

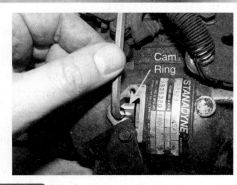

FIGURE 20-13 The fuel limiter leaf spring is accessed through the side of the injection pump.

▶ TECHNICIAN TIP

Fuel cleanliness is of the utmost importance to distributor pumps' operation. A single particle of dirt lodged in the delivery valve will stop all injections and prevent the engine from starting. When replacing fuel filters for distributor pumps, it is particularly important that only the cleanest fuel should enter the injection pump, and special care must be taken to prevent any dirt from entering the filter.

Air Purge

Air or fuel vapor entrained in fuel entering the pump can interfere with fuel pressurization. To prevent this, a small vent connects the hydraulic head through a short vertical passage to the governor linkage area. This arrangement permits any air and a small quantity of fuel into the governor area. A fuel return line connected to the pump returns some fuel to the supply tank, permitting vapor removal from the pump. A wire located in the vent controls the quantity of fuel returned to the tank. The diameter of the wire is chosen during calibration of the pump on a flow bench.

Speed and Light Load Advance Mechanisms

An automatic timing advance mechanism is incorporated in the design of the distributor injection pump. This is needed to achieve the appropriate injection timing for engine speed and load conditions. When the engine is lightly loaded and operating at high speed, the injection timing should advance.

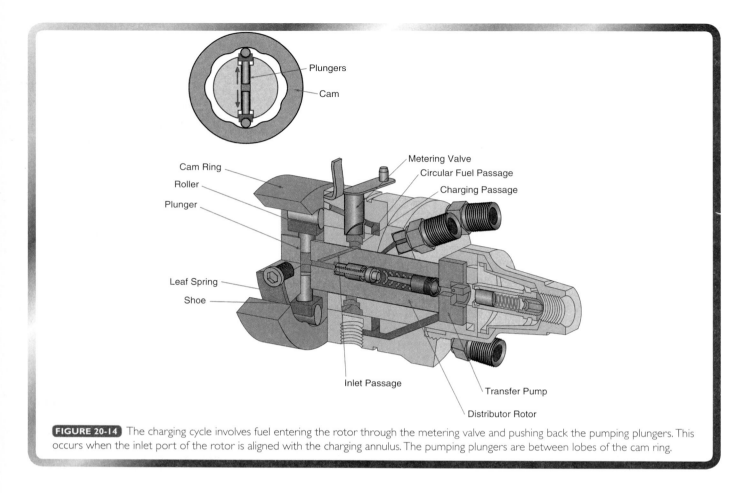

FIGURE 20-14 The charging cycle involves fuel entering the rotor through the metering valve and pushing back the pumping plungers. This occurs when the inlet port of the rotor is aligned with the charging annulus. The pumping plungers are between lobes of the cam ring.

Conversely, heavily loaded engines operating at low speed should use retarded injection timing for optimal combustion and performance. By rotating the cam ring, the contact point of the shoes and rollers with the cam ring can change and pressurization of fuel can begin sooner or later. Rotation of the cam ring is accomplished by balancing internal pump housing pressure applied to one side of a movable servo piston that has transfer pump pressure applied on the opposite side of the piston.

A change in engine speed or load will cause the timing mechanism to retard or advance injection timing. To alter timing under load, a light load lever located beneath the throttle will retard timing by pushing on a valve that causes fuel pressure to move the sliding servo piston to a retarded position **FIGURE 20-16**. The light load lever is actuated by a cam below the throttle lever. Increasing load on the engine will result in the throttle pedal being depressed proportionally farther, resulting in retarded timing.

To change the timing as a function of engine speed, the sliding hydraulic servo piston attached at a single point below the cam ring will rotate the cam ring. The position of the cam ring is determined by the balance between fuel pressure inside the injection acting on one side of the piston and fuel pressure from in transfer pump. Transfer pump pressure moves the piston into an advanced injection timing position while charging annulus pressure moves the piston to a retarded position. At low speed and light load, transfer pump pressure is low. This also means pressure applied to one side of the sliding piston is low. Similarly, pump housing pressure is also

low (approximately 10 psi [69 kPa]) which is applied against the opposite side of the sliding servo piston; thus, little timing change occurs. When engine speed increases without a load, transfer pump pressure will increase, moving the servo piston to a more advanced position while overcoming housing pressure. If the throttle is depressed farther because of increasing load, a valve located in the servo piston and actuated by the light load lever begins to reduce the fuel allowed to the advanced side of the servo piston, limiting pressure and causing timing to retard **FIGURE 20-17**.

Housing Pressure Cold-Start Advance Mechanism

It is important to understand that internal housing pressure within the pump will cause changes to injection timing by moving the sliding servo piston and changing the cam ring position. During cold engine operation, it is desirable to advance injection timing to eliminate white smoke and misfires due to ignition delay (cold cylinders take longer to ignite and burn fuel). Retarded timing is necessary during cranking as it permits the piston to rise farther during compression stroke before injection. Retarded timing during cranking ensures adequate heat is present in the cylinder to ignite fuel for easier starting during cranking.

The use of a __housing pressure cold-start advance (HPCA) mechanism__ compensates for the need for advanced

FIGURE 20-15 The rollers contact the lobes of the cam ring, pressurizing fuel for delivery. Fuel flow to all cylinders is through a single delivery valve in the rotor.

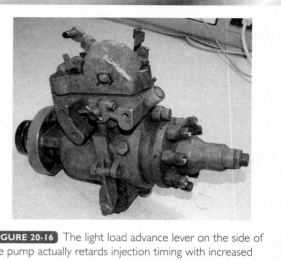

FIGURE 20-16 The light load advance lever on the side of the pump actually retards injection timing with increased accelerator pedal travel.

injection timing after starting. The HPCA mechanism uses a solenoid-operated piston, located under the top cover of the injection pump, to open the restriction fitting for the fuel return passageway. The HPCA solenoid opens a check valve in the fitting, which returns fuel in the pump housing to the tank, which lowers housing pressure and changes injection timing.

Opening the return fitting check valve HPCA solenoid plunger causes a drop in housing pressures, which reduces the pressure differential across the servo piston. Transfer pump pressure will rotate the cam ring to a more advanced position without causing housing pressure to oppose servo piston movement.

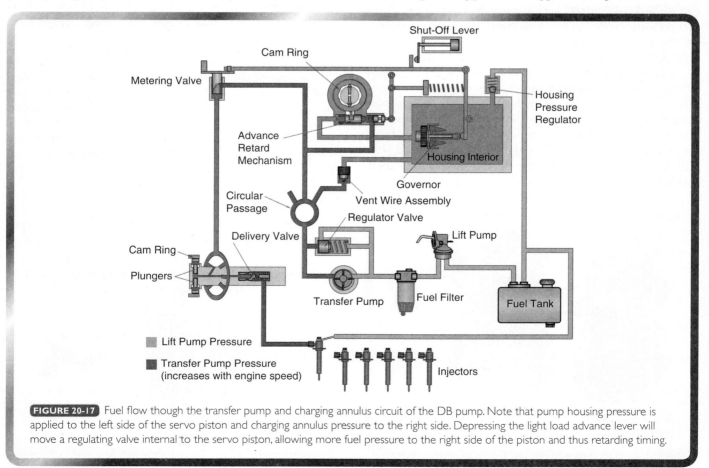

FIGURE 20-17 Fuel flow though the transfer pump and charging annulus circuit of the DB pump. Note that pump housing pressure is applied to the left side of the servo piston and charging annulus pressure to the right side. Depressing the light load advance lever will move a regulating valve internal to the servo piston, allowing more fuel pressure to the right side of the piston and thus retarding timing.

This pressure change can advance timing typically from 2 to 6 degrees after the engine starts. When power is applied to the HPCA solenoid, a minimum of 2 degrees of advance must take place. Good pumps typically advance by 4 degrees.

Current to the HPCA and fast idle solenoid mechanism is applied using an electrical thermostatic switch located in the cooling system. Until coolant temperature reaches approximately 100°F (38°C), power will be supplied to the HPCA and fast idle solenoid, which increases engine rpm and produces a sharper, louder combustion noise.

The shut-off solenoid, when activated by battery voltage, permits the governor linkage to move from a no-fuel position. Without current, a spring forces the governor linkage to shut off fuel flow through the metering valve **FIGURE 20-18**.

> ### ▶ TECHNICIAN TIP
>
> A restricted return line fitting or restriction in the fuel return line from the pump will not allow housing pressure to drop. The result is that the injection timing will retard too far, causing low power, rough running, black smoke, and even stalling. When checking the pump for problems, remove and inspect the restrictor fitting to determine whether it is clogged. Clean and reinstall the fitting if it is blocked, then retest the pump or recheck the symptoms.

Light Load Advance Check

Quick checks of the HPCA mechanism involve first measuring fuel pressure inside the injection pump at wide open throttle (WOT) and comparing against original equipment manufacturer (OEM) specifications.

A light load lever operated by a cam on the throttle linkage operates to retard injection timing as load increases. While moving this lever with a screwdriver, there should be a perceptible increase in smoke and a softer combustion noise as the timing is retarded. The engine may also begin to stumble and misfire. The lever should also be checked to determine if it has seized. Current applied to the HPCA solenoid must also produce a timing advance. This check should be performed only after the engine has warmed up.

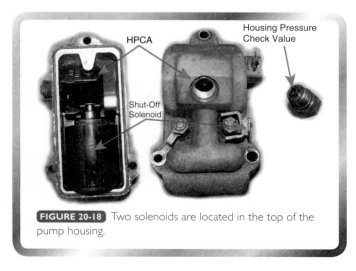

FIGURE 20-18 Two solenoids are located in the top of the pump housing.

Governor

Engines using mechanical distributor injection pumps most often have a min/max or automotive governor. This means that the governor controls high idle and idle speed. The operator controls fueling between the speed ranges of high idle and idle speed. When cold starting, the throttle must be depressed all the way to the floor and released to part throttle to set the governor to a full-fuel position for starting. Three springs are located in the governor housing to control governor spring tension at idle, part throttle, and heavy-load conditions. The metering valve regulates the fuel quantity admitted into the rotor to supply the pumping plungers with fuel. Movement of the metering valve is controlled by the governor. The position of the metering valve is a function of force applied by the governor spring, which is compressed by the throttle lever and the governor lever. A maximum fuel stop adjustment is located on the outside of the governor housing that controls tension of the heavy–load, high-speed governor spring **FIGURE 20-19**. All-speed or variable speed governors are available for off-highway applications.

▶ Diagnostics Testing

Problems associated with low power, hard starting, and stalling indicate the low-pressure fuel supply system should be tested. The tests that should be performed include:

- Fuel supply pressure test performed at idle and high idle
- Fuel pump volume test
- Fuel return restriction pressure test
- Leaking lift-pump valve test
- Injection pump and transfer pump tests

Accelerator Linkage Check

Any low-power complaint should be investigated by first checking whether the throttle moves to maximum, wide-open position. The accelerator linkage may or may not be equipped with a throttle breakover or override mechanism. This feature prevents excess pressure from being applied to the throttle shaft through the throttle lever, which would prematurely wear out the bushings and seals on the throttle shaft.

Pump Leaks

Pump seal leaks can occur when the pump is cold. This condition can cause fuel to drain out of the pump, causing hard

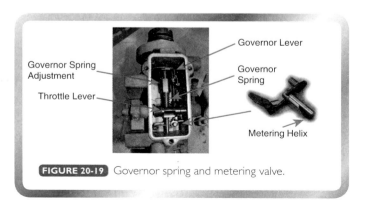

FIGURE 20-19 Governor spring and metering valve.

or prolonged starting. Cold leaks are noted by the presence of fuel in the intake manifold valley when the engine is cold. These leaks will often disappear after the engine is warmed up.

Injection Timing Checks

A locating pin will establish correct alignment of the injection pump to the front gear train timing gear during replacement, but it's best to ensure more precise timing through additional steps. There are factory-scribed hash marks on the pump and also on the engine adapter housing. Align the marks during initial start-up after pump replacement **FIGURE 20-20**. After alignment is set, dynamic timing of the pump is necessary.

GM recommends the use of a **luminosity probe** threaded into the glow plug hole of the first cylinder. This probe will sense the combustion event using a photoelectric eye in the luminosity probe. The pump hold-down bolts are loosened and the pump is rotated a few degrees while the engine is running to obtain accurate injection timing according to manufacturer specifications.

The use of a line pressure sensor to measure pump-to-engine timing is another technique to check dynamic timing. The line pressure sensor is used to detect the injection event by sensing the swelling of the injector line. The sensor, called an injection line pulse adaptor, is a **piezoelectric pressure transducer**. As a piezoelectric device, it generates current that is converted into a signal used by the inductive timing light or a magnetic probe to measure engine position relative to injection line pressure. When the line swells, the timing light flashes on the crankshaft pulley, indicating engine position **FIGURE 20-21**. The pump mounting is loosened to allow a few degrees of rotation of the pump for final adjustments.

The HPCA should also be evaluated as part of a diagnostic check or during pump replacement. Applying current to the HPCA solenoid at 2000 rpm should obtain a minimum of 1 degree of timing advance; 4 degrees of advance is more common in properly functioning pumps.

FIGURE 20-20 The scribe marks made on the injection pump and the drive gear housing should be aligned when a pump is initially installed.

Measuring Dynamic Injection Pump Timing

Distributor injection pump timing is changed using internal transfer fuel pump pressure. Housing pressure is altered during the warm-up period to advance injection timing. Bosch VE and Stanadyne DB pumps use electrical cold-start switches to produce advanced timing. A control valve mounted on the side of the VE pump overrides the pressure regulator to increase transfer pump pressure and advance injection timing. Stanadyne pumps use a housing pressure cold-start advance (HPCA) valve, which drops injection pump pressure by lifting a return fitting check ball off its seat. Lifting the check ball reduces housing pressure to near zero, enabling the transfer

FIGURE 20-21 An injection line pulse adapter is used to convert injection line swelling into an electrical signal for use with a timing light.

pump pressure on one side of the timing advance piston to easily rotate and advance the cam ring. Measuring dynamic pump timing should be done whenever low-power complaints, hard-starting complaints, or complaints about exhaust smoke are reported.

To measure dynamic injection pump timing, follow the steps in SKILL DRILL 20-1.

Measuring Pump Housing Pressure

The capability and condition of an internal transfer pump determines whether an adequate supply of fuel will be available at the correct pressure to the pumping plunger(s) within distributor injection pumps. More importantly, the injection timing mechanism is dependent on internal transfer pressure to operate at the correct pressure. This test should be performed if the pump has failed the timing test outlined in Skill Drill 20-1. A worn-out internal transfer pump will cause the engine to run rough; produce black, grey, or white exhaust emissions; and have low power and high fuel consumption.

To measure pump housing pressure, follow the steps in SKILL DRILL 20-2.

▶ Bosch Mechanical Distributor Pumps

Bosch distributor pumps that use sleeve metering and an axial piston pumping plunger are the second most common type of distributor pump design. These are rugged, durable pumps capable of withstanding harsher operating conditions due to their larger reciprocating pumping plunger and wider cam plate. For the same reason, these pumps are capable of producing higher

injection pressures while supplying more fuel to each cylinder through individual delivery valves. This next section examines the construction and operation of mechanical Bosch distributor pumps.

Bosch VE Pump Applications

Bosch has manufactured a number of different models of distributor pumps since the 1960s. In addition to their successful and wide use in industrial, marine, and off-road applications, many of these pumps have found their way into North American automotive applications. The Bosch VE pump used in early model Cummins 5.9L (360 cubic inch) engines, for example, is commonly found in off-road equipment and many medium-duty vehicles manufactured by Ford, Freightliner, and Dodge FIGURE 20-22. This pump uses a reciprocating axial piston to pressurize fuel and sleeve metering principles, which varies the end of injection to control injection delivery quantities. A hydraulic timing advance mechanism, which is similar to the mechanical Stanadyne DB system, varies the BOI timing. An electronic version with similar construction and operational characteristics as the mechanical VE pump is the VP-37 used on engines such as the 1.9L (116 cubic inch) VW TDI. In the VP-37, the sliding sleeve or control collar that regulates the sleeve metering functions is operated electronically. The Bosch VP-44 is another electronic distributor pump popularized by the Cummins ISB and is covered in the Electronic Distributor Type Injection Pumps chapter.

The VE pump is a compact, lightweight distributor pump that is capable of the highest injection pressures and output volumes of any distributor fuel injection system. The older VE

SKILL DRILL 20-1 Measuring Dynamic Injection Pump Timing

1. Attach a piezoelectric injection line clamp pressure transducer to injection line 2. Make sure to clean the line area where the clamp is attached with some sand paper. Attach the alligator clip for the transducer to engine ground.

2. Attach the inductive clamp of an ignition timing light to the pressure transducer inductive loop. The timing light should be the strobe type used to check spark ignition timing.

3. Mark the crankshaft pulley top dead center (TDC) indicator to highlight scribe marks for TDC.

4. Start the engine and allow it to run until it reaches operating temperature.

5. If required by the pressure transducer manufacturer, apply an offset correction factor to the timing light timing indicators. The offset number is the correction factors used to account for the lag time between the current induced in the line sensor by injection line swelling and the moment when the timing light flashes. A common offset value is −20 degrees.

6. Operate the engine at 2000 rpm or at the speed the OEM requires when injection timing is measured. Observe and record injection timing.

7. Bypass the cold-start switch with a jumper wire to activate the cold-start solenoid in the injection pump. Observe and record the injection timing.

8. Compare the observed injection timing with the OEM's specifications. If the timing is incorrect, loosen the pump mounting bolts and rotate the pump to achieve the correct timing specifications. If timing does not advance as the engine speed increases, recommend an injection pump replacement or overhaul.

9. Compare the timing advance with and without the cold-start mechanisms energized. There should be a change of at least 2 degrees. If injection pump timing does not advance when the cold-start mechanisms are energized, recommend an injection pump replacement or overhaul.

SKILL DRILL 20-2 Measuring Pump Housing Pressure

4 Start the engine and let it idle to purge air from the pump hosing that may have entered when the screw was removed. After engine speed has stabilized, move the throttle to the wide-open position.

5 Record the internal pump housing pressure. A typical specification for a DB pump is 90–120 psi (621–827 kPa).

6 If pump housing pressure is too high, remove the pump return line restriction fitting and clean it.

7 Retest and observe and record the internal pump housing pressure.

8 If the pump hosing pressure is too low, recommend a pump replacement or overhaul.

9 On Bosch VE pumps, the injection advance curve is controlled by pump housing pressure. Housing pressure is measured at the return line fitting, which has an integral pressure regulator.

1 Thoroughly clean the injection pump housing to prevent any dirt contamination of sensitive fuel system components.

2 On DB pumps, remove the transfer pump cover lock screw from the head of the pump.

3 Insert the purpose-made adapter into the distributor head of the pump and connect the adapter to a 0–160 psi (0–1103 kPa) pressure gauge.

10 Insert the line pressure adapter and measure pressure there. Housing pressure increases with engine speed; for example, housing pressure may be 44 psi (303 kPa) at 1000 rpm and 75 psi (517 kPa) at 2000 rpm. Consult the OEM's specifications to compare observes and expected values.

---

mechanical pumps could produce injection pressures as high as 4500–11,760 psi (310–811 bar). Power output is in the vicinity of 35 hp (30 kW) per cylinder.

VE Pump Construction

This pump found its way into many diesel engine applications because of its compact and rugged design. Using about half the number of parts as an inline pump, it is not only a simpler design, but it also reduces the pump's weight. VE pumps use sleeve-metering principles and an axial-arranged pumping plunger to pressurize fuel **FIGURE 20-23**.

The main components of the pump include the following:

- Vane transfer pump and pressure regulating valve
- Flyweight governor
- Hydraulic timing advance mechanism
- Shut-off device
- Air–fuel ratio control or aneroid used on turbocharged engines
- Distributor head with high-pressure pump
- Delivery valves
- Cam plate
- Distributor plunger
- Electric shut-off solenoid
- Cold-start advance device (KSB)

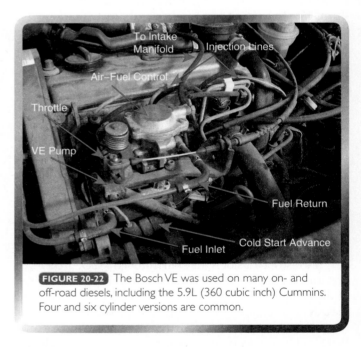

FIGURE 20-22 The Bosch VE was used on many on- and off-road diesels, including the 5.9L (360 cubic inch) Cummins. Four and six cylinder versions are common.

VE Pump Operation

The design innovation of the VE pump can be seen in its unique use of a single reciprocating pump plunger driven by a cam plate.

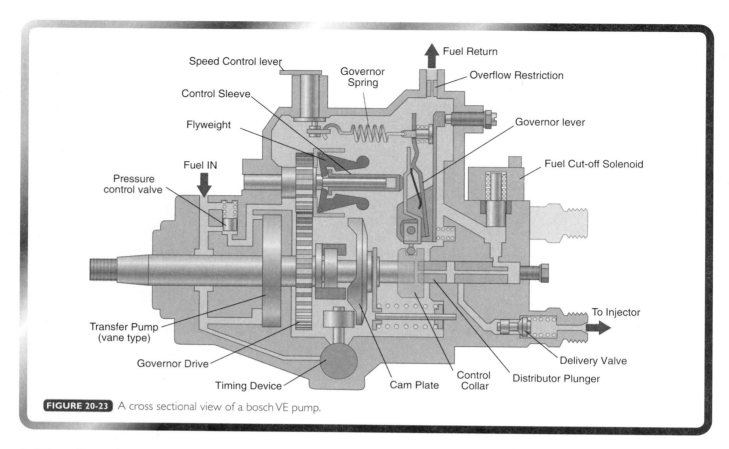

FIGURE 20-23 A cross sectional view of a bosch VE pump.

A sliding collar on the pump plunger moves back and forth to open and close a fuel spill valve, which regulates metering. This sliding collar is a sleeve-like device that gives the pump its metering mechanisms name—sleeve metering. In this next section, VE pump construction and operation is examined along with fuel circuits; learning these concepts will help technicians better understand VE pumps so they can more effectively diagnose and service these pumps.

Pumping Plunger Construction

One of the most critical elements to understanding the operation of the VE pump is the axial pumping plunger. An axial piston is oriented along the pump's centerline, which is different from the radial pump that has plungers oriented at 90 degrees to the pump's centerline. The pumping plunger has some similarity to a radial piston pump's rotor shaft in terms of its construction. However, in the VE pump, the plunger has only three kinds of slots or openings: fill slots, distributor slot, and spill port **FIGURE 20-24**.

The fill slots permit fuel to enter the pumping chamber. The number of fill slots corresponds to the number of engine cylinders.

The distributor slot is the point through which pressurized fuel exits for delivery to the injectors. This slot is near the end of the plunger and is connected to a passageway drilled along the axis of the plunger, which transmits a pressurized column of fuel to the injectors. Because only one cylinder can fire at a time, there is only one distributor slot in the plunger. As the plunger rotates, the distributor slot will align with passageways drilled in the head of the distributor pump, connecting it to delivery valves and fittings for the injector lines.

The spill port is a small, round opening drilled through the plunger at 90 degrees to the shaft. It connects to a passageway that travels nearly the full length of the plunger, connecting the pressurized end of the plunger to the distributor slot. It is the spill port that vents high-pressure fuel from the pumping chamber at the end of the injection event, thus regulating the quantity of fuel delivered to the cylinders. The movement and position of the control sleeve over the spill port determines when the injection event ends.

The output volume and pressure of the pump depends on the diameter of the pumping plunger. Plunger diameter will vary between engine models based on the power rating and emission requirements of the engine. The plunger size is designated in the pump serial number.

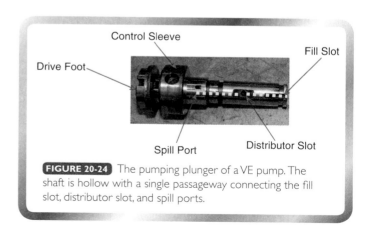

FIGURE 20-24 The pumping plunger of a VE pump. The shaft is hollow with a single passageway connecting the fill slot, distributor slot, and spill ports.

Plunger Movement

It is important to understand that the pumping plunger has two movements when the engine is operating. First, it rotates within the hydraulic distributor head to cover and uncover the fill and discharge ports, though not simultaneously. Secondly, the plunger reciprocates or moves back and forth along the pump axis as it follows the cam profile of the cam plate. The term axial piston pump denotes this kind of piston action. This means the plunger will reciprocate along the pump's axis six complete times during one rotation of the pump in a six cylinder engine.

> ### ▶ TECHNICIAN TIP
>
> Remember that distributor and inline injection pumps operate at one-half engine rpm. When installing injection pumps, it is sometimes possible to time the injection to the cylinder 360 degrees out of phase to the correct cylinder for injection. To prevent this from happening, remove the valve cover and make sure the valve's bridges for the first cylinder are both loose if the pump is timed to the first cylinder. This applies to both inline and distributor pumps.

Distributor Plunger Drive and Cam Plate

The cam of the VE pump is a circular plate with the cam lobes on the face of the plate. It is not inside a ring like the radial plunger pumps discussed in the previous section. Rollers that follow the cam profile of the cam plate cause the plunger to move in and out in a direction along the pump axis **FIGURE 20-25**. The profile of the plate controls the rate of fuel delivery and is unique to each engine model and its emission requirements.

The pump drive mechanism is attached to the cam plate and causes the plate to rotate. Passing through the plate is the plunger foot that connects the driveshaft to the plunger, thus rotating the plunger. A set of springs force the rollers against the cam plate. The springs act on the rollers and plunger through a yoke. The springs also ensure the pumping plunger returns to the cam plate bottom dead center (BDC).

Fuel Flow

The VE pump contains its own transfer pump that may be used to draw fuel from a tank. However, most vehicles will use another electric or mechanical transfer pump to supply low-pressure fuel to the pump. In such cases, a vane transfer pump is located near the pump's drive end. Four vanes are located inside an eccentric ring, and centrifugal force pushes the vanes outward against the ring, trapping and carrying fuel to the kidney-shaped recess at the outlet side of the pump. A spring-loaded, spool-like valve is located in the pump outlet and regulates maximum fuel pressure. Excess fuel flow is redirected by the pressure-regulating valve back to the vane pump inlet. Internal fuel pressure will vary from approximately 35 psi (241 kPa) at idle to a maximum of approximately 115 psi (8 bar) at high idle. Like other distributor pumps, this pressure regulation is critical for proper operation of the hydraulically operated injection timing mechanism and for charging the pressure chambers with adequate pressure for good performance.

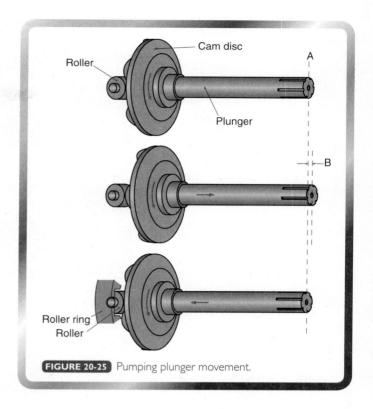

FIGURE 20-25 Pumping plunger movement.

A separate overflow valve or pressure regulator will also allow a regulated quantity of fuel to leave the pump; the fresh overflow fuel cools and lubricates the pump. Air or fuel vapor entrained in the fuel can also be removed through this device.

Fuel Pressurization

When fuel leaves the transfer pump, it enters the main pump cavity. From the main pump cavity, fuel can enter the pumping plunger high-pressure chamber when one of the fill slots aligns and uncovers the fill port in the distributor head. As the plunger begins to simultaneously rotate and move forward, reducing the volume in the pressure chamber due to cam plate action, the fill port is closed and fuel begins to pressurize. The plunger continues to rotate while fuel pressurizes within the pressure chamber and passageway inside the plunger. The plunger rotation uncovers the discharge port in the distributor head with the distributor slot. Pressurized fuel can then pass from the pressure chamber, through the plunger, out the distributor slot, and travel to the injector line fittings through the delivery valve. This means a column of high-pressure fuel now extends from the pressure chamber in the distributor head, through the plunger and delivery port passage, and all the way to the injector nozzle **FIGURE 20-26**.

Metering

A perpendicular passage is drilled along the axis of the plunger, forming a T-junction that intersects with the passage through the plunger center. This hole is called the spill port. A close-fitting ring called the **control sleeve** slides along the plunger to

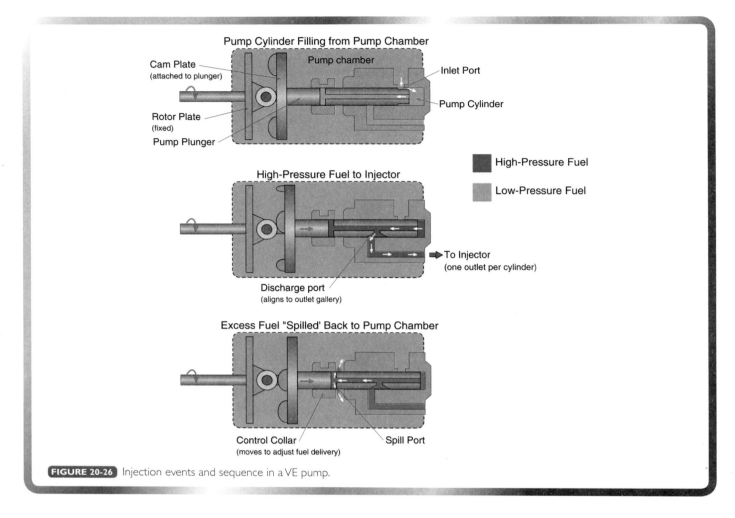

FIGURE 20-26 Injection events and sequence in a VE pump.

open or close the spill port. If the control sleeve uncovers the spill port, fuel pressurized during injection is vented into the pump housing, and injection ends. By varying the distance the plunger travels when the spill port is either open or closed, the delivery quantity of injection can change. Opening the spill port early in the plunger's stroke ends injection sooner, which means less fuel is injected. Uncovering the spill port later in the stroke increases the quantity of fuel injected.

A round recessed hole in the control sleeve permits a lever to connect the sleeve with the governor **FIGURE 20-27**. To regulate injection quantity, the governor will move the control sleeve, also called the spill ring, back and forth along the plunger, thus changing the point when fuel is spilled and injection ends. The pump's governor controls fuel delivery by altering the position of the spill port relative to the position of the control sleeve. Moving the sleeve away from the pressure chamber end of the plunger to the drive end decreases fuel delivery. Moving the control sleeve toward the pressure chamber end of the plunger increases fuel delivery **FIGURE 20-28**.

Delivery Valve Operation

Contained at each injector line fitting on the distributor head is a delivery valve for each cylinder. The delivery valves provide a crisp, sharp end to injection by preventing secondary injections

FIGURE 20-27 A lever on the governor moves the control sleeve along the plunger's axis. The position of the control sleeve regulates the quantity of fuel injected.

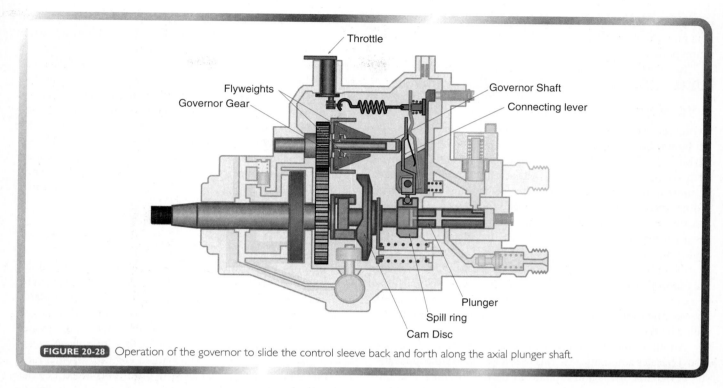

FIGURE 20-28 Operation of the governor to slide the control sleeve back and forth along the axial plunger shaft.

caused from the retention of high pressure in the fuel line just after injection ends. By lowering the line pressure to a few hundred pounds (kilograms) of pressure, the injector nozzle valve remains closed while residual pressure in the line minimizes the time required to rebuild pressure for the next injection. Defective delivery valve operation results in rough running and low power.

Electric Fuel Shut-Off

A solenoid and plunger located in the fuel supply passageway to the pressure chamber cuts off fuel delivery unless the solenoid is energized. When de-energized, a spring-loaded plunger will block fuel delivery to the pressure chamber. The electromagnet in the solenoid pulls the plunger out of the connecting passageway, permitting fueling of the pressure chamber.

Advance Mechanism

A timing mechanism operating on principles similar to radial plunger pumps such as the Stanadyne DB is also used in the VE pump. A piston connected to the cam plate moves the plate back and forth to retard and advance the beginning of the injection event. Because injection timing requires advancing with increasing engine speed, the pressure from the transfer pump will move the piston to advance timing proportional to engine speed. A spring located on the opposite side of the advance piston opposes piston movement through transfer pump pressure **FIGURE 20-29** .

Adjusting Static Pump-to-Engine Timing

The most precise procedure for establishing correct pump-to-engine timing on a Bosch VE pump involves the use of a dial

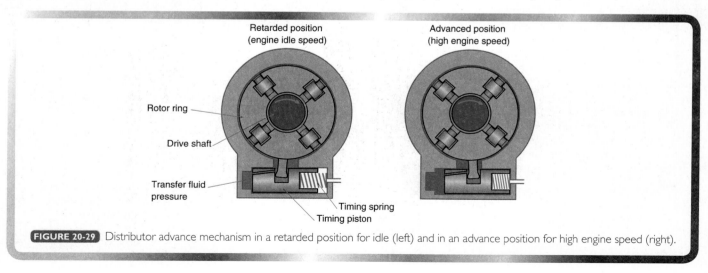

FIGURE 20-29 Distributor advance mechanism in a retarded position for idle (left) and in an advance position for high engine speed (right).

indicator to measure axial plunger travel. Bosch supplies charts that provide a corresponding crankshaft position for a given pump plunger lift travel.

To adjust static pump-to-engine timing, follow the steps in SKILL DRILL 20-3. These steps are for Bosch VE model pumps.

Cold-Start Advance Device

To provide better cold operation, less smoke, and fewer misfires, VE pumps are equipped with one of several types of **cold-start advance (KSB) devices** (KSB is an acronym for the German term for cold-start advance). All of these devices operate by moving the cam plate to an advance position through the sliding piston of the hydraulic advance mechanism. Typically, a KSB device will advance pump timing by approximately 2.5 degrees when cold, and take away the advance when the engine is warmed.

Older VE pump models used a cable to operate linkage on the pump that moved the timing advance piston. The position of a cam in relation to the piston could be varied depending on how far the cable, located in the passenger compartment, was pulled by the operator.

Another older variation of the cold-start advance mechanism operates automatically. This uses a wax pellet-like thermostat device that melts and expands to move cam linkage and to move the sliding piston of the cam plate.

The newer, most common version of an electric cold-start advance mechanism uses an electrically heated element inside the pump housing to change the internal pump pressures applied to the advance piston. By controlling the fuel pressure to the advance piston, injection timing can be retarded or advanced. An engine-mounted thermal switch supplies a current to the electric heating element located inside a modified pressure-control valve. An expansion element at the pressure regulator will regulate the amount of fuel allowed to bypass the internal vane pumps, which is normally applied to the timing advance piston FIGURE 20-30. The KSB valve is commonly incorporated into VE pumps used by Cummins for Dodge Ram trucks.

Air–Fuel Ratio Control

To minimize black smoke or particulate matter (PM) emissions, the quantity of fuel delivered to the cylinders needs to be modulated in proportion to the quantity of air mass available for combustion. On both turbocharged and non-turbocharged engines, fuel can reach the cylinder much faster and in greater quantity than the air needed to burn the fuel. To prevent excessive smoke production in turbocharged engines, air–fuel ratio control (AFRC) devices are used. Non-turbocharged engines with VE pumps use a hydraulic torque control module built into

SKILL DRILL 20-3 Adjusting Static Pump-to-Engine Timing

Static Timing in Degrees Before TDC	Plunger Travel in mm
10.0	3.25
10.5	3.35
11.0	3.45
11.5	3.55
12.0	3.65
12.5	3.7
13.0	3.8
13.5	3.9
14.0	4.0

1 Position the crankshaft at TDC for cylinder 1 and mark the engine position on the front crank pulley. If the engine uses a timing pin, locate cylinder 1 TDC using the method described in Skill Drill 19-3.

2 Remove the center plug from the pump's distributor head and install a purpose-made dial indicator. The dial face is capable of indicating movement of ±20 mm with the dial marked in increments of 0.01 mm. An inner dial will measure 1 mm in one rotation with a total indicator travel of 10 mm.

3 Rest the dial indicator extension piece on the axial pumping plunger in the pump.

4 With the engine at TDC for cylinder 1, bar the engine over counterclockwise one quarter of a turn, or until the dial indicator needle movement stops. Zero in the dial indicator needle.

5 Bar the engine over in a clockwise rotation while pressing on the timing pin or while having an observer precisely stop the engine at TDC. When the engine is at TDC for cylinder 1, stop and note dial indicator travel.

6 Compare the dial indicator movement with the OEM's specifications or the chart in this box.

7 If the injection pump is not within the OEM's specifications, loosen the pump mounting bolts and rotate the pump housing until the dial indicator pointer matches the specifications for the correct engine position. For example, an engine with pump to injection timing of 10° before TDC should have a dial indicator movement of 5.25 mm.

8 Tighten the pump mounting nuts; reinstall and reattach the pump parts.

9 Run the engine and recheck its operation

10 When properly timed, the pump-to-engine alignment marks used to static time the pump will be closely, if not exactly, aligned. These marks are etched into the pump housing and engine front cover.

FIGURE 20-30 The KSB regulates fuel pressure to the timing advance piston.

manifold boost pressure increases, the pin moves down with the diaphragm. This condition allows the maximum amount of governor travel to increase proportionally because of the increasingly smaller diameter of the pin. A return spring under the diaphragm will return the diaphragm to a position that limits the governor's maximum fuel-stop position. Rotating the pin will change the governor's position to obtain maximum fuel delivery for that particular rpm. A tamper-proof adjustment screw controls pin position. This screw is adjusted at the factory, usually to a twelve-o'clock position in relation to the pump, and then broken off.

Under the AFRC diaphragm and spring is also a star wheel adjuster that alters the spring tension for the full-load delivery rate. Turning the star wheel upward (i.e., counterclockwise) will increase the spring tension. If the star wheel is adjusted to a point at which spring tension too high, the delivery rate pin cannot move completely downward under boost to a maximum fuel position. Consequently, the rate at which the fuel injection rate increases under acceleration will slow, and the engine feels lazy. Conversely, turning the star wheel clockwise will increase the injection rate during acceleration, providing improved throttle response.

Maximum Fuel-Stop Adjustment

Beneath the AFRC at the distributor head of the pump is the full-fuel stop adjustment screw. This screw contacts the governor control lever, limiting the maximum fuel position in the pump. Turning the tamper-proof screw counter clockwise will increase maximum engine fueling, increasing engine torque. Driveline damage, excessive emissions, and high exhaust gas temperatures can result when this setting is moved from factory adjustment.

the governor. The device essentially modulates, or slows, the increase in injection delivery quantity based on engine speed. This means the quantity of fuel available for combustion will not reach maximum pump output whenever the throttle is suddenly accelerated. Instead, the fuel rate is gradually increased.

On turbocharged engines, the AFRC device modulates the quantity of fuel injected based on intake manifold pressure **FIGURE 20-31**. This device is located on top of the injection pump. The aneroid contains a spring-loaded diaphragm that is connected to an eccentric tapered pin, also called a delivery rate pin. The movement of the delivery rate pin up or down regulates the full fuel-stop position of the governor. When

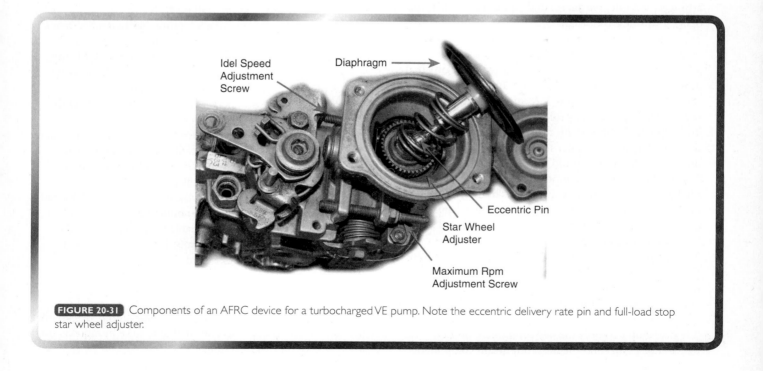

FIGURE 20-31 Components of an AFRC device for a turbocharged VE pump. Note the eccentric delivery rate pin and full-load stop star wheel adjuster.

Wrap-Up

Ready for Review

▶ When they were introduced, mechanical distributor injection pumps provided the diesel engine with wider applications in automotive, agriculture, and heavy equipment products by significantly reducing the cost, size, and weight of diesel engines.

▶ Distributor injection pump development propelled diesel engines into wider use.

▶ Distributor injection pump systems have fallen into disuse because they have been supplanted by unit injection and common rail systems.

▶ Distributor injection pumps were especially popular with farm equipment manufacturers.

▶ The design simplicity of distributor injection pumps accounts for their success; only half the numbers of parts are required to manufacturer a distributor injection pump in comparison to inline versions producing the same engine horsepower.

▶ One disadvantage of distributor injection pumps is that using a single pumping element not only limits power output and pressure, but it also has the potential for wearing out sooner in comparison to multiple plunger injection systems.

▶ Using a single fuel pressurizing pumping element also limits the fuel volume output of a distributor pump.

▶ Distributor injection pumps can be classified by the type of fuel metering system they use; there are two designs commonly used: opposed plunger and sleeve metering.

▶ The opposed plunger design uses pumping plungers arranged at 90-degree angles to the pump driveshaft that operates inside a cam ring.

▶ The axial plunger pump design uses a single reciprocating plunger located along the pump axis.

▶ While the two distributor pump designs appear distinctly different, opposed and axial piston pump designs have several features in common, including a rotating shaft with a drilled passageway for fuel through its axis.

▶ The original distributor injection pump design was developed by Roosa Master in the 1950s; the original pump configuration evolved into several other models.

▶ The most popular distributor injection pump design is the DB2 pump; the main components of the DB2 are the driveshaft, distributor rotor, transfer pump, pumping plungers, cam ring, hydraulic head, governor, and an injection timing advance mechanism.

▶ The pump's driveshaft rotates inside a tube pressed into the pump housing; one end of the shaft engages the fuel distributor rotor and turns the rotor shaft, while the other end is connected to the engine drive gear and turns the pump at one-half engine speed.

▶ The distributor rotor is the key component of the distributor pump, and the most important components of the rotor are two, three, or four opposed pumping plungers which are used to pressurize fuel for injection.

▶ By connecting the cam ring to a movable plunger at a single point near the pump's bottom, BOI timing is varied.

▶ Filtered fuel is drawn into the pump by a positive-displacement vane internal transfer pump located at the end of the hydraulic head.

▶ An automatic timing advance mechanism is incorporated in the pump design; this is needed to achieve the appropriate injection timing for engine speed and load conditions.

▶ During cold engine operation, it is desirable to advance injection timing to eliminate white smoke and misfires due to ignition delay (cold cylinders take longer to ignite and burn fuel); retarded timing is necessary during cranking because it permits the piston to rise farther during compression stroke before injection.

▶ The governor in distributor injection pumps is generally a min/max design, sometimes referred to as an automotive governor; this means that the governor controls high-idle and idle speed while the operator controls fueling in between these two ranges.

▶ Bosch has manufactured a number of different models of distributor pumps, including the Bosch VE pump; this pump uses a reciprocating axial piston to pressurize fuel and sleeve metering principles that vary the EOI to control injection delivery quantities.

▶ One of the most critical elements to understanding the operation of the VE pump is the axial pumping plunger, which has three kinds of slots: a set of fill slots, the distributor slot, and the spill port.

▶ The pumping plunger of a VE pump has two movements when the engine is operating: first, it rotates within the hydraulic distributor head to cover and uncover fill and distributor discharge ports, though not simultaneously; secondly, the plunger reciprocates, or moves back and forth, along the pump axis as it follows the profile of the cam plate.

▶ The VE pump contains its own transfer pump, which may be used to draw fuel from a tank; however, most vehicles will use another electric or mechanical transfer pump to supply low-pressure fuel to the pump.

▶ To minimize PM emissions, the quantity of fuel delivered to the cylinders needs to be modulated proportionally to the quantity of air mass available for combustion; AFRC devices are used primarily on turbocharged engines to prevent excessive smoke production.

Vocabulary Builder

axial piston pressurization A distributor pump design that uses a reciprocating plunger located along the pump axis used to pressurize fuel for injection.

cam plate A multi-lobed rotating plate in an axial plunger injection pump used to produce a reciprocating movement of the axial plunger.

cam ring A ring with lobes arranged on its internal diameter that is used to force opposing pumping plungers together to produce an injection event.

cold-start advance (KSB) device A device that provides better cold operation, less smoke, and fewer misfires. It operates by moving the servo piston of the hydraulic advance mechanism.

control sleeve A close-fitting ring that slides along the axial plunger to open or close the spill port.

delivery valve A valve that operates as a one-way check to allow fuel to remain at relatively high pressure in the fuel injection line while ensuring that fuel pressure will drop far enough below nozzle-opening pressure to prevent secondary injections caused by reflecting fuel pulsations in the injector line.

housing pressure cold-start advance (HPCA) mechanism A mechanism that is used to advance injection timing when an engine is cold.

inlet metering The use of a helical groove on the metering valve in an opposed plunger metering system to regulate fuel delivery to the pumping plungers.

luminosity probe A probe threaded into the glow plug holes of the first cylinder that senses the light produced by a combustion event. The probe is used to help adjust injection pump timing during initial installation.

opposed plunger pressurization A distributor pump design that uses two or four plungers arranged opposite one another inside a cam ring to pressurize fuel; also known as radial piston pressurization.

piezoelectric pressure transducer A sensor clamped to an injection line that transduces injection line pressure pulses into electrical signals. The signals are used to activate a timing light when checking or adjusting dynamic injection pump timing.

sleeve metering A form of metering that uses a sliding control sleeve or ring fitted to an axial plunger. The control sleeve position determines when the injection event ends by spilling fuel from the axial plunger.

vane pump A device that pressurizes fuel inside the pump housing.

Review Questions

1. A _____ is a close-fitting ring that slides along the axial plunger to open or close the spill port.
   a. control sleeve
   b. vane pump
   c. delivery valve
   d. piezoelectric pressure transducer

2. A(n) _____ is a sensor clamped to an injection line that converts injection line pressure pulses into electrical signals.
   a. control sleeve
   b. vane pump
   c. piezoelectric pressure transducer
   d. inlet meter

3. A(n) _____ is a device that pressurizes fuel inside the pump housing.
   a. delivery valve   c. control sleeve
   b. vane pump   d. inlet meter

4. A _____ is a device that operates as a one-way check to allow fuel to remain at relatively high pressure in the fuel injection line while ensuring that fuel pressure will drop far enough below nozzle-opening pressure to prevent secondary injections caused by reflecting fuel pulsations in the injector line.
   a. delivery valve
   b. control sleeve
   c. vane pump
   d. piezoelectric pressure transducer

5. _____ is the use of a helical groove on the metering valve in an opposed plunger metering system to regulate fuel delivery to the pump plungers.
   a. Injection timing   c. Outlet metering
   b. Plunging   d. Inlet metering

6. The development of _____ advanced diesel engine production into more widespread use.
   a. injection pumps   c. rotors
   b. governors   d. axial pistons

7. The _____ regulates the amount of fuel delivered to the pumping plungers to match engine speed and load conditions.
   a. cam ring   c. axial piston
   b. governor   d. annulus

8. A _____ located in the end of the rotor's axial passageway operates like a one-way check valve during the discharge of fuel.
   a. flyweight
   b. pressure control valve
   c. delivery valve
   d. distributor plunger

9. The _____ has lobes corresponding to the number of engine cylinders and surrounds the shoe and rollers of the rotor.
   a. cam ring   c. cam plate
   b. axial piston   d. delivery valve

10. Bosch VE pumps use _____ of parts as an inline pump.
    a. the same number
    b. about twice the number
    c. about half the number
    d. about a quarter the number

ASE-Type Questions

1. Technician A says distributor pumps use a single pumping element to deliver fuel to all cylinders. Technician B says distributor pumps use multiple pumping elements to deliver fuel to all cylinders. Who is correct?
   a. Technician A
   b. Technician B
   c. Both Technician A and Technician B
   d. Neither Technician A nor Technician B

2. Technician A says the cam plate in a distributor pump is the equivalent of the camshaft in a multiple plunger pump. Technician B says the cam plate in a distributor pump is the equivalent of the camshaft in a single plunger pump. Who is correct?
   a. Technician A
   b. Technician B
   c. Both Technician A and Technician B
   d. Neither Technician A nor Technician B

3. Technician A says some electronic versions of the DB2 pump use three opposed plungers. Technician B says they do not use more than two opposed plungers. Who is correct?
   a. Technician A
   b. Technician B
   c. Both Technician A and Technician B
   d. Neither Technician A nor Technician B

4. Technician A says a timing advance mechanism is incorporated in the design of the distributor injection pump. Technician B says it is an automatic timing advance mechanism. Who is correct?
   a. Technician A
   b. Technician B
   c. Both Technician A and Technician B
   d. Neither Technician A nor Technician B

5. Technician A says the axial pump plunger diameter varies between engine models based on the power rating of the engine. Technician B says the axial pump plunger diameter varies between engine models based on the emission requirements of the engine. Who is correct?
   a. Technician A
   b. Technician B
   c. Both Technician A and Technician B
   d. Neither Technician A nor Technician B

6. Technician A says the fuel limiter leaf spring is accessed through the bottom of the injection pump. Technician B says the fuel limiter leaf spring is accessed through the side of the injection pump. Who is correct?
   a. Technician A
   b. Technician B
   c. Both Technician A and Technician B
   d. Neither Technician A nor Technician B

7. Technician A says the axial piston design uses pumping plungers arranged at 90-degree angles to the pump driveshaft, which operates inside a cam ring. Technician B says the radial piston design uses pumping plungers arranged at 90-degree angles to the pump driveshaft. Who is correct?
   a. Technician A
   b. Technician B
   c. Both Technician A and Technician B
   d. Neither Technician A nor Technician B

8. Technician A says to provide better cold operation and less smoke, VE pumps are equipped with one of several types of KSB devices. Technician B says the KSB devices also lead to fewer misfires. Who is correct?
   a. Technician A
   b. Technician B
   c. Both Technician A and Technician B
   d. Neither Technician A nor Technician B

9. Technician A says the most popular application of the opposed plunger distributor injection pump design is the model DS pump. Technician B says the model DS pump was used by GM in V6 automobile engines. Who is correct?
   a. Technician A
   b. Technician B
   c. Both Technician A and Technician B
   d. Neither Technician A nor Technician B

10. Technician A says Robert Bosch invented the first distributor pump. Technician B says Henry Ford invented the first distributor pump. Who is correct?
    a. Technician A
    b. Technician B
    c. Both Technician A and Technician B
    d. Neither Technician A nor Technician B

CHAPTER 21
Electronic Signal Processing Principles

NATEF Tasks

Electrical/Electronic Systems

General Electrical Systems
- Check frequency and pulse-width signal in electrical/
electronic circuits using appropriate test equipment.
(pp 607, 612–615)

Knowledge Objectives

After reading this chapter, you will be able to:
1. Identify and describe the functions, construction, and
application of electronic control modules. (pp 604–606)
2. Identify and explain the advantages of electronic
signal processing over mechanical system control.
(pp 604–607)

3. Identify and describe the operating principles
of electronic signal processing systems used in
electrical system control on commercial vehicles.
(pp 607–608)
4. Identify and describe the types of electrical signals
and associated terminology. (pp 608–615)

Skills Objectives

There are no skills objectives for this chapter.

▶ Introduction

Today's commercial vehicles are often described as computers on wheels, and technicians are just as likely to use a computer as they will a wrench to service them. Not a single vehicle system operates without complete or at least some degree of electronic control. This has not always been the case. Until recent years, mechanical devices such as levers, springs, linkage, gears, cables, or bellows-controlled system operation. Electronic systems using microcontroller- and microprocessor-based control now provide operational capabilities far exceeding any mechanical system capabilities and can do this with greater precision, efficiency, and reliability. The dominance and sophistication of electronic control makes skill development related to servicing this technology one of the most important priorities for successful technicians. Understanding the operating principles of electronic control systems is foundational for choosing diagnostic strategies, using service tools effectively, and making sound repair recommendations.

▶ Benefits of Electronic Control

Electronic control offers many benefits to today's commercial vehicles, including increased power and efficiency, enhanced reporting capabilities, telematics, increased safety, programmable features, and self-diagnostic capabilities.

Increased Power and Efficiency

Diesel engines were the first commercial vehicle systems transformed by electronic controls **FIGURE 21-1**. Engines had reached their limit of efficiency and the next logical step was to apply electronic controls already used on gasoline engines. The immediate benefits of these refinements to engine operation are lower engine emissions, improved fuel economy, increased reliability, and enhanced performance. Smarter engines continue to deliver ever-increasing power from smaller displacements, quieter operation, and longer service intervals in addition to needing less maintenance. The increased costs of some of these features are offset through improved engine efficiency. Many of the electronic control systems have in fact lowered the cost of vehicle production while adding more features with the improved operating benefits. In comparison to mechanical controls, electronic controls enable far greater flexibility to adjust fuel injection metering, injection rate, and timing over a large number of operating conditions. When engine operational problems leading to excess emissions do occur, self-monitoring and self-diagnostic capabilities of electronic controls can identify the problem, alert the operator, and revert to operating modes that minimize noxious emission production.

TABLE 21-1 shows the increase in power output per cubic inch of displacement and lowering of emissions achieved through advanced technology and electronic control of the fuel system.

Information Reporting Capabilities

Life cycle costs of operating vehicles with these engines is further reduced through the ability of the engine control systems to interface with tablets and Windows-based diagnostic and service software. Service technicians, particularly in fleet operations, can access a wealth of diagnostic and service data much faster and with more precise detail than before **FIGURE 21-2**. Trip reports from the vehicle ECM (electronic control module) extracted during scheduled maintenance intervals report

▶ You Are the Technician

A number of vehicles have arrived at your shop with a list of apparently unrelated complaints: speedometer needles that begin to bounce at 55 mph (90 kph) cruise controls that do not work, automatic transmissions that shift erratically, dozens of ABS codes for components and circuits that have no faults, and rough running engines. On one of the vehicles, when performing some pinpoint tests with a digital multimeter, you accidentally set the meter to read AC and not DC voltage. You are surprised to discover close to 4 volts of AC current are superimposed on the system's 12-volt DC current. Realizing that the only component that could produce AC current is the alternator, you disconnect the alternator and find the AC voltage has disappeared along with the unusual electrical system complaints. To repair the problem, the alternator is replaced and so are the vehicle's batteries, which all tested defective. As you prepare to document the diagnosis and justify the parts replacement on the work orders, consider the following questions:

1. What shop equipment could be used to capture and record the AC voltage signal frequency and waveform to document the problem?
2. Would the ECM be processing the correct data from some sensor inputs if AC voltage accompanies the DC voltage inputs? Explain your answer.
3. After gaining the experience repairing these vehicles, what checks would you recommend in future for diagnosing electrical problems that may be related to electrical signal interference?

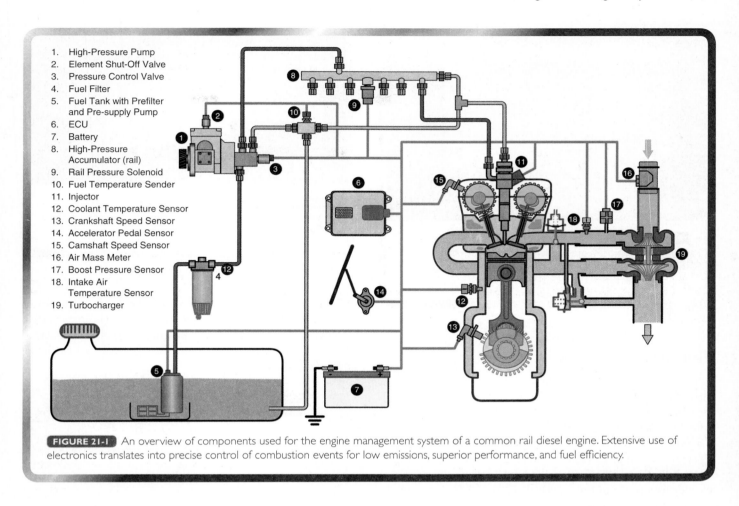

1. High-Pressure Pump
2. Element Shut-Off Valve
3. Pressure Control Valve
4. Fuel Filter
5. Fuel Tank with Prefilter and Pre-supply Pump
6. ECU
7. Battery
8. High-Pressure Accumulator (rail)
9. Rail Pressure Solenoid
10. Fuel Temperature Sender
11. Injector
12. Coolant Temperature Sensor
13. Crankshaft Speed Sensor
14. Accelerator Pedal Sensor
15. Camshaft Speed Sensor
16. Air Mass Meter
17. Boost Pressure Sensor
18. Intake Air Temperature Sensor
19. Turbocharger

FIGURE 21-1 An overview of components used for the engine management system of a common rail diesel engine. Extensive use of electronics translates into precise control of combustion events for low emissions, superior performance, and fuel efficiency.

details such as diagnostic fault codes, fuel consumption, idle time, emission system performance, and vehicle abuse statistics **FIGURE 21-3**.

TABLE 21-1: Increase in Power Output per Cubic Feet of Displacement

Engine Model	1988—7.3L IDI Diesel	2015—6.7L Powerstroke
Horsepower	180 hp	440 hp
Torque	338 ft/lb @ 1,600 rpm	860 ft/lb @ 1,600 rpm
NO_x emissions	2.5 grams/bhp	0.07 grams/bhp
Intake air flow @ 3,330 rpm	360 cubic feet/minute	732 cubic feet/minute
Exhaust flow @ 3,300 rpm	1,080 cubic feet/minute	1,499 cubic feet/minute
Fuel system	Mechanical distributor pump	Bosch piezoelectric injectors CP4.2 Common Rail Pump Electronic

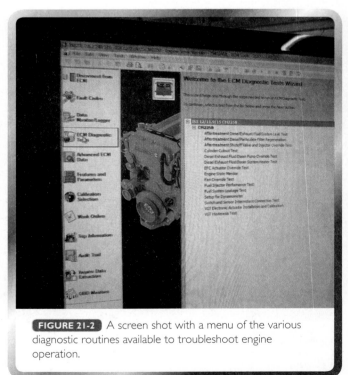

FIGURE 21-2 A screen shot with a menu of the various diagnostic routines available to troubleshoot engine operation.

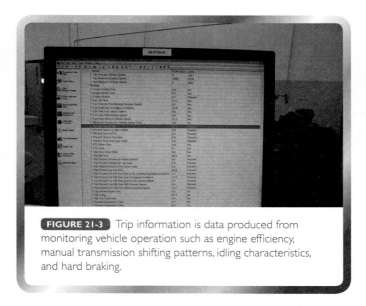

FIGURE 21-3 Trip information is data produced from monitoring vehicle operation such as engine efficiency, manual transmission shifting patterns, idling characteristics, and hard braking.

Telematics

In addition to the obtaining vehicle and trip information downloaded at scheduled maintenance intervals, ECM data can be collected and modified by other means **FIGURE 21-4** . When equipped with the correct vehicle interface devices, vehicle and engine diagnostics can be performed from distant locations **FIGURE 21-5** . Telematics, a branch of information technology, uses specialized telecommunication applications for long-distance transmission of information to and from a vehicle **FIGURE 21-6** . For example, when vehicles are equipped with radio-satellite or cellular-based vehicle communications, a technician or equipment manager can remotely monitor any information about the vehicle, engine, or product the vehicle is carrying that is available from the vehicle network data link connector. Messages can be sent back and forth between the vehicle and a central dispatch location. For example, if low on fuel, a list of nearby fuel stops can be generated with the least interference or delay to a trip. A GPS can report vehicle location to a dispatcher as well as display fuel stop locations.

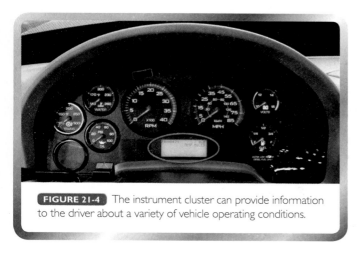

FIGURE 21-4 The instrument cluster can provide information to the driver about a variety of vehicle operating conditions.

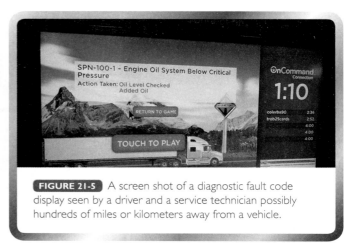

FIGURE 21-5 A screen shot of a diagnostic fault code display seen by a driver and a service technician possibly hundreds of miles or kilometers away from a vehicle.

A fault code can be evaluated to determine if immediate repairs are needed. For large fleet operations, short-range wireless technology allows diagnostics and programming of vehicles when they are in the vicinity of a maintenance or equipment facility for increased productivity.

Safety

The use of electronic engine and vehicle management provides for enhanced vehicle and occupant safety and security. If a vehicle is involved in a collision, a call can be made to an emergency dispatch. Engine systems can be monitored for operating conditions having destructive potential. Low oil pressure, high intake, or coolant temperatures are commonly monitored conditions that can initiate an adaptive response to prevent catastrophic failure or damage. Dangerous operating conditions can trigger the engine to shut down, derate power, or simply warn the operator. The microprocessor power train control makes it possible to build in features that will protect the power train from damage due to excessive torque or speed as well. Hard braking and speeding are other measurable conditions monitored by management systems to ensure road safety.

Programmable Vehicle Features

Service technicians and operators can take advantage of programmable electronic controls. Programmable software provides flexibility to engines, transmissions, and body accessories for adaptation to specific job applications, enhancing vehicle productivity, longevity, and driver comfort. Programmable changes may include things as simple as idle shut-down timers, cruise control, or maximum vehicle speed limits to adding safety interlocks preventing the vehicle from moving if a door is open, a boom is raised, or outriggers are extended **FIGURE 21-7** .

Power and torque rise profiles are easily altered electronically. Depending on the application, it is beneficial to performance and fuel economy to have maximum torque appear over different rpm ranges. Instead of replacing an injection pump and turbocharger to change engine power characteristics,

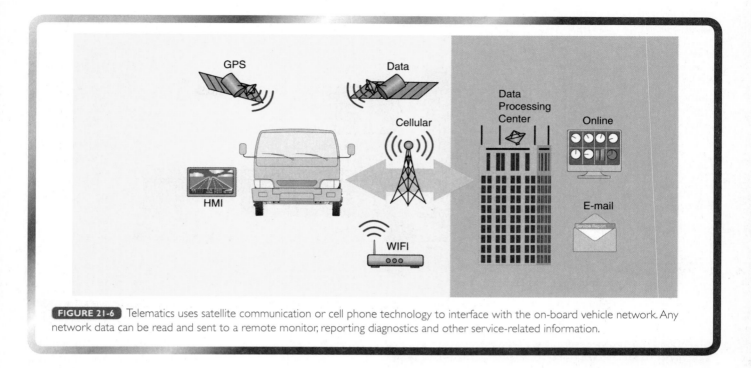

FIGURE 21-6 Telematics uses satellite communication or cell phone technology to interface with the on-board vehicle network. Any network data can be read and sent to a remote monitor, reporting diagnostics and other service-related information.

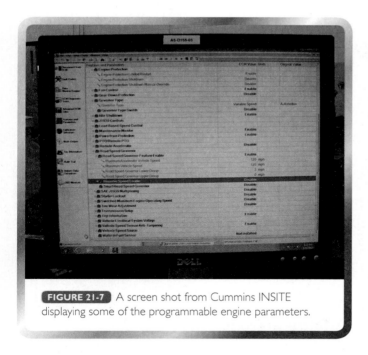

FIGURE 21-7 A screen shot from Cummins INSITE displaying some of the programmable engine parameters.

electronically controlled engines are recalibrated with new software instructions. In a few minutes with some keystrokes, a stock vehicle chassis can be reprogrammed to operate as an ambulance, an on-highway tractor, dump truck, bus, rental truck, or recreational vehicle.

Self-Diagnostic Capabilities

Electronic systems do not have many moving parts to wear out, but the systems can be complex. Diagnostics on electronically controlled vehicle systems can be performed easily, often with fewer tools and in less time than on mechanical systems **FIGURE 21-8**. When something goes wrong with a component or circuit, it can be extremely time-consuming and difficult to identify the problem without some built-in self-diagnostic capabilities. Built into electronic control systems is a self-monitoring function with capabilities to check operation of circuits and electrical devices, evaluate whether voltages are out of range, the rationality of data, and system functionality. Problems are quickly identified as they occur. The presence of faults is communicated through the malfunction indicator lamps. An engine may even lose power or derate to prevent excessive emission production, engine damage and provide an incentive to have the condition repaired. Electronic service tools assists the technicians to perform off-board diagnostics, that is, perform pinpoint checks to precisely identify system faults. Software-based diagnostics deliver huge amounts of data about system operation, enabling service technicians to identify problems more quickly than with mechanical systems. Since modules, sensors, and actuators are more compact, they are replaced quickly with minimal training and experience required **FIGURE 21-9**.

▶ Elements of Electronic Signal Processing Systems

At first glance, operation of electronic control systems looks mysterious, using a variety of sensors, wires, electrical actuators, and electronic modules moved with invisible electrical signals. However, to understand how electronic control systems operate it is helpful to observe that any

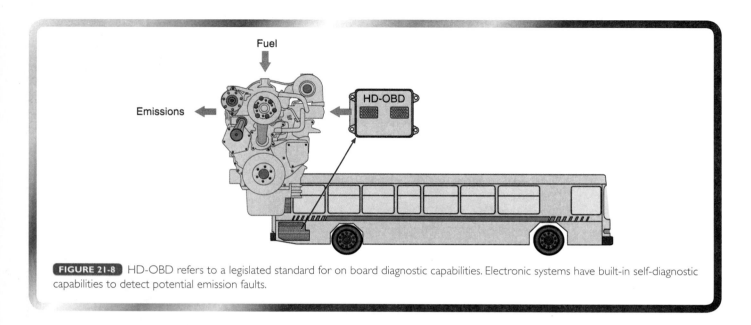

FIGURE 21-8 HD-OBD refers to a legislated standard for on board diagnostic capabilities. Electronic systems have built-in self-diagnostic capabilities to detect potential emission faults.

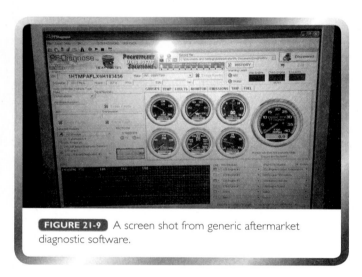

FIGURE 21-9 A screen shot from generic aftermarket diagnostic software.

system functions can be broken down into three major divisions:

- Sensing
- Processing
- Output or actuation **FIGURE 21-10**

Sensing Functions

Sensing functions collect data about operational conditions or the state of a device by measuring some value such as temperature, position, speed, pressure, flow, and angle. Sensors are devices designed to collect specific data in an electronic format.

Processing

Processing refers to the control system element that collects sensor data and determines outputs based on a set of instructions or program software. Operational algorithms, which are simply

mathematical formulas used to solve problems, are included in the software that determines the steps taken when processing electrical data.

Outputs

The outputs of a system are functions performed by electrical signals produced by the processor. These may be signals to operate anything from a digital display of numeric or alphabetic information, current to operate solenoids or injectors, actuators, motors, lights, or other electromechanical devices **FIGURE 21-11**.

▶ Types of Electrical Signals

Before looking at the elements of the electronic management system, it is first important to look at types of electrical signals used in information processing systems **FIGURE 21-12**.

Three types of electrical signals commonly used as either inputs and or outputs in electronic engine control applications are:

- Analog
- Digital
- Pulse-Width Modulation (PWM)

Analog Signals

An **analog signal** is electric current that is proportional to a continuously changing variable. Analog signals then will have a changing value of voltage, amperage frequency, or amplitude. For example, temperature changes continuously. A thermometer measuring temperature change can represent every possible temperature with the movement of liquid in a glass or a hand on a dial. An analog electrical signal would represent the smallest change in temperature proportional to the movement of liquid or hand on the dial.

Measurement of alternating electrical current is another example of an analog signal. Variable reluctance-type sensors

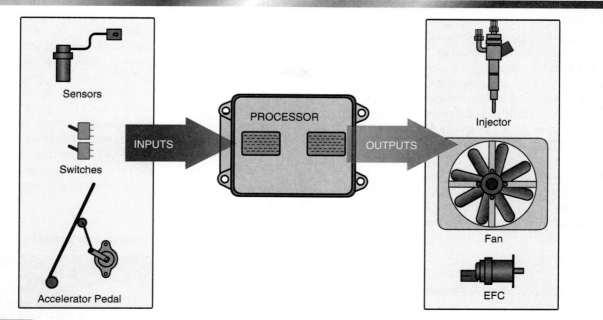

FIGURE 21-10 All engine management systems process electrical signals in three distinct stages: data collection from sensor inputs; data processing inside an electronic control module; and output devices; which are electrically operated.

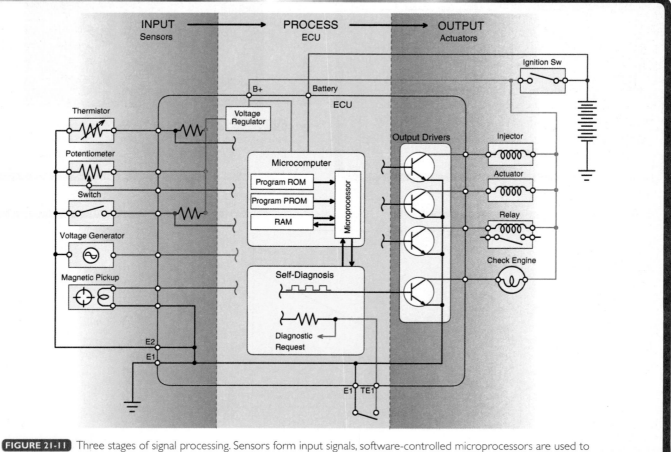

FIGURE 21-11 Three stages of signal processing. Sensors form input signals, software-controlled microprocessors are used to manipulate data, while electrically operated output devices carry out instructions of the processor.

such as wheel speed or some engine position sensors will produce an alternating current. Changing wheel or engine speeds will continuously alter the frequency of current polarity change leaving the sensor. The intensity of the voltage will further continuously vary with speed.

A throttle position sensor is another example where analog data can be collected. The electrical signal produced by the sensor varies proportionally to pedal angle. A continuously changing voltage output from the sensor will vary with the driver input **FIGURE 21-13**.

Outputs can be analog as well. The intensity of a light or sound in an output device such as a lamp or speaker can be produced by varying voltage and frequency of an electrical signal. A light is dimmed or brightened by increasing or decreasing current to a bulb. An analog signal representing sound produces loudness and pitch by varying the voltage and frequency current to a speaker.

Digital Signals

In contrast to analog signals, __digital signals__ do not vary in voltage, frequency, or amplitude. Instead, they are electrical signals that represent data in discrete, finite values. This means the data is broken down into separate or smaller meaningful values. For example, the movement of hands on an analog clock will represent time in every possible value. However, a digital watch represents time in finite values such as seconds. A digital multimeter represents data the same way. The numerical display for an electrical measurement is represented as a fixed number **FIGURE 21-14**. In contrast, an analog meter would measure the same electrical value using a sweeping needle on a scale.

FIGURE 21-14 This digital multimeter data represents resistance as a fixed precise value. Smaller changes in resistance—several places to the right of the decimal—are not measurable.

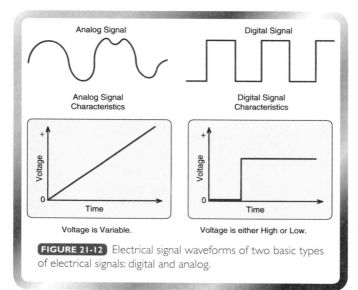

FIGURE 21-12 Electrical signal waveforms of two basic types of electrical signals: digital and analog.

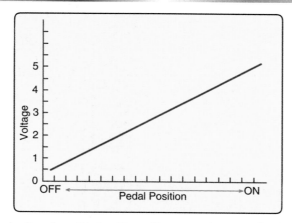

FIGURE 21-13 The signal voltage from this throttle position sensor is a type of analog data. An infinite number of values for voltage exist between idle and wide open throttle.

A more common understanding of digital signals describes them representing data using only two conditions or values. This can be on or off, yes or no, 1 or 0, open or closed, up or down, etc. Binary code is an example of a digital signal. Every number from 0 to infinity and the letters of the alphabet letters are represented by a combination of 0s and 1s. Binary code easily lends itself to use in microprocessor circuits where processing large amounts of alphabetic or numerical data, represented in strings of 0s or 1s is performed.

Computerized power train management systems process information electronically using digital signals and binary code. This means that all information, whether analog or alphabetic is converted into 1s and 0s. Using long strings of 1s and 0s may seem cumbersome, but just as the Morse code tapped out on telegraphs could send information using only dots and dashes, the 1s and 0s of binary code can satisfactorily convey all kinds of information **FIGURE 21-15**. The difference between digital and Morse code is in the speed and accuracy of electronic processing. Processing millions and billions of 1s and 0s per second is something digital electronics can do to compensate for the cumbersomeness of using only 1 and 0 to communicate alphanumeric data.

Bits and Bytes

A **bit** is a shortened term for binary digit. This is the smallest piece of digital or binary information and is represented by a single 0 or 1. As illustrated in Figure 21-15, a **byte** is a combination of 8 bits. The speed data is processed in the engine control module, also called ECM or ECU, is measured in bits. The number of bits it can process during one central processing unit (CPU) clock cycle classifies power train ECMs and computers. Desktop or laptop computers often use 64-bit processors. A Pentium IV processor is 32 bits, whereas a late model ECM will have 16-bit or 32 bit capability. A 3.0-MHz processor will have 3 million clock cycles per second, which means a 32-bit processor processes 96 million bits of data per second. While the clock speeds and bit size of the processors in an engine ECM are smaller than an average desktop, so is the programming code. The capabilities of an engine ECM may appear to lag a personal computer, but the PC operates using hundreds of complex software programs. An engine or power train control microprocessor that operates using only one program with much simpler software code to process information

and produce output signals has enormous processing capability **FIGURE 21-16**. Today's vehicle processors have many times the digital processing capabilities of the on-board computers used to send Apollo rockets to the moon.

Serial Data

While discussing binary code and digital signals it is useful to understand what serial data is. The term serial data originates from the way data is transmitted. It is in series, one bit after another along a single or pair of wires. When serial digital data is transmitted using a pair of wires, each wire will transmit a voltage pulse represented as a rectangular waveform. The wires will have a **differential voltage**, which means the voltage on the wire pair is a mirror opposite voltage when transmitting serial data **FIGURE 21-17**. A large differential

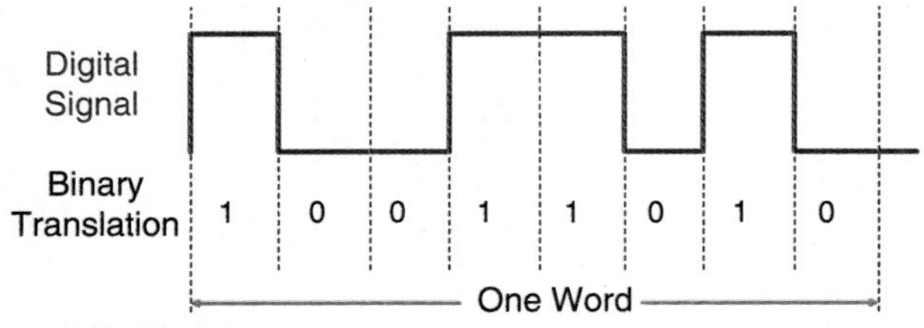

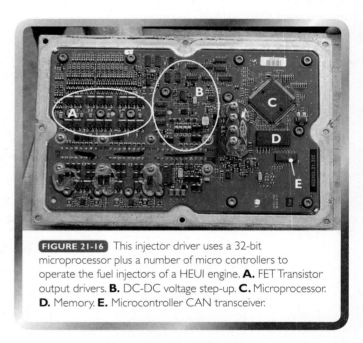

FIGURE 21-16 This injector driver uses a 32-bit microprocessor plus a number of micro controllers to operate the fuel injectors of a HEUI engine. **A.** FET Transistor output drivers. **B.** DC-DC voltage step-up. **C.** Microprocessor. **D.** Memory. **E.** Microcontroller CAN transceiver.

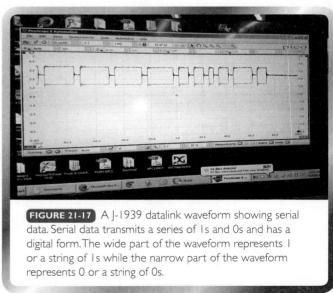

FIGURE 21-17 A J-1939 datalink waveform showing serial data. Serial data transmits a series of 1s and 0s and has a digital form. The wide part of the waveform represents 1 or a string of 1s while the narrow part of the waveform represents 0 or a string of 0s.

FIGURE 21-15 A bit is the smallest piece of digital information that is either a 1 or a 0. A byte is a unit of 8 bits. Binary code represents letters and numbers in strings of 1s and 0s. Digital data can be represented as 0s and 1s.

voltage pulse represents a 1 while a small differential voltage pulse represents 0. Serial data is used to transmit information from one electronic module to another. On-board data networks share information and control vehicle operation using serial data. More important to the technician, electronic service tools will use serial data to receive and send data. The rate at which serial data is transmitted is referred to as the baud rate. **Baud rate** refers to the number of data bits transmitted per second.

Analog to Digital Conversion

Because electronic processing units can only handle binary digital data, analog signals are converted to digital signals in a process called **analog to digital conversion** (FIGURE 21-18). To convert analog signals to digital binary information, special circuits, known as buffers or analog to digital (AD) converters, are used (FIGURE 21-19). To convert an analog signal, the electronics do a couple of things. First, the changing analog signal is sampled or divided up into segments like a loaf of bread. In one second of time, the varying analog signal could be sampled 10, 100, or even 1000 times (FIGURE 21-20). Each of these segments will represent a specific voltage value. The finer or more accurate the processor wants the data to be, the more frequent the sampling rate, resulting in better signal resolution or fidelity. Each of the segments will be assigned a digital value that is translated into a binary number. MP3 files are an example of an analog (wave file) to digital conversion.

A digital wave file could be sampled 64K times a second or 128K times a second or more. The higher fidelity—the faithfulness to the original analog signal—is achieved at the more frequent sample rate.

▶ TECHNICIAN TIP

The current used in the electronic control systems system is generally DC voltage. Radio frequency interference (RFI) induced into the system by magnetic fields of high-voltage power lines, radio transmitters, and even a microwave would be AC voltage. The signal processing systems of ECM input conditioning circuits generally recognize and ignore these types of signals. This does not mean all electromagnetic interference goes unnoticed. Magnetic fields can induce voltage in signal wires and cause confusion for signal processing units producing numerous types of unintended consequences.

Pulse-Width Modulation

An electrical signal that shares similar characteristics with both a digital and analog signal is the pulse-width-modulated (PWM) electrical signal (FIGURE 21-21), (FIGURE 21-22), (FIGURE 21-23). **Pulse-width modulation** refers to a signal that varies in "ON" and "OFF" time. That means it is digital in one aspect because it represents data in two states only—either

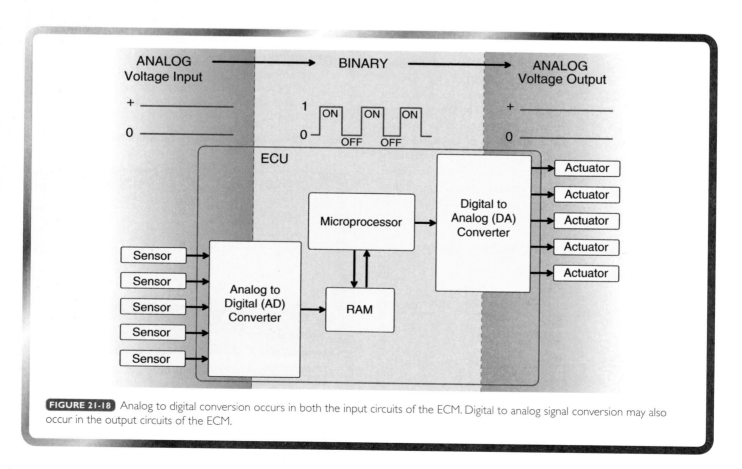

FIGURE 21-18 Analog to digital conversion occurs in both the input circuits of the ECM. Digital to analog signal conversion may also occur in the output circuits of the ECM.

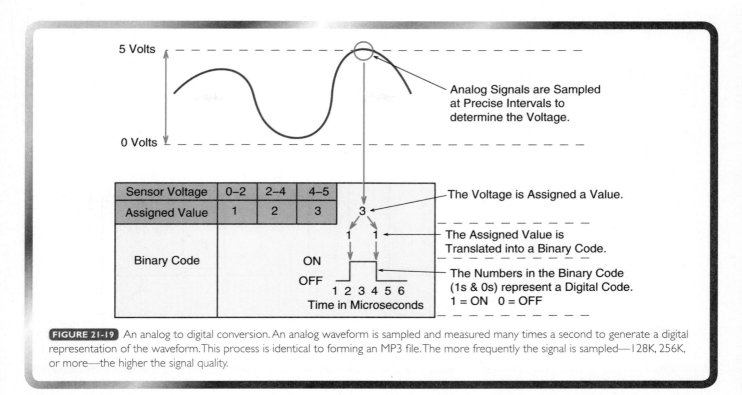

FIGURE 21-19 An analog to digital conversion. An analog waveform is sampled and measured many times a second to generate a digital representation of the waveform. This process is identical to forming an MP3 file. The more frequently the signal is sampled—128K, 256K, or more—the higher the signal quality.

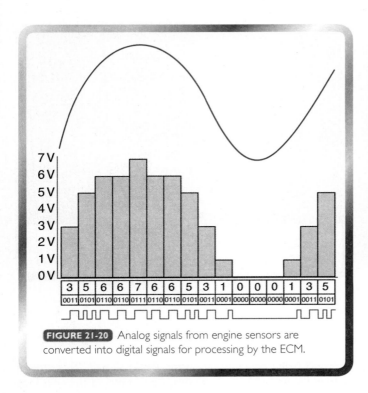

FIGURE 21-20 Analog signals from engine sensors are converted into digital signals for processing by the ECM.

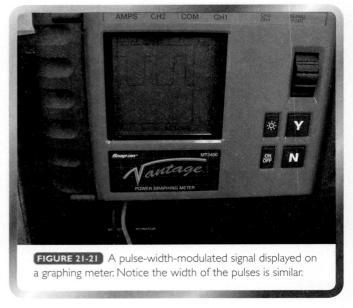

FIGURE 21-21 A pulse-width-modulated signal displayed on a graphing meter. Notice the width of the pulses is similar.

on or off, or high or low. However, information is also conveyed by the amount of time the signal stays on or off. Time on or off is variable, which gives it an analog characteristic. The units for measuring pulse width are always expressed in units of time. Time is the measure of how long the signal is high or on.

To understand PWM, consider a light illuminated by a PWM signal. In one second of time the light may be cycled on and off once. If the signal is applied for one-quarter of the second, the pulse width would be 0.25 seconds wide **FIGURE 21-24**.

Common examples of devices using PWM signals are solenoids, injectors, and light circuits. A PWM signal units of measurement are typically milliseconds. PWM signals are commonly used as an output signal of an ECM. For example, the current supplied to a fuel injector or the pressure regulator of a HEUI

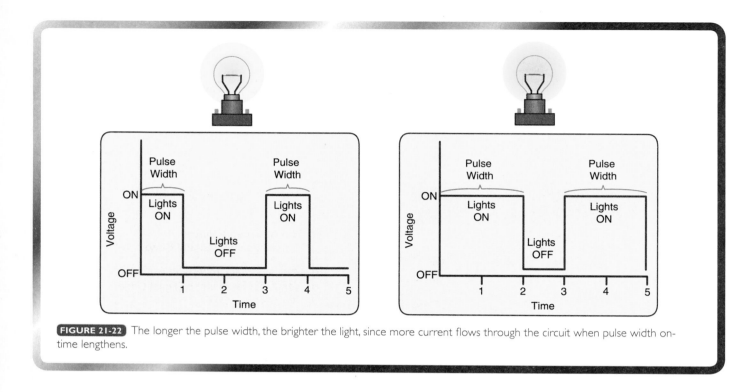

FIGURE 21-22 The longer the pulse width, the brighter the light, since more current flows through the circuit when pulse width on-time lengthens.

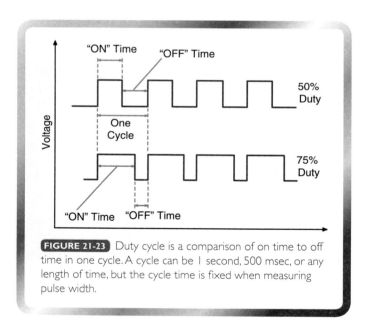

FIGURE 21-23 Duty cycle is a comparison of on time to off time in one cycle. A cycle can be 1 second, 500 msec, or any length of time, but the cycle time is fixed when measuring pulse width.

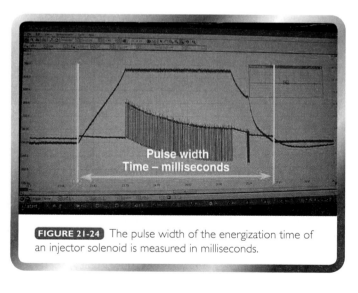

FIGURE 21-24 The pulse width of the energization time of an injector solenoid is measured in milliseconds.

or common rail pump is changed by varying the on-time of the electromagnetic control valve **FIGURE 21-25**, **FIGURE 21-26**. Output drivers of microprocessors are types of switches, usually switching transistors, which produce PWM signals to operate devices in an "ON" or "OFF" state **FIGURE 21-27**, **FIGURE 21-28**. The microprocessor device can also easily vary the duration time of a driver opening and closing.

Some manufacturers use sensors that use PWM signals to transmit data. Caterpillar uses throttle position sensors that will transmit pedal position data using PWM signals. This type of data is unaffected by voltage drops encountered through long runs of wiring harnesses and multiple connectors between the sensor and ECM.

Duty Cycle

Related to the term pulse width is duty cycle, illustrated in **FIGURE 21-23**. <u>Duty cycle</u> is another unit for measurement for PWM signals. While a pulse width is measured in time, duty

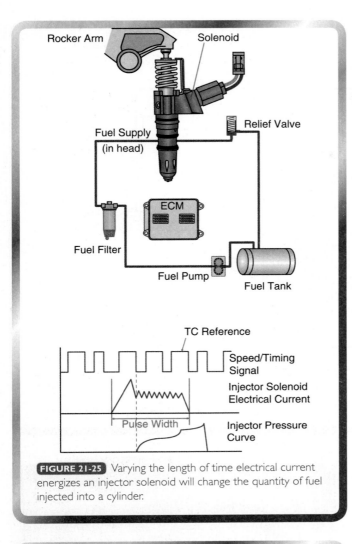

FIGURE 21-25 Varying the length of time electrical current energizes an injector solenoid will change the quantity of fuel injected into a cylinder.

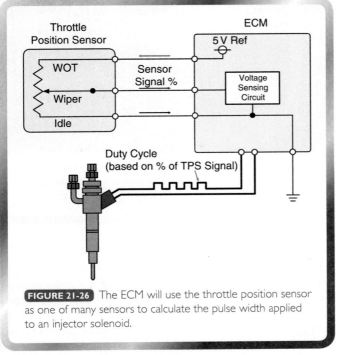

FIGURE 21-26 The ECM will use the throttle position sensor as one of many sensors to calculate the pulse width applied to an injector solenoid.

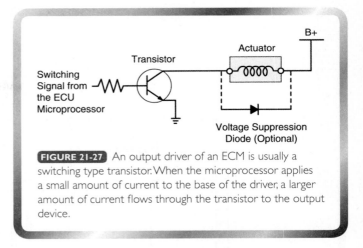

FIGURE 21-27 An output driver of an ECM is usually a switching type transistor. When the microprocessor applies a small amount of current to the base of the driver, a larger amount of current flows through the transistor to the output device.

cycle is measured as a percentage—on-time versus off time. Duty cycle refers to the percentage of time a PWM signal is high or on, in comparison to off time FIGURE 21-29 . One on and off time for a PWM signal represents one cycle. Duty cycle units are expressed as a percentage of cycle time. For example, if the pulse width is 0.8 seconds and the off time is 0.2 seconds, a cycle is 1 second in length. This means the duty cycle is 80%. A 100% duty cycle means the signal is on all the time, while a 0% duty cycle is off. Another way of expressing this relationship is signal off time versus on time. A signal that is applied for three-quarters of a cycle is 75% duty cycle.

What is different about duty cycle in comparison with PWM is where the signal is used. Duty cycle is commonly used to measure the time a signal is applied to an output device operating at a fixed frequency, whereas pulse width measures a signal applied to devices operating at a varying frequency interval. For example, an engine may speed up and slow down, so the pulse width or time an injector is energized will vary with speed. It is practical to measure actuation time only, since it is difficult to always know the frequency of a cycle—rpm, in this instance. Depending on engine speed, 10 or 20 injections may take place in 1 second, making it practical to only measure pulse width.

Consider, however, an electrohydraulic pressure regulator. This device will have a PWM signal applied to close a valve and increase pressure. Removing the signal will cause pressure to decrease. The time the signal is applied is broken into fixed time intervals. Therefore, a solenoid for this device may be on for 0.20 seconds out of fixed 1 second intervals. This would give it a pulse width of 0.20 seconds but a duty cycle of 20%. Pulse width could increase or decrease changing duty cycle FIGURE 21-30 . To practically interpret system operation, a measurement of duty cycle is more meaningful.

Frequency

Frequency is the number of events or cycles that occur in a period, usually one second. The units of measure for frequency are **hertz (Hz)**, which is the number of cycles per second. A common application for frequency measurements is for alternating current. When current switches from positive to negative, one cycle is completed FIGURE 21-31 .

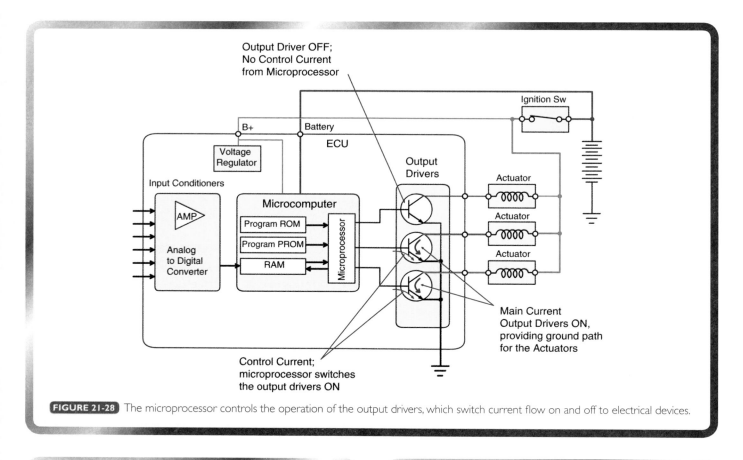

FIGURE 21-28 The microprocessor controls the operation of the output drivers, which switch current flow on and off to electrical devices.

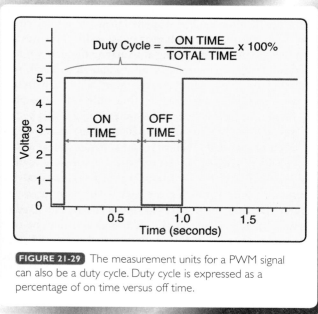

FIGURE 21-29 The measurement units for a PWM signal can also be a duty cycle. Duty cycle is expressed as a percentage of on time versus off time.

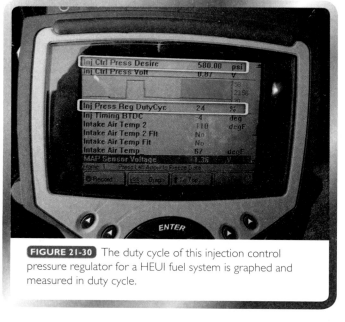

FIGURE 21-30 The duty cycle of this injection control pressure regulator for a HEUI fuel system is graphed and measured in duty cycle.

▶ Processing Function

Processing electronic signals used in vehicle management systems is the function of electronic control modules. Referred to as the electronic control module, a microprocessor or microcontroller is the heart of the control unit. Made from hundreds if not hundreds of thousands of transistors contained in a semiconductor chip, the integrated circuit chips making up microprocessors and various controllers will contain a minimal amount of memory plus input and output circuits. Microprocessors have more memory, which gives them the capability to perform advanced calculations and follow software-based instructions **FIGURE 21-32**. In contrast microcontrollers are

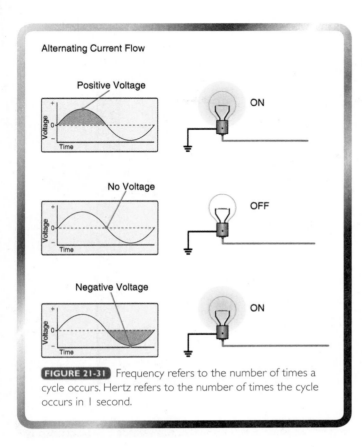

FIGURE 21-31 Frequency refers to the number of times a cycle occurs. Hertz refers to the number of times the cycle occurs in 1 second.

FIGURE 21-32 Integrated circuits used on a late model HD Mercedes Benz engine control module. **A.** Microcontroller. **B.** RAM and ROM memory. **C.** Flash memory. **D.** Microprocessor.

less capable, and carry out specific functions built into the chip design. An ECM will contain several types of memory, output drivers that control the operation of electrically operated devices such as injectors and relays as well as complex signal conditioning circuits for information processing functions. An ECM will contain a transceiver which enables it to receive and send communication signals to an on-board vehicle network.

Several types of integrated circuit devices or "chips" are on-board a typical ECM, which are essential to processing and ECM operation:

- The clock
- Microprocessor
- Microcontrollers
- A-D converter
- Memory

CPU Clock

The clock is an oscillator inside the microprocessor that controls how fast instruction stored in memory are processed **FIGURE 21-33**. It is like the drum beat that controls the pace of the work in the microprocessor. The clock speed is measured in hertz (or megahertz, or gigahertz). With each cycle of the clock, the microprocessor will perform a set of tasks. Obviously, the faster the clock speed, the greater number of instructions processed per second.

Computer Memory

Several types of memory are used in an ECM depending on its application. Some memory is used to store data from sensors since the ECM cannot process all sensor data simultaneously **FIGURE 21-34**. Other types of memory are required to store the instructions for operating the microprocessor. This memory would store software code to give the ECM its unique operational characteristics. Common categories of memory include:

- Read only memory (ROM)
- Random access memory (RAM)
- **Programmable read only memory (PROM)**
- Electrically erasable programmable read only memory (EEPROM)
- Flash memory or nonvolatile RAM (NVRAM), which is a ROM/RAM hybrid that can be written to but which does not require power to maintain its contents

Read Only Memory (ROM)

Read only memory (ROM) is used for permanent storage of instructions and fixed values used by the ECM that control the microprocessor. Information stored in the ROM would include algorithms such as how to calculate the pulse width for the injectors or the horsepower ratings for the vehicle. Other fixed values would identify a maximum engine rpm, the temperature value for an engine overheat condition, or the type of transmission. The ECM reads the instructions, but it cannot write to or change the instructions contained in ROM. ROM data is stored by the manufacturer. ROM memory is permanent and is not lost even if power to the computer is interrupted. This means the memory is **non-volatile** **FIGURE 21-35**.

Random Access Memory (RAM)

Random access memory (RAM) is a temporary storage place for information that needs to be quickly accessed. Input data from sensors is commonly stored in RAM waiting processing

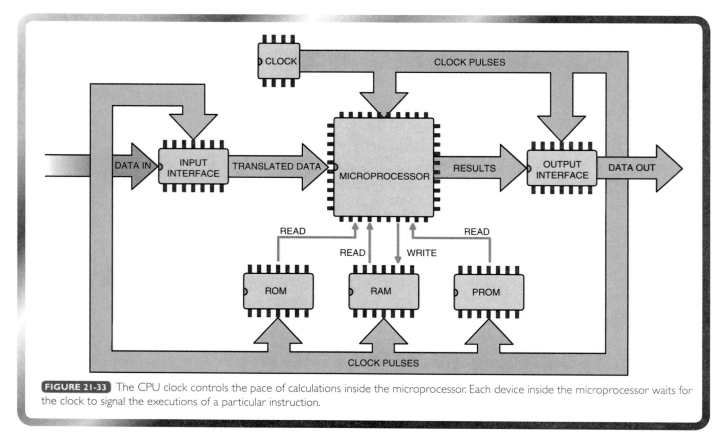

FIGURE 21-33 The CPU clock controls the pace of calculations inside the microprocessor. Each device inside the microprocessor waits for the clock to signal the executions of a particular instruction.

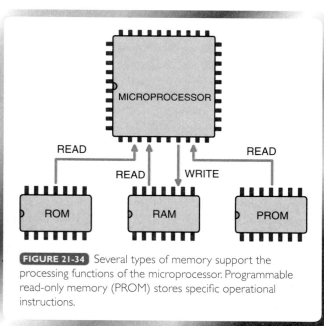

FIGURE 21-34 Several types of memory support the processing functions of the microprocessor. Programmable read-only memory (PROM) stores specific operational instructions.

by the ECM. RAM memory is both readable and writable. Most RAM memory is designed to be lost when power is interrupted, such as turning the ignition key off. That is why RAM is often referred to as temporary storage of memory. However, RAM can be stored in the ECM after the key is shut off. Non-volatile RAM holds its information even when the power is removed.

Volatile RAM will be erased when the power is removed. If volatile RAM receives its power from the ignition key, its memory is lost when the ignition is turned off. If battery power is used to keep the RAM memory intact when the key is off, it is also known as **keep alive memory (KAM)**.

EEPROM and Flash Memory

Electrically erasable programmable read only memory (EEPROM) was developed to allow manufacturers to change the software operating the ECM electronically rather than physically fix it into the ECM during its design and construction.

In recent years flash memory, which is non-volatile, is EEPROM memory. This is almost identical to the type used on a USB memory stick. It has enormous shock resistance and durability and is able to withstand intense pressure, extremes of temperature, and immersion in water, which are conditions found in commercial vehicles. It also offers the convenience of easily reprogramming or recalibrating the ECM, also known as **flashing** or flash programming. Flash programming involves the installation of look-up tables in the ECM. Look-up tables are used by the ECM to solve mathematical problems called algorithms. An example of a simple algorithm would solve the problem of how fast is the vehicle traveling. The mathematical formal for speed would be distance/time. More complex algorithms involve calculating how much fuel to inject, when to inject fuel, or how long the injector should be energized. The look-up table provides specific data to help solve the problems for a specific engine.

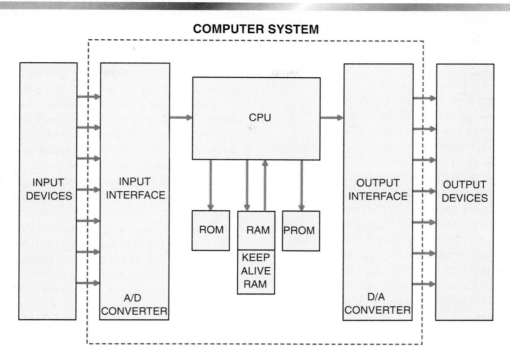

FIGURE 21-35 Non-volatile memory means the information is not lost when power to the ECM is disconnected or the ignition is switched off. Keep alive memory refers to memory that is retained only due to a constant supply of current to the ECM when the ignition is switched off.

▶ TECHNICIAN TIP

Microcontrollers and microprocessors are types of integrated circuits. The distinction between them is related to their capabilities. Engines, transmissions, and ABS electronic control modules use **microcontrollers**. This is a special-purpose processor with limited capabilities, designed to perform a set of specific tasks. Reading sensor data and using logic gates to perform calculations and determine outputs required for the application such as energize a relay or injector solenoid, are examples. Executing instructions stored in the memory of EEPROMs enhances the function of sophisticated microcontrollers. The controller's tasks, however, are limited to a specific application such as controlling the engine's operation. In contrast, a most sophisticated engine, ABS, or other ECMs use microprocessors that are capable of executing logic and supporting a larger number of devices making-up the ECM. Microprocessors will also use an operating system such as Windows, Linux, or Android, enabling the addition of multiple software programs to handle a larger variety of tasks.

Wrap-Up

Ready for Review

▸ Electronic systems using microprocessor- and microcontroller-based control provide operational capabilities far exceeding any mechanical system. The dominance and sophistication of electronic control makes skill development related to servicing this technology one of the most important priorities for successful technicians.

▸ Diesel engines were the first commercial vehicle systems transformed by electronic controls. The immediate benefits of these refinements to power train control include lower engine emissions, improved fuel economy, increased reliability, and enhanced performance.

▸ Service technicians, particularly in fleet operations using medium-duty engines, can access a wealth of diagnostic and service information much faster and with more precise detail than before.

▸ Telematics, a branch of information technology, uses specialized applications for long-distance transmission of information to and from a vehicle. Messages can be sent back and forth between the vehicle and a central dispatch location.

▸ The use of electronic engine and vehicle management provides for enhanced vehicle and occupant safety and security.

▸ Programmable software provides flexibility to engines, transmissions, and body accessories to adapt to; adaptation to specific job applications; and enhanced vehicle productivity, longevity, and driver comfort. Programmable features include idle shut-down timers, cruise control, maximum vehicle speed limits, and safety interlocks that prevent the vehicle from moving if a door is open, a boom is raised, or outriggers are extended.

▸ Built-in electronic management systems allow vehicles to check the operation of circuits and electrical devices, evaluate the rationality of data, and identify problems as they occur. The presence of faults is communicated through the malfunction indicator lamps, electronic service tools, or Windows-based diagnostic software.

▸ Electronic control systems can be broken down into three major divisions: sensing, processing, and output or actuation.

▸ Sensing functions collect data about operational conditions or the state of a device by measuring some value such as temperature, position, speed, pressure, or flow.

▸ Processing collects sensor data and determines outputs based on a set of instructions or program software.

▸ The outputs of a system are functions performed in response to electrical signals produced by the processor.

▸ Three types of electrical signals commonly used as either inputs or outputs in electronic engine control applications are analog, digital, and PWM.

▸ An analog signal is an electric current that is proportional to a continuously changing variable.

▸ In contrast to analog signals, digital signals do not vary in voltage, frequency, or amplitude. Instead, they are electrical signals that represent data as binary values, such as on-off, 0 or 1, yes-no, up-down, and open-closed.

▸ Binary code is an example of a digital signal. "Bit" is a shortened term for binary digit. This is the smallest piece of digital or binary information and is represented by a single 0 or 1. A byte is a combination of 8 bits.

▸ Serial data is used to transmit information from one electronic module to another. On-board data networks share information and control vehicle operation using serial data.

▸ Because electronic processing units can only handle binary digital data, analog signals are converted to digital signals by special circuits known as buffers or AD converters.

▸ An electrical signal that shares similar characteristics with both a digital and analog signal is the PWM electrical signal. PWM refers to a signal that varies in on and off time. A PWM signal is typically measured in milliseconds.

▸ Duty cycle is another unit of measurement for PWM signals, and it refers to the percentage of time a PWM signal is on versus the time it is off. Duty cycle is commonly used to measure the time a signal is applied to an output device operating at a fixed frequency, whereas pulse width measures a signal applied to devices operating at a varying frequency interval.

▸ Frequency is the number of events or cycles that occur in a period. The unit of measure for frequency is hertz (Hz), which is the number of cycles per second.

▸ ECMs are microprocessors or microcontrollers that process electrical signals. Several types of integrated circuit devices on-board a typical ECM are essential to processing and ECM operation.

▸ The CPU clock is an oscillator inside the microprocessor that controls how fast instructions stored in memory are processed. It is like the drum beat that controls the pace of the work in the microprocessor. The clock speed is measured in hertz (or megahertz or gigahertz).

▸ Several types of memory are used in an ECM, depending on its application. Some memory is used to store data from sensors because the ECM cannot process all sensor data simultaneously. Other types of memory are required to store the instructions for operating the microprocessor.

▸ Common categories of memory include ROM, RAM, PROM, EEPROM, and flash memory (a ROM/RAM hybrid that can be written to but does not require power to maintain its contents).

Vocabulary Builder

analog signal An electric current that is proportional to a continuously changing variable.

analog to digital conversion The process when an analog waveform is sampled and measured many times a second to generate a digital representation of the waveform.

baud rate The rate at which serial data is transmitted.

bit The smallest piece of digital information that is either a 1 or 0.

byte A unit of 8 bits.

differential voltage Refers to the voltage difference on a wire pair when one wires voltage is the mirror opposite voltage. A wide separation between the voltage pulses represents a 1 and a narrow separation represents a 0.

digital signals   Electrical signals that represent data in discrete, finite values. Digital signals are considered as binary meaning it is either on or off, yes or no, high or low, 0 or 1.

duty cycle   The percentage of time a PWM signal is ON in comparison to OFF time.

electrically erasable read only memory (EEPROM)   Non-volatile memory technology that is used to store operating instructions or programming for an ECM.

flashing   Reprogramming or recalibrating the ECM. Information is stored in the ECMs memory.

frequency   The number of events or cycles that occur in a period, usually 1 second.

hertz (Hz)   The unit for electrical frequency measurement, in cycles per second.

keep alive memory (KAM)   Memory that is retained by the ECM when the key is off.

microcontroller   A special-purpose processor with limited capabilities, designed to perform a set of specific tasks.

non-volatile memory   Memory that is not lost when power is removed or lost.

programmable read only memory (PROM)   Memory that stores programming information and cannot be easily written over.

pulse-width modulation (PWM)   An electrical signal that varies in on and off time.

random access memory (RAM)   A temporary storage place for information that needs to be quickly accessed.

read only memory (ROM)   Memory used for permanent storage of instructions and fixed values used by the ECM that control the microprocessor.

telematics   A branch of information technology that uses specialized applications for long-distance transmission of information to and from a vehicle.

volatile memory   A type of data storage that is lost or erased when the ignition power is switched off.

Review Questions

1. _____ is a non-volatile memory technology that is used to store operating instructions or programming for an ECM.
   a. Keep alive memory (KAM)
   b. Electrically erasable programmable read-only memory (EEPROM)
   c. Random access memory (RAM)
   d. Read-only memory (ROM)

2. _____ is memory used for permanent storage of instructions and fixed values used by the ECM that control the microprocessor.
   a. Read-only memory (ROM)
   b. Random access memory (RAM)
   c. Programmable read-only memory (PROM)
   d. Keep alive memory (KAM)

3. _____ is memory that is retained by the ECM when the key is off.
   a. Read-only memory (ROM)
   b. Random access memory (RAM)
   c. Keep alive memory (KAM)
   d. Programmable read-only memory (PROM)

4. _____ is memory that stores programming information and cannot be easily written over.
   a. Random access memory (RAM)
   b. Keep alive memory (KAM)
   c. Electrically erasable programmable read-only memory (EEPROM)
   d. Programmable read-only memory (PROM)

5. _____ is a temporary storage place for information that needs to be quickly accessed.
   a. Read-only memory (ROM)
   b. Random access memory (RAM)
   c. Keep alive memory (KAM)
   d. Electrically erasable programmable read-only memory (EEPROM)

6. The presence of _____ is communicated through the malfunction indicator lamps.
   a. faults
   b. outputs
   c. buffers
   d. trips

7. To convert analog signals to digital binary information special circuits, known as _____ or analog to digital converters, are used.
   a. faults
   b. outputs
   c. buffers
   d. trips

8. Programmable _____ provides flexibility to engines, transmissions, and body accessories for adaptation to specific job applications.
   a. software
   b. analog
   c. memory
   d. management

9. ROM, RAM, and PROM are examples of different types of computer _____.
   a. software
   b. analog
   c. management
   d. memory

10. A _____ report provides details such as diagnostic fault codes, fuel consumption, idle time, and emission system performance.
   a. fault   c. buffer
   b. trip   d. binary

ASE-Type Questions

1. Technician A says a trip report only provides details about fuel consumption, idle time, and emission system performance. Technician B says the trip report can be extracted from a vehicle's body control module during scheduled maintenance. Who is correct?
   a. Technician A
   b. Technician B
   c. Both Technician A and Technician B
   d. Neither Technician A nor Technician B

2. Technician A says every number from 0 to infinity and the letters of the alphabet can be represented by a combination of 0s and 1s using binary code. Technician B says every number from 1 to infinity and the alphabet letters can be represented using binary code. Who is correct?
   a. Technician A
   b. Technician B
   c. Both Technician A and Technician B
   d. Neither Technician A nor Technician B

3. Technician B says in as little as a couple of hours a stock vehicle chassis can be programmed to operate as an ambulance, an-on highway tractor, dump truck, or bus. Technician B says a vehicle chassis can be programmed to operate as any of those in just a few minutes with a few keystrokes. Who is correct?
   a. Technician A
   b. Technician B
   c. Both Technician A and Technician B
   d. Neither Technician A nor Technician B

4. Technician A says sensing functions collect data about operational conditions or the state of a device by measuring some values such as temperature or speed. Technician B says the sensing functions collect data about operational conditions or the state of a device by measuring some values such as position or pressure. Who is correct?
   a. Technician A
   b. Technician B
   c. Both Technician A and Technician B
   d. Neither Technician A nor Technician B

5. Technician A says when serial digital data is transmitted using a pair of wires, each wire will transmit a voltage pulse represented as a triangular waveform. Technician B says when serial digital data is transmitted using a pair of wires, each wire will transmit a voltage pulse represented as a rectangular waveform. Who is correct?
   a. Technician A
   b. Technician B
   c. Both Technician A and Technician B
   d. Neither Technician A nor Technician B

6. Technician A says the units for measuring pulse width are always expressed in units of time. Technician B says the term frequency refers to the number of data bits transmitted per second. Who is correct?
   a. Technician A
   b. Technician B
   c. Both Technician A and Technician B
   d. Neither Technician A nor Technician B

7. Technician A says a microprocessor or microcontroller is the heart of the control unit. Technician B says the microprocessor or microcontroller is also referred to as the electronic control module. Who is correct?
   a. Technician A
   b. Technician B
   c. Both Technician A and Technician B
   d. Neither Technician A nor Technician B

8. Technician A says random access memory is readable only. Technician B says random access memory is writable only. Who is correct?
   a. Technician A
   b. Technician B
   c. Both Technician A and Technician B
   d. Neither Technician A nor Technician B

9. Technician A says the number of events or cycles that occur in a period, usually two seconds, is called frequency. Technician A says the number of events or cycles that occur in a period, usually one second, is called frequency. Who is correct?
   a. Technician A
   b. Technician B
   c. Both Technician A and Technician B
   d. Neither Technician A nor Technician B

10. Technician A says a bit is the smallest piece of digital or binary information. Technician B says the bit is represented by a single 0 or 1. Who is correct?
    a. Technician A
    b. Technician B
    c. Both Technician A and Technician B
    d. Neither Technician A nor Technician B

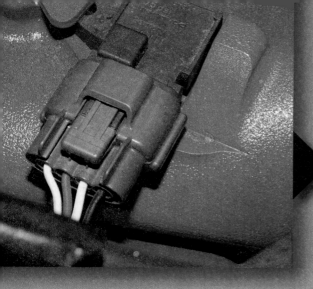

CHAPTER 22
Sensors

▶ NATEF Tasks

Diesel Engines

General
- Check and record electronic diagnostic codes. (pp 650–651)

Fuel System

Electronic Fuel Management System
- Inspect and test switches, sensors, controls, actuator components, and circuits; adjust or replace as needed. (pp 646–650)

Electrical/Electronic Systems

General Electrical Systems
- Check continuity in electrical/electronic circuits using appropriate test equipment. (pp 642–643, 652)
- Check applied voltages, circuit voltages, and voltage drops in electrical/electronic circuits using appropriate test equipment. (pp 648–649)

▶ Knowledge Objectives

After reading this chapter, you will be able to:
1. Identify and describe the operating strategies of electronic signal processing systems used in electrical system control on commercial vehicles. (pp 625–641)
2. Identify and describe the functions, construction, and application of electronic sensors used to produce electrical signals for electronic control systems. (pp 625–641)
3. Recommend and describe diagnostic procedures for sensors used in electronic control systems. (pp 641–653)

▶ Skills Objectives

There are no skills objectives for this chapter.

► Introduction

Devices that convert one form of energy into another are called transducers. Sensors are a type of transducer that convert physical conditions or states into electrical data. Pressure, temperature, angle, speed, mass, etc. are just a few of the changing physical variables about which sensors supply electrical data to processors. A distinction is made between sending units and sensors. Sensors provide information to electronic control units, whereas sending units provide information to instrument gauges.

► Types of Sensors

An enormous number of sensor types exist to measure diverse types of data required by increasingly sophisticated vehicle management systems.

- Accelerometers for vehicle dynamic control and airbags
- Pressure sensors for engine oil, fuel, crankcase, and intake boost
- Position sensors for wheel speed, camshafts, crankshafts, and pedal position
- Humidity sensors for adjusting air–fuel ratio control and cabin comfort control
- Sunlight and rain/moisture sensors
- Distance sensors for near obstacle detection and collision avoidance
- Magnetoresistive (MR) sensors that use the earth's magnetic field to operate vehicle electronic compasses and navigation systems
- Torque sensors
- Fuel level sensors
- Oil quality sensors
- Temperature sensors
- Coolant level sensors
- Barometric pressure sensors

- Mass airflow sensors
- Engine knock sensors
- Exhaust gas—NO_x, ammonia, and oxygen sensors
- Yaw sensors using the Coriolis effect to sense yaw rates
- Global positioning sensors for GPS

Active Versus Passive Sensors

All the types of sensors listed above are more simply classified other ways. For example, a sensor is considered active or passive depending on whether they use power supplied by the electronic control module (ECM) to operate. **Active sensors** use a current supplied by the ECM to operate while **passive sensors** do not **FIGURE 22-1**.

Other classifications of sensors include:

- Resistive sensors: rheostats, potentiometers, thermistors, piezoresistive sensors, Wheatstone bridge pressure sensors
- Voltage generators: oxygen sensors, NO_x sensors, ammonia sensors, variable reluctance sensors, piezoelectric sensors
- Switches
- Variable capacitance pressure sensors

Reference Voltage

Reference voltage (Vref) refers to a precisely regulated voltage supplied by the ECM to sensors. Reference voltage value is typically 5 volts direct current (VDC), but some manufacturers use 8 or 12 volts. The use of a reference voltage is important in processor operation, because the value of the variable resistor can be calculated by measuring voltage drop when another resistor with a known voltage input is connected in series with it. In **FIGURE 22-2**, +5Vref is used in the calculations performed by an ECM. Reference voltage also supplies

► You Are the Technician

A customer has brought a truck to your shop complaining that the engine will occasionally not accelerate. Sometimes, after the throttle pedal is pushed multiple times, the engine will only idle. Other times the engine drops to idle while the vehicle is moving in traffic. Sometimes the problem corrects itself after the ignition key is cycled; other times the throttle starts operating correctly on its own. After checking for fault codes, you learn the truck has had codes erased at another shop. You suspect the problem is in the accelerator position sensor (APS), but you wonder if the problem could be in the wiring or the fuel system, or if it's a power derate condition caused by some other fault. After carefully inspecting the wiring harness and connectors to the APS, you believe they are in good condition. You connect a software-based vehicle diagnostic program to the vehicle data link to monitor the APS. There are three APS signals displayed with different voltages on each sensor. Consider the following as you proceed:

1. Does this APS use an idle validation switch?
2. What complaint would the driver have if one, two, or three of the APS voltages were incorrect?
3. How will you determine if the APS has a fault?

active sensors with current to operate integrated circuits contained inside the sensor. Switches will also use +5Vref to signal the ECM.

Switches as Sensors

Switches are the simplest sensors of all, because they have no resistance in the closed position and infinite resistance in the open position. Switches are categorized as sensors whenever they provide information to an electronic control system. The data may indicate a physical value such as open or closed, up or down, high or low (e.g., a coolant level sensor or oil pressure switch), or it may indicate on and off (e.g., a brake light switch).

Switches as Digital Signals

The simplest digital signal is a single pole single throw (SPST) switch. It is found in either an open or closed state. The on/off, open/closed state data provided by this switch can provide input information to an ECM required for decision making. For example, the decision to start an engine based on whether a transmission is in neutral or the clutch is disengaged depends on the signal from a switch **FIGURE 22-3**. A zero-volt signal would present as an open switch, while 12 volts would present as a closed switch. Ignition, brake, or door switches provide similar data to ECMs to answer simple yes or no, open or closed, on or off questions posed by operating software.

FIGURE 22-1 This opened pressure sensor is an active sensor. Note the integrated circuit used to change the sensed physical data into an electrical signal used by the ECM.

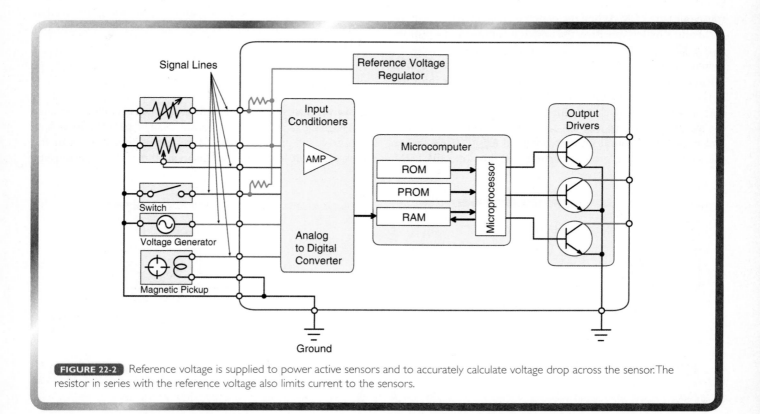

FIGURE 22-2 Reference voltage is supplied to power active sensors and to accurately calculate voltage drop across the sensor. The resistor in series with the reference voltage also limits current to the sensors.

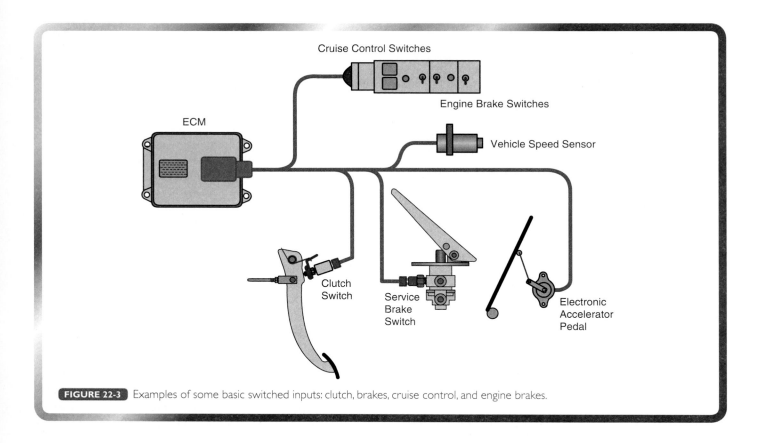

FIGURE 22-3 Examples of some basic switched inputs: clutch, brakes, cruise control, and engine brakes.

Pull-Up and Pull-Down Switches

Switches are further categorized by their connection to a current source and the ECM. When the switch is connected between the ECM and a battery positive, the switch it is known as a **pull-up switch** **FIGURE 22-4** . A circuit inside the module monitoring the switch connection will measure the voltage drop across a fixed resistor inside the ECM. The voltage data will provide information to processing circuits that will determine whether the circuit or switch is open, closed, out of range, or shorted to ground.

A **pull-down switch** is connected between the ECM and a negative ground current potential **FIGURE 22-5** . When the switch is closed, ground current will flow into the ECM.

A circuit inside the ECM monitoring the switch connection will also measure voltage drop across a fixed resistor. Once again, voltage data will provide information to processing circuits that will determine whether the circuit or switch is open, closed, out of range, or shorted to a positive current potential.

Resistive Sensors

Resistive sensors are a class of sensors that will condition or change a voltage signal applied to the sensor. Many types of resistive sensors exist, and pressure, temperature, and position sensors are the most common. Some of these sensors are three-wire active sensors.

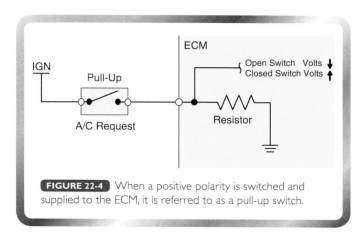

FIGURE 22-4 When a positive polarity is switched and supplied to the ECM, it is referred to as a pull-up switch.

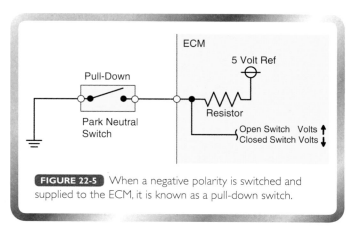

FIGURE 22-5 When a negative polarity is switched and supplied to the ECM, it is known as a pull-down switch.

Thermistors

A **thermistor** is a temperature-sensitive variable resistor commonly used to measure coolant, oil, fuel, and air temperatures. The name itself combines the words thermal and resistor. Thermistors are two-wire sensors that change resistance in proportion to temperature. This means thermistors provide analog data to processing circuits. When the sensor is measuring air temperature such as in an intake manifold, the sensor is often constructed with a plastic body to minimize heat transfer from surrounding metal. When used to measure coolant or oil temperature, the sensor element is enclosed in a brass case to make it more responsive to temperature change **FIGURE 22-6**.

Thermistors are semiconductor devices with no moving parts. Two types of thermistors exist: negative and positive temperature coefficient. In a negative temperature coefficient (NTC) thermistor, the resistance decreases as the temperature increases **FIGURE 22-7**. In a positive temperature coefficient

FIGURE 22-6 Three thermistor applications. **A.** For intake manifold temperature. **B.** For coolant temperature. **C.** For intake manifold temperature. Note the semiconductor material in the fast response, air-intake thermistor.

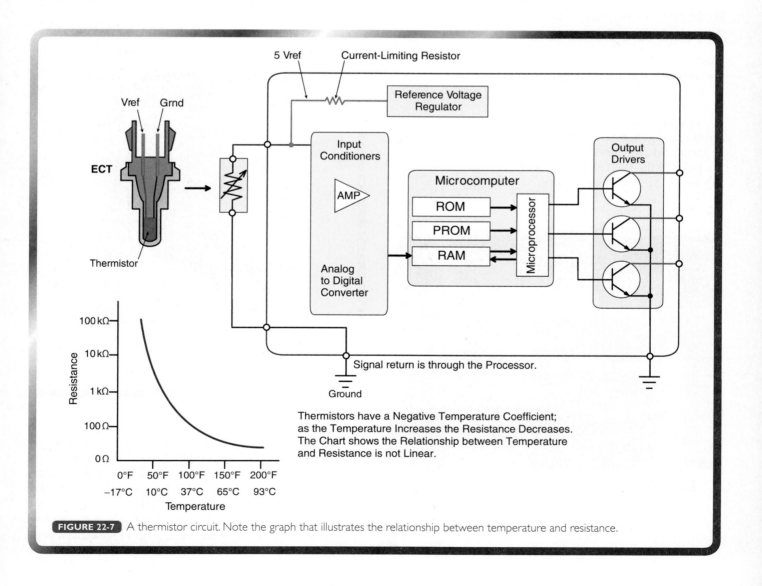

FIGURE 22-7 A thermistor circuit. Note the graph that illustrates the relationship between temperature and resistance.

(PTC) thermistor, the resistance increases as the temperature increases **FIGURE 22-8**.

The most common type of thermistor is an NTC, in which the sensor's resistance goes down as the temperature goes up. So, when the sensor is cold, the sensor resistance is high, and the ECM measures a lower return signal voltage in comparison to reference voltage. The voltage drop across the sensor is interpreted as a temperature value. Likewise, when the engine warms, the internal resistance of the sensor decreases and causes a proportional increase in the return signal voltage.

Rheostats

Rheostats are also two-wire variable resistance sensors. They are not commonly used as input devices to an ECM but are instead used to signal sending units such as for fuel level and oil pressure **FIGURE 22-9** and **FIGURE 22-10**. Rheostats use a variable sliding contact moving along a resistive wire. When current passes through the resistive wire, the sliding contact will conduct current flow from the wire. Current intensity at the sliding contact will vary depending on its position along the resistive wire.

Reference Voltage Sensors— Three-Wire Sensors

Three-wire sensors, regardless of how they appear or what function they perform, have a common wiring configuration: they all have ground, signal return, and positive voltage reference wire leads **FIGURE 22-11**.

One wire provides reference voltage to the sensor. If it is an active sensor, reference voltage will supply current to operate an integrated chip inside the device. Reference voltage is also produced by the ECM as a comparison point for voltage calculations associated with sensor data.

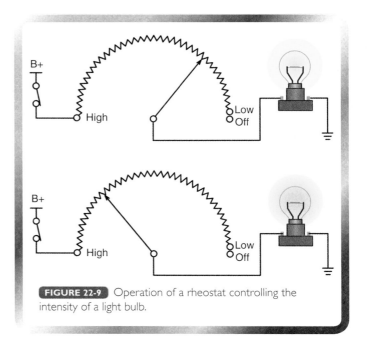

FIGURE 22-9 Operation of a rheostat controlling the intensity of a light bulb.

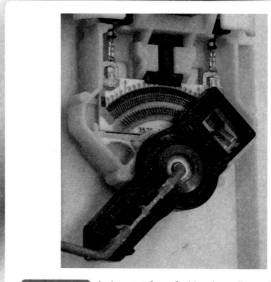

FIGURE 22-10 A rheostat for a fuel level sending unit. The wiper-whiskers transfer current from one resistive track to another. Signal return is supplied by the wipers.

FIGURE 22-8 Thermistors found in **A.** diesel particulate filters (DPFs) and **B.** selective catalyst reduction systems are often **C.** PTC thermistors. NTC thermistor material could not withstand the heat encountered when regenerating the DPF.

The second sensor wire provides a negative ground signal through the ECM and not to engine ground. This ECM return or ground is also called zero volt return (ZVR) and is identical to engine ground except it is free of any type of electrical interference. Active sensors will use the ZVR or negative ground for the other source of current to operate the sensor. In resistive sensors, the ZVR acts as a reference point to measure voltage drop across the sensor.

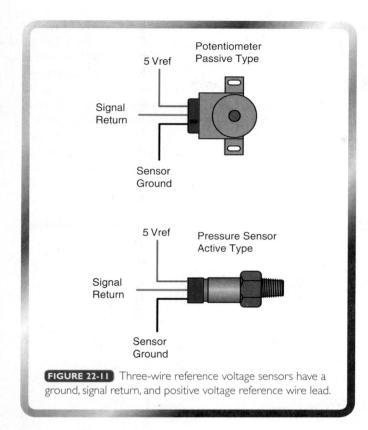

FIGURE 22-11 Three-wire reference voltage sensors have a ground, signal return, and positive voltage reference wire lead.

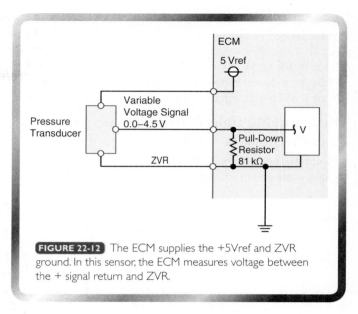

FIGURE 22-12 The ECM supplies the +5Vref and ZVR ground. In this sensor, the ECM measures voltage between the + signal return and ZVR.

The third wire is a signal return from the sensor. This circuit provides a positive voltage proportional to the physical value measured by the sensor. If pressure is the physical input measured, the signal wire data will carry an analog voltage signal proportional to pressure. Typically, low voltage of, for example, 0.8 volts will represent little to no pressure, while 3.9 volts will represent high pressure depending on the range of the sensor.

The advantage of using three-wire sensors is that they provide comprehensive diagnostic information about the sensor and its circuit operation. Sending units can be constructed with reduced complexity and expense and yet still provide the ECM with data to operate an engine, transmission, or other device. However, sending units lack the capability to self-monitor circuit operation. Consider an open or shorted to ground signal wire from a single-wire sensor. In this case there is no means by which the ECM could accurately evaluate the situation. The wire could be broken or rubbed though, and still the unit voltage data received by the ECM would not be different from normal. It is very labor intensive to find an electrical fault based on only an operational symptom—no fault codes or malfunction indicator lights are available to identify a circuit problem.

The ECM does have capabilities to monitor and diagnose two- and three-wire sensor circuits to an extent not possible with single-wire sensors. By monitoring the voltage range of the ground return path, signal voltage, and reference voltage, the ECM can determine if the sensor and circuit are functioning correctly **FIGURE 22-12**.

Sensor values can be compared with expected values to determine if the data is rational. An explanation of how sensors and electronic circuits perform self-diagnostics and generate codes is covered in the On-Board Diagnostics chapter.

Potentiometers

<u>Potentiometers</u> are similar to rheostats in that they vary signal voltage depending on the position of a sliding contact or wiper moving across a resistive material. They are three-wire sensors with the signal wire connected to the internal wiper. Potentiometers supply analog data to processing circuits.

A common application of a potentiometer is a position sensor such as the throttle position sensor (TPS) **FIGURE 22-13**. This sensor is connected to a throttle pedal and provides data regarding the driver's desired engine speed or power output by measuring pedal angle or travel. The ECM will measure the voltage drop between the ground return circuit and the signal wire to calculate pedal position. Voltage produced from the signal wire will be proportional to the pedal travel. This means that at idle or part throttle, the voltage at the signal wire will be low. Increasing pedal travel will produce increasing voltage to the signal wire as the sensor's internal wiper moves closer to the +5Vref end of the resistive element. When the pedal returns to idle, the wiper will have less voltage because it is farther way from the +5Vref wire and the current pathway is longer and therefore more resistive.

Idle Validation Switches and Throttle Position Sensors

A short circuit or incorrect data from the TPS, also called the accelerator position sensor (APS), can potentially cause uncontrolled acceleration of an engine. For safety reasons, manufacturers will build an additional safety system to verify throttle position. One common throttle safety system is the <u>idle validation switch (IVS)</u>. This circuit uses two switches: at idle, one switch will be open and the other closed. Off idle, the switches change state, which means the normally open switch closes, and the normally closed switch opens **FIGURE 22-14**. This data is used by the ECM to verify the driver has in fact moved the accelerator pedal and the circuit is not malfunctioning. At idle, the state of the switch must correspond to the TPS voltage sensed by the ECM. If the expected position sensor voltage and IVS position do not match, the ECM will revert engine speed to idle or not allow the engine rpm to increase beyond idle speed.

Dual- and Multiple-Path Throttle Position Sensors

To improve reliability of a TPS and validate accelerator position signals, some manufacturers are replacing the single TPS sensor track with a dual-track or even three-path TPS. The voltage of one sensor pathway is compared with another to verify that the sensor is operating at expected values **FIGURE 22-15**. If there is an unexpected difference between the voltage signals, the engine will only operate at idle speed. If one or even two of the resistive tracks wears out, the engine may still accelerate normally, but an APS fault is logged and the yellow fault warning indicator lamp will illuminate. Dual-path TPSs are potentiometers. Hall effect TPSs are even more reliable, because they have no moving parts. This throttle position sensor uses an AC magnetic field to induce current in a rotor moved by the throttle pedal. A circuit

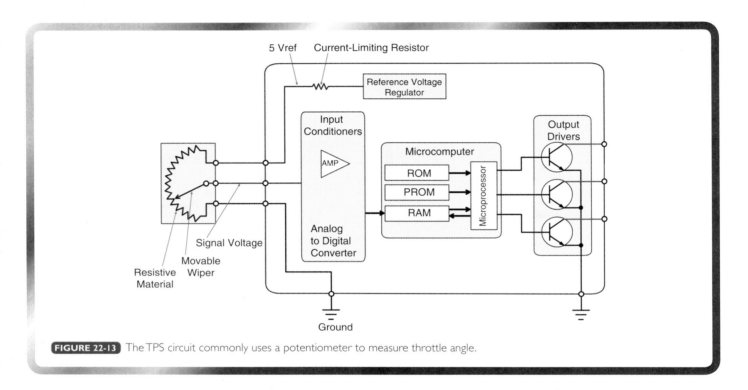

FIGURE 22-13 The TPS circuit commonly uses a potentiometer to measure throttle angle.

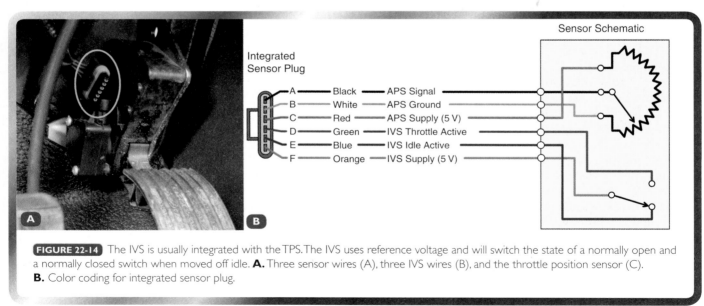

FIGURE 22-14 The IVS is usually integrated with the TPS. The IVS uses reference voltage and will switch the state of a normally open and a normally closed switch when moved off idle. **A.** Three sensor wires (A), three IVS wires (B), and the throttle position sensor (C). **B.** Color coding for integrated sensor plug.

is used to convert the rotor's position into pedal position. This type of noncontact TPS sensor has no sliding friction parts to wear out **FIGURE 22-16**.

Pressure Sensors

Pressure measurements, such as intake manifold boost, barometric pressure, and oil and fuel pressure, use two types of sensor technology: variable capacitance sensors and strain gauge resistive sensors. These are both active sensors that produce analog output signals.

Strain Gauge

A strain gauge measures small changes in the resistance of tiny wires caused by stretching or contraction. Construction of this type of pressure-sensing device uses resistive wires, called strain gauge wires, embedded in a flexible glass block. Behind the block may be a vacuum chamber to provide a reference point of zero for measurement of absolute pressure. If the device measures gauge pressure, the chamber will have atmospheric pressure as the reference value of zero.

When the glass plate flexes under pressure, the small resistive wires in it will change dimensions slightly. As the plate distorts due to pressure changes, it changes the resistance of the wires slightly **FIGURE 22-17**. A Wheatstone bridge electrical

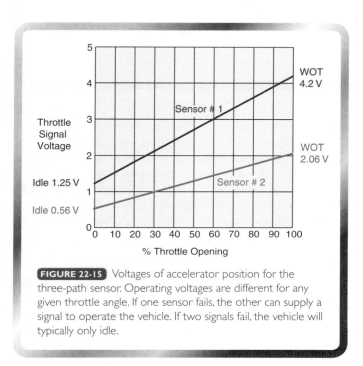

FIGURE 22-15 Voltages of accelerator position for the three-path sensor. Operating voltages are different for any given throttle angle. If one sensor fails, the other can supply a signal to operate the vehicle. If two signals fail, the vehicle will typically only idle.

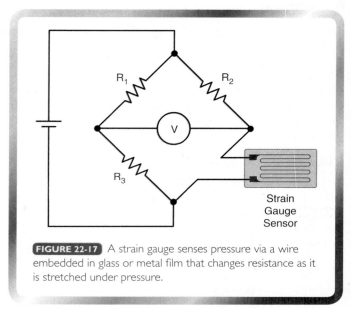

FIGURE 22-17 A strain gauge senses pressure via a wire embedded in glass or metal film that changes resistance as it is stretched under pressure.

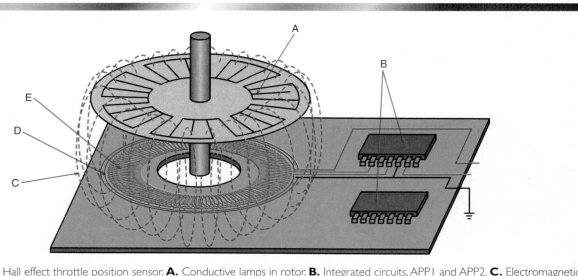

FIGURE 22-16 Hall effect throttle position sensor. **A.** Conductive lamps in rotor. **B.** Integrated circuits, APP1 and APP2. **C.** Electromagnetic field lines of force. **D.** Stator excitation coils. **E.** Stator receiver coils.

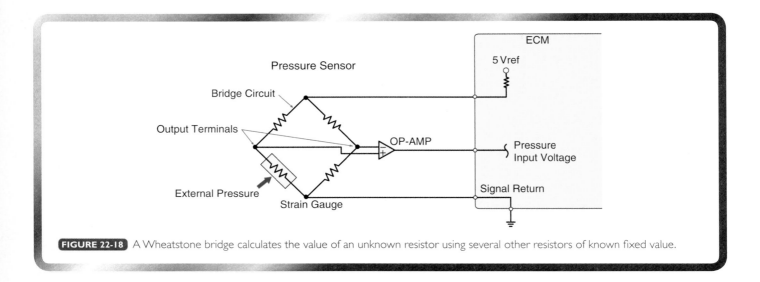

FIGURE 22-18 A Wheatstone bridge calculates the value of an unknown resistor using several other resistors of known fixed value.

circuit, which measures changes in resistance of an unknown variable resistor, is used to measure this small change in resistance of the strain gauge wires **FIGURE 22-18**. By measuring this small change in the wires' resistance, the pressure applied to the plate is determined.

Piezoresistive Sensors

Piezoresistive sensors rely on the ability of certain mineral crystals to produce voltage or change resistance when compressed **FIGURE 22-19**. Rather than using a strain gauge wire construction, these sensors have a piezoresistive crystal arranged with a Wheatstone bridge to measure the change in resistance of the piezo crystal. These sensors produce analog electrical signals.

The advantage of these sensors is their ability to measure very high pressures. Because of the sturdiness of the crystal, piezo

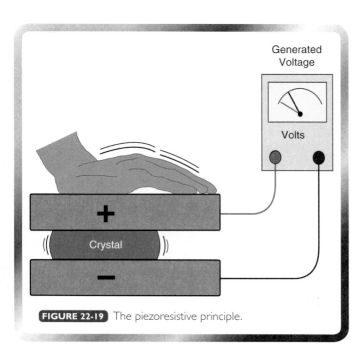

FIGURE 22-19 The piezoresistive principle.

sensors are better adapted to measuring vibration and dynamic or continuous pressure changes. Knock sensors measuring abnormal combustion signals are a common application of piezoresistive sensors. Another type of piezoresistive sensor uses mineral crystals arranged on a substrate of silicon **FIGURE 22-20**. The crystals behave as a semiconductor to produce electrical signals that are amplified and conditioned by internal circuits. Silicon-based piezoresistive sensors are very sensitive to slight pressure changes.

Variable Capacitance Pressure Sensor

A variable capacitance pressure sensor is an active sensor that measures both dynamic and static pressure. Though they are more expensive to manufacturer than a piezoresistive or strain gauge sensor, the variable capacitance pressure sensor offers a greater range of measurement flexibility and more accurate readings. Because it is an active sensor, the stronger circuit signals to the ECM are not as vulnerable to voltage drop or electromagnetic interference.

Variable capacitance sensors use the distance between two plates, or dielectric strength, inside the sensor to measure pressure **FIGURE 22-21**. One plate diaphragm will move in response to intake manifold, oil, fuel, or some other physical pressure being measured. The other plate is fixed and has on one side a reference vacuum or pressure chamber to calibrate it for accurate pressure readings. As pressure increases or decreases, the distance between the two plates will change. An electrical charge is applied to the fixed plate, and the time it takes to charge the plate is measured. Charging time will change proportionally to the dielectric strength between the plates. An electronic circuit in the chip integrated inside the sensor measures the changing voltage/time value produced by the flexing plate and outputs an analog electrical signal of less than 5 volts.

Voltage Generators

This category of sensors is passive and produces an analog signal of varying voltage or AC frequency. Variable reluctance and galvanic sensors are two examples of voltage-generating sensors. While the gas sensors used on today's diesel engines are active sensors with modules that produce and condition signals,

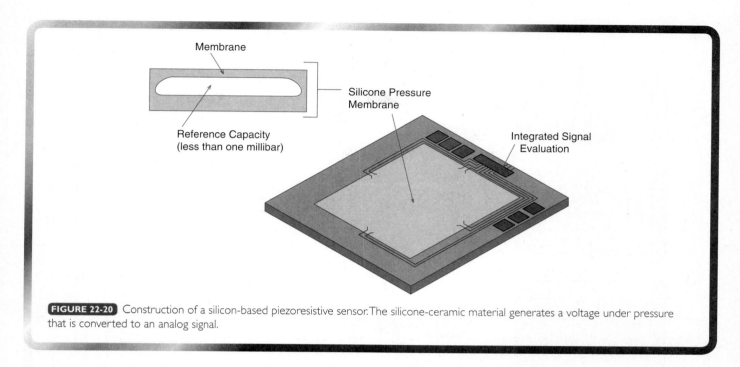

FIGURE 22-20 Construction of a silicon-based piezoresistive sensor. The silicone-ceramic material generates a voltage under pressure that is converted to an analog signal.

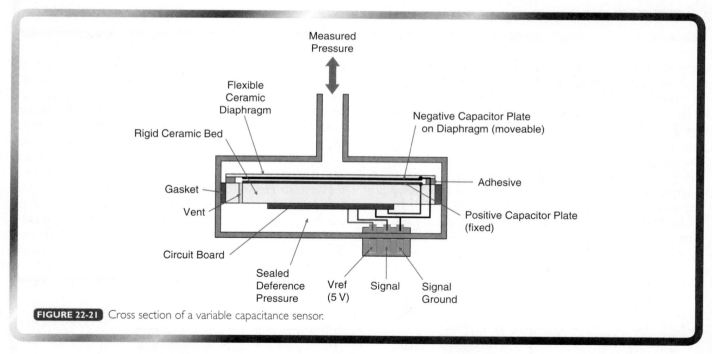

FIGURE 22-21 Cross section of a variable capacitance sensor.

the operating principle is still a galvanic reaction that produces voltage. Exhaust stream gas sensors are used to measure oxygen, NO_x, or ammonia gases in the exhaust stream. On diesel engines, data from oxygen sensors is commonly used to adjust exhaust gas recirculation (EGR) rates and sometimes to adjust the intake throttle plate position to control the operation of exhaust aftertreatment systems. Ammonia and NO_x sensors are used to identify faults in the exhaust aftertreatment systems on most diesels from 2010 and later. Ammonia sensors are more frequently used on diesel engines from 2015 and later.

Variable Reluctance Sensors

Variable reluctance sensors are two-wire sensors used to measure rotational speed. Wheel speed, vehicle speed, engine speed, and camshaft and crankshaft position sensors are their most common applications **FIGURE 22-22**. Signals from the camshaft and crankshaft position sensors are used to calculate engine position for determining the beginning of engine firing order and injection timing. The camshaft gear has raised lugs that generate waveform signals to identify top dead center (TDC) for each cylinder. When graphed against time, the AC waveform produced

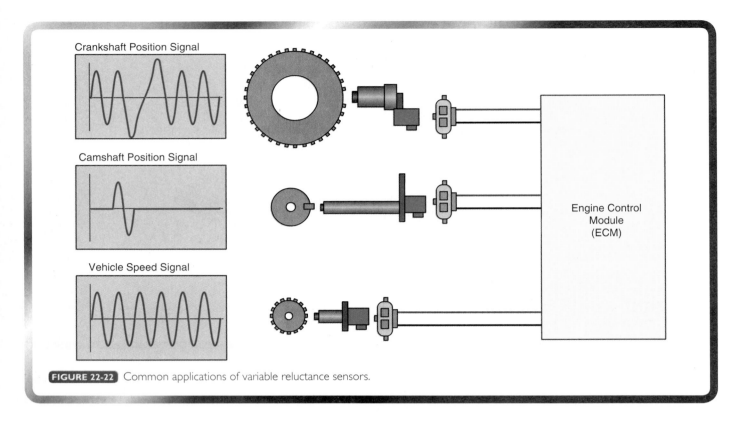

FIGURE 22-22 Common applications of variable reluctance sensors.

by the sensor data is used to precisely calculate not only engine speed but also degrees of crankshaft rotation **FIGURE 22-23**.

The ability of a material to conduct or resist magnetic lines of force is known as reluctance. Variable reluctance sensors use changing sensor reluctance to induce current flow by changing magnetic field strengths inside the sensor. A variable reluctance sensor is constructed with two main elements: a coil of narrow-gauge wire wrapped many times around a permanent magnet, and a reluctor ring (also called the sensor wheel, pulse wheel, or tone wheel), which has soft iron teeth and rotates on a shaft **FIGURE 22-24**. Because ferrous metals, particularly soft iron, have low reluctance and air has high reluctance to magnetic lines of force, the strength of the sensor's magnetic field

expands and collapses as the reluctor ring's iron teeth pass across the sensor's magnet. By changing the density of magnetic lines of force, alternately expanding and contracting the magnetic field when a gear tooth or gap passes by the sensor, current is induced in the wire coil around the sensor magnet. Increasing reluctor wheel speed increases the voltage induced in the sensor. A small air gap of approximately 0.02–0.03" (0.51–0.76 mm) is maintained between the sensor and the reluctor wheel. Too much or too little air gap will prevent the sensor from detecting tooth movement. Software inside the ECM will detect and count the number of teeth passing by the sensor to calculate shaft speed.

If the processing circuits track how many teeth complete one rotation of the shaft, rpm is easily calculated. If the engine

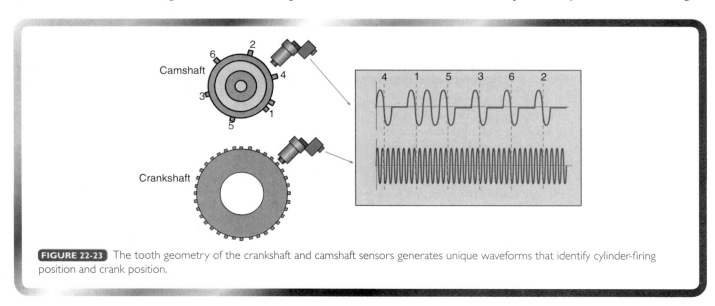

FIGURE 22-23 The tooth geometry of the crankshaft and camshaft sensors generates unique waveforms that identify cylinder-firing position and crank position.

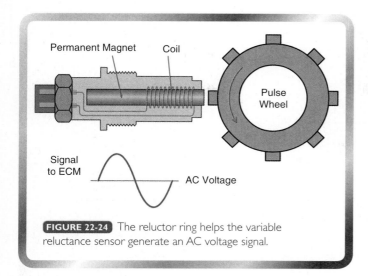

FIGURE 22-24 The reluctor ring helps the variable reluctance sensor generate an AC voltage signal.

software can divide the number of teeth passing by the sensor per unit of time, it can precisely calculate the number of degrees of crankshaft rotation.

Hall Effect Sensors

Like variable reluctance sensors, **Hall effect sensors** are commonly used to measure the rotational speed of a shaft. Though they are more complex and expensive to manufacture than variable reluctance sensors, Hall effect sensors have the advantage of producing a digital signal square waveform and have strong signal strength at low shaft rotational speeds. This is especially useful when cranking an engine when engine rpm is slow. The durability and accuracy of the digital signal is preferred when more precise injection event timing is necessary, which is why most engines today use Hall effect sensors.

The operation principle of a Hall effect sensor is simple: current flow through a Hall effect material is made from semiconductive material that changes resistance in the presence of a magnetic field **FIGURE 22-25**. When current is applied to a Hall effect material, no conduction occurs. However, in the

presence of a magnetic field, the material will conduct current. The electrical signal output from the sensor material is analog, but circuits within the sensor will convert and amplify the rising and falling voltage into a square-shaped electrical waveform **FIGURE 22-26**.

To produce the signal from the Hall effect sensor, two configurations are used. The most common arrangement is the use of a metal interrupter ring or shutter and a permanent magnet positioned across from the sensor. Because ferrous metals have a lower magnetic reluctance than air, magnetic lines of force from a magnet placed opposite the sensor will flow through the metal shield rather than the sensor. Gaps in the interrupter ring will allow magnetism to penetrate the sensor, changing current flow through the Hall effect material. Attaching the interrupter ring to a moving shaft provides rotational speed information to the control module.

Another configuration for the Hall effect sensor incorporates the magnet into the sensor itself. When a gear tooth or other ferrous metal trigger is present near the sensor, the magnetic field expands. Movement of the ferrous trigger or tooth away from the magnet causes magnetic field contraction. This pulsing magnetic field generates the signal within the sensor **FIGURE 22-27**.

Oxygen Sensors

Oxygen sensors are used to measure air–fuel ratio in order to calibrate EGR flow rates and air–fuel ratios for exhaust aftertreatment devices. Diesel engines use a heated planar, wideband, zirconium-dioxide (ZrO_2) dual-cell oxygen sensor. This sensor technology is different from the narrow-band oxygen sensor technology used commonly on gasoline engines operating at stoichiometric air–fuel ratios. Wide-band oxygen sensors are used in diesel engines because they use lean-burn combustion systems, which normally leaves an excess of air in the exhaust. Rather than producing a sharply falling and rising voltage near 0.5 volts, with 2% exhaust oxygen content found in gasoline engines, wide-band sensors produce a voltage proportional to a widely varying oxygen level **FIGURE 22-28**. The type of ceramic sensing element commonly used by wide-band sensors is

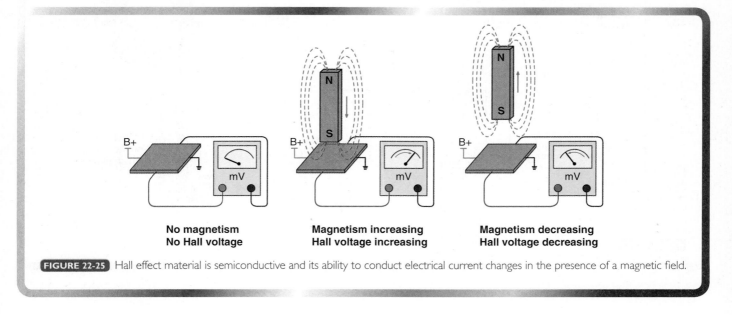

**No magnetism
No Hall voltage**

**Magnetism increasing
Hall voltage increasing**

**Magnetism decreasing
Hall voltage decreasing**

FIGURE 22-25 Hall effect material is semiconductive and its ability to conduct electrical current changes in the presence of a magnetic field.

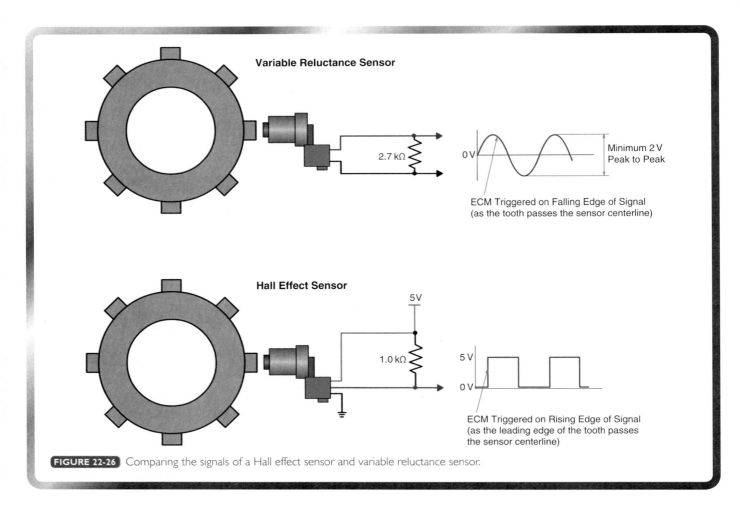

FIGURE 22-26 Comparing the signals of a Hall effect sensor and variable reluctance sensor.

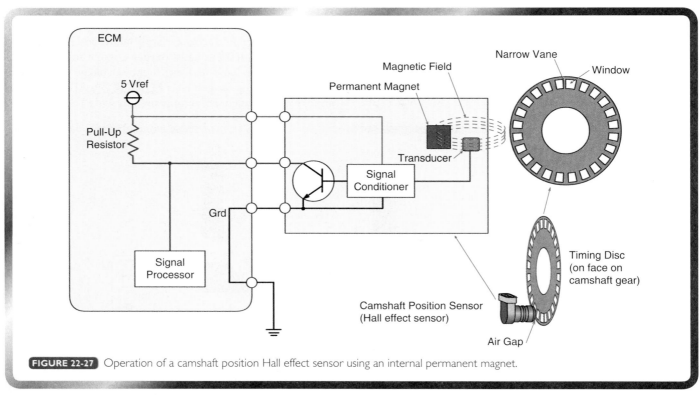

FIGURE 22-27 Operation of a camshaft position Hall effect sensor using an internal permanent magnet.

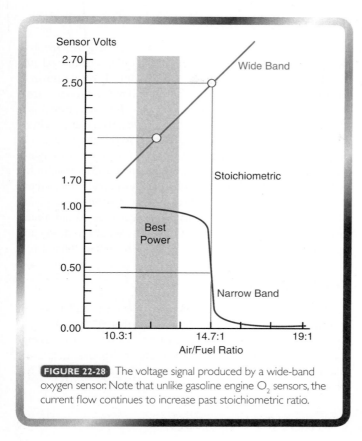

FIGURE 22-28 The voltage signal produced by a wide-band oxygen sensor. Note that unlike gasoline engine O_2 sensors, the current flow continues to increase past stoichiometric ratio.

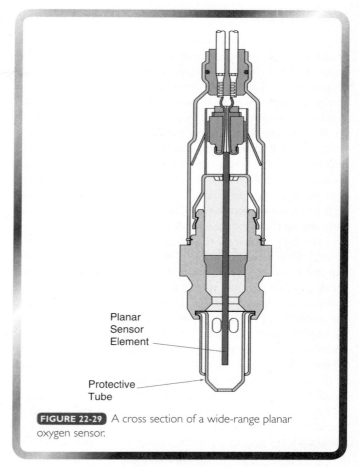

FIGURE 22-29 A cross section of a wide-range planar oxygen sensor.

a platinum-coated oxide of zirconium (Zr). An important property of this ceramic is that it conducts oxygen ions when voltage is applied at high temperatures.

Diesel oxygen sensors are **wide-range planar sensors**, which means they are flat rather than thimble-shaped like the sensors used on older gasoline-fueled engines **FIGURE 22-29**. They are also wide-band, which means they generate a signal with a wide air–fuel ratio between 0.7:1 and infinity. When heated to over 1200°F (700°C), the sensor becomes electrically conductive to oxygen ions. Because the oxygen content in the exhaust sample chamber is less than the oxygen concentration in the atmosphere, the oxygen content absorbed by the platinum coating on the ZrO_2 ceramic that contacts the exhaust and the coating that contacts the air will be slightly different **FIGURE 22-30**. This chemical difference in the sensor ceramic generates a voltage proportional to the oxygen content in the exhaust stream. The greater the difference in oxygen content, the higher the voltage. This voltage is produced because of the galvanic effect in which dissimilar metals in the presence of an electrolyte will produce electric current. Using the voltage produced across the two coatings, an amplifier circuit, called an oxygen pump cell circuit, will transfer excess electrons from the coating in the exhaust gas chamber to an electron-depleted electrode in the atmospheric reference chamber. The amount of current used to transfer these electrons is proportional to air–fuel ratio, and a circuit will precisely calculate air–fuel ratios based on the amount of current required to balance the voltage differential.

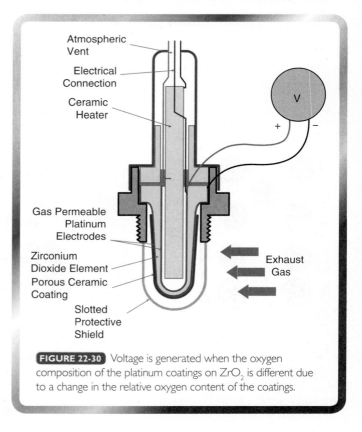

FIGURE 22-30 Voltage is generated when the oxygen composition of the platinum coatings on ZrO_2 is different due to a change in the relative oxygen content of the coatings.

NO_x Sensors

NO_x **sensors** are used to evaluate the operation of selective catalyst reduction (SCR) systems. These sensors measure NO_x from the engine and NO_x from the tailpipe, and should verify a dramatic drop in NO_x emissions. NO_x sensors are constructed and operate similarly to wide-range planar oxygen sensors using ZrO_2 ceramic substrate, except different concentrations of alloys are used in the NO_x sensor's platinum sensor walls. Also, NO_x sensors include a chamber that first removes excess oxygen, then separates NO_x into nitrogen and oxygen, and then pumps the resulting oxygen through the chamber walls. The two-chamber shape and multilayered platinum element enable these sensors to differentiate with high precision oxygen ions originating from nitric oxide (NO) from among the oxygen ions present in the exhaust gas.

The NO_x sensor's ZrO_2 chamber, which is the size of a thumbnail, is heated to 1200°F (700°C). It is housed in a metal can that has a hole for exhaust gas entrance. The chamber walls break apart the NO into nitrogen and oxygen components. The amount of oxygen produced at this stage is proportional to the amount of NO. ZrO_2 ceramic substrate will pump oxygen through the wall when a current is placed on both sides of the chamber wall. As oxygen is pumped from the first chamber, the amount of oxygen can be measured as it passes through the wall of the second chamber because it generates a voltage proportional to its concentration. Because the oxygen ions originated only from NO_x, an accurate measure is derived for NO_x in the exhaust gas. A module connected to the sensor conditions the electrical signal to represent a value for the amount of NO_x sensed in the exhaust stream **FIGURE 22-31**.

Ammonia Sensors

An NO_x SCR system used on late-model diesel engines involves injecting urea, a colorless and odorless liquid, into the exhaust stream. Exposed to exhaust heat, the urea quickly breaks down to form ammonia, which reacts with NO_x and renders it into harmless nitrogen, water, and oxygen molecules. However, ammonia is a noxious substance and should not escape into the atmosphere. The potential for ammonia to be released to the atmosphere has led to the required use of an ammonia sensor for most engines produced since 2014. The **ammonia sensor** provides data to the ECM that is used to determine whether ammonia is detected out of an anticipated range. Constructed like a wide-range planar NO_x or oxygen sensor, an ammonia sensor uses an aluminum oxide substrate rather than a ZrO_2 planar element to detect and generate a voltage for ammonia in a range from 0 to 100 ppm.

Soot Sensors

Another new sensor introduced in 2014 is a particulate sensor that measures any soot present in the exhaust. This sensor is a type of variable capacitance sensor that uses soot to change the dielectric strength between two charged plates. Increasing amounts of soot or particulate matter will reduce the dielectric strength and the electric charge the plates can store.

Mass Airflow Sensors

The mass airflow (MAF) sensor is a device that measures the weight of air entering the engine intake. Its unique design also

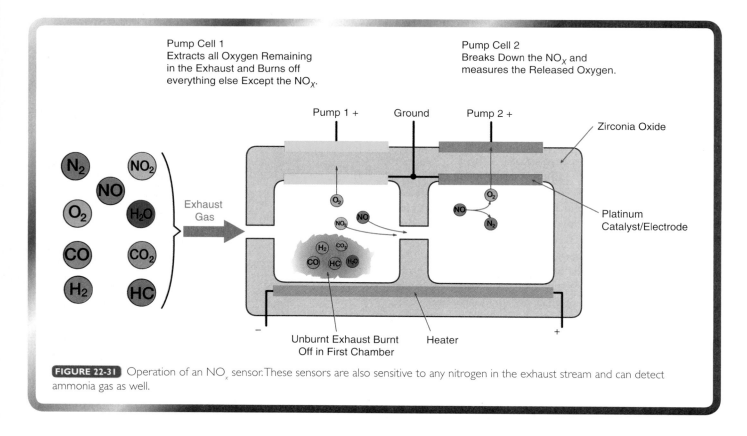

FIGURE 22-31 Operation of an NO_x sensor. These sensors are also sensitive to any nitrogen in the exhaust stream and can detect ammonia gas as well.

reports data about air density and, to some extent, the vapor content.

MAF sensors are common on engines operating at stoichiometric air–fuel ratios. However, on the diesel engines operating with an excess air ratio, the MAF is used as part of the heavy-duty on-board diagnostics (HD-OBD) component monitor for the EGR. A variety of electrical signals originate from MAF sensors, but all work using a hot wire operating principle. Heated platinum wires or a thin film of silicon nitride embedded with several heated platinum wires are located in the intake air stream. A heating circuit maintains a fixed voltage drop across the wires, maintaining a constant resistance and temperature of the wires regardless of the airflow in the intake system. This means that if a voltage drop of 5 volts is maintained across the heated wire, more current needs to flow through the wire if it cools faster due to increased airflow. Similarly, if airflow drops, less current is needed to maintain the same voltage drop across the wire **FIGURE 22-32**. Circuits internal to the MAF measure the variation in current flow proportional to the cooling effect of air mass. Due to the large valve overlap characteristic of diesel engines, some intake air may be forced back out in pulses from the intake system. MAF sensors on some engines use a reverse airflow detection circuit. Because colder air is denser than warmer air, manufacturers will also use an air temperature sensor to provide additional data for calculations to compensate for the change in air mass **FIGURE 22-33**.

Output Circuits

Output circuits, or output control devices, consist of display devices, serial data for network communication, and electromagnetic operator devices. The two basic types of operators are solenoids and relays. Injectors will use solenoids to meter fuel and adjust the timing of injection events.

Transistors inside the ECM are most often used to open or close circuits controlling these operators. A small amount of current flowing from the microprocessor through the transistor base will control the output devices by supplying either a ground or battery current to complete a circuit **FIGURE 22-34**. Output drivers use field effect transistors (FETs) that are switched either on or off with very small voltages and produce little heat, which makes them ideal for output drivers.

▶ Sensors and Position Calculations

Engine control systems need to determine the correct cylinder and point in the combustion cycle for injection. In order to send an electrical signal to fire the injectors, the ECM needs to know two things:

1. *Crankshaft position.* The ECM must know the exact position of the crankshaft in reference to TDC, that is, the number of degrees the crankshaft has rotated since it turned past TDC.

2. *Cylinder identification.* This information is necessary to determine in which cylinder the injection event should take place, based on cylinder stroke position. Once the ECM can determine when the first cylinder has reached TDC compression stroke, it can use the engine firing order stored in memory to fire the remaining cylinders in the correct sequence. However, because the crankshaft rotates through 720 degrees of a four-stroke operating cycle, or two rotations of the crankshaft, cylinder stroke for any given cylinder can only be determined after the camshaft has passed through at least one revolution. To measure crankshaft position and identify cylinder stroke to begin a firing sequence, manufacturers have developed a number of strategies using either variable reluctance or Hall effect sensors.

FIGURE 22-32 Heated wires that change resistance as airflow across the sensor increases or decreases. Air mass is calculated based how much electrical current is required to cancel the cooling effect of airflow across a heated wire.

FIGURE 22-33 A combination pressure and temperature sensor is used to calculate air mass entering an engine using a speed density algorithm. Note the two white signal wires.

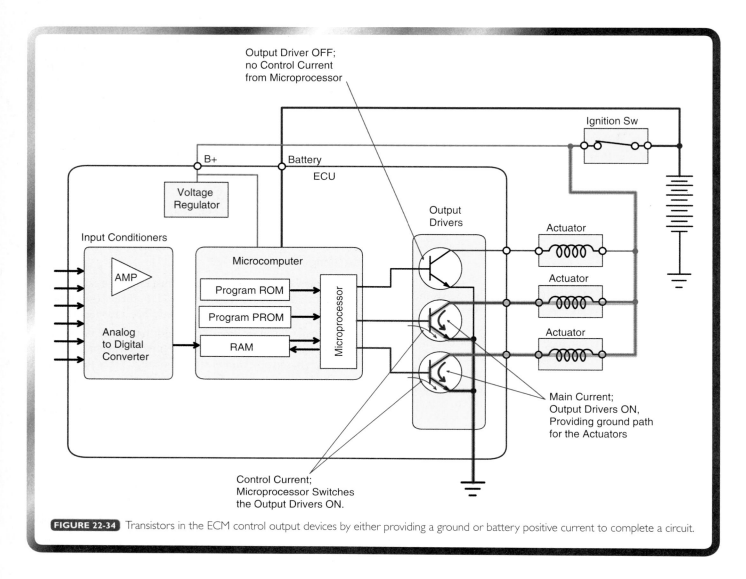

FIGURE 22-34 Transistors in the ECM control output devices by either providing a ground or battery positive current to complete a circuit.

Single Engine Position Sensor

Teeth or raised lugs on a cam gear that turns at one-half engine speed can generate signals using a Hall effect or variable reluctance sensor. A number of evenly spaced reluctor teeth, corresponding to the number of cylinders an engine has, will produce a waveform or pattern that can be used to calculate the rotational velocity and engine position. This means that for every tooth that passes over the sensor, the ECM can calculate a specific number of degrees of crank or camshaft rotation has occurred. Counting the signals produced by reluctor wheel teeth and measuring the time elapsed between signals generated by the sensor allows the ECM to precisely calculate engine rotation in fractions of degrees.

Evenly spaced reluctor ring teeth or lugs, however, will not identify the cylinder stroke position. To identify TDC of the first cylinder's compression stroke, the cam gear may use an additional tooth or lug to identify the stroke position of each cylinder. A seventh tooth or lug on the cam gear of a six-cylinder engine could correspond to TDC of the first cylinder's compression stroke. Alternatively, a manufacturer may remove a tooth from

a reluctor wheel. The longer time between two teeth is detected by the ECM's analysis of the sensor's waveform and will identify cylinder stroke as, say, TDC of the first cylinder **FIGURE 22-35**. Variations of this basic strategy include using one or two narrower teeth or an odd arrangement of teeth that corresponds to a particular engine position for a given waveform. It should be noted that the additional or missing tooth strategy may require as many as three crankshaft revolutions before the ECM can determine what the cylinder stroke position is.

Using Two Sensors

A better strategy than using a single sensor on the camshaft is to use both camshaft and crankshaft position sensors. The advantage that two sensors provides is improved precision in calculating crankshaft position. Using only the camshaft sensor, error is introduced due to backlash between the crankshaft and camshaft gears. Worn gears can result in a significant amount of gear train backlash, producing unacceptable error in reporting crankshaft position. Using the crank sensor, the ECM can determine exactly where the position of the piston is **FIGURE 22-36**.

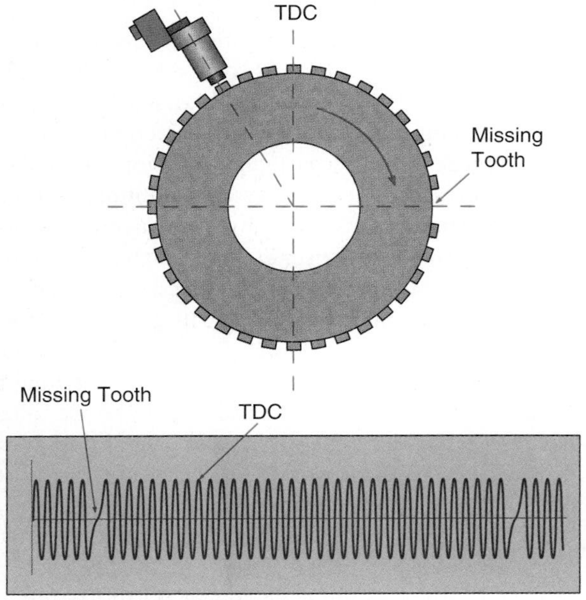

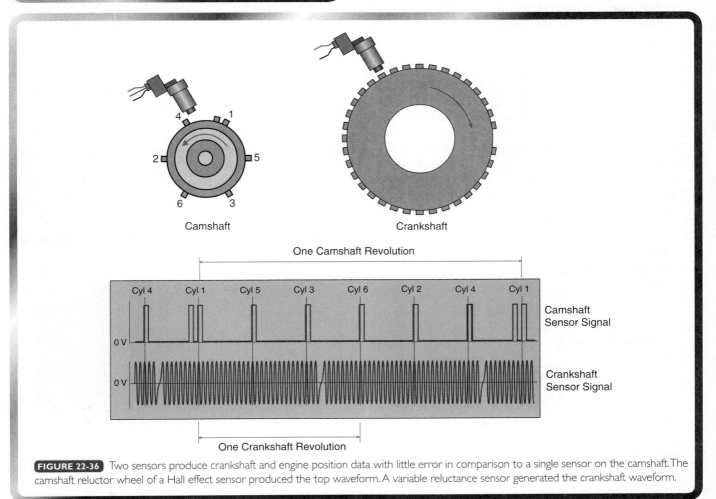

FIGURE 22-35 The waveform produced by a camshaft gear with a missing tooth on the signal generator wheel.

Cylinder Misfire and Contribution Detection

The crankshaft of a diesel engine will speed up and slow down with each power and compression stroke in the engine. The waveform that is generated from the engine position sensor(s) can determine the rotational velocity of the crank. A cylinder that is misfiring or producing little power in comparison to the other cylinders will turn more slowly, resulting in fewer teeth passing the position sensor per unit of time. Analyzing sensor waveforms using edge detection software algorithms, the ECM can determine how much power each cylinder is contributing to overall performance. Similarly, a loss of compression in a cylinder results in less crankshaft deceleration during an operating cycle. The ECM may change injection quantities to even out cylinder contribution based on data from the crankshaft and camshaft position sensors.

▶ Sensor Fault Detection Principles

Technicians are often called upon to diagnose fault codes associated with sensors or sensor circuits. Understanding how sensor-related faults are detected and the diagnostic strategies

FIGURE 22-36 Two sensors produce crankshaft and engine position data with little error in comparison to a single sensor on the camshaft. The camshaft reluctor wheel of a Hall effect sensor produced the top waveform. A variable reluctance sensor generated the crankshaft waveform.

used by an ECM will help you stay focused when performing pinpoint checks.

Sensors and On-board Diagnostics

Electronic control systems have self-diagnostic capabilities to identify faults in circuits and sensors. Without the ability of an ECM to monitor circuit operation, diagnosing faults would become an extraordinarily difficult task, requiring the technician to manually perform voltage, resistance, and current measurements for every circuit with the potential to produce a particular symptom of system malfunction. Waveforms from sensors producing varying frequencies, pulse-width modulation, digital, or sine wave would also require a staggering amount of time and resources to analyze.

Because all vehicles are required by emission legislation to monitor engine and other system operations for faults that could produce excessive emissions, evaluating sensor operation is a critical function of the HD-OBD system. Three major categories of fault codes identified by engine manufacturer diagnostics (EMD) and HD-OBD are:

1. *Out of range faults*. These faults primarily check sensor voltages, and in a few cases, they also check current draw to determine whether the sensor or associated circuits are open or have shorts. Voltages should be within 85% of reference voltage. That means for most sensors operating with a 5 Vref, signal voltages should not fall below 0.5 volts or above 4.5 volts **FIGURE 22-37** .

2. *Rationality, plausibility, or logical faults*. Manufacturers use different terms to describe the same fault detection strategy whereby the validity or accuracy of sensor data is evaluated by comparing sensor voltages with expected values. Most often, sensor data from several more sensors or measurement systems is compared with data from a particular sensor to see if the data makes sense (that is, that it's logical or rational). Another name given to these types of faults is in-range faults, because the sensor could produce signal voltages that are not

above or below a fault threshold voltage but the sensor may have failed and is supplying incorrect data.

3. *Functionality faults*. HD-OBD systems are required to evaluate the operation of at least 12 to 14 other major emission systems, such as the exhaust aftertreatment, boost pressure, and EGR. Simple or elaborate fault detection strategies are used to check whether a particular emission system is functioning correctly. The major system monitors, as they are called, depend on sensor data to function, but they do not specifically check the sensor except to analyze the influence of sensor data on a system. For example, if a system could not enter closed loop operation because the sensor data was out of range, irrational, or had some problem with its operation such as abnormal operating frequency or switching time or defective waveform, the sensor would be identified as having a fault. NO_x sensor faults are a common example in which the sensor is working properly but, due to some other incorrect system function, and the sensor is producing higher NO_x levels, the sensor is identified as defective. In many cases, the NO_x sensor is identified as being faulty but problems with a catalytic converter, EGR valve, or restricted air intake systems will produce what appears to be an in-range fault but the problem actually lies outside the sensor.

Comprehensive Component Monitor

The comprehensive component monitor (CCM) is one of the system monitors required for EMD and HD-OBD systems. It is a continuous monitor that constantly checks for malfunctions in any engine or emission-related electrical circuit or component providing input or output signals to an ECM. Electrical inputs and outputs are evaluated for circuit continuity and shorts by measuring voltage drops in a circuit. The monitor is also responsible for performing rationality checks of sensors. For example, if an oil pressure sensor indicated the engine had 40 psi (276 kPa) of oil pressure and the engine was stopped, the data would not make sense and therefore a rationality fault would be stored.

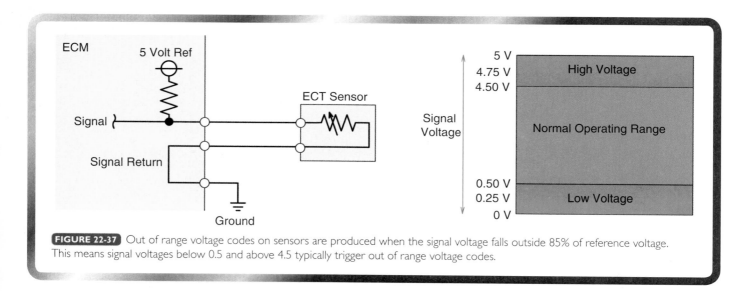

FIGURE 22-37 Out of range voltage codes on sensors are produced when the signal voltage falls outside 85% of reference voltage. This means signal voltages below 0.5 and above 4.5 typically trigger out of range voltage codes.

Another example would be that of a coolant temperature sensor that indicated the coolant was warm, say 140°F (60°C), but all other sensors such as oil, fuel, air inlet, and transmission temperatures were at –20°F (-29°C) and the engine had just started after cold soaking for 20 hours. Such a code could be triggered by plugging in a block heater, or it might indicate a defective sensor. Rationality codes need careful pinpoint diagnostic tests to determine if a sensor is defective or some outside influence is affecting sensor data.

Outputs such as injector solenoids, relays, and dosing valves are evaluated by the CCM for opens and shorts by monitoring a feedback circuit from the field effect transistor (FET), or "smart driver" associated with the output circuit. Smart FETs, as they are called, are FETs designed to supply data about the amount of amperage passing through the transistor gate **FIGURE 22-38**. These same gates can operate as virtual fuses that can disconnect power to the circuit if current flow is excessive. CCM codes use fault mode indicators (FMIs) developed by the Society of Automotive Engineers (SAE) that indicate how an electrical circuit has failed **TABLE 22-1**. Out of range voltage codes that are the most common when sensors and circuits are open or shorted include FMI 3 and 4. J1587 and J1939 SAE rationality codes are 0, 1, and 2. J1939 also adds FMI codes 15–18, 20, and 21 for rationality-related faults. Codes 8–10 are used to report problems with waveforms from sensors or systems. Codes 5 and 6 are used by smart drivers detecting excessive or insufficient amperage in a circuit. Only FMI codes 11–14, 19, and 31 are not used by the CCM.

Circuit Monitoring—Voltage Drop Measurement

The way in which switch operation is monitored inside helps provide a foundation for other circuits to monitor sensors. Two basic types of switch inputs to the ECM are pull-up and pull-down switches. The terms pull-up and pull-down are often used to describe whether current through a circuit is supplied by the positive or negative current polarity. Pull-up means current is originating from a positive voltage source, and pull down from a negative source. In the case of switches, pull-up switches supply a positive battery voltage input while pull-down supply a ground or negative voltage input **FIGURE 22-39**. Inside the ECM, a current-limiting resistor is connected in series with either of the switch types. This current-limiting resistor splits the voltage drop across the resistor and switch contacts. Voltage will drop across the current-limiting resistor when switch contacts are opened or closed. A high-impedance microcontroller capable of measuring voltage between an internal ECM ground and the resistor is connected in series with the current-limiting resistor, which enables a voltage reading. This means that voltage drop across the current-limiting resistor, whether it is a pull-up or pull-down switch, is measured by a voltmeter. Switch status

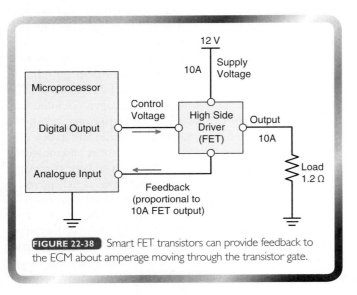

FIGURE 22-38 Smart FET transistors can provide feedback to the ECM about amperage moving through the transistor gate.

TABLE 22-1: Society of Automotive Engineers (SAE) J1939 Failure Mode Identifier (FMI)

FMI	SAE Text
0	Data valid but above normal operational range—most severe level
1	Data valid but below normal operational range—most severe level
2	Data erratic, intermittent, or incorrect
3	Voltage above normal or shorted to high source
4	Voltage below normal or shorted to low source
5	Current below normal or open circuit
6	Current above normal or grounded circuit
7	Mechanical system not responding or out of adjustment
8	Abnormal frequency or pulse width or period
9	Abnormal update rate
10	Abnormal rate of change
11	Root cause not known
12	Bad intelligent device or component
13	Out of calibration
14	Special instructions
15	Data valid but above normal operating range—least severe level
16	Data valid but above normal operating range—moderately severe level
17	Data valid but below normal operating range—least severe level
18	Data valid but below normal operating range—moderately severe level
19	Received network data in error
20–30	Reserved for SAE assignment
31	Condition exists

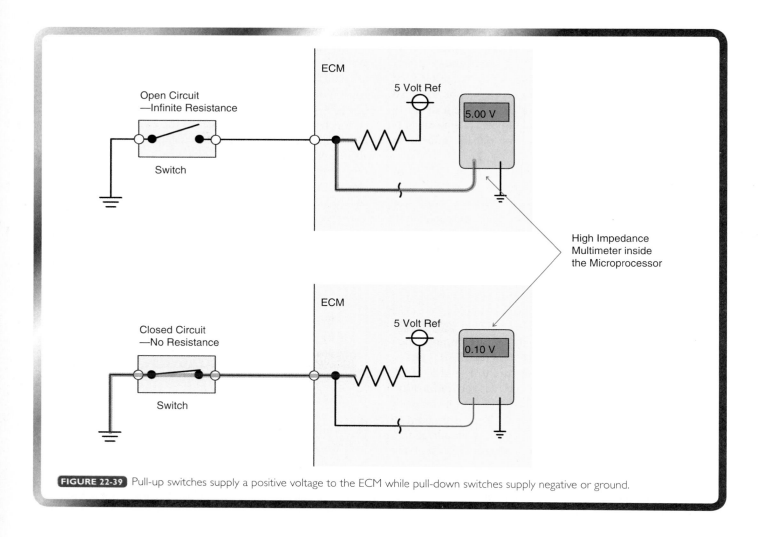

FIGURE 22-39 Pull-up switches supply a positive voltage to the ECM while pull-down switches supply negative or ground.

(i.e., whether open or closed) is determined by measuring the voltage dropped across the current-limiting resistor.

Pull-Up Resistors

When two resistors are connected in series, the greatest voltage drop takes place across the resistor with the highest resistance. The remaining resistor will drop the remaining voltage in a circuit. This is predicted by Kirchhoff's law, which states the sum of the voltage drops in a circuit equals source voltage **FIGURE 22-40**. Because the microcontroller inside the ECM that measures voltage has very high resistance, it behaves like the largest of the resistors in a circuit. A pull-up resistor will have most voltage drop measured after the current-limiting resistor when the switch is open, because it places the microcontroller in series with the resistor. In this case, only a small amount of voltage is dropped by the current-limiting resistor and the most voltage through the highly resistive microcontroller to an internal ground. When the switch is closed, the very low resistance across the contacts will cause the most current to flow through the switch contacts and the series connected current-limiting resistor. Almost no current flows through the highly resistive microcontroller, because the microcontroller has much higher

resistance compared to the pull-up resistor and switch, which are connected in series.

Smart-Diagnosable Switches

Disconnected switches, shorted switch wiring, and resistive switch contacts cannot be diagnosed using open or closed diagnostic logic. To differentiate a disconnected switch from an open switch, resistors are placed in series or in parallel with the switch **FIGURE 22-41**. This enables the microcontroller to identify problems in the wiring between the switch and ECM for failures such as shorted to ground or open circuited wiring. When properly connected in a functioning circuit, the resistor incorporated into the switch in series will have a calibrated resistance sensed by the microcontroller and measured as a specific voltage drop. If a switch has a resistor connected in parallel across its contacts, opening the switch provides a specific voltage drop measured by the microcontroller. If the switch wiring is shorted to ground, to battery positive, or simply disconnected, programmed logic within the microcontroller will identify the voltage reading as different from the switch resistance when opened or closed and log the appropriate fault code **FIGURE 22-42**. Pull-up resistors can be connected in series with the switches to further enhance the diagnostic capabilities of the microcontroller. Clutch, brake light, or AC pressure switches often use these arrangements because of their critical functions.

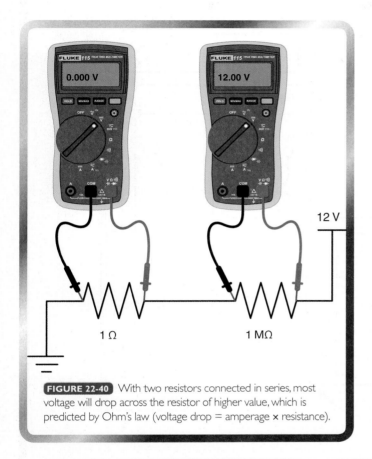

FIGURE 22-40 With two resistors connected in series, most voltage will drop across the resistor of higher value, which is predicted by Ohm's law (voltage drop = amperage × resistance).

Regulated Reference Voltage (Vref)

Regulated voltage supplied to sensor circuits is called reference voltage (Vref) and is important for several reasons. First, a stable and precise voltage is necessary for accurate voltage drop calculations used to determine the unknown resistance value of a sensor. Without the regulated voltage supply, changes in system voltage would produce sensor error. Current-limiting resistors are supplied a voltage lower than battery Vref to prevent excessive current flow through the microcontroller circuit if wiring becomes shorted. Vref values are typically 5 volts. (There are some exceptions: Caterpillar uses 8 volts on some control systems.) An internal ground called zero-volt reference (ZVR) is just as important. All sensors using reference voltage return current through the control module and not to chassis ground. Variations in voltage at chassis ground would produce error in voltage drop calculations, resulting in incorrect signal voltages. The internal ground is also filtered and "cleaned," meaning it is free from electromagnetic interference.

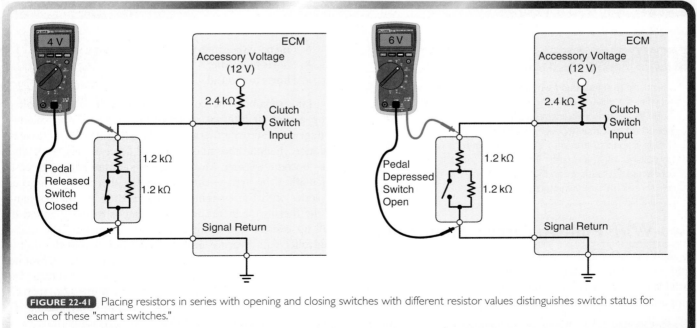

FIGURE 22-41 Placing resistors in series with opening and closing switches with different resistor values distinguishes switch status for each of these "smart switches."

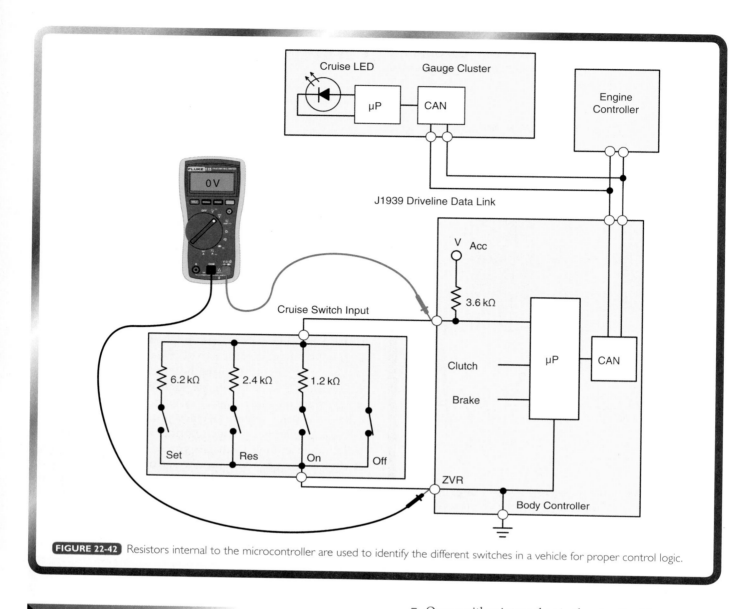

FIGURE 22-42 Resistors internal to the microcontroller are used to identify the different switches in a vehicle for proper control logic.

Just as Vref to sensors and switch circuits is regulated to typically +5 volts, a regulated ground circuit is provided through control modules. All sensors using reference voltage need a regulated ground return circuit through the control module and never to chassis ground to prevent electrical interference and variations to voltage measurements. The control module in turn is connected to chassis ground, which is the only way the electronic control system can function effectively.

Two-Wire Pull-Up Circuit Monitoring

To identify faults and measure signal voltage, thermistors are often connected to internal pull-up resistors. Thermistors are variable resistors that change resistance with temperature. These temperature-sensing devices are monitored for:

- Resistance to validate normal signal voltage and detect out of range faults

- Opens, either internal or in the circuit wiring
- Shorts to power
- Shorts to ground

Like switches, the control module will measure voltage drop across an internal current-limiting resistor to calculate voltage drop across a thermistor. NTC thermistors increase resistance when they become colder and decrease resistance when they become warmer. Measuring temperature is performed by calculating the voltage drop across the thermistor connected in series with the current-limiting resistor. As the resistance of the thermistor increases, less voltage is dropped across the pull-up resistor and more across the thermistor. The microcontroller will measure more voltage drop across the pull-up resistor when the thermistor becomes less resistive. Unwanted extra resistance in the circuit will produce a higher voltage drop across the sensor, generating colder temperatures. An open circuit (high resistance) will read the coldest temperature possible. Circuit monitoring fault detection is typically designed to recognize sensor resistance values within approximately 85%

of the voltage supplied from the pull-up resistor to be within normal range, and voltage readings outside of that range are recognized as abnormal **FIGURE 22-43**. Normal signal range used to diagnose most sensor circuits covers the entire operating range of the sensor signal, and the circuit should always have some resistance whether hot or cold. A disconnected sensor will have infinite resistance, and no voltage is dropped across the thermistor. In these circumstances, the voltage reading by the circuit's microcontroller will see maximum voltage between its internal ground and the current-limiting resistor. An open sensor or disconnected open wiring will produce an SAE fault code description of "out of range high or shorted high" (FMI 3) **FIGURE 22-44**.

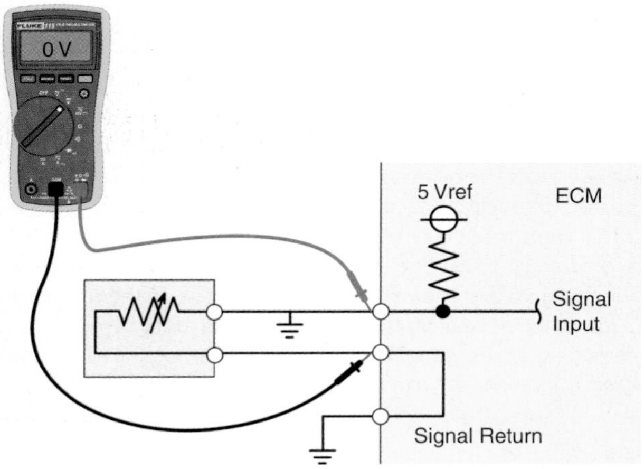

The manufacturing and SAE FMI code descriptions point to the higher voltage sensed by the microcontroller because no voltage is dropped by the disconnected or open thermistor circuit and all voltage is now dropped by the microcontroller. Note that the sensor signal wire that is shorted to positive battery voltage or another +5-volt supply will generate an identical fault code as an open circuited signal wire **FIGURE 22-45**. The logic used by the microcontroller that senses no or little voltage drop across the pull-up resistor could be caused by a positive voltage supply shorted to the signal wire. The ZVR could also be open and produce the same voltage readings by the microcontroller. Both conditions require appropriate pinpoint testing to isolate the fault.

If a thermistor signal wire is rubbed through and making contact to chassis ground, more current will flow through the signal circuit and the fault code description typically includes:

- Out of range low or shorted low (FMI 4)
- Signal wire shorted to sensor return or battery negative (OEM code)
- Signal source shorted to ground (OEM code)

Excessive current flow across the pull-up resistor connected in series with the grounded circuit means low or no voltage is measured between the pull-up resistor and the signal wire. Because most current will flow through the short to ground, little current will flow through the microcontroller, and the voltage drop will be less than 0.5 volts. This explains why the code description given is out of range low or shorted low (FMI 4). Diagnostic logic programmed into the microcontroller points to a short to ground, causing excessive voltage drop across the current-limiting resistor of more than 85% of the voltage supplied to the resistor **TABLE 22-2**.

Manufacturers can go beyond SAE minimum standards for reporting faults using J1939 protocols and add additional fault code descriptions using their own coding system. In the case of the disconnected thermistor, an enhanced code could carry

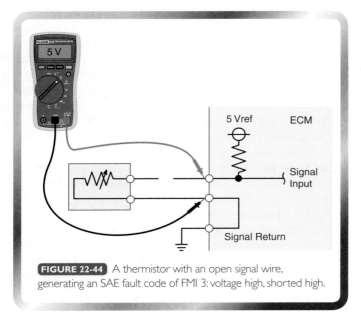

FIGURE 22-43 Circuit monitoring of thermistors involves measuring the voltage drop after a pull-up resistor. Fault code reports out of range signals at approximately 85% of Vref. This FMI 3 description is voltage high or shorted high.

FIGURE 22-44 A thermistor with an open signal wire, generating an SAE fault code of FMI 3: voltage high, shorted high.

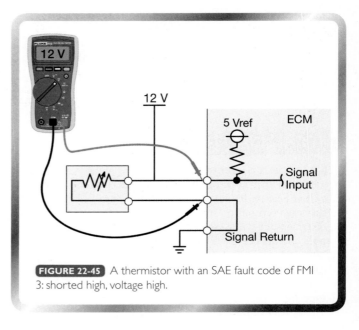

FIGURE 22-45 A thermistor with an SAE fault code of FMI 3: shorted high, voltage high.

TABLE 22-2: Out-of-Range Voltage Fault Code Descriptions Using a Pull-Up Resistor (i.e., two-wire NTC thermistor)

Condition	Observation	Code Description
Sensor disconnected	Signal voltage higher than 4.5 volts	FMI 3: Out of range high, shorted high
Signal wire shorted to positive voltage (12v battery or +5 volts reference)	Signal voltage higher than 4.5 volts	FMI 3: Out of range high, shorted high
Sensor open	Signal voltage higher than 4.5 volts	FMI 3: Out of range high, shorted high
Sensor signal wire shorted to ground	Signal voltage lower than 0.5 volts	FMI 4: Out of range low, shorted low
Sensor internally shorted to ground or ZVR	Signal voltage lower than 0.5 volts	FMI 4: Out of range low, shorted low

a code description such as "signal wire shorted to sensor supply" or "short to battery volt," "signal source shorted to voltage source," "open return," or "signal circuit."

> **TECHNICIAN TIP**

Pressure, temperature position, and other sensors can share a +5 Vref or ZVR wire. Return is the equivalent to chassis ground through the control module, which is free of electromagnetic interference and is regulated to provide the cleanest signal path. Problems in the reference voltage or signal return path can cause unusual problems and multiple fault codes from all the sensors. "Shorted high or low" and "voltage high or low" are typical fault code descriptions produced if sensors share common Vref and ZVR pathways. This happens because the voltage supplied to the sensors has changed. Less than +5 volts or the absence of a ZVR distorts the ECM's ability to properly sense correct signal voltages. If the return is connected to chassis ground, voltage fluctuations and electromagnetic interference can sometimes distort electrical signals and measurement of voltage drops across the sensor circuits. A single defective sensor may have an internal short circuit to ground and +5 volts, which can interfere with the operation of all sensors. Disconnecting a defective sensor can sometimes cause the multiple fault codes to disappear. The use of an LED diode installed in series with the ZVR circuit at each sensor can detect a malfunctioning circuit or device because the polarity-sensitive LED will light in both directions when connected to the defective sensor.

> **TECHNICIAN TIP**

Just because a control module does not log a fault code does not mean that no problems exist in the electronic control system. Because the normal signal range (within 85%) used to diagnose most sensor circuits spans the entire operating range of the sensor, it is possible for the sensor to produce a signal that does not measure the actual operating condition and therefore will not be identified with a fault code. A good strategy to identify problems is to monitor signal voltage using a scanner or software data list while comparing observed values with expected values reported in a shop manual.

> **TECHNICIAN TIP**

Quick-testing to determine whether a fault code is generated by defective wiring, pin connectors, or sensor can be performed using jumper wires. While monitoring sensor signal voltage using an electronic service tool, the signal voltage values should change when either disconnecting the sensor or jumping sensor signal wires to ZVR or +5 Vref. If no change is observed when momentarily grounding the signal wire or supplying the signal wire with +5 Vref, the wiring or pin connections in the circuit are suspect. Some manufacturers recommend using a calibrated resistor in series with the jumper wire when performing these tests to prevent damage to sensitive control modules.

Three-Wire Sensor Circuit Monitoring

Three-wire circuits, whether digital or analog, passive or active, use a reference voltage, signal, and ZVR wire, also referred to as ground return by some manufacturers. Voltage out of range faults (FMI 3 and 4) are detected when the signal voltage from a sensor typically exceeds 0.5–4.5 volts out-of-range fault threshold **TABLE 22-3**. The majority of three-wire sensors typically measure signal voltage between the positive voltage on the signal wire and the ZVR wire across a pull-down resistor **FIGURE 22-46**. However, some active three-wire sensors such as Hall effect sensors and several manufacturers of pressure sensors supply variable resistance ground path for a +5-Vref from the ECM through the sensor's ZVR **FIGURE 22-47**.

In this case, measuring signal voltage with three-wire sensors involves using a pull-up or pull down resistor located in the ECM. In the case of a circuit using a pull-down resistor, a voltage-measuring microcontroller connected in parallel across the pull-down resistor measures voltage drop across the resistor between the positive signal wire and the negative ZVR. Because there is only one pull-down resistor, all the voltage supplied by the signal wire will be dropped across the pull-down resistor. This means that a defective active type sensor will have a fault code of FMI 4 for low voltage or shorted low if the +5 Vref and ZVR circuits are open **FIGURE 22-48**. Because no current is supplied to the active sensor with either an open Vref or ZVR, internal

TABLE 22-3: Out-of-Range Voltage Fault Code Descriptions Using a Pull-Down Resistor (i.e., three-wire potentiometer)

Condition	Observation	Code Description
Sensor disconnected	Signal voltage lower than 0.5 volts	FMI 4: Out of range low, shorted low
Signal wire shorted to positive voltage (12v battery or +5 Vref)	Signal voltage higher than 4.5 volts	FMI 3: Out of range high, shorted high
Sensor open	Signal voltage lower than 0.5 volts	FMI 4: Out of range low, shorted low
Sensor signal wire shorted to ground	Signal voltage lower than 0.5 volts	FMI 4: Out of range low, shorted low
Sensor internally shorted to ground or ZVR	Signal voltage lower than 0.5 volts	FMI 4: Out of range low, shorted low

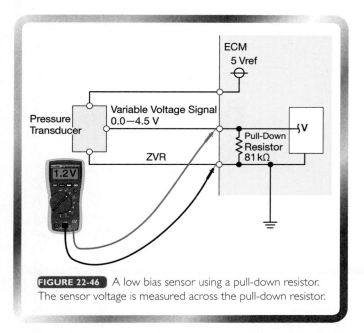

FIGURE 22-46 A low bias sensor using a pull-down resistor. The sensor voltage is measured across the pull-down resistor.

sensor circuits cannot operate and supply a varying signal voltage. Voltage in this case would be 0, which is below the 0.5-volt fault threshold for low voltage. A short to ground signal wire will produce an identical shorted low, voltage low FMI fault code.

If the sensor supplies a ground path for a signal circuit from the ECM containing a pull-up resistor carrying +5 volts, a disconnected sensor will produce a voltage high, shorted high FMI fault code. In this instance, the active sensor cannot work and provide an electronically variable resistance to ZVR for the current supplied through the pull-up resistor. This means the microcontroller will see +5 volts on the signal wire and produce a fault code of FMI 3: voltage high, shorted high, as illustrated in **FIGURE 22-47**.

High- and Low-Bias Sensors

Whenever a sensor is disconnected or open, the out of range voltage code will either be out of range high or low. If the arrangement of the pull-up resistor causes signal voltage to go high when disconnected, it is considered a high-bias resistor. That is, it has a bias or tendency to produce a fault code of out-of-range high, voltage high, or FMI 3. If the tendency for a sensor circuit is to produce a voltage low code when disconnected, it is considered a low-bias sensor. Generally, high-bias sensors

use a pull-up resistor and low-bias sensors monitor signal voltage with a pull-down resistor.

Circuits using pull-up and pull-down resistors have the added advantage of limiting excessive current flow to a sensor to protect the wiring, sensor, or control module if a short to ground or battery positive takes place. Excessive current flow would be reduced by the resistor when a fault condition exists. By limiting excessive current flow during shorted conditions in sensor circuits, Vref and ZVR circuits are protected as well.

More comprehensive circuit monitoring also takes place between the Vref and ZVR in some but not all control systems. Open, shorted to ground, or shorted to voltage source or resistive circuit pathways result in fault codes for these circuits. Because ZVR is common to the sensors, problems with the reference voltage to a specific sensor circuit may only be detected.

▶ **TECHNICIAN TIP**

After performing a repair to an electronic control system, the repair should be validated before returning a vehicle to service to confirm the fault code does not reappear. In HD-OBD systems, repair validation requires operating the circuit or device under the enabling conditions for a major system monitor to run and obtain a system readiness code. Make sure the conditions to operate the device or run the monitor are met during the testing procedure. These procedures are outlined in the service manual. Double check that no codes are pending or waiting to illuminate a malfunction indicator lamp (MIL). Occasionally, diagnostic codes can be set during routine service procedures or by problems outside the electronic control system. Always clear codes and confirm that they reset prior to circuit troubleshooting. Comprehensive monitor codes on HD-OBD vehicles often only require cycling the ignition switch on and off after a repair is completed to extinguish the MIL light.

▶ **TECHNICIAN TIP**

Tools required for fault isolation pinpoint testing include a Digital Volt Ohm Meter (DVOM) and some test leads or jumper wires. Proper break-out harness or pin connectors are needed to access the various connectors and components to be tested. Using improper tools can result in damage to pins and connectors and faulty meter reading, causing misleading diagnosis and produce even more diagnostic codes.

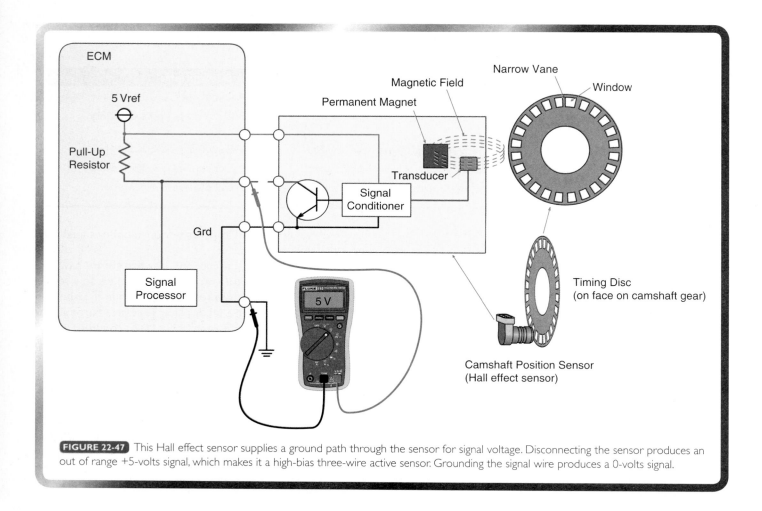

FIGURE 22-47 This Hall effect sensor supplies a ground path through the sensor for signal voltage. Disconnecting the sensor produces an out of range +5-volts signal, which makes it a high-bias three-wire active sensor. Grounding the signal wire produces a 0-volts signal.

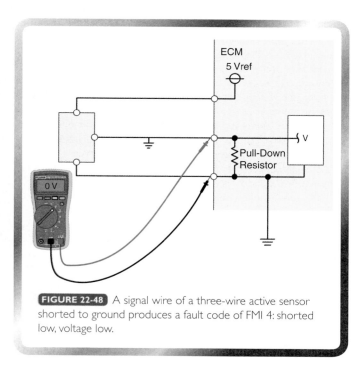

FIGURE 22-48 A signal wire of a three-wire active sensor shorted to ground produces a fault code of FMI 4: shorted low, voltage low.

▶ TECHNICIAN TIP

If an intermittent fault is suspected, a physical check of the suspect circuit can be performed by flexing connectors and harnesses at likely failure points while monitoring the circuit with a multimeter or oscilloscope. Graphing meters with glitch testing capabilities can identify and record the circuit fault in microseconds. If the problem is related to temperature, vibration, or moisture, the circuit or control module can be heated, lightly tapped, or even sprayed with water to simulate the failure conditions. Some testing software features pull test capabilities, which can provide an audible alert when brief interruption in circuit voltages takes place when pulling or bending wiring harnesses.

Low- and High-Side Driver Faults

A large variety of electrical devices such as relays, motors, and injectors depend on current supplied from a control module to operate. When supplying a negative polarity or ground to a device, current is switched through a transistor called a low-side driver. Similarly, switching transistors supplying positive DC voltage are referred to as high-side drivers. Two techniques are used to detect opens, shorts, high resistance, and excessive current draw in these circuits. Current-limiting resistors used to measure voltage drop in the output circuit much like in sensor circuits are used to evaluate circuit performance. Another method involves direct measurement of output current using smart FETs **FIGURE 22-49**. In these circuits, the drain-to-source current flows are measured through a special feedback circuit to the microcontroller. Time on and amperage are used to set fault codes. FMIs 5 and 6 are produced when amperage exceeds out of range thresholds. FMI 5, current below normal or open, is produced if little or no amperage flows through the output circuit. FMI 6, current above normal or grounded, indicates a short to grounded circuit with high current flow **FIGURE 22-50**. For example, an injector that is supplied 2 amps at 70 volts using a high-side driver would be considered open if no current flowed or shorted to ground if amperage exceeded, say, 5 amps.

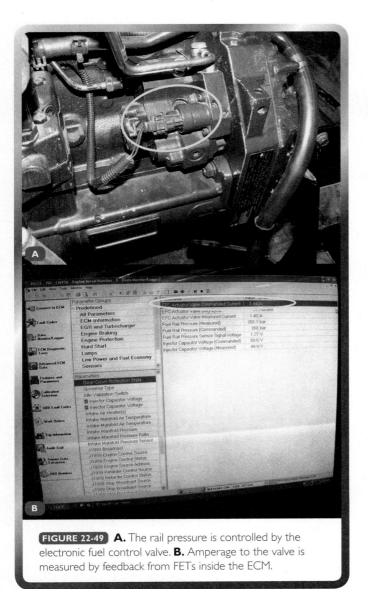

FIGURE 22-49 **A.** The rail pressure is controlled by the electronic fuel control valve. **B.** Amperage to the valve is measured by feedback from FETs inside the ECM.

FIGURE 22-50 Circuit monitoring of FET output drivers for self-diagnostic fault monitoring.

TECHNICIAN TIP

To validate a repair, start the engine and let it idle for one minute. The ECM will turn off the red MIL light whenever the diagnostic monitor has run. If it is a CCM evaluating electrical circuits, the light will switch off immediately when this diagnostic monitor runs and passes. For other faults, the ECM will turn off the MIL after three consecutive ignition cycles in which the diagnostic runs and passes.

Maintenance of Sensors

The on-board diagnostic system capabilities are limited and can only narrow a fault to a circuit or system. After that, the technician must identify what the nature of the problem is that produced the diagnostic fault code. Servicing of sensor faults involves performing pinpoint electrical tests and making other observations to identify precisely where and what caused the fault. This stage of diagnostic testing is called off-board diagnostics.

Diagnostic Testing of Pressure Sensors

Diagnostic tests of pressure sensors are similar to other strategies for evaluating three-wire sensors. Onboard diagnostic systems will identify problems in the circuits. Scan tools can then measure real-time data to observe abnormal but in-range functional problems and retrieve fault codes associated with the circuits **TABLE 22-4**. Pinpoint tests using break-out harnesses are performed on live circuits, too. Resistance tests are used to identify shorted or open wires in harnesses to these sensors. However, because these are active sensors with sensitive

TABLE 22-4: Fault Code Descriptions for a Two- or Three-Wire Sensor

Condition	Observation	Code Description
In-range voltage but signal not valid	No rationality or plausibility when data compared with normal system behavior or other sensor inputs	In-range fault

electronic circuits, it is not possible to perform resistance tests on the sensors themselves.

Safety

Never use a 12-volt jumper wire connected to battery positive to quick-check sensor harnesses. The ECM can easily be damaged by this method.

Diagnostic Testing of Thermistors

The range of resistance values of a thermistor varies by manufacturer and what temperature range the sensor measures. The change in resistance is not linear or directly proportional to temperature, either **TABLE 22-5**. At the low and high ends of temperature range, small changes in temperature produce large changes in resistance while changes in midrange temperature values produce smaller changes to sensor resistance. Several temperature and resistance values are supplied by the manufacturer to properly evaluate a thermistor when testing using an ohmmeter.

Diagnostic Testing of Variable Reluctance Sensors

Variable reluctance sensors are two-wire passive sensors. The coil of wire surrounding a magnet should be tested for continuity

TABLE 22-5: The Inverse and Nonlinear Relationship Between Temperature and Resistance of a Thermistor

Temperature		Resistance
°Celsius	°Fahrenheit	Ohms
100	210	185
70	160	450
38	100	1600
20	70	3400
−4	40	7500
−7	20	13,500
−18	0	250,000
−40	−40	100,700

and its resistance measured. Resistance is high because there are hundreds of wire winding turns and the wire diameter is very small. The output of the sensor can be measured with an alternating-current voltmeter. As the reluctor speed increases, the voltage produced by the sensor will rise proportionately.

A broken magnet will cause a low voltage reading. Likewise, an improper air gap between the sensor and reluctor will cause sensor output failure. Iron filings at the magnet of the sensor will also cause an inadequate change in sensor reluctance, generating insufficient voltage. Simply removing, cleaning, and reinstalling the sensor can sometimes correct inadequate or erratic sensor signals.

Variable reluctance sensor operation can often be evaluated from a scan tool or waveform graphing meter. For example, if an engine speed sensor is defective, engine speed data cannot be observed from a scanner. Graphing meters can compare known good sensor waveforms with observed waveforms to detect sensor faults.

Diagnostic Testing of Hall Effect Sensors

Diagnostic testing of Hall effect sensors will follow similar diagnostic strategies for any other three-wire active sensor **FIGURE 22-51**. Out of range faults on the sensor can be pinpoint tested with a voltmeter by first verifying +5 Vref and ZVR are available to the sensor **FIGURE 22-52**. After disconnecting the sensor and harness plug, a quick check to differentiate between a defective sensor and defective wiring harness is to short the +5 Vref to the signal return circuit. While monitoring sensor voltage using software or a scanner connected to the diagnostic data link connector, the signal voltage will show 5 volts or an "on" state. If

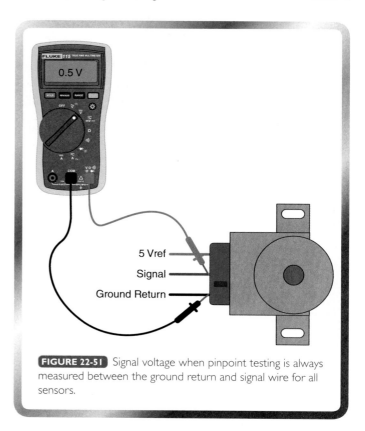

FIGURE 22-51 Signal voltage when pinpoint testing is always measured between the ground return and signal wire for all sensors.

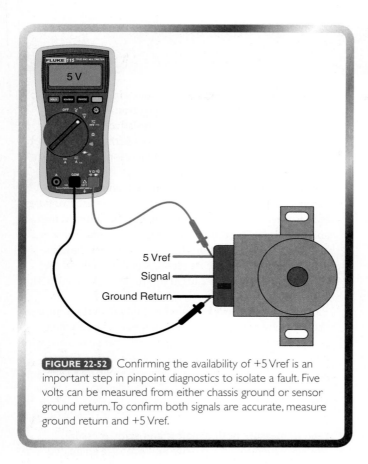

FIGURE 22-52 Confirming the availability of +5 Vref is an important step in pinpoint diagnostics to isolate a fault. Five volts can be measured from either chassis ground or sensor ground return. To confirm both signals are accurate, measure ground return and +5 Vref.

there is no change in the voltage, the wiring harness or connector plugs are likely defective. Shorts of any of the circuit wires to ground, battery voltage, or to one another are checked using either an ohmmeter when the vehicle battery is disconnected or measuring voltages in the sensor harness when the circuit is live.

Another important check of Hall effect sensors is made using a graphing meter. Sometimes the circuit-board within the sensor can fail and produce a waveform unrecognizable to the ECM, such as when the edges of a normally square waveform are not sharp and well defined. This often happens during hot soak period, and the vehicle will not start until the engine cools. A graphing meter allows examination of the waveform for comparison between known good waveforms.

Diagnostics of Mass Airflow Sensors

MAF sensors produce waveforms or data that can be observed by using a graphing meter. Sensor operation can also be monitored using a scanner, OEM software, or a multimeter with a break-out harness. Diagnostics of MAF sensors will follow those of any three-wire active sensor. It is also important to remember turbulence and airflow velocity variations can give false signals. For example, dirty heater wires or hot film or film wires can cause incorrect readings. Screens placed within the sensor to reduce turbulence can catch debris. These parts will require cleaning or replacement to restore proper operation. If the heater wire is intermittently breaking open, tapping the sensor to disconnect the wire will reveal the glitch if the sensor output is observed on a graphing meter or scanner.

Wrap-Up

Ready for Review

▶ Devices that convert one form of energy into another are called transducers. Sensors are a type of transducer because they convert physical conditions or states into electrical data. Pressure, temperature, angle, speed, and mass are just a few of the physical variables about which sensors supply electrical data to processors.

▶ A sensor is considered active or passive depending on whether it uses power supplied by the ECM to operate.

▶ Reference voltage refers to a precisely regulated voltage supplied by the ECM to sensors. It is significant to processor operation because the value of the variable resistor can be calculated by measuring voltage drop across the resistor with a known input voltage.

▶ Other classifications of sensors include resistive sensors, voltage generators, switch sensors, variable capacitance pressure sensors, and piezo-pressure and piezoresistive sensors.

▶ Switches are the simplest sensors of all because they have no resistance in the closed position and infinite resistance in the open position. Switches are categorized as sensors whenever they provide information to an electronic control system.

▶ The simplest digital signal is a single pole single throw (SPST) switch. It is found in either an open or closed state.

▶ When a switch is connected between the ECM and a battery positive, it is known as a pull-up circuit. A pull-down circuit is constructed when current to the switch is connected between the ECM and a negative ground current potential.

▶ Resistive sensors belong to the class of sensors that condition or change a voltage signal applied to the sensor. Many types of resistive sensors exist.

▶ A thermistor is a temperature-sensitive variable resistor commonly used to measure coolant, oil, fuel, or air temperature. The most common type of thermistor is a negative temperature coefficient (NTC) thermistor.

▶ Rheostats are two-wire variable resistance sensors. They are not commonly used as input devices to an ECM but instead are used for sending units such as fuel level, oil pressure, and some temperature gauges.

▶ Three-wire sensors, regardless of how they appear or what function they perform, have a common wiring configuration. The first wire provides reference voltage to the sensor. The second wire provides a negative ground signal to the ECM. The third wire is a signal return from the sensor. The advantage of using three-wire sensors is that they provide comprehensive diagnostic information about the sensor and its circuit operation.

▶ Potentiometers are similar to rheostats in that they vary signal voltage depending on the position of a sliding contact or wiper moving across a resistive material. However, they are three-wire sensors with the signal wire connected to the internal wiper. Potentiometers supply analog data to processing circuits.

▶ Pressure measurements such as intake manifold boost, barometric pressure, and oil and fuel pressure use two types of sensor technology. One is a variable capacitance sensor and the other uses strain gauge resistive sensors. These are both active sensors that produce analog output signals.

▶ Strain gage measurements record small changes in the resistance of tiny wires caused by stretching or contraction of the wires.

▶ Piezoresistive sensors rely on the ability of certain mineral crystals to produce voltage or change resistance when compressed. Rather than using a strain gauge resistor wire construction, these sensors use a piezoresistive crystal arranged with a Wheatstone bridge to measure the change in resistance of the piezo crystal. The advantage of these sensors is their ability to measure very high pressures.

▶ A variable capacitance sensor is an active pressure sensor used to measure both dynamic and static pressure.

▶ Voltage generators are passive and produce an analog signal of varying voltage or AC frequency.

▶ Variable reluctance sensors are used to measure rotational speed. Wheel speed, vehicle speed, engine speed, and camshaft and crankshaft position sensors are common applications of these sensors.

▶ The ability of a material to conduct or resist magnetic lines of force is known as reluctance. Variable reluctance sensors use changing sensor reluctance to induce current flow by changing magnetic field strengths inside the sensor.

▶ Like variable reluctance sensors, Hall effect sensors are commonly used to measure rotational speed of a shaft. Though they are more complex and expensive to manufacture than variable reluctance sensors, they produce a digital signal square waveform and have strong signal strength at low shaft rotational speeds.

▶ Oxygen sensors are used adjust EGR flow on diesels and exhaust oxygen content for exhaust aftertreatment devices.

▶ NO_x sensors are constructed and operate similarly to wide-range planar oxygen sensors, except that different concentrations of alloys are used in the sensor walls.

▶ Constructed like a wide-range planar NO_x or oxygen sensor, an ammonia sensor uses an aluminum oxide substrate rather than a ZrO_2 element to detect and generate a voltage for ammonia in a range from 0 to 100 ppm.

▶ The mass airflow (MAF) sensor measures the weight of air entering the engine intake. Its unique design also reports data about air density, and to some extent, the vapor content.

▶ MAF sensors are common on engines operating at stoichiometric air–fuel ratios. However, on diesel engines operating with an excess air ratio, the MAF is used as part of the HD-OBD component monitor for the EGR. A variety of electrical signals originate from MAF sensors, but all work using a hot-wire operating principle.

▶ Output control devices consist of display devices, serial data for network communication, and operators—electromagnetic devices that transform electrical current into movement. Two basic types of operators are solenoids and relays.

▶ ECMs need to determine the correct cylinder and point in the combustion cycle for injection. To send an electrical signal for firing the injectors, the ECM needs to know two things: crankshaft position and the stroke a cylinder is on.

▶ Using teeth or raised lugs on a cam gear that turns at one-half engine speed can generate engine position data using a Hall effect or variable reluctance sensor.

▶ A better strategy than using a single sensor on the camshaft is to use both a camshaft and crankshaft position sensor. The advantage that using two sensors provides is improved precision in calculating crankshaft position.

▶ The crankshaft of a diesel engine will speed up and slow down with each power and compression stroke in the engine. The waveform generated from the engine position sensor(s) can determine the rotational velocity of the crank. Analyzing sensor waveforms using edge detection software algorithms, the ECM can determine how much power each cylinder is contributing to overall performance.

▶ A thermistor's resistance value varies by manufacturer and the substance being measured.

▶ Variable reluctance sensors are two-wire passive sensors. The output of the sensor can be measured using an alternating-current voltmeter. As the reluctor speed increases, the voltage produced by the sensor will rise proportionately.

▶ Hall effect sensors can be tested and diagnosed in a similar way to any three-wire active sensor.

▶ MAF sensors produce waveforms that can be observed by using a graphing meter. Sensor operation can also be monitored using a scanner or a multimeter. Diagnostics of MAF sensor follow those of any three-wire active sensor.

Vocabulary Builder

active sensor   A sensor that uses a current supplied by the ECM to operate.

ammonia sensor   A sensor used in selective catalyst reduction (SCR) that provides data to the ECM that is used to determine if ammonia values are out of anticipated range.

Hall effect sensor   A sensor commonly used to measure the rotational speed of a shaft; they have the advantage of producing a digital signal square waveform and have strong signal strength at low shaft rotational speeds.

idle validation switch (IVS)   A circuit used for safety reasons that is used to verify throttle position.

NO sensor   A sensor that detects oxygen ions originating from nitric oxide from among the other oxygen ions present in the exhaust gas.

passive sensor   A sensor that does not use a current supplied by the ECM to operate.

piezoresistive sensor   A sensor that uses a piezoresistive crystal arranged with a Wheatstone bridge to measure the change in resistance of the piezo crystal; these sensors are adapted to measuring vibration and dynamic or continuous pressure changes.

potentiometer   A variable resistor with three connections—one at each end of a resistive path, and a third sliding contact that moves along the resistive pathway.

pull-down switch   A switch connected between the ECM and a negative ground current potential.

pull-up switch   A switch connected between the ECM and a battery positive.

reference voltage (Vref)   A precisely regulated voltage supplied by the ECM to sensors; the value is typically 5 VDC, but some manufacturers use 8 or 12 volts.

rheostat   A variable resistor constructed of a fixed input terminal and a variable output terminal, which vary current flow by passing current through a long resistive tightly coiled wire.

thermistor   A temperature-sensitive variable resistor commonly used to measure coolant, oil, fuel, and air temperatures.

variable capacitance pressure sensor   An active sensor that measures both dynamic and static pressure.

variable reluctance sensor   A sensor used to measure rotational speed, including wheel speed, vehicle speed, engine speed, and camshaft and crankshaft position.

wide-range planar sensor   A type of sensor technology that uses a current pump to calculate relative concentrations of oxygen, nitric oxide, and ammonia in exhaust gases.

Review Questions

1. The _____ is a sensor that does not use a current supplied by the ECM to operate.
   a. passive sensor
   b. hall effect sensor
   c. yaw sensor
   d. variable capacitance sensor

2. A _____ is a variable resistor with three connections—one at each end of a resistive path, and a third sliding contact that moves along the resistive pathway.
   a. rheostat
   b. thermistor
   c. potentiometer
   d. passive sensor

3. A _____ is a temperature-sensitive variable resistor commonly used to measure coolant, oil, fuel, and air temperatures.
   a. rheostat
   b. thermistor
   c. potentiometer
   d. hall effect sensor

4. A _____ is a sensor commonly used to measure the rotational speed of a shaft.
   a. potentiometer
   b. thermistor
   c. passive sensor
   d. Hall effect sensor

5. A _____ is a variable resistor constructed of a fixed input terminal and a variable output terminal, which vary current flow by passing current through a long resistive tightly coiled wire.
   a. rheostat
   b. thermistor
   c. passive sensor
   d. Hall effect sensor

6. _____ are a type of transducer that convert physical conditions or states into electrical data.
   a. Thermistors
   b. Resistors
   c. Generators
   d. Sensors

7. Diesel oxygen sensors are wide-range _____ sensors, which means they are flat rather than thimble-shaped.
   a. planar
   b. variable reluctance
   c. piezoresistive
   d. Hall effect

8. Several temperature and resistance valves are supplied by the manufacturer to properly evaluate a _____ when testing using an ohmmeter.
   a. rheostat
   b. thermistor
   c. potentiometer
   d. passive sensor

9. In a _____ temperature coefficient thermistor, the resistance decreases as the temperature increases.
   a. low
   b. positive
   c. negative
   d. high

10. For safety reasons, manufacturers will use a an idle _____ switch to verify throttle position.
   a. open
   b. pull-up
   c. validation
   d. single throw

ASE-Type Questions

1. Technician A says that switches are the simplest sensors of all. Technician B says it is because they have no resistance in the closed position and infinite resistance in the open position. Who is correct?
   a. Technician A
   b. Technician B
   c. Both Technician A and Technician B
   d. Neither Technician A nor Technician B

2. Technician A says three wire sensors have a common wiring configuration if they perform the same functions. Technician B says that three wire sensors, regardless of how they appear or what function they perform, have a common wiring configuration. Who is correct?
   a. Technician A
   b. Technician B
   c. Both Technician A and Technician B
   d. Neither Technician A nor Technician B

3. Technician A says hall effect throttle position sensors are less reliable than dual-path throttle position sensors. Technician B says hall effect throttle position sensors are more reliable than dual-path throttle positions because of their moving parts. Who is correct?
   a. Technician A
   b. Technician B
   c. Both Technician A and Technician B
   d. Neither Technician A nor Technician B

4. Technician A says the potential for ammonia to be released to the atmosphere has led to the required use of an ammonia sensor for most engines produced since 2016. Technician B says ammonia sensors have been required for most engines since 2012. Who is correct?
  a. Technician A
  b. Technician B
  c. Both Technician A and Technician B
  d. Neither Technician A nor Technician B

5. Technician A says output circuits consist of display devices and serial data for network communication. Technician B says that they also consist of electromagnetic operator devices. Who is correct?
  a. Technician A
  b. Technician B
  c. Both Technician A and Technician B
  d. Neither Technician A nor Technician B

6. Technician A says rationality codes indicate if a sensor is defective. Technician B says the rationality codes need careful pinpoint diagnostic tests to determine if a sensor is defective or if some outside influence is affecting sensor data. Who is correct?
  a. Technician A
  b. Technician B
  c. Both Technician A and Technician B
  d. Neither Technician A nor Technician B

7. Technician A says a broken magnet on a variable reluctance sensor will cause a low voltage reading. Technician B says a broken magnet on a variable reluctance sensor will cause a high voltage reading. Who is correct?
  a. Technician A
  b. Technician B
  c. Both Technician A and Technician B
  d. Neither Technician A nor Technician B

8. Technician A says when a switch is connected between the ECM and the battery positive, the switch is known as an open switch. Technician B says when a switch is connected between the ECM and the battery positive, the switch is called a single throw switch. Who is correct?
  a. Technician A
  b. Technician B
  c. Both Technician A and Technician B
  d. Neither Technician A nor Technician B

9. Technician A says knock sensors that measure abnormal combustion signals are a common application of piezoresistive sensors. Technician B says knock sensors that measure abnormal combustion signals are a common application of Wheatstone bridge sensors. Who is correct?
  a. Technician A
  b. Technician B
  c. Both Technician A and Technician B
  d. Neither Technician A nor Technician B

10. Technician A says a variable capacitance pressure sensor is an active sensor that uses the distance between two plates inside the sensor to measure both dynamic and static pressure. Technician B says a variable reluctance sensor is an active sensor that uses the distance between two plates inside the sensor to measure both dynamic and static pressure. Who is correct?
  a. Technician A
  b. Technician B
  c. Both Technician A and Technician B
  d. Neither Technician A nor Technician B

CHAPTER 23
Electronic Distributor Injection Pumps

▶ NATEF Tasks

Diesel Engines

General

- Check engine no cranking, cranks but fails to start, hard starting, and starts but does not continue to run problems; determine needed action. (pp 673–677)

- Identify engine surging, rough operation, misfiring, low power, slow deceleration, slow acceleration, and shutdown problems; determine needed action. (pp 673–677)

Knowledge Objectives

After reading this chapter, you will be able to:

1. Identify and describe the construction and application of electronic distributor pumps. (pp 659–676)
2. Identify and describe the operating principles of electronic distributor pumps. (pp 659–676)
3. Describe and explain diagnostic procedures for electronic distributor pumps. (pp 675–679)

Skills Objectives

After reading this chapter, you will be able to:

1. Perform a TDC offset relearn. (p 671) SKILL DRILL 23-1
2. Measure transfer pump fuel pressure and volume in a VP-44 pump. (p 677) SKILL DRILL 23-2
3. Inspect and replace a CAPS injector quill tube. (p 679) SKILL DRILL 23-3

► Introduction

The demand for cleaner engine emissions, increased engine power, quieter operation, and better fuel economy has propelled the development of even more efficient fuel injection systems. Refinement of diesel injection systems has involved applying principles of electronic signal processing to conventional fuel systems. This means that early mechanical distributor pumps have sophisticated electronic metering, injection timing, and governing controls added to their basic construction and operation. In this chapter, the construction features and operating principles for common applications of electronically controlled distributor pumps are reviewed.

► Fundamentals of Electronic Distributor Injection Pumps

The evolution of diesel engine technology demanded by increasingly stringent exhaust emission legislation has ended the use of distributor pumps in automotive on-highway applications in North America. The use of partial- and full-authority electronic controls, where timing and metering functions are performed electronically to varying degrees, extended applications of the distributor pump to 2002 model year vehicles. However, because of tighter emission standards, no distributor pumps are used on current model vehicles in North America. In 2002, GM introduced the common rail Duramax to replace the electronic distributor pump for its 6.5L (397 cubic inch) diesel. Cummins introduced common rail fuel systems, which replaced the Cummins Accumulator Pump System (CAPS) for Cummins' six cylinder C-series engines used in heavy-duty, on-road, and agricultural applications and many motorhome applications. Ford and Navistar International discontinued the use of the distributor injection pump with the introduction of the hydraulically actuated electronic unit injection (HEUI) PowerStroke, or T-444E, in 1993.

Bosch's popular mechanical VE pump, used by Cummins' 5.9L (360 cubic inch) B-Series diesels from 1989 to 1993, was replaced with the P7100 series Bosch inline injection pump. Then, from January 1998 to mid-2002, Cummins used a full-authority electronic distributor pump, the **Bosch VP-44**, popularized by the Dodge Ram diesel **FIGURE 23-1**. Many off-road engine manufacturers continue to use this pump today to meet Tier 4 emission standards. Cat and Case are two notable examples. The VP-44 has a vane internal transfer pump common to all other distributor pumps, but, in contrast to the single axial piston plunger of these pumps, pressurization of fuel

FIGURE 23-1 The Bosch VP-44 distributor pump.

► You Are the Technician

A customer has brought his pick-up truck to you with complaints about stalling, rough idle, low power, engine noise, and excessive white exhaust smoke. He's replaced most of the fuel system parts (including the electronic distributor injection pump, glow plugs, glow-plug controller, lift pump, and injectors) to try correcting the problem himself. To diagnose the problem, you start with basic checks of the fuel system, fuel quality, and base engine mechanics. The engine is in good condition, there is no problem with the fuel, and you found no fuel system fault codes. During a road test, you notice that the symptoms appear when the engine is accelerated hard. You re-inspect the fuel system and notice that a recently replaced fuel return line between the engine and frame rail is too long and folded into a Z shape. When the engine is accelerated and twists in the engine compartment due to torque reaction, the return hose actually kinks, preventing fuel from returning to the tank. Shortening the hose and properly routing it along the frame corrects the problem. While preparing to write up the job description on the work order, consider the following:

1. Provide an explanation to describe the reasons a restriction in the injection pump fuel return line would produce the symptoms the truck had.
2. Describe how the problem caused by the restricted fuel return could be measured or verified.
3. How would a restricted fuel return line from the injection pump change injection timing?

is accomplished using radial-opposed pumping plungers, much like the older mechanical Stanadyne DB pumps. A smaller, electronic version of the VE pump was used by Volkswagen for industrial engines and its earlier automobiles and smaller commercial vehicles. The **Bosch VP-37** was used in VW automobile products in North America until 2003 when the Pumpe Düse, a unit injection system, was introduced for the Golf, Jetta, and the new Beetle **FIGURE 23-2**. The VP-37 is an electronic pump with construction and operational characteristics similar to the mechanical VE pump.

Obsolescence of Mechanical Injection Systems

The design simplicity of mechanical distributor injection pumps accounted for much of their success. Mechanical distributor pumps used as few as half the number of parts as inline versions, but they still produced the same engine horsepower (hp).

However, injection pressures are low in mechanical injection systems. Injection pressures range from 5110 psi (352 bar) in the oldest mechanical Bosch VE models to 6716 psi (463 bar) in the DB-2 pump used on GM 6.2/6.5L (378/397 cubic inch) and Ford 6.9/7.3L (421/445 cubic inch) engines. In comparison, full-authority Stanadyne DS electronically governed pumps used on GM 6.5L (397 cubic inch) engines have an injection pressure of 13,140 psi (906 bar), and the VP-44 pump used on Cummins B-series engines has injection pressures of 16,060 psi (1107 bar). Lower injection pressures used by mechanical distributor pumps make them less favorable for reducing emissions. In comparison to today's fuel systems, these earlier mechanical fuel systems could only crudely vary injection quantity and timing for changing engine speed and load conditions. In addition

to injection pressure, other variables affecting combustion quality and emissions, such as atmospheric, could not be processed to modify injection strategies to reduce emissions and noise while improving fuel economy, power, and performance.

▶ Types of Electronic Distributor Injection Pumps

In addition to the updated electronic versions of the mechanical pumps examined in the Mechanical Distributor Type Injection Pumps chapter, several other electronically controlled distributor pumps had widespread use as more and more diesel engines began to be used by lighter, more powerful, small displacement diesels used in light- and medium-duty industrial, off-road, and on-highway applications. This next section will survey the variety of distributor pumps engine technicians may encounter.

DS-4 Electronic Injection Pumps

The **Stanadyne DS-4** full-authority distributor was introduced by GM for its 6.5L (397 cubic inch) turbo diesel in 1994 **FIGURE 23-3** and **FIGURE 23-4**. Three generations of the pump were built. After the introduction of the first pump, a second-generation pump was introduced in mid-1997, and a third-generation pump went into production in mid-1999. The adaptation of electronic controls to the pump allows for more accurate adjustment of delivery quantities and timing. The Chevrolet G-van equipped with the 6.5L (397 cubic inch) diesel used this pump from 1994 through

FIGURE 23-2 The Bosch VP-37 injection pump.

FIGURE 23-3 The Delphi (formerly Stanadyne) DS-4 distributor injection pump.

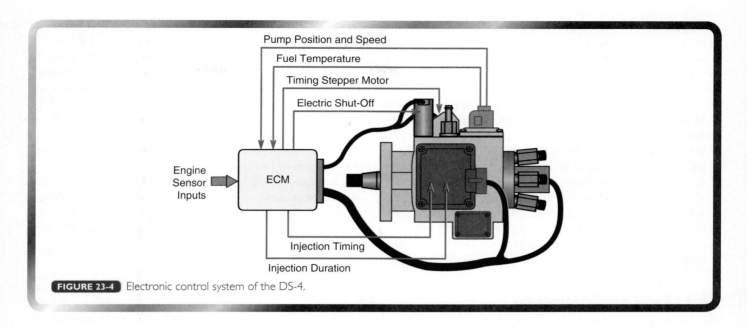

FIGURE 23-4 Electronic control system of the DS-4.

mid-2001, the CK 2500 and 3500 series trucks used it until mid-2001, and the 1500 series vehicles used it only until 1998.

The adaptation of electronic controls to the pump provided flexibility to more accurately adjust delivery quantities and timing than what mechanical systems were capable of. Control of the pump by the power train control module (PCM) also meant that fuel and timing could be optimally adjusted for any condition sensed by the PCM, including engine speed, load, exhaust gas recirculation (EGR) gas flow rates, coolant, fuel and air intake temperature, and atmospheric and boost pressure. The DB-2 mechanical pump that the DS-4 replaced had a variable beginning and fixed ending to injection, whereas the fill-spill cycle of the DS pump enables both a variable beginning and end of injection.

In addition to improved emission characteristics, this electronic control of injection provides for better idle quality, noise levels, cold-weather starting, and fuel economy. In fact, when compared to gasoline-fueled engines offered in the truck lineup, the 6.5L (397 cubic inch) engine with a DS pump could produce 20–80% better fuel economy while boasting the highest torque output of any engine in its class with 420 ft-lb (569 Nm) of twisting force. While the pump is not capable of supplying a pilot injection event, the fuel system does use throttle pintle injector nozzles, which means they can influence the rate of the injection event.

The DS pump also enabled the 6.5L (397 cubic inch) engine to be compliant with OBD-II legislation. Enhancements to the PCM in 1996 provided a 50% increase in memory. In 1998, both misfire detection and **adaptive cylinder balance** were added. The adaptive cylinder balance feature measures the power output of each cylinder at idle using changes in the crankshaft velocity detected by the pump's optical pump speed/position sensor. Adjustments to fuel delivery for each cylinder are made to increase or decrease power for any cylinder. The result is smoother engine operation achieved by minimizing power variations between each cylinder's power contributions.

Pump electronics also provided electronic cruise control and fast idle engine control for power take-off (PTO) devices.

A simple switch can set idle speed to 1070 revolutions per minute (rpm), 1360 rpm, or 1600 rpm.

Specifications

To understand pump construction and operation as well as differentiate this pump from other distributor injection pumps, it is helpful to know the specifications of the Stanadyne DS-4 full-authority distributor pump, which include:

- Capacities to 25 BHP (19 kW) per cylinder
- Peak injection pressures to 13,000 psi (896 bar)
- Electronic spill control with 12-volt solenoid actuators for timing and fuel metering control
- Four pumping plungers driven by an internal cam ring (hence the 4 in the DS-4 model designation)
- Pump-mounted solenoid driver with poppet valve closure detection
- High-resolution pump-mounted optical sensor tracking encoder
- Engine speed capability to 5000 rpm

Two different electronic distributor pumps are available to satisfy the requirements of light- and medium-duty emission standards. The basic difference is the shape of the cam profiles of the cam ring. Injection rate is controlled through a slightly different profile of the two cam rings.

Bosch Electronic Distributor Injection Systems

Bosch has manufactured a number of different models of distributor pumps since the 1960s. In addition to their successful and wide use in industrial, marine, and off-road applications, many of these pumps have found their way into North American automotive applications. These include the Bosch VE mechanical pump used in early-model Cummins 5.9L (360 cubic inch) engines found in many medium-duty vehicles manufactured by Ford and Freightliner as well as the 1989–1993 Dodge Ram diesels. This pump uses reciprocating <u>axial piston pressurization</u> and sleeve metering principles, which varies the end of injection to control injection delivery quantities. An axial piston distributor pump has a pumping plunger that reciprocates along the axis of the pump and uses a cam plate to move the plunger back and forth. An electronic version with construction and operational characteristics similar to the mechanical VE pump is the VP-37. The sliding sleeve or control collar that regulates the sleeve metering functions is electronically operated in the VP-37. This pump model was used in Volkswagen four, five, and six cylinder turbocharged direct injection (TDI) products from the late 1990s until 2004, when it was replaced by the unit injector or Pumpe Düse injection system. The VP-29/30 pump, which has a smaller output but higher injection pressure, is popular in many European vehicles.

VP-37 Axial Piston Injection Pump

The electronic successor to the mechanical VE injection pump is the VP-37 **FIGURE 23-5**. Many similarities in construction exist between the operation of the mechanical VE pump and the Bosch VP-37 distributor injection pump, reflecting its origins. A quick review of the Bosch VE pump's operating principles may help the readers understand VP-37 operation.

Like the VE, the VP-37 uses a reciprocating axial piston to pressurize fuel. The VP-37 injection pump is used on many European diesels, including Volkswagen TDI engines. It is also used in North American TDI engines, including 1.9L (116 cubic inch) four cylinder 90 hp (67 kW) and 110 hp (82 kW) engines.

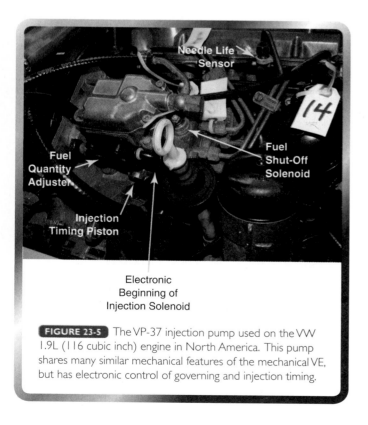

FIGURE 23-5 The VP-37 injection pump used on the VW 1.9L (116 cubic inch) engine in North America. This pump shares many similar mechanical features of the mechanical VE, but has electronic control of governing and injection timing.

The VP-37 pump is a drive-by-wire fuel system design **FIGURE 23-6**. This means there is no mechanical linkage between the accelerator pedal and the injection pump. Metering and injection timing functions are all electronically controlled. This system also uses a <u>needle lift sensor</u>, which provides a reference signal to the ECM for the beginning of injection (BOI) by providing information about movement of the nozzle valve. A correction factor to account for injection lag is applied to the injection timing of the remaining cylinders based on information supplied by this sensor.

A cogged timing belt drives the pump on Volkswagen TDI and industrial diesel engines. A larger 11-mm pumping plunger is used on automatic transmissions to obtain higher injection pressures of 11,760 psi (811 bar) with a pressure wave reflection of as much as 19,845 psi (1368 bar).

Governing Features

The basic construction features of the VP-37 pump that are used to pressurize fuel remain the same. The major difference is the use of an electronic governor to regulate injection quantity and electronic control of injection timing. These new electronic governing features include:

1. Adaptive strategy: Unlike purely mechanical systems, fuel metering and timing in electronic pumps are independent of mechanical governor characteristics and hydraulic behavior. For example, mechanical governor springs and linkage can wear out and change tension, which can compromise engine performance, emissions, and fuel economy. Engine electronics, particularly OBD-II–compliant systems, can measure changes taking place in a fuel system and adapt injection events to compensate for system deterioration. Injection lag, the time delay between pressurization of fuel and injection, can also interfere with accurate injection timing. Using a needle lift sensor, which detects the beginning of injection, permits a correction factor to be applied to this variable to achieve far more precise injection timing.

2. Closed-loop feedback: More features to improve performance, emissions, and fuel economy are integrated into operating algorithms. For example, purely mechanical systems cannot correct for fuel, coolant, oil, or intake air temperatures, but electronic systems can. The use of feedback loops provides for more accurate metering and injection timing over the engine's entire life. To get a better idea of how closed-loop feedback improves operation, consider the control sleeve position actuator and position sensor as an example of closed-loop feedback engine control. The control sleeve slides along the pump axial piston to spill fuel at the end of the injection event. Moving the control sleeve changes data supplied to the ECM by the position sensor. In turn, the actuator moving the control sleeve can make fine adjustment to better position the control sleeve to obtain an optimal fuel quantity and end of injection. Very accurate fuel metering is enabled, as the sensor provides data to the ECM about the position of the fueling mechanism because precise adjustments are made to the quantity of fuel injected. The beginning of injection control solenoid and needle lift sensor also provide feedback

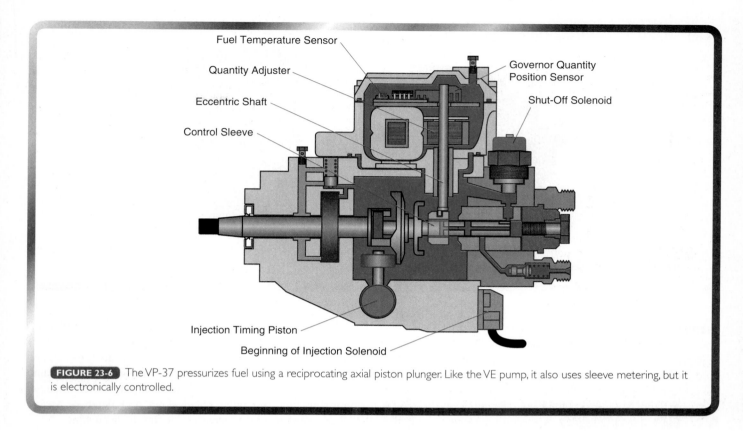

FIGURE 23-6 The VP-37 pressurizes fuel using a reciprocating axial piston plunger. Like the VE pump, it also uses sleeve metering, but it is electronically controlled.

data to the ECM so it can make changes needed for precise timing and metering. Because data points from these sensors and actuators are compared with unchanging values stored electronically in fuel-timing maps contained in the ECM, these variables are unaffected by wear and time to the degree that mechanical systems are.

3. Anti-shudder control: Drivability features such as anti-bucking dampening or **anti-shudder** control of longitudinal vehicle oscillation can be built into software-based operating algorithms. The anti-shudder feature prevents rapid changes in engine speed using the electronically controlled actuator if the throttle is moved too quickly. To suppress engine shudder, the ECM needs to know whether the clutch is engaged or disengaged. Using input from the clutch switch, the injection quantity can be briefly reduced when the clutch is first engaged.

4. Idle speed control: The fuel system can adjust idle speed metering to each individual cylinder to avoid rough and shaky engine idle. By monitoring the engine speed sensor, changes in engine speed velocity caused by unequal cylinder contributions are minimized by shot-to-shot modification of injected quantities to each cylinder.

VP-44 Radial Piston Electronic Distributor Pump

Another distributor pump commonly used in North American and European vehicles is the VP-44 **FIGURE 23-7**. A series of four different VP-44 pumps have been developed to meet different emission standards, adding features such as pilot injection. This pump has applications in the Cummins ISB used also by

Freightliner and in the Dodge Ram from January 1998 to 2003, when it was replaced by the common rail fuel system. The VP-44 pump has a vane internal transfer pump common to all other distributor pumps. However, rather than a single axial piston plunger, these distributor pumps use **radial piston pressurization** of fuel, which is accomplished using radial-opposed pumping plungers similar to the Stanadyne pumps. Electronic control of metering is also accomplished using a solenoid-actuated spill valve.

The Bosch VP-44 is another popular distributor pump used in small high-speed diesel engine applications in passenger vehicles and light- to medium-duty commercial diesels. A series of four pumps with progressive improvements and new features have been developed since the mid-1990s. This pump, like the VP-37, uses full-authority electronic control with advanced features to enhance drivability, performance, and fuel economy while reducing emissions. In North America, the John Deere 6.8L (415 cubic inch) diesel, numerous Case tractors, and construction equipment engines built by Caterpillar use this pump as well. However, the most popular North American application for this injection system is in the Cummins ISB engine. The VP-44 is much less complicated internally than the P7100, and it has fewer finely machined parts. Like the VE pump, the VP-44 is completely fuel lubricated. Later pumps are capable of controlled area network (CAN) communication, which enables better integration with other on-board electronic control modules to control the power and torque very precisely across the entire rpm range. This contrasts with mechanically governed engines, which have their power and torque controlled at torque peak and rated power rpm, but power and torque can often vary from published figures between those two engine speeds.

FIGURE 23-7 The VP-44 pump is used on many European and North American diesels. In North America, the Cummins 5.9L (360 cubic inch) diesel used this injection pump from 1998 until 2003.

Features

The VP-44 is a radial piston pump with construction and operating features similar to the Stanadyne DS pump. Depending on the model, two, three, or four pumping plungers are arranged around the pump rotor, pressurizing fuel internally to between 16,060 psi (1107 bar) and 20,440 psi (1409 bar), depending on the model **FIGURE 23-8** and **FIGURE 23-9**. A thermistor located inside the pump housing permits temperature compensation of fuel timing and metering by the fuel pump control module (FPCM).

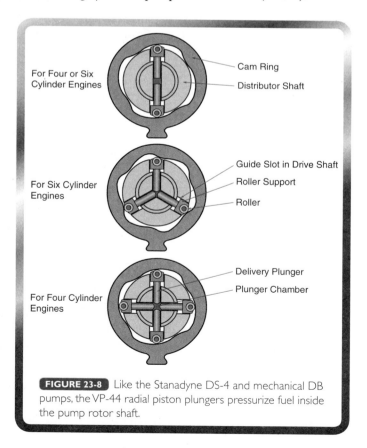

FIGURE 23-8 Like the Stanadyne DS-4 and mechanical DB pumps, the VP-44 radial piston plungers pressurize fuel inside the pump rotor shaft.

The pump is capable of pilot injection using its electronically controlled high-pressure metering control valve. The ability to rapidly change fuel delivery quantities permits it to dampen bucking or the longitudinal oscillations of a vehicle during rapid changes to the throttle. It can accomplish this by instantaneously increasing fuel as engine speed slows and decrease fueling slightly as engine speed increases due to vehicle bucking.

The ability to rapidly change fueling also permits the system to provide adaptive cylinder balance. This permits the pump to vary injection quantities to each cylinder during idle and low-speed engine operation. It does this by measuring the changes to engine speed produced by the power contributions from each cylinder. This means if a cylinder is not producing adequate power in comparison to other cylinders, the amount of fuel delivered can be slightly increased to smooth engine idle quality.

The injection control is performed by two electronic processors. A **fuel pump-mounted fuel pump control module (FPCM)** and the ECM. This arrangement is necessary for a couple of reasons. One is that the metering solenoids, which use as much as 20 amps of current, could cause overheating of electronic components if mounted with many other electronic components in the engine ECM. To minimize this possibility, the high-current drivers for the solenoid are included in the FPCM and are cooled by low-pressure fuel entering the fuel pump. Secondly, the high current flow to the metering control solenoid can cause electrical interference with some electronic components. Locating the high-current switching device on the pump minimizes this possibility as well. The processors' fuel system functions are divided with the ECM collecting senor data and providing a fueling quantity based on engine speed and load factors, while the FPCM determines injection timing with the ability to modify injection delivery quantities. The processor arrangement necessitates the use of one of the more unique features of the pump: communication between the pump and the ECM is done through a two-wire data bus. Information that passes between the ECM and FPCM over this CAN can integrate vehicle and engine operation.

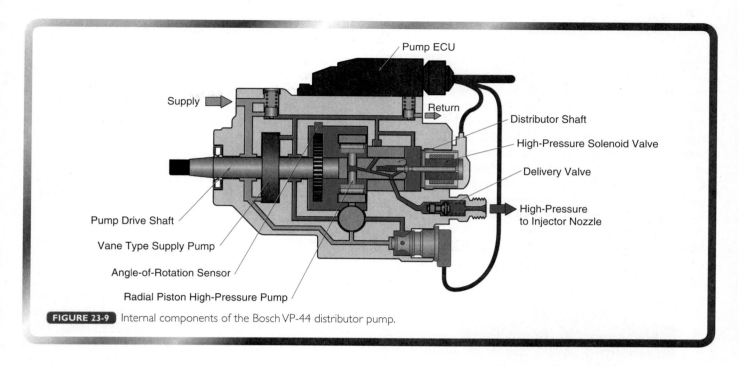

FIGURE 23-9 Internal components of the Bosch VP-44 distributor pump.

► Components and Operation of Electronic Distributor Injection Pumps

Distributor pumps are constructed with modular parts. This means that major pieces of the pumps are relatively easily to replace, so the entire pump does not need to be rebuilt or replaced at a specialty shop. Understanding the construction and operation of various distributor pumps means that technicians can better diagnose and service these fuel systems in the shop and more quickly turn around vehicles that arrive for repair.

DS-4

The DS pump, as noted earlier, is an updated version of the older mechanical Stanadyne DB pump. These pumps are highly serviceable, which enables technicians to repair the pumps, rather than specialty shops. Examining the construction and operating features of these pumps will enable technicians to develop diagnostic and service skills related to this pump model.

Components

The DS pump is operated by the PCM or power train control modules that control both engine and transmission operation. The pump contains the following major components.

Fuel-Metering Control Solenoid

This electromagnetic device is located inside the pump's hydraulic head. It opens and closes a spill control valve inside the pump to control the quantity of fuel entering the pumping chambers of the four opposed plungers of the pump rotor. When open, fuel can enter the pumping chamber. When closed, metering of fuel ends because no more fuel can enter the pumping chamber. Closing the spill control valve when the engine is rotating begins injection.

Pump-Mounted Fuel Solenoid Driver

A **fuel solenoid driver (FSD)** is an electronic control module that contains a pair of high-current switching transistors that send electrical signals to the fuel-metering control solenoid located inside the hydraulic head of the pump **FIGURE 23-10**. At 1800 rpm, the **pump-mounted driver (PMD)**, which is a control module that supplies electrical signals to control the operation of the spill valve, switches the solenoid switches on and off approximately 7200 times a minute, which generates a significant amount of heat.

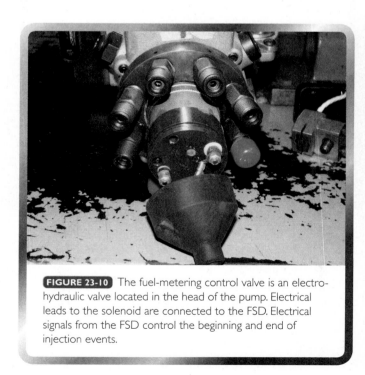

FIGURE 23-10 The fuel-metering control valve is an electro-hydraulic valve located in the head of the pump. Electrical leads to the solenoid are connected to the FSD. Electrical signals from the FSD control the beginning and end of injection events.

Optical Sensor Tracking Encoder

An **optical sensor tracking encoder (OSTE)** combines an optical fuel temperature with a pump position sensor **FIGURE 23-11**. Using the OSTE enables data collection of a reliable, defined pattern of light-and-dark to determine the position of the pump's rotor shaft. This device supplies the PCM with data regarding pump speed, rotor position, cam ring position, and fuel temperature. A disc or trigger wheel is attached to the pump rotor to provide signal data to the OSTE to track pump speed and position. The wheel has two sets of slots: 512 perforations around the circumference of the wheel provide high-resolution data regarding pump speed and precise engine position that is used to calculate injection timing events; another set of eight perforations, seven round and one rectangular, provide data regarding cylinder position and stroke identification **FIGURE 23-12**.

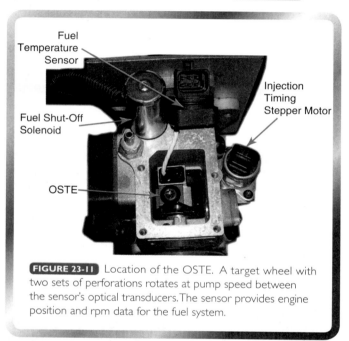

FIGURE 23-11 Location of the OSTE. A target wheel with two sets of perforations rotates at pump speed between the sensor's optical transducers. The sensor provides engine position and rpm data for the fuel system.

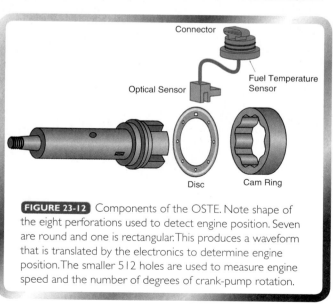

FIGURE 23-12 Components of the OSTE. Note shape of the eight perforations used to detect engine position. Seven are round and one is rectangular. This produces a waveform that is translated by the electronics to determine engine position. The smaller 512 holes are used to measure engine speed and the number of degrees of crank-pump rotation.

Injection Timing Stepper Motor

The injection timing stepper motor in the DS-4 replaced the servo-piston plunger assembly in the DB-2 pump, which controlled engine timing by rotating the pump's cam ring. Used in conjunction with another servo piston like the DB pump, the **injection timing stepper (ITS) motor** regulates internal pump housing fuel pressure used to retard and advance injection timing **FIGURE 23-13**.

Engine Shut-Off Solenoid

This solenoid device is located on the top of the injection pump and shuts the engine off when current is removed from the solenoid.

Operation

Several stages of fuel pressurization, filling, metering and distribution are involved in the operation of the DS pump.

Fill Cycle—Pressurization

At initial engine start, the fuel lift pump that is under PCM control continuously supplies fuel to the injection pump at pressure between 5.8 and 8.7 psi (40 and 60 kPa) **FIGURE 23-14**. From the lift pump, fuel enters the vane internal transfer pump. This pump varies the pressure of fuel inside the injection pump

FIGURE 23-13 Location of the ITS motor used to electronically control injection timing by hydraulic-servo rotation of the cam ring inside the pump.

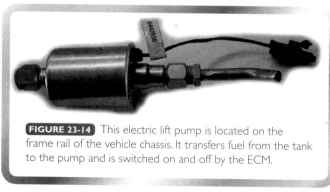

FIGURE 23-14 This electric lift pump is located on the frame rail of the vehicle chassis. It transfers fuel from the tank to the pump and is switched on and off by the ECM.

proportionally to engine speed. At idle, fuel pressure is between 20 and 30 psi (138 and 207 kPa) while maximum pressure is between 100 and 125 psi (689 and 862 kPa) at high idle. A pressure regulator valve with a viscosity-compensating feature regulates maximum transfer pump pressure by redirecting excess fuel volume back to the transfer pump inlet. Like the DB-2 pump, a vent wire is located in the DS pump, which also allows air and fuel vapor to vent from the hydraulic head into the governor housing.

Distribution and Metering

Fuel travels through the hydraulic pump head to a charging annulus or circular ring, which supplies fuel pressurized by the internal transfer pump to a passageway drilled along the length of the rotor. The charging annulus has eight slots in an eight-cylinder engine. These slots can align with two inlet ports

to the rotor. A passage within the rotor will carry fuel to the pressure chamber between the pumping plungers forcing the plungers apart.

Stages of Injection

The stages of injection are:

1. Filling: The rotor inlet ports align with slots in the charging annulus, which fills the fuel cavity between the pumping plungers, pushing the plungers apart. Because the solenoid is off, fuel also enters the fill-spill chamber **FIGURE 23-15**.

2. End of filling: The rotor ports have turned and are now out of alignment with the annulus slots. The FSD closes the fuel control valve, and fuel cannot enter the fill-spill chamber. As the rotor turns, the plungers ramp up onto the lobe of the cam ring, which begins to pressurize fuel inside the rotor **FIGURE 23-16**.

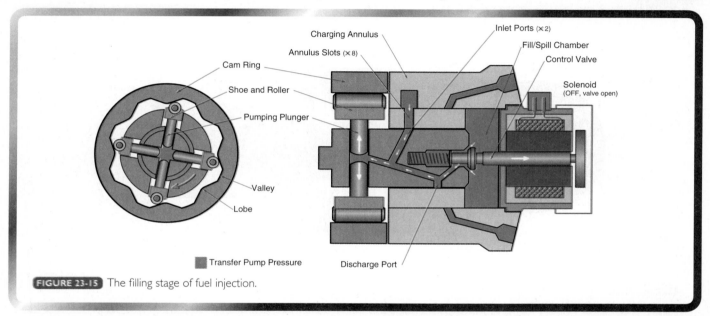

FIGURE 23-15 The filling stage of fuel injection.

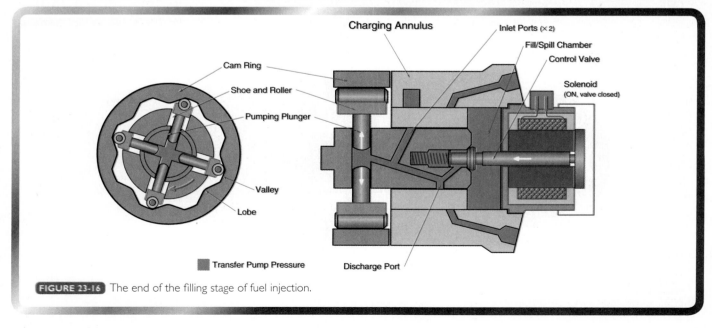

FIGURE 23-16 The end of the filling stage of fuel injection.

3. Metering: The rotor turns, and the pumping plungers are pushed inward by the cam ring lobes. The discharge port of the rotor aligns with passageways in the distributor head, directing fuel to the correct cylinder in the firing sequence **FIGURE 23-17**.

4. Spilling: The fuel control solenoid is deactivated and high-pressure fuel in the discharge passageway is vented into the fill-spill chamber. This event ends injection **FIGURE 23-18**. Because the fuel control valve is open, fuel can enter the fuel fill-spill chamber located at the end of the rotor. The spill chamber is maintained at pressure equal to the output of the transfer pump pressure. Unlike the DB-2 pump, the DS-4 pumping chamber is always pressurized with fuel, and the pumping plungers will move outwardly to their maximum travel when between cam lobes. Pressurization of fuel

begins after the fuel control solenoid is closed and when the plungers ramp onto the cam ring lobe. As the plungers pressurize fuel, the discharge ports of the rotor align with passages to each injector line fitting in the hydraulic head. Injection will continue until an electrical signal to the fuel solenoid opens a spill valve that connects the discharge port to a spill-fill chamber. When opened, injection effectively ends. The fuel metering control valve also doubles in function as a delivery valve.

Injection Timing

Injection timing of the DS pump is managed by the ITS motor. This motor partially substitutes the function of the advance/retard sliding piston in the DB-2 pump. A sliding, spring-loaded piston is still connected to the cam ring, enabling the beginning

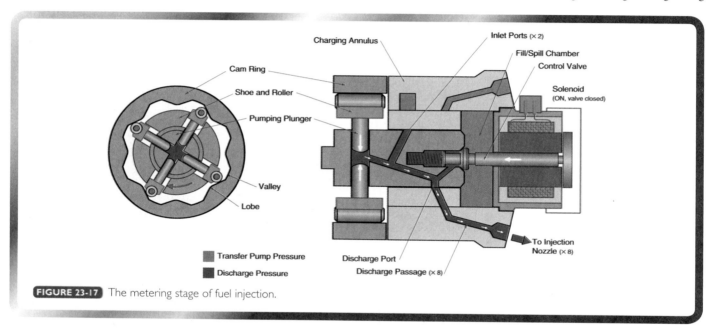

FIGURE 23-17 The metering stage of fuel injection.

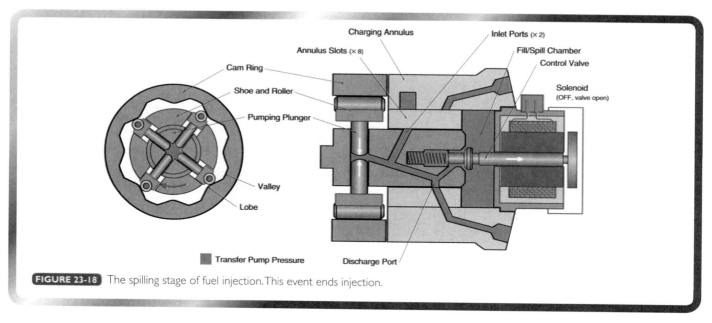

FIGURE 23-18 The spilling stage of fuel injection. This event ends injection.

of injection timing to be advanced or retarded. However, the electronically controlled ITS motor operates linkage connected to a servo valve controlling fuel pressure to one side of the sliding servo piston. Fuel pressure generated by the transfer pump opposes the opposite side of the servo piston. Depending on the position of the servo valve, more or less fuel pressure will act on a sliding piston that rotates the cam ring through a pin. Electric signals from the PCM will move the ITS motor linkage in and out of the motor to modulate hydraulic pressure applied to the servo piston. Spring pressure and fuel pump housing pressure counteracting servo valve movement will cause the sliding piston to move the cam ring to a retard position when no current is applied to the ITS motor. Conversely, an electric signal applied to the ITS is required to advance timing.

Excessively high return fuel pressure will dramatically affect pump operation like the DB-2 pump. However, unlike the DB-2, which will stall with a restricted fuel return line, the fuel pressure regulator inside the DS pump housing make it less sensitive to return-line restrictions.

Fuel Injector Driver Circuit

The PMD or FSD supplies a current-regulated signal to the fuel-metering control solenoid that regulates the length of time over which injection takes place **FIGURE 23-19**. The PCM supplies two pulse-width–modulated (PWM) signals to the solenoid. Only one is necessary, but the other is a redundant signal to increase circuit reliability if a poor electrical connection or other problem interferes with circuit operation. A third or return PWM signal is supplied from the driver to the PCM and is returned from the fuel-metering control solenoid. This signal is used to monitor fuel-metering control solenoid position. This return signal is used to modify the BOI signal to the FSD/PMD. A circuit in the FSD analyzes the slight change in the electrical waveform received from the solenoid when the control valve closes. The movement of the metering control valve will change the solenoid's magnetic reluctance, which in turn affects the PWM electrical signal returned to the drive module. The PCM will recalculate a BOI time and supply this information to the FSD to correct injection lag time caused by electrical resistances, slow-building magnetic fields, or deterioration of the fuel-metering control solenoid. This arrangement ensures even more accurate control of injection events.

Fuel Rate Calibration Resistor

Connected between two terminals of the driver module is a **fuel rate calibration resistor**. This resistor provides data to the drive module regarding the flow rate of the pump **FIGURE 23-20**. The concept driving this resistor is similar to that of a trim code of a unit injector. Each pump supplies slightly different injection quantities of fuel because of manufacturing variations. The PMD or FSD needs to compensate for these changes if accurate metering of fuel is to be accomplished. It is important to remember that the resistor is matched to the pump and not the drive module. This means that the drive module that incorporates the resistor cannot be switched between pumps or a fault code may be logged. Changing the resistor or using an incorrect resistor of higher resistance value is occasionally used to slightly increase engine power output at full load.

> ▶ **TECHNICIAN TIP**
>
> Transferring the FSD or PMD fuel rate calibration resistor to the replacement parts should take place whenever a pump is replaced or whenever a PMD is replaced.

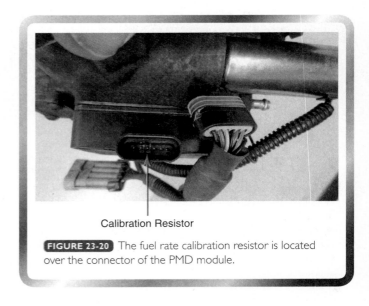

Calibration Resistor

FIGURE 23-20 The fuel rate calibration resistor is located over the connector of the PMD module.

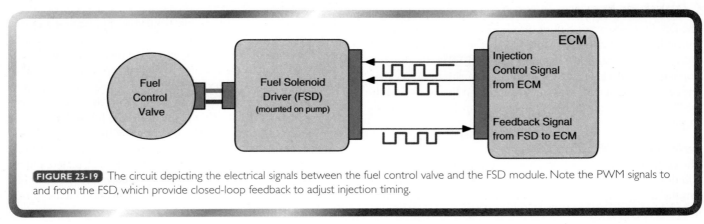

FIGURE 23-19 The circuit depicting the electrical signals between the fuel control valve and the FSD module. Note the PWM signals to and from the FSD, which provide closed-loop feedback to adjust injection timing.

Fuel Temperature Sensor

The fuel temperature sensor is used to maintain consistent fuel delivery volumes to compensate for changes to fuel viscosity caused by temperature fluctuations. Hot fuel tends to leak through pump clearances more easily. The low density of hot fuel also contributes to decreased power output. This leads to low-power complaints. If the PCM measures fuel temperature, a correction factor is applied to the fueling to correct fuel delivery rates.

Optical Sensor Tracking Encoder

This sensor is one of the most important PCM inputs for determining fuel timing. How much fuel, when it is injected, and length of injection forms PCM fueling strategies using data provided by the sensor. Data from this sensor also identifies misfire detection cylinder imbalance problems.

The PCM also compares data from this sensor with crankshaft position to account for minor variations between pump-to-engine timing. During initial start-up, the pump top dead center (TDC) signal and engine TDC signal are compared. Clearances and backlash in between the crankshaft and pump drive gear can lead to injection timing errors. If more than a couple degrees of variation in pump-to-engine timing are detected, a fault code is logged.

Crank Position Sensor   Three-Wire Hall Effect

FIGURE 23-21 A three-wire Hall effect sensor is used to measure crank position on the 6.5L (397 cubic inch) GM diesel. Coordinating data from this sensor and the OSTE provides input for timing and metering injection events.

When replacing an injection pump, the pump-to-engine timing must be correctly adjusted to obtain correct operating injection timing. Once established, the PCM will electronically change the injection timing based on a presumed relationship between the pump and engine position. To precisely adjust pump-to-engine timing the "TDC Offset Learn" feature on a scanner such as a Tech-II is used. When prompted, the PCM will examine the signals from the crank and OSTE. If the pump is installed correctly, the TDC offset value should be between −0.25 and −0.75 degrees. That means the pump and crank gear TDC indicators must correspond to the same position within ±1 degree of variation. If the value is not within specified range, the injection pump must be loosened and rotated to obtain the correct value. If adjusted incorrectly, a fault code P1214 (crankshaft position variation not learned) will illuminate the check engine light.

Crankshaft Position Sensor

The DS-4 pump's crankshaft position sensor is a Hall effect sensor, which means it measures the speed of rotation of four teeth located on the crankshaft sprocket **FIGURE 23-21**. In conjunction with the OSTE sensor, the crankshaft position senor calculates engine speed and position. Signals from the crank and the OSTE sensor are compared to detect pump-to-engine timing variations.

Performing a TDC Offset Relearn

The crank position sensor on an engine with an electronic distributor pump is used to correct any error in pump-to-engine timing through a process called TDC offset relearn. Electronic distributor pumps like the Stanadyne DS pump on GM 6.5L

(397 cubic inch) engines can have incorrect pump-to-engine timing when the pump is replaced. If the variation between the injection pump's calculation of engine position and the position measured by the crank position sensor exceeds ±2 degrees, a fault code is set. The TDC offset relearn is used to establish the correct pump-to-engine timing and eliminate the code. This procedure is also used whenever the power train control module, crank position sensor, or engine are replaced.

To perform a TDC offset relearn, follow the steps in **SKILL DRILL 23-1**.

VP-37 Components and Operation

To understand the operation of the VP-37 fuel pump system, it is helpful to first identify the major components and their functions.

Needle Lift Sensor

The needle lift sensor is an electromagnet built using a coil of wire supplied with a constant current by the ECM. A pressure pin extension connected to the end of the nozzle valve will move up and down with the opening and closing of the nozzle valve. When it lifts, the change in the magnetic field reluctance produces a distortion in the electrical signal to the magnetic coil. The ECM then detects this point of needle lift and accurately determines the point of BOI. By coordinating this signal with the data from the crankshaft position sensor and fuel timing maps stored in the ECUM the injection lag is calculated. Differences between measured BOI and expected values stored in fuel map memory are then used to apply a correction factor to BOI for the remaining cylinders.

SKILL DRILL 23-1 Performing a TDC Offset Relearn

1. Using a suitable scan tool with TDC offset relearn capabilities, clear any fault codes. Run the engine until it reaches operating temperature. After it reaches operating temperature, the power train control monitor PCM will try to automatically learn a new TDC offset. The revised TDC offset will overwrite the previous TDC offset.

2. Shut the engine off and turn the ignition switch to the on position with the engine off (KOEO).

3. Fully depress the throttle pedal for at least 45 seconds.

4. Turn the ignition switch to the off position for 30 seconds.

5. Restart the engine and navigate to the scan tool's diagnostic menu used to verify that TDC offset has been cleared to zero.

6. Operate the engine at less than 1500 rpm and observe the TDC offset parameter displayed on the scan tool; it should be between −0.25 to −0.75. If the TDC offset is within specifications, the pump is properly positioned to establish correct pump-to-engine timing and relearn procedure is complete.

7. If the TDC offset position is not within specifications, the injection pump needs to be rotated.

8. To rotate the injection pump, loosen the injection pump mounting nuts and turn the pump toward the driver's side of the vehicle if the offset is positive. Turn the pump to the passenger side of the vehicle if the offset is negative.

9. Recheck the TDC offset parameter displayed on the scanner to verify that the correct offset is established.

Control Sleeve Position Sensor

The control sleeve operates to meter the injection quantity by controlling the end of the fuel pressurization event, just as it does in the mechanical VE pump. To electronically control the sleeve, its position must first be determined via a **control sleeve position sensor**. Another name for this pump sensor, which more accurately reflects its function, is the governor position sensor. The equivalent of this sensor in partial-authority inline pumps is the rack position sensor. The control sleeve position sensor measures the angle of rotation of the cam-shaped lever operating the control sleeve. The movement of the metal ring creates disturbances in the A/C-induced magnetic field of the iron core. Electrical signals produced by the changing magnetic field are detected by a circuit in the ECM, which translates this information into position data. Like the VE pump, a sliding control sleeve on the pump plunger controls the quantity of fuel injected by opening or closing the spill port in the fuel pressure chamber. Linkage connected to the sleeve operates like a bell crank, rotating to slide the sleeve for metering of injection quantity **FIGURE 23-22**.

The sensor is a non-contact device, which means it is free from wear. Sensor data is generated by electronically evaluating changes to magnetic field strength caused by a movable hoop surrounding an iron core conducting alternating current. This design provides exceptionally reliable operation which is free from fluctuations caused by temperature and electromagnetic interference.

Fuel Quantity Solenoid

The **fuel quantity solenoid**, also known as the quantity adjuster, is an electronic actuator that moves the control sleeve adjusting shaft. Movement of the adjuster is proportional to the amount of current passing through the solenoid. The greater the current flow, the farther the control sleeve shaft moves. A spring counters the force of the solenoid movement to return it to an idle fuel quantity position. The control sleeve position is a balance between spring and solenoid force. Current from the ECM adjusts the position of the control sleeve for the correct injection quantity from zero to maximum delivery rate. A feedback loop regarding the position of the quantity adjuster works in conjunction with the control sleeve position sensor. The ECM will adjust the signal to the solenoid based on feedback from the position sensor.

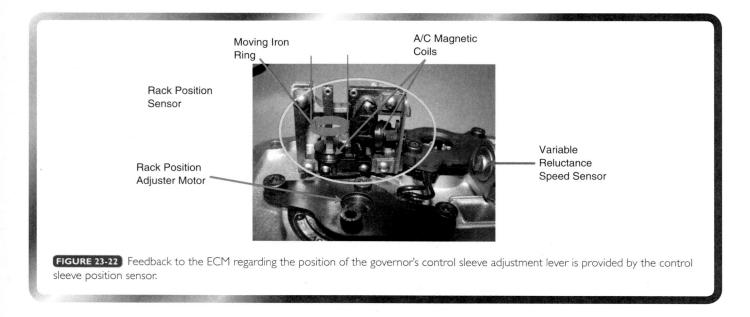

FIGURE 23-22 Feedback to the ECM regarding the position of the governor's control sleeve adjustment lever is provided by the control sleeve position sensor.

Start of Delivery Solenoid

The point when fuel injection begins is influenced by various operating conditions, such as engine starting response, injection lag time, engine speed, engine load, intake air temperature, and coolant temperature, and it also depends on performance and emission requirements. To achieve the optimal point during engine rotation for injection, an actuator is used to vary the start of injection. Using engine sensor data and fuel timing maps, the ECM calculates and delivers an electrical signal to the start of delivery solenoid, thus adjusting beginning of injection timing.

In the VE pump, internal fuel pressure influences injection timing. A sliding piston connected to the cam plate will rotate the cam ring to an advanced BOI as pressure increases. As pump speed increases, pressure produced by the internal vane pump increases proportionally. It is much the same in the VP-37 pump, but fuel pressure applied to the sliding piston is instead regulated by a solenoid. A PWM signal applied to the solenoid can vary the pressure applied to the piston, thus causing the BOI timing to advance or retard. Spring pressure retards timing, while fuel pressure will advance timing.

Limp Home and Substitute Functions

Rather than have the engine fail to operate at all when a problem with the engine control system occurs, an operating strategy called limp home mode permits operation with limited power under a number of scenarios. For example, if the engine speed sensor fails, the ECM will substitute the BOI signal from the needle lift sensor for the speed sensor. Reduced quantities of fuel are injected under these circumstances, as with other sensor failures, but the vehicle can be driven to a repair facility. In instances in which vehicle and passenger safety would be compromised if the engine were allowed to run (for example, in the instance of a fuel quantity solenoid or control sleeve position sensor failure), the fuel shut-off device will cut off fuel delivery and stop the engine.

Brake Pedal Switch Input

The ECM uses inputs from two brake pedal switches to minimize fueling during braking. This feature enhances safety and fuel economy to prevent fueling of the engine when brakes are applied at wide open throttle (WOT) position. It is important that these switches are set up correctly, because fuel cut-off can occur at the wrong time and cause the engine to stall when not braking. The switch may also become faulty, which could result in random initiation of fuel cut-off.

VP-44 Components and Operation

Because the VP-44 is an electronically controlled radial piston distributor pump, many of its construction and operating features are similar to those in other opposed-plunger metering systems, particularly the Stanadyne DS pump. However, the VP-44 does have several features that enable even more accurate electronic control over injection timing and metering. The fast-acting electromagnetic metering control solenoid also permits the use of pilot injection for reduction of combustion noise and oxides of nitrogen (NO_x) emissions. Different models with two, three, or four radial opposed pumping plungers facilitate changes to fuel delivery pressure and volume. The VP-44 used on the ISB engine has three opposed plungers. Like any other distributor pump, the VP-44 turns at camshaft or one-half engine speed to supply an injection to each cylinder as the engine completes one four-stroke combustion cycle. The following are descriptions of the major components of the low- and high-pressure fuel system.

Low-Pressure Fuel Supply Components

Fuel supply to the injection pump is usually handled by a low-pressure intermediate pump. Inside the injection pump, a vane pump is used to change the volume and pressure of fuel supplied to the pump proportional to engine speed **FIGURE 23-23**. This variable pressure is necessary to operate the

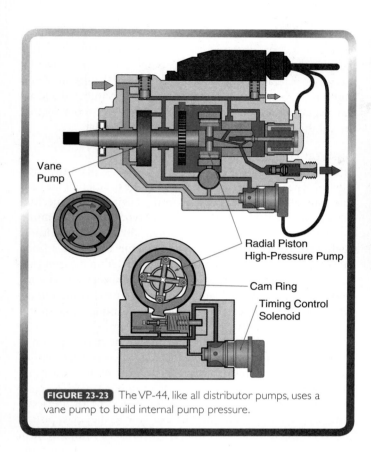

FIGURE 23-23 The VP-44, like all distributor pumps, uses a vane pump to build internal pump pressure.

FIGURE 23-24 Large fuel supply and return lines are needed on the VP-44 pump to return 70% of fuel back to the tank.

timing mechanism. A maximum internal pressure of 300 psi (207 bar) is produced by the vane pump at maximum pump speed. A pressure regulator controls outlet fuel pressure to the metering and timing control devices. Any excess fuel volume from the pressure regulator is routed back through the inlet of the vane pump.

Because pressurization of fuel produces heat, fuel is circulated through the pump and returned to the tank for cooling purposes. To accomplish this, 70% of fuel flow to the pump returns to the tank through the overflow valve. Like other overflow valves, it regulates the quantity of fuel returned to tank. If any air or vapor is entrained in the fuel supply or enters after a filter change, certain features in the overflow valve will purge the vapor from the pump and send it back to the tank with the fuel return **FIGURE 23-24**.

High-Pressure Components

The high-pressure section of the VP-44 pump resembles the operation of Stanadyne's DS-4 pump in terms of the use of opposed plungers to pressurize fuel and a rotary shaft that supplies fuel circuits to and from the plungers. Variations to metering and timing of the injection events are outlined in this next section.

Opposed Plunger High-Pressure Pump

The opposed piston plungers are arranged at 90 degrees to the rotor shaft inside a cam ring. A set of shoes and rollers for each plunger transfers the shape of the cam profile to the plungers as they rotate inside the cam ring. The version of the VP-44 pump used on the Cummins ISB engine has three opposed plungers

carried by the rotor. Four-plunger models use a pair of short and long plungers to prevent interference with one another when the cam ring compresses the plungers simultaneously. As the pump rotor turns, the cam lobes force the rollers and shoes against the plungers that pressurize the fuel. A column of pressurized fuel is then built up in a passageway drilled along the axis of the rotor. A single opening in the rotor, called the distributor slot, directs the pressurized fuel column to the appropriate cylinder through a discharge port in the head of the pump.

High-Pressure Metering Valve Solenoid

An electromagnetic solenoid valve is located at the fuel's entry point in the pump rotor. A needle valve operated by the solenoid opens and closes the passageway connecting fuel pressurized by the vane pump to the pumping plunger pressure chamber. When opened by a signal from the FPCM, fuel enters the rotor through an annular passage around the rotor **FIGURE 23-25**. Fuel passes around the solenoid-operated needle valve and fills the pump pressure chamber with fuel. This action pushes the pumping plungers against the shoes and rollers. When the electrical signal is removed from the metering control valve solenoid, the shape of the needle valve combined with fuel pressure around the valve rapidly closes the passageway to the pressure chamber. Continued rotation of the rotor compresses the plungers inside the cam ring, and fuel pressure builds in the pressure chamber. When the distributor slot in the rotor aligns with a high-pressure outlet in the hydraulic head of the pump, the high-pressure fuel column is connected to the injector nozzle through high-pressure fittings on the pump.

Opening the metering valve again will end injection and start a fill cycle. Pressure in the rotor is bled off to the low-pressure side of the pump. This dumping of high-pressure fuel produces pressure pulsations that are dampened by a pulsation dampener located in the head of the pump. Injection quantity is determined by the length of time the metering valve is closed. Metering valve operation combined with the movement of the

FIGURE 23-25 The FPCM connects to an angle of rotation sensor and outputs to the injection timing and metering solenoids.

cam ring can vary the injection timing from TDC to as much as 40 degrees before TDC. When the engine key is turned to the off position, no signal is supplied to the metering solenoid valve, so no injection pressure can be developed and the engine stops.

Electronic Pilot Injection

The design of the metering solenoid and the needle valve provides for very precise and rapid control of the injection event, and electronic control of pilot injection is accomplished with the VP-44 pump. Electronic pilot injection permits the use of conventional multi-orifice injector nozzles in the VP-44 pump, as compared to the throttling pintle injectors used on the 6.5L (397 cubic inch) GM diesel and the two-stage needle injectors used with the VP-37 pumps to achieve injection rate shape control.

Beginning of Injection Event Detection

A circuit within the FPCM analyzes the signal to the metering valve solenoid and can detect the instant the needle valve closes and injection begins. For this reason, an injector needle motion or lift sensor is not necessary to identify BOI. However, Bosch does provide the option of using this sensor with some pump VP-44 pump models.

Delivery Valves

Each cylinder fitting in the hydraulic head of the pump uses a delivery valve. These valves maintain a residual injector line pressure between injections to minimize injection lag. Lowering line pressure required to open the nozzle valve prevents secondary injections caused by reflection of the pressure wave traveling

back and forth between the closed needle valve and delivery valve. An electric lift pump (used on Cummins ISB, for example) permits bleeding of air from the pump after filter changes by momentarily cranking the engine and leaving the key in the on position. A 25-second fuel pump purge cycle is initiated and air can be purged from the system by cracking two or more injector lines at the engine side of the high-pressure fuel line.

Injection Timing Control

In electronic distributor type injection pumps, like other distributor type injection pumps, changing the position of the cam ring causes incremental changes to the beginning of injection timing. Also similar to other distributor type pumps, the timing mechanism is controlled both hydraulically and electronically. Fuel pressure developed by the vane pump is applied to one side of a spring-loaded piston that is connected to the cam ring through a single pin. The position of this master piston controls the location of the cam ring lobes relative to the pumping plungers. Hydraulic pressure advances timing while spring pressure retards timing.

Modulating the hydraulic pressure to the master piston is the job of a timing control solenoid valve. An arrangement of springs and a servo piston cause fuel pressure to the master piston to increase and advance injection timing.

The timing control valve controls fuel flow to the servo piston. When it is closed, no fuel can flow to the servo piston, which results in retarded timing. Opening the timing control valve allows fuel to flow through the servo piston and push the master piston to advance timing.

During cranking, the master piston is held in the retarded position by a return spring. Injection would occur at TDC under these conditions. During cranking, however, the vane pump pressure increases and pressure is applied to the master piston by opening the timing control valve. Fuel pressure applied to the master piston compresses the spring, moving the cam ring to an advanced position. This rotates the cam ring and causes the rollers to contact the pistons sooner and deliver fuel earlier to advance injection timing.

Angle of Rotation Sensor

A variable-reluctance sensor and trigger wheel locked to the pump drive shaft provide data regarding instantaneous pump speed and engine position. This fuel pump increment angle time system, as it is called, is used to calculate the beginning and end of fuel delivery based on pump position. The trigger wheel has teeth, and each one corresponds to 3 degrees of engine rotation. A missing tooth on the wheel also corresponds to TDC for each cylinder. The signal supplied by this system provides information to the FPCM and ECM to precisely determine engine position and determine fuel timing. With this data, the FPCM sends a signal to the timing control valve to adjust timing.

To accomplish adaptive cylinder balance, variations in cylinder contributions are measured by detecting changes to crankshaft velocity. The pump can then adjust fuel delivery quantity to each injector to produce smooth idle conditions. Cylinders requiring too much adjustment to injection quantity will cause fault codes and illumination of the malfunction indicator lamp.

Pump Timing Offset

To adjust the pump timing to compensate for minor position differences that can cause injection timing errors, comparisons are made between fuel pump shaft position and crankshaft position sensor data. Once every pump revolution, the ECM receives a reference pulse from the crank position sensor that indicates TDC of the first cylinder. By comparing this reference pulse from the ECM to the pump's speed sensor, marking TDC, the FPCM can measure any discrepancy between the pump's and engine's positions. The FPCM learns where the first cylinder's TDC event occurs and adjusts timing accordingly. If the difference between the pump position and engine position becomes too great, a fault will be logged in the FPCM. In the event the crankshaft position signal data is lost, the FPCM will substitute the injection pump position signal to operate the engine.

Pump Drive Keyway and Injection Timing

On Cummins ISB engines using the VP-44 pump, the fuel pump drive key is matched to the injection pump for correct timing. A number stamped on the pump data plate must correspond to the number stamped into the woodruff key on the drive shaft. This feature ensures even more precise injection timing accuracy.

Electronic Control Module

On Cummins 5.9L (360 cubic inch) engines, electronic control of the fuel system is performed by the engine-mounted ECM and the FPCM. Essentially, the ECM is responsible for calculating fuel delivery quantity based on engine speed and load conditions. Injection timing functions are performed by the FPCM. The ECM collects data from engine and vehicle sensors that are used to calculate fuel quantity using algorithms and maps located in the ECM. Other data is received by the FPCM and timing calculations are performed there as well. With the exception of a fuel temperature sensor located in the injection pump, the FPCM receives no data from engine or vehicle sensors. Instead, the ECM sends information over a two-wire control area network (CAN) data bus to the FPCM.

Sensor data collected by the ECM relevant to calculating correct injection timing and metering include:

- Coolant temperature
- Intake manifold temperature
- Lubrication oil temperature
- Vehicle speed data
- Crankshaft position data
- Camshaft position sensor
- Accelerator position data
- Intake manifold boost pressure sensor
- CAN data bus
- Operator switches such as cruise, PTO, or fast idle controls

On some OBD-II–compliant engines using the VP-44, an MAF sensor is used for EGR flow calculations and air–fuel ratio control.

Some operating conditions have priority over other sensor inputs. For example, low coolant temperature will prevent the engine from going to full throttle regardless of input from other devices. This engine protection feature, which monitors abuse conditions, also provides cold-weather engine protection.

Fuel Pump Control Module

The primary function of the FPCM is intelligent fuel timing and injection quantity adjustment. However, the pump is not able to operate without data from the ECM. To aid in efficient diagnosis of hard- and no-start conditions, the nine-pin connector on the injection pump can be disconnected and a special tool called an electrical harness can be used to substitute signals from the ECM to the pump. This facilitates a differential diagnosis between problems with the vehicle's electrical system (i.e., differentiating CAN problems from pump problems) **FIGURE 23-26** .

Controlling both the metering and timing control solenoids, the FPCM processes data from the angle of rotation sensor and fuel temperature sensor along with ECM data. It can modify injection quantity and injection rate commended by the ECM.

Heat developed by the actuator drivers on the pump module is removed by fuel circulating through the pump.

Original Equipment Manufacturer Low-Pressure Fuel Transfer Pump

A brief discussion of the original equipment manufacturer (OEM) fuel transfer pump is necessary for complete coverage of the VP-44 pump. Controlled by the ECM, the electric vane transfer pump mounted on the engine uses PWM signals to provide two duty cycles: full speed when the engine is running and half speed during cranking to prevent over pressurization of the injection pump, which can keep the injection pump

FIGURE 23-26 The VP-44 pump has a connector that can be replaced with another harness to provide power to the pump when diagnosing hard-start complaints.

from operating. Excessive internal pump pressure during cranking can prevent the pumping plungers from being forced outward, thus limiting full delivery quantity during cranking **FIGURE 23-27**.

The pump is self-priming and needs no mechanical priming. During cranking, the pump pressure is limited to 7 psi (48 kPa) and then increases to 10 psi (69 kPa) after the engine starts. During the first two seconds when the key is moved to the on position, the pump will operate and then shut off. If the engine is cranked and not started, the transfer pump operates for 25 seconds and shuts off. If the engine shuts down without the key being turned to the off position, a safety feature prevents the pump from operating to prevent fuel leaks in case a broken fuel line was the cause of shut-down.

► Maintenance of Electronic Distributor Injection Pumps

The modular construction of electronically controlled distributor injection pumps enables technicians to replace parts in the field, rather than sending the pumps to specialized shops for repair. The following section outlines some diagnostic and repair procedures for electronically controlled distributor injection pumps.

PMD/FSD Failures

Problems with the drive module are often due to overheating. The engine will often fail to start, stall, or experience low power when hot. Cooling the module will likely help get a stalled vehicle restarted. Aftermarket kits to relocate the module and attach a heat sink are available to improve module reliability. One aftermarket manufacturer has produced a module with military-grade electronics to increase module durability.

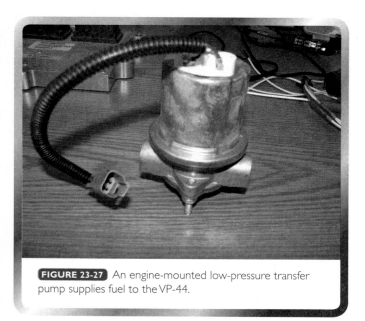

FIGURE 23-27 An engine-mounted low-pressure transfer pump supplies fuel to the VP-44.

Faulty Needle Lift Sensor

A sticking or faulty needle lift sensor can cause unusual issues. The engine will operate, but maximum engine speed is reduced because a substitute value is given for BOI, and sluggish operation and low-power complaints result. Additionally, the instrument glow plug light may illuminate.

Hard Starting

Air in the fuel system caused by filter replacement can be bled from the system during the 25-second purge cycle. By momentarily cranking the engine and disconnecting at least two injector lines, the fuel pressure produced by the pump is adequate to open the delivery valves to purge the pump and lines of air.

VP-44 Pump Failures

The VP-44 is OBD-II–compliant, meaning its sensors and actuators are monitored by the ECM to detect failures or other conditions that can cause excessive emissions. The VP-44 does not inject fuel when the throttle is closed and the engine speed is above idle (i.e., when decelerating or coasting). During these conditions, no fuel is passing through to cool and lubricate the rotor turning in the head of the pump. It is believed by some repair facilities that this condition, when prolonged, can lead to the rotor seizure in the distributor head, causing the drive plate to break and the engine to quit. Fuel transfer pump failures can reduce fuel flow through the pump, resulting in pump failure. Again, this problem is believed to be caused by reduced pump cooling and lubrication.

The use of biodiesel blended above 5% concentrations and ethanol additive to diesel fuel are not recommended by Cummins Engine Company.

Measuring Transfer Pump Fuel Pressure and Volume in a VP-44 Pump

VP-44 pumps require an above-average fuel flow to keep the fuel temperature in the pump low. Pressurizing fuel produces high fuel temperatures, which can reduce fuel viscosity. Fuel viscosity is important to these fuel-lubricated pumps. Pump housing wear accelerates due to lubrication problems caused by low fuel flow through the pump. To maintain more than adequate fuel flow, the fuel transfer pump is important because it maintains effective positive fuel flow through the injection pump. Note also that low fuel pump pressure will generate fault codes.

To measure transfer pump fuel pressure and volume in a VP-44 pump, follow the steps in **SKILL DRILL 23-2**.

► Cummins Accumulator Pressure System

One other significant distributor injection pump is the Cummins Accumulator Pump System (CAPS), which was used on Cummins six cylinder 8.3L (506 cubic inch) C-series and 8.9L (543

SKILL DRILL 23-2 Measuring Transfer Pump Fuel Pressure and Volume in a VP-44 Pump

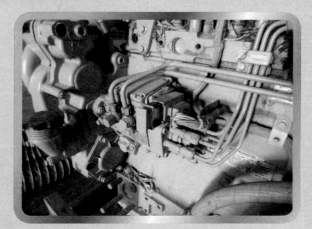

1. Inspect all fuel lines for kinks, leaks, and other damage.

2. Connect a fuel pressure gauge to the fuel filter pump outlet using an adapter fitting.

3. Start and run the engine. Test drive the vehicle. Normal fuel pressure should be 14–15 psi (97–103 kPa) at moderate road speeds. Fuel pressure should never fall below 10 psi (60 kPa), even if the engine seems to run well at that pressure.

4. Snap the throttle to wide open throttle while observing the fuel pressure. Pressure should not fall below 12 psi (83 kPa), and should quickly return to 14–15 psi (97–103 kPa). If the pressure falls below 12 psi (83 kPa), recommend a fuel filter replacement and further pump pressure volume testing.

5. To measure pump volume output and pressure, connect a 36" (91 cm) piece of clear plastic hose to the filter outlet and route it to a fuel container.

6. Turn the ignition key to the on position. The electric transfer pump should operate and stop after 2 seconds.

7. Briefly engage the starter without starting the engine to supply an engine rpm signal to the ECM. The electric lift pump should run for 25 seconds and stop.

8. Observe and measure the fuel volume from the fuel filter. Compare the output volume with the manufacturer's specifications. The fuel should be free of any air bubbles.

9. If fuel volume is less than the manufacturer's specification, measure the pressure drop across the fuel filter. Compare this with OEM's specifications, which should require a drop of less than 5 psi (34 kPa). Clean filters generally have a pressure drop of less than 1 psi (7 kPa). Excessive drop means the filter is restricted. If the pressure drop is acceptable, but the fuel volume is less than the OEM's specifications, measure the inlet pressure to the external transfer pump in inches (centimeters) of mercury (Hg). If the restriction is higher than the OEM's specifications (generally less than 6" [15 cm] Hg) a restriction exists between the transfer pump and the fuel tank.

10. Measure the pressure between the electric transfer pump and the fuel filter with the key on and engine off. High pressure indicates a restricted fuel filter. Low pressure indicates inadequate transfer pump output volume, which requires pump replacement.

---

cubic inch) L-series engines **FIGURE 23-28**. These pumps were introduced in 1998 and used until the high-pressure common rail system replaced CAPS in 2004. Many of these pumps are still in use in on- and off-highway applications, agricultural equipment, and motorhomes. The advantage of the CAPS system is that it can electronically regulate injection pressures even at low engine speeds by using an accumulator to store high-pressure fuel. Two relatively large pistons incorporated into the pump pressurize fuel any time the engine is running. Because the pistons can oversupply the injection system, surplus fuel is stored at electronically controlled injection pressure in the accumulator. Because electronic controls, and not engine speed, regulate injection pressures, the CAPS system is considered a sub-type of common rail fuel systems.

CAPS Operation Overview

In CAPS, fuel is pressurized to injection pressure by a pair of pumping plungers. High-pressure fuel is delivered to the cylinders through a distributor pump head using a rotor driven at one-half engine speed. A rotor shaft with an inlet and outlet fuel drilling transfers high-pressure fuel to the distributor head as it

FIGURE 23-28 CAPS was used on Cummins six cylinder 8.3L (506 cubic inch) C-series and 8.9L (543 cubic inch) L-series engines from 1998 to 2004.

rotates in the pump housing. The position of the rotor directs pressurized fuel to one of six drillings in the distributor housing. At the outlet of each drilling is a fuel pump delivery valve; each injector line has a delivery valve. Correct pump-to-engine timing is established by a small dowel pin on the pump's drive shaft, which fits into the engines' front gear train drive gear in only one place. An electronically controlled injection control valve controls injection timing and delivery quantity.

CAPS Construction

Cummins constructs the CAPS fuel system as a modular fuel system, which enables it to be easily serviced in the field for rapid turn-around of repairs when they are needed, without the use of a specialty repair shop. CAPS has six sections:

- Gear pump
- Camshaft housing
- High-pressure accumulator
- Distributor head
- Rate shape tube
- Injector control valve (ICV)

The gear pump serves as an internal fuel transfer pump that pulls fuel from the tank and delivers it at 160 psi (11 bar) to the pumping plungers, which pressurize fuel to injection pressure. The gear pump is driven by the pump camshaft through an internal coupling. When operating, the gear pump shaft rotates a rotor in the distributor head of the pump, directing fuel to the appropriate cylinder in the firing order. Fuel from the gear pump that supplies the pumping plungers is driven by a camshaft with three lobes for each plunger. Unlike other distributor pumps, the CAPS camshafts are lubricated with engine oil, which allows them to support higher injection pressure without accelerated wear. Oil lubrication of the camshaft also means the pump can tolerate fuels with low lubricity and alternative fuels without concern about damaging the camshaft. Roller type cam followers attached to the plungers further extend pump reliability and service life.

Injection Pressure Control

The top of the CAPS has two electronically controlled pumping control valves, one above each pumping plunger **FIGURE 23-29**. When the normally open valves are not energized, transfer fuel from the gear pump fills the plunger chambers during their downward strokes. As the plungers move upward, fuel is normally pushed out of the plunger cylinders back to the gear pump unless the control valve is energized. When the control valve is energized, fuel is directed toward the accumulator, where spring-loaded pistons in six cavities hold fuel under pressure. Fuel is prevented from returning to the plungers by one-way check valves. A 0–24,000 psi (0–1655 bar) pressure sensor provides feedback to the ECM to maintain the desired pressure in the accumulator by varying the pulse width of the electrical signal applied to the control valves. Because pressurizing fuel makes it very hot, temperature sensing capabilities are combined with the pressure sensor to supply fuel temperature data to the ECM.

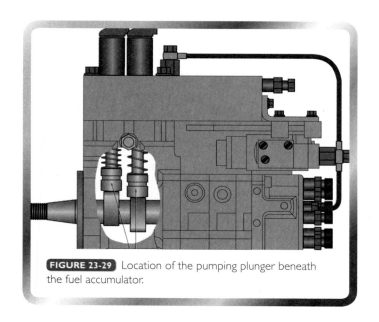

FIGURE 23-29 Location of the pumping plunger beneath the fuel accumulator.

Injection Event Control

After pressure control of the fuel injection event is established by the pressure control valves in the accumulator, timing of the injection event is the next task of CAPS. A uniquely designed injection control valve located in the distributor head of the pump regulates the beginning and ending of the injection event as well as injection quantity control. The valve controls the flow of fuel between the accumulator and pump rotor, distributing fuel to each of the six cylinders through the distributor head of the pump. This valve is capable of three directions of control. In a non-energized state, the normally closed valve blocks fuel delivery to the rotor shaft and distributor pump head. Energized using PWM current, the valve opens the passageway from the accumulator to the rotor through internal drillings. De-energizing the valve causes fuel pressure supplied to the injectors to drop and end injection. The valve's two-piece construction, which uses an electromagnetically controlled outer section and an inner section with a spring-loaded pin, controls fuel flow to either the distributor rotor or the low-pressure fuel drain. Opening and closing the valve completes one injection event. The amount of time the control valve is energized and the pressure in the accumulator will determine how much fuel is injected during the valve's one-time opening and closing in each injection event. A pressure regulator between the drain and tank return circuit helps maintain consistent injection pressure between injection events.

Rate Shape Control

A steel tube called the rate shape tube supplies fuel to the injection control valve. The line has some rate shaping capabilities due to the elasticity of the line, which helps produce a ramp-shaped injection discharge curve. Fuel enters the rate shape tube through a snubber valve. The snubber valve behaves like a delivery valve in an inline injection pump by allowing only one-way fuel movement into the rate shape fuel line and maintaining a residual line pressure at the end of each injection event. Any metal particles in this valve will cause rough engine operation, misfires, low power, and no-start conditions. The position of the rotor directs pressurized fuel to one of six drillings in the distributor housing. At the outlet of each drilling is a fuel pump delivery valve.

Block Mounted Electric Lift Pump

A lift pump is used to prime the pump for faster start-ups and to bleed filters after replacement. This pump operates for approximately 30 seconds after the key is switched on. After the engine is started, the gear transfer pump supplies fuel to the distributor pump without assistance from the priming pump.

Inspecting and Replacing a CAPS Injector Quill Tube

The Cummins CAPS system uses a steel tube known as a quill tube to connect the injector with the high-pressure fuel lines.

The quill connects to the injection supply line at one end outside the cylinder head. At the injector end, it uses a crush-fit sealing surface to stop high-pressure fuel from leaking out and around the injector. One of the most common failures on high-pressure fuel systems that use quill tubes, particularly common rail systems, is a leak between the quill tube and the injector. Leaks in this area will produce a high fuel return flow rate and a no-start condition as high-pressure fuel leaks to the fuel return passage in the cylinder head. Quill tubes that have been leaking will often have invisible scoring or etching at the leak path. The procedure used to install the injector and tube is very critical. Failure to properly follow a specific sequence of steps to install the tube during installation of an injector will cause a repeat failure.

To inspect and replace a CAPS injector quill tube, follow the steps in **SKILL DRILL 23-3**.

SKILL DRILL 23-3 Inspecting and Replacing a CAPS Injector Quill Tube

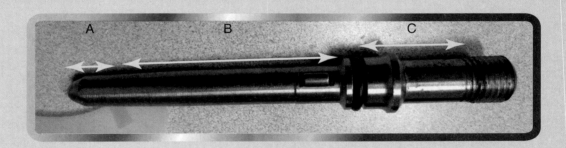

1. Clean any carbon from the injector sleeve bore and from the injector seat. Thoroughly clean the injector if it is being reused.

2. Inspect the injector sealing seat where the quill tube meets the injector. An uneven seating surface, pitting, etching, or scoring will produce injector leakage. Clean the injector sealing area with electrical contact cleaner. This liquid evaporates quickly and is cleaner than brake cleaner.

3. Lubricate the injector sealing O-rings and the injector sleeve with engine oil.

4. Lightly install and seat the injector with by lightly tapping it with a soft-faced hammer. Correctly align the injector's ball bearing or alignment pin with the sleeve in the head.

5. Inspect the new quill tube. Examine it for burrs or deformation around the inlet and outlet ends of the connector. Check the tube's edge filter for signs of plugging. Clean the tube end with brake cleaner. Install a new O-ring on the tube and lubricate it.

6. Install the quill tube into the cylinder head and lightly seat the tube. Use the manufacturer's specifications for tightening to the first stage torque, which is measured in in-lb (Nm). This procedure helps align the injector and tube.

7. Use the manufacturer's specifications to snug down the injector hold-down bolt to the first stage of torque.

8. Tighten the quill tube to the second stage torque tightening to begin to seat the tube into the injector seat.

9. Torque the injector hold-down bolt to specifications. This will seat the injector into the bore and seal the injector against the sealing washer at the bottom of the injector sleeve.

10. Torque the quill tube to specifications to seat the tube into the injector's high-pressure fuel connector.

11. Re-torque the injector hold-down bolt and quill tube. Reconnect the high-pressure fuel line to the quill tube and torque to the manufacturer's specifications to prevent damage from over-torqueing the injector line seat and leaking due to a loose line fitting.

12. Run the engine and check for rough running, leaks, and misfire conditions. A prolonged cranking condition may require measuring the fuel return volume when the engine is running to check for a further quill tube leakage.

Wrap-Up

Ready for Review

- The demand for cleaner engine emissions, increased engine power, quieter operation, and better fuel economy have propelled the development of more efficient fuel-injection systems.
- Because of tighter emission standards, distributor pumps are no longer used on vehicles in North America.
- The design simplicity of mechanical distributor injection pumps accounted for their success. However, injection pressures are low in these systems.
- The introduction of electronic controls to the pump enabled the flexibility to adjust delivery quantities and timing more accurately than was possible in mechanical systems. Idle quality, noise levels, cold-weather starting, and fuel economy were also improved.
- Pump electronics also provide electronic cruise control and fast idle engine control for PTO devices. A simple switch can set idle speed to 1070 rpm, 1360 rpm, or 1600 rpm.
- Two different pumps satisfy the emission requirements of light- and medium-duty emission standards. The basic difference lies is the shape of the cam ring's profile.
- Bosch has manufactured a number of different distributor pump models since the 1960s. In addition to their widespread use in industrial, marine, and off-road applications, many of these pumps have found their way into North American automotive applications.
- The electronic successor to the mechanical VE injection pump is the Bosch VP-37.
- In the Bosch VP-37, fuel metering and timing are independent of mechanical governor characteristics and hydraulic behavior. With mechanical governors, springs and linkage can wear out and change tension. Engine electronics, particularly OBD-II–compliant systems, can measure changes taking place in a fuel system and adapt injection events to compensate for system deterioration.
- In the Bosch VP-37, feedback loops provide for more accurate metering and injection timing over the entire engine life. The anti-shudder control of longitudinal vehicle oscillation prevents rapid changes in the engine speed using the electronically controlled actuator if the throttle is moved too quickly.
- Another popular distributor pump for small, high-speed diesel engine applications in passenger vehicles and light- to medium-duty commercial vehicles is the Bosch VP-44.
- The Bosch VP-44 is a radial piston pump with construction and operating features similar to the Stanadyne DS-4 pump. Depending on the model, two, three, or four pumping plungers are arranged around the pump rotor, pressurizing fuel internally to between 16,060 psi (1107 bar) and 20,440 psi (1409 bar).

- The Stanadyne DS-4 pump is operated by the PCM. The pump contains the following major components: fuel metering control solenoid, pump mounted fuel solenoid, driver optical sensor tracking encoder, injection timing stepper motor, and engine shut-off solenoid.
- Several stages of fuel pressurization, filling, metering, and distribution are involved in the operation of the Stanadyne DS-4 pump.
- At initial engine start, the fuel lift pump continuously supplies fuel to the injection pump at a pressure between 5.8 and 8.7 psi (40 and 60 kPa). From the lift pump, fuel enters the vane internal transfer pump. A pressure-regulator valve with a viscosity-compensating feature regulates maximum transfer pump pressure.
- Fuel travels through the hydraulic pump head to a charging annulus, or circular ring, which supplies fuel to a passageway drilled along the length of the rotor.
- Because the fuel control valve is open, fuel can enter the fuel fill-spill chamber located at the end of the rotor.
- The injection timing of the Stanadyne DS-4 pump is managed by the ITS motor. This motor partially substitutes the function of the advance/retard sliding piston in the DB-2 pump.
- The pump-mounted injector driver or fuel solenoid driver supplies a current-regulated signal to the fuel-metering control solenoid that regulates the length of time over which injection takes place. The PCM supplies two PWM signals to the solenoid. A third signal is supplied from the driver to the PCM, which is returned from the fuel control solenoid.
- A circuit in the FSD analyzes the slight change in the electrical waveform received from the solenoid when the control valve closes. The movement of the metering control valve changes the solenoid's magnetic reluctance, which in turn affects the PWM electric signal returned to the drive module. The PCM recalculates a beginning injection time and supplies this information to the FSD to correct injection lag time.
- A calibration resistor is connected between two terminals of the driver module. This resistor provides data to the drive module regarding the flow rate of the pump.
- The fuel temperature sensor is used to maintain consistent fuel delivery volumes and compensate for changes to fuel viscosity caused by temperature fluctuations.
- The OSTE is one of the most important PCM inputs for determining fuel timing.
- The crankshaft position sensor is a Hall effect sensor, meaning it measures the speed of rotation of four teeth located on the crankshaft sprocket.
- The major components of the Bosch VP-37 fuel system include the mass airflow (MAF) sensor, needle lift sensor,

control sleeve position sensor, fuel quantity solenoid, and start of delivery solenoid.

▶ Rather than have the engine fail to operate at all when a problem with the engine management system occurs, an operating strategy called limp-home mode permits operation, though with limited power, under a number of scenarios.

▶ The ECM uses inputs from two brake pedal switches to minimize fueling during braking. This feature enhances safety and fuel economy to prevent fueling of the engine when brakes are applied at WOT position.

▶ Given that the Bosch VP-44 is an electronically controlled radial piston distributor pump, many of its construction components and operating features are similar to other opposed plunger metering systems—particularly the Stanadyne DS-4 pump.

▶ Fuel supply to the injection pump is usually handled by a low-pressure intermediate pump. Inside the injection pump, a vane pump is used to change the volume and pressure of fuel supplied to the pump proportional to engine speed. This variable pressure is necessary to operate the timing mechanism.

▶ Opposed piston plungers are arranged at 90 degrees to the rotor shaft inside a cam ring. A set of shoes and rollers for each plunger transfers the shape of the cam profile to the plungers as they rotate inside the cam ring.

▶ An electromagnetic solenoid valve is located at the entry point of fuel to the pump rotor. A needle valve operated by the solenoid opens and closes the passageway, connecting fuel pressurized by the vane pump to the pumping plunger pressure chamber.

▶ Continued rotation of the rotor compresses the plungers inside the cam ring, and fuel pressure builds in the pressure chamber. When the distributor slot in the rotor aligns with a high-pressure outlet in the hydraulic head of the pump, the high-pressure fuel column is connected to the injector nozzle through high-pressure fittings on the pump.

▶ Opening the metering valve again ends injection and starts a fill cycle. Injection quantity is determined by the length of time the metering valve is closed.

▶ The designs of the metering solenoid and the needle valve provide for very precise and rapid control of the injection event.

▶ Each cylinder fitting in the hydraulic head of the pump uses a delivery valve. These valves maintain a residual injector line pressure between injections to minimize injection lag.

▶ A variable-reluctance sensor and a trigger wheel locked to the pump drive shaft provide instantaneous data regarding pump speed and engine position. This fuel pump increment angle time system is used to calculate the beginning and end of fuel delivery based on pump position.

▶ Comparisons are made between the fuel pump shaft position and crankshaft position sensor data to adjust the pump timing and thus compensate for minor positional differences.

▶ The primary function of the FPCM is intelligent fuel timing and injection quantity adjustment. However, the pump is not able to operate without data from the ECM. To aid in efficient diagnosis of hard- and no-start conditions, the nine-pin connector on the injection pump can be disconnected, and an electrical harness can be used to substitute signals from the ECM to the pump.

▶ Controlled by the ECM, the electric vane transfer pump mounted on the engine uses PWM signals to provide two duty cycles: full speed when the engine is running and half speed during cranking.

▶ Problems with the drive module are often due to overheating. The engine will often fail to start, experience stalling, or have low power when hot.

▶ A sticking or faulty needle lift sensor can cause unusual issues. The engine will operate, but maximum engine speed will be reduced, causing sluggish operation and low-power complaints.

▶ Air in the system caused by filter replacement can be bled from the system during the 25-second purge cycle.

▶ The Bosch VP-44 is OBD-II–compliant, meaning that sensors and actuators are monitored by the ECM to detect failures or other conditions that can cause excessive emissions.

Vocabulary Builder

adaptive cylinder balance A feature that measures the power output of each cylinder at idle using speed changes in the crankshaft velocity detected by the optical pump speed/position sensor.

anti-shudder A feature that prevents rapid changes in the engine speed using the electronically controlled actuator if the throttle is moved too quickly.

axial piston pressurization A distributor pump design that uses a pumping plunger that reciprocates along the axis of the pump and uses a cam plate to move the plunger back and forth.

Bosch VP-37 An electronic pump with similar construction and operational characteristics to the mechanical VE pump.

Bosch VP-44 A full-authority distributor pump that has a vane internal transfer pump common to all other distributor pumps, but, rather than a single axial piston plunger, pressurization of fuel is accomplished using radial-opposed pumping plungers.

control sleeve position sensor A sensor used in electronic governors of Bosch VP34 pumps used to provide closed loop feedback about control sleeve position.

fuel pump-mounted fuel pump control module (FPCM) A control module mounted on a distributor pump that controls the operation of a spill valve.

fuel quantity solenoid The control valve in a DS distributor pump head used to control injection quantities delivered by the pump.

fuel rate calibration resistor A unit connected between two terminals of the driver module that provides data to the drive module regarding the flow rate of the pump.

fuel solenoid driver (FSD) An electronic control module that contains a pair of high-current switching transistors that send electrical signals to the fuel metering control solenoid located inside the hydraulic head of the pump.

injection timing stepper (ITS) motor Used in conjunction with a sliding servo piston, this device regulates internal pump fuel pressure used to retard and advance injection timing.

needle lift sensor A sensor that provides a reference signal to the ECM for BOI by providing information about movement of the nozzle valve.

optical sensor tracking encoder (OSTE) A device that combines an optical fuel temperature and pump position sensor and supplies the PCM data regarding pump speed, rotor position, cam ring position, and fuel temperature.

pump mounted driver (PMD) A control module that supplies electrical signals to control the operation of the spill valve.

radial piston pressurization A distributor pump design that uses opposed plunger metering. Plungers move inside a cam ring to pressurize fuel.

Stanadyne DS-4 A full-authority distributor first introduced in 1994; three generations of the pump were built. The adaptation of electronic controls to the pump enabled the flexibility to adjust delivery quantities and timing more accurately than mechanical systems.

Review Questions

1. A _____ is a full-authority distributor pump that has a vane internal transfer pump common to all other distributor pumps, but, rather than a single axial piston plunger, pressurization of fuel is accomplished using radial-opposed pumping plungers.
   a. Bosch VP-44
   b. Bosch VP-37
   c. Stanadyne DS-4
   d. GM DB-2

2. A _____ is a full-authority distributor first introduced in 1994 and the adaptation of electronic controls to the pump enabled the flexibility to adjust delivery quantities and timing more accurately than mechanical systems.
   a. Bosch VP-44
   b. Stanadyne DS-4
   c. Bosch VP-37
   d. GM DB-2

3. _____ is a distributor pump design that uses opposed plunger metering. Plungers move inside a cam ring to pressurize fuel.
   a. Stanadyne SD-4
   b. Bosch VP-44
   c. Axial piston pressurization
   d. Inline piston pressurization

4. A(n) _____ is an electronic pump with similar construction and operational characteristics to the mechanical VE pump.
   a. Bosch VP-37
   b. Bosch VP-44
   c. Stanadyne DS-4
   d. axial piston pressurization

5. _____ is a distributor pump design that uses a pumping plunger that reciprocates along the axis of the pump and uses a cam plate to move the plunger back and forth.
   a. Radial piston pressurization
   b. Stanadyne DS-4
   c. Axial piston pressurization
   d. Bosch VP-44

6. The fuel quantity solenoid is an electronic actuator that moves the control sleeve adjusting shaft of the _____.
   a. DB-2
   b. DS-4
   c. VP-44
   d. VP-37

7. The _____ pump is capable of pilot injection using its electronically controlled high-pressure metering control valve.
   a. Bosch VP-37
   b. Bosch VP-44
   c. Stanadyne DS-4
   d. GM DB-2

8. The _____ motor regulates internal pump housing fuel pressure used to retard and advance injection timing.
   a. injection timing stepper
   b. injection timing piston
   c. axial piston
   d. radial piston

9. The _____ wheel has 512 perforations around the circumference of the wheel.
   a. control sleeve position sensor
   b. injection timing stepper motor
   c. OSTE
   d. fuel solenoid driver

10. The _____ pump's crankshaft position sensor is a hall effect sensor, which means it measures the speed of rotation of four teeth located on the crankshaft sprocket.
    a. DS-4
    b. VP-44
    c. VP-37
    d. GM DB-2

ASE-Type Questions

1. Technician A says that the third generation of the Stanadyne DS-4 pump went into production in 1999. Technician B says that the second generation of the Stanadyne DS-4 pump went into production in 1999. Who is correct?
   a. Technician A
   b. Technician B
   c. Both Technician A and Technician B
   d. Neither Technician A nor Technician B

2. Technician A says mechanical control of injection provides better noise levels. Technician B says electronic control of injection provides better fuel economy, noise levels, and idle quality. Who is correct?
   a. Technician A
   b. Technician B
   c. Both Technician A and Technician B
   d. Neither Technician A nor Technician B

3. Technician A says because of tighter emission standards, very few distributor pumps are used on current model vehicles in North America. Technician B says that because of tighter emission standards, no distributor pumps are used on current model vehicles in Europe. Who is correct?
   a. Technician A
   b. Technician B
   c. Both Technician A and Technician B
   d. Neither Technician A nor Technician B

4. Technician A says mechanical distributor pumps used as few as half the number of parts as inline versions, but still produced the same engine horsepower. Technician B says that because mechanical distributor pumps used as few as half the number of parts as inline versions, they produced less engine horsepower. Who is correct?
   a. Technician A
   b. Technician B
   c. Both Technician A and Technician B
   d. Neither Technician A nor Technician B

5. Technician A says with the use of an electronic governor the fuel system can adjust idle speed metering to each individual cylinder. Technician B says that this will avoid rough and shaky engine idle. Who is correct?
   a. Technician A
   b. Technician B
   c. Both Technician A and Technician B
   d. Neither Technician A nor Technician B

6. Technician A says the injection control of a Bosch VP-44 is performed by one electronic processor, an ECM. Technician B says the injection control of a Bosch VP-44 is performed by two electronic processors, the ECM and a fuel pump-mounted fuel pump control module. Who is correct?
   a. Technician A
   b. Technician B
   c. Both Technician A and Technician B
   d. Neither Technician A nor Technician B

7. Technician A says the injection timing of the DS pump is managed by the injection timing stepper motor. Technician B says the injection timing of the DS pump is managed by the fuel pump control module. Who is correct?
   a. Technician A
   b. Technician B
   c. Both Technician A and Technician B
   d. Neither Technician A nor Technician B

8. Technician A says the CAPS fuel system is difficult to service in the field. Technician B says that because the CAPS fuel system is modular, it is easily serviced in the field. Who is correct?
   a. Technician A
   b. Technician B
   c. Both Technician A and Technician B
   d. Neither Technician A nor Technician B

9. Technician A says the DS-4 pump's crankshaft position sensor is a hall effect sensor. Technician B says the hall effect sensor measures the speed of rotation of four teeth located on the crankshaft sprocket. Who is correct?
   a. Technician A
   b. Technician B
   c. Both Technician A and Technician B
   d. Neither Technician A nor Technician B

10. Technician A says the stages of injection of a DS pump include filling, end of filling, and spilling. Technician B says the stages of injection of a DS pump include filling, end of filling, beginning of injection, and spilling. Who is correct?
    a. Technician A
    b. Technician B
    c. Both Technician A and Technician B
    d. Neither Technician A nor Technician B

CHAPTER 24
Electronic Unit Injectors and Unit Pumps

NATEF Tasks

Diesel Engines

General

- Check engine no cranking, cranks but fails to start, hard starting, and starts but does not continue to run problems; determine needed action. (pp 705–707)
- Identify engine surging, rough operation, misfiring, low power, slow deceleration, slow acceleration, and shutdown problems; determine needed action. (pp 700–707)

Cylinder Head and Valve Train

- Inspect injector sleeves and seals; measure injector tip or nozzle protrusion; determine needed action. (pp 706–708)

Fuel System

Electronic Fuel Management System

- Interface with vehicle's on-board computer; perform diagnostic procedures using electronic service tool(s) (to include PC-based software and/or data scan tools); determine needed action. (pp 703–704)
- Check and record electronic diagnostic codes and trip/operational data; monitor electronic data; clear codes; determine further diagnosis. (pp 693–694, 704)
- Perform on-engine inspections, tests, and adjustments on electronic unit injectors (EUI); determine needed action. (pp 688–689, 703–706)
- Remove and install electronic unit injectors (EUI) and related components; recalibrate ECM (if applicable). (p 705)

Knowledge Objectives

After reading this chapter, you will be able to:

1. Explain the operating principles of the electronic unit injection and unit pump systems. (pp 687–698)
2. Identify and describe the construction features, types, and application of the electronic unit injection and unit pump systems. (pp 697–703)
3. Describe the inspection and testing procedures for electronic unit injection and unit pump systems. (pp 702–710)
4. Recommend service and maintenance for electronic unit injection and unit pump systems. (pp 702–710)

Skills Objectives

After reading this chapter, you will be able to:

1. Perform a cylinder cut-out test. (p 706)
   SKILL DRILL 24-1
2. Replace an EUI injector. (p 707) SKILL DRILL 24-2

3. Measure injector tip protrusion. (p 708)
   SKILL DRILL 24-3
4. Replace an injector cup. (p 710) SKILL DRILL 24-4

▶ Introduction

The demands for cleaner engine emissions, increased power, quieter operation, and better fuel economy have helped inspire the development of even more efficient fuel injection systems than older mechanical pump-line-nozzle (PLN) systems or mechanical unit injection. Like older mechanical unit injectors, an **electronic unit injector (EUI)** meters, pressurizes, and injects fuel directly into the combustion chamber. The first major use of EUI systems began in 1984 in Detroit Diesel's Series 92 two-stroke engines. Detroit's EUI took the 1930s mechanical unit injector design and replaced the metering components with a solenoid energized by the electronic control module (ECM) and an electrically controlled spill valve. This design enables the functions of fuel pressurization, injection timing, atomization, and fuel distribution to be accomplished using an ECM to time and govern injection events using electrical signals supplied to the injector. With greenhouse gas (GHG) emission legislation requiring better fuel economy from diesel engines, common rail fuel systems, which have better rate shaping capabilities, will replace EUI systems by 2017.

▶ Fundamentals of Electronic Unit Injectors

Unit injectors are installed directly into the cylinder head centrally located in each combustion chamber FIGURE 24-1 . To build injection pressure to higher levels than PLN systems, the injector is driven by the engine camshaft with a dedicated injector lobe FIGURE 24-2 .

EUI Advantages

There are many EUI advantages. They include high injection pressure, reduced injection lag, higher power output, lower emissions, and service advantages.

High Injection Pressure

Overhead cam engines directly actuate the EUI through only a rocker lever. The move to wider injector lobes and more durable overhead cam designs has enabled a higher degree of fuel pressurization compared to other systems. A dedicated camshaft lobe that drives the unit injector is generally the widest to distribute the high loading forces developed through pressurizing fuel to pressures as high as 38,000 psi (2620 bar) FIGURE 24-3 . To withstand the extreme pressure loading on the camshaft by the EUI, the wider injector lobe uses a roller cam follower to reduce friction. The roller is a hardened steel or steel-ceramic alloy and the cam lobe is hardened FIGURE 24-4 . This configuration is also one of the most efficient hydraulic and mechanical fuel system arrangements providing low parasitic energy losses. Until the recent introduction of amplified common rail (ACR), EUIs had the highest spray-in pressures of any fuel injection system. The

▶ You Are the Technician

A 2009 class 8 tractor has arrived at your shop with symptoms including rough running, low power, high fuel consumption, and a DPF that requires frequent regeneration. The injectors were recently replaced at another shop to repair a similar set of symptoms. After performing routine visual inspections of the vehicle, you check for diagnostic fault codes and find none related to the fuel system. When performing a cylinder balance and cut-out test you find the variation between contributions of several cylinders is close to 20%. Some cylinders are normal, others have close to normal contribution, and the remaining cylinders need a lot of extra fuel to balance. You proceed to check the low-pressure fuel system to verify correct fuel rail pressure, but the lines and fuel filter are not restricted. Finally, you remove the engine valve cover and discover that several valves have too much clearance. Before proceeding any further with diagnostic tests, consider the following:

1. Could maladjustment of the injectors cause any damage to the injectors?
2. What symptoms would likely be present if the only fault was that the fuel pressure to the injectors was draining back to the tank due to a defective fuel pressure regulator?
3. Describe the effects on fuel system operation if the low-pressure system was supplied air-entrained fuel because of a loose suction side fuel line fitting.

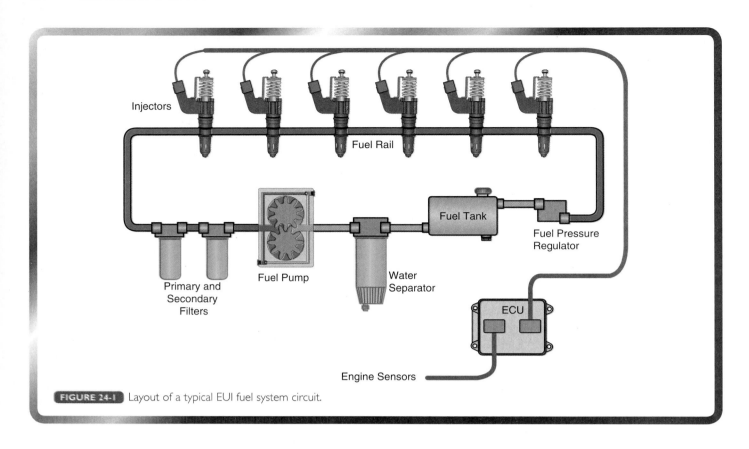

FIGURE 24-1 Layout of a typical EUI fuel system circuit.

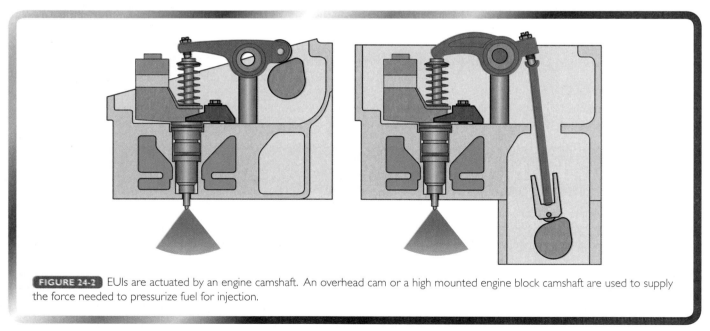

FIGURE 24-2 EUIs are actuated by an engine camshaft. An overhead cam or a high mounted engine block camshaft are used to supply the force needed to pressurize fuel for injection.

newest EUIs, such as the **Delphi E3 EUI**, can only now rival the ACR systems with approximately the same injection pressures of 35,000–38,000 psi (2412–2620 bar) depending on the manufacturer. This compares with conventional common rail (CR) injection systems with maximum 30,000-psi (2068-bar) spray-in pressures with 33,000-psi (2275-bar) unit injection used by the Cummins HPI-TPI ISX engines. It should be noted that high spray-in pressures are still dependent on engine speed in many unit injection systems. That means at low engine speed, proportionally lower injection pressures are available because cam-plunger velocities must be at their fastest to achieve the highest spray-in pressures. One exception is the Delphi E3 EUI, which can electronically vary injection pressure over all engine speeds using a second electrically operated control valve.

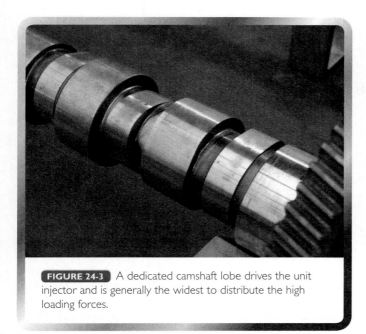

FIGURE 24-3 A dedicated camshaft lobe drives the unit injector and is generally the widest to distribute the high loading forces.

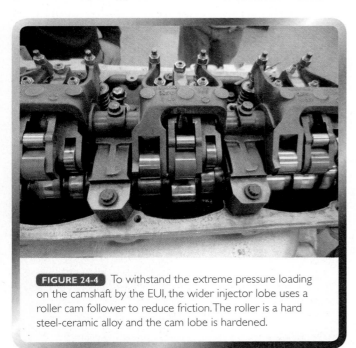

FIGURE 24-4 To withstand the extreme pressure loading on the camshaft by the EUI, the wider injector lobe uses a roller cam follower to reduce friction. The roller is a hard steel-ceramic alloy and the cam lobe is hardened.

Reduced Injection Lag

Actuating the injectors with an overhead camshaft permits the least amount of <u>injection delay</u> because there are no pushrod tubes to bend, injector lines to swell, or delivery vales to lift. The short distance pressurized fuel travels translates into reduced injection lag, unlike other high-pressure fuel systems in which pressure waves travel through lines, contributing to a time lag between pressurizing fuel and injecting it. Eliminating injection lag provides for more precise injection timing and metering. In some older, heavy-duty diesel engine applications, the EUI may be driven through a pushrod actuating mechanism. These longer, hollow pushrods can bend and flex, which produces more injection lag and variations to injection timing. The short, solid steel pushrods in engines with high-mounted camshafts minimize this bending and flexing **FIGURE 24-5** .

Higher Power Output

The extremely fine spray produced by unit injectors results in one of the best combinations of fuel atomization and distribution available. EUI engine combustion conditions enable leaner, more efficient cylinder combustion with the extremely fine "fog" mixture of air and fuel. Consequently, unit injectors can produce more power and torque for a given quantity of fuel without a penalty to fuel consumption and emissions. This explains why unit injection has long been the high-pressure system of choice for heavy-duty diesels.

Lower Emissions

EUIs contain between 5 and 13 spray holes, which, along with high pressurization, enable fuel droplet sizing of less than 20 microns. This provides for improved emissions characteristics, including less particulate matter (PM), hydrocarbons (HC), and carbon monoxide (CO). Finer atomization promotes tolerance of exhaust gas recirculation (EGR) flow into the combustion mixtures and the use of retarded engine timing for NO_x reduction.

Service Advantages

Compared to older, non-electronic injection systems, EUIs offer the following advantages:

- Virtually adjustment-free design
- All parts, including injectors, sensors, ECM's, wiring harnesses, serviceable in any shop rather than a specialized fuels shop
- Faster repair times

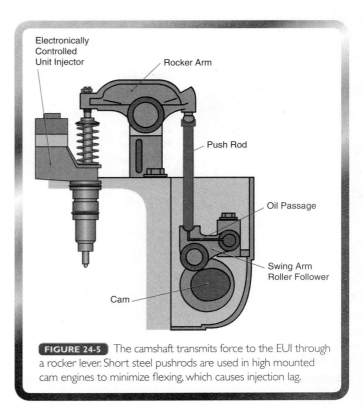

FIGURE 24-5 The camshaft transmits force to the EUI through a rocker lever. Short steel pushrods are used in high mounted cam engines to minimize flexing, which causes injection lag.

Construction of EUIs

EUIs are mechanically pressurized using electronic control of governing, timing, and metering functions. Conventional unit injector consists of several basic elements:

1. The spring-loaded plunger and barrel assembly to pressurize fuel inside the injector.

2. A poppet valve, known also as a spill control valve that regulates the buildup of pressure inside the injector.

3. An electric solenoid or cartridge valve that controls the movement of the poppet valve or spill control valve. Linkage such as a stator or solenoid pin may also directly connect the solenoid to the poppet valve in some injectors.

4. Fuel inlet and return passageways. The fuel inlet is supplied low-pressure fuel by the transfer pump. The return passageway permits fuel which has circulated through the injector to flow back to the supply tank. Because the injector is located in the cylinder head, where engine heat is picked up by not only the fuel but by injectors which also are heated through pressurization of fuel, it is important that a steady circulation of fuel passes through the injector to remove heat.

5. The nozzle valve at the injector tip is like a conventional nozzle valve opening at 3500–5000 psi (241–345 bar) in most injectors. This provides for improved atomization as well as a crisp beginning and end of injection characteristics.

EUI Operating Principles

First-generation EUIs used a single electrically controlled poppet or **spill control valve (SCV)** that opened and closed to control the beginning and end of the injection event **FIGURE 24-6**. Fuel passageways drilled though the cylinder head supply the injectors with fuel from a low-pressure transfer circuit. Another, separate

fuel return circuit in a passage drilled through the head is used by some manufacturers. O-rings on the injector seal the fuel passageways around the injector to prevent low-pressure fuel leakage into the block deck or into the combustion chamber. A third O-ring separates low-pressure fuel supply and return fuel pressure from one another. A high-mounted camshaft or overhead camshaft supply the actuation force to pressurize fuel in the injector. To prevent wear caused by the sliding action of the rocker lever against the injector tappet, an articulating joint is used instead. This "elephant foot" joint pivots, preventing sliding friction between the injector tappet and rocker lever **FIGURE 24-7**.

Injection Metering and Timing

All electronic unit injectors share common operating principles **FIGURE 24-8**. An electrical signal based on an algorithm stored in the ECM is sent by the ECM to the unit injector's solenoid-actuated SCV to regulate the injection timing and quantity of fuel delivered for combustion. Injection is performed by switching the injector's solenoid valve on and off while the camshaft forces the injector plunger down into the barrel and pressurizes the fuel **FIGURE 24-9**. The quantity of fuel delivered during injection is a function of both electrical signal time and plunger velocity, which is dependent on engine speed. This means that the time or duration the injector solenoid is energized is only one factor determining the injection quantity. A longer electrical signal applied to the solenoid generally translates into more fuel injected. However, the faster the engine rotates, the greater the distance of plunger travel per unit of time. Consequently, more fuel is injected at higher engine speed if the time the solenoid is energized remains constant.

Suction (Fill) Stroke

Fuel rail passages drilled into the cylinder head supply low-pressure fuel to each injector. Supply circuits are arranged to ensure consistent fuel temperature between injectors. Fuel flows through the drilled passage or fuel rail into the pressure chambers within

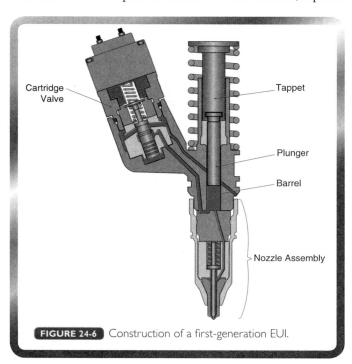

Cartridge Valve

Tappet

Plunger

Barrel

Nozzle Assembly

FIGURE 24-6 Construction of a first-generation EUI.

FIGURE 24-7 An articulating "elephant foot" joint between the rocker arm and top of the injector prevents any wear between the two components.

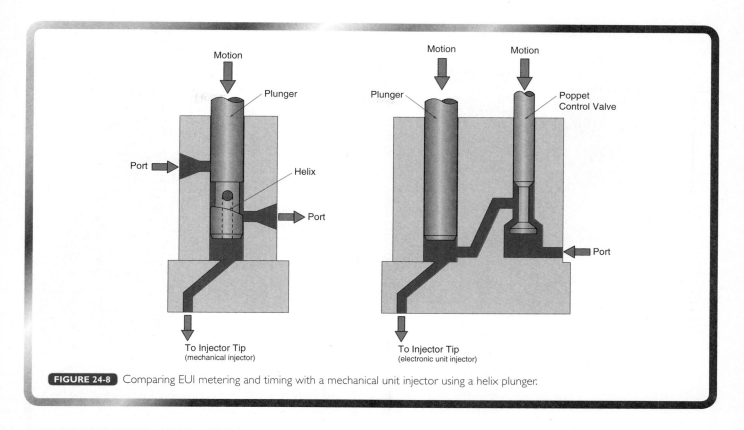

FIGURE 24-8 Comparing EUI metering and timing with a mechanical unit injector using a helix plunger.

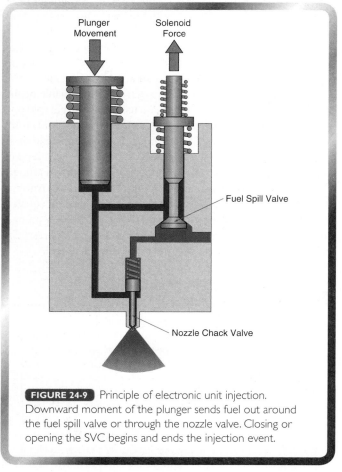

FIGURE 24-9 Principle of electronic unit injection. Downward moment of the plunger sends fuel out around the fuel spill valve or through the nozzle valve. Closing or opening the SVC begins and ends the injection event.

the injector to cool the injector and purge any vapor from the fuel circuits. The injector plunger is driven by the camshaft through a stroke determined by the injector plunger's travel adjustment. On the plunger's upward stroke, the low-pressure fuel supplied to the injector fills the cavity created beneath the plunger. Fuel can enter this cavity through the open SVC **FIGURE 24-10**.

Main Injection

The injector plunger will begin its downward stroke as the camshaft rotates onto the **outer base circle** of the cam lobe, which is one of two circles that outline the cam profile. Fuel below the injector plunger will be forced out of the injector through the fuel supply rail **FIGURE 24-11**. Without a signal from the ECM to the solenoid, the plunger will bottom out its stroke and the suction cycle will repeat with no pressurization or delivery of fuel **FIGURE 24-12**.

When the ECM does send an electrical signal to the solenoid, the poppet or SVC will close the fuel passageway to the rail, causing trapped fuel to pressurize beneath the injector plunger. As the plunger continues its downward stroke, fuel pressure builds inside the injector. Pressurized fuel forces the nozzle valve open, and fuel injection begins **FIGURE 24-13**. Maximum injection pressures occur near the end and not the beginning of plunger travel. This maximum pressure point usually coincides with when the solenoid valve is de-energized.

Residual Stroke

Injection will continue until the solenoid is de-energized. De-energization will allow the SVC to open, causing the pressure to collapse beneath the plunger. Fuel beneath

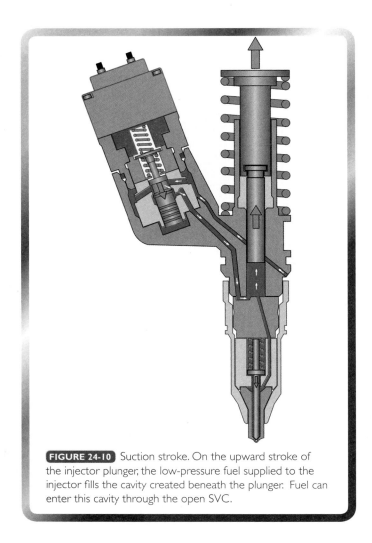

FIGURE 24-10 Suction stroke. On the upward stroke of the injector plunger, the low-pressure fuel supplied to the injector fills the cavity created beneath the plunger. Fuel can enter this cavity through the open SVC.

the plunger then drains back to the fuel inlet or to a separate return passage. As a result, the nozzle valve closes abruptly, terminating injection.

EUI Adjustment

EUI plunger travel requires adjustment to ensure that the plunger almost bottoms out but does not contact the bottom of the plunger barrel when the camshaft is on its outer base circle. Similarly, when the camshaft lobe is on its **inner base circle**, some preload is required on the injector plunger. The inner base circle is the circular part of the camshaft that does not include the lobe. This preload should only provide enough pressure to allow oil to enter the clearances between the rocker levers, push tubes, or elephant foot. Too much pressure prevents oil from lubricating the joints and causes premature wear. There is no lash allowed on unit injectors because it could easily break a yoke and clevis attached to the plunger and below the injector tappet. Allowing lash in the injector adjustment will cause the yoke and clevis to cycle back and forth with high force and ultimately break. Adjustment procedures vary between manufacturers and are performed according to a maintenance schedule, at overhaul, when engine brakes are adjusted, or when indicated by a low-power complaint. Newer injectors are designed with linkage that contacts the injector upper plunger articulates to

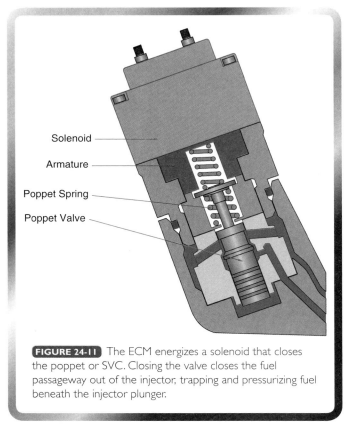

FIGURE 24-11 The ECM energizes a solenoid that closes the poppet or SVC. Closing the valve closes the fuel passageway out of the injector, trapping and pressurizing fuel beneath the injector plunger.

minimize the sliding contact wear that non-articulating joints have. In non-articulating joints, the rocker arm slides across the top of the plunger tappet and wears much more quickly.

A few styles of injectors have electronically variable beginning to injection but a mechanical end using an internal spill port that opens when plunger travel passes a particular point in the injector. The Cummins CELECT injector is one example of an injector with a variable beginning and fixed ending of injection. Adjusting these injectors is critical to provide maximum amount of fuel yet still maintain some preload on the injector. Another reason to precisely adjust injector plunger travel is to adequately pressurize fuel. Because fuel pressurization varies with plunger stroke travel, a maladjusted injector may not only not pressurize fuel enough, but also prevent proper atomization of fuel.

▶ TECHNICIAN TIP

Timing pins, torque and turn, step gauges, and a variety of other devices are used to adjust plunger travel. A specific adjustment sequence is used in an engine depending on whether the injector is adjusted by bottoming out the upper plunger or simply adjusting injector preload when the plunger is on the camshaft's inner base circle (off the cam lobe). It is critical to turn the engine in the correct direction and identify the correct cylinder to begin the adjustment sequence. Engines may require one, two, or four complete rotations to adjust all injectors and valves. Beginning an injector adjustment on the wrong injector can cause significant damage, if not catastrophic failure, to the engine and valve train.

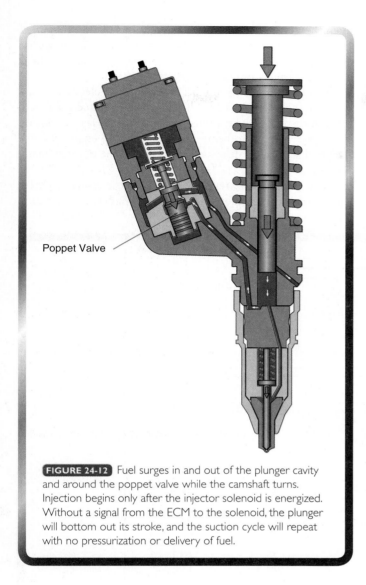

FIGURE 24-12 Fuel surges in and out of the plunger cavity and around the poppet valve while the camshaft turns. Injection begins only after the injector solenoid is energized. Without a signal from the ECM to the solenoid, the plunger will bottom out its stroke, and the suction cycle will repeat with no pressurization or delivery of fuel.

Poppet Valve

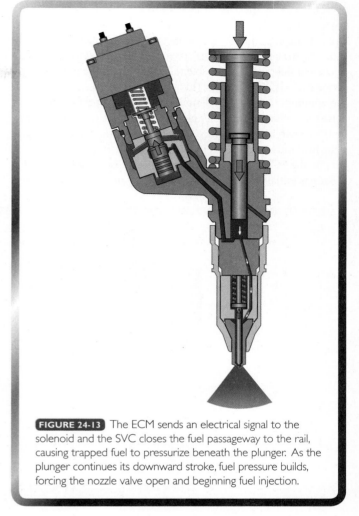

FIGURE 24-13 The ECM sends an electrical signal to the solenoid and the SVC closes the fuel passageway to the rail, causing trapped fuel to pressurize beneath the plunger. As the plunger continues its downward stroke, fuel pressure builds, forcing the nozzle valve open and beginning fuel injection.

Safety

EUIs are not likely to be involved in run-away engine operation like mechanically governed systems are. In the event of an injector malfunction, only one uncontrolled injection can happen. For example, if the solenoid valve remains open, no injection can take place, because the fuel flows back into the fuel return circuit. Because the poppet valve is normally open, it is also impossible to cause pressure to build below the plunger. If the solenoid or poppet valve is stuck closed, no fuel can enter the high-pressure chamber. In this instance, only a single injection can take place.

Electronic Signal Processing

The EUI and the ECM work together to achieve precise injection timing and fuel quantities using principles of electronic signal processing. Sensors collect data regarding engine position and operating conditions (i.e., intake, fuel, oil, and coolant temperatures, boost pressure, engine speed, network communication inputs from other control modules, and most importantly, driver input) **FIGURE 24-14**. The ECM collects and processes the data using operating algorithms, fuel timing maps, and calibration files stored in its memory to decide the exact injection timing and fuel quantity necessary to obtain best performance, lowest emissions, and highest fuel economy.

Pulse-Width Modulation

There are a variety of output signals produced by the ECM, but the current energizing the EUI is unique. A signal type known as a pulse-width modulated (PWM) current drives the injector solenoids. PWM current is a pulsing DC voltage signal that either is on or off, which gives it a digital characteristic. However, unlike digital signals that are only in one of two states (i.e., on or off, yes or no, high or low, one or zero), PWM signals vary in the amount of time they are on or off. This means that current to the solenoid will be switched on and then off for varying amounts of time, typically measured in milliseconds. Because engine speed is constantly varying, there is no fixed period for the PWM signal, so the energization time has no duty cycle like other PWM signals **FIGURE 24-15**.

Current Ramping and Injector Response Time

Another feature of the PWM signal is the use of a peak and hold current-shaping strategy to operate the injector solenoid. This current-shaping strategy, called **current ramping**, refers to the buildup of current flow through the solenoid coils during the initial energization period **FIGURE 24-16**. This is necessary to decrease heating of the windings to increase solenoid reliability and performance and solve the problem of the solenoid coils' **inductive reactance**. When coils are energized to produce magnetic fields, the expanding magnetic field induces current flow in the opposite direction of current sent by the ECM to build a magnetic field. Consequently, injector solenoids initially are highly resistive during the energization phase when the magnetic field begins to build up. Current is induced in the solenoid windings, which oppose ECM current energizing the solenoid. The resistance to initial current flow is referred to as inductive reactance or inductive resistance.

Inductive reactance briefly produces high electrical resistance in the solenoid coil when current is initially applied. While measured in brief milliseconds, it does delay the closing of the poppet valve to begin injection. At high engine speeds, even milliseconds of delay will allow the engine to rotate many degrees.

Slow poppet valve response to the electric signal results in injection delay or variations in injection timing between operating

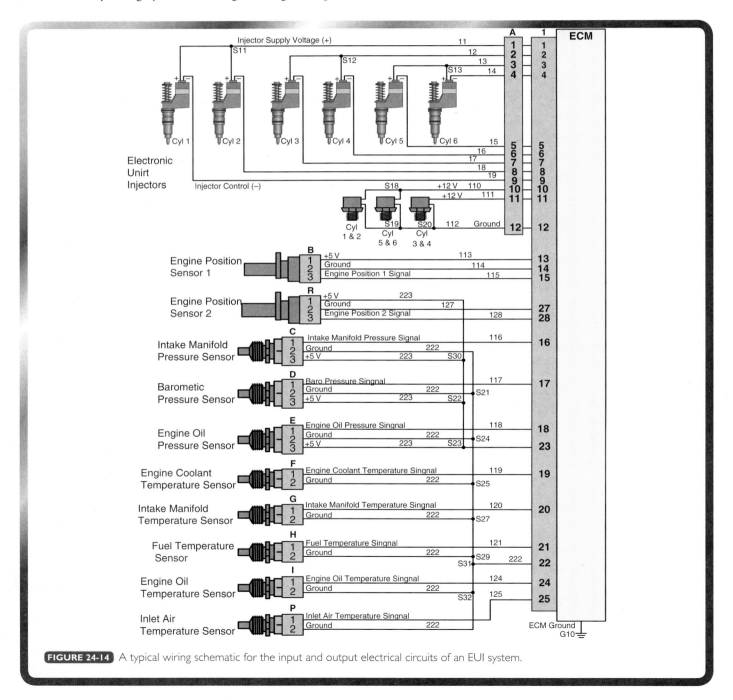

FIGURE 24-14 A typical wiring schematic for the input and output electrical circuits of an EUI system.

System

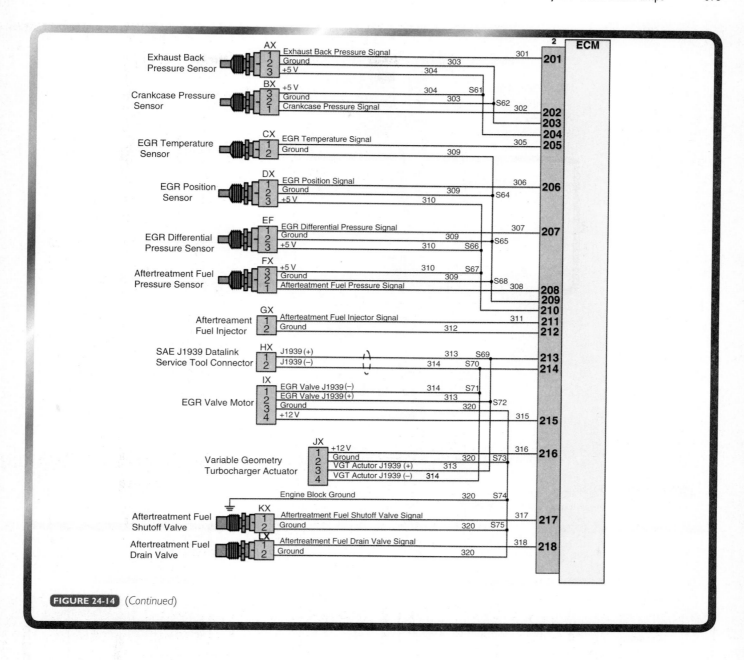

FIGURE 24-14 (Continued)

cycles, each injector, and shot-to-shot fuel delivery **FIGURE 24-17**. Solenoid coil temperature changes, battery voltage levels, and circuit resistance can further aggravate injection timing problems. Delay periods can approach as much as 15 milliseconds, which at high engine rpm can cause substantial discrepancy between calculated and actual injection timing for a combustion event taking place in as little as 0.003 seconds **FIGURE 24-18**.

Until the magnetic field is stationary, the solenoid coil will have significant resistance. To quickly overcome this resistance, higher injector voltage shortens the time required to build and stabilize the magnetic field. After the magnetic field has stabilized, less current is required to overcome injector coil resistance and keep the poppet valve closed. Maintaining the current at high levels after the magnetic field is stabilized would only overheat the coil. To prevent coil overheating, the ECM

will drop the current flow to the injector enough to remain in hold mode **FIGURE 24-19**.

Manufacturers monitor response time to injectors in order to make adjustments to timing for each cylinder. One technique to accomplish this involves the ECM measuring the time it takes for current to rise to the desired value. To do this, the ECM monitors the voltage drop across the injector current supply wires by monitoring the voltage drop across an internal resistor in the ECM that is connected in series with the injector circuit. Kirchhoff's law, which states that the sum of the voltage drops equals source voltage, predicts that if two or more resistors are connected in series, the greatest voltage drop takes place across the resistor with the highest resistance. Because the injector winding resistance changes during the time it is energized, the voltage drop across the resistor inside the ECM will

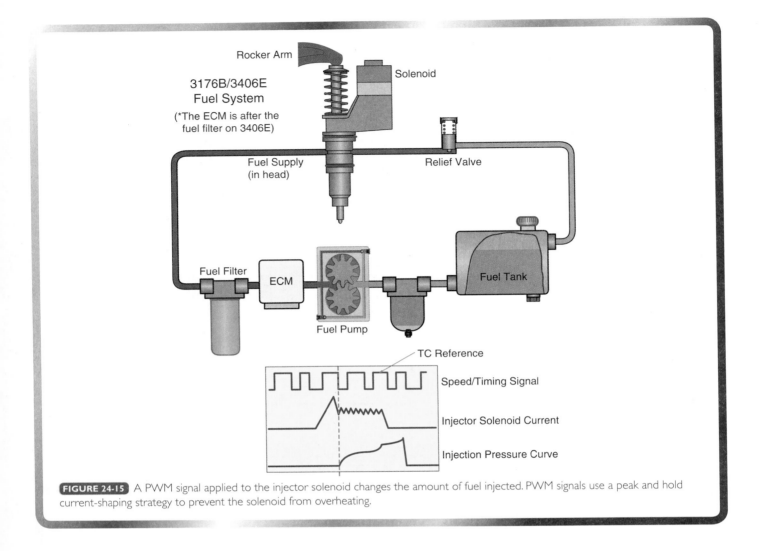

FIGURE 24-15 A PWM signal applied to the injector solenoid changes the amount of fuel injected. PWM signals use a peak and hold current-shaping strategy to prevent the solenoid from overheating.

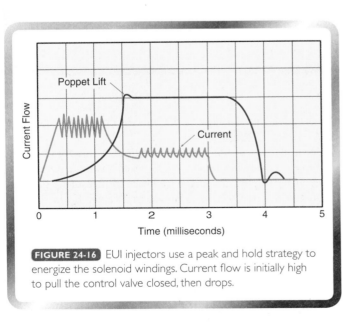

FIGURE 24-16 EUI injectors use a peak and hold strategy to energize the solenoid windings. Current flow is initially high to pull the control valve closed, then drops.

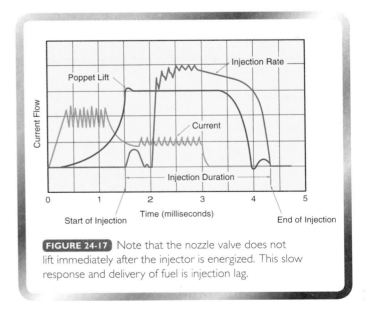

FIGURE 24-17 Note that the nozzle valve does not lift immediately after the injector is energized. This slow response and delivery of fuel is injection lag.

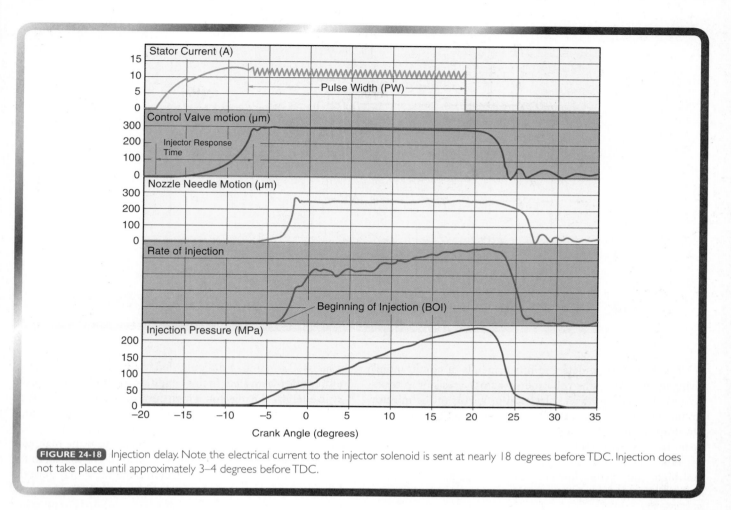

FIGURE 24-18 Injection delay. Note the electrical current to the injector solenoid is sent at nearly 18 degrees before TDC. Injection does not take place until approximately 3–4 degrees before TDC.

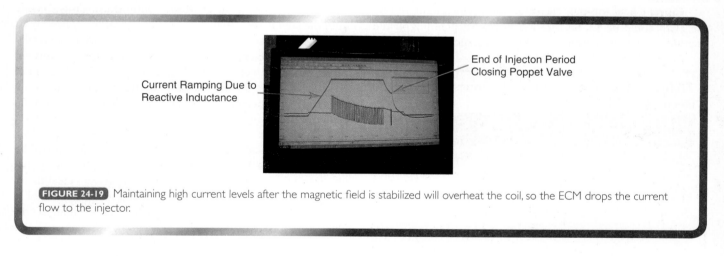

FIGURE 24-19 Maintaining high current levels after the magnetic field is stabilized will overheat the coil, so the ECM drops the current flow to the injector.

change accordingly **FIGURE 24-20**. When measured by the ECM, the voltage drop across the internal resister will go up as injector coil resistance goes down. Generally, a specific voltage drop (for example, 4 volts) across the internal resistor will indicate the voltage dropped across the injector windings (in this example, 8 volts). At a predictable voltage drop, enough current is flowing through the windings to produce a magnetic field strong enough to close the control valve. The ECM will not only measure voltage drop, but also the time it takes to reach a threshold voltage needed to close the control valve. For example, if the specific voltage is 8 volts across the injector windings, the ECM will monitor how long it takes to reach 8 volts. Because the time required to reach the specific voltage drop will vary slightlybased on a wide range of operating conditions, a correction factor is applied to the time, measured in degrees of crankshaft rotation, when the ECM closes the driver circuit and energizes the injector.

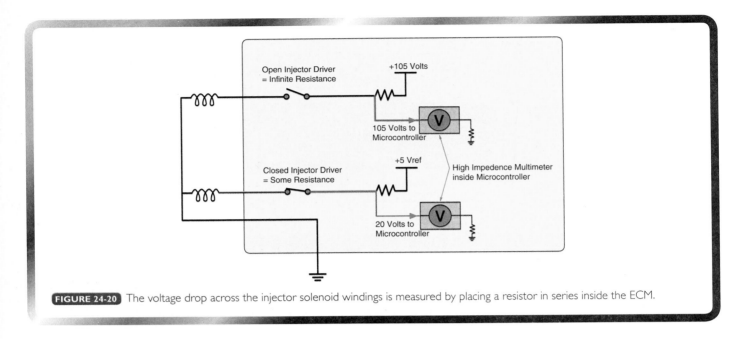

FIGURE 24-20 The voltage drop across the injector solenoid windings is measured by placing a resistor in series inside the ECM.

It is helpful to understand this principle of circuit monitoring by measuring the voltage drop across a resistor in series because it is used to detect electrical problems in the injector circuit. On-board diagnostic systems will monitor the voltage drop to determine if the injector solenoid windings are open, too resistive (loose connections, burnt wires), or short circuited. Fault codes such as voltage high, voltage low, current high, and current low are fault codes generated by measuring the voltage drop across injector windings and circuits **TABLE 24-1**.

Current flow through each injector circuit monitored by the ECM could be 12, 50, 70, or 105 volts depending on the manufacturer. If low current flow is detected, such as that caused by an open winding or disconnected wiring, a low current diagnostic code is activated. In this condition, the ECM continues to try to energize the injector. If high current flow is detected, such as that caused by shorted or grounded wiring, a diagnostic code is activated. In this condition, the ECM will disable the injector solenoid circuit to prevent further damage from the high current flow through the wiring or the injector driver circuit in the ECM. Depending on the manufacturer, the ECM may periodically try to energize the injector to determine whether the fault may have corrected itself. If the short or grounded circuit is not corrected or repaired, the ECM will continue using this strategy until the fault is corrected.

High resistance in an injector solenoid circuit generally occurs when the engine is warmed up. Loose or intermittent wiring problems will happen when the engine is vibrating under heavy load. Carefully inspect the condition of the wiring, harnesses, and connectors for chafing when this problem occurs before replacing injectors.

Caterpillar is an example of a manufacturer that provides a distinct electrical diagnostic test to check the injectors. The Injector Solenoid Test is performed with the key on and engine off. Each injector solenoid can be briefly activated, creating an audible click as the control valve closes when the solenoid is activated. Cat ET will indicate the status of the solenoid as OK, Open, or Short.

TABLE 24-1: Diagnostic Trouble Codes for EUI Electrical Circuits

J1939 Fault Code	Codes Description
651-5	Engine Injector Cylinder 1 current below normal
651-6	Engine Injector Cylinder 1 current above normal
652-5	Engine Injector Cylinder 2 current below normal
652-6	Engine Injector Cylinder 2 current above normal
653-5	Engine Injector Cylinder 3 current below normal
653-6	Engine Injector Cylinder 3 current above normal
654-5	Engine Injector Cylinder 4 current below normal
654-6	Engine Injector Cylinder 4 current above normal
655-5	Engine Injector Cylinder 5 current below normal
655-6	Engine Injector Cylinder 5 current above normal
656-5	Engine Injector Cylinder 6 current below normal
656-6	Engine Injector Cylinder 6 current above normal

▶ TECHNICIAN TIP

Most EUI injectors share a common ground wire with one or two other injectors. If two injectors are misfiring and have current low codes, check the ground return circuit for opens to the ECM. For the same reason a shorted or high current fault will take out an injector paired with a fault injectors or sharing common wiring.

Injector Response Time

The strategy of tracking time variations between the voltage drops for each injection is called <u>injector response time</u>. If a response time of 5 milliseconds is measured, the ECM will energize the injector 5 milliseconds earlier for the next injection event. Injector response is tracked for each cylinder and from shot to shot.

Injector response time is an important piece of diagnostic information. If injectors have different resistances, have bad connectors, or become overheated, their response time will lengthen. Monitoring response time indicates whether a problem is developing with an injector or the injector has failed. Individual injector response times should remain relatively consistent from one cylinder firing to the next. Wide variations in response time (typically ± 0.2 milliseconds) for one injector at a steady engine rpm may indicate an electrical problem. This could include a faulty alternator emitting excessive AC voltage ripple, resistive or broken electrical connections, or binding solenoid components.

A different method to calculate response time evaluates slight changes in the electrical signals originating from the injector. Their injection response can be designated as the <u>beginning of injection period (BIP)</u> **FIGURE 24-21**. This corresponds to the closing of the solenoid poppet valve. When the poppet valve closes, it changes the strength of the solenoid's magnetic field, which in turn produces a slight change in coil resistance, or voltage drop. The ECM can detect this change of current through the solenoid coils using a <u>BIP detection circuit</u>. Using this data, the actual start of delivery is corrected for timing the next injection event. Heavy-duty on-board diagnostics (HD-OBD) engines will measure the point when crankshaft acceleration begins, which corresponds to the beginning of injection. Consistent crankshaft acceleration rates and the point when acceleration begins due to combustion events are tracked, and adjustments to injection quantity and timing are made using the crank position sensor data.

Rate-Shaping Technology

Rate shaping is not easily accomplished electronically in EUIs. EUI magnetic solenoid coils introduce the problems associated with reactive inductance, and only enough time is available for a single injection event during a combustion cycle. Mechanical rather than electrical strategies are used to produce a pilot injection event. However, the size, weight, and inertia of the poppet valve and cartridges can be reduced to begin and end injection faster. Newer injectors use smaller, low-mass, low-inertia solenoids and poppet valves. Hydraulically balanced nozzle valves using servo hydraulic actuators, which open and close the nozzle valve by tipping the hydraulic forces applied to the top and bottom of the nozzle valve, can also speed up injection events. Piezoelectric actuators, currently used in only a few unit injectors, enable injectors to cycle as many as 10,000 times per minute, completing a full injection event in 1–2 milliseconds. Pilot injection events take place in as few as 10 microseconds (1/1000 of a millisecond).

Calibration Codes

Because variations between flow rates of injectors can occur due to manufacturing tolerances, identical injectors deliver different quantities of fuel despite using the same PWM signal. Injection variations produce inconsistent cylinder pressures and cylinder imbalance, creating rough engine operation and emission problems. To correct this condition, manufacturers will flow test all injectors and compare them against a nominal standard value. Depending on whether the injector flows more or less fuel, a numbered or alphanumerical value is applied to the injector. This injector <u>calibration code</u>, also called a fuel trim code or E-trim, is entered into ECM injector data so corrections to fuel rate control can be made electronically **FIGURE 24-22**. The process can be very elaborate with some manufacturers. For example, Caterpillar ACERT service injectors are accompanied by a CD that contains injector information needed to install the correct injector code during injector replacement. This data is uploaded into the ECM look-up tables when the injector is replaced. Some late-model engines will not energize an injector, and will instead misfire, unless the correct calibration code is entered into the ECM.

▶ Recent Types of Electronic Unit Injectors

With emission standards requiring decreasing production of noxious emissions, better EUI design was needed to prevent the formation of emissions in an engine's cylinders. Rate-shaped injection capabilities, finer atomization, higher spray-in pressures, increased reliability, injector durability when using ultra-low-sulfur fuel, and HD-OBD requirements are a few of the major factors that demanded improvements to EUI design. This next section looks at more recent EUI injectors that were developed to meet emission standards and expectations for improved performance.

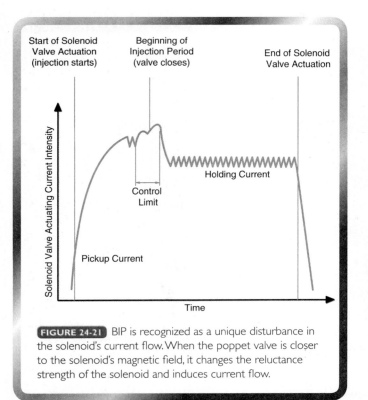

FIGURE 24-21 BIP is recognized as a unique disturbance in the solenoid's current flow. When the poppet valve is closer to the solenoid's magnetic field, it changes the reluctance strength of the solenoid and induces current flow.

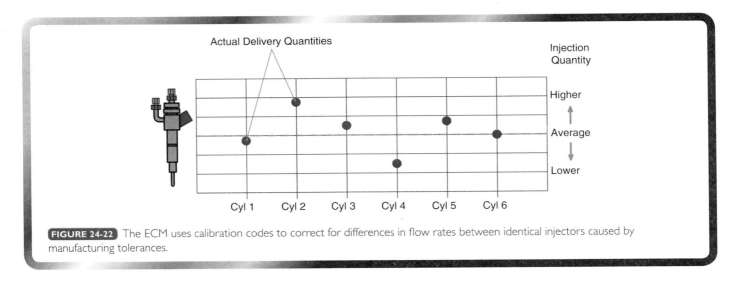

FIGURE 24-22 The ECM uses calibration codes to correct for differences in flow rates between identical injectors caused by manufacturing tolerances.

TECHNICIAN TIP

The internal manufacturing tolerances of the latest EUI injectors can be measured down to 1 micron (μ). To ensure reliability and long injector life, no abrasive contamination should enter an EUI fuel system. To prevent contaminants from entering the injectors, fuel is filtered down to 2 μ by most secondary filters on EUI systems. However, another common way for abrasive contaminants to enter an EUI fuel system is during engine repair and replacement. It is recommended that sealing or fuel blanking caps are used on lines and fittings opened to the atmosphere during service. Always keep sealing caps on all new components and lines until the moment before installation.

Detroit N3 Injector

One of the first EUIs capable of multiple injections was used by Detroit Diesel S60 DDEC V engines. Detroit's in-house name for this model of EUI is N3. The N3 was a forerunner of the Delphi E3 used by Detroit beginning in 2004. While somewhat similar in appearance, the major difference between the two injectors, which are both manufactured by Delphi, is that the N3 used a single electromagnetic solenoid while the E3 uses two **FIGURE 24-23** .

The use of a low-mass **nozzle control valve (NCV)** and a hydraulically balanced nozzle valve give this injector the capability of supplying a single pilot injection event followed by a

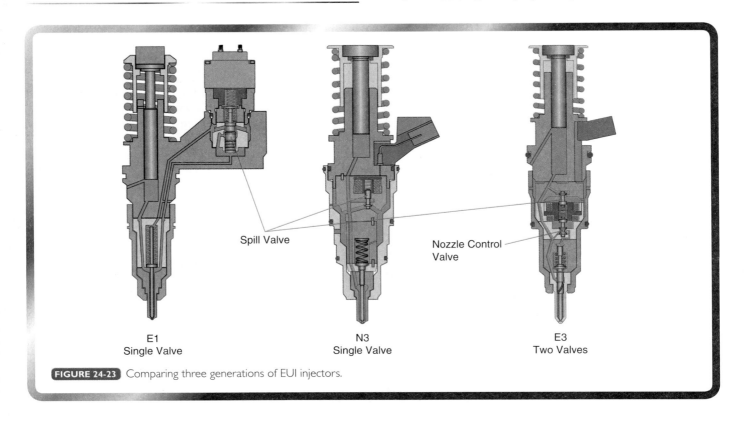

E1
Single Valve

N3
Single Valve

E3
Two Valves

FIGURE 24-23 Comparing three generations of EUI injectors.

main injection event. The use of the solenoid to only tip the balance of high-pressure fuel acting above and below the valve is done to take advantage of faster acting, more powerful hydraulic pressure. The use of the small movement produced by the electromagnetic solenoid to control the greater hydraulic force classifies this injector as having a servo actuator **FIGURE 24-24**.

N3 EUI Construction

The major similarity between the N3 and E3 injectors is the inline concept of arranging the control valve within the injector body, concentric with the injector centerline. This places the NCV and solenoid just below the pump and above the nozzle mechanisms. The NCV is much smaller than previous valves and the electromagnetic solenoid uses proprietary metals that provide a rapid buildup and collapse of a strong magnetic field. Using approximately 50 volts to operate, the solenoid needs to move the nozzle valve only a small amount to open and close the control valve regulating fuel flow through a fuel passageway above the nozzle valve. The NCV is normally open and closes only to build injection pressure. High-pressure fuel below the nozzle valve, supplied to the nozzle tip through a diagonal cut around the valve's circumference, is used to lift the valve from its seat when pressure below the nozzle valve is increased. A 40% reduction in the number of parts and an injector with half the weight of the previous E1 generation of injectors is achieved using this control valve configuration. Placing the valve as close as it is to the nozzle also helps create a more responsive injector with substantially less lag after electrical signals are applied to the solenoid.

High-Pressure Operation

The N3 injector's spray-in pressure can reach up to 35,000 psi (2413 bar). With the inline concept. the NCV or module is positioned under the plunger, making the overall envelope of the N2 smaller than previous injectors **FIGURE 24-25**. Energizing and closing the control valve determines the beginning of injection and end of injection. The time the solenoid is energized and the speed of plunger travel, which varies with engine rpm, meters the amount of fuel injected. Like other EUIs, fuel pressure is generated by the downward movement of the injector plunger. The NCV is double acting, which means that when not energized, the NCV remains open, allowing fuel below the plunger to move in and out of the injector to the fuel inlet from the cylinder head fuel drilling. Fuel in a pressure chamber above the nozzle valve is only at the same low pressure as the fuel supply to the injector. When energized, the NCV closes, blocking the fuel passage below the plunger to the fuel inlet. Pressure then builds in the injector and fuel can leave the injector tip once it overcomes the spring pressure that is holding the nozzle valve on its seat.

The unique design of the NCV enables some volume of high-pressure fuel at the end of the injection event to close the nozzle by directing high-pressure fuel to a pressure chamber above the nozzle. At almost the same time when high-pressure fuel is applied to close the nozzle, the valve opens a passage below the plunger to vent pressurized fuel back to the injector's return circuit. This slightly staggered sequence of operations is sometimes referred to as split phase operation. Just as highly pressurized fuel first closes the nozzle and then vents pressurized fuel to return during de-energization, energizing the solenoid first closes the return passage below the plunger and then opens the pressure chamber above the nozzle to allow free

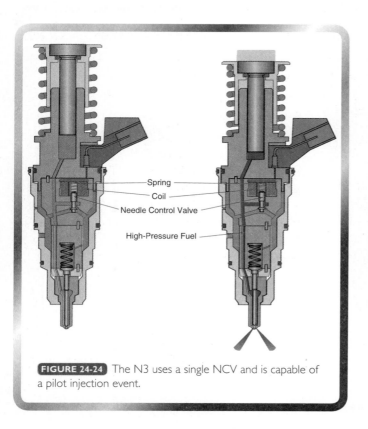

FIGURE 24-24 The N3 uses a single NCV and is capable of a pilot injection event.

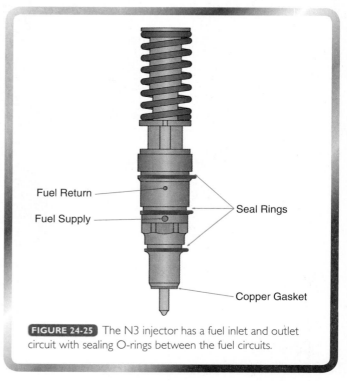

FIGURE 24-25 The N3 injector has a fuel inlet and outlet circuit with sealing O-rings between the fuel circuits.

upward movement of the nozzle valve. Using two separate energization events, the injector can respond fast enough to produce a pilot injection event.

Delphi E3 Diesel Electronic Unit Injector

The Delphi E3 Diesel EUI was introduced for 2002 EGR-equipped diesel engine on-highway heavy-duty applications. A version of the E3 is available for cam-in block engines, but the most common configuration uses the engine's overhead camshaft. What is unique about the Delphi E3 EUI is its dual control valve, four-wire design that enables high-speed, ultra-high-pressure operation (up to 37,000 psi [2551 bar]) with rate-shaped injection capabilities. This means the injector provides pilot-, post-, and split-injection events as well as ramped, low-NO_x injection profiles.

Benefits

The Delphi E3 EUI has several benefits, including the following:

- High-speed dual-valve operation for accurate control of injection events
- Ultra-high injection pressure for optimized combustion and reduced need for particulate and selective catalytic reduction (SCR) aftertreatment
- Lightweight, compact design for enhanced efficiency (15 lb [7 kg] for six cylinder engines)
- Multiple injection capability with programmable shot-to-shot injection control

- Programmable variable nozzle opening and closing pressure
- On-board diagnostic and calibration trimming capability
- 621,000-mile (1,000,000 km) durability
- 40% fewer parts than previous unit injector (E1)
- Meets emission standards for US 07 and US 10 and beyond.

Applications

The Delphi E3 diesel EUI is suitable for 9–16L (549–976 cubic inch) heavy-duty diesel engines used for on- and off-highway applications. Examples of applications include Mercedes MBE 4000; Volvo D11, 13, 7, and 16; Mack MP-7 and MP-8; and Caterpillar C-13 C-15 engines. Currently it is one of two remaining fuel systems in use; the other is the common rail system.

Features

The Delphi E3 diesel EUI has two independent, fast-response precision actuators that can electronically change the injection pressure from 5000 to 37,000 psi (345 to 2551 bar) and adjust fuel delivery timing and duration on a per-shot basis.

Older EUI systems integrate a pump and plunger into each injector and locate the injection control solenoid on the side of the injector body. While the design is effective and has acceptable injector response, the offset forged body causes it to be both bulky and complicated to manufacture. The E3 uses an inline compact body and new technology that integrates two control valves within the injector body **FIGURE 24-26** and **FIGURE 24-27**. It is smaller than conventional injector bodies and uses 40% fewer parts.

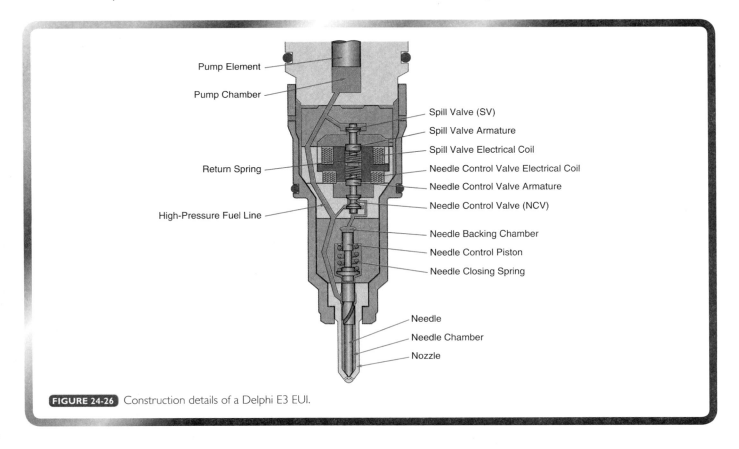

Pump Element
Pump Chamber
Return Spring
High-Pressure Fuel Line

Spill Valve (SV)
Spill Valve Armature
Spill Valve Electrical Coil
Needle Control Valve Electrical Coil
Needle Control Valve Armature
Needle Control Valve (NCV)
Needle Backing Chamber
Needle Control Piston
Needle Closing Spring
Needle
Needle Chamber
Nozzle

FIGURE 24-26 Construction details of a Delphi E3 EUI.

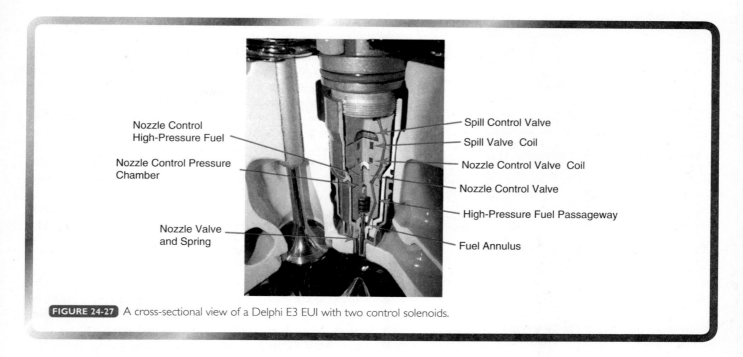

FIGURE 24-27 A cross-sectional view of a Delphi E3 EUI with two control solenoids.

The shorter fuel circuits of the E3 enable more accurate fuel metering and improved injector responsiveness. Two valves are used by the injector. One is an NCV, which allows the injector to operate like a conventional hydraulically balanced nozzle valve like those used in common rail injectors. The NCV is electronically controlled by the engine or fuel injection control module to vary injection timing and metering. The second solenoid located above the NCV is a spill control valve (SCV). This valve operates to change injection pressure as needed to meet operating requirements. When energized, the normally open valve will cause fuel pressure to build up in the injector body until the NCV is energized and injection takes place **FIGURE 24-28**.

Operation

The E3 injector uses two magnetic solenoids: the NCV, which is normally closed, and the normally opened SCV. Current from the ECM is needed to close or open either. Injection pressure regulation and timing and metering events are controlled by the coordination or phasing of SCV and NCV action.

Pressurization

To begin injection, the injector camshaft will move to the outer base circle and begin to push the injector plunger downward. No pressurization can take place until the SCV closes. At the correct time, the magnetic field of the wire coil above SCV will close. Closing the SCV traps fuel beneath the plunger and the passages leading to the nozzle valve. Fuel pressure increases as the plunger continues its downward stroke.

Injection

Fuel pressure created by closing the SCV is applied to the top of the nozzle valve. Pressurized fuel prevents the nozzle valve from lifting from its seat, and fuel pressure continues to build inside the injector. Fuel pressure is also applied to the bottom

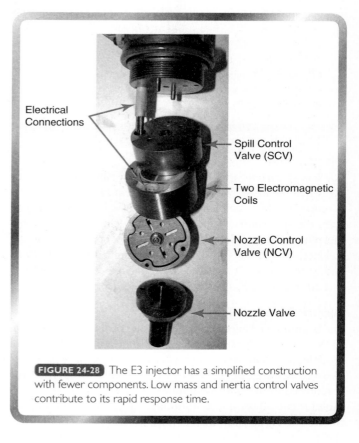

FIGURE 24-28 The E3 injector has a simplified construction with fewer components. Low mass and inertia control valves contribute to its rapid response time.

of the nozzle valve in the area of the annulus. When the NCV is energized, fuel pressure is drained from above of the nozzle valve. After the pressure balance below and above the nozzle valve changes, the nozzle valve lifts, allowing pressurized fuel to spray into the combustion chamber **FIGURE 24-29**.

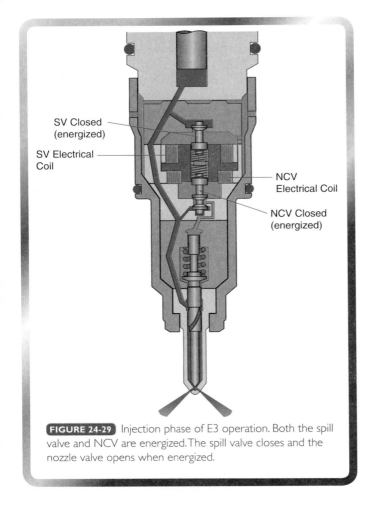

SV Closed (energized)

SV Electrical Coil

NCV Electrical Coil

NCV Closed (energized)

FIGURE 24-29 Injection phase of E3 operation. Both the spill valve and NCV are energized. The spill valve closes and the nozzle valve opens when energized.

Injection End

The PWM current applied to the control valves is discontinued when the ECM switches off the current to the injector. The de-energized SCV coil allows a beveled washer-like spring to open the spill control valve, allowing trapped fuel to pass to a fuel return circuit. When fuel pressure is low enough, the nozzle valve closes and ends injection. Fuel is spilled from the NCV and spring pressure closes the nozzle valve. Fuel from the NCV is returned through a low-pressure fuel return circuit.

Injector Response Time

The beginning of injection and metering of the fuel in relation to the crankshaft position are regulated by a dedicated control module. Injection begins soon after the control valve is closed. The valve closing point known as the injector response time is returned to the control module. This information is used to monitor and adjust injection timing, which helps to minimize injector-to-injector variation in injection timing. The amount of fuel injected depends on the pulse width stored in the calibration, which determines how long the SCV remains closed. This means the longer the pulse width, the longer the valve is closed and the more fuel is injected.

Calibration Code

Another example of electronic correction of response time and fuel flow factors is used by the Delphi E3 calibration or

trim code. Etched into the top of the injector and printed in a laser-etched machine code on the electrical connector is an alphanumeric calibration code **FIGURE 24-30** . This code is used by the ECM to adjust timing and fuel flow through the injector.

Each injector is tested after it is manufactured and is measured against a nominal or average beginning of injection pressurization (BIP), end of injection point, and idle quality factor. This creates the calibration codes that allow the ECM to identify the injector response time and qualify its idle performance. The codes have been picked at random to minimize the probability of using a code to intentionally overfuel an engine to increase power output.

It is critical that the injector code is programmed into the ECM if an injector is replaced, or reinstalled in another cylinder.

Electronic Unit Pumps

Also referred to as a unit pump system (UPS), an **electronic unit pump (EUP)** combines elements of PLN injection systems and unit injectors. Each cylinder uses a separate camshaft-driven high-pressure pump to pressurize fuel for injection **FIGURE 24-31** . Connecting the pump to the nozzle is a high-pressure fuel line **FIGURE 24-32** . The pump operates using principles similar to the unit injector. A roller reduces friction between the pumping element and dedicated camshaft lobe.

EUP injection systems have permitted the adaptation of high-pressure electronically controlled injection systems to engines previously using inline pump injection systems without extensive engine modifications. Control of the solenoid by the engine ECM is identical to the unit injector. Slightly lower injection pressures are used by EUPs and the use of the line is a barrier to the electronic rate shaping EUIs are capable of. Metering and timing of the fuel is regulated by the electronic engine control system, which actuates the solenoid poppet control valve to block the existing of fuel through the injector unit pump during the pump's plunger stroke. When the solenoid poppet valve

FIGURE 24-30 The injector calibration code on this injector is used to identify the calibration file to upload into the injector.

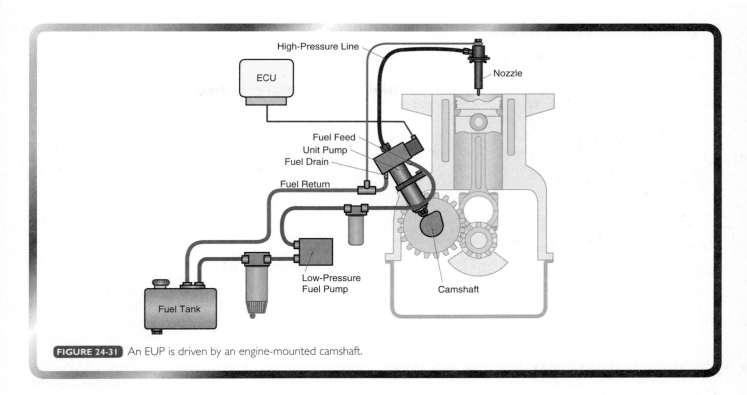

FIGURE 24-31 An EUP is driven by an engine-mounted camshaft.

closes, fuel is trapped in the injector unit pump plunger and can leave only through the high-pressure fuel line connected to the injector. Fuel supply to each EUP is provided by a low-pressure supply transfer system. The supply fuel pump delivers fuel at low pressure to the fuel filter, then to the individual fuel injection pumps. The continuous fuel flow through the injector unit pump prevents vapor pockets from collecting in the fuel system and cools the injector unit pump parts. A fuel return line collects unused fuel circulating through the pumps and empties it back into the fuel tank. The use of the flange mount on the side of the engine block above the camshaft provides for convenient service or field replacement of pumps.

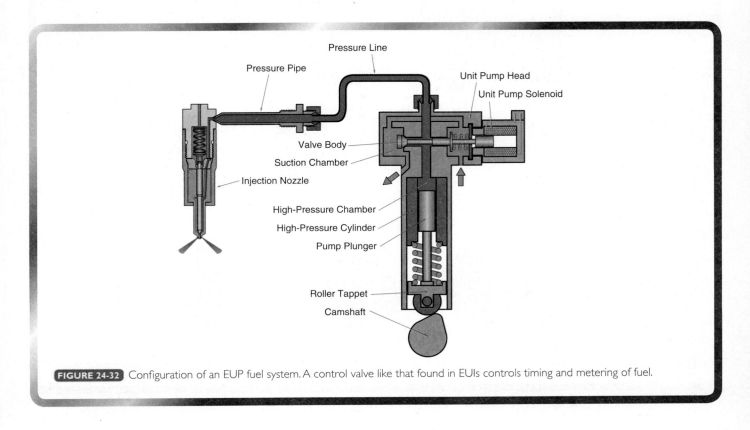

FIGURE 24-32 Configuration of an EUP fuel system. A control valve like that found in EUIs controls timing and metering of fuel.

▶ Maintenance of EUIs and Unit Pumps

EUI systems in operation are adjustment free and require little maintenance except during engine overhaul or replacement due to failure. Older injectors do wear, with plungers and barrels having increasing internal back leakage, leading to poor pressurization and low power. Nozzle spray holes also become larger after thousands of gallons (liters) of fuel have passed though the nozzle tip. Larger spray droplets lead to increased emissions and fuel consumption. This next section will look at injector failures and maintenance practices associated with injector replacement.

Water Contamination

Water contamination is very common in EUIs failures and is therefore a great concern. Water contamination can cause injector plungers to lose lubrication, which causes premature wear and seizing **FIGURE 24-33**. Water may be introduced into the fuel supply during fueling when warm, moisture-laden air condenses on the cold metal walls of fuel storage tanks and dissolves into the fuel after condensing on the cooler surface of the fuel. The effects of water in diesel fuel can be serious. Because water cannot pass easily through nozzle orifices, water can accumulate below the nozzle valve, vaporize, and then cause a tip to blow off an injector **FIGURE 24-34** and **FIGURE 24-35**. Water causes galling and seizure of injector plungers because it disrupts the lubricating film strength of fuel **FIGURE 24-36**. Water can combine with sulfur in the fuel to form corrosive acids.

Fine Abrasives

Dirt is a fine abrasive and can cause premature wear and shortened injector life. The poppet or SCV is easily scored, worn, and damaged by the continuous abrasive action of dirt. Black or gray smoke, low power, and high fuel consumption are the result of abrasive wear **FIGURE 24-37**. While most filters can remove particles down to 10 microns in size, the most damaging dirt particles are 5–7 μ in size. Micro-glass filters are the preferred filter medium for EUIs. These filters have a nominal rating of 2 μ at 90% efficiency.

Fuel Temperature

Diesel fuel provides cooling of the injection system. However, fuel temperature may vary considerably due to engine operating temperature. As fuel temperature increases, fuel viscosity decreases, which in turn decreases the lubrication capabilities of the fuel. Fuel returning to the tank can, under some circumstances, exceed its flash point and become dangerous. When the injection system is operated with elevated fuel temperatures, the injectors will operate at reduced internal clearances. As a result, dirt and smaller particulate material may cause injection durability concerns. Installing a fuel cooler or operating with fuel

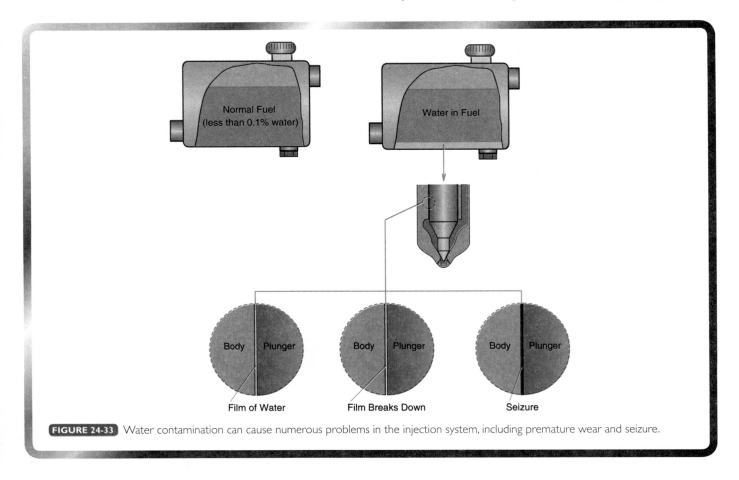

FIGURE 24-33 Water contamination can cause numerous problems in the injection system, including premature wear and seizure.

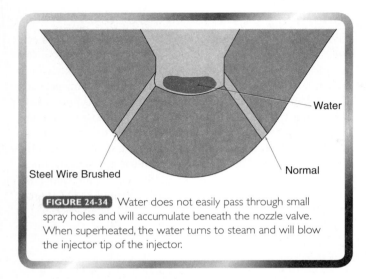

FIGURE 24-34 Water does not easily pass through small spray holes and will accumulate beneath the nozzle valve. When superheated, the water turns to steam and will blow the injector tip of the injector.

FIGURE 24-35 Water accumulating below the nozzle valve was superheated into steam and destroyed the injector tip. The radial lines from the nozzle valve tip are the remains of the spray holes.

FIGURE 24-36 High water content in the fuel caused the upper plunger to seize this injector.

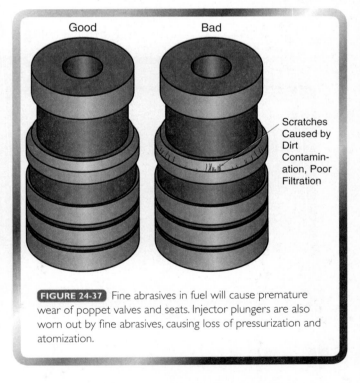

FIGURE 24-37 Fine abrasives in fuel will cause premature wear of poppet valves and seats. Injector plungers are also worn out by fine abrasives, causing loss of pressurization and atomization.

tanks above half-full may also help eliminate concern. Maintaining acceptable fuel temperatures will help fuel injection systems to function properly.

Testing EUIs

Bench testing EUIs is neither practical in the field nor recommended by OEMs. If an injector is suspected to be defective, performing a <u>cylinder cut-out test</u> or <u>cylinder contribution test</u> can identify the bad injector. Using manufacturers' diagnostic software, a cylinder cut-out or contribution test involves cutting out (removing an electrical signal to) one or pairs of cylinders at a time to determine what difference is made to engine performance. A cylinder contribution test, also called a cylinder balance test, compares cylinder pressures to one another and measures the contribution each cylinder makes. If an injector is defective or a cylinder is making little contribution, the crankshaft speed as measured by the crank or cam position sensor will slow down during the power stroke of that particular cylinder. The value of the speed change is compared to other cylinders to calculate a percentage of cylinder contribution. One hundred percent would be considered an ideal value. A cylinder contributing more than 100%, while not necessarily defective, is probably slightly overfueling. Cylinders contributing 0% or less may likely have a defective injector or some other mechanical defect. Alternatively, software can measure the change in fueling to other injectors required to compensate for a cut-out cylinder. For example, when cut out, a defective cylinder would not require the ECM to increase fueling to the remaining injectors to maintain engine speed. However, a good cylinder when cut out will require fuel compensation by the remaining cylinders to maintain engine speed. The software can measure the changes to fueling as each cylinder is cut out to calculate the relative contribution each cylinder is making to engine output.

If no software or electronic service tool is available to measure cylinder contribution, an infrared, non-contact thermometer is a helpful diagnostic tool. After speeding the engine to mid-throttle position or higher (if practical and after following safety precautions), the temperature of each cylinder at the exhaust manifold is measured. Underperforming cylinders will register lower temperatures than good cylinders. At least a 70–100°F variation between cylinders should be observed before suspecting any defect. A suspected bad injector can be swapped with a known good injector to differentiate between a defective injector and some other cylinder condition.

Performing a Cylinder Cut-Out Test

To determine whether a defective EUI injector is causing a cylinder to misfire, all OEM software contains a cylinder cut-out routine. This test can be used to identify a cylinder with a fault, such as a defective injector, or other mechanical damage, such as a broken piston ring, loose wrist pin, scored cylinder, bent connecting rod, or misadjusted valves. This test can be combined with a cylinder balance test or an injector solenoid test, which is used to identify an open circuit or a short circuit in the injector solenoids. The injector solenoid test activates the injector solenoids, which produce an audible click when activated. Software will report the status of each solenoid as OK, Open, or Shorted.

To perform a cylinder cut-out test, follow the steps in **SKILL DRILL 24-1** .

SKILL DRILL 24-1 Performing a Cylinder Cut-Out Test

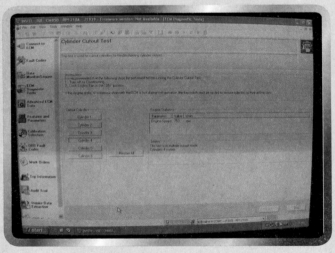

1. Start the engine and bring it to operating temperature.

2. Connect the vehicle to OEM software or a suitable replacement that can perform a cut-out test.

3. Check for fault codes; if there are any fault codes, correct them before proceeding.

4. Cylinder cut-out test results will be inaccurate if the engine load changes during the test. It is important to leave the engine fan, air compressor, air conditioning, and other sources of loads either applied or off to keep loads stable during testing. If possible, manually switch on the engine fan or disconnect the fan control solenoid. Disable the air conditioning or switch it to defrost mode. Build up vehicle air pressure and make sure there are no major leaks.

5. Navigate to cylinder cut-out testing using the diagnostic menu.

6. Adjust and hold the engine at a speed above idle for best results; 1000 rpm is ideal and can be set using the PTO switch or fast idle switch.

7. For a manual cut-out test, select a cylinder and cut it out using the software commands. Listen for a change in engine speed and noise changes when the cylinder is cut out. No change in speed indicates a dead or misfiring cylinder. Wait for at least 5 seconds between each cylinder cut out. Leave the cylinder cut out for at least 15 seconds when testing.

8. To perform double cut-out tests, disable companion cylinders for double cut outs: 1 and 6, 2 and 5, and 3 and 4. Alternatively, for triple cut-out testing, cut out cylinders 1, 2, and 3, wait 15 seconds, and then switch the cylinders back on. Repeat for cylinders 4, 5, and 6 after resuming for 5 seconds.

9. Cylinders that are overfueling will cause the greatest amount of fueling increase in other cylinder when the overfueling cylinder is cut out. Similarly, a cylinder that is not contributing, or that has low contribution, will produce the smallest increase in fueling in the other cylinders when the low power cylinder is cut out.

10. Multiple cylinder cut-out testing can be used to look for torque variations between cylinder pairs or triplets if torque data is supplied by the OEM software. Problems with fuel flow that affect multiple cylinders, or wiring harness resistances that affect cylinder banks, are more easily detected using multiple cylinder cut-out testing.

11. If a defective injector is suspected, the injector can be moved to another cylinder. If the low contribution defect follows the injector, the problem is likely the injector. If the problem remains in the same cylinder after switching an injector, a mechanical problem is indicated.

Replacing an EUI Injector

To replace an EUI injector, follow the steps in **SKILL DRILL 24-2**.

Measuring Injector Tip Protrusion

Injector tip protrusion is the distance that the tip of an EUI injector extends from the deck of the cylinder head. The correct amount of tip protrusion is required for the best spray pattern and fuel distribution in the combustion bowl. Excessive protrusion can result in tip-to-piston contact; insufficient protrusion can prevent proper fuel distribution. Cylinder head casting irregularities and variations in sealing washer thicknesses and between injectors may produce different amounts of tip protrusion. Each injector must be checked, and the amount of injector protrusion must be recorded for comparison. Specialty tools are available to check tip protrusion while the head is installed by measuring the injector cup dimensions with the injector removed. When the head is removed, a dial indicator is used to check the amount of tip protrusion.

To measure injector tip protrusion, follow the steps in **SKILL DRILL 24-3**.

SKILL DRILL 24-2 Replacing an EUI Injector

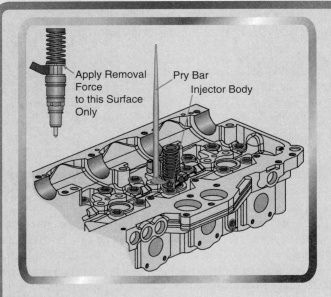

Apply Removal Force to this Surface Only — Pry Bar — Injector Body

1. Power wash and clean the valve rocker cover and the area around the cover.

2. Drain the fuel from the cylinder head. The return fitting or another plug at the rear of the cylinder head should be removed to drain fuel. Blow compressed air (less than 40 psi [276 kPa]) into the fitting for 30 seconds to help drain fuel. All fuel must be removed from the cylinder head before any injectors are removed; this will prevent a hydrostatic lock in the engine. Fuel will enter the cylinder as the injector is removed because fuel in the rail and cross drillings will drain into the piston's combustion chamber. After the piston's combustion bowl is filled with fuel, it cannot be drained, and it could potentially lock the cylinder when the engine is cranked. If a hydrostatic lock occurs, the connecting rod and valves could be bent, and the cylinder wall could even crack due to high cylinder pressure.

3. Remove the two rocker shaft bolts and the rocker shaft that contains the rocker lever for the EUI.

4. Disconnect the wiring terminals or unplug the wiring connector from the injector. Record the injector's calibration code.

5. Remove the injector hold-down bolts and clamp if they are accessible.

6. Consult the OEM's service information to identify the recommended tools and procedure for pulling the injector from the injector cup. Generally, there is a specific point on the injector where pressure should be applied with a small pry bar or heel bar to pull the injector from the injector bore.

7. Ensure that all O-rings and the copper sealing washer at the injector's tip are removed from the engine. Cover the injector hole opening with a clean shop towel to prevent dirt from getting into the injector bore.

8. Clean the injector bore with a wire brush. Inspect the injector and injector bore for damage. It is ideal to remove any debris from the injector bore with a shop vacuum.

9. If the fuel system is contaminated, drain and refill the fuel tanks with clean, fresh fuel and replace the fuel filters.

10. If a replacement injector is used, install new O-rings. Take care to install an O-ring of the correct color, and install any back-up washers in the correct position on the injector. When installing the sealing washer, the concave side should face downward if it is curved.

11. Lubricate the injector O-rings with engine oil.

12. Lubricate the injector plunger tappet beneath the injector plunger spring with oil to prevent wear during initial start-up.

13. Align the injector with the bore and install the hold-down clamp. Install the injector after firmly seating it with a light tap from a soft-faced hammer. Torque the injector hold-down bolts to the manufacturer's specifications.

14. Reinstall the rocker arms and shafts, and reconnect the fuel line fittings in the cylinder head.

15. Adjust the intake and exhaust valves, valve bridges, and injector plunger travel using the correct OEM procedure.

16. Using OEM software, change or update the injector calibration code with the code corresponding to the correct cylinder.

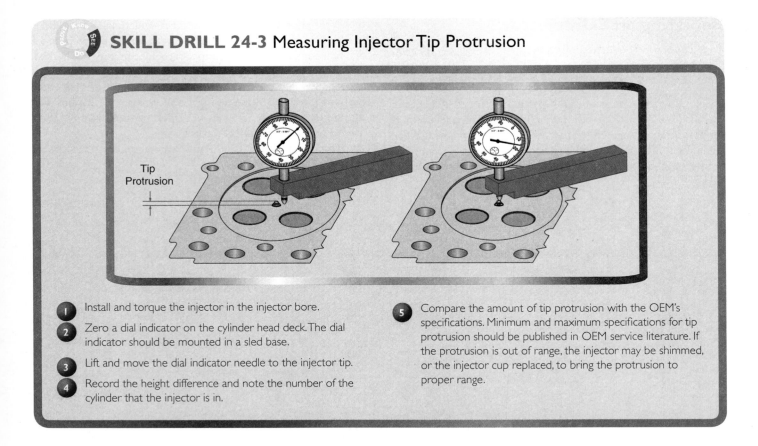

SKILL DRILL 24-3 Measuring Injector Tip Protrusion

1. Install and torque the injector in the injector bore.

2. Zero a dial indicator on the cylinder head deck. The dial indicator should be mounted in a sled base.

3. Lift and move the dial indicator needle to the injector tip.

4. Record the height difference and note the number of the cylinder that the injector is in.

5. Compare the amount of tip protrusion with the OEM's specifications. Minimum and maximum specifications for tip protrusion should be published in OEM service literature. If the protrusion is out of range, the injector may be shimmed, or the injector cup replaced, to bring the protrusion to proper range.

Fuel Rail Pressure Regulator

One common cause of no-start, hard start, and low power complaints is the pressure regulator for the fuel rail supply. This rail, which is a drilled passageway through the cylinder head, regulates fuel pressure, prevents fuel drain back, and is necessary to maintain a continuous flow of fuel through the injectors to cool and remove vapor from the injectors **FIGURE 24-38**.

The regulator is typically a restriction orifice combined with a spring-loaded pressure-regulating valve using calibrated spring tension. At low speeds, the regulator helps maintain fuel pressure in the rail to effectively supply the EUIs with an adequate fuel volume. At higher engine speeds, the regulator is wide open and the restriction orifice allows rail pressure to increase as the injectors need more fuel supplied to provide engine power. When the engine is shut off, the regulator check valve closes to prevent fuel from draining back to the fuel tank, which would allow air to enter the injectors. Fuel additives can deteriorate the nylon material forming the check valve and seat. Dirt particles, pieces of O-rings, and even filter lint can enter the valve and prevent it from closing. In this case, rail pressure may drop below acceptable values at low-speed engine operation. More commonly, the engine is hard to start and may not start at all if air has entered the rail through the open check valve. If equipped with a hand primer pump, the pump will feel spongy while priming the system due to air in the rail. Fuel pressure measured after the secondary filter should have some residual pressure long after the engine is shut down. In these cases, the filter gasket could first be checked to determine whether it may be improperly installed with a misaligned, missing, or extra gasket. But it is important to remove, clean, and inspect the check valve if the fuel pressure in the head has leaked down. To increase power output, some operators may incorrectly drill out the restriction fitting to obtain more engine power. In such cases, the size of the restriction orifice should be checked to determine whether the restriction size is correct for the engine.

Leaking check valves in the hand primer pump can also cause fuel pressure to leak down from the cylinder head. Fuel will pass through the priming pump from the head back to the inlet of the fuel transfer pump, which is also equipped with a bypass valve. While wear and age can deteriorate the check valves, and dirt can hold a valve open, excessive use of fuel conditioner, which damages nylon parts in the check valves of the pressure regulator and hand priming pump, is more commonly the cause.

Injector Cups and O-Rings

Injector cups aid the cooling of EUIs by circulating coolant around unit injectors. The cups, which are made from brass or stainless steel, transfer heat from combustion and pressurization of fuel to the engine coolant. Because the cups are exposed to coolant, corrosion due to poor cooling system maintenance

Fuel Pressure Regulator
and Return Check Valve

Return Fuel Restriction

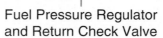

FIGURE 24-38 Faulty restriction fittings containing pressure-regulating valves are common cases of hard- or no-start conditions.

and cavitation erosion caused by combustion-related vibration of the cup can perforate the cups and allow fuel into the engine coolant **FIGURE 24-39**. Because transfer pump pressure is higher than coolant pressure, fuel will always fill the cooling system rather than allow coolant into the oil. When inspecting

FIGURE 24-39 An injector cup corroded by cavitation erosion.

a coolant reservoir, high coolant level combined with fuel contamination points directly to leaking injector cups.

If cups are leaking outside the area exposed to circulating fuel, combustion gases can leak into the cooling system, leading to over-pressurization of the system. Some engines are also prone to allowing pressurized combustion gas leakage into the cup area, bypassing the sealing washer at the injector tip. If the combustion gases push by the sealing O-rings around the injector, air can be introduced into the fuel supply in the cylinder head leading to low power, rough running, and stalling complaints. Fuel pressure fault codes are also produced if combustion gases leak into the low-pressure fuel supply within the cup.

When installing injectors, it is important to liberally lubricate the injector O-rings with engine oil. Without lubrication, injectors O-rings will roll when installed and quickly produce leaks. If the top O-ring leaks, fuel can spill onto the top of the cylinder head deck and contaminate engine oil.

Replacing an Injector Cup

Injector cups require replacement during cylinder head reconditioning and whenever fuel is found in engine coolant. Brass cups are better able to transfer heat from the injector to the coolant. Stainless steel cups have superior corrosion resistance. Cups are installed in a variety of ways. Brass cups are pressed into the cylinder head and swaged, or expanded, in the head, which is like flaring and helps to seal the cup in the injector bore. Sealant, a striking tool, and a swaging tool are used to seat and seal the cup in the head. Other engines use threaded cups with sealing O-rings to help maintain a coolant- and gas-tight seal in the cup.

To replace an injector cup, follow the steps in **SKILL DRILL 24-4**.

SKILL DRILL 24-4 Replacing an Injector Cup

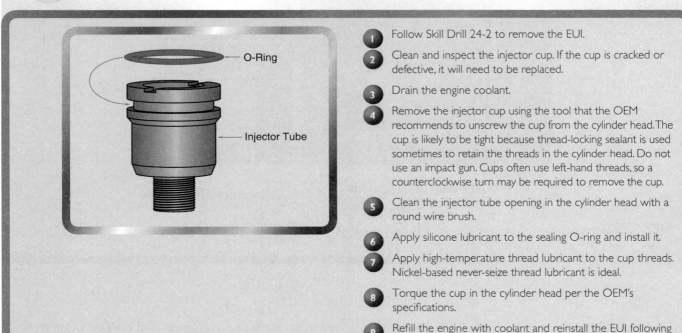

1. Follow Skill Drill 24-2 to remove the EUI.

2. Clean and inspect the injector cup. If the cup is cracked or defective, it will need to be replaced.

3. Drain the engine coolant.

4. Remove the injector cup using the tool that the OEM recommends to unscrew the cup from the cylinder head. The cup is likely to be tight because thread-locking sealant is used sometimes to retain the threads in the cylinder head. Do not use an impact gun. Cups often use left-hand threads, so a counterclockwise turn may be required to remove the cup.

5. Clean the injector tube opening in the cylinder head with a round wire brush.

6. Apply silicone lubricant to the sealing O-ring and install it.

7. Apply high-temperature thread lubricant to the cup threads. Nickel-based never-seize thread lubricant is ideal.

8. Torque the cup in the cylinder head per the OEM's specifications.

9. Refill the engine with coolant and reinstall the EUI following Skill Drill 24-2.

Wrap-Up

Ready for Review

▸ Like older mechanical unit injectors, electronic unit injectors (EUIs) inject fuel directly into the combustion chamber. However, EUIs use a solenoid and electrically controlled spill valve instead of mechanical metering components.

▸ In EUIs, fuel pressurization, injection timing, atomization, and fuel distribution are integrated into a single injector body component. An ECM sends PWM electrical signals to the injector to control metering and injection timing events.

▸ EUIs are installed directly into the cylinder head. To build injection pressure to higher levels than pump-line-nozzle (PLN) systems, the injector is driven by the engine camshaft with a dedicated injector lobe.

▸ Overhead cam engines directly actuate the EUI through a rocker lever. The move to wider and more durable overhead cam designs has enabled a higher degree of fuel pressurization compared to other systems. This configuration is also one of the most efficient hydraulic and mechanical fuel system arrangements, providing low parasitic losses.

▸ Actuating the injectors using an overhead camshaft permits the least amount of injection delay, because there are no push-tubes to bend, injector lines to swell, or delivery vales to lift.

▸ The extremely fine spray produced by unit injectors results in one of the best combinations of fuel atomization and distribution. Consequently, unit injectors can produce more power and torque for a given quantity of fuel without a penalty to fuel consumption and emissions.

▸ Conventional unit injectors consist of several basic elements: a spring-loaded plunger and barrel assembly, a spill control valve (SCV) (also known as a poppet valve or solenoid needle valve), an electric solenoid or cartridge valve, fuel inlet and return passageways, and a nozzle valve at the injector tip.

▸ Regardless of type, all unit injectors share common operating principles.

▸ Injection is performed by switching the injector's solenoid valve on and off while the camshaft forces the injector plunger down into the barrel. The quantity of injected fuel delivered is a function of both electrical signal time and plunger velocity, which is dependent on engine speed.

▸ Fuel rail passages integrated into the cylinder head supply low-pressure fuel to each injector. Fuel flows through the rail into the pressure chambers to cool the injector and purge any vapor from the fuel circuits. The injector plunger, driven by the camshaft, moves through a stroke determined by the injector plunger travel adjustment. On its upward stroke, the low-pressure fuel supplied to the injector fills the cavity created beneath the plunger.

▸ The injector plunger begins its downward stroke as the camshaft rotates onto the outer base circle of the cam lobe. If the solenoid is not energized, fuel below the injector plunger is forced out of the injector through the fuel supply rail.

▸ When the ECM sends an electrical signal to the solenoid, the poppet closes the fuel passageway to the fuel rail, causing trapped fuel to pressurize beneath the injector plunger. As the plunger continues its downward stroke, fuel pressure builds inside the injector. Pressurized fuel forces the nozzle valve open, and fuel injection begins.

▸ Injection continues until the solenoid is de-energized.

▸ Unit injection systems are not likely to be involved in run-away engine operation. In the event of an injector malfunction, only one uncontrolled injection will occur.

▸ The EUI and ECM achieve precise injection timing and fuel regulation through principles of electronic signal processing. The ECM processes sensor data regarding engine position and operating conditions using operating algorithms, fuel timing maps, and calibration files. The ECM then transmits electrical signals to the EUI to control injection timing and fuel quantity necessary to obtain the best performance, lowest emissions, and highest fuel economy.

▸ The ECM uses a pulse-width modulation (PWM) signal to operate the injector solenoid via a peak and hold current-shaping strategy.

▸ Injector response time is an important piece of diagnostic information. If injectors have excessively high or low resistances, have bad connectors, or become overheated, their response times will fall outside the expected limits. Monitoring response time can indicate that a problem is developing within an injector or that the injector has failed.

▸ Rate shaping is not easily accomplished electronically, so mechanical strategies are used to produce pilot injection events in many EUIs.

▸ Manufacturers flow test all injectors and compare them against a nominal standard value. Depending on whether the injector flows more or less fuel, a numerical or alphanumerical fuel trim code is applied to the injector. This injector calibration code is entered into the ECM injector data.

▸ The Delphi E3 EUI was introduced in mid-year 2002 for EGR-equipped diesel engines. Benefits include high-speed, dual-valve operation, ultra-high injection pressure, a lightweight and compact design, and more. The Delphi E3 is suitable for 9–16L heavy-duty diesel engines used in on- and off-highway applications.

▸ A Delphi injector Detroit named the N3 was used prior to the Delphi E3 injector. It used a single nozzle control valve (NCV), but was capable of a pilot injection event.

▶ The E3 injector uses two magnetic solenoids: the NCV, which is normally closed, and the spill control valve (SCV), which is normally open. The nozzle valve is hydraulically balanced and the control valves are servo hydraulic valves.

▶ To begin injection, the injector camshaft moves to the outerbase circle and begins to push the injector plunger downward. No pressurization can take place until the SCV closes.

▶ Fuel pressure created by the closing of the SCV is applied to the top of the nozzle valve. Fuel pressure is also applied to the bottom of the nozzle valve in the area of the annulus. The nozzle valve lifts when the pressure balance above and below it changes, allowing pressurized fuel to spray into the combustion chamber.

▶ The PWM current applied to the control valves is discontinued when the control module switches off the current to the injector. The de-energized SCV coil allows trapped fuel to pass to a fuel return circuit. When fuel pressure is low enough, the nozzle valve closes and ends injection.

▶ Injection initiation and fuel metering are regulated by a dedicated control module. The longer the pulse width, the longer the SCV is closed and the more fuel is injected.

▶ Water may be introduced into the fuel supply during fueling if warm, moist air condenses on the cold metal walls of fuel storage tanks or dissolves into the cooler fuel. The effects of water in diesel fuel can be serious.

▶ Dirt can cause premature wear and shortened injector life. The spill or poppet valve is easily scored, worn, and damaged by the continuous abrasive action of dirt.

▶ Diesel fuel temperatures vary considerably due to engine operating temperatures. As fuel temperature increases, fuel viscosity decreases and injectors operate at reduced internal clearances. Maintaining proper fuel temperatures helps ensure proper function of the fuel injection system.

▶ Bench testing of EUIs is neither practical in the field nor recommended by OEMs. If an injector is suspected defective, performing a cylinder cut-out or contribution test can identify the bad injector.

▶ Unit injection pumps are often referred to as a unit pump system (UPS) because they combine elements of PLN injection systems and unit injectors.

Vocabulary Builder

beginning of injection period (BIP) The closing of the solenoid poppet valve.

BIP detection circuit A circuit that allows the ECM to detect the closing of the poppet valve.

calibration code A numbered or alphanumerical value applied to the injector that provides information about unique fuel flow rates through the injector; also known as E-trim, injector code, or a fuel trim code.

current ramping The buildup of current flow through the solenoid coils during the initial energization period.

cylinder contribution test A test that compares cylinder pressures to one another and measures the contribution each cylinder makes; also known as a cylinder balance test or a relative compression test.

cylinder cut-out test A test where power to a solenoid is removed during engine operation using a service software or electronic service tool. The test is used to identify misfiring or noisy cylinders.

Delphi E3 EUI A type of EUI that uses a dual-control valve, four-wire design, which enables high-speed, ultra-high-pressure operation with rate-shaped injection capabilities.

electronic unit injector (EUI) A unit injector that injects fuel directly into the combustion chamber. Timing, metering, pressurization, and distribution of fuel are all integrated into a single injector body.

electronic unit pump (EUP) An single cylinder injection pump that combines elements of PLN injection systems and unit injectors; also referred to as a unit pump system (UPS).

inductive reactance Current induced in a coil of a solenoid's windings which opposes ECM current when initially energized; also known as inductive resistance.

injection delay The time lag between the start of fuel pressurization for injection and the point when fuel is actually injected.

injector response time The strategy of tracking time variations between the voltage drops for each injection.

inner base circle One of two circles that outline the cam profile. The inner base circle refers to the circular part of the camshaft that does not include the lobe.

nozzle control valve (NCV) A valve that allows the injector to operate like a conventional hydraulically balanced nozzle valve, like those used in common rail injectors; this valve is electronically controlled by the engine or fuel injection control module to vary injection timing and metering.

outer base circle One of two circles that outline the cam profile. The outer base circle refers to the circular part of the camshaft that includes the lobe.

spill control valve (SCV) A valve that operates to change injection pressure as needed to meet operating requirements. The normally open valve, when energized, will cause fuel pressure to build up in the injector body until the nozzle control valve is energized and injection takes place.

Review Questions

1. A _____ is a test used to identify a misfiring cylinder.
   a. cylinder cycling test
   b. cylinder leakage test
   c. cylinder cut-out test
   d. cylinder calibration test

2. The _____ operates to change injection pressure as needed to meet operating requirements.
   a. spill control valve
   b. nozzle control valve
   c. journal
   d. crankpin

3. Actuating the injectors with an overhead camshaft permits the least amount of injection _____.
   a. protrusion
   b. lash
   c. spill
   d. delay

4. The injector plunger begins its downward stroke as the camshaft rotates onto the _____ base circle of the cam lobe.
   a. inner
   b. outer
   c. upper
   d. lower

5. Allowing _____ in the injector adjustment will cause the yoke and clevis to cycle back and forth with high force and ultimately break.
   a. lash
   b. pressure
   c. suction
   d. protrusion

6. A signal type known as a _____ modulated current drives the injector solenoids.
   a. voltage drop
   b. inductive resistance
   c. inversion
   d. pulse-width

7. Cylinder head casting irregularities and variations in sealing washer thicknesses and between injectors may produce different amounts of injector tip _____.
   a. lash
   b. delay
   c. protrusion
   d. spill

8. The poppet or SCV is easily scored, worn, and damaged by the continuous abrasive action of _____.
   a. dirt
   b. water
   c. air
   d. heat

9. First-generation EUIs used a single electrically controlled poppet or _____ valve that opened and closed to control the beginning and end of the injection event.
   a. needle control
   b. spill control
   c. nozzle control
   d. plunger control

10. When the poppet valve closes, it changes the strength of the solenoid's magnetic field, which in turn produces a slight change in coil resistance, or _____.
    a. voltage drop
    b. response time
    c. current ramping
    d. inductive resistance

ASE-Type Questions

1. Technician A says the Delphi E3 EUI can electronically vary injection pressure over all engine speeds using a second electrically operated control valve. Technician B says EUIs currently offer the highest spray-in pressures of any fuel injection system. Who is correct?
   a. Technician A
   b. Technician B
   c. Both Technician A and Technician B
   d. Neither Technician A nor Technician B

2. Technician A says EUI injectors use a peak and hold strategy to energize the solenoid windings. Technician B says high resistance in an injector solenoid circuit generally occurs when the engine is warmed up. Who is correct?
   a. Technician A
   b. Technician B
   c. Both Technician A and Technician B
   d. Neither Technician A nor Technician B

3. Technician A says that electronic unit pump injection systems in operation are adjustment-free and require little maintenance except during engine overhaul or replacement due to failure. Technician B says EUI plunger travel is adjustable. Who is correct?
   a. Technician A
   b. Technician B
   c. Both Technician A and Technician B
   d. Neither Technician A nor Technician B

4. Technician A says electronic unit injectors contain between 1 and 5 spray holes. Technician B says electronic unit injectors contain between 5 and 13 spray holes. Who is correct?
   a. Technician A
   b. Technician B
   c. Both Technician A and Technician B
   d. Neither Technician A nor Technician B

5. Technician A says the outer base circle is the circular part of the camshaft that does not include the lobe. Technician B says the inner base circle is the circular part of the camshaft that includes the lobe. Who is correct?
   a. Technician A
   b. Technician B
   c. Both Technician A and Technician B
   d. Neither Technician A nor Technician B

6. Technician A says the problem of inductive reactance in the solenoid coils is solved by using a current-shaping strategy called current ramping. Technician B says the problem of inductive reactance in the solenoid coils is solved by using a current-shaping strategy called inversion. Who is correct?
   a. Technician A
   b. Technician B
   c. Both Technician A and Technician B
   d. Neither Technician A nor Technician B

7. Technician A says a unit pump is used by the ECM to adjust timing and fuel flow through the injector. Technician B says a calibration code is used by the ECM to adjust timing and fuel flow through the injector. Who is correct?
   a. Technician A
   b. Technician B
   c. Both Technician A and Technician B
   d. Neither Technician A nor Technician B

8. Technician A says if an injector is suspected to be defective, performing a cylinder cut-out test can identify the bad injector. Technician B says if an injector is suspected to be defective, performing a cylinder contribution test can identify the bad injector. Who is correct?
   a. Technician A
   b. Technician B
   c. Both Technician A and Technician B
   d. Neither Technician A nor Technician B

9. Technician A says valve bodies transfer heat from combustion and pressurization of fuel to the engine coolant. Technician B says nozzle valve tips transfer heat from combustion and pressurization of fuel to the engine coolant. Who is correct?
   a. Technician A
   b. Technician B
   c. Both Technician A and Technician B
   d. Neither Technician A nor Technician B

10. Technician A says water can accumulate below the nozzle valve, vaporize, and cause a tip to blow off an injector. Technician B says oil can accumulate below the nozzle valve, vaporize, and cause a tip to blow off an injector. Who is correct?
   a. Technician A
   b. Technician B
   c. Both Technician A and Technician B
   d. Neither Technician A nor Technician B

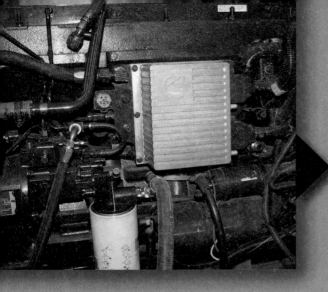

CHAPTER 25
Cummins Unit Injection Systems

> ## Knowledge Objectives

After reading this chapter, you will be able to:

1. Identify and describe Cummins unit injection systems. (pp 716–733)
2. Define and explain terminology associated with Cummins unit injection systems. (pp 716–733)
3. Describe the purpose and operating principles of Cummins unit injection systems. (pp 716–733)
4. Identify and describe the types, styles, construction, and applications of Cummins unit injection systems. (pp 716–733)
5. Identify and explain inspection and diagnostic procedures for Cummins unit injection systems. (pp 716–733)

Skills Objectives

After reading this chapter, you will be able to:

1. Adjust valves and injectors on a CELECT engine. (p 721) SKILL DRILL 25-1

2. Adjust valves and injectors on an ISX engine. (p 727) SKILL DRILL 25-2

3. Check for air in fuel. (p 731) SKILL DRILL 25-3

▶ Introduction

Clessie Cummins founded Cummins Engine Company and is recognized as having introduced the diesel to North America. In 1929, he drove from Indiana to New York in a Packard city automobile and used only $1.39 worth of fuel and drew wide attention to diesel engines for the first time. In 1931, he won the Indianapolis 500 using another hand-built diesel-powered car.

Cummins Engine Company is a global company leading the production of light-, medium-, and heavy-duty diesel engines. Several popular unit injection systems have been used by Cummins since the 1950s. The first was a **pressure time (PT) injection system** used until the early 1980s. The operating principles of this system were used in the ISX high-pressure injection system, which was used by the ISX engine until 2010. The PT system was later modified and reintroduced as a partial-authority system called **partial-authority Cummins engine (PACE)**. Partial-authority systems combine elements of a traditional mechanical system but use an electronic governor instead of a mechanical one.

PACE combined the mechanical PT pump with an electronic fuel control valve on the outlet of the fuel pump that varied pressure supplied to unit injectors. The Cummins Electronic, or **CELECT**, fuel system was a full-authority system introduced in 1990. By the late 1990s, electronic control systems advanced even farther with the introduction of the third generation of Cummins electronic systems, called the **Interact System (IS)**. In the IS, the electronic control module (ECM) processed all sensor and switch inputs to send signals to the fuel system, vehicle, and engine control devices using network communication for the first time. This system was given its name because it could integrate with other vehicle control systems, such as the transmission, braking system, and traction control system.

▶ Types of Cummins Unit Injection Systems

This section will briefly examine the PT unit injection system because its operating principles are used by the ISX **high-pressure injection, time-pressure injection (HPI-TPI)** system (**ISX** is a Cummins engine family prefix). The HPI-TPI is a unique fuel system with open-nozzle injectors that use a plunger. This system also uses a centrally located injector. In this system, metering and injection timing are controlled by varying fuel pressures supplied to the injector.

▶ You Are the Technician

A dump truck with a 2009 ISX engine has arrived at your shop for low power, engine rpm surging, and rough running. After performing routine visual inspections, you check for diagnostic fault codes and find none related to any engine system. You perform a cylinder cut-out test, but you can't precisely identify any problematic cylinder. When you measure temperatures at the exhaust manifold, you find there isn't much difference in the temperatures at the exhaust ports of each cylinder. Next you check the rail pressure using original equipment manufacturer (OEM) software and discover the pressure is erratic. It surprises you that there isn't a fault code for the data readings from the sensor, but you conclude the problem may not be serious enough to produce a code. The OEM service manual suggests using a symptom-based diagnostic strategy. You also think to check the valve and injector adjustment and wonder if the gear pump or fuel system valves in the integrated fuel system module (IFSM) could have a problem. The service manual advises that you begin by checking the low-pressure fuel system to verify it is functioning correctly. As you continue following the diagnostic steps outlined by the manufacturer, consider the following:

1. Could misadjusted unit injectors explain the symptoms?
2. What symptoms would likely be present if the low-pressure system was supplied air with fuel because of a loose suction side fuel line fitting?
3. Describe the effects on a fuel system if small amounts of air were present in the fuel.

CELECT unit injectors used by popular engines such as the N-14, M-11, and L-10E will be discussed as well. Remember that unit injectors incorporate pressurization, timing, metering, and atomization functions into a single component or unit, which gives the fuel system its unit injection system name.

Cummins PT Injection System

The Cummins PT injection system meters fuel for injection by changing fuel pressure and the time pressurized fuel is available to the injectors FIGURE 25-1. By varying fuel pressure and the time available to inject, which varies according to engine speed, fuel rate is adapted to meet constantly changing operator demands for engine power output. The two most important elements of the PT system are the injectors and the PT pump. The injectors are supplied fuel by the PT pump. Varying pump output pressure changes the amount of fuel supplied to the injectors, which decreases or increases the amount of fuel injected. For example, if fuel pressure is increased and time available for injection is held constant, more fuel is injected into the cylinders by the injectors because fuel at higher pressure fills injectors faster. Similarly, when the time to supply pressurized fuel to the injectors is increased (such as when engine speed drops under load), and fuel pressure is held constant, more fuel is supplied and injected because the fuel has more time to fill the injector. Injectors and pumps have changed over the years to accommodate increased engine power and emission standards, but PT system operation has fundamentally stayed the same.

PT Components

While the PT system has long been discontinued, its simple operating principles are shared by other contemporary Cummins fuel systems. Understanding the operation of the PT system provides foundational information that helps technicians understand, diagnose, and service other Cummins fuel systems. The enormous number of these engines produced for off-road applications, and their extreme durability, also means that some

technicians will encounter these fuel systems in machinery as diverse as rock crushers, farm equipment, power generators, and marine engines.

PT Pump

This PT system changes fuel pressure supplied to the injector using an engine-driven low-pressure gear pump FIGURE 25-2. The pump receives mechanical inputs including throttle position from the driver's throttle pedal, engine speed from the pump drive gear, and boost pressure from a line connecting the pump to the intake manifold. These three basic inputs are used to mechanically vary the pressure of fuel exiting the pump based on driver demand, engine speed, and load conditions. An electric shut-off valve with a mechanical override is located at the pump outlet and used to stop and start the engine. A long throttle shaft through the pump varies fuel pressure supplied to the injectors by a gear pump. Moving the throttle from idle to full throttle changes the size of an orifice passageway between the throttle and pressurized fuel passageway in the pump. A hydraulic governor with a centrifugal flyweight mechanism modifies fuel pressure to regulate minimum and maximum engine speed and the amount of torque rise.

PT Injectors

PT injectors are unique in that they are open-nozzle injectors. Unlike closed-nozzle injectors, which have a spring holding the nozzle valve on its seat, open nozzles use a plunger held off its seat by a heavy spring FIGURE 25-3 and FIGURE 25-4. Injection takes place when an engine-driven camshaft pushes the injector plunger down into the injector bore, forcing fuel out the injector tip. Injection ends when the injector plunger crushes into the injector seat FIGURE 25-5.

Time allowed for supplying fuel to the injectors is regulated by the injector plunger, which opens and closes a metering orifice. Available time for fuel metering is determined by engine speed, because the injector plunger is driven by the engine camshaft. At lower engine rpm, more time is allowed for fuel to flow under pressure into the injector body. To increase fuel delivery at higher engine speeds and loads when less time is available to fill the injector with fuel, fuel pressure supplied to the injector must increase. At idle, fuel pressure may be approximately 30 psi (207 kPa). Under full load and torque, fuel pressure is 130–200 psi (9–14 bar), depending on the engine model and power output. The diameter of the metering inlet orifice is carefully selected to match the engine power rating. A larger orifice will admit more fuel to the injector, while a smaller orifice will not allow the injector to fill as rapidly.

CELECT and CELECT Plus

Cummins CELECT was the first generation of full-authority electronic engine control. The second generation, **CELECT Plus**, was introduced several years later. CELECT Plus uses additional sensors, a faster and more capable ECM, and additional programmable engine controls FIGURE 25-6. CELECT Plus also had the added benefit of being compatible with J-1957 network communication through a six-pin data link connector (DLC) located in the cab.

CELECT systems meter and time the injection event using a unit injector FIGURE 25-7. While similar to other

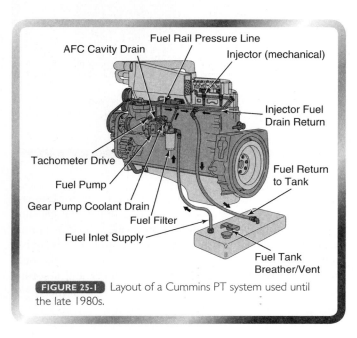

FIGURE 25-1 Layout of a Cummins PT system used until the late 1980s.

AFC Cavity Drain
Fuel Rail Pressure Line
Injector (mechanical)
Injector Fuel Drain Return
Fuel Return to Tank
Fuel Tank Breather/Vent
Fuel Inlet Supply
Fuel Filter
Gear Pump Coolant Drain
Fuel Pump
Tachometer Drive

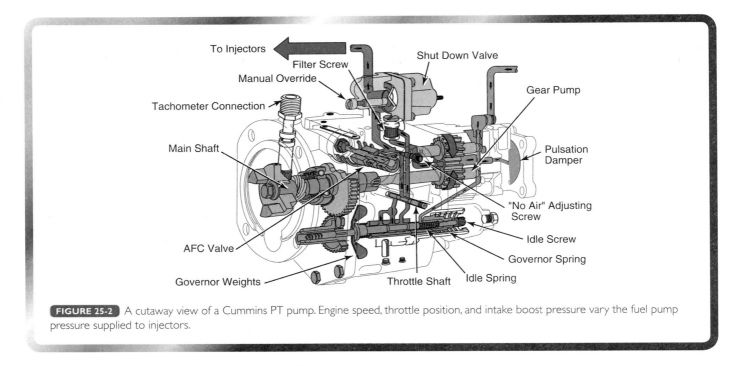

FIGURE 25-2 A cutaway view of a Cummins PT pump. Engine speed, throttle position, and intake boost pressure vary the fuel pump pressure supplied to injectors.

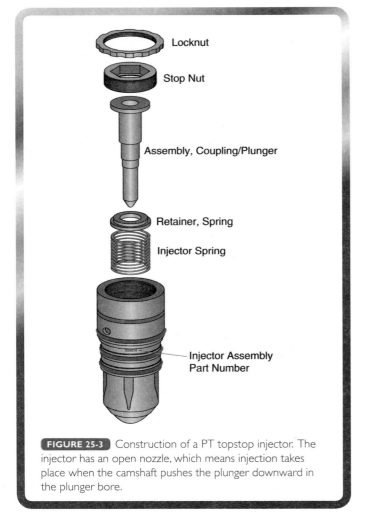

FIGURE 25-3 Construction of a PT topstop injector. The injector has an open nozzle, which means injection takes place when the camshaft pushes the plunger downward in the plunger bore.

FIGURE 25-4 The removable PT plunger is held off the plunger seat by a spring. The camshaft drives fuel out the open nozzle using the plunger.

electronic unit injectors (EUIs) the CELECT injector uses two internal plungers: a **timing plunger** (the upper plunger) and a **metering plunger** (the lower plunger) **FIGURE 25-8**. Timing and metering functions are performed by applying two pulse-width modulated (PWM) signals of close to 75 volts, once during upward stroke of the injector plunger and a second during the downward stroke.

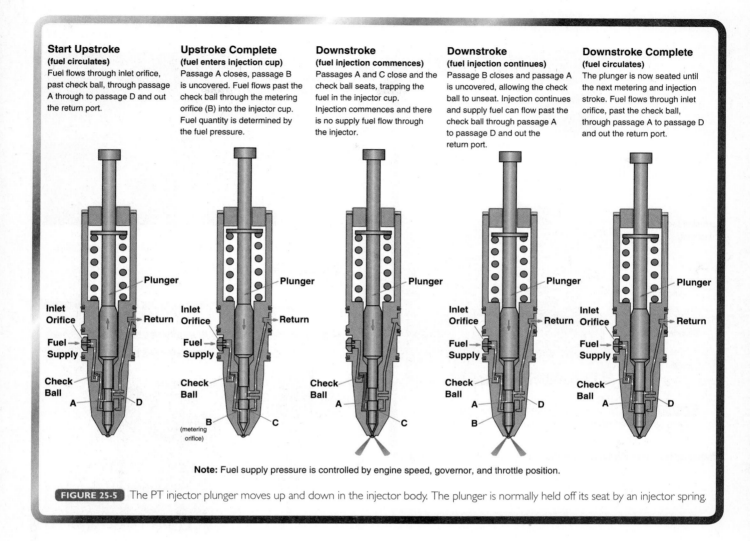

Start Upstroke
(fuel circulates)
Fuel flows through inlet orifice, past check ball, through passage A through to passage D and out the return port.

Upstroke Complete
(fuel enters injection cup)
Passage A closes, passage B is uncovered. Fuel flows past the check ball through the metering orifice (B) into the injector cup. Fuel quantity is determined by the fuel pressure.

Downstroke
(fuel injection commences)
Passages A and C close and the check ball seats, trapping the fuel in the injector cup. Injection commences and there is no supply fuel flow through the injector.

Downstroke
(fuel injection continues)
Passage B closes and passage A is uncovered, allowing the check ball to unseat. Injection continues and supply fuel can flow past the check ball through passage A to passage D and out the return port.

Downstroke Complete
(fuel circulates)
The plunger is now seated until the next metering and injection stroke. Fuel flows through inlet orifice, past the check ball, through passage A to passage D and out the return port.

Note: Fuel supply pressure is controlled by engine speed, governor, and throttle position.

FIGURE 25-5 The PT injector plunger moves up and down in the injector body. The plunger is normally held off its seat by an injector spring.

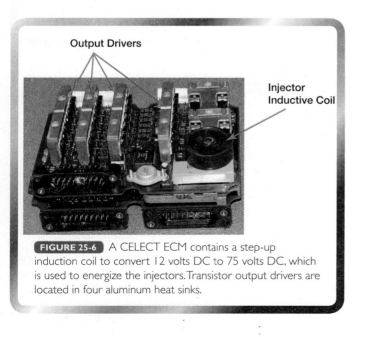

FIGURE 25-6 A CELECT ECM contains a step-up induction coil to convert 12 volts DC to 75 volts DC, which is used to energize the injectors. Transistor output drivers are located in four aluminum heat sinks.

CELECT Components

The CELECT system uses an engine-driven gear pump to pull fuel from the fuel tanks **FIGURE 25-9**. The fuel from the tank first passes through a single fuel filter and then into an ECM cooler plate. Because under-hood temperatures and heat from the electronics can shorten component life, additional fuel cooling extends the ECM's reliability.

Fuel then enters a gear pump that looks somewhat similar to the older PT system **FIGURE 25-10**. The pump output pressure is regulated to deliver fuel at a pressure of approximately 150 psi (10 bar) to a fuel rail drilled through the cylinder head. The rail supplies the injectors with a continuous supply of fuel at a constant pressure. This high volume pump quickly picks up fuel from the tank after a filter replacement and no hand or electric primer is used on the low-pressure fuel system. When the ignition is switched on, a 12-volt signal from the ECM opens a normally closed solenoid located on top of the gear pump, enabling fuel to flow to the rail drilled through the cylinder head.

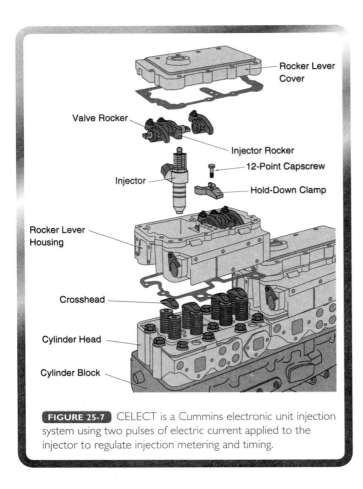

FIGURE 25-7 CELECT is a Cummins electronic unit injection system using two pulses of electric current applied to the injector to regulate injection metering and timing.

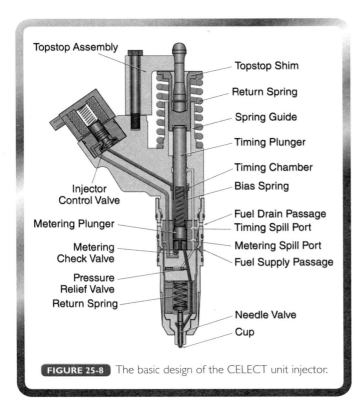

FIGURE 25-8 The basic design of the CELECT unit injector.

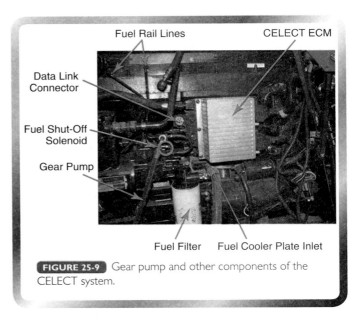

FIGURE 25-9 Gear pump and other components of the CELECT system.

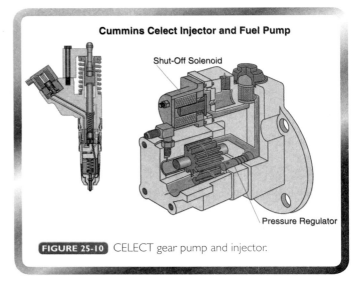

FIGURE 25-10 CELECT gear pump and injector.

▶ TECHNICIAN TIP

Some devices switched on and off by the ECM have sensitive output drivers. Drivers are switching transistors located in the ECM. Some older ECM drivers are very sensitive to current applied externally to the driver circuits and are easily damaged. Shorting out or jumping output connectors should be avoided on many older ECMs to prevent accidental destruction of ECM electronics.

Adjusting Valves and Injectors on a CELECT Engine

Cummins CELECT and CELECT Plus system injectors were used on Cummins electronically controlled engines between 1990 and 2001 in L, M, and N series engines. The injectors are adjusted when the injector cam lobe follower has just crossed over the injector lobe's outer base circle. Unlike other engines, this point corresponds to an engine position of approximately

45 degree after TDC. Because the adjustment is performed on the high point of the injector lobe, the injector rocker lever has ended downward movement of the injector plunger into the injector. Both the valves and injector are adjusted at the same time for an individual cylinder. Injector adjustment is accomplished by bottoming out the plungers in the injector and then lifting them slightly. This means at TDC, the plungers will bottom out completely in the injector. All overhead (valve and injector) adjustments must be made when the engine is cold (any stabilized coolant temperature at 60°C [140°F] or below).

To adjust valves and injectors on a CELECT engine, follow the steps in **SKILL DRILL 25-1**. Always consult OEM service information and follow the prescribed procedures using the correct tools.

Injection Operation Overview

The CELECT injector contains an electrically operated control valve like other EUIs. Injection takes place when a PWM signal closes the normally open control valve during the injector plunger's downward stroke. An engine-driven camshaft supplies

SKILL DRILL 25-1 Adjusting Valves and Injectors on a CELECT Engine

Accessory Pulley Position	Cylinder to Adjust	Rocker Lever Position	Rocker Lever Position for Companion Cylinder
A	1	Both levers loose	Cylinder 6 Intake lever tight Exhaust lever just slightly loose
B	5	Both levers loose	Cylinder 2 Intake lever tight Exhaust lever just slightly loose
C	3	Both levers loose	Cylinder 4 Intake lever tight Exhaust lever just slightly loose
A	6	Both levers loose	Cylinder 1 Intake lever tight Exhaust lever just slightly loose
B	2	Both levers loose	Cylinder 5 Intake lever tight Exhaust lever just slightly loose
C	4	Both levers loose	Cylinder 3 Intake lever tight Exhaust lever just slightly loose

1. Power wash the engine and clean the valve rocker cover and the area around the cover. Ensure that the vehicle wheels are chocked and the park brake is applied. The transmission should be in neutral in order to bar the engine during adjustment.

2. Remove the engines valve cover(s).

3. Rotate the engine to the correct position to begin the valve and injector adjustment. A 1 5/16" (33 mm) socket can be placed over a nut on the accessory drive pulley to rotate the engine. Positioning the engine is done by aligning markings on the accessory drive pulley and engine front cover. Three letters are stamped into the accessory drive gear: A, B, and C. These markings are 120 degrees apart. Do not confuse any of these letters for a TDC marking, which can be found on some drive pulleys. Rotate the engine to align the letter A with a line scribed into the front cover or a raised arrow stamping.

4. Confirm that the engine is positioned correctly to perform a valve and injector adjustment for the selected cylinder. The cylinder being adjusted should have finished compression stroke and should be 45 degrees past TDC during the power stroke. Both valves should be closed, and the rocker levers should have operating clearance that leaves them loose when they are shaken by hand. The companion cylinder will have finished exhaust stroke and begun intake stroke. Always confirm engine position by comparing the valve–rocker lever positions of pairs of companion cylinders.

5. Check the torque on the injector hold-down bolts. Most torque settings are close to 45 ft-lb (61 Nm).

6. Loosen the lock nut on the injector adjustment screw and bottom the injector plunger out three to four times to remove fuel beneath the timing plunger. This is done by tightening and loosening the injector adjustment screw.

7. Using an in-lb (Nm) torque wrench, bottom the injector adjustment screw into the injector and tighten the screw to 25 in-lb (3 Nm).

8. Back out the adjusting screw two flats or 120 degrees.

9. Tighten the lock nut.

10. Using specifications for valve adjustment clearances obtained from OEM service literature or the emission decal on the engine, adjust the clearances between the rocker lever and valve bridges using a thickness or feeler blade.

11. Rotate the engine to the next cylinder in the firing order and perform the valve and injector adjustment. Ensure that the engine is rotated in the correct direction of rotation and double check the position of the rocker levers. When on A position, the two end cylinders are adjusted. B position allows adjustment of the next two cylinders closer the engine center. C position allows adjustment of the two center cylinders. Two complete crankshafts rotations and accessory drive rotations are required to adjust all valves and injectors.

12. Reinstall the compression release housings if they were removed and adjust the clearances between the slave pistons and valve bridges. Use OEM specifications to establish the correct clearance by rotating the engine and positioning it in the same sequence as a valve and injector adjustment. This means the slave piston clearance is adjusted for cylinder 1 or 6, but not both at the same time, in A position. B position allows the slave piston adjustment on cylinder 2 or 5. C position allows the slave piston adjustment on cylinder 3 or 4.

the force to pressurize fuel for injection. Fuel trapped below the metering plunger pressurizes fuel within the injector body to lift a closed nozzle valve from its seat. The start of injection and injection quantity are electronically controlled.

Key components inside the injector are a timing plunger, an <u>injector control valve</u>, and a metering plunger. The length of time that the solenoid is energized on the upward stroke determines how much fuel is metered for injection. When the control valve is de-energized and opens during the plunger's downward stroke determines the timing or beginning of the injection event. Unlike other unit injectors, the ending of the injection event is not determined electronically; instead it is performed mechanically at a fixed point using a spill port.

Injection Metering

While CELECT injectors look like unit injectors built by other manufacturers, the double pulse operation and fixed ending of the injection event means they operate very differently. Understanding the injector's operation helps technicians understand some unusual type of failures these injectors may experience. During injection metering, the following steps occur:

1. Both the metering piston and timing plunger are bottomed in the injector. The normally open solenoid-operated control valve is closed by electrical current. This is the beginning of metering **FIGURE 25-11** .

2. The rotating engine camshaft moves the injector rocker lever to the camshaft's inner base circle. As the cam follower moves down the cam lobe, the injector's upper (timing) plunger travels upward. Spring pressure and fuel pressure entering the injector force the timing and metering plungers upward. Pressurized fuel enters the injector by unseating the lower check ball. Upward plunger travel fills the injector metering chamber as long as the control valve is energized and upward movement of the metering and timing plungers take place. Fuel pressure acting against the bottom of the metering plunger forces the plunger to maintain contact with the timing plunger **FIGURE 25-12** .

3. Metering ends when the ECM de-energizes the injector control valve, causing it to open. Pressurized fuel then flows through the open injector control valve into the upper timing chamber, which stops any further upward travel of the metering plunger **FIGURE 25-13** . The small bias spring in the timing chamber ensures that the metering plunger remains stationary while the timing plunger continues upward movement due to camshaft rotation. Fuel pressure below the timing plunger flowing past the open control valve together with bias spring force against the metering piston maintain fuel pressure below the metering plunger, keeping the lower metering check ball seated. The timing plunger may continue to move upward and continue to fill the timing chamber, but in the CELECT system, a precisely

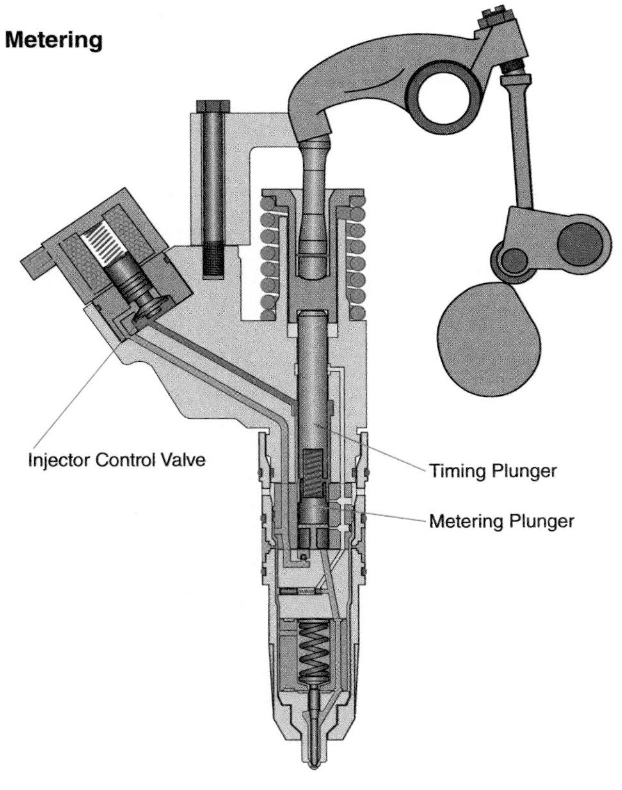

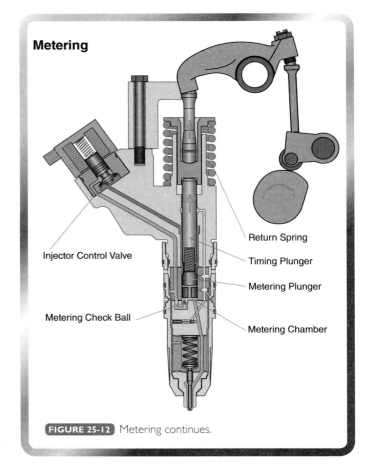

Metering

Injector Control Valve

Timing Plunger

Metering Plunger

FIGURE 25-11 The beginning of metering.

Metering

Injector Control Valve

Return Spring

Timing Plunger

Metering Plunger

Metering Check Ball

Metering Chamber

FIGURE 25-12 Metering continues.

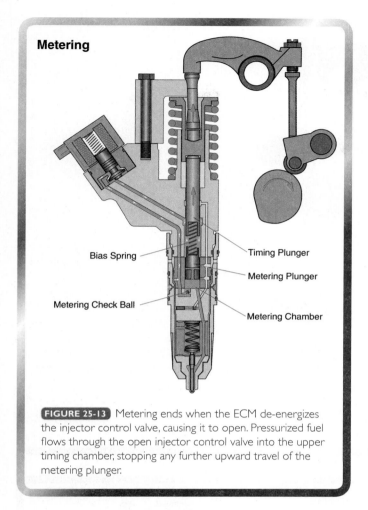

Metering

FIGURE 25-13 Metering ends when the ECM de-energizes the injector control valve, causing it to open. Pressurized fuel flows through the open injector control valve into the upper timing chamber, stopping any further upward travel of the metering plunger.

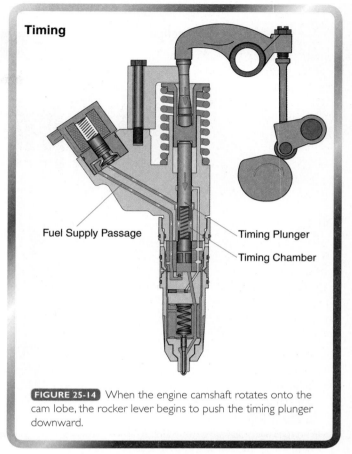

Timing

FIGURE 25-14 When the engine camshaft rotates onto the cam lobe, the rocker lever begins to push the timing plunger downward.

metered quantity of fuel is already trapped in the metering chamber ready for injection.

4. When the engine camshaft rotates onto the cam lobe, the rocker lever begins to push the timing plunger downward. The injectors control valve remains open, and fuel is pushed out from the timing chamber past the control valve and into the fuel rail. Fuel continues to spill out the timing chamber until the control valve is energized again, which prevents any more fuel from escaping from the timing chamber **FIGURE 25-14**. Closing the control valve causes fuel in the timing chamber to act like a solid hydraulic column between the timing plunger and metering piston. As a result, the metering plunger is forced downward along with the timing plunger. Fuel pressure rapidly builds in the metering chamber, and at approximately 5000 psi (345 bar) the nozzle valve opens against spring pressure and injection begins.

5. Injection continues until the spill passage of the downward-moving metering plunger uncovers the timing spill port. Fuel pressure in the timing chamber drops, ending injection. After the timing spill port is uncovered, the upper edge of the metering piston uncovers the metering spill port, enabling fuel below the metering plunger to escape to the fuel return passageway through the cylinder head and back to the tank. This event ends the injection cycle **FIGURE 25-15**.

Summary

Metering ends when the injector control valve opens during upward plunger travel. This means opening the control valve sooner during upward plunger travel results in less fuel metered for injection, whereas opening the control valve later during upward plunger travel results in more fuel metered for injection.

Closing the injector control valve during downward plunger travel determines the starting point for beginning the injection event. This means closing the control valve sooner during the downward plunger stroke results in advanced injection timing, whereas closing the injector control valve later during the downward plunger stroke results in retarded injection timing **FIGURE 25-16**.

The Interact systems found on the M-11 engine take advantage of the faster processor speeds and incorporate double pulse of the injector control valve to open the injector control valve once more during the downward plunger stroke. This event allows fuel to escape the metering chamber for a second time, enabling higher metering accuracy for the injection event.

Cummins Integrated System Engine Controls

In 1997, Cummins introduced its third generation of EUIs called the Interact System (IS) **FIGURE 25-17**. While other electronic control systems preceding the IS used the engine ECM as

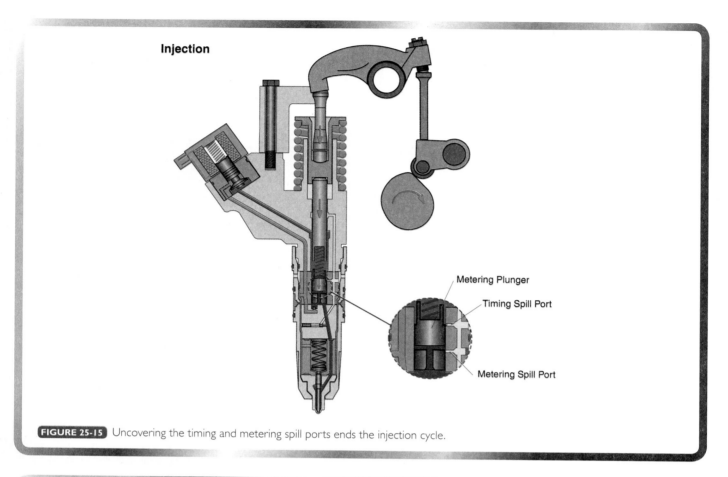

Injection

Metering Plunger
Timing Spill Port
Metering Spill Port

FIGURE 25-15 Uncovering the timing and metering spill ports ends the injection cycle.

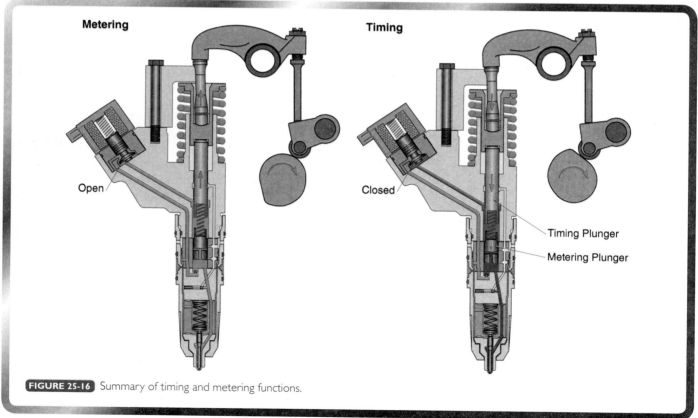

Metering

Open

Timing

Closed

Timing Plunger
Metering Plunger

FIGURE 25-16 Summary of timing and metering functions.

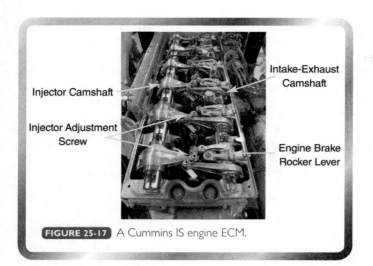

FIGURE 25-17 A Cummins IS engine ECM.

the center of the system, the IS could interact with other vehicle control systems, such as transmissions, braking systems, and traction control systems using the J-1939 on-board network in addition to the J-1957/1708 network. This meant that the ECM could now interact with other modules using very high-speed data transmission not only to read and send messages to other modules, but it could give up some exclusive control of the engine and fuel system when needed, too.

With the IS, the ECM communicates with service tools and some other vehicle controllers through a Society of Automotive Engineers (SAE) J-1939 on-board vehicle network. For example, the transmission control module could message the engine ECM to reduce engine speed to enable faster shifting between gears. The anti-lock braking system (ABS) or traction control system could also command a change to engine rpm or disengage the engine brake if a wheel slip or lock-up condition was sensed. Many changes to the IS, including processor speed, memory capacity, programming capabilities, programmable sensor features, the number of pins and connectors, the

module's own cooling abilities, and integration with other systems, have evolved yearly since its introduction.

Cummins small-, medium-, and large-bore engines received this system in the late 1990s. Instead of designating engines series as B, C, L, and M engines, engines families gained the prefix IS (or ISB, ISC, ISL, ISM, ISX, and so on). The newer common rail X-15 and X-12 engines also use the IS system. A common ECM with the prefix CM (i.e., CM840, CM870, and so on) is used across all Cummins engine families, with the exception of Dodge Ram Cummins engines. The Dodge Ram ECM, built by Motorola, is constructed to specifications using different software and network communication protocols. The N-14 kept the CELECT Plus system, but was not produced after 2000.

HPI-TPI System Description

Until 2009, Cummins 15L (915 cubic inch) ISX and **Signature 600** used a unique fuel system called high-pressure injection time pressure injection (HPI-TPI). The system has much in common with the CELECT and old PT systems. For example, the HPI-TPI injectors are an open-nozzle design using a plunger similar to earlier PT injectors. Unlike closed-nozzle designs using a nozzle valve to seal the spray holes, open nozzles allow combustion gases to mix in the injector cup before the plunger pushes the fuel–air mixture out the spray holes (and as a result, the engine maintains that "old PT system sound"). Like the PT system, metering and injection timing are controlled by varying fuel pressure supplied to the injector.

HPI-TPI systems use a centrally located injector. It is important to note there are no electrical connections or solenoids on the injector. The ISX HPI-TPI engines use two overhead camshafts. One cam is used to actuate the valves and engine brake. Pressurization of the fuel for injection, up to 33,000 psi (2275 bar) in later years, is accomplished by a plunger actuated exclusively by the second, overhead camshaft **FIGURE 25-18** .

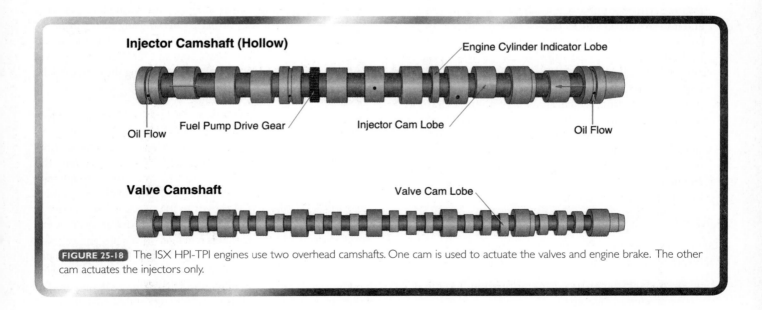

FIGURE 25-18 The ISX HPI-TPI engines use two overhead camshafts. One cam is used to actuate the valves and engine brake. The other cam actuates the injectors only.

Similarities also exist between the HPI-TPI system and CELECT system. For example, like the CELECT system, the HPI-TPI system uses separate timing and metering plungers to control the injection events. However, where the old CELECT system used a single injector control valve, the HPI-TPI system uses a separate timing and metering solenoid to control injection events in not one but three cylinders. Timing and metering solenoids now vary fuel pressure through two hydraulic circuits connected to the injectors. Pressure in the circuits is capable of varying injection timing and injection quantity from shot to shot and cylinder to cylinder.

HPI-TPI Unique Features

Software features that number in the hundreds are used by Cummins engines. The introduction of the Cummins ISX HPI-TPI introduced several unique controls that were firsts, including:

1. Engine Torque Limit Switch: The engine torque limit switch allows the operator to switch to a software-controlled lower torque output limit to protect auxiliary equipment such as power take-off (PTO) devices. Damage to drivelines is further minimized by limiting engine toque output at low speeds. The maximum torque value is programmable and entered through an electronic service tool called INSITE, under the powertrain protection feature.

2. Governor Type Switch: The governor type switch allows the operator to change between a variable speed (VS) and automotive governor. Automotive governors are desirable for on-highway use, because they provide better fuel mileage and more feedback to the driver regarding terrain and load conditions. VS governors are used to operate PTO devices and prevent wild swings in engine speed. They also help prevent and dampen vehicle surge and bucking when the clutch is initially engaged under heavy-loaded conditions. Governor selection can take place between a cab throttle pedal and remote throttle, such as those used by a concrete mixer.

3. Load-Based Speed Control: Cummins offers a patented design feature intended to improve fuel economy, lower vehicle noise, and improve driver satisfaction by controlling engine speed (rpm) based on operating conditions. Offered on all ISX and ISM engines, load-based speed control (LBSC) promotes efficient operation by limiting engine speed when conditions require low or intermediate power. This feature is similar to progressive shifting, which limits maximum engine speed depending on which gear the driver has selected. Progressive shifting is bypassed when climbing grades and higher engine speeds (up to 2000 rpm) are allowed. Without this feature, a truck climbing a long grade would potentially lose maximum engine rpm by downshifting. Ultimately, the vehicle would lose the power needed to climb the grade.

INSITE

INSITE is a service tool for Cummins electronic engine control systems. INSITE can be used to:

- Program customer-specified information into the ECM (parameter and features)

- Troubleshoot and diagnose engine problems
- Program factory-specified parameters such as engine power or rated speed
- Transfer new or update calibration files to the ECM
- Create and view trip reports

INSITE Monitor Mode

The INSITE monitor mode is a useful troubleshooting aid that displays the key ECM inputs and outputs. This feature can be used to spot constant or abnormally fluctuating values.

HPI-TPI Components

The Cummins HPI-TPI is a modular fuel system that uses the same components across all engine power ratings. Modular construction helps speed up diagnosis, repair, or replacement of major components in the field. Actuators, gear pumps, and valves are easily removed and replaced without the need for specialized service facilities or equipment.

Adjusting Valves and Injectors on an ISX Engine

Cummins ISX HPI-TPI injectors were used on Cummins ISX engines between 1998 and 2010. These injectors are adjusted when the injector cam lobe follower has just crossed over the injector lobe's outer base circle. This position corresponds to approximately 45 degrees after TDC. Because the adjustment is performed on the high point of the injector lobe, the injector rocker lever has ended downward movement of the injector plunger into the injector. The valves, injector, and engine brake are adjusted at the same time for an individual cylinder. Injector adjustment is accomplished by bottoming out the injector plungers and then lifting them slightly from the injector cup at the bottom of the injector. When operating, the injector plunger will actually crush into the injector cup at TDC, providing a crisp ending to injection. Improperly adjusting the injector by allowing too much plunger travel will cause the plunger to penetrate the injector cup, breaking the injector tip. Inadequate plunger travel will allow combustion products into the cup, coking of fuel, and rapid plunger wear due to combustion abrasives. This adjustment should ideally be done when the engine is warm.

To adjust valves and injectors on an ISX engine, follow the steps in **SKILL DRILL 25-2**. Always consult OEM service information and follow the prescribed procedures using the correct tools.

Integrated Fuel System Module

The HPI-TPI system consists of six high-pressure unit injectors and an integrated fuel system module (IFSM) containing timing and metering actuators that perform electronic control of metering and timing **FIGURE 25-19**. When energized, the actuators open and allow fuel to flow to the injectors through separate timing and metering fuel rails drilled through the cylinder head **FIGURE 25-20**. PWM signals to the actuators control injection quantity and injection timing. A cam-driven gear pump supplies pressurized fuel that is regulated by a 250-psi regulator valve integrated into the IFSM. A single 10-μ low-pressure micro-glass filter with a fuel–water separator is used along with various sensors to collect engine and driver inputs. Compared to other manufacturers, this is a coarser level of final fuel filtration.

SKILL DRILL 25-2 Adjusting Valves and Injectors on an ISX Engine

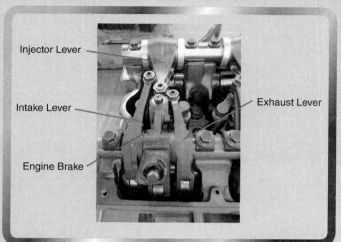

Injector Lever

Intake Lever

Engine Brake

Exhaust Lever

1. Power wash the engine and clean the valve rocker cover and the area around the cover. Ensure that the vehicle wheels are chocked and the park brake is applied. The transmission should be in neutral in order to bar the engine during adjustment.

2. Remove the engines valve cover.

3. Rotate the engine to the correct position to begin the valve and injector adjustment. Removing the oil filler cap from the engine front cover will reveal a 0.75" (19 mm) square recess in the front idler gear, which can be used to bar the engine with a ¾" (19 mm) ratchet. Positioning the engine is done by aligning markings on the accessory drive pulley and the engine front cover. Three letters are stamped into the accessory drive gear: A, B, and C. These markings are 120 degrees apart. Do not confuse any of these letters for a TDC marking, which can be found on some drive pulleys. Some early engines used the markings Brake A 1-6, Brake B 2-5, and Brake C 3-4. Rotate the engine to align the letter A to a line scribed into the front cover or a raised arrow stamping.

4. Identify the rocker levers. Each cylinder has four rocker levers: the injector lever, intake valve lever, exhaust valve lever, and engine brake rocker lever. The intake valve lever is always the longest and the injector rocker levers are only located on the left camshaft, the side of the engine where the IFSM is mounted.

5. Confirm that the engine is positioned correctly to perform the adjustment for the selected cylinder. The cylinder being adjusted should have finished compression stroke and should be 45 degrees past TDC during the power stroke. Both valves should be closed, and the rocker levers should have operating clearance that leaves them loose when they are shaken by hand. The companion cylinder will have finished exhaust stroke and begun intake stroke. Always confirm engine position by comparing the valve–rocker lever positions of pairs of companion cylinders.

6. Check the torque on the injector hold-down bolts. Most torque settings are close to 45 ft-lb (61 Nm).

7. Loosen the lock nut on the injector adjustment screw and bottom the injector plunger out three to four times to remove any fuel beneath the timing or metering plungers. This is done by tightening and loosening the injector adjustment screw.

8. Using an in-lb (Nm) torque wrench, bottom the injector adjustment screw into the injector and tighten the screw to 71 in-lb (8 Nm). The torque wrench must be a dial type and not a click type wrench.

9. Hold the injector lever adjusting screw and tighten the adjusting screw locknut.

10. Using specifications for valve adjustment clearances obtained from OEM service literature or the emission decal on the engine, adjust the clearances between the rocker lever and valve bridges using a thickness or feeler blade.

11. Rotate the engine to the next cylinder in the firing order and perform the valve and injector adjustment for that cylinder. Ensure that the engine is rotated in the correct direction of rotation and double check the position of the rocker levers. When on A position, the two end cylinders are adjusted. B position allows adjustment of the next two cylinders closer the engine center. C position allows adjustment of the two center cylinders. Two complete crankshafts rotations and accessory drive rotations are required to adjust all valves and injectors.

12. Record and report the initial and final valve clearances.

The open nozzle feature, the absence of a poppet-style control valve in the injector, plus other aspects of injector design allow the fuel system to tolerate larger dirt particles with no adverse consequences. As mentioned before, the system is controlled by a sophisticated ECM that uses stored algorithms to regulate metering and timing events based on various factors and operating conditions such as throttle pedal position; dash switches; air, fuel, oil, and coolant temperatures; barometric air pressure; engine speed and cam position; intake boost pressure; exhaust gas recirculation (EGR) and turbocharger data; plus inputs from other networked control modules.

Fuel Flow

The best way to understand the operation of the HPI-TPI system is to examine fuel flow through the IFSM and then look at injector construction and operation.

1. Low-Pressure System Circuit: Fuel flows first through an optional fuel water pre-filter before entering the IFSM. When

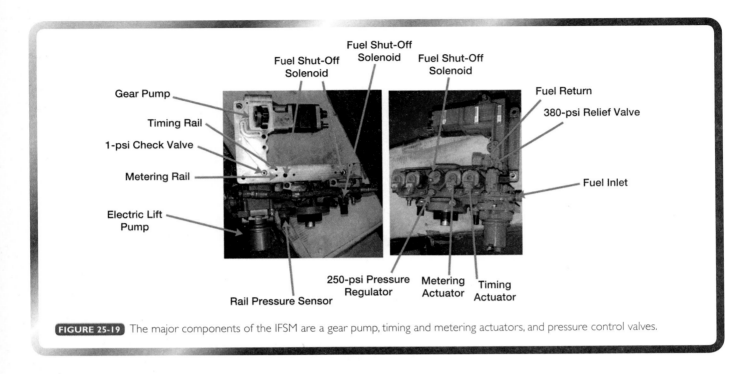

FIGURE 25-19 The major components of the IFSM are a gear pump, timing and metering actuators, and pressure control valves.

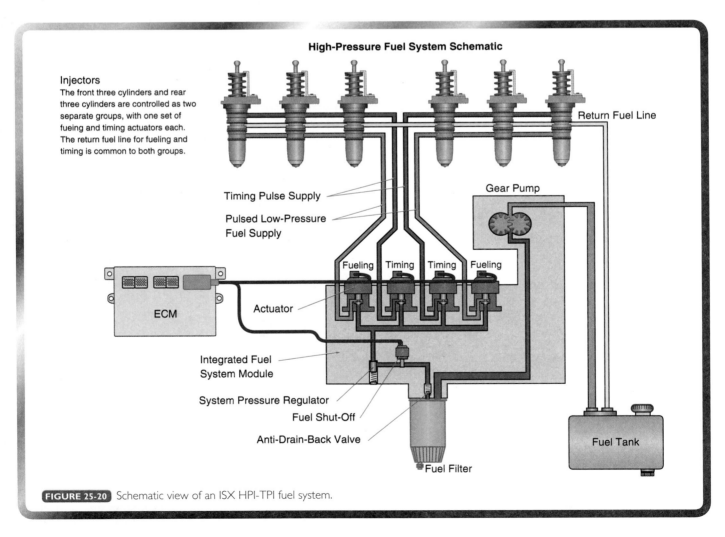

FIGURE 25-20 Schematic view of an ISX HPI-TPI fuel system.

the ignition key is first switch on, fuel continues to flow into an **electric lift pump**. The electric pump runs for the first two minutes after the key is switched on to quickly supply the gear pump for faster starting. At 1 psi (7 kPa) of pressure, a valve in the IFSM housing opens to a small amount of electric lift pump output to purge air from the gear pump inlet in the housing and flow back to the fuel return line and back to the fuel tank. After the engine starts, the gear pump pulls fuel directly from the IFSM fuel inlet fitting past an anti-drain-back valve just above the electric pump.

2. Medium-Pressure Circuit: The cam-driven gear pump supplies the high-volume and constant pressure required by the HPI-TPI system. After leaving the gear pump, fuel flows down through the IFSM and into a **380-psi high-pressure relief valve** between the gear pump and the filter **FIGURE 25-21**. The pressure relief valve is there to prevent severe damage from high fuel pressure in the event of a fuel shut-off valve failure or other blockage in the IFSM circuit. If fuel does flow through the pressure relief valve, it is returned to the tank return line connected to the IFSM. Pressurized fuel flows to the IFSM-mounted secondary fuel filter and from there to the fuel shut-off valve controlled by the IS ECM. A passage in the IFSM then moves fuel through a 250-psi (17-bar) fuel pressure regulator valve **FIGURE 25-22**. Excess fuel supplied by the fuel pump is returned to the gear pump inlet by the regulator. On earlier engines with a fuel cooled ECM fuel would pass through a cooler plate before heading to the gear pump inlet. Newer ECMs depend on air for cooling only.

3. Timing and Metering Actuators: Fuel pressure of 250 psi (17 bar) is supplied constantly to the two pairs of timing and metering actuators: a pair of timing and metering actuators for the front engine bank of three cylinders and a pair for the rear bank **FIGURE 25-23**. A PWM signal is sent by the ECM to the actuators to regulate fuel pressure to the injectors.

FIGURE 25-22 A 250-psi (17-bar) pressure-regulating valve is located below the fuel shut-off valve.

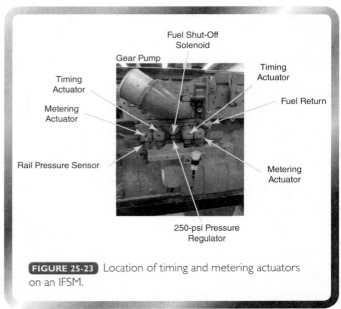

FIGURE 25-23 Location of timing and metering actuators on an IFSM.

FIGURE 25-21 A 380-psi (26-bar) high-pressure relief valve.

Actuators are normally closed solenoids switching on and off when a PWM signal is applied. When energized, the actuators open and allow fuel to flow to the injectors through separate timing and metering fuel rails drilled through the cylinder head.

Regulating fuel pressure to the injectors through timing and metering rail is controlled by the ECM using a PWM signal. Pressure to each bank is commanded separately to modify timing and metering quantities. Given a firing order of 1-5-3-6-2-4, each bank alternates injection events. This means enough time between injections exists to allow changing fuel pressures to each injector from shot to shot and cylinder to cylinder. As the camshaft rotates through the firing order, each injector in one bank or the other is pressurized to correspond to timing and metering actuator cycles. Only one plunger will pressurize fuel in an injector to produce an injector event as the firing order alternates between the front and rear banks.

When the engine is shut down, the fuel can absorb heat, causing the fuel to expand. Fuel trapped between the actuators and the injectors could push fuel through the open injector into the cylinder. This could result in a hydrostatic lock or at least increased cranking resistance and hard starting when the engine is warm. To prevent this, a small vent passage with a 0.008″ (0.2032 mm) opening is drilled between the metering supply rail and the fuel return back to the tank in the IFSM **FIGURE 25-24**. A check valve in each metering actuator drains fuel but maintains residual pressure in the metering passage to prevent fuel from completely draining to the return line.

Checking for Air in Fuel

Air leaks can cause major problems with fuel systems. Air can enter the fuel system through loose line fittings, cracked tank pick-up tubes, or leaking filter gaskets. Air leaks will only occur on the suction side of the fuel system between the fuel pump and tank pick-up. On Cummins engines, gear pumps have a high fuel volume output and return as much as 300 gallons (1136 liters) of fuel per hour back to the tank at rated speed. When the engine is operating, the gear pump pulls fuel through a single filter mounted on the pump or IFSM. This means long sections of lines are under negative pressure, which can potentially produce leaks. The high pump volume will help purge air

from the fuel system, but small bubbles of air entrained in the fuel are compressible and give the fuel an elastic-like quality. When this happens, pressure sensors will change erratically and have high pressure spikes as air is compressed and released. Engine will run rough and surge (that is, engine rpm will move up and down automatically or even shut down due to lack of fuel). When the engine shuts down, it can be cranked for some time, start, run well for a few minutes, and then begin to run rough with unstable engine speed. Two techniques are used to detect whether there are leaks in the system. The first is a vacuum test.

To check for air in fuel, follow the steps in **SKILL DRILL 25-3**.

Injectors

The most recent HPI-TPI injectors can spray in fuel up to 33,000 psi (2275 bar). A separate injector camshaft provides the actuation force on injector plungers to pressurize fuel. Four sealing O-rings on the injector body separate the fuel timing, metering, and fuel return passages **FIGURE 25-25**. No electrical connectors attach to the injector. Instead, electronic control of metering and timing are performed through timing and metering actuators **FIGURE 25-26**.

The most important parts of the injector to observe include:

- Upper plunger
- Timing plunger
- Lower plunger

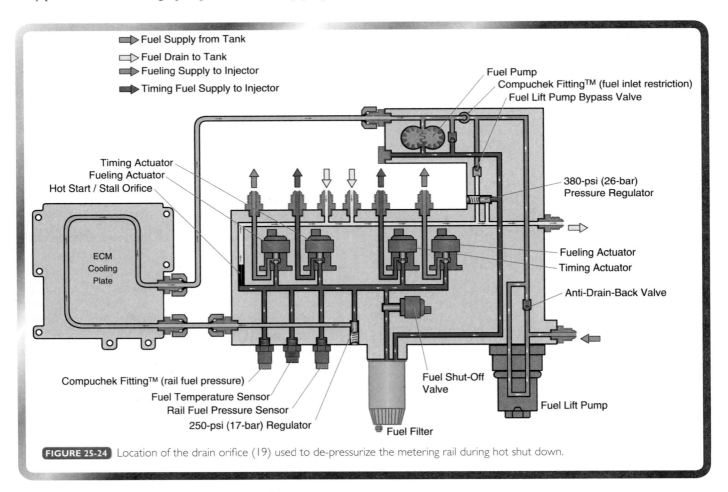

FIGURE 25-24 Location of the drain orifice (19) used to de-pressurize the metering rail during hot shut down.

SKILL DRILL 25-3 Checking for Air in Fuel

1. Connect a vacuum gauge between the engine gear pump and the suction-side fuel pick-up line.

2. Start and run the engine at rated speed. The vacuum gauge should increase to as much as 10" (25 cm) Hg; 1–6" (3–15 mm) Hg is normal.

3. After shutting down the engine, observe the vacuum gauge. The gauge reading should not be changed after 5–10 minutes.

4. If the gauge reading drops to 0 after 5–10 minutes, an inline site glass can be installed to verify the presence of air.

5. Install an inline site glass that enables observation of the suction-side fuel stream entering the lift pump.

6. Start and run the engine to check for vapor in the site glass. Some small bubbles passing through the glass are generally acceptable. Large bubbles that continuously pass through the glass indicate a suction-side line leak.

7. Tighten all line fittings; inspect all lines for cracking or abrasions. Remove and inspect the fuel tank pick-up tube.

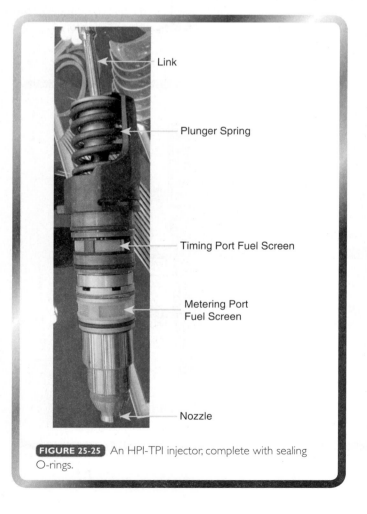

FIGURE 25-25 An HPI-TPI injector, complete with sealing O-rings.

HPI-TPI Injector

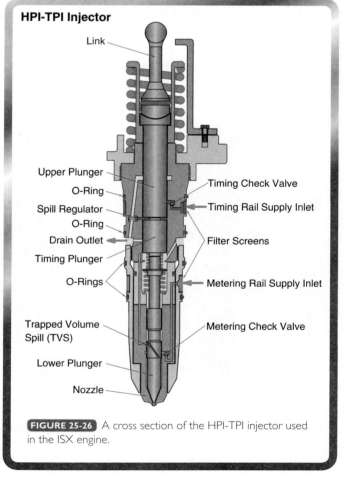

FIGURE 25-26 A cross section of the HPI-TPI injector used in the ISX engine.

- Timing rail supply inlet
- Metering rail supply inlet
- Fuel return circuit or drain outlet

Injector Operation

Injector operation follows the steps below:

1. Metering
   - At the end of the exhaust stroke, all parts of the injector are mechanically loaded by the outer base circle of the injector cam lobe. The lower plunger is pressed tightly against the nozzle seat by the upper and timing plungers.
   - As the cam lobe begins to move to its inner base circle, all three injector plungers begin moving upward together due to pressure from the lower and upper plunger springs. Upward movement continues until the lower plunger contacts a mechanical stop. The lower plunger spring holds it against the stop. The **metering rail supply inlet** is uncovered by the lower plunger, and fuel from the metering rail enters the injector cup below the lower plunger. Note: fuel will not enter the injector until the metering actuator is pulsed and fuel is supplied to the metering rail for those injectors. A check valve ensures only one-way movement of fuel to prevent fuel from flowing back to the metering rail when the lower plunger begins its downward travel. Fuel accumulates in the cavity below the lower plunger. This accumulation is the sum of injection fuel quantity and depends on the

rail pressure adjusted by the metering actuator and time available to fill the injector cup **FIGURE 25-27** .

2. Timing
   - When the upper injector plunger has reached it maximum upward travel, the timing plunger contacts a stop. The timing fuel actuator opens and supplies fuel to the **timing rail supply inlet**. Fuel enters the timing chamber below the timing plunger through a calibrated orifice. Fuel pressure then pushes the timing plunger downward for a precisely timed actuator pulse length.
   - The cam lobe rotates to its outer base circle, pushing down on the upper plunger. Increased pressure closes the timing check valve to prevent fuel from draining back to the fuel rail. All three plungers move together due to the solid column of fuel below the timing plunger. Injection begins when the lower plunger reaches the fuel accumulated in the injector cup. Continued downward movement of all the injector plungers crushes the lower plunger into the injector cup, producing the crispest end to injection of any fuel system.

3. Advancing and retarding injection timing: Injection begins sooner if timing rail pressure is high and lengthens the fuel column below the timing plunger. A longer fuel column means the upper plunger contacts the timing plunger sooner, which advances injection timing. Lower pressure supplied to the timing chamber will shorten the height of the fuel column below the timing plunger and retard the beginning of injection.

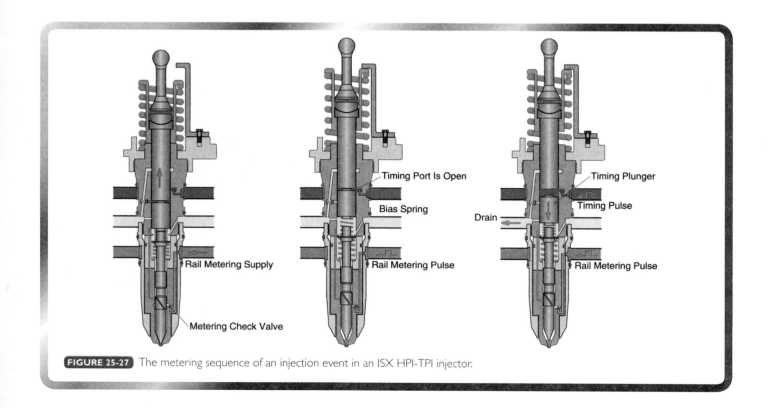

FIGURE 25-27 The metering sequence of an injection event in an ISX HPI-TPI injector.

- The **trapped volume spill (TVS) port** in the injector enables a crisp end to injection. When the timing plunger uncovers the TVS port, fuel pressure is released to the low-pressure **fuel return circuit**. The fuel circuit, also known as the drain outlet, returns fuel to the tank from the injectors and IFSM. A check valve ensures one-way movement of fuel. The lower plunger is held tightly against the nozzle seat by the spill pressure above the timing plunger.

- The injector is mechanically loaded once more at the end of the exhaust stroke by the cam lobe. Timing and metering pulses supply an alternate bank of cylinders FIGURE 25-28 .

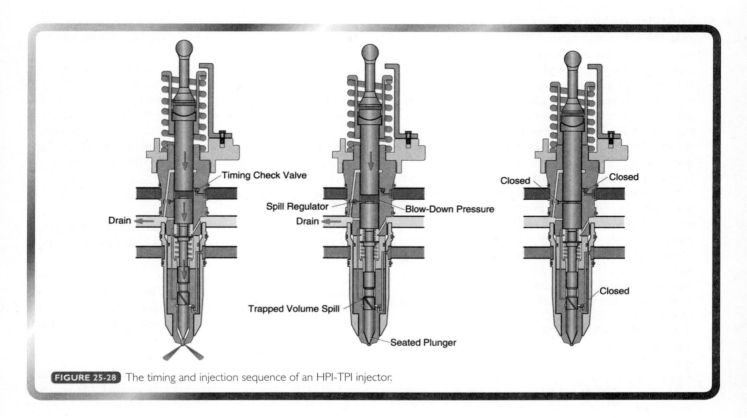

FIGURE 25-28 The timing and injection sequence of an HPI-TPI injector.

Wrap-Up

Ready for Review

- Cummins Engine Company is a leading medium- and large-bore diesel engine company.
- The Cummins pressure time (PT) unit injection system was used until the early 1980s, when the company introduced a partial-authority system called PACE. The CELECT fuel system was a full-authority system introduced in 1990.
- The PT unit injection system's operating principles are used by high-pressure injection time-pressure injection (HPI-TPI) systems.
- By varying the fuel pressure and the time available to inject (which changes due to engine speed), the fuel rate in the Cummins PT fuel system adapts to meet requirements for engine power output.
- The PT pump changes the fuel pressure supplied to the injector through a medium-pressure engine-driven gear pump. It uses mechanical inputs from the driver's throttle pedal, engine speed from the drive gear, and boost pressure from a line connecting the pump to the intake manifold. These three basic inputs are used to calculate the appropriate fuel pressure leaving the pump. An electric shut-off valve is located at the pump outlet to stop and start the engine.
- PT injectors are unique in that they are open-nozzle injectors. Unlike closed-nozzle injectors, which have a spring holding the nozzle valve on its seat, open-nozzle injectors use a plunger held off its seat by a heavy spring.
- Injection takes place when an engine-driven camshaft pushes the injector plunger down into the injector bore, pushing fuel out of the injector tip. Injection ends when the injector plunger crushes into the injector seat.
- Time allowed for supplying fuel to the injectors is regulated by the injector plunger, which opens and closes a metering orifice. Available time for fuel metering is

734 SECTION IV DIESEL FUEL AND FUEL SYSTEMS

determined by engine speed, because the injector plunger is driven by the engine camshaft.

▶ Varying PT pump output pressure changes the amount of fuel supplied to the injectors, which in turn decreases or increases the amount of fuel injected.

▶ Cummins CELECT was the first generation of full-authority electronic engine control. CELECT Plus was introduced several years after CELECT appeared in the early 1990s. The basic concept of CELECT systems is to meter and time the injection event using two separate metering and timing plungers inside a unit injector.

▶ The CELECT injector contains an electrically operated control valve like other unit injectors, but operates very differently. Injection takes place when a PWM signal closes the normally open control valve during the injector plunger's downward stroke. The start of injection and injection quantity are electronically controlled.

▶ Opening the injector control valve during upward plunger travel ends metering. Opening the control valve sooner during upward plunger travel results in less fuel metered for injection. Opening the control valve later during upward plunger travel results in more fuel metered for injection.

▶ Closing the injector control valve during downward plunger travel determines the starting point for the injection event. This means that closing the control valve sooner during the downward plunger stroke results in advanced injection timing. Closing the injector control valve later during the downward plunger stroke results in retarding injection timing.

▶ The third generation of Cummins electronic unit injection systems, the Interact System (IS), can integrate with other vehicle control systems using a J-1939 on-board network and a J-1957/1708. The ECM communicates with service tools and some other vehicle controllers through SAE J-1939 network communication.

▶ The IS system is currently used across all on-highway engine families from Cummins.

▶ Until 2009, Cummins 15L ISX and Signature 600 engines used a unique fuel system called high-pressure injection time-pressure injection (HPI-TPI). This system, which uses a centrally located injector, has much in common with the CELECT and old PT systems.

▶ The HPI-TPI system consists of six high-pressure unit injectors and an integrated fuel system module (IFSM). The best way to understand the operation of the HPI-TPI system is first to examine fuel flow through the IFSM and then look at injector construction and operation.

▶ The most recent HPI-TPI injectors can spray in fuel up to 33,000 psi (2275 bar). No electrical connectors attach to the injector. Instead, metering and timing are controlled through actuators.

▶ The HPI-TPI's engine torque limit switch allows the operator to switch to a lower torque output limit to protect auxiliary equipment.

▶ The governor type switch allows the operator to change between a variable speed (VS) and automotive governor.

▶ Offered on all ISX and ISM engines, load-based speed

control (LBSC) enhances fuel economy in lightly loaded operations while enabling full power output when the transmission is downshifted while climbing steep grades.

▶ INSITE is a service tool for Cummins electronic engine control systems. The INSITE monitor mode is a useful troubleshooting aid that displays the key ECM inputs and outputs.

▶ CELECT systems use an engine-driven gear pump to pull fuel from the vehicle's fuel tanks. The fuel from the tank first passes through a single fuel filter and then into an ECM cooler plate. Fuel then enters a gear pump regulated to deliver fuel at a pressure of approximately 150 psi (10 bar) to a fuel rail. The fuel rail through the cylinder head supplies the injectors with a continuous supply of fuel at a constant pressure. When the ignition is switched on, a 12-volt signal from the ECM opens a normally closed solenoid located on top of the gear pump, enabling fuel to flow to the rail.

Vocabulary Builder

250-psi regulator valve A valve integrated into the integrated fuel system module that regulates fuel rail pressure to 250 psi (17 bar).

380-psi high-pressure relief valve A valve between the gear pump and the filter in the integrated fuel system module that prevents severe damage from high fuel pressure in the event of a fuel shut-off valve failure or other blockage in the fuel circuit.

CELECT The first generation of full-authority electronic engine control introduced by Cummins in 1990.

CELECT Plus A full-authority electronic engine control based on CELECT that uses several additional sensors; a faster, more capable ECM; and additional programmable controls.

electric lift pump A pump that runs for the first two minutes after the key is switched on to quickly supply the gear pump for faster starting.

fuel return circuit The fuel circuit that returns fuel to the tank from the injectors and IFSM; also known as the drain outlet.

high-pressure injection, time-pressure injection (HPI-TPI) A unique fuel system with injectors that have an open-nozzle design using a plunger. This system also uses a centrally located injector. In this system, metering and injection timing are controlled by varying fuel pressure supplied to the injector.

injector control valve A key component inside a CELECT injector; when the control valve is de-energized and opens determines the timing or beginning of the injection event.

INSITE A service tool for Cummins electronic engine control systems.

Interact System (IS) The third generation of Cummins electronics; this system could integrate with other vehicle control systems, such as the transmission, braking system, and traction control system.

ISX A Cummins engine family prefix.

load-based speed control (LBSC) A patented design feature that promotes efficient operation by limiting engine speed during low and intermediate power requirements to encourage more transmission upshifting.

metering plunger The lower plunger in either the CELECT injector or HPI-TPI injector; also known as the lower plunger.

metering rail supply inlet The opening in the HPI-TPI injector that admits fuel to the cavity below the lower metering plunger.

partial-authority Cummins engine (PACE) A partial-authority system that combines the mechanical PT pump with an electronic fuel control valve on the outlet of the fuel pump, which varies pressure supplied to unit injectors.

pressure time (PT) injection system A Cummins unit injection system used until the early 1980s.

Signature 600 A premium ISX engine that produces the highest engine power output and has several key components built with extra durability.

timing and metering actuators Components that perform electronic control of metering and timing; when energized, the actuators open and allow fuel to flow to the injectors through separate timing and metering fuel rails drilled through the cylinder head.

timing plunger The upper plunger in either the CELECT injector or HPI-TPI injector; also known as the upper plunger.

timing rail supply inlet The opening in the HPI-TPI injector that admits fuel to the cavity below the upper timing plunger.

trapped volume spill (TVS) port A component in the injector that enables a crisp end to injection; when the timing plunger uncovers the TVS port, fuel pressure is released to the low-pressure fuel return.

Review Questions

1. _____ is a unique fuel system where metering and injection timing are controlled by varying fuel pressure supplied to the injector.
   a. High-pressure injection, time-pressure injection
   b. CELECT
   c. INSITE
   d. Partial-authority

2. The _____ is the upper plunger in either the CELECT injector or the HPI-TPI injector.
   a. metering plunger
   b. timing plunger
   c. coupling plunger
   d. assembly plunger

3. _____ is a service tool for Cummins electronic engine control systems.
   a. HPI-TPI
   b. CELECT
   c. INSITE
   d. CELECT Plus

4. _____ is the first generation of full-authority electronic engine introduced by Cummins in 1990.
   a. CELECT Plus
   b. INSITE
   c. HPI -TPI
   d. CELECT

5. The _____ is the lower plunger in either the CELECT injector or the HPI-TPI injector.
   a. coupling plunger
   b. metering plunger
   c. timing plunger
   d. assembly plunger

6. CELECT systems meter and time the injection event using a(n) _____ injector.
   a. fuel
   b. unit
   c. PT
   d. HPI-TPI

7. In the _____ system the metering rail supply inlet is uncovered by the lower plunger, and allows fuel to enter the injector cup.
   a. HPI-TPI   c. INSITE
   b. CELECT   d. PT

8. The injector plunger in the _____ injector actually crushes into the injector cup providing a crisp end to injection.
   a. HP1-TPI   c. INSITE
   b. CELECT   d. PT

9. _____ is a Cummins engine family prefix.
   a. SX   c. SI
   b. IS   d. ISX

10. A premium _____ engine produces the highest engine power output and has several key components built with extra durability.
    a. ISX   c. IS
    b. SX   d. X

ASE-Type Questions

1. Technician A says the first unit injection system used by the Cummins Engine Company was the pressure time injection system. Technician B says the first unit injection system used by the Cummins Engine Company was the Interact System. Who is correct?
   a. Technician A
   b. Technician B
   c. Both Technician A and Technician B
   d. Neither Technician A nor Technician B

2. Technician A says the Cummins PT injection system pump receives pressure inputs from the pump drive gear. Technician B says the Cummins PT injection system pump receives electrical inputs from the throttle pedal. Who is correct?
   a. Technician A
   b. Technician B
   c. Both Technician A and Technician B
   d. Neither Technician A nor Technician B

3. Technician A says the pump output pressure of the CELECT system is regulated to deliver fuel at a pressure of approximately 100 psi (7 bar) to a fuel rail drilled through the cylinder head. Technician B says the pump output pressure of the CELECT system is regulated to deliver fuel at a pressure of approximately 200 psi (14 bar) to a fuel rail drilled through the cylinder head. Who is correct?
   a. Technician A
   b. Technician B
   c. Both Technician A and Technician B
   d. Neither Technician A nor Technician B

4. Technician A says the Cummins CELECT system injectors were used on Cummins electronically controlled engines between 1990 and 2001. Technician B says the Cummins CELECT injection takes place when a PWM signal closes the normally open control valve during the injector plunger's downward stroke. Who is correct?
   a. Technician A
   b. Technician B
   c. Both Technician A and Technician B
   d. Neither Technician A nor Technician B

5. Technician A says when the accessory drive pulley and the engine front cover are aligned with the letter "B," the engine is positioned correctly to perform a valve and injector adjustment on cylinder number 2. Technician B says when the accessory drive pulley and the engine front cover are aligned with the letter "B," the engine is positioned correctly to perform a valve and injector adjustment on cylinder number 5. Who is correct?
   a. Technician A
   b. Technician B
   c. Both Technician A and Technician B
   d. Neither Technician A nor Technician B

6. Technician A says that the most recent HPI-TPI injectors can spray in fuel up to 15,000 psi (1034 bar). Technician B says that the most recent HPI-TPI injectors can spray in fuel up to 33,000 psi (2275 bar). Who is correct?
   a. Technician A
   b. Technician B
   c. Both Technician A and Technician B
   d. Neither Technician A nor Technician B

7. Technician A says the upper injector plunger in the HPI-TPI injector enables a crisp end to injection. Technician B says the trapped volume spill port in the HPI-TPI injector enables a crisp end to injection. Who is correct?
   a. Technician A
   b. Technician B
   c. Both Technician A and Technician B
   d. Neither Technician A nor Technician B

8. Technician A says a partial-authority system combines elements of a traditional mechanical system but uses an electronic governor. Technician B says a partial-authority system combines elements of a traditional mechanical system but uses a mechanical governor. Who is correct?
   a. Technician A
   b. Technician B
   c. Both Technician A and Technician B
   d. Neither Technician A nor Technician B

9. Technician A says the timing fuel actuator of the HPI-TPI system opens and supplies fuel to the timing rail supply inlet. Technician B says the timing fuel actuator of the HPI-TPI system opens and supplies fuel to the metering rail supply inlet. Who is correct?
   a. Technician A
   b. Technician B
   c. Both Technician A and Technician B
   d. Neither Technician A nor Technician B

10. Technician A says CELECT systems meter and time the injection event using a PT injector. Technician B says CELECT systems meter and time the injection event using a unit injector. Who is correct?
    a. Technician A
    b. Technician B
    c. Both Technician A and Technician B
    d. Neither Technician A nor Technician B

CHAPTER 26
HEUI Injection Systems

NATEF Tasks

Diesel Engines

General

- Identify engine fuel, oil, coolant, air, and other leaks; determine needed action. (pp 744, 763–766)
- Observe engine exhaust smoke color and quantity; determine needed action. (pp 763–766)
- Check engine no cranking, cranks but fails to start, hard starting, and starts but does not continue to run problems; determine needed action. (pp 744, 756, 763–766)
- Identify engine surging, rough operation, misfiring, low power, slow deceleration, slow acceleration, and shutdown problems; determine needed action. (pp 744, 747, 755, 763–766)

Fuel System

Electronic Fuel Management System

- Interface with vehicle's on-board computer; perform diagnostic procedures using electronic service tool(s) (to include PC-based software and/or data scan tools); determine needed action. (p 766)
- Perform on-engine inspections and tests on hydraulic electronic unit injectors (HEUI) and system electronic controls; determine needed action. (pp 763–766)
- Perform on-engine inspections and tests on hydraulic electronic unit injector (HEUI) high-pressure oil supply and control systems; determine needed action. (pp 763–766)

Knowledge Objectives

After reading this chapter, you will be able to:

1. Describe the functions and construction of hydraulically actuated electronic unit injector (HEUI) fuel systems and subsystem components. (pp 738–745)
2. Identify and describe various types of HEUI fuel systems. (pp 744–757)
3. Explain the operation of HEUI fuel systems. (pp 756–764)
4. Identify and describe inspection, testing, and diagnostic procedures for HEUI fuel systems. (pp 764–768)
5. Recommend maintenance, reconditioning, or repairs of HEUI fuel systems. (pp 764–768)

Skills Objectives

After reading this chapter, you will be able to:

1. Replace a HEUI injector. (766) SKILL DRILL 26-1
2. Perform an ICPR test. (768) SKILL DRILL 26-2

▶ Introduction

One of the first and largest evolutionary steps of modern high-pressure diesel injection technology was the development of the hydraulically actuated electronic unit injection (HEUI) system. In the 1980s, manufacturers began exploring technical solutions for upcoming emission standards, and they realized that mechanically governed fuel systems had several handicaps. The primary disadvantage of traditional mechanical systems is their reliance on either an engine-mounted camshaft or a camshaft, cam plate, or cam ring inside an injection pump to pressurize fuel. Camshafts used to move plungers inside unit injectors or injection pumps worked well for years, but camshafts driven at engine speed impose limits to injection pressure at low rpm. Because much higher injection pressures are required to reduce emissions, radical alternatives to the camshaft-driven injection systems needed development.

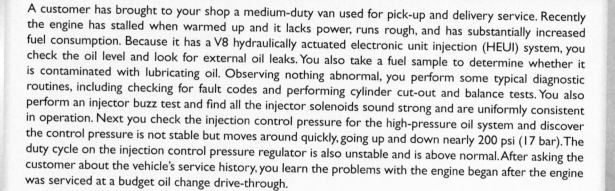

You Are the Technician

A customer has brought to your shop a medium-duty van used for pick-up and delivery service. Recently the engine has stalled when warmed up and it lacks power, runs rough, and has substantially increased fuel consumption. Because it has a V8 hydraulically actuated electronic unit injection (HEUI) system, you check the oil level and look for external oil leaks. You also take a fuel sample to determine whether it is contaminated with lubricating oil. Observing nothing abnormal, you perform some typical diagnostic routines, including checking for fault codes and performing cylinder cut-out and balance tests. You also perform an injector buzz test and find all the injector solenoids sound strong and are uniformly consistent in operation. Next you check the injection control pressure for the high-pressure oil system and discover the control pressure is not stable but moves around quickly, going up and down nearly 200 psi (17 bar). The duty cycle on the injection control pressure regulator is also unstable and is above normal. After asking the customer about the vehicle's service history, you learn the problems with the engine began after the engine was serviced at a budget oil change drive-through.

1. List two likely causes for an unstable duty cycle on the injection control pressure regulator and explain how they would produce the driver's complaints.
2. What problems could potentially cause the engine to be difficult to start after the engine is warmed up?
3. What should be the first service recommendation you make before performing any further engine diagnostic work?

A second problem of conventional mechanically governed fuel systems is their limited capability to adapt injection events to continuously changing engine and vehicle operating conditions. Engine operating conditions such as load; coolant, fuel, and intake air temperatures; intake boost and atmospheric pressures; vehicle speed; exhaust gas recirculation (EGR) flow; and many other factors require unique injection timing and <u>injection rate control</u>, which is the control of fuel delivery into the cylinder during an injection event. Better control of injection rate and timing has helped diesels obtain 99% reduction in noxious emissions today compared to engines built in the early 1990s.

Engines today cannot operate in isolation from other vehicle systems, either. Inputs from systems such as collision avoidance, exhaust emission aftertreatment, traction control, anti-lock braking, stability control, climate control, vehicle security, power take-off, and many others are designed to work interactively with the engine to enhance safety, passenger convenience, and comfort. Mechanically governed injection systems simply cannot achieve the flexibility injection events require nor interact with other control systems using an on-board network connecting control modules together.

▶ Fundamentals of HEUI Systems

HEUI injection systems have replaced the mechanical force produced by an injection pump or engine camshaft to pressurize fuel for injection. Instead, pressurized engine oil is used to produce the high injection pressures and fuel rate control needed to achieve improved performance from engines with almost undetectable emissions and superior fuel economy. This next section examines the operating principles and basic construction of HEUI fuel systems that form this contemporary high-pressure injection system.

Advantages of HEUI Systems

HEUI systems were developed and adopted because of the distinct advantages of using a hydraulic system instead of an injection system's mechanical camshaft. This first section looks at some of the reasons for the development and use of HEUI systems in on-highway diesel engines from 1993 to 2010.

Electronic Control of Injection Pressure

The biggest shortcoming of mechanically governed fuel systems is their inability to adequately pressurize fuel at low engine speeds. High injection pressures are needed over all engine speeds to achieve the best atomization and distribution of fuel in the combustion chamber. Because fuel plunger velocities in camshaft-pressurized injection systems are directly proportional to engine speed, injection pressures are tied to engine speed. Plungers move relatively slowly at low engine rpm, so maximum injection pressures are also low at low engine rpm. Slow plunger movement simply does not provide high enough injection pressure to reduce emissions. What is needed is an injection system capable of pressurizing fuel independent of engine speed **FIGURE 26-1**. The HEUI system was developed to do just that—to develop peak injection pressure without relying on engine speed to build fuel pressure **FIGURE 26-2**. This means that HEUIs have maximum spray-in pressure available whether the engine

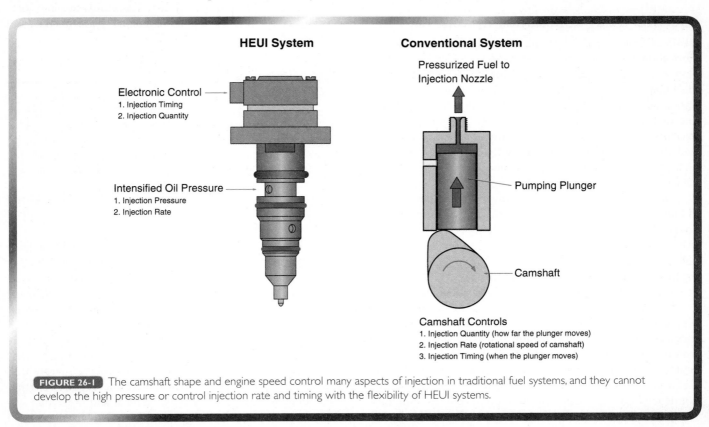

HEUI System

Electronic Control
1. Injection Timing
2. Injection Quantity

Intensified Oil Pressure
1. Injection Pressure
2. Injection Rate

Conventional System

Pressurized Fuel to Injection Nozzle

Pumping Plunger

Camshaft

Camshaft Controls
1. Injection Quantity (how far the plunger moves)
2. Injection Rate (rotational speed of camshaft)
3. Injection Timing (when the plunger moves)

FIGURE 26-1 The camshaft shape and engine speed control many aspects of injection in traditional fuel systems, and they cannot develop the high pressure or control injection rate and timing with the flexibility of HEUI systems.

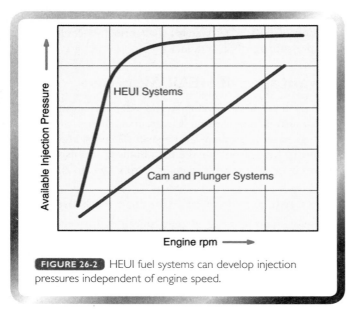

FIGURE 26-2 HEUI fuel systems can develop injection pressures independent of engine speed.

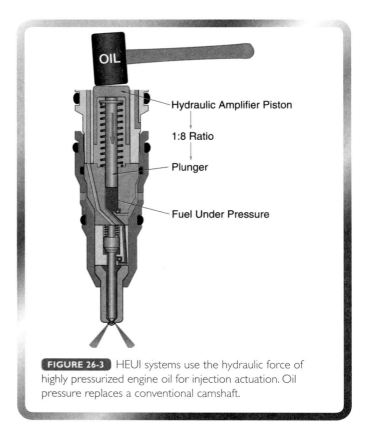

FIGURE 26-3 HEUI systems use the hydraulic force of highly pressurized engine oil for injection actuation. Oil pressure replaces a conventional camshaft.

is operating at idle or maximum rpm. During hard acceleration or sudden load changes at low speeds, the system can instantly adjust fuel pressurization to produce the combustion conditions needed to generate power while minimizing emissions. Electronic control of injection events such as timing, metering, and pressurization allows these functions to be completely adjustable. Instead of using cam lobes, springs, flyweights, and levers, HEUI engines use electronic engine sensors, software code, microprocessors, and electrical signals to control injection events with more precision than any previous system.

Injection Using Lubrication System Oil

HEUI systems use the hydraulic force of highly pressurized lubrication oil rather than a mechanical camshaft to actuate plungers and pressurize fuel for injection **FIGURE 26-3**. Because the functions of pressurization, metering, timing, and atomization are all incorporated into a single injector body, HEUI injectors are classified as unit injectors. These uniquely designed injectors are supplied with low-pressure fuel and highly pressurized engine oil. Using lubricating system oil, an engine-driven high-pressure oil pump increases lube oil pressure to up to 4000 psi (276 bar) in the latest HEUI system.

Oil supplied to the injectors provides the actuation force to inject fuel. However, even oil pressurized to a few thousand pounds (bar) of pressure cannot directly apply the force needed to inject fuel. To reach that level, oil pressure is further multiplied inside the injector using an amplifier piston to give HEUIs the capability to achieve maximum injection pressures of 23,000–28,500 psi (1586–1965 bar), depending on the engine model.

Injection pressures are varied by regulating the oil pressure supplied to the injectors. Electronically varying oil pressures enables control of injection pressure to match engine operational requirements. Highest pressure is available when needed at low engine rpm or any engine speed and load condition. Because HEUI system oil pressure is electronically regulated and does not depend on high engine speed to produce maximum injection pressure, HEUI systems are classified as a subtype of the common rail fuel system. High pressure injection capabilities combined with electronic control of timing and injection rate ensures the fine atomization of fuel, low emissions, low combustion noise, highly responsive engine performance, and improved fuel economy **FIGURE 26-4**.

▶ TECHNICIAN TIP

Modern diesels need the ability to regulate injection pressures according to engine operating conditions. By changing injection pressure, the rate at which fuel is injected into the combustion chamber is altered. Injection rate control is needed primarily to lower engine emissions, but it also significantly influences combustion pressure and fuel consumption. Rate control is therefore a critical function of all contemporary fuel injection systems.

Modular Construction

HEUI system components are interchangeable with a large variety of engine sizes, cylinders, and applications. Whether the engine is used in power generation, off-road equipment, an ambulance, a pick-up, a delivery vehicle, or a dump truck, many of the same components are used. This modular construction feature of HEUI system components permits HEUI adaption to a specific engine application by simply changing software programming. The flexibility of HEUI systems for use in a variety of chassis and engine configurations contrasts sharply with mechanically governed injection systems that required specialized configuration of injectors, governors, and other fuel system components for each engine model and application. HEUI

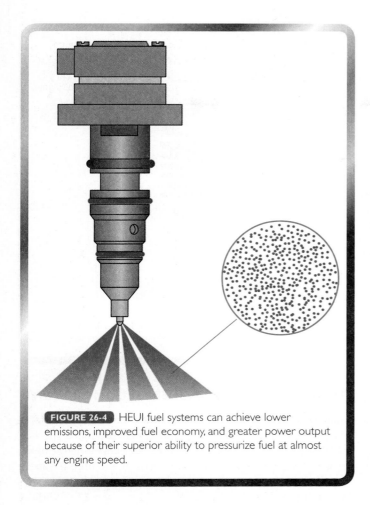

FIGURE 26-4 HEUI fuel systems can achieve lower emissions, improved fuel economy, and greater power output because of their superior ability to pressurize fuel at almost any engine speed.

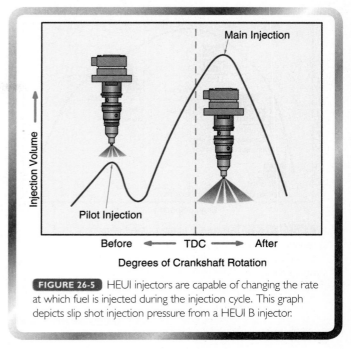

FIGURE 26-5 HEUI injectors are capable of changing the rate at which fuel is injected during the injection cycle. This graph depicts slip shot injection pressure from a HEUI B injector.

injectors and other system components are easily replaced by technicians when service is required and require no adjustment.

Quieter Engine Operation

Consecutive developments in HEUI technology have allowed for improved ability to shape the rate of fuel injection, which further reduces combustion noise and emissions for quieter, cleaner engine operation. Beginning with some 1996 models, first-generation HEUI injectors use pilot or split shot injection. **Split shot injection**, also called pre-injection metering (PRIME) in Caterpillar engines, is an injection strategy that delivers fuel in two distinct events during one combustion cycle **FIGURE 26-5**. The first event, called **pilot injection**, delivers a small quantity of fuel typically 8 to 10 degrees before the main injection. Fuel from the first, smaller injection begins to burn just as the second much larger main injection occurs. The time required to ignite the main

injection is significantly shortened, which reduces the characteristic combustion noise from diesel engines caused by ignition delay. Shortening ignition delay also means injection timing can be retarded. When the main injection event begins to burn sooner and more quickly using pilot injection, the main injection event can take place later, or in other words, be retarded. The advantage of delaying the beginning of the main injection is a reduction of oxides of nitrogen (NO_x) emissions. Less fuel is in the cylinder at TDC, which causes a sharp spike in cylinder pressure, creates NO_x-forming combustion conditions. The main injection event can also have an injection rate that is shaped like a slope (more commonly called ramped injection rate). With a ramped injection rate there is a more gradual buildup of fuel injected into the cylinder, which results in a gentler rise in cylinder pressure **FIGURE 26-6**.

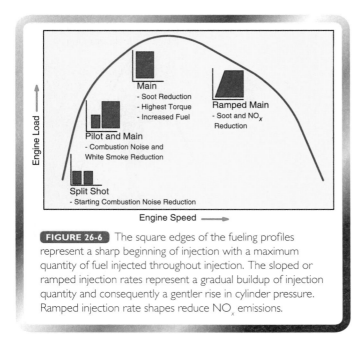

FIGURE 26-6 The square edges of the fueling profiles represent a sharp beginning of injection with a maximum quantity of fuel injected throughout injection. The sloped or ramped injection rates represent a gradual buildup of injection quantity and consequently a gentler rise in cylinder pressure. Ramped injection rate shapes reduce NO_x emissions.

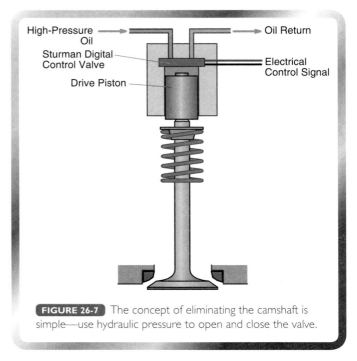

FIGURE 26-7 The concept of eliminating the camshaft is simple—use hydraulic pressure to open and close the valve.

Electro-Hydraulic Valve Operation (Cam-Less Diesel Engines)

HEUI technology also provides the potential to integrate valve-train operation into the high-pressure oil actuation system. Instead of using a camshaft to operate valves, electro-hydraulic actuation of intake and exhaust valves is possible using the HEUI high-pressure oil pump **FIGURE 26-7**. The concept of the cam-less diesel, prototyped in 1998 by Navistar, is appealing for the number of interesting advantages it offers. These advantages are explained in the Navistar chapter.

Applications of HEUI Injection Systems

Collaboration between Navistar, which builds International brand trucks and engines, and Caterpillar produced the first HEUI system in 1993. The Ford 7.3L (444 cubic inch) Power-Stroke, which was built for Ford by Navistar and branded as the T-444E for International, is one of the earliest and most popular applications of HEUI technology. More than 2.5 million of these engines were manufactured from the early 1990s until its discontinuation in 2003. In fact, for several years, two out of every three Ford F-250 and larger trucks were equipped with this engine **FIGURE 26-8**.

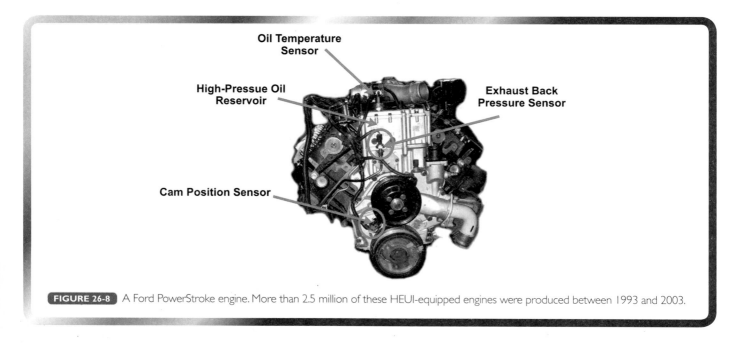

FIGURE 26-8 A Ford PowerStroke engine. More than 2.5 million of these HEUI-equipped engines were produced between 1993 and 2003.

Caterpillar produced HEUI systems for on-highway engines until 2007 when the HEUI system was superseded by high-pressure common rail systems. Numerous medium- and heavy-duty CAT diesel engines used in both on- and off-highway applications employed several styles of HEUI injectors. CAT's off-road heavy 3408E and 3412E engines also used HEUI systems **FIGURE 26-9**. CAT's largest applications for HEUI are the 3116 and 3126 engines found in GMC Topkicks, Ford, Sterling, and Freightliner truck chassis. The 3126 engine was replaced in 2001 with the C7. The HEUI system used by the C7 and C9 ACERT had a CAT-developed injector designated the **HIB-300** that was used until 2007.

Navistar also used HEUI for its DT series of engines, the DT-466 and 530, and the HT 570. Navistar used HEUI in the V6 VT-275 and MaxxForce 5, 7, 9, and 10 until late 2010, when it was replaced by Bosch common rail systems. Second generation HEUI, termed **Gen II HEUI** or G2, is a more recent refinement of HEUI technology and the product of a partnership between Siemens AG, Navistar, and Sturman Industries. The Gen II injector uses digital valve technology **TABLE 26-1**.

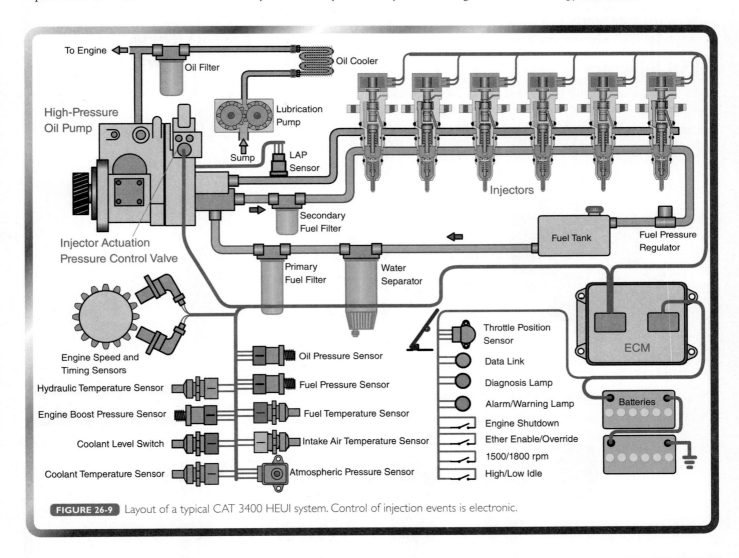

FIGURE 26-9 Layout of a typical CAT 3400 HEUI system. Control of injection events is electronic.

TABLE 26-1: Popular HEUI Truck Applications

HEUI Injector	Navistar Application	Ford Application	Caterpillar Application
HEUI A	T-444E (7.3L [444 cubic inch])	7.3L (444 cubic inch) PowerStroke	3116
HEUI B	T-444E (7.3L [444 cubic inch]) DT 466, 530, 570 (Inline 6s from 446 to HT-570 CID)	7.3L (444 cubic inch) PowerStroke	3126
Gen II	VT-365 VT-275 DT 466, 530, HT-570	6.0L (366 cubic inch) PowerStroke	N/A
Caterpillar Gen II HI-300	N/A	N/A	C7 ACERT C9 ACERT

► Components of HEUI Injection Systems

The HEUI system has four major subsystems:

- HEUI injectors
- Low-pressure oil system
- High-pressure injection actuation system
- Electronic control system

A low-pressure supply system provides fuel to the injectors at the correct pressure and free of water, vapor, and other contaminants **FIGURE 26-10**. Fuel supply pressure is regulated to 30–80 psi (207–552 kPa) on most systems.

HEUI Injectors

HEUI injectors use highly pressurized engine oil to provide injection force. Four basic variations of these injectors exist

FIGURE 26-11. Beginning in 1996, International/Ford and Caterpillar used the split shot or PRIME injector. The first variation, called the **HEUI A** injector, is the earliest HEUI injector without split shot or pilot injection capabilities **FIGURE 26-12**. The second variation, called the **HEUI B** injector, is distinguished by the white solenoid **FIGURE 26-13**. Caterpillar also manufactured their own distinct injector design on the 3116 and 3126A engines that used a side-mounted solenoid and high-pressure jumper tubes

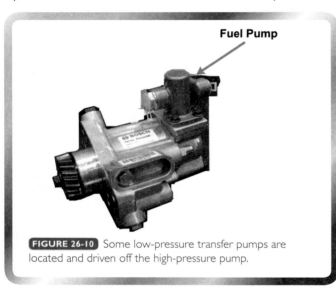

FIGURE 26-10 Some low-pressure transfer pumps are located and driven off the high-pressure pump.

FIGURE 26-12 This HEUI A injector is identified by its black solenoid and does not have split shot capabilities.

Generation II   HEUI - A 250   HEUI - B 250   CATHIB-300

FIGURE 26-11 Common HEUI injectors.

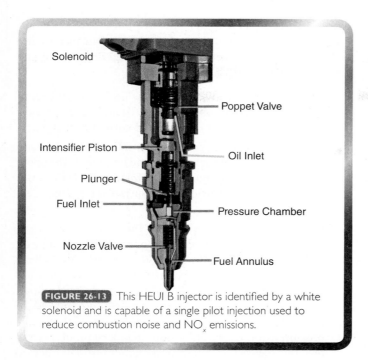

FIGURE 26-13 This HEUI B injector is identified by a white solenoid and is capable of a single pilot injection used to reduce combustion noise and NO_x emissions.

Solenoid

Poppet Valve

Intensifier Piston

Oil Inlet

Plunger

Fuel Inlet

Pressure Chamber

Nozzle Valve

Fuel Annulus

to supply oil. Caterpillar's injector has a larger plunger bore and greater fuel delivery volume capabilities than Ford and Navistar's injectors.

The third variation of HEUI is the Gen II or digital valve injector **FIGURE 26-14**. This injector is used in 6.0L (365 cubic inch) VT-365 engines. The more compact design allows the use of four valves per cylinder engine design. Using two solenoids—one to open and one to close high-pressure oil supply—gives the injectors a faster response time and rate-shaping capabilities covering a full range of engine speed and load conditions. Three electronically controlled injection events are possible in

the Gen II injector, which incidentally uses less energy than previous models.

Caterpillar developed and used a fourth variation of HEUI injector, the HIB-300 for the ACERT C-7 and C-9 engines **FIGURE 26-15**. This injector has a number of unique features:

- Electronic control of a pilot, main, and post-combustion injection events.
- Compact shape that permits a centralized location above the piston for symmetrical distribution of fuel.
- Five different combinations of injection rate shapes, including a square and ramped main injection.
- A low-mass poppet valve capable of performing electrically signaled multiple injection events.

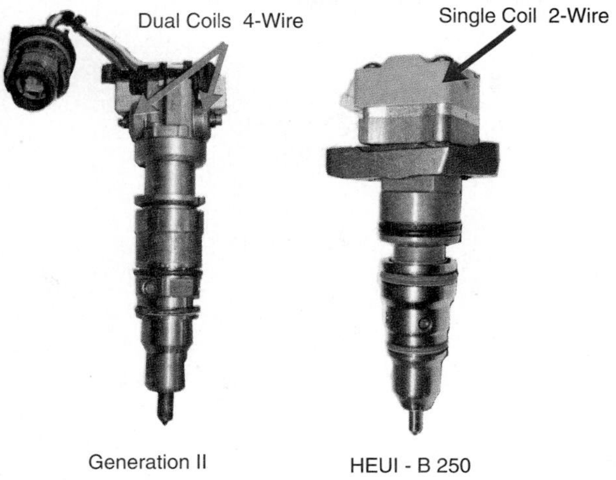

HEUI A and B

HEUI A and B injectors have two grooves on the outside of the body for receiving fuel and high-pressure oil from rails drilled in the cylinder head **FIGURE 26-16**. Sealing the grooves to maintain pressure around the injector are replaceable sets of O-rings. The top set of O-rings seals oil pressure and consists of two individual rings: a steel back-up ring and a square cushion seal. A single middle, round O-ring separates fuel and oil pressure. A bottom round O-ring seals fuel below the groove where fuel is delivered to the injector. Finally, a copper sealing washer around the injector tip seals combustion gases in the cylinder. Two hold-down bolts are used to position and clamp the injector. Only one bolt requires removal to extract the injector for service.

Dual Coils 4-Wire

Single Coil 2-Wire

Generation II

HEUI - B 250

FIGURE 26-14 This 6.0L (365 cubic inch) injector is a Gen II HEUI. The two electromagnetic coils and other design features give it improved injection rate-shaping capabilities.

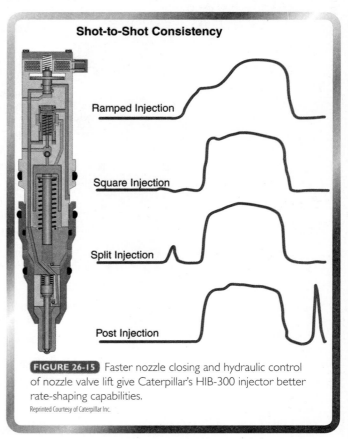

Shot-to-Shot Consistency

Ramped Injection

Square Injection

Split Injection

Post Injection

FIGURE 26-15 Faster nozzle closing and hydraulic control of nozzle valve lift give Caterpillar's HIB-300 injector better rate-shaping capabilities.

Reprinted Courtesy of Caterpillar Inc.

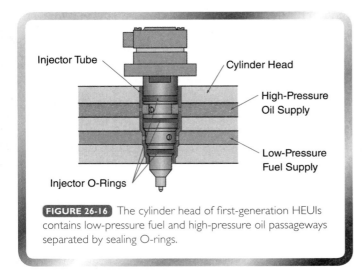

FIGURE 26-16 The cylinder head of first-generation HEUIs contains low-pressure fuel and high-pressure oil passageways separated by sealing O-rings.

▶ TECHNICIAN TIP

High-pressure oil is separated from the fuel circulating in the cylinder head by an O-ring. O-ring leakage can allow high-pressure oil to leak either up and onto the cylinder head deck or into the fuel rail. Oil in fuel and high oil consumption indicate O-ring leakage between fuel and oil passageways. Leakage of pressurized oil upward, past the O-rings, typically results in hard starting when hot, low engine power, and rough running.

Components

Both HEUI A and B split shot injectors have four major components that operate together for precise metering, timing, and rate control **FIGURE 26-17**.

1. High-voltage electric solenoid: This device controls poppet valve operation. The solenoid requires approximately 110–115 volts DC and 7–15 amps of current to energize.

2. Poppet valve: The **poppet valve** controls oil flow into and out of the injector. It has an upper and lower seat. The upper seat controls oil drainage from the injector while the lower seat controls the admission of pressurized oil into the injector **FIGURE 26-18**.

3. Intensifier piston and plunger: The **intensifier piston**, also known as the amplifier piston, multiplies the lube oil pressure, which is regulated to 480–3400 psi (33–234 bar). Depending on the manufacturer and engine model, the top surface area of the intensifier piston is seven to ten times larger than the bottom plunger diameter. Because high-pressure oil is applied to the top of the piston, hydraulic pressure is multiplied at the bottom by a factor of seven to ten. This means fuel below the amplifier piston is injected at a factor seven to ten times higher than oil pressure. For example, 2000 psi (138 bar) of oil pressure supplied to the injector could produce 20,000 psi (1379 bar) of injection pressure with an amplifier piston that uses a ratio of 10:1.

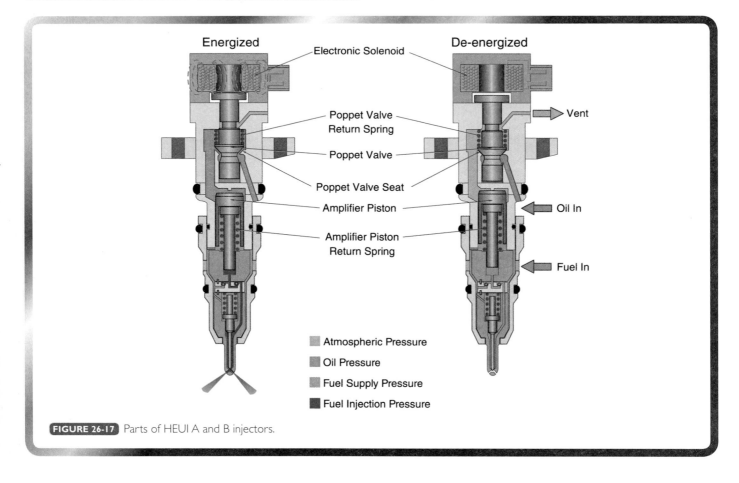

FIGURE 26-17 Parts of HEUI A and B injectors.

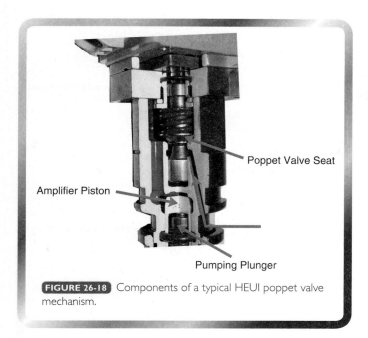

FIGURE 26-18 Components of a typical HEUI poppet valve mechanism.

Labels: Poppet Valve Seat, Amplifier Piston, Pumping Plunger

4. Nozzle assembly: The nozzle is a multi-orifice design operating to atomize and distribute fuel into the combustion chamber. Nozzle opening pressure is approximately 2700 psi (186 bar) in early injectors and more than 5500 psi (379

bar) in later injectors. The large size of the earlier injectors prevented a central location above the piston. This meant the injector could only be positioned at an offset angle and used in only two-valve or three-valve engines, such as the three-valve CAT 3126B.

Stages of Injection

HEUI injection can be understood by examining the three stages of injection: fill cycle, injection, and end of injection.

Pressurized oil supplied to the injector provides the force to pressurize fuel inside the injector. The operation of the high-pressure oil system is covered in the High-Pressure Actuation Systems section of this chapter.

1. Fill cycle: During this part of the injection cycle, the lower seat of the poppet valve is blocking high-pressure oil from entering the injector. The internal components are in their relaxed, spring-loaded positions. No electrical current is applied to the injector solenoid. The plunger and intensifier piston have returned to the top of the barrel. Fuel, pressurized to 30–80 psi (207–552 kPa) by the low-pressure transfer system, enters the injector through a passageway located just above the bottom groove of the injector. A fuel-fill check valve unseats and allows fuel to fill the plunger cavity below the intensifier piston **FIGURE 26-19**.

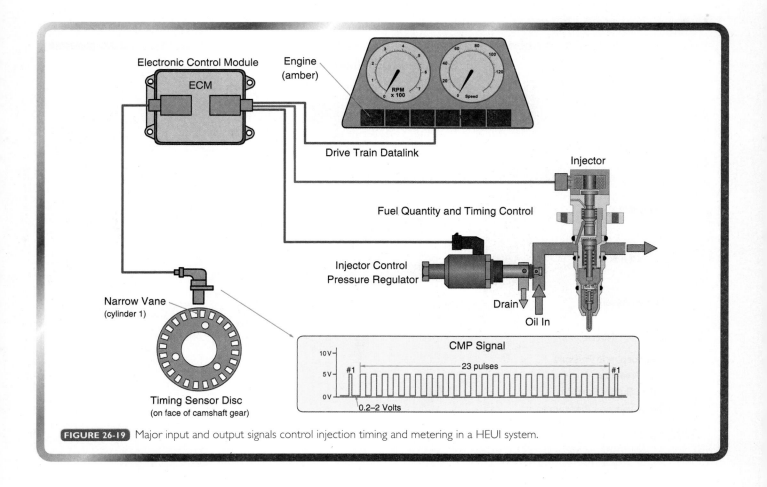

FIGURE 26-19 Major input and output signals control injection timing and metering in a HEUI system.

2. Injection: During the injection cycle, current will energize the solenoid, and the corresponding magnetic field overcomes spring tension that previously held the poppet onto its lower seat. A piece of connecting linkage or armature between the poppet valve and solenoid lifts the valve from its seat. When the poppet lifts, the oil drain path at the upper poppet valve seat is closed. High-pressure oil pushes past the poppet valve to the top of the intensifier piston. High-pressure oil, now over the amplifier piston, pressurizes fuel in the cavity beneath the plunger. Pressurized fuel travels to the nozzle valve, causing the valve to lift beginning at 2700–5500 psi (186–379 bar). Maximum oil pressure is 2300–3400 psi (159–234 bar) **FIGURE 26-20** .

3. End of injection: The injection cycle ends when the solenoid is de-energized. The magnetic field that held the poppet valve open collapses, and spring tension forces the return of the poppet valve against its seat. High-pressure oil can no longer enter the injector, and oil now spills out the oil drain path beneath the solenoid around the upper poppet valve seat. The sudden oil pressure drop above the intensifier piston combined with spring tension and fuel pressure beneath the plunger force the plunger upward in its bore. The fuel-delivery check valve remains closed and maintains residual transfer pump fuel pressure in the injector body **FIGURE 26-21** .

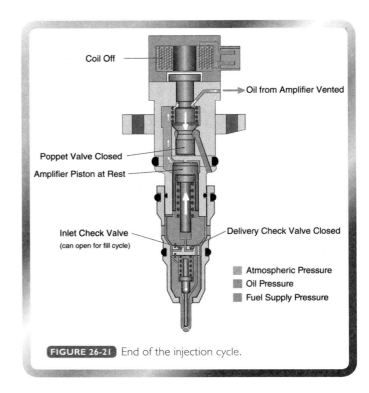

FIGURE 26-21 End of the injection cycle.

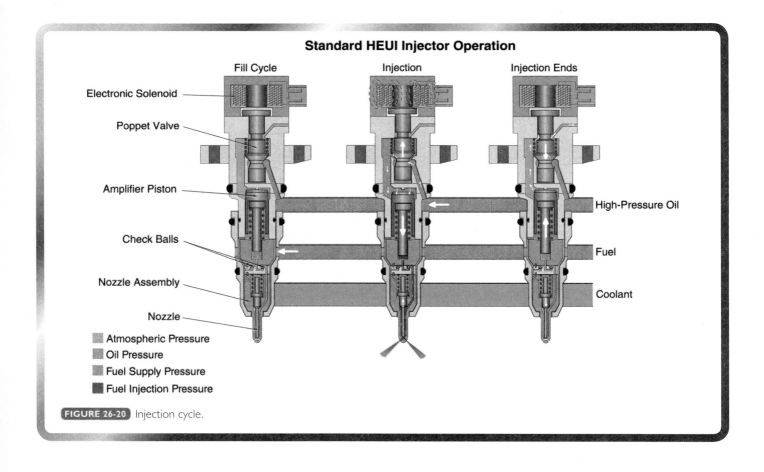

FIGURE 26-20 Injection cycle.

Metering

Injection quantity is determined by the amount of plunger travel. Two factors determine how far the plunger will travel:

1. Injector solenoid on-time: The longer the solenoid is energized, the more time is available to push the amplifier piston and injector plunger down the plunger bore.
2. Oil pressure: The higher the oil pressure applied to the amplifier piston, the faster the plunger will travel for a given amount of time.

Longer energizing time for the solenoid will result in greater quantities of fuel injected into the combustion chamber. If oil pressure is increased, the injection rate also increases proportionally. Therefore, if the on-time of the electrical signal applied to the injector remains constant, but oil pressure increases, the injection quantity increases. Conversely, increasing energization time to the injector but decreasing oil pressure results in less fuel injected. During engine operation, these two variables of solenoid on-time and oil pressure continually change depending on operating conditions and driver demand.

Injection Timing

Varying injection timing is accomplished by changing the point during the combustion cycle when energization of the injector solenoid begins and ends. Injection timing is calculated by the ECM primarily using sensor input from the crank or cam position sensors and engine calibration files stored in a look-up table in the ECM's memory.

Safety

To prevent damage to HEUI injectors after replacement, the Association of Diesel Specialist (ADS) recommends priming the high-pressure oil galleries with oil before attempting to start the engine. This is accomplished by disconnecting the cam position sensor and cranking the engine over for two consecutive starting cycles of 30 seconds each. It is estimated that a quarter of all Gen II injectors returned for warranty are damaged as a result of prolonged cranking without oil.

▶ TECHNICIAN TIP

When replacing or servicing HEUI injectors, oil and fuel must be drained from the cylinder heads first or it will drain into the cylinder when the injector is removed. A hydrostatic lock will occur in the engine after an injector is reinstalled if oil and fuel are not first removed. A hydrostatic lock when cranking can result in damage to the starter, pistons, connecting rods, and valves.

Injection Rate Control

Injection rate refers to the quantity of fuel injected per degree of crank angle rotation. Rate control is the ability of the fuel system to adjust the quantity of fuel injected during the injection sequence. Engine designers have discovered that if injection rates are properly matched for a given engine load, speed, or operating condition, it will result in improvements to emissions, fuel economy, power, and noise levels.

HEUI injection systems have the unique capability to change the rate of fuel delivery. Because oil pressure to the injector is electronically controlled by the ECM, changing oil pressure will change injection rate without any requirement to change the on-time of the injector solenoid. So, at higher oil pressure, the rate of fuel delivery is at greater. This is because high oil pressure applied to the intensifier piston will drive the plunger farther and faster per degree of crank rotation.

Pressurization is also independent of engine speed. Whether at idle or maximum engine speed, the output pressure of the high-pressure oil pump can instantly change by varying the electrical signal applied to the high-pressure pump pressure regulator. Typically at idle, actuation pressure is low to minimize combustion noise caused by ignition delay. When the driver demands more fuel, such as during hard acceleration, the actuation oil pressure will instantly and sharply increase to better atomize and quickly distribute the larger injection quantities.

▶ TECHNICIAN TIP

Oil quality is critical to effective HEUI operation. If oil contains air, it will take on elastic properties and not be able to properly pressurize injectors, which adversely affects injection pressurization and timing. Poor fuel economy, low power, and stalling are typical operator complaints caused by air entrainment of oil. Antifoaming additives used in oil for HEUI engines are necessary to prevent air bubbles from forming and staying in the oil. With use, the anti-foaming additives deplete and the oil requires changing.

HEUI B Split Shot and PRIME Injectors

These injectors have the unique capability to inject a small quantity of fuel to the combustion chamber 8–10 degrees before the main injection. This pilot injection, also known as split shot or PRIME injection, will begin to burn before the main injection arrives. The result is a combustion chamber with a burning flame front used to quickly ignite fuel in the main injection. Split shot injection strategy shortens the ignition delay and operates to provide the following benefits:

- Lower combustion chamber noise: This is especially evident at idle when prolonged ignition delay causes knocking sound characteristic of diesel engines. The hotter combustion chamber will shorten the amount of time required for ignition of the main injection, thus minimizing or even eliminating ignition delay.
- Lower NO_x emissions: The shortened ignition delay allows for retarded injection timing. Because the main injection delivery quantity will ignite faster, the beginning of injection can be delayed longer. The result is a less intense pressure spike after top dead center (TDC) in the cylinder, which in turn reduces NO_x formation.
- Fewer particulate emissions: Increased pre-ignition heat and temperature in the cylinder accelerates combustion

reactions, which helps fuel burn more completely and cleanly. The result is a more efficient burn evidenced by cleaner emissions and improved fuel economy.

Split Shot Injector Operation

By midyear 1999, all PowerStroke, Caterpillar, and International brand vehicles used HUEI injectors with split shot injection to meet stricter emission standards. Though the injector incorporates only a slight change in the plunger and barrel to accomplish this fueling strategy, injection timing does change in engines using this injector. Because timing is retarded to produce low NO_x emissions, older HEUI A and newer HEUI B injectors are not interchangeable because they require different fuel-timing maps stored in the ECM.

The injector barrel includes a new relief port that allows injection pressure to bleed back to fuel supply pressure. The amplifier piston has several small holes drilled through the bottom that intersect with a groove machined around the outer circumference of the plunger (FIGURE 26-22). When the relief port in the barrel aligns with the groove around the circumference of the plunger, a momentary drop in pressure beneath the plunger occurs. This briefly, but effectively, stops injection.

To split the injection event and deliver a pilot fuel pulse, the injector solenoid is energized once during the entire injection sequence. The amplifier piston is forced downward in the barrel and the lower edge of the plunger covers the spill port, pressurizing fuel, unseating the delivery check valve, and forcing fuel out the nozzle tip. After traveling far enough to inject less than

FIGURE 26-22 The amplifier piston of a split shot injector. The circumferential groove relieves fuel pressure below the plunger, and the holes in the bottom of the plunger connect with the circumferential groove.

$3 mm^3$ of fuel, the groove and relief port align temporarily after fuel delivery begins. At this point, the plunger's spill groove provides a passage for fuel to move from below the plunger, into the groove, and pass into the spill port in the barrel. High-pressure fuel is then released into the low-pressure fuel supply system, momentarily ending injection (FIGURE 26-23).

The amplifier piston's plunger continues to move downward in its stroke as long as the injector solenoid continues to

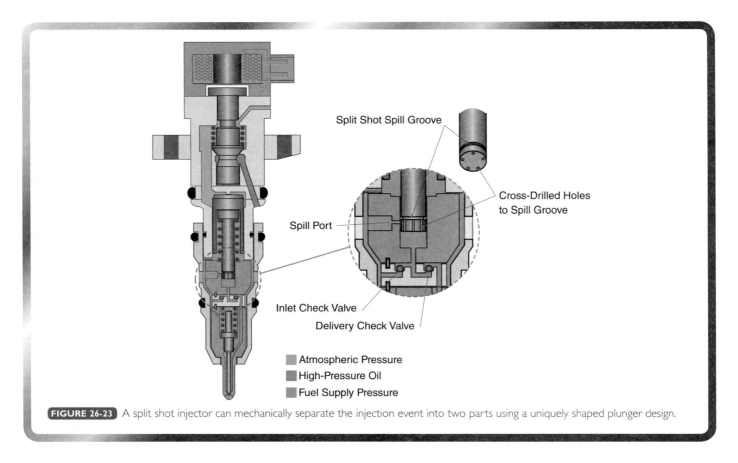

FIGURE 26-23 A split shot injector can mechanically separate the injection event into two parts using a uniquely shaped plunger design.

be energized. Injection pressure redevelops when the plunger's groove passes the relief port. The plunger continues to move downward, delivering fuel until the end of injection. Covered by the descending plunger, fuel cannot escape through the plunger into the relief port. Injection will then resume and main injection takes place as long as the amplifier piston is forced downward by oil pressure **FIGURE 26-24**.

▶ TECHNICIAN TIP

High injection pressures improve mixture preparation and combustion quality. This in turn provides the following benefits:

- Reduced exhaust smoke at higher engine speed; because smaller fuel droplets ignite and burn faster, higher engine operating speeds are possible.
- Improved fuel economy due to more complete combustion of smaller and well mixed fuel droplets.
- Minimized particulate formation caused by incompletely burned carbon.
- Increased combustion chamber ability to tolerate retarded injection timing because smaller fuel droplets ignite and burn faster.
- Increased combustion tolerance for the use of EGR used to reduce NO_x emissions.
- Reduced exhaust smoke at higher engine loads; more fuel plus finer atomization means more torque with less smoke.

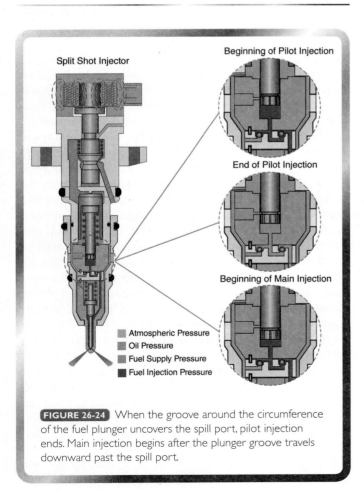

FIGURE 26-24 When the groove around the circumference of the fuel plunger uncovers the spill port, pilot injection ends. Main injection begins after the plunger groove travels downward past the spill port.

Gen II HEUI Systems

The second-generation (also called G2 or Gen II) injector uses what is termed <u>digital control valve</u> technology. This valve technology replaced the poppet valve used in the HEUI A and B designs. The digital nature of the valve refers to the position of the control valve: it is either open or closed. The digital valve's advantage is much faster operation than the poppet valve in earlier injectors, lending the injector the capability of delivering three electronically controlled injection events in one combustion cycle.

Control of injection control oil pressure is accomplished by two electromagnetic coils and a spool valve. Four external electrical pins supply the coils current to operate at 48 volts and 20 amps per coil, which is a lower voltage than other HEUI injectors. However, the time current is applied to the coils is as little as 400 microseconds. That is 400 millionths—not thousandths—of a second **FIGURE 26-25**. The longest energization time used for cold starting is 5.8 milliseconds during cranking. This contrasts with HEUI A and B injectors, which require at least 500 milliseconds to build up a magnetic field strength adequate to close the poppet valve. Dramatically shorter energization time means the coils can operate cooler. The electrical signals for a HEUI B injector use a peak and hold current strategy to keep coil heating low. Opening the poppet valve uses more current flow than holding the poppet valve open **FIGURE 26-26**. Most importantly, the coil and spool valve design enable the electrical signals to rapidly control the quantity of fuel injected over more of the injection cycle. This rate-shaping capability is critical to obtaining low emissions without sacrificing performance and fuel economy. The new control valve design provides for a smaller compact injector allowing the use of four valves per cylinder—two intake and two exhaust **FIGURE 26-27**.

What is also unique about the digital valve is its dependence on residual magnetism to move the control valve. The control valve, which resembles a hydraulic spool valve, does not use springs to center or return the valve to one end of the barrel in which it operates. Instead, residual magnetism produced by the short pulse of DC electrical current will indefinitely hold the valve in an open or closed or position. When a second pulse of electrical current is applied to the opposing coil, the valve will move in the opposite direction. It is not magnetic fields but pressurized lube oil that supplies the force needed to physically open and close the valve. By using residual magnetic energy as the triggering force and hydraulics as the driving force, the valve operates more quickly, using less energy and generating less heat than its predecessors. This digital valve overcomes the technological barriers of rapidly switching the injection event on and off using very high-pressure fluid flowing at extreme speeds with the advantage of reduced coil response time.

Sophisticated proprietary materials used in constructing the valve create exceptionally strong residual magnetic forces. During one early lab demonstration of the digital valve's operation, participants had to use a pry bar to move the control valve being held in place with only residual magnetism.

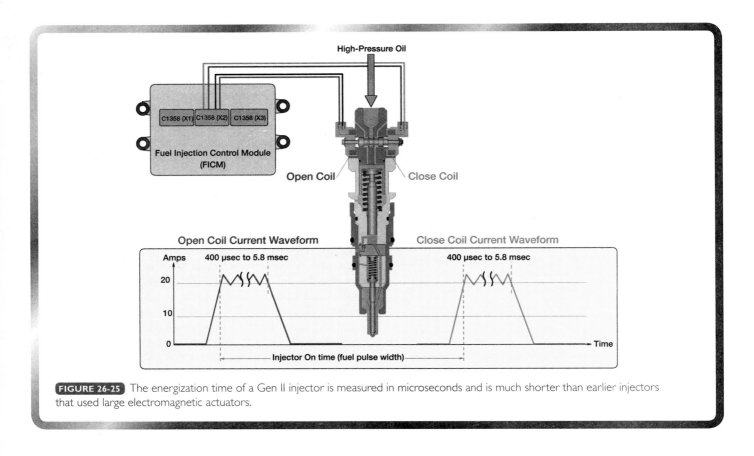

FIGURE 26-25 The energization time of a Gen II injector is measured in microseconds and is much shorter than earlier injectors that used large electromagnetic actuators.

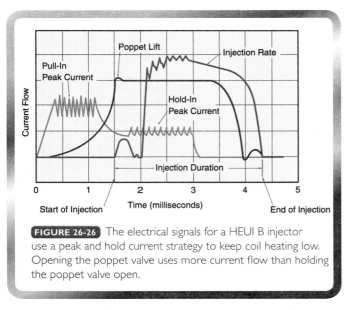

FIGURE 26-26 The electrical signals for a HEUI B injector use a peak and hold current strategy to keep coil heating low. Opening the poppet valve uses more current flow than holding the poppet valve open.

Construction

Inside the injector, the digital control valve consists of two coils: an open coil and a closed coil. A spool valve moves from side to side controlled only by magnetic forces **FIGURE 26-28**. Total movement of the valve is only 0.017" (0.4318 mm). The valve has only two positions. When open, it allows oil to flow from the high-pressure oil rail into the injector, pushing the intensifier piston and plunger downward. In the closed position, it allows oil to drain out of the injector. Two coils, rather than one, control oil flow, enabling much faster operation. Because the decay of a magnetic field is not necessary to end injection, the injector is capable of more injections, accurately metered and spaced very close together.

Similar to the operation of earlier HEUI injector amplifier pistons, the Gen II injector's intensifier piston multiplies fuel pressure below the fuel plunger. The intensifier has a surface area 7 to 10 times greater than the plunger diameter, depending on the engine and year of manufacture. A mechanical pressure relief valve in the actuation oil system opens at 4000 psi (276 bar). The relief valve limits oil pressure in the event of a malfunctioning injection pressure regulator. Given the operating range of pressurized oil, these systems theoretically can operate at up to 34,000 psi (2344 bar) of injection pressure. In service they operate just below 29,000 psi (1999 bar).

The plunger and barrel assembly develop injection pressure similar to the HEUI A and B injectors. Earlier injectors used a coating of tungsten carbide on the plunger to reduce the possibility of scuffing from poor fuel quality, water contamination, and the effects of ultra-low-sulfur diesel (ULSD) fuel. Later injectors used a silicon carbide coating with the proprietary name diamond-like carbon (DLC) coating. A new clevis over the fuel plunger has eliminated failures encountered in earlier injectors. These injectors cannot be interchanged with older injectors.

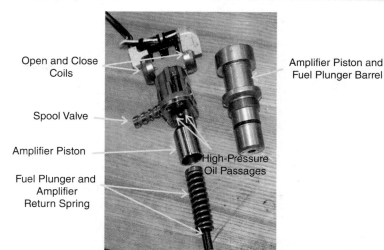

FIGURE 26-27 Internal components of the Gen II injector. Two coils controlling spool valve movement create a faster injector response time.

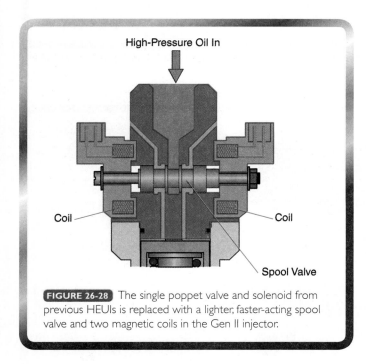

FIGURE 26-28 The single poppet valve and solenoid from previous HEUIs is replaced with a lighter, faster-acting spool valve and two magnetic coils in the Gen II injector.

High-pressure oil is supplied to the Gen II injectors through a high-pressure <u>oil manifold</u> or rail externally attached to the top of the injectors **FIGURE 26-29**. The rail incorporates hydraulic wave-dampening devices called <u>acoustic wave attenuation (AWA)</u> to minimize a rhythmic "cackling" noise at idle caused by high-pressure pump pressure waves synchronizing with injection events **FIGURE 26-30**. During the brief pressure spike, injection pressures sharply rise and create the unusual combustion noise due to momentarily high spray-in pressure. Early-model engines used a straight rail. Later models introduced a wavy high-pressure oil rail with higher oil capacity and dual AWA fittings in each rail.

Injection Cycle

The injector has three main events during an injection cycle: fill, main injection, and end of main injection.

1. Fill cycle: This event begins with the spool valve in the closed position, preventing oil from entering the injector. Low-pressure fuel regulated to 45–50 psi (310–345 kPa) enters the injector through fuel rails in the cylinder head. After entering the injector through the fuel inlet located in a groove around the injector body, fuel fills the cavity below the plunger **FIGURE 26-31**.

2. Main injection: An electrical signal energizes the open coil, moving the spool valve to the open position. This allows high-pressure oil to begin forcing the intensifier piston and plunger downward. A fuel inlet check ball closes, causing pressurization of fuel below the intensifier piston plunger. The pressurized fuel begins to lift the nozzle valve at approximately 3100 psi (214 bar) **FIGURE 26-32**.

3. End of injection: After the correct amount of fuel is delivered based on the time the injector digital valve has been left open, the close coil is pulsed with current for 800 microseconds. This moves the spool valve from an open to a closed position. High-pressure oil is blocked from entering the cavity above the intensifier piston. Oil above the intensifier piston leaves the injector through an exhaust port. Fuel pressure below the plunger and spring force returns the intensifier to its initial position. The nozzle valve simultaneously closes, and injection abruptly ends after delivering fuel **FIGURE 26-33**.

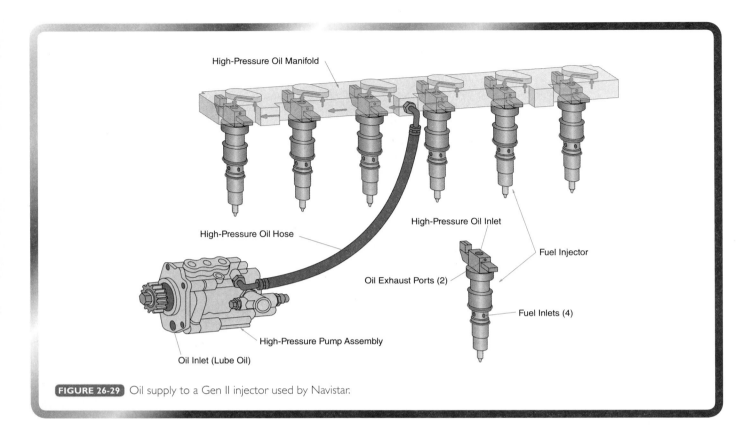

FIGURE 26-29 Oil supply to a Gen II injector used by Navistar.

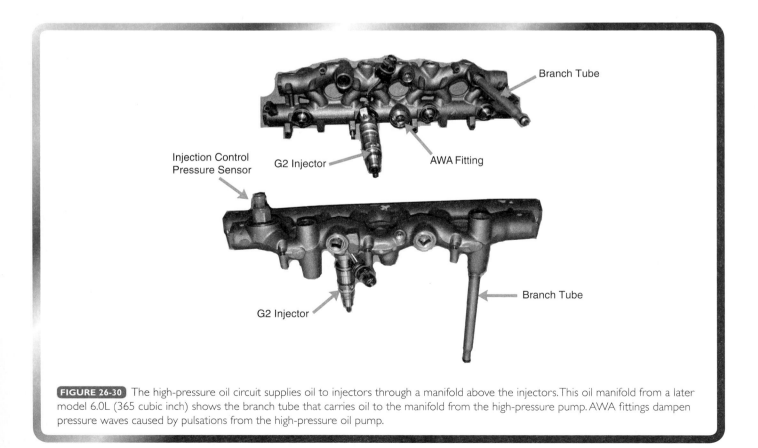

FIGURE 26-30 The high-pressure oil circuit supplies oil to injectors through a manifold above the injectors. This oil manifold from a later model 6.0L (365 cubic inch) shows the branch tube that carries oil to the manifold from the high-pressure pump. AWA fittings dampen pressure waves caused by pulsations from the high-pressure oil pump.

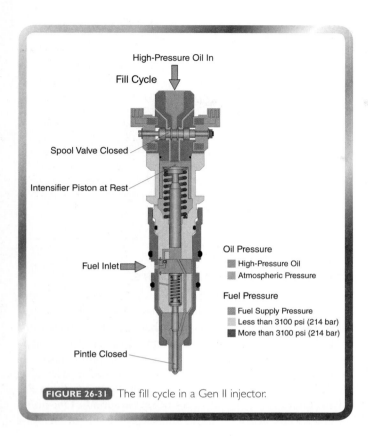

FIGURE 26-31 The fill cycle in a Gen II injector.

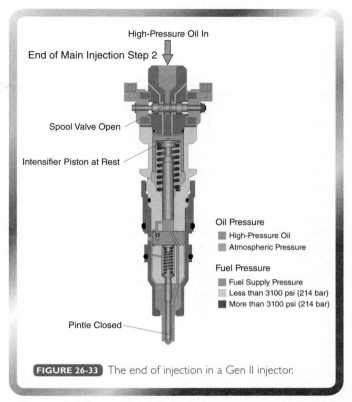

FIGURE 26-33 The end of injection in a Gen II injector.

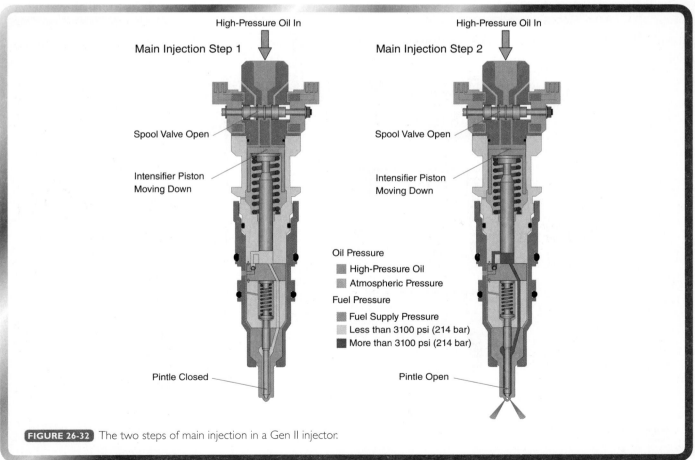

FIGURE 26-32 The two steps of main injection in a Gen II injector.

Metering Timing and Rate Control

Similar to previous HEUI injectors, the Gen II plunger's travel determines injection quantity. Plunger travel, however, is determined not by the amount of time the open or close coils are energized but by the length of time the digital valve is left open. The open coil needs only one electrical pulse to remain in its position. The opposite close coil requires energizing to change the position of the spool valve and remain closed. Varying injection timing is accomplished by changing the specific time during crankshaft rotation to cycle the open and close coils.

To change the rate of fuel delivery, the oil pressure to the injector is electronically varied by the ECM. At higher pressure, the rate of fuel delivery is proportionally greater because the force acting on the plunger is increased. The plunger will then displace more fuel per degree of crankshaft rotation at high pressure. Pressurization is independent of engine speed, so high pressures are available at low engine speed operation if needed.

Rate control or shaping is achieved through more than just varying the oil pressure. The Gen II injector is also able to rapidly open and close the spool valve several times during the course of one injection sequence. Injection events such as pilot, main, and post-combustion injections are accomplished electronically and not mechanically as in HEUI B injectors. Software instructions contained in the ECM can send several pulses to the digital valve control coils within one injection cycle. This enables execution of several injection events within one injection cycle **FIGURE 26-34** .

Caterpillar H1B-300 Injectors

The Caterpillar H1B-300 injector was developed for the C7 and and C9 ACERT series engines. The injector is capable of five different injection rate shapes and an electrically controlled pilot injection. Two unique features of the injector are the low mass poppet valve, which responds faster to electrical signals, and the hydraulically balanced nozzle valve **FIGURE 26-35** and **FIGURE 26-36** . Hydraulically balanced nozzle valves simply have hydraulic pressure at two points. One point is fuel pressure below the valve and the other is high pressure

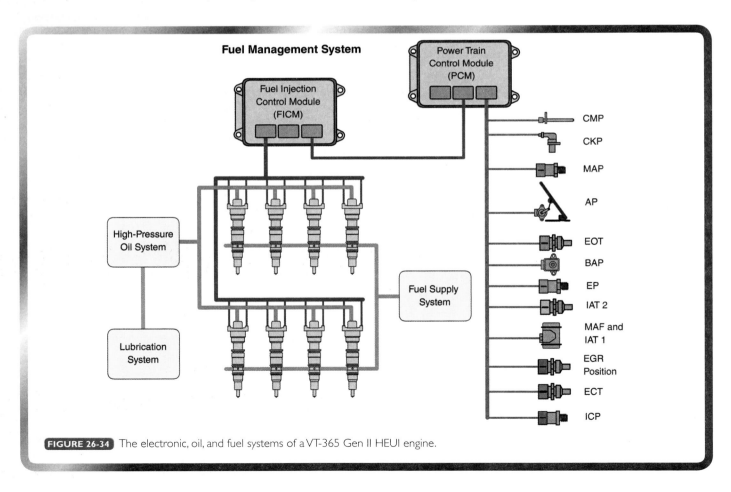

FIGURE 26-34 The electronic, oil, and fuel systems of a VT-365 Gen II HEUI engine.

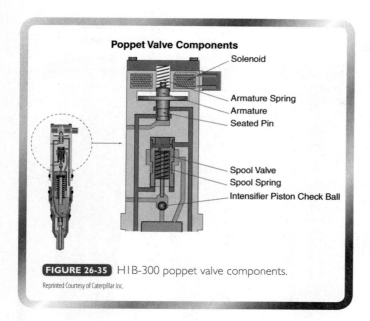

FIGURE 26-35 H1B-300 poppet valve components.

Reprinted Courtesy of Caterpillar Inc.

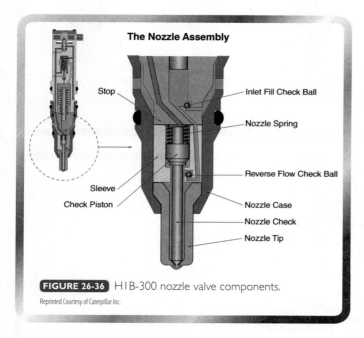

FIGURE 26-36 H1B-300 nozzle valve components.

Reprinted Courtesy of Caterpillar Inc.

oil above the nozzle valve, holding the valve onto its seat along with the nozzle spring. Changing the pressure on either side of the nozzle valve causes it to either open or close. Faster nozzle opening and closing is achieved by using more rapid acting, powerful hydraulic force than nozzle spring pressure to close the nozzle.

H1B-300 Injection Cycle

During the fill cycle, high-pressure fuel and oil enters the injector through passageways in the cylinder head. Fuel travels to the cavity below the amplifier piston while pressurized oil is applied to two sides of the poppet valve and to the top of the nozzle valve holding it closed.

When the poppet valve is energized, the valve lifts, closing off the high-pressure oil passageway and applying pressure to the nozzle valve. Lifting of the poppet valve opens a passageway, allowing pressurized oil above the nozzle valve to drain to a low-pressure oil return. Meanwhile, the spool valve above the amplifier piston is opened simultaneously by the loss of high-pressure oil holding it closed. When the spool valve opens, high pressure oil is directed to the top of the amplifier piston, and injection begins **FIGURE 26-37**.

Pilot, main, and post-combustion injection events are controlled by the electrical signals to the poppet valve. Oil pressure determines the shape of the injection rate to be either ramped for low NO_x or squared for power.

▶ TECHNICIAN TIP

Depending on outside temperatures, Caterpillar C7 and C9 engines can use either 10W-30 or 15W-40 oil. Because the viscosity of the two oils changes high-pressure system operation, a removable plug in the wiring harness is used to indicate to the ECM the viscosity of oil used. The ECM then uses a different set of calibrations and look-up table values to adjust system operation.

High-Pressure Actuation Systems

The high-pressure oil actuation system used by HEUI systems has several major subsections:

- Low-pressure oil supply
- Oil reservoirs
- High-pressure pump
- Injection control pressure regulation

Low-Pressure Oil Supply System

All HEUI engines share lubrication oil with the engine's lubrication system. The lubrication system supplies oil to the separate high-pressure oil system used to actuate injectors. Connecting the two oil systems ensures adequate capacity of oil for the high-pressure circuit. Two configurations are used to supply the high-pressure pump: the short-circuit supply and the filtered supply.

Short-Circuit Supply

An oil circuit directly connects the engine's lubrication system to an oil reservoir supplying the high-pressure oil pump **FIGURE 26-38**. Because this circuit does not pass through a filter, but instead connects the engine's main oil gallery to the reservoir, it is called a short-circuit supply. Short-circuit supply to the high-pressure system ensures a rapid filling of the reservoir subsequent to an oil change, during starting, or when the engine is cold. Without it, prolonged engine cranking may be required. A one-way check ball prevents oil from draining back to the crankcase when the engine is not operated. Early HEUI engines used this arrangement, but it has one main disadvantage. Unfiltered crankcase oil contaminated with dirt or metal will pass through the injectors, causing rapid wear or failure of injectors and the high-pressure pump.

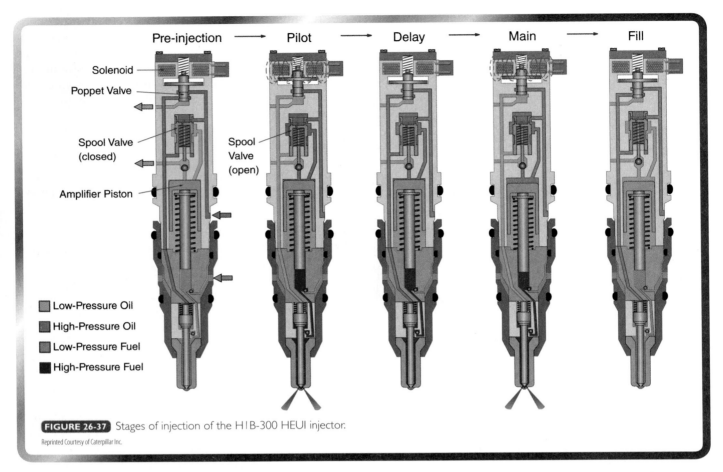

FIGURE 26-37 Stages of injection of the H1B-300 HEUI injector.

Reprinted Courtesy of Caterpillar Inc.

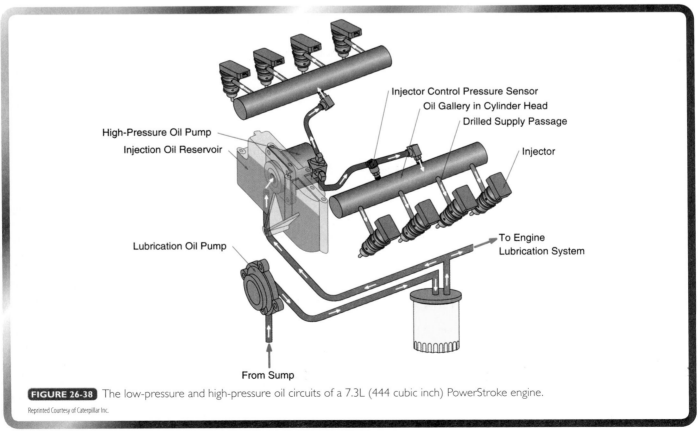

FIGURE 26-38 The low-pressure and high-pressure oil circuits of a 7.3L (444 cubic inch) PowerStroke engine.

Reprinted Courtesy of Caterpillar Inc.

Filtered Supply

Later designs of HEUI systems corrected the problem of short-circuit oil supply by using oil filtered by the engine to supply the high-pressure circuit **FIGURE 26-39**. This ensures only filtered oil, free of dirt and other contaminants, reaches the injector. Both short-circuit and filtered systems use a storage reservoir to hold oil during intervals when the lubrication system may not be capable of supplying enough oil to operate the high-pressure actuation circuit. Reservoirs with a capacity of approximately 0.26 gallon (1 liter) are incorporated into high-pressure pumps or cavities in the engine. Caterpillar uses an accumulator reservoir system for its HEUI A and B engines to store oil for its high-pressure pump **FIGURE 26-40**. During an oil change, none of this oil can be drained from the accumulator or reservoir.

> ### ▶ TECHNICIAN TIP
>
> Unfiltered oil containing abrasives or coolant will cause rapid wear of the amplifier piston plunger and seals, leading to premature injector failure. Dirt commonly enters lube oil through air intake leaks, leaking gaskets, and missing oil filler caps. Even in filtered systems, metal particles from injectors and high-pressure pumps can migrate through the circuit and cause injector failure. After any pump or injector failure, always drain and inspect the oil from the high-pressure rails or galleries. Pouring oil onto a paper towel or cloth can help identify whether metal particles are contaminating the high-pressure oil circuit.

High-Pressure Actuation Circuit

The high-pressure oil actuation system delivers engine oil under high pressure to pressurize fuel for injection. Another name for the circuit is the injection control circuit. A high-pressure oil pump connected to the reservoir increases the lube oil's pressure to levels usable by the injectors. These pumps are commonly gear-driven, fixed-displacement, piston, swash-plate, or axial piston pumps. Lines or tubes will connect the pump output to oil galleries or manifolds delivering oil to the injectors.

High-Pressure Pumps

Drive torque used to pressurize oil in the high-pressure pump is provided by the engine. Because the pump output is not phased with the injection event, little torque is required to operate the pump in comparison to other injection systems.

Caterpillar uses an innovative **high efficiency pump (HEP)** on the C7 and C9 engines. Like other variable output HEUI pumps, output pressure is matched to pressure desired by the ECM based on operating conditions (i.e., load, speed, temperature, and so on) and OEM-specific fuel maps stored in the ECM. The HEP uses a PWM-controlled displacement control valve, which adjusts pump displacement volume rather than output volume by changing the effective stroke of a swash plate pump **FIGURE 26-41**. Regulating injection control pressure with a variable displacement pump minimizes power consumed by driving the pump because the pump supplies only as much oil as the engine requires. The HEP's efficiency is further enhanced in that it does not change the pump's swash plate angle using the high-force control valve common to other pumps. Instead, a sliding collar on the pump's driveshaft moves to open or close a helix groove containing an oil circuit that adjusts the swash plate angle.

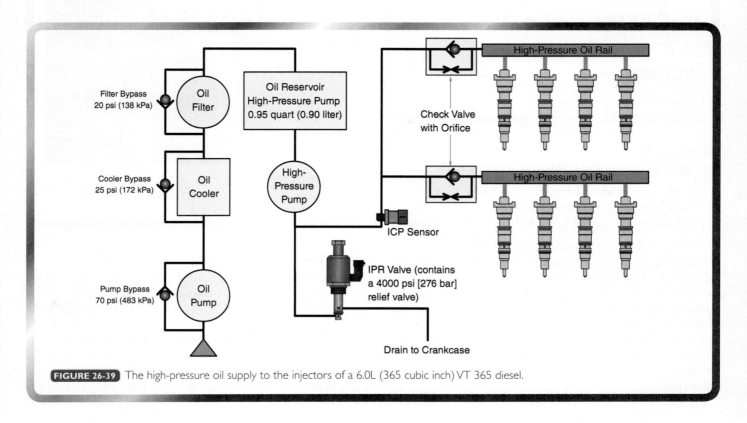

FIGURE 26-39 The high-pressure oil supply to the injectors of a 6.0L (365 cubic inch) VT 365 diesel.

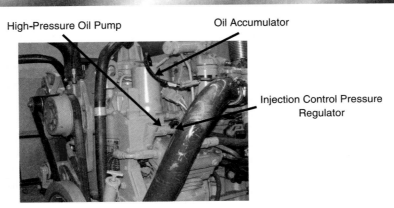

FIGURE 26-40 Caterpillar 3126 uses an accumulator reservoir system. Oil cannot be drained from the accumulator, which supplies oil to the high-pressure pump, when the low-pressure supply is inadequate.
Reprinted Courtesy of Caterpillar Inc.

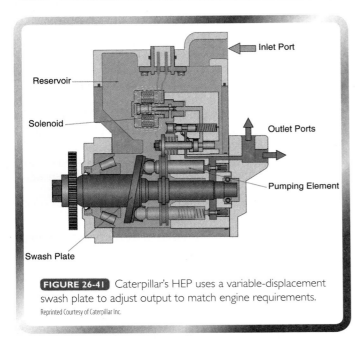

FIGURE 26-41 Caterpillar's HEP uses a variable-displacement swash plate to adjust output to match engine requirements.
Reprinted Courtesy of Caterpillar Inc.

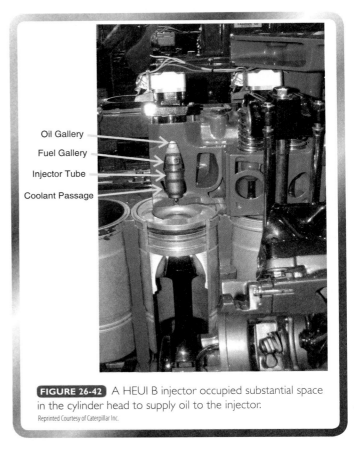

FIGURE 26-42 A HEUI B injector occupied substantial space in the cylinder head to supply oil to the injector.
Reprinted Courtesy of Caterpillar Inc.

Oil Manifolds

Pressurized oil is supplied to injectors several ways:

- Oil galleries drilled through the cylinder head
- Jumper tubes connecting oil galleries to injectors
- Cast iron oil manifolds attached to the top of the injectors

The use of oil manifolds supplying oil through the top of the injectors eliminates the problem with O-ring leakage when oil is supplied though the cylinder head. Earlier HEUI injectors encountered O-ring deterioration from heat, vibration, and chemical attack when oil is supplied through cross-drillings in the cylinder head. The diameter of injectors, such as Gen II injectors, could be reduced with oil supply from manifolds connected to the top of injectors **FIGURE 26-42**. A compact injector profile permits the use of a centralized injector location in four valve cylinders.

Injection Control Pressure Regulator

A variety of sensor inputs are used to calculate oil pressure, which is regulated using an ECM-controlled, pulse-width modulated **injection control pressure regulator (ICPR)** **FIGURE 26-43**. Caterpillar's term for the same device is injection actuation pressure control valve (IAPCV). This device is an electrically operated spool valve that moves in response to the strength of a magnetic field. By changing the current flow through a coil surrounding the spool valve, the oil pressure

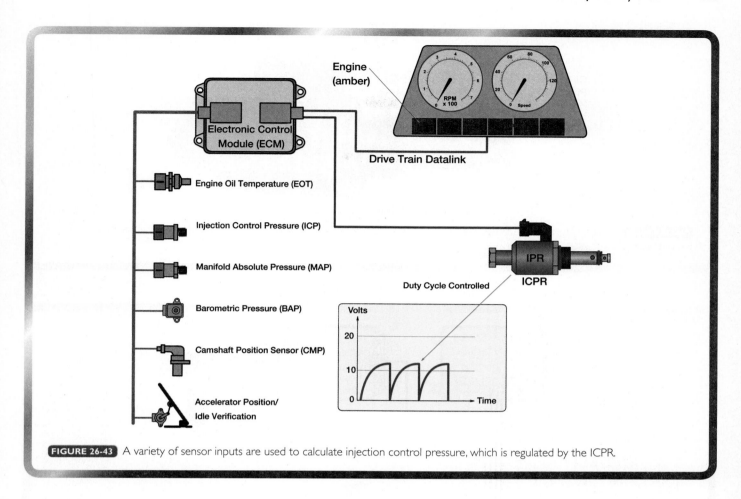

FIGURE 26-43 A variety of sensor inputs are used to calculate injection control pressure, which is regulated by the ICPR.

for injection actuation is adjusted. Pressure is usually low at idle and increases with engine speed and load conditions **FIGURE 26-44**. When not building pressure, the spool valve will direct oil back to the oil sump **FIGURE 26-45**. To build pressure, the spool valve closes the passage to the sump and directs oil to the injectors.

To provide feedback to the ECM regarding injection control pressure, a sensor is located in the high-pressure oil circuit. This sensor, the **injection control pressure (ICP) sensor**, provides closed-loop feedback to the ECM about whether the oil pressure is too low or high **FIGURE 26-46**. The ECM can change the amount of current to the ICPR coil and adjust oil pressure **FIGURE 26-47**. A feedback loop is formed between the ICP sensor, the ICPR, and the ECM. Loss of this sensor signal will usually cause the injection oil pressure to operate at a factory default value based on a predetermined PWM signal to the regulator **FIGURE 26-48**.

A minimum of 325–500 psi (22–34 bar) is usually required to start HEUI engines. When running, the oil pressure will vary depending on the engine calibration and model. However, oil pressure should remain relatively stable for any given operating condition. During hard acceleration and under full load conditions, injection control pressure will reach maximum pressures. Lowest pressures are encountered during warm idle.

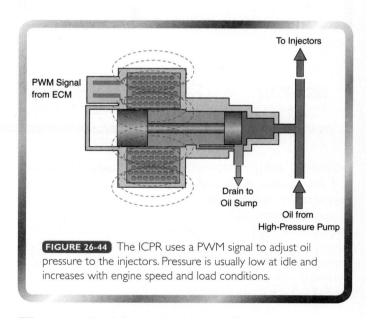

FIGURE 26-44 The ICPR uses a PWM signal to adjust oil pressure to the injectors. Pressure is usually low at idle and increases with engine speed and load conditions.

Electronic Management System

Information processing in HEUI engines is similar to that in other electronically governed diesels. Input devices collect data and send electrical signals to the ECM. The ECM processes the

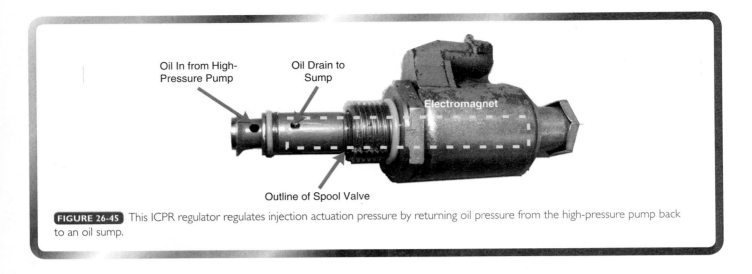

FIGURE 26-45 This ICPR regulator regulates injection actuation pressure by returning oil pressure from the high-pressure pump back to an oil sump.

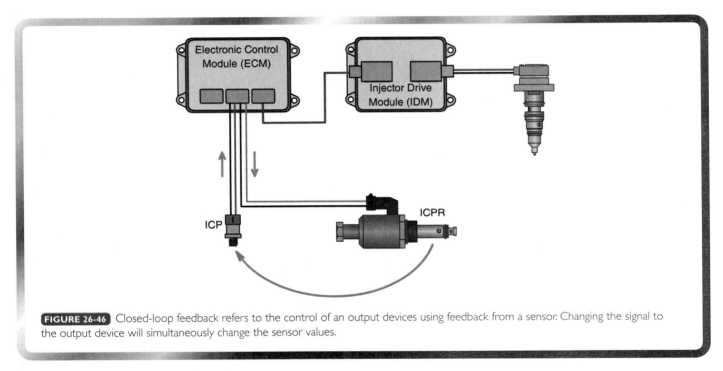

FIGURE 26-46 Closed-loop feedback refers to the control of an output devices using feedback from a sensor. Changing the signal to the output device will simultaneously change the sensor values.

information and generates outputs based on control algorithms and data contained in look-up tables stored as part of the engine calibration and software instructions. Electrical signals to output devices such as the injectors and ICPR are primary outputs. The ECM is also connected to the vehicle network allowing other modules to share data and interact with the engine's ECM. For example, early Navistar trucks use a vehicle personality module (VPM) to interact with the ECM providing the following features:

- Speed-setting limits for road, cruise, and PTO
- Programmable idle shutdown options
- Programmable engine protection shutdown options

- Remote variable PTO speed control
- Remote throttle for engine speed control outside the cab (as in boom trucks)
- Viewing of vehicle and trip data for trip hours, distance traveled, and fuel used
- Control of rated rpm
- Control of rated horsepower
- Retarder inhibiting for automatic transmissions equipped with vehicle retarders
- Torque limit for powertrain protection

Later International vehicles incorporated the engine, vehicle, and injector drive modules into a single controller.

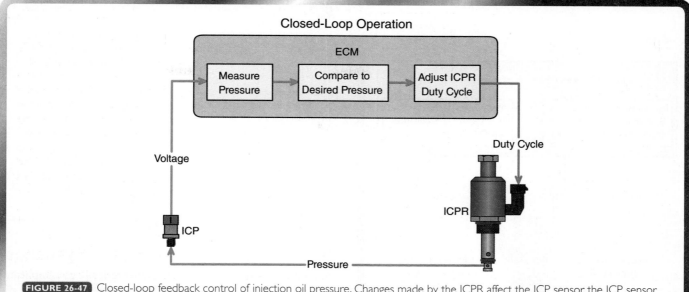

FIGURE 26-47 Closed-loop feedback control of injection oil pressure. Changes made by the ICPR affect the ICP sensor, the ICP sensor sends data to the ECM, which compares sensed data with desired values. Changes to the electrical signal are made if pressure is above or below desired value.

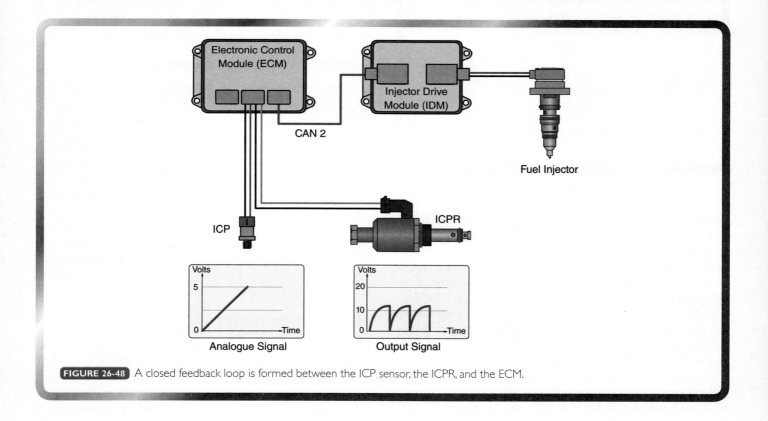

FIGURE 26-48 A closed feedback loop is formed between the ICP sensor, the ICPR, and the ECM.

Injector Drive Modules

Because the HEUI injectors require substantial amounts of current—as much as 115 volts 8 amps for HEUI A and B injectors and 48 volts 20 amps for Gen II injectors, a separate control module is often used to minimize electrical interference in the ECM.

The purpose of the __injector drive module (IDM)__, also called the FICM on Gen II HEUI, is to operate and monitor injector operation. Current is stepped up in the FICM using step-up transformers **FIGURE 26-49**. Capacitors store current used to energize the injectors **FIGURE 26-50**. The FICM module stores

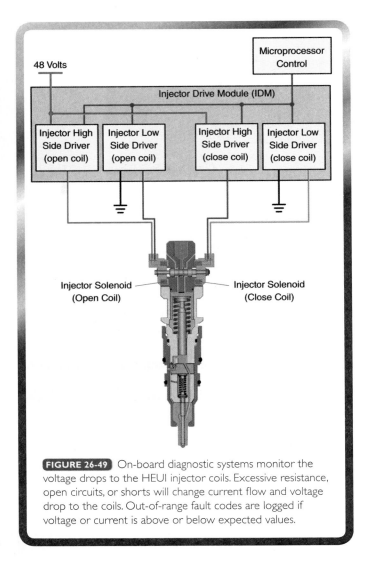

FIGURE 26-49 On-board diagnostic systems monitor the voltage drops to the HEUI injector coils. Excessive resistance, open circuits, or shorts will change current flow and voltage drop to the coils. Out-of-range fault codes are logged if voltage or current is above or below expected values.

information such as engine firing order and operating and diagnostic software instructions. Using network communication, data is exchanged between the ECM and injector control module. Two control signals from the ECM are supplied to the injection control module: the fuel delivery control signal (FDCS) and the cylinder identification (CID) signal. The FDCS is an ECM-commanded engine rpm and is used by the IDM to calculate injection timing and injection duration or energization time of the injector. The CID signal indicates engine position and is used to establish the beginning of the firing sequence. Because the firing order sequence is built into the injection control module, it can begin the injection sequence after learning when a particular cylinder is at TDC and the end of the compression stroke. An electronic feedback signal is used to send information back to the ECM in the form of diagnostic trouble codes (DTC) about the injection control module and injectors. DTCs include faults such as opens, shorts, misfires, and other electrical faults. Caterpillar engines do not require a separate IDM. All engine functions are integrated into the proprietary Advanced Digital Engine Module (ADEM) or ECM.

Excessive engine idle is very destructive to diesel engines. During idle, low combustion temperatures and pressures produce exhaust slobber—a mixture of soot, unburned fuel, and oil—creating soot loading in engine oil. To prevent damage to HEUI engines caused by engine idle, oil and coolant temperatures are monitored to enable cold-weather protection mode. When the potential for damage from excessive cold idle are present, the engine rpm is automatically elevated and injection timing changes. Cold-weather protection will not permit excessive loading of a cold engine, either. If an engine is heavily loaded before the engine is adequately warmed up, piston skirts can collapse and oil can thicken, causing damage from poor lubrication.

▶ Maintenance of HEUI Systems

Maintaining a HEUI fuel system is theoretically uncomplicated because there is no regular maintenance scheduled for the system. However, pressurizing fuel using engine oil introduces new variables to maintenance considerations related to problems with oil contamination and performing diagnostics on the high-pressure oil circuits when problems do occur. The following section examines some common issues related to diagnosing problems with and servicing HEUI fuel systems.

Replacing a HEUI Injector

If G2 injectors misfire, fail to deliver the correct quantity of fuel, are worn out or contaminated, or have sticking control valves, then they may require replacement. Stickage, the condition in which the spool valve will not properly move due to deposits or fouling caused by soot-thickened oil, may sometimes be cleaned using aftermarket solvents. If software updates and oil changes do not correct stickage, the condition can cause misfires when the engine is cold. When this occurs, an injector replacement is required.

To replace a HEUI injector, follow the steps in **SKILL DRILL 26-1**. These steps are for replacing a G2 injector in a 6.0L (365 cubic inch) PowerStroke engine. Always consult OEM service literature first to identify the most correct procedures using prescribed tooling.

HEUI Diagnostics

Because HEUI injectors operate using pressurized engine oil, diagnostic checks of the high-pressure oil system are unique compared with other fuel systems. Specialized diagnostic routines and strategies are required to identify problems with oil quality and the components controlling pressurization of engine oil.

Injection Control Pressure Problems

The high-pressure oil pumps on HEUI engines have a finite delivery volume **FIGURE 26-51**. This means the output volume of the pump matches the quantity required by the injectors when they are operating at their maximum output. The system

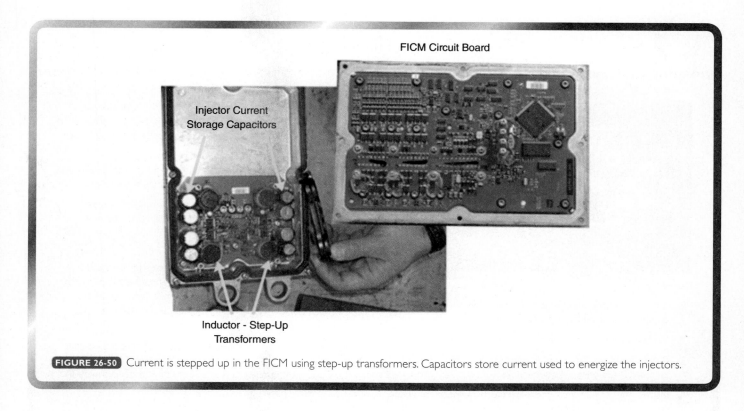

FICM Circuit Board

Injector Current
Storage Capacitors

Inductor - Step-Up
Transformers

FIGURE 26-50 Current is stepped up in the FICM using step-up transformers. Capacitors store current used to energize the injectors.

is designed to allow some extra delivery volume, but on many engines this volume is not adequate if there are leaks in the high-pressure oil systems. This means that if there is a leak in the injection control system, engine performance is significantly impacted. For example, system leaks can occur when oil leaks around injector O-rings, oil lines, fittings, through defective poppet valves, or from a worn high-pressure oil pump. These leaks will produce complaints related to rough running, low power, high fuel consumption, hard starting, and failure to start.

Symptoms of high-pressure oil leakage include:

- Large difference between hot and cold starting times, particularly a quick cold start and long hot start
- Loss of power when hot
- Low power
- High fuel consumption
- Oil consumption
- Blue exhaust smoke, especially on startup

Oil Quality

Because the HEUI fuel injectors are electronically controlled and use high-pressure lube oil for actuation, understanding the operation of the oil system is necessary to diagnose possible performance complaints. Oil quality is critical for the same reason. The correct viscosity and grade of oil are important for proper HEUI operation. Oil that has little or no antifoaming additive will cause aeration of oil. Aerated oil will not properly transmit pressure and motion, which leads to drivability complaints such as stalling and low power.

Oil contaminated with water, fuel, dirt, or particulate matter will lead to premature injector wear and malfunction. Common causes of dirt contamination of oil are improperly installed or incorrect air filters and loose or missing oil filler caps.

Oil viscosity influences the operation of the HEUI systems, too. Caterpillar uses a removable electrical jumper plug on C7 and C9 engines to correct actuation system variables when using either 15W-40 or 10W-40 engine oil. Oil thickened by excessive soot loading will interfere with proper injector control valve operation, particularly in cold weather and during start-up.

▶ TECHNICIAN TIP

Lubrication oil used in HEUI engines must have the proper level of antifoaming additive, which quickly releases air bubbles from oil. Antifoaming additive depletes with distance traveled, so HEUI engines are sensitive to overextended oil change intervals. The antifoaming additive is also affected by chemicals in room-temperature vulcanized (RTV) silicone used as gasket material. After engine service, such as resealing the oil pan using RTV silicone, adding additional antifoaming additive is recommended. Oil-displacing RTV silicone is recommended for resealing engine parts such as oil pans and engine front covers.

Testing the Oil Actuation Circuit

HEUI oil systems are divided into two sections: the low-pressure system and the high-pressure system. The low-pressure system supplies the high-pressure system with oil, and problems in either system will effect engine operation.

SKILL DRILL 26-1 Replacing a HEUI Injector

1 Clean the engine and remove the valve cover on the cylinder bank with the defective cylinder.

2 Remove the bolts holding the oil manifold.

3 Remove the hex head bolt holding the oil stand pipe to the oil manifold, and lift the oil manifold from the injectors.

4 Inspect the oil inlet area of the injectors for metal filings, which indicate a failure of the high-pressure oil pump. If the pump has failed, replace the pump, remove all injectors, and flush the high-pressure oil system with solvent. Failure to replace the pump and flush the system will cause any new injectors to fail in a short time.

5 Pour out oil from the oil manifold, preferably onto a paper shop towel, to further check for metal filings. Also, note the stain the oil leaves on the towel. Fuel in the oil will leave a large, clear-appearing stain around the oil ring on the paper towel.

6 Inspect the condition of the inlet injector O-rings. Any nicked, torn, or damaged O-ring requires an injector replacement, because the O-ring is not serviceable separately.

7 Disconnect the injector's electrical connector and push the injector connector back into the rocker housing using a 3/4" (19mm) 12-point socket.

8 Loosen and unscrew the Torx bolt in the injector hold-down clamp. Removing the injector hold-down bolt will unseat and lift the injector from its bore. Note: Do not pry on the injector, because the injector coils can be easily damaged.

9 Clean the injector bore and cup with a purpose-made wire brush and wipe with a lint-free shop cloth. Ensure the copper sealing gasket for the injector tip is removed.

10 Lubricate the injector O-rings with engine oil before installation. Transfer the hold-down clamp to the new injector. Remove any oil in the hold-down bolt hole, as oil will prevent the bolt from seating the injector.

11 Install and tighten the injector in place with the hold-down bolt. Torque the hold-down bolt; seating the injector with the correct amount of pressure is needed to transfer heat, prevent nozzle tip distortion, and ensure a good combustion seal.

12 Fill the injectors with engine oil and lubricate the oil inlet tubes on the oil manifold. Seat the manifold carefully by hand after installing a new O-ring on the stand pipe. If the manifold is not carefully seated, the inlet O-ring will be damaged, which will result in an oil pressure leak. The engine will likely be hard to start when warm.

13 Replace the fuel and oil filters and change the engine oil using the recommended grade and specification of oil.

14 Disconnect the cam and crank position sensors before attempting to start the engine. Crank the engine for two consecutive periods of 30 seconds with a 2-minute cooldown period between each crank interval. This will ensure the injector control valves are properly lubricated before being moved, which will help prevent premature injector failure.

15 Update the engine with any revised calibration for the injectors or control system.

Diagnostic Tests to Detect System Leakage

Oil leakage from the high-pressure oil circuit in HEUI engines is one of the most common complaints and detrimental to engine operation. Even small losses of oil from HEUI systems are noticeable and can be easily detected by technicians using the proper diagnostic techniques and tools.

Measuring the Duty Cycle of the ICPR

The ICPR is a pulse-width modulated oil pressure control valve that reports its electrical signal as a percentage of duty cycle on all scanners and OEM software. An unusually high duty cycle indicates the ECM is compensating for oil leakage by increasing the on-time for the pressure regulator. Longer on-time or an increased percentage of duty cycle means less oil returns to the sump, and more oil is delivered to the high-pressure circuit. Observing actual duty cycle and comparing it to expected values is one of the most useful tests to detect oil leakage **FIGURE 26-52** .

The on-board diagnostic systems will detect abnormal operation of injection actuation control, alerting technicians to faults with codes such as:

- Injection control pressure above system working range
- Injection control pressure above specifications with engine off
- Injection control above/below desired level
- injection control sensor values out of range

FIGURE 26-51 The three-piston pump on this DT MaxxForce engine pressurizes engine oil to operate the injectors. The injection control pressure regulator is located at the rear of the pump.

Performing an ICPR Test

Leaks in the HEUI high-pressure oil system or worn oil pumps are indicated by an above-average injection control pressure duty cycle. In the case of a leak, the ICPR will need to close further and block oil return to the oil sump to send more oil to the injectors. In the case of a worn pump, less oil can be allowed to return to the sump to build oil pressure, because oil pump volume output is reduced when the pump is worn.

To perform an ICPR test, follow the steps in SKILL DRILL 26-2.

Measuring System Pressure Loss

When pressurized with oil, high-pressure circuits should be able to retain pressure for hours with no significant drop. A hand-operated or electrically operated oil pump can be used to verify the sealing capabilities of the high-pressure circuit. Alternatively, air pressure can be used to pinpoint leaks in O-rings at branch tubes, oil pumps, and oil manifolds.

Visual Inspection of Fuel for Contamination

A visual check can determine whether oil is bypassing injector O-rings and entering the fuel. In early-generation HEUI engines, if the middle O-ring has failed, oil will push its way into the low-pressure fuel circuit, where it is either injected with fuel or returned to the tank with return fuel.

▶ TECHNICIAN TIP

A defective HEUI O-ring will allow high-pressure oil to push through to the low-pressure fuel supply system. Oil is recirculated back to the fuel tank with fuel and will darken the fuel.

Visual Inspection for Oil Leaks

Leaking injector O-rings, jumper tubes, and manifolds can be identified during engine operation. Oil leaking around an injector is not normal and indicates O-ring leakage. It is easy to detect oil leaks by moving a piece of paper around jumper tubes. This method also eliminates the danger of oil penetrating the skin. Plugged oil filter screens on ICPR regulators will also limit or cut-off all oil supply to the injectors.

Air Entrained in Oil

Oil containing many air bubbles will not properly transmit injection force through the amplifier piston. Air entrained in oil is also detected by measuring the duty cycle of the pressure regulator, as oil containing high amounts of air will cause the ICPR duty cycle to lengthen. Air also causes injection control pressure to become unstable, and wide variations to control pressure are observed when the engine is running.

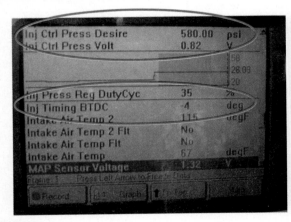

FIGURE 26-52 The duty cycle of the ICPR regulates oil pressure to the injectors. Observing oil pressure stability and the duty cycle provides important diagnostic information.

Another diagnostic test to determine whether oil is aerating is performed by monitoring the injection control pressure while operating the engine at high idle for three minutes. If oil begins to aerate, the duty cycle of the ICPR will increase, rather than fall. This happens because the control system compensates for a loss in pressure caused by aeration of oil. In Caterpillar engines, a diagnostic menu enables a technician to change the injection control pressure by stepping it up or down. The oil pressure's stability and the duty cylinder needed to maintain the oil pressure is carefully checked against expected values. Once again, too long an on-time for the ICPR and unstable oil pressure point to problems with oil quality, worn high-pressure pumps, or high-pressure oil leakage.

SKILL DRILL 26-2 Performing an ICPR Test

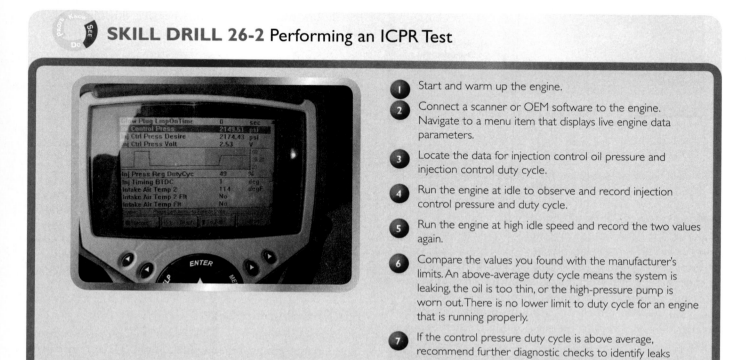

1. Start and warm up the engine.

2. Connect a scanner or OEM software to the engine. Navigate to a menu item that displays live engine data parameters.

3. Locate the data for injection control oil pressure and injection control duty cycle.

4. Run the engine at idle to observe and record injection control pressure and duty cycle.

5. Run the engine at high idle speed and record the two values again.

6. Compare the values you found with the manufacturer's limits. An above-average duty cycle means the system is leaking, the oil is too thin, or the high-pressure pump is worn out. There is no lower limit to duty cycle for an engine that is running properly.

7. If the control pressure duty cycle is above average, recommend further diagnostic checks to identify leaks caused by defective injector O-rings or worn pumps.

Wrap-Up

Ready for Review

- One of the first and largest evolutionary steps of modern high-pressure diesel injection technology was the development of hydraulically actuated electronic unit injection (HEUI) systems.
- The primary disadvantage of traditional mechanical systems was their reliance on a camshaft to pressurize fuel. A second disadvantage was their limited capability to adapt injection events to continuously changing engine and vehicle operating conditions.
- The HEUI system was developed to ensure peak injection pressure independent of engine speed, meaning that maximum spray-in pressure is available whether the engine is operating at idle or maximum rpm.
- During hard acceleration or sudden load changes at low speeds, the system can instantly adjust fuel pressurization to best match combustion conditions while minimizing emissions.
- Instead of using cam lobes, springs, flyweights, and levers to operate, HEUI systems use sensors, software code, microprocessors, and electrical signals, achieving more precise control of injection events than any previous system.
- HEUI systems replace the mechanical camshaft with highly pressurized lubrication oil. This oil actuates the plungers that pressurize fuel for injection. Oil pressure is multiplied inside the injector using an amplifier piston.
- Because the functions of pressurization, metering, timing, and atomization are all incorporated into a single injector body, HEUI injectors are classified as unit injectors.
- Injection pressures are regulated by varying the oil pressure supplied to the injectors. This regulation of oil pressures enables control of injection pressure to match engine operational requirements.
- HEUI system components are interchangeable with a large variety of engine sizes, cylinders, and applications. Whether the engine is used in power generation, off-road equipment, an ambulance, a pick-up, a delivery vehicle, or a dump truck, many of the same components are used.
- Developments in HEUI technology have improved the ability to shape the rate of fuel injection, thus reducing combustion noise and emissions for quieter, cleaner engine operation.
- HEUI technology provides the potential to integrate valve-train operation into the high-pressure oil actuation system. Instead of using a camshaft to operate valves, electro-hydraulic actuation of intake and exhaust valves is possible.
- The HEUI system has four major subsystems: the HEUI injectors, a low-pressure oil system, a high-pressure injection actuation system, and an electronic control system.
- HEUI injectors use highly pressurized engine oil to provide injection force. Four basic variations of these injectors exist.
- Both type A and B split shot injectors have four major components that operate together for precise metering, timing, and rate control. The components are the high-voltage electric solenoid, the poppet valve, the intensifier piston and plunger, and the nozzle assembly.
- The three stages of injection in the HEUI A and B injector are the fill cycle, injection, and the end of injection. Injection quantity is determined by the amount of plunger travel.
- Injection timing adjustments are made by changing the points at which energization of the injector solenoid begins and ends. Optimal injection timing is calculated by the ECM.
- Injection rate refers to the quantity of fuel injected per degree of crank angle rotation. Rate control is the ability of the fuel system to adjust the quantity of fuel injected during the injection sequence.
- HEUI B split shot and PRIME injectors can inject a small quantity of fuel to the combustion chamber 8–to–10 degrees before the main injection. This pilot injection begins to burn before the main injection arrives. The result is a combustion chamber with a burning flame front that quickly ignites fuel in the main injection.
- The second-generation (Gen II or G2) injector uses digital control valve technology. This valve technology replaced the poppet valve used in HEUI A and B injectors. When open, this valve allows oil to flow from the high-pressure oil rail into the injector, pushing the intensifier piston and plunger downward. When closed, it allows oil to drain out of the injector.
- Gen II injector operation is similar to the earlier HEUI injector amplifier piston, also called the intensifier piston. The difference between the surface area on top of the piston and the bottom multiplies fuel pressure below the piston.
- The Gen II injector has three main events during an injection cycle: fill, main injection, and end of main injection.
- Similar to other HEUI injectors, the Gen II plunger travel determines injection quantity. To change the rate of fuel delivery, the oil pressure to the injector is electronically controlled by the ECM. The Gen II injector is able to rapidly open and close the spool valve several times during the course of one injection sequence, resulting in extremely precise rate control.
- The high-pressure oil actuation system used by HEUI systems has several major subsystems: a low-pressure oil supply, oil reservoirs, a high-pressure pump, and injection control pressure regulation.
- All HEUI engines share lubrication oil with the engine's lubrication system. Lube oil supplies the separate high-pressure oil supply capacity of oil for the high-pressure circuit.

▶ Two configurations are used to supply the high-pressure pump from the oil reservoirs: a short-circuit supply and a filtered supply.

▶ The high-pressure oil actuation system (or injection control circuit) delivers engine oil under high pressure to actuate the fuel injectors.

▶ The drive torque used to pressurize oil in the high-pressure pump is provided by the engine. Because the pump output is not phased with the injection event, low torque (in comparison to other injection systems) is required to operate the pump.

▶ Oil pressure is regulated using an ECM controlled, pulse-width modulated pressure regulator. This injection control pressure regulator (ICPR) device is an electromagnetically controlled spool valve that moves in response to the strength of a magnetic field. The oil pressure for injection actuation is adjusted as the ECM changes the current flow through a coil surrounding the spool valve.

▶ These engines' information-processing functions are similar to those of other electronically governed diesels. Input devices collect data and send electrical signals to the ECM. The ECM processes the information and generates outputs based on control algorithms, stored data, and software instructions.

▶ Because the HEUI injectors require substantial amounts of current, a separate control module is often used to minimize electrical interference in the ECM.

▶ If there is an oil leak in a HEUI control system, engine performance will be significantly affected. Leaks can cause rough running, low power, high fuel consumption, and even failure to start.

▶ Because the HEUI fuel injectors are electronically controlled and use high-pressure lube oil for actuation, oil quality is critical. The correct viscosity and grade of oil are important to proper HEUI operation. Oil contaminated with water, fuel, dirt, or other contaminants will lead to premature wear and malfunctioning injectors.

▶ An unusually high duty cycle indicates that the ECM is compensating for oil leakage by increasing on-time for the pressure regulator. Longer on-time means that less oil returns to the sump and more oil is delivered to the high-pressure circuit. Observing the actual duty cycle and comparing it to the expected values is one of the most useful tests to detect oil leakage.

▶ Technicians must use visual checks to determine if oil is bypassing injector O-rings and entering the fuel.

▶ Leaking injector O-rings, jumper tubes, and manifolds are sometimes located during engine operation. Oil leaking around an injector is not normal and indicates O-ring leakage.

▶ Oil containing many air bubbles will not properly transmit injection force through the amplifier piston. Air also causes injection control pressure to become unstable. Air entrained in oil can be detected by measuring the duty cycle of the pressure regulator. Oil containing high amounts of air will cause the ICPR duty cycle to lengthen. Another diagnostic test is to monitor the injection control pressure while operating the engine at high idle for three minutes. If oil begins to aerate, the duty cycle of the ICPR will increase.

Vocabulary Builder

acoustic wave attenuation (AWA) A hydraulic wave-dampening device that minimizes a rhythmic cackling noise at idle caused by high-pressure pump pressure waves synchronizing with injection events.

cam-less diesel A system that uses electro-hydraulic actuation of intake and exhaust valves instead of using a camshaft to operate valves.

digital control valve The valve technology that replaced the poppet valve used in the HEUI A and HEUI B designs; the digital nature of the valve refers to the position of the control valve—it is either open or closed.

Gen II HEUI The newer generation of HEUI that replaced the poppet valve and solenoid with a lighter, faster-acting spool valve and two magnetic coils; also known as G2 HEUI.

HEUI A The earliest HEUI injector without split shot or pilot injection capabilities.

HEUI B A later version of the first-generation HEUI injectors with PRIME metering or split shot, pilot injection capabilities.

HIB-300 Caterpillar's second-generation HEUI injector.

high-efficiency pump (HEP) An innovative oil pump used by Caterpillar in which output pressure is matched to the pressure desired by the ECM based on operating conditions (i.e., load, speed, temperature, and so on) and OEM-specific fuel maps stored in the ECM using a PWM-controlled displacement control valve.

injection control pressure regulator (ICPR) An electrically operated spool valve that moves in response to the strength of a magnetic field; by changing the current flow through a coil surrounding the spool valve, the oil pressure for injection actuation is adjusted.

injection control pressure (ICP) sensor A sensor located in the high-pressure oil circuit that provides closed-loop feedback to the ECM about whether the oil pressure is too low or high.

injector drive module (IDM) A module on some first-generation and Gen II HEUIs that operates and monitors injector operation. It stores information such as engine firing order and operating and diagnostic software instructions; also known as the fuel injection control module (FICM) on later models of HEUI engines.

injection rate control The control of fuel delivery volume per degree of crank angle rotation into the cylinder during an injection event.

intensifier piston A piston that multiplies the force of high pressure oil pressure and is used to pressurize fuel to injection pressure; also known as the amplifier piston.

oil manifold A component that supplies oil through the top of the injectors and eliminates the problem with O-ring leakage when oil is supplied though the cylinder head.

pilot injection A small injection event taking place 8–10 degrees before the main injection event.

poppet valve A valve that controls the flow of oil into and out of HEUI A and B injectors.

split shot injection An injection strategy that delivers fuel in two distinct events during one combustion cycle; also known as pre-injection metering (PRIME) and pilot injection.

Review Questions

1. The _____ is the technology that replaced the poppet valve used in the HEUI A and HEUI B designs.
   a. split shot injection
   b. digital control valve
   c. cam-less diesel
   d. injection rate control

2. _____ is a system that uses electrohydraulic actuation of intake and exhaust valves to operate valves.
   a. Cam-less diesel
   b. Injection rate control
   c. Split shot injection
   d. Injection control pressure regulation

3. _____ is an injection strategy that delivers fuel in two distinct events during on combustion cycle.
   a. Cam-less diesel
   b. Injection control pressure regulator
   c. Injection rate control
   d. Split shot injection

4. The _____ is an electrically operated spool valve that moves in response to the strength of a magnetic field.
   a. injector drive module
   b. injection control pressure regulator
   c. digital control valve
   d. injection rate controller

5. The energization time of a(n) _____ injector is measured in microseconds.
   a. HEUI A
   b. HIB-300
   c. Gen II HEUI
   d. HEUI B

6. Lower combustion chamber noise, Lower NO_x emissions, and fewer particulate emissions are benefits to using a(n) _____.
   a. cam-less diesel
   b. injection rate control
   c. split shot injection strategy
   d. digital control valve

7. The HEUI B injector is distinguished by its _____ solenoid.
   a. silver
   b. gray
   c. black
   d. white

8. Fuel below the _____ is injected at a factor 7 to 10 times higher than oil pressure.
   a. injector drive model
   b. amplifier piston
   c. fuel injection control module
   d. fuel plunger

9. The _____ injector uses digital valve technology.
   a. Gen II HEUI
   b. HEUI A
   c. HEUI B
   d. HIB-300

10. The _____ is capable of five different injection rate shapes and an electrically controlled pilot injection.
    a. Gen II HEUI
    b. HIB-300
    c. HEUI A
    d. HEUI B

ASE-Type Questions

1. Technician A says the only benefit to using a split shot injection strategy is lower combustion chamber noise. Technician B says that there are other benefits to using the split shot injection strategy, including lower NO_x emissions and fewer particulate emissions. Who is correct?
   a. Technician A
   b. Technician B
   c. Both Technician A and Technician B
   d. Neither Technician A nor Technician B

2. Technician A says the purpose of the amplifier piston is to operate and monitor injector operation. Technician B says the purpose of the injector drive module and the fuel injection control module is to operate and monitor injector operation. Who is correct?
   a. Technician A
   b. Technician B
   c. Both Technician A and Technician B
   d. Neither Technician A nor Technician B

3. Technician A says the Gen II HEUI injector uses sequential valve technology. Technician B says the Gen II HEUI uses digital valve technology. Who is correct?
   a. Technician A
   b. Technician B
   c. Both Technician A and Technician B
   d. Neither Technician A nor Technician B

4. Technician A says the HIB-300 injector is capable of four different injection rate shapes and an electrically controlled pilot injection. Technician B says the HIB-300 injector is capable of three different injection rate shapes and an electrically controlled pilot injection. Who is correct?
   a. Technician A
   b. Technician B
   c. Both Technician A and Technician B
   d. Neither Technician A nor Technician B

5. Technician A says the use of oil manifolds supplying oil through the top of the injectors eliminates the problem with O-ring leakage when oil is supplied through the cylinder head. Technician B says oil viscosity influences the operation of the HEUI systems. Who is correct?
   a. Technician A
   b. Technician B
   c. Both Technician A and Technician B
   d. Neither Technician A nor Technician B

6. Technician A says the advantage of retarding the main injection is a reduction of oxides of nitrogen emissions. Technician B says a reduction in cylinder pressure is the advantage of retarding the main injection. Who is correct?
   a. Technician A
   b. Technician B
   c. Both Technician A and Technician B
   d. Neither Technician A nor Technician B

7. Technician A says HEUI engines use electronic engine sensors to control injection. Technician B says HEUI engines use cam lobes to control injection. Who is correct?
   a. Technician A
   b. Technician B
   c. Both Technician A and Technician B
   d. Neither Technician A nor Technician B

8. Technician A says an oil circuit that does not pass through a filter is called a short-circuit supply. Technician B says the short-circuit supply connects the main oil gallery to the reservoir. Who is correct?
   a. Technician A
   b. Technician B
   c. Both Technician A and Technician B
   d. Neither Technician A nor Technician B

9. Technician A says HEUIs have the capability to achieve maximum injection pressures of 29,000-32,000 psi. Technician B says HEUIs have the capability to achieve maximum injection pressures of 33,000-39,000 psi. Who is correct?
   a. Technician A
   b. Technician B
   c. Both Technician A and Technician B
   d. Neither Technician A nor Technician B

10. Technician A says the HEUI system used by the C7 and C9 ACERT had a Caterpillar-developed injector designated the HIB-300. Technician B says the HEUI system used by the C7 and C9 ACERT had a Caterpillar-developed injector designated the HEUI B. Who is correct?
    a. Technician A
    b. Technician B
    c. Both Technician A and Technician B
    d. Neither Technician A nor Technician B

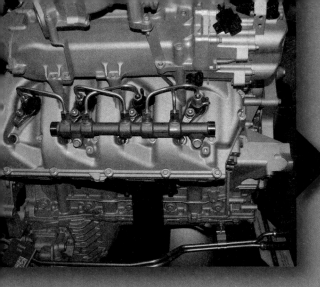

NATEF Tasks

Diesel Engines

General

- Identify engine fuel, oil, coolant, air, and other leaks; determine needed action. (pp 800–805)
- Check engine no cranking, cranks but fails to start, hard starting, and starts but does not continue to run problems; determine needed action. (pp 798, 800, 803–804)
- Identify engine surging, rough operation, misfiring, low power, slow deceleration, slow acceleration, and shutdown problems; determine needed action. (pp 786, 800, 803)
- Check and record electronic diagnostic codes. (pp xxx–xxx)

Fuel System

Electronic Fuel Management System

- Interface with vehicle's on-board computer; perform diagnostic procedures using electronic service tool(s) (to include PC-based software and/or data scan tools); determine needed action. (pp 800–805)
- Check and record electronic diagnostic codes and trip/operational data; monitor electronic data; clear codes; determine further diagnosis. (p 804)
- Perform on-engine inspections and tests on high pressure common rail (HPCR) type injection systems; determine needed action. (pp 800–806)

Knowledge Objectives

After reading this chapter, you will be able to:

1. Describe the functions and construction of common rail fuel systems and subsystem components. (pp 774–801)
2. Explain the operation of common rail fuel systems. (pp 774–801)
3. Identify and describe various types of common rail fuel systems. (pp 777–796)
4. Identify and describe inspection, testing, and diagnostic procedures for common rail fuel systems. (pp 801–808)
5. Recommend maintenance, reconditioning, or repairs of common rail fuel systems. (pp 801–808)

Skills Objectives

After reading this chapter, you will be able to:

1. Measure injector back leakage. (pp 806)
   SKILL DRILL 27-1
2. Measure injector back leakage from defective injectors without individual return lines to return

fuel through the cylinder head. (pp 806)
   SKILL DRILL 27-2
3. Measure fuel leakage from other fuel system components. (pp 807) **SKILL DRILL 27-3**

▶ Introduction

Common rail fuel injection is the most recent development in high-pressure injection systems, and it is currently used by the majority of diesel engines. First used in European automotive production in 1997, the features and benefits of common rail fuel systems have made it the injection system of choice for all light- and medium-duty and most heavy-duty on-highway diesel engines, plus a large portion of tier-four non-road engines.

▶ Fundamentals of Common Rail Fuel Systems

The basic concept of common rail injection is simple: supply fuel at injection pressure to a fuel nozzle that electrically controls the injection event **FIGURE 27-1**. Although the concept of supplying a constant high-pressure fuel supply to individual injectors is not new, the technology used to switch fuel delivery on and off at

pressures now in excess of 37,500 psi (2586 bar), while precisely metering the correct quantity of fuel for injection, was a breakthrough in manufacturing achievements. The system's metering precision, spray-in pressures, and injection event control enable dramatic reduction in exhaust emissions and fuel consumption while enabling performance superior to spark ignition engines. The common rail system's modular design lends flexibility for adaptation to any new or updated diesel engine design.

Common Rail Advantages

Switching high-pressure fuel with the metering precision required for diesel engine operation was the primary technological barrier to developing common rail (CR) injection systems. Current CR injection system pressures operate as high as 30,000–37,500 psi (2068–2586 bar). Multiple injection events take place during a combustion cycle and last less than 1 millisecond. In fact, many injections events take place in less than 500 microseconds.

You Are the Technician

A transit bus with a common rail engine won't start and has been towed to your shop. For some time, the engine has had prolonged cranking time before it would start. After performing visual inspections for external fuel leaks, adequate fuel level in the tank, and the condition of wiring harnesses, you measure the fuel rail pressure and find its pressure is zero. From there you begin to follow the engine manufacturer's troubleshooting steps and check for fault codes. There are a variety of codes indicating the rail pressure has been out of range dozens of times. Then you verify the low-pressure fuel supply system is supplying clean fuel at the correct volume and pressure to the high-pressure pump. The diagnostic steps indicate you should next measure back leakage from the cylinder head, high-pressure pump, and pressure relief valve on the fuel rail while the engine is cranking. As you perform the test, you discover the fuel returning from the cylinder head to the fuel tank is excessive and outside specifications. Consider the following:

1. List and describe three possible causes of excessive back leakage of fuel from the cylinder head.
2. Describe the procedure you will use to identify the source of the excessive fuel return.
3. If the complaint began shortly after a fuel injector was installed, list several possible explanations for the back leakage being out of specification.

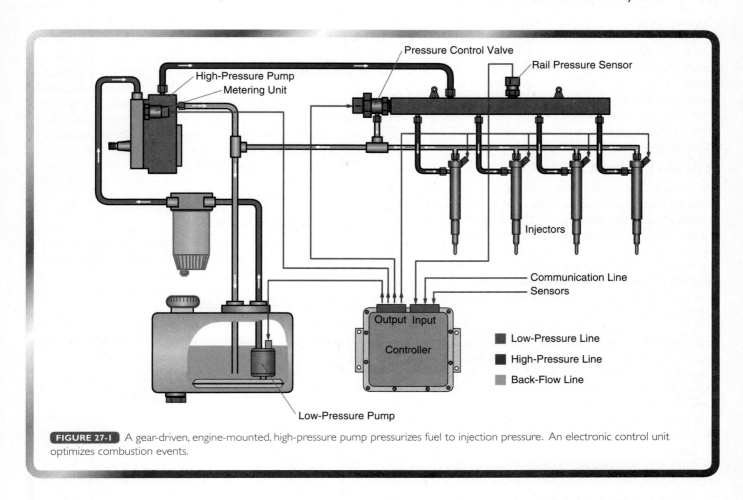

FIGURE 27-1 A gear-driven, engine-mounted, high-pressure pump pressurizes fuel to injection pressure. An electronic control unit optimizes combustion events.

Injection timing is accurate to within one-hundredths of a degree of crankshaft rotation, while shot-to-shot variations between injection quantities are well under 0.5 mm³. Enormous technical and manufacturing advances have enabled common rail systems to not only meet these rigid requirements but have combined to secure a place for diesel technology in the future.

The following sections describe the features of the CR system that make it the fuel system of choice for today's diesel engines.

Pressurization of Fuel Independent of Engine Speed

Modern common rail (CR) refers to a classification of high-pressure fuel injection systems in which pressurization of fuel is accomplished independently of engine speed. This means that regardless of engine rotational speed and load, fuel injection pressure is matched to optimal values required for the most efficient combustion, lowest emissions, highest power output, and best fuel economy **FIGURE 27-2**. Injection pressures in CR systems are also higher and more consistent during the injection event than a cam and plunger fuel pressurization systems.

Higher Pressurization

CR systems provide the highest injection pressures of any current injection system. The fourth generation of CR systems,

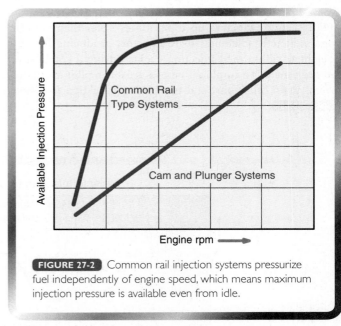

FIGURE 27-2 Common rail injection systems pressurize fuel independently of engine speed, which means maximum injection pressure is available even from idle.

the <u>**amplified common rail (ACR)**</u> injection system, reaches 37,500 psi (2586 bar). The ACR system uses a two-stage amplification of fuel pressure inside the injector that provides improved power output with lower emissions, noise, and fuel consumption, and produces a unique shape to the injection rate profile. Denso is developing CR systems with approximately 45,000 psi (3102 bar) maximum pressure. High pressurization enhances distribution and atomization of fuel in the combustion chamber for faster, leaner air–fuel mixing and lower soot formation. The result is comparatively better fuel economy, fewer emissions, improved combustion quality, and increased power.

Multiple Injection Events

The concept of switching pressurized fuel on and off with an injector-mounted solenoid has been used for decades on spark-ignition engines using multiport fuel injection. Pressures in those systems are generally below 100 psi (69 kPa). However, operating a fuel injection system at tens of thousands of pounds (bar) of pressure with the accuracy required of diesel injection made the development of CR systems difficult. Magnetic actuators are slow, especially when they are required to move relatively heavy fuel control valves inside an injector. To overcome this obstacle, CR injectors use electrical energy as the triggering or tipping force to harness the faster response and more powerful hydraulic force to control injection events. In fact, the term *servo-hydraulic actuator* given to CR injectors describes the force multiplication taking place inside a CR injector. The word *servo* refers to a control system that converts a small mechanical force or movement into a much greater force or movement. In servo-hydraulic CR injectors, control valves operate more quickly while using less energy.

Early CR injectors could manage two or three injection events during one combustion cycle. Currently, the fastest piezo CR injector can produce eight separate injection events during one combustion cycle, injecting fuel in less than 0.0001 second, which is up to six times faster than conventional magnetic solenoid valves. Injectors producing as many as eight flexibly timed injection events during a combustion cycle can include a combination of at least two pilot injections, several main injections, and two post-combustion injections **FIGURE 27-3** .

Injection Rate Shaping

The greatest advantage CR injection offers is injection <u>rate shaping</u> capabilities. CR systems can optimize the injection rate to best match engine operating conditions. Substantial reductions in exhaust emissions and fuel consumption without hurting performance result from changing injection discharge volume during the injection event. The shape of the injection discharge curve is unique to each speed and load condition **FIGURE 27-4** and **FIGURE 27-5** . Varying the injection pressure, the number of events, and when the events occur is a feature exclusive to CR injection.

Modular System Design

A shared fuel rail and separate modular components used in CR systems means the fuel system is easily adapted to different engine types. Injectors, high pressure pumps, fuel rails, and programmable ECMs are interchangeable across a wide array of engine platforms **FIGURE 27-6** .

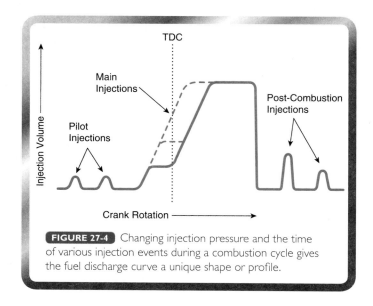

FIGURE 27-4 Changing injection pressure and the time of various injection events during a combustion cycle gives the fuel discharge curve a unique shape or profile.

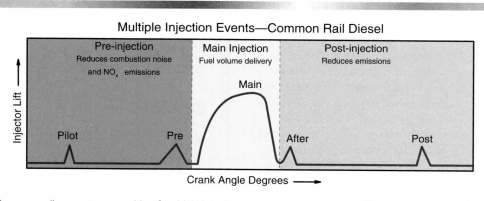

FIGURE 27-3 Common rail systems are capable of multiple injection events during one combustion cycle. This graph shows five different injection events during one combustion cycle.

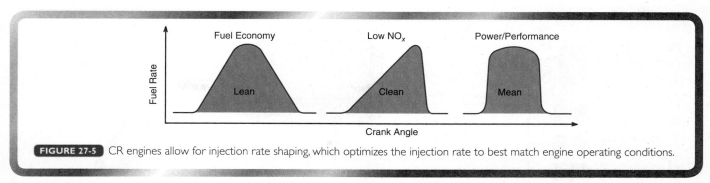

FIGURE 27-5 CR engines allow for injection rate shaping, which optimizes the injection rate to best match engine operating conditions.

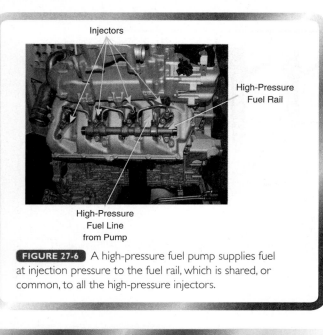

FIGURE 27-6 A high-pressure fuel pump supplies fuel at injection pressure to the fuel rail, which is shared, or common, to all the high-pressure injectors.

Safety

Never crack open an injector line on a CR system with the engine running. This is a common practice in pump-line-nozzle (PLN) injection systems to detect misfiring cylinders. However, because the fuel pressure rail is common to all cylinders in a CR system, it will not identify a misfire. Instead, opening a fuel line will drop fuel pressure to all injectors. These systems can develop pressures as high as 30,000 psi (2068 bar); fuel can stream out at this high pressure, which will easily cut and penetrate the skin and cause serious bodily harm, and may even lead to blood poisoning. Appropriate safety equipment should be worn to prevent injury.

Safety

Never attempt repairs of high-pressure fuel leaks while an engine is in operation! Instead, gradually decrease fuel pressure by slowly loosening a covered line or a specialized line dedicated to bleeding pressure gradually from the system. These lines have a diagonal groove cut into the fitting threads to allow fuel to leak from the fitting before the line is disconnected. When checking for leaks, use a piece of cardboard rather than your hand to detect the origin of spraying fuel.

Defining Features of High-Pressure Common Rail

What is generally referred to today as a common rail injection system is more precisely termed high-pressure accumulator rail system or high-pressure common rail (HPCR). The defining features of HPCR injection systems are:

- A tube or rail that stores fuel pressurized to match optimal injection pressure for any given engine speed or load condition. Fuel injectors are connected to the rail with individual lines, which means the injectors share fuel pressure supplied from the rail. The shared fuel rail lends the system the name *common* rail.
- Electrical actuators incorporated into each fuel injector that control the opening and closing of a nozzle valve for metering, timing, and rate shaping of injection events.
- An engine-driven high-pressure fuel pump that pressurizes fuel transfer pressure to injection pressure and supplies the high-pressure fuel rail. Because the rail can store enough fuel volume at injection pressure to supply several injection events, it is also called an accumulator rail.
- Microprocessor control of fuel system operation **FIGURE 27-7**.

Electronic pressure regulation of the high-pressure pump permits injection pressures to vary with speed and load conditions with maximum pressures available from idle speed. Combined with operational features of the unique CR fuel injector, the most flexible rate shaping of injection events are possible with HPCR fuel systems. CR systems pressurizing fuel are otherwise primarily classified by the type of injector at the heart of the system **FIGURE 27-8**.

Regardless of the manufacturer, current CR systems share several elements **FIGURE 27-9**:

- High-pressure stage consisting of fuel pump with pressure regulator
- High pressure fuel rail with rail pressure sensor and pressure-regulating valves
- Fuel injectors
- Electronic control system
- Short fuel lines connecting a pressurized fuel rail to the injectors

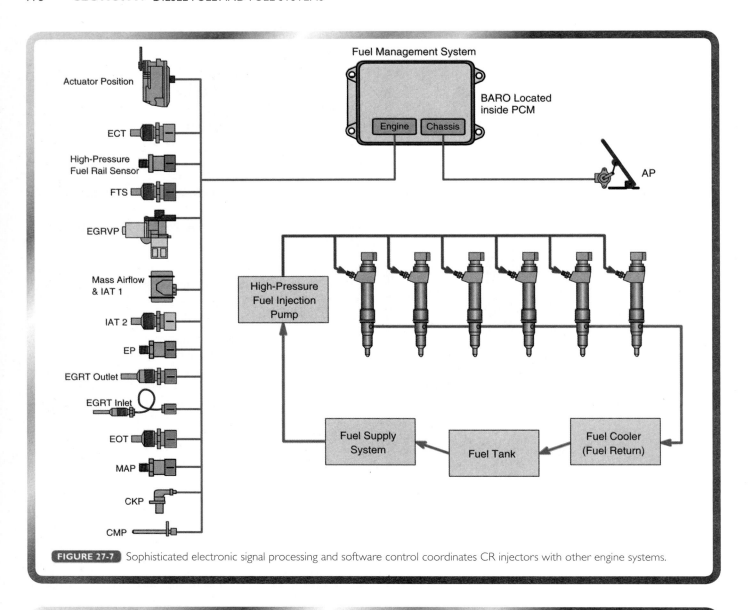

FIGURE 27-7 Sophisticated electronic signal processing and software control coordinates CR injectors with other engine systems.

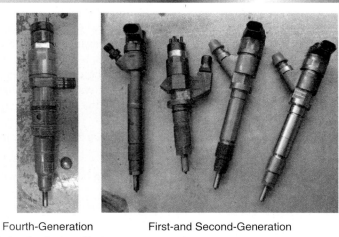

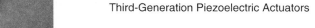

Third-Generation Piezoelectric Actuators

Fourth-Generation   First-and Second-Generation
Hydraulically Amplified   Servo Actuators

FIGURE 27-8 There are four generations of common rail injectors, which incorporate technology for faster switching, better rate shaping, lower emissions, improved fuel economy, and power output.

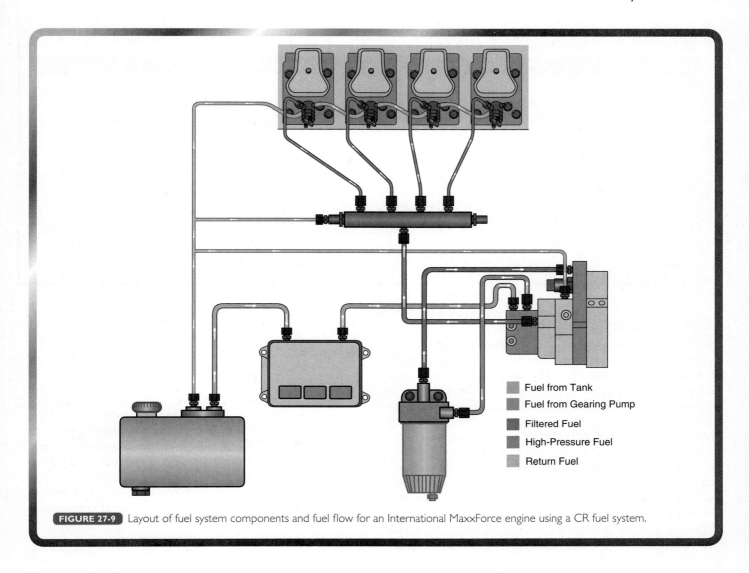

FIGURE 27-9 Layout of fuel system components and fuel flow for an International MaxxForce engine using a CR fuel system.

Legend:
- Fuel from Tank
- Fuel from Gearing Pump
- Filtered Fuel
- High-Pressure Fuel
- Return Fuel

► Types of CR Fuel Systems

While the principles of common rail systems are the same for all injection systems, applications range from small automotive engines to large, heavy-duty engines in ships and locomotives. To suit an engine's power requirements, CR systems use a variety of high-pressure pumps with different flow and pressure outputs, injectors with a variety of control valves and injection rate capabilities. This next section outlines the range of system designs used by today's engines.

Injector Requirements

All CR injectors are designed with the following common requirements:

- Flexible injection pressure independent of engine speed
- Very high injection pressure for optimal fuel atomization and distribution
- Flexible timing of beginning and end of injection
- Flexible timing of multiple injections
- Small, consistent injection quantities for pilot and post-injection sequences
- Rapid nozzle valve opening velocities to provide highest momentum to fuel spray for finest atomization
- Low injection rate during ignition delay period to minimize combustion noise
- Rapid increase in injection rate after the start of combustion
- Rapid decrease in injection rate at the end of injection accompanied by high nozzle valve closing velocity to maintain finest fuel atomization and minimize nozzle dribble
- Compact design to permit centralized location of injector in combustion chamber

Types of Common Rail Injectors

There are three main types of CR injectors with a variety of subcategories. With each new generation there are improvements to hydraulic control, increased pressurization, greater timing precision, and number of injection events with successive generations **TABLE 27-1**.

TABLE 27-1: Successive Development of CR Systems

Injector Generation	Pump	Injector	Injector Technology	Maximum Pressure	Application
Generation 1 Bosch	N/A	CRI-1	Ball valve	19,845 psi (1368 bar)	Automobile
Generation 2	CP2 CP3	CRI-2	Ball valve	23,520 psi (1622 bar)	Commercial vehicle
Generation 3	CP4.1, 4.2	CRI-3	Piezoceramic actuator	29,400 psi (2027 bar)	Commercial vehicle
Generation 4 HADIS	CPN5	CRSN-4 CRI-4	Spindle valve (amplified common rail)	36,750 psi (2534 bar)	Commercial vehicle
Generation 1 Denso	N/A	N/A	N/A	21,315 psi (1470 bar)	Automotive
Generation 2 Denso	HP2, HP3, HP4	N/A	N/A	26,460 psi (1824 bar)	Automotive/commercial
Delphi Multec	N/A	N/A	Servo-hydraulic	36,750 psi (2534 bar)	Automotive commercial
Delphi Direct Acting	N/A	DFI3	Piezoceramic actuator	36,750 psi (2534 bar)	Automotive/commercial
Siemens	N/A	N/A	Piezoceramic actuator	21,750 psi (1500 bar)	Automotive

Electro-Hydraulic Solenoids

CR injectors use solenoid valves relying on electromagnetic servo-hydraulic principles to control injection events **FIGURE 27-10**. These injectors are manufactured by Bosch, Delphi, and Denso. Though the technology is older, electro-hydraulic control of CR injectors is used on most current medium- and heavy-duty diesels for a number of reasons, including cost and durability. Servo-hydraulic actuators are more durable than piezoceramic actuators, which have greater wear rates. While servo-hydraulic mechanisms do wear, particularly ball valves in first- and second-generation injectors, the sliding motion of piezoceramic layers over one another during injection events shortens the life of the piezoceramic actuators. Longer or taller stacks of the material are needed to extend the service life. A second reason for using servo-hydraulic actuators on medium- and heavy-duty diesels is that the engine speeds are lower.

Because most heavy-duty engines do not commonly exceed 2100 rpm, the servo-hydraulic actuators are able to respond faster and with an adequate number of injection events.

Piezoceramic Electric Actuators

Instead of using electromagnetic coils to control injector operation, hundreds of thin piezoceramic wafers can form the actuator mechanism for improved control of injection events **FIGURE 27-11** and **FIGURE 27-12**. These materials will instantly change shape when electric signals are applied. Evidence for the fast response time of piezoceramic actuators is seen in the construction of high-frequency speaker tweeters used in sound systems. Current applied to piezoelectric crystals is

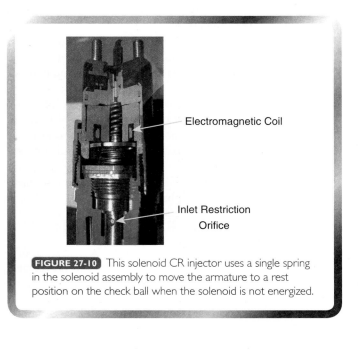

FIGURE 27-10 This solenoid CR injector uses a single spring in the solenoid assembly to move the armature to a rest position on the check ball when the solenoid is not energized.

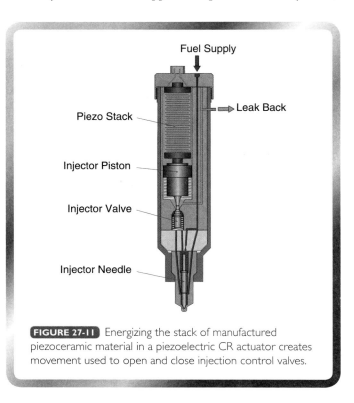

FIGURE 27-11 Energizing the stack of manufactured piezoceramic material in a piezoelectric CR actuator creates movement used to open and close injection control valves.

Ceramic
Piezoelectric Stack

FIGURE 27-12 This direct-acting CR injector places a piezoelectric actuator close to the injector nozzle for faster and more accurate response.

used to move a speaker cone at very high frequencies where electromagnet coils and permanent magnet configurations of other speakers are not capable. Using piezoceramic materials crystals rather than magnetic actuators avoids the problem of injection lag caused by slow build-up and collapse of magnetic fields and reactive inductance **FIGURE 27-13**. Without magnetic fields, piezoceramic actuators respond much more rapidly to current flow. The material also has a polarity, which means the polarity of the charge applied to the stack will increase or decrease the stack length. Sending DC current in one direction and then reversing the polarity causes instantaneous change in the injector's control valve **FIGURE 27-14**. With a faster response time, more injection events can take place during a combustion cycle with a shorter interval between injections than with servo-hydraulic actuators **FIGURE 27-15**. Bosch, Delphi, Denso, and Siemens manufacture piezoceramic injectors.

Hydraulically Amplified Common Rail

Hydraulically amplified CR injectors are the most recent CR innovation and were introduced in 2008. Bosch calls this system **hydraulically amplified diesel injection system** or **HADIS** **FIGURE 27-16**. These injectors are used by Detroit Diesel in the DD series heavy-duty diesel engines using the amplified common rail (ACR) fuel system **FIGURE 27-17**. CRI-4 injectors (Bosch's model name for to Detroit's ACR injectors)

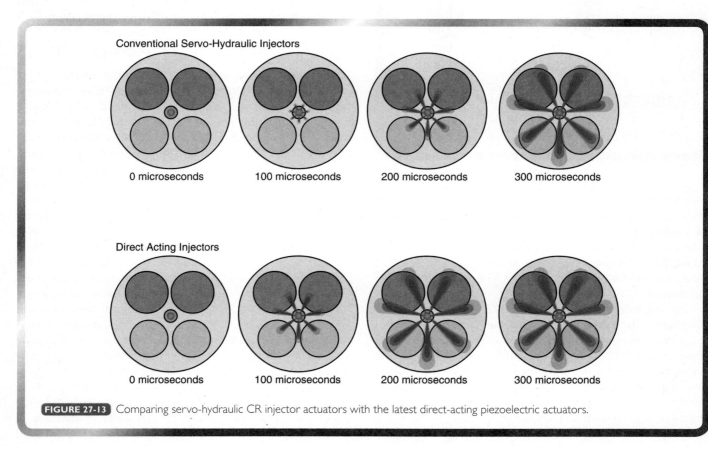

FIGURE 27-13 Comparing servo-hydraulic CR injector actuators with the latest direct-acting piezoelectric actuators.

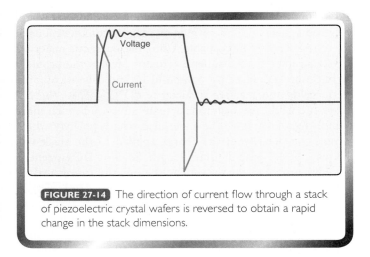

FIGURE 27-14 The direction of current flow through a stack of piezoelectric crystal wafers is reversed to obtain a rapid change in the stack dimensions.

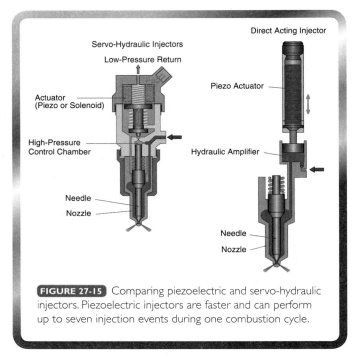

FIGURE 27-15 Comparing piezoelectric and servo-hydraulic injectors. Piezoelectric injectors are faster and can perform up to seven injection events during one combustion cycle.

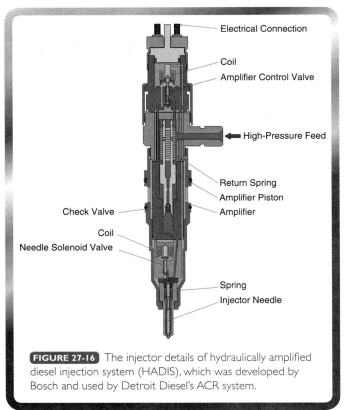

FIGURE 27-16 The injector details of hydraulically amplified diesel injection system (HADIS), which was developed by Bosch and used by Detroit Diesel's ACR system.

are currently capable of injection pressures as high as 37,500 psi (2586 bar) by multiplying pressure inside the injector using an amplifier piston. This concept of pressure intensification is similar to HEUI fuel systems, though one major exception is that the HEUI system uses high-pressure oil as the force to pressurize fuel for injection, and the CRI4 uses high-pressure fuel instead.

An amplifier piston inside the CRI4 injector multiplies fuel pressure by a factor of 2:1. One significant advantage of using internal pressure amplification is lowered mechanical stress on fuel system components such as pumps, lines, and valves due to a reduction in fuel pressure outside the injector. Two-stage amplification of fuel pressure inside this injector provides improved power output with lower emissions, less noise, and reduced fuel consumption. A unique injection rate shape is also within the capabilities of this system. More

detailed coverage of Detroit's ACR system and the operation of this injector are included in the Detroit Diesel chapter.

Bosch Common Rail Injectors

Bosch has developed four generations of CR injectors, three of which are currently in production vehicles. Passenger vehicles used first-generation CRS1 systems, which had a maximum injection pressure of 19,580 psi (1350 bar) and were capable of three injection events per combustion cycle. The CRS2 introduced in 2001 sprays in fuel at a maximum pressure of 23,210 psi (1600 bar) and is capable of as many as four injection events per cycle. A revised actuator design allows the second-generation CRS2 to respond to electrical signals faster and with greater precision. The third-generation CRS3 replaced electromagnetic solenoids with rapid-switching piezoceramic inline injectors. Bosch claims these injectors offer advantages of up to 20% lower emissions, 5% more power, 3% lower fuel consumption, and engine noise reduction of up to 3 decibels (dB). The faster acting injector permits shorter firing intervals between injections and even more accurate fuel metering. Adaptive cylinder balance, the strategy used to adjust cylinder pressures by modifying shot-to-shot, cylinder-to-cylinder injection quantities, is now performed over all engine speeds, not just at idle. The fourth generation is called a coaxial injector, and it uses two rows of spray holes in the nozzle tip. Modulating the voltage to the injector actuating mechanism enables different amounts of nozzle lift, which in turn changes which row of spray holes

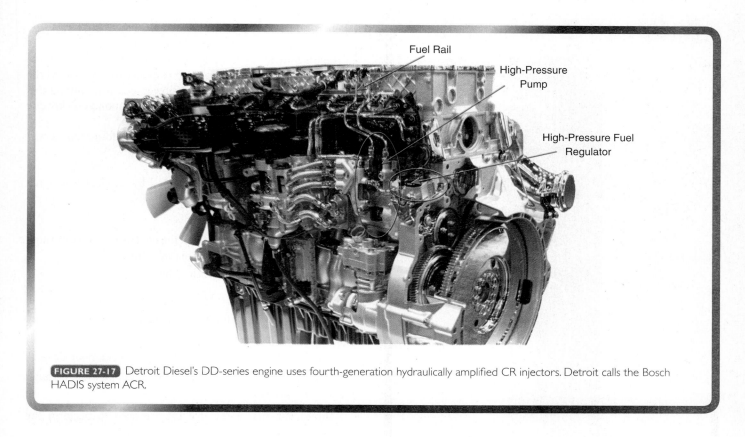

FIGURE 27-17 Detroit Diesel's DD-series engine uses fourth-generation hydraulically amplified CR injectors. Detroit calls the Bosch HADIS system ACR.

are used for injection **FIGURE 27-18**. These nozzles are able to better match fuel distribution to operating conditions.

CRS1 and CRS2: Hydraulically Balanced Nozzle Valves

CR injectors are capable of faster response due in large part to the use of hydraulically balanced nozzle valves. Hydraulically balanced nozzle valves work by applying high-pressure fuel simultaneously to both ends of a nozzle valve. If the injector is constructed with slightly more surface area on top of the nozzle valve, fuel pressure will keep the nozzle seated when

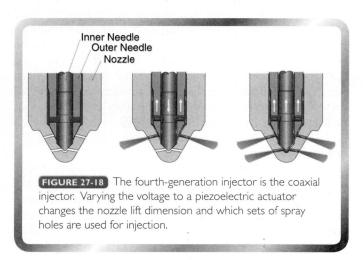

FIGURE 27-18 The fourth-generation injector is the coaxial injector. Varying the voltage to a piezoelectric actuator changes the nozzle lift dimension and which sets of spray holes are used for injection.

the engine is running. To begin an injection event and lift the nozzle valve, the slight pressure difference between the top and bottom of the valve needs only to be tipped so the pressure acting below the nozzle valve is slightly higher than pressure above. As with a conventional nozzle, high-pressure fuel lifts the nozzle. But to seat the nozzle valve and end an injection event, the pressure difference is tipped again with hydraulic pressure rather than spring force. Using high-pressure fuel closes the nozzle valve much faster than spring force. This is why nozzle springs in CR injectors are much smaller and lighter than conventional hydraulic nozzles **FIGURE 27-19**.

In Bosch's first- and second-generation CR systems, the injection events are controlled by changing the balance of hydraulic pressure acting on the nozzle needle valve using a magnetic solenoid inside the injectors. Conventional fuel systems use only high-pressure fuel to lift the nozzle valve and begin injection, but close with spring pressure. All CR injectors use high-pressure fuel to both lift and seat the nozzle valve. The ingenuity of using hydraulic pressure to both begin and end injection events gives CR injectors the ability to operate with the speed and precision they are known for. Hydraulically balanced nozzles, also called hydraulically suspended nozzles, use the small control force of the solenoid's magnetic field to tip the balance between powerful fuel rail hydraulic forces acting on the top and bottom of the injector.

Another term given to the force multiplication achieved using an electrically operated solenoid is servo action. **Servo-hydraulic** actuators multiply small electromagnetic actuator

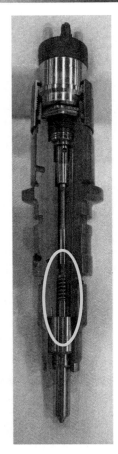

FIGURE 27-19 The nozzle spring is much smaller in a CR injector because hydraulic force does most of the work to close and seat the nozzle valve, rather than the nozzle valve spring force.

valve movement to control high-pressure injection pressures **FIGURE 27-20**.

While all common rail actuators use some kind of servo action in their control valves, servo actuators generally use electromagnetism to operate the valve. Several types of servo-hydraulic actuators are used to open and close nozzle valves. For example, Bosch uses ball valves and Siemens uses a mushroom-shaped valve. Delphi uses spindle-shaped control valves, which are also hydraulically balanced and capable of switching speeds, supplying as many as five injection events during an injection sequence. Spindle-shaped control valves are highly durable, which makes them ideal for heavy-duty diesels operating for very long distances, with thousands of engine hours between overhauls. In a de-energized state, the spindle will allow the cavity above the nozzle valve to fill with pressurized fuel from the pressure fuel rail. Energizing the valve's electromagnetic windings and moving the spindle valve very slightly causes high-pressure fuel above the nozzle in the pressure chamber to vent to the fuel return circuit **FIGURE 27-21**. Because high-pressure fuel, either below the spindle valve when it is de-energized or surrounding the valve when

it is energized, helps move the valve, servo action and force multiplication are achieved in the actuator mechanism.

Engines with lower maximum speeds can use servo-hydraulic injectors because injector response time is not as critical when rated engine speeds are slower as it is in automotive diesel engines, which require injectors that respond quickly due to their higher maximum engine rpm.

Bosch CR1 and CR2 injectors use a four-step servo-hydraulic operation to inject fuel.

1. The magnetic solenoid is actuated by an electrical signal from the control module.
2. A servo-hydraulic valve opens.
3. Fuel pressure is released from the control chamber through a small drain to low-pressure fuel return.
4. Rail pressure lifts the nozzle valve.

Ending injection is similar:

1. The electrical signal is removed from the magnetic solenoid.
2. The servo-hydraulic valve closes.
3. The drain hole from the pressure control chamber closes.
4. The pressure chamber fills with fuel at rail pressure through a small restriction orifice.

Three elements of the injector are used to perform the injection functions:

- A conventional multi-orifice spray nozzle
- A servo-hydraulic system
- A solenoid control valve

CRS1 Operation

To complete an injection event, the nozzle valve is held on its seat by the control rod or control plunger. Denso calls this component a command piston **FIGURE 27-22**. Regulating the movement of the control rod is a column of high-pressure fuel above the control rod balanced against the high-pressure fuel acting against the nozzle valve below the rod. Injection can only begin when hydraulic pressure above the control rod is relieved. Fuel pressure acting below the nozzle valve will push the nozzle upward against the control rod, allowing fuel to leave the spray holes of the nozzle. Similarly, injection ends when hydraulic pressure above the control plunger pushes the nozzle valve back onto its seat. Flow of high-pressure fuel through the drain orifice changes the small pressure differential necessary to open and close the nozzle valve. The use of an electrically controlled ball valve in the servo mechanism permits rapid control of injection events in the nozzle **FIGURE 27-23**.

Pre-injection

In a resting state with no current applied to the injector solenoid, the drain orifice is closed by spring force acting on the ball valve. Fuel pressure developed by the high-pressure pump builds in the pressure chamber above the control rod holding the control rod against the nozzle valve. The force of fuel pressure against the control rod firmly seats the nozzle valve.

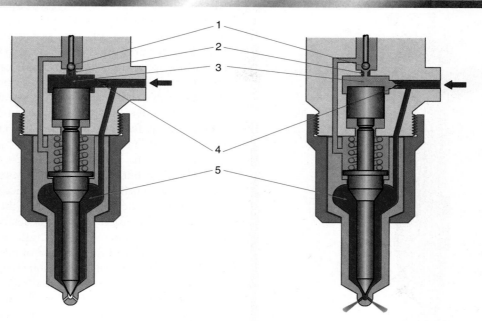

FIGURE 27-20 Fuel under high pressure is simultaneously applied to the fuel annulus (5) below the nozzle valve and the high-pressure chamber (3) above the nozzle valve. A slightly larger surface area above the nozzle valve combined with nozzle spring pressures hold the nozzle valve on its seat. When the ball valve (1) is lifted from its seat, fuel drains to the low-pressure fuel return circuit through the drain orifice (2). Pressure then drops above the nozzle valve, enabling fuel pressure to lift the nozzle valve and begin injection. When the ball valve is seated, fuel enters the inlet restriction orifice (4) and refills the pressure chamber above the nozzle valve. Hydraulic force quickly seats the nozzle valve.

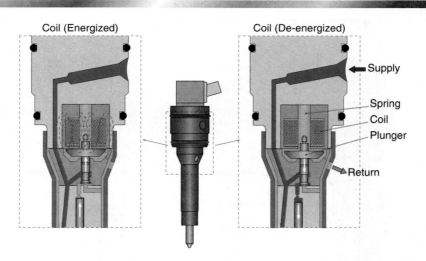

FIGURE 27-21 The spindle valve used by Delphi nozzles is a servo-hydraulic actuator that uses principles of hydraulic balance to rapidly open and close. It controls a hydraulically balanced nozzle valve.

Fuel pressure supplied to the injector by the fuel rail and lines simultaneously builds at the nozzle annulus, which is the circular chamber below the nozzle valve, but it is unable to lift the nozzle valve due to the pressure applied by the control rod.

Beginning of Injection

The injector solenoid is energized with current supplied by the fuel injector control module (FICM). In Bosch injectors, this initial amount of current can be as much as 90 volts DC, but it is typically closer to 75 volts with an average of 50 volts

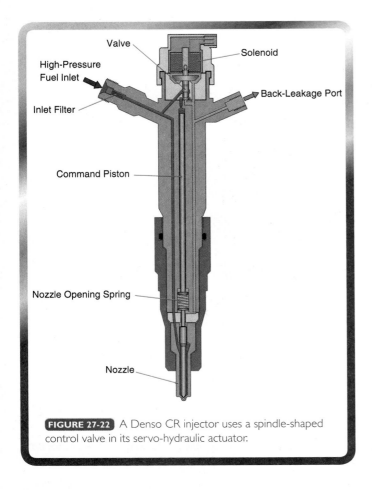

FIGURE 27-22 A Denso CR injector uses a spindle-shaped control valve in its servo-hydraulic actuator.

when the ball valve is lifted **FIGURE 27-24**. Capacitors store the charge for injection events. The magnetic force lifts the spring-loaded armature and ball valve sealing the drain orifice. Fuel flows from the pressure chamber through the drain orifice and into the low-pressure fuel return circuit leading back to the fuel tank. Consequently, pressure above the control rod drops, and the pressure below the nozzle valve immediately forces the nozzle valve from its seat to begin injection. The fully lifted nozzle valve sprays fuel into the combustion chamber at a pressure equal to the fuel rail.

The pressure drop in the pressure chamber above the control rod is controlled by the difference in the sizes of the inlet and outlet orifices. The drain orifice will always be larger than the inlet orifice to open and close the nozzle valve. While the speed of the nozzle valve lift is determined by the difference of flow rates between the drain and inlet orifices, too large a difference will slow the end of injection. Likewise, too little a difference in orifice diameters will slow the beginning of injection. The nozzle differential ratio, which is the difference in the surface area of the nozzles fuel acts on before the nozzle lifts and the wider cross-sectional area of the nozzle after it lifts, also controls nozzle lifting and closing pressures. The differential ratio ensures the nozzle opening pressure is always higher than closing pressure.

End of Injection

When current to the solenoid is shut off, the over-stroke spring inside the armature forces the check ball over the outlet orifice to close it. Closing the drain orifice causes fuel pressure to build

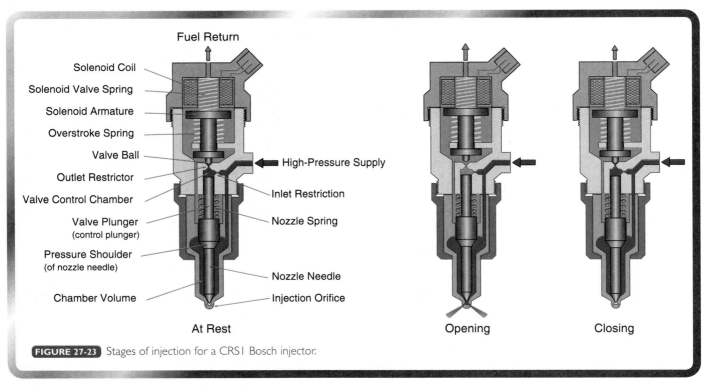

FIGURE 27-23 Stages of injection for a CRS1 Bosch injector.

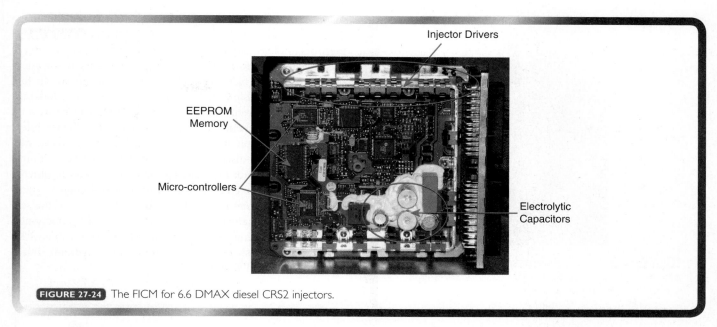

FIGURE 27-24 The FICM for 6.6 DMAX diesel CRS2 injectors.

in the pressure chamber, forcing the control rod against the nozzle valve. This effectively and rapidly ends injection as the nozzle valve is forced back against its seat using high fuel pressure. The nozzle valve closing speed is determined by the flow through the inlet orifice.

CRS2 Operation

The difference between the CRS1 and CRS2 injectors is in the armature. In the CRS1, a single spring returns the armature to a resting position, whereas the CRS2 uses two springs. The mass of the armature with the two-spring arrangement is reduced, and an over-springing effect is eliminated. CRS2 injectors can return to resting position more rapidly, thereby ending injection more quickly, which allows shorter intervals between injection events **FIGURE 27-25** and **FIGURE 27-26**.

▶ **TECHNICIAN TIP**

Corrosion, wear, or microscopic dirt particles in the ball seat of the drain/bleed orifice of CR injectors can cause major problems. Continuous leakage of fuel to the low-pressure return can prevent the needle valve from seating properly. Depending on the severity of the problem, this condition could:

- Allow the injector to continuously spray, causing the engine to run away
- Cause injector misfire
- Drain the injector and fuel rail of fuel, which can fill the cylinder with fuel during shut-down and cause a hydraulic lock on start-up
- Generate a fault code indicating an undefined leak in the fuel rail.

To identify a leaking ball valve or faulty injector, many manufactures recommend measuring the quantity of fuel retuned from the injectors. Too much leakage from a particular injector generally indicates ball/drain seat defect. Dirt and contaminants in the inlet orifice will cause identical problems.

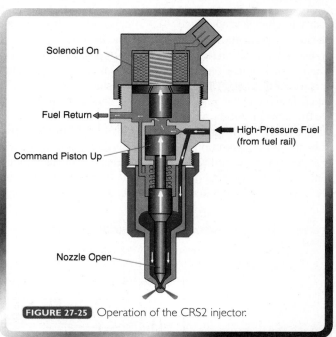

FIGURE 27-25 Operation of the CRS2 injector.

▶ **TECHNICIAN TIP**

Even the tiniest particles of dirt can prevent injector fittings from properly sealing. This is especially true with quill tube connections. It is recommended to always clean connecting surfaces with electrical contact cleaner before joining high-pressure fittings and lines.

CRS3 Piezo Injectors

Piezo technology is incorporated into all manufacturers' newer CR injectors. Piezo technology involves the replacement of magnetic solenoids with special piezoceramic material that has the

FIGURE 27-26 Two CRS2 injectors. CRS2 injectors have a more compact actuator for faster injection switching. One injector has a fuel return through the top.

shape. Movement of the stacked discs is harnessed to change the balance of hydraulic forces inside the injector **FIGURE 27-28**. Piezo technology enables the fastest switching time for injectors; it currently allows up to eight injection events in one injection sequence. In fact, piezoceramic actuators can switch fuel on and off in as little as 0.0001 second (100 microseconds). In comparison, an electromagnet's response time can be as long as 15,000 microseconds (15 milliseconds). The shorter interval between multiple injection events enables very precise rate shaping of the fuel discharge curve and even more exact control over metering. Better rate shaping capabilities result in quieter, more fuel efficient, cleaner, and more powerful engine operation. Using piezoceramics further reduces the mass of the servo-hydraulic mechanism. Bosch claims a 75% mass reduction in the CRS3's piezoceramic actuator. The CRS3 injector weighs 9.5 ounces (270 grams), as compared to the servo-hydraulic injector's 17.3 ounces (490 grams).

ability to change shape under the influence of electric current. Because no magnetic fields are induced, no **inductive resistance** or reactance (the current induced that opposes ECM current when initially energized) is produced when using piezoelectric actuators **FIGURE 27-27**. Piezoelectric crystals therefore enable much faster injector response than magnetic actuators. These are the same piezoceramic materials that can also generate electrical current when squeezed. Spark igniters used in gas barbeques are another common application for these piezo materials.

When piezoceramics are used in injectors, an electric current is passed through a **piezoceramic actuator** made of multiple layers of ceramic discs that are stacked together and change

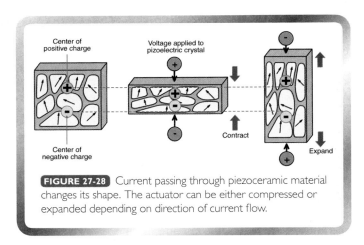

FIGURE 27-28 Current passing through piezoceramic material changes its shape. The actuator can be either compressed or expanded depending on direction of current flow.

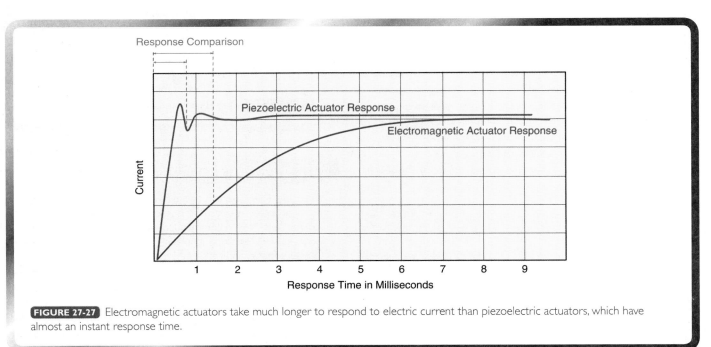

FIGURE 27-27 Electromagnetic actuators take much longer to respond to electric current than piezoelectric actuators, which have almost an instant response time.

A slice of piezoceramic material 0.02″ (508 microns [μ]) thick expands only about 0.00002″ (0.5 μ) when it reaches approximately 140 volts of electricity. By putting together hundreds of the wafers, the movement is summed together, adding up to a few thousandths of an inch of movement FIGURE 27-29. Third-generation Bosch injectors use as much as 250 volts to open and require electrical linesmen gloves as a safety precaution when working on some systems.

Not only do piezoceramic injectors have a faster response time for shorter injection lag, they also have added capabilities. Variable nozzle lift is one such special feature. By applying only a little current to the piezo stack, it only moves slightly. More current will move the stack further. By varying the current, the crystals expand proportionally more or less, enabling the use of variable lift nozzle valves. A smaller nozzle lift provides additional rate shaping capabilities, such as a longer injection duration, which sprays fuel into a cylinder over a greater number of degrees of crankshaft rotation.

CRS3 injectors made by Bosch are used in high-speed diesels such as the Ford 6.4L (391 cubic inch), which was later replaced by the midyear 2011 6.7L (409 cubic inch) PowerStroke engine (codenamed Scorpion) and the 2010 GM 6.6L (403 cubic inch) Duramax. PowerStroke CR injector nozzles made by Bosch each have eight holes and are programmed to provide five injections per combustion cycle. During cruise operation, only three or four injections are used. Two pilot injections minimize combustion noise and allow for retardation of injection timing for NO_x control. Post-combustion injections minimize soot formation by keeping cylinder temperatures and pressures high during the latter part of the power stroke. No late post-combustion injections are used to heat the exhaust after-treatment system.

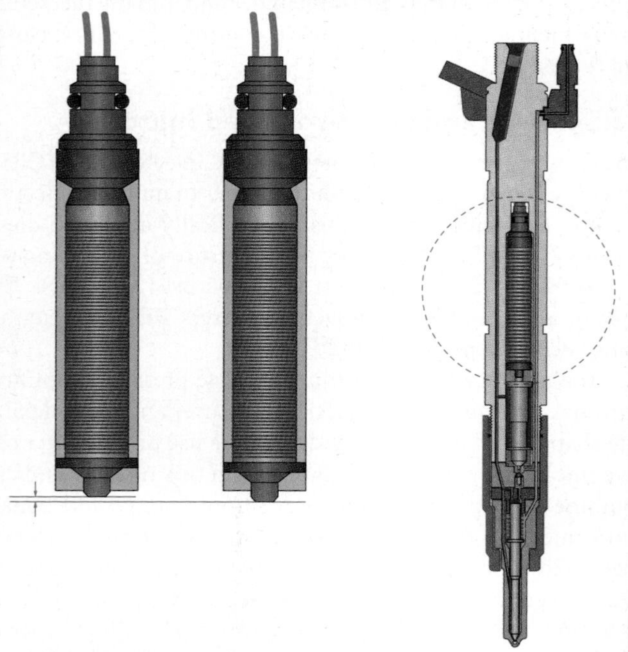

Piezo CRS3 Operation

Movement of the nozzle needle valve is controlled in a similar way to CRS1 and CRS2 injectors. That is, the balance of hydraulic pressure above the needle valve is changed. Applying current to the stacked piezoceramic wafer produces the movement and is summed and transmitted to a servo valve that controls hydraulic pressure acting directly upon the top of the nozzle valve FIGURE 27-30.

Beginning of Injection

The injector uses a servo valve that has two seats—one that closes the high-pressure fuel passage and another that controls the passage to a low-pressure fuel return to the tank. In a resting position, the nozzle valve is closed by fuel rail pressure exerted by the control chamber. When the piezoceramic actuator is activated by electrical current, it expands and causes the servo valve to move downward, closing a fuel passage supplying pressurized fuel to the control chamber. At the same time, the double-seated servo valve opens the fuel passage to the low-pressure return circuit. Fuel pressure drops in the control chamber, which flows to the fuel return passageway now opened around the servo valve. As fuel pressure in the control chamber drops, the nozzle valve is allowed to lift due to higher fuel pressure beneath the nozzle valve. Two restrictor orifices regulate fuel into and out of the control chamber. A narrower inlet restriction orifice to the control chamber prevents the chamber from filling faster than the rate fuel drains from the control chamber.

End of Injection

The end of injection takes place when the current polarity to the piezoceramic actuator is reversed, and the piezo stack contracts. The servo valve reopens the high-pressure fuel passage supply to the control chamber and simultaneously closes the low-pressure return fuel passageway. Rail pressure then builds in the control chamber, forcing the nozzle valve to its seat. Even more rapid closing of the nozzle is also accomplished by the reversal of fuel flow through a drain orifice. Fuel can fill the control chamber through both the inlet and drain orifice when the servo vale is retracted and returns to its seat against the passage for the low-pressure return circuit. The ratio of surface area above the nozzle valve in the control chamber in comparison to the surface area below the nozzle valve causes the nozzle valve to close rapidly and firmly against the nozzle valve seat.

Placing the piezoceramic stack closer to the nozzle valve minimizes injection lag caused by transmitting forces along the length of the injector through hydraulic or mechanical means. Although piezo actuators have many advantages, one disadvantage is that these actuators do wear out faster and generally will not last as long as servo-hydraulic actuators that use a ball and seat or spindle control valve. The continuous flexing and sliding movement of the ceramic discs against

FIGURE 27-29 Expanding stacks of piezoelectric crystals are used to operate third-generation Bosch CR actuators. Note the crystals expand when energized and push downward.

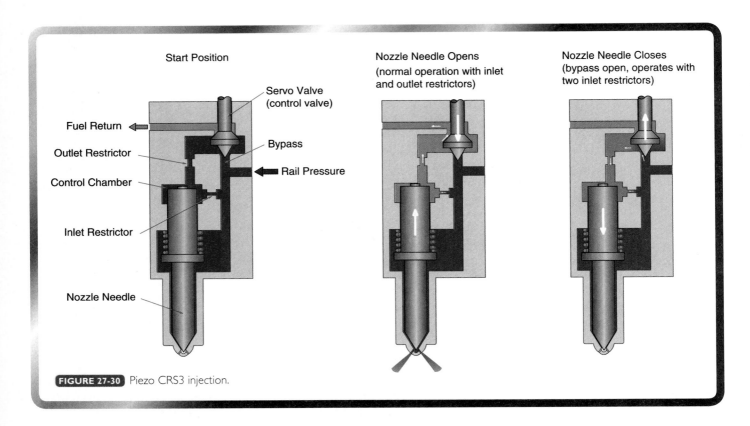

FIGURE 27-30 Piezo CRS3 injection.

one another produces friction, which wears the discs thin. To compensate for this problem, disc stacks are made longer to increase actuator reliability and longevity. On-board diagnostic algorithms measure this deterioration and help compensate for wear over the lifespan of the injector. However, to give the piezo actuator the same longevity as the best servo-hydraulic injector, the stack of discs would need to be unpractically long.

► **TECHNICIAN TIP**

One problem with electromagnetic actuators is the long response time required to build a magnetic field strong enough to move valves inside an actuator. Current used to build a magnetic field in a coil induces current flow opposing the current that initially energizes the actuator coil. Current flow opposing coil voltage is induced through magnetic self-induction. Current induction takes place because as the electromagnetic field expands, it cuts across the coils of the actuator. This effect is called inductive reactance. Eventually current used to energize the coil will produce a stable magnetic field that no longer expands. When this happens, inductive reactance stops. It can take as long as 15 milliseconds to establish a stable magnetic field. Longer response time contributes to injection lag.

CRS3 Hydraulic Coupler

The Bosch CRS3 injector incorporates a hydraulic coupler that carries out additional functions **FIGURE 27-31**. It first transfers and amplifies the intensity of the piezoceramic disc deflection to the servo control valve in the injector. Secondly, it compensates for changes to the length of the actuator mechanism caused by thermal expansion. Finally, it prevents the injector from continuously delivering fuel if an electrical fault occurs. In this case, fuel will leak out of the control chamber and into the fuel return side of the injector unless the servo control valve is first closed and reopened.

CRS4: Hydraulically Amplified Injector

One of two types of fourth-generation CR injectors is the CRS4, which uses an internal hydraulic amplifier to multiply injection pressure at a ratio of 2:1. This hydraulically amplified diesel injector (HADIS) will step up rail pressure of approximately 18,750 psi (1293 bar) to inject at 37,500 psi (2586 bar). This injector is currently used in Detroit Diesel's DD series engines using ACR systems **FIGURE 27-32**.

The primary benefit of the two-stage pressure amplification concept is its higher injection pressures and more flexible rate shaping capabilities provided by the use of two actuators. Five injection events are produced from this injector and can combine multiple pilot injections: boot, ramp, and square main injection rate shapes, as well as several post-injection events. This means an ideal injection discharge rate shape can be achieved for every operating condition to reduce fuel consumption and noxious emissions while providing superior engine performance. Currently this series of engines has the best in class fuel efficiency for class 8 vehicles.

Another advantage of pressure amplification takes place only inside the injector. The highest injection pressure is limited to the injector nozzle where the maximum pressure is required,

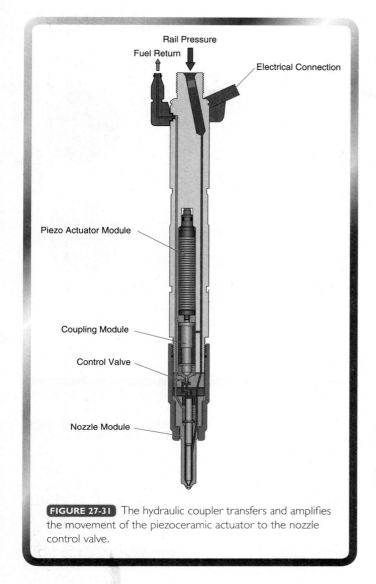

Rail Pressure
Fuel Return
Electrical Connection
Piezo Actuator Module
Coupling Module
Control Valve
Nozzle Module

FIGURE 27-31 The hydraulic coupler transfers and amplifies the movement of the piezoceramic actuator to the nozzle control valve.

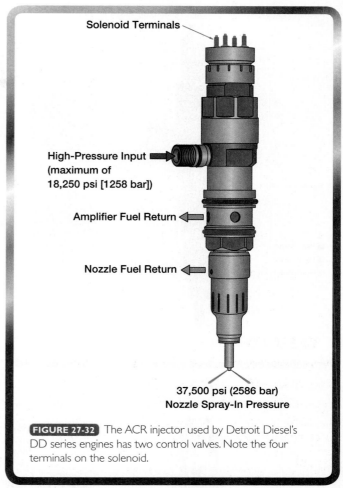

Solenoid Terminals
High-Pressure Input (maximum of 18,250 psi [1258 bar])
Amplifier Fuel Return
Nozzle Fuel Return
37,500 psi (2586 bar) Nozzle Spray-In Pressure

FIGURE 27-32 The ACR injector used by Detroit Diesel's DD series engines has two control valves. Note the four terminals on the solenoid.

instead of producing the pressure from the high-pressure pump and storing it in lines and the fuel rail. Larger pumps, lines, and fuel rails are not needed because pressures there are lower than 20,000 psi (1379 bar).

Development of this injector began as search for a lower-cost alternative to piezoceramic injectors while still using the more durable servo-hydraulic actuators. Bosch wanted to design a servo-hydraulic solenoid valve injector with injection performance close to piezo injectors that also cost less. The solution was the development of a simplified control valve. The new valve is a slotted, spindle-shaped control valve referred to as the pressure-compensated flow control valve. In comparison to ball valve technology, the new valve has lower mass with reduced lift distance for faster response. Several versions of the injector have been produced, with the latest release in 2012 capable of 37,500 psi (2586 bar) spray-in pressure. The injector is used with a two-piston high-pressure pump, the CPN5-12/2, and its own unique high-pressure fuel rail.

Pressure Amplification

The ACR injector has two control valves: the needle solenoid control valve (NSV) and the amplifier control valve (ACV). The NSV is nearest the nozzle and operates to control nozzle valve lift by changing the balance of hydraulic force above the nozzle. When there is no injection the NSV blocks the flow of rail pressure fuel from above the nozzle valve. Rail pressure is applied to both the top and bottom of the nozzle valve, keeping it firmly seated due to a slight difference in surface area pressure below and above the nozzle valve **FIGURE 27-33**. This valve operates throughout the entire engine operating range to begin and end injection, time the event, and meter the injection quantity. The normally closed ACV in the fuel injector regulates the balance of hydraulic pressure above and below an amplifier piston. When the ACR injector is in a non-amplified state, the needle control valve is lifted from it seat by draining fuel pressure from above the valve after current is applied to the control valve magnetic coil. Fuel pressure above the nozzle valve drains to low-pressure fuel return, and injection begins **FIGURE 27-34**. When activated, the ACV releases fuel pressure below the amplifier piston to the low-pressure fuel return circuit. During pressure amplification, the ACV drains fuel pressure

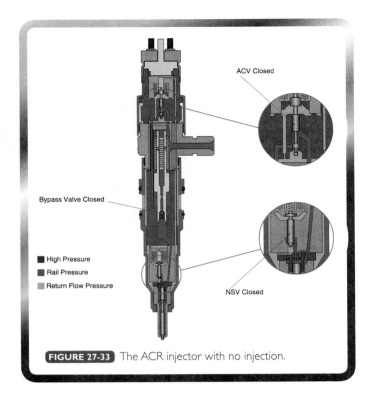

FIGURE 27-33 The ACR injector with no injection.

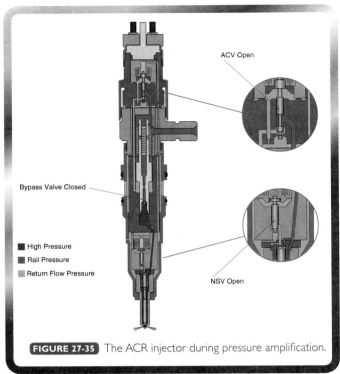

FIGURE 27-35 The ACR injector during pressure amplification.

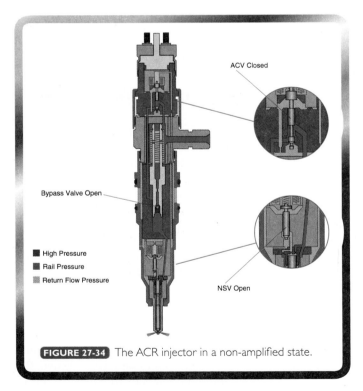

FIGURE 27-34 The ACR injector in a non-amplified state.

from below the amplifier piston to fuel return. Rail pressure above the amplifier piston forces the piston downward, pressurizing fuel to a very high pressure. A bypass valve supplying rail pressure to the injector is closed and only highly pressurized fuel is supplied to the nozzle valve **FIGURE 27-35**. Venting fuel pressure below the piston allows high-pressure fuel above the piston to force the piston plunger downward, pressurizing fuel below the piston. The surface area above the amplifier piston is twice the area below the piston, which multiplies injection pressure by a factor of 2:1. This means the amplifier piston doubles the rail pressure supplied to the nozzle valve. Without energizing the ACV, fuel from the rail uses a bypass circuit to flow through a check ball to the NSV. With the use of two solenoids in the injector, two fuel return circuits connect to the injectors in the cylinder head **FIGURE 27-36**.

Rate Shaping

The injection rate after needle opening can be varied between the three different shape profiles called boot, ramp, and square **FIGURE 27-37**. Controlling the time when the two valves are energized enables a flexible nozzle lift and injection rate shaping. At low speed, up to 930 rpm, no amplification takes place. This injection rate minimizes combustion noise. Above 930 rpm, amplification takes place to enable increased engine power output using a low-NO$_x$ ramped injection rate shape.

CRI4 Coaxial Variable Nozzle

Another fourth-generation injector concept from Bosch is the CRI4-PV injector. It uses a nozzle featuring two rows of spray holes in the nozzle tip. This **coaxial variable nozzle injector**, or variable geometry injector, contains a two-stage nozzle lift

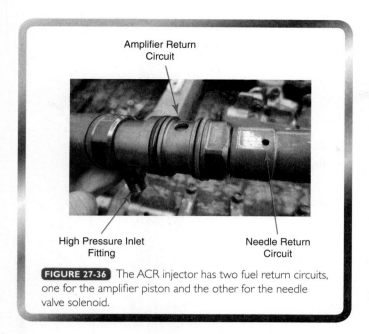

FIGURE 27-36 The ACR injector has two fuel return circuits, one for the amplifier piston and the other for the needle valve solenoid.

Siemens CR Injectors

Siemens has developed and manufactured piezo injectors since 2001 for a variety of original equipment manufacturers. The most significant North American application for this European-tested CR fuel system and injectors is in the 6.4L engine produced by Navistar and used in the Ford PowerStroke **FIGURE 27-39**.

Overview

The Siemens CR injector uses a conventional six-hole nozzle valve that opens inwardly when the hydraulic balance of the nozzle valve is higher below the nozzle. In this injector, as in the Bosch injectors, hydraulic forces are balanced with piezoceramic actuator movement tipping the balance by reducing fuel pressure above the nozzle valve. Also like Bosch injectors, a control rod or piston holds the nozzle valve on its seat, preventing the nozzle valve from lifting.

Fuel pressure in a chamber above the control piston regulates the movement of the control piston. Draining fuel pressure to the low-pressure return side of the fuel system begins injection while increasing pressure above the control piston ends injection **FIGURE 27-40**.

A piezoceramic actuator in the Siemens injector uses multiple stacked piezo crystal discs that expand longitudinally when electrically energized. The response rate is close to 0.1 milliseconds and designed for five injection events per combustion cycle in the Ford engine. The expansion of the crystals results in a linear motion that pushes against a

with two levels of spray holes **FIGURE 27-38**. A lower row is used for low-speed delivery at low pressurization. A second row of spray holes adds to injection delivery volume by combining with the low-speed spray holes during high pressurization and high-speed, heavy-load operating conditions. This design permits either row of nozzles to be opened independently, which optimizes mixture preparation to achieve a more homogenous distribution of fuel and air in the cylinder.

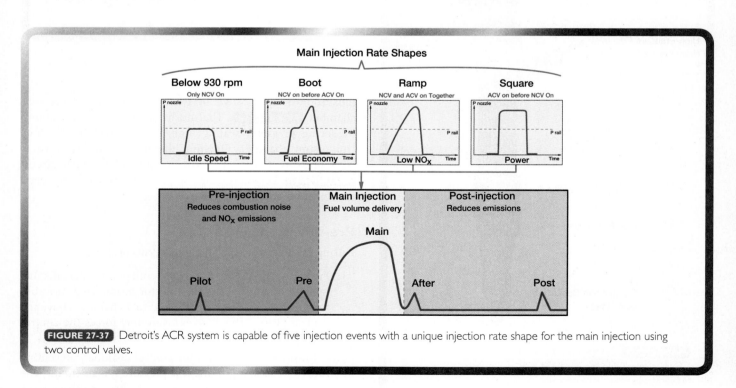

FIGURE 27-37 Detroit's ACR system is capable of five injection events with a unique injection rate shape for the main injection using two control valves.

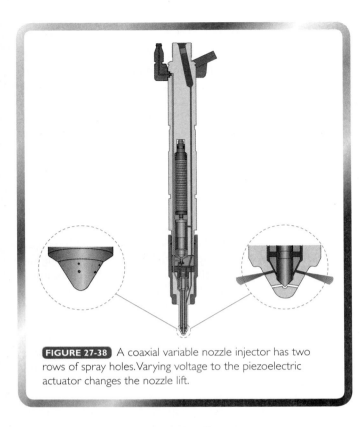

FIGURE 27-38 A coaxial variable nozzle injector has two rows of spray holes. Varying voltage to the piezoelectric actuator changes the nozzle lift.

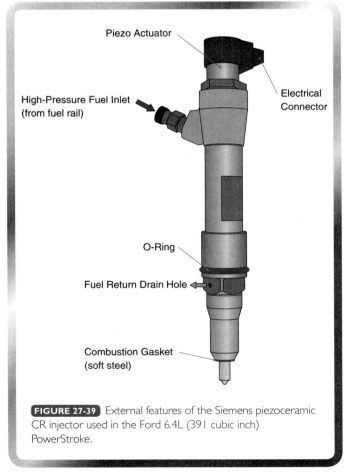

FIGURE 27-39 External features of the Siemens piezoceramic CR injector used in the Ford 6.4L (391 cubic inch) PowerStroke.

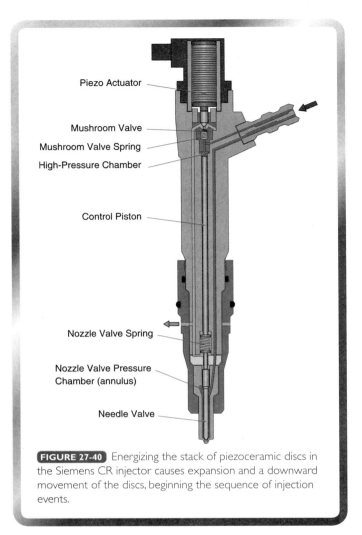

FIGURE 27-40 Energizing the stack of piezoceramic discs in the Siemens CR injector causes expansion and a downward movement of the discs, beginning the sequence of injection events.

mushroom-shaped valve to drain fuel from the pressure chamber **FIGURE 27-41**. The mushroom valve is held closed by spring pressure, sealing high-pressure fuel in the control piston chamber. Opening the mushroom valve vents high pressure fuel to the low-pressure fuel return circuit **FIGURE 27-42**. De-energizing the piezoceramic actuator ends the injection event.

Pre-injection

During pre-injection, the following events occur:

1. Fuel pressurized by the high-pressure pump enters the fuel rail and is supplied to each injector fitting. High-pressure fuel flows to the nozzle valve and to a chamber above the control piston. This high-pressure fuel forces the control piston downward against the top of the nozzle valve.

2. A mushroom valve seals the control chamber, preventing fuel from escaping to the low-pressure return circuit. The mushroom valve spring forces the mushroom valve against its seat.

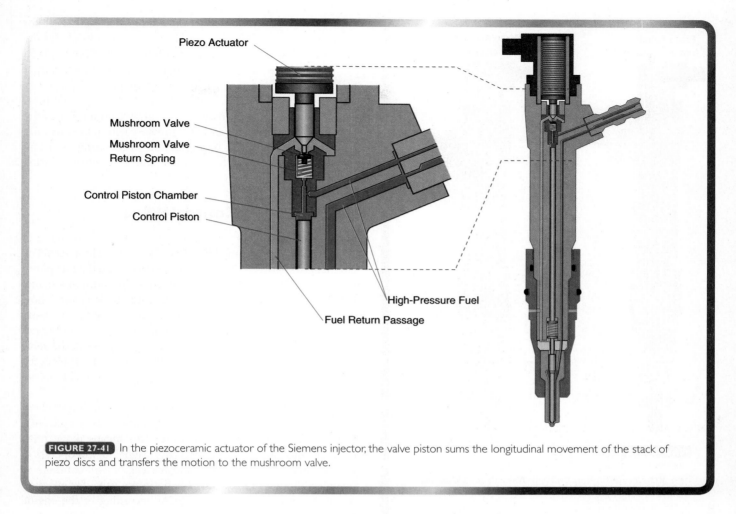

FIGURE 27-41 In the piezoceramic actuator of the Siemens injector, the valve piston sums the longitudinal movement of the stack of piezo discs and transfers the motion to the mushroom valve.

3. The larger surface area above the control piston applies greater pressure than the force of the fuel against the nozzle valve annulus.

Injection

The events that occur during injection include:

1. When the piezoceramic actuator is energized by electrical current, the valve piston below the actuator transfers movement of the piezo stack to the mushroom valve. This action opens the mushroom valve, causing fuel pressure in the control chamber to drain into the low-pressure fuel return circuit.

2. Pressure below the nozzle valve is higher than the fuel pressure in the control chamber. The nozzle valve lifts and injection begins.

3. High-pressure fuel has to enter the control piston control chamber through a narrow restriction. Fuel cannot enter the pressure chamber fast enough to replenish fuel venting to the fuel return circuit around the mushroom valve. This causes the pressure in the control chamber to continually fall, and the injection event continues. Fuel from the pressure control chamber passes through a drilled passageway in the injector and out into a fuel return passageway in the cylinder head.

End of Injection

The injection event is complete after the following events occur:

1. The ECM de-energizes the piezoceramic actuator to cause a rapid return of the actuator to a resting position. Spring pressure closes the mushroom valve, causing pressure to build in the control piston chamber.

2. The pressure in the control chamber forces the control piston downward against the nozzle valve, seating the nozzle valve and ending injection.

▶ Components of Common Rail Fuel Systems

Pumps, pressure control valves, and pressure regulators are used by all common rail systems. Major differences exist between these components depending on the size of the engine, fuel system pressure control strategy, and manufacturer designs. This next section will cover some of the more common construction and operational details of common rail system components.

High-Pressure Pump

High-pressure fuel pumps develop the pressure required for injection under all engine operating conditions, including quick

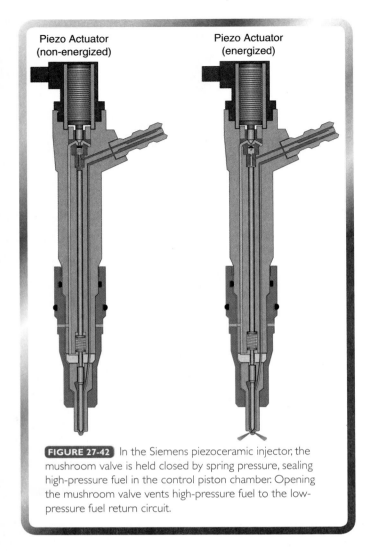

FIGURE 27-42 In the Siemens piezoceramic injector, the mushroom valve is held closed by spring pressure, sealing high-pressure fuel in the control piston chamber. Opening the mushroom valve vents high-pressure fuel to the low-pressure fuel return circuit.

Piezo Actuator (non-energized)

Piezo Actuator (energized)

starting of the engine. Single- and multiple-plunger pumps are also used in CR systems **FIGURE 27-43**. Low-cost single-plunger pumps are typically used in small displacement four-cylinder engines, while two-, three-, and even four-cylinder pumps are used in engines with higher fuel volume requirements. These pumps are cam actuated using inlet and outlet valves to control pump flow **FIGURE 27-44**. An electronically controlled fuel pressure regulator valve will vary pump output pressures as commanded by the ECM. Earlier generations of piston pumps supplied more fuel than could be delivered by the injectors during idle and part-load engine operation. To reduce parasitic power loses produced by pumping fuel needlessly and to keep fuel temperatures low, pumps now use inlet volume metering, which means only the amount of fuel needed by the engine passes through the high-pressure pumps **FIGURE 27-45**. The valve regulates fuel supplied to the pump and maximum pump output pressure.

There are several successive generations of pumps in existence, each having higher pressurization capabilities and greater refinements. The CP2 Bosch pump is a two-piston pump used on commercial vehicles. The CP3 pump is a third-generation axial piston pump used with second-generation CRS2 injectors.

A fourth generation of pumps, designated the CP4.1 for single piston and CP4.2 for two pistons, has steel heads for the pumping cylinders bolted to an aluminum body **FIGURE 27-46**.

Beginning with many 2010 engines, the fourth-generation high-pressure pumps are timed so the peak pressure pulses are phased with the injection events. Without phasing, peak injection pressures are not possible. Matching the pump pressure pulses results in a more consistent pressure within the fuel rails. If the pump is removed, timing marks on the pump gear and camshaft gear are used to correctly time components during reinstallation.

Rail Pressure Control Valve

A rail pressure control valve is used to regulate the quantity of fuel admitted into a pump **FIGURE 27-47**. A closed loop feedback circuit exists between the rail pressure sensor and the fuel pump regulator **FIGURE 27-48**. A direct current pulse width modulated (PWM) signal applied to the pressure regulator determines how much fuel is either supplied to the pump, returned to the tank, or returned to the pump inlet based on the signal from the rail pressure sensor. When no electrical energy is present, the valve is closed, forcing all pump output to the fuel rail. Increasing the length of the PWM signal opens the valve, and pressure to the fuel rail drops.

The fuel pressure control valve operates on a duty cycle of between 5% and 95%. A higher percentage of duty cycle corresponds to a lower pump pressure. This means if the pressure regulator should lose its electrical signal, it will operate at a wide-open or default value, and the engine will continue to operate although run roughly. The optimum value for injection pressure is coordinated by the ECM according to the engine speed and load conditions.

With some engine control systems, the pressure regulator acts as a fuel temperature sensor. Resistance of the coil within the regulator is proportional to fuel temperature, permitting fuel temperature to be inferred from the actuator's resistance.

Two fuel rail pressure regulators are used on late model engines. The inlet volume metering valve remains located on the injection pump and is typically a normally closed PWM-controlled valve. A second pressure control valve is located on a fuel rail and has a normally open PWM solenoid. A PWM signal is applied to this regulator to control the amount of fuel returned to the fuel tank. The pressure control valve on the fuel rail is typically used at low engine speed, during idle conditions, and at engine start-up when fuel temperature is low. The volume control valve on the pump is used to regulate fuel pressure under most other conditions.

A third mode of operation allows fuel rail pressure to be regulated by a combination of the pressure control valve and the volume control valve when fuel delivery volumes are low. Two regulators are used to provide the faster, more accurate control of fuel pressure needed for precise fuel metering and low emissions. This control is especially needed during engine over-run conditions when the vehicle is "driving" the engine. The heavy-duty onboard diagnostics (HD-OBD) system monitors the operation of the two regulators to detect when there

FIGURE 27-43 High fuel volume and a maximum commanded rail pressure of 37,709 psi (2600 bar) at 1800 rpm requires this X15 common rail system to use a multiple-plunger, high-pressure pump. The pump's camshaft is oil lubricated to extend durability.

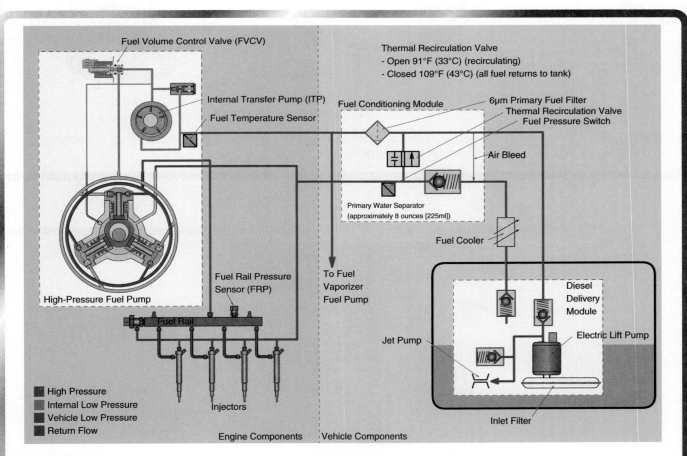

FIGURE 27-44 Note this high-pressure pump is supplied fuel through a fuel volume control valve. This regulates inlet fuel volume, which in turn controls output pressure.

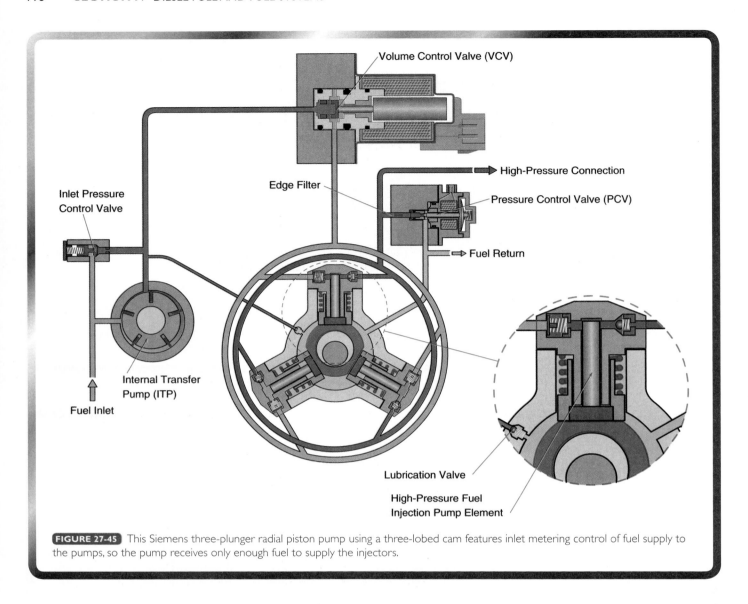

FIGURE 27-45 This Siemens three-plunger radial piston pump using a three-lobed cam features inlet metering control of fuel supply to the pumps, so the pump receives only enough fuel to supply the injectors.

FIGURE 27-46 Fourth-generation Bosch pumps like this CP4.2 are used with third-generation injectors.

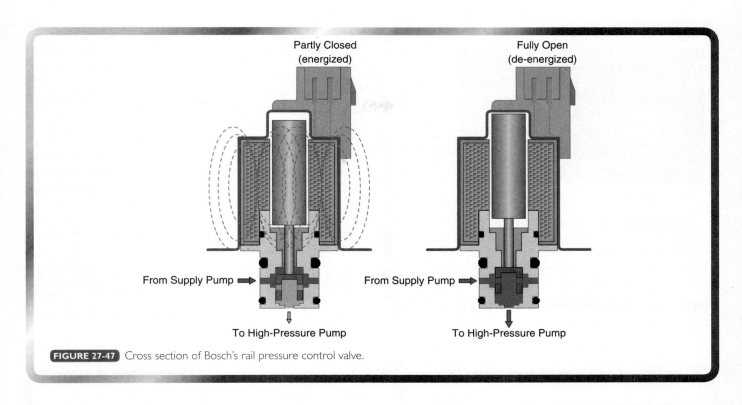

Partly Closed
(energized)

Fully Open
(de-energized)

From Supply Pump ➡

From Supply Pump ➡

To High-Pressure Pump

To High-Pressure Pump

FIGURE 27-47 Cross section of Bosch's rail pressure control valve.

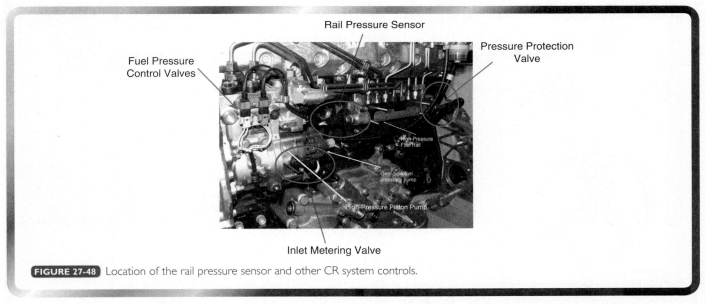

Rail Pressure Sensor

Fuel Pressure
Control Valves

Pressure Protection
Valve

High-Pressure
Fuel Rail

Gear-type fuel
pressurly pump

High-Pressure Piston Pump

Inlet Metering Valve

FIGURE 27-48 Location of the rail pressure sensor and other CR system controls.

is an excessive deviation from the desired fuel pressure, when the ECM has reached a control limit, or when the minimum or maximum allowable rail pressures are exceeded **FIGURE 27-49**.

▶ TECHNICIAN TIP

Air trapped in fuel will cause prolonged or hard starting of the engine. Electric or hand primer pumps are used on CR systems to purge air from filters during service and to ensure a rapid start of the engine. Installing filters dry and priming them after service ensures that only filtered fuel will reach dirt-sensitive CR injectors. Running an engine out of fuel and prolonged cranking

without first priming high-pressure pumps will damage the pumps. Damaged pumps may fail immediately or within hours or days after such abuse.

Inlet Volume Metering Control

The high-pressure pump is driven at one-half engine speed and coupled to the engine through a gear drive mechanism. The torque required to turn the high-pressure pump is as little as 12 ft-lb (16.27 Nm). This is one-ninth the drive torque required for a distributor injection pump. However, at 2000 rpm, a pump

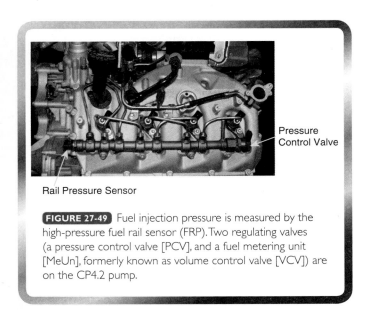

FIGURE 27-49 Fuel injection pressure is measured by the high-pressure fuel rail sensor (FRP). Two regulating valves (a pressure control valve [PCV], and a fuel metering unit [MeUn], formerly known as volume control valve [VCV]) are on the CP4.2 pump.

pressurizing fuel to 23,000 psi (1586 bar) will use almost five horsepower. Pressurizing fuel and returning a large portion of it back to the tank negatively impacts both engine power output and fuel economy. To minimize this parasitic loss, newer pumps have inlet metering capabilities to increase engine power output and fuel economy. For example, Bosch pumps provide the capability for one of the pumping elements to electrically switch off **FIGURE 27-50**. A solenoid attached to a pin on one inlet valve can hold the inlet check valve open, resulting in no compression of fuel during pump operation. Closed-loop feedback from the rail pressure sensor controls an electrohydraulic pressure control valve located on the pump's inlet valve. Less energy is expended when lower injection pressures are required, and minimal quantities of fuel pass through the pump, leading to further gains in fuel economy.

Another benefit of reducing the quantity of fuel pressurized by the pump is it eliminates unnecessary heating of fuel during pressurization. Delphi reports its system improves fuel economy by as much as 3% and eliminates the need for expensive fuel coolers.

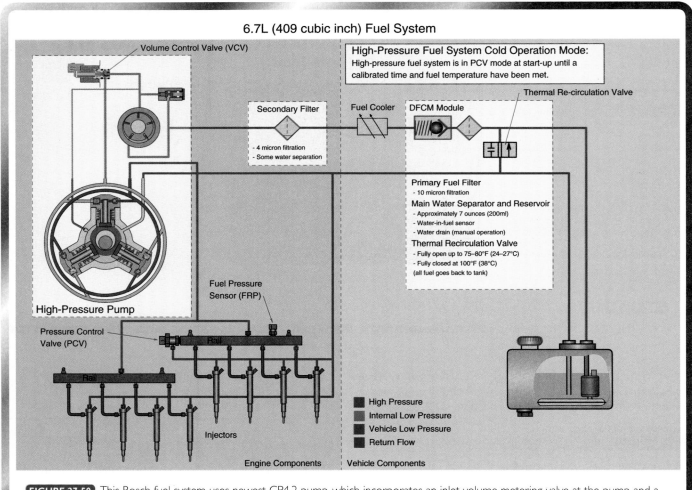

FIGURE 27-50 This Bosch fuel system uses newest CP4.2 pump, which incorporates an inlet volume metering valve at the pump and a pressure control valve on the left fuel rail.

High-Pressure Fuel Rail

The fuel rail is a thick-walled reservoir, most often in the form of a cylindrical tube, for highly pressurized fuel used for eventual supply for the injectors. The rail is continuously filled with pressurized fuel supplied by the high-pressure fuel pump. It not only stores pressurized fuel, but it also provides some dampening action for the pressure pulsations of the high-pressure pump. Throttling valves or restriction orifices inside the rail also act as pulsation dampeners.

Pressure-Protection Valve

All fuel rails contain a mechanical pressure-limiting or pressure-protection valve **FIGURE 27-51**. In the event of over-pressurization of the fuel rail due to pressure control valve failure, it opens and returns fuel to the fuel return circuit. It has a feature that permits a slight delay in pressure release until maximum rail pressure exceeds a predetermined safety factor. Typically this is approximately 3000 psi (207 bar) above maximum rail pressure **FIGURE 27-52**. On some engines the valve is incorporated into the function block with the rail pressure sensor. Most others install the valve on the fuel rail. Siemens piezoceramic injectors have an integrated pressure-relief valve.

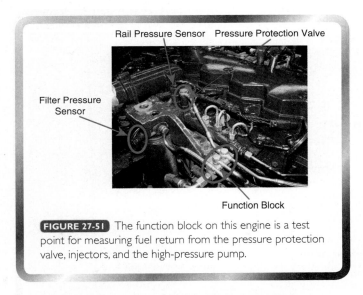

FIGURE 27-51 The function block on this engine is a test point for measuring fuel return from the pressure protection valve, injectors, and the high-pressure pump.

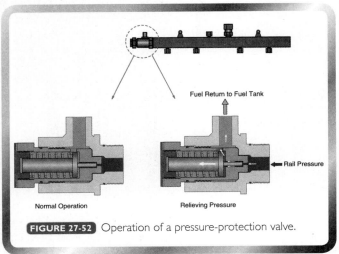

FIGURE 27-52 Operation of a pressure-protection valve.

Fuel Rail Pressure Sensor

This sensor is mounted in the high-pressure fuel rail and provides data to the ECM for closed-loop adjustment to the pressure control regulator. The sensor is usually a three-wire, variable capacitance sensor using a 5-volt reference signal. It operates in a closed-loop mode with the pressure regulator, meaning data from this sensor provides feedback to the ECM, which in turn adjusts the length of the pulse width signal to the pressure control valve. Closed-loop operation means no other input data than that provided by the rail pressure sensor is used to adjust the pressure in the fuel rail.

Flow-Limiting Valve

In the event of an injector failure causing continuous flow of fuel through the injector, a mechanical safety valve shuts off the flow of fuel to the failed injector. Flow-limiting valves can be threaded into the fuel rail for each injector. The fuel line to the injector connects with the flow-limiting valve. The valve is constructed with a plunger and spring assembly that acts like a throttling device with a precisely defined flow rate. During normal operation, the flow-limiting valve's plunger will reciprocate back and forth inside its housing during each injection. If flow rates exceed the preset limit, the plunger will seal against its seat, remaining there until the engine is switched off and fuel flow to the injector stops.

▶ Service and Maintenance of Common Rail Fuel Systems

Common rail injection systems deliver exceptional reliability. When fuel-related problems do occur, the on-board diagnostic system will quickly detect defective system operation. Because the construction and operation of common rail systems are unique, specialized service practices and diagnostic techniques are used to pinpoint problems with the system. This next section will examine some common diagnostic and service practices for non-amplified common rail systems. Diagnostic information for amplified common rail systems is covered in the Detroit Diesel chapter.

Service Precautions for CR3 Injectors

CR3 injectors operate a high voltage, which can peak at up to 240 volts DC. Operating voltage is up to 160 volts at 20 amps, which is in contrast to 50 volts for CR1 and CR2 injectors. A brightly color-coded injector harness warns against contact when the ignition key is on. When working on CR3 systems, certified insulated gloves are required. The expiration date of the gloves should be checked before using to ensure functionality.

On-Board Diagnostics for Common Rail Fuel Systems

EPA10 emission standards have mandated production of the cleanest diesels ever. Emission levels from the exhaust pipes of these engines cannot even be detected with shop-grade emission analyzers because end of life cycle emission thresholds are close to zero. To monitor and maintain the emissions levels to their current standard, the HD-OBD legislation requires manufacturers to detect any potential malfunction that could cause emissions to rise above legislated standards.

The fuel system is one area in particular monitored by the HD-OBD system, and there are several specific strategies used to identify faults on CR systems. These include:

- Fuel system pressure control
- Fuel mass observer
- Injection timing
- Fuel balancing control
- Injector voltage
- Pressure wave correction factor
- Zero fuel mass calibration

Fuel System Monitors—Fuel System Pressure Control

The CR fuel system monitor monitors fuel system pressure to verify it is operating within an expected range **FIGURE 27-53**.

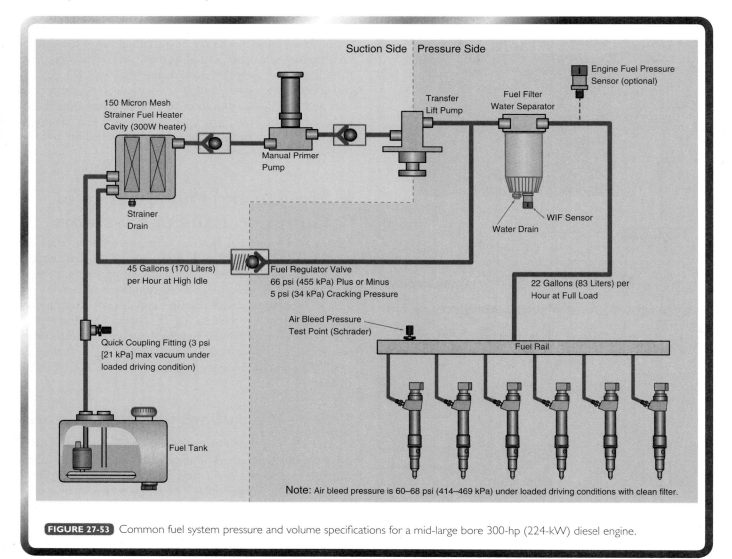

FIGURE 27-53 Common fuel system pressure and volume specifications for a mid-large bore 300-hp (224-kW) diesel engine.

The rail pressure sensor is checked and deviations of the fuel pressure control valve and volume control valve are evaluated. One particular problem CR systems can have is related to excessive fuel flow. A higher PWM signal applied to the inlet volume control valve and lower than anticipated rail pressure sensor values will indicate a fuel leak. A fuel system leak causes hard start, no start, and/or low power conditions. Often an injector with excessive fuel back leakage due to worn or defective ball valves and seat will cause the malfunction indicator lamp (MIL) light to illuminate under heavy loads or at highway cruising speed **FIGURE 27-54**. A worn, eroded, or dirty ball seat will cause the injector to leak or to stay open and inject fuel continuously. Similarly, filter lint or dirt can clog the pressure control valve passageway in the injector, causing the injector to stick open. Due to the extreme fuel pressures on CR systems, fuel lines may not always be reusable. Deformable fuel line ends are intended for one-time use only and may leak if retightened. Incorrectly tightened injector lines can form leak paths for high-pressure fuel **FIGURE 27-55**.

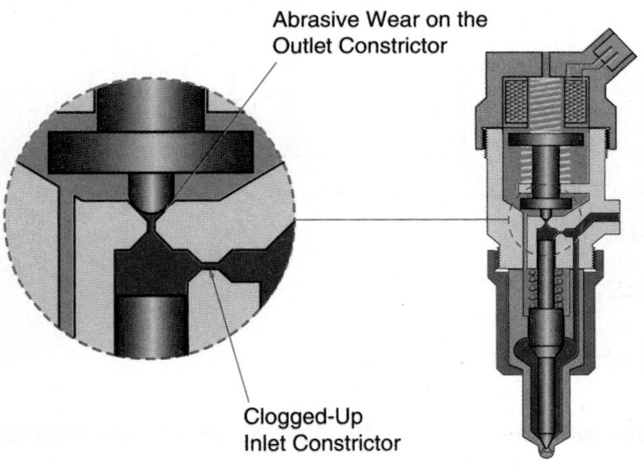

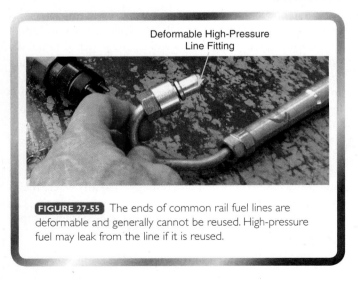

FIGURE 27-54 Good filtration is critical to CR injector function.

Abrasive Wear on the Outlet Constrictor

Clogged-Up Inlet Constrictor

Deformable High-Pressure Line Fitting

FIGURE 27-55 The ends of common rail fuel lines are deformable and generally cannot be reused. High-pressure fuel may leak from the line if it is reused.

To identify the source of the leak, it is important to understand that there are three fuel return flows that can be measured to identify the faulty component:

- Injector fuel return
- High-pressure pump return
- High-pressure relief valve return

Isolating and measuring the quantity of fuel returning to the tank is a process of elimination to determine if various components are operating within specified values **FIGURE 27-56**. For example, if an injector is suspected of having excessive fuel return due to a defect, that injector can be isolated after measuring the total return flow from all injectors. If the return flow is substantially reduced after blocking the injector, it is likely that the injector is defective **FIGURE 27-57**. Worn injector ball seats, back leakage from around the nozzle valve, pressure protection valves, and high-pressure pumps will return excess fuel. Quill tubes, which are steel tubes in the cylinder head that supply rail pressure, can make poor contact with the injector and form leak paths **FIGURE 27-58**. Unless the injector is installed carefully following the manufacturer's instructions, using the correct torque and installation sequence, the tube can fail to crush seal into the sealing seat of the injector. Fuel pressure will leak out of the rail when the engine is off and generate fuel leakage codes. Fuel return from the cylinder head is measured to identify injectors returning excess fuel. Injectors are isolated using a specialized cap in the fuel rail fitting to the injectors. To isolate a defective injector, its high-pressure fuel line is blocked. If fuel return from the head drops to normal, the blocked injector is identified.

TECHNICIAN TIP

Fuel pressure of 3500–4500 psi (241–310 bar) is needed to start most Bosch CR systems. Hard starts and failure to start are often caused by fuel pressure leaking down into the fuel rail. Common leak paths are quill tubes and defective ball valves in injectors, which allow fuel to drain to the return circuit through the injector. When diagnosing these conditions, always check the rail pressure. If the system does not hold pressure, there are leaks.

Measuring Injector Back Leakage

Leaking control valves are responsible for venting high-pressure fuel to the low-pressure fuel return and are the most common failure in common rail injectors. The control valves, which regulate the hydraulic balance across the nozzle valve, can fail due to wear, corrosion, and abrasive fuel contamination. Highly pressurized fuel can leak past the valves, which increases the volume of fuel return from the injectors. When the control valve leakage is severe, high-pressure fuel in the fuel rail can leak to the fuel return, enabling the nozzle valve to lift from its seat. If this takes place, fuel leaks out of the nozzle tip and into the combustion chamber and may cause the engine to run away, the cylinder to misfire, and the nozzle to drip. It can even fill the cylinder with fuel when the engine is shut off. Measuring fuel return volume from each nozzle is generally the most effective way to identify leaking injectors.

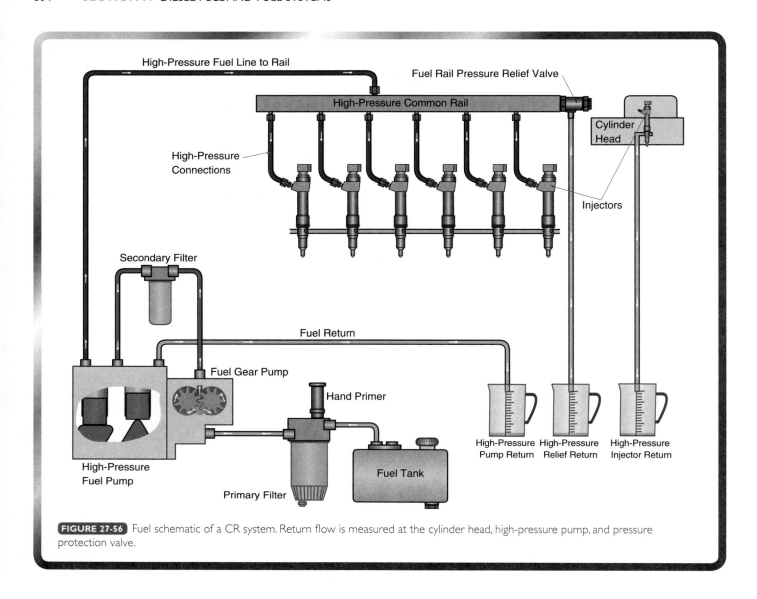

FIGURE 27-56 Fuel schematic of a CR system. Return flow is measured at the cylinder head, high-pressure pump, and pressure protection valve.

To perform an injector back leakage check, several methods are used depending on the engine and injector design.

To measure injector back leakage, follow the steps in **SKILL DRILL 27-1**.

The differences between a high-pressure pump's fuel pressure regulator pulse width for commanded rail pressure and measured rail pressure identify fuel leaks to the on-board diagnostic system. The pulse width becomes shorter as rail pressure increases. These are not external leaks, but leakage of fuel back to the fuel tank. High-pressure pumps are too often replaced because they cannot keep up with fuel leakage from the high-pressure system when under heavy loads. Often, the particulate filter will require frequent regeneration if the leakage is from defective injectors, because the injectors' nozzle tips leak if they are not quickly closed.

To measure injector back leakage from defective injectors without individual return lines to return fuel through the cylinder head, follow the steps in **SKILL DRILL 27-2**.

Measuring Fuel Leakage from Other Fuel System Components

A normal crank-to-start time for a common rail injection system is usually around 3–5 seconds. On some engines, including Cummins engines, the injectors will not be switched to the On or Off position until the fuel rail pressure reaches a minimum threshold pressure. A prolonged cranking period or no-start condition can be caused by leaks in the high-pressure fuel system. Cranking re-primes the fuel system and purges air from injectors. Leaking ball valves in the injectors are one cause of leakage, but there are others. Leaking quill tubes, defective valves in the high-pressure pump, and leaking rail pressure protection valves are some other common areas. Leakage will generate fault codes that require pinpoint testing to identify where fuel is bypassing the injectors.

To measure fuel leakage from other fuel system components, follow the steps in **SKILL DRILL 27-3**.

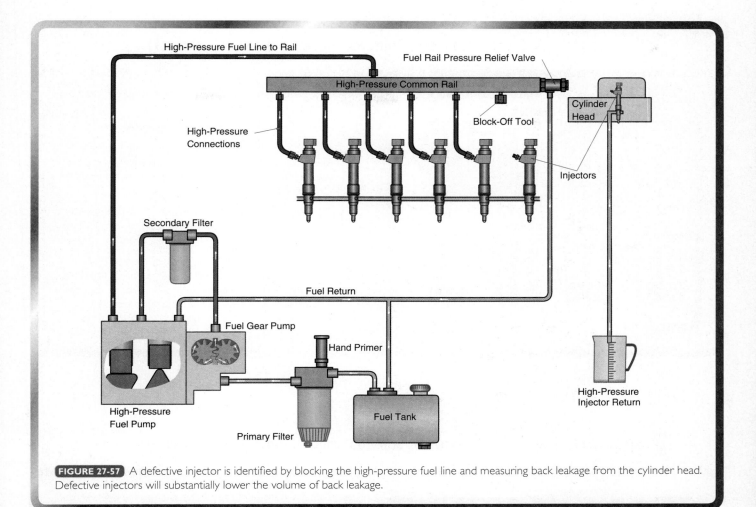

High-Pressure Fuel Line to Rail

Fuel Rail Pressure Relief Valve

High-Pressure Common Rail

High-Pressure
Connections

Block-Off Tool

Cylinder
Head

Injectors

Secondary Filter

Fuel Return

Fuel Gear Pump

Hand Primer

High-Pressure
Fuel Pump

Primary Filter

Fuel Tank

High-Pressure
Injector Return

FIGURE 27-57 A defective injector is identified by blocking the high-pressure fuel line and measuring back leakage from the cylinder head. Defective injectors will substantially lower the volume of back leakage.

TECHNICIAN TIP

When servicing injectors, it is critical that the injector calibration file matches the injector position in the engine. The code must be read from the injector and installed in one or more ECMs using an electronic service tool such as a handheld scanner or PC-based software. A swapped injector—one moved to another hole without changing the calibration file—or a replacement injector will cause the engine to run roughly. On HD-OBD engines the wrong injector calibration code will illuminate the MIL light.

TECHNICIAN TIP

Determining the correct calibration code for a common rail injector requires specialized equipment to measure and test the injector. Injector OEMs only possess the equipment and design details used to assign a calibration code. If injectors are rebuilt and internal components are replaced, the old calibration code will not apply. Failure to use a correct calibration code can result in excessive emissions, generate fault codes, and produce rough running complaints.

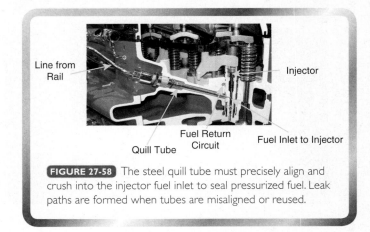

Line from
Rail

Injector

Fuel Return
Circuit

Quill Tube

Fuel Inlet to Injector

FIGURE 27-58 The steel quill tube must precisely align and crush into the injector fuel inlet to seal pressurized fuel. Leak paths are formed when tubes are misaligned or reused.

Fuel Mass Observer

A fuel mass observer (FMO) is an algorithm used to detect deviations from normal delivery volumes from all injectors. On engines equipped with oxygen sensors, the percentage of oxygen in the exhaust is compared to an expected oxygen percentage based upon fuel rate, boost pressure, and EGR flow. If oxygen content differs substantially from an expected model of exhaust gas content, a code is set.

SKILL DRILL 27-1 Measuring Injector Back Leakage (Method 1)

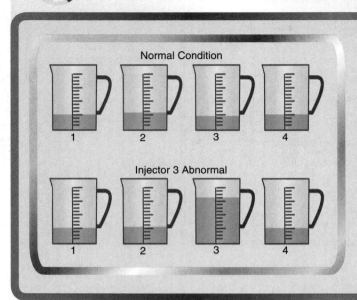

Normal Condition

1 2 3 4

Injector 3 Abnormal

1 2 3 4

1. Remove the fuel return hose from each injector and install jumper tubes to return line fittings.

2. Connect the jumper tube injector return hoses to a set of graduated cylinders.

3. Start and run the engine at idle. Measure and record the volume of fuel accumulating in the graduated cylinders for 3 minutes.

4. Operate the engine at high idle speed for 2 minutes. Measure and record the volume of fuel accumulating in the graduated cylinders.

5. Compare fuel accumulations to manufacturers' specifications. Generally, a defective injector will flow three times the minimum return rate. No fuel return indicates a defective injector solenoid. Injector replacement is recommended in either condition.

SKILL DRILL 27-2 Measuring Injector Back Leakage (Method 2)

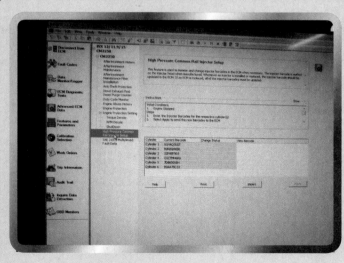

2. Collect and measure the fuel return from the cylinder head. If the return is abnormal, one or more injectors may be leaking internally due to defective ball valves, or a quill tube may be leaking.

3. Shut off the engine and disconnect cylinder 1's injector line at the fuel rail. Install a purpose-made cap on the rail fitting to block fuel flow.

4. Start and run the engine again in the fuel leakage diagnostic mode or at high idle.

5. Collect, measure, and record the volume of fuel returned from the cylinder head while the injector is blocked.

6. Repeat the fuel collection and measurement procedure for each cylinder in the engine.

7. Compare collected return volume. Note any cylinder that had an above-average drop in fuel return volume when its fuel line was blocked. This cylinder likely has a defective injector or quill tube. Alternatively, measure and record fuel return when multiple fuel lines are blocked and compare with OEM specifications for each cylinder.

1. Connect OEM software to the data link adapter and navigate to the fuel leakage diagnostic menu. Enable the fuel leakage test to raise the rail pressure to maximum pressure at idle. Alternatively, operate the engine at high idle.

SKILL DRILL 27-3 Measuring Fuel Leakage from Other Fuel System Components

1 Verify the fuel rail pressure remains high with the engine stopped. Connect a scanner or OEM service tool to the data link connector and observe the rail pressure. A good system will maintain rail pressure for weeks at values close to where they were when the engine was shut off. If rail pressure falls off quickly or goes to less than several hundred psi (bar) in a few hours, there is a high-pressure system leak.

2 Remove the valve cover and inspect individual injectors carefully for evidence of fuel leaks.

3 Navigate to the diagnostic menu of the OEM software and request a fuel leakage test. Run the engine in the fuel leakage test mode, which increases rail pressure to its maximum value.

4 Connect a clear plastic hose to the function block or return line of the high-pressure pump. Collect and measure the fuel volume in graduated cylinders with the engine running in fuel leakage test mode or at high idle. Record your observations.

5 Connect a clear plastic hose to the function block or fuel return line for the rail pressure relief valve. Collect and measure the fuel volume in graduated cylinders with the engine running in fuel leakage test mode or at high idle. Record your observations.

6 If an engine doesn't have individual return lines, but does have return passageways through the cylinder head, measure injector leakage. Connect a clear plastic hose to the function block or fuel return line for the injector return from the cylinder head. Collect and measure the fuel volume in graduated cylinders with the engine running in fuel leakage test mode or at high idle. Record your observations.

7 Compare the fuel accumulations to the manufacturers' specifications. Generally, a defective high-pressure pump or rail pressure relief valve will return excessive fuel if it is worn out or defective.

Injection Timing

The camshaft and crankshaft position sensors evaluate when the beginning of combustion takes place by measuring crankshaft acceleration rates. If the correction to injection timing deviates significantly, a fault code can be set.

Fuel Balance Control

Fuel balance control (FBC) is a strategy used by the ECM to adjust fuel delivery quantities to each cylinder to achieve consistent pressures among all cylinders. Changes in crankshaft speed due to variations in cylinder pressure are measured. The amount of fuel injected to each cylinder is then adjusted up or down to minimize the difference between cylinders until crankshaft speed is consistent from cylinder to cylinder. Large variations to correct pressure differences are identified as a fuel balance fault.

Injector Voltage

Injector voltages are measured at the beginning and end of the energization period. Significant changes in expected voltage and the energization time are identified as faults.

Pressure Wave Correction Factor

Pressure wave correction refers to a correction factor applied to a specific injector's electrical pulse width as a result of rail pressure changes. Each injector has unique flow characteristics based on electrical response time and manufacturing tolerances **FIGURE 27-59**. The procedure is used to assign a correction factor or calibration code to the injector as it measures injection quantities under different injection pressures. A calibration code etched into the injector is used by the ECM to correct fueling variations. During engine assembly or when the injector is replaced the code must be entered into the engine ECM.

Zero Fuel Mass Calibration

Just as mechanical manufacturing tolerance for injectors requires changes to injector energizing time, injector wear also changes injector operating characteristics. Injector deterioration contributes to increased emissions, calling for a recalibration of the stored correction factors that compensate for unique operational behavior. Fuel mean value adaptation (FMA) is a term used to describe the control module's automatic recalibration of the injector during service to compensate for wear and deterioration. Without a strategy to recalibrate an injector, a vehicle could pass out of compliance with emission standards and emission system durability requirements. The process of recalibrating injectors during service is called **zero fuel mass calibration (ZFC)**. A common technique for accomplishing ZFC correction occurs during vehicle deceleration. Calibration occurs when the engine is driven only by the vehicle's kinetic energy and no fuel is injected into the cylinders. Fuel rail pressure is adjusted to a specific value. With no movement of the throttle position sensor from idle position and the engine in an over-run condition, the ECM will

begin to increase energization time to a single injector. When a measurable engine speed increase is detected, the ideal energizing time stored in the ECM based on initial calibration codes is compared to the actual time to produce the engine speed change. Mathematical comparisons made between the two values result in a change to the stored correction factors. Each time the conditions for ZFC are met, another injector is recalibrated.

In the future, pressure sensors installed in the cylinder to measure combustion pressure will be used to provide more accurate data for injector calibration.

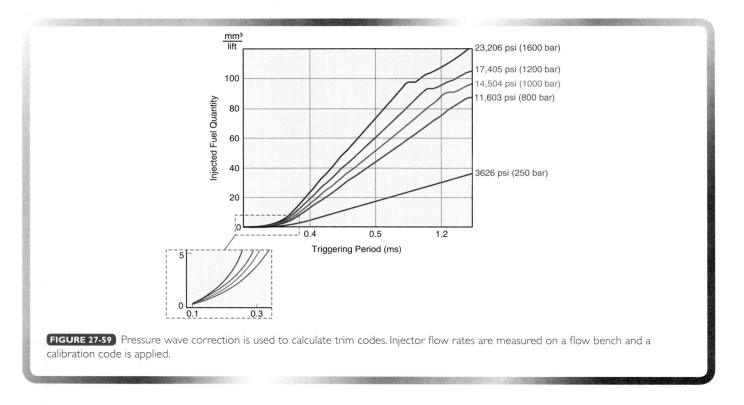

FIGURE 27-59 Pressure wave correction is used to calculate trim codes. Injector flow rates are measured on a flow bench and a calibration code is applied.

Wrap-Up

Ready for Review

▸ Common rail (CR) fuel injection is the most recently developed high-pressure injection system used by the majority of current diesel engines.

▸ The basic concept of CR injection is to supply fuel at injection pressure to a fuel nozzle that electronically controls the injection event.

▸ Diesel fuel injection systems that rely on engine-driven camshafts to pressurize fuel cannot meet legislated emission targets.

▸ Modern CR refers to a classification of high-pressure fuel-injection systems in which pressurization of fuel is accomplished independently of engine speed. This means that regardless of engine rotational speed and load, fuel injection pressure is matched to optimal values required

for the most efficient combustion, lowest emissions, and superior fuel economy.

▸ Enormous technical and manufacturing accomplishments have enabled CR systems to not only meet rigid requirements, but have combined to secure a place for diesel technology in the future.

▸ CR systems are capable of multiple injection events during one engine cycle.

▸ The biggest advantage CR injection offers is injection rate-shaping capabilities. Making substantial reductions in exhaust emissions and fuel consumption without hurting performance requires a changing injection discharge volume during the injection event.

▸ Separate modular components used in CR systems means the fuel system is easily adapted to different engine types.

▶ There are three main types of CR injectors: electrohydraulic solenoids, piezoceramic actuators, and hydraulically amplified using servo-hydraulic valves.

▶ Bosch has developed four generations of CR injectors; three are currently in production.

▶ In the first and second generations of Bosch's CR injectors, the injection events are controlled by changing the balance of hydraulic pressure acting on the nozzle needle valve using magnetic solenoids inside the injectors.

▶ The third generation of Bosch's CR injectors uses stacks of piezoceramic wafers to control injection events inside the injector.

▶ Piezo technology enables the fastest switching time for injectors, currently allowing up to seven injection events in one injection sequence.

▶ One of the biggest problems with electromagnetic actuators is the long response time required to build a magnetic field strong enough to move valves inside an actuator. Longer response time contributes to injection lag.

▶ One of Bosch's fourth-generation CR injectors is the CRS4, also referred to as HADIS, uses an internal hydraulic amplifier to multiply injection pressure by 2:1. One benefit of the two-stage pressure amplification concept is that the highest pressure is limited to the injector nozzle where the maximum pressure is required instead of the high pressure pump, lines, and fuel rail.

▶ Another fourth-generation injector concept from Bosch is the CRI4-PV injector. It uses a nozzle featuring two rows of spray holes in the nozzle tip. This design permits either row of nozzles to be opened independently, which optimizes mixture preparation to achieve a more homogenous distribution of fuel and air in the cylinder.

▶ Siemens has developed and manufactured piezo injectors since 2001 for a variety of OEMs. The injector uses a conventional six-hole nozzle valve which operates using the principle of hydraulically balancing the nozzle valve.

▶ The fuel system generally referred to today as a common rail injection is more precisely termed high-pressure accumulator rail or high-pressure common rail (HPCR). Combined with operational features of the unique CR fuel injector, the most flexible rate shaping of injection events are possible with HPCR fuel systems.

▶ High-pressure fuel pumps develop the pressure required for injection under all engine operating conditions, including for quick starting of the engine.

▶ The volume and pressure control valves use a PWM electrical signal to regulate fuel pressure in the fuel rail.

▶ The high-pressure pump is driven at one-half engine speed and coupled to the engine through a gear drive mechanism. To minimize parasitic loss, newer pumps have inlet metering capabilities to reduce fuel heating and improve fuel economy.

▶ The fuel rail is a thick-walled reservoir for highly pressurized fuel used to supply fuel to the injectors. It is continuously filled with pressurized fuel supplied by the high-pressure fuel pump. Not only can the rail store pressurized fuel, but it also provides some dampening action for the pressure pulsations of the high-pressure pump.

▶ On many systems a pressure-limiting valve is a mechanical valve that serves the same function as an over-pressure protection valve. In the event of over-pressurization of the fuel rail, it opens and fuel flows to the fuel return circuit.

▶ A fuel rail pressure sensor is mounted in the high-pressure fuel rail and provides data to the ECM for closed-loop adjustment to the fuel pressure control regulator.

▶ In the event of an injector failure causing continuous flow of fuel through the injector, a mechanical safety valve shuts off the flow of fuel to the failed injector. Flow-limiting valves are threaded into the fuel rail for each injector.

Vocabulary Builder

amplified common rail (ACR) Two-stage amplification of fuel pressure inside the injector that provides improved power output with lower emissions, noise, and fuel consumption, and that produces a unique shape to the injection rate profile.

coaxial variable nozzle injector A fourth-generation injector concept from Bosch that contains a two-stage nozzle lift with two rows of spray holes. This design permits either row of spray holes to be opened independently, which optimizes mixture preparation to achieve a more homogenous distribution of fuel and air in the cylinder.

fuel balance control (FBC) A strategy used by the ECM to adjust fuel delivery quantities to each cylinder to achieve consistent pressures among all cylinders. Crankshaft speed data is used to make corrections to the volume of fuel injected in each cylinder.

fuel mean value adaptation (FMA) A correction factor made to an injector's energization time based on changes in fuel delivery rates caused by wear and deterioration.

hydraulically amplified diesel injection system (HADIS) A fourth-generation CR injector that uses an internal hydraulic amplifier to multiply injection pressure by 2:1; also referred to as CRS4.

inductive resistance Current induced that opposes ECM current when initially energized; also known as inductive reactance.

piezoceramic actuator An actuator composed of piezoceramic discs that change shape and in turn change the balance of hydraulic forces inside the injector; this type of actuator can switch fuel on and off in as little as 0.0001 second.

pressure wave correction (PWC) The process used to produce a calibration code for a common rail injector. A correction factor is applied to a specific injector's electrical pulse width to adapt the injector to an engine based on manufacturing tolerances between injectors.

rate shaping Optimizing the injection discharge curve to best match engine operating conditions.

servo-hydraulic To use a small movement of an electrically operated control valve to manipulate much larger and powerful hydraulic forces.

zero fuel mass calibration (ZFC) The process of recalibrating injectors during service to compensate for wear and deterioration.

Review Questions

1. The process of recalibrating injectors during service to compensate for wear and deterioration is _____.
   a. zero fuel calibration
   b. pressure wave correction
   c. fuel mean value adaptation
   d. amplified common rail

2. _____ is measured at the beginning and end of the energization period.
   a. Injector voltage
   b. Injector flow
   c. Injector resistance
   d. Injector amperage

3. _____ is the two-stage amplification of fuel pressure inside the injector that provides improved power output with lower emissions, noise, and fuel consumption, and that produces a unique shape to the injection rate profile.
   a. Amplified common rail
   b. Fuel mean value adaptation
   c. Pressure wave correction
   d. Coaxial variable nozzle injection

4. _____ is the process used to produce a calibration code for a common rail injector.
   a. Amplified common rail
   b. Fuel main value adaptation
   c. Zero fuel mass calibration
   d. Pressure wave correction

5. A fourth-generation injector concept from Bosch containing a two-stage nozzle life with two rows of spray holes is called _____.
   a. Amplified common rail
   b. Pressure wave corrector
   c. Fuel mean value adapter
   d. Coaxial variable nozzle injector

6. The term _____ describes the force multiplication taking place inside a CR injector.
   a. spring coil
   b. split shot
   c. servo-hydraulic actuator
   d. cam and plunger

7. Bosch has developed _____ generations of CR injectors.
   a. two
   b. three
   c. four
   d. five

8. _____ Bosch injectors use as much as 250 volts to open.
   a. First-generation
   b. Second-generation
   c. Third-generation
   d. Fourth-generation

9. The _____ injector incorporates a hydraulic coupler that carries out additional functions.
   a. Bosch CR1
   b. Bosch CR2
   c. Bosch CRS3
   d. Bosch CRS4

10. With some engine control systems, the pressure regulator acts as a(n) _____.
    a. temperature sensor
    b. injector fuel return
    c. high-pressure pump return
    d. high-pressure relief valve return

ASE-Type Questions

1. Technician A says high pressurization enhances the atomization of fuel in the combustion chamber. Technician B says high pressurization enhances the distribution of fuel in the combustion chamber. Who is correct?
   a. Technician A
   b. Technician B
   c. Both Technician A and Technician B
   d. Neither Technician A nor Technician B

2. Technician A says that currently, the fastest piezo CR injector can produce 4 separate injection events during one combustion cycle. Technician B says that currently, the fastest piezo CR injector can produce 10 separate injection events during one combustion cycle. Who is correct?
   a. Technician A
   b. Technician B
   c. Both Technician A and Technician B
   d. Neither Technician A nor Technician B

3. Technician A says that hydraulically amplified diesel injection systems are currently capable of injection pressures as high as 37,500 psi (2586 bar). Technician B says that hydraulically amplified diesel injection systems are currently capable of injection pressures as high as 35,000 psi (2413 bar). Who is correct?
   a. Technician A
   b. Technician B
   c. Both Technician A and Technician B
   d. Neither Technician A nor Technician B

4. Technician A says that servo actuators used by Siemens to open and close nozzle valves are spindle-shaped. Technician B says that servo actuators used by Siemens to open and close nozzle valves are mushroom-shaped. Who is correct?
   a. Technician A
   b. Technician B
   c. Both Technician A and Technician B
   d. Neither Technician A nor Technician B

5. Technician A says that to identify the source of a fuel system leak, you should measure pressure at the injector fuel return. Technician B says that to identify the source of a fuel system leak, you should measure pressure at the high-pressure pump return. Who is correct?
   a. Technician A
   b. Technician B
   c. Both Technician A and Technician B
   d. Neither Technician A nor Technician B

6. Technician A says that with some engine control systems, the pressure regulator acts as a fuel temperature sensor. Technician B says that with some engine control systems, the pressure regulator acts as a bypass valve. Who is correct?
   a. Technician A
   b. Technician B
   c. Both Technician A and Technician B
   d. Neither Technician A nor Technician B

7. Technician A says the term servo-hydraulic actuator describes the force multiplication taking place inside a modular HEUI. Technician B says the term servo-hydraulic actuator describes the force multiplication taking place inside a CR injector. Who is correct?
   a. Technician A
   b. Technician B
   c. Both Technician A and Technician B
   d. Neither Technician A nor Technician B

8. Technician A says the injector solenoid is energized with current supplied by the fuel injector command piston. Technician B says the injector solenoid is energized with current supplied by the fuel injector control module. Who is correct?
   a. Technician A
   b. Technician B
   c. Both Technician A and Technician B
   d. Neither Technician A nor Technician B

9. Technician A says a piezoceramic actuator can switch fuel on and off in as little as 0.01 second. Technician B says a piezoceramic actuator can switch fuel on and off in as little as 0.001 second. Who is correct?
   a. Technician A
   b. Technician B
   c. Both Technician A and Technician B
   d. Neither Technician A nor Technician B

10. Technician A says the fourth-generation CRS4 uses an internal hydraulic amplifier to multiply injection pressure at a ratio of 4:1. Technician B says the fourth-generation CRS4 uses an internal hydraulic amplifier to multiply injection pressure at a ratio of 3:1. Who is correct?
    a. Technician A
    b. Technician B
    c. Both Technician A and Technician B
    d. Neither Technician A nor Technician B

SECTION V

Air Induction and Exhaust Systems

CHAPTER 28

Air Induction Systems

NATEF Tasks

Diesel Engines

General
- Observe engine exhaust smoke color and quantity; determine needed action. (pp 817, 824, 833, 836–837)
- Check and record electronic diagnostic codes. (pp 818–822)

Air Induction and Exhaust Systems
- Perform air intake system restriction and leakage tests; determine needed action. (p 836)
- Perform intake manifold pressure (boost) test; determine needed action. (p 836)

- Check air induction system: piping, hoses, clamps, and mounting; service or replace air filter as needed. (pp 833–837)
- Inspect intake manifold, gaskets, and connections; replace as needed. (pp 821–822, 825, 838–839)

Preventive Maintenance and Inspection

Engine System
Air Induction and Exhaust System
- Inspect and service crankcase ventilation system. (pp 820–823)

Knowledge Objectives

After reading this chapter, you will be able to:

1. Define and explain engine terminology associated with air intake and crankcase ventilation systems. (pp 816–839)
2. Identify and explain the mechanisms that form crankcase emissions. (pp 816–821)
3. Identify and explain the purpose and operating principles of air intake systems for diesel engines. (pp 816–825)
4. Describe the functions, construction, types, styles, and applications of diesel engine intake systems and crankcase ventilation systems. (pp 816–835)
5. Identify air intake system and crankcase ventilation system components. (pp 825–835)
6. Describe and explain methods for performing inspections and diagnostic procedures on diesel intake systems and crankcase ventilation systems. (pp 835–839)
7. Recommend maintenance or repairs of diesel engine intake systems and crankcase ventilation systems. (pp 835–839)

Skills Objectives

After reading this chapter, you will be able to:

1. Diagnose a high crankcase pressure code. (p 824) **SKILL DRILL 28-1**
2. Measure air filter restriction. (p 838) **SKILL DRILL 28-2**
3. Pressure test the air induction system. (p 838) **SKILL DRILL 28-3**

You Are the Technician

As an equipment technician working for a road construction company, a major maintenance concern is the amount of dirt and dust that can quickly restrict air filters or enter the engine through air induction or crankcase leaks. During the first preventative maintenance inspections of the major construction season, you randomly select a number of engines to perform a scheduled oil sample (SOS) test. Results have returned and several of the engines have unusually high levels of silicon, lead, copper, and iron in the oil. One possible cause for the unusually high levels flagged by the oil analysis lab is the possibility of an air induction system leak. You realize the equipment needs to be brought in for inspection and the remaining equipment in the fleet needs more careful and specific inspections of their air induction systems. Before planning your next steps, consider the following:

1. Explain why higher than expected levels of iron, silicon, lead, and copper would indicate a leak in an air induction system.
2. Identify the areas and list the components that urgently need inspection.
3. Describe what further complaints could be expected if the air induction system leaks are not identified and repaired.

▶ Introduction

Burning fuel turns diesel engines into air-consuming machinery, and diesel engines use far more air than similarly displaced gasoline engines. The diesel engine's abundant consumption of air makes it sensitive to air quality and requires a sophisticated air-handling system. Understanding the design, operation, and maintenance practices associated with the air induction system is important because problems with engine air quality and induction system supply have a major impact on emissions, noise, performance, and engine durability. Significant new performance and emissions technology is also associated with air induction systems such as the crankcase ventilation system. This chapter will explain the air supply requirements of diesel engines; air induction system operation, construction features, and maintenance; and crankcase ventilation systems.

▶ Fundamentals of Air Induction Systems

Diesel engines use lean burn combustion systems and have intake airflow that exceeds that of spark-ignition (SI) engines many times over. In SI engines, intake airflow only needs to satisfy the operating demands of a stoichiometric air–fuel ratio for gasoline. The airflow in a diesel engine has several other purposes, which mean diesel intake systems require higher air-handling capacity. With its high airflow requirements, engine operation becomes much more sensitive to air quality and the condition of the air that enters the combustion chambers. This next section will examine the construction and operating features of a diesel engine's intake air system.

Air Supply Requirements

While it is easy to understand that diesel engines need lots of air to support good combustion quality, there are other aspects of intake airflow critical to engine operation and performance that are not so obvious. These aspects can be easily overlooked when combustion quality and power-related complaints are reported. This section will describe the air quality and airflow requirements for diesel engines to help technicians understand how each affects engine operating efficiency.

Excess Air Supply

To support efficient combustion with minimal emissions, diesel engines need an adequate supply of air that is clean, dry, fresh, and relatively cool. Diesel engines require an excess supply of air relative to the quantity needed to completely burn fuel in the cylinders. For example, a diesel engine of 350 horsepower (hp) (361 kilowatts [kW]) typically requires an air intake capacity of close to 1000 cubic feet per minute (CFM) (28.3 cubic meters per minute [m³/min]). A 325 hp 6.0 liter (L) PowerStroke will use 732 CFM (20.7 m³/min) at 3300 revolutions per minute (rpm). This expands to an exhaust volume of 1500 CFM (42.5 m³/min) at 3300 rpm. A gasoline-fueled engine typically requires 160 CFM (4.5 m³/min) airflow for the same hp **TABLE 28-1**.

TABLE 28-1: Comparing Diesel and Gasoline Intake Airflow

	6.0L (366 cubic inch) PowerStroke	6.0L (366 cubic inch) Gasoline
Airflow at 3300 rpm	732 CFM (20.7 m³/min)	160 CFM (4.5 m³/min)
Exhaust Volume	~1500 CFM (42.5 m³/min) at 3300 rpm Exhaust temperature: 350–500°F (177–260°C) at engine pipe	2000 CFM (56.6 m³/min) at 6000 rpm Exhaust temperature: 1400°F (760°C)

Diesel engines require excess air for complete and clean combustion, to cool piston crowns and exhaust valves, and to meet diesel fuel's high stoichiometric ratio. Large amounts of intake air are required to achieve good combustion. Because diesels have a short amount of time for atomizing, distributing, vaporizing, and heating fuel vapors, it is important that the fuel find enough air to contact and react with the oxygen. Therefore, the more air in the combustion chamber, the greater likelihood the fuel completely burns **FIGURE 28-1**.

Excess air is also necessary for the cooling of critical cylinder components in a diesel. Because the flame temperature of diesel is near 3990°F (2199°C), intense combustion heat will easily melt pistons and burn valves **FIGURE 28-2**. Adding air volumes allows dilution of the combustion gases. Extra air can lower peak cylinder temperatures. Engines lacking sufficient airflow will naturally have increased exhaust and combustion chamber temperatures.

Excess air provides a greater expansion ratio for combustion gases, which are used to increase cylinder pressure and push down the piston. When excess air is lacking, the consequence is low power due to lower combustion pressure.

▶ TECHNICIAN TIP

When adding performance accessories that increase injected fuel quantities, monitoring exhaust gas temperature with a pyrometer is critical. Less excess air will be available for diluting the heat of combustion gases when additional fuel is burned in the cylinder. Monitoring exhaust gas temperatures avoids potentially destructive cylinder heat loads. Increased airflow is necessary when increasing power output by injecting more fuel to completely burn fuel. Larger intake and exhaust systems improve airflow. Increasing turbocharger boost pressure also lowers excessive combustion temperatures.

The best emissions are obtained from gasoline engines operating using a **stoichiometric ratio** of 14.73:1. Stoichiometric ratio refers to the mass of air required to completely consume fuel in the combustion chamber with no air or fuel remaining after combustion. Diesel-engine combustion is lean and stratified and does not operate at stoichiometric ratio. This means combustion regions near the injector spray pattern will be fuel

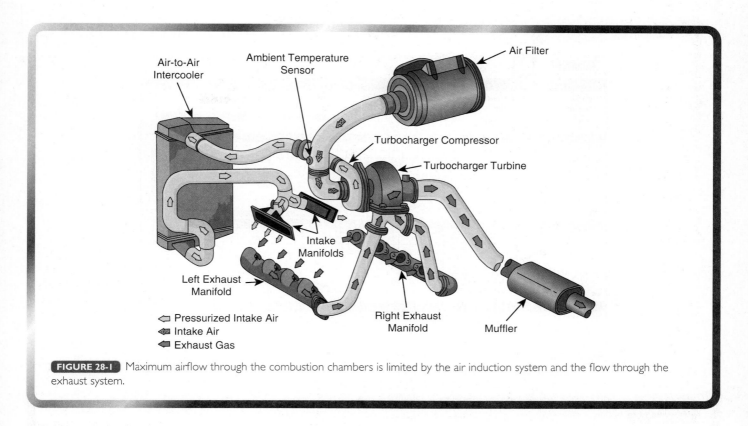

FIGURE 28-1 Maximum airflow through the combustion chambers is limited by the air induction system and the flow through the exhaust system.

FIGURE 28-2 This piston burned as a result of overheating. Excess air dilutes combustion heat and cools exhaust valves during the valve overlap period.

rich, whereas the overall chamber air–fuel ratio is lean. Ignition begins in the regions where the air–fuel ratio is closest to stoichiometric ratio and combustion flames move out from these points, consuming fuel in the cylinder. The carbon-to-hydrogen ratio of diesel fuel, which is higher than many other fuels, means it requires more oxygen, which attaches carbon bonds, to burn completely. Stoichiometric ratios are always measured in weight and not volume, so, depending on the grade, diesel fuel will require a minimum of 15–22 pounds (lb) (7–10 kilograms) of air to burn 1 lb (0.5 kg) of fuel.

Necessity of Clean Air

Clean, filtered air is critical to engine operation to prevent damage and rapid wear from abrasive dirt particles. Dirt ingestion into an engine, referred to as dusting out, can take place through small openings in the intake system and from poor filtration. Incorrect or misaligned air filters and loose hose clamps can also allow dirt leakage into an engine.

Dirt carrying abrasive material damages engines because the abrasives will stick to the oil film on cylinder walls and act as a lapping compound, accelerating ring and cylinder wall wear. From there, dirt will wash into the lubrication system, where it remains in suspension unless filtered out by the oil filter. Some engines do not use a filtered oil supply for piston cooling nozzles, turbocharger bearings, and oil supply to hydraulically actuated electronically controlled unit injectors (HEUIs). Oil contamination in these instances can lead to catastrophic failures or costly repairs **FIGURE 28-3**.

An engine oil analysis is the best choice for detecting leaks in the negative pressure side of the air intake system. This section includes intake components between the turbocharger inlet and air filter. The presence of silica, the element that makes up sand, in the oil sample indicates a leak. Engine oil analysis should not replace a visual inspection of all hoses and clamps for proper installation and alignment during regular services.

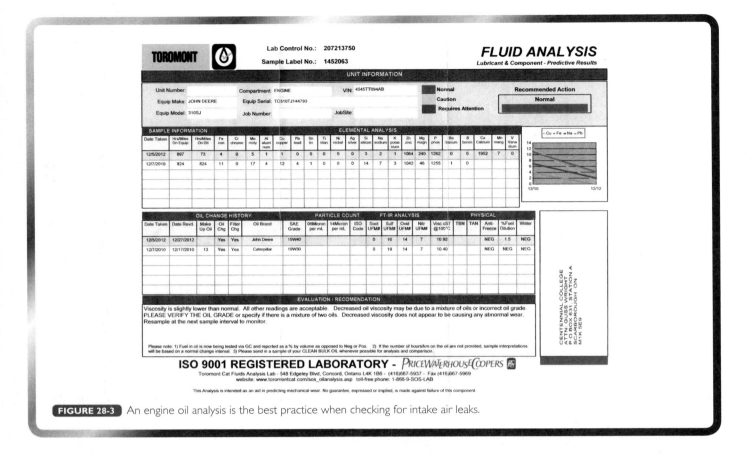

FIGURE 28-3 An engine oil analysis is the best practice when checking for intake air leaks.

TECHNICIAN TIP

Leaks caused by loose clamps or misaligned hoses and pipes between the turbocharger and air filter will pull dirt into the engine. Leaks in the turbocharger will push air out of the pipes, making the dirt ingestion unlikely. Dirt can also enter through missing oil filler caps, dipstick tubes and seals, and leaking gaskets and seals if crankcase pressure becomes low. Never check for leaks with flammable gases or liquids. Backfire through the intake system ignited by hot intake gases produced during the valve overlap period is a major safety hazard.

Effects of Air Inlet Temperature

Optimal air inlet temperatures are essential to good performance and low emissions. Atmospheric pressure, ambient temperature, and humidity affect power because the number of oxygen molecules entering the cylinder will vary with a change in any of these factors. Colder temperatures increase air density and the number of oxygen molecules for a given volume **FIGURE 28-4**. The Society of Automotive Engineers (SAE) created SAE J1349, a standard method for correcting hp and torque, to ensure uniformity of test results to compensate for changes to air pressure, humidity, and air temperature. These corrections are often referred to as **standard day factors**.

The SAE standard day factors adjust calculations of power output measurements to an atmospheric pressure of 29.23 inches of mercury (inHg) (99 kilopascals [kPa]), a temperature of 77°F (25°C), and 0% humidity. Generally, a 10°F change above or below the standard factor results in a 1% power gain or loss. For example, a 50°F increase in inlet temperature will result in a 5% power loss. Power gains occur when air inlet temperature is lower. However, an opposing factor to the power gain from cooler ambient temperatures is very low air inlet temperatures, which can also produce lower pre-ignition temperatures, resulting in reduced fuel vaporization, longer ignition delay time, and reduced power **TABLE 28-2** and **FIGURE 28-5**. Diesel-engine design is generally optimized for air inlet temperatures of approximately 60–90°F (15–32°C).

Air inlet temperature also affects combustion and exhaust temperatures. Exhaust temperatures change approximately 3°F for every 1°F change in air inlet temperature. For example, an increase of air inlet temperature of 100°F will increase exhaust temperature as much as a 300°F. Because the formation of oxides of nitrogen (NO_x) accelerates with high combustion temperatures, the use of charge air cooling is important to reduce NO_x formation.

Effects of Humidity

It is important for the technician diagnosing performance complaints to understand that water vapor or humidity in the air displaces oxygen. A room with a 50% relative humidity at 68°F (20°C) will have more oxygen than a room with

FIGURE 28-4 Compare the amount of oxygen the atmosphere contains when air temperature is hot **(A)** and when it is cold **(B)**.

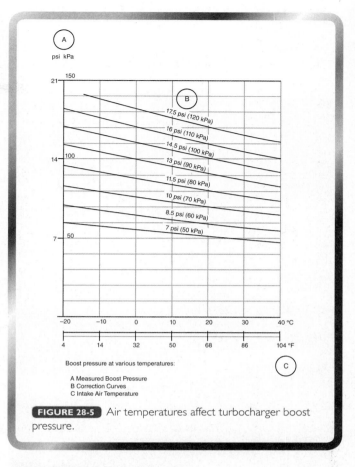

FIGURE 28-5 Air temperatures affect turbocharger boost pressure.

TABLE 28-2: Standard Day Factors SAE J1349

Atmospheric pressure	29.23 inHg (99 kPa)
Temperature	77°F (25°C)
Humidity (relative)	0%

80% relative humidity will have at the same temperature. For every water molecule entering the room, one air molecule leaves.

Warmer temperatures can also dissolve more water than cooler air temperatures. You may notice this effect on hot, humid days as you become short of breath faster when physically active. This happens because higher humidity reduces oxygen in the air **FIGURE 28-6**. Engines experience similar problems when high ambient temperatures are combined with high humidity. The result is often lower power output and higher levels of exhaust smoke. For this reason, diesel emission testing using SAE J1687 protocols—the Snap-Acceleration test—is restricted when temperatures exceed threshold limits, which are just over 80°F (27°C).

> ## TECHNICIAN TIP
>
> The combustion chamber is depleted of oxygen under wet, humid conditions. Hot days will dissolve more water vapor than cool days, which decreases engine power output and increases hydrocarbon (HC), carbon monoxide (CO), and PM emissions. Electronic engines can compensate for increased temperature but not depleted oxygen levels. Some of the newest engines use humidity sensors to correct air–fuel–EGR ratios changed by humidity. Expect an increase in visible emissions from older diesel engines on hot, humid days.

Diesel Air Intake System Design

Air intake system design is important to minimize noise and the quantity of dirt and water entering the air filter **FIGURE 28-7**. Ideally, air intakes should have minimal bending and smooth interior surfaces for maximum airflow. Plastic or rubber tubes are frequently used because they transfer little heat, resist corrosion, and can dampen intake noise better than metal tubes. To maximize airflow to the cylinders, intake manifolds use large runners.

Effects of Airflow Deficiencies

Lack of sufficient airflow to an engine can result in these conditions:

- Low turbocharger or intake boosts pressure
- Higher exhaust temperatures caused by inadequate dilution of combustion gases by fresh air

- Incomplete combustion due to poor contact between fuel and air
- Lower fuel economy caused by poor combustion quality
- Low power complaints caused by poor combustion quality

- Visible exhaust emissions caused by poor combustion quality
- Increased exhaust emissions caused by poor combustion quality
- Shorter valve and piston life due to high heat loads in the cylinders caused by an absence of excess air
- Increased lube oil use due to the intake manifold vacuum drawing oil from the intake valve guides and the turbocharger center housing into the combustion chamber **FIGURE 28-8**

Most electronically controlled engines are equipped with a variety of air inlet–system sensors to identify a problem in the intake system. The on-board diagnostic (OBD) system will set diagnostic trouble codes (DTCs), which may cause the engine's electronic control module (ECM) to adopt engine protection or adaptive strategies to compensate for the problem. For example, the engine protection system collects and monitors data from the intake manifold temperature sensor. High intake

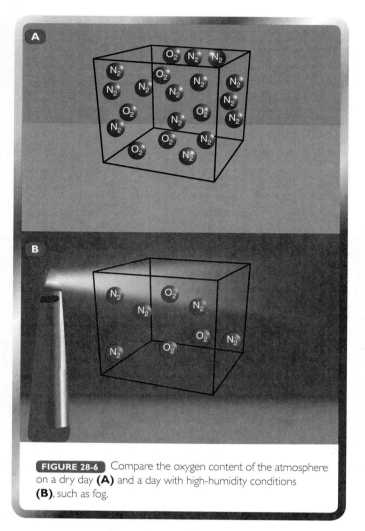

FIGURE 28-6 Compare the oxygen content of the atmosphere on a dry day **(A)** and a day with high-humidity conditions **(B)**, such as fog.

FIGURE 28-7 The plastic air filter housing of this Freightliner engine receives intake airflow from a passage just below the windshield.

- If a correctly adjusted engine has an intake air restriction of "50"(127 cm)H_2O," particulate emissions increase 75% (CO, 28%).

- If engine is overfueled, and otherwise adjusted properly, particulates (PM) increase by 44% (CO, 247%).

- If, however, the two fault situations are combined, particulate matter emissions increase by more than 1000% (CO, 446%) above the baseline value.

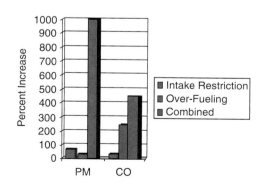

FIGURE 28-8 This chart shows the effect of plugged or restricted air filters on engine emissions for hydro-mechanical fuel systems.

temperatures will cause the engine to shut down or derate if temperatures exceed a threshold value **FIGURE 28-9**. In this example, if intake manifold temperatures exceed 190°F (88°C), the engine fan will switch on; if intake temperatures reach 210°F (99°C), a 20% power derate will occur, and it will become a 40% derate if the temperature remains high. High intake temperatures can cause thermal damage to exhaust valves and cylinder components. To prevent damage, the engine power needs to be derated if temperatures exceed threshold values.

▶ Fundamentals of Crankcase Ventilation Systems

Not all of the air that enters the engine leaves through the exhaust system. Some air ends up in the crankcase of the engine and must be removed to prevent engine damage. This next section examines the problem of crankcase pressure and cylinder blow-by, which produces it. Emission control systems associated with the crankcase are also covered.

Type and Origin of Crankcase Emissions

Gases escaping past piston rings, called blow-by, can accumulate in the engine crankcase, pressurizing the engine and contaminating lube oil. Unless blow-by pressure is relieved, oil leakage or blown seals and gaskets can result **FIGURE 28-10**. Engine blow-by will pick up oil mist from oil cooling nozzles, oil thrown off bearings, and vaporized oil from piston cooling.

▶ TECHNICIAN TIP

Crankcase oil vapors are classified as PM and must be considered as a part of a vehicle's overall emissions. PM emissions as high as 0.7 g/bhp-hr can be found during idle conditions from some diesel engines. This exceeds the exhaust PM standard of 0.1 g/bhp-hr and 0.5 g/bhp-hr for non-methane hydrocarbons (NMH) for 2002 heavy-duty diesel engines. Crankcase vapors from 2007 and later engines are included in total PM emissions, and manufacturers no longer vent vapors directly to the atmosphere.

Tier II 2007 Crankcase Emission Requirements

Considerable efforts and technology have been employed to reduce PM emissions from diesel engine exhaust. Exhaust emissions are now diminished to the point where oil droplets and combustion blow-by from the crankcase are a more significant source of PM emissions than the exhaust. Stringent emission standards have been put in place to reduce crankcase emissions.

One method to clean up blow-by emissions is to recycle crankcase emissions back into the intake manifold. This is known as a **closed crankcase ventilation system**. Another solution to crankcase oil carryover into the intake system is to use multistage filter systems or centrifugal oil-air separators. Coalescing filter devices are designed to **coalesce** (collect) and return lube oil to the engine crankcase and filter out any soot before releasing the air to the atmosphere **FIGURE 28-11** and **FIGURE 28-12**. While these filters have a very long service life, the filter is monitored

FIGURE 28-10 The road draft tube is an open crankcase ventilation system that vents blow-by gases to the atmosphere. Legislation eliminated such crankcases beginning in 2007.

Combination Four-Wire Pressure and Temperature Sensor

Mass Air Flow Sensor

Intake Air Noise Silencer

Air Filter Restriction Gauge

FIGURE 28-9 A combined temperature and pressure sensor is indicated by the four wires connecting this sensor, which provides air intake temperature data and restricts inlet airflow.

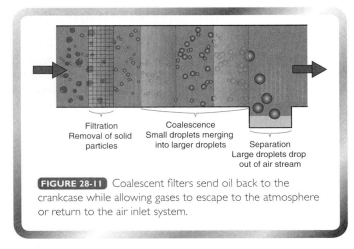

FIGURE 28-11 Coalescent filters send oil back to the crankcase while allowing gases to escape to the atmosphere or return to the air inlet system.

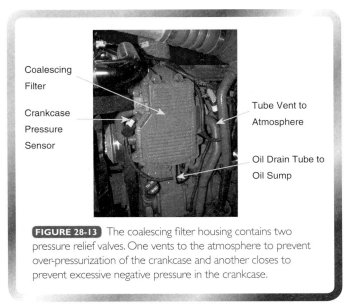

FIGURE 28-13 The coalescing filter housing contains two pressure relief valves. One vents to the atmosphere to prevent over-pressurization of the crankcase and another closes to prevent excessive negative pressure in the crankcase.

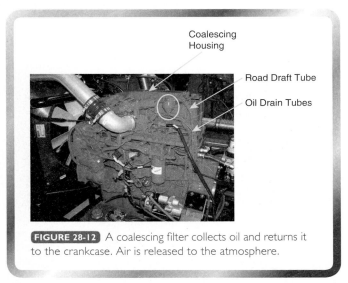

FIGURE 28-12 A coalescing filter collects oil and returns it to the crankcase. Air is released to the atmosphere.

using a crankcase pressure sensor that warns of filter plugging that results in engine damage, such as blown seals or gaskets **FIGURE 28-13**. Two valves are used in many of the coalescing filters used by Cummins to prevent over-pressurization of the crankcase and excessive negative pressure. If the crankcase is connected to the inlet of the turbocharger, excessive negative

pressure can lower crankcase pressure too much and allow dirt to be drawn into the engine through seals and gaskets. A plugged, or even frozen, filter will produce high crankcase pressure, which will blow gasket and seals **FIGURE 28-14**. Coalescing filters and centrifugal oil separators that return oil to the sump have the added benefit of reducing oil consumption.

Centrifugal-type oil-coalescing devices are another mechanism used to separate oil from air. These devices use engine oil pressure to spin a canister that contains crankcase vapors. Liquid oil drains back to the oil sump while the canister releases air **FIGURE 28-15** and **FIGURE 28-16**.

Diagnosing High Crankcase Pressure Codes

In an engine with coalescing filters, the pressure inside the crankcase is measured by the crankcase pressure sensor. Depending on how high the pressure is, a high crankcase pressure code may have moderate to severe fault modes.

To diagnose a high crankcase pressure code, follow the steps in **SKILL DRILL 28-1**.

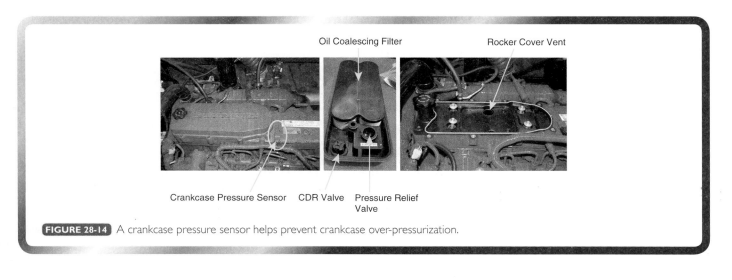

FIGURE 28-14 A crankcase pressure sensor helps prevent crankcase over-pressurization.

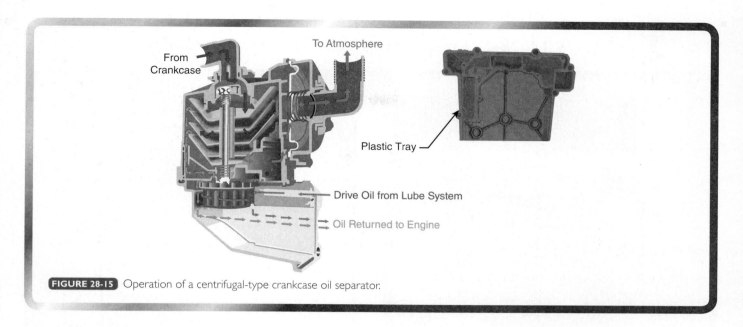

FIGURE 28-15 Operation of a centrifugal-type crankcase oil separator.

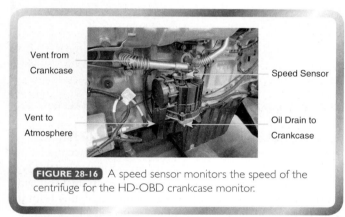

FIGURE 28-16 A speed sensor monitors the speed of the centrifuge for the HD-OBD crankcase monitor.

▶ Types of Crankcase Ventilation Systems

Crankcase emissions can smell unpleasant to vehicle users. They are also a source of particulate emissions and oil leaks from the engine. Depending on the engine displacement, emissions standards in place during the vehicle's production, and engine application, a variety of crankcase ventilation systems are used. Some systems are designed primarily to meet what engineers call sociability demands of customers (that is, the vehicle should not smell or drip oil). Other systems are designed primarily to eliminate crankcase vapors as simply and efficiently as possible. This next section details the construction and operation of crankcase ventilation systems developed to meet a range of important design criteria.

Open Crankcase Ventilation

In gasoline-fueled engines, crankcase vapors are a major source of hydrocarbon emissions because they contain fuel that leaks past the rings during the compression stroke. For this reason, crankcase vapors are recycled into the intake manifold of these engines and burned. However, in a diesel engine, blow-by leaking past the rings consists primarily of air. Because most blow-by occurs during the compression stroke, and diesel engine cylinders contain only air during compression stroke, mostly air leaks into the crankcase, plus a smaller amount of exhaust gas. Traditional ventilation of the diesel crankcase simply required a tube connecting the crankcase to the atmosphere, an arrangement known as an **open crankcase ventilation system**. Common terms for this ventilation device are **road draft tube** or crankcase ventilation tube. A metal strainer is usually incorporated into the tube to separate out oil mist picked up from oil throwoff and vapors from the crankshaft bearings and piston cooling nozzles. Open crankcase ventilation is configured differently in engines built after 2007. A road draft tube is still used, but oil and particulate are removed before venting the vapor to the atmosphere.

Recycling Crankcase Vapors

Crankcase vapors contain oil vapors and combustion by-products, which can make them unpleasant to vehicle users. To eliminate unpleasant odors and oil leakage from tubes, it can be practical to recycle crankcase vapors back into the engine intake manifold. This is accomplished using two methods.

Closed Crankcase Ventilation

One method for recycling crankcase vapors is closed-route routing. In this method, crankcase vapors are drawn into the air intake through a tube connecting the crankcase to the intake system somewhere between the air filter and the turbocharger or intake manifold. A metal mesh filter separates oil mist from the crankcase blow-by through coalescence. Because diesel engines do not produce significant intake vacuum, locating the ventilation tube at this point maintains the crankcase pressure

SKILL DRILL 28-1 Diagnosing High Crankcase Pressure Codes

1. Inspect all crankcase ventilation hoses for kinks or restrictions.

2. If equipped, inspect the oil drain tube and oil drain check valve for restrictions.

3. Check the crankcase pressure sensor for damage.

4. Remove the crankcase filter cover and check to see the filter is properly installed. Replace the crankcase ventilation filter. In cold weather, the filter may become frozen and produce high pressure codes.

to the equivalent of the negative pressure produced by the air filter restriction **FIGURE 28-17**.

While this is a simple method, it has disadvantages. On turbocharged engines, oil mist in the blow-by gases can foul turbocharger compressor wheels and fill aftercoolers with oil. However, using the correct grade of lube oil, which is changed at the appropriate service intervals, will not impair the turbocharger operation. Technicians need to be aware that oil accumulations on the compressor wheel and housing are normal using this type of ventilation system. Intercoolers can also accumulate oil. Normally, as much as 2–3 quarts (2–3 L) of oil originating from the crankcase can be drained from an intercooler **FIGURE 28-18**.

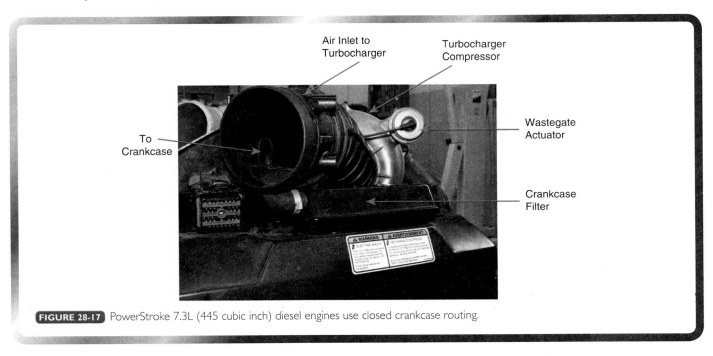

FIGURE 28-17 PowerStroke 7.3L (445 cubic inch) diesel engines use closed crankcase routing.

FIGURE 28-18 Oil carryover from this engine's closed crankcase ventilation system will cause oil seepage from intake air piping. This condition is normal and does not indicate a reason for turbocharger replacement.

FIGURE 28-19 The CDR valve on this turbocharged 6.5L (397 cubic inch) Chevy directs crankcase vapors from the right valve cover into the air inlet upstream of the turbocharger.

Crankcase pressure is another issue. It can lower to the point where dirt is pulled in through seals and gaskets, contaminating engine oil.

TECHNICIAN TIP

Turbocharger compressor wheels coated in oil do not indicate a failed turbocharger. In closed crankcase ventilation systems, oil vapors from the crankcase will collect in the turbocharger compressor housing and intake manifold. Intercoolers will also accumulate oil carried over from the crankcase.

Crankcase Depression Regulator

The second method for recirculating crankcase emissions to the intake manifold is through the use of a **crankcase depression regulator (CDR)** **FIGURE 28-19**. This device regulates, or meters, the quantity of blow-by back into the engine's intake manifold. The advantage of this valve is its ability to maintain a slight negative pressure over the entire speed range of the engine, which is desirable because high crankcase pressure tends to produce oil leakage from gaskets and seals. However, too much vacuum will pull oil into the intake manifold and dirt through the engine seals and gaskets, potentially dusting out the engine. The CDR typically maintains crankcase vacuum at 0–1″ (0–2.5 cm) of water at idle and 3–4″ (7.6–10.2 cm) at 2000 rpm.

The valve regulates crankcase pressure using a spring-loaded diaphragm. When the engine is running, slight negative intake vacuum pulls blow-by gas through the valve and past the open diaphragm. When vacuum in the crankcase exceeds spring tension of the valve, the valve closes, blocking further reduction in crankcase pressure. If crankcase pressure increases or intake vacuum decreases, the valve will open again **FIGURE 28-20**.

▶ Components of Air Induction Systems

Air intake systems are made up of more than just filters and some piping. Electronic engine controls need to adapt engine operation to the quality of the intake air. The following section looks at common electronic input devices located in the air intake systems used on contemporary diesel engines.

Intake Air Sensors

Contemporary diesels use a variety of air intake sensors to match operating conditions with engine-control strategies. Atmospheric pressure, humidity, temperature, and air filter restrictions can significantly affect engine performance and emissions. Precise measurement of air mass into the engine is needed to adjust EGR rates and injection quantities.

Barometric Pressure Sensor

The barometric pressure sensor, or ambient air pressure sensor, provides data regarding ambient air pressure for altitude compensation. This sensor provides data to adjust fuel rates, glow plug on-time, injection timing, and EGR flow depending on altitude or atmospheric pressure. This is necessary to prevent excessive exhaust emissions or performance complaints when atmospheric pressure is low. This sensor is used on non-EGR-equipped engines to prevent turbocharger overspeed at high altitudes. Because turbochargers turn faster when the air is less dense, the barometric pressure sensor input will be used to reduce the quantity of fuel injected, thus lowering turbocharger speeds and preventing overspeed damage.

Intake Manifold Air Temperature Sensor

Data from the intake manifold air temperature sensor is used to modify fuel injection timing and fuel rates to minimize

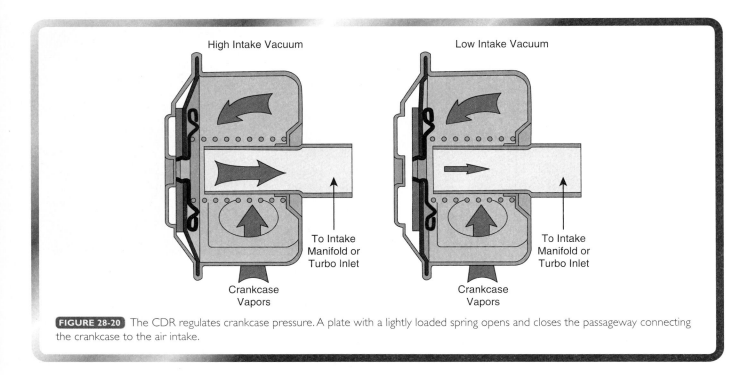

FIGURE 28-20 The CDR regulates crankcase pressure. A plate with a lightly loaded spring opens and closes the passageway connecting the crankcase to the air intake.

emissions. Low intake temperatures will result in advanced injection timing to compensate for longer ignition delay periods **FIGURE 28-21**. A high intake temperature requires retarding injection timing and lower injection rates to minimize emissions. This sensor can also detect excessive intake temperature caused by conditions such as externally restricted aftercoolers, which could lead to thermal damage in the engines. Engine software used by the engine protection system can be enabled to derate, or cut back, injection quantities to prevent this damage.

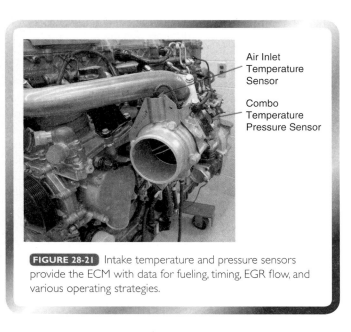

FIGURE 28-21 Intake temperature and pressure sensors provide the ECM with data for fueling, timing, EGR flow, and various operating strategies.

▶ TECHNICIAN TIP

Excessive black or gray smoke emissions may be the result of restricted air inlet systems or inadequate airflow into the engine. Always investigate possible air inlet restrictions, such as plugged filters, blocked intercoolers, collapsed air intake hoses, and incorrect valve adjustments as possible causes of excessive visible smoke emissions.

Manifold Absolute Pressure Sensor

Data from the manifold absolute pressure (MAP) sensor, which is also called the intake boost pressure sensor, is used to sense engine load and adjust fuel rates. If there is inadequate airflow, the boost levels will lower and less fuel is injected. MAP sensors are active three-wire pressure sensors that typically use a variable capacitance-type construction to convert intake manifold pressure into an electrical signal. The MAP sensor coordinates with the manifold temperature sensor to calculate the air mass entering the engine's cylinders. The ECM uses boost pressure and intake manifold temperature data as inputs for a speed-density algorithm to calculate the air mass entering the cylinders. Using air pressure, temperature, engine speed, and volumetric efficiencies of an engine for any given engine speed, the ECM can precisely calculate the weight of the air entering the engine and adjust fuel rates accordingly. Volumetric efficiency refers to the theoretical volume of air pulled into cylinders compared to actual volume **FIGURE 28-22**.

Mass Airflow Sensor

Mass airflow (MAF) sensors measure the weight of air entering the engine. Located after the air filter and before the turbocharger, this device is a stand-alone sensor for calculating

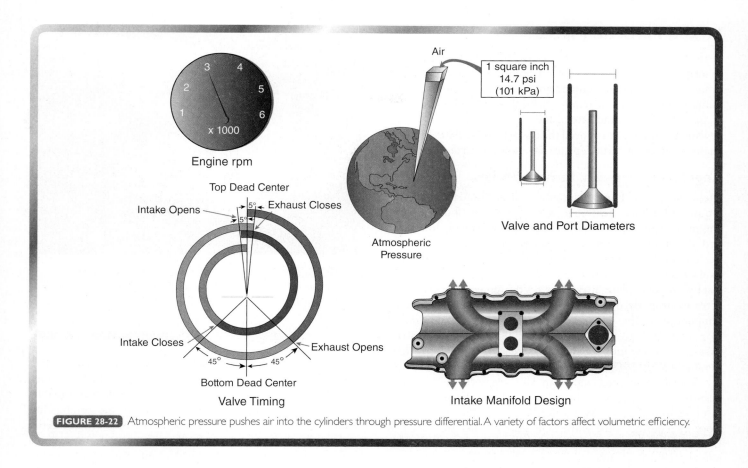

FIGURE 28-22 Atmospheric pressure pushes air into the cylinders through pressure differential. A variety of factors affect volumetric efficiency.

air mass. The MAF replaced the speed density system, which required both a pressure and a temperature sensor. Both sets of sensors are often found together on an engine to compare calculations for intake air mass to ensure that the data from the MAF and speed density system are rational or correct. In addition to measuring the weight of air, the location and operation of an MAF sensor can enable it to detect air inlet restrictions caused by a restricted air filter or intake when pressure drops below a threshold value **FIGURE 28-23**. Intake manifold pressure pulses produced by the large valve overlap of most diesels can cause backflow across the sensor and produce incorrect data. Positioning the sensor farther from the engine minimizes sensor error.

MAF sensors typically use heated platinum or "hot-wire" construction. The circuit operating the MAF sensor sends a current to the wire and maintains a continuously fixed voltage drop to the wire. When air flows past the wire, the wire cools, decreasing its resistance. Cooling the wire causes more current to flow through the heater circuit. The ECM will measure the change in current required to heat the wire and maintain a fixed resistance. The amount of current used to heat the wire to a specific resistance is directly proportional to the mass of air flowing past the sensor. For example, if air density increases due to an increase in air pressure or a decrease in temperature while the air volume remains constant, the denser air will remove more heat from the wire, indicating a higher mass airflow.

MAFs are used primarily on HD-OBD and OBD-II diesels to detect intake air problems and to calculate EGR flow. The

FIGURE 28-23 An MAF sensor on the intake air pipe of a MaxxForce engine.

strategy used by manufacturers is to measure the airflow rate with the MAF and compare it to expected values. When EGR flow increases because exhaust gas is recycled, a proportional decrease of fresh airflow into the engine occurs.

Intake Throttle Plates

Diesel engines do not use a throttle plate to control engine speed or torque output. Because diesel engines require large excess air ratios, intake manifold runners are designed to flow the maximum quantity of air. Generally, each cylinder will breathe from a large plenum common to all the cylinders. However, recent developments have introduced the use of throttle plates in diesel engines. Intake air throttle plates have several purposes.

Regulating Exhaust Temperatures

Diesel particulate filters required for all 2007 and later engines require additional heat that is not normally found in the engine exhaust. For example, during low-speed, low-load, and idle conditions, an excessive amount of air is drawn into the engine in proportion to the small injection quantities. Consequently, combustion and exhaust temperatures are low. Catalyzed particulate filters that need high exhaust temperatures to properly operate cannot function with low exhaust temperatures. The addition of the electronically controlled **intake throttle valve** will, under certain conditions, restrict excessive airflow into the engine, increasing exhaust gas temperatures **FIGURE 28-24**.

Vehicles equipped with lean NO_x traps (LNTs), or NO_x adsorbers, similarly need the exhaust to be depleted of oxygen in order to regenerate. When necessary, the throttle plate will close as required while extra EGR gas and fuel are added to the exhaust stream. Removing oxygen from the exhaust stream allows chemical reactions to convert NO_x emission stored in the LNTs to take place **FIGURE 28-25**.

Control of Combustion Turbulence for Optimized Emission Reduction

Throttled air intakes optimize air turbulence into the combustion chambers for any given load and speed condition. To

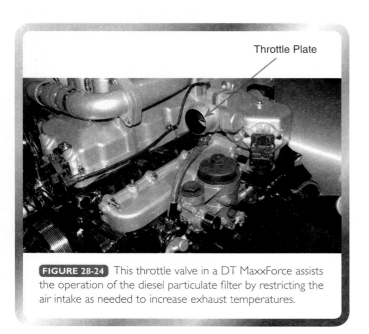

FIGURE 28-24 This throttle valve in a DT MaxxForce assists the operation of the diesel particulate filter by restricting the air intake as needed to increase exhaust temperatures.

FIGURE 28-25 Volvo and Mack engines use a specialized air diverter valve that allows boosted hot air to warm intake air, increasing the exhaust temperatures for catalyzed particulate filters.

achieve lowest emissions, best performance, and fuel economy, air and fuel must be dispersed and mixed as evenly as possible, with turbulence evening out regions where the combustion chamber is fuel rich. While much of this mixing function is the work of the shape of the combustion chamber bowl, it tends to disperse fuel vertically. But airflow into the cylinder mixes fuel horizontally. Using a **tangential intake port** with both intake valves, which admits air into the cylinder at an angle, makes a high degree of intake swirl, or turbulence, possible. Varying the amount of intake swirl is achievable by opening or closing one of the intake ports on these four-valve engines. High swirl is needed to reduce formation of carbon monoxide, hydrocarbon, and particulate emissions at low- to mid-speed operating conditions. Closing or only partially opening one intake runner enhances swirl. At high speed, the intake runner valve is fully opened for maximum airflow into the cylinders **FIGURE 28-26**.

Increasing EGR Flow

Throttle plates are used on some EGR-equipped diesels to increase the rate of exhaust gas flow into the cylinders under some conditions. Because diesels do not have an intake manifold vacuum, negative intake pressure produced by an electrically operated throttle valve draws more gas into the intake air. The EGR inlet to the intake manifold is located downstream of the plate, which is electrically actuated to limit fresh air intake while lowering the pressure in the intake manifold, which increases EGR flow rate **FIGURE 28-27**.

Reducing Engine Shudder

High compression ratios characteristic of diesel engines produce a pronounced shaking motion in the engine during shutdown. This effect is caused by air compression in the cylinders, which turns compressed air, making it behave like a coiled spring.

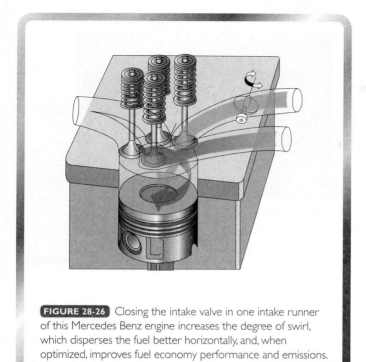

FIGURE 28-26 Closing the intake valve in one intake runner of this Mercedes Benz engine increases the degree of swirl, which disperses the fuel better horizontally, and, when optimized, improves fuel economy performance and emissions.

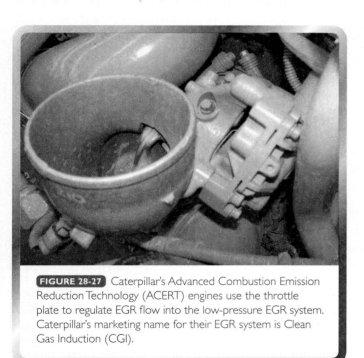

FIGURE 28-27 Caterpillar's Advanced Combustion Emission Reduction Technology (ACERT) engines use the throttle plate to regulate EGR flow into the low-pressure EGR system. Caterpillar's marketing name for their EGR system is Clean Gas Induction (CGI).

Without enough inertia to move the piston through the top dead center (TDC) of the compression stroke, the engine rotation will slow and then reverse repeatedly until all rotational energy is expended.

Accessory drive belts may squeal as the belt direction changes rapidly. Components such as the alternator have some resistance due to residual magnetism. Shutting the intake valve

the moment the ignition is shut off prevents air from entering the engine, which produces a smooth stop to engine rotation. One-way clutches on the alternator pulley are sometimes used to further reduce belt slippage noise.

Intake Air Noise Reduction

Unlike gasoline-fueled engines, diesel engines are able to use a large amount of valve overlap to enhance engine breathing and performance characteristics **FIGURE 28-28**. Valve overlap refers to the time when the intake and exhaust valves are both open near the end of exhaust stroke and the beginning of the intake stroke. In a gasoline-fueled engine, large amounts of valve overlap causes low intake vacuum and allows raw fuel to leave the cylinder during scavenging. In a diesel engine, this valve-timing configuration takes advantage of gas inertia and turbocharged intake pressure to pack more air into the cylinders during the intake stroke and improves exhaust gas scavenging at the end of the exhaust stroke.

The disadvantage of large amounts of valve overlap is the production of loud exhaust pulses that travel through the intake manifold, especially at low engine speeds. To minimize this potentially annoying feature, resonator boxes or chambers may be located in the air induction system to allow exhaust pulses to expand and dissipate, which cancels intake noise **FIGURE 28-29**.

▶ TECHNICIAN TIP

The EPA regulates noise levels from trucks and other vehicles as noise emissions. Modifications to intake and exhaust systems may cause a vehicle to no longer be compliant with emissions standards for noise.

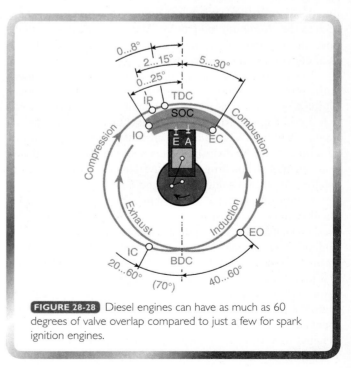

FIGURE 28-28 Diesel engines can have as much as 60 degrees of valve overlap compared to just a few for spark ignition engines.

FIGURE 28-29 The stock intake pipe for the Dodge Ram's 5.9L (360 cubic inch) Cummins engine uses a center section designed to dampen intake air noises, such as turbo whistle.

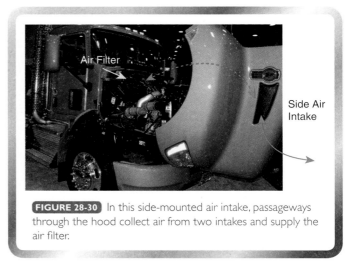

FIGURE 28-30 In this side-mounted air intake, passageways through the hood collect air from two intakes and supply the air filter.

Air Intake Filtering

Dirt, moisture, and other contaminants must be removed from the intake air to prevent engine damage and performance complaints. To minimize contaminant loading of the air filter and water ingestion into the engine, intake systems can be designed in a number of ways. A pre-cleaner will typically remove 80–90% of all airborne contaminants.

A frontal air intake, known as ram air, can take advantage of increased air pressure at highway speeds to assist charging the cylinders. However, the system also allows road salt, water, and dirt into the inlet. Water containing dissolved road salt is especially destructive because it can pass through the air filter and into the air induction system, causing corrosion of components such as the aluminum intercooler. Aluminum oxide eventually finds its way into the cylinders and dramatically accelerates wear of cylinder walls and rings.

The use of side-mounted intakes, such as inside fenders, is the preferred method to minimize water and dirt ingestion **FIGURE 28-30**. Water and dirt have greater inertia than air and will not change direction as easily and be drawn into the air intake. Deflectors located on the air inlet can enhance removal of contaminants by diverting water, snow, and dirt past the air inlet opening. When little room is available beneath the hood or cab for a filter, an outside air filter and housing is used.

Ejector tubes located at the elbows of inlet air tubes and in air filter housings assist in the removal of water and dirt that does enter the induction system. Heavier particles will tend to migrate to a particular location in the tube, where they can exit through these one-way flow-type devices. While most vehicles will locate the air inlet to pull air from outside of the vehicle, some vehicles, depending on application, will also provide the option of collecting air from underneath the hood. This arrangement causes air inlet temperatures to increase. This feature has benefits in very cold ambient conditions or where snow can enter an external inlet because the vehicle is used as a plough.

Most air filter housings also feature construction that imparts a twisting or cyclonic action to airflow, such as **cyclonic-style pre-cleaner tubes**, which pre-clean intake air by spinning dirt out of the airflow to prevent it from entering the filter. Spinning the air as it enters a filter helps separate dirt, water, snow, and fog through centrifugal force. Once thrown against the inside of a filter housing, the particles will gravitate to the bottom of the housing and drop out of the airflow rather than fill the filter media. Narrow intake air tubes impart a twisting motion to rapidly flowing intake air through toroidal action. Toroidal action is the motion imparted to gases and liquids that's observed when draining a sink. In filters that have multiple inlet tubes, toroidal action will separate heavier particles from clean air **FIGURE 28-31**.

Air Filters

An air filter is essential to obtaining clean air for cylinder combustion. Air filter selection and performance criteria are based on the dust environment in which the engine operates, the available space for installation and service, and the filter service interval. A number of materials are used to manufacture air filters. Polyurethane, cellulose, and oil-wetted cotton gauze are some of the most common filter media types **FIGURE 28-32**.

There are three critical criteria for evaluating the filter effectiveness: efficiency, capacity, and restriction. Efficiency is a filter's dirt-stopping capability. Its measurement is the percentage of dirt particles captured by the filter. A 100% efficient filter will stop all dirt particles from entering the engine intake air. Efficiency is rated for a specific size of particle. A filter operating at 98% efficiency will pass 200 times more dirt than one operating at 99.9% efficiency **TABLE 28-3**. As a filter loads with more dirt, efficiency and restriction (pressure drop) increase. This is referred to as the positive filtration principle.

Capacity reflects the dirt-holding ability of a filter. The amount of dirt a filter can hold before it requires replacement

FIGURE 28-31 Tubes impart a twisting motion to intake airflow, which then separates air from heavier contaminant particles using centrifugal force.

FIGURE 28-32 Examples of different filters: cellulose paper-type **(A)**, oil-wetted cotton gauze **(B)**, and synthetic fiber **(C)**.

TABLE 28-3: Comparison of Filtration Efficiency, Dirt-Holding Capability, and Airflow of Eight Paper Air Filter Elements

Dust Holding Capacity	Pressure Drop, (in. H₂O)	0.5 Micron % Efficient	5 Micron % Efficient	10 Micron % Efficient	≥ 15 Micron % Efficient	Average % Efficient
0.3 oz (8 g)	5.2	99.82	93.50	99.87	100	97.36
3.9 oz (111 g)	5.8	99.55	97.98	99.87	100	99.15
8 oz (228 g)	6.6	99.66	98.67	99.66	99.98	99.36
14.6 oz (413 g)	8.3	99.94	99.98	99.94	99.98	99.97
18.7 oz (530 g)	9.9	99.99	99.92	99.96	100	99.96
21.7 oz (614 g)	12.3	99.40	99.95	99.96	100	99.97
26.7 oz (756 g)	18.5	99.90	99.90	99.96	99.96	99.94
28.4 oz (805 g)	23.8	99.98	99.92	99.66	100	99.87
Dust Type		Fine	Fine	Fine	Fine	Fine

determines its capacity. Restriction is how much airflow occurs through a filter. As airflow increases, a pressure differential across the filter develops. Air filter restriction is measured in inches (centimeters) of water column.

Cellulose Paper Filters

To evaluate filter effectiveness, the ISO 5011 standard (formerly SAE J726) establishes a precise filter-testing procedure using measurements under controlled conditions. Tests performed by independent labs demonstrate paper or cellulose fiber filters have the greatest efficiency and capacity. Paper filter efficiencies rank in the range above 99% among most brands, with many between 99.5% and 99.9%.

Paper filter elements are made from compressed cellulose fibers and chemically treated to resist water damage. Pleats in the filter paper increase the surface area and capacity of the filter. Aluminum wire mesh inside and outside of the filter element provides a structural skeleton for the filter. It also removes larger solid particles and prevents them from entering or damaging filtration media.

The spaces between the cellulose fibers provide microscopic openings the air must pass through. As dirty air flows through these pores, these holes become plugged. Once a pore is plugged, the air will find an alternate route through the filter. The larger pores tend to plug up faster because greater air volumes flow through those channels. The smaller holes in the filter media will plug up later **FIGURE 28-33**. Consequently, the longer a filter is in service, the more efficient air filtration becomes.

> ### ▶ TECHNICIAN TIP
>
> Avoid over-servicing filters to obtain the most efficient filtration because a new filter will pass more dirt than a used one. However, as the filter collects more dirt, its resistance to airflow increases and airflow resistance increases. Eventually, hp and fuel economy decrease. Ideally, the media must be thick and/or the fibers must be tightly compressed and dense to load the most dirt and obtain efficient filtration.

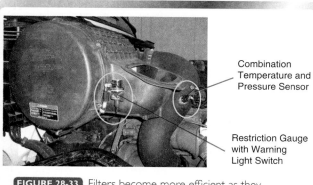

FIGURE 28-33 Filters become more efficient as they become restricted. Larger holes in filter media will plug with dirt first, and then progressively smaller holes with become blocked. .

Cotton Gauze Filter Media

Cotton gauze–type filters with special oil to enhance dirt-capturing ability have become popular to performance enthusiasts. The gauze's microfibers absorb the oil. The advantage of this filter is that it separates contaminating particles with less physical obstruction than typical paper elements. However, an ISO 5011 test evaluating one brand of this filter media places its efficiency at less than 90% and notes it does not have as much dirt-holding capacity as many paper filters. Oil wetting of the cotton gauze can contaminate intake sensors.

Nanofiber PowerCore Filters

PowerCore filters are a wall flow-type filter element. This newer filter technology uses a synthetic web-like fiber to cover a specially formulated cellulose material. The fine size of the fiber cover is why the filter media is referred to as *nanofiber*. This covering material allows dirt to imbed into the fiber overlay rather than into the cellulose. This feature extends filter service life and improves filtration efficiency. Donaldson has developed this media and a long-life low-restriction filter. When shaped similarly to corrugated cardboard, the air passageways through the filter are arranged in flutes, with one end alternately blocked on each flute **FIGURE 28-34**. Air must pass through the wall of the flute to enter the intake. This straight-through design passes air with less restriction. PowerCore filters have the additional advantage of drastically reducing filter size while increasing dirt-holding capacity. The smaller air filter footprint is especially advantageous when underhood room is limited **FIGURE 28-35** and **FIGURE 28-36**.

Intake Performance Accessories

Because diesel engines are air-breathing machines, any performance enhancement that increases power or efficiency will usually involve increased combustion air. Technicians are often called upon to provide advice and recommendations about the use of, or even install some of, these performance devices. The following section outlines the operation of some common intake air modifications to help technicians better understand how these accessories function.

Nitrous Oxide Systems

Nitrous oxide (N_2O, not to be confused with oxides of nitrogen, such as NO, NO_2, NO_3, and NO_4) will disintegrate into oxygen and nitrogen components in a combustion chamber at 565°F (296°C). Because it contains more than twice as much oxygen as a cubic foot of air, adding a **nitrous oxide system (NOS)**, which supplements intake air with N_2O, can supply a power boost if additional fuel is burned to use up the oxygen in the cylinder. The excess air diesels need in order to operate would require tremendous amounts of N_2O for just a few seconds of operation, making it somewhat impractical to use in diesels as compared to gasoline-fueled engines.

Propane Toppers

Some diesel enthusiasts buy a **propane enrichment system**, commonly called a propane topper. It introduces propane into the

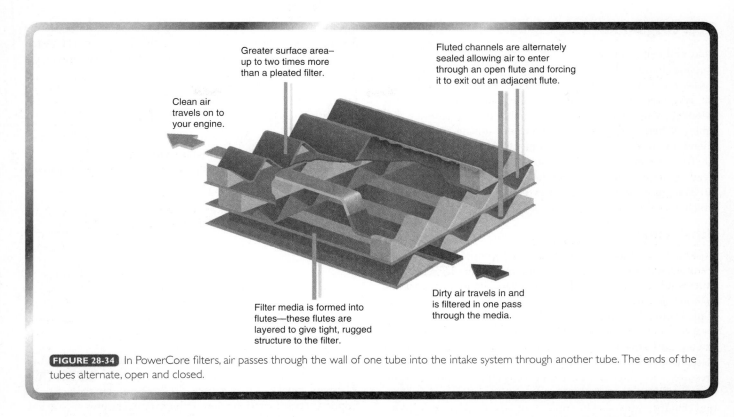

Clean air travels on to your engine.

Greater surface area—up to two times more than a pleated filter.

Fluted channels are alternately sealed allowing air to enter through an open flute and forcing it to exit out an adjacent flute.

Filter media is formed into flutes—these flutes are layered to give tight, rugged structure to the filter.

Dirty air travels in and is filtered in one pass through the media.

FIGURE 28-34 In PowerCore filters, air passes through the wall of one tube into the intake system through another tube. The ends of the tubes alternate, open and closed.

FIGURE 28-35 PowerCore filters can hold more dirt, improve filtration efficiency, and are more compact than conventional paper filters.

FIGURE 28-36 This air filter features a cyclonic type of inlet. It is located outside the hood because underhood space is limited.

intake air through a solenoid-controlled orifice. The propane will increase power output by using up oxygen left over in the cylinders. A propane cylinder weighing approximately 30 lb (14 kg) or more is stored on the vehicle and supplies the propane. The propane topper is often seen in racing or tractor-pulling competitions.

Water-Methanol Injection

Diesel performance enthusiasts occasionally use water-methanol systems to lower combustion chamber temperatures through water-methanol injection. The addition of water to the chamber will lower combustion temperatures to prevent engine damage when operating near maximum threshold temperatures. When water and methanol, a type of alcohol, are injected into the intake system, the process of vaporization absorbs heat from the intake air and reduces its temperature. Reducing intake air temperatures helps to further reduce peak combustion temperatures. Water-methanol injection uses fumigation, which is a process of sending vapors into the air intake.

Starting Aids

Cold ambient temperatures reduce pre-ignition heat or compression temperatures in the engine cylinders during cold start-up. Other problems occur when operating in cold ambient temperatures. When engines are cold, cranking time is extended. This puts stress on the starting motor, batteries, and cables. When battery capacity is reduced during cold weather operation, an engine must start quickly, or it may not start at all. To avoid the problem of a no-start condition due to cold weather, diesel engines will use starting aids to warm the intake air. Warming intake air increases compression temperatures, which improves the ability of an engine to start quickly.

Ethyl Ether

In older diesel engines, liquid ether, when sprayed into the intake manifold, was commonly used to start cold engines **FIGURE 28-37**. Ether is suited to assist starting compression-ignition engines due to its low auto-ignition temperature, 320°F (160°C), and flammability. Even at low temperatures, liquid ether will readily turn to a vapor and burn over a wide range of concentrations. Because its auto-ignition temperature is much lower than an average for diesel fuel, 520°F (271°C), ether will ignite at lower compression pressures and temperatures. The burning ether provides an ignition source for diesel fuel when it is injected into the combustion chamber. Ether can be sprayed into the intake system with a can or metered using capsules or an ether injection system. The electrical system will use a cold start switch that will not allow the ether to be inadvertently injected at temperatures above the freezing point. The operator can press the dash-mounted switch to initiate the delivery of a fixed quantity of ether into the intake manifold prior to cold starting the engine.

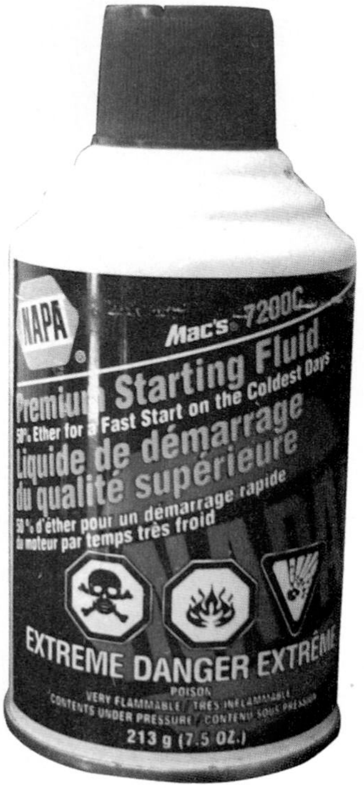

Ethyl Ether Properties

Ethyl ether has the following properties:

- Flash point: −49°F (−45°C)
- Auto-ignition temperature: 320°F (160°C)
- Flammable limits in air, percent by volume: 1.9% lower limit; 36% upper limit

Safety

Because ether is highly flammable, it should never be sprayed into an engine using glow plugs or electric intake heaters. Unless these devices are disabled, the ether will burn explosively in the intake manifold with potentially catastrophic results, including personal injury or death.

Electric Intake Heaters

Heating intake air is another technique to reduce cold-start emissions and improve engine-starting characteristics **FIGURE 28-38**. Warming intake air increases pre-ignition temperatures, an important consideration when ambient temperatures are too low, to allow normal ignition of fuel during start-up conditions. Heating intake air can also shorten ignition delay time. The additional intake heat has the effect of reducing fuel knock and white smoke caused by cylinder misfires. Less soot and HCs are produced during cold start and warm-up using intake heaters. Electric **intake air heaters** connected to circuits monitoring engine temperature are commonly used on diesel engines **FIGURE 28-39**. Low engine temperatures will activate the heating element circuit, allowing the heater to warm intake air during starting and warm-up operation. Under boost conditions, when the intake air is heated by turbocharging, intake heaters are de-energized. Barometric sensors are used to prolong heating time at high altitudes, where air is less dense and will not hold as much heat.

FIGURE 28-37 Ethyl ether is used as a starting aid because its auto-ignition temperature is lower than diesel fuel.

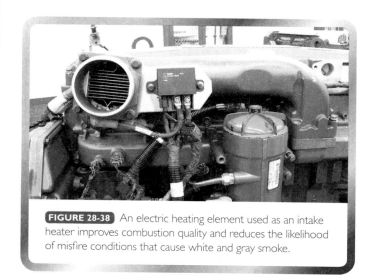

FIGURE 28-38 An electric heating element used as an intake heater improves combustion quality and reduces the likelihood of misfire conditions that cause white and gray smoke.

▶ Maintenance of Air Induction and Crankcase Ventilation Systems

Air intake service is often considered to be a matter of filter replacement. Knowing when to replace filters and how to properly evaluate filter service life helps reduce unnecessary replacement and the costs associated with these largest of engine filters. This next section also outlines other inspections of the intake system that technicians should be familiar with.

Air Filter Service

Air filter servicing should be determined by the amount of filter restriction. A manufacturer will require replacement of the filter element when its maximum allowable restriction is reached.

As an air filter element becomes loaded with contaminants, the vacuum or restriction increases on the engine side, or clean side, of the air filter. This pressure differential across the element is measured in inches (centimeters) of water. A water manometer or Magnehelic gauge calibrated in inches of water best records restriction **FIGURE 28-40** and **FIGURE 28-41**.

The element should not be serviced based on visual observation, because this usually leads to over-servicing or unnecessary filter replacement. Sometimes filters can appear clean but, in fact, are too restrictive. Filter minders or restriction gauges are usually located on air filter housing to evaluate filter restriction. If no gauge is present, a test port is usually located on the filter housing to connect a test instrument.

Some vehicles are equipped with electronic restriction gauges or switches. An **air filter restriction gauge** in the air filter housing is connected to the instrument cluster to warn the driver to service the element **FIGURE 28-42**.

On turbocharged engines, filter restriction is measured at rated speed with the engine under load. Manufacturers may also publish specifications for restrictions on turbocharged engines measured at high idle, but the restriction data will be higher when measured under load **FIGURE 28-43**. The restriction limit of most turbocharged diesel engines is a maximum of 12–15″ (30–38.1 cm) water column under full load before a penalty to fuel economy takes place.

On **naturally aspirated engines**, or engines that use only atmospheric pressure and not pressurized air to charge the cylinders with air, restriction is measured at rated rpm regardless of load. Naturally aspirated engines will operate at a maximum of 6–8″ (15–20 cm) of water column **TABLE 28-4**.

Measuring Air Filter Restriction

Air filter restriction is an important factor used to determine when to replace air filters. Visual methods of measuring air filter restriction do not accurately evaluate whether a filter is plugged or still has significant service life remaining.

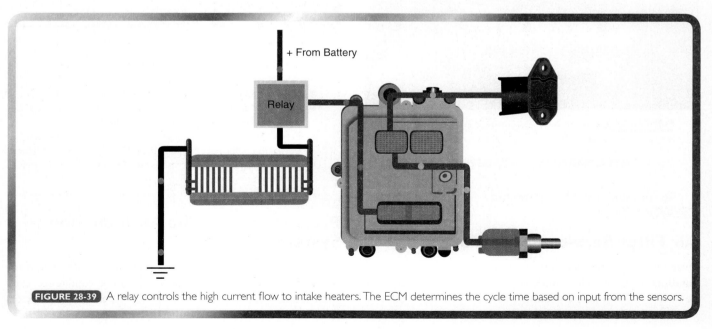

FIGURE 28-39 A relay controls the high current flow to intake heaters. The ECM determines the cycle time based on input from the sensors.

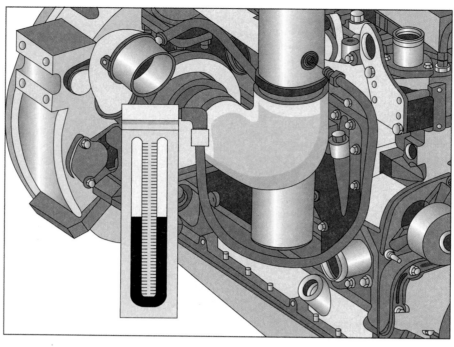

FIGURE 28-40 A water manometer measures air filter restriction.

Measure Restriction in this Pipe

FIGURE 28-41 A Magnehelic gauge measures air filter restriction in inches (millimeters) of water column.

To measure air filter restriction, follow the steps in **SKILL DRILL 28-2**.

Air Filter Service Precautions

Over-servicing filter elements can lead to problems. Excessive handling may cause element damage, or an incorrect filter may be installed. Air intake contamination from filter dust can also occur.

Do not remove element for inspection. Such inspections can do more harm than good to the engine. Sealing gaskets can be torn or damaged when removed, and ridges of dirt on the gasket sealing surface can drop into the clean side of the filter when the gasket is released. Some filter housings use an inner filter element to keep dirt and other contaminants from falling into the air intake system of the engine while the outer filter is being serviced.

TECHNICIAN TIP

To ensure proper filtration of air, keep the following in mind:

- Never use a warped air filter cover on filter housings.
- Do not use a dented filter element.
- Never substitute an incorrect element model number.
- Never rap an element to clean it; this only destroys filter elements and embeds some dirt even deeper.
- Never clean a filter with compressed air; compressed air will thin out or tear filter paper leading to dirt leakage into the engine.
- Always clean out the filter housing and moisture drains before installing a new filter.

Pressure Testing the Air Induction System

A leaking air induction system will pull dirty intake air into the engine, which leads to rapid engine dust-out conditions. Dirt-contaminated oil can quickly destroy some types of HEUI injectors and other internal components that do not receive filtered oil.

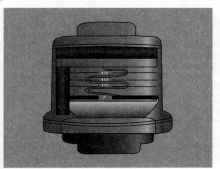

"5–10" (13–25 cm)"
Normal clean filter. (initial restriction varies with each system design.)

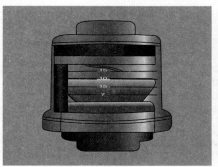

"15–18" (38–46 cm)"
The filter element is loading up with contaminants, but still has much useful life left. Fuel consumption is probably increasing.

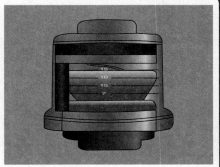

"20–25" (51–64 cm)"
The filter element should be replaced. The engine is probably using more fuel with slight loss of power. This upper limit will vary depending on whether equipment is diesel or gasoline fueled, and your fuel consumption experience.

FIGURE 28-42 An air filter restriction gauge is useful for alerting the driver or technician to service the air filter element.

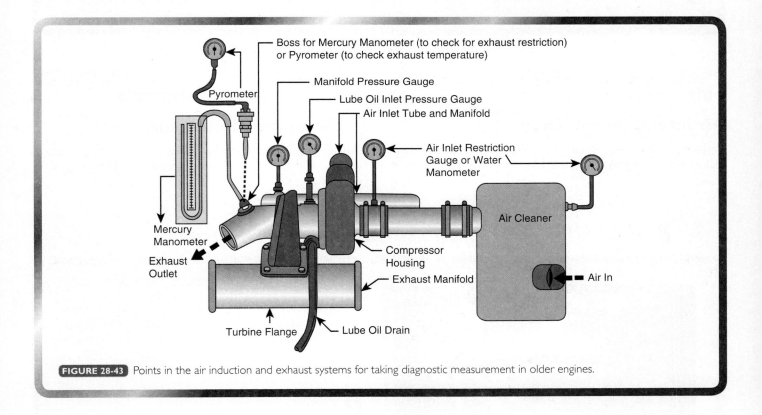

FIGURE 28-43 Points in the air induction and exhaust systems for taking diagnostic measurement in older engines.

TABLE 28-4: Air Filter Service Life Probabilities

Usage	Application	Expected Service Life, Distance	Expected Service Life, Time
Light duty	Pick-up and delivery, city/highway	40,000 miles (64,374 km)	900 hours
Medium duty	Off-road gravel trucks, electric generators	80,000 miles (128,748 km)	1600 hours
Heavy duty	Highway trucks	More than 100,000 miles (160,934 km)	2000+ hours

SKILL DRILL 28-2 Measuring Air Filter Restriction

PRESSURE CONVERSION

Unit	inH$_2$O	cmH$_2$O	inHg	cmHg	psi	kg/cm^2	atm	kPa
1 inH$_2$O	1	2.54	0.0735	1.866	0.0361			0.248
1 inHg	13.6	34.544	1	2.54	0.491	0.0345	0.0334	3.386
1 psi	27.7	70.104	2.036	5.171	1	0.0703	0.068	6.8948
1 kg/cm^2	393.73	1000.0	28.96	73.55	14.22	1	0.9678	101.28
1 atm	407.19	1033.0	29.92	75.96	14.70	1.033	1	....
1 kPa	4.01	10.18	0.295	0.750	0.145	0.026	....	....

1. Connect a Magnehelic gauge to the clean side of the air filter. A Magnehelic gauge measures pressures in units of water column. An electronic pressure transducer or a gauge with long plastic lines is needed.

2. Place the engine under load during a road test to operate the engine at maximum boost pressure.

3. Observe and record maximum filter restriction.

4. Recommend air filter replacement if restriction is more than 12–15″ (30–38 cm) of H$_2$O.

To pressure test the air induction system, follow the steps in **SKILL DRILL 28-3**.

Air Intake System Diagnostics

Problems with the air intake system are accompanied by complaints of black or gray smoke and low power in engines without particulate filters. There are several potential causes for these complaints that can be investigated **TABLE 28-5**.

Intake System Inspection

Visually inspect the air intake system to make sure it is intact. Inspect all ducts, pipes, hoses, tubing, and elbows used to

 SKILL DRILL 28-3 Pressure Testing the Air Induction System

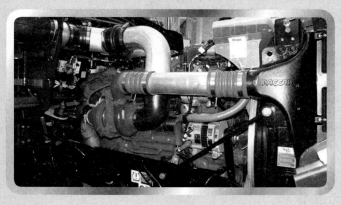

3. Connect a supply of pressurized air that is regulated to 5–8 psi (34–55 kPa) to the intake system. Removing the filter restriction gauge is an easily accessible point to pressurize the air intake system. Higher pressure will rupture the bag and rotate the engine if an intake valve is open. The engine may need to be rotated to a position where a cylinder is not on valve overlap and allowing the air to pass through to the exhaust system.

4. Inspect the intake pipes and clamps for leaks. Spray down the connections between the filter and turbocharger inlet with soapy water.

5. Retighten loose clamps, realign hoses as necessary, and repair any detectable air leaks. Leaks on the pressurized side of the intake system after the turbocharger are not a concern, because pressurized air will push dirt out rather than pull it in.

1. Remove the air filter and wrap it in a large, heavy-duty plastic garbage bag.

2. Reinstall the air filter into the filter housing.

TABLE 28-5: Guidelines for Investigating the Air Induction System

Cause	Correction/Diagnostic
Complaints associated with operational problems 1. Operation while overloaded or at excessive speed 2. Excessive idle 3. Operation during extreme ambient temperature 4. High altitude on naturally aspirated engines	Advise operator
Air induction system problems 1. Restricted air filter 2. Restricted charge air cooler 3. Collapsed air induction hose 4. Air intake manifold or charge air system leak 5. Turbocharger defective 6. Incorrect turbocharger 7. Malfunctioning EGR system	Check air inlet system Measure air filter restriction Check air inlet hoses and clamps Clean air inlet system Pressure-test air inlet and charge air system Check for air inlet system noises and loose clamps Check charge air cooler for internal restrictions Check turbocharger operation and for physical damage Measure turbocharger boost pressure on road test Inspect and repair EGR system
Mechanical system problems 1. Worn camshaft lobes 2. Exhaust system restriction 3. Low compression from worn cylinder components, damaged or misadjusted valves 4. Incorrect valve adjustment	Perform compression tests Measure cylinder leak-down Measure crankcase blow-by pressure Measure exhaust system back pressure Remove and inspect cylinder head Perform valve and injector adjustment
Fuel system problems 1. Incorrect grade of fuel 2. Over-fueling 3. Worn injectors 4. Incorrect injection timing 5. Low injection pressures 6. Low fuel viscosity 7. Engine control system problem 8. Incorrect injector adjustment 9. Tampering 10. Incorrectly calibrated engine	Check fuel quality Check throttle position sensor or linkage for maximum wide-open position Check and adjust fuel timing Check for engine fault codes Pressure-volume test of fuel pump Test injection pump on a comparator bench Test fuel nozzles Adjust injector calibration Re-flash engine ECM with correct calibration Perform valve and injector adjustment

interconnect the system. Inspect components for damage, misalignment, and leakage.

Some intake system components require noise-related inspection:

- Air cleaner housing
- Air cleaner element
- Turbocharger
- Charge air cooler and clamps
- Intake manifold

Also inspect all intake system fasteners, brackets, and clamps for damage and tightness.

Testing the CDR Valve

Engine oil leaks or excessive oil in the intake manifold indicates the CDR valve needs testing. First evaluate the engine to determine if there is excessive blow-by caused by a worn-out engine. Excessive blow-by caused by worn cylinder walls, piston rings, and valve guides will overwhelm the CDR valve, causing engine oil leaks, and push lube oil into the intake manifold with blow-by gas.

During crankcase pressure testing, which is the best procedure to evaluate the condition of cylinder components, the CDR valve is blocked and blow-by gases leave through a calibrated orifice. If blow-by is within acceptable limits, the CDR valve is reconnected and crankcase pressure is re-evaluated. At idle, a water manometer or magnehelic gauge connected to the oil dipstick tube should indicate a negative pressure of less than 1" (2.5 cm) of water column. At high idle no-load condition, the crankcase vacuum should be no more than 3–4" (7.6–10 cm) of water column.

Wrap-Up

Ready for Review

▶ Diesel engines use far more air than similarly displaced gasoline engines. The diesel's abundant consumption of air makes it sensitive to air quality and requires a sophisticated air-handling system.

▶ Problems with engine air quality and induction system supply have a major impact on emissions, noise, performance, and engine durability.

▶ To support efficient combustion with minimal emissions, diesel engines need an adequate supply of air that is clean, dry, fresh, and relatively cool. Diesel engines also require an excess supply of air relative to the quantity needed to completely burn fuel in the cylinders.

▶ Because diesels have a short amount of time for atomizing, distributing, vaporizing, and heating fuel vapors, it is important that the fuel find enough air to contact and react with the oxygen.

▶ Excess air is also necessary to cool critical cylinder components in a diesel; intense combustion heat will easily melt pistons and burn valves.

▶ A diesel engine requires 15–20 lb (7–9 kg) of air to burn 1 lb (0.5 kg) of fuel.

▶ Clean, filtered air is critical to engine operation to prevent damage and rapid wear from abrasive dirt particles. Dirt ingestion into an engine, referred to as dusting out, can take place through small openings in the intake system and from poor filtration.

▶ Optimal air inlet temperatures are essential to good performance and emissions. Atmospheric pressure, ambient temperature, and humidity affect power because the number of oxygen molecules entering the cylinder will vary with a change in any of these factors.

▶ Air inlet temperature also affects combustion and exhaust temperatures. Exhaust temperatures can change approximately 3°F for every 1°F change in air inlet temperature.

▶ Water vapor displaces oxygen in the air, which means the combustion chamber is depleted of oxygen under wet and humid conditions.

▶ Air intakes' design is important to minimize noise and the quantity of dirt and water entering the air filter. Air intakes ideally should have minimal bending and smooth interior surfaces for maximum airflow.

▶ Gases escaping past piston rings, called blow-by, will pick up oil mist from oil cooling nozzles, oil thrown off bearings, and oil vaporizing from piston cooling. Oil vapors from the crankcase are classified as PM emissions.

▶ Traditional ventilation of the diesel crankcase requires simply a tube connecting the crankcase to the atmosphere. This arrangement for crankcase ventilation is known as an open crankcase ventilation system.

▶ Due to the increasing stringency of emission standards, manufacturers no longer vent vapors directly to the atmosphere. One method to clean up blow-by emissions is to recycle crankcase emissions back into the intake manifold. This is known as a closed crankcase ventilation system. One method to recirculate crankcase emissions to the intake manifold is through a CDR.

▶ Another solution to crankcase oil carryover into the intake system is to use multistage filter systems.

▶ Most electronically controlled engines are equipped with a variety of air inlet system sensors to identify a problem in the intake system. DTCs will be set by the OBD system and may cause the engine ECM to adopt engine protection or adaptive strategies to compensate for the problem.

▶ The barometric pressure sensor, or ambient air pressure sensor, is used to provide data regarding ambient air pressure for altitude compensation.

▶ Data from the intake manifold air temperature sensor is used to modify fuel injection timing and fuel rates to minimize emissions.

▶ The MAP sensor, also called the intake boost pressure sensor, is used to sense engine load and adjust fuel rates. If airflow is inadequate, the boost levels will lower and less fuel is injected.

▶ MAF sensors measure the weight of air entering the engine. In addition, the location and operation of an MAF sensor can detect air inlet restrictions caused by a restricted air filter or intake when pressure drops below a threshold value.

▶ Diesel engines do not use a throttle plate to control engine speed or torque output. However, recent developments have introduced the use of throttle plates in diesel engines for several other purposes, including regulating exhaust temperatures, controlling combustion turbulence for optimized emission reduction, increasing EGR flow, and reducing engine shudder.

▶ Resonator boxes or chambers may be located in the air induction system, which allows exhaust pulses to expand and dissipate, canceling intake noise. Resonator boxes can also suppress turbocharger noise, but special devices and configuration of the intake system also serve this function.

▶ Dirt, moisture, and other contaminants must be removed from the intake air to prevent engine damage and performance complaints. Intake systems can be designed in a number of ways to minimize the entry of moisture and dirt entry, which minimizes contaminant loading of the air filter and water ingestion into the engine.

▶ Using side-mounted intakes, such as inside fenders, is preferred to frontal air intakes to minimize water and dirt ingestion.

▶ Deflectors located on the air inlet can enhance removal of contaminants by diverting water, snow, and dirt past the air inlet opening.

- Ejector tubes located at the elbows of inlet air tubes and in air filter housings assist in the removal of water and dirt that does enter the induction system.
- Using an air filter is essential to obtaining clean air for cylinder combustion. Air filter selection and performance criteria are based on the dust environment in which the engine operates, the available space for installation and service, and the filter service interval.
- Three critical criteria to evaluate the effectiveness of filters are efficiency, capacity, and restriction.
- A number of materials are used to manufacture air filters. Polyurethane, cellulose, and oil-wetted cotton gauze are the most common filter media.
- Air filter servicing should be determined by the amount of filter restriction. A manufacturer will require replacement of the filter element when its maximum allowable restriction is reached.
- Several intake performance accessories can be added to diesels, including nitrous oxide systems, propane toppers, and water-methanol injection.
- To avoid the problem of a no-start condition due to cold weather, diesel engines will use starting aids to warm the intake air. Warming intake air increases compression temperatures, which improves the ability of an engine to start quickly.
- Problems with the air intake system are accompanied by complaints of black or gray smoke and low power in engines without particulate filters.

Vocabulary Builder

air inlet restriction gauge A pressure sensor that measures the negative pressure between the air filter and turbocharger.

closed crankcase ventilation system A method of cleaning up blow-by emissions by recycling crankcase emissions back into the intake manifold.

coalesce The process of collecting together oil in crankcase vapors to separate it from the vapors.

crankcase depression regulator (CDR) A device that regulates, or meters, the quantity of blow-by emissions back into the engine's intake manifold.

cyclonic-style pre-cleaner tubes A component of the air intake system that pre-cleans intake air by spinning dirt out of the airflow to prevent it from entering the filter.

fumigation A process of sending vapors into the air intake, such as in the case of water-methanol injection systems.

intake air heater A device that heats intake air to reduce cold-start emissions, improve engine-starting characteristics, shorten ignition delay time, improve combustion quality, and reduce the likelihood of misfire conditions that cause white and gray smoke.

intake throttle valve A valve located at the inlet of the intake manifold and used to restrict airflow into the engine and increase exhaust aftertreatment temperatures.

mass airflow (MAF) sensor A device that measures the weight of air entering the engine and detects air inlet restrictions caused by a restricted air filter or intake when pressure drops below a threshold value.

naturally aspirated An engine that uses only atmospheric pressure and not pressurized air to charge the cylinders with air.

nitrous oxide system (NOS) A system that supplements intake air with nitrous oxide (N_2O) to supply additional oxygen in the cylinder to burn more fuel.

open crankcase ventilation system A traditional ventilation system for the diesel crankcase that vents the crankcase directly to the atmosphere.

propane enrichment system An aftermarket performance accessory that introduces propane into the intake air through a solenoid-controlled orifice to increase power output by using up excess oxygen left over in the cylinders; also known as a propane topper.

road draft tube The tube that connects the crankcase to the atmosphere in an open crankcase ventilation system; also known as a crankcase ventilation tube.

standard day factors Engine test standards for ambient temperature, atmospheric pressure, and humidity. Manufacturer measurements of horsepower and torque must be made using standard day factors to ensure uniformity of test results.

stoichiometric ratio The mass of air required to completely burn all fuel in the combustion chamber so no fuel or air remains after combustion.

tangential intake port An intake port design that admits air into the cylinder at an angle to impart more swirl, or turbulence, to charge air.

volumetric efficiency A comparison between measured cylinder volume and the volume of air actually filling a cylinder; expressed as a percentage.

water-methanol injection A system that sprays water and methanol into the intake system to absorb heat from the intake air, which helps to reduce peak combustion temperatures.

Review Questions

1. The _____ engine uses only atmospheric pressure and not pressurized air to charge the cylinders with air.
   - **a.** closed crankcase
   - **b.** open crankcase
   - **c.** naturally aspirated
   - **d.** artificially aspirated

2. The _____ is the mass of air required to completely burn all fuel in the combustion chamber so no fuel or air remains after combustion.
   - **a.** aspiration ratio
   - **b.** saturation ratio
   - **c.** effectiveness ratio
   - **d.** stoichiometric ratio

3. _____ is a process of sending vapors into the air intake, such as in the case of water-methanol injection systems.
   a. Positive filtration
   b. Fumigation
   c. Ventilation
   d. Restriction

4. To prevent damage, the engine power needs to be _____ if temperatures exceed threshold values.
   a. derated
   b. restricted
   c. increased
   d. aspirated

5. Excessive _____ pressure can lower crankcase pressure too much and allow dirt to be drawn into the engine through seals and gaskets.
   a. positive
   b. negative
   c. barometric
   d. atmospheric

6. The _____ pressure sensor provides regarding ambient air pressure for altitude compensation.
   a. stoichiometric
   b. barometric
   c. manifold absolute
   d. airflow

7. An electronically controlled _____ valve will, under certain conditions, restrict excessive airflow into the engine, increasing exhaust gas temperatures.
   a. exhaust manifold
   b. intake manifold
   c. turbocharger compressor
   d. intake throttle

8. _____ is a method of cleaning up blow-by emissions by recycling crankcase emissions back into the intake manifold.
   a. Coalescing
   b. Closed crankcase ventilation
   c. Fumigation
   d. Open crankcase ventilation

9. _____ is a comparison between measured cylinder volume and the volume of air actually filling a cylinder; expressed as a percentage.
   a. Standard day factors
   b. Volumetric efficiency
   c. Stoichiometric ratio
   d. Ambient pressure

10. The _____ is the tube that connects the crankcase to the atmosphere in an open crankcase ventilation system; also known as a crankcase ventilation tube.
    a. road draft tube
    b. drain tube
    c. air-to-air intercooler
    d. crankcase depression regulator

ASE-Type Questions

1. Technician A says that a diesel engine of 350 horsepower typically requires an air intake capacity of close to 500 cubic feet per minute. Technician B says that a diesel engine of 350 horsepower typically requires an air intake capacity of close to 1500 cubic feet per minute. Who is correct?
   a. Technician A
   b. Technician B
   c. Both Technician A and Technician B
   d. Neither Technician A nor Technician B

2. Technician A says the best choice for detecting leaks in the positive pressure side of the air intake system is an engine oil analysis. Technician B says the best choice for detecting leaks in the negative pressure side of the air intake system is an ultrasonic test. Who is correct?
   a. Technician A
   b. Technician B
   c. Both Technician A and Technician B
   d. Neither Technician A nor Technician B

3. Technician A says that the number of oxygen molecules entering the cylinder will vary with a change in atmospheric pressure. Technician B says that the number of oxygen molecules entering the cylinder will vary with a change in ambient temperature. Who is correct?
   a. Technician A
   b. Technician B
   c. Both Technician A and Technician B
   d. Neither Technician A nor Technician B

4. Technician A says that plastic or rubber tubes are frequently used for air intake construction because they resist corrosion better than metal tubes. Technician B says that plastic or rubber tubes are frequently used for air intake construction because they dampen intake noise better than metal tubes. Who is correct?
   a. Technician A
   b. Technician B
   c. Both Technician A and Technician B
   d. Neither Technician A nor Technician B

5. Technician A says that in a diesel engine, blow-by leaking past the rings consists primarily of oil. Technician B says that in a diesel engine, blow-by leaking past the rings consists primarily of air. Who is correct?
   a. Technician A
   b. Technician B
   c. Both Technician A and Technician B
   d. Neither Technician A nor Technician B

6. Technician A says that the mass airflow sensor measures the weight of air entering the engine. Technician B says that the barometric pressure sensor measures the weight of air entering the engine. Who is correct?
   a. Technician A
   b. Technician B
   c. Both Technician A and Technician B
   d. Neither Technician A nor Technician B

7. Technician A says that when water and methanol is injected into the intake system, the process of vaporization absorbs heat from the intake air and reduces its temperature. Technician B says that when ethyl ether is injected into the intake system, the process of vaporization absorbs heat from the intake air and reduces its temperature. Who is correct?
   a. Technician A
   b. Technician B
   c. Both Technician A and Technician B
   d. Neither Technician A nor Technician B

8. Technician A says that Diesel engines require an excess supply of oil relative to the quantity needed to completely burn fuel in the cylinders. Technician B says that Diesel engines require an excess supply of air relative to the quantity needed to completely burn fuel in the cylinders. Who is correct?
   a. Technician A
   b. Technician B
   c. Both Technician A and Technician B
   d. Neither Technician A nor Technician B

9. Technician A says that a restriction gauge in the air filter housing is connected to the instrument cluster to warn the driver to service the element. Technician B says that an ambient temperature sensor in the air filter housing is connected to the instrument cluster to warn the driver to service the element. Who is correct?
   a. Technician A
   b. Technician B
   c. Both Technician A and Technician B
   d. Neither Technician A nor Technician B

10. Technician A says that oil accumulations on the compressor wheel and housing are normal when using an open crankcase ventilation system. Technician B says that oil accumulations on the compressor wheel and housing are normal when using a closed crankcase ventilation system. Who is correct?
   a. Technician A
   b. Technician B
   c. Both Technician A and Technician B
   d. Neither Technician A nor Technician B

CHAPTER 29
Fixed Geometry and Wastegated Turbochargers

▶ NATEF Tasks

Diesel Engines

General
- Listen for engine noises; determine needed action. (pp 860–861)
- Identify engine surging, rough operation, misfiring, low power, slow deceleration, slow acceleration, and shutdown problems; determine needed action. (pp 851, 855, 861–863)

Engine Block
- Remove, inspect, service, and install pans, covers, gaskets, seals, wear rings, and crankcase ventilation components. (pp 863–868)

Lubrication Systems
- Inspect turbocharger lubrication systems; determine needed action. (pp 860–865)

Air Induction and Exhaust Systems
- Inspect turbocharger(s), wastegate, and piping systems; determine needed action. (pp 859–866)
- Remove and reinstall turbocharger/wastegate assembly. (pp 852–853)

▶ Knowledge Objectives

After reading this chapter, you will be able to:
1. Describe the purpose and functions of turbochargers. (pp 845–849)
2. Explain operating principles of turbochargers. (p 850)
3. Identify and describe the construction, types, styles, and application of turbochargers. (pp 852–861)
4. Identify and explain inspection, maintenance, and diagnostic procedures used for turbochargers. (pp 861–868)
5. Recommend service and repairs of turbochargers. (pp 861–868)

Skills Objectives

After reading this chapter, you will be able to:

1. Measure turbocharger radial bearing clearance. (p 863) **SKILL DRILL 29-1**
2. Measure turbocharger axial bearing clearance. (p 864) **SKILL DRILL 29-2**
3. Measure wastegate movement. (p 866) **SKILL DRILL 29-3**
4. Inspect for turbine seal leakage. (p 867) **SKILL DRILL 29-4**

▶ Introduction

Turbochargers are air pumps driven by exhaust energy to supply additional air for combustion. Using exhaust gases to drive a centrifugal type pump recovers exhaust energy that would normally be wasted to the atmosphere and instead uses it to enhance engine operating efficiency. More importantly, as air breathing machines turbochargers exert a huge influence on diesel engine performance. Squeezing more air into engine cylinders adds the potential to burn more fuel and increase power output. Engine emissions, noise characteristics, and fuel economy are also improved by turbochargers.

▶ Fundamentals of Turbochargers

Because fuel requires a minimum amount of air to completely burn, every engine reaches a limit where the addition of more fuel produces no increase in power because it cannot breathe in enough air. Instead, black exhaust smoke, decreasing fuel economy, and high exhaust temperatures result in proportion to the absence of air and excess fuel supplied to the cylinders. However, if more air mass is packed into the combustion chamber along with additional fuel, greater combustion force is produced with an increased power output from each cubic inch (or centimeter) of engine displacement. Higher cylinder pressures, in turn, translate into more torque.

Turbochargers are essentially air pumps driven by exhaust gas energy to supply additional air flow to an engine. Exhaust gases drive a turbine wheel, which is connected to a **compressor wheel** (an air pump driven by centrifugal force) through a common shaft **FIGURE 29-1**. Normally, the exhaust gas energy would vent directly to the atmosphere. Instead, the turbochargers recover some of that energy to improve engine efficiency.

You Are the Technician

A tandem axle straight truck has arrived at your shop with a complaint about intermittent noise and low power. After performing typical visual inspections, you take the vehicle for a road test to verify the complaint. When the engine is warmed up and under hard acceleration, you hear what sounds like a screeching sound that resembles the noise of tires being locked and dragged on pavement. Releasing the accelerator pedal causes the noise to disappear. Returning to the shop, you remove the air intake boot to the turbocharger and look into the compressor housing to inspect the turbocharger compressor wheel and housing for damage. A compressor wheel making contact with the compressor housing would account for both complaints from the driver. It's somewhat difficult to be sure there is no physical contact between the compressor and turbine wheel, so you are intending to perform further inspection procedures to determine if there is a problem with the turbocharger and in particular whether there is too much bearing wear. As you begin to plan your next steps, consider the following:

1. List and describe the inspection procedures for measuring turbocharger bearing wear.
2. What would cause premature center housing support bearing failure and how would it affect the compressor wheel?
3. What service recommendations would you make to the customer to prevent the likelihood of a repeat failure of the turbocharger bearings after a turbocharger replacement is made?

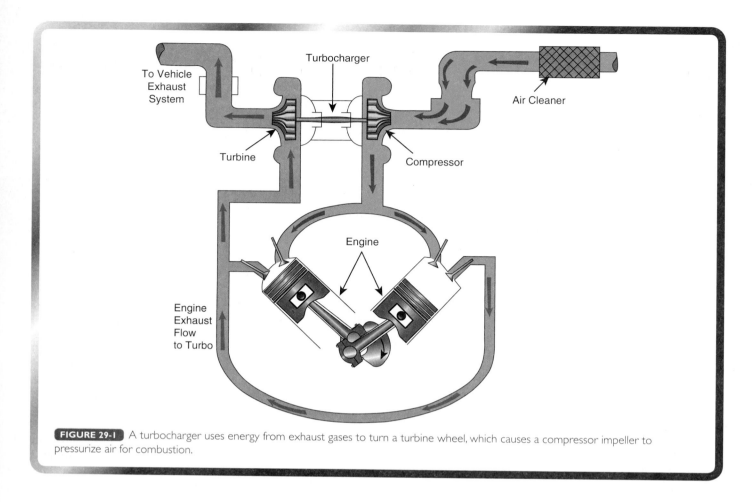

FIGURE 29-1 A turbocharger uses energy from exhaust gases to turn a turbine wheel, which causes a compressor impeller to pressurize air for combustion.

When these turbocharger wheels turn at high speed, the compressor can supply air to the combustion chambers at pressure above atmospheric. This fills the cylinders with more air mass than they are naturally capable of holding. Functionally then, turbochargers can serve as an alternative to engine displacement.

The idea of an exhaust-driven air pump to supply additional air to diesel engines was patented by Alfred Büchi in 1905. At first, the idea was not well received until the usefulness of the device for aircraft was discovered. During World War I and World War II, the **boost pressure normalization** feature of turbocharging enabled aircraft engines to fly at higher altitudes with no power loss in comparison to low altitude flying. Subsequently, the application of turbochargers to diesel engines became widespread beginning in the 1950s when design and metallurgical advances made more economical and compact devices possible.

Increasing the air supply pressure for combustion above atmospheric pressure is known as supercharging **FIGURE 29-2**. Turbochargers are a variety of **superchargers**, engines that pressurize the air intake system above atmospheric pressure. The term turbocharger is derived from the device's use of turbine type centrifugal pumps. Some engines use an engine-driven positive displacement-type air pump commonly, though incorrectly, called a supercharger. This pump is more correctly known as a rootes blower **FIGURE 29-3**. Rootes blowers are driven by the engine

directly through the gear train. The aluminum lobes pull atmospheric air into the blower and around the outside cover. Pressurized air is supplied to the cylinder intake air ports. Engines not equipped with superchargers have cylinders charged with air at atmospheric pressure and are classified as **naturally aspirated**.

Functions of Turbochargers

While supplying additional air to the cylinders is a turbocharger's most obvious purpose, there are other engine functions served by a turbocharger that improve engine performance and reduce emissions. Many of the additional functions are indirectly fulfilled by improving combustion quality. The other jobs that turbochargers perform are important reasons to add turbocharging to a vehicle to enhance engine efficiency.

Increasing Volumetric Efficiency

Turbochargers are widely used on diesel engines to improve their power output while decreasing engine size and displacement. By charging the cylinders at higher than atmospheric pressure, commonly known as boosting, more air can enter the cylinders during the intake stroke. Boosting of intake air pressure dramatically improves the volumetric efficiency (VE) of an engine to more than 300% and more than doubles its power output. Charging the cylinders with additional air mass alone does

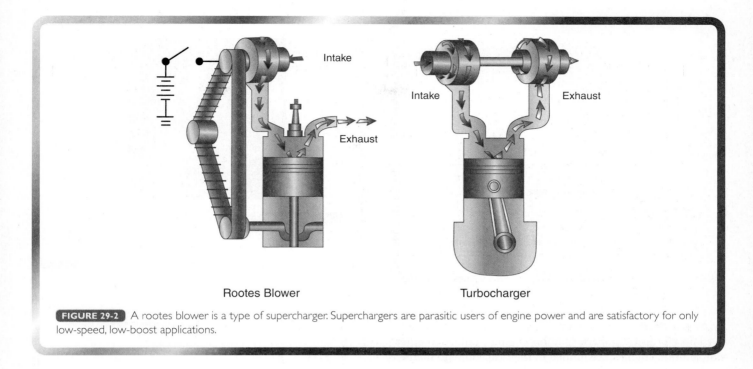

FIGURE 29-2 A rootes blower is a type of supercharger. Superchargers are parasitic users of engine power and are satisfactory for only low-speed, low-boost applications.

FIGURE 29-3 Rootes blowers are positive displacement-type air pumps driven by the engine directly through the gear train.

not increase power output. Extra air mass, however, does allow for more fuel per combustion cycle, which in turn, increases the amount of combustion pressure produced from each cylinder.

Consider that a naturally aspirated engine, that is an engine without a pressurized intake air system, has a VE of 75–85%. This means the cylinders fill to 75–85% of their total volume under the best conditions. A 1-liter (61-cubic inch) cylinder displacement would fill with 750–850 milliliters (46–52 cubic inches) of air without a turbocharger.

Consider again the same engine operated at 20 psi (138 kPa) of boost pressure and 85% VE. With a bore stroke of 3.75″ × 4.0″ (9.5 cm × 10 cm), this engine will double its compression pressure from 300 psi (21 bar) during cranking rpm (when no boost exists) to 600 psi (41 bar) when operating at 20 psi (138 kPa) of boost pressure. A 6.0-liter (366-cubic inch) Power Stroke engine operating at 3300 rpm would have a VE of 100% if airflow was 9911 liters (604,800 cubic inches) per minute. However, published specifications indicate its airflow is 20,728 liters (1,265,000 cubic inches) per minute, meaning the engine cylinders fill to more than two times their original volume when turbocharged.

Current turbochargers are easily able to boost up to three times atmospheric pressure, or approximately 45 psi (310 kPa). Series turbochargers boost to as much as 65 psi (448 kPa). Turbochargers are playing an increasing role in obtaining increased power output from engines with ever-decreasing displacements while reducing emissions and fuel consumption.

Detonation and Turbocharging

Diesel engines are well suited to turbocharging because greater boost pressure produces higher compression pressures and temperatures. Theoretically, diesel engines can have as much boost without detonating or having pre-ignition damage that high compression pressures cause in spark ignition engines. In fact, increases in cylinder air mass produce better combustion quality. This is not always efficient though, because more energy is needed to compress larger masses of air with diminishing increase to power output beyond 23:1 compression ratios **FIGURE 29-4**. Miller cycle engines can get around this problem

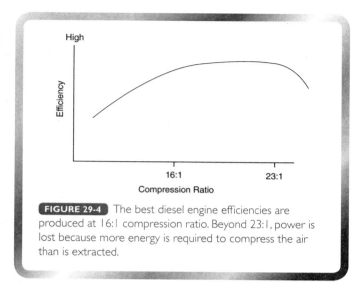

FIGURE 29-4 The best diesel engine efficiencies are produced at 16:1 compression ratio. Beyond 23:1, power is lost because more energy is required to compress the air than is extracted.

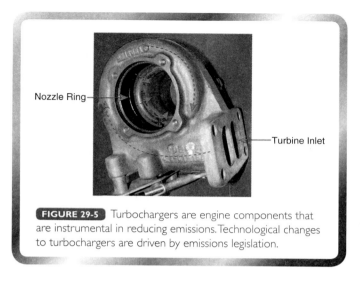

FIGURE 29-5 Turbochargers are engine components that are instrumental in reducing emissions. Technological changes to turbochargers are driven by emissions legislation.

by using progressively later intake valve closing with increasing boost pressures. Spark ignition engines, unlike compression ignition engines, are limited in their capability to increase intake charge pressure. Because fuel enters the cylinder during intake stroke, the heat developed by the air charge during compression stroke can ignite the fuel air mixture before the spark occurs. This abnormal combustion is referred to as detonation. Diesel engines, however, have the ability to operate using wide air–fuel ratios. This is because diesel fuel burns at leaner air–fuel mixtures than gasoline, and the stratified nature of diesel combustion enables lean burn combustion.

Emissions Reduction

Development of turbocharger technology is driven by demands of increasingly stringent emission standards. Turbochargers contribute to cleaner engine emissions in a number of ways.

First, by increasing the air mass in the cylinder, compression pressures and temperatures will increase. Increasing the magnitude of these factors results in accelerating combustion's chemical reactions. Fuel reacts more quickly and completely with oxygen. This, in turn, lowers the production of hydrocarbons (HC), carbon monoxide (CO) and particulate matter (PM) **FIGURE 29-5**.

Because turbochargers deliver more air to the combustion chamber, combustion quality is enhanced through improved contact between air and fuel. Some diesel engines use turbochargers primarily for this reason. Light-duty diesel engines built in the late 1990s supply only 4–8 psi (28–55 kPa) of boost pressure to the engine with the addition of a turbocharger. Power output from these changed-up designs is generally minimal.

Emission production dramatically declines when turbochargers are added **FIGURE 29-6**. After a few seconds under load, only a clear heat wave should be observed from the exhaust pipe of a turbocharged vehicle. No visible emissions should be observed for any vehicle built in compliance to 1998 emission standards.

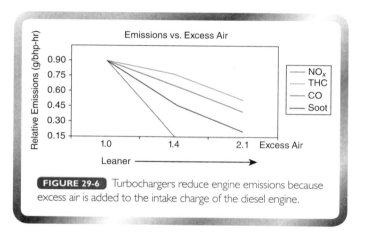

FIGURE 29-6 Turbochargers reduce engine emissions because excess air is added to the intake charge of the diesel engine.

▶ TECHNICIAN TIP

Some turbochargers are designed not to increase power output but to reduce emissions and normalize intake air pressure. Pressurized intake manifolds promote improved scavenging and charging of cylinders during the valve overlap period when fresh intake air is pushed across the chamber from the intake port and out the exhaust port, effectively purging the cylinder of exhaust gases. The added airflow has a secondary but important function to cool the piston crown and exhaust valves.

Carbon Dioxide Reduction

Helping diesel engines develop greater power output from engines with smaller displacement has the indirect effect of reducing carbon dioxide (CO_2) emissions. Lighter engines mean not only less overall vehicle weight but also as much as a 20% reduction in CO_2 emissions. Using exhaust energy to drive more air into the cylinders makes turbocharged diesel engines more efficient because the engine does not expend energy pulling air into the cylinders. Leaner air–fuel mixtures provided by turbochargers increase fuel economy because of higher cylinder pressures and improved combustion quality. Smaller engines have less internal resistances in comparison to larger engines.

Reduced Engine Noise Emissions

Another indirect benefit of turbocharging is lower noise emissions from an engine. Noisy exhaust pulses emitted from exhaust ports are chopped up by the turbocharger's turbine wheel. Reduced exhaust noise emissions require lighter muffling of the exhaust system. Turbocharging similarly dampens intake air noise. Exhaust pulses, which normally travel up the intake manifold during valve overlap, are dampened by the turbocharger's compressor wheel. This explains why naturally aspirated air intakes on diesel engines are noisier than turbocharged engines. A more compact engine design also translates into a smaller surface area to radiate noise, which further makes turbocharged diesel engines operate more quietly than non-turbocharged engines. Higher-torque engines can turn more slowly at highway speeds further reducing noise. Turbocharger whistle, the noise a high-speed turbine produces, offsets noise reduction.

Altitude Compensation—Normalization

Atmospheric pressure drops with increasing altitude. High altitudes with low atmospheric pressure are commonly encountered on North American and European highways. Unlike naturally aspirated engines, turbocharged engines do not lose power with increasing altitude because turbochargers speed up with higher altitude. Aircraft engines first demonstrated the usefulness of this feature in World War II. As aircraft flew higher, power output would naturally drop with altitude because naturally aspirated engines lose approximately 3% of power per 1000 feet of altitude (−0.5 psi/1000 ft [−3.4 kPa/305 m]) due to the drop in atmospheric pressure and air density. Thousands of turbochargers, which allowed aircraft to operate at higher altitudes with heavier loads and greater power output than naturally aspirated engines, were produced.

Because atmospheric pressure pushes air into cylinders, diesel engines without turbochargers experience the same difficulties as aircraft engines. At higher altitudes, such as when crossing a mountain passage, power is substantially reduced when pulling requirements caused by steep grades are at their highest. Turbocharged engines, however, have the ability to compensate for this condition by maintaining boost pressure in spite of lower atmospheric pressure. Turbine and compressor wheel speeds actually increase because of lower atmospheric pressure. The effect is due to the greater pressure differential across the turbine wheel as atmospheric pressure decreases. This, in turn, causes a greater pressure difference between the turbine inlet and outlet. When the difference becomes larger, the turbine wheel will turn faster. This means that the lower the atmospheric pressure, the higher the turbine speeds that are produced. When turbine speed increases, the compressor wheel speed increases as well. With higher compressor wheel speeds, boosted intake manifold pressures will remain relatively consistent with the same engine load factors found at sea level. Normalization is the term given to the turbocharger's ability to compensate for altitude change.

Barometric pressure sensors are used on turbocharged electronically controlled diesel engines to prevent overspeeding of the turbochargers. Because turbochargers spin faster at higher altitudes, under some conditions, the turbocharger can overspeed causing turbo failure. The barometric pressure sensor prevents overspeeding by cutting back fueling by as much as 15% at very high altitudes. Reduced injection quantities lower exhaust energy and consequently reduce turbocharger speed.

It is important for the exhaust system to operate with minimal backpressure. Undersized exhaust pipes and mufflers, dents and numerous bends cause exhaust backpressure to increase. If backpressure increases after the turbine wheel, the pressure differential between the turbine inlet and exhaust pipe diminishes, causing the turbocharger to slow down.

Engine Design Changes for Turbocharging

To take advantage of turbocharging, several engine design changes are required compared to naturally aspirated engines. Typically, the amount of valve overlap and the length of the intake stroke are increased to take advantage of higher intake air pressure and velocity. Higher cylinder pressures produced by turbocharging often require lower compression ratios than naturally aspirated engines. Heavier connecting rods, pistons, and crankshafts are also necessary to support increased cylinder pressure and power output. Higher cylinder pressures will also require improved head gaskets and cylinder head clamping forces to seal higher combustion pressure.

Turbocharger Operation

Turbochargers operate by converting exhaust energy into mechanical energy that in turn forces more air into the engine. The amount of energy in the exhaust is determined primarily by the temperature and mass of exhaust gas leaving the cylinders. While most of the combustion energy is used to push the piston downward in the cylinder, some energy is left over when the exhaust valve opens and combustion gas exits the exhaust port. This gas has not yet expanded to the maximum volume for its temperature. It is the energy of this unexpanded exhaust gas that causes the pressure to drive the turbine wheel.

At idle, exhaust energy is lowest because the quantity of fuel burned is minimal. However, when the operator demands increased power output, more fuel is injected and energy, in the form of high temperature and pressure exhaust, enters the exhaust manifold at the end of power stroke. Narrow exhaust manifold runners prevent the exhaust gas from expanding, and the diminishing diameter of the turbine housing increases pressure as exhaust gases flow into the turbine housing **FIGURE 29-7**. When the exhaust gases reach the turbine nozzle ring, only then can it expand, because the exhaust pipe is near atmospheric pressure. The force of exhaust gas expansion across the turbine wheel pushes the turbine wheel. This explains why turbine housings become hotter than the exhaust manifold when the engine is under load. The temperature of exhaust gas falls when it crosses the turbine by as much as 200–300°F, and its pressure falls to near atmospheric value in the exhaust pipe. Temperature changes in the turbine housing demonstrate that exhaust gas continues to compress as the turbine volute becomes smaller **FIGURE 29-8**.

As more fuel and air are added to the combustion reaction, the energy content of the exhaust gas increases. Highest turbocharger speeds and output pressure are reached when the most fuel is injected at the highest engine rpm. This point coincides with peak horsepower or rated engine rpm **FIGURE 29-9**.

FIGURE 29-7 On turbocharged engines, the exhaust manifolds are narrow to prevent exhaust gas expansion until the exhaust reaches the turbocharger nozzle ring.

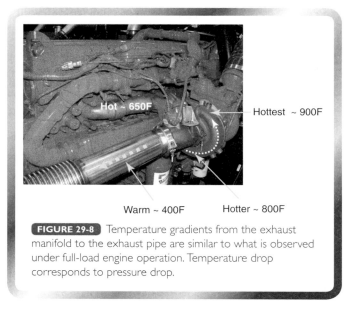

Hot ~ 650F
Hottest ~ 900F
Warm ~ 400F
Hotter ~ 800F

FIGURE 29-8 Temperature gradients from the exhaust manifold to the exhaust pipe are similar to what is observed under full-load engine operation. Temperature drop corresponds to pressure drop.

Turbo Lag

Turbo lag is experienced by a driver as a delay between stepping on the accelerator of the engine and the point when the engine responds with power proportional to driver demand. Turbocharger inertia and friction are responsible for some lag, but emission control strategies are also a significant factor contributing to lag. The fuel system could inject maximum amounts of fuel instantly into the cylinder, but adequate air to support combustion must charge the cylinders as well. Without adequate air to support combustion, excessive black smoke and other emissions are produced as well as lag. To minimize the formation of excess emissions during these load transition conditions, the governor system can only allow slight overfueling of the engine. Therefore, increasing injection quantities to bring the engine power or speed to operator-demanded levels takes place incrementally. Once enough air is available, the fuel system can add slightly more fuel to speed-up the turbocharger even further. With increased boost pressure, more fuel is added, and a cycle of adding fuel to produce more intake boost and then adding more fuel again is established. This cycle is referred to as spooling **FIGURE 29-10**.

The shortest amount of lag time is desirable because it affects emissions and the operator's perception of performance. Prolonged spooling or lag causes an engine to be perceived as lacking power, although that is not the case. Short lag times also reduce emission production because the overfueling period during acceleration is reduced as well. Air–fuel ratio controls associated with the governor use boost pressure as an input to limit injection quantities until adequate air mass is available to sustain combustion. Rootes blowers do not have any lag time.

Factors affecting turbo lag include:

- Size of the turbine housing: Smaller housings will spin the turbine faster with smaller amounts of exhaust energy. Larger housings will increase turbo lag time.

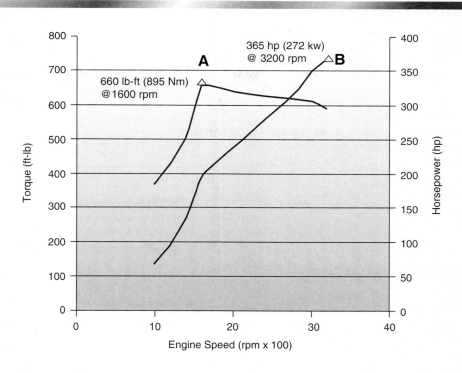

FIGURE 29-9 This torque–energy curve indicates where peak torque and horsepower occur. Point A corresponds to maximum injection quantity and cylinder pressure. Point B is maximum horsepower and turbocharger airflow. Turbocharger speed is fastest at this point.

- The mass of the turbine and compressor wheels: Lighter and smaller wheels accelerate and rotate faster. Compressor wheels are made of lightweight aluminum or titanium alloys, while turbine wheels are made of steel super alloys with high nickel content. Many turbine wheels also incorporate ceramic materials to lighten the wheel mass while improving heat resistance. Smaller wheels with less mass have the least amount of lag caused by inertia and can spin faster.

- Ball bearing versus sleeve center housing bearings: Ball bearings require up to 50% less energy and shorten lag time by as much as 15% **FIGURE 29-11** .

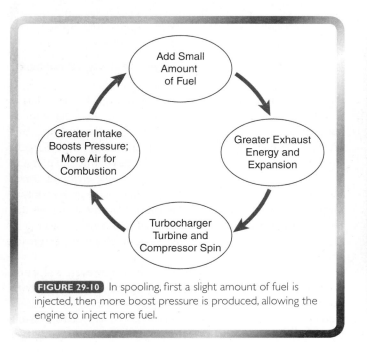

FIGURE 29-10 In spooling, first a slight amount of fuel is injected, then more boost pressure is produced, allowing the engine to inject more fuel.

FIGURE 29-11 Ball bearings are used by some manufacturers to improve durability, reduce turbo lag, and minimize turbocharger noise.

▶ Types of Turbochargers

A variety of turbocharger designs have been developed in response to increasing demands for improvements to engine performance, power output, and emission reduction. Basic types of turbochargers and configurations discussed in this chapter include:

- Fixed geometry turbochargers
- Wastegated turbochargers
- Variable geometry turbochargers, also referred to as variable vane turbochargers or variable nozzle turbochargers, among other names
- Parallel turbocharging
- Series or sequential turbocharging
- Single sequential turbocharging
- Asymmetrical turbochargers

Fixed Geometry Turbochargers

Fixed geometry turbochargers are turbochargers without boost pressure controls. The name is derived from the fact that the housings and components have unchanging dimensions. This traditional type of turbocharger technology was primarily used until the late 1980s when wastegated turbochargers began to displace fixed geometry turbochargers.

Disadvantages of Fixed Geometry Turbochargers

If an engine is operated at only one speed or load factor, a single turbocharger could be well matched to the fuel settings and airflow requirements to produce the best combustion quality. This is often the case for heavy-duty diesel engines in highway trucks that will cruise at a particular speed most of the time. However, to produce power at all speed ranges requires a turbocharger to provide adequate boost pressure under both low- and high-load factors FIGURE 29-12 . Because the amount of exhaust energy is low when an engine is lightly loaded, a fixed geometry turbocharger can produce little boost at low speeds. From an emissions perspective this is problematic, because without turbo boost, air–fuel ratios are also low at low-speed operation, which results in high PM, HC, and CO emissions.

Wastegated Turbochargers

A wastegated turbocharger is a solution to the problems of sluggish, low-power performance and high emissions at low engine speeds. These turbochargers are similar to fixed geometry turbochargers except they possess an exhaust bypass valve (called a wastegate) in the turbine housing. This valve allows exhaust gases to bypass the turbine and directly enter the exhaust pipe, thus "wasting" some of the exhaust energy FIGURE 29-13 . These turbochargers are designed to turn faster at lower engine load factors, increasing power density, or power output per liter (or cubic inch) of displacement, of small-bore engines at low speed while minimizing turbocharger lag.

The concept of a wastegated turbocharger is to build small turbine housing with a lightweight, low-inertia turbine wheel

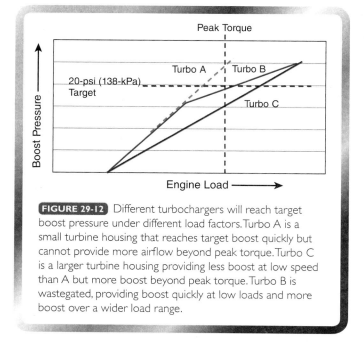

FIGURE 29-12 Different turbochargers will reach target boost pressure under different load factors. Turbo A is a small turbine housing that reaches target boost quickly but cannot provide more airflow beyond peak torque. Turbo C is a larger turbine housing providing less boost at low speed than A but more boost beyond peak torque. Turbo B is wastegated, providing boost quickly at low loads and more boost over a wider load range.

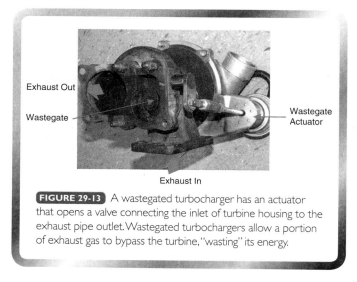

FIGURE 29-13 A wastegated turbocharger has an actuator that opens a valve connecting the inlet of turbine housing to the exhaust pipe outlet. Wastegated turbochargers allow a portion of exhaust gas to bypass the turbine, "wasting" its energy.

that can rotate faster and accelerate more quickly than larger wheels and housings. By making the turbine housing smaller, less exhaust gas energy is required to spin the turbine. This produces faster turbocharger speeds at smaller engine loads. Consequently, higher compressor discharge volume and pressure is available at low speed and load conditions, enabling corresponding increased fuel injection rates to provide greater output torque at lower engine speeds. Smaller displacement engines will not need to turn as fast to produce what is known as power density—more torque at lower speeds—a desirable characteristic for small diesel engines.

Making the turbine housing smaller, however, will cause exhaust backpressure to climb, limiting the engine's ability to breathe and produce further power gains as the engine increases load and speed. The turbine wheel can also overspeed and damage the turbo. At high turbocharger speeds, the turbocharger may not move air effectively. High exhaust gas temperatures and potential engine damage is another consequence of restricted exhaust causing reduced air intake flow.

To prevent the development of these undesirable conditions, a wastegated turbocharger vents a portion of the exhaust gas to the atmosphere before unacceptable exhaust backpressure and turbine speed develop. To accomplish this, wastegated turbochargers are constructed with an internal passageway in the turbine housing controlled by a bypass valve. When the valve is closed, the turbocharger is capable of building boost pressure. When the valve is open, exhaust is allowed to move directly from the turbine housing inlet to its outlet. Thus, exhaust gases effectively bypass the turbine and pass directly to the exhaust pipe FIGURE 29-14. Because the exhaust energy is not harnessed by the turbine, it is wasted, hence the term wastegated turbocharger.

▶ **TECHNICIAN TIP**

Never plug or prevent a wastegate actuator from opening to gain more power. This can lead to premature turbocharger failure due to overspeeding of the turbine. Lubrication breaks down and the bearings contact the journal surfaces during overspeed conditions. Preventing a wastegate from opening can also lead to excessive heat load in the cylinders causing damage to the pistons and valves, overloading of the intercooler, and an increase of NO_x emissions.

Wastegate Controls

For the wastegated turbocharger to operate effectively, the wastegate is designed to open at a predetermined boost pressure. Failure to open will cause the turbine speed to exceed speed limits, damaging the bearing and fatiguing the turbine wheel. Turbocharger failure will result if the wastegate is seized closed or tampered with to prevent it from opening. Most wastegates

will use air- or vacuum-operated actuators to operate the wastegate FIGURE 29-15.

Actuators will commonly use a spring operating against a diaphragm to close the wastegate. Many wastegates are normally closed by relatively weak spring pressure and opened by stronger boost pressure. This often leads to the wastegate sticking or binding in a partially open position. A line connecting the turbocharger compressor discharge or intake manifold air pressure to one side of the diaphragm will push the actuator open against spring pressure. When the predetermined boost pressure is reached the wastegate will begin to open, preventing any further build-up of exhaust pressure and limiting any further increase in the output of the turbocharger. Weak actuator spring pressure will prevent the wastegate from closing if the bushings and linkage are gummed or have excessive carbon deposits. In this case, the turbocharger will not build boost pressure again, and a low power complaint is the result. Springs can also be weakened by exhaust heat and may require adjustment on some turbochargers. Wastegates often have an adjustment mechanism to compensate for spring deterioration.

Some wastegates are normally open, and the actuator closes the wastegate. With this arrangement, vacuum and electronic controls will operate the actuator. The advantage of normally open wastegates is that overboosting is prevented and the wastegate will operate more frequently, minimizing the likelihood of linkage seizing..

HD-OBD and Actuators

Accurate control of turbo boost pressure is critical to minimizing engine emissions. To compensate for deterioration in operation and inaccuracy of mechanical actuator controls, heavy-duty on-board diagnostics (HD-OBD) engines use electronic control of wastegate operation FIGURE 29-16. A closed-loop feedback between the boost pressure sensor and the operation of the wastegate ensures the engine can adapt to any

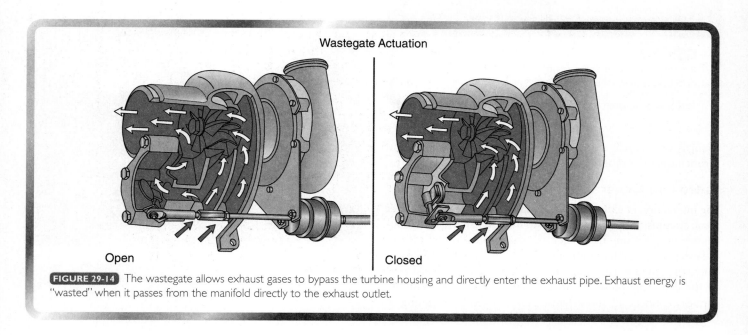

Wastegate Actuation

Open

Closed

FIGURE 29-14 The wastegate allows exhaust gases to bypass the turbine housing and directly enter the exhaust pipe. Exhaust energy is "wasted" when it passes from the manifold directly to the exhaust outlet.

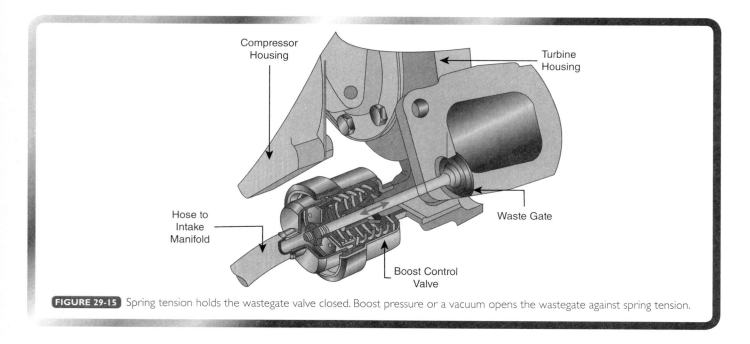

FIGURE 29-15 Spring tension holds the wastegate valve closed. Boost pressure or a vacuum opens the wastegate against spring tension.

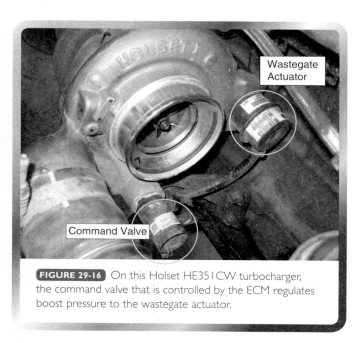

FIGURE 29-16 On this Holset HE351CW turbocharger, the command valve that is controlled by the ECM regulates boost pressure to the wastegate actuator.

changes or lifecycle deterioration of wastegate actuators and turbocharger operation.

Pulse and Constant Pressure Turbochargers

The interaction of exhaust pulses in the exhaust manifold under some circumstances is detrimental to the efficiency of the turbocharger on diesel engines. When an exhaust pulse initially leaves the exhaust port, it has high pressure. As the exhaust stroke finishes, though, a partial vacuum is created at the exhaust port by the departing pulse due to gas inertia. If exhaust manifold runners connect all the exhaust pulses together, blending of high- and low-pressure pulses occurs. This means high-pressure

exhaust pulses can enter cylinders just finishing exhaust stroke. These conditions will affect engine and turbocharger efficiency, particularly in inline six cylinder engines.

To prevent this from happening, turbocharged diesel engines use split exhaust manifolds and pulse-type turbochargers. This means that a barrier in the exhaust manifold separates the front three and back three cylinders. Likewise, the turbocharger turbine housing is divided into two volutes. This way, exhaust pulses are kept separated until they reach the turbine nozzle. Pulse-type turbocharger configurations provide for shorter turbo lag, higher boost pressure, and better exhaust gas scavenging. Pulse-type turbochargers can be identified by their dual inlets to the turbine housing **FIGURE 29-17** and **FIGURE 29-18**.

FIGURE 29-17 Pulse turbochargers have two separate exhaust volutes and split exhaust manifolds to prevent exhaust pressure pulses from canceling one another.

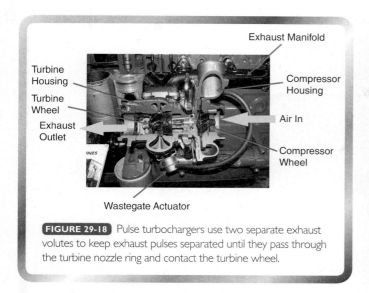

Turbine Housing

Turbine Wheel

Exhaust Outlet

Exhaust Manifold

Compressor Housing

Air In

Compressor Wheel

Wastegate Actuator

FIGURE 29-18 Pulse turbochargers use two separate exhaust volutes to keep exhaust pulses separated until they pass through the turbine nozzle ring and contact the turbine wheel.

Turbochargers without separate volutes for front and rear cylinders are called constant pressure turbochargers. These can be identified by the single turbine inlet.

Variable Geometry Turbochargers

<u>Variable geometry turbochargers (VGTs)</u>, also referred to as variable nozzle turbochargers (VNTs) and variable vane turbochargers (VVTs), are turbochargers with the capability of changing boost pressure independent of engine speed and load **FIGURE 29-19**. While having slightly different operating mechanisms, this category of turbocharger permits electronic control of boost pressure by the engine ECM. The primary advantages of VGTs are that they have very fast turbocharger response times and an ideal matching of airflow to combustion requirement. VGTs are necessary for engines equipped with high-pressure cooled exhaust gas recirculation (CEGR) because they can increase exhaust backpressure above boosted intake manifold pressure, which is necessary to mix EGR exhaust gases into the intake manifold. (See the Exhaust Gas Recirculation chapter.)

Parallel Turbocharging

When two turbochargers are used, they can be arranged with the air output either supplying the cylinders directly, or with the output of one turbocharger supplying the compressor wheel input of a second turbocharger. When two turbochargers are used to directly supply the cylinders, such as in the case of a V-bank engine, one turbocharger is located on each cylinder bank. This arrangement is called paralleling, or simply <u>parallel turbocharging</u>. Large industrial diesels such as those used in electric power generation use parallel turbocharging **FIGURE 29-20**.

Series Turbocharging

Fixed geometry, wastegated, and variable geometry turbochargers have output limits when used on engines with wide torque band. A large turbocharger for a high-output engine will not operate well at low speed and load conditions. To

FIGURE 29-19 This variable geometry turbocharger has an actuator mechanism located near the center housing that changes the volume of exhaust gases allowed to pass through the turbine housing.

compensate for this problem, <u>series turbocharging</u> involves the use of two differently sized turbochargers. The compressor output of one is directly connected to the compressor inlet of the other. This arrangement multiplies the maximum boost pressure of the turbochargers. Output from a smaller high-pressure turbocharger that responds quickly at low engine speeds is supplemented at medium speeds and loads by the larger low-pressure turbocharger **FIGURE 29-21**. A constant high boost pressure is available across the widest possible range of engine speeds.

Other Turbocharger Configurations

There are two other turbocharger configurations: series sequential and asymmetrical turbochargers. <u>Series sequential turbochargers</u> use a single turbine wheel to drive to compressor that rotates in two separate compressor housings. This type of turbocharger was popularized by the 6.7L (409 cubic inch) Ford PowerStroke, which used two different shapes of compressor wheels and housings to provide boost pressure for two different engine speed and load conditions.

<u>Asymmetrical turbochargers</u> resemble fixed geometry or wastegated turbochargers, but have exhaust volutes of two different diameters. Detroit's DD series engines use asymmetrical turbochargers to increase exhaust backpressure from the narrower volute that supplies the EGR system with exhaust gases.

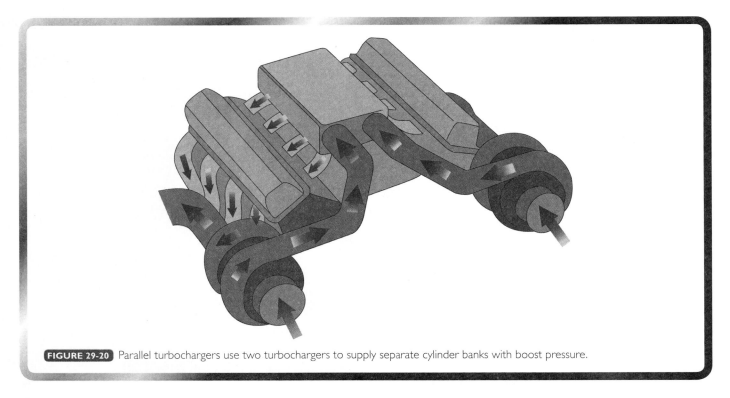

FIGURE 29-20 Parallel turbochargers use two turbochargers to supply separate cylinder banks with boost pressure.

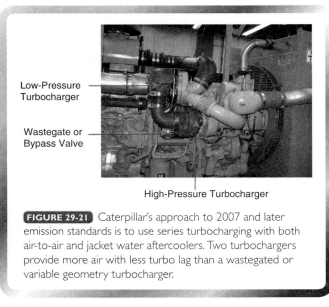

Low-Pressure Turbocharger

Wastegate or Bypass Valve

High-Pressure Turbocharger

FIGURE 29-21 Caterpillar's approach to 2007 and later emission standards is to use series turbocharging with both air-to-air and jacket water aftercoolers. Two turbochargers provide more air with less turbo lag than a wastegated or variable geometry turbocharger.

► Components of Turbochargers

Turbochargers are constructed in three parts. The two most significant parts are the turbine, or hot side, and the compressor, or cold side. A third part, the center housing, is positioned between the compressor and turbine housing. The center housing locates the shaft connecting the compressor and turbine along with bearings supporting the shaft.

The inlet to the turbine is located on the outside radius of the turbine housing and attaches to the exhaust manifold. The outlet of the turbine connects to the vehicle exhaust pipe. Air flows into the turbocharger through the compressor inlet located at the center of the compressor wheel. On the outside radius of the compressor housing is the compressor discharge or outlet that connects to either the intercooler or intake manifold **FIGURE 29-22**.

Turbine and Compressor Housing Shapes

Both the compressor and turbine housings are shaped like a scroll or snail shell; this shape is also called a volute. The turbine housing becomes progressively smaller as exhaust gas travels from the inlet at the exhaust manifold to an exit slot, called the nozzle, where exhaust flows across the turbine wheel and finally out into the exhaust system **FIGURE 29-23**. This diminishing diameter in the turbine housing causes exhaust gas pressure to multiply as it travels to the narrow nozzle. By varying the size of the turbine housing and the nozzle opening, the speed and flow characteristics of the turbine can change. Correct matching of the turbine housing and engine exhaust flow is important for effective turbocharger operation.

The **compressor housing**, which houses the compressor wheel, is shaped like the turbine housing but with opposite direction of gas flow. Air first enters the compressor housing after passing through the air filter by contacting the compressor wheel's inducer. Driven by the turbine shaft, the inducer creates a low-pressure area to draw air into the housing. The air then moves across the compressor fins to the exducer, where centrifugal force throws it through a slot called the diffuser, or tongue. Air velocity slows and builds pressure inside the increasing diameter of the compressor housing. The volume of air supplied to the engine is determined by a number of factors, including the geometry of the compressor wheel, compressor wheel speed, and housing shape **FIGURE 29-24**. The A/R ratio is a numerical

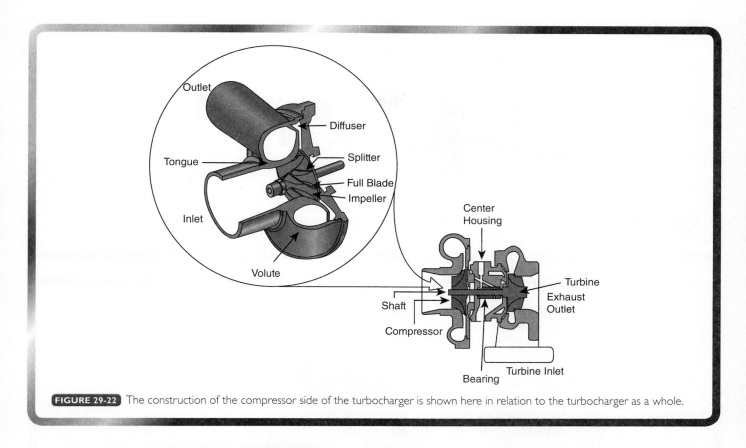

FIGURE 29-22 The construction of the compressor side of the turbocharger is shown here in relation to the turbocharger as a whole.

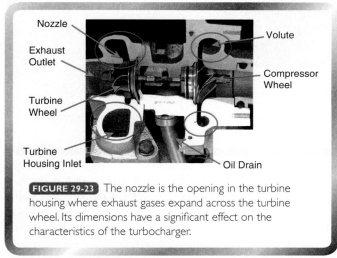

FIGURE 29-23 The nozzle is the opening in the turbine housing where exhaust gases expand across the turbine wheel. Its dimensions have a significant effect on the characteristics of the turbocharger.

representation of the diameter of the inlet opening to the volute compared to the radius of the volute.

A/R Ratio

Turbochargers must be precisely matched to a particular engine's fuel injection rate setting and engine displacement to achieve the correct boost pressure for the engine's design. For example, the fastest turbocharger speed producing the highest boost pressure should correspond to an engine's peak horsepower with minimal exhaust backpressure. Every horsepower rating and torque rise profile in an engine family uses a uniquely sized turbocharger on engines using fixed geometry turbochargers. Matching the turbocharger to the engine ensures that the airflow from the turbocharger will match the engine fuel rates **FIGURE 29-25** .

Turbine housing that is too small does not allow enough exhaust gas flow at high engine loads and speeds. This results in excessive exhaust backpressure producing low-power complaints and engine overheating. Turbine housing that is too large will produce inadequate boost pressure at low-speed operation, because large quantities of exhaust energy are needed to drive the turbocharger.

Similarly, the compressor wheel and housing need to be properly matched to produce adequate airflow across all engine speed ranges without over- or under-boosting. An incorrectly matched turbocharger can lead to either too little or too much boost for the engine. Possible consequences of turbocharger discharge pressure being too low include:

- Low power
- Poor fuel economy due to poor combustion quality
- Increased exhaust temperature due to inadequate excess air to dilute combustion temperature
- Increased smoke emissions from PM production
- Increased HC, PM, and CO emissions
- Damage to pistons, valves, and turbocharger caused by excessive thermal loads

Possible consequences of turbocharger boost pressure being too high include:

- Poor fuel economy due to excess air factor
- Increase NO_x emissions due to excessive cylinder pressures

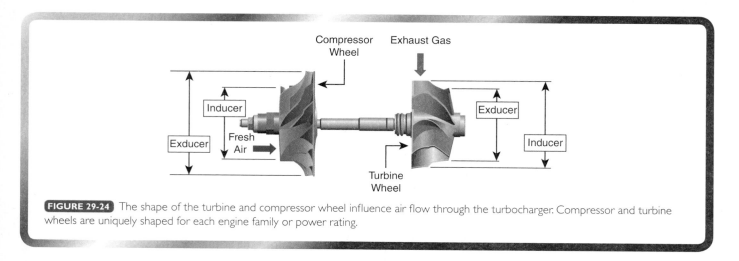

FIGURE 29-24 The shape of the turbine and compressor wheel influence air flow through the turbocharger. Compressor and turbine wheels are uniquely shaped for each engine family or power rating.

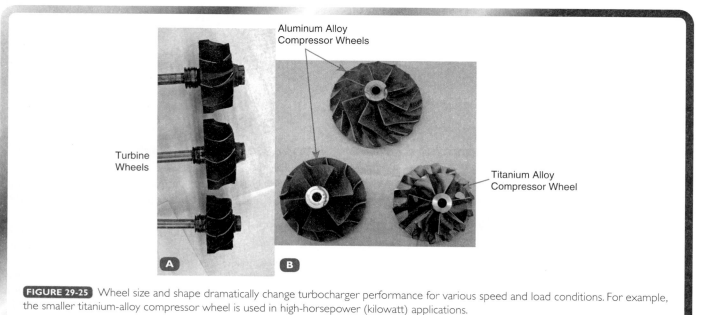

FIGURE 29-25 Wheel size and shape dramatically change turbocharger performance for various speed and load conditions. For example, the smaller titanium-alloy compressor wheel is used in high-horsepower (kilowatt) applications.

- Turbocharger bearing failure and turbocharger wheel fatigue problems caused by overspeeding turbocharger
- Damaged or blown intercooler pipes
- High inlet air temperatures caused by intercooler heat load increase
- Damage to cylinder, pistons, and valves caused by high thermal loads
- Engine power derating by engine monitoring system due to high inlet manifold temperatures

The most important factors determining turbocharger performance characteristics are the size and shape of the compressor and turbine wheels and their respective housing sizes **FIGURE 29-26**. Critical to the flow through the housings is the ratio between the area of the compressor or turbine housing inlet to the radius of the housing. These factors are summarized in the **A/R ratio**, which is often stamped into fixed geometry turbocharger housing **FIGURE 29-27**. The A factor of the A/R ratio is the area of either the compressor or turbine inlet. The R factor of the A/R ratio is the radius of the housing. A small A/R ratio for the turbine housing means the housing is restrictive to exhaust gas but will rotate faster than a housing having a large A/R ratio. A small A/R ratio will provide better torque and airflow at low engine speeds and load factors but at the expense of high-speed, high-load operation. The opposite is true for a turbocharger housing cast with a larger A/R ratio. When replacing turbochargers, the A/R ratio should not be interchanged. However, in some applications where the engine is operated frequently at high altitude, changing the A/R ratio by increasing turbine and compressor housing sizes may improve performance.

To improve turbocharger efficiency, a ported shroud compressor inlet can be used. This is a construction feature incorporated into the compressor housing that allows some airflow to exit the compressor wheel and return into the air inlet. Recirculating air flow allows a larger compressor wheel to be used for higher airflow requirements without allowing air in the compressor volute to backflow or surge

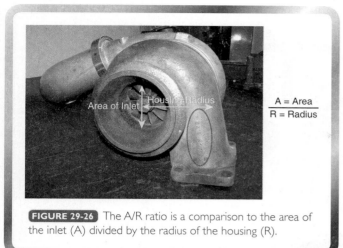

FIGURE 29-26 The A/R ratio is a comparison to the area of the inlet (A) divided by the radius of the housing (R).

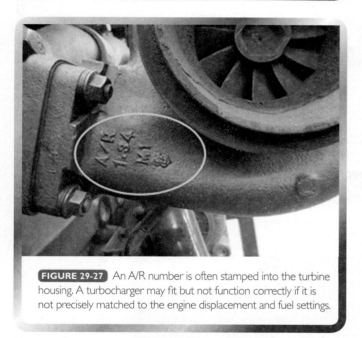

FIGURE 29-27 An A/R number is often stamped into the turbine housing. A turbocharger may fit but not function correctly if it is not precisely matched to the engine displacement and fuel settings.

out of the housing at low speeds. Using a ported shroud can have some negative effects on compressor efficiency at slow speeds, but improves efficiency at higher compressor wheel speeds.

Center Housing and Bearings

The turbocharger center section typically consists of two common configurations: plain sleeve-type bushings and angular ball bearings.

Plain Sleeve-Type Bushings

Traditionally, turbochargers used a gray cast iron housing to support a full floating bearing system for the turbine and compressor shaft. Small turbochargers can rotate at speeds up to 180,000 rpm, and medium engines will rotate in the vicinity of 100,000–130,000 rpm. Bearings, shafts, oil seals, and housing tolerances are manufactured with precision and durability suitable for this high-speed operation.

Two bearings support the shaft at each end of the center housing **FIGURE 29-28**. These bearings are full floating, meaning they rotate on the shaft and inside the housing. Oil holes in the bearings ensure an adequate oil film is available between the shaft and bearing **FIGURE 29-29**. The bearings are manufactured from bronze or brass bearing alloys. Shaft bearing journals are induction hardened and machined for dimensional accuracy and finished for high-speed operation.

To control endplay or axial movement of the turbine shaft, a thrust bearing and hardened steel thrust collar is located at the compressor end of the shaft. When assembled, the center-housing rotating assembly (CHRA) is dynamically balanced, and metal is removed from the underside of the turbine and compressor wheel to achieve vibration-free operation **FIGURE 29-30**. Because components are not normally match marked, any disassembly of the CHRA requires rebalancing.

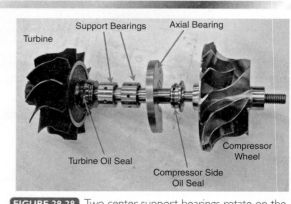

FIGURE 29-28 Two center support bearings rotate on the turbine shaft and in the housing. The thrust bearing controls turbine shaft endplay.

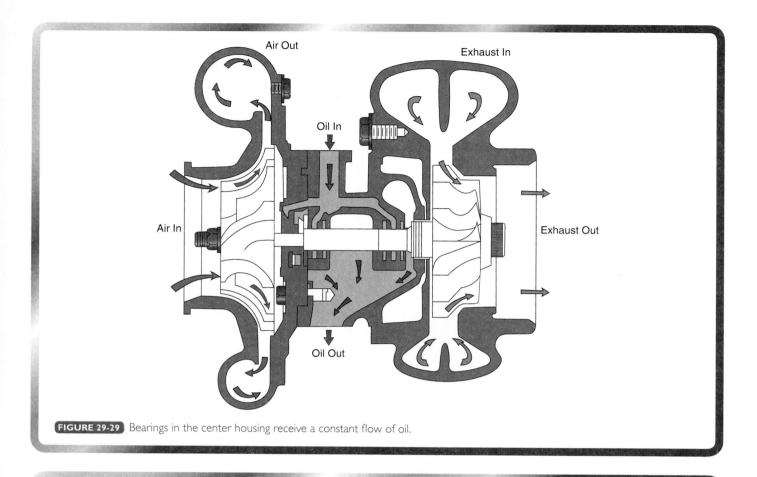

FIGURE 29-29 Bearings in the center housing receive a constant flow of oil.

FIGURE 29-30 Metal removal from turbocharger turbines and compressor wheels is performed to balance components rotating at very high speeds.

▶ TECHNICIAN TIP

Balancing turbochargers is accomplished using a machine known as a vibration sorting rig. These machines use compressed air to spin turbochargers and correctly determine where weight needs to be removed or added to the compressor or turbine wheel.

Angular Ball Bearing Turbochargers

In angular ball bearing turbochargers, also called cartridge ball bearing turbochargers, the center housing support consists of a single sleeve cartridge ball bearing system that contains a set of angular contact ball bearings at each end. Using an angular type ball bearing eliminates the need for a thrust bearing because endplay is controlled by the ball and race assembly rather than a sleeve. Advantages of the ball bearing system over the sleeve-type bearings include:

- Reduced oil flow: Ball bearing designs reduce the amount of oil required to provide adequate lubrication. Not only does this reduce the likelihood of bearing coking during hot shutdown but less cumulative damage will take place during minimal lube conditions during start-up. Reduced oil flow in the center housing minimizes seal leaks, too.
- Reduced turbocharger lag: Ball bearings reduce turbine friction by as much as 50%, thus reducing lag times by 15%.
- Reduced vibration and noise: Ball bearing turbochargers dampen shaft movement much better than sleeve bearings, which require two oil clearances: between the shaft and bearing and between the bearing and housing.

Water-Cooled Center Housing

Many turbochargers use engine coolant passing through passages cast into the center housing to remove heat. When the engine is shut down, coolant circulates using convection currents. Heat from the housing warms the water causing lighter, less dense coolant to rise and leave the housing while drawing cooler coolant from the engine block **FIGURE 29-31**.

▶ Maintenance of Turbochargers

Turbocharger support shaft and axial bearings not only enable the turbine shaft to rotate freely with little friction but also prevent excessive movement of the compressor and turbine wheels inside the turbocharger housings. Bearing wear will allow axial (end-to-end) and radial (up-and-down) movement of the wheels and allow them to touch the housings. If this happens, catastrophic failure of the turbocharger takes place **FIGURE 29-32**. Maintaining a close operating clearance to the

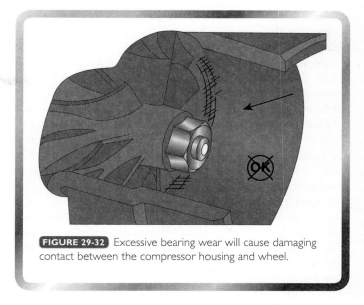

FIGURE 29-32 Excessive bearing wear will cause damaging contact between the compressor housing and wheel.

housing is needed to prevent gas leakage around the wheels and to maintain turbocharger efficiency. Little tolerance for bearing wear means the turbocharger should be regularly inspected before problems occur.

Bearing Inspection

With the intake system disconnected from compressor housing, it is possible to visually check for excess bearing axial and radial clearances. If light finger pressure applied sideways against the compressor wheel causes contact between compressor and housing, the bearings and or shaft are worn **FIGURE 29-33**. Turbocharger replacement or repair must be made if this condition is detected before catastrophic consequential damage occurs.

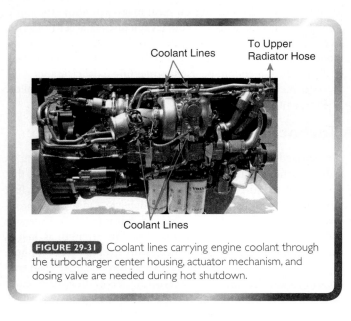

FIGURE 29-31 Coolant lines carrying engine coolant through the turbocharger center housing, actuator mechanism, and dosing valve are needed during hot shutdown.

FIGURE 29-33 Radial bearing play can be checked by lifting the turbine shaft against the housing while rotating the shaft. Excessive damage is indicated by compressor or turbine wheel contact with the housing.

Another technique to check and measure radial play is to measure the clearance between the compressor wheel and housing. Pushing the compressor wheel downward and sliding a feeler blade in between the wheel and housing measures minimum clearance FIGURE 29-34. Moving the compressor wheel upwards and re-measuring the clearance enables a calculation for bearing radial play. Subtracting the largest from the smallest clearance measured provides an indication of radial bearing wear. Because the measurement of radial play is a projection of the bearing clearance to the end of the turbine shaft, the clearance varies between manufacturers but measurements can be compared against manufacturer specifications.

Axial endplay is usually measured with a dial indicator. Moving the turbine shaft back, zeroing the dial indicators, and then moving the shaft forward enables measurement of axial play. While radial play is easily detected when moving the turbine shaft, any axial play should not be felt but only observed with a dial indicator.

Measuring Turbocharger Radial Bearing Clearance

Two different sets of turbocharger bearings are responsible for keeping the turbine and compressor wheels properly positioned in their respective housings. Excessive wear in either of these bearings can potentially cause catastrophic turbocharger and engine failures. Measuring axial and radial bearing clearances is an important estimate of turbocharger service life and can pinpoint imminent failures. Worn center support bearings can lead to more turbocharger noise, which resembles a characteristic whistling sound as the shaft vibrates.

To measure turbocharger radial bearing clearance, follow the steps in SKILL DRILL 29-1. An alternate method for checking radial clearance is to use a dial indicator to measure the turbine shaft movement through the center housing FIGURE 29-35.

FIGURE 29-34 One technique to measure radial clearances is to insert a feeler blade into the gap left when the compressor wheel is lightly pressed toward the housing.

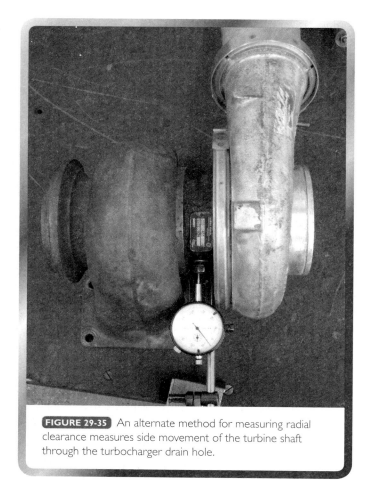

FIGURE 29-35 An alternate method for measuring radial clearance measures side movement of the turbine shaft through the turbocharger drain hole.

This method can only be used if the turbine shaft is accessible through the center housing.

Measuring Turbocharger Axial Bearing Clearance

A turbocharger's thrust bearing controls the turbine shaft's axial endplay. Excessive bearing oil clearances will allow the compressor or turbine wheel to contact the turbocharger housings. Axial clearance cannot be measured by feel because the amount of acceptable clearance is too small for any technician to detect. A dial indicator should be used to measure axial clearance.

To measure turbocharger axial bearing clearance, follow the steps in SKILL DRILL 29-2.

Turbocharger Lubrication

Pressurized lube oil circulates through the center housing to lubricate the bearings and help remove heat. It is important that oil reaches the turbocharger in sufficient volume within the first few seconds of operation to prevent damage. Oil must be properly filtered and should never exceed 250°F (121°C). Excessive oil temperature can cause the loss of oil film strength as well as cause the oil to burn or coke, which forms an abrasive compound. Coking abrasives cause damage to the turbocharger shaft and bearings FIGURE 29-36. Newer classifications of diesel engine oils are very resistant to coking, and synthetic oil does not coke at all.

SKILL DRILL 29-1 Measuring Turbocharger Radial Bearing Clearance

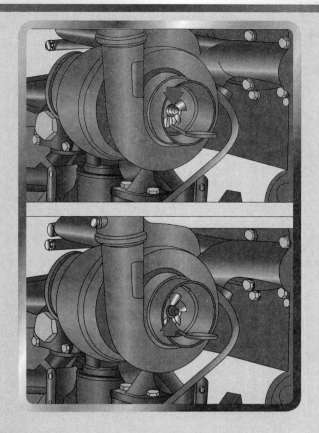

1. With the engine off, remove the intake air piping.

2. Inspect the area between the compressor wheel and housing for evidence of contact. Make a careful inspection, particularly if an operator has reported an engine noise complaint.

3. Rotate the compressor wheel; while rotating, check for any binding or roughness.

4. Grasp the compressor wheel retaining nut between your fingers and move the wheel up and down and back and forth. Any contact between the compressor wheel and housing indicates that the center support bearings are excessively worn and the turbocharger should be replaced.

5. If there is no contact between the compressor wheel and housing, rotate the compressor wheel while applying a slight amount of side pressure to the wheel. Again, any contact or roughness while rotating the wheel indicates the turbocharger should be removed from service. Contact in one spot only may indicate the compressor housing is misaligned. Loosen any band clamps or retention bolts to realign the housing and recheck.

6. To measure center support bearing wear, push down on the compressor wheel with moderate finger pressure while inserting the thickest feeler blade that will fit between the wheel and housing. Record the thickness of the feeler blade.

7. Repeat the same procedure while lifting the compressor wheel. Record the thickness of the feeler blade inserted in the same place while the compressor wheel is lifted in the opposite direction.

8. Subtract the smaller feeler blade size from the larger feeler blade size and compare the results against the manufacturer's specifications. report the bearing clearance and make a service recommendation.

Two oil seals are used in the turbocharger: one inside the thrust bearing and another on the turbine shaft. These seals are cast iron and appear like piston rings. Broken or worn seals can cause a tremendous amount of oil to be pumped into the turbine or compressor housings, enough that other drivers travelling behind an engine with defective turbocharger seals will need wipers to see through their windshield **FIGURE 29-37**.

▶ TECHNICIAN TIP

Whenever an engine has operated under load, it is important to let the engine idle for 1–3 minutes to remove heat from the turbine and center housing. Failure to do so can result in oil coking inside the center housing. Water-cooled center housings allow coolant to circulate after shutdown to prevent oil coking. Synthetic oils do not coke, and newer oil classifications require diesel oil to be highly resistant to coking.

After replacing a turbocharger it is important to pre-lube the center housing before operating the engine. This is accomplished by adding oil to the inlet of the housing while slowly rotating the turbocharger shaft **FIGURE 29-38**.

Turbocharger Servicing

Many turbochargers are replaced unnecessarily due to poor engine diagnostics and other troubleshooting procedures. The turbocharger boost pressure test is the most efficient method to confirm a low-power complaint. This is easily accomplished by accelerating the engine to a wide-open throttle (WOT) from low road speeds and measuring the boost pressure while under load. The boost will rise to a peak pressure and then quickly fall off after reaching rated rpm under load. Boost pressure then falls as the vehicle reaches higher road speeds and the load is reduced.

If boost fails to reach its specification, the turbocharger should not be changed until other diagnostic tests are made. Analysis of air

SKILL DRILL 29-2 Measuring Turbocharger Axial Bearing Clearance

1. Place a magnetic-base dial indicator on the engine block; if the turbocharger is off the engine, place the indicator on the turbine housing.

2. Place the dial indicator needle's extension piece at the center of the compressor wheel's retaining nut.

3. Push the shaft forward in the turbine housing with moderate finger pressure.

4. Zero the dial indicator.

5. Push the compressor wheel rearwards or pull on the turbine shaft with moderate finger pressure.

6. Observe and record the dial indicator movement. Compare the axial bearing clearances with the manufacturer's specifications and make a service recommendation.

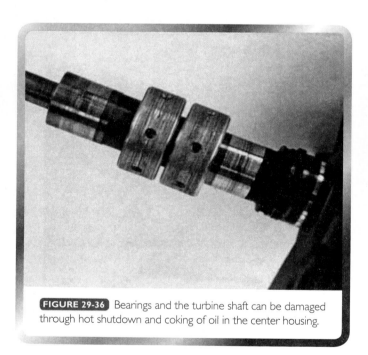

FIGURE 29-36 Bearings and the turbine shaft can be damaged through hot shutdown and coking of oil in the center housing.

FIGURE 29-37 A damaged or broken oil seal on a turbine wheel causes tremendous amounts of oil to pass into the turbine housing.

induction, exhaust and fuel systems, and other potential causes of low power should take place first to ensure they are properly functioning. Power-up devices that increase engine power beyond factory settings can also lead to turbocharger damage from overspeed and overheated turbine wheels. Turbine wheels should have sharp, distinct edges. When overheated and glowing, the metal literally boils away from the edges and rounds them **FIGURE 29-39** .

Actuator Checks

Bushings on wastegates can seize due to the corrosive effects of heat and exhaust gases. Low-power complaints can be caused by wastegates that are seized open, and turbocharger damage can result when wastegates do not open. To inspect for these conditions, boost pressure can be measured when a vehicle is under load. Failure to reach a specified boost pressure means further inspection of the wastegate mechanism is necessary. Alternatively, air pressure or vacuum can be applied to the actuator mechanism to check its movement against manufacturer's specifications. Accurate adjustment of the actuator is critical to ensure optimum performance, low emissions, and prevention of potential turbocharger and engine failures.

FIGURE 29-38 Bearings must be pre-lubricated after replacing a turbocharger. Rotate the compressor wheel slowly while filling the center housing with oil through the oil feed line.

Melted Turbine Blades

FIGURE 29-39 The tips of this turbine wheel are melted and damaged from overheating due to a common rail injector that was stuck open. Blade edges become rounded and thinner when overheated.

TECHNICIAN TIP

Periodically check wastegate actuator movement against opening pressures. Exposure to intense exhaust heat will weaken some actuator springs, causing the gate valve to prematurely open leading to low-power complaints. Similarly, moving actuators during a preventive maintenance inspection will minimize the likelihood of a wastegate seizing open.

Measuring Wastegate Movement

Turbocharger wastegates can malfunction by failing to open or close. A wastegate stuck partially open will fail to build boost pressure and will cause a low-power complaint. Wastegate springs can weaken from use and heat, leading to premature opening of the wastegate. A wastegate stuck closed will cause the turbine to overspeed and can lead to premature bearing failure.

To measure wastegate movement, follow the steps in **SKILL DRILL 29-3**.

Fuel System Checks

Recommended fuel system checks include:

- Low-pressure transfer system pressure and volume
- Full throttle reached on both mechanical and electronic systems
- Injection timing
- Injector adjustment
- Injectors and other high-pressure fuel system components correctly matched to the engine
- Engine misfiring or low cylinder contributions
- Injector spray pattern and nozzle opening pressures

- Air–fuel ratio devices function correctly, i.e., no leaking aneroid lines and gaskets and defective manifold pressure sensors

Air Induction System Checks

Recommended air induction system checks include:

- Filter restrictions
- Correct size of air filter
- Intercooler leaks and restrictions
- Valve adjustment
- EGR system operation
- Intake manifold throttle plate

Exhaust System Checks

Recommended exhaust system checks include:

- Excessive exhaust backpressure
- Correct OEM (original equipment manufacturer) exhaust system components
- Exhaust system fitted with components following the recommendation of the engine manufacturer
- Exhaust leaks on exhaust manifold
- Seized backpressure regulators or exhaust brakes

Turbocharger Checks

Recommended turbocharger checks include:

- Wastegate actuator movement and adjustment
- Correctly matched turbocharger, i.e., correct A/R ratio or turbocharger part number for the engine
- Bearing inspections, i.e., contact between turbine and compressor wheels with housings
- Correct A/R ratio

SKILL DRILL 29-3 Measuring Wastegate Movement

1 Road test the vehicle under load and accelerate the vehicle hard to produce maximum boost pressure while monitoring the intake manifold pressure sensor.

2 Compare maximum boost pressure to the manufacturer's specifications to determine whether wastegate operation should be checked. Note: Other defective conditions related to the high- and low-pressure fuel system operation, intake leaks, engine condition, and so on can produce low boost conditions.

3 Connect an adjustable air pressure regulator to the wastegate supply hose. Apply a calibrated amount of air

pressure to the wastegate actuator, usually around 20 psi (138 kPa). Check the air hose, fitting connections, and actuator diaphragm for leaks.

4 Close the air supply shut-off valve. The pressure should hold at the specified pressure. If not, repair the leak or replace the wastegate actuator or turbocharger.

5 Set up a dial indicator at the end of the wastegate actuator rod to measure travel. Adjust the dial indicator so it only contacts the actuator rod end, and zero the dial indicator reading.

6 Check the manufacturer's specifications and prepare to slowly apply a calibrated amount of air pressure to the actuator.

7 Slowly switch the air pressure supply on and off several times and observe the actuator's opening and closing supply air pressure. The dial indicator will begin to move at each point.

8 Observe and record the air pressure where dial indicator movement begins as the air pressure is slowly applied and released. Compare opening and closing pressures with the manufacturer's specifications.

9 Measure the total amount of actuator rod travel using the same steps above. Observe and record total actuator movement.

10 Compare your findings with specifications and make a service recommendation based on whether the opening and closing pressures and dial indicator movement are within specifications. Note: A sticking and binding wastegate will not move until the actuator air pressure is close to zero.

Turbocharger Failures

A number of operating conditions can cause premature failures of turbochargers. Common defects include air inlet leaks, oil leaks, bent or broken compressor wheel blades, and worn bearings.

Air Inlet Leaks

Air inlet leaks can erode and pit the compressor wheel and dull the edges of the compressor wheel. Eventually, the engine will lose power and have excessive blow-by and emissions due to "dusting out," a condition where the cylinder components are worn out from abrasives entering the engine.

Oil Leaks

Turbocharger oil leaks should be carefully differentiated from leaks caused by excessive crankcase pressure, oil originating from engine cylinders, restricted air filters, and excessive idling. The possible causes of oil leaks are numerous:

- Gas pressure assists in keeping oil inside the center housing. When idling, a minimum amount of pressure is needed inside the compressor housing or oil can leak past oil seals on the compressor and turbine shaft and into the housings.

- Excessive crankcase pressure pushes can also push oil from the center housing into the turbine and compressor housings.
- A highly restricted air filter can cause oil to be pulled from the compressor center housing and into the engine.
- Oil can leak from a defective turbine seal or compressor seal.

Removing exhaust manifolds and running the engine can differentiate between oil originating from the engine or the turbocharger. An ultraviolet tracing dye in the engine can be used along with a black light to detect oil originating from leaking turbine seals. After running the engine for 20 minutes and removing the exhaust pipe at the turbocharger, oil seen leaking around the turbine wheel indicates a leaking turbine seal **FIGURE 29-40**.

Inspecting for Turbine Seal Leakage

Turbochargers are often unnecessarily replaced for suspected oil seal leakage due to oil being in the engine exhaust or contaminating a particulate filter. Oil leakage from the turbocharger turbine seal should be differentiated from oil originating from the engine cylinders. Worn or damaged cylinder

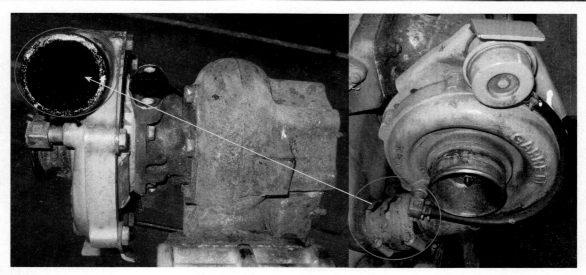

FIGURE 29-40 Turbochargers should not leak oil from the compressor or turbine housings. This engine had excessive blow-by and idle time resulting in a fouled compressor wheel. Only the outlet (not the inlet) was slobbered.

components or excessive engine idle can produce excessive slobber, which does not justify turbocharger replacement. Also, new or rebuilt engines that have not completed a break-in period will also leak oil at these points. However, worn engines with high crankcase pressure or excessive blow-by will push oil out the turbocharger seals.

To inspect for turbine seal leakage, follow the steps in **SKILL DRILL 29-4**.

 SKILL DRILL 29-4 Inspecting for Turbine Seal Leakage

1. Inspect the exhaust manifold joints and the area on the engine block below the exhaust manifold. Oil leakage or slobber present at these points likely indicates oil originating from the engine and not the turbocharger.

2. Add oil tracing dye, which is visible using an ultraviolet (UV) light, to the engine oil and run the engine to operating temperature. Run the engine at idle for 10–20 minutes.

3. Allow the engine exhaust to cool.

4. Remove the exhaust pipe from the turbocharger and use a UV light to inspect the area around the turbocharger outlet. Any accumulations of bright yellow- or green-colored dye at the turbine outlet likely indicates a defective turbocharger seal.

5. Remove the turbocharger oil drain tube to inspect for blockage. If the engine oil tube is not blocked and the engine has acceptable crankcase pressure, make a service recommendation to replace the turbocharger.

Bent Compressor Wheel Blades

Bent compressor blades are caused by the ingestion of soft materials such as shop rags or filter gaskets **FIGURE 29-41**. Broken compressor blades are caused by the ingestion of hard material such as a bolt or nut.

Broken Compressor Wheel Blades

Broken compressor wheel blades are caused by ingestion of a hard material like a bolt or nut.

Worn Bearings

Worn bearings can be caused by the hot shutdown of the engine, coolant in the oil, overextended oil service intervals, failure to pre-lube the turbocharger after replacement, low oil pressure, and excessive oil temperature.

Safety

When working around running engines with the air inlet piping removed from the turbocharger, always install a guard cover over the turbocharger inlet. Compressor wheels are very sharp and turn at a very high speed even at idle. Fingers are easily sliced off if they come in contact with the spinning turbocharger wheels. Also, turbochargers are very easily damaged with any contact with debris or clothing.

FIGURE 29-41 Bending of the compressor wheel blades is caused by ingestion of soft material such as gaskets, rags, or even water.

Wrap-Up

Ready for Review

▸ Turbochargers are air pumps driven by exhaust energy to supply additional air for combustion. Using exhaust gases to drive a centrifugal-type pump recovers exhaust energy that would normally be wasted and uses it to enhance efficiency.

▸ Turbochargers exert a huge influence on diesel engine performance. Squeezing more air into engine cylinders adds the potential to burn more fuel and increase power output. Engine emissions, noise characteristics, and fuel economy are also improved by turbochargers.

▸ Because fuel requires a minimum amount of air to completely burn, every engine reaches a limit where the addition of more fuel produces no increase in power because it cannot breathe in enough air.

▸ If more air mass is packed into the combustion chamber along with additional fuel, greater combustion force is produced with an increased power output from each cubic inch (or centimeter) of engine displacement.

▸ Increasing the air supply pressure for combustion above atmospheric pressure is known as supercharging. Turbochargers are a variety of superchargers.

▸ Turbochargers are widely used on diesel engines to improve their power output while decreasing engine size and displacement.

▸ Diesel engines are well suited to turbocharging because greater boost pressure produces higher compression pressures and temperatures. Theoretically, the diesel engine can handle unlimited boost without detonating or having pre-ignition damage.

▸ Turbochargers contribute to cleaner engine emissions in a number of ways. For example, helping diesel engines develop greater power output from smaller displaced engines has the indirect effect of reducing CO_2 emissions.

▸ Another indirect benefit of turbocharging is lower noise emissions from an engine. Noisy exhaust pulses emitted from exhaust ports are chopped up by the turbocharger's turbine wheel.

▸ Unlike naturally aspirated engines, turbocharged engines do not lose power with increasing altitude because turbochargers speed up with higher altitude.

▸ Turbochargers operate by converting exhaust energy into mechanical energy that in turns forces more air into the engine. The amount of energy in the exhaust is determined mainly by the temperature and mass of exhaust gas leaving the cylinders.

▸ More fuel and air added to the combustion reaction means greater energy content of exhaust gas.

▸ Turbo lag is experienced by a driver as a delay between stepping on the accelerator of the engine and the point when the engine responds with power proportional to driver demand. Turbocharger inertia and friction are responsible for some lag, but emission control strategies are also a significant factor contributing to lag.

▸ A variety of turbocharger designs have been developed in response to increasing demand for improvements to engine performance, power output, and emission reduction.

▸ Fixed geometry turbochargers are turbochargers without boost pressure controls. The name is derived from the fact that the housings and components have unchanging dimensions.

▸ Wastegated turbochargers are similar to fixed geometry turbochargers, except they possess an exhaust bypass valve in the turbine housing. This valve allows exhaust gases to bypass the turbine and directly enter the exhaust pipe, thus "wasting" some of the exhaust energy.

▸ For the wastegated turbocharger to operate effectively, the wastegate is designed to open at a predetermined boost pressure. Failure to open will cause the turbine speed to exceed speed limits, damaging the bearing and fatiguing the turbine wheel.

▸ Accurate control of turbo boost pressure is critical to minimizing engine emissions. To compensate for deterioration in operation and inaccuracy of mechanical actuator controls, HD-OBD engines use electronic control of wastegate operation.

▸ To prevent exhaust pulses from affecting engine and turbocharger efficiency, turbocharged diesel engines use split exhaust manifolds and pulse-type turbochargers.

▸ Variable geometry turbochargers have the capability to change boost pressure independent of engine speed and load.

▸ Series turbocharging involves the use of two differently sized turbochargers. The compressor output of one turbocharger is directly connected to the compressor inlet of another turbocharger, which multiplies the maximum boost pressure of the turbochargers.

▸ Turbochargers are constructed in three parts. The two most significant parts are the turbine, or hot side, and the compressor, or cold side. A third part, the center housing, is positioned between the compressor and turbine housing.

▸ Both the compressor and turbine housings are shaped like a scroll or snail shell, also called a volute, which becomes progressively smaller. This diminishing diameter in the turbine housing causes exhaust gas pressure to multiply as it travels to the narrow nozzle.

▸ The most important factors determining turbocharger performance characteristics are the size and shape of the compressor and turbine wheels and their respective housing sizes. Critical to the flow through the housings is the ratio between the area of either the compressor or

turbine housing inlets in comparison to the radius of the housing. These factors are summarized in the A/R ratio.
- The center section of a turbocharger typically consists of two common configurations: plain sleeve-type bushings or angular ball bearings.
- Many turbochargers use engine coolant passing through passages cast into the center housing to remove heat.
- Bearing wear in turbochargers will allow axial (end-to-end) and radial (up-and-down) movement of the wheel, allowing them to touch the housings. If this happens, catastrophic failure of the turbocharger takes place.
- Many turbochargers are replaced unnecessarily due to poor engine diagnostics and other troubleshooting procedures. The turbocharger boost pressure test is the most efficient method to confirm a low-power complaint.
- A number of operating conditions can cause premature failures of turbochargers. Common defects include air inlet leaks, oil leaks, bent or broken compressor wheel blades, and worn bearings.

Vocabulary Builder

A/R ratio The ratio between the area (A) of either the compressor or turbine inlets to the radius (R) of the housing.

asymmetrical turbocharger A turbocharger with volutes of two different sizes. Asymmetrical turbochargers are used by Detroit DD series engines.

boost pressure normalization The feature of a turbocharger that maintains boost pressure even as the engine climbs to higher altitudes with low air density.

compressor housing The housing that encloses the compressor wheel.

compressor wheel A centrifugal-type air pump attached to the turbine wheel. The compressor wheel uses centrifugal force to compress air.

fixed geometry turbocharger A turbocharger without boost pressure controls; the name is derived from the fact the housings and components have unchanging dimensions.

naturally aspirated An engine that uses only atmospheric pressure and not pressurized air to charge the cylinders with air.

parallel turbocharger The use of two turbochargers that share the exhaust energy from an engine's exhaust manifold. The output of both turbochargers is connected directly to the intake manifold of the engine to increase airflow into the engine.

series turbocharging Using two differently sized turbochargers where the compressor outlet is connected to the inlet of a second compressor.

single sequential turbocharger (SST) A turbocharger design that uses a single turbine wheel and two compressor wheels. Together the compressor wheels supply a greater volume of air to the intake manifold.

supercharger An engine that pressurizes the air intake system above atmospheric pressure.

transient emissions Emissions produced temporarily when the engine load or speed is increased, such as when accelerating or upshifting gears.

turbo lag A delay between driver demand for power and the point when the engine responds with power proportional to driver demand.

variable geometry turbocharger (VGT) A turbocharger with the capability of changing boost pressure independent of engine speed and load; also known as variable nozzle turbocharger (VNT) and variable vane turbocharger (VVT).

wastegate An exhaust bypass valve in the turbine housing that allows exhaust gases to bypass the turbine and directly enter the exhaust pipe, thus "wasting" some of the exhaust energy.

Review Questions

1. A(n) _____ is a turbocharger with volutes of two different sizes.
   a. asymmetrical turbocharger
   b. parallel turbocharger
   c. fixed geometry turbocharger
   d. variable geometry turbo charger

2. A(n) _____ is a turbocharger design that uses a single turbine wheel and two compressor wheels.
   a. asymmetrical turbocharger
   b. series sequential turbocharger
   c. fixed geometry turbo charger
   d. variable geometry turbocharger

3. In a turbocharger, exhaust gases drive a turbine wheel, which is connected to a(n) _____ through a common shaft.
   a. exhaust outlet
   b. turbine
   c. splitter
   d. compressor wheel

4. Engines not equipped with superchargers have cylinders charged with air at atmospheric pressure and are classified as _____.
   a. naturally aspirated
   b. series sequential
   c. asymmetrical
   d. pulse

5. Undersized exhaust pipes and mufflers, dents and numerous bends cause exhaust _____ to increase.
   a. compressor wheel speed
   b. barometric offset
   c. backpressure
   d. hydrocarbons

6. Because the amount of exhaust energy is low when an engine is lightly loaded, a(n) _____ turbocharger can produce little boost at low speeds.
   a. variable geometry
   b. fixed geometry
   c. asymmetrical
   d. parallel

7. Turbocharger failure will result if the _____ is seized closed or tampered with to prevent it from opening.
   a. impeller
   b. wastegate
   c. volute
   d. diffuser

8. Turbocharger _____ is a condition where the turbocharger passes oil into the exhaust system.
   a. backpressure
   b. aspiration
   c. turbo lag
   d. slobber

9. Using an _____ type ball bearing as a center housing support eliminates the need for a thrust bearing because endplay is controlled by the ball and race assembly rather than a sleeve.
   a. asymmetrical
   b. axial
   c. angular
   d. antiquated

10. Many turbochargers use engine _____ passing through passages cast into the center housing to remove heat.
    a. coolant
    b. slobber
    c. spooling
    d. aspiration

ASE-Type Questions

1. Technician A says a fixed geometry turbocharger has the capability of changing boost pressure independent of engine speed and load. Technician B says a variable geometry turbocharger has the capability of changing boost pressure independent of engine speed and load. Who is correct?
   a. Technician A
   b. Technician B
   c. Both Technician A and Technician B
   d. Neither Technician A nor Technician B

2. Technician A says that a roots blower is a positive displacement-type air pump driven by the engine directly through the gear train. Technician B says that a roots blower is a positive displacement-type air pump driven by a viscous coupler. Who is correct?
   a. Technician A
   b. Technician B
   c. Both Technician A and Technician B
   d. Neither Technician A nor Technician B

3. Technician A says that diesel engines that develop greater power output with smaller displacement have the indirect effect of reducing carbon dioxide emissions. Technician B says that diesel engines that develop greater power output with smaller displacement have the indirect effect of reducing carbon monoxide emissions. Who is correct?
   a. Technician A
   b. Technician B
   c. Both Technician A and Technician B
   d. Neither Technician A nor Technician B

4. Technician A says altitude variation is the term given to the turbocharger's ability to compensate for altitude change. Technician B says barometric offset is the term given to the turbocharger's ability to compensate for altitude change. Who is correct?
   a. Technician A
   b. Technician B
   c. Both Technician A and Technician B
   d. Neither Technician A nor Technician B

5. Technician A says compressor wheels are made out of titanium alloys. Technician B says compressor wheels are made out of lightweight aluminum. Who is correct?
   a. Technician A
   b. Technician B
   c. Both Technician A and Technician B
   d. Neither Technician A nor Technician B

6. Technician A says that a pulse turbocharger is a solution to the problems of sluggish, low-power performance and high emissions at low engine speeds. Technician B says that a symmetrical turbocharger is a solution to the problems of sluggish, low-power performance and high emissions at low engine speeds. Who is correct?
   a. Technician A
   b. Technician B
   c. Both Technician A and Technician B
   d. Neither Technician A nor Technician B

7. Technician A says the volume of air supplied to the engine by the turbocharger is determined by the geometry of the compressor wheel. Technician B says the volume of air supplied to the engine by the turbocharger is determined by the compressor wheel speed. Who is correct?
   a. Technician A
   b. Technician B
   c. Both Technician A and Technician B
   d. Neither Technician A nor Technician B

8. Technician A says that when turbocharger discharge pressure is too low, it can cause an increase in carbon monoxide emissions. Technician B says that when turbocharger discharge pressure is too high, it can cause an increase in nitrogen oxide emissions. Who is correct?
   a. Technician A
   b. Technician B
   c. Both Technician A and Technician B
   d. Neither Technician A nor Technician B

9. Technician A says the compressor housing is shaped like the turbine housing but with opposite direction of gas flow. Technician B says the compressor housing is shaped differently from the turbine housing but with the same direction of gas flow. Who is correct?
   a. Technician A
   b. Technician B
   c. Both Technician A and Technician B
   d. Neither Technician A nor Technician B

10. Technician A says that the exhaust manifold becomes hotter than turbine housings when the engine is under load. Technician B says that turbine housings become hotter than the exhaust manifold when the engine is under load. Who is correct?
    a. Technician A
    b. Technician B
    c. Both Technician A and Technician B
    d. Neither Technician A nor Technician B

NATEF Tasks

Diesel Engines

General

- Listen for engine noises; determine needed action. (pp 881, 884)
- Identify engine surging, rough operation, misfiring, low power, slow deceleration, slow acceleration, and shutdown problems; determine needed action. (pp 883–884)
- Check and record electronic diagnostic codes. (pp 878–884)

Cooling System

- Inspect turbocharger cooling systems; determine needed action. (pp 882–885)

Air Induction and Exhaust Systems

- Inspect turbocharger(s), wastegate, and piping systems; determine needed action. (pp 881–884)
- Inspect turbocharger(s) (variable ratio/geometry VGT), pneumatic, hydraulic, electronic controls, and actuators. (pp 881–884)

Knowledge Objectives

After reading this chapter, you will be able to:

1. Describe the purpose and functions of variable geometry and series turbochargers. (pp 874–875, 886–891)
2. Identify and describe the types, construction, and applications of variable geometry and series turbochargers. (pp 875–883, 886–891)
3. Explain the operating principles of variable geometry and series turbochargers. (pp 875–883, 886–891)
4. Identify and explain inspection, testing, and diagnostic procedures on variable geometry turbochargers. (pp 883–886)
5. Describe the purpose and functions of a charge air cooler (CAC). (p 889)

Skills Objectives

After reading this chapter, you will be able to:
1. Replace a VGT actuator. (pp 885) **SKILL DRILL 30-1**
2. Run a turbocharger bounce test. (pp 886) **SKILL DRILL 30-2**
3. Check VPOD output pressure. (pp 887) **SKILL DRILL 30-3**

▶ Introduction

Variable geometry turbochargers (VGTs), also known as variable nozzle turbochargers (VNTs) or variable vane turbochargers (VVTs), are technologically advanced alternatives to fixed geometry and wastegated turbochargers. VGTs were designed to meet emissions targets by supplying pressurized air to the combustion chamber faster and driving EGR gas into the cylinders. VGTs electronically vary boost pressure and exhaust backpressure by changing the size of the nozzle ring in the turbine housing. Series turbochargers are an alternative to VGTs. In series turbocharging, the output of one turbocharger is connected to the inlet of a second. This results in boost pressure multiplication. This next section will examine the purpose, construction, and operation of VGTs and series turbochargers, which have displaced fixed and wastegated turbochargers.

▶ Fundamentals of Variable Geometry Turbochargers

A VGT is a turbocharger capable of changing boost pressure or electronically varying boost and exhaust backpressure independently of engine speed and load. The electronic control module (ECM) calculates values for and then adjusts turbocharger mechanisms to achieve optimal boost and exhaust backpressure.

VGT Purpose

The primary purpose for using VGTs has to do with the operation of exhaust gas recirculation (EGR) systems. Adding EGR systems to most 2002 and later engines was necessary to meet lower oxides of nitrogen (NO_x) emission standards. As much

---

You Are the Technician

A 2006 city transit bus with an automatic transmission often makes a "woofing" noise when decelerating. While performing typical visual inspections, you notice the exhaust pipe emits black and gray smoke when the engine accelerates and when it idles. You also verify the engine noise. Realizing the bus has a high-pressure cooled exhaust gas recirculation (HP-CEGR) system, you check for diagnostic fault codes and find numerous actuator codes and intake boost pressure-related fault codes. While you intend to use the manufacturer's diagnostic fault tree to establish which fault code to investigate first, and you follow manufacturer diagnostic routines, you realize this complaint is common. The noise is likely due to turbocharger surge, which is caused by overboost. Surge produces noise from the turbocharger when high-intake air pressure pushes back through the compressor wheel when the engine cannot use all the air mass produced by high-boost pressure.

1. What position are the turbocharger vanes in when turbocharger surge takes place?
2. Provide two or more explanations for incorrect vane position from the variable geometry turbocharger (VGT).
3. List and explain other possible causes that need investigating that could explain why the bus emits black and gray exhaust smoke.

as 50% of the intake charge can be exhaust gas, with intake air as the remaining percentage. To replace intake air with exhaust gases, high exhaust gas pressure is needed to overcome intake air boost pressure to displace fresh air intake mass. As much as 80 psi (552 kPa) of exhaust backpressure may be required to force enough exhaust gas into the fresh air intake charge. To build adequate exhaust backpressure and make an EGR system work, VGT turbochargers are used. Using electronic controls, the turbocharger's resistance to exhaust flow can be increased to create more exhaust backpressure. Exhaust backpressure is built up in the exhaust manifold, where a cooler or an EGR control valve redirects it into the intake manifold, where it mixes with the fresh air charge. Because exhaust gases are cooled and pressurized, VGTs are used in these exhaust gas recirculation systems known as **high-pressure cooled EGR (HP-CEGR)** **FIGURE 30-1** and **FIGURE 30-2** .

A primary advantage of using VGTs is a fast turbocharger response time with minimal **turbo lag**, which is a delay from the driver's demand for power from the engine to the point when the engine responds with power proportional to the driver's demand. Shorter turbo lag time means fewer emissions are produced while the turbocharger spools, or speeds up. Because exhaust backpressure controls the turbocharger speed, boost pressure is also controlled electronically and can build to higher pressures than conventional turbochargers **FIGURE 30-3** .

VGTs can reduce the number of turbocharger options carried by a manufacturer and provide end users with the ability to change engine power levels without requiring turbocharger replacement. Software control means optimal boost pressure is available over a much wider engine speed range, not in a narrow range of engine load. Higher torque output from smaller engines at low and high rpm with varying loads is easily achieved with VGTs.

VGTs have been used since the 1980s, but their complexity and cost have prevented widespread use. Improved fixed geometry and wastegated turbocharger designs during that time also reduced the need to bring VGTs to market **FIGURE 30-4** .

Turbo Lag, VGTs, and Emissions

Turbocharger design also affects turbo lag. Larger turbocharger compressor housings are needed to produce greater airflow for better performance and reduced emissions. Turbine housings also need to be larger to enable more exhaust flow produced by higher horsepower (hp) engines. Larger turbine and compressor wheel mass, along with bigger housings, mean the turbocharger will take longer to spool, causing extended turbo lag time. Electronic turbocharger controls and the shape of both turbine and compressor housings provide an extended operational range for the VGT compared with other turbocharger technology. High turbine speed is available using little or considerable exhaust gas flow with the type of electronically controlled adjustments built into VGT designs. Very high compressor wheel speeds providing high boost pressure are available at low engine load and speed conditions. Compared with fixed geometry turbochargers, VGTs have an even greater impact on minimizing engine size while increasing power output and reducing exhaust emissions across the entire engine operating range.

When the engine is accelerated rapidly, VGTs reach target boost pressure faster than conventional turbochargers, which virtually eliminates turbo lag and improves throttle response.

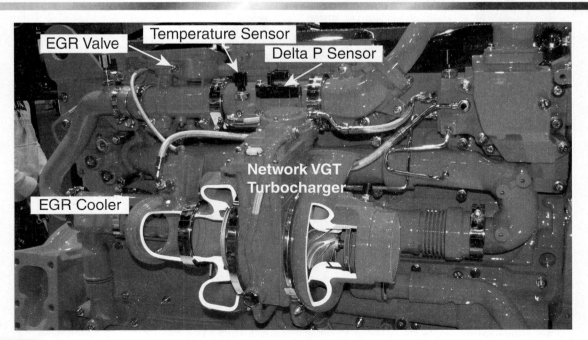

FIGURE 30-1 VGTs are used with HP-CEGR systems to increase exhaust backpressure, which is needed to mix exhaust gases with boosted fresh-air intake.

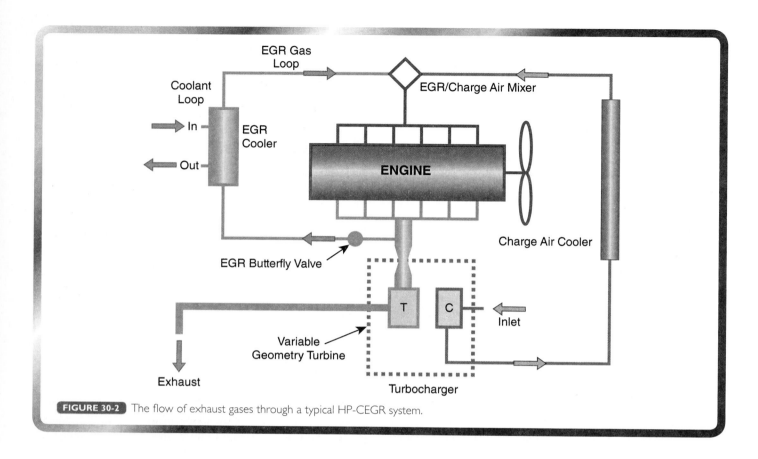

FIGURE 30-2 The flow of exhaust gases through a typical HP-CEGR system.

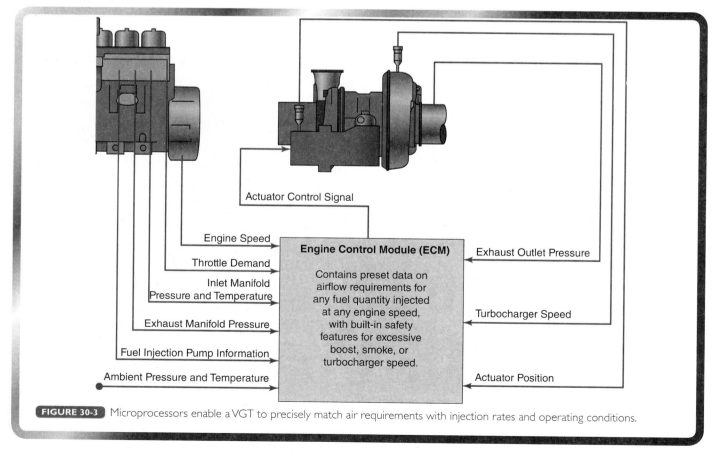

FIGURE 30-3 Microprocessors enable a VGT to precisely match air requirements with injection rates and operating conditions.

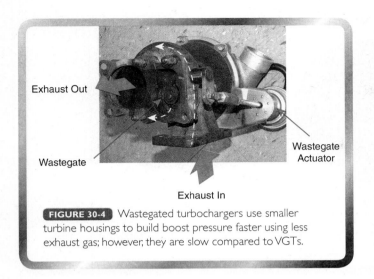

FIGURE 30-4 Wastegated turbochargers use smaller turbine housings to build boost pressure faster using less exhaust gas; however, they are slow compared to VGTs.

The brief exhaust smoke and other emissions associated with older diesels when changing gears or accelerating is gone because VGTs can almost instantly increase boost pressure to supply air needed for combustion. Late-model VGTs have a response time of as little as 0.5 seconds.

▶ VGT Components

Several different types of construction are used by VGT manufacturers to achieve the variable boost and exhaust backpressure engines need. All of the construction styles have in common the ability to change the size of the turbine housing nozzle ring where exhaust gases converge on the turbine wheel. This next section will examine the construction details of the mechanism used to vary the turbine volute's nozzle ring and the methods used to move the mechanism that opens and closes the nozzle ring exit area.

Variable Nozzle Opening

Turbochargers are built along two designs. VGTs vary the opening size of the turbine nozzle that directs exhaust gas onto the turbine wheel. By narrowing the width of the nozzle opening, the turbine speed and exhaust backpressure increase. This same effect is observed by holding a finger over the end of a garden hose to increase the pressure of water coming out of the hose. An electric actuator regulates the size of nozzle opening. As the actuator closes the nozzle to narrow its width, turbine speed and boost pressure rapidly increase as exhaust backpressure rises. This effect is produced with minimal engine load or exhaust energy. Even at low speed and load operation, VGTs achieve relatively higher boost pressure, unlike fixed geometry or wastegated turbochargers.

Opening the nozzle produces the opposite effect—more exhaust gas flow will take place across the turbine, but the turbine speed and exhaust backpressure will decrease **FIGURE 30-5**. This is like taking your finger off the end of a garden hose—flow increases but pressure drops. By varying the width of the nozzle opening with an actuator, turbine power can be adjusted to provide just enough energy to drive the compressor wheel at the desired boost level for any engine speed and load condition **FIGURE 30-6**.

The VGT concept uses vanes, which are also referred to as airfoils, around the circumference of the turbine wheel. Vanes operate to change the cross-sectional area that exhaust gas flows through to vary the amount of pressure crossing the turbine wheel before it reaches the low-pressure exhaust pipe **FIGURE 30-7**. A configuration like this is also referred to as a variable nozzle because the vanes change the amount of exhaust flow through the nozzle ring via signals from an ECM supplied to an actuator on the turbocharger.

Electronic Control of Exhaust Backpressure

Since 2002 in North America and 2004 in Europe and other parts of the world, EGR systems on most diesels take advantage of the VGT's ability to control exhaust backpressure. Because a fixed geometry turbocharger's turbo boost pressures are close to exhaust manifold pressure as a result of valve overlap, a

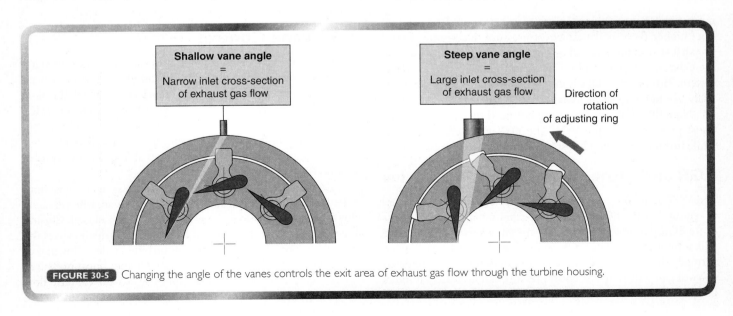

FIGURE 30-5 Changing the angle of the vanes controls the exit area of exhaust gas flow through the turbine housing.

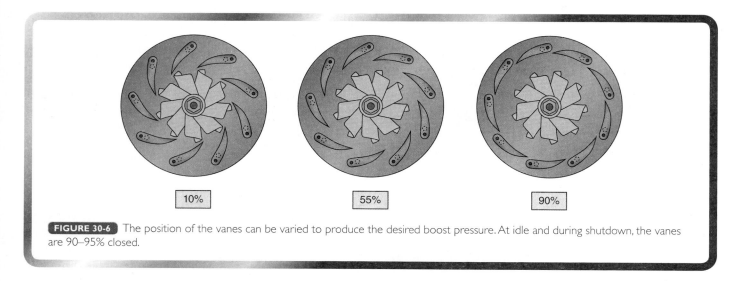

FIGURE 30-6 The position of the vanes can be varied to produce the desired boost pressure. At idle and during shutdown, the vanes are 90–95% closed.

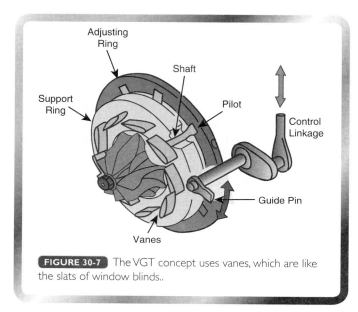

FIGURE 30-7 The VGT concept uses vanes, which are like the slats of window blinds..

mechanism is necessary to increase exhaust gas pressure to a level higher than intake air boost pressure. Electronic control of exhaust backpressure allows VGTs to build gas pressure in the exhaust manifold and push exhaust gas into the air intake system. This means intake boost pressure is controlled electronically through regulating exhaust backpressure.

Note that EGR gas flow does not need to accompany high boost pressure from the VGT. The EGR valve can fully close while turbine speed and boost pressure reach maximum limits.

EGR and Other VGT Operation Modes

The VGT actuator is adjusted to increase exhaust backpressure as required by the EGR system. The exhaust backpressure forces more EGR gas flow into the EGR circuit, where the EGR valve will ultimately regulate EGR mass flow. Exhaust gas flowing through the EGR valve regulates the quantity of recirculated exhaust gas, which means boost pressure can increase without a corresponding increase in the EGR flow.

To improve engine braking, the VGT actuator can narrow the nozzle opening and increase exhaust backpressure if the engine calibration enables the turbocharger to act as an exhaust brake. Boost and compression pressure increase accordingly to create higher compression pressures and increase engine drag when using the engine compression release brake. This takes place because high boost pressure requires more energy to compress intake air. When backpressure is higher, the engine has to work even harder to push exhaust out the exhaust manifold.

Using a VGT as part of an engine braking strategy requires heavier housings to reduce the amount of creep, or expansion, taking place under high temperatures and pressures. The tension of the exhaust valve spring needs to increase to reduce the likelihood of exhaust backpressure forcing an exhaust valve open when any piston is near top dead center.

Narrowing the nozzle opening can also increase backpressure at cold idle to quicken engine warm-up. Under these conditions, the cooling system absorbs more heat because high exhaust backpressure causes gases to linger longer at a higher temperature in the exhaust ports of the cylinder head.

VGT Vane Control

The most common VGT design rotates vanes or vanes arranged similar to slats in a window blind around the turbine wheel. The vanes surround the turbine wheel and control the flow of exhaust gas across the turbine wheel. Vanes are mounted in the turbine housing with one end pinned to the housing. Another pin connects the other end to a plate called a **unison ring**. Rotation of the unison ring causes all the vanes to revolve around the fixed pivot point.

Rotation of the vanes changes boost pressure by controlling exhaust turbine inlet pressure. At low engine load, when exhaust flow and energy are low, the vanes are partially closed. Closing the vanes increases the exhaust backpressure, which causes the exhaust to push harder against the turbine blades. This makes the turbine wheel spin faster, generating higher boost pressure.

As engine speed and load increase, so do exhaust flow and energy. Under these conditions, the vanes open to reduce pressure against the turbine and hold boost steady—or reduce it as needed.

Sliding Nozzle Control

Holset turbochargers, used primarily by engine manufacturer Cummins, have a sliding nozzle ring to change the opening in the turbine housing, which regulates exhaust gas flow onto the turbine wheel FIGURE 30-8 . Closing the nozzle speeds up the turbine wheel and increases backpressure. Opening the nozzle slows down the wheel and decreases backpressure FIGURE 30-9 . Maintaining optimal boost pressure as the engine speed and load changes is a function of opening or closing the sliding nozzle. The sliding nozzle creates a limitless number of turbine geometry configurations of a fixed geometry turbocharger.

Electric VGT Actuator Mechanisms

Fast response of the turbocharger to engine speed and load changes is the objective of the actuator mechanism. Several mechanisms are used to change vane position; electric motors and hydraulic devices are the most common types of actuators. Air actuators were initially more common on heavy-duty diesels. Network control of the VGT provides other vehicle system the ability to supply input information

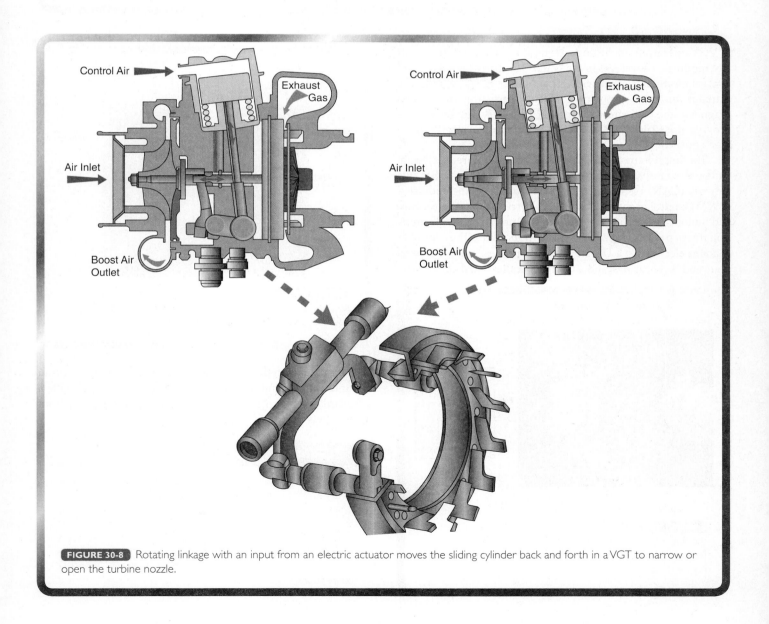

FIGURE 30-8 Rotating linkage with an input from an electric actuator moves the sliding cylinder back and forth in a VGT to narrow or open the turbine nozzle.

Sliding Nozzle In   Sliding Nozzle Out

FIGURE 30-9   The Holset sliding nozzle VGT. The width of the nozzle area is changed.

to VGT operation, including aftertreatment and traction control modules. Newer VGTs are "smart" and rely on networked control modules and use electric actuators **FIGURE 30-10**. The actuator includes a position sensor consisting of a small magnet and a Hall effect sensor **FIGURE 30-11**. The sensor can provide closed-loop feedback to the module to vary the actuator's position.

The Smart Remote Actuator (SRA), manufactured by Delphi and used extensively on newer engines, combines controller area network (CAN) communication with a pulse-width-modulated (PWM) control of the brushless DC electric motor. The controls and motor operate similarly to a stepper motor to provide precision rotary position control of turbocharger vanes. The controller contains electronics, a DC stepper motor, a gear train with steel gears and ball bearings, and a microprocessor-based closed-loop

FIGURE 30-11   Actuators contain a Hall effect sensor, stepper motor, microcontrollers, a variety of drivers, some memory, and a CAN transceiver.

position control. In the event of an electrical system malfunction, the unit has a default position even without power to provide a safeguard position. Moving the actuator requires a signal from the ECM via the CAN.

▶ TECHNICIAN TIP

VGT control modules are generally connected to the CAN on a vehicle and not controlled directly by the ECM. This is because other control systems may need to send messages directly to the turbocharger. Because a shorted VGT module can disable the entire CAN and prevent retrieval of any system information, including fault codes, it is important to not overlook the module when disconnecting modules to identify defective network connections.

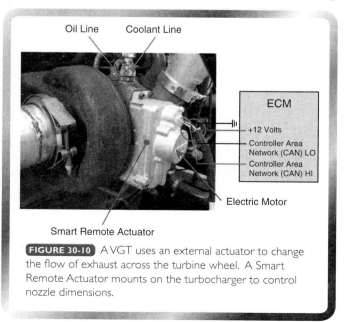

FIGURE 30-10   A VGT uses an external actuator to change the flow of exhaust across the turbine wheel. A Smart Remote Actuator mounts on the turbocharger to control nozzle dimensions.

When the ignition key is first cycled, many stepper motor devices operating throttle plates, VGT actuators, and EGR motors perform a self-calibrating "sweep." Dash gauges using stepper motors do the same thing. The stepper motors produce a noise when they relearn travel limits. A Hall effect device in the control modules evaluates whether the minimum and maximum sweep is complete. Without seeing the VGT linkage performing a complete sweep, a fault code may be set for the actuator position.

Hydraulic Actuators

Pressurized engine oil acting against a hydraulic servo piston accomplishes hydraulic actuation **FIGURE 30-12** and **FIGURE 30-13**. A PWM vane position–control solenoid varies oil pressure applied to the actuator piston to move the turbocharger's unison ring. Typically, the actuator piston will move a geared rack mechanism that, in turn, rotates a pinion gear to reposition the vanes. The vanes are fully opened when no oil flow is commanded to move the servo piston and close as oil pressure increases through the vane position–control solenoid valve.

On some engines using hydraulic turbocharger actuators, an analog position sensor with a movable tip rides on the vane actuator cam and measures the vane position to provide feedback to the control module. The sensor harness includes a module with an AC frequency generator that pulses a coil in the sensor. A moving iron core in the sensor will change the magnetic field strength of the coil, which the module analyzes and converts to a digital signal and sends to the ECM. For example, the actuator in 6.6L (403 cubic inch) Duramax engines uses oil pressure to move the vane adjustment

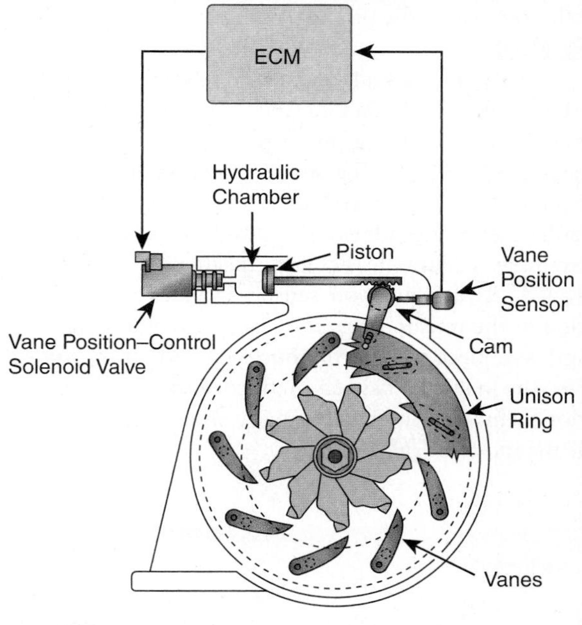

FIGURE 30-13 Hydraulic control-valve operation on the DMAX VGT. A vane position sensor provides closed-loop feedback to the ECM regarding control valve and vane positions.

mechanism. The actuator incorporates a position sensor and a servo valve to control oil pressure to either side of the hydraulic servo chamber **FIGURE 30-14**. The DMAX Garrett turbocharger has an electronic signal conditioning circuit in the connector module. A sliding iron pin in the vane position sensor changes the strength of a magnetic field. Movement of the pin up and down on a cam provides a

FIGURE 30-12 A hydraulic vane position actuator on a 6.0L (366 cubic inch) PowerStroke engine.

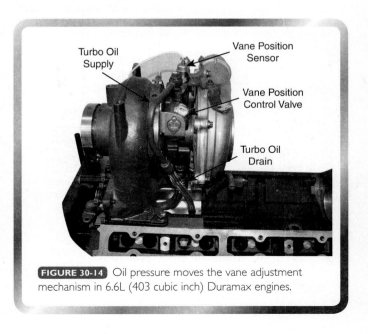

FIGURE 30-14 Oil pressure moves the vane adjustment mechanism in 6.6L (403 cubic inch) Duramax engines.

magnetic field strength proportional to vane position. The module transduces the pin position into a signal for the ECM **FIGURE 30-15**.

On hydraulic actuators used on smaller displacement Navistar engines, the end of the VGT control valve has a mechanical cam follower to provide positional feedback to a sensor **FIGURE 30-16**. The sensor functions in a closed-loop feedback circuit. The control valve supplies oil pressure to the hydraulic servo and adjusts the position of the unison ring. For example, a Duramax actuator mechanism is hydraulically controlled. A vane position sensor provides feedback for the position of the unison ring. The sensor changes magnetic field strength as a piece of soft iron moves up and down inside a coil of wire. The magnetic field strength corresponds to unison ring position, which is interpreted by a signal processing circuit inside the module **FIGURE 30-17**.

VGT Sensors

Like any electronically controlled device that has a mechanical output, the electronic control system needs to find out whether the electrical control signals are accomplishing their intended purpose. To achieve precise control, the turbocharger mechanism must provide electronic feedback about the turbocharger's operation in order for the electronic control system to adjust turbocharger operation. This process of applying an electric signal then measuring the system response is called closed-loop feedback.

Turbo Speed Sensor

Many turbochargers have a speed sensor in the center housing **FIGURE 30-18**. Turbine speed data is used to adjust the actuator position and monitor the turbocharger operation. Speed data is also critical for preventing turbocharger overspeed conditions. The speed sensor is the equivalent of the wastegate used to prevent overspeed

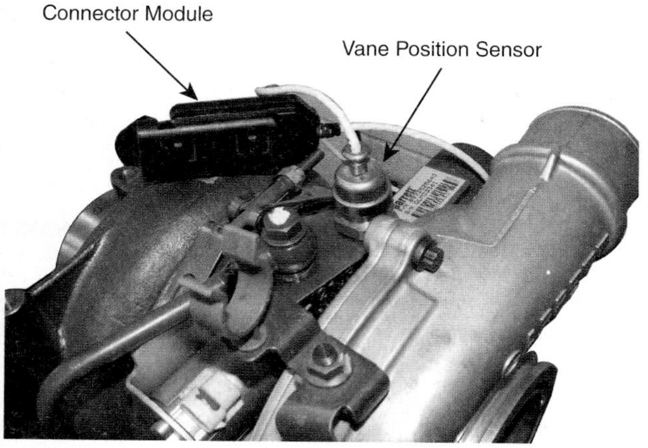

FIGURE 30-15 The connector module in the DMAX Garrett turbocharger transduces the pin position into a signal for the ECM.

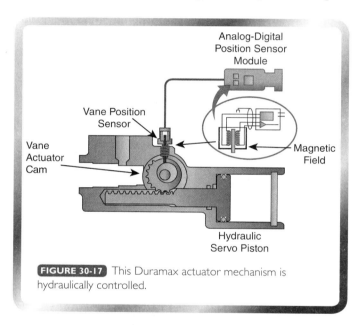

FIGURE 30-17 This Duramax actuator mechanism is hydraulically controlled.

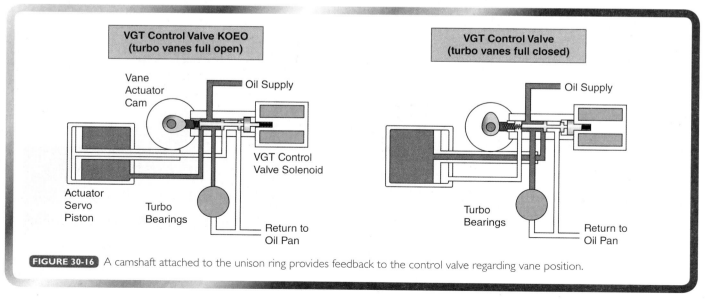

FIGURE 30-16 A camshaft attached to the unison ring provides feedback to the control valve regarding vane position.

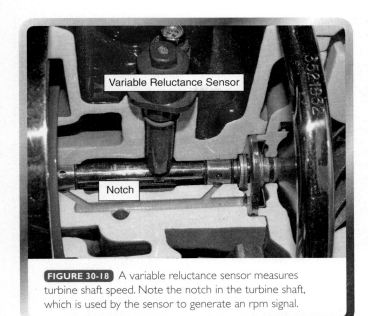

FIGURE 30-18 A variable reluctance sensor measures turbine shaft speed. Note the notch in the turbine shaft, which is used by the sensor to generate an rpm signal.

conditions in wastegated turbochargers. If overspeed is detected, the ECM will open the vanes in the VGT to slow turbine speed.

The heavy-duty on-board diagnostics (HD-OBD) system will monitor turbo operation using the speed sensor. When functional monitors evaluate the performance of the EGR system and the turbocharger, they measure turbine speed change and compare it with expected values when the actuator is moved. If measurements are outside expected ranges, an actuator fault code is set.

Exhaust Back-Pressure Sensor

An exhaust back-pressure sensor can provide data regarding exhaust manifold pressure. Data supplied by the sensor is used to calculate the correct vane position. This sensor is also important to EGR system calculations for exhaust mass flow. The HD-OBD system will use the exhaust back-pressure data to check the rationality of data from other sensors. This means boost pressures, turbine speed, or actuator position may be compared to validate that the data from those sensors is within an expected range and emission systems are functioning correctly.

Cooling VGT Center Housings and Module

The bearing housing of the turbocharger and the variable geometry actuator usually contains engine coolant passages. Minimizing bearing wear is more critical in VGTs because the compressor wheel runs closer to the housing, which improves efficiency. Bearing wear will quickly cause the compressor wheel to touch the housing and destroy the turbo. Circulating coolant through the VGT actuator housing reduces the operating temperature of the internal electronics, which increases the reliability of the vane and actuator mechanisms. During the hot-soak period, when engine temperatures rise after the engine is switched off, convection currents circulate coolant to remove excess heat. During actuator service to replace the motor or control module, drain engine coolant before removing the module.

▶ VGT Maintenance

Seized or binding actuators are major problems for VGTs. Soot in the vane or sliding nozzle can collect and prevent proper VGT functioning. Excessive idle time and low-speed and low-load operating conditions increase accumulations of gummy residue in the turbocharger. Without high exhaust pressure and temperatures to clean out the mechanism, the turbocharger vanes and actuation mechanisms begin to stick and operate erratically.

A "woofing" sound from the air intake when the engine is rapidly accelerated and decelerated is one symptom of a slow-responding actuator. This sound, referred to as **chuffing**, is the effect of turbo surge, a condition created when the turbocharger spins very fast and the engine rpm falls more quickly than the turbocharger boost pressure. The high boost pressure inside the compressor housing will flow back through the turbocharger compressor wheel, creating the woof sound effect.

A sticking nozzle ring will eventually overload the electric motor in the VGT actuator and cause it to burn out. Electronic modules in the SRA can also fail.

SRA Service

Replacing motors and modules in the actuator requires the ECM to learn the actuator's new position. After removing the SRA from the turbocharger, move the sector gear in the turbocharger that rotates the VGT vanes back and forth. Check wear in the control mechanism **FIGURE 30-19**. An alignment pin is often installed in the sector gear to fix its location in the housing **FIGURE 30-20**. Remove the pin, being careful not to move the sector gear. Next, before installing the actuator mechanism onto the sector gear, use original equipment manufacturer (OEM) software to command the actuator to learn the new maximum and minimum sweep limits. Next, assemble the two parts for a final step—the OEM software commands the complete actuation mechanism to recalibrate and learn the final sweep range. Learning maximum and minimum sweep are necessary to compensate for VGT deterioration due to wear.

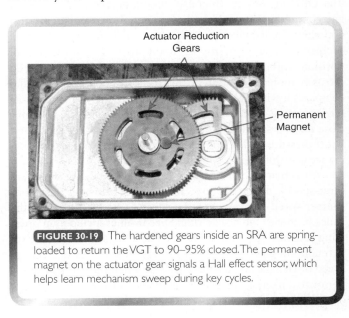

FIGURE 30-19 The hardened gears inside an SRA are spring-loaded to return the VGT to 90–95% closed. The permanent magnet on the actuator gear signals a Hall effect sensor, which helps learn mechanism sweep during key cycles.

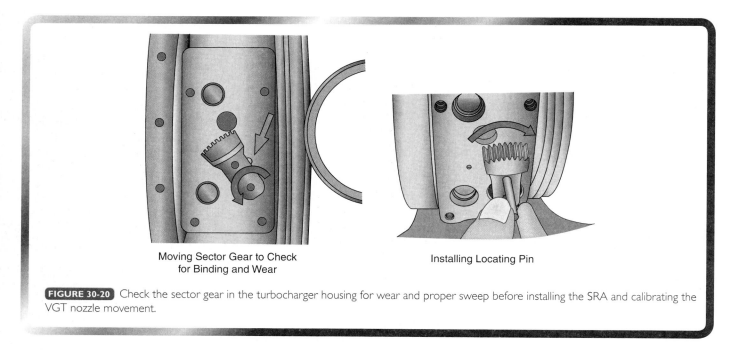

Moving Sector Gear to Check
for Binding and Wear

Installing Locating Pin

FIGURE 30-20 Check the sector gear in the turbocharger housing for wear and proper sweep before installing the SRA and calibrating the VGT nozzle movement.

When the ignition key is cycled, VGTs generally recalibrate and learn the sweep limits. A small permanent magnet and a Hall effect sensor on the circuit board identify these positions. Error codes for failure to calibrate accompany seized or sticking actuators.

Replacing a VGT Actuator

Diagnostic fault codes may indicate that an SRA requires replacement. To replace a VGT actuator, follow the steps in **SKILL DRILL 30-1**. The procedure shown is specific to Delphi SRAs. Follow the manufacturer's instructions for products from other OEMs.

VGT Diagnostics

The OBD system continuously monitors the VGT to detect any condition that could lead to potential increases in exhaust emissions. Fault codes are set for any sensor or actuator electrical problems, under- or overboost conditions, and the boost control position. Turbocharger response to nozzle ring movement is an intrusive monitoring strategy that measures boost pressure and compares it with expected values while driving. When the correct operating conditions are met, the vanes or nozzle ring may close for 2–3 seconds to measure the turbocharger's speed and boost pressure to determine whether the turbocharger's performance is within the acceptable operating range.

An actuator's performance can be tested using manufacturer-specific diagnostic software. This test measures the turbocharger speed change when the actuator closes and opens the vanes or moves the nozzle ring. Speed values included in operating software will determine whether the control mechanism is functioning properly. A turbocharger that does not change speed or changes to an expected value when the actuator test is performed likely has a defect associated with the turbocharger or control circuits.

The Bounce Test

The turbocharger actuator position can be commanded during key-on, engine-off (KOEO) tests. Measure the actuator position or air pressure supplied to the actuator to validate correct operation **FIGURE 30-21**. Another operational strategy to evaluate the turbocharger actuator response is monitoring boost pressure. Actuator movement should produce changes to the intake manifold pressure. Carbonized slobber in the turbine housing is the most common problem affecting actuator movement. In most cases, the turbocharger can be disassembled, cleaned, lubricated, and reassembled for service. Excessive force used to move

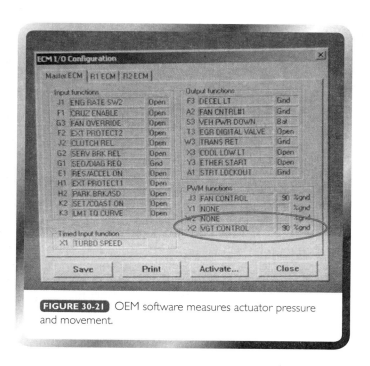

FIGURE 30-21 OEM software measures actuator pressure and movement.

SKILL DRILL 30-1 Replacing a VGT Actuator

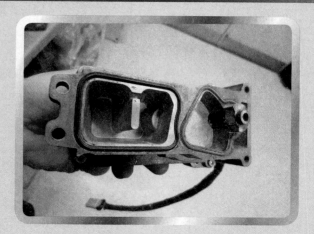

1 Drain the engine coolant and disconnect the SRA coolant lines.

2 Remove the retaining screws from the SRA and disconnect the wiring harness to complete SRA removal.

3 Inspect the VGT mechanism operation. First, hold and shake the sector gear inside the turbocharger to check for excessive movement, which would indicate a failed bearing in the sector shaft. Sweep the sector gear back and forth several times. After initially moving it several times, it should move freely. If it does not sweep freely, the turbocharger will require replacement or disassembly, cleaning, inspection, and lubrication of vane linkage.

4 Rotate the turbocharger sector gear clockwise by hand and insert a ⅕″ (5 mm) locking pin, typically supplied in the service kit, through the gear and into a reference hole in the bearing housing. If the pin does not insert into the reference hole in the turbocharger, the turbocharger will require replacement or disassembly, cleaning, inspection, and lubrication of vane linkage.

5 Rotate the sector gear counter-clockwise and ensure that the flat side of the gear aligns across the diameter of a smaller 0.1″ (2.5 mm) sight hole, if the hole is present. Alternatively, measure the sweep of the sector gear using wear gauges, which correspond to specific models of turbochargers.

6 Lubricate the sector gear and drive gear of the electric actuator.

7 Align the actuator drive gear with the turbocharger sector shaft. This process is done using software to position the electric actuator with the turbocharger sector gear. OEM software or the turbocharger manufacturer's software, such as Holset Aspect™, can be used.

8 Connect the electric actuator to the wiring harness or harness of the test software.

9 Initiate a pre-installation or calibrate actuator command from service tool software. The actuator drive gear will move to its correct position. Do not move the actuator drive gear after this point.

10 Align the sector shaft with the pin placed in the reference pin hole. Remove the pin and do not rotate the sector gear after this point. The pre-positioning of each gear allows attachment of the electric actuator to the turbocharger housing.

11 Attach the actuator to the turbocharger housing.

12 Initiate an actuator calibrate or self-calibrate command from the chosen service tool menu.

13 Disconnect the electronic service tool and reconnect the engine system harnesses. Connect the coolant lines and refill the cooling system. The turbocharger assembly is now ready to return to service.

---

the vanes is sensed by an increase in amperage or pulse width supplied to the actuator electric motor. High current flow to an electric motor is flagged as a potential for an actuator failure.

The actuators of VGTs with external linkage can be checked by performing a bounce test. With the ignition key switch in the off position, the turbocharger linkage should be easily moved to the fully open position. The linkage should move smoothly. Releasing the linkage will cause the spring-loaded actuator mechanism to move the linkage to the vanes-closed position. Properly operating actuator linkage and vanes will contact the closed position and cause the linkage to bounce at least once, if not two or three times.

Running a Turbocharger Bounce Test

Diagnostic fault codes and complaints associated with the turbocharger actuator, low power, poor throttle response, boost pressure, exhaust backpressure issues, and exhaust smoke indicate

that the turbocharger actuator may not be properly responding. A bounce test is used to inspect the actuator operation on a turbocharger with external linkage, such as those made by Garett.

To run a turbocharger bounce test, follow the steps in **SKILL DRILL 30-2**.

Linkage Movement Test

When the turbocharger fails the bounce test, the next step to determine whether the problem is in the vanes or with the actuator is the linkage movement test. For this test, disconnect and move the linkage through its range of motion, which will indicate whether the vane mechanism is binding.

Actuator Voltage Test

If the turbocharger passed the linkage test and the vane mechanism is not binding, the actuator likely failed. Using a breakout

SKILL DRILL 30-2 Running a Turbocharger Bounce Test

1. Perform a linkage pre-cycle test. Observe the turbocharger actuator linkage while cycling the key switch to the On position. The linkage should smoothly complete a full sweep at KOEO. No partial or erratic movement is permissible. Several successful completions of this test indicate that the turbocharger actuator is operating satisfactorily and no further tests are required. If the turbocharger does not properly complete the linkage pre-cycle test, a linkage bounce test or movement test is required.

2. With the key and engine off, push the actuator linkage with finger pressure to the opposite end of travel and release it. The linkage should move smoothly with slight spring resistance, then return to its original position. Good linkage will bounce two or three times when it returns; however, the linkage does not need to bounce when it returns to the stop to pass this test.

3. If the linkage sticks, operates erratically, drags, or does not return to its starting position, the vane mechanism is likely the problem. This will require a turbocharger replacement or disassembly, cleaning, and lubrication with a high-temperature anti-seize compound. Occasionally, the turbocharger actuator motor may be defective and should be disconnected from the linkage to verify whether it is turning properly when rotated to the end of its travel.

4. If the turbocharger passes the linkage bounce test, further electrical diagnostic checks are needed to determine the reason for the unresponsive actuator.

harness or proper pins to back-probe the turbocharger actuator electrical connection, measure the power and ground wire voltage when cycling the key on and off. Observe battery voltage when the ignition key is switched on. If battery voltage occurs, the actuator is defective.

▶ TECHNICIAN TIP

Carbonized turbocharger slobber around the moving actuator mechanisms hinders vane and sliding nozzle movement, which is the most common complaint from VGTs that set fault codes. Excessive idle time and poor quality, low-cetane fuel are common causes of seized actuator mechanisms. The measurement and evaluation of VGT actuator movement varies by manufacturer. In some cases where mechanisms are external, a bounce test of linkage or a visual evaluation of actuator operation can be performed. The amount of amperage supplied to the electric motor will also vary with resistance encountered by vane movement.

Checking VPOD Output Pressure

Diagnostic fault codes and complaints about low power, exhaust smoke, and chuffing noise point to problems with the Detroit VGT. A variable pressure output device (VPOD) regulates air pressure to the turbocharger actuator. A defective VPOD often can produce fault codes and drivability symptoms.

To check VPOD output pressure, follow the steps in **SKILL DRILL 30-3**.

▶ Fundamentals of Series Turbocharging

While VGTs have become common in many diesel engines, single-stage and variable geometry turbocharging have limits. Increasing torque requirements at all engine speeds requires more airflow. Larger housings can provide greater air mass, but only at high engine load and high speed conditions. The opposite is true for smaller housings. To overcome the limits

SKILL DRILL 30-3 Checking VPOD Output Pressure

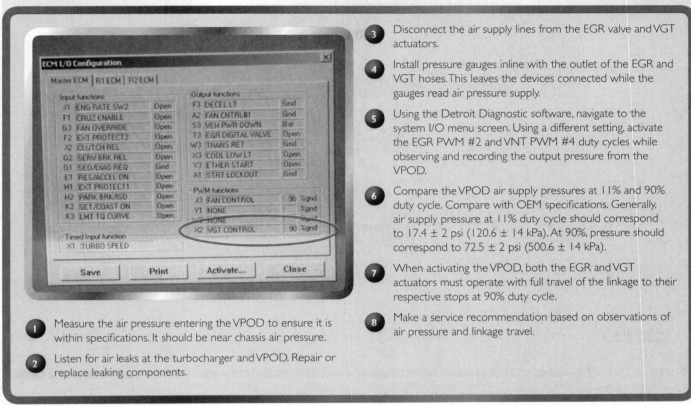

3 Disconnect the air supply lines from the EGR valve and VGT actuators.

4 Install pressure gauges inline with the outlet of the EGR and VGT hoses. This leaves the devices connected while the gauges read air pressure supply.

5 Using the Detroit Diagnostic software, navigate to the system I/O menu screen. Using a different setting, activate the EGR PWM #2 and VNT PWM #4 duty cycles while observing and recording the output pressure from the VPOD.

6 Compare the VPOD air supply pressures at 11% and 90% duty cycle. Compare with OEM specifications. Generally, air supply pressure at 11% duty cycle should correspond to 17.4 ± 2 psi (120.6 ± 14 kPa). At 90%, pressure should correspond to 72.5 ± 2 psi (500.6 ± 14 kPa).

7 When activating the VPOD, both the EGR and VGT actuators must operate with full travel of the linkage to their respective stops at 90% duty cycle.

8 Make a service recommendation based on observations of air pressure and linkage travel.

1 Measure the air pressure entering the VPOD to ensure it is within specifications. It should be near chassis air pressure.

2 Listen for air leaks at the turbocharger and VPOD. Repair or replace leaking components.

of single-stage and variable geometry turbocharging, manufacturers use two turbochargers connected in series **FIGURE 30-22**. The pressurized air outlet of a larger, high-pressure turbocharger compressor housing is connected to the air inlet of a smaller, low-pressure turbocharger compressor housing. This means the boost pressure from the first-stage turbocharger is multiplied by the second-stage turbocharger.

A **series turbocharger** can be used with a low-pressure, cooled EGR system, where the turbocharger does not increase exhaust backpressure for the system **FIGURE 30-23**. Low-pressure EGR uses an intake throttle plate to drag in EGR gas and limit intake airflow. Without the need for high exhaust backpressure, a VGT turbocharger is not necessary.

Series turbochargers use different sizes of compressor and turbine housings designated as high-pressure and low-pressure turbochargers. The high-pressure turbocharger has a smaller turbine and compressor housing than the low-pressure turbocharger. A relatively smaller turbine housing responds quickly to increased engine load, with virtually no lag at low speeds. Boost pressure increases rapidly at low speeds and load conditions using the smaller turbine housing of the high-pressure turbo.

Output pressure from the low-pressure compressor housing directs air into the high-pressure turbocharger. Air enters the low-pressure compressor housing first because it encounters little resistance inside the larger housing. Under load, the high-pressure compressor turbocharger will reach maximum boost pressure and turbine speed more quickly. Due to its size limitations, the high-pressure turbine and compressor wheel cannot spin any faster, so the second low-pressure turbocharger begins to receive increasing exhaust gas flow because an exhaust bypass valve or wastegate on the high-pressure turbocharger directs more exhaust energy into the low-pressure turbocharger. Turbine speed does not change in the high-pressure turbocharger because a wastegate, or exhaust bypass valve, diverts exhaust gases away from the high-pressure turbocharger's turbine wheel into the low-pressure turbocharger. As boost pressure from the low-pressure turbocharger increases with faster turbine speed, the high-pressure turbocharger will remain at the same speed and multiply the inlet boost pressure supplied by the low-pressure turbocharger.

Arranged in a series like this, multiplication of the output pressure occurs and causes boost pressure to increase to levels higher than either turbocharger could achieve alone. The mass of air moved and pressures developed are also substantially greater than what could be produced with a single-stage turbocharger or a VGT.

Splitting the pressurization of the charge air between two turbochargers allows both to operate at optimal efficiency

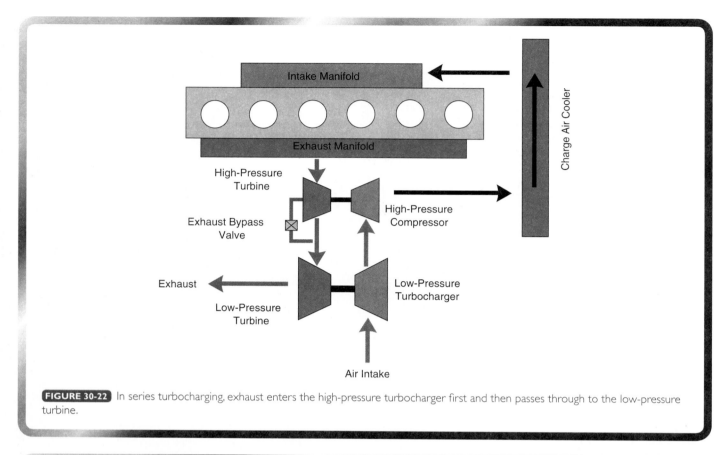

FIGURE 30-22 In series turbocharging, exhaust enters the high-pressure turbocharger first and then passes through to the low-pressure turbine.

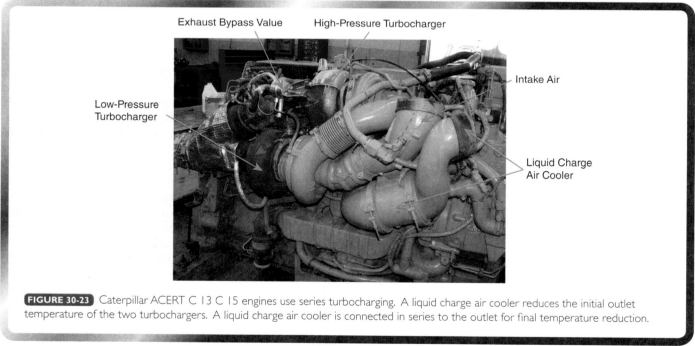

FIGURE 30-23 Caterpillar ACERT C 13 C 15 engines use series turbocharging. A liquid charge air cooler reduces the initial outlet temperature of the two turbochargers. A liquid charge air cooler is connected in series to the outlet for final temperature reduction.

because the housing and wheel sizes are not a compromise for performance over a wide engine-load range. Series turbochargers can also operate at lower pressure ratios. Pressure ratio is a comparison of the pressure at the compressor inlet and outlet. With series turbochargers, a compression ratio of 2–2.5 for each stage means lower rotating speeds, which improves the reliability of the bearings and other rotating parts.

On most series turbocharged diesels, the high-pressure turbocharger is wastegated to prevent overspeeding **FIGURE 30-24**. Its smaller housing cannot handle high exhaust flow, so the

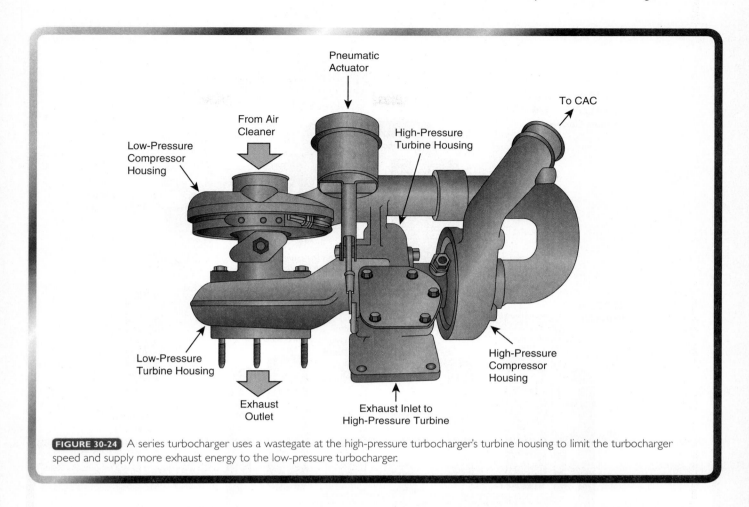

FIGURE 30-24 A series turbocharger uses a wastegate at the high-pressure turbocharger's turbine housing to limit the turbocharger speed and supply more exhaust energy to the low-pressure turbocharger.

wastegate directs exhaust flow to the low-pressure turbine housing. Other engine configurations use valves in the exhaust and intake system to balance exhaust and intake flow.

A common engine configuration uses a VGT as a low-pressure turbocharger and adds a fixed geometry high-pressure turbocharger to supply higher boost pressure when engine loads and speeds are higher **FIGURE 30-25**.

▶ Types of Series Turbochargers

While all series turbochargers share the same operating principles, they are built a variety of ways. How they are arranged on the engine and the types of control mechanisms used can be quite different. A variation of the series turbocharger is single sequential turbocharging, which is one of the latest innovations in turbocharger technology.

Single Sequential Turbocharging

Ford's 6.7L (409 cubic inch) PowerStroke diesel, code-named Scorpion Diesel, uses a unique, patented **single sequential turbocharger (SST)** design, which is also known as a VNT™ DualBoost Turbo turbocharger, and integrates two turbochargers into a single component. The innovative unit essentially uses one turbine wheel and two compressor wheels mounted back-to-back onto a single turbine shaft. The single-piece compressor housing is divided, with a compressor wheel spinning in each half. Two air inlets supply the high- and low-pressure compressor wheels in the DualBoost model, but only a single pressurized outlet supplies air to a liquid intercooler. The turbine housing uses a hydraulically actuated variable geometry mechanism to regulate turbine speed. An electronically controlled wastegate enables even smaller turbine housing for faster response times.

SST Operation

The DualBoost's unique operation begins with fresh intake air entering the low- and high-speed compressor inlets **FIGURE 30-26**. Crankcase vapors are drawn into the air inlet as fresh air passes through the lower intake manifold, which contains a crankcase vent. Pressurized air leaves a single outlet and passes through a liquid **charge air cooler (CAC)**. Also known as aftercooling and intercooling, the CAC is a system that removes excess heat from the air charging the cylinders. After being cooled by the engine's colder secondary liquid cooling system, air is distributed to the intake manifolds after EGR gas mixes with the airflow. Because the outlet of one turbo is not directly fed to the inlet of the other, as in true series turbochargers, this design is an SST.

In this design, boost pressure does not occur. Instead, the shape of the compressor wheel and the high-pressure turbocharger housing add air volume to the output of the low-pressure

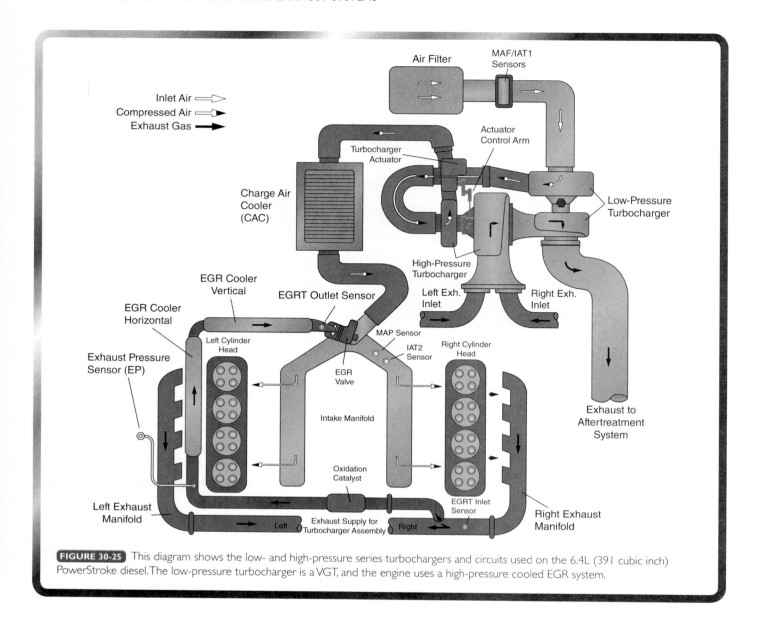

FIGURE 30-25 This diagram shows the low- and high-pressure series turbochargers and circuits used on the 6.4L (391 cubic inch) PowerStroke diesel. The low-pressure turbocharger is a VGT, and the engine uses a high-pressure cooled EGR system.

turbocharger when turbine shaft speeds are great enough to efficiently use the larger compressor wheel and housing configuration. Faster spooling from the smaller turbocharger and high air volume give the engine airflow characteristics of a larger turbo from a more compact package **FIGURE 30-27**. Ford uses this configuration to enable the use of "reversed" intake and exhaust flow through the cylinder heads. Rather than placing the exhaust ports on the outboard side of the cylinder heads, where they are traditionally found, the exhaust ports are inboard. The short connection to the turbocharger narrows the profile of the engine and improves the turbocharger's thermal efficiency with short runs of exhaust from inboard ports to the engine valley, where the turbocharger is located.

Five-Stroke Miller Cycle Engines

High boost pressures produced by series turbocharging enables the use of late intake valve closing to provide an engine efficiency increase of approximately 15%. Miller cycle engines use a mechanism to hold the intake valve open longer under high boost conditions so the engine does not need to work as hard compressing air. On Caterpillar's Advanced Combustion Emission Reduction Technology (ACERT) engines, the device is called a variable intake valve actuator (VIVA). Depending on engine operating conditions, the engine oil–operated VIVA will hold the intake valve open longer as boost pressure increases. Late intake valve closing effectively reduces the length of the compression stroke,

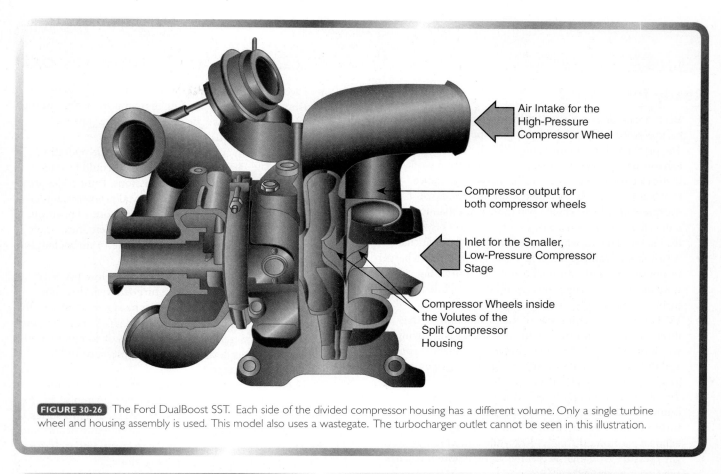

FIGURE 30-26 The Ford DualBoost SST. Each side of the divided compressor housing has a different volume. Only a single turbine wheel and housing assembly is used. This model also uses a wastegate. The turbocharger outlet cannot be seen in this illustration.

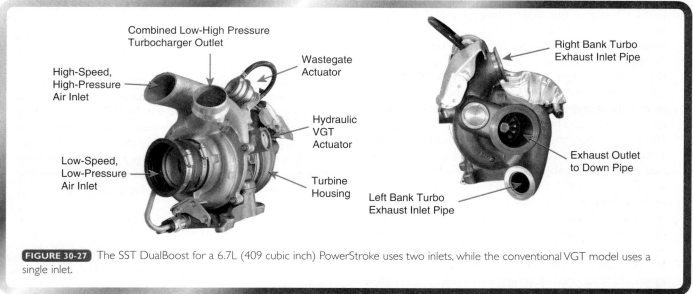

FIGURE 30-27 The SST DualBoost for a 6.7L (409 cubic inch) PowerStroke uses two inlets, while the conventional VGT model uses a single inlet.

which means fewer degrees of crankshaft rotation are needed to com press air. The extra air volume provided by higher boost delivered by series turbochargers packs the cylinder with the same amount of air mass as a conventional turbocharger but with a shorter, less power robbing compression stroke.

The advantage of the Miller cycle is that less compression work is done by the engine because the turbochargers do more work compressing air. Additional cooling of the air intake using jacket water aftercooling (JWAC) and an air-to-air charge air cooler means combustion temperatures are lowered for reduced NO_x emissions. Miller cycle engines are also referred to as a five-stroke cycle because the compression stroke is divided into two phases—normal intake-valve closing and late intake-valve closing.

Wrap-Up

Ready for Review

▶ VGTs are capable of electronically varying boost and exhaust backpressure independently of engine speed and load.

▶ The primary purpose for using VGTs is to build adequate exhaust backpressure to make the EGR system work.

▶ Using electronic controls, the turbocharger's resistance to exhaust flow can be increased to create more exhaust backpressure, which is built up in the exhaust manifold and redirected through either a cooler or an EGR control valve into the intake manifold, where it mixes with the fresh air charge.

▶ A primary advantage of using VGTs is a fast turbocharger response time with minimal turbo lag. Shorter lag time means fewer emissions are produced while the turbocharger spools, or speeds up.

▶ VGTs vary the opening size of the turbine nozzle that directs exhaust gas onto the turbine wheel. Narrowing the width of the nozzle opening increases the turbine speed and the exhaust backpressure. Widening the opening produces the opposite effect.

▶ The VGT concept uses a set of vanes, which are also known as airfoils, located around the circumference of the turbine wheel. Vanes change the cross-sectional area that exhaust gas flows through to vary the amount of exhaust-gas pressure crossing the turbine wheel before it reaches the low-pressure exhaust pipe.

▶ EGR gas flow does not need to accompany high boost pressure from the VGT. The EGR valve can fully close while turbine speed and boost pressure reach maximum limits.

▶ To improve engine braking, the VGT actuator can narrow the nozzle opening and increase exhaust backpressure if the engine calibration enables the turbocharger to act as an exhaust brake. High boost pressure requires more energy to compress intake air.

▶ Holset turbochargers, used primarily by Cummins, have a sliding nozzle ring to change the opening in the turbine housing, which regulates exhaust gas flow onto the turbine wheel. Changing the width of the nozzle opening increases or decreases the turbine speed.

▶ Several mechanisms change vane position. Electric motors or hydraulic devices are the most common actuators. The objective of the actuator mechanism is fast response of the turbocharger to engine speed and load changes.

▶ Hydraulic actuation is accomplished using pressurized engine oil acting against a hydraulic servo piston.

▶ Many turbochargers have a speed sensor in the center housing. Turbine speed data is used to adjust the actuator position and monitor the turbocharger operation.

▶ An exhaust back-pressure sensor can provide data regarding exhaust manifold pressure. Data supplied by the sensor is used to calculate the correct vane position.

▶ The bearing housing of the turbocharger and the variable geometry actuator usually contain engine coolant passages. Circulating coolant through the VGT actuator housing reduces the operating temperature of the internal electronics to increase the reliability of the vane and actuator mechanisms.

▶ The OBD system continuously monitors the operation of the VGT to detect any condition that could lead to potential increases in exhaust emissions. Fault codes are set for any sensor or actuator electrical problems, under- or overboost conditions, and the boost control position.

▶ While VGTs are common in many diesel engines, single-stage turbocharging and variable geometry turbocharging have limits.

▶ A series turbocharger can be used with a low-pressure cooled EGR system, where the turbocharger does not increase exhaust backpressure for the system. Without the need for high exhaust backpressure, a VGT is unnecessary.

▶ Series turbochargers use different sizes of compressor and turbine housings designated as high-pressure and low-pressure turbochargers.

▶ As boost pressure from the low-pressure turbocharger increases, the high-pressure turbocharger simply multiplies the inlet boost pressure. Arranged in a series like this, multiplication of the output pressure occurs and causes boost pressure to increase to levels higher than either turbocharger could achieve alone.

▶ Splitting the pressurization of the charged air between two turbochargers allows both to operate at optimal efficiency because the housing and wheel sizes are not a compromise for performance over a wide engine-load range.

▶ An SST integrates two turbochargers into a single component. A single housing unit supports two compressor wheels, which reduces space requirements.

▶ High boost pressures produced by series turbocharging enable the use of late intake valve closing to provide an engine efficiency increase of approximately 15%. Miller cycle engines use a mechanism to hold the intake valve open longer under high boost conditions so the engine does not need to work as hard compressing air.

Vocabulary Builder

charge air cooler (CAC) The system responsible for removing excess heat from the air charging the cylinders; also known as aftercooling and intercooling.

chuffing The sound a VGT turbocharger can produce when actuator response is slow. Chuffing is caused by turbocharger surge.

high-pressure cooled EGR (HP-CEGR) An exhaust gas recirculation system that depends on a VGT to build exhaust backpressure. EGR gas is cooled by a liquid cooler.

series turbocharger A turbocharger that uses two differently sized turbochargers connecting the compressor outlet of one turbocharger into the compressor housing inlet of a second turbocharger; in this system output from a smaller high-pressure turbocharger, which responds quicker at low engine speeds, is supplemented at heavier engine speeds and loads by the larger low-pressure turbocharger.

single sequential turbocharger (SST) A unique turbocharger design with one turbine wheel and two compressor wheels operating in separate housings. The two compressor wheels share a common turbine shaft. This system is also known as the DualBoost system used by Ford.

turbo lag A delay from the driver's demand for power from the engine to the point when the engine responds with power proportional to driver demand.

unison ring A device used by VGT turbochargers to rotate the nozzle ring vanes together simultaneously.

variable geometry turbocharger (VGT) A turbocharger with the capability of changing boost pressure or electronically varying boost and exhaust backpressure independent of engine speed and load; also known as a variable nozzle turbocharger (VNT) or a variable vane turbocharger (VVT).

Review Questions

1. _____ is the sound a VGT turbocharger can produce when actuator response is slow.
   a. Ringing   c. Chuffing
   b. Whistling   d. Knocking

2. _____ is an exhaust gas recirculation system that depends on a VGT to build exhaust backpressure.
   a. Charge air cooler
   b. High-pressure cooled EGR
   c. Charge air heater
   d. Low-pressure cooled EGR

3. VGTs vary the opening size of the turbine _____ that directs exhaust gas onto the turbine wheel.
   a. nozzle   c. support
   b. unison   d. adjusting ring

4. VGTs use vanes, which are also referred to as _____, around the circumference of the turbine wheel
   a. links   c. guide pins
   b. housings   d. airfoils

5. The VGT actuator is adjusted to increase exhaust _____ as required by the EGR system.
   a. backpressure   c. turbo surge
   b. emissions   d. throttle response

6. Holset turbochargers use a _____ nozzle ring to change the opening in the turbine housing.
   a. stationary
   b. sliding
   c. magnetic
   d. unison

7. A(n) _____ is used by VGT turbochargers to rotate the nozzle ring vanes together simultaneously.
   a. adjusting ring
   b. sliding ring
   c. support ring
   d. unison ring

8. _____ is a delay from the driver's demand for power from the engine to the point when the engine responds with power proportional to driver demand.
   a. Turbo lag
   b. Pressure drop
   c. Inlet restriction
   d. Aspiration

9. Duramax engines use _____ pressure to move the vane adjustment mechanism.
   a. linkage
   b. throttle
   c. air
   d. oil

10. On hydraulic actuators used on smaller displacement Navistar engines, the end of the VGT control valve has a(n) _____ cam follower to provide positional feedback to a sensor.
    a. hydraulic
    b. electronic
    c. mechanical
    d. pneumatic

ASE-Type Questions

1. Technician A says the heavy-duty on-board diagnostics system monitors turbo operation using a speed sensor. Technician B says the heavy-duty on-board diagnostics system monitors turbo operation using a mass airflow sensor. Who is correct?
   a. Technician A
   b. Technician B
   c. Both Technician A and Technician B
   d. Neither Technician A nor Technician B

2. Technician A says the sound referred to as chuffing is caused by pressure drop. Technician B says the sound referred to as chuffing is caused by turbo surge. Who is correct?
   a. Technician A
   b. Technician B
   c. Both Technician A and Technician B
   d. Neither Technician A nor Technician B

3. Technician A says a linkage movement test is used to inspect the actuator operation on a turbocharger with external linkage. Technician B says a bounce test is used to inspect the actuator operation on a turbocharger with internal linkage. Who is correct?
   a. Technician A
   b. Technician B
   c. Both Technician A and Technician B
   d. Neither Technician A nor Technician B

4. Technician A says variable geometry turbochargers (VGTs) are also known as variable nozzle turbochargers. Technician B says variable geometry turbochargers (VGTs) are also known as variable vane turbochargers. Who is correct?
   a. Technician A
   b. Technician B
   c. Both Technician A and Technician B
   d. Neither Technician A nor Technician B

5. Technician A says that adding EGR systems to most 2002 and later engines was necessary to meet lower NOx emission standards. Technician B says that adding EGR systems to most 2002 and later engines was necessary to meet lower CO emission standards. Who is correct?
   a. Technician A
   b. Technician B
   c. Both Technician A and Technician B
   d. Neither Technician A nor Technician B

6. Technician A says VGTs often have a built-in safety default position, which is approximately 50-60% open. Technician B says VGTs often have a built-in safety default position, which is approximately 75-80% closed. Who is correct?
   a. Technician A
   b. Technician B
   c. Both Technician A and Technician B
   d. Neither Technician A nor Technician B

7. Technician A says a compound turbocharger can be used with a low-pressure, cooled EGR system where the turbocharger does not increase exhaust backpressure for the system. Technician B says a series turbocharger can be used with a low-pressure, cooled EGR system where the turbocharger does not increase exhaust backpressure for the system. Who is correct?
   a. Technician A
   b. Technician B
   c. Both Technician A and Technician B
   d. Neither Technician A nor Technician B

8. Technician A says series turbochargers use different sizes of compressor and turbine housings designated as high-pressure turbochargers. Technician B says series turbochargers use different sizes of compressor and turbine housings designated as low-pressure turbochargers. Who is correct?
   a. Technician A
   b. Technician B
   c. Both Technician A and Technician B
   d. Neither Technician A nor Technician B

9. Technician A says turbocharger response to nozzle ring movement is an intrusive monitoring strategy that measures boost pressure and compares it with expected values while driving. Technician B says turbocharger response to nozzle ring movement is an intrusive monitoring strategy that measures throttle response and compares it with expected values while driving. Who is correct?
   a. Technician A
   b. Technician B
   c. Both Technician A and Technician B
   d. Neither Technician A nor Technician B

10. Technician A says Miller cycle engines are referred to as a five-stroke cycle because the compression stroke is divided into five phases. Technician B says Miller cycle engines are referred to as a five-stroke cycle because the compression stroke is divided into two phases. Who is correct?
    a. Technician A
    b. Technician B
    c. Both Technician A and Technician B
    d. Neither Technician A nor Technician B

CHAPTER 31
Exhaust Gas Recirculation

NATEF Tasks

Diesel Engines

Air Induction and Exhaust Systems
- Inspect exhaust gas recirculation (EGR) system, including EGR valve, cooler, piping, filter, electronic sensors, controls, and wiring; determine needed action. (pp 905, 909–911)

Knowledge Objectives

After reading this chapter, you will be able to:
1. Explain operating principles of diesel engine exhaust gas recirculation system components. (pp 897–898)
2. Describe the functions, construction, and application of diesel engine exhaust gas recirculation systems. (pp 901–911)
3. Describe and explain methods for performing inspection and diagnostic procedures on diesel engine exhaust gas recirculation systems. (pp 905–911)
4. Recommend maintenance or repairs on diesel engine exhaust gas recirculation systems. (pp 912–913)

Skills Objectives

After reading this chapter, you will be able to:
1. Inspect an EGR cooler for leaks. (p 907) SKILL DRILL 31-1
2. Test a pressure sensor. (p 911) SKILL DRILL 31-2
3. Test an EGR valve. (p 913) SKILL DRILL 31-3

► Introduction

The application of exhaust gas recirculation (EGR) to diesel engines is a long established, proven technology used to achieve greener and cleaner diesel engines. By reintroducing exhaust gas back into the cylinders, a major reduction in exhaust emissions of oxides of nitrogen (NO_x) is achieved. EGR technology has been used for nearly four decades on gasoline-fueled engines but applied to heavy-duty diesel engines only since 2002. While diesel engines make up only 4–6% of all motor vehicles, studies once estimated that they contributed to over 50% of all NO_x emissions **FIGURE 31-1**. Today, diesel engines emit almost no detectable NO_x emissions. While EGR is effective in reducing NO_x formation from the cylinders of engines, the introduction of EGR has required many changes to engine design, operation, and maintenance requirements.

► Fundamentals of EGR

EGR is an in-cylinder emission reduction strategy. That means EGR is used to prevent the formation of NO_x emissions during the combustion process rather than remove NO_x in the exhaust system. Understanding the mechanisms of NO_x formation helps explain the various reasons for EGR system design, construction, and operation.

NO_x Forming Conditions

EGR reintroduces exhaust gas into engine cylinders to reduce peak cylinder pressure and temperature; high cylinder pressures and temperatures produce NO_x. Normally, nitrogen gas, which constitutes slightly more than 75% of the atmosphere, stays out of combustion reactions. However, combustion temperatures above 2500°F (1371°C) will cause reactions between oxygen and nitrogen to take place. In addition to heat, squeezing molecules together under high pressure, compression, and combustion conditions also creates a greater likelihood of chemical reactions forming various types of molecules containing nitrogen and oxygen. Collectively, these nitrogen and

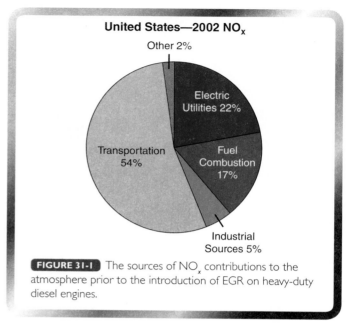

FIGURE 31-1 The sources of NO_x contributions to the atmosphere prior to the introduction of EGR on heavy-duty diesel engines.

oxygen compounds are referred to as NO_x and may consist of a variety of gases, including NO, NO_2, NO_3, and NO_4.

__Nitric oxide (NO)__, a colorless gas, is the most abundant type of NO_x initially produced during diesel combustion. However, because NO is an unstable and highly reactive gas, it begins to combine with oxygen immediately after combustion has ended. Post-combustion __nitrogen dioxide (NO_2)__ is a reddish-brown gas formed when NO binds to oxygen. The presence of a noxious reddish brown tint to the atmosphere over cities when the winds are light indicates an abundance of NO_2 emissions. NO_2 should not be confused with nitrous oxide (N_2O), an anesthetic gas that is also used in racing to increase a gasoline-fueled engine's power output. When NO_x breaks down in the presence of sunlight and heat, it converts to nitrogen and ozone gas (O_3), which is a primary component of smog **FIGURE 31-2**. NO_x emissions are toxic to the environment and human health.

You Are the Technician

A 2002 city transit bus has a prematurely worn engine. After less than 240,000 miles (386,243 kilometers [km]) and 6000 hours of engine operation, the rings and cylinder walls are worn out and the engine has low power. You have been asked to investigate possible causes for the accelerated wear. Many buses in the fleet are not providing the service life that older buses with similar engines provided. You perform an oil analysis and find no special clues except a very high amount of soot. Service records confirm that oil services were performed well within recommended limits. You begin to wonder whether there might be an electronic control module (ECM) calibration issue that is causing injection timing to be incorrect and contributing to the soot in the oil. Someone suggests to you that the EGR system may have a problem. Before proceeding further, consider the following:

1. Explain why a defect in the EGR system could cause excessive soot in engine oil.
2. Explain why a defect in the EGR system could lead to premature ring and cylinder wall wear.
3. What checks of the EGR system would you perform to determine whether the EGR system is functioning correctly?

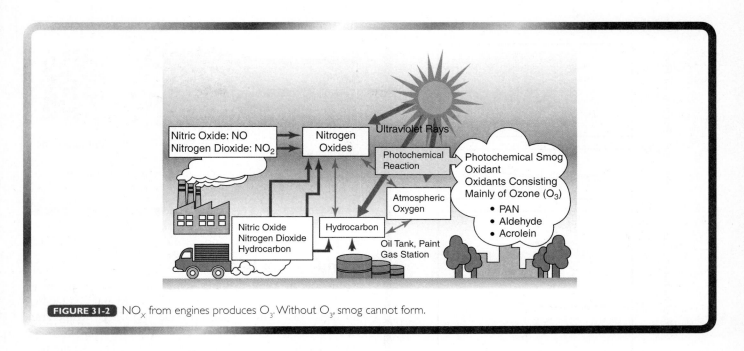

FIGURE 31-2 NO_x from engines produces O_3. Without O_3, smog cannot form.

Diesel Combustion and NO_x

NO_x formation is a major emission problem with diesel engines due to higher compression ratios, cylinder pressure, and temperature **FIGURE 31-3**. This is especially true for turbocharged diesel engines where the combination of additional air and fuel produce more power from each cubic unit of cylinder displacement. Additionally, diesel combustion is stratified. This means the combustion chamber has regions where air–fuel ratios vary widely. Areas within the combustion chamber where rich fuel mixtures burn hotter will also contribute to NO_x formation. This contrasts with gasoline-fueled engines where lean mixtures contribute to NO_x formation. In gasoline-fueled engines, lean mixtures cause the combustion flame to travel slower than normal, which results in abnormally high cylinder pressure near top dead center (TDC) because more fuel burns at once as a result of uncontrolled combustion.

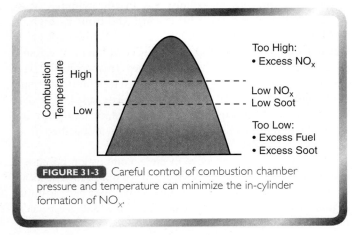

FIGURE 31-3 Careful control of combustion chamber pressure and temperature can minimize the in-cylinder formation of NO_x.

EGR System Operation

While the design, construction, and operation of different EGR systems are unique, the basic mechanisms used to reduce NO_x formation in the cylinders are the same. The principle behind all EGR systems is to disrupt the chemical processes that form NO_x. Replacing combustion oxygen with EGR gas is one strategy used by all EGR systems. EGR gas displaces air from the cylinder charge, and EGR systems are designed to replace a portion of the cylinder air charge with EGR gas **FIGURE 31-4**.

It is important to note, though, that increased boost pressure is used on EGR engines, meaning the same amount of oxygen is available in the cylinder to keep power output comparable with non-EGR engines. More gas mass ends up in the cylinder with higher compression pressure but lower peak combustion pressure and temperature. Higher injection pressures are also necessary to create better atomization for the combustion event to tolerate EGR gas without producing even more emissions. In addition to higher turbocharger pressure, several operating conditions need to be first met before NO_x reduction can take place.

Conditions for Enabling EGR Delivery

Because the greatest amount of NO_x is formed when cylinder pressure and temperatures are high, EGR systems at a minimum monitor engine speed and load conditions to meter the correct amount of exhaust gas into the engine intake.

During cold weather or while the engine is idling, minimal or no EGR flow usually takes place. During warm-up, condensation of corrosive exhaust can take place in EGR coolers, so flow is minimized or disabled during that period. When high coolant temperatures exist, the EGR flow may also

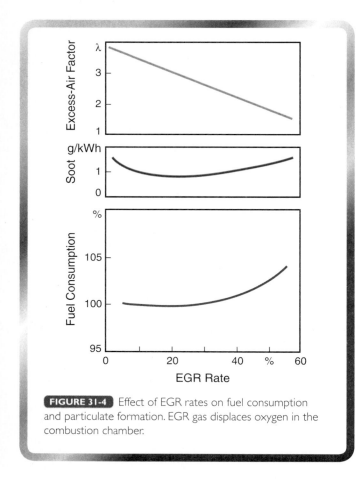

FIGURE 31-4 Effect of EGR rates on fuel consumption and particulate formation. EGR gas displaces oxygen in the combustion chamber.

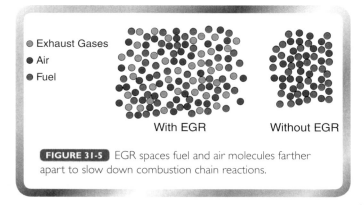

FIGURE 31-5 EGR spaces fuel and air molecules farther apart to slow down combustion chain reactions.

be disabled because cooling of exhaust gas in EGR coolers can contribute to overheated engine operation. High altitude or low barometric pressures may also be a condition to disable EGR operation because EGR flow under these conditions could significantly deteriorate combustion quality and engine performance.

Pressure Reduction

EGR reduces NO_X emission formation for several reasons. One means is through lowering peak cylinder pressure. Higher cylinder pressure increases the likelihood of chemical reactions by squeezing the molecules together. Cylinder pressure that increases the speed of chemical reactions is distinctly higher in diesel engines due to higher compression ratios, turbocharging, and fuel rates. However, exhaust gas is relatively inert, having little usable oxygen and high amounts of carbon dioxide (CO_2) and nitrogen. Because the exhaust gas cannot directly enter into the combustion process, it slows down the combustion speed by spacing oxygen and fuel molecules farther apart **FIGURE 31-5**. Chain reactions between oxygen and fuel take longer, which results in a slower pressure rise in the cylinder. The sharp spike in cylinder pressure characteristic of older non-EGR engines is diminished in EGR engines. A by-product of lower peak cylinder pressure is reduced combustion noise resulting in quieter engine operation.

Temperature Reduction

Reduction in peak cylinder temperature is also produced using EGR. The flame temperature of close to 4000°F (2204°C) for diesel fuel is more than the 2500°F (1371°C) temperature threshold required to begin NO_X formation. While there are regions in the cylinder where temperature may spike momentarily to this level, reducing the peak combustion temperature to below 2500°F (1371°C) minimizes NO_0 formation. Above 2500°F (1371°C), NO_X forms exponentially with twice as much NO_X produced for every 100°F temperature increase above this threshold temperature.

EGR use reduces temperature two ways. One way is through its ability to slow down combustion speed, which not only causes a pressure drop but also a temperature drop. Combustion temperatures are not as intense or as hot because the air/fuel mixture will burn more slowly over a larger number of degrees of crankshaft rotation. This means the push against the top of the piston is both longer and gentler. Injection timing may be advanced in many EGR engines to enable adequate burn time for the slower combustion speeds. To capture more of the energy and optimize the release of EGR-diluted combustion, the stroke length of many EGR engines is lengthened. Engines that had smaller displacement before EGR often had the crank throws lengthened and the cylinder displacement increased slightly **FIGURE 31-6**.

The second mechanism for heat reduction is the heat-absorbing properties of exhaust gas in the cylinder. Most cooled EGR systems cool the exhaust gas from as high as 1000°F (538°C) to just over 400°F (204°C). While EGR gas is warmer than intake air, CO_2 (a major constituent of exhaust gas) also has high specific heat properties. This means CO_2 can absorb larger amounts of heat without a temperature increase compared to gases with lower specific heat. <u>Specific heat</u> is the amount of heat required by a gas, solid, or liquid to produce a temperature change of 1°F within a specified time period **FIGURE 31-7**.

EGR is especially effective in diesel combustion because it can reduce temperature and pressure in regions of intense localized heat where most NO_X formation occurs. These NO_X-forming regions tend to be fuel rich and air lean where EGR is especially effective.

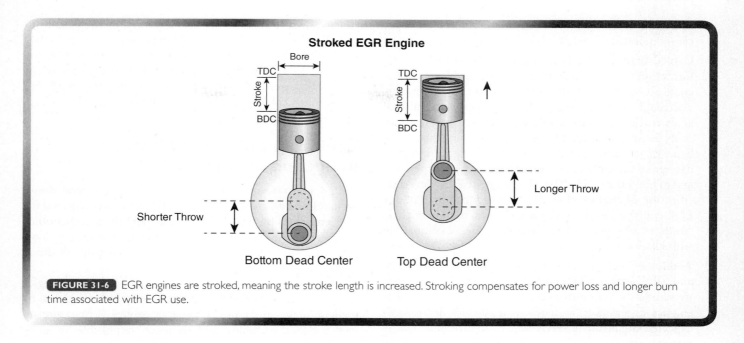

FIGURE 31-6 EGR engines are stroked, meaning the stroke length is increased. Stroking compensates for power loss and longer burn time associated with EGR use.

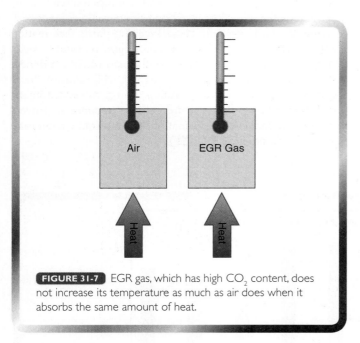

FIGURE 31-7 EGR gas, which has high CO_2 content, does not increase its temperature as much as air does when it absorbs the same amount of heat.

Drawbacks of EGR Usage

While EGR is one of the most effective in-cylinder solutions for reducing NO_X emissions, there are a few drawbacks:

1. EGR does reduce the potential peak cylinder pressure and air and fuel charge produced without EGR gas. This means engine torque and power output will fall unless other engine operating strategies and design compensate for EGR use. Fuel economy and power penalties are supposed to be negligible under most operating conditions using EGR. However, users comparing pre- and post-EGR engines are reporting a 1–10% fuel economy penalty. It is important to note,

however, that throttle response is improved and combustion noise is reduced because of associated technologies used to support EGR.

2. EGR is an excellent method for reducing emissions, but it taxes the engine lubricating oil more than ever. New lubricating oil specifications are developed for EGR engines to handle the extra contamination of lubrication oil from recycling exhaust gas back into the cylinder **FIGURE 31-8**. Exhaust contaminants such as particulate will stick to the lubrication oil on the cylinder wall and are then scraped into the crankcase creating higher soot loading of the oil. Cylinder wear increases because soot is an abrasive. Uneven distribution of EGR gas between cylinders can wear out one

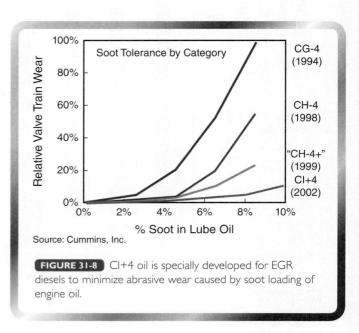

Source: Cummins, Inc.

FIGURE 31-8 CI+4 oil is specially developed for EGR diesels to minimize abrasive wear caused by soot loading of engine oil.

or more cylinders faster. Soot entering the intake valves causes premature wear of intake valves and seats as well.

3. Cooled EGR also leads to water condensation and the formation of higher sulfuric and nitric acid levels in the combustion chamber after reactions take place between water and combustion gases. If not properly neutralized, acids in the oil can corrode any exposed metal, especially the soft lead overlay of bearings exposing the copper beneath. To minimize these problems, higher levels of detergents are added to the oil to keep soot in suspension and to neutralize acids. The API designated this new classification of engine oil as CI+4, introduced in 2002 for EGR-equipped engines. Current CJ-4 oil used in engines equipped with particulate filters is backward compatible with CI+4 oil.

4. Additional wear of cylinder components piston rings and valve seats is also reported with EGR. Until durability standards were introduced in 2004, some early EGR engines experienced as much as a 20–30% decrease in expected engine life in severe service applications such as transit buses. However, the use of harder ring and cylinder wall materials, hardened valve seats, and other advanced materials have corrected many of these earlier problems. Break-in periods for engines are now as long as 12,000 miles (20,000 km) compared with just a few thousand miles or kilometers for pre-EGR engines.

5. <u>Cooled EGR (CEGR)</u>, where exhaust gas passes through an engine coolant heat exchanger, adds additional heat load to the cooling system and engine compartment. Larger radiators, water pumps, and cooling systems are required to transfer the heat absorbed by the coolant to the atmosphere. Underhood temperature is much higher with EGR engines due to increased heat rejection by the cooling system. Heat rejection refers to the amount of heat transferred to the coolant rather than converted into mechanical force driving down the pistons.

Limitations of Other NO_x Reduction Strategies

EGR is an emission-control technology with several drawbacks. However, given the progressive reductions required for NO_x emissions by emission legislation and the fact that other NO_x reduction technologies and operating strategies have reached their limits, EGR is necessary on virtually all diesel engines.

For example, two common NO_x-reducing strategies already in use on pre-EGR engines are retarded injection timing and intake-air cooling. Charge air coolers (CACs) already reduce intake air temperature as much as possible. In addition, injection timing in many pre-EGR engines is already near TDC, and further retarding injection timing would degrade fuel economy, performance, and cause excessive particulate matter (PM) formation. Soot contamination of engine oil would rise to unacceptable levels as well. However, the use of EGR combined with retarded injection timing reduces NO_x while allowing for a nominal degree of advanced injection timing. Advanced injection timing in turn produces better throttle response, improved fuel economy, reduced PM formation, and less soot contamination of lubrication oil **FIGURE 31-9** .

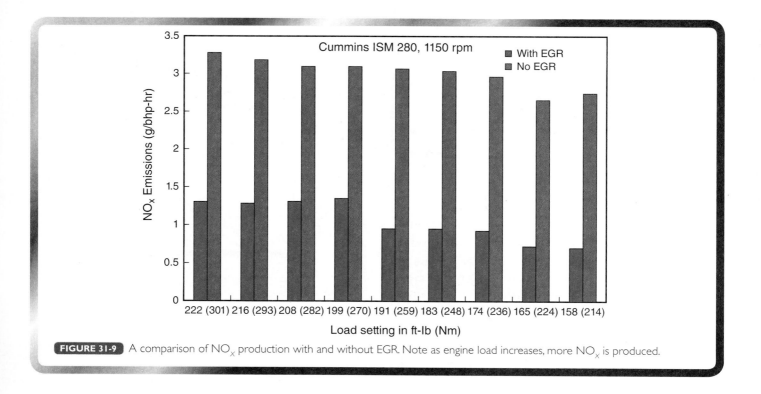

FIGURE 31-9 A comparison of NO_x production with and without EGR. Note as engine load increases, more NO_x is produced.

► Types of EGR

EGR rates are much higher in diesel engines than in gasoline-fueled engines. Flow rates by intake volume for 2007 model year low-NO$_x$ engines are in the vicinity of 20–35%, while engines can handle rates as high as 40%. Navistar introduced engines for the 2010 model year without liquid selective catalyst reduction (SCR). These engines have massive EGR delivery rates of up to 50% according to some reports. Older EGR engines built before 2002 with less aggressive emission reductions have lower EGR rates (10–20%). This compares with gasoline-fueled engines, which may use an EGR rate that rarely exceeds 12%.

Since the introduction of liquid SCR systems, which break down NO$_x$ in the exhaust system, manufacturers have depended less on in-cylinder NO$_x$ reduction strategies. Reduced EGR rates and a return to more advanced injection timing on SCR-equipped engines have improved fuel economy **TABLE 31-1**.

Several types of EGR delivery systems exist to introduce exhaust gas uniformly into the cylinders. Types of EGR delivery systems used on medium- and heavy-duty diesels include:

- High-Pressure Cooled
- Low-Pressure Cooled

Less frequently used EGR systems used on a few heavy-duty diesel, light-duty, and off-road engines include:

- Internal EGR
- External Non-Cooled
- External Cooled

Internal EGR

While not commonly used, some engine manufacturers will use a variety of internal types of EGR systems. This means no external EGR controls are used, but exhaust gas is reintroduced into the cylinders through a change to exhaust valve timing. By leaving the exhaust valve open longer during the intake stroke, exhaust gas is drawn back into the cylinder during intake stroke **FIGURE 31-10**. Another method is to add a "bump" to the exhaust cam lobe that cracks open the exhaust valve briefly during the intake stroke to draw exhaust gas into the cylinder along with the intake air charge. These internal methods, however, result in poor mixing with the intake air and excessive EGR rates at low speeds. With the introduction of variable valve timing, these problems may be minimized.

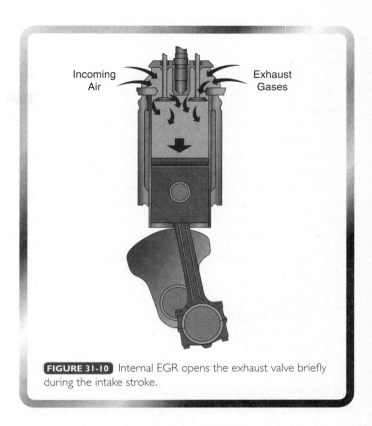

FIGURE 31-10 Internal EGR opens the exhaust valve briefly during the intake stroke.

External EGR Non-Cooled

External EGR uses a metering valve and control circuits to deliver exhaust gas into the intake manifold. The GM 6.5L (397 cubic inch) diesel is an example of this system. The engine uses a turbocharger with a vacuum-operated EGR valve located in the intake plenum. A passageway in the intake manifold routes exhaust gas from the cylinder head to the valve. Exhaust gas is driven into the intake manifold through the exhaust backpressure in the exhaust system. The **exhaust back-pressure (EBP) sensor** measures pressure in the exhaust manifold.

Even on turbocharged engines, exhaust backpressure is higher than intake boost pressure. The EGR pedestal location and venturi in the intake are designed to create a low-pressure area using intake airflow. Exhaust gas is drawn into the intake from the valve at this point.

High-Pressure Cooled

The technological evolution to more elaborate EGR systems found on current diesel engines has taken place for a number of reasons. Primarily, with more stringent legislative requirements for emission reductions from diesel engines, manufacturers have had to ensure precise control of mixture formation to achieve emission reductions. Fuel rates, air, and exhaust gas mass must be carefully measured and balanced for efficient, powerful, low-emission combustion. To accomplish this, a number of additional sensor and actuator circuits are required to accurately meter EGR rate proportional to other combustion elements. For example, too high an EGR rate will starve the combustion process of adequate oxygen, driving up production

TABLE 31-1: EGR Rates for Diesel Engines

Light EGR	10–20%	Older Light Duty
Heavy EGR	20–35%	2002–2010 Medium and Heavy Duty
Moderate EGR	15–25%	2010+ SCR
Massive EGR	35–50% or more	2010+ Navistar Non-SCR

of carbon monoxide (CO), hydrocarbon (HC), and PM emissions. However, too low an EGR rate will not obtain the required emission reductions.

The necessity of meeting engine manufacturer's diagnostic (EMD), heavy-duty on-board diagnostic (HD-OBD), and on-board diagnostic II (OBDII) requirements to monitor emission systems operation also increases the complexity of the EGR system. To validate the correct operation of the EGR system, the HD-OBD system must ensure the EGR system is properly functioning to achieve its intended emission reductions.

EGR gas derived from the exhaust manifold and pressurized to overcome intake boost pressure is called **high-pressure cooled EGR (HP-CEGR)** `FIGURE 31-11`. Typical components of cooled EGR systems include:

- Variable Geometry Turbocharger (VGT)
- EGR Cooler
- EGR Mixer
- EGR Valve
- Exhaust Transfer Tubing
- Intake Mixing Device
- Input Sensors
- Output Devices

Turbocharging and Cooled EGR Systems

The use of EGR creates several problems for intake air handling. First, the addition of exhaust gas will reduce power output. Second, EGR will displace some oxygen. To compensate for this problem, newer model EGR engines increase the total gas volume in a cylinder while adding inert exhaust gas. As total gas volume in the combustion chamber increases, cooler but higher peak pressure is produced in the cylinder to help compensate for the horsepower loss. While an increase in gas volume and cylinder pressure occurs, NO_X formation does not because the expansion

of burning fuel takes place at a lower temperature and over more degrees of crankshaft rotation than in non-EGR engines.

EGR engines are typically stroked, meaning increased stroke length is used with longer crank throws. More leverage on the crank due to a lengthened throw and the longer distance travelled by the piston converts more combustion energy into mechanical force than leaving engine dimensions unchanged. Changing cylinder dimensions combined with a gentler increase in combustion pressure means peak engine torque is produced at 100–200 revolutions per minute (rpm) higher than traditional non-EGR engines.

Another problem with turbocharged EGR engines is supplying the necessary volume of exhaust gas to the pressurized intake manifold. Exhaust gas pressure needs to be at least as high as, if not higher than, intake pressure to achieve adequate exhaust flow into the cylinders. While low-pressure EGR systems incorporate an electronically controlled throttle plate to produce a pressure drop in the intake manifold, drawing exhaust gas into the intake airflow, all manufacturers have relied upon VGTs to pressurize exhaust gas `FIGURE 31-12`.

Unlike conventional turbocharger technology, a **variable geometry turbocharger (VGT)**, also known as variable nozzle turbocharger (VNT) and variable vane turbocharger (VVT), can vary boost pressure and exhaust backpressure independently of engine speed. (See the Fixed Geometry and Wastegated Turbochargers chapter and the Variable Geometry and Series Turbochargers chapter.)

Low-Pressure EGR Systems

An alternate strategy to HP-CEGR is to draw EGR gas into the cylinders through either the turbocharger inlet or after the turbocharger between a throttle plate and intake manifold. Referred to as **low-pressure EGR**, NO_X emissions are reduced 5–64%. These systems are considered more efficient because exhaust backpressure is lower and a single fixed geometry turbocharger can be used `FIGURE 31-13` and `FIGURE 31-14`. Some light-duty systems combine low- and high-pressure EGR to obtain even lower NO_X emissions while increasing efficiency.

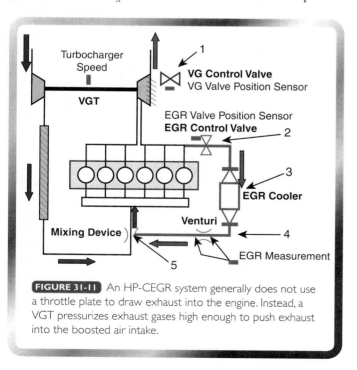

FIGURE 31-11 An HP-CEGR system generally does not use a throttle plate to draw exhaust into the engine. Instead, a VGT pressurizes exhaust gases high enough to push exhaust into the boosted air intake.

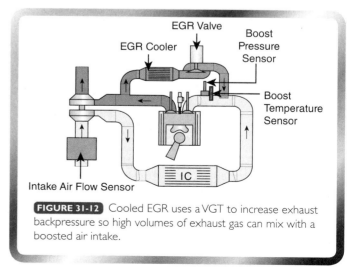

FIGURE 31-12 Cooled EGR uses a VGT to increase exhaust backpressure so high volumes of exhaust gas can mix with a boosted air intake.

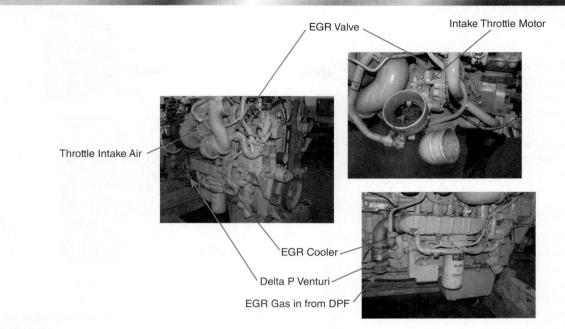

FIGURE 31-13 Caterpillar ACERT C-13, C-15, and C-16 engines use low-pressure EGR systems. Exhaust gas is drawn into the cooler and intake manifold using a throttled intake.

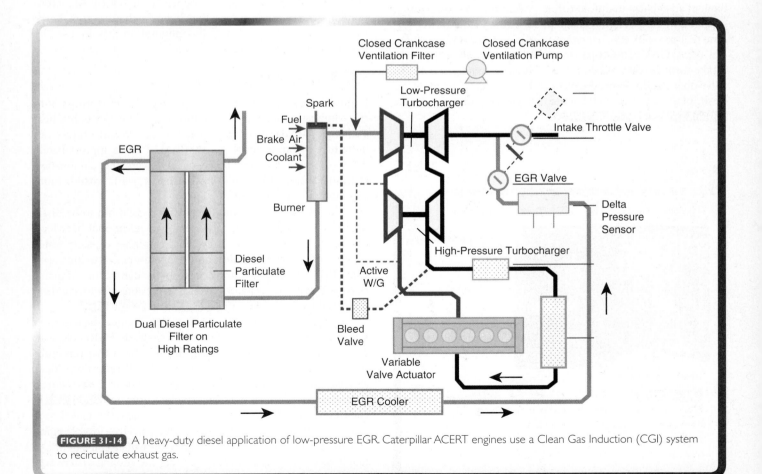

FIGURE 31-14 A heavy-duty diesel application of low-pressure EGR. Caterpillar ACERT engines use a Clean Gas Induction (CGI) system to recirculate exhaust gas.

Advantages and Disadvantages of Using Low-Pressure EGR

Advantages of using low-pressure EGR include:

- Improved mixing of EGR and intake air—especially at low speeds and during acceleration
- Cleaner intake charge when using a particulate filter for less soot loading of oil and associated wear from soot injection
- Improved reduction in NO_X emission compared to high-pressure EGR
- Increased engine efficiency due to lower exhaust back-pressure

Disadvantages of using low-pressure EGR include:

- Potential higher formation of combustion gas condensates in the EGR cooler and charge air cooler
- Potential for damage to the turbocharger from higher heat loads and damaging exhaust particles if exhaust is drawn into the turbocharger inlet

Detroit Diesel's DD series engines use a unique type of low-pressure EGR system with lower rates of EGR flow. The engine does not use a VGT to develop exhaust backpressure. Instead, one of the volutes of the turbocharger is made intentionally smaller to restrict the flow of exhaust gas in the front bank of an exhaust manifold runner. Additional backpressure is supplied when an engine is equipped with an axial power turbine that recovers exhaust energy and converts it into mechanical force. Flow of EGR gas into the engine is aided using an intake throttle plate. When more EGR gas is required, the EGR valve opens and the throttle plate will close slightly to allow less fresh intake air charge and more exhaust flow into the engine **FIGURE 31-15** and **FIGURE 31-16** .

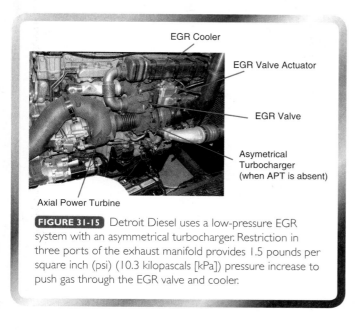

FIGURE 31-15 Detroit Diesel uses a low-pressure EGR system with an asymmetrical turbocharger. Restriction in three ports of the exhaust manifold provides 1.5 pounds per square inch (psi) (10.3 kilopascals [kPa]) pressure increase to push gas through the EGR valve and cooler.

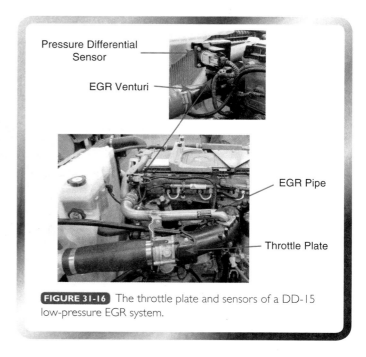

FIGURE 31-16 The throttle plate and sensors of a DD-15 low-pressure EGR system.

▶ Components of Exhaust Gas Recirculation

Operation of the EGR system depends on several key components to cool and control the flow of exhaust gases. Large variations in design and system configuration that are used by various manufacturers are examined in this next section.

EGR Coolers

Engine manufacturers cool EGR gas before recirculating it into the combustion chambers. Exhaust gas is sent through a heat exchanger circulating engine coolant where its temperature can be reduced from as much as 1000°F (538°C) to approximately 425°F (218°C). Cooling the exhaust lowers the combustion chamber temperature and allows exhaust gas to absorb more combustion chamber heat.

The use of EGR cooling means more heat has to be dissipated by the engine cooling system. The additional heat load on the cooling system typically requires higher-capacity water pumps and radiators. Underhood temperature is also increased using EGR coolers, meaning hoses, engine compartment materials, and even hood paint have to be capable of withstanding increased temperatures **FIGURE 31-17** and **FIGURE 31-18** .

Design requirements for EGR coolers include the ability to self-clean. To resist corrosion by exhaust gas acids, EGR coolers are constructed of stainless steel **FIGURE 31-19** . To further minimize the potential for plugging and corrosion, EGR operating strategies often prevent EGR gas flow in cold ambient temperatures, i.e., below 40°F (4°C) and during engine warm-up **FIGURE 31-20** . Failures of coolers due to cracking from frequent thermal expansion and contraction or corrosion are indicated by a loss of engine coolant. Engine coolant can be found in the exhaust pipe or intake manifold of the engine. Pressure testing the cooling system will reveal coolant leaks into the cooler gas passageway.

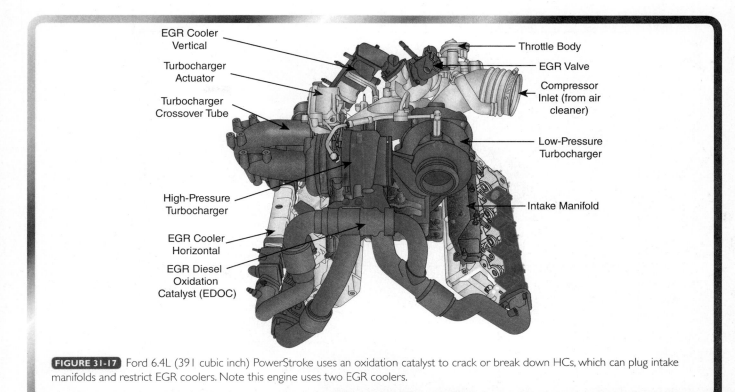

FIGURE 31-17 Ford 6.4L (391 cubic inch) PowerStroke uses an oxidation catalyst to crack or break down HCs, which can plug intake manifolds and restrict EGR coolers. Note this engine uses two EGR coolers.

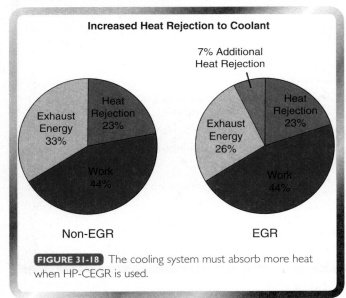

FIGURE 31-18 The cooling system must absorb more heat when HP-CEGR is used.

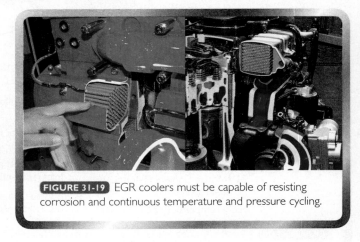

FIGURE 31-19 EGR coolers must be capable of resisting corrosion and continuous temperature and pressure cycling.

Inspecting an EGR Cooler for Leaks

EGR coolers most often fail due to the constant thermal expansion and contraction cycles caused by exhaust heat and exhaust backpressure produced by the turbocharger. Although some diagnostic fault codes may be produced by leaking coolers, other symptoms of an EGR cooler leak include the loss of coolant without external leaks, high sodium levels in scheduled oil samples, an over-pressurized cooling system, and white smoke with a sweet odor.

To inspect an EGR cooler for leaks, follow the steps in **SKILL DRILL 31-1**.

TECHNICIAN TIP

Plugged intake manifolds can occur on some engines using EGR while encountering extended periods of low-load or idling. Increasing the cetane rating of the fuel helps prevent this condition. Adding cetane booster may minimize intake plugging of some engines using low-cetane fuel. Newer EGR coolers are built with a "floating" heat exchanger inside the cooler housing. The cooler bundle is attached to the housing only through contact with O-rings. This enables the cooler to expand and contract, which reduces the likelihood of the cooler bundle cracking due to frequent thermal cycling.

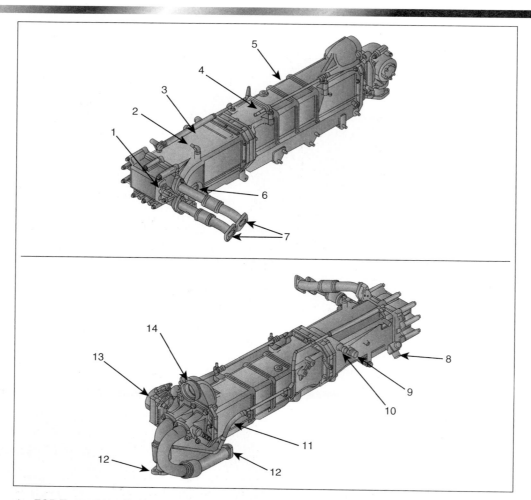

1. EGR Temperature Sensor
2. EGR Cooler Air Bleed (to deaeration tank)
3. EGR Cooler (low-temperature stage)
4. EGR Valve Coolant Return Line (to deaeration tank)
5. High-Temperature EGR Cooler

6. Intake Manifold Temperature (IMT)
7. EGR Cooler Outlet Tube (2) (gases)
8. Low-Temperature EGR Cooler Inlet (coolant)
9. Engine Coolant Temperature 2 (ECT2) Sensor

10. Low-Temperature EGR Cooler Outlet (coolant)
11. EGR Valve Coolant Supply Line
12. EGR Cooler Inlet Tubes (gases)
13. EGR Valve
14. EGR Coller Inlet (coolant)

FIGURE 31-20 Navistar engines use EGR coolers with two heat exchangers. More precise regulation of intake air temperature is enabled by controlling the temperature of coolant flowing in either heat exchanger.

EGR Mixer

Exhaust gas recirculation systems require a device to blend recirculated exhaust gas and intake charge air. This ensures an equally proportioned amount of recirculated exhaust gas and air is delivered to all cylinders. Some engines simply use the turbulence of the intake manifold and/or valve port design to swirl air and exhaust together for even blending **FIGURE 31-21** and **FIGURE 31-22**.

To pull adequate amounts of exhaust gas into an engine, some engine models have used an electronically controlled throttle plate to create low pressure in the intake to draw in exhaust gas. The throttle also operates to limit airflow into the engine, which can adjust the portion of air and exhaust gas.

Other engines will use a mixer. Two different styles of mixing devices are commonly used:

1. A venturi style mixer creates a pressure drop through a restriction or venturi located in the intake manifold. EGR gas is injected into the low-pressure area created by the venturi, where mixing occurs.

2. Another type of mixer is a fluted style mixer. In this design, gas evenly blends into the intake stream around the circumference of the inlet of the intake manifold.

SKILL DRILL 31-1 Inspecting an EGR Cooler for Leaks

Coolant Ports

Exhaust Ports

1. Pressurize the cooling system. Disconnect and remove the clamps at each end of the EGR cooler.

2. Visually examine the EGR cooler inside. The presence of gooey black liquid is an indicator of an internal leak.

3. Disconnect and remove the EGR valve from its bore. A gooey black residue covering the valve indicates an EGR cooler leak.

4. Inspect the EGR bore for white coolant residue. White streaking indicates coolant additives have leaked from coolant emitted by the EGR cooler.

5. After visually inspecting the engine for coolant leaks during a pressure test, the EGR cooler can be disconnected and removed.

6. Using purpose-made test adapters, plug the exhaust inlet and outlet ports with purpose-made plugs.

7. Using shop air pressure regulated to 20 psi (138 kPa), pressurize the cooler exhaust ports.

8. Immerse the cooler in a water tank or check the coolant ports for leaking air using soapy water. Any air leaks indicate a cracked EGR cooler.

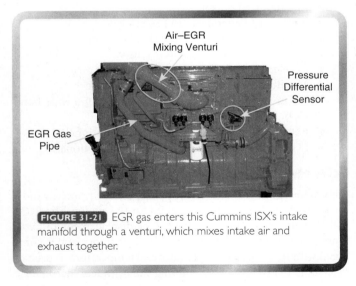

FIGURE 31-21 EGR gas enters this Cummins ISX's intake manifold through a venturi, which mixes intake air and exhaust together.

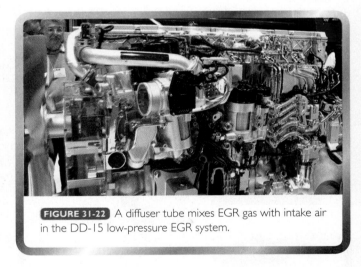

FIGURE 31-22 A diffuser tube mixes EGR gas with intake air in the DD-15 low-pressure EGR system.

EGR Valves

Central to the EGR system is the valve that meters the quantity of EGR flow into the intake manifold. The valve does this by regulating exhaust flow through the valve connecting a passageway between the exhaust system and the intake manifold. Valves may be located on either the hot side between the exhaust manifold and cooler or the cold side between the cooler and intake manifold.

EGR Valve Features

Requirements of EGR valve design incorporate features to:

- Minimize carbon contamination or coking of internal passageways
- Clean carbon contamination from the valve seat through high valve opening and closing
- Quicken response times to accurately meter exhaust gas flow for various engine operating conditions.

To operate quickly, EGR valve mechanisms operate using solenoids and DC stepper motors or DC motor actuators. EGR valves commonly use single or dual outwardly opening poppet valves **FIGURE 31-23** and **FIGURE 31-24**. The valves are sized to meet flow requirements of the engine. Valve opening and closing forces have increased substantially from earlier valves to prevent valve sticking caused by carbon build-up.

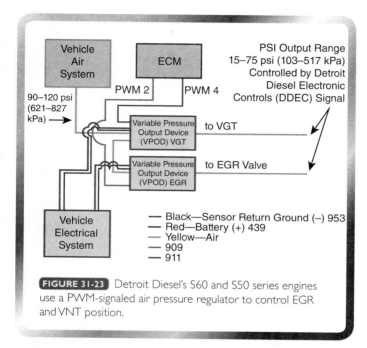

FIGURE 31-23 Detroit Diesel's S60 and S50 series engines use a PWM-signaled air pressure regulator to control EGR and VNT position.

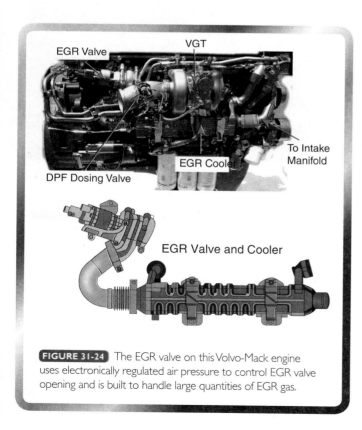

FIGURE 31-24 The EGR valve on this Volvo-Mack engine uses electronically regulated air pressure to control EGR valve opening and is built to handle large quantities of EGR gas.

Manufacturers will use electrically operated valves or, for increased valve force, air pressure. Detroit uses a valve that receives an air signal from a variable pressure output device. This is a pulse-width-modulated (PWM) air regulator that sends varying air pressure to both the turbocharger actuator and the EGR valve. Closed-loop feedback about the valve's operation includes the EGR gas mass measurement system **FIGURE 31-25**.

EGR System Input Sensors

Because the quantity of EGR flow must be precisely matched to engine speed and load and operating conditions, a number of input and control devices are used to accurately meter EGR into the cylinders. The sensors will provide the ECM with data about the quantity of air and exhaust, the conditions that would enable and disable EGR flow, and diagnostic data for the OBD system.

To calculate the quantity of exhaust gas for optimal engine operation and emission reduction, the mass of exhaust gas required and delivered to the cylinders is measured by input sensors. Three common circuit configurations are used. A **wide-band heated oxygen sensor (HOS)** provides feedback to the ECM about EGR flow rates. A **mass airflow (MAF) sensor** measures the weight of air entering the engine and can detect air inlet restrictions caused by a restricted air filter or intake when pressure drops below a threshold value. A **delta pressure (delta P) differential sensor** measures the pressure drop across a venturi.

The following sensor inputs are used to calculate required and actual mass of EGR flow into the engine.

- Engine speed sensor
- Intake air temperature (IAT) sensor
- Engine coolant temperature (ECT) sensor
- Barometric pressure (BARO) sensor
- Accelerator pedal position (APP) sensor
- Manifold absolute pressure (MAP) sensor
- Either an MAF sensor, a delta P sensor, or a wide-band HOS
- Exhaust back-pressure (EBP) sensor (optional)
- EGR cooler outlet temperature sensor (optional)

EGR Mass Calculations

The engine speed and accelerator pedal position primarily indicate how much EGR mass is required for the engine. The ECM will have look-up data tables for engine displacement and volumetric efficiency for any given rpm. This information, combined with intake manifold pressure and temperature, is used to determine the weight of air entering the cylinders. Barometric pressure, coolant, and intake air temperature measurements will determine whether the EGR system should be enabled based on ambient and engine-operating conditions. The ECM will adjust the EGR valve position based on calculations of intake air mass and required EGR mass. Measurement of the actual amount of exhaust gas delivered to and from a closed loop feedback circuit for the EGR valve is performed by several mechanisms:

1. Using an MAF sensor
2. Using a delta P sensor
3. Using oxygen sensors

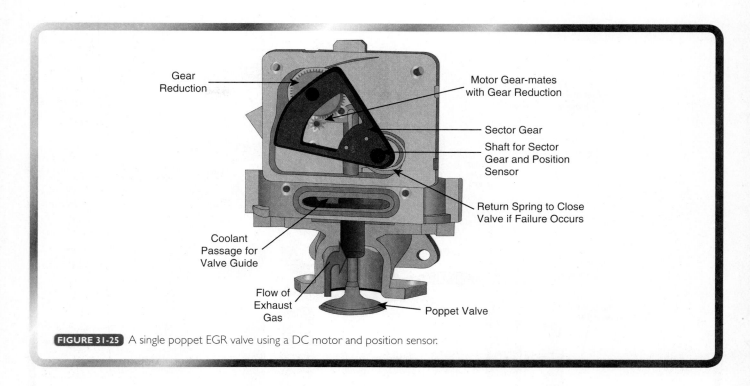

FIGURE 31-25 A single poppet EGR valve using a DC motor and position sensor.

MAF Sensor and EGR Flow Calculations

The MAF sensor is located upstream of the EGR flow into the engine. This means the mass of exhaust gas flow corresponds to reductions in intake airflow because intake air supply is supplanted by EGR flow. Using the MAF sensor, the HD-OBD or OBDII system detects and measures whether correct EGR flow is enabled based on a reduction in airflow into the engine.

Pressure Differential Measurement of EGR Flow

Another method to measure EGR mass involves the use of a pressure differential sensor and a temperature sensor. In these systems, EGR gas flows through a venturi, which has a sensor measuring the pressure on its inlet and outlet sides. When EGR flow rate is low, little pressure drop occurs across the venturi. At high EGR flow, such as when the EGR valve is opened further, the venturi becomes more restrictive to the flow and the pressure differential increases. Combined with gas temperature data from a temperature sensor, data from the pressure differential sensor can accurately measure the mass of EGR flow **FIGURE 31-26**.

A closed feedback loop is formed using data from the combined delta pressure sensor and intake manifold temperature sensor along with the EGR valve position **FIGURE 31-27**. A speed density measurement system uses data from the pressure differential sensor and exhaust temperature to calculate EGR mass flow. The delta pressure differential sensor measures EGR gas pressure drop across a venturi. Much like measuring amperage in an electrical circuit using circuit resistance and voltage, the speed density calculation can predict EGR gas mass based on gas pressure drop across the venturi. The pressure differential becomes greater as gas mass flow increases through the venturi.

Testing a Pressure Sensor

A three-wire active sensor, such as the Delta P sensor used by the EGR system, may require a pinpoint voltage test to determine whether or not it is defective. The internal circuit needs to be biased, or energized, to measure its voltage when it is not connected to the wiring harness, and voltages cannot be read from the screen of a service tool.

To test a pressure sensor, follow the steps in **SKILL DRILL 31-2**. This procedure can be applied to most pressure sensors, particularly Hall effect sensors.

Heated Oxygen Sensors

An EGR flow rate into the engine that keeps the exhaust gas oxygen concentration at 14% is optimal for low emissions and engine performance. Oxygen sensors, also called lambda sensors, are used by some manufacturers as feedback devices for EGR controls **FIGURE 31-28**. If exhaust gas oxygen content falls above or below 14–16%, the EGR system will automatically adjust EGR flow into the cylinder to compensate for the oxygen content change. This is not unlike the function of the oxygen sensor on gasoline engines, which is used to adjust air fuel ratios to achieve stoichiometric combustion. Oxygen gas content will fall with increased EGR gas flow and will rise with reduced EGR gas flow. When oxygen sensors are replaced, a calibration routine is usually used prior to operating the engine. Bosch sensors have a resistor in the connector fitting and the engine ECM needs to know its value to make corrections to sensor data. The sensor itself is connected and then held in the air to "learn" new values for barometric pressure and atmospheric oxygen content. These values are used recalibrate the sensor in use to compensate for sensor deterioration as the sensor ages.

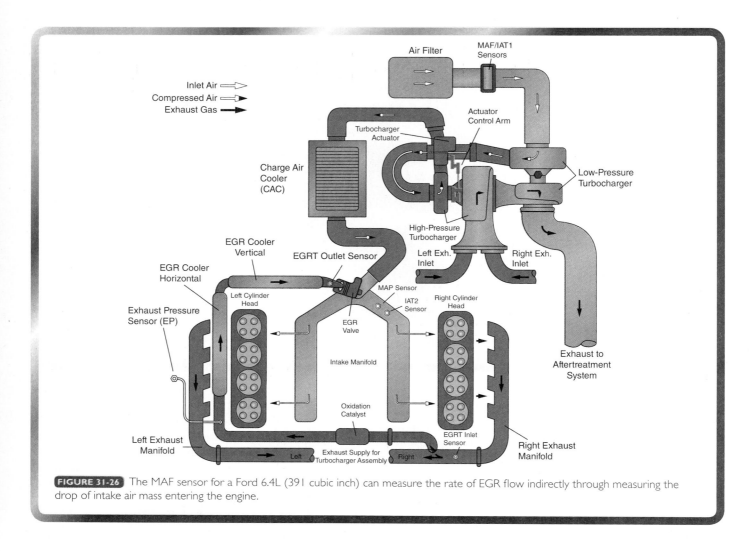

FIGURE 31-26 The MAF sensor for a Ford 6.4L (391 cubic inch) can measure the rate of EGR flow indirectly through measuring the drop of intake air mass entering the engine.

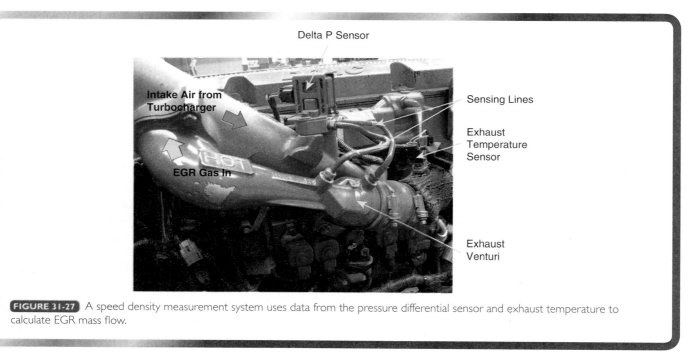

FIGURE 31-27 A speed density measurement system uses data from the pressure differential sensor and exhaust temperature to calculate EGR mass flow.

SKILL DRILL 31-2 Testing a Pressure Sensor

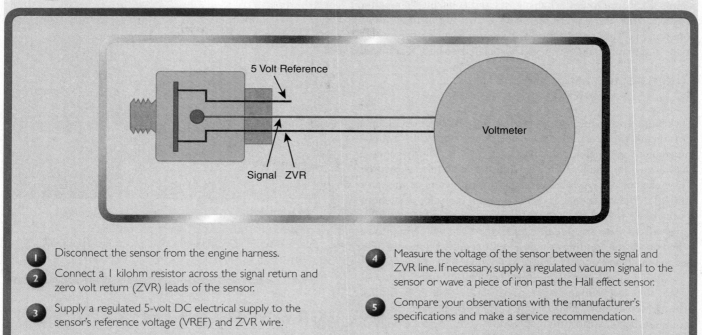

1. Disconnect the sensor from the engine harness.

2. Connect a 1 kilohm resistor across the signal return and zero volt return (ZVR) leads of the sensor.

3. Supply a regulated 5-volt DC electrical supply to the sensor's reference voltage (VREF) and ZVR wire.

4. Measure the voltage of the sensor between the signal and ZVR line. If necessary, supply a regulated vacuum signal to the sensor or wave a piece of iron past the Hall effect sensor.

5. Compare your observations with the manufacturer's specifications and make a service recommendation.

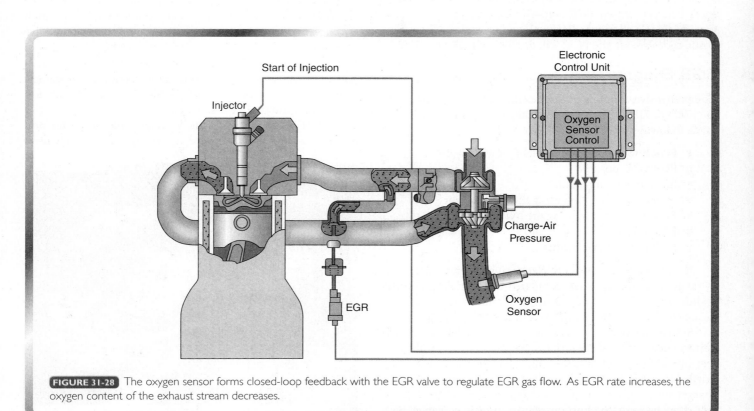

FIGURE 31-28 The oxygen sensor forms closed-loop feedback with the EGR valve to regulate EGR gas flow. As EGR rate increases, the oxygen content of the exhaust stream decreases.

► Maintenance of EGR Systems

EGR systems are one of the most common causes of engine complaints. Exposure to hot exhaust gases and constantly changing pressures and temperatures can shorten the life of many EGR components. This next section will examine some of the diagnostic and maintenance strategies associated with EGR systems.

Diagnostics for External, Non-Cooled EGR

A vacuum gauge and scan tool are required for EGR system diagnostics. To perform electrical pinpoint tests, a high-impedance multimeter is also necessary. At idle, after the engine has warmed up, the vacuum signal to the EGR valve should be 5–7 inches of mercury (inHg) (13–18 centimeters of mercury [cmHg]). The mechanical vacuum pump supplies a vacuum source of 15 inHg (38 cmHg). The vacuum signal to the EGR valve will increase for higher engine speed and load conditions. When operating conditions require reduced EGR flow, the EGR vent solenoid will dump vacuum in the line to the EGR valve.

The on-board diagnostic (OBD) system monitors the EGR system for electrical and operational faults. The EGR control pressure sensor information can be read by a scan tool and should indicate atmospheric pressure with the key on and engine off. Electrical faults with sensor circuits such as the throttle position circuit and engine speed sensor can be determined by monitoring these circuits with a scan tool. Significant differences between sensed EGR control vacuum and commanded vacuum signal will trigger diagnostic trouble codes. When diagnostic codes are set, the PCM will disable the EGR operation.

EGR Diagnostics

Comprehensive component monitoring of the EGR system by the EMD or HD-OBD system typically detects malfunctioning in the following areas:

- EGR flow rate using the delta P or MAF sensor
- EGR valve position
- EGR cooler temperature
- Intake boost pressure using the MAP sensor
- Boost temperature using the IAT sensor
- EBP sensor
- EGR system performance

If any data or circuits have electrical problems, data is out of range or irrational when compared to other data, and the malfunction indicator lamp (MIL) will illuminate and a diagnostic trouble code (DTC) will be stored **FIGURE 31-29**.

System behavior is measured against a model of expected performance by HD-OBD systems. For example, under the correct operating conditions, the OBD diagnostic manager may briefly open the EGR valve and measure the drop in turbocharger speed against expected values. The turbocharger speed will drop because combustion temperature is cooler at high EGR flow rates. Delta P flow change, EGR valve position, and MAF change could also be sensed. When the diagnostic manager has evaluated EGR system operation, it reports the monitor has run and no faults were detected.

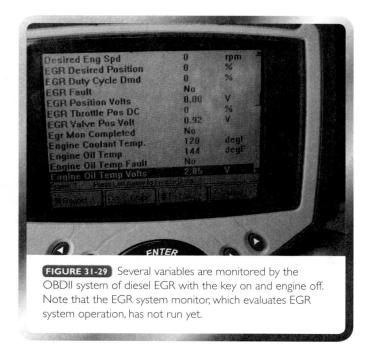

FIGURE 31-29 Several variables are monitored by the OBDII system of diesel EGR with the key on and engine off. Note that the EGR system monitor, which evaluates EGR system operation, has not run yet.

EGR Valve Diagnostics

In some systems, a variable resistance type position sensor is incorporated into the EGR valve to provide feedback to the EGR controls about the position of the valve. Differences between the valve's commanded position in comparison to actual position are measured to apply a position correction. Failure of the valve to position correctly will generate fault codes associated with EGR system operation. To increase the reliability of the position sensor, coolant may circulate through the valve to reduce heat from the exhaust gas flow **FIGURE 31-30**. Heat shields can also attach to the motor for the same purpose.

The EGR control circuit will also perform electrical diagnostics of the EGR valve according to comprehensive

FIGURE 31-30 EGR coolers often have vent valves, the highest point in the cooling system. After servicing, air must be bled from the system to purge air from the coolers.

component monitoring required of HD-OBD. For example, the position sensor and motor circuit are measured for resistance, voltage, short circuits, and out-of-range values.

EGR System Performance Checks

Some common diagnostic tests to evaluate the operation of the EGR system include the EGR valve override test and the VGT manual override test.

The EGR manual override test allows the service technician to override the EGR valve position by commanding different EGR valve positions and monitoring the actual position feedback from the valve. The technician can electronically measure the amount of valve movement and listen for changes to engine operation. This test is used to determine if the EGR valve is sticking, stuck in one position, or not actuating the full amount of travel.

Because the VGT is an integral part of the EGR system, the service technician should evaluate its operation. Usually with the engine at idle, the VGT vanes or nozzle will move from a closed to an open position. Measurements are taken of turbo speed during this operation. If the turbocharger speed increase does not meet a minimum value, troubleshooting of the air handling system is required.

Testing an EGR Valve

EGR valve operation is evaluated by the OBD system by observing the change in turbocharger speed when the valve opens and closes. The EGR valve will lower turbocharger boost pressure when enabled, because there is less expansion of the exhaust gases. The following procedure can be used on some engines with diagnostic menu items to open and close the EGR valve.

To test an EGR valve, follow the steps in **SKILL DRILL 31-3**.

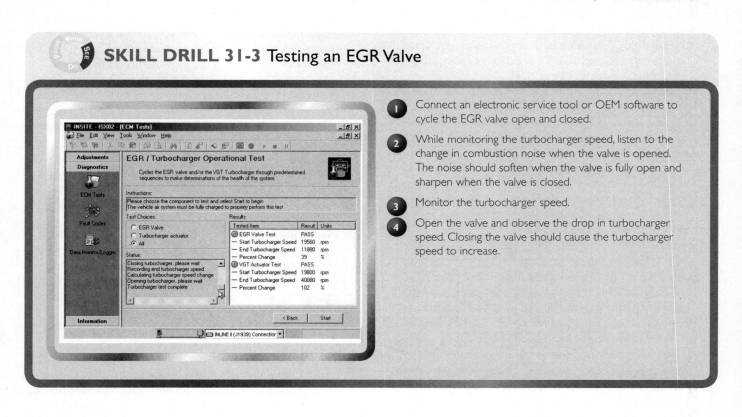

SKILL DRILL 31-3 Testing an EGR Valve

1. Connect an electronic service tool or OEM software to cycle the EGR valve open and closed.

2. While monitoring the turbocharger speed, listen to the change in combustion noise when the valve is opened. The noise should soften when the valve is fully open and sharpen when the valve is closed.

3. Monitor the turbocharger speed.

4. Open the valve and observe the drop in turbocharger speed. Closing the valve should cause the turbocharger speed to increase.

Wrap-Up

Ready for Review

▶ Exhaust gas circulation (EGR) technology reduces the formation of oxides of nitrogen (NO_x) from the cylinders of engines by reintroducing exhaust gas into the engine's cylinders.

▶ The introduction of EGR has required many changes to engine design, operation, and maintenance requirements.

▶ EGR is used to prevent the formation of NO_x emissions during the combustion process rather than remove NO_x in the exhaust system.

▶ EGR reintroduces exhaust gas into engine cylinders to reduce peak cylinder pressure and temperature—conditions that produce NO_x.

▶ While the design, construction, and operation of different EGR systems are unique, the basic mechanisms used to reduce NO_x formation in the cylinders are the same. The principle behind all EGR systems is to disrupt the chemical processes that form NO_x.

▶ While EGR systems are designed to replace a portion of the cylinder air charge with EGR gas, increased boost pressure is used on EGR engines; this means that the same amount of oxygen is available in the cylinder to keep power output comparable with non-EGR engines.

▶ EGR systems monitor engine speed and load conditions to meter the correct amount of exhaust gas into the engine intake.

▶ During idle, cold weather, or engine operation, minimal or no EGR flow usually takes place. During warm-up, condensation of corrosive exhaust can take place in EGR coolers, so flow is minimized or disabled during that period.

▶ EGR reduces NO_x emission formation by lowering peak cylinder pressure. Because exhaust gas cannot directly enter into the combustion process, it slows down the combustion speed by spacing oxygen and fuel molecules farther apart. Chain reactions between oxygen and fuel take longer, which results in a slower pressure rise in the cylinder.

▶ EGR use reduces temperature two ways. One way is through its ability to slow down combustion speed, which not only causes a pressure drop but also a temperature drop. The second way is due to the heat-absorbing properties of exhaust gas in the cylinder.

▶ By reducing the potential peak cylinder pressure, EGR use will make engine torque and power output fall unless other engine-operating strategies and design compensate for EGR use.

▶ EGR taxes the engine lubricating oil. New lubricating oil specifications have been developed for EGR engines to handle the extra contamination of lubrication oil from recycling exhaust gas back into the cylinder.

▶ Cooled EGR, where exhaust gas passes through an engine coolant heat exchanger, adds additional heat load to the cooling system and engine compartment. Larger radiators, water pumps, and cooling systems are required to transfer the heat absorbed by the coolant to the atmosphere.

▶ Cooled EGR leads to water condensation and the formation of higher sulfuric and nitric acid levels in the combustion chamber after reactions take place between water and combustion gases.

▶ Given the progressive reductions required for NO_x emissions by emission legislation and the fact that other NO_x-reducing technologies and operating strategies have reached their limits, EGR is necessary on virtually all diesel engines.

▶ Several types of EGR delivery systems exist to introduce exhaust gas uniformly into the cylinders. Types of EGR delivery systems used on medium- and heavy-duty diesels include high-pressure cooled EGR and low-pressure cooled EGR. Less frequently used EGR systems are used on a few heavy-duty, light-duty, and off-road engines and include internal EGR, external non-cooled EGR, and external cooled EGR.

▶ In an internal EGR system, no external EGR controls are used, but exhaust gas is reintroduced into the cylinders through a change to exhaust valve timing. These internal methods result in poor mixing with the intake air and excessive EGR rates at low speeds.

▶ External EGR uses a metering valve and control circuits to deliver exhaust gas into the intake manifold. Exhaust gas is driven into the intake manifold through the exhaust backpressure in the exhaust system.

▶ To achieve emission reduction, fuel rates, air, and exhaust gas mass must be carefully measured and balanced for efficient, powerful, low-emission combustion. A number of additional sensor and actuator circuits are required to accurately meter EGR rate proportional to other combustion elements.

▶ Supplying the necessary volume of exhaust gas to the pressurized intake manifold is a problem for turbocharged EGR engines. Manufacturers have relied upon VGTs, which can vary boost pressure and exhaust backpressure independently of engine speed.

▶ EGR gas derived from the exhaust manifold and pressurized to overcome intake boost pressure is called high-pressure EGR.

▶ An alternate strategy to high-pressure EGR is to draw EGR gas into the cylinders through either the turbocharger inlet or after the turbocharger between a throttle plate and intake manifold; this is referred to as low-pressure EGR.

▶ Some light-duty systems combine low- and high-pressure EGR to obtain even lower NO_x emissions while increasing efficiency.

▶ Engine manufacturers cool EGR gas before recirculating it into the combustion chambers. Cooling the exhaust lowers combustion chamber temperature and allows exhaust gas to absorb more combustion chamber heat.

▶ Exhaust gas recirculation systems require a device to blend recirculated exhaust gas and intake charge air. Some engines simply use the turbulence of the intake manifold and/or valve port design to swirl air and exhaust together for even blending.

▶ Central to the EGR system is the valve that meters the quantity of EGR flow into the intake manifold. Valves may be located on either the hot side (between the exhaust manifold and cooler) or the cold side (between the cooler and intake manifold).

▸ A number of input and control devices are used to accurately meter EGR into the cylinders. Three common circuit configurations are used: a wide-band heated oxygen sensor (HOS), a mass airflow (MAF) sensor, or a pressure differential (delta P) sensor.

▸ Engine speed and accelerator pedal position primarily indicate how much EGR mass is required for the engine.

▸ Using the MAF sensor, the OBDII system detects and measures whether correct EGR flow is enabled based on a reduction in airflow into the engine.

▸ Another method to measure EGR mass involves the use of a pressure differential sensor and a temperature sensor.

▸ An EGR flow rate into the engine that keeps the exhaust gas oxygen concentration at 14% is optimal for low emissions and engine performance. Oxygen sensors are used by some manufacturers as feedback devices for EGR controls.

▸ EGR system behavior is monitored and measured against a model of expected performance by HD-OBD systems.

▸ Some common diagnostic tests to evaluate the operation of the EGR system include the EGR valve override test and the VGT manual override test.

Vocabulary Builder

cooled EGR (CEGR) A system that cools EGR exhaust gas by passing it through an engine coolant heat exchanger.

delta pressure differential sensor A sensor that measures the pressure drop across two points in a gas circuit. In an EGR system, the delta P sensor measures the pressure drop across a venturi.

exhaust back-pressure (EBP) sensor A sensor that measures pressure in the exhaust manifold. The sensor can be used to perform diagnostic tests and provide closed-loop feedback control of the VGT actuator position.

high-pressure cooled EGR (HP-CEGR) A system in which EGR gas is pressurized in the exhaust manifold by a VGT turbocharger. Exhaust gas pressure is driven above intake boost pressure.

low-pressure EGR A system in which EGR gas is drawn into the cylinders through either the turbocharger inlet or after the turbocharger between a throttle plate and intake manifold.

mass airflow (MAF) sensor A device that measures the weight of air entering the engine and can detect air inlet restrictions caused by a restricted air filter or intake when pressure drops below a threshold value.

nitric oxide (NO) An unstable, highly reactive, colorless gas. It is the most abundant type of NO_x produced during diesel combustion. It is a noxious respiratory irritant.

nitrogen dioxide (NO_2) A reddish-brown gas formed from nitric oxide and oxygen. It is a noxious respiratory irritant.

specific heat The amount of heat required by a gas, solid, or liquid to produce a temperature change of 1°F within a specified time period.

variable geometry turbocharger (VGT) A turbocharger with the capability of changing boost pressure and exhaust backpressure independent of engine speed and load; also known as variable nozzle turbocharger (VNT) and variable vane turbocharger (VVT).

wide-band heated oxygen sensor (HOS) An exhaust gas sensor that provides feedback to the ECM about EGR flow rates.

Review Questions

1. The _____ is a sensor that measures pressure in the exhaust manifold.
   a. exhaust back pressure (EBP) sensor
   b. delta pressure differential sensor
   c. wide-band heated oxygen sensor (HOS)
   d. gear and position sensor

2. _____ is a reddish-brown gas formed from nitric oxide and oxygen.
   a. Nitrous oxide   c. Carbon monoxide
   b. Ozone gas   d. Nitrogen dioxide

3. The _____ is a sensor that measures the pressure drop across two points in a gas circuit.
   a. exhaust back-pressure (EBP) sensor
   b. wide-band heated oxygen sensor (HOS)
   c. delta pressure differential sensor
   d. gear and position sensor

4. Replacing combustion _____ with EGR gas is a strategy used by all EGR systems.
   a. oxygen   c. carbon
   b. nitrogen   d. ozone

5. Heat _____ refers to the amount of heat transferred to the coolant rather than converted into mechanical force driving down the pistons.
   a. combustion   c. blend
   b. rejection   d. differential

6. Symptoms of an EGR cooler leak include high _____ levels in scheduled oil samples, and white smoke with a sweet odor.
   a. glycol   c. sodium
   b. carbon   d. ozone

7. A(n) _____ measures the weight of air entering the engine and can detect air inlet restrictions caused by a restricted air filter or intake when pressure drops below a threshold value.
   a. mass airflow sensor
   b. delta pressure differential sensor
   c. wide-band heated oxygen sensor
   d. exhaust back-pressure sensor

8. Oxygen sensors, also called _____ sensors, are used by some manufacturers as feedback devices for EGR controls.
   a. mass airflow   c. lambda
   b. internal   d. external

9. The principle behind all EGR systems is to disrupt the chemical processes that form _____.
   a. carbon monoxide   c. oxides of Nitrogen
   b. carbon dioxide   d. hydrogen dioxide

10. Injection timing may be advanced in many EGR engines to enable adequate burn time for the slower _____ speeds.
    a. rejection   c. emission
    b. combustion   d. differential

ASE-Type Questions

1. Technician A says that by reintroducing exhaust gas back into the cylinders, a major reduction in exhaust emissions of oxides of nitrogen is achieved. Technician B says that by reintroducing exhaust gas back into the cylinders, a major reduction in exhaust emissions of carbon dioxide is achieved. Who is correct?
   a. Technician A
   b. Technician B
   c. Both Technician A and Technician B
   d. Neither Technician A nor Technician B

2. Technician A says the most abundant type of NO_x initially produced during diesel combustion is nitrous oxide. Technician B says the most abundant type of NO_x initially produced during diesel combustion is nitric oxide. Who is correct?
   a. Technician A
   b. Technician B
   c. Both Technician A and Technician B
   d. Neither Technician A nor Technician B

3. Technician A says the amount of heat required by a gas, solid, or liquid to produce a temperature change of 1°F within a specified time period is called focused heat. Technician B says the amount of heat required by a gas, solid, or liquid to produce a temperature change of 1°F within a specified time period is called latent heat. Who is correct?
   a. Technician A
   b. Technician B
   c. Both Technician A and Technician B
   d. Neither Technician A nor Technician B

4. Technician A says cooled EGR leads to the formation of higher nitric acid levels in the combustion chamber after reactions take place. Technician B says cooled EGR leads to the formation of higher sulfuric acid levels in the combustion chamber after reactions take place. Who is correct?
   a. Technician A
   b. Technician B
   c. Both Technician A and Technician B
   d. Neither Technician A nor Technician B

5. Technician A says that too low of an EGR rate will not obtain the required emission reductions. Technician B says that too low of an EGR rate will starve the combustion process of adequate oxygen. Who is correct?
   a. Technician A
   b. Technician B
   c. Both Technician A and Technician B
   d. Neither Technician A nor Technician B

6. Technician A says a fluted style mixer evenly blends gas into the intake stream around the circumference of the inlet of the intake manifold. Technician B says a cyclone style mixer evenly blends gas into the intake stream around the circumference of the inlet of the intake manifold. Who is correct?
   a. Technician A
   b. Technician B
   c. Both Technician A and Technician B
   d. Neither Technician A nor Technician B

7. Technician A says that measurement of the actual amount of exhaust gas delivered to and from a closed loop feedback circuit for the EGR valve is performed by a mass airflow sensor. Technician B says that measurement of the actual amount of exhaust gas delivered to and from a closed loop feedback circuit for the EGR valve is performed by oxygen sensors. Who is correct?
   a. Technician A
   b. Technician B
   c. Both Technician A and Technician B
   d. Neither Technician A nor Technician B

8. Technician A says that EGR rates are much lower in diesel engines than in gasoline-fueled engines. Technician B says that EGR rates are much higher in diesel engines than in gasoline-fueled engines. Who is correct?
   a. Technician A
   b. Technician B
   c. Both Technician A and Technician B
   d. Neither Technician A nor Technician B

9. Technician A says that when NO_x breaks down in the presence of sunlight and heat, it converts to carbon and oxygen gas. Technician B says that when NO_x breaks down in the presence of sunlight and heat, it converts to nitrogen and ozone gas. Who is correct?
   a. Technician A
   b. Technician B
   c. Both Technician A and Technician B
   d. Neither Technician A nor Technician B

10. Technician A says that EGR coolers send exhaust gas through a heat exchanger where its temperature can be reduced from as much as 1000°F (538°C) to approximately 212°F (100°C). Technician B says that EGR coolers send exhaust gas through a heat exchanger where its temperature can be reduced from as much as 1000°F (538°C) to approximately 650°F (343°C). Who is correct?
   a. Technician A
   b. Technician B
   c. Both Technician A and Technician B
   d. Neither Technician A nor Technician B

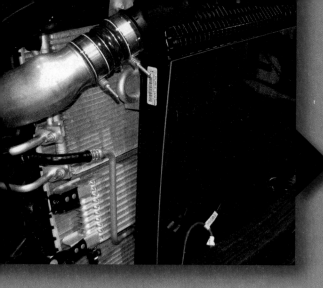

CHAPTER 32
Charge Air Cooling

NATEF Tasks

Diesel Engines

General
- Identify engine fuel, oil, coolant, air, and other leaks; determine needed action. (pp 921–924)

- Listen for engine noises; determine needed action. (p 921)

Air Induction and Exhaust Systems
- Inspect, clean, and test charge air cooler assemblies; replace as needed. (pp 921–926)

Knowledge Objectives

After reading this chapter, you will be able to:
1. Describe the purpose and functions of charge air coolers. (pp 918–920)
2. Identify and describe the types, construction, and applications of charge air coolers. (pp 920–923)

3. Identify and explain inspection, testing, and diagnostic procedures on charge air coolers. (pp 923–928)

Skills Objectives

After reading this chapter, you will be able to:
1. Pressure test a CAC. (pp 926) **SKILL DRILL 32-1**
2. Test a CAC for internal restriction. (pp 927) **SKILL DRILL 33-3**

3. Inspect a CAC for external restrictions. (pp 928) **SKILL DRILL 32-2**

► Introduction

Charge air cooling, aftercooling, and intercooling are interchangeable terms for removing excess heat from the air charging, or filling, the cylinders **FIGURE 32-1**. Charge air cooling is an important technology for reducing oxides of nitrogen (NO_x) emissions. Other benefits include improved fuel economy, power output, and maximum injection rates. Either ambient (outside) air or engine coolant passing though heat exchangers are the mechanisms for removing heat from the pressurized intake air. A **heat exchanger** transfers heat from coolant to the atmosphere. A chassis-mounted **air-to-air aftercooler (ATAAC)** cools using ambient air **FIGURE 32-2**. This type of system is often called a **charge air cooler (CAC)**; it is also known as an aftercooler or intercooler. A **jacket water aftercooler (JWAC)** cools using engine coolant instead of air.

► Fundamentals of Charge Air Cooling

On turbocharged engines, air intake temperatures rise dramatically with boost pressure. High intake air temperatures negatively affect emissions, engine durability, and performance. Loss of air density and increased cylinder temperatures accompanying higher intake air temperatures are the main factors causing these problems. Because pressurizing a gas increases its temperature, intake air temperature is raised proportional to its compressed pressure **FIGURE 32-3**. Additionally, when gas temperatures increase, molecules spread farther apart, so the gas loses density. This means a cubic foot (meter) of air, when heated, contains fewer oxygen molecules and weighs less than when it is not heated.

The relationship between temperature and pressure can be predicted using mathematical equations. Consider the following examples:

- If intake or under-hood intake air temperature is 75°F (24°C) at atmospheric pressure (15 psi [103 kPa] at sea level), the turbo outlet temperature will be 285°F (141°C) at 20 psi (138 kPa) boost pressure.
- If the inlet air temperature to the turbocharger climbs to 100°F (38°C), the discharge temperature will be 320°F (160°C).
- A boost pressure of 30 psi (207 kPa) produces an outlet temperature of 358°F (181°C) with an intake

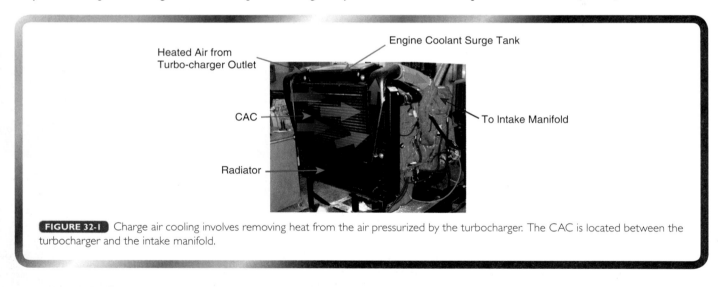

FIGURE 32-1 Charge air cooling involves removing heat from the air pressurized by the turbocharger. The CAC is located between the turbocharger and the intake manifold.

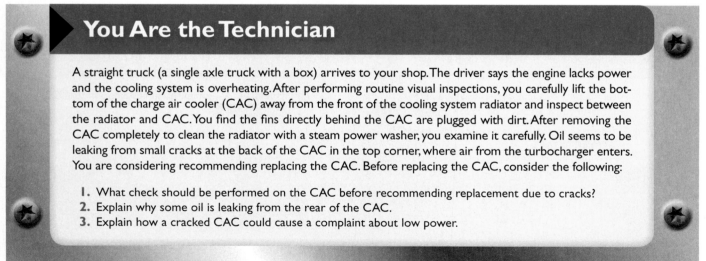

You Are the Technician

A straight truck (a single axle truck with a box) arrives to your shop. The driver says the engine lacks power and the cooling system is overheating. After performing routine visual inspections, you carefully lift the bottom of the charge air cooler (CAC) away from the front of the cooling system radiator and inspect between the radiator and CAC. You find the fins directly behind the CAC are plugged with dirt. After removing the CAC completely to clean the radiator with a steam power washer, you examine it carefully. Oil seems to be leaking from small cracks at the back of the CAC in the top corner, where air from the turbocharger enters. You are considering recommending replacing the CAC. Before replacing the CAC, consider the following:

1. What check should be performed on the CAC before recommending replacement due to cracks?
2. Explain why some oil is leaking from the rear of the CAC.
3. Explain how a cracked CAC could cause a complaint about low power.

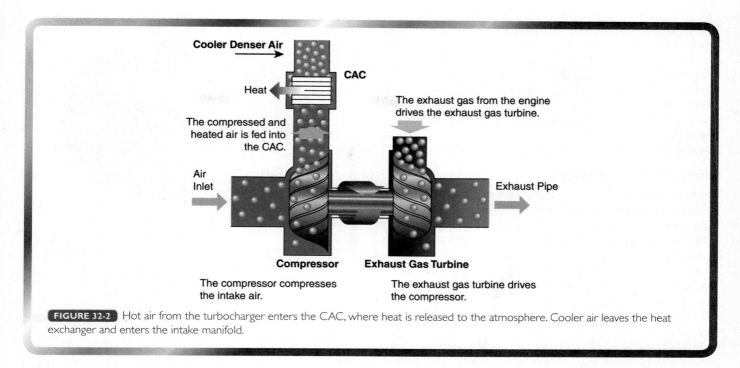

FIGURE 32-2 Hot air from the turbocharger enters the CAC, where heat is released to the atmosphere. Cooler air leaves the heat exchanger and enters the intake manifold.

temperature of 75°F (24°C) and an outlet temperature of 396°F (202°C) with an intake temperature of 100°F (38°C).

- A 250-horsepower (hp) (186-kilowatt [kW]) engine will develop only 240 hp (179 kW) if the air temperature is 130°F (54°C) using the same quantity of fuel.

Problems with High Intake Air Temperatures

Low Air Density

A high cylinder-charging air temperature lowers air density and results in poorer combustion quality. As air molecules spread farther apart, less oxygen is available to support combustion and the air mass available to cool cylinder components drops. For every 10°F temperature increase above 60°F (16°C), the changes to air density and oxygen content result in a power loss.

Power decreases 1% for every 10°F above 90°F (32°C). Without a cool air mass traveling across the piston crown from the intake to the exhaust valve during the valve overlap period, the piston crown and exhaust valve become very hot. The loss of air's cooling effect leads to higher cylinder heat loads and shorter engine life.

Higher Combustion Temperatures

Increases in the intake charge temperature lead to significantly higher combustion and exhaust temperatures. This exhaust temperature increase is disproportional to the air inlet temperature increase, with small increases in air inlet temperature often producing even larger changes to exhaust temperature. Generally, a 3-to-1 ratio exists, with every 1°F increase in charge-air temperature producing a 3°F increase in exhaust temperature. However, many factors affect this relationship,

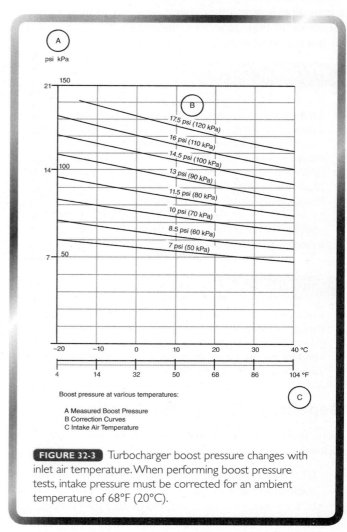

Boost pressure at various temperatures:

A Measured Boost Pressure
B Correction Curves
C Intake Air Temperature

FIGURE 32-3 Turbocharger boost pressure changes with inlet air temperature. When performing boost pressure tests, intake pressure must be corrected for an ambient temperature of 68°F (20°C).

including fuel rates, excess air ratio, air density, and engine compression ratio. The exhaust temperature should never exceed 1250–1300°F (677°C–704°C) or damage to valves and pistons will occur **FIGURE 32-4**. The normal exhaust temperature is less than 900°F (482°C). Very hot exhaust gases will also cause the thin outer edges of the turbocharger turbine to glow and eventually melt. If charge air cooling reduces thermal loading of the cylinders, larger quantities of fuel can be injected to develop more power from the same engine displacement.

Higher NO_x Emissions

Increases to charge air temperatures result in higher combustion chamber temperatures, which increase the production of NO_x emissions. Normally, nitrogen, which makes up approximately 77% of the composition of air, remains inert and uninvolved in combustion processes. At temperatures above approximately 2500°F (1371°C), and because of high cylinder pressures, nitrogen will react with oxygen to produce nitrogen–oxygen compounds collectively known as NO_x.

Beginning in 1988, the Environmental Protection Agency (EPA) in the United States introduced increasingly strict emissions standards for NO_x. EURO stage 1 standards were introduced in 1992. The cooling of intake air, which drops combustion temperatures, goes a long way to minimizing the formation of these emissions, making the CAC an important emission-control device.

> ### ► TECHNICIAN TIP
>
> The first year for legislated reductions to diesel emissions was 1988. Until that time, diesels needed to meet only a standard for exhaust opacity during a throttle snap test. In 1990, NO_x emissions dropped from approximately 11 grams per brake horsepower-hour (g/bhp-hr) (15 grams per kilowatt-hour [g/kW-hr]) for heavy-duty on-highway diesels to 6 g/bhp-hr (8 g/kW-hr). During this time, almost every medium- and heavy-duty diesel vehicle began being equipped with charge air cooling to bring NO_x to these levels. Without cooling intake air adequately, combustion temperatures rise and produce exponential increases in NO_x.

> ### ► TECHNICIAN TIP
>
> CACs are large air-handling components and vulnerable to damage. Leaking and cracking often cause complaints of low power. Cracks can easily develop in these devices due to constant thermal cycling from hot to cold. When investigating such complaints, always inspect and test the CAC for leaks.

Benefits of Charge Air Cooling

Cooling the intake air charge to the cylinders accomplishes the following important benefits:

1. If increases air density and oxygen content, which improves combustion quality. More oxygen in the cylinders means better contact between fuel and oxygen for efficient, clean combustion.

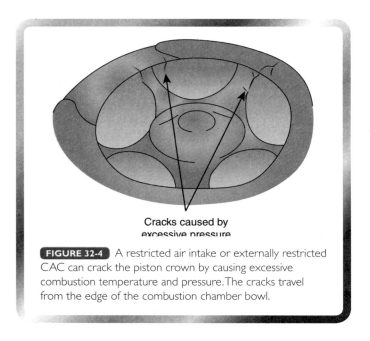

FIGURE 32-4 A restricted air intake or externally restricted CAC can crack the piston crown by causing excessive combustion temperature and pressure. The cracks travel from the edge of the combustion chamber bowl.

2. CACs provide additional air mass for cooling valves and pistons. Denser air means the air can remove more heat from valves and pistons during valve overlap. Adding air mass to the cylinders dilutes the heat produced during combustion for lower cylinder temperatures.

3. Denser, cooler air improves fuel economy up to 5% due to improved combustion qualities. The simple addition of a CAC does not produce more power—that requires more fuel and air. However, because cooling of intake air improves combustion quality, the potential to slightly increase power does exist **FIGURE 32-5**.

4. CACs enable higher injection rates, which means more fuel enters the cylinders. Higher injection rates translate into greater power density, which means the engine can produce more power per cubic inch (centimeter) of cylinder displacement. Because the additional fuel can push cylinder thermal loads to their maximum threshold, cooling charge air can reduce combustion and exhaust temperatures by diluting combustion heat with cooler, denser air mass. This makes it possible to gain power while minimizing the risk of engine damage using higher injection rates.

5. CACs reduce NO_x emissions by lowering peak cylinder temperatures and pressures through cooling the charge air.

► Types of Charge Air Cooling

Heat exchangers are used to transfer heat from the air charge to either the atmosphere or cooling system. Efficient and effective heat transfer is necessary to keep engine emissions low and prevent engine damage. Many different names are given to these heat exchangers. This next section will examine the construction and operation of two major categories of charge air coolers: liquid coolers, which use engine coolant as a heat transfer medium, and air coolers, which use atmospheric airflow as a cooling medium.

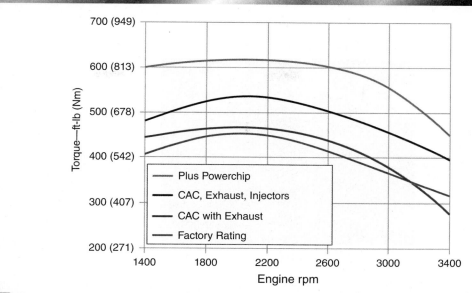

FIGURE 32-5 The addition of a CAC and larger exhaust only offers marginal power improvement. Engines with CACs usually have more power, but CACs do not increase power output.

JWAC

A JWAC lowers intake temperatures by passing the boost air through a water-type heat exchanger. A JWAC is capable of lowering the turbocharger boost air temperature from approximately 300°F (149°C) to approximately 200°F (93°C).

Older, mechanically-governed engines often use a JWAC, positioned inside the intake manifold **FIGURE 32-6**. The advantage of a mechanically governed fuel system is that the injection timing can be calibrated around a relatively constant air inlet temperature. This type of cooling is still popular on marine diesel engines. Today, JWACs are used in series turbocharger applications, where very high boost pressures produce even hotter intake air temperatures. Air intake temperatures are first lowered by a JWAC before passing through an ATAAC **FIGURE 32-7**. When a JWAC is used to cool air between each stage of turbocharging, it is often referred to as **interstage cooling** or intercooling.

FIGURE 32-6 This JWAC, located inside the intake manifold of a mechanically governed engine, uses engine coolant to lower intake air temperatures. The outlet of the turbocharger is connected to the intake manifold with a tube.

> ### TECHNICIAN TIP
>
> When servicing the cooling system of an engine using a JWAC, bleeding air from the cooler is important. The cooler is a high point in the cooling system, so air can become trapped in the cooler and prevent proper functioning. Series turbocharged engines using JWACs transfer more heat to the cooling system and therefore require more vigilant maintenance of the cooling system.

ATAAC

The most popular method of cooling intake air is to use an air-to-air heat exchanger, which is often referred to as an ATAAC or ATA. Moving the heated charge air through an ATAAC can drop the temperature from more than 400°F (204°C) to 90–110°F (32–43°C) with an outside temperature of 75°F (24°C) **FIGURE 32-8**. The exact temperature reduction depends on the ambient air temperature and the volume of airflow across the cooler core. A properly functioning CAC has a maximum temperature differential of 30°F between air intake temperature and outside air when airflow is 30 mph (48 km/h). Most coolers have an efficiency of approximately 80%, which means they reduce intake temperatures to no more than 30–40°F above outside temperatures.

Air-to-air aftercooling requires relatively high airflow across the cooler to remove heat. Therefore, a winter front, which is a

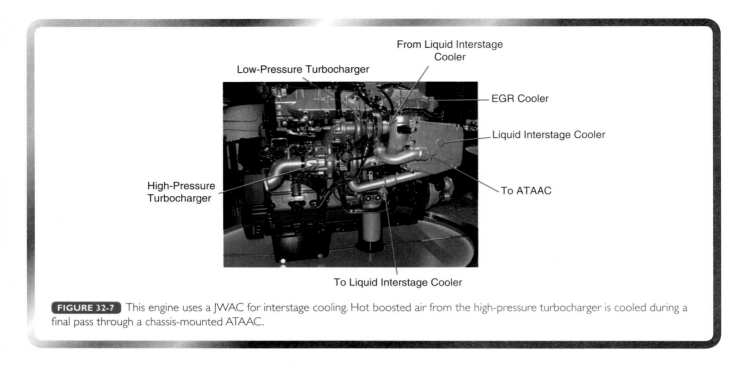

FIGURE 32-7 This engine uses a JWAC for interstage cooling. Hot boosted air from the high-pressure turbocharger is cooled during a final pass through a chassis-mounted ATAAC.

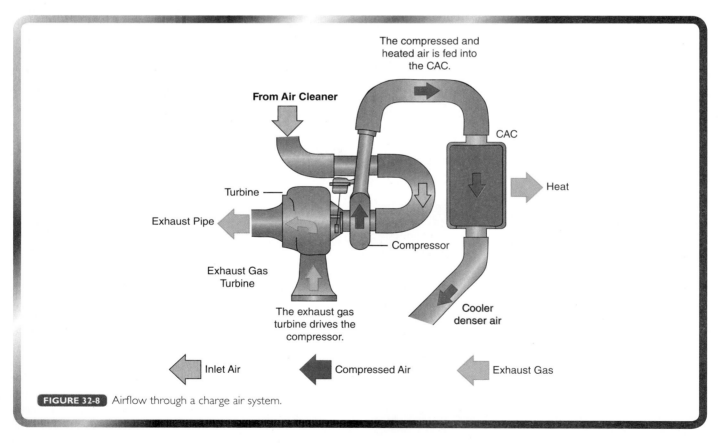

FIGURE 32-8 Airflow through a charge air system.

radiator cover used in cold weather operation, should not be used with an ATAAC. If a winter front must be used to maintain cab heat, never close it completely. At least 20% airflow must remain flowing across the cooler, even in the coldest weather **FIGURE 32-9**.

Most engine manufacturers using electronic controls monitor air intake manifold temperatures as a part of the engine protection system. High intake temperatures will cause the engine to derate power or even shut down.

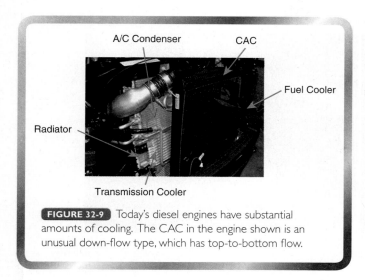

FIGURE 32-9 Today's diesel engines have substantial amounts of cooling. The CAC in the engine shown is an unusual down-flow type, which has top-to-bottom flow.

▶ ATAAC Components

Most ATAACs are constructed of aluminum for maximum heat transfer and strength **FIGURE 32-10**. To achieve optimum cooling, the inlet and outlet of the cooler may have different

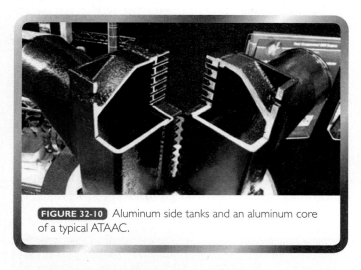

FIGURE 32-10 Aluminum side tanks and an aluminum core of a typical ATAAC.

diameters to slow the airflow through the cooler and maximize heat transfer.

As the temperature in the cooler drops, a corresponding pressure drop occurs. A cooler pressure drop from side to side should not typically exceed more than 3 psi (21 kPa). If the pressure drops more than this, check the cooler for internal restrictions and leaks **FIGURE 32-11**.

Cooler Mounting

Because coolers are often made from aluminum, they expand and contract when heated and cooled. For this reason, the cooler's mounting system is designed to allow for thermal cycling. For example, washers on both sides of mounting bolts may include a spring type washer and nylon-like washers, which allow the cooling to slide. Give special care to manufacturers' mounting instructions to avoid damaging the cooler.

Hoses and Clamps

ATAACs use unique connector hoses that are often color coded to differentiate the hot and cold sides of the cooler. These hoses are made of chemically stable, durable silicone material. Clamps with smooth underside surfaces prevent damage to the hose. Spring-operated clamps are preferred because they can maintain a constant torque on the hose regardless of the dimensional variations produced by temperature extremes **FIGURE 32-12**.

Underhood noises during heavily loaded operating conditions can be pinpointed to leaking clamps and hoses. A sudden drop in CAC pressure from a blown clamp can cause the turbocharger compressor wheel to draw oil into the compressor housing, which can be misidentified as a defective turbocharger.

▶ Charge Air Cooling Maintenance

Continuous pressure and temperature changes exert tremendous stress on coolers, which often results in cracks or some type of leak. Coolers can also become internally and externally restricted from debris or liquids passing through the cooler.

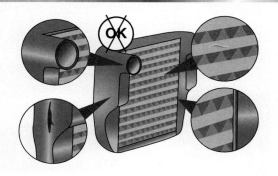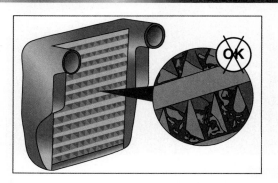

FIGURE 32-11 Check CACs for cracks in cooler tubes and the joint between the tanks and tubes. Inspect for external restrictions in front and behind the intercoolers.

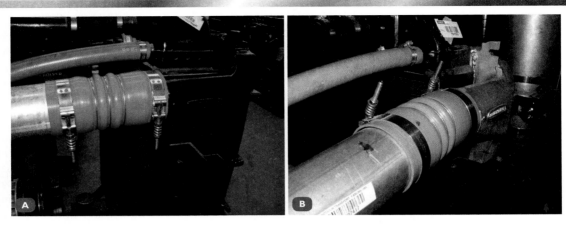

FIGURE 32-12 CAC hoses are made from different materials depending on whether the hose is on the hot or cool side. The materials are color coded.

This section will examine some of the common problems and maintenance practices associated with CACs.

ATAAC Testing and Servicing

CACs can fail for a number of reasons, which can lead to air inlet restriction, excessive emissions, and high exhaust and cylinder temperatures. Internal or external restrictions of the CAC can cause low power. Electronic engines will often derate power output when intake manifold temperatures are high because high intake manifold temperatures can cause severe heat damage to cylinder components and turbochargers **FIGURE 32-13**.

ATAAC Service Conditions

Leakage

Thermal cycling can stress a CAC until it cracks. The stress is compounded because aluminum has a much higher expansion coefficient than other metals. Cracks are common in areas of the cooler where inlet temperatures are highest and at the joint between the inlet tank and cooler tubes **FIGURE 32-14**. Replacement is not always the expected service recommendation for this condition because the size of some cracks does not justify cooler replacement. Because the CAC is pressurized and the turbocharger produces excess air, the CAC can tolerate small cracks without allowing dirt into the engine intake.

Pressure Testing

Small cracks do not warrant CAC replacement because dirt ingestion into the engine through a crack is not likely when a cooler is pressurized. Additionally, if the engine is using excess air for combustion, some leakage is permissible before the air loss affects the engine performance. Considering these variables, many manufacturers do not recommend replacing the

FIGURE 32-13 Electric air intake heaters minimize cold-start and warm-up emissions. The ECM will disconnect these devices when the engine is under boost pressure and intake air temperatures need lowering.

FIGURE 32-14 This CAC has elongated slots at its mounting locations to allow for expansion and contraction. Mounting hardware cannot be too tight and prevent movement.

cooler if the leak is small. Until the leak is significant, engine performance is not compromised.

Instead, pressure-testing a CAC to determine the magnitude of air volume lost is the most important criterion for justifying cooler replacement. After isolating and pressurizing the cooler to the manufacturer's specifications, check the rate of leakage against acceptable limits. Manufacturers typically recommend pressurizing the cooler to 30 psi (207 kPa) and measuring the rate of leakage by observing the pressure drop. A drop in pressure of less than a 5 psi (34 kPa) in 15 seconds is an acceptable leak limit for a variety of manufacturers **FIGURE 32-15**.

Pressure Testing a CAC

CACs can leak and allow loss of charge air mass, which reduces engine power and increases exhaust temperature and emissions. Low-power complaints should include a pressure test of the CAC. Some leakage is acceptable, because an overabundance of air mass entering the engine cylinders and some cracking of the cooler is unavoidable due to frequent thermal cycling.

To pressure test a CAC, follow the steps in **SKILL DRILL 32-1**.

Safety

Always secure pressure-testing adapters used to seal CAC pipes with safety chains. Under pressure, these adapters can slip with explosive force and cause vehicle damage, severe personal injury, or even death.

Internal Restrictions

CAC core restriction has a variety of causes. For example, a shredded air filter gasket or ingestion of water or oil can reduce airflow inside a cooler core. Oil can accumulate because crankcase emissions can pass through the cooler and condense oil **FIGURE 32-16**. Turbochargers wisp a small quantity of oil, which can easily accumulate inside a core. Any dirt getting through an air filter can stick to the oily core tubes and further restrict airflow. A failed turbo may leave a large quantity of oil and even debris inside the cooler **FIGURE 32-17**.

After a turbo failure, flushing a cooler thoroughly is important to prevent ingestion of debris into an engine. Lubrication oil loaded inside a cooler core can lead to an engine's destruction because a diesel engine can easily run on aspirated engine oil. Excess oil in the CAC supplies the engine with an unregulated external fuel source, which leads to the destruction of many engines.

FIGURE 32-16 This image shows oil weeping from a charge air pipe clamp. It is normal for oil to accumulate around joints.

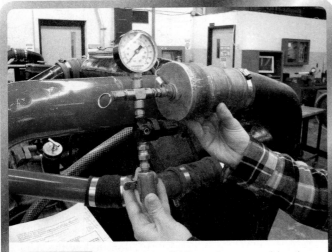

FIGURE 32-15 Leak-testing a CAC requires pressurizing the cooler to 30 psi (207 kPa) using a pressure regulator, then shutting off the air supply to measure the leak.

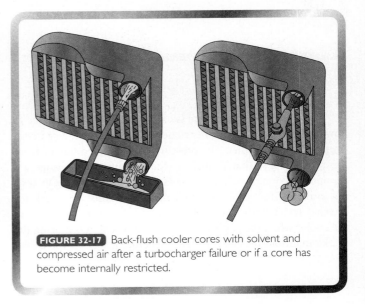

FIGURE 32-17 Back-flush cooler cores with solvent and compressed air after a turbocharger failure or if a core has become internally restricted.

SKILL DRILL 32-1 Pressure Testing a CAC

1. Disconnect the CAC inlet and outlet pipes.

2. Connect purpose-made adapters to the CAC pipe hoses. One adapter has a drain valve and the other has a quick-connect fitting.

3. Connect an air pressure regulator to the test adapter plug and pressurize the cooler to 30 psi (207 kPa).

4. Shut off the air pressure supply to the regulator and count the number of seconds it takes for the cooler to drop 5 psi (34 kPa).

5. Generally, any leak that allows a pressure drop of more than 5 psi (34 kPa) in 15 seconds is too large.

6. Make a service recommendation based on manufacturer's specifications and the observed time it took for a pressure drop in the cooler.

To evaluate whether there is excessive internal resistance to flow because of an internal restriction exists, complete a **pressure drop test** of the cooler. The pressure drop test is different from the pressure test that evaluates whether any cooler leaks are significant enough to justify replacement. Pressure drop testing evaluates the cooler for internal restrictions. To check for internal restrictions, measure the inlet and outlet pressures of the cooler when the engine is under load. While monitoring the intake manifold pressure, install a separate gauge on the cooler inlet or turbocharger outlet. Usually, a drop in pressure of no more than 3 psi (21 kPa) is acceptable. However, compare test results against manufacturer's specifications for acceptable limits.

Testing a CAC for Internal Restrictions

CACs can internally accumulate oil, water, debris, and even ice. The result is a loss of air mass due to the internal restriction.

To test a CAC for internal restriction, follow the steps in SKILL DRILL 32-2 .

SKILL DRILL 32-2 Testing a CAC for Internal Restrictions

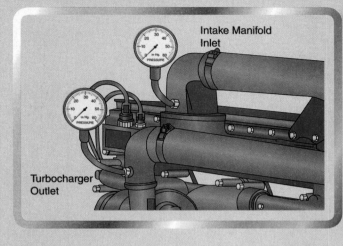

Intake Manifold Inlet

Turbocharger Outlet

1. Connect two direct-reading pressure gauges or a pressure gauge with two separate, switchable inputs to the intake manifold and turbocharger outlet.

2. Road test the vehicle while loading the engine to achieve maximum boost pressures. This is done by accelerating the engine at full throttle while the transmission is a couple of gear steps above where it should be.

3. While the engine lugs down and the turbocharger moves through peak boost pressure, observe and record the pressure at both points in the induction systems.

4. Compare the results against the manufacturer's specifications. Generally, no more than 6 inHg (15 cmHg) or 3 psi (21 kPa) of pressure drop is unacceptable.

5. Make a service recommendation based on observations of the pressure differential across the CAC. The CAC may require draining or back-flushing with solvent to clean the restriction.

External Restrictions

Winter fronts, bug screens, and blocked coolant radiators and air conditioner condensers can restrict external airflow over the CAC. Sometimes, a small leak in the cooler will allow oil to migrate out, creating adhesive surfaces for road dust to cling to behind the cooler. While a quick visual inspection of a cooler might show no signs of restriction, the area directly behind the cooler may be completely blocked.

This type of restriction would also not allow sufficient airflow across the radiator, causing the engine to overheat or resulting in high engine coolant temperatures. Engine emissions and cylinder heat loads would increase proportional to the degree of air restriction over the CAC.

To diagnose an external restriction, a **temperature differential test** can identify a loss of cooling across a cooler. The vehicle needs to travel at least 30 mph (48 km/h). Normally, the difference between the ambient temperature and the intake manifold temperature should not be more than 20–30°F. For comparative purposes, the Cummins air temperature differential test limits the temperature difference to no more than 50°F with an airflow of at least 30 mph (48 km/h) across the cooler.

Inspecting a CAC for External Restrictions

CAC efficiency is monitored by the HD-OBD or OBD-II system. CAC efficiency is calculated by measuring the temperature differential between the CAC's inlet and outlet. A large differential indicates a properly functioning CAC. An externally restricted cooler that is plugged with debris, covered with cardboard or a winterfront, or located in front of a blocked radiator will generate efficiency codes or produce engine protection codes. The latter happens when intake manifold temperatures become too high, which can result in valve and piston damage.

To inspect a CAC for external restrictions, follow the steps in SKILL DRILL 32-3 .

TECHNICIAN TIP

Testing the CAC temperature differential can be easily accomplished on a road test with an electronic diagnostic tool. Usually, original equipment manufacturer software or a handheld diagnostic code reader can monitor intake manifold temperature, which you can compare with the known ambient temperature. Make sure to load the engine by operating it under full throttle, up a grade, or in a higher gear than the vehicle would normally operate.

SKILL DRILL 32-3 Inspecting a CAC for External Restrictions

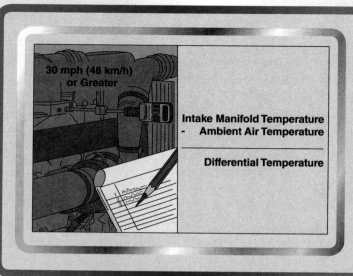

1. Measure the ambient temperature.

2. Road test the vehicle and load the engine to produce peak boost pressures. Ensure the road speed is faster than 30 mph (48 km/h) to obtain good airflow across the cooler.

3. Monitor the intake manifold temperature sensor and record the intake air temperature in the manifold at peak boost.

4. Subtract the intake manifold air temperature from ambient temperature, and compare that with the manufacturer's specifications.

5. Based on test observations, make a service recommendation for cleaning the CAC or radiator. Generally, the temperature differential should not exceed 30°F.

Wrap-Up

Ready for Review

▶ Charge air cooling, aftercooling, and intercooling are interchangeable terms describing the system responsible for removing excess heat from the air charging, or filling, the cylinders.

▶ Charge air cooling is an important technology for reducing NO_x emissions.

▶ Charge air cooling improves fuel economy, power output, and the maximum injection rates an engine can use.

▶ The mechanisms for removing heat from the pressurized intake air include ambient (outside) air or engine coolant passing though heat exchangers. An ATAAC uses ambient air for cooling. A JWAC uses engine coolant to cool intake air.

▶ High intake air temperatures negatively affect emissions, engine durability, and performance by decreasing air density and increasing cylinder temperature.

▶ High cylinder-charging air temperatures result in lower air density with fewer oxygen molecules available for combustion and, therefore, poorer combustion quality. Power loss due to high inlet air temperatures is 1% for every 10°F above 90°F (32°C).

▶ Increases in the intake charge temperature result in significantly higher combustion and exhaust temperatures. Very hot exhaust gases can damage valves and pistons and will also cause the thin outer edges of the turbocharger turbine to glow and eventually melt.

▶ Cooling the intake air charge to the cylinders increases air density and oxygen content for improved combustion quality. More oxygen in the cylinders means better contact between fuel and oxygen for efficient, clean combustion.

▶ Charge air cooling provides additional air mass for cooling valves and pistons. Denser air means the air is heavier and can remove more heat from valves and pistons during valve overlap.

▶ Denser, cooler air improves fuel economy up to 5% due to improved combustion qualities.

▶ Charge air cooling allows more fuel to reach cylinders and provides higher power output per cubic inch (or centimeter) of cylinder displacement.

▶ JWAC lowers intake temperature by passing the boost air through a water-type heat exchanger. Today, JWACs are used in series turbocharging applications, where very high boost pressures produce even hotter intake air temperatures.

▶ The most popular method of cooling intake air is an air-to-air-type heat exchanger, which is an ATAAC and works by moving the heated charge air through an air-cooled heat exchanger.

▶ Most ATAACs are constructed of aluminum for maximum heat transfer and strength. To achieve optimum cooling, the inlet and outlet of the cooler may have different diameters to slow the airflow through the cooler to maximize heat transfer.

▶ Because coolers are often made from aluminum, they expand and contract when heated and cooled, so the cooler mounting system is designed to allow for thermal cycling.

▶ ATAACs use unique connector hoses that are often color coded to differentiate the hot and cold sides of the cooler. These hoses are made of chemically stable, durable silicone material.

▶ CACs can fail for a number of reasons, which can lead to air inlet restriction, excessive emissions, and high exhaust and cylinder temperatures. Internal or external restrictions to the CAC can cause low power.

▶ Thermal cycling can stress a CAC until it cracks. Cracks are common in areas of the cooler where inlet temperatures are highest and at the joint between the inlet tank and cooler tubes.

▶ Pressure-testing a CAC to determine the magnitude of air volume lost is the most important criterion for justifying cooler replacement. Small cracks do not warrant replacement.

▶ CAC core restriction has a variety of causes. For example, a shredded air filter gasket or ingestion of water or oil can reduce airflow inside a cooler core. A pressure drop test can determine whether excessive internal resistance to flow is because of an internal restriction.

Vocabulary Builder

air-to-air aftercooler (ATAAC) A system that uses ambient air to remove heat from the pressurized intake air.

charge air cooler (CAC) The system responsible for removing excess heat from the air charging the cylinders, which is known as charge air cooling, aftercooling, and intercooling; also known as an aftercooler and intercooler.

heat exchanger A system that transfers heat from coolant to the atmosphere.

interstage cooling The use of a liquid charge air cooler between two turbochargers connected in series. The air output of the first turbocharger is cooled before entering the second turbocharger.

jacket water aftercooler (JWAC) A system that uses engine coolant to remove heat from the pressurized intake air.

pressure drop test A test that measures internal restrictions of the intercooler core.

temperature differential test A test that measures cooler efficiency or whether the cooler is possibly externally restricted.

Review Questions

1. The _____ is a system that transfers heat from coolant to the atmosphere.
   a. coolant exchanger
   b. charge air cooler
   c. interstage cooler
   d. jacket water aftercooler

2. A system that uses engine coolant to remove heat from pressurized intake air is called a(n) _____.
   a. charge air cooler
   b. air-to-air aftercooler
   c. heat exchanger
   d. jacket water aftercooler

3. _____ is a system that uses ambient air to remove heat from the pressurized intake air.
   a. Interstage cooling
   b. Air-to-air aftercooler
   c. Jacket water aftercooler
   d. Charging air cooler

4. The use of a liquid charge air cooler between two turbochargers connected in series is called _____.
   a. heat exchanging
   b. charge air cooling
   c. interstage cooling
   d. jacket water cooling

5. The _____ is the system responsible for removing excess heat from the air charging the cylinders.
   a. charge air cooler
   b. air-to-air intercooler
   c. heat exchanging
   d. jacket air aftercooler

6. When gas temperatures increase, molecules spread farther apart, so the gas loses _____.
   a. mass
   b. density
   c. volume
   d. pressure

7. Increased air density and oxygen content improves _____ quality.
   a. transfer
   b. cycling
   c. combustion
   d. compression

8. Thermal _____ can stress a CAC until it cracks.
   a. cycling
   b. failure
   c. combustion
   d. transfer

9. High intake temperatures will cause the engine to _____ power or even shut down.
   a. transfer
   b. fail
   c. cycle
   d. derate

10. After a turbo _____, flushing a cooler thoroughly is important to prevent ingestion of debris into an engine.
    a. cycling
    b. failure
    c. transfer
    d. combustion

ASE-Type Questions

1. Technician A says a cubic foot of air contains fewer oxygen molecules when it is heated than it does when it is not. Technician B says a cubic foot of air, when heated, weighs less than when it is not heated. Who is correct?
   a. Technician A
   b. Technician B
   c. Both Technician A and Technician B
   d. Neither Technician A nor Technician B

2. Technician A says that prior to 1985, diesels needed to meet only a standard for exhaust opacity during a throttle snap test. Technician B says that diesels needed to meet only a standard for exhaust opacity during a throttle snap test prior to 1988. Who is correct?
   a. Technician A
   b. Technician B
   c. Both Technician A and Technician B
   d. Neither Technician A nor Technician B

3. Technician A says when an ATAAC is used to cool air between each stage of turbocharging, it is often referred to as intercooling. Technician B says during cold weather operation ATAACs require the use of a radiator cover called a winter front to maintain cab heat. Who is correct?
   a. Technician A
   b. Technician B
   c. Both Technician A and Technician B
   d. Neither Technician A nor Technician B

4. Technician A says CAC efficiency is calculated by measuring the temperature differential between the CAC's inlet and outlet. Technician B says because CACs are pressurized and the turbocharger produces excess air, CACs can tolerate small cracks without allowing dirt into the engine intake. Who is correct?
   a. Technician A
   b. Technician B
   c. Both Technician A and Technician B
   d. Neither Technician A nor Technician B

5. Technician A says to evaluate whether there is excessive internal resistance to flow because of an internal restriction, you must complete a pressure test. Technician B says a pressure drop test must be completed to evaluate whether there is excessive internal resistance to flow because of an internal restriction. Who is correct?
   a. Technician A
   b. Technician B
   c. Both Technician A and Technician B
   d. Neither Technician A nor Technician B

6. Technician A says cooler cores should be back-flushed with coolant after a turbocharger failure or if a core has become internally restricted. Technician B says cooler cores should be back-flushed with solvent, coolant, and compressed air after a turbocharger failure or if a core has become internally restricted. Who is correct?
   a. Technician A
   b. Technician B
   c. Both Technician A and Technician B
   d. Neither Technician A nor Technician B

7. Technician A says a pressure test should be used to determine justification for the replacement of a CAC. Technician B says justification for the replacement of a CAC is best determined using a temperature differential test. Who is correct?
   a. Technician A
   b. Technician B
   c. Both Technician A and Technician B
   d. Neither Technician A nor Technician B

8. Technician A says underhood noises during heavily loaded operating conditions can be pinpointed to improper cooler mounting. Technician B says underhood noises during heavily loaded operating conditions can be pinpointed to a defective turbocharger. Who is correct?
   a. Technician A
   b. Technician B
   c. Both Technician A and Technician B
   d. Neither Technician A nor Technician B

9. Technician A says a properly functioning CAC has a maximum temperature differential of 30 degrees Fahrenheit between air intake temperature and outside air when airflow is 30 mph. Technician B says a properly functioning CAC has a maximum temperature differential of 35 degrees Fahrenheit between air intake temperature and outside air when airflow is 48 km/h. Who is correct?
   a. Technician A
   b. Technician B
   c. Both Technician A and Technician B
   d. Neither Technician A nor Technician B

10. Technician A says if the side to side pressure in an ATAAC drops more than 3 psi, you should check the cooler for internal restrictions and leaks. Technician B says if the side to side pressure in an ATAAC drops more than 4 psi, you should check the cooler for internal restrictions and leaks. Who is correct?
    a. Technician A
    b. Technician B
    c. Both Technician A and Technician B
    d. Neither Technician A nor Technician B

CHAPTER 33
Exhaust Aftertreatment Systems

NATEF Tasks

Diesel Engines

General

- Inspect fuel, oil, diesel exhaust fluid (DEF) and coolant levels, and condition; determine needed action. (pp 946–947, 950–951)

Air Induction and Exhaust Systems

- Inspect exhaust aftertreatment devices; determine needed action. (pp 948–951)

Preventive Maintenance and Inspection

Engine System

Air Induction and Exhaust System

- Inspect diesel exhaust fluid (DEF) system, to include tanks, lines, gauge pump, and filter. (pp 950–951)
- Inspect selective catalyst reduction (SCR) system; including diesel exhaust fluid (DEF) for proper levels, leaks, mounting, and connections. (pp 948–951)

Knowledge Objectives

1. Describe the functions, construction, and application of diesel exhaust emission aftertreatment systems. (pp 933–950)
2. Explain the principles of operation of diesel exhaust emission aftertreatment systems. (pp 933–950)
3. Describe and explain methods for performing inspection and diagnostic procedures on diesel exhaust emission aftertreatment systems. (pp 950–953)
4. Recommend maintenance or repairs on diesel exhaust emission aftertreatment systems. (pp 950–953)

Skills Objectives

After reading this chapter, you will be able to:
1. Perform an active regeneration procedure. (p 950)
   SKILL DRILL 33-1
2. Perform a forced DPF regeneration. (p 951)
   SKILL DRILL 33-2
3. Replace a DPF. (p 952) **SKILL DRILL 33-3**

▶ Introduction

Greener and cleaner diesel engines now use a variety of emission-reduction technologies centered in the exhaust system. These include **exhaust gas recirculation (EGR)** (a technology that reduces oxides of nitrogen [NO_x] by mixing exhaust gas with fresh intake air), **diesel particulate filters (DPFs)** (which trap black carbon soot and other particulate matter [PM]), and a variety of catalytic converters that remove hydrocarbons (HCs), carbon monoxide (CO), and NO_x. **Selective catalyst reduction (SCR)** is an exhaust aftertreatment system designed to break down NO_x in the exhaust system into harmless substances using a **catalyst**, a material that speeds up or slows down chemical reactions without entering the reaction. SCR using a liquid **urea** (an ammonia-carrying molecule that breaks down in hot exhaust gas) injection, **lean NO_x traps (LNTs)** (a catalyst mechanism that selects and destroys only NO_x emissions without the use of liquid diesel exhaust fluid; also referred to as hydrogen-SCR and NO_x adsorbers), and **NO_x adsorber catalysts (NACs)** (a unique catalyst material that stores NO_x emissions and then decomposes the NO_x under specialized exhaust conditions) are leading technologies for NO_x cleanup centered in the exhaust system. These systems represent the latest developments in diesel technology, and while complex in design and function, they are easily understood using a systematic approach, examining the construction and operation of each device associated with removing specific exhaust emissions **FIGURE 33-1**.

▶ Fundamentals of Exhaust Emission Aftertreatment Systems

To meet Tier II Environmental Protection Agency (EPA) emission standards scheduled for 2007 and 2010, drastic reductions in diesel emissions were necessary. From 2004 to 2007, and again in 2010, standards required a reduction in emissions of almost 90% **FIGURE 33-2**. Because in-cylinder, engine-based emission control strategies are inadequate to meet emission reduction targets, the exhaust system became the focal point for technology to remove harmful emissions.

Exhaust aftertreatment devices, such as catalytic converters, that convert CO, HCs, and NO_x have been successful. They have been used since the early 1970s on spark-ignition, gasoline-fueled engines, but their application to diesel engine exhaust reduction presents some unique technical difficulties. Cold exhaust temperatures and excess air content in diesel exhaust (relative to gasoline counterparts) are the biggest technical challenges with diesel catalysts.

▶ Types of Exhaust Emission Aftertreatment Systems

Catalytic converters speed up chemical reactions of noxious exhaust emissions and change them into harmless combustion by-products. Exhaust heat, along with special metals (e.g., platinum and palladium) embedded into a base or substrate (e.g., ceramic or sintered metal), is a typical element of a catalytic converter. The many types of converters are classified according to the noxious emission converted or the type of chemical reaction that takes place in the catalyst material. The different kinds of converters include:

- Diesel oxidation
- Catalyzed DPF
- SCR
- LNT
- NO_x adsorbers **TABLE 33-1** and **TABLE 33-2**

Diesel Oxidation Converters

An oxidation catalytic converter causes oxygen (O_2) to chemically combine with noxious emissions such as HC and CO **FIGURE 33-3**. The oxidation process is like flameless combustion

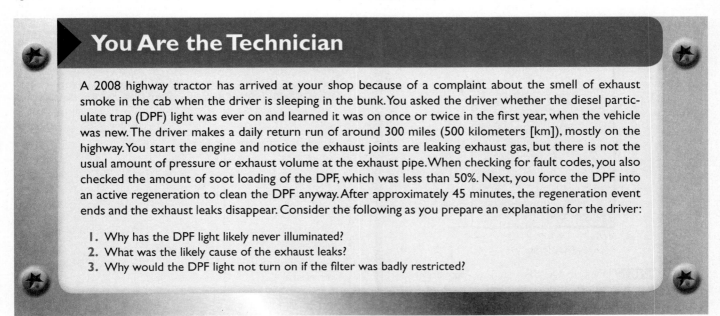

You Are the Technician

A 2008 highway tractor has arrived at your shop because of a complaint about the smell of exhaust smoke in the cab when the driver is sleeping in the bunk. You asked the driver whether the diesel particulate trap (DPF) light was ever on and learned it was on once or twice in the first year, when the vehicle was new. The driver makes a daily return run of around 300 miles (500 kilometers [km]), mostly on the highway. You start the engine and notice the exhaust joints are leaking exhaust gas, but there is not the usual amount of pressure or exhaust volume at the exhaust pipe. When checking for fault codes, you also checked the amount of soot loading of the DPF, which was less than 50%. Next, you force the DPF into an active regeneration to clean the DPF anyway. After approximately 45 minutes, the regeneration event ends and the exhaust leaks disappear. Consider the following as you prepare an explanation for the driver:

1. Why has the DPF light likely never illuminated?
2. What was the likely cause of the exhaust leaks?
3. Why would the DPF light not turn on if the filter was badly restricted?

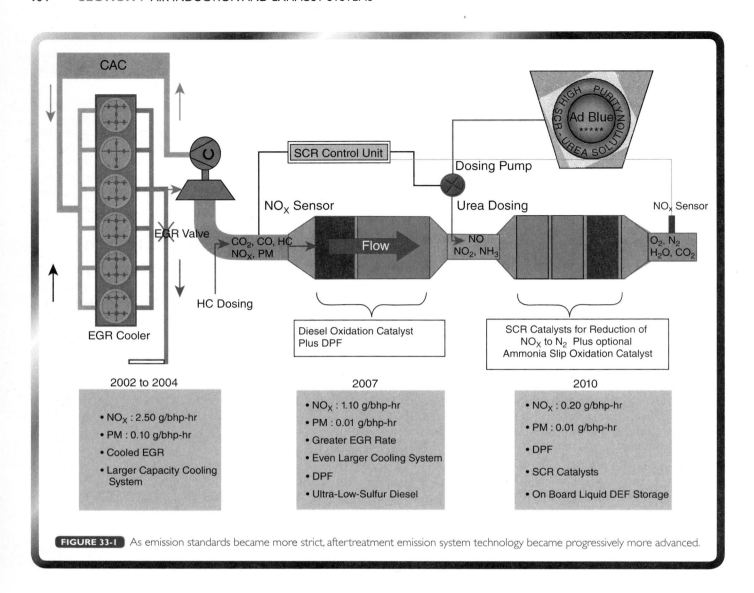

FIGURE 33-1 As emission standards became more strict, aftertreatment emission system technology became progressively more advanced.

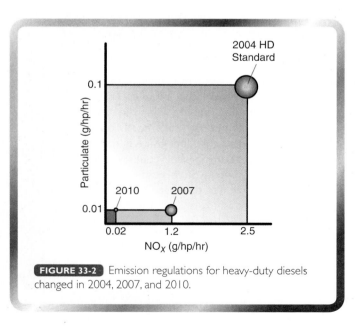

FIGURE 33-2 Emission regulations for heavy-duty diesels changed in 2004, 2007, and 2010.

TABLE 33-1: Exhaust Catalyst Reactions

Technology	Gasoline Engines	Diesel Engines
Two-way (oxidation) catalytic converters	CO, HCs	CO, HCs, particulate matter (PM)
Three-way catalytic converters	CO, HCs, NO_x	N/A
SCR	N/A	NO_x
NO_x adsorber catalytic converters	N/A	NO_x
Diesel particulate filters	N/A	CO, HCs, PM
Four-way (combined) diesel catalytic systems	N/A	CO, HCs, PM, NO_x

TABLE 33-2: Summary of Exhaust Catalytic Technology for Diesel Engines

Catalyst Technology	Reaction Type	Reduced Emissions
Diesel oxidation catalyst (DOC)	Oxidation	CO, HCs, PM, including SOF and odor
SCR	Selective catalytic reduction by urea	NO_x
Lean NO_x Catalyst (LNC) $DeNO_x$ converters	Selective catalytic reduction by HCs	NO_x, CO, HCs, PM
LNT	Adsorption (trapping) of NO_x from lean exhaust followed by release and catalytic reduction under rich- fuel, oxygen-lean conditions	NO_x, CO, HCs

FIGURE 33-3 An oxidation converter with a silicon carbide substrate is attached to this 3406C Caterpillar engine. This configuration is commonly used in underground mining for powering air compressors and other machines with a hydro-mechanical fuel system.

of these emissions inside the converter, which turns the emissions into water (H_2O) and carbon dioxide (CO_2). Diesel oxidation converters also decrease the mass of diesel PM emissions 5–90% by oxidizing some of the carbon in the particulate. Because oxidation converters clean up two noxious emissions, they are called two-way converters.

Catalyst Substrate

Oxidation converters consist of a stainless steel canister that usually contains a ceramic material formed into a honeycomb-like structure called a substrate or catalyst support. There are no moving parts, only a huge area created over the surface of the substrate. The substrate has a coating—called a washcoat—of catalytic precious metals, such as platinum or palladium. This is the active material that causes the chemical reaction between noxious emissions and O_2 in the exhaust after combustion.

The ceramic substrate used by diesel oxidation catalysts (DOCs) is a flow-through type. This means channels through the ceramic are parallel to one another and travel from one end of the catalyst brick to the other. Low-temperature-design diesel catalysts need a minimum temperature of 400°F (204°C) before O_2 can oxidize, or burn, CO and HCs (gaseous and liquid). This process also reduces the characteristic pungent diesel odor caused by unburned HC aromatic molecules in the exhaust. In summary, the reactions are as follows:

$$CO + O_2 = CO_2 + H_2O$$
$$HC + O_2 = CO_2 + H_2O$$

Problems with Diesel Catalyst Technology

Diesel catalyst technology is not without problems. The first difficulty in cleaning up diesel exhaust using oxidation catalytic converters is the relative coolness of diesel exhaust temperatures. Unlike gasoline-fueled engines, the lean burn combustion strategy of a diesel engine means exhaust gas is diluted with excess air, reducing its temperature. Even under moderate to heavy loads, the exhaust temperature of many diesels rarely rises above 300–400°F (149–204°C). A conventional oxidation catalytic converter found on a gasoline-fueled vehicle requires exhaust temperatures as high as 500°F (260°C) to effectively operate, which means conventional oxidation converter operation in a diesel is ineffective.

In addition, the level of sulfur in diesel fuel negatively affects the temperature level at which chemical reactions in some catalytic materials occur. The use of close-coupled oxidation converters minimizes the problem of cool exhaust temperatures by locating the converter as close as possible to the exhaust manifold. However, new catalyst materials developed uniquely for diesels enable the effective use of low-temperature oxidation of HC and CO emissions.

Low-Temperature Oxidation Catalysts

New designs of oxidation catalytic converters are able to burn HC and CO emissions even at low temperatures. One significant oxidation catalyst technology incorporates HC-trapping materials into a crystalline-shaped catalyst substrate called zeolite, which is similar to filtering sand used for pools. Iron or copper mixed with zeolite are commonly used in North American catalysts. This material functions like a molecular sieve, trapping the noxious emissions while letting exhaust gas pass through the substrate wall. When HCs are emitted from the combustion chamber, this converter substrate captures them. The zeolite will then adsorb HCs when exhaust temperature are low, such as during engine idle or part throttle. However, when the exhaust temperature increases when under load, the HCs are released from the substrate and oxidized by the platinum-based washcoat catalyst. These converters begin to catalyze at approximately 360°F (182°C), which is much lower than traditional catalyst substrate materials.

Low-temperature oxidation catalysts will typically reduce emissions of HC by 50% and CO by 40%. Operation of these converters is even more efficient when ultra-low sulfur diesel (ULSD) fuel is used. Efficiencies for HC conversion using ULSD are greater than 90%.

DPFs

The primary purpose of a DPF is to remove soot and other solid particles from diesel exhaust, rendering the exhaust completely smokeless. While diesel engines have been virtually smokeless since 2002, the DPF eliminates the smallest microscopic particles down to 50 nanometers. Introduced for the 2007MY, the DPF is needed to meet the 90% reduction in particulate emission compared to 2002 levels.

The concept for removing PM is relatively simple. Soot and other exhaust-borne particles must pass through a wall-flow-type filter, which traps them before reaching the exhaust outlet. Wall-flow filter media permits only the gas portion of the exhaust to pass through the filter material **FIGURE 33-4**. This technology is effective enough to remove up to 99% of solid PM from the engine exhaust. Because PM is composed of some non-solid matter, overall efficiencies are slightly less than this.

Trapped soot and other particles collected on the walls of the filter will eventually plug the filter and produce high exhaust backpressure. Regeneration, a renewal process, purges soot from the filter and cleans it. In all DPFs, this process involves burning the soot out of the filter **FIGURE 33-5**.

Regeneration

Heat for regeneration comes from two sources. One method is through natural chemical reactions in the catalysts. The other method involves supplemental heating of the DPF with fuel or another heat source.

Passive Regeneration

Passive regeneration occurs if the engine is operated under sufficient load to increase exhaust temperatures to 482°F (250°C) or

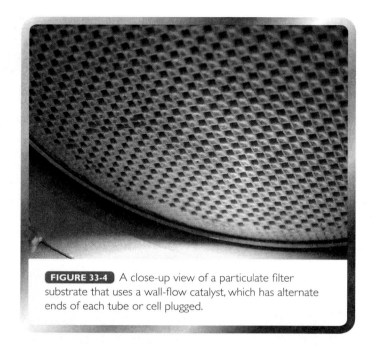

FIGURE 33-4 A close-up view of a particulate filter substrate that uses a wall-flow catalyst, which has alternate ends of each tube or cell plugged.

hotter. O_2 will combine with soot to eliminate soot when the DPF is hot enough, producing CO_2. Passive regeneration also uses nitric oxide (NO), which is normally produced in the combustion chamber. Converting NO to nitrogen dioxide (NO_2) produces heat. NO_2 also combines with soot to produce CO_2 and nitrogen (N_2) **FIGURE 33-6**. Supplemental heating of the DPF using electrical heating elements is possible but not currently used by any manufacturer. In heavy-duty Class 8 vehicles operating mostly on highways, passive regeneration takes place more than 85% of the time.

Passive regeneration looks like this:

$$\text{Combustion with } O_2\text{: Soot} + O_2 = CO_2 + \text{Heat}$$
$$\text{Combustion with } NO_2\text{: Soot} + NO_2 = CO_2 + N_2 + \text{Heat}$$

Conditions necessary for passive regeneration require the vehicle to be driven faster than 30 miles per hour (mph) (48 kilometers per hour [km/h]) for 20–30 minutes for a full regeneration to occur. Passive regeneration occurs without any intervention by or awareness of the driver.

To enhance passive regeneration, many diesel engines are equipped with throttle plates that restrict airflow into the engine to increase exhaust temperature. Reducing airflow limits the dilution of exhaust gas with excess air, which would normally lower exhaust temperature. Some manufacturers also intentionally lower boost pressure from variable geometry turbochargers (VGTs). This has the same effect as restricting air intake flow. A post-combustion injection of fuel into the exhaust stream contributes approximately 45% of the increase in exhaust temperature. Electronically controlled throttle plates contribute approximately 35%, and 10% of the remaining heat comes from the VGT, which will change exhaust temperatures by altering intake boost and **exhaust backpressure** at idle. Exhaust backpressure is exhaust pressure buildup in the exhaust system, and it can occur before or after the turbocharger. While the process of passive regeneration is supposed to be transparent to the driver, lowering boost pressure or throttling the air intake to increase exhaust temperatures can

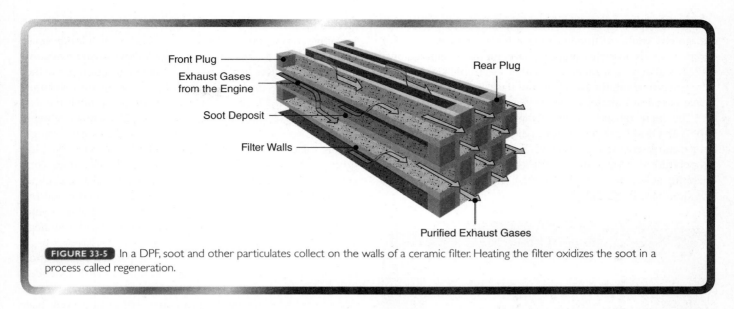

FIGURE 33-5 In a DPF, soot and other particulates collect on the walls of a ceramic filter. Heating the filter oxidizes the soot in a process called regeneration.

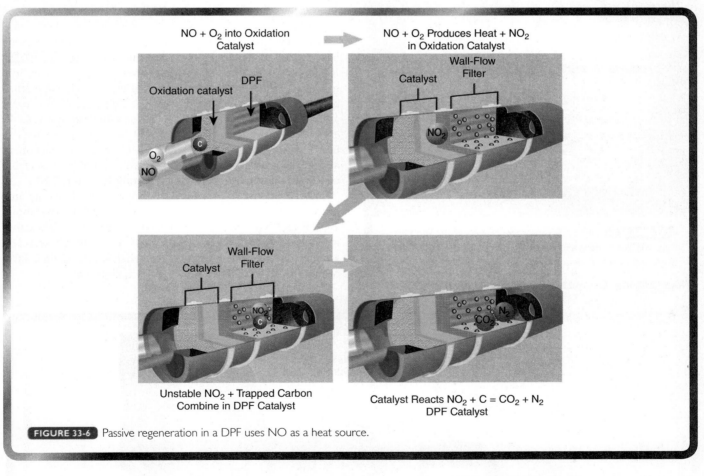

FIGURE 33-6 Passive regeneration in a DPF uses NO as a heat source.

limit engine power output. For this reason, some manufacturers install a warning light or display information on a driver display unit to inform the driver that passive regeneration is taking place.

Prolonged low-load operation, which prevents the DPF from passively regenerating, also requires an alert for the driver to change driving style. A warning light alerts the driver to increase engine speed and load by driving faster than 45 mph

(70 km/h) for 20–30 minutes to quickly regenerate the filter. However, the minimum speed of 30 mpg (48 km/h) is generally not enough for regeneration after the DPF is soot loaded.

The DPF warning light is normally off. When on, it alerts the driver to change the engine's duty-cycle, or driving mode, to increase heat in the exhaust system. That means rather than stop-and-go driving, a steady, moderate speed is necessary. If a change in engine operation is not possible, such as in stop-and-go city traffic or underground mine operation, an **active regeneration** is possible using original equipment manufacturer (OEM) software, a scanner, or another electronic service tool. A regeneration inhibit switch in the dash is more commonly toggled to allow a stationary active regeneration to occur.

The high exhaust system temperature (HEST) warning light is an OEM light that indicates higher than normal exhaust temperatures during regeneration. For example, if the exhaust temperature is greater than 750°F (400°C) and the vehicle is operating at less than 5 mph (8 km/h), the HEST warning light will illuminate **FIGURE 33-7**.

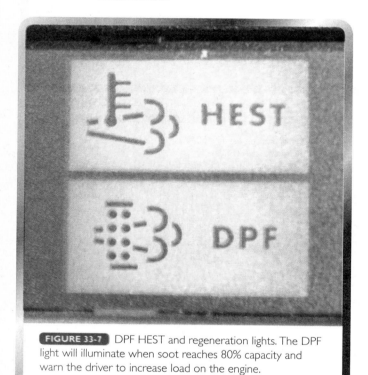

FIGURE 33-7 DPF HEST and regeneration lights. The DPF light will illuminate when soot reaches 80% capacity and warn the driver to increase load on the engine.

Active Regeneration

In active regeneration, the DPF is heated by adding small amounts of fuel to the exhaust stream. A downstream oxidation converter produces heat through a catalytic reaction of the fuel **FIGURE 33-8**. Flameless combustion of fuel in the oxidation converter heats the DPF as exhaust gas passes through the oxidation converter into the DPF. Fuel for supplemental heating is supplied two ways: One is to inject fuel into the exhaust using a dosing valve. Located in the exhaust after the turbocharger, the dosing valve operates like a fuel injector under electronic control module (ECM) control. Another, less popular, technique is to use a post-combustion injection event from common rail injectors to supply fuel. The problems associated with biofuel contamination of engine oil has almost eliminated this strategy since 2012.

Active regeneration occurs only if passive regeneration cannot maintain or reduce the soot level in the DPF. Extended idling of a vehicle, prolonged low-speed, low-load operation, or delivery vehicles making frequent short trips can prevent passive regeneration from lowering DPF soot levels.

Active regeneration only takes place when a fault code for excessive soot loading is set because accumulations of soot have exceeded an anticipated threshold value **FIGURE 33-9**. It is important to remember that this level is based on theoretical models of DPF soot loading given a variety of engine operating conditions, such as fuel consumption and duty cycle. Soot levels are not measured values because sensor values are not reliable enough to measure the degree of soot loading. Sensor data is used only to validate the DPF system behavior and correct operation. Data readings that exceed expected thresholds will set fault codes and illuminate the malfunction indicator lamp (MIL).

During active regeneration, the supplemental heating and burning soot will cause the DPF's temperature to rise above 1000°F (550°C). On light- and medium-duty vehicles, active regeneration needs OEM service tools or a properly featured scanner. A fault code is typically set when soot loading is 80% or more, and the DPF warning lamp will illuminate.

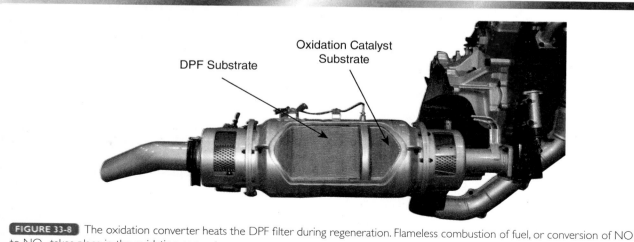

FIGURE 33-8 The oxidation converter heats the DPF filter during regeneration. Flameless combustion of fuel, or conversion of NO to NO_2, takes place in the oxidation converter.

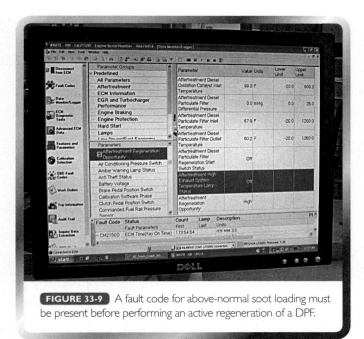

FIGURE 33-9 A fault code for above-normal soot loading must be present before performing an active regeneration of a DPF.

TECHNICIAN TIP

Active regeneration is determined by an algorithm that predicts when soot loading will reach a particular threshold value and is not measured by pressure drop across the DPF filter. Activation of a warning light is based on an anticipated level of soot accumulation, not a measured quantity.

Problems with theoretical models regularly occur in the field when the DPF is almost completely plugged and no DPF warning light or prompt for active regeneration is given. Performing a forced regeneration using software will clear the soot from the DPF and restore normal system functioning.

There are two common active regeneration strategies: from the injectors and from a dosing valve. In the injectors strategy, the ECM will command additional injections from common rail injectors before bottom dead center (BBDC) or just after bottom dead center (ABDC) during the exhaust stroke. Fuel is vaporized in the exhaust gas, where it undergoes flameless combustion reactions in the oxidization catalyst. One major drawback to this technique is fuel dilution of engine oil because fuel can pass the piston rings with other blow-by gases. Biodiesel fuels present special problems because they can accelerate the deterioration of engine oil **FIGURE 33-10**.

When active regeneration occurs after activating the dosing valve, which is also called the seventh injector or the HC doser, supplemental heating of the DPF occurs by spraying fuel directly into the exhaust after the turbocharger. The fuel is then catalyzed in the oxidation converter upstream of the DPF filter **FIGURE 33-11**. Flameless combustion will raise the DPF substrate temperature.

Active stationary regeneration or active driving regeneration can take place depending on the manufacturer's options. If an active stationary regeneration, also called a parked regeneration, takes place, the vehicle must be parked away from any environment that may potentially ignite due to exhaust heat from the regeneration event (for example, garbage in a landfill, tall grass and other

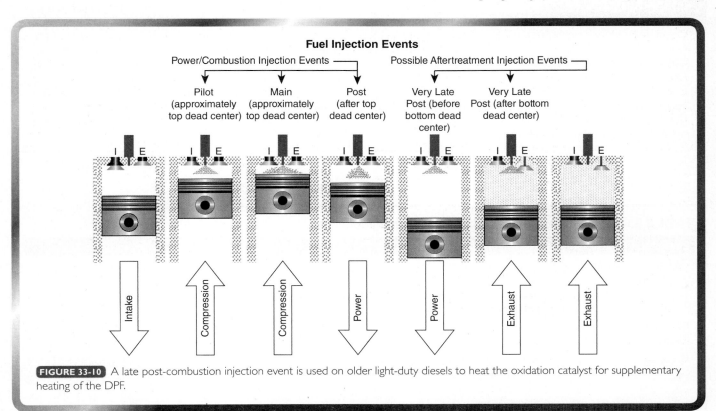

FIGURE 33-10 A late post-combustion injection event is used on older light-duty diesels to heat the oxidation catalyst for supplementary heating of the DPF.

HC Doser

Coolant Lines

FIGURE 33-11 The dosing valve sprays fuel into the exhaust, where it undergoes flameless combustion in the oxidation converter. Exhaust gas passing through the oxidation converter carries heat into the DPF, which combusts soot to regenerate, or renew, the filter.

FIGURE 33-12 The double-walled pipe end is designed to draw fresh, cool outside air into the exhaust outlet to dilute the intense exhaust heat encountered during DPF regeneration.

vegetation, or near fuel islands) **FIGURE 33-12**. The regeneration inhibit switch must be depressed for 5 seconds after the control module has verified safe conditions for an active regeneration are met. These conditions include no vehicle speed, the transmission in neutral, and the brakes applied **TABLE 33-3** and **TABLE 33-4**.

TECHNICIAN TIP

Occasionally, DPFs will regenerate too frequently, even constantly. One common cause is defective fuel injectors. Leaking injectors dribbling fuel will cause DPFs to load very quickly, prompting regeneration. Check for and repair any fuel-related problems before making repairs to the DPF aftertreatment system. Too frequent regeneration will overheat and melt or crack a DPF filter. A filter loaded with ash that needs cleaning or replacement will also frequently attempt to regenerate.

TECHNICIAN TIP

To actively regenerate a DPF, a code indicating high soot loading must be set. If the DPF light is on, the driver can initiate an active regeneration by toggling a regeneration inhibit switch on the dash. On light-duty vehicles that weigh less than 14,000 lb (6350 kg) GVWR, only OEM software or a properly featured scanner can be used to force an active regeneration of a DPF. These vehicles are not equipped with a regeneration inhibit switch. Before an active regeneration will take place, the vehicle usually must be stationary, in neutral, with the parking brakes applied. Whenever a new green DPF is installed, an active regeneration should be forced. This enhances the DPF's soot storage capacity.

TABLE 33-3: Features of Active and Passive Regeneration

Features	Active Regeneration	Passive Regeneration
General information	• Requires a temperature of approximately 1112°F (600°C) • Excess HCs and O_2 in exhaust stream provide fuel to raise temperature of catalyst	• NO_2-based • Reaction occurs beginning at 482°F (250°C) • NO_2 is a powerful oxidant.
Gas used in regeneration reaction	• O_2 in exhaust gas stream • Stand-alone catalyzed DPF with oxidation converter	• NO_2 is made from NO in exhaust stream and requires an oxidation converter with the DPF
Initialization	• OEM or aftermarket software • Stored fault and toggled inhibit switch • Only on 14,000 lb (6350 kg) GVWR and below	• When exhaust temperatures and exhaust gas are adequate to promote oxidation of soot

TABLE 33-4: Exhaust Surface Temperatures

Exhaust Surface	Normal Temperature	Regeneration Temperature
Pipe surface ahead of the particulate trap	600–800°F (316–427°C)	600–1000°F (316–538°C)
Surface of the particulate trap	350°F (177°C)	500°F (260°C)
Pipe surface at the top of the particulate trap	600°F (316°C)	900°F (482°C)
Exhaust temperature at tailpipe exit	750°F (399°C)	1150°F (621°C)

TECHNICIAN TIP

After soot loading reaches 100% of the DPF capacity, the DPF warning light generally begins to flash and an alarm may sound. The yellow check engine light will also illuminate and a 15% power derate condition will happen to encourage service. When loading reaches 120%, the engine will shut down and DPF regeneration should not take place. Soot in the DPF could cause a thermal runaway, melting and severely damaging the substrate.

DPF Catalyst Substrate

DPF catalyst substrate is available in different materials. Cordierite, a ceramic-like material, is a common and inexpensive material used for many converters in North America. Silicon carbide is more durable than cordierite, and capable of tolerating higher exhaust regeneration temperatures, but it is considerably more expensive. Metal foil converters are popular in Europe. These are made from sintered metal, which is porous and foamed and reduces exhaust backpressure. Sintered metal foil catalyst substrate can handle 2.5 times more ash than ceramic-based substrates, which promises to make the filter as long-lasting as the vehicle's normal service life before servicing is needed to remove the ash from the filter. When metal foil converters are used, vehicle owners should incur no additional costs for DPF service or aftermarket part replacement during the normal life of the vehicle **FIGURE 33-13**.

Because the substrate is a wall-flow material, ash accumulates in the DPF filter tubes. Ash is inorganic, which means it has no carbon content to burn. Ash accumulates in the filter as engine oil is burned. Oil additives, which contain ash, will find their way into the DPF filter. Too much ash will plug a DPF just as too much soot will. Because ash cannot be burned off during regeneration, the filter requires removal and cleaning. Filters are removed from the vehicle and back-flushed with a combination of vacuuming and pulses of compressed air **FIGURE 33-14**. The service interval for DPF filter cleaning depends on the size of the filter and the amount of oil an engine burns **FIGURE 33-15**. Low-ash oils are mandatory for diesel engines that use DPFs to prevent premature plugging with ash.

TECHNICIAN TIP

When handling DPF and other catalytic converters, take care to prevent damage to converters through rough handling. Water entering a DPF with ash loading will harden to a concrete-like material and prevent flow through the DPF, which will cause high exhaust backpressure.

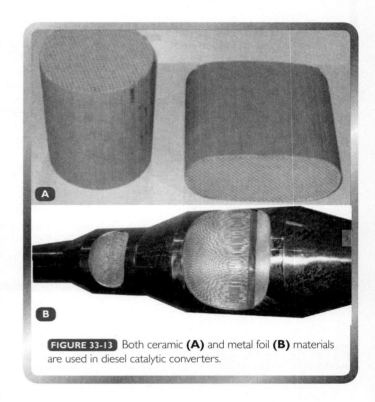

FIGURE 33-13 Both ceramic **(A)** and metal foil **(B)** materials are used in diesel catalytic converters.

FIGURE 33-14 The amount of ash accumulated in a DPF over the course of one year.

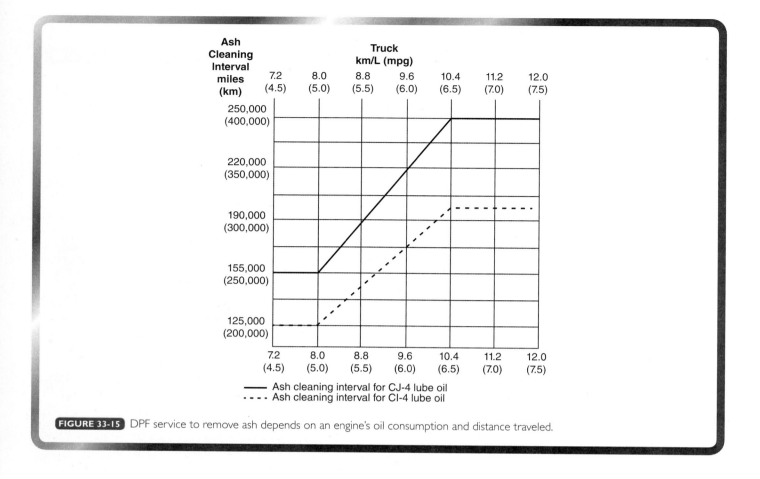

FIGURE 33-15 DPF service to remove ash depends on an engine's oil consumption and distance traveled.

TECHNICIAN TIP

DPFs are made from several removable sections to allow for disassembly. The particulate filter will accumulate ash over time that cannot be removed through regeneration. Depending on oil consumption and quality, service may require removing and disassembling the DPF to clean out the accumulated ash. Commercial equipment reverse flushes the DPF filter with compressed air while also vacuuming and collecting the dust for safe disposal. Replacement service filters are usually filters that have undergone cleaning at another facility.

SCR

SCR is a process where liquid urea is sprayed into the exhaust stream to destroy NO_x molecules. Diesel exhaust fluid (DEF) is the generic name of the liquid, which is a clear, nontoxic, and nonflammable combination of water and urea. The urea mixes with the exhaust gas and decomposes to form ammonia (NH_3), which reacts with NO_x. This is a **reduction reaction**—which removes O_2 from NO_x molecules, converting them into N_2 and O_2. An **oxidation reaction** adds O_2 to HCs and CO to produce H_2O and CO_2 plus heat **FIGURE 33-16** and **FIGURE 33-17**.

A catalytic converter is not necessary for any of these reactions. However, passing the mixture over a substrate platinum

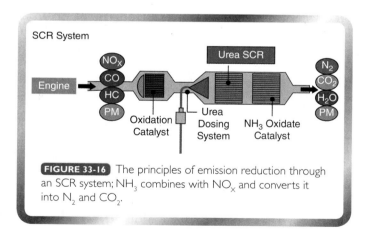

FIGURE 33-16 The principles of emission reduction through an SCR system; NH_3 combines with NO_x and converts it into N_2 and CO_2.

catalyst causes a reduction reaction to happen faster and at lower temperatures. Because reduction reactions cannot normally take place in the oxygen-rich environment of lean exhaust and specifically target NO_x, urea is said to selectively combine with NO_x, giving SCR its name.

SCR Advantages and Disadvantages

The advantage of SCR technology is that it enables the lowest fuel consumption of existing exhaust aftertreatment technologies

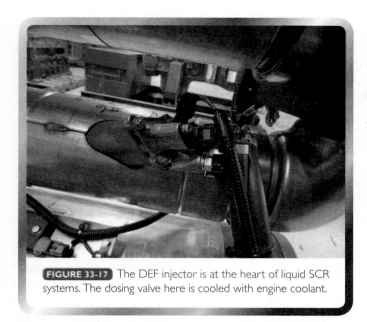

FIGURE 33-17 The DEF injector is at the heart of liquid SCR systems. The dosing valve here is cooled with engine coolant.

while improving power output, engine durability, and longevity. SCR is essentially better than in-cylinder processes to reduce emissions.

Until the development of SCR, manufacturers in North America had to depend on increased EGR flow and retarded injection timing to reduce NO_x. These strategies increase soot production and lower power output. Because SCR cleans up exhaust emissions, less EGR is necessary and injection timing is advanced, which optimizes power and fuel economy.

Advanced injection timing and lower EGR rates accompanying the use of SCR have other benefits:

- Reduced active regenerations of soot filter plus advanced injection timing produces less soot.
- Higher specific power output per cubic inch displacement
- Longer engine life from:
  - Lower cylinder pressures because the turbocharger compressor pressure ratio is reduced to compensate for power lost using EGR gas
  - Lower piston speeds because stroking a block to compensate for power lost to EGR is not necessary (stroking = longer piston stroke)
- Increased reliability from:
  - Reduced heat loads with lower EGR rates
  - Diminished soot loading of oil
  - Fewer DPF regenerations

SCR also tolerates sulfur in the fuel. In addition to eliminating over 90% of NO_x emissions, SCR catalysts installed upstream of the DPF typically convert 20–40% of particulate matter (PM) to CO_2 and H_2O. In Europe, liquid SCR has been used since 2005, enabling diesel-powered vehicles there to reduce both NO_x and PM emissions to meet European emission standards without a particulate filter.

DEF consumption is typically 1–4% of total fuel consumption, depending on driving habits, load, and road conditions. The average is 2%. The EPA durability regulations for emission systems include the provision that emission-related maintenance cannot occur before 100,000 miles (160,934 km) of use (150,000 miles [241,402 km] for medium- and heavy-duty engines) or before 100,000-mile (160,934-km) intervals thereafter. Because the SCR catalyst in a urea SCR system does not function without a reducing agent, manufacturers must satisfy the five guidelines to maintain vehicle compliance according to EPA guidance if the DEF level is depleted:

- Driver warning system (i.e., a dash warning light)
- Driver inducement (i.e., reduced engine power, fuel filler lockout, no restarting after fueling if DEF is depleted)
- System identification of incorrect reducing agent—the system would identify if its reservoir were filled with only water or other liquid
- Tamper-resistant design—the warning, driver-inducement, and operational systems (i.e., sensor wiring and dosing injector) are not easily deactivated
- Durable design—the system must operate effectively to 120,000 or 150,000 miles (193,121 or 241,402 km), depending on certification criteria

Liquid SCR storage requires additional precautions for low temperatures. DEF can freeze at 12°F (−11°C). As a result, the storage tank and lines require heating and insulating **FIGURE 33-18**.

Location of DPF and SCR Catalysts

Catalysts are configured in two ways. The DPF is upstream or downstream of the SCR.

DPF Upstream of the SCR

Placing the DPF upstream of the SCR is the most common configuration for two reasons. First, heat energy required for regeneration is minimized because the DPF is closer to the engine's exhaust ports. As a result, active regeneration requires less fuel and passive regeneration can occur more easily. Second, more NO_2 is available for passive regeneration when the DPF is upstream of the SCR rather than downstream.

Placing the DPF upstream of the SCR does have a risk. High DPF regeneration temperatures can damage catalysts **FIGURE 33-19**.

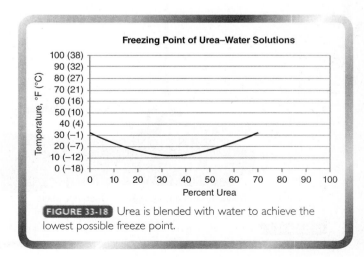

FIGURE 33-18 Urea is blended with water to achieve the lowest possible freeze point.

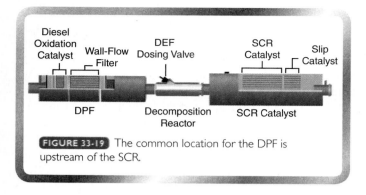

FIGURE 33-19 The common location for the DPF is upstream of the SCR.

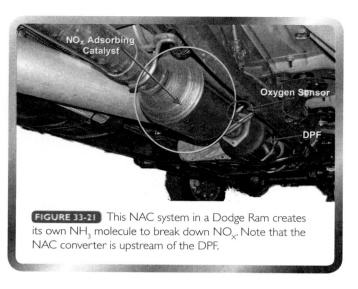

FIGURE 33-21 This NAC system in a Dodge Ram creates its own NH_3 molecule to break down NO_x. Note that the NAC converter is upstream of the DPF.

DPF Downstream of the SCR

Sometimes, the DPF is placed downstream of the SCR because this configuration can minimize the need for regeneration of the DPF. That is because an SCR catalyst will eliminate substantial amounts of soot before reaching the DPF **FIGURE 33-20**.

The primary disadvantage of downstream DPF placement is cooler exhaust temperature. The relatively cool exhaust temperature even after cold start-up limits the effectiveness of the DPF catalyst.

NO_x Adsorbing and Lean NO_x Traps

NO_x adsorber technology is a catalyst strategy for removing NO_x in the low-temperature, oxygen-rich exhaust environment of diesel engines **FIGURE 33-21**. Adsorber means the NO_x emissions are adsorbed, or temporarily trapped and stored, by the catalyst material. The stored NO_x is removed in a two-step

reaction by temporarily inducing an oxygen-depleted, fuel-rich exhaust condition **FIGURE 33-22**. Moving the exhaust O_2 concentration from high to low, or lean, during regeneration conditions lends the system the name lean NO_x trap (LNT). Other names for this technology include $DeNO_x$ or hydrocarbon-SCR.

The main advantage of this catalytic converter is that the system requires no maintenance. It requires no onboard storage of liquid urea. Cleaning up emissions in the exhaust minimizes the use of power robbing, fuel-consuming in-cylinder operating strategies to prevent NO_x formation. Injection timing, EGR rate, boost pressure, and other variables can be optimized for

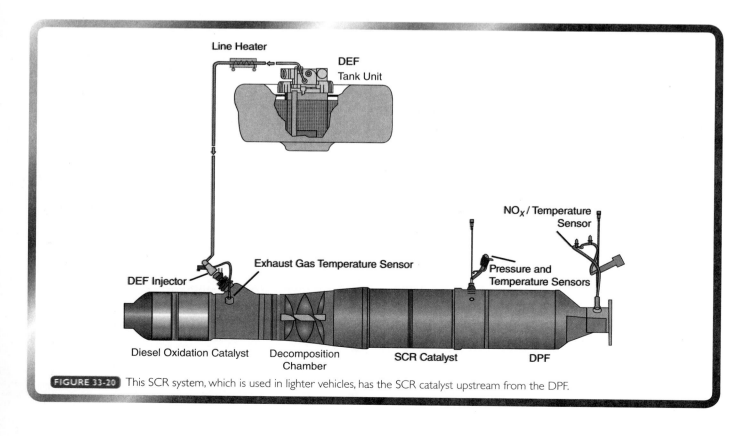

FIGURE 33-20 This SCR system, which is used in lighter vehicles, has the SCR catalyst upstream from the DPF.

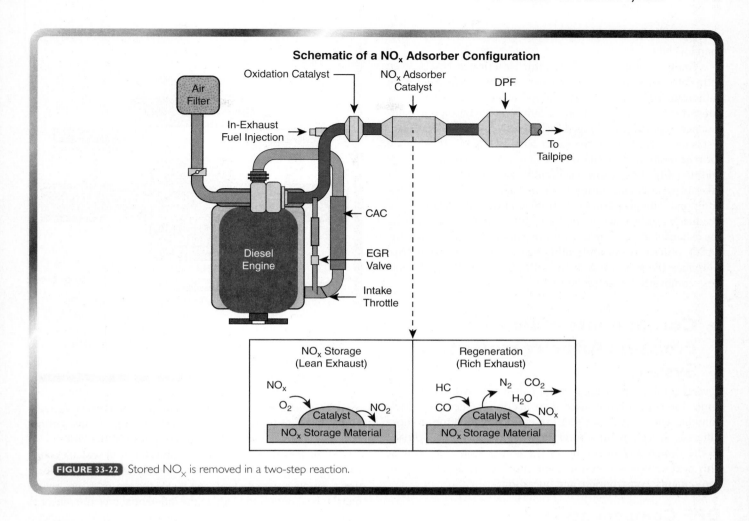

Schematic of a NO$_x$ Adsorber Configuration

FIGURE 33-22 Stored NO$_x$ is removed in a two-step reaction.

increasing power output while reducing fuel consumption. A number of North American diesels currently use LNTs, including the 2500 Dodge Ram that has a Cummins diesel.

Dodge Ram markets this technology as part of the wider range of NO$_x$-reducing emission systems known as **BlueTec**, which includes both **AdBlue** and DeNO$_x$. NACs are not effective for large diesel engines with high exhaust volumes and are used mainly in small and medium diesels **FIGURE 33-23**.

DeSO$_x$ Reactions

NAC aftertreatment has two major drawbacks. One is the requirement for additional fuel to activate system catalysts, which can penalize fuel economy. The increased consumption of fuel during rich operation needed to reduce NO$_x$ produces a fuel penalty of 3–5%. However, these numbers are offset by the improved fuel consumption and power produced from optimized injection timing, rate shaping, and other operating

▶ **TECHNICIAN TIP**

BlueTec is Dodge Ram's name for its two NO$_x$-reducing systems used in its European and North American diesel engines. AdBlue is liquid based. DeNO$_x$ uses an oxidizing catalytic converter and particulate filter combined with an NO$_x$ adsorber.

▶ **TECHNICIAN TIP**

There are two selective catalyst mechanisms that only select and destroy NO$_x$ emissions. One is called hydrogen-SCR and is used in LNTs. The second type of SCR uses liquid DEF, which is sprayed directly into the exhaust stream.

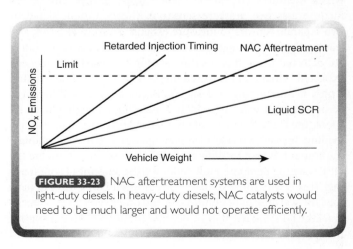

FIGURE 33-23 NAC aftertreatment systems are used in light-duty diesels. In heavy-duty diesels, NAC catalysts would need to be much larger and would not operate efficiently.

strategies that favor increased power and fuel economy rather than low NO$_x$ formation.

Another problem is that sulfur deactivates NACs, even ultra-low diesel fuel at 15 parts per million (ppm). Hydrogen sulfide stored in the catalyst material will eventually cause the converter to lose its effectiveness. Sulfur regeneration is a maintenance step where prolonged fuel-enriched heating of the catalyst is necessary to burn the sulfur out of the NAC. The interval for regeneration is based on the amount of fuel consumed. The additional heating, known as desulfurization mode, or **DeSO$_x$**, takes place after consuming 1–2 tanks of fuel. In some vehicles, additional late post-combustion injection events take place to produce a DeSO$_x$ reaction, replacing the normal two to intensify the exhaust temperature during a regeneration of the NAC. The DeSO$_x$ process is intermittently interrupted during some trips to reduce the soot levels in the DPF caused by the additional post-combustion injection of fuel.

► Components of Exhaust Emission Aftertreatment Systems

Several configurations are used for exhaust aftertreatement systems. The configuration used depends on whether the vehicle complies with EPA07 or EPA10 standards. In addition to those differences, each manufacturer has a slightly different approach to the design and operation of these aftertreatment systems. This next section will examine common aftertreatment system components, construction, and operation.

DPF Components

DPF systems require more than just filters to work. A variety of sensors and controls are needed to ensure safe and efficient operation, as well as monitor the DPF operation as an HD-OBD requirement.

Differential Pressure Sensor

A differential pressure sensor measures the exhaust pressure at the DPF inlet and outlet and supplies that data to the ECM, which measures DPF performance **FIGURE 33-24**. The sensor incorporates two pressure sensors with one output signal or two separate sensors to measure exhaust pressure entering and leaving the DPF. Plugged, restricted, cracked, or missing filters are detected using this pressure sensor. Comparisons between expected values and measured pressure will determine whether a filter is functioning as designed. Because pressure differences across the filter will vary widely depending on engine load and speed, the Delta P sensor data is not used to measure soot or ash loading. Instead, a model of system operation is used to estimate the amount of soot loading; this model is used to illuminate the DPF warning light and fault codes for the amount of soot loading. This is why some vehicles with plugged DPFs will not have the DPF warning light illuminated and other vehicles will regenerate the DPF too frequently. Because the aftertreatment control module estimates soot and ash loading based on an expected

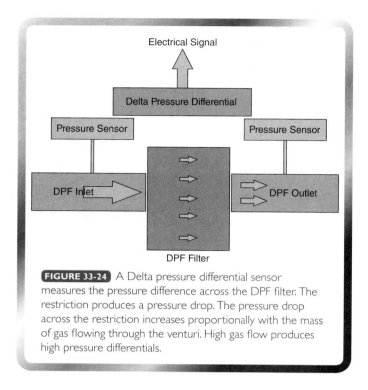

FIGURE 33-24 A Delta pressure differential sensor measures the pressure difference across the DPF filter. The restriction produces a pressure drop. The pressure drop across the restriction increases proportionally with the mass of gas flowing through the venturi. High gas flow produces high pressure differentials.

model of performance, fuel rates, other engine defects, extreme operating conditions, or poorly developed algorithms will not correctly estimate the actual amounts of soot in the DPF.

Deviations from expected Delta P values will set fault codes, when caused by missing or drilled out substrate. The sensor location prevents water condensation inside the sensor. Long, hollow metal tubes connect the DPF to the differential pressure sensor to reduce exhaust gas temperature and prolong sensor life. Temperature sensor data combined with Delta P data is used to measure gas mass flowing through the DPF using a speed-density algorithm.

Temperature Sensors

To manage the regeneration functions of the DPF, detect faults, and alert the driver of usual operating conditions, most DPFs use three temperature sensors. These are located at the oxidation catalyst inlet, between the oxidation catalyst and DPF filter and the DPF outlet **FIGURE 33-25** and **FIGURE 33-26**. If DPF temperatures are too high, the DPF substrate can melt or crack. Regeneration is terminated at temperatures greater than 1472°F (800°C). If temperatures are too low, regeneration will not be complete and not burn the soot. Excessive soot loading of the DPF above 120% can lead to excessively high DPF temperatures and fire or damage in the filter. After 120% loading, the DPF cannot be actively regenerated and must be removed to service.

A theoretical model of how the temperature and Delta P sensors should respond under various operating conditions is compared against measured values. Deviations between expected and actual values will set fault codes.

Liquid SCR Components

The EPA10 emission standards reduced permissible NO$_x$ emissions to almost undetectable levels. In-cylinder solutions, such

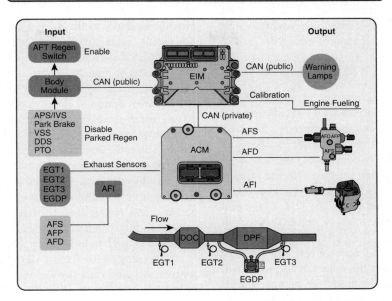

Big Bore Engine AFT Functional Diagram

- Engine Interface Module (EIM)
- Aftertreatment Control Module (ACM)
- Accel Pedal Sensor/Idle Validation Switch (APS/IVS)
- Vehicle Speed Sensor (VSS)
- Driveline Disconnect Switch (DDS)
- Power Take Off Switch (PTO)
- Exhaust Gas Temperature 1 (EGT1) Sensor
- Exhaust Gas Temperature 2 (EGT2) Sensor
- Exhaust Gas Temperature 3 (EGT3) Sensor

- Exhaust Gas Differential Pressure (EGDP) Sensor
- Diesel Oxidation Catalyst (DOC)
- Diesel Particulate Filter (DPF)
- Aftertreatment Fuel Injector (AFI)
- Aftertreatment Fuel Supply (AFS) Valve
- Aftertreatment Fuel Drain (AFD) Valve
- Aftertreatment Fuel Pressure (AFP) Sensor
- Controller Area Network (CAN)

FIGURE 33-25 Navistar aftertreatment systems on MaxxForce engines use a variety of input and output devices.

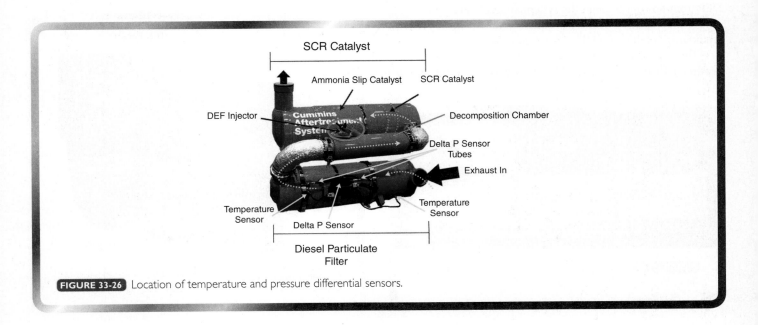

FIGURE 33-26 Location of temperature and pressure differential sensors.

as increased use of EGR and improved high-pressure injection systems, helped reduce NO_x levels, but the most significant system to clean up NO_x is the SCR. SCR targets, or specifically selects, NO_x emissions for elimination. Liquid SCR uses an ammonia-containing molecule called urea that combines with NO_x molecules to convert NO_x into harmless nitrogen.

DEF

DEF is a nontoxic, nonpolluting, nonhazardous, and nonflammable solution made up of water and urea. DEF is colorless and relatively stable chemically, which makes it safe to handle. DEF is a precise combination of 32.5% urea and 67.5% deionized water. DEF is stored in a separate onboard tank, and its rate of use is 1–4% of fuel use (50:1). When injected into the exhaust stream as a fine mist upstream of an SCR catalyst, it vaporizes and decomposes to form NH_3 and CO_2. The NH_3 is the end product and converts the NO_x to harmless N_2 and H_2O (through thermolysis) in the SCR catalyst.

The concentration of urea and water gives DEF the best freeze protection and ensures both the urea and the water will freeze at the same rate, preventing the fluid from become diluted or over-concentrated as it thaws. Because DEF does freeze, heaters in the reservoirs and on lines ensure rapid delivery in cold-weather operation **FIGURE 33-27**. When the vehicle shuts down, the DEF pump will reverse the flow of DEF and pull fluid out of the lines, returning it to the reservoir. The EPA permits fault detection systems up to 40 minutes after engine startup to move DEF to the injector in cold weather to accommodate frozen DEF.

In North America, the American Petroleum Institute (API) has established a performance standard for DEF used in liquid SCR systems. If contamination of DEF is suspected, use a refractometer to measure its density and to evaluate the quality of DEF. DEF's specific gravity should be 1.310–1.3843 at 68°F (20°C). DEF should be clear and smell like ammonia. The most recent SCR systems use a DEF quality sensor. This sensor uses tuning forks or optical sensors to accurately measure DEF's density to prevent contaminated DEF from flowing through the system and potentially damaging other aftertreatment sensors. Measurement of DEF quality is also a requirement of the latest HD-OBD standards.

The amount of DEF used is carefully metered to be proportional to the amount of NO_x produced. Current systems dose the exhaust system with DEF based on a probability of NO_x in the exhaust system predicted by engine operating factors and software stored in the ECM. Systems built since 2010 use an NH_3 or NO_x sensor to evaluate performance and not to provide feedback to the ECM **FIGURE 33-28**. These sensors do not usually form closed-loop feedback with the dosing injector, but only detect SCR problems such as incorrect fluid, poor DEF quality, or high NO_x levels. Dosing is done using an algorithm that predicts the amount of DEF needed to eliminate NO_x. One exception to closed-loop feedback takes place during dosing when the NO_x sensor at the tailpipe outlet detects any slippage or waste of ammonia (NH_3) out of the exhaust pipe. In that instance, the dosing injector can reduce the amount of DEF entering the exhaust system. Because NH_3 is a noxious emission, an **ammonia slip** catalyst is used to break down excess NH_3 into harmless nitrogen and water. High temperatures are needed to perform this reaction, so the temperature sensors in the SCR catalyst supply data that prevents DEF dosing until the catalysts are warm enough to break down NO_x and NH_3 **FIGURE 33-29**.

Beginning in 2015, most HD vehicles began using two new sensors. An ammonia slip sensor located after the SCR detects only high NH_3 levels after the SCR catalyst. A soot sensor located after the DPF detects faults in the DPF filter that could allow particulate to bypass the filter.

▶ TECHNICIAN TIP

Filling a low DEF reservoir with water may be tempting because the fluid is colorless. Never add water or any other fluid to the DEF reservoir. Doing so may damage the aftertreatment system. Adding water to the DEF reservoir will change the DEF concentration levels, which may affect SCR efficiency and will raise the freezing temperature and change other characteristics of the diesel DEF. The potential exists where the SCR system components can be damaged during cold weather operation or lead to a derate condition or even a failure of the engine to start at all.

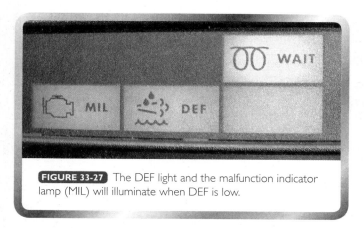

FIGURE 33-27 The DEF light and the malfunction indicator lamp (MIL) will illuminate when DEF is low.

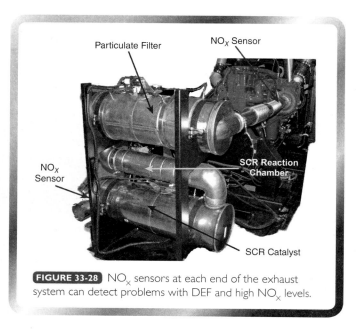

FIGURE 33-28 NO_x sensors at each end of the exhaust system can detect problems with DEF and high NO_x levels.

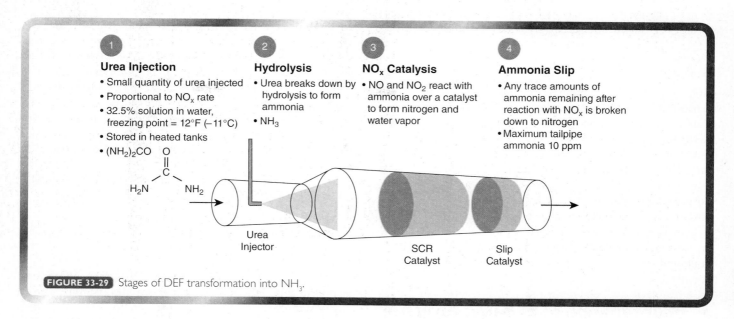

1 Urea Injection
- Small quantity of urea injected
- Proportional to NO_x rate
- 32.5% solution in water, freezing point = 12°F (−11°C)
- Stored in heated tanks
- $(NH_2)_2CO$

2 Hydrolysis
- Urea breaks down by hydrolysis to form ammonia
- NH_3

3 NO_x Catalysis
- NO and NO_2 react with ammonia over a catalyst to form nitrogen and water vapor

4 Ammonia Slip
- Any trace amounts of ammonia remaining after reaction with NO_x is broken down to nitrogen
- Maximum tailpipe ammonia 10 ppm

Urea Injector

SCR Catalyst

Slip Catalyst

FIGURE 33-29 Stages of DEF transformation into NH_3.

TECHNICIAN TIP

Long-term storage (i.e., more than 6 months) of DEF in a vehicle is not recommended. DEF will slowly undergo chemical change. Shelf life of DEF is expected to be 18 months. Complete scheduled testing of the DEF to ensure that its concentration does not fall below specification. Maintain DEF storage temperature at 23–77°F (−5–25°C). DEF consumption is approximately 2–5% of fuel consumption, depending on several factors, including vehicle operation, duty cycle, geography, and load rating. That ratio with diesel is 50:1, so for every 50 gallons (gal.) (189 liters [L]) of diesel fuel burned, 1 gal. (4 L) of DEF is consumed.

NO_x Sensors

NO_x sensors do not provide closed-loop feedback to meter the correct amount of DEF. However, NO_x sensors detect incorrect concentrations of DEF emitted by dosing injectors and other emission-related faults. For example, water in the DEF reservoir will not produce a drop in NO_x between the NO_x sensor located at the outlet of the turbocharger and the exhaust pipe outlet. Failure of the system to convert NO_x will generate multiple fault codes. When this occurs, a set of inducements, including a progressive engine derate, warning lights, and audible alerts, will warn the driver to have the SCR system repaired, especially if the DEF tank is empty or a serious emissions-related fault exists. A DEF warning light or gauge will alert the driver before the onboard storage of DEF is depleted. Refueling is a frequent trigger for severe inducement. If the DEF reservoir has remained empty for more than 10 hours, or has a severe SCR fault, a vehicle could have 75% of torque before refueling. If more diesel fuel than 5% of the fuel tank's capacity is added, but the reservoir is still without DEF, the engine will start, but vehicle speed will be limited to 5 mph (8 km/h).

The NO_x sensors are solid-state electronics, wide-range planar zirconia oxide type. A sensor has two chambers. The first chamber pumps O_2 out of the exhaust gas when current is passed through the sensor walls while heated to 1202°F (650°C). NO and

NO_2 are separated in the second chamber. The platinum coatings of each cell wall change as a result of differing chemical compositions, which in turn produces different levels of voltage depending on the composition of NO_x gases in each chamber. A differential voltage measured between the two chambers and outside air provides a value for the amount of NO_x in the exhaust stream. A module connected to the sensor operates the sensor and conditions the electrical signal supplied to either the engine control system or a separate aftertreatment module **FIGURE 33-30**.

NAC/LNT Components

LNTs and NACs produce NH_3 in the engine exhaust using a unique combination of HC dosing, high EGR flow, and reduced oxygen content. The ability to produce NH_3 in the exhaust

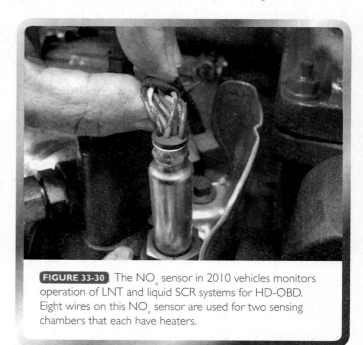

FIGURE 33-30 The NO_x sensor in 2010 vehicles monitors operation of LNT and liquid SCR systems for HD-OBD. Eight wires on this NO_x sensor are used for two sensing chambers that each have heaters.

system has the advantage of not requiring the extra maintenance of filling a reservoir.

Sensor Function

NO_x and O_2 sensors monitor the lean–rich cycling of the exhaust. NO_x sensors are upstream of the NAC or LNT catalyst. Data from these sensors estimates the loading of the catalyst. A wide-range oxygen sensor is located at the outlet of the catalysts. Data from this sensor helps ensure almost no O_2 content is in the exhaust stream during the brief regeneration period. Another downstream NO_x sensor measures NO_x output for on-board diagnostics (OBD) fault detection. If levels of NO_x rise too much, the NAC or LNT may not be operating correctly and a fault code is set.

Temperature sensors evaluate exhaust operation against an expected model of behavior. The sensors identify system faults and whether a set of predetermined conditions are met to regenerate the NAC or LNT or continue $DeSO_x$.

▶ Maintenance of Exhaust Emission Aftertreatment Systems

Performing an Active Regeneration Procedure

When DPF soot loading exceeds 80%, the DPF light will illuminate. This is a warning to the driver to change the driving conditions to passively regenerate the DPF. Typically, the vehicle needs to be driven faster than 45 mph (72 km/h) for at least 20 minutes to reduce the soot load. A parked regeneration can be performed using the dash mounted inhibit switch only after the soot loading has increased to the point where the DPF warning lamp is on. Without meeting this condition, an active regeneration cannot be performed. Only a forced regeneration can be done using an electronic service tool or OEM software. Another name for an active regeneration is a parked regeneration procedure.

To perform an active regeneration procedure, follow the steps in **SKILL DRILL 33-1**.

Performing a Forced DPF Regeneration

A forced regeneration of a DPF is an active regeneration initiated using an electronic service tool or OEM software. Several circumstances require the forced regeneration of a DPF, which a technician initiates. One example is a light-duty diesel vehicle, which, at less than 14,000 lb (6350 kg) GWVR, does not have the capability to allow the operator to actively regenerate the DPF if soot loading becomes excessive. Another example is a heavy-duty vehicle that cannot operate for a sustained time period at speeds fast enough to passively regenerate a DPF; a vehicle such as this would also require a forced regeneration in

---

 SKILL DRILL 33-1 Performing an Active Regeneration Procedure

1 The DPF warning lamp must be illuminated before an active regeneration can be performed.

2 Verify that enabling conditions are met: the engine should be fully warmed up with a coolant temperature hotter than 185°F (85°C). The engine must be at slow idle; the DPF cannot be regenerated if the engine is in fast idle or PTO mode.

3 The aftertreatment control module must verify that the parked regeneration can be performed safely. It will request cycling of the park brake, clutch, and neutral start switch.

4 In order for an active regeneration to occur, the transmission must be in neutral, the park brake applied, and no vehicle speed can be sensed.

5 With the engine running, press and hold the DPF inhibit/regeneration switch to the On position for 5 seconds and release it. The engine speed will increase and the DPF lamp will typically go out once the regeneration event begins.

6 The regeneration will take approximately 20–40 minutes. It is complete when the engine returns to low idle and the DPF lamp remains off. The length of time the regeneration event takes depends on the amount of soot loading in the DPF. The aftertreatment control system will end the regeneration event when the DPF inlet and outlet temperatures are nearly the same, which means there is no longer any consumable soot in the DPF. Note: If the DPF lamp comes back on after the procedure, the regeneration has failed and requires further diagnostic checks.

7 To cancel or inhibit an active regeneration procedure, hold the DPF switch to the On position for 5 seconds and release. An active regeneration will stop if the key is turned to the Off position, the vehicle is put into gear, or the parking brake is released.

a service facility. Refuse trucks, sightseeing buses, vehicles operating in mines, and mining equipment are a few examples of heavy-duty engines that require forced regenerations.

Whenever a DPF filter is installed, a forced regeneration should be performed to increase its soot-loading capacity. More critically, a forced regeneration is required after a vehicle has derated in power due to excessive soot loading. If the DPF warning light is flashing and accompanied by the amber check engine light or stop engine light, the vehicle must be parked, and a forced regeneration must be performed.

To perform a forced DPF regeneration, follow the steps in **SKILL DRILL 33-2**.

DPF Service—Ash Loading

The regeneration process incinerates PM. However, an ash residue remains in the filter. Ash consists primarily of incombustible by-products from lubrication oil consumption. Because regeneration will not burn off the ash, the DPF will need to be removed from the vehicle and cleaned or replaced **FIGURE 33-31**.

The EPA requires that the first cleaning should not occur before 150,000 miles (241,402 km). Subsequent cleaning can take place every 100,000 miles (160,934 km) after that. Actual cleaning intervals depend on the vehicle operating cycle and oil consumption, with the longest cleaning intervals obtained using low-ash CJ-4 lubrication oils with only 1% ash content.

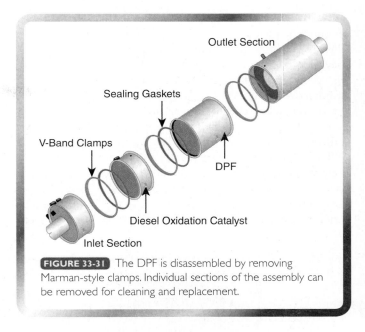

FIGURE 33-31 The DPF is disassembled by removing Marman-style clamps. Individual sections of the assembly can be removed for cleaning and replacement.

Replacing the DPF

Removing ash from the DPF is a maintenance item. The DPF must be periodically removed and cleaned because inorganic ash cannot be burned. Ash removal is different from regeneration,

---

SKILL DRILL 33-2 Performing a Forced DPF Regeneration

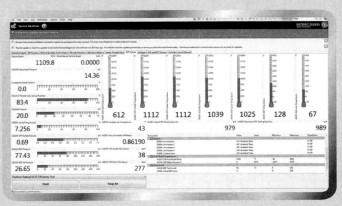

to reach a coolant temperature of 130°F (54°C) before executing commands to regenerate the DPF.

4 Carefully observe other instructions given by the service software or electronic service tool to meet pre-conditions necessary before regeneration can begin. For example, on light-duty vehicles a quarter tank of fuel is generally required before regenerating, or the hood must be closed. On heavier vehicles, the PTO or fast idle should not be engaged. The transmission must be in neutral, the park brakes applied, and no vehicle speed should be sensed.

5 If the vehicle is equipped with a regeneration inhibit switch, ensure that the switch is not in the Inhibit position.

6 Ensure that the engine is operating at slow idle speed. Note whether the clutch, brake, and neutral start switch are cycled to verify that the vehicle is in a proper state to safely begin a regeneration.

7 Command the aftertreatment control system to regenerate. The regeneration will take approximately 20–40 minutes. Once regeneration is complete and the engine returns to low idle, the DPF lamp should be switched off. If the DPF lamp comes back on, the regeneration failed and further diagnostic procedures need to be performed.

1 With the ignition switch On and the engine running, connect an electronic service tool to the vehicle's data link connector.

2 Check for active diagnostic fault codes. On a number of engines, EGR faults and other engine malfunctions prevent an active regeneration from taking place. Diagnostic faults detected during the regeneration will often cause the event to abort.

3 Warm up the engine to enable the software to execute a command for active regeneration. Many engines need

and it involves removal of the filter in order to use compressed air combined with a vacuum system to blow the ash from the filter and capture the ash for disposal. One or two DPF filters may require cleaning. For example, Detroit Diesel's One Box system contains two DPF filters which require disassembly of box covers to access **FIGURE 33-32** Each manufacturer has a recommended schedule for cleaning a DPF. DPF removal and cleaning, or installation of a remanufactured filter, is indicated whenever a turbocharger failure has occurred, the DPF is regenerating too frequently and no other engine faults are present, or exhaust backpressure becomes too high. High backpressure leads to low engine power and increased fuel consumption. Diagnostic fault codes and an illuminated malfunction indicator lamp may also indicate DPF replacement.

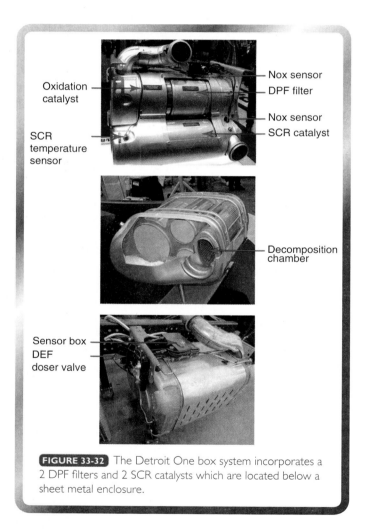

FIGURE 33-32 The Detroit One box system incorporates a 2 DPF filters and 2 SCR catalysts which are located below a sheet metal enclosure.

A common fault code description includes "diesel particulate filter efficiency below threshold." After the DPF is replaced, the ash load needs to be reset to zero to enable the aftertreatment system to calculate the next interval for DPF service life.

To replace a DPF, follow the steps in **SKILL DRILL 33-3**.

SCR Service

Early SCR systems can completely deplete the DEF before a fault code is set. After operating for more than 10 hours, the vehicle will derate power. Another 10 hours of operation allows the vehicle to only idle. Simply filling the DEF reservoir will not allow the vehicle to return to normal operation because the active SCR code is removed only after the SCR monitor runs. Because it is a non-continuous monitor, a service tool must erase the code because the monitor will not run at idle. An alternative is to use an OEM electronic service tool to perform an SCR system refill activation. When used in this mode, the service tool will force a quick refill detection strategy after the DEF reservoir has been refilled. SCR systems phased in until 2015 have increasingly stringent thresholds for fault detection and limitations on how long the SCR system can operate without DEF fluid.

SCR maintenance includes many other service procedures:

- SCR visual leak check: Use this test to pressurize the SCR system to visual check for leaks.
- SCR system emptying: Use this test to depressurize the SCR system and empty the DEF from system lines, as well as to place the system into a known default state to check the HD-OBD monitor operation.
- SCR parameter reset: Use this test to reset the SCR system data following an SCR catalyst replacement. Because HD OBD requires the ability to compensate for system wear and deterioration, new values for the SCR temperature and pressure sensor require learning.
- SCR dosing measurement test: Use this test to visually verify the SCR dosing injector is flowing the correct quantity of DEF; a container collects and measures the quantity and flow of DEF from the injector after it is commanded to dose a specific quantity of DEF.

▶ TECHNICIAN TIP

After refilling a depleted DEF reservoir, the SCR fault code may need erasing before the vehicle will operate normally. This is because the OBD system SCR monitor will not run if the engine has derated to idle.

SKILL DRILL 33-3 Replacing the DPF

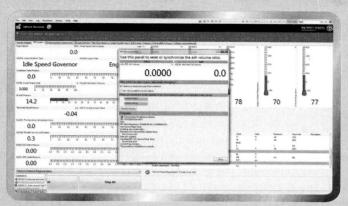

1 Disconnect and remove the Marman-style band clamps holding the removable DPF filter in the DPF filter canister.

2 Scrape and clean the filter gasket surfaces of the filter canister.

3 Reinstall the new or rebuilt filter with new gaskets. Carefully note the direction of exhaust flow through the DPF filter during installation.

4 Perform a forced regeneration of the new or green filter to increase soot-loading capacity.

5 Reset the ash accumulator according to the OEM service procedures. An example from Detroit Diesels requires a technician to choose "Diesel Particulate Filter (DPF) ash accumulator" from the Actions menu of DDI service software.

6 Follow the dialog boxes for entering the new filter serial number, the type of filter installed (new or replacement), and the current vehicle mileage.

7 Follow these installation tips:
- Use only manufacturer-recommended filter cleaning procedures. Do not use cleaning solvents on filters; they do not work and are likely to damage the filter and solidify ash in the filter passageways.
- Do not use a shop compressor in an open area to clean a filter.
- Use a transmission jack or floor jack to help maneuver the filter from the underside of the vehicle.
- Do not steam clean the DPF; water will turn ash to a concrete-like material.
- Oil-contaminated filters are generally not reusable, but may be recovered through baking in an industrial oven to remove the oil.
- Do not drop the filter element on the shop floor to remove ash.
- DPF ash must be handled and disposed as a hazardous waste.
- Make sure that filter elements are installed in the correct direction of flow.

Wrap-Up

Ready for Review

- Diesel engines now use a variety of emission reduction technologies centered in the exhaust system, including EGR, DPFs, catalytic converters, SCR, LNTs, and NACs.
- While the latest developments in diesel technology are complex in design and function, they are easily understood using a systematic approach, examining the construction and operation of each device associated with removing exhaust emissions.
- Because in-cylinder, engine-based emission control strategies were inadequate to meet emission reduction targets, the exhaust system became the focal point for technology to remove harmful emissions.
- Catalytic converters speed up chemical reactions of noxious exhaust emissions and change them into harmless combustion by-products. Several types of converters exist and are classified according to the noxious emission converted or the type of chemical reaction taking place in the catalyst material.
- An oxidation catalytic converter refers to the type of catalyst that causes O_2 to chemically combine with noxious emissions such as HCs and CO, turning the emissions into H_2O and CO_2.
- Oxidation converters consist of a stainless steel canister containing a ceramic material formed into a honeycomb-like structure called a substrate or catalyst support. The substrate has a coating of active material that causes the chemical reaction between noxious emissions and oxygen remaining in the exhaust after combustion.
- The first difficulty in cleaning up diesel exhaust using oxidation catalytic converters is the relative coolness of diesel exhaust temperatures. However, new catalyst materials have been developed for diesels that enable the effective use of low-temperature oxidation of HC and CO emissions.
- The primary purpose of a DPF is to remove soot and other solid particles from diesel exhaust, rendering the exhaust completely smokeless. To remove soot and other exhaust-borne particles, exhaust gas passes through a wall-flow filter, which traps PM before reaching the exhaust outlet.
- Trapped soot and other particles collected on the walls of the DPF will eventually plug the filter, producing high exhaust backpressure. To clean the DPF, regeneration, a renewal process, purges soot from the filter; this process involves burning the soot out of the filter.
- Heat for regeneration is provided two ways: one is through natural chemical reactions in the catalysts, which produce heat; the other involves heating the DPF with fuel or another heat source.
- SCR is a process where an ammonia-containing liquid is sprayed into the exhaust stream to destroy NO_x molecules. DEF is the generic name of the liquid, which is a clear, nontoxic, and nonflammable combination of water and urea.
- The advantage of SCR technology is that it enables the lowest fuel consumption of existing exhaust aftertreatment technologies while improving power output, engine durability, and longevity.
- Two configurations are used for the location of the DPF and the SCR: the DPF can be upstream or downstream of the SCR; locating the DPF upstream of the SCR is the most common configuration.
- NO_x adsorber technology is a catalyst strategy for removing NO_x in the low-temperature, oxygen-rich exhaust environment of a diesel engine. In this system, NO_x emissions are absorbed, or temporarily trapped and stored, by the catalyst material; the stored NO_x is removed in a two-step reaction.
- Moving the exhaust gas O_2 concentration from high to low, or from lean to a temporarily rich condition, is the strategy used in LNT; other names for this technology include $DeNO_x$ or hydrocarbon-SCR.
- A differential pressure sensor measuring the exhaust pressure at the DPF inlet and outlet supplies data to the ECM used to measure DPF performance. Deviations from expected values will set fault codes.
- To manage the regeneration functions of the DPF, detect faults, and alert the driver of usual operating conditions, most DPFs use three temperature sensors, which are located at the oxidation catalyst inlet.
- NO_x sensors provide closed-loop feedback to meter the correct amount of DEF in SCR systems. The sensors detect incorrect concentrations of DEF, emitted from dosing injectors, and other emission-related faults.
- In NAC and LNT systems, NO_x and O_2 sensors monitor the lean-rich cycling of the exhaust to estimate the loading of the catalyst.
- DPFs require service for ash loading. Regeneration will not burn off DPF ash, so the DPF will need to be removed from the vehicle and cleaned or replaced.
- SCRs require service after refilling a DEF reservoir that has been depleted. The SCR fault code may need erasing before the vehicle will operate normally. Erasing is necessary because the OBD system SCR monitor will not run if the engine has derated to idle.

Vocabulary Builder

active regeneration A process in which soot is burned inside the DPF through supplemental heating of the DPF filter.

AdBlue A liquid-based NO_x-reducing system Dodge Ram uses in its European and North American diesel engines.

ammonia slip NH_3 that escapes from the SCR catalyst and into the atmosphere.

BlueTec DaimlerChrysler's name for its two NO_x-reducing systems used in their European and North American diesel engines.

catalyst A material that speeds up or slows down chemical reactions without entering the chemical reactions.

DeSO$_x$ A sulfur-reducing reaction used in NAC and LNT systems to remove sulfur from catalyst material. Sulfur in diesel fuel tends to contaminate catalysts and reduces their effectiveness unless a DeSO$_x$ reaction takes place.

diesel particulate filter (DPF) A device installed in the exhaust system to filter out black carbon soot and other particulates from the exhaust stream.

exhaust backpressure Exhaust pressure build-up in the exhaust system. The pressure can be before or after the turbocharger.

exhaust gas recirculation (EGR) An NO_x reduction technology that mixes exhaust gas with fresh intake air.

lean NO$_x$ trap (LNT) A catalyst mechanism that selects and destroys only NO_x emissions without the use of liquid diesel exhaust fluid. Also referred to as hydrogen-SCR and NO_x adsorbers.

NO$_x$ adsorber catalyst (NAC) A unique catalyst material that stores NO_x emissions and then decomposes the NO_x under specialized exhaust conditions.

oxidation reaction Reactions that add O_2 to HCs and CO to produce H_2O, CO_2, and heat.

passive regeneration A process where relatively low-temperature chemical reactions take place in the exhaust catalysts to oxidize soot into CO_2 and H_2O. Passive reactions take place when the DPF is hot enough under normal vehicle operation; this occurs when sufficient load and engine speed produce exhaust inlet temperatures above 482°F (250°C).

reduction reaction Reactions that remove oxygen from NO_x molecules, converting NO_x into N_2 and O_2.

selective catalyst reduction (SCR) system An exhaust aftertreatment system that decomposes NO_x molecules using ammonia NH_3.

urea An ammonia-carrying molecule that breaks down in hot exhaust gas.

Review Questions

1. _____ is a process where relatively low-temperature chemical reactions take in the exhaust catalysts to oxidize soot into CO_2 and H_2O.
   a. Passive regeneration
   b. Active regeneration
   c. Reduction reaction
   d. Oxidation regeneration

2. _____ is an exhaust aftertreatment system that decomposes NO_x molecules to form NH_3.
   a. Reduction reaction
   b. Oxidation reaction
   c. Active regeneration
   d. Selective catalyst reduction system

3. The process in which soot is burned inside the DPF through supplemental heating of the DPF filter is called _____.
   a. passive regeneration
   b. active regeneration
   c. reduction reaction
   d. oxidation regeneration

4. _____ is a reaction that removes oxygen from NO_x molecules, converting NO_x into N_2 and O_2.
   a. Active regeneration
   b. Reduction reaction
   c. Passive regeneration
   d. Oxidation reaction

5. _____ is a reaction that adds O_2 to HCs and CO to produce H_2O, CO_2, and heat.
   a. Oxidation reaction
   b. Reduction reaction
   c. Active regeneration
   d. Passive regeneration

6. A renewal process called _____ purges soot from the diesel particulate filter and cleans it.
   a. absorption
   b. regeneration
   c. decomposition
   d. reduction

7. Catalytic converters speed up _____ of noxious exhaust emissions and change them into harmless combustion by-products.
   a. regeneration
   b. differential pressure
   c. chemical reactions
   d. reduction reactions

8. Oxidation converters can clean up _____ noxious emission(s).
   a. one
   b. two
   c. three
   d. four

9. Oxidation converters contain a ceramic material formed into a honey-comb-like structure called a(n) _____.
   a. urea
   b. zeolite
   c. substrate
   d. absorber

10. Active stationary regeneration is also called _____.
   a. parked regeneration
   b. active regeneration
   c. passive regeneration
   d. reduction regeneration

ASE-Type Questions

1. Technician A says warm exhaust temperatures and excess air content in diesel exhaust are the biggest technical challenges with diesel catalysts. Technician B says cold exhaust temperatures and excess air content in diesel exhaust are the biggest technical challenges with diesel catalysts. Who is correct?
   a. Technician A
   b. Technician B
   c. Both Technician A and Technician B
   d. Neither Technician A nor Technician B

2. Technician A says active regeneration is only possibly using original equipment manufacturer software, a scanner, or another electronic service tool. Technician B says the need for active regeneration is determined by measuring the pressure drop across the DPF filter. Who is correct?
   a. Technician A
   b. Technician B
   c. Both Technician A and Technician B
   d. Neither Technician A nor Technician B

3. Technician A says the regeneration inhibit switch must be depressed for 5 seconds after the control module has verified safe conditions for an active regeneration are met. Technician B says the regeneration inhibit switch must be depressed for 3 seconds after the control module has verified safe conditions for an active regeneration are met. Who is correct?
   a. Technician A
   b. Technician B
   c. Both Technician A and Technician B
   d. Neither Technician A nor Technician B

4. Technician A says an advantage of selective catalyst reduction technology is that it enables the lowest fuel consumption of existing exhaust aftertreatment technologies while improving power output. Technician B says other advantages include the improvement of engine durability and longevity. Who is correct?
   a. Technician A
   b. Technician B
   c. Both Technician A and Technician B
   d. Neither Technician A nor Technician B

5. Technician A says NAC aftertreatment systems are only used in heavy-duty diesels. Technician B says sulfur regeneration is a maintenance step where prolonged fuel-enriched heating of the catalyst is necessary to burn the sulfur out of an NAC. Who is correct?
   a. Technician A
   b. Technician B
   c. Both Technician A and Technician B
   d. Neither Technician A nor Technician B

6. Technician A says catalytic converters are classified according to the noxious emission converted. Technician B says catalytic converters are classified according to the type of chemical reaction. Who is correct?
   a. Technician A
   b. Technician B
   c. Both Technician A and Technician B
   d. Neither Technician A nor Technician B

7. Technician A says because oxidation converters clean up two noxious emissions, they are called two-way converters. Technician B says exhaust gas recirculation converters clean up two noxious emissions, they are called two-way converters. Who is correct?
   a. Technician A
   b. Technician B
   c. Both Technician A and Technician B
   d. Neither Technician A nor Technician B

8. Technician A says the primary purpose of a p-trap is to remove soot and other solid particles from diesel exhaust, rendering the exhaust completely smokeless. Technician B says the primary purpose of a washcoat is to render the exhaust completely smokeless. Who is correct?
   a. Technician A
   b. Technician B
   c. Both Technician A and Technician B
   d. Neither Technician A nor Technician B

9. Technician A says SCR catalysts typically convert 20 to 40% of particulate matter to CO_2 and H_2O. Technician B says SCR catalysts eliminate over 90% of NO_x emissions. Who is correct?
   a. Technician A
   b. Technician B
   c. Both Technician A and Technician B
   d. Neither Technician A nor Technician B

10. Technician A says sintered metal foil catalyst substrate can handle 2 times more ash than ceramic-based substrates. Technician B says sintered metal foil catalyst substrate can handle 3 times more ash than ceramic-based substrates. Who is correct?
    a. Technician A
    b. Technician B
    c. Both Technician A and Technician B
    d. Neither Technician A nor Technician B

CHAPTER 34
Exhaust Systems and Engine Retarders

NATEF Tasks

Diesel Engines

Air Induction and Exhaust Systems
- Check exhaust backpressure; determine needed action. (p 967)
- Inspect exhaust manifold, piping, mufflers, and mounting hardware; repair or replace as needed. (pp 959–960)

Engine Brakes
- Inspect and adjust engine compression/exhaust brakes; determine needed action. (pp 967, 969, 971–974)

- Inspect, test, and adjust engine compression/exhaust brake control circuits, switches, and solenoids; determine needed action. (pp 971–974)
- Inspect engine compression/exhaust brake housing, valves, seals, lines, and fittings; determine needed action. (pp 967, 971–974)

Knowledge Objectives

After reading this chapter, you will be able to:
1. Explain the principles of operation of diesel exhaust systems and engine-based braking systems. (pp 958–959)
2. Describe the functions, construction, and application of diesel exhaust systems and engine-based braking systems. (pp 959–973)
3. Describe and explain methods for performing inspection and diagnostic procedures on diesel exhaust systems and engine-based braking systems. (pp 973–976)
4. Recommend maintenance or repairs on diesel exhaust systems and engine-based braking systems. (pp 973–976)

Skills Objectives

After reading this chapter, you will be able to:
1. Adjust the exhaust brake. (p 969) **SKILL DRILL 34-1**
2. Adjust a Caterpillar compression release brake. (p 971) **SKILL DRILL 34-2**
3. Adjust engine brake programmable parameters. (p 976) **SKILL DRILL 34-3**

▶ Introduction

Diesel exhaust systems were traditionally relatively simple in design, with a pipe and a muffler to quiet exhaust and carry it away from the engine. However, as with other vehicle systems, exhaust systems on modern diesel-powered vehicles have become increasingly sophisticated due to the introduction of emission-reduction technologies. Greener and cleaner diesel engines now use a variety of emission-reduction technologies centered in the exhaust system. This chapter will review other, non-emission-related functions of the exhaust system, including compression-release brakes, service and diagnostic techniques for the exhaust, engine-based braking systems, and **exhaust brakes**, which are engine brakes that work by placing a restriction in the exhaust system that increases backpressure, causing the engine to exert a retarding force against the driveline.

▶ Fundamentals of Engine Exhaust Systems

In addition to playing a role in reducing noxious emissions, exhaust systems perform a number of other important functions. On diesel-powered vehicles and equipment, the exhaust system is associated with the following functions:

- Collecting and removing hot exhaust gases from engine cylinders
- Minimizing noise emissions from exhaust pulses
- Powering turbochargers
- Reducing exhaust noise
- Quenching sparks
- Removing solids from exhaust gas
- Engine braking
- Promoting faster coolant warm-up

Exhaust Systems and Engine Breathing

Perhaps because it is only heard and little seen, the exhaust system's contribution to engine performance can be easily underestimated. However, an engine's ability to draw a fresh air charge for combustion relies on the efficiency of its exhaust system. What goes in must come out is a principle basic to engine breathing **FIGURE 34-1**. This means that if exhaust gases are not removed with as little resistance as possible, the cylinders will not properly fill because combustion gas pressure builds up

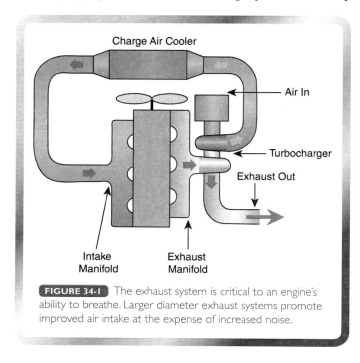

FIGURE 34-1 The exhaust system is critical to an engine's ability to breathe. Larger diameter exhaust systems promote improved air intake at the expense of increased noise.

▶ You Are the Technician

A highway coach bus arrives at your shop with the complaint the engine brakes work intermittently and are weak when they do operate. Using the manufacturer's service literature, you begin performing diagnostic tests of the electrical circuits and solenoid control valves. One brake solenoid out of three has an open circuit. The clearance between the slave pistons and exhausts valves is excessive, which probably contributes to the weak brake performance. During testing, you check the operation of the throttle pedal and discover the voltage at idle is inconsistent, sometimes as much as 1.5 volts, sometimes 0.8 volts, which is the manufacturer's specification. You also check programmable parameters associated with the brake and note the compression release brake is configured to apply only after the service brakes are applied momentarily and not automatically whenever the brake is on and the clutch and throttle pedals are up. As you prepare to report to the customer with estimates and recommendations for repairs, consider the following:

1. What effect do you think the inconsistent throttle pedal voltage at idle may have on the engine-brake operation?
2. What other service procedures would you recommend to the customer that could take place while you replace the control valve solenoid?
3. How would the programmed setting for the engine-brake operation affect the customer's complaint about the brake operation?

in the exhaust system. With exhaust gas pressure backed up in a restrictive exhaust system, cylinders cannot be swept clear of exhaust before the next combustion cycle, and the exhaust gas pressure in the cylinders will resist engine rotation during the exhaust stroke.

Installing an exhaust system that can efficiently collect and discharge combustion gas is an important element of vehicle design and improved engine performance. Therefore, changes or enhancements to engine components affecting output power should be accompanied with a careful evaluation of the exhaust system's ability to handle additional exhaust gas volume produced by increased horsepower (hp).

Exhaust Backpressure

Exhaust systems that do not properly remove exhaust gases are said to have backpressure. **Exhaust backpressure (EBP)** is resistance to exhaust gas flow from the engine. Resistance results from a variety of restrictions:

- Undersized pipes, mufflers, and **resonators** (a resonator is a device in the exhaust system that provides additional dampening and tuning of exhaust noise)
- Blockage in exhaust pipes, mufflers, and emission-control devices
- Bent or kinked pipes
- Seized exhaust brakes
- Improper system design
- Incorrect repair procedures
- Soot- and ash-loaded diesel particulate filters (DPFs)

High EBP in addition to performance complaints leads to a number of other detrimental operating conditions, including the following:

1. High exhaust valve temperatures caused by inadequate flow of fresh, cool air intake charge over the exhaust valve, especially during the valve overlap period
2. Overheating of cooling systems caused by transfer of heat energy from slow-moving exhaust gases lingering near the exhaust ports into the cylinder head
3. Excessive crankcase pressure from exhaust gas pressure retained in the cylinder that leaks past piston rings and enters the crankcase, making EBP contribute to increased volume of engine blow-by
4. Excessive exhaust emissions produced by poor combustion quality caused by high EBP; exhaust gases left in the cylinder at the end of the exhaust stroke will displace oxygen and increase particulate matter (PM), hydrocarbon (HC), and carbon monoxide (CO) emissions
5. Low turbocharger speed and boost pressure, which results from a reduction in the pressure differential across the turbine
6. Damage to pistons and valves because high backpressure can force exhaust gases to open an exhaust valve with a weak valve spring and cause contact between pistons and exhaust valves

Limits to acceptable backpressure in most diesels are 3″ (8 cm) of mercury or 14″ (36 cm) of water column as measured with a **water manometer**. Performance complaints are noticeable at 30–40″ (76–102 cm) of water. For this reason, the exhaust system is designed, and must be maintained, to minimize EBP.

Exhaust Systems and Noise Emissions

Engine exhaust is a major contributor to total vehicle noise **FIGURE 34-2** . Pressure pulses from exhaust leaving the cylinder head ports generate significant noise emissions, which are regulated by their own unique emission standards. Currently, the maximum allowable noise level for light-duty cars and trucks is 80 decibels (dB). For this reason, exhaust systems are designed to discharge exhaust gas as quietly as possible to the perimeter of the vehicle.

▶ Types of Engine Exhaust Systems
Horizontal Exhaust Systems

A **horizontal exhaust system** routes the exhaust components under the chassis and aims the outlet pipe downward toward the ground or to the rear of the vehicle. This type of exhaust system is the most common on light- and medium-duty diesel-powered vehicles. The entire exhaust system is connected to the underbody of the vehicle through flexible suspension elements designed to reduce vibration to the passenger compartment and allow movement of the engine during torque reaction **FIGURE 34-3** .

Dual exhaust can be configured to achieve better flow and noise reduction from higher displacement engines. Using a

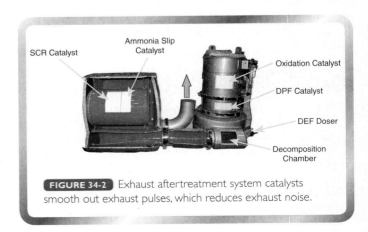

FIGURE 34-2 Exhaust aftertreatment system catalysts smooth out exhaust pulses, which reduces exhaust noise.

FIGURE 34-3 Horizontal exhaust systems are not damaged by interference with tunnels and low overhead bridges.

horizontal exhaust system does have some disadvantages. One is shortened muffler life from road splash caused by thermal shock, which produces cracks in the system. Water can easily accumulate in the muffler and combine with exhaust gases to produce corrosive acids. Corroded and rusted exhaust pipes and mufflers occur and require replacement more often on horizontal exhaust systems than on vertical systems. Exterior noise emissions can also be more pronounced because of the exhaust's proximity to bystanders and passengers. And road dust and exhaust fumes can be more of a nuisance due to outlet location. To prevent recirculation of exhaust into the cab or even into the air intake system, outlets should be located as far as possible to the rear of the vehicle. Locating the outlet behind the tires causes a negative pressure at the outlet, which promotes better flow. An angle of 30–45 degrees cut at the end of the outlet pipes also creates a negative pressure when air is passing over the outlet during highway cruising speeds.

In Europe, horizontal systems are used because they will not interfere with tunnels and low bridges, which are frequently encountered when driving there. The downsides of a horizontal system are that it has a shortened exhaust system life and it releases noxious emissions beneath the cab and at curb levels.

▶ TECHNICIAN TIP

The exhaust outlet on a bus should not exit on what is called the "open side" of a bus, where passengers get on and off the bus. Also, exhaust emissions should not be directed where people might wait around a bus. Horizontal exhaust systems on buses should use an outlet with curved elbows to direct exhaust gases down and away from the chassis. Alternatively, the exhaust outlet should be directed to the driver's side or road side of the vehicle.

Vertical Exhaust Systems

Heavy-duty vehicles use a different exhaust system than light- and medium-duty diesel-powered vehicles. In a heavy-duty vehicle, a **vertical exhaust system** directs exhaust gases upward, into the atmosphere **FIGURE 34-4**. Advantages of vertical exhaust systems include lower noise levels because they aim the exhaust noise and fumes away from passengers and street-level bystanders. In addition, muffler size is not constrained as much as it is on horizontal exhaust systems, where space limitations prevent the use of a large unit. Vertical exhaust systems generally have longer life due to improved drainage of water and corrosive acids. Some vehicle owners consider the vertical stack

FIGURE 34-4 Vertical exhaust systems can incorporate the latest aftertreatment technology. This system for heavy-duty equipment incorporates a DPF and selective catalyst reduction.

more aesthetically pleasing. Disadvantages of vertical exhaust systems include:

- Noise transmission to cab unless properly supported
- Clearance problems between the cab fifth-wheel and trailers that minimize the swing radius of the trailer
- Greater vulnerability to damage from overhead hazards

► Components of Engine Exhaust Systems

The exhaust system traverses the chassis from the exhaust manifolds to the exhaust pipe at the end of the vehicle. A variety of components are used to safely remove the heated gases while keeping noise levels to a minimum. This next section examines the construction and operation of various exhaust system components.

Exhaust Manifolds

The **exhaust manifold** collects exhaust gases from each cylinder of the cylinder head. Exhaust manifolds are divided and split between front and rear cylinder banks on four- and six-cylinder engines to prevent interference of exhaust pulses between front and rear cylinders **FIGURE 34-5**. This arrangement not only improves exhaust scavenging but is also necessary to optimize turbocharger performance. Without this, high-pressure pulses released at the initial opening of the exhaust valve and low-pressure exhaust gases present at the end of another cylinder's exhaust stroke would cancel one another inside the exhaust manifold. So in an engine having a standard 1-5-3-6-2-4 firing order, as cylinder 1 finishes the exhaust stroke, number 5 begins. Both pressure waves would merge in a single piece manifold. Depending on the valve timing, high-pressure exhaust gases from cylinder 5 could push into cylinder 1. However, high-pressure exhaust gases are needed to drive the turbocharger

turbine, and turbocharger performance is enhanced when pressure pulses are sequentially transmitted through the turbine housing. This is accomplished only when manifolds are divided and separate gas pressure from multiple cylinders.

Manifolds are often multipiece to accommodate thermal expansion. A piston ring-like seal will separate sections of exhaust manifold, allowing it to creep while sealing exhaust gases inside the manifold **FIGURE 34-6**. Cast iron is the material of choice because it is heat resistant and durable, and because it dampens noise well. Manifolds may or may not be sealed with a gasket material. Alignment of multipiece cylinder heads and smoothness of sealing surfaces are critical on manifolds without gaskets to prevent exhaust gas leakage.

The exhaust manifold usually provides the location for mounting the turbocharger. While this is not always the case, turbocharger performance is enhanced when exhaust gases do not travel far from the combustion chamber, which causes them to lose energy through expansion and cooling. Occasionally, exhaust manifold runners are designed to tune exhaust pulse travel into the turbocharger. Tuning means to optimize the length and shape of the manifold runner to take advantage of dynamics produced by exhaust pulse pressure waves. By altering the length of the runner from the exhaust port to the turbocharger, the exhaust pulses are distributed more evenly and sequentially to the turbine wheel. Tuned manifolds keep short the runner for the cylinder farthest from the turbocharger, while the closest runners are lengthened.

Exhaust Pipes

Exhaust systems should be made of durable materials to resist the corrosive effects of exhaust gases and heat. Piping is made of galvanized or aluminized steel. Stainless steel piping has high heat resistance and is used for maximum longevity. In addition to being constructed for durability, exhaust pipes need to be the appropriate size. A diameter of exhaust pipe that is too large will result in more noise and have little impact on improving engine efficiency. A diameter that is too small will result in power-robbing, engine-damaging backpressure.

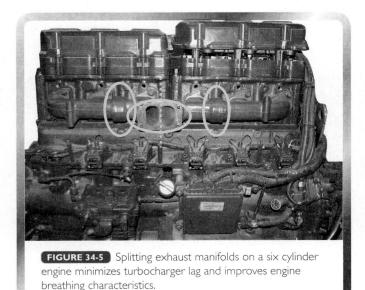

FIGURE 34-5 Splitting exhaust manifolds on a six cylinder engine minimizes turbocharger lag and improves engine breathing characteristics.

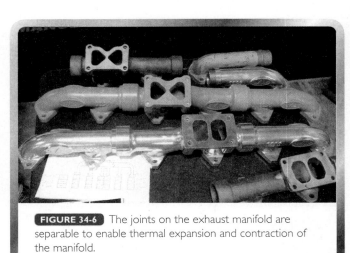

FIGURE 34-6 The joints on the exhaust manifold are separable to enable thermal expansion and contraction of the manifold.

Keep exhaust system length, as well as bends and elbows in the exhaust system, to a minimum to reduce backpressure. The greater the length and the greater the number or sharpness of bends, the slower exhaust gases will flow through the system. Resistance to exhaust-gas flow increases backpressure.

It should be noted that long exhaust systems, such as those found on school buses, can consume more lubrication oil. High-pressure exhaust pulses moving down the exhaust pipe leave pressure areas in their wake that are very low. Low-pressure areas at the exhaust valve stems and turbochargers tend to drag oil out of these components and into the exhaust stream. On older, worn engines, these vehicles will produce a characteristic blue smoke ring during deceleration

Care must be taken to isolate engine vibration away from the exhaust system and to provide for expansion when the system is hot. A **flex pipe** may be used between the engine pipe and the rest of the exhaust system to absorb twists and movement of pipe caused by engine torque reaction **FIGURE 34-7**.

The service life of flex pipe is improved if it is installed in a relaxed position. Stretching and compressing flex pipe during initial installation will reduce life span because these movements limit the material's ability to absorb vibration and thermal expansion. A well-supported exhaust system will reduce the noise generated by the vibration of exhaust pipes and the muffler shell.

Mufflers and Resonators

A muffler is the exhaust system's primary component for minimizing noise. Mufflers reduce exhaust noise by allowing the expansion of the exhaust pressure pulse. Using a series of baffles, or perforated tubes, dissipates the pressure pulse energy after it passes through the muffler, creating a smooth flow of gases out the tailpipe. Mufflers packed with fiberglass material are designed to absorb even more noise from the exhaust. On turbocharged diesel engines, mufflers do not need to be highly dampened because the turbine wheel chops up pressure pulses, which decreases exhaust noise.

A resonator is a device in the exhaust system that looks like a small muffler. Resonators provide additional dampening and tuning of exhaust noise. Resonators are especially effective when space constraints limit the size of muffler that can be configured for a chassis. Resonators have minimal impact on EBP.

Exhaust aftertreatment devices, such as DPFs, SCRs, and oxidation catalysts, can eliminate the need for a muffler. That is because these devices dampen pressure pulsations, which reduces exhaust noise **FIGURE 34-8**.

Muffler size is critical to reducing noise emissions while minimizing backpressure. A minimum of approximately seven times engine displacement is required for the volume of a turbocharged diesel engine muffler. Muffler volumes smaller than this will increase backpressure. Mufflers that are too large will increase noise emissions. Higher horsepower engines with high fuel and airflow rates from the turbocharger require dual exhaust stacks to supply enough expansion volume for exhaust gases to reduce backpressure. Vehicle manufacturers using engines from another manufacturer should follow the engine manufacturer's recommendation for exhaust system requirements. Cases exist where vehicles have been built with poorly designed and undersized exhaust systems, causing performance-related complaints not directly related to the engine.

Exhaust System Accessories

Spark Arrestors

Engines can accumulate carbon deposits in the cylinder and in the exhaust system. When loosened and discharged, these hot carbon particulates can ignite fires if discharged in off-road conditions, such as grass fields and woodlands. In fact, several U.S. states require spark arrestors on any vehicle traveling off road. To prevent fires, spark arrestors are often placed at the end of the exhaust system. The **spark arrestor** is usually a screen covering the exhaust outlet. When large incandescent carbon particles make contact with this screen, they are trapped and the flow of exhaust gases pounds them into smaller pieces, which cools them **FIGURE 34-9**.

EBP Regulators

The superior thermal efficiency of the direct-injection diesel combustion chamber has one drawback—slow coolant warm-up when

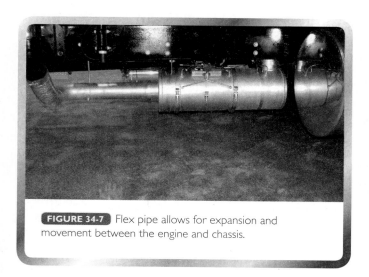

FIGURE 34-7 Flex pipe allows for expansion and movement between the engine and chassis.

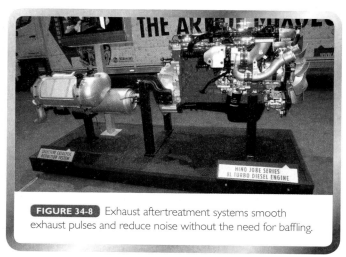

FIGURE 34-8 Exhaust aftertreatment systems smooth exhaust pulses and reduce noise without the need for baffling.

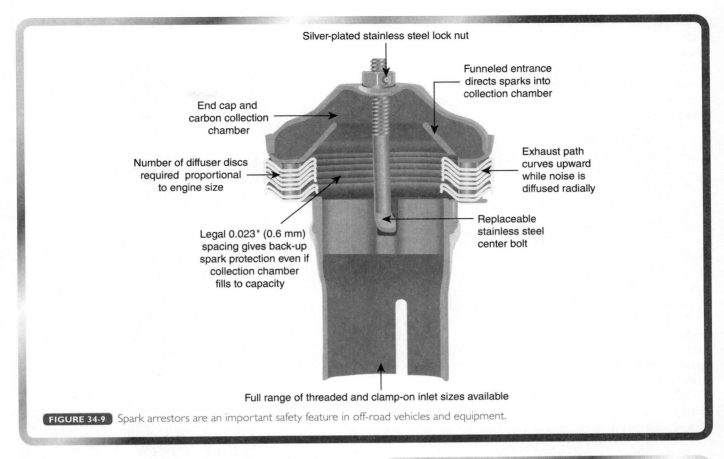

Silver-plated stainless steel lock nut

Funneled entrance directs sparks into collection chamber

End cap and carbon collection chamber

Exhaust path curves upward while noise is diffused radially

Number of diffuser discs required proportional to engine size

Replaceable stainless steel center bolt

Legal 0.023" (0.6 mm) spacing gives back-up spark protection even if collection chamber fills to capacity

Full range of threaded and clamp-on inlet sizes available

FIGURE 34-9 Spark arrestors are an important safety feature in off-road vehicles and equipment.

the engine is at idle or low engine load. The primary reasons are excess air factor at idle and small injection quantities combined with a combustion chamber having a small chamber surface area compared to combustion volume. This means little heat energy from the combustion chamber transfers to the engine coolant, so the engine will not warm—or is slow to warm—to operating temperature at idle. To modify this characteristic, an **EBP regulator** increases exhaust pressure inside the diesel engine's exhaust manifolds. Doing this causes the exhaust gases to linger longer around the exhaust ports and transfer their heat to the cooling system.

Operation of EBP Regulators

Older engines often use bimetallic or vacuum-operated controls to modulate the opening of a butterfly valve located in the exhaust pipe just after the manifold. An electric or vacuum-operated switch in the cooling system would open and close the device via a light spring pressure.

A more contemporary example of an EBP regulator is found on the 7.3L (445 cubic inch) PowerStroke or optionally on the T444E Navistar engine **FIGURE 34-10**. Raising EBP on these engines provides more heat to the coolant for cab heating and defrosting when ambient air temperature is below 45°F (7°C) and engine oil temperature is below 167°F (75°C) and during low-load, low-speed operating conditions. The major component is a butterfly valve located at the outlet of the turbocharger. An EBP regulator valve operated by engine oil actuates the butterfly valve. When signaled by the electronic control module (ECM), the EBP regulator valve will direct oil pressure to a servo piston that closes the butterfly valve. Inputs to the circuit

Wastegate Actuator

EBP Regulator Actuator

Butterfly Valve

FIGURE 34-10 In this EBP regulator, an oil-operated control valve moves the butterfly valve to a closed position to speed engine warm-up.

include the EBP sensor, which is located in a tube connected to the exhaust manifold, an air intake sensor, and an engine oil temperature sensor.

Each time the engine starts, the butterfly valve is cycled from fully closed to open to prevent seizure of bushings in the turbocharger housing. After cycling at start-up, other conditions cause the butterfly valve to close:

- Intake air temperature is less than 37°F (3°C)
- Oil temperature is 32–140°F (0–60°C)
- As the oil temperature rises during engine operation, the ECM will modulate the valve position, opening it proportional to the rising oil temperature

Volvo Exhaust Pressure Governor

To increase combustion temperatures during cranking and improve warm-up characteristics, Volvo uses an **exhaust pressure governor (EPG)**, which also reduces cold start emissions. The concept is simple: an air-operated piston restricts exhaust flow in the exhaust pipe just after the turbocharger **FIGURE 34-11**.

Ideal combustion chamber temperatures can be reached by cranking the engine while increasing EBP. Fuel is not injected during the first four to seven cranking revolutions to minimize formation of HC emissions and to avoid the cooling effect of excess fuel in the combustion chamber **FIGURE 34-12**.

After the EPG is activated during engine rotation, combustion temperatures increase further to reduce the likelihood of misfires and excessive HC emissions, visible as white or gray smoke during the warm-up period:

1. The engine cranks without fuel for 4–7 revolutions.
2. The backpressure regulator closes during the cranking period.

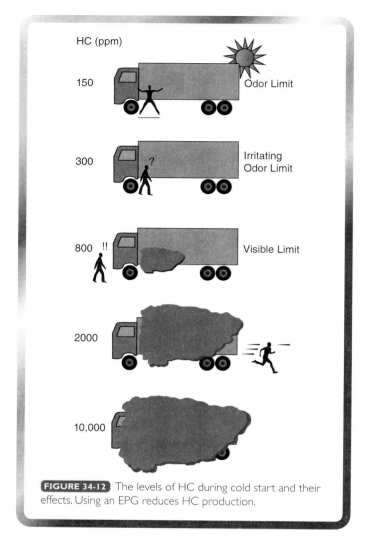

FIGURE 34-12 The levels of HC during cold start and their effects. Using an EPG reduces HC production.

3. Higher exhaust (actually air) pressure is in the combustion chamber and increases combustion chamber temperatures.
4. Fuel is injected.

Note that the combustion chamber temperature must reach the flash point of the fuel. This is achieved by cranking the engine without injection.

An insufficient number of crankshaft rotations will not provide the correct temperature, and too many rotations without starting may annoy the driver. Excessive battery current is used, too, which could damage the starter and other starting system circuits **FIGURE 34-13**.

Combustion chamber temperatures can be increased further by keeping the EPG closed after the engine starts. This not only speeds up engine warm-up, it also reduces cold-start emissions. If the backpressure is too high, the engine can produce black smoke.

The ECM controls the EPG **FIGURE 34-14**. The ECM collects data from the starter key, parking brake, and power take-off (PTO) switches. An ECM-controlled air relay supplies vehicle air pressure to the EPG. Releasing the parking brake or activating the PTO will automatically disengage the EPG.

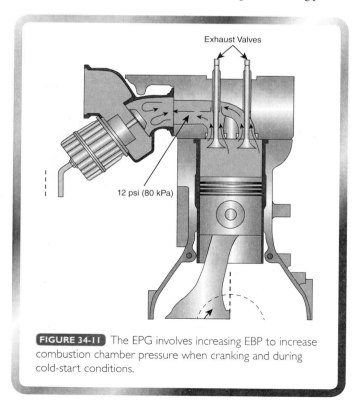

FIGURE 34-11 The EPG involves increasing EBP to increase combustion chamber pressure when cranking and during cold-start conditions.

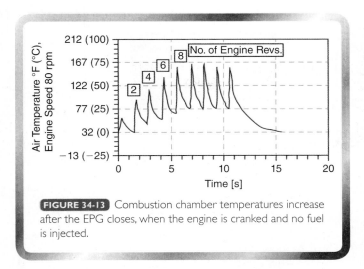

FIGURE 34-13 Combustion chamber temperatures increase after the EPG closes, when the engine is cranked and no fuel is injected.

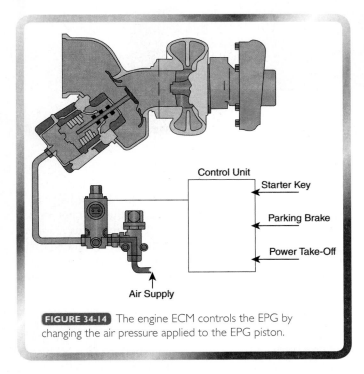

FIGURE 34-14 The engine ECM controls the EPG by changing the air pressure applied to the EPG piston.

During engine braking, the EPG will have two air pressure steps applied to the governor piston. This enhances the effect of the compression release engine brake.

Pyrometers and Exhaust Gas Temperature

A **pyrometer** is a temperature gauge designed to measure exhaust gas temperatures (EGTs) above those measurable by an ordinary thermometer or thermistor. A pyrometer provides warning data regarding excessively high combustion temperatures. Restricted air intake or overfueling will increase exhaust temperatures. Slow speeds while driving uphill in low gear means little airflow across an intercooler, which can contribute to high exhaust temperatures **FIGURE 34-15**.

A pyrometer consists of a thermocouple probe placed in the exhaust as close as possible to the exhaust ports. EGT is normally measured after the turbo and is called turbine outlet temperature. If the probe is positioned before the turbine section of the turbocharger, the EGT may also be called the turbine inlet temperature. On a diesel, the probe is mounted in the exhaust manifold or immediately after the turbine outlet of the turbocharger. The probe is connected to a voltmeter gauge, which is located in the cab. A thermocouple typically will generate approximately 29 microvolts for every 1°F change.

Some technicians fear installing the pyrometer thermocouple in the exhaust manifold in the event the probe will break or burn off and blow into the turbocharger. This would cause serious damage that could break the turbine and the turbine shaft, sending broken pieces of the compressor wheel into the intake system of the engine, where even more damage could occur. However, quality pyrometers feature thermocouples that are sheathed in stainless steel and can withstand temperatures up to 2500°F (1371°C) to prevent such an occurrence.

Note that when the EGT is measured after the turbine, the turbine outlet temperature at full throttle or under a heavy load typically would be 250–500°F (121–260°C) lower than the EGT measured in the exhaust manifold. Note the following as well:

- Maximum normal exhaust port temperature is 950°F (510°C)
- Damage will occur after 1250°F (677°C)

Under sustained excessive EGT, the square corners at the outer ends of the turbine, where the material is thinnest, can become incandescent and melt. The result is a rounding off of the corners. If the tips melt, the turbine wheel will become unbalanced and damage the turbocharger bearings, which may cause shaft failure and destroy the turbine and compressor wheels. Excessive EGT can also erode or crack the turbine housing. In extreme cases, the additional heat energy of high EGT can drive the turbocharger into an overspeed condition that exceeds the designed operating speed. When this happens, either the turbine wheel or the compressor wheel may burst. Excessive EGT, if sustained, will damage the pistons. Damage can include deformation, melting, burning, holes, and cracking.

Engine-Based Braking Systems

Engine-based brakes can be classified into two categories:

- Compression release
- Exhaust

Exhaust Brakes

Diesels are popular because they have more pulling power and low-speed torque than other engine types and because they will do the work using less fuel. However, with a gross vehicle weight rating limit of 80,000 lb (36,287 kg) for a 6x4 tractor trailer, the service brakes can be severely overloaded. In this respect, diesel engines are at a disadvantage compared with gasoline-fueled engines because engine braking in a gasoline engine is better than a diesel engine. This is because gasoline

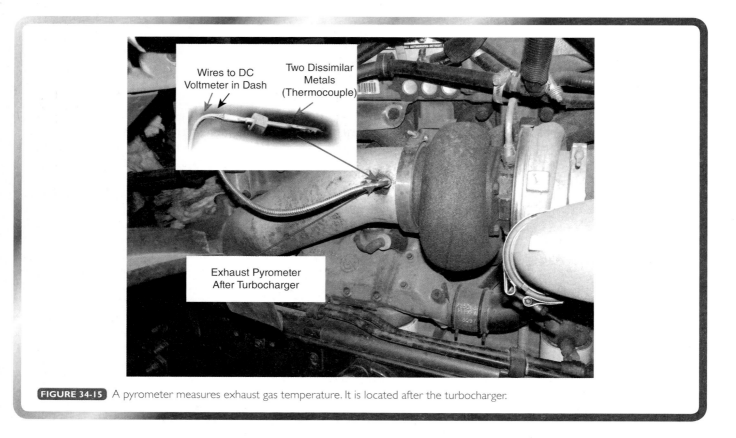

Wires to DC Voltmeter in Dash

Two Dissimilar Metals (Thermocouple)

Exhaust Pyrometer After Turbocharger

FIGURE 34-15 A pyrometer measures exhaust gas temperature. It is located after the turbocharger.

engines have throttle plates that produce what is known as a pumping loss. Pumping loss is energy expended by the engine when attempting to pull air around a closed throttle plate (and pushing exhaust gases out of the cylinders). In hilly or mountainous terrain, the gasoline engine with its throttle plate closed will have a better natural retarding force than the diesel engine. Therefore, less demand is placed on the service brakes to slow down a vehicle with a gasoline engine.

To compensate for the natural loss of engine braking, aftermarket exhaust brakes can be installed on vehicles with diesel engines to improve their braking ability **FIGURE 34-16**. The concept of the exhaust brake is relatively simple. A fixed or variable restriction is placed in the exhaust system increases backpressure, which causes the engine to exert a retarding force against the driveline **FIGURE 34-17**. Typically, this involves using a small butterfly in the exhaust pipe **FIGURE 34-18**. An electric-pneumatic solenoid will open and close the butterfly valve. An integral wastegate, or bypass port, prevents exhaust gas pressure from climbing too high and possibly opening exhaust valves or over-pressurizing a turbocharger, if equipped **FIGURE 34-19**. Because high exhaust pressure can cause exhaust valves to stay open, higher valve spring pressure is recommended for some engines using exhaust brakes. The disadvantage of increasing valve spring tension is that doing so increases the potential for wear of valve faces and seats.

Exhaust Brake Controls

Exhaust brakes will typically have controls allowing them to operate only when the accelerator pedal is at idle position and the clutch is engaged. Electronic engines will use throttle position sensor data to determine whether the throttle is closed. A clutch switch also provides data to the ECM regarding clutch position. In addition to a throttle pedal, the operator uses a manual toggle switch to turn the brake on and off as required. A second toggle switch determines the level of braking—high medium, or low. When an operator wants to speed engine warm-up, he or she can switch on the exhaust brake to promote a quicker increase to coolant temperature.

Adjusting the Exhaust Brake (Off-Idle Pressure Test)

An exhaust brake's backpressure is measured to ensure the brake is adjusted correctly for optimal engine braking. The brakes are adjusted at the factory and usually do not need adjustment. However, if braking is not adequate, the brake may need adjustment if an adjustment is available.

To adjust the exhaust brake, follow the steps in **SKILL DRILL 34-1**.

Variable Geometry Turbocharger Braking

Variable geometry turbochargers (VGTs) can be calibrated to operate as exhaust brakes. On light- and medium-duty vehicles, during deceleration, the transmission torque converter will remain locked and the turbocharger vanes will close, restricting exhaust gas flow. Heavier turbocharger housings prevent turbocharger distortion under the high internal heat and pressure encountered during breaking. When road surfaces are slippery, the wheels can also lock because the engine is resisting driveline movement. To prevent the vehicle from performing more

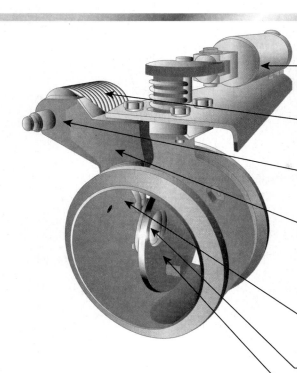

Sealed air cylinder
Hard, coated stainless steel cylinder with stainless steel shaft and high-performance seals throughout

Automatic low rpm adjustment
Optimum retarding performance maintained by maximizing exhaust back pressure throughout the entire rpm range

Maximum allowable exhaust back pressure limit
Factory preset and designed to meet standards and requirements set by the engine manufacturer

Arcor® nitrided housing and components
Industry exclusive process that increases resistance to wear and corrosion, strengthens and adds lubricity

Precision mounting surface
Both contacting surfaces are machined, which eliminates the need for gaskets

Free-flow exhaust
When not activated, exhaust flow is unrestricted and won't interfere with power output

No overpressure potential
Enlarged orifice design

90-degree closing, non-contacting butterfly valve
Guarantees engine safety with special design to prevent sticking

FIGURE 34-16 An exhaust brake restricts exhaust gas flow in the exhaust pipe, generating backpressure in the engine, which produces a retarding force that resists driveline rotation.

PRXB Exhaust Brake Operation

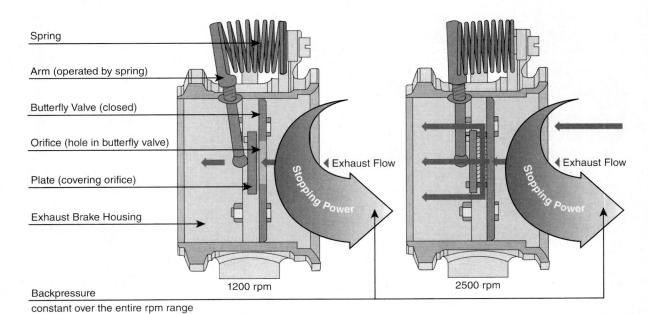

Spring

Arm (operated by spring)

Butterfly Valve (closed)

Orifice (hole in butterfly valve)

Plate (covering orifice)

Exhaust Brake Housing

Exhaust Flow

Stopping Power

1200 rpm   2500 rpm

Backpressure
constant over the entire rpm range

FIGURE 34-17 A variable-orifice exhaust brake uses a spring-loaded restrictor valve that maintains constant exhaust backpressure.

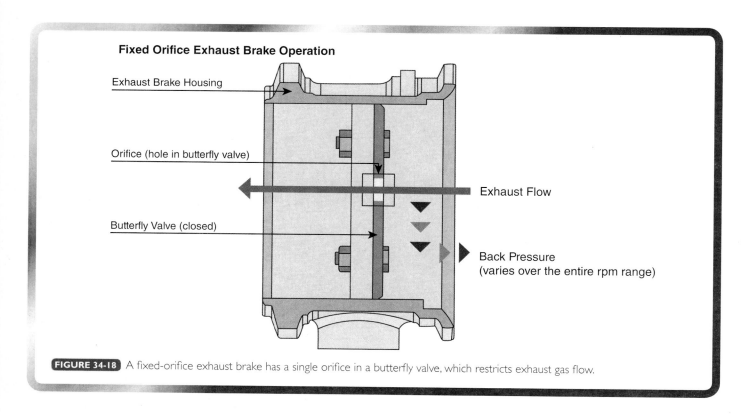

FIGURE 34-18 A fixed-orifice exhaust brake has a single orifice in a butterfly valve, which restricts exhaust gas flow.

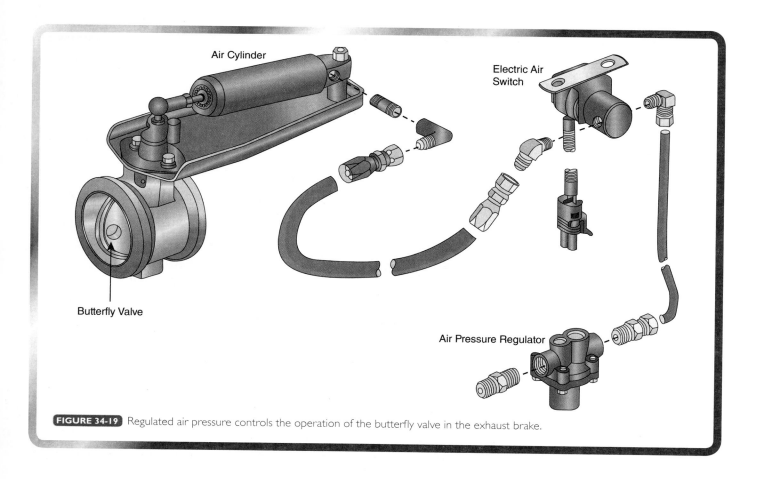

FIGURE 34-19 Regulated air pressure controls the operation of the butterfly valve in the exhaust brake.

SKILL DRILL 34-1 Adjusting the Exhaust Brake (Off-Idle Pressure Test)

1 Connect a purpose-made exhaust back-pressure gauge to a long hose to view backpressure in the cab of the vehicle.

2 With the exhaust brake engaged and the engine at idle, measure the exhaust backpressure at the test port on the brake valve. Consult the manufacturer's specifications for backpressure. Generally, a pressure below 13 psi (90 kPa) is inadequate. The exhaust system should be checked for leaks and the EGR system should be checked for a malfunction to determine whether exhaust gas pressure is escaping through an EGR valve that is stuck open.

3 If the exhaust back pressure is more than 25 psi (172 kPa), an adjustment of the spring-loaded stop bolt is necessary. Loosen the stop bolt jam nut and turn the bolt counterclockwise to lengthen the bolt and reduce the spring tension applied to the butterfly valve. Retest idle backpressure.

4 Measure off-idle backpressure by operating the vehicle at highway speed on a downhill grade. Compare your observations with the manufacturer's specifications. The backpressure should not exceed the maximum backpressure recommended by the OEM. Carbon buildup in variable orifice brakes will tend to increase backpressure with use and time. Off-idle backpressure is set by adjusting the air pressure regulator, which will increase or decrease off-idle exhaust backpressure. Lowering the air pressure will decrease the maximum backpressure and vice versa.

5 If off-idle adjustments are performed, recheck the idle pressure adjustment and correct as necessary.

---

like a sled and losing maneuverability, the anti-lock braking system will monitor wheel speed and disengage the turbocharged engine-based braking **FIGURE 34-20**.

TECHNICIAN TIP

Engine brakes retard driveline motion by making the engine more resistant to rotation through the drive train. Slippery conditions can cause wheel lockup and steering loss. To prevent this, the anti-lock braking system (ABS) monitors wheel speed for lockup conditions. If lockup occurs, the engine braking system will disengage automatically via messages sent over the vehicle network. Older engines used an electrical relay that would cut power to the engine brake after receiving a ground signal from the ABS module.

Compression Release Brakes

Only diesel engines have **compression release brakes**. Approximately 70% of heavy-duty vehicles produced in North America are equipped with compression release engine brakes. These brakes are most common on engines with a displacement of 3 gallons (gal) (11 liters [L]) and greater. The operation of an engine brake produces a sudden release of the compressed air from the cylinder by quickly opening the exhaust valve near top dead center (TDC) of the compression stroke, dissipating the energy used to compress air.

Two factors cause the engine to retard the speed of the vehicle. First, the diesel's high compression ratio (as much as 17.5:1 in on-highway engines) uses energy to compress the intake air to 500–1800 pounds per square inch (psi) (34–124 bar) inside the cylinders. The higher pressures are found in

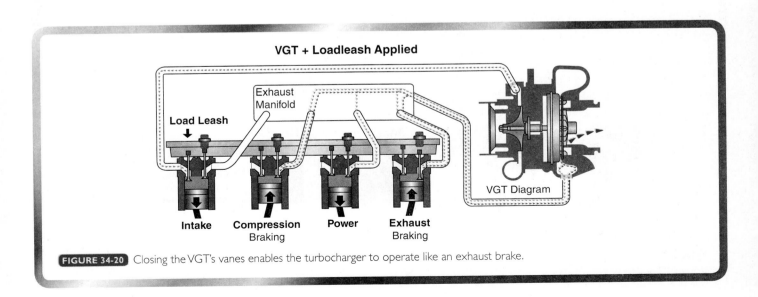

FIGURE 34-20 Closing the VGT's vanes enables the turbocharger to operate like an exhaust brake.

turbocharged engines rotating near maximum governed speeds. Energy used to compress the air is lost when the exhaust valve opens near TDC. The effect can be compared to wasting the energy in a compressed spring. When compressing a spring, normally it will rebound after the pressure compressing it is released. In the engine, not opening the exhaust valve will allow the energy stored in the compressed air to simply push the piston downward during the power stroke, even if no fuel is injected. Opening the exhaust valve dissipates energy used to compress this air.

The loss of this energy from combustion or the natural "spring" force of air as it rebounds and pushes the piston back down into the cylinder is also lost. During the downward piston movement, in what would have been the power stroke, no fuel is injected and the engine pulls almost a vacuum in the cylinder. This is the second cause for the engine's resistance: Because the vehicle driveline is connected to the engine, the vehicle speed is naturally retarded. To effectively slow the vehicle, the clutch must be engaged in standard transmissions, and the torque converter must be locked in automatic transmissions. Without a standard transmission and direct connection to the engine, this type of braking is not possible, so a driveline or transmission retarder is required **FIGURE 34-21**.

Advantages of Compression Brakes

Braking power available through a truck's service brakes is dramatically reduced as the brake shoe temperature increases. The supplemental retarding power provided by engine brakes enables a truck or bus operator to control vehicle speed on long downgrades without overheating the vehicle's service brakes. Compression release braking reduces the danger of brake fade. Using an engine brake leads to lower maintenance costs by extending the change interval of brake lining. Compression release brakes have additional benefits:

- They can be combined with cruise control settings to prevent vehicle overspeed
- Drivers using standard non-synchronized transmissions make faster and easier upshifts and downshifts because the engine and transmission main shaft speeds will quickly match using compression release braking
- Highly compressed air moving across the injector nozzles helps keep injector nozzles cleaner
- Engine brakes can also reduce driveline shock loading

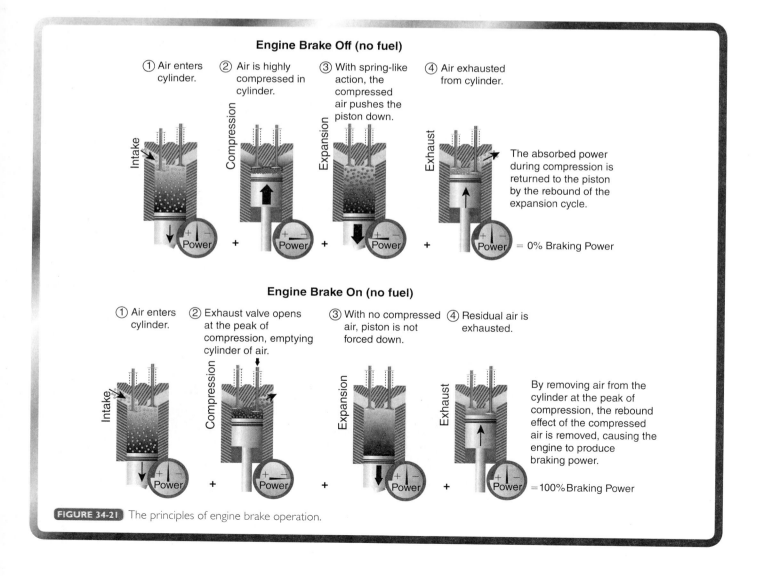

FIGURE 34-21 The principles of engine brake operation.

Safety

Brakes should never be used on reduced friction coefficient surfaces—wet, snowy, and/or icy surfaces—because the operator may lose control of the vehicle. Brakes are automatically disabled by the ABS module if a wheel lockup is sensed.

Adjusting a Caterpillar Compression Release Brake

After the valve and injector adjustment is completed, the clearance between an engine brake's slave piston and the contact point on the exhaust valve crosshead is adjusted. Then, the engine brake housings are reinstalled and torqued. Finally, the engine brake slave piston clearance is adjusted, making it the last procedure when performing a complete top-end adjustment.

To adjust a Caterpillar compression release brake, follow the steps in **SKILL DRILL 34-2**. The procedure shown is specific to Caterpillar. Follow the manufacturer's instructions for products from other OEMs.

Principle of Conventional Brake Operation

Controlling the opening of the exhaust valve depends on the type of brake used by an engine. On older four-stroke cycle engines with unit injectors, the movement of the injector push-rod or lever actuates the brake action **FIGURE 34-22**. Newer engines use a separate cam lobe or specialized exhaust cam profile to provide the force needed to open the exhaust valve.

Two major components of an engine brake are the master piston and the slave piston. Much like hydraulic brakes **master and slave cylinders**, pushing on the master cylinder moves the slave cylinder. In conventional compression release brakes, the brake housing uses a solenoid that, when energized, traps oil between the master and slave pistons. An injector push tube will push on the master cylinder, which causes the slave piston to push down on an exhaust valve or valve bridge to open the valve. Up-and-down movement of the injector push tube opens and closes the exhaust valve just before TDC at the end of compression stroke **FIGURE 34-23** and **FIGURE 34-24**.

Two-Lobed Camshaft

Another technique for operating a compression release brake is to use an exhaust cam lobe with a regular cam lobe lift for the exhaust valve opening and closing. A second smaller cam lobe bumps the exhaust valve open near TDC **FIGURE 34-25**. Normally, this second lobe will not open or close the valve. However, under braking conditions, the rocker lever of many compression release brakes uses a hydraulic link that is much like a hydraulic valve lifter. Pressurized oil entering the rocker lever removes operating clearances, and **decompression lobes** open and close the exhaust valve near TDC **FIGURE 34-26**.

SKILL DRILL 34-2 Adjusting a Caterpillar Compression Release Brake

1. The compression brake adjustment provides specifications for a cold engine. The engine should be allowed to cool before performing an adjustment procedure.

2. All clearances between the slave piston and the exhaust valve bridges are made when the exhaust valves are closed.

3. Position the engine at TDC for cylinder 1 by installing a threaded 3/8" (9.5 mm) bolt in the bell housing cover and locking the flywheel at TDC. The bolt hole is accessed on the right side of the engine, opposite the starter motor. When the engine is at TDC, remove the access plug thread the bolt into the flywheel.

4. Verify the correct cylinder is chosen to begin performing adjustments. Shaking the rocker levers on cylinders 6 and 1 should indicate the rocker levers are both tight on cylinder 6 and both loose on cylinder 1. The cylinder 1 slave piston can be adjusted.

5. Insert a feeler blade of the correct thickness between the slave piston and valve bridge. Tighten the adjusting screw for the slave piston until you feel a light drag on the feeler blade. Lock the valve adjustment screw and torque the lock nut to specifications. Recheck the clearance between the slave piston and valve bridge.

6. Complete the adjustment the same way for cylinders 3 and 5.

7. Remove the timing pin from the flywheel and rotate the engine 360 degrees. This position will place the piston of cylinder 6 at the TDC at the end of its compression stroke. Both rocker levers should be loose on cylinder 6. Perform the same procedure to adjust cylinders 2, 4, and 6.

8. Remove the timing bolt from the flywheel after all slave piston adjustments have been performed and reinstall the valve covers.

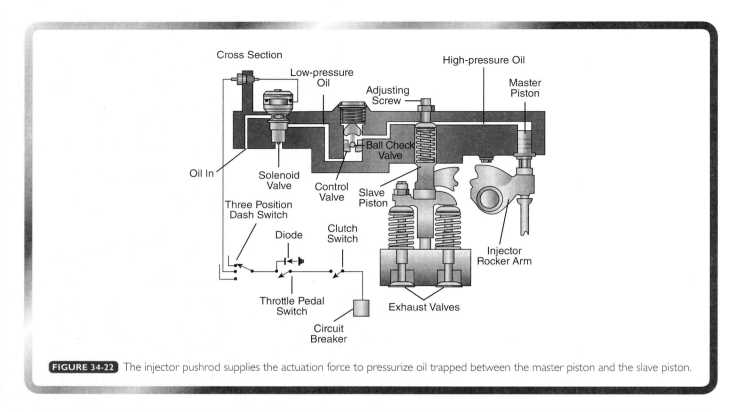

FIGURE 34-22 The injector pushrod supplies the actuation force to pressurize oil trapped between the master piston and the slave piston.

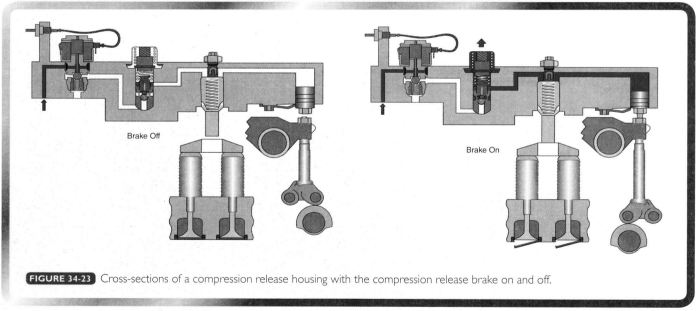

FIGURE 34-23 Cross-sections of a compression release housing with the compression release brake on and off.

To get valve actuation from the small lobe, a solenoid will energize and trap oil in the rocker shaft. Trapping oil causes oil pressure to build in the rocker lever containing the link that pumps up the hydraulic link. The specially ground profile on the cam shaft lifts the exhaust valve off its seat, releasing the compressed air. Internal exhaust brakes like this typically run with efficiencies of 80–110%.

Engine cooling fans may be activated during braking to increase drag. This can add 15–40 hp (11–30 kilowatts [kW]) to engine drag.

The Volvo compression release brake uses three bump profiles on the exhaust lobe. One is to open the exhaust valve at the end of power stroke. Another is to open the exhaust valve at the end of compression stroke for compression release. The third, called the charging lobe, cracks open the exhaust lobe during the intake stroke to admit additional pressurized exhaust gas into the cylinder. The additional exhaust mass increases cylinder pressure, particularly if the exhaust brake is simultaneously engaged. Much more retarding force is produced when the charging lobe admits the exhaust gas along with the intake air charge.

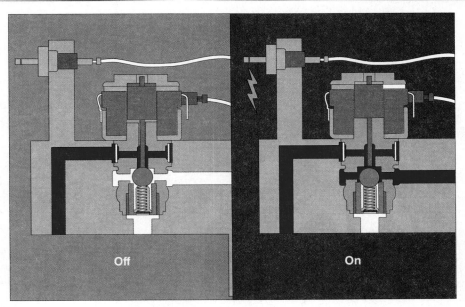

FIGURE 34-24 A solenoid will energize when the compression brake is engaged, trap oil in the compression brake housing, and cause oil pressure to build there.

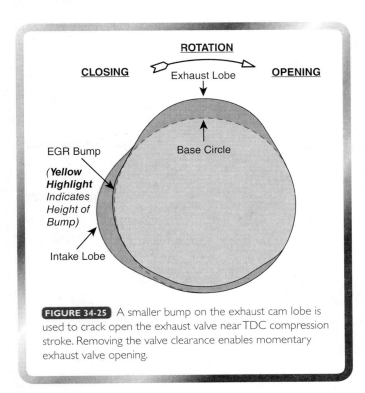

FIGURE 34-25 A smaller bump on the exhaust cam lobe is used to crack open the exhaust valve near TDC compression stroke. Removing the valve clearance enables momentary exhaust valve opening.

Newer engines use a separate lobe to operate the compression release brake. The lobe is next to an exhaust lobe. A separate rocker lever following the brake lobe will connect with the exhaust rocker lever to push it down at the correct time to open the exhaust valve during braking **FIGURE 34-27**.

Double-Pump Compression Release Brakes

Even more effective engine braking can take place on exhaust gas recirculation engines by opening the exhaust valve during the intake stroke. Exhaust gases in the manifold, which are pressurized by the VGT, will fill the cylinder with even more gas mass for improved braking **FIGURE 34-28**.

Compression Brake Controls

On electronically-controlled engines, the ECM controls compression release brake operation. The brake, clutch, throttle position, idle validation switch, vehicle speed sensor, and ABS module are typical inputs for control. A number of strategies can be programmed by the customer. For example, the brake can be set up to activate only above a vehicle speed threshold or to maintain vehicle speed when coasting down a grade. Remember the brake will not operate unless the driver has his or her foot off the throttle and has released the clutch pedal.

Engine Brakes and Noise

Opening the exhaust valve during braking can create high noise levels because of the cylinder pressures when the exhaust valve is opened. Better exhaust mufflers are needed when using a compression release brake. Operating with a damaged or open exhaust system adds 22 dB to the 101 dB of noise the brake is already producing **TABLE 34-1**.

▶ Maintaining Engine Brakes
Adjusting Engine Brake Programmable Parameters

Three different modes of engine retarder operation can be custom programmed on a Caterpillar engine. These

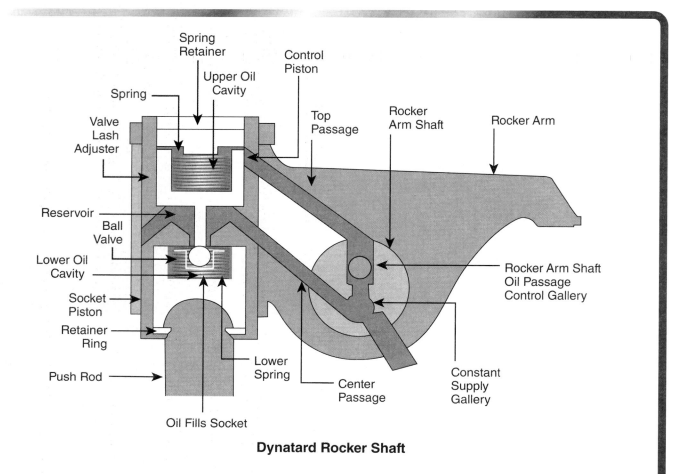

Dynatard Rocker Shaft

FIGURE 34-26 A hydraulic link, something like a hydraulic lifter, is incorporated into the exhaust rocker lever of an engine with a decompression cam lobe.

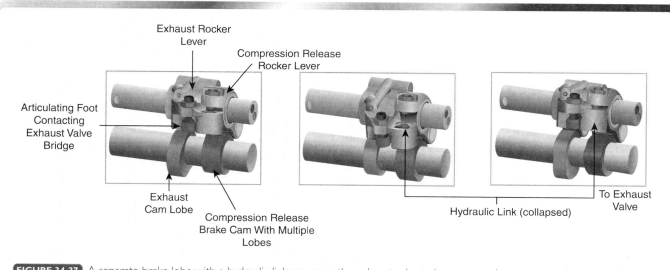

FIGURE 34-27 A separate brake lobe with a hydraulic link can open the exhaust valve twice: once to decompress and a second time to admit exhaust gas into the cylinder during intake stroke.

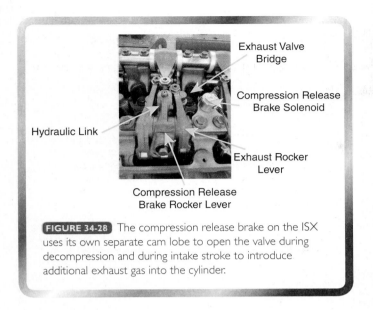

FIGURE 34-28 The compression release brake on the ISX uses its own separate cam lobe to open the valve during decompression and during intake stroke to introduce additional exhaust gas into the cylinder.

software-controlled engine brake features are similar to features used by other diesel engine manufacturers. Manual, Coast, and Latch are customer-programmable engine retarder parameters.

To adjust engine brake programmable parameters, follow the steps in **SKILL DRILL 34-3**. The procedure shown is specific to Caterpillar. Follow the manufacturer's instructions for products from other OEMs.

Servicing Engine Brakes

When servicing engine brakes, clutch and throttle switches may require adjustments to enable the brake to operate correctly. Electronically controlled brakes may require a minimum road speed and engine rpm to enable the brake. In addition, slave pistons require adjustments to maintain some clearance between them and the exhaust valves or bridge. Inadequate clearance could cause the valves to hit the pistons and produce poor brake operation. Tune-up kits are available for brakes and

should be included in regularly scheduled engine maintenance **TABLE 34-2**.

Adjust slave piston clearances between the exhaust valves after adjusting intake and exhaust valve clearances. A clearance is established between the slave piston and exhaust valve when adjusting the compression release brake operation **FIGURE 34-29**.

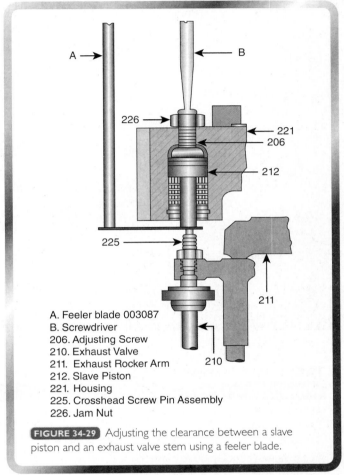

A. Feeler blade 003087
B. Screwdriver
206. Adjusting Screw
210. Exhaust Valve
211. Exhaust Rocker Arm
212. Slave Piston
221. Housing
225. Crosshead Screw Pin Assembly
226. Jam Nut

FIGURE 34-29 Adjusting the clearance between a slave piston and an exhaust valve stem using a feeler blade.

TABLE 34-1: Comparison of Truck Exhaust Noise Level

VEHICLE DRIVE BY CONDITION	Resulting Sound Level	Increase in Sound Level over One Truck
When…		
1 properly muffled truck drives by	80 dBA	Baseline
2 property muffled trucks drive by together	83 dBA	+3 dBA
4 property muffled trucks drive by together	86 dBA	+6 dBA
8 property muffled trucks drive by together	89 dBA	+9 dBA
16 properly muffled trucks drive by together	92 dBA	+12 dBA
32 properly muffled trucks drive by together	95 dBA	+15 d&A
64 properly muffled trucks drive by together	98 dBA	+18 dBA
1 28 properly muffled trucks drive by together	101 dBA	+21 dBA
1 truck operating with straight slacks drives by alone	101 dBA	+21 dBA

SKILL DRILL 34-3 Adjusting Engine Brake Programmable Parameters

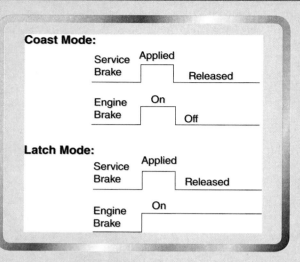

Coast Mode:

Service Brake — Applied / Released

Engine Brake — On / Off

Latch Mode:

Service Brake — Applied / Released

Engine Brake — On

① Connect the vehicle's data link adapter to the OEM software launched from a laptop or desktop computer cart. For example, the Caterpillar Electronic Technician software is used to adjust engine parameters and is available from the Cat Service Information System software suite.

② Navigate to the vehicle configuration menu and select the menu item for cruise control parameters.

③ Within the cruise control parameters, select retarder mode and note the drop-down selection for Manual, Latch, and Coast.

④ Determine which application best suits the vehicle's operation. Highway coaches, line-haul runs with long or steep grades, and intercity freights require different settings for optimal driver comfort and reduced service brake wear. Review the following application descriptions to select the most appropriate application:

- Manual mode: The engine compression release brake is enabled regardless of whether the cruise control switch is on. The brake will activate when the following conditions are met: the retarder switch is on, the engine speed is faster than 800 rpm, and the throttle pedal is released at idle.
- Coast mode: The engine brake is enabled only when the cruise control switch is on and the service brake pedal is applied. When the pedal is released, the brake disengages.
- Latch mode: The engine brake is enabled only when the cruise control switch is on and the service brake pedal is applied. Releasing the service brake pedal does not disengage the engine brake. The engine brake will remain enabled until another input, such as the accelerator or clutch pedal, is pushed, the engine speed drops below 800 rpm, or the engine brake switch is turned off.

TABLE 34-2: Troubleshooting a Jacobs Engine Brake

Problem	Possible Cause	Correction
Engine will not start	Solenoid valve stuck in "on" position.	With electrical current off, check the solenoid valve. If the solenoid valve is in the "on" position (solenoid cap down), replace the solenoid.
Engine brake will not operate	1. No power or insufficient power to the engine brake; 12 volts DC minimum is required. Check for: blown fuses; brittle, chafed, or broken wiring; broken, misadjusted, or open switches; corroded wire connectors; etc. 2. Faulty ECM or control module electronic engines. 3. Solenoid valve tab arcing to ground. 4. Low engine oil pressure; 25 psi (172 kPa) oil pressure minimum, measured at the engine brake, is required for proper operation.	1. Repair, as required. 2. Check and repair, if necessary, as outlined in the engine manufacturer's service manual. 3. Replace if necessary. 4. Repair as outlined in the engine manufacturer's service manual.
Engine brake slow to operate or braking action weak	1. Engine oil cold and thick. 2. Improper slave piston adjustment. 3. Slave piston binding in its bore. 4. Solenoid valve seal ring damaged. 5. Solenoid valve screen clogged. 6. Master piston stuck. 7. Control valves binding in housing bore, or malfunctioning.	1. Allow the engine to warm up before using the engine brake. 2. Adjust. 3. Replace if scored or damaged. 4. Replace. 5. Clean or replace. 6. Replace if scored or damaged. 7. Remove the control valve and check the body for scoring or damage. Replace if necessary. Make sure that the check ball is seating and can be removed off its seat. Make sure that there is spring pressure against the ball.

Wrap-Up

Ready for Review

▶ Exhaust systems on modern diesel-powered vehicles are increasingly sophisticated due to the introduction of emission-reduction technologies.

▶ On diesel-powered vehicles and equipment, the following functions are associated with the exhaust system: collecting and removing hot exhaust gases from engine cylinders, minimizing noise emissions from exhaust pulses, powering turbochargers, reducing exhaust noise, quenching sparks, removing solids from exhaust gas, engine braking, and promoting faster coolant warm-up with EBP devices.

▶ An engine's ability to draw a fresh air charge for combustion relies on the efficiency of its exhaust system. Installation of an exhaust system that can efficiently collect and discharge combustion gas is an important element to vehicle design and improving engine performance.

▶ Exhaust systems that do not properly remove exhaust gases have backpressure, which is resistance to exhaust gas flow from the engine. This can lead to performance complaints and detrimental operating conditions.

▶ Engine exhaust is a major contributor to total vehicle noise, which is regulated by unique emission standards. For this reason, exhaust systems are designed to discharge exhaust gas as quietly as possible to the perimeter of the vehicle.

▶ There are two main types of engine exhaust systems: horizontal, which route the exhaust components under the chassis and have the outlet pipe aimed downward (toward the ground) or toward the rear of the vehicle, and vertical, which direct exhaust gases upward and into the atmosphere.

▶ Exhaust manifolds are divided and split on four and six cylinder engines to prevent interference of exhaust pulses between front and rear cylinders. This not only improves exhaust scavenging but is necessary to optimize turbocharger performance.

▶ Exhaust pipes need to be durably constructed and appropriately sized.

▶ Keep exhaust system length, as well as bends and elbows in the exhaust system, to a minimum to reduce backpressure. The greater the length and the greater the number of bends or sharpness of bends, the slower exhaust gases will flow through the system.

▶ A muffler is the exhaust system's primary component for minimizing noise. Mufflers diminish exhaust noise by allowing the expansion of the exhaust pressure pulse within the muffler.

▶ A resonator is a device in the exhaust system that looks like a small muffler. Resonators provide additional dampening and tuning of exhaust noise.

▶ To prevent fires, spark arrestors are often placed at the end of the exhaust system. The spark arrestor is usually a screen covering the exhaust outlet. When large incandescent carbon particles make contact with this screen, they are trapped and the flow of exhaust gases pounds them into smaller pieces, cooling them through this process.

▶ A diesel engine will not warm to operating temperature at idle. To modify this characteristic, a number of diesel engines have used EBP regulators, which increase exhaust pressure inside the engine's exhaust manifolds. Doing this causes the exhaust gas to linger longer around the exhaust ports and transfer its heat to the cooling system.

▶ To increase combustion temperatures during cranking and improve warm-up characteristics, Volvo uses an EPG.

▶ A pyrometer is a temperature gauge designed to measure EGTs above those measurable by an ordinary thermometer or thermistor. A pyrometer provides warning data regarding excessively high combustion temperatures.

▶ Diesel engines do not naturally help vehicle braking. Service brakes can be severely overloaded. To compensate for the natural loss of engine braking, aftermarket exhaust brakes can be installed on vehicles to improve their braking ability.

▶ Exhaust brakes will typically have controls that allow them to operate only when the accelerator pedal is at idle position and the clutch is engaged.

▶ VGTs can be calibrated to operate as exhaust brakes.

▶ Compression release engine brakes are only used on diesel engines. The operation of a compression brake produces a sudden release of the compressed air from the cylinder by quickly opening the exhaust valve near TDC of the compression stroke.

Vocabulary Builder

charging lobe A component that admits extra gas exhaust volume into the cylinder before compression.

compression release brakes Engine brakes that work by causing a sudden release of the compressed air from the cylinder by quickly opening the exhaust valve near TDC of the compression stroke, dissipating the energy used to compress air.

decompression lobe A component that lifts the exhaust rocker lever near TDC to release engine compression.

exhaust backpressure (EBP) The pressure produced in an exhaust system by restrictions to exhaust gas flow.

exhaust backpressure (EBP) regulator A device that increases exhaust pressure inside the engine's exhaust manifolds to cause the exhaust gas to linger longer around the exhaust ports and transfer its heat to the cooling system.

exhaust brake An engine brake that works by placing a restriction in the exhaust system, which increases backpressure, causing the engine to exert a retarding force against the driveline.

exhaust manifold A component that collects exhaust gases from each cylinder of the cylinder head.

exhaust pressure governor (EPG) An EBP regulating device that speeds up engine warm-up and reduces cold start engine emissions.

flex pipe A component used between the engine pipe and the rest of the exhaust system to absorb twists and movement of pipe caused by engine torque reaction.

horizontal exhaust system An exhaust system that routes the exhaust components under the chassis and has the outlet pipe aimed downward toward the ground or to the rear of the vehicle.

master and slave cylinders Pistons used in engine brakes to transfer motion from the injector rocker lever to the exhaust valves. The master piston follows the injector profile.

pyrometer A temperature gauge designed to measure exhaust temperatures. The pyrometer is a thermocouple device that generates electric current proportional to its temperature.

resonator A device in the exhaust system that looks like a small muffler. This device provides additional dampening and tuning of exhaust noise.

spark arrestor A screen covering the exhaust outlet that prevents fires by trapping large incandescent carbon particles. Exhaust gas flow pounds these particles into smaller pieces and cools them in the process.

vertical exhaust system An exhaust system that directs exhaust gases upward, into the atmosphere.

water manometer A slack u-tube device used to measure EBP using inches of water column.

Review Questions

1. The _____ is a device that provides additional dampening and tuning of exhaust noise.
   a. resonator
   b. pyrometer
   c. flex pipe
   d. decompression lobe

2. The component that lifts the exhaust rocker lever near TDC to release engine compression is called a _____.
   a. flex pipe
   b. charging lobe
   c. decompression lobe
   d. resonator

3. A _____ is a temperature gauge designed to measure exhaust temperatures.
   a. resonator
   b. pyrometer
   c. charging lobe
   d. decompression lobe

4. A component that admits extra gas exhaust volume into the cylinder before compression is called a _____.
   a. flex pipe
   b. resonator
   c. decompression lobe
   d. charging lobe

5. A _____ is a component used between engine pipe and the rest of the exhaust system to absorb twists and movement of pipe caused by engine torque reaction.
   a. resonator
   b. pyrometer
   c. flex pipe
   d. charging lobe

6. Installing an _____ that can efficiently collect and discharge combustion gas is an important element of vehicle design and improved engine performance.
   a. EBP regulator
   b. exhaust system
   c. exhaust pressure governor
   d. air pressure regulator

7. Approximately _____ of heavy-duty vehicles produced in North America are equipped with compression release engine breaks.
   a. 60%
   b. 65%
   c. 70%
   d. 75%

8. The service life of a _____ is improved if it is installed in a relaxed position.
   a. decompression lobe
   b. pyrometer
   c. resonator
   d. flex pipe

9. A _____ exhaust system routes the exhaust components under the chassis and aims the outlet pipe downward toward the ground or to the rear of the vehicle.
   a. horizontal
   b. vertical
   c. diagonal
   d. pulse-type

10. Limits to acceptable backpressure in most diesels are at 3" of mercury or _____ of water column as measured with a water manometer.
   a. 11"
   b. 12"
   c. 13"
   d. 14"

ASE-Type Questions

1. Technician A says high exhaust backpressure can lead to high exhaust valve temperatures and excessive exhaust emissions. Technician B says high exhaust backpressure can lead to low turbocharger speed and boost pressure. Who is correct?
   a. Technician A
   b. Technician B
   c. Both Technician A and Technician B
   d. Neither Technician A nor Technician B

2. Technician A says higher horsepower engines with high fuel and airflow rates from the turbocharger require resonators to supply enough expansion volume for exhaust gases to reduce backpressure. Technician B says air coolers are required to supply enough expansion volume for exhaust gases to reduce backpressure in these cases. Who is correct?
   a. Technician A
   b. Technician B
   c. Both Technician A and Technician B
   d. Neither Technician A nor Technician B

3. Technician A says an EBP regulator is used to actuate a butterfly valve. Technician B says when an EBP regulator is used to actuate a butterfly valve, it increases exhaust pressure inside a diesel engine's exhaust manifolds. Who is correct?
   a. Technician A
   b. Technician B
   c. Both Technician A and Technician B
   d. Neither Technician A nor Technician B

4. Technician A says Volvo uses an EBP governor to increase combustion temperatures during cranking and improve warm-up characteristics. Technician B says Volvo uses a compression brake to increase combustion temperatures during cranking and improve warm-up characteristics, which also reduces cold start emissions. Who is correct?
   a. Technician A
   b. Technician B
   c. Both Technician A and Technician B
   d. Neither Technician A nor Technician B

5. Technician A says aftermarket exhaust brakes can be installed on vehicles with diesel engines to improve their braking ability. Technician B says aftermarket hydraulic brakes can be installed on vehicles with diesel engines to improve their braking ability. Who is correct?
   a. Technician A
   b. Technician B
   c. Both Technician A and Technician B
   d. Neither Technician A nor Technician B

6. Technician A says vertical exhaust systems are most commonly used on light- and medium-duty diesel-powered vehicles. Technician B says an engine's ability to draw a fresh air charge for combustion relies on the efficiency of its exhaust system. Who is correct?
   a. Technician A
   b. Technician B
   c. Both Technician A and Technician B
   d. Neither Technician A nor Technician B

7. Technician A says when 3 properly muffled trucks drive by together the resulting noise level will be +6 dBA higher than the noise level of a single truck. Technician B says when 4 properly muffled trucks drive by together the resulting noise will be +4 dBA higher than the noise level of a single truck. Who is correct?
   a. Technician A
   b. Technician B
   c. Both Technician A and Technician B
   d. Neither Technician A nor Technician B

8. Technician A says the Volvo compression release break uses three bump profiles on the exhaust lobe. Technician B says the Volvo compression release break uses only two bump profiles on the exhaust lobe. Who is correct?
   a. Technician A
   b. Technician B
   c. Both Technician A and Technician B
   d. Neither Technician A nor Technician B

9. Technician A says without a standard transmission and direct connection to the engine compression release braking would require a driveline retarder. Technician B says without a standard transmission and direct connection to the engine compression release braking would require a transmission retarder. Who is correct?
   a. Technician A
   b. Technician B
   c. Both Technician A and Technician B
   d. Neither Technician A nor Technician B

10. Technician A says low-pressure areas at the exhaust valve stems and turbocharges tend to drag oil out of these components and into the exhaust stream. Technician B says high-pressure areas at the exhaust valve stems and turbocharges tend to drag oil out of these components and into the exhaust stream. Who is correct?
    a. Technician A
    b. Technician B
    c. Both Technician A and Technician B
    d. Neither Technician A nor Technician B

EGR Data

gine Run Time	00:05:26
GR Solenoid Command	19 %
sired EGR Position	15 %
GR Position Sensor	15 %
GR Position Sensor	1.45 Volts
GR Learned Minimum Pos	0 %
GR Cooler Temp. Sen. 1	142 °C
GR Cooler Temp. Sen. 2	92 °C
irflow Leak Equivalenc	1.99 : 1
	5 / 33 – ▼

GR Learned Minimum Position

Select Items	DTC	Quick Snapshot	More

NATEF Tasks

Diesel Engines

General
- Check and record electronic diagnostic codes. (pp 993–1002)

Fuel System
Electronic Fuel Management System
- Locate and use relevant service information (to include diagnostic procedures, flow charts, and wiring diagrams). (pp 981, 1001–1002)

- Inspect and test switches, sensors, controls, actuator components, and circuits; adjust or replace as needed. (pp 982–995)
- Interface with vehicle's on-board computer; perform diagnostic procedures using electronic service tool(s) (to include PC-based software and/or data scan tools); determine needed action. (pp 993–1002)
- Check and record electronic diagnostic codes and trip/operational data; monitor electronic data; clear codes; determine further diagnosis. (pp 993–1002)

Knowledge Objectives

After reading this chapter, you will be able to:
1. Identify and describe legislative requirements of engine manufacturer's diagnostic and heavy-duty on-board diagnostic (HD-OBD) systems. (pp 981–984)
2. Differentiate between on- and off-board diagnostics. (pp 982–994)
3. Identify and describe features of on-board diagnostic (OBD) strategies. (pp 982–983)
4. Identify and describe circuit monitoring strategies for out-of-range fault detection. (pp 982–985)
5. Identify and describe principles of fault detection and diagnosis for commercial vehicle electronic control systems. (p 984)
6. Describe and explain standards for assigning fault codes to circuit faults. (pp 993–1002)

Skills Objectives

There are no skills objectives for this chapter.

▶ Introduction

Technicians servicing today's commercial vehicles will be just as likely to use a computer as a screw driver to perform repairs. Electronic systems using microprocessors control every chassis, engine, and drive train system and provide operational capabilities far exceeding any mechanical system—and with greater precision, efficiency, and reliability.

Although electronics offer many advantages and benefits over mechanical controls, a new challenge is to identify and repair quickly any failure in systems that operate with increasing invisibility using electronic signals and software-based operating systems. To prevent a problem as simple as a broken wire from requiring huge number of labor hours to identify and repair, electronic systems have self-diagnostic capabilities. These self-diagnostic capabilities extend to the emission systems, which also must operate flawlessly for the normal service life of the vehicle to maintain almost undetectable emission levels from the latest engines.

▶ Fundamentals of HD-OBD

The dominance of electronics makes skill development related to servicing electronic control technology one of the most important priorities for successful technicians. Understanding the operating principles of electronic control systems is foundational for choosing diagnostic strategies, using service tools effectively, and making sound repair recommendations. Nowhere are these skills more important than in comprehending and troubleshooting the operation of the HD-OBD system. This unique system is responsible for maintaining a vehicle's compliance with emission standards. The comprehensive monitoring of the vehicle performed by the HD-OBD system means electronic-related faults requiring service will be identified by the OBD system.

Development of HD-OBD

The term **on-board diagnostics (OBD)** has two meanings for the technician. The simplest, most familiar definition is the diagnostic function of electronic control systems to identify or self-diagnose system faults and report fault codes. The second meaning is the legislated standards for maximum vehicle emissions levels. The legislation also establishes requirements for maintaining the lowest vehicle emissions and alerting the operator if any fault occurs that could potentially cause emissions to increase above specific thresholds or levels.

The legislation did not pop up overnight, however. It evolved over time and in stages, as we will discuss in this section.

OBD

Emission standards established for diesels beginning in the late 1970s have required a level of precision for engine control only possible through the extensive use of electronics. Electrical devices now perform the work once done by fuel system camshafts, levers, springs, flyweights, and other assorted mechanical devices. Because of the invisible nature of electronic signals and the operation of microprocessors executing thousands of lines of software code, many hours would be spent to identify simple problems such as a broken wire or faulty sensor if these systems did not have self-diagnostic capabilities. This self-diagnostic capability, referred to as the OBD system, was originally developed by manufacturers to enable technicians to service electronic controls. Beginning in 2007, emission legislation began requiring OBD systems to monitor the operation of emission control systems and alert the vehicle operator to any potential emission increase above threshold standards. When a malfunction is detected, diagnostic information is stored for retrieval by a technician to assist in the diagnosis and repair of the malfunction **FIGURE 35-1**.

▶ You Are the Technician

You are at a customer's yard to diagnose a problem with a brand-new Class 8 highway tractor. The vehicle will start and run, but the engine will not accelerate above idle speed. After starting the engine, a red warning light immediately flashes for 30 seconds before the engine shuts down. You perform typical visual inspections of the vehicle, examine the exhaust system and wiring harnesses, and check for fuel coolant air and oil leaks. The selective catalytic reduction (SCR) tank is three-quarters full according to the dash gauge and when visually verifying the level. Nothing seems amiss, but you realize that certain emission-related and engine protection system-related faults will produce these symptoms. Without being able to easily return to the shop with the vehicle to access diagnostic software and service information, finding the fault that is causing the severe engine power de-rate conditions and shutdown is challenging. Before calling for a tow truck to bring the tractor to the shop, consider the following:

1. What two procedures, other than using original equipment manufacturer (OEM) or other diagnostic software, can you use to retrieve fault codes?
2. Explain why the red engine warning lamp (the stop engine lamp) flashes before the engine shuts down.
3. Are SAE J-1939 fault codes retrievable from this vehicle without OEM software? Explain your answer.

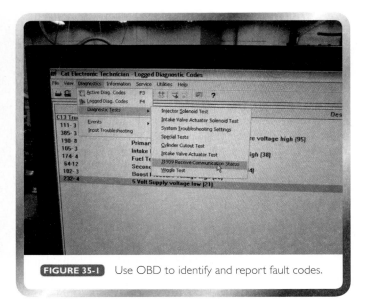

FIGURE 35-1 Use OBD to identify and report fault codes.

Engine Manufacturer's Diagnostic Systems

Before 2007, legislated standards for OBD systems were required for passenger cars, light-duty trucks, and medium-duty vehicles and engines with a gross vehicle weight of up to 14,000 lb (6350 kg). While a form of OBD was always used by all heavy-duty diesel engine manufacturers for electronically controlled engines, in 2007, the Environmental Protection Agency (EPA) began establishing standards for detecting faults in the emissions system that were not only for electronic controls of engine, power train, and other chassis systems. A preliminary standard to the 2010 HD-OBD standard was called an engine manufacturer's diagnostic (EMD) system. The introduction of particulate filters, crankcase ventilation (CV) systems, and exhaust gas recirculation (EGR) systems in 2007 added a level of complexity to emissions systems needing monitoring to ensure they were properly functioning. The EMD standard had fewer standardized legal requirements and was less comprehensive than HD-OBD. However, EMD does continuously monitor circuit continuity and performs functional monitoring of the fuel injection system, exhaust gas recirculation (EGR), and particulate filter. A malfunction indicator lamp (MIL) was introduced for 2010 engines. The "useful life," or durability, requirement is included in the latest HD-OBD system and was incorporated in 2004 emissions legislation. Useful life standards required for diesel-powered vehicles meant manufacturers had to ensure engines complied with emissions standards over time and distance, not just on the day a representative engine from a particular engine family met emissions standards. Useful life requirements for diesel engines are:

- Light duty: 110,000 miles (177,028 km) or 10 years
- Medium duty: 185,000 miles (297,729 km) or 10 years
- Heavy duty: 435,000 miles (700,065 km) or 10 years

HD-OBD

In December 2006, the EPA revised EMD legislation by mandating more comprehensive OBD systems that functionally monitor emissions-control systems and components. Beginning with model year 2010 with a phase-in period until 2016, HD-OBD is a significant update to EMD. Unlike the sensor and limited functionality monitoring of EMD, HD-OBD is a model-based diagnostic system that uses advanced algorithms similar to artificial intelligence to identify emissions-related faults. Legislation also includes a "right-to-repair" provision for the truck/bus repair industry, directing manufacturers to make available any information necessary to perform repairs or maintenance on OBD systems and other emissions-related engine components. All OBD standards are developed by SAE International and adopted by the EPA. Engines must maintain 90–95% reduction to emissions output over the normal engine life cycle. Technical amendments to HD-OBD standards are regularly made, and legislation is updated based on SAE revisions.

Class 8 vehicle sales account for almost half of all truck sales. HD-OBD applies to approximately three-quarters of all truck and bus sales. Emissions reduction from this group, making up 5% of registered vehicles, accounts for approximately 23% of fuel consumption for all vehicles and makes a large impact on emissions levels **TABLE 35-1**.

Self-Diagnostic Capabilities and Approaches

Electronic systems do not have many moving parts to wear out, but the systems can be complex. When something goes wrong with a component or circuit, identifying the problem without some built-in self-diagnostic capabilities can be extremely time consuming and difficult. Consider what steps would be needed to identify a problem as simple as a bent pin on a control module or a broken or worn wire on today's vehicle. Many hours, if not days, would be needed to trace every individual circuit while performing voltage and resistance checks. With built-in self-monitoring functions, electrical systems can check circuits and electrical devices, evaluate the accuracy of sensor data, and identify problems as they occur. The system records and reports when, where, and how faults occurred, enabling diagnostics on electronically controlled vehicle systems to be performed easily, often with fewer tools and in less time than on mechanical systems **FIGURE 35-2**.

TABLE 35-1: Heavy-Duty Vehicle Sales

Weight Class	2000–2001 U.S. Average Retail Sales (Units)
3: 10,001–14,000 lb (4536–6350 kg)	104,686
4: 14,001–16,000 lb (6351–7257 kg)	49,727
5: 16,001–19,500 lb (7258–8845 kg)	26,763
6: 19,501–26,000 lb (8846–11,793 kg)	46,799
7: 26,001–33,000 lb (11,794–14,968 kg)	107,089
8: 33,001+ lb (14,969 kg)	175,584
Total Class 4 and Above	405,962

FIGURE 35-2 HD vehicles that conform to the 2014 emissions standard for European trucks and buses have a 16-pin diagnostic link connector identical to the OBD-II for light-duty vehicles.

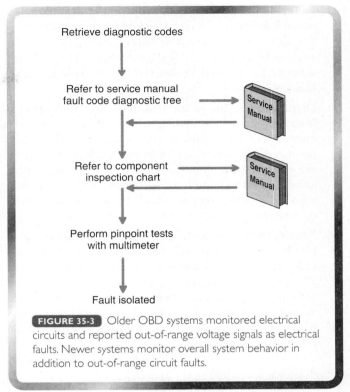

FIGURE 35-3 Older OBD systems monitored electrical circuits and reported out-of-range voltage signals as electrical faults. Newer systems monitor overall system behavior in addition to out-of-range circuit faults.

The system can take one of two self-diagnostic approaches to identifying faults. The system can either use traditional self-diagnostic strategies or use a model-based approach.

Traditional self-diagnostic strategies focus on specific areas of commercial vehicle control, such as the engine, anti-lock braking, traction control, and transmissions. In vehicles where only a few control modules are used and communicate with one another, out-of-range-type fault codes and off-board fault isolation methods are adequate.

System self-diagnostic checks are generally performed by limit checking of sensors or circuit data. For example, if the signal voltage produced by a coolant temperature sensor exceeds the limits of normal operation, the system will generate an out-of-range electrical fault code **FIGURE 35-3**. The code will point to a general circuit problem requiring off-board pinpoint testing to determine whether it is the sensor, wiring, or even a disconnected or missing sensor. As system complexity evolved, the technician performed off-board diagnostics after the on-board system identified a fault. Using flow charts for a specific diagnostic code (e.g., troubleshooting diagnostic trees) in more sophisticated electronic control systems became more time consuming and sometimes ineffective, resulting in high levels of "no-fault-found."

Manufacturers have also discovered incorrect component replacement and increased warranty costs are associated with high reliance on off-board diagnostic testing by technicians using service literature. Furthermore, data from a sensor as simple as the coolant temperature is even more critical to operation because monitors that evaluate emissions-control devices will run only after an engine has reached operating temperature. The cooling system operation could be within normal range, but the cooling sensor itself may not respond properly.

Model-based diagnostics compare system and component behaviors to expected patterns of operation. In addition to fault detection and isolation, the model-based approach also analyzes and categorizes the fault using advanced algorithms.

System problems are generally identified without interfering with system operation by substituting suspected data from a sensor or device with a backup or default data set.

Diagnostic Definitions

A variety of terms are used to categorize abnormal system operation:

1. **Fault**: A fault is a deviation of at least one characteristic property of the system from its standard behavior. Low battery voltage, excessive oil pressure, and a missing sensor input are examples of faults. Depending on how quickly a fault occurs and whether it persists, faults are classified in four categories:

   - *Active*: This type of faults is currently taking place and is uninterrupted in action. Sudden component or circuit problems are generally active faults. An illuminated malfunction indicator light (MIL) or check engine light (CEL) indicates an **active fault**.
   - *Historical*: This type of fault, which is also called inactive, took place at one time but was corrected and is no longer active. A sensor that was temporarily disconnected is an example of a **historical fault**. Amber check engine lights can also indicate the presence of historical faults.
   - *Intermittent*: This type of fault is not ongoing and can be both active and historical. Loose connectors or poor pin contact can cause an **intermittent fault**.
   - *Incipient*: This type of fault is the result of system or component deterioration. An exhaust particulate filter filling with ash is an example of an **incipient fault**.

2. **Failure**: This refers to a fault that permanently interrupts a system's ability to perform a required function under specified operating conditions. Open or shorted circuits, cylinder misfires, or a seized variable geometry turbocharger (VGT) actuator are examples of failures. Failures produce active fault codes.

3. **Disturbance**: This is an unknown and uncontrolled input acting on the system. Electromagnetic interference, loss of mass, fluid or gas leakage from a hydraulic or pneumatic system, or excessive mechanical friction are examples of unknown or uncontrolled disturbances affecting system inputs. Low coolant level in a system without a level sensor could be an example of a disturbance.

4. **Fault detection**: This is a diagnostic strategy to determine whether faults are present in the system. An electronic control module will continuously check for voltage drops for all input and output circuits. Emissions system monitors are typical examples of a fault detection strategy used to evaluate a systems operation based on a model of expected behavior compared with actual performance of individual components or systems.

5. **Fault isolation**: This involves determining the location of the fault. Fault isolation is best accomplished using a diagnostic fault tree supplied by the manufacturer **FIGURE 35-4**. Examples of fault isolation include pinpoint electrical testing using a voltmeter, an ohmmeter, or commanding actuator tests.

6. **Fault accommodation**: This happens when a fault is detected. Fault accommodation, which is also known as an adaptive strategy, reconfigures the system operation or substitutes suspect data with default data to maintain normal system functionality even with the fault. One example is a newer engine that continues to run after it has lost data from a defective crank or the cam position sensor. The control modules will substitute a value derived from data from the other sensor to keep the engine running, although not as well. For example, a defective mass airflow sensor data could be replaced by intake manifold pressure and temperature data.

▶ Types of HD-OBD Monitors

To detect conditions that can increase emissions levels beyond Federal Test Procedure (FTP) thresholds, the HD-OBD system monitors individual components and major engine

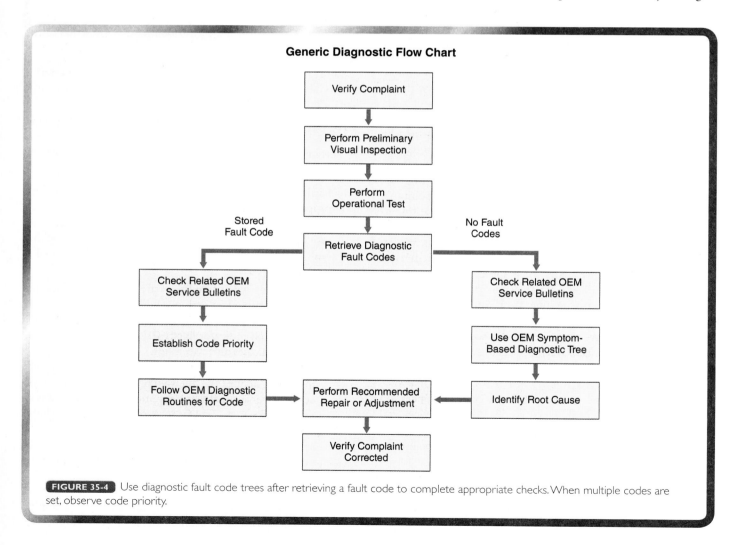

Generic Diagnostic Flow Chart

FIGURE 35-4 Use diagnostic fault code trees after retrieving a fault code to complete appropriate checks. When multiple codes are set, observe code priority.

emissions-control systems. Validating the operation of individual components that make up an emissions system is not enough because coordinated operation of numerous inputs and outputs form a distinct emissions-control system. What is more important is that everything is working together, and that is the job of a monitor. To identify an emissions system failure, the OBD software uses a testing procedure to detect a specific system malfunction. Testing the operation of individual emissions system components using an organized procedure is known as a monitor. The OBD executive, or supervisor, function executes the diagnostic procedure used by the monitor and evaluates the system operation. This function is located in the engine control module (ECM), which consists of specialized software algorithms. The OBD executive determines when and how to run the emissions monitor.

When all the major system monitors have run, a vehicle is considered to have completed a drive cycle. An HD-OBD system executes, or runs, monitors once every eight hours of engine operation. Currently, monitors used by the diesel HD-OBD system can be divided into several general types:

1. **Threshold monitoring**: This is directly measuring the level of emissions using a sensor to identify a noxious emission. Ammonia, particulate matter (PM), or oxides of nitrogen (NO$_x$) sensors are examples of input devices for threshold monitors **FIGURE 35-5**.

2. **Functionality monitoring**: This is evaluating an emissions system to ensure it is operating correctly. Monitoring is generally based on a computerized model of expected or desired system behaviors developed in an OEM laboratory or through field tests. Monitoring usually includes evaluating multiple electrical signals from various sensors and performing a test during normal engine operation to evaluate system response. Moving a VGT actuator and measuring boost pressure would be an example of a simple-functional monitor that evaluates whether a system is responding correctly.

3. **Rationality, or plausibility, monitoring**: This involves evaluating the accuracy of an electrical input signal compared with other available data. For example, a coolant temperature sensor should sense a temperature similar to an oil or air temperature sensor at initial start-up if an engine has not operated for several hours. If a large difference between sensor data exists or the data does not match the engine operating conditions, such as no oil pressure when the engine is running or fuel temperature considerably colder than ambient temperature, the data is considered irrational, or implausible. Rationality faults are also called logical faults.

4. **Electrical circuit continuity monitoring**: This monitoring measures voltage drops and signal and ground return voltage from sensors or output devices to validate circuits are not open or shorted to ground and battery voltage. These types of faults produce out-of-range voltage codes. Field effect transistors (FET) sense the amount of amperage used by a circuit to detect overcurrent or undercurrent conditions caused by open or shorted circuits.

FIGURE 35-5 The NO$_x$ sensor is an example of a component used for threshold monitoring.

5. **Out-of-range monitoring**: This monitoring is different from out-of-range voltage codes. Out-of-range monitors validate sensor data to verify a system is operating within an expected range for a given operating condition. Out-of-range monitoring is important to enable other OBD monitors to operate. Coolant temperatures are commonly evaluated for proper response to engine warm-up. If the cooling system is slow to warm up, it is out of range.

HD-OBD legislation for diesels also includes the following features:

- An MIL
- Standardized 9-pin **diagnostic link connector (DLC)** in the driver area. The DLC is the connection point for electronic service tools used to access fault code and other information provided by chassis electronic control modules. World Wide Harmonized Diagnostic OBD (WWHD-OBD)—compliant systems use a 16-pin connector.
- Standardized emissions-related fault codes for all manufacturers
- Reading of fault codes by aftermarket electronic test equipment (i.e., scanners) for emissions system diagnosis (enabled with standardized network communication protocols)
- Display of standard emissions-related data by aftermarket electronic service tools

- Indication of the operating conditions in which a fault occurred, a feature called freeze-frame data
- Standardized names and abbreviations of components and systems
- Evaluation of the functional capability of emissions-related sensors and actuators
- Evaluation of the functions of emissions-related input and output devices for electrical-related faults (e.g., short circuit to battery positive)
- Evaluation of the rationality of emissions-related input signals and components operation, which means the accuracy of an input signal is validated while in the range of normal operation and when compared with all other available information
- Monitoring of the operation of specific emissions-related systems to validate operation. Diesel engines have unique system monitors. A readiness code is displayed once the monitor has completed a functional test of a system and found no fault **FIGURE 35-6** .

The EMD or the HD-OBD emissions system monitors major engine systems that influence the production of emissions **TABLE 35-2** . Major system monitors are essentially diagnostic strategies used to determine if an emissions system is performing properly. The **OBD manager**, software that identifies fault codes

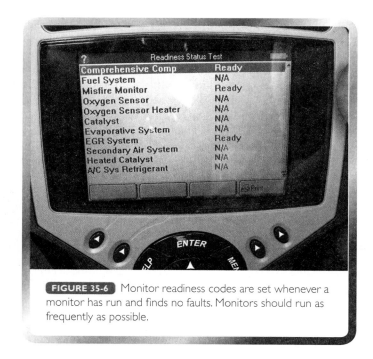

FIGURE 35-6 Monitor readiness codes are set whenever a monitor has run and finds no faults. Monitors should run as frequently as possible.

TABLE 35-2: OBD Emissions Thresholds for Diesel-Fueled/Compression-Ignition Engines Meant for Placement in Applications Greater than 14,000 Pounds (6364 Kilograms) GVWR (G/BHP+Hr)

Component	NMHC (Non-Methane Hydrocarbons)	CO	NO$_x$	PM
Model Years 2010–2012				
NO$_x$ aftertreatment system			+0.6	
Diesel particulate filter (DPF) system	2.5x			0.05/+0.04
Air–fuel ratio sensors upstream of aftertreatment devices	2.5x	2.5x	+0.3	0.03/+0.02
Air–fuel ratio sensors downstream of aftertreatment devices	2.5x		+0.3	0.05/+0.04
NO$_x$ sensors			+0.6	0.05/+0.04
"Other monitors" with emissions thresholds	2.5x	2.5x	+0.3	0.03/+0.02
Model Years 2013 and Later				
NO$_x$ aftertreatment system			+0.3	
Diesel particulate filter (DPF) system	2x			0.05/+0.04
Air–fuel ratio sensors upstream of aftertreatment devices	2x	2x	+0.3	0.03/+0.02
Air–fuel ratio sensors downstream of aftertreatment devices	2x		+0.3	0.05/+0.04
NO$_x$ sensors			+0.3	0.05/+0.04
"Other monitors" with emissions thresholds	2x	2x	+0.3	0.03/+0.02

Source: U.S. Government Publishing Office, Electronic Code of Federal Regulations, Title 40, Chapter 1, Subchapter C, Part 86, Subpart A, Section 86.010-18, http://www.ecfr.gov

and ensures emissions systems are operating correctly, regularly evaluates malfunctions in the emissions systems unique to diesel engines.

Major System Monitors

Diagnostic monitoring of diesel engines is broken down into separate, specific hardware systems that are responsible for some specialized aspect of engine operation and emissions-control. The high-pressure injection system and the EGR system are examples of systems that have a major monitor associated with their operation. Each of these major engine systems is assigned a monitor that tests and evaluates the system to determine whether it is functioning properly to maintain the low emissions for which the system was designed. Generally, the monitor detects conditions that would cause an emissions increase of 1.5 times the FTP for emissions testing. However, diesel engines use higher FTP thresholds for exhaust aftertreatment systems. Monitors are not required for a system where failure of a component cannot cause an increase above 1.5 times the emission limit or the failure will not cause a detectable change in emission levels. In this case, functional monitoring is required to simply ensure the system is operating within an acceptable performance range. An example of this would be a diesel particulate filter. No sensor currently measures soot from a failed diesel particulate filter (DPF). Instead, a functional monitor is used that has a diagnostic strategy to detect whether the filter is present and operational using a combination of exhaust system pressure and temperature sensors. The OBD executive evaluates the filter by comparing the measured and expected temperature and pressure values, rather than emission levels, based on a model of DPF operation (TABLE 35-3).

HD-OBD legislation requires 14 mandatory major system monitors for diesel engines. If equipped with the applicable system, the following systems have monitors associated with their operation:

- Fuel
- Cold-start emissions strategy
- EGR
- Misfire
- Boost pressure
- Cooling
- Crankcase ventilation (CV)
- Comprehensive component
- Variable valve timing (VVT)

Aftertreatment monitors include:

- DPF
- Lean-NO_X Trap (LNT) or NO_X adsorber
- SCR
- Diesel oxidation catalyst (DOC)
- Exhaust gas sensors

Major emissions system monitors include:

1. Fuel system
   - Fuel pressure
   - Fuel-injection quantity
   - Multiple fuel-injection event performance
   - Fuel-injection timing
   - Closed-loop feedback controls
2. Misfire monitoring
   - Must detect misfire occurring continuously in one or more cylinders during idle
3. EGR system
   - EGR flow rate
   - EGR response rate
   - EGR cooling system
   - Feedback control
   - EGR cooler performance
   - Closed-loop feedback controls
4. Boost pressure control systems
   - Underboost and overboost malfunctions
   - Wastegate operation
   - Slow response (VGT systems only)
   - Charge air undercooling
   - Closed-loop feedback controls
5. Cold-start emissions strategies
   - Glow plugs or intake heater on-time
   - Glow plugs and intake air heaters enabled
6. Diesel exhaust aftertreatment systems: Monitor requires faults to be detected before emissions exceed standards for any of the following systems:
   - Oxidation catalyst
   - Lean NO_X catalyst

TABLE 35-3: Diesel Threshold Capability by Year (Multiple of FTP Standard)

Emissions System Monitor	Hydrocarbons(HCs)	NO_X	PM
Catalyst (three-way, oxidation, NO_X SCR, or NO_X adsorber)	2007: 3–5x 2010: 2.5–3x 2013: 1.75x	2007: 3–5x 2010: 2.5–3x 2013: 1.75x	N/A
PM filter	N/A	N/A	2007: 5x 2010: 4x 2013: pending
All others (EGR, fuel system, etc.)	2007: 2.5–3.5x 2010: 2–3x 2013: 1.5x	2007: 2.5–3.5x 2010: 2–3x 2013: 1.5x	2007: 2.5–5x 2010: 2–4x 2013: 1.75–2x

- SCR catalyst
- NO$_x$ trap
- PM trap

7. Variable Valve Timing (VVT) system: VVT system, once used by Caterpillar ACERT engines, are related to achieving the commanded valve timing and/or control within a crank angle and/or lift tolerance and to detecting slow system response prior to emissions exceeding the thresholds for other monitors. Malfunctions are monitored whenever fault conditions are met rather than monitored once per trip.

8. Engine cooling system: Cooling system malfunctions are related to slow warm-up times, which can prevent other monitors from running because coolant is not at the appropriate temperature. Proper thermostat functions and engine coolant temperature sensor readings are measured and must be reached within a specific time. Monitoring is performed monitored once per drive cycle.

9. Crankcase Ventilation (CV) system: The CV system is checked for system operation and integrity. The manufacturer may not monitor for disconnections between the crankcase and the CV valve, provided the CV system is designed to use connections that are resistant to failure and tampering.

Comprehensive Component Monitor

The comprehensive component monitor (CCM) tracks electrical circuits operating power train components that can cause a measurable emissions increase during any reasonable driving conditions or:

1. Are used for other OBD monitors

2. Are required to monitor input components for circuit and rationality faults

3. Are required to monitor output components for functional faults

The CCM is not tied to emissions thresholds. Any electrical problem will cause the MIL to illuminate.

Continuous and Non-Continuous Monitors

An emissions system may be monitored continuously or non-continuously. A non-continuous monitor requires certain conditions to be met before evaluation of an emissions system. For example, the vehicle may need to be above a particular road speed, the engine at a specific temperature, or there may even need to be an adequate level of fuel in the tank before a monitor can run. A monitor may not run if the altitude is too high, or a power take-off is operating, or some other condition is present that could jeopardize the safety of an operator or damage the vehicle. To provide an understanding of monitor operation, the following are examples of several HD-OBD monitors, along with a description of the monitor strategy and testing conditions needed to enable or activate each monitor.

Misfire Detection Monitor

Cylinder misfire occurs when a cylinder fails to produce combustion pressure similar to other engine cylinders **FIGURE 35-7** . Causes can include poor compression, improper fuel delivery, or mechanical engine failure. Because engine misfires can cause hydrocarbons and carbon monoxide (CO) emissions, the OBD system must evaluate engine operation to determine whether misfires are occurring. The threshold for diesel misfire detection is 4% per 1000 crankshaft revolutions. This corresponds to 40 misfires per 1000 revolutions per minute (rpm).

The misfire detection monitor is intermittent. Data from the engine sensors include oil temperature, crankshaft position (CKP), injection quantity, exhaust pressure, intake air

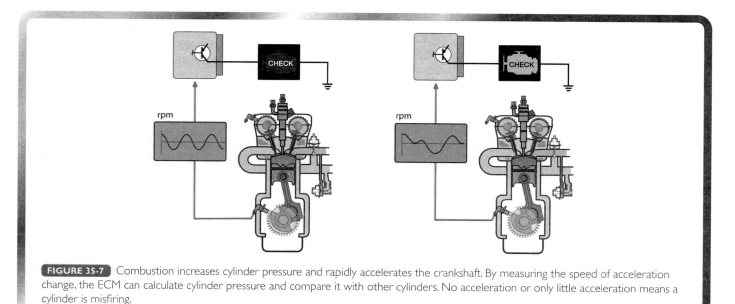

FIGURE 35-7 Combustion increases cylinder pressure and rapidly accelerates the crankshaft. By measuring the speed of acceleration change, the ECM can calculate cylinder pressure and compare it with other cylinders. No acceleration or only little acceleration means a cylinder is misfiring.

temperature, and fuel level input. This data ensures certain conditions are met when detecting a misfire, such as distinguishing whether a vehicle is low on or out of fuel, warmed up and running, or lugging under load.

Misfire Monitor Operation

The crank position (CKP) sensor is a primary input in determining cylinder misfire. The CKP sensor produces data by sensing the movement of the teeth on a wheel located on the crankshaft. The ECM uses the speed at which the wheel passes by the sensor to calculate the time between CKP tooth edges. This data supplies rotational velocity of the crankshaft. By comparing the accelerations of each cylinder event, the ECM calculates the pressure produced from each cylinder. Cylinders producing less power will have fewer teeth pass by the CKP senor per unit of time compared with cylinders with normal or higher cylinder pressure. When the power contribution from a particular cylinder is less than an expected value and other criteria for enabling the misfire monitor are met, the cylinder is determined to have misfired. Loss of compression, worn rings, and bent connecting rods can be diagnosed by the fine resolution produced by many CKP teeth and diagnostic strategies of the latest OEM software.

EGR System Monitor

A more complex type of on-board diesel monitor is the EGR monitor. To maintain lowest production of NO_X emissions, EGR gas is recycled from the exhaust to the intake manifold, which lowers peak combustion temperatures and pressures. Failure of the EGR system to perform as it should will result in high NO_X emissions or poor performance and misfire conditions.

HD-OBD requirements for the diesel EGR monitor include detecting the following faults before emissions exceed HD-OBD thresholds:

- EGR flow rate
- EGR response rate
- EGR cooling system performance

An additional operational check includes detecting if a normally closed-loop EGR system fails to enter a closed loop or defaults to an open loop.

EGR Monitor Operation

A large variety of mechanical and electrical functions and conditions need to be evaluated by the EGR monitor, so inputs and operating strategies to check its operation are more elaborate. The electronic and mechanical functionality of the EGR valve, the EGR valve actuator, the VGT, the EGR valve position sensor, and other sensors (e.g., barometric pressure, intake boost, exhaust pressure, mass airflow, oil temperature, air inlet temperature) provide input to this monitor. Even the efficiency of the EGR cooler must be checked by the monitor to determine if the EGR system is operating correctly. Efficiency monitoring is usually accomplished by comparing exhaust gas temperature entering and leaving the cooler. Little temperature change means low cooler efficiency. The elements and components of the EGR system and associated circuits are first evaluated by the monitor before EGR flow is evaluated.

If a mass airflow sensor is used on the engine as part of the EGR monitor strategy, the following is a typical method to evaluate EGR flow. First, when normal EGR rates are being commanded and when the engine enters into either one of two specified operating ranges, a flow measurement is performed. Essentially, the intake air mass airflow (MAF) sensor will detect less fresh airflow into the engine when the EGR is enabled because EGR gas replaces fresh air intake **FIGURE 35-8** and **FIGURE 35-9**. The difference in flow with and without the

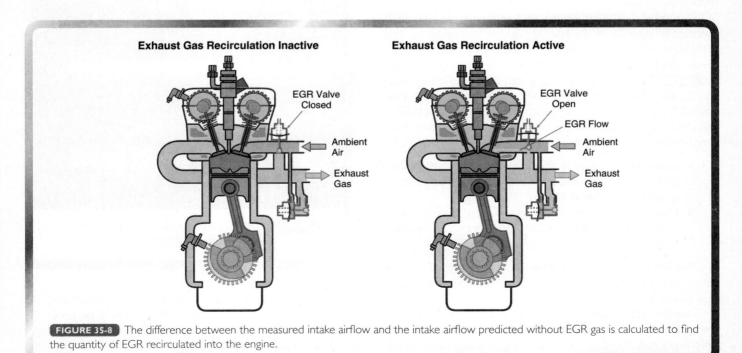

FIGURE 35-8 The difference between the measured intake airflow and the intake airflow predicted without EGR gas is calculated to find the quantity of EGR recirculated into the engine.

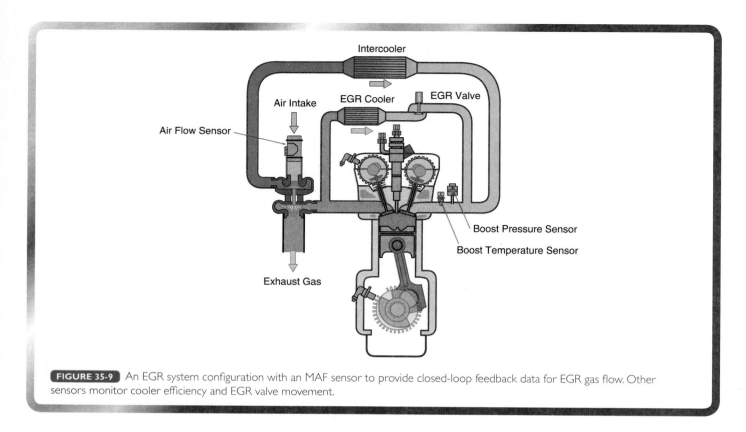

FIGURE 35-9 An EGR system configuration with an MAF sensor to provide closed-loop feedback data for EGR gas flow. Other sensors monitor cooler efficiency and EGR valve movement.

EGR occurs because EGR gas bypasses the MAF sensor and goes directly into the intake manifold. Two engine operating ranges are used for taking measurements to ensure an adequate amount of EGR is being supplied as requested by the engine management system and compared with an expected quantity. The variation between the quantity of EGR gas actually metered and the expected quantity by the OEM is used to determine if there is insufficient or excessive EGR gas flow.

The most basic conditions and sequence for the EGR monitor to operate occur after all the circuits, sensors, and actuators have been evaluated for correct operating range values or checked for opens and shorts and the engine is warmed up **FIGURE 35-10**. When the engine has entered the following conditions, the monitor evaluates commanded EGR flow against the actual quantity of gas inside the intake manifold as calculated by the intake temperature sensor and intake pressure sensor:

- Condition 1: The EGR flow commanded is greater than 20% and engine speed is 1000–2200 rpm. The injection quantity is 0.0006–0.0022 in³ (10–35 mm³).
- Condition 2: The EGR flow commanded is greater than 20% and engine speed is 2200–3000 rpm. The injection quantity is 0.003–0.007 in³ (50–110 mm³).

The limits of variations between actual and expected flow values stored in the ECM/PCM are based on engine speed and load conditions.

Another technique to monitor EGR flow is to command the EGR valve to fully open when the correct drive-cycle conditions are met. Typically, when cruising at steady speed above

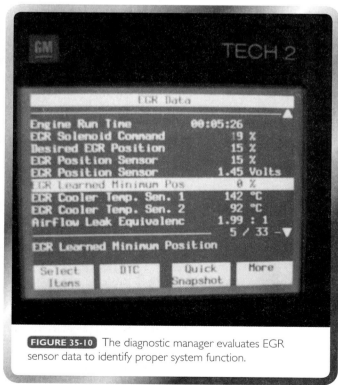

FIGURE 35-10 The diagnostic manager evaluates EGR sensor data to identify proper system function.

50 mph (80 kph), the EGR valve is opened briefly and the turbocharger speed is measured. High EGR flow cools the exhaust gas temperature and substantially lowers turbocharger speed. If the turbocharger speed falls to an expected range, the

EGR system monitor is complete, which means no faults were detected and the EGR system is functioning correctly.

Fuel System Monitors

Fuel system monitors are required to detect faults associated with the high-pressure injection system before emissions exceed OBD emissions thresholds. To do this, manufacturers will typically evaluate fuel system pressure control, fuel injection quantity, and fuel injection timing.

Fuel system monitors on common rail engines evaluate fuel pressure control by comparing expected pressure values in the fuel rail with actual pressure measured using a pressure sensor. For example, worn injectors of a common rail fuel system will set a fault indicating a loss of fuel pressure based on the shorter pulse width applied to the pressure regulator required to maintain fuel pressure in the fuel rail. Because more fuel will bypass a worn nozzle valve or other internal parts of the injectors, the fuel system will detect this as a pressure leak.

Fuel-injection quantity is monitored and calculated by measuring crankshaft speed fluctuations. Crankshaft speed is proportional to cylinder pressures, which are controlled by the amount of fuel burned inside the cylinder.

Fuel-injection timing is typically monitored by comparing a specific point when crankshaft rotational velocity suddenly increases compared with the expected angle of rotation stored in memory. Additionally, on unit injector fuel systems, signal evaluation circuits in the ECM can detect changes in the injector coil inductive signal corresponding to the beginning of injection. The needle lift sensor provides input for some electronic distributor systems.

Additional fuel monitor requirements include detecting faults of closed-loop feedback systems when they fail to enter closed loop or default to open loop.

A closed loop between the rail pressure sensor and the fuel pressure regulator is an example of a normally closed-loop system on a common rail engine. Problems with the signals or data will force the ECM to move out of closed-loop operation and use an adaptive strategy. Injector voltage is measured at the beginning and end of the injection event to check for faults in injector solenoids or electrical circuits energizing the injector.

Boost Pressure Control Monitoring

OBD diesel monitor requirements for the boost control include detecting faults before emissions exceed 1.5 times FTP emissions test standards under the following conditions:

- Underboost and overboost malfunctions
- Slow response (VGT systems only)
- Charge air undercooling

Additional requirements include detecting faults of closed-loop feedback systems if they fail to enter closed loop or default to open loop. Underboost and overboost malfunctions are typically detected by comparing expected boost pressure values stored in the engine control module (ECM) with actual boost pressure measured by the boost pressure sensor.

Slow turbocharger response times (VGT systems only) are evaluated by measuring the time the turbocharger takes to reach expected boost pressure, which is done by the boost pressure sensor and/or the turbine speed sensor. Temperature sensors located at the inlet and outlet of the intercooler or intake manifold temperature sensors evaluate charge air cooling effectiveness.

Cooling System Monitor

Other OBD monitors and emissions systems, such as the EGR, are enabled only after the engine reaches operating temperature. Engine temperature is also a variable that affects transmission shift points and injection timing. Because defective thermostats and engine temperature sensors will negatively affect engine operation, the OBD system also monitors the operation of the cooling system. The operating strategy of the cooling system monitor typically involves comparing actual operating temperature with a warm-up model based on start-up temperature, ambient conditions, and driving time. If the engine fails to reach operating temperature within a reasonable time, the monitor will set a fault. The monitor may also compare values of the coolant sensor with values of other temperature sensors, such as the oil or transmission, to check the rationality of the data.

TECHNICIAN TIP

Adding auxiliary heaters for passenger compartments can cause the cooling system monitor to indicate a fault. Taking heat out of the cooling system during engine warm up will delay the time to warm-up, which will illuminate the MIL.

Crankcase Ventilation (CV) System

The HD-OBD requires monitoring of the CV system of a diesel. Particulate emissions from oil vapor and blow-by gases are no longer permitted to be vented directly to the atmosphere. A plugged CV filter could also lead to engine damage from blown seals as well as oil leakage from other gaskets and engine seals. OBD crankcase ventilation system monitoring consists primarily of detecting the presence of the coalescing filter, if equipped; an open crankcase due to a missing or damaged gasket or oil fill cap; or disconnection of the ventilation system.

Aftertreatment System Monitors

Two common aftertreatment systems are diesel particulate filter (DPF) monitoring and SCR monitoring.

DPF

DPF monitoring includes the following:

- Filter performance
- Frequent regeneration
- Non-methane HC conversion
- Incomplete regeneration
- Missing substrate
- Active regeneration fuel delivery
- Closed-loop feedback control

Any disconnected sensors, missing catalysts, or invalid data will cause the MIL to illuminate. Monitoring of the DPF also includes the operation of the hydrocarbon (HC) dosing system to determine whether it is delivering fuel. Monitoring of the system operation is performed by a combination of temperature and pressure sensors **FIGURE 35-11**.

When the hydrocarbon dosing valve sprays raw fuel into the exhaust system, the fuel undergoes flameless combustion in the oxidation catalyst, which raises the temperature of the exhaust gas. The temperature change in and out of the exhaust system catalysts is monitored to determine whether the catalysts are operating within an expected temperature range. Missing, broken, deactivated, or tampered catalysts will not meet target temperature values, which will produce fault codes. The delta pressure (Delta P) sensor measures the pressure differential across the DPF and essentially checks for missing or damaged catalysts. This sensor does not influence when an active regeneration event takes place. Active regeneration events are based on models of expected soot loading that are derived from the amount of fuel burned, operating conditions, time or distance elapsed since the previous regeneration, and so on. The Delta P sensor will measure filter performance by comparing measured and estimated restrictions after a regeneration event. If the values match, the system determines the filter has proper efficiency when trapping soot. A new type of soot or sensor introduced in 2015 performs as a threshold monitor for the DPF. The sensor is located downstream of the DPF filter and detects any carbon based particulate in the exhaust stream.

SCR Monitor

SCR monitoring ensures the SCR is capable of converting NO_x emissions. Two NO_x sensors measure concentrations of NO_x upstream and downstream of the SCR. When the temperature sensors in the SCR indicate the catalyst is at proper operating temperature, the monitor compares the NO_x sensor differences over time to calculate NO_x catalyst efficiency and deterioration. If the diesel exhaust fluid (DEF) dosing system is not operating correctly, the monitor will detect the absence of NO_x conversion and set fault codes, typically for identifying faults in the entire SCR system.

A DEF quality sensor can now determine the quality of DEF fluid by measuring its density. Using tuning fork technology, ultra-high frequency vibrations produced in the sensor will move at a precise rate based on fluid density.

Fault codes in the SCR system will produce de-rate conditions, depending on their severity. Running a vehicle with no DEF fluid in the reservoir will eventually cause the engine to only idle and could keep the engine from starting **TABLE 35-4**. **FIGURE 35-12** refers to fault lamps in the instrument cluster to alert the driver to faults in the exhaust aftertreatment system.

▶ Maintaining HD-OBD

Maintaining the HD-OBD system is critical in order to identify and address emissions system deterioration and remedy failures. Technicians must understand how to use off-board

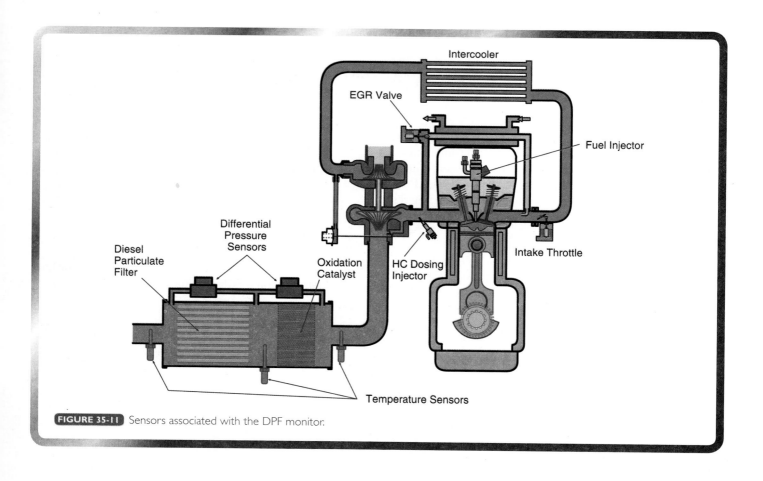

FIGURE 35-11 Sensors associated with the DPF monitor.

TABLE 35-4: OBD Emissions Thresholds for Diesel-Fueled/Compression-Ignition Engines Meant for Placement in Applications Greater than 14,000 Pounds (6364 Kilograms) GVWR (G/BHP+Hr)

| Condition | Notification | | De-Rate | Deactive Warning and De-Rate |
	EMD+	HD-OBD		
>10% full	None	None	None	None
Minimum 10% full	DEF solid	DEF solid	None	Fill DEF tank to a minimum of 10% above stage 1
Minimum 5% full	DEF flash	DEF flash	None	Fill DEF tank to a minimum of 10% above stage 2
From minimum of 2.5% to before tank is empty	DEF flash, Amber solid	DEF flash, Amber solid	25% torque derate	Fill DEF tank to a minimum of 10% above stage 3
Lack of DEF detected by loss of prime	DEF flash, Amber solid	DEF flash, Amber solid, MIL	25% torque derate	Fill DEF tank to a minimum of 10% above stage 3
Empty, after the engine had been shut down intentionally or in extended idle	DEF flash, Amber solid, Red solid	DEF flash, Amber solid, Red solid	25% torque derate and vehicle speed limited to 5 mph (8 kph)	System will return to stage 3 after doser is able to build pressure

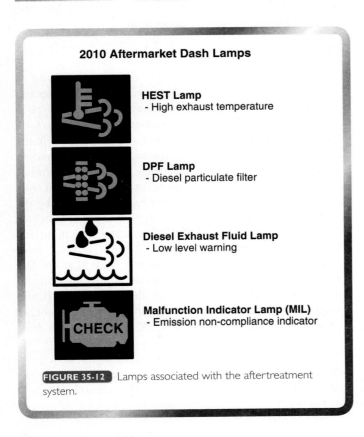

2010 Aftermarket Dash Lamps

HEST Lamp
- High exhaust temperature

DPF Lamp
- Diesel particulate filter

Diesel Exhaust Fluid Lamp
- Low level warning

Malfunction Indicator Lamp (MIL)
- Emission non-compliance indicator

FIGURE 35-12 Lamps associated with the aftertreatment system.

diagnostics and interpret readiness and diagnostic trouble codes in order to diagnose a system properly and make appropriate repairs.

Off-Board Diagnostics

When electrical faults or system problems occur in commercial vehicle control systems, electronic control modules log **diagnostic trouble codes (DTCs)** in the system memory, which are read through an instrument display cluster, a **blink code**, or retrieved by a scanner or personal computer connected to the vehicle DLC. OBD is the self-diagnostic checks by the control modules that measure circuit voltages, resistances, rationality, and other variables. More sophisticated OBD systems monitor system behavior to detect smaller faults faster. **Off-board diagnostics** and repair occur when the technician retrieves codes and vehicle data as a starting point to diagnose system problems. During off-board diagnostics, the technician may monitor system operation, perform actuator tests, pinpoint electrical tests, and inspect components. Remotely assisted diagnostics using **telematics** is also a type of off-board diagnostics. Telematics is a branch of information technology that uses specialized applications for long-distance transmission of information to and from a vehicle **FIGURE 35-13**.

Readiness Code

Depending on the OEM, some provision is made to validate whether a component or emissions system generating a DTC has been repaired or corrected. After a repair has been made, operating the vehicle under conditions that cause an emissions system monitor to self-check validates whether a successful repair has been completed. An HD-OBD service tool displays a readiness code indicating that a monitor has completed its functionality

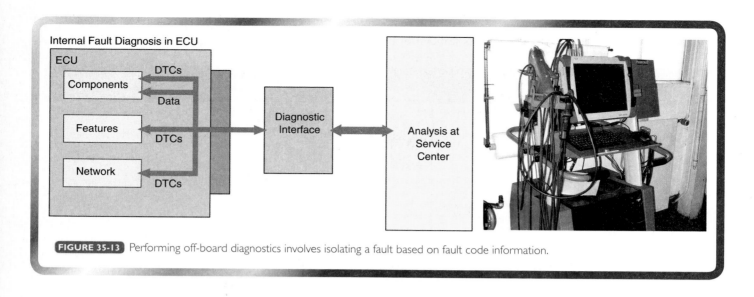

FIGURE 35-13 Performing off-board diagnostics involves isolating a fault based on fault code information.

test and no fault was found. Each monitor requires a unique set of drive-cycle operating conditions to be met before it can properly run and evaluate the performance of an emissions system.

When an HD-OBD readiness code validates the system that has been repaired, no other fault codes associated with the system should be active. However, a message such as "system not ready" or "monitor incomplete" or "monitor not run" is displayed if the repair is not successful, or if the emission system has not met the conditions needed to enable the monitor to run.

> ### ▶ TECHNICIAN TIP
>
> After repairing a fault associated with the engine or power train, the codes should be cleared and the vehicle road tested, which involves operating the vehicle under the conditions necessary for a monitor to run (i.e., warmed up and cruising at highway speed). Recheck the vehicle for codes after the road test, before returning the vehicle to the customer. The monitor associated with the repaired fault should indicate it has "run" or is "ready."

> ### ▶ TECHNICIAN TIP
>
> Note that two-trip B-type DTCs take two drive cycles before they are logged. This means two test drives are required to ensure malfunctions have been corrected.

Emissions System Deterioration

The HD-OBD is primarily an emissions-driven diagnostic system. For diesel engines, the threshold for alerting the driver and setting a fault code generally occurs any time a condition is sensed that could cause noxious emissions to exceed the legislated FTP emissions standards 1.5 times. Higher thresholds are used for aftertreatment systems, with progressively lower threshold standards for the latest vehicle models. While malfunctions in the engine cause excessive emissions, problems

with other vehicle systems also can cause the vehicle to exceed the threshold for emissions. Adaptive strategies can compensate for system deterioration. For example, wastegated turbochargers have metal springs in their actuators. Heat and time will weaken the springs so closed-loop feedback between the wastegate and the boost pressure sensor compensate for system deterioration. Common rail injectors are regularly checked using zero-fuel adaptation, which automatically updates the calibration file during vehicle deceleration.

DTCs

The HD-OBD system sets three types of codes: A, B, and C. Type A DTCs are the most critical emissions-related faults and will illuminate the MIL with only one occurrence. If a Type A code is set, the HD-OBD can store it several ways. Type A codes are generally stored in the ECM historical memory. To help the technician diagnose the problem, the code has a failure record associated with it, such as a time and date stamp of when the last failure occurred, whether the code occurred since the last code clearing event, or whether the failure has occurred during the current ignition cycle. Furthermore, Type A codes have freeze-frame data, which is a record of all other sensor data occurring when the fault was detected.

Type B codes are emissions-causing faults that are less serious than type A faults and must occur at least once on two consecutive trips before the MIL will illuminate. The MIL will also go out if a Type A or Type B DTC problem does not reoccur after a predetermined number of drive cycles (e.g., 3–5 drive cycles—varies by OEM).

Type C DTCs are non-emissions-related codes, or enhanced codes. Enhanced codes also cover non-emissions-related failures that occur outside the engine control system.

Freeze-Frame Data

The freeze-frame data the ECM stores will provide a snapshot of the engine operating conditions present at the time the malfunction was detected. This information should be stored when a pending DTC is set. If the pending DTC matures to a MIL-on DTC, the manufacturer can choose to update or retain the freeze-frame data stored in conjunction with the pending DTC. Likewise, any freeze-frame data stored in conjunction with a pending or MIL-on DTC should be erased upon erasure of the DTC.

HD-OBD Emissions Codes

The OBD executive is an element in the emissions system's operational strategy that manages the DTCs and operating modes for all diagnostic tests related to emissions systems. It can be referred to as the "traffic cop" of the diagnostic system, managing DTC storage and MIL illumination. Note that the HD-OBD MIL light is yellow, unlike the light-duty OBD-II system, which is red.

Control modules that contribute to maintaining emissions compliance must be connected to the controlled area network bus (CAN-bus) using SAE J-1939 standards for communication and network operation **FIGURE 35-14** and **FIGURE 35-15**.

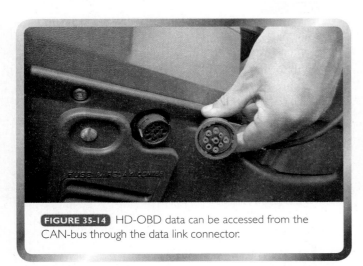

FIGURE 35-14 HD-OBD data can be accessed from the CAN-bus through the data link connector.

CAN-bus modules performing emissions diagnostics will include the following types:

- Engine ECM
- Vehicle electronic control unit
- Aftertreatment control module
- Aftertreatment NO_x sensors
- Engine VGT
- EGR control module
- Anti-lock braking system (ABS)/traction control

> ### TECHNICIAN TIP
>
> To validate a repair for a fault detected by the Comprehensive Component Monitor, start the engine and let it idle for one minute. The ECM will turn off the yellow MIL when the diagnostic monitor has run. If a CCM is evaluating electrical circuits, the light will switch off after the MIL has illuminated for five seconds. For other faults, the ECM will typically turn off the MIL after three consecutive ignition cycles that the diagnostic monitor runs and passes.

Two protocols exist for identifying fault codes on heavy-duty commercial vehicles. The first is J-1587 using a J-1708 two-wire data bus. J-1587 began being used by heavy-duty and most medium-duty vehicles built after 1985. Up to 1995, individual OEMs used their own unique diagnostic connectors. J-1587, used primarily from 1996 to 2001, is easily identified by the 6-pin diagnostic connectors. Beginning in 2001, most OEMs switched to a more sophisticated J-1939 standard recognized by a 9-pin diagnostic connector. Both the J-1587/1708 and the J-1939 network connections are found in the 9-pin DLC. A specific standard exists in both protocols for identifying faults detected by the CAN-bus modules.

Proprietary Blink and Flash Codes

Manufacturers are not bound to report faults exclusively using CAN-bus codes. Specialized equipment and systems can use

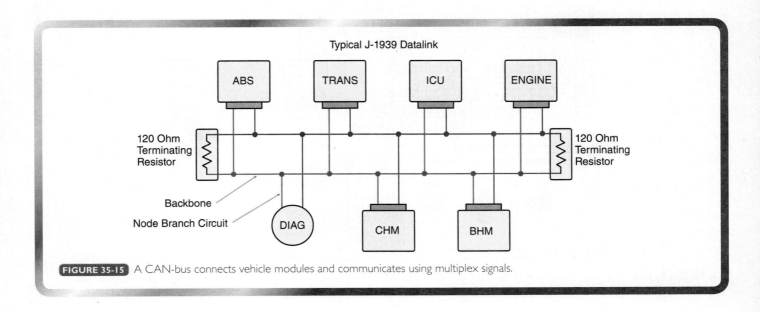

FIGURE 35-15 A CAN-bus connects vehicle modules and communicates using multiplex signals.

proprietary codes, meaning the OEM is free to define its own non-emissions-related fault codes. Blink codes are dash lights that will blink, or flash, proprietary fault codes using the red and amber engine warning lights FIGURE 35-16.

Two- and three-digit codes commonly report faults. A typical arrangement to obtain blink codes based on a proprietary code will require switching on a diagnostics switch. A warning lamp flashes to indicate a fault code. Next, the stop lamp flashes out the hundredth, tenth, and single digits of the fault code. A short pause separates the flashing of each digit, and a longer pause separates codes. Warning lamps may switch between active and inactive codes by flashing either the red for active or yellow warning light for inactive. If no fault codes are active, the warning lamps remain lit. Late-model International trucks do not use a diagnostic switch to obtain blink codes. Instead, the ignition key is switched on while the engine is off, the park brake is applied, and the cruise control switch and resume switches are depressed simultaneously to produce diagnostic blink codes. Rather than using a diagnostic switch, other vehicles may require creating the correct conditions—such as key-on engine-off (KOEO), park brakes set, or depressing the cruise ON and RESUME switches—to prompt engine blink codes. Instrument clusters are network devices can also receive and report fault codes in the absence of a readily available service tool.

J-1587 Fault Code Construction

The SAE developed the fault code reporting standard referred to as J-1587. Six- and nine-pin diagnostic connectors carry J-1587 codes, but six-pin connectors do not include J-1939, the latest protocol. J-1587 fault codes are specifically constructed to help technicians easily isolate faults. The codes have four parts:

- Message identifier (MID) (also called module identifiers)
- Parameter identifier (PID)
- System identifier (SID)
- Fault mode identifier (FMI) FIGURE 35-17.

Other fault code identifiers specific to an OEM may include the following:

- Proprietary parameter identification (PPID) is an OEM identification of a parameter or value used only by that manufacturer.
- Proprietary subsystem identification description (PSID) is an OEM-unique component identification.

A **message identifier (MID)** identifies which module is reporting the fault. MIDs are the first byte or character of each message that identifies which control module on the J-1587 serial communication link originated the information. A standard list of message or module identifiers exists for all vehicles regardless of manufacturer FIGURE 35-18 and TABLE 35-5.

A **system identifier (SID)** indicates a specific failed component or replaceable subsystem associated with a fault. There are several SIDs TABLE 35-6.

A **parameter identifier (PID)** is a value or identifier of an item being reported with fault data. J-1957 uses hundreds of PIDs TABLE 35-7.

The **fault mode identifier (FMI)** describes the type of failure detected in the subsystem and identified by the PID or SID TABLE 35-8. The FMI and the PID or SID, not both, combine to form a J-1957 diagnostic code. The general format of a fault message is MID-PID/SID–FMI. Now consider code 128-101-002. It breaks down as follows:

- 128: engine
- 101: intake boost pressure
- 002: data erratic, intermittent, or incorrect.

OEM proprietary fault codes would include the following:

- 54: Detroit Diesel
- 84: Caterpillar
- 115: Cummins

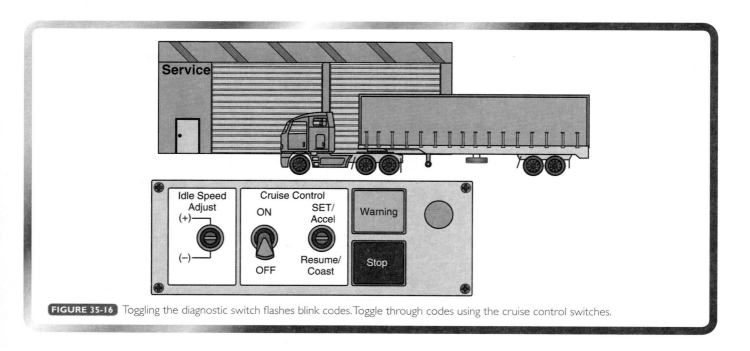

FIGURE 35-16 Toggling the diagnostic switch flashes blink codes. Toggle through codes using the cruise control switches.

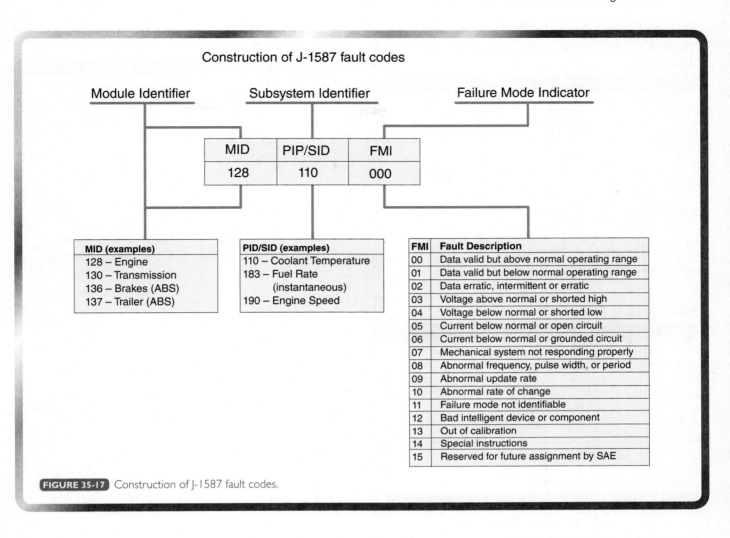

Construction of J-1587 fault codes

Module Identifier   Subsystem Identifier   Failure Mode Indicator

MID	PIP/SID	FMI
128	110	000

MID (examples)
128 – Engine
130 – Transmission
136 – Brakes (ABS)
137 – Trailer (ABS)

PID/SID (examples)
110 – Coolant Temperature
183 – Fuel Rate
         (instantaneous)
190 – Engine Speed

FMI	Fault Description
00	Data valid but above normal operating range
01	Data valid but below normal operating range
02	Data erratic, intermittent or erratic
03	Voltage above normal or shorted high
04	Voltage below normal or shorted low
05	Current below normal or open circuit
06	Current below normal or grounded circuit
07	Mechanical system not responding properly
08	Abnormal frequency, pulse width, or period
09	Abnormal update rate
10	Abnormal rate of change
11	Failure mode not identifiable
12	Bad intelligent device or component
13	Out of calibration
14	Special instructions
15	Reserved for future assignment by SAE

FIGURE 35-17 Construction of J-1587 fault codes.

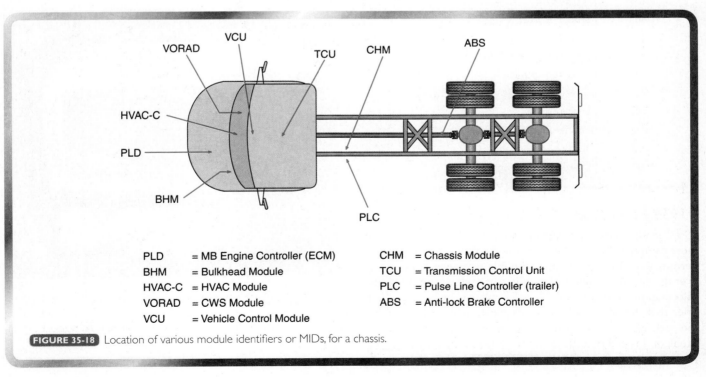

PLD	= MB Engine Controller (ECM)	CHM	= Chassis Module
BHM	= Bulkhead Module	TCU	= Transmission Control Unit
HVAC-C	= HVAC Module	PLC	= Pulse Line Controller (trailer)
VORAD	= CWS Module	ABS	= Anti-lock Brake Controller
VCU	= Vehicle Control Module		

FIGURE 35-18 Location of various module identifiers or MIDs, for a chassis.

TABLE 35-5: Common MIDs Standard Across All Vehicles

MID	Description
128	ECM
130	Transmission control unit
136	ABS
140	Instrument cluster unit
180	Off-board diagnostics
181	Satellite
190	Climate control module
229	Collision avoidance
231	Cellular

TABLE 35-6: Example SIDs

SID	Description
001	Injector cylinder 01 (on/off)
034	Reverse switch (open/closed)
100	Oil pressure or lubrication system
101	Boost pressure
103	Transmission range (high/low)

TABLE 35-7: Example PIDs

PID	Description
25	Air conditioner system status A2
33	Clutch cylinder position
40	Engine retarder
41	Cruise control switch status
91	Percent engine throttle
92	Percent engine load
93	Output torque
98	Engine oil level
100	Engine oil pressure
102	Turbo boost pressure
105	Intake manifold temperature

TABLE 35-8: Example FMIs

FMI	Description
0	Data valid but above the normal working range
1	Data valid but below the normal working range
2	Intermittent or incorrect data
3	Abnormally high voltage or short circuit to higher voltage
4	Abnormally low voltage or short circuit to lower voltage
5	Abnormally low current or open circuit
6	Abnormally high current or short circuit to ground
7	Incorrect response from a mechanical system
8	Abnormal frequency
9	Abnormal update rate
10	Abnormally strong vibrations
11	Unidentifiable fault
12	Faulty module or component
13	Calibration values outside limits
14	Special instructions
15	Reserved for future use

J-1939 Fault Code Construction

J-1939 codes have construction similar to J-1957 but are far more comprehensive. J-1939 uses the CAN-bus protocol, which permits any electronic control module to transmit a message over the network when the bus is idle or not transmitting other information. Similar to J-1957, every message includes an identifier that defines who sent it, what data is contained within the message, and the priority, or seriousness, of the fault or problem. Instead of a PID and SID, J-1939 uses only a **suspect parameter number (SPN)** **FIGURE 35-19**. The SPN is the

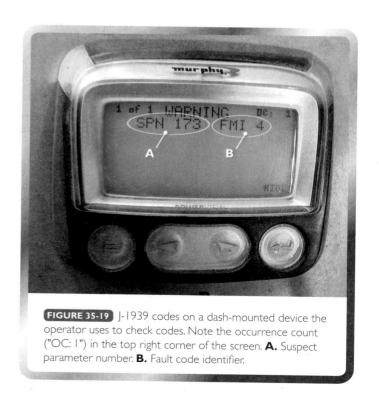

FIGURE 35-19 J-1939 codes on a dash-mounted device the operator uses to check codes. Note the occurrence count ("OC: 1") in the top right corner of the screen. **A.** Suspect parameter number. **B.** Fault code identifier.

smallest identifiable fault. Next, a failure mode indicator (FMI) notes the type of failure that has been detected.

The **source address (SA)** field designates the control module that is sending the message `TABLE 35-9` and `TABLE 35-10`.

Suspect Parameter Number

The suspect parameter number (SPN) combines elements of J-1957 PIDs and SIDs. The SPN is used for multiple diagnostic purposes:

- Identifying the least repairable subsystem that has failed
- Identifying subsystems and/or assemblies that may not have completely failed but may be exhibiting abnormal operating performance
- Identifying a particular event or condition that requires reporting

TABLE 35-9: Example J-1939 SAs

SID	Description
1	Engine
3	Transmission
11	Brakes or ABS controller
47	Headway controller for collision avoidance system

TABLE 35-10: Comparing J-1939 and J-1587 Fault Codes

J-1939	J-1957
Source address (SA)	Message identifier (MID)
Suspect parameter number (SPN) (thousands of combinations)	Parameter identifier (PID) (hundreds of combinations)
N/A	System identifier (SID)
Fault mode indicator (0–31)	Fault mode indicator (0–15)

- Reporting a component and nonstandard failure mode `FIGURE 35-20` and `TABLE 35-11`

J-1939 FMI

The FMI defines the type of failure detected in the subsystem identified by an SPN. The failure may not be an electrical failure but may instead be a subsystem failure or condition needing to be reported to the service technician and, perhaps, the operator. Conditions can include system events or statuses `TABLE 35-12` and `TABLE 35-13`.

Occurrence Count

The occurrence count (OC) represents the number of times a fault combination of SPN/FMI has taken place.

Parameter Group Number

SPN, source addresses, and FMI information are part of a larger J-1939 message called the **parameter group number (PGN)**. PGN information includes commands, data, requests, acknowledgments, and negative acknowledgments, as well as fault codes. The package of serial data is transmitted over the

TABLE 35-11: Example SPNs

SPN	Description
031	Transmission range position
156	Injector timing rail 1 pressure
190	Engine speed
512	Driver's demand engine—percent torque
513	Actual engine—percent torque
639	J-1939 network
899	Engine torque mode
1483	Source address of controlling device for engine control
1675	Engine starter mode
2432	Engine demand—percent torque

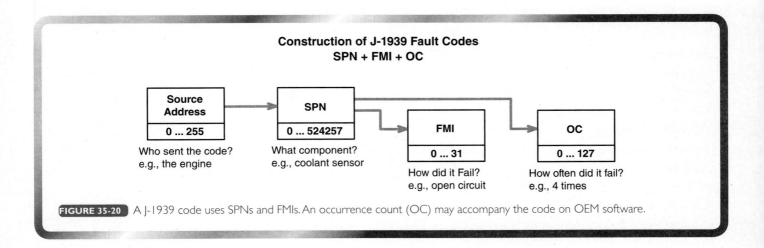

Construction of J-1939 Fault Codes
SPN + FMI + OC

Source Address
0 ... 255
Who sent the code?
e.g., the engine

SPN
0 ... 524257
What component?
e.g., coolant sensor

FMI
0 ... 31
How did it Fail?
e.g., open circuit

OC
0 ... 127
How often did it fail?
e.g., 4 times

FIGURE 35-20 A J-1939 code uses SPNs and FMIs. An occurrence count (OC) may accompany the code on OEM software.

TABLE 35-12: SAE J-1939 FMIs

FMI	SAE Text
0	Data valid but above normal operational range—most severe level
1	Data valid but below normal operational range—most severe level
2	Data erratic, intermittent, or incorrect
3	Voltage above normal or shorted to high source
4	Voltage below normal or shorted to low source
5	Current below normal or open circuit
6	Current above normal or grounded circuit
7	Mechanical system not responding or out of adjustment
8	Abnormal frequency or pulse width or period
9	Abnormal update rate
10	Abnormal rate of change
11	Root cause not known
12	Bad intelligent device or component
13	Out of calibration
14	Special instructions
15	Data valid but above normal operating range—least severe level
16	Data valid but above normal operating range—moderately severe level
17	Data valid but below normal operating range—least severe level
18	Data valid but below normal operating range—moderately severe level
19	Received network data in error
20–30	Reserved for SAE assignment
31	Condition exists

TABLE 35-13: Comparison of J-1939 SPN and J-1708/J-1587 Fault Codes

Description	J-1939		J-1708/J-1587	
	PGN	SPN	MID	PID
Percent load at current speed	61433	92	128	92
Engine speed (rpm)	61444	190	128	190
Distance	65248	245	128	245
Engine hours	65253	247	128	247
Coolant temperature	53262	110	128	110
Oil temperature	65262	175	128	175
Fuel delivery pressure	65263	94	128	94
Oil pressure	65263	100	128	100
Speed	65265	84	128	84
Fuel rate	65266	183	128	183
Instantaneous fuel economy	65266	184	128	184
Ambient air temperature	65269	171	128	171
Turbo boost	65270	102	128	102
Air filter differential pressure	65270	107	128	107
Exhaust gas temperature	65270	173	128	173

continued on next page

TABLE 35-13: Comparison of J-1939 SPN and J-1708/J-1587 Fault Codes, continued

Description	J-1939		J-1708/J-1587	
	PGN	SPN	MID	PID
Net battery current	65271	114	128	114
Battery voltage	65271	168	128	168
Transmission oil temp	65272	171	128	171
Brake application pressure	65274	116	128	116
Brake primary pressure	65274	117	128	117
Brake secondary pressure	65274	118	128	118
Hydraulic retarder pressure	65275	119	128	119
Hydraulic retarder oil temperature	65275	120	128	120
Fuel level	65276	96	41	96

CAN-bus. SPNs are assigned to each individual parameter within the PGN. This means each PGN will contain a different set of SPNs. For example, PGN 61444 is the electronic engine controller 1. Hundreds of possible messages can originate from this component because of the number of sensors and complexity of the system and its operation FIGURE 35-21 and TABLE 35-14.

PGN 61444 includes the following SPNs:

- Engine torque mode
- Driver's demand engine—percent torque
- Actual engine—percent torque
- Engine speed
- Engine starter mode
- Engine demand—percent torque

TABLE 35-14: Example PGNs

PGN	Description
61441	Electronic Brake Controller 1 (EBC1)
61442	Electronic Transmission Controller 1 (ETC1)
61444	Electronic Engine Controller 1 (EEC1)
65225	Service Information (SERV)

Message Priority

To prevent message signals from canceling out one another, signal collisions are avoided through an arbitration process that takes place while the PGN identifier is transmitted. The lower

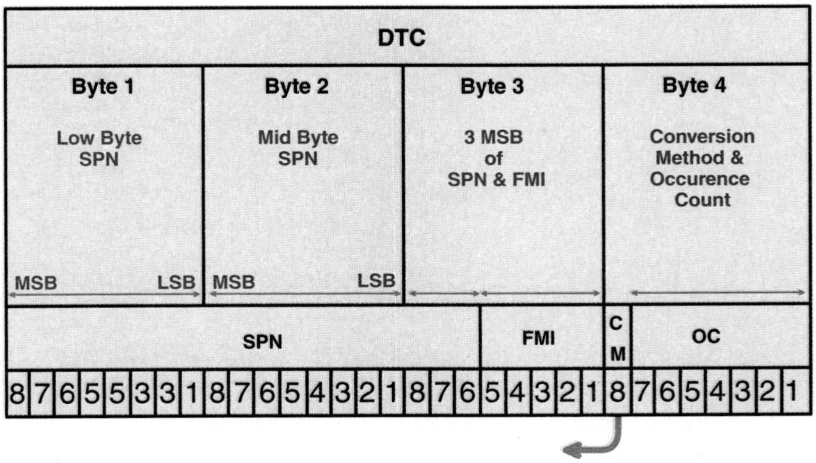

FIGURE 35-21 A J-1939 fault code is 29 bits long. The check sum (CM) field is a function of the other numbers in the code. If another module reads the code and the CM does not match, the data is rejected.

the first number is in the message, the greater importance attached to the information, requiring all other modules to listen while the information is transmitted:

- Highest priority: This is used for situations that require immediate action by the receiving device in order to provide safe vehicle operation (e.g., braking systems). This level of priority is only used in safety critical conditions.
- High priority: This is used for control situations that require prompt action in order to provide safe vehicle operation (e.g., a transmission performing an upshift, which requires a change in engine speed to control gear synchronization of damage to clutch packs) **TABLE 35-15**.

TABLE 35-15: Priority Fault Codes

Priority	Description
1 and 2	Reserved for messages that require immediate access to the bus
3 and 4	Reserved for messages that require prompt access to the bus in order to prevent severe mechanical damage.
5 and 6	Reserved for messages that directly affect the economical or efficient operation of the vehicle
7 and 8	All other messages not fitting into the previous priority categories

Wrap-Up

Ready for Review

▶ Emissions standards set for diesels beginning in the late 1970s have required a level of precision for engine control possible only through the extensive use of electronics. The OBD system was originally developed by manufacturers to diagnose faults with electronic controls.

▶ Since 2007, emissions legislation has required OBD systems to monitor the operation of emissions-control systems and alert the vehicle operator to any emission-related faults producing excessive emissions above threshold standards.

▶ In the United States, the EPA revised EMD legislation by mandating more comprehensive OBD system monitors that functionally monitor emissions-control systems and components. Beginning with model year 2010, with a phase-in period until 2016, HD-OBD is a significant update to EMD.

▶ Electronic systems do not have many moving parts to wear out, but the systems can be complex. When something goes wrong with a component or circuit, identifying the problem without some built-in self-diagnostic capabilities can be extremely time consuming and difficult.

▶ With built-in electronic self-monitoring functions, electrical systems possess the capability to check the operation of circuits and electrical devices, evaluate the rationality of data, and identify problems as they occur.

▶ Traditional self-diagnostic strategies focus on specific areas of commercial vehicle control, such as the engine, anti-lock braking, traction control, and transmissions.

▶ Model-based diagnostics compare system and component behaviors to expected patterns of operation.

▶ A fault is a deviation of at least one characteristic property of the system from its standard behavior.

▶ A failure is a fault that permanently interrupts a system's ability to perform a required function under specified operating conditions.

▶ A disturbance is an unknown and uncontrolled input acting on the system.

▶ Fault detection is a diagnostic strategy to determine whether faults are present in the system.

▶ Fault isolation is determining the location of the fault.

▶ When a fault is detected, fault accommodation, which is also known as an adaptive strategy, reconfigures the system operation or substitutes suspect data with default data to maintain normal system functionality even with the fault.

▶ To detect conditions that can increase emissions levels beyond FTP thresholds, the OBD system monitors individual components and major engine emissions-control systems. Monitors used by the diesel HD-OBD system can be divided into several general types:

threshold, functionality, rationality or plausibility, electrical circuit continuity, and out of range.

▶ The diagnostic manager, software that identifies fault codes and ensures emissions systems are operating correctly, regularly evaluates emission- related systems and components to detect faults in the emissions systems.

▶ Diagnostic monitoring of diesel engines is broken down into separate, specific hardware systems that are responsible for some specialized aspect of engine operation and emissions-control. The high-pressure injection system and the EGR system are examples of systems that have a major monitor associated with their operation.

▶ Emissions systems may be monitored continuously or non-continuously.

▶ The CCM continuously monitors electrical circuits operating powertrain components. The CCM is not tied to emissions thresholds.

▶ Because engine misfires can cause HC and CO emissions, the OBD system must evaluate engine operation to determine whether misfires are occurring.

▶ A more complex on-board diesel monitor is the EGR monitor. HD-OBD requirements for the diesel EGR monitor include detecting the following faults before emissions exceed HD-OBD thresholds: EGR flow rate, EGR response rate, and EGR cooling system performance.

▶ Fuel system monitors are required to detect faults associated with the high-pressure injection system before emissions exceed OBD thresholds.

▶ Underboost and overboost malfunctions are typically detected by comparing expected boost pressure values stored in the ECM with actual boost pressure measured by the boost pressure sensor.

▶ Because defective thermostats and engine temperature sensors will prevent running of other emissions system monitors, the OBD system also ensures the cooling system warms up quickly to the correct temperature.

▶ When electrical faults or system problems occur in commercial vehicle control systems, electronic control modules log DTCs in the system memory, which are read through an instrument display cluster or blink codes or retrieved by a scanner or personal computer connected to the vehicle DLC.

▶ For diesel engines, the threshold for alerting the driver and setting a fault code generally occurs any time a condition is sensed that could cause noxious emissions to exceed the legislated FTP emissions standards 1.5 times.

▶ HD-OBD requires monitoring of the CV system of a diesel.

▶ Type A DTCs are the most critical emissions-related faults and will illuminate the MIL with only one occurrence.

▶ Type B DTCs are emissions-causing faults that are less serious than type A faults and must occur at least once on two consecutive trips before the MIL will illuminate.

▶ Types C DTCs are non-emissions-related codes, or enhanced codes. Enhanced codes also cover non-emissions-related failures that occur outside the engine control system.

▶ The SAE developed the fault code reporting standard referred to as J-1587.

▶ J-1939 uses the CAN-bus protocol, which permits any electronic control module to transmit a message over the network when the data bus is idle or not transmitting other information. Every message includes an identifier that defines who sent it, what data is contained within the message, and the priority, or seriousness, of the fault or problem.

Vocabulary Builder

active fault A fault that is currently taking place and uninterrupted in action.

blink code A method of providing fault code data for a specific system that involves counting the number of flashes from a warning lamp and observing longer pauses between the light blinks.

diagnostic link connector (DLC) The connection point for electronic service tools used to access fault code and other information provided by chassis electronic control modules.

diagnostic trouble code (DTC) A code logged by the electronic control module when electrical faults or system problems occur in commercial vehicle control systems.

fault mode identifier (FMI) The type of failure detected in the SPN, PID, or SID.

historical fault A fault that took place at one time but that is now corrected and no longer active.

incipient fault A fault that is the result of system or component deterioration.

intermittent fault A fault that is not ongoing and can be both active and historical.

message identifier (MID) Also called module identifier, the electronic control module that has identified a fault. J-1587 protocols use MIDs.

OBD manager Software that identifies fault codes and ensures emissions systems are operating correctly.

off-board diagnostics Procedures to isolate a fault based on fault code information, including retrieving fault code information, monitoring system operation, performing actuator tests and pinpoint electrical tests, and inspecting components.

on-board diagnostics (OBD) Self-diagnostic capabilities of electronic control modules that allow them to evaluate voltage and current levels of circuits to which they are connected and determine if data is in the correct operational range.

out-of-range monitoring Validating sensor data to verify a system is operating within an expected range for a given operating condition.

parameter group number (PGN) A package of serial data transmitted over the CAN network that includes SPN, source addresses, and FMI, as well as commands, data, requests, acknowledgments, negative-acknowledgments, and fault codes.

parameter identifier (PID) A value or identifier of an item being reported with fault data.

source address (SA) The field that designates which control module is sending the message.

suspect parameter number (SPN) A numerical identifier that defines the data in a fault message and the priority of the fault.

system identifier (SID) A fault code used by J-1587 protocols that identifies which subsystem has failed.

telematics A branch of information technology that uses specialized applications for long-distance transmission of information to and from a vehicle.

Review Questions

1. A(n) _____ is a fault that took place at one time but that is now corrected and no longer active.
   a. incipient fault   c. active fault
   b. historical fault   d. intermittent fault

2. A fault that is the result of system or component deterioration is called a(n) _____.
   a. active fault   c. intermittent fault
   b. historical fault   d. incipient fault

3. A(n) _____ is a fault that is not ongoing and can be both active and historical.
   a. intermittent fault   c. transient fault
   b. incipient fault   d. preliminary fault

4. A(n) _____ is the type of failure detected in the SPN, PID, or SID.
   a. active fault   c. incipient fault
   b. fault mode identifier   d. intermittent fault

5. A fault that is currently taking place and uninterrupted in action is called a(n) _____.
   a. incipient fault   c. historical fault
   b. active fault   d. intermittent fault

6. The threshold for diesel misfire detection is 4% per _____ crankshaft revolutions.
   a. 800   c. 1,200
   b. 1,000   d. 1,500

7. A(n) _____ is a deviation of at least one characteristic property of the system from its standard behavior.
   a. isolation   c. readiness
   b. fault   d. occurrence

8. Fault _____ is best accomplished using a diagnostic fault tree supplied by the manufacturer.
   a. monitoring   c. readiness
   b. management   d. isolation

9. A _____ self-diagnostic strategy focuses on specific areas of commercial vehicle control, such as the engine, anti-lock braking, traction control, and transmissions.
   a. non-traditional   c. comprehensive
   b. traditional   d. standard

10. A diesel exhaust fluid quality sensor can now determine the quality of DEF fluid by measuring its _____.
   a. volume   c. mass
   b. density   d. temperature

ASE-Type Questions

1. Technician A says priority fault codes 1 and 2 are reserved for messages that require prompt access to the bus in order to prevent severe mechanical damage. Technician B says fault codes 3 and 4 are reserved for messages that require prompt access to the bus in order to prevent severe mechanical damage. Who is correct?
   a. Technician A
   b. Technician B
   c. Both Technician A and Technician B
   d. Neither Technician A nor Technician B

2. Technician A says a suspect parameter number is the smallest identifiable fault. Technician B says the parameter group number is the smallest identifiable fault. Who is correct?
   a. Technician A
   b. Technician B
   c. Both Technician A and Technician B
   d. Neither Technician A nor Technician B

3. Technician A says suspect parameter number, source addresses, and failure mode indicator information are part of a larger J-1939 message called the parameter group number. Technician B says those things are part of a larger J-1939 message called the subsystem identification number. Who is correct?
   a. Technician A
   b. Technician B
   c. Both Technician A and Technician B
   d. Neither Technician A nor Technician B

4. Technician A says a system identifier is the first byte or character of each message that identifies which control module on the J-1939 serial communication link originated the information. Technician B says a system identifier is the first byte or character of each message that identifies which control module on the J-1587 serial communication link originated the information. Who is correct?
   a. Technician A
   b. Technician B
   c. Both Technician A and Technician B
   d. Neither Technician A nor Technician B

5. Technician A says the J-1587/1708 and the J-1939 network connections are found in the 6-pin DLC. Technician B says both the J-1587/1708 and J-1939 network connections are found in the 12-pin DLC. Who is correct?
   a. Technician A
   b. Technician B
   c. Both Technician A and Technician B
   d. Neither Technician A nor Technician B

6. Technician A says type B diagnostic trouble codes are emissions-causing faults that must occur at least once on two consecutive trips before the malfunction indicator light (MIL) will illuminate. Technician B says type A diagnostic trouble codes are emissions-causing faults that must occur at least once on two consecutive trips before the malfunction indicator light (MIL) will illuminate. Who is correct?
   a. Technician A
   b. Technician B
   c. Both Technician A and Technician B
   d. Neither Technician A nor Technician B

7. Technician A says diesel particulate filter (DPF) monitoring is a common aftertreatment system monitor. Technician B says another common aftertreatment system monitor is selective catalyst reduction (SCR) monitoring. Who is correct?
   a. Technician A
   b. Technician B
   c. Both Technician A and Technician B
   d. Neither Technician A nor Technician B

8. Technician A says HD-OBD requirements for the diesel EGR monitor include detecting EGR response rate before emissions exceed HD-OBD thresholds. Technician B says HD-OBD requirements for the diesel EGR monitor also include flow rate and cooling system performance before emissions exceed HD-OBD thresholds. Who is correct?
   a. Technician A
   b. Technician B
   c. Both Technician A and Technician B
   d. Neither Technician A nor Technician B

9. Technician A says HD-OBD legislation for diesels does not include standardized 9-pin DLC in the driver area. Technician B says the HD-OBD legislation for diesels includes the 9-pin DLC in the driver area, as well as standardized names and abbreviations of components and systems and reading of fault codes by aftermarket electronic test equipment. Who is correct?
   a. Technician A
   b. Technician B
   c. Both Technician A and Technician B
   d. Neither Technician A nor Technician B

10. Technician A says the HD-OBD standards have fewer standardized legal requirements and are less comprehensive than the EMD standards. Technician B says all OBD standards are developed by SAE International and adopted by the EPA. Who is correct?
    a. Technician A
    b. Technician B
    c. Both Technician A and Technician B
    d. Neither Technician A nor Technician B

SECTION VI

OEM Service Information and Engine Systems

CHAPTER 36
Navistar

NATEF Tasks

Diesel Engines

Air Induction and Exhaust Systems
- Inspect turbocharger(s), wastegate, and piping systems; determine needed action. (p 1013)
- Inspect turbocharger(s) (variable ratio/geometry VGT), pneumatic, hydraulic, electronic controls, and actuators. (p 1013)
- Inspect exhaust gas recirculation (EGR) system including EGR valve, cooler, piping, filter, electronic sensors, controls, and wiring; determine needed action. (p 1019)

Fuel System

Electronic Fuel Management System
- Interface with vehicle's on-board computer; perform diagnostic procedures using electronic service tool(s) (to include PC-based software and/or data scan tools); determine needed action. (p 1019)
- Check and record electronic diagnostic codes and trip/operational data; monitor electronic data; clear codes; determine needed action. (p 1031)

Knowledge Objectives

After reading this chapter, you will be able to:
1. Identify recent Navistar engine products. (pp 1011–1012)
2. Identify and explain key operating principles and functions of Navistar engine control systems. (pp 1012–1022)
3. Identify unique features and operations of Navistar exhaust aftertreatment systems. (pp 1022–1024)
4. Describe and explain the operation of Navistar's low-pressure fuel transfer systems. (pp 1024–1029)
5. Identify and explain key operating principles and functions of Navistar Diamond Logic® on-board networks. (pp 1029–1032)

Skills Objectives

After reading this chapter, you will be able to:

1. Calibrate a Navistar oxygen sensor. (p 1021)
   SKILL DRILL 36-1

2. Isolate fuel rail pressure leakage. (p 1030)
   SKILL DRILL 36-2

3. Access Navistar OEM DTCs. (p 1033)
   SKILL DRILL 36-3

▶ Introduction

Navistar International Corporation is one of the largest North American producers of medium- and heavy-duty truck chassis. The corporation traces its roots to the farm equipment industry when McCormick Harvesting Machine Company joined with William Deering's Deering Harvester Company and three other smaller firms in 1902 to form the International Harvester (IH) Company. The company was so successful at selling farm equipment that by 1910, it was the fourth largest company in the United States. In 1933, IH produced its first diesel engine, the D-40, which was a four-cylinder, four-cycle, overhead valve using an indirect injection (IDI) fuel system. IH began producing commercial trucks in 1937. The company also introduced the first engine with a wet sleeve block. This meant that engines with worn, scored, or damaged cylinders did not need to be removed from a chassis to be rebored and repaired. Instead, replaceable cylinder sleeves enabled engines to be rebuilt quickly and efficiently. Regarded as revolutionary and the greatest single improvement made on a truck engine, replaceable cylinder sleeves have become almost standard on heavy-duty diesel engines **FIGURE 36-1**.

One of IH's most well-known line of products is its V8 diesels. In the early 1980s, IH introduced the 6.9 liter (L) (421 cubic inch), an IDI V8 engine, as an engine option for Ford 3/4-ton (680 kilogram [kg]) trucks and vans. The engine was hugely successful, selling millions as the original V8 transitioned to a 7.3 IDI, to a 7.3 direct injection (DI) known as the **PowerStroke**, and then to the 6.0L (366 cubic inch) in 2003. International Harvester, which became Navistar in the mid-1980s, ended its partnership with Ford after the production of the 6.4L (391 cubic inch). Ford then began to make its own in-house design PowerStroke diesels in 2009, the 6.7L (409 cubic inch) PowerStroke.

In the early 1980s, financial troubles led to major company restructuring at IH and discontinuation of the International Travelall SUV and the Scout line of trucks. The greatest change took place in 1984, when IH sold the agricultural business to the Tenneco subsidiary of Case, which also acquired the IH brand. The name International Harvester was dropped and the reorganized company became Navistar. Navistar uses the name International in its branding of diesel engines and truck product lines, but the company replaced the old IH logo with the symbolic diamond highway insignia, which became Navistar's new company logo.

▶ You Are the Technician

A customer brings a 2010 MaxxForce DT to your shop with a GEN2 HEUI system. The customer says the engine lacks power and takes a long time to accelerate to speed. You begin diagnosis by performing a key-on test, which is the first test required by Navistar. The water-in-fuel warning lamp flashes for about eight seconds and goes out, which indicates there are no water-in-fuel problems. Next, you visually inspect the vehicle and the engine compartment. You check fluid levels and look for leaks, disconnected wiring, and restrictions in the exhaust system and air filter. Everything is satisfactory. When checking diagnostic fault codes, you find codes related to the intake air boost pressure and the variable geometry turbocharger (VGT) actuator. With the engine off, you perform a bounce test of the turbocharger linkage and find it stiff to move and binding the vanes in a fully open position. You remove the turbocharger and clean and lubricate the VGT vane mechanism. After reinstalling the turbocharger, the actuator linkage bounces well and you take the vehicle for a road test. The low power symptoms are still present. You return to the shop and continue to try and diagnose the complaint.

1. List two steps you missed when attempting to diagnose whether the turbocharger was likely the root cause of the low power.
2. Explain why the position of the turbocharger vanes would produce low power and slow acceleration.
3. How much voltage is supplied to the turbocharger actuator when the ignition switch is in the off position?

FIGURE 36-1 This DT 466 engine has replaceable cylinder sleeves.

FIGURE 36-2 Navistar produces the WorkStar, a vocational severe service chassis.

FIGURE 36-3 Navistar is a major supplier of the defense industry, providing purpose-made vehicles and equipment.

Today, Navistar is a holding company that owns the manufacturer of International brand commercial trucks, <u>Maxx-Force</u> brand diesel engines, IC Bus school and commercial buses, and Workhorse brand chassis for motor homes and step vans **FIGURE 36-2**. Navistar has also had a successful business producing purpose-made vehicles for the defense industry **FIGURE 36-3**. Purpose-made vehicles are customized vehicles manufactured for specific, but highly unique, applications.

Navistar's International Truck and Engine Corporation partnered with the Eaton Corporation to become the first company to enter the hybrid commercial truck market, with the International DuraStar Hybrid diesel-electric truck. Navistar's Diamond Logic on-board vehicle network, introduced in 2001, advanced the use of a controller area network (CAN) chassis and cab electrical system, which distributed control of the electrical system through multiple control modules. The change to software control of the electrical system enabled customization of electrically controlled vehicle accessories plus the addition of a long list of safety and convenience features. A series of OnCommand™ support systems offers customers advanced vehicle telematics control, fleet management solutions, and online training and education opportunities.

Navistar's current line of truck products includes the following offerings:

- Medium Duty
  - International TerraStar Class 4-5 conventional cab
  - International CityStar LCF (low-cab forward) cab-over
  - International DuraStar Class 6-7 conventional cab
- Class 8
  - International LoneStar conventional cab
  - International ProStar+ conventional cab
  - International 9000 Series conventional cab
  - International TranStar conventional cab

- Severe Service
  - International PayStar conventional cab
  - International WorkStar conventional cab

The longevity of Navistar's 3000, 4000, 7000, and 8000 series trucks is exceptional, with this truck series replacing the venerable S-line chassis in the early 1990s. A heavy-duty cab-over-engine tractor built in partnership with Mahindra has replaced Navistar's own Class 8 cab-over-engine chassis, which has declined in popularity in North America, mainly due to changes in vehicle length laws **FIGURE 36-4**.

FIGURE 36-4 Navistar's cab-over-engine chassis was at one time one of the best-selling heavy-duty tractors.

▶ Navistar Engines

Navistar has manufactured dozens of engine lines over the years, incorporating cutting-edge technology and innovation with Navistar's own unique technological features. Navistar began using the hydraulically actuated electronic unit injector (HEUI) system extensively in the V8 and DT series engines. In 2003, Navistar developed a second-generation HEUI capable of multi-shot rate-shaped injection with Siemens, a major original equipment manufacturer (OEM) supplier in Europe and North America. Navistar then introduced several common rail engines beginning in 2007 to help meet the EPA07 emission standards. Navistar originally resisted the industry move to liquid selective catalytic reduction (SCR) used by almost every other engine manufacturer to meet EPA10 emission standards. The company believed drivers did not want the aggravation of adding yet another liquid to a reservoir. Its solution was to use more exhaust gas recirculation (EGR) to meet the 90% reduction of oxides of nitrogen (NO_x) required by 2010. At the outset, the concept seemed strategically sound. However, implementation of the complex technology was plagued with trouble and damaged the reputation of Navistar, according to industry observers. The rapid development of a wide variety of untested emission reduction strategies followed on the heels of the trouble-stricken 6.0L (365 cubic inch) engine product, afflicting the PowerStroke brand. Navistar has since abandoned the use of massive EGR rates to reduce NO_x and switched its entire line of Class 8 trucks to liquid SCR aftertreatment. The N-series engines now use liquid SCR systems. The company produced the last HEUI engine in 2010 using emission credits accumulated through years of producing cleaner engines that met emission standards earlier than required.

Navistar leads the industry in the innovative use of quiet and exceptionally strong composite graphite iron (CGI) engine blocks. **SinterCast**, Navistar's name for its CGI engine block construction, improves performance, fuel economy, and durability while reducing engine weight, noise, and emissions. The Maxx-Force 7L (427 cubic inch), 13L (793 cubic inch), and 15L (915 cubic inch) engines were the first engines in Navistar's lineup to use this lightweight block technology. Navistar has since dropped the 15L (915 cubic inch) engine, which was designed in collaboration with Caterpillar and used in Caterpillar CT series trucks. The 13L (793 cubic inch) engine is used in its place **TABLE 36-1**, **TABLE 36-2**, **TABLE 36-3**, and **TABLE 36-4**.

TABLE 36-1: Navistar's Early Engines

Engine and Displacement	Fuel System	Engine Type	Production Years
6.9L (421 cubic inch)	(Pump-Line-Nozzle) PLN	V8	1983–1985
7.3L (445 cubic inch)	PLN	V8	1986–1992
DT 360, 5.9L (360 cubic inch)	PLN	I-6	1984–1997
DT 408, 6.7L (408 cubic inch)	PLN	I-6	1994–1997
DT/HT 466, 7.6L (466 cubic inch)	PLN	I-6	1978–1997
DT/HT 530, 8.7L (530 cubic inch)	PLN	I-6	1994–1997
DT/HT 570, 9.3L (570 cubic inch)	PLN	I-6	1994–1997

TABLE 36-2: Navistar's HEUI Engines

Engine and Displacement	Fuel System	Engine Type	Production Years
7.3L (446 cubic inch)	GEN I	V8	1994–2003
DT/HT 466, 7.6L (466 cubic inch)	GEN I	I-6	1994–2003
DT/HT 530, 8.7L (530 cubic inch)	GEN I	I-6	1994–2003
VT 275, 4.5L (275 cubic inch)	GEN II	V6	2003–2006
VT 365, 5.9L (365 cubic inch)	GEN II	V8	2003–2006
DT/HT 466, 7.6L (466 cubic inch)	GEN II	I-6	2003–2010
DT/HT 530, 8.7L (530 cubic inch)	GEN II	I-6	2003–2010

TABLE 36-3: Navistar's Common Rail Engines

Engine and Displacement	Engine Type	Production Years
MaxxForce 5, 4.5L (274 cubic inch)	V6	2007–current
MaxxForce 7, 6.4L (391 cubic inch)	V8	2007–current
MaxxForce DT, 7.6L (466 cubic inch)	I-6	2010–current
MaxxForce 9, 9L (549 cubic inch)	I-6	2010–2013
MaxxForce 11, 10.5L (640 cubic inch)	I-6	2010–2013
MaxxForce 13, 12.4L (756 cubic inch)	I-6	2010–2013
MaxxForce 15, 15L (915 cubic inch)	I-6	2010–2013

TABLE 36-4: SCR Exhaust Aftertreatment System Engines

Engine and Displacement	Fuel System	Production Years
N-9, 9L (549 cubic inch)	Common rail	2013–current
N-10, 10.5L (641 cubic inch)	Common rail	2013–current
N-13, 12.4L (756 cubic inch)	Common rail	2013–current

Navistar's CGI blocks all feature main bearing and connecting rod bearing caps that use split fracture manufacturing techniques, which Navistar terms Sure Lock technology. Main bearing caps are scribed with a laser and hydraulically split after the main bearing bore is line bored. The unique separation pattern enables more precise alignment of bearing caps for improved bearing oil control and crankshaft alignment. Much of Navistar's technology is covered in other sections of this textbook. This chapter examines some of the major technological features unique to Navistar, including the following:

- Air management systems (AMSs)
- Exhaust aftertreatment systems
- Fuel systems
- Diamond Logic electrical system
- OnCommand telematics

▶ AMSs—Mid-Bore Engines

The AMS encompasses all the controls that regulate the air and EGR gas entering and exiting the combustion chamber of the engine. This means the masses of EGR gas and intake air need individual measurements to correctly meter and blend under all engine speed and load conditions. Mid- and large-bore engines use three distinctly different AMSs. Mid-bore engines (i.e., the 2002–2010 MaxxForce DT 466, 9, and 10) all use a single VGT and an air-to-air charge cooler. In 2010, the engines received a series turbocharger system with a combination of air-to-air charge cooling and one or two liquid intercoolers. Since 2007, the medium- and large-bore 11L (671 cubic inch), 13L (793 cubic inch), and 15L (915 cubic inch) engines use series turbocharging combined with a liquid charge air cooler (CAC). Looking first at the earlier EGR engines built in 2002–2010, the early I-6 mid-bore engine AMS consists of the following components:

- Air filter assembly
- Intake air temperature sensor
- VGT
- Exhaust back-pressure sensor
- CAC

The EGR system consists of the following components:

- Exhaust manifold
- Intake manifold
- EGR mixer duct
- Intake manifold absolute pressure sensor
- Intake manifold air temperature sensor
- EGR valve
- Closed crankcase breather

Variable Geometry Turbocharging

At the center of the AMS system used in 2002–2006 is the VGT, which is responsible for building boost pressure and creating the exhaust backpressure needed to drive the exhaust gas pressure above the intake air charge pressure **FIGURE 36-5**. Like any turbocharger, the VGT uses the expansion pressure of the exhaust gases to turn the turbine wheel. The VGT compressor wheel is located at the opposite end of the turbine shaft and spins in a separate compressor wheel housing, where it compresses the incoming air using high-speed centrifugal force imparted to the air by the compressor wheel. Intake air enters the turbocharger through the air filter, where its temperature is measured. A filter minder gauge measures excessive restriction across the filter, which indicates a need for filter replacement.

Intake Boost and Exhaust Back-Pressure Control

To change the speed of the turbine wheel, exhaust backpressure is varied by opening and closing movable vanes surrounding the turbine wheel **FIGURE 36-6**. When the vanes are closed, little exhaust can move through the turbine housing, which increases backpressure. Higher exhaust backpressure will spin the turbine wheel faster, much like holding a finger over the opening of a garden hose to increase the water's velocity. In addition to increasing turbine speed, closing the vanes also increases the compressor wheel speed, which boosts pressure. Opening the vanes reduces backpressure, slowing the turbocharger and reducing boost pressure. Rotating the vanes together is a unison ring inside the turbine housing that connects to a stepper motor-driven actuator.

The actuator is a controller area network (CAN) device. It both transmits and receives information over the vehicle's CAN. This means the engine control module (ECM) and other modules, such as the EGR controller or aftertreatment controllers, can command the VGT position and receive data from it. Moving the actuator enables electronic control of intake boost and exhaust backpressure to match engine speed and load conditions.

While a position sensor inside the turbocharger actuator self-calibrates the turbocharger every time the ignition switch is

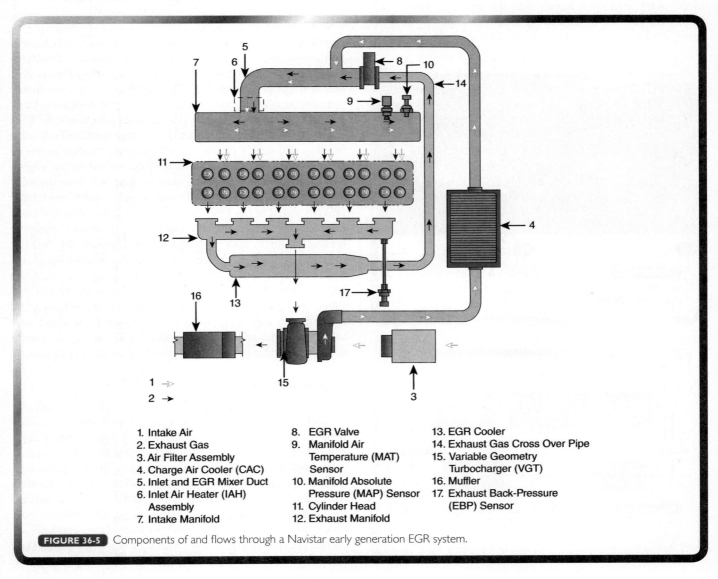

1. Intake Air
2. Exhaust Gas
3. Air Filter Assembly
4. Charge Air Cooler (CAC)
5. Inlet and EGR Mixer Duct
6. Inlet Air Heater (IAH) Assembly
7. Intake Manifold
8. EGR Valve
9. Manifold Air Temperature (MAT) Sensor
10. Manifold Absolute Pressure (MAP) Sensor
11. Cylinder Head
12. Exhaust Manifold
13. EGR Cooler
14. Exhaust Gas Cross Over Pipe
15. Variable Geometry Turbocharger (VGT)
16. Muffler
17. Exhaust Back-Pressure (EBP) Sensor

FIGURE 36-5 Components of and flows through a Navistar early generation EGR system.

cycled, positioning of the turbocharger vanes is part of a closed-loop system that uses the exhaust back-pressure sensor to monitor exhaust backpressure and supply the data to the ECM. Based on tables inside the ECM and algorithms calculating the optimal turbocharger backpressure, the ECM will review back-pressure data and determine whether it is above, below, or equal to target backpressure. Depending on the answer, the actuator control module will open, close, or do nothing to vane position **FIGURE 36-7**. The temperature of pressurized intake air will increase to minimize further NO_x emissions. An air-to-air charge air cooler mounted in front of the cooling system radiator will cool the air. An EGR cooler also cools exhaust gases. The cooler passes engine coolant through a heat exchanger, where coolant will absorb heat from the exhaust to lower combustion temperatures.

Opening and Closing VGT Vanes

Opening and closing VGT vanes is primarily determined by the amount of exhaust backpressure needed to supply exhaust gas to the EGR system. If more EGR gas is needed, the EGR valve will open and the VGT vanes will close to build backpressure to the point where it is higher than the intake air boost pressure. Increasing the exhaust backpressure and opening the EGR valve will meter more exhaust gases into the cylinder charge.

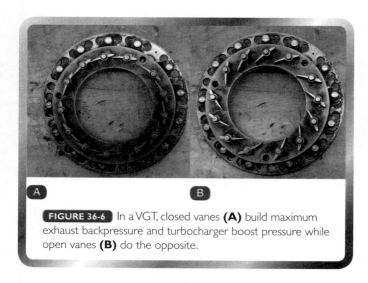

FIGURE 36-6 In a VGT, closed vanes **(A)** build maximum exhaust backpressure and turbocharger boost pressure while open vanes **(B)** do the opposite.

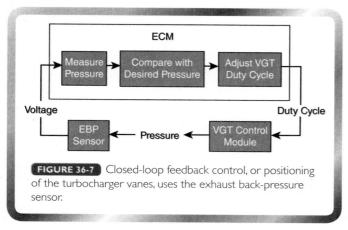

FIGURE 36-7 Closed-loop feedback control, or positioning of the turbocharger vanes, uses the exhaust back-pressure sensor.

Opening the vanes accomplishes the opposite. Opening VGT vanes decreases backpressure and boost pressure. VGT vanes also open during high-speed and high–engine load conditions because more exhaust energy is available to drive the turbine wheel than is needed. If the vanes do not open, excessive turbocharger boost pressure can damage cylinder components, decrease engine efficiency, and stress the EGR cooler with excessively high exhaust pressure.

During low-speed or low–engine load conditions, little exhaust energy is available to build boost pressure. To squeeze the most energy from the exhaust, the VGT vanes are moved toward the closed position. Closing the vanes will increase turbine shaft speed, producing higher boost and exhaust backpressure. The default position for the actuator vanes is closed when power is removed from the turbocharger or the key is off. More air goes to the combustion chamber to avoid excessive emissions if a failure occurs. The vanes are also closed near idle. This strategy enables boost pressure to build quickly when the engine is put under load because the actuator does not take time to move the vanes closed.

EGR Metering

The EGR valve on the early AMS was a dual poppet valve located on the cooled side of the EGR cooler. Dual poppet valves have two paths for exhaust to flow and a higher exhaust mass flow than a single poppet valve **FIGURE 36-8**. A DC stepper motor controls the opening and closing of the valve to regulate exhaust flow into the intake manifold. A microcontroller inside the EGR valve monitors three Hall effect sensors that read the EGR valve position and supply data to the EGR control module mounted on the engine ECM. The module is connected to the engine ECM through the CAN bus. Based on feedback from the EGR valve, the EGR module will send a pulse-width-modulated (PWM) signal to the EGR motor, causing it to rotate and close or open the valve. Precise valve positioning is obtained using the feedback from the Hall effect sensors. The engine ECM, the EGR module, and the EGR valve itself perform the closed-loop operation of the valve. Based on feedback from the engine ECM to the EGR module, the EGR module will interpret engine ECM CAN signals and position the valve. Once the valve is positioned, the EGR module will supply data to the engine ECM about new valve positions, and the engine ECM will once again decide whether the valve should open more, less, or stay in position.

Calculation of EGR Flow

Algorithms determine EGR valve positioning based on calculations of EGR flow-based intake boost pressure, intake manifold temperature, and exhaust backpressure. A speed density algorithm determines the mass of gases entering the cylinders using data about the engine's volumetric efficiency, speed, intake manifold temperature, and pressure. Calculations for the algorithm use data from the pressure and temperature sensors to measure the weight and density of the intake charge. Determining how much gas is entering the cylinders per second uses engine revolutions per minute (rpm) and volumetric efficiency tables. Data from the intake air temperature sensor and boost pressure also

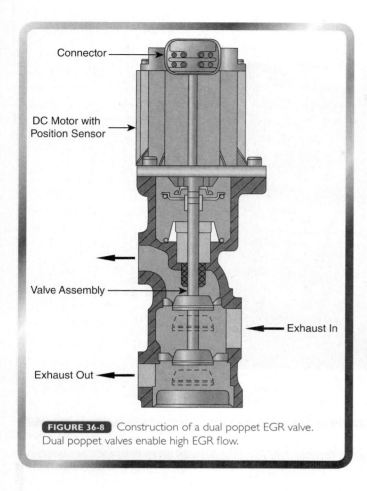

FIGURE 36-8 Construction of a dual poppet EGR valve. Dual poppet valves enable high EGR flow.

Labels: Connector; DC Motor with Position Sensor; Valve Assembly; Exhaust Out; Exhaust In

figure into the speed of the turbocharger, increasing or decreasing turbine speed to regulate boost pressure.

Diagnosing Turbocharger Actuator Codes

Turbocharger vanes can often seize as a result of excessive engine slobber from idling or low-load and low-speed conditions. Often, if the vanes have seized, the actuator motor will burn out attempting to move the binding or seized linkage. Occasionally, the cause is a defect in the printed circuit board, but that failure still requires a complete actuator replacement. Three tests can determine the problems with the actuator:

- Bounce test: With the ignition key switched to the off position, try to move the turbocharger linkage to the fully open position. The linkage should move smoothly. Releasing the linkage will cause the spring-loaded actuator mechanism to move the linkage to the vanes closed position. Properly operating actuator linkage and vanes will contact the closed position and bounce at least once, if not two or three times.
- Linkage movement test: Failing the bounce test, the next step to determine whether the problem is in the turbocharger vanes or actuator is disconnecting the linkage. Moving the linkage through its range of motion will indicate whether the vane mechanism is binding.

- Actuator voltage test: If the turbocharger passed the linkage movement test and the vane mechanism is not binding, the actuator likely failed. Using a breakout harness or proper pins to back probe the turbocharger actuator electrical connection, the power and ground wire voltage is measured when cycling the key on and off. Battery voltage should be observed when the ignition key is switched on. If battery voltage is observed, the actuator is defective.

Crankcase Ventilation

After 2006, engine crankcases were no longer permitted to be ventilated to the atmosphere. On mid-bore engines, a coalescing filter was placed in the breather tube. Oil and air are separated by the filter, with oil returning to the sump through a check valve. The check valve prevents crankcase gases from venting to the atmosphere through the breather tube. When enough oil sits on the check valve, the valve opens and drains oil from the oil collection tube **FIGURE 36-9** and **FIGURE 36-10**.

TECHNICIAN TIP

EGR coolers have tubes, surrounded by coolant, that exhaust gases travel through. Constant pressure and temperature changes can crack EGR coolers. If coolant leaks from an EGR cooler, it will leak into the exhaust manifold or the intake manifold. Loss of coolant and sweet smelling exhaust gases are indicators of EGR cooler leaks. To verify the cooler is leaking, manufacturers recommend removing and pressure testing the cooler with air. Pressurizing the coolant side of the cooler and placing the cooler in a water tank will quickly reveal leaks, which are indicated by air bubbles emerging from the cooler.

Intake Throttle Valve

The introduction of diesel particulate filters in 2007 brought an intake throttle valve (ITV), which is installed between the charge air cooler and the intake manifold, ahead of the EGR inlet. The ITV's purpose is to reduce excess airflow into the cylinder during particulate filter regeneration events. Decreasing airflow means less dilution of exhaust gases takes place with cooler air. The exhaust temperatures at idle increase close to 200°F (93°C) with the intake throttle closed. Increasing exhaust temperatures accelerate chemical reactions in the aftertreatment system, which does not normally take place in the cool, air-rich exhaust of a diesel. The throttle actuator receives a signal from the engine ECM to open or close. A throttle position sensor provides feedback about the throttle position. An electric intake heater is also installed to preheat intake air during cold start and warm-up conditions. The intake heater reduces the amount of soot and hydrocarbons normally accompanying engine warm-up.

Series Two-Stage Turbocharged Engines

Using two turbochargers connected in series can provide a faster increase in boost pressure and the potential to provide

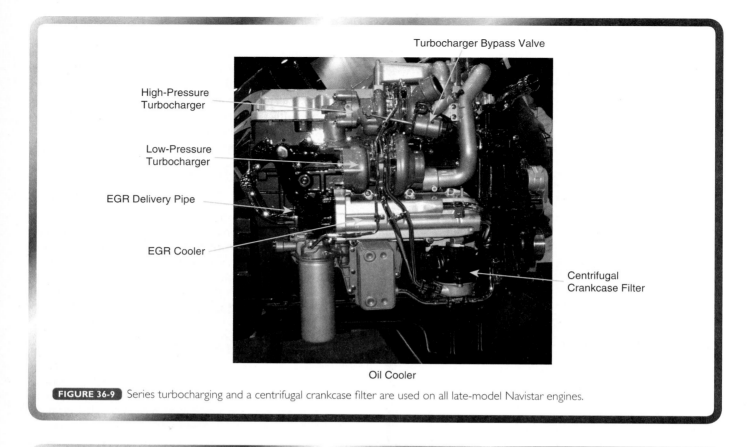

FIGURE 36-9 Series turbocharging and a centrifugal crankcase filter are used on all late-model Navistar engines.

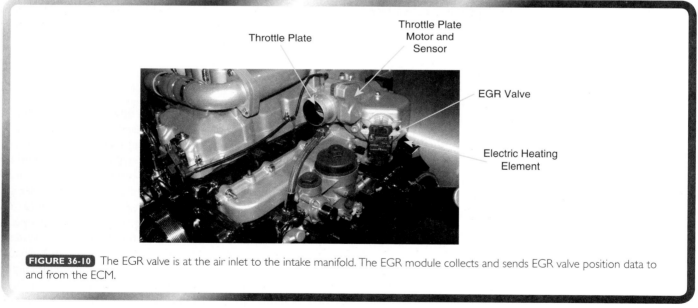

FIGURE 36-10 The EGR valve is at the air inlet to the intake manifold. The EGR module collects and sends EGR valve position data to and from the ECM.

higher overall boost pressures. With a faster increase in boost pressure, the throttle response is quicker. Using higher boost pressures also increases the power density of an engine (i.e., the engine can burn proportionally more fuel as more air fills a cylinder). Higher cylinder pressures translate into greater torque and power output for every cubic inch of engine displacement.

With series turbocharging, the compressor output pressure of one turbocharger feeds into the compressor inlet of another turbocharger **FIGURE 36-11**. The effect is a multiplication of boost pressure, not an addition of output pressure of the two turbochargers. Navistar's two-stage turbochargers produce approximately 50 pounds per square inch (psi) (345 kilopascals [kPa]) of boost. This compares with approximately 35 psi (241 kPa) maximum boost from a VGT on similar-sized engines. Using two turbochargers produces a wider range of high-boost pressure over all engine speeds.

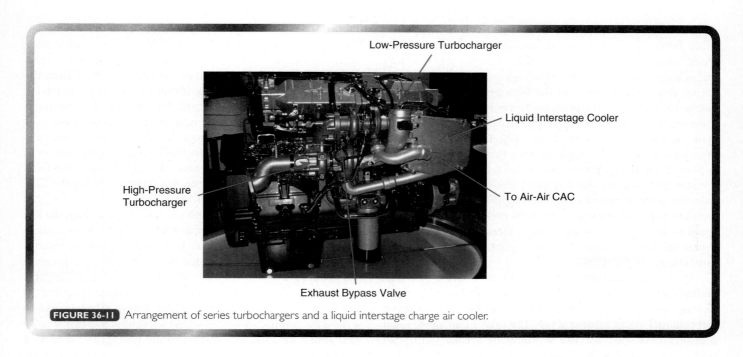

High-Pressure Turbocharger

Low-Pressure Turbocharger

Liquid Interstage Cooler

To Air-Air CAC

Exhaust Bypass Valve

FIGURE 36-11 Arrangement of series turbochargers and a liquid interstage charge air cooler.

Both turbochargers can turn slower when two are used, which extends turbocharger life.

Series turbocharging can reduce emissions. Higher cylinder temperatures and pressures lower production of hydrocarbon (HCs), carbon monoxide (CO), and particulate matter (PM) emissions. To reduce NO_x production, which increases with cylinder temperatures and pressures, retarded injection timing and increased EGR rate are needed. Increasing the flow of relatively inert exhaust gas into the intake air charge slows the release of heat during the combustion process. Burn time is distributed over a larger number of degrees of crank rotation, and cylinder pressures do not spike after the ignition delay period. The use of pilot and rate-shaped injection further contributes to reduced NO_x formation. Cooling the boost pressure between each stage lowers the intake charge temperature to minimize NO_x formation.

> ## TECHNICIAN TIP
>
> Series turbochargers use high- and low-pressure turbochargers. The low-pressure turbocharger boosts pressures at high speeds, while the high-pressure turbocharger builds boost at low speeds. Air enters the compressor housing of the larger, low-pressure turbocharger, where it passes into the smaller, high-pressure turbocharger. This multiplies boost pressure. Exhaust gas enters the high-pressure turbocharger first, where it passes to the low-pressure turbocharger. The high-pressure turbocharger will always use a wastegate or exhaust bypass valve to limit turbocharger overspeed.

High- and Low-Pressure Turbochargers

Series turbochargers use different sizes of compressor and turbine housings, which are designated as high-pressure and low-pressure turbochargers **FIGURE 36-12**. The low-pressure turbocharger has larger turbine and compressor housings. It receives exhaust energy left over after passing through the high-pressure turbocharger. The high-pressure turbocharger has smaller turbine and compressor housings. The smaller, high-pressure turbocharger, builds boost pressure quickly at low speeds because its smaller turbine housing needs less exhaust energy to speed up the turbine wheel and has less turbine shaft inertia. The high-pressure turbocharger gives the engine a quicker throttle response because it increases speed quickly when the engine load increases, with virtually no lag at low speeds. Boost pressure increases rapidly at low-speed and low load conditions using this turbocharger.

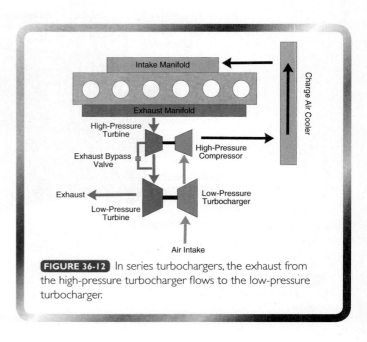

FIGURE 36-12 In series turbochargers, the exhaust from the high-pressure turbocharger flows to the low-pressure turbocharger.

The high-pressure turbocharger will reach its maximum speed faster and cannot provide enough airflow under high-speed, high-load conditions. The second, low-pressure turbocharger takes over where the high-pressure turbocharger output stops. Air supplied to the high-pressure turbocharger passes through the low-pressure turbocharger first because it encounters little resistance inside the larger housing. Under load, the low-pressure turbocharger begins to supplement air pressure supplied to the high-pressure turbocharger. As boost pressure from the low-pressure turbocharger increases, the high-pressure turbocharger speed remains stable, but boost pressure rises due to the increased air pressure supplied to the inlet of the high-pressure turbocharger. The high-pressure turbocharger's speed is limited by a wastegate, also referred to as an exhaust bypass valve, which redirects exhaust gases to the low-pressure turbocharger **FIGURE 36-13**.

When turbochargers are arranged in a series like this, multiplication of the turbocharger output pressure takes place, causing boost pressure to increase to levels higher than either turbocharger could achieve alone. The mass of air moved and pressures developed are also substantially greater than what could be produced with a single-stage or even a VGT turbocharger. By splitting the pressurization of the air charge between two turbochargers, both can operate at optimal efficiency range. Multiplication of pressure between stages of boost means lower rotating speeds for improved reliability of the bearings and other rotating parts.

Airflow

Air enters the low-pressure turbocharger after first passing through the air filter. Because the low-pressure turbocharger increases air pressure and temperature, the air passes through a low-pressure charge air cooler (LPCAC), or interstage cooler, which is between the low- and high-pressure turbochargers **FIGURE 36-14**. Cooled and compressed air then flows from the LPCAC into the high-pressure turbocharger compressor inlet, where its pressure is boosted even further. Heated, compressed air flows from the high-pressure turbocharger compressor outlet into the high-pressure air-to-air charge air cooler, where it is cooled. The engine throttle valve (ETV) regulates the amount of air entering the cylinders. Because the ETV is upstream from the EGR gas duct into the intake, opening and closing the ETV changes the ratio of EGR gas to air.

A series of temperature and pressure sensors along the airflow path into the engine provides data to the ECM to regulate boost pressure control. Because both turbochargers are wastegated, the ECM will position the wastegates using air pressure supplied by a PWM air control valve (ACV) **FIGURE 36-15**. When little or no boost is required, air pressure is applied to both wastegates to open them, which allows exhaust gases to bypass the turbine wheels. To increase boost pressure, the ACV will reduce air pressure supplied to the wastegates based on a PWM signal provided by the ECM and data collected from temperature and pressure sensors.

The wastegates are spring-loaded to close and receive air pressure signals from the ACV to open. A safety feature built into the boost pressure controls enables boost pressure to pass through the ACV and open the wastegates in the event the ACV did not work. Normally, air pressure supplied by the air reservoirs and regulated to 43 psi (296 kPa) is used to open the wastegates. Boost pressure higher than this means even if the ACV control did not open, boost pressure is enough to open

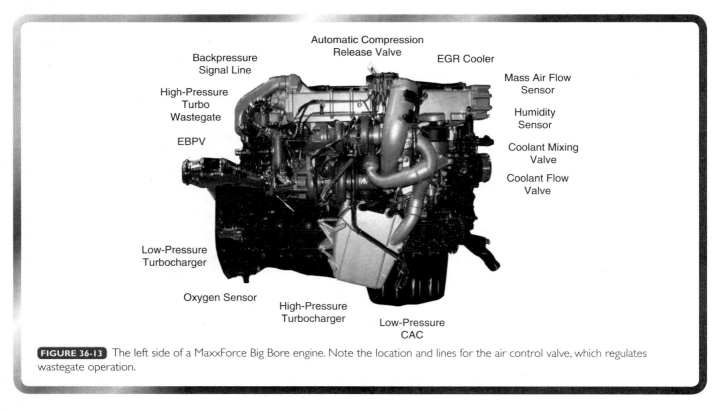

Backpressure Signal Line

Automatic Compression Release Valve

EGR Cooler

High-Pressure Turbo Wastegate

Mass Air Flow Sensor

Humidity Sensor

EBPV

Coolant Mixing Valve

Coolant Flow Valve

Low-Pressure Turbocharger

Oxygen Sensor

High-Pressure Turbocharger

Low-Pressure CAC

FIGURE 36-13 The left side of a MaxxForce Big Bore engine. Note the location and lines for the air control valve, which regulates wastegate operation.

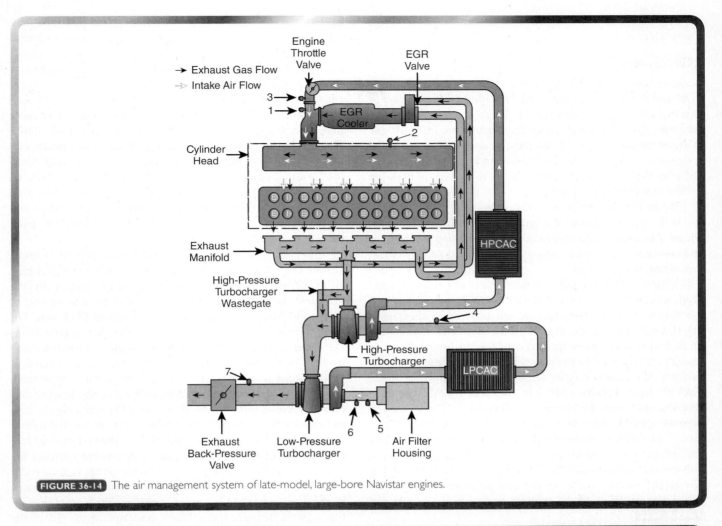

FIGURE 36-14 The air management system of late-model, large-bore Navistar engines.

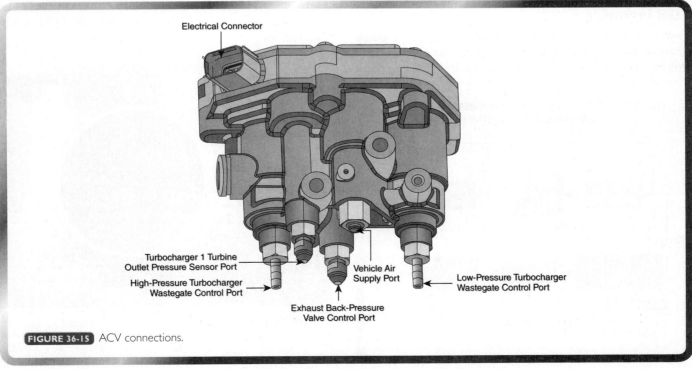

FIGURE 36-15 ACV connections.

the wastegate and prevent damage to the turbochargers or the charge air coolers.

EGR System

Because Navistar MaxxForce engines use higher amounts of EGR gases to eliminate the need for liquid SCR, an exhaust aftertreatment system favored by other manufacturers, the Navistar system has a high flow rate of recirculated exhaust gas. Without the use of a VGT to increase exhaust backpressure, the system relies on an exhaust back-pressure valve (EBPV) located just after the low-pressure turbocharger to pressurize EGR gas to flow into the intake manifold.

When the EGR valve is open, exhaust gas passes through the EGR cooler and into the intake air duct below the ETV, where it is mixed with charge air. The combined exhaust gas and charge air then passes into the intake manifold, where it is drawn into the cylinders.

After combustion, exhaust gases enter the exhaust manifold, where they can flow through the EGR valve back into the intake or leave through the exhaust pipes after passing through the turbocharger turbine housings. The EBPV located at the low-pressure turbocharger turbine outlet can restrict exhaust flow to the exhaust pipe and increase exhaust backpressure. Increasing backpressure forces more EGR gas through the EGR valve when it is open. The EBPV is air actuated and controlled by air pressure from the ACV. When the valve is opened, exhaust gas is released. Closed-loop operation of the EBPV is controlled by the ECM using the ACV and the turbocharger 1 turbine outlet pressure (TC1TOP) sensor. This sensor is located in the ACV and connected through a line to the exhaust outlet of the low-pressure turbocharger. When the EBPV is open, exhaust backpressure is released **FIGURE 36-16**.

EGR Metering

Two methods are used to measure EGR flow. One method Navistar uses in its MaxxForce engines incorporates data from oxygen sensors. By measuring the amount of exhaust gas oxygen, the ECM can calculate whether more or less EGR flow is required. Low oxygen content would mean too much EGR gas is flowing, whereas high oxygen content means not enough EGR gas is entering the cylinders. An exhaust gas oxygen (EGO) sensor on diesels is a wide band type that measures a larger range of oxygen content than sensors typically found on gasoline engines. The EGO sensor has a heater element that heats the sensor to an operating temperature of 1436°F (780°C). During engine warm-up, the EGO sensor heater element switches on only after the engine coolant reaches 104°F (40°C) and the exhaust gas temperature reaches 212°F (100°C) for more than 30 seconds. When it is within normal operating temperatures where the data is accurate, the EGR system will move to closed-loop control of EGR flow based on data from the EGO sensor.

The other way to measure EGR flow is with a mass airflow (MAF) sensor located in the air intake of the engine **FIGURE 36-17**. Because EGR gas displaces oxygen in the cylinders, a drop in fresh air intake airflow for a given engine speed and load condition indicates increased EGR flow. For example, an engine using 1000 cubic feet per minute (cfm) (1699 cubic meters per hour [m/hr]) of air at 1200 rpm with no EGR flow would experience a drop in fresh air intake flow proportional to an increase of EGR flow. If the engine fresh intake flow dropped to 1000 cfm (1699 cubic m/hr), then 200 cfm (340 cubic m/hr) of EGR gas would be entering the cylinders with the 1000 cfm (1699 cubic m/hr) of air. The heavy-duty on-board diagnostics (HD-OBD) system can compare the two calculations of EGR flow to determine whether the system is functioning properly and to check the rationality of sensor data. A large discrepancy between measurements made by the oxygen and MAF sensors could indicate a problem with the sensors. Because water vapor can displace oxygen in the intake air, the engine is equipped with a humidity sensor to correct any error in measuring gas mass content caused by high humidity.

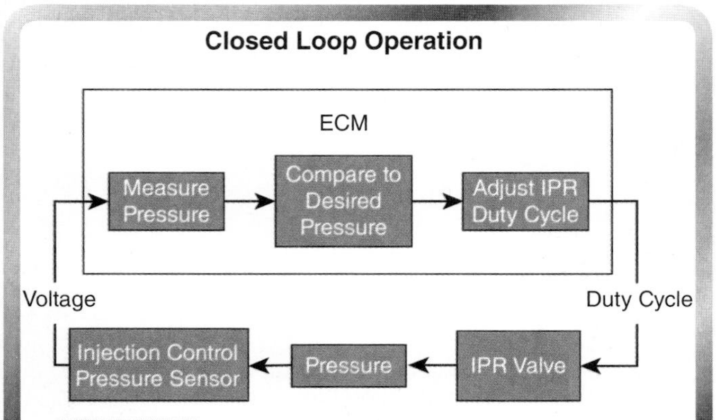

Closed Loop Operation

ECM

Measure Pressure → Compare to Desired Pressure → Adjust IPR Duty Cycle

Voltage   Duty Cycle

Injection Control Pressure Sensor ← Pressure ← IPR Valve

FIGURE 36-16 Exhaust backpressure and EGR valve position are controlled by closed-loop feedback using exhaust-based engine sensors.

FIGURE 36-17 Navistar's MAF sensors use a heated wire to measure airflow in grams per second.

Calibrating a Navistar Oxygen Sensor

Navistar uses oxygen sensors to make adjustments to the EGR gas mass flow. The Bosch sensor has an integrated calibration resistor located in the connector on the plug end. On HD-OBD engines, the emission diagnostic manager must correct for system deterioration factors to ensure engine compliance with emissions standards. The oxygen sensor will deteriorate and needs to self-calibrate to maintain accuracy. During installation, this wideband sensor requires learning an initial calibration before it can be used, which serves as a reference point for future self-calibrating corrections.

To calibrate a Navistar oxygen sensor, follow the steps in **SKILL DRILL 36-1**. The oxygen calibration procedure generally involves using Navistar ServiceMaxx software.

EGR Coolers

An important part of Navistar's emissions-reduction strategy is precise control of intake air pressure, air, and EGR flow rates and temperatures. Part of this strategy uses a two-stage EGR cooler, with high- and low-temperature coolers incorporated into a single unit **FIGURE 36-18**.

Optimizing intake air temperature and density helps the combustion temperature operate in a low NO_x zone and improves combustion efficiency. A low-temperature EGR cooling circuit is needed to better control the temperature of EGR gas entering the cylinders. Additional cooling of EGR gas is performed by a low-temperature radiator (LTR) located in front of the main cooling system radiator **FIGURE 36-19**. This three-pass LTR is positioned so the final coolant pass is cooled with lower-temperature air. It is thermostatically controlled to operate near 100–110°F (38–43°C) in contrast with the main cooling radiator operating at 200°F (93°C). When charge air temperatures are high, more coolant will flow through the LTR and supply both the LPCAC and the EGR low-temperature circuit with coolant. The coolant mixer valve (CMV) and the coolant flow valve (CFV) control coolant flow through the low-temperature EGR cooler and the LPCAC. Depending on operating conditions the CMV sends coolant through the low-temperature EGR cooler and the LPCAC, after passing through the LTR located in front of the main coolant radiator. When charge temperatures are low, the LPCAC can function as an air temperature heater as well. A coolant flow valve (CFV) will bypass the LTR and send coolant directly to the LPCAC **FIGURE 36-20**.

It is important to note that MaxxForce 11 and 13 engines have no coolant passages between the engine block and the cylinder head through the cylinder head gasket. This design eliminates any possible coolant leak from the cylinder head gasket. Coolant in and out of the block and cylinder head is directed through external pipes to the high-temperature stage of the EGR cooler, where it travels parallel with exhaust flow. A passage from the EGR cooler to the thermostat housing enables coolant to flow to the radiator **FIGURE 36-21**.

Cold Start Assist

In addition to using an electric heating element in the air inlet of the intake manifold, Navistar also uses a cold start assist system **FIGURE 36-22**. With the use of a glow plug integrated with a fuel injector, a small amount of diesel fuel is sprayed and ignited in the air intake during cold-weather start-up **FIGURE 36-23**. The main component, a cold start fuel igniter (CSFI) contains a glow plug–like heating element, a vaporizer tube, and a vaporizer filter enclosed in a protective sleeve with holes that allow air to pass through to the heating element. A high-current relay called the cold start relay provides current to the CSFI

SKILL DRILL 36-1 Calibrating a Navistar Oxygen Sensor

Wide Band Oxygen Sensor

1. Verify there are no oxygen sensor circuit faults before sensor replacement. The sensor may be defective, but wiring and connectors cannot have faults.

2. With the sensor removed from the exhaust system, first connect the oxygen sensor to the engine harness before running the oxygen sensor calibration procedure. Leave the sensor outside the exhaust system.

3. From the ServiceMaxx software, select "Run O_2 Sensor Calibration procedure."

4. Turn on the ignition switch, turn off the engine, and run the calibration procedure.

5. After calibration is complete, install the oxygen sensor in the exhaust system.

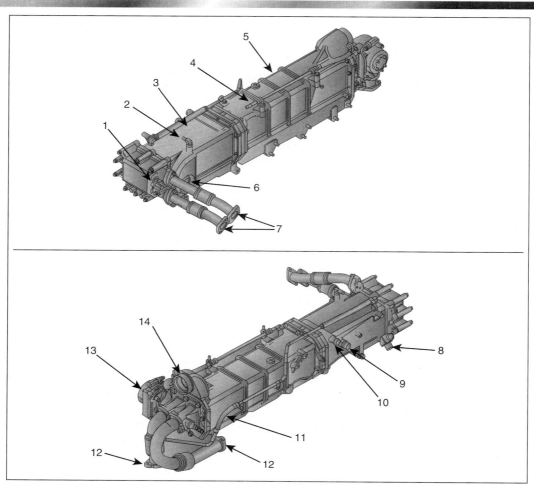

1. EGR Temperature Sensor
2. EGR Cooler Air Bleed (to deaeration tank)
3. EGR Cooler (low-temperature stage)
4. EGR Valve Coolant Return Line (to deaeration tank)
5. High-Temperature EGR Cooler

6. Intake Manifold Temperature (IMT)
7. EGR Cooler Outlet Tube (2) (gases)
8. Low-Temperature EGR Cooler Inlet (coolant)
9. Engine Coolant Temperature 2 (ECT2) Sensor

10. Low-Temperature EGR Cooler Outlet (coolant)
11. EGR Valve Coolant Supply Line
12. EGR Cooler Inlet Tubes (gases)
12. EGR Valve
12. EGR Coller Inlet (coolant)

FIGURE 36-18 Navistar uses a two-pass EGR cooler, which can vary the temperature of the EGR gas metered into the intake air flow. This strategy helps achieve very precise control of combustion temperatures for low emissions.

when signaled by the ECM. When ambient temperatures are colder than 50°F (10°C), the heater element is energized for 35 seconds. This happens after the ignition key is switched on and the wait-to-start lamp is illuminated. As that light goes out and the driver cranks the engine, fuel from the low-pressure supply system is piped to the CSFI, vaporizing and igniting when it contacts the heater element. Once the engine starts, the CSFI will continue to operate for as long as four minutes or as long as the wait-to start light is flashing. If the driver accelerates the vehicle during this time, the CSFI and the wait-to-start light will shut off.

▶ Navistar Exhaust Aftertreatment Systems

Navistar chose a different pathway than the rest of its industry to achieve emission compliance for the EPA10 low-NO_x standards. While the entire heavy-duty diesel engine industry used an on-board liquid SCR system, which sprayed diesel exhaust fluid (DEF) into the exhaust stream, Navistar decided to meet the standards with in-cylinder solutions that prevented NO_x formation. The idea of minimizing NO_x formation to eliminate an exhaust-based system to reduce engine NO_x required a much

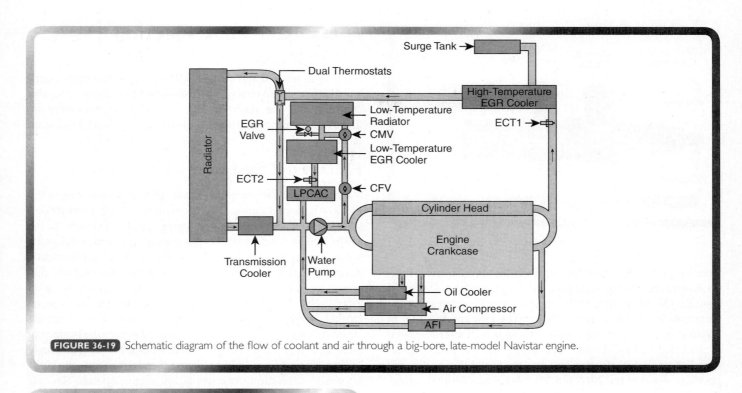

FIGURE 36-19 Schematic diagram of the flow of coolant and air through a big-bore, late-model Navistar engine.

FIGURE 36-20 Location of the coolant control valves on a large-bore Navistar block.

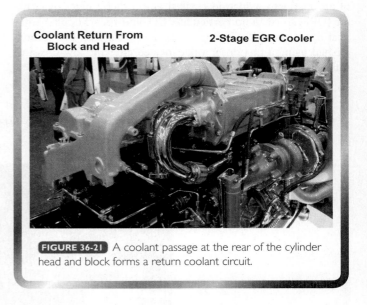

FIGURE 36-21 A coolant passage at the rear of the cylinder head and block forms a return coolant circuit.

more complex air management control system to regulate combustion temperatures and pressures. Later, Navistar abandoned the in-cylinder solutions and incorporated liquid SCR systems. This next section examines exhaust aftertreatment systems that Navistar used to meet the EPA07 and EPA10 standards.

No Liquid SCR

Before 2012, Navistar took a different approach than other manufacturers to meeting the EPA10 emission standards. The company did not believe it was necessary to add more aggravation and inconvenience to operating commercial vehicles by filling another fluid reservoir, so instead of using a liquid SCR exhaust aftertreatment system, Navistar attempted to engineer its engines to meet the low NO_x EPA10 requirement of 0.2 grams per brake horsepower-hour (g/bhp-hr) of NO_x, using only its In-Cylinder Technology without SCR aftertreatment. That pathway to compliance has since been abandoned and all the Class 8 engines and the 9L (549 cubic inch), 10L (610 cubic inch), 11L (671 cubic inch), and 13L (793 cubic inch) engines

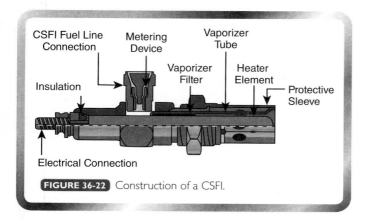

FIGURE 36-22 Construction of a CSFI.

have a liquid SCR system that uses Cummins Emissions Solutions products. At the same time, Navistar announced it would drop its 15L (915 cubic inch) engine and offer customers the Cummins X 15 common rail engine. The new combination of Navistar engine technology with Cummins SCR aftertreatment is marketed as In-Cylinder Technology Plus (ICT+). Engines with ICT+ met EPA10 emissions standards and the greenhouse gas rules ahead of the 2014 and 2017 deadlines. More information about this aftertreatment system is found in the Exhaust Aftertreatment Systems chapter.

Prior to 2012, Navistar used a conventional arrangement of an upstream oxidation catalyst and a diesel particulate filter (DPF) to clean up particulate, CO, and HCs. Supplemental heating of the DPF during active regenerations was accomplished using a fuel doser valve located after the low-pressure turbocharger **FIGURE 36-24** .

▶ Navistar Fuel Injection Systems

Navistar developed and used HEUI in many of its engines until late 2010, when all engines were designed to use high-pressure common rail. The MaxxForce 11, 13, and 15 engines were the first to use common rail systems developed by Bosch beginning in 2007.

HEUI Fuel Systems

Navistar, in collaboration with Caterpillar, produced one of the first and largest evolutionary steps of modern high-pressure diesel injection technology by developing the HEUI system. In the 1980s, when manufacturers began exploring technical solutions for upcoming emission standards, they realized mechanically governed fuel systems had several handicaps. The primary disadvantage of traditional mechanical systems is their reliance on a camshaft driven by the engine or an injection pump to pressurize fuel. Much higher injection pressures are required to reduce emissions, and injection events are needed to vary the beginning and end of injection. Injection systems needed to also uncouple injection pressurization from engine speed to generate the highest possible injection pressures at low engine speeds. Navistar developed the HEUI system to replace the mechanical camshaft with highly pressurized lubrication oil, which is used instead of cam lobes to actuate plungers pressurizing fuel for injection. An amplifier piston in the latest G2 injectors multiplies oil by a factor of 10:1 to produce close to 30,000 psi (2068 bar) of injection pressure. Because the functions of pressurization, metering, timing, and atomization are all incorporated into a single injector body, HEUI injectors are classified as unit injectors.

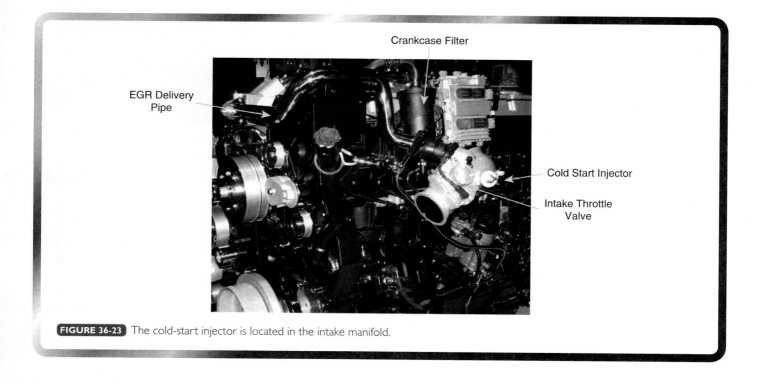

FIGURE 36-23 The cold-start injector is located in the intake manifold.

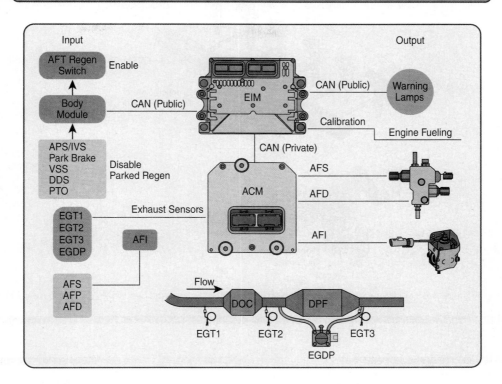

Big Bore Engine AFT Functional Diagram

- Engine Interface Module (EIM)
- Aftertreatment Control Module (ACM)
- Accel Pedal Sensor/Idle Validation Switch (APS/IVS)
- Vehicle Speed Sensor (VSS)
- Driveline Disconnect Switch (DDS)
- Power Take Off Switch (PTO)
- Exhaust Gas Temperature 1 (EGT1) Sensor
- Exhaust Gas Temperature 2 (EGT2) Sensor
- Exhaust Gas Temperature 3 (EGT3) Sensor

- Exhaust Gas Differential Pressure (EGDP) Sensor
- Diesel Oxidation Catalyst (DOC)
- Diesel Particulate Filter (DPF)
- Aftertreatment Fuel Injector (AFI)
- Aftertreatment Fuel Supply (AFS) Valve
- Aftertreatment Fuel Drain (AFD) Valve
- Aftertreatment Fuel Pressure (AFP) Sensor
- Controller Area Network (CAN)

FIGURE 36-24 Functional diagram of the AFT system used by Navistar prior to 2012.

The system was one of the first electronically controlled diesel engines to be capable of varying injection pressures independently of engine load. Combined with pilot injection capabilities, HEUI systems were the first fuel systems capable of injection rate shape control **FIGURE 36-25** and **FIGURE 36-26**.

Electro-Hydraulic Valve Operation in Cam-less Diesel Engines

HEUI technology also provides the potential to integrate valve-train operation into the high-pressure oil actuation system. Instead of using a camshaft to operate valves, electro-hydraulic actuation of intake and exhaust valves is possible using the HEUI high-pressure

oil pump. Navistar created a prototype of the cam-less diesel in 1998. The design has a number of interesting advantages:

- Variable valve timing and valve lift would provide ultimate control of engine breathing. Instead of a compromised design of the valve train operation as a consequence of unchanging camshaft profile, intake and exhaust flow could be better matched to engine load and speed conditions. Electro-hydraulic control using software to optimize valve train operation would allow the engine to produce the lowest emissions and best performance characteristics without the constraints of a mechanical, fixed geometry camshaft.

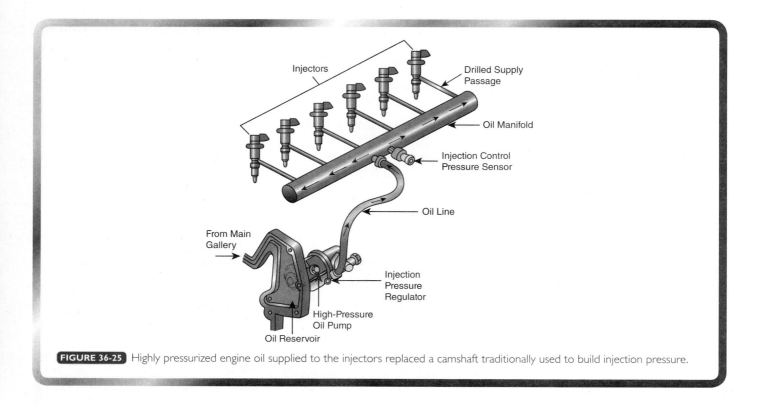

FIGURE 36-25 Highly pressurized engine oil supplied to the injectors replaced a camshaft traditionally used to build injection pressure.

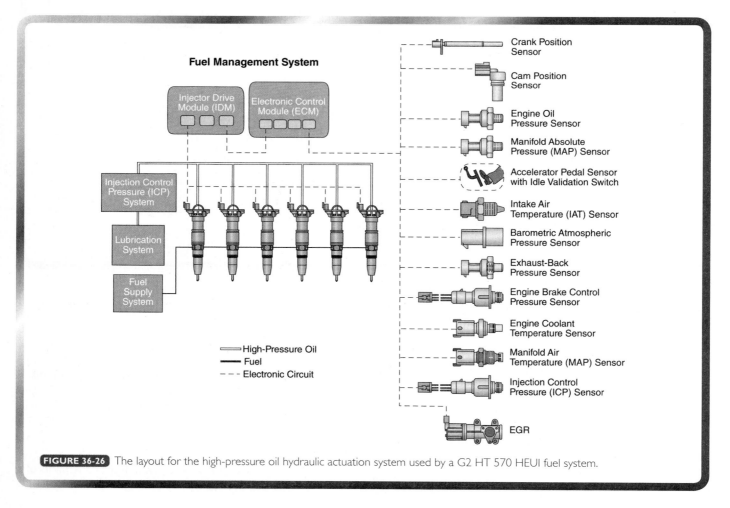

FIGURE 36-26 The layout for the high-pressure oil hydraulic actuation system used by a G2 HT 570 HEUI fuel system.

- An internal compression release brake feature could be incorporated into engine operation with no additional components.
- Hydraulic actuation of valves permits the use of compression-less starts, enabling the use of smaller starting motors and fewer batteries. An engine can be easily cranked with exhaust valves slightly open, allowing high initial cranking rpm with minimal starting motor torque. Shortly after the engine begins cranking, closing the valves in one or all cylinders at the correct time would start the engine.
- Cam-less diesels are capable of displacement on demand, which means cylinders can be cut out with minimal parasitic loss of power until they are needed. Hydraulically actuated valve operation also enables the use of engine-based compression release braking systems without the additional components required of conventional compression release brakes FIGURE 36-27 . The HEUI fuel injector is also integrated into this system, and both use the same high-pressure oil supply.

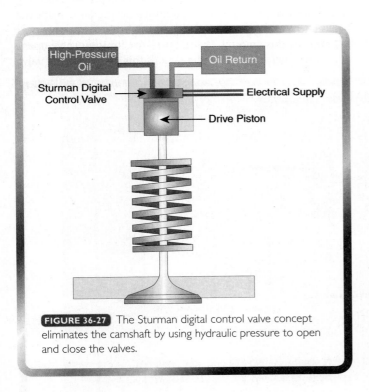

FIGURE 36-27 The Sturman digital control valve concept eliminates the camshaft by using hydraulic pressure to open and close the valves.

HEUI Applications

International used HEUI for its DT series of engines: the 466, the 530, and the 570. International has also used HEUI in VT-275, MaxxForce DTs, and MaxxForce 5, 7, 9, and 10 engines. The second generation of HEUI, termed GEN II or G2, refined HEUI technology. A partnership between Navistar, Siemens AG, and Sturman Industries produced digital valve technology. Digital valve technology uses two control solenoids in the injector to either allow filling or emptying of the pressure chamber above the amplifier piston. The 6.0L (365 cubic inch) PowerStroke engine, or VT-365, in International brand trucks uses this new injector design. International produced a 4.5L (275 cubic inch) V6 version of the VT-365 V8 for use in military vehicles and the Ford CF, a medium-duty class 4-5 cab-over series chassis. Navistar also supplied the Perkins 1300Edi HEUI engines and Daimler-Detroit Diesel branded Series 40 engine, which use an HEUI fuel system.

The most successful HEUI engine was Navistar's T-444E, a 7.3L (444 cubic inch) engine produced for Ford between model years 1993.5 and 2003.5. Navistar manufactured more than 2.5 million of these engines. In fact, two out of every three Ford F-250 and larger trucks were equipped with this engine. Between model years 2003.5 and 2006, the 6.0L (365 cubic inch) PowerStroke, branded the VT-365 by International, used the G2, which was not produced in collaboration with Caterpillar. Navistar continued to supply HEUI engines until the production of the VT365 ended in 2006 TABLE 36-5 .

More comprehensive coverage of HEUI fuel systems is included in the HEUI Injection Systems chapter.

High-Pressure Common Rail Fuel Systems

Common rail systems are one of only two remaining injection systems used on commercial diesels that can meet emission standards while providing superior fuel economy and performance unheard of in previous generations of diesels. The basic concept of common rail injection is simple—supply fuel at injection pressure to a fuel nozzle that electrically controls the injection event. While the concept of supplying a constant high-pressure fuel supply to individual injectors is not new, the technology to switch fuel delivery on and off at pressures now in excess of 36,000 psi (2482 bar) involves breakthrough technological and manufacturing achievements. The systems metering precision, spray-in pressures, and injection event control enable

TABLE 36-5: Types of HEUI Fuel Systems

HEUI Injector	Navistar	Ford	Caterpillar
HEUI-A	T-444E	7.3L (444 cubic inch) PowerStroke	3116
HEUI-B	T-444E DTs 466, 530, 570	7.3L (444 cubic inch) PowerStroke	3126
GEN II	VT-365 VT-275 DTs 466, 530, 570	6.0L (365 cubic inch) PowerStroke	N/A
Caterpillar second-generation HI-300	N/A	N/A	C7 ACERT C9 ACERT

dramatic reduction in exhaust emissions and fuel consumption while offering engine performance superior to gasoline-powered vehicles. Common rail modular design lends great flexibility to adaptation on any new or updated diesel engine design. Pressurization of fuel and injection are separate functions in the common rail injection system.

The Bosch second-generation servo hydraulic injectors used by Navistar systems allowed for up to three injections per combustion cycle (FIGURE 36-28). Out of the three, the first injection is a pilot injection designed to reduce combustion noise and emissions by delivering a small amount of fuel into the cylinder 8–10 degrees before the main injection event. This shortens the ignition delay period and enables the delivery of the main injection event to take place later, which means injection timing can be retarded to reduce NO_x formation. Following the main injection event, which is the second of three injections, the third post main injection event keeps cylinder temperatures high to minimize soot formation.

Injection Pressure Control

The electronically controlled injection pressure can be generated by the high-pressure pump at any engine speed. Injection pressures are produced by a high-pressure pump driven by a gear train. They are regulated by the fuel pressure control valve (FPCV) located on the high-pressure pump. Injection timing

and quantities are calculated in the ECM and delivered by an electrically controlled servo valve on the injector. A fuel rail pressure sensor provides closed-loop feedback to the FPCV. The ECM will reposition the FPCV if rail pressures are above or below desired values. The FPCV is a PWM actuator located in the suction side of the high-pressure pump and regulates the output fuel pressure. A 100% duty cycle PWM signal sent by the ECM produces very little fuel pressure delivered, while a 0% duty cycle PWM causes the high-pressure pump to produce maximum injection pressure.

Fuel Rail

The fuel rail is located along the engine and is designed to store some fuel volume and reduce pressure pulsation produced by the piston-type high-pressure pump (FIGURE 36-29). A constant fuel pressure in the fuel rail is available to all the injectors, which lends the name "common rail" to the fuel system. High-pressure fuel lines connect the fuel rail and injectors. A hard steel line called the quill tube connects to a centrally located injector. Another line connects the quill tube to the high-pressure fuel rail.

In the event of a failure of the FPCV, a rail pressure limiting valve is located in the fuel rail that limits fuel pressure inside the fuel rail to 37,710 psi (2600 bar). If the high-pressure pump output exceeds this amount, the rail pressure limiting valve opens and allows fuel to return to the tank. If this pressure relief valve

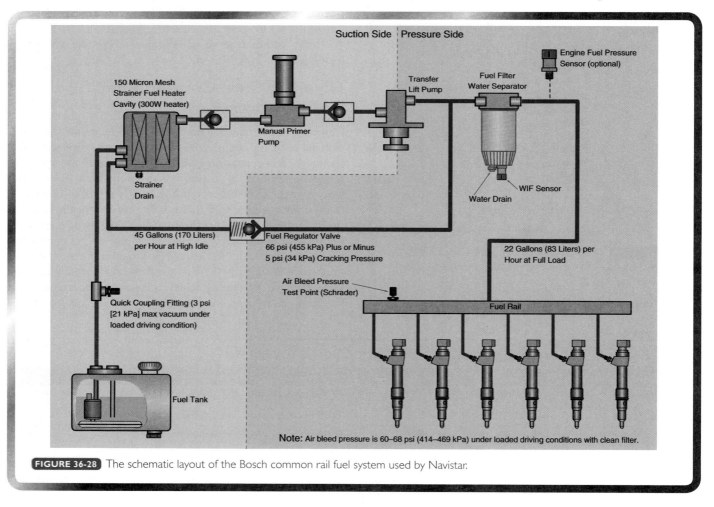

FIGURE 36-28 The schematic layout of the Bosch common rail fuel system used by Navistar.

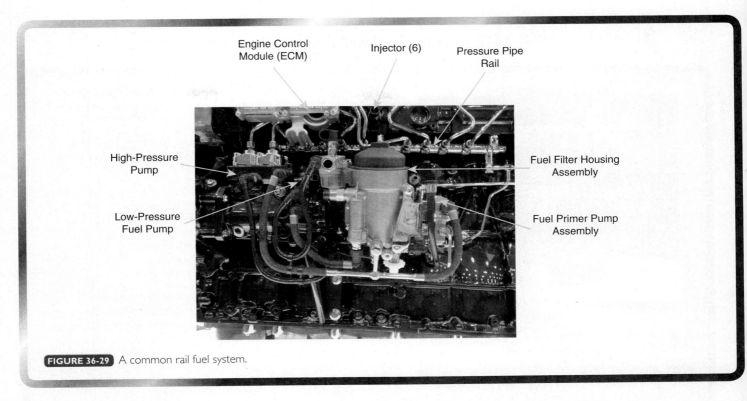

Engine Control Module (ECM)

Injector (6)

Pressure Pipe Rail

High-Pressure Pump

Low-Pressure Fuel Pump

Fuel Filter Housing Assembly

Fuel Primer Pump Assembly

FIGURE 36-29 A common rail fuel system.

does open, fuel pressure in the pressure rail drops to approximately 15,954 psi (1100 bar).

Isolating Fuel Rail Pressure Leakage

The high-pressure fuel system can have extremely high pressure that needs draining before servicing. The ECM on Navistar common rail engines commands a blank shot injection process that drains the high-pressure fuel rail whenever the ignition key is switched off. Verify that system pressure is below 500 psi (34 bar) using ServiceMaxx software before disconnecting any high-pressure fuel line.

Common rail engine fault codes for fuel rail pressure leakage are often caused by defective injectors. Fuel return flow increases from defective injectors, which will set a fuel rail pressure leakage code.

To isolate fuel rail pressure leakage, follow the steps in **SKILL DRILL 36-2**.

▶ Diamond Logic Electrical System

Navistar was the first major truck producer to move to the use of a CAN control of the cab and chassis electrical system. Navistar's version of a multiplex-controlled electrical system is called Diamond Logic **FIGURE 36-30** and **FIGURE 36-31**. This type of control is not like older electrical systems, with point-to-point connections between cab switches and electrical devices such as horns, lights, and a starter motor. Instead, driver inputs to a central electrical system control module are one of several control inputs used to operate electrical devices. Inputs from the engine ECM, the anti-lock braking system, the transmission controller,

and other modules on the vehicle supply electrical data that is processed by software in the form of ladder logic embedded into a central electrical system control module. This central module is much like a body electrical system control module used for years by automobile manufacturers. International calls its electrical system control module an electrical system controller (ESC).

Since 2001, the Diamond Logic electrical system has enabled custom programmable chassis electronics, which provides control and communication between a truck's specialized body equipment and customizable cab electrical system control. More than 200 factory-available electrical system templates can be programmed to accommodate the addition of chassis installation equipment for everything from fire and ambulance bodies to adding hydraulic controls for boom trucks or pickup and waste vocational truck bodies. With the use of Navistar's Diamond Logic Builder software, customers can add even more specialized electrical system functions at dealers.

ESC

The ESC module operates circuits such as headlights, taillights, windshield wipers, and the A/C system controls. Using field effect transistors (FET) as output drivers, the high amperage transistors supply +12 volts and 20 amps from high side drivers and supply a ground circuit to operate coils and relays. Up to three remote power modules (RPMs) supply additional programmable current output to body equipment. The RPMs communicate with the ESC using CAN. The RPMs have a high amperage battery supply, which distributes as much as 80 amps of current to programmable output pins. For example, if an electric hydraulic motor requires current flow, the driver would activate a switch in the dash that provides an input to the ESC,

SKILL DRILL 36-2 Isolating Fuel Rail Pressure Leakage

1 Cap cylinder 1's high-pressure line connector with an OEM-prescribed high-pressure rail plug.

2 Disconnect the fuel return line from the cylinder head and run a clear plastic hose to the line. Place the other end of the plastic line into a graduated cylinder to measure fuel volume.

3 Start the engine and operate it at low idle. Once fuel flow and volume are steady, measure the return volume for exactly 1 minute.

4 Repeat the procedure for cylinders 2–5 by continuing to cap off one injector supply fitting at a time until the excessive leak is isolated.

5 Compare the fuel return volume to Navistar's specifications. The normal expected volume for fuel returned for connected cylinders may resemble the following:
- Five connected injectors: 16–18 mL
- Four connected injectors: 12–16 mL
- Three connected injectors: 8–12 mL
- Two connected injectors: 8–10 mL

6 If the observed results are much higher than manufacturer's specifications, the defective injector(s) will produce a normal return volume when capped. When connected, return fuel volume will exceed specifications. If the fuel volume is within specifications, replace the injector tube and high-pressure connector body for cylinder 6.

7 Replace the defective injector(s) and retest the system.

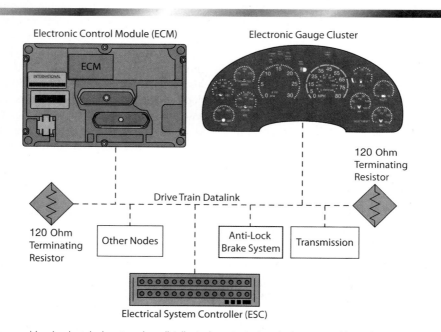

FIGURE 36-30 The Diamond Logic electrical system is a distributed-control electrical system with various modules operating electrical devices and circuits. The CAN network enables communication between modules.

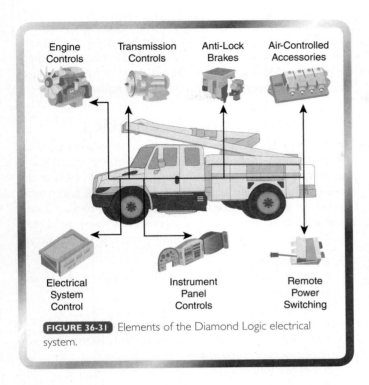

Engine Controls · Transmission Controls · Anti-Lock Brakes · Air-Controlled Accessories

Electrical System Control · Instrument Panel Controls · Remote Power Switching

FIGURE 36-31 Elements of the Diamond Logic electrical system.

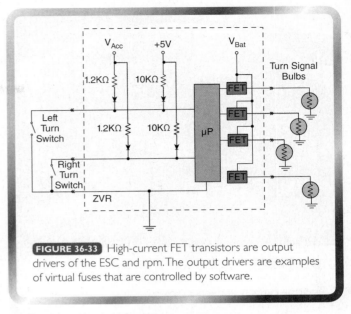

FIGURE 36-33 High-current FET transistors are output drivers of the ESC and rpm. The output drivers are examples of virtual fuses that are controlled by software.

which then signals the RPM, which switches current flow on and off to the electric motor as programmed into the software for the motor operation **FIGURE 36-32**.

Output circuits with FET use what are known as virtual fuses. A circuit for each output driver will monitor the amperage through an FET. If the current exceeds the programmed limit for the circuit, power is temporarily disconnected. The frequency and duration of the power supplied to the driver is shortened until the circuit is finally disconnected. Restoring power requires repairing the cause of the high current draw and cycling the ignition switch on and off **FIGURE 36-33**.

FIGURE 36-32 A remote power module located on the frame rail provides a connection point for electrical accessories for truck or bus bodies.

Because other modules can influence electrical system response, the electrical system uses a distributed electrical system control. For example, the driver may switch on only the wipers, but the low-beam headlights may also be activated for safety reasons. Data supplied by the ABS module regarding vehicle speed may cause the door locks to close when the vehicle is moving faster than 5 miles per hour (mph) (8 kilometers per hour [km/h]) to protect occupants. Optional dash-mounted switch packs provide information to the ESC over a CAN data link. After a vehicle leaves the assembly plant, an auto body builder or dealer technicians can program optional switch functions and add features.

Electronic Gauge Cluster

The electronic gauge cluster (EGC) is another important element of the Diamond Logic electrical system. It contains warning lamps, gauges, and audible alarms that alert the driver when an element is operating in an unsafe range, such as low fuel, low voltage, low oil pressure, or high coolant temperature **FIGURE 36-34**. A speaker provides a clicking sound when using the turn signals that simulates the noise made by older flasher relay. Gauges use stepper motors for extreme accuracy to rotate the needles in analog gauges. Fault codes and other vehicle information can be presented on the liquid crystal display used for the driver's information center in the gauge cluster. The efficiency of using multiplex CAN control is seen with only seven wires connecting to the gauge cluster, which is considerably fewer than the more than 90 required by previous instrument clusters.

Accessing Navistar OEM Diagnostic Trouble Codes

The cruise control switches mounted in the steering wheel can be used to enable the ECM to display the active and inactive diagnostic trouble codes (DTCs) in the instrument cluster or by using the red stop engine light (SEL) and yellow check engine

FIGURE 36-34 The EGC is a CAN device that can receive and send messages across the network. Gauges use highly accurate digital type stepper motors.

light (CEL). All Navistar OEM codes are three digits. Code 111 indicates no fault codes are stored. During normal start-up tests, the SEL and CEL lights turn on and then turn off, unless a fault is detected. If the ECM detects an active fault, the CEL light remains on.

To access Navistar OEM DTCs, follow the steps in **SKILL DRILL 36-3**.

Air Solenoid Module

CAN-connected remote air solenoid modules (ASMs) electronically control the non-braking chassis air system and air-operated accessories **FIGURE 36-35**. An ASM may contain four or seven electric over air solenoids, which receive current from the RPM or the ESC. The ESC will supply 10 amps of current to both the +12 volt and ground side of the ASM circuits. Anytime an electrical fault is detected, the ESC will disconnect power to

the circuit. After several attempts to reconnect the circuit, this virtual fuse will finally need to be reset by cycling the ignition switch off, then on again. Devices controlled by the ASM include the power divider lock, differential axle lock, sliding fifth-wheel lock release, air horn, and air suspension dump valve.

▶ OnCommand Telematics

OnCommand is Navistar's comprehensive set of software solutions to manage fleet operations. Parts, service information, and preventative maintenance scheduling are just of few of the features offered to OnCommand users **FIGURE 36-36**. For technicians, an online service information system provides access to up-to-date service and parts information based on vehicle identification number (VIN), including access to the following:

- Wiring diagrams
- International brand and IC Bus service manuals and bulletins
- Fault code index
- iKNow*—extensive diagnostic database
- VIN-based information about warranty history and part numbers of components
- Service tool catalog
- Warranty administration
- Service letters
- Vehicle operator manuals

Service software from Navistar includes the following elements:

1. ServiceMaxx, a software-based diagnostic system used for all electronically controlled MaxxForce engines. Menu items include the following options:
   - Display active/inactive diagnostic trouble codes and operating data.
   - Perform "engine off" and "engine running" diagnostic tests.

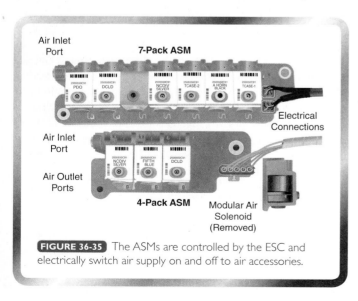

FIGURE 36-35 The ASMs are controlled by the ESC and electrically switch air supply on and off to air accessories.

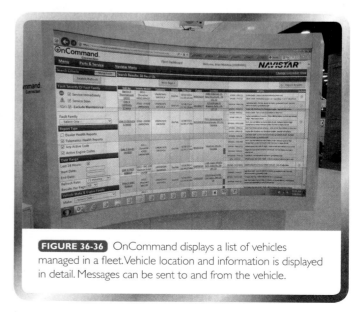

FIGURE 36-36 OnCommand displays a list of vehicles managed in a fleet. Vehicle location and information is displayed in detail. Messages can be sent to and from the vehicle.

SKILL DRILL 36-3 Accessing Navistar OEM DTCs

Using the LCD Display

1. Set the parking brake and turn the ignition key to the On position.

2. Press and release the CRUISE ON button and the RESUME/ACCEL button simultaneously. If no active faults are logged, the instrument cluster LCD odometer will display "NO FAULT."

3. If the ECM detects an active fault, the yellow CEL light will remain on.

4. Switch off the ignition key to end the instrument cluster's diagnostic mode.

Using Blink Codes (Flashing SEL and CEL Lights)

1. Set the parking brake and turn the ignition key to the On position.

2. Press and release the CRUISE ON and the RESUME/ACCEL buttons simultaneously twice within 3 seconds.

3. If faults are detected, the standard key-on, engine-off (KOEO) test will run to cycle system outputs, and codes will begin to flash. The red SEL light will flash or blink once to indicate the beginning of active DTCs. Then, the yellow CEL light will flash or blink repeatedly indicating an active DTC code.

4. Count the yellow CEL flashes/blinks in sequence. After each number of the three-digit blink code is flashed, a short pause will occur. For example, two flashes and a pause would indicate the number 2. Two flashes and a pause, three flashes and a pause, and one flash and a pause would indicate DTC 231.

5. When there is more than one DTC is stored, the red SEL light will flash once more following the yellow CEL flashes to indicate the beginning of another active DTC.

6. After all DTCs have been flashed or blinked, the red SEL lamp will flash three times to indicate the end of messages.

7. To repeat the DTC transmission, again push both cruise control buttons simultaneously twice and the ECM will re-transmit the stored DTCs.

Clearing Inactive DTCs

1. Set the parking brake and turn the ignition key to the On position.

2. Press and hold the CRUISE ON button and the RESUME/ACCEL button simultaneously.

3. While holding down both the cruise buttons, depress and release the accelerator pedal three times within 6 seconds.

4. Release both cruise buttons.

5. Ensure that the inactive codes are cleared. (If no active DTCs are present, the red SEL light should flash 111.)

- Record snapshots of the engine operation.
- Perform extensive troubleshooting using cylinder cut-out and injector disable tests.

2. Diamond Logic Builder (DLB) Fleet is another software-based service for diagnosing electrical system faults and customizing electrical systems. The software displays vehicle electrical signals in graphical and text format and reads and displays vehicle diagnostic trouble codes as well as vehicle features and parameters.

3. Instrument panel cluster (IPC) diagnostic software is for programming the instrument panel on medium- and heavy-duty IPCs. Adjustments and diagnostic checks of the IPC can ensure accurate instrument cluster gauge readings and be used to make changes to tire and axle ratios after tire and axle changes have been made.

Wrap-Up

Ready for Review

▶ Navistar International Corporation is one of the largest North American producers of medium- and heavy-duty truck chassis.

▶ International Harvester (a previous name for Navistar) introduced the first engine with a wet sleeve block. Regarded as revolutionary and the greatest single improvement made on a truck engine, replaceable wet cylinder sleeves have become almost standard on heavy-duty diesel engines.

▶ Today, Navistar is a holding company that owns the manufacturer of International brand commercial trucks, MaxxForce brand diesel engines, IC Bus school and commercial buses, and WorkStar brand chassis for motor homes and step vans.

▶ Navistar has manufactured dozens of engine lines over the years, incorporating cutting-edge technology and innovation with Navistar's own unique technological features.

▶ The AMS regulates air and EGR gases entering and exiting the combustion chamber of the engine. Navistar used the AMS operation as an engineering approach to meeting EPA10 standards to avoid using liquid SCR and to carefully control intake air to help prevent in-cylinder formation of NO_x emissions.

▶ At the center of the AMS system used 2002–2006 is the VGT, which is responsible for building boost pressure and creating the exhaust backpressure needed to drive the exhaust gas pressure above the intake air charge pressure.

▶ To change the speed of the turbine wheel in the VGT, exhaust backpressure is varied by opening and closing movable vanes surrounding the turbine wheel. When the vanes are closed, little exhaust can move through the turbine housing, which increases backpressure. Opening the vanes reduces backpressure, slowing the turbochargers and reducing boost pressure.

▶ Opening and closing VGT vanes is primarily determined by the amount of exhaust backpressure needed to supply exhaust gas to the EGR system.

▶ EGR valve positioning is based on algorithms that calculate EGR flow based on intake boost pressure, intake manifold temperature, and exhaust backpressure.

▶ Using two turbochargers connected in a series can provide a faster increase in boost pressure and the potential to provide higher overall boost pressures. Navistar's two-stage turbochargers produce approximately 50 psi (345 kPa) of boost. A VGT on an engine of similar size produces approximately 35 psi (241 kPa) maximum boost.

▶ Series turbocharging, because of higher cylinder temperatures and pressures, can reduce some emissions, including HCs, CO, and PM.

▶ Navistar MaxxForce engines use higher amounts of EGR gases to eliminate the need for liquid SCR. In 2012, Navistar began using liquid SCR on its large-bore engines to meet emission standards for NO_x.

▶ Two methods are used to measure EGR flow. One method Navistar uses in its MaxxForce engines incorporates data from oxygen sensors. The other method to measure EGR flow is to use an MAF sensor located in the air intake of the engine.

▶ An important part of Navistar's emissions-reduction strategy is precise control of intake air pressure, air, and EGR flow rates and temperatures. Part of this strategy uses a two-stage EGR cooler, with high- and low-temperature coolers incorporated into a single unit.

▶ In addition to using an electric heating element in the air inlet of the intake manifold, Navistar also uses a cold start assist system.

▶ Before 2012, Navistar took a different approach than other manufacturers to meeting the EPA10 emission standards. Instead of using a liquid SCR exhaust aftertreatment system, Navistar attempted to engineer its engines to meet the low NO_x EPA10 requirement using only its In-Cylinder Technology without SCR aftertreatment.

▶ Navistar, in collaboration with Caterpillar, produced one of the first and largest evolutionary steps of modern high-pressure diesel injection technology by developing the HEUI system.

▶ In 2003, Navistar developed a second-generation HEUI capable of multi-shot rate-shaped injection with Siemens, a major OEM supplier in Europe and North America.

▶ Common rail systems are one of only two remaining injection systems used on commercial diesels that can meet emission standards while providing superior fuel economy and performance unheard of in previous generations of diesels. Navistar systems use Bosch second-generation electrohydraulic servo injectors.

▶ OnCommand is Navistar's comprehensive set of software solutions to manage fleet operations. Parts, service information, and preventative maintenance scheduling are just of few of the features offered to OnCommand users.

Vocabulary Builder

MaxxForce A brand of diesel engines owned by Navistar.

PowerStroke Navistar's name for its mid-bore V-block diesel engines.

SinterCast Navistar's name for its CGI engine block construction.

Review Questions

1. Navistar leads the industry in the innovative use of quiet and exceptionally strong composite _____ engine blocks.
   a. stainless steel
   b. aluminum
   c. graphite iron
   d. titanium alloy

2. The _____ system encompasses all the controls that regulate the air and EGR gas entering and exiting the combustion chamber of the engine.
   a. air management
   b. common rail
   c. indirect injection
   d. biodiesel

3. Properly operating actuator linkage and vanes will contact the closed position and _____ at least once, if not two or three times.
   a. knock
   b. bend
   c. pop
   d. bounce

4. With _____ turbocharging, the compressor output pressure of one turbocharger feeds into the compressor inlet of another turbocharger.
   a. parallel
   b. series
   c. fixed geometry
   d. variable geometry

5. A low-temperature EGR _____ circuit is needed to better control the temperature of EGR gas entering the cylinders.
   a. condensing
   b. compressing
   c. cooling
   d. heating

6. Navistar developed the _____ system to replace the mechanical camshaft with highly pressurized lubrication oil, which is used instead of cam lobes to actuate plungers pressurizing fuel for injection.
   a. MAXX
   b. HEUI
   c. biodiesel
   d. common rail

7. The ESC module operates circuits such as headlights, taillights, windshield wipers, and the A/C system controls, using _____ transistors as output drivers.
   a. field effect
   b. grown junction
   c. fused junction
   d. epitaxial planar

8. The actuator on a _____ turbocharger can both transmit and receive information over the vehicle's controller area network.
   a. series
   b. wastegate
   c. fixed geometry
   d. variable geometry

9. Increasing the exhaust _____ and opening the EGR valve will meter fewer exhaust gases into the cylinder charge.
   a. backpressure
   b. temperature
   c. slobber
   d. air-fuel ratio

10. Pressurization of fuel and injection are separate functions in the _____ system.
    a. HEUI
    b. biodiesel
    c. indirect injection
    d. common rail injection

ASE-Type Questions

1. Technician A says the PowerStroke is Navistar's mid-bore V-block diesel engine. Technician B says the MaxxForce is Navistar's mid-bore V-block diesel engine. Who is correct?
   a. Technician A
   b. Technician B
   c. Both Technician A and Technician B
   d. Neither Technician A nor Technician B

2. Technician A says International Harvester introduced the first engine with a wet sleeve block. Technician B says International Harvester introduced the first engine with a compression ignition system. Who is correct?
   a. Technician A
   b. Technician B
   c. Both Technician A and Technician B
   d. Neither Technician A nor Technician B

3. Technician A says that algorithms determine EGR valve positioning based on intake manifold temperature. Technician B says that algorithms determine EGR valve positioning based on exhaust backpressure. Who is correct?
   a. Technician A
   b. Technician B
   c. Both Technician A and Technician B
   d. Neither Technician A nor Technician B

4. Technician A says that turbocharger vanes can often seize as a result of excessive engine backpressure from revving or high-load and high-speed conditions. Technician B says that turbocharger vanes can often seize as a result of excessive engine slobber from idling or low-load and low-speed conditions. Who is correct?
   a. Technician A
   b. Technician B
   c. Both Technician A and Technician B
   d. Neither Technician A nor Technician B

5. Technician A says that when turbochargers are arranged in a series, the air passes through an interstage cooler. Technician B says that when turbochargers are arranged in a series, the air passes through a low-pressure charge air cooler. Who is correct?
   a. Technician A
   b. Technician B
   c. Both Technician A and Technician B
   d. Neither Technician A nor Technician B

6. Technician A says that Navistar uses air-fuel ratio meters to adjust the EGR gas mass flow. Technician B says that Navistar uses temperature sensors to adjust the EGR gas mass flow. Who is correct?
   a. Technician A
   b. Technician B
   c. Both Technician A and Technician B
   d. Neither Technician A nor Technician B

7. Technician A says the MaxxForce 11, 13, and 15 engines were the first to use indirect injection systems. Technician B says the MaxxForce 11, 13, and 15 engines were the first to use common rail systems. Who is correct?
   a. Technician A
   b. Technician B
   c. Both Technician A and Technician B
   d. Neither Technician A nor Technician B

8. Technician A says that Navistar's version of a multi-plex-controlled electrical system is called Diamond Logic. Technician B says that Navistar's version of a multiplex-controlled electrical system is called STAR logic. Who is correct?
   a. Technician A
   b. Technician B
   c. Both Technician A and Technician B
   d. Neither Technician A nor Technician B

9. Technician A says that the actuator on a variable geometry turbocharger can only transmit information over the vehicle's controller area network. Technician B says that the actuator on a variable geometry turbocharger can both transmit and receive information over the vehicle's controller area network. Who is correct?
   a. Technician A
   b. Technician B
   c. Both Technician A and Technician B
   d. Neither Technician A nor Technician B

10. Technician A says that after 2001, engine crankcases were no longer permitted to be ventilated to the atmosphere. Technician B says that after 2006, engine crankcases were permitted to be ventilated to the atmosphere. Who is correct?
   a. Technician A
   b. Technician B
   c. Both Technician A and Technician B
   d. Neither Technician A nor Technician B

CHAPTER 37
Detroit Diesel

NATEF Tasks

Diesel Engines

General

- Check engine no cranking, cranks but fails to start, hard starting, and starts but does not continue to run problems; determine needed action. (p 1048)
- Identify engine surging, rough operation, misfiring, low power, slow deceleration, slow acceleration, and shutdown problems; determine needed action. (p 1042)

Electronic Fuel Management System

- Interface with vehicle's on-board computer; perform diagnostic procedures using electronic service tool(s) (to include PC-based software and/or data scan tools); determine needed action. (p 1064)
- Check and record electronic diagnostic codes and trip/operational data; monitor electronic data; clear codes; determine needed action. (p 1064)

Knowledge Objectives

After reading this chapter, you will be able to:

1. Identify and differentiate between various models of Detroit Diesel engines. (pp 1038–1041)
2. Describe the construction features of Detroit Diesel engines. (pp 1038–1041)
3. Describe construction features and differentiate between various types of Detroit Diesel injectors and low-pressure fuel systems. (pp 1043–1053)
4. Explain the operation of electronic unit injectors used by Detroit Diesel. (pp 1043–1053)
5. Describe the fuel circuits and trace the flow of fuel through amplified common rail (ACR) fuel systems. (pp 1055–1064)
6. Describe and explain the operation of high-pressure ACR injection systems. (pp 1055–1064)
7. Identify the purpose and explain the operation of an axial power turbine. (pp 1062–1064)

Skills Objectives

After reading this chapter, you will be able to:
1. Adjust valves and injectors on an S60 engine. (p 1048) **SKILL DRILL 37-1**
2. Adjust valves and brakes on DD series engines. (p 1065) **SKILL DRILL 37-2**
3. Perform a fuel system integrity check. (p 1066) **SKILL DRILL 37-3**

▶ Introduction

Daimler Trucks North America (DTNA) is known for its Detroit Diesel engine brand, which the investment group Daimler AG and off-road engine maker MTU Friedrichshafen acquired in 2006. In the commercial vehicle transportation industry, Detroit Diesel has an iconic history as a leading producer of diesel engines for a broad range of applications, including marine, off-road heavy equipment, truck, bus, power generation, and locomotive. For decades, Detroit Diesel powered every type of commercial equipment with its legendary two-stroke cycle "screaming Jimmies," which became popular during World War II, when they powered landing craft, tanks, trucks, and other defense applications. Today, the Detroit Diesel brand is distinguished by its innovative, market-leading DD13, DD15, and DD16 engines, truck axle production, and DT12 automated manual transmission **FIGURE 37-1**.

General Motors (GM) created Detroit Diesel in 1938 to produce diesel engines after the company experimented with the development of unit injectors for marine and locomotive diesel engines. Charles Kettering, who is widely esteemed as the industry's greatest automotive genius for the products and technologies he developed, promoted the creation of the new engine division for GM. While the engine the new division developed was originally intended for GM's own line of trucks, the engine proved to be one of the most versatile platforms ever produced. The first of five series of two-stroke engines, the 71 series, was revolutionary in the 1930s. Its two-stroke operating cycle made the engine compact. Today, the 71 continues to have one of the best horsepower-to-weight ratios **FIGURE 37-2**.

The 71's high-speed capabilities (more than 2500 revolutions per minute [rpm]) were astonishing, exceeding competitors at its introduction and for years to come. Using a **rootes blower** to

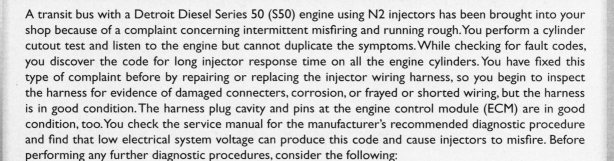

You Are the Technician

A transit bus with a Detroit Diesel Series 50 (S50) engine using N2 injectors has been brought into your shop because of a complaint concerning intermittent misfiring and running rough. You perform a cylinder cutout test and listen to the engine but cannot duplicate the symptoms. While checking for fault codes, you discover the code for long injector response time on all the engine cylinders. You have fixed this type of complaint before by repairing or replacing the injector wiring harness, so you begin to inspect the harness for evidence of damaged connecters, corrosion, or frayed or shorted wiring, but the harness is in good condition. The harness plug cavity and pins at the engine control module (ECM) are in good condition, too. You check the service manual for the manufacturer's recommended diagnostic procedure and find that low electrical system voltage can produce this code and cause injectors to misfire. Before performing any further diagnostic procedures, consider the following:

1. What operating conditions or circumstances encountered by an urban transit bus in the course of a normal day might produce low battery voltage?
2. List at least three electrical system defects outside the engine that could cause low system voltage.
3. What unique operating or design feature of Detroit Diesel's N2 injector make it sensitive to low system voltage?

FIGURE 37-1 Side view of a DD13 engine by Detroit Diesel.

FIGURE 37-3 Detroit Diesel's two-stroke engine does not use intake valves. The rootes blower, a type of supercharger, pushes air into the cylinders through ports in the liner.

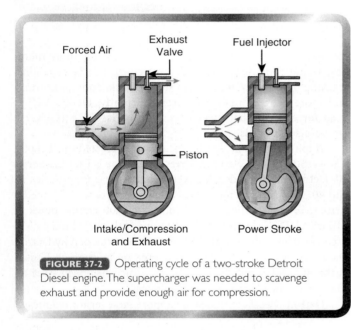

FIGURE 37-2 Operating cycle of a two-stroke Detroit Diesel engine. The supercharger was needed to scavenge exhaust and provide enough air for compression.

FIGURE 37-4 A rootes blower provides the air required to start the engine during cranking.

supercharge the air intake of the engine was technology Kettering brought from the farm where he was raised FIGURE 37-3 . These high-volume positive displacement air pumps, which were originally used to move grain from harvesting machinery to silos, enabled the two-stroke cycle to work in diesels and the engine to achieve power density that was vastly superior to other diesel engines of its day. A rootes blower supplied the minimum 3 pounds per square inch (psi) (21 kilopascals [kPa]) during cranking to the engine's air boxes or liner port that was required to start the engine FIGURE 37-4 . Unit-type injectors Kettering had refined went into the 71 series, which was also the first modularly constructed engine. The 71 designated the swept cylinder volume of the engine's dry liners, which were used with common pistons, connecting rods, injectors, and other standardized parts to configure engines into blocks of four, six, eight, and twelve cylinders that were in-line or V type. By flipping around the camshaft, and reversing the direction of rotation for the coolant, fuel, and oil pumps, the engine could be made to turn clockwise (right-hand rotation—the engine turns clockwise when viewed from the flywheel) or counterclockwise (left-hand rotation—the engine turns counterclockwise when viewed from the flywheel), an invaluable feature for marine engines.

Later, other modular engines joined the 71 series, including the 53, 92, 110, and 141. They worked so well that, even after decades of production, most of the parts had not changed. The engines were fabulously popular in urban buses using automatic transmissions, trucks, highway coaches, and off-road equipment until the early 1980s, when other four-stroke engine manufacturers pulled ahead of two-stroke Detroit Diesel engines in terms of power output and durability.

To stay competitive, GM developed a completely new four-stroke cycle overhead camshaft engine using full-authority electronic engine controls. The electronics were mostly borrowed from its automotive engines to create the Series 60 (S60) engine, which GM officially introduced in 1987. Earlier versions of electronic unit injection were introduced in the 92 series two-stroke engines.

Until 1965, Detroit Diesel was actually the GM Diesel Division. The company became its own entity that year and was later sold to Roger Penske in 1988, almost immediately after the release of the S60 engine. After the change of ownership, Detroit Diesel marketed the S50 engine, which removed two cylinders from S60 and added a balance shaft to minimize torsional vibration—the speeding up and slowing down of a crankshaft due to deceleration compression strokes and acceleration during power strokes **FIGURE 37-5**. A balance shaft is a rotating shaft with an eccentric weight that offsets torsional vibration. A version of the S60 appeared in late 1985 with a two-module control system known as DDEC I. DDEC is an abbreviation for Detroit Diesel electronic controls. DDEC I was first used on two-stroke electronically controlled unit injectors before the engines were discontinued from the on-highway market. DDEC II appeared in 1987 as a single ECM system. DDEC III launched in 1994 with faster processor speeds and more features and memory **FIGURE 37-6**. With each new stage of tightening of emission regulations, Detroit Diesel added electronic control systems. DDEC IV was

FIGURE 37-6 The inside of a DDEC III ECM. Simplified 12-volt electronics from GM's car divisions led to using electronic engine control in heavy-duty diesels for the first time.

introduced in 1998. It had even faster processing, more memory, a built-in battery for a real-time clock, J-1939 capability, tracking of special vehicle data through back-door audit trails, and more programmable features. Currently, DDEC VIII is used for engines that meet Greenhouse Gas 2014 (GHG14) emissions standards.

A joint venture is with Navistar, which created the T-444E, a PowerStroke marketed as a Series 30, and the DT466E, a Series 40. Detroit also branded MaxxForce engines as their Series 30 and 40. A Series 55 engine was a joint venture with Mercedes Benz (MB) that joined the in-line Series 400 engine block of MB with DDEC electronics. This engine and others built by MB used electronic unit pumps, a system first developed by Detroit Diesel in the early 1980s but never used on its engines. United Technologies bought the technology, which has been used on Mack and other Mercedes truck engines.

Detroit Diesel continues to support these legacy engines:

- S50: 8.5 liter (L) (519 cubic inch) in-line four cylinder developing 250–350 horsepower (hp) (186–261 kilowatt [kW]) and 725–1150 foot-pound (ft-lb) of torque (983–1559 Newton meter [Nm]).
- S60: 11.1 L (677 cubic inch), 12.7 L (775 cubic inch), later stroked to become the 14 L (854 cubic inch) in-line six cylinder developing 400–665 hp (298–496 kW) and 1250–1650 ft-lb of torque (1695–2237 Nm).
- Mercedes-Benz Engine (MBE) 900: 7.2 L (439 cubic inch) in-line six cylinder developing 350 hp (261 kW) and 860 ft-lb (1166 Nm) of torque.
- MBE 4000: 12.8 L (781 cubic inch), in-line six cylinder developing 350–450 hp (261–336 kW) and 1350–1550 ft-lb (1830–2102 Nm) of torque.

DTNA purchased a smaller off-road engine manufacturer, MTU Friedrichshafen, which is now known as MTU America

Balance Shaft

FIGURE 37-5 The Detroit S50 engine is a four cylinder version of the S60. A gear-driven balance shaft smoothed out torsional vibration, which is stronger in a four cylinder engine.

and is part of the DTNA corporate structure. The company manufactures very large diesel engines that are used in locomotive and marine applications. In terms of legacy support for the two-stroke cycle engines, the production line for the two-stroke engines by DTNA at Outer Drive in Detroit, Michigan remains intact to produce engines for the military. Because so many of these engines are still in use in the equipment of armies around the world, the Detroit manufacturing plant has strategic value and remains capable of ramping up production if needed.

▶ Detroit S60/S50

Detroit Diesel produced the S60 in three displacements: 11.1L (677 cubic inch), 12.7L (775 cubic inch), and a 14L (854 cubic inch) 550 hp (405 kW). When the company discontinued the 11.1L (677 cubic inch), the 12.7L (775 cubic inch) became the most popular engine (**FIGURE 37-7**). The S60 became the top-selling engine in the truck market in 1993 when it broke 50% market share for the first time, only a few years after the company nearly went bankrupt. By 2009, Detroit Diesel had built more than 1 million S60 engines. With the introduction of exhaust gas recirculation (EGR), Detroit Diesel stroked the 12.7L to become the 14L in 2007 and dropped the 12.7L. The S50 is a four cylinder version of the S60 with a balance shaft. The S50 was an economical alternative to developing a completely new engine for use in the large-engine market for transit buses, motor homes, marine applications, emergency vehicles, medium-duty trucks, and industrial and off-road equipment (**FIGURE 37-8**). Built between 1993 and 2004, S50 engines shared most of the same parts as S60 engines. S50s were also produced as alternative fuel engines and could operate on compressed or liquid natural gas fuel.

Electronic Engine Control

Measuring engine rpm and identifying cylinder 1's top dead center (TDC) position is necessary to determine when to

FIGURE 37-7 A view of the right side of a 2009 Detroit S60 engine.

FIGURE 37-8 This S50 engine, which is installed in a bus engine module, is being readied for service. The S50 was a popular engine for urban transit buses.

energize the injectors and for how long. Detroit Diesel engines were the first electronic diesels to use crankshaft and camshaft position sensors to calculate injection timing and measure injection quantity (**FIGURE 37-9**). Using a camshaft position sensor, you can identify cylinder position and where the firing order should begin. Detroit Diesel uses different names for these sensors. <u>Synchronous reference sensor (SRS)</u> is Detroit Diesel's name for the camshaft position sensor. <u>Timing reference sensor (TRS)</u> is Detroit Diesel's name for the crankshaft position sensor.

When the engine is initially cranked for starting, the TRS sensor detects cylinder 1's position using a specially marked reluctance wheel attached to the crankshaft. The synchronous reference sensor helps the ECM differentiate whether the paired cylinders (i.e., 1 or 6) were on the overlap or ending compression stroke and beginning the power stroke. A pin on the large bull gear, which is the main gear transferring crankshaft rotation to the camshaft, signals cylinder 1's end of compression stroke (**FIGURE 37-10**).

Because the bull gear has the timing pin indicator on its rear face, every two engine revolutions will generate one pulse in the cam sensor and indicate when cylinder 1 has reached TDC end of compression stroke. Using this data, which is synchronized with the TRS data, the ECM can calculate and begin to send electrical signals to fire the injectors. The signal is based on the firing order of the engine (1-5-3-6-2-4 on in-line six cylinder engines). By counting the number of teeth that pass the TRS, the firing impulses can be timed correctly because the ECM knows the precise position of the crankshaft. After the engine has started, the SRS signal is ignored and the ECM will send an injection command signal every 36 pulse counts of the TRS. Loosening or disconnecting the SRS sensor will not affect engine operation when running, but doing so will prevent the engine from starting.

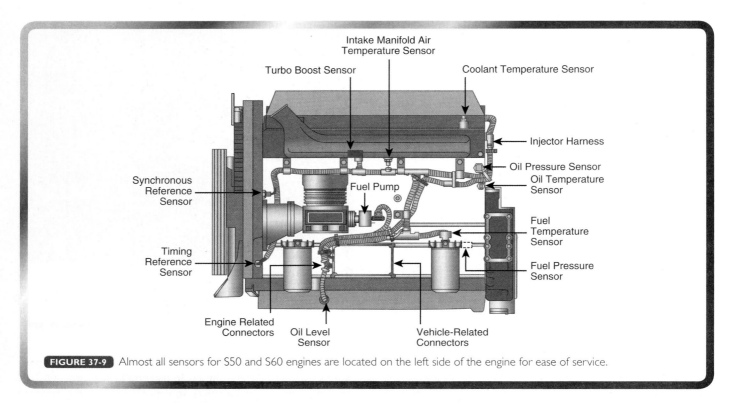

FIGURE 37-9 Almost all sensors for S50 and S60 engines are located on the left side of the engine for ease of service.

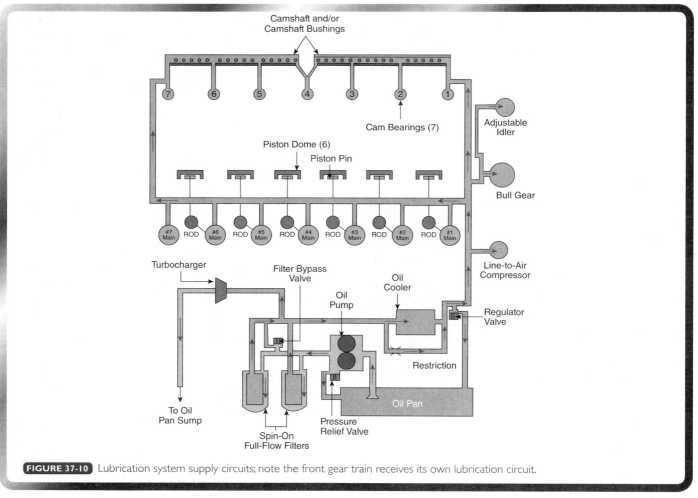

FIGURE 37-10 Lubrication system supply circuits; note the front gear train receives its own lubrication circuit.

Fuel System

Detroit Diesel S50 and S60 engines have an overhead camshaft to achieve high injection pressures of up to 28,000 psi (1931 bar). The camshaft can directly actuate the injectors through a rocker lever without the bending and flexing that would take place if the force to pressurize fuel were transferred through a pushrod. With the direct action of the camshaft on the injector, higher injection pressures are available with little injection lag **FIGURE 37-11** .

The S60 has used three types of electronic unit injectors (EUIs). The first-generation injector, designated N2, used a **poppet-type control valve** to regulate the beginning and end of injection. This mushroom-shaped valve operates under the influence of a magnetic field to open and close an injector spill port. One injection event is produced per combustion cycle. GM designed the first generation of engines to operate on 12-volt electronics that include the injectors. The ECM's entire power consumption, which includes the current to drive the injectors, is less than 5 amps at wide-open throttle and 1–2 amps at idle.

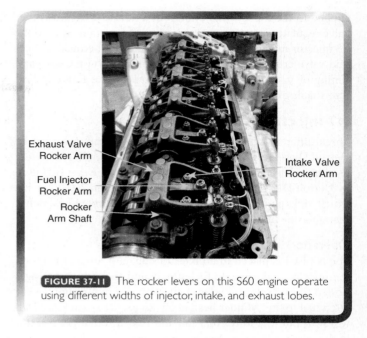

FIGURE 37-11 The rocker levers on this S60 engine operate using different widths of injector, intake, and exhaust lobes.

The second type of injector, the N3, was introduced on the EGR engines in 2002 **FIGURE 37-12** . It uses a faster-acting low-mass, low-inertia control valve and operates at 50 volts. The nozzle valve is hydraulically balanced, which means the solenoid controls the tipping point between more powerful fuel pressure above and below the nozzle valve. Delphi manufactured the N3. In 2007, Delphi introduced the third type of injector, the E3, to meet EPA07 emission standards. The E3 has two sophisticated low-mass, low-inertia solenoids. One solenoid controls a **hydraulically balanced nozzle valve**, a fast-acting nozzle valve that opens and closes by slight changes in the fuel pressure

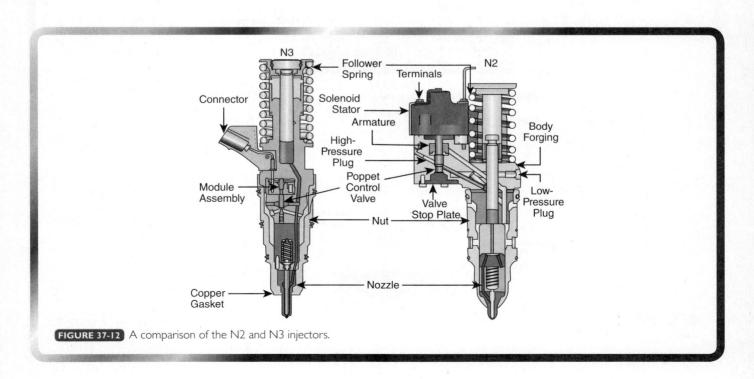

FIGURE 37-12 A comparison of the N2 and N3 injectors.

applied to the top and the bottom of a nozzle valve. The other valve regulates injection pressure. Adding a second valve to the E3 injector made it superior to the N3 injector because the second valve enabled electronic control of injection pressure and timing of injection events, which enhanced the E3's injection rate-shaping capabilities.

N2 Injectors

Three different types of electronic unit injectors are used by Detroit Diesel in addition to the amplified common rail system used in its latest engines. The N2 injector was the first EUI used by Detroit Diesel; it was superseded by the N3 in 2002. The E3, which looks similar to the N3, has two control solenoids, rather than just one like the N3.

Operation

The N2 EUI is placed in an injector cup, and three O-rings on the injector seal separate fuel-supply and fuel-return passages drilled through the cylinder. A fuel transfer pump supplies filtered fuel to the cylinder head at 60–85 psi (414–586 kPa). Fuel will flow into the lower fuel rail and pass through the injector to the return rail before returning to the tank. At the rear of the cylinder head in the upper rail is a check valve combined with a restriction fitting. Residual fuel pressure is held in the return rail to prevent **back leakage** of fuel to the tank, which would allow air to enter the injector. Back leakage is a general term used to describe any fuel circuit or component that supplies or transports fuel from the engine to the fuel tank. A defective check valve would cause a hard-start or no-start condition. The restriction orifice is a calibrated size to allow enough fuel to return to the fuel tank and carry heat and fuel vapors produced

by warm fuel from the injectors **FIGURE 37-13**. A restriction in the return fitting that is too small allows the fuel to overheat, which produces low power. A restriction that is too large prevents pressure from building up in the cylinder head fuel supply rail to charge the injectors with enough fuel.

Stages of Injection

The N2 poppet injector has four stages **FIGURE 37-14**. They are:

- Fill: During this stage, the injector lobe allows the injector plunger to lift; then fuel is pulled into the plunger cavity from the supply rail through an opening in the injector. Fuel continues to fill the plunger cavity as long as the plunger moves upward.
- Spill: This stage begins when the injector plunger begins to move downward as the injector lobe lifts the injector rocker lever. At approximately 120 degrees before TDC, during the compression stroke, the injector cam lobe starts to actuate the injector rocker arm. Fuel below the plunger spills back into the fuel return drilled in the cylinder heads as long as the injector is not energized.
- Injection: The overhead camshaft pressurizes fuel for injection. The ECM energizes the injector solenoid to begin the injection event. Energizing the solenoid closes the poppet valve using a magnetic field. If the injector is not energized, fuel is pushed out of the injector to the supply and return circuits. Energizing the solenoid prevents fuel from leaving the cavity below the injector plunger, and trapped fuel builds pressure to the point when the injector nozzle valve overcomes nozzle spring force, holding the nozzle against its seat. When nozzle

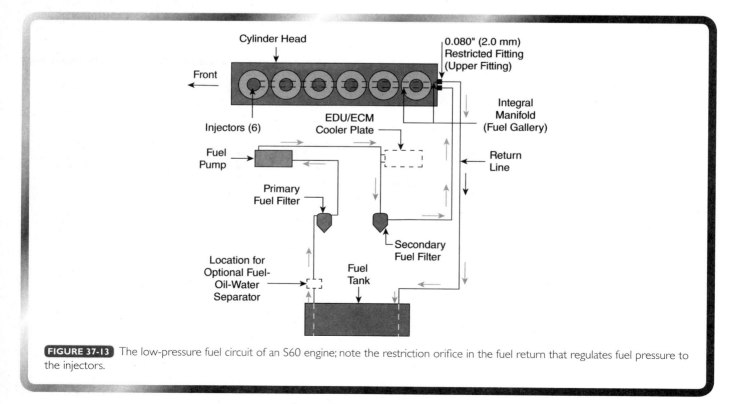

FIGURE 37-13 The low-pressure fuel circuit of an S60 engine; note the restriction orifice in the fuel return that regulates fuel pressure to the injectors.

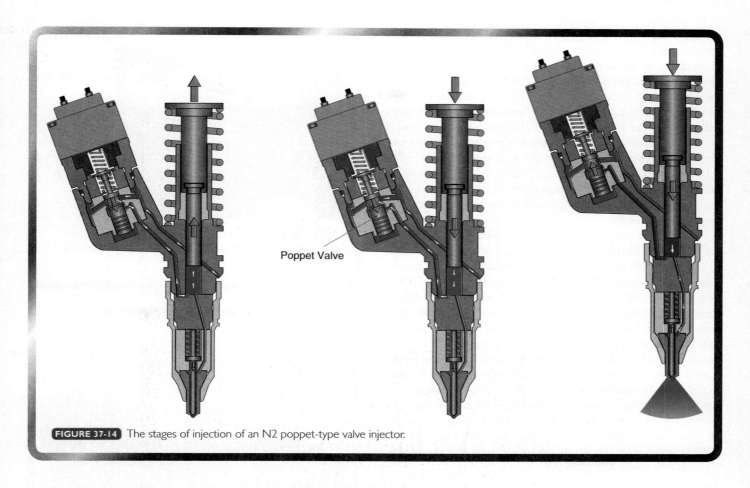

FIGURE 37-14 The stages of injection of an N2 poppet-type valve injector.

Poppet Valve

opening pressure is reached, highly pressurized fuel travels through the injector and out the nozzle valve as long as the injector plunger moves downward and the poppet valve remains closed.

- Pressure relief: Injection ends when the solenoid is de-energized and the poppet valve opens. Fuel below the plunger is pushed out into the fuel return rail because transfer pump pressure prevents most of the fuel from re-entering the supply rail. The plunger reaches the bottom of its stroke, ending the pressure relief stage. The fill stage begins again when the injector lobe allows injector spring force to retract the injector plunger and follow the rocker arm upward.

Injector Response Time

Because the voltage operating the injector solenoid is comparatively low, the time for the magnetic field to saturate, or build inside the windings, is longer. This means the N2 poppet valve takes more time to open and close. Its large mass also contributes to prolonged injection delay. As a result, the point when the injectors begin and end the injection event varies substantially due to small variances in electrical resistance from injector to injector. This variation in coil saturation time causes unacceptable changes to injection timing because the beginning of injection depends on magnetic field strength. To correct for timing variations, the DDEC monitors the electrical signal energizing each injector to determine how long the magnetic field takes to

close and open the poppet valve. A unique "blip" in the electrical signal monitored by the ECM also indicates when the poppet valve has closed. The blip is caused by the change in magnetic field reluctance when the poppet valve suddenly moves nearer the solenoid windings.

The time it takes for each injector to build a magnetic field strong enough to operate the valve is the **injector response time (IRT)**. This time can be observed on electronic service tools and is helpful to diagnose weak injectors or problems in injector circuits. The DDEC will vary when energizing the solenoid begins and ends based on IRT feedback from the injectors. Adjusting the time to begin each injection will ensure a consistent beginning and ending of combustion pressure in order to maintain clean emissions and smooth engine operation. Excessive response time is caused by such things as low battery voltage or poor electrical connections in the injector circuits. A long IRT will generate a fault code.

The length of time the injector solenoid is energized is referred to as the pulse width. Detroit Diesel equipment is unique because it measures electrical pulse width in degrees of crankshaft rotation rather than in milliseconds or duty cycle, which are standard measurements.

Injector Calibration Codes

Beginning in 1998 with DDEC III and IV, the N2 injectors began using two-digit fuel injector calibration codes. These injector codes, **calibration codes**, or fuel trim codes, as they are sometimes called, are alpha and/or numeric information assigned to a specific injector used by the ECM to correct for manufacturing tolerances of an injector. The codes are necessary to maintain emission compliance of the engines. Injectors produced at the same plant using the same machinery are not consistent. Each injector will have manufacturing tolerances that produce variations in its flow rate. Some of the variations are due to nozzle opening pressure differences, spray hole and plunger diameter variations, or different amounts of electrical resistances in the solenoids. If injectors deliver different quantities of fuel when the same pulse width is applied to all the injectors, cylinder pressures will be uneven and cause the engine to run rough.

The biggest problem, though, is the types of emissions that are formed by changes in cylinder temperature and pressure. A cylinder with higher combustion pressures will produce more nitrogen oxides (NO_x) and less particulate matter (PM). The opposite will happen in a cylinder with lower cylinder pressures. To correct inconsistent delivery volume, a calibration code between 1 and 99 is assigned to each injector after it is bench tested to measure flow variations. The numbers have no predictable pattern that would allow someone to increase power output from the engine. The ECM will simply use the number to make a correction to the injector pulse width to achieve consistent combustion pressure. When changing the injector, the calibration code must be assigned to the new injector using an electronic service tool or original equipment manufacturer (OEM) software. If the wrong codes are used, the engine will typically idle rough **FIGURE 37-15**.

N2 Valve and Injector Adjustments

Detroit Diesel S50 and S60 engines do not have any external indicator for TDC of cylinder 1 or 6. To adjust the valves and injectors, observe the valve rocker lever/cam follower positions to determine piston position **FIGURE 37-16**. Valve overlap between the intake and exhaust valves is used to determine TDC piston position in one cylinder. When overlap is found, its companion cylinder, the cylinder where piston movement is matched, will have its intake and exhaust valve clearances adjusted. Intake and exhaust valves are adjusted together on the companion cylinder to the cylinder on overlap. For example, all in-line six cylinder engines use the firing order 1-5-3-6-2-4. Cylinders 1 and 6, 2 and 5, and 3 and 4 are paired in travel. If both intake and exhaust valve rocker levers are tight on cylinder 6 (i.e., they have no operating clearances), cylinder 6 is finishing the exhaust stroke and beginning the intake stroke because both valves are slightly open. This means cylinder 1, which is cylinder 6's companion, is finishing compression and beginning the power stroke. The valves for cylinder 1 can be adjusted. Turning the engine more than 360 degrees would place cylinder 6 in the correct position for valve adjustment. However, the engine is turned only 120 degrees, and in the correct direction of rotation, to position the next cylinder for a valve adjustment. If cylinder 1 was adjusted, one-third of a rotation brings up the next cylinder in the firing order, cylinder 5, for adjustment. To verify the engine position and the cylinder selection are correct, cylinder 5's companion cylinder is 2.

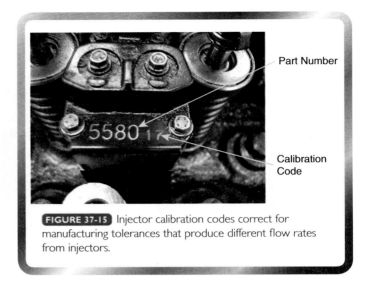

FIGURE 37-15 Injector calibration codes correct for manufacturing tolerances that produce different flow rates from injectors.

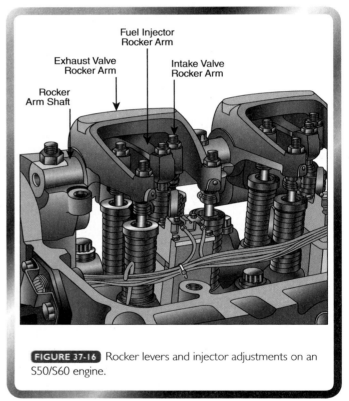

FIGURE 37-16 Rocker levers and injector adjustments on an S50/S60 engine.

Cylinder 2 should have two tight rocker levers, while 5 should have two loose rocker levers.

Injectors are adjusted in a similar manner. Observing the cylinder on overlap determines the correct cylinder for adjusting injector height **FIGURE 37-17**. However, the cylinder selected for injector adjustment is always the cylinder that is one ahead in the firing order of the cylinder whose valves are being adjusted. This means that if cylinder 1's valves are adjusted, the injector for cylinder 5 is adjusted at the same time. When the engine is rotated 120 degrees forward in the correct rotation, the valves on cylinder 5 and the injector on cylinder 3 are adjusted.

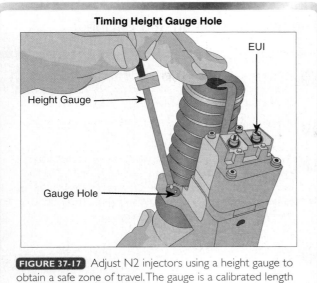

Timing Height Gauge Hole

EUI

Height Gauge

Gauge Hole

FIGURE 37-17 Adjust N2 injectors using a height gauge to obtain a safe zone of travel. The gauge is a calibrated length for each series of injectors.

▶ TECHNICIAN TIP

When rotating an engine to adjust valves and injectors, one of the most critical tasks is identifying the correct cylinder to begin adjusting. If the wrong cylinder is selected, the engine will be damaged by valve-to-piston contact and incorrect injector adjustment. Remember, pistons travel in pairs for proper engine balance, so each piston in a six cylinder engine has a companion. When rotating the engine, turning it in the correct direction is also crucial. The correct cylinder may have been selected, but turning the engine in the wrong direction will position the engine incorrectly and result in damage. When rotating an engine in the correct direction, the exhaust valve will be the first to open when both valves are closed in a cylinder. If the intake valve opens, you are turning the engine in the wrong direction.

Use a **height gauge** to adjust N2 injectors. The gauge will establish the correct amount of injector plunger travel. Adjusting injector height places the injector in a safe zone of travel. Because all injectors operate with a slight amount of preload, or pressure, applied to the injector spring, no operating clearances should be observed at the injector. If there is clearance between the injector rocker lever and the injector upper plunger, the plunger mechanism will be damaged quickly and broken by repeated and abrupt contact with the upper plunger stop. Too much preload on the injector plunger could allow the plunger to bottom out in the injector and damage it. Excessive preload will not allow oil between parts such as the injector cam follower and roller, which will cause rapid cam and cam follower wear. Specifications for the valve clearance and correct gauge height are part of the emissions information located on the emissions decal.

Worn or damaged S50 and S60 injectors cannot be rebuilt in the field and must be replaced. However, injectors can be removed, cleaned, and inspected. The external injector O-rings and return spring are replaceable and available in service kits **TABLE 37-1**.

TABLE 37-1: Sequence of Adjusting Valves and Injectors on an S60 Engine

Cylinder on Overlap	Firing Order	Valves Adjustment	Injector Adjustment
6	1	1	5
2	5	5	6
4	3	6	3
1	6	3	2
5	2	2	4
3	4	4	1

Adjusting Valves and Injectors on an S60 Engine

On S50 and S60 Detroit Diesels that use N2 injectors, the valves and injectors have a unique adjustment procedure that uses valve overlap as a reference point to correctly position the engine and select the appropriate valve and injector to adjust. No external marking on the engine identify TDC. Instead, the engine is rotated until a pair of rocker levers simultaneously moves up and down during the valve overlap period. This means that, if cylinder 6 exhaust and intake rocker levers are both tight when they are shaken with hand force, then the companion cylinder to 6, which is cylinder 1, will have two loose levers. In that instance, cylinder 1 intake and exhaust valves are adjusted.

To adjust valves and injectors on an S60 engine, follow the steps in **SKILL DRILL 37-1**.

N3 Injectors

Detroit introduced the N3 injector to help meet the lower NO_x and particulate emissions standards mandated for 2002. The advanced design and spray-in capabilities ensured that the combustion process could tolerate mixing EGR gas with air and fuel in the cylinder while delivering lower emissions. New injection rate-shaping capabilities enabled the use of retarded injection timing and multiple-shot injection.

Construction and Operation

The N3 has a faster, more precise injector response than the N2 because of its lighter-weight nozzle valve and a uniquely designed single low-mass, low-inertia **nozzle control valve (NCV)**, which controls the balancing of hydraulic pressure on either side of a hydraulically balanced nozzle valve. The faster-acting NCV, which used spindle control valve technology rather than a ball valve, enabled the use of pilot injection. The injector can supply higher injection pressures of close to 30,000 psi (2068 bar), which results in cleaner emissions. Unlike the N2 injector, which used a larger, bulky external solenoid and poppet valve, the NCV is not external. Rather, it is located inside the injector body. Incorporating the NCV into the main injector body enables it to change the state of hydraulic balance above and below the nozzle valve.

Like common rail injectors, which use hydraulically balanced nozzle valves, the NCV's primary function is to alter the

SKILL DRILL 37-1 Adjusting Valves and Injectors on an S60 Engine

1. Bar the engine over in the correct direction of rotation. Most engines turn counterclockwise when viewed from the flywheel and clockwise when viewed from the front.

2. Rotate the engine until a pair of cylinders on overlap is identified.

3. Adjust the intake and exhaust valves on the companion cylinder of the overlapped cylinder (see Table 37-2 to find the correct companion cylinder). The valves are adjusted by loosening an adjusting screw and inserting a feeler blade of the correct thickness between the rocker lever and valve stem.

4. While the engine remains in the same position, adjust the injector in the cylinder that is next in the firing order.

5. Use the correct timing tool height gauge to adjust plunger travel. A small hole beside the injector spring locates the height tool. A shoulder on the gauge should sweep across the top of the injector to remove an oil film. Loosen and turn the injector adjusting screw to obtain the correct plunger height.

balance of pressurized fuel applied to the bottom and top of the nozzle valve. Hydraulic forces are more powerful and act faster than magnetic fields. The injector design takes advantage of tremendous force multiplication achieved using NCV movement only as a triggering force for hydraulic pressure to begin and end injection events. When mechanical force multiplication takes place in a hydraulically operated device, its effect is called servo action **FIGURE 37-18**.

To understand its operation, it is important to understand that the injector's NCV is a three-port, two-position valve **FIGURE 37-19**. The NCV is located between the high-pressure passage that supplies fuel to the nozzle tip and the low-pressure fuel return circuit. Energizing the normally open NCV solenoid pulls the valve downward to close a spill passage for highly pressurized fuel while simultaneously opening a passage for highly pressurized fuel above the nozzle valve and allowing it to drain to the low-pressure fuel supply.

Stages of Injection
The stages of N3 injection are as follows:

- Fill: When the injector plunger lifts as it follows the injector rocker lever, a fuel supply port pulls fuel into the cavity below the plunger. Fuel passes through the area surrounding a narrow stem of the NCV and into the plunger cavity. The cavity fills as long as the NCV is de-energized and the rocker lever is moving upward.
- Spill: As the camshaft injector lobe rotates and begins to push the injector plunger downward, fuel is pushed out from below the plunger cavity and into the fuel supply rail. Unless the solenoid is energized, fuel will

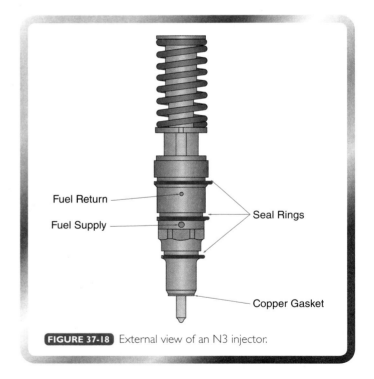

FIGURE 37-18 External view of an N3 injector.

continue to spill out of the injector and no injection will take place.
- Injection: Energizing the NCV solenoid does three things. First, the valve blocks the passage between the fuel supply port and the internal high-pressure injection circuit. The injector's electromagnetic solenoid, located

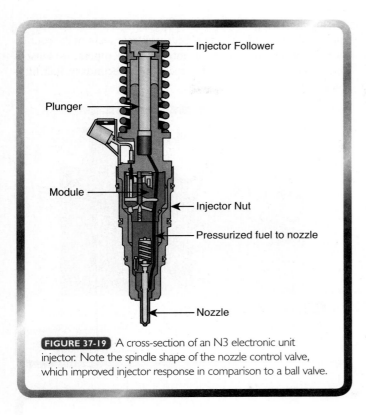

FIGURE 37-19 A cross-section of an N3 electronic unit injector. Note the spindle shape of the nozzle control valve, which improved injector response in comparison to a ball valve.

Labels in figure: Injector Follower, Plunger, Module, Injector Nut, Pressurized fuel to nozzle, Nozzle

N3 Maintenance

The N3 injector is adjusted on the injector lobe's outer base circle, which is the lobe of the camshaft. The inner base circle is the area of the camshaft where no lift takes place, which is opposite the outer base circle of the camshaft lobe.

Detroit Diesel recommends the following procedure for the most accurate adjustment of the injector:

1. Locate a cylinder where both valves are closed and the injector lobe is beginning its downward movement.
2. Place a dial indicator on the injector cam roller and continue to rotate the engine in the correct direction of rotation.
3. Rotate the engine until the dial indicator movement shows no more camshaft lobe lift.
4. At the point where maximum camshaft lobe lift is found, the injector plus the intake and exhaust valves can be adjusted together.
5. Rotate the engine in the correct direction of rotation and repeat the adjustment procedure for the next cylinder in the firing order (i.e., 1-5-3-6-2-4).

To adjust the injector, follow these steps:

1. Loosen the locknut at least two turns to free the adjusting screw.
2. Tighten the adjusting screw until the injector plunger bottoms out.
3. Torque the adjusting screw to 40 in-lb (4.5 Nm) to verify the plunger has bottomed out.
4. Back out the adjusting screw three-quarters of a turn. This moves up the plunger approximately 0.03125″ (0.79 mm).
5. To complete the injector adjustment, tighten the locknut and torque to 30–35 ft-lb (41–47 Nm) **TABLE 37-2** .

Injector O-Ring and Injector Cup Maintenance

The injector cups and O-rings are serviceable parts associated with the unit injector. To prevent O-ring damage during injector installation, Detroit Diesel recommends using a thin coat of clean diesel fuel. This antifreeze base lubricates O-rings and other types of elastomer seals that are not oil

below the NCV, pulls the valve down to block the spill passageway. Second, fuel pressure begins to build below the plunger cavity and reaches injection pressure quickly. Pressurized fuel is applied to both the top and bottom of the nozzle valve. The surface area at the top of the nozzle valve is slightly larger than the surface area below the nozzle valve. This arrangement is necessary because the larger surface area combined with nozzle spring force is required to keep the nozzle valve seated. Third, fuel drains from a pressure chamber above the nozzle valve. Movement of the NCV downward simultaneously vents fuel from the nozzle pressure chamber as it blocks the passage of fuel to the fuel supply port. Draining pressurized fuel from above the nozzle valve shifts the balance of hydraulic pressure exerted against the nozzle valve. Because the fuel pressure below the nozzle valve has become much higher than the pressure above it, the nozzle lifts and allows highly pressurized fuel to exit spray holes in the injector tip. The quantity of fuel metered depends on the plunger velocity and the length of time the NCV is closed. As the engine turns faster, the distance the plunger travels per unit of time lengthens proportionally.

■ Depressurization: When the NCV is de-energized, the passage between the high-pressure circuit inside the injector and the low-pressure fuel supply opens. Fuel pressure below the nozzle valve suddenly drops, and the nozzle spring forces the nozzle onto its seat and ends injection. The injector plunger may continue downward, but fuel will spill from the plunger cavity and into the injector's fuel inlet.

TABLE 37-2: Sequence of Adjusting Valves and Injectors Using N3 Injectors

Overlap Cylinder	Cylinder Number	Adjust Valves on Cylinder Number	Adjust Injector on Cylinder Number
1	1	6	2
5	5	2	4
3	3	4	1
6	6	1	5
2	2	5	3
4	4	3	6

compatible. If the O-rings are cut or damaged, the symptoms will depend on which O-ring is defective. O-rings can deteriorate from combustion heat caused by a leaking copper washer sealing the injector tip. If the upper two O-rings are defective, return fuel can leak onto the deck of the cylinder head and dilute engine oil **FIGURE 37-20**. A lower O-ring leak could allow compression or compression gases to enter the return fuel.

Replace O-rings whenever the unit injector is removed. Apply oil to the plunger located behind the injector return spring before installation to prevent damage during initial start-up **FIGURE 37-21** and **FIGURE 37-22**.

A residual amount of fuel pressure must remain in the cylinder head to prevent air from entering the injector. At the rear of the cylinder head, a check valve in the fuel return circuit prevents fuel from leaking back to the tank. If it is held open by a piece of O-ring or debris, starting the engine will be difficult and cranking times will be prolonged. During fuel filter service, a quarter-turn shutoff valve at the filter prevents fuel from draining through the open filter header when it is closed **FIGURE 37-23**. Failure to shut the valve will allow fuel to drain from the cylinder head and cause hard starting. The valve should always be closed before replacing the fuel filter and opened before starting

the engine. The gear-type transfer pump will prevent fuel drain back on the fuel supply side because the gear teeth make contact with the pump housing. Also, note the fuel temperature sensors and quick connect fitting for measuring secondary fuel filter outlet pressure.

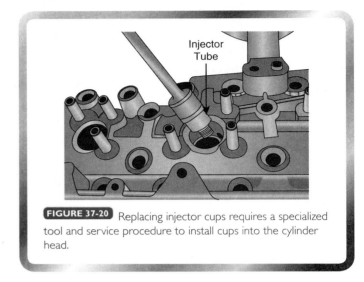

FIGURE 37-20 Replacing injector cups requires a specialized tool and service procedure to install cups into the cylinder head.

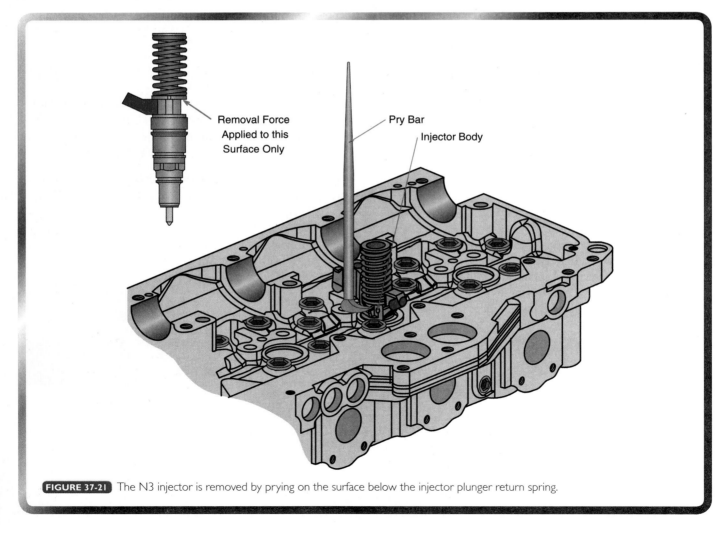

FIGURE 37-21 The N3 injector is removed by prying on the surface below the injector plunger return spring.

FIGURE 37-22 The plunger of a freshly cleaned injector should be lubricated with engine oil before operating for the first time. Lubricating the injector prevents scuffing damage to the injector plunger.

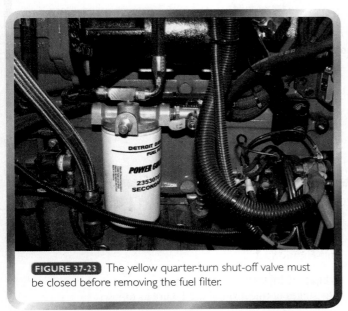

FIGURE 37-23 The yellow quarter-turn shut-off valve must be closed before removing the fuel filter.

Delphi E3 Injector

The E3 injector that developed from the N3 to meet **EPA07 emission standards** is intended for use on engines with 9–16 L (549–976 cubic inch) of displacement **TABLE 35-3**. The EPA set these standards for 2007, which are similar to Euro 5, for medium- and heavy-duty diesel engines. Caterpillar used the E3 injector in its on-highway truck engines until 2009. Volvo and Mack truck engines continue to use the E3 today.

TABLE 35-3: A Comparison of N3 and E3 Injectors

	N3	E3
Plunger diameter range	0.36–0.4375″ (9–11 mm)	0.36–0.4375″ (9–11 mm)
Stroke range	Up to 0.7″ (18 mm)	Up to 0.7″ (18 mm)
Engine cylinder capacity	1.5–2.6 L (92–159 cubic inch)	1.5–2.6 L (92–159 cubic inch)
Peak pressure	29,008 psi (2000 bar)	36,259 psi (2500 bar)
Weight	2.4 lb (1.1 kg)	2.4 lb (1.1 kg)
Drive voltage	50 volts	50 volts
Target emissions standard	Euro III and EPA02/04	Euro IV, V, and VI; EPA07, EPA10, and beyond
Number of solenoids	1	2

The E3's additional control valve provides significant new features for the injector. In contrast with the N3, Delphi's **E3 EUI** has a dual control valve that enables high-speed, ultra-high-pressure operation (as much as 37,000 psi [2500 bar]) with rate shaped injection events. The injection pressures, pilot injections, post-main injections, split injections, and ramped injection profiles are all electronically controlled. A version of this injector is available for cam-in block engines, but the most common application is for engines using overhead camshafts.

Delphi lists a number of advantages to using the E3:

- Faster injector response, with more accurate control of injection events using the dual solenoid design
- Ultra-high injection pressure—37,000 psi (2500 bar) for the highest combustion quality and reduced soot loading of the diesel particulate filter (DPF)
- A weight savings of 15 lb (7 kg) in six cylinder engines due to a lighter, more compact design compared with the N2 injector
- Multi-shot rate shaped injection capabilities with shot-to-shot electronic injection control
- Electronic control of injection nozzle opening and closing
- Durable for 621,371 miles (1,000,000 km)
- Fewer parts (40% less) than the N2 unit injector

Construction and Operation

The operation of the E3 is somewhat similar to the N3 in that the nozzle valve opens and closes using a hydraulic balanced nozzle valve **FIGURE 37-24**. Like the N3, force multiplication, or servo hydraulic action, rather than simple electromagnetic control, is used to perform injection events with more powerful, faster-acting hydraulic pressure. Rather than using these principles with one solenoid, servo action is initiated with two solenoids. The injector's two small electromagnetic control valves provide the small triggering force to manipulate

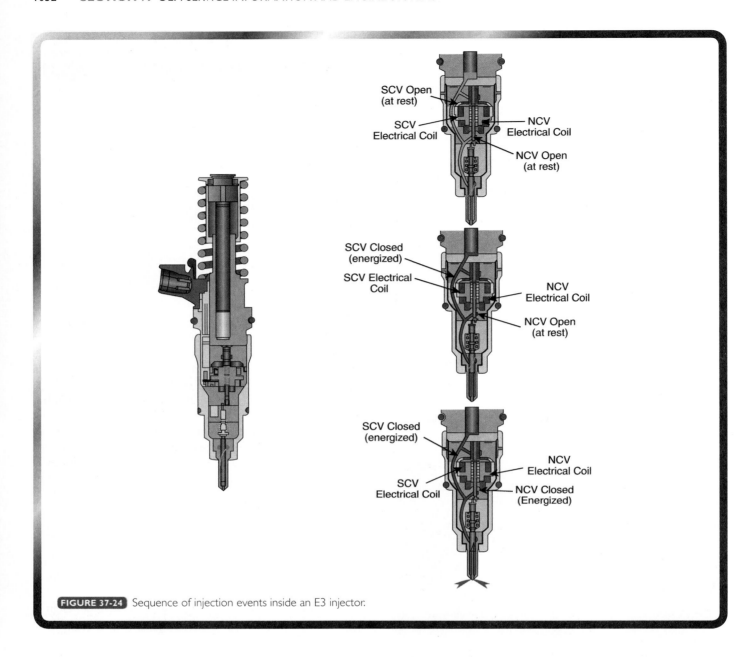

FIGURE 37-24 Sequence of injection events inside an E3 injector.

hydraulic pressures during an injection event. The additional control valve in the compact injector package is a **spill control valve (SCV)**. This valve is normally open and regulates the injection pressure available at the nozzle tip. Energizing the SCV closes the valve, which causes injection pressure to build. The NCV is normally closed and determines when the nozzle valve lifts and closes. Energizing the NCV to open the nozzle valve allows high-pressure fuel in a chamber above the nozzle valve to drain. De-energizing the NCV ends the injection event, and the nozzle is closed using high-pressure fuel combined with nozzle spring force.

Varying the time between the closing of the SCV and the opening of the NCV changes the injection pressure. A shorter interval between SCV closing and NCV opening supplies lower spray pressures. The opposite action occurs when the SCV closes much sooner than the NCV, allowing more time for pressure to build in the injector. The quantity of fuel metered is a function of time energized, fuel pressure, and engine speed.

Stages of Injection

The stages of injection of the E3 are as follows:

- Fill: When the injector lobe rotates to its inner base circle, the injector plunger follows the rocker lever. Just as in the N3 injector, fuel supplied to the injector through the fuel rail in the cylinder head begins to fill the cavity below the plunger. Filling continues as long as the plunger is moving upward and the SCV is open.
- Spill: Downward movement of the plunger caused by contact with the rocker shaft and outer base circle of the camshaft lobe pushes fuel out of the plunger cavity. Fuel passes back into the fuel rail and flows around the

normally open spill valve. Because neither of the control valves is energized, no injection takes place.

- Injection: Injection begins when the ECM, which is a generic term for the **motor control module (MCM)**, sends DC current to the SCV, which closes it. Blocking the passage to the fuel rail causes fuel pressure to build rapidly in the injector. Injection cannot take place until the NCV is energized. Depending on calculations done in the control module, the NCV is energized, which drains high-pressure fuel from the chamber above the nozzle valve. Fuel pressure in the chamber and below the nozzle valve varies with the time difference between closing the SCV and opening the NCV. Both valves will open and close multiple times during the injection event to control the injection pressure and the rate of fuel discharged from the injector tip. While the ECM or the MCM controls injection pressures, maximum nozzle opening pressures will not exceed approximately 17,000 psi (1172 bar). There are a number of incidents where failure of the NCV to open will actually cause the injector body to split open under the ultra-high internal pressures.
- Depressurization: The injection event ends when the control valves are de-energized. Fuel will spill out of the injector as long as the injector plunger moves downward. When the injector camshaft lobe has moved off its outer base circle, the plunger will move upward and begin the fill stage to repeat the cycle. As with the other Detroit Diesel injectors, response time is monitored to adjust the timing of electrical signals to the injector. The MCM controls the shot-to-shot and cylinder-to-cylinder variations in delivery quantities. This means cylinder pressures will be consistent to prevent the formation of different emissions, which will vary according to cylinder pressure and temperature. Without the programmable calibration codes for each injector and the ability to perform adaptive cylinder balance through the entire engine operating range, emissions would increase substantially.

▶ DD Series Engines

In 2007, as the S60 platform was reaching the end of its twenty-year life cycle, Detroit Diesel launched its DD engine platform beginning with the double overhead cam DD15 engine. After discontinuing the S60 in 2009, the company introduced the DD13, DD15 TC, and DD16 engines for 2010. These engines share a similar structure and a similar design on the engine block. The engines use a unique Bosch **amplified common rail (ACR)** high-pressure injection system that multiplies the fuel rail pressure inside the injectors. The following globally marketed engines use ACR:

- DD13: a dual overhead camshaft, 12.8 L (781 cubic inch) in-line six cylinder, developing 350–470 hp (261–350 kW) and 1250–1650 ft-lb (1695–2237 Nm) of torque **FIGURE 37-25**
- DD15: a dual overhead camshaft, 14.8 L (903 cubic inch) in-line six cylinder, developing 455–505 hp (339–377 kW) and 1550–1750 ft-lb (2102–2373 Nm) of torque

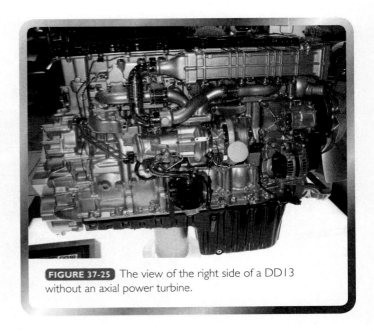

FIGURE 37-25 The view of the right side of a DD13 without an axial power turbine.

- DD16: a dual overhead camshaft, 15.6 L (952 cubic inch) six cylinder, developing 475–600 hp (354–447 kW) and 1850–2050 ft-lb (2508–2779 Nm) of torque

The DD15AT is identical to the DD15TC (TC means turbocharged), except the DD15AT uses an **axial power turbine (APT)** in addition to a fixed geometry turbocharger. The APT has a turbine wheel to capture normally wasted exhaust energy and convert it into mechanical power. The device is connected to the engine's rear gear train, after the turbocharger, and will supply up to 50 hp (37 kW) of additional power under full-load conditions. In addition to providing more power, less fuel burns. The engine also boasts a fast torque response, reaching 90% of peak torque in 1.5 seconds. This compares with 4.4 seconds in competitive engines.

Anticipating the **EPA10** and Euro 6 emissions standards, which required a 90% reduction in NO_x, Daimler Trucks embarked on another clean-sheet development program for a new engine platform. In 2007, Detroit Diesel unveiled the first engine in its new platform of heavy-duty engines. The DD15 represented a new generation of diesel engines and a business strategy of producing a globally coordinated engine development and production network.

Developed jointly by Daimler Trucks in Germany, Japan, and the United States, Detroit Diesel reported the DD series was one of the largest investments ever made in a development program for an engine. Engines are built in all three countries. The initial DD series program, which includes the DD13, DD15, and DD16, has close to a 90% parts commonality **FIGURE 37-26**. Three initial products conceived for the DD engine platform include the 12.8 L (781 cubic inch) DD-13, which began production in 2009, the 2007 DD15, and, more recently, the DD15TC, which replaced the 14.8L (903 cubic inch) S60, and the 15.6L (952 cubic inch) DD16, which hit the market in 2010. The engines replaced the MBE 4000 and S50/S60 engines used

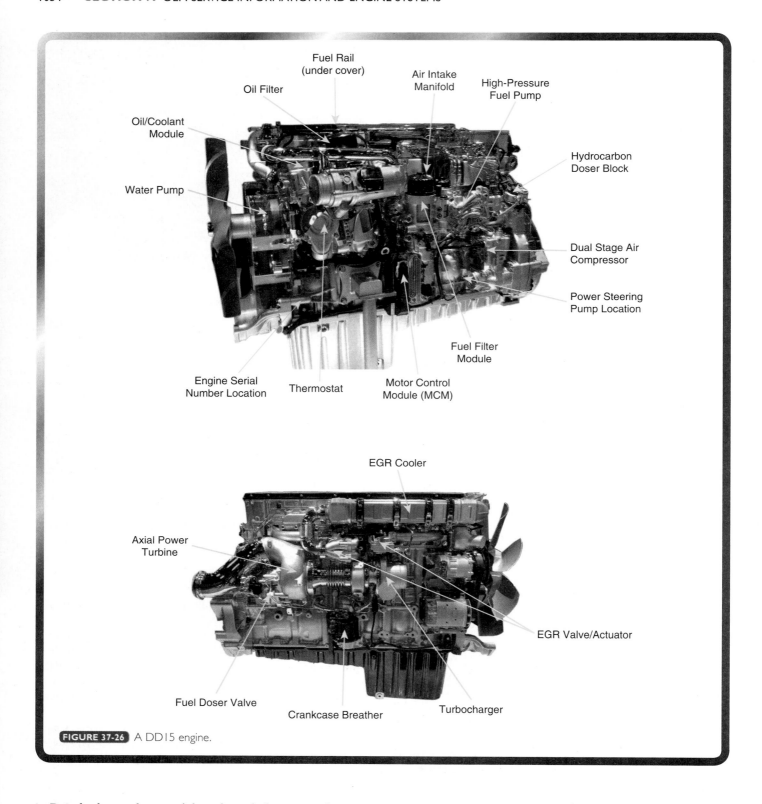

FIGURE 37-26 A DD15 engine.

in Daimler heavy-duty truck brands, including Mercedes Benz and Mitsubishi Fuso.

New and lighter engines, the DD5 and DD8, will be offered beginning in 2016 throughout DTNA's truck and bus products, which include Freightliner, Western Star, and Thomas Built buses. The engines were GHG certified in 2013, one year ahead of the GHG14 schedule.

DD Series Features

The DD series engines are nearly identical in construction features. With four valves per cylinder, two hollow overhead camshafts, and a fourth-generation Bosch-built ACR high-pressure injection system, the engines have gained a solid reputation for outstanding fuel economy, powerful performance, and smooth operation. Compared with the older S60 engine, the DD15 produces 75% better torque response, achieving 90% peak torque in only 1.5 seconds. The engine block is constructed from conventional gray cast iron and uses compression ratios as high as 18.4:1.

DD15 and DD16 engines use an innovative APT that converts normally wasted exhaust energy into mechanical energy. Detroit Diesel claims the APT's turbocharger-like technology reduces fuel consumption by up to 5% and provides as much as an additional 50 hp (37 kW) under optimal conditions, such as during heavy load operation **FIGURE 37-27**.

While DD engines are designed to be EGR engines, their low EGR rates allow the engines to operate without complex variable geometry turbochargers. Backpressure for the EGR system is minimal. The **asymmetrical turbocharger (AT)** provides the backpressure. The AT has one turbine volute that is smaller than the other in order to increase exhaust backpressure for the EGR system. EGR gas is supplied to the EGR valve only from the front three cylinders. The smaller of the two turbine volutes collects the gas.

DDEC Electronic Control

Detroit Diesel introduced the DDEC VI electronic engine control system for the DD15 to help meet EPA07 emission standards. The system exerts full authority electronic control over engine functions, regulating injection timing and quantity through two solenoids in each of the six ACR injectors. DDEC VI uses an engine-mounted MCM and a **common power train controller (CPC)** located inside the cab. The CPC is an electronic control module used to store and process vehicle- and application-specific information. The two modules communicate through a proprietary data link. The CPC broadcasts data over the on-board network using SAE J-1587 and J-1939 protocols. Detroit Diesel added an **aftertreatment control module (ACM)** in 2010; this electronic control module processes sensor

FIGURE 37-27 The APT uses a turbine with a hydrodynamic clutch to convert exhaust energy to drive the rear gear train.

data and controls the outputs of the DPF and the selective catalytic reduction (SCR) system. GHG engines rely on DDEC VIII.

The CPC receives a variety of vehicle data from the cab, such as throttle position and switch information from the brakes, the cruise, the clutch, and the dash. It also receives information from other network modules, including the anti-lock braking system. Vehicle program data specific to an application is stored in the CPC—for example, governor settings, whether there is remote throttle, power take-off (PTO) information and safety interlocks for outriggers, power dividers, and air suspension systems. Stored parameters include idle speed; maximum engine rpm, torque, and horsepower settings; and any other programmable parameters set by the customer and the factory. The CPC analyzes data using algorithms and then transmits information to the MCM, which controls outputs to the engine. The CPC will also receive engine sensor data collected by the MCM.

The MCM monitors engine sensor data, CPC data, and data from network communication to process outputs signals for the engine. Outputs include calculating injection timing and quantity, then energizing the injectors, operating relays for intake heaters, or sending signals to actuators such as the intake manifold throttle or EGR valve.

The **heavy-duty on-board diagnostic (HD-OBD) executive** function is located in the MCM. This software program runs monitors and makes decisions concerning the on-board diagnostic system. When the MCM detects an HD-OBD fault or an engine protection fault, it selects an appropriate strategy to execute, such as de-rate or shut down. Or the MCM might use an adaptive strategy such as data substitution or something as simple as turning on a multifunction indicator lamp.

ACR Injector

To create a faster-acting, less expensive, and more durable common rail (CR) injector as an alternative to the piezoelectric actuators, Bosch developed the fourth-generation **CRI4 injector**, which is another name for the ACR injector, for the heavy-duty diesel engine market. The **hydraulically amplified direct injector (HADI)** is an injector made specifically for heavy-duty diesel engines. HADI is Bosch's term for the ACR injector supplied to DD series engines. Unlike light-duty diesel engines, heavy-duty systems are less concerned about combustion noise characteristics than reducing fuel consumption and providing high power output. The technical challenge to creating an injector comparable to piezoelectric performance was building low-cost servo hydraulic control valves that could deliver multiple injection events. The solution came in the form of an injector with two control valves that operate using principles of hydraulic balance, or pressure compensation, which also control a hydraulically balanced nozzle valve.

Bosch's HADI is capable of five injection events per combustion cycle and two-stage pressure amplification, which doubles the injection pressure supplied by a fuel rail. The injector also provides a unique and flexible boot-shaped injection rate to match a variety of operating conditions **FIGURE 37-28**. According to Bosch, during amplification mode, the injector produces

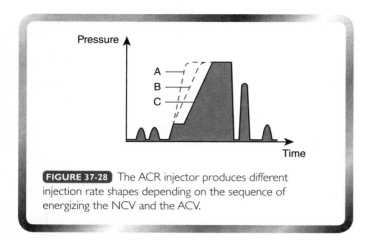

FIGURE 37-28 The ACR injector produces different injection rate shapes depending on the sequence of energizing the NCV and the ACV.

a maximum injection pressure of approximately 35,500 psi (2450 bar). During non-amplified mode, injection pressures are capable of reaching 19,500 psi (1350 bar) **FIGURE 37-29**. Detroit Diesel's service literature reports lower injections pressures.

▶ TECHNICIAN TIP

Hearing a different sound for a DD engine at idle than at above idle is normal. ACR injection systems have two modes of operation. Each produces a different combustion noise during engine operation. In non-amplified mode, which is below 940 rpm, the engine is relatively quiet. Raising engine speed above idle causes the injector to switch to amplified mode, which changes combustion characteristics and produces a different engine sound.

ACR Injection

ACR Injector Construction and Operation
At the heart of Detroit Diesel's ACR or amplified pressure common rail system (APCRS) is a CR injector with a hydraulic

FIGURE 37-29 The ACR injector used in DD13, DD15, and DD16 engines.

amplification stage **FIGURE 37-30**. The injector can operate like a conventional CR injector when conditions require it, plus multiply injection pressure inside the injector by a 2:1 ratio when commanded. Typically, the amplification mode of operation is not enabled until the engine speed exceeds 940 rpm. The injectors, which are connected to the MCM with four wires, have two servo hydraulic control valves. One, the NCV, regulates the hydraulic balance acting on the nozzle valve to open and close the nozzle much like the N3 and E3 injectors. The other, an ACV, is located near the top of the injector and is part of the amplifier control module, which is made up of a number of mechanical components.

Pressure amplification takes place only inside the injector, which has the advantage of reducing mechanical stress from ultra-high-pressure loads inside the high-pressure pump, the common fuel rail, and the high-pressure fuel lines. With pressure amplification taking place only in the injector, there is less likelihood of fuel leaks from the lines, the high-pressure fuel pump, and the fuel rail. The high-pressure pump does, however, need to produce greater output volume to keep up with increased fuel flow through the injector's ACV.

Because the injector uses two control valves, the NCV and the ACV, it also uses two fuel return circuits. The needle, or nozzle, return and amplifier piston return circuits exit the cylinder head at the rear of the engine, just above the high-pressure pump.

Non-Amplified Injection Mode
Pressurized fuel from the rail enters the injector through jumper lines to the injector, which is centered above the combustion chamber **FIGURE 37-31**. Fuel at rail pressure flows to the injector nozzle

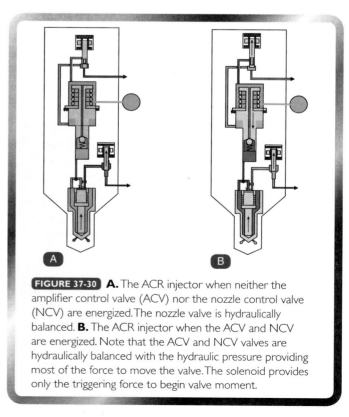

FIGURE 37-30 **A.** The ACR injector when neither the amplifier control valve (ACV) nor the nozzle control valve (NCV) are energized. The nozzle valve is hydraulically balanced. **B.** The ACR injector when the ACV and NCV are energized. Note that the ACV and NCV valves are hydraulically balanced with the hydraulic pressure providing most of the force to move the valve. The solenoid provides only the triggering force to begin valve moment.

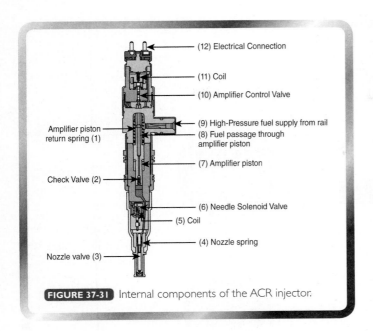

FIGURE 37-31 Internal components of the ACR injector.

- (12) Electrical Connection
- (11) Coil
- (10) Amplifier Control Valve
- Amplifier piston return spring (1)
- (9) High-Pressure fuel supply from rail
- (8) Fuel passage through amplifier piston
- (7) Amplifier piston
- Check Valve (2)
- (6) Needle Solenoid Valve
- (5) Coil
- (4) Nozzle spring
- Nozzle valve (3)

pressure to hold the nozzle against its seat, producing an effective seal. A two-port pressure chamber contains fuel pressure on top of the nozzle valve. One port is an inlet from the supply fuel at rail pressure. The other, a drain port, is sealed by an inward-opening NCV valve that opens when energized to allow pressurized fuel to drain to the low pressure **nozzle return circuit**, a fuel pathway from the ACR injectors leading to the low-pressure fuel module.

When the MCM supplies current to the NCV (6), fuel pressure in the pressure chamber above the injector nozzle (8) is allowed to drain through the injector nozzle return circuit. The injector nozzle (8) lifts due to the rail pressure acting on the bottom of the nozzle, which also overcomes nozzle spring pressure (7) that is holding the nozzle valve closed. Injection begins with fuel at rail pressure exiting the injector tip through six spray holes (GHG injectors use seven nozzle spray holes). When the MCM de-energizes the NCV (6), the pressure in the control chamber above the injector nozzle (8) builds again, forcing the nozzle valve to move rapidly against its seat (8). Spring and hydraulic pressures hold the nozzle valve against its seat (7) **FIGURE 37-32** and **FIGURE 37-33**.

Amplified Injection Mode

The amplifier control module uses a stepped amplifier piston, which has a surface area twice that of the area below the piston. Fuel at rail pressure is supplied to the injector above the amplifier piston whenever the engine is operating **FIGURE 37-34**. Fuel at rail pressure is also supplied to a cavity below the

valve fuel annulus (8) through the center of the amplifier module (4) and passes through a check valve (5) located at the bottom of the amplifier piston (4). Pressurized fuel is applied to the top and the bottom of the nozzle valve, as with the N3 and E3 injectors. A slightly higher surface area on top of the nozzle valve enables fuel

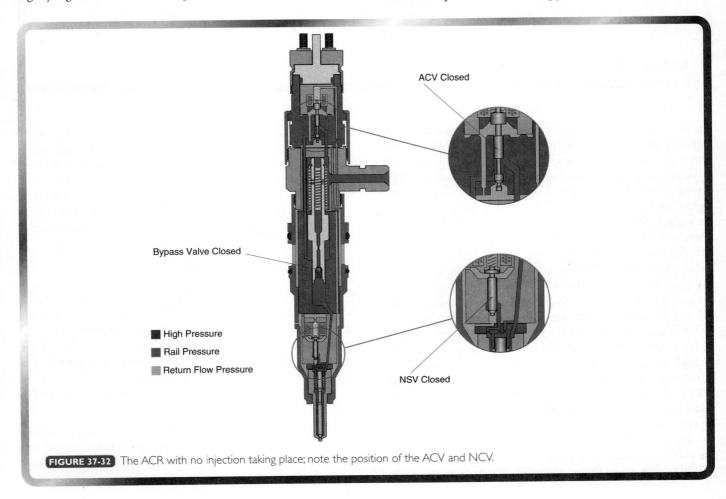

- ACV Closed
- Bypass Valve Closed
- NSV Closed
- ■ High Pressure
- ■ Rail Pressure
- ■ Return Flow Pressure

FIGURE 37-32 The ACR with no injection taking place; note the position of the ACV and NCV.

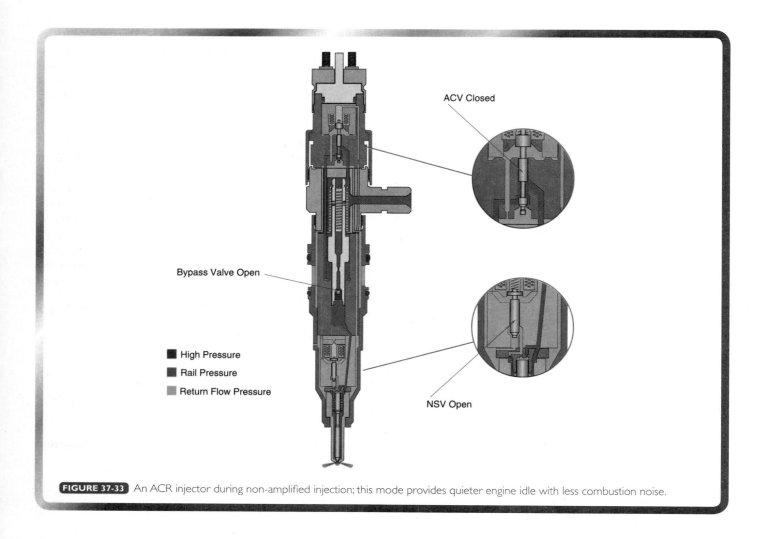

ACV Closed

Bypass Valve Open

- ■ High Pressure
- ■ Rail Pressure
- ■ Return Flow Pressure

NSV Open

FIGURE 37-33 An ACR injector during non-amplified injection; this mode provides quieter engine idle with less combustion noise.

amplifier piston (4). A slightly higher surface area below the amplifier piston ensures fuel rail pressure pushes the amplifier piston upward when no amplification takes place. The ACV regulates movement of the amplifier piston. The ACV (1) is a three-port, two-position valve. When the ACV is energized, two events can take place. The first is the ACV movement uncovers a passage for pressurized fuel below the amplifier piston to drain to the low-pressure amplifier fuel return circuit. A pressure differential is created between the top and the bottom of the amplifier piston. After the pressure differential is produced, the amplifier piston is driven downward, pressurizing fuel in the cavity below it (red). This pressurized fuel closes the check valve in the center of the amplifier piston and fuel below the piston is forced at twice the rail pressure to the nozzle valve tip, where it is available for injection. ACV opening is accelerated by high-pressure fuel acting below the valve after initial valve movement is produced by an electromagnet. While fuel is supplied to the nozzle at twice the rail pressure, injection can only take place when the NCV is energized and has allowed the nozzle valve to open.

Injection ends when the NCV closes the drain passage from the pressure chamber above the nozzle valve, allowing pressure to build again above the nozzle valve. Nozzle spring force and

fuel pressure drive the nozzle valve closed. To return the amplifier piston to its state where pressurized fuel is present above and below the piston, the MCM de-energizes the ACV. A small amount of spring pressure in the solenoid initially moves the valve downward. To speed up the ACV closing, the initial ACV movement uncovers a small fuel passage supplying pressurized fuel to a groove around the ACV. Pressurized fuel provides the force to quickly drive the ACV valve to a closed position.

Rate Shaped Injection Discharge

One of the interesting and unique advantages of the ACR injector is the variety of shapes the injection discharge curve can take when the timing of the ACV and NCV openings are staggered or synchronized. The injector is capable of controlling pilot and post-main injection events electronically, but the shape of the main injection discharge curve is substantially altered by the sequence for energizing the NCV and the ACV.

Three main injection rate shapes are available to best match engine operating conditions:

1. Square: energizing the ACV before the NCV; square injection rate shapes are ideal for producing highest torque output and are most often used at higher engine speeds under heavy load operation.

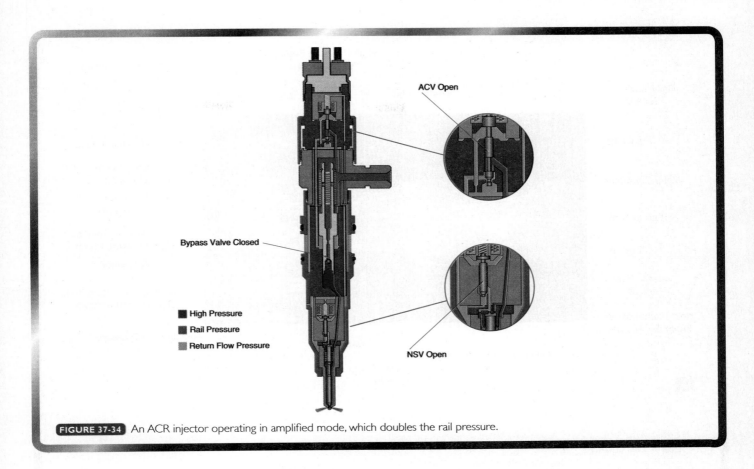

FIGURE 37-34 An ACR injector operating in amplified mode, which doubles the rail pressure.

2. Ramped: energizing the ACV and the NCV simultaneously; ramped injection rate shapes are best for reducing NO$_x$ and are used at moderate engine speeds.

3. Boot: energizing the ACV after the NCV; boot-shaped injection rate shapes are best for providing low fuel consumption and are most often used during lower engine speeds.

Low-Pressure Fuel System

Two low-pressure fuel system modules supply the ACR system. Between 2007 and 2012, a die-cast module manufactured by Parker-Racor used three filters. The company made two versions of this system, the V5 and the V7. Two replaceable cartridge filters and a prescreen filter were used in both modules. In 2012, Mahle began making a cast aluminum module for GHG engines, which uses a single replaceable cartridge and a prescreen filter. The Mahle fuel module comes in two versions: KM53 and KM63. All filter modules are supplied by a low-pressure gear-type fuel pump mounted on the rear of the high-pressure pump and that is driven through the high-pressure pump **FIGURE 37-35**. A bypass valve in the low-pressure pump allows fuel to bypass a stopped gear pump and continue through the system. This valve is needed to enable the fuel system to be primed when the engine is stopped. After the engine is started, the gear pump pulls fuel from the fuel tank. Fuel entering the module first flowed from the fuel filter module into a cooling plate beneath the MCM. Fuel re-enters the fuel filter module and first passes into the fuel 0.004″ (100 microns [μ]) prescreen filter. A check

ball located at the fuel inlet of the fuel pre-filter prevents fuel drain back from the suction line into the fuel tank. Cleaned fuel is pulled into the gear pump and then returns to the module through another line.

Parker-Racor Fuel Module

In the Parker-Racor module, fuel leaves the low-pressure pump and returns to the filter module and into a water separator. Gravity and centrifugal force separate water from the fuel, and the water settles to the bottom of the module and drains through a manual drain valve. A water-in-fuel module monitors the water level at the bottom of the water separator and switches a light from green to red when too much water has accumulated. If the module requires draining, the MCM can transmit a message to a warning light in the cab **FIGURE 37-36**.

After passing through the water separator, fuel flows upward through the center of a 0.0004″ (10 μ) primary filter and into the module cavity. Fuel will pass through a 0.0002″ (5 μ) secondary filter in the module before flowing to the quantity control valve on the high-pressure pump. The quantity control valve is a pulse-width modulated inlet metering valve on the high-pressure pump of Detroit Diesel's ACR system. Its operation controls the pressure supplied to the high-pressure fuel rail.

Lines from the fuel module connect to the high-pressure pump through a fuel manifold. Passages in the manifold direct fuel through a low-and-high-pressure bypass circuit in the high-pressure pump.

Rail Pressure Sensor

Final Filter

Water Separator

Return to Tank

Fuel In

Water-in-Fuel Sensor

Heat Exchanger to Fuel Filter Module

Injector

High-Pressure Fuel Rail

Transfer Tube

High-Pressure Feed Lines with Damper

PLV Return

Pressure Limiting Valve (PLV)

Amplification Return Line

Needle Return Line

Emergency Pump Lubrication Line

Doser Block Assembly Fuel Supply

Low-Pressure Feed to High-Pressure Pump

Quantity Control Valve

Low-Pressure Return from High-Pressure Pump

Suction- Low-Pressure Feed

Fuel to Heat Exchanger (MCM)

Amplification Return into Prefilter

Pre-filter

Low-Pressure Pump

Low-Pressure Supply to Filter Module

A

Needle Return Line (Banjo Connection)

Final Filter Water Coalescer

Pre-filter

Hand Primer Pump

PLV Return Line

LPPO Sensor

Fuel Cooler Plate (backside of module—Coolant in connection crank case)

Priming Port Location

Coolant Return

Fuel Inlet

AMP Return

Fuel Temp Sensor

HC Doser Supply Line

HC Doser Pressure Regulator

New HPP Inlet

New HPP Outlet

New LP—Flange and Lines

Manual Water Drain (turn clockwise to close)

Shallow Water Drain Bowl with WIF Sensor

Fuel Outlet Return to Tank

B

FIGURE 37-35 **A.** An early three-filter, die-cast Parker-Racor fuel module. **B.** A later two-filter, loss foam–cast Mahle filter housing.

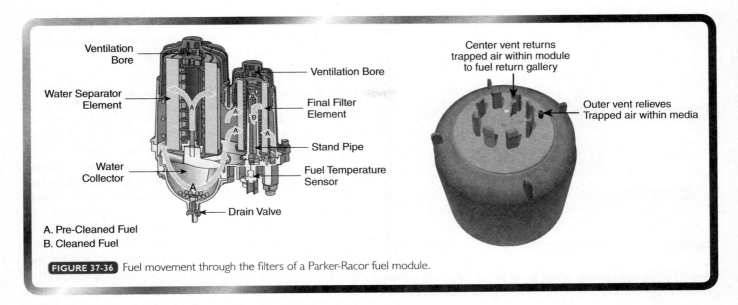

A. Pre-Cleaned Fuel
B. Cleaned Fuel

FIGURE 37-36 Fuel movement through the filters of a Parker-Racor fuel module.

A fuel temperature sensor located on the bottom of the fuel filter supplies temperature data to the MCM. Ventilation passages in the module enable trapped vapors to return to the fuel tank through the fuel return line. Two pressure regulators in the module housing limit maximum fuel pressure inside the module.

High-Pressure Pump

The quantity control valve meters the fuel supplied to the high-pressure pump. The valve receives a pulse-width modulation (PWM) signal from the MCM to regulate the rail pressure based on closed-loop feedback between the rail pressure sensor, the MCM, and the quantity control valve **FIGURE 37-37**. Two pistons inside the high-pressure pump pressurize fuel. Each piston has a line connecting the pump outlets to the fuel rail. Two roller tappets on the double-lobed cams of the camshaft produce reciprocating action of the pistons **FIGURE 37-38** and **FIGURE 37-39**. The gear ratio between the pump and engine produces four pressure strokes for each engine revolution. A quantity control valve on the pump regulates fuel supply to the pump. This valve is normally open and is also responsible for shutting off the fuel supply to the pump during engine-off conditions. Increasing the duty cycle of the PWM current to the pump lowers the rail pressure, and reducing the PWM duty cycle increases the rail pressure. During the initial key on to key off, when the engine is shut down, the quantity control valve current increases to maximum duty cycle to stop the flow of fuel to the high-pressure pump. After the engine is shut down and if the key is on for a period of time, the PWM signal drops to 0%.

Two-Stage Valve

The two-stage pressure control valve is another valve is located in the high-pressure pump after the quantity control valve. The two-stage valve has three functions. First, it opens and closes a fuel return passage back to the fuel tank when fuel supplied to the high-pressure pump inlet exceeds 189 psi (13 bar). To promote quicker starting of the engine when fuel pressure supplied to the pump is low, the valve closes to supply more

fuel to the high-pressure pump when cranking the engine. The two-stage valve also ensures fuel is supplied to the crankcase of the high-pressure pump if the quantity control valve shuts off, such as when decelerating or motoring. Because the fuel pump

FIGURE 37-37 The MCM is mounted on the engine. It uses a fuel cooler plate that is supplied with fuel from the fuel module.

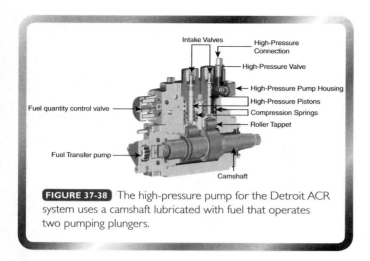

FIGURE 37-38 The high-pressure pump for the Detroit ACR system uses a camshaft lubricated with fuel that operates two pumping plungers.

camshaft is fuel lubricated, a steady supply of fuel through the pump is necessary to prevent pump damage **FIGURE 37-40** .

Fuel Cooler

Fuel leaving the needle valve return and amplifier piston return circuits is hot because it was pressurized during injector operation. A fuel cooler lowers fuel temperature before returning the fuel into the filter module, where it mixes with cool fuel. The cooler is located in the engine block, behind the fuel module. Engine coolant circulating around the cooler lowers the fuel temperature from 212°F (100°C) to the temperature of the engine coolant. Returning fuel from the cooler to the module reduces work for the low-pressure gear pump, which reduces mechanical energy losses.

Fuel Rail

The high-pressure fuel rail has a pressure relief vale that opens if the maximum rail pressure is exceeded. Leakage from the valve on early systems begins at 15,592 psi (1075 bar) and opens fully

at 18,130 psi (1250 bar). Later model relief valves open at 20,015 psi (1380 bar). A rail pressure sensor provides closed-loop feedback to the ECM and to the quantity control valve.

DD Series Air Management System

One of the unique devices originally introduced on the DD15 engine is the APT. Under ideal conditions, the APT can convert exhaust energy that is normally wasted into as much as 50 hp (37 kW) and transfer the power to the engine's rear-mounted gear train. Located after the turbocharger, the APT uses a turbine wheel to produce rotational movement along the turbine shaft. Rotational speed can be as high as 78,000 rpm at high altitude. Because the high speed cannot be applied directly to the gear train, a hydrodynamic clutch, which is similar to an automatic transmission's torque converter, converts the high turbine shaft speed into torque that is supplied to a gear reduction system and then to an output gear. APT torque is transferred to the crankshaft through the rear gear train. Exhaust backpressure produced by the APT drives EGR gases into the cylinders. Typical exhaust backpressure from the APT ranges 1.3–1.8 psi (9–12.4 kPa). Maximum EGR pressure is closer to 8 psi (55 kPa).

Later DD15 and DD16 engines made the APT available as an option. DD15AT engines use the APT, while DD15TC use the asymmetrical turbocharger to create backpressure for the EGR system **FIGURE 37-41** .

Intake Throttle

All the DD series engines use an __intake throttle valve__ to increase exhaust temperatures needed to assist the DPF regeneration strategies. When the throttle is closed, less fresh outside air is available to dilute the heat in the exhaust. When idling, exhaust temperatures rise from a low of 130°F (54°C) to more than 300°F (149°C) with a 95% closed throttle. During active regenerations, the

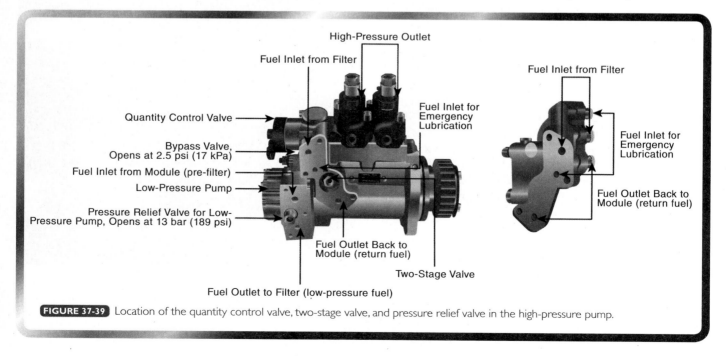

FIGURE 37-39 Location of the quantity control valve, two-stage valve, and pressure relief valve in the high-pressure pump.

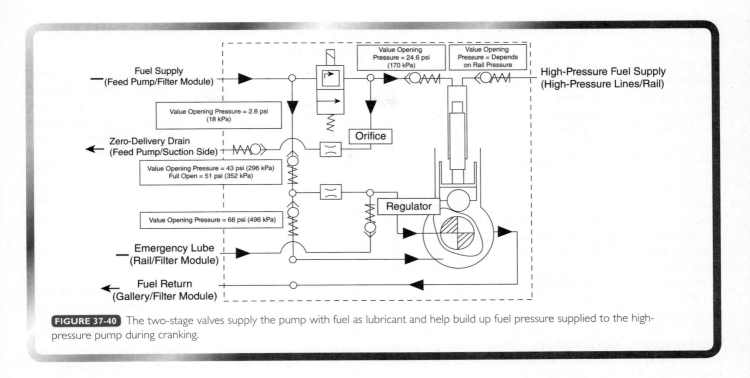

FIGURE 37-40 The two-stage valves supply the pump with fuel as lubricant and help build up fuel pressure supplied to the high-pressure pump during cranking.

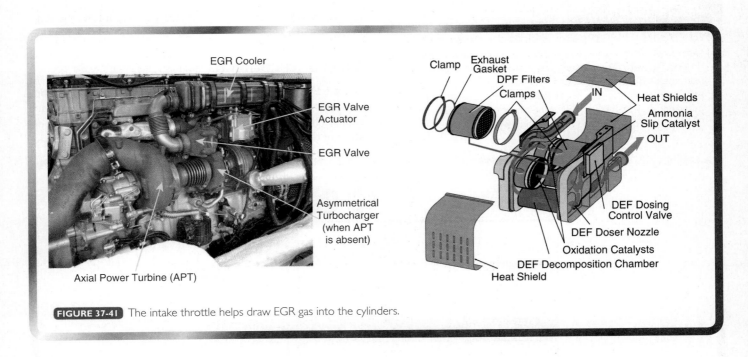

FIGURE 37-41 The intake throttle helps draw EGR gas into the cylinders.

throttle will also close to increase exhaust temperatures needed to speed up the regeneration process. When the ignition key is initially switched on, a self-test is performed on the intake throttle valve to learn maximum and minimum throttle positions.

GHG14 Aftertreatment Devices

The <u>GHG14 aftertreatment device (ATD)</u> has changed to an airless dosing system. GHG14 ATD is Detroit Diesel's name for aftertreatment system components that use electrically controlled diesel exhaust fluid (DEF) pumps and fluid dosing of the SCR rather than air pressure. The SCR system consists of an ACM, a DEF tank, a DEF pump, an airless DEF dosing unit, and an SCR module. DEF is pumped to the airless dosing unit through a high-pressure DEF line at 145 psi (10 bar). The DEF dosing unit injects a fine mist of atomized DEF into the SCR module to convert NO_x present in the exhaust stream into water vapor and nitrogen (N_2).

EPA10/GHG14 Diesel Exhaust Fluid System Anti-Tampering Feature

The HD-OBD system monitors for faults in DEF system components and monitors the DEF supply pressure. If the HD-OBD detects that components critical to the SCR or the DEF supply system are disconnected or malfunctioning, or if the diagnostics detect abnormal system pressures that indicate a DEF supply blockage, the malfunction indicator lamp (MIL) will illuminate and the control system will begin a time and mileage count. If the sensors detect that the SCR system has been tampered with, the MIL illuminates to warn the driver, and engine performance is limited, with a 55 miles per hour (mph) (90 kilometers per hours [km/h]) speed limit. If the system fault is not corrected, the stop engine light will illuminate and a 5 mph (8 km/h) speed limit will be applied during non-driving conditions. Similar warnings and penalties will result when insufficient urea quantity is present **FIGURE 37-42**.

A four-light bar segment indicates the DEF level in 25% increments. Low DEF levels will trigger a decrease in the engine's performance, as will using improper DEF fluid. In an empty or ignored state and when the diesel fuel tank is filled without filling the DEF tank, the vehicle's speed will be limited to 5 mph (8 km/h) until DEF is detected in the DEF tank.

▶ TECHNICIAN TIP

For EPA10 only, the DEF purge cycle is used to protect the DEF system from freezing. The purge cycle starts right after the key is shut off. The vehicle's air system is used to evacuate excess DEF from the DEF metering unit and nozzle supply hose. During the purge cycle, air can be heard leaking, which should not be mistaken as a leak. It is normal for the air pressure gauge to drop 9–12 psi (62–83 kPa) during this routine with the engine off.

Adjusting Valves and Brakes on DD Series Engines

Normal valve adjustment service intervals for DD series engines requires the first valve adjustment at 100,000 miles (160,934 km), the second at 500,000 miles (804,672 km), and then every 500,000 miles (804,672 km) after. In engine hours, this distance corresponds to a valve adjustment at 2565 hours, at 12,825 hours, and then every 12,825 hours after. Whenever the cylinder head or camshafts have been disturbed, the valve adjustment should be performed.

To adjust valves and brakes on DD series engines, follow the steps in **SKILL DRILL 37-2**.

Performing a Fuel System Integrity Check

The fuel system integrity check (FSIC) diagnostic test runs the fuel system through several specialized operational conditions to identify problems with the low- and high-pressure fuel system. A data log kept on the computer used to perform the test records important information needed to analyze fuel system operation. The FSIC test can pinpoint failed components or an incorrect aspect of the system without removing and testing individual components.

To perform a fuel system integrity check, follow the steps in **SKILL DRILL 37-3**.

Virtual Technician

Detroit Diesel uses **Virtual Technician**, a telematics communications package used to exchange information between a vehicle chassis and a central dispatch, which monitors the operation of the vehicle. It is an OEM-specific on-board diagnostics

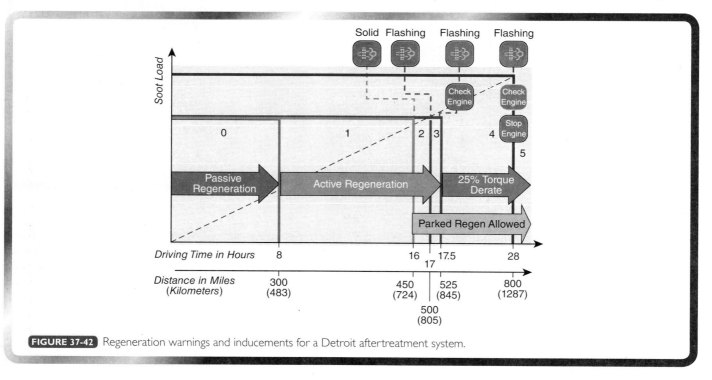

FIGURE 37-42 Regeneration warnings and inducements for a Detroit aftertreatment system.

SKILL DRILL 37-2 Adjusting Valves and Brakes on DD Series Engines

Exhaust Valve
Adjusting Screw

Engine Brake Valve
Clearance

Intake Valve
Adjustment Screw

Three-Lobed Exhaust
Cam Lobe

1. Steam clean the engine and lock out the ignition switch for safety.

2. Remove any components that would interfere with removing the valve cover, such as the air cleaner housing and turbocharger inlet hose. Refer to the OEM's procedures.

3. After removing the rocker cover, bar the engine over until cylinder 1 is at TDC at the end of compression stroke. Shake the rocker levers on cylinders 1 and 6 to verify. Cylinder 1 should have two loose levers while 6 should have two tight levers.

4. Using a feeler gauge, adjust the intake valve lash clearances on the intake rocker levers for cylinders 1, 2, and 4 to the manufacturer's specifications. The intake valves are all on one side of the engine and driven by a separate camshaft from the exhaust and engine brake camshaft. The specifications can be found on the engine's emission decal. A typical specification is 0.016" (0.4 mm). All the adjusting screws in direct contact with the exhaust and intake valves.

5. Adjust the valve lash clearances on the exhaust rocker levers for cylinders 1, 3, and 5.

6. Bar the engine over 360 degrees and repeat the procedure by adjusting the intake valve lash on cylinders 3, 5, and 6. The exhaust valve clearances can be adjusted on cylinders 2, 4, and 6.

7. Adjust the engine brake rocker lever clearances after each exhaust valve lash has been set. This is done by rotating the engine until the cylinder to be adjusted has reached its maximum intake valve lift. By observing the bottoming out of the rocker lever travel, the engine can be properly positioned to adjust the engine brake adjusting screws.

8. When the engine brake rocker arm begins to make contact with the exhaust valve, set the lash using the engine brake rocker arm adjusting screw. The clearance is set between the slave piston and the exhaust vale rocker lever. A typical clearance is 0.1614" (4.1 mm).

9. Adjust the brake lash clearances in the cylinder sequence of the engine firing order: 1, 5, 3, 6, 2, and 4.

10. Torque the lock nut valve adjusting screws to specifications and reassemble the engine.

(OBD) system feature. When an MIL illuminates, Virtual Technician collects snapshot data before, during, and after a fault code event. The tool then sends freeze-frame data to Detroit Diesel Customer Support Center, where technicians diagnose the problem and make service recommendations. Virtual Technician also has an optional Visibility Package that captures latitude, longitude, time, and odometer readings for enabled vehicles. The system records vehicle stops, speeds, routes, distance traveled, excessive idling, fuel consumption, and other onboard events.

SKILL DRILL 37-3 Performing a Fuel System Integrity Check

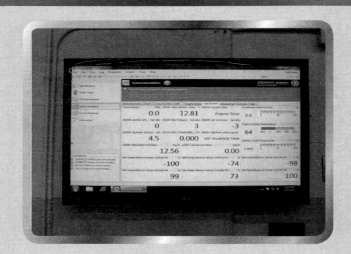

1 With a vehicle that has a fuel system–related complaint or diagnostic fault code, connect Detroit software to the vehicle with Detroit's DDL version 7.06 or newer.

2 Locate the diagnostic fault code and use it to direct you to the FSIC diagnostic routine.

3 For older three-filter systems, remove the doser pressure regulator and install a prescribed fuel pressure test plug.

4 Navigate in Detroit's DDL to Service Routines and select the Fuel System Integrity Check (FSIC) tab. Then, have the software execute Automatic FSIC.

5 Follow the instructions on screen to prepare the engine conditions to enable the FSIC test. For example, the engine requires a minimum operating temperature to begin the test.

6 Allow the FSIC diagnostic routine to complete.

Review the Automatic FSIC section.

7 Return to the initial diagnostic flow chart that directed fault code troubleshooting to the FSIC Routine.

8 Once the routine completes, review the automatic rail pressure bleed-off test time and fuel temperature rise under Automatic Rail Pressure Bleed-Off Test.

Automatic FSIC

The Automatic FSIC routine runs the engine through a diagnostic routine that begins at 600 rpm and climbs progressively to 850, 950, 1500, and finally 1800 rpm. After 1800 rpm, the engine speed falls to 600 rpm and the fuel rail pressure is increased to 11,800 psi (800 bar) for 20 seconds. Subsequently, the engine will shut down.

At 600 rpm, the low-pressure fuel system is monitored and the amount of fuel filter loading is calculated using the pressure difference between the low-pressure fuel sensor and the fuel compensation pressure sensor in the doser block. To get an accurate pressure differential measurement in the first-generation filter system, a plug is placed in the doser block.

At higher rpm, the engine MCM will monitor the quantity control valve current and the rail pressure, which should be stable at all engine speeds. If everything is operating correctly, then moving from 850 to 950 rpm should enable the pressure amplification to take place and have no impact on the low-pressure system pressures.

Automatic Rail Pressure Bleed-Off Test

At higher engine rpm, the automatic fuel rail pressure bleed-off test begins. During this test, the amount of time for the rail pressure to drop after the engine shuts off is recorded and compared with expected values. A faster-than-expected rail pressure bleed-off time could indicate a leak in one of the following:

- High-pressure pump (pumping elements)
- High-pressure fuel lines from the pump to the fuel rail or injector lines
- Fuel rail pressure sensor or pressure limiting valve
- Internal amplifier or needle leakage to the fuel return circuit
- Internal amplifier or needle leakage into the cylinders

Also during the test, the change in fuel temperature from the lowest to highest is monitored to check for low-pressure fuel system restrictions in the fuel module.

Wrap-Up

Ready for Review

▶ In the commercial vehicle transportation industry, Detroit Diesel has an iconic history as a leading producer of diesel engines for a broad range of applications, including marine, off-road heavy equipment, truck, bus, power generation, and locomotive.

▶ Detroit Diesel was conceived in 1938 by General Motors to produce diesel engines after the company experimented with the development of unit injectors for marine and locomotive diesel engines.

▶ Today, the Detroit Diesel brand is distinguished by its innovative, market-leading DD13, DD15, and DD16 engines, truck axle production, and DT12 automated manual transmission.

▶ Detroit Diesel's S60 became the top-selling engine in the truck market in 1993 when it broke the 50% market share for the first time, only a few years after the company nearly went bankrupt. By 2009, Detroit Diesel had built more than 1 million S60 engines.

▶ Detroit Diesel engines were the first electronic diesels to use crankshaft and camshaft position sensors to calculate injection timing and measure injection quantity.

▶ Detroit Diesel S50 and S60 engines have an overhead camshaft to achieve high injection pressures of up to 28,000 psi (1931 bar).

▶ The S60 used three types of electronic unit injectors.

▶ The first-generation injector used on S60 engines was the N2, which used a poppet-type control valve to regulate the beginning and end of injection.

▶ The second type of injector used on S60 engines, the N3, was introduced on the EGR engines in 2002. It uses a faster-acting low-mass, low-inertia control valve and operates at 50 volts.

▶ The E3 was the third type of injector used on S60 engines. Delphi introduced it in 2007 to meet EPA07 emission standards. The E3 has two sophisticated low-mass, low-inertia solenoids.

▶ Detroit Diesel is unique in that it measures electrical pulse width in degrees of crankshaft rotation rather than milliseconds or duty cycle.

▶ Detroit S50 and S60 engines do not have any external indicator for TDC for cylinder 1 or 6. Adjustment of the valves and injectors is performed by observing valve rocker lever/cam follower positions to determine piston position.

▶ In 2007, as the S60 platform was reaching the end of its twenty-year life cycle, Detroit Diesel launched its DD engine platform, beginning with the double overhead cam DD15 engine.

▶ DD engines use a unique third-generation Bosch ACR injection system.

▶ New and lighter engines, the DD5 and DD8, will be offered beginning in 2015 throughout DTNA's truck and bus products, which include Freightliner, Western Star, and Thomas Built buses.

▶ The DD series engines are nearly identical in construction features: four valves per cylinder, two hollow overhead camshafts, and a fourth-generation Bosch-built ACR high-pressure injection system.

▶ Detroit Diesel introduced the DDEC VI electronic engine control system for the DD15 to help meet EPA07 emission standards. The system exerts full authority electronic control over engine functions, regulating injection timing and quantity through two solenoids in each of the six ACR injectors.

▶ To create a faster-acting, less expensive, and more durable CR injector as an alternative to the piezoelectric actuators, Bosch developed the fourth-generation CRI4 injector for the heavy-duty diesel engine market.

▶ At the heart of Detroit's ACR or amplified pressure common rail system (APCRS) is a CR injector with a hydraulic amplification stage. The injector can operate like a conventional CR injector when conditions require it, plus multiply injection pressure inside the injector by a 2:1 ratio when commanded.

▶ One of the unique devices originally introduced on the DD15 engine is the APT. Under ideal conditions, the APT can convert exhaust energy that is normally wasted into as much as 50 hp (37 kW) and transfer the power to the engine's rear-mounted gear train.

▶ All the DD series engines use an intake throttle valve to increase exhaust temperatures needed to assist the DPF regeneration strategies.

▶ Detroit Diesel uses Virtual Technician, an OEM-specific on-board diagnostics system feature.

Vocabulary Builder

aftertreatment control module (ACM) An electronic control module used to process sensor data and control the outputs for the DPF and the SCR system.

amplified common rail (ACR) A high-pressure injection system that multiplies the fuel rail pressure inside the injector.

asymmetrical turbocharger (AT) A type of turbocharger that has one turbine volute made smaller than the other in order to increase exhaust backpressure for the EGR system.

axial power turbine (APT) A device located after the turbocharger that uses a turbine wheel to capture exhaust energy and convert it into usable engine power.

back leakage A general term used to describe any fuel circuit or component that supplies or transports fuel from the engine to the fuel tank.

balance shaft A rotating shaft having an eccentric weight that is used to offset torsional vibration produced by an engine.

calibration codes Alpha and or numerical information assigned to a specific injector used by the ECM to correct for manufacturing tolerances of an injector; also called injector codes or fuel trim codes.

common power train controller (CPC) An ECM used to store and process vehicle- and application-specific information.

CRI4 injector Another term for the amplified common rail injector.

E3 EUI A type of electronically controlled unit injector containing a nozzle control valve and spill control valve. Delphi manufactures E3 injectors for several OEM engine producers.

EPA07 emissions standards The emissions standards set by the EPA for medium- and heavy-duty diesel emissions in 2007. These standards are similar to Euro 5.

EPA10 emission standards The emissions standards set by the EPA for medium and heavy-duty diesel emissions in 2010. These standards are similar to Euro 6.

ethylene glycol A fluid used as an antifreeze base and to lubricate O-rings and other types of elastomer seals that are not oil compatible.

GHG14 aftertreatment device (ATD) Detroit Diesel's term for aftertreatment system components that use electrically controlled DEF pumps and fluid dosing of the SCR rather than air pressure.

heavy-duty on-board (HD-OBD) executive A software program inside the MCM used to run monitors and make decisions about concerning the on-board diagnostic system.

height gauge A tool used by technicians that is used to adjust the plunger travel of a unit injector for Detroit Diesel N2 injectors.

hydraulically amplified direct injection (HADI) Bosch's term used for the ACR injector supplied to DD series engines.

hydraulically balanced nozzle valve Fast-acting nozzle valve that opens and closes by slight changes in fuel pressure applied to the top and bottom of a nozzle valve.

injector response time (IRT) The time it takes for each injector to build a magnetic field strong enough to operate the valve.

intake throttle valve A valve used to regulate the quantity of fresh air entering the cylinders of an engine.

left-hand rotation engine An engine that turns counterclockwise when viewed from the flywheel.

motor control module (MCM) The electronic control module used by Detroit Diesel to control engine operation. The MCM receives sensor input, processes information using operating algorithms, and produces output signals.

nozzle control valve (NCV) The valve that controls the balancing of hydraulic pressure on either side of a hydraulically balanced nozzle valve; it opens and closes the nozzle valve.

nozzle return circuit A fuel pathway from the ACR injectors leading to the low-pressure fuel module, which drains fuel from the NCV; also known as a needle return circuit.

poppet control valve A mushroom-shaped valve used by unit injectors that operates under the influence of a magnetic field to open and close an injector spill port.

quantity control valve The pulse-width modulated inlet metering valve used on the high-pressure pump of Detroit Diesel's ACR system. Its operation controls the pressure supplied to the high-pressure fuel rail.

right-hand rotation engine An engine that turns clockwise when viewed from the flywheel.

rootes blower A high-volume positive displacement air pump used to pressurize intake air for Detroit Diesel two-stroke cycle diesels.

spill control valve (SCV) One of two control valves used in E3 and ACR injectors, which are used to vary spray in pressure of injectors. The timing of the SCV operation lowers or increases injection pressures.

supercharger Any mechanical device used to pressurize the intake air above atmospheric pressure. Superchargers include rootes blowers and turbochargers.

synchronous reference sensor (SRS) Detroit Diesel's term for a camshaft position sensor.

timing reference sensor (TRS) Detroit Diesel's term for a crankshaft position sensor.

torsional vibration The speeding up and slowing down of a crankshaft due to deceleration during compression strokes and acceleration during power strokes.

virtual technician A brand name for telematics communications package used to exchange information between a vehicle chassis and a central dispatch monitoring the operation of a vehicle.

Review Questions

1. _____ is a type electronically controlled unit injector containing a nozzle control valve and spill control valve.
   a. E3 EUI
   b. EPA05
   c. DDEC IV
   d. S60H

2. A(n) _____ is a device located after the turbocharger that uses a turbine wheel to capture exhaust energy and convert it into usable engine power.
   a. amplified common rail
   b. balance shaft
   c. valve overlap
   d. axial power turbine

3. The Detroit Diesel S50 engine is a four-cylinder version of the S60 model with an added _____ to minimize torsional vibrations.
   a. rocker arm shaft
   b. balance shaft
   c. amplifier piston
   d. nozzle spring

4. When the Detroit Diesel engine is initially cranked for starting, the _____ sensor detects cylinder 1's position using a specially marked reluctance wheel attached to the crankshaft.
   a. timing reference
   b. Parker-Racor
   c. valve overlap
   d. spill control

5. The additional control valve in the E3 compact injector package is a(n) _____ valve that regulates the injection pressure available at the nozzle tip.
   a. check
   b. amplifier control
   c. spill control
   d. needle solenoid

6. Backpressure for the EGR system of a Detroit Diesel DD series engine is provided by a(n) _____ turbocharger.
   a. series
   b. wastegate
   c. fixed geometry
   d. asymmetrical

7. The _____ control valve meters the fuel supplied to the high-pressure pump.
   a. quantity
   b. aftertreatment
   c. amplifier
   d. spill

8. A four-light bar segment indicates the _____ fluid level in 25% increments.
   a. coolant
   b. oil
   c. diesel exhaust
   d. hydraulic

9. On S50 and S60 Detroit Diesels that use N2 injectors, the valves and injectors have a unique adjustment procedure that uses _____ as a reference point to correctly position the engine and select the appropriate valve and injector to adjust.
   a. turbo lag
   b. valve overlap
   c. timing reference
   d. axial power

10. By flipping around the _____, and reversing the direction of rotation for the coolant, fuel, and oil pumps, a modular engine could be made to turn clockwise or counterclockwise.
    a. turbocharger
    b. rocker arm shaft
    c. balance shaft
    d. camshaft

ASE-Type Questions

1. Technician A says that the Detroit Diesel N3 used a spindle type nozzle control valve that enabled the use of pilot injection. Technician B says that the Detroit Diesel N3 used a butterfly type nozzle control valve that enabled the use of pilot injection. Who is correct?
   a. Technician A
   b. Technician B
   c. Both Technician A and Technician B
   d. Neither Technician A nor Technician B

2. Technician A says the Delphi E3 electronic unit injector was developed to meet EPA05 emission standards. Technician B says the Delphi E3 electronic unit injector was developed to meet EPA09 emission standards. Who is correct?
   a. Technician A
   b. Technician B
   c. Both Technician A and Technician B
   d. Neither Technician A nor Technician B

3. Technician A says that the Detroit Diesel DD series engines, which includes the DD13, DD15, and DD16, have close to a 75% parts commonality. Technician B says that the Detroit Diesel DD series engines have close to a 90% parts commonality. Who is correct?
   a. Technician A
   b. Technician B
   c. Both Technician A and Technician B
   d. Neither Technician A nor Technician B

4. Technician A says that the first-generation Detroit Diesel electronic unit injector, designated N2, used a poppet-type control valve to regulate the beginning and end of injection. Technician B says that the first-generation Detroit Diesel electronic unit injector, designated N2, used a spiral control valve to regulate the beginning and end of injection. Who is correct?
   a. Technician A
   b. Technician B
   c. Both Technician A and Technician B
   d. Neither Technician A nor Technician B

5. Technician A says the synchronous reference sensor (SRS) is Detroit Diesel's term for a crankshaft position sensor. Technician B says the synchronous reference sensor (SRS) is Detroit Diesel's term for a camshaft position sensor. Who is correct?
   a. Technician A
   b. Technician B
   c. Both Technician A and Technician B
   d. Neither Technician A nor Technician B

6. Technician A says that a left-hand rotation engine is an engine that turns counterclockwise when viewed from the flywheel. Technician B says that a left-hand rotation engine is an engine that turns clockwise when viewed from the flywheel. Who is correct?
   a. Technician A
   b. Technician B
   c. Both Technician A and Technician B
   d. Neither Technician A nor Technician B

7. Technician A says a height gauge is a tool used by technicians that is used to adjust the plunger travel of a unit injector for N2 injectors. Technician B says a torque wrench is used to verify that the injector plunger has bottomed out on E3 EUI injectors. Who is correct?
   a. Technician A
   b. Technician B
   c. Both Technician A and Technician B
   d. Neither Technician A nor Technician B

8. Technician A says a Parker-Racor module is a high-volume positive displacement air pump used to pressurize intake air for Detroit Diesel two-stroke cycle diesels. Technician B says a rootes blower is a high-volume positive displacement air pump used to pressurize intake air for Detroit Diesel two-stroke cycle diesels. Who is correct?
   a. Technician A
   b. Technician B
   c. Both Technician A and Technician B
   d. Neither Technician A nor Technician B

9. Technician A says Detroit Diesel uses a telematics communications package called OnStar to exchange information between a vehicle chassis and a central dispatch. Technician B says Detroit Diesel uses a telematics communications package called Fleet Watch to exchange information between a vehicle chassis and a central dispatch. Who is correct?
   a. Technician A
   b. Technician B
   c. Both Technician A and Technician B
   d. Neither Technician A nor Technician B

10. Technician A says that DDEC VI electronic engine control system for the DD15 was introduced to help meet EPA07 emission standards. Technician B says that the DDEC VI electronic engine control system for the DD15 uses an engine-mounted MCM and a common power train controller located inside the cab. Who is correct?
    a. Technician A
    b. Technician B
    c. Both Technician A and Technician B
    d. Neither Technician A nor Technician B

CHAPTER 38
Caterpillar

NATEF Tasks

Diesel Engines

General
- Check and record electronic diagnostic codes. (p 1094)

Cylinder Head and Valve Train
- Inspect electronic wiring harness and brackets for wear, bending, cracks, and looseness; determine needed action. (p 1092)

Fuel System
Electronic Fuel Management System
- Interface with vehicle's on-board computer; perform diagnostic procedures using electronic service tool(s)

(to include PC-based software and/or data scan tools); determine needed action. (p 1094)
- Check and record electronic diagnostic codes and trip/operational data; monitor electronic data; clear codes; determine further diagnosis. (p 1094)
- Using electronic service tool(s), access and interpret customer programmable parameters. (pp 1092–1094)

Knowledge Objectives

After reading this chapter, you will be able to:

1. Outline the development of Caterpillar engine manufacturing. (pp 1073–1075)
2. Classify Caterpillar engine models according to original equipment manufacturer (OEM) descriptions. (pp 1073–1075)
3. Identify and describe unique construction features of Caterpillar engines. (pp 1075–1078)
4. Identify and describe Caterpillar fuel system types and operation. (pp 1078–1086)
5. Outline and explain the flow of fuel through Caterpillar low-pressure fuel systems. (p 1082)
6. Identify Caterpillar Service Information Systems (Cat SIS) and telematics control. (pp 1084–1085)
7. Identify and describe the purpose of Caterpillar E-trim injector codes. (pp 1084–1085)

8. Describe and explain adjustable parameters for Caterpillar engines and fuel systems. (pp 1085–1086)
9. Describe features of Caterpillar's Advanced Combustion Emissions Reduction Technology (ACERT). (pp 1086–1094)
10. Identify the purpose and explain the operation of the Miller operating cycle. (pp 1087–1088)
11. Identify and describe the purpose and function of variable intake valve actuation (VIVA). (pp 1087–1088)
12. Describe the purpose and operation of series turbochargers. (p 1088)
13. Describe the purpose and operation of clean gas induction (CGI) systems. (pp 1089–1090)
14. Describe the purpose and operation of Caterpillar regeneration systems (CRS). (pp 1091–1093)

Skills Objectives

After reading this chapter, you will be able to:

1. Exchange injectors. (p 1095) **SKILL DRILL 38-1**
2. Program or update the flash file. (p 1095) **SKILL DRILL 38-2**

3. View Caterpillar proprietary diagnostic codes. (p 1096) **SKILL DRILL 38-3**

You Are the Technician

A customer has brought a highway coach bus with a 2009 C13 to your shop. The engine is misfiring and running roughly. During a preliminary inspection, you find the sediment bowl of the fuel water separator full of water. In draining some of the fuel tanks through a drain plug located in the bottom of the tank, you find several liters of water were contained in the tank. You perform a cylinder cut-out test using Cat ET, and cylinders 5 and 6 made no power contribution. To eliminate the possibility of a misfire originating in damaged cylinder components, you have decided to exchange injectors 1 and 6 first, then perform another cut-out test before swapping 2 and 5. However, after removing the valve cover, you discover the injector plungers are seized with both plungers compressed downward. Suspecting the injectors were damaged by water in the fuel system, you recommend replacement of all six injectors, filter changes, and flushing the low-pressure fuel system with clean fuel. After getting the customer's consent to perform the work, consider the following:

1. Outline the steps you would use to drain and remove water from the low-pressure fuel system.
2. What is different about the procedure used to exchange injectors from one cylinder to another and simply replacing a defective injector with a new one?
3. Provide several reasons for recommending replacement of all six injectors.

► Introduction

Caterpillar is well-known global manufacturer of construction and mining equipment, diesel and natural gas engines, power generators, and diesel-electric locomotives. Its roots as an off-road equipment manufacturer began with the invention of a movable track on crawler tractors. Benjamin Holt invented the movable track to solve the problem of heavy steam-powered tractors sinking into the rich topsoil in the soft earth of California farmland. Instead of placing boards in front of tractor wheels, he replaced the wheels with a set of wooden tracks bolted to chains. Distributing the weight of the equipment over the crawler track gave the equipment exceptional maneuverability capabilities and the equipment's movement, which resembled that of a caterpillar, became synonymously attached to products built by the Holt Manufacturing Company **FIGURE 38-1**. After merging with another tractor manufacturer, the Best Manufacturing Company, the combined enterprise produced caterpillar tractors and incorporated as Caterpillar Tractor Company. Caterpillar developed its first diesel engine, the D9900, in 1931. The engine was colossal in size—it weighed 5175 lb (2347 kg) while producing only 89 horsepower (hp) (66 kilowatts [kW]) at 700 rpm. However, it significantly improved power output, reliability, and fuel economy in comparison to gasoline-fueled alternatives and other competitors' diesels engines.

► Caterpillar Innovation

Caterpillar introduced many innovations to diesel engines that were considered frivolous by other manufacturers in the 1930s. Features like enclosed pushrods, camshaft bearings, and oil bath air cleaners enabled the engines to operate reliably beyond 3000 hours. Because the engines were designed for rugged tractor operation, truck owners looking for high output torque, fuel economy, and better durability began re-powering trucks with Caterpillar diesels removed from tractors or purchased directly from Caterpillar. The first Caterpillar diesel built for trucks was the D468, produced in 1939. The six cylinder D468 was rated for 90 hp (67 kW) at 1800 rpm and was sold with a matching transmission. Prior to this, only one truck in 10,000 had a diesel engine, and the D468 rose from obscurity with its reputation of operating on $5 fuel cost per day.

Caterpillar's focus on building diesel engines allowed the company to promote improvements in fuel and engine oil quality, which they continue to set standards for today. Caterpillar had several industry firsts, including introducing turbocharging in 1955, the first dual overhead cam engine in 1967, and the world's only hydraulic engine retarder in 1973. Development of hydraulically actuated, electronically controlled unit injection (HEUI) using engine oil to pressurize fuel in 1993 represents one of the largest technological leaps forward for diesel engines. The HEUI system not only enabled electronic control to vary the beginning and end of injection timing for cleaner emissions and improved engine performance, but could vary injection pressure independently of engine speed to better match operating conditions and use multiple injection events during a combustion cycle **FIGURE 38-2** and **FIGURE 38-3**.

FIGURE 38-1 The Caterpillar company name is derived from the caterpillar-like movement of tracked equipment invented by the Holt Manufacturing Company, a company which later was incorporated into Caterpillar.

More recently, in 2004, Caterpillar introduced series turbocharging and variable valve timing to heavy-duty engines, which enabled the use of a <u>Miller combustion cycle</u>. Miller cycle engines essentially change the timing of the intake valve closing. By closing the valve later, less energy is needed to compress the air charge before combustion takes place. A large mass of intake air can still charge the cylinders, even though the intake valve closes later during the compression stroke, because the series turbocharging will increase intake boost pressure, which fills the cylinder faster with more air pressure. Power needed to compress air is derived from the normally wasted exhaust gas energy rather than using energy from the crankshaft.

To compete in an ever-increasing global market, Caterpillar acquired Perkins Diesel in 1998. Engines made using the combined manufacturing and development resources of Caterpillar and Perkins are sometimes amusingly called "Perkapillar" engines. The addition of Perkins Diesel, a supplier to Caterpillar since the 1970s, is claimed to have made Caterpillar the world's largest diesel engine manufacturer, building products in 51 North American facilities and in 65 other locations in 23 countries around the world. In 1997, Caterpillar also acquired the marine division of Maschinenbau Kiel, or MaK, of Germany and markets marine diesel engines through this new division.

Caterpillar Engine Models

Since the production of its first diesel engine in the 1930s, Caterpillar has excelled as a supplier of diesel engines to a wide variety of industries, including heavy-duty trucking, off-road equipment, construction, mining, forestry, buses, and power generation. Caterpillar engines are esteemed as a premium engine product, garnering a reputation for reliable, durable operation with outstanding product support. In fact, for years rankings by independent surveys like JD Power consistently

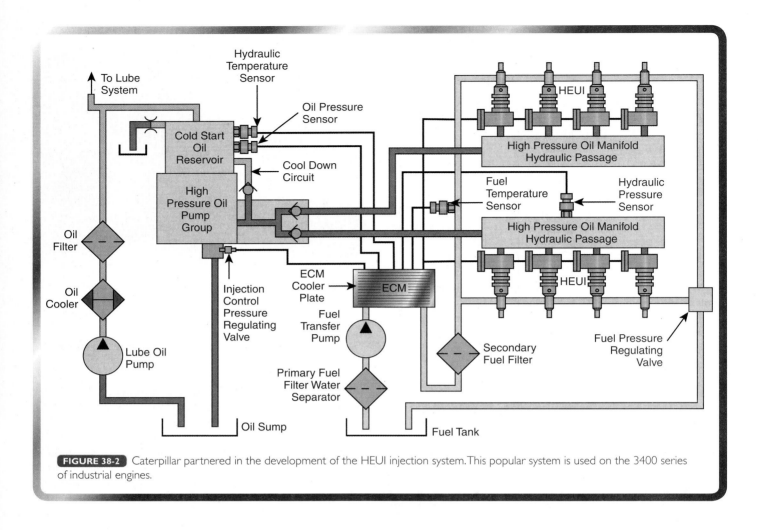

FIGURE 38-2 Caterpillar partnered in the development of the HEUI injection system. This popular system is used on the 3400 series of industrial engines.

HIA 250   Cat HIB 300   Generation 2

FIGURE 38-3 Comparing Caterpillar's HEUI injector with other HEUI injectors.

placed Caterpillar heavy-duty diesel engines first in measures of customer satisfaction and quality.

Caterpillar is a vertically integrated manufacturer that produces all of the components making up its product. As such, Caterpillar designs and manufactures its own engines **FIGURE 38-4**. However, production of on-highway engines delivered to other truck and bus makers ended in 2009 as the EPA-10 emission standards were introduced and Caterpillar had decided not to develop engines to meet those new standards. Instead of supplying other truck makers, Caterpillar introduced its new CT series of vocational trucks in collaboration with Navistar, which supplied engine and chassis parts. The CT660 and CT681 used Navistar's 11L, 13L, and 15L MaxxForce engines. And while the Navistar engines are EPA-10 certified, the truck was designed primarily for severe service vocational off-road applications, such as in dump trucks and concrete mixers **FIGURE 38-5**. The latest models of CT series trucks use only the 13L engine with power ratings up to 550 hp (410 kW). Caterpillar's own CX31 transmission is mated to the engine and vehicles are equipped with a selective catalytic reduction (SCR) aftertreatment system.

FIGURE 38-4 Caterpillar is a vertically integrated manufacturer of equipment and manufactures engines for the off-road machinery it also produces.

FIGURE 38-5 The CT truck series is manufactured by Caterpillar for severe service vocational use.

Caterpillar has not abandoned support of its extensive on-highway engine products, which are still found in its off-road equipment. To distinguish engine families, model numbers for Caterpillar have gone through several changes. In 1974 Caterpillar began to use a four-digit system. The first digit is designated a 3 to identify diesel engines. The next digit indicated to which engine family or market the engine belonged. That meant that for most of the 1990s the second number was a 1, 2, 3, 4, or 5. Popular on-highway diesel engines models were designated 3100, 3200, 3300, 3400, and 3500. A second digit of 0 indicated the engine was a small-bore Perkins engine. The last digit indicated the number of cylinders. Common six cylinder truck engines were 3126, 3176, 3306, and 3406. The 3208 engine was an eight cylinder engine popular in off-highway equipment that was also used in some trucks. For some, but not all, the middle two digits designated the cylinder displacement. Engines like the 3126 and 3116 had 1.2L (73 cubic inch) and 1.1L (67 cubic inch) displacement per cylinder, respectively. (The 3406 was an exception to this general rule.) Additional letters following the four digits identified models with incremental upgrades or revisions to an engine technology. For example, successive generations of the popular 3406, an on-highway, high-horsepower engine with approximately 14.5L (885 cubic inch) of total displacement was identified with the letters A, B, C, and E. The 3406E was a version with electronic unit injectors, and A, B, and C engines used a hydromechanical injection pump.

A story is told that in the mid-1990s, the president of Freightliner asked Caterpillar executives why its numbering system made little sense. He suggested a system that used the letter C for Caterpillar followed by the liter displacement of the engine. Caterpillar changed the names for its on-highway engines to C10, C12, and C15. This was in addition to the mid-bore engines, the 3126 and 3116. With the introduction of **Advanced Combustion Emissions reduction Technology (ACERT)** in 2003, the hyphen was dropped and the engines were stroked (meaning the piston stroke was lengthened) to accommodate new exhaust gas recirculation (EGR) systems called **clean gas induction (CGI)**. New ACERT engine models indicating their displacements were the C7, C9, C11, C13, and C15 **FIGURE 38-6**. Caterpillar also used an arrangement number that matches a bill of material for parts used to construct an engine. In addition to an engine model and serial number, the arrangement number is used when ordering parts to differentiate a parts breakdown list for identical engine models with different construction features **FIGURE 38-7**.

▶ Engine Construction Features

Engine Blocks

Caterpillar mid- and large-bore engines all use induction-hardened wet sleeves in cast iron engine blocks. Blocks have high tensile strength and use serpentine crankcase contours to increase rigidity, which in turn reduces noise and vibration without increasing weight. Deep skirt blocks are used by Caterpillar exclusively with a crankshaft stiffening plate attached to the oil pan rails on higher horsepower models. The 3176 was the first

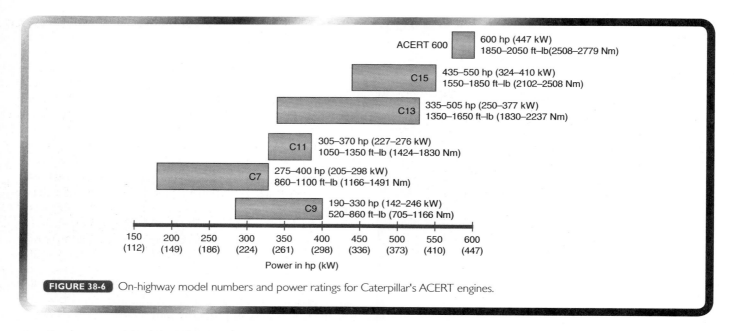

FIGURE 38-6 On-highway model numbers and power ratings for Caterpillar's ACERT engines.

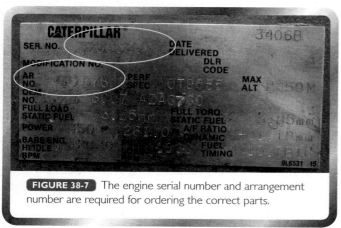

FIGURE 38-7 The engine serial number and arrangement number are required for ordering the correct parts.

Caterpillar engine to use mid-stop liners. The liner had only the top half surrounded in coolant, which enabled a smaller engine water jacket for reduced engine weight. These engines, along with 3406 and C15, used a Caterpillar patented **spacer plate**, which was placed between the cylinder head and block deck. The intention of the spacer plate is to assist in reducing stresses on the liner flanges, which cause cracking in the liner ledge, counterbore, and liner flange. No liner counterbore or ledge is used in these engines. Instead, the liner flange sits directly on the top of the engine block. The spacer plate is machined to snuggly fit around the liner flanges **FIGURE 38-8**. The spacer, which is just a few thousandths of an inch thinner than the liner flange, surrounds the liner flange as it sits directly on top of the block deck **FIGURE 38-9**. When the cylinder head is installed, the

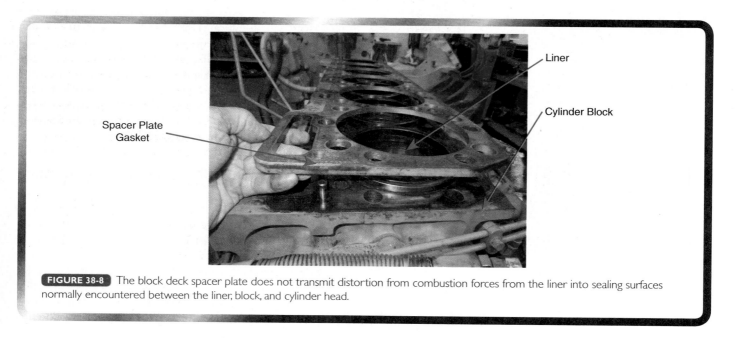

FIGURE 38-8 The block deck spacer plate does not transmit distortion from combustion forces from the liner into sealing surfaces normally encountered between the liner, block, and cylinder head.

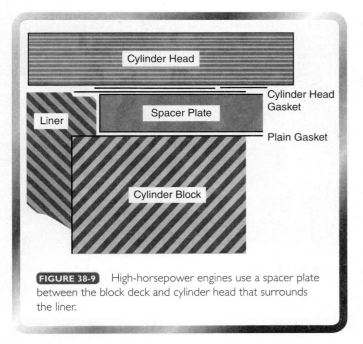

FIGURE 38-9 High-horsepower engines use a spacer plate between the block deck and cylinder head that surrounds the liner.

head will exert clamping force directly to the top of the liner and hold it firmly in place against the block deck. Because a counterbore is not cut into the block deck, the height of the liners with uniform flange thickness is much more consistent than liners placed in machined counterbores or on ledges, which have more height variation due to manufacturing machining tolerances. More uniform force is applied by the cylinder head to clamp the liners, creating less distortion of the liner to cylinder head sealing surface when combustion forces are high. The use of the spacer plate next to the liner flanges makes the liner less sensitive to height variations that lead to combustion and coolant leaks. If the liner does move and wear a groove into the block deck, the deck can be machined and a hardened steel insert can be installed to restore the correct projection height of the liner

FIGURE 38-10. When a steel spacer plate encounters any kind of wear or damage, it can be more easily replaced than machining the block deck or liner counterbores.

Cylinder Heads

On higher horsepower engines, Caterpillar uses an overhead camshaft, which enables higher injection pressure due to direct transfer of camshaft actuation force to the injector plunger. Without transmitting force through a pushrod, overhead camshafts can achieve higher injection pressures with the least amount of injection lag caused by flexing pushrods. One drawback is the amount of gear backlash produced when transmitting crankshaft force through multiple gears to the cam gear. In addition to the synchronization error between the crankshaft and camshaft rotation, torsional vibration transmitted to the cam gear produces an additional synchronization error of between 4 and 6 degrees. To minimize gear noise, wear, and synchronization problems, Caterpillar uses a dampening system feature on the cam gear called a **pendulum gear dampener** **FIGURE 38-11**. Unlike regular balancers, pendulum dampeners provide torsional vibration control by producing counterbalance forces that directly cancel the forces producing torsional vibration. Steel rollers called centrifugal pendulums fit loosely into a specific number of holes in the overhead cam drive gear. The rollers store and release energy back into the cam gear as it speeds up and slows down due to torsional speed changes. A patented mathematical algorithm is used to calculate roller size, hole size, and gear size to obtain optimum roller movement during compression strokes when the crank slows down and during acceleration events in power strokes. Movement of the rollers back and forth minimizes camshaft velocity changes. Caterpillar claims the pendulum dampener provides a smoother-running engine and increases valve train stability while offering more accurate injection timing. Pendulum gear dampeners have the added advantage of being lighter than conventional dampeners.

OEM Specifications for flatness on over the entire block surface are typically within 0.004" (0.102 mm) and vary no more than 0.002" (0.051 mm) over any 6" (15.24 cm) section of surface.

Damage to the liner seat area should be no more than 0.001" (0.025 mm) deep in any particular spot, and should be no more the half the width of the seat.

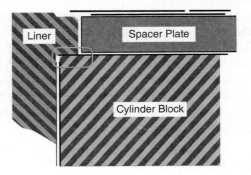

FIGURE 38-10 Cylinder liners can wear into the block deck and may require cutting and insertion of shims to maintain correct liner protrusion.

FIGURE 38-11 The pendulum gear on the overhead camshaft minimizes torsional vibration transmitted to the camshaft.

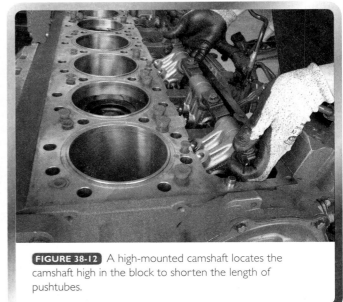

FIGURE 38-12 A high-mounted camshaft locates the camshaft high in the block to shorten the length of pushtubes.

In overhead camshaft engines, the camshaft is driven by an adjustable idler gear, which is turned by a fixed idler gear, and the fixed idler gear is turned by a cluster idler gear in the front gear train. Correct gear backlash is achieved by locking the cam gear and moving the adjustable idler gear held in place with bolts passing through a plate with elongated holes. Correct synchronization of cam to crank position is made using timing marks on the crankshaft and idler gear. When done correctly, the gear alignment and backlash adjustment will establish proper synchronization between the piston movement and the valve action.

The alternative to using an overhead camshaft is to use a camshaft located in the engine block but to locate the shaft as close as possible to the cylinder block deck. In **high-mounted cams**, pushrods or solid pushtubes are used, but shorter and solid tubes will flex less and transmit more force **FIGURE 38-12**.

Cylinder heads are a one-piece cast iron unit. When the camshaft is located within the cylinder head, its rigidity is improved. Steel-backed aluminum bearings are pressed into each cam bushing journal. Engine thermal efficiency is enhanced by the use of stainless steel thermal sleeves positioned in each exhaust port. The sleeves reduce the amount of heat transferred to the cooling system and instead increase exhaust energy to power the turbocharger. Electronic unit injectors are located in a stainless steel injector sleeve pressed into the cylinder head injector bores. The use of stainless steel prevents cavitation erosion from the cooling system **FIGURE 38-13**.

▶ Fuel Systems

Caterpillar has used three types of electronic fuel injection systems since the late 1980s: electronic unit injection (EUI), hydraulic actuated electronic unit injection (HEUI), and

FIGURE 38-13 Corroded injector tubes caused by cavitation erosion.

common rail. The first engine with full-authority electronic unit injectors was the 3176, which was first produced in 1988 when Caterpillar introduced electronic controls on the new 3176A and the 3406 programmable electronic engine controls (PEEC) engine. The 3406 PEEC was a partial authority system, which meant it was not a drive-by-wire fuel system but an electronically governed pump-line-nozzle (PLN) fuel system. The PEEC electronic control module (ECM) were replaced in 1993 by 40-pin second-generation **Advanced Diesel Engine Management**, or ADEM II. (No highway engines used an ADEM I ECM because it was used only in off-road engines.) By 1998, the introduction of 70-pin ADEM III ECM enabled J-1939 on-board network communication. The ECM also had more processing capabilities and greater versatility of programming inputs and outputs. The 140-pin ADEM 4 was introduced for ACERT engines and was used until the last 2009 on-highway engines were produced. All the ECMs have various versions offering air or fuel cooling, different amounts of memory, and varying support for engines with large numbers of cylinders and output devices **FIGURE 38-14** and **FIGURE 38-15**.

Mechanically Actuated Electronically Controlled Unit Injector Fuel System

The **mechanically actuated electronically controlled unit injector (MEUI)** is Caterpillar's term for what were previously known as electronic unit injectors (EUI) **FIGURE 38-16**. This injection system uses the engine camshaft located either in the cylinder head or engine block to pressurize fuel for injection pressure. The ECM regulates the amount of fuel injected into the cylinders according to preprogramed software instructions. When a solenoid on each injector is energized by electrical current supplied by the ECM, fuel is injected. The quantity, timing, and duration of the injection event is controlled by varying the pulse-width modulated (PWM) electrical signal supplied to the injectors.

The EUI system used in its C13 and C15 engines is identical to the Detroit Diesel Delphi E3 injectors described in the Electronic Unit Injectors and Unit Pumps chapter. Caterpillar does use a tool unique from the E3 to adjust the injector height to achieve safe plunger travel **FIGURE 38-17**. For some C15 engines, the height gauge has a yoke that surrounds the injector body and has a precision-length pin attached to the yoke. When the engine is on the inner base circle of the injector cam lobe, or off the outer cam lobe, the injector height is adjusted by measuring the dimension from the top of the cylinder head deck to a machined ledge of the fuel injector body. Identifying top dead center (TDC) on most Caterpillar engines to adjust valves and injectors is performed by removing a pipe plug on the right side of the engine bell housing on the side facing the front of the engine **FIGURE 38-18**. When the flywheel is rotated, a 0.3125″ (7.9375 mm) or 0.375″ (9.525 mm) bolt can be threaded into the rear of flywheel when the engine has reached TDC for cylinder 1. Another pipe plug can be removed to insert a turning tool to rotate the engine.

HEUI System

Collaborating with Navistar in the 1980 and 1990s, Caterpillar developed HEUI A and B fuel systems. Later, Navistar worked instead with Siemens to produce a second-generation HEUI system with a dual solenoid injector. Caterpillar continued HEUI development and independently produced the H1B-300 injector (see the Hydraulically Actuated Electronic Unit Injector Systems chapter). The Caterpillar H1B-300 was developed for the C7 and C9 ACERT series engines and was used until 2003 when Caterpillar introduced its common rail fuel system. The H1B-300 injector is capable of five different injection rate shapes and an electrically controlled pilot injection. Two unique features of the injector are the low-mass poppet valve, which responds faster to electrical signals, and the hydraulically balanced nozzle valve. Hydraulically balanced nozzle valves simply have hydraulic pressure applied to two nozzle surfaces, one for highly pressurized fuel below the nozzle valve and the other for slightly higher hydraulic pressure above the nozzle valve to hold the valve on its seat. Changing the balance of hydraulic pressure applied to either side of the nozzle valve causes it to either open or close.

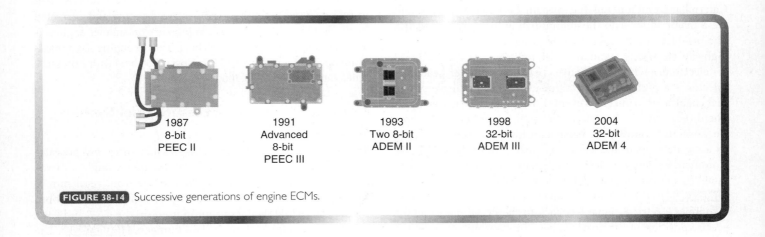

1987	1991	1993	1998	2004
8-bit	Advanced	Two 8-bit	32-bit	32-bit
PEEC II	8-bit	ADEM II	ADEM III	ADEM 4
	PEEC III			

FIGURE 38-14 Successive generations of engine ECMs.

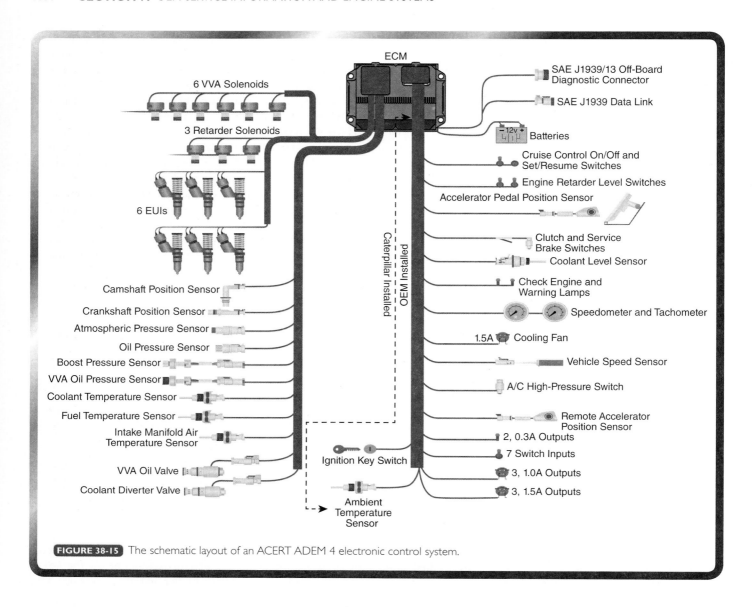

FIGURE 38-15 The schematic layout of an ACERT ADEM 4 electronic control system.

Caterpillar Common Rail

Caterpillar's C9.3, C6.6, and C4.4 engines are built using the Caterpillar common rail fuel system designed by Continental, a major supplier to the automotive industry **FIGURE 38-19**. The products are ACERT engines designed to meet tier 4 off-highway emissions standards. All three engines use ADEM A4 electronics with a four-valve cross-flow cylinder head. The injector is a piezoelectric actuator using a direct drive design that enables more injection events during the combustion cycle. The direct drive design places the actuator closer to the nozzle valve and controls the balance of hydraulic pressures used to accurately open and close the nozzle valve **FIGURE 38-20**. Continental's injector design is the first of its kind that can establish an injection rate shape pattern for each injection event **FIGURE 38-21**. What is also unique to the piezo actuator is that it supplies electrical signal feedback to the ECM, reporting the precise position of the nozzle valve. This capability enables the

fuel system to modify the injection rate to best control the combustion events in each cylinder while easily compensating for injector deterioration. Over time the smallest variations or drift in fuel delivery discharge volumes are detected and corrected by the system. Maximum system pressure on smaller engines is approximately 23,000 psi (1586 bar). The C9 engine has a maximum operating pressure of 27,550 psi (1900 bar) with a pressure relief valve setting of 33,300 psi (2296 bar).

Common Rail High-Pressure Fuel System Overview

The fuel system consists of a high-pressure and a low-pressure fuel circuit. The high-pressure pump is either a single- or two-plunger pump configuration driven by the front gear train of the engine. The smaller C4.4 pump camshaft has two lobes on the cam while the larger pump used on the C6.6 and C9.3 has three lobes for each of the two plungers **FIGURE 38-22**. The

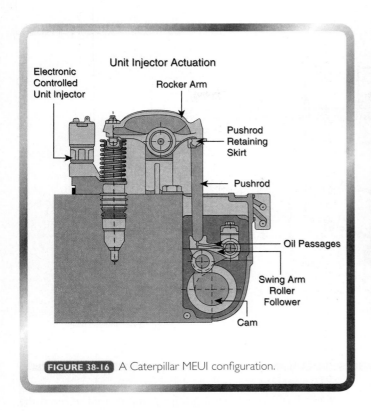

FIGURE 38-16 A Caterpillar MEUI configuration.

FIGURE 38-18 Two pipe plugs can be removed from the bell housing to insert a timing pin to lock cylinder 1 at TDC and another plug to insert a pinion tool to rotate the engine.

FIGURE 38-17 A pinion turning tool and a C15 injector height adjustment tool.

pump is lubricated by the engine oil and not by diesel fuel, which allows the use of a wider range of fuels without the concern for loss of the lubricity needed to prevent rapid wear of the camshaft lobe. Fuel is supplied to the pump after the secondary fuel filter. Pump output pressure is achieved using spill control valves for each pumping chamber. The electrically controlled spill valves are normally opened and closed only by an electrical signal from the ECM. Without current supplied to the valves, the valves are open and the pump does not build pressure.

One or both valves can operate, depending on how much output volume is required. For example, when the larger pump is operating at a lower output range, such as at 25–50% of maximum output, the spill valves can be energized to allow only one pump cylinder assembly to produce pressure and supply pressurized fuel to the rail. This strategy reduces parasitic power loss and overheating of fuel caused by unnecessary pumping of fuel. Two pump pistons together can supply fuel at 50–100% of output volume. Interestingly, the spill valves are actuated asynchronously or at irregular intervals when output volume is higher. This is done to smooth pump output pressure and minimize pressure fluctuations. In a normal piston pump, pressure above the plunger is much lower at the beginning of the stroke and peaks near the end of plunger travel. Energizing the spill valves at irregular intervals achieves more consistent or balanced hydraulic forces above each plunger and prevents torque reversal in the pump caused by extreme fuel pressures. For example, one valve might be energized to spill at 45 degrees before TDC and another at 90 degrees to achieve correct rail pressure and a more even delivery pressure. A pump speed and position sensor is used by the ECM as an input for an algorithm to calculate the best points in the pump rotation and plunger position to reduce pressure spikes and troughs. Because the pump rotates at the same speed as the engine and precise spill valve timing is needed to correct pressure wave irregularities, the pump position is phased or timed to the engine during installation **FIGURE 38-23**.

It is important to note that unlike other common rail systems, which hold fuel pressure after the engine is shut down, the normally open common rail pump actuators will allow fuel to drain from the rail within a minute of engine shutdown.

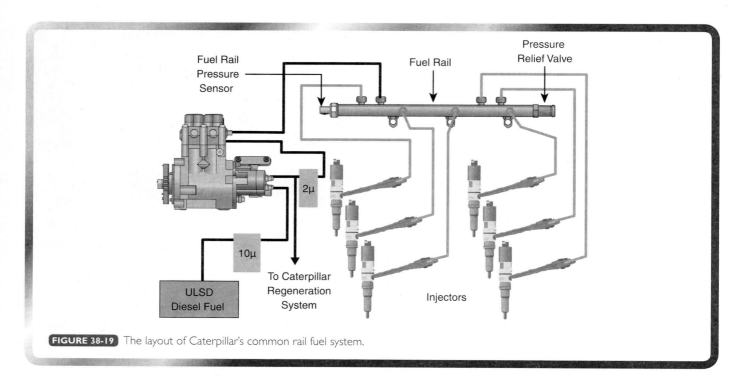

FIGURE 38-19 The layout of Caterpillar's common rail fuel system.

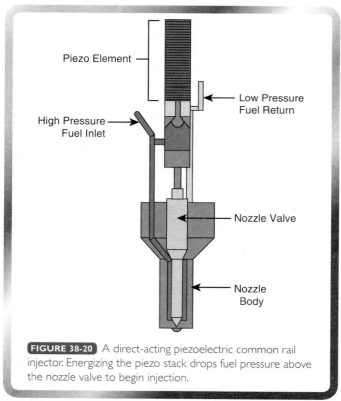

FIGURE 38-20 A direct-acting piezoelectric common rail injector. Energizing the piezo stack drops fuel pressure above the nozzle valve to begin injection.

Low-Pressure System

ACERT common rail engines are equipped with a two-filter filtration system to protect the dirt-sensitive fuel system from abrasive wear and contamination. A gear-type transfer pump is mounted at the rear of the high-pressure pump and pulls fuel from the primary filter and fuel-water separator before pushing fuel into the secondary filter. A hand primer pump is used to bleed the fuel system and fill fuel filters after filter replacement. On some equipment, electric fuel pumps are also used in the fuel tanks. Bleed valves in the system help remove air, and high-pressure lines should never be opened to bleed the system. High-pressure line replacement is recommended if lines are disconnected. A thermo-recirculating fuel valve is located at the tank, which helps regulate the temperature of fuel supplied to the system. Warm fuel returned from the engine is mixed with fuel from the tank to increase the temperature of cold fuel, or it is simply returned directly to the tank if the fuel from the tank is warm.

Direct Drive Piezo Injectors

Continental's direct drive piezo injector uses a piezo crystal stack of more than 300 thin ceramic wafers to mechanically actuate the pressure control valve regulating nozzle movement. The stack is mechanically connected to the control valve through a push pin. When switching current is applied, the piezo wafers expand, moving the spindle control valve and draining fuel pressure acting on the control rod linkage holding the nozzle valve closed **FIGURE 38-24**. As the balance of fuel pressure on either side of the nozzle valve tips, fuel pressure below the nozzle valve forces the valve upward against the control rod, opening the injector nozzle within milliseconds. The extremely rapid injector response time enables up to seven injections per combustion cycle. Better rate shape control of the combustion events means fewer emissions, improved performance, and superior fuel economy. In comparison to previous common rail systems, Continental reports a 3% improvement in fuel economy accompanied by a 35% reduction in NO_x and particulate emissions. Steel quill tubes connect the centrally located injectors to fuel lines, which are in turn connected to the fuel rail.

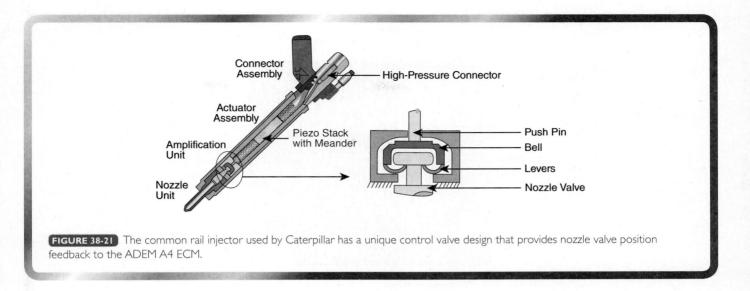

FIGURE 38-21 The common rail injector used by Caterpillar has a unique control valve design that provides nozzle valve position feedback to the ADEM A4 ECM.

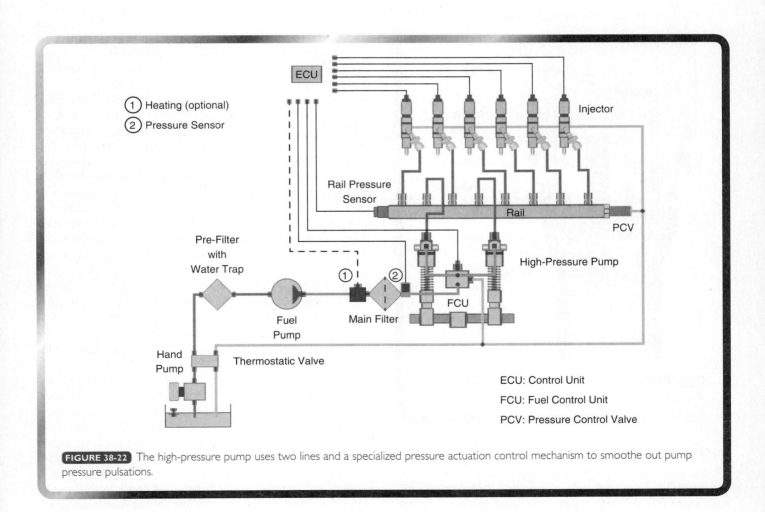

FIGURE 38-22 The high-pressure pump uses two lines and a specialized pressure actuation control mechanism to smoothe out pump pressure pulsations.

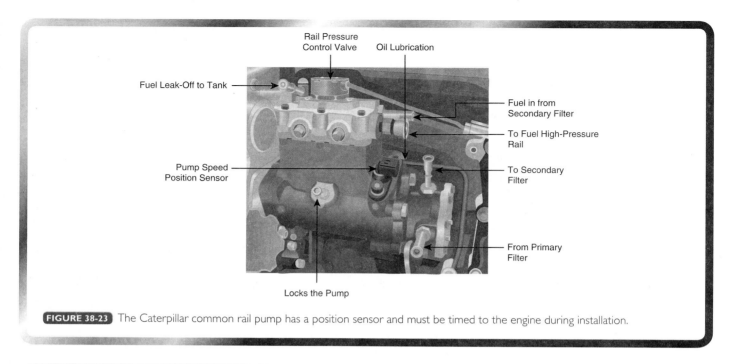

FIGURE 38-23 The Caterpillar common rail pump has a position sensor and must be timed to the engine during installation.

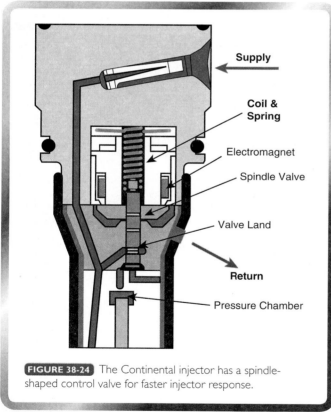

FIGURE 38-24 The Continental injector has a spindle-shaped control valve for faster injector response.

Injector Trim Codes

All injectors, including Caterpillar's, have slight construction variations due to manufacturing tolerances that result in differences in fuel delivery volumes. For example, even though injectors are made using identical processes on the same assembly line, changes in the size of very small internal injector passageways, coil resistances, spray hole diameter, length and smoothness, plunger clearances, and many other factors inevitably happen as machine tooling wears or the quality of parts changes. If the same electrical signal is applied to identical injectors supplied with exactly the same fuel pressure, no two injectors will produce precisely identical delivery volumes. The result is uneven cylinder pressures, which do not significantly affect engine performance but produce excessive emissions. To correct for variations in flow rates between injectors, Caterpillar assigns an **E-trim** code to compensate for variations in injection quantity **FIGURE 38-25**. The code is used by the ECM to change the timing and duration of the electrical signal used to energize the injector. E-trim codes, like all other calibration codes, are generated by testing injectors on fuel flow benches. Injectors are typically placed in a fixture and operated for a set number of cycles. The quantity of fuel delivered by the injectors is measured and compared against baseline data for identical injectors. If the injector is slightly above or below a benchmark for flow rate, a specific code is assigned to the injector. After the injector is installed in the engine, or subsequent to an ECM replacement, the injector calibration code is entered into the ECM's fueling information, where software can compensate for flow differences.

Whenever Caterpillar ECMs are recalibrated, a process Caterpillar refers to as **flashing**, the calibration file must properly match the engine and ECM. Every flash file contains a unique **personality module code** that corresponds to the horsepower rating, engine family and the emission certification of the flash file. Caterpillar requires technicians to record two numbers when replacing an injector or ECM: an injector serial number and the injector confirmation code are located on the injector and are needed to install the correct E-trim file in the ECM **FIGURE 38-26** and **FIGURE 38-27**. Using proprietary service software called **Caterpillar Electronic Technician (Cat ET)**,

FIGURE 38-25 The injector calibration code used for this HI300 injector is 1544.

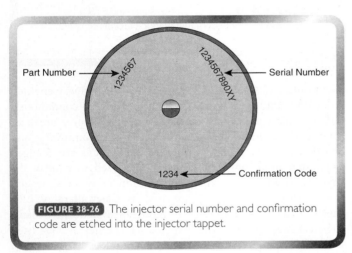

FIGURE 38-26 The injector serial number and confirmation code are etched into the injector tappet.

Part Number

Serial Number

Confirmation Code

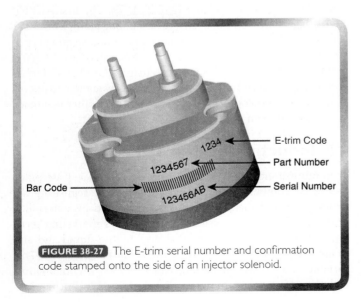

FIGURE 38-27 The E-trim serial number and confirmation code stamped onto the side of an injector solenoid.

E-trim Code

Part Number

Serial Number

Bar Code

the serial number is entered into the appropriate menu item in the <u>**Caterpillar Service Information System (Cat SIS)**</u>. Cat ET is the software used to perform Caterpillar electronic service or diagnostics. It is part of Cat SIS, which can be used as a web-based system or using DVDs to access all of Caterpillar's product information, service bulletins, and service manuals. The calibration file for the injector is downloaded from the company's web-based servers or from a DVD when web access is not available and installed in the ECM. To prevent tampering with calibration files or to verify the correct file is downloaded into the ECM, the software may prompt the technician to supply the confirmation code to ensure the technician has actually handled the injector. The confirmation code is a randomly generated code that matches a specific serial number or set of serial numbers. If the confirmation code and serial number do not match, the file will not upload to the ECM. If Cat ET displays a four-digit E-trim code, use the four-digit confirmation code on the injector. If Cat ET displays a 12-digit injector serial number, enter the injector serial number, then load the new flash file for that serial number.

TECHNICIAN TIP

When a flash file is loaded into a new ECM, the file's personality module code is stored in its memory. If a different flash file is later loaded, the two codes are compared. If the updated personality module code is not compatible with the original code, the flash file upload will stop and the ECM will not allow any file to be written to it. A Caterpillar diagnostic 630-2 code is activated with the description "Personality Module Code," and the ECM becomes "bricked" and will only allow the engine to idle. Unless a factory-authorized password is obtained to unlock the ECM, it becomes unusable and will require replacement.

TECHNICIAN TIP

E-trim or injector calibration codes are assigned to and printed on each injector during production. The alphanumeric code is recorded by the technician during installation. The code is stored in the ECM using a diagnostic service tool. Failure to store the correct value for each cylinder can result in rough running condition and a fault code that illuminates the MIL light. Caterpillar fault code 268-02 along with the fault description "Injector Trim" typically means the ECM has detected a compatibility problem between the injector and its trim code.

Fuel Injection Parameters

Programmable software inside the ECM regulates fuel delivery and establishes limits on the amount of fuel injected into a cylinder. Several unique fueling control parameters are used by Caterpillar to govern injection. One governor limit used by Caterpillar is the <u>**FRC limit**</u>, or fuel rate control limit. This variable, which is reported in cubic millimeters, refers to the maximum quantity of fuel that can be injected for a given engine speed and load condition. When observed using an electronic service tool, the FRC number appears to change when the engine is operating. This happens because the number is a limit to the amount of fuel that can be injected based on intake manifold air pressure and engine rpm. To prevent overfueling and smoke or other emissions, the FRC limit is continuously calculated and used to control the air–fuel ratio. A higher intake manifold air pressure allows the ECM to increases the FRC limit because more air is present in the cylinders to support combustion. When the ECM increases the FRC limit, more fuel is not necessarily injected; it simply reports the new calculation. The FRC limit is a useful diagnostic tool that can help identify problems with emissions and engine fueling or air intake problems.

Rated fuel limit is another limit to the maximum amount of fuel required to produce the engine's horsepower at rated rpm, which is the maximum engine speed achievable under load. Exceeding rated speed will produce excess emissions because the combustion process will run out of time to completely burn fuel if the speed limit is exceeded. Exceeding rated fuel limit will produce excessive emissions because the air–fuel ratio will become too rich. Rated speed, rated fuel, and FRC limits are stored or calculated by the engine software and can only be changed by the manufacturer.

Two other fueling parameters used only by Caterpillar are **full load setting (FLS)** and **full torque setting (FTS)**. These numbers correspond to two points on an electronic torque rise curve or fuel map. The FTS locates a data point on the torque curve map for a specific rpm for peak torque and the maximum amount of fuel an engine will inject at peak torque. The FLS number also refers to a coordinate on the same curve for a maximum engine rpm limit and fuel quantity at rated speed. Together the two numbers for power at peak torque and power at rated rpm establish the torque rise of an engine. The numbers do not follow any particular pattern and are in a sense encrypted to prevent them from being easily altered by unauthorized tampering. If an engine is being re-rated for a change in horsepower or adjusted for use in another application, the numbers need to be changed. For example, removing an engine from a highway tractor and placing it into a vocational vehicle such as a dump truck chassis will require a change to the FLS and FTS **FIGURE 38-28**. Similarly, changing tire diameters or rear axle ratios, or modifying the engine to produce more or less power requires supplying the factory with specific information such as the tire size, axle ratio, transmission information, ECM time, and personality module codes to allow the factory to generate new correct FLS and FTS numbers. If the numbers are not correctly chosen, or the wrong ones have been programmed into the ECM based on incorrectly supplied data, the engine can lose or increase power, the fuel economy will be altered, and other performance problems will result. The maximum cylinder pressure can also be exceeded and the engine can be destroyed due to cracked or burnt pistons.

▶ ACERT

To meet the 2004 EPA emissions requirements, Caterpillar introduced what they referred to as Advanced Combustion Emissions Reduction Technology (ACERT), which is a marketing term used to collectively describe all the emissions strategies Caterpillar

FIGURE 38-28 The fuel parameters FLS and FTS correspond to points on a fuel map for fuel quantity and speed at peak torque and rated speed.

uses to meet EPA regulations for on- and off-highway engines. From 2004 until today, ACERT engines have been continuously refined to more precisely control the mass and temperature of air entering the cylinders, cylinder pressures, injection timing, and injection quantity. Combustion chamber designs are changed and faster, more powerful ECMs are utilized to control the engine and additional exhaust aftertreatment systems. Several major pieces of technology are used by Caterpillar's ACERT engines that center around the air induction system and exhaust aftertreatment systems. The first ACERT engines in 2004 used series turbocharging along with **variable intake valve actuation (VIVA)**, a type of variable valve timing that changes the time it takes the intake valve to close **FIGURE 38-29**. The first ACERT engines also used additional charge air cooling along with more sophisticated fuel injection systems with the rate-shaping capabilities needed to meet standards for lower emissions. In 2007, particulate filters and EGR systems were introduced on Caterpillar's vehicles. Caterpillar's other processes allowed them to put off using these technologies until several years after other manufacturers needed them to meet emissions requirements.

Air Induction Systems

To minimize emissions produced in the cylinder, Caterpillar optimized combustion conditions by precisely regulating air temperature and mass. The three systems used by Caterpillar to do this are its CGI system, which is Cat's marketing term for an EGR system; a system that uses both a liquid and air-to-air charge air cooler to reduce intake air temperatures; and variable intake valve actuation, which works in combination with the additional charge air cooling and series turbocharging.

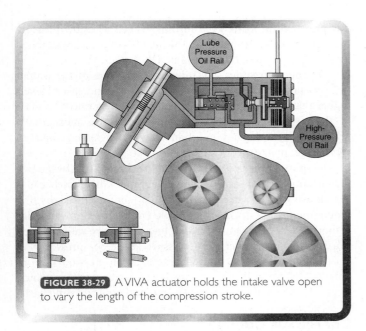

FIGURE 38-29 A VIVA actuator holds the intake valve open to vary the length of the compression stroke.

Variable Intake Valve Actuation

<u>Variable intake valve actuation (VIVA)</u> is used with series turbocharging on heavy-duty on-highway engines and operates to control cylinder pressures. With VIVA, the intake valve closing is variable and the intake valve is held open much longer. The principle of using late intake valve closing, referred to as the Miller cycle, was developed in the 1940s. Miller cycle engines change the length of the compression stroke by changing the point in the operating cycle when the intake valve closes. Doing this enables Miller cycle engines to reduce NO_x emissions by as much as 30% after using a cooler intake air charge. Miller cycle engines also provide efficiency increases by allowing advanced injection timing and reducing the energy needed to compress air during the shortened compression stroke. Series turbocharging is used in ACERT engines to perform more of the job of compressing the intake air charge rather than using energy derived from the crankshaft. In fact, some Caterpillar ACERT engines will increase turbocharger boost to close to 65 psi (448 kPa). At this pressure, more air can be packed into the cylinders in a shorter amount of time. So, instead of closing the intake valve at 120–140 degrees before TDC, the intake closes at 120–53 degrees before TDC and still packs enough air mass into the cylinders. Under those conditions, the engine does not need to work as hard to compress air. Cooling pre-ignition air temperatures lowers the peak cylinder temperatures to a level below that needed to form NO_x.

When using VIVA, the Miller cycle does not work at low-speed, low-load operation because there would be no gain in efficiency in leaving the intake valve open later than normal. Electronic controls are needed to change the timing of the intake valve closing to enable conventional intake valve timing at low speeds and shorten the compression stroke at high speeds. In Caterpillar engines, the VIVA mechanism uses oil pressure to actuate a small piston, which is used to hold the intake valve open until the ECM determines when to close it **FIGURE 38-30**. The VIVA system is supplied oil pressure through a normally closed control valve that is electrically opened when the oil temperature is above 68°F (20°C) and the engine operates at 1100–2100 rpm at 20–100% torque. On the VIVA unit, the actuation solenoids are normally open. This means engine oil is supplied to the VIVA pistons continuously. Without energizing the actuator solenoids, the oil pressure, even though low, would extend the pistons when the intake valve is open. However, the force of the intake valve springs pushes the piston back into its bore when the intake valve closes. To hold the intake valve open, the actuation solenoid valve is energized, preventing oil from escaping from above the extended piston. When held open, the intake valves are held open 0.118" (3 mm). The intake valve remains open until the actuator solenoid is de-energized by the ECM.

FIGURE 38-30 The VIVAs use oil pressure to hold the intake valve open longer as engine boost pressure increases.

Two valves inside the VIVA control intake valve bounce when the intake rocker lever closes and the snubber valve controlling the velocity of the intake valve is de-energized. Because the VIVA can also incorporate the engine compression release brake on some engine models, additional control valves and solenoids are included in the VIVA housing.

Series Turbocharging

Series turbochargers use different sizes of compressor and turbine housings designated as high-pressure and low-pressure turbochargers. The low-pressure turbocharger has a smaller turbine and compressor housing than the high-pressure turbocharger. Its relatively smaller turbine housing responds quickly to engine load and minimal exhaust gas energy with virtually no lag at low speeds. Boost pressure increases rapidly at low speed and load conditions using this turbo **FIGURE 38-31**.

To supply air to the low-pressure turbocharger, fresh intake air is first pulled into the high-pressure turbocharger compressor housing because it encounters little resistance due to its larger housing. Output from the high-pressure turbocharger then passes into the inlet of the low-pressure turbocharger compressor housing. Under initial load, the low-pressure compressor turbocharger will reach maximum boost pressure and turbine speed quickly. However, due to its smaller size, the low-pressure turbine and compressor wheel cannot spin any faster and the second, high-pressure turbocharger begins speeding up as exhaust gas energy increases under engine load. As air inlet pressure supplied to the low-pressure turbocharger from the larger high-pressure turbocharger increases, boost pressure is multiplied in the low-pressure turbocharger. The low-pressure turbocharger turbine speed does not change because a wastegate or exhaust bypass valve diverts exhaust gases away from the low-pressure turbocharger's turbine wheel. The low-pressure turbocharger simply multiplies the inlet boost pressure supplied by the high-pressure turbocharger.

Arranged in series like this, multiplication of the output pressure takes place, causing boost pressure to increase to levels higher than either turbocharger could achieve alone. The mass of air moved and pressures developed are also substantially greater than what could be produced with single-stage or even variable geometry turbochargers (VGT).

By splitting the pressurization of the charge air between two turbochargers, both can operate at optimal efficiency because the housing and wheel sizes are not compromised by the requirement to perform over a wide engine load range. Series turbochargers can also operate at lower pressure ratios, which is a comparison between the pressure at the compressor inlet and outlet. With series turbochargers, a compression ratio of only 2–2.5:1 for each stage means lower rotating speeds, which improves the reliability of the bearings and other rotating parts.

Charge Air Cooling

Charge air coolers assist in the control of air intake temperature. Two coolers, a jacket water pre-cooler (JWPC) and an air-to-air-charge air cooler (ATAAC), reduce the temperature of boosted intake air. The JWPC, which circulates engine coolant, is used to cool the air before it enters the ATAAC after it leaves the low-pressure turbocharger. To prevent over cooling of the engine coolant during low load operation, coolant flow through the JWPC is blocked if the coolant temperature is below 20 °C (68 °F). An electrically controlled bypass valve is energized, and coolant cannot enter the JWPC. If the coolant temperature is above 20 °C (68 °F), the coolant bypass valve is opened enabling flow through the JWPC **FIGURE 38-32**.

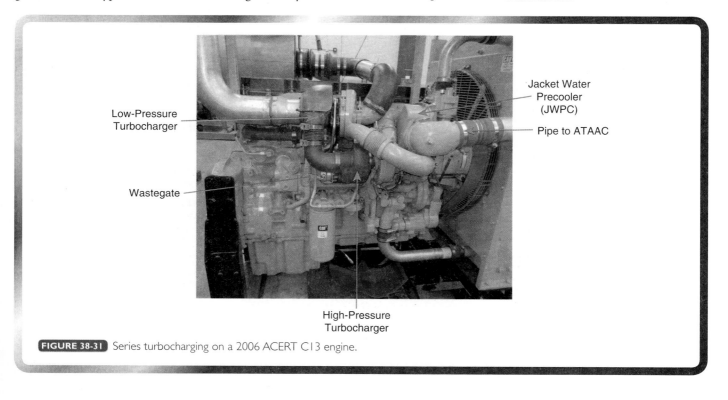

FIGURE 38-31 Series turbocharging on a 2006 ACERT C13 engine.

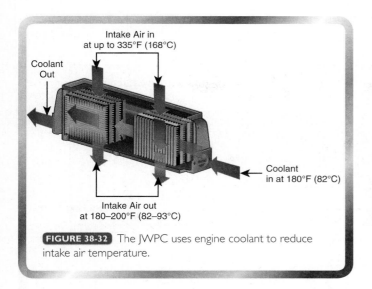

FIGURE 38-32 The JWPC uses engine coolant to reduce intake air temperature.

Clean Gas Induction

To meet EPA07 NO_x requirements, Caterpillar ACERT engine technology added a diesel particulate filter (DPF) for particulate matter (PM) reduction and cooled exhaust gas recirculation (CEGR). Caterpillar marketed the EGR system as CGI because it only recirculated exhaust gas derived after the DPF. This meant that no soot or other particulate is contained in the EGR gas,

which could contribute to abrasive wear of the intake valves, cylinder walls, or piston rings, or contribute to further soot loading of the engine oil. With less exhaust soot reintroduced into the cylinders through EGR, oil that becomes contaminated with soot scraped into the crankcase by the piston rings will have less contamination, and oil changes can be extended.

On heavy-duty engines, Caterpillar uses a low pressure EGR system that draws EGR gas from downstream of the DPF into the low-pressure turbocharger **FIGURE 38-33**. This system is unlike most other heavy-duty engines that use a high-pressure cooled EGR system using VGTs to create high-exhaust backpressure needed to drive large amounts of exhaust gas into the cylinders. On mid-range engines like the C7 and C9, Caterpillar uses a VGT high-pressure cooled EGR system.

The CGI system on heavy-duty diesels consists of a CGI line connecting the outlet of the DPF to the EGR cooler on the engine. A venturi combined with a pressure differential and temperature sensor between the CGI tube and cooler is used to measure the mass of EGR flow. As more exhaust gas is drawn into the engine, the pressure drop across the venturi increases proportionally to gas mass flow. Pressure sensor data combined with temperature data provide a measurement of gas density that is used by a speed density algorithm contained in engine software to calculate gas mass flow **FIGURE 38-34**.

After passing through the EGR cooler, which lowers exhaust temperature using engine coolant, EGR gas is metered into the engine through the electro-hydraulically controlled

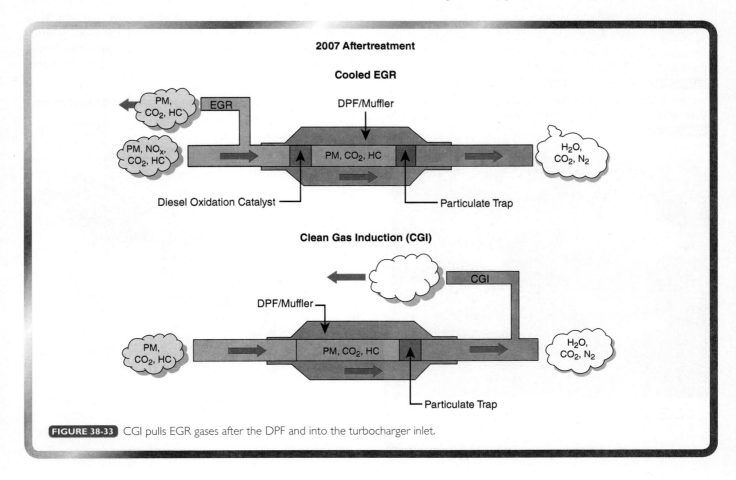

FIGURE 38-33 CGI pulls EGR gases after the DPF and into the turbocharger inlet.

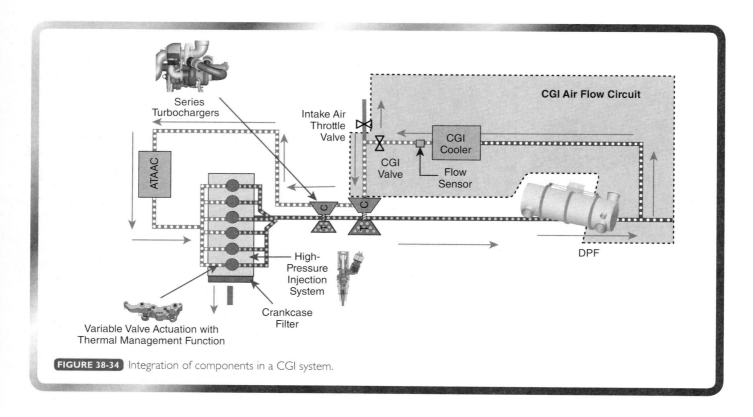

FIGURE 38-34 Integration of components in a CGI system.

CGI valve **FIGURE 38-35**. The valve contains a mixing door that controls the balance between fresh intake air entering the turbocharger inlet and the CGI passage containing exhaust gas. When no EGR flow is required, the mixing door on the valve completely seals off the CGI intake passage while allowing unobstructed flow of fresh air into the turbocharger inlet **FIGURE 38-36**. As more EGR flow is demanded, the mixing door opens progressively wider, increasing flow from the CGI cooler while progressively obstructing fresh air intake flow **FIGURE 38-37**.

Exhaust Aftertreatment

For 2004 ACERT engines, Caterpillar used an oxidation converter similar to the technology used by spark ignition gasoline fueled engines. Due to diesel's cooler, air-rich exhaust, an aluminum oxide (Al_2O_3) wash coat is applied to the catalyst

FIGURE 38-35 EGR gas is metered into the air intake using a valve that opens a passage to the EGR cooler.

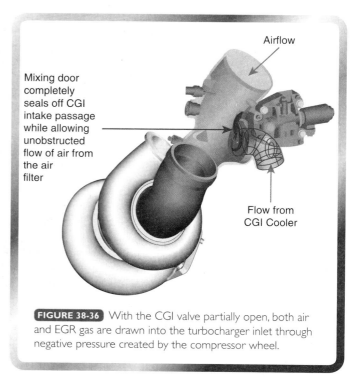

FIGURE 38-36 With the CGI valve partially open, both air and EGR gas are drawn into the turbocharger inlet through negative pressure created by the compressor wheel.

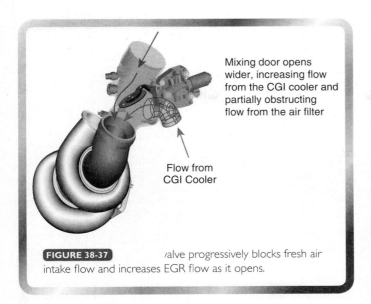

FIGURE 38-37 ...valve progressively blocks fresh air intake flow and increases EGR flow as it opens.

substrate to give it more absorption area. The wash coat is a water-based slurry containing metals such as platinum and palladium that act as a catalyst to speed up the breakdown of noxious emissions. Because aluminum oxide provides more surface area to absorb emissions, it improves the catalyst efficiency by storing emissions on its surface when the catalyst is cold.

Caterpillar Regeneration System

In 2007, Caterpillar introduced its DPF system called the **Caterpillar regeneration system (CRS)**. Like other DPF systems it uses a wall-flow filter to trap soot. To prevent the filter from plugging with soot, the filter can be regenerated two ways. One method is through a catalytic acceleration of soot oxidation using natural exhaust heat that is present when the engine is loaded. A second process, which complements the passive regeneration process that does not need engine control system intervention, is an active regeneration of the DPF. Active regeneration involves periodic supplemental heating of the catalyst by superheating engine exhaust gas using a device that operates similarly to the furnace of a flame thrower FIGURE 38-38 . Diesel fuel is injected into the

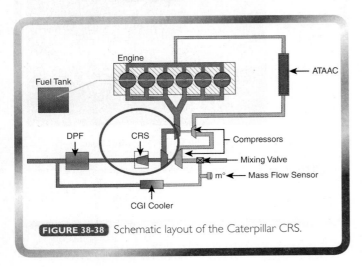

FIGURE 38-38 Schematic layout of the Caterpillar CRS.

exhaust stream after the turbocharger, where its vaporization is enhanced using a swirl plate. Fuel mixed with supplemental air flow is ignited by a spark plug. The additional exhaust heat drives up the temperature of the catalyzed cordierite particulate filter substrate burning-off any trapped soot. No late post-combustion in the cylinder injection event is used, as it is common in other DPF systems. There is no oxidation catalyst in the DPF housing either because supplemental heating is performed by the after-treatment regeneration device (ARD) head. Engines rated for less than 500 hp (373 kW) require only one DPF, while engines with 550 hp (410 kW) require dual filters. Caterpillar also offers a variety of warning lights and switches. A standard DPF warning lamp is used to inform the driver to change driving habits or initiate an active regeneration of the DPF. A high exhaust temperature light and a derate lamp indicate engine shut-down is imminent due to extreme operating conditions.

The DPF contains inlet and outlet exhaust temperature sensors plus a pressure differential sensor to measure the pressure drop across the DPF filter. These sensors are used to comply with emissions system manufacturer diagnostics (EMD) to detect defects or abnormal operation of the DPF that could produce excessive emissions FIGURE 38-39 . Missing or broken catalyst substrate will produce unexpected pressure differences across the DPF, which will generate fault codes. Inactive substrate or abnormal system operation can likewise produce unexpected temperature changes that will generate fault codes or illuminate warning lights alerting the operator to excessive exhaust temperatures.

The CRS uses a number of additional devices and sensors to ensure the proper elements are available for supplemental heating. A **hydra combustion air valve (HCAV)** combined with a pressure differential sensor to measure the pressure drop across a venturi calculates the amount of supplemental air flow supplied to the exhaust during active regeneration events FIGURE 38-40 . A CRS control valve is used by the ECM to regulate air flow to the exhaust based on data from the pressure differential sensor. A variety of fuel control valves regulate fuel flow to the ARD to supply a pilot and main fuel supply to the device FIGURE 38-41 . Temperature sensors monitor the ARD flame length and the operation of the ARD. To maintain a clean fuel nozzle in the ARD head, the nozzle is purged with compressed air after an active regeneration event.

Regeneration Strategies

An example of the operation of the CRS for an on-highway C13 provides insight to the operation of the DPF. Before a parked or stationary regeneration can occur, the following conditions must be met:

- Check that the exhaust outlet is clear of any combustible debris such as grass, tree branches, or garbage. The DPF warning lamp is illuminated either on solid or flashing.
- While making a service brake application, cycle the automated transmission shift selector by pressing NEUTRAL—DRIVE—NEUTRAL. Then leave in NEUTRAL.
- While making a service brake application, cycle the park brake ON—OFF—ON and leave the park brake applied.

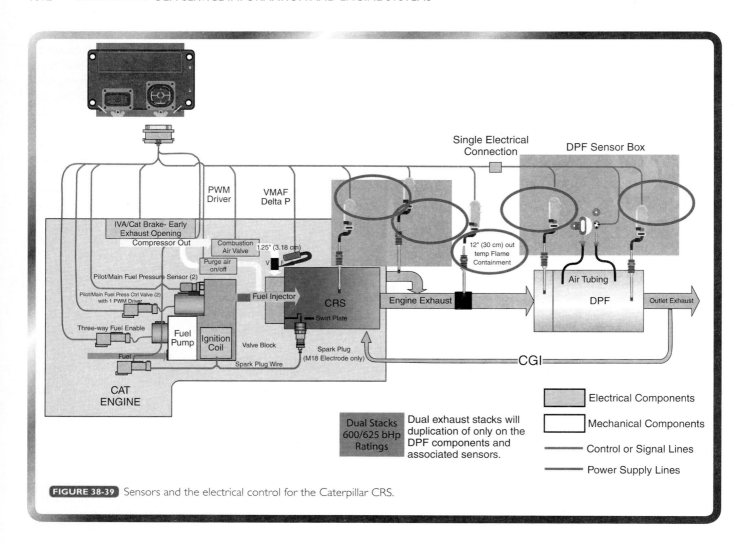

FIGURE 38-39 Sensors and the electrical control for the Caterpillar CRS.

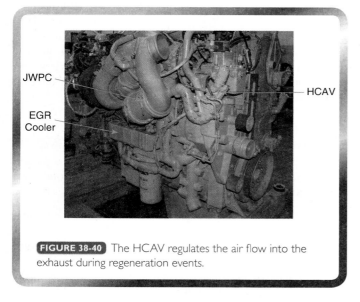

FIGURE 38-40 The HCAV regulates the air flow into the exhaust during regeneration events.

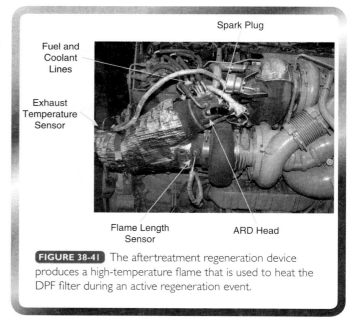

FIGURE 38-41 The aftertreatment regeneration device produces a high-temperature flame that is used to heat the DPF filter during an active regeneration event.

- Turn off the air-conditioning/HVAC system OFF.
- Ensure vehicle speed is 0 mph.
- Run the engine at low idle, release the service brake, and ensure that engine coolant temperature is above 140°F (60°C).
- Press the regeneration switch to the INITIATE position for 5 seconds and release. Do not move the switch to the REGEN INHIBIT position.

During a normal stationary regeneration event, the DPF lamp will turn OFF for the duration of regeneration and engine rpm will rise to 1400 rpm. The engine cooling fans will turn ON. As the exhaust system heats up, the high exhaust temperature (HET) lamp will light up after 3 minutes of operation and remain illuminated until the exhaust temperature falls below a predetermined threshold after the regeneration has taken place. The regeneration events will last 20–40 minutes depending on the level of soot load in the DPF. Once completed, the engine rpm will return to idle and the cooling fans will switch off. If the regeneration needs to be disabled, the regeneration switch can be toggled to the INHIBIT position for 5 seconds, or the ignition switch can be turned off FIGURE 38-42.

Caterpillar Electronics

All CT series trucks come equipped with a standard telematics system called Product Link. Product Link also includes a management system that tracks vehicle operation in real time, alerting for pending service intervals and service checklists to schedule preventive maintenance. Fuel consumption, location, service history, odometer readings, and operating hours update wirelessly. Even working versus idle time, movement outside authorized areas, and alerts can be configured to identify abuse and harsh operation and minimize inefficient vehicle use.

Caterpillar Service Information System (SIS) is a software suite that contains not only searchable service information specific to products, but also has diagnostic software called Caterpillar Electronic Technician or Cat ET. SIS also contains engine calibration files for reflashing an engine's ECM with new look-up tables and operating algorithms. SIS software can supply service letters and technical service bulletins, extract and download trip information data used to help manage equipment operation, look up and order parts, and even send part order requests online.

Caterpillar Sensors

Caterpillar sensors can sometimes use a reference voltage other than +5 Vref. For example, 8- and 12-volt sensors are commonly used for throttle position sensors. The ECM monitors the signal voltage from the sensor in order to detect a problem in the circuit. J-1939 fault codes are used in addition to Caterpillar's own fault codes. What is different with Caterpillar's sensor faults is the use of high- and low-bias measurements of signal voltage. Most other manufactures use high-bias sensors for two-wire sensors such as thermistors. This means an open circuit will produce a fault mode indicator (FMI) of 3 that is described as shorted high or voltage high. Disconnecting a two-wire Caterpillar thermistor sensor, however, will produce an FMI of 4, which is described as voltage low or shorted low. Furthermore, the circuit monitoring is different with a unique arrangement of pull-up and pull-down resisters for fault detection. Conditions that cause a low-voltage code with an FMI of 4 include moisture in a connector and melted or worn insulation that allows the sensor wires to connect and create a short circuit. These

Event	Condition	
HET Lamp is illuminated	Vehicle speed less than 5 mph (8 km/h), exhaust temperature greater than 842°F (450°C)	
DPF Lamp is illuminated	DPF greater than 63% loaded	
Check Engine Lamp is illuminated	DPF greater than 75% loaded	
Stop Engine Lamp is illuminated	DPF 100% loaded	
Manual Regen Switch	Activate when DPF lamp is illuminated	
Disable Switch	Always active	

FIGURE 38-42 The operation of lights and switches for the Caterpillar CRS.

conditions would produce the same FMI 4 code in other manufacturer's diagnostics.

Conversely, most active three-wire sensors used by other manufacturers are low-bias sensors, which produce an FMI of 4 when disconnected. The opposite is true of a Caterpillar active three-wire sensor. When disconnected, these sensors will produce a shorted high or voltage high FMI of 3. This means they are high-bias type sensors. Whenever checking Caterpillar sensors, remember that they have a much longer bounce period to detect a fault and will not log a code for 30 seconds after a fault has occurred. So, when jumping sensor pins and wiring harnesses to quickly check faults, 30 seconds will elapse before a code will change from and FMI of 3 to 4 or vice versa. Reference voltage and zero volt return or ground circuits are also monitored by Caterpillar electronics. Any open Vref or sensor ground will produce a fault code FIGURE 38-43 .

► Maintenance of Caterpillar Vehicles

Exchanging Injectors

Moving an injector from one cylinder to another can help determine if a combustion-related problem was caused by an injector or a mechanical condition in the cylinder. If two injectors currently installed in the engine are exchanged between cylinders, the injector trim files can also be quickly exchanged using the Exchange command on the Injector Trim Calibration screen within Cat ET. Select the two injectors that will be exchanged and press the OK button. After the transaction has taken place, a field within Cat ET called the tattletale will

increase by one. A tattletale is Caterpillar's method for indicating how many times a particular parameter or operation was performed. Tattletales are specific to the ECM and are helpful when diagnosing ECM-related problems caused by incorrect or inadvertent changes to programmable parameters. If a complaint for a poorly performing engine has coincided with a parameter change, the tattletale will easily identify the altered parameter, which enables the technician to quickly and correctly reset.

To exchange injectors, follow the guidelines in SKILL DRILL 38-1 .

Programming or Updating the Flash File

Flash programming is a method of programming or updating the flash file in an ECM. Cat ET can be utilized to program a new flash file into the ECM. The programming is accomplished by transferring the data from a PC to the ECM.

To program a flash file, follow the guidelines in SKILL DRILL 38-2 .

Viewing Caterpillar Proprietary Diagnostic Codes

Caterpillar uses two-digit proprietary diagnostic codes in addition to J-1939 fault codes. The Caterpillar codes can be obtained by counting the blinks or flashes of the check engine light (CEL), which correspond to code digits.

To view Caterpillar proprietary diagnostic codes, follow the steps in SKILL DRILL 38-3 .

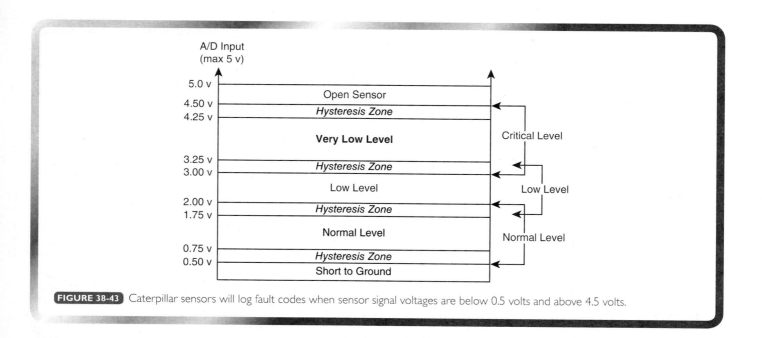

FIGURE 38-43 Caterpillar sensors will log fault codes when sensor signal voltages are below 0.5 volts and above 4.5 volts.

SKILL DRILL 38-1 Exchanging Injectors

1. Record the injector serial number and the injector confirmation code for each injector.

2. Click on Service Software Files in Cat SIS Web.

3. Enter the serial number for the injector in the search field.

4. Download the injector trim file to the PC. Repeat this procedure for each injector as required.

5. Connect Cat ET to the data link connector (DLC).

6. Select the following menu options on Cat ET:
   - Service
   - Calibrations
   - Injector Trim Calibration

7. Select the appropriate cylinder.

8. Click the Change button.

9. Select the appropriate injector trim file from the PC.

10. Click the Open button.

11. If you are prompted by Cat ET, enter the injector confirmation code into the field. Note: The injector serial number and the injector confirmation code are located on the injector. Cat ET may require the entry of injector confirmation code during this process. Cat ET will prompt you for the code if necessary.

12. Click the OK button. The injector trim file is loaded into the ECM.

13. Repeat the procedure for each cylinder as required.

SKILL DRILL 38-2 Programming a Flash File

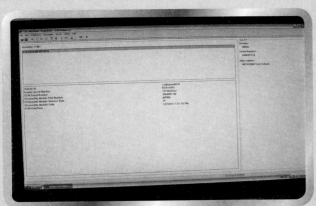

1. Obtain the part number for the new flash file. Note: If you do not have the flash file's part number, use the Flash File Search tool on the Service Technician Workbench (STW). Alternatively, use the Flash Software Files feature on Cat SIS Web. You must have the engine serial number in order to search for the flash file's part number.

2. Connect Cat ET to the DLC.

3. Turn the ignition key on and engine off. Do not start the engine.

4. Select WinFlash from the Utilities menu on Cat ET. Note: If WinFlash will not communicate with the ECM, refer to troubleshooting without a diagnostic code.

5. Select the engine ECM under the Detected ECMs.

6. Click the Browse button in order to select the part number of the flash file that will be uploaded or flashed into the ECM.

7. When the correct flash file is selected, click the Open button.

8. Verify that the file values match the application. If the file values do not match the application, search for the correct flash file.

9. When the correct flash file is selected, click the Begin Flash button. Cat ET will indicate when flash programming has been successfully completed.

10. Start the engine and check for proper operation.

11. Access the Configuration screen under the Service menu in order to determine the parameters that require programming. Look under the Tattletale column. All of the parameters should have a tattletale of 1 or more. If a parameter has a tattletale of 0, adjust that parameter.

SKILL DRILL 38-3 Viewing Caterpillar Proprietary Diagnostic Codes

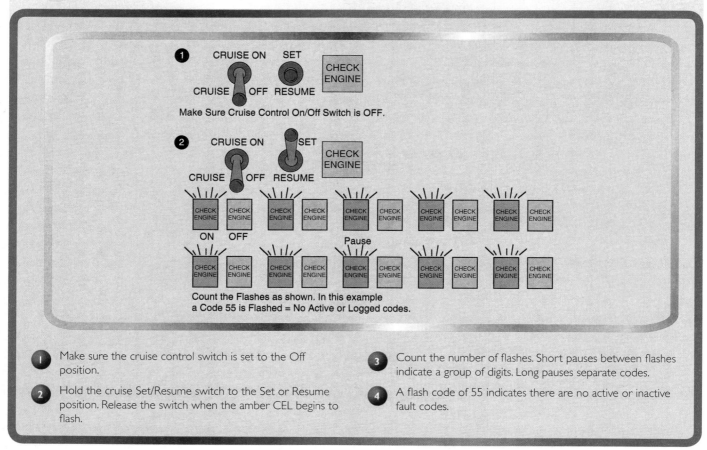

1. Make sure the cruise control switch is set to the Off position.

2. Hold the cruise Set/Resume switch to the Set or Resume position. Release the switch when the amber CEL begins to flash.

3. Count the number of flashes. Short pauses between flashes indicate a group of digits. Long pauses separate codes.

4. A flash code of 55 indicates there are no active or inactive fault codes.

Wrap-Up

Ready for Review

▶ Caterpillar is a well-known global manufacturer of construction and mining equipment, diesel and natural gas engines, power generators, and diesel-electric locomotives.

▶ Caterpillar introduced many innovations to diesel engines that were only considered luxuries by other manufacturers in the 1930s, such as enclosed pushrods, camshaft bearings, and oil bath air cleaners.

▶ Caterpillar introduced series turbocharging and variable valve timing to heavy-duty engines in 2004, which enabled the use of a Miller combustion cycle.

▶ Caterpillar is a vertically integrated manufacturer that produces all of the components making up its product and designs and manufactures its own engines.

▶ Caterpillar mid- and large-bore engines all use induction-hardened wet sleeves in cast iron engine blocks that have high tensile strength and use serpentine crankcase contours to increase rigidity.

▶ On higher horsepower engines, Caterpillar uses an overhead camshaft that enables higher injection pressure due to direct transfer of camshaft actuation force to the injector plunger.

▶ Caterpillar has used three types of electronic fuel injection systems since the late 1980s: electronic unit injection (EUI), hydraulically actuated electronic unit injectors (HEUI), and common rail.

▶ Caterpillar collaborated with Navistar in the 1980s and 1990s to develop HEUI A and B fuel systems.

▶ Caterpillar's C9.3, the C6.6 and C4.4 engines are built using the Caterpillar common rail fuel system designed by Continental, a major supplier to the automotive industry.

▶ To correct for variations in flow rates between injectors, Caterpillar assigns an E-trim code to compensate for variations in injection quantity. The code is used by the ECM to change the timing and duration of the electrical signal used to energize the injector.

▶ Programmable software inside the ECM regulates fuel delivery and establishes limits on the amount of fuel injected into a cylinder. Several unique fueling control parameters are used by Caterpillar to govern injection.

▶ The FRC limit, which is reported in cubic millimeters, refers to the maximum quantity of fuel that can be injected for a given engine speed and load condition.

▶ Two other fueling parameters used only by Caterpillar are full load setting (FLS) and full torque setting (FTS). These numbers correspond to two points on an electronic torque rise curve.

▶ To meet the 2004 EPA emissions requirements, Caterpillar introduced what they referred to as Advanced Combustion Emissions Reduction Technology (ACERT), which is a marketing term used to collectively describe all the emission strategies Caterpillar uses to meet EPA regulations for on- and off-highway engines.

▶ The first ACERT engines in 2004 used series turbocharging along with variable intake valve actuation (VIVA), a type of variable valve timing that changes the time the intake valve closes.

▶ In ACERT, additional charge air cooling is used along with more sophisticated fuel injection systems with the rate-shaping capabilities needed to meet standards for lower emissions.

▶ To meet EPA-07 NO_x requirements, Caterpillar ACERT engine technology added a diesel particulate filter (DPF) for PM reduction and cooled exhaust gas recirculation (CEGR).

▶ To minimize emissions produced in cylinder, Caterpillar optimizes combustion conditions by precisely regulating air temperature and mass.

▶ All CT series trucks come equipped with a standard telematics system called Product Link. Product Link also includes a management system that tracks vehicle operation in real time and alerts for pending service intervals and service checklists to schedule preventive maintenance.

Vocabulary Builder

Advanced Combustion Emissions Reduction Technology (ACERT) A name given to a wide variety of Caterpillar's emissions reduction technologies.

Advanced Diesel Engine Management (ADEM) Caterpillar's marketing name for its series of engine ECMs.

Caterpillar Electronic Technician (Cat ET) A piece of software within Caterpillars SIS system which performs engine diagnostic tests and changing of engine control parameters.

Caterpillar Regeneration System (CRS) Caterpillars marketing name given to its exhaust particulate filter system.

Caterpillar Service Information System (Cat SIS) A suite of Caterpillar software providing engine diagnostics, parts listings and service information.

clean gas induction (CGI) Caterpillar's marketing name given to its exhaust gas recirculation system.

E-trim The marketing name given by Caterpillar to describe the injector calibration code assigned to Caterpillar injectors.

flashing The process of uploading a new engine calibration file. A calibration file contains unique set of data or look-up tables needed by engine operating algorithms to control a particular engine model.

FRC limit Fuel rate control limit refers to the maximum quantity of fuel allowed for injection under a specific operating condition.

full load setting (FLS) A calibration number used to determine the maximum amount of fuel injected at rated speed. Along with the FTS, it shapes the engine's torque rise curve or slope.

full torque setting (FTS) A calibration number used to determine the maximum amount of fuel injected at peak torque. Along with the FLS, it shapes the engine's torque rise curve or slope.

high-mounted cams Refers to the location of an engine camshaft near the engine block deck. High-mounted camshafts enable the use of shorter, less heavy pushrods.

hydra combustion air valve (HCAV) An air supply valve used to regulate additional airflow into the exhaust system to support heating and regeneration in the exhaust aftertreatment system.

mechanically actuated electronically controlled unit injector (MEUI) Caterpillar's name for camshaft actuated electronic unit injectors.

Miller combustion cycle A modified four-stroke engine operating cycle that varies the closing of the intake valve.

pendulum gear dampener A patented camshaft gear design used for dampening torsional vibration transmission to the camshaft.

personality module code An engine ECM identification number used to determine which engine calibrations are allowed to be uploaded or flashed into the ECM.

spacer plate A plate located between the engine block deck and cylinder head used on high-horsepower Caterpillar engines. The plate reduces stress transmitted to the cylinder liners.

variable intake valve actuation (VIVA) A type of variable timing that changes the time it takes the intake valve to close.

Review Questions

1. A _____ is a calibration number used to determine the maximum amount of fuel injected at peak torque.
   a. full load setting
   b. full torque setting
   c. Miller combustion cycle
   d. Caterpillar Regeneration System

2. The calibration number used to determine the maximum amount of fuel injected at rate speed is called the _____.
   a. full load setting
   b. full torque setting
   c. Miller combustion cycle
   d. Caterpillar Regeneration System

3. Caterpillar named its _____ the Caterpillar Regeneration System.
   a. emission reduction system
   b. combustion trapping system
   c. exhaust particulate filter system
   d. clean gas induction system

4. A(n) _____ is a modified four-stroke engine operating cycle that varies the closing of the intake valve.
   a. advanced combustion emissions reduction technology
   b. full load setting
   c. Caterpillar Regeneration System
   d. Miller combustion cycle

5. _____ is a name given to a wide variety of Caterpillar's emissions reduction technologies.
   a. Caterpillar Regeneration System
   b. Advanced Combustion Emissions Reduction Technology
   c. Emission reduction system
   d. Clean gas induction system

6. Clean gas induction system is the name Caterpillar uses to identify its _____.
   a. exhaust gas recirculation system
   b. combustion trapping system
   c. emission reduction system
   d. clean gas induction system

7. On 2004 ACERT engines, Caterpillar used a(n) _____ converter similar to the technology used by spark ignition gasoline fueled engines.
   a. consumption
   b. cavitation
   c. oxidation
   d. recirculation

8. All CT series trucks come equipped with a standard _____ called Product Link.
   a. service information system
   b. telematics system
   c. executive management system
   d. diagnostic analysis system

9. The use of a _____ next to the liner flanges makes the liner less sensitive to height variations that lead to combustion and coolant leaks.
   a. pipe plug
   b. variable intake
   c. common rail
   d. spacer plate

10. Electronic unit injectors are located in a stainless-steel injector sleeve to prevent _____ erosion from the cooling system.
    a. cavitation
    b. oxidation
    c. regeneration
    d. combustion

ASE-Type Questions

1. Technician A says Caterpillar was the first company in the industry to introduce turbocharging. Technician B says Caterpillar was the first company in the industry to introduce dual overhead cam engines. Who is correct?
   a. Technician A
   b. Technician B
   c. Both Technician A and Technician B
   d. Neither Technician A nor Technician B

2. Technician A says Caterpillar named its exhaust gas recirculation system the environmental system. Technician B says Caterpillar uses the name Emission reduction system to identify its exhaust gas recirculation system. Who is correct?
   a. Technician A
   b. Technician B
   c. Both Technician A and Technician B
   d. Neither Technician A nor Technician B

3. Technician A says the 140-pin ADEM 4 ECM was introduced for ACERT engines and was used until the last 2009 on-highway engines were produced. Technician B says the 140-pin ADEM III was introduced for ACERT engines and was used until the last 2009 on-highway engines were produced. Who is correct?
   a. Technician A
   b. Technician B
   c. Both Technician A and Technician B
   d. Neither Technician A nor Technician B

4. Technician A says every flash file contains a unique personality module code that corresponds to the horsepower rating, engine family, and the emission certification of the flash file. Technician B says every flash file contains a unique E-trim code that corresponds to the horsepower rating, engine family, and the emission certification of the flash file. Who is correct?
   a. Technician A
   b. Technician B
   c. Both Technician A and Technician B
   d. Neither Technician A nor Technician B

5. Technician A says fuel consumption rate is a fueling parameter used by Caterpillar that corresponds to a point on an electronic torque rise curve or fuel map. Technician B says the full load setting is a fueling parameter used by Caterpillar that corresponds to a point on an electronic torque rise curve or fuel map. Who is correct?
   a. Technician A
   b. Technician B
   c. Both Technician A and Technician B
   d. Neither Technician A nor Technician B

6. Technician A says Caterpillar's first diesel engine, the D9900 produced only 89 horsepower at 700 rpm. Technician B says Caterpillar's first diesel engine, the D9900, weighed 5175 pounds. Who is correct?
   a. Technician A
   b. Technician B
   c. Both Technician A and Technician B
   d. Neither Technician A nor Technician B

7. Technician A says the H1B-300 injector is capable of three different injection rate shapes and an electrically controlled pilot injection. Technician B says the H1B-300 injector is capable of four different injection rate shapes and an electrically controlled pilot injection. Who is correct?
   a. Technician A
   b. Technician B
   c. Both Technician A and Technician B
   d. Neither Technician A nor Technician B

8. Technician A says the continental's duo-servo actuated common rail injector design is the first of its kind that can produce three different injection rate shapes. Technician B says unlike other common rail systems, Caterpillar's normally open common rail pump actuators will allow fuel to drain from the rail within a minute of engine shutdown. Who is correct?
   a. Technician A
   b. Technician B
   c. Both Technician A and Technician B
   d. Neither Technician A nor Technician B

9. Technician A says when using variable intake valve actuation, the Miller cycle does not work during low-speed, low-load operation. Technician B says when using a variable intake valve actuation, the Miller cycle does work during low-speed, low-load operation. Who is correct?
   a. Technician A
   b. Technician B
   c. Both Technician A and Technician B
   d. Neither Technician A nor Technician B

10. Technician A says Caterpillar sensors have a much longer bounce period to detect a fault and will not log a code for 25 seconds after a fault has occurred. Technician B says Caterpillar sensors have a much longer bounce period to detect a fault and will not log a code for 35 seconds after a fault has occurred. Who is correct?
    a. Technician A
    b. Technician B
    c. Both Technician A and Technician B
    d. Neither Technician A nor Technician B

CHAPTER 39
Volvo–Mack and PACCAR

Knowledge Objectives

After reading this chapter, you will be able to:

1. Outline the development of Volvo–Mack and PACCAR engine manufacturing. (pp 1102–1125)
2. Classify Volvo–Mack and PACCAR engine models according to original equipment manufacturer (OEM) descriptions. (pp 1102–1109, 1124–1125)
3. Identify and describe unique features of Volvo–Mack and PACCAR. (pp 1102–1130)
4. Identify and describe unique construction features of Volvo–Mack and PACCAR engines. (pp 1102–1130)
5. Identify service software used by Volvo–Mack and PACCAR. (pp 1103–1104, 1128–1130)
6. Describe and explain the purpose of adjustable parameters for Volvo–Mack engines and fuel systems. (pp 1108–1112)
7. Identify and describe Volvo–Mack and PACCAR fuel system types and operation. (pp 1109–1112, 1125–1128)
8. Outline and explain the flow of fuel through Volvo–Mack low-pressure fuel systems. (p 1110)
9. Identify and describe the purpose of an exhaust pressure governor (EPG). (pp 1113–1114)
10. Differentiate between internal EGR and high-pressure cooled EGR systems. (pp 1118–1121)
11. Describe the purpose and operation of internal EGR systems. (p 1118)
12. Describe the operation of Volvo–Mack and PACCAR aftertreatment systems. (pp 1117–1125, 1128–1130)
13. Identify the consequences of tampering with the aftertreatment system. (pp 1121–1124)

Skills Objectives

After reading this chapter, you will be able to:

1. Bleed a Volvo–Mack fuel system. (p 1112) **SKILL DRILL 39-1**
2. Drain the charge air cooler. (p 1124) **SKILL DRILL 39-2**
3. Adjust for engine idle shutdown. (p 1130) **SKILL DRILL 39-3**

You Are the Technician

A customer has brought a 2014 Mack dump truck with a low power complaint to your shop. After performing a preliminary inspection of the vehicle, you find there are numerous fault codes associated with the selective catalytic reduction (SCR) system. These faults include codes for the NO$_x$ sensors, diesel exhaust fluid (DEF) quality, a dosing valve failure, DEF pumps, and so on. After closer inspection of the SCR system you find a DEF dosing line to the dosing valve is pinched closed by a pair of locking pliers. After removing the pliers and filling the DEF reservoir, the SCR system becomes functional again. When the fault codes are erased and the engine is operated to run the aftertreatment monitor, the repair to the SCR system is validated with a readiness code. While writing a description on a work order for the diagnosis and work performed, consider the following:

1. What was the likely cause of the low power complaint?
2. Why might there be numerous other aftertreatment SCR fault codes caused by a blocked DEF line?
3. Explain why it is important to erase the fault codes and have the SCR emission monitor run before returning the vehicle to the customer.

▶ Introduction

Volvo, Mack, Kenworth, and Peterbilt are major North American truck and bus manufacturers that all have large European stakeholders. Volvo and Mack are a single corporate entity, while Kenworth and Peterbilt are part of PACCAR, Inc., a global producer of premium medium- and heavy-duty trucks. PACCAR, with headquarters in Bellevue, Washington, has design and manufacturing divisions that include Netherlands-based DAF Trucks and the UK-based Leyland Trucks. Engines used by these companies have designs originating in Europe, which is reflected in a number of construction features including compact profiles to fit into smaller engine compartments of cab over vehicles and unique cold-weather operational features intended for use in northern European climates. These diesels also have numerous weight-reducing features along with low emissions and superior fuel efficiency. These features help adapt the engines for the European market with its higher sensitivity to the environment and fuel costs, which are among the most expensive in the world.

▶ The Volvo Group Trucks

With headquarters in Gothenburg, Sweden, Volvo is an integrated manufacturer of heavy-duty vehicles and engines and is ranked the world's second-largest heavy-duty truck brand behind Daimler Trucks. Volvo built its first truck in Sweden in 1928, but it is one of the most recent additions to North American truck manufacturing. Volvo gained a major presence in the North American market in the 1970s after it bought the assets of White Motor Company, a maker of trucks and farm equipment. In 1986, Volvo expanded further after entering into a joint venture with General Motors' heavy truck division to form a new company, the Volvo GM Heavy Truck Corporation. Nameplates for vehicles they sold included Volvo, White, GMC, and Autocar. In the 1990s the remaining shares of GM's truck division were purchased by Volvo with the new organization becoming Volvo Trucks of North America, with main operations located in Greensboro, North Carolina.

The European quality, reliability, and fuel efficiency of Volvo trucks increased the brand's popularity among customers for long-distance freight, construction, and pick-up delivery operations. During the 1990s, Volvo also purchased Prevost buses, a Canada-based manufacturer of transit buses, luxury touring coaches, specialty bus conversions, and shells for high-end motorhomes. One of the largest evolutionary steps of the company came in 2000, when Volvo acquired Renault Vehicles Industry (RVI), which also had previously purchased Mack Trucks. The deal made Volvo the largest European heavy vehicle maker but required dropping their popular low-cab-over-engine (LCOE) vehicles to satisfy European financial regulators. Mack and Volvo remained distinctive brands until 2009 when the company was reorganized into Volvo Group Trucks. Mack operations were joined together with Volvo, but both vehicles continue to be manufactured as distinctive models within the group but share common chassis and engine components. Though similar, Mack's and Volvo's engine systems and features still carry different names and acronyms. The Volvo Group includes Nissan Diesel Trucks and Renault Trucks plus the manufacture of buses, construction equipment, and marine and industrial engines.

Volvo Engine Lineup

Volvo made a popular D7 7L (427 cubic inch) engine for its medium-duty LCOE vehicles and a D9 for truck, bus, marine, and off-road applications. However, Volvo is best known in the bus and truck industry for its earlier D12 12L (732 cubic inch) engine introduced in 1993, which Volvo claims was the highest-selling heavy-duty diesel engine model in the world in 2005. Four models of the D12 were used in North America. The D12-A was an overhead camshaft, inline six cylinder engine with multiple-piece cylinder heads (one for each cylinder). The D12-C is a single-piece cylinder head **FIGURE 39-1** and **FIGURE 39-2**. The overhead camshafts on all Volvo engines have a viscous torsional dampener to improve valve timing **FIGURE 39-3**. It was the first European electronically controlled engine with electronic unit injectors in an engine and had a very high 17.3:1 compression ratio. The off-road

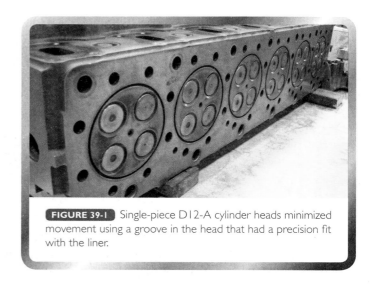

FIGURE 39-1 Single-piece D12-A cylinder heads minimized movement using a groove in the head that had a precision fit with the liner.

FIGURE 39-2 Liners for the Volvo D12 had a ridge that fit into a groove of the cylinder head and centered the head on the engine block.

FIGURE 39-3 A viscous torsional dampener is integral to the front camshaft gear of Volvo overhead camshaft engines.

model had an even higher compression ratio of 18.1:1. The D12-A and D12-B, which had minor differences in the fuel system, were manufactured from 1993 to 1998. A D12-C was made from 1998 to 2002. The D12-C differs from earlier versions with a completely redesigned single-piece cylinder head, front timing gears, and the addition of a <u>**stiffening plate**</u> bolted to the crankcase oil pan

FIGURE 39-5 The stiffening plate bolted to the oil pan rails of the D12-C minimized crankcase distortion in engines with higher power output.

FIGURE 39-4 The front timing gears of a Volvo D12 engine.

rails **FIGURE 39-4** and **FIGURE 39-5**. The modest output of the D12-A and B engines was increased to 460 hp (343 kW) in the C engine. A D12-D used from 2002 to 2005 featured a dual-solenoid Delphi E3 unit fuel injector having ultra-high fuel injection pressure (UHFP), with maximum fuel injection pressures increased to 35,000 psi (2413 bar)—20% over the Volvo D12-B. Volvo's <u>**V-pulse EGR**</u> system used only in vocational trucks and industrial engines did not use a variable geometry turbocharger (VGT) to increase exhaust backpressure. Instead, the natural exhaust pressure pulsation in the exhaust manifold passing through a set of one-way check valves delivered recirculated exhaust gases to the engine intake to achieve NO_x reductions.

Volvo engine electronics were initially called the <u>**VECTRO**</u> electronic control system and had self-diagnostic capabilities that went through increasing stages of sophistication with each new set of emission regulations. In 2000, the VECTRO system received J-1934 on-board network communication capabilities. Volvo used a diagnostic and service programing package called <u>**Volvo Computer-Aided Diagnostics Systems (VCADS)**</u>. By

2007 the engine electronics were adapted to handle the additional requirements of the exhaust aftertreatment system operation. This later system, termed **Advanced Electronics Engine Management System(EMS)**, incorporated aftertreatment system control into the engine ECM, which in turn regulated the operation of a separate aftertreatment control module. Volvo's current diagnostic software is called **Premium Tech Tool**.

New Generation Volvo D Engines

In 2006 Volvo introduced an entirely the new family of Volvo and Mack diesels: the D11, D13, and D16 engines designed to meet the EPA-07 emissions standards. Volvo's D-series engines correspond to the Mack Power or MP engines, which are the MP7, MP8, and MP10 `TABLE 39-1` and `FIGURE 39-6`. Together all the Volvo engines share a 94% parts commonality in design and function. Basic features of the engines include an inline six cylinder overhead cam design using EMS, a rear engine-mounted gear train with an overhead camshaft, and the dual solenoid Delphi E3 injector `FIGURE 39-7`. The Delphi injector, described in the Electronic Unit Injectors and Unit Pumps chapter, used **ultra-high-pressure injection (UHPI)**, up to 35,000 psi (2413 bar) injection pressures with the ability to perform multiple injection events `FIGURE 39-8`. A cooled high-pressure exhaust gas recirculation (EGR) system with a Holset VGT operates with an electronically regulated oil pressure actuated EGR valve. Volvo continued to use its own successful and reliable engine braking system, the Volvo exhaust brake (VEB), integrated with the exhaust rocker lever that resembles the operation of the D12 engine brake system.

▶ Mack Trucks

When thinking about tough, rugged, heavy-duty vocational trucks, one of the first associations people make is to the Mack nameplate. Mack's reputation goes back a century when Mack trucks were purchased by the British government to run troop supplies in World War I. Soldiers nicknamed the supply vehicle the "Bulldog Mack" due to the blunt hoods that resembled an English bulldog's snout. The name stuck with the truck and the bulldog emblem was made the official corporate logo in 1922.

FIGURE 39-6 The Mack Power MP series engines share a common platform with Volvo's engines. This MP8 corresponds to Volvo's D13 engine.

Today, the Mack bulldog emblem is still found on the front of all Mack trucks: A gold-plated bulldog hood ornament indicates the entire truck is made of Mack components `FIGURE 39-9`. A chrome-plated bulldog designates trucks constructed using another manufacturer's transmission, engine, rear axles, or suspension system.

Mack Engine Innovation

Originally a streetcar builder, Mack's roots as a truck maker go back to 1907, when the Mack brothers built their first truck to diversify their manufacturing expertise. Its long heritage is marked with many innovative firsts, such as the use of drive shafts rather than chain drive powertrains. Power brakes, air suspension cabs, the use of charge air cooling, and the development of high torque rise engines are some of Mack's achievements. It was also one of the first engine manufacturers to use engine air and oil filters, doing so as early as 1918.

TABLE 39-1: Comparing Mack MP Engines and Volvo D-Series Engines

Mack Model	Volvo Model	Displacement	Power	Torque
MP7 (Current)	D11	10.8L (659 cubic inch) 17.0:1	Mack 325–405 horsepower (hp) (242–302 kilowatts [kW]) Volvo 365–405 hp (727–302 kW)	1200–1560 ft-lb (1627–2115 Nm) 1250–1550 ft-lb (1695–2102 Nm)
MP8 (Current)	D13	12.8L (781 cubic inch) 16.0:1	Mack 415–505 hp (309–377 kW) Volvo 375–500 hp (280–373 kW)	1480–1780 ft-lb (2007–2413 Nm) 1450–1750 ft-lb (1966–2377 Nm)
MP10 (Current)	D16	16.1L (982 cubic inch) 16.0:1	Mack 515–605 hp (384–451 kW) Volvo 500–600 hp (373–447 kW)	1880–2060 ft-lb (2549–2793 Nm) 1860–2050 ft-lb (2522–2779 Nm)
N/A	D12 (A, B, & C) (1993–2006)	12.1L (738 cubic inch)	Up to 460 hp (343 kW)	1350–1650 ft-lb (1830–2237 Nm)
E7 E-TECH (1987–2006)	E7 E-TECH (1987–2006)	11.9 L (726 cubic inch)	Up to 454 hp (339 kW)	1200–1660 ft-lb (1627–2251 Nm)

With the development of <u>high torque rise engines</u> in the early 1960s, Mack pioneered the concept of <u>gear fast run slow</u> engine operation **FIGURE 39-10**. This design strategy takes advantage of the diesel engine's very high, low-rpm torque to run a vehicle at highway speeds using fuel-efficient, low engine speed engine operation. Mack's line of high torque rise engines, marketed first as Maxidyne engines, operated in a range of 1050–1700 rpm, at first using an unconventional large stepped five-speed transmission. The class 8 highway tractor's transmission was complemented by Mack's very low rear axle ratios to move the truck at highway speeds. Transmission gearing, tire sizes, and rear axle ratios enabled the truck to cruise just above <u>peak torque</u> rpm, the point at which cylinder pressures are highest. When encountering a hill or increasing load, lowering vehicle speed, rather than downshifting, simultaneously causes engine rpm to lower. But rather than lose load moving power, the engine transitions more quickly into the peak torque

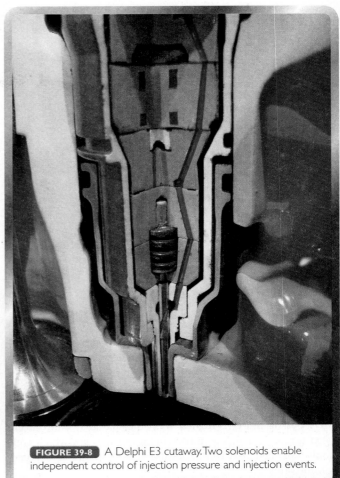

FIGURE 39-8 A Delphi E3 cutaway. Two solenoids enable independent control of injection pressure and injection events.

FIGURE 39-7 Mack and Volvo 2007+ engines use a rear gear train.

FIGURE 39-9 The gold-plated Mack bulldog hood ornament indicates the truck is made exclusively from Mack components.

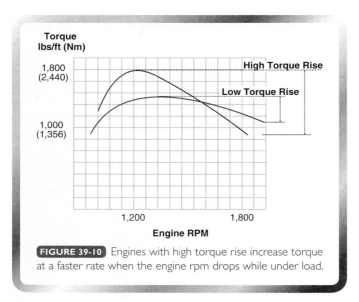

FIGURE 39-10 Engines with high torque rise increase torque at a faster rate when the engine rpm drops while under load.

FIGURE 39-11 Mack's E-TECH block uses cross-bolted main bearing caps, which increases block strength and reduces the size of the crankcase.

FIGURE 39-12 Mack E7s used mid-stop liners for reduced water jacket and engine block size.

range where engine load pulling ability is best. The increase in engine torque encountered at peak torque operating range allows the driver to remain in top gear longer without having to downshift to increase torque. If downshifting is minimized, engine rpm remains low and is accompanied with superior fuel economy and faster vehicle speeds than an engine operating at higher speeds with greater gear reduction. This peak torque "sweet spot" where pulling power is highest was not separated from cruising speed torque as much as other engines of the day, which commonly operated between 1800 and 2300 rpm using 10-speed transmissions.

Mack E7 E-TECH Engine

Mack engines used in low-speed vocational operations, rather than in on-highway trucks, were called Econodyne engines. Prior to being acquired by Volvo, successful engines made by Mack included the Econodyne E6, an 11L (672 cubic inch) inline 6 engine, and the E7 introduced in 1987, which was 11.9L (728 cubic inch). Mack also produced a powerful V8 diesel designated E9, which was a 16.4L (998 cubic inch) engine producing in excess of 500 hp (373 kW). Used in military applications such as tanks, the engine produced over 700 hp (522 kW). The E7 used mid-stop cylinder liners, a cross-bolted engine block, and other weight-saving features, which made it one of the lightest engines, reducing engine weight by as much as 800 lb (363 kg) compared to competitors' engines **FIGURE 39-11** and **FIGURE 39-12**. While more than 90% of class 8 diesel engines are rated between 300 and 450 hp (224 and 336 kilowatts [kW]), Mack's E7 12L (732 cubic inch) engine had power output of up to 454 hp (339 kW). This made the engine not only versatile, but allowed it to fit in smaller conventional chassis and vocational trucks with short hoods and setback front axles, and it could also haul heavier loads. Mack's E-TECH engine was a further refinement of its E7 pump-line-nozzle (PLN) injection pump. Four primary design features that differentiate the E-TECH engine from the E7 engine included replacement of the PLN injection pump with a Bosch electronic unit pump (EUP) fuel injection system, a V-MAC III electronic engine control system, a

serpentine poly V-belt drive system, and the J-Tech engine brake manufactured by Jacobs **FIGURE 39-13**. After merging with Volvo, Mack engine platforms were the same for 2007 midyear, when the 11L (671 cubic inch) MP7, 13L (793 cubic inch) MP8, and 16L (976 cubic inch) MP10 became available.

VMAC Fuel Systems

To meet standards for the first big reduction in engine emissions, Mack developed a partial-authority electronically controlled injection pump-line-nozzle (PLN) fuel system exclusively for the E7 engine. This first-generation vehicle management and control system, or VMAC I, was adapted to a Bosch P-7100 injection pump **FIGURE 39-14**. It replaced the internal mechanical governor with an electronically controlled governor and a

FIGURE 39-13 Bosch EUPs are used in the E-TECH engine. The pumps are engine camshaft actuated.

hydraulically controlled variable advance injection timing system. The injection timing advance system was termed the <u>**Econovance variable injection timing system**</u>. The VMAC II system introduced in 1994 included 30 programmable operating features such as trip-recording functions, driver event and maintenance logging to cruise control, PTO operation, idle shutdown, and emergency shutdown features.

The electronic road speed governor improved fuel economy and included self-diagnostics functions to identify fault codes. VMAC III was used from 1998 through to 2005 and dropped the multiple-plunger injection pump and adopted unit injection pump systems. VMAC IV was used from 2005 to 2009 and included a driver instrument panel display that allowed reading and erasing of diagnostic trouble codes (DTCs) and access to numerous maintenance monitors **FIGURE 39-15**.

The VMAC system used two electronic control units: a vehicle control unit in the cab (VECU) and an engine ECM (EECM) mounted on the engine block. Two distinctly different emission reduction strategies were used by Mack to meet the EPA emission requirements starting in October 2002, known as Mack ASET AI and AC. ASET is an acronym for <u>**application-specific engine technology**</u>. For on-highway vehicles such as the Vision and CH series vehicles, Mack ASET AC relied on the use of high-pressure cooled exhaust gas recirculation (HP-CEGR) technology. For its vocational trucks including the Granite, RD, RM, and DM chassis, ASET AI used an internal EGR system that incorporated an additional bump on the exhaust camshaft to briefly open the exhaust valves during intake stroke and allow exhaust gas to enter the cylinder.

CCRS Unit Pump System

Beginning in 2001, Mack began to phase in their unit pump system on the E-TECH engine. The inline multiple plunger pumps were replaced with Bosch manufactured unit pumps, which extended the lifecycle of the E7 block. Fuel is supplied to the unit pump through a fuel gallery passing through the block **FIGURE 39-16**. Unit pumps with wide cam lobes and roller-type cam followers reduced friction and have greater ability to inject fuel at higher pressure with increased fuel system durability. The pumps had rate-shaping capabilities, which means they could control the rate fuel is delivered into the cylinders.

FIGURE 39-14 The partial-authority governor replaced the mechanical governor mechanism with electrical components. Note the speed sensor, rack position sensors, and brushless torque motor that move the control rack.

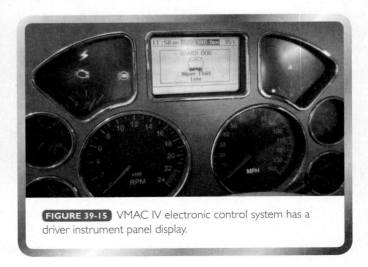

FIGURE 39-15 VMAC IV electronic control system has a driver instrument panel display.

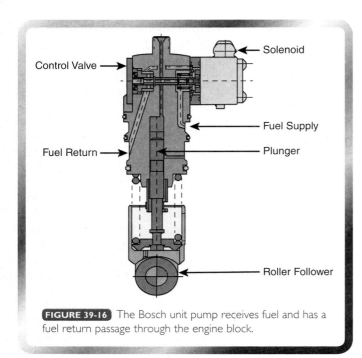

Control Valve

Solenoid

Fuel Supply

Fuel Return

Plunger

Roller Follower

FIGURE 39-16 The Bosch unit pump receives fuel and has a fuel return passage through the engine block.

For this reason, the system was called the **current-controlled rate shaping (CCRS)** fuel system.

The CCRS fuel system used two injection phases—essentially, a pilot and main injection event. The low-inertia stepped shaped control valve provided a boot sequence or pilot injection before the main injection. The boot sequence occurred just after the control valve began to move and allowed a small amount of fuel to pass across the control valve seat **FIGURE 39-17**. As the valve continued to open, a greater volume of fuel could enter the injection line and supply the bulk of the fuel for the

combustion event. The boot sequence enabled a shorter ignition delay period, which allowed main injection timing to be retarded and reduced the spike in cylinder pressures that usually follow a main injection event without a pilot injection. Mack claimed the system improved highway fuel economy, low speed idle stability, and engine braking performance.

Mack Power Engines

The first Mack Power (MP) engine brought to market-sharing Volvo platforms was the 11L (671 cubic inch) MP7. Like the MP8 and MP10 engine platforms that followed, it uses a rear-mounted gear train, an HP-CEGR system, the dual-valve Delphi E3 unit injector with UHPI, and a single overhead camshaft using four valves per cylinder **FIGURE 39-18**. Mid-stop wet sleeve cylinders help reduce engine weight and single-piece steel pistons enable it to withstand very high cylinder pressures and temperatures giving the engine tremendous power density (that is, produce maximum power from every cubic inch of displacement).

Each of the MP engine models fall within three engine families: the Econodyne for on-highway applications demanding the best fuel economy, the Maxidyne for vocational and construction vehicles, and the Maxicruise for multipurpose vehicles. Newer MP engines have **multi-torque** capabilities, which Mack and Volvo call the Eco-Torque Performance feature. Multi-torque capabilities means the engines have two different peak torque curves: a higher peak torque curve can be used on steep grades while a lower peak torque curve is used over regular terrain. The lower peak torque curve is the default when in the top two gears. The multi-torque capability is enabled only when the engine is in cruise mode. To enable feature unique to Mack and Volvo, a mass-based variable torque programmable parameter must be enabled.

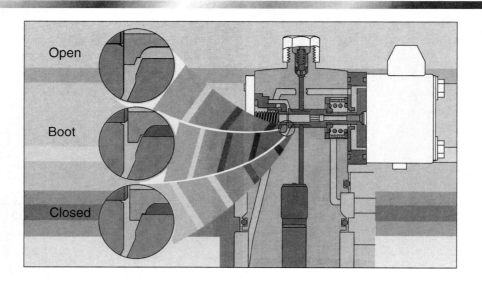

Open

Boot

Closed

FIGURE 39-17 The Bosch unit pumps on E-TECH engines have rate-shaping capability provided by the stepped shape of the control valve and seat.

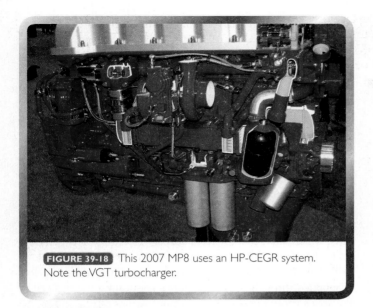

FIGURE 39-18 This 2007 MP8 uses an HP-CEGR system. Note the VGT turbocharger.

Mass-Based Variable Torque

Mass-based variable torque (MBVT) is an engine governor control function that automatically adjusts engine torque output to match vehicle weight. Heavier vehicles climbing steep grades require more torque, and the feature provides more torque under these conditions. The downside to having higher torque output is increased fuel consumption. To provide more fuel efficiency when lighter loads are hauled, the vehicle control system senses the load conditions and reduces maximum available torque. Throttle position, boost pressure, and the time under load help calculate whether the increased fueling is permissible. On vehicles equipped with the I-Shift transmission, which is Volvo's own automated transmission, an inclination sensor provides input data to indicate the road's grade to ensure maximum engine power is available. One effect of MBVT technicians need to be aware of is a loss of power under more fuel-efficient operation may be noticeable to the driver. The vehicle may not pull as well to remain fuel efficient under some conditions, which ultimately amounts to less than 1 minute longer travel time per trip hour. If a driver complains about poor acceleration or low power, particularly when hauling empty, it's important to determine whether the feature is enabled to differentiate between other causes of low power or to properly educate the driver. The MBVT feature is viewed, enabled, and modified using the parameter programming function within Premium Tech Tool.

Another feature included in the MBVT is the Eco-Torque. Eco-Torque operates identically to the droop function of mechanical and electronic governors, which are described in more detail in the Governors chapter. Essentially, droop refers to the governor function that improves fuel economy by reducing the maximum amount of fuel injected as the engine reaches rated speed. A higher percentage of governor droop means less fuel is injected as the engine speed approaches rated speed. When cruise control is engaged, the Eco-Torque feature causes the vehicle to travel a little slower in order to save fuel. When traveling downhill, the vehicle is allowed to travel a little faster than wet speed to compensate for trip time lost on uphill climbs.

The MBVT feature provides three different droop settings for Eco-Torque: small, medium, and best, with the best setting only available with the I-Shift transmission.

▶ Volvo–Mack Fuel Systems

All current Mack and Volvo engines use electronic unit injectors. Mack's E7 E-TECH used unit pumps driven by an engine-mounted camshaft. Volvo D12 engines used first-generation unit injectors manufactured by Delphi that had a single electrically energized control valve. Even using electronically controlled unit pumps, which are capable of high injection pressures, they have the disadvantage of introducing longer injection lag time and variations in injection timing due to the line connecting the pump and nozzle. Line swelling during the pressurization stage and pressure wave transmission through the fuel lines introduced too much variability to injection events needed to obtain low engine emissions.

Delphi E3 Unit Injector

The Delphi E3 injector is used across all Mack MP engines, the Volvo D12-C, and 2007 and later D-series engines. More detailed injector operation is described in the Electronic Unit Injectors and Unit Pumps chapter. The E3 has two solenoid valves to vary injection pressure and injection timing. Because of their compact size, the injectors can be centrally located, vertically between the four valves, and are held in place by a yoke. The lower part of the injector is held against the injector sleeve, surrounded by coolant to help cool the injector. Two O-rings are used to seal a fuel passage into the injector. Fuel is supplied by the low-pressure fuel system through a single fuel gallery drilled along the length of the cylinder head.

Delphi E3 Unit Injector Operation

The overhead camshaft provides the mechanical force used to pressurize fuel within the injector's pump section. Two electrically energized control valves in the injector's valve actuation section control the beginning and end of injection timing as well as the pressure at which injection occurs. The injector's nozzle valve is hydraulically balanced like in common rail injectors. This means fuel pressure above and below the nozzle valve primarily controls the nozzle opening and closing. Tipping the state of balance between the two hydraulic forces above and below the valve either opens or closes the valve much faster than a nozzle spring.

During upward movement of the injector plunger, fuel enters the injector during the fill stage. On the downward movement of the plunger, fuel spills back to the fuel rail unless the injector is energized. If the normally open spill control valve (SCV) is energized, fuel return to the fuel rail is blocked and pressure builds up in the injector. Pressure will build until the normally closed nozzle control valve (NCV) is energized. Energizing the nozzle valve will begin the injection event. During pressure build-up phase, the closing SCV allows a high pressure to build on top of the nozzle valve and keep it closed. Once the desired injection pressure is reached, which is determined by a control algorithm, the NCV solenoid is opened and releases fuel pressure above the nozzle holding it closed. Atomized fuel will then spray out the injector into the combustion chamber at extremely high pressure. Injection ends when the SCV and NCV are de-energized.

Injector Trim Codes

There are three identification markings on the injector electrical connector. One is the part number, the second is the injector calibration or trim code, and the third number is a manufacturing number **FIGURE 39-19**. When replacing or moving one or more injectors, the engine ECM must use the new trim code for the injector in the correct cylinder to properly correct variations to delivery quantities unique to every injector. These variations are caused by manufacturing tolerances allowed during injector manufacturing. The trim code is entered into ECM memory using the parameter programming feature in Premium Tech Tool.

Low-Pressure Fuel System

Engine fuel systems are divided into low- and high-pressure zones. The low-pressure zone filters and supplies clean, vapor-free fuel to the high-pressure unit injectors at the correct pressure, volume, and temperature. In systems using a particulate filter, additional fuel is supplied to the hydrocarbon dosing system, which Volvo calls the **7th injector**. Because injectors meter fuel delivery to the engine based on volume, heated fuel can reduce engine power because it is less dense.

Low-Pressure System Fuel Flow

All MP and Volvo engines use a common flow pressure fuel system configuration. The supply pump pulls fuel from the fuel tank fuel to the engine usually using pick-up tubes in top-draw fuel tanks. Fresh, cool fuel from the tank circulates through a cooler plate located on the back of the ECM to increase ECM reliability. From the cooler plate, fuel moves to the fuel filter housing, which contains a pre-filter with a fuel water separator. The primary filter's 20–40 micron size filter media removes larger dirt particles. After passing through the pre-filter and separator, fuel is pulled into the gear-type fuel transfer pump. Two valves are found in the supply pump **FIGURE 39-20**. One valve is an anti-drain back valve or no-return valve that prevents fuel from draining back to the tank when the engine is not running. The no-return flow check valve opens to allow fuel to bypass the pump gears when the hand primer is used. The second valve in the transfer pump is a pressure protection or relief valve that allows fuel to return to the suction side of the pump if fuel pressure becomes too high, such as when a fuel filter becomes blocked or restricted.

The transfer pump pushes pressurized fuel into the secondary filter, which filters 3–5 micron particulates. From there, fuel travels to the rear of the cylinder head and passes through a fuel rail drilled along the length of the cylinder head. Fuel to the injectors is supplied through internal drillings connecting the fuel rail to the area surrounding the two injector O-rings **FIGURE 39-21**. An overflow valve that serves as a pressure-regulating valve is located near the front of the cylinder head. The valve regulates fuel pressure supplied to the injectors to approximately 50 psi (345 kPa).

To prevent the loss of engine power as fuel temperature increases, fuel temperature correction can be factored into the ECM's calculation of injection quantity. Another additional strategy is to add fuel cooler, but they can add to engine cost and complexity. Fuel returns from the cylinder head and back to the fuel filter housing to mix with fuel entering the primary filter. This mixing strategy is used to keep fuel cooler entering the cylinder head. Because the low-pressure system draws only the amount of fuel needed to operate the high-pressure system, fuel temperature increases and flow volume is kept to a minimum. Volvo believes this return-less fuel system configuration is better at supplying cooler fuel without an additional fuel cooler than returning large amounts of fuel to the tank after it is preheated in the cylinder head.

FIGURE 39-19 The trim code for an E3 is etched into the injector's electrical connector.

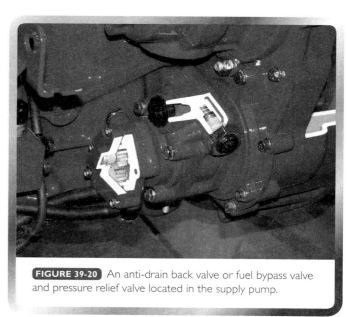

FIGURE 39-20 An anti-drain back valve or fuel bypass valve and pressure relief valve located in the supply pump.

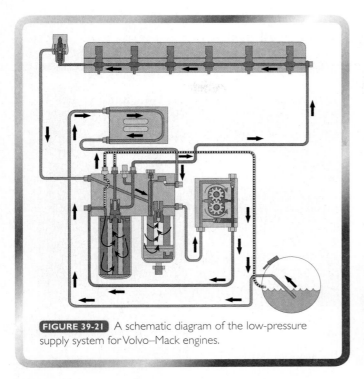

FIGURE 39-21 A schematic diagram of the low-pressure supply system for Volvo–Mack engines.

Automatic Air Bleeding

Unlike older fuel systems, fuel filters do not need to be bled after replacement. Two valves in the filter header, one for each fuel filter, mechanically close when the filters are removed to prevent fuel from draining out of the fuel filter headers **FIGURE 39-22**. Additionally, two return line passageways above the secondary filter purge air from the filters and return it to the fuel tank within two minutes of engine start-up. An air purge valve above the clean side of the secondary filter begins to purge the filter after the engine has run for two minutes. A hand primer pump is used to help purge and prime the fuel filters when replacement takes place. A pressure sensor in the filter header of the newer Volvo–Mack engines monitors outlet fuel pressure and will trigger a fault event if fuel pressure is sensed below a minimum threshold value.

FIGURE 39-22 The fuel filter head contains a fuel output pressure sensor and valves that prevent fuel from draining from the header when the filters are removed.

On older D12 engines, two air bleed screws are opened to purge air from the filter housing and the cylinder head after a filter change **FIGURE 39-23** and **FIGURE 39-24**. The fuel filter is bled first using a hand priming pump. The cylinder head is bled next. Corrosion of injector tubes can lead to air in the cylinder head, producing misfire codes and low fuel pressure codes. Identifying the origin of the gas leakage in the cylinder head is performed using clear plastic tubing spliced into the fuel system at various points.

Bleeding a Volvo–Mack Fuel System

Volvo–Mack engines have two fuel system bleeder screws: one on the fuel filter and the other on the cylinder head. MP series engines and Volvo D series engines have two fuel system bleeder screws on

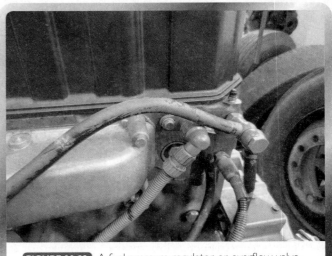

FIGURE 39-23 A fuel pressure regulator or overflow valve and bleeder screw are located at the rear of the cylinder head of this D12 engine.

FIGURE 39-24 A bleeder screw for the fuel filter is used to bleed the filter after a service on a D12 engine.

SKILL DRILL 39-1 Bleeding a Volvo–Mack Fuel System

1 Clean around the bleeder screws on the fuel filter housing and cylinder head.

2 Connect a plastic hose to the fuel filter housing bleeder screw. Open the bleeder screw and pump the hand primer until clean fuel runs out of the hose. Tighten the bleeder screw while fuel is still running out.

3 Attach the bleeder hose to the rear cylinder head bleeder screw and remove any air using the same techniques in Step 2. Move to the front of the cylinder head and bleed that screw the same way.

4 Start the engine and allow it to run at fast idle, or with the PTO engaged, for about 5 minutes to remove air from the system. Recheck the fuel system for leaks.

the cylinder head. These screws are used to bleed the fuel system after a filter is replaced or other low-pressure system work.

To bleed a Volvo–Mack fuel system, follow the steps in **SKILL DRILL 39-1**.

▶ Volvo–Mack Electronics

Multiple electronic control units (ECUs) are used on Volvo–Mack engine chassis. These include the ECM, instrument control module (ICM), vehicle electronic control unit (VECU), transmission control module (TCM), gear selector control module (GSCM), and aftertreatment control module (ACM). Together, these modules form the vehicle controlled area network (VCAN), which enables communication between modules to control a variety of engine, vehicle, and cab functions **FIGURE 39-25**. The engine controlled area network (ECAN) controls a variety of functions related to operation of the engine, plus it coordinates with the ACM to control the emission aftertreatment system (EATS) to operate aftertreatment devices **FIGURE 39-26**. The VECU controls other vehicle-related functions associated with the engine such as all programmable parameters, accessory relay controls, and idle shutdown functions.

The modules connected to the VCAN have onboard diagnostic (OBD) capabilities that operate to detect faults or abnormal operating conditions that could potentially increase vehicle emissions **FIGURE 39-27**. When the modules detect a fault or abnormal operating condition, the fault will be logged and the malfunction indicator lamp (MIL) will light up to

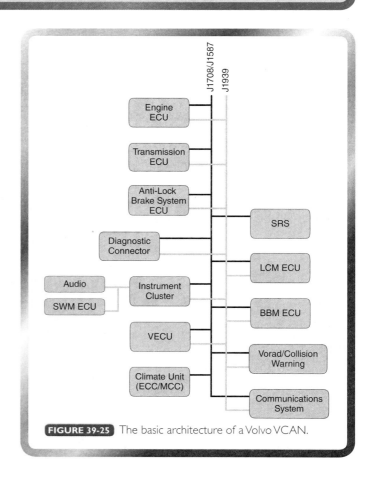

FIGURE 39-25 The basic architecture of a Volvo VCAN.

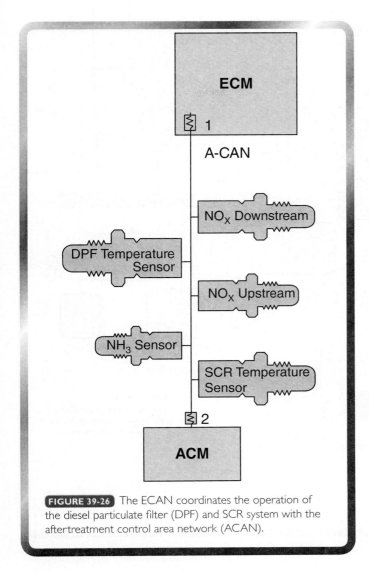

FIGURE 39-26 The ECAN coordinates the operation of the diesel particulate filter (DPF) and SCR system with the aftertreatment control area network (ACAN).

alert the operator to the presence of a fault. The engine ECM may initiate the engine shutdown procedure if the system determines that an engine protection system fault that could damage the engine has occurred. Alternatively in other situations, serious emission-related faults will cause the OBD system to enter **derate mode**. The derate mode allows continued vehicle operation with lower power output or limited vehicle speed, but the system may also substitute a sensor or signal value that requires reduced performance. Diagnostic trouble codes (DTCs) logged and stored in module memory can later be read to assist fault diagnostic checks. The VECU and ECM are dependent on each other to perform their specific control functions. The ECM serves as a gateway module for all diagnostic trouble codes and descriptions from the VECU, NO_x sensor modules, and the VGT-smart remote actuator (SRA) module. The use of a scan tool or Premium Tech Tool is necessary to perform diagnostic work as well as clearing of any DTCs that can no longer be cleared using the vehicle's instrument cluster digital display and turn signal stalk switch control **FIGURE 39-28**.

▶ Exhaust Pressure Governor and Engine Brake

Another unique feature of the Volvo D12 engine is the use of an **exhaust pressure governor (EPG)**. The EPG has four important functions:

1. To speed engine warm-up and keep the engine at normal operating temperature when engine is idling.
2. To help reduce cold start and warm-up hydrocarbon emissions.
3. To operate as an exhaust brake to supplement the compression release engine brake operation.
4. To apply exhaust system backpressure during idle EGR function.

The EPG is mounted to the turbocharger housing at the exhaust outlet and all engine exhaust gas passes through the EPG's normally open shutter before exiting the exhaust pipe **FIGURE 39-29**. Regulated air pressure of 7–110 psi (48–758 kPa) is supplied to the EPG through a PWM control valve that adjusts air pressure to close the shutter.

Start and Warm-Hold EPG Operation

Since direct injection combustion chambers use excess air, the exhaust and cylinder temperatures are naturally low. The result is diesel engines do not warm up when idling and, in fact, will cool from operating temperatures when idling. As a manufacturer from Northern Europe, Volvo has developed a strategy to maintain engine heat when idling when heat from cab and bunk heaters are needed. When coolant temperature is below approximately 157°F (55°C) and the parking brakes are applied, the EPG shutter will close. The effect of closing the shutter increases exhaust backpressure, which in turn prevents exhaust gases, which are primarily air, from escaping the cylinders. Exhaust temperatures inside the cylinder and manifold rise to approximately 200°F (93°C) and more heat transfers to the cooling system. The flow of exhaust gases is not completely blocked by the EPG because a number of holes in the shutter allow some of the exhaust gases to flow through. A carefully calculated shutter area and air pressure applied to the shutter's piston will allow the shutter to open if the exhaust pressure is too high. Closing the shutter for the warm-hold strategy will take place approximately 5 seconds after the engine starts.

Idle Hydrocarbon Reduction

Restricting exhaust gas flow from the cylinders also increases compression pressure, which promotes higher pre-ignition temperatures. The advantage during cold-start operation is reduction of unburned hydrocarbon emissions producing white and blue exhaust smoke. This smoke will always accompany combustion when the temperature of cylinders is too low. To keep the hydrocarbon emissions even lower, Volvo will delay the beginning of injection during the cold-start cranking period. As many as seven revolutions of the engine may take place during cranking to increase cylinder temperatures before injecting fuel. Heat retained by the cylinder produced through compression heating will improve combustion quality and

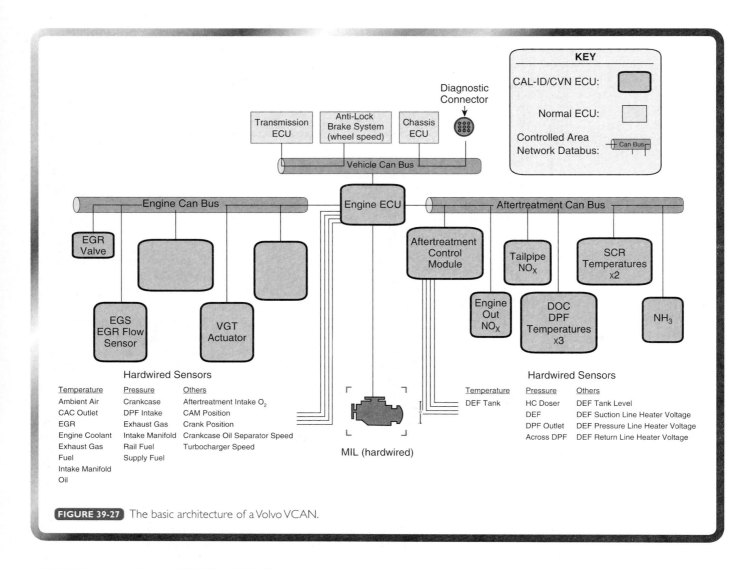

FIGURE 39-27 The basic architecture of a Volvo VCAN.

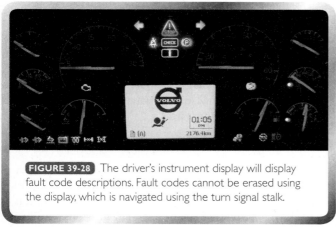

FIGURE 39-28 The driver's instrument display will display fault code descriptions. Fault codes cannot be erased using the display, which is navigated using the turn signal stalk.

reduce smoke right after startup and until the start-warm-up feature is activated.

An electric intake preheater is used on engines that do not preheat the engine with several crank rotations before injecting fuel on startup. The high current draw preheater will cycle on for up to 25 seconds when air or coolant temperatures are below 50°F (10°C). After the engine starts, the heater will remain energized for the same amount of time used during the preheat cycle.

▶ Volvo Engine Brake

Volvo uses a uniquely designed engine retarding system combining two different systems, the exhaust brake incorporated into the EPG and the compression brake. Operating on principles like other compression release brakes, the exhaust valve is opened slightly near the end of TDC on compression stroke **FIGURE 39-30**. Rather than using a separate cam lobe or lobe of an injector or adjacent intake or exhaust valve, Volvo uses three lobes on its exhaust cam lobe to lift the exhaust valve from its seat. The first and largest lobe is the exhaust lobe used to open the exhaust valve at the end of power stroke. On engines with the Volvo engine brake (VEB), the camshaft has two additional smaller lobes: an induction or intake lobe and decompression lobe. The size of the lobes sharing the same camshaft profile provides a lift height of 0.032″ (0.813 mm) above the camshaft's inner base circle. When projected to the end of the exhaust rocker lever, the exhaust valve will open approximately 0.043″ (1.092 mm).

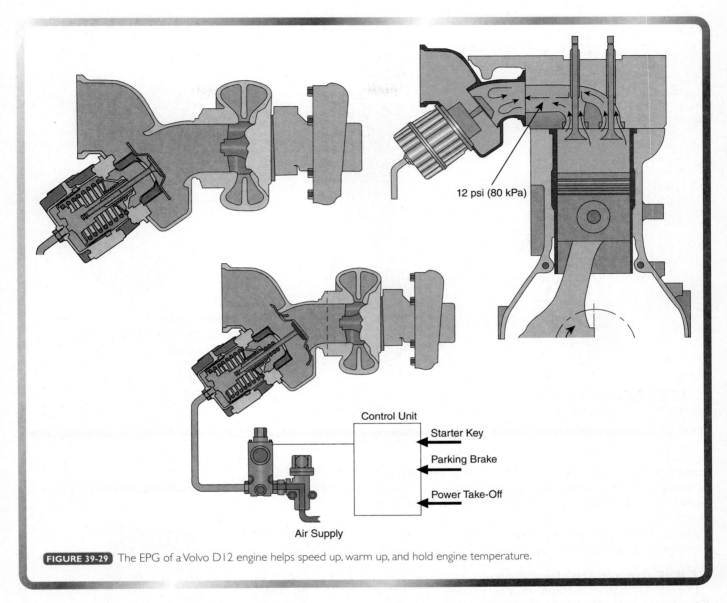

12 psi (80 kPa)

Control Unit

Starter Key

Parking Brake

Power Take-Off

Air Supply

FIGURE 39-29 The EPG of a Volvo D12 engine helps speed up, warm up, and hold engine temperature.

The induction lobe is located on the camshaft to bump open the exhaust valve at the end of the intake stroke and to admit additional exhaust gases into the cylinder after filling with intake air. The decompression lobe opens the exhaust valve near the end of the compression stroke.

VEB Camshaft

During the exhaust gas induction phase, high exhaust pressure in the exhaust manifold can enter the cylinder and supplement the gas volume charging the cylinder during compression stroke. Positioning of the decompression lobe is designed to open the exhaust valve at the end of the compression stroke. During normal engine operation when the cylinders are not braking, the lobes have no operational effectiveness—essentially they do nothing. Clearances in the valve train provided by the valve adjustment will take up any movement of the rocker lever by the additional lobes and not actuate the exhaust valve. That means the larger exhaust lobe of the camshaft will open and close the

exhaust valve only once during the operating cycle. However, if the valve clearance becomes zero, these two extra lobes will open and close the exhaust valve two additional times during a combustion cycle. To enable the compression release operation, Volvo has developed and patented exclusive technology to add and remove clearances on the exhaust rocker lever. Additionally, the EPG works to combine its engine retarding capabilities with the compression release mechanism. Supplemental engine braking is achieved during the exhaust stroke using the backpressure created when the exhaust gas flow is blocked by the EPG. In the VEB, both the compression release and EPG systems can operate at the same time and independently of one another.

Compression Brake Operation

The compression uses an oil-operated control valve connected between the engine oil pressure supply and the rocker arm shaft. Its purpose is to change oil pressure supplied to the rocker arms when the engine is running. Under nonbraking conditions, oil

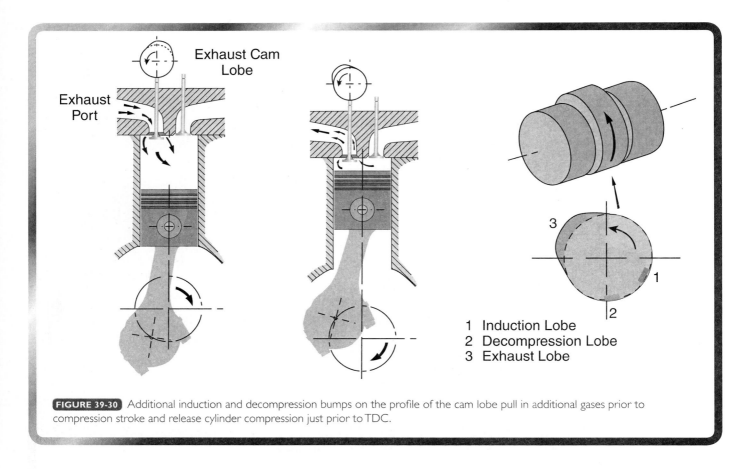

Exhaust Cam Lobe

Exhaust Port

3 Induction Lobe
1
2 Decompression Lobe
3 Exhaust Lobe

1 Induction Lobe
2 Decompression Lobe
3 Exhaust Lobe

FIGURE 39-30 Additional induction and decompression bumps on the profile of the cam lobe pull in additional gases prior to compression stroke and release cylinder compression just prior to TDC.

pressure to the rocker arm shaft is 14.5 psi (100 kPa) but can be increased to 29 psi (200 kPa) by energizing a solenoid valve located inside the braking control valve. The solenoid changes the pressure balance of a pressure-limiting valve inside the control valve. Activating the solenoid drains oil from one side of the control valve to increase oil pressure supplying the rocker shaft.

VEB Exhaust Rocker Arms

The exhaust rocker arms on an engine with a compression brake are larger because they contain a check valve, pressure-limiting valve, and plunger at the valve bridge end of the rocker lever **FIGURE 39-31** and **FIGURE 39-32**. When oil pressure from the control valve is low, a light pressure spring holds the rocker arm at the rest position against the exhaust valve bridge. Engine oil can flow freely through the non-return valve in the rocker arm in both directions. During braking, when oil pressure increases to 29 psi (200 kPa), the pressure-limiting valve inside the rocker arm opens and oil can exit only through a small hole in the plunger. The result is downward movement of the plunger, which eliminates any valve lash clearance. Oil cannot be pushed back through the arm by the plunger force because a check valve blocks the passage. This means the rocker lever plunger operates like a solid hydraulic column and can transmit camshaft actuation force to the exhaust valve bridge.

Valve clearance is greater on engines without a compression brake because the induction and decompression lobes must not open the exhaust valve. In VEB-equipped engines, more rugged

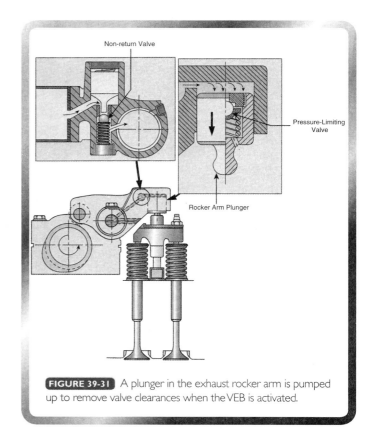

Non-return Valve

Pressure-Limiting Valve

Rocker Arm Plunger

FIGURE 39-31 A plunger in the exhaust rocker arm is pumped up to remove valve clearances when the VEB is activated.

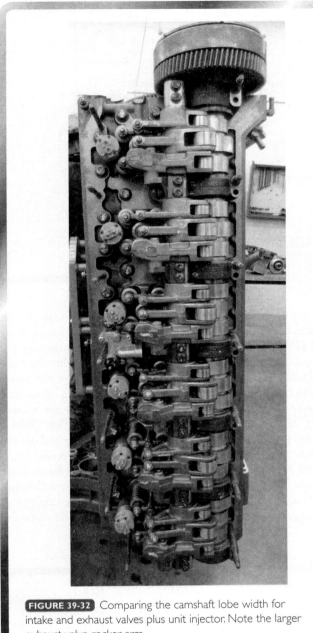

FIGURE 39-32 Comparing the camshaft lobe width for intake and exhaust valves plus unit injector. Note the larger exhaust valve rocker arm.

FIGURE 39-33 There is no adjustment screw on the exhaust rocker lever, which is unlike the injector and intake lever. Shims are used on the exhaust valve bridge to adjust exhaust valve clearances.

shims with greater surface area are used to adjust valve clearances **FIGURE 39-33**. Volvo does not recommend using more than two shims to obtain proper valve clearance.

Enabling Conditions

Like other engine brakes, the VEB will be enabled only under the following conditions:

- The engine brake is activated by the dash switch.
- The accelerator pedal is released.
- Engine rpm must be greater than 1100.
- The clutch pedal is released.

- Boost pressure is lower than 22 psi (150 kPa).
- The PTO must not be activated.
- There is no engine brake disable input from the anti-lock brake system (ABS) module due to a wheel lock-up event.
- Vehicle speed is greater than 2 mph (3.2 km/h).
- The engine near operating temperature.

The brake can also be configured to automatically engage if the vehicle exceeds a specified cruise control limit. The speed above the set cruise control limit can be further modified to apply the VEB between 4 and 20 mph (6.4 and 32 km/h) above the cruise control set speed.

Dash switches can be either a two-position or three-position type. For a two-position HI/LO switch, the HI position selects both the exhaust brake and the compression brake. In the LO position, only the exhaust brake is selected. A three-position switch is nearly the same except it incorporates a brake OFF position. When the exhaust brake is used, the air control pressure applied to EPG is about 109 psi (8 bar). Restricting the flow of exhaust gases creates exhaust backpressure between the EPG shutter and the piston crowns. Greater force is required to push exhaust out from the cylinder, which increases the engine retarding effect. This effect is multiplied at higher engine speeds during exhaust braking. Higher backpressure also fills the cylinders with more gas during the induction phase.

▶ Exhaust Gas Recirculation Systems

Volvo–Mack engines use three EGR systems. The first was introduced by Volvo in 2002 and was called the V-pulse system. V-pulse depends on natural exhaust gas pulses plus reed valves to regulate EGR flow. Another system is referred to as an internal EGR (I-EGR) system, described below, which is used for vocational and off-road engines. All of the most recent engines use conventional high-pressure cooled EGR gas with some unique components. Later 2007 Mack and Volvo engines share a common EGR system configuration.

Internal EGR (I-EGR)

This system is also called a switchable **internal exhaust gas recirculation (I-EGR)** system, and operates using principles similar to the VEB by using the oil-controlled exhaust rocker lever of the VEB. When EGR gas recirculation is required, the exhaust rocker lever with a hydraulic plunger is supplied with pressurized oil. A bump on the cam lobe enables exhaust gases to enter the cylinder during the intake stroke using a short, second exhaust valve lift event **FIGURE 39-34** and **FIGURE 39-35**. The I-EGR system is electronically controlled by the EMS and its operation based on meeting low NO_x requirements under various engine operating conditions.

V-Pulse I-EGR

The earliest EGR system used by Volvo on the D12-C engine, called V-pulse, does not use a high-pressure EGR system but

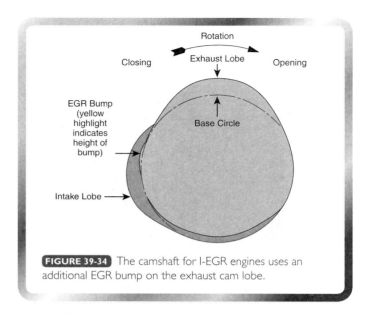

FIGURE 39-34 The camshaft for I-EGR engines uses an additional EGR bump on the exhaust cam lobe.

does use cooled EGR gas and depends on natural pressure pulses in the exhaust system to supply exhaust gases to the intake manifold **FIGURE 39-36**. In a pulsed EGR system, a portion of the exhaust gas is metered by two poppet EGR valves into the EGR cooler. After the exhaust gas temperature is reduced in the cooler, it flows through a set of reed valves, which are thin, plate-type one-way check valves **FIGURE 39-37**. These valves are located at the end of the EGR cooler and do two things: they prevent boosted intake air from flowing into the EGR cooler and out the exhaust manifold, and they ensure gases leave the cooler when natural high-pressure pulses are emitted by the exhaust valve opening. Pressure peaks in exhaust pressure occur as a result of initial exhaust valve opening and then pressure diminishes the longer the valve is open. Cooled exhaust gases flow into the

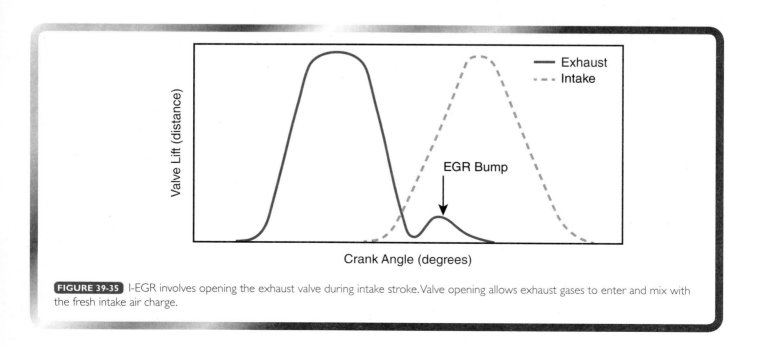

FIGURE 39-35 I-EGR involves opening the exhaust valve during intake stroke. Valve opening allows exhaust gases to enter and mix with the fresh intake air charge.

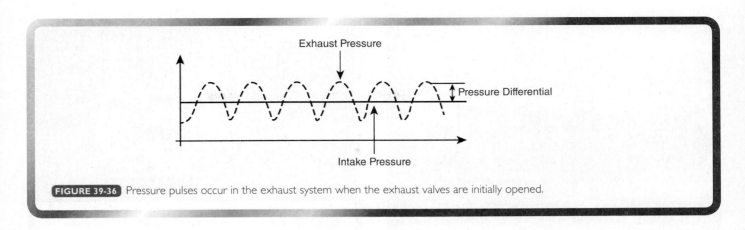

FIGURE 39-36 Pressure pulses occur in the exhaust system when the exhaust valves are initially opened.

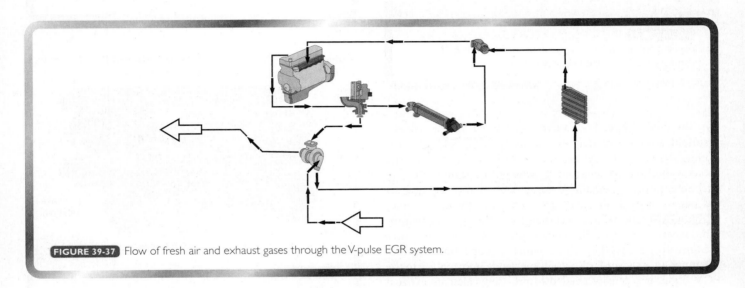

FIGURE 39-37 Flow of fresh air and exhaust gases through the V-pulse EGR system.

intake charge mixing chamber where they combine with fresh, pressurized intake air exiting the charge air cooler. The quantity of recirculated EGR gases is regulated by the EGR valves and varies with engine operating conditions. Maximum EGR flow takes place under high engine loads.

High-Pressure Cooled EGR

Volvo–Mack engines use a conventional EGR system that has been adopted by many manufacturers. The system uses a VGT to build exhaust backpressure needed to push enough EGR gas into the pressurized intake air. A speed density measurement system calculates the mass of EGR flow through a venturi pipe in the EGR tubing **FIGURE 39-38**. What is unique is the oil actuated EGR valve that uses a pressure balanced piston to regulate EGR flow. The valve is supplied by two ports from the exhaust manifold. Exhaust pressure acts on both sides of the piston assembly, which means little force is needed to open the valve. An internal spool valve controlled by a PWM solenoid diverts engine oil to apply pressure on either side of shaft for a powerful piston driven by oil pressure **FIGURE 39-39**. The piston moves the EGR valve to the correct point to precisely position the valve

for control of the exhaust gas circulated through the engine. The pressure-balanced oil-actuated design results in a valve that is less likely to stick and is well cooled by engine oil even though it is exposed to hot exhaust gases.

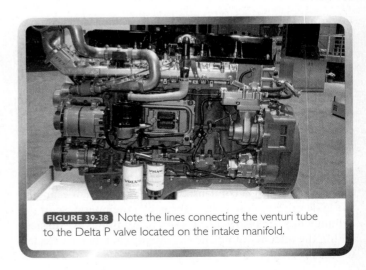

FIGURE 39-38 Note the lines connecting the venturi tube to the Delta P valve located on the intake manifold.

FIGURE 39-39 The Volvo–Mack EGR valve has two oil line connections and an electrical connector for the PWM-controlled pressure balanced valve.

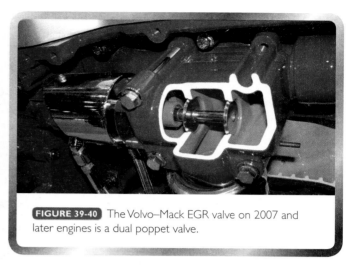

FIGURE 39-40 The Volvo–Mack EGR valve on 2007 and later engines is a dual poppet valve.

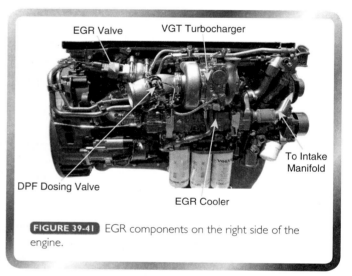

EGR Valve   VGT Turbocharger

To Intake Manifold

DPF Dosing Valve

EGR Cooler

FIGURE 39-41 EGR components on the right side of the engine.

The dual poppet EGR valve is mounted on the exhaust manifold and is activated by the ECM **FIGURE 39-40**. Positioning the valve on the rear section of the exhaust manifold protects the EGR cooler from exhaust pulses at high pressure encountered during engine braking. A portion of the exhaust gas passes through the EGR valve and into the EGR cooler **FIGURE 39-41**. The exhaust gas then flows through the venturi tube, where a pressure differential pressure sensor measures pressure drop across the venture, which is proportional to flow. A temperature sensor is also used to provide information to the ECM about gas density needed to precisely calculate exhaust mass flow and provide closed-loop feedback to position the EGR valve. The actual amount of EGR recirculated depends on engine load, engine coolant temperature (ECT), and other various factors.

Intake Manifold Corrosion

Intake manifold corrosion and possibly some engine damage can take place when moisture-laden exhaust gases are allowed to condense in the intake manifold. To prevent engine damage, the engine ECM uses a number of variables such as rpm, torque load, ambient temperature, inlet manifold temperature, and EGR flow to calculate the dew point in the inlet manifold. This refers to the temperature at which condensation of warm corrosive exhaust gases on engine and intake manifold surfaces can take place. The ECM will then position the EGR valve to flow EGR gas to maintain a temperature above the dew point. Under other conditions, EGR flow is stopped when condensation might occur. For example, the EGR valve is closed when the coolant temperature in the cylinder head is below 122°F (50°C). Additionally, surfaces within the inlet manifold and the mixing chamber are treated to resist corrosion.

EGR Diagnostics

The ECM commands the EGR valve position and monitors current used by the EGR valve. An abnormally high reading indicates a sticking or seized EGR valve. The ECM also validates that a command was sent and that the valve was positioned and moved correctly. If the valve is jammed, or does not respond correctly when commanded, the ECM sets fault codes. EGR cooler efficiency is evaluated by comparing cooler outlet temperature with exhaust and engine coolant temperature.

Exhaust Aftertreatment System

Volvo–Mack 2007 engine models used a uniquely shaped diesel particulate filter (DPF). The compact DPF is mounted on the frame behind the right front wheel and contains an oxidation catalyst upstream from a wall flow DPF filter plus sensors **FIGURE 39-42**. When there is no space to place the compact DPF, such as in refuse trucks and cab overs, a vertical back of cab (VBOC) DPF is used. A VBOC DPF is

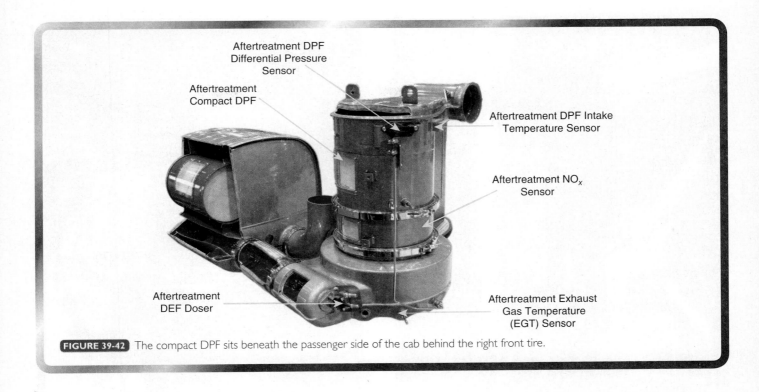

Aftertreatment DPF
Differential Pressure
Sensor

Aftertreatment
Compact DPF

Aftertreatment DPF Intake
Temperature Sensor

Aftertreatment NO$_x$
Sensor

Aftertreatment
DEF Doser

Aftertreatment Exhaust
Gas Temperature
(EGT) Sensor

FIGURE 39-42 The compact DPF sits beneath the passenger side of the cab behind the right front tire.

mounted on a frame support behind the cab **FIGURE 39-43** and **FIGURE 39-44**. One or two DPF filters are used for VBOC mounting, depending on engine power output. Events in the aftertreatment system are signaled by the ACM, which is in turn regulated by the engine ECM. Communication between the ACM and other smart J-1939-compliant sensor modules takes place over a separate CAN network for the after-treatment system. DPFs in both systems are sized to meet or exceed the EPA service interval regulations of 150,000 miles (240,000 km) or 4500 hours. The normal DPF catalyst filter element expected cleaning or replacement interval is 250,000 miles (400,000 km).

Spark-Assisted VBOC Regeneration

The MP7 with a VBOC is designed to meet EPA10 emissions standards and requires a spark-assisted DPF system. For trucks in stop-and-go operating conditions, such as refuse trucks, there is not enough heat maintained in the exhaust to allow passive regeneration to effectively take place. Using the spark-assisted VBOC DPF system, air from the intake manifold and diesel fuel are mixed with exhaust gases in a combustion chamber where spark plug ignites the mixture. This technique supplies the needed supplemental heating of the DPF filter to oxidize PM and soot in the DPF.

Continuous Dosing Valve Air Purge

When an active regeneration of the DPF is required, supplemental heating by the oxidation converter of the DPF takes place by dosing the exhaust gases with fuel. For all EPA10 engines using

both the compact and VBOC DPF, a continuous air purge system is used to remove any fuel remaining in the hydrocarbon dosing valve after an active DPF regeneration **FIGURE 39-45**. This means that anytime the engine is running there is a regulated 32-psi (221-kPa) flow of air through a one-way check valve to the dosing valve located in the exhaust just after the turbocharger. Compressed air for purging the dosing valve is supplied by the chassis air system. An air shutoff valve prevents air leakage into the fuel system when the ignition is switched to the off position.

When an active regeneration event is to take place, fuel will pass through a separate one-way check valve and also enter the same line supplying air to the dosing valve. A pressure sensor signal will monitor air pressure in the fuel-air line to ensure the dosing valve is functioning correctly and not blocked. After this takes place, fuel and air are both supplied to the dosing valve for the regeneration event.

Turbocharger Compressor Bypass Valve

In most Volvo–Mack engine applications for EPA10 and later vehicles, there is a requirement to increase exhaust tempera-tures necessary to speed up catalytic reactions in the after-treatment systems. While other manufacturers use throttle plates to restrict intake air flow to keep the DPF warm for passive regeneration, Volvo–Mack engines instead use a **tur-bocharger compressor bypass valve** **FIGURE 39-46**. This valve connects the turbocharger outlet back to the turbocharger inlet, which recirculates outlet air back into the inlet. The recirculating action is initiated when a solenoid is energized by the ECM to activate the bypass valve. As the turbocharger compresses fresh intake air, its temperature will increase, and

FIGURE 39-44 The DPF and SCR systems are both incorporated into this VBOC aftertreatment system.

FIGURE 39-43 The VBOC DPF is commonly found on medium-duty cab overs. The NO$_x$ sensor and SCR outlet temperature sensor are near the exhaust stack outlet.

it is redirected back into the turbocharger for more compression and heating. Some of the recirculated air will pass through the engine and produce higher exhaust temperatures. Boost pressure is reduced when the bypass valve is operational, which means the action only takes place at low-speed low-load conditions.

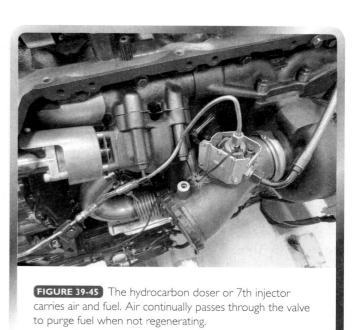

FIGURE 39-45 The hydrocarbon doser or 7th injector carries air and fuel. Air continually passes through the valve to purge fuel when not regenerating.

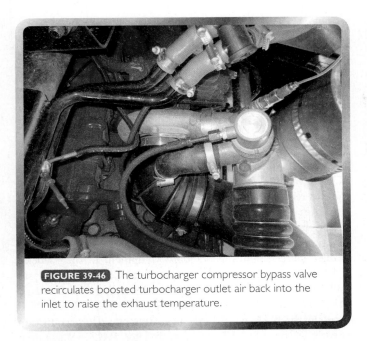

FIGURE 39-46 The turbocharger compressor bypass valve recirculates boosted turbocharger outlet air back into the inlet to raise the exhaust temperature.

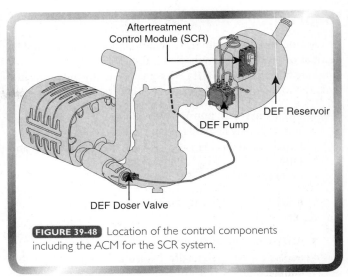

FIGURE 39-48 Location of the control components including the ACM for the SCR system.

SCR Operation

Like other aftertreatment systems, the SCR system is controlled by the ECM, which communicates with a separate aftertreatment control module (ACM) signaling the DEF dosing system **FIGURE 39-47** . When instructed by the engine ECM to dose the SCR system, the ACM uses the signal from the DEF tank level sensor indicating the DEF solution is above the set minimum level and then activates the DEF pump, which forces filtered DEF solution into the DEF dosing valve **FIGURE 39-48** . After a number of operating criteria have been met, such as the dosing pressure has reached 75 psi (517 kPa) and the SCR catalyst temperature has reached a minimum threshold, the ECM will supply the ACM with data regarding the volume of DEF to use to dose the SCR. A return line on the doser valve returns excess DEF back to the reservoir. When the ignition is switched off,

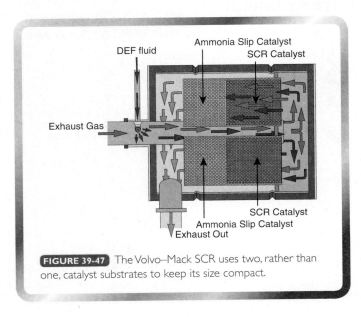

FIGURE 39-47 The Volvo–Mack SCR uses two, rather than one, catalyst substrates to keep its size compact.

DEF fluid is pulled by the reverse operation of the DEF pump back into the reservoir. This action, which takes as long as 90 seconds, prevents freezing and crystallization of DEF in lines of the SCR system.

SCR Sensor Disconnected Tampering Type

The EPA requires that the aftertreatment systems should be capable of detecting tampering and derate the engine if the fault persists. How the faults are detected and the specifics about system response are up to individual manufacturers. For Volvo–Mack engines, when an SCR tampering fault is active for more than one hour, texts on the driver information display (DID) screen appears. Texts associated with these tampering faults include:

- Aftertreatment Control Module (ACM) Disconnected
- Aftertreatment NO_x Sensor Disconnected
- DEF Pump Disconnected
- DEF Dosing Valve Disconnected
- DEF Tank Level Sensor
- Disconnected DEF Supply Line to DEF Pump Disconnected
- DEF Return Line Blocked or Plugged

If tampering DTCs are logged, the following derate schedule takes place:

- After initial detection and 10 hours of engine operation, the result is a 25% torque reduction.
- After more than 40 hours and the vehicle is refueled more than 15%, a 5-mph (8 km/h) road speed limit is imposed. The vehicle has to be stationary before the 5-mph (8 km/h) limit becomes active.

A failure of the system NO_x sensors to identify a proper drop in NO_x readings in the aftertreatment system will trigger a poor DEF quality fault. This might be caused by adding the wrong fluid, water, or even diesel fuel to the DEF reservoir. If poor DEF quality is detected during a second HD-OBD monitoring drive cycle, the vehicle will derate to 5 mph (8 km/h) after the vehicle has been stationary for 20 minutes.

Incorrectly Filling DEF Reservoirs

In addition to DEF quality DTs, Volvo–Mack have identified a number of problems encountered if the DEF reservoir and fuel tanks are filled incorrectly. If DEF is inadvertently put in the fuel tank, the following complaints can be reported:

- Engine may run poorly or not at all
- Injectors may be damaged
- Exhaust system corrosion between the turbocharger and DPF
- OBD DTCs

If diesel fuel is added to the DEF reservoir, the following may result:

- Aftertreatment SCR system damage
- SCR catalyst chemically "poisoned" and irreversibly damaged
- Emissions related fault codes

► TECHNICIAN TIP

The DEF dosing valve is a sensitive component that should be handled carefully during removal and installation. Closely observe that inlet and outlet connections have quick-release couplings of different sizes to prevent incorrect connection. Check the dosing system using Premium Tech Tool. When changing a DEF pump or DEF dosing valve, always ensure that the system is depressurized. Always detach the DEF hoses before disconnecting the electrical connectors to prevent DEF spillage from entering the connectors. Wrap the electrical and DEF connections. Seal the system so that the DEF does not crystallize if the system is disconnected for more than a few hours.

Draining the Charge Air Cooler

The charge air cooler on the Volvo chassis passes air from the turbocharger outlet to the top of the cooler and draws cooled air from the bottom of the cooler. Oil and water can accumulate in the cooler.

To drain the charge air cooler, follow the steps in **SKILL DRILL 39-2**.

► PACCAR History

PACCAR Inc. started as Seattle Car Manufacturing Company in 1905. In 1917, it merged with a Portland-based competitor and was renamed Pacific Car and Foundry Company, known as PACCAR. Kenworth became part of the PACCAR group after it was purchased in 1945. Kenworth, a well-known premium-quality truck manufacturer was the first American manufacturer to offer diesel engines as standard equipment in their trucks. In 1954, PACCAR acquired the Dart Truck Company of Kansas City, Missouri, and the Peterbilt Motors Company of Oakland, California. In 1996 the company acquired DAF Trucks N.V. based in the Netherlands after first attempting the acquisition as early as the mid-1980s. Two years later, PACCAR acquired UK-based Leyland Trucks for its light- and medium-duty trucks, which ranged in gross vehicle weight (GVW) from 6.6–49 tons (6–44 metric tons). With the additional nameplates and design and manufacturing capabilities, PACCAR currently ranks second in in the United States and third globally in the number of heavy vehicles produced, behind only Daimler AG in the U.S. market.

► PACCAR MX-13 and MX-11 Engines

PACCAR has several engines under its nameplate. A PX series of engines is produced through its partnership with Cummins. Those engines include the PX-6, which is based on the

---

 SKILL DRILL 39-2 Draining the Charge Air Cooler

1. Remove the drain plug from the bottom of the cooler.
2. Drain the cooler liquids and residue into a pan.
3. Start the engine and accelerate the engine to high idle for 1 minute to push any remaining oil and water out of the cooler.
4. Reinstall the drain plug.

Cummins ISB, the PX-8, which is the Cummins ISC, and the 8.9L (543 cubic inch) PX-9, which is the ISL engine.

The PACCAR MX-13 and MX-11, introduced in 2010 and 2015, respectively, mark the entry of PACCAR into the North American heavy-duty engine market **FIGURE 39-49** and **FIGURE 39-50**. Both engines are clean sheet design, which PACCAR partnered with Cummins to produce. While it is predominantly a PACCAR product, many Cummins engine components are used in the MX engines.

PACCAR's extensive investment in the design and production of its MX engines has produced some industry firsts. Most notably, the cylinder block and cylinder head are made from **compacted graphite iron (CGI)**. CGI material resembles cast iron, except the process uses iron granules that are molded and electrically heated under pressure to form these backbone engine components. The result is a material that is stronger, more resilient to bending fatigue, and far more resilient to thermal fatigue than traditional gray cast iron. CGI blocks can be manufactured to be lighter while maintaining high strength and durability. PACCAR claims the MX-13 engine is 150 lb (68 kg) lighter than a comparable gray-iron engine and 325 lb (147 kg) lighter than the Cummins ISX. Because CGI has noise-absorbing capabilities, combustion noise levels are also three times quieter at idle and approximately 1½ times quieter at 55 mph (88 km/h) and 70 mph (113 km/h), according to PACCAR.

The MX-13 is available in the range of 380–510 hp (283–380 kW) with up to 1850 ft-lb (2508 Nm) of torque. The 10.8L (659 cubic inch) MX-11 is almost 400 lb (181 kg) lighter than the MX-13, but it was only introduced in North America in 2015 for Kenworth trucks. The MX-11 was first put into service in Europe in 2013. The MX-11 is available in ratings from 282–440 hp (210–328 kW) with 1550 ft-lb (2102 Nm) of torque.

Unique Engine Features

Electronically controlled, engine camshaft-driven unit pumps by Delphi were used on the original MX-13; however, both engines began using ultra-high-pressure common rail (UHPCR) systems in 2013. The common rail system is capable of producing injection pressures of 36,300 psi (2503 bar) **FIGURE 39-51**.

Both engines use liquid SCR systems in combination with EGR. The MX-11 engine cylinder heads feature two hollow design overhead camshafts driving four valves per cylinder. This contrasts with the MX-13, which uses a high-mounted camshaft. One advantage of the cam-in-block is it offers is a more ideal location of head bolts for effective clamping force without the interference of an overhead camshaft. The gear train is rear mounted in the MX-13.

To help meet newer greenhouse gas (GHG) emission standards, the latest engines have water pumps with a two-speed electromagnetic coupling to reduce fuel consumption.

FIGURE 39-49 An early PACCAR MX-11 engine.

FIGURE 39-50 A circa-2010 PACCAR MX-13 engine.

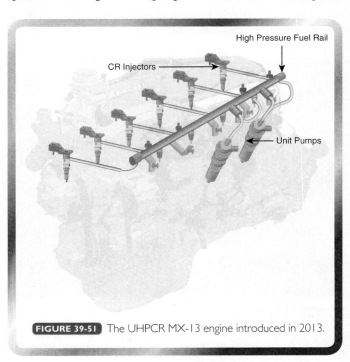

High Pressure Fuel Rail

CR Injectors

Unit Pumps

FIGURE 39-51 The UHPCR MX-13 engine introduced in 2013.

Additionally, the air compressors also use electromagnetic clutches controlled by the engine ECM, which uses software-controlled engagement to allow compressor loading (building up air pressure) to take place as much as possible during deceleration.

Fractured Bearing Caps

The MX engines use <u>fractured cap technology</u> for the main bearing caps and connecting rods. This technique involves laser-etching a parting line along the bearing cap, and the parts are pulled apart using force fracturing with a hydraulic ram. The resulting parting surface produced by force fracturing leaves a unique three-dimensional mating surface. The unique mating of each part produces a much more precise concentric bearing bore for improved oil control in the bearings. No movement takes place on the parting surfaces, so the possibility of fretting or wear on the bearing cap mating surfaces is eliminated **FIGURE 39-52**.

> ### ▶ TECHNICIAN TIP
>
> Cleanliness is critical when handling fracture-split bearing caps. Mating surfaces must be carefully cleaned before assembling. Any dirt or damage between the cap surfaces will reduce the precision fit alignment and potentially cause catastrophic bearing and engine damage. If the cap is installed in the wrong location or backward, any application of pressure can irreversibly damage the connecting rod or main baring cap. Both cap and rod or block are marked with journal numbers to help correctly match up the parts.

MX Fuel Systems

PACCAR used Delphi EUPs on its first-generation MX-13. Like Bosch pumps, the Delphi units were driven by the camshaft mounted in the engine block with interconnecting high-pressure fuel delivery lines connected to the nozzle in the cylinder head **FIGURE 39-53**. The EUP, which is capable of close to 30,000 psi (2068 bar) injection pressure used control valves similar to the single-solenoid EUI product line and are capable of meeting EPA10 emission standards. Delphi offs a system that can be used together with either Delphi's mechanical injector (single-valve system) or the Delphi Smart Injector for Diesel Engines (dual-valve system).

Unit Pump Common Rail

In 2013, PACCAR introduced its new common-rail fuel-injection system for the MX engines with injection pressures of up to 36,000 psi (2482 bar) to replace the MX-13 unit injector system **FIGURE 39-54** and **FIGURE 39-55**. What is unique to the Delphi CR system is the use of two unit pumps to develop rail pressure for the injectors. The injectors are also use servo-hydraulic injectors rather than piezoelectric actuation. The injector control valve is a patented design built to deliver the speedy response time of a piezoelectric control but with the longer durability and ruggedness of servo-hydraulic switching of the injection events **FIGURE 39-56**.

Unit Pumps

Two unit pumps are used on the engine to supply the fuel volume and injection pressure to the injectors. The simple piston pump uses a roller lifter that is mounted above a three-lobed camshaft that provides three pump strokes for every two crank rotations. The pumps operate out of phase with one another,

FIGURE 39-52 The parting surfaces of a split-fractured rod are unique and must be carefully aligned during assembly.

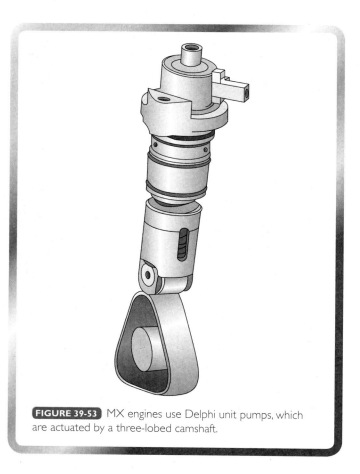

FIGURE 39-53 MX engines use Delphi unit pumps, which are actuated by a three-lobed camshaft.

with each completing a stroke while the other plungers are bottomed out. Fuel enters the injector through a fuel gallery and passes into an internal inlet metering valve. After drawing fuel into the plunger through a downward stroke, a pump pressure event begins when the plunger travels upward in a barrel, and the ECM energizes the unit pump solenoid to close the inlet metering valve. Fuel cannot escape back into the fuel gallery and the plunger pushes fuel out of the unit pump body into the fuel rail. The pumping event will end when the roller lifter passes the top of the camshaft lobe and begins its downward travel. The inlet metering valve will open again while the check valve in the pump outlet closes to prevent fuel in the rail from flowing back. Specialized algorithms regulate the volume of fuel supplied to the rail by admitting only the exact amount of fuel into the unit pump for pressurization. Steel tubes supplying fuel to the centrally located injectors are integrated into the cylinder head to reduce external leaks.

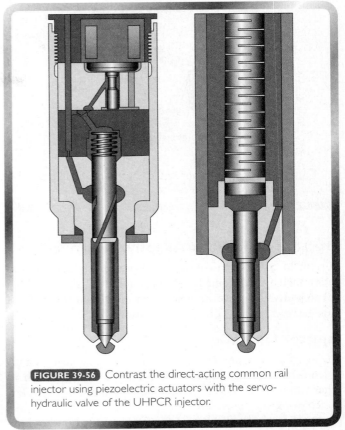

FIGURE 39-56 Contrast the direct-acting common rail injector using piezoelectric actuators with the servo-hydraulic valve of the UHPCR injector.

FIGURE 39-54 Note the location of the two unit pumps and rail for the MX-13 UHPCR engine.

FIGURE 39-55 Components of the MX UHPCR fuel system.

Since the amount of fuel pressurized in the fuel rail depends on the duration of the effective pump stroke, the sooner the inlet metering valve solenoid is energized during the up stroke of the pump plunger, the more (mg/stroke) fuel is supplied to the rail. The rail has a pressure sensor that provides closed-loop control with the inlet metering solenoids on the unit pumps. A comparison is made between the actual rail pressure and expected rail pressure calculated by the ECM. Rail pressure is then adjusted by pumping more or less fuel to the rail with the common rail pump units **FIGURE 39-57**. A PWM-controlled rail pressure relief valve is used to protect the fuel system if a malfunction in the rail pressure control circuit occurs. It's adjusted to relieve rail pressure if it exceeds 47,138 ± 4351 psi (3250 ± 300 bar). The rail pressure relief valve is integrated into the fuel rail and is not serviceable as a separate part. During normal rail pressure control, the valve's normal duty cycle keeps the valve closed. The duty cycle to keep the relief valve closed varies with commanded rail pressure. This means the opening pressure can vary with engine speed, fuel temperature, and other operating conditions. If the relief valve opens, fuel is diverted into the inlet side of the low-pressure fuel system pump. If the pressure relief valve loses an electrical signal due to an open circuit, the normally closed valve opens at approximately 4641 ± 1015 psi (320 ± 7 bar).

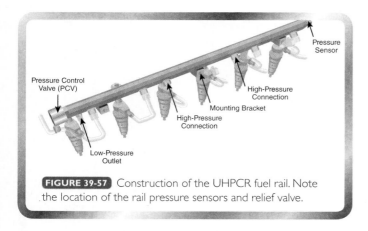

FIGURE 39-57 Construction of the UHPCR fuel rail. Note the location of the rail pressure sensors and relief valve.

Pressure Relief Valve Adaptive Learning

Current to control the common rail pressure release valve is determined by the engine ECM and is stored in its memory. If a rail pressure relief valve is replaced, the stored value in the ECM must be reset with DAVIE service software.

Injector Operation

The injector has a simple but efficient design that enables multiple injection events during the combustion cycle. As with all other common rail injectors, a pressure-balanced nozzle is key to achieving the speed and responsiveness needed for multiple injection events. Fuel rail pressure is supplied on both the top and bottom of the nozzle valve with the surface area above the valve being slightly greater than the fuel pressure acting on the nozzle valve annulus surface. Energizing the nozzle control valve (NCV) opens a low-pressure drain passage to the fuel return for pressurized fuel holding the nozzle valve closed. Simultaneously, the valve blocks the internal passage from the fuel rail supplying fuel to close the nozzle. Injection begins within 3 microseconds after the injector is energized and ends when the NCV is de-energized. High-pressure fuel from the fuel rail rapidly re-enters a chamber above the nozzle valve to force the nozzle back onto its seat.

Injector Codes

Every fuel injector is calibrated during production to compensate for any production tolerances. An injector calibration code is etched on the surface of the electrical connector for the injector. These injector codes must be saved in the ECM with DAVIE if one or more injectors have been replaced or moved to another position. Injector codes also need to be re-entered into any new engine ECM if it is replaced. If wrong codes or no codes are entered, the engine may derate and DTCs are stored because the discrepancy between an injector's previous performance and current performance is detected by the ECM.

To validate fuel system or other emission-related repair, the vehicle must be driven until the coolant temperature is at least 158°F (70°C). Once the minimum coolant temperature is reached, the vehicle is driven at a minimum speed of 50 mph (80 km/h) in the highest gear possible with the engine speed at 1100–1500 rpm and the cruise control set. This test

is best performed on a flat road with a loaded vehicle, but if engine load is not high it is advised to activate as many engine accessories as possible to increase the load (i.e., turn on electrical accessories, AC system, and engine fan). The vehicle should be driven to run all the HD-OBD monitors, which is about 3–5 miles (5–8 km) or through three separate 1-mile (1.5-km) stages if a steady 3–5 miles (5–8 km) trip is unavailable TABLE 39-2 .

Diagnostic Software—DAVIE

PACCAR uses a service diagnostic tool called DAVIE. DAVIE is a European acronym for DAF Vehicle Investigation Tool. In North America, it refers to Diagnostic Analysis for Vehicle Interface Equipment. Regardless, DAVIE is a software package and vehicle communication interface used to communicate with the engine ECM. DAVIE can enable the following:

- Review diagnostic codes
- Review sensor and actuator data
- Perform tests
- Program customer parameters
- Reflash the programming of the engine ECM

EGR Flow

A speed density measurement system and oxygen sensor is used to adjust and monitor EGR flow on the latest MX-13 engine FIGURE 39-58 . The pressure differential sensor measures the EGR gas pressure before and after a venturi in the EGR pipe located between the EGR cooler and the intake manifold. To increase the reliability of the Delta-P sensor, it is cooled by engine coolant. The EGR pressure difference sensor contains two internal pressure sensors with electronics. An oxygen sensor and an NO_x sensor are located immediately after the turbocharger. Too little EGR flow will cause exhaust oxygen content to rise, while too much causes oxygen content to lower. To validate the correct EGR flow and monitor the fuel system

FIGURE 39-58 A 2013+ MX-13 engine with gas sensors located after the turbocharger.

TABLE 39-2: HD-OBD Drive Cycle for 2013+ PACCAR MX Engines

Verification Cycle	Procedure
Power-Up/Electrical	With the brakes set and the ignition switched to the ON position with the engine off, wait 10 seconds for the system to initialize and run diagnostics.
Start-Up	With the park brakes applied, start the engine and run it for 2 minutes at idle.
System Initiation	Operate the truck under normal driving conditions until the coolant temperature reaches a minimum of 150°F (66°C). This test cycle can be performed with a loaded trailer or bobtail.
Transient	With the System Initiation cycle complete, under moderate engine load (A/C and fan both ON), perform a series of brief accelerations, starting from a low to a progressively higher speed until reaching a top speed of 40 mph (75 km/h). Once 40 mph (75 km/h) is reached, perform several decelerations from a high to a progressively lower low speed until reaching 10 mph (16 km/h). Perform this cycle five times.
Steady State	While driving the vehicle on a flat road grade while under load, switch on the A/C and engine fan to increase engine load. With the System Initiation cycle complete, operate the vehicle to a minimum speed limit of 50 mph (80 km/h), with the highest gear possible while the engine speed is 1100–1500 rpm. Set the cruise control. Operate the vehicle for approximately 3–5 miles (5–8 km) or in three separate 1-mile (1.5 km) increments if a steady operational speed is not possible over a 3–5 miles (5–8 km) mile trip.
DEF Doser & SCR	Perform the same procedure outlined for the Steady State cycle. Using DAVIE service software, select the following monitor values to record: Exhaust Temperature Before SCR Exhaust Temperature After SCR Pump Module Once the SCR temperatures have reached a minimum of 536°F (280°C), continue the remainder of this cycle in high idle. The monitored Pump Module value will indicate when dosing starts. Allow dosing to occur for a minimum of 15 minutes. Check the recorded values after the driving has been completed to verify temperatures and dosing.
Overrun	With the System Initiation cycle complete, proceed to a road with minimum speed limit of 50 mph (80 km/h). While remaining within the legally posted speed limit, get the truck in the highest gear possible with the engine speed at a minimum of 1800 rpm. Once the target engine speed has been reached, leave the truck in gear and release the accelerator pedal, allowing the truck to coast until the engine speed has reached 900 rpm. Perform this cycle four times. For Eaton Ultrashift transmissions, idle drop can only go to 1000 rpm. For Alison Autoshift transmission, this test will not be able to be conducted.
DPF & DOC	This test can take up to 45 minutes to 1 hour to complete. Start the truck and using cruise control, bump and set the idle to 1500 rpm. Connect DAVIE, and go to DPF Regeneration test. Follow the prompts to complete a Stationary Regeneration.
Cold Soak	The truck must remain off (key to OFF and the engine OFF) for 8–10 consecutive hours. Wait for this time to elapse before continuing. Perform the Electrical & Power-Up cycle. Perform the Start-Up cycle.

operation, the wide-band planar-type oxygen sensor measurements are compared against expected values. Too much or too little flow will trigger fault codes.

Backpressure Valve Control

PACCAR uses a **backpressure valve (BPV)** on its MX engines to create exhaust backpressure for engine braking and increase exhaust backpressure to supply the EGR system and decrease the exhaust gas flow in the exhaust system to assist heating the exhaust aftertreatment system FIGURE 39-59. By lowering the amount of exhaust flow, less intake air is drawn into the engine, producing an increased exhaust temperature. The BPV actuator is a smart remote actuator that communicates with the on-board network. While it is controlled by the engine ECM, it provides diagnostic information for its input and output circuits, which include:

- Stepper motor position and current flow
- Output shaft position
- ECU printed circuit board temperature
- Power supply voltage

After the ignition is switched on, the valve position is 100% open until the actuator is closed by the engine ECM. The failsafe unpowered and position of the valve is controlled by a spring inside the smart remote actuator. If a fault is detected, the BPV moves to the failsafe wide open position.

FIGURE 39-59 An air-operated BPV and a coolant cooled EGR valve.

Adjusting for Engine Idle Shutdown

The engine idle shutdown timer (EIST) is a valuable tool used to limit idle time and improve fuel economy. However, during extreme weather conditions, Paccar engines can be programmed to respond to engine coolant temperatures, which allows for longer uninterrupted warm-up time intervals. Temperature overrules allow the engine to idle while coolant, oil, and fuel temperatures are below calibrated settings. Several options are available to change the weather and operating conditions to determine how long the engine is allowed to idle. These include resetting the countdown to engine shutdown based on the accelerator pedal, clutch pedal, parking brake, service brake, and engine load. Also, the following are customer programmable settings for the EIST: ambient air temperature overrule, EIST in PTO mode, and EIST engine load overrule.

To adjust for engine idle shutdown, follow the steps in **SKILL DRILL 37-3**.

 SKILL DRILL 37-3 Adjusting for Engine Idle Shutdown

1. Open PACCAR Engine Pro (PEP), which is a North American software application used for making changes or adjusting engine parameters.

2. Select Engine Idle Shutdown Timer (EIST) from the list of programmable parameters.

3. Select Feature Options and choose the new setting within the Max-Min parameter range.

Wrap-Up

Ready for Review

- Volvo, Mack, Kenworth, and Peterbilt are major North American truck and bus manufacturers with large European stakeholders. Volvo and Mack are a single corporate entity, while Kenworth and Peterbilt are part of PACCAR, Inc., a global producer of premium medium- and heavy-duty trucks.
- Engines used by these companies have designs originating in Europe which are reflected in a number of construction features. These include compact profiles to fit into smaller engine compartments of cab over vehicles and unique cold-weather operational features that reflect engine operation intended for use in northern European climates.
- Volvo is an integrated manufacturer of heavy-duty vehicles and engines and is ranked the world's second-largest heavy-duty truck brand behind Daimler Trucks.
- One of Volvo's largest evolutionary steps came in the 2000 when Volvo acquired Renault Vehicles Industry (RVI), which also had previously purchased Mack Trucks. The deal made Volvo the biggest European heavy vehicle maker.
- Volvo is best known in the bus and truck industry for its D12 12L (732 cubic inch) engine, which was introduced in 1993.
- In 2006, Volvo introduced an entirely the new family of Volvo diesels: the D11, D13, and D16 engines, which were designed to meet the EPA07 emissions standards.
- Mack's roots as a truck maker extend to 1907 when the first truck built by the Mack brothers as part of an effort to diversify manufacturing expertise after originally building streetcars.
- When not used for on-highway trucks, Mack engines used in low-speed vocational operations were called Econodyne engines.
- To meet the first big reduction in engine emissions standards, Mack developed a partial authority electronically controlled injection pump-line-nozzle (PLN) fuel system, which it used exclusively on the E7 engine.
- Beginning in 2001, Mack began to phase in their unit pump system on the E-TECH engine.
- The first of the MP engines brought to market sharing Volvo platforms was the 11L (671 cubic inch) MP7. Newer MP engines have multi-torque capabilities, which means they have two different peak torque curves. To enable this feature unique to Mack and Volvo, a mass-based variable torque (MBVT) programmable parameter must be enabled.
- MBVT is an engine governor control function that automatically adjusts engine torque output to match vehicle weight.

- All current Mack and Volvo engines use electronic unit injectors. Mack's E7 E-TECH used unit pumps driven by an engine mounted camshaft. Volvo D12 engines used first-generation unit injectors manufactured by Delphi that had a single electrically energized control valve.
- All MP and Volvo engines use a common flow pressure fuel system configuration.
- Multiple electronic control units (ECUs) are used on Volvo–Mack engine chassis. These include the engine control module (ECM), instrument control module (ICM), vehicle electronic control unit (VECU), transmission control module (TCM), gear selector control module (GSCM), and the aftertreatment control module (ACM).
- Another unique feature of the Volvo D12 engine is the use of an exhaust pressure governor (EPG).
- Volvo uses a uniquely designed engine retarding system combining two different systems, the exhaust brake incorporated into the EPG and the compression brake.
- Volvo–Mack engines use three EGR systems: the V-pulse system, the internal or I-EGR system, and a conventional high-pressure cooled EGR system with some unique components.
- PACCAR Inc. started as Seattle Car Manufacturing Company in 1905. In 1917, it merged with a Portland-based competitor and was renamed as Pacific Car and Foundry Company. Kenworth became part of the PACCAR group after it was purchased in 1945.
- PACCAR ranks second in the United States and third globally in number of heavy vehicles produced, behind only Daimler AG in the U.S. market.
- PACCAR has several engines under its nameplate. The PACCAR MX-13, introduced in 2010, and MX-11, in 2015, are new engines, marking the entry of PACCAR into the North American heavy-duty engine market.
- The MX engines use fractured cap technology for the main bearing caps and connecting rods.
- PACCAR used Delphi EUPs on its first-generation MX-13. In 2013 PACCAR introduced its new common-rail fuel-injection system for the MX engines with injection pressures of up to 36,000 psi (2482 bar) to replace the MX-13 unit-injector system.
- PACCAR uses a service diagnostic tool called DAVIE, which is a software package and vehicle communication interface used to communicate with the engine ECM.

Vocabulary Builder

7th injector   Volvo–Mack's name for a hydrocarbon dosing valve that sprays diesel fuel into the exhaust system after the turbocharger. The 7th injector is used to help supplement the heating of the exhaust aftertreatment system.

advanced electronics engine management system (EMS) The latest generation of electronic control used by Volvo–Mack engines.

application-specific engine technology (ASET) Mack's suite of emission-control technologies that have specific application for on-highway and vocational vehicles.

backpressure valve (BPV) A valve located after the turbocharger on MX-13 engines used to create exhaust backpressure for engine braking, increase exhaust backpressure to supply the EGR system, and decrease the exhaust gas flow in the exhaust system to assist in heating the exhaust aftertreatment system.

compacted graphite iron (CGI) A material used to construct engine blocks. CGI is lighter, stronger, and more resistant to bending and twisting forces than conventional cast iron.

current-controlled rate shaping (CCRS) A marketing name given by Mack for a Bosch electronic unit pump high-pressure injection system

DAVIE Service and diagnostic software used by PACCAR. It is an acronym for DAF Vehicle Investigation Tool. In North America DAVIE refers to Diagnostic Analysis for Vehicle Interface Equipment.

derate mode The reduction of power output by 25% or more in response to an emission-related engine fault code or an engine protection fault code.

Econovance variable injection timing system A partial-authority fuel system used by Mack trucks. The inline injection pump had an electronically controlled governor and an electrohydraulic mechanism used to electronically vary injection timing.

exhaust pressure governor (EPG) A device used by Volvo to restrict exhaust gas flow from the engine. Increasing backpressure raises engine operating temperature at idle, reduces hydrocarbon emissions, and can supplement the engine-based compression release brake.

fractured cap technology A technique used by PACCAR to create a precision fit between connecting rod and main bearing caps. The caps are formed by scribing a parting line on the caps and then breaking the caps apart to form two separate parts.

gear fast run slow A fuel-efficient operating strategy used to take advantage of a diesel engine's low rpm torque. The differential gear ratios are intentionally low to enable high road speed at low engine rpm.

high torque rise engine An engine that has a sharp increase in torque as engine rpm drops from cruising speed when under heavy loads.

internal exhaust gas recirculation (I-EGR) An EGR system used on vocational vehicles that opens the exhaust valve momentarily during the intake stroke to recirculate exhaust gas into the cylinders.

mass-based variable torque (MBVT) An software-based torque control system that automatically adjusts engine torque output to match vehicle weight and load conditions. MBVT improves fuel efficiency and performance.

multi-torque An engine with the capability of changing its torque rise based on operating conditions. Commonly higher engine torque output is enabled in cruise mode.

peak torque The engine rpm where cylinder pressures are highest.

Premium Tech Tool The latest generation of service software used by Volvo–Mack to diagnose fault codes, adjust programmable parameters, and provide any other electronic support for the vehicle and engine control system

stiffening plate A steel plate attached to the oil pan rails to minimize vibration and torsional movement of the crankcase in high-horsepower engines.

turbocharger compressor bypass valve A valve used by Volvo–Mack engines to assist heating of intake air at idle. Turbocharger outlet pressure is recirculated back into the compressor inlet to repressurize intake air and raise its temperature

ultra-high-pressure injection (UHPI) Volvo–Mack's name for a high-pressure injection system using Delphi's E3 unit injector.

VECTRO An acronym for Volvo electronic control system for engine electronics.

Volvo Computer-Aided Diagnostics Systems (VCADS) A diagnostic software system used by Volvo to adjust and troubleshoot engine fault codes. The system is also used to adjust programmable parameters and perform any electronic support of the vehicle and engine control system.

V-pulse EGR An internal EGR system used by Volvo that uses cooled EGR gas and depends on natural pressure pulses in the exhaust system to supply exhaust gases to the intake manifold.

Review Questions

1. A _____ is an engine with the capability of changing its torque rise based on operating conditions.
   a. multi-torque
   b. high torque rise
   c. mass-based variable torque
   d. low torque

2. _____ is Volvo-Mack's name for a hydrocarbon dosing valve that sprays diesel fuel into the exhaust system after the turbocharger.
   a. MackForce
   b. Gear fast run slow
   c. 7th injector
   d. Econovance variable injection timing system

3. The _____ is an engine that has a sharp increase in torque as engine rpm drops from cruising speed when under heavy loads.
   a. multi-torque
   b. high torque rise engine
   c. 7th injector
   d. gear fast run slow

4. A fuel-efficient operating strategy used to take advantage of a diesel engine's low rpm torque is a _____.
   a. high torque rising system
   b. multi-torque
   c. 7th injector
   d. gear fast run slow

5. A(n) _____ is a partial authority fuel system used by Mack trucks.
   a. 7th injector
   b. Econovance variable injection timing system
   c. gear fast run slow
   d. multi-torque

6. Premium Tech Tool is the name of _____'s current diagnostic software.
   a. PACCAR
   b. International
   c. Volvo
   d. Delphi International

7. The overhead camshafts on all Volvo engines have a(n) _____ torsional dampener to improve valve timing.
   a. viscous
   b. active
   c. fractured
   d. electronic

8. All MP and Volvo engines use a(n) _____ pressure fuel system configuration.
   a. ultra-high
   b. partial-authority
   c. rate shaping
   d. common flow

9. On engines with the Volvo _____ the camshaft has two additional smaller lobes: an induction or intake lobe and decompression lobe.
   a. rocker arm
   b. engine break
   c. unit pump
   d. fractured cap

10. When a(n) _____ regeneration of the DPF is required, supplemental heating by the oxidation converter of the DPF takes place by dosing the exhaust gases with fuel.
    a. viscous
    b. high-pressure
    c. active
    d. low-pressure

ASE-Type Questions

1. Technician A says PACCAR, Inc. is a global producer of medium- and heavy-duty trucks. Technician B says both Kenworth and Peterbilt are part of PACCAR, Inc. Who is correct?
   a. Technician A
   b. Technician B
   c. Both Technician A and Technician B
   d. Neither Technician A nor Technician B

2. Technician A says in 2006 PACCAR introduced an entirely new family of diesels, the D11, D13, and D16 engines designed to meet the EPA-07 emissions standards. Technician B says in 2006 in Volvo and Mack introduced an entirely new family of diesels, the D11, D13, and D16 engines designed to meet the EPA-07 emissions standards. Who is correct?
   a. Technician A
   b. Technician B
   c. Both Technician A and Technician B
   d. Neither Technician A nor Technician B

3. Technician A says Mack engines used in low-speed vocational operations were called Econodyne engines. Technician B says Econodyne engines were used in on-highway trucks. Who is correct?
   a. Technician A
   b. Technician B
   c. Both Technician A and Technician B
   d. Neither Technician A nor Technician B

4. Technician A says the VMAC system introduced in 1994 included 30 programmable operating features such as trip-recording functions, PTO operation, idle shutdown, and emergency shutdown features. Technician B says the VMAC III system introduced in 1994 included 30 programmable operating features such as trip-recording functions, PTO operation, idle shutdown, and emergency shutdown features. Who is correct?
   a. Technician A
   b. Technician B
   c. Both Technician A and Technician B
   d. Neither Technician A nor Technician B

5. Technician A says the AI emission reduction strategy relied on the use of high-pressure cooled exhaust gas recirculation strategy. Technician B says the ASET AF emission reduction strategy relied on the use of high-pressure cooled exhaust gas recirculation strategy. Who is correct?
   a. Technician A
   b. Technician B
   c. Both Technician A and Technician B
   d. Neither Technician A nor Technician B

6. Technician A says the normal DPF catalyst filter element expected cleaning or replacement interval on a Volvo-Mack engine is 200,000 miles. Technician B says the normal DPF catalyst filter element expected cleaning or replacement interval on a Volvo-Mack engine is 250,000 miles. Who is correct?
   a. Technician A
   b. Technician B
   c. Both Technician A and Technician B
   d. Neither Technician A nor Technician B

7. Technician A says accidentally adding diesel fuel to the DEF reservoir may result in damaged injectors. Technician B says accidentally adding diesel fuel to the DEF reservoir may result in aftertreatment SCR system damage. Who is correct?
   a. Technician A
   b. Technician B
   c. Both Technician A and Technician B
   d. Neither Technician A nor Technician B

8. Technician A says PACAAR's engine idle shutdown timer can be adjusted to reset the countdown to the engine shutdown based on the accelerator pedal and parking brake. Technician B says PACAAR's engine idle shutdown timer can be adjusted to reset the countdown to the engine load. Who is correct?
   a. Technician A
   b. Technician B
   c. Both Technician A and Technician B
   d. Neither Technician A nor Technician B

9. Technician A says together all the Volvo-D series engines share a 90% parts commonality in design and function. Technician B says together all the Volvo-D series engines share a 94% parts commonality in design and function. Who is correct?
   a. Technician A
   b. Technician B
   c. Both Technician A and Technician B
   d. Neither Technician A nor Technician B

10. Technician A says mass-based variable torque is an engine governor control function that automatically adjusts engine torque output to match vehicle weight. Technician B says the high torque rise is an engine governor control function that automatically adjusts engine torque output to match vehicle weight. Who is correct?
   a. Technician A
   b. Technician B
   c. Both Technician A and Technician B
   d. Neither Technician A nor Technician B

SECTION VII

Engine Electrical, Hybrid Drive Systems, and Alternate Fuels

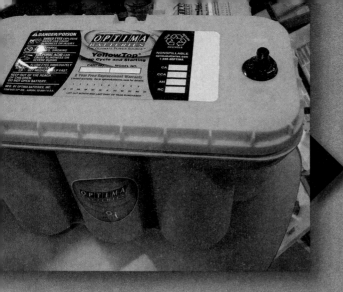

CHAPTER 40
Commercial Vehicle Batteries

NATEF Tasks

There are no NATEF tasks for this chapter.

Knowledge Objectives

After reading this chapter, you will be able to:

1. Describe the purpose and applications of batteries. (pp 1139–1141)
2. Identify and describe the construction and types of lead–acid batteries. (pp 1142–1147)
3. Identify and describe the features of lithium, nickel-cadmium, and nickel-metal hydride batteries as well as ultra capacitors. (p 1142)
4. Identify and describe the purpose, operation, and application of battery types. (p 1142)
5. Define battery terminology and explain battery ratings. (pp 1147–1149)
6. Recommend the correct size, type, and rating of replacement batteries. (pp 1149–1150)
7. Identify and explain chemical reactions in lead–acid batteries during charging and discharging. (pp 1150–1151)

Skills Objectives

There are no skills objectives for this chapter.

► Introduction

Batteries are the most essential component in a vehicle's electrical system. Not only do batteries provide starting power for engines and operating electrical accessories, they play a critical role in proper operation and longevity of many other electrical components. The recent development of medium- and heavy-duty hybrid drive vehicles has added to the battery's list of jobs. In addition to their traditional functions, batteries must now supply energy to electric drive motors and help recover energy during braking. Today's technicians need to know a lot more about the various types of batteries they will encounter, how those batteries work, as well as what should be done to maintain, test, and work safely with them.

► What Is a Battery?

Batteries are not devices that store electricity. In reality, they just convert chemical energy into electrical energy and vice versa. When connected to an electrical load, such as a light or electric motor, chemical reactions taking place inside the battery force electrons from the negative to the positive terminal of the battery though the load. Flow of electricity will end when the battery's chemical energy is depleted by the electrical loads in the circuit. The single direction electrons flow during discharge means a battery is a source of direct current (DC).

Battery Classifications

Batteries can be classified into two basic categories: primary and secondary. In a **primary battery**, chemical reactions are not reversible, and the battery cannot be recharged. In contrast, **secondary batteries** are rechargeable **FIGURE 40-1**. By reversing the direction of current and pushing electricity back into the

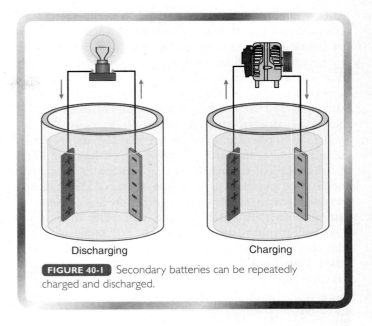

FIGURE 40-1 Secondary batteries can be repeatedly charged and discharged.

Discharging   Charging

battery, the chemical reactions that originally produced electrical current are renewed, allowing the secondary battery to be used over and over again. For this reason, secondary batteries based on the principles of galvanic reaction are the most practical for use in automotive applications. A **galvanic reaction** is a chemical reaction in which electricity is generated when two dissimilar metals are placed in an electrolyte.

Galvanic Batteries

The term *battery* more accurately refers to a collection of electrochemical cells connected together. A discovery made more

---

► You Are the Technician

As a technician with many years of service in your truck and heavy equipment dealership, you've been asked to join the health and safety committee. Your experience working in a shop environment has made you conscious of the importance of using safe working practices and making workplace safety a top priority. One of the initiatives of the health and safety committee is implementing the best safety practices to use while working with batteries. In fact, development of an in-house policy in addition to OSHA requirements originates from a recent incident where one worker was injured by an exploding battery while jump-starting a vehicle. As you are considering the various procedures that should be rigorously followed in the shop to avoid any accidents, injuries, or damage to customer vehicles and property.

1. What are the major safety issues related to working with batteries?
2. What protective equipment should you use when filling batteries or checking cell electrolyte with a hydrometer?
3. Outline a sequence of actions a technician should follow while jump-starting a vehicle.

than two hundred years ago by a medical experimenter named Galvani found that electricity is produced when two dissimilar metals are placed in an electrolyte. **Electrolyte** refers to any liquid that conducts electric current. For example, pure water will not conduct current. Tap water, however, will. That's because tap water often contains minerals and chlorine, so tap water is an electrolyte. Water containing salt, acids, or alkaline solutions is an even better conductor of electricity. The dissimilar metals placed in an electrolyte form electrodes—which are the points of the battery forming the positive and negative electrical poles. Chemical action between the electrolyte and electrodes strips electrons from one metal electrode and adds electrons to another electrode. That process develops the battery's polarity. After Galvani, another experimenter named Volta built the first battery by alternately stacking copper and zinc plates separated with a piece of saltwater-soaked cardboard. Volta named it a "voltaic pile" after demonstrating its electrical properties.

TECHNICIAN TIP

Galvanic reactions are observed in many places. Corrosion is one example of a galvanic reaction. The cooling system of an engine contains water (an electrolyte) and dissimilar metals like copper injector tubes, cast iron blocks, aluminum water pump housings, and so on. Metals losing electrons disintegrate while other metals remain unaffected. However, the electron transfer between the metals through coolant is easily observed by placing a voltmeter with one lead in the coolant and the other on the engine block or other metal part. (Corrosion inhibitors in the cooling system work by minimizing the loss of electrons from metals.) On trailers, aluminum side plates are insulated with a piece of non-conductive Mylar or insulating tape to electrically isolate the plate from steel I-beams supporting the floor. For the same reason, when aluminum and steel disc wheels are placed together on the same wheel end, they are separated with a plastic or nylon gasket to minimize corrosion caused by galvanic reactions.

A battery consists of two dissimilar metals: an insulator material separating the metals and an electrolyte, which is an electrically conductive solution. The material from which the electrodes are made and the type of electrolyte determine the voltage potential of a battery. The area of the plates making up each positive and negative electrode determines the capacity or amperage of a battery.

The traditional commercial vehicle battery type is the lead–acid battery. It is available in a variety of sizes and designs to meet the requirements for various applications. For example, the battery used for starting a vehicle's engine is different from the battery used for a boat, golf cart, or bulldozer. Each requires unique design characteristics based on its applications. Batteries for commercial vehicles using diesel engines are designed to supply high amperage to the starting motor for short periods of time. In contrast, a deep cycle battery is intended for use where its current is almost completely depleted, supplying smaller, continuous loads over longer periods of time.

TECHNICIAN TIP

Maintaining a strong negative ground on a vehicle will minimize chassis corrosion caused by galvanic reaction. You may notice most corrosion takes place at positive battery posts and at the end of non-insulated, positively charged wires. This happens because positively charged wire ends and battery posts are deficient of electrons. Oxygen and molecules in road salt are examples of substances that easily provide those electrons to electron-depleted metal and then are electrically bound to positive terminals and wire ends. Some military equipment and off-road heavy equipment from Europe use a positive ground system to protect the exposed wiring on starters, alternators, and wiring harnesses from the effects of corrosion. Electrical system reliability is enhanced at the expense of chassis corrosion, which instead attacks large heavy steel chassis components.

Battery Functions

Batteries similar to those shown in **FIGURE 40-2** have traditionally been used in heavy vehicles to provide starting current and operate electrical accessories if the engine is not running.

And, although supplying electric current for starting is the most obvious function for a battery, it's important to consider the other jobs the battery performs that are critical to proper electrical system operation. Battery functions on medium- and heavy-duty commercial vehicles include:

1. **Providing electrical energy to the vehicle whenever the engine is not running.** When the engine is running, a properly designed and operational charging system will supply electrical current to meet most electrical demands and charge the battery. For today's heavy vehicles and equipment, the limitation on, or even elimination of, engine idle means batteries need to supply electrical current for prolonged periods to devices such as electro-hydraulic pumps for hydraulic brakes, power steering, coolant pumps, and air conditioning compressors. Hybrid electric vehicles are now commonplace in urban transit. Hybrid electric transit buses are dependent on battery-supplied electrical current to operate all electrical devices, including electric drive motors and all electrical accessories, for much longer periods than conventional vehicles using accessories driven by an internal combustion engine.

2. **Providing electrical energy to operate the starter motor, ignition, and other electrical systems during cranking.** Other devices, such as hydraulic or air starter motors, could be used to start engines. However, even electronically controlled diesel injection systems require current to operate during cranking. When electric starter motors are used, batteries must be capable of delivering high current flow for short periods of time. Batteries used for cranking purposes have unique construction features and are commonly termed **starting, lighting, and ignition (SLI) batteries**. Commercial equipment, particularly diesel-powered equipment, will use multiple batteries, called a bank of batteries, connected in series or parallel to produce adequate starting current.

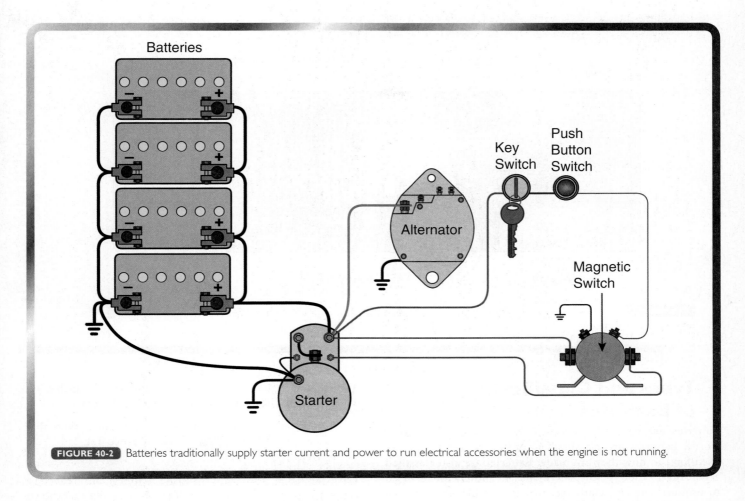

FIGURE 40-2 Batteries traditionally supply starter current and power to run electrical accessories when the engine is not running.

3. **Providing extra electrical power whenever power requirements exceed the output of the charging system.** High current demands are occasionally placed on the electrical system. For example, when an engine is idling, the charging system current output is low. Current flow to blower motors operating at high speed for heating or air conditioning systems, lighting circuits, and other electrical devices can exceed the output of the charging system. To maintain proper operation of these circuits, the batteries should be sized to provide adequate current.

4. **Storing energy over long periods of time. Even when vehicles are not in use for extended periods of time, the battery is still expected to deliver current to start a vehicle.** Today, heavy vehicles and equipment have numerous <u>key-off electrical loads</u>. These are current draws on the battery when the ignition is switched off. Also called <u>parasitic draw</u>, this battery current is required to continually operate vehicle security systems, GPS devices, and computer memory for multiple electronic control modules, entertainment systems, and other electrical accessories requiring constant power.

5. **Acting as an electric shock absorber for the vehicle's electrical systems.** The use of microprocessors and microcontrollers in almost every vehicle system makes today's heavy equipment sensitive to fluctuations in voltage. Operating on current in the millivolt range, stray and uneven electrical current can interfere with and even damage the operation of these sensitive electronic devices. The operation of common components such as alternators, switches, and electrical devices with inductive coils regularly produces this type of electrical interference. Batteries help minimize fluctuations in a vehicle electrical system by absorbing and smoothing variations in electrical current.

6. **Operating electric drive traction motors.** The development of hybrid electric vehicles (HEVs) has created new functions in addition to the traditional purposes of batteries. In HEVs, batteries must provide even higher amounts of current for longer periods of time to operate electric traction motors used to propel the vehicle, as illustrated in **FIGURE 40-3**. The same battery is also used to store energy recovered by the drive motors during braking. HEVs require new battery chemistry and construction to extend battery life, reduce weight, increase energy density, charge more quickly, and discharge and charge more frequently while delivering higher amounts of current flow for extended periods of time. Batteries must accomplish these goals in the harsh operating environment and duty cycle of commercial vehicles. At the same time, batteries must perform with greater and more consistent reliability than ever before. New types of batteries and battery-management systems are used to help meet these operational demands.

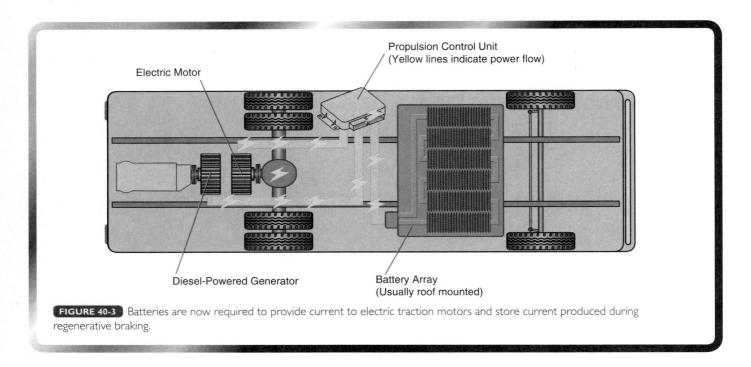

Electric Motor

Propulsion Control Unit
(Yellow lines indicate power flow)

Diesel-Powered Generator

Battery Array
(Usually roof mounted)

FIGURE 40-3 Batteries are now required to provide current to electric traction motors and store current produced during regenerative braking.

▶ Types and Classification of Batteries

Batteries are generally classified by application. In other words, batteries are classified according to what they are used for and how they are made. Batteries are also classified according to the type of plate materials and chemistry used to produce current. Until recently, lead–acid batteries have been the only battery technology used in commercial vehicles. While the search for more durable and reliable lead–acid batteries has brought innovation to that category of batteries, the development of hybrid drive vehicles has resulted in the introductions of different types of battery technology such as nickel–metal hydride and lithium batteries. Other chemistries will be further discussed in the Advanced Battery Technologies chapter.

Lead–Acid Batteries

Lead–acid batteries have been developed commercially for over 130 years and are a mature, reliable, and well-understood technology. They are also the most common battery used in the transportation industry. Lead–acid batteries deliver high rates of current with a higher tolerance for physical and electrical abuse compared to other battery technology. These batteries hold a charge well and when stored dry—without electrolyte—the shelf life is indefinite. Relatively simple compared to other battery technologies, lead–acid batteries are also the least expensive to manufacture in terms of cost per watt of power.

Contributing to the popularity of lead–acid batteries is the fact that they are available in a wide range of sizes and capacities from many suppliers worldwide. Lead–acid batteries can be classified by their construction and application. Six types of construction are found in on-highway commercial vehicles, but the basic chemical action is identical in all, including:

- Flooded cell, including low maintenance (like that shown in **FIGURE 40-4**) or maintenance free.
- Deep cycle flooded cell.

Valve-regulated lead–acid (VRLA) battery, also called a **sealed lead–acid (SLA)** or recombinant battery, like that shown in **FIGURE 40-5**, is a category that includes:

- Flooded
- Gel cell
- Absorbed glass mat (AGM)
- Spiral cell (Optima batteries)

FIGURE 40-4 A typical low- or no-maintenance SLI battery.

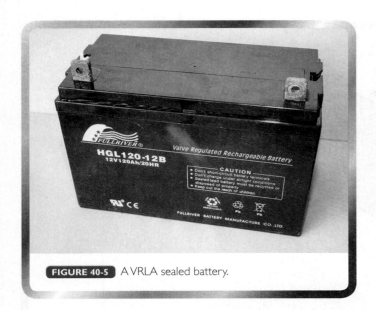

FIGURE 40-5 A VRLA sealed battery.

Starting, Lighting, and Ignition Batteries

Among the categories of lead–acid batteries, the most common use is for starting, lighting, and ignition (SLI). SLI batteries are designed for one short-duration deep discharge of up to 50% depth of discharge (DOD) during engine cranking. Discharging is quickly followed by a charging period, and a full charge is maintained. The operating requirements of an SLI battery are very different from traction batteries used in hybrid electric vehicles. Traction batteries are rechargeable batteries used for propulsion in hybrid electric vehicles. Though identical in appearance, SLI batteries are also constructed differently than deep cycle batteries.

Deep Cycle—Deep Discharge

Deep cycle batteries are used to deliver a lower, steady level of power for a much longer period of time than an SLI type battery. Furthermore, battery plate construction and charging and discharging characteristics of deep cycle batteries are different from SLI type batteries. In heavy vehicles, deep cycle batteries are used to supply current to constantly powered accessories like driver and vehicle communication devices. Deep cycle batteries also supply power to wave inverters, which in turn supply alternating current (AC) to appliances such as refrigerators, TVs, or laptop chargers. In addition, deep cycle batteries are also used to power accessory lighting, electric winches, and tailgates. This type of battery will typically use a battery isolator system that separates the main vehicle electrical system from the deep cycled battery circuit. The charging system will replenish the deep cycle battery charge but cannot be accessed by the main vehicle electrical circuits.

▶ Battery Construction and Operation

The basic components of a battery are its case, terminals, plates, and electrolyte. Even though the construction of batteries can vary depending on their type and application, these basic components remain the same. It is important that the correct size, type, and construction are selected for the application. Before selecting a battery for a particular application, the technician needs to answer a number of questions. For example, is the requirement for a starting battery or a deep cycle battery used to supply electrical accessories? Is the battery working in extremes of temperature? Is it a high vibration environment? What electrical load does the battery need to supply and for how long? What case and terminal configuration is required?

This section examines battery construction and discusses how those questions and their answers aid in the selection of the correct battery for an application. This section will also explain the charge and discharge cycle of a battery.

Flooded Lead–Acid Batteries

Flooded lead–acid batteries refer to battery cell construction where the electrodes are made from thin lead (Pb) plates submersed in liquid electrolyte. Two dissimilar compositions of lead form the positive and negative electrodes FIGURE 40-6. Sponge lead, which is lead made porous with air bubbles, forms the negative plate. Lead dioxide (PBO_2) is the active material of the positive plate.

The electrodes and electrolyte of a lead–acid battery cell produce 2.1 volts. Connecting cells together in series allows batteries to be produced in a variety of output voltage. This means a fully charged 12-volt battery, in fact, will produce 12.6 volts with no electrical loads by connecting six cells together. 24-volt systems are commonly used in heavy-duty off-road equipment, urban transit buses, highway coaches, and by the military. These are combinations of 12-volt batteries connected in series to produce 24 volts.

Adding Amperage and Voltage

The amount of amperage a battery supplies is a function of the surface area of the plates. To increase the amperage deliverable from a battery, the surface area or number of plates needs to increase. Plates are connected together in parallel within each cell to increase the amperage or capacity of a battery. Positive plates are connected only to other positive plates within each cell and likewise with negative plates. Plate straps for each cell set of positive and negative plates are joined through a connector to another strap in adjacent cells. There are two rows of these inter-cell straps and connectors. In a 12-volt battery, six positive plate straps are linked in series to six negative plate straps, alternating a positive strap to negative strap as each cell is connected FIGURE 40-7. The last cell in the series circuit will contain one of the battery posts, either positive or negative. Strap connections between the cells are made either through the cell partitions in the case or over the top of the partition.

Separator Plates

To prevent the battery positive and negative plate from touching and short circuiting, separator plates are placed between each plate in every cell. Separator plates are very thin, porous, glass-fiber materials allowing electrolyte to diffuse freely throughout the cell and at the same time prevent plate contact.

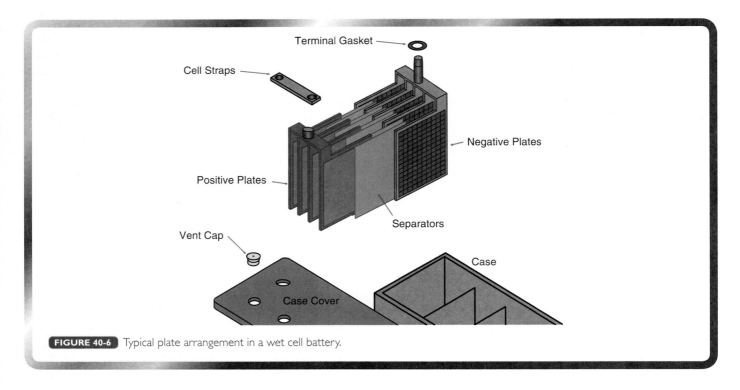

FIGURE 40-6 Typical plate arrangement in a wet cell battery.

FIGURE 40-7 Interconnections between all six cells in a battery, showing the most negative and positive points of the battery.

▶ TECHNICIAN TIP

SLI batteries are designed and constructed to deliver a short, high-amperage burst of current for starting. Using a deep cycle battery to replace an SLI battery can cause damage to starting motors and conductors through a condition known as low-voltage burn-out. This happens when battery voltage drops very low while supplying high cranking amperage to the starting motor. Because the deep discharge battery cannot maintain as high an output voltage, the excessive amperage produces resistance and heat in motors, cables, and connection windings, leading to burn-out. (See the Heavy-Duty Starting Systems and Circuits chapter for a complete explanation.)

Deep Cycle Versus SLI Battery Construction

SLI batteries are designed to produce a quick burst of energy for starting and should not be discharged less than 50% before recharging. Deeply discharging SLI batteries dramatically shortens their service life. Ideally, the longest service life is achieved when this battery is discharged no more than 5% and quickly recharged **FIGURE 40-8**.

In contrast, deep cycle batteries are made for deep discharging by continuous but light electrical loads until completely discharged. To optimize SLI battery characteristics, plates are made thin to fit more plates in each cell. More and thinner plates

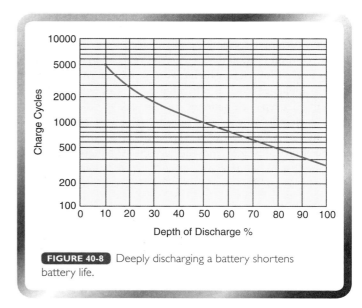

FIGURE 40-8 Deeply discharging a battery shortens battery life.

translate into higher available amperage due to increased plate surface area. However, continuous discharge of SLI batteries for prolonged periods of time will cause the current flow to overheat, distort, and warp the thin plates. Similarly, charging SLI batteries from a deeply discharged state can cause plates to overheat, dramatically shortening battery life. The primary difference between deep cycle batteries and SLI is the thickness of the plates **FIGURE 40-9**. Deep cycle plates are thicker to resist distortion during a discharge/charge cycle. However, thicker plates mean fewer plates compared to an SLI battery with identical dimensions. Thicker plate batteries also have higher resistance during high amperage charging and discharging in comparison to SLI batteries.

Electrolyte

Lead–acid battery electrolyte is a mixture of 36% sulfuric acid and 64% water. The specific gravity of water is 1.000. (**Specific gravity** is a measure of density.) Sulfuric acid has a specific gravity of 1.835, which means it is much heavier than water. Combined, the sulfuric acid and water solution has a specific gravity of 1.265. This makes it an electrolyte 1.265 times heavier than plain water. During charging and discharging, the specific gravity of the electrolyte changes. When discharging occurs, sulfate from the sulfuric acid enters both positive and negative plates. Oxygen also leaves the positive plate and combines with hydrogen left around in the electrolyte by the departing sulfate. This means the electrolyte has increasingly more water content and less acid during discharge, as illustrated in **FIGURE 40-10**. The process reverses during charging when sulfate is electrically driven from the plates and renters the electrolyte. Measuring the specific gravity or density of an electrolyte, therefore, is a good measure of battery state of charge (SOC).

Flooded cell batteries can be manufactured with or without an electrolyte. Dry batteries (without electrolyte) can be stored on the shelf for extended periods without the fear of sulfation and are lighter to transport. For this reason electrolyte is often only added to the battery at the point of sale.

When the specific gravity of battery acid is too low, such as when a battery is discharged, it may freeze in colder climates. An electrolyte that has lost water and is, therefore, over concentrated with acid can accelerate corrosion of battery grids to which lead plate material is bonded.

It is important to note that sodium bicarbonate (baking soda, not baking powder) is an effective way to neutralize electrolyte spills. Using a power washer, for example, will reduce the concentration of acid but not neutralize it. Squirting a mixed solution of ammonia and water on spilled battery acid will also neutralize the acid. Water and ammonia will also evaporate, leaving no mess to clean up.

A squeeze bulb and float type **hydrometer**, like the one shown in **FIGURE 40-11A**, is an instrument used to measure the density or the specific gravity of liquids. It also can be used to measure the specific gravity of batteries. A refractometer is an optical device that measures the density of coolant and battery electrolyte. When a drop of liquid is placed beneath the lens of the device, and then held up against a bright light source, a graduated scale in the view finder indicates the battery's specific gravity. A refractometer is shown in **FIGURE 40-11B**. **TABLE 40-1** indicates the various specific gravity and voltage readings for flooded lead–acid batteries. Electronic hydrometers enable faster, temperature-compensated measurement of the battery's state of charge. Remember that battery acid is highly corrosive, so when using these devices, properly protect yourself by wearing eye protection, a rubber apron, and acid-resistant gloves, particularly when handling electrolyte.

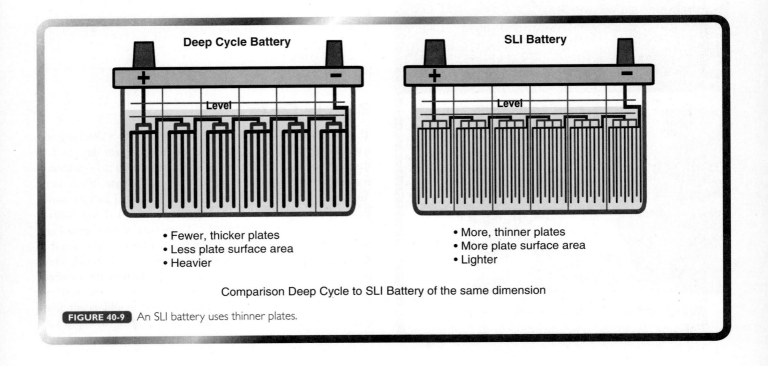

Comparison Deep Cycle to SLI Battery of the same dimension

FIGURE 40-9 An SLI battery uses thinner plates.

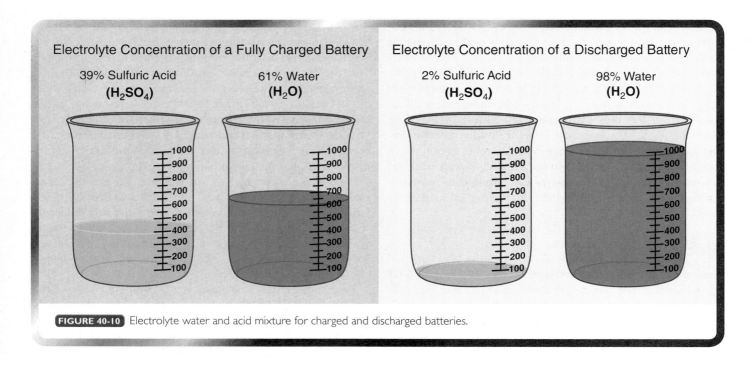

Electrolyte Concentration of a Fully Charged Battery

39% Sulfuric Acid
(H_2SO_4)

61% Water
(H_2O)

Electrolyte Concentration of a Discharged Battery

2% Sulfuric Acid
(H_2SO_4)

98% Water
(H_2O)

FIGURE 40-10 Electrolyte water and acid mixture for charged and discharged batteries.

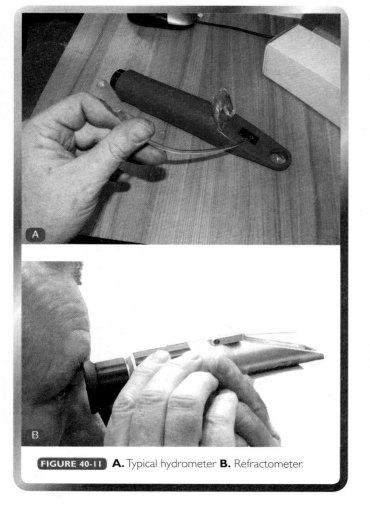

FIGURE 40-11 **A.** Typical hydrometer **B.** Refractometer.

TABLE 40-1: State of Charge as Indicated by Specific Gravity and Voltage Reading for Flooded Cell Batteries*

Open Circuit Voltage	Specific Gravity	Percentage of Charge
12.65 or greater	1.265 (minimum)	100
12.45	1.225	75
12.24	1.190	50
12.06	1.155	25
11.89	1.120	0

*AGM voltages will differ.

Battery Cases

The battery case is usually made of polypropylene. Ribbing and irregular features on the outside of the case are designed to increase the length of resistive electrical conductive pathways made when dirt and water accumulate on the case. These accumulations can allow current to drain from the battery posts. Each of the six cells in a 12-volt battery is sealed and electrolytes cannot move between cells. A gap between the plates and the bottom of each cell forms a sediment trap, as illustrated in **FIGURE 40-12**. The trap collects battery plate material that sheds during operation. Vibration and deeply discharging a battery accelerate the loss of plate material and reduce the battery's capacity. Without the trap, plate material would accumulate and potentially short circuit the plates, leading to rapid self-discharge of the battery.

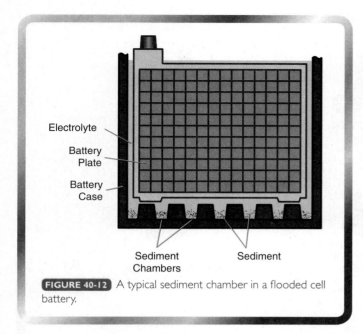

FIGURE 40-12 A typical sediment chamber in a flooded cell battery.

Labels: Electrolyte, Battery Plate, Battery Case, Sediment Chambers, Sediment

During charging and discharging, batteries produce hydrogen and oxygen gas caused by the break-down of water through a process called hydrolysis. These gases require venting and are an explosion hazard. In older flooded batteries, each cell used a cap to vent gases, add water to the electrolyte level, and permit inspection of the electrolyte with a hydrometer. Low-maintenance batteries use a small, single vent near the top of the battery. Extra electrolyte is added to these batteries to compensate for water loss over the expected lifetime of the battery. Low-maintenance batteries have advanced plate material that result in less water loss than conventional flooded batteries. Nonetheless, a removable plug is often still used to allow access to the electrolyte during testing and servicing.

Sizing and Terminal Configuration

Batteries for commercial vehicles are available in a wide variety of sizes. Manufacturers build their batteries to an internationally adopted Battery Council International (BCI) group number. BCI group numbers are established according to the physical

case size, terminal placement, terminal type, and polarity. For example, battery terminals used in medium- and heavy-duty commercial applications use a top post, threaded stud, or "L" terminal, with combinations of each of these types. **TABLE 40-2** classifies various heavy-duty commercial battery groups.

Other designations relate to the battery terminal configuration, which refers to the shape and location of the positive and negative terminals on the battery, as illustrated in **FIGURE 40-13**. Different types of battery posts are also available for batteries, including top post, threaded stud, side terminal, or "L" terminal, as well as combinations of each of these types.

▶ TECHNICIAN TIP

To help identification and prevent incorrect connection to post-type batteries, the positive terminal is 1/16" (1.6 mm) larger than the negative terminal. Because terminals are only soldered to the cell straps and anchored by the polyethylene case, they are vulnerable to damage if abused. Prying and hammering on posts are common types of abuse that will break the seal between the post and case and damage the connection to the plate strap.

Battery Ratings

The **electrical capacity** of a battery is the amount of electrical current a lead–acid battery can supply. Common battery capacity ratings used by North American manufacturers are established by the BCI and the Society of Automotive Engineers (SAE). Technicians will encounter other rating systems depending on the origin of the vehicle and while using some testing equipment, including:

- Japanese Industrial Standard (JIS)
- EN (European Norms) Standard
- DIN (Deutsches Institut für Normung)
- IEC (International Electrotechnical Commission) Standard

There are several methods used to rate lead–acid battery capacity. The three most common are cold cranking amps (CCA), cranking amps (CA), and reserve capacity. **Cold cranking amps (CCA)** is a measurement of battery capacity, in amps,

TABLE 40-2: Heavy-Duty Commercial Batteries Groups (12-Volt)						
BCI Group Size	Length (mm)	Width (mm)	Height (mm)	Length (inches)	Width (inches)	Height (inches)
4D	527	222	250	20 3/4	8 3/4	9 7/8
6D	527	254	260	20 3/4	10	10 1/4
8D	527	283	250	20 3/4	11 1/8	9 7/8
28	261	173	240	10 5/16	6 13/16	9 7/16
29H	334	171	232	13 1/8	6 3/4	9 1/8 10
30H	343	173	235	13 1/2	6 13/16	9 1/4 10
31	330	173	240	13	6 13/18	9 7/16

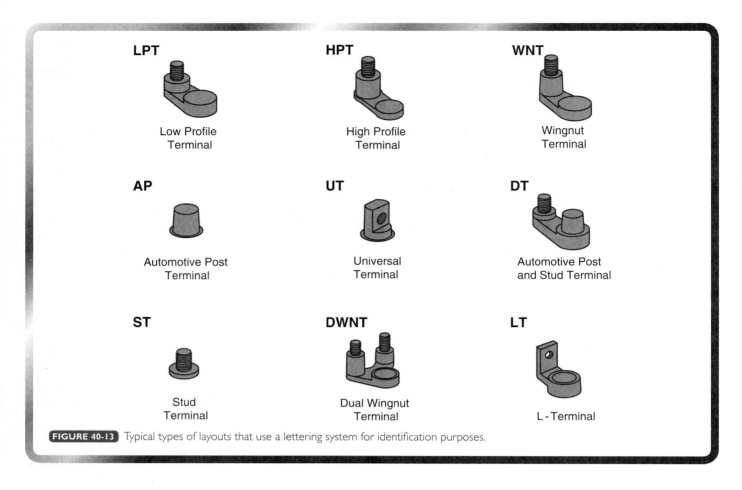

FIGURE 40-13 Typical types of layouts that use a lettering system for identification purposes.

that a battery can deliver for 30 seconds while maintaining a voltage of 1.2 volts per cell (7.2 volts for a 12-volt battery) or higher at 0°F (−18°C) **FIGURE 40-14**. **Cranking amps (CA)** measure the same thing, but at a higher temperature: 32°F (− 0°C). A 500-CCA battery has about 20% more capacity than a 500-CA battery.

Reserve capacity is the length of time, in minutes, a battery can be discharged under a specified load of 25 amps at 80°F (26.7°C) before battery cell voltage drops below 1.75 volts per cell (10.5 volts for a 12-volt battery). This measure is modeled on estimates of how long an automobile could be driven after an alternator fails with electrical loads from headlights and other loads before the ignition system fails.

FIGURE 40-14 Battery ratings are indicated on battery label. **A.** Date code. **B.** Battery ratings CCA, CA, and RC.

TECHNICIAN TIP

Early commercial vehicles with minimal electrical loads used 6-volt batteries for a 6-volt electrical system. In the 1950s, 12-volt systems and batteries became widely used. 24-volt systems are made from combinations of 12-volt batteries connected in series to produce 24 volts. Operating with higher voltages means less amperage will flow through electrical circuits and connections yet maintain the same power levels. With less amperage traveling through conductors, the reliability of the vehicle's electrical system improves because connections and cables do not heat nearly as much from high amperage flow. The size of components and wire diameters are reduced as well.

Amp-hour is a measure of a battery's capacity. Specifically, it is a measure of how much amperage a battery can continually supply over a 20-hour period without the battery voltage falling below 10.5 volts. Amp-hour is measured at 80°F (26.7°C)— the temperature at which lead–acid batteries perform best.

A battery with a 200 amp-hour rating would deliver 10 amps continually for 20 hours (20 hours × 10 amps). This is an important rating when selecting a deep cycle battery.

Multiple-Battery Configurations

Batteries can be connected together to supply either more amperage or more voltage. Diesel engines, which require more cranking torque, will either connect batteries in parallel, like those illustrated in **FIGURE 40-15** to supply more cranking amperage, or in series to supply higher voltage. For example, if two 600-CCA 12-volt batteries were connected in parallel, the batteries' potential output would be 1,200 CCA at 12 volts. If the batteries are connected in series, the batteries' voltage output is added together even though the cranking amperage remains the same. That means, if two 600-CCA 12-volt batteries were connected in series, the batteries' potential output would be 600 CCA at 24 volts.

Battery Selection

Factors that determine the battery rating required for a vehicle include the current needed for key-off loads, operating electrical accessories, the engine type (diesel or spark ignited), the engine size, and climate conditions under which equipment must operate.

In cold weather, battery power drops drastically because the electrolyte thickens and cold temperatures slow chemical activity inside the battery. In colder weather, engines are also harder to crank due to increased resistance from oil thickening. It is calculated that engine resistance increases between 50% and 250% in the winter compared to the summer, as illustrated in **FIGURE 40-16**. Simultaneously, available battery current can drop as much as 75%. As batteries age, their capacity drops too.

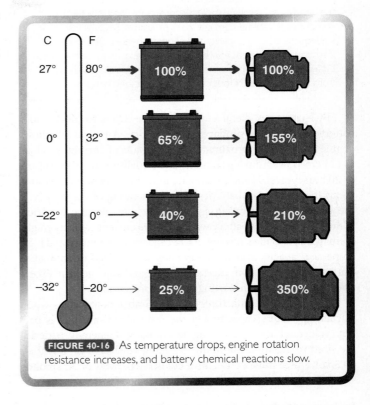

FIGURE 40-16 As temperature drops, engine rotation resistance increases, and battery chemical reactions slow.

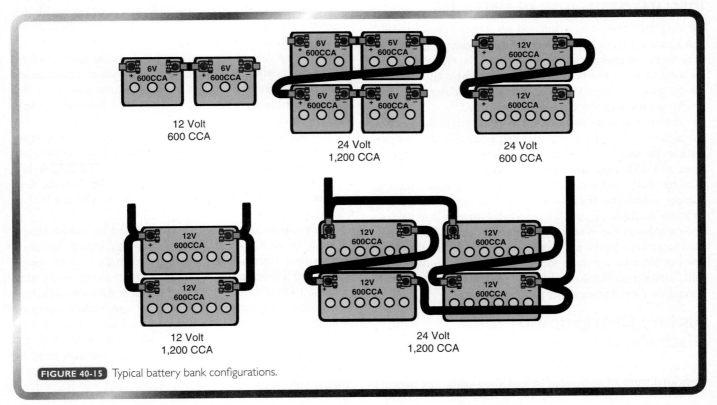

FIGURE 40-15 Typical battery bank configurations.

▶ **TECHNICIAN TIP**

Equipment with excessive battery capacity (too many CCAs) can lead to premature failure of the starter motor and starter drive due to excessively high torque. Excessive battery CCA increases the amperage through cables, connections, and starter circuit components, causing damage from resistance heating. However, inadequate battery capacity will shorten battery life from deep discharging. Equipment may even fail to start in cold weather or as batteries age. Starter motors, cables, and circuits can be damaged from low-voltage burn-out caused by undersized batteries.

BCI estimates diesel engines require 220% to 300% more battery power than a similar gasoline engine. A typical 15L diesel engine today uses approximately 10,000 watts of current (or close to 12 horsepower) during cranking and initially needs 15,000 watts, or 20 horsepower. Vehicle manufacturers make recommendations about the capacity of batteries. The CCA rating of the battery is the most important rating considered when selecting batteries. Although selecting a battery with excessive current capacity might seem like a good idea, it is not. Extra capacity is expensive and high amperage capacity available from batteries can lead to premature starter drive failure from excessive torque and damage from excessive amperage through starting circuit connections.

Equipment manufacturers use a number of variables when calculating battery capacity, but the most significant one is battery voltage at the end of engine cranking. Generally batteries are sized to ensure a minimum cranking voltage of no less than 10.5 volts after three consecutive cranking periods of 30 seconds with a 2-minute cool-down period between each cranking period.

Internal Resistance of Batteries

All electrical devices have internal resistance—even batteries. Not all battery types have the same internal resistance, however. A battery's internal resistance depends on the types of materials used to make the plates and the chemical composition of the electrolyte. A battery's internal resistance determines how quickly a battery can be charged or discharged.

Batteries with a relatively low internal resistance, such as a standard lead–acid battery, can be charged quickly, and they can also be discharged quickly to supply a lot of current over a short period of time. This makes them ideal for use in vehicles as starter batteries because they can supply the high discharge current required by the starter motor to start the vehicle. Batteries are available with a lower internal resistance than that of a lead–acid battery, such as the newer lithium batteries now being used in battery banks for electric and hybrid vehicles. These types of batteries are more expensive than the standard lead–acid battery, and their lower internal resistance is generally not needed for everyday starter motor applications.

Battery Charging and Discharging Cycle

Battery plates are made of two different compositions of lead fabricated from paste bonded to lead alloy grids. The negative plate uses lead (Pb) and the positive plate uses lead peroxide (PbO_2). Antimony, calcium, or other metals are alloyed with the lead grid material to minimize corrosion of the lead by acidic electrolyte. Because the plates are made of dissimilar metals, the addition of electrolyte will cause galvanic reactions in each cell.

In a fully charged condition, the positive plate material is predominantly lead peroxide (PbO_2), and the negative plate is sponge lead. The composition of the electrolyte is 64% water and 36% sulfuric acid. Chemical interactions between the plates and electrolyte strip electrons from the positive plate and add electrons to the negative plate. That produces a 12.6-volt difference between the battery terminals. A lead–acid battery will remain in this condition without a load applied. However, due to activity of chemical reactions, a slow rate of self-discharge occurs, which will eventually discharge the battery. This self-discharge rate is dependent on temperature and the selection of materials used during manufacturing. In hot climates, complete self-discharge is measured in weeks. Cold slows down chemical reactions, so the self-discharge rate can take almost two years in colder climates.

When a load is applied across the battery, electrons moving from the negative to the positive terminal accelerate galvanic reactions. This process is illustrated in **FIGURE 40-17A**. Both plates and the electrolyte composition change as a result of electron movement. Oxygen atoms in the positive plate move into the electrolyte while the sulfate part of the acid moves into the positive plate, changing the cell from lead peroxide (PbO_2) to lead sulfate ($PbSO_4$). On the negative plate, sulfate also moves into the plate material, forming lead sulfate ($PbSO_4$). The electrolyte becomes less acidic and turns to water, as sulfate leaves and hydrogen in the electrolyte combines with oxygen driven from the positive plate.

Galvanic reaction in a battery will stop under two circumstances. One is if the battery has the electrical load removed. This halts chemical reactions caused by movement of electrons from one battery terminal to the other. Electron movement also stops when the positive and negative plates become saturated with sulfate in a process called **sulfation**.

When charging a lead–acid battery, the chemical reactions used to produce current are reversed, restoring the plate and electrolyte to its charged condition **FIGURE 40-17B** While charging, sulfate is driven from both plates back into the electrolyte. Oxygen in the electrolyte recombines with the lead in the positive plate.

The chemical action is accomplished by connecting a charger or an alternator (DC current), stripping the positive post of electrons and forcing them back into the negative terminal. Charging voltage needs to be sufficiently high enough to overcome a battery's natural resistance to current flow. Most charging systems maintain a maximum charging voltage of approximately 0.5-volts above battery voltage. This explains why the charging system set point for most 12.65-volt batteries is around 14.2-volts. Higher voltages used by battery chargers push more current into the battery at a higher amperage.

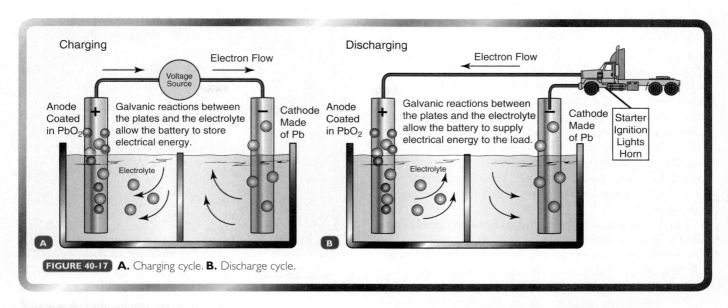

FIGURE 40-17 **A.** Charging cycle. **B.** Discharge cycle.

> ▶ **TECHNICIAN TIP**
>
> If a battery is completely discharged, the similar chemical composition of both plates permits the battery polarity to be reversed if connected incorrectly to a charger or charging system. The battery will charge up with reverse polarity. If a battery with reverse polarity is reconnected to a vehicle, the results are disastrous. Burnt wiring, blown fuses, and alternator damage will quickly result, leading to a potential vehicle fire.

Plate Sulfation

Sulfate is driven off battery plates when charging, as shown in **FIGURE 40-18A**. However, if a battery is left in a discharged state for a long period of time, continually undercharged, or left partially charged, the soft sulfate turns to a hardened crystalline form, as shown in **FIGURE 40-18B**. Hard sulfate cannot be driven from the plates.

This means the battery cannot be recharged and the remaining active plate material develops a high resistance to charging. The latest innovation to lead–acid battery technology incorporates black-carbon graphite foam into the plate paste to prevent sulfation damage. Graphite-foam carbon increases plate strength and surface area, which translates into greater power density and durability.

Battery Gassing

During charging and discharging, water in the electrolyte is broken apart into its constituent hydrogen and oxygen. This process, called **electrolysis**, releases both gases. Battery electrolyte is depleted through the loss of water by electrolysis. If battery electrolyte is too low, the plates dry out, and the increased acid concentration of electrolyte permanently damages the grids. Severe **gassing** occurs when cell charging voltage is pushed beyond 2.4 volts or severe discharge takes place, such as when a wrench or piece of metal is laid across battery terminals.

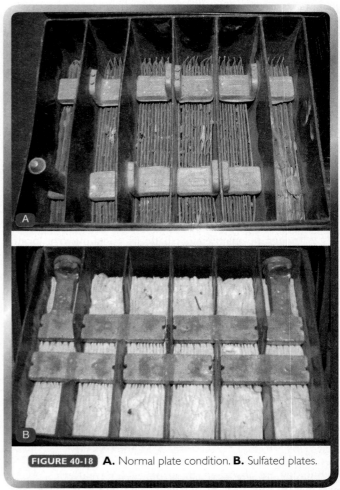

FIGURE 40-18 **A.** Normal plate condition. **B.** Sulfated plates.

Low- and No-Maintenance Batteries

The use of antimony alloy in the plate grids of conventional flooded battery technology minimizes grid corrosion and allows these batteries to accept up to 10 times more overcharging than newer low- or no-maintenance batteries. Unfortunately, antimony alloyed grids cause excessive gassing, resulting in substantial water loss. No- or low-maintenance battery technology solves that problem.

Introduced in the middle 1970s, no- and low-maintenance batteries reduce or eliminate the antimony content in grids. Calcium is used primarily now to replace antimony but barium, cadmium, or strontium is also used. No-maintenance batteries eliminate all the antimony, whereas low-maintenance batteries contain a reduced level of antimony content (approximately 2%). No- and low-maintenance batteries still require venting and need a large electrolyte reserve area above the plates to compensate for some water loss.

Another recent advance in grid composition involves the addition of silver into the calcium-lead alloy. Silver alloy has demonstrated a very high resistance to grid growth and corrosion. Thus, silver alloy significantly lengthens battery life in high heat and severe service conditions.

The advantages of low- or no-maintenance batteries include:

- Less water usage
- Less grid corrosion
- Less gassing
- Lower self-discharge rate
- Less terminal corrosion because less corrosive gas is emitted from the vents

The disadvantages of low- and no-maintenance batteries include:

- A lower electrical reserve capacity
- Often a shorter life expectancy
- Grid growth/expansion when exposed to high temperatures
- More quickly discharged by parasitic losses
- Difficulty accepting a boost when completely discharged

Although no-maintenance batteries contain a vent located beneath the top cover, the battery tops are completely sealed. Delco, which introduced the first no-maintenance battery, uses a built-in hydrometer that has colored balls. These balls will rise or fall in the electrolyte depending on the electrolyte density, thereby providing an indication of the state of charge. To boost these batteries from a completely discharged state, a small charge is recommended for about 10 minutes to begin the hydrolytic process of breaking water into hydrogen and oxygen. After that, the batteries are capable of receiving a higher rate of charge.

Low-maintenance batteries may look completely sealed, but they will usually have a means of adding water if required. Often the caps are concealed under a plastic cover that is removed to reveal cell caps that can be unscrewed **FIGURE 40-19**.

The latest and most advanced commercial vehicle battery technology are **absorbed glass mat (AGM) batteries**. AGMs provide improved safety, efficiency, and durability over existing battery types. The electrolyte is absorbed into a fine glass mat, as shown in **FIGURE 40-20**, preventing it from sloshing or

FIGURE 40-19 The spiral cell Optima battery is an example of an AGM-type battery.

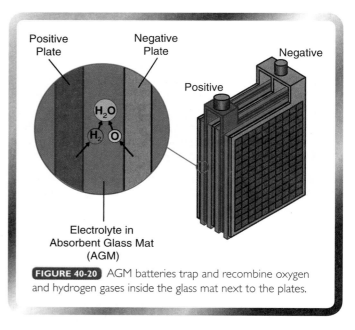

FIGURE 40-20 AGM batteries trap and recombine oxygen and hydrogen gases inside the glass mat next to the plates.

separating into layers of heavier acid and water. The fiber first helps by enhancing gas recombination rather than simply venting gas to the atmosphere and lowering electrolyte levels. AGM material also possesses low electrical resistance. As a result, it can deliver more cranking amperage and absorb up to 40% more charging current than conventional lead–acid, leading to faster charging. Higher cell voltage and sensitivity to overcharging requires special service consideration. Those topics will be covered in the Advanced Battery Technologies and Servicing Commercial Vehicle Batteries chapters.

Wrap-Up

Ready for Review

- There are two types of batteries. Primary batteries cannot be recharged; secondary batteries are rechargeable.
- Secondary batteries operate using the principles of galvanic reaction and are the most practical for use in commercial vehicle applications.
- Through a galvanic reaction, electricity is produced when two dissimilar metals are placed in an electrolyte.
- Batteries have traditionally been used in heavy vehicles to provide starting current and operate electrical accessories if the engine is not running.
- Batteries are classified by use, application, and chemistry used within the battery. Although lead–acid batteries are most prevalent, hybrid-drive vehicles also make use of nickel-metal hydride and lithium batteries.
- Lead–acid batteries deliver high rates of current with a higher tolerance for physical and electrical abuse compared to other battery technology. These batteries hold a charge well and when stored dry—without electrolyte—the shelf life is indefinite.
- Regardless of battery construction, all batteries have the same basic components: case, terminals, plates, cell straps, and electrolyte.
- A starting-lighting-ignition battery can supply very high discharge currents while maintaining a high voltage, which is useful when cold starting. A lead–acid battery gives high power output for its compact size, and it is rechargeable.
- Starting, lighting, and ignition batteries (SLI) are designed for a single short-duration deep discharge during engine cranking. Deep cycle batteries provide lower amperage current continually for electrical devices and accessories.
- Lead–acid batteries can be manufactured with electrolyte or dry. Dry batteries can be stored on the shelf for extended periods without the fear of sulfation and are lighter to transport.
- During charging and discharging, batteries produce hydrogen and oxygen gas caused by the break-down of water through a process called hydrolysis. These gases require venting and are an explosion hazard.
- Batteries can be configured into battery banks in cases where larger current or higher-voltage batteries are required.
- Battery temperature plays an important role in the performance of a battery and lead–acid batteries have ideal operating temperature range. A battery's internal resistance depends on the types of materials used to make the plates and the chemical composition of the electrolyte. A battery's internal resistance determines how quickly a battery can be charged or discharged.

Vocabulary Builder

absorbed glass mat (AGM) battery A battery in which electrolyte is absorbed in a fine glass mat that prevents prevent the solution from sloshing or separating into layers of heavier acid and water.

amp-hour A measure of how much amperage a battery can continually supply over a 20-hour period without the battery voltage falling below 10.5 volts.

cold cranking amps (CCA) A measurement of the load, in amps, that a battery can deliver for 30 seconds while maintaining a voltage of 1.2 volts per cell (7.2 volts for a 12-volt battery) or higher at 0°F (−18°C).

cranking amps (CA) A measurement of the load, in amps, that a battery can deliver for 30 seconds while maintaining a voltage of 1.2 volts per cell (7.2 volts for a 12-volt battery) or higher at 32°F (– 0°C).

deep cycle battery A battery used to deliver a lower, steady level of power for a much longer time.

electrical capacity The amount of electrical current a lead-acid battery can supply.

electrolysis The use of electricity to break down water into hydrogen and oxygen gases.

electrolyte An electrically conductive solution.

flooded lead–acid battery A lead–acid battery in which the plates are immersed in a water–acid electrolyte solution.

galvanic reaction A chemical reaction that produces electricity when two dissimilar metals are placed in an electrolyte.

gassing A situation that occurs when overcharging or rapid charging causes some gas to escape from the battery.

hydrometer An instrument used to measure the specific gravity of liquids.

key-off electrical loads Unwanted drain on the vehicle battery when the vehicle is off. Also called *parasitic draw*.

parasitic draw Unwanted drain on the vehicle battery when the vehicle is off. Also called *key-off electrical load*.

primary battery A battery in which chemical reactions are not reversible and the battery cannot be recharged.

reserve capacity The time, in minutes, that a new, fully charged battery at 80°F (26.7°C) will supply a constant load of 25 amps without its voltage dropping below 10.5 volts for a 12-volt battery.

sealed lead–acid battery A battery that does not have a liquid electrolyte nor requires the addition of water. Also called a *valve-regulated lead–acid battery (VRLA)* or *recombinant battery*.

secondary battery A rechargeable battery.

specific gravity A measurement of the density of a substance.

starting, lighting, and ignition (SLI) battery A battery designed for one, short-duration, deep discharge of up to 50% depth of discharge (DOD) during engine cranking.

sulfation A chemical reaction that results in the soft sulfate turning to a hardened crystalline form that cannot be driven from the plates in the battery.

traction battery A rechargeable battery used for propulsion in hybrid electric vehicles.

valve-regulated lead–acid (VRLA) battery A type of sealed lead–acid battery used in heavy-duty equipment. It does not require the addition of water. Also called a *sealed lead–acid battery (SLA) or recombinant battery.*

Review Questions

1. A measurement of the load, in amps, that a battery can deliver for 30 seconds while maintaining a voltage of 1.2 volts per cell or higher at 32°F (0°C) is called _____.
   a. cold cranking amps (CCA)
   b. cranking amps (CA)
   c. amp-hour
   d. reserve capacity

2. _____ is the time, in minutes that a fully charged battery at 80°F (26.7°C) will supply a constant load of 25 amps without its voltage dropping below 10.5 volts for a 12-volt battery.
   a. reserve capacity
   b. electrical capacity
   c. amp-hour
   d. cranking amp

3. _____ is a measurement of the load, in amps, that a battery can deliver for 30 seconds while maintaining a voltage of 1.2 volts per cell or higher at 0°F (-18°C).
   a. Electrical capacity
   b. Amp-hour
   c. Cranking amps
   d. Cold cranking amps

4. The amount of electrical current a lead acid battery can supply is called _____.
   a. reserve capacity
   b. electrical capacity
   c. amp-hour
   d. cranking amps

5. _____ is a measure of how much amperage a battery can continually supply over a 20-hour period without the battery voltage falling below 10.5 volts.
   a. Cold cranking amps
   b. Cranking amps
   c. Amp-hour
   d. Electrical capacity

6. The single direction electrons flow during discharge means a battery is a source of _____ current.
   a. direct
   b. indirect
   c. primary
   d. secondary

7. Corrosion is one example of a _____ reaction.
   a. chemical
   b. primary
   c. galvanic
   d. resistance

8. A battery's internal _____ determines how quickly a battery can be charged or discharged.
   a. resistance
   b. traction
   c. deep cycle
   d. recombinant

9. Connecting cells together in _____ allows batteries to be produced in a variety of voltage.
   a. sequence
   b. series
   c. order
   d. tandem

10. The amount of _____ a battery supplies is a function of the surface area of the plates.
    a. voltage
    b. amperage
    c. resistance
    d. power

ASE-Type Questions

1. Technician A says automotive battery capacity is rated by cranking amps and cold cranking amps. Technician B says automotive battery capacity is rated by reserve capacity. Who is correct?
   a. Technician A
   b. Technician B
   c. Both Technician A and Technician B
   d. Neither Technician A nor Technician B

2. Technician A says the Battery Council International group numbers are established according to terminal placement and type. Technician B says the Battery Council International group numbers are established according to physical case size. Who is correct?
   a. Technician A
   b. Technician B
   c. Both Technician A and Technician B
   d. Neither Technician A nor Technician B

3. Technician A says a squeeze bulb and float type hygrometer is an instrument used to measure the density or the specific gravity of batteries. Technician B says a squeeze bulb and float type hydrometer is an instrument used to measure the density or the specific gravity of batteries. Who is correct?
   a. Technician A
   b. Technician B
   c. Both Technician A and Technician B
   d. Neither Technician A nor Technician B

4. Technician A says the electrodes and electrolyte of a lead acid battery cell produce 2.1 volts. Technician B says the electrodes and electrolyte of a lead acid battery cell produce 3.2 volts. Who is correct?
   a. Technician A
   b. Technician B
   c. Both Technician A and Technician B
   d. Neither Technician A nor Technician B

5. Technician A says current demands on the battery when the ignition is switched off are called stray currents. Technician B says current demands on the battery when the ignition is switched off are called key-off electrical loads or parasitic draw. Who is correct?
   a. Technician A
   b. Technician B
   c. Both Technician A and Technician B
   d. Neither Technician A nor Technician B

6. Technician A says deep cycle batteries are used for propulsion in hybrid electric vehicles. Technician B says recombinant batteries are used for propulsion in hybrid electric vehicles. Who is correct?
   a. Technician A
   b. Technician B
   c. Both Technician A and Technician B
   d. Neither Technician A nor Technician B

7. Technician A says water containing salt and acids would be considered an electrolyte. Technician B says water containing alkaline solutions would be considered an electrolyte. Who is correct?
   a. Technician A
   b. Technician B
   c. Both Technician A and Technician B
   d. Neither Technician A nor Technician B

8. Technician A says lead acid batteries are not all that common in the transportation industry. Technician B says lead acid batteries are the most common battery used in the transportation industry. Who is correct?
   a. Technician A
   b. Technician B
   c. Both Technician A and Technician B
   d. Neither Technician A nor Technician B

9. Technician A says the primary difference between deep cycle batteries and SLI batteries is the thickness of the plates. Technician B says the plates are connected together in series to increase the amperage or capacity of the battery. Who is correct?
   a. Technician A
   b. Technician B
   c. Both Technician A and Technician B
   d. Neither Technician A nor Technician B

10. Technician A says temperature does not affect battery power. Technician B says in warm weather, battery power drops because the electrolyte thickness and warm temperatures slow chemical activity inside the battery. Who is correct?
    a. Technician A
    b. Technician B
    c. Both Technician A and Technician B
    d. Neither Technician A nor Technician B

CHAPTER 41
Advanced Battery Technologies

NATEF Tasks

There are no NATEF tasks for this chapter.

Knowledge Objectives

After reading this chapter, you will be able to:

1. Identify and describe the features of lithium and nickel-metal hydride batteries, and ultra-capacitors. (pp 1157–1164)

2. Identify and describe common battery failures. (p 1164)
3. Identify and explain the operation of battery isolators, low voltage disconnect, charge equalizers, and battery management systems. (pp 1164–1168)

Skills Objectives

There are no skills objectives for this chapter.

▶ Introduction

The demand for advanced battery technology in commercial vehicles is growing. Not only do the increasingly popular hybrid electric vehicles require advanced batteries, heavy-duty commercial vehicles also have a greater need for electrical storage capacity to run accessories. Several key factors are at play in determining which application of a variety of battery technologies to use on commercial vehicles, including:

- Energy density—FIGURE 41-1—expressed in Watt-hour per kilogram (Wh/kg) and Watt-hour per liter (Wh/L)
- Energy efficiency—the ability to convert charging current into storage capacity
- Life span—measured by the number of charge/discharge cycles as a function of depth of discharge
- The state of charge window—the availability of usable battery voltage
- Cost in dollars per kWh

▶ Types of Advanced Batteries

The major battery technologies used in heavy-duty commercial vehicles are nickel–metal hydride (NiMH), lithium, and lead–acid. Each technology has distinct capabilities, which we will discuss in this section. TABLE 41-1 compares the capacities of different battery types.

Nickel–Metal Hydride Battery

Nickel–metal hydride (NiMH) batteries are used not only in consumer electronics but are also a preferred battery chemistry for hybrid drive vehicles. That is because NiMH batteries are relatively lightweight and have high power output and long

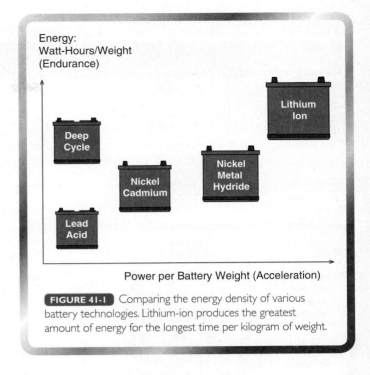

FIGURE 41-1 Comparing the energy density of various battery technologies. Lithium-ion produces the greatest amount of energy for the longest time per kilogram of weight.

life expectancy. Allison Ev heavy-duty hybrids use these as well as many automotive electric hybrid systems. NiMH batteries provide twice the energy storage of lead–acid by weight, but only half the power output—at 1.2 volts/cell compared to 2.1 volts/cell for lead–acid batteries. As illustrated in FIGURE 41-2, a unique alloy of rare earth metal, which has an unusual ability to absorb hydrogen, forms the metal hydroxide negative electrode. The positive electrode is made of nickel oxide ($NiOH_2$). The electrolyte is composed of potassium hydroxide, which is an alkaline.

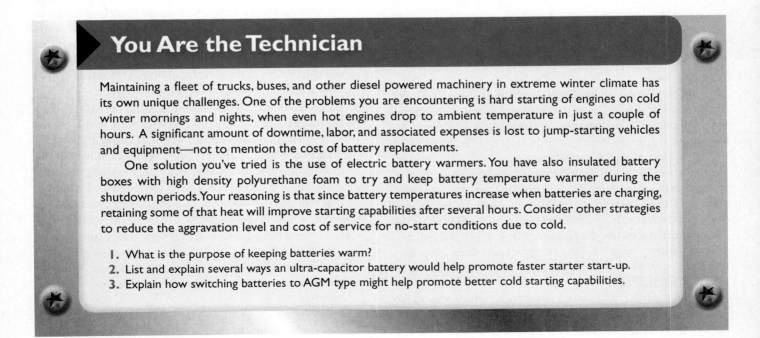

▶ You Are the Technician

Maintaining a fleet of trucks, buses, and other diesel powered machinery in extreme winter climate has its own unique challenges. One of the problems you are encountering is hard starting of engines on cold winter mornings and nights, when even hot engines drop to ambient temperature in just a couple of hours. A significant amount of downtime, labor, and associated expenses is lost to jump-starting vehicles and equipment—not to mention the cost of battery replacements.

One solution you've tried is the use of electric battery warmers. You have also insulated battery boxes with high density polyurethane foam to try and keep battery temperature warmer during the shutdown periods. Your reasoning is that since battery temperatures increase when batteries are charging, retaining some of that heat will improve starting capabilities after several hours. Consider other strategies to reduce the aggravation level and cost of service for no-start conditions due to cold.

1. What is the purpose of keeping batteries warm?
2. List and explain several ways an ultra-capacitor battery would help promote faster starter start-up.
3. Explain how switching batteries to AGM type might help promote better cold starting capabilities.

TABLE 41-1: Comparison of Properties for Different Battery Chemistries

Range Battery type	Voltage/cell	Cost Watt/hour	Energy Density Watt-hour/kg	Joules/kg	Watt-hour/liter
Lead–acid	2.1 volts	Lowest = 1	41	146,000	100
NiMH	1.2 volts	6 times lead–acid	95	340,000	300
Li-Ion	~4.0 volts	25 times lead–acid	128	460,000	230
Ultra-capacitors	~2-3 volts	4–5 times lead–acid	30–60	–	–
Diesel Fuel	–	–	–	–	10,942

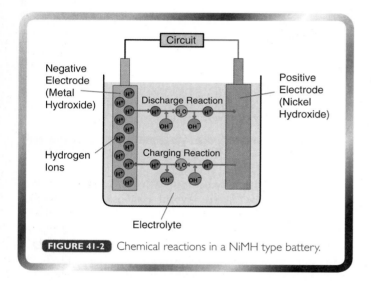

FIGURE 41-2 Chemical reactions in a NiMH type battery.

Lithium-Ion Battery

Lithium-ion batteries were developed for commercial use in the early 1990s. Since then, they have been used in laptops, cell phones, and other consumer electronic devices. Lithium-ion (Li-ion) batteries are secondary batteries and are not the same as disposable, primary-type lithium batteries, which contain metallic lithium.

Like conventional batteries, Li-ion batteries have electrodes and use an electrolyte. Unlike conventional batteries, the chemical reactions in Li-ion batteries are not galvanic, and the material separating the electrodes is a gel, salt, or solid material. With no liquid electrolyte, Li-ion batteries are immune to leaking. Currently there are dozens of different cell chemistries used to produce lithium-ion batteries. The voltage, capacity, life cycle, and safety characteristics of a lithium-ion battery can change dramatically depending on the choice of material for the anode, cathode, and electrolyte. Regardless of their specific chemistry, lithium batteries have a higher energy density than other battery types such as lead–acid, nickel–cadmium, and NiMH, as shown in **FIGURE 41-3**.

Popular Li-ion chemistries incorporate electrodes made from lithium combined with phosphate, cobalt, carbon, nickel, and manganese oxide. Lithium–phosphate chemistry

demonstrates the most promising attributes for electric and hybrid-electric vehicle batteries in transportation applications. For example, **FIGURE 41-4** shows a transit bus with battery tubs containing lithium batteries. The tubs and the battery management system are both located on the roof of the vehicle. Note that the stairs used to access the rooftop battery tubs have been specially designed for this purpose. A123 Systems produces lithium–phosphate batteries ($LiFePO_4$ chemistry) for use in heavy-duty hybrid and electric vehicles produced by BAE Systems, Navistar, Eaton, and Magna Steyr.

There are several advantages to using lithium-ion batteries in on-highway vehicles, including:

1. The best power-to-weight ratio compared to other battery technology. For example, the replacement of lead–acid batteries on a BAE-Orion Hybrid transit bus with equivalent lithium-ion, reduces battery pack weight from 4100 lb (1865 kg) to 1000 lb (455 kg). Li-ion batteries have twice the power density per kilogram of weight compared to NiMH chemistry (Bulletin from the Toronto Transit Commission).

2. Li-ion batteries have higher cell voltages—with as much as 5 volts in some designs. A typical cell voltage averages between 3.3 and 4.2 volts, which means fewer Li-ion cells are required to form high voltage batteries. It also translates into fewer vulnerable and resistive cell connections and reduced electronics in the battery management system. One lithium cell can replace three nickel–cadmium (NiCad) or NiMH cells, which have a cell voltage of only 1.2 volts.

3. Li-ion cells maintain a constant voltage for over 80% of their discharge curve. In comparison, conventional lead–acid batteries maintain voltage until only 50% discharged. Therefore, in a Li-ion battery, more stored energy is usable over longer periods to supply electrical accessories or to crank an engine frequently and faster before becoming effectively discharged. It also means that a smaller capacity battery can be used to supply a vehicle's power needs.

4. Li-ion batteries operate well over wide temperature ranges −60°F (−51°C) to 167°F (+75°C). Cold slows down chemical reactions in other battery technology. However, cold temperatures do not slow the non-galvanic reactions in Li-ion batteries.

5. Charging characteristics of Li-ion batteries are superior to other batteries. In consumer electronic devices, Li-ion

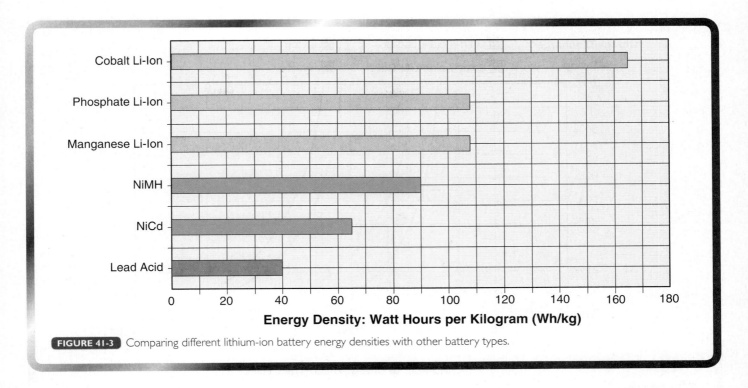

FIGURE 41-3 Comparing different lithium-ion battery energy densities with other battery types.

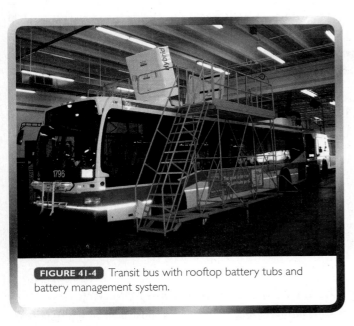

FIGURE 41-4 Transit bus with rooftop battery tubs and battery management system.

batteries have demonstrated the capacity to re-charge as much as 90% within five minutes. That speed is a distinct advantage for the efficiency of regenerative braking used by electric and hybrid electric vehicles. Once charged, Li-ion batteries self-discharge at a very low rate.

6. Li-ion batteries have low internal resistance and can discharge their current four times faster when compared to lead–acid batteries. In addition, high discharge and charge rates do not wear out a Li-ion battery to the extent that charge and discharge cycles reduce the lifespan of other

types of batteries. Currently, typical Li-ion batteries can withstand 1200 charge–discharge cycles in comparison to 500–800 cycles for lead–acid and 1500 for NiMH, as illustrated in the chart shown in **FIGURE 41-5**. Li-ion batteries last for millions of micro-discharge cycles. A micro-discharge cycle occurs when the charge is maintained between 40% and 80%. In contrast, lead–acid batteries last the longest only when discharged less than 5%.

While Li-ion technology appears to have every advantage over other battery technology, use of Li-ion technology is restricted by a number of limitations. Extensive investment and research are currently aimed at correcting serious limitations to the use of Li-ion technology in automotive applications. As a result, a variety of Li-ion chemistries are now competing for widespread use, each with unique advantages and disadvantages.

One disadvantage of current Li-ion battery technology is cost. Li-ion batteries cost eight times more than conventional lead–acid batteries for each kilowatt of power produced per hour. However, continuous innovation and increasing production are steadily dropping the price differential.

Chemical stability of Li-ion batteries is also a concern. Some batteries are destroyed at high temperatures and are known to overheat and even catch fire when overcharged or damaged. Other Li-ion batteries are ruined if completely discharged. The highly reactive chemistry of the Li-ion cell requires special safety precautions to prevent physical or electrical abuse of the battery. To maintain the cells within design operating limits, a microprocessor-controlled battery management system is required for Li-ion batteries to prevent damage and extend life cycle. Electronic controls add costs to production.

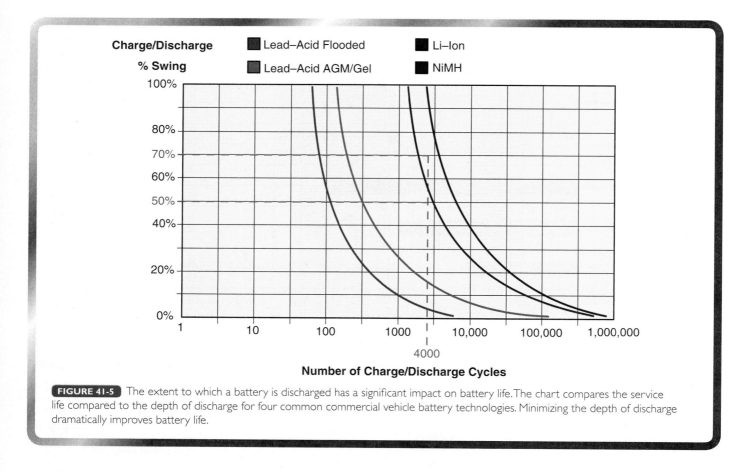

FIGURE 41-5 The extent to which a battery is discharged has a significant impact on battery life. The chart compares the service life compared to the depth of discharge for four common commercial vehicle battery technologies. Minimizing the depth of discharge dramatically improves battery life.

Valve-Regulated Lead–Acid Batteries (VRLA)

Recall from the Commercial Vehicle Batteries chapter that valve-regulated lead–acid batteries (VRLA) are sealed lead–acid batteries that do not have a liquid electrolyte and do not require the addition of water. That design has numerous advantages. Plate and electrolyte technology used in VRLAs result in lower self-discharge rates because VRLAs typically lose only 1% to 3% of their charge per month. This compares to lead antimony grid batteries having a self-discharge rate of 2% to 10% per week and with 1% to 5% per month for batteries using lead calcium grids.

Since VRLA batteries are completely sealed, they can be installed in any position without leaking—even under water. Sealing the battery eliminates the need to replenish the electrolyte or to check specific gravity. Battery state of charge is determined through voltage checks.

Other advantages of VRLA batteries include:

- No required specific gravity readings or adjustments
- No need to add distilled water
- No acid or lead to deal with in wash water
- No cable corrosion
- No tray corrosion
- No corrosive gas in battery compartment to damage electronics
- The longest service life of all battery types

- The highest cranking amps, even at low temperature
- The fastest recharge possible
- The highest vibration resistance
- 400 full cycles (80% DOD)
- Triple the life of traditional lead–acid batteries

There are two common types of VRLA battery—absorbed glass mat (AGM) and gel. Additionally, a spiral cell battery, which is a variation of AGM technology, has actually become the more recognizable of the AGM-type batteries. Each of these VRLA batteries is discussed in greater detail in the following sections.

Absorbed Glass Mat (AGM) Battery

Absorbed glass mat batteries, as illustrated in **FIGURE 41-6**, feature a unique and highly absorbent, thin glass fiber plate separator that absorbs the electrolyte like a sponge. The fiberglass-like plate separator, or mat, material gives the battery its AGM name. These batteries eliminate water loss through a process called oxygen recombination. No vents are used. Instead, the battery case is pressurized constantly to between 1 and 4 psi (6.9 and 27.6 kPa). Because of the special properties of the glass mat, pressurizing the battery causes 99%+ of the hydrogen and oxygen gases to recombine back into water when recharging. A piece of foil in place of a traditional vent cap allows the battery gases to vent only under severe conditions such as during overcharging when voltage is greater than 15 volts. If venting

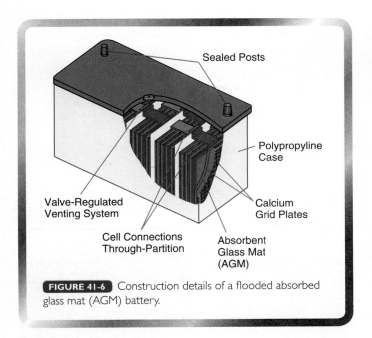

FIGURE 41-6 Construction details of a flooded absorbed glass mat (AGM) battery.

occurs, the battery is likely damaged, and the cell will dry out like any other cell. Charging above 2.7 volts per cell, the battery is severely damaged.

Advantages to AGM Batteries

Absorbed glass mat batteries have several advantages. AGM cell design places plates and separator mats closer together, which lowers the battery's internal resistance. A more efficient and faster chemical reaction between battery electrolyte and the plates can take place using the unique boron–silicate glass mat separator plate. Lower resistance and faster reactions means AGM batteries can charge up to five times the rate of conventional lead–acid batteries. AGM cells produce slightly more voltage: 12.80–13.0 volts open circuit voltage compared to 12.65 for conventional flooded lead–acid. As a result, AGMs deliver more amperage at higher voltage when cranking. **TABLE 41-2** compares the state of charge and open-circuit voltage of flooded, gel, and AGM batteries.

Glass mat plate separators used in AGMs absorb mechanical shock better than other batteries. The vibration-resistant

battery can, therefore, be used in operating conditions where other battery plates would quickly be destroyed. In one study, a fleet compared 68 trucks with conventional flooded batteries to 69 trucks with AGM batteries. Thirty-four months later, 113 of the flooded batteries had been replaced compared to eight of the AGM designs.

Service Precautions with AGM Batteries

AGM cells are extremely sensitive to damage from overcharging and require chargers that will limit charging voltage to between 14.4 and 14.6 volts maximum at 68°F (20°C). Using conventional shop taper chargers, which can charge at up to 18 volts, will destroy an AGM battery. Sustained charging at 15 volts will also cause the battery to overheat and gas excessively due to electrolysis. Instead, a smart charger, such as the one shown in **FIGURE 41-7**, should be used. A **smart charger** is a battery charger with an internal microcontroller used to regulate charging rates and times. It is an intelligent, temperature-compensated charger with an "AGM" setting. Because cell voltage is slightly higher for AGM batteries, a vehicle's charging system voltage may need adjustment to keep it in range between 13.8 and 14.4 volts maximum at 68°F (20°C) for optimum performance and service life. Voltage regulator settings on some vehicles are too high for AGM batteries and may require adjustment. The higher open-circuit voltage also means that AGM batteries cannot be mixed with other battery types to prevent unequal charging and shortened battery life. Without access to the electrolyte, AGM state of charge can only be determined by measuring battery voltage.

The depth of discharge also affects the life cycle of batteries. In general, the deeper the discharge between charges, the shorter the life cycle of batteries. **TABLE 41-3** compares the depth of discharge against the number of charge/discharge cycles that can be expected from different battery chemistry types.

FIGURE 41-7 Only microprocessor-controlled, or "smart," chargers should be used to charge AGM batteries.

TABLE 41-2: State of Charge Versus Open Circuit Voltage

Charge	Open Circuit Voltage		
Flooded	Gel	AGM	
100%	12.65	12.85	12.80
75%	12.40	12.65	12.60
50%	12.20	12.35	12.30
25%	12.00	12.00	12.00
0%	11.80	11.80	11.80

TABLE 41-3: Comparison of Depth of Discharge Cycle to Battery Life for Different Battery Chemistries

Depth of Discharge (%)	Gel: Cycle Life	AGM: Cycle Life	Flooded Lead–Acid: Cycle Life	Li-Ion	NiMH
100	450	200	30–150	Potentially ruined/damaged with some Li-ion chemistries	500–3000 (demonstrated only)
80	600	250			
50	1000	500	500	2000	
25	2100	1200			
10	5700	3200	2000	Millions +	300,000+ (demonstrated only)

Safety

AGM batteries are very sensitive to overcharging, as they will gas excessively and burst cell vents. Intelligent chargers that limit maximum charging voltage to 14.6 volts are required. Traditional taper chargers (used by most shops) that have an adjustable charging amperage setting should not be used to charge AGM batteries because taper chargers increase charging amperage to batteries by raising voltage to over 15 volts—and as much as 18 volts in some conditions.

Spiral Cell Optima Batteries

In the late 1980s, AGM battery technology advanced further with the introduction of spiral-wound plate technology. A typical spiral-wound cell battery is shown in **FIGURE 41-8**. **Spiral-wound cell batteries** are AGM batteries in every way except that the electrodes for each cell are not made of rectangular plates. Instead, two long, thin, lead plates—the positive and negative electrodes—are coiled into a tight spiral cell with an absorbent micro-glass mat placed between the plates absorbing the electrolytes, as illustrated in **FIGURE 41-9**. Replacing multiple plates with two coiled electrodes reduces internal battery resistance even further, thus enabling higher charging absorption rates for faster charging and higher discharge rates. These batteries also use higher internal gas pressures than other AGM batteries.

> **TECHNICIAN TIP**
>
> Many commercial vehicles use several batteries connected in parallel, or series and parallel, to supply adequate current for starting and operating electrical accessories. It is not a good practice to mix battery types or old and new batteries within battery banks for several reasons. First, slight open-circuit voltage differences exist between battery types caused by variations in plate and electrolyte composition. Similarly, variations exist in the internal resistances of different types of batteries. All these changes produce different discharge and charging characteristics. In a mixed set of batteries, some batteries will discharge quicker at higher rates of current. Others will not accept a charge easily. Those differences quickly lead to shorter battery life, undercharged, and eventually dead batteries in a set of batteries.

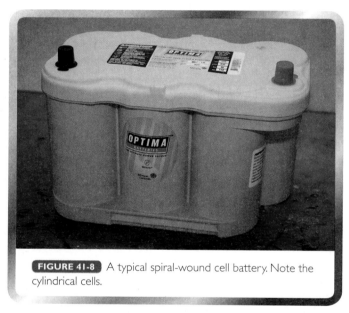

FIGURE 41-8 A typical spiral-wound cell battery. Note the cylindrical cells.

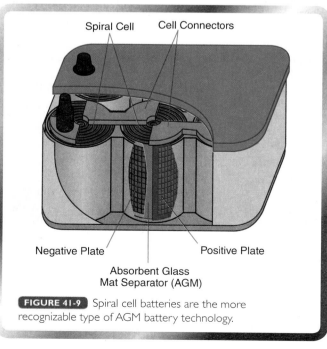

FIGURE 41-9 Spiral cell batteries are the more recognizable type of AGM battery technology.

Spiral cell batteries are produced in three categories, designated by the color of the battery's top cover.

- Red top—a 12-volt SLI battery
- Blue top—a deep cycle battery
- Yellow top—a combination deep cycle and SLI or leisure battery

Gel Cell

Just as battery plate and grid materials technologies have advanced to allow more powerful, lighter, and longer-lasting lead–acid batteries, electrolyte technology has also evolved. In the mid-1960s, spill-proof batteries were introduced using gel cells. Gel cell batteries are created by adding silica powder to the electrolyte, which turns the liquid into the consistency of petroleum jelly, hence the name "gel cells." A fully charged gel cell battery will have an open-circuit voltage of at least 12.85 volts and, like AGM cells, gel batteries are sensitive to overcharging and can be ruined by overcharging.

Ultra-capacitors

Compared to more traditional capacitors, ultra-capacitors are a new generation of high-capacity and high-energy density capacitors. Capacitors are electrical devices well known for their ability to temporarily store short bursts of electrical energy. For example, capacitors suppress and smooth voltage fluctuations, or ripple, from alternators. Capacitors also suppress radio static when connected across the power line-in. Ultra-capacitors are capable of supplying large bursts of energy and quickly recharging themselves, which make them ideal for use in modern vehicles. Ultra-capacitors are particularly advantageous in situations requiring regenerative braking and in frequent stop-start systems, such as in electric and hybrid vehicles.

Ultra-capacitors have a very low internal resistance when compared to lead–acid batteries. Consequently, ultra-capacitors deliver and absorb high-energy currents much more readily. In hybrid vehicles, using regenerative braking applications, typical batteries are slow to absorb a charge, thus limiting the maximum recovery of energy. Ultra-capacitors do not have this problem and are quickly recharged when depleted. This also makes them ideal for plug-in hybrid technology because they would allow vehicles to recharge in seconds—not hours! Furthermore, unlike other battery technologies, ultra-capacitors are not worn out by continuous charge and discharge cycles. Whereas other battery technologies can be cycled between 200 and several thousand times, ultra-capacitors can be cycled literally millions of times!

An ultra-capacitor is constructed using two electrodes (plates), an electrolyte, and a separator plate, as illustrated in FIGURE 41-10A. The dielectric material is double layered—not single as in conventional capacitors—and is made from a porous carbon. While the construction features are similar to a cell of a galvanic-type battery, the method by which it stores electrical energy is different. Ultra-capacitors store electrical energy within electrostatic fields (electrostatically) and do not produce electricity through electrochemical reactions. Like any

capacitor, the main factors that determine how much electrical energy an ultra-capacitor can store are as follows:

- Plate/electrode surface area—the greater the plate area, the higher the capacity.
- Distance between the plates—the closer the plates are, the higher the capacity.
- Electrical properties of the dielectric insulating layer separating the electrodes—some materials have better storage properties within capacitors than others.

A popular ultra-capacitor type battery is the Maxwell ESM Ultra series FIGURE 41-10B. Having the same dimensions as a group 31 battery, it can also produce 1800 CCA for 3 seconds and is unaffected by the cold. Three terminals are used. Two are for charging the battery, and a third connects directly to the starter motor. An internal battery control module regulates the charging rate to each cell and performs diagnostic tests.

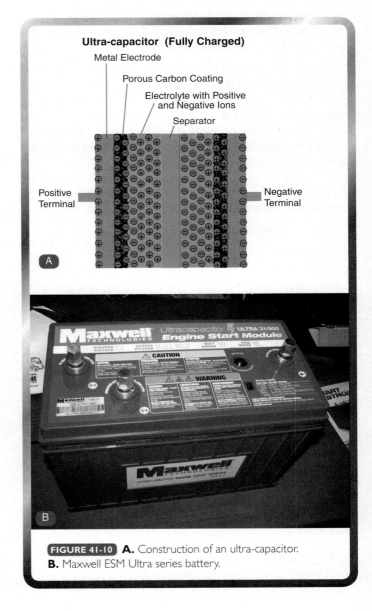

FIGURE 41-10 **A.** Construction of an ultra-capacitor. **B.** Maxwell ESM Ultra series battery.

Ultra-capacitors are currently used to assist batteries for the first 1.5 seconds during cranking where they can supply an additional 2000 amps of current to supplement the starter batteries, as illustrated in **FIGURE 41-11**. That supplement increases starter torque and speed. when cranking amperage is highest during the initial starter engagement.

▶ Battery Management Systems

Battery failure is a costly service issue for commercial vehicles. Weak batteries can lead to premature failure of starting and charging system components and loss of service caused by no-start conditions. The severe operating conditions and use of multiple batteries in many commercial vehicles contributes to shortened battery life. To minimize the expense and disruption due to battery failures, various electrical devices and systems are used to manage battery performance. **Battery management systems (BMSs)** are designed to perform the following functions:

- Protect the cells or the battery from damage
- Prolong the life of the battery
- Maintain the battery in a state of charge to perform the work for which it was specified

The development of commercial hybrid-vehicle applications places more demands on batteries and requires sophisticated battery management systems for sensitive battery technology. Components of the battery management system include battery isolators, low-voltage disconnects, battery balancers and equalizers, and battery monitors. Each of these components is discussed in the following sections.

Battery Isolators

Many commercial vehicles use multiple batteries that can be separated according to function. For example, consider a vehicle with one battery bank of starting, lighting, and ignition (SLI) batteries for the starting and main vehicle operating system and another set of batteries for auxiliary deep cycle batteries for accessories or systems that may be required to operate after the engine is shut down. Permanently connecting all the battery banks in parallel could cause the SLI battery to become discharged if a continual electrical load is placed on the auxiliary deep cycle batteries for extended periods. This would prevent the vehicle from starting.

Battery isolator systems, or **split charge relays**, as illustrated in **FIGURE 41-12**, enable charging of an auxiliary battery by the vehicle charging system and electrical separation of the auxiliary battery from the starting circuit when the engine shuts down. Separation of the main starting and auxiliary batteries can take place automatically during charging and discharging. Battery isolation systems range from simple, isolating solenoids, or relays, to complex battery management systems that monitor charge rates and voltages for both the SLI and auxiliary batteries.

Low-Voltage Disconnect (LVD)

Low-voltage disconnects (LVD) are devices that monitor battery voltage and disconnect non-critical electrical loads when the battery voltage level falls below a preset threshold value. LVD devices preserve battery current to a level adequate to start the vehicle's engine when key-off loads or other parasitic draws

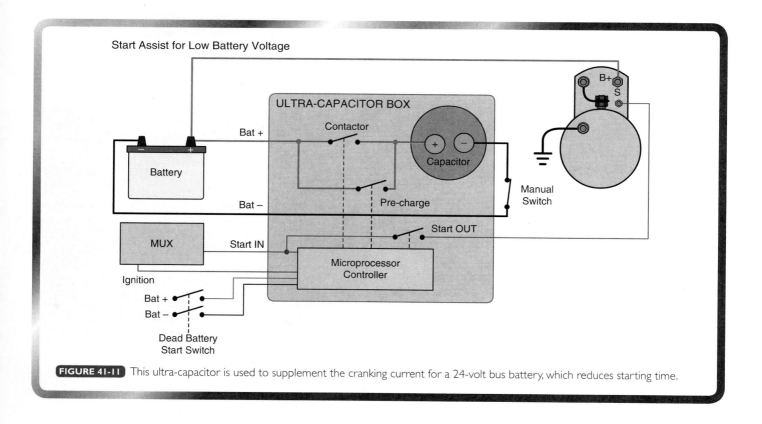

FIGURE 41-11 This ultra-capacitor is used to supplement the cranking current for a 24-volt bus battery, which reduces starting time.

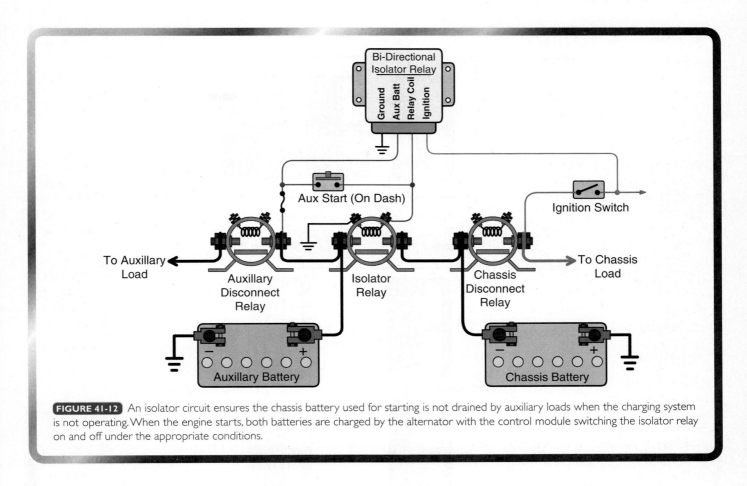

FIGURE 41-12 An isolator circuit ensures the chassis battery used for starting is not drained by auxiliary loads when the charging system is not operating. When the engine starts, both batteries are charged by the alternator with the control module switching the isolator relay on and off under the appropriate conditions.

are draining the battery. LVD devices then reconnect the electrical loads when the battery level is restored to a high enough voltage—for example, when the alternator begins charging above 12.6 volts. No intervention is required by the vehicle operator to protect the batteries, as the LVD automatically disconnects and reconnects the load. An audible warning typically alerts the operator before a disconnect event occurs, which is generally between 12.0 and 12.2 volts. LVDs can be integrated with the vehicle's power distribution system and will progressively shed loads as battery voltage drops.

Battery Balancers and Equalizers

Higher cranking amperage and greater electrical loads in commercial equipment require two or more batteries connected either in series, for 24-volt electrical systems, or in parallel, in 12-volt systems. Charging and discharging resistance changes with battery use and the electrical distance from the alternator. For example, longer battery cables and more electrical connections are almost unavoidable in many vehicles. This means one or more batteries in a bank gets undercharged, which in turn leads to undercharging and progressive plate sulfation. Sulfation, in turn, increases battery resistance, causing the battery to become weaker **FIGURE 41-13** .

Balancers (sometimes called battery equalizers), illustrated in **FIGURE 41-14** , attempt to adjust battery voltage to compensate for unequal charges in multiple batteries. Equalizers are found in many commercial applications using 24-volt charging systems, including transit and tour buses, private coaches, off-highway equipment, yachts, and alternative energy systems.

In multiple battery configurations, whether connected in series or in parallel, batteries will eventually charge and discharge unevenly, shortening battery life. For example, you may often discover that while testing two 12-volt batteries connected in parallel, one battery will become completely dead while the other stays in good condition. When testing three batteries, one will be good, another fair, and the third defective. The defective battery is always the farthest from the alternator in terms of electrical distance.

There are two methods of correcting this common condition of unequal charge and discharge rates. One is to regularly rotate the batteries and exchange their positions in the configuration. Another method is to use a battery equalizer. Also, remember to check the equipment manufacturer's recommendation for connecting battery cables. Properly connecting cables is one way to minimize the charge and discharge imbalances between batteries.

Various configurations of charge equalizers enable:

- Charging 12-volt batteries from a 24-volt charging system
- Charging 24-volt batteries from a 12-volt charging system
- Charging series-connected 12-volt batteries at 24 volts and providing a 12-volt output for 12-volt chassis electrical loads

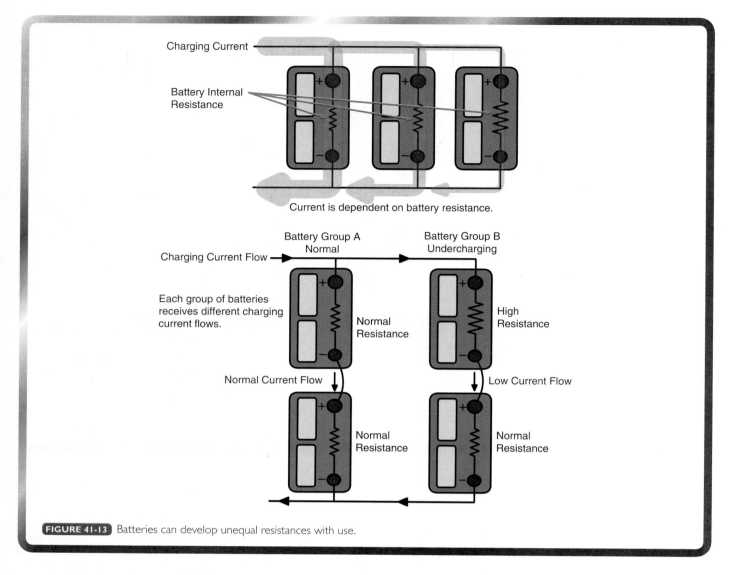

FIGURE 41-13 Batteries can develop unequal resistances with use.

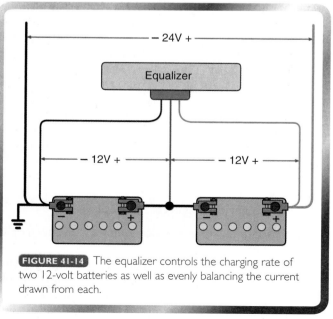

FIGURE 41-14 The equalizer controls the charging rate of two 12-volt batteries as well as evenly balancing the current drawn from each.

- Balanced battery charging of 12-volt batteries from 24 volts to within a difference of 0.1 volts
- Balanced draining of batteries to supply a 12-volt load so that each battery is depleted to within a difference of 0.1 volts

A common bus configuration has 12-volt batteries connected to the equalizer that interfaces the batteries with the 24-volt alternators, as illustrated in **FIGURE 41-15**. The equalizer will sense battery voltage and drive a higher charge rate into weaker batteries and less current into stronger batteries. The voltage balance and charge acceptance rate of each battery is kept to within 0.1 volts under light loads and within 0.5 volts at full loads. When the voltage of Battery A is higher than that of Battery B, the battery equalizer switches to standby mode. This means no power is transferred from its 24-volt alternator input to its 12-volt output. If a 12-volt load is present, and Battery A's voltage decreases to just below the voltage of Battery B, the battery equalizer activates and transfers sufficient current from Battery B to Battery A, satisfying the load and maintaining an equal voltage and charge in both batteries.

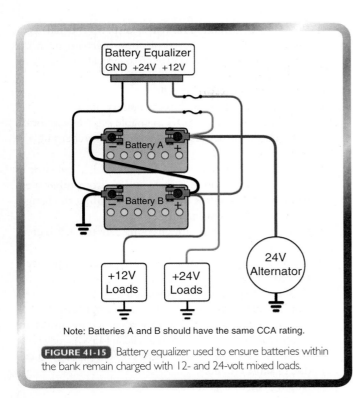

Note: Batteries A and B should have the same CCA rating.

FIGURE 41-15 Battery equalizer used to ensure batteries within the bank remain charged with 12- and 24-volt mixed loads.

More complex systems, like that illustrated in **FIGURE 41-16**, can have both battery isolation and battery equalization across multiple banks. For example, auxiliary or house batteries used in motor homes and chassis batteries are isolated from each other when the alternator is not charging, but are connected together so both banks charge when the alternator is charging—along with battery equalization for each bank.

Charge equalization is critical for series-connected battery cells in hybrid vehicle applications. The higher voltage in hybrid-drive systems requires very long, series strings of batteries pushing battery performance to extremes. Without battery management systems incorporating charge equalization, batteries banks would quickly fail.

Battery Monitors

Hybrid commercial vehicles use battery monitors to collect battery data for display to the operator and service technician. The data that is typically collected includes:

- Temperature of each battery or pack
- Voltage of the pack
- Rate of charge or discharge

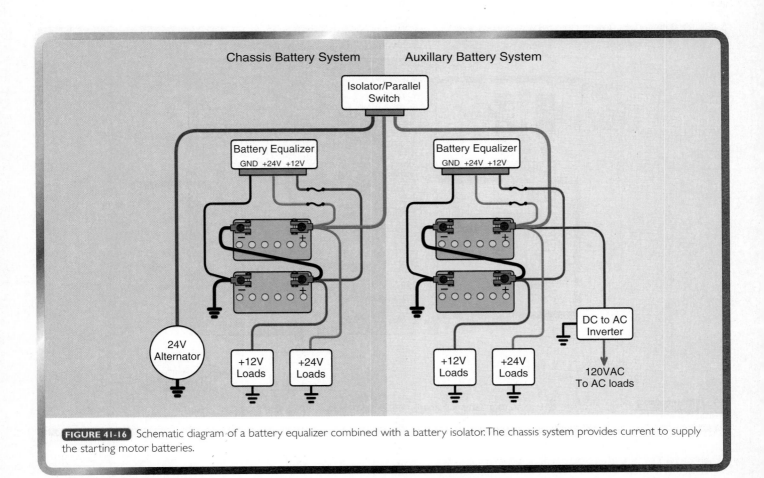

FIGURE 41-16 Schematic diagram of a battery equalizer combined with a battery isolator. The chassis system provides current to supply the starting motor batteries.

Hybrid Battery Management Systems

Hybrid-drive battery management is much more demanding than the previously described battery management devices. Batteries in these applications work in a demanding and harsh environment because of rapidly changing charging and discharging conditions, such as when the vehicle accelerates using electric motors and charges during regenerative braking. Li-ion and NiMH batteries are best charged to between 40% and 70% of full capacity to allow absorption of current generated during braking and to extend their lifecycle. An on-board battery management system, like that illustrated in FIGURE 41-17, will perform some, but not necessarily all, of the following functions:

- Monitoring the state of charge (SOC) of the battery and battery cells that compose the battery banks; this function is often the equivalent of a fuel gauge distance to empty reading
- Maintaining the state of charge (SOC) of all the cells with both voltage and amperage protection against overcharging and undercharge conditions
- Providing service and diagnostic information on the condition of the batteries and cells; this includes recording battery service and diagnostic data (battery voltage readings, temperature, hours, faults, out of tolerance conditions)

- Providing information for driver displays and alarms
- Providing an emergency protection mechanism in the event of damage, uncontrolled overheating, or other abuse condition
- Isolating the batteries or cells
- Charge equalization within the battery bank
- Adjusting the battery SOC to enable regenerative braking charges to be absorbed without overcharging the battery
- Communicating with the on-board vehicle network to receive information and instructions from other electronic vehicle-control units and responding to changes in the vehicle operating mode
- Calculating the optimum charging rate to each battery and or cell
- Enabling adaptive strategies or emergency "limp-home" mode in case of battery failure
- Provide reverse polarity protection
- Control temperature-dependent charging; some batteries can be damaged by charging when temperatures are lower than 32°F (0°C) or above 100°F (45°C)
- Discharge current protection to prevent damage to cell due to short circuits
- Depth of discharge cut-off

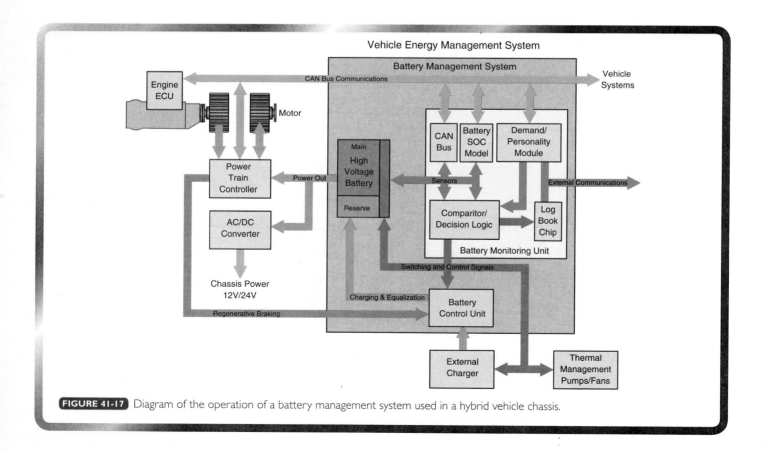

FIGURE 41-17 Diagram of the operation of a battery management system used in a hybrid vehicle chassis.

Wrap-Up

Ready for Review

- Energy density, energy efficiency, life span, the state of the charge window, and the cost in dollars per kWh are all factors in determining the battery technology to use on heavy-duty commercial vehicles.
- The major battery technologies used in heavy-duty commercial vehicles are nickel-metal hydride (NiMH), lithium, and lead–acid. Each technology has distinct capabilities.
- NiMH batteries are relatively lightweight and have high power output and long life expectancy, making them a preferred technology for hybrid drive vehicles.
- Lithium-ion (Li-ion) batteries are secondary batteries. They are not galvanic, nor do they use an electrolyte solution. Rather, they use a gel, salt, or solid material that replaces electrolyte, so they are immune to leaking.
- Valve-regulated lead–acid (VRLA) batteries do not use a liquid electrolyte and are completely sealed. As such, they can be installed in any position without leaking.
- Absorbed glass mat (AGM) batteries use a pressurized battery case that helps recombine oxygen and hydrogen when the battery is recharged. These batteries have a lower internal resistance and a more efficient and faster chemical reaction.
- A spiral-wound cell battery is a special type of AGM battery that reduces internal resistance even further.
- Ultra-capacitors are capable of supplying large bursts of energy and quickly recharging themselves—which make them ideal for use in modern vehicles. As such, they are particularly advantageous in situations requiring regenerative braking and frequent stop-start systems, such as in electric and hybrid vehicles.
- Compared to lead–acid batteries, ultra-capacitors have very low internal resistance and are very quick to absorb a charge.
- To minimize and prevent battery failure, many vehicles incorporate a battery management system to protect the cells, prolong battery life, and maintain the battery in a state of charge.
- Battery isolation systems allow the multiple batteries in a battery bank to be separated according to function.
- When multiple batteries are connected in parallel, batteries will eventually charge and discharge, unevenly shortening battery life. Batteries should, therefore, be rotated through the different positions in the battery compartment or a balancer (equalizer) should be used to compensate for unequal charges in multiple batteries.
- Hybrid-drive battery management is much more demanding than the conventional battery management devices due to the harsher environment in which hybrid-drive batteries operate (e.g., rapidly changing charging and discharging conditions).

Vocabulary Builder

absorbed glass mat (AGM) battery   A type of lead acid battery that uses a thin fiberglass plate to absorb the electrolyte; prevents the solution from sloshing or separating into layers of heavier acid and water.

balancers   A device designed to adjust battery voltage to compensate for unequal charges in multiple batteries. Also called *battery equalizers*.

battery equalizers   A device designed to adjust battery voltage to compensate for unequal charges in multiple batteries. Also called *balancers*.

battery isolator systems   A system designed to separate the main starting battery and the auxiliary battery. Also called a *split charge relay*.

battery management system (BMS)   A system of electrical devices used to manage battery performance.

gel cell battery   A type of battery to which silica has been added to the electrolyte solution to turn the solution to a gel-like consistency.

lithium-ion (Li-ion) battery   A type of battery that does not use a galvanic reaction and in which a gel, salt, or solid material replaces the electrolyte solution.

low-voltage disconnect (LVD)   A device that monitors battery voltage and disconnects non-critical electrical loads when battery voltage level falls below a preset threshold value.

nickel–metal hydride (NiMH) battery   A battery in which metal hydroxide forms the negative electrode and nickel oxide forms the positive electrode.

smart charger   A battery charger with microprocessor-controlled charging rates and times.

spiral-wound cell battery   A type of AGM battery in which the positive and negative electrodes are coiled into a tight spiral cell with an absorbent micro-glass mat placed between the plates.

split charge relay   A system designed to separate the main starting battery and the auxiliary battery. Also called a *battery isolator system*.

ultra-capacitor   A new generation of high-capacity and high-energy density capacitors

Review Questions

1. The _____ battery is a type of lead acid battery that uses a thin fiberglass plate to absorb the electrolyte.
   a. gel cell
   b. lithium-ion
   c. spiral-wound
   d. absorbed glass mat

2. The _____ battery is a battery in which metal hydroxide forms the negative electrode and nickel oxide forms the positive electrode.
   a. gel cell
   b. lithium ion
   c. absorbed glass mat
   d. nickel-metal hydride

3. The _____ of a battery is measured by the number of charge/discharge cycles as a function of depth of discharge.
   a. life span
   b. shelf life
   c. polarity
   d. voltage

4. Lithium-ion batteries have low internal _____ and can discharge their current four times faster when compared to lead acid batteries.
   a. charge
   b. resistance
   c. amperage
   d. life span

5. _____ batteries eliminate water loss through a process called oxygen recombination.
   a. Absorbed glass mat
   b. Nickel-cadmium
   c. Lithium-ion
   d. Deep cycle

6. Absorbed glass mat cells are extremely sensitive to damage from overcharging and should be charged using a _____ charger.
   a. quick
   b. trickle
   c. smart
   d. relay

7. A(n) _____ is capable of supplying large bursts of energy and quickly recharging, which makes them ideal for use in modern vehicles.
   a. ultra capacitor
   b. battery isolator
   c. smart charger
   d. split charge relay

8. A _____ battery is an absorbed glass mat battery in every way except that the electrodes for each cell are not made of rectangular plates.
   a. gel cell
   b. lithium-ion
   c. spiral-wound cell
   d. nickel-cadmium

9. Devices that monitor battery voltage and disconnect noncritical electrical loads when the battery voltage level falls below a preset threshold value are called low-voltage _____.
   a. equalizers
   b. disconnects
   c. relays
   d. resistors

10. Hybrid commercial vehicles use battery _____ to collect battery data for display to the operator and service technician.
    a. monitors
    b. equalizers
    c. relays
    d. chargers

ASE-Type Questions

1. Technician A says energy efficiency is expressed in watt-hour per kilogram (Wh/kg) and watt-hour per liter (Wh/l). Technician B says the ability to convert charging current into storage capacity is known as energy density. Who is correct?
   a. Technician A
   b. Technician B
   c. Both Technician A and Technician B
   d. Neither Technician A nor Technician B

2. Technician A says that nickel-cadmium battery chemistry produces the highest amount of voltage per cell. Technician B says that lithium-ion battery chemistry produces the highest amount of voltage per cell. Who is correct?
   a. Technician A
   b. Technician B
   c. Both Technician A and Technician B
   d. Neither Technician A nor Technician B

3. Technician A says lithium-ion batteries are used primarily in laptops, cell phones, and other consumer electronic devices. Technician B says nickel-cadmium batteries are used primarily in laptops, cell phones, and other consumer electronic devices. Who is correct?
   a. Technician A
   b. Technician B
   c. Both Technician A and Technician B
   d. Neither Technician A nor Technician B

4. Technician A says one lithium cell can replace five NiCad or NiMH cells. Technician B says one lithium cell can replace four NiCad or NiMH cells. Who is correct?
   a. Technician A
   b. Technician B
   c. Both Technician A and Technician B
   d. Neither Technician A nor Technician B

5. Technician A says that the advantage to using valve-regulated lead acid batteries is that there is no corrosive gas in the battery compartment. Technician B says that the advantage to using valve-regulated lead acid batteries is that there is no need to add distilled water. Who is correct?
   a. Technician A
   b. Technician B
   c. Both Technician A and Technician B
   d. Neither Technician A nor Technician B

6. Technician A says a leisure spiral cell battery will have a yellow top cover. Technician B says a deep cycle spiral cell battery will have a blue top cover. Who is correct?
   a. Technician A
   b. Technician B
   c. Both Technician A and Technician B
   d. Neither Technician A nor Technician B

7. Technician A says a balancer will sense battery voltage and drive a higher charge rate into weaker batteries and less current into stronger batteries. Technician B says an equalizer will sense battery voltage and drive a higher charge rate into weaker batteries and less current into stronger batteries. Who is correct?
   a. Technician A
   b. Technician B
   c. Both Technician A and Technician B
   d. Neither Technician A nor Technician B

8. Technician A says nickel–metal hydride batteries provide twice the energy storage of lead acid batteries by weight, but only half the power output. Technician B says nickel–metal hydride batteries provide twice the energy storage of lead acid batteries by weight, with twice the power output. Who is correct?
   a. Technician A
   b. Technician B
   c. Both Technician A and Technician B
   d. Neither Technician A nor Technician B

9. Technician A says lithium-ion batteries cost ten times more than conventional lead acid batteries for each kilowatt of power produced per minute. Technician B says lithium-ion batteries cost eight times more than conventional lead acid batteries for each kilowatt of power produced per hour. Who is correct?
   a. Technician A
   b. Technician B
   c. Both Technician A and Technician B
   d. Neither Technician A nor Technician B

10. Technician A says that the deeper the discharge between charges, the shorter the life cycle of the battery. Technician B says that the deeper the discharge between charges, the longer the life cycle of the battery. Who is correct?
    a. Technician A
    b. Technician B
    c. Both Technician A and Technician B
    d. Neither Technician A nor Technician B

NATEF Tasks

Electrical/Electronic Systems

General Electric Systems Page
- Identify parasitic (key-off) battery drain problems; perform tests; determine needed action. (p 1184)

Battery
- Inspect, clean, and service battery; replace as needed. (p 1177)
- Inspect and clean battery boxes, mounts, and hold downs; repair or replace as needed. (p 1177)
- Inspect, test, and clean battery cables and connectors; repair or replace as needed. (p 1177)

- Determine battery state of charge using an open circuit voltage test. (p 1179)
- Perform battery capacitance test; determine needed action. (p 1180)
- Identify battery type; perform appropriate battery load test; determine needed action. (p 1181)
- Charge battery using appropriate method for battery type. (p 1183)
- Jump start a vehicle using jumper cables and a booster battery or appropriate auxiliary power supply using proper safety procedures. (p 1184)
- Identify and test low-voltage disconnect (LVD) systems; determine needed repair. (p 1185)

Knowledge Objectives

After reading this chapter, you will be able to:
1. Identify safety equipment and safe work practices for servicing batteries. (pp 1174–1175)
2. Identify and describe failure modes of batteries. (pp 1175–1176)
3. Recommend battery replacement based on battery testing procedures. (pp 1176–1180)
4. Identify and describe procedures and equipment used to test lead–acid batteries. (pp 1176–1180)

Skills Objectives

After reading this chapter, you will be able to:
1. Inspect, clean, fill, or replace the battery, battery cables, clamps, connectors, hold-downs, and battery boxes. (pp 1177) **SKILL DRILL 42-1**
2. Perform a battery state of charge test. (p 1179) **SKILL DRILL 42-2**
3. Perform a conductance test on a battery. (p 1180) **SKILL DRILL 42-3**
4. Perform a load test on a battery. (p 1181) **SKILL DRILL 42-4**
5. Charge a commercial battery. (p 1183) **SKILL DRILL 42-5**
6. Jump-start a commercial vehicle. (p 1184) **SKILL DRILL 42-6**
7. Measure parasitic draw on a battery. (p 1184) **SKILL DRILL 42-7**
8. Identify and test a low-voltage disconnect. (p 1185) **SKILL DRILL 42-8**

▶ Introduction

Batteries should be the starting point when diagnosing complaints such as hard starting, slow cranking, or no-start complaints FIGURE 42-1. Battery testing is also indicated when lights dim when an engine idles or when other electrical problems occur. Battery testing is also recommended whenever an alternator is replaced. A variety of instruments and tools are used to evaluate the condition of vehicle batteries, and a number of procedures are commonly used to service batteries during maintenance checks. These techniques are covered in this chapter.

Traditional comprehensive maintenance and testing of batteries includes the following evaluation methods:

- Visual inspection, cleaning, filling, and battery replacement
- State of charge testing using a voltmeter
- Cell voltage checks
- Load or capacity testing
- Conductance or impedance testing
- Charging batteries
- Jump-starting vehicles
- Measuring parasitic draw

Batteries should be evaluated visually first before proceeding with any other significant tests. Visual checks include checking the electrolyte level if it is possible. Most batteries today are sealed, low- or no-maintenance type, which prevents this procedure.

Another basic maintenance task is to make sure the exterior case is dry and free of dirt. Dirt on top of the battery can actually cause premature self-discharge of the battery as current "leaks" across the path of dirt or grime. Grime and vapors from a battery can become conductive and drain the battery over time. To tell if the surface of the battery is leaking current, use a digital volt-ohm meter (DVOM), like the one shown in FIGURE 42-2, set to

FIGURE 42-1 Regular battery maintenance reduces downtime.

"volts" to measure the voltage on the surface of the top of the battery. You can do this by placing the black lead on the negative battery post and rubbing the red lead around the top of the battery, measuring the voltage present there. Any voltage exceeding 0.5 volts means the battery should be washed down with water. Do not use mixtures of diluted ammonia or baking soda, as they can enter the battery cells and contaminate electrolyte.

Batteries should be fully charged to perform properly and prolong their service life. A weakened battery causes the alternator to work harder charging batteries and shortening its life. Lower current level available to the starter will lead to low-voltage burn-out of the starter, too. State of charge will be covered in detail in the section Testing Battery State of Charge and Specific Gravity.

▶ You Are the Technician

Maintaining a fleet of trucks, buses, and other diesel-powered machinery in hot climates presents unique challenges. One of the problems you are frequently encountering is hard starting of engines due to dead batteries. Within a few months, many of the batteries have become defective, usually just one out of two batteries or two out of three batteries in a multiple-battery configuration. One battery is usually in good condition. A significant amount of downtime, labor, and associated expenses is lost to jump-starting vehicles and equipment in addition to the cost of battery replacements. From your experience working in other areas and even during cooler months, you associate hot weather with more frequent battery failures. Even if the batteries do not fail during hot weather, the first cold morning after a long season of heat often produces many no-start conditions. Consider strategies to reduce the aggravation level and cost of service for no-start conditions due to the effects of high temperatures on batteries.

1. Why do batteries fail more quickly in hot climates?
2. How can you determine if batteries are sulfated?
3. Identify several maintenance procedures used to minimize battery failure due to sulfation.

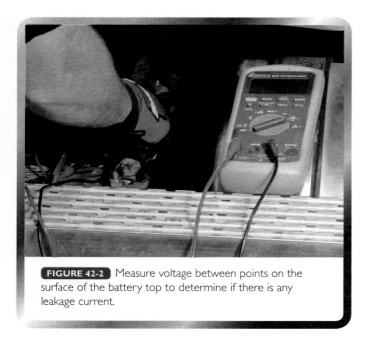

FIGURE 42-2 Measure voltage between points on the surface of the battery top to determine if there is any leakage current.

▶ **TECHNICIAN TIP**

Treatments specifically designed to coat battery terminals should be applied to battery terminals to prevent corrosion and resistance from developing at battery connections. These treatments are not electrically conductive and will not attack cable insulating materials. Many other types of grease, such as chassis grease, are electrically conductive and will lead to battery self-discharge and even corrosion of battery terminals.

Electrolyte level and condition are also important factors in battery service life. Electrolyte condition is checked at the same time specific gravity is evaluated. Electrolyte level and condition will be discussed further in the section Electrolyte Level and Condition.

The section Battery Inspecting, Testing, and Maintenance covers several tests can be used to determine battery service life and identify reasons for battery failure. Load or capacity tests determine the ability of a battery to deliver cranking amperage and will be discussed in detail in the section Testing Battery Capacity. Conductance testing, or impedance testing, has replaced this method for evaluating battery capacity and will be covered in the section Testing Battery Conductance. Testing for sulfation is not performed as part of a regular battery evaluation but only to validate a diagnosis of sulfation. The procedure is discussed in the section Performing a Sulfation (Three-Minute Charge) Test.

Parasitic draw testing and case drain or leakage testing are other means to detect conditions that cause batteries to lose their charge. A parasitic drain of battery current should be no more than 0.5 amps of current. An inductive ammeter placed on either battery cable with all vehicle accessories off will easily measure and detect excessive draw. Wet and dirty batteries will leak voltage, too. Placing one voltmeter lead on a battery post and the other lead on the case will identify voltage leaks exceeding 0.5 volts. Battery cases should be cleaned and dried to remove electrically

conductive grime from the case. Parasitic draw will be discussed in greater detail in the section Measuring Parasitic Draw.

▶ Battery Service Precautions

Nearly 6000 people in the United States are recently reported to have suffered eye injuries from batteries, according to Prevent Blindness America organization. Safety should be the first priority when working around and servicing batteries. Batteries are dangerous for a couple of reasons. First, electrolyte inside lead-acid batteries is corrosive. Acid on skin, in eyes, on clothing, or on paint will burn, causing bodily harm and vehicle damage. Also, an explosive gas mixture consisting of hydrogen and oxygen is produced during charging and discharging of the battery. Ensure the following precautions are followed to reduce the risk when working with batteries:

- Always wear protective clothing such as rubber gloves and goggles or full-face shields when handling batteries. When handling a battery or checking electrolyte levels, wear a rubber apron to protect clothing from splashed battery acid. If acid contacts your skin or eyes, flush with water immediately.
- Never wear any conductive jewelry (neck chains, watches, or rings) when working on or near batteries, as they may provide an accidental short-circuit path for high currents.
- Do not smoke, weld, or grind metal near batteries since sparks may ignite the explosive gas mixture.
- Never create a low-resistance connection or short across the battery terminals.
- Never disconnect a battery charger, jumper cables, or power booster from a battery when charging or jump-starting. Sparks will occur when disconnected and can result in battery explosions. Shut the power booster off. Disconnect the chassis ground clamp which is away from the battery first. Connect the ground clamp last when boosting.
- Charge batteries in a well-ventilated area.

Always remove the negative or ground terminal first when disconnecting battery cables, because this procedure reduces the possibility of a wrench creating a short circuit between any positive voltage wiring and the chassis ground.

- All battery cable connections to the battery terminals need to be properly tightened. Loose connections are resistive and may cause sparks.
- Never set a wrench or other tool on a battery, as doing so can cause short battery terminals, leading to gassing, overheating, and an explosion in an alarmingly short period.

▶ **TECHNICIAN TIP**

Always connect and disconnect the main battery ground first. If there are other ground cables connected to the battery for the engine and other electronic control modules, connect these grounds last. When additional grounds are either connected or disconnected and the main battery ground is NOT connected, voltage spikes could occur and may damage electronic control modules.

▶ Causes of Battery Failure

According to several studies, 52% of vehicle break-downs or failures to provide service are caused by batteries. Battery failures are by far the leading cause for service break-downs, with tires being the next most common (15%), followed by engines (8%). The two most common complaints concerning batteries are that they will either not charge or not hold a charge. Batteries may suddenly fail through the loss of a cell or open circuits within the internal connections. Batteries may also slowly fail over time through the gradual loss of capacity caused by plate deterioration.

Sulfation

According to a study, of all lead–acid batteries returned to the manufacturer under warranty, close to half were found to have no defect. Of those found defective, close to 80% were caused by sulfation. Sulfation can be observed when a white colored substance coats and swells, as shown in **FIGURE 42-3**. It occurs when batteries are subjected to prolonged undercharge conditions. During normal use, soft sulfate crystals form and dissipate as part of the normal charge and discharge cycle. During periods of prolonged undercharge, the sulfate converts to hard crystals and deposit on the negative plates. During subsequent charging, the hardened sulfate cannot be driven from the plate and reduces the active area of plate material. Sulfation also increases the internal resistance of a battery. This means higher charging voltage is needed to regenerate active plate material when charging. Pulse-type battery chargers have a setting for potentially reconditioning batteries that may have been sitting for periods of time in an undercharged state.

Common reasons for sulfation include:

1. *Leaving batteries too long in a state of discharge*—Soft sulfation occurring during normal discharge turns to hard sulfate crystals over time. Batteries should be recharged as soon as possible after discharging. Key-off loads, also called parasitic drains, contribute to sulfation caused by prolonged discharge.

FIGURE 42-3 Sulfate on the top of the plates of a lead–acid battery.

2. *Undercharging of a battery*—High resistance at battery connections, particularly in batteries connected in series or parallel, leads to undercharging of cells. Incorrect charging system voltage can also cause undercharging.

3. *High ambient temperatures*—Temperatures in excess of 100°F (39°C) speeds-up chemical activity inside a battery, accelerating the self-discharge of a battery. It is calculated that a new, fully charged, flooded battery would most likely not start an engine if continuously exposed to 110°F (47°C) in as little as 30 days. Significantly higher rates of battery failures occur in warm regions of North America than in cold areas. To minimize self-discharge, batteries are best stored in cool, dry places.

4. *Low electrolyte level*—Battery plates exposed to air will dry out and prevent transfer of sulfate from the plate material back into electrolyte during charging. Adding acid to a battery will not recover a dead battery. Instead, it will increase the concentration of sulfate in the battery.

Performing a Sulfation (Three-Minute Charge) Test

Sulfation is indicated using a three-minute battery charge test. This test is not performed as part of a regular battery evaluation but only to validate a diagnosis of sulfation. This battery test requires charging the battery at 30–40 amps for three minutes, while measuring the battery voltage with the charger on. If the voltage rises above 15.5 volts, the battery is excessively resistive and is likely sulfated.

Vibration

Excessive vibration can cause open circuits in the internal battery connections and "shed" or shake loose plate material, which settles to the bottom of the battery case. **Shedding** reduces the plate surface area and therefore reduces capacity. Shedding may also produce short circuits between the bottom of positive and negative plates.

Electrolyte Level and Condition

Low electrolyte level exposes the plates to air, preventing the transfer of sulfate from the plate material back into the electrolyte during charging. It is critical to maintain the correct acid-water mix of electrolyte. If electrolyte level is lost through evaporation, then distilled water should be added. If electrolyte is lost due to spillage, then the battery should be topped up with electrolyte.

Plates and grids that are damaged are often detected by examining the electrolyte. Gray or dirty electrolyte in any cell renders a battery defective. Although voltage and electrolyte readings may be satisfactory, contaminants even in one cell will cause the battery to self-discharge quickly. Series connections between cells will cause even one dead or defective cell to discharge all other cells in the battery. Electrolyte condition is checked at the same time specific gravity is evaluated.

Grid Corrosion

Grid corrosion, like that illustrated in **FIGURE 42-4**, takes place primarily in the positive grid and is accelerated by overcharging

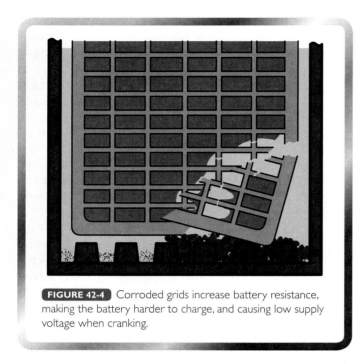

FIGURE 42-4 Corroded grids increase battery resistance, making the battery harder to charge, and causing low supply voltage when cranking.

and high temperatures. When corrosion takes place, grid resistance increases during charging and discharging. Grids are the foundation and the electrical conducting layer for the battery plate. Although grids are alloyed with antimony, calcium, or sometimes barium to minimize the corrosive effects of the electrolyte, grids do disintegrate. The mud-like lead paste attached to grids also falls apart when grids corrode.

▶ Battery Inspecting, Testing, and Maintenance

As noted earlier, batteries last longer if they are properly maintained. In fact, one of the most common causes of vehicle no-starts is dirty or corroded battery cables. Inspecting, cleaning, and filling (if not maintenance free) are common tasks that should be performed every six months to one year on top-post batteries, and one to two years on side-post batteries. During periodic maintenance, batteries should be checked for proper ventilation. All slide mechanisms on battery trays should work properly. Battery cables should be inspected for rubbing or binding. Battery terminals should be tight and show no evidence of overheating. Always coat battery terminals with a dielectric sealer to prevent corrosion.

Batteries should be evaluated visually first before proceeding with any other significant tests. Visual checks include:

- Cracks
- Bulges—Indicate batteries have either overheated or been frozen
- Cable connections—Connections should be clean, tight, acid resistant, and show no signs of heat damage
- Battery hold-downs—Loose or missing hold downs cause plate shedding

- Dirty case—Causes current to leak out of batteries
- Leaks
- Electrolyte level—Level should be above the plates
- Electrolyte appearance—Liquid should be clear; a brownish color indicates the plates maybe damaged or the electrolyte contaminated

To inspect, clean, fill, or replace the battery, battery cables, clamps, connectors, and hold-downs, follow the guidelines in **SKILL DRILL 42-1**.

Testing Battery State of Charge and Specific Gravity

Although the capacitance test is the industry standard to evaluate battery condition, other tests may still be used. One of those tests is the state of charge test. <u>State of charge (SOC) testing</u> tells you how charged or discharged a battery is, not how much capacity it has.

A fully charged battery should have an open-circuit voltage of 12.65 volts. If the battery has been recently charged, a light load applied to the battery for a minute will remove a surface charge. Open-circuit voltage is consequently affected by the battery specific gravity. About 1/10-volt change occurs for every 10°F below 80°F. **TABLE 42-1** shows state of charge as indicated by specific gravity and voltage reading.

Voltage reading can also identify defective cells. Using a multi-meter, place one meter lead on either terminal of the battery, and dip the other lead into battery electrolyte (if accessible). The meter should record a change of 2.1 volts for each cell when moving across the battery.

The state of charge is best evaluated by measuring the density of electrolyte in each cell using either a bulb-type hydrometer or refractometer. The specific gravity (SG) of electrolyte indicates the state cell charge. Cells should not have wide variations. If the SG reading between the highest and lowest cell is more than 0.050 points, the battery is defective. For example if the highest SG is 1.265 points in one cell and only 1.210 in the lowest, the battery is scrap. **FIGURE 42-5A** and **FIGURE 42-5B** show two different tools used to measure battery specific gravity. A refractometer is shown in Figure 42-5B.

> ### ▶ TECHNICIAN TIP
>
> When performing a state of charge test, keep these tips in mind:
>
> - When filling a battery that is not fully charged, never fill it to the top of the full line, as charging the battery will raise the electrolyte level.
> - Small amounts of electrolyte in the hydrometer may leak out, potentially damage and corrode parts and battery terminals.
> - Do not inadvertently remove electrolyte from one cell or add it to another cell when testing; doing so will cause incorrect readings.

SKILL DRILL 42-1 Inspecting, Cleaning, Filling, or Replacing the Battery, Battery Cables, Clamps, Connectors, Hold-Downs, and Battery Boxes

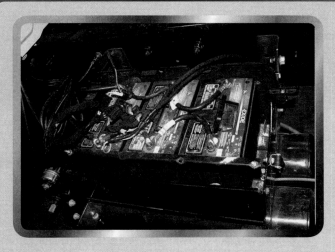

1 Always remove the cable clamp from the negative terminal first. Then remove the positive terminal clamp. While they are disconnected, bend the cables back, or if necessary, tie them out of the way so that they cannot fall back and touch the battery terminals accidentally.

2 Remove the battery hold-downs or other hardware securing the battery. Depending on the type of vehicle, you will need to unbolt, unscrew, or unclip the restraint and move it away from the battery.

3 Keeping it upright, remove the battery from its tray and place it on a clean, level work surface. Visually inspect the battery for damage, cracks, bulges, loose or leaking posts, and so on. If any are found, the battery will need to be replaced.

4 Measure the voltage on the top of the battery with a DVOM. Place the black lead on the negative post and move the red lead across the top of the battery until you find the highest reading. The higher the voltage reading, the larger the potential drain.

5 Check the electrolyte level and its appearance.

6 Carefully clean the case of the battery, hold-downs, and battery tray and box either by (a) washing them or by (b) wiping them down with damp paper towels if the battery and tray are not very dirty. It is best to wear rubber gloves while doing this in case any corrosive electrolyte has leaked from the battery. Safely dispose of the paper towels.

7 Clean the battery posts or screw terminals with a battery terminal tool. On lead posts and terminals, the preferred tool is a scraper style, since it is designed to produce smooth surfaces that are more airtight when clamped together. Do not use the wire-brush style of battery terminal tool, which leaves rougher surfaces that are more likely to corrode.

8 Clean the cable terminals with the same battery terminal tool or wire brush. Examine the battery cables for fraying or corrosion. If the damage looks extensive, the cables and terminals should be replaced.

9 Reinstall the cleaned and serviced battery. Reinstall the hold-downs and make sure the battery is securely held in position. If a new battery needs to be installed, be sure to compare the outside dimensions as well as the type of terminals and their locations prior to installation. These must meet the original manufacturer's specifications.

10 Reconnect the positive battery terminal and tighten it in place. Once the positive terminal is finished, reconnect the negative terminal and tighten it.

11 Coat the terminal connections with anti-corrosive paste or spray to keep oxygen from the terminal connections. Verify that you have a good electrical connection by starting the vehicle.

TABLE 42-1: State of Charge as Indicated by Specific Gravity and Voltage Reading

Open Circuit Voltage	Specific Gravity	Percentage of Charge
12.65 or greater	1.265 (minimum)	100
12.45	1.225	75
12.24	1.190	50
12.06	1.155	25
11.89	1.120	0

Unlike the reading from a refractometer, the hydrometer's reading must be corrected for electrolyte temperature. The density of battery electrolyte changes with temperature and 1.265 is only the density of electrolyte at 80°F (27°C). To correct for temperature effects on specific gravity, add or subtract 4 points to the reading either above or below 80°F (27°C) for every 10°F (6°C) temperature change. (For example add 0.004 for temperatures at 70°F or at 21°C.) Because the hydrometer draws electrolyte into it to raise a float, the electrolyte level must be at least slightly above the top of the plates. If it is not, then distilled water will need to be added and the battery fully charged. To perform a battery state of charge test, follow the guidelines in **SKILL DRILL 42-2**.

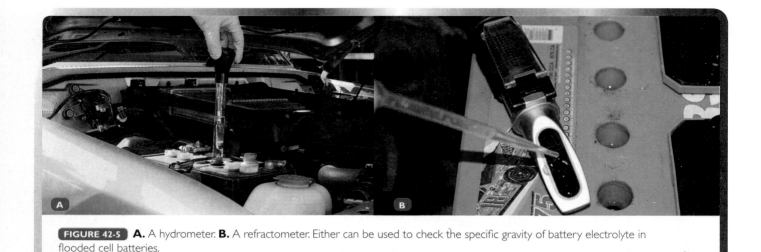

FIGURE 42-5 **A.** A hydrometer. **B.** A refractometer. Either can be used to check the specific gravity of battery electrolyte in flooded cell batteries.

Testing Battery Conductance

Evaluating a battery's condition using hydrometers, refractometers, and load testers provides reasonably accurate results if the instruments are used correctly and the battery is tested under proper conditions. In the field, however, batteries often need charging for hours before they can be tested, and SOC testing is time consuming.

In cold weather, testing on equipment outside presents other problems, too. In the last 15 years, several rapid-test battery testers have emerged that eliminate the need for SOC and discharge-type testing. Referred to collectively as conductance testers, this equipment performs a measurement of the amount of active plate surface area available for chemical reaction. Active plate surface, as measured by conductivity, is a reliable indication of a healthy battery, as it corresponds directly to battery capacity. Also referred to as impedance testing, the AC equivalent to resistance, battery plate conductance declines as the battery fails.

All manufacturers are now requiring the use of a conductance test instead of a high-amperage load test in order for warranty coverage to be considered. A **conductance test** determines the battery's ability to produce current. Many of the testers have integrated printers and, for the battery to be warranted, a printout of the test result has to accompany the returned battery. Advantages of conductance testing are as follows:

- It does not require any battery discharge activity
- It requires only minimal technician involvement, as only two clip-on connectors are attached to the battery terminals during the test
- It is fast—the testing can usually be performed in under two minutes
- Low-frequency AC does not affect battery
- Conductance testing does not prematurely age the battery
- It is safe—no heat or gassing is produced

- Conductance testing can be repeated immediately to verify result
- Batteries can be evaluated in a state of discharge; some testers only require as little as 2 volts of battery voltage to qualify the battery
- The testing method is endorsed by all electrical standards testing organizations including Battery Council International (BCI)
- Printed read-outs can be supplied to the customer or accompany warranty claims **FIGURE 42-6**

The most common type of conductance tester works by applying an AC voltage of a known frequency and amplitude across the battery. The battery's response to the signal is interpreted by a microprocessor inside the test unit. Conductance, or acceptance of the AC voltage, is measured by comparing the shape of the AC waveform exiting the battery to the waveform sent into the battery. The closer the waveforms match, the better the conductivity of the battery.

The most sophisticated testers today analyze, lead acid, Li-ion, and NiMH batteries using a microprocessor containing algorithms that match waveforms from known battery configurations. These analyzers can identify not only the type and condition of a battery, but also the manufacturer and other battery details.

To conductance test a battery, follow the guidelines in **SKILL DRILL 42-3.**

> ### TECHNICIAN TIP
>
> Never use steel bolts, nuts, washers, etc. on battery terminals when using conductance testers. Instead, only use the lead adapters supplied with the conductance tester. The materials and any coatings on other hardware will interfere with the signals sent through the battery and affect the tester's accuracy. Conductance testing is best suited for SLI batteries and may not provide accurate results for deep cycle batteries using thicker plate.

SKILL DRILL 42-2 Performing a Battery State of Charge Test

1. If the battery is not a sealed unit, it will have individual or combined removable caps on top. Remove them and look inside to check the level of the electrolyte. If the level is below the tops of the plates and their separators inside, add distilled water or water with a low mineral content until it covers them. Be careful not to overfill the cells; they could "boil" over when charging. If water is added, the battery will need to be charged to ensure the newly added water mixes with the electrolyte before measuring the specific gravity.

2. Using a hydrometer designed for battery testing, draw some of the electrolyte into the tester and look at the float inside it. A scale indicates the battery's relative state of charge by measuring how high the float sits in relation to the fluid level. A very low overall reading (1.150 or below) indicates a low state of charge. A high overall reading (about 1.280) indicates a high state of charge. The reading from each cell should be the same. If the variation between the highest and lowest cell exceed 0.050, the battery is defective and should be replaced. Be sure to consult temperature correction tables if the battery electrolyte temperature is not at or around 80°F (27°C).

3. Using the refractometer, place one or two drops of electrolyte on the specimen window and lower the cover plate. Make sure the liquid completely covers the specimen window. If not, add another drop of electrolyte:
   - Look into the eyepiece with the refractometer under a bright light.
   - Read the scale for battery acid. The point where the dark area meets the light area is the reading. Compare the readings with the values given in step 2.

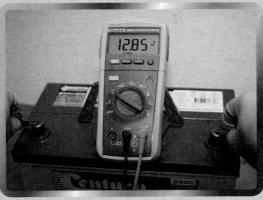

4. For open circuit voltage testing with a DVOM, perform the following actions: (a) With the engine not running, select the "volts DC" position on your DVOM and attach the probes to the battery terminals (red to positive, black to negative). (b) With all vehicle accessories switched off and the battery near 80°F (27°C), the voltage reading should be 12.65 volts if the battery is fully charged. This may be slightly lower at cooler temperatures.

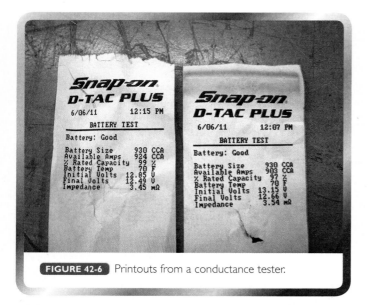

FIGURE 42-6 Printouts from a conductance tester.

Testing Battery Capacity

Traditionally, the load test was used to evaluate a battery's capacity, but the test has become less popular due to the overwhelming advantages of conductance testing.

The **load test** determines the ability of a battery to deliver cranking amperage and is based on the battery CCA rating. For example, a 1000 CCA battery can deliver 1000 amps at 0°F (–18°C) for 30 seconds, while maintaining a voltage of 7.2 volts. During a load test, only half the CCA rating is applied as an electrical load for 15 seconds.

A battery must be at least 75% charged to perform a capacity test, so SOC must be first evaluated before proceeding. A carbon pile is used to simulate the high amperage electrical load on the battery. At the end of 15 seconds, after one-half the CCA

rating has been applied, battery voltage must not fall below 9.6 volts. If it does, the battery is scrap. Because temperature affects battery voltage, 0.1 volts is subtracted from the failure threshold voltage level of 9.6 volts for every 10°F below 70°F.

Another way to think of a load test is that you are testing the battery's ability to produce the high starting current, while maintaining enough voltage to operate the engine's electronic control systems.

If the battery fails the load test after it has had its state of charge properly qualified, the battery should be discarded. No attempt should be made to recharge and re-load test after it has failed the first time. To load test a battery, follow the guidelines in **SKILL DRILL 42-4**.

Charging Batteries

Batteries go dead for a variety of reasons. Parasitic drains, self-discharge, or battery leakage are common reasons a battery may quickly lose its charge. A number of different chargers are available to recharge dead batteries, each with its own advantages and disadvantages.

Battery Charger Types

Differentiating between the types of battery chargers is useful for determining the best method for recharging a battery, given its condition and other operating variables. The most common types of chargers include constant-voltage chargers, constant-current chargers, taper-current chargers, pulsed chargers, and intelligent chargers.

- **Constant-voltage chargers**, like the one shown in **FIGURE 42-7**, are direct current (DC) power supplies that use a step-down transformer and a rectifier to convert AC voltage to DC voltage for charging. As the name suggest, output voltage is constant between 13 and 14 volts.

 SKILL DRILL 42-3 Conductance Testing a Battery

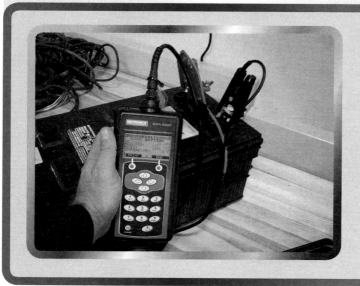

1. Consult manufacturers' procedures and guidelines for the battery being tested and tester being used.
2. Isolate batteries if they are connected in a bank so that they can be individually tested.
3. Identify the type of battery, size, and voltage for input into the test unit.
4. Save information and input as required into the test unit.
5. Run the test.
6. Analyze the result by comparing them to manufacturer specifications.
7. Print or record results of the battery test. Repeat steps if multiple batteries are to be tested.

SKILL DRILL 42-4 Load Testing a Battery

1 With the tester controls off and the load control turned to the off position, connect the tester leads to the battery. Observe the correct polarity and be sure the leads fully contact the battery terminals.

2 Place the inductive amps clamp around either the black or the red tester cables in the correct orientation.

3 Verify that the battery's state of charge is more than 75% before beginning the test. Also measure the battery's temperature to make any correction to the cut-off voltage threshold.

4 If you are using an automatic load tester, enter the battery's CCA and select "test" or "start." If you are using a manual load tester, calculate the test load, which is half of the CCA. Turn the control knob or press the "start" button.

5 Maintain calculated load of 1/2 the CCA rating for 15 seconds while watching the voltmeter. At the end of the 15-second test load, read the voltmeter and immediately turn the control knob off. At room temperature, the voltage must be 9.6 volts or higher at the end of the 15-second load. If the battery is colder than room temperature, correct the battery failure threshold voltage against temperature. Close to 1/10 volt lower is allowed for every 10°F below 70°F. Using the results from the test, determine any necessary action.

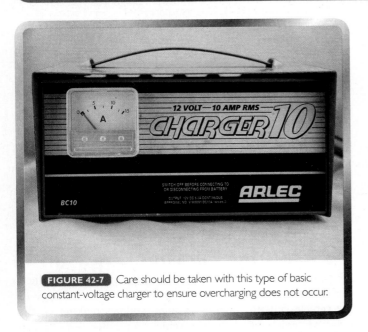

FIGURE 42-7 Care should be taken with this type of basic constant-voltage charger to ensure overcharging does not occur.

A manual switch may allow the voltage setting to increase or decrease to change the charge rate. These designs are found in inexpensive chargers and must be used with care because they can cause overcharging of batteries. **Trickle chargers**, which charge a battery at a low amperage rate, are made following this design. Slow charging or trickle charging a battery is less stressful on a battery than fast charging because a low amperage charge does not excessively heat and gas a battery.

- **Constant-current chargers** automatically vary the voltage applied to the battery to maintain a constant amperage flow into the battery. These vary the voltage to maintain the constant current into the battery as its resistance changes. Also called series chargers, several batteries can be connected together in series and charged together. These are premium, high-end chargers not commonly found in service facilities.

- **Taper-current chargers**, like that shown in **FIGURE 42-8**, are the most common found in repair shops. Either constant voltage or constant amperage is applied to the battery through a manually adjusted current selection switch. Charger current only diminishes as the cell voltage increases. These chargers can cause serious damage to batteries through overcharging if the charge current is adjusted too high. Timers can automatically shut-off the charger to prevent this condition.

- **Pulsed chargers** are recommended to recover sulfated batteries and send current into the battery in pulses of one-second cycles. Varying the voltage and length of time a pulse is applied to the battery controls the charging rate. During the charging process, a short rest period of 20 to 30 milliseconds between pulses improves the quality of chemical reactions in the battery.

- An **intelligent charger's** output varies with the sensed condition of a battery. This means the charger, like the one shown in **FIGURE 42-9**, will monitor battery voltage and temperature and vary its output based on these variables. The charger will also calculate the optimal charge current and vary it over the charging period depending on the type

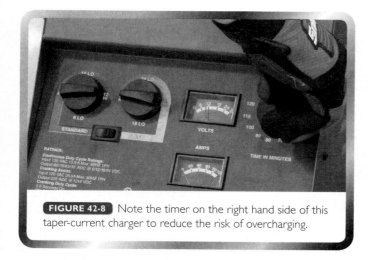

FIGURE 42-8 Note the timer on the right hand side of this taper-current charger to reduce the risk of overcharging.

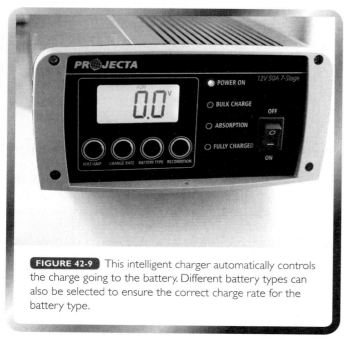

FIGURE 42-9 This intelligent charger automatically controls the charge going to the battery. Different battery types can also be selected to ensure the correct charge rate for the battery type.

of battery connected to it. Charging terminates when the voltage, temperature, or charge time indicates a full charge. VRLA batteries are best suited to these types of chargers. These chargers can be left connected indefinitely without overcharging since they can maintain a float charge. This means the charging voltage floats at zero or a very minimal charge voltage until it senses that the battery voltage has fallen and then resumes charging.

Removing the negative battery terminal while charging a battery reduces the risk of burning up any electronic devices on the vehicle if the ignition key is switched on.

Charging Battery Banks: Series or Parallel

Manufacturers install multiple batteries in most heavy-duty commercial vehicles to provide additional cranking amperage. Knowing how the batteries are connected together will determine how to properly connect a battery charger. Batteries can be connected in series or parallel. Batteries connected in series are connected in line with each other, with the positive of one connected to the negative of the other. Batteries connected in parallel are connected side by side, with positive connected to positive and negative to negative.

To charge a 24-volt set of batteries, a 24-volt charger is needed to charge all the batteries at the same time. If you only have a 12-volt charger, you will have two options: either charge one battery at a time, or reconnect the batteries so they are connected in parallel. To charge batteries, follow the guidelines in **SKILL DRILL 42-5**.

Safety

When connecting jumper cables, a spark will almost always occur on the last connection you make. That is why it is critical that you make the last connection on the chassis away from the battery and any other flammables. A spark also occurs when you disconnect the first jumper cable connection, so that also needs to be the connection somewhere on the chassis.

- Keep your face and body as far back as you can while connecting jumper leads.
- Do not connect the negative cable to the discharged battery because the spark may blow up the battery.
- Use only specially designed heavy-duty jumper cables to start a vehicle with a dead battery. Do not try to connect the batteries with any other type of cable.
- Always make sure you wear the appropriate personal protective equipment (PPE) before starting the job. Remember, batteries contain sulfuric acid, and it is very easy to injure yourself.
- Always follow any manufacturer's personal safety instructions to prevent damage to the vehicle you are servicing.

▶ Jump-Starting Vehicles

Jump-starting a vehicle is the process of using one vehicle with a charged battery to provide electrical energy to start another vehicle that has a discharged battery. Because starting a vehicle requires a high amount of electrical energy, jump-starting a vehicle can put stresses on both vehicles.

To jump-start commercial vehicles, follow the guidelines in **SKILL DRILL 42-6**.

▶ Measuring Parasitic Draw

All modern vehicles have a small amount of current draw when the ignition is turned off. This charge is used to run some of the vehicle systems, such as various modules making up the onboard vehicle network. The vehicle computer systems also require a small amount of power to maintain the computer memory while the vehicle is off. The parasitic current draw should be a relatively small amount of current, since excessive draw will discharge the battery over a short amount of time.

Parasitic current draw does not necessarily immediately drop to its lowest level the instant the ignition is turned off. This usually occurs over a period of time as various systems go into hibernation or sleep mode, which can take up to a few hours. Consult the manufacturer's service information to determine the maximum

SKILL DRILL 42-5 Charging Commercial Batteries

1. Determine the voltage of the system that needs charging. If you are charging a 12-volt battery, use the 12-volt setting on the charger. If you are charging a 24-volt battery, or two 12-volt batteries connected in series, use the 24-volt setting on the charger, if it has one.

2. Identify the positive and negative terminals. Never simply use the color of the cables to determine the positive or negative terminals; use the + and − or the Pos and Neg marks.

3. Visually inspect the battery to ensure there are no cracks, holes, or damage to the casing.

4. Verify that the charger is unplugged from the wall and turned off. Connect the red lead from the charger to the positive battery terminal. Connect the black lead from the charger to the negative battery terminal.

5. Check the settings on the charger and verify that they are correct for what you are charging.

6. Turn the charger on and select the automatic setting, if equipped. Select the rate of charge. A slow charger usually charges at a rate of less than 5 amperes. A fast charger charges at a much higher ampere rate depending on the original battery state of charge; a fast charge should be carried out only under constant supervision.

7. Verify that the voltage and amperage the charger is putting out is proper.

8. Once the battery is charged, turn the charger off. Disconnect the black lead from the negative battery terminal and then the red lead from the positive battery terminal.

9. Allow the battery to stand for at least five minutes before testing the battery. Using a load tester or hydrometer, test the charged state of the battery.

allowable parasitic current draw and the time period, after the ignition is turned off, that it takes the modules to go to sleep.

Parasitic current draw can be measured in several ways, the most common being the process of using an ammeter capable of measuring milliamps and inserting it in series between the battery post and the battery terminal. The ammeter is usually put in series with the negative battery lead. If the vehicle is equipped with systems or modules that will require electronic memory to be maintained, follow the procedure for identifying modules that lose their initialization during battery removal and maintain or restore electronic memory functions. Note that the timers may reset during the process of disconnecting the battery terminal and connecting the ammeter in series, so you may have to wait for the timers to go back to sleep. If excessive parasitic draw is measured, disconnect fuses or systems one at a time while monitoring parasitic current draw to determine the systems causing excessive draw.

Disconnecting the battery can be avoided if a sensitive low-current (that is, milliamps) clamp is available. The low-amp **current clamp** measures the magnetic field generated by a very small current flow through a wire or cable. Placing the low-amp current clamp around the negative battery cable will allow you to measure the parasitic draw. If excessive parasitic draw is measured, disconnect fuses or systems one at a time while monitoring parasitic current draw to determine the systems causing the excessive draw. To measure parasitic draw with a parasitic load test, follow the guidelines in SKILL DRILL 42-7.

▶ Identify and Test Low-Voltage Disconnect Systems

Low-Voltage Disconnect (LVD) systems disconnect a battery load when the voltage of the battery falls below a preset threshold. By doing this, they protect the battery from being excessively discharged and the vehicle from starting. The voltage threshold is normally set between 12.2 and 12.4 volts. Once the battery voltage rises above the set threshold, as it does when the vehicle starts and the alternator commences charging, the load is reconnected automatically. In many cases, LVDs will also incorporate an audible alarm and visual warning light to alert the operator before disconnection occurs.

LVDs are connected in series with the load. They are tested by varying the amount of input voltage around the threshold settings and checking the switching of the output or load to determine if the device switches on and off at the correct voltages. Testing can be conducted on the vehicle or off the vehicle on a test bench. The LVD is tested on the vehicle by monitoring the input and output, or load voltage, with a DVOM while placing a load across the battery to reduce battery voltage. At the threshold point, the device should turn the power off to the output or load. If two DVOMs are not available, a test lamp may be used to indicate when the output or load voltage drops away as the device switches off, although you should also check the output voltage at some point to ensure the load is receiving full battery

SKILL DRILL 42-6 Jump-Starting Commercial Vehicles

- Then connect the black jumper lead to the negative terminal of the charged battery. The negative terminal is the one with the minus sign.
- Connect the other end of the negative lead to a good ground on the chassis of the vehicle with the discharged battery, and as far away as possible from the battery.
- DO NOT connect the lead to the negative terminal of the discharged battery itself; doing so may cause a dangerous spark.

3 Try to start the vehicle with the discharged battery. If the booster battery does not have enough charge or the jumper cables are too small in diameter to do this, start the engine in the booster vehicle and allow it to partially charge the discharged battery for several minutes. Try starting the first vehicle again with the booster vehicle's engine running.

1 Position the charged battery close enough to the discharged battery that it is within comfortable range of your jumper cables. If the charged battery is in another vehicle, make sure the two vehicles are not touching.

2 Always connect the leads in this order:
- First, connect the red jumper lead to the positive terminal of the discharged battery in the vehicle you are trying to start. The positive terminal is the one with the plus sign.
- Next, connect the other end of this lead to the positive terminal of the charged battery.

4 Disconnect the leads in the reverse order of connecting them. Remove the negative lead from the chassis ground away from the battery. Then disconnect the negative lead from the booster battery. Next remove the positive lead from the booster battery, and lastly, disconnect the other positive end from the battery in the vehicle you have just started. If the charging system is working correctly and the battery is in good condition, the battery will be recharging while the engine is running. Note, a deeply discharged set of batteries can cause the alternator to charge at an excessively high rate for too long and damage the alternator.

SKILL DRILL 42-7 Measuring Parasitic Draw on a Battery

1 Research the parasitic draw specifications in the appropriate service information for the vehicle you are diagnosing. Typically this is between 0.035 amps and 0.050 amps (35–50 milliamps).

2 Connect the low-current clamp around (or insert the ammeter in series with) the negative battery cable and measure the parasitic draw. Compare the parasitic draw with specifications.

3 Disconnect the circuit fuses one at a time to determine the cause of excessive parasitic current draw. Determine any necessary actions.

voltage when the LVD has the load turned on. Compare the threshold voltages for turn on and off with the manufacturer's specifications. The units are usually sealed and are not serviceable, although some units may provide a means for adjusting threshold voltages.

The LVD can also be tested off vehicle using a variable voltage power supply. When using a variable voltage power supply to test an LVD, you duplicate the connections made on the vehicle with the power supply taking the place of the battery. You must ensure that the power supply is capable of supplying enough current to operate the LVD and any load you connect to it on the bench. Once the unit is connected to the power supply and load, as per manufacturer requirements, you can slowly increase and decrease the power supply voltage to test the threshold voltages at which the LVD switches on and off the output or load. To identify and test a low voltage disconnect system, follow the guidelines in SKILL DRILL 42-8.

▶ Battery Recycling

Disposal is a critical issue at the end of every battery's service life. Batteries contain many environmentally damaging chemicals and neurotoxic lead. If they find their way into a landfill, the lead can contaminate the soil and groundwater. For this reason, recycling of batteries is mandatory. Many municipalities require battery recycling and levy a "core charge" on every new lead–acid battery sold. The core charge is refunded if an old battery is brought in and exchanged for the new one. This process helps prevent batteries from being discarded in landfills. Check local laws and regulations to ensure that batteries are disposed of correctly.

 SKILL DRILL 42-8 Identifying and Testing a Low-Voltage Disconnect (LVD)

1. Research the LVD specifications such as the wiring schematic, device operation, and threshold voltages in the appropriate manufacturer's information.

2. Check the unit on the vehicle for appropriate power and grounds as per the manufacturer's specifications. If no battery voltage is present on the input side of the LVD, check fuses or circuit breakers for correct operation. Rectify any power or ground issues before proceeding to check LVD threshold voltages.

3. If you are testing the unit on a test bench, remove the unit from the vehicle and connect both power and grounds to the unit as per manufacturer's specifications.

4. Connect a DVOM to the input or battery side connection of the LVD and a second DVOM or test lamp to the output or load side connection. Note the voltage readings on both the input and output of the LVD.

5. Vary the battery voltage by connecting a variable load to the vehicle battery if testing in the vehicle or adjust the voltage if using a variable voltage power supply for bench testing.

6. Note the DVOM readings of the threshold voltages from the input of the LVD as the unit turns the load or output on and off. Compare the voltage readings with manufacturer's specifications. If the unit does not meet specifications, adjust the threshold voltage if adjustment is possible. If the unit is not adjustable or cannot be adjusted to manufacturer's specifications, then the unit will need to be replaced.

7. Connect an appropriate load to the output or load side of the LVD and recheck the threshold voltages to ensure the unit is capable of supplying the current with minimal voltage drop between the input and output or load.

8. Check the operation of any warning lights or bulbs fitted to the unit, ensuring they turn and off as the output or load of the LVD is turned on and off. Report any recommendations and return the unit to normal operation.

Wrap-Up

Ready for Review

▶ Testing the batteries should be the starting point when diagnosing complaints such as: hard starting, slow cranking, or no start; when lights dim when an engine idles or other electrical problems occur; and whenever an alternator is replaced.

▶ Keeping the battery and terminals clean is one of the best maintenance practices for batteries.

▶ Safety should be the first priority when working around and servicing batteries. The electrolyte inside lead–acid batteries is corrosive and can cause injury to skin and eyes and can cause damage to clothing and the vehicle's parts.

▶ Batteries also produce an explosive gas mixture of hydrogen and oxygen during charging and discharging of the battery.

▶ Batteries fail suddenly due to the loss of a cell or open circuits within the internal connections. Batteries also fail gradually through loss of capacity caused by age, sulfation, extremes in operating temperature, vibration, low electrolyte levels, and grid corrosion.

▶ Inspecting, cleaning, and filling (if not maintenance free) are common tasks that should be performed every six months to one year on top-post batteries and one to two years on side-post batteries.

▶ The reverse current flow can damage some or all of the electronic control units (ECUs) throughout the vehicle, so it is critical to connect the battery correctly to prevent sending the current in the reverse direction through the electrical system.

▶ The capacitance test is the preferred test of battery condition.

▶ State of charge testing indicates how charged or discharged a battery is. Low-maintenance or no-maintenance type batteries may not provide access to the electrolyte in the cells for state of charge testing.

▶ Technicians use hydrometers and refractometers to measure the specific gravity of the electrolyte in the battery during a state of charge test.

▶ Load testing has long been used to test a battery's capacity and internal condition, but is no longer used. Manufacturers now insist on conductance testing for batteries, particularly any battery returned under warranty.

▶ There are a number of different battery charger types available for charging batteries: constant-voltage, constant-current, taper-current, pulsed charger, and intelligent chargers.

▶ Even with the ignition turned off, all modern vehicles have a small amount of current draw used to run some of the vehicle systems, such as the on-board network modules.

▶ The parasitic current draw should be a relatively small amount of current, since excessive draw will discharge the battery over a short amount of time.

▶ Correct disposal of batteries by recycling them is good for the environment and the precious metals can be reclaimed for reuse.

Vocabulary Builder

conductance test A type of battery test that determines the battery's ability to conduct current.

constant-current charger A battery charger that automatically varies the voltage applied to the battery to maintain a constant amperage flow into the battery.

constant-voltage charger A direct current (DC) power that is a step-down transformer with a rectifier to provide the DC voltage to charge.

current clamp A device that claps around a conductor to measure current flow. It is often used in conjunction with a digital volt-ohm meter (DVOM).

intelligent charger A battery charger that varies its output according to the sensed condition of the battery it is charging.

load test A battery test that subjects the battery to a high rate of discharge, and the voltage is then measured after a set time to see how well the battery creates that current flow.

pulse charger A battery charger that sends current into the battery in pulses of one-second cycles; used to recover sulfated batteries.

shedding A process that reduces the plate surface area and therefore reduces capacity. Shedding may also produce short circuits between the bottom of positive and negative plates.

state of charge test A test that indicates how charged or discharged a battery is, not how much capacity it has.

taper-current charger A battery charger that applies either constant voltage or constant amperage to the battery through a manually adjusted current selection switch.

trickle charger A battery charger that charges at a low amperage rate.

Review Questions

1. A _____ is a battery charger that charges at a low amperage rate.
   a. trickle charger
   b. intelligent charger
   c. taper-current charger
   d. constant-voltage charger

2. A(n) _____ is a battery charger that varies its output according to the sensed condition of the battery it is charging.
   a. trickle
   b. intelligent charger
   c. constant-current charger
   d. constant-voltage charger

3. A _____ drain of battery current should be no more than 0.5 amps of current.
   a. positive
   b. normal
   c. negative
   d. parasitic

4. Always remove the _____ or first when disconnecting battery cables.
   a. negative
   b. positive
   c. trickle
   d. pulsed

5. A three-minute battery charge test can be used to verify a diagnosis of _____.
   a. grid corrosion
   b. shedding
   c. sulfation
   d. calcification

6. Excessive _____ can cause open circuits in the internal battery connections and "shed" or shake loose plate material, which settles to the bottom of the battery case.
   a. discharge
   b. vibration
   c. conductance
   d. load

7. A _____ test will tell you how charged or discharged a battery is, not how much capacity it has.
   a. state of charge
   b. conductance
   c. discharge
   d. load

8. The _____ of electrolyte indicates the state cell charge.
   a. conductance
   b. volume
   c. weight
   d. specific gravity

9. A _____ test determines the ability of a battery to deliver cranking amperage and is based on the battery CCA rating.
   a. state of charge
   b. load
   c. conductance
   d. discharge

10. Batteries connected in _____ are connected side by side, with positive connected to positive and negative to negative.
    a. parallel
    b. series
    c. unison
    d. variance

ASE-Type Questions

1. Technician A says that any voltage exceeding 0.5 volts between the negative battery post and the top of the battery indicates that the battery is leaking current due to excessive dirt or grime. Technician B says that any voltage exceeding 0.25 volts between the negative battery post and the top of the battery indicates that the battery is leaking current due to excessive dirt or grime. Who is correct?
   a. Technician A
   b. Technician B
   c. Both Technician A and Technician B
   d. Neither Technician A nor Technician B

2. Technician A says that to clean dirt and grime from the top of a battery you should use a mixture of diluted ammonia and baking soda. Technician B says that if a battery fails a load test after it has had its state of charge properly qualified, the battery should be recharged and tested again. Who is correct?
   a. Technician A
   b. Technician B
   c. Both Technician A and Technician B
   d. Neither Technician A nor Technician B

3. Technician A says that subjecting a battery to prolonged undercharge conditions can cause oxidation. Technician B says that subjecting a battery to prolonged undercharge conditions can cause sulfation. Who is correct?
   a. Technician A
   b. Technician B
   c. Both Technician A and Technician B
   d. Neither Technician A nor Technician B

4. Technician A says that calcification takes place primarily in the positive grid and is accelerated by overcharging and high temperatures. Technician B says that grid corrosion takes place primarily in the positive grid and is accelerated by overcharging and high temperatures. Who is correct?
   a. Technician A
   b. Technician B
   c. Both Technician A and Technician B
   d. Neither Technician A nor Technician B

5. Technician A says a fully charged battery should have an open-circuit voltage of 6.25 volts. Technician B says a fully charged battery should have an open-circuit voltage of 24 volts. Who is correct?
   a. Technician A
   b. Technician B
   c. Both Technician A and Technician B
   d. Neither Technician A nor Technician B

6. Technician A says the state of charge is best evaluated by measuring the density of electrolyte in each cell using a refractometer. Technician B says the state of charge is best evaluated by measuring the density of electrolyte in each cell using a bulb-type hydrometer. Who is correct?
   a. Technician A
   b. Technician B
   c. Both Technician A and Technician B
   d. Neither Technician A nor Technician B

7. Technician A says that if a battery has an open circuit voltage of 12.24 and a specific gravity reading of 1.190 it would indicate that the battery has a 50% state of charge. Technician B says that if a battery has an open circuit voltage of 12.24 and a specific gravity reading of 1.190 it would indicate that the battery has a 100% state of charge. Who is correct?
   a. Technician A
   b. Technician B
   c. Both Technician A and Technician B
   d. Neither Technician A nor Technician B

8. Technician A says a conductance test performs a measurement of the amount of active plate surface area available for chemical reaction. Technician B says a state of charge test will tell you how charged or discharged a battery is. Who is correct?
   a. Technician A
   b. Technician B
   c. Both Technician A and Technician B
   d. Neither Technician A nor Technician B

9. Technician A says an intelligent charger can be left connected indefinitely without overcharging since it can maintain a float charge. Technician B says an intelligent charger cannot be left connected indefinitely without overcharging because it does not maintain a float charge. Who is correct?
   a. Technician A
   b. Technician B
   c. Both Technician A and Technician B
   d. Neither Technician A nor Technician B

10. Technician A says the voltage threshold of a low-voltage disconnect system is normally set between 6.2 and 6.4 volts. Technician B says the voltage threshold of a low-voltage disconnect system is normally set between 12.2 and 12.4 volts. Who is correct?
    a. Technician A
    b. Technician B
    c. Both Technician A and Technician B
    d. Neither Technician A nor Technician B

CHAPTER 43

Heavy-Duty Starting Systems and Circuits

NATEF Tasks

Diesel Engines

Engine Block

- Inspect flywheel/flexplate (including ring gear) and mounting surfaces for cracks and wear; measure runout; determine needed action. (pp 1209, 1212, 1214)

Electrical/Electronic Systems

Starting Systems

- Perform starter circuit cranking voltage and voltage drop tests; determine needed action. (p 1212)

- Inspect and test components (key switch, push button, and/or magnetic switch) and wires and harnesses in the starter control circuit; replace as needed. (pp 1213–1214)
- Inspect and test starter relays and solenoids/switches; replace as needed. (p 1214)
- Remove and replace starter; inspect flywheel ring gear or flex plate. (pp 1213–1215)

Knowledge Objectives

After reading this chapter, you will be able to:

1. Identify and describe the various classification and construction features of heavy-duty starting motors and circuits. (pp 1190–1193)
2. Explain operating principles of DC motors. (pp 1193–1196)
3. Identify and describe the major components of a starting system. (pp 1197–1202)
4. Identify and explain the purpose and function of starting system control components. (pp 1202–1205)

5. Identify and describe the procedures for performing an on-vehicle starting system test. (p 1208)
6. Identify and describe test procedures for starting system components. (pp 1208–1212)
7. Identify and explain the causes of starter system failures. (p 1209)
8. List and explain maintenance procedures for starting systems and circuits. (pp 1212–1215)

Skills Objectives

After reading this chapter, you will be able to:

1. Measure starter draw. (p 1211) **SKILL DRILL 43-1**
2. Measure the voltage drop in a starter circuit. (p 1212) **SKILL DRILL 43-2**
3. Inspect and test the starter control circuit. (p 1213) **SKILL DRILL 43-3**

4. Inspect and test relays and solenoids. (p 1213) **SKILL DRILL 43-4**
5. Remove and replace a starter motor and inspect the ring gear or flex plate. (1214) **SKILL DRILL 43-5**
6. Overhaul a starter motor. (p 1215) **SKILL DRILL 43-6**

▶ Introduction

Dozens of electric motors are found in heavy vehicles operating a variety of devices from electric seats, fuel and coolant pumps, fan blower motors, and even instrument gauges. The largest of all these electric motors is the starter motor, like the one shown in **FIGURE 43-1**. The starting system provides a method of rotating (cranking) the heavy vehicles, internal combustion engine (ICE) to begin the combustion cycle. The starter is designed to work for short periods of time and must crank the engine at sufficient speed for it to start. Modern starting systems are very effective provided that they are well-maintained.

FIGURE 43-1 Typical starter motor cross section.

Understanding and maintaining starting systems is important since diagnosing "no-start" conditions are costly in terms of vehicle downtime and component costs if they are "over-repaired" or haphazardly investigated. In fact, various manufacturers have noted that between 55% and 80% of all starters returned for warranty were not defective. Vehicle and passenger safety can be jeopardized if the starting system is not properly repaired and maintained. Interlocked circuits, which prevent the engine from starting under various operating conditions, and the high current supplied by multiple starting batteries are just a few of the safety concerns with this system.

▶ Fundamentals of Starting Systems and Circuits

The starting/cranking system consists of the battery, high- and low-amperage cables, a solenoid, a starter motor assembly ring gear, and the ignition switch. On ECM-controlled starting systems, the ECM enables the operation of a relay to energize the starter circuit. Data supplied by other on-board network modules, along with control algorithms in the module, determine when and for how long the starter will crank. A control circuit determines when and if the cranking circuit will function.

During the cranking process, two actions occur. The pinion of the starter motor engages with the flywheel ring gear, and the starter motor then rotates to turn over, or crank, the engine. The starter motor is an electric motor mounted on the engine block or transmission. It is typically powered by a 12- or 24-volt battery and is designed to have high rotational torque at low speeds. The starter cables are the heaviest conductors in the vehicle because they carry the high current needed by the starter motor. The starter motor causes the engine flywheel

▶ You Are the Technician

The cost of a no-start condition in the fleet of diesel-powered equipment you maintain is extraordinarily high. Equipment productivity, labor hours, and driver and operator time are all lost. In addition, customer aggravation increases, as does the expense of resolving no-start conditions. At the specific direction from management to end or dramatically reduce the number of no-start complaints, you begin to analyze some of the common root cause of the starting system failures. Reviewing service records for the repaired equipment, you discover that the starting motors are frequently burned-out and cable terminals are loose and often burned as well. You also notice that there doesn't seem to be a specific preventative maintenance schedule in place to evaluate the condition of the starting system. It is only when the equipment does not start that the problems are identified, but that occurs too late to prevent disruption of operations. As you consider what steps to take to prevent the no-start complaints, answer the following questions.

1. Explain how the conditions that cause low-voltage burn-out actually damage starting motors and starting-motor connections.
2. What maintenance practices would you recommend to prevent low-voltage burn-out of starting motors and connections?
3. What trend would you observe regarding the voltage and amperage measurements made during a starter draw test if a starter were beginning to fail due to burnt brushes, armature, and field windings?

and crankshaft to rotate from a resting position and keeps them turning until the engine fires and runs on its own.

High-compression-ratio diesel engines with large displacements require high amounts of electrical current, so multiple batteries are connected together to supply more amperage or voltage. To supply more cranking amperage in a 12-volt system, batteries are connected in parallel. Adding more batteries increases the amount of amperage available for cranking, but the system voltage remains the same. Connecting batteries in series increases available voltage, but amperage supplied to the starter remains the same.

Demands on Today's Starting Systems

Today's heavy-vehicle engines demand the most from starter motors since emission reduction strategies have increased engine cylinder pressures during cranking. Anti-idling laws, which require drivers to reduce the amount of time their engine idles, require modern starter motors to crank warm and more mechanically resistive engines many more times than before. Start-stop energy reducing drive systems and hybrid drive vehicles place even more strain on starter motors.

In spite of the increasing demands, new designs of starter motors and systems controls are enabling starters to last longer and increase output torque while substantially reducing motor weight. A typical example of this is the improvements and changes that have occurred to Delco Remy™ starter motors in recent times. The Delco Remy™ 40MT **FIGURE 43-2A** weighs 66 lb (30 kg), and the 39MT weighs only 30 lb (14 kg) yet produces more cranking torque with much greater reliability **FIGURE 43-2B**. The 37MT is the latest, third-generation starter using a gear reduction drive system to multiply torque output. The 37 MT weighs approximately 50 lb (23 kg). All three starters are used on engines from 10 to 15L displacement **FIGURE 43-2C**. Minimum life expectancy for a starter now is 4 years with 7000 start cycles.

Most starting systems have only a single starter motor to crank the engine. In large displacement engines, where the starting demands are higher, two starter motors may be required to crank the engine over.

Starter Motor Classification

Electric starter motors were first installed in the 1912 Cadillac cars to replace hand-operated engine cranks. While electric motors were invented decades before this, the concept that made electric starters practical was the idea of building motors to operate at high amperage levels for a few seconds and not burn out. The Dayton Electric Company, later shortened and called DELCO™, pioneered the use of high-current-draw motors that enabled the starter to develop a tremendous amount of torque. The motors were unlike any compact electric motors of the day, which were all designed for continuous operation.

Using a small pinion gear, the starter motor rotates the engine through a ring gear attached to the flywheel. When the starter motor begins to turn, the pinion teeth quickly line up with the flywheel teeth and rotate the engine at a minimum of 125 rpm for a 4-stroke diesel engine to an average of 200–250 rpm. In gasoline

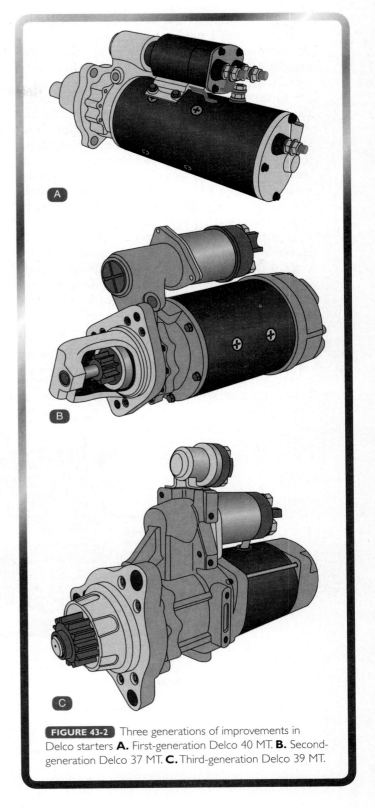

FIGURE 43-2 Three generations of improvements in Delco starters **A.** First-generation Delco 40 MT. **B.** Second-generation Delco 37 MT. **C.** Third-generation Delco 39 MT.

engines, the ratio between the flywheel ring gear and pinion gear is anywhere between 10 and 15:1. Diesel engines use 18:1 to 25:1, with 20:1 being most common.

Currently, there are three major categories of electric starters used in heavy vehicles.

- **Direct drive**—The motor armature directly engages the flywheel through a pinion gear. In this arrangement, as illustrated in **FIGURE 43-3**, the only gear torque multiplication is between the pinion gear and the ring gear.
- **Reduction gear drive**—The motor multiplies torque to the starter pinion gear by using an extra gear between the armature and the starter drive mechanism. The gear reduction allows the starter to spin at a higher speed with lower current, while still creating the required torque through the reduction gear to crank the engine. The reduction drive of this type of starter motor is approximately between 3.3:1 and 5.7:1. These types of starters, like that illustrated in **FIGURE 43-4**, can be identified by an offset drive housing to the motor housing.
- **Planetary gear reduction drive**—Another type of gear reduction system, the planetary gear system, illustrated in **FIGURE 43-5**, reduces the starter profile using a planetary gear set rather than a spur type gear to multiply motor torque to the pinion gear. Gear reduction starters can reduce starter weight by more than 50%.

Direct drive starters are becoming less common due to their larger size, heavier weight, and higher current requirements. The use of gear reduction and planetary gear reduction starter

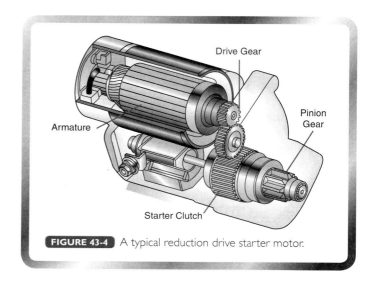

FIGURE 43-4 A typical reduction drive starter motor.

designs means the motor will require less current, is more compact, and is lighter—while increasing cranking torque. Higher motor speeds used in these units result in potentially less motor damage than direct drive units because less current is needed to produce torque The disadvantage of the smaller starter profile

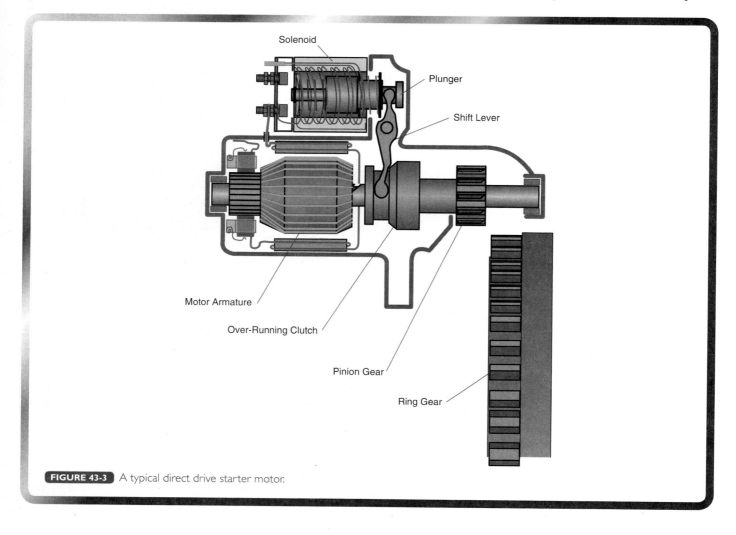

FIGURE 43-3 A typical direct drive starter motor.

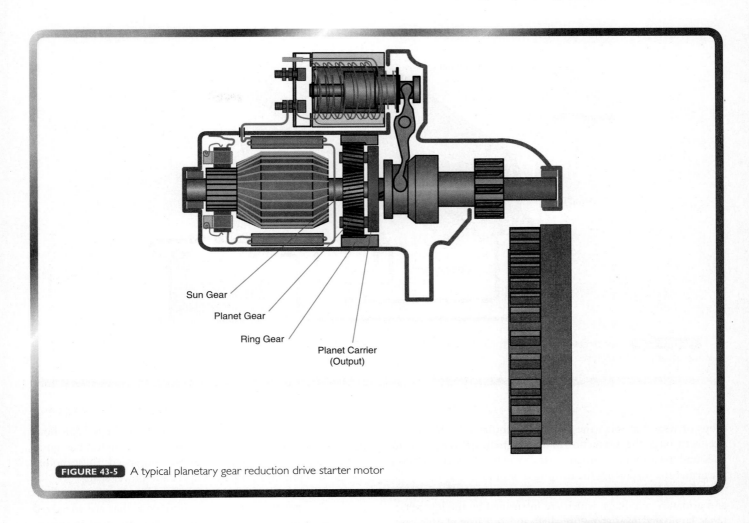

FIGURE 43-5 A typical planetary gear reduction drive starter motor

Sun Gear

Planet Gear

Ring Gear

Planet Carrier (Output)

in comparison to direct drive starters is the inability to tolerate high heat loads caused by prolonged engine cranking.

Pneumatic, or air starters, like that shown in **FIGURE 43-6**, are another type of starter motor used on some older diesel engines, particularly two-stroke Detroits, which need a minimum of 200 cranking rpm to start. The system consists of a geared air motor, starting valve, and a pressure tank. Compressed air from a dedicated reservoir tank is used to spin the motor after the operator pushes a spring-loaded dash mounted air valve. A set of reduction gears between the motor and pinion gears multiplies motor torque while engaging the flywheel ring gear. Once running, the engine recharges the starter reservoir tank.

DC Motor Principles

All electric motors operate using principles of magnetic attraction and repulsion. Because like magnetic poles repel one another and unlike poles attract, it is possible to arrange magnetic poles within the motor to be continuously in a state of repulsion and attraction. That produces the motor action.

The magnetic fields are produced either by permanent magnets or electromagnets, which use coils or loops of conductors with electric current flowing through them to create magnetic fields. Two magnetic fields are required for motor action: one surrounds the motor armature and is called the field

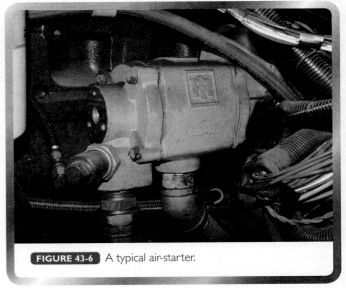

FIGURE 43-6 A typical air-starter.

winding, and the other is in the rotating armature, as illustrated in **FIGURE 43-7**. The magnetic field in the field is produced by permanent magnets but in all heavy-duty applications by strong electromagnets. The armature's magnetic field is generated in

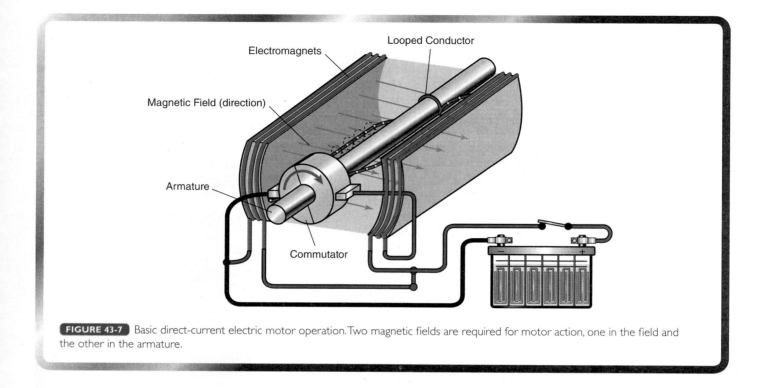

FIGURE 43-7 Basic direct-current electric motor operation. Two magnetic fields are required for motor action, one in the field and the other in the armature.

loops of wire that form the armature windings. Motor action occurs through the interaction of the magnetic fields of the field coils and the armature, which causes a rotational force to act on the armature, producing the turning motion.

Heavy-duty starter motors use electromagnets in the field and armature windings, which are intensified by the low reluctance laminated iron armature shaft and soft iron starter case. Motors used for smaller applications, such as blower and wiper motors, may use permanent magnets for the field and electromagnets for the armature. Permanent magnet field starter motors are not used in medium or heavy-duty starter applications.

Regardless of its design, a starter motor consists of housing, field coils, an armature, a commutator and brushes, end frames, and a solenoid-operated shift mechanism. Major variations between starters are in the starter drive mechanism, with most starters using a gear-reduction drive rather than a direct-drive configuration.

▶ Types of DC Motors

Direct current motors are categorized by the arrangement of electromagnetic circuits producing magnetic forces of repulsion and attraction. Common electric motor classification used in heavy vehicles includes:

- Series—Field and armature windings are connected in series. These motors develop the highest torque and are used as starting motors.
- Shunt (parallel wound)—Field and armature windings are connected in parallel. These motors develop less torque but maintain a constant speed. They are often used as blower motors.

- Compound—Field and armature windings have both series and parallel connections. The motor has good starting torque and stable operating speed. These motors are commonly used in wipers and power seats.
- Stepper—The field is made from an electromagnet and the armature has two or more coils that are energized by a microcontroller. These motors are used in instrument clusters gauges, turbochargers, and EGR actuators where high precision movement is required.

Series Motors

The series and shunt motor are the two most common types found in the automotive industry. **FIGURE 43-8** shows the current flow circuits through a series and shunt motor. Note the difference in the way the current flows through the fields. Series motors are called "series" because the field and armature windings are connected in series. So, current will flow through the field windings first and then to the armature windings before leaving the armature through the positive brush. This means current first passes from the negative chassis ground, through a brush, and into the armature. Current leaves from another brush and passes into the field coils before returning to the battery positive. Because it is a series circuit, any unwanted resistance inside the motor, whether it is a burnt contact or loose brush, will reduce current flow throughout the entire motor circuit.

Series-wound motors are primarily used in starter motors because they develop the greatest amount of torque at zero rpm, which is ideal for developing break-away torque needed to crank a stopped engine. As magnetic field strength is always proportional to amperage and not voltage, the initial amperage

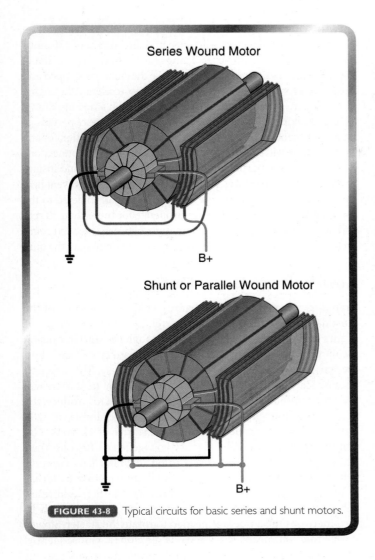

FIGURE 43-8 Typical circuits for basic series and shunt motors.

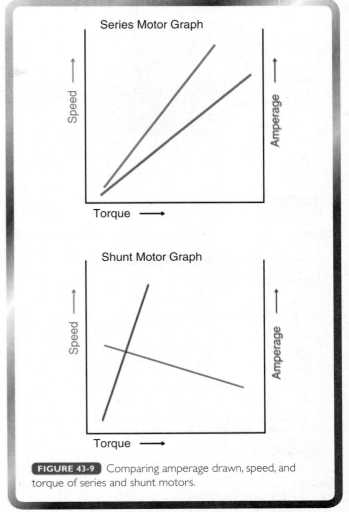

FIGURE 43-9 Comparing amperage drawn, speed, and torque of series and shunt motors.

drawn by a series motor produces the most torque. In comparison, as illustrated in FIGURE 43-9, shunt motors produce less torque than series motors but do not drop as much speed as torque diminishes. This makes them ideal for applications like blower motors.

Series Motor Current Flow

The current flow for a series motor, such as the one illustrated in FIGURE 43-10, is as follows:

1. Current first enters the motor through the brush connected to negative chassis ground. Current passes through the armature via the commutator and leaves through the second brush connected to the field winding. A magnetic field is created in the armature.

2. Current passes through the windings of the field coils. The laminated iron making up the pole shoes intensifies the magnetic field strength. The direction the winding is wound around the pole shoe establishes the polarity of the pole shoe. The field windings are wound in directions opposite to one another to produce a like pole to the armatures, which always opposes the magnetic pole produced in the armature.

3. The forces of repulsion between the field coil and armature cause the armature to turn.

4. Each armature winding is connected to a pair of segments on the commutator. The commutator turns with the armature, causing the stationary brushes to continuously connect with a new armature winding as the armature rotates. This arrangement enables the forces of repulsion to constantly reposition to maintain starter motor rotation.

Series Motor Operational Characteristics

Series wound motors also are self-limiting in speed due to the development of a **counter-electromotive force (CEMF)**. CEMF is produced by the spinning magnetic field of the armature, which induces current in the opposite direction of battery current through the motor. Battery current and CEMF current both flow through a motor at the same time but in opposite directions. The faster the motor turns, the higher the CEMF, and the less current is drawn from the battery. Higher voltage from cranking batteries produces greater motor speed and more CEMF. FIGURE 43-11 illustrates the relationship between motor speed, torque, and amperage draw.

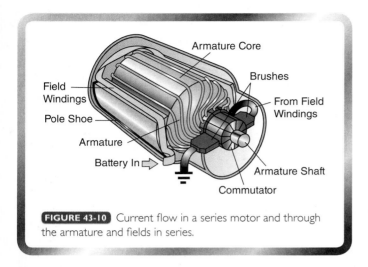

FIGURE 43-10 Current flow in a series motor and through the armature and fields in series.

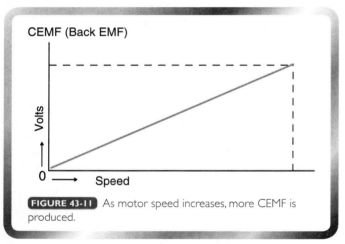

FIGURE 43-11 As motor speed increases, more CEMF is produced.

Consider the following relationship between armature speed, CEMF, amperage, and torque for a series starter motor:

- The faster the armature spins, the greater the CEMF current induced in the opposite polarity of battery voltage.
- The starter draws less current from the battery as it spins faster due to CEMF resistance.
- Since less current is used at higher speeds, magnetic fields will weaken and starter torque drops off.
- Slower motor speeds mean less CEMF resistance to current flow through the starter and higher battery amperage drawn by the starter.
- Greatest torque is produced at low speed since the motor will draw the highest amperage.

▶ TECHNICIAN TIP

Weak and discharged batteries are a starting motor's worst enemy because they can cause low-voltage burn-out. Low battery voltage will prevent the starter from spinning as fast as it should, which reduces CEMF—a starter's internal resistance when operating. With lower internal resistance, the starter will draw more amperage than it should, which leads to heat damage to starter windings, solenoids, and external circuits.

Amperage drawn by a starter at normal room temperature with a fully charged battery will range from an average of 350 amps for a 7-liter engine to 800 or 900 amps for a 15-liter engine. Initial starting amperage is much higher because the engine is stopped and needs more torque from the starting motor to accelerate the engine from 0 rpm to cranking speed. Because of the high amperage drawn during cranking, the starter can only operate for short periods of time before cooling. Heat produced by continuous operation for any length of time will cause serious damage to the motor. Connections become loose and burnt. Some will even melt. Brushes and insulation will become burned as well as motor windings. To prevent heat damage, armature windings are brazed rather than soldered to the commutator. The starter must never operate for more than 30 seconds at a time and should rest for 2 minutes between extended crank cycles. This permits the heat to dissipate without damage to the unit.

Low-Voltage Burn-Out

Cranking an engine with low battery voltage causes one of the most damaging conditions for a starter. **Low-voltage burn-out** occurs when excess amperage flows through the starter, causing the motor to burn out prematurely. When battery voltage is low, the starter will use even more amperage to rotate. This happens because starters are constant power devices. That is, starters will use any combination of voltage and amperage to produce the necessary output power, rated in watts. For example, if 7200 watts of power is needed to operate a starter at 12 volts, 600 amps is needed. If available battery voltage fell to 10 volts, then 720 amps would be needed according to Watts Law (watts = volts × amperage). Increasing amperage drawn from batteries, in turn, increases batteries' internal resistance. Increased resistance causes available voltage to drop even further, which in turn increases the amperage needed to rotate the starter. Slower starter rotation means less CEMF is developed. Consequently, amperage through the starter climbs even more. To prevent damage to the starter, cables, solenoid, and switches from low voltage, several design and maintenance practices are required.

- Correct battery sizing. Batteries must be sized according to their CCA to maintain a cranking voltage of no less than 10.5 volts after three consecutive cranking periods lasting 30 seconds. The appropriate two-minute cooling period is included in this estimation.
- Correct sizing of battery cables. Dedicated battery negative and positive cables are needed for heavier starting systems. Cable diameters should be sized for maximum amperage capacity using OEM recommendations. Double cables are needed when using four or more starting batteries.
- Using overcrank protection switches. Thermal protection switches may be located in the starter housing and connected in series with the starter solenoid ground circuit. When hot, the switch opens and prevents the starter solenoid from operating until the starter is sufficiently cooled.
- Using voltage sensitive starter control circuit relays. Starter relays are produced that will disengage when battery voltage falls below a predetermined level, thus disconnecting the starter circuit. Alternatively, an

electronic control module (ECM), which supplies current to energize the starter, can monitor battery voltage, enabling the ECM to disconnect the starter relay when battery current falls too low during cranking. Disconnect voltage is approximately 7.2 volts.

- Using ultra-capacitors. Ultra-capacitors are a recent application of organic capacitors used to provide cranking assist to HD starters. Up to 1800 amps of current can rapidly discharge for a brief moment to provide battery assist to the starting motor. As illustrated in **FIGURE 43-12**, ultra-capacitors connected in parallel to the battery provide a high initial current to the starter to speed up the armature rotation. Supplementing the available amperage to the starter during the initial cranking period reduces the likelihood of a low-voltage burn-out due to low CEMF when armature speed is reduced

▶ TECHNICIAN TIP

Battery capacity is specifically designed to meet the cranking requirements of the engine. An under-capacity set of batteries will not be capable of delivering the required current flow to the starter motor while still maintaining sufficient battery voltage. The batteries may cause low-voltage burn-out of the starter and damage the starter circuit. It may also create a situation where there is insufficient voltage available to operate the engine's ECM during cranking. Although not as common a problem, excessive battery capacity can also damage the starter motor by supplying too much amperage while cranking. This can create a situation in which excessive torque is produced from the starter motor, damaging the starter drive and ring gear.

▶ Components of Starters

Regardless of the motor design, a starter motor consists of housing, field coils, an armature, a commutator, brushes, end frames, and a solenoid-operated shift mechanism. Major variations between starters are in the starter drive mechanism. Some starters use a gear-reduction drive, while others use a direct drive configuration. Still other starter motors, called axial starter motors, are a type of direct drive starter. Axial starter motors use an axial sliding armature to engage the pinion with the flywheel. This type of starter will be discussed later in this chapter.

Starter Housing and Field Coils

The starter housing, or frame, encloses and supports the internal starter components, protecting them and intensifying the magnetic fields produced in the field coils. Housings and pole shoes are made from soft iron, which conducts magnetic fields with less resistance than air or other materials, which concentrates the magnetic field produced in the fields, making a more powerful magnet. In the starter housing shown in **FIGURE 43-13**, field coils and their pole shoes are securely attached to the inside of the iron housing. The field coils are insulated from the housing and are connected to a terminal, called the motor terminal, which protrudes through to the housing. Fields will have a "North" or "South" magnetic polarity facing inward or outward depending on the direction of current flow. The magnetic flux of the pole shoes is illustrated in **FIGURE 43-14**.

Field coils are connected in series with the armature windings through the starter brushes. In a four-brush starter motor,

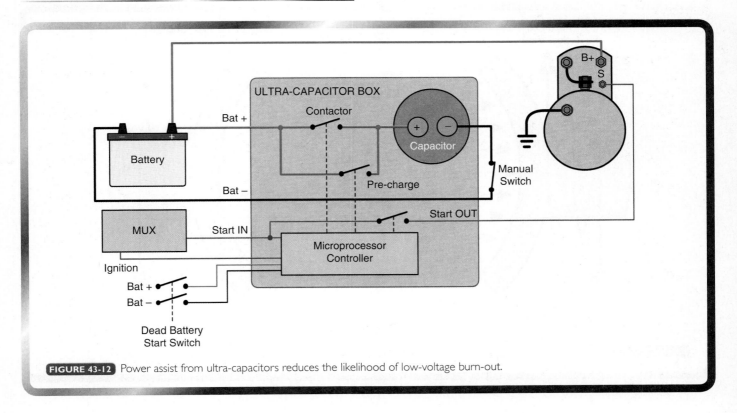

FIGURE 43-12 Power assist from ultra-capacitors reduces the likelihood of low-voltage burn-out.

two brushes are used to connect the field coils to the armature and the other two brushes connect to ground to complete the series circuit.

Armature

The **armature** is the only rotating component of the starter. Armatures, like that shown in **FIGURE 43-15**, have three main components: the shaft, windings, and the commutator.

FIGURE 43-13 A set of starter motor fields, windings, and housing.

Armature Shaft and Windings

Different from the thin wire used in shunt motors, armature windings are made of heavy, flat, copper strips that can handle the heavy current flow of the series motor. The windings are made of numerous coils of a single loop each. The sides of these loops fit into slots in the armature core or shaft, but they are insulated from it with insulating strips and varnish applied to the winding before placement. Each slot contains the side of one half of a coil and a commutator segment. In a four-brush motor, each half of a coil is wound at 90-degrees to each other. The coils connect to each other at the commutator so that current flows through all of the armature windings at the same time.

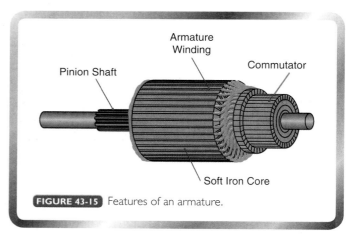

FIGURE 43-15 Features of an armature.

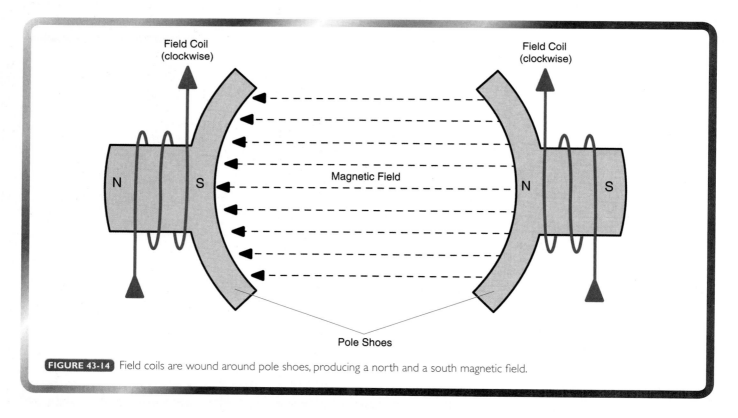

FIGURE 43-14 Field coils are wound around pole shoes, producing a north and a south magnetic field.

This arrangement generates a magnetic field around each armature winding. The interaction between the armature and field windings' magnetic fields produces a torque or twisting force that turns the armature.

Commutator and Commutation

The commutator assembly presses onto the armature shaft. It is made up of heavy copper segments separated from each other and the armature shaft by insulation. The commutator segments connect to the ends of the armature windings. Starter motors have four or more brushes that ride on the commutator segments and carry the heavy current flow from the stationary field coils to the rotating armature windings via the commutator segments. A brush holder holds the brushes in position.

The commutator's role is to switch the direction of current flow through each armature coil as the armature rotates, thereby maintaining the rotary movement by ensuring the magnetic pole in the field winding is always the same as the pole in the armature winding opposite it. For a simple explanation of how a commutator works, consider a basic motor with a single loop of wire. When current flows in a conductor, an electromagnetic field is generated around it. If the conductor is placed in a stationary electromagnetic field with current flowing through the field in the opposite direction, the two magnetic fields will oppose one another, and the conductor will be repelled or pushed away from the stationary field. Reversing the direction of current flow in the conductor will cause the conductor to move in the opposite direction. This is known as the motor effect and is greatest when the current-carrying conductor and the stationary magnetic field are at right angles to each other.

By switching the direction of current flow through the conductor at the right time, the conductor can be continuously pushed away from one field winding and pulled towards another, as illustrated in **FIGURE 43-16**. The turning motion is called the motor effect and causes the loop to rotate until it is at 90 degrees to the magnetic field. To continue rotation, the direction of current flow in the conductor must be reversed. A commutator is used to continually reverse the current flow to maintain rotation of the loop, as illustrated in **FIGURE 43-17**. For example, a commutator consists of two semicircular segments that are connected to the two ends of the loop and are insulated from each other. Carbon brushes provide a sliding connection to the commutator to complete the circuit and allow current to flow through the loop.

This continuously changing direction of current through the loop maintains a consistent direction of rotation of the loop. To achieve a uniform motion and torque output, the number of loops must be increased. The additional loops smooth out the rotational forces. A starter motor armature has a large number of conductor loops and therefore has many segments on the commutator. A simple multi-loop motor is depicted in **FIGURE 43-18**.

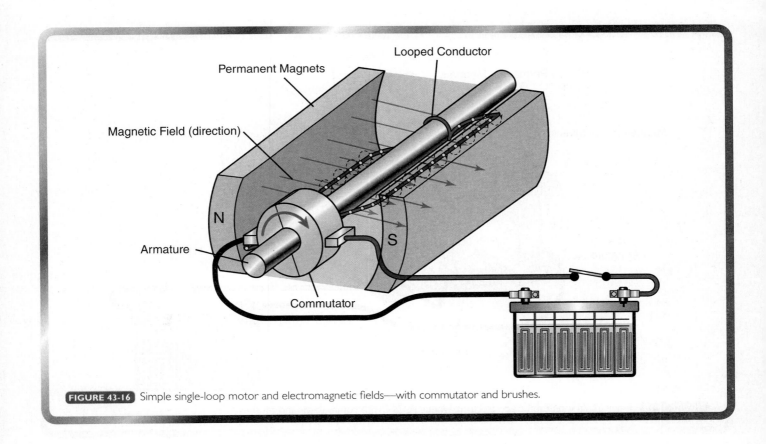

FIGURE 43-16 Simple single-loop motor and electromagnetic fields—with commutator and brushes.

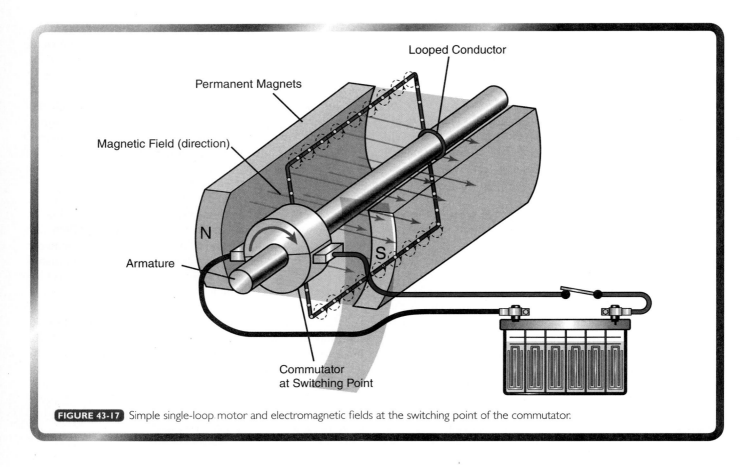

FIGURE 43-17 Simple single-loop motor and electromagnetic fields at the switching point of the commutator.

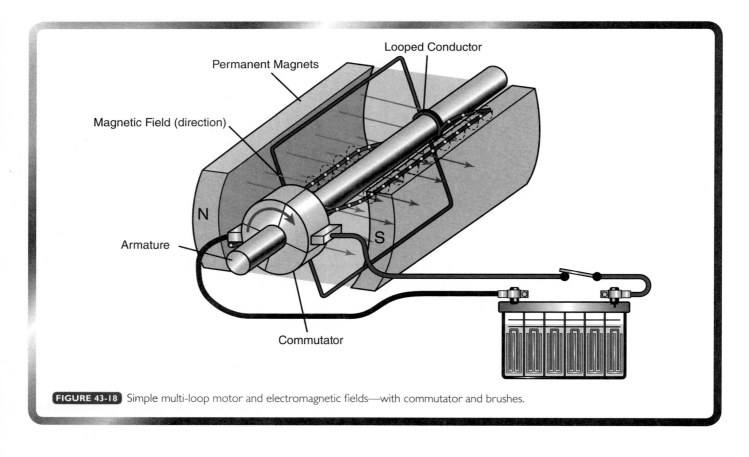

FIGURE 43-18 Simple multi-loop motor and electromagnetic fields—with commutator and brushes.

Solenoid and Shift Mechanism

The solenoid on the starter motor performs two main functions:

1. It switches the high current flow required by the starter motor on and off.

2. It engages the starter drive with the ring gear.

The solenoid-operated shift mechanism is mounted in a case that is sealed to keep out oil and road splash, as in **FIGURE 43-19**. In direct-drive starters, the case is flange mounted to the starter motor case and contains two electromagnets around a hollow core. A movable iron plunger is installed in the hollow core. Energizing the electromagnets pulls the iron plunger, which, in turn, moves a shift lever, engaging the drive pinion gear. This is illustrated in **FIGURE 43-20**. At the same time, moving the iron core also closes a set of contacts to connect battery current with the motor terminal, directing full battery current to the field coils and starter motor armature for cranking power. The starter pinion gear will engage the flywheel ring gear before energizing the motor terminal to prevent damage to either gear from spinning teeth, as illustrated in Figure 43-20.

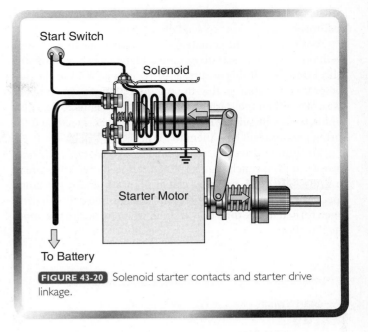

FIGURE 43-20 Solenoid starter contacts and starter drive linkage.

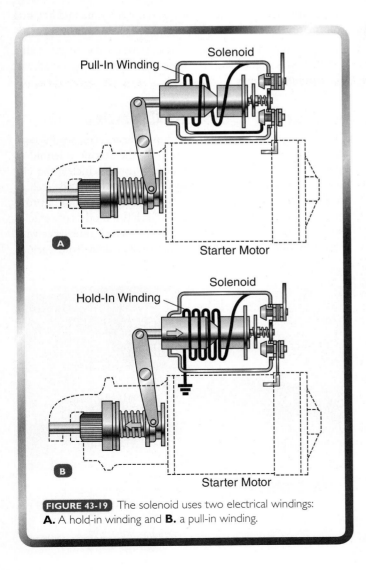

FIGURE 43-19 The solenoid uses two electrical windings: **A.** A hold-in winding and **B.** a pull-in winding.

TECHNICIAN TIP

A solenoid is an electromagnet that is used to perform work and has mechanical action. A solenoid is made with one or two coil windings wound around an iron tube. When electrical current is passed through the coil windings, it creates electromagnetic force that creates linear action pushing or pulling an iron core. When the core is connected to a lever or other mechanical device, the solenoid can put this mechanical movement to practical use. For example, it may engage the pinion of the starter motor with the flywheel; shift gears in electronically controlled transmissions; shut off air, fuel, or oil supplies; engage engine and exhaust brakes; move the fuel rack in a diesel engine; and so on. Solenoids can also close contacts, such as the solenoid contact in a starter motor solenoid.

TECHNICIAN TIP

Low battery voltage produces starter chatter—the rapid cycling of the solenoid plunger in and out of engagement. This happens because the thinner windings of the hold-in circuit are more sensitive to voltage drop than pull-in windings. When the solenoid closes the connection between the battery and motor terminal, the available voltage also drops due to the increased amperage flow from the battery.

Starter Drive Mechanisms

The starter drive transmits the rotational force from the starter armature to the engine via the ring gear that is mounted on the engine flywheel or torque converter. Armature rotation is transferred to the pinion gear through a variety of mechanisms.

Direct-drive starters, which diesel engines used exclusively for many decades, transferred torque directly to the pinion gear.

Today, gear reduction starters using both planetary and spur-gear mechanisms have replaced direct drives.

With a solenoid-actuated, direct-drive starting system, teeth on the pinion gear do not immediately mesh with the flywheel ring gear. If this occurs, a spring located behind the pinion gear compresses so that the solenoid plunger can complete its stroke. When the starter motor armature begins to turn, the pinion teeth will quickly line up with the flywheel teeth and the spring pressure will help them to mesh FIGURE 43-21.

The pinion drive gear is attached to a roller-type, one-way, or overrunning clutch that is splined to the starter armature as in FIGURE 43-22. A one-way clutch is in all pinion gears and operates like a ratchet to protect the starter motor. It will drive when turned in one direction and slip when turned in the opposite direction.

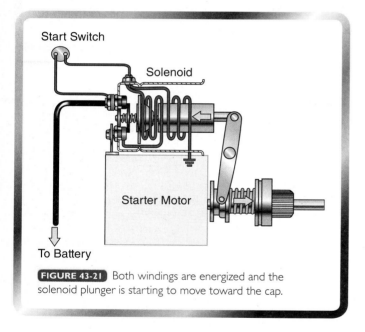

FIGURE 43-21 Both windings are energized and the solenoid plunger is starting to move toward the cap.

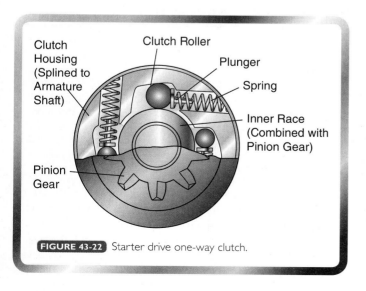

FIGURE 43-22 Starter drive one-way clutch.

When the engine starts and runs, the starter motor would be damaged if it remained connected to the engine through the flywheel. The ring gear-to-pinion gear ratio, which multiplies starter torque, also multiplies the starter's speed when driven by the engine. At idle, with a 20:1 gear ratio, the starter's armature will turn 14,000 rpm or more, which will destroy the armature windings. To prevent this, the one-way overrunning clutch allows the pinion gear to spin—but not turn the armature if it remains or is accidentally engaged with the flywheel. When the solenoid is de-energized, the shift assembly is pulled away from the flywheel through spring pressure FIGURE 43-23.

Most heavy-vehicle starters will have a pinion clearance adjustment to ensure the pinion engages fully with the flywheel while maintaining a clearance from the drive end housing. Starter motors will usually use one of the following three methods for providing pinion clearance adjustment, as illustrated in FIGURE 43-24. Proper adjustment of the mechanism is important to prevent damage to the flywheel teeth.

1. An eccentric shift fork pin, which is turned until the correct pinion clearance is measured and then locked off by a lock nut
2. Shims, which are placed between the solenoid and housing to adjust pinion clearance
3. A screw or nut on the solenoid core where it connects to the shift fork; tightening and loosening the screw or nut adjusts pinion clearance

▶ Starter Control Circuits

The starter control circuit, in its most basic form, would have an ignition switch directly controlling the starter solenoid to operate the starter motor. In modern heavy vehicles, the circuits are more complex, as relays and control circuits such as transmission neutral and clutch switches are added to improve reliability and the safety of vehicles. The latest models of vehicles use an electrical system control module, which interfaces with the on-board vehicle network that receives data from various

FIGURE 43-23 Ring gear damage can result from poorly adjusted pinion clearance or engagement of the pinion while the ring gear is rotating.

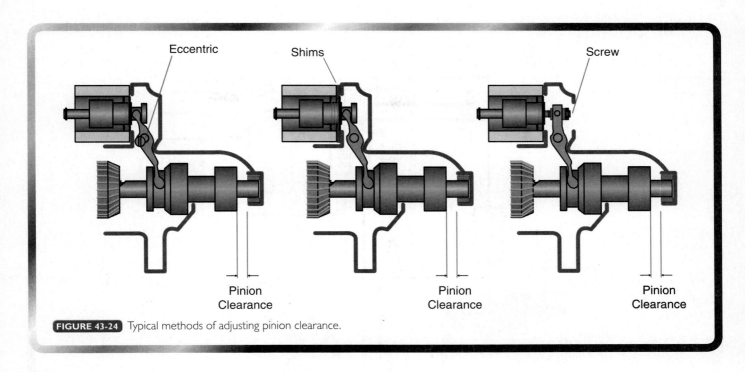

FIGURE 43-24 Typical methods of adjusting pinion clearance.

sensors, and various sensors to control the operation of the starter control circuit.

Solenoid Control Relay

Since it is neither practical nor safe to have large battery and starter cables routed in the cab of a vehicle, the starter control circuit allows the operator to use a small amount of battery current provided by the ignition switch to control the flow of a large amount of current in the starting circuit. The control circuit may also have a provision for locking out the starter engagement if the engine is running or the starter has overheated. Safety switches, also called neutral safety switches **FIGURE 43-25A**, can be located in either of two places in the control circuit—interrupting either the ground or battery positive of the starter relay **FIGURE 43-25B**. Placing the transmission in PARK or NEUTRAL or depressing the clutch will close the starter control circuit so current can flow to the relay switch. The safety switch can also be connected between the relay switch and its ground so that the switch must be closed before current can flow from the magnetic switch to ground.

ECM controlled circuits use the ignition key as an input device and control the starter operation by supplying a ground to the starter relay. The starter relay is the point in the starting system where the control circuit and starter solenoid circuit join. Because starter solenoids can consume between 30 and 60 amps, relays are needed to switch low current from the ignition switch or starter button to energize the starter solenoid circuit. Starter relays are a type of intermittent duty relay. This means they are not intended for continuous operation or operation longer than a minute. The intermittent duty relay has heavy, large-gauge windings in the control circuit capable of producing strong magnetic fields, which are less sensitive to voltage drop during cranking.

As there is a relatively high amount of amperage drawn by the starter solenoid itself, solenoid circuits have a minimum of one relay to switch current flow to the solenoid circuit. The relay may be controlled by a separate push button located in the dash or by an ignition key switch. On electronically controlled engines, it is more common to have the circuit controlled by a start button than the key switch. Having a start button prevents voltage drops through the switch. Likewise, a start button also prevents voltage spikes from the magnetic field collapse of the relay's coil that could travel back to other ignition circuits through the key **FIGURE 43-26**.

The ignition switch has other jobs besides controlling the starting circuit. The ignition switch normally has at least four separate positions: Accessory, Off, On (Run), and Start. There may be a separate position for "proving-out," which test illuminates on-dash lights and gauges. When a vehicle has a push-button starter switch, battery voltage is available to the button switch only when the ignition switch is in the ON position. When the starter pushbutton is pushed, current flows through the control circuit to the starter relay.

Relays use electromagnets to close contacts and act like a switch. Larger relays are sometimes referred to as "mag" switches.

Overcrank Protection (OCP)

Some starter motors are equipped with an **overcrank protection (OCP) thermostat**. The thermostat, as illustrated in **FIGURE 43-27**, monitors the temperature of the motor. If prolonged cranking causes the motor temperature to exceed a safe threshold, the thermostat will open the relay circuit and the current to the solenoid is interrupted.

ADLO Lockout

Another device that may be used within the starter control circuit is **automatic disengagement lockout (ADLO)**, like that

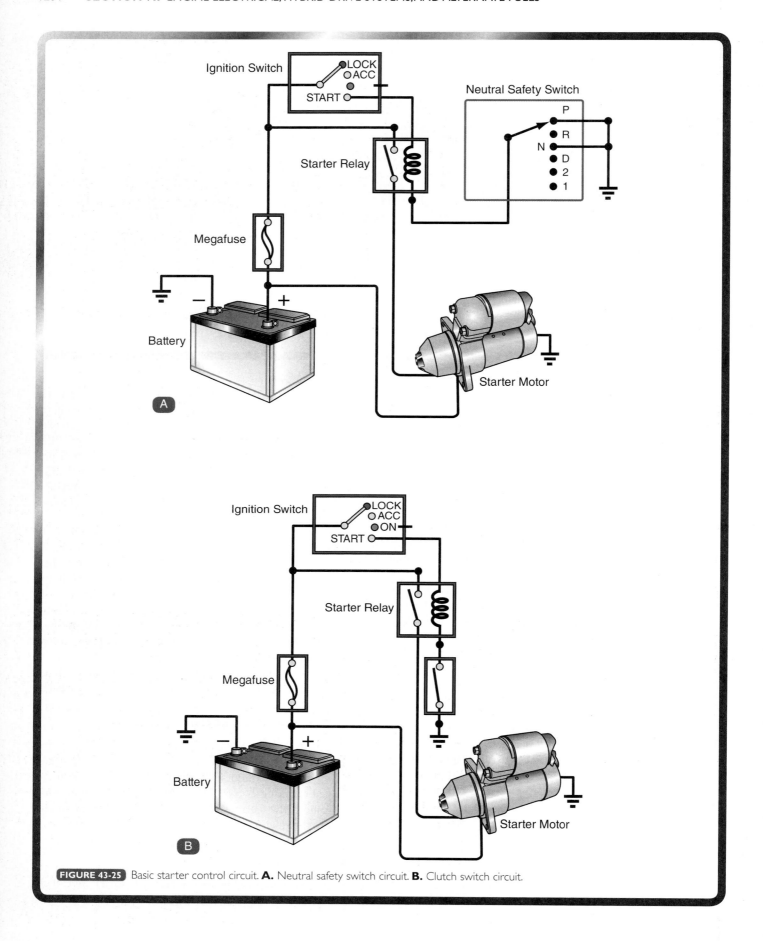

FIGURE 43-25 Basic starter control circuit. **A.** Neutral safety switch circuit. **B.** Clutch switch circuit.

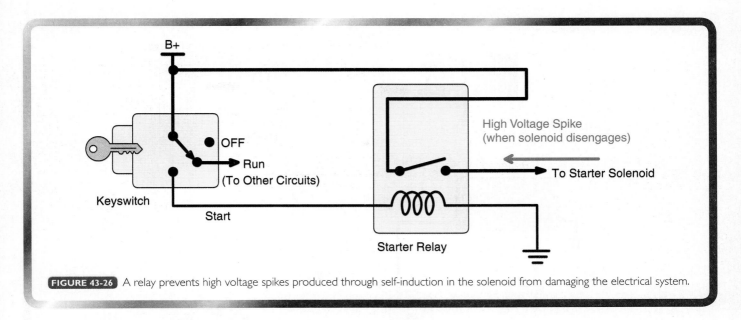

FIGURE 43-26 A relay prevents high voltage spikes produced through self-induction in the solenoid from damaging the electrical system.

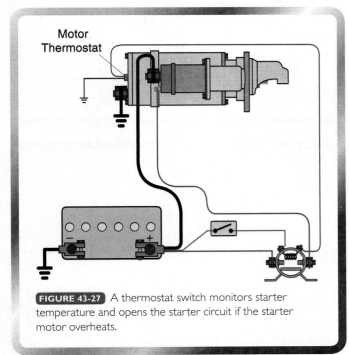

FIGURE 43-27 A thermostat switch monitors starter temperature and opens the starter circuit if the starter motor overheats.

illustrated in **FIGURE 43-28**. The ADLO circuit prevents the starter motor from operating if the engine is running. It does this by using a **frequency-sensing relay** connected to the alternator, which detects AC current only when the alternator is charging. The ADLO relay contacts are connected in series in the starter motor control circuit. If the engine is running, the relay prevents starter engagement and disengages the starter if the key switch is left engaged too long after the engine starts.

Voltage-Sensing Relay

Because starters can be damaged from low battery voltage, some companies find the solution is to prevent the starter from cranking when the battery voltage is too low. This also has the additional benefit of preventing prolonged cranking. The voltage-sensing relay, as illustrated in **FIGURE 43-29**, is connected in series to the solenoid control circuit. When the battery voltage drops below 7.2 volts while cranking, the voltage-sensing relay will typically open-circuit the starter relay circuit.

Series-Parallel Electrical Systems—Split Load

Series Parallel Electrical Systems, or spilt load as it is generally called, use two, four, or six 12-volt batteries connected in series through an equalizer to supply most of the vehicle's electrical systems. Buses and heavy equipment are common examples of vehicles using split loads for several reasons. Large engines with high starter torque requirements will use 24-volt starters. Other electrical devices using large amounts of power benefit from 24 volts, as their size and the gauge of electrical wire supplying current is smaller.

Conducting less amperage also means resistance in circuits is reduced, with less damage and loosening of electrical connections. On buses, the 24-volt supply powers the majority of the vehicle's electrical components, while on other vehicles, 12 volts may supply the exterior lighting or other 12-volt accessories. Batteries are recharged by a 24-volt alternator, and current is redistributed by a battery equalizer to ensure the batteries charge at an equal rate **FIGURE 43-30**.

▶ Starting System Testing

The starting system requires testing when the engine will not crank, cranks slowly, cranks intermittently, or when the starter motor will not turn. Various manufacturers report that between 55% and 80% of defective starters returned for warranty work normally when tested. That points to poor or incomplete diagnosis of the starting and related systems and circuits. The starting system is just part of the overall vehicle's electrical and

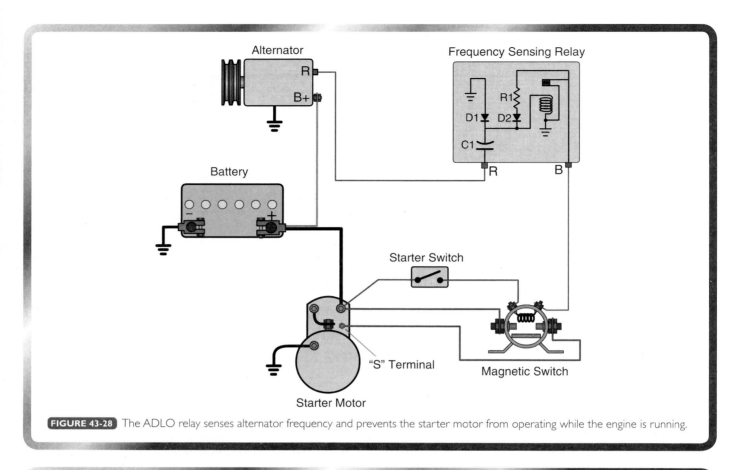

FIGURE 43-28 The ADLO relay senses alternator frequency and prevents the starter motor from operating while the engine is running.

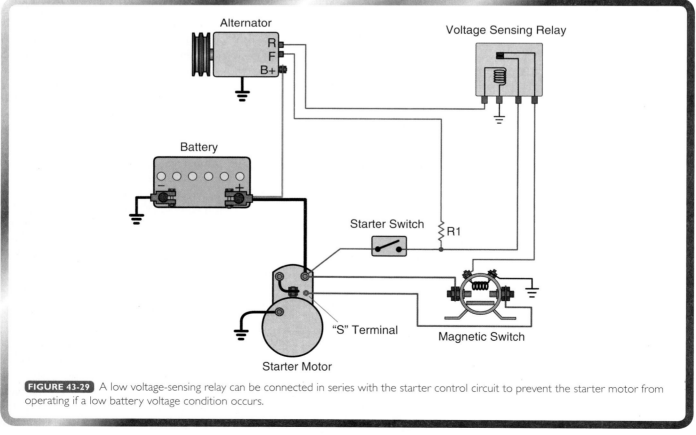

FIGURE 43-29 A low voltage-sensing relay can be connected in series with the starter control circuit to prevent the starter motor from operating if a low battery voltage condition occurs.

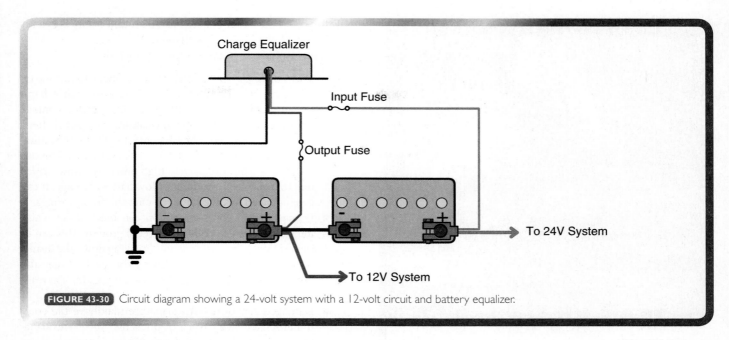

FIGURE 43-30 Circuit diagram showing a 24-volt system with a 12-volt circuit and battery equalizer.

mechanical system. As such, there are areas of overlap between the various electrical and mechanical systems on the vehicle. For example, the starter system makes use of the batteries to supply power for starting, but the charging system needs to provide an adequate charge to ensure there is enough power to start the engine. At the same time, the engine's mechanical condition will affect the load on the starter motor. So, when testing the starting system, also bear in mind that other electrical systems and mechanical items may require inspection to ensure a successful repair.

Because cranking torque produced from a starting motor is also affected by the condition and charge of the battery, the condition of the battery needs to be qualified first before performing starting systems checks. Battery checks include:

- Verifying the battery voltage matches the voltage rating of the starter motor
- Ensuring that cranking amperage (CA or CCA) of the batteries meet or exceed OEM recommendations
- Verifying that the state of charge is not lower than 50% and that open circuit voltage is not less than 12.4 volts or 24.8 volts
- Measuring the batteries' capacity through load testing or conductance testing

For information on how to undertake battery checks, review the Servicing Commercial Vehicle Batteries chapter.

Differentiating Between Electrical and Mechanical Problems

Whether a slow-crank or a no-crank condition, failure to crank over properly can be caused by electrical or mechanical problems. For example, slow cranking could result from an electrical fault such as high resistance in the solenoid contacts. This problem could be resolved by replacing the starter with a new or remanufactured unit. But the slow-crank condition could also be caused by a mechanical engine fault such as a spun main bearing that is causing a lot of drag on the crankshaft and preventing the starter from cranking it over at normal speed. In this case, the entire engine will need to be rebuilt.

TECHNICIAN TIP

Low battery voltage and weak batteries are the primary cause of stress to starters and of excessive starter amperage draw. Faulty batteries will also stress charging circuits, as an alternator is forced to continually charge a weak battery. Liquid starting aids can also produce engine "kick-back" and apply extreme twisting forces to the motor. Heat from overcranking and vibration from loose mountings are other leading causes of starter damage **FIGURE 43-31**.

As you can imagine, telling customers that they need a new starter motor when in fact they need a new engine (costing 10 to 20 times as much money) will not make them very happy with you. It is important to be able to differentiate between the two types of faults so that a wrong diagnosis can be avoided and the problem fixed appropriately the first time. Typical electrical problems that can cause starting system problems include loose, dirty, or corroded terminals and connectors, a discharged or faulty battery, a faulty starter motor, or a faulty control circuit.

Mechanical problems that may cause starting system problems include seized pistons or bearings, hydrostatic lock from liquid in the cylinder(s) (for example, a leaky fuel pressure regulator or water ingestion during off-road operation), incorrect injection or valve timing, a seized alternator or other belt-driven device, and so on. Gathering as much customer and vehicle information as possible will assist in narrowing down the options of what is causing the fault.

A slow-crank condition accompanied by a high draw could be due to a fault in the starter or to engine mechanical fault. If a

FIGURE 43-31 A burned solenoid contact disc caused by low available voltage.

mechanical fault is suspected, check the oil and coolant for signs of contamination. If the coolant and oil are mixing, suspect a head gasket or cracked head/block issue. If the oil and coolant are not contaminated, turn the engine over by hand to see if it is tight compared with a similar engine that is known to be good. If it is harder to turn than it should be, remove the accessory drive belt, spin each of the accessories, and try to turn the engine over again. If it is still hard to turn over, you will have to go deeper in your visual inspection and start disassembling components based on the information you have gathered along the way. For example, if the crankshaft cannot be turned a complete revolution, remove the injectors and see if liquid is ejected out of one or more cylinders. If so, the engine was hydrolocked and you will need to determine the cause. If no liquids are ejected, then you will need to disassemble the engine further until you determine the cause of the mechanical resistance.

The important thing to remember is that slow-crank and no-crank conditions can be caused by both electrical and mechanical faults, so do not jump to conclusions. You need to identify the root cause of the fault through tests so that you can advise the customer on what is needed to repair the vehicle.

Starter Motor Tests

The inspection and measurement procedures used to diagnose starting system complaints should be symptom based. That is, a flow chart should be used to begin a proper sequence of pinpoint checks recommended by the OEM. Symptoms include intermittent and no start, slow cranking, prolonged cranking, starter chatter, or starter noise. Any diagnostic procedure should begin with qualifying the condition of the batteries and inspecting all battery cables, grounds, and connections. Information on

how to undertake battery checks can be found in the Servicing Commercial Vehicle Batteries chapter.

Faults within the starter motor may include:

- Worn brushes—Intermittent starter operation or starter operation that resumes after it is tapped with a hammer indicates brushes with poor commutator contact. Poor contact could be due to weak spring tension after a brush wears out. Poor brush contact with the commutator can also be caused by loss of brush spring tension due to heating from excessively high amperage flow—often due to prolonged cranking or low battery voltage. It can be evidenced by blued or even charred brush springs.
- Damaged field coils—Insulation can break down, causing shorts between coils or shorts to ground. This can be caused by age, by contaminants breaking down the insulation, or by excessive current flow. Excessive heat may also cause connections to be melted, creating additional resistance in the circuit.
- Damaged armature—An armature may have the commutator excessively worn or unevenly worn. The armature may also develop shorts between the windings, shorts to ground, and opens between windings and the commutator. A test instrument called a growler is used to test an armature.
- Worn bushings or bearings—Sintered brass bushings or, in some cases, bearings are used to suspend the armature in the starter case. Because motor efficiency is dependent on having the smallest clearance between the armature and field coils, any wear of bushing or bearings will cause contact between the armature and field coils. Worn bushing or bearings will cause excessive current draw that can be observed during a starter draw test.

Use **TABLE 43-1** to assist in diagnosing starting system problems. Always consult manufacturers' information before commencing any work.

The tests explained in the following sections include:

- Available voltage test
- Measuring starter current draw
- Measuring starter circuit voltage drop
- Inspecting and testing the starter control circuit
- Inspecting and testing relays and solenoids

Available Voltage Test

If the starting system complaint is slow cranking, the available voltage test is recommended. This test measures the amount of voltage at the starter battery positive cable and ground stud on the starter, if equipped. Minimum available voltage to the starter must not fall below 10.5 volts after three consecutive cranking periods of 30 seconds, with a 2-minute cooling period between each cranking period. If the voltage falls below 10.5 volts, the electrical system may not have adequate current to energize injectors or operate ECMs even though cranking speed is adequate.

To measure available voltage, first disable the engine from starting by removing a fuse for the ECM, disabling the shut-off solenoid, or alternative method. Then, connect a voltmeter

TABLE 43-1: Starting System Diagnosis Chart

Concern	Possible Cause	Remedy
Engine cranks slowly, does not start	Discharged battery	Charge; test and replace if necessary
	Very low temperature	Allow battery to warm up; check circuits and battery
	Battery cables too small or poor connections	Install correct battery cables or clean and replace connections
	Defective starter motor	Test; repair or replace as needed
	Engine malfunction	Check engine for low oil or mechanical problems
Solenoid clicks, chatters	Loose or corroded battery terminals	Remove, clean, reinstall
	Battery discharged	Charge; test and replace if necessary
	Wiring problem inside solenoid	Replace solenoid
Lights stay bright, vehicle does not crank	Open circuit in starter	Disassemble and repair or replace starter
	Open circuit or high resistance in circuit	Check solenoid, relays, and neutral start switch or clutch switch; repair or replace if needed
	Open circuit in safety switch	Check; repair or replace switch
Lights dim greatly, vehicle does not crank	Discharged or malfunctioning battery	Charge and test battery; replace if necessary
	High resistance at battery connection	Clean and tighten terminal connections
	Loose or corroded battery terminals	Remove, clean, reinstall
	Very low temperature	Allow battery to warm up; check circuits and battery
	Pinion not engaging ring gear	Check for damaged parts and alignment of starter
	Solenoid engaged but not cranking	Check starter motor and connections
	Pinion jammed—starter and flywheel out of alignment	Check pinion and gear teeth
	Stuck armature in starter	Replace or repair starter
	Short in starter	Check engine for low oil or mechanical problem
	Engine malfunction	Charge and test battery; replace if necessary
Lights out, vehicle does not crank	Poor connection (probably at battery or earth)	Clean cable clamp and terminal; tighten clamp
	Open circuit	Clean and tighten connections; replace wiring if necessary
	Discharged or faulty battery	Charge and test battery; replace battery if necessary
Whine or siren sound just after starting	Overrunning clutch defective	Repair or replace as needed
	Solenoid plunger sticking	Repair or replace solenoid
	Weak return spring	Replace spring
	Damaged flywheel ring gear teeth	Remove and replace
	Pinion jammed, too tight – starter and flywheel out of alignment	Check pinion alignment with gear teeth; shim if necessary
Starter turns, engine does not	Pinion not engaging – starter and flywheel out of alignment	Check pinion alignment with gear teeth; shim if necessary
	Pinion slipping	Replace or repair starter
	Damaged flywheel ring gear teeth	Remove and replace
Pinion disengages slowly when engine starts	Solenoid plunger sticking	Repair or replace solenoid
	Overrunning clutch defective	Repair or replace as needed
	Weak return spring	Replace spring
	Pinion jammed, too tight – starter and flywheel out of alignment	Check pinion alignment with gear teeth; shim if necessary

between the starter ground stud and battery positive terminal on the solenoid. While cranking the engine, measure and record the amperage and voltage and evaluate the results.

Starter Current Draw Testing

Testing starter motor current draw is the best indicator of overall cranking system performance. Manufacturers will specify the current draw for starter motors, and any tests must be performed with a fully charged and correct capacity battery for the vehicle. Starter motors can be tested in two ways: on vehicle or off vehicle. The on-vehicle test is usually called a starter draw test, while the off-vehicle test is called a no-load test. Manufacturers will provide specifications for one or both of the tests.

If the starting system complaint is slow cranking, a starter draw and available voltage test is recommended using the following steps:

1. The engine is disabled from starting by removing a fuse for the ECM, disabling the shut-off solenoid or alternative method.
2. A voltmeter is connected between the starter ground stud and battery positive terminal on the solenoid.
3. An inductive type amp clamp is placed over the either battery cable to the starter.
4. While cranking, the amperage and voltage are measured and recorded.

Results are compared with the manufacturer's specifications found in a shop manual. Properly charged batteries with adequate capacity should not allow available voltage to fall below 10.5 volts during cranking **FIGURE 43-32** .

If cranking speed is low, and amperage measured is below normal but available voltage is high, the starting motor or starting circuit has high resistance. Worn brushes or loose or burnt internal connections could cause this condition.

If amperage drawn by the starting motor is high and available voltage low, the starter may be defective internally, the engine seizing or resistive, or the battery voltage low. Shorted field coils caused by the armature contacting the coils are a likely cause of an internal defect. Low available voltage to the starter may also be the cause. Undersized cables, loose connections, or a corroded and highly resistive connection will reduce available voltage to the starter, causing excessive amperage draw. Each electrical connection and cable in the starter circuit needs to be measured for voltage loss due to excessive resistance in this situation. Small resistances will become larger as amperage increases predicted by Joule's Heating Law. Resistive wire or connections will drop voltage and heat up at the same time. By using a carbon pile to load cables and circuits to 500 amps, voltage loss should not total more than 5% in a 12-volt circuit (0.5 volts), with no more than 2% loss in any single cable.

There is no "fixed" amount of amperage draw for each and every engine. However, no more than one amp per cubic inch of engine displacement should be observed. Manufactures will publish some guidelines for an engine or starter configuration. The amount of amperage will vary, however, due to the following reasons:

- Engine displacement—larger engines require more torque to turn and consequently more cranking amperage
- The compression ratio may change the amount of cranking torque

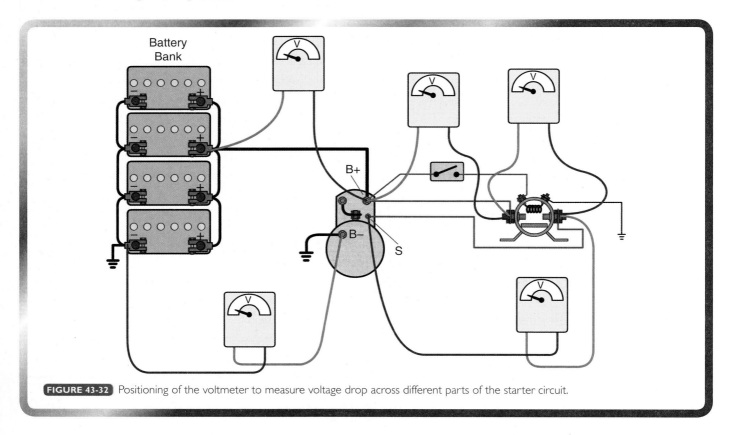

FIGURE 43-32 Positioning of the voltmeter to measure voltage drop across different parts of the starter circuit.

- The type of starter—direct drive or gear reduction will change the amount of amperage used
- Mechanical condition of engine—loose or tight due to varying mechanical conditions such as temperature, amount of lubrication, wear, bearing or piston seizure, ring condition, and combustion chamber deposits
- The starter drive-to-flywheel ratio
- The condition of the battery

To test the starter draw, follow the guidelines in **SKILL DRILL 43-1**.

Testing Starter Circuit Voltage Drop

The electrical circuit of the starter motor consists of a high-current circuit and a control circuit. The high-current circuit consists of the battery, main battery cables to the starter motor solenoid, solenoid contacts, and heavy ground cables back to the battery from the engine and chassis. The control circuit activates the solenoid and can ECM controlled. Voltage drop can occur across both the high-current and control circuits.

A voltmeter is used to measure voltage drop across all parts of the circuit. A voltmeter with a minimum/maximum range setting is very useful when measuring voltage drop because it will record and hold the maximum voltage drop that occurs for a particular operation cycle. Small resistance and poor connections are magnified when high amperage passes through the circuit—resistances that will not be observable when low amperage current passes through a circuit.

Voltage drop is tested while the circuit is under load. The voltmeter is connected in parallel across the component or part of the circuit that is to be tested for voltage drop. This means the voltmeter would be connected on either side of a terminal connection or either end of a cable. For example, to measure the voltage drop across

a battery terminal, one voltmeter lead would touch the battery post, while the other end would touch the wire of the battery cable connected to the terminal, as close as possible to the post. When the starter is cranked, or a load applied through a carbon pile load tester, any resistance will be observed as a voltage reading. A high voltage reading indicates excessive resistance. Similarly, a voltmeter with long leads can be connected to each end of a battery cable. When the starter is cranked, cable resistance is observed with a voltmeter reading. In both cases, the voltmeter is simply measuring the voltage or pressure differential between two points.

To test starter circuit voltage drop, follow the guidelines in **SKILL DRILL 43-2**.

> ### TECHNICIAN TIP
>
> A faulty battery will affect voltage drop tests, so always ensure that the battery is fully charged and in good condition before performing tests.

Inspecting and Testing the Starter Control Circuit

The starter control circuit activates the starter solenoid, and the starter solenoid activates the starter motor. If there is a problem in the starter control circuit, the vehicle will likely not crank over at all, or maybe intermittently. The control circuit is made up of the battery, ignition switch, neutral safety switch (automatic vehicles), clutch switch (manual vehicles), starter relay, and solenoid windings. If the starter is controlled by the ECM, then you must be aware of all of the circuits, such as the immobilizer circuit and the ECM itself.

 ## SKILL DRILL 43-1 Testing Starter Draw

1. Research the specifications for the starter draw test. Place an inductive type amp clamp over either the positive or negative cable. It doesn't matter which starter cable is measured, as it is a series circuit, so amperage will be the same at any point in the circuit.

2. Connect the AVR voltmeter leads to the battery or at the starter.

3. Make sure all of the appropriate wires are inside the clamp and the clamp is completely closed.

4. Disable the engine from starting by removing a fuse from the engine ECM or disabling the injection system shut-off solenoid.

5. With the engine disabled, crank the engine and record the amps and volts as soon as the amps stabilize.

6. Compare the readings with the specifications and determine any necessary actions.

SKILL DRILL 43-2 Testing Starter Circuit Voltage Drop

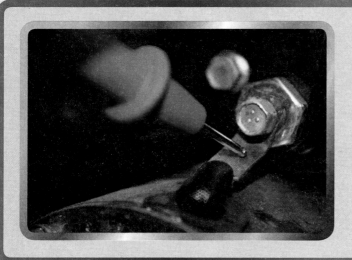

1. Set the DVOM to volts. Connect the black lead to the positive battery post and the red lead to the positive battery terminal on the starting motor.

2. Crank the engine and read the maximum voltage drop for the positive side of the circuit. Connect the black lead to the negative battery post and the red lead to the negative terminal or starting motor ground stud. Crank the engine and read the voltage drop.

3. If the voltage drop is more than 0.5 volts on either side of the circuit, use the voltmeter and wiring diagram to isolate the voltage drop. Conduct further voltage drop tests across individual components and cables. Determine any necessary actions.

To inspect and test the starter control circuit, follow the guidelines in SKILL DRILL 43-3.

▶ TECHNICIAN TIP

The starter relay bypass test is a quick method of determining if the relay is operational. This test should be performed when the starter motor does not crank when the ignition is in the start position (or when the starter button is depressed). Connect a jumper wire between the battery and starter terminal on the relay. This connection bypasses the control circuit of the relay, so the engine should crank. If the engine cranks with the jumper installed, check to see whether current is supplied to the relay when the ignition key or starter button is in the crank position. If current is available to the relay, check the ground supplying the control circuit to determine whether it is properly connected or resistive. If the control circuit is properly energized, and the starter cranks when the jumper wire is used, the starter relay is defective. If the starter motor still does not crank, check the cables and other circuits to the starter.

Inspecting and Testing Relays and Solenoids

The starting system typically contains solenoids and relays that activate the control circuit. The solenoid is mounted on the starter motor, while one or more of the starter circuit relays are found on the starter, or firewall.

Before performing any tests, ensure that the vehicle battery is charged and in good condition. The manufacturer's wiring diagrams should be checked to determine the circuit operation, identification, and location of all components in the starter circuit.

Relays must be tested in two or three ways depending on the relay. The simplest test is to measure the resistance of the relay winding. If it is out of specifications, the relay will need to be replaced. If it is OK, the contacts will need to be tested for an excessive voltage drop. The best way to do this is by using an adapter that fits between the relay and the relay socket. This will allow the

normal circuit current flow to flow through the contacts so that a voltage drop measurement can be taken. Any excessive voltage drop across the relay contacts will require the replacement of the relay. The last test is used only on relays with a suppression diode in parallel with the relay winding. Connect a reasonably fresh 9-volt battery across the relay winding terminals in one direction, and then switch polarity by turning the battery around. If the diode is good, the relay should click in one direction and not in the other. If it clicks in both directions, the diode is shorted. If it does not click in either direction, the relay winding is open or the diode is open.

Solenoids are tested by measuring the voltage drop between the battery terminal and motor terminal. The first test to perform is a voltage drop test across the solenoid contacts. Place the red lead on the solenoid B-positive input and the black lead on the solenoid B-positive output. The voltage drop should be less than 0.5 volts for a 12-volt system and less than 1.0 volts for a 24-volt system. If not, replace the starter assembly. Testing of the solenoid winding requires partial disassembly of the solenoid. Therefore, it is usually best to disconnect the control circuit connector from the solenoid and use a jumper wire to activate the solenoid. If the solenoid and starter operate, there is probably a fault in the vehicle's control circuit that needs further testing. If the solenoid or starter does not work (and the circuit is grounded), then the starter is likely faulty and will need to be replaced.

To inspect and test relays and solenoids, follow the guidelines in SKILL DRILL 43-4.

Removing and Replacing a Starter, and Inspecting the Ring Gear or Flex Plate

The starter motor will need to be removed to check for on-bench testing, poor drive engagement, or starter motor overhaul or replacement. The starter motor may be mounted in difficult-to-access locations. In some cases, other vehicle parts may need to be

SKILL DRILL 43-3 Inspecting and Testing the Starter Control Circuit

1. Use a DVOM to measure voltage between the solenoid control circuit terminal on the solenoid (R) terminal and the housing of the starter while the engine is cranking.

2. If the voltage is less than 10.5 volts, measure the voltage drop between the R terminal and the relay.

3. If the voltage drop is less than 0.5 volts, measure the voltage drop on ground side of the relay control circuit.

4. If the voltage drop is higher than 0.5 volts on either side of the circuit, use the wiring diagram to guide you in isolating the voltage drop on that side of the circuit. Continue conducting voltage drop tests across individual components and cables.

5. If the voltage drops are within specifications on both sides of the circuit, the resistance of the solenoid pull-in and hold-in windings will need to be measured. If out of specifications, the solenoid or starter motor and solenoid will need to be replaced.

SKILL DRILL 43-4 Inspecting and Testing Relays and Solenoids

3. Activate the relay while measuring the voltage across the relay winding. If it is near battery voltage, the control circuit wiring is OK.

4. Measure the voltage across the contacts with the relay not activated. This should read near battery voltage if both sides of the switched circuit are OK. If not, perform voltage drop tests on each side of the switch circuit.

5. Activate the relay while measuring the voltage drop across the contacts. If it is more than 0.5 volts, the relay will need to be replaced.

6. To test a starter solenoid, measure the voltage drop across the solenoid contact terminals with the key in the crank position. If it is more than 0.5 volts, replace the solenoid or starter assembly.

7. If the solenoid does not click with the key in the crank position, remove the electrical connection for the control circuit at the solenoid.

8. Use a jumper wire to apply battery voltage to the control circuit terminal on the solenoid and see if the solenoid clicks. If it does, then there is likely a fault in the control circuit wiring. If the solenoid still does not click (and the circuit is grounded), then the solenoid windings or starter brushes are likely worn (sometimes tapping on the starter while the key is turned to the crank position will free up the brushes enough that the pull-in winding can operate). Determine any necessary actions.

1. To test a relay, measure the resistance of the relay winding and compare with specifications. If the relay is out of specifications, replace it.

2. Use a relay adapter to mount the relay on top of the relay socket so you can check the control circuit wiring and perform voltage drop tests on the contacts.

removed before the starter itself can be removed. Access to both the topside and underside of the vehicle may be required to remove mounting bolts. It may also be necessary to have another technician assist you to remove the heavy starter motor from vehicle.

To remove and replace a starter motor and inspect the ring gear or flex plate, follow the guidelines in **SKILL DRILL 43-5**.

Overhauling a Starter Motor

Overhauling a starter motor requires the disassembly and checking of all component parts. The starter motor component parts should also be cleaned and replaced or repaired and lubricated as necessary. Always mark the position of the housings in relation to each other before commencing disassembly. This ensures that the housings are correctly aligned when reassembled. Each starter motor is unique and may require slightly different disassembly and overhaul procedures. Always consult the manufacturer's procedures for the specific starter motor on which you are working.

Note that the assembly procedure is the reverse of disassembly. When assembling, be sure to correctly lubricate all lubrication points. Check the manufacturer's procedure for the lubrication points and type of lubricant.

Once the starter motor has been disassembled into its component parts, conduct the following tests for each component as follows:

- Solenoid:
  - Test the resistance and current draw of the pull-in and hold-in windings.
  - Check for the free movement of the iron core.
  - Check contacts and terminal end cap for wear and cracks. Make replacements if necessary.

- Drive and yoke:
  - Visually inspect the drive engagement yoke for wear and damage. Replace if there is excessive wear.
  - Check the drive clutch for slippage. If there is excessive slippage, replace the drive.
- Brushes:
  - Check the length of the brushes with the manufacturer's specifications and replace if necessary.
  - Check the brush springs for tension, brush movement in the brush holder, and the insulation of the brush holder.
  - Field windings: Visually check the insulation for cracks or damage. Check for short circuits through the field insulation and case by connecting a 110-volt test lamp between the field coil and case. If the lamp lights, there is a short circuit. If the field insulation fails, the field will need to be replaced or reinsulated.
- Armature:
  - Check the armature on a growler for shorts between windings. Using a thin metal strip, rotate the armature. A vibrating strip means the armature is shorted and requires replacement. However, before condemning it, check to ensure there are no shorts between the commutator segments. Retest if you find any.
  - Also check the armature insulation to ground using an insulation tester or the insulation tester fitted to the growler. Use an insulation test no higher than 110 volts for a 12- or 24-volt armature. Note that to pass an insulation test, the armature needs to be dry and free of contaminants.
  - If the armature fails either test, it must be replaced.

 SKILL DRILL 43-5 Removing and Replacing a Starter Motor and Inspecting the Ring Gear or Flex Plate

1. Locate and follow the appropriate procedure in the service manual.

2. Disconnect the battery ground and electrical connections to the starter motor.

3. Loosen the mounting bolts, leaving them in place until you are ready to remove the starter motor.

4. Remove the starter motor by supporting its weight while the mounting bolts are removed. You may need assistance to support the weight of the starter while this step is being conducted.

5. Examine the starter drive for any wear to the drive teeth.

6. Using a work light, inspect the ring gear or flex plate teeth for damage. Slowly turn the engine over while checking the ring gear or flex plate, ensuring the circumference is inspected. In difficult-to-see locations, an engine borescope may provide assistance. Report and report any damage to the ring gear.

7. Reinstall the starter motor by reversing the steps used in steps 1 through 4 above.

- Machine the commutator in a lathe if it is worn.
- Check the armature shaft for wear or damage to the bearing surfaces. Also check the drive splines for wear or damage. Check the laminations for damage. Check the shaft to ensure it is not bent. Check the windings to ensure they are not damaged or bent. Any damage to the above items will mean the armature needs to be replaced.

■ Housings:
- Check the housings for damage or wear. Replace if they are cracked or broken.

■ Bushes:
- Check the bushings for wear using the armature bearing surfaces. Replace the bushings if they are worn.
- When replacing bushings, use soft bush drifts to drive or press the bushes into and out of the housing.
- Oil-sintered bushings before fitting them into housing.
- Some bushings may require machining to size once they are fitted into the housing.

Once the starter motor has been overhauled, it should be tested on a starter test bench with a full load if possible. If a full load test is not possible, conduct a no-load bench test as per the procedure in this chapter. To overhaul a starter motor, follow the guidelines in SKILL DRILL 43-6.

Engine and Starter Rotation

When observing engine rotation, many technicians often note the front engine pulley/harmonic balancer turns clockwise. However, not all engines are mounted in-line with the driveline (e.g., "V" drives). Some engines are mounted sideways in a vehicle and some are mounted at the rear and sideways. Since there is an abundance of configurations including engines in heavy-duty stationary applications, the SAE references engine rotation from the flywheel end of the engine. Most automotive engines are LEFT-HAND or CCW counterclockwise rotation.

The location and position of the starter on the engine can determine which direction the engine is cranked. Starter drive mechanism and the cut of the teeth will be changed along with helix features of the armature that may move the drive.

 SKILL DRILL 43-6 Overhauling a Starter Motor

1. Locate and follow the appropriate procedure in the service manual.
2. Remove the solenoid and the yoke securing pin.
3. Remove the bearing end cap and circlip from the brush end of the starter motor if it is fitted.
4. Remove the through bolts holding the starter motor together.
5. Prize the starter motor apart while checking for any remaining screws or bolts.
6. Remove the brushes from the brush holder if necessary.
7. Slide the armature out of the main casing.
8. Remove the drive circlip and remove the drive assembly.

9. Clean, test, and inspect all component parts. Use specialized testers where necessary; for example, growler to test the armature, insulation tester to test fields and armature, and DVOM to check resistances of solenoid windings.
10. Replace any faulty components. You may need to arrange for the commutator to be machined to make it true.
11. Remove and replace the bushings into the end housing. Ensure bushes are pre-oiled if they are the sintered type. Bushings will need to be driven or pressed out and in using a bushings drift.
12. If the brushes require replacement, disconnect or de-solder them, and replace them.
13. Reassemble the drive to the armature, ensuring it is appropriately lubricated.
14. Reassemble the armature into the main case and locate the brushes. At this stage, the drive yoke and securing pin may need to be fitted. In some cases, the securing pin is not fitted until after the armature is in place.
15. Assemble the main case and end housing securing with the through bolts.
16. Reassemble the solenoid, its connections, and the brush end armature circlip. Ensure the appropriate lubrication if fitted.
17. Check to ensure that all components are fitted and the drive and armature are free to move.
18. Test the starter motor in the test bench.
19. Clean the work area and return tools and materials to proper storage.

Wrap-Up

Ready for Review

▸ The starting system provides a method of rotating (cranking) the vehicle's engine to begin the combustion cycle.

▸ Diesel engines require large starter current draw, so several batteries are often connected in parallel of series to increase available cranking amperage or voltage.

▸ New designs of starter motors and systems controls are enabling starters to last longer and increase output torque while substantially reducing motor weight.

▸ There are three major categories of electric starters used in heavy vehicles: direct drive, reduction, and planetary gear reduction.

▸ The three most common types of DC motors found in commercial vehicles are series, shunt, and compound motors.

▸ Series motors are called "series" because the current pathway through various components inside the motor is in series. Because it is a series circuit, any unwanted resistance inside the motor, whether it is a burnt contact or loose brush, will reduce current flow throughout the entire motor circuit.

▸ Series wound motors also are self-limiting in speed due to the development of a counter-electromotive force (CEMF) that induces current in the opposite direction of battery current through the motor.

▸ Cranking an engine with low battery voltage is destructive to a starter motor.

▸ Regardless of the motor design, a starter motor consists of housing, fields, an armature, a commutator, brushes, end frames, and a solenoid-operated shift mechanism.

▸ Some starter motors are equipped with overcrank protection thermostats that will open the relay circuit and interrupt the current to the solenoid if prolonged cranking causes the motor temperature to exceed a safe threshold.

▸ Another protection device for the starter control circuit is the automatic disengagement lockout, which prevents the starter motor from operating if the engine is running.

▸ Dual-voltage systems allow the vehicle to be started on 24 volts for improved electrical efficiency, while the other electrical loads operate on the more common 12 volts.

▸ The starting system is just part of the overall vehicle's electrical and mechanical system. As such, there are areas of overlap between the various electrical and mechanical systems on the vehicle.

▸ Whether a slow-crank or a no-crank condition, failure to crank over properly can be caused by electrical or mechanical problems. It is important to be able to differentiate between the two types of faults so that a wrong diagnosis can be avoided and the problem fixed appropriately the first time.

Vocabulary Builder

armature The only rotating component of the starter; has three main components: the shaft, windings, and the commutator.

automatic disengagement lockout (ADLO) A device that prevents the starter motor from operating if the engine is running.

counter-electromotive force (CEMF) An electromagnetic force produced by the spinning magnetic field of the armature, which induces current in the opposite direction of battery current through the motor.

direct drive A starter motor drive system in which the motor armature directly engages the flywheel through a pinion gear.

frequency-sensing relay A relay connected to the alternator that detects alternating current only when the alternator is charging.

low-voltage burn-out A damaging condition for starter motors in which excess current flows through the starter, causing the motor to burn out prematurely.

overcrank protection (OCP) thermostat A thermostat that monitors the temperature of the motor and opens a relay circuit to interrupt the current to the solenoid if prolonged cranking causes the motor temperature to exceed a safe threshold.

planetary gear reduction drive A type of gear reduction system in which a planetary gear set reduces the starter profile to multiply motor torque to the pinion gear.

reduction gear drive A starter motor drive system in which the motor multiplies torque to the starter pinion gear by using an extra gear between the armature and the starter drive mechanism.

Review Questions

1. The _____ is a device that monitors the temperature of the motor and opens a relay circuit to interrupt the current to the solenoid if prolonged cranking causes the motor temperature to exceed a safe threshold.
   a. automatic disengagement lockout
   b. commutator
   c. overcrank protection thermostat
   d. overcrank protection switch

2. The _____ is a device that prevents the starter motor from operating if the engine is running.
   a. ADLO
   b. ALDO
   c. OPC
   d. overcrank protection switch

3. To supply more cranking amperage in a 12-volt system, batteries are connected in _____.
   a. series
   b. parallel
   c. series-parallel
   d. rows

4. The only gear torque multiplication in a _____ starter is between the pinion gear and the ring gear.
   a. pneumatic
   b. reduction gear drive
   c. planetary gear reduction drive
   d. direct drive

5. A _____ starting system consists of a geared air motor, starting valve, and a pressure tank.
   a. hydraulic
   b. electronic
   c. pneumatic
   d. mechanical

6. Most starter motors are _____ -wound motors because they develop the greatest amount of torque at zero rpm.
   a. parallel
   b. series
   c. backward
   d. forward

7. The _____ assembly presses onto the armature shaft.
   a. commutator
   b. solenoid
   c. starter housing
   d. pole shoes

8. Testing starter motor _____ draw is the best indicator of overall cranking system performance.
   a. amperage
   b. voltage
   c. load
   d. current

9. The _____ is the only rotating component of the starter; has three main components: the shaft, windings, and the commutator.
   a. armature
   b. pinion gear
   c. clutch roller
   d. plunger

10. _____ is a starter motor drive system in which the motor armature directly engages the flywheel through a pinion gear.
    a. Shunt
    b. Direct drive
    c. Reduction gear drive
    d. Planetary gear reduction drive

ASE-Type Questions

1. Technician A says that a planetary gear reduction drive can be identified by an offset drive housing to the motor housing. Technician B says that a direct drive can be identified by an offset drive housing to the motor housing. Who is correct?
   a. Technician A
   b. Technician B
   c. Both Technician A and Technician B
   d. Neither Technician A nor Technician B

2. Technician A says that shunt-type DC motors develop more torque and maintain a constant speed. Technician B says that shunt-type DC motors develop less torque but maintain a constant speed. Who is correct?
   a. Technician A
   b. Technician B
   c. Both Technician A and Technician B
   d. Neither Technician A nor Technician B

3. Technician A says that stepper-type DC motors are used in instrument clusters' gauges, turbochargers, and EGR actuators where high precision movement is required. Technician B says that shunt-type DC motors are used in instrument clusters' gauges, turbochargers, and EGR actuators where high precision movement is required. Who is correct?
   a. Technician A
   b. Technician B
   c. Both Technician A and Technician B
   d. Neither Technician A nor Technician B

4. Technician A says that low-voltage burn-out can be prevented by using ultra-capacitors. Technician B says that low-voltage burn-out can be prevented by using overcrank protection switches. Who is correct?
   a. Technician A
   b. Technician B
   c. Both Technician A and Technician B
   d. Neither Technician A nor Technician B

5. Technician A says an armature motor winding is made of heavy, flat, copper strips. Technician B says an armature motor winding is made of lightweight, round, nickel strips. Who is correct?
   a. Technician A
   b. Technician B
   c. Both Technician A and Technician B
   d. Neither Technician A nor Technician B

6. Technician A says that it is the role of the starter housing to switch the direction of current flow through each armature coil as the armature rotates. Technician B says that it is the role of the field coil to switch the direction of current flow through each armature coil as the armature rotates. Who is correct?
   a. Technician A
   b. Technician B
   c. Both Technician A and Technician B
   d. Neither Technician A nor Technician B

7. Technician A says the pinion drive gear is attached to a roller-type one-way clutch that is splined to the starter armature. Technician B says the pinion drive gear is attached to a roller-type overrunning clutch that is splined to the starter armature. Who is correct?
   a. Technician A
   b. Technician B
   c. Both Technician A and Technician B
   d. Neither Technician A nor Technician B

8. Technician A says pinion clearance is adjusted using shims. Technician B says pinion clearance is adjusted using an eccentric shift fork pin. Who is correct?
   a. Technician A
   b. Technician B
   c. Both Technician A and Technician B
   d. Neither Technician A nor Technician B

9. Technician A says that the low voltage sensing relay is connected in parallel with the starter motor control circuit. Technician B says that the low voltage sensing relay is connected in series with the starter motor control circuit. Who is correct?
   a. Technician A
   b. Technician B
   c. Both Technician A and Technician B
   d. Neither Technician A nor Technician B

10. Technician A says that intermittent starter operation or starter operation that resumes after it is tapped with a hammer may indicate worn brushes. Technician B says that intermittent starter operation or starter operation that resumes after it is tapped with a hammer may indicate damaged field coils. Who is correct?
    a. Technician A
    b. Technician B
    c. Both Technician A and Technician B
    d. Neither Technician A nor Technician B

CHAPTER 44
Charging Systems

NATEF Tasks

Electrical/Electronic Systems

Charging System Diagnosis and Repair
- Test instrument panel mounted volt meters and/or indicator lamps; determine needed action. (pp 1235–1237)
- Identify causes of no charge, low charge, or overcharge problems; determine needed action. (p 1237)
- Inspect and replace alternator drive belts, pulleys, fans, tensioners, and mounting brackets; adjust drive belts and check alignment. (p 1238)

- Perform charging system voltage and amperage output tests; perform AC ripple test; determine needed action. (pp 1238–1239)
- Perform charging circuit voltage drop tests; determine needed action. (p 1240)
- Remove and replace alternator. (pp 1240–1242)
- Inspect, repair, or replace cables, wires, and connectors in the charging circuit. (p 1241)

Knowledge Objectives

After reading this chapter, you will be able to:
1. Identify and explain principles of electromagnetic induction. (pp 1222–1223)
2. Describe principles of current rectification. (pp 1227–1230)
3. Describe the operation of voltage regulators. (pp 1230–1232)

4. Describe techniques for electrical balancing of multiple alternators. (pp 1234–1237)
5. Identify and explain recommended procedures for diagnosing charging system complaints. (pp 1237–1240)
6. Identify tools and test instruments for evaluating charging systems. (pp 1240–1242)

Skills Objectives

After reading this chapter, you will be able to:
1. Replace a serpentine belt. (p 1238) **SKILL DRILL 44-1**
2. Perform a charging system output test. (p 1239) **SKILL DRILL 44-2**
3. Test charge a circuit voltage drop. (p 1240) **SKILL DRILL 44-3**

4. Inspect, repair, or replace connectors and wires of charging circuits. (p 1241) **SKILL DRILL 44-4**
5. Remove, inspect, and replace an alternator. (p 1242) **SKILL DRILL 44-5**
6. Overhaul an alternator. (p 1243) **SKILL DRILL 44-6**

► Introduction

Compared with older heavy vehicles, modern heavy-duty vehicles are increasingly dependent on electronic and electrical systems that require a constant and reliable supply of electrical power. As heavy-duty vehicles become more sophisticated and add more comfort and convenience items, alternators are working harder than ever to meet the demands of the electrical system. For example, years ago, a DC generator supplying 8 to 45 amps of current was all that was needed to operate lights, wipers, and horn and to charge the batteries. Today, the average 12-volt electrical system loads for a late model highway tractor add up to 150 amps at peak with an 84-amp average. School buses have a 102-amp average load, and highway coaches will use as much as 160 amps at 24 volts just to power the heating, ventilation, and air conditioning system. It is now normal for vehicles to use 200- to 300-amp alternators, like that in **FIGURE 44-1**, to supply adequate electrical system amperage at idle and charge depleted batteries. Lighting, electronic powertrain controls, power accessories, communication, telematic systems, and many smaller electrical accessories add to the load carried by contemporary alternators.

Both DC generators and alternators produce electricity by relative movement of conductors in a magnetic field. That movement induces an electrical potential or voltage within the conductors. The key difference between an alternator and a DC generator is which component rotates or moves to generate electricity. In the DC generator, the conductors that generate power rotate as part of the armature, and the armature rotates within a magnetic field created by the stationary pole shoes. In the alternator, the magnetic field is created by the rotor, which rotates within the stationary stator windings to generate electricity there. In both cases, there is relative movement between the magnetic field and the conductors.

FIGURE 44-1 A typical heavy-vehicle alternator.

► Alternator Functions

The charging system provides electrical energy for all of the electrical components on the vehicle. The main parts of the charging system, as illustrated in **FIGURE 44-2**, include the battery, the alternator, the voltage regulator (which may be integrated into the alternator), a charge warning light or voltmeter, and wiring that completes the circuits.

The battery stores an electrical charge in chemical form, acts as an electrical dampening device for variations in voltage or voltage spikes, and provides the electrical energy for cranking the engine. Once the engine is running, the alternator—which is connected to the engine and driven by a drive belt—converts some of the mechanical energy of the engine into electrical

► You Are the Technician

There is a bus that has had numerous service calls for jump-starting because the batteries often go dead. Service calls are taking place almost every day, causing a high level of aggravation to the customer and the service center where you work. On previous occasions, the batteries have been replaced. In addition, the charging system output has been measured and found to be OK. Furthermore, the presence of parasitic draws has been checked, and none were found.

The bus drivers have often been blamed for the problems, assuming that they have left lights or other accessories on, draining the battery. Out of frustration, the service manager has asked you to accompany the bus driver for a day to find out when the bus batteries drain and whether electrical loads are left on. After the bus has stopped for a 45-minute break, you find the batteries are dead. Checking the alternator, you discover that the back of the alternator where the rectifier bridge is located has become excessively hot to touch. Finally, the cause has been found. Before explaining the fault to the customer, you'll need to have answers to the following questions.

1. Why has the rectifier bridge of the alternator become hot to touch while the engine was shut down?
2. During previous checks of the charging system, what inspection procedure would have identified that fault?
3. What component has failed in the rectifier bridge? Be specific.

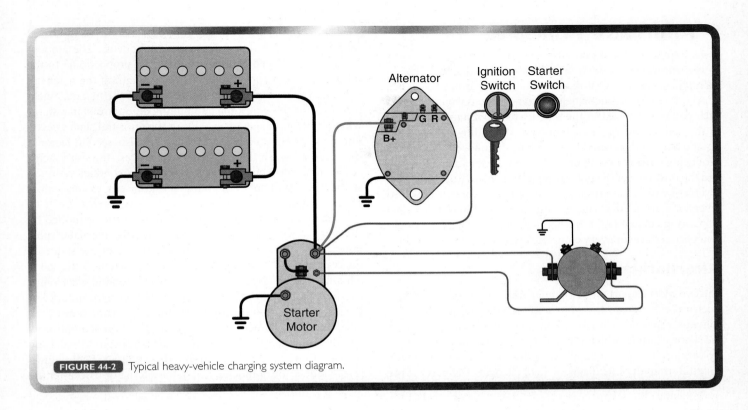

FIGURE 44-2 Typical heavy-vehicle charging system diagram.

energy to supply energy to all the electrical components of the vehicle. The alternator also charges the battery to replace the energy used to start the engine. The voltage regulator circuit maintains optimal battery state of charge by sensing and maintaining a required charging system output voltage.

Older vehicles have separate (discrete) regulators mounted on the firewall. The next generation of charging systems included regulators that were incorporated inside the alternator. More recently, electrical system control modules have been used to regulate the charging system more efficiently by controlling alternator output based on a number of parameters such as electrical load, engine load and rpm, alternator capability, battery type and temperature, fuel economy benefits, and more.

Battery technology is also altering the charging requirements of alternators. For example, more OEMs are using absorbed glass mat (AGM) batteries now because AGMs are capable of absorbing an electrical charge of up to five times faster than older flooded-type lead–acid batteries. Different battery types and variations to cell chemistry also result in differences to required charging voltages, the charging voltage profile or the charge rate over time, and the state of charge voltage readings. Modern charging systems need to adapt to these various challenges, and in many cases this is achieved through the use of ECM control over the charging system.

▶ Alternator Advantages

Alternators have not always been used on commercial vehicles. Until the 1960s, DC generators were used to supply direct current to the electrical system and charge batteries. The current produced by DC generators became inadequate as vehicle electrical loads increased. Generators were especially inefficient at low speeds, leading to a discharged battery condition after a few short trips. The development of low-cost solid-state rectifiers in the 1950s made the use of alternating current "generators" (alternators) possible. Alternators are much more efficient at producing current than DC generators. Alternating current—not DC current—is produced inside an alternator. Several pairs of diodes, referred to as the rectifier bridge, have the job of converting AC current to usable DC current.

Thanks to solid state electronics and circuitry, alternators have become the dominant design due to their superior operating characteristics compared to generators. For example:

- Alternators weigh less per ampere of output.
- Alternators have fewer moving parts.
- Alternators can produce power at engine idle speeds; generators cannot.
- Alternators can be operated at much higher speeds. Alternators use a lighter rotor compared with a heavy armature in generators.
- Alternators conduct less current through the brushes, if equipped, thus reducing wear.
- Alternators do not require current regulators; they control their own maximum amperage output.
- Alternators will produce current when rotated in either direction. Polarity from generators will change when rotated in the opposite direction. Note that cooling fans in alternators can turn only in one direction.
- Alternators allow the reduction of battery capacity due to faster recharging rate.

▶ Alternator Principles

The alternator converts mechanical energy into electrical energy by electromagnetic induction, as illustrated in **FIGURE 44-3**. In a simplified version, a bar magnet rotates in an iron yoke, which concentrates the magnetic field. A coil of wire is wound around each end of the yoke. As the magnet turns, voltage is induced in the coil, producing a current flow. When the north pole is up and the south pole is down, voltage is induced in the coil, producing current flow in one direction. As the magnet rotates and the positions of the poles reverse, the polarity of the voltage reverses as well. As a result, the direction of current flow also reverses. Current that changes direction in this way is called alternating current (AC). In this example, the change in direction occurs once for every complete revolution of the magnet.

Alternating Current

The two most important parts in an alternator used to produce electrical current are the rotor and stator winding. The rotor contains a spinning electromagnet that induces current flow in the stator winding, which is made up of numerous coils of wire. By varying the current supplied to the rotor's electromagnetic coil, the strength of its magnetic field changes. The parts of the alternator are illustrated in **FIGURE 44-4** and will be discussed in detail in the section Alternator Components. The amount of current produced from an alternator is proportional to the following four factors. The first is the strength of the magnetic field in the rotor. Increasing the strength of the magnetic field increases the force pushing and pulling on electrons in a stator winding. Stronger magnetic fields in the rotor translate directly into higher output voltage and amperage. The second factor is the speed at which the magnetic field rotates. The third factor is the angle between the magnetic field and conductors in the stator. The last factor is the number and/or size of conductors cutting magnetic lines of force.

Maximum amperage output of an alternator is limited by the speed at which an alternator rotates. As the alternator spins faster, a counter electrical current is induced in the stator by the continuously changing polarity of AC current in the stator windings. This induced current, called the counter electromotive force (CEMF), opposes any increase in current induced in the stator by the spinning rotor. At high alternator speeds, the CEMF, which is induced in the opposite direction of output current by changing AC current polarity, will be begin to equal any increase to induced stator current. The result is CEMF. CEMF acts to reduce the output current of the alternator. The faster the

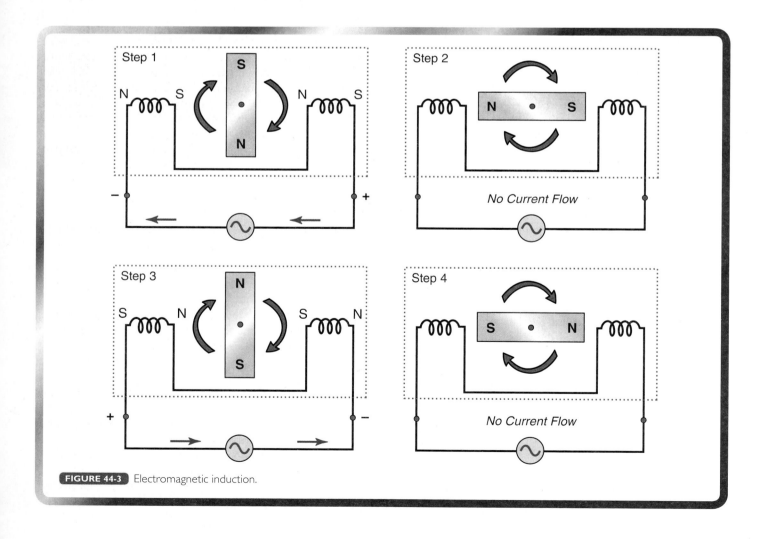

FIGURE 44-3 Electromagnetic induction.

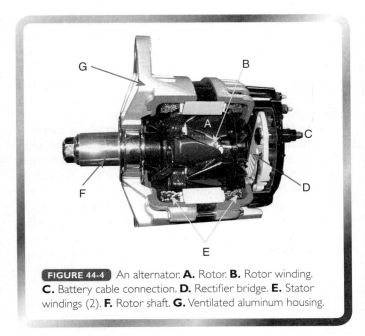

FIGURE 44-4 An alternator. **A.** Rotor. **B.** Rotor winding. **C.** Battery cable connection. **D.** Rectifier bridge. **E.** Stator windings (2). **F.** Rotor shaft. **G.** Ventilated aluminum housing.

alternator turns, the higher the CEMF produced in the stator, as shown in **FIGURE 44-5**.

Alternator Classification

Alternators can be categorized by a number of variables including whether voltage regulation is internal or external; the diameter of the housing; whether the alternator is sealed, oil cooled, or externally air cooled; amperage output; charging voltage; manufacturer; and many other factors. The SAE classifies alternator automotive mounting configurations into standards to enable the adaptation of alternators from all manufacturers to fit engines. Two common mounting types for alternators are a pad-mount alternator **FIGURE 44-6A** and a hinge-mount type **FIGURE 44-6B**.

FIGURE 44-6 **A.** Pad-mount alternator. **B.** Hinge-mount alternator.

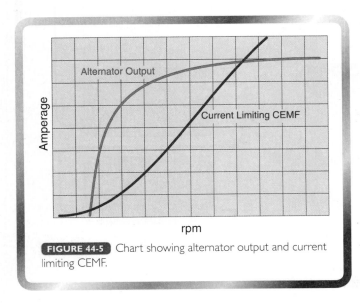

FIGURE 44-5 Chart showing alternator output and current limiting CEMF.

Alternator Output

Current Limiting CEMF

Amperage

rpm

▶ Alternator Components

Regardless of the alternator's classification, all alternators share common components. Major components of the alternator are illustrated in Figure 44-4. These include:

- Rotor—A rotating electromagnet that provides the magnetic field to induce voltage and current in the stator.
- Brushes/slip rings—Make an electrical connection to the rotor field coil to supply current from the voltage regulator.
- Stator—Stationary coils of wire in which current and voltage is induced by the magnetic field of the rotor.
- Rectifier—Converts the AC-induced voltage and current into a DC output.

- Voltage regulator—Controls the maximum output voltage of the alternator by varying the amount of current flow in the rotor and therefore the magnetic field strength.
- Cooling mechanism (air and oil)—In the case of air cooling, additional airflow is provided through the use of a cooling fan.
- End frames and bearings—Alternators have two end frames, which fit together to house the components into a single unit. One end frame contains the rotor, the drive end bearing, and drive mechanism (usually a pulley). The other end houses the stator rectifier regulator and brush assembly.
- Drive mechanism—In most cases, a pulley drive is used, but direct-gear drive mechanisms may also be employed.

Rotor

The rotor provides the rotating magnetic field that cuts the wire coils within the stator to induce the flow of electrical current in the stator. The rotor consists of an iron core that encloses a coil of many turns of wire. Each end of the wire coil is connected to one of two conductive slip rings on the rotor shaft. The wire coil and slip rings are electrically insulated from the rotor shaft. Energizing the rotor's wire coil with typically 2 to 5 amps produces an electromagnetic field beneath two halves of the soft iron core. These two halves are arranged into claws or pole pieces.

The pole pieces have two purposes. One is to intensify the electromagnetic field, and the other is to arrange magnetic lines of flux produced in the coil into poles on each claw of the rotor.

Each of the claws or pole pieces will have a stationary pole that alternates in sequence with each pole piece as north and south. A heavy alternator has more pole pieces or "claws"—typically between 12 and 16. Fourteen is a common number of claws for heavy-duty alternators. Passing current through the rotor coil magnetizes the rotor claws. Alternating poles of magnetism are formed north–south–north–south on the rotor.

The output of the alternator is determined by a couple of the alternator's physical features. The first is the size and number of windings in the stator that is cut by the magnetic lines of force. The second is the strength of the magnetic field of the rotor. Increasing or decreasing the current flow through the rotor winding will change the magnetic field strength. Usually the maximum possible amperage is 5 amps or less. Controlling the strength of the magnetic field is the job of the voltage regulator. **FIGURE 44-7** illustrates how the current flows through the rotor.

Brushes and Brushless Alternators

Regulated current to the alternator rotor is supplied through a pair of graphite brushes sliding against slip rings on the rotor shaft. The slip rings and the coil are electrically insulated from the rotor shaft. Lightweight springs help the brushes maintain contact with the slip rings. Brushes are designed to have a minimum of 95,000 miles (150,000 km) service life but eventually wear out. Dirt, fluids, engine blow-by, corrosion, and other substances can leave residues on the slip rings or gum up the brush holders, also preventing good contact.

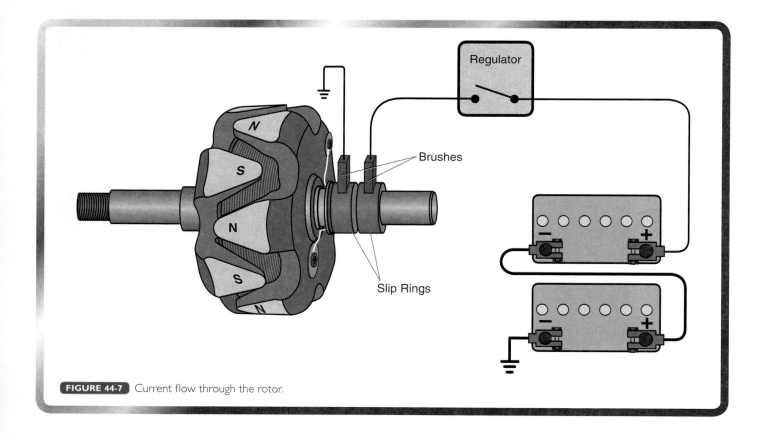

FIGURE 44-7 Current flow through the rotor.

The service life of heavy-duty alternators used needs to be extended in chassis accumulating travel distances in excess of 620,000 miles (one million kilometers). One way to extend the service life is by using brushless alternator designs such as the one illustrated in FIGURE 44-8 to bypass the problems of using brushes. Instead of locating the magnetic field coil inside a rotating rotor, these alternators use a stationary field winding bolted to the alternator end frame. The rotor's pole pieces rotate around the stationary coil. Brushes, therefore, are not required to deliver the current to the rotor. As a result, there is no need to service the brushes and slip rings.

Exciting the Alternator

While the voltage regulator will supply current to the rotor, some alternators require some residual magnetism on the rotor before current is generated. **Residual magnetism** refers to the small amount of magnetism left on the rotor after it is initially magnetized by the coil's magnetic field. Residually magnetized rotors will begin to induce current in the stator windings when the alternator starts rotating without any current passing through the rotor coil. The stator, in turn, supplies current to the voltage regulator through exciter diodes. Normal alternator operation using a regulator will resume once current is supplied to the regulator. This category of self-exciting alternators generally features a single, heavy-gauge battery cable connecting the alternator to the vehicle batteries.

FIGURE 44-8 A brushless alternator has rotating pole pieces around a stationary field winding. **A.** Rotor. **B.** Pole pieces (2). **C.** Stator windings. **D.** Stationary field coil.

Self-exciting alternators do not require the use of a circuit but may require some initial current in the rotor's coil through the "R" terminal for the first time after installation or when the engine has been sitting without running for long periods. Often, vehicles fitted with self-exciting alternators may require the engine rpm to be briefly increased after every start-up to initiate charging. Using self-exciting alternators eliminates the need for a separate circuit from the key switch to the alternator and simplifies chassis wiring.

> ## ▶ TECHNICIAN TIP
>
> Self-exciting alternators do not use a circuit connected to the ignition switch to switch on the voltage regulator and supply current to the rotor. Instead, they rely on residual magnetism found in the rotor after operating. If the alternator stays unexcited due to a prolonged shut-down period or after rebuilding, residual magnetism needs to be re-established. The "R" terminal is briefly energized with battery current using a jumper wire connected to the battery cable after the alternator starts. Once energized, the alternator will begin charging and should not need initializing with current again. Many alternators are regularly returned as defective because technicians are unaware of the procedure to excite the rotor initially.

Stator

The stator is made of loops of coiled wire wrapped around a slotted metal alternator frame. The laminated-iron stator frame channels magnetic lines of force through the conductors where current is induced by the spinning rotor. Because the wires are looped, with alternating magnetic N–S poles passing beneath the loops, alternating current is produced from the stator FIGURE 44-9. The windings are insulated from each other and also from the iron core. They form a large number of conductor loops, which are each subjected to the rotating magnetic fields of the rotor. The stator is mounted between two end housings, and it holds the stator windings stationary so that the rotating magnetic field cuts through the stator windings, inducing an electric current in the windings. To smooth the pulsating current flow, there are three distinct layers of windings offset 120 degrees in each layer from one another. This arrangement produces a more even flow of current from the alternator. The number of loops in each winding corresponds to the number of rotor poles. So, if the rotor has 14 poles, there will be 14 loops of wire in each of the three windings. Ultimately, the amount of amperage the alternator is capable of producing depends on the mass of wire in the stator. A larger stator having more loops, more turns of wire in each loop, and/or thicker wire will have higher maximum output amperage than one with fewer loops, less wire, and thinner wire. FIGURE 44-10 provides a side-by-side comparison of low- and high-output stators.

Phase Winding Connections

Two methods of connection can be used for the stator or phase windings: the Wye and Delta configurations. Both types

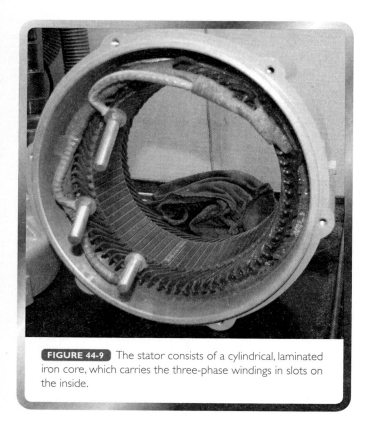

FIGURE 44-9 The stator consists of a cylindrical, laminated iron core, which carries the three-phase windings in slots on the inside.

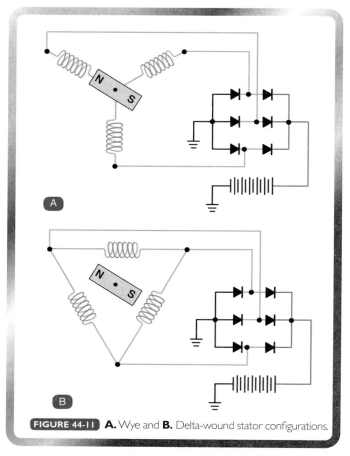

FIGURE 44-11 **A.** Wye and **B.** Delta-wound stator configurations.

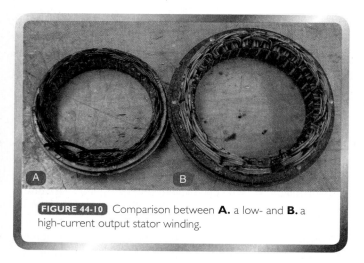

FIGURE 44-10 Comparison between **A.** a low- and **B.** a high-current output stator winding.

of windings produce three-phase AC current, but voltage and amperage outputs differ. Windings connected in a Wye-type configuration have four connection points. As the name suggests, Wye windings resemble the letter "Y" **FIGURE 44-11A**. Three ends of each of the windings are connected together to a point called the neutral junction. The other three free ends are connected to a pair of diodes in the rectifier bridge. The advantage of Wye windings is that they produce higher voltage at comparably lower rotor speeds. This means the alternator can begin charging a battery at lower engine speeds.

Delta windings, shaped like the symbol "delta," are more popular in alternators for diesel engines **FIGURE 44-11B**. These windings have only three connection points. The three junction points between the windings are connected to a pair of diodes found in the rectifier bridge. Because stator windings are connected in parallel, the resistance of Delta windings is one-third less than Wye windings. Although Delta windings do not produce as much voltage as Wye windings at same low rotor speeds, they do, however, produce substantially more amperage. Delta-wound alternators are best adapted to supply higher amperage output to charge multiple batteries and the heavy electrical loads found in trucks and buses. Combination Wye and Delta stators are rarely found in HD alternators.

Testing Stators

Stators, like rotors, are not normally serviced in a repair facility. However, when rebuilding, stators can be visually checked for burnt, cut, or nicked winding laminations. Winding junction points are checked to ensure they are solid. Continuity should exist between all junction points of the stator. An amperage draw test of each winding can be performed to check the resistance and balance of each section of winding. No continuity should exist between the windings and alternator frame. As illustrated in **FIGURE 44-12**, a stator can be tested for short circuits and open circuits. A leakage to ground test evaluates winding insulation and is also known as an insulation stress test. Stress testing involves passing high voltage, low amperage current through the windings. Any breakdown in insulation is detected when continuity exists between the windings and frame.

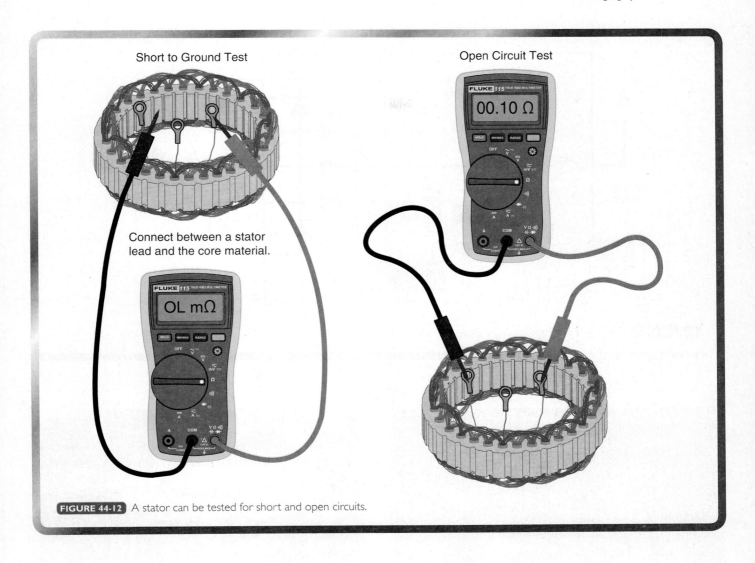

Short to Ground Test

Connect between a stator lead and the core material.

OL mΩ

Open Circuit Test

00.10 Ω

FIGURE 44-12 A stator can be tested for short and open circuits.

Rectifier

Alternators produce alternating current, which is acceptable for operating many electrical devices. However, not all AC-operated devices are cost effective to produce or efficient to operate. AC current cannot charge a battery either. Converting the AC current to usable DC current is referred to as **rectification**.

AC current is produced in the stator due to the influence of the rotors, magnetic fields. Alternating north–south poles passing over windings will alternately push and pull electrons. Moving the electrons in two different directions gives stator current flow its AC characteristic. The speed at which the lines of force cut the conductors, the angle the magnetic field cuts the stator conductors, the number of conductors, and the wire gauge will determine the amount of amperage induced in the stator.

Two diodes are connected to each wire end of either Delta- or Wye-wound stators. Each stator winding will produce one of three phases of AC current **FIGURE 44-13**. So, a minimum of six diodes is required to completely rectify all three phases of alternating current into DC current. The silicon diodes making up the rectifier behave like a one-way electrical check valve.

The two diodes connected to each winding will allow either a positive or negative current potential to appear at the output of the rectifier. If only a single diode is used at the end of the windings, only half the AC sine wave will be rectified. Two diodes enable full wave rectification **FIGURE 44-14**.

The top of the waveform is called the **alternator ripple**. A ripple that is consistent across each winding indicates that the stator windings and diodes are each creating current flow and voltage consistently. Inconsistent ripple indicates a fault in either the diodes or the stator windings. Study the illustrations carefully so that you understand the role the diode bridge plays in providing the relatively smooth DC output required by the vehicle's systems.

Rectifier Diode Problems

Heat can cause premature failures of diodes **FIGURE 44-15**. Additional cooling of rectifier bridges can be accomplished with heavier diodes and heat sinks or by connecting diodes in parallel so that six rather than three pairs accomplish the work. Another problem facing an alternator occurs when the diodes become open or shorted. An internally shorted positive diode will cause

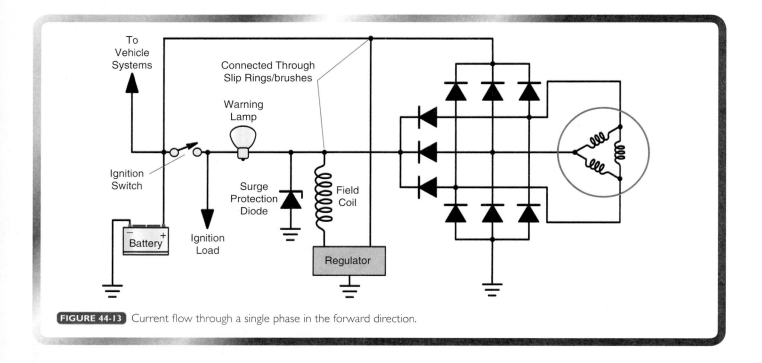

FIGURE 44-13 Current flow through a single phase in the forward direction.

FIGURE 44-14 Diode trio supplies power to the rotor circuit in most alternators. **A.** Ignition terminal. **B.** Voltage regulator. **C.** Diode trio. **D.** Stator connections (3). **E.** Rectifier bridge. **F.** Negative ground connection. **G.** Positive battery terminal. **H.** "R" terminal.

FIGURE 44-15 Rectifier in an alternator housing. Note the fins on the heat sink to remove heat.

a parasitic loss of battery current through the alternator when the engine is not running. This condition will also cause a loss of up to 67% of alternator output because it interferes with the rectification of current from two winding phases. Shorted diodes can be detected with an AC voltmeter measurement of alternator output. Generally, any more than 0.4–0.7 volts of AC current superimposed over the DC output indicate that AC current is passing through a shorted diode. Many AVRs have a diode ripple feature that detects this large AC waveform and illuminates a diagnostic light on the machine. Graphing the alternator output with a graphing meter or oscilloscope and carefully observing the pattern also indicates the condition of the diodes. An open diode will not cause as much of a loss of output as a shorted diode—only up to 33% of output—but will cause increased fluctuations or pulsing of DC output current.

When measuring alternator output using an AC (not DC) voltmeter, AC current can normally be measured. An alternator with output voltage fluctuations between 13.9 to 14.2 volts DC, for example, will produce a 0.3-volt AC current. When graphed, the waveform looks like a ripple of a wave, hence the term **AC ripple** **FIGURE 44-16**. The voltage fluctuations are produced by the differences between the peak voltage of an AC sine wave and the minimum voltage found in the trough between sine waves **FIGURE 44-17**. AC ripple is suppressed by a capacitor inside the alternator and is absorbed by the battery. If AC ripple is too great, it leads to radio noise and electromagnetic interference (EMI) in many electronic control devices **FIGURE 44-18**. For example, an engine ECM may fail to function correctly, causing the engine to run rough. An ABS module may even generate fault codes.

Smoothing Capacitors

Capacitors can be used to smooth alternator AC ripple and prevent EMI. In the alternator, one is connected across the output to act like an electric shock absorber. When the output voltage increases slightly, the capacitor will charge and absorb the new increase. When voltage drops, the capacitor will drain, topping up the output voltage and is then ready for a new charge.

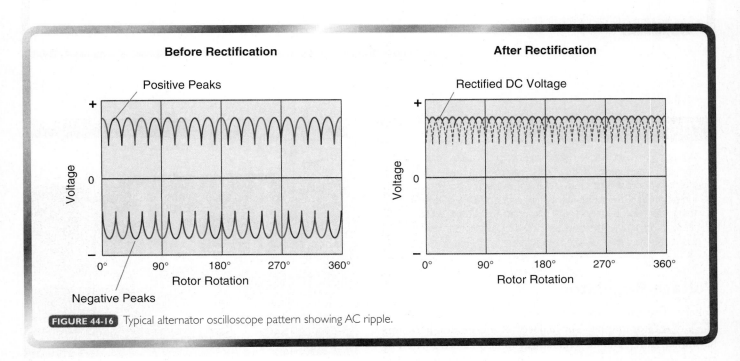

FIGURE 44-16 Typical alternator oscilloscope pattern showing AC ripple.

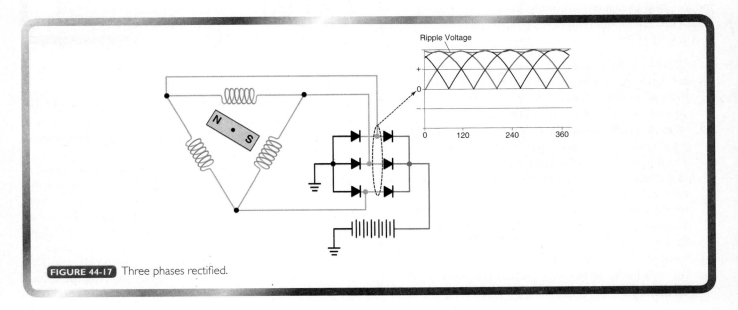

FIGURE 44-17 Three phases rectified.

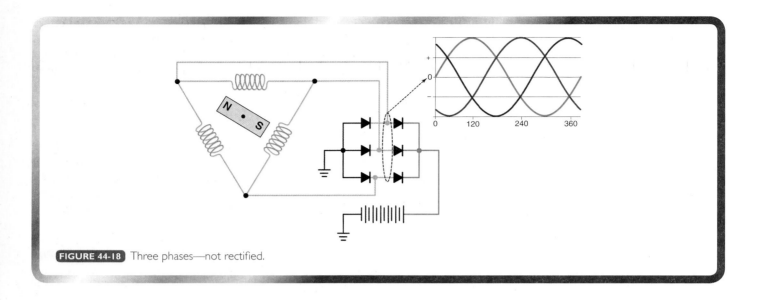

FIGURE 44-18 Three phases—not rectified.

TECHNICIAN TIP

A missing or defective alternator capacitor can cause radio noise and EMI interference with chassis electronic modules. When checking for parasitic draws, the capacitor may give a false indication of current draw as it charges for a few seconds after the battery is disconnected. If batteries are disconnected for even a short time, they will spark when connected while the capacitor charges.

Voltage Regulator

Voltage regulators are first classified as either external **FIGURE 44-19** or internal. The majority of late-model alternators have internal regulators. Regulators can also be categorized by circuit connections used to supply current to the rotor used to induce "field excitation." Knowing the type of field excitation circuit used is helpful when developing diagnostic strategies for testing alternators:

1. "A" type regulators regulate the field current by controlling the resistance through to ground. One rotor brush is connected to the alternator output or B+, and the other is connected to ground through the regulator **FIGURE 44-20**.
2. "B" type regulators control the battery positive supply to the rotor. One brush is connected directly to negative ground and the regulator varies battery positive voltage supplied to the other brush. B-type circuits are used only by external regulators. If the electronic regulator fails or develops a resistive ground due to corrosion, it commonly causes the alternator to overcharge, as system voltage is sensed through the ground and battery positive **FIGURE 44-21**.
3. Isolated field type of rotor excitation varies current through both the negative ground and battery positive **FIGURE 44-22**.

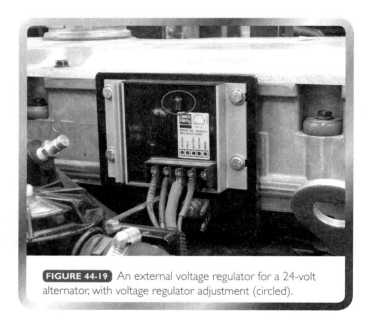

FIGURE 44-19 An external voltage regulator for a 24-volt alternator, with voltage regulator adjustment (circled).

In SI series Delco alternators, current supplied to the regulator is provided by the diode trio. These three diodes will perform single wave rectification of each phase of the alternators, windings. Single phase rectification means only a maximum of half the alternators, output can excite the rotor.

Some voltage regulators use an analog voltage signal to modulate the strength of the magnetic field. This means that the current to the rotor continuously varies. As the alternator reaches its set point, the field current gradually diminishes. Digital regulators will use a pulse-width-modulated signal to control the magnetic field strength. These alternators will have a duty cycle frequency interval of between 10 and 7000 times per second. Within that frequency interval, the voltage regulator changes the length of "on-time" current applied to

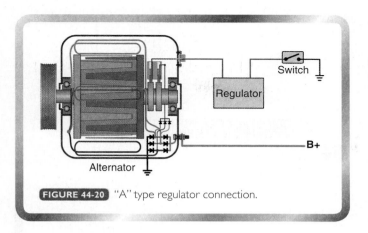

FIGURE 44-20 "A" type regulator connection.

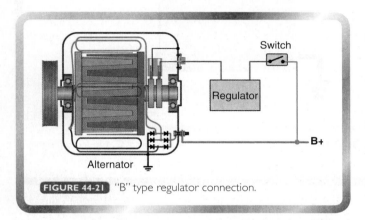

FIGURE 44-21 "B" type regulator connection.

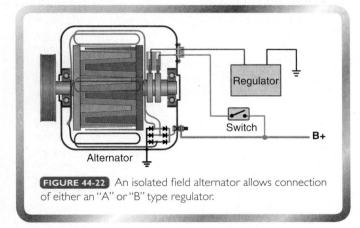

FIGURE 44-22 An isolated field alternator allows connection of either an "A" or "B" type regulator.

the rotor. Current is cycled on and off hundreds of times each second, the length of on-time increasing as higher output is required.

Output current from an alternator varies with the strength of the rotor's magnetic field. Increasing or decreasing current flow through the rotor will change output. Low current through the rotor produces low output and vice versa with high current flow. Changing electrical demands, varying engine speeds, and changing the battery all require rapid, continuous adjustments to output voltage.

Current or amperage regulation is a function of voltage regulation. To understand this, consider that an alternator's output depends on two factors. One is the regulator set-point, and the other is the vehicle's electrical system total circuit resistance. So, an electrical system with a low battery charge, and many other electrical loads switched on, has low resistance. Multiple current pathways exist, which lowers total circuit resistance. Low resistance permits high amounts of amperage to flow out of the alternator. (Remember Ohm's law: Voltage = Amperage × Resistance.) Because the alternator is connected to all these circuits, the voltage regulator will supply the highest possible current flow to the rotor for maximum magnetic field strength. As the batteries charge and some loads are turned off, less amperage is needed, as electrical system resistance increases. Because electrical system resistance increases, the system voltage will rise as amperage is reduced. When the system voltage reaches the alternator's set-point, it will turn off current to the rotor until the voltage falls again.

Stated another way, using power and Ohm's law (Power = Volts × Amps)—if 1200 watts of power are needed to supply the electrical system, the voltage-amperage combination could be 85 amps at 14.0 volts or 100 amps at 12.0 volts.

Voltage regulators controlled by the electrical system control module (ECM) are commonplace. Using engine speed, air intake temperature, coolant temperature, and other variables, the ECM will adjust charging voltage to match battery temperature. To reduce drag when cranking, no field excitation takes place until after the engine starts. Once the engine is started, current output is slowly raised to minimize rough engine operation. If battery voltage is too low, engine idle speed can be increased. Communication between the PCM and voltage regulator takes place over the CAN network **FIGURE 44-23**.

Charging System Set Point

Alternators must be capable of controlling the output of the DC current. There must be enough current to adequately charge the batteries but not so much current that it causes damage to the vehicle's electrical system. Voltage regulation for 12-volt systems will establish a maximum charging voltage, known as the set point. Charging voltage set point averages between 13.5 and 14.6 volts. This is 1.5 to 2.0 volts above 12.6-volt open-circuit voltage for a typical 12-volt battery. 24-volt systems use 27 and 28.4 volts for a typical set point. Lower charging voltages may be encountered, however, particularly on vehicles that are doing long-haul runs. It is always advisable to check manufacturer specifications for correct charging voltage ranges for the vehicle and operating conditions. Charging at voltages above 15 volts (12-volt system) and 31 volts (24-volt system) causes:

- Batteries to gas excessively
- Batteries to overheat and lose electrolyte through electrolysis
- Battery plates to shed grid material, buckle, and generally become heat damaged as the temperature rises above 125°F (52°C)

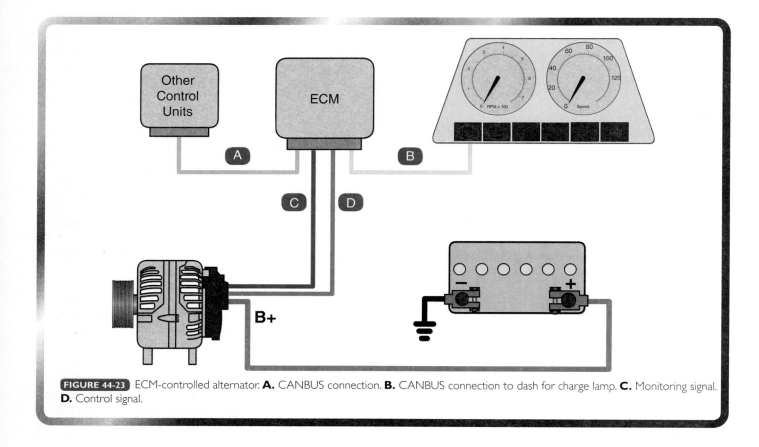

FIGURE 44-23 ECM-controlled alternator. **A.** CANBUS connection. **B.** CANBUS connection to dash for charge lamp. **C.** Monitoring signal. **D.** Control signal.

- Vehicle electrical systems, control modules, and so on, to be damaged by high voltage
- Premature and extensive bulb failure and LED light failure

Undercharging leads to battery plate sulfation and grid corrosion. This is a condition where sulfate deposited on the plates during discharge is left too long. If left long enough, sulfate turns to a hard crystalline structure and cannot be driven off by charging. Multiple battery installations are especially vulnerable to the problems of uneven charge rates causing plate sulfation.

Factors affecting the precise set point include:

- Type of batteries—Flooded batteries (standard lead acid) charge at lower voltages than no-maintenance or AGM batteries. AGM batteries are more easily damaged by overcharging.
- States of battery charge—Discharged batteries have low resistance to current compared to charged batteries. AGM batteries can absorb 40% more current than flooded and low-maintenance batteries.
- Temperature—Battery resistance to charging increases as temperatures decrease. Temperature sensors in voltage regulators can adjust set points. To warm-up the battery, Delco CS alternators charge at 16.5 volts for the first few minutes after start-up when the weather is cold.
- Drive cycle—Low-speed operation requires higher set points to keep batteries charged.

TECHNICIAN TIP

The vehicle's electrical system can be severely damaged by high-voltage spikes if batteries are disconnected accidentally or intentionally while the alternator is charging. Since the rotor's magnetic fields do not disappear immediately and the battery is unable to absorb current, output voltage can suddenly rise to levels that can damage sensitive electronic devices. Some alternators include a load-dumping feature that temporarily suppresses these high voltage spikes. This usually involves using specialized diodes in the rectifier bridges, which become resistive rather than conductive at a specific voltage level. The diodes are called transient voltage suppression (TVS) diodes. They will temporarily resist high voltage and automatically reset when the overvoltage goes away. Best practice is never to disconnect batteries when the engine is running.

Alternator Cooling

Because a significant amount of heat is produced when diodes are blocking or, more correctly, resisting current flow in one direction, the rectifier bridge is designed to absorb and radiate heat it to the atmosphere. Stator windings also produce substantial amounts of heat, which can burn the insulation and windings. Larger 24-volt alternators, such as the Delco 50DN used by buses, circulate oil through the alternator to remove heat from the rectifier and stator windings.

When operating in environments where a spark from an alternators, brush could trigger an explosion or cause a fire, the alternator is sealed, and heat is radiated through the housing. Most alternators, however, rely on air to internally cool internal components FIGURE 44-24 . If equipped with a cooling fan, the alternator must rotate in a direction that will push air through the unit. Today most cooling fans will push air through the alternator regardless of rotational direction.

Large alternators used by buses producing as much as 300 amps at 24 volts require superior cooling. In these situations, oil-cooled alternators, such as the one in FIGURE 44-25 , may be used. A minimum of 2 gallons (7.6 liters) flow per minute is required. The engine oil cooling system keeps internal engine oil temperatures below 250°F (121°C), and this can be used to cool the alternator. Alternators using oil cooling do need to be sealed well and serviced to prevent any internal shorts or sparks, which may lead to a crankcase explosion caused by ignition of volatile oil vapors inside the alternator case.

Alternator End Frames and Bearings

The alternator housings support and enclose all of the alternator components and are typically constructed from aluminum, as shown in FIGURE 44-26 . Vents within the frames provide for a large amount of airflow to assist in dissipating heat. The housings accept the bearing assemblies, which support the rotor at the drive and slip ring ends. A pulley that is driven by a belt is mounted at the end of the rotor shaft. Most slip ring end frames also house the rectifier assembly. In some cases, the negative diodes are pressed into holes in the frame to provide a ground, while the positive diodes are mounted on insulated plates.

Drive Mechanism

A drive gear, rather than a pulley, is used to couple the alternator to the engine. It requires the alternator to be bolted directly to the engine in a location where a driving gear is available. This arrangement eliminates maintenance issues around belt tension

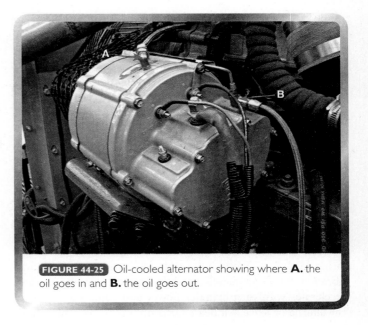

FIGURE 44-25 Oil-cooled alternator showing where **A.** the oil goes in and **B.** the oil goes out.

FIGURE 44-26 Alternator end frames enclose and support all components and allow for maximum airflow through the alternator to remove excess heat.

FIGURE 44-24 A fan attached to rotor used to cool the alternator.

and replacement but does require the alternator to be well sealed to prevent any oil leakage.

The correct gearing or pulley size needs to be selected for the alternator to ensure that the alternator does not over speed at higher engine rpm but also produces enough output at idle to cater for electrical demand. Since a highway diesel operates typically between 650 rpm and 2100 rpm, a mechanical advantage between the alternator pulley and engine speed is needed to spin the alternator fast enough. Most larger alternators are limited to 8000 rpm, which means the alternator drive ratio is precisely chosen to produce high output at idle yet stay below maximum speeds. This is particularly true as output curves tend to flatten out and brush and bearing wear increase with increasing speed.

For large-bore diesel engines found in trucks and busses, the driven ratio is approximately 2.7:1, which means that every engine rpm produces 2.7 rotor shaft revolutions. In recent years a ratio of 3:1 or even 3.1:1 is becoming common. At 2000 rpm the alternator will turn 6000 rpm. Some slow rpm diesels may use a ratio as high as 5:1 in comparison to smaller capacity, higher revving engines that use a ratio as low as 2:1.

V-type belts and pulleys have been the traditional method of driving alternators. However, to extend belt maintenance intervals, manufacturers have moved completely away from using V-type pulleys in favor of serpentine belts, like that shown in **FIGURE 44-27**, equipped with automatic tensioners. A serpentine belt is a type of multi-rib belt that is long enough to drive multiple accessories. Due to the length of the serpentine belt and the number of accessories it drives, idler pulley are required to ensure each pulley has enough wrap or surface contact with the belt. Serpentine belt systems reduce belt wear while improving the coupling force with multiple accessories.

Belt tensioners, like that shown in **FIGURE 44-28**, can be spring-loaded or hydraulic can absorb some of the torsional vibration found in diesels as the crankshaft accelerates and decelerates with each cylinder power and compression event. The alternator drive belt bears the brunt of this damaging force occurring as the engine acceleration rate changes and the alternators, mass resists the speed change. When the belt and alternator speed are out of phase, the belt is snapped and slips. This force is magnified by the 3:1 drive ratio between the crankshaft and alternator pulley. To improve belt life and mechanical efficiency, it is becoming common to use **overrunning alternator decoupler (OAD)** pulleys rather than a conventional solid pulley and tensioner. An OAD pulley uses an internal spring and clutch system that allows it to rotate freely in one direction and provide limited, spring-like movement in the other direction. The pulley acts like a shock absorber, absorbing the force associated with belt accelerations and speed reversals, enabling the alternator to free-wheel when the belt suddenly decelerates.

▶ Dual Alternators—Paralleling

Vehicles needing extra high current output at idle or those with extra electrical loads can use two or more alternators. Fire trucks, ambulances, RVs, buses, and highway tractors running extra accessories are examples where using **parallel alternators** provides a higher charging voltage at idle with more available amperage. Connecting alternators in parallel requires the output of each to be properly balanced so one will not work harder than the other and wear out. This can happen unless the alternators are exactly identical and sense the same system voltage. In practice this is difficult to achieve because even slight differences

FIGURE 44-27 A multi-rib serpentine belt.

FIGURE 44-28 A belt tensioner ensures the correct tension is applied to the belt to prevent slippage.

using the same regulators and alternators will cause one alternator to charge at a slightly higher voltage than the other. The second alternator will not charge as much, and the first alternator will wear or burn out prematurely.

Several strategies can be used to prevent that from happening:

- Use engineered systems with alternators and regulators designed to work in dual alternator systems.
- While using an amp-clamp to measure output, the alternators, if equipped with adjustable voltage regulators, are adjusted to produce the same amperage output with the lights and accessories switched-on.
- When using identical alternators matched by model and output and having the same regulators, a shunt or cable is connected between the battery positive terminals on the alternators. This helps both alternators to sense the same output current.
- A single regulator for both alternators can be used so the current supplied to the rotor is identical and should produce similar output amperage and set point.
- ECM-controlled alternators may be configured to support two alternators. In this arrangement, the ECM ensures that each alternator produces just the right amount of output for the given requirements.

▶ Alternator Wiring Connections

The terms and connections used in this section are ones commonly used for heavy vehicles. Different manufacturers may use different socket arrangements, color codes, and naming conventions for the various terminals and connectors on alternators, so it is always important to check manufacturer's wiring diagrams and naming conventions for information. The wiring requirements for alternators are relatively simple. This is particularly true for internal regulator self-exciting alternators, like that shown in FIGURE 44-29, as they only use a single battery cable. The battery positive cable is large, red, gauge wire (4AWG or larger). It connects to the battery terminal on the starter and has

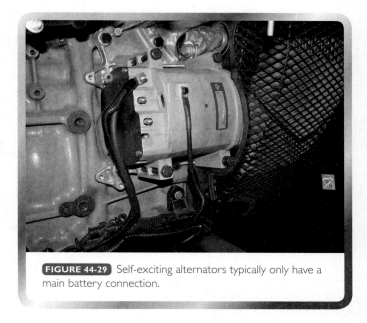

FIGURE 44-29 Self-exciting alternators typically only have a main battery connection.

voltage present at all times. Some alternators, particularly high output ones, will also have a ground or negative cable. A large-gauge wire (4AWG or larger) is connected to battery or chassis ground, as illustrated in FIGURE 44-30. This prevents the engine block from conducting hundreds of amps the alternator may produce and minimizes voltage loss.

A remote sensing connection, as illustrated in FIGURE 44-31, will also be used on some alternators and will usually be marked on the back of the alternator with an "S." The term **sensing** refers to the voltage reference point the alternator uses for regulation of the output. Many alternators reference the battery positive connection from within the alternator. Those alternators using **remote sensing** provide direct reading battery input terminal that is used for the regulator reference voltage. This allows the remote sensing terminal to be connected directly to the batteries, providing the regulator with an accurate battery reference

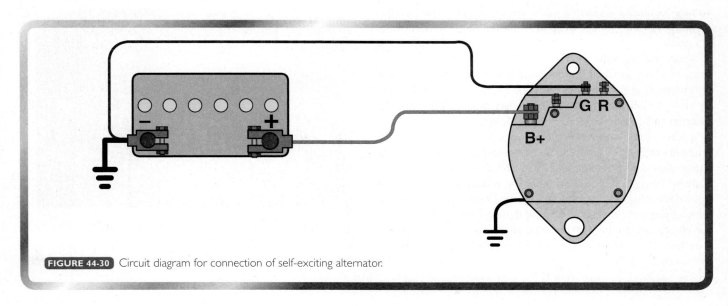

FIGURE 44-30 Circuit diagram for connection of self-exciting alternator.

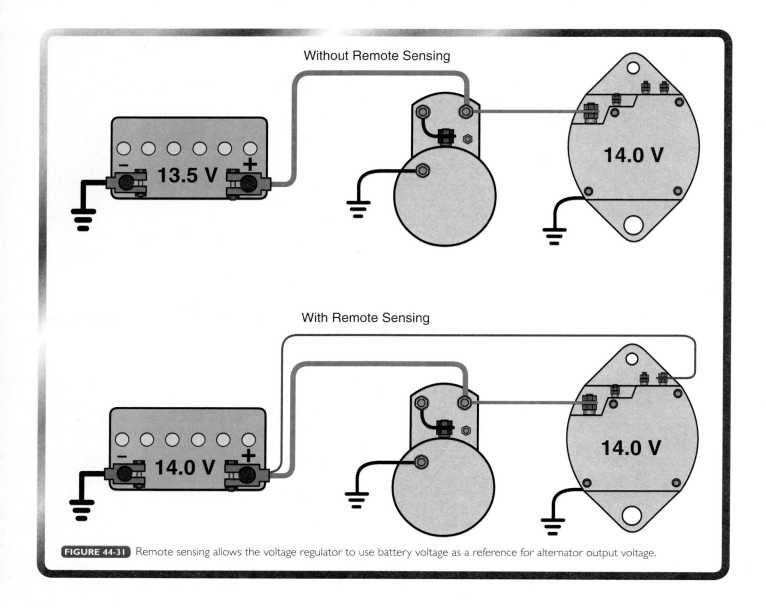

Without Remote Sensing

13.5 V

14.0 V

With Remote Sensing

14.0 V

14.0 V

FIGURE 44-31 Remote sensing allows the voltage regulator to use battery voltage as a reference for alternator output voltage.

voltage for alternator output and reducing the effect on alternator output of any voltage drop in the battery connection to the alternator.

External regulator alternators will have additional connections to allow for field connections from the regulator to the alternator, as was shown in Figure 44-19. Provision for the connection of alternator warning lights may also be fitted to both internal and external regulator alternators.

Alternators that require external excitation will have an ignition excite or "I" connection. This small gauge wire has voltage present only when the ignition switch is in the run position. Current through this wire switches the voltage regulator on. In light-duty vehicles without voltmeters in the dash and equipped with an instrument cluster warning light, current will pass from the switch and to the light into the alternator regulator to provide initial excitation of the rotors, magnetic field. In heavy-duty vehicles, however, voltmeters are used FIGURE 44-32.

FIGURE 44-32 Charging system warning lights are seldom used in trucks. Instead, voltmeters are used.

When the alternator starts charging, charging voltage appears at the "I" terminal, which provides battery positive to both sides of the light and extinguishes the charging system warning light. In situations where a charge warning light is not required, an ignition feed may be directly connected to the "I" terminal.

Another connection found on many alternators is the relay or "R" terminal. This terminal is connected directly to one phase of the stator winding. Because it is connected directly to the stator, it provides an AC signal whose frequency is related to the speed of the alternator. Because the speed of the alternator is related to engine speed, this signal can be used to operate a tachometer, hour meter, or operate a frequency-sensitive starter lock out relay to disable the cranking circuit when the engine is running. Energizing or flashing this terminal, which is the temporary connection of battery voltage, is necessary on some self-exciting alternators to magnetize the rotor for initial start-up. Since the rotor is soft iron, the rotor will maintain this magnetism once it has been initially excited. However, after rebuilding or through prolonged inactivity, the rotor may lose the residual magnetism. For this reason, the relay terminal is needed on self-exciting single wire alternators. This feature is common to some Bosch and Delco SI series alternators.

▶ Charging System Diagnosis

When diagnosing charging system problems, always start with the battery. A weak or dead battery, corroded battery cable connections, and/or damaged or worn components may cause a no-crank or slow-crank problem. Check for dirt build-up on the battery top, case damage, loose or corroded connections, or any other trouble that could drain the battery charge. Charging system malfunctions are often identified by battery condition. Use **TABLE 44-1** to assist in diagnosing charging system problems. Always consult manufacturers' information before commencing any work.

Inspecting, Adjusting, and Replacing Alternator Drive Belts, Pulleys, and Tensioners

If a problem arises with an alternator, perform a visual inspection of its drive belts, pulleys, and tensioners. An index mark on a belt tension indicates whether the belt is too loose or too tight. The tensioner arm should ideally be centered between the two stop points on the tensioner bracket.

TABLE 44-1: Charging System Diagnosis Chart

Concern	Cause	Remedy
Overcharged batteries	Resistive voltage sensing lead contact at alternator or electrical system	Repair
	Open voltage sensing circuit	Repair circuit
	Defective voltage regulator	Replace regulator
	Improperly adjusted voltage regulator	Adjust regulator
	One shorted battery in a battery bank	Replace battery
Low voltage or no-charge condition	Loose drive belts	Tighten or replace belt as necessary
	Corroded, broken, burnt, or loose wiring connections	Repair connections
	Undersize battery cables	Install proper gauge cables
	Defective batteries	Replace batteries as required
	Batteries too far from sensing lead contact	Reposition
	Missing sensing lead contact	Repair contact
	Defective voltage regulator	Replace regulator
	Improperly adjusted voltage regulator	Adjust regulator
	Defective rectifier bridge; shorted or open diodes	Replace or overhaul alternator
No magnetic field at alternator	Poor contact between brushes and slip rings	Overhaul alternator/replace brushes
	Damaged or worn brushes/slip rings	Overhaul alternator/replace brushes
	No residual magnetism present in the rotor	Overhaul/replace alternator
	Defective or improperly adjusted regulator	Adjust or replace regulator as required
	Open, shorted, or grounded rotor winding	Overhaul alternator/replace rotor
	No ignition excitation of regulator	Check and repair connection
	No current feed to internal regulator	Check and repair connection

Preventive Maintenance Practices

When performing preventative maintenance, the following areas require attention.

1. *Cleaning cable terminals, wiring, and alternator connection points or corrosion.* Alternator surfaces should be cleaned until they are free of accumulations of dirt, grease, and dust. Air passages need to be unobstructed to allow air to easily pass through. All connection points must be clean and free from corrosion since voltage is sensed from between ground and battery positive.

2. *Mounting brackets should be inspected for loose bolts and to allow correct belt alignment.* Broken and loose mounting may indicate damage from engine torsional vibration. If other accessory drive system components are functioning correctly, a sturdier model of alternator may be required.

3. *Condition of belts and belt tension. A loose belt will slip and cause undercharging.* Tensioners must be correctly aligned operating perpendicular to the belt. Multi-grooved belts should be check for cracks, which may extend completely across the belt. The back side of the belt should not be worn and glazed.

Belts can have several issues, as shown in **FIGURE 44-33**. To replace a serpentine belt, follow the guidelines in **SKILL DRILL 44-1**.

FIGURE 44-33 Failure conditions for serpentine belts.

Charging System Output Test

Vehicle charging systems are voltage regulated, which means that the alternator will try to maintain a set voltage across the electrical systems. As electrical load current increases in the vehicle systems, voltage starts to drop. The voltage regulator senses this voltage drop and increases the current output of the alternator, which in turn increases system voltage to try to maintain the correct voltage in the

SKILL DRILL 44-1 Replacing a Serpentine Belt

1. For safety reasons, disconnect the battery and set the park brake. Inspect the belt for failure. Repair any condition causing belt contamination or failure due to misalignment.

2. Familiarize yourself with the belt routing. Draw a sketch, take a picture of the belt routing, or locate the belt routing diagram in a shop manual or on the radiator module.

3. Release the belt tension to remove the belt. To release belt tension, the automatic belt tensioner is retracted away from the belt using a wrench, socket wrench, 1/2" drive or 3/8" drive ratchet.

4. Inspect the drive belt pulley system for wear. Make sure the tensioner and the pulleys operate freely, without noise or looseness, and are in perfect condition. The tensioner pulley should contact the belt squarely; if not, the tensioner should be replaced. The installation of a belt kit containing a new tensioner and drive pulleys is recommended when replacing a belt at high accumulated mileage.

5. Before installing the new belt, inspect the alignment of the pulleys to prevent severe belt wear, damage, and belt noise.

6. Route and install the new belt according to the belt routing diagram. Align the belt ribs with the pulley grooves and ensure that the belt fits squarely on each pulley and all the belt grooves fit into the pulley grooves.

7. Release the belt tensioner once again to install the belt over the tensioner pulley. The automatic tensioner will apply the correct tension to the belt. When the installation tension is correct, start the engine and observe if the belt drive and tensioning system is properly functioning.

system. The testing of an alternator output initially involves the testing of the system's regulated voltage using a voltmeter. Regulated voltage is the voltage at which the regulator is allowing the alternator to create only a small charge due to the battery being relatively charged, as evidenced by the greatly reduced current output.

Unless the batteries are deeply discharged, the vehicle headlights should not dim at idle when the alternator is operating satisfactorily. To performance test the charging system, also called a set-point test, alternator voltage and amperage is measured with the engine running at 1000–1500 rpm. With all the vehicle loads switched off and the batteries fully charged, alternator output should be 20 amps or less, and voltage should be 13.8–14.4 volts for a 12-volt system. 24-volt systems should charge between 27.8 and 28.4 volts. If the voltage is not within this range and the regulator not adjustable, the alternator is likely defective.

An alternator's performance is tested under load and measured while the engine is at 1500 rpm. A carbon pile tester is connected to the batteries, and the system is loaded until it drops to 12.5 volts. At 12.5 volts, the amperage output from the alternator is also measured. Output should generally be within 10% of the alternator's maximum rating. This means that a 200-amp alternator should deliver at least 180 amps.

To differentiate between a defective regulator and the current generating section of an alternator, a full field test of the alternator is performed. This means that the voltage regulator is bypassed, and full battery voltage is supplied briefly to the rotor slip rings. The type of alternator circuit must be identified before performing this test.

"A" circuit alternators will ground one brush. In Delco alternators, ground is done by passing a screwdriver through the "D" tab at the back of the alternator. With the screwdriver against the alternator frame and the other end on a tab of the voltage regulator, a working alternator will begin to generate current. A voltmeter is used to measure output. If voltage rises, the regulator is defective and may be replaced instead of replacing the entire alternator.

"B" circuits will use a jumper wire connected to battery positive to full-field. Isolated circuits will use two jumper wires. CAN-controlled alternators will provide diagnostic information needed to diagnose alternator problems. If current output does not rise after **full fielding**, it may indicate one of the following conditions:

- A shorted, open, or grounded rotor coil
- Stator windings shorted, open, or grounded
- Rectifier bridge shorted, open, or grounded

To perform a charging system output test, follow the guidelines in **SKILL DRILL 44-2**.

> **TECHNICIAN TIP**
>
> The battery, or battery terminals, should never be removed when the engine is running. Removing battery terminals on alternator-equipped vehicle may damage the alternator and sensitive electronic equipment fitted to the vehicle.

SKILL DRILL 44-2 Performing a Charging System Output Test

2. Start the engine, turn off all accessories, and measure the regulated voltage at around 1500 rpm. The regulated voltage is the highest voltage the system achieves once the battery is relatively charged, as evidenced by the ammeter reading less than about 20–30 amps when the amps clamp is around the alternator output cable. Typical regulated voltage specifications are wider than they used to be due to the ability of the electrical system ECM to adjust the output voltage for a wide range of conditions.

2. Operate the engine at about 1500 rpm and either manually or automatically load down the battery to 12.5 volts or 25 volts for a 24-volt system. Measure the alternator amperage output. This reading should be compared against the alternator's rated output. Normally, the maximum output should be within 10% of the alternator's rated capacity. A hot alternator may have slightly lower results.

1. Connect a charging system load tester to the battery with the red lead to the positive post, the black lead to the negative post, and the amps clamp around the alternator output wire.

Testing Charging System Circuit Voltage Drop

An excessive voltage drop in the charging system output and ground circuit tends to cause one of two problems: (1) The battery is not able to be fully charged because, although the alternator is producing the specified voltage, the voltage drop is reducing the amount of voltage to the battery, or (2) the battery is fully charged, but the alternator is working at a higher voltage to do so, potentially overheating it. Which of the two issues is occurring depends on where the voltage is sensed. If it is sensed at the alternator, then the battery will generally be undercharged. If the voltage is sensed at the battery, then the alternator will work at the higher voltage. Knowing the system will help you diagnose voltage drop issues in the output and ground circuits of the charging system.

The alternator cable voltage drop test is performed to test the positive cable for excessive resistance between the alternator and the batteries. With the engine running at 1500 rpm and the alternator loaded to 75% of its output capacity, voltage is measured at the alternator and batteries. If the voltage difference is greater than 0.25 volts in a 12-volt circuit or 0.50 volts in a 24-volt circuit, all positive and ground wire cable connections should be checked. Acceptable cable voltage drop readings are less than 0.25 volts in 12-volt system and 0.50 volts in a 24-volt system. To test charging circuit voltage drop, follow the guidelines in **SKILL DRILL 44-3**.

Inspecting, Repairing, or Replacing Connectors and Wires of Charging Circuits

When you are diagnosing charging system problems, you should always make sure you visually inspect connectors and wires of charging circuits for tightness, wear, or damage. Check the connection on the voltage regulator and the alternator for loose electrical connections or shorted wires. Move the wires around while running the engine. If the warning lamp flickers or the ammeter instrument indicates incorrect charging, the problem is in the wire being jarred. You may need to perform a voltage drop test to check wiring along the charging system path. When replacing connectors and/or wires, always refer to the appropriate manufacturer's service manual for the exact procedure. To inspect, repair, or replace connectors and wires of charging circuits, follow the guidelines in **SKILL DRILL 44-4**.

Removing, Inspecting, and Replacing an Alternator

During charging system tests, low voltage and current output problems may indicate a defective alternator. If you find that the alternator is defective, it will need to be replaced. It is the rotors, brushes, stators, rectifier bridges, and cooling fans of the alternator that work together to create magnetic fields, produce current, and charge the system.

SKILL DRILL 44-3 Testing Charging Circuit Voltage Drop

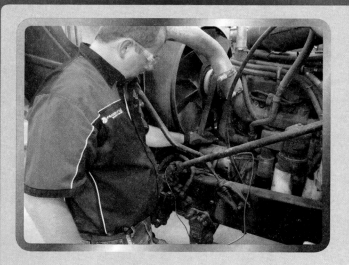

the positive post of the battery. The red probe goes on the positive battery post because, in this case, the alternator output terminal is higher voltage than the positive battery terminal. For the meter to read correctly, the leads need to be connected as listed.

2 Start the engine and turn on as many electrical loads as possible or use an external load bank to load the battery. Read the maximum voltage drop for the output circuit.

3 Move the leads to measure the voltage drop on the ground circuit by placing the black probe on the alternator case and the red probe on the negative terminal of the battery. With the engine running and the circuit still loaded, read the maximum voltage drop for the ground circuit.

4 If the measurements are excessive, check each part of the circuit for excessive voltage drops by slowly bringing the probes closer together on each section of the circuit. Determine any necessary actions.

1 Set the DVOM up to measure voltage, and select min/max if available. Connect the red probe of the DVOM to the output terminal of the alternator and the black probe to

SKILL DRILL 44-4 Inspecting, Repairing, or Replacing Connectors and Wires of Charging Circuits

1. Locate and follow the appropriate procedure and wiring diagram in the service manual.

2. Move the vehicle into the shop, apply the parking brakes, and chock the vehicle wheels. Observe lockout and tagout procedures.

3. If the vehicle has a manual transmission, place it in "neutral." If it has an automatic transmission, place it in "park" or "neutral."

4. Trace the wiring harness from the alternator to the battery and around the engine bay.

5. Check the harness and connectors for wear, damage, or corrosion.

6. Disconnect the battery negative cable if repairs are necessary.

7. Repair damaged areas with replacement cables or connectors. Ensure all harnesses are secured to prevent abrasion or damage from vibration.

8. Reconnect all harness plugs and secure all connections.

9. Reconnect the battery negative cable.

10. Check repair by visual inspection and running the vehicle.

11. Clean the work area and return tools and materials to their proper storage.

Alternators all operate on the same principle. There are, however, differences in their construction and style. Different manufacturers will usually favor different types of alternators. Always refer to the appropriate manufacturer's service manual for the specific type and style of alternator. Follow the manufacturer's instructions when installing a new alternator. To remove, inspect, and replace an alternator, follow the guidelines in SKILL DRILL 44-5.

▶ Overhauling an Alternator

Overhauling an alternator requires the disassembly and checking of all component parts. The alternator component parts should also be cleaned and replaced or repaired as necessary. The alternator is relatively simple to disassemble. You should always mark the position of the housings in relation to each other before commencing disassembly. This ensures that the housings are correctly aligned when reassembled.

Most alternators have the brushes inside the alternator, and they cannot be removed until the alternator is disassembled. However, some alternators have a brush box, which should be removed before the alternator is disassembled. Before commencing disassembly, check to see if the brushes can be removed while the alternator is in one piece. If so, undo the brush box and remove it. To disassemble the alternator, remove the through bolts with a suitable wrench or socket. Pry the housings apart; this may require a screwdriver to lever apart the housings, as they are usually a tight fit. When prying the housings apart, be careful not to damage any of the stator windings. The rotor will usually be attached to the pulley end housing. Once the alternator is separated into its two housings, further disassemble the alternator into its component parts. This may require the use of a soldering iron to remove the rectifier diodes and the brushes. The rectifier and main battery terminals will have a number of insulating bushings fitted to them. Be sure to note how the insulators are fitted for later replacement.

Once the alternator has been disassembled into its component parts, conduct the following tests for each component:

- **Housings**: Clean and check housings for cracks. If they are damaged, replace them.
- **Rotor**:
  - Check the resistance of the winding against the manufacturer's specifications. In some cases, it is also useful to check the current draw of the winding. Remember, the winding is inductive. This means it will produce a spark when power is connected or disconnected.
  - If the alternator has slip rings, check them for mechanical wear. If they are excessively worn, the slip ring assembly will need to be replaced. To do this, remove the coil wires and press off the old slip ring.

SKILL DRILL 44-5 Removing, Inspecting, and Replacing an Alternator

4 Disconnect the battery from the vehicle.

5 Disconnect wires at the connector on the alternator. Make a note of the location and any special insulating washers.

6 Loosen bolts.

7 Slide the belt off the alternator.

8 Lift the alternator out of vehicle.

9 Place a new alternator onto the engine.

10 Hand screw the bolts without tightening; connect wires first if needed.

11 After checking the condition of the belt and replacing it if needed, slip the belt on each pulley and align properly.

12 If required, adjust belt tension using belt tension gauge.

13 Tighten the bolts.

14 Reconnect the battery.

15 Start the vehicle and verify that the alternator is charging.

16 Clean the work area and return tools and materials to their proper storage.

1 Locate and follow the appropriate procedure in the service manual.

2 Move the vehicle into the workshop, apply the parking brakes, and chock the vehicle wheels. Observe lockout and tagout procedures.

3 If the vehicle has a manual transmission, place it in "neutral." If it has an automatic transmission, place it in "park" or "neutral."

Press on a new slip ring and reconnect the coil wires. You may need to machine a new slip ring in the lathe to produce a clean, round finish.

- Check bearing surfaces and pulley retaining thread for wear. Replace the rotor if they are excessively worn.

■ **Diode rectifier**: Check the diode rectifier with a diode checker. You can use a DVOM, however, a specialized alternator diode tester is recommended as it places a load on the diodes. Replace diodes if they fail the test. In some cases, individual diodes can be replaced. In others, the whole rectifier must be replaced as a unit.

■ **Regulator**: Use a regulator tester to check the regulator. Each regulator tester is slightly different, although they perform the same job. Always check the manufacturer's specifications for the correct hookup and procedure. Modern regulators are electronic and generally cannot be repaired. Replace the regulator if required.

■ **Brushes**: If fitted, brushes should be replaced whenever the alternator is overhauled. Take care when reassembling the alternator to ensure the brushes are not

damaged. Many alternators require the insertion of a pin to hold the brushes away from the slip rings as the alternator is reassembled.

■ **Bearings**: Bearings should be replaced whenever the alternator is overhauled.

■ **Pulley and fan**: Check the pulley and fan for wear and replace if necessary. When replacing the fan, ensure that it is replaced with one that operates in the same direction as the one removed.

Once the alternator has been overhauled, you will need to test it in an alternator test bench. Clamp the alternator securely in the test bench and make the electrical connections. Pay particular attention to the battery, regulator, and warning light to ensure they are connected as per the manufacturer's specifications. Run the alternator up to speed and make sure the warning light operates correctly, the alternator can generate its specified maximum current output, and the regulated voltage is according to specifications. To overhaul an alternator, follow the guidelines in SKILL DRILL 44-6.

SKILL DRILL 44-6 Overhauling an Alternator

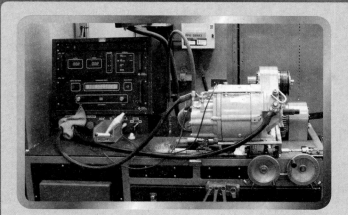

1. Locate and follow the appropriate procedure in the service manual.

2. Check to see if the brushes need to be removed first. If so, remove the brush box or regulator.

3. Remove the through bolts holding the alternator together.

4. Pry the alternator apart.

5. Disassemble the component parts from the housing. Take note of the placement of insulator bushes.

6. Clean, test, and inspect all component parts. Use specialized testers where necessary; for example, regulator tester, diode tester, and DVOM.

7. Replace any faulty components. If the slip ring assembly requires replacement, ensure the new slip ring is machined on the lathe.

8. Reassemble component parts into the housings.

9. Reassemble the alternator housings. Ensure the brushes are retained using a retaining pin to prevent damage to them.

10. Test the alternator in the alternator test bench. Ensure the warning light circuit is working and test for maximum current output and voltage regulation.

11. Clean the work area and return tools and materials to their proper storage.

Wrap-Up

Ready for Review

▶ Both DC generators and alternators produce electricity by relative movement of conductors in a magnetic field. The key difference between an alternator and a DC generator is which component rotates or moves to generate electricity.

▶ The charging system provides electrical energy for all of the electrical components on the vehicle. The main parts of the charging system include the battery, the alternator, the voltage regulator (which may be integrated into the alternator), a charge warning light or voltmeter, and wiring that completes the circuits.

▶ The alternator converts mechanical energy into electrical energy by electromagnetic induction.

▶ A single-phase stator has a single winding, which creates a single sine wave. In a typical vehicle alternator, there are three separate coils of wire composing the stator.

▶ Alternators have a built in maximum current limitation due to the counter electromotive force (CEMF) in the stator coils.

▶ Brushless alternators have greater longevity than alternators with brushes.

▶ Alternators require an initial magnetic field to be produced within the rotor to initiate the process of generating electricity. Initial excitation can be either internal or external.

▶ Wye and Delta windings produce three-phase AC current, but voltage and amperage outputs differ. The Wye configuration produces higher voltage at lower rotor speeds.

▶ Alternators are much more efficient at producing current than DC generators. Alternating current—not direct current—is produced inside an alternator.

▶ To change AC to DC, automotive alternators use a rectifier assembly consisting of two diodes for every phase of the stator winding.

▶ Alternators' voltage output is controlled by a voltage regulator. The voltage regulator regulates current output and limits maximum charging system voltage.

▶ A significant amount of heat is produced within the alternator from the rectifier, stator, and rotor windings. The two main types of cooling systems used on heavy-duty vehicle alternators are air and oil cooling.

▶ Alternators can be driven by a pulley or direct drive through a gear.

▶ Vehicles needing extra high current output at idle or those with extra electrical loads can use two or more alternators.

▶ When diagnosing charging system problems, always start with the battery. A weak or dead battery, corroded battery cable connections, and/or damaged or worn components may cause a no-crank or slow-crank problem.

Vocabulary Builder

AC ripple A pattern produced by voltage fluctuations from the alternator that create differences between the peak voltage of an AC sine wave and the minimum voltage found in the trough between sine waves.

alternator ripple The top of the waveform.

Delta windings Stator windings in which the windings are connected in the shape of a triangle.

full fielding Making the alternator produce maximum amperage output.

load-dumping A feature that allows temporary suppression of high-voltage spikes.

overrunning alternator decoupler (OAD) A pulley that uses an internal spring and clutch system that allows it to rotate freely in one direction and provide limited, spring-like movement in the other direction.

parallel alternators The practice of connecting alternators in parallel to provide higher charging voltage at idle with more available amperage.

rectification A process of converting alternating current (AC) into direct current (DC).

remote sensing Referencing the battery positive connection through an input terminal that is used for the regulator reference voltage.

residual magnetism The small amount of magnetism left on the rotor after it is initially magnetized by the coil windings' magnetic field.

self-exciting alternator An alternator that relies on the residual magnetism found in the rotor after operating as a way to switch on the voltage regulator and supply current to the rotor.

sensing The voltage reference point the alternator uses for regulation of the output.

transient voltage suppression (TVS) diodes Specialized diodes in the rectifier bridge that become resistive rather than conductive at a specific voltage level.

Wye windings Stator windings in which one end of each phase winding is taken to a central point where the ends are connected together.

Review Questions

1. _____ is a process of converting alternating current (AC) into direct current (DC).
   a. Rectification
   b. Electromagnetic induction
   c. Kinetic unification
   d. Recombination

2. _____ is the top of the waveform.
   a. Field ripple
   b. Alternator ripple
   c. Peak
   d. Valley

3. In a(n) _____, the magnetic field is created by the rotor, which rotates within the stationary stator windings to generate electricity.
   a. regulator
   b. rectifier
   c. alternator
   d. rotor

4. The voltage _____ circuit maintains optimal battery state of charge by sensing and maintaining a required charging system output voltage.
   a. alternator
   b. meter
   c. phases
   d. regulator

5. Several pairs of diodes, referred to as the _____ bridge, have the job of converting AC current to usable DC current.
   a. rectifier
   b. regulator
   c. rotor
   d. stator

6. The _____ contains a spinning electromagnet that induces current flow in the stator winding, which is made up of numerous coils of wire.
   a. battery
   b. rotor
   c. rectifier
   d. alternator

7. Regulated current to the alternator rotor is supplied through a pair of graphite _____ sliding against slip rings on the rotor shaft.
   a. windings
   b. phases
   c. brushes
   d. rings

8. Each stator winding will produce one of three _____ of AC current.
   a. fields
   b. spikes
   c. alternator ripples
   d. phases

9. A(n) _____ voltage regulator uses a pulse-width-modulated signal to control the magnetic field strength.
   a. digital
   b. analog
   c. alternating current
   d. direct current

10. Voltage regulation for 12-volt systems will establish a maximum charging voltage, known as the _____.
    a. phase
    b. set point
    c. rectification
    d. end point

ASE-Type Questions

1. Technician A says the development of low-cost solid-state rectifiers in the 1950s made the use of alternators possible. Technician B says the development of low-cost solenoids in the 1950s made the use of batteries possible. Who is correct?
   a. Technician A
   b. Technician B
   c. Both Technician A and Technician B
   d. Neither Technician A nor Technician B

2. Technician A says the alternator converts mechanical energy into electrical energy by electromagnetic induction. Technician B says the alternator converts mechanical energy into electrical energy by kinetic unification. Who is correct?
   a. Technician A
   b. Technician B
   c. Both Technician A and Technician B
   d. Neither Technician A nor Technician B

3. Technician A says the stator is made of loops of coiled wire wrapped around a slotted metal alternator frame. Technician B says the regulator is made of loops of coiled wire wrapped around a slotted metal alternator frame. Who is correct?
   a. Technician A
   b. Technician B
   c. Both Technician A and Technician B
   d. Neither Technician A nor Technician B

4. Technician A says Wye windings are stator windings in which the windings are connected in the shape of a triangle. Technician B says Delta windings are stator windings in which the windings are connected in the shape of a triangle. Who is correct?
   a. Technician A
   b. Technician B
   c. Both Technician A and Technician B
   d. Neither Technician A nor Technician B

5. Technician A says Delta windings are stator windings in which one end of each phase winding is taken to a central point where the ends are connected together. Technician B says Wye windings are stator windings in which one end of each phase winding is taken to a central point where the ends are connected together. Who is correct?
   a. Technician A
   b. Technician B
   c. Both Technician A and Technician B
   d. Neither Technician A nor Technician B

6. Technician A says a Wye-wound alternator is best adapted to supply higher amperage output to charge multiple batteries and the heavy electrical loads found in trucks and buses. Technician B says a Delta-wound alternator is best adapted to supply higher amperage output to charge multiple batteries and the heavy electrical loads found in trucks and buses. Who is correct?
   a. Technician A
   b. Technician B
   c. Both Technician A and Technician B
   d. Neither Technician A nor Technician B

7. Technician A says the amount of current produced from an alternator is proportional to the strength of the magnetic field in the rotor. Technician B says the amount of current produced from an alternator is proportional to the speed at which the magnetic field rotates. Who is correct?
   a. Technician A
   b. Technician B
   c. Both Technician A and Technician B
   d. Neither Technician A nor Technician B

8. Technician A says the two halves of the rotor's soft iron core are arranged into claws. Technician B says the two halves of the rotor's soft iron core are arranged into pole pieces. Who is correct?
   a. Technician A
   b. Technician B
   c. Both Technician A and Technician B
   d. Neither Technician A nor Technician B

9. Technician A says a minimum of 3 diodes is required to completely rectify all three phases of alternating current into direct current. Technician B says a minimum of 9 diodes is required to completely rectify all three phases of alternating current into direct current. Who is correct?
   a. Technician A
   b. Technician B
   c. Both Technician A and Technician B
   d. Neither Technician A nor Technician B

10. Technician A says DC generators are much more efficient at producing current than alternators. Technician B says most heavy-duty alternators typically contain between four and six claws. Who is correct?
    a. Technician A
    b. Technician B
    c. Both Technician A and Technician B
    d. Neither Technician A nor Technician B

CHAPTER 45

Electrical Wiring and Circuit Diagrams

NATEF Tasks

Diesel Engines

Fuel System

Electronic Fuel Management System
- Inspect and replace electrical connector terminals, seals, and locks. (pp 1251–1255)

Electrical/Electronic Systems

General Electrical Systems
- Read and interpret electrical/electronic circuits using wiring diagrams. (pp 1255–1266)

Knowledge Objectives

After reading this chapter, you will be able to:

1. Describe the elements that make up a wiring schematic (i.e., wire markings, wire size, symbols of components, grounds, relationship between components and circuits, power distribution). (pp 1248–1249)
2. Identify types and applications of electrical wiring. (pp 1248–1251)
3. Identify and describe wiring repair procedures. (pp 1252–1256)
4. Identify schematic diagram electrical symbols SAE, DIN, and Valley Forge. (pp 1255–1266)
5. Describe how to read wiring schematics. (pp 1255–1266)
6. Recommend diagnostic strategies using electrical schematics and test equipment. (pp 1255–1266)
7. Describe various uses of electrical schematics. (pp 1257–1266)
8. Identify differences between various types of electrical schematics—pictorial, isometric, block, schematic, and wiring diagrams—and power and ground distribution. (pp 1257–1266)

Skills Objectives

After reading this chapter, you will be able to:

1. Strip wire insulation. (pp 1254–1255)
2. Install a solderless terminal. (p 1255)
3. Solder wires and connectors. (p 1255)
4. Use wiring diagrams to diagnose electrical circuits. (pp 1255–1266)

▶ Introduction

Wires and wiring harnesses connect components in the vehicle's electrical system, and as such they need to be kept in good condition, free of any damage or corrosion. They carry the electrical power and signals through the vehicle to control virtually all of the systems on a vehicle. As technology in vehicles has increased, so, too, has the number of wires and cables installed on these vehicles. Although wireless communication is being used in some vehicle security, entertainment, and tire pressure monitoring systems, wires are still the dominant signal carriers in a vehicle. This chapter will cover basics about wiring, including wiring requirements, how wires are sized and coded, basic wiring repair, and types of wiring diagrams.

▶ Electric Wiring

Electrical wiring has numerous requirements specific to heavy-duty vehicles. Wiring is sized and color- and number-coded to ensure the proper wire is used for the specific application.

Wiring Requirements

Because conductors carry electron flow through the electrical system, wiring is a critical component in the electrical system. When selecting wires or cables for applications, consideration needs to be given to the following factors:

- *The amount of amperage flowing through a circuit.* Smaller wires become more resistant and heat up as amperage increases. Larger wiring increases cost and weight.
- *The operating environment.* The type of wire will differ depending on whether it is used in the engine compartment, inside the engine, inside or outside the cab, or along the chassis. Exposure to oil, grease, fuel, abrasion,

and the elements change the requirements for electrical wiring.

- *Circuit identification.* The complexities of chassis wiring necessitates the use of color coding and numbering of circuits for assembling and connecting harnesses as well as to simplify repairs.

Wire Sizing

Increasing amperage through a circuit increases resistance, as predicted by Joule's law. Circuits carrying too much current will heat to the point where they can even cause a fire. Using wires that are too small in diameter may also cause a fire. Ohm's law predicts voltage drop using the formula:

$$V_{drop} = \text{Amperage} \times \text{Resistance}$$

This means a conductor 100′ long with 0.5 ohms of resistance required to carry 10 amps of current in a 12-volt circuit will see a voltage drop of 5 volts FIGURE 45-1 . Available voltage at the end of the conductor is:

$$12 - 5 = 7 \text{ volts}$$

The same circuit carrying only 5 amps of current will drop only 2.5 volts, resulting in 9.5 available volts. Therefore, the diameter of wire for a circuit is based on the amount of amperage and the length of the circuit. Longer circuits and higher amperage require larger diameter of wire. As shown in TABLE 45-1 , as wire diameter increases, less voltage is dropped.

Two major classification systems for measuring wire diameter the American Wire Gage (AWG) and the Metric Gauge system. See FIGURE 45-2 . Both systems measure the wire size only and not the wire and insulator. The AWG system is more than a hundred years old and measures wire gauge in numbers

▶ You Are the Technician

After a positive battery cable grounded out near the alternator, high-amperage current melted the cable and burned though a number of other nearby wiring harnesses, damaging them. Several of the other harnesses also grounded through the battery cable when they were melting. Because the vehicle was relatively new, the insurance adjuster has requested the vehicle be repaired by replacing or repairing the harness as necessary. After inspecting the damage, you've determined there are two possible directions for the repairs to take. One approach is to replace the harnesses, as the vehicle has a modular harnesses system. Several major harnesses would have to be disconnected and removed and a new one reinstalled. The other approach is to replace only damaged sections of the harnesses. This second approach would be less labor intensive, and the material cost would be substantially lower. There are a number of other factors that will also guide your final decisions, but as you weigh them, consider the following:

1. Outline the various factors that will guide the selection of materials for replacing sections of the harnesses. Include information about the features of the wiring, connectors, splices, and so on.
2. Outline in the correct sequence the steps you should take to properly make multiple splices to replace wiring in a major wiring harness.
3. Identify and list the tools and any other resources you will need to make proper repairs of the wiring harness.

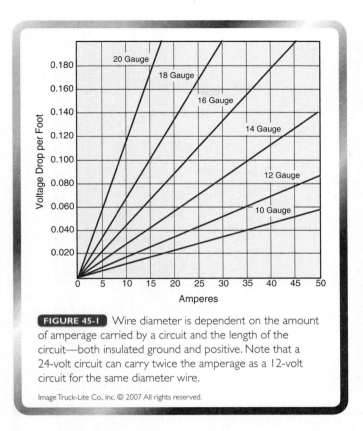

FIGURE 45-1 Wire diameter is dependent on the amount of amperage carried by a circuit and the length of the circuit—both insulated ground and positive. Note that a 24-volt circuit can carry twice the amperage as a 12-volt circuit for the same diameter wire.

every 6-gauge decrease. The gauges 00, 000, and 0000 are often used to measure battery cables and can also be written 2/0, 3/0, and 4/0, respectively.

The Metric Gauge scale measures the cross-sectional surface area of the wire and not its diameter. Sizes are rounded up to provide an even number for the wire size. For example, a 1 mm^2 wire is 0.823 mm^2, and a 2.080 mm^2 is 2.5 mm^2. In most wiring diagrams, metric-sized wire is specified in millimeters rather than metric gauge diameter. As the diameter of the wire increases in the metric standard, the gauge will also increase. This is opposite to the AWG standard, which uses a smaller gauge to indicate a larger diameter wire.

Wire Color Coding

Wire-coding systems are another useful feature of wiring to aid troubleshooting and service of electrical systems. Both colors and numbering systems designate wiring circuits, application, and even the routing of wires. The SAE also recommends color coding for circuits. For example, the J560 trailer plug connector identifies seven colors used for each lighting circuit. Wire color codes recommended by International Organization for Standardization (ISO) are partially listed in **TABLE 45-2**. Note, these are only recommendations and manufacturers will often use their own color codes.

SAE J1128 Standard

The **SAE J1128 standard** and newer ISO 6722 standard specify the dimensions, test methods, and performance requirements for single-core primary wire intended for use in road vehicle applications. Primary wire is used in low-voltage applications

from 0000 to 50. As the gauge number increases, the diameter of the wire decreases. A 0000 wire is approximately 0.5" (12.7 mm) diameter while a 10 gauge is 0.102" (2.591 mm) in diameter. Using the AWG system, the wire diameter doubles for

	24v System	12v System	10′	20′	30′	40′	50′	60′	70′	80′	90′	100′
TABLE 45-1: Total Footage of Wire from Power Source to the Most Distant Electric Lamp											
Amperage Required	2.0	1.0	18	18	18	18	18	18	18	18	18	18
	3.0	1.5	18	18	18	18	18	18	18	18	18	18
	4.0	2.0	18	18	18	18	18	18	18	16	16	16
	6.0	3.0	18	18	18	18	18	16	16	16	14	14
	8.0	4.0	18	18	18	16	16	16	14	14	14	12
	10.0	5.0	18	18	18	16	14	14	14	12	12	12
	12.0	6.0	18	18	16	16	14	14	12	12	12	12
	14.0	7.0	18	18	16	14	14	12	12	12	10	10
	16.0	8.0	18	18	16	14	12	12	12	10	10	10
	20.0	10.0	18	16	14	12	12	12	10	10	10	10
	22.0	11.0	18	16	14	12	12	10	10	10	10	8
	24.0	12.0	18	16	14	12	12	10	10	10	8	8
	30.0	15.0	18	16	12	12	10	10	10	8	8	8
	36.0	18.0	16	14	12	10	10	8	8	8	8	8
	40.0	20.0	16	14	12	10	10	8	8	8	8	6

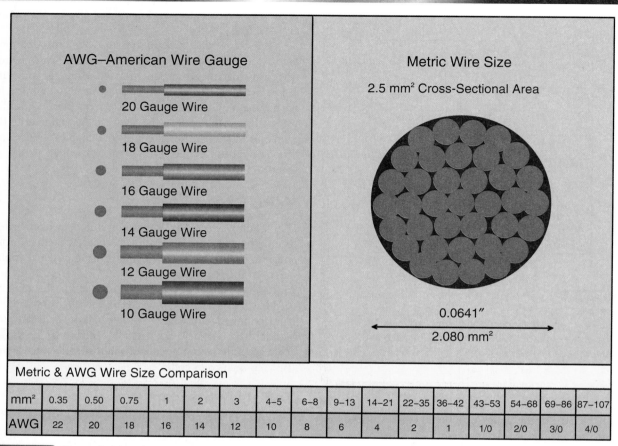

| **AWG–American Wire Gauge** |
| 20 Gauge Wire |
| 18 Gauge Wire |
| 16 Gauge Wire |
| 14 Gauge Wire |
| 12 Gauge Wire |
| 10 Gauge Wire |

Metric Wire Size

2.5 mm² Cross-Sectional Area

0.0641″
2.080 mm²

Metric & AWG Wire Size Comparison

mm²	0.35	0.50	0.75	1	2	3	4–5	6–8	9–13	14–21	22–35	36–42	43–53	54–68	69–86	87–107
AWG	22	20	18	16	14	12	10	8	6	4	2	1	1/0	2/0	3/0	4/0

FIGURE 45-2 Comparing American wire gauge system with metric. AWG represents the diameter of a wire while metric measures the cross-sectional area in mm².

under 60 volts. The number of strands a wire should have, its temperature rating, and its resistance to chemicals and resistance to oxidation are just a few standards specified. Five common types of wire for use in bus, truck, and trailer applications are classified by their insulation. These include:

- **GPT (General Purpose Thermoplastic Wire)**—Has a PVC insulation jacket and is used for general connection wiring inside a cab. Temperature rating is 176°F (80°C).
- **SXL**—Has extra-thick insulation using cross-linked polyethylene insulation to withstand operating conditions in the engine compartment where the highest heat is possible. Temperature rating is 275°F (135°C). Heat sources will cause the wire to blister like popcorn but insulation will not "melt" off wire.
- **GXL**—Uses cross-linked polyethylene insulation and, like SXL, is also used where heat, flame, and abrasion resistance is a requirement. The insulation is thinner that SXL and is used typically inside a cab or passenger compartment. Temperature rating is 275°F (130°C).
- **TXL**—Extra thin primary wire that has a cross-linked polyethylene jacket that is resistant to oil, grease, gasoline, and acids. It is used where small diameter and minimal weight are desirable. Temperature rating is 275°F (130°C).

SGR-type wire refers to starting, ground, and battery cable and is required to meet a different SAE standard than regular primary wiring. These cables use a chlorinated polyethylene (CPE) insulation, which provides the highest heat resistance of any primary wiring. Temperature rating is 194°F (90°C). <u>Parallel wiring</u> refers to a type of custom-made wiring harness that encloses multiple conductors into a single vinyl insulator covering. Parallel wiring harness is often used for a rear taillight wiring harness that includes a separate wire for stop, turn, reverse, and tail lights. The harness is typically flat, and even though wires are insulated from one another, the wiring insulation is fused together to form a single harness.

▶ TECHNICIAN TIP

Multi-stranded wire is better at conducting higher amounts of current with less resistance because it has more surface area to conduct electron flow. It is also more flexible for routing through a chassis and cab. Multi-stranded wire can break down more quickly, however, with each smaller strand being less resistant to physical damage than a larger single strand. Under the valve cover or inside the harsh operating environment of an engine, single-stranded wire is better.

TABLE 45-2: Partial Listing of Wire Color Designations by ISO

ISO Wire Color	Abbreviation	Function
Black	bk	• Ground and general purpose
Black-red	bk-r	• Battery power • Ignition • Run
Blue-dk	dkbl	• Back up light • Windshield wipers • Trailer auxiliary
Brown	br	• Tail, marker, and panel lights
Green-dk	dkg	• Right turn signal • Driver's display • Data recording • J1587 positive • J1939 negative
Orange	o	• ABS or EBS • J1587 negative
Pink	pk	• Starter control • Charging, voltmeter, or ammeter • J1922 negative
Pink-white	pk-w	• Fuel control • Indicators for speed and shut-down
Yellow	y	• Left turn signal • J1939 positive • GXL insulated wire
White	w	• Transmission • SXL insulated wire

TABLE 45-3: Examples of SAE Circuit Designations to Supplement OEM Wire Identification

Circuit Number	Circuit Description
1	Battery cable, ground
6	Battery cable, 12-volt positive
15	Starter, engine
82	Starter magnetic switch, power supply
117	Speed sensor "+", vehicle, mph (km/h)
118	Speed sensor "−", vehicle, mph (km/h)
295	Radio, AM/FM/CB
305	Ignition switch, accessory
306	Ignition switch, run position
468	Obstacle detection system (ODS), vehicle on-board radar (VORAD)
1102	Ignition buss feed
1504	Cruise control on/off
1515	Air management
1939	Data link, controls, SAE J1939

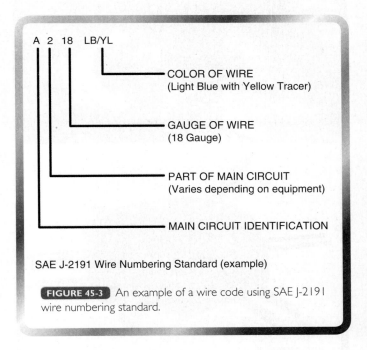

SAE J-2191 Wire Numbering Standard (example)

FIGURE 45-3 An example of a wire code using SAE J-2191 wire numbering standard.

Wire Number Coding

Chassis wiring often uses numerical codes to identify which circuit the wire belongs to, where the wire is in the circuit, which harness it belongs in, and the wire gauge and color. An SAE standard J-2191 designates standard numbers for wiring circuits for power and signal distribution systems of Class 8 trucks and tractors. **TABLE 45-3** contains examples of these circuit designations. A proprietary corporate wire identification number together with an SAE number may also be printed on the wire every six to eight inches apart. The SAE system will supplement the manufacturer's system. **FIGURE 45-3** contains an example of SAE wiring code.

Wiring Connectors

To join electrical wires to components or other circuits, terminal connections are used. The simplest connector is a terminal block that uses small studs to which ring or spade type connectors are attached and secured with machine screws. The ideal electrical connector would offer a low contact resistance, a body with high insulation value, and resistance to vibration, water, fuel, and oil.

Connectors need also to be connected and disconnected easily and repeatedly. Servicing connectors must also require only simple tooling, such as what is shown in **FIGURE 45-4**, that maintains the connectors' shape to preserve the orientation of the connectors with components. Each application requires an emphasis on connector characteristics, so there are a large variety used. Many connectors are keyed or have indexing slots to

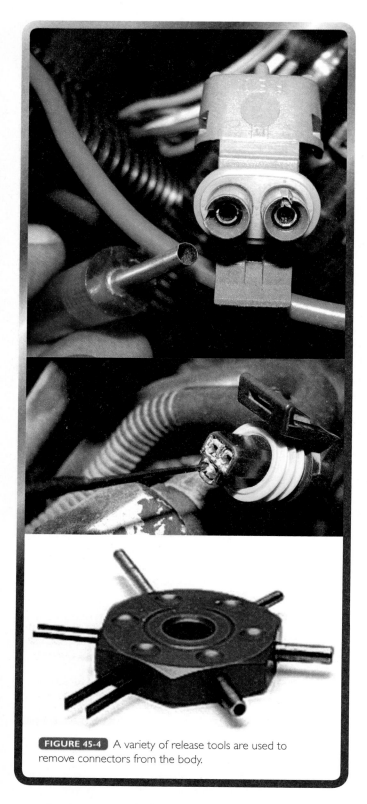

FIGURE 45-4 A variety of release tools are used to remove connectors from the body.

prevent mis-mating, which damages connectors and pins from forcing connectors together at the wrong angle or fitting into incorrectly connected connections. The connector generally has three parts: a body or housing, silicone seals to prevent water intrusion, and the terminal. Terminals are the metal part that is crimped to a wire and housed inside a connector. There are

two main types of terminals used in harness connectors—pull-to-seat and push-to-seat terminals. <u>Pull-to-seat terminals</u> are terminals that are installed by inserting the wire through the connector cavity, crimping on a terminal, and then pulling the terminal back into the connector cavity to seat it. <u>Push-to-seat terminals</u> are inserted into the back of the connector cavity to seat after the terminal is crimped to the wire.

Connector housings have male and female sides and are usually shaped so that they can be connected in only one way. Some connectors also use a connector position assurance clip (CPA) or secondary lock. This is a plastic part of the connector that assures that two connector halves will stay locked together and not work loose. **FIGURE 45-5** shows typical harness connectors. Many of these connectors are weatherproofed to keep moisture out. Special tools are usually needed to insert and remove the terminals from the connector housing.

A <u>Weather-Pack connector</u> from Delphi is an environmentally sealed push-to-seat electrical connection system supplied in one- to six-pin configurations. As illustrated in **FIGURE 45-6**, this system uses only round pin terminals and round socket terminals. The male pin end of the connector is called the tower while the female socket end is the shroud. Terminals (pin and sleeve) are tin plated and have special core wings that allow crimp-only wire attachment, eliminating the need for solder. The self-lubricating silicone connector and cavity seals are triple-ribbed. Connectors are rated at 20 amps per pin at 16 volts DC.

A <u>Metri-Pack connector</u> from Delphi is a family of electrical connection systems similar to the Weather-Pack connectors except that the terminals are flat rather than round and it is a pull-to-seat connector. **FIGURE 45-7** shows a Metri-Pack connector. Standardized male blade sizes and box-like female terminals designate the five different series of these connectors. Each series has a different current-carrying capacity. Terminals are tin plated and have special core wings that allow crimp-only connections, eliminating the need for solder. Silicone seals prevent water intrusion into the connector.

Bosch/AMP connectors use push-to-seat-type terminals. They are available in two- to six-pin configurations and rated at 9 amps per pin. Like other terminals, they use wings to crimp the wire to terminal. A metal secondary lock easily helps distinguish this connector from other types.

<u>Deutsch connectors</u>, such as illustrated in **FIGURE 45-8**, are also an environmentally sealed connector. Using solid round metal pins and hollow female sockets, Deutsch connectors are much more compact than any other connector. They occupy one quarter of the volume of the Weather-Pack connectors and one half the volume of the Bosch/AMP connectors. Rated at 15 amps per pin, they are considered a premium connector and used when reliability of the connection is of utmost importance. The DT Series of Deutsch connectors is popular on trucks and buses and is available in two- to twelve-pin configurations.

▶ Wiring Failure and Repair

After component failures, wiring and connectors are the leading causes of electrical problems. Wire chaffing, heat, oil and fuel damage, and road debris are common preventable causes

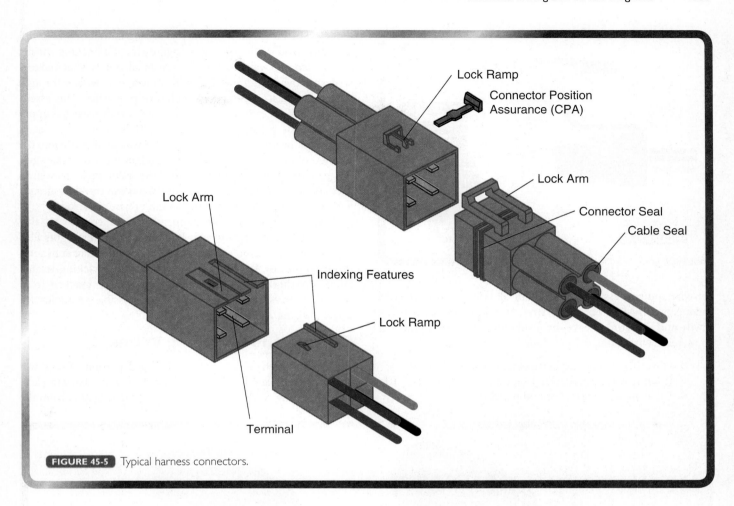

FIGURE 45-5 Typical harness connectors.

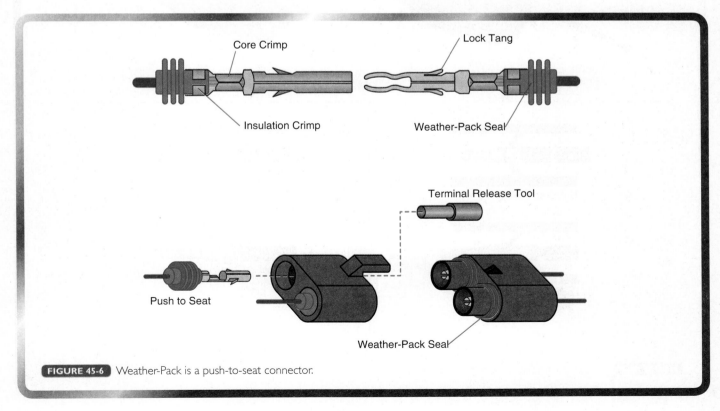

FIGURE 45-6 Weather-Pack is a push-to-seat connector.

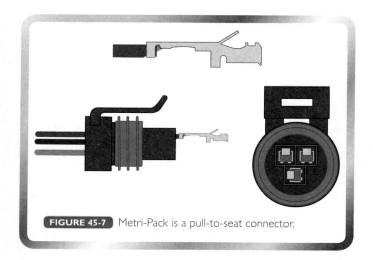

FIGURE 45-7 Metri-Pack is a pull-to-seat connector.

One of the greatest enemies to wiring is water. Water with dissolved road salt is particularly aggressive at damaging wiring. The tendency of water to "wick" inside insulation is what makes it so destructive. **Water wicking** is the movement of water through wiring due to its adhesive and cohesive properties. This essentially means water is sticky. It will easily attach itself to copper wire and has a high surface tension. That means water stays together or beads-up. Once inside a wire, water will move into the smallest openings and spaces through adhesion. More water gets dragged along inside a wire because the water sticks so well to itself. Because of the effect of wicking, water can travel far along a wire to the point where an entire length of wire is corroded.

Wicking failures often happen close to connectors due to a defective or missing seal. Punctures from test lights also lead to damage of the entire harness. A powder-like substance inside connectors or wire insulation indicates a wicking-related failure. Wiring may actually appear swollen or cracked from corrosion pressure. **TABLE 45-4** shows possible remedies for various wiring and terminal faults.

Cutting and Stripping Wires

The amount of wire cut out of a damaged portion of wire will depend on the amount needed to produce ends that are clean and free of any corrosion. After stripping the insulation from the

for wire and harness failure. Mechanical damage from repeated flexing, probing with test lights, stretching, or bending can break a wire and sometimes leave the insulation intact. Best practices to increase wiring longevity include:

- Covering wiring and harness in a protective loom
- Routing wiring away from heat sources and moving parts
- Securing wire with clips and plastic ties

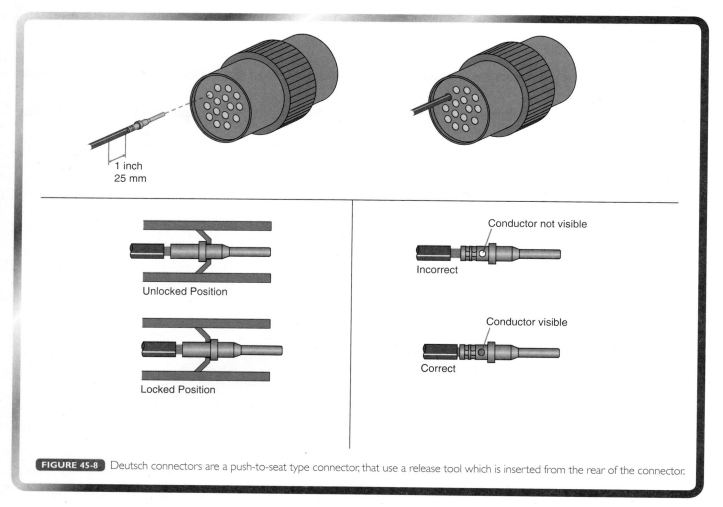

FIGURE 45-8 Deutsch connectors are a push-to-seat type connector, that use a release tool which is inserted from the rear of the connector.

TABLE 45-4: Remedies for Various Wiring Failures

Fault	Remedy
Broken wire conductor	Repair or replace
Kinked wire conductor	Repair or replace
Oil-damaged insulation	Replace
Cracked insulation	Repair if minor; otherwise replace
Melted insulation	Repair
Worn or missing insulation	Repair
Discolored insulation	Replace
Damaged connectors or terminals	Repair or replace with proper tool. Use correct replacement terminals.

remaining wire ends, the wires should appear clean and bright. Wire-stripping tools remove only the insulation and do not nick or cut wire. Dull or dirty wiring can be cleaned with fine emery-cloth sand paper. Tin-plated copper wiring used to add corrosion resistance to wiring in marine applications is commonly used in truck and bus repair, too. This wire has a dull gray appearance that cannot be cleaned. The section of wire to replace must be slightly longer than the original section removed to provide some slack.

Splicing and Soldering

Soldering wires together provides a strong mechanical and lowest electrical resistance compared to just twisting. If a connection is not soldered, wiring can move within the connection, leading to arcing and resistance which ultimately causes connection failure. To enhance the strength of the joint, wires should be joined by bending each into a double-J bend, then twisting to form a Western Union splice **FIGURE 45-9** . A small amount of solder should be applied to the tip of the soldering iron before touching the tip to the joint surface. Rosin-core solder wire is

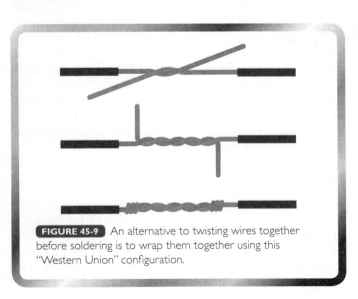

FIGURE 45-9 An alternative to twisting wires together before soldering is to wrap them together using this "Western Union" configuration.

then applied to the joint but is not brought into contact with the iron. Heat from the joint should melt the solder into the wire. This procedure avoids a cold solder joint that could cause a poor electrical connection.

Safety

Although soldering is generally thought of as a simple process, it can be very dangerous. The solder, soldering iron, and wires are very hot and can cause severe burns. Be careful what you grab or where you set hot items. Molten solder can be flicked by springy wire up into your eyes, so always wear safety glasses or goggles.

Sealing and Securing

Spliced connections need protection against water wicking. Heat-shrink tubing provides the best seal for a spliced electrical connection. Heat shrink is available in two types—double and single wall. Double-walled tubing is recommended because it has an adhesive layer between the tubing and wire. When heated, the inner layer of hot-melt adhesive turns into a watertight seal when cooled. The outer layer is generally made of flame retardant, cross-linked polyolefin. It shrinks to provide electrical and mechanical protection. Covering the wire with tape provides additional abrasion resistance to the spliced joint. Using nylon ties and insulated clips to secure the wire against movement prevents any further mechanical damage.

Crimp-Type Connectors

Faster splice repairs are made with crimp-type connectors **FIGURE 45-10** . Stripped wire ends placed inside aluminum metal tubes are squeezed together with barrel-type crimping pliers.

Crimp connectors can provide mechanical strength similar to solder but must be used with double-walled shrink tube to make the repair permanent. Color codes are used to designate wire gauge to use for shrink crimp connectors. An incorrectly sized crimp connector can become loose, leak, and fail.

▶ TECHNICIAN TIP

Heat is required to contract and seal shrink tube. Heat from a hair dryer is not adequate. Rather, a similar-looking heat gun is needed. Heat from the gun provides enough heat to melt the inner adhesive and shrink the outer layer. Propane torches and lighters will actually burn char and split shrink tube, so they are not recommended tools for activating heat-shrink tubing.

▶ Wiring Diagrams

Magneto ignition systems used at the beginning of the 1900s were the first electrical systems. With only four major components—the high-voltage magnetic, a distributor, spark plugs, and coil—identifying and connecting these components was simple. By 1911, the electrical system expanded to include a DC generator, headlamps, a battery, voltage regulator, and

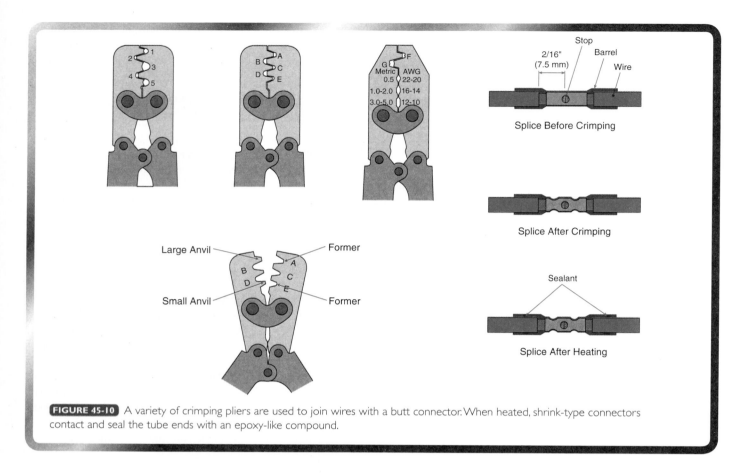

FIGURE 45-10 A variety of crimping pliers are used to join wires with a butt connector. When heated, shrink-type connectors contact and seal the tube ends with an epoxy-like compound.

switches. In 1950, the main interests were the starting, ignition, and lighting circuits. Today the types of electrical components number into the thousands—over 3000 circuits are commonly found in HD commercial vehicles!

Modern electronic controls applied to every vehicle system and networked electrical systems have increased the complexity of today's vehicles. Added to traditional vehicle systems are convenience devices, such as navigational and multimedia devices, vehicle safety and security systems, and custom electrical circuits for body builders.

The complexity of the electrical circuits and their interconnections requires electrical road maps that allow a technician to trace circuits from power supplies, through switches, components, circuit protection devices, harnesses, splices, junction blocks, connectors, and finally to ground. Technicians must be able to correctly understand and interpret a wiring diagram in order to reduce diagnostic time for electrical problems and eliminate guesswork.

▶ **TECHNICIAN TIP**

Modern vehicles have many electrical components, wiring connectors, and wires. To work on vehicles, you need an understanding of how all the components are assembled together and arranged in circuits. Electrical symbols and circuit diagrams are a way to provide this information in a logical way that represents the physical wiring harness and components attached to vehicles.

Wiring diagrams are arranged by manufacturers in a number of different styles to show with a high degree of clarity individual circuit components, connections, and their locations. The three main types of wiring diagrams include are map, isometric, and schematic diagrams.

Map Diagrams

Map or pictorial diagrams show the entire vehicle wiring circuit. Symbols for components are usually pictorial **FIGURE 45-11**. That is, the symbol looks like a component it represents. **FIGURE 45-12** contains a map diagram. Individual components and their spatial relationship to one another are not to scale and do not necessarily represent their location on the vehicle. Linear diagrams are a variation of the map diagram. Linear diagrams use pictorial representations with a mixture of schematic symbols and internal wiring. A linear diagram may start on one page and continue onto several more, mapping out individual circuits with a separate diagram.

Isometric Diagrams

Isometric diagrams are used to locate a component within a system. If the location of a component or wiring harness is unknown, this type of diagram shows the outline of a vehicle or piece of equipment where the component can be found. Various components and wiring harnesses of the electrical system are shown where they are located on the unit **FIGURE 45-13**.

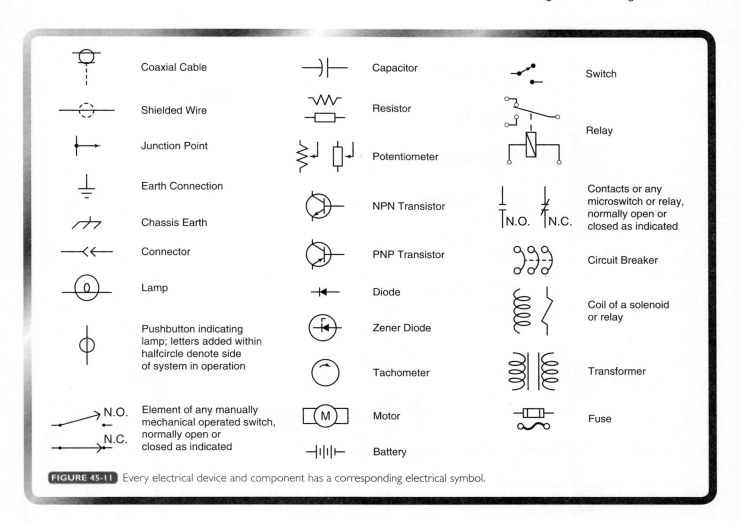

FIGURE 45-11 Every electrical device and component has a corresponding electrical symbol.

Schematic Diagrams

Schematic diagrams are line drawings that explain how a system works by using symbols and connecting lines **FIGURE 45-14**. On schematics, symbols are used to represent devices or components from simple through to complex electrical and electronic systems. There is a great deal of information represented in a small amount of space, and the reading of schematic symbols requires practice. To make them easier to use when diagnosing a problem, the diagrams are divided into sections or represent an individual system. For example, a lighting problem requires reference to the lighting section of the publication.

Schematic circuit diagrams may be supplemented with body diagrams, tables, graphs, and descriptions. Current paths are arranged to show signal or mechanical action from left to right and or top to bottom. Block diagrams are used to represent complex electronic circuitry such as electronic control modules. On these devices, no internal circuitry is shown and only inputs or outputs are depicted. Dotted lines may represent an area or some mechanical action taking place with a component.

The two most common types of schematic diagrams used today are Deutsche Institute Norm (DIN) and Valley Forge (VF). SAE symbols are used by VF, and DIN symbols are used together with DIN diagrams.

Deutsche Institute Norm (DIN) Diagrams

Many European based heavy vehicle manufacturers use Deutsche Institute Norm (DIN) diagrams **FIGURE 45-15**. In these diagrams, symbols, terminal connections numbers, line symbols, and operational status of items such as switches and relays are defined by a DIN standard. DIN diagrams may be accompanied by illustrations showing the internal circuitry of some devices. Reference coordinates are often supplied to assist in locating components.

DIN schematic diagrams are also called current track wiring diagrams because they show the power source at the top of the page and the ground points at the bottom. This format simplifies the wiring diagram and minimizes conductor and symbol overlap where they do not connect. Situated between power and ground are current tracks that contain electrical components and conductors. Symbols are used to represent components and conductors in the wiring diagrams. Arrangement of the components and circuit paths on the diagram do not usually correspond to their physical locations on the vehicle. However, newer DIN standards do indicate on which side of the vehicle a component may be located. For example, an R or L suffix after a component will designate a right- or left-side location.

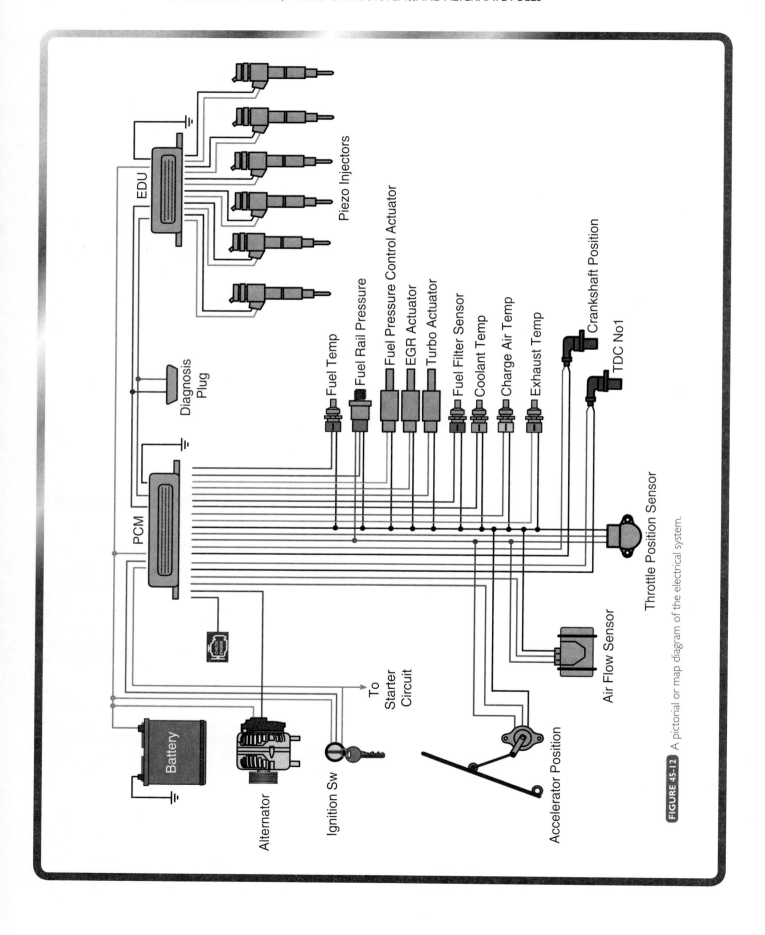

FIGURE 45-12 A pictorial or map diagram of the electrical system.

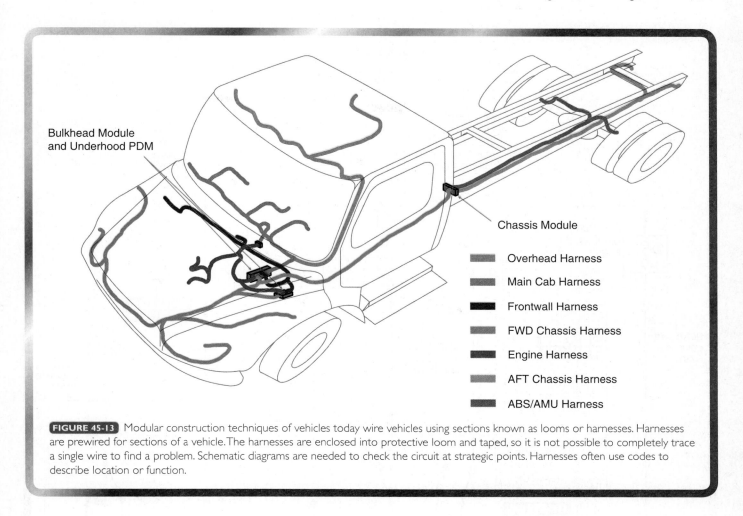

Bulkhead Module
and Underhood PDM

Chassis Module

Overhead Harness

Main Cab Harness

Frontwall Harness

FWD Chassis Harness

Engine Harness

AFT Chassis Harness

ABS/AMU Harness

FIGURE 45-13 Modular construction techniques of vehicles today wire vehicles using sections known as looms or harnesses. Harnesses are prewired for sections of a vehicle. The harnesses are enclosed into protective loom and taped, so it is not possible to completely trace a single wire to find a problem. Schematic diagrams are needed to check the circuit at strategic points. Harnesses often use codes to describe location or function.

Elements of a DIN Wiring Diagram

DIN diagrams are representative of all wiring diagrams in use today. They contain elements that every electrical circuit needs at a minimum to operate:

- Power supply
- Load
- Ground
- Conductors (usually wire)
- Circuit protection (fuse, virtual fuse)

If any of these are missing, a complete circuit is broken, and the load will not function. The ability to break down a circuit into its individual parts is the key to being able to diagnose failures in the circuit. Wiring diagrams also incorporate many standardized DIN symbols and codes used to illustrate a complete circuit **FIGURE 45-16**. These DIN unique symbols and codes can include:

- Current track numbers
- Components and devices (DIN standard 40719 and 42400)
- Terminal designations (DIN standard 72552)
- Conductors
- Connectors

FIGURE 45-17 Identifies many of the features of a DIN schematic diagram:

1. Relay location number on a relay panel.
2. Arrow. Indicates wiring circuit is continued on another page.
3. Connector designation for the relay terminal and connector panel. For example: 17/30 equals terminal 30 of relay would connect to terminal 17 of central relay panel.
4. Threaded pin on relay panel. The white circle indicates the connection is threaded.
5. Fuse indicating location and amperage. For example: S228 means fuse 28 is rated for 15 amps.
6. Reference of wire for continuing current track number.
7. Wire connection designation in wiring harness. The location of wire connections are indicated in the accompanying legend.
8a. Terminal designation on a multi-point connector.
8b. Terminal designation on a component. This number will appear on the component and/or terminal number of a multi-point connector.
9. Ground connection designation in wire harness. The locations of ground connections provided in legend.

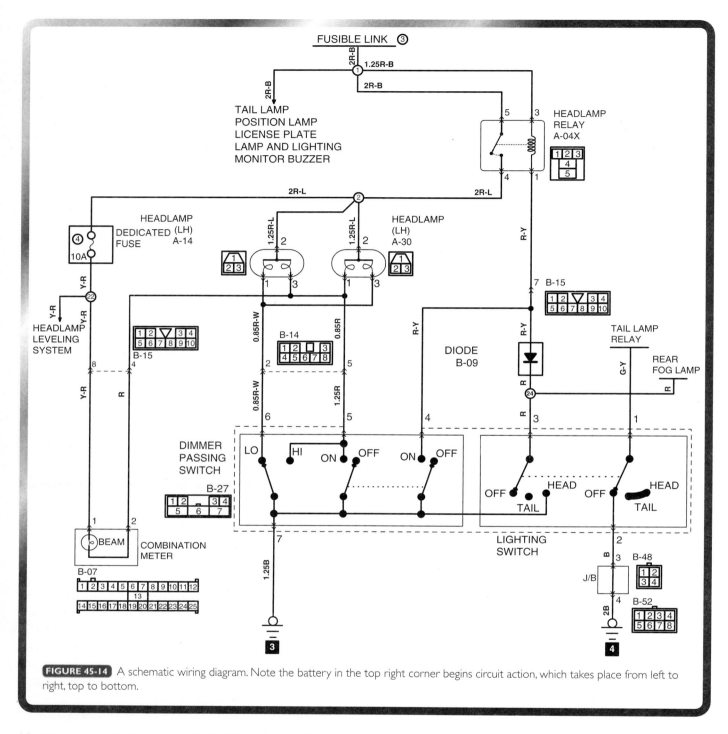

FIGURE 45-14 A schematic wiring diagram. Note the battery in the top right corner begins circuit action, which takes place from left to right, top to bottom.

10. Component designation, which follows a standardized coding. The legend at bottom of page identifies the component in this diagram.

11. Component symbols. A schematic symbol of component type.

12. Wire cross section size in mm² and wire colors.

13. Component symbol with an open side indicates the component is continued on another wiring diagram.

14. Internal connections (thin lines) and are not wires. Internal connections allow technicians to trace current flow inside a component or wiring harness.

a. Internal Harness Splice (Welded connection)

b. Physical Contact (Mounted to engine)

15. Reference of continuation of wire to component

16. Central Relay panel connectors, which depicts wiring of multipoint or single connectors on the central relay panel. For example: S3/3 equals Multi-point connector S3, terminal 3.

17. Reference of internal connection continuation. Letters indicate where connection continues on previous and/or next page.

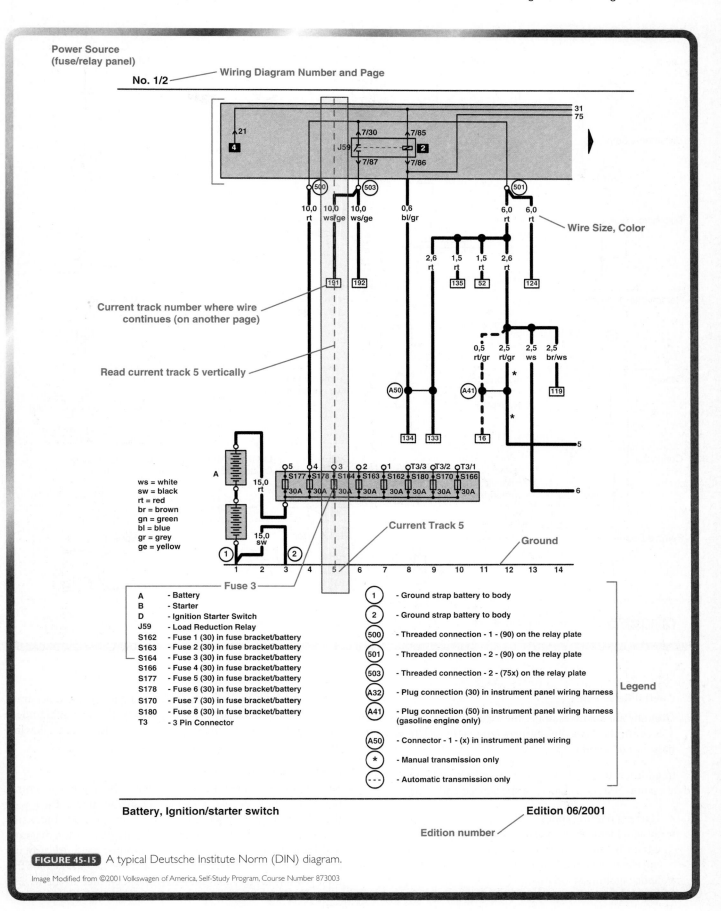

FIGURE 45-15 A typical Deutsche Institute Norm (DIN) diagram.

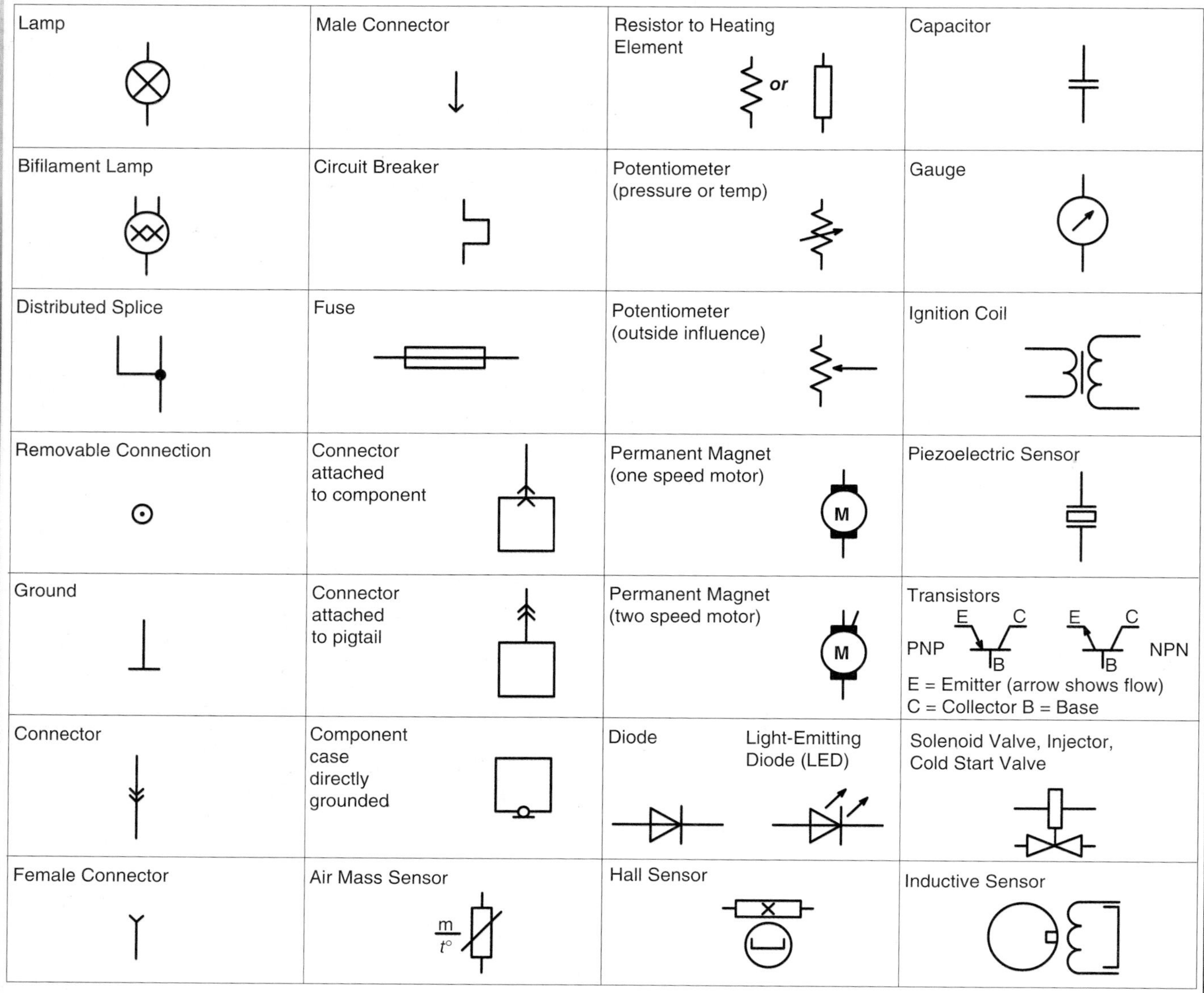

Lamp	Male Connector	Resistor to Heating Element	Capacitor
Bifilament Lamp	Circuit Breaker	Potentiometer (pressure or temp)	Gauge
Distributed Splice	Fuse	Potentiometer (outside influence)	Ignition Coil
Removable Connection	Connector attached to component	Permanent Magnet (one speed motor)	Piezoelectric Sensor
Ground	Connector attached to pigtail	Permanent Magnet (two speed motor)	Transistors PNP NPN E = Emitter (arrow shows flow) C = Collector B = Base
Connector	Component case directly grounded	Diode Light-Emitting Diode (LED)	Solenoid Valve, Injector, Cold Start Valve
Female Connector	Air Mass Sensor	Hall Sensor	Inductive Sensor

FIGURE 45-16 Some typical DIN symbols.

18. Central Relay Panel
19. Ground Path. In this example, the welded harness connection 135 connects to welded harness connection 81 to welded harness connection 42.

In addition to the above general symbols and codes, individual manufacturers will include specialized codes for:

- Harness naming codes
- System identifying codes—Indicates a system to which a circuit belongs. For example, trailer, driveline, or braking electrical circuits will have a code associated
- Splice naming standards
- Inline connector naming standards

Together these elements make up a complete and accurate wiring diagram. The key to reading wiring diagrams is in understanding the symbols. These symbols are standardized, allowing quick recognition of various components.

Power Distribution Flow

Since power flow begins at the top of a DIN diagram, a central power, fuse link, or relay panel is typically located at the top of the wiring diagram page. Circuit grounds, ground studs, and splices are located at the bottom of the diagram or the diagram will indicate the circuit ground on another page. All ground connections, whether they occur as a splice in a harness or the final ground source, are numbered and identified in the wiring diagram.

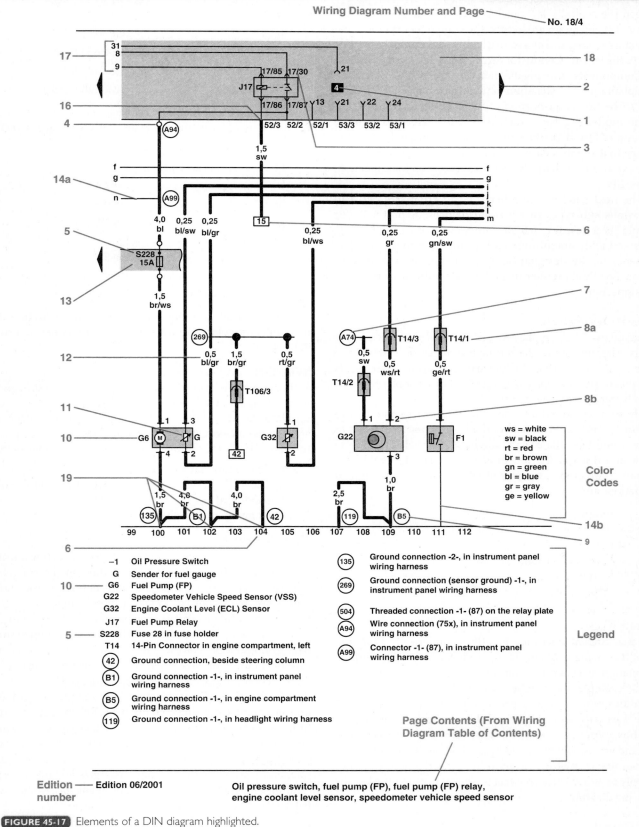

FIGURE 45-17 Elements of a DIN diagram highlighted.

Component and Device Codes

Between the central relay panel and the vehicle ground at the bottom of the diagram are located the component symbols and conductors. Components are marked with a component code listed in the legend. Conductors are marked with wire color and size. Components in wiring diagrams are given a DIN standardized alphanumeric designation for identification (DIN Standard 40717). The first letter portion of the code separates the component into basic groups. The letters A to Z are used with the exception of Q and O. The letter G, for example, will designate a device that supplies current that includes alternators, batteries, or even battery chargers. Switches receive an S designation; motors, M.

The next code is a number that differentiates between the various sub-types of electrical devices. A prefix R, for example, is a resistor, which could mean it's a glow-plug, heater element, potentiometer thermistor, and so on. The number 3 in the designation R3 will indicate sub-type of resistor. The final number in a DIN code indicates a terminal or designation.

Terminal Designation

DIN standard 72552 applies to the terminal designations for circuits. The purpose of the terminal designation system is to enable connection verification of wiring to various components when diagnosis and repair is necessary. For example, B+ indicates a battery positive terminal.

The number 30 indicates the circuit is a wire conductor to the battery positive terminal. So, the battery positive circuit to a relay would have the designation of 30. The relay would use code K and if it was the fourth of many relays it would have the symbol K4. Some examples of DIN standards for terminal designations are:

- 15 Ignition
- 30 Battery +
- 31 Ground
- 31b Switched ground
- 50 Starter control
- 53 Wiper motor +

Current Tracks

Individual current tracks are identified numerically along the base of the wiring diagram. These numbers are used to find the continuation of a conductor on another page or diagram.

For example, the number 221 inside a small box on one page indicates that the wire is continued on current track 221 on the next page with the same color and size of wire with a small box. Wires are conductors that carry current to components and are usually indicated by a solid line. A wire shown as a dashed line in a wiring diagram indicates that the wire does not apply to all vehicles. That fact is usually noted in the key for the wiring diagram.

Wire Colors

Knowing the standards for wiring colors makes the job of reading and interpreting schematics easier. Some colors and terminal designations for wiring are used across a number of standards, for example:

Red .... Battery +
Green .... Ignition (1)
Brown.. Ground (31)
Yellow....................................... Headlights (58)

In DIN diagrams, wire colors are shown as abbreviations of the German word for the color (DIN standard 47002) for example:

bl .... Blue
br .... Brown
ge .... Yellow
gn .... Green
ro .... Red
sw .... Black
li .... Violet
ws .... White

The International Organization for Standardization (ISO) uses different colors to designate circuit functions as listed in Table 45-2.

Wire Sizes on Diagrams

Wiring diagrams also indicate the wire gauge used (shown in mm^2), designating the cross-sectional area of the wire. Because standards exist for the maximum permissible voltage drop across a circuit, wire gauge is critical. If the voltage drop across the wire is too high, one or more of the following may occur:

- The circuit may overheat
- The load may not operate properly (due to low voltage condition)
- Components may be damaged

Complex Symbols

Often the internal schematic of the component is shown to allow the technician to follow current flow through the component. These internal symbols are a combination of several basic symbols. This allows the technician to take a more complex symbol and break it down into its smaller components. Even the most complex components are nothing more than a combination of smaller basic symbols. More complex components may contain complex control circuitry. In DIN schematics, this will be indicated with the symbol of a transistor in the component symbol.

A relay in a DIN schematic is an example of a combination of symbols in a single component. Relays require a signal from an outside source to activate. Relays share the component designator J with control units. The basic five-pin relay in **FIGURE 45-18** contains two separate components: a switch and a solenoid. The coil in the solenoid is energized with low current, creating a magnetic pull that closes or opens the switch. Terminal designation for a standard five-pin relay is:

- 30 Receives + battery current
- 87 Normally open contact to load
- 86 Control circuit receives a switched battery positive

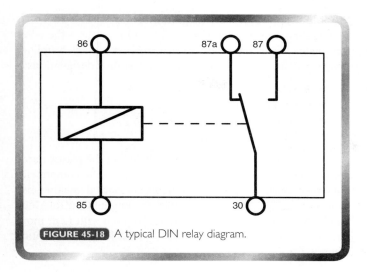

FIGURE 45-18 A typical DIN relay diagram.

- 85 Receives a switched ground to activate the solenoid winding in the relay
- 87a Normally closed contact to load

Note: All switches and relays are shown in a non-operated state.

Valley Forge Diagrams

Valley Forge (VF) wiring diagrams are used by many North American based OEMs. VF diagrams share many commonalities with DIN standards. For example, VF diagrams also show power flow from top to bottom and circuit operation from left to right, with inputs on the left and outputs on the right. VF diagrams use standards for wiring colors, circuit codes, and symbols.

A primary difference between the two types of schematic diagrams is that VF diagrams use SAE-type symbols. Conductor sizes, symbol representations, component, and terminal designations are different from DIN standards. Some of the common features shown in the Valley Forge diagram in **FIGURE 45-19** are:

1. Battery positive. Begins at top right of diagram, indicating a location to check for power.
2. Dotted line indicates the fuse location in a fuse block, but the dotted line means the component is not completely shown.
3. Thermal fuse. Circuit protection fuse size, circuit name, and location.
4. Wiring splice number indicates wires are joined. 121 indicated the splice number and "S" designate a splice.

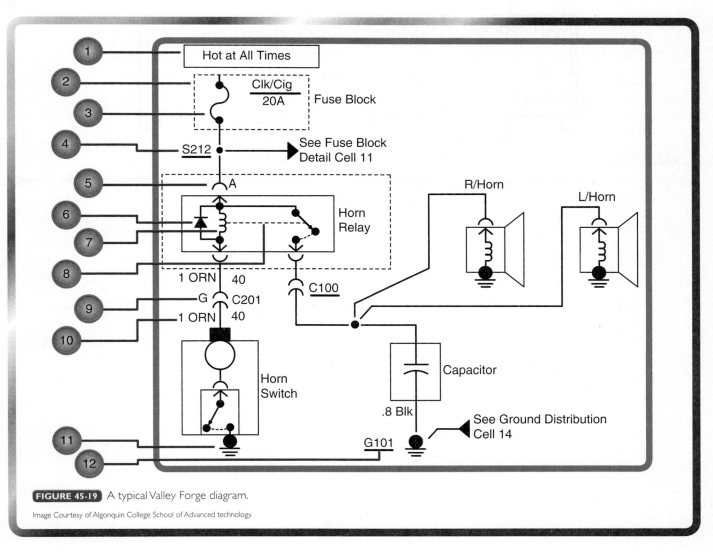

FIGURE 45-19 A typical Valley Forge diagram.

Image Courtesy of Algonquin College School of Advanced technology.

5. Terminal location designated A. It shows a connection point on the horn relay.

6. A diode for suppression of voltage spike produced when the magnetic field of the relays, coil collapses.

7. Control circuit of the relay.

8. Dotted line represents mechanical action.

9. G indicates the wire position in the connector. 201 is the circuit number. C designates it as a connector.

10. Identification of wire color, circuit number, and size. 1 indicates the wires, cross-sectional area is $1mm^2$. ORN indicates an orange wire. The wire circuit number is 40.

11. A ground symbol indicates the component itself is grounded.

12. G indicates a ground source. 101 indicates the number and location of the ground.

Module Connector Pin Assignments

Wiring diagrams tell the user at which pin numbers the wires terminate. Knowing where the wires terminate simplifies diagnosis. There are four main types of terminal designations:

- Push-on/multi-point connections
- Component/multi-point
- Central/relay panel
- Relay

Generally, pin assignments are labeled on the plastic hard-shell connector housing and/or the corresponding component. On larger connectors, pin assignments are labeled at either end of a row **FIGURE 45-20** . For example, the Engine Control Module (ECM) plug often has four to ten rows, each with 12 or more terminals. Each row will be marked on each end to facilitate diagnosis.

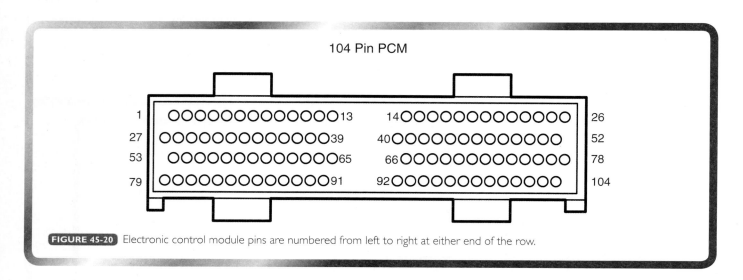

FIGURE 45-20 Electronic control module pins are numbered from left to right at either end of the row.

Wrap-Up

Ready for Review

▶ Wires and wiring harnesses carry the electrical power and signals through the vehicle to control virtually all of the systems on a vehicle.

▶ Electrical wires are used to conduct current around the vehicle. Wire can also be referred to as cable, although cable typically refers to large-diameter wire.

▶ Wiring harnesses are subject electrical noise or EMI noise. To prevent noise, some vehicles use shielded wiring harnesses.

▶ Shielded wiring harnesses can be twisted pair shielding, Mylar tape, or drain lines.

▶ Wire size relates to the correct operation of electrical circuits. Selecting a wire gauge that is too small for an application will have an adverse effect on the operation of the circuit. Selecting a wire gauge that is too large increases costs and the weight and size of wiring harnesses.

▶ The resistance of a wire affects how much current it can carry.

▶ There are two scales used to measure the sizes of wires: the metric wire gauge and the American wire gauge (AWG).

▶ Wire-coding systems are another useful feature of wiring to aid troubleshooting and service of electrical systems. Both colors and numbering systems designate wiring circuits, application, and even the routing of wires.

▶ SAE and ISO standards specify the dimensions, test methods, and requirements for single-core primary wire intended for use in road vehicle applications.

▶ Chassis wiring often uses numerical codes to identify which circuit the wire belongs to, where the wire is in the circuit, which harness it belongs in, and the wire gauge and color.

▶ Terminals installed to the wire ends provide low-resistance termination to wires. Terminals allow electricity to be conducted from the end of one wire to the end of another wire.

▶ There are two main types of terminals used in harness connectors—pull-to-seat and push-to-seat terminals. Connector housings have male and female sides and are usually shaped so that they can be connected in only one way.

▶ Wires are generally trouble free and long lasting, and any issues with wiring are more likely to be with the terminals than with the wires themselves.

▶ One of the greatest enemies to wiring is water. The tendency of water to "wick" inside insulation is what makes it so destructive.

▶ When electrical wire is joined to other wires or connected to a terminal, the insulation needs to be removed using wire-stripping tools.

▶ Solderless terminals are quick to install and effective at conducting electricity across joints that are designed to be disconnected. Connectors can also be soldered.

▶ Wiring diagrams use abstract graphical symbols to represent electrical circuits and their connection or relationship to other components in the system. They are essentially a map of all of the electrical components and their connections.

▶ Three main types of wiring diagrams are map, isometric, and schematic diagrams.

▶ The two most common types of schematic diagrams are the Deutsche Institute Norm (DIN) and the Valley Forge (VF).

▶ Schematic wiring diagrams show power supply, load, ground, conductors (wires), and circuit protection.

▶ Schematic wiring diagrams show power flow from top to bottom and circuit operation from left to right, with inputs on the left and outputs on the right.

▶ Reading a wiring diagram is like reading a road map. There are a lot of interconnected circuits, wires, and components to decipher.

Vocabulary Builder

current track Another name for a DIN diagram.

Deutsch connector A compact, environmentally sealed electrical connector that uses solid, round metal pins and hollow female sockets.

Deutsche Institute Norm (DIN) diagram A schematic wiring diagram on which symbols, terminal connection numbers, line symbols, and operational status of items such as switches and relays are defined by a DIN standard. Also called *current track*.

isometric diagram A wiring diagram used to locate a component within a system and which shows the outline of a vehicle or piece of equipment where the component can be found.

map (pictorial) diagram A wiring diagram that shows the entire vehicle wiring circuit using pictorial symbols.

Metri-Pack connector A pull-to-seat electrical connector with flat terminals instead of round.

parallel wiring A type of custom-made wiring harness that encloses multiple conductors into a single vinyl insulator covering.

pull-to-seat terminal A terminal installed by inserting the wire through the connector cavity, crimping on a terminal, and then pulling the terminal back into the connector cavity to seat it.

push-to-seat terminal A terminal inserted into the back of the connector cavity to seat after the terminal is crimped to the wire.

SAE J1128 standard A standard that specifies the dimensions, test methods, and requirements for single-core primary wire intended for use in road vehicle applications.

schematic diagram A line drawing that explains how a system works by using symbols and connecting lines.

Valley Forge (VF) diagram A schematic wiring diagram that uses SAE-type symbols.

water wicking The movement of water through wiring due to its adhesive and cohesive properties.

Weather-Pack connector An environmentally sealed push-to-seat electrical connection system supplied in one- to six-pin configurations.

Review Questions

1. A(n) _____ is a wiring diagram that shows the entire vehicle wiring circuit using pictorial symbols.
   a. map diagram
   b. isometric diagram
   c. schematic diagram
   d. valley forge diagram

2. A(n) _____ is a line drawing that explains how a system works by using symbols and connecting lines.
   a. schematic diagram
   b. map diagram
   c. isometric diagram
   d. valley forge diagram

3. Longer circuits and higher amperage require a larger _____ of wire.
   a. area
   b. bundle
   c. diameter
   d. volume

4. In most wiring diagrams, metric-sized wire is specified in _____ rather than metric gauge diameter.
   a. centimeters
   b. millimeters
   c. meters
   d. inches

5. The simplest wiring connector is a _____ that uses small studs to which ring or spade type connectors are attached and secured with machine screws.
   a. push-to-seat
   b. terminal block
   c. connector seal
   d. lock ramp

6. A _____ terminal is inserted into the back of the connector cavity to seat after the terminal is crimped to the wire.
   a. terminal block
   b. lock arm
   c. push-to-seat
   d. connector seal

7. Once inside a wire, _____ will move into the smallest openings and spaces through adhesion.
   a. air
   b. dirt
   c. electricity
   d. water

8. If a connection is not _____, wiring can move within the connection, leading to arcing and resistance, which ultimately causes connection failure.
   a. glued
   b. stamped
   c. taped
   d. soldered

9. A(n) _____ diagram may start on one page and continue onto several more, mapping out individual circuits with a separate diagram.
   a. analog
   b. digital
   c. linear
   d. modular

10. Pin _____ are generally labeled on the plastic hard-shell connector housing and/or the corresponding component.
    a. pictures
    b. indexes
    c. terminals
    d. assignments

ASE-Type Questions

1. Technician A says smaller wires become more resistant and heat up as amperage increases. Technician B says both wire classification systems measure both the sire and the insulator when determining the total diameter of a wire. Who is correct?
   a. Technician A
   b. Technician B
   c. Both Technician A and Technician B
   d. Neither Technician A nor Technician B

2. Technician A says multi-stranded wire is better at conducting higher amounts of current with less resistance. Technician B says multi-stranded wire is better at conducting higher amounts of current with less resistance is because it has more surface area to conduct electron flow. Who is correct?
   a. Technician A
   b. Technician B
   c. Both Technician A and Technician B
   d. Neither Technician A nor Technician B

3. Technician A says connector housings are shaped so they almost always can be connected in more than one way. Technician B says connector housings have male and female sides and are usually shaped so they can be connected in only one way. Who is correct?
   a. Technician A
   b. Technician B
   c. Both Technician A and Technician B
   d. Neither Technician A nor Technician B

4. Technician A says water has adhesive properties. Technician B says water is one of wiring's greatest enemies. Who is correct?
   a. Technician A
   b. Technician B
   c. Both Technician A and Technician B
   d. Neither Technician A nor Technician B

5. Technician A says color codes are used to designate wire gauge to use for soldered connectors. Technician B says color codes are used to designate wire gauge to use for shrink crimp connectors. Who is correct?
   a. Technician A
   b. Technician B
   c. Both Technician A and Technician B
   d. Neither Technician A nor Technician B

6. Technician A says schematic diagrams are used to show internal circuitry. Technician B says arrangement of the components and circuit paths on a current track diagram usually correspond to their physical locations on the vehicle. Who is correct?
   a. Technician A
   b. Technician B
   c. Both Technician A and Technician B
   d. Neither Technician A nor Technician B

7. Technician A says in a DIN program, a wire identified using the abbreviation "ge" would be green in color. Technician B says in a DIN program, the wire identified using the abbreviation "ge" would be black in color. Who is correct?
   a. Technician A
   b. Technician B
   c. Both Technician A and Technician B
   d. Neither Technician A nor Technician B

8. Technician A says the Deutsche Institute Norm (DIN) diagram shows the power source at the top of the page and the ground points at the bottom. Technician B says the pictorial diagram shows the power source at the top of the page and the ground points at the bottom. Who is correct?
   a. Technician A
   b. Technician B
   c. Both Technician A and Technician B
   d. Neither Technician A nor Technician B

9. Technician A says wires should be joined together by bending each into a double-J bend, then twisting to form a Brummel splice. Technician B says wires should be joined together by bending each into a double-J bend, then twisting to form a Western Union splice. Who is correct?
   a. Technician A
   b. Technician B
   c. Both Technician A and Technician B
   d. Neither Technician A nor Technician B

10. Technician A says a TXL wire is an extra thin primary wire that has a cross-linked polyethylene jacket. Technician B says the polyethylene jacket is resistant to oil, grease, gasoline, and acids. Who is correct?
   a. Technician A
   b. Technician B
   c. Both Technician A and Technician B
   d. Neither Technician A nor Technician B

CHAPTER 46

Hybrid Drive Systems and Series-Type Hybrid Drives

NATEF Tasks

There are no NATEF tasks for this chapter.

Knowledge Objectives

After reading this chapter, you will be able to:

1. Identify the applications and advantages and benefits of heavy-duty hybrid propulsion systems. (pp 1271–1272)
2. Explain the operating principles and differences between hybrid drive power train systems. (pp 1272–1281)
3. Explain operating principles of hydraulic launch assist (HLA) hybrid drive systems. (pp 1274–1275)
4. Identify and explain hazards of high voltage electrical circuits. (pp 1275–1278)
5. Explain operating principles of series electric propulsion drives. (pp 1278–1279)
6. Describe the construction and operation of the BAE HybriDrive propulsion system. (pp 1278–1279)
7. Describe the operating principles of a series hybrid drive train. (pp 1278–1288)
8. Identify and explain the function of the HybriDrive propulsion system components. (pp 1280–1288)
9. Outline service precautions to use when servicing the HybriDrive propulsion system. (pp 1285–1288)
10. Outline service precautions to use when servicing hybrid drive systems. (pp 1285–1288)
11. Outline basic service and maintenance procedures for the HybriDrive propulsion systems. (pp 1287–1288)

Skills Objectives

There are no skills objectives for this chapter.

▶ Introduction

Understanding the word "hybrid" as meaning mixed or combined in nature helps explain the concept of a **hybrid electric vehicle (HEV)**—a type of vehicle that combines an internal combustion engine with an electric propulsion system into a new or hybrid powertrain configuration. Hybrids are fundamentally different from **electric vehicles**, which use only electric motors to move a vehicle. A variety of hybrid drive vehicle configurations are used in commercial vehicles. In essence, hybrid propulsion systems can use any type of engine—gasoline, natural gas, diesel, turbine, or reciprocating—assisted by an electric motor to accelerate the vehicle. In all cases, the engine will drive an electric generator used to charge batteries and help power the electric motor.

▶ Fundamentals of Hybrid Drives

Hybrid electric vehicles are now employed in many commercial vehicle applications due to their capability to reduce simultaneously both fuel consumption and emissions produced from burning fuel. Estimates suggest that hybrids improve fuel consumption by between 20% and 60%, though real-world observed consumption in a number of applications is substantially less than those estimates suggest. Urban transit buses, intercity pick-up, delivery, and utility vehicles are the most common applications in which hybrid drive systems have the potential to excel. Even the military has seized on the hybrid advantage for situations where fuel economy is mission critical—for example, when supply lines are stretched, or when stealth is required.

Vehicles operating in urban driving conditions are best suited to hybrid use, as much of the energy derived from burning fuel is lost through idling and braking. Studies have shown that approximately 65% of energy used to accelerate a city bus is quickly dissipated into heat by frequent braking **FIGURE 46-1**. Garbage trucks lose 59%, while delivery vehicles picking up and moving small parcels lose half the energy produced by the engine the same way. Because hybrid drive systems are designed to produce electricity when braking, generators connected to the wheels will assist braking and store this energy in on-board batteries. In turn, the batteries will supply electric current to the traction motors for acceleration. (A **traction motor** is an electric motor that provides propulsion to a vehicle.) This feature, by which generators recover energy during braking, is called **regenerative braking**.

The inefficiencies of conventional powertrain systems are not limited to losses from idling and braking. Another inefficiency stems from idle time. Engine idle time is in the range of 50% for many vehicles operating in urban driving conditions. The stop-start feature used by some hybrid drives shuts off the engine when not in use. Also, engines required to accelerate over a wide engine rpm operating range during stop-and-go operation do not use fuel efficiently. Because hybrid drive systems can limit the rate of engine rpm change, they enable the engine to operate at its most fuel efficient, lowest emission, high torque-speed range, using less fuel while producing fewer emissions.

Other hybrid drive train advantages include:

- Increased brake life and reduced need for brake service using regenerative braking
- Extended engine life due to more favorable operating conditions
- Electric drive motors provide more torque for faster acceleration added pulling power
- Smoother acceleration

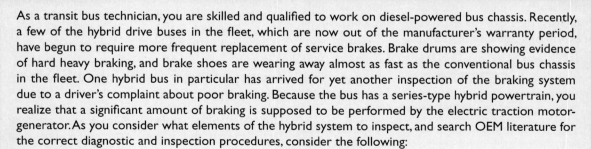

▶ You Are the Technician

As a transit bus technician, you are skilled and qualified to work on diesel-powered bus chassis. Recently, a few of the hybrid drive buses in the fleet, which are now out of the manufacturer's warranty period, have begun to require more frequent replacement of service brakes. Brake drums are showing evidence of hard heavy braking, and brake shoes are wearing away almost as fast as the conventional bus chassis in the fleet. One hybrid bus in particular has arrived for yet another inspection of the braking system due to a driver's complaint about poor braking. Because the bus has a series-type hybrid powertrain, you realize that a significant amount of braking is supposed to be performed by the electric traction motor-generator. As you consider what elements of the hybrid system to inspect, and search OEM literature for the correct diagnostic and inspection procedures, consider the following:

1. Is there some method to adjust the amount of braking performed by the regenerative braking feature of the series hybrid?
2. List some potential problems with the hybrid powertrain that may contribute to more work being performed by the regular service brakes and not the regenerative braking system.
3. During a road test of the braking system, is there some feature that you or the driver could easily see which will verify the regenerative braking is taking place?

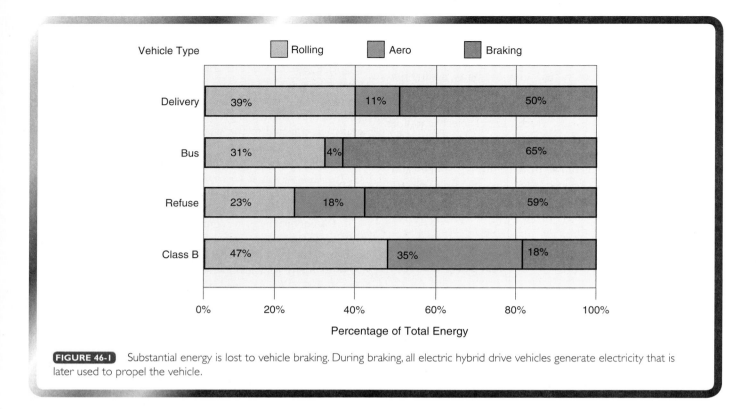

FIGURE 46-1 Substantial energy is lost to vehicle braking. During braking, all electric hybrid drive vehicles generate electricity that is later used to propel the vehicle.

- Quieter vehicle operation
- Compatible with all fuels and engine designs so no requirement to change fueling infrastructure
- All engine emissions are reduced and less exhaust after-treatment system service is required
- Minimum driver training required

▶ Types of Hybrid Drives

Even though all electric hybrid systems are configured with engines, electric motors, and batteries to propel the vehicle, not all hybrid systems are alike. Different configurations offer unique advantages. The following are the most common configurations of hybrid drive systems in use:

1. **Series drive**—Only an electric traction motor supplies torque to propel the vehicle **FIGURE 46-2**. The engine drives a generator used to charge a bank of batteries and supply current to the electric motor (e.g., BAE HybriDrive System).

2. **Parallel drive**—Both the engine and electric motor work together, blending motor and engine torque to propel the vehicle **FIGURE 46-3**.

3. **Series-parallel drive**—A more complex system enabling an engine only, an electric motor only, and a combined engine-motor operation **FIGURE 46-4** Also called a power-split configuration, the engine and motor operation is optimized for driving conditions (e.g., Arvin Meritor, Allison EV).

4. **Plug-in hybrid electric vehicle (PHEV)**—Refers to any type of hybrid electric vehicle containing a battery storage system that uses an external source to recharge the battery when the

vehicle is not in operation. These vehicles also have an ability to drive or operate for an extended period in all-electric mode, lending the alternate name of extended-range electric vehicles.

One popular type of PHEV is the municipal utility truck. These trucks typically travel shorter distances than others but are operated in residential neighborhoods continuously for extended periods, running the lift boom, powering lights, tools, and other accessories **FIGURE 46-5**.Ordinarily, the engine is required to operate hydraulic pumps or generators. Using stored battery energy allows the vehicle to operate at a job site without engine idling, which reduces emissions from idling and exposure to diesel exhaust. Vehicle operating costs are lowered by reducing fuel consumption and engine wear. In drive mode, low-speed driving conditions are ideally suited to using the electric traction motors.

Comparing Parallel and Series Systems

Compared to a parallel system, a series system requires a larger electric motor and battery pack, but a smaller internal combustion engine. A series hybrid does not require a transmission because the electric motor is capable of a wide range of speeds. The series drive system works best in frequent stop-and-go service because the electrically-driven propulsion system has high torque at low speeds, providing smooth, fast acceleration regardless of the grade. The efficiency differences between a series hybrid and conventional bus decline as average vehicle speed increases and the number of stops decreases. Parallel-drive systems are better suited to higher speeds with less stop-and-go operation.

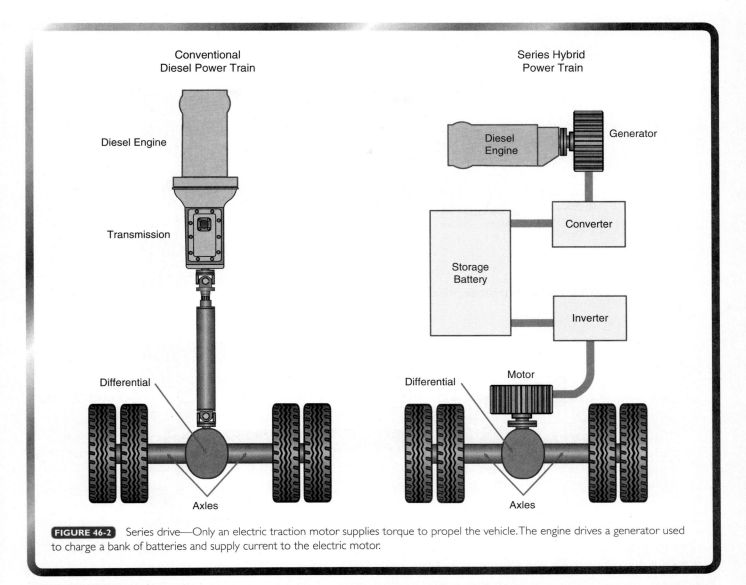

FIGURE 46-2 Series drive—Only an electric traction motor supplies torque to propel the vehicle. The engine drives a generator used to charge a bank of batteries and supply current to the electric motor.

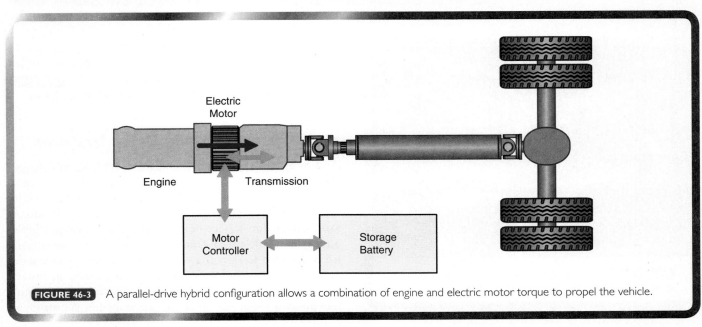

FIGURE 46-3 A parallel-drive hybrid configuration allows a combination of engine and electric motor torque to propel the vehicle.

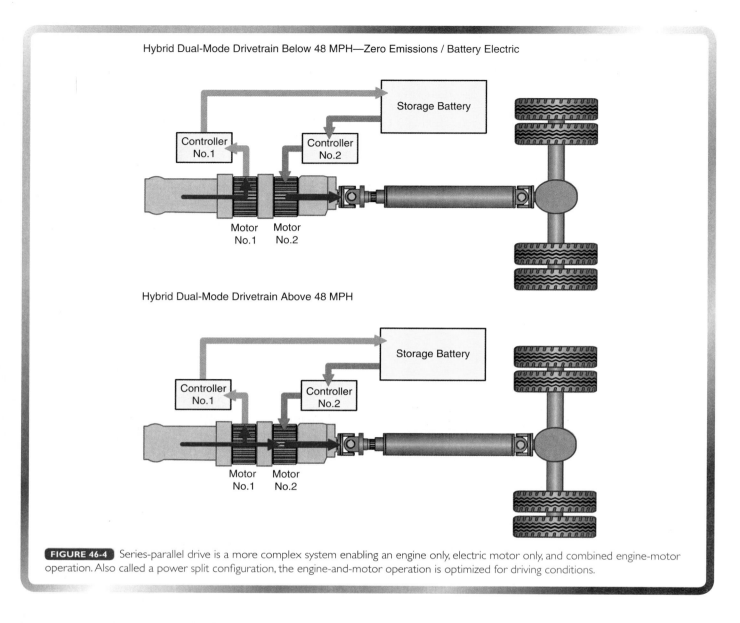

FIGURE 46-4 Series-parallel drive is a more complex system enabling an engine only, electric motor only, and combined engine-motor operation. Also called a power split configuration, the engine-and-motor operation is optimized for driving conditions.

FIGURE 46-5 Plug-in hybrid vehicles, such as this utility truck, can operate hydraulic power equipment using battery power only.

(Parallel-drive systems will be covered in the Allison EV Drive Hybrid Systems chapter.) One disadvantage of both systems is a 50–70% higher initial purchase cost. **TABLE 46-1** compares series, parallel, and series-parallel hybrid drives.

Non-Electric Hybrid Drive Systems

An alternative to electric hybrid drives is the **hydraulic launch assist (HLA)** system. The concept of HLA uses hydraulic regenerative braking to capture braking energy and help launch the vehicle during acceleration. In an HLA system, application of standard friction service brakes is prevented until just before a complete vehicle stop. During braking, friction components normally used to slow the vehicle, such as drums and shoes, are replaced by a hydraulic pump. Braking power is, instead, absorbed by the force used to pump hydraulic fluid from a low-pressure reservoir to a gas accumulator. Nitrogen gas

TABLE 46-1: Comparison of Series, Parallel, and Series-Parallel Hybrid Drives

	Driving Performance		Fuel Economy Improvement			
	Acceleration	Continuous High Output	Idling Stop	Energy Recovery	High-Efficiency Operation Control	Total Efficiency
Series	Best	Poor	Best	Best	Good	Good
Parallel	Best	Best	Good	Best	Best	Good
Series-parallel	Poor	Poor	Poor	Poor	Best	Best

● Best ◖ Good ○ Poor

inside the accumulator is compressed by the fluid to 5000 psi (34,470 kPa), which effectively absorbs the vehicle's kinetic energy and turns it into stored potential energy FIGURE 46-6. This hydraulic-over-gas capture performed by the HLA system is reported to convert close to 70% of normally lost braking energy and, at the same time, cut brake wear 50%. When it is time to accelerate the vehicle again, fluid in the high-pressure accumulator is metered to the combined driveline pump and motor where the device operates as a motor. The HLA hydraulic motor accelerates the vehicle by transmitting torque to the driveshaft.

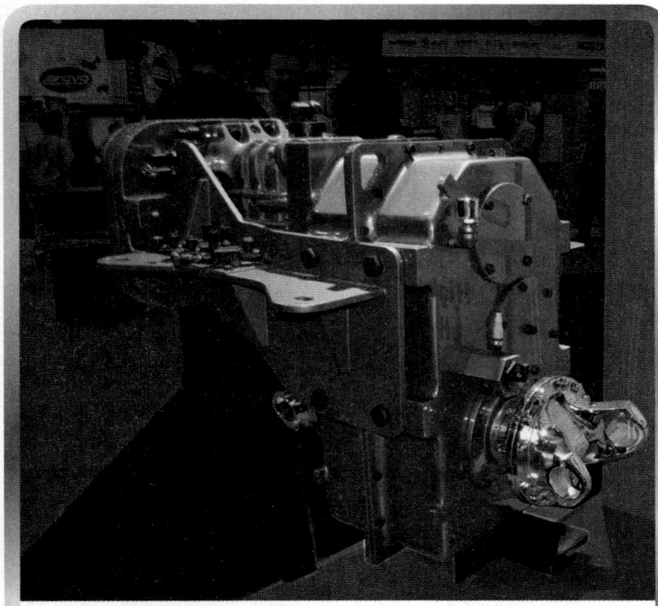

FIGURE 46-6 Eaton's hydraulic launch assist (HLA) pressurizes hydraulic fluid to capture braking energy. Pressurized fluid is used to power a hydraulic motor and launch the vehicle. The primary benefits of HLA are faster acceleration and reduced emissions and fuel consumption.

HLA systems are a parallel hybrid system, allowing the engine to drive the vehicle when the HLA is off-line. Improvements to fuel economy are estimated between 15% to 30% with corresponding reductions in emissions. HLA has two modes of operation: economy and performance. In economy mode, energy stored in the accumulator during braking is used only to initially accelerate the vehicle. Once emptied, the engine will begin to propel the vehicle. In performance mode, both the engine and accumulator will provide driveline torque until the accumulator empties. Performance mode provides more torque for 2% quicker acceleration but does not provide the same reduction to fuel consumption as economy mode. TABLE 46-2 lists some common specifications of an HLA system.

► Hybrid Drive Electrical Safety

Hybrid drive system components use lethal high-voltage power devices operating up to 900 volts and contain energy storage systems over 700 volts DC. Although systems are designed to provide safe propulsion energy under normal conditions, during accidents or servicing personal injury, death, and expensive equipment damage can occur. Unique service procedures are outlined in mandatory training courses provided by the OEM

TABLE 46-2: Specifications of a Typical HLA System

Weight of HLA system	1250 lb (568 kg)
Max pressure	5000 psi (2272 kg)
Total system oil volume	21 gallons (80 l)
Torque	2550 ft-lb (3457 Nm)
Active speed range	Up to 25 mph (40 kph)
Minimum wheelbase, single	191" (4.85 m)
Minimum wheelbase, tandem	215" (5.46 m)

and invigilated by local electrical authorities. Special tools must be used in addition to safety clothing (PPE) to ensure that the technician is kept as safe as possible during service procedures **FIGURE 46-7**.

Effects of Electric Shock

Shock hazard to the human body is a function of the type of current (AC or DC), voltage, amperage, and skin resistance. Generally, ten times the amount of DC current has the same effect as AC current. Under the right conditions, 5 milliamps of AC current can be dangerous, and 500 milliamps lethal, as electricity can affect the contraction of heart muscles and muscles controlling breathing. A level of 60Hz AC is especially lethal because it closely corresponds to heart rate and can cause the heart to beat irregularly. Higher frequency AC current conducts with less resistance than low-frequency current. At high levels, electricity generates enough heat to simply destroy nerve muscle and blood tissue. The effects of electricity can be experienced as:

- Tingling sensation (AC current)
- Burning sensation
- Muscle contractions
- Ventricular fibrillation (irregular heart rhythm)
- Cardiac arrest (heart stoppage)
- Pulmonary arrest (stopped breathing)

Reactions to electricity can have serious consequences, as a person may jump or fall in response to even a light shock. High-amperage shorts can produce blinding light, fires, and explosions. **TABLE 46-3** describes effects of different levels of electric current. **TABLE 46-4** shows the effects of electricity on different skin conditions.

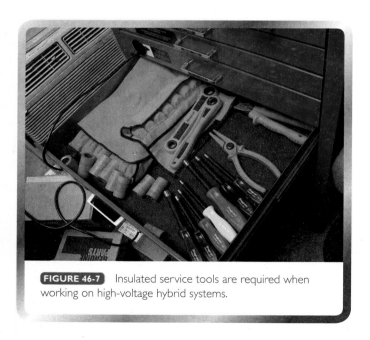

FIGURE 46-7 Insulated service tools are required when working on high-voltage hybrid systems.

TABLE 46-3: Effects of Various Levels of AC and DC Current

Effect	AC	DC
Sensation	1 milliamp at 60 Hz	5 millamps
Muscle contraction	60 milliamps at 60 Hz	300–500 milliamps
Let-go limit	10.5 milliamps	15–88 milliamps
Minimal hazard with worst case	60 V peak AC (Not RMS)	42 V
Non-lethal under most conditions	60–150 V	60–150 V

TABLE 46-4: Electrical Resistance of Skin Under Various Conditions

Skin Condition	Resistance
Open skin (wound)	500–1000 ohms
Wet skin	10,000–20,000 ohms
High ionic content wet skin (i.e., sweating)	5000–10,000 ohms
Under high voltage conditions	500 ohms

High Voltage Disconnect

Disconnecting and discharging any residual current in EV components is imperative before performing any service work. Always assume the electrical system is live, even after disconnecting the battery power supply and testing for the presence of current with an approved electrical meter. Appropriate personal protective equipment safety is necessary; glasses, footwear, and gloves should always be worn, and all jewelry removed. A long-sleeved, heavy denim shirt offers protection from inadvertent upper body electrical contact. When the ignition key is switched off, most hybrid systems use a set of relays to disconnect power from the rest of the system components. A master disconnect switch is used in bus applications and should also be switched off, effectively disconnecting the vehicle batteries from the 12/24-volt electrical system. Specialized electrical connectors in the battery storage system and power cables are provided to add another level of redundancy to power disconnect procedures. Inverters and propulsion control modules should usually be disconnected, and a waiting period of several minutes is needed to allow capacitors to discharge. Additional power disconnect verification procedures are recommended by OE system manufacturers, which should be followed. For example, a lock-out device clamped on the master disconnect switch can prevent accidental energizing of high-voltage circuits when the vehicle is being serviced **FIGURE 46-8** .

When working on the battery storage system, two persons are required in case one person is harmed or becomes incapable of removing themselves from a live electrical circuit. Scaffolding, as shown in **FIGURE 46-9** , is a must when working around or servicing overhead battery systems. In addition, non-conductive body hooks and Class D fire extinguishers are required at scaffolding level.

> ### ▶ TECHNICIAN TIP
>
> Floating ground refers to the electrical ground separation between the chassis and the high-voltage electrical system. Dedicated circuits are used for the high-voltage system current, which does not share a ground path with the low-voltage system. An electrical system isolation monitor continuously checks to ensure that a high value of electrical resistance insulates the high from the low-voltage electrical system. Any time the potential for stray currents is detected, fault codes are logged, warning lights may be illuminated, and the vehicle may even shut-down.

FIGURE 46-9 The use of purpose-built stairs and a buddy system is critical to safety when serving roof-mounted equipment tubs and batteries.

Insulated Gloves

One of the first lines of defense when it comes to preventing contact with energized electrical components and/or electrical power cables are insulating gloves, commonly known as lineman gloves **FIGURE 46-10** . OSHA requires the use of rubber insulated gloves for those persons working on or near energized circuits and/or other electrical sources that are considered either high or low-voltage applications. Lineman gloves are categorized by the amount of AC and DC voltage they have been proof-tested to in addition to the

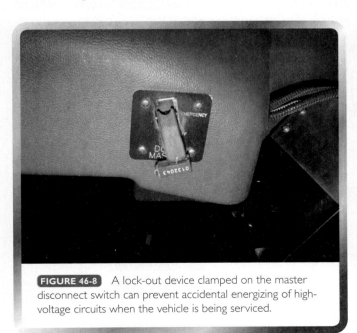

FIGURE 46-8 A lock-out device clamped on the master disconnect switch can prevent accidental energizing of high-voltage circuits when the vehicle is being serviced.

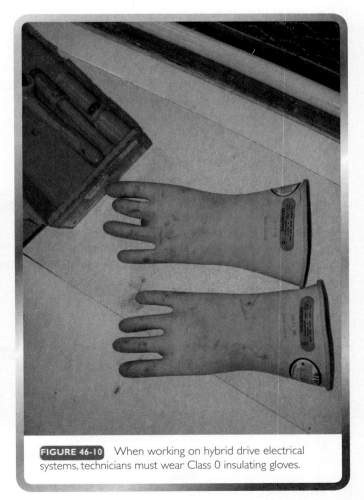

FIGURE 46-10 When working on hybrid drive electrical systems, technicians must wear Class 0 insulating gloves.

designated maximum-use voltage. The voltage protection is referenced as a Class rating, which is broken down starting with Class 00 having the lowest voltage protection up to Class 4 with highest protection. Class 0 lineman gloves recommended for use on high voltage hybrid circuits offer protection from 1500 to 5000 volts.

Routine Inspection

Routine periodic inspection of a hybrid drive system typically involves checking for the following:

- Loose bolts, mounting components, and grounding straps
- Loose, worn, or frayed electrical components
- Improperly routed or frayed vehicle electrical harnesses
- Damaged or loose hoses
- Fluid leaks
- Damaged, dented, or out-of-phase drive shafts
- Checking for fault codes or warning light illumination

Technicians must know the correct jacking and hoisting procedures prior to servicing the vehicle found in the OEM service manual.

Collisions

In the event of a collision:

- Turn off ignition switch, master, and battery isolator switches
- Inspect all EV propulsion system components for external damage
- Inspect all cooling lines and connections for leaks
- Place the vehicle in the service facility for a full checkout
- Emergency responders are recommended to use a Class 0 – 1000-volt cable cutter with a 2" (5 cm) opening size to cut power from the battery storage to the vehicle system

- Type D, smothering type fire extinguisher is recommended for fires

Lithium-ion and lead–acid batteries, if ruptured, will both produce flammable hydrogen gas. Corrosive battery acid will leak from lead–acid batteries. The chemical composition of the nickel-metal hydride battery electrolyte can cause severe burns to skin if it comes into contact with the body. It is essential that precautions are always followed if the hybrid vehicle has been in a collision because of the dangers associated with leaking batteries.

▶ Series-Type Hybrid Drive Systems

BAE HybriDrive Propulsion Systems

BAE is an aerospace and defense technology company and is also one of the leading developers and manufacturers of hybrid-drive propulsion systems for the military and heavy-duty commercial vehicles. Since 1996, BAE Systems has collaborated with Daimler in hybrid electric propulsion systems for transit buses. The company's HybriDrive series-type propulsion system is currently the best-selling heavy hybrid drive and is in service in more than 4000 transit buses in cities around the world.

HybriDrive systems are also available in parallel-type drive configurations. In 2012, BAE and Caterpillar collaborated to integrate the Caterpillar CX model transmissions into its HybriDrive parallel propulsion system. While the series system does not use a transmission, the HybriDrive parallel system is based on a single, electric, machine interfacing between the truck's engine and the CX Series transmission. This chapter focuses on the HybriDrive series system shown in **FIGURE 46-11**, as it represents one of the most common hybrid propulsion systems and also the first system, introduced back in 1998. **TABLE 46-5** compares different models of hybrid drive systems.

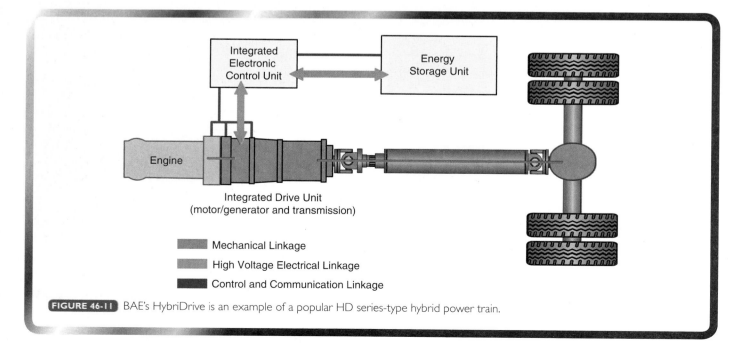

FIGURE 46-11 BAE's HybriDrive is an example of a popular HD series-type hybrid power train.

TABLE 46-5: Comparison of Different Types of Hybrid Drive Systems

	BAE Systems (HybriDrive Propulsion System)	Allison EP 40	Allison EP 50
Power	• 250 hp continuous (320 hp [239 kW] peak) • Torque 2700 lb-ft (3660 Nm) at 0 rpm	• Continuous: 280 hp (209 kW) • Rated input torque: 910 lb-ft (1235 Nm) • Rated input speed: 2300 rpm • Acceleration power: 350 hp (261 kW)	• Continuous: 330 hp (298 kW) peak • Torque: 1050 lb-ft (1423 Nm) • Rated input speed: 2300 rpm • Acceleration power: 400 hp (298 kW)
Engine	• Orion VI Transit Bus • Gen 1 Cummins B Series • Gen 2 Cummins C Series		
Electric drive motor	• Three-phase alternating current (AC) induction type	• Three-phase asynchronous induction motor/generator	• Three-phase asynchronous induction motor/generator
Motor horsepower	• 160 hp continuous using 436 VAC at 2300 rpm • 450 ft-lbs. (610 Nm) of torque at 0 rpm • 4.69:1 gear reduction produces 2100 ft-lbs (2847 Nm) of torque at 0 rpm at the output shaft yoke	• Input continuous: 280 hp (209 kW) • Rated input torque: 910 lb-ft (1235 Nm) • Rated input speed: 2300 rpm • Acceleration power: 350 hp (261 kW)	• Input continuous: 330 hp (246 kW) • Rated input torque: 1050 lb-ft (1420 Nm) • Rated input speed: 2300 rpm • Acceleration power: 400 hp (298 kW)
Generator type	• Permanent magnet	• Three-phase asynchronous induction motor/generator	• Three-phase asynchronous induction motor/generator
Energy storage type	• Sealed lead–acid (Gen 1) • Lithium-ion (Gen 2)	• Nickel-metal hydride (NiMH)	• Nickel-metal hydride (NiMH)
Voltage	• 520–700 VDC • 436 VAC continuous	• 600 VAC ESS Voltage Range: 432–780 VDC DPIM Voltage Range: 350 VDC	• 600 VAC ESS Voltage Range: 432–780 VDC DPIM Voltage Range: 350 VDC

VAC = Volts of AC current **VDC** = Volts of DC current

HybriDrive series type is available as different levels or "Generation" of hybrid systems. The differences between the systems are not obvious but, according to the manufacturer, a number of subsystems on the higher level versions have been improved including the engine, generator, propulsion control, and cooling and packaging FIGURE 46-12. The most significant difference in the systems is the energy storage components; lead-acid batteries were used in the original release of the systems, but now lithium-ion batteries are used instead on new systems.

The BAE HybriDrive series system is designed for applications requiring low average vehicle speeds and frequent stop-and-start operation. The HybriDrive parallel system is designed for use on vehicles with operating cycles having faster operating speeds and fewer frequent stops such as medium duty trucks.

HybriDrive Series Propulsion System Overview

Many buses using the BAE HybriDrive systems are coupled to a Cummins diesel engine to obtain the highest fuel efficiency with the lowest emissions. In such installations, the engine operates at a fixed speed.

Connected directly to the engine is an electrical generator used to produce electrical power for the drive motor and to charge the batteries. A single electric drive motor coupled to the driveline has two functions. As with any series hybrid-drive system, the first function is to provide all the power necessary to propel the vehicle. The second function is to create regenerative braking, which enables the generator to convert braking force into electrical current rather than to lose energy to heat through traditional friction brakes.

On-board battery banks supply electrical current needed during acceleration and store current recovered from regenerative braking. Specialized computer software operates the propulsion control system module, which electronically controls the complete system by processing input data and sending electrical output signals to all system actuators.

The batteries compose the largest part of the electrical storage subsystem. A battery monitoring subsystem maintains the charge of each individual battery and performs battery diagnostic checks.

Hybrid vehicles produce significantly lower emissions than conventional diesel-powered buses, as the energy storage system supplies power during start-up and acceleration. At these times, the diesel engine is idling.

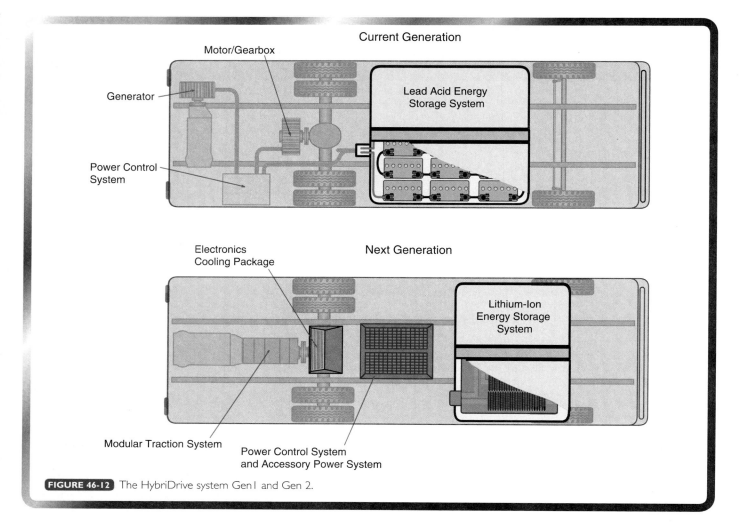

FIGURE 46-12 The HybriDrive system Gen1 and Gen 2.

► Major System Components of Series HybriDrive

HybriDrive includes the following major system components **FIGURE 46-13**

- Propulsion Control System (PCS)
- AC Traction Generator (ACTG)
- AC Traction Motor (ACTM)
- Energy Storage System (ESS) and fresh air cooling system for the ESS required for operation above 100°F (38°C)

The systems also include battery monitoring systems and current inverters, as well as diagnostic service software supplied by the manufacturer (BAE) called the Intuitive Diagnostic system (IDS). Also available is an optional data logging module that is used to record all system information available on the network data bus.

Propulsion Control System Module

The **propulsion control system (PCS) module** is the system element controlling the operation of the entire HybriDrive System **FIGURE 46-14**. It is a microprocessor based device that supplies electrical output signals based on input data collected from a vehicle's sensors, such as the accelerator position sensor, brake switch, gear range selector, and so on. **FIGURE 46-15** shows a schematic of the HybriDrive propulsion system.

Three low-voltage connectors, each with 40-pins, form the input-output interface of the PCS with the system. Critical sensor input data is also collected from the electrical generator (ACTG), the transmission (ACTM), and the energy storage system (ESS) modules and enters the PCS through the connectors.

The ignition switch is also a critical input signal that initiates system operation by "waking-up" the PCS, which, in turn, activates other system components. Software inside the PCS containing control algorithms uses sensor data to regulate engine speed and the supply of electrical current to the inverters, which determines the output torque of the traction motor.

Even the batteries' state of charge is monitored and controlled by the PCS module. Diagnostic software continuously checks the complete system operation and sends fault information as well as system status to the diagnostic connector, where it can interface with the **Intuitive Diagnostic System (IDS)** software used by service technicians.

Fault codes are retained in the PCS non-volatile memory (NVM), which means that they can only be erased using the IDS service tool. System warning lights are also outputs of the

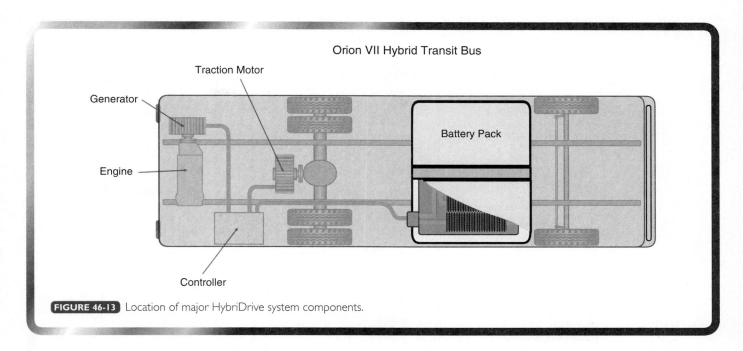

FIGURE 46-13 Location of major HybriDrive system components.

PCS. To maintain module reliability and durability, the PCS, which weighs roughly 185 lb (84 kg), is cooled using the transmission fluid.

The system uses the following inputs and outputs to operate the system at maximum efficiency:

- PCS Inputs
  - Throttle pedal
  - Brake pedal
  - Emergency override switch
  - Gear selector switch
  - Master switch
  - Master disconnect switch
  - Engine test switch
  - Brake regeneration disable switch (optional)
  - High idle switch (optional)
- PCS Outputs
  - Stop HEV indicator
  - Check HEV indicator
  - REGEN applied indicator
  - Motor over-speed warning indicator
  - HEV maintenance required indicator
  - Electric current to inverters
  - Battery state of charge control
  - Serial data via DINEX and SAE J1939 data link

AC Traction Generator (ACTG)

Connected directly to the flywheel of the engine is the **alternating current traction generator (ACTG)**, which converts mechanical energy produced by the engine into electrical current for the propulsion system **FIGURE 46-16**. This component is a permanent magnet-brushless design generator, producing three-wave AC voltage at approximately 436 volts and 600 amps maximum with 160-horsepower

FIGURE 46-14 The PCS is the central control module for the entire HybriDrive system. Three 40-pin electrical connectors and two oil-cooling lines connect to the PCS.

(119 kW) input. Generator output is partly controlled by the speed of the engine, which is regulated by the PCS to between 800 and 2300 rpm. Even though the generator is air cooled, heat produced during current production may require supplemental cooling using a fresh air plenum for vehicles operating in temperatures greater than 100°F (38°C). In addition to the 280 pound (127 kg) weight of the generator is an oil scavenging pump used to pump synthetic automatic transmission fluid for lubricating and cooling the traction motor. **FIGURE 46-17** shows a PCS with high-voltage connection points to the ACTM and ACTG.

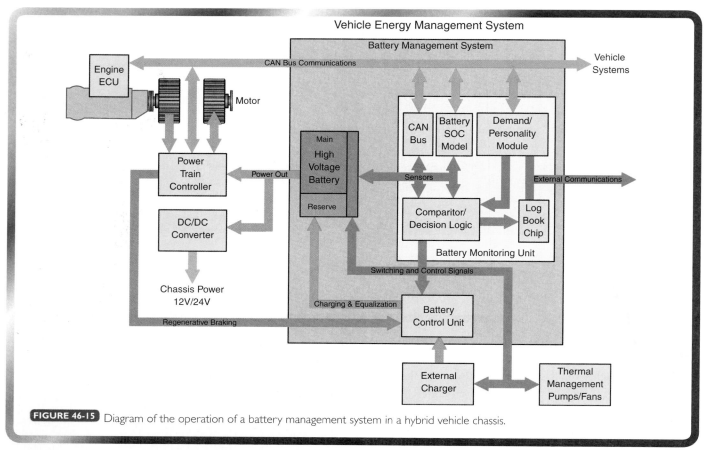

FIGURE 46-15 Diagram of the operation of a battery management system in a hybrid vehicle chassis.

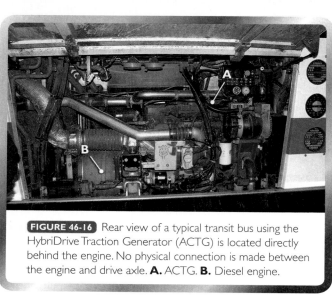

FIGURE 46-16 Rear view of a typical transit bus using the HybriDrive Traction Generator (ACTG) is located directly behind the engine. No physical connection is made between the engine and drive axle. **A.** ACTG. **B.** Diesel engine.

Safety

When power washing engines, dirt washed from the engine can easily enter the ACTG. After start-up, damage occurs quickly inside the generator due to abrasive wear from the dirt. To prevent this, always use a protective apron when cleaning the engine to prevent the entry of dirt into the air-cooled generator.

FIGURE 46-17 High voltage connection points **A.** to the ACTM-ACTG from the PCS central control module for the entire HybriDrive system. Note the electrical connectors for sensors **B.** that also connect to the PCS.

AC Traction Motor (ACTM)

The **alternating current traction motor (ACTM)** has two functions. One is to resist driveline rotation when commanded by the PCS during braking. This effectively turns the traction motor into an electrical generator, which then sends current to charge the on-board batteries. The other function is as a high-speed, three-phase, induction-type motor **FIGURE 46-18**. Induction motors work well in hybrid drive systems, as they produce the greatest amount of torque at 0 rpm, when the opposing magnetic fields in the stator and rotor are strongest. In the HybriDrive system, maximum torque is 2100 ft-lbs. (2847 Nm) of torque at 0 rpm.

The highest torque at starting is useful to accelerate the vehicle when it is necessary to overcome vehicle inertia. Induction motors also have no brushes, which eliminates reoccurring maintenance caused by wear and extends component reliability.

Maximum speed of the motor is 15,000 rpm; however a 4.69:1 gear reduction box is used to multiply torque output while reducing motor speed. With maximum current flow from both the batteries and the generator, the motor can momentarily produce up to 250 hp (186 kW) at approximately 600 VAC operating between 0 and 3200 rpm. Since the motor has three phases, or windings, in the stator, the angles between the magnetic field of the stator and rotor can be electrically altered to reverse the direction of motor rotation.

A special sensor called the **resolver** measures the rotor position and speed for the PCS to properly manage the motor operation by reducing current flow and shutting down the system as needed. Because overspeed conditions will damage the motor, the resolver is a critical sensor for the PCS. The motor is connected directly to the vehicle's differential through a standard driveshaft and yoke arrangement.

During regenerative braking, reverse torque produces current to charge the batteries, which is later used to propel the vehicle. This arrangement helps the HybriDrive to reduce fuel consumption and friction brake wear. Regenerative braking energy recovered from the ACTM is automatically reduced when the batteries are fully charged. As part of the fault protection system, two temperature sensors inside the motor are used to protect the motor against overheating **FIGURE 46-19**. The motor, which weighs 450 pounds (205 kg), is also oil cooled and lubricated with synthetic transmission fluid. **FIGURE 46-20** illustrates fluid lines to the ACTM.

Energy Storage System (ESS)

To maximize acceleration energy, the **energy storage system** supplies current to the ACTM when current demand exceeds availability from the ACTG. The ESS also stores electrical current produced during regenerative braking to maximize reductions to fuel consumption. The DC Power Link Contactor is a switch that connects the ESS to the PCS. When closed it completes the path between the Energy Storage System and PCS through the battery cables.

Elements of the ESS include battery modules, a battery management system (BMS), (the BMS manages the charging and discharging of the batteries to ensure long battery life and safe operation); an electronic cooling package (ECP), (an electronically managed cooling system for the battery modules); and system safety protection devices such as fuses and contactor switches. The original Gen 1 systems used lead–acid storage batteries, while the Gen 2 system uses lithium-phosphate ion batteries stored in tubs on the vehicle roof to keep them cooler and cleaner **FIGURE 46-21**.

Unlike hybrid drive systems used in light-duty vehicles, in heavy-duty commercial vehicles, nickel-metal hydride (NiMH) batteries are not used because they are regarded as having reached their maximum potential. Further technological advancements and cost reductions are not expected for NiMH batteries. Lithium-ion batteries are now commonplace because they offer higher energy density than NiMH batteries and do not experience adverse memory effects due to inconsistent charging. Lithium batteries also have the lowest self-discharge rate compared to other battery technologies. That is, lithium batteries will maintain a charge for a very long time when idled.

Compared with lead–acid batteries, a lithium battery pack is less than one-quarter of the weight and charges faster. Upgrading to lithium batteries reduces battery pack weight from 4100 to 1000 pounds (1818 to 455 kg), which means roof structures in buses do not need as much reinforcement and fuel consumption can decrease. Frequent charge and discharge cycles shorten battery life. Service life of lead–acid batteries is between two and three years compared to six years for lithium batteries.

The Lithium-ion energy storage system (ESS) contains a total of 16 Lithium-ion modules producing 39.6 V DC per module connected to total approximately 633 VDC. During **charge-depleting (CD) operating mode**, the vehicle is powered only—or almost only—by the energy stored in the battery. If an under-voltage condition is detected, current is diverted from the AC traction motor to the energy storage modules.

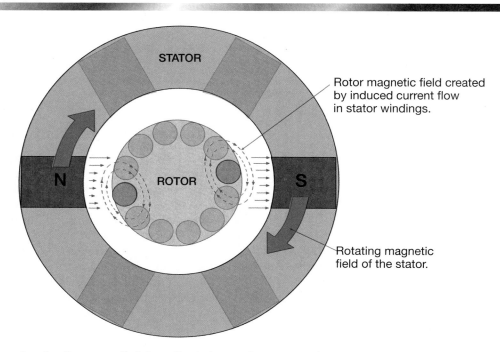

Rotor magnetic field created by induced current flow in stator windings.

Rotating magnetic field of the stator.

End view showing the magnetic interaction between the stator and two rotor segments

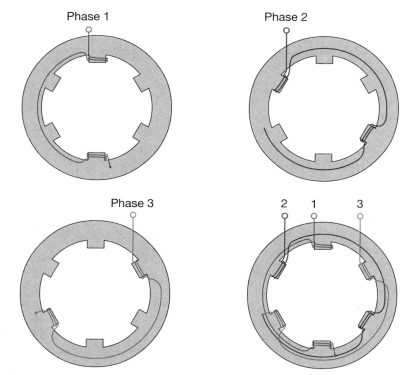

Phase 1

Phase 2

Phase 3

2 1 3

FIGURE 46-18 The ACTM is a three-phase induction motor induction which means it uses three stator winding which enables the direction of the motor to change. The polarity of each of the stator poles changes each time the AC current reverses direction. The PCS controls the phasing of stator energization, which in turn causes the motor to change direction.

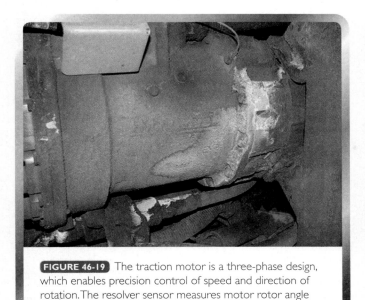

FIGURE 46-19 The traction motor is a three-phase design, which enables precision control of speed and direction of rotation. The resolver sensor measures motor rotor angle and speed.

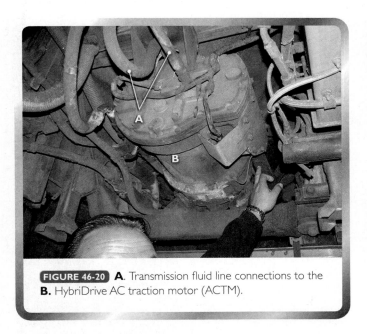

FIGURE 46-20 **A.** Transmission fluid line connections to the **B.** HybriDrive AC traction motor (ACTM).

FIGURE 46-21 **A.** Lithium-ion batteries for the energy storage system (ESS) are located in the "roof tubs." Batteries are stored on the roof to keep them cooler and cleaner. Fires and battery gassing are less likely to endanger passengers. **B.** Lithium-ion battery cells are packaged in interconnected modules of 80 volts each.

State of ESS Charge

In <u>charge-sustaining (CS) mode</u>, the batteries' state of charge (SOC) may rise and fall slightly. The SOC will, however, on the average, remain at its initial level and can be recharged through regenerative braking. Energy storage modules are kept at a 40% state of charge. This may seem low, but the batteries are required to have capacity to store regenerative braking energy extracted from the AC traction motor.

Without battery capacity, regenerative braking is automatically reduced when the ESS modules are fully charged, which causes the friction-type service brakes to work harder, dissipate more heat, and waste fuel.

A <u>master disconnect switch</u> located in the battery compartments enables technicians to disconnect the power circuit for maintenance or emergencies. This switch has a lock-out feature that prevents anyone other than the technician from reconnecting vehicle power.

The master disconnect switch is different FIGURE 46-22 from the master switch. This switch controls the vehicle electrical system allowing the lights, engine, and HybriDrive propulsion system to operate when it is switched to the on position.

Battery Monitoring System

The battery monitoring system operates to equalize charges evenly across all the battery modules. Because batteries will often have slightly different resistances to charging and discharging, the battery monitor controls the charge and discharge rate to each module.

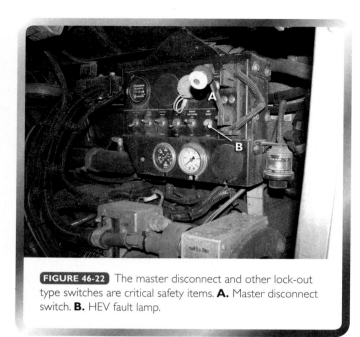

FIGURE 46-22 The master disconnect and other lock-out type switches are critical safety items. **A.** Master disconnect switch. **B.** HEV fault lamp.

Voltage to each module will change when discharging, such as under acceleration or during regenerative braking, when batteries are charged at high amperage. Defective battery modules are identified by their inability to accept a charge. The IDS service tool does not monitor individual module amperage, so module voltage is used for comparison.

For example, operative modules in good condition **TABLE 46-6** will have less internal resistance and charge at a lower voltage compared with weak or defective modules. Modules in poor condition will have the largest charging voltage differences with good modules when charge amperage is highest, such as during braking. Voltage during acceleration will drop much more compared with good modules too. Diagnostic software will flag bad battery modules under these conditions.

Current Inverters

<u>Wave inverters</u> are devices that change the shape of electrical current waves. A <u>DC-to-AC inverter</u> takes the straight, unchanging

TABLE 46-6 Condition of Good Versus Defective Battery Modules

Condition	Good Battery Modules	Defective Battery Modules
Discharge voltage at high amperage draw	Higher voltage	Lower voltage
Charging voltage at high amperage	Lower voltage	Higher voltage
Charge time	Faster	Slower
Capacity	High discharge amperage	Low discharge amperage

wave of DC current and flips, or inverts, the current's polarity to resemble an AC wave signal. Similarly, an <u>AC-to-DC inverter</u> switches the polarity of an AC current signal to resemble the straight wave polarity of DC current **FIGURE 46-23**.

Both types of current inverters are used in the HybriDrive system. AC current produced by the ACTG is rectified to 580 Volts DC to charge the batteries. To operate the ACTM 633-Volts DC, battery voltage is converted to three-phase 346-volts—phase-to-phase or line-to-line volts. The frequency of the voltage is varied to change the traction motor speed. At 250 hp (186 kW) maximum, 346 volts AC will have a maximum frequency of 500 Hz.

Intuitive Diagnostic System (IDS)

The intuitive diagnostic system is BAE's service software. It is PC based and enables technicians to connect through the J-1939 connector to:

- Monitor system parameters
- View programmable parameters and make adjustments to customer programmable parameters
- View and erase fault codes
- View fault history
- Perform diagnostic tests

The IDS is able to read data and fault codes generated by the on-board diagnostic system

- Above normal component temperature
- Under and Over Voltage conditions
- Battery Under and Over Charging
- Motor Over-Speed

The PCS monitors the system for failure conditions. Under extreme conditions the system will derate or shut-down. If failures occur and the system shuts down, a PCS (Emergency)

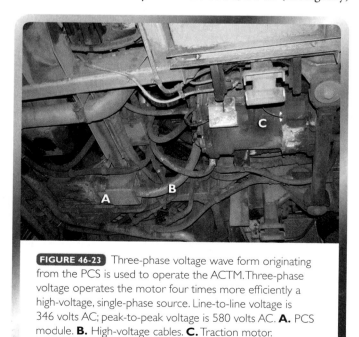

FIGURE 46-23 Three-phase voltage wave form originating from the PCS is used to operate the ACTM. Three-phase voltage operates the motor four times more efficiently a high-voltage, single-phase source. Line-to-line voltage is 346 volts AC; peak-to-peak voltage is 580 volts AC. **A.** PCS module. **B.** High-voltage cables. **C.** Traction motor.

Override Switch can be pushed and held to override most shutdown conditions for up to 10 seconds continuously and thirty seconds total. The PCS emergency override switch is used only to move a vehicle to a safe location if stalled on a roadway. Two dash lights indicate problems with the propulsion system.

The Stop HEV indicator is illuminated when an active severe fault is detected. In these circumstances the vehicle will not move unless the emergency override switch is pushed and a warning buzzer will sound. A Check HEV Indicator lights when a less serious but active fault is detected and the vehicle is operable in a de-rated condition. When inactive faults are logged by the on-board diagnostic system, the HEV Maintenance Required Indicator illuminates. This light is located in the engine compartment.

► TECHNICIAN TIP

Corrosion caused by water intrusion in the wiring harness is a common cause of HEV problems and fault codes. Contributing to the problem is the position of protective split loom around vehicle cables, which can form "drip loops." These occur when water from road spray easily enters the split loom and collects. To minimize the likelihood of this problem, always orientate split in the cable loom away from the curbside engine grate and down to allow water to drain.

Unique System Inputs

To calculate the amount of torque to apply to the rear axles, a throttle pedal position sensor provides a varying voltage signal to the PCS. Based on signal values and a throttle torque map containing look-up table values, the PCS will determine the frequency and voltage supplied to the ACTM.

Brake Pressure Sensor

A brake pressure signal is needed to calculate the amount of regenerative braking performed by the ACTM **FIGURE 46-24**. Although the braking performed by ACTG is designed to simulate the action of conventional friction brakes, the brake "feel" of regenerative brakes may be too aggressive under some situations, such as on a bus with standing passengers. For safety reasons, an adjustment to the degree of regenerative braking is possible on the HybriDrive. A scale of one to ten is used for the adjustment, with ten being the most aggressive recovery of energy for greatest efficiency. In transit applications, the setting may be set as low as between three and five.

Regeneration Disable Switch

An optional switch located near the driver is available to turn regenerative braking off for one key cycle. Slippery road conditions may be one situation for which it would be desirable to turn off the regenerative braking for better control. Wheel lock-up conditions are sensed by the ABS, which will send a message along the CAN data bus to disengage the ACTM regeneration.

When the regeneration system is on, current is produced by the ACTM and ACTG to charge the batteries to a 40% state of charge. When regen is off, the ACTG charges modules ONLY

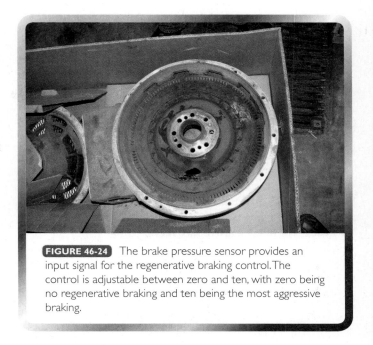

FIGURE 46-24 The brake pressure sensor provides an input signal for the regenerative braking control. The control is adjustable between zero and ten, with zero being no regenerative braking and ten being the most aggressive braking.

when vehicle is parked in neutral. A dash light informs the driver whenever any brake regeneration is taking place.

Engine Test Switch

To service the engine separately from the hybrid drive system, it is preferable to disconnect all high voltage supply and operate the engine using the throttle pedal. To accomplish this, an engine test switch is used. As a two-position toggle switch, the normal position integrates engine operation into the HybriDrive system and the vehicle responds as intended. With the switch in the engine test position, only the engine responds to the throttle pedal, and all high voltage contacts are open.

► Maintenance and Service

Preventative maintenance on the HybriDrive propulsion systems consists of inspections prescribed in the service manual and scheduled changes of coolant and traction motor oil. An air filter in the battery compartment is changed at two-year intervals. None of the major system components are rebuilt in the field but simply replaced after diagnostic tests have identified a replaceable unit.

Whenever the PCS is removed for replacement, it is a good practice to record all programmable parameters to adjust the replacement module efficiently. In addition to the electrical safety precautions outlined in the section, special tools like the ones shown in Figure 46-7 should be used when working on hybrid vehicles. Other electrical safety general procedures for component replacement include:

1. Switching off the master disconnect switch and locking out the switch until repairs are completed. Locking out the switch will prevent accidental reconnection of power during maintenance. The master disconnect switch disables the master switch and ignition signal, preventing the

engine from starting or the PCS to energize. The master disconnect also disables the contactors in PCS and ESS.

2. Disconnect and remove all ESS high voltage connectors while wearing high voltage type 0000 lineman's gloves. Connections inside the battery storage enclosure are never to be performed without specialized OEM training.

3. Disconnect and tag external harnesses, lines and cooling connections to replacement components.

4. Validate the repair after service is completed by a proper road test or by operating the component under the appropriate condition to evaluate its performance. Faults codes should be erased before testing begins to determine whether they reoccur. Before returning the vehicle to service, any fault codes should be erased once more.

Safety

Even after the master disconnect switch is opened and locked-out, the battery system has the potential to deliver a severe shock hazard since the battery modules are not de-energized by this switch. Extreme caution must always be used when working around the Energy Storage System. Before touching any electrical conductor during HybriDrive service, always verify that an electrical circuit is de-energized by using a digital multimeter (DMM).

Wrap-Up

Ready for Review

- A variety of hybrid drive vehicle configurations are used in commercial vehicles. In essence, hybrid propulsion systems can use any type of engine—gasoline, natural gas, diesel, turbine, or reciprocating—assisted by an electric motor to accelerate the vehicle.
- Hybrid electric vehicles simultaneously reduce both fuel consumption and emissions produced from burning fuel.
- Vehicles operating in urban driving conditions are best suited to hybrid use, as much of the energy derived from burning fuel is lost through idling and braking.
- The main configurations of hybrid vehicles are series, parallel, series-parallel, and plug-in hybrid vehicles.
- A series system requires a larger electric motor and battery pack, but a smaller internal combustion engine and works best in stop-and-go situations. Parallel systems are better suited to higher speeds with less stop-and-go operation.
- An alternative to electric hybrid drives is the hydraulic launch assist (HLA) system. The concept of HLA uses hydraulic regenerative braking to capture braking energy and help launch the vehicle during acceleration.
- Hybrid drive system components use lethal high-voltage power devices operating up to 900 volts and contain energy storage systems over 700 volts DC, so special tools and personal protective equipment must be used during servicing to ensure technician safety.
- BAE is an aerospace and defense technology company and is also one of the leading developers and manufacturers of hybrid-drive propulsion systems for the military and heavy-duty commercial vehicles. It manufactures series-type and parallel-type hybrids.
- HybriDrive includes the following major system components: propulsion control system (PCS); AC traction generator (ACTG); AC traction motor (ACTM); Energy Storage System (ESS)—and fresh air cooling system for the ESS required for operation above 100°F (38°C).
- The entire HybriDrive system is controlled by a microprocessor-controlled propulsion control system. Multiple inputs and outputs enable the PCS to operate the system at maximum efficiency.
- The alternating current system generator (ACTG) is a permanent magnet-brushless design generator that is air cooled.
- The alternating current traction motor (ACTM) resists driveline rotation when commanded by the PCS during braking. It also functions as a high-speed, three-phase, induction-type motor.
- Unlike hybrid drive systems used in light-duty vehicles, in heavy-duty commercial vehicles, nickel-metal hydride (NiMH) batteries are not used because they are regarded as having reached their maximum potential.
- Without battery capacity, regenerative braking is automatically reduced when the ESS modules are fully charged, which causes the friction-type service brakes to work harder, dissipate more heat, and waste fuel.
- The battery monitoring system operates to equalize charges evenly across all the battery modules. Defective battery modules are identified by their inability to accept a charge.
- HybriDrive systems use DC-to-AC and AC-to-DC inverters.
- A brake pressure signal is needed to calculate the amount of regenerative braking performed by the ACTM because the braking feel of regenerative brakes can be too aggressive in some situations, such as mass transit.
- Regenerative braking can be turned on or off by the driver.
- To service the engine separately from the hybrid drive system, it is preferable to disconnect all high voltage supply and operate the engine using the throttle pedal.

Vocabulary Builder

AC-to-DC inverter A device that switches the polarity of an AC current signal to resemble the straight wave polarity of DC current.

AC traction generator (ACTG) A device that converts mechanical energy produced by the engine into electrical current for the propulsion system.

AC traction motor (ACTM) A motor that functions as an electrical generator in a hybrid drive system.

charge-depleting operating mode (CD) A mode of operation in which the vehicle is powered only—or almost only—by the energy stored in the battery.

charge-sustaining mode (CS) A mode of operation in which the batteries' state of charge (SOC) may rise and fall slightly and energy storage modules are kept at a 40% state of charge.

DC-to-AC inverter A device that takes the straight, unchanging wave of DC current and flips, or inverts, the current's polarity to resemble an AC wave signal.

electric vehicle (EV) A vehicle in which only electric motors are used to move a vehicle.

electronic cooling package (ECP) A system of fans and electronic controls that maintains a hybrid ESS within a set temperature range.

energy storage system (ESS) A system that stores and distributes electrical current to the various components of a hybrid drive system.

hybrid electric vehicle (HEV) A type of vehicle that combines an internal combustion engine with an electric propulsion system into a new or hybrid powertrain configuration.

HybriDrive Propulsion System A series-type hybrid propulsion system developed by BAE, an aerospace and defense technology company.

hydraulic launch assist (HLA) An alternative to electric hybrid drives in which application of standard friction service brakes is prevented until just before a complete vehicle stop.

Intuitive Diagnostic System (IDS) Proprietary software system available on BAE propulsion systems to aid technicians in diagnosing service issues.

master disconnect switch A switch located in the battery compartments that enables technicians to disconnect the power circuit for maintenance or emergencies.

parallel drive A vehicle in which both the engine and electric motor work together, blending motor and engine torque, to propel the vehicle.

plug-in hybrid electric vehicle (PHEV) Any type of hybrid electric vehicle containing a battery storage system that uses an external source to recharge the battery when the vehicle is not in operation.

propulsion control system (PCS) module A microprocessor-based device that supplies electrical output signals based on input data collected from a vehicle's sensors.

regenerative braking A feature of hybrid vehicles by which generators recover energy during braking.

resolver A special sensor that measures the rotor position and speed for the PCS to properly manage the motor operation by reducing current flow and shutting down the system as needed.

series drive A vehicle in which only an electric traction motor supplies torque to propel the vehicle.

series-parallel drive A more complex system enabling an engine only, an electric motor only, and a combined engine-motor operation. Also called *power-split configuration.*

traction motor An electric motor that provides propulsion to a vehicle.

wave inverter A device that changes the shape of electrical current waves.

Review Questions

1. In _____ vehicles, both the engine and electric motor work together, blending motor and engine torque, to propel the vehicle.
   a. electric
   b. parallel drive
   c. series drive
   d. series-parallel drive

2. The _____ is a type of vehicle that combines an internal combustion engine with an electric propulsion system.
   a. HLA   c. Zero emission
   b. Hybrid electric d. All electric

3. A feature called _____ braking uses generators to recover energy during braking.
   a. plug   c. regenerative
   b. anti-lock   d. dynamic

4. The _____ system uses hydraulic regenerative braking to capture braking energy and help launch the vehicle during acceleration.
   a. mechanical launch assist
   b. vacuum launch assist
   c. magnetic launch assist
   d. hydraulic launch assist

5. In HLA _____ mode, both the engine and accumulator will provide driveline torque until the accumulator empties.
   a. performance   c. launch
   b. charging   d. regenerative

6. Disconnecting and _____ any residual current in EV components is imperative before performing any service work.
   a. charging   c. magnetizing
   b. discharging   d. storing

7. The _____ system module is the system element controlling the operation of the entire HybriDrive System.
   a. engine control
   b. hydraulic launch assist
   c. propulsion control
   d. reciprocating

8. To maximize acceleration energy, the _____ system supplies current to the ACTM when current demand exceeds availability from the ACTG.
   a. plug-in
   b. performance
   c. propulsion control
   d. energy storage

9. A(n) _____ located in the battery compartments enables technicians to disconnect the power circuit for maintenance or emergencies.
   a. master disconnect switch
   b. inverter
   c. generator
   d. converter

10. An optional regenerative braking _____ switch is located near the driver for use during slippery road conditions.
    a. master disconnect
    b. disable
    c. performance
    d. inverter

ASE-Type Questions

1. Technician A says Hybrid propulsion systems use a natural gas engine assisted by an electric motor to accelerate the vehicle. Technician B says Hybrid propulsion systems use a reciprocating engine assisted by an electric motor to accelerate the vehicle. Who is correct?
   a. Technician A
   b. Technician B
   c. Both Technician A and Technician B
   d. Neither Technician A nor Technician B

2. Technician A says that approximately 35% of energy used to accelerate a city bus is quickly dissipated into heat by frequent braking. Technician B says that approximately 50% of energy used to accelerate a city bus is quickly dissipated into heat by frequent braking. Who is correct?
   a. Technician A
   b. Technician B
   c. Both Technician A and Technician B
   d. Neither Technician A nor Technician B

3. Technician A says an advantage to using a hybrid drive train is smoother acceleration. Technician B says an advantage to using a hybrid drive train is increased brake life. Who is correct?
   a. Technician A
   b. Technician B
   c. Both Technician A and Technician B
   d. Neither Technician A nor Technician B

4. Technician A says class 3 lineman gloves are recommended for use on high voltage hybrid circuits and offer protection from 1,500 to 5,000 volts. Technician B says class 1 lineman gloves are recommended for use on high voltage hybrid circuits and offer protection from 2,500 to 3,000 volts. Who is correct?
   a. Technician A
   b. Technician B
   c. Both Technician A and Technician B
   d. Neither Technician A nor Technician B

5. Technician A says a series drive system works best in frequent stop-and-go service conditions. Technician B says a parallel drive system works best in frequent stop-and-go service conditions. Who is correct?
   a. Technician A
   b. Technician B
   c. Both Technician A and Technician B
   d. Neither Technician A nor Technician B

6. Technician A says the AC traction generator is connected directly to the flywheel of the engine. Technician B says the intuitive drive system is connected directly to the flywheel of the engine. Who is correct?
   a. Technician A
   b. Technician B
   c. Both Technician A and Technician B
   d. Neither Technician A nor Technician B

7. Technician A says that during charge depleting operation mode the vehicle is powered only—or almost only—by the energy stored in the battery. Technician B says that during intuitive operating mode the vehicle is powered only—or almost only—by the energy stored in the battery. Who is correct?
   a. Technician A
   b. Technician B
   c. Both Technician A and Technician B
   d. Neither Technician A nor Technician B

8. Technician A says a resolver type current inverter is used in the HybriDrive system. Technician B says an AC-to-DC type current inverter is used in the HybriDrive system. Who is correct?
   a. Technician A
   b. Technician B
   c. Both Technician A and Technician B
   d. Neither Technician A nor Technician B

9. Technician A says a series system requires a smaller electric motor and battery pack, but a larger internal combustion engine than a parallel system. Technician B says a series system requires a larger electric motor and battery pack, but a smaller internal combustion engine than a parallel system. Who is correct?
   a. Technician A
   b. Technician B
   c. Both Technician A and Technician B
   d. Neither Technician A nor Technician B

10. Technician A says hydraulic launch assist systems are a series-parallel hybrid system. Technician B says the degree of HybriDrive regenerative brakes can be adjusted using a scale of 1 to 10. Who is correct?
   a. Technician A
   b. Technician B
   c. Both Technician A and Technician B
   d. Neither Technician A nor Technician B

NATEF Tasks

There are no NATEF tasks for this chapter.

Knowledge Objectives

After reading this chapter, you will be able to:

1. Explain the operating principles of series-parallel electric propulsion drive. (pp 1293–1295)
2. Describe the construction and operation of Allison EP Hybrid drive system. (pp 1293–1301)
3. Identify and explain the function of the Allison EP drive system components. (pp 1294–1305)
4. Describe the operating principles of a dual mode hybrid drive train. (p 1305)
5. Outline basic service and maintenance procedures for Allison EP drive systems. (p 1306)

Skills Objectives

There are no skills objectives for this chapter.

▶ Introduction

In addition to series-type hybrids, parallel drive and series-parallel drive are two common configurations of Allison EV Drive Hybrid Systems used in heavy-duty commercial vehicles. In parallel drive hybrids, both the engine and electric motor work together, blending motor and engine torque to propel the vehicle. Series-parallel drive is a more complex system enabling an engine only, an electric motor only, and a combined engine-motor operation. Also called a power-split configuration, the engine and motor operation is optimized for driving conditions.

Arvin Meritor markets a dual-mode hybrid system specifically designed for line-haul application, but as the Allison system is the most common series-parallel hybrids, this chapter will discuss that system in greater detail.

▶ Overview of Allison EV Drive Hybrid System

EP40 and EP50 systems are model names derived for Allison's Electric Propulsion system, or alternatively Allison's Electrically Variable (EV) Drive. Although the two models are almost identical in construction and operation, the EP40 is capable of continuously delivering 280 hp (209 kW), while the EP50's output is higher at 330 hp (246 kW).

The Allison EP Drive system is primarily a parallel-type hybrid drive. Unlike series hybrid systems, such as the BAE HybriDrive, which use only an electric motor for torque, parallel systems use a transmission, which enables a combination of output torque from both the electric traction motor and engine.

A dedicated engine-mechanical pathway and an electrical motor pathway for traction torque, along with a combination of both, are possible through the power train. Allison describes the hybrid architecture as a two mode compound-split system. That is because the system's capabilities allow for only electric or only a diesel engine for traction power and an infinitely variable combination of both **FIGURE 47-1** .

Torque from both sources is blended to optimally match vehicle operating conditions and the electric propulsion-drive operating state. Its automatic transmission does not used fixed gear ratios. Instead, the power continuously varies from the engine and two electric motors when the vehicle is driving in a forward direction. When decelerating, the EP system uses regenerative braking to recover braking energy. Like other hybrids, the electric **traction motors** turn into generators, producing electric current used to charge an on-board bank of NiMH batteries. Regenerative braking slows the vehicle, like a retarder would in a conventional automatic transmission, which in turn reduces brake wear and fuel consumption.

Parallel Drive Advantages and Disadvantages

Real-world comparisons of the EP system to the series HybriDrive system show that EP offers slightly greater reduction in fuel consumption compared to the HybriDrive system operated on an identical route. The EP is capable of faster acceleration, too, if its adjustable HyGain accelerating setting feature is set up for performance. Late-model Allison H-EP40/50s also have a unique feature referred to as **smart electrification**.

▶ You Are the Technician

As a transit bus technician, you are skilled and qualified to work on diesel-powered bus chassis. Recently, a few of the hybrid-drive buses in the fleet, which are now out of the manufacturer's warranty period, have begun to receive more complaints about braking. Passengers are falling during braking, and there are even a few reports of injuries due to overly aggressive braking. Examining the service records, you notice the buses all have far less frequent brake service and foundation replacement than what is expected from a hybrid chassis. After inspecting all the brake foundation components on one particular chassis, you find them all to be in proper working condition. Inspection and test procedures performed on the air brake circuits and values all are within normal expected limits. While road testing the bus, you do find that even under very light brake pedal application force, the bus does brake very aggressively. As it is a series-parallel type hybrid powertrain, you realize that a significant amount of braking is supposed to be performed by the electric traction motor-generator. As you consider which elements of the hybrid system to inspect, and search OEM literature for the correct diagnostic and inspection procedures, consider the following:

1. List the safety procedures that should be followed before beginning any inspection of diagnostic work on an Allison EV hybrid powertrain.
2. Identify potential problems with the hybrid powertrain that may contribute to more work being performed by the regenerative braking system and not the service braking system.
3. What strategy do you think the Allison EV system uses to ensure there is an adequate buffer or storage capacity in the batteries for regenerative braking if the batteries become excessively charged?

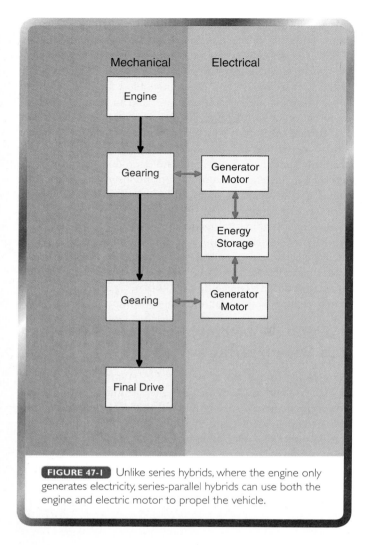

FIGURE 47-1 Unlike series hybrids, where the engine only generates electricity, series-parallel hybrids can use both the engine and electric motor to propel the vehicle.

This feature enables the system's motors to switch over to generating mode to produce as much as 300 amps at 24 volts at idle. Idle electrical generation at this magnitude is an ideal feature for buses replacing hydraulic-drive motors with current loads from electric accessories, such as the radiator cooling fan, charge air cooler fans, and hybrid drive cooling fans. Introduced in 2011, this feature uses a highly efficient solid state DC-to-DC converter **FIGURE 47-2**, eliminating the need for a traditional belt-driven alternator and associated maintenance requirements. On-board battery current is not used. Consequently, hybrid- and starting-battery life increase due to less frequent charge and discharge cycles. See **FIGURE 47-3A** and **FIGURE 47-3B**.

Despite the EP system advantages, currently less than a third of Allison EV Drive Hybrid Systems sold are Allison EP drives. The addition of the transmission and associated components adds approximately 1500 pounds (682 kg) to vehicle weight. Additional capital purchase costs are also associated with the system. **FIGURE 47-4** shows the layout of a transit bus using a series parallel-dual mode Allison EP system.

▶ System Components

The Allison EV drive system consists of the following major components:

- EV drive transmission unit
- Transmission control module (TCM)
- Vehicle control module (VCM)
- Traction motors
- Energy storage system (ESS)
- Dual power inverter module (DPIM)

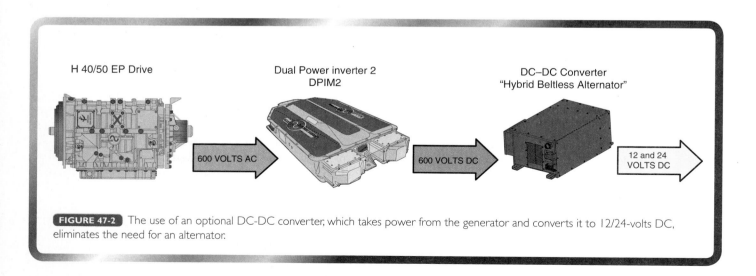

FIGURE 47-2 The use of an optional DC-DC converter, which takes power from the generator and converts it to 12/24-volts DC, eliminates the need for an alternator.

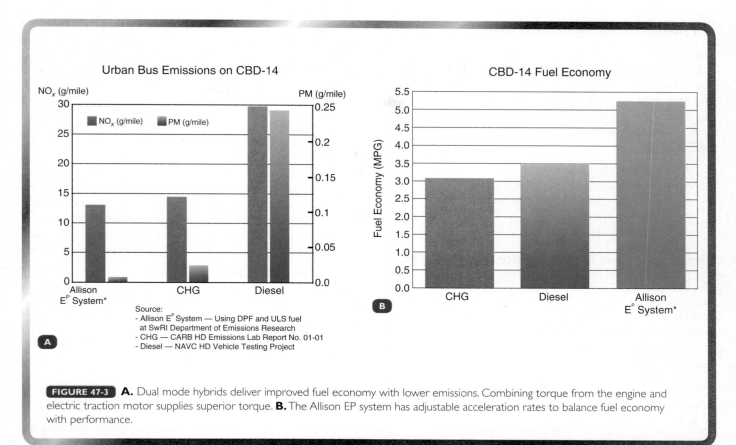

FIGURE 47-3 **A.** Dual mode hybrids deliver improved fuel economy with lower emissions. Combining torque from the engine and electric traction motor supplies superior torque. **B.** The Allison EP system has adjustable acceleration rates to balance fuel economy with performance.

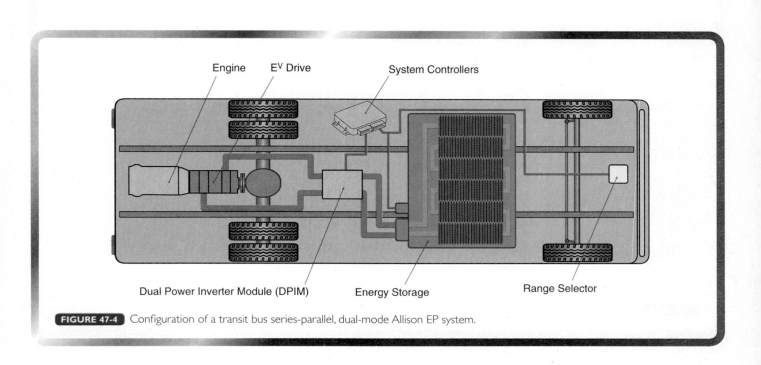

FIGURE 47-4 Configuration of a transit bus series-parallel, dual-mode Allison EP system.

EV Drive Transmission Unit

The EV Drive transmission unit provides a pathway for transmitting electric motor or engine torque (or a blend of both) using three planetary gear sets. Inside the unit, there are three planetary gear sets, two wet-type hydraulic clutches, and two motor/generators. The EV drive transmission itself consists of several standard modules illustrated in **FIGURE 47-5** and **FIGURE 47-6** :

- Input housing module
- Main (stator) housing module
- Control valve assembly/oil pan module
- Clutch housing module
- Rear cover module

Transmission Control Module (TCM)

The **transmission control module (TCM)** is one of the most important of twelve microprocessor-based controllers the EP system uses. Most of the EP system operation is directly controlled by this processing module, which collects input signals to determine electrical outputs controlling the EV transmission operation. Torque blending, adaptive hydraulic clutch control,

diagnostic system management, hydraulic oil level monitoring, and start-up and shut down routines are some of the basic important functions. In addition to J1939 CAN messages used as inputs for the TCM, a number of input circuits are connected to the TCM, such as:

- Ignition sense—Detects the ignition key switch state
- Hydraulic transmission control pressure sensors
- Transmission oil sump temperature
- Oil level sensor
- Transmission output speed
- ESS relay status
- Accelerator interlock—Disables the engine throttle, keeping it at neutral when passenger doors are open
- Fast idle switch—Increases idle speed in steps when activated
- Engine brake enable—Status of the engine brake on/off

Likewise, the TCM outputs include:

- Auxiliary function range inhibit—Prevents selection to forward or reverse range when auxiliary equipment is enabled
- Front operation—Enables vehicle start-up and operation from the driver's compartment

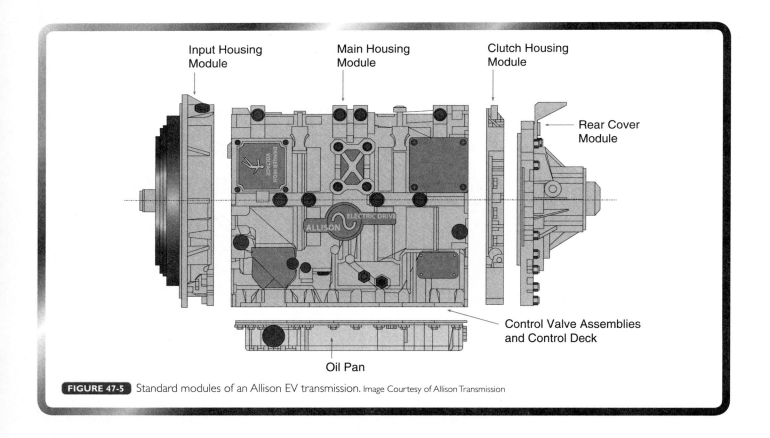

FIGURE 47-5 Standard modules of an Allison EV transmission. Image Courtesy of Allison Transmission

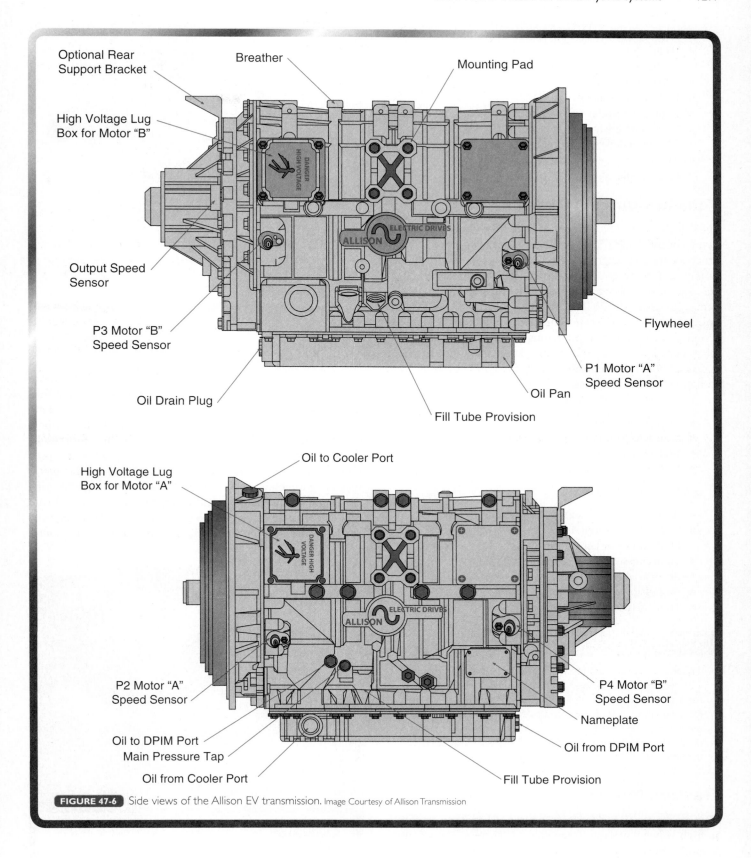

FIGURE 47-6 Side views of the Allison EV transmission. Image Courtesy of Allison Transmission.

- Remote shutdown—Requests system shutdown
- Hydraulic clutch trim solenoids (two)
- Hydraulic clutch-blocking solenoid drivers
- DPIM wake-up signal
- ESS wake-up signal
- Engine controller wake-up signal
- Speedometer signal
- Engine brake enable
- Auxiliary brake enable indicator lamp
- PTO enable

Vehicle Control Module (VCM)

The Vehicle Control Module (VCM) is the other microprocessor-based controller **FIGURE 47-7** that operates with the TCM to process data and determine electric signal outputs for the EP system and other vehicle features. Both the TCM and VCM are identical looking modules, sharing identical components. However, the VCM function concerns the vehicle-to-powertrain interface, such as limiting operation of auxiliary systems—such as rear door opening when vehicle is moving—relay control, solenoids, and warning lamp operation. The TCM and VCM both communicate over the SAE J1939 CAN network with other control modules.

VCM system inputs include:

- Vehicle switches
- Shift selector input
- Brake pressure sensor
- System override requests

Outputs include:

- Accelerator pedal sensor supply
- Shift selector serial data link
- Dash indicator lamp control
- Main pressure boost solenoid commands
- Reverse warning
- Propulsion system inhibits
- Transmission boost solenoid

▶ TECHNICIAN TIP

Allison's EP pushbutton shift selector features transmission fluid level reading. High fluid levels cause transmission fluid to contact rotating parts, aerating the fluid. Aerated fluid is compressible, resulting in low hydraulic clutch application force, slipping, and overheating. The power inverters (DPIMs) also use transmission fluid for cooling and can easily be damaged by aerated or contaminated fluid and or low fluid levels.

Traction Motors

EP systems use two electric asynchronous motors operating on high voltage, variable-frequency AC current. Both motors A and B are capable of continuously producing up to 100 hp (75 kw) and can rotate in either direction from 0 to 5000 rpm. Both motors are arranged concentrically around the transmission main-shaft, with the motor nearest the engine flywheel

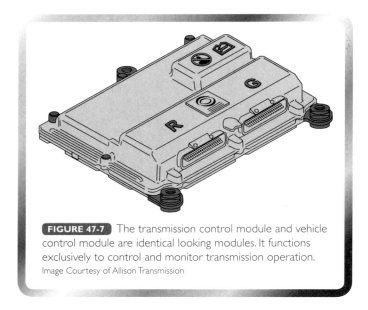

FIGURE 47-7 The transmission control module and vehicle control module are identical looking modules. It functions exclusively to control and monitor transmission operation.
Image Courtesy of Allison Transmission

called Motor A, and the rear motor near the output yoke called Motor B **FIGURE 47-8** .

The motor stator windings are pressed into the EV stator housing and the motor has two temperature sensing thermistors embedded in the winding, which supply motor temperature data to the DPIM. For service reasons, only one sensor is connected to the DPIM. In the event one fails, the sensor wiring can be connected to the spare thermistor. A Hall effect speed sensor is located in each motors' housing. These provide motor speed and direction data to the TCM. Motor A's role is to crank the engine during start-up and to supply torque to blend with Motor B. Two of the EV's three planetary gear sets (P1 and P2) are located in Motor A's housing to enable these functions.

FIGURE 47-8 Inside the Allison EV transmission there are two electric motors, which are used in either of two driving modes—low-speed or high-speed operation the rear motor, low speed, is shown here.

Motor B supplies the initial traction force when accelerating from a stop. While in reverse, Motor B is the only source of torque. The third planetary gear set is located in Motor B's housing.

When the engine start button is depressed, motor speed and direction tests are performed before the engine cranks by applying a low power input to both motors.

In an **asynchronous AC motor**, the magnetic field in the rotor is induced by induction of the magnetic field in the stationary stator FIGURE 47-9 . This explains why asynchronous

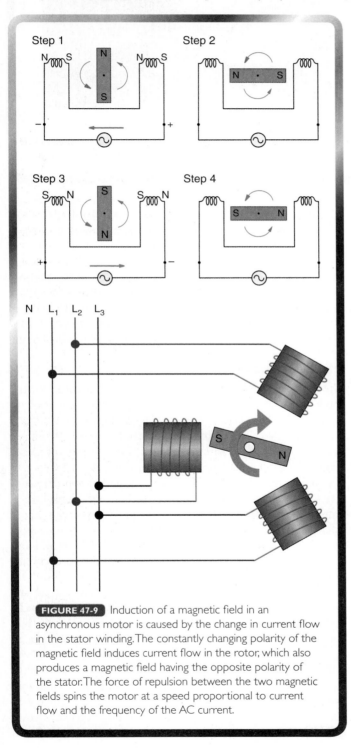

FIGURE 47-9 Induction of a magnetic field in an asynchronous motor is caused by the change in current flow in the stator winding. The constantly changing polarity of the magnetic field induces current flow in the rotor, which also produces a magnetic field having the opposite polarity of the stator. The force of repulsion between the two magnetic fields spins the motor at a speed proportional to current flow and the frequency of the AC current.

motors are sometimes called induction motors. In asynchronous motors, no brushes are used to supply current to the rotor like a DC motor. Instead, the continuously switching direction of current flow and corresponding magnetic field polarity in the stationary stator induces current flow in the rotor windings. Flow of current induced in the rotor in turn produces magnetic fields used for repulsion forces to rotate the motor rotor. Induction in both the rotor and stator takes place as the direction of AC current flow moves from zero volts to peak volts in the stator winding. The sudden change and movement of the stators, magnetic field induces current flow in the rotor winding. Because AC current continuously switches direction, the stator current will move from peak volts in one direction to zero and then to peak volts in the opposite direction. The effect of the change in direction of current flow produces a magnetic field of the opposite polarity in the rotor. Asynchronous AC motors can use wire-wound or permanent magnets in the rotor. Rotors using permanent magnets are more efficient than wire-wound motors but are much more costly to produce FIGURE 47-10 .

> ### TECHNICIAN TIP
>
> To control vehicle movement when the vehicle is stopped on an uphill grade in forward range, the EP will limit rotation of the output shaft to a near zero vehicle speed. It accomplishes this by applying reverse torque through the drive motors when the throttle is at idle stop and no service brakes are applied.

> ### TECHNICIAN TIP
>
> To simulate feedback of a conventional automatic transmission using a torque converter, creep torque is applied at closed throttle, with the service brake unapplied. Creep torque is limited to 5 mph (8 kph) and creates the impression of using a conventional powertrain system.

Energy Storage System (ESS)

ESS Function

The **energy storage system (ESS)** function is to store and supply direct current energy for the electric drive system FIGURE 47-11 . Electrical energy to charge the ESS is generated by both drive motors during regenerative braking and from Motor A in mode one when not in use for propulsion. Only 40% of the electrical energy to accelerate the bus originates from regenerative braking—the remaining energy originates from the engine.

The state of charge of the ESS is carefully controlled to maintain energy levels for accelerating but, more importantly, to maintain a buffer to allow adequate battery capacity to absorb energy during regenerative braking. This means that, under most conditions, ESS batteries are never fully charged, so battery capacity is available to store energy. Without the charge buffer to absorb energy, regenerative braking cannot be used, as it would damage the batteries through overcharging. Extra friction brake wear would take place, too. One advantage of using NiMH

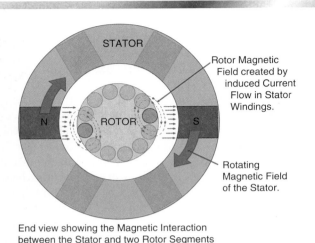

FIGURE 47-10 Three-phase motors can rotate in either direction, depending on the electrical connection to the stator. By changing which phase receives the zero-to-peak-positive or negative current direction, the positioning of the magnetic poles will influence the direction of rotor movement.

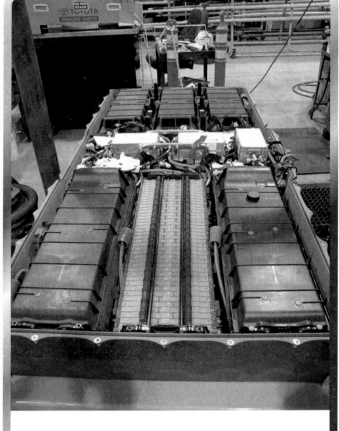

FIGURE 47-11 The energy storage system (ESS) consists of nickel-metal hydride (NiMH) batteries connected in series and parallel used to supply electric current to the motor and absorb electrical energy produced during regenerative braking.

batteries instead of other batteries is the ability of the NiMH battery to be charged and discharged repeatedly without shortening its life cycle **FIGURE 47-12**.

If the ESS SOC is reported to be too high, Motor A is run in the opposite direction of engine's rotation at idle to dissipate excess stored energy. Under these conditions, the TCM will request the engines ECM to command the exhaust brake to close, creating high engine exhaust back pressure, which converts more electric motor energy into heat and rotational force.

ESS Construction

The ESS battery tub contains 240 nickel-metal hydride (NiMH) modules weighing under 1000 lb (455 kg) operating at a voltage range of 432–780 VDC. To achieve this voltage from a 1.2-volt NiMH cell, 40 cells are arranged to form a module. Two modules are connected to form a subpack. Two parallel connected subpacks form a substring having approximately 312 volts DC. Six battery substrings form the battery group of approximately 624 VDC enclosed in separate enclosed housing called a tub. A battery control interface module (BCIM) monitors each subpack operation and condition by measuring voltage and temperature. Data from the BCIM is reported over the CAN to the TCM module, which processes data regarding SOC, temperature, cooling fan status, and diagnostic information such as fault codes.

The TCM provides to the ESS overall system control and battery protection strategies. Since charge and discharge cycles produce heat, each subpack is fan cooled. Under excessive heat conditions, a refrigerant line to the auxiliary AC cooler can be opened to reduce inlet air temperature to the batteries. To service individual subpacks, three plastic blocks connecting cables to the batteries breaks the current path to a battery substrings. High voltage DC energy passes through the ESS tubs through two high voltage connections, one positive polarity and one negative polarity. **FIGURE 47-13** shows a schematic representation of the substrings.

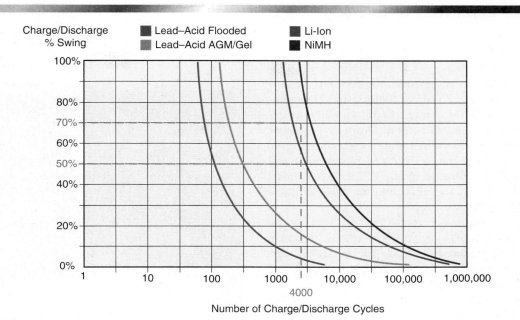

FIGURE 47-12 Note one advantage of NiMH batteries is the ability to be charged and discharged repeatedly without a shortened life cycle.

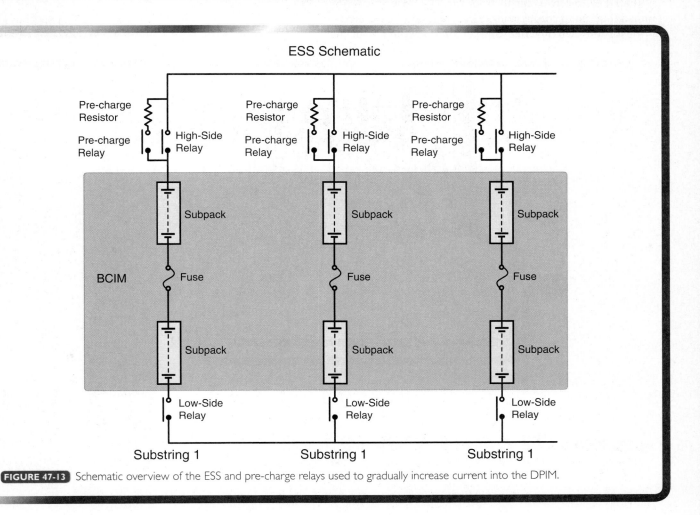

FIGURE 47-13 Schematic overview of the ESS and pre-charge relays used to gradually increase current into the DPIM.

Dual Power Inverter Module (DPIM)

DPIM Function and Construction

The main function of the <u>dual power inverter module DPIM</u> **FIGURE 47-14** is to convert energy from the ESS into AC currents used to power the EZV drive motors. To vary motor torque and speed, the DPIM also functions to modify the frequency and voltage of the AC current. During regenerative braking, AC current produced by the motors is converted to DC current used to charge the ESS batteries. As current in and out of both motors is controlled by the DPIM, two identical wave inverters are found in the DPIM housing, each dedicated to a motor **FIGURE 47-15**.

A specialized field effect transistor (FET) called an <u>insulated gate bipolar transistor (IBGT)</u> inverts DC current to three-phase, variable-frequency, and variable-voltage AC current. IGBTs are commonly used in many home appliances and sound amplifiers, which are fast-switching, voltage-controlled power transistors capable of handling current in the order of hundreds of amperes while blocking voltages up to 6000 volts. Heat generated by the IGBT is absorbed by heat sinks on each transistor and then removed by transmission fluid circulating around the heat sink.

The DPIM receives signals from the TCM over the CAN commanding motor torque and ESS current flow. Two microcontrollers for each inverter contain the necessary logic to control DPIM operation, run self-diagnostics, and communicate with the TCM. Three low-voltage connectors power and communicate with the DPIM, and three high voltage connections are made to the DPIM.

FIGURE 47-14 The Dual Power Inverter Module (DPIM) is an DC-AC and AC-DC electronic wave inverter used to power the EP drive propulsion system and charge the batteries in the Energy Storage System (ESS).

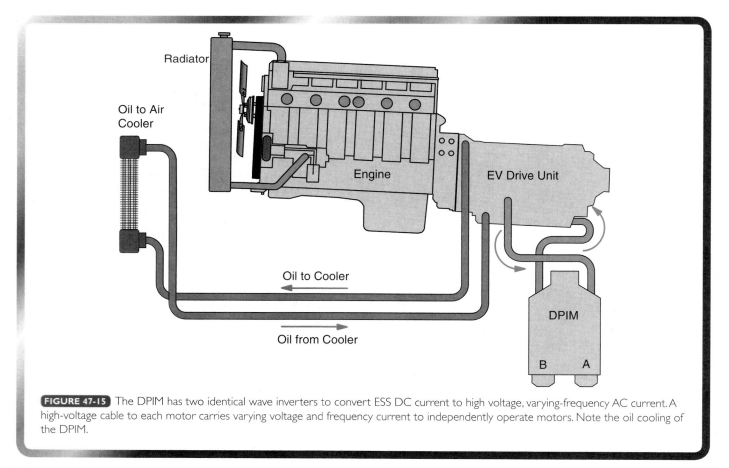

FIGURE 47-15 The DPIM has two identical wave inverters to convert ESS DC current to high voltage, varying-frequency AC current. A high-voltage cable to each motor carries varying voltage and frequency current to independently operate motors. Note the oil cooling of the DPIM.

A high-voltage DC positive and negative cable for the DPIM is connected with ESS. These high voltage circuits are isolated for use by the ESS and DPIM only and are not connected to any other positive, negative, or ground circuit. For safety reasons, DPIM self-diagnostics capabilities continuously monitor the high voltage DC circuits to ensure they remain isolated from the vehicle chassis.

DPIM Operation

A sudden in rush of DC current into the DPIM from the ESS can damage the DPIM. To enable a gradual build-up of current in the DPIM, a pair of relays located on each battery substring and a current limiting resister regulates current build-up and charging of a large voltage smoothing capacitor inside the DPIM. A fuse

is also used in this to prevent catastrophic damage from overcurrent situations. During the one-half-second start-up period, the DPIM passes through three operating conditions:

1. Initial state—All battery relays are open, and no current flows into or out of the ESS **FIGURE 47-16**

2. Pre-charge state—The battery pre-charge relay and the low-side relays are closed, allowing current to flow through the pre-charge resistor, which slowly increases voltage to charge the DPIM capacitor **FIGURE 47-17**

3. Operational state—Voltage to the DPIM reaches 400V in 200 ms, achieving 85% of ESS voltage. The high-side relays close, and pre-charge relays open to allow full voltage to the DPIM **FIGURE 47-18**.

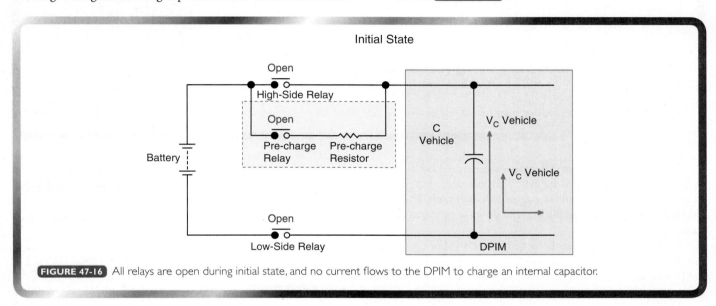

FIGURE 47-16 All relays are open during initial state, and no current flows to the DPIM to charge an internal capacitor.

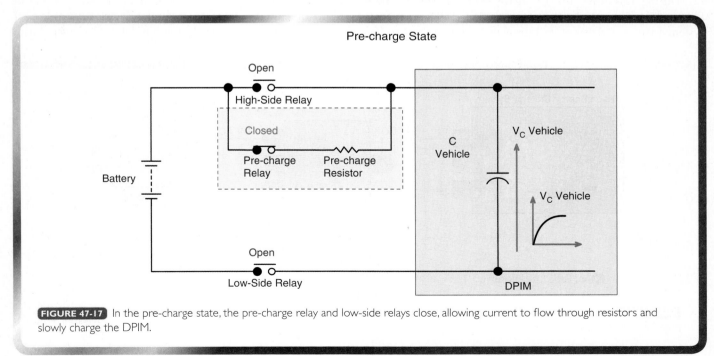

FIGURE 47-17 In the pre-charge state, the pre-charge relay and low-side relays close, allowing current to flow through resistors and slowly charge the DPIM.

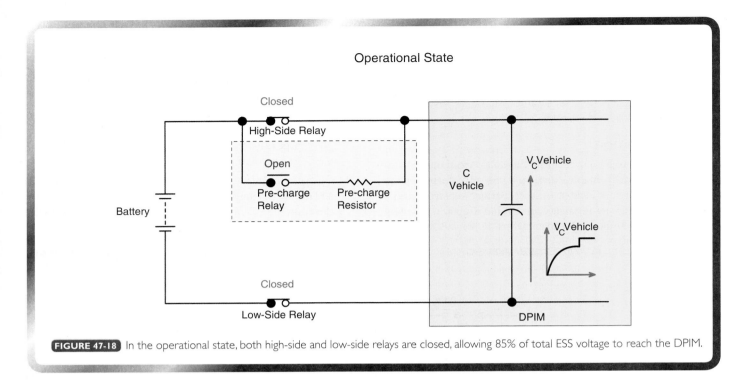

FIGURE 47-18 In the operational state, both high-side and low-side relays are closed, allowing 85% of total ESS voltage to reach the DPIM.

If a significant voltage difference is measured between the ESS and the DPIM, fault is logged. This indicates that the pre-charge sequence failed, and the engine will not crank. Voltage in the DPIM must fall to zero during shut down, eliminating safety hazards in the system.

To dissipate any residual charge in the DPIM or on the DC bus, DPIM current passes through a 10-KΩ resistor bank inside the DPIM, which is also connected to the motor stator windings that turn current to heat.

During this time, the EV drive shift selector remains illuminated for several seconds while the TCM saves the system-adaptive and diagnostic information from the last key-on event. Once information is stored and the charge depleted, the shift selector display goes out, indicating the system shut-down sequence is complete.

High Voltage Interlock Loop (HVIL)

The Allison EP uses a **high-voltage interlock loop (HVIL)** to prevent access to potentially hazardous energized electrical circuits **FIGURE 47-19**. The HVIL consists of a 12V relay control circuit routed in series to switches on cover plates located on all hybrid components where potential electrical hazards exist. When any switch in an HVIL circuit is detected as open during

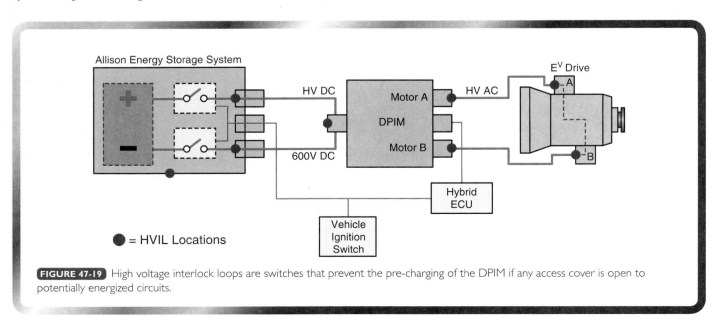

FIGURE 47-19 High voltage interlock loops are switches that prevent the pre-charging of the DPIM if any access cover is open to potentially energized circuits.

ignition key-on, the pre-charge sequence will not take place. The engine will not crank, and the STOP SYSTEM lamp will remain illuminated.

An open HVIL circuit detected during forward or reverse operation will log fault codes but does not result in an active system shutdown. However, while passing through neutral position between forward and reverse, the fault will result in system shut-down.

Safety

The HVIL disconnects power from the ESS to the DPIM but it is not to be relied on to disable the high-voltage system. Turning the ignition key off powers down the system. Specific procedures to disconnect high-voltage connections are described in OEM training programs and are to be followed before any system work is performed. Always treat the high voltage electrical system as if it is powered on. Make sure vehicle ignition is switched off, and always follow the electrical disconnect verification procedure before performing any service work where a potentially hazardous electrical current may exist.

▶ Operating Modes

Parallel hybrids can operate in various modes, for example, the capability to operate in "hush" mode. This electric-only operation minimizes noise when operating in sound sensitive areas and eliminates emissions when operating in places like long tunnels. In addition, BAE parallel hybrids can use a split-mode operation, and Arvin Meritor systems offer a dual-mode operating system.

Split-Mode Operation

The EP system has two forward modes of operation. **Mode 1** is for low-speed operation and **Mode 2** for high-speed operation. Generally, the EP control maintains Mode 2 operation until vehicle speed is under 20 or 25 mph (32 to 40 kph), at which point it will switch to Mode 1. Initially, only Motor B is used to accelerate the vehicle from rest. However, torque from the engine and Motor A are blended to supplement torque from Motor B in Mode 2. Blending torque from the motors and engine together is referred to as **compound split operation**. Exactly when the EV shifts between modes, or which torque inputs it uses, will vary based upon specific measured conditions, such as the throttle position, programmed acceleration rate, available battery current, and vehicle speed. Three planetary gear sets and two hydraulic clutches operating under electronic control of the TCM and VCM function to obtain engine-motor torque blending and forward and reverse operating modes. The split between mechanical and electric torque, EV gear ratios, and torque ratios are continuously adjusted by the TCM until maximum power output is reached. Torque blending algorithms programmed into the TCM calculate the most efficient combination to obtain best performance and lowest fuel consumption by adjusting engine speed and torque, motor speed and torque, and current consumption from power stored in the ESS

batteries. **FIGURE 47-20** illustrates the differences in acceleration between the Allison hybrid and a conventional diesel engine.

Dual-Mode Hybrid Drive

Although most hybrid systems today are designed for start-stop applications, Meritor produces a dual-mode hybrid drive train specifically designed for line haul trucks. The Meritor **dual-mode hybrid drive train** uses a relatively simple operating principle, combining both mechanical and electrical propulsion systems.

At speeds under 48 mph (77 kph), torque for vehicle propulsion is produced entirely by an electric motor supplied with current from lithium-ion batteries. At speeds in excess of 48 mph (77 kph), the drive train transitions to a diesel-engine power system, supplemented occasionally with the electric motor providing torque during hill climbs or passing—situations similar to a parallel hybrid system. Like other hybrid systems, the Meritor uses Li-ion batteries that are recharged through regenerative braking because the motor, located in series with the driveline, can switch to generation mode.

The advantages of this dual-mode system include the following:

- Fuel efficiency—Savings through regenerative braking.
- Stop-start fuel savings—Eliminates fuel consumption and emissions when vehicle is not in motion.
- Full electric, zero-emission mode in emission restricted areas.
- The electrification of accessories (e.g., air or AC compressors)—Provides further efficiency benefits, as batteries can supply continuous power during overnight rest periods, thereby eliminating the need for engine idling or other additional anti-idling systems.
- Smaller engines—Motors can supply additional acceleration boost on grades and start-up.
- Silent-mode operation

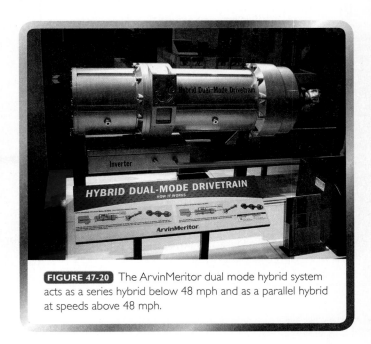

FIGURE 47-20 The ArvinMeritor dual mode hybrid system acts as a series hybrid below 48 mph and as a parallel hybrid at speeds above 48 mph.

▶ EP System Maintenance

Isolation Fault Detection

For safety reasons, Allison EP systems use an isolation fault detection monitor to identify high voltage circuit shorts to the vehicle chassis. Various diagnostic trouble codes are logged when the isolation resistance between the high voltage circuit and the chassis ground is measured at less than 50 million ohms. These fault codes are displayed on the push button PBSS display and will illuminate the HEV fault lamp.

Diagnostic Code Display

Diagnostic trouble codes (DTCs) can be viewed and cleared using the PBSS display. DTCs are displayed in the sequence in which they were logged into the TCM. All codes consist of OEM unique four-digit codes displayed as a two-digit main code followed by a two-digit sub code with more specific information about the system area where the fault has occurred. For example, the first two digits may indicate an electrical short to ground while the last two digits indicate a hydraulic pressure sensor wire.

Warning Lights

A check system warning light FIGURE 47-21 alerts the operator that an EP system fault has occurred but does not lead to a system derate or shut-down. However, a stop system warning light indicates the propulsion system will shut-down with a 30-second warning period.

A system over-temperature warning light alerts the operator when any of the EP system components are outside normal heat ranges. Over heat conditions result in reduced performance or system shut-down.

Allison DOC Service Tool

The PC-based service software for the EP system is called **Allison DOC**. (DOC is an abbreviation for diagnostic optimized connection.) Allison DOC can display logged fault codes, record snap shot data of operating conditions for later playback, and display system operating conditions in real time. The TCM contains a number of self-diagnostic routines that monitor the EP system sensors, solenoids, and speed ratios to validate that these devices are operating correctly.

Allison DOC can access and run these diagnostic routines as well. Similarly, the DPIM and ESS controllers perform diagnostic tests not conducted by the TCM, which are initiated by Allison DOC, too.

Oil Filtration

Four separate hydraulic filters are located in the EP drive transmission in the system. The filters include the:

- Suction filter screen
- Control Main filter
- Trim Solenoid filters
- Transmission fluid filter

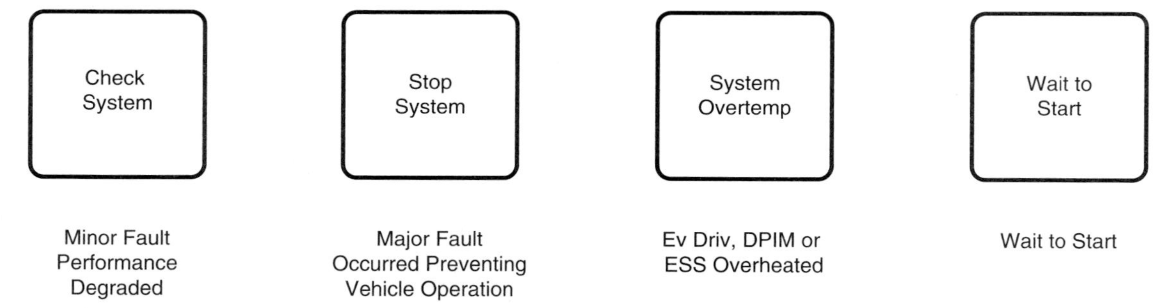

Check System	Stop System	System Overtemp	Wait to Start
Minor Fault Performance Degraded	Major Fault Occurred Preventing Vehicle Operation	Ev Driv, DPIM or ESS Overheated	Wait to Start

FIGURE 47-21 Diagnostic warning lights for the EP system.

Wrap-Up

Ready for Review

▶ Parallel drive and series-parallel drive are two common configurations of Allison EV Drive Hybrid Systems used in heavy-duty commercial vehicles.

▶ Allison makes one of the most common series-parallel hybrids.

▶ Allison describes the hybrid architecture as a two mode compound-split system that allows for only electric or only a diesel engine for traction power and an infinitely variable combination of both.

▶ Its automatic transmission does not used fixed gear ratios. Instead, the power continuously varies from the engine and two electric motors when the vehicle is driving in a forward direction.

▶ Real-world comparisons of the EP system to the series HybriDrive system show that EP offers slightly greater reduction in fuel consumption compared to the HybriDrive system operated on an identical route.

▶ Allison EV drive systems consists of an EV drive transmission unit, transmission control module (TCM), vehicle control module (VCM), traction motors, energy storage system (ESS), and a dual power inverter module (DPIM).

▶ The EV drive transmission unit provides a pathway for transmitting electric motor or engine torque (or a blend of both) using three planetary gear sets.

▶ The EV drive transmission unit includes several modules: an input housing module, main (stator) housing module, control valve assembly/oil pan module, clutch housing module, and rear cover module.

▶ Most of the EP system operation is directly controlled by the transmission control module, which collects input signals to determine electrical outputs controlling the EV transmission operation.

▶ The TCM and VCM both communicate over the SAE J1939 CAN network with other control modules.

▶ EP systems use two electric asynchronous motors operating on high voltage, variable-frequency AC current.

▶ In an asynchronous AC motor (also called an induction motor), the magnetic field in the rotor is induced by induction of the magnetic field in the stationary stator.

▶ The state of charge of the ESS is carefully controlled to maintain energy levels for accelerating. Therefore, under most conditions, ESS batteries are never fully charged, so battery capacity is available to store energy.

▶ The ESS battery tub contains multiple battery modules arranged in groups of 40 cells to create a module. Two modules are connected to form a subpack; two subpacks connected in parallel form a substring; and six substrings form the battery group.

▶ A battery control interface module (BCIM) monitors each subpack operation and condition by measuring voltage and temperature.

▶ The main function of the DPIM is to convert energy from the ESS into AC currents used to power the EZV drive motors. To vary motor torque and speed, the DPIM also functions to modify the frequency and voltage of the AC current.

▶ During the one-half second start-up period, the DPIM passes through three operating conditions: initial state, pre-charge state, and operational state.

▶ The Allison EP uses a High Voltage Interlock Loop (HVIL) to prevent access to potentially hazardous energized electrical circuits.

▶ Parallel hybrids can operate in various modes, for example, hush mode, split mode, or dual mode.

▶ Hush mode minimizes noise and eliminates emissions.

▶ Split mode involves two forward modes of operation—one for low-speed operation and one for high-speed operation.

▶ The Meritor dual-mode hybrid drive train uses a relatively simple operating principle, combining both mechanical and electrical propulsion systems.

▶ Allison EP systems use an isolation fault detection monitor to identify high voltage circuit shorts to the vehicle chassis.

▶ Diagnostic trouble codes (DTCs) are displayed in the sequence in which they were logged into the TCM.

▶ Warning lights include a check system light, a stop system light, and an over-temperature light.

▶ The PC-based service software for the EP system is called Allison DOC. It can display logged fault codes, record snap shot data of operating conditions for later playback, and display system operating conditions in real time.

Vocabulary Builder

Allison DOC PC-based service software for Allison's EP system.

asynchronous AC motor A motor in which the magnetic field in the rotor is induced by induction of the magnetic field in the stationary stator.

compound split operation Blending torque from the motors and engine together.

dual-mode hybrid drive train A hybrid system that combines both mechanical and electrical propulsion systems.

dual power inverter module (DPIM) The module responsible for converting energy from the ESS into AC currents used to power the EZV drive motors.

energy storage system (ESS) A system that stores and distributes electrical current to the various components of a hybrid drive system.

EP40/50 System Models of Allison's Electric Propulsion system. Also known as Allison's Electrically Variable (EV) Drive.

high-voltage interlock loop (HVIL) A device that prevents access to potentially hazardous energized electrical circuits.

insulated gate bipolar transistor (IGBT) A specialized field effect transistor (FET) that inverts DC current to three-phase, variable-frequency, and variable-voltage AC current.

Mode 1 In split-mode operation, the mode that is for low-speed operation.

Mode 2 In split-mode operation, the mode that is for high-speed operation.

smart electrification A feature that enables the EP 40/50 system's motors to switch over to generating mode to produce as much as 300 amps at 24 volts at idle.

traction motor An electric motor that provides propulsion to a vehicle.

transmission control module (TCM) The electronic controller that issues commands to the solenoids inside the transmission to obtain the desired range. Also known as the transmission electronic control unit (ECU).

Review Questions

1. _____ is a hybrid system that combines both mechanical and electrical propulsion systems.
   a. Dual-mode hybrid drive train
   b. Electric drive train
   c. HLA drive train
   d. ESS drive drain

2. A(n) _____ blends torque from the motors and engine together.
   a. dual power inversion
   b. compound split operation
   c. smart electrification
   d. accelerator interlock

3. The _____ is a device that prevents access to potentially hazardous energized electrical circuits.
   a. high-voltage interlock loop
   b. low-voltage interlock loop
   c. dash indicator lamp control
   d. battery boost control

4. When decelerating, the EP system uses _____ braking to recover braking energy.
   a. magnetic
   b. anti-lock
   c. hydraulic
   d. regenerative

5. The EV drive transmission unit provides a pathway for transmitting electric motor or engine torque (or a blend of both) using three _____ gear sets.
   a. planetary
   b. dual-mode
   c. regenerative
   d. asynchronous

6. Induction of a magnetic field in a(n) _____ motor is caused by the change in current flow in the stator winding.
   a. dual-mode
   b. asynchronous
   c. traction
   d. series drive

7. Electrical energy to charge the _____ is generated by both drive motors during regenerative braking and from Motor A in mode one when not in use for propulsion.
   a. dual power inversion
   b. battery boost control
   c. energy storage system
   d. smart electrification

8. A specialized field effect transistor called a(n) _____ bipolar transistor inverts DC current to three-phase, variable-frequency, and variable-voltage AC current.
   a. isolation
   b. dual-mode
   c. planetary
   d. insulated gate

9. Meritor produces a _____ hybrid drive train specifically designed for line haul trucks.
   a. dual-mode
   b. series
   c. parallel
   d. series-parallel

10. Allison EP systems use a(n) _____ fault detection monitor to identify high voltage circuit shorts to the vehicle chassis.
    a. insulation
    b. isolation
    c. module
    d. substring

ASE-Type Questions

1. Technician A says that most of the EP system operation is directly controlled by the transmission control module. Technician B says that most of the EP system operation is directly controlled by the hybrid control module. Who is correct?
   a. Technician A
   b. Technician B
   c. Both Technician A and Technician B
   d. Neither Technician A nor Technician B

2. Technician A says that remote shutdown is an output of the transmission control module. Technician B says that accelerator interlock is an output of the transmission control module. Who is correct?
   a. Technician A
   b. Technician B
   c. Both Technician A and Technician B
   d. Neither Technician A nor Technician B

3. Technician A says that the brake pressure sensor is an input of the vehicle control module. Technician B says that the propulsion system inhibits are an input of the vehicle control module. who is correct?
   a. Technician A
   b. Technician B
   c. Both Technician A and Technician B
   d. Neither Technician A nor Technician B

4. Technician A says that two parallel-connected battery subpacks form a tub having approximately 120 volts DC. Technician B says that two parallel-connected battery subpacks form a substring having approximately 312 volts DC. Who is correct?
   a. Technician A
   b. Technician B
   c. Both Technician A and Technician B
   d. Neither Technician A nor Technician B

5. Technician A says that in the dual power inverter module's initial state, both high-side and low-side relays are open, allowing 50% of total ESS voltage to reach the DPIM. Technician B says that in the dual power inverter module's operational state, both high-side and low-side relays are closed, allowing 85% of total ESS voltage to reach the DPIM. Who is correct?
   a. Technician A
   b. Technician B
   c. Both Technician A and Technician B
   d. Neither Technician A nor Technician B

6. Technician A says the dual power inverter module consists of a 24V relay control circuit routed in parallel to switches on cover plates located on all hybrid components where potential electrical hazards exist. Technician B says the high-voltage interlock loop consists of a 12V relay control circuit routed in series to switches on cover plates located on all hybrid components where potential electrical hazards exist. Who is correct?
   a. Technician A
   b. Technician B
   c. Both Technician A and Technician B
   d. Neither Technician A nor Technician B

7. Technician A says that fuel efficiency is an advantage of using the Meritor dual-mode hybrid drive train. Technician B says that smaller engines is an advantage of using the Meritor dual-mode hybrid drive train. Who is correct?
   a. Technician A
   b. Technician B
   c. Both Technician A and Technician B
   d. Neither Technician A nor Technician B

8. Technician A says that the Allison EP system has adjustable acceleration rates to balance fuel economy with performance. Technician B says that The Allison H-EP 40/50s offers a feature referred to as smart electrification that uses a highly efficient solid-state DC-to-DC converter eliminating the need for a traditional belt-driven alternator. Who is correct?
   a. Technician A
   b. Technician B
   c. Both Technician A and Technician B
   d. Neither Technician A nor Technician B

9. Technician A says a parallel drive hybrid allows you to choose between engine only, electric motor only, or combined engine-motor operation. Technician B says that at speeds in excess of 48 mph (77 kph), the dual-mode hybrid drive train transitions to an all-electric power system, supplemented occasionally by the diesel engine. Who is correct?
   a. Technician A
   b. Technician B
   c. Both Technician A and Technician B
   d. Neither Technician A nor Technician B

10. Technician A says that in the pre-charge state of the dual power inverter module all battery relays are open, and no current flows into or out of the ESS. Technician B says that an open high-voltage interlock loop circuit detected during forward or reverse operation will log a fault code and result in an active system shutdown. Who is correct?
    a. Technician A
    b. Technician B
    c. Both Technician A and Technician B
    d. Neither Technician A nor Technician B

CHAPTER 48

Alternative Fuel Properties and Characteristics

NATEF Tasks

There are no NATEF tasks for this chapter.

Knowledge Objectives

After reading this chapter, you will be able to:

1. Explain the purposes of and applications for using alternative fuels instead of diesel fuel in heavy-duty engines. (p 1311)
2. Identify common classifications of alternative fuels used to power heavy-duty engines. (pp 1313–1322)
3. Identify the selection criteria used to choose an alternative to diesel fuel. (pp 1311–1313)
4. Identify properties of the alternative fuels commonly used in heavy-duty applications. (pp 1313–1322)
5. Describe the basic construction and operating principles of engines that use alternative fuels. (pp 1317–1320)
6. Identify safety issues associated with servicing vehicles that are powered by natural gas. (pp 1322–1323)

Skills Objectives

There are no Skill Objectives for this chapter.

▶ Introduction

Alternative fuels are defined as fuels derived from sources other than petroleum. Significant interest and financial investments in developing alternative fuel sources have been, and continue to be, made to reduce air pollution, greenhouse gas (GHG) emissions, and dependency on oil imports. The total operating costs for a vehicle or fleet is another major consideration when adopting alternative fuels because fuel is the largest single operating expense for most heavy-duty vehicles. In North America, two key pieces of legislation that have driven the pursuit of commercially viable alternative fuel sources are the **Renewable Fuel Standard (RFS)** and the **Low Carbon Fuel Standard (LCFS)**. The RFS was a part of the US Energy Policy Act (EPAct) of 2005, and was expanded under the Energy Independence and Security Act (EISA) of 2007. It requires increasing amounts of fuel from renewable sources to be blended with gasoline and diesel fuel every year until 2022. **Renewable fuels** are a category of alternative fuels that are made from sources that can be replaced or reproduced. Some renewable fuels are biologically based, including those derived from vegetable oil or animal fat and fuels produced from biomass such as wood chips, grass clippings, and even algae. Unlike petroleum-based fuels, which have limited reserves and cannot be replaced once they are burned, renewable fuels can be continually produced. According to the RFS, the sources of renewable fuels used in transportation sector must emit lower levels of GHGs than the petroleum-based fuels they replace.

The LCFS, which is administered by the California Air Resources Board, reflects another aspect of the alternative fuel legislative initiatives introduced around the world to reduce GHG emissions **FIGURE 48-1**. While there are a variety of vehicle emissions that can contribute to GHGs, reducing the production of carbon dioxide (CO_2), a normal byproduct of combustion, is achievable by burning fuels with less carbon content. Reduction of CO_2 emissions, which are widely believed to be the man-made cause of global warming, can be accomplished by using fuels with lower carbon levels, including compressed natural gas (CNG), liquid natural gas (LNG), and hydrogen, or

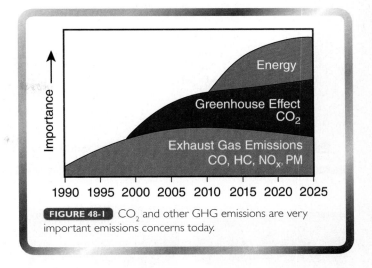

FIGURE 48-1 CO_2 and other GHG emissions are very important emissions concerns today.

electric-powered vehicles that use current from solar or wind resources **FIGURE 48-2**. The LCFS aims to reduce transportation energy consumption by 10% by 2020 compared to a 2010 baseline. When analyzing the impact a fuel has on the environment, the California Air Resources Board relies on the total lifecycle contribution of an energy source, from production, to distribution, to final consumption. In other words, it uses a "well-to-wheel" measurement of a fuel's GHG emissions.

▶ Selection Criteria for Alternative Fuels

Standards for renewable fuels and low-carbon fuels set important criteria for selecting among dozens of possible alternative fuels. Beyond that, there are many other criteria for companies, fleet operations, or even individuals to consider before switching to an alternative fuel, alternative fuel–powered vehicle, or electric or hybrid vehicle **FIGURE 48-3** and **FIGURE 48-4**. Often the choice is made based on environmental considerations because most alternative fuels produce fewer noxious

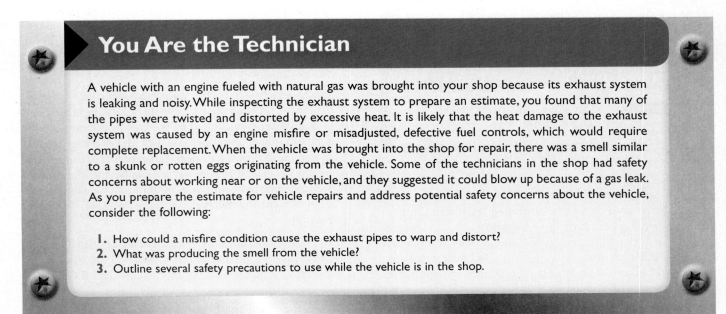

▶ You Are the Technician

A vehicle with an engine fueled with natural gas was brought into your shop because its exhaust system is leaking and noisy. While inspecting the exhaust system to prepare an estimate, you found that many of the pipes were twisted and distorted by excessive heat. It is likely that the heat damage to the exhaust system was caused by an engine misfire or misadjusted, defective fuel controls, which would require complete replacement. When the vehicle was brought into the shop for repair, there was a smell similar to a skunk or rotten eggs originating from the vehicle. Some of the technicians in the shop had safety concerns about working near or on the vehicle, and they suggested it could blow up because of a gas leak. As you prepare the estimate for vehicle repairs and address potential safety concerns about the vehicle, consider the following:

1. How could a misfire condition cause the exhaust pipes to warp and distort?
2. What was producing the smell from the vehicle?
3. Outline several safety precautions to use while the vehicle is in the shop.

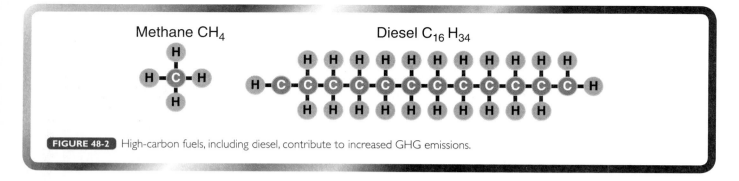

FIGURE 48-2 High-carbon fuels, including diesel, contribute to increased GHG emissions.

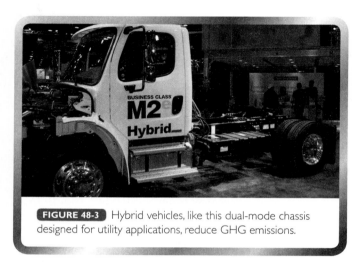

FIGURE 48-3 Hybrid vehicles, like this dual-mode chassis designed for utility applications, reduce GHG emissions.

FIGURE 48-4 This fully electric vehicle reduces GHG emissions by eliminating the internal combustion engine.

emissions. Government agencies and some corporations "go green" by using alternative fuels or vehicles as part of promoting a favorable social image or demonstrating the sustainability of an alternative fuel or vehicle. Sustainability refers to whether a vehicle or fuel, and its production and associated processes, can be maintained over the long-term. Declining petroleum reserves and access to lower cost oil produced in regions free of conflict make the use of conventional petroleum-based fuels less sustainable with every passing year.

Technical Considerations for Alternative Fuels

Technical considerations when evaluating the use of alternative fuels in commercial vehicles include:

1. Emissions

    At one time, many alternative fuels, including natural gas and biodiesel, had noxious emission characteristics that were superior to those of diesel fuel. Reductions in the production of noxious emissions, particularly in transit applications, which can have a major impact on public health, made natural gas an ideal alternative to diesel. This is not as important of a consideration today as it was a few years ago when diesel engines still had to achieve significant emission reductions. Today's diesel-fueled engines have negligible noxious emissions and all available fuels must meet the same, almost-zero, emissions output standards over the useful life of an engine. However, engines powered by natural gas can still deliver lower exhaust emissions than diesel-fueled engines without the expensive aftertreatment systems needed for use with diesel fuel. The GHG emission standards that phased in beginning in 2014, the RFS, and various low-carbon fuel standards now have more significance from an environmental standpoint than those that regulate the production of noxious emissions.

2. Power Density

    Power density is the power output per cubic inch (or cubic centimeter) of an engine over its entire operating range. Fuels with lower energy content by volume do not produce the same amount of power as those with higher energy content by volume and special strategies are required to compensate for the deficiency. Ideally, any alternative fuel should provide the same or better power output from the same engine displacement as diesel fuel.

3. Operating Costs

    Operating costs are a major factor when selecting an alternative fuel. An alternative fuel is usually more attractive to a company, fleet operation, or an individual if the initial investments to use the technology can be offset by reduced fuel expenditures, operating costs, or lifecycle costs. Some alternative fuels simply cost too much to produce to be commercially viable. If the energy inputs required to produce a fuel are high, that negates any reduction in carbon output when the fuel is finally burned. Usually, the use of an alternative fuel requires the addition of special equipment, engine and vehicle modifications, or implementation of unique maintenance practices that minimize any benefit the alternative can provide **FIGURE 48-5**. Engine reliability and durability when using alternative fuels also need to be factored into the calculation of whether the use of alternative fuels makes economic sense over a vehicle's lifecycle. If resale value is negatively affected or the vehicle breaks down more frequently as a result of using an alternative fuel, there is even less customer enthusiasm for using the fuel.

4. Capabilities

Another selection criterion when considering an alternative fuel is whether the fuel is widely available, or refueling is only available at a few specific locations, such as a yard of a truck fleet. The use of natural gas, whether CNG or LNG, is an example of fuel with limited range capability. There are few places along major transportation routes where vehicles can be easily refueled with CNG or LNG. While efforts are currently underway to improve this situation, it is not currently ideal. The availability of fueling infrastructure for any alternative fuel significantly influences the decision of customers about whether or not an alternative fuel can be used. If a vehicle operates daily on a fixed route, regularly returning to a home base for refueling is not as much as a concern as it is for a fleet operation with trucks or buses traveling long distances and returning infrequently to a yard. Related to the criterion of fuel range are issues related to fuel quality and standardization. When refueling with an alternative fuel, the fuel quality must be consistent from one location to another to ensure the engine and emission reduction systems operate correctly. ASTM International (formerly known as the American Society for Testing Materials) recently established specifications for B-100 fuel in ASTM standard D6751. Purchasers of fuel meeting this specification can expect uniform performance and quality.

► Alternative Fuels for Diesel Engines

There are three categories of alternative fuels used in diesel engines: renewable, non-renewable, and a combination of both types. There are also three different combustion systems used to burn alternative fuels. The first type ignites fuels with a spark in a diesel engine block with modified cylinder heads that accommodate spark plugs **FIGURE 48-6**. The second type is a diesel engine that uses a small pilot injection of diesel fuel to ignite an alternative fuel in the cylinder. This is known as a **wet-spark ignition system** **FIGURE 48-7**. The third type is a diesel engine that has relatively little modification and burns an alternative fuel like a conventional diesel engine burns diesel fuel. Most biofuels are used in engines that have few or no changes to their design and construction. The following examples of alternative fuels that are made from biologically derived sources are basic categories of biodiesels, which are discussed more thoroughly in the Diesel Fuel Properties and Characteristics chapter.

Biofuels

Conventional biodiesel is any fuel derived from plant material or animal fats. These fuels can produce up to a 20% reduction in GHG emissions compared to petroleum-based diesel fuel. Biodiesel can be blended with conventional petroleum-based diesel in various proportions, from 2% to 99%. A blend with 5% biodiesel is referred to as B5, a blend with 20% biodiesel is referred to as B20. Fuel made from 100% biological sources

FIGURE 48-5 This dual-fuel vehicle has an LNG storage tank in addition to a diesel fuel tank. The dual tanks increase the production and maintenance cost of the vehicle.

FIGURE 48-6 This Cummins 8.3L (506 cubic inch) engine uses a diesel engine block with a modified cylinder head that accommodates spark plugs. The spark plugs ignite natural gas.

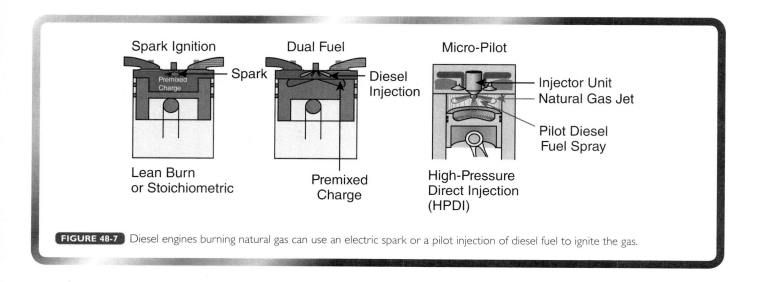

FIGURE 48-7 Diesel engines burning natural gas can use an electric spark or a pilot injection of diesel fuel to ignite the gas.

is referred to as B100 and it is an entirely renewable fuel. The various types of biodiesels are also categorized by the feedstock, or materials, used to make the fuel. Biomass-based fuels are made from everything from wood and sawdust to garbage, agricultural waste, and manure. **Cellulosic biodiesel** is derived from non-food based feedstock, like wood. More recently, oil derived from algae has been used to produce a wide variety of fuels, including diesel fuel. Its advantage is that more fuel can be produced from a smaller land mass than any other biofuel.

E-Diesel

E-diesel is a fuel made from combining petroleum-based diesel fuel and ethanol, an alcohol made from plant sugars. Ethanol is different from methanol, another type of alcohol that is made from wood. Unlike ethanol, methanol will not mix with diesel fuel. When diesel is blended with ethanol, it has some renewable fuel features. Because ethanol contains oxygen, e-diesel is described as oxygenated diesel fuel. Ethanol can be blended with petroleum-based diesel in proportions up to 15% by volume. To compensate for ethanol's physical and chemical properties, additives must be blended with e-diesel to improve its lubricity and cetane number. Also, because ethanol has a very different density than diesel fuel, it tends to separate from diesel fuel. This means that e-diesel is not stable, even when prepared through a process of **emulsification** where mechanical pressure is used to mix the two fuels.

E-diesel has lower carbon emissions and reduces particulate formation in comparison to conventional diesel fuel, but it also has a much lower flash point, which makes the fuel hazardous. Because of e-diesel's instability as a mixture, low flash point, and the use of food-based feedstock to produce ethanol, this fuel will likely only ever have niche uses.

Fischer-Tropsch Fuels

Fischer-Tropsch fuels are a category of biofuels made from substances including coal, plastic, and natural gas; these substances are first turned into a gas, and are then converted from a gas

into a liquid. Other names for these fuels include syn-gas fuel and gas-to-liquid (GTL) fuel. The Fischer-Tropsch reaction was developed in Germany, where it was extensively used during World War II. During that time, approximately 25% of the fuel Germany produced was created using the Fischer-Tropsch reaction. Out of necessity, the oil-poor but coal-rich country used the process to produce liquid fuels from feedstock such as coal.

In the Fischer-Tropsch reaction, the feedstock is heated to a temperature range of 302–572°F (150–300°C). The gases produced from heating are then condensed by pressurization, generally 1–75 psi (7–517 kPa). Depending on the amount of heat used and the pressure applied, various fuels can be made by forming hydrocarbons chains with the assistance of metal catalysts such as iron or cobalt. The use of heat and pressure to produce fuel makes the process expensive, and it is not thermally efficient. Only 50–60% more heat than what is used to produce the fuel is derived from fuels produced through the Fischer-Tropsch reaction **FIGURE 48-8**. One large-scale operation provided the U.S. military with synthetic fuels made from the Fischer-Tropsch reaction and successfully blended them with aircraft fuel. The resulting fuel was classified as a renewable because it could be made from many types of feedstock. However, because of the production cost and complexity, it will also remain a niche fuel.

Wood Pyrolysis Liquid Fuel

One promising type of renewable fuel, which is derived from biomass using the process of pyrolysis, began to be commercially developed in the 1980s. **Pyrolysis** involves heating biomass feedstock to temperatures of 842–1112°F (450–600°C) in the absence of air. Vapors are produced when the solids are heated that are then condensed and converted into a liquid bio-oil **FIGURE 48-9**. When a rapid heating process, which only lasts a few seconds, is used, the bio-oil production is called fast pyrolysis. Fast pyrolysis more efficiently converts biomass solids into a liquid bio-oil fuel product. Wood offers the greatest yield of bio-oil, which is why this fuel is also called **wood pyrolysis liquid (WPL)**.

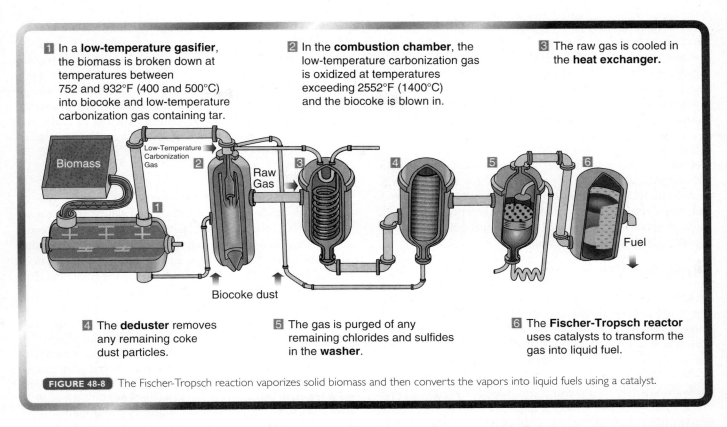

1 In a **low-temperature gasifier**, the biomass is broken down at temperatures between 752 and 932°F (400 and 500°C) into biocoke and low-temperature carbonization gas containing tar.

2 In the **combustion chamber**, the low-temperature carbonization gas is oxidized at temperatures exceeding 2552°F (1400°C) and the biocoke is blown in.

3 The raw gas is cooled in the **heat exchanger.**

4 The **deduster** removes any remaining coke dust particles.

5 The gas is purged of any remaining chlorides and sulfides in the **washer.**

6 The **Fischer-Tropsch reactor** uses catalysts to transform the gas into liquid fuel.

FIGURE 48-8 The Fischer-Tropsch reaction vaporizes solid biomass and then converts the vapors into liquid fuels using a catalyst.

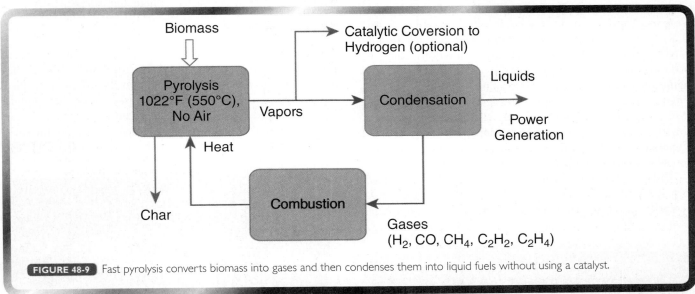

FIGURE 48-9 Fast pyrolysis converts biomass into gases and then condenses them into liquid fuels without using a catalyst.

WPL is inexpensive to produce and emits substantially fewer noxious emissions than petroleum-based diesel when burned. It promises to be the simplest and least expensive fuel to produce for diesel engines. Currently, WPL is only burned in industrial boilers and furnaces as a replacement for heavy petroleum furnace fuel. A distillation process is needed to convert bio-oil into refined transportation fuels. However, combustion research labs around the world, including the University of Toronto's Combustion Research Laboratory, are working to modify both the fast pyrolysis process to produce improved fuels with better

combustion quality. Work is also being performed by Centennial College in Toronto in partnership with the University of Toronto to learn what modifications to engine construction are necessary to achieve greater commercial value from bio-oil combustion for diesel-electric power generation.

Hydrogen

In Germany, Daimler is promoting the use of hydrogen as an alternative fuel for commercial vehicles. Rather than burning hydrogen in an engine, the gas is used to operate fuel cells by producing electricity to operate electric traction motors. Reacting hydrogen and oxygen in a fuel cell produces only heat and water vapor with no noxious emissions. If hydrogen is someday produced from renewable sources, this emission-free transportation fuel will become sustainable and more attractive. Before mass production of fuel-cell vehicles could be viable, the industry would also need to overcome the barrier of users having access to a widespread network of filling stations. Currently, a few hydrogen-powered transit buses and trucks made by Mercedes operate in California, but utilization of commercially viable hydrogen fuel cells is expected to be many years away. Manufacturers agree that in the near term natural gas, hybrid, and fully electric vehicles are effective alternatives for specific applications and zero-emission hydrogen fuel cells remain only a longer-term alternative solution.

Dimethyl Ether

Dimethyl ether (DME) is a methanol-like renewable fuel and one of the cleanest burning renewable fuels. DME has a high cetane value of 55–60, which enables smooth, quiet combustion. It also burns with no particulate matter (PM) formation and minimal oxides of nitrogen (NO_x) emissions. This is because DME has no hard-to-break carbon-to-carbon bonds **FIGURE 48-10**. Without paired carbon bonds, the oxygen in DME can easily react with carbon atoms to produce CO_2. Combustion characteristics like this allow DME-fueled engines to easily meet current emission standards without complex and expensive exhaust aftertreatment systems. Selective catalyst reduction (SCR) systems are used with DME to reduce its small amount of NO_x emissions. Specialized engine calibrations could be used instead of an SCR system, but this would result in reduced engine efficiency. With fewer combustion byproducts and simplified engine controls, compression ignition engines that use DME require less maintenance and have increased durability. DME, however, requires injection systems specifically modified to operate on DME. DME is used in current production commercial vehicles manufactured by Volvo and Mack Trucks.

DME is more commonly used as a propellant in aerosol cans; it replaced CFCs after they were banned in the 1990s. A colorless gas at room temperature, DME requires about 75 psi (517 kPa) of pressure in fuel tanks to remain in its liquid form **FIGURE 48-11**. This means storage and handling requirements of DME are similar to that of propane, because both require moderately pressurized storage tanks. DME does not require the design standards needed for CNG or cryogenic storage like LNG. Because DME has only about half the energy density of conventional diesel fuel by volume, the size of DME fuel tanks needs to be doubled to provide the same travel range as conventional diesel fuel.

DME Production

DME is a synthetic fuel that can be produced from a variety of feedstocks, including biogas, methanol, and natural gas. The most common feedstock for large-scale production of DME is natural gas. DME can be produced using a multi-step process that combines steam and natural gas, and can be competitively priced compared to diesel fuel. Because DME is made from abundant North American supplies of natural gas, its cost does not swing as widely as petroleum-based fuels. Also, because renewable sources are used to make DME, it is considered a renewable fuel with the additional benefit of having low global warming potential. One large promoter of DME is Oberon fuels, which manufacturers a skid-size unit capable of producing 3000–10,000 gallons (11,356–37,854 liters) of DME per day. With this arrangement, the problem of a fleet operation having available infrastructure to access steady supplies of DME is irrelevant for vehicles that make daily return trips to a home base where they can refuel.

Gaseous Fuels

Two gaseous fuels used in commercial vehicle applications are propane and natural gas. Both are hydrocarbons and each has a much lower carbon-to-hydrogen ratio than diesel fuel; their higher hydrogen levels make them gases rather than liquids. While both fuels are gaseous, their chemical structures are not the same, and there are many of differences between the fuels' other properties and combustion characteristics **FIGURE 48-12**.

FIGURE 48-11 This tank from a Volvo tractor keeps DME in a liquid state by pressurizing the tank.

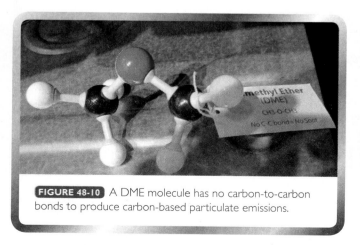

FIGURE 48-10 A DME molecule has no carbon-to-carbon bonds to produce carbon-based particulate emissions.

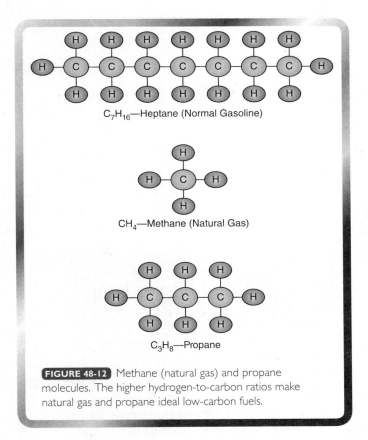

FIGURE 48-12 Methane (natural gas) and propane molecules. The higher hydrogen-to-carbon ratios make natural gas and propane ideal low-carbon fuels.

Natural gas, also called **methane**, has the chemical formula CH_4, and is lighter than air. **Propane** has the chemical formula is C_3H_8. Because propane has a higher carbon-to-hydrogen ratio, it is heavier than air **FIGURE 48-13**. Propane is extracted in small quantities from natural gas, which makes it more difficult to produce large supplies for widespread transportation consumption. Because natural gas burns with fewer noxious emissions than propane and is more widely available and cheaper than propane, propane has limited use in heavy-duty commercial engines. Instead, propane is more often used in light- and medium-duty

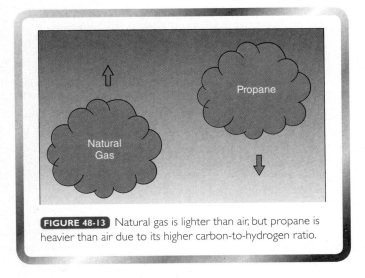

FIGURE 48-13 Natural gas is lighter than air, but propane is heavier than air due to its higher carbon-to-hydrogen ratio.

spark-ignition engines where it is stored onboard as a liquid. Propane has 70% of the power density of diesel fuel, which is superior to natural gas's 20%. The higher power density of liquid propane gas (LPG) enables the use of smaller fuel tanks compared to natural gas, which is most commonly compressed and stored in fuel tanks.

Natural Gas as a Transportation Fuel

Over the past 40 years, the interest in natural gas as an alternative fuel has tracked closely with the price differential between diesel and natural gas. In recent years, abundant amounts of natural gas have been recovered from shale rock formations using horizontal drilling techniques and fracking. The result is the plentiful availability of inexpensive natural gas while the prices of oil and diesel have both climbed. In addition to the cost advantage of natural gas, the technology used to adapt engines to burn natural gas has matured. Diesel engines are especially simple to convert or modify for natural gas operation. Two different methods are used to enable diesel engines to burn natural gas:

- Substituting diesel fuel injection systems for those that enable natural gas delivery
- Dual fuel engines that simultaneously burn diesel fuel and natural gas

Converting a diesel engine to burn only natural gas primarily involves replacing the cylinder head and diesel fuel injectors. In such a system, natural gas is mixed with air and drawn into the cylinders where it is ignited via an electric spark from a spark plug **FIGURE 48-14**. The engine's pistons are also replaced with ones that use combustion chamber bowls of different shapes that provide a lower compression ratio **FIGURE 48-15**. Because natural gas has an auto-ignition temperature of 1100–1200°F (593–649°C) and a high octane number of 130–140, it can be highly compressed without detonation or auto-ignition taking place **FIGURE 48-16**, **FIGURE 48-17**, and **FIGURE 48-18**. High auto-ignition temperatures and octane also mean that natural gas–fueled engines are easily turbocharged, which adds power density to an engine. This compensates for natural gas's lower power density compared to diesel fuel. Cummins is one of the major engine manufacturers that has developed natural gas engines using diesel engine blocks with a dedicated spark-ignition system.

The biggest technical challenge when converting an engine to natural gas combustion is controlling the higher heat loads in the cylinder. Natural gas has a **stoichiometric ratio** (which is the minimum mass of air required to completely burn all fuel in the combustion chamber so that no fuel or air remains after combustion) of 17.5:1. Burning fuel at that air–fuel ratio produces enormous amounts of heat, which can quickly burn valves and pistons. The solution is to operate the engine using a very lean burn combustion system, with air–fuel ratios up to 30:1 **FIGURE 48-19**. The additional combustion air supply helps dilute the excess combustion heat in the same way that excess air in a diesel engine reduces exhaust and combustion temperatures. The other solution, used more recently, is to burn natural gas at close to stoichiometric ratio, but recirculate high amounts of

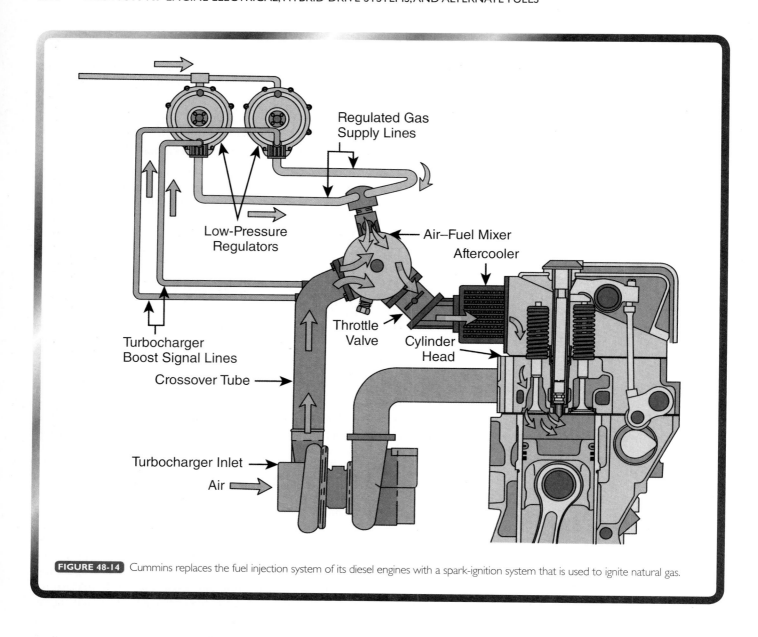

FIGURE 48-14 Cummins replaces the fuel injection system of its diesel engines with a spark-ignition system that is used to ignite natural gas.

exhaust gas into the cylinder to reduce peak temperatures and pressures.

Dual fuel engines are the second type of natural gas combustion system. In this system, diesel fuel is substituted with up to 85% natural gas **FIGURE 48-20** . No spark-ignition system is needed. Instead, a small amount of diesel fuel is injected into a conventional diesel combustion chamber to ignite a mixture of natural gas and air, which is drawn into the cylinder during the intake stroke. The use of a diesel fuel pilot injection event is also called a wet-spark ignition system. The power output in a dual fuel operation is the same as in a regular diesel operation, but it has the added advantage of providing a full diesel injection backup if the natural gas system fails or if there is no natural gas available. Engines currently retrofitted for natural gas consumption use dual fuel systems to provide diesel fuel as a fall back if natural gas prices go up or diesel fuel prices decline. Caterpillar, which has produced a variety of dual fuel engines

for on-highway, off-road, and power generation, lists the advantages of the dual fuel system as follows:

- Similar power to diesel
- Similar cooling system requirements as diesel
- Enables the use of cleaner burning, lower cost natural gas
- Increased engine life and potentially lower maintenance costs due to reduced oil contamination from combustion byproducts
- Retention of full diesel backup
- Retention of compression release engine braking capabilities
- Maintains vehicle resale value

A joint venture between Cummins and Westport, a Canada-based manufacturer of natural gas engine technology, has developed specialized fuel injectors that allow an engine to

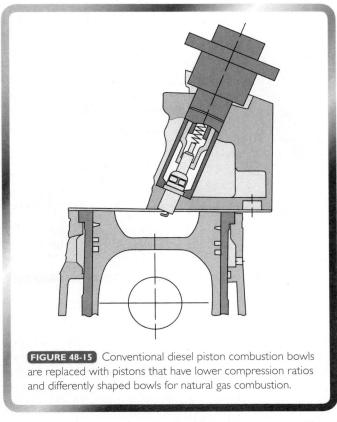

FIGURE 48-15 Conventional diesel piston combustion bowls are replaced with pistons that have lower compression ratios and differently shaped bowls for natural gas combustion.

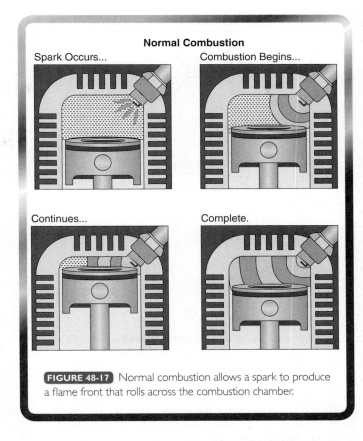

FIGURE 48-17 Normal combustion allows a spark to produce a flame front that rolls across the combustion chamber.

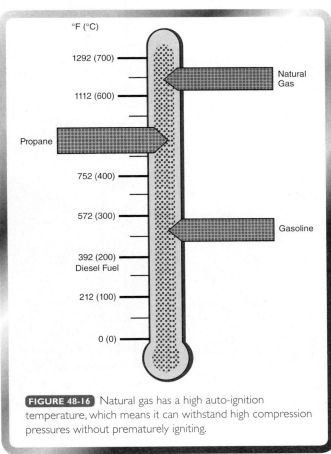

FIGURE 48-16 Natural gas has a high auto-ignition temperature, which means it can withstand high compression pressures without prematurely igniting.

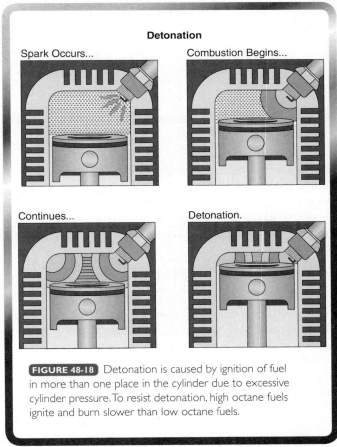

FIGURE 48-18 Detonation is caused by ignition of fuel in more than one place in the cylinder due to excessive cylinder pressure. To resist detonation, high octane fuels ignite and burn slower than low octane fuels.

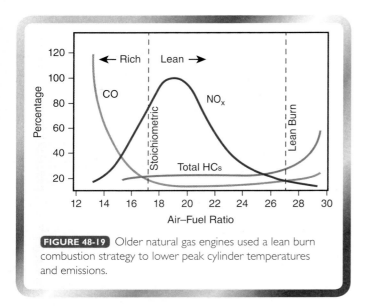

FIGURE 48-19 Older natural gas engines used a lean burn combustion strategy to lower peak cylinder temperatures and emissions.

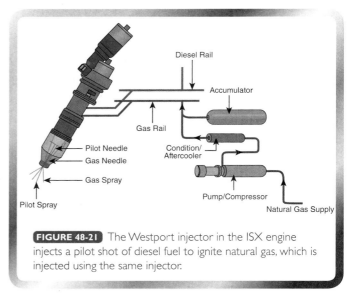

FIGURE 48-21 The Westport injector in the ISX engine injects a pilot shot of diesel fuel to ignite natural gas, which is injected using the same injector.

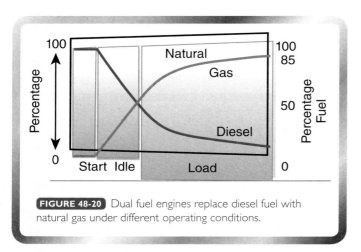

FIGURE 48-20 Dual fuel engines replace diesel fuel with natural gas under different operating conditions.

exists more readily as a gas, methane is transmitted and stored as a gas, even when compressed to more than 3000 psi (207 bar) inside a storage cylinder **FIGURE 48-22**. In this way, methane is unlike propane, which boils at −43°F (−42°C) at atmospheric pressure but converts to a liquid when compressed to 100 psi (689 kPa) at room temperature.

In its pure state, natural gas is odorless, colorless, and tasteless. It does not usually contain any toxic substances, so there is no health hazard in handling of the fuel. Heavy concentrations, however, can cause drowsiness and eventual suffocation. For safety reasons, such as preventing an accidental fire or explosion, an odorant called **mercaptan**, which has a smell similar to a skunk or rotten egg, is added in very small concentrations, such as 0.05%, so that any leak can be easily detected.

operate on up to 95% natural gas **FIGURE 48-21**. A wet-spark ignition system is used, but the injectors supply both diesel fuel and natural gas to the cylinders. However, because there are few natural gas supply stations, the use of an engine fueled primarily by natural gas creates range problems for long-distance trucking.

Properties and Characteristics of Natural Gas

The properties of natural gas, more accurately called methane, can be divided into two categories: physical properties and chemical properties. While the physical properties describe the physical aspects of the fuel (including its state, composition, weight, color, and odor) the chemical properties describe the fuel's combustion properties.

Methane is gaseous at any temperature warmer than −258°F (−161°C). At atmospheric pressure and a temperature of −258°F (−161°C), methane turns from a liquid into a gas. Because it

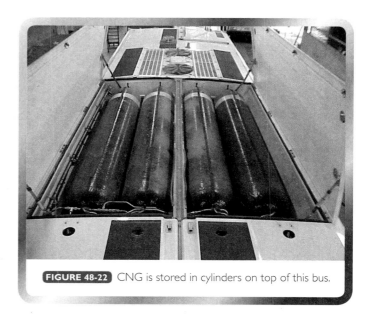

FIGURE 48-22 CNG is stored in cylinders on top of this bus.

The composition of natural gas is never constant; it can have 90–98% methane. The origin of the gas will determine its constituents. For example, bio-methane can be produced by composting garbage in landfills or sewage digesters where it is collected to operate diesel-powered electric generators or water pumps. Pulled from hundreds or thousands of feet (meters) below the earth's surface, the type of plant or animal material, which decomposed millions of years ago to form the gas, also changes its composition. However, methane is by far the largest component of natural gas. Other components can include ethane, propane, butane, pentane, nitrogen, CO_2, and traces of other gases. To maintain its high octane rating of 130–140, natural gas must be composed of at least 90% methane. Natural gas's octane rating is much higher than that of propane, which has an octane rating of 105, or good-quality, high-octane gasoline, which has an octane rating of 94.

To measure the quality of natural gas, the **Wobbe index** is especially important. The Wobbe index, also referred to as the Wobbe number, is a comparison of a gas's heating value compared to its density or specific gravity **TABLE 48-1**. Natural gas's Wobbe index changes when the content of higher density non-methane hydrocarbon increases or inert gas concentration rises.

The index that measures the knock resistance of gaseous fuels is called the **methane number**, and it uses methane and hydrogen as reference points. Methane, which has high knock resistance, is given the index 100. Hydrogen, which has low knock resistance, is given the index 0. If a particular gas mixture has a methane number of 70, its knock resistance is equivalent to that of a gas mixture of 70% methane and 30% hydrogen.

Methane is a very light fuel gas due to its high hydrogen content. At close to half the density of air, natural gas will rise if its leaks from a system. This important characteristic makes natural gas safer than most fuels because leaks quickly dissipate to the atmosphere **FIGURE 48-23**.

One problem with working with natural gas fuel is its very high ignition temperature. Bonds between the carbon and hydrogen atoms are very strong, which gives the fuel a

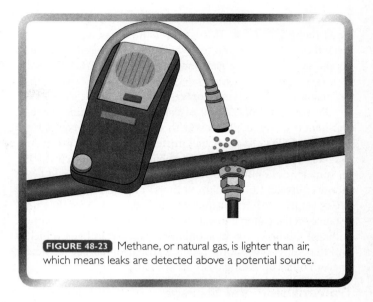

FIGURE 48-23 Methane, or natural gas, is lighter than air, which means leaks are detected above a potential source.

minimum ignition temperature of 1100–1200°F (593–649°C). More powerful ignition systems, which have higher energy output and special service practices, are required to produce and maintain higher spark plug firing voltage if a spark-ignition system is used to ignite natural gas.

Another unique combustion characteristic of methane is its range of flammability. The upper and lower range of flammability of any fuel is assigned as a percentage of air in an air–fuel mixture within which the mixture can burn. For natural gas, the lower flammability limit is 4%, while the upper limit is 16% **FIGURE 48-24**. This means that natural gas mixtures ignite within a range of 30:1 to 7:1 air–fuel ratio by weight. Compare this to gasoline, which ignites between 8:1 and 17:1, or propane, which has a 2% lower flammability limit and a 10% upper flammability limit. Methane's higher limit of flammability compared to other fuels allows for very lean air fuel mixtures when compression pressures are very high.

TABLE 48-1: Cummins Fuel Specifications for Natural Gas Engines

Methane	90%	Minimum
Ethane	4%	Maximum
Propane	1.7%	Maximum
C_4 and higher	0.7%	Maximum
C_8 and higher	0.2%	Maximum
$CO_2 + N_2$	3%	Maximum
Hydrogen	0.1%	Maximum
CO_2	0.1%	Maximum
Sulfur	10ppm	Maximum
Wobbe Index	1300–1377	Maximum
Water	4%	Maximum

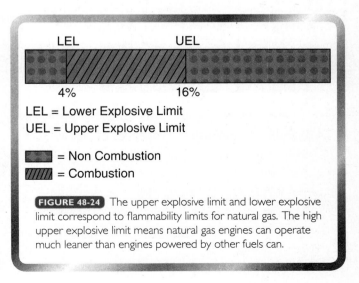

LEL = Lower Explosive Limit
UEL = Upper Explosive Limit

= Non Combustion
= Combustion

FIGURE 48-24 The upper explosive limit and lower explosive limit correspond to flammability limits for natural gas. The high upper explosive limit means natural gas engines can operate much leaner than engines powered by other fuels can.

Natural gas contains about 20% of the energy content of diesel fuel **TABLE 48-2**. This is why natural gas must be compressed or stored as liquid to give a vehicle powered by natural gas the same range as a gasoline or diesel vehicle. CNG is sold on a <u>Gasoline Gallon Equivalent (GGE)</u> basis to ensure that the customer is receiving equivalent energy value. The GGE for CNG is 5.66 lb (2.57 kg) of natural gas. This unit of measurement provides consumers with a useful tool for comparing the value of CNG to other fuel. Instead of purchasing 1 gallon (4 liters) of CNG (roughly 231 cubic inches [3785 cm]), the consumer would purchase 5.66 lb (2.57 kg), which would have energy equivalent to 1 gallon (4 liters) of gasoline **TABLE 48-3**. In use, vehicles will travel approximately 0.6–0.8 times the same distance on the gallon equivalent of CNG as they will on a liquid gallon of gasoline. On an economic basis, natural gas vehicles tend to compete best in the high fuel use fleet market segments when all other operating costs are similar.

Transmission and Storage

After natural gas is extracted, very little processing is required to make it suitable for use as a transportation fuel. First sand and dust are separated out of the raw gas. The heavier particles are removed by slowing the flow of gas to allow the heavy particles to drop out. Finer grains are removed from the gas by running it through a scrubber, which is a tank partially filled with oil. In a scrubber, the gas bubbles to the surface, but the dust is trapped in the oil.

The next step is the removal of the heavier hydrocarbons. Generally, this is accomplished by piping the gas through a scrubber tank containing mineral oil, which absorbs heavier hydrocarbons such as propane and butane. The mineral oil is then heated to vaporize the heavy hydrocarbons, which are recovered by condensation. Butane and propane are used to make LPG, and other heavier hydrocarbons are used to make gasoline.

Next, the gas is dehydrated, or freed from any water contained in it, in order to preserve the heating capacity of the gas and to protect gas pipelines from deposits and corrosion. A standardized level of dehydration is usually accomplished by passing the gas through beds of water-absorbing granules located in vertical towers. Natural gas is transported by pipeline at high pressure, which is maintained by pumping stations at regular intervals of about 93 miles (150km) along the pipeline. One concern for technicians regarding natural gas is the contamination of the gas by compressor lubricating oil. Because natural gas acts like an oil solvent, any oil removed from a compressor can travel to an engine and end up fouling sensitive fuel-metering controls. For this reason, natural gas filters are used on engines to coalesce, or separate, oil from natural gas. Once gas lines reach a city level, gas pressure drops to 30–50 psi (207–345 kPa). Pressure regulators at houses further reduce gas pressure to approximately 6–12″ (15–30 cm) of water column pressure. Because onboard gas storage systems compress natural gas to more than 3000 psi (207 bar), gas is pressurized to high pressures at filling stations in order to quickly fill CNG storage cylinders.

Liquid Natural Gas

To be practical as a transportation fuel, natural gas must either be compressed or liquefied to reduce the size of fuel storage tanks. Gas storage density is 600 times greater when natural gas is liquefied. Expressed another way, natural gas volume increases approximately 600 times when <u>liquid natural gas (LNG)</u> becomes a gas rather than a liquid. LNG is liquefied at −195°F to −260°F (−120°C to −160°C). Special vacuum-sealed, bottle-like containers called <u>Dewars</u> are required to store LNG to prevent it from turning to a gas. These Dewars are fabricated with an inner shell surrounded by super insulated vacuum space enclosed in an outer shell **FIGURE 48-25**. The insulation factor is equivalent to R-3000 (for comparison, a well-insulated house may have an R-30 insulated ceiling). After liquefaction, the power density of LNG is about 60% that of conventional diesel fuel. This means 1 gallon (3.8 liters) of LNG has an amount of energy equal to 0.6 gallon (2.2 liters) of diesel fuel. Reducing the volume of natural gas by liquefaction provides significant economic advantages for storing and transporting natural gas, which is why many gas-producing countries are constructing liquefaction facilities and ships to transport LNG to various markets. LNG is very clean because impurities such as water vapor, sulfur, and propane cannot survive the liquefaction process. For this same reason, LNG cannot be odorized because the mercaptan would solidify and not remain dissolved in the liquid.

Natural Gas Safety

In its pure state, natural gas is tasteless, colorless, and odorless. As a safety measure, it is odorized with ethyl mercaptan. The odor of ethyl mercaptan is unpleasant and similar to the odorant used in propane. The odor ensures that natural gas is detected

TABLE 48-2: Heating Properties of Natural Gas

Fuel	Units	Approximate Heating Value
Unleaded Gasoline	Btu/gallon (Btu/liter)	115,400 (436,837)
Diesel	Btu/gallon (Btu/liter)	128,980 (488,242)
CNG	Btu/lb (Btu/kg)	20,356 (9233)
CNG	Btu/cubic foot (Btu/liter)	923.7 (26,156)
Liquefied Natural Gas	Btu/gallon (Btu/liter)	78,000 (295,262)

TABLE 48-3: Combustion Properties of Natural Gas

0.0458 lb per cubic foot

923.7 Btu/cubic foot (26,156 Btu/liter)

Thermal Heat Value/GGE = 81,328.1 Btu

140 cubic feet (3964 liters) = 1 gallon (4 liters) diesel fuel

CNG mpg (km/L) = Diesel mpg (km/L) × 0.8

Octane = 130–140 points

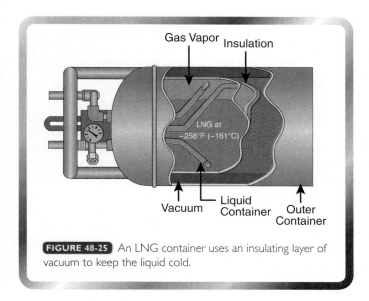

Gas Vapor   Insulation

LNG at
−258°F (−161°C)

Vacuum   Liquid
Container   Outer
Container

FIGURE 48-25 An LNG container uses an insulating layer of vacuum to keep the liquid cold.

in the atmosphere whenever its concentration reaches approximately 0.05%; this level is well below the level that will cause drowsiness or the weakest mixture that will support combustion.

Leaks and Caution

If a minor fuel leak of natural gas occurs:

- Eliminate all sources of ignition
- Switch off all engines
- Switch off all electrical devices
- Close all shutoff valves
- Allow the gas to disperse into a ventilated area
- Repair the system that was leaking

If a major fuel leak occurs, such as a fuel cylinder emptying:

- Ensure ventilation of the area surrounding the vehicle
- Evacuate the area surrounding the vehicle

- Do not operate any electric overhead doors (open doors manually only)
- Do not operate any electrical switches

Fire

In a natural gas fire, stop the fire by cutting off the fuel flow. Any secondary fire can then be put out with an extinguisher. If you cannot control the fire in this way, evacuate the area, then call the fire department and the police.

Collision Damage

In the event of a collision involving a vehicle powered by natural gas, turn off the ignition key and, if possible, close the master shut-off valve at the valve(s) of the cylinder(s). The natural gas fuel system is designed to contain fuel under high pressure. Its construction is mechanically stronger than that of its diesel or gasoline counterpart. This construction and the strict installation standards result in a system that is less likely to be damaged in a collision.

Inhalation

Natural gas is non-toxic and will not harm anyone breathing in low concentrations found near minor fuel leaks. Heavy concentrations, however, can cause drowsiness and eventual suffocation.

Vehicle Storage

Vehicles fueled with natural gas may be parked anywhere a gasoline-fueled vehicle is permitted, including underground commercial or residential parking facilities. When vehicles are stored for long periods, it is advisable to close the tank valve and run the vehicle until the natural gas in the system is depleted. While in a repair or conversion shop, shut off the master valve or cylinder valve(s) until repairs have been completed and leak tested, when natural gas is needed to run the engine.

Wrap-Up

Ready for Review

▸ Alternative fuels are defined as fuels derived from sources other than petroleum.

▸ Significant interest and financial investments in developing alternative fuel sources have been, and continue to be, made to reduce air pollution, GHG emissions, and dependency on oil imports.

▸ Renewable fuels are a category of alternative fuels that are made from sources that can be replaced or reproduced.

▸ While there are a variety of vehicle emissions that can contribute to GHGs, reducing the production of CO_2, a normal byproduct of combustion, is achievable by burning fuels with less carbon content.

▸ Reduction of CO_2 emissions, which are widely believed to be the man-made cause of global warming, can be accomplished by using fuels with lower carbon levels, including compressed natural gas (CNG), liquid natural gas (LNG), and hydrogen, or electric-powered vehicles that use current from solar or wind resources.

▸ Declining petroleum reserves and access to lower cost oil produced in regions free of conflict make the use of conventional petroleum-based fuels less sustainable with every passing year.

▸ At one time, many alternative fuels, including natural gas and biodiesel, had noxious emission characteristics that were superior to those of diesel fuel. This is not as important of a consideration today as it was a few years ago because today's diesel-fueled engines have negligible noxious emissions and all available fuels must meet the same, almost-zero, emissions output standards over the useful life of an engine.

▸ Ideally, any alternative fuel should provide the same or better power output from the same engine displacement as diesel fuel.

▸ Operating costs are a major factor when selecting an alternative fuel. An alternative fuel is usually more attractive to a company, fleet operation, or an individual if the initial investments to use the technology can be offset by reduced fuel expenditures, operating costs, or lifecycle costs.

▸ The availability of fueling infrastructure for any alternative fuel significantly influences the decision of customers about whether or not an alternative fuel can be used.

▸ There are three categories of alternative fuels used in diesel engines: renewable, non-renewable, and a combination of both types.

▸ There are also three different combustion systems used to burn alternative fuels.

▸ Conventional biodiesel is any fuel derived from plant material or animal fats. These fuels can produce up to a 20% reduction in GHG emissions compared to petroleum-based diesel fuel.

▸ E-diesel is a fuel made from combining petroleum-based diesel fuel and ethanol, an alcohol made from plant sugars. When diesel is blended with alcohol, it has some renewable fuel features.

▸ Fischer-Tropsch fuels are a category of biofuels made from substances including coal, plastic, and natural gas; these substances are first turned into a gas, and are then converted from a gas into a liquid.

▸ WPL is a promising type of renewable fuel that is derived from biomass using the process of pyrolysis.

▸ In Germany, Daimler is promoting the use of hydrogen as an alternative fuel for commercial vehicles. Rather than burning hydrogen in an engine, the gas is used to operate fuel cells by producing electricity to operate electric traction motors.

▸ Dimethyl ether (DME) is a methanol-like renewable fuel and one of the cleanest burning renewable fuels.

▸ Two gaseous fuels used in commercial vehicle applications are propane and natural gas. Both are hydrocarbons and each has a much lower carbon-to-hydrogen ratio than diesel fuel; their higher hydrogen levels make them gases rather than liquids.

▸ Propane is more often used in light- and medium-duty spark-ignition engines where it is stored onboard as a liquid.

▸ Over the past 40 years, the interest in natural gas as an alternative fuel has tracked closely with the price differential between diesel and natural gas. In recent years, inexpensive natural gas has become widely available while the prices of oil and diesel have both climbed.

▸ Diesel engines are especially simple to convert or modify for natural gas operation.

▸ In its pure state, natural gas is odorless, colorless, and tasteless. The composition of natural gas is never constant; it can have 90–98% methane. The origin of the gas will determine its constituents.

▸ The index that measures the knock resistance of gaseous fuels is called the methane number, and it uses methane and hydrogen as reference points.

▸ After natural gas is extracted, very little processing is required to make it suitable for use as a transportation fuel.

▸ Natural gas contains about 20% of the energy content of diesel fuel. To be practical as a transportation fuel, natural gas must either be compressed or liquefied to reduce the size of fuel storage tanks. Gas storage density is 600 times greater when natural gas is liquefied.

Vocabulary Builder

cellulosic biodiesel A renewable biodiesel derived from non-food based feedstock, like wood.

Dewar A vacuum-sealed, bottle-like storage container for LNG that is pressurized to approximately 100 psi (689 kPa). Dewars are fabricated with an inner shell surrounded by super insulating vacuum space enclosed in an outer shell.

dimethyl ether (DME) A methanol-like renewable fuel which is a gas at room temperature and requires pressurization to stay in liquid form.

e-diesel A category of renewable fuel made from a combination of diesel fuel and ethanol, a type of alcohol made from plant sugars.

emulsification A process where mechanical pressure is used to mix a fuel with water or another liquid.

Fischer-Tropsch fuels A category of biofuels made from substances including coal, plastic, and natural gas; these substances are first turned into a gas, and are then converted from a gas into a liquid. Unlike pyrolysis, the process used to make these fuels requires a catalyst and gas pressure to form hydrocarbon chains. Other names given to these fuels are syn-gas or gas-to-liquid (GTL) fuels.

Gasoline Gallon Equivalent (GGE) A standardized unit used to sell natural gas. It equals the energy content of 1 gallon (4 liters) of gasoline and is made up of approximately 231 cubic inches (3785 cubic centimeters) of natural gas or 5.66 lb (2.57 kg) of natural gas.

liquid natural gas (LNG) Liquefied methane that is condensed from a gas to a liquid at −195°F to −260°F (−120°C to −160°C).

Low Carbon Fuel Standard (LCFS) A standard administered by the California Air Resources Board aimed at reducing GHG emissions form the transportation sector. By reducing fuel consumption of motor vehicles by 10% by 2020 compared to a 2010 baseline less carbon emissions are expected to be emitted into the atmosphere.

mercaptan A gaseous fuel odorant that has a skunk-like or rotten egg–like smell. Mercaptan is added in very small concentrations to help detect any gaseous fuel leaks.

methane The primary constituent of natural gas. Methane's chemical formula is CH_4.

methane number A measurement of the knock resistance of gaseous fuels that do not contain octane molecules; similar to the measurement of octane. The methane number uses methane and hydrogen as reference points. Methane, which has high knock resistance, has a methane number of 100. Hydrogen, which has low knock resistance, has a methane number of 0.

propane A gaseous fuel that is heavier than air. It has the chemical formula C_6H_8. It is also referred to as liquid petroleum fuel (LPG).

pyrolysis A chemical process in which biomass feedstock is heated in the absence of air to gasify the material at temperatures of 842–1112°F (450–600°C).

Renewable Fuel Standard (RFS) A part of the US Energy Policy Act (EPAct) of 2005, which was expanded under the Energy Independence and Security Act (EISA) of 2007. It requires increasing amounts of fuel from renewable sources to be blended with gasoline and diesel fuel every year until 2022.

renewable fuels A category of alternative fuel sources that can be replaced or reproduced. Examples of renewables are biological based fuels such as those derived from vegetable oil or animal fat.

stoichiometric ratio The minimum mass of air required to completely burn all fuel in the combustion chamber so that no fuel or air remains after combustion.

sustainability The ability of an engine or fuel production process to be maintained over a long-term period.

wet-spark ignition system An engine that ignites natural gas using a pilot injection of diesel fuel.

Wobbe index (WI) A measure of gas quality made by comparing the heating value of a gas to its density or specific gravity; also called the Wobbe number.

wood pyrolysis liquid (WPL) A bio-oil liquid fuel produced from wood through pyrolysis.

Review Questions

1. _____ is a chemical process in which biomass feedstock is heated in the absence of air to gasify the material at temperatures of 842-1112°F (450-600°C).
   a. Pyrolysis
   b. Aftertreatment
   c. Wobbe index
   d. Wet-spark ignition

2. A measure of gas quality made by comparing the heating value of a gas to its density or specific gravity is called the _____.
   a. Fischer-Tropsch
   b. pyrolysis
   c. wet-spark ignition system
   d. Wobbe index (WI)

3. The _____ is an engine that ignites natural gas using a pilot injection of diesel fuel.
   a. aftertreatment system
   b. wet-spark ignition system
   c. Fischer-Tropsch
   d. Wobbe index

4. _____ is a methanol-like renewable fuel, which is a gas at room temperature and requires pressurization to stay in liquid form.
   a. Cellulosic biodiesel fuel
   b. Fischer-Tropsch fuel
   c. Dimethyl ether fuel
   d. Biomass-based fuel

5. _____ is a category of biofuels made from substances including coal, plastic, and natural gas.
   a. Fischer-Tropsch fuel
   b. Cellulosic biodiesel
   c. Biomass-based fuel
   d. E-diesel

6. The _____ aims to reduce transportation energy consumption by 10% by 2020 compared to a 2010 baseline.
   a. Low Carbon Fuel Standard
   b. Renewable Fuel Standard
   c. Diesel Exhaust Emission Standard
   d. Vehicle Emission Performance Standard

7. _____ biodiesel is derived from non-food-based feedstock, like wood.
   a. Propane
   b. Fischer-Tropsch
   c. Cellulosic
   d. Wood pyrolysis liquid

8. Power _____ is the power output per cubic inch (or cubic centimeter) of an engine over its entire operating range.
   a. temperature
   b. pressure
   c. mass
   d. density

9. E-diesel is a fuel made from combining petroleum-based diesel fuel and _____, an alcohol made from plant sugars.
   a. methane
   b. biomass
   c. natural gas
   d. ethanol

10. Finer grains sand and dust are removed from natural gas by running it through a(n) _____, which is a tank partially filled with oil.
    a. mixer
    b. scrubber
    c. aftercooler
    d. insulator

ASE-Type Questions

1. Technician A says fuel made from 100% biological sources is referred to as B100. Technician B says fuel made from 100% biological sources is an entirely renewable fuel. Who is correct?
   a. Technician A
   b. Technician B
   c. Both Technician A and Technician B
   d. Neither Technician A nor Technician B

2. Technician A says diesel engines are especially simple to convert or modify for natural gas operation. Technician B says diesel engines are rather difficult to convert or modify for natural gas operation. Who is correct?
   a. Technician A
   b. Technician B
   c. Both Technician A and Technician B
   d. Neither Technician A nor Technician B

3. Technician A says in its pure state, natural gas is toxic even though it is odorless, colorless and tasteless. Technician B says in its pure state, natural gas is odorless, colorless, tasteless, and does not usually contain any toxic substances. Who is correct?
   a. Technician A
   b. Technician B
   c. Both Technician A and Technician B
   d. Neither Technician A nor Technician B

4. Technician A says to be practical as a transportation fuel, natural gas must be compressed to reduce the size of fuel storage tanks. Technician B says to be practical as a transportation fuel, natural gas must be liquefied to reduce the size of fuel storage tanks. Who is correct?
   a. Technician A
   b. Technician B
   c. Both Technician A and Technician B
   d. Neither Technician A nor Technician B

5. Technician A says methane is a very light fuel gas due to its high oxygen content. Technician B says methane is a very light fuel gas due to its high nitrogen content. Who is correct?
   a. Technician A
   b. Technician B
   c. Both Technician A and Technician B
   d. Neither Technician A nor Technician B

6. Technician A says oil derived from algae can be produced from a small land mass than any other biofuel. Technician B says oil derived from ethanol can be produced from a small land mass than any other biofuel. Who is correct?
   a. Technician A
   b. Technician B
   c. Both Technician A and Technician B
   d. Neither Technician A nor Technician B

7. Technician A says e-diesel can be made from everything from wood and sawdust to garbage, agricultural waste, and manure. Technician B says cellulosic biodiesel can be made from everything from wood and sawdust to garbage, agricultural waste, and manure. Who is correct?
   a. Technician A
   b. Technician B
   c. Both Technician A and Technician B
   d. Neither Technician A nor Technician B

8. Technician A says the index that measures the knock resistance of gaseous fuels is called the octane number. Technician B says the index that measures the knock resistance of gaseous fuels is called the methane number. Who is correct?
   a. Technician A
   b. Technician B
   c. Both Technician A and Technician B
   d. Neither Technician A nor Technician B

9. Technician A says in a dual-fuel engine, diesel fuel is substituted with up to 75% natural gas. Technician B says in a dual-fuel engine, diesel fuel is substituted with up to 85% of natural gas. Who is correct?
   a. Technician A
   b. Technician B
   c. Both Technician A and Technician B
   d. Neither Technician A nor Technician B

10. Technician A says natural gas is a fuel with limited range capability. Technician B says ethanol is a fuel with limited range capability. Who is correct?
    a. Technician A
    b. Technician B
    c. Both Technician A and Technician B
    d. Neither Technician A nor Technician B

CHAPTER 49
Natural Gas Combustion Systems

NATEF Tasks

There are no NATEF tasks for this chapter.

Knowledge Objectives

After reading this chapter, you will be able to:

1. Identify and explain the advantages of using natural gas to fuel heavy-duty engines. (p 1329)
2. Identify the unique ignition systems used in natural gas engines and explain their requirements. (pp 1330–1333)
3. Identify and explain the operating principles of various air–fuel ratio strategies used in heavy-duty natural gas engines. (pp 1333–1334)
4. Identify the types of gas metering systems used in heavy-duty natural gas engines and describe their operation. (pp 1334–1337)
5. Describe the operation of dual-fuel gas metering systems. (pp 1336–1339)
6. Identify and describe components of natural gas storage systems. (pp 1339–1344)
7. Differentiate between liquid and gaseous natural gas fuel storage systems. (pp 1339–1344)
8. Describe how gas flows through gas storage systems. (pp 1339–1344)
9. Identify and explain the purpose of gas pressure control and safety devices. (pp 1339–1344)
10. Classify natural gas storage tanks according to their construction type. (pp 1339–1344)

Skills Objectives

After reading this chapter, you will be able to:

1. Replace the coalescing fuel filter. (pp 1343)
   SKILL DRILL 49-1

▶ Introduction

The use of natural gas as an alternative fuel gained traction in Europe, particularly in Italy, following WWII when fuels refined from petroleum oil were still in limited supply. However, natural gas, until recently, has only had a peripheral role as an engine fuel, except in market cycles when the price differential between diesel fuel and natural gas widened. One reason for the ebb and flow of interest in natural gas as an engine fuel is that the cost of converting engines to natural gas or buying new natural gas vehicles is expensive. A typical acquisition premium for a heavy-duty natural gas vehicle is close to 30% above the initial purchase price for conventional heavy-duty diesel-fueled vehicle. The range of vehicles powered by natural gas is also limited because little natural gas refueling infrastructure exists and engine power output is diminished by 10% or more in a vehicle running on natural gas.

Another reason for the low interest in natural gas vehicles is that the natural gas technology used by some original equipment manufacturers (OEMs) was not mature when it was released and some systems were unable to deliver reliable performance. This led to sharply increased vehicle operating costs. Additionally, specialized technician training and certification is mandatory for service personnel who repair or perform conversions to natural gas vehicles. In spite of the poor track record of natural gas engines, three major factors are raising general interest in natural gas as a mainstream fuel. The first is the enactment of various pieces of legislation in North America and around the world that aim to reduce production of greenhouse gas (GHG) emissions. Natural gas has a much lower carbon content compared to other fuels. With approximately a 60% reduction in particulate matter (PM) emissions and a 20% reduction in carbon dioxide (CO_2) output, natural gas engines go a long way to meeting new GHG emission standards.

The second factor is legislated requirements to use more renewable fuels. Because natural gas is available in abundant quantities and can be extracted from decomposing landfills or sewage waste, it qualifies as a renewable energy resource. The third, and most significant, factor is the price differential between natural gas and diesel fuel. With continuing drops in natural gas prices and the stubbornly high cost of diesel fuel, the higher purchase cost of a natural gas vehicle can be recovered in as little as a year and a half. A natural gas vehicle will continue to provide substantial savings over the lifetime of the vehicle.

▶ Converting Combustion Systems in Heavy-Duty Engines

Heavy-duty diesel engines are simple to convert or modify to natural gas operation. This enables heavy-duty diesel engines to maintain diesel-like reliability and performance while supplying the clean emissions and fuel economy of natural gas. Depending on an engine's ignition system and how the natural gas is delivered to the cylinders, it can often remain unchanged with the exception of the addition of the gas mixing and delivery system. Other major components (turbocharging, air handling, and electronic controls) remain the same.

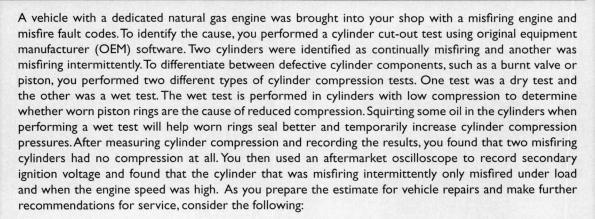

▶ You Are the Technician

A vehicle with a dedicated natural gas engine was brought into your shop with a misfiring engine and misfire fault codes. To identify the cause, you performed a cylinder cut-out test using original equipment manufacturer (OEM) software. Two cylinders were identified as continually misfiring and another was misfiring intermittently. To differentiate between defective cylinder components, such as a burnt valve or piston, you performed two different types of cylinder compression tests. One test was a dry test and the other was a wet test. The wet test is performed in cylinders with low compression to determine whether worn piston rings are the cause of reduced compression. Squirting some oil in the cylinders when performing a wet test will help worn rings seal better and temporarily increase cylinder compression pressures. After measuring cylinder compression and recording the results, you found that two misfiring cylinders had no compression at all. You then used an aftermarket oscilloscope to record secondary ignition voltage and found that the cylinder that was misfiring intermittently only misfired under load and when the engine speed was high. As you prepare the estimate for vehicle repairs and make further recommendations for service, consider the following:

1. How is ignition firing voltage different for engines fueled with natural gas? Explain why it is different.
2. If the air–fuel mixture became too rich for some reason, what effect would it have on the cylinder, valves, and turbochargers?
3. List three service precautions to follow when replacing spark plugs in natural gas engines.

Ignition Systems

In spite of the simplicity of many natural gas systems, the combustion of natural gas has several technical challenges. One is related to the ignition of natural gas. While diesel fuel will easily ignite at compressions ratios above 15:1, with 16:1 being the most common, natural gas requires a 38:1 compression ratio to achieve the cylinder temperature needed for ignition. To operate the engine, the gaseous fuel needs to be ignited either by an electrical spark or by an injection event that uses diesel fuel. When a pilot injection of diesel fuel is used, the diesel fuel ignites first and then spreads flames into the natural gas already introduced into the cylinder during the intake stroke **FIGURE 49-1**. An engine that uses a pilot injection of diesel fuel to initiate natural gas combustion is often called a **wet-spark ignition system**. An engine that combusts both diesel and natural gas together in the cylinder is referred to as a **dual-fuel engine**.

The two natural gas ignition systems each have advantages and disadvantages. Cummins Engine Company, which produces the highest number and most models of natural gas engines with 6–12L (366–732 cubic inch) displacements, uses electric spark ignition. Without a diesel injection system, these vehicles only have to carry one type of fuel and there is no duplication of fuel delivery system parts. The primary advantage of the electric spark system is that 100% natural gas is used. No other fuel or fuel system is needed.

If an electric spark ignition system is used, converting a diesel engine to burn only natural gas primarily involves replacing the cylinder head and diesel fuel injectors with a cylinder head adapted for spark plugs **FIGURE 49-2**. Pistons are also replaced with specialized pistons that have combustion chamber bowls of a different shape. These pistons provide a lower compression ratio, typically between 10:1 and 12:1 **FIGURE 49-3**. Because natural gas has an **auto-ignition temperature** (the temperature at which a fuel will ignite when heated) of 1100–1200°F (593–649°C) and a high octane number of 130–140, it can be

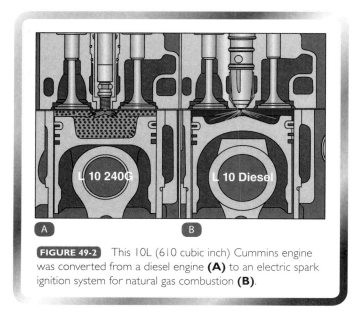

FIGURE 49-2 This 10L (610 cubic inch) Cummins engine was converted from a diesel engine **(A)** to an electric spark ignition system for natural gas combustion **(B)**.

FIGURE 49-3 A piston from an L-10 natural gas engine.

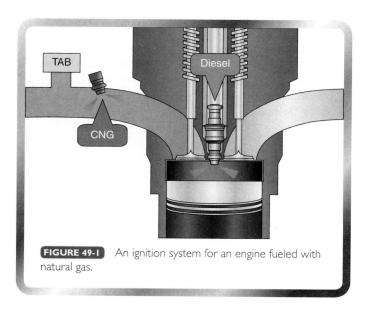

FIGURE 49-1 An ignition system for an engine fueled with natural gas.

highly compressed without the risk of **detonation** (an abnormal combustion event where an air–fuel mixture ignites before the spark plug fires) taking place. The resistance of natural gas to combustion knock can also be measured by using the **methane number** instead of octane. Natural gas engines require a methane index number of at least 90 to resist combustion knock caused by the other gases mixed with methane to form natural gas. The high auto-ignition temperatures and octane of natural gas also allow engines fueled by natural gas to be easily turbocharged, which adds power density to an engine. This helps compensate the lower heat value of natural gas in comparison to diesel fuel.

Dual-Fuel Ignition

Dual-fuel systems are popular with the aftermarket conversion industry, which has recently expanded due to increasing interest in converting heavy-duty diesel engines for natural gas. These engines can transition back and forth between natural gas and diesel fuel. The amount of natural gas used in dual-fuel engines varies, and can be as high as 70% depending on operating conditions and loads. With power output similar to that of convention diesel operation, dual-fuel engines have the advantage of providing a full diesel injection backup if the natural gas system fails or if natural gas refueling isn't available. Engines currently retrofitted for natural gas consumption use dual-fuel systems so that the vehicles can switch back to regular diesel fuel if natural gas prices go up or diesel fuel prices decline **FIGURE 49-4**.

In addition to aftermarket conversion systems that typically substitute natural gas for diesel fuel, a **High Pressure Direct Injection (HPDI)** dual-fuel system is available. This system, developed by Cummins Westport Inc., uses a unique injector that injects both diesel fuel and natural gas into the cylinder through a single injector. The injector uses a diesel pilot injection and replaces up to 95% of diesel fuel with natural gas.

Ignition System Requirements

Because the bonds between carbon and hydrogen atoms are very strong, and methane contains many of these bonds, methane is one of the hardest fuels to ignite. The energy of a spark ignition system used with natural gas is higher than ignition systems used in gasoline-fueled engines **FIGURE 49-5**. Ignition systems need to be maintained in optimal condition because there is little reserve voltage in natural gas engines. **Reserve voltage** is the difference between the voltage required to produce a spark across the spark plug gap needed to ignite the fuel and the additional voltage that can be delivered to the spark plugs. The strong bonds between carbon and hydrogen atoms are also why methane burns more slowly compared to gasoline and requires a different spark advance curve to adjust for engine speed and load conditions. Energy requirements are lowest when fuel is burning at close to stoichiometric ratio. The voltage required to ignite natural gas increases proportionally as air–fuel mixtures become leaner under load **FIGURE 49-6**.

Two other factors that increase the energy demands on natural gas ignition systems are **lean burn combustion** and the high combustion chamber turbulence produced when engines are turbocharged. With lean burn combustion, which uses more air than fuel, fuel molecules are spaced farther apart. The additional distance between the molecules makes it more difficult for chain reactions to occur between fuel and air during combustion to easily spread flames. When fuel molecules are closer, flames spread faster and jump from molecule to molecule more easily. Turbocharging has another interesting effect on the spark crossing the spark plug gap. High turbulence in the combustion chamber produced by the additional air mass actually bends and distorts the spark pathway and lengthens it.

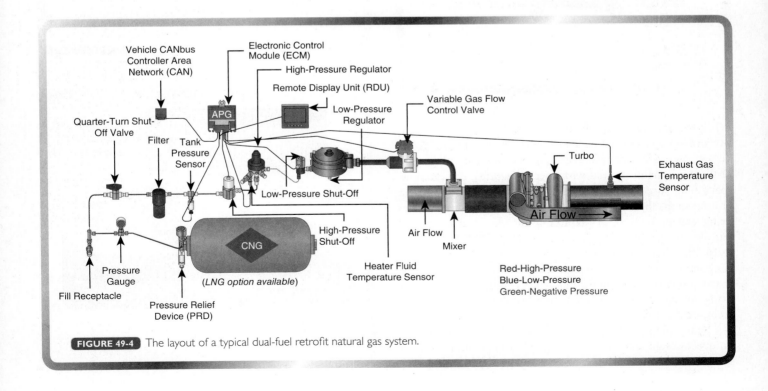

FIGURE 49-4 The layout of a typical dual-fuel retrofit natural gas system.

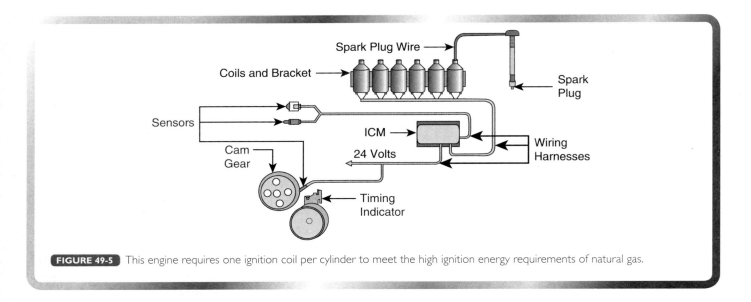

FIGURE 49-5 This engine requires one ignition coil per cylinder to meet the high ignition energy requirements of natural gas.

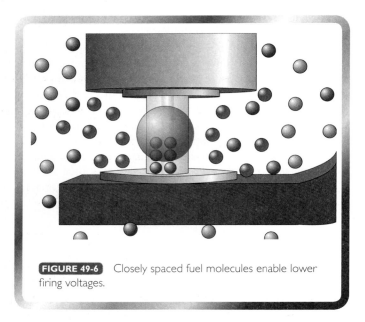

FIGURE 49-6 Closely spaced fuel molecules enable lower firing voltages.

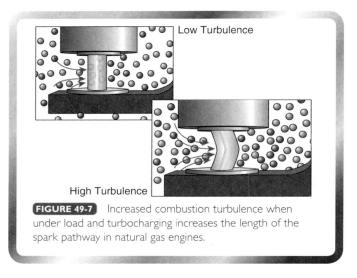

FIGURE 49-7 Increased combustion turbulence when under load and turbocharging increases the length of the spark pathway in natural gas engines.

When the pathway is lengthened, the gap becomes more resistive and more voltage is needed to bridge the gap **FIGURE 49-7**. To prevent misfires in natural gas engines, the spark plugs used in them are manufactured with special features. For example, spark plugs used in natural gas engines have electrodes and ground straps that have platinum pads, which not only reduces firing voltage because of platinum's low electrical resistance, but also makes the plugs last longer **FIGURE 49-8**. Platinum resists the chemical and mechanical erosion found in natural gas combustion chambers better than most other materials. If sharp points are maintained on a plug's platinum pad surfaces, firing voltages remain low compared to round surfaces, which are more resistive.

Spark plug boots, cables, and other insulators are also uniquely designed to withstand higher flashover and insulator breakdown caused by higher firing voltage **FIGURE 49-9**. The

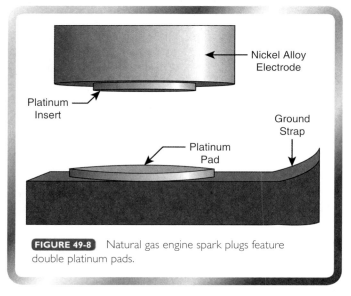

FIGURE 49-8 Natural gas engine spark plugs feature double platinum pads.

FIGURE 49-9 A heavy-duty spark plug extender and boot for a natural gas spark plug.

spark plugs for natural gas engines should never be handled with bare hands because the grease, dirt, or oil that can be transferred will cause the low resistance pathways and the plug to misfire. Plugs should be cleaned with alcohol prior to installation and handled with the paper found in the plug packing material.

Natural Gas Combustion Air–Fuel Ratio

A tougher challenge that must be handled when converting a diesel engine to a natural gas combustion system is controlling the higher heat loads in the cylinder. Diesel engines use excess air to dilute the heat of combustion, which lowers the cylinder heat loads produced by diesel fuel's approximately 4000°F (2204°C) flame temperature. Natural gas has a stoichiometric ratio of 17.5:1 and burning fuel at that air–fuel ratio produces enormous amounts of heat, which can quickly burn valves and pistons. The result is that engines burning natural gas at stoichiometric ratio have limited power, efficiency, and durability. High cylinder temperatures can also increase oxides of nitrogen (NO_x) emissions. However, due to the homogenous mixing of natural gas with air, less NO_x is produced from natural gas than from diesel fuel that is burned with very rich regions of fuel, which produces intense localized heat. In older engines, natural

gas was supplied to a mechanical air-and-gas mixing device. No air–fuel mixture feedback or adjustment controls such as oxygen sensors were used. Air–fuel ratios were not precise, particularly when gas quality changed. Three-way catalytic converters were used for emission control on these engines.

Gaseous Fuels and Power Density

Another problem of natural gas combustion is caused by the gaseous state of natural gas. While gaseous fuels easily mix with air to form homogeneous air–fuel mixtures in the engine's cylinder, which eliminates the need for cold-start enrichment that is needed by liquid fuels, gaseous fuels occupy a larger volume than liquid fuels. This means less air can enter the cylinder with gaseous fuels than with liquid fuels. The result is a limit to the amount of power a cylinder can produce from gaseous fuel relative to an injection of liquid diesel fuel. In high horsepower applications, the loss of power density due to reduced fuel and air mass can be a problem. Turbocharging engines and using richer air–fuel mixtures helps increase the power density of the latest natural gas engines **FIGURE 49-10**.

Lean Burn Combustion

Unlike spark-ignition engines fueled with gasoline, which can have detonation take place when air–fuel mixtures are lean, natural gas engines tend to have more **combustion knock** (combustion noise created by an abnormally sharp increase in cylinder pressure) and detonations when air–fuel mixtures are richer. The closer spacing of fuel molecules in rich air–fuel mixtures increases the likelihood of a rapid spread of the ignition flame front and uncontrolled combustion. One solution to the problem of engine damage caused by high combustion temperatures and detonation is to operate heavy-duty engines using a very lean burn combustion system with up to 30:1 air–fuel ratios under full load, with richer air–fuel mixtures at idle and partial load conditions **FIGURE 49-11**.

This strategy for operating turbocharged heavy-duty engines, which provides good emission characteristics and reliability, was introduced in the early 1990s. Adding more air than was needed to burn all the fuel in the cylinder helped dilute the excess combustion heat in the same way that excess air in a diesel reduces cylinder and exhaust temperatures. NO_x control

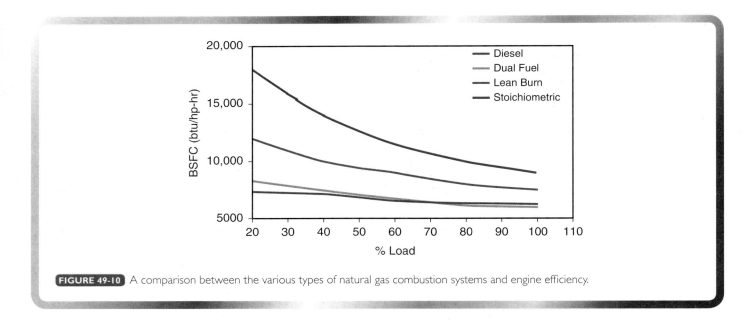

FIGURE 49-10 A comparison between the various types of natural gas combustion systems and engine efficiency.

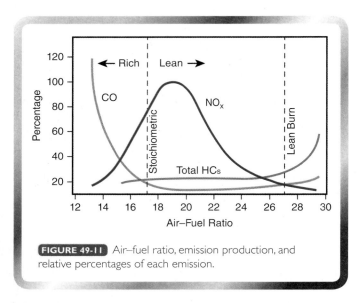

FIGURE 49-11 Air–fuel ratio, emission production, and relative percentages of each emission.

Stoichiometric Combustion with Cooled Exhaust Gas Recirculation

To meet the stricter emission standards for 2010, the other solution to reduce emissions and cylinder heat load was to burn natural gas at close to stoichiometric ratio but recirculate high amounts of exhaust gas into the cylinder to reduce peak temperatures and pressures. Spark-ignited, stoichiometric combustion with cooled exhaust gas recirculation technology involved using cooled EGR gas to replace the excess air in earlier lean burn engines **FIGURE 49-13**. The result was improved engine torque and fuel economy, particularly at low engine speeds. Cummins was one of the major engine manufacturers to develop natural gas engines using diesel engine blocks with a dedicated spark-ignition system. Using cooled EGR and stoichiometric air–fuel ratios, these late-model engines can meet the tougher EPA 10 emissions standards using three-way catalytic converters **FIGURE 49-14**. The latest engines introduced in 2015 by Cummins Westport Inc. use an injector similar to a common rail to deliver gas directly into the cylinders. This enables engines such as the ISL-G or ISB 6.7-G to meet even the near-zero California emission standards required for 2023 8 years ahead of schedule.

Gas Metering Systems

Air–fuel ratios need precise control in natural gas engines to maintain low emissions, prevent cylinder misfires, and provide good performance. Supplying the correct quantities of natural gas and air requires unique mass measuring and delivery systems. Older systems used simple mechanical controls and regulated gas delivery using intake vacuum signals and gas pressure regulators. A governor, which received inputs from the driver's accelerator pedal, engine rpm, boost pressure, and so on, electrically controlled a throttle plate moved by an electric motor. Later systems incorporated feedback controls,

was accomplished in the cylinder with this technique and no exhaust aftertreatment systems were needed. In this system, a two-way catalytic converter was installed in the exhaust system to reduce any hydrocarbon (HC) and carbon monoxide (CO) emissions, which could be produced at part throttle conditions **FIGURE 49-12**. In such a system, no NO_x catalysts could be used because the lean air–fuel mixtures would not work with a reduction catalyst, which is normally used to reduce NO_x emissions. Until the Environmental Protection Agency (EPA) 07 emission standards were introduced, lean burn combustion dominated natural gas combustion systems. In lean burn engines, fuel is metered into the cylinders using an electronically controlled metering system equipped with closed loop feedback oxygen sensors, which are used to adjust air–fuel ratios for various operating and load conditions.

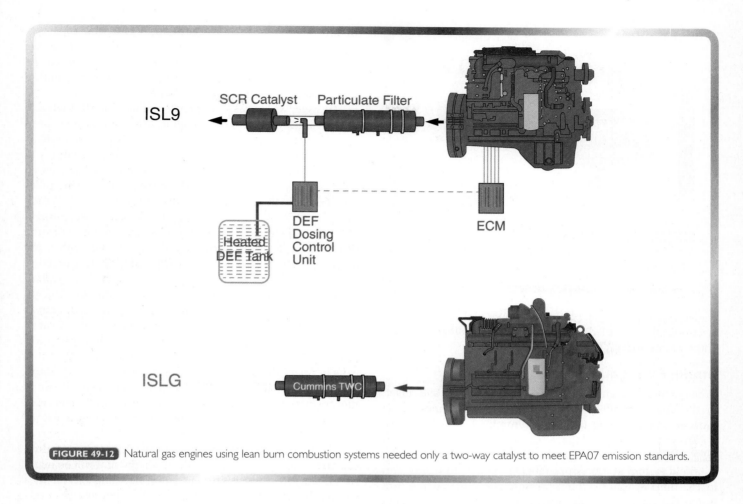

FIGURE 49-12 Natural gas engines using lean burn combustion systems needed only a two-way catalyst to meet EPA07 emission standards.

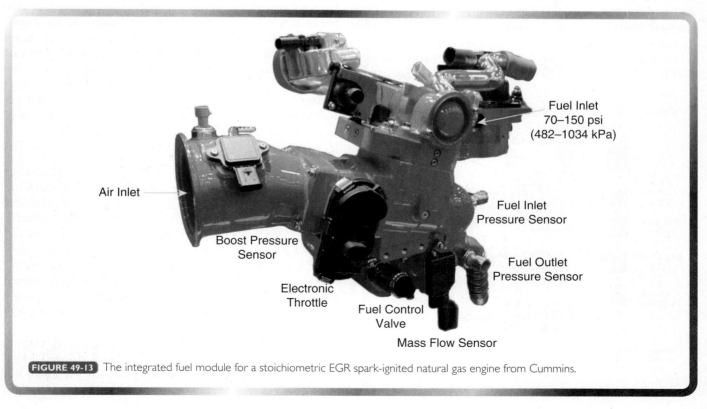

FIGURE 49-13 The integrated fuel module for a stoichiometric EGR spark-ignited natural gas engine from Cummins.

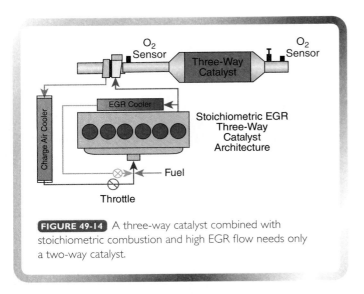

FIGURE 49-14 A three-way catalyst combined with stoichiometric combustion and high EGR flow needs only a two-way catalyst.

electronically controlled gas valves, and several different generations of injectors **FIGURE 49-15** .

Intake Fumigation

When natural gas is metered into the intake air flow and mixed in the intake manifold with air entering the cylinders, the process is called fumigation. The Cummins L-10G 240 Phase I Fuel System is representative of this type of configuration **FIGURE 49-16** . Gas is fumigated or introduced into the intake manifold system at a pressure ranging from 2″ to 6″ (51 mm to 152 mm) of water column pressure above the air pressure inside the intake manifold. Two low-pressure gas regulators are supplied fuel from the high-pressure gas storage tanks after gas pressure is stepped down using a high-pressure gas regulator. The high-pressure regulator drops storage tank pressure from more than 3600 psi (248 bar) to approximately 100 psi (689 kPa). Two regulators are necessary to supply an adequate

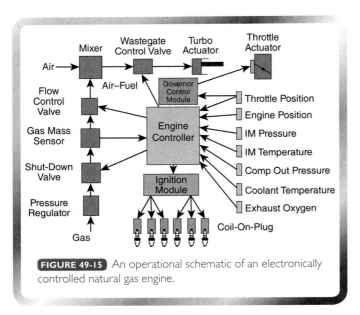

FIGURE 49-15 An operational schematic of an electronically controlled natural gas engine.

volume of gas to be used by the engine. Connected to the regulators are sensor lines that supply a signal that indicates the pressure of air of the intake system. When properly adjusted, the regulators will supply gas at a steady pressure of 2″ (51 mm) of water column above the intake pressure.

A **mixer** with a **gas control valve** adjusts the air–fuel ratio of the mixture entering the engine. At idle and low-speed operation, the fuel is metered in at close to a stoichiometric ratio. At full load and rated speed, the air–fuel ratio is in the range of 26:1. The air–fuel ratio is controlled through an air mass sensing device inside the mixer. Four sensing tubes protrude into the air stream of the mixer. One end of each tube protrudes above a spring loaded sealed the diaphragm chamber. When air flow through the mixer increases as the throttle is opened, it causes a pressure change within the diaphragm chamber of the mixer **FIGURE 49-17** . This pressure change is due to the **Bernoulli effect**, which acts like a siphon to pull air out of the chamber above the diaphragm. The gas control valve, which is metering gas into the intake air, is connected to the diaphragm and moves on and off its seat in response to diaphragm movement. The diaphragm spring will return the gas valve to its seat when no pressure differential exits between the mixer airway and the chamber area above the diaphragm **FIGURE 49-18** . Using this arrangement, small movements of the diaphragm produce only slight amounts of gas flow; large diaphragm movements produces proportionally larger flows of gas.

At relatively low intake air velocities, the pressure drop caused by the sensing tubes inside the diaphragm will be small. In this situation there is little gas flow. Increasing air velocities will produce proportionately large gas flow because the pressure difference between the area inside the diaphragm and the mixer airway is increasing. Because the diaphragm responds to the pressure differential between its chamber and the mixer airway, it will meter a quantity of gas proportional to airflow. It is important to observe that as the diaphragm lifts the gas valve, the diameter of the air passageway inside the mixer increases. This change in the cross sectional area of the mixer inlet varies the airflow into the engine and produces the change in air–fuel ratio.

Dynamic Gas Blending System

Intake fumigation is a method preferred by aftermarket conversion systems because it can use the engine's existing diesel fuel injection system to ignite fuel. Caterpillar and Cummins offer add-on systems to convert large generators and other industrial engines to natural gas by substituting up to 70% of diesel fuel with natural gas. The system, called the Dynamic Gas Blending System, is a dual-fuel application. When the engine is operating in dual-fuel mode, natural gas is drawn into the intake system through the turbocharger inlet **FIGURE 49-19** . The air–natural gas mixture from the intake is pulled into the cylinder, but with a leaner air–fuel ratio.

Near the end of the compression stroke, just before top dead center (TDC), a pilot injection of diesel fuel takes place, which ignites and in turn causes the natural gas to burn. These dual-fuel engines can operate on 100% diesel fuel or varying proportions

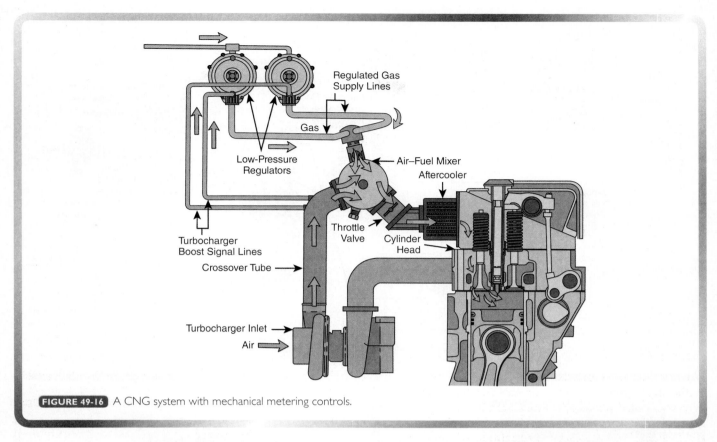

FIGURE 49-16 A CNG system with mechanical metering controls.

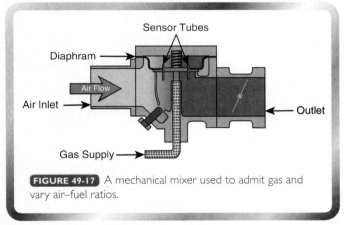

FIGURE 49-17 A mechanical mixer used to admit gas and vary air–fuel ratios.

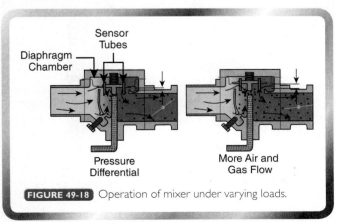

FIGURE 49-18 Operation of mixer under varying loads.

of diesel fuel and natural gas, but they cannot operate on natural gas alone. After the engine is started with diesel fuel and the intake air temperature rises with increasing boost pressure, increasing amounts of natural gas are injected into the cylinder through an electronically controlled gas valve located in the air intake valve. The proportion of diesel fuel injected decreases as greater quantities of natural gas are injected. When the quantity and quality of the natural gas changes, the electronic control software automatically adjusts the engine operation. Hardware conversion kits include the natural gas fuel system components, engine controls that can integrate with OEM electronic controls, and all software, sensors and mounting brackets. Conversion kits enable engines to meet emission standards and are certified for use by the EPA.

HPDI

Most dual-fuel engines can burn no more than 65–80% natural gas. However, the HPDI developed by Cummins Westport, Inc., which was designed based on the ISX high-pressure injection time-pressure injection (HPI-TPI) diesel injector, is capable of injecting both natural gas and diesel fuel **FIGURE 49-20**. The design enables engines to operate on up to 95% natural gas. These engines are no longer dual fuel in a traditional sense because they cannot switch to diesel-only operation using the HPDI. The injector itself was developed at the University of British Columbia and contains a unique dual nozzle valve design. The dual-fuel injector replaces the conventional diesel injector in the cylinder head, fitting into the cylinder with the same

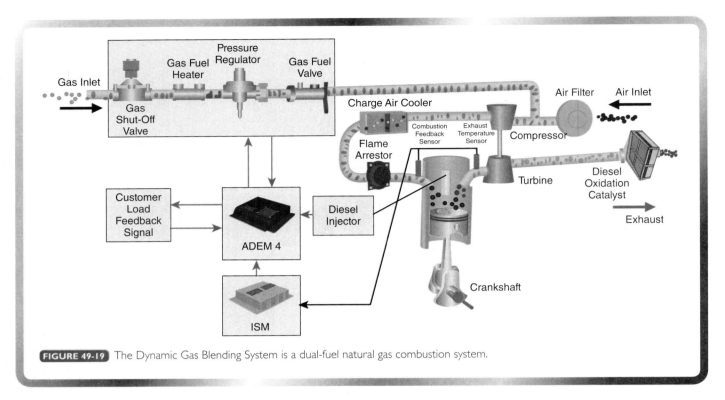

FIGURE 49-19 The Dynamic Gas Blending System is a dual-fuel natural gas combustion system.

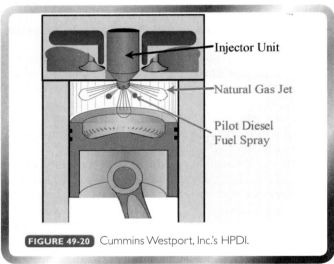

FIGURE 49-20 Cummins Westport, Inc.'s HPDI.

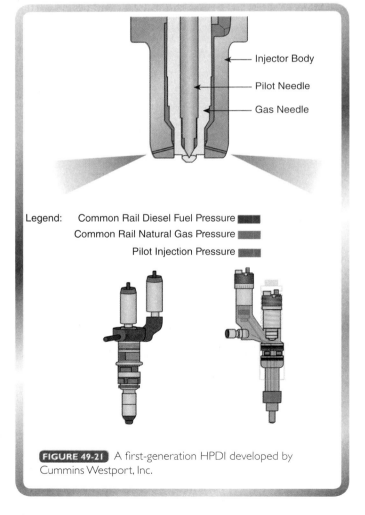

FIGURE 49-21 A first-generation HPDI developed by Cummins Westport, Inc.

compact shape **FIGURE 49-21**. The diesel nozzle at the injector's center uses a conventional inward opening, closed type nozzle. Like other common rail injectors, fuel pressure is developed by an overhead camshaft. Nozzle valve opening and closing is controlled by an electrically signaled solenoid, which regulates the state of hydraulic balance on either side of the nozzle valve. A second gas needle valve with an open center for the closed nozzle surrounds the diesel fuel nozzle valve. The gas valve's operation is also hydraulically controlled by a second solenoid. Gas and diesel fuel are supplied to the injector through separate, dedicated fuel rails. Downward movement of the overhead cam plunger drives gas into the cylinder and ends gas injection. During the gas nozzle's upward stroke, the amount of gas entering the injector is metered by varying the energization time of the solenoid.

A second-generation injector introduced in 2012 for use in the ISL-G engine uses a single control valve for both the natural gas and diesel fuel nozzle valve operation **FIGURE 49-22**. This injector's operation is again similar to a common rail injector operation. Independent control of the injection pressure, timing, and metering are accomplished by the electronic control of this injector **FIGURE 49-23**. The lower compression ratio used in this engine means it is not as thermally efficient as a diesel-only

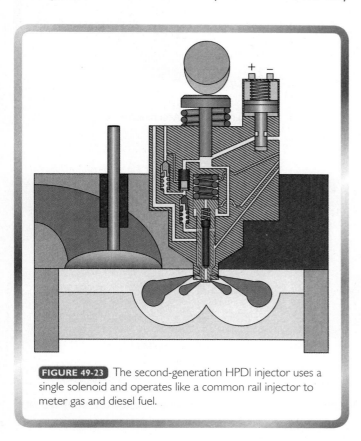

FIGURE 49-23 The second-generation HPDI injector uses a single solenoid and operates like a common rail injector to meter gas and diesel fuel.

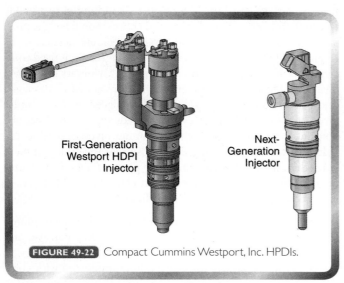

FIGURE 49-22 Compact Cummins Westport, Inc. HPDIs.

fuel system. These engines have slightly less torque, but estimates by the manufacturer for a 12L (732 cubic inch) ISX-G point to a fuel savings of $25,337/year with a 4.5 mpg (1.9 km/L) fuel economy compared with 5.0 mpg (2.1 km/L) operating on diesel fuel. And like other natural gas engines, there are substantial reductions in noise emissions along with the other environmental benefits.

In both generations of HPDIs, a hydraulically operated gas compressor removes gas from the fuel storage cylinders to transfer it to the engine, or a cryogenic pump for transferring liquefied natural gas is used **FIGURE 49-24**. The pumps enable the supply reservoirs to empty close to 90% of fuel from tanks or gas cylinders to provide extended range and efficient use of on-board gas storage capacity. High injection pressure can also be maintained at the same time—typically 3000 psi (207 bar).

▶ On-Vehicle Fueling and Storage Systems

On-board storage of natural gas can be either in the form of compressed natural gas (CNG) stored in cylinders at pressures up to 3600 psi (248 bar), or liquefied natural gas (LNG) cooled to 258°F (126°C) and pressurized to approximately 100 psi (689 kPa) in <u>Dewars</u> **FIGURE 49-25**. The choice between using CNG or cold <u>cryogenic</u> LNG, which has been turned into liquid and maintained as a liquid at very low temperatures, is based on a number of factors, including the weight of the load. The heavier CNG system can limit freight revenue. The size and weight of the fuel storage system, range required by the vehicle, and availability of CNG or LNG are all factors to consider. Because the energy density of LNG is 60% of conventional diesel fuel while CNG is only 25%, vehicles are able to haul heavier loads over longer distances using LNG. To increase the range of CNG storage, more cylinders and vehicle weight are added. Because CNG trucks do have a very short range, using CNG makes them suitable only for transit, utilities, and local or regional freight operations where they return to a yard daily for fueling. LNG trucks are better suited to longer haul freight operations, with a maximum range typically at 600 miles (966 km).

CNG Storage

Cylinders are installed in various places on a chassis. For low-floor buses, the cylinders are located on the rooftop. Rooftop storage not only allows for lower chassis ground clearance, but is safer in the event of a fire because natural gas, which is lighter than air, rises. CNG fuel systems, including cylinders, are designed to meet a variety of safety standards established by regulatory bodies. Only certified personnel can install, repair, service, or remove any part of a CNG fuel system. A qualification license is required to inspect, repair, and service natural gas–fueled vehicles.

To provide adequate range, a typical CNG system has several high-pressure storage cylinders. Cylinders are made from a number of different materials, each with its own advantages. The earliest cylinders were steel and could hold only 2400 psi

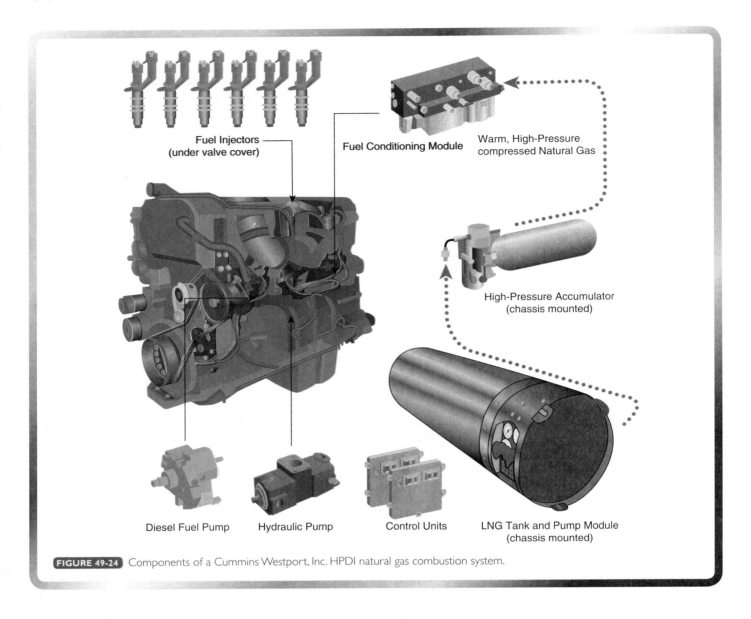

FIGURE 49-24 Components of a Cummins Westport, Inc. HPDI natural gas combustion system.

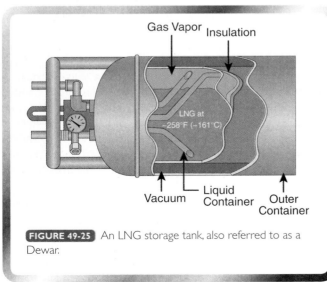

FIGURE 49-25 An LNG storage tank, also referred to as a Dewar.

(165 bar) of gas pressure. The cylinders had limited service life due to their continual expansion and contraction from gas pressure and temperature changes. These cylinders needed to be requalified for service on a regular basis. Later designs used combinations of steel, plastic, and carbon fiber. Cylinders must meet a variety of test standards to ensure they are not easily damaged and will not burst easily. A date code is placed on the cylinder label to indicate when the cylinder needs to be requalified for continued service. Requalifying a cylinder involves sending the cylinder to a special facility that pressurizes the tank and measures the amount of expansion taking place. Other test measures are used to check for any potential unseen structural failures.

There are four types of CNG cylinders:

- Type 1 cylinders are composed of only steel or aluminum. These cylinders were the earliest, least expensive, and heaviest cylinder design.
- Type 2 cylinders use a metal liner reinforced with composite glass or carbon fiber around the center of the

cylinder. Type 2 cylinders are also called hoop wrapped cylinders. The liner and the composite fiber distribute 50% of the stress produced by internal pressurization. These cylinders are lighter than Type 1 cylinders, but more expensive.

- Type 3 cylinders are constructed of a metal liner reinforced with glass or carbon fiber composite wrap around the entire tank. The cylinders most popular today are made from a fiberglass-wrapped aluminum shell. On a bus, each cylinder is approximately 100″ (254 cm) long and 15.8″ (40 cm) in diameter and weighs approximately 360 lb (163 kg). A cylinder this size can carry 1921 standard cubic feet (54 cubic meters) of CNG. When filled to capacity, a transit bus with eight cylinders will have enough fuel to operate for approximately 350 miles (563 km). While these tanks have the advantage of being lightweight, they are more expensive than Types 1 or 2 **FIGURE 49-26**.

- Type 4 cylinders are made from a plastic, gas-tight liner reinforced by composite wrapped around the entire cylinder. The entire strength of the cylinder is its composite fiber reinforcement. While this is the most lightweight tank design, it is also the most expensive in comparison to Types 1, 2, or 3.

Pressure Relief Devices

Pressure Relief Devices (PRDs) are designed to release pressure from a natural gas cylinder in the event of a fire **FIGURE 49-27**. Venting the cylinder during pressure build up will prevent the tank from explosively rupturing. PRDs can be pressure sensitive, temperature sensitive, or both. Thermally activated PRDs have a fusible material that melts at a predetermined temperature and opens a path for natural gas to release into the atmosphere. A series combination device is activated by both temperature and pressure. PRDs use a temperature-sensitive material that

FIGURE 49-26 A type 3 cylinder has serial numbers and other product information needed to certify the cylinder.

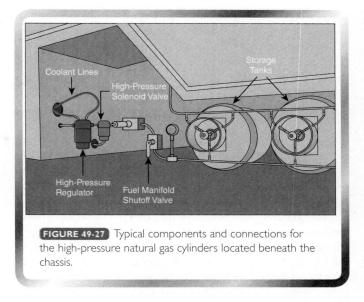

FIGURE 49-27 Typical components and connections for the high-pressure natural gas cylinders located beneath the chassis.

melts at 216–219°F (102–104°C). This allows a mechanical plunger to move inside the valve and vent all CNG from the cylinder through the vent tubes connected to the PRDs.

High-Pressure Solenoid Shutoff Valves

Each bank of cylinders has a high-pressure shutoff solenoid. The high-pressure solenoid shutoff valves are placed at the output line of the cylinder assemblies to provide fuel isolation when the vehicle is shut off. All the solenoid valves are energized open during normal operation, allowing fuel flow from the cylinders to the common fuel line. The solenoids are de-energized during refueling, on command of engine shutdown from the electronic control module (ECM), or upon activation of the fire suppression system.

Manual Shutoff Valves

A manual shutoff valve is mounted at the in-board end of each cylinder. Although normally opened, the valves can be used to isolate each cylinder individually. Closing the manual shutoff valves does not affect the operation of the PRDs. A quarter-turn manual shutoff valve is installed in the main supply line above the CNG manifold to control the fuel supply to the engine. During normal operating conditions the handle should be in the vertical (open) position. During servicing or maintenance activities, the handle should be in the horizontal (closed) position to isolate the fuel from the engine. Although the quarter-turn valve may be in the closed position, the fuel lines, cylinders, and the distribution lines are under high pressure. Prior to performing major maintenance work, always ensure that the fuel supply from the cylinders is shut off and that the pressure is released from all fuel lines.

High-Pressure Regulator

High-pressure regulators reduce the gas pressure from 3600 psi (248 bar) to approximately 100 psi (690 kPa). The pressure drop through the regulator causes the gas to absorb significant quantities of heat in order to expand and lower gas pressure.

Circulating warm engine coolant through a heating jacket in the regulator eliminates regulator freeze up. Coolant from the regulator is returned to the engine water pump. If more than one regulator is fitted in the system, the coolant lines are series connected to each regulator. The high-pressure regulator pressure is preset and not adjustable.

Lines and Pressure Gauges

There is no fuel level indicator for a CNG cylinder. The amount of fuel remaining in the cylinder is indicated by a dash-mounted low-fuel warning light. A CNG low-fuel indicator illuminates on the driver's front instrument panel whenever fuel system pressure is reduced to 500 psi (34 bar). In addition to the CNG pressure gauge located below the quarter-turn valve, an optional pressure gauge may be installed just inside the rear engine compartment door. A remote-mounted fuel filter is installed in the fuel-filling compartment at the top of the fueling assembly. This filter requires daily draining to remove any oil passed by the compressors used to pump natural gas through pipelines and fuel stations.

All fuel lines used by natural gas vehicles must conform to ASTM International (formerly known as the American Society for Testing Materials) standard A-13. A variety of tube fittings, all made from #316 stainless steel, are used to connect the fuel system. The tube fittings consist of a body, nut, front ferrule, and back ferrule **FIGURE 49-28** .

Replacing the Coalescing Fuel Filter

A natural gas fuel filter is a coalescing filter, which means it is primarily designed to remove oil from the gas. Oil readily dissolves in natural gas and will be carried through the high-pressure gas system. If oil is not removed, it will contaminate regulators and gas mass sensors. Oil should be drained from the filter through a drain valve located on the bottom of the filter housing. To replace the filter, the system needs to be depressurized.

To replace the coalescing fuel filter, follow the steps in **SKILL DRILL 49-1** .

Fuel Receptacles

Two CNG fueling receptacles are typically located on heavy-duty vehicles. Each receptacle connect to a quick-connect fitting at a fast-fill fuel station. A 0.5″ (12.7 mm) automotive style receptacle or a larger 0.75–1.0″ (19.1–25.4 mm) receptacle can be used for filling the larger fuel tanks found on heavy-duty vehicles **FIGURE 49-29** .

The filling adapter is connected to a manifold assembly that routes the fuel to and from the rooftop CNG cylinders, to the engine, and to other CNG-powered devices, such as coolant heaters on transit buses (if equipped). The manifold

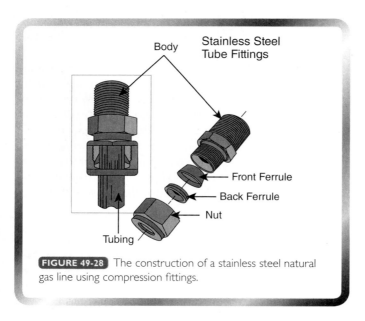

FIGURE 49-28 The construction of a stainless steel natural gas line using compression fittings.

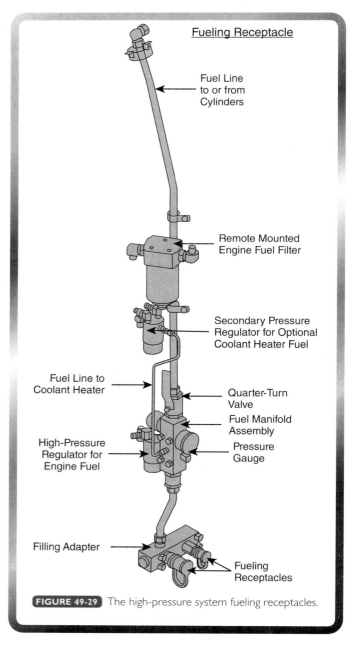

FIGURE 49-29 The high-pressure system fueling receptacles.

SKILL DRILL 49-1 Replacing the Coalescing Fuel Filter

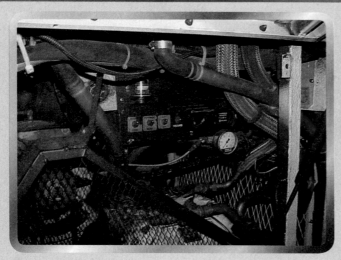

1 Shut off the vehicle.

2 Open the fuel cylinder access doors on the roof of the vehicle.

3 Turn off the manual shut-off valves at the end of each cylinder.

4 Start the engine from the engine compartment using the engine ignition and gauge box controls and run the vehicle until the engine stalls because of fuel starvation.

5 Check that the pressure gauge at the fuel filler compartment reads 0 psi (0 kPa). If the system is still pressurized, go to Step 6.

6 Place the ignition switch on the engine ignition and gauge box to the Off position to prevent the engine from igniting during Step 7.

7 Place the starter switch on the engine panel to the Start position and hold to engage the starting system. Residual natural gas from the fuel lines will now flow to the engine's air–fuel mixer, but there will be no engine ignition because the ignition switch was turned off in Step 6.

8 Check the pressure gauge in the fuel filler compartment to verify that the fuel pressure is at 0 psi (0 kPa); if not, repeat Steps 6–7.

9 Replace the coalescing fuel filter.

assembly contains a pressure gauge and a quarter-turn valve, which are used to turn off the fuel flow from the CNG cylinders **FIGURE 49-30**.

LNG Fuel Tank

LNG fuel tanks (commonly known as Dewars) are fabricated with an inner shell surrounded by super insulated vacuum space enclosed in an outer shell **FIGURE 49-31**. The insulation factor is equivalent to R-3000 (a house may have an R-30 ceiling). The tanks are made lighter to take advantage of the lower pressures maintained in the tank. An LNG tank will have a working pressure that is a maximum of 250 psi (17 bar), but 125 psi (8.6 bar) is typical. Vent valves are installed to release pressure if the liquid is absorbing heat and turning to vapor. If left for several days, some venting of the cylinders normally occurs. The fuel tanks and their supports are designed to withstand a g-force of 8g acceleration in all directions. Like CNG tanks, LNG tanks incorporate pressure relief strategies to ensure that excess fuel pressure is relieved in a controlled and safe manner in the event of an accident. After fuel leaves the tank, it passes through an LNG vaporizer, which warms cold liquid to convert it to a vapor usable by the fuel system.

LNG Leak Detection Systems

In service and fueling stations where LNG is found, a leak detection system using methane detectors is required because LNG has no odor to warn of leaks. The cold temperature of LNG would turn **mercaptan**, a gaseous fuel odorant that has a skunk-like or rotten egg–like smell, into a solid. Methane detectors are placed strategically above the refueling area. The methane

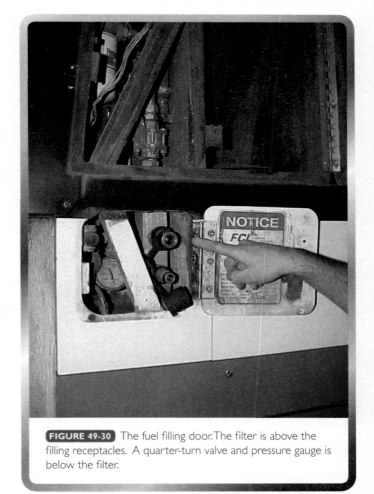

FIGURE 49-30 The fuel filling door. The filter is above the filling receptacles. A quarter-turn valve and pressure gauge is below the filter.

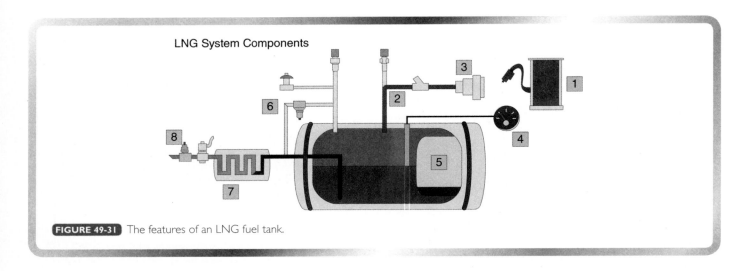

FIGURE 49-31 The features of an LNG fuel tank.

detectors provide outputs to activate alarms when certain levels of methane are detected. Most detectors are set up to alarm when 20% of the **lower flammability limit (LFL)** of methane in air is detected. LFL is the minimum concentration of fuel in air that will support combustion. Some refueling facilities have used a two-stage approach for methane detection and alarm. When 20% LFL is detected, a first level alarm is sounded. If the concentration increases, additional measures, such as shut down of the refueling system, are initiated or garage doors powered by electric motors are disabled.

Wrap-Up

Ready for Review

▶ Natural gas, until recently, has only had a peripheral role as an engine fuel.

▶ In spite of the poor track record of natural gas engines, general interest in natural gas as a mainstream fuel is rising.

▶ Heavy-duty diesel engines are simple to convert or modify to natural gas operation. This enables heavy-duty diesel engines to maintain diesel-like reliability and performance while supplying the clean emissions and fuel economy of natural gas.

▶ In spite of the simplicity of many natural gas systems, the combustion of natural gas has several technical challenges.

▶ There are two natural gas ignition systems; each has advantages and disadvantages.

▶ An engine that uses a pilot injection of diesel fuel to initiate natural gas combustion is often called a wet-spark ignition system.

▶ An engine that combusts both diesel and natural gas together in the cylinder is referred to as a dual-fuel engine.

▶ If an electric spark ignition system is used, converting a diesel engine to burn only natural gas primarily involves replacing the cylinder head and diesel fuel injectors with a cylinder head adapted for spark plugs. Pistons are also replaced with specialized pistons that have combustion chamber bowls of a different shape.

▶ Dual-fuel systems are popular with the aftermarket conversion industry, which has recently expanded due to increasing interest in converting heavy-duty diesel engines for natural gas. These engines can transition back and forth between natural gas and diesel fuel.

▶ The energy of a spark ignition system used with natural gas is higher than ignition systems used in gasoline-fueled engines.

▶ A tougher challenge that must be handled when converting a diesel engine to a natural gas combustion system is controlling the higher heat loads in the cylinder.

▶ Another problem of natural gas combustion is caused by the gaseous state of natural gas. Gaseous fuels occupy a larger volume than liquid fuels, so less air can enter the cylinder with gaseous fuels than with liquid fuels.

▶ One solution to the problem of engine damage caused by high combustion temperatures and detonation is to operate heavy-duty engines using a very lean burn combustion system with up to 30:1 air–fuel ratios under full load, with richer air–fuel mixtures at idle and partial load conditions.

▶ To meet the stricter emission standards for 2010, the other solution to reduce emissions and cylinder heat load was to burn natural gas at close to stoichiometric ratio but recirculate high amounts of exhaust gas into the cylinder to reduce peak temperatures and pressures.

▶ Air–fuel ratios need precise control in natural gas engines to maintain low emissions, prevent cylinder misfires, and provide good performance.

▶ When natural gas is metered into the intake air flow and mixed in the intake manifold with air entering the cylinders, the process is called fumigation.

▶ Intake fumigation is a method preferred by aftermarket conversion systems because it can use the engine's existing diesel fuel injection system to ignite fuel.

▶ Most dual-fuel engines can burn no more than 65–80% natural gas. However, the HPDI developed by Cummins Westport, Inc., which was designed based on the ISX high-pressure injection time-pressure injection (HPI-TPI) diesel injector, is capable of injecting both natural gas and diesel fuel.

▶ On-board storage of natural gas can be either in the form of compressed natural gas (CNG) stored in cylinders at pressures up to 3600 psi (248 bar), or liquefied natural gas (LNG) cooled to 258°F (126°C) and pressurized to approximately 100 psi (689 kPa) in Dewars.

▶ There are four types of CNG cylinders. Cylinders must meet a variety of test standards to ensure they are not easily damaged and will burst easily.

▶ Pressure Relief Devices (PRDs) are designed to release pressure from a natural gas cylinder in the event of a fire.

▶ LNG fuel tanks (commonly known as Dewars) are fabricated with an inner shell surrounded by super insulated vacuum space enclosed in an outer shell.

▶ In service and fueling stations where LNG is found, a leak detection system using methane detectors is required because LNG has no odor to warn of leaks.

Vocabulary Builder

auto-ignition temperature The temperature at which a fuel will ignite when heated.

Bernoulli effect The creation of a low-pressure area by the increased velocity of air (or a fluid). The lift of an airplane wing is a common example of the Bernoulli effect.

combustion knock A combustion noise created by an abnormally sharp increase in cylinder pressure. Knock is usually caused by detonation or pre-ignition of fuel in the cylinder by an atypical ignition source, such as a piece of hot carbon or hot spark plug insulator.

cryogenic A gas that is converted to a liquid and maintained as a liquid at a very low temperature.

detonation An abnormal combustion event where an air–fuel mixture ignites before the spark plug fires. Detonation is usually caused by high cylinder pressures, which drive up pre-ignition cylinder temperatures.

Dewar A vacuum-sealed, bottle-like storage container for LNG that is pressurized to approximately 100 psi (689 kPa). Dewars are fabricated with an inner shell surrounded by super insulating vacuum space enclosed in an outer shell.

dual-fuel engine An engine capable of combusting two different types of fuel, such as natural gas and diesel fuel.

gas control valve A valve within a mixer that responds to an electrical or vacuum signal to admit natural gas into the intake air stream.

High Pressure Direct Injection (HPDI) A dual-fuel system developed by Westport Industries that injects a small pilot injection of diesel fuel from the same injector that delivers natural gas. The bulk of this system's combustion fuel is natural gas.

lean burn combustion A combustion air–fuel mixture that uses more air than fuel, which exceeds a fuel's stoichiometric ratio.

lower flammability limit (LFL) The minimum concentration of fuel in air that will support combustion. Flammability limit units are measured in percentage by volume.

mercaptan A gaseous fuel odorant that has a skunk-like or rotten egg–like smell. Mercaptan is added in very small concentrations to help detect any gaseous fuel leaks.

methane number A measurement of the knock resistance of gaseous fuels that do not contain octane molecules; similar to the measurement of octane. The methane number uses methane and hydrogen as reference points. Methane, which has high knock resistance, has a methane number of 100. Hydrogen, which has low knock resistance, has a methane number of 0.

mixer A device used on natural gas engines to meter the correct amount of natural gas into the intake air.

reserve voltage The maximum voltage the secondary ignition system can produce to fire a spark plug.

wet-spark ignition system An engine that ignites natural gas using a pilot injection of diesel fuel.

Review Questions

1. _____ gas that is converted to a liquid and maintained as a liquid at a very low temperature.
   a. Cryogenic
   b. Detonation
   c. Lean burn combustion
   d. Bernoulli

2. _____ is an air-fuel mixture that uses more air than fuel.
   a. Stoichiometric combustion
   b. Bernoulli effect
   c. Lower flammability limit
   d. Lean burn combustion

3. The creation of a low-pressure area by the increased velocity of air (or a fluid) is called _____.
   a. lean burn combustion
   b. Bernoulli effect
   c. detonation
   d. stoichiometric combustion

4. _____ is an abnormal combustion event where an air-fuel mixture ignites before the spark plug fires.
   a. Liquid-ignition
   b. Bernoulli effect
   c. Detonation
   d. Lean burn combustion

5. _____ is the minimum concentration of fuel in air that will support combustion.
   a. Lower flammability limit
   b. Lean burn combustion
   c. Detonation
   d. Bernoulli effect

6. Natural gas has a much lower _____ content compared to other fuels.
   a. methane
   b. nitrogen
   c. hydrogen
   d. carbon

7. With _____, which uses more air than fuel, fuel molecules are spaced farther apart.
   a. stoichiometric combustion
   b. lean burn combustion
   c. detonation
   d. Bernoulli effect

8. Compressed natural gas _____ must meet a variety of test standards to ensure they are not easily damaged and will not burst easily.
   a. controls
   b. valves
   c. cylinders
   d. sensors

9. All _____ used by natural gas vehicles must conform to ASTM International standard A-13.
   a. fuel inlets
   b. fuel lines
   c. fuel control valves
   d. fuel pressure sensors

10. Liquefied natural gas is stored in _____.
    a. dewars
    b. shells
    c. containers
    d. receptacles

ASE-Type Questions

1. Technician A says Cummins Westport Inc. developed a unique HPDI injector that injects both diesel fuel and natural gas into the cylinder through a single injector. Technician B says an engine that combusts both diesel and natural gas together in the cylinder is referred to as a hybrid-diesel engine. Who is correct?
   a. Technician A
   b. Technician B
   c. Both Technician A and Technician B
   d. Neither Technician A nor Technician B

2. Technician A says spark plugs used in natural gas engines have electrodes and ground straps that have platinum pads. Technician B says the spark plugs in natural gas engines reduce firing voltage and make the plugs last longer. Who is correct?
   a. Technician A
   b. Technician B
   c. Both Technician A and Technician B
   d. Neither Technician A nor Technician B

3. Technician A says Caterpillar and Cummins offer add-on systems to convert large generators and other industrial engines to natural gas by substituting up to 85% of diesel fuel within natural gas. Technician B says Caterpillar and Cummins offer add-on systems to convert large generators and other industrial engines to natural gas by substituting up to 70% of diesel fuel within natural gas. Who is correct?
   a. Technician A
   b. Technician B
   c. Both Technician A and Technician B
   d. Neither Technician A nor Technician B

4. Technician A says a second-generation injector introduced in 2012 for use in ISL-G engines uses a dual control valve, one for natural gas and another for diesel fuel. Technician B says liquid natural gas trucks have a very short range, making them suitable only for transit, utilities, and local or regional freight operation. Who is correct?
   a. Technician A
   b. Technician B
   c. Both Technician A and Technician B
   d. Neither Technician A nor Technician B

5. Technician A says Type 2 compressed natural gas cylinders are also called hoop wrapped cylinders. Technician B says A Type 2 compressed natural gas cylinder is constructed of metal liner reinforced with glass or carbon fiber composite wrap around the entire tank. Who is correct?
   a. Technician A
   b. Technician B
   c. Both Technician A and Technician B
   d. Neither Technician A nor Technician B

6. Technician A says for low-floor buses, compressed natural gas cylinders are located at the rear of the bus. Technician B says for low-floor buses, compressed natural gas cylinders are located beneath the driver's area. Who is correct?
   a. Technician A
   b. Technician B
   c. Both Technician A and Technician B
   d. Neither Technician A nor Technician B

7. Technician A says the HPDI developed by Cummins Westport, Inc., enables engines to operate on up to 75% natural gas. Technician B says the HPDI developed by Cummins Westport, Inc., enables engines to operate on up to 95% natural gas. Who is correct?
   a. Technician A
   b. Technician B
   c. Both Technician A and Technician B
   d. Neither Technician A nor Technician B

8. Technician A says natural gas as a stoichiometric ratio of 17.5:1. Technician B says this ratio can result in burnt valves or pistons. Who is correct?
   a. Technician A
   b. Technician B
   c. Both Technician A and Technician B
   d. Neither Technician A nor Technician B

9. Technician A says the process of aspiration is when natural gas is metered into the intake air flow and mixed in the intake manifold with air entering the cylinders. Technician B says the process of fumigation is when natural gas is metered into the intake air flow and mixed in the intake manifold with air entering the cylinders. Who is correct?
   a. Technician A
   b. Technician B
   c. Both Technician A and Technician B
   d. Neither Technician A nor Technician B

10. Technician A says natural gas requires a compression ratio of 42:1 to achieve the cylinder temperature needed for ignition. Technician B says natural gas engines require a methane index number of at least 100 to resist combustion knock. Who is correct?
    a. Technician A
    b. Technician B
    c. Both Technician A and Technician B
    d. Neither Technician A nor Technician B

APPENDIX A
Units of Measure

▶ Multiples and Decimals for the Metric System

The units in the metric system are referred to as basic units. Prefixes are added to the units to expand their use. Always use the correct case when using metric measurements and prefixes. For example, 1 Mm is 1 megameter and is very different from 1 mm (millimeter).

Metric System Prefixes

Factor	Prefix	Symbol
1,000,000,000	giga	G
1,000,000	mega	M
1000	kilo	k
100	hecto	h
10	deca	da
1	No prefix	
0.1	deci	d
0.01	centi	c
0.001	milli	m
0.000001	micro	μ
0.000000001	nano	n

▶ Length

Length is a measurement of linear distance. The metric system uses millimeters (mm), centimeters (cm), meters (m), and kilometers (km). The imperial system uses inches and fractions ("), feet ('), and miles (mi). You will use length measurements frequently when replacing and repairing fasteners, determining wheelbase, shaft sizes—in short, any time you would use a ruler.

Length Conversions

1000 m = 1 km	1.61 km = 1 mi
0.62 mi = 1 km	0.304 m = 1 ft
0.39" = 1 cm	2.54 cm = 1"
0.039" = 1 mm	12.7 mm = ½"

▶ Mass

Mass is a unit or system of units by which a degree of heaviness is measured. The metric system uses grams (g), kilograms (kg), and tonnes (t). The imperial system uses ounces (oz), pounds (lb), and tons (T). In the workshop, you will use these measurements to determine the lifting capacity of equipment like hydraulic and engine hoists and floor jacks.

Mass Conversions

28.3 g = 1 oz	1 kg = 1000 g
1 lb = 16 oz	453 g = 1 lb
1 kg = 2.2 lb	1 t = 1000 kg
1 Ton = 2240 lb	0.98 tonne = 1 T
1.01 T = 1 tonne	

▶ Time

Time measurements are the same in both metric and imperial systems. However, the metric system's base unit of time is the second (s), whereas the imperial system uses the minute (min.) as its base measurement. Time is a key measurement to determine labor costs when servicing a vehicle.

Time Conversions

60 s = 1 min
1 s = 0.016 min

▶ Velocity

Velocity is the measurement of distance traveled over a period of time. The metric system uses meters/second (m/s) and kilometers/hour (km/h). The imperial system uses miles/hour (mph) and knots (kn). Velocity is used when checking speedometers, determining vehicle acceleration performance, and determining fuel consumption.

Velocity Conversions

1 kn = 1.15 mph	1 m/s = 3.6 km/h
1 mph = 0.87 kn	1 km/h = 0.27 m/s
1 mph = 1.6 km/h	1 km/h = 0.62 mph
1 kn = 1.85 km/h	1 km/h = 0.55 kn

▶ Volume

Volume is the amount of space occupied by a three-dimensional object. The metric system uses liters (l) or cubic centimeters (cc or cm^3). The imperial system uses gallons and quarts for "wet" volume and cubic feet or inches for "dry" volume. You will need to determine volume any time you fill a vehicle's reservoir with liquid. This includes fuel, coolant, oil, transmission fluid, or lubricant.

Volume Conversions

4 US quarts = 1 US gallon	1 liter = 1000 cc
1 cubic foot = 7.48 US gallons	1 cc = 0.001 liter
1 cubic foot = 6.22 UK gallons	1 liter = 0.035 cubic feet
1 US gallon = 3.78 liters	1 liter = 0.26 US gallons
1 UK gallon = 4.54 liters	1 liter = 0.21 UK gallons
1 US quart = 0.95 liters	1 liter = 1.05 quarts

▶ Area

Area is the amount of expanse of a flat or curved surface. The metric system uses square meters (m^2). The imperial system uses square inches (in^2), square feet (ft^2), and acres. You will need to understand area measurements when determining the size of wheel cylinders and brake calliper pistons.

Area Conversions

144 in^2 = 1 ft^2
1550 in^2 = 1 m^2
10.7 ft^2 = 1 m^2

▶ Electrical Units

Basic electrical measurements are volts, amperes, ohms, and watts. All these measurements are defined by Ohm's law.

Electrical units are uniform across both metric and imperial systems. You will need to know basic electrical concepts to determine electric loads, measure galvanic reactions and battery performance, and select the correct type of wiring and connections for vehicle electrical systems.

Basic Electrical Measurements

Volts (V) is the measurement of electromotive force (EMF or E).

Amperes (A) is the measurement of electrical current flow rate (I).

Ohms (Ω) is the measurement of electrical load or resistance (R).

Watts (W) is the measurement of power (P).

All of these measurements are defined by Ohm's law, which states that current flow in a circuit varies in direct proportion to changes in voltage, and in inverse proportion to changes in resistance. This is expressed in the equation:

$$E = I \times R \text{ } or \text{ } V = A \times \Omega$$

Electrical power is the product of electromotive force and current flow. This is expressed as:

$$P = I \times E \text{ } or \text{ } W = A \times V$$

▶ Pressure

Pressure is a measurement of force per unit area. The metric system uses kilopascals (kPa) and bar. The imperial system uses pounds per square inch (psi) and atmospheres. Vacuum is a term given to a pressure that is less than atmospheric pressure. The imperial system measures vacuum in inches of mercury (0 Hg) or inches of water. The metric system measures vacuum in millimeters of mercury (mm Hg). You will need to understand pressure conversions when filling tires and replacing air conditioning refrigerants or using a vacuum gauge.

Pressure Conversions

14.7 psi = 1 atmosphere	100 kPa = 1 bar
1 psi = 6.89 kPa	1″ Hg = 25.4 mm Hg
1 atmosphere = 101.3 kPa	1″ Hg = 14″ H$_2$0
1 atmosphere = 1.013 bar	760 mm Hg = 1 atmosphere

▶ Energy

Energy is used up when any physical system does work. The metric system uses calories (cal), joules (J), or kilojoules (kJ). These are also measurements of heat. The imperial systems uses British thermal units (Btu).

Energy Unit Definitions

1 cal is the amount of heat required to raise the temperature of 1 gram of water at 15°C by 1°C.

1 Btu is the amount of heat required to raise the temperature of 1 lb of water 1°F.

Energy Conversions

1 Btu = 1.05 kJ	1 kJ = 1000 J
0.0039 Btu = 1 cal	1 J = 0.0001 kJ
	1 cal = 4.18 J

▶ Temperature

Temperature is the measurement of heat intensity. The metric system uses degrees Celsius (°C) for normal use and Kelvin (K) for measurement in absolute terms. The imperial system uses degrees Fahrenheit (°F) for normal use and degrees Rankine (°R) for measurement in absolute terms.

Temperature conversions are important when you are rating thermostats and air conditioning outlets. You also need to know the optimum temperatures of cooling systems, automotive fluids, and engines.

To convert from: C to F = $32 + (C \times 1.8)$
To convert from: F to C = $(F - 32) \times 0.555$

Temperature Conversions

0°R = Absolute zero	0°K = Absolute zero
0°R = −459°F	0°K = −273°C
0°F = 459°R	0°C = 273K
0°F = −17.7°C	0°C = 32°F
100°F = 37.7°C	100°C = 212°F

▶ Torque

Torque is the twisting force applied to a shaft. The metric system uses the Newton meter (Nm). The imperial system uses the inch-pound (in-lb) and the foot-pound (ft-lb). Vehicle manufacturers specify torque settings for key fasteners on the engine and wheels. You will need to follow the specifications or you could strip threads or break bolts. Torque is also an important concept when discussing engine performance.

Torque Definitions

A Newton meter (Nm) is the twisting force applied to a shaft by a level 1 meter long with a force of 1 Newton applied to the end of the lever. (1N is equivalent to the force applied by a mass of 100.)

A foot-pound (ft-lb) is the twisting force applied to a shaft by a lever 1 foot long with a 1 pound mass on the end.

Torque Conversions

12 in-lb = 1 ft-lb
1 in-lb = 0.08 ft-lb
1 ft-lb = 1.34 Nm
1 Nm = 0.74 ft-lb
1 Nm = 8.8 in-lb

▶ Power

Power is the ability to do work. The metric system uses watts (W), kilowatts (kW), or pferdestärke (PS or metric horsepower). The imperial system uses horsepower (hp). Power measures an engine's size and performance.

Power Conversions

1 hp = 0.745 kW	1 kW = 1000 W
1 hp = 1.01 PS	1 kW = 1.36 PS
	1 kW = 1.34 hp
	1 PS = 0.98 hp

APPENDIX B

2014 NATEF Medium/Heavy Duty Truck Accreditation Task List Correlation Guide

NATEF Task List	NATEF Priority Number	Chapter
Required Supplemental Tasks		
Shop and Personal Safety		
1. Identify general shop safety rules and procedures.	N/A	3
2. Utilize safe procedures for handling of tools and equipment.	N/A	4
3. Identify and use proper placement of floor jacks and jack stands.	N/A	5
4. Identify and use proper procedures for safe lift operation.	N/A	5
5. Utilize proper ventilation procedures for working within the lab/shop area.	N/A	3
6. Identify marked safety areas.	N/A	3
7. Identify the location and the types of fire extinguishers and other fire safety equipment; demonstrate knowledge of the procedures for using fire extinguishers and other fire safety equipment.	N/A	3
8. Identify the location and use of eye wash stations.	N/A	3
9. Identify the location of the posted evacuation routes.	N/A	3
10. Comply with the required use of safety glasses, ear protection, gloves, and shoes during lab/shop activities.	N/A	3
11. Identify and wear appropriate clothing for lab/shop activities.	N/A	3
12. Secure hair and jewelry for lab/shop activities.	N/A	3
13. Demonstrate awareness of the safety aspects of supplemental restraint systems (SRS), electronic brake control systems, and hybrid vehicle high voltage circuits.	N/A	*
14. Demonstrate awareness of the safety aspects of high voltage circuits (such as high intensity discharge (HID) lamps, ignition systems, injection systems).	N/A	*
15. Locate and demonstrate knowledge of material safety data sheets (MSDS).	N/A	3
Tools and Equipment		
1. Identify tools and their usage in automotive applications.	N/A	4
2. Identify standard and metric designation.	N/A	4
3. Demonstrate safe handling and use of appropriate tools.	N/A	4
4. Demonstrate proper cleaning, storage, and maintenance of tools and equipment.	N/A	4
5. Demonstrate proper use of precision measuring tools (i.e., micrometer, dial-indicator, dial-caliper).	N/A	4
Preparing Vehicle for Service		
1. Identify information needed and the service requested on a repair order.	N/A	2
2. Identify purpose and demonstrate proper use of fender covers, mats.	N/A	2
3. Demonstrate use of the three C's (concern, cause, and correction).	N/A	2
4. Review vehicle service history.	N/A	2
5. Complete work order to include customer information, vehicle identifying information, customer concern, related service history, cause, and correction.	N/A	2

*All NATEF tasks for this standard can be found in *Fundamentals of Medium/Heavy Duty Commercial Vehicle Systems* (ISBN 978-1-2840-4116-3).

Continued on next page

NATEF Task List	NATEF Priority Number	Chapter
Preparing Vehicle for Customer		
1. Ensure vehicle is prepared to return to customer per school/company policy (floor mats, steering wheel cover, etc.).	N/A	2
Workplace Employability Skills		
Personal Standards		
1. Reports to work daily on time; able to take directions and motivated to accomplish the task at hand.	N/A	2
2. Dresses appropriately and uses language and manners suitable for the workplace.	N/A	2
3. Maintains appropriate personal hygiene.	N/A	2
4. Meets and maintains employment eligibility criteria, such as drug/alcohol-free status, clean driving record.	N/A	2
5. Demonstrates honesty, integrity, and reliability.	N/A	2
Work Habits/Ethic		
1. Complies with workplace policies/laws.	N/A	2
2. Contributes to the success of the team, assists others, and requests help when needed.	N/A	2
3. Works well with all customers and coworkers.	N/A	2
4. Negotiates solutions to interpersonal and workplace conflicts.	N/A	2
5. Contributes ideas and initiative.	N/A	2
6. Follows directions.	N/A	2
7. Communicates (written and verbal) effectively with customers and coworkers.	N/A	2
8. Reads and interprets workplace documents; writes clearly and concisely.	N/A	2
9. Analyzes and resolves problems that arise in completing assigned tasks.	N/A	2
10. Organizes and implements a productive plan of work.	N/A	2
11. Uses scientific, technical, engineering, and mathematics principles and reasoning to accomplish assigned tasks.	N/A	2
12. Identifies and addresses the needs of all customers, providing helpful, courteous, and knowledgeable service and advice as needed.	N/A	2
I. DIESEL ENGINES		
A. General		
1. Inspect fuel, oil, Diesel Exhaust Fluid (DEF) and coolant levels, and condition; determine needed action.	P-1	12, 13, 15, 33
2. Identify engine fuel, oil, coolant, air, and other leaks; determine needed action.	P-1	11, 12, 13, 15, 17, 26, 27, 32
3. Listen for engine noises; determine needed action.	P-3	8, 9, 11, 17, 29, 30, 32
4. Observe engine exhaust smoke color and quantity; determine needed action.	P-2	7, 8, 17, 18, 26, 28
5. Check engine no cranking, cranks but fails to start, hard starting, and starts but does not continue to run problems; determine needed action.	P-1	8, 15, 18, 19, 20, 23, 24, 25, 26, 27, 37
6. Identify engine surging, rough operation, misfiring, low power, slow deceleration, slow acceleration, and shutdown problems; determine needed action.	P-1	8, 9, 15, 17, 18, 19, 20, 23, 24, 25, 26, 27, 29, 30, 37
7. Identify engine vibration problems.	P-2	8, 9, 10
8. Check and record electronic diagnostic codes.	P-1	15, 22, 28, 30, 35, 38

Continued on next page

NATEF Task List	NATEF Priority Number	Chapter
B. Cylinder Head and Valve Train		
1. Inspect cylinder head for cracks/damage; check mating surfaces for warpage; check condition of passages; inspect core/expansion and gallery plugs; determine needed action.	P-2	11
2. Disassemble head and inspect valves, guides, seats, springs, retainers, rotators, locks, and seals; determine needed action.	P-3	11
3. Measure valve head height relative to deck and valve face-to-seat contact; determine needed action.	P-3	11
4. Inspect injector sleeves and seals; measure injector tip or nozzle protrusion; determine needed action.	P-3	24
5. Inspect valve train components; determine needed action.	P-1	11
6. Reassemble cylinder head.	P-3	11
7. Inspect, measure, and replace/reinstall overhead camshaft; measure/adjust end play and backlash.	P-3	11
8. Inspect electronic wiring harness and brackets for wear, bending, cracks, and looseness; determine needed action.	P-1	38
9. Adjust valve bridges (crossheads); adjust valve clearances and injector settings.	P-2	11
C. Engine Block		
1. Perform crankcase pressure test; determine needed action.	P-1	9
2. Remove, inspect, service, and install pans, covers, gaskets, seals, wear rings, and crankcase ventilation components.	P-2	9, 11, 29
3. Disassemble, clean, and inspect engine block for cracks/damage; measure mating surfaces for warpage; check condition of passages, core/expansion and gallery plugs; inspect threaded holes, studs, dowel pins, and bolts for serviceability; determine needed action.	P-2	10
4. Inspect cylinder sleeve counter bore and lower bore; check bore distortion; determine needed action.	P-2	10
5. Clean, inspect, and measure cylinder walls or liners for wear and damage; determine needed action.	P-2	9, 10
6. Replace/reinstall cylinder liners and seals; check and adjust liner height (protrusion).	P-2	10
7. Inspect in-block camshaft bearings for wear and damage; determine needed action.	P-3	10
8. Inspect, measure, and replace/reinstall in-block camshaft; measure/adjust end play.	P-3	10, 11
9. Clean and inspect crankshaft for surface cracks and journal damage; check condition of oil passages; check passage plugs; measure journal diameter; determine needed action.	P-2	10
10. Inspect main bearings for wear patterns and damage; replace as needed; check bearing clearances; check and correct crankshaft end play.	P-2	10
11. Inspect, install, and time gear train; measure gear backlash; determine needed action.	P-2	10, 11
12. Inspect connecting rod and bearings for wear patterns; measure pistons, pins, retainers, and bushings; perform needed action.	P-3	9
13. Determine piston-to-cylinder wall clearance; check ring-to-groove fit and end gap; install rings on pistons.	P-3	9
14. Assemble pistons and connecting rods; install in block; install rod bearings and check clearances.	P-2	9
15. Check condition of piston cooling jets (nozzles); determine needed action.	P-2	9
16. Inspect crankshaft vibration damper; determine needed action.	P-3	10
17. Install and align flywheel housing; inspect flywheel housing(s) to transmission housing/engine mating surface(s) and measure flywheel housing face and bore runout; determine needed action.	P-3	10
18. Inspect flywheel/flexplate (including ring gear) and mounting surfaces for cracks and wear; measure runout; determine needed action.	P-2	10, 43

Continued on next page

NATEF Task List	NATEF Priority Number	Chapter
D. Lubrication Systems		
1. Test engine oil pressure and check operation of pressure sensor, gauge, and/or sending unit; test engine oil temperature and check operation of temperature sensor; determine needed action.	P-1	12
2. Check engine oil level, condition, and consumption; determine needed action.	P-1	12
3. Inspect and measure oil pump, drives, inlet pipes, and pick-up screens; check drive gear clearances; determine needed action.	P-3	12
4. Inspect oil pressure regulator valve(s), by-pass and pressure relief valve(s), oil thermostat, and filters; determine needed action.	P-3	12
5. Inspect, clean, and test oil cooler and components; determine needed action.	P-3	12
6. Inspect turbocharger lubrication systems; determine needed action.	P-2	29
7. Determine proper lubricant and perform oil and filter change.	P-1	*
E. Cooling System		
1. Check engine coolant type, level, condition, and consumption; test coolant for freeze protection and additive package concentration; determine needed action.	P-1	13
2. Test coolant temperature and check operation of temperature and level sensors, gauge, and/or sending unit; determine needed action.	P-1	13
3. Inspect and reinstall/replace pulleys, tensioners and drive belts; adjust drive belts and check alignment.	P-1	13
4. Inspect thermostat(s), by-passes, housing(s), and seals; replace as needed.	P-2	13
5. Recover coolant, flush, and refill with recommended coolant/additive package; bleed cooling system.	P-1	13
6. Inspect coolant conditioner/filter assembly for leaks; inspect valves, lines, and fittings; replace as needed.	P-1	13
7. Inspect water pump and hoses; replace as needed.	P-1	13
8. Inspect, clean, and pressure test radiator. Pressure test cap, tank(s), and recovery systems; determine needed action.	P-1	13
9. Inspect thermostatic cooling fan system (hydraulic, pneumatic, and electronic) and fan shroud; replace as needed.	P-1	13
10. Inspect turbo charger cooling systems; determine needed action.	P-2	30
F. Air Induction and Exhaust Systems		
1. Perform air intake system restriction and leakage tests; determine needed action.	P-1	28
2. Perform intake manifold pressure (boost) test; determine needed action.	P-3	28
3. Check exhaust back pressure; determine needed action.	P-3	34
4. Inspect turbocharger(s), wastegate, and piping systems; determine needed action.	P-2	29, 30, 36
5. Inspect turbocharger(s) (variable ratio/geometry VGT), pneumatic, hydraulic, electronic controls, and actuators.	P-2	30, 36
6. Check air induction system: piping, hoses, clamps, and mounting; service or replace air filter as needed.	P-1	28
7. Remove and reinstall turbocharger/wastegate assembly.	P-3	29
8. Inspect intake manifold, gaskets, and connections; replace as needed.	P-3	28
9. Inspect, clean, and test charge air cooler assemblies; replace as needed.	P-2	32
10. Inspect exhaust manifold, piping, mufflers, and mounting hardware; repair or replace as needed.	P-2	34
11. Inspect exhaust after treatment devices; determine necessary action.	P-2	33
12. Inspect and test preheater/inlet air heater, or glow plug system and controls; perform needed action.	P-2	8
13. Inspect exhaust gas recirculation (EGR) system including EGR valve, cooler, piping, filter, electronic sensors, controls, and wiring; determine needed action.	P-2	31, 36

*All NATEF tasks for this standard can be found in *Fundamentals of Medium/Heavy Duty Commercial Vehicle Systems* (ISBN 978-1-2840-4116-3).

Continued on next page

NATEF Task List	NATEF Priority Number	Chapter
G. Fuel System		
1. Fuel Supply System		
1. Check fuel level, and condition; determine needed action.	P-1	15
2. Perform fuel supply and return system tests; determine needed action.	P-1	15
3. Inspect fuel tanks, vents, caps, mounts, valves, screens, crossover system, supply and return lines and fittings; determine needed action.	P-1	15
4. Inspect, clean, and test fuel transfer (lift) pump, pump drives, screens, fuel/water separators/indicators, filters, heaters, coolers, ECM cooling plates, and mounting hardware; determine needed action.	P-1	15
5. Inspect and test pressure regulator systems (check valves, pressure regulator valves, and restrictive fittings); determine needed action.	P-1	15, 19, 20
6. Check fuel system for air; determine needed action; prime and bleed fuel system; check primer pump.	P-1	15, 25
2. Electronic Fuel Management System		
1. Inspect and test power and ground circuits and connections; measure and interpret voltage, voltage drop, amperage, and resistance readings using a digital multimeter (DMM); determine needed action.	P-1	*
2. Interface with vehicle's on-board computer; perform diagnostic procedures using electronic service tool(s) (to include PC based software and/or data scan tools); determine needed action.	P-1	16, 24, 26, 27, 35, 36, 37, 38, 39
3. Check and record electronic diagnostic codes and trip/operational data; monitor electronic data; clear codes; determine further diagnosis.	P-1	16, 18, 24, 27, 35, 36, 37, 38
4. Locate and use relevant service information (to include diagnostic procedures, flow charts, and wiring diagrams).	P-1	35
5. Inspect and replace electrical connector terminals, seals, and locks.	P-1	45
6. Inspect and test switches, sensors, controls, actuator components, and circuits; adjust or replace as needed.	P-1	22, 35
7. Using electronic service tool(s) access and interpret customer programmable parameters.	P-1	18, 38, 39
8. Perform on-engine inspections, tests and adjustments on electronic unit injectors (EUI); determine needed action.	P-2	24, 25
9. Remove and install electronic unit injectors (EUI) and related components; recalibrate ECM (if applicable).	P-2	24
10. Perform cylinder contribution test utilizing electronic service tool(s).	P-1	16
11. Perform on-engine inspections and tests on hydraulic electronic unit injectors (HEUI) and system electronic controls; determine needed action.	P-2	26
12. Perform on-engine inspections and tests on hydraulic electronic unit injector (HEUI) high pressure oil supply and control systems; determine needed action.	P-2	26
13. Perform on-engine inspections and tests on high pressure common rail (HPCR) type injection systems; determine needed action.	P-2	27
14. Inspect high pressure injection lines, hold downs, fittings and seals; determine needed action.	P-2	19
H. Engine Brakes		
1. Inspect and adjust engine compression/exhaust brakes; determine needed action.	P-2	34
2. Inspect, test, and adjust engine compression/exhaust brake control circuits, switches, and solenoids; determine needed action.	P-3	34
3. Inspect engine compression/exhaust brake housing, valves, seals, lines, and fittings; determine necessary action.	P-3	34
II. DRIVE TRAIN		
All NATEF tasks for this standard can be found in *Fundamentals of Medium/Heavy Duty Commercial Vehicle Systems* (ISBN 978-1-2840-4116-3).		

*All NATEF tasks for this standard can be found in *Fundamentals of Medium/Heavy Duty Commercial Vehicle Systems* (ISBN 978-1-2840-4116-3).

Continued on next page

NATEF Task List	NATEF Priority Number	Chapter
III. BRAKES		
All NATEF tasks for this standard can be found in *Fundamentals of Medium/Heavy Duty Commercial Vehicle Systems* (ISBN 978-1-2840-4116-3).		
IV. SUSPENSION AND STEERING		
All NATEF tasks for this standard can be found in *Fundamentals of Medium/Heavy Duty Commercial Vehicle Systems* (ISBN 978-1-2840-4116-3).		
V. ELECTRICAL/ELECTRONIC SYSTEMS		
A. General Electrical Systems		
1. Read and interpret electrical/electronic circuits using wiring diagrams.	P-1	45
2. Check continuity in electrical/electronic circuits using appropriate test equipment.	P-1	22
3. Check applied voltages, circuit voltages, and voltage drops in electrical/electronic circuits using appropriate test equipment.	P-1	22
4. Check current flow in electrical/electronic circuits and components using appropriate test equipment.	P-1	*
5. Check resistance in electrical/electronic circuits and components using appropriate test equipment.	P-1	*
6. Locate shorts, grounds, and opens in electrical/electronic circuits.	P-1	*
7. Identify parasitic (key-off) battery drain problems; perform tests; determine needed action.	P-1	42
8. Inspect and test fusible links, circuit breakers, relays, solenoids, and fuses; replace as needed.	P-1	*
9. Inspect and test spike suppression devices; replace as needed.	P-3	*
10. Check frequency and pulse-width signal in electrical/electronic circuits using appropriate test equipment.	P-3	21
B. Battery		
1. Identify battery type; perform appropriate battery load test; determine needed action.	P-1	42
2. Determine battery state of charge using an open circuit voltage test.	P-1	42
3. Inspect, clean, and service battery; replace as needed.	P-1	42
4. Inspect and clean battery boxes, mounts, and hold downs; repair or replace as needed.	P-1	42
5. Charge battery using appropriate method for battery type.	P-1	42
6. Inspect, test, and clean battery cables and connectors; repair or replace as needed.	P-1	42
7. Jump start a vehicle using jumper cables and a booster battery or appropriate auxiliary power supply using proper safety procedures.	P-1	42
8. Perform battery capacitance test; determine needed action.	P-2	42
9. Identify and test low voltage disconnect (LVD) systems; determine needed repair.	P-2	42
C. Starting System		
1. Perform starter circuit cranking voltage and voltage drop tests; determine needed action.	P-1	43
2. Inspect and test components (key switch, push button, and/or magnetic switch) and wires and harnesses in the starter control circuit; replace as needed.	P-2	43
3. Inspect and test starter relays and solenoids/switches; replace as needed.	P-1	43
4. Remove and replace starter; inspect flywheel ring gear or flex plate.	P-1	43
D. Charging System Diagnosis and Repair		
1. Test instrument panel mounted volt meters and/or indicator lamps; determine needed action.	P-1	44
2. Identify causes of no charge, low charge, or overcharge problems; determine needed action.	P-1	44
3. Inspect and replace alternator drive belts, pulleys, fans, tensioners, and mounting brackets; adjust drive belts and check alignment.	P-1	44
4. Perform charging system voltage and amperage output tests; perform AC ripple test; determine needed action.	P-1	44

*All NATEF tasks for this standard can be found in *Fundamentals of Medium/Heavy Duty Commercial Vehicle Systems* (ISBN 978-1-2840-4116-3).

Continued on next page

NATEF Task List	NATEF Priority Number	Chapter
5. Perform charging circuit voltage drop tests; determine needed action.	P-1	44
6. Remove and replace alternator.	P-1	44
7. Inspect, repair, or replace cables, wires, and connectors in the charging circuit.	P-1	44

E. Lighting Systems

All NATEF tasks for this standard can be found in *Fundamentals of Medium/Heavy Duty Commercial Vehicle Systems* (ISBN 978-1-2840-4116-3).

F. Gauges and Warning Devices

All NATEF tasks for this standard can be found in *Fundamentals of Medium/Heavy Duty Commercial Vehicle Systems* (ISBN 978-1-2840-4116-3).

G. Related Electrical Systems

All NATEF tasks for this standard can be found in *Fundamentals of Medium/Heavy Duty Commercial Vehicle Systems* (ISBN 978-1-2840-4116-3).

VI. HEATING, VENTILATION, AND AIR CONDITIONING

A. HVAC Systems

All NATEF tasks for this standard can be found in *Fundamentals of Medium/Heavy Duty Commercial Vehicle Systems* (ISBN 978-1-2840-4116-3).

B. A/C System and Components

All NATEF tasks for this standard can be found in *Fundamentals of Medium/Heavy Duty Commercial Vehicle Systems* (ISBN 978-1-2840-4116-3).

C. Heating and Engine Cooling Systems

NATEF Task List	NATEF Priority Number	Chapter
1. Identify causes of outlet air temperature control problems in the HVAC system; determine needed action.	P-1	*
2. Identify window fogging problems; determine needed action.	P-2	*
3. Perform engine cooling system tests for leaks, protection level, contamination, coolant level, coolant type, temperature, and conditioner concentration; determine needed action.	P-1	*
4. Inspect engine cooling and heating system hoses, lines, and clamps; determine needed action.	P-1	*
5. Inspect and test radiator, pressure cap, and coolant recovery system (surge tank); determine needed action.	P-1	13
6. Inspect water pump; determine needed action.	P-1	13
7. Inspect and test thermostats, by-passes, housings, and seals; determine needed repairs.	P-2	13
8. Recover, flush, and refill with recommended coolant/additive package; bleed cooling system.	P-1	13
9. Inspect thermostatic cooling fan system (hydraulic, pneumatic, and electronic) and fan shroud; replace as needed.	P-2	*
10. Inspect and test heating system coolant control valve(s) and manual shut-off valves; determine needed action.	P-2	*
11. Inspect and flush heater core; determine needed action.	P-3	*

D. Operating Systems and Related Controls

All NATEF tasks for this standard can be found in *Fundamentals of Medium/Heavy Duty Commercial Vehicle Systems* (ISBN 978-1-2840-4116-3).

E. Refrigerant Recovery, Recycling, and Handling‡

All NATEF tasks for this standard can be found in *Fundamentals of Medium/Heavy Duty Commercial Vehicle Systems* (ISBN 978-1-2840-4116-3).

VII. Preventive Maintenance And Inspection

A. Engine System

1. Engine

All NATEF tasks for this standard can be found in *Fundamentals of Medium/Heavy Duty Commercial Vehicle Systems* (ISBN 978-1-2840-4116-3).

2. Fuel System

All NATEF tasks for this standard can be found in *Fundamentals of Medium/Heavy Duty Commercial Vehicle Systems* (ISBN 978-1-2840-4116-3).

*All NATEF tasks for this standard can be found in *Fundamentals of Medium/Heavy Duty Commercial Vehicle Systems* (ISBN 978-1-2840-4116-3).

Continued on next page

NATEF Task List	NATEF Priority Number	Chapter
3. Air Induction and Exhaust System		
1. Check exhaust system mountings for looseness and damage.	P-1	*
2. Check engine exhaust system for leaks, proper routing, and damaged or missing components to include exhaust gas recirculation (EGR) system and after treatment devices, if equipped.	P-1	*
3. Check air induction system: piping, charge air cooler, hoses, clamps, and mountings; check for air restrictions and leaks.	P-1	*
4. Inspect turbocharger for leaks; check mountings and connections.	P-1	*
5. Check operation of engine compression/exhaust brake.	P-2	*
6. Service or replace air filter as needed; check and reset air filter restriction indicator.	P-1	*
7. Inspect and service crankcase ventilation system.	P-1	28
8. Inspect diesel exhaust fluid (DEF) system, to include tanks, lines, gauge pump, and filter.	P-1	33
9. Inspect selective catalyst reduction (SCR) system; including diesel exhaust fluid (DEF) for proper levels, leaks, mounting, and connections.	P-2	33
4. Cooling System		
1. Check operation of fan clutch.	P-1	*
2. Inspect radiator (including air flow restriction, leaks, and damage) and mountings.	P-1	*
3. Inspect fan assembly and shroud.	P-1	*
4. Pressure test cooling system and radiator cap.	P-1	*
5. Inspect coolant hoses and clamps.	P-1	*
6. Inspect coolant recovery system.	P-1	*
7. Check coolant for contamination, additive package concentration, aeration, and protection level (freeze point).	P-1	*
8. Service coolant filter.	P-1	*
9. Inspect water pump.	P-1	13
5. Lubrication System		
All NATEF tasks for this standard can be found in *Fundamentals of Medium/Heavy Duty Commercial Vehicle Systems* (ISBN 978-1-2840-4116-3).		
B. Cab and Hood		
All NATEF tasks for this standard can be found in *Fundamentals of Medium/Heavy Duty Commercial Vehicle Systems* (ISBN 978-1-2840-4116-3).		
C. Electrical/Electronics		
All NATEF tasks for this standard can be found in *Fundamentals of Medium/Heavy Duty Commercial Vehicle Systems* (ISBN 978-1-2840-4116-3).		
D. Frame and Chassis		
All NATEF tasks for this standard can be found in *Fundamentals of Medium/Heavy Duty Commercial Vehicle Systems* (ISBN 978-1-2840-4116-3).		
VIII. HYDRAULICS		
All NATEF tasks for this standard can be found in *Fundamentals of Medium/Heavy Duty Commercial Vehicle Systems* (ISBN 978-1-2840-4116-3).		

*All NATEF tasks for this standard can be found in *Fundamentals of Medium/Heavy Duty Commercial Vehicle Systems* (ISBN 978-1-2840-4116-3).

GLOSSARY

250-psi regulator valve A flow control valve incorporated into the Cummins integrated fuel system module (IFSM) that regulates fuel rail pressure to 250 psi (17 bar).

380-psi high-pressure relief valve A valve between the gear pump and the filter in the Cummins integrated fuel system module (IFSM) that prevents severe damage from high fuel pressure in the event of a fuel shut-off valve failure or other blockage in the fuel circuit.

7th injector Volvo–Mack's name for a hydrocarbon dosing valve that sprays diesel fuel into the exhaust system after the turbocharger. The 7th injector is used to help supplement the heating of the exhaust aftertreatment system.

A/R ratio The ratio between the area (A) of either the compressor or turbine inlets to the radius (R) of the housing.

abrasive flow machining (AFM) A process of enhancing the flow characteristics and performance of injector nozzles by smoothing passageways through the injector and enlarging the spray holes by running an abrasive compound through the nozzles.

absolute micron rating A rating of a fuel filter that refers to the largest sized particle that the fuel filter media will allow to pass.

absorbed glass mat (AGM) battery A type of lead acid battery that uses a thin fiberglass plate to absorb the electrolyte; prevents the solution from sloshing or separating into layers of heavier acid and water.

AC ripple A pattern produced by voltage fluctuations from the alternator that create differences between the peak voltage of an AC sine wave and the minimum voltage found in the trough between sine waves.

AC traction generator (ACTG) A device that converts mechanical energy produced by the engine into electrical current for the propulsion system.

AC traction motor (ACTM) A motor that functions as an electrical generator in a hybrid drive system.

acoustic wave attenuation (AWA) A hydraulic wave-dampening device that minimizes a rhythmic cackling noise at idle caused by high-pressure pump pressure waves synchronizing with injection events.

active fault A fault that is currently taking place and uninterrupted in action.

active regeneration A process in which soot is burned inside the DPF through supplemental heating of the DPF filter.

active sensor A sensor that uses a current supplied by the ECM to operate.

AC-to-DC inverter A device that switches the polarity of an AC current signal to resemble the straight wave polarity of DC current.

adaptive cylinder balance A feature that measures the power output of each cylinder at idle using speed changes in the crankshaft velocity detected by the optical pump speed/position sensor.

AdBlue A liquid-based NO_x-reducing system Dodge Ram uses in its European and North American diesel engines.

additives Chemicals that improve the original properties of the base stock oil.

Advanced Combustion Emission Reduction Technology (ACERT) A marketing term used by Caterpillar to describe a variety of technologies used to lower emissions and increase engine efficiency.

Advanced Diesel Engine Management (ADEM) Caterpillar's marketing name for its series of engine ECMs.

advanced electronics engine management system (EMS) The latest generation of electronic control used by Volvo–Mack engines.

aeration A condition in which excessive amounts of air or steam bubbles are dissolved in coolant, diminishing the coolant's effectiveness.

aftertreatment control module (ACM) An electronic control module used to process sensor data and control the outputs for the DPF and the SCR system.

air drill A compressed air-powered drill.

air hammer A tool powered by compressed air with various hammer, cutting, punching, or chisel attachments.

air inlet restriction gauge A pressure sensor that measures the negative pressure between the air filter and turbocharger.

air nozzle A compressed-air device that emits a fine stream of compressed air for drying or cleaning parts.

air ratchet A ratchet tool for use with sockets powered by compressed air.

air-impact wrench An impact tool powered by compressed air designed to undo tight fasteners.

air-to-air aftercooler (ATAAC) A system that uses ambient air to remove heat from the pressurized intake air.

algorithm A mathematical formula used to solve a problem.

alkalis Chemical compounds that have a pH value greater than 7. They are commonly used in toy batteries and bleaches.

Allen head screw Sometimes called a cap screw, it has a hexagonal recess in the head which fits an Allen key. This type of screw usually anchors components in a predrilled hole.

Allen wrench A type of hexagonal drive mechanism for fasteners.

Allison DOC PC-based service software for Allison's EP system.

alternator ripple The top of the waveform.

American Petroleum Institute (API) An organization that develops specifications to define engine oil performance standards and standards for measuring fuel density.

ammonia sensor A sensor used in selective catalyst reduction (SCR) that provides data to the ECM that is used to determine if ammonia values are out of anticipated range.

ammonia slip NH_3 that escapes from the SCR catalyst and into the atmosphere.

amp-hour A measure of how much amperage a battery can continually supply over a 20-hour period without the battery voltage falling below 10.5 volts.

amplified common rail (ACR) A high-pressure injection system used by Detroit Diesel that multiplies the fuel rail pressure inside the injector.

analog signal An electric current that is proportional to a continuously changing variable.

analog to digital conversion The process when an analog waveform is sampled and measured many times a second to generate a digital representation of the waveform.

angle grinder A portable grinder for grinding or cutting metal.

Anisotropic An object that has unequal physical properties along its various axes. Used in head gaskets to pull heat laterally from the edge surrounding the combustion chamber to the water jacket.

anodizing A process used to harden aluminum by electrochemically reacting oxygen with aluminum.

anti-drain back valve A valve that prevents the oil in the engine from returning to the crankcase when the engine is shut down.

anti-seize compound Neutralizes a chemical reaction that can prevent threads and fasteners from sticking together and freeze spark plugs in place in aluminum cylinder blocks.

anti-shudder A feature that prevents rapid changes in the engine speed using the electronically controlled actuator if the throttle is moved too quickly.

API number A measurement of a fuel's density.

application-specific engine technology (ASET) Mack's suite of emission-control technologies that have specific application for on-highway and vocational vehicles.

armature The only rotating component of the starter; has three main components: the shaft, windings, and the commutator.

aromatic content The portion of fuel composed of a particular type of hydrocarbon molecule that is difficult ignite and burn.

articulating piston A two-piece piston design that uses a separate aluminum skirt connected to an alloy steel crown through a piston pin.

ASTM International An organization that establishes today's diesel fuel standards; formerly known as the American Society for Testing and Materials (ASTM).

asymmetrical turbocharger (AT) A type of turbocharger using turbine volutes of two different sizes. One volute is made smaller than the other in order to increase exhaust backpressure for the EGR system.

asynchronous AC motor A motor in which the magnetic field in the rotor is induced by induction of the magnetic field in the stationary stator.

atomization The process of breaking up liquid fuel into a fine mist.

auto-ignition temperature The temperature at which a fuel will ignite when heated.

automatic disengagement lockout (ADLO) A device that prevents the starter motor from operating if the engine is running.

automotive governor A governor that features an accelerator response similar to a throttle plate-controlled gasoline-fueled engine; also known as a limiting speed (LS) governor or a min/max governor. The operator has to change the throttle position in response to engine load and speed changes.

aviation snips A scissor-like tool for cutting sheet metal.

axial piston pressurization A distributor pump design that uses a reciprocating plunger located along the pump axis used to pressurize fuel for injection. The injection pump uses a cam plate to move the plunger back and forth inside the pump.

axial power turbine (APT) A device located after the turbocharger that uses a turbine wheel to capture exhaust energy and convert it into usable engine power.

back leakage A general term used to describe any fuel circuit or component that supplies or transports fuel from the engine to the fuel tank. When referred to in the context of a fuel injector, back leakage is a calibrated leakage of fuel from around the nozzle valve that is used to lubricate and cool the valve.

backpressure valve (BPV) A valve located after the turbocharger on MX-13 engines used to create exhaust backpressure for engine braking, increase exhaust backpressure to supply the EGR system, and decrease the exhaust gas flow in the exhaust system to assist in heating the exhaust aftertreatment system.

balance shaft A rotating shaft having an eccentric weight that is used to offset torsional vibration produced by an engine.

balancers A device designed to adjust battery voltage to compensate for unequal charges in multiple batteries. Also called *battery equalizers*.

ball-peen (engineer's) hammer A hammer that has a head that is rounded on one end and flat on the other; designed to work with metal items.

barrier cream A cream that looks and feels like a moisturizing cream but has a specific formula to provide extra protection from chemicals and oils.

base stock The raw mineral processed from crude oil.

battery A device that converts and stores electrical energy through chemical reactions.

battery charger A device that charges a battery, reversing the discharge process.

battery equalizers A device designed to adjust battery voltage to compensate for unequal charges in multiple batteries. Also called *balancers*.

battery isolator systems A system designed to separate the main starting battery and the auxiliary battery. Also called a *split charge relay*.

battery management system (BMS) A system of electrical devices used to manage battery performance.

baud rate The rate at which serial data is transmitted.

beginning of injection (BOI) The point when fuel delivery begins and is referenced according to the position of the crankshaft measured in degrees of crankshaft rotation.

beginning of injection period (BIP) The closing of the solenoid poppet valve.

belt routing label A label that lists a diagram of the serpentine belt routing for the engine accessories.

bench grinder (pedestal grinder) A grinder that is fixed to a bench or pedestal.

bench vice A device that securely holds material in jaws while it is being worked on.

Bernoulli effect The creation of a low-pressure area by the increased velocity of air (or a fluid). The lift of an airplane wing is a common example of the Bernoulli effect.

biocide A fuel treatment that kills microorganisms.

biodiesel Refer to fuels derived from a plant or animal source. Biodiesel is a renewable fuel made by chemically combining oils derived from soybeans (or cottonseeds, canola, etc.; animal fats; or even recycled cooking oil) with an alcohol such as methanol.

BIP detection circuit A circuit that allows the ECM to detect the closing of the poppet valve.

bit The smallest piece of digital information that is either a 1 or 0.

bleeder screw A component located in the fuel system that allows trapped air to escape from the filter when priming.

blind rivet A rivet that can be installed from its insertion side.

blink code A method of providing fault code data for a specific system that involves counting the number of flashes from a warning lamp and observing longer pauses between the light blinks.

blow-by The leakage of air past the piston rings into the crankcase.

BlueTec DaimlerChrysler's name for its two NO_x-reducing systems used in their European and North American diesel engines.

bolt A type of threaded fastener with a thread on one end and a hexagonal head on the other.

bolt cutters Strong cutters available in different sizes, designed to cut through non-hardened bolts and other small-stock material.

boost pressure normalization The feature of a turbocharger that maintains boost pressure even as the engine climbs to higher altitudes with low air density.

bore The diameter of a cylinder.

Bosch VP-37 An electronic pump with similar construction and operational characteristics to the mechanical VE pump.

Bosch VP-44 A full-authority distributor pump that has a vane internal transfer pump common to all other distributor pumps, but, rather than a single axial piston plunger, pressurization of fuel is accomplished using radial-opposed pumping plungers.

bottoming tap A thread-cutting tap designed to cut threads to the bottom of a blind hole.

brake horsepower (BHP) The actual useful horsepower available at the flywheel.

brake specific fuel consumption (BSFC) The amount of fuel required to produce one horsepower for one hour, expressed as lb per hp per hour.

break-in period The operation of an engine after it is initially assembled or rebuilt when piston ring, cylinder wall, bushing, and bearing surfaces have high initial wear as the moving surfaces conform to each other.

byte A unit of 8 bits.

calibration Adjustments of the control rack to pinion, rack travel, or rotation of barrels to ensure that that the delivery of fuel from each plunger is the same throughout the entire speed range of the pump.

calibration codes Alpha and/or numerical information assigned to a specific injector used by the ECM to correct for manufacturing tolerances of an injector; Also called injector codes, E-trim or fuel trim codes, the codes contain information about unique fuel flow rates through the injector.

cam ground piston An elliptically shaped piston that expands to a round, symmetrical shape after it is warmed up.

cam plate A multi-lobed rotating plate in an axial plunger injection pump used to produce a reciprocating movement of the axial plunger.

cam ring A ring with lobes arranged on its internal diameter that is used to force opposing pumping plungers together to produce an injection event.

cam-less diesel A system that uses electro-hydraulic actuation of intake and exhaust valves instead of using a camshaft to operate valves.

camshaft A component used by multiple plunger injection pumps that actuates plungers that pressurize fuel for injection.

carbon dioxide (CO_2) A harmless, colorless, odorless gas which is a by-product of combustion. It is also classified as a greenhouse gas (GHG).

carbon monoxide (CO) A regulated poisonous gas emission which is odorless, colorless, and tasteless. It is a by-product of incomplete combustion.

cartridge filter A filter element consisting simply of filter media unenclosed by a metal container.

castellated nut A nut with slots, similar to towers on a castle, that is used with split pins; it is used primarily to secure wheel bearings.

catalyst A material that speeds up or slows down chemical reactions without entering the chemical reactions.

Caterpillar Electronic Technician (Cat ET) A piece of software within Caterpillars SIS system which performs engine diagnostic tests and changing of engine control parameters.

Caterpillar Regeneration System (CRS) Caterpillars marketing name given to its exhaust particulate filter system.

Caterpillar Service Information System (Cat SIS) A suite of Caterpillar software providing engine diagnostics, parts listings and service information.

cavitation Erosion in cylinder block walls, heads, and liner sleeves as a result of the collapse of tiny water vapor bubbles after they are formed when coolant vaporizes on hot cylinder wall surfaces.

C-clamp A clamp shaped like the letter C; it comes in various sizes and can clamp various items.

CELECT The first generation of full-authority electronic engine control introduced by Cummins in 1990. **C**ummins **Elect**ronic.

CELECT Plus A full-authority electronic engine control based on CELECT that uses several additional sensors; a faster, more capable ECM; and additional programmable controls.

cellulosic biodiesel A renewable biodiesel derived from non-food based feedstock, like wood.

centrifugal force A force pulling outward on a rotating body.

cetane booster An additive that is marketed to reduce combustion noise and smoke, improve startability in cold weather, and increase acceleration response; also known as ignition accelerator.

cetane number (CN) A measure of the ignition quality of fuel; also known as cetane rating or cetane value.

charge air cooler (CAC) The system responsible for removing excess heat from the air charging the cylinders, which is known as charge air cooling, aftercooling, and intercooling; also known as an aftercooler and intercooler.

charge-depleting operating mode (CD) A mode of operation in which the vehicle is powered only—or almost only—by the energy stored in the battery.

charge-sustaining mode (CS) A mode of operation in which the batteries' state of charge (SOC) may rise and fall slightly and energy storage modules are kept at a 40% state of charge.

charging gallery A passageway for fuel surrounding all the barrels of the injection pump.

charging lobe A component that admits extra gas exhaust volume into the cylinder before compression.

chassis dynamometer A machine with rollers that allows a vehicle to attain road speed and load while sitting still in the shop.

chemical compound Helps prevent fasteners from loosening; it is applied to one thread, then the other fastener is screwed onto it. This creates a strong bond between them, but one that stays plastic, so they can be separated by a wrench.

chrome A bright, shiny corrosion-resistant metal; it is mostly used for decorative purposes, such as on hubcaps.

chuffing The sound a VGT turbocharger can produce when actuator response is slow. Chuffing is caused by turbocharger surge.

clean gas induction (CGI) Caterpillar's marketing name given to its exhaust gas recirculation system.

cleaning gun A device with a nozzle controlled by a trigger fitted to the outlet of pressure cleaners.

clearance volume The space remaining in a cylinder when the piston is at top dead center.

closed crankcase ventilation system A method of cleaning up blow-by emissions by recycling crankcase emissions back into the intake manifold.

closed-end wrench A wrench with a closed or ring end to grip bolts and nuts.

cloud point The temperature at which the wax in diesel fuel begins to congeal.

club hammer The club hammer is like a small mallet, with two square faces made of high-carbon steel. It is the heaviest type of hammer that can be used one-handed.

coalesce The process of collecting together oil in crankcase vapors to separate it from the vapors.

coaxial variable nozzle injector A fourth-generation injector concept from Bosch that contains a two-stage nozzle lift with two rows of spray holes. This design permits either row of spray holes to be opened independently, which optimizes mixture preparation to achieve a more homogenous distribution of fuel and air in the cylinder.

coefficient of friction (CoF) The amount of friction between two particular objects in contact; calculated by dividing the force required to move the object by the weight of the object.

cold cranking amps (CCA) A measurement of the load, in amps, that a battery can deliver for 30 seconds while maintaining a voltage of 1.2 volts per cell (7.2 volts for a 12-volt battery) or higher at 0°F (−18°C).

cold-start advance (KSB) device A device that provides better cold operation, less smoke, and fewer misfires. It operates by moving the servo piston of the hydraulic advance mechanism.

combination pliers A type of pliers for cutting, gripping, and bending.

combination wrench A type of wrench that has an open end on one end and a closed-end wrench on the other.

combustion A chemical reaction between oxygen and fuel molecules in which heat is released.

combustion knock A combustion noise created by an abnormally sharp increase in cylinder pressure. Knock is usually caused by detonation or pre-ignition of fuel in the cylinder by an atypical ignition source, such as a piece of hot carbon or hot spark plug insulator.

combustion slobber A combustion by-product from diesel engines consisting of unburned fuel, soot, and lubricating oil; also known as engine slobber or turbo slobber.

common power train controller (CPC) An ECM used to store and process vehicle- and application-specific information.

common rail A high-pressure injection system that electronically varies injection pressure, timing, and injection rate independently of engine speed.

compacted graphite iron (CGI) A material produced from powdered iron alloys squeezed into molds at high pressures and then heated to bond the metal particles together; also known as sintered graphite. The material is commonly used to construct cylinder blocks and heads since CGI is lighter, stronger, and more resistant to bending and twisting forces than conventional cast iron.

comparator bench A test bench used to evaluate pumps and make calibration adjustments to multiple plunger injection pumps and governors.

compatibility A property that allows two metals to slide against one another with minimal friction or wear.

compensation A response by the fuel system governor to a loss of contribution from one or more cylinders. The governor increases the quantity of fuel injected into the other cylinders to maintain idle speed.

complicated fracture A fracture in which the bone has penetrated a vital organ.

compound split operation Blending torque from the motors and engine together.

compression ignition (CI) A combustion mechanism that ignites fuel by using the heat derived from compressing air as an ignition source.

compression ratio A comparison between total cylinder volume and clearance volume (the space left in the cylinder when the piston is at TDC).

compression release brakes Engine brakes that work by causing a sudden release of the compressed air from the cylinder by quickly opening the exhaust valve near TDC of the compression stroke, dissipating the energy used to compress air.

compression testing A measure of the maximum pressure of engine cylinders when cranking.

compressor housing The housing that encloses the compressor wheel.

compressor wheel A centrifugal-type air pump attached to the turbine wheel. The compressor wheel uses centrifugal force to compress air.

conductance test A type of battery test that determines the battery's ability to conduct current.

constant-current charger A battery charger that automatically varies the voltage applied to the battery to maintain a constant amperage flow into the battery.

constant-voltage charger A direct current (DC) power that is a step-down transformer with a rectifier to provide the DC voltage to charge.

control rack The mechanisms used to connect the mechanical governor to the plungers in order to rotate them in unison and meter correct quantities fuel.

control sleeve A part of the fuel control mechanism in mechanical injection pumps used to connect the mechanical governor to the pumping plungers in order to rotate them and meter fuel in the correct quantities.

control sleeve When used to describe fuel control in a distributor type injection pump, a control sleeve is a close-fitting ring that slides along the axial plunger to open or close the spill port.

control sleeve position sensor A sensor used in electronic governors of Bosch VP34 pumps used to provide closed loop feedback about control sleeve position.

coolant A fluid that contains special anti-freezing and anti-corrosion chemicals mixed with water.

coolant extender An additive package that is only used with ELC, which is added at the midpoint of the coolant's life.

coolant label A label that lists the type of coolant installed in the cooling system.

cooled EGR (CEGR) A system that cools EGR exhaust gas by passing it through an engine coolant heat exchanger.

copper A non-ferrous, pure metal that can be alloyed (combined) with other metals but is not combined with iron.

counter-electromotive force (CEMF) An electromagnetic force produced by the spinning magnetic field of the armature, which induces current in the opposite direction of battery current through the motor.

crankcase depression regulator (CDR) A device that regulates, or meters, the quantity of blow-by emissions back into the engine's intake manifold.

crankcase pressure test A measurement of the amount of cylinder blow-by; this indicates the sealing ability of the piston rings and cylinder walls.

cranking amps (CA) A measurement of the load, in amps, that a battery can deliver for 30 seconds while maintaining a voltage of 1.2 volts per cell (7.2 volts for a 12-volt battery) or higher at 32°F (−0°C).

crankpin The crankshaft journal which attaches the connecting rod to the crankshaft.

crankshaft The component that converts the reciprocating action of the pistons to a rotational movement and revolves inside the crankcase portion of the engine block.

crankshaft throw The distance between the centerline of the main bearing journal and crankpin journal.

crevice volume The area above the top compression ring between the piston crown and the cylinder wall.

CRI4 injector Another acronym used to identify an amplified common rail injector.

cross-arm A description for an arm that is set at right angles or 90° to another component.

cross-bolted block A variation of the deep-skirt block that uses additional horizontally placed bolts to connect the crankcase walls of the block to the main bearing caps; also known as a tie-bolted or bolster-bolted block.

cross-cut chisel A type of chisel for metal work that cleans out or cuts key ways.

cross-flow cylinder head A head design with the intake and exhaust manifolds located on opposite sides of an inline engine to improve engine breathing characteristics.

cross-hatch A cylinder wall finish of fine intersecting lines that are used to retain oil.

cryogenic A gas that is converted to a liquid and maintained as a liquid at a very low temperature.

current clamp A device that claps around a conductor to measure current flow. It is often used in conjunction with a digital volt-ohm meter (DVOM).

current ramping The build-up of current flow through the solenoid coils during the initial energization period.

current track Another name for a DIN diagram.

current-controlled rate shaping (CCRS) A marketing name given by Mack for a Bosch electronic unit pump high-pressure injection system

curved file A type of file that has a curved surface for filing holes.

cyclonic-style pre-cleaner tubes A component of the air intake system that pre-cleans intake air by spinning dirt out of the airflow to prevent it from entering the filter.

cylinder block The largest structure of an engine, which encloses the cylinders and provides a rigid frame to support the cylinders or cylinder liners, crankshaft, oil and coolant passages, and, in many engines, the camshaft.

cylinder contribution test A test that compares cylinder pressures to one another and measures the contribution each cylinder makes; also known as a cylinder balance test or a relative compression test.

cylinder cut-out test A test where power to a solenoid is removed during engine operation using a service software or electronic service tool. The test is used to identify misfiring or noisy cylinders.

cylinder displacement The volume displaced by the piston as it moves from TDC to BDC.

cylinder glazing A condition that occurs when lubricating oil is first baked and then smoothed into the cross-hatch of the cylinder wall. Cylinder glazing prevents the cylinder wall from retaining oil and reduces the ability of rings to seal.

cylinder head gasket The component that maintains the seal around the combustion chamber at peak operating temperatures and pressures and keeps air, coolants, and engine oil in their respective passages over all temperatures and pressures.

cylinder leakage The percentage of gas leakage past the rings. High leakage rates are usually due to worn cylinders and rings.

DAVIE Service and diagnostic software used by PACCAR. It is an acronym for DAF Vehicle Investigation Tool. In North America DAVIE refers to Diagnostic Analysis for Vehicle Interface Equipment.

DC-to-AC inverter A device that takes the straight, unchanging wave of DC current and flips, or inverts, the current's polarity to resemble an AC wave signal.

dead-blow hammer A type of hammer that has a cushioned head to reduce the amount of head bounce.

decompression lobe A component that lifts the exhaust rocker lever near TDC to release engine compression.

deep cycle battery A battery used to deliver a lower, steady level of power for a much longer time.

deep-skirt block A block configuration with a bottom edge that extends well below the crankshaft's centerline.

delivery valve A valve that operates as a one-way check to allow fuel to remain at relatively high pressure in the fuel injection line while ensuring that fuel pressure will drop far enough below nozzle opening pressure to prevent secondary injections caused by reflecting fuel pulsations in the injector line.

Delphi E3 EUI A type of EUI that uses a dual-control valve, four-wire design, which enables high-speed, ultra-high-pressure operation with rate-shaped injection capabilities.

delta pressure differential sensor A sensor that measures the pressure drop across two points in a gas circuit. In an EGR system, the delta P sensor measures the pressure drop across a venturi.

Delta windings Stator windings in which the windings are connected in the shape of a triangle.

depth micrometers A micrometer that measures the depth of an item such as how far a piston is below the surface of the block.

derate mode The reduction of power output by 25% or more in response to an emission-related engine fault code or an engine protection fault code.

DeSO$_x$ A sulfur-reducing reaction used in NAC and LNT systems to remove sulfur from catalyst material. Sulfur in diesel fuel tends to contaminate catalysts and reduces their effectiveness unless a DeSO$_x$ reaction takes place.

detonation An abnormal combustion event where an air–fuel mixture ignites before the spark plug fires. Detonation is usually caused by high cylinder pressures, which drive up pre-ignition cylinder temperatures.

Deutsch connector A compact, environmentally sealed electrical connector that uses solid, round metal pins and hollow female sockets.

Deutsche Institute Norm (DIN) diagram A schematic wiring diagram on which symbols, terminal connection numbers, line symbols, and operational status of items such as switches and relays are defined by a DIN standard. Also called current track.

Dewar A vacuum-sealed, bottle-like storage container for LNG that is pressurized to approximately 100 psi (689 kPa). Dewars are fabricated with an inner shell surrounded by super insulating vacuum space enclosed in an outer shell.

diagnostic link connector (DLC) The connection point for electronic service tools used to access fault code and other information provided by chassis electronic control modules.

diagnostic trouble code (DTC) A code logged by the electronic control module when electrical faults or system problems occur in commercial vehicle control systems.

diagonal-cutting pliers Cutting pliers for small wire or cable.

dial bore gauge A precision measuring tool used to measure the amount of taper wear in a cylinder.

dial indicators A dial that can also be known as a dial gauge, and as the name suggests, has a dial and needle where measurements are read.

diaphragm pump A common type of fuel transfer pump used to supply fuel at low pressure.

die A device used to cut threads on a bolt or shaft.

die stock handle A handle for securely holding dies to cut threads.

diesel coolant additive (DCA) An additive used to treat cooling systems to reduce the effects of cavitation erosion.

diesel particulate filter (DPF) A exhaust emission aftertreatment device installed in the exhaust system to filter out black carbon soot and other particulate from the exhaust stream.

differential voltage Refers to the voltage difference on a wire pair when one wires voltage is the mirror opposite voltage. A wide separation between the voltage pulses represents a 1 and a narrow separation represents a 0.

digital control valve The valve technology that replaced the poppet valve used in the HEUI A and HEUI B designs; the digital nature of the valve refers to the position of the control valve—it is either open or closed.

digital signals Electrical signals that represent data in discrete, finite values. Digital signals are considered as binary meaning it is either on or off, yes or no, high or low, 0 or 1.

dimethyl ether (DME) A methanol-like renewable fuel which is a gas at room temperature and requires pressurization to stay in liquid form.

direct drive A starter motor drive system in which the motor armature directly engages the flywheel through a pinion gear.

direct injection (DI) A diesel combustion chamber design that has a piston-formed combustion bowl and a multi-orifice nozzle.

dislocation The displacement of a joint from its normal position; it is caused by an external force stretching the ligaments beyond their elastic limit.

distillation The process of boiling petroleum oil to separate oil molecules into fractions or cuts based on the boiling point temperature of each fraction.

distribution The mixing of fuel and air in the cylinders during the injection event.

double flare A seal that is made at the end of metal tubing or pipe.

double-insulated Tools or appliances that are designed in such a way that no single failure can result in a dangerous voltage coming into contact with the outer casing of the device.

dowel pins Used to keep components in place where shearing forces are high, such as valve plates on high-pressure pumps.

down speeding A strategy that takes advantage of a diesel engine's high torque output at low engine speeds by lowering drive axle gear ratios. The engine operates at lower rpm while operating at highway speeds.

drift punch A type of punch used to start pushing roll pins to prevent them from spreading.

drill chuck A device for securely gripping drill bits in a drill.

drill press A device that incorporates a fixed drill with multiple speeds and an adjustable worktable. It can be free-standing or fixed to a bench.

drill vice A tool with jaws that can be attached to a drill press table for holding material that is to be drilled.

droop The change or difference in engine speed caused by a change in load.

dry sleeve block A block designed with a bored or honed hole in the block that allows no coolant contact with the cylinder sleeve.

dual mass flywheel (DMF) A two-piece flywheel design that incorporates specialized torsional dampening springs.

dual power inverter module (DPIM) The module responsible for converting energy from the ESS into AC currents used to power the EZV drive motors.

dual-fuel engine An engine capable of combusting two different types of fuel, such as natural gas and diesel fuel.

dual-mode hybrid drive train A hybrid system that combines both mechanical and electrical propulsion systems.

durability requirements Legislated standards for engine durability that require noxious engine emissions to remain below set thresholds through the expected useful life of an engine.

dusting out A condition where dirt is drawn into an engine; this causes premature abrasive wear of the cylinder walls and rings.

duty cycle The percentage of time a PWM signal is ON in comparison to OFF time.

dynamic timing Changes in pump timing when an engine is running.

dynamometer A device that measures engine or vehicle road speed and torque to calculate engine power.

E3 EUI A type of electronically controlled unit injector containing a nozzle control valve and spill control valve. Delphi manufactures E3 injectors for several OEM engine producers.

ear protection Protective gear worn when the sound levels exceed 85 decibels, when working around operating machinery for any period of time, or when the equipment you are using produces loud noise.

Econovance variable injection timing system A partial-authority fuel system used by Mack trucks. The inline injection pump had an electronically controlled governor and an electrohydraulic mechanism used to electronically vary injection timing.

e-diesel A category of renewable fuel made from a combination of diesel fuel and ethanol, a type of alcohol made from plant sugars.

effective stroke The distance the plunger moves between fill port closing and spill port opening.

elasticity The amount of stretch or give a material has.

electric lift pump A pump that runs for the first two minutes after the key is switched on to quickly supply the gear pump for faster starting.

electric vehicle (EV) A vehicle in which only electric motors are used to move a vehicle.

electrical capacity The amount of electrical current a lead–acid battery can supply.

electrically erasable read only memory (EEPROM) Non-volatile memory technology that is used to store operating instructions or programming for an ECM.

electrolysis The use of electricity to break down water into hydrogen and oxygen gases.

electrolyte An electrically conductive solution.

electronic control module (ECM) A device containing a microprocessor that processes electronic input signals according to software-based mathematical algorithms. The ECM then produces output signals based on processed information to control engine operation.

electronic cooling package (ECP) A system of fans and electronic controls that maintains a hybrid ESS within a set temperature range.

electronic unit injectors (EUI) An electrically controlled injector incorporating timing, metering, atomization, and pressurization functions into a single unit or injector body.

electronic unit pump (EUP) An single cylinder injection pump that combines elements of PLN injection systems and unit injectors; also referred to as a unit pump system (UPS).

emission monitor A diagnostic strategy used by the engine control module to evaluate whether emission-related systems are functioning correctly.

emulsification A process where mechanical pressure is used to mix a fuel with water or another liquid.

Energy Independence and Security Act (EISA) Legislation that requires the increased use of renewable fuels.

energy storage system (ESS) A system that stores and distributes electrical current to the various components of a hybrid drive system.

engine hoist A small crane used to lift engines.

engine manufacturer diagnostics (EMD) A pre-HD-OBD standard for an on-board diagnostic system used to detect emission related faults.

Environmental Protection Agency (EPA) Federal government agency that deals with issues related to environmental safety.

EP40/50 System Models of Allison's Electric Propulsion system. Also known as *Allison's Electrically Variable (EV) Drive*.

EPA07 emissions standards The emissions standards set by the EPA for medium- and heavy-duty diesel emissions in 2007. These standards are similar to Euro 5.

EPA10 emission standards The emissions standards set by the EPA for medium and heavy-duty diesel emissions in 2010. These standards are similar to Euro 6.

ethanol Alcohol-based fuel made from starches and sugars.

ethylene glycol The base chemical from which the majority of anti-freezes are made.

E-trim The marketing name given by Caterpillar to describe the injector calibration code assigned to Caterpillar injectors.

exhaust backpressure Exhaust pressure build-up in the exhaust system between the cylinders and the exhaust system outlet.

exhaust backpressure (EBP) The pressure produced in an exhaust system by restrictions to exhaust gas flow.

exhaust backpressure (EBP) regulator A device that increases exhaust pressure inside the engine's exhaust manifolds to cause the exhaust gas to linger longer around the exhaust ports and transfer its heat to the cooling system.

exhaust back-pressure (EBP) sensor A sensor that measures pressure in the exhaust manifold. The sensor can be used to perform diagnostic tests and provide closed-loop feedback control of the VGT actuator position.

exhaust brake An engine brake that works by placing a restriction in the exhaust system, which increases backpressure, causing the engine to exert a retarding force against the driveline.

exhaust gas recirculation (EGR) An NO_x-reduction technology that mixes exhaust gas with fresh intake air.

exhaust manifold A component that collects exhaust gases from each cylinder of the cylinder head.

exhaust pressure governor (EPG) An EBP regulating device that speeds up engine warm-up and reduces cold start engine emissions. Volvo uses this device to increase backpressure which raises engine operating temperature at idle, reduces hydrocarbon emissions, and can supplement the engine-based compression release brake.

extended-life coolant (ELC) Several types of long-life coolant formulations containing an anti-corrosion additive package that does not deplete; also known as long life coolant (LLC).

external bleeding The loss of blood from an external wound; blood can be seen escaping.

external combustion engine An engine that burns fuel outside the engine cylinders.

fast chargers A type of battery charger that charges batteries quickly.

fasteners Devices that securely hold items together, such as screws, cotter pins, rivets, and bolts.

fatty acid methyl ester (FAME) Biodiesel produced through transesterification.

fault mode identifier (FMI) The type of failure detected in the SPN, PID, or SID.

feather key Used to prevent the free rotation of gears or pulleys on a shaft; usually attached to levers that have to slide along a shaft to allow engagement of a part. The connection is a positive fitting and serves to transmit torques and revs, for example, on the drive shaft of a belt pulley.

feeler gauges Also called feeler blades; flat metal strips used to measure the width of gaps, such as the clearance between valves and rocker arms.

ferrous metals Metals that use iron as an alloying agent. Cast iron, steel, and stainless steel are the main categories of iron alloys used in the automotive industry.

fill and spill ports Posts on either side of a barrel through which fuel enters or leaves the barrel's assemblies.

fillet radius A circular machining applied to the surface between the journal and the crankshaft cheek that strengthens the crankshaft and minimizes the possibility of a fracture.

finished rivet A rivet after the completion of the riveting process.

fire rings Steel rings integrated into the cylinder head gasket nearest the combustion chambers that provide extra sealing to seal in the high combustion pressures.

first aid The immediate care given to an injured or suddenly ill person.

first-degree burns Burns that show reddening of the skin and damage to the outer layer of skin only.

Fischer-Tropsch fuels A category of biofuels made from substances including coal, plastic, and natural gas; these substances are first turned into a gas, and are then converted from a gas into a liquid. Unlike pyrolysis, the process used to make these fuels requires a catalyst and gas pressure to form hydrocarbon chains. Other names given to these fuels are syn-gas or gas-to-liquid (GTL) fuels.

Fischer-Tropsch reaction A process used to create synthetic liquid diesel fuel from vaporized hydrocarbons.

fixed geometry turbocharger A turbocharger without boost pressure controls; the name is derived from the fact that the housings and components have unchanging dimensions.

flare-nut wrench A type of closed-end wrench that has a slot in the box section to allow the wrench to slip through a tube or pipe. Also called a flare tubing wrench.

flash point The temperature at which fuel will produce an adequate amount of vapor that will ignite if exposed to an open source of ignition such as a spark or flame.

flashback arrestor A spring-loaded valve installed on oxyacetylene torches as a safety device to prevent flame from entering the torch hoses.

flashing The process of uploading a new engine calibration file. A calibration file contains unique set of data or look-up tables needed by engine operating algorithms to control engine operation. Flash information is stored in the ECMs memory.

flat washers Spread the load of bolt heads or nuts as they are tightened and distribute it over a greater area. They are particularly useful in protecting aluminum alloy.

flat-nosed pliers Pliers that are flat and square at the end of the nose.

flat-tip screwdriver A type of screwdriver that fits a straight slot in screws.

flex pipe A component used between the engine pipe and the rest of the exhaust system to absorb twists and movement of pipe caused by engine torque reaction.

flooded lead–acid battery A lead–acid battery in which the plates are immersed in a water–acid electrolyte solution.

forcing screw The center screw on a gear, bearing, or pulley puller. Also called a jacking screw.

forged pistons Pistons made from aluminum alloy billets that are stamped into shape by forging dies.

forward leakage Leakage of an injector nozzle from the spray holes, which indicates that the nozzle valve-to-seat seal is poor.

fractions The different petroleum products that make up a barrel of oil, which are separated by the distillation process.

fractured cap technology A technique used by PACCAR to create a precision fit between connecting rod and main bearing caps. The caps are formed by scribing a parting line on the caps and then breaking the caps apart to form two separate parts.

FRC limit Fuel rate control limit refers to the maximum quantity of fuel allowed for injection under a specific operating condition.

frequency The number of events or cycles that occur in a period, usually 1 second.

frequency-sensing relay A relay connected to the alternator that detects alternating current only when the alternator is charging.

fuel (gasoline, diesel) A derivative of crude oil.

fuel balance control (FBC) A strategy used by the ECM to adjust fuel delivery quantities to each cylinder to achieve consistent pressures among all cylinders. Crankshaft speed data is used to make corrections to the volume of fuel injected in each cylinder.

fuel heater A device that warms fuel to keep wax dissolved in the fuel.

fuel hydrometer A tool used to measure fuel density and identify its API number.

fuel mean value adaptation (FMA) A correction factor made to an injector's energization time based on changes in fuel delivery rates caused by wear and deterioration

fuel pump-mounted fuel pump control module (FPCM) A control module mounted on a distributor pump that controls the operation of a spill valve.

fuel quantity solenoid The control valve in a DS distributor pump head used to control injection quantities delivered by the pump.

fuel rate Fuel consumption expressed as the quantity of fuel consumed per hour.

fuel rate calibration resistor A unit connected between two terminals of the driver module that provides data to the drive module regarding the flow rate of the pump.

fuel return circuit The fuel circuit that collects fuel from the injectors, fuel pump, and relief valves and returns the fuel to the tank.

fuel solenoid driver (FSD) An electronic control module that contains a pair of high-current switching transistors that send electrical signals to the fuel metering control solenoid located inside the hydraulic head of the pump.

fuel–water separator A device that removes water from fuel by coalescing small water droplets into large ones that eventually fall out of the less-dense fuel into a sump.

fulcrum The point around which a lever rotates and that supports the lever and the load.

full fielding Making the alternator produce maximum amperage output.

full load setting (FLS) A calibration number used to determine the maximum amount of fuel injected at rated speed. Along with the FTS, it shapes the engine's torque rise curve or slope.

full torque setting (FTS) A calibration number used to determine the maximum amount of fuel injected at peak torque. Along with the FLS, it shapes the engine's torque rise curve or slope.

full-authority governing A system in which all metering and timing functions use principles of electronic signal processing to regulate engine fueling; also known as electronic engine management.

fumigation A process of sending vapors into the air intake, such as in the case of water-methanol injection systems.

galvanic reaction A chemical reaction that produces electricity when two dissimilar metals are placed in an electrolyte.

garter spring A metal spring wrapped circularly around the inside of a lip seal to keep it in constant contact with the moving shaft.

gas control valve A valve within a mixer that responds to an electrical or vacuum signal to admit natural gas into the intake air stream.

gas welding goggles Protective gear designed for gas welding; they provide protection against foreign particles entering the eye and are tinted to reduce the glare of the welding flame.

gasket scraper A broad, sharp, flat blade to assist in removing gaskets and glue.

Gasoline Gallon Equivalent (GGE) A standardized unit used to sell natural gas. It equals the energy content of 1 gallon (4 liters) of gasoline and is made up of approximately 231 cubic inches (3785 cubic centimeters) of natural gas or 5.66 lb (2.57 kg) of natural gas.

gassing A situation that occurs when overcharging or rapid charging causes some gas to escape from the battery.

gas-to-liquid (GTL) fuel Fuel derived from using the Fischer-Tropsch reaction.

gear fast run slow A fuel-efficient operating strategy used to take advantage of a diesel engine's low rpm torque. The differential gear ratios are intentionally low to enable high road speed at low engine rpm.

gear pullers A tool with two or more legs and a cross-bar with a center forcing screw to remove gears.

gear pump A positive displacement fuel supply pump that sweeps fuel around the gear housing between pump gear teeth and can pressurize the output side to very high pressure.

gear-down protection A parameter that limits engine speed if the engine speed is too high for a particular road speed.

gel cell battery A type of battery to which silica has been added to the electrolyte solution to turn the solution to a gel-like consistency.

gelling When the paraffin or wax content of the fuel causes fuel to become too viscous to properly flow through filters and lines due to low temperatures.

Gen II HEUI The newer generation of HEUI that replaced the poppet valve and solenoid with a lighter, faster-acting spool valve and two magnetic coils; also known as G2 HEUI.

GHG14 aftertreatment device (ATD) Detroit Diesel's term for aftertreatment system components that use electrically controlled DEF pumps and fluid dosing of the SCR rather than air pressure.

Gibb-head key Used to prevent the free rotation of gears or pulleys on a shaft; designed to be pulled out easily and are used when a gear or a pulley has to be attached to a shaft.

governor A device that regulates the quantity of fuel injected into the cylinders.

greenhouse gas (GHG) Gases that are classified as contributing to global warming because they trap heat in the atmosphere.

grinding wheels and discs Abrasive wheels or flat discs fitted to bench, pedestal, and portable grinders.

ground The return path for electrical current in a vehicle chassis, other metal of the vehicle, or dedicated wire.

Hall effect sensor A sensor commonly used to measure the rotational speed of a shaft; they have the advantage of producing a digital signal square waveform and have strong signal strength at low shaft rotational speeds.

harmonic vibration A vibration that sends pressure waves moving back and forth along the crankshaft.

hazard Anything that could hurt you or someone else.

hazardous environment A place where hazards exist.

hazardous material Any material that poses an unreasonable risk of damage or injury to persons, property, or the environment if it is not properly controlled during handling, storage, manufacture, processing, packaging, use and disposal, or transportation.

headgear Protective gear that includes items like hairnets, caps, or hard hats.

heat buildup A dangerous condition that occurs when the glove can no longer absorb or reflect heat and heat is transferred to the inside of the glove.

heat exchanger A system that transfers heat from coolant to the atmosphere.

heat rejection The transfer of heat into the cooling system from the combustion chamber.

heavy-duty on-board (HD-OBD) executive A software program inside the MCM used to run monitors and make decisions about concerning the on-board diagnostic system.

heavy-duty on-board diagnostics (HD-OBD) The most recent EPA standard for detecting emission-related faults in heavy-duty vehicles.

height gauge A tool used by technicians that is used to adjust the plunger travel of a unit injector for Detroit Diesel N2 injectors.

hertz (Hz) The unit for electrical frequency measurement, in cycles per second.

HEUI A The earliest HEUI injector without split shot or pilot injection capabilities.

HEUI B A later version of the first generation HEUI injectors with PRIME metering or split shot, pilot injection capabilities.

HIB-300 Caterpillar's second-generation HEUI injector.

high idle The maximum speed at which an engine turns without a load.

High Pressure Direct Injection (HPDI) A dual-fuel system developed by Westport Industries that injects a small pilot injection of diesel fuel from the same injector that delivers natural gas. The bulk of this system's combustion fuel is natural gas.

high resistance Describes a circuit or components with more resistance than designed.

high torque rise engine An engine that has a sharp increase in torque as engine rpm drops from cruising speed when under heavy loads.

high-efficiency pump (HEP) An innovative oil pump used by Caterpillar in which output pressure is matched to the pressure desired by the ECM based on operating conditions (i.e., load, speed, temperature, and so on) and OEM-specific fuel maps stored in the ECM using a PWM-controlled displacement control valve.

high-mounted cams Refers to the location of an engine camshaft near the engine block deck. High-mounted camshafts enable the use of shorter, less heavy pushrods.

high-pressure cooled EGR (HP-CEGR) An exhaust gas recirculation system uses cooled exhaust gas and depends on a VGT to build exhaust backpressure above intake boost pressure. EGR gas temperatures are reduced by a liquid type heat exchanger.

high-pressure injection, time-pressure injection (HPI-TPI) A unique fuel system with injectors that have an open-nozzle design using a plunger. This system also uses a centrally located injector. In this system, metering and injection timing are controlled by varying fuel pressure supplied to the injector.

high-voltage interlock loop (HVIL) A device that prevents access to potentially hazardous energized electrical circuits.

historical fault A fault that took place at one time but that is now corrected and no longer active.

hollow punch A punch with a center hollow for cutting circles in thin materials such as gaskets.

homogeneous charge compression ignition (HCCI) engine A low-emission, experimental type of CI combustion system that pulls air and fuel into the cylinder during intake stroke.

horizontal exhaust system An exhaust system that routes the exhaust components under the chassis and has the outlet pipe aimed downward toward the ground or to the rear of the vehicle.

horsepower (hp) A measure of engine power, which is a function of both torque and engine speed.

housing pressure cold-start advance (HPCA) mechanism A mechanism that is used to advance injection timing when an engine is cold.

hunting A rhythmic change in engine rpm at idle speed caused by uneven delivery of fuel; also known as loping.

hybrid electric vehicle (HEV) A type of vehicle that combines an internal combustion engine with an electric propulsion system into a new or hybrid powertrain configuration.

hybrid organic acid technology (HOAT) A combination of IAT and OAT with nitrites added, making it suitable for use in both light- and heavy-duty systems.

HybriDrive Propulsion System A series-type hybrid propulsion system developed by BAE, an aerospace and defense technology company.

hydra combustion air valve (HCAV) An air supply valve used to regulate additional airflow into the exhaust system to support heating and regeneration in the exhaust aftertreatment system.

hydraulic hoist A type of hoist that the vehicle is driven onto that uses two long, narrow platforms to lift the vehicle.

hydraulic jack A type of vehicle jack that uses oil under pressure to lift vehicles.

hydraulic launch assist (HLA) An alternative to electric hybrid drives in which application of standard friction service brakes is prevented until just before a complete vehicle stop.

hydraulic nozzle holder The nozzle body that encloses the nozzle assembly containing passageways connecting the high-pressure injection line to the nozzle valve.

hydraulically amplified diesel injection system (HADIS) The term used by Bosch to describe a fourth-generation CR injector using an internal hydraulic amplifier to multiply injection pressure by 2:1; also referred to as CRS4 injector or amplified common rail (ACR).

hydraulically balanced nozzle valve A fast-acting nozzle valve design that opens and closes by slight changes in fuel pressure applied to the top and bottom of a nozzle valve.

hydrocarbon (HC) A molecule, often a fuel, composed of hydrogen and carbon atoms.

hydrometer An instrument used to measure the specific gravity of liquids.

hydroscopic The ability to mix and absorb water.

hydrostatic lock A condition that occurs when fluids in the cylinder of an engine prevent the engine from rotating.

hygroscopic When brake fluid absorbs water from the atmosphere.

hypereutectic piston A piston that has high silicon content (16–20% silicon).

idle An engine's minimum operational speed.

idle validation switch (IVS) A circuit used for safety reasons that is used to verify throttle position.

ignition delay The time period between the beginning of fuel injection and actual ignition of fuel in a combustion chamber.

impact driver A tool that is struck with a blow to provide an impact turning force to remove tight fasteners.

in-block camshaft An engine that has only the valves, rocker levers, and bridges located in the cylinder heads above the piston; the camshaft is located in the engine block. The cam may be a low or high mounted type. Also called a pushrod engine.

incipient fault A fault that is the result of system or component deterioration.

indirect injection (IDI) A diesel combustion chamber that uses a pre-combustion chamber formed in the cylinder head and a pintle nozzle.

induction hardening A heat treatment process that involves passing alternating electric current through coils of heavy-gauge wire surrounding the material to be hardened; through magnetic induction, heat is produced in the metal, which is then quenched with water to produce a hard, wear-resistant metal surface.

inductive reactance Current induced in a coil of a solenoid's windings which opposes ECM current when initially energized; also known as inductive resistance.

inductive resistance Current induced that opposes ECM current when initially energized; also known as inductive reactance.

injection control pressure (ICP) sensor A sensor located in the high-pressure oil circuit that provides closed-loop feedback to the ECM about whether the oil pressure is too low or high.

injection control pressure regulator (ICPR) An electrically operated spool valve that moves in response to the strength of a magnetic field; by changing the current flow through a coil surrounding the spool valve, the oil pressure for injection actuation is adjusted.

injection delay The time lag between the start of fuel pressurization for injection and the point when fuel is actually injected.

injection lag The time delay that occurs between the start of fuel pressurization and the moment when injection actually takes place; also known as injection delay.

injection quantity adjustment (IQA) A feature that allows software to compensate for pressure variations in cylinders; also known as the E-trim, adaptation value, or the injector calibration code.

injection rate The quantity of fuel injected per degree of crank angle rotation. It is reported as the position of the crankshaft when the injection begins.

injection rate control The control of fuel delivery volume per degree of crank angle rotation into the cylinder during an injection event.

injection timing stepper (ITS) motor Used in conjunction with a sliding servo piston, this device regulates internal pump fuel pressure used to retard and advance injection timing.

injector control valve A key component inside a CELECT injector; when the control valve is de-energized and opens determines the timing or beginning of the injection event.

injector drive module (IDM) A module on some first-generation and Gen II HEUIs that operates and monitors injector operation. It stores information such as engine firing order and operating and diagnostic software instructions; also known as the fuel injection control module (FICM) on later models of HEUI engines.

injector response time (IRT) The time it takes for an electronic unit injector to build a magnetic field strong enough to move the injection control valve and to begin an injection event.

inlet metering The use of a helical groove on the metering valve in an opposed plunger metering system to regulate fuel delivery to the pumping plungers.

inner base circle One of two circles that outline the cam profile. The inner base circle refers to the circular part of the camshaft that does not include the lobe.

inorganic additive technology (IAT) A diesel engine cooling system conditioner containing non-carbon-based corrosion inhibitors such as phosphates, borates, and silicate.

inside micrometer Micrometer that measures inside dimensions.

INSITE A service tool for Cummins electronic engine control systems.

instant start glow plug system (ISS) A recent development in glow plug technology that uses two heating elements connected together in series. A steel-like sheath covers the heating elements and rapidly heats to starting temperature in as little as 2 seconds.

insulated gate bipolar transistor (IGBT) A specialized field effect transistor (FET) that inverts DC current to three-phase, variable-frequency, and variable-voltage AC current.

intake air heater A device that heats intake air to reduce cold-start emissions, improve engine-starting characteristics, shorten ignition delay time, improve combustion quality, and reduce the likelihood of misfire conditions that cause white and gray smoke.

intake throttle valve A valve used to regulate the quantity of fresh air entering the cylinders of an engine.

integrated pressure-sensing glow plug A glow plug that includes a pressure sensor that measures cylinder pressure for closed-loop feedback of combustion pressure.

intelligent charger A battery charger that varies its output according to the sensed condition of the battery it is charging.

intensifier piston A piston that multiplies the force of high pressure oil pressure and is used to pressurize fuel to injection pressure; also known as the amplifier piston.

Interact System (IS) The third generation of Cummins electronics; this system could integrate with other vehicle control systems, such as the transmission, braking system, and traction control system.

intermediate tap One of a series of taps designed to cut an internal thread. Also called a plug tap.

intermittent fault A fault that is not ongoing and can be both active and historical.

internal bleeding The loss of blood into the body cavity from a wound; there is no obvious sign of blood.

internal combustion engine An engine that burns fuel inside the cylinders.

internal exhaust gas recirculation (I-EGR) An EGR system used on vocational vehicles that opens the exhaust valve momentarily during the intake stroke to recirculate exhaust gas into the cylinders.

interstage cooling The use of a liquid charge air cooler between two turbochargers connected in series. The air output of the first turbocharger is cooled before entering the second turbocharger.

Intuitive Diagnostic System (IDS) Proprietary software system available on BAE propulsion systems to aid technicians in diagnosing service issues.

isochronous governor A governor that is able to maintain more precise engine speed control than other types of governors.

isometric diagram A wiring diagram used to locate a component within a system and which shows the outline of a vehicle or piece of equipment where the component can be found.

ISX A Cummins engine family prefix.

jack stands Metal stands with adjustable height to hold a vehicle once it has been jacked up.

jacket water aftercooler (JWAC) A system that uses engine coolant to remove heat from the pressurized intake air.

keep alive memory (KAM) Memory that is retained by the ECM when the key is off.

key-off electrical loads Unwanted drain on the vehicle battery when the vehicle is off. Also called *parasitic draw*.

labor guide A guide that provides information to make estimates for repairs.

ladder-frame block A block design with sides that extend exactly to the centerline of the crankshaft bearings and a separate, additional section that attaches to the crankcase and the oil pan and incorporates the main bearing caps into one unit.

leak-off lines Lines at the injectors that collect fuel and return it to the fuel tank.

lean burn combustion Combustion that uses an excess amount of air to burn fuel. The cylinder is considered fuel lean and air rich. Air–fuel ratios are above stoichiometric ratio.

lean NO$_x$ trap (LNT) A catalyst mechanism that selects and destroys only NO$_x$ emissions without the use of liquid diesel exhaust fluid. Also referred to as hydrogen-SCR and NO$_x$ adsorbers.

left-hand rotation engine An engine that turns counterclockwise when viewed from the flywheel.

lift to port closure The position where the pumping plunger just begins to cover the fill and spill port.

lip-type dynamic oil seal A seal with a precisely shaped dynamic rubber lip that is held in contact with a moving shaft by a garter spring. An example would be a valve seal or camshaft seal.

liquid natural gas (LNG) Liquefied methane that is condensed from a gas to a liquid at −195°F to −260°F (−120°C to −160°C).

lithium-ion (Li-ion) battery A type of battery that does not use a galvanic reaction and in which a gel, salt, or solid material replaces the electrolyte solution.

load controller A mechanism that improves ride quality and reduces emissions by modulating increases and decreases in fueling to prevent vehicle bucking and jerking during acceleration and deceleration; also known as a pulse dampener.

load test A battery test that subjects the battery to a high rate of discharge, and the voltage is then measured after a set time to see how well the battery creates that current flow.

load-based speed controls A feature that supplies increased torque and sometimes more engine rpm when climbing hills with heavy loads, and also reduce torque when it senses the vehicle is unloaded or only lightly loaded.

load-dumping A feature that allows temporary suppression of high-voltage spikes.

locking pliers A type of plier where the jaws can be set and locked into position.

lockout/tagout A safety tag system to ensure that faulty equipment or equipment in the middle of repair is not used.

Low Carbon Fuel Standard (LCFS) A standard administered by the California Air Resources Board aimed at reducing GHG emissions form the transportation sector. By reducing fuel consumption of motor vehicles by 10% by 2020 compared to a 2010 baseline less carbon emissions are expected to be emitted into the atmosphere.

lower flammability limit (LFL) The minimum concentration of fuel in air that will support combustion. Flammability limit units are measured in percentage by volume.

low-pressure EGR A system in which EGR gas is drawn into the cylinders through either the turbocharger inlet or after the turbocharger between a throttle plate and intake manifold.

low-sulfur diesel (LSD) Diesel fuel with a maximum sulfur content of 0.05% mass or 500 ppm.

low-voltage burn-out A damaging condition for starter motors in which excess current flows through the starter, causing the motor to burn out prematurely.

low-voltage disconnect (LVD) A device that monitors battery voltage and disconnects non-critical electrical loads when battery voltage level falls below a preset threshold value.

lubricity A fuel's lubricating quality.

lugging An abuse condition where an engine is operated under heavy load below an acceptable operating speed range.

luminosity probe A probe threaded into the glow plug holes of the first cylinder that senses the light produced by a combustion event. The probe is used to help adjust injection pump timing during initial installation.

machine screw A screw with a slot for screwdrivers.

Magnehelic gauge A gauge that measures both pressure and vacuum using inches or a water column as a measuring unit.

magnetic pickup tools An extending shaft, often flexible, with a magnet fitted to the end for picking up metal objects.

main bearing journals The crankshaft surfaces located along the crankshaft centerline supported by the main bearing caps.

major side thrust Piston side thrust caused by cylinder pressure and the angle of the connecting rod during power.

malfunction indicator lamp (MIL) A dash-mounted warning light used to alert the driver when an emission-related fault is detected by the on-board diagnostic system.

mandrel The shaft of a pop rivet.

mandrel head The head of the pop rivet that connects to the shaft.

map (pictorial) diagram A wiring diagram that shows the entire vehicle wiring circuit using pictorial symbols.

mass airflow (MAF) sensor A device that measures the weight of air entering the engine and detects air inlet restrictions caused by a restricted air filter or intake when pressure drops below a threshold value.

mass-based variable torque (MBVT) A software-based torque control system that automatically adjusts engine torque output to match vehicle weight and load conditions. MBVT improves fuel efficiency and performance.

master and slave cylinders Pistons used in engine brakes to transfer motion from the injector rocker lever to the exhaust valves. The master piston follows the injector profile.

master disconnect switch A switch located in the battery compartments that enables technicians to disconnect the power circuit for maintenance or emergencies.

MaxxForce A brand of diesel engines owned by Navistar.

measuring tapes A flexible type of ruler and a common measuring tool.

mechanical fingers Spring-loaded fingers at the end of a flexible shaft that pick up items in tight spaces.

mechanical governor A governor that regulates the quantity of fuel injected by the high-pressure injection pump using flyweights and spring tension.

mechanical jacks A type of vehicle jack that uses mechanical leverage to lift a vehicle.

mechanically actuated electronically controlled unit injector (MEUI) Caterpillar's name for camshaft actuated electronic unit injectors.

mercaptan A gaseous fuel odorant that has a skunk-like or rotten egg–like smell. Mercaptan is added in very small concentrations to help detect any gaseous fuel leaks.

message identifier (MID) Also called module identifier, the electronic control module that has identified a fault. J-1587 protocols use MIDs.

metering Measurement of the correct quantity of fuel for each cylinder required for various speed and load conditions demanded of the engine.

metering plunger The lower plunger in either the CELECT injector or HPI-TPI injector; also known as the lower plunger.

metering rail supply inlet The opening in the HPI-TPI injector that admits fuel to the cavity below the lower metering plunger.

methane The primary constituent of natural gas. Methane's chemical formula is CH_4.

methane number A measurement of the knock resistance of gaseous fuels that do not contain octane molecules; similar to the measurement of octane. The methane number uses methane and hydrogen as reference points. Methane, which has high knock resistance, has a methane number of 100. Hydrogen, which has low knock resistance, has a methane number of 0.

methanol A fuel made from wood or cellulose.

Metri-Pack connector A pull-to-seat electrical connector with flat terminals instead of round.

microcontroller A special-purpose processor with limited capabilities, designed to perform a set of specific tasks.

micro-finish etching A piston skirt finish where many fine lines are machined into the skirt to retain oil.

micrometers Precise measuring tools designed to measure small distances and are available in both millimeter (mm) and inch calibrations.

micron (μ) A unit of measure equal to 0.001 mm.

middle distillates A fraction or cut produced in the distillation process, such as jet fuel or diesel.

Miller combustion cycle A modified four-stroke engine operating cycle that varies the closing of the intake valve.

Miller cycle An operating cycle that uses late intake valve closing and varies the closing of the intake valve.

minor side thrust Piston side thrust caused by compression pressure and the angle of the connecting rod.

mixer A device used on natural gas engines to meter the correct amount of natural gas into the intake air.

Mode 1 In split-mode operation, the mode that is for low-speed operation.

Mode 2 In split-mode operation, the mode that is for high-speed operation.

MONOTHERM piston A one-piece piston design made entirely of alloyed steel, which has a compact height and a large reduction of material between the skirt and crown.

Morse taper A tapered mounting shaft for drill bits and chucks in larger drills and lathes.

motor control module (MCM) The electronic control module used by Detroit Diesel to control engine operation. The MCM receives sensor input, processes information using operating algorithms, and produces output signals.

multigrade oil A blend of a several different oils with different viscosities; also known as multiweight oil.

multilayer steel (MLS) gasket A method of sealing the cylinder head to the engine block using multiple thin layers of cold-rolled, spring-grade stainless steel coated with elastomeric (rubber) material.

multilayer steel (MLS) head gasket A gasket composed of multiple layers of steel which may be coated with a rubberlike substance that adheres to metal surfaces. MLS gaskets are typically used between the cylinder head and the cylinder block.

multi-orifice nozzle A fuel nozzle that uses multiple spray holes to distribute and atomize fuel.

multi-torque An engine with the capability of changing its torque rise based on operating conditions. Commonly higher engine torque output is enabled in cruise mode.

Nanoslide technology A plasma spray welding technique developed by Mercedes-Benz to coat cylinder walls with a tool-grade hardness iron alloy.

naturally aspirated An engine that uses only atmospheric pressure, not pressurized air, to charge the cylinders with air.

needle lift sensor A sensor that provides a reference signal to the electronic control module (ECM) for the beginning of injection (BOI) by providing information about movement of the nozzle valve.

needle-nosed pliers Pliers with long tapered jaws for gripping small items and getting into tight spaces.

nickel–metal hydride (NiMH) battery A battery in which metal hydroxide forms the negative electrode and nickel oxide forms the positive electrode.

nippers Pliers designed to cut protruding items level with the surface.

Ni-Resist insert A stainless steel–nickel alloy insert placed in aluminum pistons in the compression ring groove. The insert minimizes groove wear caused by ring movement.

nitrated-organic acid technology (NOAT) An ELC using OAT with nitrates added.

nitric oxide (NO) An unstable, highly reactive, colorless gas. It is the most abundant type of NO_x produced during diesel combustion. It is a noxious respiratory irritant.

nitriding The process of hardening a metal's surface by heating the metal and slowly cooling or quenching the metal surface with cyanide salts.

nitrogen dioxide (NO_2) A reddish-brown gas formed from nitric oxide and oxygen. It is a noxious respiratory irritant.

nitrous oxide system (NOS) A system that supplements intake air with nitrous oxide (N_2O) to supply additional oxygen in the cylinder to burn more fuel.

nominal micron rating The minimum particle size a fuel filter is expected to remove.

non-ferrous metals Pure metals such as copper; can also be used in alloys.

non-volatile memory Memory that is not lost when power is removed or lost.

NO_x adsorber catalyst (NAC) A unique catalyst material that stores NO_x emissions and then decomposes the NO_x under specialized exhaust conditions.

NOX sensor A sensor that detects oxygen ions originating from nitric oxide (NOX) from among the other oxygen ions present in the exhaust gas.

nozzle chatter A high-pitched noise or chirping sound produced by the high-speed cycling of the nozzle valve opening and closing with contact between the valve and seat.

nozzle control valve (NCV) The valve that controls the balancing of hydraulic pressure on either side of a hydraulically balanced nozzle valve; it opens and closes the nozzle valve in common rail type injectors.

nozzle differential ratio The ratio between the surface area of the nozzle valve that is acted upon by high-pressure fuel when the valve is closed compared to the nozzle valve area when the nozzle valve is unseated.

nozzle opening pressure (NOP) The pressure required to unseat the nozzle valve and begin the injection of fuel. Also known as valve opening pressure (VOP).

nozzle return circuit A fuel pathway from the ACR injectors leading to the low-pressure fuel module, which drains fuel from the NCV; also known as a needle return circuit.

nozzle valve A valve in the nozzle that seals the end of the nozzle tip when it is not injecting fuel; also known as a needle valve.

nut A fastener with a hexagonal head and internal threads for screwing on bolts.

Nylock nut Keeps the nut and bolt done up tightly; can have a plastic or nylon insert. Tightening the bolt squeezes it into the insert, where it resists any movement. The self-locker is highly resistant to being loosened.

OBD manager Software that identifies fault codes and ensures emissions systems are operating correctly.

Occupational Safety and Health Administration (OSHA) Government agency created to provide national leadership in occupational safety and health.

octane number A measurement of the ignition characteristics of gasoline.

off-board diagnostics Procedures to isolate a fault based on fault code information, including retrieving fault code information, monitoring system operation, performing actuator tests and pinpoint electrical tests, and inspecting components.

offset screwdriver A screwdriver with a 90° bend in the shaft for working in tight spaces.

offset vice A vice that allows long objects to be gripped vertically.

oil manifold A component that supplies oil through the top of the injectors and eliminates the problem with O-ring leakage when oil is supplied though the cylinder head.

oil quality sensor An electrical device that measures the amount of soot loading in engine oil.

oil seal Any seal used to seal oil in and dirt, moisture, and debris out.

on-board diagnostics (OBD) Self-diagnostic capabilities of electronic control modules that allow them to evaluate voltage and current levels of circuits to which they are connected and determine if data is in the correct operational range.

opacity A measure of the percentage of light blocked by exhaust smoke which is used to evaluate exhaust gas density.

open circuits Describes a circuit that has a break and no current can flow.

open crankcase ventilation system A traditional ventilation system for the diesel crankcase that vents the crankcase directly to the atmosphere.

open fracture A fracture in which the bone is protruding through the skin or there is severe bleeding.

open-end wrench A wrench with open jaws to allow side entry to a nut or bolt.

operator's manual A document that contains information about a vehicle, which is a valuable source of information for both the owner and the technician.

opposed plunger pressurization A distributor pump design that uses two or four plungers arranged opposite one another inside a cam ring to pressurize fuel; also known as radial piston pressurization.

optical sensor tracking encoder (OSTE) A device that combines an optical fuel temperature and pump position sensor and supplies the PCM data regarding pump speed, rotor position, cam ring position, and fuel temperature.

organic acid technology (OAT) A category of ELC containing carbon-based corrosion inhibitors.

Otto cycle An engine operating cycle consisting of four strokes: intake, compression, power, and exhaust.

outer base circle One of two circles that outline the cam profile. The outer base circle refers to the circular part of the camshaft that includes the lobe.

out-of-range monitoring Validating sensor data to verify a system is operating within an expected range for a given operating condition.

outside micrometer Measures the outside dimensions of an item.

overcrank protection (OCP) thermostat A thermostat that monitors the temperature of the motor and opens a relay circuit to interrupt the current to the solenoid if prolonged cranking causes the motor temperature to exceed a safe threshold.

overflow valve A low-pressure fuel system pressure regulating valve for an injection pump that uses a ball and spring assembly. The overflow valve helps purge vapor from fuel and keeps fuel temperatures cool inside the pump.

overhead camshaft engine An engine that has the camshaft located in the cylinder head.

overrun The inability of a governor to keep the engine speed below the high idle speed when it is rapidly accelerated.

overrunning alternator decoupler (OAD) A pulley that uses an internal spring and clutch system that allows it to rotate freely in one direction and provide limited, spring-like movement in the other direction.

over-square engine An engine with a stroke that is shorter than the cylinder bore dimension.

oxidation reaction Reactions that add O_2 to HCs and CO to produce H_2O, CO_2, and heat.

oxides of nitrogen (NOX) A category of noxious emissions made up of oxygen and nitrogen.

oxyacetylene torch Used mainly as a cleaning agent in the commercial vehicle industry.

ozone A noxious gas molecule composed of three oxygen molecules.

paraffin A type of wax dissolved in diesel fuel.

parallax error A visual error caused by viewing measurement markers at an incorrect angle.

parallel alternators The practice of connecting alternators in parallel to provide higher charging voltage at idle with more available amperage.

parallel drive A vehicle in which both the engine and electric motor work together, blending motor and engine torque, to propel the vehicle.

parallel flow head A head design that features intake and exhaust manifolds on the same side of the engine and short, large ports that are joined together to provide a more compact engine design with adequate airflow to the cylinders; also known as the uniflow design.

parallel keys Used to prevent the free rotation of gears or pulleys on a shaft and can be used to secure a gearwheel on its shaft.

parallel turbocharger The use of two turbochargers that share the exhaust energy from an engine's exhaust manifold. The output of both turbochargers is connected directly to the intake manifold of the engine to increase airflow into the engine.

parallel wiring A type of custom-made wiring harness that encloses multiple conductors into a single vinyl insulator covering.

parameter group number (PGN) A package of serial data transmitted over the CAN network that includes SPN, source addresses, and FMI, as well as commands, data, requests, acknowledgments, negative-acknowledgments, and fault codes.

parameter identifier (PID) A value or identifier of an item being reported with fault data.

parasitic draw Unwanted drain on the vehicle battery when the vehicle is off. Also called *key-off electrical load*.

parent bore block A block design that has holes cast and bored in the block for the cylinders with the pistons inserted directly into these holes; also known as a no-sleeve block.

partial-authority Cummins engine (PACE) A partial-authority system that combines the mechanical PT pump with an electronic fuel control valve on the outlet of the fuel pump, which varies pressure supplied to unit injectors.

partial-authority fuel system A mechanical fuel system that has adapted some electronic controls to extend the design usefulness, particularly where stricter emission regulations require cleaner combustion.

particulate matter (PM) A category of noxious emissions made up of liquid or solid particles. Black exhaust soot is a common PM emission.

parts program A computer software program for identifying and ordering replacement vehicle parts.

parts specialist The person who serves customers at the parts counters.

passive regeneration A process where relatively low-temperature chemical reactions take place in the exhaust catalysts to oxidize soot into CO_2 and H_2O. Passive reactions take place when the DPF is hot enough under normal vehicle operation; this occurs when sufficient load and engine speed produce exhaust inlet temperatures above 482°F (250°C).

passive sensor A sensor that does not use a current supplied by the ECM to operate.

peak torque The engine speed at which cylinder pressures are highest.

peening A term used to describe the action of flattening a rivet through a hammering action.

pendulum gear dampener A patented camshaft gear design used for dampening torsional vibration transmission to the camshaft.

pendulum vibration absorber A dampener that provides torsional vibration control by producing forces that directly cancel the forces producing torsional vibration.

performance curve A line graph that plots engine torque, fuel consumption, and horsepower against engine speed.

personal protective equipment (PPE) Safety equipment designed to protect the technician, such as safety boots, gloves, clothing, protective eyewear, and hearing protection.

personality module code An engine ECM identification number used to determine which engine calibrations are allowed to be uploaded or flashed into the ECM.

petroleum distillates Fuel produced from distilling crude oil.

phasing An injection pump adjustment procedure that is made when the remaining pumping elements are adjusted to obtain lift to port closure (in 60° intervals for a six cylinder pump) after the initial setting on cylinder 1.

Phillips screwdriver A type of screwdriver that fits a head shaped like a cross in screws; also called Phillips head screwdriver.

photochemical smog A type of air pollution that gives the atmosphere a hazy, reddish-brown color.

piezoceramic actuator An actuator composed of piezoceramic discs that change shape and in turn change the balance of hydraulic forces inside the injector; this type of actuator can switch fuel on and off in as little as 0.0001 second.

piezoelectric pressure transducer A sensor clamped to an injection line that transduces injection line pressure pulses into electrical signals. The signals are used to activate a timing light when checking or adjusting dynamic injection pump timing.

piezoresistive sensor A sensor that uses a piezoresistive crystal arranged with a Wheatstone bridge to measure the change in resistance of the piezo crystal; these sensors are adapted to measuring vibration and dynamic or continuous pressure changes.

pilot injection A small injection event taking place 8°–10° before the main injection event.

pin punch A type of punch in various sizes with a straight or parallel shaft.

pinion gear The component that is engaged by the control rack to rotate the plunger drive vane.

pintle nozzle A fuel nozzle that sprays fuel through a single hole.

piston slap A noise in the engine produced by large operating clearances between a piston and cylinder wall. Piston slap is most often heard when an engine is cold.

planetary gear reduction drive A type of gear reduction system in which a planetary gear set reduces the starter profile to multiply motor torque to the pinion gear.

plasma catalytic converters A new catalytic converter technology that uses high-frequency alternating current to destroy noxious emissions in the exhaust system.

pliers A hand tool with gripping jaws.

plug-in hybrid electric vehicle (PHEV) Any type of hybrid electric vehicle containing a battery storage system that uses an external source to recharge the battery when the vehicle is not in operation.

plunger and barrel assembly The elements making up the high-pressure pumps in a multiple plunger injection pump.

pneumatic jacks A type of vehicle jack that uses compressed gas or air to lift a vehicle.

policy A guiding principle that sets the shop direction.

polyalphaolefin (PAO) A manmade base stock (synthetic) used in place of mineral oil. PAO molecules are smaller and more consistent in size, and no impurities are found in this oil because it is derived through chemical process.

pop tester A tool used by technicians that supplies pressurized fuel to injector nozzles which is used to evaluate the condition of fuel nozzles.

poppet control valve A mushroom-shaped valve used by unit injectors that operates under the influence of a magnetic field to open and close an injector spill port.

poppet valve A valve that controls the flow of oil into and out of HEUI A and B injectors.

pop-rivet gun A hand tool for installing pop rivets.

portable lifting hoists A type of vehicle hoist that is portable and can be moved from one location to another.

port-helix metering A mechanism to meter fuel that uses reciprocating plungers and a camshaft to pressurize fuel; rotating the helix groove in the pumping plungers in relation to the spill port controls fuel metered to the injectors.

Potentiometer A variable resistor with three connections—one at each end of a resistive path, and a third sliding contact that moves along the resistive pathway.

pour point The temperature at which fuel will no longer flow through lines and filters because of wax.

power density The power an engine produces for its displacement.

power tools Tools powered by electricity or compressed air.

PowerStroke Navistar's name for its mid-bore V-block diesel engines.

Premium Tech Tool The latest generation of service software used by Volvo–Mack to diagnose fault codes, adjust programmable parameters, and provide any other electronic support for the vehicle and engine control system

pressure drop test A test that measures internal restrictions of the intercooler core.

pressure time (PT) injection A Cummins unit injection system used until the early 1980s.

pressure washer/cleaner A cleaning machine that boosts low-pressure tap water to a high-pressure output.

pressure wave correction (PWC) The process used to produce a calibration code for a common rail injector. A correction factor is applied to a specific injector's electrical pulse width to adapt the injector to an engine based on manufacturing tolerances between injectors.

pressure wave reflection The movement of a pressure wave back and forth along the length of an injector line. Like the sloshing of water in a tub, the pressure wave bounces back and forth between the nozzle and high pressure pump.

pressurization Compressing fuel to the degree required for an injection event.

prick punch A punch with a sharp point for accurately marking a point on metal.

primary balance Balance achieved when the crankshaft counterweights offset the weight of the piston and connecting rod assembly.

primary battery A battery in which chemical reactions are not reversible and the battery cannot be recharged.

primary filter The first filter in the fuel stream from the fuel tank.

primary sources People who have direct experience with the same or a similar problem.

prime mover A term used for engines in off-road equipment, locomotives, and electrical generators.

priming A process that removes any air that may have entered the fuel system and prevents introduction of unfiltered fuel into the system

procedure A list of the steps required to get the same result each time a task or activity is performed.

programmable parameter A measurable value about engine system operation that can be changed using service software (e.g., maximum vehicle speed).

programmable read only memory (PROM) Memory that stores programming information and cannot be easily written over.

progressive shifting A programmable parameter that limits engine speed until a minimum road speed is reached. Progressive shifting encourages a driver to shift gears sooner to save fuel.

propane A gaseous fuel that is heavier than air. It has the chemical formula C_6H_8. It is also referred to as liquid petroleum fuel (LPG).

propane enrichment system An aftermarket performance accessory that introduces propane into the intake air through a solenoid-controlled orifice to increase power output by using up excess oxygen left over in the cylinders; also known as a propane topper.

propulsion control system (PCS) module A microprocessor-based device that supplies electrical output signals based on input data collected from a vehicle's sensors.

propylene glycol An anti-freeze base that is non-toxic and environmentally friendly.

pry bars (crowbars) A high-strength carbon-steel rod with offsets for levering and prying.

pull-down switch A switch connected between the ECM and a negative ground current potential.

pullers A generic term to describe hand tools that mechanically assist the removal of bearings, gears, pulleys, and other parts.

pull-to-seat terminal A terminal installed by inserting the wire through the connector cavity, crimping on a terminal, and then pulling the terminal back into the connector cavity to seat it.

pull-up switch A switch connected between the ECM and a battery positive.

pulse charger A battery charger that sends current into the battery in pulses of one-second cycles; used to recover sulfated batteries.

pulse-width modulation (PWM) An electrical signal that varies in on and off time.

pump mounted driver (PMD) A control module that supplies electrical signals to control the operation of the spill valve.

pumping loss The energy used by an engine to move intake and exhaust gases in and out of the cylinders.

punches A generic term to describe a high-strength carbon-steel shaft with a blunt point for driving. Center and prick punches are exceptions and have a sharp point for marking or making an indentation.

push-to-seat terminal A terminal inserted into the back of the connector cavity to seat after the terminal is crimped to the wire.

pyrolysis A chemical process in which biomass feedstock is heated in the absence of air to gasify the material at temperatures of 842–1112°F (450–600°C).

Pyrometer A temperature gauge designed to measure exhaust temperatures. The pyrometer is a thermocouple device that generates electric current proportional to its temperature.

quantity control valve The pulse-width modulated inlet metering valve used on the high-pressure pump of Detroit Diesel's ACR system. Its operation controls the pressure supplied to the high-pressure fuel rail.

radial piston pressurization A distributor pump design that uses opposed plunger metering. Plungers move inside a cam ring to pressurize fuel.

random access memory (RAM) A temporary storage place for information that needs to be quickly accessed.

ratchet A generic term to describe a handle for sockets that allows the user to select direction of rotation. It can turn sockets in restricted areas without the user having to remove the socket from the fastener.

ratcheting screwdriver A screwdriver with a selectable ratchet mechanism built into the handle that allows the screwdriver tip to ratchet as it is being used.

rate shaping Optimizing the injection discharge curve to best match engine operating conditions.

rated horsepower The power output of an engine measured at the maximum engine speed.

rated speed An engine's maximum speed with a load.

rate-shaped injection An injection strategy that carefully regulates the amount of fuel injected into a cylinder per degree of crank angle rotation.

rattle gun The most common air tool in a shop; also called the air-impact wrench or impact gun.

rawl pins Often used to hold components on rotating shafts. They are a type of shear pin, used when excessive force is used to avoid further damage to a component.

read only memory (ROM) Memory used for permanent storage of instructions and fixed values used by the ECM that control the microprocessor.

reciprocating engine An engine that uses pistons moving up and down in a cylinder. A crankshaft converts the up-and-down motion into rotational movement.

rectification A process of converting alternating current (AC) into direct current (DC).

reduction gear drive A starter motor drive system in which the motor multiplies torque to the starter pinion gear by using an extra gear between the armature and the starter drive mechanism.

reduction reaction Reactions that remove oxygen from NO_x molecules, converting NO_x into N_2 and O_2.

reference voltage (Vref) A precisely regulated voltage supplied by the ECM to sensors; the value is typically 5 VDC, but some manufacturers use 8 or 12 volts.

refrigerant label A label that lists the type and total capacity of refrigerant that is installed in the A/C system.

regenerative braking A feature of hybrid vehicles by which generators recover energy during braking.

remote sensing Referencing the battery positive connection through an input terminal that is used for the regulator reference voltage.

Renewable Fuel Standard (RFS) Legislation that requires the use of more biologically based fuels from renewable sources.

renewable fuels A category of alternative fuel sources that can be replaced or reproduced. Examples of renewables are biological based fuels such as those derived from vegetable oil or animal fat.

repair order A form used by shops to collect information regarding a vehicle coming in for repair, also referred to as a work order.

reserve capacity The time, in minutes, that a new, fully charged battery at 80°F (26.7°C) will supply a constant load of 25 amps without its voltage dropping below 10.5 volts for a 12-volt battery.

reserve voltage The maximum voltage the secondary ignition system can produce to fire a spark plug.

residual magnetism The small amount of magnetism left on the rotor after it is initially magnetized by the coil windings' magnetic field.

resolver A special sensor that measures the rotor position and speed for the PCS to properly manage the motor operation by reducing current flow and shutting down the system as needed.

resonator A device in the exhaust system that looks like a small muffler. This device provides additional dampening and tuning of exhaust noise.

respirator Protective gear used to protect the wearer from inhaling harmful dusts or gases. Respirators range from single-use disposable masks to types that have replaceable cartridges. The correct types of cartridge must be used for the type of contaminant encountered.

reverse-flow cylinder heads A cylinder head with no exhaust manifolds on the outside of the cylinder head; instead, short exhaust runs are fed directly to the turbocharger located in the V between the cylinder banks.

rheostat A variable resistor constructed of a fixed input terminal and a variable output terminal, which vary current flow by passing current through a long resistive tightly coiled wire.

right-hand rotation engine An engine that turns clockwise when viewed from the flywheel.

road draft tube The tube that connects the crankcase to the atmosphere in an open crankcase ventilation system; also known as a crankcase ventilation tube.

rollover valve A valve located on the fuel tank that prevents fuel from draining from the fuel tank vent line in the event of a rollover accident.

rootes blower A high-volume positive displacement air pump used to pressurize intake air for Detroit Diesel two-stroke cycle diesels.

SAE J1128 standard A standard that specifies the dimensions, test methods, and requirements for single-core primary wire intended for use in road vehicle applications.

safe working load (SWL) The maximum safe lifting load for lifting equipment.

safety data sheet (SDS) A sheet that provides information about handling, use, and storage of a material that may be hazardous.

sand or bead blasters A cleaning system that uses high-pressure fine particles of glass bead or sand.

scheduled oil sampling (SOS) An extremely detailed analysis of the condition of the engine and quality of the engine oil.

schematic diagram A line drawing that explains how a system works by using symbols and connecting lines.

scissor gear Two separate spring-loaded gears incorporated into a single unit to reduce gear rattle caused by torsional vibration.

screw extractor A tool for removing broken screws or bolts.

screws Usually smaller than bolts and are sometimes referred to as metal threads. They can have a variety of heads and are used on smaller components. The thread often extends from the tip to the head so they can hold together components of variable thickness.

secondary balance Balance achieved when the movement of one piston counterbalances the movement of another, result in smoother running engines.

secondary filter The second filter in the fuel stream from the fuel tank.

secondary sources Secondhand information compiled from a variety of sources.

second-degree burns Burns that involve blistering and damage to the outer layer of skin.

selective catalyst reduction (SCR) An exhaust aftertreatment technology that targets and breaks down NO$_x$ emissions into harmless substances in the exhaust system using ammonia.

self-exciting alternator An alternator that relies on the residual magnetism found in the rotor after operating as a way to switch on the voltage regulator and supply current to the rotor.

self-tapping screw A screw that cuts down its own thread as it goes. It is made of hard material that cuts a mirror image of itself into the hole as you turn it.

sending units An electrical device, usually a variable-resistance rheostat, that supplies a voltage signal to an analog-type dash gauge proportional to the fuel level.

sensing The voltage reference point the alternator uses for regulation of the output.

series drive A vehicle in which only an electric traction motor supplies torque to propel the vehicle.

series turbocharger A turbocharger that uses two differently sized turbochargers connecting the compressor outlet of one turbocharger into the compressor housing inlet of a second turbocharger; in this system output from a smaller high-pressure turbocharger, which responds quicker at low engine speeds, is supplemented at heavier engine speeds and loads by the larger low-pressure turbocharger.

series turbocharging Using two differently sized turbochargers where the compressor outlet is connected to the inlet of a second compressor.

series-parallel drive A more complex system enabling an engine only, an electric motor only, and a combined engine-motor operation. Also called *power-split configuration*.

serrated edge shake-proof washer A washer that is used to anchor smaller screws.

service campaign and recall A corrective measure conducted by manufacturers when a safety issue is discovered with a particular vehicle.

service history A complete list of all the servicing and repairs that have been performed on a vehicle.

servo-hydraulic To use a small movement of an electrically operated control valve to manipulate much larger and powerful hydraulic forces.

shedding A process that reduces the plate surface area and therefore reduces capacity. Shedding may also produce short circuits between the bottom of positive and negative plates.

shock Inadequate tissue oxygenation resulting from serious injury or illness.

shop or service manual Manufacturer's or after-market information on the repair and service of vehicles.

short circuits Describe a condition in which the current flows along an unintended route.

shot-peened A technique that uses small steel balls to blast metal surfaces in order to close up any small cracks or pores, which have the potential to become larger.

Signature 600 A premium ISX engine that produces the highest engine power output and has several key components built with extra durability.

simple fracture A fracture that involves no open wound or internal or external bleeding.

single flare A sealing system made on the end of metal tubing.

single sequential turbocharger (SST) A unique turbocharger design with one turbine wheel and two compressor wheels operating in separate compressor housings. The two compressor wheels share a common turbine shaft. This system is also known as the DualBoost system is used by Ford Powerstroke engines.

SinterCast Navistar's name for its CGI engine block construction.

sleeve metering A form of metering that uses a sliding control sleeve or ring fitted to an axial plunger. The control sleeve position determines when the injection event ends by spilling fuel from the axial plunger.

sliding T-handle A handle fitted at 90° to the main body that can be slid from side to side.

slipper skirt piston A piston design that has a portion of the skirt removed on both non-thrust sides of the piston to provide clearance for the crankshaft counterweights.

slow charger A battery charger that charges at low current.

smart charger A battery charger with microprocessor-controlled charging rates and times.

smart electrification A feature that enables the EP 40/50 system's motors to switch over to generating mode to produce as much as 300 amps at 24 volts at idle.

snap ring pliers A pair of pliers for installing and removing internal or external snap rings.

Society of Automotive Engineers (SAE) viscosity ratings An oil performance criteria that indicates oil's flow characteristics.

socket An enclosed metal tube commonly with 6 or 12 points to remove and install bolts and nuts.

solvent A highly flammable liquid that can dissolve other substances.

solvent tank A tank containing solvents to clean vehicle parts.

soot loading A condition that occurs when engine oil dissolves combustion soot.

source address (SA) The field that designates which control module is sending the message.

spacer plate A plate located between the engine block deck and cylinder head used on high-horsepower Caterpillar engines. The plate reduces stress transmitted to the cylinder liners.

spark arrestor A screen covering the exhaust outlet that prevents fires by trapping large incandescent carbon particles. Exhaust gas flow pounds these particles into smaller pieces and cools them in the process.

specific heat The amount of heat required by a gas, solid, or liquid to produce a temperature change of 1°F within a specified time period.

speed brace A U-shaped socket wrench that allows high-speed operation. Also called a speeder handle.

speed nut A nut usually made of thin metal; it does not need to be held when started but it is not as strong as a conventional nut. A fast and convenient way to secure a screw.

spill control valve (SCV) A valve that operates to increase or decrease injection pressure as needed to meet operating requirements. The normally open valve, when energized, will cause fuel pressure to build up in the injector body until the nozzle control valve is energized and injection takes place.

spill timing A procedure that can be performed on an engine to verify or adjust pump-to-engine timing. The procedure is also used on a comparator bench to establish correct lift to port closure.

spin-on filter Filter media enclosed in a metal can that is threaded onto a filter header.

spiral-wound cell battery A type of AGM battery in which the positive and negative electrodes are coiled into a tight spiral cell with an absorbent microglass mat placed between the plates.

split ball gauge (small hole gauge) A gauge that is good for measuring small holes where telescoping gauges cannot fit.

split charge relay A system designed to separate the main starting battery and the auxiliary battery. Also called a *battery isolator system*.

split fracture connecting rod A technique used to form a mating surface between a connecting rod and cap. The mating surfaces are not machined but are produced by fracturing the big end of the rod along a line scribed into the rod.

split shot injection An injection strategy that delivers fuel in two distinct events during one combustion cycle; also known as pre-injection metering (PRIME) and pilot injection.

sprain An injury in which a joint is forced beyond its natural movement limit.

spray-wash cabinet A cleaning cabinet that sprays solvent under pressure to clean vehicle parts.

spring washer A washer that compresses as the nut tightens; the nut is spring loaded against this surface, which makes it unlikely to work loose. The ends of the spring washer also bite into the metal.

sputter bearing The latest technology in bearing overlay material, which deposits a metal overlay surface onto a bearing backing that is three times harder than conventional overlay. This complex process involves spray welding in a vacuum and is used to make a bearing that has the highest ability to carry a load over any other bearing.

square engine An engine with an equal stroke and bore dimensions.

square file A type of file with a square cross-section.

square thread A thread type with square shoulders used to translate rotational to lateral movement.

Stanadyne DS-4 A full-authority distributor first introduced in 1994; three generations of the pump were built. The adaptation of electronic controls to the pump enabled the flexibility to adjust delivery quantities and timing more accurately than mechanical systems.

standard (imperial) system Bolts, nuts, and studs can have either metric or imperial threads. They are designated by their thread diameter, thread pitch, length, and grade. Imperial measures are in feet, inches, and fractions of inches. Most countries use metric.

standard day factors Engine test standards for ambient temperature, atmospheric pressure, and humidity. Manufacturer measurements of horsepower and torque must be made using standard day factors to ensure uniformity of test results.

state of balance The state of mechanical governor flyweights when flyweight force equals spring force.

state of charge test A test that indicates how charged or discharged a battery is, not how much capacity it has.

static timing Pump timing that is adjusted when an engine is stopped.

steel ruler A ruler that is made from stainless steel. Stainless steel rulers commonly come in 30 mm, 60 mm, and 1 meter lengths.

stiffening plate A steel plate attached to the oil pan rails to minimize vibration and torsional movement of the crankcase in high-horsepower engines.

stoichiometric ratio The minimum mass of air required to completely burn all fuel in the combustion chamber so that no fuel or air remains after combustion.

straight edges A measuring device generally made of steel to check how flat a surface is.

straight grinder A powered grinder with the wheel set at 90° to the shaft.

straight vegetable oil (SVO) Unrefined vegetable oil used as fuel made from plants such as soybeans, jatropha, and palms.

stratified combustion Combustion that burns fuel in layers of varying air–fuel ratios.

stroke The distance traveled by the piston from the top to the bottom of the cylinder.

stroke ratio A comparison between the bore diameter and stroke distance of a cylinder, also known as squareness.

stud A type of threaded fastener with a thread cut on each end, as opposed to having a bolt head on one end.

sulfuric acid A type of acid that when mixed with pure water forms the basis of battery acid or electrolyte.

supercharger Any mechanical device used to pressurize the intake air above atmospheric pressure. Superchargers include rootes blowers and turbochargers.

supplemental coolant additive (SCA) An additive used to treat cooling systems to reduce the effects of cavitation erosion and optimize cooling system performance.

supporting statement A statement that urges the speaker to elaborate on a particular topic.

suspect parameter number (SPN) A numerical identifier that defines the data in a fault message and the priority of the fault.

sustainability The ability of an engine or fuel production process to be maintained over a long-term period.

synchronous reference sensor (SRS) Detroit Diesel's term for a camshaft position sensor.

synthetic diesel Fuel made through the Fischer-Tropsch reaction.

synthetic oil Oil made from base stock that is synthetically derived or manufactured.

system identifier (SID) A fault code used by J-1587 protocols that identifies which subsystem has failed.

tab washer A washer that gets its name from the small tabs that are folded back to secure the washer. After the nut or bolt has been tightened, the washer remains exposed and is folded up to grip the flats and prevent movement.

tangential intake port An intake port design that admits air into the cylinder at an angle to impart more swirl, or turbulence, to charge air.

tap A term used to generically describe an internal thread-cutting tool.

tap handle A tool designed to securely hold taps for cutting internal threads.

taper key Used to prevent the free rotation of gears or pulleys on a shaft; used to anchor a pulley to a shaft or a disc to a driving shaft.

taper pins Used to position parts on a shaft; for example, gears, pulleys, and collars.

taper tap A tap with a tapper; it is usually the first of three taps used when cutting internal threads.

taper-current charger A battery charger that applies either constant voltage or constant amperage to the battery through a manually adjusted current selection switch.

tappet A components used by multiple plunger injection pumps to produce low friction reciprocating motion of the plungers.

technical service bulletin (TSB) Information issued by manufacturers to alert technicians of unexpected problems or changes to repair procedures.

telematics A branch of information technology that uses specialized applications for long-distance transmission of information to and from a vehicle.

telescoping gauge Gauge used for measuring distances in awkward spots such as the bottom of a deep cylinder.

temperature differential test A test that measures cooler efficiency or whether the cooler is possibly externally restricted.

tensile strength The amount of force required before a material deforms or breaks.

test certificate A certificate issued when lifting equipment has been checked and deemed safe.

thermal efficiency The amount of energy an engine converts into mechanical energy compared to what could theoretically be extracted from a pound of fuel.

thermal efficiency The ability of an engine to convert the energy content of fuel into mechanical force. Thermal efficiency is measured by making a comparison between the amount of energy released during combustion and energy available at the engine flywheel.

thermistor A temperature-sensitive variable resistor commonly used to measure coolant, oil, fuel, and air temperatures.

thread chaser A device similar to a die that cleans up rusty or damaged threads.

thread pitch The coarseness or fineness of a thread as measured by the distance from the peak of one thread to the next, in threads per inch.

thread repair A generic term to describe a number of processes that can be used to repair threads.

three Cs Concern (the concern, or problem, with the vehicle); cause (the cause of the concern); and correction (fixing the problem).

throttle pintle nozzle A type of injector that changes the rate of injection from the nozzle through the shape of the nozzle valve; also called a delay nozzle.

Tier 1, 2, 3, and 4 emission standards Consecutive phases of increasingly cleaner off-road emission standards.

timing In the high-pressure injection system, the beginning of the injection event in the combustion cycle relative to crank rotation.

timing and metering actuators Components that perform electronic control of metering and timing; when energized, the actuators open and allow fuel to flow to the injectors through separate timing and metering fuel rails drilled through the cylinder head.

timing chain A steel chain connecting the crankshaft assembly to the camshaft assembly.

timing gear A sprocket attached to the crankshaft assembly and the camshaft assembly.

timing pins Tools used lock and injection pump or engine in position to obtain correct pump to engine timing.

timing plunger The upper plunger in either the CELECT injector or HPI-TPI injector; also known as the upper plunger.

timing rail supply inlet The opening in the HPI-TPI injector that admits fuel to the cavity below the upper timing plunger.

timing reference sensor (TRS) Detroit Diesel's term for a crankshaft position sensor.

tin A metal most often used as a corrosion-resistant coating in automotive applications.

tin snips Cutting device for sheet metal; works in a similar fashion to scissors.

ton miles per gallon A measure used for new fuel efficiency standards that is calculated by measuring the vehicle weight in tons, multiplying by the distance traveled in miles, and then dividing by the volume of fuel consumed measured in gallons. The metric equivalent of ton miles per gallon is grams per ton.

top dead center (TDC) The highest point the piston travels in a cylinder.

torque A measurement of rotational, or twisting, force transmitted through the crankshaft to the flywheel.

torque angle A method of tightening bolts or nuts based on angles of rotation.

torque control The regulation of fuel entering the cylinders to produce an appropriate amount of torque for a given engine speed.

torque elasticity The ability of an engine to produce the torque needed to accelerate from medium to high engine speed while under load.

torque plate A device that limits maximum control rack travel in a mechanical injection pump; also called a full load stop.

torque rise The difference between peak torque and torque at rated speed.

torque specification Describes the amount of twisting force allowable for a fastener or a specification showing the twisting force from an engine crankshaft; supplied by manufacturers.

torque to yield (TTY) A method of tightening bolts just beyond their yield point or the point at which they will not return to their original length.

torque wrench A tool used to measure the rotational or twisting force applied to fasteners.

torque-to-yield (TTY) bolts Bolts that are tightened using the torque-to-yield method.

torque-turn A method that requires a bolt to receive an initial preload using a torque wrench; afterward, the bolt is turned several additional degrees, flats, or turns.

torsional vibration The rhythmic speeding up and slowing down of the crankshaft due to deceleration during compression strokes and acceleration during power strokes of the engine cylinder.

torx bolt Often found in vehicle engines in places such as cylinder heads to blocks, where particular tightening sequences are require.

total acid number (TAN) The acidity of an oil. Certain contaminants cause engine oil to increase in acidity, which is measured using the TAN index.

total base number (TBN) The measurement of a lubricant's reserve alkalinity, which aids in the control of acids formed during the combustion process.

total cylinder displacement The volume of all of the cylinders in an engine. To find total cylinder displacement, multiply the displacement of one cylinder by the total number of cylinders.

total cylinder volume The sum of the cylinder displacement plus clearance volume.

traction motor An electric motor that provides propulsion to a vehicle.

transesterification A process that replaces glycerin in vegetable oil or animal fat with alcohol molecules.

transient emissions Emissions produced temporarily when the engine load or speed is increased, such as when accelerating or upshifting gears.

transient voltage suppression (TVS) diodes Specialized diodes in the rectifier bridge that become resistive rather than conductive at a specific voltage level.

transmission control module (TCM) The electronic controller that issues commands to the solenoids inside the transmission to obtain the desired range. Also known as the transmission electronic control unit (ECU).

trapezoidal pin bushing A pin bushing design in which the bearing surfaces absorbing combustion forces are wider on the connecting rod and piston to improve piston and connecting rod load bearing capabilities.

trapped volume spill (TVS) port A component in the injector that enables a crisp end to injection; when the timing plunger uncovers the TVS port, fuel pressure is released to the low-pressure fuel return.

trickle charger A battery charger that charges at a low amperage rate.

trunk piston A piston design that is dimensionally longer than it is wide, with a full piston skirt.

tube-flaring tool A tool that makes a sealing flare on the end of metal tubing.

tubing cutter A hand tool for cutting pipe or tubing squarely.

tunnel-bore block A block that has the main bearing bores and block formed into one solid structure for maximum block rigidity and strength.

turbo lag A delay between driver demand for power and the point when the engine responds with power proportional to driver demand.

turbocharger Exhaust-driven device that compresses air to pressurize the air intake of an engine.

turbocharger compressor bypass valve A valve used by Volvo–Mack engines to assist heating of intake air at idle. Turbocharger outlet pressure is recirculated back into the compressor inlet to repressurize intake air and raise its temperature

twist drill A hardened steel drill bit for making holes in metals, plastics, and wood.

two-stroke engine An engine that uses an operating cycle that is completed using two piston strokes and one crank rotation.

ultra capacitor A new generation of high-capacity and high-energy density capacitors

ultra-high-pressure injection (UHPI) Volvo–Mack's name for a high-pressure injection system using Delphi's E3 unit injector.

ultra-low-sulfur diesel (ULSD) Fuel that has a maximum sulfur content of 15 ppm.

under-square engine An engine with a stroke that is longer than the cylinder bore.

unison ring A device used by VGT turbochargers to rotate the nozzle ring vanes together simultaneously.

urea An ammonia-carrying molecule that breaks down in hot exhaust gas.

useful life requirement Emissions legislation that requires an engine to remain below maximum emission thresholds for its normal expected service life.

V blocks Metal blocks with a V-shaped cutout for holding shafts while working on them. Also referred to as vee blocks.

validating statement A statement that shows common interest in the topic being discussed.

Valley Forge (VF) diagram A schematic wiring diagram that uses SAE-type symbols.

valve overlap The number of degrees of crankshaft rotation when both the intake and exhaust valves are open. Overlap occurs at the end of the exhaust stroke and the beginning of the intake stroke.

vane-type pump A pump that uses a set of rotating vanes inside an eccentric shaped housing o to pressurize fuel.

variable capacitance pressure sensor An active sensor that measures both dynamic and static pressure.

variable geometry turbocharger (VGT) A turbocharger with the capability of changing boost pressure independent of engine speed and load; also known as variable nozzle turbocharger (VNT) and variable vane turbocharger (VVT).

variable intake valve actuator (VIVA) A device used by Caterpillar ACERT engines to vary the timing of intake valve closing.

variable orifice nozzle A type of nozzle that is under development, which has two rows of spray holes that regulate the delivery rate, spray angle, and spray hole size with a variable lift nozzle valve; also known as a coaxial nozzle.

variable reluctance sensor A sensor used to measure rotational speed, including wheel speed, vehicle speed, engine speed, and camshaft and crankshaft position.

variable speed governor A governor that controls engine speed based only on accelerator pedal position; also known as an all-speed governor.

VECTRO An acronym for Volvo electronic control system for engine electronics.

vehicle emission control information (VECI) label A label used by technicians to identify engine and emission control information for the vehicle.

vehicle hoist A type of vehicle lifting tool designed to lift the entire vehicle.

vehicle safety certification (VSC) label A label certifying that the vehicle meets the Federal Motor Vehicle Safety, Bumper, and Theft Prevention Standards in effect at the time of manufacture.

vernier caliper An accurate measuring device for internal, external, and depth measurements that incorporates fixed and adjustable jaws.

vertical exhaust system An exhaust system that directs exhaust gases upward, into the atmosphere.

virtual technician A brand name for telematics communications package used to exchange information between a vehicle chassis and a central dispatch monitoring the operation of a vehicle.

viscosity A measure of oil's resistance to flow which characterizes a fluids thickness or ability to flow.

viscosity index (VI) A measurement of the total amount of change in an oil's viscosity due to temperature.

viscosity index (VI) improver An additive that prevents oil from thickening when cold and thinning when hot.

volatile memory A type of data storage that is lost or erased when the ignition power is switched off.

volatile organic compound (VOC) Any carbon-containing molecule that is highly reactive.

volatility The quantity of fuel evaporating at a particular temperature.

volumetric efficiency A comparison between the measured cylinder volume and the volume of air actually filling a cylinder; this measurement is expressed as a percentage.

Volvo Computer-Aided Diagnostics Systems (VCADS) A diagnostic software system used by Volvo to adjust and troubleshoot engine fault codes. The system is also used to adjust programmable parameters and perform any electronic support of the vehicle and engine control system.

V-pulse EGR An internal EGR system used by Volvo that uses cooled EGR gas and depends on natural pressure pulses in the exhaust system to supply exhaust gases to the intake manifold.

wad punch A type of punch that is hollow for cutting circular shapes in soft materials, such as gaskets.

warding file A type of thin, flat file with a tapered end.

warp anchor A block design that has the cylinder head and the cylinder block bolted together by tie bolts; sliding steel sleeves, which are locked in the block, accept the cylinder head bolt from one side and the tie bolt from the other.

wastegate An exhaust bypass valve in the turbine housing that allows exhaust gases to bypass the turbine and directly enter the exhaust pipe, thus "wasting" some of the exhaust energy.

water manometer A slack u-tube device used to measure EBP using inches of water column.

water wicking The movement of water through wiring due to its adhesive and cohesive properties.

water-in-fuel (WIF) module A device that illuminates a warning light that informs the operator to drain or service the fuel–water separator.

water-in-fuel (WIF) sensor A detector that uses an electrical conductivity probe to sense a specific level of water in fuel and cause a dash-mounted light to illuminate; this light or warning alerts the vehicle operator of the need to drain water from the fuel–water separator.

water-methanol injection A system that sprays water and methanol into the intake system to absorb heat from the intake air, which helps to reduce peak combustion temperatures.

water-pump pliers Adjustable pliers with parallel jaws that allow you to increase or decrease the size of the jaws by selecting a different set of channels.

Weather-Pack connector An environmentally sealed push-to-seat electrical connection system supplied in one- to six-pin configurations.

wet sleeve block A block designed with a number of large holes into which the cylinder sleeves are inserted; coolant has direct contact with the outside of the sleeve and there is no supporting cylinder bore structure.

wet stacking The appearance of engine slobber on an exhaust stack as a result of prolonged engine idle.

wet-spark ignition system An engine that ignites natural gas using a pilot injection of diesel fuel.

wide-band heated oxygen sensor (HOS) An exhaust gas sensor that provides feedback to the ECM about EGR flow rates.

wide-range planar sensor A type of sensor technology that uses a current pump to calculate relative concentrations of oxygen, nitric oxide, and ammonia in exhaust gases.

Wobbe index (WI) A measure of gas quality made by comparing the heating value of a gas to its density or specific gravity; also called the Wobbe number.

wood pyrolysis liquid (WPL) A bio-oil liquid fuel produced from wood through pyrolysis.

Wye windings Stator windings in which one end of each phase winding is taken to a central point where the ends are connected together.

yield point The point at which a bolt is stretched so hard that it fails; it is measured in pounds per square inch (psi) or kilopascals (kPa) of bolt cross-section.

zero fuel mass calibration (ZFC) The process of recalibrating injectors during service to compensate for wear and deterioration.

INDEX